2008
ALMANAC

110TH CONGRESS
2ND SESSION

VOLUME LXIV

JAN AUSTIN, EDITOR
MELINDA W. NAHMIAS, PRODUCTION

Congressional Quarterly Inc.
1255 22nd Street, N.W.
Washington, D.C. 20037

"By providing a link between the local newspaper and Capitol Hill we hope Congressional Quarterly can help to make public opinion the only effective pressure group in the country. Since many citizens other than editors are also interested in Congress, we hope that they too will find Congressional Quarterly an aid to a better understanding of their government."

Foreword, Congressional Quarterly, Vol. I, 1945
Henrietta Poynter, 1901-1968
Nelson Poynter, 1903-1978

SUMMARY TABLE OF CONTENTS

APPENDIXES

TABLE OF CONTENTS

CHAPTER 1 — INSIDE CONGRESS

CHAPTER 2 — APPROPRIATIONS

CHAPTER 3 — AGRICULTURE, REGULATORY POLICY & TRANSPORTATION

CHAPTER 4 — BUDGET & TAXES

CHAPTER 5— CONGRESSIONAL AFFAIRS

CHAPTER 6— DEFENSE, FOREIGN POLICY, INTELLIGENCE & TRADE

CHAPTER 7 — ECONOMIC AFFAIRS

CHAPTER 8 — ENERGY & ENVIRONMENT

CHAPTER 9 — HEALTH, EDUCATION, EMPLOYMENT & LABOR, & LEGAL AFFAIRS

CHAPTER 10 — POLITICS & ELECTIONS

Appendixes

Chapter 1

INSIDE CONGRESS

A Year of Partisanship, Financial Crises and History Made at the Polls

LAWMAKERS RETURNED to Washington in January ready for what they knew would be a year of partisan skirmishing in advance of the November elections. What they were not prepared for was the extraordinary series of events that would unfold in the late summer and fall, as the scope of the financial and economic crisis facing the country began to sink in and Barack Obama shattered early expectations to be elected the nation's first African-American president.

Democrats started the session with a less ambitious agenda than in the previous year, gambling that they would come out of the election with bigger majorities in Congress and a Democrat in the White House. They put much of the appropriations process on hold rather than give into President Bush on cuts to domestic spending, and they essentially abandoned efforts to force Bush to begin withdrawing troops from Iraq.

On a handful of important occasions, Democratic and Republican leaders and the White House worked together in ways they had not in the past, particularly when it came to addressing the crisis in the financial system and the economy.

But overall, with the election in sight, partisanship on Capitol Hill was as high as it had been in any recent year, a reality that was reflected in the high percentage of votes that divided the two parties and in the tendency of individual lawmakers to side with their fellow caucus members. The year provided the capstone for an era under Bush that was the most polarized period since Congressional Quarterly began examining partisan voting in 1953.

Republicans used parliamentary guerilla tactics to bring their issues to the fore in a Congress that was tightly controlled by the Democratic leadership. Their chief success was in putting Democrats on the spot over domestic energy production. After hammering away at the issue for months, Republicans ultimately forced the majority to lift a 26-year-old moratorium on drilling off the Pacific and Atlantic coasts.

Democratic leaders in both chambers carried out their own parliamentary maneuvers to protect their caucuses from having to take difficult votes, while painting Republicans as obstructionists. The majority had an easier time in the House, where Speaker Nancy Pelosi, D-Calif., and other top Democrats could get floor rules that limited the time for debate and blocked GOP amendments. They also used suspension of the rules, a procedure that barred Republicans from offering amendments or motions to recommit a bill for the purpose of adding GOP-backed language.

In the Senate, Democrats' 51-49 majority, counting two independents that voted with the caucus, required Majority Leader Harry Reid, D-Nev., to win over enough Republicans to reach the 60 votes needed

to cut off filibusters. Often, he simply pulled bills from the floor.

As the year progressed, however, the pre-election partisanship was overshadowed by the increasingly dire news on the economy. The housing market had collapsed, throwing the financial services industry into chaos and freezing credit markets. Frightened consumers were cutting spending, especially for big-ticket items like cars. Manufacturing and retail cutbacks brought job losses. Unemployment was spiraling upward, and the stock prices were plunging.

By mid-September, lawmakers were in uncharted waters, facing a crisis in the financial industry and an economy in free fall. There was no road map, and partisan lines were blurred, with a free-market-centric Republican administration demanding unprecedented government intervention.

Lawmakers were unnerved by the pressure to make decisions of such magnitude with so little time for debate, but a majority feared the alternative would be worse. In early October, Congress granted Treasury the authority to use a staggering $700 billion in an effort to rescue the financial services industry, after allowing up to $800 billion to salvage mortgage finance giants Fannie Mae and Freddie Mac.

The votes were difficult for members. Their constituents were angry over losing their jobs and their homes or learning about others who had. They were angry that money in their 401(k) accounts was evaporating, that gas cost $4 a gallon and that the government was spending billions for what many saw as a bailout of rich Wall Street brokers who had gotten the country into the mess in the first place.

The fact that the meltdown had occurred on their watch, combined with Bush's unpopularity, left Republicans scrambling to limit their losses on Nov. 4. Democrats added to their majorities in both chambers, and voters made the historic choice of electing Obama, the nation's first African-American president.

The second session of the 110th Congress convened on Jan. 4. The House adjourned on Oct. 3 for the election campaign, although the Senate remained in pro forma session. Congress reconvened Nov. 17-20 for a lame-duck session and returned Dec. 8-10 to consider a bailout for auto companies.

AVOIDING A SPENDING SHOWDOWN

Setting up a potential face-off with Bush, Democrats adopted a budget resolution (S Con Res 70) in early June that called for $20.1 billion more in fiscal 2009 discretionary spending for domestic programs than the president said he would accept. A similar decision the year before had led to an appropriations showdown, in which Bush

Leaders: 110th Congress, 2nd Session

SENATE

President of the Senate: Vice President Dick Cheney
President Pro Tempore: Robert C. Byrd, D-W.Va.

Democrats

Majority Leader	Harry Reid, Nev.	Steering and Outreach		
Majority Whip	Richard J. Durbin, Ill.	Committee Chairwoman	Debbie Stabenow, Mich.
Caucus Vice Chairman	Charles E. Schumer, N.Y.	Chief Deputy Whip	Barbara Boxer, Calif.
Policy Committee Chairman	Byron L. Dorgan, N.D.	Democratic Senatorial Campaign		
Conference Secretary	Patty Murray, Wash.	Committee Chairman	Charles E. Schumer, N.Y.

Republicans

Minority Leader	Mitch McConnell, Ky.	Policy Committee Chairwoman	Kay Bailey Hutchison, Texas
Minority Whip	Jon Kyl, Ariz.	Chief Deputy Whip	John Thune, S.D.
Conference Chairman	Lamar Alexander, Tenn.	National Republican Senatorial		
Conference Vice Chairman	John Cornyn, Texas	Committee Chairman	John Ensign, Nev.

HOUSE

Speaker of the House: Nancy Pelosi, D-Calif.

Democrats

Majority Leader	Steny H. Hoyer, Md.	Democratic Congressional Campaign		
Majority Whip	James E. Clyburn, S.C.	Committee Chairman	Chris Van Hollen, Md.
Caucus Chairman	Rahm Emanuel, Ill.	Steering and Policy Committee		
Caucus Vice Chairman	John B. Larson, Conn.	Co-Chairwoman	Rosa DeLauro, Conn.
Assistant to the Speaker	Xavier Becerra, Calif.	Co-Chairman	George Miller, Calif.
Senior Chief Deputy Whip	John Lewis, Ga.		

Republicans

Minority Leader	John A. Boehner, Ohio	Conference Secretary	John Carter, Texas
Minority Whip	Roy Blunt, Mo.	Policy Committee Chairman	Thaddeus McCotter, Mich.
Conference Chairman	Adam H. Putnam, Fla.	Chief Deputy Whip	Eric Cantor, Va.
Conference Vice Chairwoman	Kay Granger, Texas	National Republican Congressional		
		Committee Chairman	Tom Cole, Okla.

made good on a threat to veto domestic spending bills that exceeded his budget request and forced Democrats to back down in order to get an omnibus appropriations bill enacted before Congress adjourned.

But Democratic leaders signaled early in the year that they had no intention of reliving that experience. Instead, they planned to leave most, if not all, of the domestic spending bills to be completed after Bush was no longer president.

David R. Obey, D-Wis., chairman of the House Appropriations Committee, stopped holding markups in late June after his panel approved five of the 12 annual fiscal 2009 bills; the House passed only one — for military construction and the Department of Veterans Affairs (VA). Senate appropriators disposed of nine bills before they stopped work in late July; none of the bills reached the floor.

Instead, Congress cleared a continuing resolution (PL 110-329) at the end of September that combined the three security-related bills — the measure for military construction and the VA and those for the departments of Defense and Homeland Security. For the other nine, the stopgap bill provided funding through March 6, 2009, mostly at fiscal 2008 levels.

BACKING OFF ON THE WAR

Anti-war congressional Democrats and their limited number of GOP allies were a chastened lot in 2008, after finding themselves un-

able in 2007 to force Bush's hand on the Iraq War. Largely because they were short of the 60 votes needed to overcome GOP filibusters in the Senate, Democrats backed away from serious attempts to force a deadline for withdrawing most combat troops from Iraq. In the end, they settled for a handful of provisions limiting U.S. funding of programs to rebuild Iraq.

● **War appropriations.** The closest that war critics came to legislating troop withdrawal deadlines was during consideration of a supplemental spending bill (PL 110-252) that was enacted in June. And that was not very close.

The House-passed version would have required a withdrawal of most troops beginning 30 days after enactment and ending in 18 months. It would have set minimum standards for training and equipping troops before they were deployed, required congressional approval of any U.S.-Iraq security pact governing the presence of U.S. troops in Iraq after 2008 and required Iraqis to match U.S. reconstruction funds and subsidize U.S. fuel costs, among other provisions.

But the Senate rejected an attempt to bring up the House's war policy riders and voted down a weaker version that would have expressed the nonbinding "sense of Congress" that troop withdrawals should be completed, with certain exceptions, by June 2009. The provisions also included troop readiness standards, requirements that Iraq shoulder

more of its rebuilding costs and a mandate that Congress approve the U.S.-Iraq security pact that was being negotiated.

The final bill contained none of the major limits on war activities that Democrats had hoped to impose at the start of the 110th Congress. The only war provisions to survive were a requirement that U.S. reconstruction aid be matched dollar for dollar by the Iraqi government and a ban on the use of military construction funds to establish permanent bases in Iraq.

The $186.5 billion bill provided $161.8 billion for the wars in Iraq and Afghanistan, close to Bush's request. It also included $24.7 billion for domestic programs, foreign aid, military construction and disaster aid. Democrats tacked on two of their legislative priorities — the expansion of GI bill education benefits for veterans and an extension of unemployment benefits, which were accounted for separately.

● **Defense authorization.** The fiscal 2009 defense authorization bill, enacted in October (PL 110-181), contained a small number of war-related policy provisions, including a prohibition on using Pentagon funds for most Iraqi infrastructure projects. It required the U.S. government to begin negotiating a cost-sharing agreement for U.S.-Iraq military operations and to ensure that Baghdad paid for its own security costs. Heeding a presidential veto threat, negotiators backed away from a House-passed provision that would have required congressional approval for the U.S.-Iraq security pact. Instead, the bill mandated a report on the subject.

● **Detainee interrogation.** Members of both chambers made a concerted effort to require the CIA and other intelligence agencies to abide by the same restrictions on interrogation tactics that were imposed on the military. The provisions, which were included in the fiscal 2008 intelligence authorization bill, would have barred the agencies from using harsh techniques such as "waterboarding," or simulated drowning. The White House said the provisions would tie the CIA's hands and give terrorists information that could help them counter U.S. interrogation tactics. Bush vetoed the fiscal 2008 intelligence authorization bill in March, and the House fell short of the two-thirds majority required to override him.

The Senate Select Intelligence Committee tried again, approving a fiscal 2009 intelligence bill that included the same language, but the House committee disagreed, saying it was more important to get the bill signed into law. The White House threatened to veto both bills, anyway, and the legislation was never finished.

VICTORIES AND COMPROMISES

Democrats were able to use their control in both chambers to win enactment of several pieces of legislation that had stalled when Republicans were in the majority. But those Democratic victories often required compromise — usually with Republicans or Bush, but sometimes among themselves.

● **Higher education.** For the first time in a decade, Congress cleared a major overhaul of the Higher Education Act, the law governing federal aid for post-secondary education. Although Bush raised numerous objections to the bill as it made its way through Congress, he signed it in mid-August (PL 110-315). The law, which was originally enacted in 1965 to help students from low-income families afford a college education, had not been renewed since 1998.

The 2008 bill renewed the law for five years, with a number of changes. It authorized increases in federal financial aid for programs such as Pell grants. It barred private lenders from giving schools financial perks to get on their "preferred lender" lists and instituted penalties for states that cut funding for higher education.

The House and Senate both passed versions of the bill by large majorities. The chief difference was over a House proposal to reduce aid to states that cut back their own contributions to public colleges and universities. GOP senators were opposed to the provision, but supporters prevailed after conferees modified the programs that would be affected by the potential cuts.

● **Amtrak.** Democrats sealed a deal that led to the first reauthorization of Amtrak in more than a decade. The last authorization, enacted in 1997, had expired in 2003. Since then, Congress had provided just enough money in the annual appropriators bills to keep the national passenger rail line limping along. The Bush administration, joined by fiscal conservatives, insisted that any new authorization be tied to a restructuring that would wean the cash-strapped railway from government subsidies by turning key portions over to the private sector. Most Democrats viewed the rail line as a public responsibility and backed increases in federal funding combined with improvements in management.

The House passed an Amtrak reauthorization in June, the first time it had done so in 11 years. The proposal was based on a compromise between James L. Oberstar, D-Minn., chairman of the Transportation and Infrastructure Committee, and the panel's ranking Republican, John L. Mica of Florida. Mica agreed to a higher funding level than Bush had proposed, while Oberstar agreed to include language allowing private companies to bid on building a high-speed rail line in the Northeast Corridor. Mica was an ardent supporter of such a line and said only the private sector had the capability to build it.

The Senate had passed an Amtrak reauthorization bill in 2007 that rejected privatization, but the House prevailed. Mica helped persuade Bush, who had threatened to veto the bill, to sign it into law (PL 110-432) in October. The measure authorized $13 billion over five years for Amtrak, including operating and capital grants, plus $1.6 billion for rail safety and an additional $1.5 billion over 10 years for Washington, D.C.'s Metro subway system.

● **Medicare doctors' fees.** Democrats mustered the votes to override Bush's veto of a controversial bill to prevent a scheduled 10.6 percent cut in pay rates for doctors who participated in Medicare. The override enacted the bill into law (PL 110-275) in mid-July.

The White House and many Senate Republicans opposed the bill, primarily because most of the cost was offset by reducing funds for Medicare Advantage, a GOP-championed program that allowed private managed-care plans to provide benefits to seniors in place of the government.

The House passed the bill by an overwhelming majority in June. But Senate Democrats failed twice to invoke cloture and prevent a filibuster. They finally succeeded in July, but only after Edward M. Kennedy, D-Mass., made a dramatic appearance in the chamber to cast his vote. Kennedy, who had been out of Washington during treatment for brain cancer, drew a standing ovation as he walked onto the floor and put the vote over the top, with several members switching. That outcome foreshadowed the Senate's later vote to override Bush's veto.

● **Veterans' education benefits.** Congress provided the first major update in GI education benefits in nearly 25 years after the plan was inserted into the emergency war supplemental spending bill. The measure provided tuition aid for veterans who had served since Sept. 11, 2001, along with living stipends and other assistance. The program

Highlights: 110th Congress, 2nd Session

CONGRESS DID

- Grant the Treasury secretary authority to spend up to $700 billion to acquire financial assets in the hope of shoring up the economy.
- Authorize a financial lifeline for Fannie Mae and Freddie Mac as part of a mortgage relief bill, including a $300 billion trust fund for the Federal Housing Administration to help home borrowers refinance.
- Provide tax rebates of $600 for most individuals as part of a $152 billion effort to stimulate the economy.
- Lift limitations on offshore oil drilling.
- Expand the reach of the Americans with Disabilities Act.
- Require insurers to offer mental health and addiction benefits equal to traditional medical benefits.
- Enact the biggest expansion in nearly 25 years of educational benefits for veterans.
- Enhance the government's electronic surveillance power.
- Clear an Amtrak reauthorization bill that included substantial increases in passenger rail funding and additional safety measures.
- Expand the president's plan to fight AIDS and other infectious diseases overseas.
- Increase the statutory limit on federal borrowing twice, first to $10.6 trillion and nine weeks later to $11.3 trillion.
- Clear a $611.1 billion defense authorization bill, which included $68.6 billion for the wars in Iraq and Afghanistan.
- Boost spending on nutrition programs, preserve crop subsidies and expand conservation programs in a five-year rewrite of the farm bill enacted over a presidential veto.

CONGRESS DID NOT

- Finish any of the eight domestic spending bills or the foreign aid appropriations bill for fiscal 2009, freezing spending for most programs in those measures at fiscal 2008 levels until March.
- Enact a permanent change to avoid millions of taxpayers being subjected to the alternative minimum tax.
- Change the Medicare cost containment formula, which, since 2002, required Congress to take annual action to avoid a cut in physician reimbursement rates.
- Act on legislation to limit carbon emissions in an effort to slow global warming.
- Complete legislation giving the Food and Drug Administration broad authority to regulate tobacco products.
- Reauthorize federal intelligence programs for fiscal 2009.
- Set a deadline for the withdrawal of U.S. troops from Iraq.
- Pass a second economic stimulus bill that focused on the creation of jobs through infrastructure projects.
- Enact a U.S.-Colombian free-trade agreement.
- Expand the rights of workers to file wage-discrimination lawsuits.

was expected to cost as much as $62 billion over 10 years.

Virginia Democrat Jim Webb, a former Marine and Vietnam War veteran who served as secretary of the Navy in the Reagan administration, championed the GI bill in 2007. In February 2008, he joined John W. Warner, R-Va., also a former Navy secretary as well as a previous chairman of the Senate Armed Services Committee, to revise the bill and make it more palatable to fiscally conservative senators.

The Bush administration and the Pentagon warned that generous education benefits for veterans who served as little as three years of active-duty service could create retention problems for U.S. military forces. Sen. John McCain of Arizona, the GOP presidential nominee, tried to get support for an alternative that would have required more service time before the benefits could be used. And fiscal conservative "Blue Dog" Democrats in the House refused to support the benefits unless they were offsets by increased tax revenue. But that was a nonstarter in the Senate, where Republicans who opposed tax increases had the clout to stop it.

Democratic leaders in the House and Senate were ultimately able to sway Republicans by using the war supplemental as leverage and by agreeing to allow veterans to transfer their educational benefits to other family members if they were so inclined. Most of the Blue Dogs reluctantly went along despite the lack of offsets.

● **Mental health parity.** It took a compromise between House and Senate Democrats to enact a mental health parity law that lawmakers and mental health advocates had pushed for more than a decade.

Under the legislation, insurers had to offer benefits for mental health and addiction treatment that were equal to those provided for other health services. The requirement applied only to insurance plans that covered mental health and addiction treatment.

The main controversy was over how specific to be in identifying the conditions that the insurers would have to cover.

The Senate, led by Kennedy and Pete V. Domenici, R-N.M., passed a bill in 2007 that was the result of lengthy negotiations among stakeholders and did not specify precisely which mental illnesses would be covered. In March 2008, Kennedy's son, Democratic Rep. Patrick J. Kennedy of Rhode Island, fought off business and insurance lobbyists to win House passage of a version that required plans that offered mental health benefits to cover the full range of disorders outlined by the American Psychiatric Association.

Although lawmakers on each side were strongly wedded to their approaches, they managed to reach an agreement in September. The final bill did not require that specific conditions be covered, although it set up studies to make sure that certain conditions were not left out. Unlike the Senate bill, it did not preclude more stringent state parity laws. The compromise was enacted in the year-end continuing resolution.

● **Unemployment insurance.** Democrats succeeded in providing additional federal unemployment benefits to workers who had exhausted their regular 26 weeks of state-administered compensation.

The first extension, enacted in June as part of the war supplemental,

was a compromise negotiated by House Democrats and Republicans. It provided an extra 13 weeks of federal benefits, as Democrats wanted, but left out a House-passed plan for an additional 13 weeks for those in the hardest-hit states. The bill also required 20 weeks of work before a jobless worker could collect the extended benefits — a restriction House Republicans fought to include.

With unemployment at 6.6 percent and rising, lawmakers gave bipartisan support to a second extension that was enacted as a stand-alone bill in November (PL 110-449). The measure added seven weeks of federal benefits to the 13 weeks provided in June. Unlike the earlier law, it included an additional 13 weeks of benefits for people who had worked in states with unemployment rates of 6 percent or higher.

● **Genetic discrimination.** After more than a decade of debate, Congress cleared legislation to bar employers and health insurers from discriminating on the basis of genetic information, such as data about cancer or heart disease risk.

Strong opposition from business groups had stymied the legislation when the House was under Republican control. When Democrats took over in 2007, the House passed a genetic discrimination bill by a virtually unanimous vote. But in the Senate, opponent Tom Coburn, R-Okla., agreed to drop a hold on the measure in 2008 only after Democrats agreed to add what he called a "firewall" to protect employers from excessive lawsuits under the bill. Bush signed the bill in May (PL 110-233), after lawmakers agreed to allow the military to collect genetic information in order to identify soldiers' remains.

FINDING COMMON GROUND

Sometimes, despite the intense polarization in both chambers, lawmakers found themselves in agreement.

● **Farm bill.** The combination of farm aid programs, rural conservation and increased nutrition aid for low-income Americans drew strong bipartisan backing for a $289 billion, five-year farm bill. Hard bargaining was required, particularly over establishing eligibility for farm subsidies and setting caps on farm payments, but the compromise won by large margins in both chambers.

Bush vetoed the bill in May, after arguing for months that it was too expensive and did not go far enough to curtail farm subsidies. Both chambers voted to override him, enacting the measure into law (PL 110-234). Lawmakers repeated the exercise in June (PL 110-246), after restoring trade provisions that were mistakenly omitted the first time.

Senate Republicans supported the override by an almost 3-to-1 margin. House Republicans backed it 100-94.

● **Americans with Disabilities Act.** Democrats, Republicans and the White House were on the same page when it came to revising the Americans with Disabilities Act in response to a series of Supreme Court rulings that lawmakers said narrowed the scope of protections under the act. The court had ruled that disabled people who corrected or mitigated the effect of their disability — for example, by using medication or hearing aids — were not protected by the law in decisions about hiring, firing or job performance. The bill, signed in September (PL 110-325), stated that such mitigation did not affect the person's qualification under the ADA. It also clarified that an individual with a vision problem was not considered disabled if the impairment could be corrected by eyeglasses.

The revisions were largely the result of negotiations by an unorthodox coalition of business groups and advocates for the disabled. Once the House agreed to drop an attempt to create a new definition for "disabled," the bill had so much support that both chambers passed it by voice vote in September. Bush's father, President George Bush, had signed the original act in 1990.

● **Global HIV/AIDS.** Republicans and Democrats in Congress also joined forces with the White House to enact a five-year, $48 billion reauthorization (PL 110-293) of a Bush program to fight global AIDS and related diseases. A compromise brokered by Howard L. Berman, D-Calif., chairman of the House Foreign Affairs Committee, in advance of House passage averted a controversy that could have sidetracked the bill. In exchange for a higher funding level of $50 billion — Bush initially requested $30 billion — Democrats dropped language that would have linked family planning groups closer to HIV/AIDS services, a proposal that conservatives said would open a back door to funding overseas abortions. Another provision that satisfied both sides required balanced funding for abstinence, fidelity and condom programs, replacing language that had specified that one-third of the funding go to abstinence education.

PRIORITIES LEFT UNFINISHED

Although Democrats maintained an exceptional level of party unity during the session, particularly in the House, they were unable to prevail on some of their signature issues. That was usually, though not always, due to their narrow majority in the Senate.

● **Climate change.** A Senate debate on climate change fizzled in June, leaving Democrats without a chance to debate one of their top legislative priorities. Reid was unable to win a cloture vote that would have prevented a GOP filibuster on a wide-ranging bill by Barbara Boxer, D-Calif., that aimed to set a comprehensive national policy on global warming. It included a cap on greenhouse gas emissions and a market-based trading program to help companies meet the cap. It also would have collected trillions of dollars in fees from polluters over the following four decades to pay for clean-energy programs.

Although Democrats did not expect the measure to pass, they had hoped for a thorough floor debate.

● **Wage discrimination.** Buoyed by a White House veto threat, Senate Republicans succeeded in blocking a House-passed bill that was aimed at reversing a 2007 Supreme Court decision on wage discrimination. The court ruled, in *Ledbetter v. Goodyear Tire & Rubber Co.*, that under the Civil Rights Act of 1964, a worker filing suit for pay discrimination had to do so within 180 days of the date of the alleged discrimination.

Reid tried to bring the legislation up in April, but supporters could not rally enough GOP moderates to get the 60 votes needed to avert a filibuster and proceed to the bill.

● **Tobacco regulation.** A struggle for jurisdiction between Democratic committee chairmen in the House, combined with strenuous opposition by tobacco-state lawmakers, halted a Democratic-led effort to authorize the Food and Drug Administration to regulate tobacco products. The Energy and Commerce Committee approved the bill, but Ways and Means claimed jurisdiction over tax provisions and insisted on offsets. They finally broke the gridlock in late July, with the help of Henry A. Waxman, D-Calif., the bill's champion. That led to an overwhelming vote for passage in the House at the end of July, sending the measure to the Senate.

There, however, the legislation stalled, this time permanently. Richard M. Burr, R-N.C., who fought it when the Health, Education, Labor and Pensions Committee approved it in 2007, vowed to do all he could to delay the bill. With the days ticking down to adjournment, lawmak-

110th Congress, 2nd Session: By the Numbers

The second session of the 110th Congress began at noon on Jan. 4, 2008. The House adjourned sine die at noon on Jan. 3, 2009. The Senate adjourned sine die at 10 a.m. on Jan. 2, 2009. Following are some statistical comparisons of activities in the two chambers over the past decade:

		2008	2007	2006	2005	2004	2003	2002	2001	2000	1999	1998
Days in session	Senate	184	189	138	159	133	167	149	173	141	162	143
	House	119	164	101	140	110	133	123	142	135	137	119
Time in session *(hours)*	Senate	988	1,376	1,028	1,222	1,032	1,454	1,043	1,236	1,018	1,184	1,095
	House	891	1,478	850	1,067	879	1,015	772	922	1,054	1,125	999
Average length of daily session *(hours)*	Senate	5.4	7.3	7.4	7.7	7.8	8.7	7.0	7.1	7.2	7.3	7.7
	House	7.5	9.0	8.4	7.6	8.0	7.6	6.3	6.5	7.8	8.2	8.4
Public laws enacted[1]		285	175	321	161	300	198	269	108	410	170	241
Bills and resolutions introduced	Senate	1,590	3,033	2,302	2,616	1,318	2,398	1,558	2,212	1,546	2,352	1,321
	House	3,225	6,194	2,451	5,703	2,338	4,616	2,711	4,318	2,701	4,241	2,254
	Total	**4,815**	**9,227**	**4,753**	**8,319**	**3,656**	**7,014**	**4,269**	**6,530**	**4,247**	**6,593**	**3,575**
Roll call votes	Senate	215	442	279	366	216	459	253	380	298	374	314
	House[2]	690	1,186	543	671	544	677	484	512	603	611	547
	Total	**905**	**1,628**	**822**	**1,037**	**760**	**1,136**	**737**	**892**	**901**	**985**	**861**
Vetoes		4	7[3]	1	0	0	0	0	0	7[3]	5	5

SOURCE: Congressional Record   [1]Bills signed into law during congressional session   [2]Includes quorum calls   [3]Includes pocket vetoes

ers focused on other priorities, and the Senate never took it up.

• **Domestic surveillance.** Democratic efforts to confront Bush over electronic surveillance laws ended in July, with the White House the clear winner and Democrats dropping the fight for the rest of the Bush presidency.

Bush signed the bill the day after it cleared (PL 110-261) in a Rose Garden ceremony attended primarily by GOP lawmakers, who were close to unanimous in their support of the bill.

Many Democrats agreed with the administration on the need to update FISA to reflect developments in electronic communications, but they wanted more restrictions to protect American's civil liberties, and most House Democrats opposed the retroactive immunity.

Few votes caused as much anguish for Democrats, but they had been unable to agree among themselves on an alternative proposal. With the White House and congressional Republicans ratcheting up the pressure, arguing that Democratic delays were compromising national security, 105 Democrats voted for passage in the House, and 21 Democrats joined all Republicans in the Senate to clear the bill.

Bush had made a rewrite of the Foreign Intelligence Surveillance Act (FISA) a legislative priority, and the final measure gave him the two things he wanted most: enhanced executive branch spying authority and the almost-certain dismissal of lawsuits against the telecommunications companies that had participated in a warrantless surveillance program carried out by the National Security Agency (NSA) under his authority.

TAX BATTLES

After skirmishing throughout most of the 110th Congress over whether to pair extended tax breaks with revenue-raising offsets, lawmakers cleared a $107 billion tax package that was attached to the financial services rescue bill. The measure renewed a number of popular tax provisions that were known as "extenders" because of Congress' habit of extending them one year at a time to limit the cost. It also provided a one-year adjustment to the alternative minimum tax (AMT) to prevent it from reaching millions of additional middle-income taxpayers. And it included tax incentives for producing and using energy from alternative sources.

House Democrats insisted on complying with pay-as-you-go requirements, which they had added to House rules at the start of the 110th Congress. Republicans were equally adamant that Congress not increase taxes to offset the tax breaks. They could do little in the House, but they forced cloture votes in the Senate to stop the House bills from reaching the floor. Instead, the Senate passed bills with only partial offsets, which the House in turn rejected.

The stalemate continued until October, when the Senate seized the chance to insert its tax package into the must-pass, $700 billion financial services rescue bill that was enacted in October.

The final bill provided about $149.2 billion in tax breaks, offset by $42.2 billion in revenue-raisers. The key components included the AMT adjustment, the extension of tax breaks such as the popular research and development credit for businesses, and energy incentives such as tax breaks for developing wind and solar power. A single provision accounted for more than half the offsets by curtailing the ability of hedge fund managers to avoid taxes on large amounts of money by getting it as deferred compensation in offshore tax havens.

GOP WINS ON OFFSHORE DRILLING

Congressional Republicans scored their biggest victory of the year by forcing Democrats to drop the ban on drilling for oil and gas off

the Atlantic and Pacific coasts. It was the first time since 1982 that the offshore drilling ban, which was part of the annual Interior Department appropriations bill, was allowed to lapse.

Democrats' energy polices focused on reducing energy demand and developing alternative-energy sources, while protecting the environment. But with prices at the pump topping $4 per gallon in June and July, the public became increasingly receptive to the GOP message that the country needed to produce more domestic oil and gas — even though production would not begin for almost a decade.

Democrats were caught off guard by the swift change in public sentiment, and Republicans took every opportunity to try to maneuver them into taking uncomfortable votes on oil-drilling amendments. The House Appropriations Committee stopped marking up spending bills in June, after GOP members tried to force votes on drilling. In the Senate, Republicans blocked the Democrats' floor agenda for much of July, demanding that senators debate and vote on GOP energy proposals. Reid refused to allow such amendments and accused the Republicans of being obstructionist.

Republicans staged daily protests on the House floor during the August recess, saying Congress should return to deal with energy issues. Public-opinion surveys showed support for drilling was climbing. Delegates to the Republican National Convention erupted into a chant of "Drill, baby, drill!" as their vice presidential nominee, Alaska Gov. Sarah Palin, extolled the advantages of domestic oil production.

House Democratic leaders backed off in September, passing a bill that would have allowed some offshore drilling. But the measure had no legs in the Senate. Democrats finally gave up in late September, accepting GOP demands to drop the offshore drilling moratorium as the price for clearing the continuing resolution. The measure also allowed the expiration of a ban on drilling in the Rocky Mountain West for oil shale.

FINANCIAL CRISIS TAKES CENTER STAGE

The severity of the financial and economic crisis facing the country came into focus only gradually, and lawmakers continually found themselves behind the curve. The circumstances were unlike anything they had experienced before, and even top officials, such as Treasury Secretary Henry M. Paulson Jr. and Ben S. Bernanke, chairman of the Federal Reserve, had difficulty wrapping their minds around it.

When the subprime mortgage market collapsed in 2007, many experts said the fallout could be contained. But as the weeks went by in early 2008, it became increasingly evident that the problem had infected the economy and was threatening financial institutions not only in the United States but worldwide. At the end of the year it would be determined that the economy was in recession going back to December 2007.

● **Stimulus bill.** Congress' first response was a $151.7 billion economic stimulus bill, enacted in February (PL 110-329). The primary aim was to boost consumer confidence by providing tax rebates of up to $600 to eligible individuals ($1,200 for couples filing jointly). The bill also included tax provisions to encourage business investments. Enactment of the bill was one of the few truly bipartisan accomplishments of the 110th Congress. It was the result of a deal negotiated by Pelosi; Minority Leader John A. Boehner, R-Ohio; and administration officials. Leaders of both parties said that taxpayers and markets around the world were waiting for the U.S. government to take some action.

Senate Democrats tried to broaden the bill to include energy tax breaks and extend unemployment benefits, among other things. But the pressure to get money into people's pockets pushed them to accept the House bill with a few changes.

● **Fannie Mae, Freddie Mac.** During the spring and summer, the House Financial Services and Senate Banking, Housing and Urban Affairs committees worked on legislation to bring greater scrutiny to mortgage lenders and companies that sold mortgage-backed securities. A central feature of the evolving bill was a new regulatory regime for Fannie Mae and Freddie Mac.

Then, in an event for which lawmakers were completely unprepared, Paulson announced July 13 that he needed immediate and virtually open-ended authority from Congress to protect Fannie and Freddie from collapse. Together, the two government-sponsored enterprises owned or guaranteed about $5 trillion of the $12 trillion in mortgages issued on U.S. houses, and it was feared that their collapse would further damage the weakened housing industry and throw international debt markets into chaos. A precipitous fall in the companies' share prices during the previous week had prompted the government to act.

Despite anxiety about the enormous cost of the plan, the virtually unfettered authority it would give the Treasury and the precedent it could set, lawmakers took just two weeks to clear a bill that gave Paulson virtually everything he sought (PL 110-289). The measure also included a negotiated version of the mortgage bill that lawmakers had been working on for months.

The bill effectively allowed Treasury to borrow $800 billion, although the Congressional Budget Office put the likely cost at $25 billion, saying the very existence of the government backstop was likely to reassure the markets enough that the funds would never be needed.

The mortgage market continued to deteriorate, however, and enactment of the bailout did little to reassure investors. On Sept. 7, barely five weeks after the bill became law, the Treasury announced that it had put both Fannie and Freddie into conservatorships and would funnel as much as $200 billion into the companies to keep them functioning.

● **Financial services rescue.** If lawmakers were taken aback by the need to salvage Fannie and Freddie, they were stunned in mid-September when Paulson and Bernanke asked Congress for $700 billion for a Troubled Asset Relief Program (TARP) that they said would allow the Treasury to buy worthless mortgage-backed assets from damaged banks and investment firms. The value of those assets was deemed negligible because of the rising number of foreclosures and the volume of subprime home loans that were in danger of default. As a result, banks had tightened their lending standards, and Paulson and Bernanke warned that the resulting freeze in the credit markets would cripple the broad economy.

During the two weeks that preceded the request, the Treasury had allowed Lehman Brothers Holdings Inc., the fourth-largest Wall Street investment house, to go bankrupt. Bank of America Corp. had acquired Merrill Lynch, which was on the verge of bankruptcy, in a deal encouraged by federal officials. And the Fed and Treasury had started bailing out American International Group Inc., the world's largest insurance company.

The prospect of spending such a huge amount of taxpayer money to bail out what many saw as fat cats who had caused the crisis was immensely unpopular with the public and with members of Congress.

Still, it was a shock when, shortly before leaving to campaign, the

Eight Years, A Dozen Bush Vetoes

PRESIDENT BUSH VETOED 12 BILLS during his two terms in office. Just one veto came in the first six years of his presidency, a period when Republicans controlled both chambers. During the last two years of his presidency, he vetoed 11 bills sent to him by the Democratic-controlled 110th Congress.

Congress overrode four of his vetoes, a procedure that requires a two-thirds majority of those voting in both chambers. The override automatically enacts the bill into law. House leaders tried but failed to override six other vetoes, which made it unnecessary for the Senate to vote.

109TH CONGRESS, SECOND SESSION

July 19, 2006. The bill (HR 810) would have expanded federal funding for stem cell research. An override attempt in the House failed, 235-193, on July 19 (286 needed). *(House vote 388, 2006 Almanac, p. H-120)*

110TH CONGRESS, FIRST SESSION

May 1, 2007. The supplemental spending bill (HR 1591) for the wars in Iraq and Afghanistan would have set a date for redeploying U.S. troops and imposed other restrictions on the war. An override attempt in the House failed, 222-203, on May 2 (284 needed). Bush signed a later version without the policy prescriptions (PL 110-28). *(House vote 276, 2007 Almanac, p. H-94)*

June 20, 2007. This was Congress' second attempt to expand federal funding for stem cell research (S 5). Congress did not challenge Bush's veto.

Oct. 3, 2007. Bush said the bill to expand children's health insurance (HR 976) would move the program beyond its goal of helping poor children. An override attempt in the House failed, 273-156, on Oct. 18 (286 votes needed). *(House vote 982, 2007 Almanac, p. H-312)*

Nov. 2, 2007. Bush rejected the popular water resources development bill (HR 1495) as too costly and expansive. The House overrode the veto, 361-54, on Nov. 6. The Senate followed, 79-14, on Nov. 8, enacting the bill into law (PL 110-114). *(House vote 1040, Senate vote 406, 2007 Almanac, pp. H-330, S-78)*

Nov. 13, 2007. Bush vetoed the fiscal 2009 spending bill for the departments of Labor, Health and Human Services, and Education (HR 3043) to demonstrate that he would not accept bills that exceeded his spending cap. An override attempt in the House failed, 277-141, on Nov. 15 (279 votes needed). *(House vote 1122, 2007 Almanac, p. H-356)*

Dec. 12, 2007. A modified version of the children's health insurance bill (HR 3963) was no more palatable to Bush than the first. An override attempt in the House failed, 260-152, on Jan. 23, 2008 (275 votes needed). *(House vote 22, p. H-10)*

Dec. 28, 2007. Bush pocket vetoed the fiscal 2008 defense authorization bill (HR 1585) by withholding approval after Congress adjourned. Congress changed one small provision, and the revised bill was enacted (PL 110-181) on Jan. 28, 2008.

110TH CONGRESS, SECOND SESSION

March 8, 2008. Bush rejected the fiscal 2008 intelligence authorization bill (HR 2082) largely because it would have restricted CIA interrogation tactics. An override attempt in the House failed, 225-188, on March 11 (276 votes needed). *(House vote 117, p. H-38)*

May 21, 2008. This popular bill (HR 2419) reauthorized federal farm, nutrition, rural conservation and food aid programs for five years. Bush objected that it did not do enough to limit farm subsidies. The House overrode the veto, 316-108, on May 21. The Senate agreed, 82-13, on May 22, enacting the bill into law (PL 110-234). *(House vote 346, p. H-112; Senate vote 140, p. S-30)*

June 18, 2008. Due to a clerical error in the first farm bill, Congress cleared and Bush vetoed a revised version (HR 6124). The House voted to override him, 317-109, on June 18; the Senate followed suit, 80-14, the same day, enacting the bill into law (PL 110-246). *(House vote 417, p. H-138; Senate vote 151, p. S-33)*

July 15, 2008. This bill (HR 6331) blocked a scheduled cut in payments to doctors who treated Medicare patients. Bush's main objection was that the cost was offset with cuts to a GOP-backed health program. The House overrode him, 383-41, on July 15. The Senate voted to override, 70-26, the same day, enacting the measure into law (PL 110-275). *(House vote 491, p. H-164; Senate vote 177, p. S-39)*

House voted down a bill to authorize the funds. Wall Street reacted with disbelief, and the Dow Jones Industrial Average suffered its worst point drop in history. The Senate quickly stepped in to salvage the bailout, adding sweeteners such as the package of popular tax extensions, mental health parity legislation and an increase in the limit on federal insurance for bank deposits. The House cleared the revised bill, and Bush signed it the same day (PL 110-343).

The final bill authorized an initial $250 billion in funds for TARP, an additional $100 billion following a certification from the president that the money was needed, and a further $350 billion if the president requested it and Congress did not object. While the delicate compromise essentially left the Treasury's broad asset-buying powers intact, it included some provisions to safeguard the taxpayers' money.

Less than two weeks after the bill was signed, Paulson announced that market conditions had worsened significantly and that buying troubled assets would not work. Instead, Treasury planned to use authority included in the new law to inject capital directly into banks by purchasing stock.

● **Auto loans.** Even as lawmakers were struggling over the $700 billion bailout bill, Congress agreed to finance a $25 billion loan to the Big Three automakers: General Motors Corp., Chrysler LLC and Ford Motor Co. Democratic leaders included the provision in the continuing resolution after intense lobbying by the companies' chief executives. The bill appropriated $7.5 billion to cover the cost of the loan, which had been authorized in the 2007 Energy Act (PL 110-140) to help the Big Three retool to produce more fuel-efficient vehicles.

The auto companies returned in November and again in December

to request more money, this time from TARP, to help stave off bankruptcy. The House agreed, but the Senate refused.

In the end, the Bush administration reluctantly agreed to use TARP funds to provide $17.5 billion in low-interest, short-term loans to GM and Chrysler in return for concessions and restructuring. Ford said it did not need money at the time. Bush's decision left the job of finding longer-term solutions to the incoming Obama administration.

MAKING HISTORY ON NOV. 4

Never far from the lawmakers' minds, even as they confronted the nation's economic and financial straits, was the Nov. 4 election. From the Iowa caucuses in January to Election Day, Democrats were caught up in their presidential primary and election campaigns. The primaries quickly became a competition between two precedent-breaking candidates — Sen. Hillary Rodham Clinton, the expected winner and potential first woman president, and Sen. Obama, a relative political newcomer seeking to become the first African-American in the Oval Office.

Obama had to engage in a bruising battle through the final primaries on June 3 before he could declare victory. McCain, by contrast, wrapped up the Republican nomination in early March and was free to turn to his election campaign.

Many factors contributed to the election outcome, among them Obama's appeal to the youth vote, his tactical flexibility and highly organized grass-roots campaign, and his obvious command of the issues. McCain hit high points, but overall he ran a relatively disorganized campaign, appeared inconsistent on some issues and was saddled with the fact that the economic tailspin had occurred on the watch of a Republican president.

Obama's victory, which had once seemed impossible, electrified the nation, as the relatively young but immensely confident president-elect began laying out his ambitious plans for his new administration. The Bush administration handled the transition with grace, consulting closely with Obama and his advisers in handling the economic crisis and other issues.

Democrats also added to their majorities in both chambers. Although they fell short in their long-shot quest to win the 60 seats needed to dominate the Senate, their net gain of at least seven seats brought their number to 58, counting the two independents. One race, in Minnesota, was undecided at the end of the year.

In the House, Democrats solidified their control with a net gain of 21 seats, making it the second consecutive election in which the party gained a significant number of House seats. The party's success was fueled by the ever-deepening public disapproval of Bush and the Republican Party in general and by a surge in Democratic turnout spurred by Obama's winning presidential campaign.

Republicans — who had expected to lose seats almost from the start of the campaign cycle two years earlier, given Bush's unpopularity — expressed a measure of relief that their losses were not greater.

ORGANIZING FOR THE 111TH

Lawmakers of both parties met in Washington in November to organize for the next Congress.

House Democrats re-elected their leaders by acclamation Nov. 18. Pelosi, Majority Leader Steny H. Hoyer of Maryland and Whip James E. Clyburn of South Carolina had no opposition. John B. Larson of Connecticut was unopposed in his move up from vice chairman of the caucus to the chairman's slot, replacing Rahm Emanuel of Illinois, who was leaving to serve as White House chief of staff in the Obama administration.

In the only contested race among House Democrats, Xavier Becerra of California bested Marcy Kaptur of Ohio, the longest-serving Democratic woman in the House, for the job of vice chairman.

In a high-profile vote with important policy implications, the Democratic Caucus voted Nov. 20 to depose John D. Dingell of Michigan, the legendary dean of the House, as chairman of the Energy and Commerce Committee. They handed the gavel to Henry A. Waxman of California, who had begun his campaign for the job immediately after the Nov. 4 election. "It was like Zeus and Thor in there, hurling lightning bolts at each other," George Miller of California said after the caucus decision.

Waxman was a staunch advocate of strong clean-air protections and stringent fuel efficiency and energy conservation measures, while Dingell had been a fierce protector of the U.S. auto industry, which was crucial to the economy of his home state.

House Republicans elected Boehner to a second term as minority leader, defeating Dan Lungren of California. Boehner's team for the 111th was more conservative than the outgoing roster of GOP leaders, with members of the Republican Study Committee (RSC) winning some top positions. Eric Cantor of Virginia was chosen minority whip, and Mike Pence of Indiana became House Republican Conference chairman. The two RSC members were unopposed and had Boehner's backing.

In the Senate, Democrats retained their leadership, with Reid as majority leader.

Republicans kept in place the lineup that had evolved in 2008, headed by Minority Leader Mitch McConnell of Kentucky. Other members included Jon Kyl of Arizona, who had taken over as minority whip when Trent Lott of Mississippi left at the end of 2007 to join a lobbying firm, and Lamar Alexander of Tennessee, who had moved into Ensign's previous job as conference chairman.

BUSH WINDS DOWN PRESIDENCY

Bush took less and less of a public role as he prepared for the end of his presidency. Paulson was the driver of the administration's efforts to cope with the financial crisis As the year ended, Bush seemed to have faded from view. It was Obama who was talking publicly about meeting the challenges facing the country and lobbying for a new eoncomic stimulus bill in the next Congress. ∎

Chapter 2

APPROPRIATIONS

Democrats Put Off Most FY '09 Bills To Avoid Domestic Spending Cuts

DEMOCRATIC LEADERS SIGNALED EARLY in the year that they did not plan to finish the fiscal 2009 appropriations bills if it meant engaging in a veto fight with President Bush. They were determined to avoid a replay of the previous year's showdown, when Bush forced the Democrats to accept his limit on discretionary spending and back down on their domestic spending goals. (2007 *Almanac, p. 2-3*)

"I'm not about to waste the time of this committee or of this Congress . . . with a needless eight-month squabble over numbers if the president simply intends to stick by his original budget, not changing a dollar," Democrat David R. Obey of Wisconsin, chairman of the House Appropriations Committee, told his panel in February.

In a sure sign of the trouble ahead, Democrats adopted a budget resolution (S Con Res 70) in June that gave appropriators a discretionary total of $1.012 trillion for the 12 fiscal 2009 bills — $20.1 billion more than Bush requested.

The Senate did not pass a single annual fiscal 2009 appropriations bill. The House passed only one, for military construction and the Department of Veterans Affairs (VA).

Instead, Congress cleared a continuing resolution (PL 110-329) built around the final versions of the three security-related bills — Defense, Homeland Security and Military Construction-VA. For agencies covered by the remaining nine bills, the resolution continued funding through March 6, 2009. Most accounts were frozen at fiscal 2008 levels, although a few programs were singled out for increases. They included the Low Income Home Energy Assistance Program, Pell grants, wildfire suppression and the 2010 census.

The measure also provided $22.9 billion in emergency funds for states that had suffered hurricane damage, flooding and other natural disasters, as well as $7.5 billion to finance a $25 billion loan program for the Big Three automakers.

EARLY COLLAPSE

Although Democrats had planned to halt work on the appropriations bills at some point, pre-election sparring between the two parties hastened the breakdown.

The turning point came June 26, when Republicans on the House Appropriations Committee disrupted a planned markup of a bill to fund the departments of Labor, Health and Human Services, and Education in an attempt to force a vote on offshore drilling. The move was part of a campaign by Republicans to put Democrats on the spot over GOP proposals to increase domestic drilling at a time when gas prices were rising and voters were increasingly receptive to producing more oil at home.

Obey abruptly adjourned the session and refused to have additional full committee markups. "It's stunts like this that make people hate Washington," Obey said, adding, "I'll see them in September on a CR," a reference to the continuing resolution. In the end, however, the Republicans forced Democrats to drop a moratorium on offshore drilling as the price for getting the CR enacted.

The House committee had approved five of the 12 fiscal 2009 spending bills; the Senate panel disposed of nine before it stopped work in late July. While 2008 was the most extreme example, the breakdown of "regular order" in handling the spending bills had become a pattern, one that tended to strengthen the role of the majority party's leadership, the Appropriations chairmen and the White House.

The last time things had gone by the book — meaning all of the individual appropriations bills were enacted by the start of the new fiscal year — was 1994. In 2004, Congress rolled nine measures into one just before Thanksgiving. The following year, the bills were finished, one by one, but not until Dec. 21. In 2006, Republicans essentially gave up and turned the process over to the incoming Democratic majority. And in 2007, all 11 of the non-defense bills were stapled together and signed the day after Christmas.

WAR SUPPLEMENTAL

Before starting on the regular fiscal 2009 spending bills, Congress had to assemble and clear a supplemental appropriations bill for the wars in Iraq and Afghanistan that Bush would sign (PL 110-252). That meant Democrats had to drop a number of House-passed war policy prescriptions. The Senate cleared the $186.5 billion in June. Most of the money was for Defense Department war activities, but lawmakers added funds for other purposes and attached several unrelated bills. The final package contained:

● **War funding.** $161.8 billion to cover Pentagon costs related to operations in Iraq and Afghanistan — $95.9 billion for the remainder of fiscal 2008, and $65.9 billion for the first part of fiscal 2009. The bill included a requirement that the Iraqi government match U.S. reconstruction aid dollar for dollar and a ban on the use of funds to establish permanent bases in Iraq. The bill did not set a timetable for the withdrawal of U.S. troops, as House Democrats had sought.

● **Disaster aid.** $5.8 billion to strengthen New Orleans levees and $2.7 billion for relief from floods and tornadoes in the Midwest.

● **Military construction.** $4.6 billion for military construction, including base-closing costs.

● **Other domestic programs.** A total of $1 billion in unrequested funds for the Food and Drug Administration, the Federal Bureau of Prisons, census cost overruns and other accounts.

● **Foreign aid.** $8.8 billion over two years for refugee assistance in Iraq and elsewhere, drug enforcement in Central America and Mexico, embassy security, and international economic support. The bill also provided $1.2 billion over two years for international food aid.

● **GI Bill.** An expansion of education benefits for servicemembers who had served on active duty since Sept. 11, 2001, at an estimated cost of $796 million in fiscal 2008-09.

● **Unemployment benefits.** Up to 13 weeks of federal unemployment benefits for workers who had exhausted their regular 26 weeks of compensation.

● **Medicaid.** A moratorium on seven Medicaid regulations issued by the Bush administration to narrow some services, limit others eligible for federal reimbursements and end accounting maneuvers used by the states. ∎

Appropriations Mileposts
110th Congress — Second Session

Bill	House Action	Senate Action	House Final	Senate Final	President Signed	Story
FY 2009 Agriculture* (House draft, S 3289)	Subcommittee approved draft 6/19/08	Committee approved S 3289 7/17/08				2-5
FY 2009 Commerce-Justice-Science* (HR 7322, S 3182)	Committee approved HR 7322 6/25/08	Committee approved S 3182 6/19/08				2-7
FY 2009 Defense (House, Senate drafts; enacted in HR 2638 — PL 110-329)	Subcommittee approved draft 7/30/08	Subcommittee approved draft 9/10/08	Passed HR 2638 9/24/08	Cleared HR 2638 9/27/08	9/30/08	2-9
FY 2009 Energy-Water* (HR 7324, S 3258)	Committee approved HR 7324 6/25/08	Committee approved S 3258 7/10/08				2-12
FY 2009 Financial Services* (HR 7323, S 3260)	Committee approved HR 7323 6/25/08	Committee approved S 3260 7/10/08				2-15
FY 2009 Homeland Security (HR 6947, S 3181; enacted in HR 2638 — PL 110-329)	Committee approved HR 6947 6/24/08	Committee approved S 3181 6/19/08	Passed HR 2638 9/24/08	Cleared HR 2638 9/27/08	9/30/08	2-17
FY 2009 Interior-Environment* (House draft)	Subcommittee approved draft 6/11/08					2-20
FY 2009 Labor-HHS-Education* (House draft, S 3230)	Subcommittee approved draft 6/19/08	Committee approved S 3230 6/26/08				2-21
FY 2009 Legislative Branch* (House draft)	Subcommittee approved draft 6/23/08					2-23
FY 2009 Military Construction-VA (HR 6599, S 3301, enacted in HR 2638 — PL 110-329)	Passed HR 6599 8/1/08	Committee approved S 3301 7/17/08	Passed HR 2638 9/24/08	Cleared HR 2638 9/27/08	9/30/08	2-24
FY 2009 State-Foreign Operations* (House draft, S 3288)	Subcommittee approved draft 7/16/08	Committee approved S 3288 7/17/08				2-27
FY 2009 Transportation-HUD* (House draft, S 3261)	Subcommittee approved draft 6/20/08	Committee approved 7/10/08				2-29
FY 2009 Continuing Resolution (HR 2638— PL 110-329)			Passed HR 2638 9/24/08	Cleared HR 2638 9/27/08	9/30/08	2-3
War Supplemental (HR 2642— PL 110-252)	HR 2642 5/15/08	HR 2642 5/22/08	Passed HR 2642, amended 6/19/08	Cleared HR 2642 6/26/08	6/30/08	2-32

* Appropriations extended through 3/6/09 under fiscal 2009 continuing resolution (HR 2638 — PL 110-329).

Extra Spending for Food Programs

HOUSE AND SENATE appropriators began work on a fiscal 2009 Agriculture spending bill, but the measure did not reach the floor in either chamber. Programs covered by the bill were kept operating through March 6, 2009, under a short-term continuing resolution (PL 110-329) enacted Sept. 30. Most accounts got the same amount under the stopgap law as they did in fiscal 2008, although several programs were singled out for extra funding.

The fiscal 2008 spending law (PL 110-161) provided $18.1 billion in discretionary funds for the Agriculture Department and agencies such as the Food and Drug Administration (FDA) and the Commodity Futures Trading Commission. Discretionary budget authority — the funding over which the appropriators had control — accounted for about 25 percent of the overall bill. The remainder was mandatory spending for a variety of programs such as crop supports, nutrition and conservation. *(2007 Almanac, p. 2-7)*

Appropriators in both chambers planned to increase the discretionary funding available under the bill in fiscal 2009. The House Agriculture Appropriations Subcommittee approved a draft bill in June that included $20.6 billion, about a 14 percent increase over fiscal 2008 and 10 percent more than President Bush sought. The full Senate Appropriations Committee followed suit in July, approving a slightly smaller bill with $20.4 billion in discretionary appropriations, 13 percent above the previous year and 9 percent more than requested.

Further progress on the legislation was halted, mainly by Democratic leaders' decision to put off the domestic spending bills until the next administration to avoid a veto fight with Bush, who vowed not to sign bills that exceeded his requests.

Although the stopgap bill eliminated most of the increases sought by the appropriators, several areas that were priorities in the early bills got special attention in the year-end law.

▶ $6.68 billion to the Women, Infants and Children (WIC) nutrition program, or $680 million above the fiscal 2008 level, to soften the blow of the economic downturn on families. The program supplements the diets of low-income pregnant and postpartum women and their young children.

▶ Authority for the FDA to spend an additional $150 million in fiscal 2009 funds that were appropriated under the war supplemental spending bill (PL 110-252). Food safety issues had taken on added importance in the aftermath of a nationwide salmonella scare and deaths tied to contaminated doses of the blood-thinning drug heparin made in China. Both committees proposed increases, and the White House upped its FDA request by $265 million on June 9, acknowledging that additional money was needed for import safety initiatives.

▶ $163 million for the Commodity Supplemental Food Program, a nutrition program for low-income seniors that the president proposed eliminating.

▶ $403 million in emergency funds for disaster recovery, mainly for emergency conservation programs.

BILLS: House draft, S 3289

....

LEGISLATIVE ACTION:

House Appropriations subcommittee approved draft by voice vote June 19.

Senate Appropriations Committee approved S 3289 (S Rept 110-426), 29-0, on July 17.

LEGISLATIVE ACTION
HOUSE SUBCOMMITTEE ACTION

The Agriculture Appropriations Subcommittee gave voice vote approval June 19 to a draft bill that included $20.6 billion in discretionary spending, which was about $2.5 billion more than was provided for fiscal 2008 and $1.9 billion more than Bush requested.

Connecticut Democrat Rosa DeLauro, the subcommittee's chairwoman, said that $1.3 billion of the increase over Bush's budget went to restoring the president's proposed cuts. "This mark is, in essence, a back to basics," she said.

Some subcommittee Republicans said the measure was too expensive when taxpayers nationwide were struggling economically. The full Appropriations Committee's ranking Republican, Jerry Lewis of California, applauded the bill's funding increases for nutrition programs but said he disapproved of the total cost of the measure. Because the bill did not reach the full committee, it was not formally introduced and no report was filed. However, a subcommittee summary highlighted the following increases:

▶ About $6.65 billion for WIC, $550 million more than requested and $630 million above fiscal 2008 spending.

▶ $2.1 billion for the FDA, about $5 million more than Bush's request, including the additional $265 million he requested in June.

▶ $848 million for Natural Resources Conservation Service operations, $54 million more than requested and $14 million above the fiscal 2008 level.

The panel ignored a number of White House proposals, such as requests to eliminate direct loans for single-family housing and to dismantle the Commodity Supplemental Food Program, which the panel said aided almost a half-million low-income senior citizens.

The measure included a number of policy provisions, some of which rankled Republicans. The draft called for the National School Lunch Program to purchase meat solely from facilities enrolled in the Agriculture Department's animal identification program, which registered where each cow, chicken and pig was born, sold and slaughtered.

It also proposed eliminating an Agriculture Department rule that allowed China to process chicken raised in the United States and then export the processed poultry back to America. DeLauro said the agency could not verify that the manufactured products coming back were actually made from U.S. chicken.

A full Appropriations Committee markup was tentatively scheduled for the following week but never occurred.

SENATE COMMITTEE ACTION

The Senate Appropriations Committee approved a $96.7 billion Agriculture spending bill (S 3289 — S Rept 110-426) by a vote of 29-0 on July 17 that included a provision to ease travel to Cuba, language that had repeatedly drawn White House veto threats.

The measure included $20.4 billion in discretionary spending for fiscal 2009, $1.7 billion more than Bush requested and $2.3 billion

WHERE THE MONEY GOES — FISCAL 2009 APPROPRIATIONS
AGRICULTURE

S 3289 (S Rept 110-426); House draft

	(figures are in thousands of dollars of new budget authority)		
	Fiscal 2008 appropriations	Fiscal 2009 Bush request	Senate committee approved
GRAND TOTAL	$90,916,423	$94,765,269	$96,736,226
Discretionary spending	$18,093,000	$18,743,000	20,435,000
MAIN COMPONENTS			
Domestic nutrition programs	60,056,845	64,125,763	65,011,562
Food stamps program	39,782,723	43,348,804	43,437,304
Child nutrition programs	13,901,513	14,455,683	14,455,683
Nutrition for women, infants and children	6,020,000	6,100,000	6,750,000
Agriculture programs	24,450,902	24,304,630	24,412,241
Rural economic and community development	2,333,957	2,135,732	2,887,855
International food aid	1,213,525	1,228,661	1,228,661
Food and Drug Administration	1,716,770	2,046,203	2,051,397

SOURCE: Senate Appropriations Committee

above the fiscal 2008 total. The amount was about $190 million less than the House subcommittee proposed.

"Now is not the time to cut or eliminate programs that invest in the growth of our nation and support nutritional assistance to Americans who are suffering from a shrinking economy," said Appropriations Chairman Robert C. Byrd, D-W.Va.

Targeted areas of investment included food and drug safety, nutrition assistance, global food aid, rural rental assistance and agency facilities. The bill included:

▶ $2.1 billion for FDA operations, including buildings and facilities. That was $5 million more than Bush requested and $335 million more than fiscal 2008 funding.

Committee member Tom Harkin, D-Iowa, who chaired the Senate Agriculture, Nutrition and Forestry Committee, worked with Herb Kohl, D-Wis., chairman of the Agriculture Appropriations Subcommittee, on language in the spending bill that directed the FDA to leverage the extra funding to track food from production to consumption, a Harkin aide said.

On July 15, Harkin wrote a letter to Health and Human Services Secretary Michael O. Leavitt saying, "The inability of FDA and [the Centers for Disease Control and Prevention] to trace food products from farm to fork has been called into question by the salmonella outbreak." He urged the FDA to "move quickly to establish a strong trace-back system using its authority" under current law or immediately advise Congress on its needs if the agency lacked the proper authority.

▶ $974 million for the Agriculture Department's Food Safety and Inspection Service, $22 million more than Bush requested.

▶ $6.75 billion for WIC, $730 million above the fiscal 2008 level and $650 million more than Bush requested. The committee said the amount above the president's request would allow an additional 400,000 people to receive services under the program.

▶ $867 million for Natural Resource Conservation Services operations.

Like the House panel, the committee funded a number of programs that Bush wanted to eliminate, including direct loans for single-family housing and the Commodity Supplemental Food Program.

During the markup, the committee:

▶ Adopted an amendment by Tim Johnson, D-S.D., to bar funding to import meat, ruminants or swine from Argentina until the Agriculture Department certified to Congress that every region of that country was free of foot-and-mouth disease, a viral infection affecting cattle and swine.

The issue, which occupied much of the discussion during the markup, arose because the Agriculture Department was preparing to declare Argentina's southern Patagonia region free of the disease, which would exempt beef produced in that region from a blanket ban on imports of Argentine beef. There had been no foot-and-mouth outbreaks in Patagonia since 1976, but critics argued that Argentina had difficulty in dealing with the disease and that imports from any part of a country with a poor record of animal disease should be barred.

▶ Approved by voice vote an amendment by Byron L. Dorgan, D-N.D., to authorize general licenses for travel to Cuba for agricultural purposes. A similar amendment had been included in the Senate's Agriculture bill in each of the previous five fiscal years but drew veto threats and never made it into law. ■

Increase Goes Toward 2010 Census

LAWMAKERS' EFFORTS to provide more funding for state and local law enforcement became one of the casualties of the breakdown in the fiscal 2009 appropriations process.

House and Senate appropriators began work on the annual bill to fund the Commerce and Justice departments, NASA, and several other agencies. But the legislation did not reach the floor in either chamber, and funding for the programs covered by the bill was extended at fiscal 2008 levels through March 6, 2009, under a continuing resolution that President Bush signed Sept. 30 (HR 2638 — PL 110-329)

Fiscal 2008 Commerce-Justice-Science appropriations (PL 110-161) — on which the short-term funding was based — provided a total of about $53.7 billion, with $51.8 billion for discretionary programs. Bush asked Congress for $54.1 billion in discretionary funds for fiscal 2009, a 4 percent increase.

Appropriators in both chambers set out to provide a bigger increase. The House committee approved a bill in June that would have provided $56.9 billion in discretionary funding, nearly 10 percent above the fiscal 2008 level and 6 percent more than Bush's request. The Senate committee went further, approving a bill the same month that called for $57.9 billion for discretionary programs, 2 percent above the amount in the House version.

Both committees rejected attempts by Bush to reduce or eliminate several popular law enforcement grant programs, including the Community Oriented Policing Services (COPS) program and Byrne formula grants for local police.

Although the continuing resolution froze most funding at fiscal 2008 levels until Congress could agree on a full-year bill in 2009, it did provide a handful of increases.

The Census Bureau, which was part of the Commerce Department, was funded at an annual level of $2.9 billion — about $1.7 billion above fiscal 2008 funding — to help it prepare for the 2010 census. Bush initially requested $2.6 billion, or double the amount the bureau received in fiscal 2008. On June 9, Bush asked for an additional $546 million. Census takers were going to use paper questionnaires, not hand-held computers as originally planned, to gather information from residents who did not mail back forms — a decision that increased expected costs for the census by as much as $3 billion.

Both the Senate and House Appropriations committees said they received the request too late to include it in their spending bills.

LEGISLATIVE ACTION
HOUSE COMMITTEE ACTION

The House Appropriations Committee approved its bill (HR 7322 — H Rept 110-919) by voice vote June 25 in a session that was largely devoid of policy fights over issues, such as gun rights, that had punctuated the debate in previous years. The Commerce-Justice-Science Subcommittee, which wrote the bill, approved it by voice vote June 12.

The $56.9 billion in discretionary funding was $5.1 billion above the fiscal 2008 level and $2.7 billion more than Bush requested.

BOX SCORE 2009 FISCAL YEAR

COMMERCE-JUSTICE-SCIENCE

BILLS: HR 7322, S 3182

LEGISLATIVE ACTION:

Senate Appropriations Committee approved S 3182 (S Rept 110-397), 29-0, on June 19.

House Appropriations Committee approved HR 7322 (H Rept 110-919) by voice vote June 25.

Appropriators once again rejected Bush's push to reduce or eliminate several popular law enforcement programs. The bill called for $3.1 billion for state and local law enforcement grants, nearly $450 million more than fiscal 2008 spending. Bush proposed a cut of $1.6 billion.

Within that total, the bill included $627 million for the COPS program, a $40 million increase over fiscal 2008, and $550 million for the Edward Byrne Memorial Justice Assistance Grant program, more than triple the $170 million enacted for fiscal 2008. The president did not request funding for either program in his budget.

The Census Bureau, which Subcommittee Chairman Alan B. Mollohan, D-W.Va., called "the elephant in the room," would have gotten $2.6 billion from the Commerce total, in line with the president's initial budget and more than double the $1.2 billion enacted for fiscal 2008.

The National Oceanic and Atmospheric Administration (NOAA), also part of the Commerce total, would have received nearly $4.3 billion, an increase of about $355 million above fiscal 2008 and $150 million above the request.

Funding for other science activities included $17.8 billion for NASA, about $460 million above fiscal 2008 spending and $155 million more than requested. For the National Science Foundation, the committee proposed $6.9 billion, which matched the president's request and was $790 million more than fiscal 2008 spending.

The most contentious part of the markup came when Republican John Culberson of Texas, tried to bar Arizona's U.S. attorney, Diane J. Humetewa, from spending funds for travel outside Arizona or "any non-official purpose" until the attorney general determined that she was prosecuting at least 25 percent of the human trafficking, drug trafficking and illegal immigration cases referred by the Border Patrol. Culberson withdrew the amendment, but he attacked the federal prosecutor for having what he described as a lax prosecution rate for such crimes.

Ed Pastor, D-Ariz., said that Humetewa had "a distinguished track record" and that Arizona needed more federal resources to help combat those crimes. "To say that she's not willing to prosecute is absurd," Pastor said.

The committee approved several amendments by voice vote, including proposals by:

▶ Appropriations Chairman David R. Obey, D-Wis., to require the Justice Department to use a peer review process for its discretionary grant programs. Obey pointed to recent news reports about alleged mismanagement of some Justice grants.

▶ Mark Steven Kirk, R-Ill., to require the attorney general and the Homeland Security secretary to report to the Appropriations committees within a year on the three international drug gangs that were determined to "present the greatest threat to law and order in the United States" and to establish a national strategy to crack down on those gangs.

WHERE THE MONEY GOES — FISCAL 2009 APPROPRIATIONS
COMMERCE-JUSTICE-SCIENCE

HR 7322 (H Rept 110-919); S 3182 (S Rept 110-397)

(figures are in thousands of dollars of new budget authority)

	Fiscal 2008 appropriations	Fiscal 2009 Bush request	House committee approved	Senate committee approved
GRAND TOTAL	$53,734,969*	$55,929,033	$59,036,421	$60,100,709
Discretionary spending	51,803,000	54,131,519	56,857,909	57,900,000
MAIN COMPONENTS				
Justice Department	23,591,916	23,088,915	25,438,765	25,788,555
FBI	6,657,689	7,108,091	7,108,091	7,270,131
Federal Prison System	5,425,488	5,533,889	5,733,889	5,973,889
State and Local Law Enforcement	2,682,000	1,072,747	3,129,100	3,136,100
NASA	17,309,400	17,614,200	17,768,967	17,814,000
Commerce Department	6,856,534	8,216,518	8,706,889	9,402,384
NOAA	3,896,484	4,103,913	4,252,640	4,445,921
National Science Foundation	6,065,000	6,854,100	6,854,100	6,854,100

*Includes emergency appropriations.

SOURCE: House and Senate Appropriations committees

SENATE COMMITTEE ACTION

The Senate Appropriations Committee approved its bill (S 3182 — S Rept 110-397) by a vote of 29-0 on June 19. The Senate bill included $57.9 billion in discretionary funding, about $3.8 billion more than Bush requested and $6.1 billion more than enacted in fiscal 2008. The Commerce-Justice-Science Subcommittee had approved a draft of the bill by voice vote June 18.

The amount exceeded that in the House bill by about $1 billion, with some of the increase used to boost funding for Justice and the Census Bureau.

The amount for state and local law enforcement was $3.1 billion, about the same as in the House bill. The total included $580 million for Byrne grants for local police, $30 million more than in the House version, and $600 million for the COPS program, about $30 million less than in the House version.

The appropriations measure was approved with little debate and no amendments beyond a manager's amendment. As on the House side, the Senate panel's markup of the Commerce-Justice-Science bill in recent years had been characterized by heated debates over policy riders concerning firearms and English-only workplaces.

Barbara A. Mikulski, D-Md., chairwoman of the subcommittee, said she supported a potential investigation by the Homeland Security and Governmental Affairs Committee into allegations that favoritism might have played a role in the distribution of competitive Justice Department grants for law enforcement.

But Mikulski had said she was trying to keep policy riders out of the bill, including one that she had pushed aggressively the previous year to allow broader access to gun trace data for civil lawsuits.

The bill also included:

▶ $25.8 billion for the Justice Department, which was $400 million more than in the House bill.

▶ $9.4 billion for the Commerce Department, $700 million more than in the House bill.

▶ $3.2 billion from Commerce for the Census Bureau, $550 million more than in the House measure.

▶ $4.4 billion from Commerce for NOAA, which was $200 million more than in the House bill.

▶ $17.8 billion for NASA, the same as in the House bill. ∎

Defense Gets Full Year of Funding

A \$487.7 BILLION FISCAL 2009 Defense spending bill became law without being considered on the floor of either chamber. The measure was enacted as part of a year-end continuing resolution that was signed into law Sept. 30 (HR 2638 — PL 110-329).

The Defense bill provided \$4 billion less in discretionary funds for the Pentagon than President Bush requested but \$28.4 billion more than was appropriated under the fiscal 2008 law (PL 110-116), not counting supplemental funding for the wars in Iraq and Afghanistan. The bill also included an additional \$279 million in mandatory funding for CIA retirement and disability benefits. *(2007 Almanac, p. 2-14)*

The legislation generally followed the fiscal 2009 defense authorization bill (PL 110-417), which cleared Sept. 27. *(Defense authorization, p. 6-3)*

The appropriations bill provided generously for weapons programs, soldiers' pay and benefits, and readiness and equipment needs, while leaving major program decisions to the next administration. It provided more than was requested for equipment depleted by the war in Iraq, including new combat vehicles and new battle gear for the Army National Guard and reserve, while appropriating less than Bush sought for missile defense and other futuristic programs.

The bill included no emergency funding for operations in Iraq and Afghanistan or language calling for the withdrawal of U.S. forces from Iraq.

John P. Murtha, D-Pa., chairman of the House Defense Appropriations Subcommittee, said the bill was meant to direct the Pentagon to look past the Iraq and Afghanistan wars toward urgent needs at home and future threats abroad.

"This lack of strategic foresight has left our armed forces in a degraded state of readiness, has left our military facilities in disrepair, and has left many Defense acquisition programs broken or badly damaged," Murtha said.

Appropriations subcommittees in both chambers approved versions of the bill, but the measures went no further. Democratic leaders had said they hoped to send the bill to the president, but they put off action and ended up not having the time to finish it before the new fiscal year began Oct. 1.

Instead, they attached full-year fiscal 2009 funding for the Pentagon, as well as for the departments of Homeland Security and Veterans Affairs, to a continuing resolution that froze most funding for the rest of the government through March 6, 2009.

Republicans decried their exclusion from the process of drafting the overall package, but they said the Defense portion was written in a bipartisan manner and did not change much after the subcommittees weighed in.

"It's a terrible process, there's no excuse for this process, and I totally object," said C.W. Bill Young of Florida, ranking Republican on the House subcommittee. "But I am satisfied with the Defense appropriations bill; it's a good bill."

BOX SCORE 2009 FISCAL YEAR

DEFENSE

BILL: HR 2638 — PL 110-329

LEGISLATIVE ACTION:

House included the Defense bill in an amendment to HR 2638, adopted 370-58, on Sept. 24.

Senate cleared HR 2638, 78-12, on Sept. 27.

President signed Sept. 30.

HIGHLIGHTS

The fiscal 2009 Defense bill provided \$114.4 billion for military personnel (\$452 million less than requested), \$152.9 billion for operations and maintenance (\$1.9 billion less than requested), \$101.1 billion for weapons procurement (\$1.1 billion less than requested), \$80.5 billion for research and development (\$905 million more than requested), and \$25.8 billion for the Defense Health Program (\$1 billion more than requested).

The total for the bill actually could be figured in a number of ways. Appropriators said they provided a net total of \$543.6 billion for the Pentagon, but that included \$65.9 billion from a separate emergency supplemental law (PL 110-252) enacted in June. Excluding those funds brought the total to \$477.6 billion. The Pentagon also was slated to get nearly \$10.4 billion in permanently appropriated funds for retiree health benefits. When those funds were included, the total came to \$488 billion — \$487.7 billion in discretionary funds and \$279 million in mandatory spending.

The following are major components of the Defense bill:

● **Aircraft.** Appropriations included:

▸ F-22A Raptor. \$2.9 billion for 20 of the Air Force's next-generation, premier fighters, intended to replace the F-15 and designed to have both air-to-air and air-to-ground fighter capabilities. The bill also provided \$523 million in unrequested funds for the advance components for an additional lot of 20 aircraft in fiscal 2010. Bush requested \$3.1 billion for 20 planes but no funds for future aircraft.

▸ F-35 Joint Strike Fighter. \$6.7 billion, as requested, for development and procurement of the F-35. But Congress allocated funds to buy 14 planes instead of the 16 requested and set aside \$430 million for a program to develop a second, competing engine for the plane. The administration opposed the second engine, but Congress argued annually that competition would improve the final product. The aircraft, which had been subject to huge cost overruns, was planned as an affordable, next-generation, multirole fighter based on a common airframe and components to be used by the Air Force, Navy and Marine Corps.

▸ Aerial refueling tanker. \$894 million, as requested, to continue development of a new Air Force refueling tanker to replace the KC-135. The Pentagon announced in September that a new round of competitive bidding to build the tanker would be put off until the next administration took office. The first selection had been canceled after the Government Accounting Office (GAO) concluded that the Air Force had bungled the bidding process and called for it to start over. Congress put the funds into a tanker replacement fund that could be used when a new manufacturer was chosen.

● **Shipbuilding.** The bill funded the following major Navy vessels:

▸ CVN-21. \$3.9 billion, about equal to the request, for long-lead procurement of the CVN-21, the Navy's next-generation nuclear aircraft carrier scheduled to be delivered to the fleet in 2014.

▸ LPD-17 amphibious ship. \$933 million, \$830 million more than requested, for the 10th LPD-17 *San Antonio*-class ship.

WHERE THE MONEY GOES — FISCAL 2009 APPROPRIATIONS

DEFENSE

HR 2638 — PL 110-329

(figures are in thousands of dollars of new budget authority)

	Fiscal 2008 enacted*	Fiscal 2009 Bush request	Fiscal 2009 enacted
GRAND TOTAL*	**$460,303,497**	**$481,648,058**	**$477,644,889**
Total after scorekeeping**	459,594,497	492,019,058	488,015,889
Discretionary appropriations	459,331,997	491,739,858	487,736,689
MAIN COMPONENTS			
Operations and maintenance	140,062,158	154,847,272	152,949,705
Military personnel	105,292,237	114,896,340	114,443,890
Procurement	98,201,598	102,132,287	101,051,708
Research, development, testing	77,271,482	79,615,941	80,520,837
Defense Health Program	23,458,692	24,799,202	25,825,832

*Excludes emergency appropriations.
**Scorekeeping adjustment consists mainly of the addition of permanently appropriated funding for future retiree health benefits.

SOURCE: House and Senate Appropriations committees

▶ Littoral Combat Ship. $1 billion for two of the coastal-combat ships, which were small, specialized variants of the DD(X) family of future surface-combat ships. Bush requested $920 million.

▶ *Virginia*-class submarine. $3.5 billion, slightly more than requested, for procurement of the next of the attack submarines, which were slated to replace retiring *Los Angeles*-class subs and constitute the bulk of the future attack-submarine force.

▶ DDG-1000. $2.5 billion, as requested, for procurement of the Navy's next-generation destroyer, but Congress held back about $1 billion of the funds to be used toward a second vessel in fiscal 2010; the administration wanted to devote the funding to one ship.

● **Missile defense.** Almost $10 billion for missile defense, slightly less than requested. The total included funding for the deployment of a national missile defense system based in Alaska and California. It also included funds for a third interceptor site in Eastern Europe; the project faced skepticism from NATO and criticism from Russia.

● **Future Combat Systems.** $3.6 billion, roughly equal to Bush's request, for the Future Combat Systems, the Army's next generation of combat vehicles and weapons systems.

● **Military pay.** Funding for a 3.9 percent pay increase for military personnel, 0.5 percent more than Bush requested. Authorization for the increase was enacted in the defense authorization law. The bill also provided $72 million in unrequested funds for a new initiative to pay troops $500 for every month their term of service was involuntarily extended in 2009.

● **Defense Health Program.** $25.8 billion for the Defense Health Program, $1 billion more than requested and $2.4 billion above the fiscal 2008 level. Congress included $300 million for traumatic brain injury and mental health programs.

● **Other provisions.** Among thousands of other provisions, the bill:

▶ Required the Defense secretary to report to Congress within 180 days of enactment on plans for a potential closure of the detention facility at Guantánamo Bay, Cuba.

▶ Appropriated $434 million for the Nunn-Lugar program, which aided in dismantling nuclear weapons in the former Soviet Union.

▶ Appropriated $750 million in unrequested funds for National Guard and reserve equipment.

▶ Provided $750 million in unrequested funds for urgent intelligence, surveillance and reconnaissance needs identified by the Defense secretary's intelligence task force.

▶ Appropriated $266 million, $123 million less than requested, for a headquarters for a new U.S. Africa Command. A location had not been found yet.

▶ Renewed provisions in the fiscal 2008 law prohibiting torture.

LEGISLATIVE ACTION
HOUSE SUBCOMMITTEE ACTION

The House Defense Appropriations Subcommittee approved a $487.7 billion draft of the spending bill in a closed-door session July 30. There reportedly were no amendments.

The unnumbered draft bill proposed to:

▶ Fully fund the president's $6.7 billion request for the Joint Strike Fighter program but shift $785 million away from production, with $430 million devoted to the continued development of a second engine and $320 million used to allow additional testing.

▶ Allocate $893 million for the Air Force's troubled aerial refueling tanker program. Murtha said the bill would direct the Pentagon, which had taken control of the rebid from the Air Force, to follow GAO's recommendations when organizing the new competition. But the draft also included language directing the Pentagon to consider "industrial base concerns" in their evaluation, a nod to Boeing Co., which argued that its selection would bolster national security by keeping more jobs and production from going overseas.

▶ Provide funds to procure 20 F-22 fighters, plus an extra $523 million to buy long-lead items for 20 additional aircraft. Without those funds, the F-22A production line was due to close after 2009.

▶ Fully fund Bush's $3.6 billion request for the Army's Future Combat Systems.

▶ Add $1.6 billion in unrequested funds for an LPD-17 transport ship.

▶ Provide an unrequested $398 million for advance procurement of an additional *Virginia*-class submarine.

▶ Provide no funds for a third DDG-1000 destroyer, after the Navy said it wanted to halt production following the completion of two prototype vessels. The bill did include $450 million in advance procurement funds.

▶ Fully fund the Navy's Littoral Combat Ship program, which had also faced cost overruns and delays.

▶ Fund a 3.9 percent pay raise and add $1.2 billion to the personnel budget to make up for jettisoning the administration's plan to increase fees and co-payments for the Tricare health care system.

In a new initiative, Murtha's panel added $600 million to give a salary bonus to all personnel who had been held involuntarily past the end of their enlistments through the Pentagon's stop-loss program. Each soldier affected since October 2001 would receive an extra $500 per month.

On the policy side, the bill called for a report from the secretary of Defense on his plans to close the detention facility at Guantánamo and move those prisoners to U.S. facilities. It also required that war costs be included in the following year's budget request, a provision that became law in the fiscal 2007 defense authorization bill (PL 109-364) but had been met only partially by the Bush administration.

Murtha said other war policy provisions would be added when the full committee met, including language to require that troops be given time at home equal to the length of their deployments and that they be fully trained and equipped before being deployed.

Jerry Lewis of California, ranking Republican on the full committee, noted that the bill would provide less than the president requested while some of the non-security-related spending bills received multibillion-dollar increases. "This bill represents a substantial increase over last year, but cutting the funding from the Defense request to funnel it elsewhere should not be the priority," Lewis said.

Murtha said he had been promised a full committee markup and floor time for his bill in early September. But by then it was clear that there would not be enough time to pass the bill in both chambers and reconcile the differences before the month was over.

SENATE SUBCOMMITTEE ACTION

The Senate Defense Appropriations Subcommittee approved its unnumbered $487.7 billion draft bill by voice vote Sept. 10.

Subcommittee Chairman Daniel K. Inouye, D-Hawaii, said the bill would fund the purchase of 14 of the 16 F-35 fighters Bush requested for fiscal 2009 and add $495 million for a second engine. It would also fund advance procurement to keep open production lines for the F-22A fighter and the DDG-51 destroyer.

He said the National Guard and reserve would receive $750 million more than the president requested for equipment. Near-term missile defense programs would get an increase of $150 million above the president's request. Unlike the House appropriators, the Senate panel included full funding for a third DDG-1000 destroyer.

Thad Cochran of Mississippi, the committee's ranking Republican, said the bill largely mirrored the president's request. The measure would fully fund the Army's Future Combat Systems and add $750 million to the request for intelligence, surveillance and reconnaissance capabilities, he added.

The bulk of the debate at the markup was over two amendments.

Pete V. Domenici, R-N.M., successfully added language to limit the amount of enriched uranium that Russia could export commercially to the United States. Under the amendment, once an existing agreement with Moscow expired, no more than 20 percent of the enriched uranium needed by the United States could come from Russia. The amount could increase to 25 percent if Russia took steps to "down-blend," or transform, weapons-grade uranium into commercially viable forms. Domenici said Russia was delivering about 40 percent of the uranium the United States used to fuel nuclear reactors.

"I think it makes common sense that we should develop our own uranium resources and not be dependent on Russia for years to come," he said.

Dianne Feinstein, D-Calif., initially objected but was finally won over by Domenici's arguments. The amendment was adopted by voice vote.

Byron L. Dorgan, D-N.D., offered an amendment to rescind some funds previously appropriated for Iraqi reconstruction in light of Iraqi oil surpluses. Dorgan estimated that $1 billion would be rescinded. Cochran said that to reclaim money Congress had already promised would set a bad precedent.

"If we are going to have any credibility at all as a partner . . . it's shortsighted at best and dangerous at worst," he said.

The proposal was rejected, 9-10.

Senate Majority Leader Harry Reid, D-Nev., said he was looking for ways to get the bill done in September, but he never scheduled floor time.

FINAL ACTION

With the end of the fiscal year approaching, Democratic leaders attached a compromise version of the bill, worked out by House and Senate appropriators, to the continuing resolution, which put funding for much of the rest of the government on autopilot for about five months.

The House voted, 370-58, on Sept. 24 to adopt the entire continuing resolution as an amendment to HR 2638. The Senate cleared the bill, 78-12, on Sept. 27. *(House vote 632, p. H-212; Senate vote 208, p. S-46)* ∎

Chambers Split on Nuclear Programs

THE HOUSE AND SENATE Appropriations committees approved separate versions of the fiscal 2009 Energy-Water spending bill, but the legislation became caught in a broader collapse of the appropriations process and went no further. Instead, funding for the Department of Energy, the Army Corps of Engineers and the Interior Department's Bureau of Reclamation was extended at fiscal 2008 levels through March 6, 2009, under a continuing appropriations resolution signed into law Sept. 30 (PL 110-329).

Both committees proposed $33.8 billion — $33.3 billion of which was discretionary spending — when they wrote their fiscal 2009 Energy-Water bills. The discretionary total was $2.4 billion, or 8 percent, more than the agencies covered by the bill got the previous year. President Bush requested $31.2 billion in discretionary funds, an increase of about 1 percent over fiscal 2008. *(2007 Almanac, p. 2-18)*

Both committees emphasized their rejection of proposals by Bush to cut funding for renewable-energy and energy efficiency programs.

The chief difference between the bills produced by the two Appropriations committees was over the Energy Department's nuclear programs, including nuclear weapons and non-proliferation activities. In what had become an annual dispute, Senate appropriators proposed an increase of nearly 10 percent over the previous year while the House panel sought to keep funding virtually the same as in fiscal 2008.

In its report on the bill, the House panel said it had a "dim view" of Bush's request for the National Nuclear Security Administration, which sought to boost spending on U.S. atomic weapons while cutting funds for international efforts to prevent the spread of nuclear materials to risky owners. The House report called the U.S. nuclear stockpile "hyper sufficient" while noting that "a single failure of nuclear non-proliferation could have an impact on U.S. national security that would be almost immeasurably large."

Senate appropriators rejected the House's proposal for cuts and vowed to fight for the nuclear labs. Their prospects for winning the battle were diminished, however, by the fact that the most vocal supporter of the labs in the Senate — Republican Pete V. Domenici of New Mexico — was retiring at the end of 110th Congress and would not be present when the final decisions were made in 2009.

Though the continuing resolution kept most programs running at fiscal 2008 levels, it added $250 million for the Energy Department's weatherization program to help low-income families reduce energy costs with better home insulation. Bush wanted to eliminate the program, but it had strong support in Congress.

LEGISLATIVE ACTION
HOUSE COMMITTEE ACTION

The House Appropriations Committee gave voice vote approval to its Energy-Water bill (HR 7324 — H Rept 110-921) on June 25. The Energy-Water Appropriations Subcommittee had approved a draft of the bill by voice vote without amendment June 17. Before the bill could reach the floor, however, the appropriations process ground to a

---

BOX SCORE 2009 FISCAL YEAR **ENERGY-WATER**

BILLS: HR 7324, S 3258

LEGISLATIVE ACTION:

House Appropriations Committee approved HR 7324 (H Rept 110-921) by voice vote June 25.

Senate Appropriations Committee approved S 3258 (S Rept 110-416), 28-0, on July 10.

---

halt in the House as Republicans began offering offshore-oil-drilling amendments to other spending bills.

Subcommittee Chairman Peter J. Visclosky, D-Ind., worked closely with ranking Republican David L. Hobson of Ohio, who said he supported the measure "100 percent." Both were generally skeptical of the Energy Department's management of major projects and demanded that the Bush administration provide a better plan for modernizing and downsizing the nuclear weapons complex, which they said still dated from the Cold War era.

The bill's $33.3 billion in discretionary funds was about $2.1 billion more than Bush requested and $2.4 billion above fiscal 2008 enacted levels. Major elements of the House bill included:

● **Energy.** $27.2 billion for the Energy Department, $2.7 billion more than the fiscal 2008 level and $1.3 billion more than Bush's request. Within the department's budget, the bill recommended:

▸ $8.8 billion for the National Nuclear Security Administration, $274 million less than the president requested. The total included $6 billion for weapons activities, $582 million less than requested. It also included $1.5 billion for non-proliferation programs — particularly those intended to keep nuclear material away from terrorists — which was $283 million more than Bush requested.

▸ $495 million, the amount Bush requested, for the disposal site for domestic and military nuclear waste at Yucca Mountain in Nevada.

▸ $5.4 billion for Pentagon environmental cleanup programs, $76 million more than was spent in fiscal 2008 and $128 million more than Bush requested

▸ $2.5 billion for renewable-energy and energy efficiency programs, nearly $1.3 billion more than requested. The committee said the bill included $500 million for initiatives to find new sources of domestic energy and reduce consumption through conservation and investments in vehicle technology.

▸ $250 million for the weatherization assistance program that Bush wanted to kill, a $23 million increase above fiscal 2008.

● **Army Corps of Engineers.** $5.3 billion for the corps to carry out popular water and infrastructure projects, $256 million below fiscal 2008 spending. Bush asked for $4.7 billion, a cut of about $846 million from the previous year's funding.

In its report, the committee criticized the administration for its proposed cuts to the corps' budget. "Last year, this committee characterized the budget request for the corps as woefully inadequate; this year, the budget request borders on irresponsible," the report said. "This administration has clearly not learned the lessons of the Gulf Coast hurricanes and the Minnesota highway bridge collapse."

Corps water projects, carried out in districts across the country, were virtually sacrosanct in Congress. When Bush vetoed a bill authorizing funds for the projects in November 2007, Congress easily overrode him, making the bill one of just four that were enacted over a veto during Bush's eight years in office. *(2007 Almanac, p. 18-3)*

● **Interior.** $957 million, $193 million below the fiscal 2008 level, for

WHERE THE MONEY GOES — FISCAL 2009 APPROPRIATIONS
ENERGY-WATER

HR 7324 (H Rept 110-921); S 3258 (S Rept 110-416)

(figures are in thousands of dollars of new budget authority)

	Fiscal 2008 appropriations	Fiscal 2009 Bush request	House committee approved	Senate committee approved
GRAND TOTAL	**$31,508,398**	**$31,720,700**	**$33,799,000**	**$33,767,000**
Discretionary appropriations	30,888,000	31,186,700	33,265,000	33,258,000
MAIN COMPONENTS				
Energy Department	24,489,102	25,892,888	27,204,820	27,016,658
Atomic energy defense activities	15,113,140	15,995,350	15,322,269	16,457,779
National Nuclear Security Admin.*	8,810,285	9,097,262	8,823,243	9,665,770
Defense environmental cleanup	5,349,325	5,297,256	5,425,202	5,771,506
Science	4,017,711	4,721,969	4,861,669	4,640,469
Nuclear waste disposal**	386,440	494,742	494,742	388,390
Army Corps of Engineers	5,587,087	4,741,000	5,331,000	5,300,000
Interior Department	1,150,913	793,799	957,479	1,126,799

*Includes nuclear weapons and non-proliferation activities.   ** Includes civilian and military waste; the latter is also included under atomic energy defense activities.

SOURCE: House and Senate Appropriations committees

dams, canals, water treatment and other projects in the West. Bush asked for $794 million.

While the committee proposed more spending than Bush wanted for many programs, it also sought to reduce funds for several projects favored by the White House. The committee:

▶ Rejected Bush's recommendation to nearly double the size of the Strategic Petroleum Reserve, providing $173 million, about half the amount Bush requested and $14 million below fiscal 2008 funding.

▶ Provided no money for the Global Nuclear Energy Partnership, a Bush initiative aimed at recycling spent nuclear fuel to power a new generation of atomic generators while preventing terrorists from obtaining weapons-grade material. The president requested $302 million for the program.

▶ Rejected for a second straight year any funding for the Reliable Replacement Warhead, a next-generation nuclear weapons program backed by the White House.

▶ Provided none of the $145 million requested for new "pits," or fissile cores, for the W88 nuclear warhead, saying the warhead was outdated and should be put out of service.

The committee's report included a lengthy list of the earmarked projects in the bill, along with their sponsors, as required by the House. The Energy-Water bill was traditionally among the most heavily earmarked of the annual appropriations measures.

Several sections of the bill made reference to earmarked accounts in an effort to circumvent a January executive order directing federal agencies to ignore earmarks that appeared only in committee reports.

SENATE COMMITTEE ACTION

The Senate Appropriations Committee voted, 28-0, on July 10 to approve an Energy-Water bill (S 3258 — S Rept 110-416) that included $842 million more than the House panel recommended for nuclear programs. The added funding was a victory for Domenici, who had a long record of fighting for the national energy laboratories based in his state, including the nuclear weapons facility at Los Alamos.

"Senator, I've long admired your moxie," said Appropriations Chairman Robert C. Byrd, D-W.Va. "We'll miss your knowledge. We'll miss your experience. And I will miss your friendship."

The bill's $33.3 billion in discretionary funds was virtually the same as in the House version. Like the House measure, the Senate bill proposed boosts in funding for renewable-energy and energy efficiency programs that the White House had recommended cutting. The bill included:

● **Energy.** $27 billion for the department, an increase of $2.5 billion over fiscal 2008 spending, but less than the $27.2 billion in the House bill. The total included:

▶ $9.7 billion for the National Nuclear Security Administration, about $855 million above the previous year's level and $842 million more than in the House bill. The total included $6.5 billion for weapons activities, $488 million more than in the House bill, and $1.9 billion for non-proliferation programs, $379 million more than House appropriators approved.

▶ $388 million for the Yucca Mountain nuclear waste disposal site, $107 million less than the House proposed and Bush requested.

▶ $5.8 billion for defense environmental cleanup programs, about $422 million more than the fiscal 2008 appropriation and $346 million less than in the House bill.

▶ $1.9 billion for energy efficiency and renewable-energy programs, $205 million above the previous year's spending and $591 million less than in the House version.

▶ $200 million for the weatherization program, $50 million less than in the House bill.

● **Corps of Engineers.** $5.3 billion, the same called for in the House bill and roughly $600 million more than requested.

● **Interior.** $1.1 billion, a slight increase over fiscal 2008 and $169 million more than in the House version. Byrd called water programs "our nation's most neglected infrastructure."

The committee also:

▶ Rejected Bush's plan to double the size of the Strategic Petroleum Reserve, providing $205 million, $139 million less than requested and

$33 million more than the House panel proposed.

▸ Provided no funding for the Reliable Replacement Warhead.

▸ Included $145 million requested by the administration for new pits for the W88 nuclear warhead.

During the markup, Domenici spoke at length about his 25 years on the committee and the funding he had helped procure for advanced nuclear weapons, non-proliferation programs, and next-generation nuclear energy and waste-recycling programs. He had been a member of the Appropriations Committee since 1983 and either chairman or ranking member of the Energy-Water Subcommittee since 1995. "I have witnessed tremendous change on this subcommittee since I joined," Domenici said. "And I am extraordinarily proud of the work performed by the Department of Energy, including the three national security labs, the dozen Office of Science laboratories and three energy laboratories."

Energy-Water Subcommittee Chairman Byron L. Dorgan, D-N.D., made it clear he would continue to fight for the labs. "Our laboratories are our national jewels and treasures," he said. ■

Lawmakers Seek to Ease Cuba Travel

THE HOUSE APPROPRIATIONS Committee approved a $44.4 billion fiscal 2009 Financial Services spending bill in June, and Senate appropriators followed suit in July, approving a similar $44.8 billion measure. Congress took no further action on the bill, however, and funding for programs covered by the annual legislation was extended through March 6, 2009, at fiscal 2008 levels under a stopgap spending bill (PL 110-329) signed Sept. 30.

The Financial Services bill covered a diverse set of federal agencies, the judiciary, the White House and the District of Columbia. The Senate version also included the Commodity Futures Trading Commission, which was covered in another House spending bill.

About half the funding each year was for mandatory programs — mainly civil service pension plans and retiree health benefits administered by the Office of Personnel Management. The remainder was discretionary funding that lawmakers could allocate among the agencies. Most of it went to the Treasury Department.

The fiscal 2008 law (PL 110-161), which was the basis for the agencies' funding during the first five months of the new fiscal year, provided $20.7 billion in discretionary budget authority. House appropriators wanted to provide about 9 percent more in fiscal 2009. The Senate committee bill called for almost 10 percent more. *(2007 Almanac, p. 2-22)*

Both versions contained policy provisions that rankled the White House, including the easing of restrictions on travel to Cuba and a prohibition on spending federal money on a private IRS debt collection program. Similar provisions on Cuba and IRS debt collection were left out of the fiscal 2008 bill in the face of strong administration opposition.

Both also called for a 3.9 percent cost-of-living increase for federal civilian employees, a boost over President Bush's proposed 2.9 percent increase and the same amount that was ultimately approved for military personnel under the defense authorization law (PL 110-417).

Both would have continued a policy set in the fiscal 2008 law of allowing the District of Columbia to use its own local funds on a needle-exchange program for drug users. Bush opposed the policy. The House bill would have barred spending to implement a Federal Communications Commission (FCC) ruling that allowed one company to own both a newspaper and a television or radio station in the same market.

LEGISLATIVE ACTION
HOUSE COMMITTEE ACTION

The House Appropriations Committee approved a Financial Services bill (HR 7323 — H Rept 110-920) by voice vote June 25 that retained a number of controversial policy provisions written by the Financial Services Subcommittee. The subcommittee approved the bill by voice vote June 17. By the time of the full committee markup, however, the House appropriations process was coming to a halt and the bill never reached the floor.

The $44.4 billion bill included $22.5 billion in discretionary fund-

BOX SCORE 2009 FISCAL YEAR

FINANCIAL SERVICES

BILLS: HR 7323, S 3260

LEGISLATIVE ACTION:

House Appropriations Committee approved HR 7323 (H Rept 110-920) by voice vote June 25.

Senate Appropriations Committee approved S 3260 (S Rept 110-417), 29-0, on July 10.

ing, $1.8 billion more than was appropriated in fiscal 2008 and $188 million more than Bush's request.

More than half the total, $12.6 billion, was allotted to the Treasury Department, about $315 million more than in the previous year and $115 million more than Bush's request. As always, most of the department's funding — $11.4 billion in this case — was for the IRS. The bill included $60 million more than requested for taxpayer services and an amount equal to the request for enforcement. It proposed cutting $44 million from the IRS's business system modernization budget compared with fiscal 2008 funding.

The bill called for $712 million as a federal payment to the District of Columbia, $102 million above fiscal 2008 funding and $45 million more than Bush wanted. The payment was made primarily in lieu of taxes on the large amount of federal real estate in the city.

The committee endorsed a series of policy provisions that had drawn White House opposition in the past. They included proposals to:

▶ Allow family members of Cubans to travel to the communist-controlled country once a year, rather than once every three years. The definition of immediate family would have been expanded to include first cousins, aunts, uncles, nieces and nephews. Subcommittee Chairman José E. Serrano, D-N.Y., said the provision was a concession not to the Cuban government but to Cuban-Americans.

▶ Change trade policy to allow Cuba to pay for agricultural imports upon arrival. Under existing policy, Cuba had to pay for imports before they left U.S. ports.

Debbie Wasserman Schultz, D-Fla., said the Cuba provisions were a concession to a dictatorial government and asked for support in removing the language when the bill reached the House floor.

▶ Bar funds for an IRS program that allowed private debt collectors to pursue some unpaid taxes. The House had passed a bill (HR 5719) in April to eliminate the program, but it went no further. Opponents of privatized collection, including the union representing IRS employees, argued that federal workers could perform the task more efficiently and safely. Republicans said the program allowed the IRS to go after tax delinquents it would otherwise not pursue.

▶ Place a one-year moratorium on a Bush administration initiative that encouraged agencies to contract out some operations to private business.

▶ Prohibit the use of funds in the bill to implement the FCC ruling that allowed one company to own both a newspaper and a television or radio station in the same market. In May, the Senate had voted to nullify the rule. "There should have been a lot more limitations on ownership a long time ago," said House Appropriations Chairman David R. Obey, D-Wis. "It's the only vehicle around."

▶ Reject a Bush administration proposal to remove provisions enacted in the 2008 spending law that allowed the District of Columbia to spend local funds for a needle-exchange program and for lobbying Congress for a voting representative or for statehood.

The committee narrowly defeated a proposal to create a commis-

WHERE THE MONEY GOES — FISCAL 2009 APPROPRIATIONS

FINANCIAL SERVICES

HR 7323 (H Rept 110-920); S 3260 (S Rept 110-417)

(figures are in thousands of dollars of new budget authority)

	Fiscal 2008 appropriations	Fiscal 2009 Bush request	House committee approved	Senate committee approved
GRAND TOTAL	**$44,639,154**	**$44,196,913**	**$44,406,639**	**$44,750,883**
Discretionary spending	20,710,266	22,337,274	22,525,000	22,870,000
MAIN COMPONENTS				
Treasury Department	12,262,800	12,462,724	12,577,599	12,699,443
Internal Revenue Service	11,094,519	11,361,509	11,398,464	11,524,848
Executive Office of the President	679,959	695,529	697,444	748,083
Federal Judiciary	6,246,074	6,721,191	6,524,837	6,517,619
Office of Personnel Management	21,110,266	20,357,911	20,358,411	20,362,475
District of Columbia	609,853	666,918	711,745	722,023

SOURCE: House and Senate Appropriations committees

sion to look at the growing gap between anticipated revenue and the costs of major entitlement programs such as Medicare and Social Security, which had sparked an impassioned debate.

The committee narrowly rejected an amendment by Frank R. Wolf, R-Va., that would have added the text of a separate bill (HR 3654) aimed at creating such a commission. The panel would have been charged with developing legislation to limit the growth in entitlement spending, as well as to examine the implications of foreign ownership of the U.S. debt instruments that finance the deficit. The proposal was rejected, 31-32.

"The Chinese hold a large portion of our debt," said Wolf, who cosponsored the entitlement bill with Jim Cooper, D-Tenn. "They are our banker. The Saudis . . . are our bankers. Our country is facing a terrible crisis, and we have to deal with it."

The sponsors were energized by the narrow vote and made plans to put together a group of three Republicans and three Democrats to address issues raised in the committee. Questions included whether the commission would delegate congressional responsibility to the executive branch and require Congress to vote on the panel's recommendations under a fast-track system. Obey said the Rules Committee would not have allowed the provision to be considered on the floor because of jurisdictional concerns.

SENATE COMMITTEE ACTION

The Senate Appropriations Committee approved a $44.8 billion version of the bill (S 3260 — S Rept 110-417) by a vote of 29-0 on July 10. The panel's Financial Services and General Government Subcommittee approved the bill, 9-0, on July 9. The $22.9 billion in discretionary funds in the bill was $2.2 billion more than fiscal 2008 spending and $533 million more than Bush had requested.

Like the House bill, the measure contained several provisions that were sharply opposed by the White House. Foremost among them were proposals to relax the rules on family visits to Cuba and permit travel to Cuba for the purpose of marketing and selling agriculture and medical goods. Richard J. Durbin, D-Ill., the chairman of the subcommittee, said the bill would restore the rights of families to visit relatives in Cuba

to pre-2004 levels by allowing a trip once a year rather than once every three years, an unlimited stay rather than a 14-day stay and a spending limit of $170 per day rather than $50 per day. Subcommittee ranking Republican Sam Brownback of Kansas said the provision was "very sensitive" and needed additional consideration.

The bill allocated $12.7 billion to the Treasury Department, about $120 million more than the House committee proposed. It was about $435 million more than fiscal 2008 spending and $235 million more than the administration's request. The IRS was slated to get $11.5 billion, including nearly $5.1 billion for enforcement and $2.2 billion for taxpayer services.

The measure included a $722 million federal payment to the District of Columbia, $10 million more than in the House bill and $55 million above the level requested by the president.

Durbin said funding for the District of Columbia's school voucher program would be continued but that the program would have to be reauthorized before the money could be spent. He said his concerns were that voucher schools had been found to be unsafe, had teachers without college degrees and had not been proven successful.

Durbin also included $95 million for the Consumer Product Safety Commission, which was $15 million more than both fiscal 2008 spending and Bush's request. The committee said the funding was sufficient to pay for a database for consumer complaints, as well as to hire additional staff for the inspector general, for new rule-making, and for inspections in China and other parts of Asia.

Among other policy prescriptions, the bill proposed to:

► Prohibit spending any funds in the bill on the IRS program that allowed private debt collectors to pursue some unpaid taxes.

► Allow the District of Columbia to use its own local funds on a needle-exchange program for drug users.

► Halt any new privatization studies or job competitions, in an effort to allow the next president to determine federal workforce policies.

The bill did not contain the House prohibition on using funds to implement the FCC ruling allowing one company to own both a newspaper and a television or radio station in the same market. ■

Full-Year Homeland Bill Enacted

FUNDING FOR HOMELAND SECURITY was a priority for lawmakers, particularly in an election year. As a result, Congress provided full-year fiscal 2009 appropriations for the Department of Homeland Security at a time when many agencies got only stopgap funding until early March 2009.

The Homeland Security spending bill was one of three fiscal 2009 measures attached to the short-term continuing resolution, which froze funding for most other government programs at fiscal 2008 levels. The other full-year bills were for Defense and Military Construction-VA. President Bush signed the package into law Sept. 30.

The bill appropriated $41.2 billion for the Homeland Security Department. Of the total, $40.1 billion was discretionary funding — $2.4 billion, or nearly 7 percent, more than Bush requested. The remainder was mandatory spending. The department also gained access to an additional $2.2 billion for Project Bioshield, a program created to spur the development of drugs and other countermeasures against biological weapons. The money had been appropriated in fiscal 2004 (PL 108-90) on the condition that it not be released until fiscal 2009.

The House and Senate Appropriations committees approved versions of the bill in June that would have provided discretionary funding of $39.9 billion and $40.1 billion, respectively. The differences between the bills were minor, but neither measure reached the floor. As a result, the White House did not issue policy statements on them, but the administration generally warned that fiscal 2009 spending bills that exceeded the president's request would be vetoed.

Most of the increase in discretionary spending over Bush's request — about $2 billion in the final bill — was used for grants to help state and local governments prepare for and respond to terrorist attacks. Bush and many Republicans argued that the states already had received billions of dollars for homeland security and that a slowdown in new appropriations was warranted. Democrats maintained the additional funding still was needed because the states and cities were at the front line of homeland security.

Harold Rogers of Kentucky, the top Republican on the House Homeland Security Appropriations Subcommittee, said he could support the final bill, especially after Democrats worked to adopt changes he favored, such as increased funds for border security fencing. "It's a good, sturdy, steady bill," he said.

Among other things, the final bill included funds to pay for 4,361 new border protection personnel in the Customs and Border Protection agency and 1,400 more detention beds for Immigration and Customs Enforcement. It also provided $775 million for border fencing and technology and $404 million for container security.

Not all programs received more than Bush sought. Funding for two that had not met lawmakers' expectations — US-VISIT, a program that screened foreigners entering and exiting the United States, and the Domestic Nuclear Detection Office — came in below the request. US-

BOX SCORE 2009 FISCAL YEAR

HOMELAND SECURITY

BILL: HR 2638 — PL 110-329

....

LEGISLATIVE ACTION:

Senate committee approved S 3181 (S Rept 110-396), 29-0, on June 19.

House committee approved HR 6947 (H Rept 110-862) by voice vote June 24.

House included the Homeland bill in an amendment to HR 2638, adopted 370-58, on Sept. 24.

Senate cleared HR 2638, 78-12, on Sept. 27.

President signed Sept. 30.

VISIT received $300 million, 23 percent less than Bush wanted. The Domestic Nuclear Detection Office got $514 million, 9 percent less than requested.

The bill required the department to report to Congress on the implementation of US-VISIT and other programs, and it blocked the department from implementing a new personnel system.

HIGHLIGHTS

The following are major components of the Homeland Security section of the continuing resolution:

● **Customs and Border Protection.** $9.8 billion in discretionary appropriations — about $330 million, or 4 percent, above Bush's request and 24 percent more than was provided under the fiscal 2008 law. The bureau was expected to take in an additional $1.4 billion in fees, mainly for inspections, bringing the total to $11.3 billion. Although the bill included $775 million for fencing along the U.S.-Mexico border, it withheld $400 million until the Appropriations committees received and approved a detailed plan for expenditures. The department also was required to meet certain consultation requirements in existing law.

● **Immigration and Customs Enforcement.** $5 billion in discretionary appropriations — an increase of $240 million, or 5 percent, over Bush's budget and 19 percent above fiscal 2008 funding, including emergency appropriations. An additional $300 million in fees brought the total available to $5.3 billion. About $1 billion was set aside to identify and deport illegal immigrants convicted of crimes. And $2.5 billion of the amount in the account for salaries and expenses was dedicated to detention and removal operations.

● **FEMA.** $7 billion for the Federal Emergency Management Agency — $1.4 billion or nearly 26 percent more than requested and about 4 percent more than fiscal 2008 appropriations, not counting more than $2.9 billion in emergency disaster appropriations for that year.

The total included:

▶ $4.2 billion for homeland security grants, mostly for state and local governments and for training, nearly double the $2.2 billion that Bush requested. The grants included assistance to big cities considered at high risk for terrorist attacks, funds to be distributed among all states, and assistance for firefighters and port and transit security.

▶ $1.3 billion for disaster relief, about $620 million or 4 percent less than requested and about the same as in the fiscal 2008 law, although FEMA got an additional $2.9 billion for disaster relief that year.

● **Transportation Security Administration.** $4.4 billion for the TSA, an increase of about 8 percent above fiscal 2008 funding and 7 percent more than requested. An additional $2.6 billion in anticipated fees brought the total available to the agency to $7 billion. Aviation security accounted for more than half the total, with $2.4 billion in appropriations and $2.3 billion in fees. Of the total, $3.9 billion was set aside for screening operations.

WHERE THE MONEY GOES — FISCAL 2009 APPROPRIATIONS

HOMELAND SECURITY

HR 2638 — PL 110-329

(figures are in thousands of dollars of new budget authority)

	Fiscal 2008 enacted*	Fiscal 2009 Bush request	House committee approved	Senate committee approved	Fiscal 2009 enacted
GRAND TOTAL**	$38,746,643	$38,849,658	$41,136,745	$41,313,745	$41,225,245
Discretionary spending	35,099,172	37,621,913	39,929,000	40,108,800	40,069,873
MAIN COMPONENTS					
Customs and Border Protection**	10,807,504	10,935,334	11,142,326	11,188,994	11,268,886
Immigration and Customs Enforcement**	4,968,217	5,046,905	5,112,171	5,288,210	5,288,210
Transportation Security Administration**	6,813,510	7,101,553	6,963,527	6,886,677	6,977,358
Coast Guard	8,631,695	9,071,386	9,206,449	9,216,181	9,361,052
Secret Service	1,385,496	1,414,346	1,370,845	1,418,004	1,412,954
Federal Emergency Management Agency	9,706,470	5,544,711	7,407,425	7,327,997	6,962,906

*Includes emergency appropriations.
**Includes fees.

SOURCE: House and Senate Appropriations committees

● **U.S. Coast Guard.** $9.4 billion, about $290 million or 3 percent more than Bush wanted and 9 percent above the previous year's level. Congress included $1 billion for the Integrated Deepwater Systems modernization program, the Coast Guard's multibillion-dollar program to replace aging ships and aircraft. That was about $250 million or 32 percent above fiscal 2008 funding and $44 million more than Bush sought.

LEGISLATIVE ACTION
HOUSE COMMITTEE ACTION

The House Appropriations Committee approved a $41.1 billion bill (HR 6947 — H Rept 110-862) by voice vote June 24 that included $39.9 billion in discretionary funding — $2.3 billion more than Bush's request. The Homeland Security Subcommittee, which drafted the bill, had approved it by voice vote June 11.

The committee proposed withholding about $1.4 billion — including funding for fencing along the U.S.-Mexico border — until the department submitted planning documentation to Congress. "We require the department to provide an analysis of its proposed infrastructure and technology solution for individual border segments," said David E. Price, D-N.C., chairman of the Homeland Security Subcommittee. Price said the department would be required "to manage its programs efficiently and robustly and to ensure that programs comply with all laws before they begin operations."

The bill proposed:
▸ $11.1 billion for Customs and Border Protection, including fees.
▸ $5.1 billion for Immigration and Customs Enforcement, including fees.
▸ $7 billion for TSA, including fees.
▸ $9.2 billion for the Coast Guard, including $934 million for Deepwater.
▸ $7.4 billion for FEMA, including $4.2 billion for state and local grants and training.

Democrats' demand to require more accountability to Congress on border fence construction drew strong opposition from Republicans. Among other things, the bill proposed to withhold $400 million until the committee received and approved a detailed expenditure plan. The committee report on the bill said the initial fiscal 2008 plan "did not provide the information and level of detail required. Some requirements were completely ignored, including the comparison of alternatives to fencing as a means to achieve effective control on the border. The Committee directs [the bureau] to comply fully with the requirements of the law in its fiscal year 2009 expenditure plan."

An attempt by Rogers to strip out the language was defeated on a 27-36 party-line vote. "The onerous consultation requirements and the detailed analysis hurdles are so pervasive, it seems like the bill is determined to actually stop the border fence in its tracks," Rogers said. "This is clearly, to me, oversight gone overboard."

Price said there was nothing "illegitimate" or "obstructive" about the requirements and said the department had $352 million available for building fences. "Careful analysis is needed; billions of dollars are at stake," Price said.

The committee adopted an amendment by Price to allow the TSA to determine whether an airport needed to participate in a pilot program requiring vetting of airport employees who worked beyond security checkpoints to ensure they were eligible to work. Price offered his plan as a substitute for a Republican proposal to limit access to secured airport areas to employees who had been verified as American citizens or permanent residents.

The committee gave voice-vote approval to:
▸ An amendment by Rogers to dedicate $5 million for FEMA to study the effectiveness of homeland security grants for police, firefighters, emergency medical services, ports and public transportation services.
▸ An amendment by Price to allocate $5.7 million for Immigration and Customs Enforcement's cybercrime investigation operations, with offsetting funding reductions to be determined later.
▸ An amendment by Tom Latham, R-Iowa, to provide roughly

$94 million in emergency funding for loans to Midwestern states recently ravaged by major floods.

SENATE COMMITTEE ACTION

The Senate Appropriations Committee approved a $41.3 billion version of the bill (S 3181 — S Rept 110-396) by a vote of 29-0 on June 19. The total included $40.1 billion in discretionary funding, which was only about $180 million more than in the House committee version. The Homeland Security Subcommittee approved a draft of the bill by voice vote June 18.

The committee agreed to provide $4.1 billion for grants for police, fire and emergency personnel, rejecting Bush's proposal to cut the grants by nearly 50 percent from the previous year.

"We plan to send the president a bill that exceeds his request, and I hope that he again has the wisdom to sign it," said Robert C. Byrd, D-W.Va., the chairman of the Appropriations Committee and its Homeland Security Subcommittee. Bush signed Homeland Security bills that provided more than he sought in fiscal 2007 and 2008.

The Senate bill included:

▸ $11.2 billion for Customs and Border Protection, including fees, which was $40 million more than in the House bill. The total included $775 million for border fencing, infrastructure and related technology and $403 million for construction of Border Patrol facilities and repairs to land-border ports of entry.

▸ $5.3 billion for Immigration and Customs Enforcement, including fees. The total was $166 million above the House number.

▸ $9.2 billion for the Coast Guard, with about $1 billion for Deepwater. The figures were about the same as in the House bill.

▸ $7.3 billion for FEMA, about $80 million less than called for in the House bill.

▸ $6.9 billion for TSA, counting fees, about the same called for in the House bill.

The committee gave voice vote approval to a manager's amendment containing proposals mainly from Democrats. It included a proposal by Byrd and ranking Republican Thad Cochran of Mississippi that struck language in the bill that would have required Customs and Border Protection to submit plans for southern border fencing projects to the committee before it could receive $175 million in related funding. It also included language by Mary L. Landrieu, D-La., instructing the administration to reimburse police, fire and criminal justice facilities damaged by hurricanes Katrina and Rita for any eligible costs.

Dianne Feinstein, D-Calif., said she would probably introduce an amendment on the Senate floor to require the department to verify both the arrival and departure of foreign visitors under the Visa Waiver Program. Feinstein said the program, which allowed residents from 27 countries to enter the United States without a visa, was "the soft underbelly" in Homeland Security because the department only confirmed departures. ∎

Republicans Force End to Drilling Ban

APPROPRIATORS HAD BARELY gotten started on the fiscal 2009 Interior Department spending bill when the whole House appropriations process broke down. A continuing resolution (PL 110-329), signed Sept. 30, kept programs covered by all the unfinished fiscal 2009 bills operating at fiscal 2008 levels through March 6, 2009.

The Interior bill also funded the EPA, U.S. Forest Service, Smithsonian and other cultural institutions. The only action on the bill was a markup in the House Appropriations Subcommittee on Interior, Environment and Related Agencies.

The panel's draft bill included $27.9 billion in discretionary funding — $1.3 billion, or 5 percent, more than was appropriated in fiscal 2008 (PL 110-161). President Bush had asked for $25.8 billion.

Norm Dicks, D-Wash., chairman of the subcommittee, said he wanted to restore funding to a number of programs that had been subject to years of cuts under the Bush administration.

The draft included a controversial provision that would have forced oil and natural gas companies to renegotiate offshore-drilling leases that granted royalty relief in 1998 and 1999, costing taxpayers billions. Democratic appropriators wrote the provision into the fiscal 2008 House Interior bill, but Senate appropriators rejected the plan and it was left out of the final bill in conference. *(2007 Almanac, p. 2-30)*

Republicans had an oil-drilling proposal of their own: They wanted to expand domestic energy production, including oil and gas drilling off the Pacific and Atlantic coasts.

They had been trying to force votes on the issue in both chambers, hoping to force Democrats to back down or to have to defend their position in the November election.

In what ranking Republican Jerry Lewis of California acknowledged was "highly unusual," Republicans attempted to substitute the text of the Interior-Environment bill into the Labor-Health and Human Services-Education spending measure, which was scheduled for a markup in the full committee. The purpose was to make amendments on domestic energy production in order. Lewis said it was the only way they could debate the Interior bill. "I have it from very good sources that they do not have the intent to bring up the [Interior measure] unless they have the votes to kill the energy amendments," Lewis said.

Chairman David R. Obey, D-Wis., responded by calling off the June 26 committee markup and refusing to consider any more fiscal 2009 bills. He said Republicans were trying to disrupt the appropriations process for political reasons. "It won't be just one amendment. They will have amendment after amendment after amendment. This is filibuster by amendment," he said.

In the end, larger disputes between Democrats and the White House over domestic funding led Democratic leaders in both chambers to put off finishing the bills until Bush was out of office.

Although Republicans lost the battle, they later forced Democrats to drop longstanding language in the Interior bill that had banned most new drilling off the Atlantic and Pacific coasts. It was their price for allowing Congress to finish the continuing resolution in time for the Oct. 1 start of the new fiscal year. *(Offshore drilling, p. 8-3)*

BOX SCORE 2009 FISCAL YEAR INTERIOR-ENVIRONMENT

BILL: House draft

LEGISLATIVE ACTION:

House Interior-Environment Appropriations Subcommittee approved draft bill by voice vote June 11.

LEGISLATIVE ACTION
HOUSE SUBCOMMITTEE ACTION

The House Interior-Environment Appropriations Subcommittee approved its draft of the fiscal 2009 bill by voice vote June 11.

Dicks proposed substantial increases for programs to benefit American Indians, including $3.6 billion for the Indian Health Service, a 7.5 percent boost over fiscal 2008, and $2.4 billion for the Bureau of Indian Affairs, a 5 percent increase. Dicks said some of the increases would go to recruit health professionals and help tribes deal with methamphetamine and domestic violence issues.

Democrats rejected a Bush proposal to slash funding for the Clean Water State Revolving Loan Fund, which helped states pay to upgrade wastewater treatment facilities. The bill called for $850 million, $161 million above the enacted level and $295 million above the request.

Other proposed funding in the draft included:

● **Interior Department.** $10.5 billion, 6 percent more than the fiscal 2008 level and 7 percent more than Bush requested. Besides the Bureau of Indian Affairs the funding included:

▸ $1.4 billion for the U.S. Fish and Wildlife Service, 5 percent above fiscal 2008 and 11 percent more than requested. Dicks said he included $469 million, a $35 million increase over fiscal 2008, for refuges run by the National Wildlife Refuge System. Dicks said that 200 refuges had "no staff at all to protect the wildlife and serve the visitor."

▸ $2.1 billion for National Park Service operations, slightly less than requested but nearly 8 percent above fiscal 2008 spending.

● **EPA.** $7.8 billion for the EPA, a 5 percent increase over fiscal 2008 and nearly 10 percent more than requested.

● **Forest Service.** $2.6 billion for the Agriculture Department's Forest Service, excluding fire fighting programs, which was a 4 percent increase over fiscal 2008 and 22 percent more than Bush sought. Dicks said Bush's proposal to cut $400 million would have "devastated" the service. The draft also included $3 billion for wildland fire activities coordinated between the Interior Department and the Forest Service.

● **Arts.** $791 million for the Smithsonian Institution, a 16 percent above fiscal 2008, and $160 million each for the National Endowments for the Arts and the Humanities, an 11 percent increase for each.

Most of the debate centered on an amendment by John E. Peterson, R-Pa., to allow oil and natural gas drilling between 50 and 200 miles off the Pacific and Atlantic coasts and in the eastern Gulf of Mexico. The amendment, rejected, 6-9, would have ended a longstanding moratorium on such drilling.

Peterson called expanded drilling the most important legislative issue in his time in office. He touted the safety record of the oil and gas industries in drilling in deep water, saying there has not been an offshore drilling accident since 1969.

Dicks responded that the Minerals Management Service estimated that 82 percent of the known natural gas reserves and 79 percent of the known oil reserves in the outer continental shelf were in areas open for drilling. Dicks also chastised the Commodity Futures Trading Commission for "not doing its job" in looking into speculation as a reason for increased oil costs. ∎

Pell Grants, LIHEAP Get Boosts in CR

FUNDING FOR THE departments of Labor, Health and Human Services (HHS) and Education was frozen at fiscal 2008 levels through March 6, 2009, under a continuing resolution enacted Sept. 30 (HR 2638 — PL 110-329).

Like the other fiscal 2009 bills for domestic programs, the Labor-HHS-Education measure was a casualty of a breakdown in the appropriations process. Democratic leaders signaled early in the year that they would put off the spending bills until the next administration rather than accept President Bush's limits on domestic spending. Pre-election sparring between Republicans and Democrats also contributed to the collapse.

Although discretionary spending accounted for only about 25 percent of the bill, it was still far more than was provided in any of the other spending bills, except for Defense. The remainder of the funding was for mandatory programs, such as Medicare and Medicaid, over which appropriators had virtually no control.

Fiscal 2008 funding for programs under the Labor-HHS-Education bill totaled $600.5 billion, with about $144.8 billion for discretionary programs. With some exceptions, funding for the first five months of fiscal 2009 was continued at that level. *(2007 Almanac, p. 2-34)*

Bush had requested $145.4 billion for discretionary programs in fiscal 2009, an increase of less than 1 percent. But appropriators in both chambers approved significantly more.

Versions of the bill approved in June by the House Labor-HHS-Education Appropriations Subcommittee and the full Senate Appropriations Committee would have increased fiscal 2009 discretionary funding to $153.1 billion, about 6 percent more than provided under the fiscal 2008 law (PL 110-161) and 5 percent more than Bush wanted.

The cost alone set the legislation up for an almost certain veto. Senate Democrats further antagonized the administration by including a provision that would have negated a controversial administration directive, sent to state health directors in August 2007, establishing new requirements for receiving federal funding for their children's health insurance programs. Many states saw the new mandates as onerous and lobbied Congress to step in. The Government Accountability Office had said the directive was illegal.

Progress on both versions ended for the year on June 26, when Republicans on the House Appropriations Committee tried to use the bill as a means to force votes on expanding domestic oil drilling. At that point, Appropriations Chairman David R. Obey, D-Wis., halted further action on that and most of the other spending bills. Obey had the support of Speaker Nancy Pelosi, D-Calif., who fiercely opposed oil drilling off the coast of California and did not want to allow Republicans any opportunity to score a victory on the issue in an election year.

Although the continuing resolution (CR) kept most accounts at fiscal 2008 levels, it did include increases for a few programs. For example, the Pell grant program for low-income college students received $16.8 billion, not as much as appropriators had approved but up $2.6 billion from fiscal 2008. The Low Income Home Energy As-

BOX SCORE 2009 FISCAL YEAR

LABOR-HHS-EDUCATION

BILLS: House draft, S 3230

LEGISLATIVE ACTION:

House Appropriations subcommittee approved draft bill by voice vote June 19.

Senate Appropriations Committee approved S 3230 (S Rept 110-410), 26-3, on June 26.

sistance Program (LIHEAP) to assist the poor with home energy bills got $5.1 billion, an increase of $2.5 billion and almost double the amount provided in fiscal 2008 or approved by either Appropriations panel.

There was no extra funding in the CR for the National Institutes of Health (NIH), which was kept at its fiscal 2008 level of $29.2 billion. Bush had proposed no increase, but appropriators in both chambers wanted at least $1 billion more for the agency responsible for funding much of the nation's biomedical research.

LEGISLATIVE ACTION
HOUSE SUBCOMMITTEE ACTION

The House Labor-HHS-Education Appropriations Subcommittee gave voice vote approval June 19 to a $626.5 billion draft Labor-HHS-Education bill. The $153.1 billion in discretionary spending was $7.8 billion more than Bush wanted and $8.3 billion more than in the fiscal 2008 law.

The biggest increases in the draft included:

▶ $30.4 billion for NIH, $1.2 billion above the fiscal 2008 law. Bush had requested a freeze at the fiscal 2008 level.

▶ $17.3 billion for Pell grants, $3.1 billion above the fiscal 2008 level and about $395 million more than Bush wanted. The amount was enough to increase the maximum grant amount by $169, to $4,410.

▶ $7.1 billion for the Head Start early childhood education program, $1.6 billion above fiscal 2008 funding and $1.5 billion more than requested. However, the panel did not include any advance funding for the following year. Both the fiscal 2008 law and Bush's budget included an additional $1.4 billion for that purpose.

▶ $2.8 billion for LIHEAP, $200 million above fiscal 2008 spending and $770 million more than requested.

HOUSE COMMITTEE ACTION

The full Appropriations Committee attempted to mark up the bill June 26, but the session adjourned in chaos after Republicans tried to maneuver the panel into voting on proposals to expand oil and gas drilling. It was one of many times during the year that Republicans sought ways to demonstrate their support for more domestic drilling while forcing their Democratic critics to cast votes they hoped would alienate voters already upset by high gasoline prices.

When Obey brought up the Labor-HHS-Education bill, Jerry Lewis of California, the senior Republican on the panel, stood and said he was offering a "highly unusual" amendment — one that would strip the bill's text and replace it with the text of the Interior-Environment spending bill. Debating the Interior-Environment measure would have opened the door for drilling amendments.

"I believe that it would be unconscionable to leave for the Fourth of July recess without doing anything to address skyrocketing gas prices," Lewis said.

"It's stunts like this that make people hate Washington," Obey retorted.

WHERE THE MONEY GOES — FISCAL 2009 APPROPRIATIONS
LABOR-HHS-EDUCATION

House draft; S 3230 (S Rept 110-410)

(figures are in thousands of dollars of new budget authority)

	Fiscal 2008 appropriations	Fiscal 2009 Bush request	House subcommittee approved	Senate committee approved
GRAND TOTAL	$600,467,001	$618,688,815	$626,531,029	$626,474,029
Discretionary spending	144,840,500	145,353,786	153,121,000	153,139,000
MAIN COMPONENTS				
Department of Health and Human Services	476,596,497	493,613,789	498,881,421	498,039,493
Medicare	188,445,000	195,308,000	195,308,000	195,308,000
Medicaid state grants	208,920,725	221,035,069	221,035,069	221,035,069
National Institutes of Health	29,229,524	29,229,524	30,379,524	30,254,524
Children and Family Services	8,970,491	8,493,210	9,305,723	9,184,205
Department of Education	62,055,509	63,027,229	66,590,258	65,473,145
Education for the disadvantaged Title I grants	13,898,875	14,304,901	14,454,901	14,529,901
Special education grants	10,947,511	11,284,511	11,551,5111	11,424,511
Department of Labor	14,608,917	13,451,707	15,129,564	15,263,189

SOURCE: House Labor-HHS-Education Appropriations Subcommittee; Senate Appropriations Committee

John E. Peterson, R-Pa., tried to offer an amendment to Lewis' amendment that would have allowed oil and gas drilling between 50 and 200 miles offshore in the Pacific, Atlantic and Eastern Gulf of Mexico. Republicans also planned to offer amendments to open the Arctic National Wildlife Refuge to drilling and to allow a leasing program for oil shale in Western states. Peterson said Democrats were "afraid" of votes to expand domestic oil production.

At that point, Norm Dicks, D-Wash., moved that the committee adjourn. The motion prevailed, 35-27, and the meeting ended. An angry Obey threatened to call off the whole appropriations process. "I'll see them in September on a CR," he said of the Republicans.

SENATE COMMITTEE ACTION

The Senate Appropriations Committee approved a similar bill (S 3230 — S Rept 110-410) by a vote of 26-3 on June 26. Like the House version, the measure would have appropriated $626.5 billion, including $153.1 billion in discretionary spending. The Labor-HHS-Education Subcommittee, which drafted the bill, approved it by voice vote June 24.

The full committee gave voice vote approval to amendments by:

▶ Frank R. Lautenberg, D-N.J., to negate the Aug. 17, 2008, directive telling state health directors of new requirements they had to meet before enrolling families making more than 250 percent of the federal poverty level, or $53,000 for a family of four, in the federally assisted children's health insurance program.

▶ Wayne Allard, R-Colo., to direct the NIH to take steps toward developing a new standard for conflicts of interest for scientists who received NIH grant funding but do their research outside of the NIH.

Because of the blowup in the House, however, prospects for the bill were uncertain. Senate Majority Whip Richard J. Durbin, D-Ill., said he did not expect the Senate to vote on any of the annual spending bills during the summer except for the Defense bill.

Increases above fiscal 2008 levels in the bill included:

▶ $30.3 billion for NIH, an increase of about $1 billion over fiscal 2008 and Bush's request but about $125 million less than in the House draft.

▶ $16.9 billion for Pell grants, $2.7 billion more than in the fiscal 2008 law but about $50 million less than requested and $445 million less than in the House draft. It was enough to raise the maximum grant to $4,310.

▶ $5.7 billion for Head Start, about $225 million more than the program got in fiscal 2008, plus $1.4 billion in advance funding for fiscal 2010. The total was about the same as in the House draft.

▶ $2.6 billion for LIHEAP, equal to fiscal 2008 funding and $570 million more than requested but $200 million less than in the House version.

The Senate Appropriations Committee agreed with House appropriators in proposing to eliminate funding for Reading First, a program begun under Bush that once provided $1 billion a year to school districts to help elementary school students improve their reading skills. The Education Department's inspector general had found the program plagued by scandal, and the department had published research showing that the program failed to improve reading scores.

The Senate bill also targeted other Bush priorities. It proposed to cut funding for abstinence-only sex education at schools by 25 percent, to $85 million; Bush had requested $141 million. It proposed cutting grants to faith-based groups made through the Compassion Capital Fund to $43 million, 19 percent below fiscal 2008 funding and 43 percent less than Bush had sought. ∎

Funding for Congress a Non-Starter

LAWMAKERS ARE NEVER comfortable with the image of funding their own operations before clearing at least one of the year's other spending bills. For fiscal 2009, that meant virtually no work was done on the Legislative Branch appropriations measure.

In the end, only the security-related spending bills for fiscal 2009 were completed. Funding for the legislative branch, like that for all federal domestic agencies, was continued at fiscal 2008 levels through March 6, 2009, under a continuing resolution enacted Sept. 30 (PL 110-329).

The Legislative Branch bill funded the operations of the House, Senate and various congressional agencies such as the Government Accountability Office (GAO), Congressional Budget Office (CBO), Capitol Police and Library of Congress.

The House Appropriations subcommittee responsible for the bill approved a draft in June, but that was as far as the measure went. A few days later, a blowup in the full committee over GOP oil-drilling amendments brought an end to the committee's action for the year. The prospects for the bill had appeared dim in any case: Democratic leaders indicated early in the year that they would start the appropriations process but not send President Bush spending bills that he would veto.

The fiscal 2008 legislative branch spending law (PL 110-161) provided $3.97 billion. House and Senate appropriators had informally agreed on roughly $4.4 billion for fiscal 2009. *(2007 Almanac, p. 2-39)*

LEGISLATIVE ACTION
HOUSE SUBCOMMITTEE ACTION

The House Legislative Branch Appropriations Subcommittee approved a draft of the fiscal 2009 bill by voice vote June 23. The measure proposed funding of $3.4 billion for the legislative branch, excluding spending devoted to the Senate, which traditionally added its costs

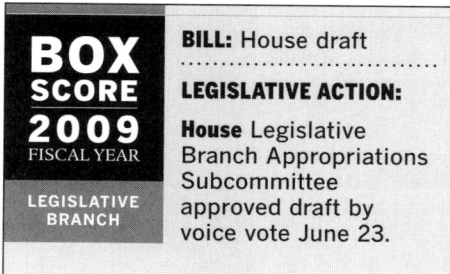

BOX SCORE 2009 FISCAL YEAR

LEGISLATIVE BRANCH

BILL: House draft

LEGISLATIVE ACTION:

House Legislative Branch Appropriations Subcommittee approved draft by voice vote June 23.

later. The total in the House draft consisted of about $1.2 billion for House operations and $2.5 billion for related agencies, which were jointly controlled by both chambers.

Senate appropriators did not mark up a companion bill, but aides said it would have allotted approximately $800,000 for Senate-side operations.

The House subcommittee put off a decision on whether Congress should foot the cost of visitors' bus rides between Union Station and the entrance of the new Capitol Visitor Center, leaving the matter for the full committee. The distance was only a few blocks to the Capitol, making it an easy walk for the physically fit, but not for everyone.

Because the draft was not approved by the full committee, the bill was not formally introduced and no report was filed.

In her opening statement, subcommittee Chairwoman Debbie Wasserman Schultz, D-Fla., said the legislative branch faced a $1.4 billion backlog of critical infrastructure projects, "including many health and safety items, as well as a growing strain on our agencies' ability to provide the support we need to sustain our reinvigorated oversight efforts."

The chairwoman said the draft included about $517 million for the GAO, an $8.5 million boost over fiscal 2008 funding. She said the increase would enable the GAO to rebuild its staff, which she said was at the lowest level in the agency's history.

Wasserman Schultz said the draft included a $1 million increase to build up CBO's ability to analyze health care issues and provide more timely cost estimates. CBO received $37 million in fiscal 2008.

The subcommittee also said the draft would provide $34.5 million, up from $12.5 million in fiscal 2008, for the Library of Congress to convert talking books for the blind to digital format so that the project could be completed in three years instead of six. ■

Bill Boosts Health Care for Veterans

VETERANS' HEALTH CARE programs got a substantial boost under the fiscal 2009 spending bill for the Department of Veterans Affairs (VA) and Pentagon military construction activities. The bill was incorporated into the year-end continuing resolution, which President Bush signed into law on Sept. 30 (HR 2638 — PL 110-329), just in time for the start of the new fiscal year.

The Military Construction-VA title provided a record $119.6 billion. The total included $72.9 billion in discretionary spending — $3.5 billion more than Bush requested and $4.2 billion above fiscal 2008 spending, counting emergency funds. (2007 Almanac, p. 2-41)

The remainder of the bill was mandatory spending for veterans' pensions and other benefits required under existing law. The estimated amount needed for those programs had grown by $2.3 billion since fiscal 2008 and by about $745 million since Bush issued his budget in February.

Virtually all of the extra discretionary spending above the president's request went to the VA, which received $47.6 billion, or about $2.8 billion more than requested. Veterans' health care got the biggest portion of the increase ($1.8 billion), followed by VA construction projects ($850 million).

The money for veterans was the driving force behind the bill, making it the only fiscal 2009 spending measure passed as a separate bill by either chamber. An increase in the number of veterans wounded in Iraq and Afghanistan continued to put financial strain on veterans' health programs. In addition, medical improvements and innovations enabled seriously wounded veterans to survive in greater numbers than before, further raising the costs of the health care systems.

"A vote for this bill is a vote of respect, respect for those who have given so much in service to our nation in uniform," Chet Edwards, D-Texas, told his colleagues. Edwards, who chaired the House Military Construction-VA Appropriations Subcommittee, said the bill also meant "better housing, more day care centers and modernized training facilities."

The White House warned that if the final bill provided more than requested for the VA, the amount would have to be cut from other bills so that overall fiscal 2009 appropriations did not exceed Bush's budget. But the Military Construction-VA bill turned out to be one of only three fiscal 2009 measures completed before Congress adjourned. The other two — for the departments of Defense and Homeland Security — were enacted in the continuing resolution as well. Funding for the nine other bills was continued at fiscal 2008 levels.

Senate appropriators approved a $119.7 billion version of the bill in mid-July, and the House passed a $118.7 billion version in August.

HIGHLIGHTS

The following are the major funding components of the Military-Construction-VA portion of the law:

● **Veterans Affairs.** $94.4 billion — $47.6 billion in discretion-

BOX SCORE 2009 FISCAL YEAR

MILITARY CONSTRUCTION-VA

BILL: HR 2638 — PL 110-329

LEGISLATIVE ACTION:

Senate committee approved S 3301 (S Rept 110-428), 29-0, on July 17.

House passed HR 6599 (H Rept 110-775), 409-4, on Aug. 1.

House included Military Construction-VA bill in an amendment to HR 2638, adopted 370-58, on Sept. 24.

Senate cleared HR 2638, 78-12, on Sept. 27.

President signed Sept. 30.

ary funding and $46.7 billion for mandatory programs. The discretionary total was 6 percent more than Bush requested and 9 percent above fiscal 2008 funding, which included about $4.3 billion in emergency appropriations. The total included:

▶ VA health care. $41 billion for the Veterans Health Administration (VHA), about 5 percent more than requested and 10 percent above the previous year's appropriation. The bill assumed that fees would pay for an additional $2.5 billion for the agency. Bush's request and the fiscal 2008 bill also assumed offsetting fees.

Funding included $510 million for trauma and health research and other studies to improve the quality of life for injured and aging veterans. Appropriators said the bill also included $1.6 billion for next-generation prosthetics and sensory aids for veterans, $3.8 billion for specialty mental health care, and about $580 million for substance abuse programs.

▶ VA benefits. $46.9 billion, virtually all of it mandatory, for pensions and other benefits handled by the Veterans Benefits Administration. The total was 5 percent above fiscal 2008 spending.

● **Defense Department.** $25 billion, mainly for military construction and base closing. The total was about 3 percent more than requested and just slightly above the previous year's spending and included:

▶ Military construction. $12.1 billion to construct and maintain military facilities on bases, a reduction of about $560 million from fiscal 2008 but 7 percent more than requested. More than half the funds added to Bush's request were for the National Guard and reserve.

▶ Family housing. $3.2 billion, 10 percent above the previous year's funding but slightly less than Bush requested, to construct and maintain military family housing.

▶ BRAC. $9.2 billion for the ongoing costs of base realignment and closure, particularly for the 2005 round. The amount was 5 percent more than fiscal 2008 spending but about 3 percent less than requested.

LEGISLATIVE ACTION
HOUSE COMMITTEE ACTION

The House Appropriations Committee approved a $118.7 billion Military Construction-VA bill (HR 6599 — H Rept 110-775) by voice vote June 24. The total included $72.7 billion in discretionary spending, $3.4 billion more than Bush requested. The Military Construction-VA Subcommittee, which drafted the measure, approved it by voice vote June 12.

● **Veterans Affairs.** The committee allocated $93.7 billion for the VA, $47.7 billion of which was discretionary appropriations. The discretionary total was $2.9 billion above Bush's request.

Much of the increase was for veterans' health programs, which were slated to get a total of $40.8 billion, $1.6 billion more than requested. The committee said the VHA expected to treat more than 5.8 million

WHERE THE MONEY GOES — FISCAL 2009 APPROPRIATIONS

MILITARY CONSTRUCTION-VA

HR 2638 — PL 110-329

(figures are in thousands of dollars of new budget authority)

	Fiscal 2008 enacted*	Fiscal 2009 Bush request	House passed	Senate committee approved	Fiscal 2009 enacted
GRAND TOTAL	$113,152,934	$115,344,081	$118,726,081	$119,742,925	$119,607,925
Discretionary spending	68,665,000	69,347,156	72,729,156	73,000,000	72,865,000
MAIN COMPONENTS					
Defense Department	24,875,344	24,400,239	24,800,239	24,744,390	25,049,583
Military construction	12,681,112	11,362,876	11,741,876	11,682,418	12,117,688
Family housing	2,878,490	3,203,455	3,166,455	3,216,750	3,157,760
Base Realignment and Closure	8,810,166	9,458,763	9,538,763	9,460,077	9,223,990
Veterans Affairs	88,111,519	90,761,057	93,685,057	94,792,750	94,351,057
Veterans Benefits Administration	44,642,822	46,155,162	46,155,162	46,901,162	46,901,162
Veterans Health Administration	37,201,220	39,178,503	40,783,270	41,078,232	40,958,903

*Totals include emergency appropriations.

SOURCE: House and Senate Appropriations committees

patients in 2009, 40,000 more than in 2008.

Funding for the Veterans Benefits Administration was mandatory, and it was estimated at the time to be $46.2 billion.

● **Defense Department.** Defense construction programs were to get $24.8 billion, just $400 million more than requested, including:

▸ $11.7 billion for construction for the military services, about $380 million more than requested. The committee said the increase was due primarily to the costs of implementing and preparing for planned increases in the size of the Army and Marine Corps.

▸ $3.2 billion for family housing, about the same as requested.

▸ $9.5 billion for BRAC, slightly more than requested. Most of the funding was to implement the 2005 round of base closures.

HOUSE FLOOR ACTION

The House passed the bill, 409-4, on Aug. 1, shortly before members left for the monthlong August recess. *(House vote 563, p. H-190)*

The White House issued a statement July 30 that fell just short of threatening a veto. As it had the previous year, the Office of Management and Budget (OMB) warned that if Congress increased funding in the bill above the president's request, it had to reduce spending on other appropriations bills to stay in line with the White House's top-line discretionary number of $991.6 billion. Otherwise, Bush would veto any of the bills that exceeded his request.

"The bill is laden with costly earmarks and contains overall excessive spending, as well as other objectionable provisions," a statement from OMB said.

"I do not understand the values," Edwards said, "that would suggest, during a time of war, we provide tax breaks for people making over $1 million a year, but we cannot afford to provide the health care our veterans deserve and the housing our troops need. I believe our veterans, military families, and the American family will be as offended by this veto threat as I am."

The bill was the only regular fiscal 2009 measure to reach the House floor as a stand-alone bill. The appropriations process had been stalled since late June, when Appropriations Chairman David R. Obey,

D-Wis., halted work on the spending bills after a partisan fight over oil drilling broke out at a markup. Obey relented slightly in late July, saying, "We'll just put [the Military Construction-VA bill] up and see if people behave responsibly."

The energy issue emerged during the debate on the rule for floor debate. The House adopted the rule by a vote of 230-186 on July 31, with just four Republicans voting with the majority. Republicans objected that the rule restricted their ability to propose amendments spontaneously as the debate progressed and limited their opportunities to propose opening the Arctic National Wildlife Refuge and areas off the Atlantic and Pacific coasts to oil and gas drilling. *(House vote 550, p. H-184)*

House Minority Leader John A. Boehner, R-Ohio, still tried to attach an amendment that embodied the GOP energy plan, including an end to a moratorium on offshore drilling. Boehner's proposal was ruled out of order as an effort to include authorizing language in an appropriations bill.

Most other GOP attempts to attach drilling language were equally unsuccessful. However, an energy-related amendment by Jeb Hensarling, R-Texas, was adopted by voice vote. It called for barring the use of funds in the bill to enforce a 2007 law (PL 110-140) that prohibited federal agencies from procuring alternative fuels that produced more emissions than conventional fuels, unless they were being used for research.

Before final passage, the House rejected, 63-350, an attempt by Jeff Flake, R-Ariz., and John Campbell, R-Calif., to delete 103 earmarks totaling $621.8 million. *(House vote 560, p. H-188)*

SENATE COMMITTEE ACTION

The Senate Appropriations Committee approved a $119.7 billion bill (S 3301 — S Rept 110-428) on July 17 that included $72.9 billion in discretionary funding. The measure, approved by a vote of 29-0, was about $1 billion larger than the House-passed version. About $745 million of the additional spending was the result of an increase in the estimated cost of mandatory veterans' benefits.

"I'm tired of veterans getting the short end of the stick," Military Construction-VA Subcommittee Chairman Tim Johnson, D-S.D., said in a statement. "Patriotism is more than saluting the flag. It is also supporting the troops by honoring the promises we made to them."

The bill included:

● **Veterans Affairs.** $94.8 billion for the VA, including $47.9 billion in discretionary funding. About $41.1 billion of the total was for veterans' health care services, including facility maintenance and research.

● **Defense Department.** $24.7 billion for the Pentagon, virtually the same as in the bill passed by the House. The total included $11.7 billion for military construction, $3.2 billion for family housing and $9.5 billion for BRAC.

Committee Chairman Robert C. Byrd, D-W.Va., asked Bush to back down from his threat to veto other bills if the total exceeded his budget request. The Military Construction-VA bill is "in excess of the president's request because the president's requests are inadequate,"

Byrd said. "Now is not the time to cut or eliminate programs that . . . provide medical assistance to veterans."

FINAL ACTION

With the end of the fiscal year approaching, Democratic leaders attached the Military Construction-VA, Defense and Homeland Security bills to the continuing resolution, which essentially put funding for the rest of the government on autopilot for about five months. Democratic leaders had assumed all along that final action on domestic spending would be put off until the following year to avoid Bush's promised veto. But they put the security bills on a separate track to avoid election-year charges that they were ignoring national security needs.

The House voted 370-58 on Sept. 24 to adopt the entire continuing resolution as an amendment to HR 2638. The Senate cleared the bill, 78-12, on Sept. 27. *(House vote 632, p. H-212; Senate vote 208, p. S-46)* ■

Bills Seek Aid Boost for Global Health

APPROPRIATORS IN BOTH chambers approved versions of a fiscal 2009 State Department-Foreign Operations spending bill that upset conservatives by proposing increased funding for family planning programs and looser restrictions on the money. However, the language, like the legislation itself, went no further. Instead, Congress funded programs covered by the bill at fiscal 2008 levels through March 6, 2009, under a continuing resolution signed Sept. 30 (PL 110-329).

The full Senate Appropriations Committee and a House subcommittee approved versions of the fiscal 2009 bill in July that totaled $36.8 billion, all but about $150 million of which was discretionary spending. The total was about 4 percent more than the $35.3 billion appropriated in fiscal 2008 (PL 110-161) and 4 percent below President Bush's request of $38.4 billion. *(2007 Almanac, p. 2-45)*

Reflecting Democrats' impatience with Bush's signature foreign aid program, the Millennium Challenge Corporation (MCC), both bills included significantly less than the $2.2 billion that Bush had requested. Critics said the MCC, a bilateral aid program aimed at fostering democracy and free-market economies, had been too slow to spend money and was sitting on hefty reserves.

Meanwhile, conservatives in both chambers raised concerns over proposed increases for the United Nations Population Fund, known as the UNFPA, which they said helped fund abortions in countries including China. They also objected to legislative language, including proposals to relax some restrictions on the funding.

Both the House and Senate measures would have left in place a longstanding law (PL 99-88) that allowed the administration to bar money from going to organizations that supported coerced abortion or forced sterilization. But they would have made exceptions for certain UNFPA activities, such as supplying emergency obstetric care, preventing unintended pregnancy, treating fistula and opposing genital mutilation. Since 2002, the Bush administration had withheld $235 million from the UNFPA based on the restriction.

Although the continuing resolution essentially froze funding at fiscal 2008 levels, the supplemental war spending bill (PL 110-252) enacted in June provided about $8.8 billion in additional foreign aid funds for fiscal 2008 and 2009. *(Supplemental, p. 2-32)*

The extra foreign aid in the supplemental included:

▶ $170 million in fiscal 2009 military financing for Israel, keeping the United States on track to meet a 10-year, $30 billion security agreement with Israel signed in August 2007. The $170 million made up the difference between $2.38 billion provided in the continuing resolution and the $2.55 billion that the pact called for in fiscal 2009.

▶ $465 million for a three-year, $1.4 billion counternarcotics program with Mexico and Central America known as the Merida Initiative. The bill dropped some restrictions that Mexican officials viewed as an infringement on their sovereignty but withheld some money contingent on a report to Congress on Mexican human-rights issues.

▶ $696 million for refugee assistance in Iraq and elsewhere.

The supplemental also allowed the president to waive the so-

BOX SCORE 2009 FISCAL YEAR

STATE-FOREIGN OPERATIONS

BILLS: House draft, S 3288

LEGISLATIVE ACTION:

House Appropriations subcommittee approved draft bill by voice vote July 16.

Senate Appropriations Committee approved S 3288 (S Rept 110-425), 28-1, on July 17.

---

called Glenn amendment (PL 103-236) to the Arms Export Control Act, thereby allowing the use of U.S. equipment and funding in dismantling North Korea's nuclear reactor at Yongbyon and disposing of its radioactive material.

LEGISLATIVE ACTION
HOUSE SUBCOMMITTEE ACTION

The House State-Foreign Operations Subcommittee approved its draft of the bill by voice vote July 16. Because the full Appropriations Committee never approved the draft, the bill was not officially filed and there was no report. The subcommittee released some information on the measure.

It said the $36.6 billion in discretionary spending included:

▶ $809 million in operating expenses for the U.S. Agency for International Development, about $40 million above Bush's request and $180 million above the fiscal 2008 level.

▶ $5.5 billion for global HIV/AIDS activities, $500 million more than Bush sought. Still, it was significantly less than called for in a five-year, $48 billion global AIDS reauthorization law enacted in July (PL 110-293). *(HIV/AIDS, p. 6-9)*

▶ $1.9 billion for global health and child survival, $283 million above Bush's request and about $150 million above fiscal 2008.

▶ $600 million for family planning. The total included $60 million for the UNFPA, compared with $40 million in the fiscal 2008 law. The draft also would have waived some restrictions on the funding.

▶ $2.4 billion in military financing for Israel, about equal to the previous year's funding and $170 million less than requested.

▶ $1.3 billion in military financing and $200 million in economic aid for Egypt, both equal to Bush's request. Military financing was just slightly more than provided in fiscal 2008, but the economic aid was about half the previous year's amount.

▶ $1 billion for Afghanistan, equal to Bush's request.

▶ $697 million in total aid to Jordan, about $160 million above the president's request.

▶ $1.5 billion for the MCC, equal to fiscal 2008 funding but about $700 million less than Bush had sought.

▶ $778 million for humanitarian and peacekeeping aid to Sudan.

▶ New language requiring a report from the State Department on its implementation of sanctions against Iran, as well as a report from the Treasury Department on the activities of foreign subsidiaries of U.S. companies trading with and investing in Iran.

During the markup, the subcommittee:

▶ Defeated by voice vote an attempt by Dave Weldon, R-Fla., to drop the UNFPA provision and return to the $40 million appropriation and the tighter restrictions contained in the fiscal 2008 law. Subcommittee Chairwoman Nita M. Lowey, D-N.Y., said there were guidelines on how U.S. money could be used and that no funds would go to forced abortions.

▶ Defeated, 6-9, an amendment by ranking Republican Frank R. Wolf of Virginia that would have stripped $65 million of the funding for Jordan and added $100 million for embassy security. Lowey argued

WHERE THE MONEY GOES — FISCAL 2009 APPROPRIATIONS
STATE-FOREIGN OPERATIONS

S 3288 (S Rept 110-425); House draft

	Fiscal 2008 appropriations*	Fiscal 2009 Bush request	Senate committee approved
(figures are in thousands of dollars of new budget authority)			
GRAND TOTAL	**$35,342,643**	**$38,375,675**	**$36,777,100**
Discretionary spending	32,799,000	38,216,575	36,620,000
MAIN COMPONENTS			
State Department**	11,503,667	12,235,857	12,235,663
Diplomatic and consular programs	5,322,719	5,364,269	5,290,000
Bilateral economic assistance	16,845,397	17,822,329	16,846,137
Global Health and Child Survival	6,491,082	6,356,830	6,740,000
Economic Support Fund	2,974,959	3,153,743	3,098,904
Millennium Challenge Corporation	1,544,388	2,225,000	254,000
Foreign Military Financing	4,551,970	4,812,000	4,479,000
International financial institutions	1,259,363	2,053,305	1,749,241

*Totals include emergency appropriations.
**Total includes the Broadcasting Board of Governors.

SOURCE: Senate Appropriations Committee; House table not available

that Jordan was one of America's important allies in the Middle East and that a severe cut in funding would destabilize the country.

▸ Rejected, 7-8, an amendment by Joe Knollenberg, R-Mich., that would have stripped funding for Azerbaijan, due to what Knollenberg called that country's "saber rattling" against Armenia. Lowey said she did not want Congress to take sides in the dispute and that the draft bill contained a "balance" of aid for the two countries.

SENATE COMMITTEE ACTION

The Senate Appropriations Committee approved its State-Foreign Operations bill (S 3288 — S Rept 110-425) by a vote of 28-1 on July 17. There were no amendments. The bill included:

▸ $12.2 billion for State Department operations, close to the president's request and $730 million above the fiscal 2008 level. The committee said the increase would support a request for 500 additional positions, many of which would be used for posts that had been depleted by the shift of positions to Iraq over the previous five years.

The measure proposed withholding some funds until the department implemented recommendations from its inspector general aimed at improving internal controls over access to passport files. It had been reported in March that the passport files of several presidential candidates had been breached.

▸ $5.1 billion for global HIV/AIDS activities, a step below the House's $5.5 billion but about $120 million above the fiscal 2008 level. The amount was equal to Bush's request.

▸ $254 million for the MCC, a sharp drop from the $1.5 billion provided in fiscal 2008 and included in the House draft and a fraction of Bush's $2.2 billion request.

▸ $520 million for family planning, including $45 million for the UNFPA.

Kansas Republican Sam Brownback, who cast the lone vote against the bill, criticized the funding and policy provisions related to the U.N. organization.

"There was language put in that would allow funds to be used in countries that have, through UNFPA, forced abortions, forced sterilizations," Brownback said, citing Vietnam and North Korea as other offending countries where UNFPA worked.

Unlike the House draft, the Senate bill included a provision to overturn the so-called Mexico City policy, which prohibited funding for groups that performed or promoted abortion overseas.

Among its other policy provisions, the Senate bill would have required Iraq to match U.S. reconstruction money dollar for dollar and would have required that the United States oppose loans from international banks to Zimbabwe. ∎

Debate Centers on Highway Funding

THE FISCAL 2009 SPENDING bill for the departments of Transportation and Housing and Urban Development (HUD) went no further than the Appropriations Committee in the Senate and the Transportation-HUD Appropriations Subcommittee in the House.

Like all of the domestic appropriations bills, the measure remained unfinished at the end of the session. Congress kept the programs under the bill going at fiscal 2008 levels through March 6, 2009, as part of a continuing resolution (PL 110-329) enacted Sept. 30.

The fiscal 2008 Transportation-HUD law (PL 110-161) totaled $102.6 billion, excluding emergency funds, with $48.8 billion in discretionary funds. *(2007 Almanac, p. 2-49)*

The Senate Appropriations Committee approved a $109.4 billion fiscal 2009 bill July. The measure included $53.3 billion in discretionary funds; most of the rest came from trust funds, primarily the Highway Trust Fund. The discretionary total was $4.5 billion or 9 percent more than provided in fiscal 2008 and $2.7 billion or 5 percent more than President Bush requested.

The House Transportation-HUD Appropriations Subcommittee approved a $108.7 billion draft bill in June, but the full Appropriations Committee never took it up. The subcommittee said the draft would provide about $55 billion in discretionary funding.

The two panels took opposite positions on one major transportation issue: how to replenish the nearly defunct federal Highway Trust Fund. The trust fund was fed by fuel excise taxes, principally the 18.4-cents-per-gallon federal gasoline tax. The funds were then distributed to states to be used for maintaining highways and bridges. Funding levels for those programs were guaranteed in the 2005 surface transportation law (PL 109-59). *(2005 Almanac, p. 18-3)*

However, gasoline tax revenue was not expected to keep pace with inflation or growing transportation demands, leading to declining cash balances in the fund. Both the Office of Management and Budget and the Congressional Budget Office projected that the trust fund would run $3.7 billion into the red in fiscal 2009.

The Highway Trust Fund also included a smaller account for mass transit. Bush proposed borrowing about $3.2 billion from that account and using it for highway programs in fiscal 2009, but transportation advocates dismissed that as a "rob Peter to pay Paul" solution.

Although additional funding for discretionary programs covered by the annual Transportation-HUD bill was on hold until early 2009, the continuing resolution provided $850 million in emergency spending for the Federal Highway Administration to help repair roads and bridges damaged by disasters.

Congress subsequently cleared a separate bill (PL 110-318) that transferred $8 billion from the general fund to the highway account. *(Highway Trust Fund, p. 3-18)*

Overall, the Bush administration called for a 2 percent reduction in fiscal 2009 Transportation spending compared with the previous year, with $36.3 billion for highways, about 5 percent less than Congress appropriated in fiscal 2008. Amtrak would have gotten a 40 percent

BILLS: House draft, S 3261

....

LEGISLATIVE ACTION:

House Appropriations subcommittee approved draft bill by voice vote June 20.

Senate Appropriations Committee approved S 3261 (S Rept 110-418), 28-0, on July 10.

cut to $800 million from $1.3 billion in fiscal 2008. Bush proposed to reduce capital grants for the rail service by $325 million and eliminate operating subsidies. Amtrak would have had to request money for capital investments through the Efficiency Incentive Grants account and would not have received the funds unless certain benchmarks were reached.

Bush wanted to increase funding for the Federal Aviation Administration (FAA) by about 1 percent to $14.6 billion.

Housing programs would have gotten an increase of $1.4 billion, or 4 percent, to $39.1 billion under Bush's budget.

LEGISLATIVE HISTORY
HOUSE SUBCOMMITTEE ACTION

The House Transportation-HUD Appropriations Subcommittee approved its $108.7 billion draft of the spending bill by voice vote June 20. The total included $55 billion for discretionary programs.

The panel rejected proposals to bail out the Highway Trust Fund, saying it was a job suited to the authorizing committees, not the appropriators. "This shortfall is not of this committee's making," said John W. Olver, D-Mass., chairman of the subcommittee.

The 2005 highway law, Olver said, "overcommitted the dedicated revenues available for surface transportation, and I am hopeful the authorization and tax writing committees will be able to make up the shortfall as we continue to move this bill forward."

The subcommittee's ranking Republican, Joe Knollenberg of Michigan, warned that appropriators alone could not fix the nation's transportation troubles. "We're at a crossroads. We're digging a hole that we might not be able to climb out of," he said. "To fix this problem is going to take the full Congress."

Because the full committee did not take up the draft, the measure was never formally introduced and no report was filed. The subcommittee issued a summary, but comparisons with other figures were difficult.

● **Transportation.** The draft called for $66.7 billion for the Transportation Department, about 80 percent of it money from the trust funds. The proposal included:

▸ $37.9 billion for highways, keeping with the guarantees in the 2005 highway law.

▸ $10.3 billion for public transit services, which the panel said was about $1 billion above fiscal 2008 spending. The total included $1.8 billion for new commuter transit lines.

▸ $15.4 billion for the FAA, about $850 million more than the agency got in fiscal 2008. Bush asked for $14.6 billion, about $20 million above the fiscal 2008 level. The panel provided $1.1 billion for aviation safety, including a $16 million increase for 200 additional aviation safety inspectors. The FAA funds also included $3.5 billion for the Airport Improvement Program and $130 million for the Essential Air Service program, which provided subsidies to small airports that serve local needs.

▸ $1.4 billion for Amtrak, including $114 million for back pay for

WHERE THE MONEY GOES — FISCAL 2009 APPROPRIATIONS
TRANSPORTATION-HUD

S 3261 — S Rept 110-418

	Fiscal 2008 appropriations	Fiscal 2009 Bush request	Senate committee approved
	(figures are in thousands of dollars of new budget authority)		
GRAND TOTAL	$102,564,749*	$102,839,933	$109,438,855
Discretionary spending	48,821,000	50,622,520	53,325,000
MAIN COMPONENTS			
Transportation Department	64,708,126	63,494,202	66,795,556
Federal Aviation Administration	14,524,439	14,643,000	15,430,833
Federal Highway Administration	38,067,896	36,252,728	38,032,507
Federal Transit Administration	9,491,642	10,135,407	10,225,815
Amtrak	1,325,000	800,000	1,503,200
Department of Housing and Urban Development	37,636,952	39,075,451	42,363,811
Tenant-based rental assistance	16,391,000	15,881,000	16,703,000
Community planning and development	10,547,390	6,942,740	7,940,205

* Excludes emergency appropriations

SOURCE: Senate Appropriations Committee; House table not available

union employees who had worked without a pay increase for eight years. The fiscal 2008 law provided $118 million less.

● **HUD.** The draft included $41.6 billion for the department, which received particular attention because of the housing crisis that had already forced millions of homeowners into foreclosure. "It has become painfully clear that the often-overlooked importance of affordable rental housing must once again become an integral part of the nation's housing policies," Olver said.

The panel rejected a number of Bush's proposed cuts to affordable-housing programs. The measure included:

▸ $16.6 billion for the Section 8 tenant-based housing program, which Olver said was enough to make sure no one would lose the vouchers they already had. "I wish we could do more," Olver said, "but we did our best given the limited resources."

▸ $4 billion, $1 billion more than requested, for Community Development Block Grants, which gave states funds for affordable housing, anti-poverty programs and infrastructure development.

▸ $120 million for the HOPE VI program, which helped to rehabilitate or replace dilapidated public housing. Bush and some congressional Republicans wanted to eliminate the program.

SENATE COMMITTEE ACTION

The Senate Appropriations Committee approved its version of the Transportation-HUD bill by a vote of 28-0 on July 10, rejecting the decision by the House panel not to take on the trust fund issue. The bill would have transferred $8 billion from the general fund to the highway fund.

The $109.4 billion measure (S 3261 — S Rept 110-418) included $53.3 billion in discretionary funding.

Patty Murray, D-Wash., chairwoman of the Transportation-HUD Subcommittee, said she and Christopher S. Bond of Missouri, the panel's ranking Republican, agreed to fix the trust fund problem in the spending bill after numerous other attempts to address the problem had failed. The most recent attempt was in a short-term FAA

authorization bill (HR 6327).

● **Transportation.** The bill called for $66.8 billion for the department — $3.3 billion more than the White House requested and $2.1 billion more than fiscal 2008 funding. The total included:

▸ $38 billion for the Federal Highway Administration, $35 million below fiscal 2008 spending and $1.8 billion more than requested.

▸ $15.4 billion for the FAA, about $907 million above the fiscal 2008 level and $790 million more than requested. The committee included $34 million more than Bush requested for air traffic control operations, $12 million more for procurement and $32 million more for the FAA's safety oversight.

▸ $1.5 billion for Amtrak, nearly double what the president requested for the passenger rail company and $180 million above fiscal 2008 funding.

▸ $10.2 billion for the Federal Transit Administration, $730 million more than in fiscal 2008 and $90 million more than requested. The total included $8.3 billion for formula and bus grants and $1.8 billion for the New Starts program, which invested in new transit systems.

● **HUD.** The committee approved $42.4 billion for HUD programs, $4.7 billion above fiscal 2008 funding and $3.3 billion more than the White House requested. The total included:

▸ $32.8 billion for public and Indian housing, $2.6 billion more than fiscal 2008 spending and $2.5 billion more than requested. Much of the increase was for project-based rental assistance.

▸ $3.9 billion for Community Development Block Grants, $890 million more than the president requested and $23 million above fiscal 2008 appropriations.

▸ $500 million more than requested for Section 8 tenant-based housing.

▸ $100 million for HOPE VI public housing, equal to fiscal 2008 spending. Bush requested no funds.

The committee approved by voice vote an amendment by Wayne Allard, R-Colo., to designate $10 million for the American Dream Down Payment Initiative, signed into law in 2003 (PL 108-186). A

spokesman for Allard said the program, which helped low-income families make down payments on homes, had gotten lost among other housing initiatives in years past. This year Allard wanted to ensure that money was specifically set aside for the program, which he helped create.

● **Mexican trucks.** Much of the debate during the Senate markup involved an embattled Transportation pilot program that allowed some Mexican truck companies to send vehicles more than 25 miles across the U.S. border.

The committee adopted, 20-9, an amendment by Byron L. Dorgan, D-N.D., to prohibit the use of any money in the bill to implement the program.

The fiscal 2008 appropriations law contained language blocking the Bush administration from proceeding with the program during that year, but the Transportation Department had been accused of ignoring the provision.

Christopher S. Bond, R-Mo., warned the committee that halting the pilot program might prompt Mexico to retaliate by imposing fees and tariffs on U.S. goods. "I regret that farmers and other exporters are going to pay the price for it," Bond said.

Critics of the program said it threatened American jobs and lacked safety precautions such as testing drivers for drugs, conducting criminal background checks or compiling a database of driving records. ■

President Prevails on War Funding

AFTER WEEKS OF SHUTTLING sections of the legislation back and forth between the two chambers, Congress in June cleared a $186.5 billion supplemental spending bill, primarily for U.S. operations in Iraq and Afghanistan. President Bush, who prevailed in a battle over the contents of the bill, signed the measure into law on June 30 (HR 2642 — PL 110-252).

Final action on the fiscal 2008-2009 measure was hastened, in part, by warnings from the Defense Department that it would run out of funds for operations and personnel in early July.

The bill provided $161.8 billion for Pentagon operations in Iraq and Afghanistan, including $65.9 billion in "bridge" funds for the first few months of 2009. Another $24.7 billion went to domestic programs; foreign aid; military construction; and disaster aid, including money for Midwest flood and tornado relief and reconstruction of levees destroyed by Hurricane Katrina.

The spending was treated as emergency funding and did not count against congressional limits on discretionary appropriations.

Democrats also attached unrelated legislation to expand education assistance for veterans, extend federal unemployment benefits by 13 weeks and postpone seven proposed Medicaid regulations for a year. The cost of those provisions was accounted for separately.

Bush's request for emergency funds totaled about $183.9 billion. It included $166.1 billion for the Pentagon — $100.1 billion that had not yet been appropriated for fiscal 2008, plus $66.1 billion as a down payment for fiscal 2009. It also included $5.8 billion for levee reconstruction in Louisiana.

To expedite action, House leaders brought the measure directly to the floor, bypassing the committee stage and using an unneeded fiscal 2008 appropriations bill (HR 2642) as a vehicle. In a process that would be repeated several times, the leadership divided the provisions into separate amendments, a tactic that allowed anti-war Democrats to vote against the war funds while supporting the extended unemployment benefits, extra spending for domestic programs and other provisions. Democratic leaders assumed that while many House Republicans would oppose the non-war-funding amendment, they would provide enough votes to pass the war funds. Republicans were not always willing to oblige.

The amendments went back and forth between the chambers until a bipartisan group of House leaders reached an agreement with the White House shortly before the Memorial Day break. Although the House deal met the president's demands, it left many Democrats disappointed. Although they were realistic about the urgency of clearing the funding for the troops, several senators vowed to return with a second supplemental later in the year that would provide some of

BOX SCORE
2008-09 FISCAL YEARS
WAR SUPPLEMENTAL

BILL: HR 2642 — PL 110-252

LEGISLATIVE ACTION:

House on May 15 adopted a war policy amendment to HR 2642, 227-196. It adopted a funding amendment for domestic and other programs, 256-166, and rejected a war funding amendment, 141-149.

Senate on May 22 adopted amendments to HR 2642 on war funding, 70-26, and on domestic and other programs, 75-22.

House on June 19 agreed to the Senate's war funding amendment, 268-155, and adopted a compromise on domestic and other programs, 416-12.

Senate on June 26 agreed to the domestic amendment, 92-7, clearing the bill.

President signed June 30.

the domestic spending that was dropped in the final agreement.

HIGHLIGHTS

The following are the main components of the supplemental:

● **War funding.** $161.8 billion to cover costs related to operations in Iraq and Afghanistan — $95.9 billion for the remainder of fiscal 2008 and $65.9 billion for the first part of fiscal 2009.

● **Iraq policy provisions.** A requirement that reconstruction aid from the U.S. Agency for International Development be matched dollar for dollar by the Iraqi government. The bill also prohibited the use of funds to establish permanent bases in Iraq.

● **Disaster aid.** $5.8 billion to strengthen New Orleans levees and $2.7 billion for relief from floods and tornadoes in the Midwest.

● **Military construction.** $4.6 billion, $1.6 billion more than requested, for military construction, including base-closing costs.

● **Other domestic programs.** $1 billion in unrequested funds for the Food and Drug Administration, the Federal Bureau of Prisons, census cost overruns and other programs.

● **Global food aid.** $1.2 billion over two years for international food aid through the PL 480 program, about $500 million more than requested.

● **Bilateral aid.** $8.8 billion over two years for refugee assistance in Iraq and elsewhere, drug enforcement aid in Central America and Mexico, embassy security, and international economic support. The total was $165 million more than requested.

● **Veterans' education benefits.** Expanded education benefits for servicemembers who had served on active duty since Sept. 11, 2001. It was the largest expansion of the GI Bill program since World War II. The cost was put at $796 million for fiscal 2008 and 2009.

● **Unemployment benefits.** Up to 13 weeks of federal unemployment benefits for workers who had exhausted their existing compensation. The extension was estimated to cost a total of $12.6 billion in fiscal 2008 and 2009.

● **Medicaid.** A moratorium on seven Medicaid regulations issued by the Bush administration that were aimed at narrowing certain services, limiting others eligible for federal reimbursements and ending some accounting maneuvers used by the states.

LEGISLATIVE ACTION
HOUSE FLOOR ACTION

The House sent its version of the supplemental to the Senate on May 15, following a series of three roll-call votes on separate amendments. While the process allowed Democrats to oppose the war while supporting other spending, the complex strategy also handed Republicans an opportunity to disrupt some of the leadership's plans.

Instead of voting for the war funding amendment, as the Democrats had expected, many Republicans voted "present," forcing Democrats to rely on their own majority to adopt the amendment. But with many anti-war Democrats opposed to further war funding, the amendment failed. As a result, the legislation went to the Senate without the core funding provisions.

The other two amendments, both of which were adopted, prescribed changes in the administration's Iraq War policies and tacked on a domestic spending package that also included extended unemployment benefits, expanded veterans' education benefits and a surtax on the very wealthy to offset the costs of the program.

Jim Nussle, director of the White House Office of Management and Budget, criticized the bill and promised that the president would reject it. The Democrats "insisted on tax increases, higher spending and tying the hands of our military commanders," Nussle said in a statement. "Those are misplaced priorities, and the president will veto this bill."

● **War funding.** The war funding amendment would have provided $162.5 billion for Pentagon operations in Iraq and Afghanistan — $96.6 billion for fiscal 2008 and $65.9 billion for fiscal 2009. But with a majority of Democrats voting "no" and 132 Republicans voting "present," it was rejected, 141-149. *(House vote 328, p. H-106)*

The GOP strategy was devised by Mike Pence of Indiana and members of the conservative Republican Study Committee (RSC). It was purely symbolic — the Senate was expected to restore the war funding — but the RSC wanted to demonstrate just how dependent Democrats were on GOP votes to keep money for the troops flowing. House Republican leaders were apparently apprehensive, but they acquiesced. "Today Republicans voted 'present' on the troop-funding bill to expose a cynical ploy by the Democrat majority to play politics with our troops," said Minority Leader John A. Boehner, R-Ohio.

Appropriations Chairman David R. Obey, D-Wis., maintained that the Democrats had won, noting that most of them opposed further funding of the war anyway.

● **Iraq policy.** The second amendment, which focused on war policy, was adopted, 227-196, with almost all Democrats voting "yes" and almost all Republicans opposed. *(House vote 329, p. H-106)*

The amendment included provisions to:

▸ Require the president to begin withdrawing combat troops from Iraq within 30 days of enactment, with a goal of having most troops out by Dec. 31, 2009.

▸ Require that troops sent to Iraq meet the Pentagon definition of "fully mission capable," prohibit troops from being deployed longer than Pentagon guidelines recommended and require the Pentagon to abide by its policies on home time between deployments.

▸ Require that any agreement with the Iraqi government that committed U.S. forces be ratified by the Senate and be specifically authorized in law. The Bush administration was trying to negotiate a status-of-forces agreement with Iraq to provide a legal basis for the continued presence and operation of U.S. armed forces in that country once the existing U.N. Security Council mandate expired on Dec. 31, 2008.

▸ Require that U.S. reconstruction aid to Iraq be matched dollar for dollar by the Iraqi government and that Iraq partially reimburse the United States for the cost of fuel used by U.S. troops.

▸ Prohibit the establishment of permanent U.S. bases in Iraq.

▸ Prohibit interrogation techniques not authorized by the relevant Army field manual, and require that the International Red Cross be given access to military detainees.

● **Domestic and other programs.** The third amendment was adopted 256-166, with almost all Democrats voting "yes," joined by 32 Republicans. With that vote, the measure was sent to the Senate. *(House vote 330, p. H-106)*

The amendment included:

▸ Expanded education benefits for veterans equivalent to a four-year education at a public university for those who had spent 36 months on active duty. Benefits would be scaled back for veterans with shorter time on active duty. The language was based on a bill (S 22) introduced by Sen. Jim Webb, D-Va. The White House opposed the Webb bill, arguing that its generous offerings could hurt retention in the military.

▸ A 0.47 percent surtax on modified adjusted gross income above $500,000 ($1,000,000 for joint filers), to offset the cost of the expanded GI Bill benefits. The surtax was crucial for House "Blue Dogs," a group of 49 fiscally conservative Democrats who had delayed action on the bill and threatened to defect if it included new veterans' benefits without paying for them.

▸ The 13 weeks of extended federal unemployment benefits, plus the additional 13 weeks in states with high unemployment rates.

▸ A moratorium on the seven Medicaid regulations.

▸ $5.8 billion to strengthen New Orleans levees.

▸ $9.9 billion for international food, disaster and refugee aid.

▸ $4.6 billion for military construction.

SENATE COMMITTEE ACTION

As the House was voting on its amendments May 15, the Senate Appropriations Committee was marking up a version of the bill that added billions for domestic programs. Democratic leaders had tried to avoid a Senate markup, but West Virginia Democrat Robert C. Byrd, chairman of the Appropriations panel, insisted on putting his panel's stamp on the bill.

Unlike the House, Senate appropriators did not attempt to stay within Bush's aggregate request total of $183.9 billion. Byrd said the draft he brought to the markup totaled $193 billion. He defended his committee's prerogatives, saying, "The president claims that by adding money for America to this bill, we are holding money for the troops hostage. What hogwash."

Although Byrd asked for restraint in the markup, the committee adopted more than 20 provisions that added both policy language and at least another $1.1 billion to the bill's cost.

The legislation was structured as three separate amendments — for war funding, Iraq policy prescriptions and domestic programs — which appropriators planned to add to HR 2642 on the floor. All three amendments were approved by voice vote.

● **Domestic and other programs.** Provisions in Byrd's first amendment included:

▸ The 13-week extension of federal unemployment benefits, plus the additional 13 weeks for workers in high-unemployment states.

▸ The delay in implementing the seven Medicaid regulations.

▸ Webb's proposal to expand GI Bill education benefits.

▸ $10.4 billion for Hurricane Katrina and Rita recovery efforts.

▸ $1 billion for low-income housing energy assistance. The committee added the language, proposed by Jack Reed, D-R.I., by a vote of 20-9.

▸ $1.25 billion for global food aid.

▸ $1.2 billion for science programs at NASA, the National Science Foundation, the National Institutes of Health and the Energy Department.

▸ $490 million for Byrne grants to assist state and local law

enforcement agencies, $275 million for the Food and Drug Administration, $451 million for the Federal Highway Administration's emergency relief program, $400 million to help rural counties where federal timber royalties had declined, and smaller amounts for a number of other accounts.

▸ A lengthy section of immigration provisions added during the markup. California Democrat Dianne Feinstein proposed a temporary five-year program to provide so-called H-2A visas to emergency agricultural workers who agreed to work 100 days a year in agriculture and pay a fine of $250, plus processing fees. Her proposal was adopted 17-12.

An amendment by Barbara A. Mikulski, D-Md., adopted 23-6, was aimed at renewing an expired law that previously allowed an increase in the availability of non-farm H-2B seasonal-worker visas by granting a waiver for returning workers from the statutory cap of 66,000. The waiver had expired in September, and employers who relied on summer business feared they would not be able to find enough temporary employees.

Other amendments adopted during the markup included a $300 million increase in aid to Jordan, $50 million to track unregistered sex offenders, $100 million to fight drug crimes on the U.S.-Mexico border and a ban on the use of federal money to pay contractors who avoided taxes by incorporating overseas.

Thad Cochran of Mississippi, the panel's ranking Republican, wondered aloud whether the committee's work would find its way into the final bill. "I have little confidence that the recommendations being made today will even be brought before the Senate," he said.

Majority Leader Harry Reid, D-Nev., who wanted a less expansive amendment, indicated that Byrd might not have the final word.

● **War funding.** The next amendment proposed $168.9 billion for operations in Iraq and Afghanistan.

● **Iraq War policies.** Policy prescriptions, which were contained in the third amendment, included a requirement that units deployed for combat be fully mission-capable; a time limit on combat deployments; a prohibition on permanent bases in Iraq; a statement that the U.S. mission in Iraq should shift to counterterrorism, training and supporting Iraqi forces and force protection by June 2009; and a requirement that Iraq provide partial reimbursement for fuel used by U.S. troops.

SENATE FLOOR ACTION

On May 22, the Senate passed a revised version of the bill that was assembled on the floor and left out some of the committee's most controversial provisions. The convoluted process was orchestrated by Democratic leaders in what they said was an effort to reach across the aisle and get enough votes to send the measure back to the House. The Senate never took an actual vote on passage. Rather, it agreed to the House amendments, with further amendments.

● **Domestic programs.** In a surprise move, Democrats raised a point of order against their own committee's amendment on domestic programs, effectively killing it. Senators then agreed, 75-22, to a scaled-back amendment written by the leadership that dropped much of the committee-approved authorizing language, such as the long list of immigration provisions, as well as the $1.2 billion for science programs. *(Senate vote 137, p. S-30)*

The leadership version retained the expanded education benefits for veterans, the extension of unemployment compensation and the delay of the seven Medicaid rules issued by the Bush administration

— all of which were also included in the House version. The amendment also included the $10.4 billion for hurricane recovery, $1 billion for the Low Income Home Energy Assistance Program and $1.25 billion for global food aid.

In a major difference with the House bill, the Senate measure did not include the 0.47 percent surtax on higher incomes to offset the cost of expanding GI benefits.

● **War funding.** The leadership combined the committee's war-funding and Iraq policy prescriptions into a single amendment, which the Senate rejected, 34-63. Having demonstrated that the war restrictions could not pass in the Senate, Reid then put forward a war-funding-only amendment that called for $165.4 billion in supplemental war funds — $95.5 billion in fiscal 2008 and $65.9 billion in fiscal 2009. The amendment had virtually no restrictions on war funds, calling instead for a number of reports to Congress. It was adopted, 70-26. *(Senate votes 138, 139, p. S-30)*

COMPROMISE/FINAL ACTION

After weeks of negotiations, and with the Pentagon running short of money, House Democrats struck a deal the week of June 16 with the White House and the chamber's GOP leadership. "This agreement has required significant compromise by both sides," acknowledged Obey, who was the chief Democratic negotiator.

The bill included the president's entire request for war funding, without any of the House's proposed restrictions on the deployment of U.S. troops in Iraq. Senate leaders were not involved with the negotiations, and most of the Senate's domestic spending add-ons were dropped. Senate Democrats reluctantly accepted the compromise, but Byrd predicted there would be a second supplemental, devoted to domestic spending.

The $186.5 billion bottom line for fiscal 2008 and 2009 did not include the costs of extending unemployment benefits or expanding the GI Bill for veterans. "The cost of the bill, frankly, is high, but it's a price of freedom," Boehner said.

The House agreed to the compromise June 19 in the form of two amendments. It voted 268-155 to adopt the war spending amendment, which provided $165.4 billion, as the Senate had proposed. The second amendment, adopted 416-12, provided $24.7 billion for a range of domestic, foreign aid and military construction accounts. It included the unemployment and GI provisions. And it reduced the war funding total by $3.6 billion. *(House votes 431, 432, p. H-144)*

The administration endorsed the package the day of the House votes. "We urge both the House and Senate to immediately pass this bipartisan agreement," the White House said in a statement of administration policy.

The Senate did not need to vote on the first amendment because it was identical to the one senators had adopted May 22. The chamber adopted the second amendment, 92-7, on June 26, clearing the bill for the president. *(Senate vote 162, p. S-35)*

The following are among the compromises made in the final bill:

● **War funding.** The $161.8 billion for operations in Iraq and Afghanistan that resulted from the two amendments, was $3.6 billion less than the Senate had approved and about $700 million less than in the House bill.

The compromise barred the use of funds for permanent bases in Iraq and required the Pentagon to begin equal cost sharing with the Iraqi government for reconstruction projects. But it did not include any policy restrictions on how the war funding could be spent — a

key concession to the White House. Most of the proposed restrictions on a status-of-forces agreement were also dropped, although the bill prohibited the use of funds for a U.S.-Iraq agreement that subjected U.S. forces to the jurisdiction of the Iraqi courts.

● **Domestic and other programs.** The $24.7 billion provided in the second amendment was about $6.9 billion more than the administration requested. However, $3.6 billion of the total was paid for with money cut from the war funding.

The main components of the second amendment were:

▸ $8.5 billion for disaster relief — the $5.8 billion that Bush requested for levees in Louisiana, plus $2.7 billion added by Congress for the Federal Emergency Management Agency disaster relief fund, Army Corps of Engineers and Small Business Administration to address recent flooding and tornadoes in the Midwest.

▸ $10.1 billion for foreign aid programs, including $1.2 billion for food aid, $374 million to help support international peacekeeping missions, $220 million for international disaster assistance in places such as Myanmar and $390 million to fight international narcotics trafficking.

▸ $4.6 billion for military construction projects, including $1.3 billion to support the 2005 round of base realignment and closure and about $980 million for military hospitals.

▸ The moratorium, through March 2009, on the seven Medicaid regulations. Some of the regulations eliminated payment for some rehabilitation services for Medicaid beneficiaries, such as children in foster care; limited state Medicaid payments to public hospitals, thereby limiting federal matching payments; barred compensation for state child welfare agencies that provided Medicaid services; prohibited the use of Medicaid funds for the transportation of school-age Medicaid patients to and from school; and barred use of the funds for administrative activities performed by a school employee.

The others proposed to limit state taxes on Medicaid providers by redefining what the Centers for Medicare and Medicaid Services considered to be an allowable provider tax, outlaw Medicaid payments for graduate medical education, and limit Medicaid payments to hospitals and nursing homes that serviced Medicaid patients.

▸ A permanent expansion of GI Bill education benefits for veterans who served after Sept. 11, 2001, at an estimated cost of $12.6 billion through fiscal 2018. Under the program, which was a permanent entitlement, eligible veterans could get a payment equal to what in-state residents would pay at the most costly public institution in the state, as well as a monthly stipend for housing. The bill also provided for the federal government to match assistance in veterans' tuition made by private institutions. Eligibility was based on time of service.

Negotiators dropped the House plan to offset the cost with a surtax on wealthy taxpayers, a decision that did not go over well with the House Blue Dogs. Not only was the offset removed, but Democrats also agreed to a White House proposal to allow veterans to transfer this benefit to family members, which was likely to add $10 billion to its cost.

But most of the Blue Dogs chose to express their opposition to the decision by voting against the rule (H Res 1284) governing the floor debate and not against the supplemental itself. The rule was adopted, 342-83. Forty Democrats voted against the rule, but only three cast "nay" votes on the domestic spending amendment, which included the veterans' education benefits. *(House vote 429, p. H-142)*

▸ An extension of unemployment benefits that was less generous than in either the original House or Senate versions. The bill provided a 13-week extension for all states — with no additional benefits in high jobless areas — and required that individuals work at least 20 weeks to be eligible to collect the extended federal benefit. House Republicans fought to make these changes.

Among the Senate items dropped in the compromise were $1 billion for low-income home energy assistance, $490 million for law enforcement grants and $451 million for the Federal Highway Administration's emergency relief program. The amendment still contained a small amount of funding for domestic discretionary programs, including $150 million for the Food and Drug Administration for food and medical product safety, $178 million for the Bureau of Prisons for incarceration costs, and $210 million for census cost overruns.

The long list of scrapped items prompted several Senate Democrats to call for another supplemental bill focused on domestic needs. "I have every reason to believe the committee will meet again to consider a second supplemental," Byrd said. ■

Chapter 3

Agriculture, Regulatory Policy & Transportation

Following a Protracted Money Fight, Farm Bill Enacted Over Bush Veto

AFTER NEARLY A YEAR and a half of debate, Congress cleared a new, five-year farm bill and overrode a presidential veto to enact it into law.

President Bush objected to the cost of the measure and pushed for sharp reductions in farm subsidies, arguing that generous aid to farmers was not needed at a time of high crop prices and farm revenue. But support in both chambers for a less-stringent bill was strong enough to rebuff him.

A clerical glitch that left a section on international trade out of the first version sent to the White House forced Congress and Bush to repeat the process. The first bill was enacted over Bush's veto May 22 (HR 2419 — PL 110-234). But the operative version was enacted June 18 (HR 6124 — PL 110-246).

The measure was expected to result in a net $289 billion in outlays over five years for farm, nutrition, conservation and other related programs. At least two-thirds of the funding was for nutrition activities such as food stamps and school lunches for low-income children. The measure tightened income eligibility limits for farm payments, expanded the food stamp program, expanded conservation programs and offered new incentives for alternative energy.

The previous farm law (PL 107-171), enacted in 2002, expired in September 2007 and had been kept alive through a series of six short-term extensions. The House passed its original version of the new five-year bill in July 2007, and the Senate passed an amended bill in December 2007. Although the two chambers largely agreed on program reauthorizations, negotiations over the final version dragged on for months. *(2002 Almanac, p. 4-3; 2007 Almanac, p. 3-3)*

The bill's price tag — specifically its cost compared with a March 2007 baseline from the Congressional Budget Office (CBO) — was the source of nearly every hurdle, stalemate and fight along the way. The fiscal 2008 budget resolution (S Con Res 21) instructed the House and Senate Agriculture committees to stay within the five- and 10-year CBO baseline limits when they wrote the new farm bill. They could add up to $20 billion, but the extra spending would have to be offset by cuts in other mandatory programs or by tax increases.

The baseline was an estimate of what it would cost if Congress simply extended the 2002 law for five years under projected economic and market conditions. CBO put the total cost at $284 billion in outlays over five years and $604 billion over 10 years.

CBO's calculations put particular pressure on the amount available for agricultural subsidies in fiscal 2008 through 2012. Within the baseline total, CBO projected that spending on food stamps

BOX SCORE

BILLS: HR 2419 — PL 110-234; HR 6124 — PL 110-246.

LEGISLATIVE ACTION:

House adopted the conference report on HR 2419, 318-106, on May 14.

Senate cleared the bill, 81-15, on May 15.

President vetoed May 21.

House passed HR 2419 over president's veto, 316-108, on May 21 (two-thirds required).

Senate enacted the bill over president's veto, 82-13, on May 22 (two-thirds required).

House passed HR 6124, 306-110, on May 22.

Senate cleared HR 6124, 77-15, on June 5.

President vetoed June 18.

House passed HR 6124 over president's veto, 317-109, on June 18 (two-thirds required).

Senate enacted the bill over president's veto, 80-14, on June 18 (two-thirds required).

would increase by about $29.9 billion if the 2002 law were extended for five years and that conservation spending would grow by about $5.7 billion. By contrast, the agency assumed that the cost of commodity subsidies would fall by about $22.7 billion, compared with the previous five years. That was based on an assumption that farmers would get higher crop prices in the next five-year period, which would reduce the need for farm subsidies.

CBO found that the House-passed bill exceeded the baseline by $5.7 billion over five years; the Senate-passed version was over by $5.3 billion. The two bills differed substantially in the kind and amount of taxes and other offsets that they proposed to make up the difference.

What ensued was an extended fight over spending levels and acceptable offsets that forced lawmakers to make tough choices about which programs to cut back, which to increase and how to pay for the added costs.

After months of negotiations, House and Senate conferees reached agreement on most provisions of the multi-year bill May 7. As negotiators released details the following day, Agriculture Secretary Ed Schafer reiterated the administration's veto threat, saying farm subsidies in the bill were still far too generous.

It took conferees another five days to complete their work and file the conference report. Among the last issues resolved were how to pay for the extra spending and how far to go in limiting farm payments.

Disaster aid, nutrition, conservation and alternative energy topped the list of programs that benefited from increased spending in the bill. Some of the extra costs were offset by cutting other programs below the CBO baseline. The largest reductions were in crop insurance ($3.9 billion over five years and $5.6 billion over 10 years) and commodity supports ($1.7 billion over both five and 10 years). Much of the reduction in crop insurance was achieved through shifts in timing for receipts and expenditures. The cuts in commodity programs also came in part from timing shifts, as well as from reducing the percentage of a farmer's acreage that was eligible for direct payments.

Even with the reductions, CBO said the cost of the final bill exceeded the baseline by about $5 billion over five years and $10 billion over 10 years.

The conferees used an accounting maneuver to cover the five-year cost. Congress offset the 10-year cost by extending customs user fees. Some Republicans sharply opposed the tax increases, and Bush cited them in his veto message.

HIGHLIGHTS

The following are highlights of the new farm law:

● **Farm program reauthorization.** The law reauthorized crop support programs from the 2002 law including:

▸ Direct, or fixed, payments based on the farmers' acreage and the type of crops they grew.

▸ Countercyclical payments, which went to farmers of major crops when the market price for their crops fell below a target price defined in the law.

▸ Marketing loans, which allowed producers to borrow from the government using their crops as collateral until they sold their harvests.

▸ Loan-deficiency payments, which allowed farmers to forgo the marketing loan when market prices fell below loan prices and to receive payments equal to the difference between the loan and the market price.

● **Farm income limits.** Conferees struggled to set an adjusted gross income eligibility level that could get through Congress but still satisfy Bush. The president had threatened to veto the bill unless Congress prohibited anyone making more than $200,000 a year from getting crop subsidies.

Aides said a compromise cap of $500,000 was part of the discussion at one point, but conferees ultimately went for a more complicated formula that distinguished between farm and non-farm income and set limits based on a three-year average. The result was a $500,000 limit on non-farm income for all commodity benefits and a $750,000 cap on farm income for those receiving direct payments.

Previously, the limit for benefits was $2.5 million for those who got less than 75 percent of their income from farming. The House proposed changing that to a $500,000 limit for those who received less than 67 percent of their income from farming, with an absolute limit of $1 million. The Senate would have started with a $2.5 million cap, declining to $750,000 by the end of the five-year period.

Although the final deal did not satisfy Bush, it represented a major compromise between Southern lawmakers, who tended to represent larger farming operations, and Midwestern lawmakers, who largely spoke for farmers with much smaller incomes.

● **Payment limits.** The law made no change to the previous limits of $40,000 in direct payments and $65,000 in countercyclical payments to qualified farmers. However, the overall cost was expected to drop by about $300 million because of a provision that reduced the portion of farmed acreage on which a farmer could collect direct payments from 85 percent to 83.3 percent. Conferees retained provisions in the 2002 law that allowed farmers to double the limits on direct and countercyclical payments if their spouses also farmed.

The bill contained no limit on marketing loans, which were capped under the 2002 law at $75,000 ($150,000 for a couple farming the same land).

The law eliminated the so-called three-entity rule, which had allowed farmers to collect full payments on one farm plus 50 percent of the payment limit on two more farms. That rule was replaced by a "direct attribution" requirement that did not restrict the number of farms in which a producer could have a share but specified that the total amount of direct and countercyclical payments that the individual received could not exceed the caps.

● **Countercyclical payments.** In addition to reauthorizing the existing price-based countercyclical program, the law created a new, optional countercyclical program based on revenue. The new ACRE program tied payments to producers to a state's revenue level for a crop. Participants had their rates for direct payments and marketing loans reduced, and they had to remain in the program for the duration of the farm bill.

● **Dairy.** Two milk price support programs — the Milk Income Loss Contract Program and the Dairy Export Incentive Program — were extended through fiscal 2012.

● **Nutrition.** The act authorized $188.9 billion for domestic nutrition programs over five years, a net increase of $2.9 billion in outlays above the CBO baseline. Most of the increase went to expanding food stamp benefits and easing the eligibility rules. Other significant increases went to providing emergency food aid and fresh fruit and vegetables for schools.

● **Conservation.** The law authorized $24.1 billion for conservation programs, a $2.7 billion increase over the baseline, not counting related revenue increases and offsets. It reauthorized most programs from the 2002 law, including the conservation reserve, wetlands and grasslands program, and the Environmental Quality Incentives Program. It prohibited farmers with adjusted gross incomes of more than $1 million from receiving conservation payments.

● **Disaster aid.** A total of $3.8 billion was provided for new agriculture disaster programs in fiscal 2008 through 2012, mainly for crop and livestock losses. The Senate had proposed a permanent trust fund for agriculture disaster aid, with $5.1 billion authorized over five years. The House bill had no comparable proposal.

● **Country-of-origin meat labeling.** The measure reaffirmed an existing law that required that all meat have a country-of-origin label beginning in September 2008. The label had to specify whether the product was from U.S.-raised and -slaughtered animals, was of completely foreign origin, or contained meat from more than one country, such as in some ground beef. Meat labeling was originally mandated in the 2002 farm law, but Congress had twice delayed its implementation except in the case of fish, which was already being labeled.

● **Energy.** The law put a major focus on developing advance biofuels made from stock such as switch grass. It authorized $1 billion for new research, development, loan and incentive programs, including about $320 million in loan guarantees for biorefineries for advanced biofuels and $35 million to help ethanol facilities reduce their use of fossil fuels. It also authorized $1 billion in discretionary funds, which were up to appropriators to provide.

● **Farm bill offsets.** Virtually all of the 10-year cost of the law was offset by an extension of customs user fees through Sept. 20, 2015, a revenue-raiser favored by the Bush administration that had not been in either chamber's version of the bill.

But that money was not due to start coming in until 2015, after the existing customs authorization expired. Under the budget resolution, Congress had to pay for increases over the CBO baseline in both the five-year and 10-year periods. To overcome the five-year shortfall, conferees required corporations with assets of at least $1 billion to shift some of their estimated tax payments from fiscal 2013 to the last quarter of fiscal 2012. That was expected to boost revenue by $4.5 billion in the 2008-12 period but reduce it by a similar amount after that.

● **Tax package.** The farm bill was also a vehicle for a package of tax reductions, mainly to encourage conservation and alternative energy, that totaled $1.7 billion over 10 years. The tax breaks were accompanied by revenue-raisers slated to bring in $2 billion over the same period, more than offsetting the cost of the cuts. The surplus was used to pay for a small number of trade provisions.

The most expensive tax breaks included a new credit for producing cellulosic biofuel (at a 10-year cost of $403 million), authorization for tax-exempt bonds to finance forest conservation ($250 million over 10 years) and a deduction for expenses related to the Endangered Species Act ($283 million over 10 years).

The main revenue-raiser was a reduction in the existing federal tax credit for ethanol, which was expected to generate $1.2 billion in revenue over 10 years. Beginning in 2009, the credit was slated to drop from 51 cents per gallon to 45 cents per gallon. Also, a 54-cents-per-gallon duty on imported ethanol was extended for two years.

A provision that prohibited farmers who received commodity payments from using more than $300,000 in farm losses to reduce other income for tax purposes was expected to bring in about $480 million over 10 years.

The House had opposed the energy and conservation tax credits. Speaker Nancy Pelosi, D-Calif., said they would use up potential offsets that were far too scarce as Democrats struggled to abide by their pay-as-you-go budget rules. Others objected to the cost and the fact that many of the credits would be temporary, which meant they would require extensions in a year or two. Representatives voted, 400-11, on April 9 to instruct House conferees to oppose any provision that would result in a tax increase. But Senate conferees, who had pressed for a $2.4 billion package of tax cuts, insisted the credits were needed to win votes for the farm bill in their chamber. (House vote 175, p. H-56)

Both chambers had to abandon some of their biggest revenue proposals. The Senate could not get House support for a plan to raise $10 billion over 10 years by codifying the "economic substance" doctrine, a judicial precedent that disallowed shelters that did not result in real economic benefit but merely provided tax savings. The House had to give up a plan to raise $7.5 billion over 10 years by barring so-called earnings stripping, a practice by which foreign-owned companies that operated subsidiaries in the United States reduced their tax liability by shifting U.S. income to a country with lower tax rates.

Lawmakers also gave up on a plan to require stockbrokers and mutual funds to report the cost basis of securities sold to their customers, after the White House warned that Bush would veto the measure if it included the provision. The proposal was estimated to raise about $6 billion over 10 years by improving taxpayers' compliance in reporting their capital gains.

● **Trade.** The extra funds from the revenue-raisers paid for the cost of several trade provisions, including extending the Caribbean Basin Initiative, with expanded preferences for Haiti. The trade section also included language to comply with a 2005 World Trade Organization (WTO) decision that a U.S. cotton program violated trade rules. However, the WTO ruled June 2 that U.S. subsidies for cotton producers still failed to comply with trade obligations.

LEGISLATIVE ACTION
FINAL ACTION/FIRST VETO OVERRIDE

Brushing aside the veto threats, the House adopted the conference report on the bill (H Rept 100-667) by a vote of 318-106 on May 14, and the Senate cleared the bill the next day, 81-15. One hundred Republicans in the House and 35 in the Senate voted for the bill. (House vote 315, p. H-102; Senate vote 130, p. S-28)

The president returned the measure to Congress without his signature May 21, saying in a statement that it "continues subsidies for the wealthy and increases farm bill spending by more than $20 billion, while using budget gimmicks to hide much of the increase." (Text, D-12)

Later the same day, the House voted 316-108 to override the veto. The Senate agreed, 82-13, on May 22. With more than two-thirds voting in favor, the bill was enacted over the president's veto. (House vote 346, p. H-112; Senate vote 140, p. S-30)

SECOND BILL/VETO OVERRIDE

The bill's 18-month saga was not quite over, however. Because of a clerical mistake, Congress had to repeat the process, clearing a new bill (HR 6124) and overriding a second veto. The problem stemmed from an error by a House enrollment clerk, who dropped one of the bill's 15 titles — covering trade and international food assistance — before sending the bill to the White House.

Democrats initially considered passing a stand-alone bill with just the missing title, but Republicans protested that Congress would be inviting a constitutional challenge to the 14 titles already enacted because that bill was incomplete. Democratic leaders agreed, although some of them insisted publicly that the GOP was making too much of the situation.

The House passed a new bill (HR 6124) that was identical to the 15-title, $289 billion version that cleared May 15. The 306-110 vote came on May 22, shortly before lawmakers recessed for Memorial Day. The measure was passed under suspension of the rules, a procedure that prohibited amendments. (House vote 353, p. H-114)

An attempt by Minority Leader John A. Boehner, R-Ohio, to force an ethics committee investigation into the way the bill was handled was tabled, or killed, 220-188. Republicans were particularly annoyed that the bill managers in the House — Agriculture Chairman Collin C. Peterson, D-Minn., and ranking Republican Robert W. Goodlatte of Virginia — had discovered the omitted title hours before they went to the House floor for the veto override vote without telling members about it. (House vote 352, p. H-114)

Senate action was stalled for a time by Republicans Tom Coburn of Oklahoma and Jim DeMint of South Carolina, who objected to the cost and to the inclusion of provisions unrelated to agriculture. But the logjam was broken with an agreement allowing them floor time to express their concerns, and the Senate cleared the bill, 77-15, on June 5. (Senate vote 144, p. S-31)

The president reprised his role June 18, saying in his veto message that Congress should have taken the opportunity to modify "certain objectionable, onerous and fiscally imprudent provisions." (Text, D-13)

Later the same day, the House voted, 317-109, to override the veto, and the Senate followed suit, 80-14. Once again, the votes in both chambers exceeded the needed two-thirds majority, and the bill was enacted into law over the president's veto. (House vote 417, p. H-138; Senate vote 151, p. S-33)

The action was the third successful veto override during the Bush presidency — and the second for the farm bill. In 2007, Congress enacted a water projects bill over the president's veto (PL 110-114). ∎

[PROVISIONS]
Farm Law Reshapes Subsidies

THE FOLLOWING ARE MAJOR PROVISIONS of the five-year farm bill enacted over the president's veto on June 18 (PL 110-246).

COMMODITY PROGRAMS
● **Fixed payments.** The law reauthorized through 2012 direct payments, which farmers received regardless of actual crop prices.

● **Market loans.** The law renewed marketing loans and deficiency payments for major commodity crops, including soybeans, corn, cotton, rice and wheat, for the 2008 through 2012 crop years. But it adjusted the price levels at which farmers would become eligible for such loans if the market prices of their crops fell below levels specified in the bill. The program allowed farmers to use their crops as collateral for federal loans to cover their crop production costs. If the crop sold for less than the loan rate, farmers could repay the government at the lower rate. Deficiency payments covered the difference between the going rate for the crop and the assistance loan rate.

● **Countercyclical payments.** The countercyclical program, which paid farmers when the price of their crop dropped below a statutory target price, was extended through the 2012 crop year. The target prices for several crops, including grain sorghum, barley, oats, soybeans and other oil seeds, were to increase beginning in 2010.

● **State-based countercyclical payments.** Beginning in the 2009 crop year, farmers had the option of choosing a new program, dubbed ACRE, as an alternative to the countercyclical program. Those who did so had to remain in the program through 2012 and forgo 20 percent of the direct payment rate and 30 percent of the marketing assistance loan rate for the crops. Participants would receive a government payment when revenue for the crop fell below a target based on 90 percent of the five-year state average yield (excluding the years with the highest and lowest yields) times the two-year national average price for the crop. ACRE revenue payments would be made on 85 percent of the acreage planted with the covered commodity or with peanuts. For the 2009, 2010 and 2011 crop years, payment would be made on 83.3 percent of the planted acres.

● **Repeal of the "three entity" rule.** The law prohibited farmers from collecting subsidies on more than one property. Previously, they could collect money on up to three properties. However, the new allow still allows the limits to be doubled if the farmer had a spouse who also farmed.

● **Sugar programs.** Sugar growers got a loan rate increase of a quarter-cent a year for three years, which meant the loan rate for cane sugar would go up to 18.75 cents and the loan rate for beet sugar would go up to 24 cents. The bill also continued the marketing allotment program, which allowed some sugar imports every year, while ensuring that domestic sugar cane and beet producers provided most of the sugar used by U.S. consumers.

● **Limits on payments.** Farmers making more than a three-year average of $750,000 a year in gross adjusted farm income were no longer eligible for direct payments. Those making more than a three-year average of $500,000 in non-farm-related income could not collect any subsidies. A farmer who fell within both categories could make up to $1.25 million a year and collect the full array of government supports.

● **Income eligibility.** As under the 2002 law, an individual farmer could collect no more than $40,000 per year in direct payments and no more than $65,000 in countercyclical payments. A couple could collect up to double the combined amount, or $210,000, if both spouses were actively engaged in farming. The law did not continue previous limits on marketing loan benefits.

● **Dairy programs.** The Milk Income Loss Contract program, which paid farmers when dairy prices dropped below a government-set target, was extended through 2012. The law continued the government purchase of cheese, butter and nonfat dry milk. It also re-established the Dairy Forward Pricing program, which allowed dairy farmers to voluntarily enter into forward contracts with milk handlers. This was an agreement to sell a quantity of milk at a certain price for an agreed upon period of time, allowing milk producers to lock in prices early.

● **Fruit and vegetables.** As under previous law, farmers were prohibited from growing fruit and vegetables on land that was enrolled in commodity crop programs. That helped fruit and vegetable farmers by keeping prices for their produce relatively high and limiting competition in the market. However, the law also established a pilot program to allow farmers in seven states to grow certain fruits or vegetables meant for processing on enrolled land.

● **Direct attribution of farm payments.** All agricultural subsidies would be directly attributed to the person who receives them. Lawmakers said this would bring more transparency to the system and ensure that owners were not receiving multiple payments.

CONSERVATION PROGRAMS
● **Conservation Reserve Program.** The law reduced enrollment in the program to 32 million acres through 2012. Participants received government payments for taking highly erodible and sensitive land out of production. A new program would allow a portion of the enrolled acreage to be used for grazing or crop production, if the land was being given to a new or socially disadvantaged farmer or rancher. A farmer could not receive more than $200,000 over five years for all contracts.

● **Wetlands Reserve Program.** The voluntary program, which paid farmers for preserving wetlands, was extended through 2012, and the maximum enrollment was increased to more than 3 million acres. New payment schedules provided for easements valued at less than $500,000 a year to be paid out over a period of up to 30 years and easements valued at more than $500,000 to be paid out between five and 30 years. The USDA could grant waivers to give lump sum payments on easements over $500,000.

● **Environmental Quality Incentives Program (EQIP).** The law increased funding by $3.4 billion for the program, which paid ranchers to improve water and soil quality on their land. Farmers using conservation practices related to organic certification became eligible for payments. The legislation also improved the evaluation process for applications and established a program to help ranchers improve water quality. Participating farmers could get a maximum of $300,000 in EQIP payments over six years, but the USDA could grant waivers up to $450,000 over the same period.

● **Conservation Security Program.** The act increased funding for the program by about $1.1 billion, allowing enrollment of about 13 million acres a year, and added private forests to land eligible for the program. Participants received government subsidies when they used soil-saving and habitat-conservation techniques on working lands. The law also restructured the program to encourage producers to implement additional conservation practices.

● **Grassland Reserve Program.** The law reauthorized the program through 2012 and allowed the enrollment of an additional 1.2 million acres. Under the program, created in the 2002 farm law, ranchers and other private grassland owners entered 10-, 15- and 20-year contracts that barred development of the land and preserved grassland ecosystems.

● **Other conservation funding.** The law authorized $438 million in new funding for the Chesapeake Bay region. It created a $50 million Open Fields Program to help state governments and Native American tribes open private land to public hunting and fishing, and it doubled the authorization for the Farm Protection Program to $773 million.

● **Payment limits.** Farmers collecting more than $1 million in non-farm income could not receive conservation payments, though the USDA could waive the rule in cases where it would prevent the protection of particularly environmentally sensitive land.

TRADE PROGRAMS

● **Local purchase pilot program.** The law created a pilot program to allow the government to use about $60 million to purchase in-country food for hungry people abroad.

● **McGovern-Dole international food program.** The McGovern-Dole program was reauthorized and given about $84 million in mandatory funding to subsidize school lunches for hungry children abroad.

● **Market Access Program.** The law authorized $200 million a year for the program, which helped U.S. farmers and exporters promote their products in other countries. Part of the funds — about $37 million over five years — was dedicated to helping fruit and vegetable growers overcome sanitation issues that kept them from exporting their produce.

● **Global Crop Diversity Trust.** The U.S. Agency for International Development was authorized to contribute funds to the Global Crop Diversity Trust, an organization that collected and stored seeds in case of a major natural disaster.

● **Softwood Lumber Act.** The law required lumber importers to declare that their imports met the terms of international agreements and set penalties for importers who violated the new rules, among other things.

● **Caribbean trade.** Trade preferences under the Caribbean Basin Initiative were extended for two years, though fiscal 2010.

● **Haiti trade.** The law expanded the scope of trade preferences for Haiti by making it easier for Haitian apparel to qualify for duty-free access to the United States.

NUTRITION PROGRAMS

● **Food stamps.** For the first time in years, Congress increased the minimum amount households were allowed to deduct from their annual gross income in determining their benefits. The limit was increased from $134 per month to $144 per month, with inflation adjustments in subsequent years. The cap excluded retirement and education savings in addition to special combat pay. The law also increased the asset limits for individual food stamp recipients by indexing them to inflation.

The law increased the minimum benefit for food stamp recipients, which expected to be of particular help to senior citizens. Other changes to the food stamp program included renaming it the Supplemental Nutrition Assistance Program; providing new authority for the USDA to combat fraud in the program; and ending the use of food stamp coupons in favor of Electronic Benefit Transfer cards, which could also be used at some farmers' markets.

● **Emergency Food Assistance Program.** Funding for the program, which provided states with food and other resources to stock food banks, was increased by $1.3 billion.

● **Support for child and senior nutrition.** The law also extended the Commodity Supplemental Food Program for seniors who needed additional assistance; increased funding for a snack program for school children by $1 billion and expanded it to all 50 states; and reauthorized the Women, Infants and Children Program, which was funded through annual discretionary appropriations.

FARM CREDIT

● **Loans for farmers.** The law authorized an increase of about $400 million, to $4.2 billion, for direct and guaranteed loans to help farmers make down payments and to operate their farms. The limit for the loans was increased from $200,000 to $300,000. The interest rate was set at 1.5 percent or at 4 percent below regular rates, whichever was greater. The law also reduced the borrower down payment to 5 percent from 10 percent, and increases the USDA portion of a loan to 45 percent from 40 percent.

● **Conservation loans.** A conservation loan and loan guarantee program was established for farmers who carried out qualified conservation projects. The government would guarantee 75 percent of the principal loan amount, with a priority given to young and socially disadvantaged farmers.

● **Beginning farmer program.** The law expanded a program that guaranteed loans made by a private seller of a farm or ranch to qualified beginning farmers or ranchers. The two-year limit on payment guarantees under the program was increased to three years. The seller was given the option of taking the three-year guarantee or a standard 90 percent guarantee. The program, originally a pilot, was made permanent, expanded nationwide and broadened to include socially disadvantaged buyers. The maximum purchase price for the farm or ranch was set at $500,000.

● **Other programs for socially disadvantaged and beginning farmers.** The law increased the number of loans that could be given to young and disadvantaged farmers and fixed the interest rate for those loans at 1.5 percent or at 4 percent below regular rates, whichever was greater. Farmers could get a down payment requirement as low as 5 percent.

RURAL DEVELOPMENT

● **Water and wastewater programs.** The law authorized about $120 million to fund pending applications for rural infrastructure programs, including Waste Disposal Grants and Rural Water and Wastewater Circuit Rider programs, which helped lower water and waste disposal operating costs in small towns, and the Emergency and Imminent Community Water Assistance Grants program, which helped towns improve the quality of their drinking water.

● **Rural health care programs.** The Rural Firefighters and Emergency Medical Service Assistance Program, which supported emergency

services in rural areas, was reauthorized, and a 911 access program for small towns was expanded.

● **Rural broadband, telephone and energy.** To better target rural and underserved areas, the law limited large companies from getting broadband loans and grants under the Rural Electrification Act. The loan would have to serve an area where at least 25 percent of the households could only get service from one provider. The measure also provided for bond guarantees for telephone or electrification purposes, and grants to bring alternative energy to small towns. It directed the Federal Communications Commission and the USDA to develop a comprehensive broadband strategy for rural areas and authorized $25 million annually through fiscal 2012 for a new National Center for Rural Telecommunications.

● **Rural employment and business development.** A new, $15 million rural micro-enterprise program was created to provide grants for training and marketing, among other things. Additionally, the law authorized about $10 million in grants to help disabled people get jobs in rural areas. The Rural Business Investment Program, which provided grants for rural business investment companies, was reauthorized through 2012 at $50 million. The law also established a new investment program to allow multi-community regions to invest in rural development projects.

RESEARCH PROGRAMS

● **National Institute of Food and Agriculture.** The law reorganized offices in charge of applied research, extension and education programs at the institute and created new offices to develop new programs and track ongoing agriculture research.

● **Agriculture and food research**. A new research program, the Agriculture and Food Initiative, was created under the act to support fundamental and applied research and research that supported entrepreneurship and business development. The program — authorized at $700 million annually in 2008 through 2012 — would provide grants to colleges and universities, agriculture experiment stations and other organizations doing farm-related research.

● **Energy research.** The act authorized $50 million in each of fiscal years 2008 through 2012 to establish a new bio-energy and biobased products research initiative that will award competitive grants for on-farm biomass crop research and the dissemination of results. It directs the Agriculture secretary to establish a best-practices database on the production, harvest, transport and storage of various biomass crops. It also authorized competitive grants for on-farm energy efficiency research and extension projects aimed at improving the energy efficiency of agricultural operations.

● **Minority researchers.** The law made historically black and Native American universities a priority for research funding, expanded funding to Hispanic colleges and universities, created an endowment fund for Hispanic universities, and made Hispanic universities eligible for research programs.

● **Specialty crops.** The law provided $230 million for research grants on fruits and vegetables, $25 million for produce safety grants, and $78 million for organic produce research. Some funding — about $23 million — was targeted for fighting food-borne illnesses.

FORESTRY

● **Healthy Forests Reserve Program.** The law authorized $39 million over four years for the program, which helped property owners preserve endangered species.

● **Training for minorities.** A new grant program was established to help train Hispanics and other underserved groups in forestry careers.

● **Emergency Forestry Conservation Reserve Program.** The program, which helped land owners restore forests after a natural disaster, was extended.

● **Community forest and open space conservation program.** The law established a new program to provide communities with grants to buy forest and park land for public use.

ENERGY PROGRAMS

● **Rural Energy for America Program.** A new program authorized by the law provided grants and loan guarantees to farmers and rural small businesses to purchase renewable fuel systems and make energy efficiency improvements to their operations. The program was to get $250 million in mandatory funding over four years, part of which would go to grants for energy experts to help farmers and businesses do energy audits.

● **Biorefinery assistance.** The law authorized grants and loan guarantees for the construction and retrofitting of biorefineries to produce advanced biofuels — non-corn-based biofuels such as those from cellulose, sugar and waste products. It authorized grants for up to 30 percent of the cost of pilot biorefineries and loan guarantees to support 90 percent of the principal and interest on loans to develop and construct commercial-scale biorefineries. The aim of the program was to accelerate commercial production of advanced biofuels.

● **Biomass research and development.** The law provided about $120 million over four years in mandatory spending for a program that provided competitive funding for research projects on biofuels and biobased chemicals and products. It authorized an additional $1 billion in discretionary funds for the program over four years.

● **Bioenergy Program.** About $300 million was authorized for the Bioenergy Program, which provided incentives to expand production of advanced biofuels made from farm and forestry waste and manure, among other things.

● **Biomass crop assistance.** The law established a program to provide financial assistance to promote the development of new biofuels made from cellulosic products. The program included contracts with farmers and forestry companies to grow cellulosic crops and incentives to harvest, store and transport those crops to production facilities.

● **Biobased markets program.** A new voluntary program was created to recognize agencies, contractors and farmers that used significant amounts of biobased products. The purpose was to help farmers label biobased products as "USDA Certified Biobased Products" and help the federal government establish procurement preferences for those products.

● **Forest and wood fuels.** The law authorized $60 million over four years for a competitive research and development program to encourage use of forest biomass for energy. Another $20 million was authorized for a new program of grants to state and local governments to develop ways to use wood scraps for energy.

● **Biofuels infrastructure assessment.** The USDA was directed to work with the EPA and the Department of Energy on a study to determine how best to expand the production, transport and distribution of biofuels.

● **Sugar ethanol program.** A new program was established to allow the government to buy U.S. sugar equal to any excess in imports in order to maintain market prices above support levels. The sugar would be sold to be turned into ethanol. The change was meant to address a

provision in the North American Free Trade Agreement eliminated tariffs on Mexican sugar.

HORTICULTURE AND ORGANIC AGRICULTURE

● **Farmers' market promotion.** The law expanded the use of food stamps at farmers' markets and provided $33 million in grants for market advertising and for the expansion of markets, roadside stands and other community farm programs. It also included $3 million to bring produce to underserved urban areas.

● **Pest and disease management.** The law authorized $377 million for pest and disease control. It directed collaboration between federal and state governments to do a better job of detecting plant pests and disease earlier, as well as mandating an audit-based certification system between growers and the government.

● **Honey bees.** To combat losses in the honey market, the bill extended a marketing loan program for beekeepers that provided income support if the market price of honey fell below 69 cents per pound. The law also dedicated $10 million a year to research on colony collapse, which was threatening honey bees.

● **National Clean Plant Network.** About $20 million in new funding was provided for a strategy to keep plants free from pests and diseases.

● **Miscellaneous provisions.** About $22 million was provided for a USDA cost-share program to mitigate the costs farmers incurred while seeking organic certification. The law also provided $5 million for organic marketing data collection and publication. Fruit and vegetable growers would be eligible for $466 million in grant money for marketing, research, disease management and food safety. In the future, the USDA was to include produce in its census of agriculture; the department also was directed to conduct a feasibility study on whether to establish a federal marketing order for Haas avocados. Asparagus growers who lost money between 2004 and 2007 from competing imports could collect part of $15 million in government funding.

LIVESTOCK

● **Country-of-origin labeling.** The law kept in place a requirement that all meat be labeled by Sept. 30, 2008, to indicate the country where the animal was raised. Meat could be labeled as originating in the United States only if the animal was born here or was in the country before July 15, 2008. The law added goat meat and chicken to the list of meat that had to be labeled. It also added macadamia nuts and peanuts to the list of products that had to be labeled.

● **Livestock contracts.** Those who raised livestock or poultry were allowed to decline mandatory arbitration before entering into contracts with meat processors. Livestock producers said they were being put out of business by costly arbitration and often did not have enough money to take their case to court. The bill also required the department to develop criteria to decide whether there was market discrimination against smaller poultry and pig operations.

● **Packers and Stockyards Act.** The USDA was to compile an annual report detailing investigations and potential violations of the act.

● **Interstate shipment of meat.** Some meat inspection facilities participating in state meat and poultry inspection programs could receive federal inspection from state inspectors and ship products across state lines.

● **Miscellaneous livestock provisions.** The law authorized $10 million for the National Sheep Industry Improvement Center, created a voluntary trichinae certification program, authorized cooperative agreements to carry out aquatic animal health plans to detect and control disease in aquaculture species, and required a study to evaluate animal manure as a source of fertilizer and the potential impact on consumers.

CROP INSURANCE

Sections of the crop insurance program, which insures against weather losses and falling prices, were cut to provide savings for other parts of the farm bill. Lawmakers also used "timing shifts," such as requiring farmers to pay premiums earlier, starting in 2012.

● **Administrative and operating subsidies.** The law reduced by 2.3 percent the reimbursements to private crop insurance companies for administrative and operating expenses, saving about $929 million. It allowed a 50 percent restoration in states where the loss ratio is greater than 1:2.

● **Investigating fraud and abuse.** New funding was authorized for a USDA investigation into crop insurance records to identify fraud.

● **Organic crop insurance.** The USDA was required to compare production risks for conventional and organic crops and to reduce premium surcharges on organic crops if the analysis demonstrated no difference. The study was also to look at organic produce prices in the marketplace so those prices could be incorporated in the crop insurance options available for organic crops.

● **Standard Reinsurance Agreement.** The law authorized the USDA to conduct periodic renegotiations of its Standard Reinsurance Agreement, which required the government to share in any program losses experienced by the private insurers that administered the federal crop insurance program. The purpose of the reinsurance was to make it viable for the companies to offer crop insurance in all regions of the country, including high-risk areas. The law required that the agreements be renegotiated every five years beginning in 2011.

COMMODITY FUTURES

● **CFTC authorization.** The law reauthorized the Commodity Futures Trading Commission (CFTC) through 2013 and strengthened the agency's oversight of commodity derivatives and futures trading.

● **Foreign currency transactions.** The law clarified that the CFTC had authority to regulate foreign currency transactions and combat fraud. Retail foreign exchange dealers had to register with the CFTC and comply with its rules. The law also strengthened qualifications and capital requirements for futures merchants and foreign-exchanges dealers.

● **Energy speculation.** In an effort to guard against speculation in energy markets, the law set record-keeping requirements for electronic energy traders and required them to provide an audit trail. It also set up monitoring aimed at detecting market manipulation and increased financial penalties for such manipulation and excessive speculation.

● **Market manipulation.** Traders violating CFTC rules would face higher penalties in some cases and would face felony charges if they failed to comply with cease-and-desist orders. Previously, noncompliance was subject to a misdemeanor charge.

TAX PROVISIONS

● **Customs user fees.** The largest revenue raiser was an extension of Customs user fees through fiscal 2017, expected to bring in receipts of $10 billion over 10 years.

● **Ethanol tax credits.** Starting in 2009, the tax credit for manufacturers of ethanol fuel would be reduced from 51 cents per gallon to 45 cents per gallon, increasing tax revenue by $1.2 billion over five years. Other ethanol provisions were expected to bring in a total of $206 million

over five years and $211 million over 10 years. The increases would be reduced somewhat by a new $1.01-a-gallon credit for producing ethanol from cellulosic feedstocks that would cost $348 million over five years and $403 million over 10 years.

● **Limitation of farming losses claimed on tax returns.** The law limited the farming losses that could be used to offset non-farm business income to the greater of $300,000 or the net farm income the taxpayer had received over the previous five years. The provision was expected to bring in $206 million over five years and $479 million over 10 years.

● **Endangered species.** A tax deduction for property owners who took steps to preserve endangered species on their land was expected to cost $72 million over five years and $283 million over 10 years.

● **Conservation Reserve Program payments.** The act excluded Conservation Reserve Program payments from self-employment taxes for retired or disabled individuals, costing $84 million over five years and $192 million over 10 years.

● **Taxation of qualified timber gain and timber REIT provisions.** The law provided an alternative minimum tax rate of 15 percent for gains on some timber harvests. Previously, timber sales were eligible for capital gains treatment. It also modernized timber real estate investment trusts by clarifying that gains from timber sales held for less than one year qualified as income, and it changed safe harbors for timber property sales. The expected cost was $184 million over five years and $221 million over 10 years.

● **Forest conservation bonds.** A new program allowed the issuance of $500 million in timber conservation bonds so nonprofits could buy forest land for conservation, at a cost of $250 million over five years.

MISCELLANEOUS

● **Socially disadvantaged farmers.** The law set aside $75 million in mandatory funding for programs to educate and support poor farmers. The USDA was required to seek to bring more disadvantaged producers into their programs and provide an annual report to Congress on its progress. The department was required to establish an Office of Advocacy and Outreach to develop diversity in the farming industry; the office was charged with providing a liaison to groups that represented low-income migrant and seasonal workers, ensuring that farmworkers were treated well on the job and that their needs were met during disasters and emergencies. A minority farmer and rancher advisory committee would be established to conduct civil rights activities and ensure that minorities were participating in farm programs.

● **Farm Service Agency offices.** No agency office could be closed or relocated within two years of the law's enactment.

● **Office of Homeland Security.** A new USDA office was created to develop interagency emergency response plans and coordinate with the Department of Homeland Security. A new communications center would prepare for emergencies such as animal disease outbreaks or agro-terrorism.

● **Animal welfare.** Animal fighting penalties and penalties under the Animal Welfare Act were increased, and dogs younger than six months could no longer be imported from other countries.

● **Disaster aid.** The law provided for a four-year, $3.8 billion disaster trust fund for farmers who lost crops or livestock to flood, fire, drought and other natural disasters. Ranchers and farmers had to have crop insurance to participate. ■

Law Modifies Toy Safety Standards

A MAJOR REWRITE OF SAFETY standards for toys and other consumer goods was enacted as part of a five-year reauthorization of the Consumer Product Safety Commission. Congress cleared the bill in July, and President Bush signed it into law Aug. 14 (HR 4040 — PL 110-314).

Michigan Democrat John D. Dingell, chairman of the House Energy and Commerce Committee, called the measure "the most significant overhaul . . . since the creation of the Consumer Product Safety Act some 40 years ago."

The legislation authorized $626 million for the agency in fiscal 2010 through 2014, modified toy safety requirements, provided whistleblower protections to private workers, gave states more consumer protection authority and increased damage awards in product safety cases. It also required the commission to review and adopt widely accepted international product safety standards or write its own similar standards if the international standards were deemed inadequate.

The House passed a three-year overhaul bill without a single dissenting vote in December 2007. The action was spurred by a rash of product recalls that included Chinese-made toys pulled from shelves before the holiday shopping season because they contained dangerous levels of lead. *(2007 Almanac, p. 12-8)*

The Senate passed a seven-year authorization bill in March 2008 that was the result of a bipartisan compromise and contained what some consumer protection advocates said were tougher provisions on lead content, penalties, consumer information and other issues.

The chief disagreement in the House-Senate conference on the bill concerned phthalates, a family of chemicals that make plastic soft and durable. The Senate-passed bill would have banned six phthalates in children's products, while the House version was silent on the issue.

After months of talks, House and Senate negotiators reached agreement on a final bill in late July.

HIGHLIGHTS

The following are major provisions of the new product safety law:
- **Authorization.** The measure authorized $626 million for the commission over five fiscal years — $118 million in 2010, $116 million in 2011, $124 million in 2012, $132 million in 2013 and $136 million in 2014.
- **General toy standards.** The law required the commission to adopt widely recognized safety standards set by the non-governmental ASTM International as interim product safety standards, pending an assessment. Within two years, the commission was to issue new rules based on the international standards unless it found them inadequate. In that case, the commission had to write its own, more stringent standards. The law also required third-party testing of certain children's products and authorized the commission to inspect manufacturers' proprietary laboratories.
- **Plastics.** The legislation permanently outlawed use of three of the

BOX SCORE

BILL: HR 4040 — PL 110-314

LEGISLATIVE ACTION:

Senate passed HR 4040, after substituting the text of S 2663, 79-13, on March 6.

House adopted the conference report on HR 4040 (H Rept 110-787), 424-1, on July 30.

Senate cleared the bill, 89-3, on July 31.

President signed Aug. 14.

phthalates in children's toys and child care articles and temporarily banned three others pending further study and rulemaking. There was some evidence that children could ingest phthalates by putting toys in their mouths, causing problems related to reproduction, especially with boys.
- **Lead.** The law phased in restrictions aimed at reducing the permissible lead level in children's products to the lowest level that was technically feasible. The cap was set at 0.06 percent of the item's weight beginning 180 days after enactment, dropping to 0.03 percent after one year and to 0.01 percent or as close as feasible after three years. The lead level for paint was to be reduced from 600 parts per million to 90 parts per million one year after enactment.
- **Product identification.** Companies that manufactured children's products were required to place distinguishing marks on the product and the packaging to aid in identifying recalled items.
- **ATV safety.** Domestic and foreign manufacturers of all-terrain vehicles sold in the United States were required to meet U.S. safety standards. U.S. manufacturers already complied with voluntary standards, but critics said foreign manufacturers often skirted such precautions. The standards, put into statute by the bill, effectively banned all three-wheel ATVs, which critics claimed were more prone to rollovers than four-wheel models.
- **Product safety database.** The law directed the commission to create a publicly available, searchable database on the safety of consumer products. It required the Government Accountability Office to study the general utility of the database and recommend steps to increase its use.
- **Penalties.** The maximum civil penalty for each violation of consumer product laws was increased to $100,000 from $8,000. The maximum for a series of related violations was increased to $15 million from $1.8 million. The commission was authorized to seek asset forfeiture as a penalty for criminal violations. The measure also removed a requirement in existing law that directors, officers and agents of a company had to know about the company's violations to be subject to fines or penalties.
- **Whistleblower protections.** The measure provided whistleblower protections for employees of private companies who reported violations of product safety rules.
- **State enforcement.** State attorneys general were authorized to obtain appropriate injunctions against toy manufacturers that were allegedly in violation of the law. States were required to notify the commission prior to filing any action and to give the commission 30 days to respond to or assist with an action.

LEGISLATIVE ACTION
SENATE FLOOR ACTION

The Senate passed HR 4040 by a vote of 79-13 on March 6, after inserting a manager's amendment based on a bill (S 2663) sponsored by Mark Pryor, D-Ark. *(Senate vote 41, p. S-11)*

Two days before passing the bill, senators voted, 57-39, to table (or kill) an attempt by Jim DeMint, R-S.C., to substitute the House version of the bill. Pryor argued that the Senate measure had more enforcement, more transparency and "more comprehensive reform" than the House version. *(Senate vote 37, p. S-11)*

"I believe the Senate spoke pretty loudly when we rejected the House bill," said Amy Klobuchar, D-Minn., a cosponsor of the Senate measure.

During several days of debate, the Senate also:

▸ Adopted by voice vote an amendment by Dianne Feinstein, D-Calif., to ban the use of three types of phthalates in all children's toys and three others from toys that children put in their mouths.

▸ Adopted, 96-0, an amendment by Klobuchar to prohibit agency employees or commissioners from accepting payment or reimbursement for travel or lodging from anyone with interests before the commission. Instead, it proposed to authorize up to $1 million annually for travel and other expenses for employees to attend meetings and other functions. (Similar provisions were included in the final bill.) *(Senate vote 38, p. S-11)*

▸ Tabled, 51-45, an amendment by John Cornyn, R-Texas, to prohibit state attorneys general from entering into contingency fee agreements for legal or expert witnesses in civil cases related to federal consumer product safety rules. *(Senate vote 39, p. S-11)*

▸ Tabled, 56-39, an amendment by David Vitter, R-La., to permit winning parties in civil cases related to consumer product safety rules to recover reasonable costs and attorney fees. *(Senate vote 40, p. S-11)*

House members watched the Senate debate carefully. In a letter to Pryor, Dingell and Bobby L. Rush, D-Ill. — the chairman of the Energy and Commerce Subcommittee on Commerce, Trade and Consumer Protection — they said the House bill had been "repeatedly mischaracterized." They disputed claims that the Senate bill promoted more transparency than the House version by mandating creation of a public database of consumer complaints, saying their plan would require the commission to submit a detailed plan to Congress for expanding its complaints database.

Dingell and Rush said the House wanted to protect whistleblowers but preferred to do it in a comprehensive bill instead of in a "potentially inconsistent agency-by-agency fashion." However, the two also pointed to many similarities between the bills.

CONFERENCE/FINAL ACTION

House and Senate negotiators announced July 28 that they had resolved the last of the issues that had mired negotiations on the bill. A breakthrough on restricting the use of phthalates cleared the way for a deal. A major holdout on the phthalates provision, Rep. Joe L. Barton, R-Texas, said conferees "reached a sensible compromise" that "every member of the conference committee can support."

The House adopted the conference report (H Rept 110-787) by a vote of 424-1 on July 30. The Senate cleared the measure, 89-3, the next day. *(House vote 543, p. H-182; Senate vote 193, p. S-43)*

Among the compromises:

▸ The agreement prohibited the sale of children's toys or child care articles that contained more than 0.1 percent of three phthalates — di-(2 ethylhexyl) phthalate (DEHP), dibutyl phthalate (DBP) or benzyl butyl phthalate (BBP). Items that contained more than 0.1 percent of three others — diisononyl phthalate (DINP), diisodecyl phthalate (DIDP), or di-n-octyl phthalate (DnOP) — were temporarily prohibited pending a report and a new rule.

▸ The restriction on lead in products intended for children age 12 and younger began at 0.06 percent of the item's weight, as opposed to the stricter 0.03 percent required in the Senate bill. After that, the threshold was reduced quicker than in the House bill, reaching 0.01 percent in three years, rather than four as specified in the House version.

▸ Conferees included a strengthened version of the Senate provision directing the commission to create an online database to allow people to search consumer reports and official accounts of product-related injuries and risks.

▸ The compromise included the Senate's whistleblower protections; there were none in the House version.

▸ Conferees also sparred over mandatory toy safety standards. The final agreement went significantly further than the early House and Senate versions of the bill by adopting the ASTM International standards on an interim basis and directing the commission to make them the basis of its rules or to write tougher standards if necessary. The earlier bills had simply directed the commission to review the adequacy and effectiveness of the international standards.

"This is not a perfect bill," Barton said, "but it is a very, very good bill. It's a strong bill and it will protect America's children." ∎

Chambers Differ on Wind Coverage

ATTEMPTS TO UPDATE the National Flood Insurance Program fell by the wayside in 2008, a casualty of Congress' foreshortened election-year schedule and disagreements over several issues such as adding wind coverage. Instead, the existing law was extended through March 6, 2009, as part of the year-end continuing resolution that funded departments covered by unfinished appropriations bills. President Bush signed that measure into law Sept. 30 (HR 2638 — PL 110-329).

The National Flood Insurance Program, created in 1968, was supported by premium revenue for nearly two decades until 2005, when Hurricanes Katrina, Rita and Wilma devastated New Orleans and other parts of the Gulf Coast. The claims resulting from the disasters overwhelmed the program, far outstripping the premium income and leaving the program nearly $17.5 billion in debt to the U.S. Treasury.

Congress amended the program's pre-2005 statutory borrowing limit of $1.5 billion three times after the hurricanes, raising it to $3.5 billion, then to $18.5 billion and finally to $20.8 billion (PL 109-106).

The program protected about 5.5 million property owners in case of flood damage, and its previous authorization was due to run out at the end of fiscal 2008. Lawmakers hoped to use the reauthorization to put the program on a sounder financial footing.

The House easily passed a five-year reauthorization bill (HR 3121) in September 2007. The Senate Banking, Housing and Urban Affairs Committee approved a separate version (S 2284), also covering five years, in October 2007, but floor action was put off until 2008. *(2007 Almanac, p. 16-4)*

Both bills would have allowed the Federal Emergency Management Agency, which administered the flood insurance program, to increase premium rates by 15 percent a year, up from 10 percent under existing law. Both proposed to phase out premium subsidies for second homes and commercial property built before 1974, when flood insurance maps went into effect and properties already in areas designated as flood zones were given subsidies. About 25 percent of all insured properties still had subsidized premiums.

Both measures also would have increased civil penalties for lenders who did not ensure that owners who were required to purchase flood coverage did so.

The most significant differences between the House and Senate bills included:

▸ A controversial House provision to allow optional "multi-peril" policies that would cover both flood and wind damage. The expansion was proposed by Gene Taylor, D-Miss., whose Gulf Coast home was destroyed in Hurricane Katrina and who later sued his insurance company for denying his wind-damage claim. Gulf Coast lawmakers considered it the most important aspect of improving the national program, but critics said such a move would interfere with private markets and increase the government's liability exposure. The Senate rejected an amendment to add wind coverage, and the proposal drew a White House veto threat.

▸ A Senate provision to forgive the debt incurred by the program as a result of the 2005 hurricanes. Democrat Christopher J. Dodd of Connecticut, chairman of the Banking panel, said debt-forgiveness was a critical part of putting the program back on sound financial footing.

The proposal was a problem in the House, where Democrats had instituted pay-as-you-go budget rules that would have required that the huge cost be offset. The House bill would have increased the program's borrowing authority to $21.5 billion.

▸ A House proposal to expand coverage limits from $350,000 to $470,000 for residences and from $500,000 to $670,000 for commercial property. Gulf state lawmakers wanted the extra coverage. The Senate bill did not have a similar provision.

Efforts to bring the Senate bill to the floor in 2008 were blocked by Louisiana's senators, Republican David Vitter and Democrat Mary L. Landrieu, along with Mississippi Republican Roger Wicker, who placed holds on the measure. Their objections centered on the lack of wind coverage and other issues important to their hurricane-prone region, such as the more restrictive limits on maximum coverage levels. They held out until May, when, with some concessions, they let action on the bill proceed.

LEGISLATIVE ACTION
SENATE FLOOR ACTION

The Senate finally ended the long stalemate, passing HR 3121 by a vote of 92-6 on May 13, after substituting the language of its own bill. The actual breakthrough came May 6, when the Senate voted 90-1 to invoke cloture on a motion to proceed to the bill. *(Senate votes 125, 116, pp. S-27, S-25)*

An attempt by the Senate to waive budget rules so that the debt-forgiveness provision could remain in the bill was approved, 70-26. Tom Coburn, R-Okla., had raised a budget point of order against the provision unless the cost was offset. *(Senate vote 121, p. S-26)*

Gulf coast senators won some changes but lost on the big issues. During the debate, the Senate:

▸ Rejected, 19-74, an amendment by Wicker that would have expanded the flood insurance program to include coverage for wind damage. *(Senate vote 117, p. S-25)*

Environmentalists, consumer organizations and insurers urged senators to oppose the expanded coverage, saying it could cost taxpayers billions while providing incentives to build homes and businesses in environmentally fragile areas subject to frequent hurricanes and other storms.

▸ Rejected, 27-66, an amendment by Vitter and Landrieu that would have increased maximum coverage limits under the program to correspond to those in the House bill. *(Senate vote 118, p. S-25)*

▸ Rejected, 23-69, an amendment by Vitter and Landrieu to allow a longer phase-in period for property owners who were required to pay higher premiums under the bill because new flood mapping put their properties in a higher-risk category. The amendment would have mirrored the House bill by lengthening the period to five years from the two years in the Senate bill. *(Senate vote 119, p. S-25)*

"If a property is at greater risk under those new flood maps," said Vitter, "premiums would go up. They should go up. But I do think we need to temper that with a reasonable time period over which to spread out that increase."

▸ Rejected, 30-62, a Landrieu amendment to strike a provision requiring that residents in areas protected by levees and dams buy flood

insurance. Instead, Landrieu proposed a study to assess the risk for properties protected by such structures. *(Senate vote 120, p. S-26)*

Dodd agreed to add a provision sponsored by Landrieu that would boost oversight of insurance companies as they determined whether storm damage was caused by privately covered wind damage or federally covered water damage. That amendment was adopted by voice vote. But Landrieu still voted against the legislation, saying in a statement that it would place "a great burden on Louisianans" and that she hoped that the final bill would more closely mirror the House version. ∎

Conflicting Interests Kill Tobacco Bill

A BILL TO GIVE THE Food and Drug Administration (FDA) the authority to regulate tobacco products passed in the House. But a companion measure approved by a Senate committee never reached the floor, and the legislation died at the end of the Congress.

Democrats had promised a strong push in the 110th Congress to give the FDA sweeping new powers to regulate tobacco products, including nicotine levels, packaging, sales and marketing.

While both bills would have allowed the FDA to regulate tobacco and nicotine levels, they would not have empowered the agency to ban cigarettes or to force the elimination of nicotine from tobacco products. Still, public health groups supported the bill, with the expectation that it would decrease smoking rates and reduce tobacco-related illnesses and deaths.

Market leader Philip Morris USA, maker of Marlboro cigarettes, supported the legislation, saying FDA regulation "would bring predictability and clear standards to the tobacco industry in the United States." But second-level tobacco companies such as Lorillard and R.J. Reynolds fiercely opposed the legislation, saying it would enable Philip Morris to gain a near monopoly because the larger company could more easily afford regulation and essentially lock in its share of sales.

Although almost all lawmakers had come to agree that tobacco was a dangerous product and hardly any of them publicly defended the industry, opponents said it was inappropriate to have the FDA regulate the substance because the agency could never certify a tobacco product as safe.

In the Senate, Edward M. Kennedy, D-Mass., teamed up in the first session with Texas Republican John Cornyn to win approval for their bill (S 625) in the Health, Education, Labor and Pensions (HELP) Committee, despite the determined opposition of tobacco-state lawmakers such as Republican Richard M. Burr of North Carolina.

The real fight was waged in the House, where Democratic committee chairmen vied over jurisdictional claims. The bill was championed by sponsor Henry A. Waxman, D-Calif., and won the approval of the Energy and Commerce Committee in March. But others, mainly Ways and Means Chairman Charles B. Rangel, D-N.Y., wanted a crack at sections of the bill before it went to the floor.

The chairmen finally broke the gridlock in late July, setting up an overwhelming vote for passage in the House.

But the bill stalled in the Senate, where Burr and other tobacco-state senators vowed to do all they could to delay it. They were joined by Republican Michael B. Enzi of Wyoming, who did not like the bill because it would not phase out sales of tobacco products altogether. Other Senate Republicans, including Orrin G. Hatch of Utah and Johnny Isakson of Georgia, also wanted a stricter bill.

With days ticking down in the legislative session and lawmakers focused on other priorities, the Senate never took it up.

BACKGROUND

Efforts to allow the FDA to regulate tobacco went back more than a decade. The FDA first tried to assert control over tobacco products as part of a broad effort under the Clinton administration to curb teen smoking. The agency issued regulations in 1996 to prohibit the sale of tobacco products to people younger than 18 and strictly limit tobacco advertising.

But in 2000, the Supreme Court prohibited the FDA from enforcing the requirements, ruling that Congress had not granted the agency such power. The decision was widely viewed by anti-tobacco lawmakers as an invitation for Congress to act.

In 2004, the Senate endorsed a compromise plan that paired FDA regulation of tobacco with a multibillion-dollar buyout aimed at gradually easing farmers out of the tobacco business. Supporters said that combining the two proposals, which had very different constituencies, was the only way to get either through the Senate. Senators adopted the combined plan as an amendment to a corporate tax bill. But House opponents, led by Majority Leader Tom DeLay, R-Texas, dropped the FDA regulations from the final bill, while including the bailout for farmers (PL 108-357). *(2004 Almanac, p. 13-5)*

SENATE COMMITTEE ACTION IN 2007

The HELP Committee approved Chairman Kennedy's bill (S 625) by a vote of 13-8 on Aug. 1, 2007, and he said he hoped it would reach the floor sometime after that year's August recess.

The bill would have given the FDA authority over most tobacco advertising and over many ingredients in cigarettes, as well as the ability to regulate, or at least disclose, the ingredients of cigarettes. It would have subjected to scrutiny industry claims about "light" and "low tar" cigarettes and limited or eliminated advertising targeted toward children. It would have required the agency to hire a much larger staff. The costs would have been paid for with a "user fee" on tobacco companies amounting to about 2.5 cents per pack of cigarettes.

Opposition from tobacco-state senators and from Enzi, the panel's ranking Republican, had stalled two previously scheduled markups. Opponents Burr and Tom Coburn of Oklahoma argued that the FDA was not the best agency for the job, given the bill's focus on advertising and marketing. Coburn said the Federal Trade Commission (FTC) might be better suited to regulate the industry's advertising claims.

The committee agreed to add language by Enzi to put new, bold health warnings on tobacco packaging that featured color pictures and graphics akin to warnings on cigarette packs in Canada and the Netherlands. Enzi also won an amendment to bar the use of cloves, which appealed particularly to young people, in tobacco products marketed in the United States.

The panel defeated several attempts by Burr, a former House member whose Winston-Salem-based district was home to employees of R.J. Reynolds, to strip some regulatory powers from the legislation.

LEGISLATIVE ACTION
HOUSE SUBCOMMITTEE ACTION

The House Energy and Commerce Health Subcommittee approved Waxman's bill in a tumultuous session March 11, 2008.

The bill proposed to authorize the FDA to regulate tobacco companies' marketing practices, evaluate their product claims, control nicotine levels in products and dictate warning labels. Like the Senate version, it required tobacco companies to pay user fees to cover the cost of regulating their products, as drug companies did. And it did not seek to allow the FDA to ban tobacco.

Chairman Frank Pallone Jr., D-N.J., had been forced to abandon an earlier markup, in part because of fierce GOP opposition to a provision that would have allowed the Congressional Budget Office to set an annual percentage increase in the tobacco user fee, with the extra funds going to the Treasury. Democrats said the provision was necessary to meet pay-as-you-go rules and make the bill budget neutral, but Republicans argued that the fees amounted to a tax and, therefore, fell outside the committee's jurisdiction.

The subcommittee approved two GOP amendments by voice vote. Ranking member Nathan Deal of Georgia won approval for a requirement that all regulations stemming from the bill undergo the usual rule-making process. Deal was concerned the legislation might allow for an expedited regulatory process. Michael C. Burgess of Texas added a requirement that tobacco regulation be funded entirely from user fees and that the FDA be barred from shifting money from other areas if user fees were insufficient.

But all GOP attempts to make major changes to the bill or delay the proposed regulations were rejected.

HOUSE COMMITTEE ACTION

The full Energy and Commerce Committee approved a revised version of the bill (HR 1108 — H Rept 110-672) by a vote of 38-12 on April 2.

Chairman John D. Dingell, D-Mich., made a number of changes that diffused some of the GOP hostility to the bill and made it a more bipartisan measure. Panel Republicans complimented the chairman for negotiating with them; 11 of them supported the bill. Dingell's revisions, made in a manager's amendment that was adopted by voice vote, also persuaded several small tobacco companies and the National Association of Convenience Stores to drop their opposition.

Twelve Republicans still voted against bill, however; some of them cited the measure's potential effect on the FDA itself. "It is incongruous that the FDA would be able to regulate a product that is as inherently dangerous as tobacco," said Burgess, who voted against approval. "If we're going to regulate tobacco, I think it should be done at the Federal Trade Commission and not as a health issue at the Food and Drug Administration," said Joe L. Barton of Texas, the ranking Republican on the committee.

Under Dingell's amendment:
▶ The user fees would be assessed by the Health and Human Services Department (HHS) and would be dedicated only to the FDA's tobacco activities.
▶ The FDA would have more time to comply with the bill. HHS would be required to issue a rule implementing the law six months after it was enacted. The original bill required a rule within 30 days.
▶ Convenience stores won provisions requiring the regulation of tobacco sales beyond over-the-counter transactions — putting them on the same footing as Internet and mail order retailers.
▶ Before prohibiting stores from selling tobacco products or issuing fines for violations, the government would have to consider whether those retailers had programs in place to prevent sales of tobacco products to minors and whether they had been subject to state fines.
▶ Tobacco companies employing fewer than 350 people won provisions giving them more time to comply with product-testing and reporting requirements in the bill and allowing them to jointly purchase laboratory testing services.
▶ Growers won provisions requiring that foreign-produced tobacco be subject to the same limits on pesticides and other chemicals and meet the same standards the FDA applied to domestic tobacco.
▶ Tobacco opponents won language to ensure that tobacco companies would not be able to claim that "smoke-free" or similarly labeled products had lower health risks.

The committee rejected nine GOP amendments, including one by Burgess that would have allowed the FDA to ban tobacco outright.

Steve Buyer of Indiana and Mike Rogers of Michigan offered five amendments that would have delayed implementation of the bill for up to 10 years after its enactment, saying the delay was needed to give the FDA time to improve its regulation of food, drugs, medical devices and overseas factories.

The agency had been beleaguered in recent years by reports that it could not adequately fulfill its existing responsibilities. Democrats largely agreed but said the answer was to fix the agency's problems, not to abandon giving it authority over tobacco products.

The committee adopted by voice vote three Republican amendments, which removed language that critics said might have allowed the FDA to award no-bid research grants; required the FTC to study whether the tobacco industry would become more concentrated and less competitive should the bill become law; and required the government to study the health effects of "cross-border trade in tobacco products," including smuggled and counterfeit products.

HOUSE FLOOR ACTION

The House passed the bill by a vote of 326-102 on July 30 under suspension of the rules, a procedure that barred amendments and required a two-thirds vote for passage. The margin was large enough to override a threatened presidential veto. (House vote 542, p. H-182)

Democratic infighting had tied up the bill for months, with the Ways and Means and Natural Resources committees making claims on tax and tribal government provisions, respectively.

The gridlock was broken in late July, just as Congress was preparing to recess. Waxman found a new $300 million offset for the bill by attaching an unrelated piece of legislation (HR 6500) that he had introduced regarding the Federal Thrift Savings Plan. That satisfied Rangel. Waxman and Dingell also removed or altered the Indian affairs provisions.

The House debate on the bill grew heated at times, especially after Minority Leader John A. Boehner, R-Ohio, weighed in. "Most people who smoke in America probably don't need the federal government to tell them that smoking isn't good for their health," railed Boehner, a cigarette smoker. "This is a bone-headed idea! A bone-headed idea! How much government do we need?"

Dingell quickly fired back in unusually personal terms. "This leg-

islation is on the floor because people are killing themselves smoking these evil cigarettes! And the distinguished gentleman, the minority leader, is going to be amongst the next to die!" Dingell yelled.

"I am trying to save him, as the rest of us are, because he is committing suicide every time he puffs on one of those," Dingell concluded, refusing to yield to Boehner for a response.

The White House issued its veto threat the day the House voted. It said the bill would "undermine one of the nation's premier public health and regulatory institutions and potentially lead the public to mistakenly conclude some tobacco products are safe." The administration argued that the bill would divert the FDA from its primary responsibilities, such as reviewing new pharmaceutical drugs and overseeing food safety. The White House also objected to the proposed user fees on cigarettes, calling them "a new tax that would be paid disproportionately by low-income individuals."

Industry lobbyists fighting the bill counted — accurately, as it turned out — on opponents in the Senate and the brief time left on the legislative schedule to kill the bill. ■

Amtrak Reauthorization Enacted

FOR THE FIRST TIME in more than a decade, Congress reauthorized Amtrak, the national passenger rail line. The legislation combined substantial increases in authorized passenger rail funding with new rail-safety measures. President Bush signed the measure into law Oct. 16 (HR 2095 — PL 110-432).

The law authorized $13 billion over five years for Amtrak programs and another $1.6 billion for rail safety. An additional $1.5 billion was authorized over 10 years for grants for the Washington Metropolitan Area Transit Authority, which runs the Metro subway system.

The last Amtrak authorization (PL 105-134) had been enacted in 1997 and expired at the end of fiscal 2002. Congress continued to provide funding through the annual appropriations bills, but there was an ongoing tug of war between those who thought Amtrak should become a private enterprise and others who regarded rail as a federal responsibility. (1997 Almanac, p. 3-22)

The Bush administration sought minimal to zero funding for Amtrak each year, arguing the government should wean the rail line off federal subsidies and move it toward privatization. Under Republican control, the House typically backed the proposed budget cuts, while the Senate supported more generous funding. In the end, Amtrak usually received just enough to limp along.

In fiscal 2008, Amtrak asked for $1.7 billion, and Bush requested $900 million, including $100 million for intercity rail. Congress appropriated $1.3 billion for Amtrak (PL 110-161).

In the first session of the 110th Congress, the Senate passed a six-year, $11.4 billion Amtrak reauthorization bill (S 294) that rejected privatization proposals. The House passed an expanded reauthorization measure (HR 6003) in June 2008 that would have authorized $14.4 billion for Amtrak and related rail investments for five years, with limited private-sector competition on high-speed rail.

The House named conferees in preparation for formal negotiations on the bill, but Senate leaders were blocked from doing so. Instead, House and Senate negotiators reached an informal agreement on the $13 billion Amtrak reauthorization, including controversial privatization provisions, and folded them into a stalled rail-safety

| **BOX SCORE** | **BILL:** HR 2095 — PL 110-432 |

LEGISLATIVE ACTION:

House passed Amtrak reauthorization bill (HR 6003 — H Rept 110-690), 311-104, on June 11.

Senate passed safety bill (HR 2095), amended, by voice vote Aug. 1.

House agreed to Senate amendment, with an amendment adding Amtrak provisions, by voice vote Sept. 24.

Senate cleared HR 2095, 74-24, on Oct. 1.

President signed Oct. 16.

bill (HR 2095).

The House had passed that bill in October 2007, and the Senate passed an amended version in August 2008. The legislation gained new urgency after a Sept. 12 collision between a passenger train and a freight train in California that killed 25 people and injured dozens more.

"With a combination of Republicans and Democrats looking to the future, we have been able to just keep Amtrak's nose above water over these intervening years," Democrat James L. Oberstar of Minnesota, chairman of the House Transportation and Infrastructure Committee, said the day the House passed its bill. "Today we change that model."

Bush was not happy with the legislation. The White House had opposed the Senate bill and threatened to veto the House-passed version because of its cost and because it did not seek to restructure Amtrak. The administration's own proposal, issued in the 109th Congress, would have split Amtrak into three entities: a private company to provide infrastructure maintenance and operations for the Northeast Corridor between New York and Washington, a second company to operate the trains, and a government corporation to hold the Amtrak name and logo and the right of access to existing routes on lines owned by the freight railroads.

But the majorities that voted for the bill in both chambers were large enough to override a veto, and John L. Mica of Florida, the ranking Republican on the House Transportation and Infrastructure Committee, worked to persuade Bush to back the bill, saying that it would hold Amtrak more financially accountable than before and allow some small-scale privatization of high-speed rail lines.

HIGHLIGHTS

The following are some of the main provisions of the bill:
● **Passenger rail.** The passenger rail section:
▸ Authorized $13 billion over five years (fiscal 2009 through 2013) for Amtrak and federal passenger rail programs, including $5.3 billion for capital grants to Amtrak, $2.9 billion for operating grants and $1.4 billion to retire Amtrak's debt. The authorization also included $1.9 billion over five years for intercity passenger rail service grants.

▸ Directed the Transportation Department to solicit bids for the financing, design, construction, operation and maintenance of a high-speed intercity rail system within one of 11 high-speed rail corridors that included the Northeast Corridor, and authorize $5 million for preliminary engineering. Any proposal that satisfied criteria set in the bill would be subject to review and recommendation by a special commission before a contract was signed.

▸ Called on the department to create a pilot program under which a rail carrier that owned tracks that were used by Amtrak could bid on providing passenger services over that route in lieu of Amtrak for up to five years. Preference was to be given to bidders seeking to operate routes that were identified as among the five worst-performing Amtrak routes.

▸ Authorized $1.5 billion over five years for grants to states and Amtrak to develop high-speed rail lines that could accommodate speeds of 110 mph or more.

▸ Required a plan to restore Northeast Corridor infrastructure to good repair.

▸ Authorized $1.5 billion over 10 years for capital and maintenance grants for the Washington Metropolitan Area Transit Authority.

● **Rail safety.** The rail-safety section included provisions that:

▸ Authorized $1.6 billion over five years (fiscal 2009 through 2013) for rail-safety programs, including $1.3 billion for the Federal Railroad Administration.

▸ Required each Class I railroad carrier, as well as intercity and passenger train companies, to submit plans to have positive train control systems in place by the end of 2015 that could sense impending collisions and stop the trains. It authorized $50 million a year to help implement the technology.

▸ Capped rail workers' on-duty and "limbo" time — the time during which workers traveled to the location where they officially completed their shifts or remained on a train after a shift ended — at 276 hours per month, barred shifts longer than 12 hours, and required that workers receive at least 10 consecutive off-duty hours every 24 hours. Total per-month limbo time was reduced from 40 hours to 30 hours.

▸ Authorized $3 million annually for highway-rail grade-crossing safety grants and $5 million annually in grants for safety improvements to railroad infrastructure.

▸ Increased maximum civil penalties for certain rail-safety violations from $10,000 to $25,000. For grossly negligent violations, the maximum penalty increased from $20,000 to $100,000.

LEGISLATIVE ACTION

HOUSE COMMITTEE ACTION: AMTRAK

The House Transportation and Infrastructure Committee gave voice vote approval May 22 to a $14.4 billion, five-year Amtrak reauthorization bill (HR 6003 — H Rept 110-690). The panel's Subcommittee on Railroads, Pipelines and Hazardous Materials had approved it by voice vote two days earlier.

"Europe has invested $350 billion in rail," Oberstar told his committee. "We need to do the same."

The bill was the result of a bipartisan agreement between Oberstar, who was no fan of privatization, and Mica, who in the past had supported significant budget cuts for Amtrak. Mica agreed to the higher funding level; Oberstar accepted Mica's proposal to allow private companies to bid on building a high-speed rail line in the Northeast Corridor.

Mica was an ardent supporter of a high-speed rail line in the cor-

ridor that could compete with airline travel. "Amtrak doesn't have the capability to put in high-speed," he said. "The private sector is going to have to do that."

The $14.4 billion authorization included $6.7 billion for capital expenses ($4.2 billion in grants for Amtrak and $2.5 billion in grants to states to develop intercity rail service). The total also covered $3 billion for operations, including money to help Amtrak repay the millions of dollars it owed unionized workers for the nearly eight years they worked without a wage increase, and $1.8 billion for grants to develop high-speed rail corridors.

The bill included a requirement that the Transportation secretary solicit bids to design, construct and operate an initial high-speed rail system operating between Washington, D.C., and New York City, subject to review by a special commission. This allowed bids from private companies. After reporting to Congress on a successful bid for the Northwest Corridor, the secretary could consider private-sector proposals for other high-speed rail projects.

To alleviate tensions between freight and passenger rail lines, the bill proposed creating federal guidelines for negotiations over rights of way. Amtrak experienced significant delays when waiting for freight trains to pass, costing the passenger line millions of dollars.

Although no members spoke in opposition to the bill, Mica acknowledged that some Republicans would balk at its cost.

HOUSE FLOOR ACTION: AMTRAK

Despite a presidential veto threat, the House passed the bill June 11 by a vote of 311-104. It was the first time the House had passed an Amtrak authorization bill in 11 years. Lawmakers subsequently inserted the provisions into S 294, the 2007 Senate-passed bill, in preparation for going to conference. *(House vote 400, p. H-132)*

During the debate, the House:

▸ Adopted, 295-127, an amendment by Thomas M. Davis III, R-Va., to add to the total authorization $1.5 billion for the Washington Metropolitan Area Transit Authority to provide for capital needs on the Metro transit system. *(House vote 398, p. H-130)*

▸ Adopted by voice vote an amendment by Adam Smith, D-Wash., to require Amtrak to engage in good-faith discussions with commuter rail and public transportation entities operating on the same tracks.

▸ Rejected, 150-275, an amendment by Pete Sessions, R-Texas, that would have prohibited Amtrak from spending money on the Sunset Limited, a long-distance route between Los Angeles and New Orleans. Sessions said it was "the worst performing long-distance route." *(House vote 397, p. H-130)*

▸ Adopted by voice vote a manager's package by Oberstar that included language to bar the use of funds in the bill to employ illegal immigrants.

Although the privatization language helped win some GOP support, it did not satisfy the Bush administration. The White House issued a statement June 9, two days before the floor vote, saying that Bush's senior advisers would recommend a veto of the House bill because it did not require "any meaningful reforms in Amtrak's governance or operations" and would not allocate resources based on the demand for rail service.

SENATE FLOOR ACTION: RAIL SAFETY

The Senate passed an amended version of HR 2095 — the rail-safety bill that the House had passed in 2007 — by voice vote Aug. 1. The measure proposed a six-year authorization of the Federal Railroad

Administration (fiscal 2009 through 2014) and authorized $1.4 billion over that period, plus funds for grant programs. The House version was a four-year authorization (fiscal 2008 through 2011) with a $1.1 billion authorization plus grant money.

Both of the bills included increases in the number of rail-safety inspection and enforcement personnel and included steps toward implementing positive train control systems. Both also proposed modifying hours-of-service requirements for rail workers in an effort to limit worker fatigue and improve safety. Oberstar, the son of a union official, had long championed stronger limits on the number of hours that railroad employees could work.

The House version would have reauthorized the Federal Railroad Administration four years (2008 through 2011) and authorized a total of $1.1 billion, plus money for grants.

It included provisions to increase from eight hours to 10 hours the minimum rest time for railroad workers during a 24-hour period, prohibited shifts of more than 12 hours and required 24 consecutive hours off each week.

It also limited limbo, or "deadhead," time to 10 hours per month. Under existing law, limbo time did not count against hours-of-service limits. The Bush administration called the provision "overly prescriptive" but stopped short of issuing a veto threat.

Many of the provisions of the Senate bill were similar. However, the Senate version proposed to cap rail workers' total on-duty and limbo time at 276 hours per month. It would have required time off for employees who were in limbo for more than 12 consecutive hours and limited to three hours the time a railroad employee could spend on a train after working a 12-hour shift. Like the House bill, it also would have prohibited railroads from communicating with workers during rest hours, except to inform them of some emergency.

A floor amendment by Frank R. Lautenberg, D-N.J., who sponsored the Senate version, increased leave time for employees who worked more than five consecutive days. For six consecutive days of work, an employee would receive two days off; for every seven consecutive days, an employee would receive three days of leave.

FINAL ACTION: AMTRAK AND RAIL SAFETY

The House took up the Senate-amended bill on Sept. 24 and replaced the text with a complete substitute worked out in informal House-Senate negotiations. The compromise was adopted by voice vote. The Senate cleared the combined bill, 74-24, on Oct. 1. (*Senate vote 210, p. S-46*)

Lawmakers had been ready to hold a conference on the Amtrak bill (S 294), but Tom Coburn, R-Okla., blocked Senate leaders from appointing conferees. Coburn strongly opposed the House provision authorizing $1.5 billion for improvements to the Washington Metro subway system. "He thinks that's the mother of all earmarks," an aide said. "If there's money for D.C. Metro, the senator will object to it."

Although Coburn continued to oppose the legislation, Reid won a vote Sept. 29 to invoke cloture, which limited further debate on the bill and paved the way for final action. The vote was 69-17, well above the 60 votes needed for cloture. (*Senate vote 209, p. S-46*)

The following are some of the main compromises made during the negotiations.

▸ The major sticking point in the Amtrak portion of the bill was the House proposal to allow private bids on a high-speed rail line in the Northeast Corridor. Mica said there was no room for compromise on the language. Lautenberg, one of Amtrak's staunchest allies, said he would fight to keep Mica's provision out of the final bill, although he stopped short of saying he would seek to kill the measure if he failed. The argument during informal meetings ended up being whether the Northeast Corridor, Amtrak's most profitable line, should be bid first. Some senators said it made more sense to allow private companies to invest in struggling corridors elsewhere. The compromise was to allow private companies to bid on any one of 11 corridors.

▸ The $13 billion, five-year Amtrak authorization was closer to the House provision. The $1.6 billion five-year authorization for rail-safety programs was more than either chamber recommended.

▸ Like the Senate bill, the final measure capped the total on-duty and limbo time for rail workers at 276 hours per month. Like both measures, it limited shifts to 12 hours and required that workers receive at least 10 consecutive hours off duty in a 24-hour period.

The measure gradually reduced the allowable limbo time from 40 hours per month to 30 hours per month. The final bill also extended hours-of-service standards to contractors. And it gave the Transportation Department the authority to reduce the maximum hours of service or increase the minimum period of rest based on scientific and medical research.

▸ The increases in civil penalties for certain rail-safety violations were similar to those in the original House bill. ■

$8 Billion Added to Highway Fund

THE FEDERAL HIGHWAY TRUST FUND, which was nearing bankruptcy, was rescued when Congress cleared legislation to transfer $8 billion from the Treasury's general fund into the highway account. President Bush signed the bill into law Sept. 15 (HR 6532 — PL 110-318).

The Bush administration had adamantly opposed attempts by Congress to replenish the highway fund, which was projected to face a shortfall in 2009. When the House passed an $8 billion bill in July, the White House issued a veto threat, calling it a "gimmick and a dangerous precedent that shifts costs from users to taxpayers at large."

But the impending depletion of the trust fund, which seemed to take the administration by surprise, led officials in September to urge lawmakers to pass the legislation immediately.

The highway fund was financed primarily by an 18.4-cents-a-gallon federal excise tax on gasoline. Revenues were declining as Americans drove less and switched to more fuel-efficient vehicles in response to soaring gas prices. The administration opposed using money from the Treasury to make up the shortfall, proposing instead that the highway fund borrow $3.2 billion from a separate mass transit account. Lawmakers rejected the proposal as a "rob Peter to pay Paul" solution.

● **Stalled in the Senate.** Efforts by Senate Finance Chairman Max Baucus, D-Mont., and others to push the highway fund replenishment through the Senate were blocked by fiscal conservatives who op-

posed adding to the deficit or using tax increases to offset the cost.

One major push came on a bill (HR 2881) to reauthorize the Federal Aviation Administration (FAA). Baucus and Charles E. Grassley of Iowa, the ranking Republican on the Finance Committee, tried to add provisions transferring $8 billion to the highway fund, offset primarily by a 5-cent increase in an oil-spill tax. Republicans derailed the FAA bill on the Senate floor, complaining mainly about the trust fund proposal and the taxes used to offset it. An attempt to limit debate by invoking cloture failed May 6, and the FAA bill went no further.

Baucus also tried unsuccessfully to add the Highway Trust Fund plan to a bill to renew popular expiring tax provisions.

After seeing earlier attempts fail, Senate appropriators decided in July to include an $8 billion replenishment in a draft of the fiscal 2009 Transportation-Housing and Urban Development spending bill. House appropriators had opted in June not to include the fund, saying that fixing the trust fund was a job for authorizers and did not belong in a spending bill. Congress did not finish any of the domestic appropriations bills, so the difference was not resolved. (*Appropriations, p. 2-29*)

● **Easy House passage.** On July 23, the House passed a bill (HR 6532), sponsored by Ways and Means Chairman Charles B. Rangel, D-N.Y., to inject $8 billion from the general fund into the Highway Trust Fund. Despite a White House veto threat issued the day of the vote, lawmakers backed the bill by a vote of 387-37 — substantially more than the two-thirds majority required to override the president. (*House vote 518, p. H-174*)

A handful of fiscal conservatives voted against the measure, saying it would only add to the nation's deficit, but most supported it. "I wish, as one of the strongest conservatives in the House, to have some other alternative to bring you today, but I do not have that," said John L. Mica of Florida, ranking Republican on the House Transportation and Infrastructure Committee. Mica voted for the bill.

● **Administration about-face.** Senate action seemed uncertain until Sept. 5, when Transportation Secretary Mary E. Peters announced that the Highway Trust Fund would run dry by the end of the month,

much sooner than expected, and urged Congress to act quickly to send the bill to Bush.

"At current spending rates, we will start the new fiscal year on Oct. 1 with a zero balance in the trust fund, and will continue to spend more than we take in," Peters said. The surprise announcement came about a month after the Office of Management and Budget said the highway account would have about $4.3 billion when the fiscal year ended Sept. 30.

Peters said that because the trust fund was so close to zero, the Transportation Department would have to start within a week changing the way it reimbursed states by cutting checks less often or paying them on a pro rata basis.

● **Senate comes around.** Baucus said he was "encouraged that the administration is acknowledging the urgent need" for highway funds, and he urged "senators who have blocked this vital funding until now to get out of the way."

Three days later, a handful of Senate Republicans blocked an attempt by Majority Leader Harry Reid, D-Nev., to clear the House-passed bill by voice vote. Judd Gregg, R-N.H., argued that using taxpayers' money instead of gasoline-tax revenue to pay for highway construction was "a really terrible precedent."

But the combined pressure from the White House, state governments, and powerful contracting and road-building lobbyists was hard to resist, as was members' concern that highway dollars keep flowing to their areas.

Gregg and fellow Republicans Tom Coburn of Oklahoma and Jim DeMint of South Carolina eventually lifted their hold, agreeing to a deal that gave them 90 minutes to debate the bill but did not allow them to offer amendments. The senators said they reluctantly acquiesced because states and highway construction workers should not be punished because the highway fund was in trouble.

The Senate passed the bill by voice vote Sept. 10 with an amendment that released the funds as soon as the bill was signed. The House cleared the revised measure, 376-29, the next day. (*House vote 587, p. H-198*) ■

Chapter 4

Budget & Taxes

Democrats Greet Bush's Last Budget Proposal With Patient Opposition

PRESIDENT BUSH SENT HIS LAST FULL BUDGET to Capitol Hill on Feb. 4, requesting $3.1 trillion for the federal government in fiscal 2009. The event elicited familiar protests from Democrats who had scoffed at Bush's budget recommendations for seven years but were able to do little beyond making minor changes around the edges.

Bush once again asked that domestic discretionary spending be essentially frozen at existing levels while seeking big increases for defense, homeland security programs and foreign assistance. He called for some reductions in the expected costs of Medicare, Medicaid and other entitlement programs. And he recommended that his signature tax cuts — the centerpiece of his economic agenda in his first term — be made permanent before they expired in 2010.

Bush had won a spending showdown with Democrats at the end of 2007 by threatening to veto an 11-bill omnibus appropriations package if it exceeded his fiscal 2008 spending ceiling. This time, however, Democrats had the option of waiting out Bush in the hope that the November election would bring a Democrat to the White House and spell the end of Republican fiscal policies.

"The president really had us over a barrel last year on the appropriations bills," said Senate Majority Leader Harry Reid, D-Nev. "But he doesn't have us over a barrel this year, because either President [Hillary Rodham] Clinton or [Barack] Obama will be the president in less than a year." He indicated that Congress could pass a short-term continuing resolution to keep the government open until Inauguration Day. *(2007 Almanac, p. 2-3)*

Bush again proposed cuts in a number of programs that were popular with Democrats, such as sewage treatment and transportation projects and local law enforcement grants. Overall, he proposed eliminating or reducing spending on 151 programs for a savings of $18.2 billion in fiscal 2009, but Congress had rejected many of the ideas in the past.

For instance, as he had the previous year, the president called on Congress to terminate the Agriculture Department's Commodity Supplemental Food Program, which provided nutrition assistance for pregnant women, children and the elderly, arguing that needed aid was already being provided through food stamps and other programs. Congress rejected the request in fiscal 2008 and was expected to do so again.

Bush requested some increases in domestic spending for administration priorities. For example, he asked Congress to renew the 2002 education law known as the No Child Left Behind Act and requested $14.3 billion, a 3 percent increase, for Title I programs that funded most of the initiative's efforts.

Democrats criticized the budget for omitting several major items that affected the defi-cit. For example, the administration assumed a one-year provision to restrict the reach of the alternative minimum tax (AMT), at a cost of more than $60 billion in fiscal 2009. But it did not assume further limits on the tax in later years, an unrealistic assumption, as it would have meant allowing the AMT to affect millions of additional taxpayers.

Also, the administration included $70 billion for war operations in Iraq and Afghanistan for fiscal 2009 and nothing for later years. For fiscal 2008, Bush had requested $196.4 billion for the wars. The budget also included $6 billion in emergency disaster aid funds.

The White House's Office of Management and Budget (OMB) wrote the president's budget. In March, the Congressional Budget Office (CBO) issued its own analysis. Congress traditionally used CBO's numbers, and they are used in the following description as well. CBO calculated the spending and tax changes against a baseline that assumed the continuation of existing law, adjusted for projected economic conditions.

HIGHLIGHTS OF BUSH'S BUDGET

● **Discretionary spending.** Bush called for a $991.6 billion cap on discretionary spending, the budget authority that appropriators could allocate as they saw fit. The total, which did not include emergency war funding or disaster aid, was $37 billion, or 3.8 percent, more than fiscal 2008 spending. All of the proposed increase and more was for Defense, Homeland Security and international affairs. The request included:

▸ $537.8 billion for Defense, not counting emergency war money. CBO said was a 7.2 percent increase over fiscal 2008.

▸ $37 billion for Homeland Security, an 7.8 percent increase.

Fiscal 2009 Budget Totals

President Bush's fiscal 2009 budget request as estimated by the White House and as calculated by the Congressional Budget office (CBO).

Fiscal years, in billions of dollars

	Estimated 2008	2009	2010	Proposed 2011	2012	2013
Budget Authority						
Bush	$3,013	$3,026	$3,064	$3,192	$3,267	$3,348
Outlays						
Bush	2,931	3,107	3,091	3,171	3,222	3,399
CBO	2,933	3,041	3,082	3,169	3,215	3,363
Revenue						
Bush	2,521	2,700	2931	3,076	3,270	3,428
CBO	2,537	2,699	2900	3,040	3,215	3,342
Deficit						
Bush	-410	-407	-160	-95	+48	+29
CBO	-396	-342	-182	-129	*	-21

*Between -$500 and zero.

SOURCES: Office of Management and Budget; Congressional Budget Office

Economic Forecasts Compared

	2008	2009	2010	2011	2012	2013
Real GDP growth						
Administration	2.7%	3.0%	3.0%	2.9%	2.8%	2.8%
Administration 2007	3.0	3.1	3.0	3.0	2.9	
CBO January	1.7	2.8	3.5	3.4	2.9	2.6
Blue Chip January	2.2	2.7	2.8	2.9	2.9	2.8
Inflation (CPI)						
Administration	2.7	2.1	2.3	2.3	2.3	2.3
Administration 2007	2.6	2.5	2.4	2.3	2.3	
CBO January	2.9	2.3	2.2	2.2	2.2	2.2
Blue Chip January	2.9	2.3	2.3	2.3	2.3	2.3
Unemployment						
Administration	4.9	4.9	4.8	4.8	4.8	4.8
Administration 2007	4.8	4.8	4.8	4.8	4.8	
CBO January	5.1	5.4	5.1	4.8	4.8	4.8
Blue Chip January	5.0	5.0	4.8	4.8	4.8	4.8
Three-month Treasury bills						
Administration	3.7	3.8	4.0	4.1	4.1	4.1
Administration 2007	4.6	4.4	4.2	4.1	4.1	
CBO January	3.2	4.2	4.6	4.7	4.7	4.7
Blue Chip January	3.4	3.9	4.5	4.5	4.5	4.5
10-year Treasury notes						
Administration	4.6	4.9	5.1	5.2	5.3	5.3
Administration 2007	5.1	5.2	5.3	5.3	5.3	
CBO January	4.2	4.9	5.2	5.2	5.2	5.2
Blue Chip January	4.3	4.8	5.2	5.2	5.2	5.2

This comparison of forecasts from the Bush administration, the Congressional Budget Office (CBO) and the Blue Chip consensus of private economists uses annual percentage changes in inflation-adjusted gross domestic product (GDP) and the consumer price index (CPI). The unemployment rate and the Treasury bill and note interest rates are annual averages. The administration forecast (including that from 2007) assumes enactment of President Bush's budget and therefore is not strictly comparable with those of CBO and the Blue Chip consensus.

SOURCES: Office of Management and Budget, Congressional Budget Office, Blue Chip Economic Indicators

▸ $453.9 billion for non-Defense, non-Homeland Security programs, excluding emergency funds, a $13 billion, 3 percent increase over fiscal 2008. A few programs were singled out for big increases, leaving deep cuts for many domestic accounts. For example, Bush proposed a 16 percent increase for international affairs and 14 percent more for veterans' programs but a 6.5 percent cut for natural resources programs.

● **War funds.** $70 billion in fiscal 2009 as partial funding for operations in Iraq and Afghanistan and other anti-terrorism activities.

● **Mandatory spending.** CBO said Bush's proposed changes in entitlement programs would reduce net mandatory spending by $11 billion in fiscal 2009 and $143 billion over 10 years (fiscal 2009 through 2018), compared with the costs projected for existing programs.

The biggest reduction — $481 billion over 10 years — was from proposed changes to Medicare, including rate reductions for many of the services covered by the hospital insurance (Part A) and supplementary medical insurance (Part B) programs and from premium increases to higher-income beneficiaries for Part B services and the prescription drug benefit (Part D).

Bush also proposed spending cuts for Medicaid, combined with increases for the State Children's Health Insurance Program, resulting in a net reduction of $24 billion in mandatory spending over 10 years.

At the same time, the budget included increases in mandatory outlays for other programs, such as a $126 billion increase for the refundable portions of the earned income and child tax credits going to people who made too little to owe taxes. Bush's proposal to establish voluntary individual accounts for workers that would replace some Social Security benefits was expected to increase net outlays by $287 billion in 2012 through 2018.

● **Taxes.** Bush called for tax cuts that CBO said would amount to $94 billion in fiscal 2009 and a net $2.1 trillion over 10 years. (CBO used estimates from Congress' Joint Committee on Taxation. Joint Tax subsequently issued estimates that included the impact of the proposed tax changes on outlays and showed costs of $836.1 billion over five years and $2.2 trillion over 10 years.) The main revenue proposals were:

▸ A permanent extension of the 2001 and 2003 tax cuts (PL 107-16, PL 108-27), most of which were scheduled to expire Dec. 31, 2010, compared with existing law. The provisions included reduced individual tax rates, elimination of the so-called marriage penalty, a 15 percent rate on dividends and capital gains, repeal of the estate tax, and a child credit of $1,000. CBO said that keeping the provisions in place would cost the Treasury about $2.3 trillion over 10 years (2009 through 2018).

▸ A one-year extension through 2008 of provisions that exempted millions of middle-income Americans from the AMT, a system intended to ensure that the wealthy did not escape paying their taxes. CBO estimated the revenue loss at a combined total of $55 billion in 2009 and 2010.

▸ A new standard deduction for taxpayers who bought health insurance — $15,000 for taxpayers with family coverage and $7,500 for those with single coverage. CBO said the change would cost about $17 billion in 2009 but begin generating revenue in 2011, resulting in an 10-year increase of $429 billion.

▸ A permanent, modified 20 percent tax credit for business costs for research and development above a specified level, at an estimated cost of $5 billion in 2009 and $105 billion over 10 years.

▸ An end to the taxes on most air transportation, including domestic airline tickets, beginning in 2010. The taxes financed the Airport and Airway Trust Fund. The change was projected to reduce revenues by $87 billion over 10 years. They would be replaced with fees on commercial aviation that would help offset discretionary spending for air traffic control services.

▸ Proposals to improve tax collection, which the administration was counting on to bring in an additional $26.8 billion in revenue over 10 years. About half the revenue was attributed to a proposal to require banks and other institutions to report annually to the IRS the aggregate reimbursements made to merchants for credit card transactions.

● **Deficit.** CBO projected a $342 billion fiscal 2009 deficit (2.3 percent of the gross domestic product) under Bush's budget,

Bush's Fiscal 2009 Proposal by Agency

Following are totals for new budget authority and expected outlays for Cabinet departments and major federal agencies. Fiscal 2008 amounts are based upon enacted appropriations, plus requested supplemental appropriations and minus proposed rescissions. Totals include both discretionary and mandatory spending, some of which is permanently appropriated.

in millions of dollars

	BUDGET AUTHORITY			OUTLAYS		
	2007 Actual	2008 Estimate	2009 Proposed	2007 Actual	2008 Estimate	2009 Proposed
Legislative branch	$4,300	$4,418	$5,132	$4,308	$4,586	$4,962
Judiciary	6,180	6,461	6,942	6,006	6,161	6,981
Agriculture	91,831	92,242	96,985	84,437	94,764	94,753
Commerce	7,767	7,604	8,919	6,476	8,151	9,246
Defense — military	602,999*	670,517*	588,290*	529,875*	583,057*	651,162*
Education	68,265	66,590	64,883	66,372	68,046	63,500
Energy	21,686	21,223	22,292	20,116	23,209	23,325
Health and Human Services	658,421	717,126	733,298	672,035	709,381	738,633
Homeland Security	39,718	41,144	40,122	39,172	42,340	44,297
Housing and Urban Development	35,364	40,401	39,432	45,561	52,269	45,630
Interior	10,354	10,457	9,584	10,490	11,081	10,239
Justice	24,771	24,370	23,697	23,349	25,026	26,520
Labor	47,624	49,111	53,131	47,544	49,652	54,192
State	17,094	22,937	19,238	13,747	18,892	22,103
Transportation	65,994	63,437	57,138	61,697	68,662	71,104
Treasury	492,744	522,493	549,964	490,605	520,163	547,801
Veterans Affairs	79,575	87,961	91,194	72,820	86,643	91,815
Army Corps of Engineers	7,046	5,571	10,483	3,918	7,211	8,772
Other defense — civil programs	47,188	49,019	51,162	47,113	49,067	51,220
Environmental Protection Agency	7,533	7,426	7,044	8,259	7,541	7,999
Executive Office of the President	390	336	355	2,956	2,079	528
General Services Administration	93	245	496	31	357	722
International assistance	51,377	15,987	18,381	12,770	15,224	16,451
NASA	16,275	17,104	17,600	15,861	17,318	18,137
National Science Foundation	6,069	6,156	6,977	5,529	6,256	6,414
Office of Personnel Management	61,633	66,538	70,842	58,450	64,173	67,213
Small Business Administration	528	251	663	1,175	530	825
Social Security Administration						
(On-budget)	56,663	59,438	65,117	54,917	60,035	66,341
(Off-budget)	569,627	599,176	629,566	566,846	596,528	626,442
Other independent agencies						
(On-budget)	15,523	19,851	22,770	12,919	17,466	18,817
(Off-budget)	8,899	3,079	3,801	5,093	935	1,071
Allowances	—		- 543	—	—	- 495
Undistributed offsetting receipts	- 260,206	- 285,581	- 289,365	- 260,206	- 285,581	- 289,365
(On-budget)	- 141,904	- 158,183	- 153,731	- 141,904	- 158,183	- 153,731
(Off-budget)	- 118,302	- 127,398	- 135,634	- 118,302	- 127,398	- 135,634
TOTALS	$2,863,325*	$3,013,088*	$3,025,590*	$2,730,241*	2,931,222*	$3,107,355*

* For all three fiscal years, the overall totals and the amounts for the category of defense-military include emergency supplemental spending for military activities in Iraq and Afghanistan.

NOTE: Figures may not add because of rounding.

SOURCE: Office of Management and Budget

compared with $407 billion (2.7 percent of GDP) estimated by OMB. CBO projected a balanced budget in fiscal 2012; the OMB said there would be a $48 billion surplus. CBO projected a cumulative five-year deficit of $674 billion; OMB estimated it at $585 billion.

Until 2008, relatively strong economic growth had pushed up both corporate and individual tax receipts, which helped produce three straight years of declining deficits. The fiscal 2007 deficit was $162 billion.

ECONOMIC OUTLOOK

Despite rising fears of recession on Capitol Hill and Wall Street, the White House based its budget on relatively optimistic economic assumptions. OMB projected 2.7 percent growth in GDP in fiscal 2008. CBO had calculated in January that GDP would expand by a much slower 1.7 percent in 2008, while the Blue Chip Consensus, an average of about 50 top private industry economists, was forecasting economic growth of 2.2 percent.

CBO's projections were critical because lawmakers used them, not the estimates in the Bush budget, for their tax and spending decisions.

The White House acknowledged that if economic growth turned out to be 1 percentage point lower than expected and unemployment were to rise, the fiscal 2008 deficit would increase by $16.4 billion, as tax receipts fell by $13.8 billion and spending increased by $2.6 billion, particularly for unemployment benefits.

The five-year cumulative effect of 1 percentage point less growth would be a $251 billion rise in the deficit, the White House said. Those projections were based on a single-year slowdown in the economy. A long-term drop in output could raise the deficit by more than $700 billion over five years, according to administration estimates.

Treasury Secretary Henry M. Paulson Jr. defended the administration's economic assumptions at a Feb. 6 hearing, saying the forecast had been made in November. He said the slower rate of growth predicted by CBO would lead to added costs of about $10 billion to $15 billion.

White House, CBO and Blue Chip forecasters all expected the economy to pick up somewhat after 2008, although the administration remained the most optimistic — for example, projecting GDP growth of 3 percent in 2009, compared with the 2.8 percent expected by CBO and the 2.7 percent expected in the Blue Chip projections.

Administration inflation projections were more in sync with those of other analysts. OMB expected a 2.7 percent inflation rate in 2008, as measured by the consumer price index, while CBO and Blue Chip forecasters projected slightly higher inflation at 2.9 percent. Inflation tends to subside as the economy slows, but not always. Fed officials were somewhat concerned that global price pressures and a weak dollar would cause inflation to accelerate in the United States.

The White House expectation of 4.9 percent unemployment was

Deficit Breaks Record

THE FEDERAL DEFICIT for fiscal 2008, which ended Sept. 30, reached a record high of $458.6 billion — $297.9 billion more than in fiscal 2007. The fiscal 2008 total was the result of $2.983 trillion in outlays and $2.524 trillion in receipts. The outlays were up 9.3 percent from fiscal 2007, while receipts fell by 1.7 percent.

The White House's Office of Management and Budget (OMB) attributed the reduced receipts to the economic stimulus package enacted in February (PL 110-185), particularly the tax rebates, and the declining state of the economy, which resulted in lower individual and corporate tax revenues. It said the increase in outlays had a variety of causes, mostly related to the economy and growth in defense spending.

The previous record in dollar terms was the $412.7 billion deficit recorded in fiscal 2004. The red ink had declined to $160.7 billion in fiscal 2007.

The news for the year was also glum when viewed in terms of the overall size of the economy. The deficit increased to 3.2 percent of the gross domestic product in fiscal 2008 from 1.2 percent the year before. OMB said that, as a percentage of GDP, the fiscal 2008 deficit was the largest since the 3.6 percent of GDP recorded in fiscal 2004, but well below the post-war peak of 6 percent in fiscal 1983.

In Bush's fiscal 2009 budget, issued in February, OMB estimated that the fiscal 2008 deficit would equal $410 billion. The budget office lowered that to $389 billion in its July midsession view of the budget. The Congressional Budget Office projected a lower deficit figure of $396 billion in March but raised it to $407 billion in September.

somewhat lower than that of other analysts. CBO put the rate at 5.1 percent, while the Blue Chip consensus was that it would reach 5 percent.

A HOLDING PATTERN

Administration officials made numerous appearances on Capitol Hill following the release of the budget. But while there were some tense exchanges between congressional Democrats and the White House, the debate had the feel of two teams playing out the clock in a game they knew would soon end.

Even the debate over war funding eventually had both sides acknowledging that regardless of what was in the budget, the next president would determine what would be spent in future years. ■

Budget Calls for Domestic Increase

HOUSE AND SENATE Democrats agreed in May to a $3.034 trillion fiscal 2009 budget resolution (S Con Res 70), allowing appropriators to begin a largely symbolic effort to assemble the annual spending bills.

The resolution, written by the Democratic majority and adopted with virtually no Republican support, set a $1.012 trillion limit on fiscal 2009 discretionary spending — $20.1 billion more than President Bush requested. Democrats wanted all of the increase to go to domestic programs.

A similar decision in 2007 resulted in a showdown with Bush and congressional Republicans over appropriations that the president ultimately won. This time, however, Democratic leaders responded to warnings that Bush would veto the bills by indicating they would hold them until after the election, which they hoped would bring one of their own to the White House in 2009. (2007 Almanac, p. 2-3)

Although the annual budget resolution did not require the president's signature or become law, it established guidelines for congressional spending and tax decisions. And the debate gave both parties an opportunity to make appeals to voters on fiscal issues.

Much of the House debate focused on Bush administration tax cuts enacted in 2001 (PL 107-16) and 2003 (PL 108-27), which were due to expire at midnight on Dec. 31, 2010. Bush's cuts included a new 10 percent tax bracket, special low rates on dividends and capital gains, a larger child credit, so-called marriage penalty relief, and repeal of the estate tax. Although the budget resolution made room for extending reductions that benefited low- and middle-class taxpayers, it assumed that the other cuts would be allowed to expire or that Congress would offset the costs with revenue-raisers, a difficult task. (2001 Almanac, p. 18-3; 2003 Almanac, p. 17-3)

"This agreement, we believe, will strengthen the economy and create jobs," said Senate Budget Chairman Kent Conrad, D-N.D. "It will do that by investing in energy, in education and infrastructure. It will expand health coverage for our kids. It will provide tax cuts for the middle class."

But Republicans portrayed Democrats as spendthrifts bent on raising taxes. "As American families and small businesses face increasing food prices, rising health care costs and gas prices that are nearly $4 per gallon, the very last thing they need is a higher tax bill," declared House Minority Leader John A. Boehner, R-Ohio. "But that is exactly what this Democratic budget would deliver: a $683 billion tax hike that will impact every taxpayer — from single filers and families to small-business owners and seniors. No one is immune from the Democrats' largest tax hike in American history."

The House and Senate adopted their initial versions of the resolution on March 13 and 14, respectively. The main differences were a $5.5 billion discrepancy over the limit on discretionary spending ($4 billion counting advance appropriations and other adjustments) and the way the two bills proposed paying for a one-year extension of adjustments to the alternative minimum tax (AMT). The House pro-

---

BOX SCORE

BILL: S Con Res 70

LEGISLATIVE ACTION:

House adopted H Con Res 312 (H Rept 110-543), 212-207, on March 13. It later inserted the text as an amendment to S Con Res 70.

Senate adopted S Con Res 70 (S Print 110-39), 51-44, on March 14.

Senate agreed to the conference report on S Con Res 70 (H Rept 110-659), 48-45, on June 4.

House agreed to the conference report, 214-210, on June 5.

---

vided for a reconciliation bill that would offset the revenue loss; the Senate's plan included no such language and assumed the AMT extension would add to the federal deficit.

HIGHLIGHTS

The following are highlights of the conference report on the fiscal 2009 budget resolution as adopted by both chambers.

● **Discretionary appropriations.** The $1.012 trillion cap on discretionary spending set the amount of money appropriators could divide among the 12 regular fiscal 2009 spending bills in so-called 302(b) allocations. It was about $20.1 billion more than the $991.6 billion in Bush's budget. However, the resolution also allowed $28.9 billion in advance fiscal 2010 appropriations, $3.5 billion more than Bush sought, plus nearly $1 billion for "program integrity" initiatives to counter fraud and tighten spending. Counting those funds, the resolution allowed $24.5 billion more than Bush sought for discretionary budget authority.

The resolution recommended a breakdown of the discretionary funding by programs, but those numbers were not binding. It concurred with Bush's request for $537.8 billion in non-emergency defense spending, a category that included nuclear weapons activities at the Energy Department.

● **Deficit/surplus.** The budget resolution included a deficit number of $340.4 billion in fiscal 2009, decreasing to $209.8 billion in 2010 and $73 billion in 2011 before being replaced by a $21.9 billion surplus in 2012. According to the Congressional Budget Office (CBO), Bush's budget would have resulted in a $342.3 billion fiscal 2009 deficit turning into a balanced budget in fiscal 2012.

● **Taxes.** The revenue levels in the budget resolution were based on the assumption that most of the 2001 and 2003 tax cuts would expire, as scheduled, in 2010. If they were extended beyond that date, it assumed that the costs would be fully offset through tax increases or spending cuts. CBO estimated that allowing the tax cuts to expire would increase revenue by $683 billion over five years.

The resolution did allow for the extension without offsets of some tax provisions, including the $1,000-per-child child tax credit, the 10 percent income tax bracket and provisions addressing the marriage penalty, as well as an overhaul of the estate tax.

It also assumed that Congress would pass a one-year bill to limit the expansion of the AMT, which otherwise would reach a growing number of middle-class taxpayers, but that the revenue loss would be offset.

● **Mandatory spending.** The final resolution assumed $1.945 trillion in outlays for mandatory programs in fiscal 2009, which anticipated the effects of the 2008 farm bill (PL 110-246). It ignored cuts proposed by Bush in the Medicaid program, assumed that funding for Medicare would follow the CBO baseline and rejected private accounts for Social Security. It also did not include House provisions that would have required authorizing committees to find savings in mandatory programs

that could be packaged into a reconciliation bill.

● **Budget enforcement.** The resolution assumed that spending and tax bills would be subject to House and Senate pay-as-you-go budget rules, which required that any legislation reducing federal revenue or increasing mandatory spending be offset by reductions in other mandatory spending or increased federal revenue.

If pay-as-you-go rules were waived, it was assumed that the resulting deficit would instead be offset through efforts to improve tax collection and end abusive tax shelters.

The measure also included a "trigger mechanism" similar to one in the fiscal 2008 budget resolution (S Con Res 21). The trigger applied to bills or conference reports that reduced revenue over a five-year period below CBO's baseline calculation of what existing programs would cost, adjusted for inflation and other factors. Those bills would be subject to a separate point of order in the House, unless they were contingent on certification that their cost through fiscal 2013 would not exceed the lesser of $340.6 billion or 80 percent of the budget surplus for both 2012 and 2013.

● **Debt limit.** The resolution set the stage for raising the statutory debt limit by $800 billion, to $10.615 trillion, by the end of the year. The House did not have to vote on the increase: Under the so-called Gephardt Rule, adoption of the budget resolution automatically passed legislation to increase the statutory debt limit. The Senate, however, had to take a separate vote to clear the measure. *(Debt limit, p. 4-9)*

LEGISLATIVE ACTION
HOUSE COMMITTEE ACTION

The House Budget Committee approved its initial version of the resolution (H Con Res 312 — H Rept 110-543) on March 6. The party-line vote of 22-16 came in the early morning, after a long session the previous day. The measure included:

● **Discretionary spending.** A $1.014 trillion cap on fiscal 2009 discretionary budget authority, $22.4 billion more than requested, plus $27.6 billion in advance appropriations, $2.2 billion more than Bush proposed.

The resolution assumed an additional $70 billion in emergency funds for the wars in Iraq and Afghanistan in fiscal 2009, but none beyond that, and $5.8 billion, as requested, for hurricane repairs in Louisiana. The committee rejected Bush's recommendations for cuts in domestic programs, such as local law enforcement and some health care aid, and ignored his annual call for fees to help cover veterans' health care programs.

● **Taxes.** Revenue levels were based on the assumption that any changes to the AMT would be fully offset. The resolution also allowed for extensions after 2010 of middle-class tax cuts, including the child tax credit, marriage penalty relief, 10 percent tax bracket and deduction for state and local sales taxes, as long as they were fully offset.

● **Deficit.** A $340.4 billion deficit, turning into surpluses of $178.2 billion in fiscal 2012 and $158 billion the following year.

● **Reconciliation.** Instructions to the Ways and Means Committee to report two reconciliation bills, a privileged type of legislation that could not be filibustered in the Senate. The first would allow a one-year adjustment to the AMT, offset by revenue increases through 2013. The second was a bill to achieve $750 million in savings over six years from mandatory programs. The expectation was that the savings would be used to make changes to Medicare, but the legislation could serve as a vehicle for making a wide range of changes as long as the net savings met the requirement.

The conservative Blue Dog wing of the Democratic Caucus pushed hard to ensure that offsets for the AMT patch could move through the reconciliation process. They had been frustrated in 2007 at their inability to offset the cost of a similar bill, despite the pay-as-you-go rules that Democrats had instituted as evidence they would govern in a fiscally responsible manner. *(2007 Almanac, p. 7-10)*

The issue of taxes dominated the debate. "Our budget doesn't raise taxes by one penny," said Budget Chairman John M. Spratt Jr., D-S.C. He said that because Bush's tax cuts would not expire until the end of 2010, the actual decision was two years away. "When they do expire, if the budget is still deep in deficit, both parties will have to decide which tax cuts to extend," Spratt said.

Republicans scoffed at this argument. "This budget increases taxes, and you can't spin your way out of it," said Paul D. Ryan of Wisconsin, the panel's ranking Republican. Republicans also chided Democrats for not including any plans for reducing the long-term costs of entitlement programs.

The committee rejected more than two dozen GOP amendments on party-line votes, including:

▶ A proposal to place a moratorium on earmarks — specific projects requested by members — for the remainder of the 110th Congress and create a joint select committee to study the earmark process. The amendment, which was offered by Republican Study Committee leaders Jeb Hensarling of Texas and John Campbell of California, was rejected, 16-21.

Rosa DeLauro, D-Conn., argued that earmarks had grown for a dozen years under GOP majorities and that Democrats had implemented a series of steps to improve the earmark process, such as making the sponsors public. "When earmarks served the Republicans well, they could not get enough," she said.

▶ An amendment to provide for a reconciliation bill that would cut taxes by $683 billion for fiscal 2009-2013, about the cost of extending the 2001 and 2003 tax cuts in 2010. The proposal, by Ryan, was rejected, 16-21.

▶ An amendment by Jo Bonner of Alabama to direct Congress to cut entitlement programs to achieve a savings of $77 billion in fiscal 2009-2013. Veterans' programs and Social Security would have been exempted from the cuts. It was rejected, 15-22.

▶ A proposal by Scott Garrett of New Jersey to instruct Ways and Means to extend the AMT patch for one year without offsets, which was rejected, 16-22.

HOUSE FLOOR ACTION

The House adopted the resolution, 212-207, on March 13, after rejecting substitutes offered by Republicans, the Congressional Black Caucus and the Congressional Progressive Caucus. No Republicans voted for the measure. The House later agreed to adopt S Con Res 70 after substituting its own text, a step needed in order to go to conference with the Senate. *(House vote 141, p. H-44)*

During debate on H Con Res 312, the House:

▶ Rejected, 157-263, the GOP alternative. Ryan, who offered the substitute, said the plan would cap discretionary spending at $973 billion in fiscal 2009. It assumed an extension of the 2001 and 2003 tax cuts and provided for reconciliation legislation to reduce mandatory spending by $412.5 billion over five years. It also called for a moratorium on earmarks. Four Democrats voted for the measure; 38 Republicans voted against it. *(House vote 140, p. H-44)*

▶ Rejected, 98-322, a plan offered by Barbara Lee, D-Calif., on behalf

of the Congressional Progressive Caucus. No Republicans voted for the plan, which called for a redeployment of U.S. military personnel and contractors from Iraq by the end of fiscal 2009. It also assumed repeal of the 2001 and 2003 tax cuts for the wealthiest 1 percent of U.S. households and the elimination of certain corporate tax provisions. It called for more funding for transportation, the environment, education, housing, health care and job training. *(House vote 138, p. H-44)*

▸ Rejected, 126-292, a Congressional Black Caucus substitute offered by Carolyn Cheeks Kilpatrick, D-Mich. It assumed a repeal of the 2001 and 2003 tax cuts for any portion of a taxpayer's income that exceeded $200,000. It also assumed the repeal of certain corporate tax provisions, as well as increased funding for health care, education, job training programs and veterans' benefits and services. No Republicans voted for the amendment. *(House vote 137, p. H-44)*

SENATE COMMITTEE ACTION

The Senate Budget Committee approved its version of the budget (S Con Res 70 — S Print 110-39) by a vote of 12-10 on March 6, the same day the House panel acted. The vote came at the end of a two-day markup. The chief differences concerned the total for discretionary spending and whether to require offsets for a one-year AMT fix.

The Senate resolution included:

● **Discretionary spending.** A total of $1.008 trillion in fiscal discretionary spending to be allocated to the appropriators, not counting $70 billion in emergency war funds and $5.8 billion for hurricane recovery. The cap was $5.5 billion lower than under the House resolution, but $6.8 billion more than Bush requested. In addition, the resolution allowed for $29.4 billion in advance appropriations for fiscal 2010, $3.3 billion more than proposed. Like the House version, it rejected administration proposals to cut domestic programs and add fees for veterans.

● **Deficit.** A projected deficit of $366.3 billion in fiscal 2009, turning into surpluses of $176.7 billion in 2012 and $159.9 billion in 2013.

● **Taxes.** Provision for a one-year patch for the AMT in 2008, without requiring offsets. The resolution also assumed that some tax cuts, including marriage penalty relief, the child tax credit, the 10 percent bracket and the reduced estate tax rate, would be extended after 2010 without offsets. Democrats said that would reduce the projected surplus to $40 billion in 2012 and $10 billion in 2013. Budget writers assumed that other tax incentives for purposes such as education and energy conservation could be paid for by clamping down on delinquent taxpayers and shutting down certain tax shelters and offshore tax havens.

● **Stimulus.** Provision for a $35 billion economic stimulus package, leaving the door open for possible housing relief, unemployment insurance benefits, infrastructure projects and expanding the food stamp program. The House resolution did not provide for such a package. Congress had already cleared a $151.7 billion fiscal 2008 stimulus bill (PL 110-185). *(Stimulus, p. 7-17)*

● **Reconciliation.** No reconciliation instructions.

● **Budget enforcement.** A point of order against legislation that would cause any increase in the deficit. An existing point of order was limited to legislation that would add more than $5 billion to the deficit after 10 years.

As in the House, the debate centered on tax cuts. Conrad argued that Democrats could provide some new or extended tax breaks by cracking down on those who did not pay their taxes. Republicans scoffed at that approach as unrealistic. "Ah, the tax gap, the magic

Debt Limit Raised Twice

TWICE DURING THE YEAR, Congress agreed to raise the statutory limit on the federal debt — first to $10.615 trillion and nine weeks later to $11.315 trillion. Both times, the increase was enacted as part of legislation aimed at shoring up major financial institutions in hopes of preventing the economy from slipping into a deep recession.

The debt ceiling had been increased seven times since 2002, usually giving members of both parties a chance to assail each other's fiscal policies. But in 2008 the combined increase of $1.5 trillion caused little debate.

The issue was overshadowed by the larger debate over the government's unprecedented and extremely costly efforts to help the struggling financial sector and thaw frozen credit markets.

Congress first raised the debt ceiling in July, by $800 billion to $10.615 trillion, as part of a law that gave the government the ability to take over mortgage giants Fannie Mae and Freddie Mac. The debt limit probably would have had to increase regardless, but the expectation that the Treasury would use the authority provided in the law to shore up the two companies required an increase in the amount of federal debt the government could carry.

The House agreed, 272-152, on July 23 to a compromise amendment to the bailout bill for Fannie and Freddie that included a debt limit increase. The Senate cleared the mortgage rescue bill, 72-13, on July 26, and President Bush signed it into law July 30 (HR 3221 — PL 110-289). *(House vote 519, p. H-174; Senate vote 186, p. S-42)*

In October, Congress cleared a bill authorizing the Treasury Department to spend $700 billion as part of an effort to unfreeze credit markets and keep the financial sector from collapsing. The expectation that the Treasury would use the money required a $700 billion increase in the statutory debt ceiling, bringing it to $11.315 trillion. The Senate passed the rescue bill, 74-25, on Oct. 1, and the House cleared it, 263-171, on Oct. 3. Bush signed the bill Oct. 3 (HR 1424 — PL 110-343). *(Senate vote 212, p. S-47; House vote 681, p. H-230)*

The debt subject to the statutory limit includes government savings bonds, publicly traded securities bought on Wall Street, and special securities held by trust fund accounts that finance government programs such as Social Security and Medicare. If the debt were allowed to run up against the statutory ceiling, the Treasury would be unable to pay interest on bonds and existing notes or borrow more funds. As a result, no matter how intense the partisan squabbling, Congress had always cleared an increase in time to avoid a crisis.

In one of their parting shots at the outgoing administration, Democrats noted that the federal debt had increased from $5.8 trillion at the start of fiscal 2001 to more than $10.6 trillion during the Bush presidency. Democrats controlled Congress for two of those years, however. Many economists and observers warned that the amount of debt on the books could constrain the policies that President-elect Barack Obama would be able to implement.

tax gap," said the committee's ranking Republican, Judd Gregg of New Hampshire.

On war funding, Democrats argued that the one-year provision in the resolution was realistic because they wanted to start withdrawing troops, but Republicans said the $70 billion still would not meet the needed spending. "Even if you want to cut off funding to troops in the field, you gotta to pay to get them back here," Gregg said.

Among the many votes taken during the markup, the committee:

▸ Rejected a Gregg amendment intended to prevent Democrats from using a reconciliation bill to boost government spending while meeting the required deficit-reduction target through large offsets. The Senate resolution did not contain reconciliation instructions, but Republicans worried the House would succeed in getting its instructions into the conference report.

▸ Rejected, 10-11, an amendment by Charles E. Grassley, R-Iowa, to exempt a 2008 AMT patch from pay-as-you-go rules.

▸ Rejected, 11-12, an amendment by Jeff Sessions, R-Ala., to exempt any bill or report that would extend tax relief from budget points of order on the floor.

▸ Adopted by voice vote a Gregg amendment to bar legislation that increased spending outside the 10-year budget window in any 10-year period.

SENATE FLOOR ACTION

The Senate adopted the resolution, 51-44, early March 14 after voting on dozens of amendments in a marathon 15-hour session. *(Senate vote 85, p. S-18)*

All 100 senators were on hand for a lengthy string of roll call votes, including Senate Appropriations Chairman Robert C. Byrd, D-W.Va., who was released from the hospital the night of March 12 in time to attend the session.

Republicans continued to paint the Democratic plan as a prescription for tax increases and overspending. "We need a budget that understands that it's not our money," said Gregg. "It's not the federal government's money."

In a high-profile debate, senators rejected a one-year moratorium on individual members' projects, or earmarks, although many members had pledged previously to cut the number of earmarks in the annual appropriations bill. The amendment, by Jim DeMint, R-S.C., was defeated on a procedural vote, 29-71. *(Senate vote 75, p. S-16)*

On other amendments, none of which were binding, the Senate:

▸ Adopted, 99-1, a proposal by Finance Chairman Max Baucus, D-Mont., to allow the extension of tax breaks aimed at lower-income households, such as the 10 percent tax bracket, the $1,000 child tax credit and marriage penalty relief. Wisconsin Democrat Russ Feingold cast the lone "no" vote. *(Senate vote 42, p. S-12)*

▸ Rejected, 47-52, a proposal by Lindsey Graham, R-S.C., to extend the rest of the 2001 and 2003 tax cuts, including reduced rates for capital gains and dividends. *(Senate vote 43, p. S-12)*

▸ Rejected, 49-51, an amendment by Arlen Specter, R-Pa., to reduce the AMT rate from 28 percent to 24 percent — the rate in effect before 1993 — without offsetting its cost. *(Senate vote 48, p. S-12)*

▸ Rejected, on a 50-50 tie, an amendment by Senate Minority Whip Jon Kyl, R-Ariz., to allow $5 million of an estate to be exempt from the estate tax and set a maximum tax rate of 35 percent on the rest. *(Senate vote 50, p. S-13)*

Republican Wayne Allard of Colorado targeted Democratic presidential contender Barack Obama of Illinois by offering an amendment that called for a $1.4 trillion increase in taxes over five years, arguing that that amount would be needed to cover the policy proposals Obama had made on the campaign trail. The amendment was rejected, 0-97. "I think this is beneath the dignity of the Senate," Conrad said. *(Senate vote 62, p. S-14)*

CONFERENCE/FINAL ACTION

House and Democratic negotiators agreed on a compromise budget resolution May 20. The Senate adopted the conference report (S Con Res 70 — H Rept 110-659) by a vote of 48-45 on June 4. Two Republicans — Olympia J. Snowe and Susan Collins of Maine — supported the measure. The House followed suit the next day, adopting the report, 214-210, with no GOP support. *(Senate vote 142, p. S-31; House vote 382, p. H-124)*

The final $1.012 trillion ceiling on regular fiscal 2009 discretionary spending was about $2.3 billion less than the House had proposed but $3.2 billion more than the Senate had recommended. The $28.9 billion limit on advance fiscal 2010 appropriations was $1.3 billion more than in the House measure but just $500 million less than the Senate approved.

House Democrats prevailed on paying for a one-year fix for the AMT: The conference report assumed that the cost in lost revenue would be offset. ■

Hill Does Battle Over Tax 'Extenders'

AFTER NEARLY TWO YEARS of skirmishing over offsets, Congress cleared a $107 billion tax package that provided an extension of popular tax provisions, incentives for the production and use of alternative energy and a one-year fix for the alternative minimum tax (AMT). The tax provisions were enacted after they were attached to a $700 billion financial services rescue bill. President Bush signed the measure into law Oct. 3 (HR 1424 — PL 110-343).

Lawmakers from both parties agreed on many of the tax breaks, but they had been locked in a fight over whether to pair them with revenue-raisers to offset the cost.

House Democrats instituted a pay-as-you-go rule at the start of the 110th Congress that required offsets for any new tax cuts or entitlement spending, and they insisted that any tax package comply.

Republicans rejected the idea, arguing that the extension of existing tax provisions was not the same as new tax cuts and did not need to be offset. Republicans were outvoted in the House, but the Democrats' narrow majority in the Senate and the need for 60 votes to prevent a filibuster enabled Senate Republicans to make their position stick.

The fight devolved into a procedural stalemate: House Majority Leader Steny H. Hoyer, D-Md., refused to consider a bill that did not comply with the pay-as-you-go rule, while Senate Republicans forced repeated cloture votes to stop House-passed tax bills from reaching the Senate floor. The battle ended when the Senate added its provisions to the must-pass financial services rescue bill, forcing House Democrats to accept far fewer offsets than they wanted.

The final bill provided about $149.2 billion in tax breaks, offset by $42.2 billion, which brought the net total to $107 billion.

Three main categories of tax benefits were central to the debate and to the final legislation:

● **"Extenders."** Debate over so-called tax extenders was a leftover from 2007, when Congress adjourned without pushing popular provisions such as the research and development tax credit and the optional deduction for state sales taxes beyond their Dec. 31, 2007, expiration date. Some provisions affected businesses, and others benefited individuals. They routinely expired after one or two years, and Congress almost always extended them — retroactively if the expiration date had already passed.

● **Energy incentives.** Another set of tax breaks was aimed at encouraging the production and use of alternative-energy sources. Some were extensions of expiring benefits, such as a tax credit for producing electricity from wind and solar power and a benefit for purchasing energy-efficient appliances. Other proposals were new, such as assistance for state energy conservation projects and a tax

---

BOX SCORE

BILL: HR 1424 — PL 110-343

LEGISLATIVE ACTION:

House passed HR 5351, 236-182, on Feb. 27.

Senate passed HR 3221 with energy provisions, 84-12, on April 10.

House passed HR 6049 (H Rept 110-658), 263-160, on May 21.

House passed HR 6275, 233-189, on June 25.

Senate passed HR 6049, amended, 93-2, on Sept. 23.

House passed HR 6983, 376-47, on Sept. 23.

House passed HR 7005, 393-30, on Sept. 24.

House passed HR 7006, 419-4, on Sept. 24.

House passed HR 7060, 257-166, on Sept. 26.

Senate passed HR 1424, amended, 74-25, on Oct. 1.

House cleared HR 1424, 263-171, on Oct. 3.

President signed Oct. 3.

---

credit for plug-in hybrid cars.

● **AMT.** Limiting the reach of the AMT was a perpetual issue for Congress. The AMT was created to prevent the rich from paying minimal or no taxes. Taxpayers subject to the AMT had to calculate how much they would pay in taxes if they did not count many of their credits and deductions. They could exempt a set amount from the new total before calculating what they would pay using the higher AMT rates. The amount due was the higher of the two tax totals.

However, alternative tax calculations had not been adjusted for inflation, so the AMT covered a growing number of middle-class taxpayers each year. In 2008, for example, the tax was calculated to reach an additional 22 million couples or individuals. As a result, lawmakers felt compelled to provide an annual "patch" that raised the exemption.

Republicans argued that the AMT was never intended to cover middle-class taxpayers, so blocking its growth should not be seen as a tax increase. In 2007, Congress cleared a one-year AMT extension without offsets (PL 110-166) after Senate Republicans blocked two House-passed versions that included revenue increases. (2007 Almanac, p. 7-10)

Similarly, strong opposition from Senate Republicans forced the House to drop a fully offset package of energy tax incentives from an energy bill enacted at the end of 2007 (PL 110-140). (2007 Almanac, p. 10-3)

HIGHLIGHTS

Following are some of the many components of the tax package that was attached to the financial bailout bill (HR 1424). The costs and offsets were calculated by Congress' Joint Committee on Taxation and covered fiscal years 2009 through 2018. (Detailed provisions, p. 4-14)

● **Energy taxes.** The bill extended and revised a long list of energy credits and other tax benefits, mostly to encourage energy conservation and spur the production and use of alternative fuels. The total cost of $16.9 billion was fully offset. Provisions included:

▸ Extension of energy production incentives, including credits for producing electricity from renewable sources such as wind, solar power and biomass. (Cost: $10.9 billion)

▸ Extension and creation of tax breaks for domestic energy, including credits for producing biodiesel and renewable diesel, and for plug-in hybrid cars. (Cost: $2.6 billion)

▸ Extension of tax incentives for energy conservation and efficiency. (Cost: $3.5 billion)

▸ A variety of revenue-raisers worth $17 billion, many of which targeted the oil and gas industry.

● **AMT.** The bill provided a one-year patch for the 2008 tax year,

costing $64.1 billion from the loss of anticipated tax revenue.

● **Tax extenders.** The bill extended a long list of expired or expiring tax breaks for individuals and businesses at a total cost of $48.4 billion. The provisions included:

▸ $11.5 billion in extensions through 2009 of benefits for individual taxpayers, including deductions for state and local sales taxes, tuition costs and teachers' classroom supplies.

▸ $36.9 billion in extensions through 2009 of a range of business tax benefits. More than half the cost — $19.1 billion — was for extending the research and development credit.

● **Additional tax benefits.** The bill also included about $10.9 billion in various other tax benefits, such as a reduction in the income threshold for those eligible for the refundable child tax credit.

● **Disaster relief.** $8.8 billion in tax relief for areas affected by disasters such as Midwestern flooding and Hurricane Ike.

● **Offset.** The extensions were partially offset by a single provision that was estimated to bring in $25.2 billion by curtailing the ability of senior executives such as hedge fund managers to avoid taxes on large amounts of money by getting it as deferred compensation in offshore tax havens.

LEGISLATIVE ACTION

The following are examples of the back-and-forth between the chambers on the elements of tax legislation.

HOUSE ENERGY TAXES

The House started early, passing a tax bill (HR 5351) on Feb. 27 that was aimed at encouraging investment in renewable-energy technologies. It proposed $17.6 billion in tax breaks, fully offset by revenue-raisers that targeted the oil and gas industry. The vote was 236-182, with all but 17 Republicans voting "nay." *(House vote 84, p. H-28)*

The bill was made up of $8.6 billion in energy production incentives and $9.1 billion to encourage conservation. The most expensive tax benefit was the extension and expansion of a credit for producing electricity from renewable resources, at a cost of $6.6 billion over 11 years. Others included a credit for plug-in hybrid vehicles ($1.3 billion), approval for energy conservation bonds ($1.9 billion), and the extension and modification of a credit for energy-efficient homes ($1.5 billion). The bill also included an extension of tax credits for wind and solar energy and renewed incentives for constructing renewable-fuel pumps at gasoline stations.

To pay for the bill, Democrats included provisions to repeal a manufacturing deduction for five major oil and gas companies and change how energy companies' foreign earnings were taxed.

The deduction for domestic manufacturers, enacted as part of a 2004 corporate tax law (PL 108-357), replaced an export subsidy that was being phased out.

The bill proposed removing Chevron Corp., BP, Shell, Exxon Mobil Corp. and ConocoPhillips from the list of manufacturers that qualified for the tax break, which equaled 6 percent of income, climbing to 9 percent in 2010, and freezing the deduction at 6 percent for smaller companies. The change was expected to generate $13.6 billion over 10 years.

The rest of the revenue came mostly from a provision to change the tax treatment of energy companies' foreign earnings.

The timing for the Democrats was ideal. Oil futures topped $102 a barrel for the first time on the day the bill passed, before closing at $99.64 on the New York Mercantile Exchange. The average price of a gallon of regular gasoline was $3.13, with experts predicting it could rise to $4 a gallon by spring.

But the administration quickly threatened to veto the bill. "This targeted tax increase would reduce the nation's energy security rather than improve it," the White House statement said. "Industries should be taxed on a level playing field, and that field should be leveled by lowering rates, not by raising them."

The Senate did not take up the bill.

SENATE ENERGY TAXES

Democrats on the Senate Finance Committee had tried in January to include an energy tax package in an economic stimulus bill (PL 110-185), but under pressure from Republicans and the White House, they removed it from the final version of that legislation.

In April, however, the Senate agreed to attach an $8.3 billion package of energy tax breaks to a high-profile bill (HR 3221) aimed at relieving the mortgage crisis. The amendment — offered by John Ensign, R-Nev., and Maria Cantwell, D-Wash. — had no offsets. It was adopted, 88-8, on April 10. The mortgage bill then passed, 84-12. *(Senate votes 95, 96, p. S-21)*

The largest items were provisions to extend and modify tax credits for the production of renewable energy (at a cost of $3.7 billion over 11 years), for residential energy efficiency improvements ($1.8 billion), and for investment in solar energy and fuel cells ($1.8 billion).

Unwilling to budge, the House stripped out the energy provisions before passing an amended version of the mortgage relief bill and sending it back to the Senate.

HOUSE ENERGY TAXES/TAX EXTENSIONS

Two weeks later, the House combined energy tax breaks and the extension of other expired or expiring tax breaks into a $54.1 billion bill (HR 6049 — H Rept 110-658) that was fully offset. The measure passed, 263-160, on May 21. Thirty-five House Republicans supported the bill, but Republicans declared it "dead on arrival" in the Senate. *(House vote 344, p. H-112)*

The bill contained $17.1 billion in energy tax incentives, including $7 billion for a one-year extension of credits for producing renewable energy from wind, biomass and other sources. The energy taxes were combined with $5.3 billion in extensions affecting individual taxpayers, $21.6 billion in extensions for business and $10 billion in other tax breaks. The most expensive of the extenders were a one-year renewal of the research and development credit (costing $8.8 billion over 11 years) and a one-year extension of the "active-finance exception," which allowed financial services firms and manufacturers with overseas financing arms to defer taxes on foreign income from those operations until profits were repatriated (costing $4 billion).

The measure also included several new tax provisions. One, which was stripped out of the tax law (PL 110-166) enacted in December 2007, would lower the income floor for families eligible to receive a refundable child credit for 2008 (costing $3.1 billion). Homeowners who did not itemize their deductions would get a temporary deduction of $350 ($700 for married couples) for property taxes in addition to their standard deduction (costing $1.2 billion).

All of the offsets — $54.3 billion worth— came from two provisions. One was a requirement that executives with certain offshore deferred-compensation arrangements count money in those plans as income immediately. The other proposed a delay in rules (PL 108-357) that gave multinational corporations more flexibility in how they allocated

their interest expenses.

Republicans tried to force changes in the bill, moving to recommit it with instructions to add an AMT patch, lengthen the extension of several tax breaks and strip out the offsets. The motion failed, 201-220. "We don't object to extending the expired provisions of the tax code," said Jim McCrery of Louisiana. But he said Republicans strongly opposed the offsets, which he said "would lead to a huge tax increase over the next 10 years." *(House vote 343, p. H-110)*

"There's only two options here," said Hoyer, who had strong support from the fiscally conservative "Blue Dog" Democrats. "We can pay for" extending the tax breaks, "or our children can pay for it."

Before the House vote, the Bush administration issued a veto threat against the bill, citing the offsets and several other provisions, including the temporary standard deduction for property taxes.

HOUSE AMT BILL

The partisan skirmishing over offsets continued in June, when the House passed a one-year AMT patch (HR 6275 — H Rept 110-728). The $61.5 billion cost was fully offset with various revenue-raisers. The bill passed by a vote of 233-189 on June 25. Ten Republicans joined virtually all the Democrats in supporting the bill; some of the 10 were leaving Congress, and others were facing tough re-election battles. *(House vote 455, p. H-152)*

The Ways and Means Committee had approved the bill June 8 by a strict party-line vote of 22-16.

The bill contained four major revenue-raisers. The largest was a proposal to tax carried interest — or profit-sharing income — of private-equity managers and others as ordinary income rather than at the lower capital gains rate. The other provisions proposed to repeal the manufacturing deduction for major oil and gas companies, tighten rules on foreign-owned companies that used tax treaties to reduce their tax burdens and require credit card issuers to report more information to the IRS about purchases at merchants.

"Enacting an AMT patch today when we don't pay for it would simply shift that $62 billion from the middle class onto their children and their grandchildren," said Peter Welch, D-Vt.

Republicans argued that the patch maintained the tax status quo and should not be paired with tax increases, which they said would hurt the struggling economy. Before passage, the House rejected, 199-222, a GOP motion to recommit the bill with a requirement that the offsets be dropped. *(House vote 454, p. H-150)*

The day before the vote, the White House issued a veto threat citing the bill's tax increases.

SENATE ENERGY/EXTENDERS/AMT BILL

After a summer of failed cloture votes on proceeding to the House tax-extenders bill (HR 6049), the Senate voted overwhelmingly Sept. 23 in favor of a bipartisan tax package that combined the extensions with energy incentives and AMT relief and was partially offset. The plan was a relatively fragile compromise negotiated by Max Baucus, D-Mont., and Charles E. Grassley, R-Iowa, the chairman and ranking member of the Finance Committee. The Senate substituted the compromise for the House text and passed the bill, 93-2. *(Senate vote 205, p. S-45)*

The bill, which contained many of the same tax benefits included in the other bills, was broken into two parts: The first was a fully offset set of energy tax incentives. The second combined a partially offset extenders section, which pushed expiration dates to the end of 2009, and a one-year AMT patch and disaster tax relief that had no

offsets. The bill also included a variety of provisions designed to please particular lawmakers, including mental health parity legislation, the extension of a rural county payments program, and tax breaks for oil-shale refining, Alaskan fishermen and farming equipment. *(Mental health parity, p. 9-5)*

The Senate took three votes on elements of the package before passing it. The first was on an $18.3 billion energy tax package that was fully offset with revenue-raisers that mainly targeted the oil and gas industry. It was adopted, 93-2. *(Senate vote 202, p. S-45)*

Next, the Senate voted on a one-year adjustment to the AMT, with offsets, which was rejected 53-42. By agreement, 60 votes were needed for adoption. *(Senate vote 203, p. S-45)*

Having demonstrated that they would not accept the offsets, senators adopted a package that included the AMT patch at a cost of $61.8 billion over 10 years with no offsets. It also contained another $68.1 billion in tax benefits over 10 years, such as a two-year extension of the research and development credit for businesses ($3.1 billion); nearly $9 billion in tax breaks for disaster victims; an expansion of the child tax credit ($3.1 billion); and mental health parity legislation ($3.9 billion). The amendment was partially offset by the $25.2 billion expected to come from altering deferred-compensation rules.

The amendment was adopted after the Senate voted, 84-11, on a procedural motion by Baucus that waived budget-related objections. *(Senate vote 204, p. S-45)*

"I would hope when this matter goes to the House of Representatives, that they take [account] . . . of how difficult it has been for us to get this passed," Majority Leader Harry Reid, D-Nev., said after the bill passed. "I say to my friends on the other side of the Capitol, don't send us back something else. We can't get it passed."

HOUSE FOUR-BILL RESPONSE

Rejecting the pleas, House Democrats quickly pulled the compromise apart and sent a four-bill barrage back to the Senate.

▸ On Sept. 24, the House passed an AMT patch (HR 7005) with no offsets. It was estimated to cost $64.6 billion over 10 years. The vote was 393-30. *(House vote 634, p. H-214)*

▸ Also on Sept. 24, the House voted 419-4 to pass a set of tax breaks (HR 7006) for individuals and businesses hit by natural disasters, mainly from storms and flooding in the Midwest. It had no offsets and was estimated to cost $8.1 billion over 10 years. The AMT and disaster bills were considered under suspension of the rules, which meant Democrats did not have to formally waive the House's pay-as-you-go rule. *(House vote 635, p. H-214)*

▸ On Sept. 26, the House passed the most expensive of the bills (HR 7060), a fully offset $60.3 billion measure that combined about $14.3 billion in incentives for renewable energy with the extension of numerous expired or expiring tax breaks at cost of $42.1 billion. An additional $3.9 billion in miscellaneous tax provisions included an $8,500 threshold for the child tax credit. The vote was 257-166. *(House vote 649, p. H-218)*

Ways and Means Chairman Charles B. Rangel, D-N.Y., had insisted that the bill be fully paid for, and he cobbled together a set of revenue-raising provisions. The biggest — estimated to bring in $6.7 billion over 10 years — was a requirement that brokers who reported the proceeds from a customer's sale of a security also report the basis, or amount the customer paid to purchase the security. The purpose was to give the IRS information that could be used to check whether taxpayers accurately reported their capital gains.

Other revenue provisions included higher taxes on the oil and gas industry, the provision targeting certain offshore deferred-compensation plans and a further delay of rules to help multinational corporations that paid interest in multiple countries.

The White House issued a veto threat against the bill and urged the House to accept the Senate version.

Earlier, on Sept. 23, the House passed a mental health parity bill (HR 6983) by a vote of 376-47. *(House vote 625, p. H-210)*

FINAL BILL

On Sept. 29, as the House prepared to leave for the election campaign, Hoyer reiterated that he would not consider the Senate-passed bill. But just hours later, the House inadvertently handed the Senate an opportunity to emerge victorious from the two-year tax policy fight. In a vote that stunned the financial markets, the House rejected a $700 billion rescue package (HR 3997), which the administration said was critical to addressing the nation's financial crisis. That moved action to the Senate, where Democratic leaders added the Senate's energy, extenders and AMT provisions to a re-vised bailout bill (HR 1424) as sweeteners intended to make it more palatable to House opponents.

The Senate passed the bill Oct. 1 by a vote of 74-25, giving the House a take-it-or-leave-it choice. House Democrats reluctantly accepted the Senate's version as the price for completing the bill, and the House cleared the measure 263-171 on Oct. 3. *(Senate vote 213, p. S-47; House vote 681, p. H-230)*

Tax lobbyists who had all but concluded that Congress would adjourn for the election, if not the year, without extending the expir-ing tax breaks, reacted quickly to the Senate's action, adding to the lobbying campaign that had been launched to sway ambivalent House members to back the overall package.

The final Senate bill was a bipartisan compromise, but that was not enough to mollify the House. "It was not [a] responsible thing to do," Hoyer said of the Senate's endgame. "You can't tell me they couldn't have gotten that thing through the Senate without that in there," said prominent Blue Dog Mike Ross, D-Ark., referring to the tax package.

Fiscal conservatives were not the only ones in the House frustrated by being forced to vote on the Senate's tax package. Liberal Democrats were disgruntled, particularly over the Senate's energy tax provisions, which contained more incentives for coal than they wanted and pro-vided a new break for oil-shale refining. Those provisions had been absent from House versions of energy-tax legislation.

The House also lost out on the disaster-relief provisions. The Ways and Means bill would have provided a consistent set of tax breaks for disaster victims from 2008 through 2011, regardless of where they lived. The Senate bill, written largely by Grassley, created a national disaster program, but only for 2008 and 2009. The Senate bill also gave Midwest flood victims a more generous collection of tax assistance, modeled on the legislation (PL 109-73) enacted shortly after Hurri-cane Katrina in 2005. Residents of the hurricane-battered Gulf Coast also got tax breaks beyond the national program.

Perhaps most important for House members, who carefully guarded their tax-writing prerogative, was the fact that the Senate strategy succeeded. "I hope that this Senate gamble is not accepted as some new constitutional attitude by their leadership," Rangel said in a statement. "We have a process in the House.... Apparently, in the Senate, they just decide what can get 60 votes and insist the House follow suit." ■

[PROVISIONS]
Details of the Tax Package

THE FOLLOWING ARE THE MAJOR TAX PROVISIONS attached to the financial services rescue bill enacted Oct. 3 (HR 1424 — PL 110-343). All cost and revenue estimates are for 10 years (fiscal 2009 through 2018) as calculated by the Joint Committee on Taxation. *(Financial rescue, p. 7-3)*

ALTERNATIVE MINIMUM TAX
● **One-year AMT "patch."** The law included a temporary increase in the amount of income that was exempt when individuals calculated whether they had to pay alternative minimum tax (AMT) rates, rather than regular rates. The exemption was increased from $33,750 to $46,200 for unmarried individuals and from $45,000 to $69,950 for married couples filing jointly. The change, dubbed the AMT patch, was aimed at preventing an estimated 22 million additional taxpayers from falling under the AMT in 2008. It was expected to cost the government $61.8 billion in lost revenue.

● **Incentive stock options.** The law also included a $2.3 billion provision to help taxpayers affected by a quirk in the AMT. Many taxpayers were forced to pay taxes on paper gains that resulted from exercising incen-tive stock options, even if they received relatively little cash. A 2006 law (PL 109-432) allowed those taxpayers to reclaim the extra taxes paid over five future years when they did not make enough to pay the AMT.

The new law allowed that process to occur over two years and waived penalties and interest associated with this scenario.

ENERGY TAX INCENTIVES
● **Production tax credit.** The main tax incentive for generating electric-ity from wind and refined coal was extended for one year, applying to projects placed in service by Dec. 31, 2009. Other energy sources, including geothermal power, hydropower and trash combustion, got a two-year extension, through the end of 2010. Electricity generated from tides and waves also became eligible for the tax credit.

● **Solar energy.** A 30 percent investment tax credit for solar energy and certain fuel cells was extended for eight years, applying to projects placed in service through 2016. The law also removed a $2,000 cap on a similar credit for residential-scale solar projects and allowed residential wind turbines (capped at $4,000) and geothermal heat pumps (capped at $2,000) to become eligible for the tax credit.

● **Coal production.** The law provided $1.5 billion in tax credits for proj-ects that produced electricity from coal and met targets for sequestering the resulting carbon dioxide. To qualify for the credit, advanced coal electricity projects were required to sequester 65 percent of their carbon, while coal gasification projects had to sequester 75 percent. The law also created a tax credit for capturing carbon dioxide — $10 per ton if it was

injected into wells to recover oil and $20 per ton if it was permanently stored. Producers of coal used to make coke for steel production got a new tax credit of $2 per barrel-of-oil equivalent.

● **Fuels.** A $1-per-gallon credit for production of biodiesel was extended through 2009. The law also extended through 2010 a 30 percent tax credit for fueling-station pumps that dispensed natural gas or ethanol and expanded the credit to cover electric-recharging stations. It also allowed certain investments in many cellulosic biofuels, not just ethanol, to qualify for a 50 percent write-off.

● **Bond authority.** The law allocated $800 million in Clean Renewable Energy Bonds. The bonds provided tax-advantaged financing for facilities owned by electric cooperatives, public power companies, and state and local governments that produced electricity from renewable sources. The law also created a category of tax-advantaged bonds, setting aside $800 million for state and local governments to use for projects designed to reduce greenhouse gas emissions. Both types of bonds provided investors with tax credits.

● **Refineries.** The law extended for two years, through 2013, a 2005 provision that allowed refinery owners to deduct half the cost of capital improvements that increased refinery capacity or that allowed certain non-conventional fuels to be processed. The law also added oil shale and tar sands to the fuels eligible for the refining credit.

● **Energy efficiency.** The law contained a series of provisions to encourage energy efficiency and conservation. They included extensions of a tax credit for energy-efficient improvements to existing homes through 2009, a similar initiative for commercial buildings through 2013, a program for energy-efficient appliances through 2010 and one for energy-efficient new homes through 2009.

● **Smart meters.** Electric meters that provided more detailed information about consumption could be depreciated on a 10-year schedule, instead of a 20-year schedule, giving an incentive to utility companies that wanted to deploy the new meters.

● **Recycling.** Companies that bought equipment for collecting and processing certain recyclable materials could get accelerated depreciation, allowing them to recover their costs more quickly.

● **Plug-in vehicles.** The law included a new tax credit for plug-in vehicles that typically ranged from $2,500 to $7,500. The credit would be reduced after the 250,000th such vehicle was produced.

OFFSETS FOR ENERGY TAX BENEFITS

● **Oil and gas offsets.** Most of the cost of the energy tax breaks was offset by revenue increases targeting the oil and gas industry. A manufacturing deduction scheduled to jump from 6 percent of profit to 9 percent in 2010 was frozen at 6 percent for income from oil and gas activities, raising an estimated $4.9 billion. The oil spill liability tax was increased from 5 cents per barrel to 8 cents per barrel through 2016, and then up to 9 cents per barrel in 2017, raising $1.7 billion. The law also altered the treatment of oil companies' foreign income in a way that would force higher taxes on income earned from transporting and refining oil, generating another $2.2 billion.

● **Securities basis reporting.** Starting with certain stocks purchased in 2011, securities brokers were required to report their customers' basis, or cost of purchasing the stocks, to the IRS. The provision was estimated to raise $6.7 billion over 10 years by preventing investors from overstating their cost basis and thus understating their profit subject to capital gains taxes.

● **Other offsets.** The law extended through 2018 a coal excise tax of $1.10 per ton from underground mines and 55 cents per ton from sur-

face mines, raising $1.3 billion to replenish the Black Lung Disability Trust Fund. It also extended a 0.2 percent surtax under the Federal Unemployment Tax Act for one year, bringing in $1.5 billion.

BUSINESS EXTENSIONS

● **Research and development.** The law extended the research and development tax credit through 2009. It also modified the credit, increasing the credit percentage under an alternative structure from 12 percent to 14 percent in 2009 and repealing a different alternative structure. The total cost was estimated at $19.1 billion.

● **Restaurant and retail depreciation.** The law extended accelerated depreciation for certain leased retail and restaurant space through 2009. It provided the same 15-year depreciation schedule (instead of 39 years for most real estate) for retail owners and new restaurants starting in 2009. The total cost was put at $8.7 billion.

● **Active-finance exception.** Financial services companies that operated overseas and manufacturers with overseas financing arms could continue to treat their income as active in 2009, allowing them to defer taxes on that income at a cost to the Treasury of $4 billion.

● **Straight extensions.** The law included extensions through 2009 of dozens of provisions that benefited a variety of targeted groups, including companies that cleaned up contaminated "brownfields," owners of motor sports tracks, homebuyers in the District of Columbia and short-line railroads.

INDIVIDUAL TAX-BREAK EXTENSIONS

● **Sales tax deduction.** Taxpayers could deduct sales taxes — according either to a formula or to actual receipts — for two additional years (2008 and 2009) as an alternative to deducting state and local income taxes. The provision, which benefited residents of states with no income taxes, was expected to cost $3.3 billion.

● **Tuition.** The law extended through 2009 a deduction of up to $4,000 for tuition and related expenses, at a cost of $5.3 billion.

● **Teachers.** A $410 million provision extended through 2009 a $250 deduction for teachers who spent their own money to purchase classroom equipment. It and the tuition deduction were subtracted before calculating adjusted gross income.

● **IRAs.** People over age 70½ could continue to make up to $100,000 in tax-free charitable contributions from their individual retirement accounts in 2009, at a cost of $795 million.

● **Property taxes.** Homeowners who did not itemize their deductions got an additional standard deduction of up to $500 ($1,000 for married couples) for property taxes. A law enacted earlier in 2008 (PL 110-289) created the deduction; the new law extended it through 2009, at an estimated cost of $1.5 billion.

● **Deferred-compensation offset.** To partially pay for the extensions, the law required people with certain offshore deferred-compensation arrangements to count the deferred compensation as income at the time the money was set aside for them, rather than waiting until they took the money out. The arrangements, often used by hedge fund managers, were set up in countries with little or no taxation. The provision was expected to raise $25.2 billion.

DISASTER-RELATED PROVISIONS

● **National program.** The law created a standardized national program of disaster tax assistance, which would take effect automatically whenever the president declared a natural disaster. Previously, Congress was required to pass an emergency bill to provide the tax relief. The

new program applied to disasters in 2008 and 2009. Victims got more flexibility to deduct casualty losses and write off demolition costs. Businesses in affected areas got a 50 percent bonus depreciation and could carry their losses back five years instead of two, allowing them to get refunds for taxes paid in those years. The law also provided additional expensing for small businesses.

● **Midwest flood response.** Victims of floods in 10 Midwestern states got a separate set of tax breaks modeled after the government's response to Hurricane Katrina (PL 109-73). Key benefits included more flexible use of money in retirement accounts, additional low-income housing tax credits, extra tax-advantaged bonds for reconstruction efforts, benefits for businesses that paid employees while they were closed and looser rules for charitable contributions.

● **Gulf Coast.** In addition to the national disaster tax program, the law included targeted provisions for victims of Hurricane Ike along the Gulf Coast, including low-income housing tax credits and more tax-exempt bonds for reconstruction.

OTHER PROVISIONS

● **Child tax credit.** The law temporarily expanded the refundable child tax credit to enable families making as little as $8,500 in 2008, instead of $12,050, to receive the credit even if they owed no income taxes.

● **County payments.** The law reauthorized and funded a program of payments to rural counties with significant amounts of federal land. The payments, designed to replace a portion of federal timber revenues and help counties transition to new funding sources, was sought by lawmakers from Western states. The law allocated $3.3 billion to extend the program through fiscal 2011.

● **Film and TV production.** The law extended for one year an existing $15 million deduction for domestic film and television production — $20 million if production occurred in economically distressed areas. It also expanded the deduction to apply to bigger-budget productions and broadened the criteria for companies that could receive tax breaks for domestic investment.

● **Farm equipment.** Certain farming equipment purchased in 2009 could be depreciated over five years instead of seven.

● **Wooden arrows.** Certain wooden arrows used by children for target practice were exempted from an excise tax on arrows.

● *Exxon Valdez* **assistance.** Commercial fishermen and others receiving money from legal action related to the 1989 oil spill were allowed to average their income over three years, reducing their tax burden, and to contribute up to $100,000 to a retirement account. ■

Chapter 5

CONGRESSIONAL AFFAIRS

Alaska Sen. Stevens Loses Re-Election After Conviction on Ethics Charges

THE DEFEAT IN NOVEMBER of Alaska Republican Ted Stevens, the longest-serving Senate Republican, spared the GOP leadership and the Select Ethics Committee from a painful decision over whether to recommend disciplinary action against him. Stevens was convicted Oct. 27 on seven felony counts of lying on his Senate financial disclosure forms by omitting sizable gifts he received from Alaska business interests. Throughout the process, Stevens steadfastly maintained his innocence.

Appointed to the Senate in 1968, Stevens, 84, was one of the chamber's "old bulls," known for his gruff demeanor. He won the first of his six full six-year terms in 1970 and ranked seventh on the all-time seniority list. He was a former chairman of the Senate Appropriations Committee and took pride in directing billions of dollars in earmarked funds to his home state. By virtue of his seniority, Stevens served from 2003 to 2007 as president pro tempore of the Senate, making him third in line for the presidency.

Stevens was convicted of failing to report more than $250,000 worth of gifts from oil services company VECO Corp. and its former chief executive, Bill Allen, from 1999 to 2006. The government contended that Stevens engaged in a multi-year scheme to conceal the gifts, most of which came in the form of improvements to Stevens' Girdwood, Alaska, home.

Although top Republicans urged Stevens to resign, the Alaskan vowed to stay in office as his appeal made its way through the courts. In the meantime, he faced the toughest political fight of his career, campaigning for a seventh full term in the Senate. Late in the campaign, he appeared to be closing the gap, but on Nov. 19, after all the absentee ballots were counted, he conceded defeat to Democrat Mark Begich.

Stevens' supporters blamed his conviction, coming just days before the election, for his defeat. The conviction would ultimately be overturned in 2009 because of prosecutors' mistakes.

INDICTMENT

Stevens was indicted July 27 by a federal grand jury in Washington on seven felony counts of filing false financial disclosures from 2000 through 2006. As required by Senate Republican Conference rules, he stepped down from posts as the top Republican on the Commerce, Science and Transportation Committee; the Defense Appropriations Subcommittee; and the Homeland Security and Governmental Affairs Subcommittee on Disaster Recovery.

The first count in the indictment concerned his alleged failure to report gifts that he received from VECO, most notably labor and supplies for the renovation and improvement of his Girdwood home. The project added a new first floor, a garage, a second-story deck, a Jacuzzi and other amenities.

The FBI and the IRS, which was reportedly investigating whether VECO had covered Stevens' home renovation costs, had raided the senator's home in July 2007.

The charge stated that Stevens was fully aware of the project on his home and who was doing the work. "Stevens had multiple conversa-

tions and correspondence with Allen in which the two discussed, among other things, the work of VECO employees and contractors on the renovation project," it said.

The indictment also alleged that Stevens used his Senate position to aid VECO at the request of Allen and other company employees. It said the solicitations included "funding requests and other assistance with certain international VECO projects and partnerships, including those in Pakistan and Russia; requests for multiple federal grants and contracts to benefit VECO . . . including grants from the National Science Foundation to a VECO subsidiary; and assistance on both federal and state issues in connection with the effort to construct a natural gas pipeline from Alaska's North Slope Region."

In addition, the count alleged, Stevens and Allen arranged for Allen to transfer a new 1999 Land Rover Discovery, purchased for $44,000, to a child of Stevens' in exchange for Stevens' 1964 Ford Mustang and $5,000. The Mustang was worth less than $20,000, according to the indictment.

In failing to report the gifts, the count charged that Stevens "knowingly and intentionally sought to conceal and cover up his receipt of things of value."

The other six counts alleged that Stevens essentially amplified the violation listed in the first count in his annual Senate financial disclosure forms for the years 2001 through 2006.

Allen and former VECO Vice President Richard L. Smith had pled guilty in May 2007 to providing more than $400,000 in payments to Alaska public officials. A lobbyist, a former chief of staff to Alaska's then-governor and three Alaska state lawmakers were also convicted in the scandal, including Peter Kott, the former speaker of the Alaska House, who was convicted of extortion, bribery and conspiracy. Kott was sentenced to six years in prison.

TRIAL AND CONVICTION

Stevens' trial opened in Washington on Sept. 25, after the defense failed to have the proceedings moved to Alaska.

Allen appeared as the prosecution's star witness. He testified that he never sent Stevens a bill for the work, despite a written request from the senator in 2002, because he thought Stevens only asked for the invoice as legal cover. He said a Stevens confidant told him that Stevens did not really want to get the bill and that, "Ted's just covering his ass."

Stevens testified that he believed all the disclosure forms he filed with the Senate were accurate, that he never intended to file false forms and that he never tried to conceal gifts. He told the jury that his wife, Catherine, received and paid the bills for the renovation. Defense lawyers said their client was unaware of any renovations to his Alaska home that he did not pay for personally — and that in fact Stevens provided more than $160,000 to cover the cost of home improvements.

Prosecutors contended that VECO, not Stevens, paid nearly all the renovation's costs and that, at a minimum, the senator was required to disclose the gifts.

Stevens and his lawyers repeatedly accused prosecutors in the case of gross misconduct, and U.S. District Court Judge Emmet G. Sullivan admonished the prosecutors on several occasions, for example for redacting information favorable to Stevens from FBI notes turned over to defense lawyers before the trial started.

Sullivan stopped short of throwing out the case, as Stevens' lawyers requested, but he postponed the sentencing indefinitely while the Justice Department probed several allegations of misconduct by the prosecution.

ETHICS DILEMMA AVERTED

Stevens' vow to remain in office while he appealed his conviction made life uncomfortable for senators of both parties. A chorus of GOP senators, including presidential nominee John McCain of Arizona, called for Stevens to resign immediately. Minority Leader Mitch McConnell, R-Ky., demanded that Stevens resign before Election Day. "If he is re-elected and the felony charge stands through the appeals process, there is zero chance that a senator with a felony conviction would not be expelled from the Senate," McConnell said.

The Senate had not expelled a member since the Civil War and never for any reason other than treason. The Select Ethics Committee, which was evenly divided between Republicans and Democrats, would have had to carry out an investigation, which would be time-consuming, particularly if the panel held public hearings first. If the committee then decided to recommend expulsion, leaders would have taken it to the floor for a vote, with a two-thirds majority required for expulsion.

Expelling a convicted member after re-election also went against congressional "practice and policy," the Congressional Research Service reported. In the past, Congress had not expelled a member for

offenses if the electorate knew about them and still chose to return the person to office.

Jim DeMint of South Carolina planned to force the issue at a Nov. 18 GOP meeting by offering a resolution to eject Stevens from the Republican Conference. The other old bulls were expected to support Stevens, but others were torn. Some less-senior lawmakers were reticent about voting against him. However, with Stevens' re-election appearing increasingly unlikely, Republicans decided to wait for the outcome.

Hours later, the Alaska election results were announced, and Republicans were spared the need to take what many saw as a wrenching vote. Still, said National Republican Senatorial Committee Chairman John Ensign, R-Nev., the party would have preferred to have Stevens win re-election and deal with the aftermath than lose the seat.

On Nov. 20, colleagues on both sides of the aisle bade Stevens an emotional farewell on the Senate floor.

"I have two homes: One is right here in this chamber, and the other is my beloved state of Alaska. I must leave one to return to the other," he told them.

POSTSCRIPT

On April 1, 2009, Attorney General Eric H. Holder Jr. announced that he had concluded, after a Justice Department review, that prosecutors had withheld evidence from the defense team in the Stevens case and that it was "in the interest of justice to dismiss the indictment and not proceed with a new trial."

On April 7, Sullivan set aside the conviction. "In nearly 25 years on the bench, I have never seen anything approaching the mishandling and misconduct I have seen in this case," he said. ∎

Ethics Panels Spared Major Cases

THE HOUSE VOTED IN MARCH to create an independent outside ethics panel to review complaints filed against lawmakers by outside groups and unelected individuals.

The House's own, 10-member ethics panel — the Committee on Standards of Official Conduct — granted a request by Charles B. Rangel, D-N.Y., to launch a formal investigation into several of his alleged violations of House rules; Rangel hoped to clear his name. There were developments on several other House ethics cases during the year, including some in the courts.

The Senate Select Ethics Committee publicly closed the book on three cases that were carried over from 2007: those of Republicans Larry E. Craig of Idaho and Pete V. Domenici of New Mexico and a complaint against Republican David Vitter of Louisiana.

But the six-member panel, headed by Barbara Boxer, D-Calif., and John Cornyn, R-Texas, ended the year taking no disciplinary action in the high-profile case of Ted Stevens of Alaska, the Senate's longest-serving Republican, who was convicted Oct. 27 on seven felony counts of lying on his Senate financial disclosure forms. Stevens' defeat in the Nov. 4 election spared the Ethics committee from a painful decision over whether to recommend disciplinary action against him. (Stevens, p. 5-3)

HOUSE ETHICS

● **Independent ethics office.** The House voted 229-182 on March 11 to create an independent Office of Congressional Ethics (H Res 895) to review ethics complaints from outside individuals or groups against members, delegates, officers and employees of the House. (House vote 122, p. H-40)

The Speaker and the minority leader were responsible for jointly appointing a six-member board composed of people who were not members of Congress at the time and were not registered lobbyists. The board was meant to supplement the work of the chamber's own ethics committee, which still handled complaints filed by members of the House. The office did not affect Senate ethics procedures.

The resolution creating the board established a two-stage review process to be initiated at the joint request of two of the commissions' members who were from different parties. If three members voted to continue the matter after the initial review, the board would conduct a second-phase review, after which it would refer the matter to the ethics committee, recommending dismissal or further review.

A task force created by Speaker Nancy Pelosi, D-Calif., and headed by Michael E. Capuano, D-Mass, proposed the plan. The purpose was to make good on a 2006 House Democratic campaign promise to

"drain the swamp of corruption" in Washington.

In late July, Pelosi and Minority Leader John A. Boehner, R-Ohio, appointed former Rep. David Skaggs, D-Colo., to chair the six-member group, with former Rep. Porter Goss, R-Fla., serving as co-chairman. The other panel members were former Democratic Reps. Yvonne B. Burke of California and Karan English of Arizona; former House Chief Administrative Officer Jay Eagen; and assistant professor Allison Hayward of George Mason University School of Law in Virginia. The group met for the first time Sept. 26.

On Jan. 23, 2009, the board approved its rules and code of conduct, allowing it to begin taking complaints.

● **Rangel.** The House ethics committee agreed Sept. 24, 2008, to form a subcommittee to launch an investigation into allegations against Rangel, chairman of the Ways and Means Committee. Rangel, who denied any wrongdoing, asked for the probe to clear himself of accusations that he had violated House rules. "God bless them," Rangel said of the panel's decision to investigate. "I wish they did that two weeks ago."

Rangel sought the formal investigation after reports during the summer questioned lapses on his financial disclosure forms, his lease on four rent-controlled apartments in New York City, the use of his official parking spot in a House garage for long-term storage of a car with expired tags and the use of his official letterhead to set up meetings with potential donors to the Charles B. Rangel Center for Public Service established at the City College of New York. The New York Times subsequently reported that Rangel had failed to report and pay taxes on more than $75,000 in rental income from a villa he had owned in the Dominican Republic since 1988.

Rangel denied all allegations, although he paid the back taxes in September.

An attempt by Boehner to censure Rangel failed July 31 when 25 Republicans sided with Democrats in a 254-138 vote to table the resolution (H Res 1396). Boehner tried again in September with a resolution (H Res 1460) that would have required Rangel to step down as chairman of the tax-writing committee. The House voted 226-176, to table, or kill, the measure. *(House votes 546, 609, pp. H-184, H-204)*

On Dec. 9, acting ethics Chairman Gene Green, D-Texas, and ranking Republican Doc Hastings of Washington announced that, acting on a formal request from Rangel, the subcommittee would expand the investigation to include newspaper reports that in 2007 Rangel preserved tax breaks for an oil drilling company the same day he solicited donations from the firm for his public service center.

Pelosi said the committee would issue a report on the probe by the end of 2008, but the deadline passed with no word from the panel, which rarely commented on its investigations.

● **Renzi.** Under a 2007 House rule (H Res 451), the Feb. 22 indictment of Rick Renzi, R-Ariz., on charges of federal conspiracy, fraud, extortion and money laundering related to a land-swap deal in his home state required the ethics panel to form an investigative subcommittee, which it did Feb. 28. *(2007 Almanac, p. 5-14)*

Renzi, who refused to resign his seat, pleaded not guilty March 4; the trial was eventually put off until 2009. The investigative subcommittee decided in May to delay its inquiry at the request of the Justice Department. Renzi lost his seat in the Nov. 4 election, making the issue moot.

● **Young.** In a case that did not involve the ethics committee, the House cleared a small highway bill in April (PL 110-244) that included a provision instructing the Justice Department to look into a controversial earmark that directed money to a Florida highway project. The Senate had added the provision by a vote of 64-28 on April 17. *(Senate vote 105, p. S-23)*

Rep. Don Young, R-Alaska, had been accused of changing the earmark in the 2005 highway law (PL 109-59) after Congress cleared the legislation but before the president signed it. The change steered $10 million to study building an interchange off Interstate 75 near Fort Myers at Coconut Road. A major campaign donor and fundraiser for Young, who was Transportation and Infrastructure Committee chairman at the time, owned property near the proposed interchange.

Young voted for the 2008 bill, which made technical corrections to the highway law, although he objected to the provision calling for an investigation. Young said he had done nothing improper in connection with the earmark, which he said was backed by the community and the local congressman.

● **Mahoney.** Pelosi called for an ethics investigation into allegations that Florida Democrat Tim Mahoney paid a former employee and mistress $121,000 not to file suit against him. Mahoney said Oct. 14 that he broke no laws, and he apologized for his family's "embarrassment and heartache." Mahoney was defeated in his re-election bid Nov. 8, making that issue moot, as well.

● **McDermott.** At least one outstanding legal matter was closed during the year. Jim McDermott, D-Wash., paid more than $1.1 million to Boehner's campaign committee to compensate Boehner for attorney's fees. Boehner had sued McDermott for leaking the contents of a cell phone call that was illegally recorded in 1996. McDermott refused to apologize and argued the public had a right to know what was said in the call between Boehner and other GOP leaders, including then-Speaker Newt Gingrich of Georgia. McDermott paid his bill with money from his legal defense fund and his campaign. *(2007 Almanac, p. 5-14)*

● **Jefferson.** At year's end, outgoing-Rep. William J. Jefferson, D-La., was awaiting trial on 16 corruption-related charges stemming from allegations that he illegally brokered business deals in Africa.

The U.S. Court of Appeals for the D.C. Circuit had ruled in 2007 that much of the material the FBI had acquired in a raid on Jefferson's congressional office in May 2006 was taken in violation of the Constitution's Speech or Debate Clause. Jefferson sought to toss out nearly all of the corruption and bribery charges on the grounds that the evidence violated the constitutional protections afforded to legislators. But a three-judge panel rejected the request, saying that the grand jury that indicted Jefferson had not seen any protected material.

In December, the 4th U.S. Circuit Court of Appeals in Richmond, Va., refused to reconsider the panel's ruling, a decision that paved the way for a trial date for Jefferson, who lost his bid for a 10th term.

The House had voted in 2007 to call on the ethics committee to determine whether Jefferson should be expelled, but the panel subsequently suspended its work pending the outcome of the criminal case. *(2007 Almanac, p. 5-13)*

SENATE ETHICS INQUIRIES

● **Craig.** The Senate Select Ethics Committee admonished Craig in February, saying he brought discredit on the Senate through his actions in 2007 in an airport rest room, his attempt to withdraw a guilty plea and his unapproved use of campaign funds to pay lawyers. Craig was arrested June 11, 2007, in a rest room at the Minneapolis-St. Paul International Airport after an undercover police officer interpreted some of Craig's hand and foot motions as an invitation for sex. Craig continued efforts to withdraw his guilty plea. *(2007 Almanac, p. 5-13)*

"We consider your attempt to withdraw your guilty plea to be

an attempt to evade the legal consequences of an action freely undertaken by you — that is, pleading guilty," the six-member panel said in its Feb. 13 letter to the congressman. Craig did not seek re-election in November. "In our view, you committed the offense to which you pled guilty and you entered your plea knowingly, voluntarily and intelligently," the committee wrote. "Even if an attempt to withdraw a guilty plea under the circumstances present in this case is a course that a defendant in the state of Minnesota may take . . . it is a course that a United States senator should not take."

The panel also chided Craig for using more than $213,000 in campaign funds to pay legal and public relations fees without approval from either the Ethics panel or the Federal Election Commission. Craig later set up a legal expense fund to help defray his legal fees.

● **Domenici.** In April, the Ethics panel concluded that Domenici, another retiring Republican, did not try to influence a probe involving the construction of an Albuquerque courthouse but said the six-term senator should have known better than to contact a prosecutor on a matter related to corruption, especially during an election year.

A call by Domenici in 2006 to U.S. Attorney David Iglesias "created an appearance of impropriety that reflected unfavorably on the Senate," the committee said in an April 24 "letter of qualified admonition." There was no additional punishment.

The Justice Department fired Iglesias weeks after the 2006 elections, when Republicans lost control of Congress. The former prosecutor said he felt that Domenici was pressuring him to move faster on the probe because it involved Democrats. The incident was linked to a larger scandal in 2007 that involved the Justice Department's firing of several U.S. attorneys and contributed to the resignation of Attorney General Alberto R. Gonzales. (*2007 Almanac, p. 15-3*)

The Ethics committee launched its inquiry in March 2007, after a public-corruption interest group filed a complaint alleging that Domenici had violated Senate rules, including a rule that barred lawmakers from contacting agencies for political reasons. (*2007 Almanac, p. 5-14*)

Domenici publicly apologized for contacting Iglesias but insisted that he had "never pressured him nor threatened him in any way."

● **Vitter.** In May, the Ethics panel closed a probe of Vitter's ties to a Washington prostitution ring. A watchdog group — Citizens for Responsibility and Ethics in Washington — had filed a complaint alleging that Vitter's actions violated rules requiring conduct that reflects well upon the Senate. The committee dismissed the complaint May 8, but panel members said in a letter to Vitter that the case could be reopened "should new allegations or evidence" surface.

Vitter acknowledged in July 2007 that his telephone number appeared in the records for Pamela Martin and Associates, a since-defunct escort service run by "D.C. Madam" Deborah Palfrey that catered to an upscale Washington clientele. Vitter indicated that he had contacted the escort service before his 2004 Senate campaign.

The Senate committee said it opted not to launch an investigation because Vitter's conduct occurred while he was a member of the House, he was never charged with a crime and his behavior "did not involve use of public office or status for improper purposes." ■

Two Cabinet Secretaries Confirmed

THE SENATE CONFIRMED TWO NEW Cabinet secretaries, as well as the nomination of a highly praised general in Iraq to take over a regional military command. But there were partisan disputes throughout the year over a number of other executive branch and judicial nominations.

● **Agriculture.** The Senate confirmed Ed Schafer, President Bush's choice for Agriculture secretary, by voice vote Jan. 28, in time for him to attend Bush's final State of the Union address that night. Schafer, a Republican, served as North Dakota's governor from 1992 to 2000. He succeeded former Nebraska Gov. Mike Johanns, who left the Agriculture Department's top job in September 2007 to run a successful campaign for the Senate seat of retiring Republican Chuck Hagel.

Schafer arrived in his new post just as Congress and the White House were facing off over a new five-year farm bill. The administration threatened to veto both the House and Senate versions unless Congress did more to cut farm subsidies and make farm programs more trade-friendly. Schafer had long represented farmers who supported the existing mix of subsidies and had fought for a disaster trust fund, which the administration said it would reject.

Questioned by Democratic Sen. Tom Harkin of Iowa, chairman of the Agriculture, Nutrition and Forestry Committee, at his Jan. 24 confirmation hearing, Schafer indicated that he would not be able to support the disaster fund. "As governor of the state of North Dakota, you know, it was easy to champion my state and . . . to understand the need for this disaster assistance," Schafer said. "Now if I'm confirmed, I move into the national arena and no longer would champion any state's specific needs, but [will] look at the overall policy of the needs of this nation."

Bush ultimately vetoed the farm bill, and Congress overrode him, enacting the measure into law (PL 110-246). (*Farm bill, p. 3-3*)

● **Housing and Urban Development.** Steven C. Preston was confirmed by voice vote June 5 as secretary of Housing and Urban Development (HUD) in a deal that also allowed the confirmation of roughly 80 nominees to various boards, commissions and executive branch posts. Preston had headed the Small Business Administration (SBA) for nearly two years before Bush nominated him April 18. During his time at the SBA, he revamped the Disaster Assistance Program, which was struggling to respond to the 2005 Gulf Coast hurricanes.

Christopher J. Dodd, D-Conn., chairman of the Senate Banking, Housing and Urban Affairs Committee, had expressed concerns about Preston's lack of experience in housing-related issues. But Dodd said during Preston's confirmation hearing that he had been assured by a number of colleagues, most notably John Kerry, D-Mass., chairman of the Small Business and Entrepreneurship Committee, that Preston would be a good fit for HUD.

"You come very highly recommended," Dodd said. "You came to town without many people knowing about you, and you've scored some very significant points with the people you have worked with."

Preston succeeded the scandal-plagued Alphonso R. Jackson in a post that was central to combating the tide of home foreclosures.

White House Officials Cited for Contempt

THE HOUSE VOTED TO HOLD White House Chief of Staff Joshua B. Bolten and former White House counsel Harriet Miers in contempt of Congress for refusing to comply with House Judiciary subpoenas. Lawmakers also authorized the Judiciary Committee to seek enforcement of the subpoenas in court. A federal judge ruled in favor of the committee in July, but an appeals court stayed the ruling.

The panel had subpoenaed Bolten and Miers for documents and, in Miers' case, testimony, as part of the panel's probe of the firings of nine U.S. attorneys in 2006. President Bush invoked executive privilege and instructed Bolten and Miers not to comply with the subpoenas. *(2007 Almanac, p. 15-3)*

The House voted, 223-32, on Feb. 14 to adopt a self-executing rule (H Res 982) that directed automatic adoption of a pair of resolutions. One (H Res 979) cited Bolten and Miers for contempt. The other (H Res 980) empowered the Judiciary Committee to go to court on its own to get a judge to rule that Bolten and Miers should comply with the subpoenas. Republicans staged a walkout over the scheduling of the vote, saying that the chamber should have been debating electronic surveillance legislation, which they said was a real priority. *(House vote 60, p. H-20)*

The Judiciary Committee filed a suit in federal court in Washington, after Attorney General Michael B. Mukasey, who replaced Gonzales, refused to allow a federal prosecutor to present the contempt citation to a grand jury. On July 31, U.S. District Judge John D. Bates ruled that Bolten could not simply refuse to hand over any White House documents without at least providing a description of the relevant material. Bates also ruled that Miers could not avoid physically appearing before the Judiciary Committee. The defendants appealed, and on Oct. 7 the U.S. Court of Appeals for the District of Columbia Circuit stayed Bates' ruling pending the appeal.

The Judiciary Committee also approved a contempt of Congress resolution on July 30 against former senior White House aide Karl Rove for refusing to comply with a subpoena to appear at a hearing to testify about allegations that the Justice Department engaged in politically motivated prosecutions of Democratic officials. Rove's attorney cited executive privilege.

Jackson had announced his resignation in March amid allegations of cronyism, corruption and political favoritism.

● **Central Command.** On a vote of 95-2 on July 10, the Senate confirmed the nomination of Gen. David H. Petraeus, the former commander in Iraq, to lead the U.S. Central Command, which had authority over operations in Southwest Asia, the Middle East and North Africa. *(Senate vote 171, p. S-38)*

Despite sharp disagreements among senators about Bush's war policies, Armed Services Chairman Carl Levin, D-Mich., said Petraeus earned high marks as an architect of the "surge" strategy that raised the number of combat brigades in Iraq to focus on counterinsurgency operations. Democrats Harkin and Robert C. Byrd of West Virginia were Petraeus' only opponents.

● **Other nominations.** The smooth sailing for the Cabinet secretaries contrasted with a more contentious atmosphere for judicial and other executive branch nominees. Republicans used parliamentary tactics to slow floor action or block committees from meeting in order to protest the pace of confirmations.

Senate Democrats scheduled pro forma sessions during congressional breaks throughout the year to prevent recess appointments. A top target was Steven G. Bradbury. Bush had nominated Bradbury five times since 2005 to head the Justice Department's Office of Legal Counsel, an office responsible for providing legal advice to the rest of the government. Democrats had concerns about Bradbury's views on interrogation techniques that critics said amounted to torture.

Republicans also complained about the pace of confirmations for circuit court judges. The Senate confirmed 10 circuit judges during the 110th Congress, compared with an average of 15 during the final two years for each of the previous three presidents facing a Senate controlled by the opposite party.

Bush became somewhat more conciliatory in judicial nominations during the year. For example, in July he withdrew the nomination of Gene E.K. Pratter to the 3rd U.S. Circuit Court of Appeals. Pratter was opposed by Pennsylvania Democrat Bob Casey. Instead, Bush named Paul S. Diamond to the slot, a choice that Casey supported. Bush also nominated Helene N. White, who had first been nominated by President Bill Clinton 11 years earlier, to the 6th Circuit. She was confirmed June 24. ■

Chapter 6

DEFENSE, FOREIGN POLICY, INTELLIGENCE & TRADE

$611.1 Billion Defense Authorization Clears Congress After Long Debate

DELAYED FOR MONTHS by partisan bickering over earmarks and unrelated energy legislation, the fiscal 2009 defense authorization bill cleared just as lawmakers were preparing to adjourn for the fall campaign season. President Bush signed the measure (S 3001 — PL 110-417) on Oct. 14, making it the 43rd year in a row that the annual defense measure became law.

The bill authorized $611.1 billion and set policies for Pentagon programs and Energy Department nuclear weapons activities. The total included $68.6 billion for the wars in Iraq and Afghanistan during the initial months of fiscal 2009, but no major conditions were placed on the funding.

Although actual spending was provided by a separate appropriations measure, lawmakers considered the authorization bill must-pass legislation, especially because the Pentagon could not pay military personnel without it. For fiscal 2009, the bill authorized a 3.9 percent raise, half a percentage point more than Bush wanted. The bill was also necessary to establish new troop levels. *(Defense appropriations, p. 2-9)*

Bush requested $612.5 billion for national defense, $70 billion of which was for war-related activities. Virtually all of the $1.4 billion difference between the request and the final bill was the result of the smaller amount provided for operations in Iraq and Afghanistan.

The base authorization in the bill for Pentagon and Energy Department programs came to $542.5 billion, $895 million less than requested but about $35 billion more than in the fiscal 2008 law (PL 110-181). *(2007 Almanac, p. 6-3)*

While the bill did not eliminate any major weapons programs, it authorized less than requested for missile defense and other futuristic programs, such as the Army's Future Combat Systems, and shifted funds to replace equipment depleted by the war in Iraq, including new combat vehicles and new battle gear for the Army National Guard and Reserves. Increases also went to military pay raises and shipbuilding.

And, in what had become an annual ritual, Congress rejected Bush's proposal to pay for part of the cost of military health care services through a $1.2 billion increase in fees, premiums and drug co-payments charged to participants in the Tricare health care network.

The final bill diluted most provisions that had drawn veto threats, such as proposals to sharply limit the use of contractors in Iraq and require congressional approval of any agreement on the continued presence of U.S. forces in that country. Other provisions that the White House opposed but did not threaten to veto remained, such as language barring the Defense Department from using funds for most infrastructure projects in Iraq.

The House passed its original bill (HR 5658) in May, and the Senate Armed Services Committee approved its version (S 3001) in April.

BOX SCORE

BILL: S 3001 — PL 110-417

LEGISLATIVE ACTION:

House passed HR 5658 (H Rept 110-652), 384-23, on May 22.

Senate passed S 3001 (S Rept 110-335), 88-8, on Sept. 17.

House passed S 3001, amended, 392-39, on Sept. 24.

Senate cleared S 3001 by voice vote Sept. 27.

President signed Oct. 14.

But conflicts over unrelated amendments, particularly proposals to expand offshore oil drilling, prevented the Senate from proceeding to the bill until September. In the interim, a dispute over earmarks replaced drilling as the main obstacle to passage. Senate Republicans objected to holding a formal conference, so senior members of the two Armed Services committees negotiated a compromise in informal sessions.

In signing the bill, Bush issued a "signing statement" indicating that he reserved what he described as the executive branch's right to disregard certain provisions. These included a ban on the use of funds authorized in the measure "to exercise control of the oil resources of Iraq" and a requirement that the U.S. government initiate negotiations with Baghdad on sharing costs of combined military operations.

HIGHLIGHTS

The base Pentagon authorization of $542.5 billion included $154.3 billion for operations and maintenance; $128.7 billion for personnel; $104 billion for procurement of equipment and weapons; $77.7 billion for research, development, test and evaluation; $24.9 billion for military construction and family housing; and $16.3 billion for national security programs carried out by the Energy Department.

Details of the $611.1 billion bill included:

● **War funds.** $68.6 billion in fiscal 2009 emergency funding, which was expected to last through June or July of 2009. Virtually all the money had already been appropriated in the supplemental spending bill (PL 110-252) enacted in June. The exception was $2.1 billion authorized for six unrequested C-17 cargo aircraft. *(Supplemental, 2-32)*

The war authorization included $10.4 billion to repair and rebuild Army and Marine Corps equipment worn down by fighting in Iraq and Afghanistan. It authorized $1.7 billion for Mine Resistant Ambush Protected vehicles, which protected against bomb blasts, and $2.2 billion for continued research to combat roadside bombs.

● **Aircraft.**

▸ $3.4 billion, about $375 million more than requested, for 20 F-22 Raptors, the Air Force's controversial next-generation fighter intended to replace the F-15 and have both air-to-air and air-to-ground fighter capabilities. Unlike Bush's request, the bill dedicated about $525 million of the total to be used either for advance procurement of 20 more aircraft in fiscal 2010 or to shut down the production line, depending on what the next president wanted to do.

▸ $3.4 billion to procure 14 F-35 Joint Strike Fighter aircraft, about $300 million and two aircraft less than requested. The bill also authorized $3.6 billion for development, $495 million more than Bush requested, with the extra funds used to continue development of a second, competitive engine. Congress regarded the competition

as good for quality and price; the Pentagon opposed it as unnecessary. The F-35 was planned as an affordable, next-generation, multirole fighter based on a common airframe and components for use by the Air Force, Navy and Marine Corps.

▸ $832 million, as requested, for development of a new Air Force aerial refueling tanker — but none of the $62 million requested for advanced procurement in fiscal 2009. The tanker contract was slated to be re-bid in 2009.

The initial contract for the tanker had gone to European Aeronautic Defense and Space Co., the parent company of Airbus, the European jet manufacturer. Boeing Co., which lost out, asked the Government Accountability Office to look at the process, saying the Air Force had tilted the competition in Airbus' favor. The GAO agreed with Boeing and ordered that the competition be done over. Defense Secretary Robert M. Gates took the program away from the Air Force and subsequently delayed the new bidding until 2009.

The bill also required that if the World Trade Organization (WTO) ruled that an illegal subsidy was given to any large commercial manufacturer, such as EADS, to make the plane, the Pentagon had to factor that into the selection process. The United States had brought suit against the European Union at the WTO, claiming that European governments had injected billions of dollars in subsidies into Airbus.

● **Future Combat Systems.** $3.6 billion, about equal to the Army request, for continued development of the system, planned as an integrated set of vehicles, aircraft, radios and computers. The project had become so complex and expensive that even some supporters questioned its viability. The bill continued a requirement that the GAO and other independent consultants review the program and set numerous other requirements.

● **Ships.** $15 billion for Navy shipbuilding, about $1 billion more than requested, including:

▸ $600 million in unrequested funding for advance procurement for two LPD-17 *San Antonio*-class amphibious ships. Bush's only request was about $100 million to close down production.

▸ $920 million, as requested, for two Littoral Combat Ships — small, specialized ships tailored for fighting close to shore.

▸ $3.7 billion, as requested, for the next ship in the *Virginia* class of new attack submarines, which were replacing retiring *Los Angeles*-class submarines and were expected to constitute the bulk of the attack submarine force in the future. In addition, it authorized $300 million in unrequested funds to purchase components in preparation for building two boats per year.

▸ $2.6 billion, as requested, for one DDG-1000, the Navy's next-generation battleship.

● **Missile defense.** $10.5 billion for various missile defense programs, $410 million less than requested. The total included funding for the deployment of a long-range missile defense system based in Alaska and California, but no funds for a proposed Space Test Bed to develop and test space-based interceptors. It shifted the $10 million requested for the Reliable Replacement Warhead, a next-generation nuclear weapon, to other programs.

It also included $708 million, $246 million less than requested, to build a third interceptor site in Poland and the Czech Republic. Construction could begin only after it was approved by the host nations, and deployment could not occur until the Defense secretary certified that the interceptors worked.

● **Military pay.** A 3.9 percent pay increase for all military personnel, half a percentage point more than the administration sought, before

special pay or bonuses.

● **Health care.** $25 billion for the Defense Health Program. This was the amount Bush requested, but Congress included $1.2 billion to replace Bush's plan to increase fees, premiums and drug co-payments for participants in the military's Tricare health care system. The bill barred such increases for one year.

● **Troop levels.** Increases in troop strength, as requested. Army end strength was raised by 7,000 soldiers to 532,400. Marine Corps strength was increased by 5,000 to 194,000. The bill also increased the full-time manning level for the Army National Guard to 32,060 and the Air National Guard to 14,360.

● **Base closure.** $9.5 billion, as requested, for base realignment and closure, mainly for ongoing costs of the 2005 round.

LEGISLATIVE ACTION
SENATE COMMITTEE ACTION

The Senate Armed Services Committee approved a $612.5 billion authorization bill (S 3001 — S Rept 110-335) by a vote of 24-0 in a closed meeting April 30. The total consisted of $542.5 billion for the base budget and $70 billion for war costs.

The committee wrote language in the bill to bar Pentagon spending on major reconstruction work in Iraq and to lay the groundwork for Baghdad to start paying its own military bills, as well as some of Washington's expenses.

"The policies and funding decisions in this bill are designed to reduce our nation's strategic risk by helping to restore the readiness of the military services to conduct the full range of their assigned missions as soon as possible," Chairman Carl Levin, D-Mich., said in a statement.

Highlights of the Senate authorization included:

● **War funding.** $70 billion, with separate accounts for Iraq ($49.6 billion), Afghanistan ($19.9 billion) and war-related military construction ($500 million). The total also included $2.1 billion to buy six C-17s.

● **Health care.** $24.8 billion for the Defense Health Program. The bill made up for the $1.2 billion in extra fees, premiums and drug co-payments assumed by Bush but not included in the bill.

● **Ships.**

▸ $3.5 billion for construction and long-lead components for the next *Virginia* sub, plus $79 million to prepare for two boats per year.

▸ $2.6 billion, as requested, to buy one DDG-1000 destroyer.

▸ $273 million for partial procurement of an LDP-17 amphibious ship and none of the funds that Bush requested to close down the production line.

● **Missile defense.** $954 million, as requested, for antimissile weapons and facilities in Poland and the Czech Republic. The fiscal 2009 funds could not be spent to deploy or operate the missiles until the two countries' parliaments ratified the deployment and the Pentagon certified that realistic tests showed that the missile "has a high probability of accomplishing its mission in an operationally effective manner."

● **Future Combat Systems.** $3.6 billion, as requested, to continue development and procurement.

● **Aircraft.**

▸ $3.5 billion for the F-22, including $497 million that could be used either for parts for new F-22s or to begin closing down the production line.

▸ $893 million to begin development of the new aerial tanker. The development funds included the $62 million that Bush had wanted to use for procurement.

• **Earmarks, outsourcing.** A provision stating that members' projects listed in the committee report were to be considered as authorized by the bill and were "binding on agency heads." Bush had issued an executive order in January that directed government agencies to disregard earmarks unless they were specified in the enacted text of a bill.

The Senate bill also prohibited the Defense Department from conducting a public-private competition before expanding the civilian workforce to address gaps in the number and skills of the workforce.

HOUSE COMMITTEE ACTION

The House Armed Services Committee approved its version of the authorization bill (HR 5658 — H Rept 110-652) by a vote of 61-0 in a lengthy and sometimes-heated markup on May 15. Like the Senate version, the authorization totaled $612.5 billion — $542.5 billion for the base budget, plus $70 billion in war funding.

The committee rejected amendments that would have authorized several hundred million dollars — requested by the president but left out of the bill — for the antimissile shield in Europe and for the Army's Future Combat Systems.

The bill proposed shifting billions of dollars requested by Bush for futuristic weapons systems to more immediate battlefield priorities and the pay and health care needs of military families. "This bill continues the committee's commitment to restoring the readiness of our military as its first priority," said Chairman Ike Skelton, D-Mo.

The committee also allowed room for billions of dollars in earmarks for ship and airplane programs that would create jobs in members' districts.

Highlights of the House bill included:

• **War funding.** $70 billion to conduct military operations in Iraq and Afghanistan for the first few months of fiscal 2009. The total included $3.9 billion in unrequested funds to buy 15 C-17 cargo planes.

• **Health care.** $24.7 billion for the Defense Health Program, with none of $1.2 billion in increased fees, premiums and drug co-payments proposed by Bush.

• **Ships.**

▸ $4.1 billion for construction and long-lead components for the next ships in the *Virginia* class of submarines, including $722 million for advance procurement to move up the construction of a second boat to fiscal 2010.

▸ None of the $2.6 billion requested to buy the next DDG-1000 land-attack ship. Instead, the bill authorized $400 million to be used either for procurement of long-lead materials for the next DDG-1000 or to restart procurement of two DDG-51-class destroyers.

▸ None of the funds requested to close down the production line for the LPD-17 amphibious ship. Instead, appropriators proposed authorizing $1.8 billion in unrequested funds to procure one vessel.

▸ $840 million for Littoral Combat Ship procurement, $80 million less than requested.

• **Missile defense.** $582 million, $372 million less than requested, for the antimissile weapons and facilities in Poland and the Czech Republic. Conditions for using the funds were similar to those in the Senate bill but were not limited to fiscal 2009 spending.

• **Aircraft.**

▸ $3.1 billion for 20 F-22 fighters, equal to the request, plus $523 million for unrequested funds to procure parts for 20 more planes, pending a decision by the next president.

FY '08 Authorization Exempts Iraq Lawsuits

CONGRESS ACTED SHORTLY after the start of the session to clear a revised fiscal 2008 defense authorization bill. President Bush signed the measure into law Jan. 28 (HR 4986 — PL 110-181).

The legislation replaced an earlier bill (HR 1585) that Bush had refused to sign in December 2007. The new version was nearly identical, except for language effectively exempting the Iraqi government from litigation stemming from the regime of Saddam Hussein. *(2007 Almanac, p. 6-3)*

The Iraqi government had objected to provisions that gave individuals enhanced rights to sue nations designated by the State Department as sponsors of terrorism. Iraq faced claims by several of Saddam's American victims, including former prisoners of war from the 1990-91 Gulf War. U.S. officials feared that Iraqi assets in U.S. capital markets, totaling some $25 billion, could be frozen during litigation if the original bill became law. The Bush administration said a potential freeze of those assets would harm Iraq's reconstruction and stabilization efforts.

The House passed the revised bill, 369-46, on Jan. 16, and the Senate cleared it, 91-3, on Jan. 22. *(House vote 11, p. H-6; Senate vote 1, p. S-4)*

The $696.4 billion authorization included $189.5 billion for war operations in Iraq and Afghanistan. Although the Defense appropriations bill had been enacted two months earlier (PL 110-116), the authorization bill still set polices for Defense Department programs and nuclear weapons activities in the Energy Department. More important for members of Congress, it determined pay and benefit levels for military personnel.

Senate Armed Services Chairman Carl Levin, D-Mich., noted that the bill contained language expressing the sense of Congress that the State Department should work directly with the Iraqi government to address the claims of American soldiers and citizens who suffered under the former regime. "We expect that the Department of State will actively pursue such compensation from Iraq," Levin said.

▸ $832 million, as requested, to begin systems design and demonstration of the aerial tanker, but none of the $62 million for advance procurement in fiscal 2009. The committee said Air Force officials said they did not need the money in 2009.

• **Future Combat Systems.** $3.4 billion, $200 million less than requested, to continue development and procurement of the Future Combat Systems. The committee said in its report that the concerns it had expressed the previous year had "only grown more acute." The panel cited schedule delays, the escalating cost, and the competing need for funds for other Army programs.

• **Earmarks, outsourcing.** A provision stating that the bill was exempt from Bush's January executive order directing federal agencies to disregard earmarks unless they were specified in the enacted text of a bill.

The committee also proposed a moratorium until Sept. 30, 2011, on any public-private competitions for Pentagon jobs performed by civilian employees.

During the markup, the committee:

▶ Rejected, 24-34, an attempt by Terry Everett of Alabama, the ranking Republican on the Strategic Forces Subcommittee, to restore the $372 million cut from Bush's request for antimissile sites in Poland and the Czech Republic.

"We don't believe the American people should be digging holes in Poland for a system that will eventually cost over $4 billion when we don't have ratified and signed agreements with their government," argued Ellen O. Tauscher, D-Calif., chairwoman of the Strategic Forces Subcommittee. Duncan Hunter of California, the ranking Republican on the full committee, disagreed: "This reduction sends a terrible signal to our foreign friends . . . who have supported us in this endeavor. . . . I also wonder about the message this reduction sends to Russia and Iran," he said.

▶ Rejected, 25-34, an amendment by Trent Franks, R-Ariz., to add $100 million for the Multiple Kill Vehicle program, designed to launch several interceptor warheads at once to defeat multiple incoming missiles or decoys.

▶ Rejected, 23-33, an amendment by H. James Saxton of New Jersey, the ranking Republican on the Air and Land Forces Subcommittee, to restore a $200 million cut from the $3.6 billion requested for the Future Combat Systems. The Senate bill covered the full request.

HOUSE FLOOR ACTION

The House passed the $612.5 billion bill by a vote of 384-23 on May 22, after adopting two amendments aimed at setting ground rules for a status-of-forces agreement being negotiated with Iraq to replace the U.N. mandate, which was due to expire at the end of the year. *(House vote 365, p. H-118)*

The White House issued a statement of administration policy on the day of the vote that included a long a list of provisions and potential amendments that would result in a veto of the bill. The House adopted several of the amendments anyway. They included:

▶ A requirement that a U.S.-Iraq agreement specify that Iraq would have to pay for certain costs of the U.S. military presence there. The language was part of a package of amendments adopted by voice vote.

▶ An amendment by Barbara Lee, D-Calif., adopted 234-183, to require congressional authorization for any agreement obligating the U.S. military to defend Iraq. Lee said that the Iraqi parliament was expected to ratify the agreement, and that it was only right that U.S. legislators do the same. *(House vote 359, p. H-116)*

▶ An amendment by Rush D. Holt, D-N.J., and Tauscher, adopted 218-192, to require that interrogations of detainees be videotaped. *(House vote 362, p. H-118)*

▶ An amendment by David E. Price, D-N.C., adopted, 240-168, to bar the use of contractors as interrogators. *(House vote 361, p. H-118)*

▶ An amendment by John M. Spratt Jr., D-S.C., adopted by voice vote to require the director of national intelligence to send Congress an annual update of intelligence findings on Iran's nuclear weapons program. The White House objected to the amendment but did not include it in the veto threat.

Other items cited in the veto warning included the moratorium on public-private competition for Defense Department jobs; restrictions on the Pentagon's ability to procure goods and services from foreign sources; a rejection of Bush's executive order on earmarks; and substantial cuts from the administration request for missile defense programs, including the system in Poland and the Czech Republic.

Democrats turned back a number of Republican amendments, including:

▶ A proposal by Franks, rejected 186-229, to restore the $719 million cut from Bush's missile defense request and direct the funds toward medium-range antimissile systems, rather than the European system or programs aimed at intercepting intercontinental missiles. *(House vote 356, p. H-116)*

▶ An amendment by Steve Pearce of New Mexico, rejected 145-271, that would have restored the $10 million requested by Bush for the Reliable Replacement Warhead. *(House vote 358, p. H-116)*

SENATE FLOOR ACTION

In a last-minute push, the Senate passed its bill by a vote of 88-8 on Sept. 17, leaving only a few days to write the final legislation before Congress' scheduled Sept. 26 adjournment. *(Senate vote 201, p. S-44)*

The bill's fate was not clear until Sept. 16 when Majority Leader Harry Reid, D-Nev., mustered just enough votes to invoke cloture, thereby limiting the remaining debate to 30 hours. The vote was 61-32, one more than the 60 needed. *(Senate vote 200, p. S-44)*

With the time about to run out, senators skipped the hundreds of amendments that had been filed, from an Iran sanctions proposal to language praising Bush's "surge" in Iraq.

Levin had initially tried to bring up the bill at the end of July, but wrangling over Republicans' insistence on offering domestic oil drilling amendments prevented the leadership from getting enough votes to proceed before the August recess.

On Sept. 8 — their first day back — senators agreed 83-0 to invoke cloture and take the parliamentary step of proceeding to the bill. *(Senate vote 197, p. S-44)*

Two days later, lawmakers began to dispense with amendments, but by then, a dispute over the earmark language had surfaced as the main obstacle to passage.

One of the most controversial proposals was an attempt by Republican Jim DeMint of South Carolina to delete the provision specifying that earmarks listed in the report were part of the bill. DeMint — backed by the Senate's top Republican, Mitch McConnell of Kentucky, and Tom Coburn, R-Okla., a leading anti-earmark crusader — promised to hold up work on the bill until he got a vote on his amendment.

Levin said he would be willing to print the earmarks in the bill itself but that it would take at least four days to accomplish, putting the chances of finishing before Congress adjourned in jeopardy.

In the meantime, the Senate:

▶ Adopted, 94-2, an amendment by Bill Nelson, D-Fla., to repeal a requirement in existing law that the survivors of military personnel killed in action had to offset the amount of benefits they received from the Defense Department by the amount they got from the Department of Veterans Affairs. Nelson and others had tried for eight years to repeal the offset. The Senate had passed the provision repeatedly, but it had been deleted in conference because of its cost: $6.9 billion over a decade in mandatory spending. It was not included in the final bill. *(Senate vote 199, p. S-44)*

▶ Rejected, 39-57, an amendment by David Vitter, R-La., to authorize an additional $271 million for testing and procuring parts for antimissile systems. *(Senate vote 198, p. S-44)*

▸ Adopted by voice vote an amendment by Patrick J. Leahy, D-Vt., to extend from three years to five years the statute of limitations on contractor fraud in theaters of war, including the conflicts in Iraq and Afghanistan.

The White House issued a veto warning Sept. 9 aimed primarily at provisions that would restrict the Pentagon's ability to hire private contractors and limit their role in the war. Among the items cited were provisions to restrict the use of contractors as security guards in combat zones, bar the use of contractors to interrogate detainees, require changes in the structure of military intelligence operations and limit public-private competition for Pentagon jobs.

FINAL ACTION

The final version of the bill was written by the senior members of the House and Senate Armed Services committees.

The compromise took the form of a House amendment to S 3001. The House passed the amended bill by a vote of 392-39 on Sept. 24. Democratic leaders took the unusual step of bringing the measure to the floor under suspension of the rules, which barred amendments and required a two-thirds vote for passage. The Senate easily cleared the bill by voice during a Saturday session on Sept. 27, enabling Congress to send the $611.1 billion measure to Bush before lawmakers left to campaign. *(House vote 631, p. H-212)*

● **White House-opposed provisions.** The leaders eliminated or rewrote a number of the provisions cited in the White House veto threats, including:

▸ Language in both bills to ban the use of private contractors to interrogate detainees held in U.S. military facilities. Instead, a nonbinding sense-of-Congress provision stated that one year after enactment, the Pentagon should develop the resources needed to ensure that all such interrogations could be conducted by government personnel rather than contract employees.

▸ A House requirement that all intelligence interrogations of detainees be videotaped. It was replaced with a sense-of-Congress statement that such interrogations should be videotaped.

▸ A House requirement that any status-of-forces agreement with Iraq be approved by Congress, either as a treaty or as a bill enacted into law. The managers' statement on the bill said that it was already "well-established" that such an agreement had to be approved by Congress. Instead, the president was required to send Congress a report on any pact with Iraq on the future of U.S. forces in that country.

▸ Prohibitions on public-private competition for Pentagon jobs.

▸ A provision in both bills to prohibit private security contractors from performing "inherently governmental functions" on combat zones. The final bill expressed the sense of Congress that certain functions should not be carried out by private security contractors in an area of combat operations.

However, lawmakers included other provisions opposed by the administration, as well as language aimed at continuing congressional oversight of the wars. Provisions retained included:

▸ A ban, similar to the Senate proposal, on using Pentagon funds for most Iraq infrastructure projects. The provision also required the U.S. government to begin negotiating a cost-sharing agreement for U.S.-Iraqi combined operations and to act to ensure that Iraq paid for the costs of its security forces.

▸ A Senate requirement that the Pentagon submit a detailed report to the Armed Services committees on detention operations at internment facilities and reintegration centers in Iraq.

▸ A ban on using funds authorized by the bill to establish permanent military bases in Iraq or control over Iraqi oil facilities. Both bills had versions of the ban.

▸ A House provision requiring an annual report to Congress on Iran's nuclear weapons capabilities. The president also was required to notify Congress if Iran resumed its nuclear weapons program.

▸ A provision stating that members' projects listed in the statement of managers on the bill were "authorized by law to be carried out to the same extent as if included in the text of the act, subject to the availability of appropriations." The statement said that the Government Printing Office had indicated that it would not be able to incorporate the tables into the bill in time for Congress to finish the measure before adjournment.

● **Weapons compromises.** Differences resolved in the informal negotiations included:

▸ A reduction of $246 million from the request — rather than the $372 million cut recommended by the House or the full funding in the Senate bill — to develop and construct the missile defense system in Poland and the Czech Republic. The bill contained limits on the use of funds in fiscal 2009 and beyond but allowed acquisition of long-lead-time components.

▸ $300 million added for advance procurement of a second *Virginia*-class sub, less than half what the House wanted but nearly four times what the Senate recommended.

▸ $2.6 billion, as the Senate proposed, to buy one DDG-1000 destroyer. But the bill also included $349 million for spares or advance procurement of the older DDG-51 destroyer.

▸ $600 million for advance procurement for two LDP-17 amphibious ships, a third of what the House approved but more than twice what the Senate wanted.

▸ $832 million for development of a new aerial tanker, the amount the House proposed but about $60 million below the Senate figure. Like both bills, the final version provided none of the money requested for procurement in fiscal 2009. ■

GI Bill Education Benefits Expanded

GI EDUCATION BENEFITS were significantly increased for the first time in nearly 25 years as part of an emergency war supplemental spending bill that President Bush signed June 30 (HR 2642 — PL 110-252).

The provisions created a permanent entitlement program that expanded education benefits for veterans who had served since Sept. 11, 2001. The measure was based on a bill written by Virginia Democrat Jim Webb, a former Marine and Vietnam War veteran who served as secretary of the Navy in the Reagan administration. The program was expected to cost as much as $62 billion over 10 years.

The Servicemen's Readjustment Act of 1944 (PL 78-346), as the first GI Bill was formally known, was written to provide money for college or vocational education, as well as cheap loans to buy homes and start businesses, for returning World War II veterans. The program was reworked in 1984 under the Montgomery GI Bill (PL 98-525), named for Rep. G.V. "Sonny" Montgomery, D-Miss. *(1984 Almanac, p. 56)*

Veterans said the money they received was inadequate to pay for their college educations. Active-duty servicemembers who became full-time students received up to $1,101 per month for a maximum of 36 months — a fraction of the total cost of tuition, books, and room and board at most colleges and universities.

Webb introduced his bill in 2007 on his first day in office, but the measure stagnated. In February 2008, he joined with John W. Warner, R-Va., also a former Navy secretary as well as a previous chairman of the Senate Armed Services Committee, to revise the bill and make it more palatable to Senate fiscal conservatives.

The White House and the Pentagon said repeatedly that Webb's plan to overhaul the GI Bill would hurt Pentagon efforts to retain members of the armed services and work against the government's ability to maintain an all-volunteer military. Webb called such reasoning "absurd." He said, "It is going to expand their recruiting base, and I think it would improve the active-duty military."

In a statement of administration policy released May 15, the White House said the president wanted to work with Democrats on the issue but repeated concerns about retention and complained that the bill would not allow veterans to transfer unused education benefits to family members.

In addition, "Blue Dog" Democrats, a 49-member House coalition of fiscal conservatives, opposed providing the expensive benefits without paying for them through increased tax revenues or reduced spending elsewhere in the budget.

Democratic leaders in the House and Senate were ultimately able to sway Republicans by using the war supplemental as leverage and by agreeing to allow veterans to transfer their education benefits to family members. The Blue Dogs were brought along despite the lack of offsets, which were not acceptable to Senate Republicans.

HIGHLIGHTS

The following are the main provisions of the GI Bill expansion:

● **Education benefits.** Eligible veterans were entitled to receive tuition assistance. Depending on their length of service, the amount could equal what in-state residents paid at the costliest public educational institution in the veteran's home state. Benefits were scaled back for veterans with shorter time on active duty.

Other benefits included a monthly stipend to cover housing ex-

penses, based on average housing prices in the area, and stipends for books and other required educational expenses. An additional payment of $100 per month was available for tutorial assistance, expiring after 12 months or until a total of $1,200 had been used. The bill also allowed payment for one licensing or certification test, not to exceed the lesser of $2,000 or the exam fee.

● **Eligibility and terms.** To qualify for the increased education benefits, a veteran had to have served between three months and three years of active duty after Sept. 11, 2001. National Guard and reserve members were fully eligible for the assistance. The assistance covered 36 months, equal to four academic years. The entitlement was protected if the veteran's education was interrupted by deployment or transfer, and veterans had 15 years to use the benefits. Servicemembers could transfer education benefits to their spouses and dependents.

● **Benefit levels.** Payment for tuition and stipends ranged from 40 percent to 100 percent of total costs, based on how long the veteran had served on active duty. A veteran who served three months was eligible for 40 percent of the maximum award. Six months earned 50 percent. The benefit topped out at 100 percent for those who served a 36-month tour on active duty.

● **Public/private contributions.** The measure created a program under which the federal government would provide a dollar-for-dollar match to contributions made by private colleges and universities that were more expensive.

LEGISLATIVE ACTION

Democrats in both chambers appended similar education benefits to their versions of the supplemental spending bill. The provisions were part of a domestic spending section of the bill that also included items such as extended unemployment benefits.

HOUSE, SENATE ACTION

The House approved the portion of the bill devoted to the GI benefits and numerous other domestic provisions by a vote of 256-166 on May 15. *(House vote 330, p. H-106)*

The veterans' benefits were virtually the same as those included in the final bill, with one major exception: To win the support of the Blue Dogs, the leadership included a 0.47 percent surtax on modified adjusted gross incomes above $500,000 ($1 million for joint filers), to pay for the expansion. The Blue Dogs had delayed action on the bill and threatened to defect if it included the new benefits without offsets.

The Senate sent a revised version of the domestic spending package back to the House by a vote of 75-22 on May 22. The only significant difference in the GI Bill provisions was the omission of the surtax, which Republicans rejected as a part of their general opposition to tax increases. *(Senate vote 137, p. S-30)*

Senate Republicans had offered a competing version of the GI benefits bill cosponsored by John McCain of Arizona and Lindsey Graham of South Carolina. It would have increased the monthly education benefit by $400 to $1,500, with a maximum of $2,000 per month after 12 years of service. The benefit could have been transferred to family members. The senators offered the plan May 14 as an amendment to an unrelated collective-bargaining bill (HR 980), but the Senate voted, 55-42, to table the proposal, thus killing

it. *(Senate vote 127, p. S-27)*

The final version of the supplemental was worked out by House leaders and the White House. The House adopted the domestic spending portion, 416-12, on June 19. The Senate cleared the bill, 92-6, on June 26. *(House vote 432, p. H-144; Senate vote 162, p. S-35)*

The negotiators dropped the House plan to offset the cost of the veterans' provisions with a surtax on wealthy taxpayers, a decision that did not go over well with the House Blue Dogs. Not only was the offset removed, but Democrats also agreed to a White House proposal to allow veterans to transfer the benefit to family members, which was likely to add $10 billion to its cost.

But most of the Blue Dogs chose to express their opposition to the decision by voting against the rule (H Res 1284) that governed the floor debate, and not against the supplemental itself. Forty Democrats voted against the rule, which was adopted by a vote of 342-83, but only three cast "nay" votes on the domestic spending amendment, which included the veterans' education benefit. *(House vote 429, p. H-142)* ∎

Global AIDS Programs Expanded

IN A DISPLAY OF bipartisanship that was rare in the overheated election-year atmosphere, members of both parties and the White House joined forces to enact a five-year, $48 billion reauthorization and expansion of President Bush's global AIDS program. The measure was signed into law July 30 (HR 5501 — PL 110-293).

Enactment marked the end of a seven-month legislative journey that began when the chairman of the House Foreign Affairs Committee, Tom Lantos, D-Calif. (1981-2008), drafted legislation to reauthorize the 2003 global AIDS program (PL 108-25).

The program, spearheaded by Bush, had provided AIDS drug treatment to 1.4 million people, supported care for 6.6 million and earned bipartisan praise as a foreign policy success. The original law authorized $15 billion for the first five years. As of Sept. 30, 2007, Congress had appropriated about $19 billion. Bush called for a $30 billion reauthorization.

After Lantos' death in February, California Democrat Howard L. Berman took over as chairman of the Foreign Affairs Committee and helped broker a bipartisan compromise among Democrats, Republicans and the White House that allowed all sides to sign on and take credit. In exchange for a higher funding level, Democrats dropped language that would have tied family planning groups more closely to HIV/AIDS services, which conservatives said would open a back door to funding abortion overseas.

The House and Senate made a few changes in the bill, but the deal largely held. The final bill bore Lantos' name, along with that of the Foreign Affairs Committee chairman who guided the 2003 law to enactment, Henry J. Hyde, R-Ill. (1975-2007), who died in 2007.

"The measure before the House today is a compromise — a compromise between Democrats and Republicans, between the House and the Senate, and between Congress and the executive branch," Berman said of the final bill. "The fact that compromise was achievable in this highly politicized era is a testament to the bipartisan roots of this legislation."

In addition to the funding boost, the bill was designed to shift the program from its original, "emergency" purpose toward a long-term, sustainable plan, which included expanding the programs' focus to include food aid, health care worker recruitment and special outreach

---

BOX SCORE

BILL: HR 5501 — PL 110-293

LEGISLATIVE ACTION:

House passed HR 5501 (H Rept 110-546), amended, 308-116, on April 2.

Senate passed HR 5501, 80-16, on July 16, after substituting the text of S 2731 (S Rept 110-325).

House cleared HR 5501, 303-115, on July 24.

President signed July 30.

---

to women and girls.

However, the authorization did not ensure that Congress would actually provide a funding increase. The continuing resolution enacted at the end of the year (PL 110-329) to fund all non-defense programs through March 6, 2009, provided a total of about $6 billion for global AIDS programs, slightly above the fiscal 2007 level.

"The challenge for future presidents and future Congresses will be to continue this commitment, so that we can lift the shadow of malaria and HIV/AIDS and other diseases once and for all," Bush said July 24, the day the bill cleared.

HIGHLIGHTS

Major elements of the new law:

● **Authorization.** Provided $48 billion for global HIV/AIDS programs for fiscal 2009 through 2013, including:

▸ $5 billion for malaria programs.

▸ $4 billion for tuberculosis programs.

▸ Up to $2 billion in fiscal 2009 for the Geneva-based Global Fund to Fight AIDS, Tuberculosis and Malaria and unspecified sums in fiscal 2010 through 2013. The measure continued a provision in existing law that limited the U.S. contribution to 33 percent of the total amount contributed to the fund from all other sources.

▸ $2 billion for health care, clean water and law enforcement programs for American Indians.

● **Abstinence education.** Repealed a law that required that one-third of prevention money be spent on abstinence education. Instead, the bill required a report to Congress if abstinence and fidelity programs fell below half of U.S. funds spent on prevention in a given country.

● **Prostitution.** Preserved an existing requirement that, to be eligible for aid, organizations have an explicit policy opposing prostitution.

● **Aid distribution.** Required that more than half the program's bilateral aid go toward AIDS treatment and care; 10 percent had to go to orphans and vulnerable children.

● **Targeted results.** Set goals of preventing 12 million new HIV infections worldwide and supporting treatment for 12 million individuals infected with HIV/AIDS. The number was to increase with spending and the decline of drug costs. The bill also set a target of reaching

80 percent of pregnant women for prevention of mother-to-child transmission of HIV in countries with U.S. programs.

● **Nutrition and staff.** Linked AIDS prevention and treatment programs to nutrition programs and included a goal of recruiting 140,000 new health care workers.

● **Ban on HIV-positive visitors.** Repealed a statute, in existence since 1987, that made HIV infection grounds for barring prospective immigrants, foreign students, refugees and tourists from entry into the United States.

● **Faith-based organizations.** Strengthened the "conscience clause," a provision of law that allowed faith-based organizations to opt out of endorsing or using any prevention or treatment method to which they had a religious or moral objection. The bill stated that faith-based groups would not be required to integrate with or refer people to other programs to which the organizations objected, and it barred government discrimination against faith groups based on their refusal to refer people to organizations to which they objected. The conscience clause was also extended to programs that cared for those affected by AIDS.

LEGISLATIVE ACTION
HOUSE COMMITTEE ACTION

The House Foreign Affairs Committee agreed by voice vote Feb. 27 to a bill that reflected the bipartisan compromise (HR 5501 — H Rept 110-546).

Without the compromise, the panel would have faced a battle between Democrats pushing to get rid of requirements for abstinence-only education and restrictions on family planning groups and Republicans who said such changes would funnel money to abortionists overseas. Republicans and the White House had balked at an earlier Democratic draft that would have made sweeping changes to social-policy provisions in existing law.

The administration supported the measure, although the committee proposed to authorize $50 billion over five years, $20 billion more than Bush sought. Democrats, implementing groups and even some Republicans said Bush's request would sustain existing efforts but would not expand the program.

"Although in the end we had to compromise on several items that were important to me and many Democratic members, I think this is a good bill, and I am pleased to support it," said Democrat Barbara Lee of California.

HOUSE FLOOR ACTION

The House pushed aside objections about the cost and passed the bill, 308-116, on April 2. *(House vote 158, p. H-50)*

No significant changes were made on the floor, and a GOP motion to recommit the bill to lower its cost to the $30 billion that Bush originally requested failed, 175-248. *(House vote 157, p. H-50)*

"We have people who can't take care of their own health needs and are at risk of losing their homes, and we are going to spend $50 billion in Africa?" asked Dana Rohrabacher, R-Calif.

Mike Pence, R-Ind., a fiscal conservative who supported the bill, saw it differently. "I believe it's possible to be responsible to our fiscal constraints while being obedient to our moral calling," he said.

SENATE COMMITTEE ACTION

The Senate Foreign Relations Committee approved a similar five-year, $50 billion bill (S 2731 — S Rept 110-325) on March 13 by a vote of 18-3, with the "no" votes coming from Republicans who objected

to its cost. Lawmakers were hoping to get the bill to Bush by the July 7 start of the Group of Eight summit in Japan so that he could use it to get commitments from other countries. "We wanted to get this up and out," Senate sponsor and panel Chairman Joseph R. Biden Jr., D-Del., said after the markup.

SENATE/FINAL ACTION

The Senate passed a revised version of the bill by a wide margin July 16, after turning back Republican attempts to reduce its cost and shift its focus. The 80-16 vote came after months of behind-the-scenes wrangling, three days of debate and consideration of 10 amendments. The delay deprived Bush of the chance to use the bill as a talking point in Japan. *(Senate vote 182, p. S-40)*

The House cleared the compromise bill July 24 by voting, 303-115, to adopt the Senate-passed version. *(House vote 531, p. H-178)*

Sen. Tom Coburn, R-Okla., had held up the bill since the committee markup, demanding that more than half the program's bilateral aid go toward AIDS treatment and care. Just before the July Fourth recess, Biden and the committee's ranking Republican, Richard G. Lugar of Indiana, unveiled a compromise that included Coburn's language.

Bush hailed the Senate action, praising "both sides of the aisle, who came together today to ensure that America's generosity in battling HIV/AIDS, malaria and other diseases around the globe will continue in a manner consistent with the program's successful founding principles."

During the floor debate, the Senate:

▸ Adopted by voice vote an amendment that trimmed the original $50 billion authorization for the global health plan to $48 billion and directed the other $2 billion to health care, law enforcement and drinking water programs for American Indians. This was the only sizable change made on the floor. It was backed by Indian Affairs Chairman Byron L. Dorgan, D-N.D., and other Democrats, including Biden and Hillary Rodham Clinton of New York.

▸ Rejected, 31-64, an attempt by Jim DeMint, R-S.C., to cut the bill's total cost to $35 billion. "Why, at a time when our country is in debt as far as we can see, why would we as a country create the biggest foreign aid bill in history and borrow more money — $50 billion — and send it all around the world?" DeMint asked. He said even $35 billion was too much. *(Senate vote 181, p. S-40)*

Lugar said DeMint's amendment would be "a severe blow to the United States' leadership and prestige on this issue because it would profoundly affect the calculations of individuals, groups and governments that we are trying to engage in this fight against HIV/AIDS and whose commitments are, many of them, contingent upon our action today."

▸ Adopted amendments by voice vote aimed at increasing oversight of the Global Fund and encouraging cost-sharing and transition strategies as part of agreements with recipient countries.

▸ Defeated, 32-63, an amendment by John Cornyn, R-Texas, to establish a sunset commission to propose legislation, with expedited consideration, that would abolish any global AIDS programs that Congress did not explicitly reauthorize. *(Senate vote 178, p. S-40)*

▸ Rejected, 44-51, an amendment by Judd Gregg, R-N.H., to set up an inspector general for the programs, whose rapid growth he said required more oversight. *(Senate vote 179, p. S-40)*

▸ Defeated, 28-67, an amendment by Jon Kyl, R-Ariz., to limit spending in the program's final year to $10 billion. *(Senate vote 180, p. S-40)* ■

Hill Backs Nuclear Deal With India

CONGRESS GAVE ITS APPROVAL to a U.S.-India civilian nuclear cooperation agreement in October, clearing the way for the two countries to put the pact into force. Enactment marked the end of more than three years of work and gave President Bush a foreign policy victory as his term was drawing to a close. The president signed the bill into law Oct. 8 (HR 7081 – PL 110-369).

The U.S.-India agreement allowed nuclear trade between the two countries. India agreed to a number of preconditions required by international regulators and U.S. law to engage in such trade. Among the most important was an agreement to separate its military and civilian nuclear facilities and to place the civilian, but not military, program under international oversight.

Supporters, including leaders of both parties, said the U.S.-India deal would open opportunities for U.S. businesses that would otherwise go to other nations and would cement ties with a nation that was both the world's largest democracy and a key counterweight in the region to China. Critics warned that the deal could give rogue nations a rationale for developing their own nuclear programs and that India could use the imported nuclear fuel to feed its civilian energy program while diverting its own nuclear fuel to weapons production. A number of lawmakers also expressed concern that India's close ties to Iran might lead New Delhi to assist the Iranian nuclear program.

In the end, most members of Congress supported the agreement as part of a strategic global partnership with India, but they also insisted on specific safeguards and continued congressional oversight.

Bush and Indian Prime Minister Manmohan Singh first announced plans for nuclear cooperation in 2005. In March 2006, the two leaders announced they had agreed on the details of the pact. But before Bush could sign off on a final agreement, he needed legislation that allowed him to exempt India from certain restrictions on nuclear exports under the 1954 Atomic Energy Act (PL 83-703).

In December 2006, Congress sent Bush a bill allowing the necessary waivers, but the measure also required that lawmakers be much more involved in the process than the administration had wanted. In particular, the 2006 law (PL 109-401) required the administration to bring the final U.S.-India agreement back to Congress for approval before the deal could take effect. The law also imposed a set of conditions that had to be met before Bush could use the waiver authority provided in the new law. (2006 Almanac, p. 10-5)

The two countries announced a final text in July 2007, and on Sept. 10, 2008, Bush sent the agreement to Congress. He also certified that the conditions set under the 2006 law had been met. These included a credible plan by India to separate its civilian and military nuclear facilities, an agreement between the International Atomic Energy Agency (IAEA) and India to allow inspections and other safeguards, and an agreement from the Nuclear Suppliers Group, an international body overseeing trade in nuclear reactors and fuel, to exempt India from certain restrictions.

In response to Bush's request, Congress passed the bill (HR 7081) that granted the necessary congressional approval, but it also required

---

BOX SCORE

BILL: HR 7081 – PL 110-369

....

LEGISLATIVE ACTION:

House passed HR 7081, 298-117, on Sept. 27.

Senate cleared HR 7081, 86-13, on Oct. 1.

President signed Oct. 8.

---

additional safeguards and ongoing congressional oversight, particularly on any subsequent agreement with India on reprocessing nuclear fuel.

The complicated process of exemptions from U.S. law and international agreements was due largely to India's peculiar status as a country that had tested nuclear weapons but was not officially recognized as a nuclear-weapons state. Under the international Non-Proliferation Treaty (NPT), the only nations recognized as nuclear-weapons states were those that had tested weapons before 1968. India's first weapons test was in 1974; India also had never signed the NPT.

The U.S. Atomic Energy Act specified, among other things, that the United States could engage in nuclear cooperation with a non-nuclear state only if that country opened all of its nuclear facilities to inspection by the IAEA, a step India could not be expected to take in the case of its military facilities. The U.S. law also required the termination of nuclear exports if a non-nuclear-weapons state tested nuclear weapons after 1978; India tested a weapon in 1998.

HIGHLIGHTS

The following are the major components of the 2008 bill:

● **Approval.** The bill gave Congress' approval to the United States-India Agreement for Cooperation on Peaceful Uses of Nuclear Energy.

● **Additional safeguards.** Before the Nuclear Regulatory Commission could issue licences for the sale of nuclear-related goods and services to India, the president had to certify to Congress that:

▸ India had provided the IAEA with a credible plan to separate civilian and military nuclear facilities, materials and programs and had filed a declaration regarding its civilian facilities with the agency.

▸ The required agreement between India and the IAEA on the inspection of Indian nuclear facilities, which was reached Aug. 14, 2008, had entered into force.

● **Reprocessing.** The bill gave Congress the explicit right to review and disapprove of any subsequent agreement to permit India to extract plutonium and uranium from spent reactor fuel that originated in the United States. Congress would have 30 days within which to adopt a joint resolution of disapproval. Also, the president was required to inform the appropriate congressional committees "at the earliest possible time" after any request by the Indian government to negotiate reprocessing arrangements.

Under the U.S.-India accord, before India could reprocess nuclear material, it had to set up a new reprocessing facility for civilian nuclear material, and it had to reach an agreement with Washington on the procedures to be used at the new facility.

● **Future agreements.** The bill specified that Congress could reject a presidential decision to resume nuclear trade with any country that had detonated a nuclear explosive device by adopting a joint resolution of disapproval within 60 days of the decision.

LEGISLATIVE ACTION
HOUSE ACTION

The House passed the India bill Sept. 27 by a vote of 298-117 under suspension of the rules, a procedure that barred amendments and required a two-thirds majority. *(House vote 662, p. H-222)*

Howard L. Berman, D-Calif., chairman of the Foreign Affairs Committee, expressed skepticism about the deal, voicing particular concern that India might assist Iran with its nuclear program. He considered combining the India legislation with provisions to strengthen sanctions against Iran. Pairing the two issues would have required a difficult vote for members who supported action against Iran but opposed the India deal.

But administration officials, including Secretary of State Condoleezza Rice, appealed to Congress to pass a "clean," unconditional approval of the India nuclear deal.

Berman introduced the bill after receiving personal assurance from Rice that she would seek a global ban on transferring enrichment and reprocessing technology to countries that did not already have it.

SENATE ACTION

The Senate cleared the House-passed bill (HR 7081) by a vote of 86-13 on Oct. 1. It was one of the Senate's last roll call votes of the 110th Congress. *(Senate vote 211, p. S-47)*

The Senate Foreign Relations Committee had approved an identical bill (S 3548) by a vote of 19-2 on Sept. 23. The panel rejected, 4-15, an amendment offered by Wisconsin Democrat Russ Feingold that would have required the president to certify that the Nuclear Suppliers Group had amended its guidelines to prohibit the transfer of equipment and technology related to the enrichment of uranium and reprocessing of spent nuclear fuel to any state that was not a party to the NPT. Christopher J. Dodd, D-Conn., the bill's sponsor, argued that the amendment would delay the agreement and could cause political problems with India.

During floor debate on the bill, senators rejected by voice vote an amendment by Byron L. Dorgan, D-N.D., and Jeff Bingaman, D-N.M., that would have required a cutoff of nuclear supplies to India if that country conducted another nuclear test. "We are taking apart the basic architecture of nuclear non-proliferation that has served us for many decades," Dorgan said.

Richard G. Lugar of Indiana, the ranking Republican on the Foreign Relations Committee, said that existing law already offered the same protections. "If India tests a nuclear weapon, [the agreement] is over," he said, echoing the State Department view as outlined in a letter from Rice to the House Foreign Affairs Committee. ∎

Bush Prevails on FISA Overhaul

DEMOCRATIC EFFORTS to confront President Bush over electronic surveillance laws ended abruptly in July, with the White House the clear winner and Democrats dropping the fight for the duration of the Bush presidency. Legislation overhauling the Foreign Intelligence Surveillance Act (FISA) was signed into law July 10 (HR 6304 — PL 110-261).

Bush had made a rewrite of electronic surveillance guidelines one of his legislative priorities. His main objective was to revise FISA to authorize enhanced executive branch spying powers and provide retroactive legal protection for telephone companies that had participated in a warrantless wiretapping program conducted under presidential authority by the National Security Agency (NSA).

The bill established a process that gave Bush both, although with some additional court and congressional oversight. Christopher S. Bond of Missouri, ranking Republican on the Senate Select Committee on Intelligence, said the bill ended up being essentially what Bush wanted. "There really is not much that is significantly different, save some cosmetic fixes that were requested by the majority party in the House," said Bond, who strongly supported the bill.

The legislation revamped FISA to establish new rules for the use of electronic surveillance to collect foreign intelligence, including monitoring communications involving parties on U.S. soil. It was scheduled to expire Dec. 31, 2012.

BOX SCORE

BILL: HR 6304 — PL 110-261

LEGISLATIVE ACTION:

Senate passed S 2248, amended, 68-29, on Feb. 12, then substituted the text into HR 3773.

House agreed to the Senate amendment to HR 3773, with an amendment, 213-197, on March 14.

House passed HR 6304, 293-129, on June 20.

Senate cleared HR 6304, 69-28, on July 9.

President signed July 10.

It did not explicitly grant retroactive legal immunity to the telecommunications companies, but it came close enough to satisfy the White House by creating conditions for the courts to dismiss the lawsuits. Dozens of lawsuits had been brought against the firms over their participation in the program. Aides and lawmakers considered the dismissal of the lawsuits a virtual certainty.

While Democrats agreed with the Bush administration on the need to overhaul FISA, they generally wanted more restrictions to protect Americans' civil liberties. However, they were not able to resolve differences between the two chambers over the exact role of the FISA court and whether to grant retroactive immunity.

Some Democrats opposed giving companies such as AT&T immunity for their work with the NSA, expressing concern about the legal precedent and the effect such immunity might have on potential court scrutiny of the program. The administration threatened to veto any bill that did not include such immunity, saying that leaving it out could discourage private sector cooperation with future spying programs.

With no agreement, Democrats had had little choice but to accept most of the administration's demands. A six-month law (PL 110-55) written by the White House and enacted in August 2007 broadened the government's surveillance powers, allowing intelligence agencies to immediately begin conducting warrantless surveillance of foreign

targets, whether or not they were communicating with someone in the United States. Procedures governing the surveillance had to be submitted later to the FISA court.

Democratic leaders vowed to rein in some of the provisions in a follow-up law, but they again disagreed over the FISA court's role and over retroactive immunity.

The House passed a bill (HR 3773) in November 2007 specifying that no warrant would be required for electronic surveillance of communication between parties that were not known to be "United States persons" and were reasonably believed to be located outside the country — "without respect to whether the communication passed through the United States or the surveillance device was located within the United States." Except in emergencies, the FISA court would have to approve the procedures being used before the surveillance could begin.

Warrants would still be required for electronic surveillance of foreign targets who were communicating with someone in the United States, although intelligence agencies could get "blanket" warrants covering entire groups of people. The bill did not include retroactive immunity for the telecommunications providers.

Two Senate committees approved competing versions of a separate bill (S 2248), but that measure did not reach the floor in 2007. Both panels would have allowed the attorney general and director of national intelligence (DNI) to jointly authorize up to one year of warrantless surveillance of parties reasonably believed to be outside the United States.

Among the chief differences: The Select Committee on Intelligence provided for retroactive immunity for phone companies; the Judiciary Committee version did not, but it proposed that the U.S. government replace the companies as defendant in the lawsuits.

In February 2008, the Senate passed what was essentially the Intelligence panel's version of the bill. In March, the House passed a revised version of its own bill. Democrats chose to allow the six-month 2007 bill to expire while they continued work on the overhaul. After months of negotiations failed to produce a compromise, Congress cleared the bill that gave Bush much of what he wanted.

HIGHLIGHTS

The following are among the main elements of the new FISA law:
- **Warrantless surveillance.** The law allowed the attorney general and DNI to jointly authorize up to one year of surveillance of parties that they reasonably believed were not Americans and were located outside the country. No FISA warrant was required, even if the communications were routed through the United States.
- **FISA review.** Before such surveillance could begin, the attorney general and DNI had to secure approval from the FISA court, not of the targets but of the procedures to be used. The surveillance could start prior to the FISA court review if the need was deemed urgent. The court had 30 days to determine whether the procedures met statutory guidelines on providing reasonable assurance that the target was outside the United States, preventing the targeting of communication with anyone known to be in the United States and minimizing possible disclosure of any information acquired about an American. If the procedures met the guidelines, the court would give its approval; if not, the agencies would have to comply or terminate the surveillance.
- **Domestic surveillance.** Like previous law, the measure required FISA court warrants for surveillance that targeted anyone located in the United States. A FISA warrant was also required for surveillance of Americans located outside the country.

- **Lawsuit waivers.** Federal and state courts were required to dismiss existing lawsuits against companies that assisted Bush's warrantless surveillance program if there was "substantial evidence" the companies had received written assurances that the program was legal and authorized by the president. A Senate Intelligence panel report on an earlier version of the legislation detailed the assurances that the companies had received from the Justice Department and the White House.
- **Surveillance rationale.** The law contained language stating that FISA, as modified by the new law, was "the exclusive means by which electronic surveillance and the interception of domestic wire, oral, or electronic communications may be conducted." It specified that any variations or modifications could be made only through a new statute directly addressing FISA. The aim was to prevent the administration from using legal rationales outside of FISA for surveillance activities.
- **Program reviews.** The inspectors general for the Justice Department, DNI, NSA and Defense Department were required to review the president's warrantless surveillance program and report within a year. The administration also was required to file periodic reports to Congress on the execution of the new law, disclosures of FISA court orders and other information.

LEGISLATIVE ACTION
SENATE FLOOR ACTION

On Feb. 12, the Senate passed a comprehensive FISA overhaul (S 2248), 68-29, after rejecting a series of amendments that could have turned the White House against the carefully negotiated measure. The most significant amendments would have eliminated retroactive immunity provisions. Nineteen Democrats and one independent joined 48 Republicans in support of the bill; no GOP senators voted against it. After passage, the Senate inserted the text into the bill (HR 3773) the House had passed the previous November. *(Senate vote 20, p. S-7)*

Floor debate on the Senate bill began Jan. 23, shortly after the start of the session, and stretched over three weeks. Majority Leader Harry Reid, D-Nev., started with the Intelligence committee's version, which was favored by Republicans and the White House. It included retroactive immunity and warrantless surveillance of foreign targets regardless of whether they were communicating with someone in the United States. If the FISA court later found that statutory procedural requirements were not being met, it could order the government to correct the problems within 30 days or stop the surveillance. The bill would sunset on Dec. 31, 2013.

The Senate tabled, or killed, an amendment that would have substituted the Judiciary Committee version, which omitted the retroactive-immunity provisions and would have imposed more limits on executive branch spying, including oversight authority by the FISA court. The White House warned that such an amendment could result in a veto of the bill. The vote was 60-36. *(Senate vote 2, p. S-4)*

Thereafter, the debate stalled in a partisan feud over floor procedures. A number of Democrats wanted a chance to remove the immunity language. Republicans argued that such amendments were a waste of time, especially with the impending Feb. 1 expiration of the August law looming. Minority Leader Mitch McConnell, R-Ky., tried unsuccessfully Jan. 28 to bring debate on the bill to a close and move to passage. The near-party-line vote was 48-45, 12 short of the 60 needed to invoke cloture. *(Senate vote 3, S-4)*

When work on the bill resumed, Democrats tried repeatedly without success to remove the immunity language. "This is an issue the Intelligence committee has considered very, very carefully," responded

Background on FISA

THE ORIGINAL FOREIGN INTELLIGENCE Surveillance Act (FISA) became law in 1978 in response to public outcry over the extensive use of wiretapping by the Nixon administration, as well as revelations by what became known as the Church Committee — a select congressional committee charged with investigating 40 years of covert activities — that every administration since Franklin D. Roosevelt's had authorized the use of warrantless electronic surveillance. *(1978 Almanac, p. 186)*

The law (PL 95-511) required the government to obtain a warrant from a special FISA court before it could conduct foreign surveillance in which one of the parties was a U.S. citizen. The FISA court did not have jurisdiction over intelligence operations that took place completely outside the United States. Cases that came before the court were sealed and were generally not revealed even when subsequent court cases were based on evidence obtained through the warrants.

The president could authorize electronic surveillance to collect foreign intelligence without first getting court approval for up to three days in an emergency and 15 days after a declaration of war by Congress. The government also could conduct warrantless surveillance for up to a year if the activity involved communications only among foreigners and if communications of U.S. citizens or residents were unlikely to be collected.

In December 2005, The New York Times revealed that the National Security Agency (NSA) had been secretly monitoring international telephone calls and e-mails of U.S. residents without warrants. The secret program, authorized by President Bush in the year following the Sept. 11, 2001, terrorist attacks, monitored thousands of U.S. citizens, permanent residents, tourists and foreigners in the country in order to track possible links to al Qaeda.

In January 2007, after Democrats took control of both chambers of Congress, the Bush administration announced that the NSA surveillance program had been submitted to the FISA court for approval and that the court had granted several orders. Subsequent reports indicated some effort by the court to limit surveillance of foreign communications that were routed through the United States.

On May 1, 2007, National Intelligence Director Michael McConnell called on Congress to update FISA to reflect the widespread advances in communications technology by making the law "technologically neutral." He told the Senate Select Intelligence Committee that the law should be changed to allow warrantless surveillance of foreign terrorism suspects without regard to whether they were communicating with people in the United States — essentially, one of the activities that the administration had conducted through the NSA program.

On July 28, 2007, Bush called on Congress to send him a bill that would authorize U.S. intelligence agencies to cope with "sophisticated terrorists" who used disposable cell phones, the Internet and other technologies that were not available when FISA was written.

On Aug. 4, 2007, Congress cleared a six-month Republican-written bill that gave the government significant latitude under FISA. *(2007 Almanac, p. 14-3)*

On Nov. 15, 2007, the House passed a bill to pull back some of the provisions, but the measure went no further.

John D. Rockefeller IV, D-W.Va., the chairman of the Intelligence panel and sponsor of the bill. "I and most members of the committee became convinced the companies acted in good faith, relied on the most senior legal authority of the government and cooperated because they wanted to help."

In floor action in February, the Senate:

▶ Rejected, 49-46, an attempt by Benjamin L. Cardin, D-Md., to have the bill sunset at the end of 2011 instead of 2013. *(Senate vote 7, p. S-5)*

▶ Rejected, 40-56, an amendment by Russ Feingold, D-Wis., to allow limits on the use of information on U.S. individuals if the procedures in the bill were found to be deficient. *(Senate vote 11, p. S-6)*

▶ Rejected, 38-57, a second Feingold amendment, which would have prohibited the government from wiretapping someone overseas in order to get information on a target in the United States, a practice known as reverse targeting. *(Senate vote 12, p. S-6)*

▶ Rejected, 57-41, an attempt by Dianne Feinstein, D-Calif., to tighten language stating that FISA and the new bill were the "exclusive means" of conducting domestic intelligence surveillance. The Senate had agreed to require 60 votes for adoption. Feinstein, an Intelligence panel member who had voted for the bill in committee, said she was trying to prevent a chief executive, "either now or in the future, from moving outside of this law." *(Senate vote 13, p. S-6)*

▶ Rejected, 31-67, an amendment by Connecticut Democrat Christopher J. Dodd to strike the immunity provision from the bill. Dodd had earlier said he would use every tool in his power to eliminate the language. *(Senate vote 15, p. S-6)*

▶ Rejected, 30-68, an amendment by Arlen Specter, R-Pa., to substitute the federal government for the companies as the defendant in the lawsuits against the firms that participated in the NSA warrantless surveillance. *(Senate vote 17, p. S-7)*

▶ Rejected, 41-57, an attempt by Feinstein to grant immunity to the companies on a case-by-case basis if the FISA court determined that a company acted with a reasonable belief that its role was legal. *(Senate vote 18, p. S-7)*

Finally, on Feb. 12, the Senate voted, 69-29, to limit further debate on the bill, clearing the way for passage. *(Senate vote 19, p. S-7)*

EXTENSION, EXPIRATION OF 2007 LAW

While the Senate struggled to pass its bill, Congress on Jan. 29 cleared a 15-day extension that delayed the expiration of the existing law from Feb. 1 to Feb. 16. Republicans were unhappy with the extension and called on Congress to clear the Senate bill instead. Bush signed the stopgap bill on Jan. 31 (PL 110-182) but vowed not to accept another extension.

On Feb. 13, House leaders tried to pass another, 21-day extension (HR 5349) to give the two chambers more time. But Republicans joined with a group of 34 liberal and conservative Democratic defectors to reject the bill, 191-229. Earlier in the day, Democrats had closed ranks to kill, 222-196, a GOP attempt to replace the short-term extension with the Senate-passed bill. *(House votes 54, 53, p. H-18)*

GOP lawmakers and the White House raised the specter of a hobbled intelligence community if the House did not act quickly to clear the Senate bill. But House Democrats chose to let expire the law they had reluctantly accepted in August 2007. They insisted that the intelligence community would have all the tools it needed to defend against terrorist attacks and said that if Republicans really saw the lapse as endangering the country, they should have voted for the extension.

Legal experts said the implications of an expiration were mixed. Any spying orders already in place would remain in effect long after the temporary law lapsed. At the same time, most experts agreed that the administration would have to go back to the secret FISA court to obtain warrants in cases where foreign-to-foreign communications were routed through the U.S. telecommunications infrastructure. That posed little immediate problem, they said, but if a backlog of warrant applications were to build, it could begin to have an impact.

Among experts in national security law, there was no agreement over whether telecommunications companies would still have to comply with administration surveillance demands.

And because Bush administration officials had repeatedly claimed that the president had all the authority he needed to conduct a surveillance program in the service of national security, some experts argued that the administration was likely to do as it pleased regardless of what happened in Congress.

HOUSE FLOOR ACTION

House Democratic leaders reworked their bill from November, and on March 14 the chamber adopted it, 213-197, as a substitute amendment. A mix of 12 liberal and conservative Democrats joined every Republican present in voting against the bill, which still defied the president in the way it dealt with the telecommunications companies that had cooperated in the administration's eavesdropping operations. Like the November version, the bill would have expired Dec. 31, 2009. *(House vote 145, p. H-46)*

Republicans did everything they could to force the House to accept the Senate bill, even walking out of the chamber as a group at one point. Bush castigated Democrats and said he would delay the start of a planned trip to Africa over the weekend if it would help quickly clear long-term legislation.

The rule for floor action allowed no amendments.

Debate on the bill broke along party lines, with Democrats arguing that it would grant the intelligence community all the authority it needed to spy on foreign terrorist suspects while protecting Americans' civil liberties. Republicans assailed the bill for what they said were too many restrictions on surveillance and for the absence of immunity provisions.

"The security of the country for the next two weeks we're [in recess] will not be the same as it would have been had we passed a bipartisan bill that has already passed in the Senate," said House Minority Whip Roy Blunt, R-Mo. "The only thing that can become law is the bipartisan Senate bill. This vote has no impact at all."

The revised bill included provisions to:

▶ Remove legal barriers erected by the administration to prevent the telecommunications companies from using classified information in civil court to defend themselves. Under the bill, a judge could review such evidence in private without showing it to the plaintiffs. The administration and congressional Republicans said that was no substitute for retroactive immunity.

▶ Allow phone companies to go to the FISA court to challenge

requirements from the government that they cooperate in warrantless surveillance. If the court did not find in favor of the companies, it could compel them to comply.

▶ Require that, prior to approving warrantless surveillance operations, intelligence officials certify to the FISA court that the procedures being used complied with requirements in the bill. The Senate bill required that certifications be submitted after the surveillance began.

▶ Stipulate that FISA and the bill provided the exclusive legal means by which surveillance could be conducted to gather foreign intelligence. The provision was not included in the Senate bill.

The day before the vote on passage, the House held its first secret session in 25 years, at the request of the Republicans who said they wanted to discuss classified material that would help lawmakers understand the need to clear the Senate-passed legislation.

Democrats derided the secret session; Republicans defended it and blamed Democrats for not getting more out of the meeting. But members of both parties said it was unlikely to change the outcome of the vote on the bill. A group of 21 "Blue Dog" Democrats had endorsed the Senate bill, but many of them said afterward that they were leaning toward supporting the House version. The next day, only five of them voted against the reworked measure.

FINAL ACTION

Three months after the House vote, Congress cleared a new bill (HR 6304) that was expected to lead to the dismissal of lawsuits against the accused telecommunications companies. The legislation was based on a bipartisan agreement announced June 19 and backed by the White House.

The House passed the bill, 293-129, on June 20, with the support of 105 Democrats and 188 Republicans. On July 9, 21 Senate Democrats joined all Republicans to clear the measure, 69-28. *(House vote 437, p. H-146; Senate vote 168, p. S-37)*

House Majority Leader Steny H. Hoyer, D-Md., said pressure from conservative House Democrats to adopt the Senate bill had forced Democratic leaders into a reluctant compromise. Hoyer and Blunt from the House struck the deal with Rockefeller and Bond from the Senate. Supporters said the measure was an improvement over the Senate-passed bill, which would have required less court and congressional oversight.

Bush and congressional Republicans praised the legislation. "It will help our intelligence professionals learn our enemies' plans for new attacks," Bush said. "It ensures that those companies whose assistance is necessary to protect the country will themselves be protected from liability for past or future cooperation with the government."

But the final bill proved a bitter pill for many Democrats. House members who voted against it said the expansion of executive branch surveillance powers would gut Fourth Amendment protections against unreasonable search and seizure. "This bill scares me to death," said Barbara Lee, D-Calif.

"It's not a happy occasion, but it's the work we have to do," said Speaker Nancy Pelosi, D-Calif. She said the debate on the legislation was "valuable for making the bill better, if not good enough, but certainly preferable to the alternative we have."

Before clearing the bill, the Senate voted down a trio of amendments. Feingold and Dodd managed to delay the vote until after the July Fourth recess, giving opponents one last chance to derail the legislation. But an overwhelming vote of 80-15 on June 25 to limit debate on a motion to proceed to the legislation made it all but certain

that they would not succeed. *(Senate vote 158, p. S-34)*

All three of the Democrats' amendments were aimed at modifying or eliminating the retroactive immunity. They were:

▸ A proposal by Feingold and Dodd, rejected 32-66, to strip out the immunity provisions. *(Senate vote 164, p. S-36)*

▸ A Specter amendment, defeated, 37-61, to deny retroactive immunity to a telecommunications company that aided in government surveillance activities if the court found that the intelligence activities violated the Constitution. Specter said his amendment would ensure court scrutiny of a program on which few members of Congress had been briefed. *(Senate vote 165, p. S-36)*

▸ An amendment by Jeff Bingaman, D-N.M., defeated 42-56, that would have stayed pending lawsuits against the phone companies until 90 days after Congress received an inspectors general report, required by the bill, on the warrantless surveillance program. If lawmakers took no action within 90 days, the provisions of the bill would go into effect. The purpose was to give Congress a chance to decide on immunity based on a third-party review. *(Senate vote 166, p. S-36)*

The White House opposed all three amendments, insisting any provision that jeopardized or delayed retroactive legal immunity threatened future private sector cooperation with spying programs.

Rockefeller said the bill would prevent a repeat of Bush's warrantless surveillance program by strengthening court review and congressional oversight. Senate Judiciary Chairman Patrick J. Leahy, D-Vt., disagreed. "This bill would dismiss ongoing cases against the telecommunications carriers that participated in that program without allowing a judicial review of the legality of the program," he said.

Concessions to Democrats in the final bill included:

▸ The requirement for prior court review of electronic surveillance procedures, including the targeting process and "minimization" procedures aimed at limiting the information that could be retained and disseminated on U.S. citizens — with an exception for urgent circumstances.

▸ A stronger statement that FISA and the bill were the only means by which the executive branch could conduct surveillance related to foreign intelligence and that the act could be modified only by a new statute directly addressing the executive branch's foreign intelligence surveillance authority.

▸ The requirement that inspectors general report to Congress within a year on the president's warrantless surveillance program.

Bush, who had chastised Congress throughout the debate for not sending him a bill, signed the measure the day after it cleared. "This law will play a critical role in helping to prevent another attack on our soil," he said. The Rose Garden ceremony was attended primarily by GOP lawmakers, who had been virtually unanimous in their support of the bill. ∎

Veto Threats Halt Intelligence Bill

CONGRESS ADJOURNED WITHOUT clearing a fiscal 2009 intelligence authorization bill. It was the third year in a row without a new law to update intelligence policy. Earlier in the year, lawmakers were unable to override President Bush's veto of a fiscal 2008 intelligence authorization bill.

The main obstacle in both cases was a conflict between lawmakers and the White House over efforts to require the intelligence community — including the CIA — to abide by specific limits on the methods used in interrogating detainees.

The fiscal 2008 bill included a provision that would have prohibited the intelligence agencies from using any interrogation techniques "not authorized in the United States Army Field Manual on Human Intelligence Collector Operations."

The Army manual was revised in September 2006 following enactment of the 2005 Military Detainee Act (PL 109-148), which prohibited members of the armed forces from subjecting prisoners to "cruel, inhuman or degrading treatment." *(Detainee act, 2005 Almanac, p. 2-14)*

The manual specifically prohibited harsh interrogation methods, such as simulated drowning, known as waterboarding. It also barred forcing a detainee to be naked, perform sexual acts or pose in a sexual manner; placing hoods or sacks over the head of a detainee; using duct tape over the eyes of a detainee; applying beatings, electric shock,

---

BOX SCORE

BILLS: HR 2082, HR 5959, S 2996

LEGISLATIVE ACTION:

Senate cleared HR 2082 (Conf. Rept 110-478), 51-45, on Feb. 13.

President vetoed HR 2082 March 8.

House override attempt failed, 225-188, on March 11 (two-thirds required).

Senate Intelligence Committee approved S 2996 (S Rept 110-333), 10-5, on May 1.

House passed HR 5959 (H Rept 110-665, Parts 1, 2) by voice vote July 16.

---

burns or other forms of physical pain; using military working dogs; inducing hypothermia or heat injury; conducting mock executions; and depriving a detainee of necessary food, water or medical care.

Bush vetoed the bill March 8, saying that it would tie the CIA's hands and give al Qaeda and other terrorists a public glimpse of interrogation procedures. An attempt in the House to override him failed.

The Senate Select Intelligence Committee was unwilling to back down and courted another veto by including the provision in its fiscal 2009 intelligence bill. The panel also added language to bar the CIA from using contractors to interrogate detainees. The bill never reached the Senate floor because of Republican opposition. Majority Leader Harry Reid, D-Nev., did not make it a priority for the limited fall schedule.

The House passed a companion bill in July that left out the Army manual as the basis for interrogation but included the ban on using contractors. The White House threatened to veto both bills.

All three bills would have authorized funding and prescribed policies for the 16 national intelligence agencies and the Office of the Director of National Intelligence (DNI). The agencies included the CIA, the Defense Intelligence Agency, the FBI, the National Security Agency and the National Reconnaissance Office (NRO), as well as the foreign intelligence activities of the departments of State

and Homeland Security.

The exact amount of the proposed authorizations was classified, but it was believed to exceed $40 billion. The National Intelligence Program, which excluded military intelligence operations, had a budget of $43.5 billion in fiscal 2007, the last year for which declassified totals were available. Aides and lawmakers said the bills would authorize more funding for the base intelligence budget than ever before.

LEGISLATIVE ACTION
FY 2008 BILL: SENATE FLOOR ACTION

The Senate adopted the conference report on the fiscal 2008 bill (HR 2082 — H Rept 110-478) by a vote of 51-45 on Feb. 13, clearing the measure for the president. The House had adopted the conference report, 222-199, on Dec. 13, 2007. (Senate vote 22, p. S-8; 2007 Almanac, p. 14-6)

Although it was the first time in three years that Congress had sent an annual intelligence authorization bill to the White House, the narrow vote made it clear that the Senate would not be able to override a veto.

The prohibition on using interrogation methods not authorized in the Army field manual was proposed by Dianne Feinstein of California, the No. 2 Democrat on the Senate Intelligence panel.

The conference report said that inclusion of the provision reflected "the conferees' considered judgment that the CIA's program is not the most effective method of obtaining the reliable intelligence we need to protect the United States from attack. Further, the conferees concluded that damage to international perception of the United States caused by the existence of classified interrogation procedures that apply only to CIA's program and are different from those used by the U.S. military outweighs the intelligence benefits that may result."

The provision would have ensured that the United States used only interrogation methods that would not be seen as abuse if used against an American soldier.

Democrats repeatedly invoked the name of Sen. John McCain of Arizona, the GOP presidential front-runner at the time, who wrote the original language in the Military Detainee Act. But McCain voted against the conference report. "We have said in our law . . . that we would allow the CIA to use additional techniques that were not in violation of the anti-torture convention, that were not in violation of the Geneva Conventions, that were not in violation of the Detainee Treatment Act," he said.

GOP aides said Senate Republicans decided not to raise a widely anticipated point of order to remove the interrogation provision because Bush was expected to veto the bill. But the vice chairman of the Select Intelligence Committee, Republican Christopher S. Bond of Missouri, said limiting the interrogation techniques available to the CIA would be dangerous.

FY 2008 BILL: VETO SUSTAINED

The House on March 11 rejected an attempt to override Bush's March 8 veto of the bill. The vote was 225-188, well short of the two-thirds majority — 276 in this case — that was needed. (Veto text, D-10; House vote 117, p. H-38)

Senate Intelligence Chairman John D. Rockefeller IV, D-W.Va., said he would not consider striking the language on interrogations in order to get the bill enacted. "I am not going to put my party and my conscience in jeopardy by taking out [the interrogation language]," he said. "They say you can take it out and pass it again,

and [Bush would] sign it. Not me."

Feinstein said that eventually "there will be a president that will sign it."

In his veto message, Bush said it was "vitally important" that the CIA maintain a separate and classified interrogation program. "Terrorists often are trained specifically to resist techniques prescribed in publicly available military regulations," he said, adding that "the CIA's ability to conduct a separate and specialized interrogation program for terrorists who possess the most critical information in the war on terror has helped the United States prevent a number of attacks." He also said that the attorney general had determined that the CIA methodology was "lawful under existing domestic and international law."

Bush cited other provisions as well, including a requirement that the directors of the NSA and NRO be subject to Senate confirmation, in explaining his decision to veto the bill.

FY 2009 BILL: SENATE COMMITTEE ACTION

The Senate Select Committee on Intelligence renewed its efforts to rein in administration interrogation practices in its fiscal 2009 authorization bill (S 2996 — S Rept 110-333), which was approved, 10-5, on May 1.

Feinstein won a 9-6 vote to add the Army field manual language from the vetoed bill.

The panel also adopted amendments to bar the CIA from using contractors for interrogations and to require the intelligence community to disclose detainees' identities to the International Committee of the Red Cross and give the agency access to the detainees.

Bond blamed Democrats for the failure to enact the fiscal 2008 bill and said they were repeating the process. "The provision in the final bill," Bond said, "would tie the hands of our terror fighters and could lead to the loss of information that could prevent another major attack on our homeland." He proposed issuing a more specific list of outlawed tactics instead, but the amendment was rejected.

A Feinstein spokesman argued that Bond's proposal would leave the door open for the administration to come up with other objectionable techniques. The field manual has proved effective, she said, making it a worthy basis for a clear, unified standard.

The bill also proposed the creation of posts for an inspector general and chief financial officer for the intelligence community, require Senate confirmation of several top intelligence officials and require annual reports for major acquisition programs.

Other provisions called for a bipartisan, independent commission to study intelligence collection and analysis with an eye toward future threats and the speedup of an overhaul of FBI intelligence programs.

FY 2009 BILL: HOUSE COMMITTEE ACTION

The House Select Intelligence Committee approved its version of the bill (HR 5959 — H Rept 110-665) by voice vote May 8. Unlike the Senate committee, members rejected an attempt to add the restriction on interrogation methods that could be used by the intelligence agencies.

An aide said Silvestre Reyes, D-Texas, the committee chairman, preferred to send Bush a bill he would sign.

The panel defeated an amendment by Jan Schakowsky, D-Ill., to require all federal agencies, including the CIA, to comply with the Army field manual. However, the committee adopted a Schakowsky amendment to block CIA contractors from interrogating detainees.

By a vote of 17-4, the House panel adopted an amendment by ranking Republican Peter Hoekstra of Michigan to strip out an undisclosed number of member-requested projects. The Senate bill included $25.1 million worth of such earmarks.

The bill proposed increased authorizations for human spying, including in Asia, Africa and Latin America, as well as more money for monitoring communications. The bill also sought to focus funding on nuclear counterproliferation.

FY 2009 BILL: HOUSE FLOOR ACTION

House Democrats and Republicans joined forces July 16 to pass the bill by voice vote, despite a veto threat and questions about whether disputes in the Senate could block passage in that chamber.

Reyes said that the bill was one of the chief mechanisms for ensuring congressional oversight of the intelligence agencies and that it was too important to do without.

The White House targeted various accountability and reporting provisions in the bill that it said represented overzealous congressional interference in the workings of the intelligence community. In a statement, the administration criticized provisions that would bar the CIA from using contractors to conduct interrogations, require additional information from the White House and create a statutory inspector general for the intelligence community, among others. The administration could have waived the contractor provision.

Lawmakers adopted several amendments to the bill, including provisions to:

‣ Effectively bar federal agencies from discouraging the use of certain terms, including "Islamic terrorists." The amendment, offered by Hoekstra, was adopted 249-180. *(House vote 500, p. H-168)*

‣ Require the CIA to report to the House and Senate Intelligence panels any information it had about human rights violations committed by the military government in Argentina from the mid-1970s to the mid-1980s. The proposal, offered by Maurice D. Hinchey, D-N.Y., was adopted by voice vote.

‣ Require the DNI to update members of Congress who received an October 2007 intelligence report on Iran's nuclear program about any new intelligence. Offered by Rush D. Holt, D-N.J., the amendment was adopted by voice vote.

‣ Require a National Intelligence Estimate on the sale of drugs to support terrorism. The amendment, by Mark Steven Kirk, R-Ill., was adopted, 426-2. *(House vote 501, p. H-168)*

Democrats turned aside a Republican motion by Hoekstra to recommit the bill to add language requiring a study of the national security implications of high gasoline prices. The vote was 200-225. Democrats said they supported the idea but opposed the motion because it called for the bill to be returned to the floor "promptly," which would have had the effect of taking the bill off the floor and sending it to the committee — essentially killing it. *(House vote 502, p. H-168)* ∎

U.S.-Colombia Trade Pact Sidelined

THE HOUSE DELAYED INDEFINITELY any congressional action on a free-trade agreement with Colombia, leaving that and other international trade deals negotiated by the Bush administration stalled in Congress.

Lawmakers and the president did find common ground on extending two other trade programs: a trade pact with four Andean nations and a system of duty-free imports from developing countries.

The U.S.-Colombia Free Trade Agreement promised to eliminate tariffs on more than 80 percent of Colombia-bound exports of industrial and consumer goods. But it faced opposition from Democrats and labor groups, who said the Colombian government had not done enough to reduce violence against union members. Colombia, along with GOP supporters of the pact, said Bogota had met every objection that opponents raised.

House Democratic leaders blocked consideration of a bill (HR 5724) to implement the Colombia pact by changing House rules that had guaranteed expedited consider-

BOX SCORE

BILLS: HR 5724; HR 5264 — PL 110-191; HR 7222 — PL 110-436

LEGISLATIVE ACTION:

House voted, 224-195, on April 10 to adopt a resolution (H Res 1092) suspending fast-track trade rules for the Colombia trade pact (HR 5724).

House passed the 2008 Andean Trade Preference Extension Act (HR 5264 — H Rept 110-529) by voice vote Feb. 27.

Senate cleared HR 5264 by voice vote Feb. 28.

President signed Feb. 29.

House passed the 2009 Andean Trade Preference Act extension (HR 7222) by voice vote Sept. 29.

Senate passed the Andean trade/GSP bill (HR 7222), amended, by voice vote Oct. 2.

House cleared HR 7222 by voice vote Oct. 3.

President signed Oct. 16.

ation of the measure.

Two other trade pacts — with South Korea and Panama — also remained in limbo. The White House said it would not send the Panama or South Korea deals to Capitol Hill until Congress dealt with the Colombia pact. The U.S.-Korea agreement faced criticisms from lawmakers of both parties who represented manufacturing states. They argued that South Korea had not made any concessions on non-tariff barriers, which they said shut U.S. automakers out of the Korean market. The Panama pact was seen as the least controversial of the three.

LEGISLATIVE ACTION
COLOMBIA TRADE AGREEMENT

Over vehement Republican protests, the House voted April 10 to revoke expedited treatment of the bill, effectively removing it from consideration. Democratic Speaker Nancy Pelosi of California forced the delay with an amendment to House rules (H Res 1092) after President Bush ignored her advice and on April 8 sent Congress the implementing legislation for the trade deal.

The rules change was adopted by a largely party-line vote of 224-195. *(House vote 181, p. H-58)*

Ten Democrats — most of them members of the Southern-dominated, fiscally conservative Blue Dog Coalition — joined Republicans in voting against the resolution. Six Southern Republicans voted with the majority.

Bush issued a statement saying House Democrats had chosen "a short-sighted and partisan path" that "undermined the trust required for any administration to negotiate trade agreements in the future."

Pelosi's resolution specified that the Colombia deal was not covered by provisions of the 1974 Trade Act (PL 93-618) that established fast-track trade negotiating rules. The U.S.-Colombia agreement had been negotiated in November 2006, when the last version of the fast-track rules (PL 107-210) was still in effect. *(Fast-track law, 2002 Almanac, p. 18-13)*

The fast-track law required that both chambers act within 90 legislative days after receiving legislation from the president to implement a trade deal. Congress could comment on the measure ahead of time, but once the legislation was formally submitted, it was subject to an up-or-down vote in both chambers with no amendments. The purpose was to give trading partners confidence that if they negotiated a deal with the United States, it would not be changed later.

Under the law, the procedures and timetable were rules of the House and Senate that could be changed by either chamber.

Democrats said they were frustrated that Bush sent the pact to Congress in the midst of the heated election campaign and without securing support from their party leadership. Trade legislation was politically sensitive, especially in the House, and Pelosi had warned the White House that "if brought to the floor immediately, it would lose." Democratic leaders also hoped to use the Colombia trade pact as leverage to force Bush to compromise with them on trade adjustment assistance and other programs to help laid-off workers and struggling homeowners in the slumping economy.

The GOP decried Pelosi's unprecedented procedural move, saying it would weaken a strong U.S. ally in the region and empower neighboring Venezuelan President Hugo Chavez and his anti-U.S. policies.

The House action was decisive, because legislation affecting revenue — including trade agreements — had to originate in that chamber.

ANDEAN TRADE PACT

The Senate cleared a bill by voice vote Feb. 28 that renewed trade preferences for four South American countries one day before they were set to expire. The House had passed the bill a day earlier, also by voice vote. The measure extended duty-free treatment for most goods from Bolivia, Colombia, Ecuador and Peru through the end of 2008 under the Andean Trade Promotion and Drug Eradication Act. Bush signed the measure into law Feb. 29 (HR 5264 — PL 110-191).

GOP lawmakers said the trade preferences paled in comparison with benefits that would be received if the trade pact with Colombia were enacted. Jim McCrery of Louisiana, ranking Republican on the House Ways and Means Committee, said the Colombia agreement would provide greater benefits to the United States, while strengthening labor protections in Colombia. The Andean bill was expected to reduce revenue from customs duties by an estimated $82 million in fiscal 2008 and $37 million in fiscal 2009, according to the Congressional Budget Office.

As proposed by Ways and Means Chairman Charles B. Rangel, D-N.Y., the bill would have extended the Andean preferences for 31 months. After negotiations with panel Republicans, that was scaled back to 10 months.

ANDEAN TRADE/GSP

Congress in October cleared a second extension of the Andean trade pact. The bill also extended the Generalized Systems of Preferences (GSP), a trade program that allowed duty-free entry into the United States for products from more than 100 developing countries as a means of promoting economic growth. Both programs were authorized through Dec. 31, 2009. Bush signed the measure into law Oct. 16 (HR 7222 — PL 110-436).

Sen. Charles E. Grassley of Iowa, ranking Republican on the Finance Committee, had held up the bill for several months out of dissatisfaction with anti-drug efforts in Ecuador and Bolivia. The compromise, struck by Grassley and Majority Leader Harry Reid, D-Nev., renewed trade benefits for the two countries for six months, with an additional six-month extension if they cooperated with U.S. anti-drug efforts. The Senate added the language and passed the bill by voice vote Oct. 2.

"Peru and Colombia have pursued a strong reciprocal trading relationship with the United States and are being treated accordingly. Bolivia and Ecuador have taken different paths," Grassley said. "Today's outcome gives those countries a chance to address these concerns."

The House cleared the bill by voice vote Oct. 3.

On Nov. 28, Bush suspended Bolivia's benefits under the Andean trade pact due to a lack of cooperation in anti-drug efforts. ∎

Chapter 7

Economic Affairs

Congress Clears $700 Billion Bailout Of Financial Services Industry

IN AN EXTRAORDINARY response to what was threatening to become the worst financial and economic crisis in more than half a century, Congress granted the Treasury Department authority to spend as much as $700 billion to stabilize a battered financial sector crippled by losses on housing-related assets. President Bush signed the unprecedented legislation into law Oct. 3 (HR 1424 — PL 110-343).

As originally conceived, the program would have purchased seemingly worthless mortgage-based assets from financial companies. But Treasury officials quickly abandoned that plan in favor of buying stock in troubled institutions.

The plan drew strong opposition from both sides of the aisle, not to mention the public. The House at first rejected it outright. But Congress sent Bush a finished bill 15 days after receiving the request from Treasury Secretary Henry M. Paulson Jr., whose warnings of a global financial collapse left lawmakers stunned.

The legislation was the third broad effort by Congress in 2008 to address the worsening economy — following a tax-driven stimulus bill and a measure to stem rising foreclosures. This effort grew out of a late-night meeting with congressional leaders on Sept. 18, led by Paulson and Federal Reserve Chairman Ben S. Bernanke, who pleaded for new emergency powers to respond to the deepening crisis. (*Stimulus, p. 7-17; mortgage finance overhaul, p. 7-9*)

During the two weeks that preceded the request, the Treasury had taken control of mortgage giants Fannie Mae and Freddie Mac. The fourth-largest investment bank, Lehman Brothers Holdings Inc., had been allowed to go bankrupt. The Fed and Treasury had bailed out the country's largest insurance company, American International Group Inc. And global financial conditions had deteriorated further, threatening banks, pension funds and individual investors.

Many credit markets were effectively frozen, largely because lenders held hundreds of billions of dollars in mortgage-related securities whose value had fallen sharply because of the rising number of foreclosures and the volume of subprime home loans that were in danger of default. As a result, banks tightened their lending standards — refusing even to do business with one another — and Paulson and Bernanke warned that the resulting denial of credit would cripple the broad economy.

PAULSON'S PLAN

On the evening of Thursday, Sept. 18, Paulson and Bernanke held a closed-door Capitol Hill meeting with congressional leaders, in which they outlined the depth of the economic problems. They asked for approval of a comprehensive — if not clearly defined — plan to allow the government to purchase the bulk of the essentially worthless assets of damaged banks and investment firms. "The ultimate taxpayer

BOX SCORE

BILL: HR 1424 — PL 110-343

LEGISLATIVE ACTION:

House rejected bailout, offered as an amendment to HR 3997, 205-228, on Sept. 29.

Senate passed expanded bailout package, offered as an amendment to HR 1424, 74-25, on Oct. 1.

House cleared HR 1424, 263-171, on Oct. 3.

President signed Oct. 3.

protection will be the stability this troubled asset relief program provides to our financial system, even as it will involve a significant investment of taxpayer dollars," Paulson, a former chairman of Goldman Sachs, said at a news conference the following morning.

Two days after the meeting, a three-page proposal from Paulson was circulated on the Hill. Paulson wanted a free hand to purchase a staggering $700 billion worth of so-called toxic assets from financial institutions, though the plan included provisions that would allow the Treasury to buy almost any financial instrument with the bailout money.

Treasury hoped to buy the assets through a reverse auction process, allowing market participants to set the price the government would pay for the troubled assets. After buying the assets, Treasury would hold them and sell them at a later date when the market stabilized.

Lawmakers balked at Paulson's opening bid, saying it would give the Treasury secretary nearly unfettered authority to spend huge sums of taxpayer money as he saw fit. Complaints ranged from the lack of details to the need to protect taxpayers and the absence of oversight. Many Republicans objected strongly to giving the government such a major role in the private sector.

However, given the urgency of the situation, bipartisan leaders from the House and Senate sat down with Treasury officials and others to put together a deal. The plan that came out of the talks called for the creation of the Troubled Asset Relief Program (TARP). Treasury would receive an initial $250 billion for the program and an additional $100 billion following a certification from the president that the money was needed. A further $350 billion would be available if the president requested it and Congress agreed, using an expedited procedure.

The delicate compromise essentially left intact the broad asset-buying powers Paulson sought for the Treasury, while providing some assurances to nervous lawmakers that taxpayer investments would be paid back. Safeguards included an oversight panel and authority for the Treasury to take equity positions in companies receiving assistance. The negotiated agreement also included some restrictions on executive pay for companies that got money from the bailout fund.

TENSE NEGOTIATIONS

The intense and speedy dealmaking that led to the final compromise was by all accounts torturous. "We've had a lot of pleasant words, and some that haven't always been pleasant," Senate Majority Leader Harry Reid, D-Nev., said at the end. "This is a new environment for Secretary Paulson, the political one. But it's one he's been educated in very quickly in the past week."

The administration spent the week of Sept. 21, trying to sell the TARP to skeptical lawmakers of both parties. Vice President Dick Cheney and White House Chief of Staff Joshua B. Bolten came to the

Capitol to cajole balky Republicans into supporting the plan.

Testifying on Monday and Tuesday, Sept. 22-23, and meeting privately with lawmakers on both sides of the Hill, Paulson and Bernanke implored lawmakers to give them the go-ahead.

Senate Banking Chairman Christopher J. Dodd, D-Conn., sharply criticized the Treasury proposal, calling Paulson's initial three-page draft "stunning and unprecedented in its scope and lack of detail."

"It would do nothing to help even a single family save a home, at least not up front. . . . And it would allow [Paulson] to act with utter and absolute impunity — without review," Dodd said. "After reading this proposal, I can only conclude that it is not just our economy that is at risk but our Constitution, as well."

Most Senate Republicans expressed cautious support for the bailout package, but Richard C. Shelby of Alabama, the ranking Republican on the Banking Committee, made it clear he was not sold and said Congress needed more time to develop a proper plan.

Bush went on national television Wednesday, Sept. 24, to build support for the proposal. "I know that an economic rescue package will present a tough vote for many members of Congress," Bush said in his first prime time broadcast speech in more than a year. But, he added, "The government's top economic experts warn that, without immediate action by Congress, America could slip into a financial panic, and a distressing scenario would unfold.

"More banks could fail, including some in your community. The stock market would drop even more, which would reduce the value of your retirement account. The value of your home could plummet. Foreclosures would rise dramatically. And if you own a business or a farm, you would find it harder and more expensive to get credit. More businesses would close their doors, and millions of Americans could lose their jobs."

The urgency of the financial crisis was underscored by news of the largest bank failure in U.S. history. The Federal Deposit Insurance Corporation on Sept. 25 seized Washington Mutual Inc. and sold its bank assets to J.P. Morgan Chase & Co. for $1.9 billion. The Seattle-based thrift, the nation's largest savings and loan, had been hammered by mortgage-related losses and had experienced withdrawals of $16.7 billion since Sept. 16.

Still, congressional opposition grew throughout the week, particularly among conservative Republicans who objected to the wholesale government intervention in the workings of the financial sector. Rank-and-file lawmakers from both parties were caught between the potential for a financial meltdown and the anger of constituents who viewed the administration plan as a veritable lifeboat for risk-happy Wall Street executives and speculators.

I don't think I've gotten one call or e-mail from a constituent supporting this," said Rep. Roscoe G. Bartlett, R-Md. "I've had two calls from business people who say they just want a solution; they're suffering because of the uncertainty.

In a surprise move, Republican presidential nominee Sen. John McCain suddenly announced he was suspending his campaign and returning to the Senate to help manage the deal. He challenged his opponent, Democratic Sen. Barack Obama, to do the same — which he reluctantly did after Bush invited both candidates to join with congressional leaders in a White House meeting on Thursday afternoon, Sept. 25.

The White House gathering was designed to smooth the way for a bipartisan deal based on the administration's core plan of buying mortgage-backed securities and other risky assets from financial institutions. Hours earlier, the chief congressional negotiators from both parties announced they had reached an agreement in principle.

But House Republicans caught the negotiators off-guard at the meeting by calling instead for the government to offer insurance to holders of risky mortgage-backed securities, with the holders financing the plan through premium payments.

Within hours, Paulson returned to the Hill and negotiators began trying to get the talks back on track. Minority Leader John A. Boehner of Ohio designated Minority Whip Roy Blunt of Missouri to represent the House GOP's interests.

Throughout the negotiations that followed, the underlying concept for the TARP never changed. But reaction on the Hill and in home districts was so negative that negotiators gathered late Saturday, Sept. 27, to make sure the bill they would bring to the House and Senate appealed to a bipartisan majority of lawmakers.

The congressional side of the negotiating table included a bipartisan, bicameral representation of leadership: Reid; House Speaker Nancy Pelosi, D-Calif.; House Financial Services Chairman Barney Frank, D-Mass.; and Judd Gregg of New Hampshire, the ranking Republican on the Senate Budget Committee.

Shortly after midnight on Sunday, Sept. 28, the negotiators triumphantly announced they had reached an accord. Leaders on both sides of the Capitol expressed confidence that they had the votes, and House leaders scheduled a vote for the next day. The Senate was expected to clear the measure on Wednesday, after a one-day break for the Jewish holiday of Rosh Hashana, after which lawmakers would go home to campaign.

"We've made great progress toward a deal which will work and will be effective in the marketplace and effective for all Americans," Paulson said early the next morning at a hastily convened news conference. "I think we're there."

Lamar Alexander of Tennessee, chairman of the Senate Republican Conference, urged quick passage. "Congress should approve the amended plan without delay on Monday," he said in a statement. "Otherwise, there is a real risk that credit will freeze and Americans will not be able to get car, student, auto and mortgage loans or even to cash their paychecks."

SETBACK IN THE HOUSE

The hopefulness expressed by leaders hours earlier evaporated Monday, Sept. 29, when the $700 billion bailout went down to a stunning defeat in the House. Resounding opposition from conservative Republicans, who said the huge intervention violated free-market principles, and liberal Democrats, who argued that Wall Street executives did not deserve a bailout, scuttled the rescue package. Traders on the floor of the New York Stock Exchange watched the televised vote in disbelief as the House rejected the plan, 205-228. The Dow Jones industrial average fell 777 points, the largest one-day point drop in the 112-year history of the stock index. *(House vote 674, p. H-226)*

Refusing to ask their members to shoulder the burden of passing the bill by themselves, Democratic leaders had demanded support from a majority of the minority party's members, pressuring Boehner to produce the necessary votes. In the end, two-thirds of House Republicans voted against the plan, while 60 percent of the Democrats supported it.

The lobbying to win GOP votes for the plan came from all sides. McCain called 50 to 60 House Republicans. The U.S. Chamber of Commerce, a lobbying voice often heeded by the GOP, warned that the vote would be in its annual scorecard. Bush worked the phones,

The Unfolding Financial Crisis

THE FOLLOWING ARE SOME of the major events in the collapse of the nation's financial services industry:

● **March 14.** Federal regulators step in to prevent the collapse of **Bear Stearns Cos.**, the nation's fifth-largest investment bank. The Federal Reserve extends short-term credit to the company through **J.P. Morgan Chase & Co.** Two days later, J.P. Morgan purchases Bear Stearns in a deal facilitated by the Fed. A $28.8 billion loan from the Fed plus $1.15 billion from J.P. Morgan are used to buy Bear Stearns' toxic assets, thus wiping them off the books.

● **July 11.** The Federal Deposit Insurance Corporation (FDIC) seizes **Indymac Bank** and places it in conservatorship, following a run on the already-troubled institution. It is the second-largest bank failure in U.S. history, behind Continental Illinois National Bank and Trust Co. in 1984.

● **July 13.** Treasury Secretary Henry M. Paulson Jr. announces the administration needs wide-ranging authority to shore up mortgage finance giants **Fannie Mae** and **Freddie Mac**. Two weeks later, on July 30, President Bush signs a bill (PL 110-289) authorizing Treasury to provide new credit and buy assets from the two enterprises. The law also allows the government to insure up to $300 billion worth of refinanced loans for struggling mortgage borrowers. It raises the federal debt limit by $800 billion to allow the government to borrow the necessary money.

● **Sept. 7.** Paulson announces that the financial situation at Fannie and Freddie is far worse than originally feared and that the two are being placed in government conservatorship. Treasury says it will use stock purchases, additional lending and the purchase of mortgage-backed securities issued by the two enterprises to help keep them afloat.

● **Sept. 15.** **Lehman Brothers Holdings Inc.**, the fourth-largest Wall Street investment house, files for bankruptcy after the Treasury and Fed decline to save the firm. The government action is seen as a signal that there will be no more federal bailouts.

● **Sept. 15.** **Bank of America Corp.**, which backed away from buying Lehman Brothers, announces it will acquire **Merrill Lynch** in a $50 billion deal encouraged by federal officials.

● **Sept. 16.** In a stunning reversal, the Fed steps in to extend an $85 billion line of credit to **American International Group Inc.**

(AIG), the country's largest insurance company. AIG's mounting losses are imperiling banks, pension funds and individual clients in the United States and around the world. (The loan is later reduced to $65 billion.)

Another Fed loan to AIG on Oct. 8 for $37.8 billion is later restructured, folded entirely into toxic asset purchases. In a move similar to the Bear Stearns rescue, the Fed and AIG purchase assets, sequestering them in two separate funds and allowing AIG to wipe them off its books. Residential mortgage-backed securities are bought with $22.5 billion from the Fed and $1 billion from AIG. Collateralized debt obligations insured by AIG are purchased with $30 billion from the Fed and $5 billion from AIG.

● **Sept. 19.** Treasury sets up a one-year, $50 billion program to insure money market mutual funds. The action is taken to tamp down sudden fears among investors that the funds, considered among the safest investments, may be caught up in the financial crisis.

● **Sept. 19.** Paulson attends an evening meeting on Capitol Hill where he tells congressional leaders that he needs authority to buy up to $700 billion worth of troubled mortgage-related assets to get them off the books of financial institutions in the hope of unfreezing credit markets.

● **Sept. 25.** In the largest bank failure in U.S. history, the FDIC seizes **Washington Mutual Bank** and sells its bank assets to J.P. Morgan for $1.9 billion. The bank had been hammered by mortgage-related losses and withdrawals of $16.7 billion since Sept. 16.

● **Oct. 3.** Congress clears a bill creating the Troubled Asset Relief Program (TARP), which will allow Treasury to spend the $700 billion. Bush signs the bill immediately (PL 110-343).

● **Nov. 25.** Treasury provides AIG with another infusion by purchasing $40 billion in stock using TARP funds.

● **Dec. 1.** The National Bureau of Economic Research concludes that the U.S. economy has been in a recession since December 2007.

● **Dec. 19.** The White House announces it will use TARP funds to provide $18.3 billion in short-term loans to keep **General Motors Corp.** and **Chrysler LLC** from going bankrupt. In September, Congress had provided funding for $25 billion in loans to the industry as part of the fiscal 2009 continuing resolution (PL 100-329), but the Senate blocked a bill to provide an additional $14 billion.

and his budget director, Jim Nussle, a former House Republican, kept up the push during the vote from the rear of the House chamber.

But lawmakers were also listening to the voters, and nothing in the deal assuaged concerns that the plan was nothing more than a taxpayer bailout of Wall Street. The blizzard of negative telephone calls and e-mail messages from angry constituents continued to bombard lawmakers from both parties right up to the vote.

There was also significant pushback from conservative House Republicans, especially those in the Republican Study Committee. "If you came here because you believe in limited government and the

freedom of the American marketplace, vote in accordance with those convictions," Mike Pence of Indiana, a leader of the group, told his colleagues.

Democratic leaders kept the roll call open for about 30 minutes trying to change the outcome, but the tally held.

SENATE TAKES THE REINS

Sobered by the overwhelmingly negative Wall Street response to the House vote, Senate leaders stepped in quickly to try to salvage the bailout. "We're going to stay here until we get this done," said Gregg,

the chief GOP negotiator. "Because we have to. That's our responsibility [as] members of government."

Bipartisan Senate negotiations produced a package that preserved the core of Paulson's plan but added a number of items to attract additional House votes: a mental health parity plan; a package of energy tax breaks and extensions of popular but expiring tax benefits; and an increase in the limit on federal insurance for bank deposit coverage, to $250,000 for each bank account, up from $100,000. The tax and mental health provisions had been stalled, probably for the rest of the year. *(Provisions, p. 7-7; mental health, p. 9-5; tax "extenders," p. 4-11)*

Few senators were enthusiastic about the bailout, even if they voted for it. But most saw no alternative. To underline the significance of the moment, Reid asked that all members remain seated and cast their votes from their desks, a formality used on the rarest and most momentous of occasions. On Oct. 1, the Senate agreed, 74-25, with a strong, bipartisan majority, to insert the package into a shell bill (HR 1424). Senators then passed the bill by the same tally. Presidential candidates McCain and Obama returned to Washington for the votes. *(Senate votes 212, 213, p. S-47)*

HOUSE CLEARS THE BILL

With some trepidation, but with evidence mounting that the economy was headed for recession, the House took up the measure on Oct. 3 and cleared it, 263-171, with 58 previous opponents voting yes. Of those who switched, 33 were Democrats and 25 were Republicans. *(House vote 681, p. H-230)*

Several of the vote switchers cited the new elements in the Senate package and fresh signs that the Main Street economy was under stress. The latest evidence arrived hours before the vote, when the Labor Department reported that employers had slashed 159,000 jobs in September — the ninth straight month of job losses. The unemployment rate was unchanged from August at 6.1 percent, the highest in five years. Bankers warned that credit remained exceedingly tight. And earlier in the week, the mortgage crisis claimed yet another bank. Citigroup Inc. and Wells Fargo & Co. began a bidding war over Wachovia Corp., which had a network of more than 3,000 branches across the country but a balance sheet badly impaired by billions of dollars in sour mortgages.

The addition of the tax extenders brought even more lobbying clout to the effort to sway wavering House members. From solar-energy companies to film producers and mental health advocates, interest groups with little or no stake in the original bailout bill suddenly were as keenly interested in it as the powerful financial services industry,

creating perhaps the biggest lobbying campaign of the year.

The Bush administration reiterated its support. "Passage of HR 1424 is of tremendous importance to all Americans," the White House said in an official statement of administration policy.

While many members continued to cite a high volume of negative calls, the stock market's plunge after the last vote appeared to rattle constituents worried about the effect the crisis was having on their retirement savings, particularly stock-based mutual funds and 401(k) plans. Business lobbyists also mobilized, warning that they had increasing difficulty getting credit to finance their day-to-day operations.

"I think the biggest reason for the change here," said Frank, "is the damages that started coming in . . . the reality of the economic damage." Republican Sue Myrick of North Carolina said before the vote that she would switch from no to yes after conversations during the week with small businesses in her district. "I talked to people I trust . . . good, solid businesses," she said. "They could not get credit."

Among the Democrats who switched to support the bill were several members of the Black Caucus.

"The people are afraid," said John Lewis of Georgia. "Their retirement savings are slipping away. Small businesses have no sales, no credit and are closing their doors."

Still, most of those in both parties who voted against the original bill were not swayed to switch by the new version or the economic news.

BAILOUT PURPOSE SHIFTS

Less than two weeks after the bill was signed, the rescue program began to evolve. Originally pitched as a plan to buy up troubled assets, the TARP was used mostly to inject capital directly into banks by purchasing stock. That policy, first announced Oct. 14, made the government a stockholder in troubled banks, rather than relieving the banks of toxic mortgage-backed securities.

Paulson explained the shift Nov. 12, saying that by the time the bill was enacted on Oct. 3, market conditions had "worsened considerably," making it clear that Treasury had to act quickly. "Purchasing troubled assets — our initial focus — would take time to implement and would not be sufficient given the severity of the problem," he said. The most timely approach, he said, was "to strengthen bank balance sheets quickly through direct purchases of equity in banks."

The new law had given the Treasury wide discretion to buy financial instruments, including stock, by defining troubled assets as mortgage-backed securities or "any other financial instrument."

Treasury used the first $125 billion of the TARP funds to buy shares in nine of the largest U.S. banks. ∎

[PROVISIONS]
Rescue Plan for Financial Sector

THE FOLLOWING ARE MAJOR PROVISIONS of the financial services rescue bill enacted Oct. 3 (HR 1424 — PL 110-343). The legislation also included a package of tax provisions and a mental health parity bill, which are covered separately. *(Taxes, p. 4-11; mental health parity, p. 9-5)*

TROUBLED ASSET RELIEF PROGRAM

● **Program created.** The law authorized the Treasury Department to establish a program — the Troubled Asset Relief Program (TARP) — to purchase troubled assets from financial institutions on terms and conditions determined by the secretary in accordance with this law.

● **Authorization.** The department was authorized to purchase up to $700 billion in troubled assets. Of the total, $250 billion was available for immediate release upon enactment. Another $100 billion would be available if the president certified the need for it to Congress. If the president requested the final $350 billion, Congress would have the option of passing a joint resolution — to be considered on an expedited basis — disapproving the release of the funds. If no disapproval resolution was enacted, the $350 billion would be released 15 days after the president's request.

● **Eligible assets.** The law authorized the Treasury to buy residential and commercial mortgages, and any mortgage-backed securities, obligations or other instruments that were originated before March 14, 2008. After consulting with the Federal Reserve Board and notifying Congress, the Treasury could also buy "any other financial instrument" it deemed necessary to "promote financial market stability."

● **Eligible institutions.** To be eligible to sell assets to the government, a financial institution had to have significant operations in the United States and could not be owned by a foreign government.

● **Purchase price.** The Treasury could not buy assets from an institution for more than that institution originally paid for them.

● **Consultation.** The law required Treasury to consult with the Fed, the Federal Deposit Insurance Corporation (FDIC), the Comptroller of the Currency, the Office of Thrift Supervision, and the Housing and Urban Development Department (HUD) in exercising its new authorities.

● **Sunset.** Treasury's authority to buy assets terminated Dec. 31, 2009. The Treasury secretary could extend the buying authority for up to two years after enactment after reporting to Congress on why the extension was necessary to assist American families and stabilize financial markets and how much it was expected to cost taxpayers.

● **Management and sale of assets.** Treasury was authorized to manage troubled assets purchased under the program. It could sell the assets or repackage them for sale to private investors at any time and price and under any conditions the Treasury secretary determined. Proceeds would be used to reduce the federal debt. These provisions were not subject to the sunset requirement.

● **Recouping losses.** Five years after enactment, the Office of Management and Budget, in consultation with the Congressional Budget Office, was required to submit a report to the Congress on the net amount in the TARP. If there was a shortfall, the president had to submit legislation to Congress to recoup the loss from the financial services industry.

● **Insurance of troubled assets.** After setting up the TARP, the Treasury Department was required to establish the Troubled Assets Insurance Financing Fund to guarantee the assets originated or issued prior to March 14, 2008, including mortgage-backed securities. The Treasury also was directed to develop guarantees for troubled assets still held by financial institutions. Financial institutions would be able to request that the Treasury guarantee the timely payment of the principal and interest on such assets in amounts not to exceed 100 percent of the payments.

● **Insurance premiums.** The Treasury Department would collect premiums from the financial institutions participating in the insurance program to cover anticipated claims, based on an analysis of the risk involved.

● **Warrants.** The Treasury would take warrants in a company that sold its assets into the program. The warrants would allow the government to take a non-voting equity stake in the company, providing Treasury with a share of any profits if the company made money after the government bought the troubled assets.

● **Executive compensation.** Any financial institution that sold troubled assets directly to the program would have to abide by limits on executive compensation. The limits, set by the Treasury, were to include a ban on "golden parachutes" — large benefits such as severance pay, bonuses, stock options or any combination. The limits also would include a requirement that a participating firm pay back bonuses that turn out to be based on incorrect earnings statements — a so-called claw-back provision — and a ban on compensation incentives for executives who took excessive risks.

An institution that sold more than $300 million in assets to the Treasury via an auction was prohibited from signing any new employment contracts for a senior executive officer that provided golden parachutes in the event of an involuntary termination, bankruptcy filing, insolvency or receivership.

● **Tax penalties.** The law also sought to put some limits on executive pay through changes in the tax code. An institution that sold more than $300 million in assets to the Treasury was subject to additional taxes, including a 20 percent excise tax on golden-parachute payments triggered by events other than retirement. In addition, those institutions could no longer deduct more than $500,000 in compensation per executive from the company's taxable income.

OVERSIGHT

● **Oversight board.** The law established a board — the Financial Stability Oversight Board — to review Treasury's activities. The board could make recommendations, and it could appoint a credit review committee to evaluate how the Treasury exercises its authority to buy troubled assets. The board consisted of the chairman of the Federal Reserve, the Treasury secretary, the director of the Federal Home Finance Agency, the chairman of the Securities and Exchange Commission (SEC), and the HUD secretary.

● **Reports to Congress.** The Treasury was required to report to Congress 60 days after it began exercising its new authority to buy financial instruments and every 30 days thereafter. The reports had to include an overview of actions taken by the department, the actual obligation and expenditure of the funds provided for administrative expenses, and a de-

tailed financial statement. After the Treasury bought $50 billion worth of troubled assets, it was required to provide another report describing all of the transactions made during the reporting period, how prices were set for the transactions and a justification for the purchase price. Treasury also would review the state of the financial markets and the regulatory system and report on its findings to Congress.

● **GAO oversight.** The Government Accountability Office (GAO) was tasked with conducting ongoing oversight of the activities and performance of the program and to report to Congress every 60 days. It also would determine the extent to which financial institutions' leveraging, or borrowing, and sudden de-leveraging was a factor behind the existing financial crisis.

● **Inspector general.** The law established a special inspector general for the program who would be nominated by the president and confirmed by the Senate. It provided $50 million for the office to conduct, supervise and coordinate audits and investigations. The inspector was required to submit a quarterly report to Congress summarizing the program's activities.

● **Congressional oversight.** The law established a five-member Congressional Oversight Panel to review the state of the financial markets and the regulatory system. It would be required to submit a special report on regulatory reform before Jan. 20, 2009, that analyzed the state of the regulatory system and its effectiveness at overseeing the financial system and protecting consumers. The report was to include recommendations for improvement and whether there were any gaps in existing consumer protections. The Speaker, the House minority leader, and the Senate majority and minority leaders would each appoint one board member. The fifth member would be appointed by the Speaker and Senate majority leader after consulting with the two minority leaders.

● **Deposit insurance increase.** The law temporarily increased — through Dec. 31, 2009 — the limit on FDIC and National Credit Union Administration deposit insurance to $250,000 per account from $100,000. The limit had not been increased since 1980.

● **Foreclosure mitigation.** The Treasury Department was required to implement a plan to mitigate foreclosures and to encourage lenders to modify loans or mortgages that supported mortgage-backed securities acquired under the program. The Treasury could use loan guarantees and credit enhancement to avoid foreclosure. The depart-

ment was directed to coordinate with other federal agencies that held troubled assets in order to identify opportunities to modify loans.

● **Homeowner assistance.** The law required certain other federal agencies that held mortgages, mortgage-backed securities and other assets secured by residential real estate to carry out plans to maximize assistance for homeowners. It directed them to encourage servicers of the underlying mortgages to take advantage of the HOPE for Homeowners Program and other available programs to minimize foreclosures. The provision applied to the FDIC, the Federal Housing Finance Agency and the Federal Reserve Board.

TAX AND OTHER PROVISIONS

● **Community banks.** Community banks could deduct losses from investments purchased before April 1, 2008, in mortgage finance giants Fannie Mae and Freddie Mac, which were taken over by the Treasury in September. The Joint Committee on Taxation (JCT) estimated that the provision would reduce federal revenue by more than $3 billion through fiscal 2018.

● **Forgiven mortgage debt.** The law included a three-year extension of a provision that allowed taxpayers who had their mortgage loans reduced to avoid paying taxes on up to $2 million of the forgiven debt. The exclusion, enacted in 2007 (PL 110-142), originally applied to mortgage debts discharged through the end of 2009. The JCT estimated the cost to the Treasury at more than $362 million through fiscal 2018.

● **Mark-to-market accounting.** The law restated the SEC's authority to suspend the application of mark-to-market accounting rules if it determined that doing so would serve the public interest and protect investors. Mark-to-market rules require companies to calculate the value of their holdings using the current market price, not the price they paid to acquire them. The SEC, in consultation with the Fed and Treasury, would conduct a study on mark-to-market standards, including the effects on balance sheets and the impact on the quality of financial information. The study was due to Congress within 90 days of enactment.

● **Debt limit increase.** The statutory limit on the public debt was increased to $11.315 trillion from the previous limit of $10.615 trillion. The $700 billion increase was needed to accommodate the potential cost of the new bailout program. ∎

Treasury Gets Keys to Fannie, Freddie

RESPONDING TO URGENT pleas from Treasury Secretary Henry M. Paulson Jr., Congress agreed to provide a multibillion-dollar lifeline for troubled mortgage finance giants Fannie Mae and Freddie Mac as part of a foreclosure relief bill that cleared before the August recess. President Bush signed the measure into law July 30 (HR 3221 — PL 110-289).

The essentially open-ended grant of authority to the Treasury Department to shore up Fannie and Freddie was added to the mortgage bill after Paulson and other top officials warned that the companies could fail amid the housing crisis and tightened credit markets.

The House and Senate were close to agreement on the mortgage relief bill after months of wrangling when Paulson made his request. The crisis swept away the remaining differences over the mortgage provisions.

Together, Fannie and Freddie owned or guaranteed about $5 trillion worth of the $12 trillion in mortgages issued on U.S. houses, and it was feared that their collapse would do immense damage to the weakened housing industry and throw international debt markets into chaos. The price per share for both companies, which had exceeded $60 in mid-2007 and $20 a month before Paulson's announcement, dropped below $10, cutting the market capitalization for the two companies in half and raising concerns about failure.

Paulson lobbied hard for the bailout authority, which gave the Treasury permission to buy assets from the companies, including their mortgage holdings and shares of their stock, and extend new credit to them. Lawmakers agreed with Treasury to impose no dollar limit on the lending to Fannie or Freddie or on purchases of their stock. But costs associated with the bailout were limited by the overall ceiling on government borrowing, which the bill raised by $800 billion to $10.6 trillion.

As part of the bargain to add the bailout to the mortgage relief bill, the White House dropped its veto threats against elements of the underlying measure. Some conservative Republicans worried that the government could end up being exposed to Fannie and Freddie's huge liabilities, but their objections were not strong enough to derail the legislation. The bill became law less than three weeks after Paulson's surprise request. *(Detailed provisions, p. 7-13)*

The chief architects of the bill on the Senate side were Christopher J. Dodd, D-Conn., chairman of the Banking, Housing and Urban Affairs Committee, and the committee's ranking Republican, Richard C. Shelby of Alabama. In the House, the job fell to Barney Frank, D-Mass., the chairman of the Financial Services Committee.

When Paulson asked Congress for the bailout authority, he said he did not think he would need to use it because the very fact that the government was backing the firms would be enough to reassure

BOX SCORE

BILL: HR 3221 — PL 110-289

....

LEGISLATIVE ACTION:

Senate passed HR 3221, amended, 84-12, on April 10.

House passed HR 3221, through three motions to concur, with new amendments, 266-154, 322-94, 256-160, on May 8.

Senate agreed, 79-16 on June 25 to insert the Dodd-Shelby substitute to HR 3221.

Senate passed HR 3221, by agreeing, 76-10, on June 25 to strip Senate energy package, and agreeing, 63-5, on June 11 to drop House tax and state law provisions.

House passed HR 3221 through a motion to concur that added the Fannie Mae and Freddie Mac rescue provisions, 272-152, on July 23.

Senate cleared the bill, 72-13, on July 26.

President signed July 30.

the markets. The Congressional Budget Office (CBO) said the new authority could cost the federal government $25 billion over the following two fiscal years, but the agency said the chances were "probably better than 50 percent" that a bailout wouldn't be necessary.

But the mortgage market continued to deteriorate, and enactment of the bailout did little to reassure investors — especially those that had loaned more than $1.5 trillion to the two companies. On Sept. 7, barely five weeks after the bill became law, the Treasury announced that it had put both Fannie and Freddie into conservatorships and would funnel as much as $200 billion into the companies to keep them functioning.

A new HOPE for Homeowners program, created under the bill to help borrowers avoid foreclosure by refinancing mortgages at lower rates, turned out to be too complicated and never got off the ground. By Feb. 3, 2009, only 451 people had applied.

HIGHLIGHTS

Following are highlights of the combined Fannie-Freddie and mortgage relief bill:

● **Federal bailout authority.** The bill gave the Treasury Department temporary emergency authority to buy securities issued by Fannie Mae and Freddie Mac, including stock, if the purchase would provide stability to the financial markets, prevent disruptions in the availability of mortgage finance and protect taxpayers. The authority was set to expire at the end of 2009, and the government's purchase of stock was limited by the statutory federal debt ceiling. But Treasury could hold on to its purchases indefinitely or sell them.

● **New regulator.** A new, independent agency — the Federal Housing Finance Agency — was created to regulate Fannie Mae, Freddie Mac and the Federal Home Loan Bank System. The agency, which replaced the Office of Federal Housing Enterprise Oversight, could place these entities into conservatorship or receivership in the event of a financial crisis. The new agency was officially established Sept. 2.

● **Loan limits.** The size of individual mortgage loans that Fannie and Freddie could buy was increased to a maximum of $625,000. The economic stimulus law (PL 110-185), enacted in February, included this increase for loans originated by Dec. 31, 2008. *(Stimulus, p. 7-17)*

● **Affordable-housing trust fund.** A new affordable-housing trust fund was created, financed by Fannie and Freddie, to support homeownership by low-income families and to increase the supply of rental housing.

● **Community Development Block Grants.** The bill provided $3.9 billion under the CDBG program to help state and local governments buy abandoned and foreclosed homes and residential property.

● **FHA overhaul.** The bill permanently increased the maximum loan that the Federal Housing Administration (FHA) could insure

to $417,000 from $362,790. For high-cost residential areas, the maximum was increased to $625,000. It also increased down payment requirements and prohibited the FHA from offering risk-based mortgages for one year.

● **HOPE for Homeowners.** The bill created a temporary program administered by the FHA and authorized $300 billion in loan guarantees through fiscal 2011 to help at-risk borrowers refinance into viable mortgages.

● **Lender regulation.** A new Nationwide Mortgage Licensing System and Registry was created, and brokers were required to register in order to originate mortgage loans.

● **Debt limit increase.** The bill raised the federal debt limit by $800 billion, bringing it to $10.6 trillion, to accommodate the potential cost of bailing out Fannie and Freddie. *(Debt limit, p. 4-9)*

● **Tax provisions and offsets.** The bill provided $15.1 billion in housing tax deductions and other benefits through 2018, along with provisions to increase revenue by $18.6 billion over the same period.

BACKGROUND
REGULATING FANNIE AND FREDDIE

Lawmakers had tried repeatedly to impose new rules on Fannie Mae and Freddie Mac, but disagreements over creating a new federal regulator and limiting the firms' portfolios — combined with Fannie and Freddie's legendary lobbying clout — had stymied every effort.

The two companies played a critical role in creating a secondary housing market. They purchased mortgages from banks, giving them the money to make new loans at lower rates than might otherwise be available — a role that had led Democrats to support the firms for many years. Fannie and Freddie bundled the mortgages into packages that became the basis for mortgage-backed securities. Over time they had become involved in more complicated transactions, buying and selling complex, unregulated financial instruments such as derivatives to hedge against risks. The management of the companies was also a problem: In 2003 and 2004, multibillion-dollar accounting scandals led to the ouster of top executives in both companies.

Lawmakers worried about the complex portfolios and about the inability of the existing regulator, the tiny Office of Federal Housing Enterprise Oversight, to police the mortgage finance giants. Although Fannie and Freddie were public corporations, they were originally chartered by Congress as government-sponsored enterprises (GSEs), a status that created an implied guarantee of federal support The thought that taxpayers might be on the hook, in the event the GSEs failed, was a major motivator for Congress to act.

● **108th Congress.** In October 2003, a bill to split oversight of the companies between the Department of Housing and Urban Development and a new Treasury agency stalled in the House Financial Services Committee, after the White House came out against it, saying it did not go far enough. In April 2004, the Senate Banking, Housing and Urban Affairs Committee approved a bill to create a new safety and soundness regulator that could raise minimum capital requirements for the GSEs. But the measure was derailed by partisan tensions, lobbying and disagreement over how to regulate the two companies. *(2003 Almanac, p. 4-8; 2004 Almanac, p. 3-3)*

● **109th Congress.** The House passed a GSE regulation bill in 2005, and the Senate Banking committee approved a similar measure. Both proposed creating an independent regulator, but there were disagreements over a House provision to require the companies to contribute 5 percent a year to a new affordable-housing fund and a Senate plan

to allow the regulator to restrict Fannie and Freddie's portfolios. The legislation went no further. *(2005 Almanac, p. 3-11)*

● **110th Congress.** In May 2007, the House passed a bill (HR 1427) to establish a strong new federal regulator — the Federal Housing Finance Agency — with broad powers to set capital levels and portfolio limits for Fannie and Freddie and to place them into conservatorship or receivership in the event of a financial crisis. It also proposed a new Federal Housing Fund to support affordable housing, financed by a percentage of Fannie and Freddie's portfolios. The Senate did not act on the bill in 2007. *(2007 Almanac, p. 7-8)*

HOUSING MARKET COLLAPSE

In the fall of 2007, lawmakers' immediate priority shifted from regulating the mortgage finance giants to addressing the collapse in the subprime mortgage market that had begun reverberating through the economy. Most of the legislation was aimed at preventing a repeat of the boom in subprime mortgages and getting credit flowing to homebuyers at a time when lenders were increasingly reluctant or unable to make new loans. Subprime mortgage loans carried low initial interest rates, allowing borrowers to buy more expensive homes than they could afford. But the rates were adjustable, and when they started to ratchet up, hundreds of thousands of homeowners faced foreclosure. In the eyes of lawmakers, the culprits included subprime lenders who pushed the mortgages, and investors, whose sales of securities based on the loans fueled the subprime market. Some also blamed homeowners who bought homes they could not afford.

▶ **FHA overhaul.** Both chambers passed bills (HR 1852, S 2338) in the fall of 2007 aimed at expanding the ability of the FHA to guarantee mortgage loans. The Depression-era agency protected lenders against losses if a borrower defaulted on a mortgage loan. That guarantee allowed lenders to offer better terms than they otherwise would, enabling lower-income borrowers to purchase a home. The bills proposed increasing outdated limits on the size of loans the agency could insure and making other changes to allow the FHA to give more borrowers an alternative to subprime loans. The House bill also included an affordable-housing fund, championed by Frank. *(2007 Almanac, p. 7-7)*

▶ **Lender regulation.** The House in November 2007 passed a bill by Frank (HR 3915) to overhaul the regulation of mortgage lenders. It included a national licensing system for mortgage brokers, minimum standards for home loans and a requirement that firms that packaged the loans share in the liability. Dodd introduced a similar bill, which was never marked up. Unlike Frank's bill, it would have made the investor who bought the mortgage-backed securities liable for losses and would not have pre-empted state law. *(2007 Almanac, p. 7-5)*

▶ **Bankruptcy relief.** The House Judiciary Committee approved a bill (HR 3609) in December 2007 that differed from the others because it was aimed at helping existing subprime borrowers who were in trouble. It would have allowed bankruptcy judges to change the terms of a mortgage for a primary residence. *(2007 Almanac, p. 7-6)*

LEGISLATIVE ACTION

In February 2008, the two chambers began writing and rewriting an increasingly broad bill to ease the mortgage crisis. Huge bank losses, resulting from rising foreclosures and a parallel drop in home prices, were leading to a series of major bankruptcies and takeovers. Fearing that the problem would escalate, lawmakers decided early in the ses-

sion that it was critical to help struggling homeowners refinance their mortgages and to take other steps to bolster the housing market. The resulting legislation drew on all of the bills begun in 2007.

SENATE FLOOR ACTION

After nearly three months of maneuvering and negotiation, the Senate voted, 84-12, on April 10 to pass a mortgage relief bill that was devoted mainly to overhauling FHA lending policies and providing tax benefits to businesses hurt by the mortgage crisis. The leadership used a House-passed energy bill (HR 3221) to get around the requirement that tax provisions originate in the House. The Senate deleted the energy language and replaced it with the Senate mortgage package. *(Senate vote 96, p. S-21)*

The bill was a bipartisan compromise brought to the floor April 3 by Dodd and Shelby. Majority Leader Harry Reid, D-Nev., and Minority Leader Mitch McConnell, R-Ky., issued a joint statement supporting the measure.

Among other things, the Dodd-Shelby deal dropped proposed bankruptcy language that had led Republicans to stall the measure for weeks. The provision, backed by consumer advocates and many Democrats, would have allowed bankruptcy judges to modify subprime mortgages, including reducing the outstanding principal. Under existing law, judges could modify mortgages on vacation homes but not on primary residences.

Democratic backers said the change would help hundreds of thousands of struggling homeowners keep their homes. Republicans, the White House and the lending industry argued that it would hurt all borrowers because lenders would raise their interest rates to offset the chance that a loan could be modified. An attempt to restore the bankruptcy language was tabled (killed), 58-36. *(Senate vote 88, p. S-19)*

Democrats also agreed to add provisions, such as tax breaks for homebuyers and builders and a major revision of the FHA's mortgage insurance program, to attract support.

Elements of the Senate-passed bill, many of them drawn from the 2007 legislation, included:

▶ Increases in the loan limits for FHA-backed loans, including further increases in high-cost areas.

▶ $4 billion in Community Development Block Grants to purchase and rehabilitate foreclosed properties in the hardest-hit areas. Both of those provisions were Democratic priorities.

▶ A provision, avidly sought by homebuilders, to allow businesses to use net operating losses in 2008 and 2009 to offset profits from four prior years and receive tax refunds. Existing law allowed a two-year carryback.

▶ A $7,000 tax credit, spread over two years, for people who purchased foreclosed homes.

▶ An additional standard deduction in 2008 of $500 ($1,000 for joint filers) for taxpayers who paid state or local property taxes but did not itemize on their federal return.

▶ $10 billion in private-activity bond authority for use in refinancing subprime loans and providing mortgages for first-time homebuyers and for multifamily rental housing.

▶ An $8.3 billion package of extensions of expiring tax breaks for renewable energy and energy efficiency, which was added at the last minute by a vote of 88-8. The amendment, offered by John Ensign, R-Nev., and Maria Cantwell, D-Wash., was certain to raise problems in the House because it included no revenue provisions to offset the cost. House Democrats were adamant about paying for tax breaks

and had incorporated the requirement into House rules, but Senate Republicans rejected offsets as tax increases. *(Senate vote 95, p. S-21)*

HOUSE FLOOR ACTION

The House passed a much broader version of HR 3221 on May 8, by agreeing to the Senate version with three amendments that, taken together, replaced the Senate provisions. The result was a bill that included a new, strong, independent regulator for Fannie Mae and Freddie Mac, along with the affordable-housing fund.

● **Housing provisions.** The principal amendment combined several of the bills passed in 2007 with a new measure to help refinance at-risk mortgages. The amendment was adopted, 266-154, which was short of the two-thirds majority that would be needed to override a veto. *(House vote 301, p. H-98)*

Major elements of the first amendment included:

▶ An independent agency, the Federal Housing Finance Agency, to regulate Fannie, Freddie and the Federal Home Loan Bank System with the power to place these entities into conservatorship or receivership in the event of a financial crisis. The amendment would also raise the GSE's conforming loan limit for homes in high-cost areas.

▶ An affordable-housing fund financed from Fannie and Freddie's portfolios. Only very low-income families would be eligible for assistance from the fund.

▶ Increases in the loan limits for FHA-backed loans, with a further increase for homes in high-cost areas.

▶ An expanded FHA program to help borrowers threatened with foreclosure on their primary residence refinance to new, affordable, fixed-rate, government-backed mortgages. The Financial Services Committee had approved this part of the package as a separate bill (HR 5830) on May 1. It included a $300 billion authorization for the new loan guarantees and required both the lenders' and the borrowers' voluntary participation and agreement to take losses.

The Bush administration opposed the FHA rescue plan, arguing that it would bail out real estate speculators and the lenders who made bad loans in the first place. Although members of his party broke ranks, House Minority Leader John A. Boehner, R-Ohio, sided with the Bush administration, saying Democrats "are forcing responsible homeowners and taxpayers to pick up a $300 billion tab to bail out scam artists, speculators and reckless borrowers."

● **Tax package.** The second amendment, designed to relieve the tax burden on new and struggling homeowners, was adopted, 322-94. *(House vote 302, p. H-98)*

It was based on a bill (HR 5720 — H Rept 110-606) approved by the Ways and Means Committee on April 9. Chairman Charles B. Rangel, D-N.Y., described the measure as consumer-friendly compared with the Senate version, which took a more industry-targeted approach. In particular, the House bill did not include the net operating loss carryback provision. Rangel also did not include the Senate's energy tax package.

The tax amendment, which was fully offset, included:

▶ A refundable tax credit of up to $7,500 for first-time homebuyers that would serve as a zero-interest, 15-year loan. The proposal was broader than the Senate plan, which applied only to foreclosed properties.

▶ An additional standard deduction in 2008 for non-itemizers who paid property taxes. The amount — $350 for individuals and $700 for joint filers — was smaller than in the Senate bill.

▶ Authority for $10 billion in tax-exempt bonds that was similar

to the Senate plan.

▸ Revenue-raisers that offset the cost of the tax provisions — mainly by requiring that brokers report their customers' basis, or purchase cost, for securities transactions and by a one-year delay in new rules allocating interest expenses between foreign and domestic sources.

● **State laws.** The third amendment was a proposal by Brad Miller, D-N.C., and Steven C. LaTourette, R-Ohio, to specify that no provision in the bill or in either of two major federal banking statutes, the Home Owner's Loan Act and the National Bank Act, would pre-empt state laws dealing with residential foreclosures. It was adopted, 256-160. (House vote 303, p. H-98)

SENATE FLOOR ACTION

The Senate took up HR 3221, as amended by the House, in mid-June and replaced most of the text with a comprehensive substitute written by Dodd and Shelby. Senators agreed, 79-16, on June 25, to insert the Dodd-Shelby plan. (Senate vote 157, p. S-34)

The Senate then voted 76-10 on July 7 to concur in the House decision to strip out the Senate energy tax language. On July 11, it voted, 63-5, to reject the House tax amendment and the provision on state law. (Senate vote 163, p. S-36; Senate vote 173, p. S-39)

The bipartisan substitute combined provisions of HR 3221 as passed by the Senate in April — which focused mainly on FHA loan limits and tax provisions — with a draft bill that the Senate Banking committee approved May 20. The committee draft added major sections, including:

▸ A new regulator for Fannie Mae, Freddie Mac and the FHA with authority similar to that in the House bill. The regulator would have to consider the broader effect on markets in the event of a GSE failure when setting limits on the company's huge portfolios.

▸ An increase in Fannie and Freddie's conforming loan limits in high-cost housing markets.

▸ A new affordable-housing fund financed from Fannie and Freddie's portfolios.

▸ The HOPE for Homeowners program to help borrowers avoid foreclosure. Unlike the House version, the bill proposed that the $300 billion authorized for the program come from the affordable-housing fund.

▸ About $12 billion in revenue-raisers over 10 years.

During the floor debate, the Senate rejected two amendments by Christopher S. Bond, R-Mo., aimed at the heart of the bill. The first, rejected 11-77, would have prevented the use of funds from Fannie and Freddie for the affordable-housing fund. The second, which would have eliminated the HOPE for Homeowners program, was rejected, 21-69, on a procedural vote. (Senate votes 152, 153, p. S-33)

Shelby said the trust fund and the funding mechanism were vital to the measure. "Eliminating either one of these now would simply unwind the entire bill, would destroy the whole bill," he said.

HOUSE-SENATE DIFFERENCES

The two versions of the bill had become similar in many respects, but there were also significant differences that had to be resolved before a final version could be sent to Bush. For example:

▸ The House proposed delaying the start date of the new GSE regulator for six months after enactment, when a new president would be in the White House. The Senate made the effective date immediate.

▸ The House favored higher conforming loan limits for Fannie

and Freddie — the lesser of 125 percent of the median home price in a local market or $729,750. The Senate proposed to increase the limit to $625,000 in high-cost areas.

▸ The Senate, but not the House, included the $3.9 billion in CDBG grants to assist localities in buying and rehabilitating foreclosed homes. This was one of the provisions that drew a White House veto threat.

▸ The House included a fully offset package of roughly $11 billion in housing-focused tax breaks. The Senate bill included $14.5 billion in tax breaks; all but $2.4 billion were offset.

CRISIS AT FANNIE AND FREDDIE

The debate was suddenly transformed on Sunday, July 13, when Paulson asked Congress for largely unfettered authority to provide Fannie and Freddie with capital and potentially to take them over.

The two firms had taken a financial beating the week before, as investors lost confidence in the housing market and in the companies' ability to repay $1.5 trillion in loans. Given Fannie and Freddie's unique size and structure and their fundamental involvement in the U.S. and global economies, the Treasury and the Federal Reserve said they had little choice but to take action.

Lawmakers expressed trepidation at giving the Treasury such broad authority so quickly, but most thought the alternatives were more perilous. "There's nothing I know of in my 27 years that comes close to this situation," Dodd said. "We need to act on something. Inaction is not really an option."

Fiscal conservatives warned of the huge potential cost of Paulson's rescue plan. "By bailing out Fannie and Freddie as proposed, Congress would put taxpayers on the hook for billions of dollars' worth of risk," Rep. Jeb Hensarling of Texas, chairman of the conservative Republican Study Committee, said in a statement.

FINAL BILL

Details of the compromise bill came together July 22, despite warnings the previous day that the president would veto it over some of the mortgage provisions.

Lawmakers agreed to the administration's insistence that there be no dollar limit on the Treasury's lending or equity purchases, but in contrast to the administration's proposal, they made any spending subject to the statutory debt limit. They increased that limit by $800 billion to cover the cost of the bailout.

Although the legislation did not mandate preferred-shareholder status for any government equity stake in the two companies, which would ensure a priority return on a federal investment, Frank said that it would be an option in the Treasury secretary's "arsenal" should the lifeline be activated.

The legislation gave the Federal Reserve a "consultative" role to the new regulator for Fannie and Freddie but, contrary to the administration's proposal, that provision was set to expire at the end of 2009.

The cap on the size of mortgages that Fannie and Freddie could buy and package as securities was set at the lesser of 115 percent of the median home price or $625,000 in certain high-cost areas, with language aimed at allowing more homes to qualify for the programs.

House members also made some changes to the package of housing-focused tax breaks. The compromise version totaled about $15.1 billion, an increase over the Senate's $14.5 billion package.

The measure included about $18.5 billion in offsets, which covered the cost of the housing tax breaks as well as most of the cost of

the grants to states and localities to buy and rehabilitate foreclosed properties.

The legislation gained momentum July 23 when the administration reversed course and dropped its final objections to the bill, while key Senate lawmakers also endorsed the House-passed measure.

White House Deputy Press Secretary Tony Fratto said Paulson recommended that Bush sign the bill because of the urgency of providing a backstop to the mortgage finance giants in order to calm the jittery financial markets. In addition, the regulatory overhaul of Fannie and Freddie had been a longtime goal of the Bush administration.

"We're in a position where we are going to have to accept some bad policy," Fratto said.

"I don't like everything in this bill, either," said Frank. "It is incon-ceivable to me that anybody would like everything in this bill — it is a product of a very significant set of compromises."

The House voted, 272-152, on July 23 to insert the carefully assembled compromise into the mortgage relief bill. *(House vote 519, p. H-174)*

The Senate voted, 80-13, on July 25 to invoke cloture on the House amendment, a strong show of support that virtually ensured that it would be sent to the president. The Senate cleared the bill, 72-13, on July 26 in a weekend session. *(Senate votes 185, 186, pp. S-41, S-42)*

Speaking at a news conference with Dodd, Shelby characterized the measure as essential for Fannie and Freddie to weather the current financial storm.

"Without this legislation . . . I don't know if they could survive, he said, adding, "There's a lot at stake." ■

[PROVISIONS]
Details of Mortgage Finance Bill

THE FOLLOWING ARE MAJOR PROVISIONS of the mortgage finance bill, which was signed into law July 30 (HR 3221 — PL 110-289).

FEDERAL BACKSTOP
● **Stock purchase.** The Treasury Department was given temporary emergency authority to purchase securities issued by Fannie Mae and Freddie Mac — including stock — if the purchase was expected to provide stability to the financial markets, prevent disruptions in the availability of mortgage finances and protect taxpayers. The Treasury secretary was required to consider protections for the government's investment, such as limitations on existing stock dividends or executive compensation.
● **Debt limit.** The law raised the statutory limit on the federal debt to $10.6 trillion, up from $9.8 trillion. The increase set the limit for Treasury's purchase of stock.
● **Sunset.** The authority was set to expire on Dec. 31, 2009.

HOUSING FINANCE OVERHAUL
REGULATION OF GSES
● **New regulatory agency.** The law established a new, independent federal regulator, the Federal Housing Finance Agency (FHFA), with broad oversight over three government-sponsored enterprises (GSEs): the mortgage finance giants Fannie Mae and Freddie Mac, and the 12 Federal Home Loan banks.

The new agency replaced the Office of Federal Home Enterprise Oversight (OFHEO), which was responsible for regulating Fannie and Freddie. It also replaced the Federal Housing Finance Board, which oversaw the Home Loan Bank system. The OFHEO and the Federal Housing Finance Board were abolished one year after enactment.
● **Funding.** Funding for the new agency was to come through assessments on the three GSEs; it did not need an annual appropriation. The Treasury Department could invest excess funds from the assessments in government securities.
● **Agency structure.** The director of the new agency was responsible for overseeing the financial health and soundness of the three GSEs. The director was to be appointed by the president and confirmed by the Senate for a five-year term. The agency had three divisions, each headed by a deputy director: the Division of Enterprise Regulation, with oversight of Fannie and Freddie; the Division of Federal Home Loan Bank Regulation, with oversight of the Federal Home Loan banks; and Housing Mission and Goals, which would oversee the housing missions of the three GSEs.
● **Duties.** The director's principal duties included ensuring that each GSE maintained adequate capital and internal controls, fostered a healthy national housing finance market that minimized the cost of housing financing, and complied with all applicable regulations. The director could review and reject any acquisition or transfer of a controlling interest in one of the GSEs.
● **Oversight board.** The law also created a five-member Housing Finance Oversight Board to advise the director on overall strategy and policies. It was to be chaired by the director and include the secretaries of Housing and Urban Development (HUD) and Treasury and two members appointed by the president and confirmed by the Senate. Board members served four-year terms; no more than three members could be from the same political party.
● **Regulatory powers.** The director was responsible for issuing new regulations to govern the mortgage portfolios of Fannie and Freddie, which together totaled about $1.5 trillion. The purpose of the regulations was to ensure that the mortgage portfolios were backed by sufficient capital, were consistent with the GSEs' mission, and allowed for safe and sound operations. The director also had to take into account the ability of the enterprises to provide a liquid secondary market through securitization activities and the portfolio holdings in relation to the overall mortgage market, among other factors.

The FHFA had the authority to approve or modify executive compensation at the GSEs.

Any new financial products offered by the GSEs had be reviewed and approved by the regulatory agency, taking into consideration whether the product was in the public interest and whether it would interfere with the safety and soundness of the companies or the broader financial system. After a new product request had been made, there would be a 30-day period for public comments, at the end of which the director would be required to make a decision.

• **Capital requirements.** The FHFA was required to issue regulations setting risk-based capital requirements to ensure that the GSEs operated in a safe and sound manner. It was also responsible for setting minimum capital levels and could raise the levels temporarily or permanently, if needed, to preserve the safe and sound operation of Fannie and Freddie.

• **Rating system.** The GSEs were to be rated under a system similar to that used by other federal banking regulators, with four classifications: adequately capitalized, undercapitalized, significantly undercapitalized and critically undercapitalized.

• **Classification.** An undercapitalized GSE would be monitored to ensure compliance with capital restoration plans, among other requirements. The FHFA could restrict the GSE's asset growth, including the expansion of its mortgage portfolios. An undercapitalized GSE could not acquire a stake in other companies or expand new business activities without the regulator's approval.

If a GSE was found to be significantly undercapitalized, the FHFA had to take actions that could include removing the board of directors and electing a new board, dismissing directors or executives, or requiring the GSE to hire qualified management. A GSE found to be significantly undercapitalized would be barred from paying bonuses or increased salaries to its executives unless approved by the FHFA.

If a GSE was rated critically undercapitalized, the FHFA could be appointed conservator or receiver to reorganize, rehabilitate or close it. However, the regulator could not revoke the GSE's charter.

• **Enforcement.** The law set three tiers of civil monetary penalties for violations. The first tier — for violating the new law and the authorizing statutes, or engaging in unsafe and unsound practices — carried penalties of up to $10,000 per day. The second tier — for violations involving "reckless engagement in unsound business practices" and breaches of trust in sound business — carried penalties of up to $50,000 per day. The third tier — covering violations committed by an employee who engaged in unsound business practices and knowingly caused a substantial loss or substantial gain by breaking laws or regulations — brought a maximum penalty of $2 million per day.

• **Federal Reserve consultation.** The FHFA director was required to consult with the Federal Reserve chairman about risks to the financial system posed by the GSEs prior to issuing any regulation, order or guidelines on prudent management, safety and soundness, or capital requirements and portfolio standards. This requirement expired on Dec. 31, 2009.

OTHER GSE CHANGES

• **Conforming loan limits.** The law permanently raised the GSEs' conforming loan limits, which governed the size of the mortgages that the companies could purchase, in areas where the median home price exceeded the general conforming loan limit of $417,000. The size of individual mortgage loans that Fannie and Freddie could buy was increased to the lesser of 115 percent of an area's median price or $625,000. The economic stimulus law (PL 110-185), enacted in February, included this increase for loans originated between July 1, 2007, and Dec. 31, 2008.

• **Underserved markets.** Under previous law, the GSEs were supposed to purchase mortgages for households representing three income levels as measured by an area's median income (AMI): moderate income (100 percent AMI), low income (80 percent AMI), and very low income (60 percent AMI or less).

The new law redefined low-income families as those with 50 percent AMI or less, and very low-income families as those with incomes of 30 percent AMI or less.

The GSEs were required to meet new goals established by the FHFA for purchasing single-family and multifamily home mortgages for households in these categories, based on Home Mortgage Disclosure Act data by using three-year averages to determine the market. The goals were to be set annually but could be set for a multi-year period.

The GSEs were also directed to include mortgages in central cities, rural areas and other underserved housing areas, as well as loans for manufactured housing and the preservation of affordable housing.

AFFORDABLE HOUSING FUND

• **Fund creation.** The law created a new, permanent Affordable Housing Trust Fund administered by HUD and funded by proceeds from Fannie Mae and Freddie Mac. The fund's purpose was to support homeownership among low-income and very low-income families, increase investment in economically distressed areas, and increase the supply of rental and owner-occupied housing for those families.

• **GSE assessments.** Fannie and Freddie were required each year to divert 0.42 percent of the total value of newly purchased mortgages to pay for the trust fund.

However, the funding stream was to be diverted in the first few years to pay for a new program created under the bill to help borrowers avoid foreclosure. Twenty-five percent of the funds would be set aside to reimburse the government for administrative expenses associated with the borrower rescue program, known as HOPE for Homeowners. In fiscal 2009, the remaining 75 percent would go to offset the rescue program, declining to 50 percent in fiscal 2010 and 25 percent in fiscal 2011. Beginning in fiscal 2012, 75 percent of the GSE assessments would be allocated to the Affordable Housing Trust Fund.

• **Distribution formula.** HUD was responsible for devising the formula for dispersing money from the trust fund, which had to be published in the Federal Register. Grants were to be awarded to state housing agencies, housing and community development agencies, and tribally designated housing entities. None of the affordable housing funds could be used for political activities, advocacy, lobbying, counseling, travel expenses, or preparation or advice on tax returns. No more than 10 percent of the funds could be used for grantee administrative costs or expenses. The Congressional Budget Office estimated that outlays for the trust fund would total $1.6 billion in fiscal 2008 through 2013.

FEDERAL HOME LOAN BANKS

The FHFA's responsibilities included regulatory control over the Federal Home Loan Bank system. The new law reduced the number of directors on a Home Loan Bank Board to 13 from 14. Two or more banks were allowed to establish a joint office to perform banking functions that each was individually authorized to perform. The FHFA was required to create regulations to ensure that the Home Loan banks had access to the information they needed to determine joint liability. Individual Home Loan banks could merge, subject to approval from the new regulator and each of the bank's boards. The cap on director compensation was lifted, and the term was lengthened to four years from three.

MORTGAGE LICENSING

• **New licensing system.** The law set out standards for a nationwide licensing and registration system for mortgage brokers and for bank

loan officers who dealt with real estate loans. The states were encouraged to administer the system on their own, in accordance with the standards set out under the law. But if HUD found that a state-run system was deficient, the federal government was required to put a backstop licensing system in place.

- **Licensing standards.** Under the new law, a broker had to be licensed and registered by the Nationwide Mortgage Licensing System and Registry (NMLSR) in order to be a loan originator. Anyone applying for licensing and registry had to provide fingerprints, personal history and relevant experience. The applicant had to meet minimum standards to receive a license, including not having their loan originator license revoked in the previous five years, no felony conviction in the previous seven years, demonstration of financial responsibility, complete pre-licensing education, and correctly answering 75 percent of a written test developed and administered by the NMLSR.

Federal banking regulators were required to jointly develop systems for registering employees of banks as registered loan originators within one year of enactment. The bank regulators, through the Federal Financial Institutions Examination Council, were directed to coordinate with the new broker-licensing agency to establish a unique identifier for all registered loan originators. The Justice Department was authorized to provide access to criminal-history records to states for background checks on state-licensed loan originators.

- **Federal backup.** HUD was required to create a backup licensing system for states that failed to meet the minimum standards established by law or did not participate in the licensing system.
- **Fees.** Federal banking agencies, along with the new licensing agency, could charge fees to cover the costs of the program, provided the fees were not passed on to consumers.
- **Immunity.** State or HUD officials acting in good faith while administering the program were afforded civil-liability protection within the scope of their office or employment.

FORECLOSURE PREVENTION
FHA OVERHAUL

The new law updated and modernized several elements of the Federal Housing Administration, a Depression-era agency that insured mortgages made by qualified lenders to low- and moderate-income families to purchase or refinance a home. The program provided mortgage insurance to protect lenders against the risk of default on mortgages to qualified buyers, enabling the lenders to provide better terms.

- **Loan limit.** The FHA's loan limit — the maximum loan amount that the agency could insure — was permanently increased to $417,000 from $362,790. The minimum loan was raised to $271,050 from $200,160. For high-cost residential areas, the loan limit was increased to the lesser of 115 percent of an area's median home price or $625,000.
- **Premiums.** The FHA could charge upfront premiums of up to 3 percent of the original insured principal obligation and 2.75 percent for first-time homebuyers who completed a counseling program.
- **Down payment.** Down payment requirements for getting an FHA-backed loan were increased to 3.5 percent from 3 percent. Borrowers getting FHA-backed loans could not get down payment assistance from the seller. The law also set a one-year moratorium on risk-based pricing for FHA insurance products, effective Oct. 1, 2008.
- **Loan-to-value limit.** The law set the loan-to-value limit — the ratio of the fair market value of a house to the value of the loan that would finance the purchase — for FHA single-family loans at 97.75 percent

of the appraised value, plus the upfront FHA mortgage premium.

The FHA could increase single-family loan limits up to 100 percent of the appraised value of a home, plus closing costs for 36 months, in a presidentially declared disaster area.

- **Mutual Mortgage Insurance Fund.** The bill made changes to the Mutual Mortgage Insurance Fund, through which the FHA insured mortgage loans on one- to four-family residential housing. The program was self-funding, taking in premiums from mortgagors and paying claims from lenders on losses from mortgage defaults.

Under the bill, the FHA was allowed to change the premiums or underwriting standards if the fund was at risk of becoming financially unsound. The law also added four types of government-backed mortgages to the fund's responsibilities: mortgages used in conjunction with the Homeownership Voucher program; reverse mortgages insured by FHA; Hawaiian Home Lands insured mortgages; and single-family mortgages insured on Indian reservations.

- **Reverse mortgages.** The law removed the limit on the number of reverse mortgages (previously set at 275,000) that the FHA could insure. Reverse mortgages allowed homeowners age 62 and older to convert their home equity into a monthly stream of income and a line of credit to be repaid when they no longer occupied the house. The law created a uniform nationwide cap of $417,000 on reverse-mortgage loans. The FHA was required to set limits on the origination fee that could be charged for such loans. Reverse-mortgage loans were permitted in co-op units.
- **Borrower ID.** Borrowers were required to provide personal identification to receive an FHA-insured loan. Acceptable forms of identification included a Social Security card along with a photo ID issued by the federal or state government, a driver's license or ID card issued by a state in accordance with the REAL ID Act, a passport or a U.S. Citizenship and Immigration Services photo ID card.

HELP FOR BORROWERS

- **HOPE for Homeowners.** The law established a temporary government program administered by the FHA to help borrowers who could not afford their mortgage payments to avoid foreclosure. Under the program, which was authorized from Oct. 1, 2008, until Sept. 30, 2011, certain borrowers could refinance into new, FHA-insured mortgages if the lender agreed to reduce the mortgage debt. Participation in the program was voluntary and required agreement from both the borrower and the holder of the mortgage. Costs of the program were to be paid for by funds diverted from Fannie Mae and Freddie Mac.
- **Insurance limit.** The FHA was authorized to insure up to $300 billion worth of newly refinanced mortgages through fiscal 2011.
- **Procedure for getting insurance.** The process began with an applicant contacting an FHA-approved lender to refinance his or her current mortgage. The lender would determine the loan size that would meet the program's requirements, including a requirement that the borrower be able to repay the new loan. If the borrower's existing lender agreed to take a write-down on the existing loan to a level that was affordable for the borrower, the FHA lender would then pay off the discounted existing mortgage.
- **Eligibility.** Borrowers and lenders had to meet eligibility requirements to participate in the program. Only owner-occupied principal residences were eligible, and borrowers had to certify that they owned no other homes. Borrowers could not have a mortgage-debt-to-income ratio of more than 31 percent as of March 1, 2008. Borrowers

also had to certify that they had not intentionally defaulted on existing mortgages and had not obtained the existing loan fraudulently.

Lenders had to agree to waive any existing penalties or fees on the existing mortgage and to accept the proceeds from the new loan as payment in full. Holders of secondary liens — such as a home equity line — on the property also had to relinquish any claims, and borrowers could not take such loans for at least five years.

● **Other loan requirements.** If all those requirements were met, the existing lender would agree to reduce the outstanding principal on the loan. To participate in the program, the lender would have to pay the FHA a 3 percent upfront premium and would have to write down the value of the existing mortgage to no greater than 90 percent of the property's appraised value. After refinancing a mortgage, the borrower would be required to pay annual insurance premiums to the FHA that would be equal to 1.5 percent of the principal. The new loan would have a fixed interest rate and a maturity of not less than 30 years.

● **Equity share.** The borrower getting an insured loan had to agree to share a portion of the house's future appreciation with the government, both to help lower the program's cost and to prevent borrowers from unfairly profiting from the federal program.

A borrower who sold a home or refinanced the loan within five years had to share equity with the government according to the following formula: 100 percent in year one, 90 percent in year two, 80 percent in year three, 70 percent in year four, 60 percent in year five and 50 percent through the rest of the loan. A borrower who sold a home was required to share a flat 50 percent of the home's appreciated value with the government.

● **Board of directors.** The law established a new board to oversee the program, made up of the Treasury and HUD secretaries and the chairmen of the Federal Reserve and the Federal Deposit Insurance Corporation. The board is directed to issue regulations setting a "reasonable" limit on origination fees for the new loans and to establish rules to ensure that the interest rate was comparable to similar market rates.

OTHER PROVISIONS

● **Mortgage disclosure.** The law required more disclosure from lenders on the terms of mortgages, particularly adjustable-rate mortgages. A lender was required to state clearly and conspicuously that an adjustable-rate mortgage would have an interest rate that varies over time and to disclose the maximum possible payment on the mortgage.

● **Protection for servicemembers.** The law temporarily expanded a provision of the Servicemembers Civil Relief Act (PL 108-189) that required lenders to wait 90 days before they could begin foreclosure proceedings against a returning servicemember. The new law lengthened the grace period to nine months. The change applied to sales, foreclosures or seizures of property made on or after the law's enactment. A lender or loan servicer had to provide a written financial disclosure to a servicemember who failed to make a mortgage payment for two consecutive months. The expansion expired on Dec. 31, 2010.

● **Veterans.** The Department of Veterans Affairs was authorized to make improvements and structural alterations to the homes of servicemembers who had a permanent disability that required a discharge as a result of service in the line of duty.

● **Abandoned and foreclosed homes.** The law appropriated $3.9 billion for grants to states and local governments to purchase and rehabilitate abandoned and foreclosed homes. HUD was directed to develop a

formula for distributing the grants. Recipients had to use the funds within 18 months to purchase and redevelop the property. At least 25 percent of the money had to be used on properties that would house individuals or families whose incomes were below 50 percent of the area median income. Homes purchased with the funds had to be sold at a price equal to or less than the cost of buying and rehabilitating the house. Any excess revenue generated during the first five years of the program through resale, rental or redevelopment of the property had to be reinvested in rehabilitating other homes. After the five-year period, excess revenue would be deposited in the U.S. Treasury.

● **Homeowner counseling.** The law provided a total of $180 million for counseling services for homeowners facing foreclosure; $80 million was set aside for pre-foreclosure counseling, and $100 million was allocated for the Neighborhood Reinvestment Corporation until Dec. 31, 2008, for foreclosure mitigation efforts and outreach to borrowers at risk of losing their homes.

TAX PROVISIONS
HOUSING INCENTIVES

● **First-time homebuyer credit.** Under the law, first-time homebuyers would receive a refundable tax credit of up to $7,500 for purchases made between April 8, 2008, and July 1, 2009. The credit would effectively function as an interest-free loan, covering 10 percent of the purchase price of the house, up to $7,500. The credit was also "refundable," meaning that it could be claimed even if it was worth more than the taxes owed by the homebuyer. The credit was phased out for higher-income buyers, beginning at $75,000 in modified adjusted gross income for individuals ($150,000 for joint filers).

The credit had to be repaid over 15 years, meaning a participating homebuyer's taxes would increase each year by 6.67 percent of the total amount of the credit. The credit would not be available if the house qualified for the Washington, D.C., homebuyer credit, the residence was financed by a tax-exempt mortgage bond, the taxpayer was a non-resident alien or the taxpayer disposed of the house before the end of the taxable year.

The expected cost, calculated by the Joint Tax Committee, was $4.5 billion over 11 years.

● **Property tax deduction.** The law created an additional standard deduction in 2008 for state and local property taxes. Taxpayers who did not itemize could deduct up to $500 for individuals ($1,000 for joint filers) for those taxes. If the property taxes were less than the standard deduction amount, the taxpayer would claim the amount of taxes paid. The additional deduction was expected to cost $1.5 billion over 11 years.

● **Low-income-housing tax credit.** The limit on state allocations of low-income-housing tax credits was increased by 20 cents for 2008 and 2009, thus providing a limit of $2.20 per resident for those years. The program provides tax credits that can be claimed over a 10-year period for the costs of building or rehabilitating certain rental housing occupied by low-income tenants. The dollar amount used to determine credits for states with smaller populations was increased by 10 percent. These and other tax incentives for multifamily low-income housing were expected to cost $1.9 billion over 11 years.

● **Tax-exempt housing bonds.** The law authorized $11 billion in additional state-issued tax-exempt private activity bonds in 2008 for housing-related financing, and it changed certain rules regarding the bonds. The bonds are officially issued by state and local governments,

but the proceeds are used by private entities and the payment of the bonds comes from private entities. The types of private-activity bonds eligible for tax-exempt treatment included qualified mortgage bonds, qualified veterans' mortgage bonds and bonds used to finance certain residential rental projects.

The new bonds had to be used to finance new mortgages or certain residential rental properties that met low-income eligibility requirements. Some mortgage bonds could also be used to refinance adjustable-rate single-family mortgages that originated between 2002 and 2007, if a bond issuer determined that refinancing would be "reasonably likely" to cause financial hardship to the borrower. Increasing the tax-exempt bond cap in this way was expected to cost about $1.5 billion over 11 years.

● **AMT provisions.** Certain housing-related tax incentives were not covered by the alternative minimum tax (AMT). Specifically, the law allowed certain low-income-housing tax credits to be used to offset tax liability under the AMT, allowed the rehabilitation credit to be used to offset tax liability when calculating the AMT, and prevented interest earned on tax-exempt housing bonds issued after the enactment date from being treated as taxable income under the AMT. The estimated cost was $2.1 billion over 11 years.

REVENUE PROVISIONS

● **AMT credits.** Corporations were allowed to accelerate the use of certain tax credits in lieu of the bonus depreciation for certain equipment purchases. The available tax credits that could be swapped out included stored-up historic credits under the AMT, as well as research and development credits. The amount that could be obtained was capped at $30 million or 6 percent of the stored-up credits, whichever was less. The estimated cost was $996 million over 11 years.

● **Hurricane losses.** The law modified the statutory rules for the Gulf Opportunity Zone, or GO Zone, which covered the area affected by the 2005 hurricanes Katrina, Rita and Wilma. Taxpayers could file an amended tax return if they received a grant authorized under certain federal laws that reimbursed them for hurricane-related casualty losses for their primary residence after they had previously claimed a deduction for those losses on a tax return. Generally, when taxpayers were reimbursed for casualty losses in a subsequent year, they took those reimbursements into account on the return for the year in which they were received. The estimated cost was $1.3 billion over 11 years.

REVENUE OFFSETS

● **Credit card reporting.** "Payment settlement" companies, which process transactions for debit and credit cards, were required to provide certain information to the IRS and to the merchant or seller that accepted payments processed by those companies. The provision amounted to a tax compliance measure to prevent merchants from successfully avoiding taxes by under-reporting their income from credit card, debit card or third-party transactions. It was expected to raise $9.5 billion over 11 years.

● **Exclusion of gain on home sales.** The law placed a new condition on the amount of gain or profits from the sale of a home that a taxpayer could exclude from taxation. Under previous law, individual taxpayers could exclude $250,000 and couples could exclude $500,000, as long as they occupied the home as a primary residence for at least two of the previous five years. The new law specified that the taxpayer could only exclude the portion of the gain that was attributed to the period during which the home was used as a primary residence, as opposed to a second residence or a rental property. The provision, which affected sales and exchanges after Dec. 31, 2008, was expected to raise $1.4 billion over 11 years.

● **Worldwide interest allocation rules.** The act delayed for two years the effective date for a provision of the 2004 corporate tax overhaul (PL 108-357) that allowed companies to use a modified rule for allocating their interest expenses between U.S. and foreign sources when determining their foreign tax credit limitation. Implementation would take effect for taxable years beginning in 2011, rather than 2009, increasing revenue by an estimated $7.6 billion over 11 years. ■

Stimulus Bill Provides Tax Rebates

CONGRESSIONAL LEADERS of both parties claimed victory in February for their roles in clearing a short-term stimulus package designed to put money in Americans' pockets and boost the sagging economy. President Bush signed the bill into law Feb. 13 (HR 5140 — PL 110-185).

The package was the result of a deal negotiated by House Speaker Nancy Pelosi, D-Calif., Minority Leader John A. Boehner, R-Ohio, and Treasury Secretary Henry M. Paulson Jr.

The centerpiece of the bill was a plan to send checks — advance refunds on credits against taxes owed for fiscal 2008 — to most taxpayers. The credits were refundable, meaning checks were sent to many people whose income was so low that they paid little or no taxes.

The bill also provided write-off incentives to encourage businesses

BOX SCORE

BILL: HR 5140 — PL 110-185

LEGISLATIVE ACTION:

House passed HR 5140, 385-35, on Jan. 29.

Senate passed HR 5140, amended with compromise, 81-16, on Feb. 7.

House cleared the bill, 380-34, on Feb. 7

President signed Feb. 13.

to invest in new equipment. It increased the size of mortgages that Fannie Mae and Freddie Mac could purchase and that the Federal Housing Administration could insure, with the aim of assisting some families in refinancing their mortgages and helping to stabilize the housing market, which had been roiled by the subprime mortgage crisis. (*Mortgage finance overhaul, p. 7-9*)

The bipartisan agreement between House leaders and the White House, announced Jan. 24, was a notable exception to the partisan dueling that dominated the election year. It came at a time of slowing economic growth, rising unemployment and a collapse in the housing market that were giving rise to concern about a recession. Leaders of both parties said that taxpayers and markets around the world were waiting for the U.S. government to take some action.

"We know throughout the households of America that many people are living paycheck to paycheck, and they need this economy to turn around," Pelosi said. "Now we see across the world that the state of the economy in the [United States] is having an impact as well, so the urgency we feel at home is now even more urgent as we see the impact of our markets on others."

Pelosi and Boehner brought the bill directly to the House floor, bypassing the committee process. They called on members of their respective caucuses to line up behind the package, which passed overwhelmingly Jan. 29.

Despite intense pressure to clear the House bill, senators — particularly Democrats — insisted that the Senate have its say on the package. On Jan. 30, the Senate Finance Committee produced a broader bill with expanded rebates, more options for businesses, energy tax breaks and an expansion of unemployment benefits.

But lawmakers had set the Presidents Day recess as the deadline for completing the bill, and leaders of the two chambers reached a relatively quick compromise. The final bill, which won the support of most Republicans, cleared a little more than a week after it was introduced. It was expected to increase the deficit by $151.7 billion in fiscal 2008 and a total of $124.5 billion in fiscal 2008 through 2018.

HIGHLIGHTS

Following are highlights of the stimulus law, with cost estimates from the Congressional Budget Office (CBO) and Congress' Joint Committee on Taxation:

● **Individual refunds.** Payments to individuals totalling $105.7 billion in fiscal 2008 and $9.8 billion in fiscal 2009, including:

▸ Checks of up to $600 for individuals ($1,200 for couples filing jointly) who paid income taxes on wages and investment income in 2007 or 2008. Eligibility for the rebate began phasing out for individuals with more than $75,000 in adjusted gross income ($150,000 for couples).

▸ Checks of $300 for individuals ($600 for couples) who earned at least $3,000 in qualifying income in 2007 and filed a return but had no tax liability. Qualifying income included wages, Social Security benefits and payments to disabled veterans or their survivors.

▸ An additional $300 for each dependent child under age 17 for workers receiving either of the two types of credit.

▸ A requirement that taxpayers include a valid Social Security number on their tax returns in order to prevent illegal immigrants from receiving checks.

● **Business tax deductions.** Business tax benefits expected to cost $44.8 billion in fiscal 2008, declining to $7.5 billion by fiscal 2018, including:

▸ A bonus depreciation that allowed companies to deduct an additional 50 percent from their taxable income in fiscal 2008 for the cost of items that were subject to depreciation over 20 years or less. The equipment had to be purchased and put into service in 2008. The remaining value of the investment would be depreciated over the life of the item.

▸ An increase to $250,000 from $128,000 in the amount small businesses could "expense," or deduct in full, in fiscal 2008 for new property, mainly equipment. The amount was gradually reduced after the company's total investments for the year reached $800,000; previously the phaseout began at $410,000.

● **Housing provisions**. The changes, which had no net cost, were:

▸ An increase in the size of individual mortgage loans that Fannie

Mae and Freddie Mac could purchase to 125 percent of the median home price in the local market or $729,750, whichever was less. The previous limit was $417,000. The increase applied to loans originated between July 1, 2007, and Dec. 31, 2008.

▸ An increase in the limit on Federal Housing Administration (FHA) mortgage loans to 125 percent of the median home price in the local market or $729,750, whichever was less. The previous loan limit was $362,000. The FHA could increase the limit by $100,000 if it was warranted by market conditions. The provision applied to loans approved before Dec. 31, 2008.

LEGISLATIVE ACTION
HOUSE PASSAGE

The House passed the bill Jan. 29 by a lopsided 385-35 vote, one day after Bush urged support for the bipartisan agreement in his State of the Union address. He urged Congress not to "load up" the bill with additional spending. "That would delay or derail it," Bush said. "This is a good agreement that will keep our economy growing and our people working. And this Congress must pass it as soon as possible." (Text, p. D-3)

CBO put the cost at $152 billion in fiscal 2008, falling to $124 billion over 11 years.

The chief elements of the House bill were:

● **Individuals.** A basic credit of up to $600 for individuals ($1,200 for couples) would go to those who paid taxes in 2007 on wages or investment income. The check would be reduced by $50 for each $1,000 above an income threshold of $75,000 in adjustable gross income for individuals ($150,000 for couples).

Workers who earned at least $3,000 in 2007 and paid little or no income tax would be eligible for checks of $300 for individuals ($600 for couples filing jointly).

Those eligible for either refund would receive an additional $300 per dependent child living with them.

● **Businesses.** A 50 percent bonus write-off would be available for items purchased and placed in service in 2008 that were subject under existing law to depreciation over 20 years or less. The remaining value of such investments would be depreciated over the life of the item.

Small businesses would be able to write off up to $250,000 for the cost of new equipment in 2008, with the phaseout beginning when total investment for the year reached $800,000.

● **Housing.** The bill proposed a permanent increase in FHA-insured mortgage loans to a maximum of $729,750, along with a one-year increase in the loans that Fannie Mae and Freddie Mac could purchase to a maximum of $729,750.

SENATE COMMITTEE APPROVAL

The Senate Finance Committee approved a significantly expanded stimulus bill, 14-7, on Jan. 30. The add-ons pushed the estimated cost to $158.1 billion in fiscal 2008 and $155.7 billion from fiscal 2008 to 2018, raising objections from House leaders and Republicans on both sides of the Capitol.

Changes in the Senate bill included:

● **Expanded rebates.** Checks of $500 for individuals ($1,000 for couples) would go both to those who paid taxes in 2007 and those who owed no taxes but earned at least $3,000. Unlike the House bill, the measure proposed that Social Security payments count toward the $3,000 minimum. The committee said this would allow 20 million low-income senior citizens who would not be covered under the

House bill to qualify for checks. Disabled veterans living on non-taxable disability compensation would also qualify.

Committee leaders wanted to eliminate any upper limits on income eligibility for the tax rebates, but Democrats in both chambers protested. So the Finance Committee included caps but at double the levels contained in the House-passed bill. As a result, the phaseout of the rebates would start at $150,000 in gross adjusted income for individuals ($300,000 for couples).

● **Business options.** Companies would be able to choose one of three possible tax breaks:

As under the House bill, small businesses would be able to write off up to $250,000 for the cost of new equipment in 2008, with the phaseout beginning when total investment for the year reached $800,000.

Alternatively, businesses could accelerate the write-off of 50 percent of the value of new investments purchased in fiscal 2008, with a 25 percent write-off in each of 2008 and 2009. The remaining value of the investments would be depreciated under existing-law schedules.

As a third option, companies could "carry back" net operating losses from 2006, 2007 and 2008 to reduce taxable income earned during the previous five years, as opposed to the previous two years under existing law.

● **Energy tax breaks.** The bill included extensions of tax credits and deductions for wind and solar power and other renewable sources, as well as for energy-efficient buildings and appliances. The cost was estimated at $700 million in fiscal 2008 and $5.7 billion over 11 years.

Charles E. Grassley of Iowa, the Finance Committee's ranking Republican and an advocate of renewable energy, pushed for the last-minute addition of the energy provisions.

"For energy needs and economy growth, we need to continue renewable-energy provisions without interruption," Grassley said. "The high price of oil helped start the economic downturn. The stimulus package should underscore the nation's commitment to energy efficiency and alternative energy."

● **Unemployment benefits.** Under the bill, jobless workers who exhausted the standard 26 weeks of aid would be able to get 13 additional weeks of federal unemployment benefits. Those in states with high jobless rates would get another 13 weeks on top of that. The estimated cost was $10.1 billion in fiscal 2008 and $9.9 billion from fiscal 2008 to 2018.

Also during the markup, the committee adopted, 20-1, an amendment by John Kerry, D-Mass., and Gordon H. Smith, R-Ore., to expand states' ability to issue mortgage revenue bonds. It contributed $100 million to the first-year cost of the bill and $1.7 billion to the 11-year cost.

Members also agreed to make a payment to coal companies, essentially a rebate of interest paid on unconstitutionally collected taxes and any principal not yet refunded. Democrat John D. Rockefeller IV of West Virginia offered the amendment.

FINAL ACTION

After more than a week of partisan jousting, Senate Democrats gave up efforts to pass a broader bill, settling instead for a few changes to the House's measure. The Senate amendment, adopted 91-6 on Feb. 7, expanded the eligibility for rebate checks to low-income senior citizens, disabled veterans and survivors of disabled veterans, who had been left out of the House version. It also tightened language designed to prevent undocumented immigrants from receiving checks. *(Senate vote 9, p. S-5)*

After adopting the amendment, the Senate passed the revised bill, 81-16. The House cleared it, 380-34, later the same day. *(Senate vote 10, p. S-5; House vote 42, p. H-16)*

The Senate had spent days tied up in maneuvers aimed at forcing — or avoiding — votes on expanding the original House version of the bill.

Initially, Majority Leader Harry Reid, D-Nev., planned to hold a vote on the Finance Committee version, which was expected to fail. At that point, he would call up the House-passed bill and vote on targeted amendments containing pieces of the Finance bill. When he could not get GOP agreement to that plan, he signaled that senators would have to choose between the Finance Committee package and the narrower House bill.

"If the package does not pass, that's the end of the line," he said.

The turning point came Feb. 6, when Democrats fell one vote short of the 60 needed to invoke cloture, thereby limiting debate, on the Finance bill, which had been expanded to include $1 billion for extra low-income home heating assistance, added tax relief for businesses and several other provisions. Reid switched his vote to "nay" to preserve his right to offer a motion to reconsider later, leaving the tally at 58-41. *(Senate vote 8, p. S-5)*

After the cloture motion failed, Reid and Minority Leader Mitch McConnell, R-Ky., reached a deal that preserved some of the Democrats' priorities. McConnell had offered the same deal days before but was rebuffed by Reid.

"Legislation is the art of compromise, and that compromise comes very hard sometimes," Reid said.

"The best thing is to declare the big victory that we've achieved," said Finance Chairman Max Baucus, D-Mont. "This is what's achievable."

Among the provisions left out in the final bill were the temporary extension of unemployment benefits and an extension of renewable energy credits. ■

Loans Keep Automakers Afloat

STRUGGLING DOMESTIC automakers persuaded Congress to finance a $25 billion loan program as part of the fiscal 2009 stopgap spending bill enacted on Sept. 30 (HR 2638 — PL 110-329). But the companies were rebuffed when they returned seeking an immediate bailout aimed at staving off potential bankruptcies.

Given the precarious state of the auto industry and projections of large-scale layoffs, President Bush reluctantly stepped in in December to provide $17.5 billion in immediate, short-term loans. That decision left the toughest questions about the industry's future to the incoming Obama administration.

LEGISLATIVE ACTION
$25 BILLION LOAN

Following intense lobbying by the chief executive officers of the domestic automakers and their supporters in Congress, Democratic leaders included funding for the $25 billion loan as part of the fiscal 2009 continuing resolution. The massive stopgap spending bill was must-pass legislation because it was critical to keeping the government afloat after Sept. 30 in the absence of the unfinished appropriations bills.

The House leadership brought the appropriations package directly to the floor without committee action. The House easily passed it by a vote of 370-58 on Sept. 24. The Senate cleared the measure, 78-12, on Sept. 27. *(House vote 632, p. H-212; Senate vote 208, p. S-46)*

The auto provisions appropriated $7.5 billion to cover the estimated cost to the Treasury of the $25 billion loan to be administered by the Energy Department. The program was authorized in the 2007 energy law (PL 110-140) but had not been funded. The loans were authorized to help automakers retool to produce more fuel-efficient vehicles and meet new federal mileage standards.

Detroit's Big Three automakers — General Motors Corp., Chrysler LLC and Ford Motor Co. — had been talking since August with key Democrats and members of the Michigan delegation about jumpstarting the loan. The deepening U.S. recession and reduced availability of credit had compounded the longer-term financial problems facing the companies. Some were talking of a larger loan of perhaps $50 billion, but lawmakers were clearly not willing to go that far.

In September, the top executives of the Big Three automakers — G. Richard Wagoner Jr., chairman and CEO of GM; Robert Nardelli, chairman and CEO of Chrysler; and Alan Mulally, president and CEO of Ford — were on Capitol Hill urging lawmakers to act by the end of the month.

"This is very, very important to an important industry in our country," said House Speaker Nancy Pelosi, D-Calif. "It's about jobs, jobs, jobs." Senate Majority Leader Harry Reid, D-Nev., agreed, saying it was "extremely important that we do something" to help the industry.

The lobbying blitz came just as lawmakers were trying to absorb the impact of unprecedented government intervention in the financial markets that included takeovers of Fannie Mae, Freddie Mac and the

---

BOX SCORE

BILLS: HR 2638 — PL 110-329; HR 7321, HR 7005.

....

LEGISLATIVE ACTION:

House passed HR 2638, 370-58, on Sept. 24.

Senate cleared HR 2638, 78-12, on Sept. 27.

President signed Sept. 30.

House passed HR 7321, 237-170, on Dec. 10.

Senate rejected cloture on proceeding to HR 7005, a shell for the auto loans, 52-35, on Dec. 11; 60 votes were required for approval.

---

country's largest insurance company, American International Group Inc. On Sept. 18, six days before the House vote on the continuing resolution, Treasury Secretary Henry M. Paulson Jr. began his campaign for a $700 billion rescue package for the financial services industry.

Automakers and their allies took pains to separate themselves from those bailouts, stressing that they were asking for a loan that would be repaid. *(Financial services, p. 7-3)*

"Some critics will call this loan package a bailout. It is not," said John D. Dingell, D-Mich., chairman of the House Energy and Commerce Committee and a staunch supporter of the industry. "These loans amount to a little more than 1 percent of the real bailout — the one that the Bush administration wants for Wall Street at a cost of $700 billion to taxpayers," he said.

Not all Democrats were so enthusiastic. Sen. Bill Nelson of Florida voiced skepticism at a Sept. 12 Senate Energy and Natural Resources Committee energy session when Wagoner urged lawmakers to "move rapidly" on the loan. "I must admit it is hard for me to do that," Nelson said, citing the auto companies' repeated opposition to congressional efforts to raise fuel efficiency standards for cars and trucks.

Some conservative lawmakers said the auto loans were another government bailout for an industry that planned poorly. "I do not support the auto plan," said Judd Gregg of New Hampshire, the top Republican on the Senate Budget Committee. But with the heavy presence of car factories and autoworkers in the battleground election states of Michigan, Ohio and Indiana, Gregg seemed resigned. "Politics wins over policy every time here in a presidential year," he said.

BID FOR MORE AID FALLS SHORT

With the jobless rate reaching 6.6 percent in October and the auto industry in increasingly dire straits, Democratic leaders put aid to carmakers at the top of their agenda for the lame-duck session, which began Nov. 17. Help for the Big Three was one of the first things President-elect Barack Obama called for after his victory, which was aided by Michigan's 17 Electoral College votes; the state also added Democrats to the House majority.

The plan was to tap into the $700 billion financial industry bailout enacted in October (PL 110-343) to give Detroit a quick infusion of money. Although Congress had activated the $25 billion direct-loan program just six weeks earlier, the money was not expected to reach the companies for awhile because it was tied to specific plans for retooling factories and could not be used for other purposes.

Despite the momentum, however, questions remained about whether the automakers could and should survive without federal government intervention. Critics on the right and left pointed out that the companies had been troubled for decades and said the Big Three had done too little to control costs and produce products that satisfied consumer demand.

The Bush administration and congressional Republicans were united in opposing the use of the financial bailout fund, known as the Troubled Assets Relief Program (TARP), to aid the Big Three. The White House said Congress instead should relax restrictions on the $25 billion Energy Department loan.

● **November hearings.** Democratic chairmen Barney Frank of Massachusetts, head of the House Banking Housing and Urban Affairs Committee, and Christopher J. Dodd of Connecticut, who ran the Senate Banking and Infrastructure Committee, invited the CEOs of the Big Three to return to Washington in November to present their case for more federal assistance. As it turned out, the executives did not give their supporters much to work with.

In hearings held by the two committees on Nov. 18-19, the executives said vehicle sales were plunging to levels not seen since World War II and that the companies were burning through cash reserves at a rate that would leave them bankrupt within months. They were armed with findings from the Michigan-based Center for Automotive Research, a nonprofit research group that got some of its support from the industry. The group projected that, given the industry's symbiotic relationship with parts suppliers, dealers and associated businesses, a collapse of the Big Three could result in the loss of almost 3 million jobs and $150 billion in personal income in 2009 alone.

But the auto executives did little to show that they had credible plans for restructuring their companies into viable enterprises or that additional government aid would be more than a short-term fix. In a blunder that seemed to underline their lack of awareness of the mood in Congress and the country, they arrived in Washington in separate corporate luxury jets. "It's almost like seeing a guy show up at the soup kitchen in high hat and tuxedo," Frank quipped.

"I'm not an opponent of private flights by any means," said Republican Patrick T. McHenry of North Carolina, "but the fact that you flew in on your own private jet at tens of thousands of dollars of cost just for you to make your way to Washington is a bit arrogant before you ask the taxpayers for money."

As the lame-duck session came to an end Nov. 20, Pelosi, Reid and other key Democrats said they would give each of the Big Three until Dec. 2 to submit a proposal showing a path to viability that would protect taxpayers and autoworkers. If they did, committees in both chambers would hold hearings, with floor action possible the week of Dec. 8.

"Until they show us a plan, we cannot show them the money," Pelosi said.

● **December hearings.** The three CEOs returned to Washington — in hybrid cars — for a second round of hearings Dec. 4-5, where they increased their request to $34 billion. This time, they came prepared with individual restructuring plans that focused on cost cutting and developing new, more fuel-efficient product lines. The United Auto Workers (UAW) also announced concessions on a health care trust fund and on payments to laid-off workers.

"Our plan dramatically accelerates and expands the restructuring we've been driving . . . for the past several years," GM's Wagoner said in written testimony.

A number of lawmakers remained skeptical that the money would save the ailing companies. Richard C. Shelby of Alabama, the top Republican on the Senate Banking Committee, said the restructuring plans "lack a systematic presentation" of how the companies would use the federal money for their long-term survival. "If you made this presentation to get a bank loan, I suspect any loan officer would sum-

marily dismiss your request," he told the top executives Dec. 4.

GM requested a total of $18 billion in loans and credit but said it needed an immediate $4 billion loan to stay solvent through Dec. 31, and $6 billion more to keep operating through March. Chrysler LLC said it needed $7 billion by the end of the year to avoid bankruptcy. Though Ford Motor Co. requested access to a total of $9 billion in long-term loans, it said it might not need to use them.

The executives, joined by UAW president Ron Gettelfinger, implored the lawmakers not to consider bankruptcy as an option. "In the current environment, a Chapter 11 reorganization is simply not a viable option for restructuring the companies," Gettelfinger said, citing research that "has indicated that the public just won't buy vehicles from a company in bankruptcy."

"Time is of the essence. . . . I believe we could lose General Motors by the end of this month," Gettelfinger said.

Throughout the Banking Committee hearing, Dodd argued that the Treasury and the Federal Reserve were both in a position to extend funding to the ailing industry. "This would be a cleaner way for us to move," Dodd said, adding that it would give Congress time to look more carefully at other options.

As the hearings went into a second day, the Labor Department announced that the economy had lost 533,000 jobs in November, the steepest decline in 34 years. The unemployment rate rose to 6.7 percent, up from 6.6 percent in October, the highest since 1993.

● **House-passed bill shelved.** House and Senate leaders called members back the week of Dec. 8 to consider legislation granting assistance to the domestic automakers.

On Dec. 10, the House voted to make a $14 billion short-term "bridge loan" available. The bill (HR 7321) passed 237-170, with the support of 32 mostly Rust Belt Republicans. *(House vote 690, p. H-232)*

The measure was the result of intense negotiations between Democratic leaders and the White House, spurred by the enormity of the November job losses. Given the administration's refusal to use the financial services bailout fund for the automakers, Democrats relented on redirecting the $25 billion loan.

The bill directed the president to choose one or more administrators from the executive branch who would be authorized to disburse the bridge loans to the Big Three automakers. The administrators would bring together companies, unions, creditors and other players to negotiate long-term restructuring plans, which automakers would have to submit by March 31. If the administrators had not approved a company's plan by the deadline, the company's loans would be recalled immediately.

But Senate Republicans — especially those from states that were home to foreign-owned auto plants — were staunchly opposed to the bill, and White House attempts to sway them fell flat.

When it was clear that the House-passed bill would not fly, Bob Corker, the junior senator from Tennessee, emerged as the surprise GOP point man in trying to assemble an alternative. His plan would have required the automakers to reduce their debt obligations by at least two-thirds and set "a date certain" for cutting autoworkers' pay and benefits to levels equal to those paid by foreign automakers with U.S. operations, which were largely non-union.

Senators spent a day in tense bargaining sessions but were unable to reach a final deal on some of their biggest concerns, especially on the timing of concessions by union workers. "We are about three words, three words away from a deal," Corker said on the Senate floor.

But with the talks deadlocked, Reid decided to bring the effort to a close. "Although we have worked and worked — and we could spend all night tonight, tomorrow, Saturday and Sunday — we are not going to get to the finish line," he said on the floor. "That is just the way it is. There is too much difference between the two sides."

On Dec. 11, the Senate rejected, 52-35, a motion to invoke cloture on proceeding to a House tax bill (HR 7005) that was to serve as a shell for the Senate's auto bailout language. The vote was eight shy of the 60 votes needed to prevail. Immediately after, Reid said the Senate would adjourn until January with no further roll call votes. *(Senate vote 215, p. S-47)*

"I dread looking at Wall Street tomorrow. It's not going to be a pleasant sight," Reid said.

BUSH STEPS IN

Before the markets opened the next day, however, the White House announced that it was considering stepping in to prevent a collapse of the automakers.

Seven days later, on Dec. 19, Bush announced that the administration would immediately make available $13.4 billion in low-interest, short-term loans to GM and Chrysler in return for concessions and restructuring. Among other things, he said, that meant "putting their retirement plans on a sustainable footing" and "persuading bondholders to convert their debt into capital."

In an about-face, Bush said the funds would come from the $700 billion financial industry bailout program. The president said he acted because Congress had failed to do so. "The only way to avoid a collapse of the U.S. auto industry is for the executive branch to step in," he said.

The White House said an additional $4 billion would become available in February if Congress gave Treasury access to the second $350 billion tranche of the TARP funding.

Of the initial $13.4 billion, Treasury officials said, $9 billion was earmarked for GM and $4 billion for Chrysler. The second round of $4 billion would all go to GM. The plan paralleled much of the House-passed bill, giving the companies until March 31, 2009, to put restructuring plans in place or pay back the loans immediately.

Under the plan, the government would take warrants in the participating companies, and the companies would have to accept restrictions on executive compensation and issue no dividends for the life of the loans.

Obama quickly supported the administration. "Today's actions are a necessary step to help avoid a collapse in our auto industry that would have devastating consequences for our economy and our workers," Obama said. "With the short-term assistance provided by this package, the auto companies must bring all their stakeholders together — including labor, dealers, creditors and suppliers — to make the hard choices necessary to achieve long-term viability."

He urged the companies not to "squander" their chance to restructure and become competitive.

The day before his announcement, Bush said at a Washington think tank forum that he wanted to avoid leaving Obama with a major catastrophe that would further rattle financial markets. "I'm worried about a disorderly bankruptcy and what it would do to the psychology of the markets," Bush said

Asked whether a court-supervised Chapter 11 bankruptcy reorganization was an option, Bush, replied, "I think under normal circumstances, no question, the bankruptcy court is the best way to sort through credit and debt and restructuring. . . . These aren't normal circumstances. That's the problem." ■

Chapter 8

ENERGY &
ENVIRONMENT

With Rallying Cry, 'Drill, Baby, Drill,' GOP Brings End to Offshore Ban

REPUBLICANS SCORED a victory on one of their priorities for the year: ending a moratorium on new offshore oil and gas drilling. Bolstered by growing public outrage over the high price of gasoline, they succeeded in forcing Democrats to lift the 26-year-old ban, which prohibited expanded drilling off the Atlantic and Pacific coasts.

The moratorium had been included in the Interior Department appropriations bill every year since 1982. Supporters, including coastal lawmakers from both parties, said it was essential to protecting the coast from the risk of a catastrophic oil spill. Those who wanted to lift the ban argued that expanding domestic supplies of oil and gas was critical to bringing down prices and reducing a dangerous dependence on foreign oil. They also said that improved drilling techniques had greatly minimized the risk of a major oil spill.

Democrats' energy strategy focused on promoting the production and use of renewable fuels and encouraging conservation and energy efficiency. They worked through the spring and summer to produce a set of tax incentives aimed at achieving those goals, and in the fall they were able to clear a $16.9 billion energy tax package by attaching it to a massive financial services rescue bill (PL 110-343). *(Taxes, p. 4-11)*

But the Democrats were caught off guard by the swift change in public sentiment on domestic drilling driven by record gasoline prices. By July, a Pew Research Center poll found that 60 percent of voters said developing new energy sources was a higher priority than protecting the environment.

Surprised at having to play defense, Senate Majority Leader Harry Reid of Nevada, House Speaker Nancy Pelosi of California and others concentrated on preventing votes that would put their rank and file on the spot in advance of the November election — even when it meant derailing major legislation such as the annual spending bills and the defense authorization act. They cast their opponents as shills for the big oil companies, which strongly supported open drilling, and tried to redirect the debate with bills to curb energy speculation and help low-income families with heating bills.

Republicans, meanwhile, spent much of the summer hammering the Democrats, gaining traction on what they hoped would be a potent campaign issue. Day after day, GOP senators went to the floor to speak about drilling, outline amendments they wanted to offer and demand votes that would put Democrats in an uncomfortable position.

"Why is this so hard?" Christopher S. Bond, R-Mo., asked in a speech similar to many others. "Why are Democrats so desperate to deny the relief the American people need and are demanding?"

When Congress left for the August recess, Republicans staged daily

BOX SCORE

BILLS: HR 6515, S 3268, S 3186, HR 6899, HR 6604

LEGISLATIVE ACTION:

House rejected HR 6515 (leases), 244-173, on July 17 (two-thirds majority required).

Senate rejected cloture on S 3268 (futures trading), 50-43, on July 25 (60 votes required).

Senate rejected cloture on S 3186 (LIHEAP), 50-35, on July 26 (60 votes required).

Senate rejected cloture on S 3001 (defense authorization), 51-39, on July 31 (60 votes required).

House passed HR 6899 (offshore drilling), 236-189, on Sept. 16.

House passed HR 6604 (futures trading), 283-133, on Sept. 18.

protests on the House floor, as various members flew back to Washington to demand that Pelosi return the House to session and have an up-or-down vote on offshore drilling.

Pressure for action intensified when GOP presidential nominee John McCain endorsed offshore drilling. Democratic nominee Barack Obama said in early August that he would accept it as part of a larger package. A number of Democratic congressional candidates followed suit. At the Republican National Convention, delegates erupted into a chant of "Drill, baby, drill!" as their vice presidential nominee, Alaska Gov. Sarah Palin, extolled the advantages of domestic oil production.

Finally, in September, Republicans used their trump card. Before lawmakers could adjourn to campaign for the election, they had to pass a continuing resolution, or CR, to keep federal domestic agencies and foreign aid going into the new year. Nine of the 12 fiscal 2009 spending bills had fallen by the wayside. Republicans threatened to block passage of a CR unless the drilling moratorium in the Interior-Environment section was dropped. At that point, Democrats saw no alternative. In addition to omitting the moratorium, the continuing resolution (PL 110-329) allowed the expiration of a ban on drilling for oil shale in the Rocky Mountain West.

LEGISLATIVE ACTION
APPROPRIATIONS BILLS

The fiscal 2009 appropriations process effectively broke down in June, when House Democrats halted action rather than allow Republicans on the Appropriations Committee to force votes on drilling.

At a June 26 committee markup, Jerry Lewis of California, the panel's senior Republican, pressed Chairman David R. Obey, D-Wis., to promise that he would bring up the Interior-Environment spending bill immediately after the July Fourth recess. "If the gentleman wants to set the agenda of the committee, he needs to go out and get 30 Republicans elected," Obey responded.

Lewis next tried to insert the Interior bill into the measure that was scheduled for consideration — the spending bill for the departments of Labor, Health and Human Services, and Education. Republicans planned to offer several energy amendments, including proposals to expand offshore drilling, open the Arctic National Wildlife Refuge (ANWR) to drilling and allow a leasing program for oil shale in Western states.

Obey called off the markup. "I'll see them in September on a CR," he said. Republicans said Democrats were acting out of fear that the GOP amendments might be adopted, not an unrealistic outcome given voters' growing concern about high gas prices.

Acting with Pelosi's support, Obey held no further appropriations markups. Congress ultimately cleared just three fiscal 2009 spending bills: Defense, Homeland Security and Military Construction-Veterans Affairs. The need to fund the remaining departments is what made it mandatory to pass a continuing resolution.

'USE IT OR LOSE IT'

In response to persistent GOP calls for legislation to open public lands and offshore areas to new drilling, House leaders brought a series of energy-related bills to the floor in June and July.

The most contentious was what was dubbed "use it or lose it" legislation requiring that oil and gas companies with leases on federal lands drill or risk losing their leases. Democrats said oil companies already had leases on 68 million acres of government land and waters that they were not exploiting. Before talking about opening new areas, they argued, the companies should be required to use the leases they held.

In a strategy that infuriated Republicans, Pelosi brought two versions of the bill to the floor under suspension of the rules. The expedited procedure required a two-thirds vote and barred amendments, which meant Republicans could not offer drilling proposals. Both bills won a majority, but the votes fell short of the two-thirds threshold and the bills were rejected.

The first bill (HR 6251) would have required the annual sale of oil and natural gas leases on public lands, but those who held such leases would have to proceed with exploration and drilling or relinquish their leases and be barred from getting more. The measure fell, 223-195, on June 26, 56 votes short. *(House vote, p. 469, p. H-156)*

Democrats tried again the following month with a new bill (HR 6515) adding several provisions to pick up more support. They included the annual sale of oil and gas leases in the National Petroleum Reserve, a 23-million-acre territory on Alaska's North Slope where oil exploration was permitted. Other provisions would have sped up construction of oil pipelines from drilling sites in the reserve to the existing Trans-Alaska Pipeline System and prohibited the export of Alaskan oil. The bill was rejected, 244-173, on July 17, 34 votes short of the necessary two-thirds. *(House vote 511, p. H-170)*

The White House threatened to veto both versions, saying, "It is incredible that Congress is considering legislation that would reduce domestic oil supply. Congress should instead remove barriers to domestic production of oil."

The House rejected another Democratic energy bill (HR 6346), brought to the floor under suspension of the rules June 24. The measure, which was aimed at retail gasoline "price gouging," was defeated, 276-146. It would have authorized the Federal Trade Commission to impose fines and other punishments on anyone who charged "unconscionably excessive" prices for motor fuels during a presidentially declared "energy emergency." The White House issued a veto threat against it. *(House vote 448, p. H-150)*

Two Democratic energy bills passed June 26. The first (HR 6052), passed 322-98, would have provided transit agencies with grants to expand services and subsidize fares. The second (HR 6377), passed 402-19 under suspension of the rules, would have directed federal regulators to take action to tighten oversight of trading in the oil futures market. Later, on Sept. 18, the House passed a similar bill (HR 6604), by a vote of 283-133. *(House votes 467, 468, p. H-156; House vote 608, p. H-204)*

The Senate did not take up any of the measures.

SENATE STALEMATE

In the weeks before the August recess, the skirmishing over expanded drilling produced a stalemate on the Senate floor that stalled a number of bills, most notably the fiscal 2009 defense authorization measure. The standoff also prevented Democrats from bringing up several other major bills that they had hoped to pass before the break.

● **Energy futures speculation.** A bill aimed at curbing oil speculation became the focal point of the GOP campaign to get a prolonged floor debate on offshore drilling.

The bill (S 3268) would have increased staffing at the Commodity Futures Trading Commission and limited the number of futures contracts an investor could own. Democrats presented it as a first step toward bringing down gasoline prices. But Republicans said the legislation addressed only a tiny part of the problem, and they insisted on a chance to offer multiple amendments aimed at increasing domestic energy supplies.

"They want a debate that never ends," said Majority Whip Richard J. Durbin, D-Ill.

Reid used a procedure known as "filling the amendment tree," offering a string of amendments that left no room for Republicans to offer their own. He then moved to invoke cloture, a step that would have ended the GOP filibuster. The cloture motion failed, 50-43, on July 25, well short of the 60 votes that were required. *(Senate vote 184, p. S-41)*

GOP leaders vowed to use every procedural opportunity to keep debating the bill. "We'll be on this as long as it takes," said Minority Leader Mitch McConnell of Kentucky. "Senate Republicans will refuse to get off this subject. This is washing over the Democrats, and they're scrambling to avoid it."

● **Low-income heating assistance.** On the following day, July 26, Republicans turned back a cloture motion on another Democratic energy bill (S 3186), this one aimed at boosting assistance for low-income families struggling with energy costs. The measure would have nearly doubled fiscal 2008 funding for the Low Income Home Energy Assistance Program, or LIHEAP, with an infusion of $2.5 billion.

Republicans insisted that the focus should remain on amending the futures speculation bill. McConnell said Democrats were "trying to take us off the subject." The motion on proceeding to the bill failed, 50-35, 10 votes short of the number needed to invoke cloture. *(Senate vote 187, p. S-42)*

● **Defense authorization.** The biggest casualty of the partisan skirmishing in advance of the August recess was the fiscal 2009 defense authorization bill (S 3001). While members on both sides considered it must-pass legislation, the battle over oil drilling amendments pushed action into September. *(Defense authorization, p. 6-3)*

Carl Levin, D-Mich., chairman of the Armed Services Committee, worked behind the scenes to seek agreement to limit amendments. He argued that it was important to pass the defense bill early, given the busy floor schedule anticipated in September and the lack of any certainty that there would be a lame-duck session. He was supported by John W. Warner of Virginia, who was standing in as ranking Republican on the panel while McCain was out campaigning.

Reid asked for a unanimous consent agreement July 26 to allow the defense bill to come to the floor and limit amendments to those considered germane. But McConnell objected and pledged not to consent to any agreement on the bill until his demands on votes on energy legislation were addressed. "We all want to do the defense authorization bill, but right now the No. 1 issue in the country is the price of gas at the pump," said McConnell. "Why would we want to

get off that issue and go to anything else?"

On July 31, the Senate rejected a cloture motion to proceed to the bill; the vote was 51-39. *(Senate vote 195, p. S-43)*

(By the time lawmakers returned in September, partisan sparring had shifted to the earmarks issue, and the Senate cleared the bill Sept. 27.)

DEMOCRATS' DRILLING BILL

After resisting for months, House Democratic leaders responded in September by passing a bill to authorize coastal states to permit oil and gas drilling 50 miles offshore. It was a major concession designed to prevent defections by moderate members of their own caucus. The House passed the bill (HR 6899) by a vote of 236-189 on Sept. 16, with just 15 Republicans supporting it. *(House vote 599, p. H-202)*

The Senate was not expected to take up the bill, but the vote allowed House Democrats, particularly those in tight election races, to go on record in support of drilling. At the same time, the measure included Democratic priorities such as incentives for renewable energy and energy-efficient buildings, similar to those offered in a Senate tax bill.

Most Republicans said the measure was a sham because the revenue would be devoted entirely to alternative energy. They said states would be unlikely to allow drilling near their shores if they did not get any of the royalties. Lewis called it a "backdoor disincentive." The White House threatened a veto.

The bill, which Democrats described as a compromise, included provisions to:

▶ Allow oil and natural gas drilling in areas of the outer continental shelf that were 100 miles or more from the coast.

▶ Permit leases for drilling 50 to 100 miles offshore on the outer continental shelf if a state chose to allow it.

▶ Require energy companies to explore their existing oil and gas leases or lose them.

▶ Expedite oil and gas production in Alaska's National Petroleum Reserve.

▶ Keep certain areas off-limits to petroleum companies, including the eastern Gulf of Mexico off the coast of Florida and the historic Georges Bank fishery in New England.

▶ Lift a moratorium — perpetuated in the Interior Department spending bill — on an oil shale leasing program for Colorado, Utah and Wyoming, but only if each state decided to move ahead with its leases.

▶ Require utilities to generate 15 percent of their energy from renewable sources by 2020.

▶ Use the new oil and gas royalties to pay for incentives designed to promote energy efficiency, renewable energy, or carbon capture and sequestration.

The bill also included a variety of tax credits for renewables such as wind and solar energy, as well as new tax breaks for coal projects that captured carbon, fueling stations for natural gas vehicles and energy conservation.

"I don't know why my Republican colleagues can't take 'yes' for an answer," said cosponsor Gene Green, D-Texas. "If you want to drill in

our country, this is the bill."

By a vote of 191-226, the House rejected a GOP effort to delay the bill by recommitting it to the Natural Resources Committee with instructions to substitute language repealing the moratorium on drilling in the Pacific, Atlantic and the eastern Gulf of Mexico, while allowing states to restrict drilling 25 to 50 miles offshore. *(House vote 598, p. H-202)*

Nick J. Rahall II, D-W.Va., chairman of the House Natural Resources Committee, sought to reassure pro-environmentalist Democrats that lifting the moratorium would not allow oil companies to start drilling at will because the leasing process contained "built-in environmental safeguards."

"Unlike what [the Republicans] may lead us to believe," Rahall said, "lifting the moratoria does not immediately mean there's going to be drilling and certainly no immediate relief at the pump for taxpayers."

GOP DECLARES VICTORY

Democratic leaders acknowledged after the August recess that they did not have the votes to clear a resolution to keep the federal government running after Oct. 1 without dropping the moratorium language. Republicans vowed to fight any spending package that extended the drilling ban, and those in the Senate had demonstrated they had the votes to do so.

Democrats had floated the idea of including provisions from the House-passed drilling bill, but they dropped that idea and decided instead to simply eliminate the language that had imposed the ban, thereby allowing drilling as close as three miles from shore. The ban on developing oil shale deposits in the Rocky Mountains was also allowed to expire.

"Thank you to the American people for getting it right down to the point: 'Drill, drill, drill,' said they," said Sen. Pete V. Domenici, R-N.M. "And that's why we're here today, because that was finally heard by the majority party."

Policy experts and moderate Democrats said that once the ban had been lifted, it was unlikely it could ever be reinstated wholesale, even under a Democratic Congress and president.

Rahall said the "sea change" by Democrats reflected the reality of future high energy prices, relentless campaigning by the GOP and, most of all, pressure from constituents. "We have to listen to them," he said, "and that's what they're saying they want."

The Interior Department's Minerals Management Service, whose job was to lease and manage offshore energy production, said the process of completing environmental reviews, holding lease sales, conducting geologic studies and building new infrastructure could take five to 10 years before any new offshore drilling could begin.

Some lawmakers said that would give the next Congress and the new administration a chance to work out some restrictions and barriers to drilling in the newly opened waters, including strict permitting processes and environmental reviews. ■

Senate Republicans Sink Climate Bill

SENATE DEMOCRATS ABANDONED efforts to hold a floor vote on climate change legislation (S 3036), after Republicans succeeded in forcing a prolonged floor debate that had no apparent end.

The bill, which Democrats had made a priority in the 110th Congress, was aimed at establishing a comprehensive national policy to address global warming. It would have capped emissions of greenhouse gases and set up a market-based trading program for businesses to meet the cap. It would have redistributed trillions of dollars collected from polluters to industries, states and electricity consumers over the following four decades.

The chief sponsors were Democrat Barbara Boxer of California, independent Joseph I. Lieberman of Connecticut and Republican John W. Warner of Virginia. The Senate Environment and Public Works Committee, which Boxer chaired, approved the bill in late 2007. *(2007 Almanac, p. 10-6)*

While the environmental community pushed hard for the measure, even supporters acknowledged that it was an uphill battle to secure Senate passage. The scope of the bill was vast, and opponents argued it would raise the price of energy during a summer of record-high gas prices. Still, sponsors at least wanted to get the Senate on the record on several amendments that could help shape a climate change bill in the 111th Congress.

But Republicans were able to prevent the Senate from even taking up amendments, much less voting on them. As a result, the Senate never addressed issues that could be critical to any future legislation, such as the role of nuclear power or whether to pre-empt more stringent action at the state level.

HIGHLIGHTS

Following are highlights of the plan laid out in the Senate bill:

● **Greenhouse gas emission cap.** Utilities, factories, natural gas producers, petroleum refiners, producers of hydrofluorocarbons and similar facilities would have to reduce their levels of greenhouse gas emissions by 19 percent by 2020 and by 71 percent by 2050. Greenhouse gas producers would have to directly reduce their own emissions or purchase allowances from other producers that exceeded requirements. Gas producers could meet a portion of their required reduction through domestic and international offset credits, such as for planting trees. Violations would be treated as if they were violations of the Clean Air Act.

● **Trading mechanism.** A trading market for greenhouse gas allowances would be created, with oversight and regulatory boards. The market would include an automatic mechanism to reduce costs by releasing additional allowances when prices rose to unexpected levels.

● **Revenue.** The Congressional Budget Office calculated that the bill would raise $901.1 billion in revenue over 10 years from auctioning emission allowances.

● **Hardship assistance and mitigation.**

  ‣ An estimated $800 billion in tax benefits would be provided for consumers "in need of assistance related to energy costs." In addition, revenue from the cap-and-trade system would be used to provide almost $575 billion to industries for adjustment assistance and $190 billion for worker training and assistance programs.

  ‣ States, localities and Indian tribes would be eligible for an estimat-

ed $911 billion to reduce the impact of emission limits, $254 billion for adjustment assistance and $171 billion for mass transit.

  ‣ States would also be eligible for an estimated $566 billion for early action activities, $253 billion for natural resources programs and $237 billion for wildlife adaptation.

  ‣ Federal programs to alleviate the impact of climate change on natural resources would be allocated an estimated $288 billion.

● **Immediate action.** A tracking system for significant emissions from across the country would be created, with rewards to companies that took early action to reduce emissions and use renewable-energy technologies. Money would be provided for research and development of new technologies.

LEGISLATIVE ACTION
SENATE FLOOR ACTION

The Senate began June 2, voting, 74-14, to bring up S 3036 and start what promised to be the most serious congressional debate yet on how to respond to climate change. *(Senate vote 141, p. S-31)*

But hopes for that debate evaporated June 4, when Majority Leader Harry Reid, D-Nev., offered a substitute amendment by Boxer that was to serve as the base legislation. Minority Leader Mitch McConnell, R-Ky., quickly objected to a routine motion to dispense with reading the measure, forcing clerks to read the entire 500-page amendment aloud. McConnell said he was protesting the majority party's handling of the unrelated confirmation process for appellate court nominees.

When the clerks had finished more than eight hours later, an angry Reid complained about GOP delaying tactics and demanded a live quorum call, asking the sergeant at arms to compel senators to appear in the chamber. The request was rejected, 27-28. *(Senate vote 143, p. S-31)*

Reid and McConnell could not agree on how many amendments to allow. Reid proposed five amendments per side, with action completed by the end of the week. Republicans disagreed. "We shouldn't get off this bill until the July recess because of the tremendous impact it has on our country," said Bob Corker, R-Tenn. "I hope we have 40 or 50 amendments. I hope we have hundreds and hundreds of hours of debate."

Republicans particularly disliked the idea of collecting and redistributing trillions of dollars in fees from polluters, saying it would increase energy prices for Americans. The White House threatened a veto, listing dozens of objections.

Supporters said the critics were ignoring provisions designed to ease the sting of higher costs for consumers and to invest in new technologies that could drive down energy costs. "This bill, in fact, will lead us to a strong economy, with the creation of millions of new jobs," Boxer said.

When Reid attempted on June 6 to limit the debate on Boxer's amendment itself, the motion to invoke cloture was rejected, 48-36, a dozen votes short of the 60 needed. Reid pulled the bill from floor consideration, and the Senate went on to other issues. *(Senate vote 145, p. S-31)*

McConnell sought to put the onus on the Democrats. "The majority says climate change is the most important issue facing the planet," he said. "Yet they've rushed the debate on that topic and brought the bill to a premature end." ∎

Chapter 9

HEALTH, EDUCATION, EMPLOYMENT & LABOR, & LEGAL AFFAIRS

Over Veto, Lawmakers Block Pay Reduction for Medicare Doctors

CONGRESS CANCELED a scheduled 10.6 percent cut in payments to physicians who treated Medicare patients, overriding President Bush's veto. The bill froze the existing payment rates and allowed a 1.1 percent increase in 2009. The cost was offset mainly by reducing bonus payments to private plans known as Medicare Advantage. The measure became law over the president's objection on July 15 (HR 6331 — PL 110-275).

Payments to physicians who treated Medicare patients were subject to a cost control formula enacted in 1997 as part of the Balanced Budget Act (PL 105-33). The rates were based on a preset spending cap that required cuts if the cost of the health care program for the elderly and disabled exceeded the limit. *(1997 Almanac, p. 6-5)*

Since 2002, the formula had required reductions in doctors' rates, but Congress regularly stepped in to avert the cuts. In late 2007, lawmakers voted to delay for six months a 10 percent rate cut that was scheduled to go into effect Jan. 1, 2008, and to give physicians a 0.5 percent increase during that time (PL 110-173). *(2007 Almanac, p. 12-7)*

That gave Congress until July 1 to decide how to address what would have been a 10.6 percent cut. Doctors said the reduction was unaffordable and that if it took effect it might mean they would begin refusing new Medicare patients. The prospect of physicians turning away seniors on Medicare made the issue one of paramount importance to Congress.

While there was broad, bipartisan support for postponing the pay reduction, Republicans opposed paying for it through cuts to Medicare Advantage. The program, created by Republicans in the 2003 Medicare overhaul (PL 108-173), allowed private managed-care plans to provide benefits to seniors in place of the government. *(2003 Almanac, pp. 11-3, 11-10)*

The Government Accountability Office, Congressional Budget Office (CBO) and Medicare Payment Advisory Commission had all said that Medicare Advantage plans were overpaid compared with traditional Medicare, making the plans a target for Democrats.

However, the Bush administration and many Republicans regarded the private plans as the future of Medicare, enabling patient choice and providing private sector solutions for the entitlement program.

Democrats tried to cut payments to the Medicare Advantage plans in 2007, but they were thwarted by Bush's veto threat and by his GOP allies in the Senate. In 2008, House Democrats opted to see what their Senate colleagues could get through that chamber.

The first try in the Senate collapsed when Republicans blocked an attempt by Max Baucus, D-Mont., chairman of the Finance Commit-

---

BOX SCORE

BILL: HR 6331 — PL 110-275

LEGISLATIVE ACTION:

Senate rejected motion to invoke cloture on S 3101, 54-39, on June 12 (60 votes required).

House passed HR 6331, 355-59, on June 24.

Senate rejected motion to invoke cloture on HR 6331, 58-40, on June 26 (60 votes required).

Senate invoked cloture on HR 6331, 69-30, on July 9 and cleared the bill by voice vote.

President vetoed the bill July 15.

House passed the bill over the president's veto, 383-41, on July 15 (two-thirds vote required).

Senate passed the bill over the president's veto, 70-26, on July 15, thereby enacting it into law (two-thirds vote required).

---

tee, to bring up a bill (S 3101) paid for mainly through cuts to Medicare Advantage.

Anxious to demonstrate to voters that they were not dropping the ball, House leaders quickly put together their own legislation (HR 6331) and passed it overwhelmingly, handing the Senate a bill just a week before the July 1 deadline. However, Republicans were able to block Senate leaders from bringing up the House bill, and Congress left for the July Fourth recess without acting on the pay cut.

After the recess, Senate Majority Leader Harry Reid, D-Nev., again tried to bring up the House bill. This time, the effort was rescued at the last minute by the surprise appearance in the chamber of the ailing Sen. Edward M. Kennedy, D-Mass., who had been away from Washington during treatment for brain cancer. Kennedy's return drew a standing ovation and put the votes for the bill over the top. The measure cleared after several former GOP opponents voted to support it.

That did not end the fight, however: The president vetoed the bill, citing the cuts to Medicare Advantage, but both chambers voted to override him, thereby enacting the bill into law without his signature. *(Veto text, p. D-14)*

HIGHLIGHTS

The following are the main elements of the legislation, with costs and offsets estimated by CBO. The bill:

● **Medicare physician payments.** Canceled the 10.6 percent cut in payments to physicians treating Medicare patients scheduled to take effect July 1. The measure froze existing payment rates for 18 months and provided for a 1.1 percent increase in 2009. CBO said the change would cost $94 billion over both six years (fiscal 2008 through 2013) and 11 years (fiscal 2008 through 2018). After 2009, the rates would revert to the levels in prior law, requiring physicians' fees to be reduced by 21 percent in 2010.

● **Preventive and mental health services.** Expanded the coverage of preventive services for some beneficiaries and reduced the 50 percent co-payment for mental health services to 20 percent, which was the usual co-payment rate for regular medical services such as doctor visits. The combined cost was estimated at $1.9 billion over six years and $8.7 billion over 11 years.

● **Low-income beneficiaries.** Allowed more beneficiaries to qualify for low-income assistance by adjusting asset requirements. For example, the measure excluded life insurance from the asset test applied to beneficiaries. CBO estimated the cost at $2.2 billion over six years and $7.8 billion over 11 years.

● **Medicare Improvement Fund.** Created a new fund available to

the secretary of Health and Human Services to make improvements to Medicare Part A and Part B benefits. The fund replaced an earlier fund. CBO estimated that it would save $3.1 billion in 2013 but increase costs by a total of $18.9 billion over 11 years.

● **Medical suppliers.** Postponed for 18 months a Bush administration plan to require providers of home medical equipment to bid for Medicare business. The program was expected to save $1 billion a year when fully implemented. But many lawmakers were concerned about the bidding process because suppliers of the equipment — known as durable medical equipment — had complained that they were unfairly prevented from bidding or that companies unfamiliar with the business won bids. Some seniors said they worried that the confusing process could result in them losing access to needed medical equipment such as oxygen, walkers and hospital beds. The change was not expected to affect the budget.

● **Medicare Advantage.** Offset the cost of the bill primarily by reductions to Medicare Advantage. The legislation phased out "indirect medical education" payments, which went to Medicare Advantage plans that had teaching hospitals in their service area. It also required fee-for-service plans — a subset of Medicare Advantage — to establish networks with health care providers, thereby reducing costs by slowing the rate of the growth of the plans.

Previously, the fee-for-service plans were not required to have provider networks, and doctors could choose to accept or reject plan payment at the point of service. CBO estimated that the changes would reduce spending by $13.6 billion over six years and $48.7 billion over 11 years.

● **Welfare.** Extended the Temporary Assistance for Needy Families supplemental grant program though fiscal 2009. CBO estimated the extension would cost $300 million over both six years and 11 years.

LEGISLATIVE ACTION
SENATE ACTION STALLED

Senate Democrats began June 12 by trying to bring Baucus' Medicare bill (S 3101) to the floor, but Republicans denied them the 60-vote majority needed to limit debate on a motion to begin considering the legislation. The vote was 54-39. Democrats were closer than they seemed, however: Reid changed his vote to "no" to be on the winning side, a procedural move to retain his right to try again, and five Democrats missed the vote. *(Senate vote 149, p. S-32)*

The Republicans' main objection was Baucus' plan to use cuts to Medicare Advantage to pay for most of the bill.

The bill would have canceled the pay cut and instead given doctors a 1.1 percent pay increase in 2009. The bill also proposed to extend many expiring Medicare provisions, expand Medicare's coverage of preventive services and modify the rules governing eligibility for the Medicare Savings Program.

Baucus maintained that the bill would not greatly affect most Medicare Advantage plans. He said it would gradually eliminate the bonus payments some plans received for being located in areas with teaching hospitals. It also would limit the growth of private fee-for-service plans.

"By far, the best option for getting a Medicare bill done this year is the bill on which we will vote today," Baucus said.

Before the vote, Reid rejected a GOP request for a cloture vote on an alternative Medicare bill written by the senior Republican on the Finance Committee, Charles E. Grassley of Iowa. Grassley's bill would have provided doctors the same pay increase as Baucus' legislation,

but without changes to the Medicare Advantage private fee-for-service plans. To pay for his bill, Grassley would have eliminated the same bonus payments for teaching hospitals, and he would have made two small changes in Medicaid, the health entitlement for the poor, that together would have yielded about $2.8 billion in savings, according to CBO.

With the failure of the Baucus bill, Baucus and Grassley were widely expected to restart stalled negotiations on a compromise bill.

HOUSE FLOOR ACTION

Although House Democrats expected that the final bill would come from the Senate, they lost faith that Senate negotiators would send them a bill before the July Fourth recess.

On June 24, the House passed its bill (HR 6331), 355-59 — enough to overcome a presidential veto. *(House vote 443, p. H-148)*

Although the GOP leadership urged Republicans to vote against the bill, at least a dozen of them changed their votes from "nay" to "yea" as the votes were tallied. Lawmakers from both sides were hoping to go home during the recess and tell physicians and patients that they did something to keep doctors from leaving Medicare.

"This overwhelming vote should send a strong signal to the Senate," Majority Leader Steny H. Hoyer, D-Md., said in a statement.

SENATE ACTION DELAYED

Two days after the House vote, Reid tried to bring up the House bill. But the Senate refused, by a vote of 58-40, to invoke cloture to proceed to the legislation, just shy of the 60 votes needed to move on. *(Senate vote 160, p. S-35)*

"We'll be back, and you'll have another opportunity to vote for this," said Reid, who again changed his vote to "nay."

Minority Leader Mitch McConnell, R-Ky., offered a motion to extend the existing physician payment rates for 30 days, but Reid objected.

Republicans were upset at having only one option to vote — in the form of a House bill — instead of getting a chance to support a tentative compromise that Baucus and Grassley had worked out earlier in the week.

"This is a terrible way for Congress to do business," said John Cornyn, R-Texas. He called the bill "a partisan proposal here that we're being asked to take or leave."

McConnell said that Grassley would lead negotiations to produce a new Senate bill that more Republicans would support.

Congress left for the July Fourth recess, missing the July 1 deadline. The administration, however, announced it would not apply the cut immediately, instead holding doctors' claims for 10 business days — until July 15 — to give Congress more time to pass a bill. Over the recess, bill supporters, including the American Medical Association, which represents physicians, launched a flurry of political ads aimed at swaying politically vulnerable Republican lawmakers.

SENATE CLEARS BILL

Reid tried yet again July 9. The debate was filled with partisan rhetoric, and Democrats appeared to be one vote short of the 60 votes they needed — until Kennedy, who had surgery June 2 for a malignant brain tumor, made a surprise return to cast his first vote in more than six weeks. In one of the most dramatic moments of the 110th Congress, Kennedy's presence electrified the chamber. Sen. Barack Obama of Illinois, then the presumed Democratic presidential nominee, entered

with him, an arm around his shoulder. As they walked through the door, stunned fellow senators, aides and gallery watchers broke into lengthy applause.

Once Kennedy voted, nine Republicans joined him, providing a wide enough margin to invoke cloture and to override a threatened veto of the bill, with votes to spare. The cloture vote was 69-30. The Senate then cleared the bill by voice vote. *(Senate vote 169, p. S-37)*

Republicans seemed philosophical. "We've had a very dramatic moment in the room here," said Kay Bailey Hutchison of Texas. "I voted for the bill. It's not the way I would have written it."

Cornyn, who continued to criticize the bill, explained his vote for it. "It reversed the cut. That's the commitment I made to the physicians in my state," he said.

VETO OVERRIDE

Bush vetoed the bill July 15, and his veto was overridden by both chambers the same day. The House vote was 383-41, surpassing the two-thirds majority required by 100 votes. The Senate followed suit with a 70-26 vote that enacted the bill into law. *(House vote 491, p. H-164; Senate vote 177, p. S-39)* ∎

Mental Health Parity Becomes Law

AFTER MORE THAN A DECADE of effort, Congress cleared a bill requiring that mental health and addiction benefits be equal in cost and scope to traditional medical benefits. Lawmakers included the measure in a financial sector rescue package, which President Bush signed into law Oct. 3 (HR 1424 — PL 110-343).

Some, but not all, insurers offered equal benefits for mental health, and mental health advocates argued that patients needing treatment often had to pay higher co-payments and face stricter treatment limits and restrictions on out-of-network coverage.

The legislation did not require health plans to offer mental health benefits; it only applied to plans that offered both those benefits and traditional health services.

The bill was named after Sens. Paul Wellstone, D-Minn., and Pete V. Domenici, R-N.M., early advocates of mental health parity legislation. In 1996, they won enactment of the Mental Health Parity Act, which was folded into the fiscal 1997 Veterans Affairs-Housing and Urban Development Appropriations law (PL 104-204). The legislation prohibited group health plans and health insurance issuers from imposing annual and lifetime dollar limits on mental health coverage that were more restrictive than limits imposed on medical and surgical coverage.

The original law, however, did not apply to substance abuse and did not bar group health plans from limiting the number of visits to doctors' offices or increasing co-payments for those benefits. After Wellstone died in 2002, Domenici — joined by Sen. Edward M. Kennedy, D-Mass. — continued trying to expand the parity requirements.

On the House side, the campaign was led by Patrick J. Kennedy, D-R.I. — the senator's son — and Jim Ramstad, R-Minn.

Throughout much of the 110th Congress, supporters of parity legislation were locked in disagreement over how specific to be in setting requirements for insurers.

The Senate passed a mental health parity bill (S 558) in September 2007 that was the result of almost two years of meetings and negotiations led by Domenici and Kennedy that involved senators, insurance and business groups, and mental health advocates. The parties found

BOX SCORE

BILL: HR 1424 — PL 110-343

....

LEGISLATIVE ACTION:

House passed HR 1424 (H Rept 110-374), 268-148, March 5.

House passed HR 6983, 376-47, on Sept. 23.

Senate passed HR 6049, amended, 93-2, on Sept. 23.

Senate passed HR 1424, amended, 74-25, on Oct. 1.

House cleared HR 1424, 263-171, on Oct. 3.

President signed HR 1424 on Oct. 3.

common ground in part by not trying to specify precisely which mental illnesses would be covered under the bill.

Kennedy and his Senate colleagues argued that they had put together the only package that could win the endorsement of these powerful lobbies, and that the House should back it. Kennedy's son disagreed. Years of struggle with his own personal issues had convinced him that mental health and addiction patients needed stronger protections than the Senate bill afforded.

Patrick Kennedy and Ramstad worked persistently to bring a bill (HR 1424) to the House floor that would require insurers offering mental health benefits to cover a specific list of disorders outlined by the American Psychiatric Association. Business and health insurance lobbyists opposed the bill, arguing that it would impose heavy mandates on health plans, add to their costs, and discourage them from offering mental health and substance abuse benefits at all. A number of senators also were adamantly opposed to it.

Nevertheless, Kennedy in 2007 guided the measure through a legislative gantlet of subcommittee and committee markups. At each step, he and his supporters fended off GOP attempts to replace the text of the bill with the Senate version. *(2007 Almanac, p. 12-14)*

In 2008, Kennedy won easy House passage for the bill, forcing senators to reconsider their unwillingness to negotiate.

Over the next three months, the two sides negotiated a compromise. Patrick Kennedy had to give up on requiring that specific conditions be covered, but the compromise set up studies to make sure certain conditions were not left out. Unlike the Senate bill, it did not preclude more stringent state parity laws.

With the policy compromise in place, supporters turned to finding a vehicle that would carry the plan into law.

In September, the House passed a new version of the bill (HR 6983) that encompassed the compromises. The Senate added the language to a tax package (HR 6049), which it passed the same day. In the end, the Senate used HR 1424 as a vehicle for a financial sector bailout package that also included the tax provisions and the mental health language. *(Financial sector rescue, p. 7-3)*

HIGHLIGHTS

The following are major provisions of the parity law:

• **Financial requirements.** Group health plans that offered medical and surgical benefits could not impose more restrictive financial requirements — such as deductibles, co-payments and out-of-pocket expenses — for mental health and addiction care than for other services.

• **Treatment limitations.** Limits set by insurers on the scope or duration of coverage for mental health and drug addiction could not be more restrictive than those for other care, and there could not be separate treatment limits. These included limits on the frequency of treatment, the number of visits and the number of days of treatment covered.

• **Covered conditions**. The law did not specify what conditions insurers that offered mental health or drug addiction benefits had to cover. As before, those decisions were left to the insurers. The Government Accountability Office was required to send Congress two follow-up studies analyzing how insurers were covering mental health and substance use services, whether they were excluding coverage for specific diagnoses, and whether the new law affected trends in mental health and drug abuse benefits.

• **Out-of-network coverage.** Insurance plans that provided coverage for medical or surgical services from out-of-network providers were required to provide the same coverage for out-of-network mental health and substance abuse services. The benefits for those conditions had to be just as generous as the medical and surgical benefits, without higher co-pays or cost-sharing.

• **Notification.** The beneficiary had the right to be notified of the reason for being denied mental health or substance abuse benefits.

• **Small-business exemption.** Group health plans for companies with no more than 50 employees were exempt from the rules.

• **Cost exemption.** The law also exempted a group health plan if implementing the parity requirements would increase the combined one-year cost of coverage for traditional and mental health and substance abuse services by more than 2 percent in the first year and 1 percent in the second year. The exemption would occur the year after the cost increase. The increase would have to be determined and certified by a licensed actuary, and the Health and Human Services (HHS) Department could audit the books of a health plan claiming the exemption.

• **No state pre-emption.** The new law did not pre-empt stricter state mental health parity laws.

• **Compliance.** The HHS secretary was required to report to Congress every two years starting in 2012 on health plans' compliance with the law.

• **Cost.** The Joint Committee on Taxation estimated that the act would result in a loss of $3.9 billion in federal income and payroll taxes over 10 years because employees would get more of their compensation in the form of non-taxable employer-paid premiums.

LEGISLATIVE ACTION
HOUSE FLOOR ACTION

The House passed Patrick Kennedy's bill (HR 1424), by a vote of 268-148, on March 5. The measure was an amalgam of the versions approved by three separate committees in 2007 and was inserted into the bill by the rule for floor debate. (*House vote 101, p. H-32*)

Critics in both chambers argued that Kennedy's hard line in support of his legislation endangered chances of getting a mental

health parity bill into law. But many members strongly supported the measure.

House Republicans, who objected to the specific mental health coverage requirements as well as the cost offsets, offered a motion to recommit the bill. The motion, which would have substituted the Senate text, failed, 196-221. (*House vote 100, p. H-32*)

Under the House bill:

• **Parity requirements.** Health plans could not set more restrictive financial requirements or treatment limits than those for medical and surgical benefits. The requirements only applied to health plans that offered mental health or substance abuse benefits.

Benefits for out-of-network mental health treatment had to be subject to the same financial requirements and treatment limitations as other out-of-network benefits.

• **Minimum coverage.** Health plans that provided mental health and substance abuse benefits would have to cover "any mental health condition or substance-related disorder included in the most recent edition of the Diagnostic and Statistical Manual (DSM) of Mental Disorders published by the American Psychiatric Association."

• **Exemptions.** Exemptions were similar to those in the final bill for small businesses and for plans that experienced significant cost increases because of the requirements in the act.

• **Offsets.** To offset at least part of the estimated $3.9 billion cost of the bill, the measure included provisions to:

▸ Increase the Medicaid drug rebate, or discount, that pharmaceutical companies paid to state Medicaid programs from 15.1 percent to 20.1 percent. The change would cut the cost of what state programs paid for beneficiaries' drugs, in turn reducing the matching payments that the federal government made to the states.

▸ Limit the expansion of "specialty hospitals," which typically specialized in one or more surgical procedures, such as heart surgery or orthopedics, and were owned at least in part by physician investors. Physicians also would be prohibited from referring patients to hospitals in which they had an ownership interest, although existing physician-owned hospitals could be exempted from the restrictions. The change was expected to reduce the number of medical procedures and result in Medicaid savings.

• **Genetic discrimination.** The rule also attached a bill (HR 493) sponsored by Louise M. Slaughter, D-N.Y., aimed at prohibiting insurers and employers from discriminating or making business decisions using data from genetic tests. (*Genetic discrimination, p. 9-15*)

The White House issued a statement March 5 saying the administration opposed any bill that would expand mental health parity benefits beyond those laid out in the Senate legislation.

HOUSE-SENATE COMPROMISE

On Sept. 23, the House passed a new version of the mental health parity bill (HR 6983) that was the product of three months of negotiation with the Senate. The bipartisan measure passed by a vote of 376-47. (*House vote 625, p. H-210*)

Rather than passing the compromise as a separate bill, the Senate incorporated the provisions into a package containing energy incentives, tax extenders and an exemption from the alternative minimum tax. The bill (HR 6049) passed, 93-2, also on Sept. 23. (*Senate vote 205, p. S-45*)

The following are among the chief differences between the compromise and the earlier House- and Senate-passed bills:

• **Minimum coverage.** Unlike the earlier House bill, the compro-

mise did not specify which services had to be covered by a plan that offered such mental health or substance abuse benefits. Instead, it simply required that they cover such services as defined under the terms of the plan and relevant state laws.

• **Pre-emption.** Unlike the original Senate bill, the compromise did not pre-empt state mental health parity laws.

• **Offsets.** The new Senate version did not include direct cost offsets; instead, the mental health parity provisions were offset as part of the larger tax package. Under House rules, however, the cost of the legislation still had to be offset. The House bill proposed to delay, until 2013, a provision of the 2004 corporate tax overhaul (PL 108-357) that allowed companies to use a modified "worldwide interest allocation" rule for allocating their interest expenses between U.S. and foreign sources when determining their foreign tax credit limitation. In the first year that the allocation rules took effect, the amount that a

business would have to attribute to U.S. sources would increase from 30 percent to 85 percent.

FINAL BILL

On Oct. 1, the Senate passed what had become the financial industry bailout bill (HR 1424), including the parity provisions, as well as the tax provisions from its earlier measure. The vote for the package was 74-25. The House cleared it, 263-171, on Oct. 3. *(Senate vote 213, p. S-47; House vote 681, p. H-230)*

The Senate assembled the package, using the mental health parity bill as the vehicle, after the House had stunned the stock markets and others by rejecting a slightly different version of the rescue provisions. Like HR 6049, the bill offset the parity provisions as part of the tax package. The measure also included the genetic discrimination bill. ∎

Attempt to Override SCHIP Veto Fails

DEMOCRATS TRIED UNSUCCESSFULLY in January to override President Bush's veto of a bill aimed at expanding children's health insurance. It was the second time in four months they had failed to override Bush on the legislation.

The president vetoed the bill (HR 3963) on Dec. 12, 2007. On Jan. 23, 2008, the House rejected a motion to override the veto by a vote of 260-152 — 15 short of the two-thirds majority required. The vote was a reprise of an October 2007 vote, when the House rejected a Democratic motion to override Bush's veto of a virtually identical bill (HR 976), 13 votes short of the required majority. *(House vote 22, p. H-10; 2007 Almanac, p. 12-3)*

The bill, which was a top priority for Democrats in the 110th Congress, would have increased funding and expanded eligibility for the State Children's Health Insurance Program (SCHIP). Established in 1997, the program was aimed at providing health care to low-income children whose parents could not afford private insurance but were not poor enough to qualify for Medicaid. SCHIP was financed jointly by the federal government and the states within general federal guidelines; states had flexibility to create their own eligibility requirements. *(1997 Almanac, p. 6-3)*

The Congressional Budget Office (CBO) said the changes proposed by the Democrats would cost an extra $35.4 billion over five years, bringing the total cost of the program to about $60 billion. Democrats proposed paying for the increase mainly by boosting the cigarette tax by 61 cents per pack to $1 per pack. The bill's proponents said the legislation would provide health insurance to roughly 4 million additional children, for a total of about 10 million children.

Most Republicans opposed the bill. They argued the legislation would be too costly, that it would raise tobacco taxes too much, that it would draw too many middle-income families out of private insurance, that it would allow SCHIP to continue covering adults and that it would allow illegal immigrants to enroll in the program.

A statement from the White House called the legislation "misguided," saying it "would have expanded SCHIP to higher-income households while increasing taxes."

Democrats said they had responded to those concerns in the second bill, mainly by including language to cap eligibility for the program at three times the poverty level, or about $64,000 for a family of four. The revised measure also included stricter citizenship documentation requirements and a phase-out of coverage for childless adults by the end of 2008, instead of 2009.

The veto did not jeopardize the existing program. Bush had signed a law (PL 110-173) in 2007 that kept SCHIP running through March 2009 with enough money to maintain coverage at existing enrollment levels. ∎

Higher Education Overhaul Enacted

FOR THE FIRST TIME in a decade, Congress cleared a major overhaul of the law governing federal aid to higher education. Although President Bush raised numerous objections to the bill as it made its way through Congress, he signed it into law Aug. 14.

The measure (HR 4137 — PL 110-315) reauthorized the Higher Education Act through fiscal 2012. It authorized increases in federal financial aid programs such as Pell grants, required schools and lenders to provide more information to students, and barred lenders from giving schools financial perks in order to get on a "preferred lender list." It penalized states that cut funding for institutions of higher education and reauthorized teacher education programs and aid to historically minority colleges and universities.

The bill complemented two other higher education laws enacted during the 110th Congress. The first, signed in November 2007 (PL 110-84), reduced subsidies to lenders in order to boost the funds available for student aid. It was followed by a law, signed in April 2008 (PL 110-227), aimed at ensuring access to student loans in the midst of a widening credit crunch. (*Loan access, p. 9-10*)

The House passed a version of the reauthorization by an overwhelming vote in February. The Senate had passed a similar bill (S 1642) by an even more lopsided vote in July 2007. The main difference — and the main obstacle in House-Senate negotiations — was an effort by the House to penalize states that reduced their own contributions to public colleges and universities. GOP senators were staunchly opposed to the provision, but supporters prevailed in conference.

The absence of Edward M. Kennedy, D-Mass., chairman of the Senate Health, Education, Labor and Pensions (HELP) Committee, temporarily stalled the final conference agreement. Sen. Barbara A. Mikulski, D-Md., took over the committee's work on the conference report on behalf of Kennedy, who was undergoing treatment for a brain tumor.

The original Higher Education Act (PL 89-329), signed into law in 1965 as part of President Lyndon B. Johnson's Great Society program, was aimed at helping students from low-income families afford a college education. It had last been reauthorized in 1998 (PL 105-244). An attempt to renew it in 2005 was eclipsed by the urgency of responding to Hurricane Katrina. In September 2006, Bush signed a measure (PL 109-292) that extended the higher education law through June 2007. Congress passed a series of eight short-term extensions as lawmakers struggled to finish the bill.

HIGHLIGHTS

The main elements of the new law included:
- **Pell grants**. A gradual increase in the maximum Pell grant, to $8,000 per year by the 2014-15 academic year from the previous level of $5,800. The grants could be used year-round and would be accessible to part-time students.
- **State spending penalties.** A requirement that states provide at

BOX SCORE

BILL: HR 4137 — PL 110-315

LEGISLATIVE ACTION:

House passed HR 4137 (H Rept 110-500), 354-58, on Feb. 7.

Senate passed HR 4137 by voice vote July 29, after substituting the text of S 1642 (S Rept 110-231), which had passed, 95-0, on July 24, 2007.

House adopted the conference report on HR 4137 (H Rept 110-803), 380-49, on July 31.

Senate cleared the bill, 83-8, on July 31.

President signed Aug. 14.

least as much for higher education in any academic year beginning after July 1, 2008, as the average amount provided over the previous five years. Capital investments were not included. States that violated this "maintenance of effort" requirement would lose access to federal funding for College Access Challenge Grants for low-income students until they showed progress in meeting the funding goal. Grants for students with exceptional financial need were not subject to the reduction.

- **Consumer information.** A variety of online tools to help students and parents calculate net average annual costs at different colleges, which factored in student aid. The data to be posted included:
  ▸ A sortable and searchable list on the Education Department's Web site of all institutions eligible for federal aid and loans. The list was to include information such as tuition and fees, the average net price for students receiving federal student financial aid, the total amount of need- and merit-based federal, state and institutional aid to students, and the total number of students receiving aid.
  ▸ Listings on the department Web site of the 5 percent of institutions of higher education that had the highest costs, with and without student aid; the 5 percent with the largest percentage increase in those costs over three years; and the 10 percent with the lowest costs. The top 5 percent of colleges with the greatest cost increases were required to submit detailed reports to the Education secretary explaining why their costs had risen and what they would do to hold them down in the future.
  ▸ A net price calculator on the Web sites of all institutions of higher learning that received federal funds. The calculator, to be based on a model that the Education Department would develop, would show the average annual price actually charged to first-time, full-time undergraduate students, minus their student aid.
- **Lenders' ties to schools.** Tighter regulations aimed at preventing private lenders from offering inducements to schools to advertise their loans. The bill banned gifts, revenue sharing and the co-branding of loans. Students would have 30 days after a loan was approved to accept the terms and interest rates and up to three days to back out after signing a loan agreement. Students would have to obtain as much federal aid as possible before they took out private loans.
- **Lobbying ban.** Language specifying that colleges and universities could not use federal higher education funds to lobby employees of any agency, members of Congress or congressional staff in an effort to influence federal contracts, grants or loans. Schools also could not use federal aid funding to hire a registered lobbyist or pay any person or entity for securing an earmark.
- **Simplified aid application.** A new, two-page "EZ-FAFSA" — the Free Application for Federal Student Aid — in place of the existing seven-page version.
- **For-profit schools.** A two-year reprieve to private schools from having to count a $2,000 increase in federal loan limits enacted in

2008 toward a requirement that they get at least 10 percent of revenue from sources other than federal loans and other aid.

- **Armed forces benefits.** A requirement that schools readmit members of the armed forces who were called away to duty assignments elsewhere. The bill also provided interest-free deferrals on student loans for servicemembers on active duty and in-state tuition rates for servicemembers, their spouses or dependent children when they moved to a new state because of military service. Children and family members of servicemembers who had died since Sept. 11, 2001, were exempted from the family contribution requirement for Pell grant eligibility.

LEGISLATIVE ACTION
HOUSE FLOOR ACTION

The House passed its version of the bill (HR 4137 — H Rept 110-500) by a vote of 354-58 on Feb. 7. The Education and Labor Committee had approved the measure in November 2007. *(House vote 40, p. H-14)*

The bill proposed maximum Pell grants of $9,000 per year through the 2013-2014 academic year. It also called for withholding some grants to states that cut funding for higher education below the average spent in the previous five years.

During the floor debate, Republicans attempted to eliminate language reauthorizing the Fund for the Improvement of Postsecondary Education, which made grants to colleges and universities to improve the quality of higher education. For many years, lawmakers had used the program to target funds to favored higher education institutions. Republicans offered a motion to recommit the bill that would have redirected the funds to the Pell grant program, but it was rejected, 194-216. *(House vote 39, p. H-14)*

To the chagrin of student groups and the Project on Student Debt, members rejected, 179-236, a bid by Danny K. Davis, D-Ill., to make it easier for borrowers to discharge private student loans through bankruptcy. Lenders lobbied vigorously against Davis' amendment. Howard P. "Buck" McKeon of California, the ranking Republican on the Education and Labor Committee, said it would have added "uncertainty and additional risk" to lending. *(House vote 38, p. H-14)*

SENATE FLOOR ACTION

The Senate passed HR 4137 by voice vote July 29, after substituting the text of a bill (S 1642 — S Rept 110-231) that had passed, 95-0, on July 24, 2007. The step was required before the House and Senate could hold a conference on the measure.

The Senate bill proposed a smaller increase in the maximum Pell grant, raising it to $5,400 for academic year 2008-09, $5,700 for 2009-10, $6,000 for 2010-11 and $6,300 for 2011-12. It did not include penalties for states that reduced their funding for higher education.

CONFERENCE/FINAL ACTION

House and Senate negotiators reached agreement on the bill July 30. The House adopted the conference report (H Rept 110-803) by a vote of 380-49 the next day; hours later, the Senate cleared the bill by a vote of 83-8. *(House vote 544, p. H-182; Senate vote 194, p. S-43)*

The two main obstacles to reaching a deal were the dispute over penalties for states that reduced education funding and questions about the distribution of funds for historically black colleges.

Senate conferees accepted a modified version of the House's state penalties provision, after rejecting an attempt by Sen. Lamar Alexander, R-Tenn., to put it on hold until the federal funding for state special education programs met the 40 percent goal set in law. Many state governors and legislators joined Alexander in opposing the penalties.

Rep. John F. Tierney, D-Mass., made one important concession in the version he presented to the conferees. Instead of affecting states' access to the well-established Leveraging Educational Assistance Partnership grants that were awarded to students with exceptional financial need, the amendment targeted the newer College Access Challenge Grants program, which was set to expire in fiscal 2009. Those grants were available to state-sanctioned nonprofit lenders for projects helping to improve college access for low-income students.

The other snag in the talks was a lower-profile disagreement over a Senate provision making four new types of graduate programs — in the physical and natural sciences, mathematics, technology, and nursing — eligible for funding at historically black graduate institutions. Several members of the Congressional Black Caucus — along with the National Association for Equal Opportunity in Higher Education and the United Negro College Fund — worried that with no promise to increase overall funding for historically black schools, the provision would result in less money for existing programs.

The final bill created a new grant program for predominantly black institutions and authorized $75 million for it in fiscal 2009. In supporting the bill, Davis also noted that it increased authorized funding for historically black colleges to $375 million, an amount he said was almost three times the amount set in the previous law, and provided $125 million for historically black graduate institutions.

The White House, which had said it strongly opposed the bill when the House passed it, remained skeptical. White House spokesman Scott Stanzel said the administration "will want to take a good look at the legislation as it's changed in conference and see where changes might have been made" before officially taking a position on the bill. Bush signed the bill without issuing a statement. ∎

Legislation Shores Up Student Loans

CONGRESS CLEARED A BILL in May to ensure that the widening credit crunch and growing crisis in the economy did not prevent college students from getting the loans they needed to finance their education. President Bush signed the bill, which affected the 2008-09 academic year, on May 7 (HR 5715 — PL 110-227).

A second bill, which extended the provisions for the 2009-10 year, was signed into law Oct. 7 (HR 6889 — PL 110-350).

The legislation covered both loans offered directly by the federal government and those offered by private lenders with federal guarantees under the Federal Family Education Loan program. The bill increased the total amount that students and parents could borrow under the federal loan program and authorized the Education Department to purchase student loans from private lenders in order to ensure that the lenders had capital for more loans.

No eligible student had been denied a loan, but the freezing up of the credit markets and the dropping out of dozens of lenders from the program frightened lawmakers, students and aid administrators.

HIGHLIGHTS

The May bill included the following major provisions:

● **Federal loan caps.** The measure increased the annual limit on direct federal college loans by $2,000 for all students and raised the aggregate loan limit (spanning the entire course of a student's education) to $31,000 from $23,000 for dependent undergraduates and to $57,500 from $46,000 for independent undergraduates.

● **PLUS loans.** Parents who had fallen up to 180 days behind in mortgage payments or medical bills would still be able to take out PLUS loans to help finance their children's education. Under prior law, being delinquent on those bills would have made them ineligible. Also under the bill, parent borrowers could defer repayment until six months after their children left school. The federally sponsored Parent PLUS loan was a low-interest student loan for parents of undergraduate, dependent students. Parents could borrow up to the total cost of education through the loans, minus any aid they had already received.

● **Guaranteed private loans.** The bill gave the Education Department temporary authority to purchase existing loans that lenders were unable to sell to inject liquidity into the market. It also codified the "lender of last resort" program, which allowed the government to advance funds to state guarantee agencies so the agencies could make loans if more lenders drop out of the student loan program.

BOX SCORE

BILLS: HR 5715 — PL 110-227; HR 6889 — PL 110-350.

....

LEGISLATIVE ACTION:

House passed HR 5715 (H Rept 110-583), 383-27, on April 17.

Senate passed HR 5715, amended, by voice vote April 30.

House cleared, 388-21, on May 1.

President signed May 7.

House passed HR 6889, 368-4, on Sept. 15.

Senate cleared the bill Sept. 17 by voice vote.

President signed Oct. 7.

LEGISLATIVE ACTION
HOUSE ACTION

The House passed HR 5715 by a vote of 383-27, on April 17. The Education and Labor Committee had approved the measure (H Rept 110-583) by voice vote April 9. The panel's chairman, George Miller, D-Calif., was the sponsor. *(House vote 204, p. H-66)*

Education Department officials said the law needed to be in place by July, when the high season for student borrowing began.

The vote came a day after Sallie Mae, the nation's largest student lender, announced it lost $104 million in the first quarter and that almost all its new loans would be made at a loss. JPMorgan Chase & Co. and Citigroup had said they would be more selective in the schools to which they loaned money, which was interpreted as meaning they would back away from schools with high default rates — most frequently community colleges, schools that historically served minorities and others that educated many people from low-income backgrounds.

A total of 57 lenders had already dropped out of the Federal Family Education Loan program in 2008, driven away by the credit crunch.

Before approving the measure, the committee rejected, 16-21, an amendment by Tom Price, R-Ga., to include language saying that the bill would not take effect if it would result in new costs to the government without offsets.

SENATE, HOUSE FINAL ACTION

The Senate passed an amended version of the bill by voice vote April 30, and the House cleared it the following day, 388-21. *(House vote 239, p. H-78)*

The revisions, agreed to by voice vote, included language to:

▸ Sunset the Education Department's authority to designate institutions as lenders of last resort at the end of the 2008-09 academic year.

▸ Require that lenders operating under the lender-of-last-resort program be subject to the same conflict-of-interest requirements as private lenders operating under the guaranteed loan program.

▸ Clarify that the delinquency period on a mortgage payment would not disqualify a parent from accessing a PLUS loan.

▸ Require any savings generated by the bill to be used for grants to low-income math and science students with good grades.

ONE-YEAR EXTENSION

In September, Congress agreed to extend the provisions of HR 5715 for one year. The House passed the bill (HR 6889) by a vote of 368-4 on Sept. 15. The Senate cleared it Sept. 17 by voice vote. ∎

Unemployment Benefits Extended

CONGRESS TWICE EXTENDED emergency unemployment benefits in the face of the nation's growing economic crisis. The first extension was enacted June 30 as part of a supplemental spending bill for the wars in Iraq and Afghanistan. The second, a stand-alone bill, was cleared during the lame-duck session and became law Nov. 21.

The bills provided additional compensation to unemployed workers who had already exhausted their regular 26 weeks of benefits. The regular unemployment program was funded through federal and state payroll taxes and administered by the states. The additional compensation provided under the bills came from the federal government.

HIGHLIGHTS

The following are the unemployment compensation provisions contained in each of the two bills:

● **June extension.** The 2008 supplemental (HR 2642 — PL 110-252) established a temporary program for individuals who had exhausted their regular 26 weeks of compensation by March 28, 2009. The emergency program, which became effective July 6, 2008, provided up to 13 weeks of federal benefits equal to what the person had received under the regular state-run program. To qualify, the person had to have worked for 20 weeks prior to being laid off. Those who had not completed their 13 weeks of extended benefits by the March 28, 2009, cutoff were able to receive the remaining compensation.

● **October extension.** The stand-alone bill (HR 6867 — PL 110-449) added seven weeks of benefits to the 13-week compensation provided in the earlier law. The emergency benefits still applied only to workers who had used up their regular 26 weeks by March 28, 2009. Unlike the earlier law, the measure provided an extra 13 weeks of compensation to people who had worked in states with unemployment rates of 6 percent or higher.

LEGISLATIVE ACTION: JUNE EXTENSION

Lawmakers made several failed attempts to enact the first extension before successfully adding it to the supplemental.

● **Stimulus bill.** The Senate Finance Committee included a 13-week extension of federal unemployment benefits, with an additional 13 weeks in hard-hit areas, in a draft economic stimulus bill that it approved Jan. 30. The provision was one of many that made the Senate measure far more expensive than a relatively narrow stimulus bill passed by the House.

After days of partisan maneuvering, the Senate rejected the Finance Committee draft by voting down an attempt to limit debate on it. The motion to invoke cloture on the committee version failed, 58-41, on Feb. 6, largely because of objections to the overall cost. The vote was one short of the 60 needed before Reid switched his vote to "nay" for

---

BOX SCORE

BILLS: HR 2642
— PL 110-252; HR 6867
— PL 110-449

....

LEGISLATIVE ACTION:

House adopted amendment to HR 2642 that included unemployment benefits, 256-166, on May 15.

Senate adopted revised amendment to HR 2642 that included unemployment benefits, 75-22, on May 22.

House adopted amendment to HR 2642 that included unemployment benefits, 416-12, on June 19.

Senate agreed to the amendment, 92-6, on June 26, clearing HR 2642.

President signed June 30.

House passed HR 6867, 368-28, on Oct. 3.

Senate cleared HR 6867 by voice vote Nov. 20.

President signed Nov. 21.

---

parliamentary reasons. *(Senate vote 8, p. S-5)*

On Feb. 7, the Senate passed a stripped-down version of the bill (HR 5140) that omitted the unemployment benefits and many other committee provisions. The House cleared the measure the same day.

● **Stand-alone House bill.** With the stimulus bill no longer available, Democrats planned to add the unemployment compensations provisions to a fiscal 2009 supplemental war spending bill that appropriators were writing.

When work on the supplemental stalled and the Bureau of Labor Statistics reported that the May unemployment rate had risen to 5.5 percent from 5 percent the previous month, House leaders decided to bring a narrow benefits extension bill to the floor.

That measure (HR 5749 — H Rept 110-607) passed, 274-137, on June 12. *(House vote 412, p. H-136)*

The legislation, similar to the Senate Finance Committee plan, called for 13 weeks of federal unemployment benefits for workers whose 26 weeks of regular benefits had run out. An additional 13 weeks would be available in states with unemployment rates of 6 percent or higher. The Ways and Means Committee had approved the bill, 23-13, on April 16.

While both parties agreed on the need for some type of extension, Republicans argued that the Democrats' plan was too broad. They endorsed a more limited approach that targeted states with unemployment rates of 5 percent or higher and states where unemployment rates had grown by more than 20 percent in the previous year. They said their plan would apply to 22 states.

Republicans also argued that the Democrats' bill would provide a disincentive for some people to pursue work, a charge that rankled Democrats. "This is not about people sitting back home on their butts saying, 'Goody, I'm getting an unemployment check,'" said Speaker Nancy Pelosi, D-Calif.

GOP lawmakers and the White House took particular exception to the fact that the bill did not include a requirement that people work at least 20 weeks to become eligible for the extended federal benefits. Democrats said that was necessary to accommodate part-time workers and women who had been on maternity leave.

Senate leaders preferred to keep the unemployment extension as part of the supplemental bill. But House leaders were concerned that, because President Bush had threatened to veto the unemployment provisions, including them could provoke a veto fight that would slow the supplemental at a time when the Pentagon was urging quick action.

Senate Majority Leader Harry Reid, D-Nev., said he would try to bring the House-passed bill to the Senate floor by unanimous consent but would abandon it if Republicans objected. "I'm not wasting a week's time on unemployment compensation," he said. "We're going to put it in the supplemental."

● **Supplemental.** Although it took longer than Democratic leaders hoped, the supplemental spending bill became the vehicle for enacting the extension of jobless benefits into law.

The House attached a large package of domestic provisions to the supplemental that included a 13-week extension of unemployment benefits in all states, plus an additional 13 weeks in states where the jobless rate was 6 percent or higher. The House adopted the amendment on domestic programs, 256-166, on May 15. The Senate revised other parts of the amendment but left the unemployment provisions unchanged before adopting it, 75-22, on May 22. (*House vote 330, p. H-106; Senate vote 137, p. S-30*)

After weeks of negotiations, House Democrats reached agreement on the overall bill with the White House and the chamber's GOP leadership. The House agreed to the compromise on June 19 in the form of two amendments. The portion on domestic programs, including the extended unemployment benefits, was adopted, 416-12. The Senate agreed to the House amendment, 92-6, on June 26, clearing the entire supplemental for the president. (*House vote 432, p. H-144; Senate vote 162, p. S-35*)

The unemployment provisions were less generous than either chamber had proposed. They did not include extra compensation for the hardest-hit states, and the bill required 20 weeks of work before an unemployed worker could collect the extended federal benefit — a restriction that House Republicans had fought to include.

LEGISLATIVE ACTION: OCT. EXTENSION

On Sept. 26, House Democrats passed a new $61 billion stimulus bill (HR 7110) that included an additional seven weeks of federal unemployment benefits, plus another 13 weeks in states with high jobless rates. The vote was 264-158. Republicans blocked the Senate from taking up the measure. (*House vote 660, p. H-222*)

Shortly before adjourning for the campaign, House leaders put the unemployment provisions into a separate bill (HR 6867), which the House passed, 368-28, on Oct. 3. "Unemployment insurance does not simply help those struggling through tough times," said Majority Leader Steny H. Hoyer, D-Md. "Economists consider it one of the best ways to stimulate our economy." Again, Senate Republicans held up the measure, putting the issue off until the lame-duck session.

When Congress returned after the election, it was against the backdrop of a deepening economic crisis and an unemployment rate that had reached 6.6 percent in October. Republicans were ready to go along with the temporary extension, and the Senate cleared the House bill by voice vote Nov. 20, after agreeing, 89-6, to invoke cloture and proceed to the measure. (*Senate vote 214, p. S-47*)

Edward M. Kennedy of Massachusetts reiterated the Democrats' argument that the bill would have a stimulative effect on the economy. "Each dollar of unemployment benefits," he said, "generates $1.64 in economic growth. I urge my colleagues to join me in supporting this critical extension of unemployment assistance."

"This dramatic downturn in the economy and surge in unemployment convinced me to support this extension of unemployment coverage," said Republican Whip Jon Kyl of Arizona.

But Kyl made it clear that he did not buy the argument that the bill would have broader effects. "I do not believe an extension or expansion of federal unemployment benefits stimulates the economy," he said. ■

Bills Against Pay Inequity Fall Short

HOUSE DEMOCRATS PASSED two bills targeting wage discrimination, but the Senate did not act on either of them. Although the measures died at the end of the session, Democrats appeared confident that they would prevail in the next Congress.

The first bill sought to extend the period of time during which an employee could file a wage discrimination suit. The second would have made it easier for women whose pay was below that of their male counterparts to sue their employers and receive compensation.

LEGISLATIVE ACTION
LEDBETTER BILL

House Democrats passed a bill (HR 2831) in July 2007 that was intended to reverse a Supreme Court decision in a wage-discrimination case. But in April 2008, when Majority Leader Harry Reid, D-Nev., tried to bring the legislation up on the Senate floor, supporters were unable to rally enough GOP moderates to achieve the 60-vote majority needed to avert a filibuster and proceed to the bill. The cloture motion was rejected, 56-42, on April 23. (*Senate vote 110, p. S-24*)

The Supreme Court had ruled, 5-4, in *Ledbetter v. Goodyear Tire & Rubber Co.* that, under the Civil Rights Act of 1964 (PL 88-352), a

BOX SCORE

BILLS: HR 2831, HR 1338

LEGISLATIVE ACTION:

Senate rejected motion to invoke cloture on proceeding to HR 2831, 56-42, on April 23 (60 votes required).

House passed HR 1338 (H Rept 110-783), 247-178, on July 31.

worker claiming pay discrimination had to file a suit within 180 days of the date of the alleged discrimination.

The case grew out of a complaint filed in 1998 by Lilly Ledbetter, who alleged that during her 19-year career at a Goodyear Tire plant in Alabama, her supervisors conspired to pay her less than men doing substantially identical work. A federal jury awarded her back pay, but an appeals court reversed the decision. The Supreme Court ruled that Ledbetter's complaint was "untimely."

The bill would have amended the Civil Rights Act to make the 180-day statute of limitations begin anew with each discriminatory paycheck. (*1964 Almanac, p. 340*)

The April 23 Senate debate on the bill was held until 5 p.m. to ensure that Democratic presidential candidates Barack Obama of Illinois and Hillary Rodham Clinton of New York could deliver comments of support on the floor.

Backers of the legislation argued that the court decision made it too difficult for many employees to bring legitimate pay-discrimination claims and that it permanently shielded employers from liability once the initial 180-day period had elapsed.

Barbara A. Mikulski, D-Md., the most senior woman in the Senate,

sought to rally support. "Women of America: Put your lipstick on; square those shoulders. We've got a hell of a fight," she said. The bill drew strong support from several other women in the Senate, including Republicans Olympia J. Snowe and Susan Collins of Maine.

Republican opponents argued that the bill was not an anti-discrimination measure but an attempt to upend congressional intent behind the Civil Rights Act, which envisioned a statute of limitations for claims of discrimination. They said the measure would open corporations to endless lawsuits.

The White House issued a statement the day before the cloture vote warning that the president would veto the bill. It said the measure would effectively eliminate any statute of limitations, allowing employees "to bring a claim of pay or other employment-related discrimination years or even decades after the alleged discrimination occurred."

GENDER DISCRIMINATION BILL

The House passed the second bill on pay discrimination by a vote of 247-178 on July 31. However, the margin of support was not enough to overcome a threatened veto. The measure would have shifted the burden of proof in wage discrimination suits from the employee — who was required under existing law to prove that the employer's pay discrepancy was intentional — to the employer, who would have to prove it was not. (House vote 556, p. H-186)

The House Education and Labor Committee had approved the bill (HR 1338 — H Rept 110-783), 26-17, on July 24.

Under the Equal Pay Act (PL 88-38) employers taken to court for paying women less than men for the same job could raise "any factor other than sex" to justify the disparity, regardless of whether the factor was related to the employee's job or to the business.

The House-passed bill required that the employer demonstrate that the disparity was based on a factor other than gender, such as education, training or experience, that was not the result of a gender-based difference and that it was required by "business necessity." That defense would not apply if the employee could prove that an alternative employment practice existed that would serve the same business purpose without producing the pay difference and that the employer refused to adopt the alternative.

According to census data cited by bill supporters, women in 2006 made about 77 cents for every dollar earned by men, a difference that could amount to $2 million over a lifetime of earnings, retirement pay and Social Security benefits. Opponents said the disparities could be accounted for by other causes, such as women leaving the workforce to have children.

Under the bill, employees could sue for discrimination if they learned that they earned lower wages than similar workers within the same company, even if the employees worked at different locations of a business but in the same county.

Workers who won wage discrimination cases could collect compensatory and punitive damages, not just back pay and liquidity damages, and employers would be barred from retaliating against employees who discussed their pay with one another.

Republicans criticized the bill as duplicative of existing anti-discrimination standards and fodder for frivolous lawsuits. "This bill will make it easier for trial lawyers to cash in, and taxpayers should be outraged that their money is being put to such use," said Rep. Virginia Foxx, R-N.C.

The White House said the changes would "encourage discrimination claims to be made based on factors unrelated to actual pay discrimination."

Supporters said the bill would close the loophole in the Equal Pay Act. George Miller, D-Calif., the House Education and Labor chairman, said the measure was needed to avoid discrimination like that cited in the Ledbetter case.

The House adopted several amendments to the bill, including a requirement that punitive damages be awarded only to plaintiffs who proved intentional discrimination.

House Rules Committee Chairwoman Louise M. Slaughter, D-N.Y., was removed from the presiding officer's chair when Republicans objected to her cry of "Hallelujah!" when the bill passed. ■

Law Clarifies Disability Protections

PRESIDENT BUSH SIGNED a bill in September that expanded the category of those classified as disabled and included provisions to ensure that protections under the 1990 Americans with Disabilities Act (ADA) were not withheld from anyone meeting those standards.

The bill was the result of parallel efforts from the White House and Capitol Hill in response to a series of Supreme Court decisions over the previous decade that lawmakers said had narrowed the scope of the protection available under the 1990 law (PL 101-336).

The original act was intended to make it easier for people with disabilities to work and use services available to the non-disabled by requiring businesses to make accommodations, such as wheelchair ramps and wider doors and stalls in restrooms. *(1990 Almanac, p. 447)*

The court had ruled that disabled individuals who corrected or mitigated the effect of their disability — for example, through the use of medication or medical devices such as hearing aids — should not be considered disabled for the purpose of decisions relating to hiring, firing or job performance. Advocates for the disabled argued that the court's decisions created a situation in which people attempting to treat their disabilities could lose legal protections against discrimination.

An unorthodox coalition of business groups and advocates for the disabled worked behind the scenes for the better part of the 110th Congress to amend the original act. The first product of their efforts was a bill (HR 3195), introduced in 2007 by House Majority Leader Steny H. Hoyer, D-Md., and ranking Judiciary Committee Republican F. James Sensenbrenner Jr. of Wisconsin.

The bill, which passed by a sizable margin in late June 2008, would have specified in statute the categories of physical and mental ailments that could be considered disabilities for the purposes of the ADA and revised the definition of "disabled" in the original law. The bill would have changed the definition from a condition that "substantially limits" a bodily function to something that "materially restricts" such a function.

The White House was eager for the Senate to clear the measure in time for Bush to sign it July 26 — 18 years after his father signed the original law. But efforts slowed in the Senate, where lawmakers disagreed over whether to include the House's new definition of "disabled." That sent the coalition of business groups and advocates for the disabled back to the drawing board.

In September, the Senate passed a new bill (S 3406), sponsored by Tom Harkin, D-Iowa, that did not revise the definition of "disabled" but stated that the ability to mitigate the effects of the disability through means such as medication, prosthetics or hearing aids did not affect the person's qualification under the ADA.

The House cleared the Senate's bill a week later.

BACKGROUND

The following are key Supreme Court rulings cited by lawmakers as narrowing the categories of people who qualified under the ADA:

BOX SCORE

BILL: S 3406 —
PL 110-325

LEGISLATIVE ACTION:

House passed HR 3195 (H Rept 110-730, Parts 1 and 2), 402-17, on June 25.

Senate passed S 3406 by voice vote, Sept. 11.

House cleared S 3406 by voice vote, Sept. 17.

President signed Sept. 25.

▶ *Bragdon v. Abbott* (1998). When Randon Bragdon, a dentist, found a cavity in patient Sidney Abbott's gumline, he told Abbott that, because she was HIV-positive, filling the cavity in his office would be dangerous and offered to complete the procedure in a hospital. Abbott insisted the ADA entitled her to office treatment, and her lawsuit against Bragdon made it up to the Supreme Court as its first of both ADA and AIDS-related cases. Although the court agreed that HIV met the ADA's definition of a physical impairment impacting numerous life activities, it said it did not have enough evidence to rule on the risk of her condition to Bragdon's office and sent the case back to the lower courts.

▶ *Sutton v. United Air Lines Inc.* (1999). In 1992, Karen Sutton and Kimberly Hinton were rejected for pilot positions with United Air Lines because they did not meet the company's vision standard for pilots. The twin sisters were severely myopic, but with corrective measures, both functioned identically to individuals without similar impairments. They were pilots for regional carriers and claimed they were discriminated against on the basis of their vision. The Supreme Court, however, stated that the ADA's definition of disability did not include correctable physical impairments that did not substantially limit a major life activity.

▶ *Murphy v. United Parcel Service Inc.* (1999). This case, reviewed with *Sutton v. United Air Lines Inc.,* concerned Vaughn Murphy, a UPS mechanic who was fired when tests showed that his blood pressure exceeded the government's limit of what it considered safe for truck drivers. The high court ruled against Murphy, citing the same argument used in its *Sutton* decision.

▶ *Albertsons Inc. v. Kirkingburg* (1999). In a second case reviewed with *Sutton,* Oregon truck driver Hallie Kirkingburg sued his company, which fired him for failing to meet basic vision standards and refused to rehire him after he received a waiver under an experimental government program. The high court ruled that the ADA did not require a company to waive safety regulations for individual cases.

▶ *Toyota Motor Manufacturing, Kentucky Inc. v. Williams* (2002). After Ella Williams, an assembly-line worker for Toyota, was diagnosed with carpal tunnel syndrome and reassigned tasks, disputes with the company eventually led to her dismissal. Williams sued, claiming that Toyota refused to accommodate her worsening condition. The Supreme Court decided she did not prove that her physical problems prevented her from performing tasks pertinent to daily life activities.

LEGISLATIVE ACTION
HOUSE COMMITTEE ACTION

Two House committees approved identical versions of Hoyer's bill (HR 3195) on June 18. The Education and Labor Committee approved the measure, 43-1 (H Rept 110-730, Part 1). The Judiciary Committee approved it, 27-0 (H Rept 110-730, Part 2). Both votes were on June 18.

The bill explicitly rejected the relevant Supreme Court rulings. It expanded the definition of the term "disabled," which the original law described as meaning "a physical or mental impairment that substantially limits one or more of the major life activities." Hoyer's bill stated that "substantially limits" in the law meant "materially restricts." It also provided several examples of major life activities such as caring for oneself, eating, sleeping, breathing and walking.

It authorized the Equal Employment Opportunity Commission, the attorney general and the secretary of Transportation to issue regulations implementing the new definitions.

The bill reiterated protections for people with disabilities not immediately evident in the workplace — such as those involving the immune, digestive and neurological systems. It also stated that the effects of "mitigating measures," such as hearing aids and prosthetics, could not be used in weighing whether a person's disability substantially affected his or her life activities.

In response to concerns that the changes might be abused by those with minor disabilities, the bill exempted anyone with disabilities that were minor or were expected to last less than six months, as well as those whose disability could be corrected through contact lenses or eyeglasses.

The measure was hailed from both sides of the aisle as a vital piece of civil rights legislation.

The day before the two markups, the Bush administration announced a series of proposed new ADA regulations that included several specific infrastructure rules and changes, such as mandating the construction of wheelchair ramps to and from court witness stands, setting height regulations for light switches, and clarifying the types of animals that could be used in service for the disabled. The Justice Department said the changes, which had been in the planning stages for the better part of four years, would cost as much as $23 billion, a price that brought protests from businesses. Advocates for the disabled said they wanted language put into statute, adding there was a huge difference between that and regulation.

HOUSE FLOOR ACTION

Reflecting the strong bipartisan support for the bill, the House passed the measure June 25 by a vote of 402-17. (House vote 460, p. H-154)

"We never expected that people with disabilities who worked to mitigate their conditions would have their efforts held against them," Hoyer said, referring to the court rulings.

"It is better, when there is a conflict between the courts and the Congress, for the Congress to come back and say that's not what we meant," said Minority Whip Roy Blunt, R-Mo.

FINAL SENATE, HOUSE ACTION

The Senate passed Harkin's version of the bill (S 3406) by voice vote Sept. 11. The House cleared the bill Sept. 17, also by voice vote.

Much of the language was identical to that in the House-passed bill. Unlike the House version, however, it did not include a change in the definition of "disability." But it directed the courts to broadly construe the definition of "disability" and to adjudicate the merits of a disability claim and not the severity of the disability when hearing cases involving clinically certified disabled people. House leaders said they were comfortable with that change. ■

Genetic Discrimination Outlawed

AFTER MORE THAN A DECADE of debate, Congress cleared legislation to bar employers and health insurers from discriminating on the basis of genetic information. President Bush signed the bill into law May 21 (HR 493 — PL 110-233), after insisting on a handful of minor modifications.

Rep. Louise M. Slaughter, D-N.Y., who sponsored the bill, called the legislation "the most important thing I have done in my life." Slaughter, who had degrees in bacteriology and public health, had first introduced the anti-discrimination legislation in 1995, inspired by reports that people were avoiding tests for dangerous genetic conditions out of fear that the data would be used against them.

The legislation prohibited employers from using genetic screening results — data about cancer or heart disease risk, for example — in hiring, assignment or promotion decisions. It also prohibited training programs run by employers or labor unions from discriminating on the basis of genetic information.

The measure barred insurers from requiring genetic testing or making decisions on enrollment, coverage or premiums based on the results of such tests. The law applied to group health plans, individual

BOX SCORE

BILL: HR 493 — PL 110-233

....

LEGISLATIVE ACTION:

Senate passed HR 493, amended, 95-0, on April 24.

House cleared HR 493, 414-1, on May 1.

President signed May 21.

health plans and Medicare supplementary policies. And it extended the prohibitions to include genetic information on the fetus of a pregnant woman.

The Senate had passed an identical bill twice, in 2003 and 2005. But the House did not vote on genetic discrimination legislation until April 25, 2007, when it passed Slaughter's bill by a vote of 420-3.

During the previous 12 years, when the House was under GOP control, the influential U.S. Chamber of Commerce had successfully lobbied the leadership to keep the bill bottled up. Business leaders argued that the bill was unnecessary and could lead to frivolous lawsuits against businesses. They said that they should not be barred from simply collecting genetic information and that where there were documented cases of genetic discrimination, businesses had been punished in court.

Actual cases of genetic discrimination were rare, but supporters of the bill argued that the mere threat of discrimination stymied the field of genetic medicine, in which doctors targeted treatments to patients' specific genetic code. Enactment of legislation, they said, would reassure people that the results of genetic tests could not be used against

www.cq.com | 2008 CQ ALMANAC **9-15**

them, and more tests could mean more opportunities to advance genetic medicine.

The Senate Health, Education, Labor and Pensions (HELP) Committee approved its own version of the bill (S 358) on Jan. 31, 2007. The measure was sponsored by Olympia J. Snowe, R-Maine, with the support of ranking committee Republican Michael B. Enzi of Wyoming. The measure languished for more than a year, however, because of a hold placed on it by Tom Coburn, R-Okla., who said it would expose employers and insurers to undue risk of lawsuits.

Coburn ultimately lifted his hold in April 2008 after reaching a compromise with the bill's sponsors, and the Senate passed the bill by an overwhelming majority. The House cleared the amended bill, but at the last minute, the White House demanded another change affecting the military's ability to collect genetic information. That language was adopted as a separate resolution, and the bill was signed.

BACKGROUND

When the mapping of the human genome was completed in 2003, there was widespread excitement about the possibility that genetic medicine could lead to better diagnoses, treatment and even cures for diseases such as diabetes and cancer. But the advances also raised concerns that employers and insurers could discriminate against people who might be genetically predisposed to certain conditions, and that the fear of such discrimination might discourage people from undergoing genetic testing or participating in clinical studies.

Two major court cases were often cited as pointing out the potential for such discrimination. In 1998, the 9th U.S. Circuit Court of Appeals ruled unconstitutional the practice of testing certain employees for diseases related to their genetic makeup. In this case, the Lawrence Berkeley National Laboratory in California secretly tested black employees for sickle cell anemia. In a second case, the Equal Employment Opportunity Commission (EEOC) sued Burlington Northern Santa Fe Railroad on behalf of employees who claimed they had been forced to undergo genetic tests after complaining of carpal tunnel syndrome, which in rare cases could be attributed to a chromosome. The railroad settled with the EEOC and the employees in 2002, paying them $2.2 million.

Existing law provided some protection against discrimination on the basis of an individual's genetic information. The Health Insurance Portability and Accountability Act (PL 104-191) prohibited group health plans from establishing eligibility rules for individual enroll-

ment based on genetic information and prohibited group health plans from requiring individuals to pay higher premiums based on such data. In addition, under an executive order issued Feb. 10, 2000, federal employees could not be dismissed or subjected to restrictions in employment or benefits on the basis of their genetic information. The executive order also barred improper collection and unauthorized disclosure of federal employees' genetic data.

LEGISLATIVE ACTION
SENATE, HOUSE FLOOR ACTION

The Senate passed a revised version of HR 493 by a vote of 95-0 on April 24, after agreeing by voice vote to a compromise that assuaged concerns raised by Coburn and the White House. *(Senate vote 113, p. S-24)*

On May 1, the House cleared the amended bill, 414-1. *(House vote 234, p. H-76)*

The compromise was the result of two weeks of intense negotiations among aides to Snowe, Coburn, Democratic Sen. Edward M. Kennedy of Massachusetts and other members, as well as representatives from the departments of Labor and Health and Human Services. Coburn's office insisted on changing the bill language to clarify a stronger "firewall" to protect companies from excess legal jeopardy. Among other changes, the sponsors added language providing that an employer who was also acting as an insurer could not be sued twice.

Coburn also wanted to include a broad "business necessity" provision that would let employers collect and use genetic information in cases in which it was "job related and consistent with business necessity." But that proposal was unacceptable to bill sponsors, and Coburn's office agreed to drop it. Lawmakers signed off on the deal on April 22, and Coburn dropped his hold.

From there, the rails were greased. Administration officials gave assurances that the stronger "firewall" provisions met their needs, and the bill passed with Coburn voting "aye."

But proponents still had to overcome one more White House concern: The administration wanted language that would allow the military to collect genetic information in order to identify human remains.

Congress acted quickly to satisfy the administration. After clearing the bill on May 1, the House adopted a resolution (H Con Res 340) by voice vote to amend the measure by adding the language requested by the White House. The Senate adopted the resolution that night, also by voice vote. ■

Chapter 10

POLITICS & ELECTIONS

Obama Scores Decisive Victory to Be The First African-American President

BARACK OBAMA was elected Nov. 4 to be the 44th president of the United States and the first African-American to hold the nation's highest office. Obama, a Democratic senator from Illinois, won a decisive victory over John McCain, a Republican senator from Arizona — 53 percent to 46 percent in the popular vote and 365 to 173 in the Electoral College. His victory returned the White House to the Democratic Party after the tumultuous and ultimately unpopular eight-year presidency of Republican George W. Bush.

The election capped Obama's amazingly rapid political rise. He was a state legislator, little known outside his constituency on Chicago's South Side, just four years earlier when he burst onto the national stage, first with a stirring keynote address at the 2004 Democratic National Convention and then three months later with a landslide victory to take a Senate seat left open by the retirement of a Republican incumbent.

Obama's ranking among the nation's chief executives, and his prospects for winning a second term in 2012, were expected to depend on his handling of the enormous challenges that awaited him following his inauguration Jan. 20, 2009. These included a deep recession, longstanding problems in national priorities such as health care and education, and the U.S. military engagements in long-running wars in Iraq and Afghanistan.

But no wait was needed to acknowledge the historic breakthrough achieved by Obama, who permanently secured a place in the nation's political and social history the moment he declared victory at a massive outdoor Election Night victory rally in Chicago's Grant Park: the first black winner in the 220-year history of American presidential elections.

Obama, who was 47 years old when elected, was the son of a black father from Kenya and a white mother from Kansas who met in Hawaii while attending college. Such interracial marriages were extremely rare at that time, an era in which many black Americans were struggling to achieve civil rights that historically had been denied them by law in some parts of the country and by custom in others. Obama was born in August 1961, almost two years before the March on Washington where the Rev. Martin Luther King Jr. delivered his "I Have a Dream" speech, three years before the enactment of the 1964 Civil Rights Act and four years before the Voting Rights Act became law.

Obama made history just by accepting the Democratic nomination before a crowd of 84,000 in the pro football stadium in Denver on Aug. 28. No non-white candidate ever had come close to winning the nomination of one of the two major parties. The only African-American who had even run a full-fledged presidential campaign was the Rev. Jesse Jackson, in the 1984 and 1988 contests for the Democratic nomination. Jackson, a veteran of the civil rights movement, received most of his support from black voters. By contrast, Obama, with his degrees from Columbia University and Harvard Law School and experience as a constitutional law professor at the University of Chicago, personified a younger generation of black politicians who practiced what many analysts described as "post-racial" politics.

In fact, it was clear from the beginning of the campaign that Obama's themes of "change" and "hope" would attract support from millions of white Americans, with special appeal to younger voters.

This was signaled in 2007 by the big, racially mixed audiences Obama attracted prior to the primaries and caucuses that would determine the Democratic nomination. He was seeking to overcome the putative front-runner status enjoyed by New York Sen. Hillary Rodham Clinton, who also was first lady when Bill Clinton was president. And it was confirmed by his victory in the first voting of 2008, when he received 38 percent of the delegates elected by the precinct caucuses in Iowa, where blacks made up 2 percent of the population.

Obama's emergence came at a time when huge majorities of respondents told pollsters they believed the country was on the wrong track. The disenchantment with Bush and the Republican Party in general, which had abetted the Democrats' takeover of Congress in the 2006 midterm election, would weigh down Republican nominee McCain and provide valuable leeway for Obama in setting a bold agenda for national revival.

Republican presidents and presidential candidates since Ronald Reagan in 1980 had declared that government was the problem rather than an agent in solving the nation's difficulties. Even Bill Clinton, the most recent Democratic president, proclaimed, "The era of big government is over," as he ran for his second term in 1996.

Obama, though, succeeded while pledging to utilize the agencies of the federal government to address the sputtering economy and the chronic shortcoming he described in the nation's health care, education and infrastructure systems. The message gained cogency in the final weeks of the general election campaign, when the financial sector, undermined by badly flawed mortgage lending practices that had fueled a mid-decade economic boom, unraveled and pushed the economy into a recession that Obama and many in both parties characterized as the worst economic crisis since the Great Depression.

ORGANIZATIONAL SAVVY

While Obama built a massive national voting base with an activist message and a stirring rhetorical flair, his prodigious fundraising skills and instincts for grass-roots political organizing were the key factors that enabled him to overcome Clinton's advantages as the Democrats' perceived "establishment" candidate.

Obama once was a community organizer who counseled laid-off steel workers in Chicago, and he applied that ethos to his campaign for president. He teamed with chief advisers David Axelrod and David Plouffe, both veterans of Chicago politics, to build a vast network of campaign offices across the nation — including some in conservative-leaning states in the South, Midwest and Mountain West where Democrats had not vigorously competed in presidential elections for many years.

The Obama campaign also broke new ground in using high-tech tools, both at its national headquarters in Chicago and at the local level, for identifying and contacting potential Obama voters, "mining" data such as e-mail addresses and cell phone numbers to promote

By the Numbers

- Democratic Sen. Barack Obama of Illinois received 69.5 million votes (52.9 percent of all votes cast) to 59.9 million votes (45.7 percent) for Republican Sen. John McCain of Arizona. Other candidates received 1.8 million votes (1.4 percent). Obama received more votes than any presidential candidate in history, easily topping the 62 million votes that President George W. Bush won in his 2004 re-election campaign.
- Approximately 131.3 million Americans cast a vote for a presidential candidate, the most in history. The turnout on Nov. 4 was 62 percent of all eligible voters, just above the 61 percent turnout rate in the 2004 election.
- Obama's share of the national popular vote was the largest for a presidential nominee since 1988, when Republican nominee George Bush took 53.4 percent of the vote to win his first and only term, and the highest for a Democratic candidate since 1964, the year President Lyndon B. Johnson was elected with 61.1 percent of the vote.
- Obama's 7.2 percentage point margin of victory was the largest for a non-incumbent Democratic presidential candidate since 1932, when Franklin D. Roosevelt unseated President Herbert Hoover by nearly 18 percentage points.
- Obama carried 28 states and the District of Columbia, which had a cumulative 364 electoral votes. McCain won 22 states with an electoral vote allocation of 174. But the Electoral College tally was actually 365-173 because Obama won one of five electoral votes in Nebraska, where McCain outpolled Obama statewide but Obama won more votes in the congressional district that included Omaha. Nebraska was one of two states — Maine was the other — that did not use a "winner-take-all" system of awarding electoral votes, instead using a district-based system that awarded two electoral votes to the statewide winner and one electoral vote for each congressional district a candidate carried.
- Obama won nine states, totaling 112 electoral votes, that had voted for President George W. Bush in 2004: Florida (27 electoral votes); Ohio (20); North Carolina (15); Virginia (13); Indiana (11); Colorado (9); Iowa (7); Nevada (5); and New Mexico (5). Indiana and Virginia last voted Democratic for president in 1964. The other 41 states voted for the same party's nominee in 2008 as they had four years before.
- Among the 50 states, Obama took his largest vote share in Hawaii (71.8 percent), his birth state. McCain's best-performing state was Oklahoma (65.6 percent).

frequent communications and ultimately driving up voter turnout.

The candidate showed repeatedly that he was cool under pressure, lending credence to his campaign's description of him as "No Drama Obama." Yet the Democratic primary campaign identified weaknesses that raised some doubt he would prevail in November.

Hillary Clinton's superior performance among white, working-class voters, including those in "battleground states" such as Ohio and Pennsylvania, created concerns that Obama's race might prove a barrier in the general election campaign. And, while McCain wrapped up the Republican nomination in early March, Obama endured a bruising battle right through the final primaries on June 3 before he could declare victory and obtain Clinton's concession.

While most critics refrained from direct reference to race, there was a concerted effort to portray Obama as exotic or radical. Much was made of the fact that his African father was born a Muslim, and some Republicans relished enunciating the candidate's full name, Barack Hussein Obama. Conservatives also made much of a comment in February by Michelle Obama, the candidate's wife, that "for the first time in my adult life I am really proud of my country, because it feels like hope is finally making a comeback."

The effort to caricature the Obamas was captured by a cover drawing for the New Yorker magazine. It portrayed Michelle Obama — a conservatively coiffed, Princeton-educated lawyer — bearing an AK-47 rifle, sporting an outsize Afro and fist-bumping her turban-topped husband in the Oval Office beneath a portrait of the al Qaeda leader Osama bin Laden. The magazine said its intent was to ridicule the descriptions of the Obamas as radicals being spread through the right-wing rumor mill. But Democrats decried the cartoon as promulgating the very negative image the magazine was trying to mock.

During the primary campaign, Obama decided to make a major address on race relations to deflect the controversy that arose over his former pastor, the Rev. Jeremiah Wright, who had made a series of inflammatory comments about race. In the fall, Republicans sought to get political mileage out of Obama's past work on education panels in Chicago with William Ayers, a 1960s leftist radical turned college professor. Obama said he and Ayers were not personally close. However, the Republican vice presidential nominee, Gov. Sarah Palin of Alaska, took to describing him as "palling around with terrorists."

There was some irony, then, in another frequent criticism of Obama: that he had a cerebral and overly cautious approach to addressing complex policy questions. While the soaring rhetoric he employed in his speeches inspired his supporters, his answers to questions in debates and television interviews at times appeared hesitant and less than heartfelt.

GOP RATINGS SLIP

It turned out that whatever pitfalls Obama faced were outweighed by the burden that the damaged Republican Party "brand" would inflict on the GOP nominee.

As recently as 2004, the party appeared ascendant, with Bush winning re-election while the GOP maintained control of the House and expanded its Senate majority by four seats, to 55. But the party's standing already was starting to unravel by the time Bush was sworn in for his second term.

Both of the principal rationales that Bush, Vice President Dick Cheney and other administration officials had used to justify the 2003 invasion of Iraq — stockpiled weapons of mass destruction and close ties between Iraqi dictator Saddam Hussein and the al Qaeda terrorist network that perpetrated the attacks of Sept. 11, 2001 — had been proven wrong. Poor planning for post-victory pacification resulted in a conflict that was longer, far bloodier and much more expensive than Bush and fellow Republicans had predicted.

Bush's popularity already was shrinking when a botched federal response to Hurricane Katrina's devastation in New Orleans in August 2005 sent his job approval rating into a tailspin from which it never recovered. These setbacks, along with early signs that a long-running economic boom was slowing down, had cost the Republicans 30

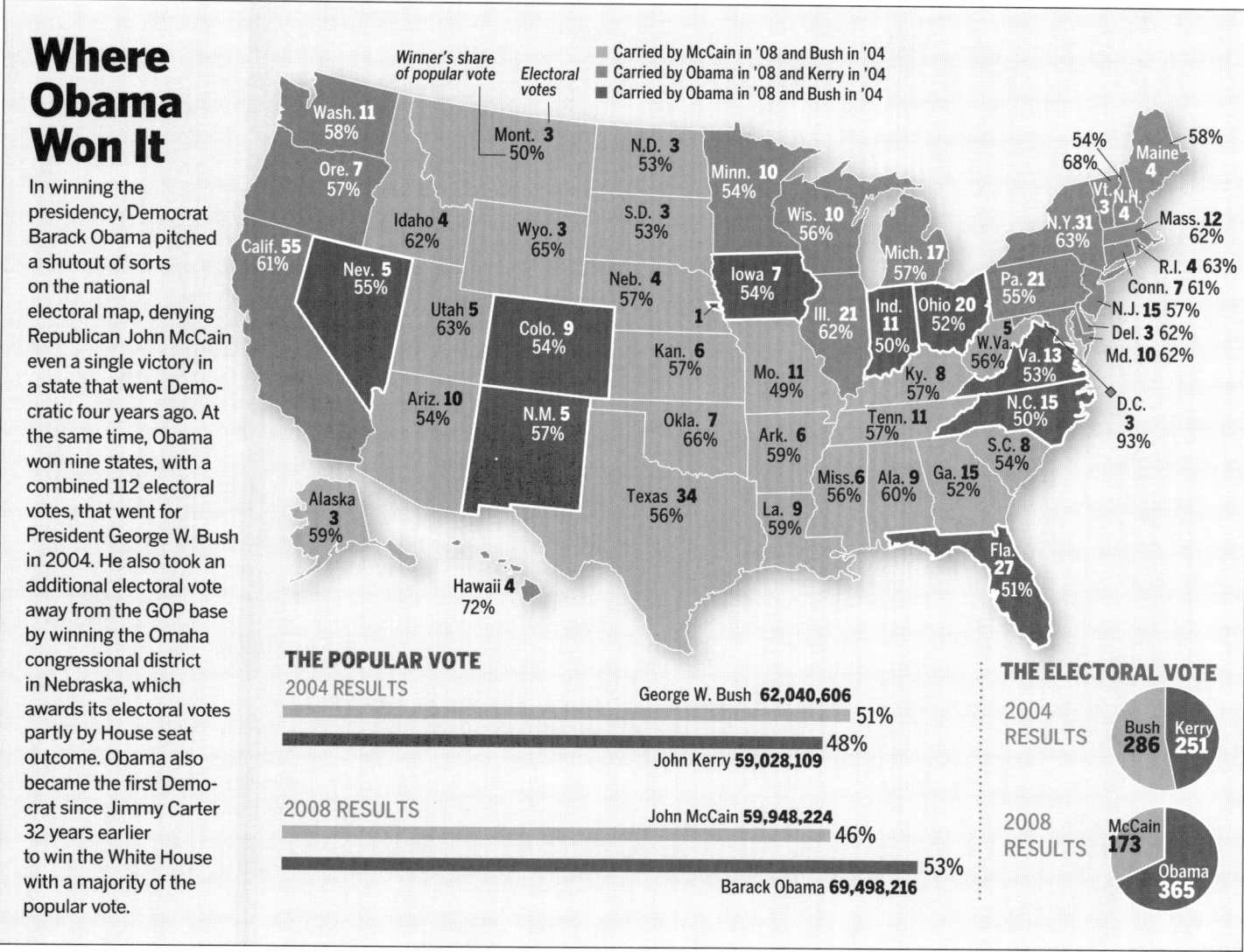

Where Obama Won It

In winning the presidency, Democrat Barack Obama pitched a shutout of sorts on the national electoral map, denying Republican John McCain even a single victory in a state that went Democratic four years ago. At the same time, Obama won nine states, with a combined 112 electoral votes, that went for President George W. Bush in 2004. He also took an additional electoral vote away from the GOP base by winning the Omaha congressional district in Nebraska, which awards its electoral votes partly by House seat outcome. Obama also became the first Democrat since Jimmy Carter 32 years earlier to win the White House with a majority of the popular vote.

Winner's share of popular vote

Electoral votes

- Carried by McCain in '08 and Bush in '04
- Carried by Obama in '08 and Kerry in '04
- Carried by Obama in '08 and Bush in '04

Wash. 11 58%
Ore. 7 57%
Calif. 55 61%
Nev. 5 55%
Idaho 4 62%
Utah 5 63%
Ariz. 10 54%
Alaska 3 59%
Hawaii 4 72%

Mont. 3 50%
Wyo. 3 65%
Colo. 9 54%
N.M. 5 57%

N.D. 3 53%
S.D. 3 53%
Neb. 4 57%
1
Kan. 6 57%
Okla. 7 66%
Texas 34 56%

Minn. 10 54%
Wis. 10 56%
Iowa 7 54%
Mo. 11 49%
Ark. 6 59%
La. 9 59%

Mich. 17 57%
Ill. 21 62%
Ind. 11 50%
Ohio 20 52%
Ky. 8 57%
Tenn. 11 57%
Miss. 6 56%
Ala. 9 60%
Ga. 15 52%
Fla. 27 51%

54% 68%
Vt. 3
N.Y. 31 63%
Pa. 21 55%
W.Va. 5 56%
Va. 13 53%
N.C. 15 50%
S.C. 8 54%

Maine 4 58%
N.H. 4
Mass. 12 62%
R.I. 4 63%
Conn. 7 61%
N.J. 15 57%
Del. 3 62%
Md. 10 62%
D.C. 3 93%

THE POPULAR VOTE

2004 RESULTS
George W. Bush **62,040,606** 51%
John Kerry **59,028,109** 48%

2008 RESULTS
John McCain **59,948,224** 46%
Barack Obama **69,498,216** 53%

THE ELECTORAL VOTE

2004 RESULTS
Bush 286
Kerry 251

2008 RESULTS
McCain 173
Obama 365

House seats, six Senate seats and control of both chambers in the 2006 midterm, with analysts accurately predicting another round of big congressional losses for the party looming in the 2008 contests.

By the onset of the presidential campaign, Bush's approval ratings were below 30 percent, and polls showed the Democrats favored by gaping margins on nearly all issues, even reducing the Republicans' traditional advantages on national and homeland security issues.

To overcome these handicaps, the GOP needed a very strong nominee running a nearly flawless presidential campaign. McCain, despite his significant political strengths, came up well short of that threshold. His biggest asset was a personal story that spoke of strength and character: a Navy aviator, shot down and seriously injured in North Vietnam at the height of that war, who survived more than five hellish years in prison camps.

That background also provided McCain with an image of expertise on defense and foreign policy issues — the central focus of his political career — that he wielded during the 2008 campaign. McCain was a strong supporter of Bush's decision to go to war in Iraq and an early advocate of the "surge" of additional U.S. troops that Bush instituted in 2007. He described Obama, who opposed the Iraq War, as naive and unprepared to serve as commander in chief.

McCain's age (he turned 72 in August 2008) was at least a subliminal issue in the contest with Obama, who was a quarter-century younger and had been in Congress fewer than four years. McCain, by contrast, won his first of two House terms in 1982 and moved to the Senate in 1986.

The other credential that McCain made a centerpiece of his campaign was his reputation for defying party orthodoxy. His campaign lionized him as the "Original Maverick."

While his overall record was conservative, McCain had broken with most Republicans on issues, perhaps most prominently in his authorship, with Democratic Sen. Edward M. Kennedy of Massachusetts, of legislation to assimilate, and in many cases enfranchise, millions of illegal immigrants — a measure reviled by conservatives as amounting to "amnesty" for lawbreakers.

But McCain, who had alienated many conservative activists when he waged a serious challenge to Bush for the 2000 nomination, reached a political crossroads in 2004. Some of his fans urged him to break away and build a new third-party movement. It also was learned that Sen. John Kerry of Massachusetts, the Democrats' nominee against Bush that year, considered asking McCain to jump parties and to be his vice presidential running mate.

McCain instead charted a course for a second presidential bid in 2008 by burnishing his bona fides as a conservative. He offered a full-

Democratic Ticket

BARACK HUSSEIN OBAMA

Residence: Chicago

Born: Aug. 4, 1961, in Honolulu

Religion: United Church of Christ

Family: Married Michelle LaVaughn Robinson in 1992; daughters Malia (born 1998) and Sasha (born 2001)

Education: Punahou School, Honolulu, graduated 1979; Occidental College, attended 1979-81; Columbia University, B.A., 1983 (political science); Harvard University, J.D., 1991

Career: Analyst, Business International Corp., New York, 1983-84; organizer, New York Public Interest Research Group, 1984-85; director, Developing Communities Project, Chicago, 1985-88; director, Illinois Project Vote, 1992; associate, Davis, Miner, Barnhill & Galland of Chicago, 1993-96; lecturer, University of Chicago Law School, 1992–2004

Political highlights: Elected as Illinois state senator for the 13th District in 1996, 1998 and 2002; lost 2000 Democratic congressional primary in Illinois' 1st House District, garnering 30 percent against incumbent Rep. Bobby L. Rush; elected to the Senate in 2004, taking 70 percent of the vote against Republican Alan L. Keyes to win the seat from which Republican Peter G. Fitzgerald retired; resigned from the Senate Nov. 16, 2008

Committees: Foreign Relations (European Affairs, chairman); Health, Education, Labor and Pensions; Homeland Security and Governmental Affairs; Veterans' Affairs

JOSEPH ROBINETTE BIDEN JR.

Residence: Wilmington, Del.

Born: Nov. 20, 1942, in Scranton, Pa.

Religion: Roman Catholic

Family: Married Jill Tracy Jacobs in 1977; one daughter, Ashley (born 1981); married Neilia Hunter in 1966; she died in 1972; children Joseph R. IV "Beau" (born 1969), Hunter (born 1970) and Amy (born 1971, died 1972)

Education: Archmere Academy, Claymont, Del., graduated 1961; University of Delaware, B.A., 1965 (history and political science); Syracuse University, J.D., 1968

Career: Public defender and then partner, Biden & Walsh, 1968-72

Political highlights: Elected to the New Castle County Council in 1970; elected to the Senate in 1972, taking 51 percent of the vote against Republican incumbent J. Caleb Boggs, who was seeking a third term; re-elected six times with at least 58 percent of the vote; resigned from the Senate Jan. 15, 2009

Committees: Foreign Relations, chairman; Judiciary (Crime and Drugs, chairman; full committee chairman, 1987-94)

---

throated endorsement for Bush at the 2004 Republican convention and ardently defended the president's prosecution of the war. He reached out to Christian conservative leaders whom he had lambasted during his 2000 campaign. And he essentially abandoned the immigration legislation he'd written with Kennedy.

The result of this maneuvering was not what McCain had hoped for. It raised serious doubts among crucial swing vote constituencies, including independent voters and "soft" Democrats, about how much of a maverick McCain really was. Yet, at the same time, he didn't much placate his harshest conservative critics, many of whom remained unenthusiastic about him right up through Election Day.

McCain did utilize his well-known name, war hero reputation and image as a "straight talker" to prevail over a crowded but relatively weak field of Republican rivals. While the front-loaded process of early primaries and caucuses enabled him to clinch the nomination by early March, his key early victories were a series of plurality wins that nonetheless netted him delegate bounties under winner-take-all rules allowed in the GOP nominating process.

By spring, the party's chances for a November victory appeared to hinge on the hope that the prolonged Democratic battle between Obama and Clinton would leave the eventual winner's campaign irreparably damaged. Instead, Clinton endorsed the victorious Obama, and they achieved reconciliation much quicker than had seemed plausible during their long and often acrimonious contest.

SUPERIOR GAMESMANSHIP

Shortly after Obama locked up the nomination, his campaign unveiled a strategy for the general election campaign focused on "spreading the playing field" by competing not only for the electoral votes of traditional battleground states— among them Ohio, Pennsylvania, Florida, Iowa and New Mexico — but in longstanding Republican presidential strongholds such as Virginia, North Carolina and Colorado.

Republicans scoffed that the Obama camp was blowing smoke in an effort to bait McCain and his party into unnecessarily spending time and money defending states that should be securely in their column. But the Republicans underestimated Obama's determination to follow through on his plan, the ability of his lavishly funded campaign to do so and the underlying weakness of the GOP's case for retaining the White House in the political atmosphere of 2008.

McCain campaigned on standard Republican arguments that he would be a better steward of voters' tax dollars and a stronger defender of national security. But his efforts to slow Obama's momentum involved a series of shifting and at times contradictory tactical moves, which contrasted — mostly unfavorably — with the Democrat's steady and unflappable demeanor.

Obama, after absorbing criticism from McCain about his lack of experience in foreign relations, embarked on a heavily publicized world tour in July that took him to the war zones of Afghanistan and Iraq and to several European capitals where Bush's foreign policies were highly unpopular. The highlight was an outdoor speech before a huge and enraptured throng in the German capital of Berlin.

Although Obama received mainly positive coverage from the U.S. press, the McCain campaign launched an ad at the end of July that derided Obama as "the world's biggest celebrity" and juxtaposed a photograph of him with images of socialite Paris Hilton and pop singer Britney Spears. It turned out to be the most successful ploy of McCain's campaign, raising questions about Obama's depth. The

Republicans returned to the theme after Obama accepted the Democratic nomination on the last Thursday in August.

Yet the very next day, after hammering Obama for months as inexperienced and as a superficial political rock star, McCain announced that his vice presidential choice was Palin — who, at 44, was younger than Obama and had spent fewer than two years as governor of Alaska, two years on a state regulatory board and six years as the mayor of a suburb of fewer than 10,000 people. After the charismatic and staunchly conservative Palin quickly proved a magnet for huge crowds of Republican loyalists, the McCain campaign turned and touted her as an even bigger celebrity than Obama. (Her notoriety was magnified by her standing as only the second woman — and first GOP woman — on a national, major-party ticket. The other was Rep. Geraldine Ferraro of New York, the 1984 Democratic vice presidential nominee.)

Despite Palin's splashy start, her choice turned out to be, at best, a wash for McCain. While her popularity among conservatives addressed one of his biggest chronic weaknesses, she turned off the crucial bloc of moderate voters and proved incapable of appealing to more liberal women who had supported Hillary Clinton and were disappointed that she did not receive the Democratic nomination. Moreover, Palin's stumbling performances in interviews and her Obama-bashing partisanship became fodder for comedians, most notably Tina Fey of NBC's "Saturday Night Live," whose dead-on impersonation of Palin was matched by her uncanny physical resemblance.

McCain's first choice as a running mate who could shake up his campaign and underscore his reputation as a maverick had been his close friend Sen. Joseph I. Lieberman of Connecticut, who continued to caucus with the Democrats in Washington even after declaring himself an independent in 2006. (He'd been the Democratic vice presidential candidate in 2000.) The two shared many of the same views on defense and foreign policy but on domestic and social policy, Lieberman was sufficiently to the left. Ultimately, McCain was convinced that such a nomination was likely to be rejected by delegates at the GOP convention in St. Paul, Minn.

Obama had moved from the outset toward a much more conventional choice for vice president. In the end, the finalists were Sen. Evan Bayh of Indiana, Gov. Tim Kaine of Virginia and Sen. Joseph R. Biden Jr. of Delaware. Biden, the chairman of the Senate Foreign Relations Committee, was chosen in part to counteract voter concerns about Obama's relative lack of foreign policy experience. Biden's modest upbringing in the Pennsylvania city of Scranton and his long rapport with white working-class voters was also expected to help seal off another of Obama's political weaknesses.

The near-collapse of the financial sector in September boosted Obama into a big lead in polls that he would not surrender. While McCain was hobbled by the fact that the economic tailspin occurred on the watch of a Republican president, his own actions underscored the downside of his improvisational approach to politics.

After first drawing heat by telling a campaign audience that "the fundamentals of the economy are sound," McCain described the situation as a crisis. Two days before his first scheduled Sept. 26 debate with Obama, McCain said he would suspend his campaign in order to return to Washington to help broker a deal on a financial industry rescue bill. He then prevailed upon Bush to convene a summit at the White House that included both the presidential candidates and congressional leaders of both parties. Obama, saying voters expected a potential president to handle more than one responsibility at a time,

Republican Ticket

JOHN SIDNEY McCAIN III

Residence: Phoenix

Born: Aug. 29, 1936, in the Panama Canal Zone

Religion: Baptist

Family: Married Cindy Lou Hensley in 1980; four children: Meghan (born 1984), John IV (born 1986), James (born 1988) and Bridget (born 1991, adopted); married Carol Shepp in 1965 and divorced in 1980; adopted her sons from a previous marriage: Douglas (born 1959) and Andrew (born 1962); one daughter, Sidney (born 1966)

Education: Episcopal High School, Alexandria, Va., graduated 1954; U.S. Naval Academy, B.S., 1958; National War College, attended 1973-74

Career: Naval aviator, 1958-67; prisoner of war in North Vietnam, 1967-73; commander, Replacement Air Group 174, Jacksonville, Fla., 1976-77; Navy liaison to the Senate, 1977-81; retired as a captain, 1981 (honors including Silver Star, Bronze Star, Legion of Merit, Purple Heart and Distinguished Flying Cross); vice president for public relations, Hensley & Co. Anheuser-Busch beer distributorship of Phoenix, 1981-82

Political highlights: Elected to the House in 1982 with 66 percent in Arizona's 1st District to succeed Republican John J. Rhodes, who retired; re-elected in 1984 with 78 percent; elected to the Senate in 1986 with 61 percent to succeed Republican Barry Goldwater, who retired; re-elected three times with at least 56 percent of the vote; sought 2000 Republican presidential nomination,

winning seven state contests and garnering 5.1 million primary votes and 239 pledged delegates

Committees: Armed Services, ranking Republican; Commerce, Science and Transportation (chairman 1997-2000 and 2003-04); Indian Affairs (chairman 1995-96 and 2005-06)

SARAH LOUISE HEATH PALIN

Residence: Wasilla, Alaska

Born: Feb. 11, 1964, in Sandpoint, Idaho

Religion: Protestant

Family: Married Todd Mitchell Palin in 1988; five children: Track (born 1989), Bristol (born 1990), Willow (born 1995), Piper (born 2001) and Trig (born 2008)

Education: Wasilla High School, graduated 1982; attended Hawaii Pacific College, North Idaho College, University of Idaho and Matanuska-Susitna College, 1982-85; University of Idaho, B.S. 1987 (journalism)

Career: Sports reporter at KTUU, KTVA and the Mat-Su Valley Frontiersman, 1987-88; commercial fishing company partner

Political highlights: Elected to the Wasilla City Council in 1982 and 1985; elected mayor in 1996 and 1999; unsuccessful candidate for GOP nomination for lieutenant governor in 2002; chairwoman, Alaska Oil and Gas Conservation Commission, 2003-04; elected governor in 2006 with 48 percent against Democratic former Gov. Tony Knowles after defeating incumbent Gov. Frank H. Murkowski in the Republican primary

2008 Presidential Election Results

STATES	ELECTORAL VOTE		POPULAR VOTE				PERCENT OF POPULAR VOTE			WINNER'S MARGIN (Percentage points)
	OBAMA	McCAIN	OBAMA	McCAIN	OTHERS	TOTAL	OBAMA	McCAIN	OTHERS	
Alabama		9	813,479	1,266,546	19,794	2,099,819	38.7	60.3	0.9	21.6
Alaska		3	123,594	193,841	8,762	326,197	37.9	59.4	2.7	21.5
Arizona		10	1,034,707	1,230,111	28,657	2,293,475	45.1	53.6	1.2	8.5
Arkansas		6	422,310	638,017	26,290	1,086,617	38.9	58.7	2.4	19.9
California	55		8,274,473	5,011,781	275,646	13,561,900	61.0	37.0	2.0	24.1
Colorado	9		1,288,576	1,073,589	39,196	2,401,361	53.7	44.7	1.6	9.0
Connecticut	7		997,772	629,428	18,385	1,645,585	60.6	38.2	1.1	22.4
Delaware	3		255,446	152,373	4,579	412,398	61.9	36.9	1.1	25.0
District of Columbia	3		245,800	17,367	2,686	265,853	92.5	6.5	1.0	85.9
Florida	27		4,282,074	4,045,624	63,046	8,390,744	51.0	48.2	0.8	2.8
Georgia		15	1,844,137	2,048,744	36,618	3,929,499	46.9	52.1	0.9	5.2
Hawaii	4		325,871	120,566	7,131	453,568	71.8	26.6	1.6	45.3
Idaho		4	236,440	403,012	15,580	655,032	36.1	61.5	2.4	25.4
Illinois	21		3,419,348	2,031,179	71,844	5,522,371	61.9	36.8	1.3	25.1
Indiana	11		1,374,039	1,345,648	31,367	2,751,054	49.9	48.9	1.1	1.0
Iowa	7		828,940	682,379	19,067	1,530,386	54.2	44.6	1.2	9.6
Kansas		6	514,765	699,655	21,452	1,235,872	41.7	56.6	1.7	15.0
Kentucky		8	751,985	1,048,462	26,061	1,826,508	41.2	57.4	1.4	16.2
Louisiana		9	782,989	1,148,275	29,497	1,960,761	39.9	58.6	1.5	18.6
Maine	4		421,923	295,273	13,967	731,163	57.7	40.4	1.9	17.3
Maryland	10		1,629,467	959,862	42,267	2,631,596	61.9	36.5	1.6	25.4
Massachusetts	12		1,904,097	1,108,854	68,034	3,080,985	61.8	36.0	2.2	25.8
Michigan	17		2,872,579	2,048,639	80,548	5,001,766	57.4	41.0	1.6	16.5
Minnesota	10		1,573,354	1,275,409	61,606	2,910,369	54.1	43.8	2.1	10.2
Mississippi		6	554,662	724,597	10,606	1,289,865	43.0	56.2	0.8	13.2
Missouri		11	1,441,911	1,445,814	37,480	2,925,205	49.3	49.4	1.3	0.1
Montana		3	231,667	242,763	15,679	490,109	47.3	49.5	3.2	2.3
Nebraska	1	4	333,319	452,979	14,983	801,281	41.6	56.5	1.9	14.9
Nevada	5		533,736	412,827	21,285	967,848	55.1	42.7	2.2	12.5
New Hampshire	4		384,826	316,534	9,610	710,970	54.1	44.5	1.4	9.6
New Jersey	15		2,215,422	1,613,207	39,608	3,868,237	57.3	41.7	1.0	15.6
New Mexico	5		472,422	346,832	10,904	830,158	56.9	41.8	1.3	15.1
New York	31		4,804,701	2,752,728	79,600	7,637,029	62.9	36.0	1.0	26.9
North Carolina	15		2,142,651	2,128,474	39,664	4,310,789	49.7	49.4	0.9	0.3
North Dakota		3	141,278	168,601	6,742	316,621	44.6	53.3	2.1	8.6
Ohio	20		2,940,044	2,677,820	90,486	5,708,350	51.5	46.9	1.6	4.6
Oklahoma		7	502,496	960,165	—	1,462,661	34.4	65.6	0.0	31.3
Oregon	7		1,037,291	738,475	52,098	1,827,864	56.7	40.4	2.9	16.3
Pennsylvania	21		3,276,363	2,655,885	62,889	5,995,137	54.7	44.3	1.0	10.3
Rhode Island	4		296,571	165,391	7,805	469,767	63.1	35.2	1.7	27.9
South Carolina		8	862,449	1,034,896	23,624	1,920,969	44.9	53.9	1.2	9.0
South Dakota		3	170,924	203,054	7,997	381,975	44.7	53.2	2.1	8.4
Tennessee		11	1,087,437	1,479,178	33,134	2,599,749	41.8	56.9	1.3	15.1
Texas		34	3,528,633	4,479,328	69,834	8,077,795	43.7	55.5	0.9	11.8
Utah		5	327,670	596,030	28,670	952,370	34.4	62.6	3.0	28.2
Vermont	3		219,262	98,974	6,810	325,046	67.5	30.4	2.1	37.0
Virginia	13		1,959,532	1,725,005	38,723	3,723,260	52.6	46.3	1.0	6.3
Washington	11		1,750,848	1,229,216	56,814	3,036,878	57.7	40.5	1.9	17.2
West Virginia		5	303,857	397,466	12,039	713,362	42.6	55.7	1.7	13.1
Wisconsin	10		1,677,211	1,262,393	43,813	2,983,417	56.2	42.3	1.5	13.9
Wyoming		3	82,868	164,958	6,832	254,658	32.5	64.8	2.7	32.2
TOTAL	**365**	**173**	**69,498,216**	**59,948,224**	**1,839,809**	**131,286,249**	**52.9**	**45.7**	**1.4**	**7.3**

'Congress' Rarely Tops a President's Résumé

Having Sen. Barack Obama of Illinois as the Democratic nominee and Sen. John McCain of Arizona as the Republican nominee created a milestone in American presidential election history: The 2008 election marked the first time when both the principal candidates in the general election were incumbent members of Congress. In fact, only 15 times previously had a sitting senator (and only twice before had a sitting House member) sought and won presidential votes in the

Electoral College. Only three of those lawmakers (a success rate of 18 percent) had won the White House, the most recent being Sen. John F. Kennedy in 1960. Historically, the odds were best for winning the presidency from a position as a former Army general: Six of 10 times, major candidates with that background triumphed. Those who had already won the White House at least once did best of all: 65 percent of the time that one of them ran, he won again.

Losers   Winners

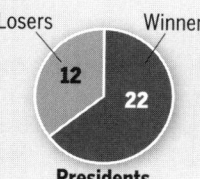 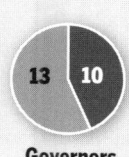 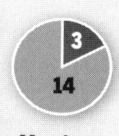   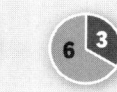 

| Presidents | Governors | Members of Congress | Generals | Vice presidents | Cabinet members | Former members of Congress | Ambassadors | Other* |

NOTES: Candidates are characterized with the jobs for which they were best known in their presidential bids. Therefore, the "presidents" category includes three former presidents attempting comebacks: T. Roosevelt in 1912, Cleveland in 1892 and Fillmore in 1856. There are also six former governors (most recently Reagan in 1980), two former vice presidents (most recently Mondale in 1984), three former Cabinet secretaries and three former diplomats. Included are all candidates who sought and received votes in the Electoral College for president. Some are in more than one category: George W. Bush, for example, is counted among the governors (his job in 2000) and the presidents (his job in 2004).

* Supreme Court justice, state judge, former mayor, utility company executive, newspaper editor and explorer

2004 SEN. JOHN KERRY of Massachusetts, **Democrat**   `LOST`
251 electoral votes *(lost to President George W. Bush)*

1996 SEN. BOB DOLE of Kansas*, **Republican**   `LOST`
159 electoral votes *(lost to President Bill Clinton)*

1972 SEN. GEORGE McGOVERN of South Dakota, **Democrat**   `LOST`
17 electoral votes *(lost to President Richard Nixon)*

1964 SEN. BARRY GOLDWATER of Arizona, **Republican**   `LOST`
52 electoral votes *(lost to President Lyndon B. Johnson)*

1960 SEN. JOHN F. KENNEDY of Massachusetts, **Democrat**   `WON`
303 electoral votes *(defeated Vice President Richard Nixon)* **

1924 SEN. ROBERT M. LA FOLLETTE of Wisconsin, **Progressive**   `LOST`
13 electoral votes *(lost to President Calvin Coolidge)*

1920 SEN. WARREN G. HARDING of Ohio, **Republican**   `WON`
404 electoral votes *(defeated Gov. James M. Cox of Ohio)*

1880 REP. JAMES A. GARFIELD of Ohio, **Republican**   `WON`
214 electoral votes *(defeated Gen. Winfield S. Hancock)*

1860 SEN. STEPHEN A. DOUGLAS of Illinois, **Democrat**   `LOST`
12 electoral votes *(lost to former Rep. Abraham Lincoln of Illinois)*

1848 SEN. LEWIS CASS of Michigan*, **Democrat**   `LOST`
127 electoral votes *(lost to Major Gen. Zachary Taylor)*

1836 SEN. HUGH LAWSON WHITE of Tennessee, **Whig**   `LOST`
26 electoral votes
SEN. DANIEL WEBSTER of Massachusetts, **Whig**
14 electoral votes
SEN. WILLIE P. MANGUM of North Carolina, **Whig**
11 electoral votes *(all lost to Vice President Martin Van Buren)*

1832 SEN. HENRY CLAY of Kentucky, **National Republican**   `LOST`
49 electoral votes *(lost to President Andrew Jackson)*

1824 SEN. ANDREW JACKSON of Tennessee, **Democratic-Republican**   `LOST`
99 electoral votes
REP. HENRY CLAY of Kentucky, **Democratic-Republican**
37 electoral votes *(both lost to Secretary of State John Quincy Adams)*

1816 SEN. RUFUS KING of New York, **Federalist**   `LOST`
34 electoral votes *(lost to Secretary of State James Monroe)*

* Resigned Senate seat after securing nomination.
** Sen. Harry F. Byrd, D-Va., was not an active candidate but took 15 electoral votes.

NOTE: Not included are members of Congress who received electoral votes in the four elections before the 12th Amendment was ratified in 1804, when electors did not designate which of their votes was for president and which was for vice president.

rejected the idea of suspending his campaign. And McCain's strategy backfired when the summit dissolved into partisan rancor. House Republicans, whom McCain had tried to persuade to vote for the legislation, instead sent it to an embarrassing defeat. A revised version was passed and enacted a few days later.

By the middle of October, Obama maintained a steady lead in national polls of mid to high single digits. More ominously for McCain, Obama moved into big leads in several states that were expected to produce competitive races.

In the end, Obama's victory followed the road map that his campaign had drawn. He swept the longstanding Democratic strongholds

of the Northeast, Illinois and the West Coast; won dominant victories in such battleground states as Pennsylvania, Michigan, Wisconsin, Minnesota, Iowa, New Mexico and New Hampshire; scored narrow but key wins for the big electoral vote prizes in Florida and Ohio, the states that had decided the previous two elections for Bush; and scored big breakthroughs in Indiana and Virginia.

He capped his sweeping victory — the strongest for a Democratic presidential nominee since incumbent Lyndon B. Johnson's 1964 landslide — by carrying the former Republican presidential stronghold of Colorado, where Obama's stadium spectacular in August had set the stage for his march into political history. ∎

Obama Upsets Clinton for Nomination

BARACK OBAMA'S ANNOUNCEMENT that he was running for president — an event that drew several thousand supporters and a big media presence to Springfield, Ill., on a frigid winter morning in 2007 — initially suggested nothing more than that he was a fast-rising and ambitious star in American politics. Hillary Rodham Clinton, a second-term senator from New York and wife of former President Bill Clinton, was widely regarded as a nearly prohibitive favorite to win the Democratic nomination.

Obama had only recently arrived on the national scene, first with a dynamic keynote address to the 2004 Democratic National Convention and later that year with a landslide election to an open Senate seat in Illinois. Clinton had been on center stage since 1992, when her husband won his first term as president. Obama was six months shy of his 46th birthday when he entered the presidential contest. Clinton, who was almost 14 years older, would repeatedly question whether Obama was experienced enough.

And while Clinton sought to break the "glass ceiling" in American politics — by becoming the first woman to win the White House — Obama appeared to face a more daunting obstacle. He was seeking to become the nation's first African-American president, and to do so within recent memory of deep and sometimes violent racial divisions that split the nation. He was born to a black father from Kenya and a white mother from Kansas in 1961, before blacks had been granted many basic civil rights under federal law.

But Obama's Feb. 10 kickoff event highlighted the political strengths that would establish him as a top-tier contender, then allow him to leap past Clinton with a series of key victories in early 2008, and finally help him to weather a comeback effort that Clinton sustained through the final primaries.

Obama exhibited the rhetorical talents that first brought him to national attention. He displayed a sense of stagecraft and an ability to draw big audiences. And he clearly articulated a theme of change at a time when most Americans disapproved of George W. Bush, the two-term Republican president, and his handling of the Iraq War, the economy and other matters.

Obama's Springfield announcement came in the city where he had been a state senator for eight years before arriving in Washington. The setting was the Old State House, where Abraham Lincoln famously declared before the Civil War, "A house divided against itself cannot stand." The climactic paragraph of the new candidate's text paid clear homage to Lincoln, who had decreed an end to slavery in the United States 144 years earlier: "Together, starting today, let us finish the work that needs to be done, and usher in a new birth of freedom on this Earth."

CLINTON'S AURA OF INEVITABILITY

Clinton's low-key announcement, three weeks before, exuded the confidence of a front-runner. She posted a video on her Web site that had been made while she sat on a couch in her home off Washington's Embassy Row. That confidence appeared well-placed. Though controversy and even an impeachment had plagued Bill Clinton's tenure in the White House and had fueled intense partisan divisions in the country, most Democrats remained fond of the 42nd president and appeared open to a sort of dynastic restoration through the nomination of his wife, the only first lady to have won elective federal office.

A USA Today-Gallup poll taken Feb. 9-11, 2007, a period that included Obama's announcement, showed Clinton leading Obama, 40 percent to 21 percent. Third, with 14 percent, was Al Gore, Bill Clinton's vice president and the party's 2000 nominee. (He ended up not running in 2008.) John Edwards, the 2004 vice presidential nominee and a former North Carolina senator, had 13 percent.

Stuck in single digits — and bound for early elimination from the nominating contest a year later — were Gov. Bill Richardson of New Mexico, who sought to become the first Hispanic president; Senate Foreign Relations Chairman Joseph R. Biden Jr. of Delaware, who ran briefly for the 1988 nomination and was ultimately chosen by Obama as running mate; Christopher J. Dodd of Connecticut, chairman of the Senate Banking, Housing and Urban Affairs Chairman and a former national party chairman; Rep. Dennis J. Kucinich of Ohio, who was running as an anti-war candidate as he had in 2004; and former Sen. Mike Gravel of Alaska, who cast himself as an iconoclastic outsider.

Clinton sought to create an aura that her nomination was inevitable, suggesting in the initial Democratic debates that the other candidates were focusing their criticism on her because she was so clearly in the lead. Yet weaknesses emerged that would prevent Clinton from clearing the field and eventually would knock her off her front-runner's perch. Although she was a strong critic of Bush's handling of the Iraq War, she angered party liberals by refusing to renounce her Senate vote in 2002 to authorize the initial invasion of the country. Her position contrasted with that of Obama, who spoke out against going to war when he was a state senator.

Clinton also fell short of gaining the support of the party establishment, which at the outset had appeared to be hers for the asking. Party rules gave hundreds of seats at the August 2008 convention in Denver to party operatives and elected officials. Clinton hoped these superdelegates would rally to her. Instead, most deferred their endorsements until after the caucuses and primaries began.

Obama's surge into contention, meanwhile, was fueled by massive fundraising, much of it Internet-based, that built upon candidates' experiences from the 2004 and 2006 elections. Obama ultimately shattered previous records by raising about $750 million overall, and he became the first candidate to opt out of the public financing system for presidential general elections (which included spending limitations) since it took effect with the 1976 election.

EARLY SETBACK VOTES FOR CLINTON

Clinton's image of inevitability was shattered when the first votes were cast. The Jan. 3 Iowa caucuses produced a victory for Obama, who took 38 percent of the precinct delegates. Clinton fell to third, with 29 percent to Edwards' 30 percent.

Suddenly the commentary turned from how quickly Clinton would dispose of her opposition to whether her campaign could survive the New Hampshire primary just five days later. Clinton fought back with renewed emphasis on her experience in national affairs, which she asserted made her ready "from Day One" to fulfill the duties of the presidency. She also challenged Obama's claim to be the true agent of political change, saying that he was a relative newcomer and outsider, while she had spent more than three decades working to better the lives of Americans.

2008 Democratic Primary and Caucus Results

	DATE	TURNOUT	CLINTON	EDWARDS	OBAMA	OTHERS	WINNER	PLURALITY
PRIMARIES								
New Hampshire	Jan. 8	287,557	39%	17%	36%	8%	*Clinton*	7,589
Michigan (*unsanctioned*)	Jan. 15	594,398	55	–	–	45	*Clinton*	90,141
South Carolina	Jan. 26	532,151	26	18	55	0	**Obama**	153,908
Florida (*unsanctioned*)	Jan. 29	1,749,920	50	14	33	3	*Clinton*	294,772
Alabama	Feb. 5	536,626	42	1	56	1	**Obama**	77,230
Arizona	Feb. 5	455,635	50	5	42	2	*Clinton*	36,375
Arkansas	Feb. 5	314,234	70	2	26	2	*Clinton*	137,660
California	Feb. 5	5,066,993	51	4	43	2	*Clinton*	421,522
Connecticut	Feb. 5	354,539	47	1	51	2	**Obama**	14,316
Delaware	Feb. 5	96,374	42	1	53	3	**Obama**	10,388
Georgia	Feb. 5	1,060,851	31	2	66	1	**Obama**	374,221
Illinois	Feb. 5	2,038,614	33	2	65	1	**Obama**	650,304
Massachusetts	Feb. 5	1,258,923	56	2	41	2	*Clinton*	193,505
Missouri	Feb. 5	822,734	48	2	49	1	**Obama**	11,237
New Jersey	Feb. 5	1,141,199	54	1	44	1	*Clinton*	112,128
New York	Feb. 5	1,862,445	57	1	40	1	*Clinton*	317,477
Oklahoma	Feb. 5	417,207	55	10	31	4	*Clinton*	98,350
Tennessee	Feb. 5	624,764	54	4	40	1	*Clinton*	83,371
Utah	Feb. 5	131,403	39	3	57	1	**Obama**	23,205
Louisiana	Feb. 9	384,346	36	3	57	4	**Obama**	83,707
District of Columbia	Feb. 12	123,994	24	0	75	1	**Obama**	63,916
Maryland	Feb. 12	878,174	36	1	61	2	**Obama**	218,454
Virginia	Feb. 12	986,203	35	1	64	0	**Obama**	278,054
Washington (*nonbinding*)	Feb. 19	691,381	46	2	51	1	**Obama**	38,368
Wisconsin	Feb. 19	1,113,753	41	1	58	1	**Obama**	192,897
Ohio	March 4	2,354,721	53	2	45	–	*Clinton*	203,851
Rhode Island	March 4	186,439	58	1	40	1	*Clinton*	33,633
Texas	March 4	2,874,986	51	1	47	1	*Clinton*	100,258
Vermont	March 4	154,960	39	1	59	1	**Obama**	32,095
Mississippi	March 11	434,071	37	1	61	1	**Obama**	106,097
Pennsylvania	April 22	2,336,480	55	–	45	–	*Clinton*	213,598
Indiana	May 6	1,278,314	51	–	49	–	*Clinton*	14,192
North Carolina	May 6	1,580,726	42	–	56	2	**Obama**	229,722
Nebraska (*nonbinding*)	May 13	94,535	47	–	49	4	**Obama**	2,691
West Virginia	May 13	359,910	67	7	26	–	*Clinton*	148,154
Kentucky	May 20	701,768	65	2	30	3	*Clinton*	249,557
Oregon	May 20	641,499	41	–	59	1	**Obama**	115,560
Idaho (*nonbinding*)	May 27	42,802	38	–	56	6	**Obama**	7,858
Puerto Rico	June 1	384,578	68	–	32	–	*Clinton*	141,662
Montana	June 3	182,421	41	–	57	2	**Obama**	28,285
South Dakota	June 3	97,797	55	–	45	–	*Clinton*	10,459
CAUCUSES								
Iowa	Jan. 3	239,000*	29%	30%	38%	3%	**Obama**	–
Nevada	Jan. 19	117,599	51	4	45	0	*Clinton*	–
Alaska	Feb. 5	8,880	25	0	75	0	**Obama**	4,480
Colorado	Feb. 5	119,831	32	0	66	1	**Obama**	40,982
Idaho	Feb. 5	21,224	17	1	80	3	**Obama**	13,225
Kansas	Feb. 5	36,731	26	0	74	0	**Obama**	17,710
Minnesota	Feb. 5	214,066	32	0	66	1	**Obama**	73,115
New Mexico	Feb. 5	149,379	49	1	48	2	*Clinton*	1,709
North Dakota	Feb. 5	19,012	37	1	61	1	**Obama**	4,677
Nebraska	Feb. 9	38,670	32	0	68	0	**Obama**	13,681
Washington	Feb. 9	244,458	31	0	68	1	**Obama**	–
Maine	Feb. 10	44,340	40	0	60	1	**Obama**	–
Hawaii	Feb. 19	37,182	24	0	76	0	**Obama**	19,512
Texas	March 4	1,000,000*	44	0	56	0	**Obama**	–
Wyoming	March 8	8,753	38	0	61	1	**Obama**	2,067

*Estimates

SOURCE: The Rhodes Cook Letter

Clinton ended up besting Obama in New Hampshire, 39 percent to 36 percent, with Edwards pushed to the brink of elimination by finishing a distant third with 17 percent.

But Clinton scored only two more clear victories in the first month of voting — in Michigan on Jan. 15 and Florida on Jan. 29 — and both primary wins were tainted by a dispute between the state parties and the Democratic National Committee (DNC). The two states had picked January dates in violation of national party scheduling rules, prompting the DNC to threaten to deny both states their delegates to the national convention. Clinton observed a DNC request not to actively campaign in Michigan, but she was the only major candidate who kept her name on the ballot and ended up with 55 percent to 40 percent for "uncommitted." Obama was on the ballot in Florida, but the same "no campaigning" rule was in effect, and the better-known Clinton won, 50 percent to 33 percent.

Obama, though, had fought Clinton to a virtual draw in the Jan. 19 caucuses in Nevada, a harbinger of his subsequent successes in organizing at the grass roots in the states that held caucuses instead of primaries. And his 28-percentage-point margin of victory in the Jan. 26 South Carolina primary showed he could both generate enormous support among black voters and cut into Clinton's support among whites. Obama prevailed despite an aggressive and at times combative involvement in that primary by Bill Clinton, starting a long-running debate within the senator's camp about the strategically appropriate campaign role for the former president.

The next milestone came Feb. 5, "Super Tuesday," designed by the party to be the climax of a front-loaded primary and caucus schedule that would surely yield a prohibitive front-runner for the nomination. Clinton's campaign was built on an expectation that she would dominate most of the day's contests. Clinton won 10, including the primaries in California and New York that were the day's biggest delegate prizes. But Obama won 13, including a primary landslide in his home state of Illinois. Beyond that, he exposed one of Clinton's crucial miscalculations: Making little effort to organize in caucus states, under the presumption that her front-runner status would be sufficient to push her to the nomination. Obama capitalized on that decision by winning six of the day's seven caucuses by lopsided margins.

TRADING VICTORIES

It quickly became apparent that Clinton's team lacked a plan for waging a competitive campaign after Super Tuesday. Obama won the next 10 primaries and caucuses, spurring a wave of superdelegates' endorsements and putting pressure on Clinton to concede so that her rival could start focusing on a general election contest against Sen. John McCain of Arizona, who by then had effectively secured the Republican nomination.

McCain had benefitted from GOP rules permitting many states to hold winner-take-all contests for convention delegates. The Democrats required states to divide their delegates proportionally among all candidates who secured at least 15 percent support. So while Obama built a delegate lead over Clinton, he remained well short of the necessary majority.

Clinton won the next two big primaries, on March 4, both on turf favorable to her. Support among working-class white voters propelled her to an 8-point margin of victory in Ohio and strong support from Hispanics helped her claim a 4-point win in Texas. Not only that, but her pivotal levels of support from those two demographic groups, both vitally important in the general election, gave Clinton an open-

ing to argue to fellow Democrats that she would have a better shot in November than would Obama.

In addition, a skit on NBC's "Saturday Night Live" that parodied alleged media favoritism toward Obama turned into a boon for Clinton. Her supporters claimed the media had been much tougher on their candidate, with some decrying what they viewed as sexism. It was also during this period that Clinton aired her most successful television advertisement. Hoping to underscore her view of her superior experience, it showed children sleeping when the White House phone rings, signaling a crisis. "It's 3 a.m., and your children are safe and asleep. Who do you want to answer the phone?"

The ensuing weeks before the April 22 Pennsylvania primary — the longest lull in the primary campaign — were the most difficult for Obama. In mid-March, videos that gained wide circulation showed the Rev. Jeremiah Wright, Obama's longtime pastor in Chicago, engaging in inflammatory rhetoric about race relations. After facing intense questioning about his ties to Wright, who by then was no longer his pastor, Obama delivered an address in Philadelphia in which he distanced himself from Wright's remarks. Obama sought to explain the anger that many black Americans felt and called for reconciliation. The March 18 speech drew mainly high praise.

It was also at this time that discussion arose about how close Obama had been to William Ayers, a Vietnam War era radical who later became a professor at the University of Illinois at Chicago and served along with Obama on boards dealing with education issues. Obama described their ties as professional, and the issue faded during the rest of the Democratic campaign, though Republicans would seek to revive it in the fall.

Obama committed his biggest campaign gaffe just before the contest in Pennsylvania, home to a large population of white, blue-collar voters. In remarks made at a private event in San Francisco but leaked to a political Web site, Obama said many working-class people who experience economic distress "get bitter" and "cling to guns or religion or antipathy to people who aren't like them." Clinton's campaign sought to capitalize on the comment, portraying Obama as an elitist. This issue, too, would get a second airing in the general election campaign.

Clinton won the primary, 55 percent to 45 percent, but her delegate gain was small. She was set back further May 6 when Obama easily won in North Carolina and held Clinton to a 1-point victory in Indiana, another state with a big working-class population.

The candidates traded wins in the closing weeks. In a final blow to Clinton, the DNC and the state Democratic parties in Michigan and Florida resolved their conflict over the disputed January primaries in a manner that diminished the importance of her victories.

Obama declared victory the night of June 3, after primaries that produced a win for him in Montana and a win for Clinton in South Dakota. He picked a symbolic location: the hockey arena in St. Paul, Minn., where Republicans would hold their September convention.

Clinton did not leave questions lingering for long about whether she would give wholehearted support to Obama, as she made a concession and endorsement speech June 7 in Washington. She also urged her supporters to back Obama during a speech at the Democratic convention in Denver, as did Bill Clinton, and made frequent campaign appearances on Obama's behalf.

In December 2008, following his election as president, Obama chose Clinton to be his secretary of State. She was confirmed to that office in January and resigned her seat in the Senate. ∎

'Maverick' McCain Wins GOP Nod

JOHN MCCAIN WON THE 2008 REPUBLICAN presidential nomination in part because he was able to revive many of the political assets he had brought to his first bid for the White House, which he lost to George W. Bush in the GOP primaries eight years before. The Arizona senator once again rallied voters who saw fortitude in his experience as a badly injured Vietnam prisoner of war. And this time, most in his party were won over by the independence they saw in his image as a "maverick," who over a quarter-century in Congress had voted a mainly conservative line that was punctuated with some highly public stands against party orthodoxy.

McCain turned 72 in August 2008 and would have been the oldest president at the time of his first inauguration. But he allayed concerns by campaigning with vigor — often aboard a bus he dubbed the "Straight Talk Express," as he had during his unsuccessful 2000 battle.

These factors would help keep him competitive in his general election campaign against Democrat Barack Obama, even though McCain was compelled all year to fight against a deepening disaffection with his Republican Party. He was running to succeed Bush, whose handling of critical issues in his second term had caused his popularity to plummet and contributed greatly to the Democrats' takeover of Congress in 2006.

But McCain did not win his party's nomination by acclamation. He faced skepticism from a sizable portion of the conservative wing that made up most of the GOP base.

The same iconoclastic image that appealed to McCain's supporters caused friction with the more conservative factions. Many on the Republican right resented McCain for his outspoken stance on certain issues, including his alliance with Democratic Sen. Edward M. Kennedy of Massachusetts in proposing immigration legislation that included a program to assimilate many of the nation's undocumented immigrants; his crusade for enactment in 2002 of a law tightening federal campaign finance rules, which many conservatives viewed as an infringement on their freedom of speech; and his conclusion, early among Republicans, that global climate change was a major environmental problem that should be met with assertive federal intervention.

Some conservatives also had seen Bush, the governor of Texas at the time, as their champion in 2000 and resented McCain for the challenge he waged then. During that contest, he described Pat Robertson and Jerry Falwell, longtime leaders of the Christian conservative movement and crucial supporters of Bush, as "agents of intolerance."

McCain sought to mend fences as he geared up for 2008, reaching out to prominent figures on the religious right. He also gave a strong speech of support for Bush at the 2004 Republican convention, lending his imprimatur of military expertise to Bush's decision a year earlier to launch the war in Iraq. These actions may have eased the doubts about McCain held by many — though not all — conservatives. But they had the less beneficial effect of raising qualms among independent and Democratic voters about how much of a maverick McCain really was.

Nearly all of his rivals in the crowded 2008 Republican field — including former Govs. Mitt Romney of Massachusetts and Mike Huckabee of Arkansas, who emerged as his leading rivals — attempted to run to McCain's right. The only candidates who clearly held views on some issues that strayed from conservative doctrine were former New York Mayor Rudolph Giuliani, who favored abortion rights and gay rights, and Rep. Ron Paul of Texas, a libertarian Republican who was alone in the GOP field in opposing the war in Iraq.

None of the other Republicans came into the contest with a national base, and none campaigned skillfully enough to overcome McCain's strengths. However, McCain's momentum was built on a string of plurality victories, most of them in winner-take-all primaries, that gave him an outsized edge in the race for delegates to the late summer Republican National Convention in St. Paul, Minn.

His success at clinching the nomination by early March masked the difficulty he would face in energizing the party's base in the fall. This played a role in McCain's decision to hand the vice presidential nomination to Gov. Sarah Palin of Alaska, who emerged as a conservative darling while drawing plenty of skepticism — even within the party — that she was inexperienced and ill-prepared for national office.

GIULIANI CHALLENGES FRONT-RUNNER STATUS

In mainstream Republican circles, McCain was the consensus front-runner for the 2008 nomination as soon as Bush won his second term in 2004. McCain was well-known from his first bid, and the populist image he honed then convinced many in the party he could reach beyond the GOP base to win over independents and even some Democrats. In addition, no one likely to run in the 2008 Republican contest could come close to matching the drama inherent in McCain's biography. The five-and-a-half years that he spent in North Vietnamese prisons after being shot down over Hanoi in an October 1967 bombing run left him with an indelible image of strength and character.

In fact, McCain's perceived status as a Navy hero had the ironic effect of almost scuttling his campaign before it got off the ground. After officially entering the race in April 2007, McCain enlisted so many eager consultants that his campaign grew top-heavy and quickly expended millions of dollars. By July the organization was nearly broke, and McCain was compelled to reduce his overhead — in part by dismissing campaign manager Terry Nelson and Rick Weaver, a longtime ally who served as chief adviser.

Things appeared to stabilize under the new leadership of Rick Davis, who ran the 2000 effort, and Steve Schmidt, who held a major role in Bush's 2004 campaign. But McCain was slipping deeply in polls on the nomination. A CBS News survey from Aug. 8 to 12, 2007, showed Giuliani with the support of 38 percent of GOP respondents; in second with 18 percent was former Sen. Fred Thompson of Tennessee, whose other career as an actor had led some Republicans to hope that, like Ronald Reagan, he could become a rallying figure for conservatives. Third with 13 percent was Romney, who once was seen as something of a center-right Republican but campaigned for president on a strongly conservative platform. McCain was fourth with 12 percent.

Giuliani stayed first in the polls through most of the year, but his front-runner status proved fragile. It was based on the stalwart image he projected in steering his city through the crisis that followed the 2001 terrorist attacks. But Giuliani referred so often to 9/11 that critics mocked him as a one-note candidate. He also became vulnerable

2008 Republican Primary and Caucus Results

	DATE	TURNOUT	GIULIANI	HUCKABEE	McCAIN	PAUL	ROMNEY	THOMPSON	OTHERS	WINNER	PLURALITY
PRIMARIES											
New Hampshire	Jan. 8	239,699	8%	11%	37%	8%	32%	1%	3%	McCain	13,038
Michigan	Jan. 15	869,169	3	16	30	6	39	4	3	Romney	80,331
South Carolina	Jan. 19	445,499	2	30	33	4	15	16	0	McCain	14,743
Florida	Jan. 29	1,949,498	15	13	36	3	31	1	0	McCain	96,829
Alabama	Feb. 5	552,155	0	41	37	3	18	0	0	Huckabee	22,899
Arizona	Feb. 5	541,035	3	9	47	4	35	2	1	McCain	68,359
Arkansas	Feb. 5	229,153	0	60	20	5	14	0	0	Huckabee	92,214
California	Feb. 5	2,932,811	4	12	42	4	35	2	1	McCain	225,517
Connecticut	Feb. 5	151,604	2	7	52	4	33	0	2	McCain	28,945
Delaware	Feb. 5	50,239	2	15	45	4	33	–	0	McCain	6,284
Georgia	Feb. 5	963,541	1	34	32	3	30	0	0	Huckabee	22,123
Illinois (nonbinding)	Feb. 5	899,422	1	16	47	5	29	1	0	McCain	169,512
Massachusetts	Feb. 5	500,550	1	4	41	3	51	0	1	Romney	51,113
Missouri	Feb. 5	588,427	1	32	33	4	29	1	1	McCain	8,355
New Jersey	Feb. 5	566,201	3	8	55	5	28	1	–	McCain	153,071
New York	Feb. 5	642,894	4	11	52	6	28	–	–	McCain	154,958
Oklahoma	Feb. 5	335,054	1	33	37	3	25	1	1	McCain	10,873
Tennessee	Feb. 5	553,815	1	34	32	6	24	3	1	Huckabee	14,813
Utah	Feb. 5	296,061	0	1	5	3	89	0	0	Romney	249,025
Louisiana	Feb. 9	161,169	1	43	42	5	6	1	1	Huckabee	2,043
District of Columbia	Feb. 12	6,211	2	16	68	8	6	–	–	McCain	3,178
Maryland	Feb. 12	320,989	1	29	55	6	7	1	1	McCain	84,438
Virginia	Feb. 12	489,252	0	41	50	4	4	1	–	McCain	45,826
Washington	Feb. 19	529,932	1	24	49	8	16	1	1	McCain	134,647
Wisconsin	Feb. 19	410,607	0	37	55	5	2	1	1	McCain	73,048
Ohio	March 4	1,095,917	–	31	60	5	3	2	–	McCain	321,331
Rhode Island	March 4	26,996	–	22	65	7	4	–	3	McCain	11,633
Texas	March 4	1,362,322	0	38	51	5	2	1	3	McCain	179,765
Vermont	March 4	39,843	2	14	71	7	5	–	1	McCain	22,719
Mississippi	March 11	143,286	1	13	79	4	2	2	1	McCain	95,131
Pennsylvania (nonbinding)	April 22	816,928	–	11	73	16	–	–	–	McCain	465,852
Indiana	May 6	412,673	–	10	78	8	5	–	–	McCain	279,135
North Carolina	May 6	517,583	–	12	74	7	–	–	7	McCain	320,067
Nebraska (nonbinding)	May 13	136,648	–	–	87	13	–	–	–	McCain	101,104
West Virginia	May 13	119,015	2	10	76	5	4	–	2	McCain	78,209
Kentucky	May 20	197,793	2	8	72	7	5	–	6	McCain	126,530
Oregon	May 20	353,476	–	–	81	14	–	–	5	McCain	234,781
Idaho	May 27	125,570	–	–	70	24	–	–	7	McCain	57,675
Montana	June 3	95,730	–	–	76	22	–	–	2	McCain	52,185
New Mexico	June 3	110,939	–	–	86	14	–	–	–	McCain	79,817
South Dakota	June 3	60,964	–	7	70	17	3	–	3	McCain	32,716
CAUCUSES											
Iowa	Jan. 3	119,188	3	34	13	10	25	13	0	Huckabee	10,933
Nevada	Jan. 19	43,578	4	8	13	13	51	8	2	Romney	16,588
Maine	Feb. 1-3	5,446	0	6	21	18	52	0	3	Romney	1,677
Alaska	Feb. 5	13,703	0	22	16	17	44	0	2	Romney	2,992
Colorado	Feb. 5	70,229	0	13	18	8	60	0	0	Romney	29,300
Minnesota	Feb. 5	62,828	0	20	22	16	41	0	1	Romney	12,164
Montana	Feb. 5	1,630	0	15	22	25	38	0	0	Romney	–
North Dakota	Feb. 5	9,785	0	20	23	21	36	0	0	Romney	1,266
West Virginia (convention)	Feb. 5	1,089	0	33	16	10	41	0	0	Huckabee	–
Kansas	Feb. 9	19,516	0	60	24	11	3	0	2	Huckabee	7,040
Washington	Feb. 9	n.a.	0	23	25	22	16	0	15	McCain	–

Note: Neither Wyoming's Jan. 5 caucus nor Hawaii's Jan. 25-Feb. 7 caucus included presidential preference polls.

SOURCE: The Rhodes Cook Letter

as conservative Republicans learned more about his three marriages and his more liberal positions on social issues.

McCain, meanwhile, found the key to his comeback in an issue that played to his strength as a longtime specialist on defense and foreign policy: the Iraq War.

McCain was a wholehearted supporter of Bush's decision to send thousands of additional troops to Iraq in a policy known as the "surge," which was carried out at a time when polling showed most Americans wanted Bush to extract all troops from the sectarian bloodletting that plagued Iraq following Saddam Hussein's downfall. But by the end of 2007, the surge appeared to have reduced violence and improved stability in Iraq, and McCain reminded GOP voters that he had been a steadfast supporter. While the vast majority of Democrats and most independents had turned against the war, most Republicans remained supportive, and McCain's position aided his rebound.

POOL OF GOP RIVALS DWINDLES

McCain still faced challenges in breaking from a Republican pack that topped out at 11 candidates, though it had been culled by the time the voting began in January 2008.

McCain, Romney, Giuliani and Thompson had been joined in the top tier by Huckabee, who rose quickly in the polls because his role as a Southern Baptist minister appealed to many conservatives. Paul had developed a fervent though relatively small following behind a platform that combined small-government conservatism with opposition to the Iraq War. Rep. Duncan Hunter of California, the chairman of the House Armed Services Committee, tried to compete with McCain for primacy on defense issues but barely registered in the polls and soon left the race. Already out were former Govs. Tommy G. Thompson of Wisconsin and James S. Gilmore III of Virginia, Sen. Sam Brownback of Kansas and Rep. Tom Tancredo of Colorado.

McCain skipped the Jan. 3 kickoff event in Iowa, which he had no chance of winning. The state's precinct caucuses tended to be dominated by the most conservative voters, and McCain was a critic of subsidies for corn-based ethanol, an alternative-fuel program highly popular in a state that produced millions of bushels of corn each year. The gamble paid off. Romney invested heavily in Iowa but finished second, with 27 percent to 30 percent for Huckabee. Thompson drew 12 percent, the same share that McCain took without campaigning.

Romney faced a must-win situation five days later in New Hampshire, which neighbors his home state. But his emphasis on Iowa had given a big head start to McCain, who had focused on New Hampshire, an open-primary state where he scored a stunning upset of Bush in 2000. McCain won the primary with 37 percent to 32 percent for Romney. Huckabee slipped to third with 12 percent.

The next big contest was Michigan's primary Jan. 15, and there was little likelihood McCain would repeat his 2000 victory over Bush: Romney was born in Detroit; his father, George Romney, was a former auto company chief executive and governor of Michigan in the 1960s; and the contest highlighted the limits of a "straight talk" approach. McCain angered many voters in the economically struggling state by saying, "There are some jobs that aren't coming back to Michigan." Romney won, 39 percent to McCain's 30 percent.

But the race permanently turned in McCain's favor with the Jan. 19 primary in South Carolina, where he had suffered a crushing defeat to Bush eight years before. Again, McCain pulled a modest plurality, but his 33 percent topped 30 percent for Huckabee, who hoped to establish himself as the candidate of the South. Thompson made a

last-stand bid for a foothold on that same turf, but he finished with 16 percent and quit the race. Romney scored only 15 percent.

McCain stirred some controversy during this period. With many conservatives agitating to crack down on illegal immigration, he said in a debate that border security had to be dealt with ahead of the future status of illegal immigrants, and he declared he would not vote again for the immigration bill he had written with Kennedy.

McCain also pushed hard to exploit his principal rival's biggest weakness: the view of many conservatives that Romney was not altogether trustworthy and was a campaign-season convert to many of the right's views. McCain's advertisements raised questions about Romney's fealty to tax cuts and the Iraq War, and Romney protested that McCain had unfairly distorted his record.

The Jan. 29 Florida primary further slowed Romney, who lost to McCain, 36 percent to 31 percent. The contest eliminated Giuliani. After plummeting in national polls, he had decided to wager his entire campaign on winning Florida, a state with a sizable population of transplanted New Yorkers. Instead, he finished third with 15 percent.

STRONG END TO PRIMARY SEASON

McCain's momentum gave him a tremendous advantage going into "Super Tuesday," the Feb. 5 climax of the front-loaded primary and caucus schedule. McCain won nine of that day's 21 contests, including the big delegate prizes of California, New York, Illinois, New Jersey and Missouri. Romney won seven, but most were in much smaller states with fewer delegates. Four days later, Romney ended his campaign with a concession speech at the annual Conservative Political Action Conference in Washington.

Though he had a dominant lead, McCain had not yet secured a majority of convention delegates. Huckabee, who had won five Super Tuesday contests, kept his campaign going in hopes that conservatives who were not thrilled with McCain might rally around him. He received some encouragement by winning Feb. 9 contests in Kansas and Louisiana, but those were his final victories.

McCain hit one more bump before clinching the nomination: a front-page story in The New York Times on Feb. 20 exploring whether the self-proclaimed political outsider was too cozy with lobbyists. The story caused a furor principally because it intimated that the senator had an extramarital affair with one such lobbyist. Both denied any impropriety, and in the end the story benefited the campaign somewhat by galvanizing sympathy for McCain's treatment by what many Republicans derided as the liberal media elite.

McCain's wins in March 4 primaries in four states, including Texas and Ohio, put him over the top and prompted Huckabee to concede. Only Paul declined to throw his support to McCain, and he ran a symbolic campaign through the end of the primary schedule in early June.

The strong roll that enabled McCain to wrap up the nomination early overshadowed an imbalance in voter turnout that was worrisome to GOP strategists. The Democratic nominating contest between Obama and Sen. Hillary Rodham Clinton of New York had drawn many more voters than the Republican side, producing much discussion that the Republicans were suffering from an "enthusiasm gap."

McCain's hopes for victory in November appeared highly dependent on the winner of the Democratic battle — not decided in Obama's favor until June — being badly bruised entering the general election campaign. But the focus of voters and the media on the Obama-Clinton showdown ended up diminishing McCain's visibility for months. ∎

No Magic Number, but More Muscle

ALTHOUGH DEMOCRATS FELL SHORT in their long-shot quest to win the 60 seats necessary to dominate the Senate in the 111th Congress, their net gain of at least seven seats in 2008 put them on the brink of that fili-buster-busting threshold. It also marked the second straight election in which Democrats dominated the Senate balloting.

The new Democratic majority of at least 58 seats — counting the two independents who had caucused with Democrats — was the largest for either party since 1994, just before Republicans gained eight seats and control of the Senate. The Democrats looked poised to secure a 59th seat if the apparent victory of Democrat Al Franken, the humorist and radio talk-show host, over one-term Republican Norm Coleman survived GOP legal challenges in 2009. *(Minnesota, p. 10-18)*

The string of Democratic victories in Senate races was remarkable. Excluding the disputed contest in Minnesota, four Republican incumbents were turned out — Ted Stevens in Alaska, John E. Sununu in New Hampshire, Elizabeth Dole in North Carolina and Gordon H. Smith in Oregon. Democrats claimed three open seats that had been held by Republicans — in Colorado, New Mexico and Virginia.

Four additional Democrats were headed to the Senate as freshmen in 2009: the appointed successors to the newly elected president, Barack Obama, a senator from Illinois elected in 2004; the new vice president, Joseph R. Biden Jr., a senator first elected from Delaware in 1972; Obama's secretary of State, Hillary Rodham Clinton, a senator first elected in New York in 2000; and Obama's Interior secretary, Ken Salazar, elected in 2004 as a senator from Colorado.

Republicans put together a strong challenge against only one incumbent Democrat, Mary L. Landrieu of Louisiana, and it failed. She won a third term by 6 percentage points. Of the 11 other Democratic senators on 2008 ballots, only New Jersey Democrat Frank R. Lautenberg was re-elected with less than 60 percent of the vote.

Democrats had many of the same advantages in the Senate campaigns as Obama did in his presidential campaign against Republican Sen. John McCain of Arizona: money, public disillusionment with Republicans and carefully calibrated candidates. The international financial crisis coming late in the campaign solidified Democratic chances.

The Democrats' advantage in campaign contributions seemed boundless. The Democratic Senatorial Campaign Committee (DSCC) reported raising $163 million in the two-year election cycle, while the National Republican Senatorial Committee (NRSC) raised $94 million. That imbalance in campaign fundraising allowed the DSCC to spend heavily in states where Republican candidates otherwise would have had a substantial money edge over their Democratic opponents.

Republicans, meanwhile, not only suffered from President Bush's low approval ratings and the accumulated mistakes of his administration, but they also were forced to defend more territory — 23 of

THE SENATE

	110th Congress		111th Congress	
Democrats	49	Democrats	56
Republicans	49	Republicans	41
Independents	2	Independents	2
		Undecided*	1

*Minnesota's election remained in litigation as of May 2009.

DEMOCRATS

Net gain	7
Freshmen**	11
Incumbents re-elected	12
Incumbents defeated	0

REPUBLICANS

Net loss	7
Freshmen	2
Incumbents re-elected	13
Incumbents defeated	4

** Includes appointees to fill post-election vacancies in Colorado, Delaware, Illinois and New York.

the 35 Senate seats on the ballot Nov. 4. The Republicans were defending so many seats because they had won the lion's share of Senate races six years earlier, in 2002. The 23-12 partisan split of Senate races was the most lopsided since 1980, when Republicans made a net gain of 12 Senate seats in a year in which they were defending just 10 Senate seats vs. the Democrats' 23.

Moreover, five Republican senators did not seek re-election in 2008, while Democrats did not have a single retirement in their ranks. It was the first time since 1990 that a party had a zero-retirement year in the Senate.

In addition to the advantages of money and terrain, experts said Democrats were able to recruit stronger candidates. The seven Democratic senators first elected in 2008 were a politically experienced bunch: two former governors, two U.S. House members, a state House Speaker, a state senator and a mayor of his state's biggest city.

RACKING UP VICTORIES

On Election Night, it was clear the Democrats had picked up seats in six states.

● **New Hampshire.** Restive Democrats had sought a heavy hitter to take on Sununu — who was finishing his first term, had a proven ability to raise money and whose well-known father, John H. Sununu, had been New Hampshire's governor for six years and White House chief of staff for President George H.W. Bush.

In the summer of 2007, Kathy Sullivan, a former chairwoman of the state Democratic Party, started a movement to recruit Jeanne Shaheen, who had been governor from 1997 through 2002, to take on Sununu six years after she lost their first senatorial matchup by 4 percentage points. New Hampshire had both staunch conservatives and liberals, and Sullivan thought Shaheen, who had run three statewide races and had a record as a moderate on fiscal and social issues, "really fit New Hampshire." Once Shaheen officially entered the race, she gained wide support from the state and national parties as well as from outside groups. Sununu trailed in polling throughout most of the year despite efforts to distance himself from Bush and the national party.

New Hampshire Republican Party Chairman Fergus Cullen blamed Sununu's decisive loss — 52 percent to 45 percent — on the national climate, saying, "There was nothing we could have done" to change the outcome.

● **North Carolina.** Kay Hagan, a state senator from Greensboro for a decade and another moderate, shocked Republicans by trouncing Dole, who had held Cabinet posts in two administrations and had succeeded conservative icon Jesse Helms in the Senate six years before. Moreover, her husband, Bob Dole, had been Senate majority leader and the GOP nominee against President Bill Clinton in 1996.

Dole's vulnerability became clear after withering DSCC ads undercut

New Senators in the 111th Congress

Alaska	Mark Begich, D	Defeated Ted Stevens, R, who sought a seventh full term
Colorado	Mark Udall, D	Elected to succeed Wayne Allard, R, who retired
Colorado	Michael Bennet, D	Appointed to replace Ken Salazar, D, who became secretary of Interior
Delaware	Ted Kaufman, D	Appointed to replace Joseph R. Biden Jr., D, who was elected vice president
Idaho	Jim Risch, R	Elected to succeed Larry E. Craig, R, who retired
Illinois	Roland W. Burris, D	Appointed to replace Barack Obama, D, who was elected president
Nebraska	Mike Johanns, R	Elected to succeed Chuck Hagel, R, who retired
New Hampshire	Jeanne Shaheen, D	Defeated John E. Sununu, R, who sought a second term
New Mexico	Tom Udall, D	Elected to succeed Pete V. Domenici, R, who retired
New York	Kirsten Gillibrand, D	Appointed to replace Hillary Rodham Clinton, D, who became secretary of State
North Carolina	Kay Hagan, D	Defeated Elizabeth Dole, R, who sought a second term
Oregon	Jeff Merkley, D	Defeated Gordon H. Smith, R, who sought a third term
Virginia	Mark Warner, D	Elected to succeed John W. Warner, R, who retired

NOTE: The outcome of the 2008 race in Minnesota between Republican incumbent Norm Coleman, R, and Al Franken, D, remained in litigation as of May 2009.

one of her key arguments — that her long tenure in Washington and extensive ties within the GOP made her an effective champion for North Carolina. The DSCC's multimillion-dollar "Rocking Chairs" commercials questioned her effectiveness and her support for Bush's policies.

At 55, Hagan was a fresh face and provided a contrast to Dole, who not only had spent 40 years in Washington but at 72 was the same age as McCain, who opponents argued was too old to run for president. Hagan is "energetic, she knows the ropes, been in politics, been a legislator, good North Carolina image," said Gary Pearce, a Democratic political consultant from Raleigh, all of which gave her a strong base.

Hagan won, 53 percent to 44 percent, on the same day that Obama became the first Democratic presidential candidate since Jimmy Carter to carry the state.

● **Oregon.** Smith has cultivated a generally moderate and independent record through two terms, and during the campaign one of his first television advertisements mentioned Obama favorably. But Oregon's increasingly strong Democratic trend allowed the somewhat low-key Speaker of the state House, Jeff Merkley of Portland, to draw even.

Smith emphasized his criticism of the Iraq War and his support for the environmentalist causes and gay rights. Merkley asserted he'd be a more reliably progressive voice on those issues. In the race between Democratic state House Speaker Jeff Merkley and Republican Smith, the incumbent did not concede that he'd lost his quest for a third term until Nov. 6, two days after the election. Merkley won with just under 49 percent of the vote, compared with 46 percent for Smith.

● **Virginia.** Democrats did not have to search far to find a candidate to compete for the seat that Republican John W. Warner was relinquishing after five terms. Mark Warner, who was no relation, had been a popular, centrist governor from 2002 through 2005 (Virginia limited its governors to a single term) and had a keen desire to run for the Senate after backing away from plans to run for president in 2008.

Republicans had few options in the state. The party's strongest candidate very well could have been Rep. Thomas M. Davis III, whose moderate tendencies might have helped him capture his Northern Virginia home base. But Davis dropped his bid after the state party decided to hold a nominating convention, an event that catered to a narrow slice of conservative activists, instead of a primary that would have involved more voters.

Another former governor, James S. Gilmore III, won the nomination but headed into the general election as a distinct underdog. Warner was by far the more popular governor and had been credited with fixing fiscal problems left by Gilmore, his predecessor. He won by 31 points — an astonishingly big margin for an open-seat race, made all the more remarkable by the fact that it was a takeaway from the incumbent party.

Virginia Republican leaders also felt the state's political climate was against them, and indeed Warner's election — combined with Obama's victory, the first by any Democratic presidential candidate in the state since 1964 — marked a departure from Virginia's conservative moorings. Northern Virginia, more Democratic than most areas of the state, continued to gain population and was largely responsible for electing two Democrats in a row to the Senate. But both were centrists; Jim Webb, elected in 2006, was a former Republican and a Reagan administration official.

● **Colorado.** Rep. Mark Udall, who had represented the liberal-leaning Boulder area for a decade, won by 10 points over Republican Bob Schaffer, a state board of education member and former congressman, to succeed Republican Wayne Allard, who retired after two terms.

Udall benefited from a nearly decade-long Democratic surge in Colorado and painted Schaffer as too conservative for the state. Udall, whose father Morris K. Udall was a legendary witty and liberal Arizona congressman (1961-91) and presidential candidate, was joined in the Senate freshman class by his first cousin from New Mexico.

● **New Mexico.** Tom Udall of Santa Fe, a House member for a decade, prevailed by 22 points against GOP Rep. Steve Pearce to take the seat that Republican Pete V. Domenici relinquished after 36 years. Udall's father, Stewart, was Interior secretary in the Kennedy administration.

Democratic candidates also took over two open Republican House seats in the state, giving their party complete control of the delegation in a state with a long history of close partisan division.

RACES HANGING FIRE

Contests in two states were not resolved for several weeks after Election Day. One went to each party.

● **Alaska.** Stevens, the longest-serving Republican senator in history, having first come to the Senate as an appointee in late 1968, conceded that he had lost his campaign for a seventh full term on Nov. 18, on his 85th birthday. An unofficial Election Day vote count

Minnesota Standoff

THE YEAR ENDED WITHOUT AN OFFICIAL winner in the Minnesota Senate contest between Republican Norm Coleman, who was seeking a second term, and Democrat Al Franken, a liberal talk-radio host and satirical author who initially gained fame as an actor and writer with NBC's "Saturday Night Live."

The race appeared to be a tossup all fall. Coleman's campaign was hampered by questions about his ethics and complicated by the strong support in Minnesota for Democratic presidential candidate Barack Obama. (Obama carried the state by 10 percentage points.) But no one was expecting the Senate race to be as close as it was — or to drag on for as long as it did.

On Nov. 18, two weeks after Election Day, a statewide canvassing report had Coleman ahead with 1,211,590 votes (41.99 percent) and Franken with 1,211,375 votes (41.98 percent) — a difference of 215 votes. Most of the rest of the ballots were for Dean Barkley, the nominee of the state's Independence Party, who served a brief appointive stint in the Senate at the end of 2002, just before Coleman began serving his term.

Because the margin separating Coleman and Franken was less than half of 1 percentage point, state law required a hand recount, which began Nov. 19 at 120 sites. Both candidates gained votes in the recount, but Franken's gains were sufficient to overcome Coleman's lead.

The recount, certified Jan. 5, 2009, determined that Franken won 1,212,431 votes and Coleman won 1,212,206 — a 225-vote margin for Franken. (In the meantime, the Senate seat officially became vacant, because Coleman's term expired Jan. 3.)

Franken declared victory, but Coleman contested the outcome in state court, alleging inconsistencies in the vote count. Republican Gov. Tim Pawlenty said he would not sign the election certificate until Coleman had exhausted his appeals.

had Stevens ahead of the Democrat Mark Begich, the mayor of Anchorage since 2003 — a surprising result, given that Stevens had been politically wounded by his conviction in federal court a week before on seven felony counts of failing to report expensive gifts from home-state business interests.

But a count of thousands of absentee ballots put Begich on top by about 4,000 votes. Stevens pushed for an early trial in hopes that he would be acquitted before the election. *(Stevens, p. 5-3)*

● **Georgia.** Republican Saxby Chambliss was elected to his second term in a runoff election on Dec. 2. On Nov. 4, he had received fewer than the 50 percent required in the state to claim outright victory over his Democratic opponent, Jim Martin, a state representative from 1983 to 2002 and the unsuccessful candidate for lieutenant governor in 2006.

Chambliss decisively out-polled Martin in the runoff election (57 percent to 43 percent), in which Martin found it difficult to replicate turnout, especially among African-Americans, without Obama on the ballot. Martin didn't appear to have any decent traction before the closing weeks of the race, when it appeared Obama might have a shot at carrying the state. Democrats had been determined to unseat Chambliss ever since his successful 2002 campaign, when his ads im-

pugned Sen. Max Cleland's patriotism. Chambliss maintains an edge, though, as the well-funded and powerful incumbent (he has the top GOP seat on the Agriculture Committee) in a conservative state.

TOP REPUBLICAN HOLDS

There were a few bright spots for Republicans:

● **Kentucky.** The party's floor leader in the Senate, Mitch McConnell, had been targeted by Democrats but managed to retain the seat he first won 24 years before, defeating Democrat Bruce Lunsford, a nursing-home entrepreneur, by 53 percent to 47 percent. In his victory speech, McConnell noted he was on his way to becoming Kentucky's longest-serving senator, and described himself as "energized and recommitted" to addressing key issues, including energy independence.

● **Maine.** Resilient GOP centrist Susan Collins easily withstood a Democratic tide in her state, which Obama carried with 58 percent of the vote. The race was perceived at the start of the campaign season as one of the Democrats' best opportunities to take away a GOP seat, but Collins won her third term with a lopsided 61 percent of the vote against Tom Allen of Portland, who had been a House member for six terms.

● **Mississippi.** Ronnie Musgrove, a relatively conservative governor from 2000 through 2003, was widely hailed as the best possible Democratic candidate, but he lost by 10 percentage points. In a state where McCain ran strongly, Roger Wicker held the seat to which he had been appointed at the end 2007, when Trent Lott quit to become a lobbyist.

THE APPOINTED NEWCOMERS

There were the four Democrats sent to the Senate by Democratic governors to succeed leaders of the new administration:

● **Delaware.** Biden was succeeded by Ted Kaufman, his former Senate chief of staff. Kaufman, whose appointment was announced Nov. 24 by outgoing Gov. Ruth Ann Minner, said that he would not run in the 2010 special election to fill the remaining four years of the six-year term that Biden won with 65 percent on the same day he was elected vice president. Biden was sworn in for his seventh term in January 2009 and resigned from the Senate five days before his inauguration as vice president.

● **Illinois.** Roland W. Burris, a former state attorney general and state treasurer, was tapped on Dec. 29 by Gov. Rod R. Blagojevich to succeed Obama, who resigned his Senate seat on Nov. 16. The move was highly controversial. Blagojevich had been arrested in early December on federal corruption charges that included an allegation that he tried to trade the Senate seat. Democratic Senate leaders initially resisted seating Burris, but ultimately relented. Burris replaced Obama as the Senate's only African-American.

● **Colorado.** Michael Bennet, the superintendent of the Denver public school system, was introduced as Salazar's successor on Jan. 3, 2009, by Gov. Bill Ritter Jr. He took office on Jan. 22 after Salazar's confirmation to run the Interior Department. Bennet is running in the regularly scheduled 2010 Senate election.

● **New York.** After Clinton said Dec. 1 that she had accepted Obama's offer to become secretary of State, it took Gov. David A. Paterson nearly eight weeks to decide on a successor. He settled Jan. 23, 2009, on Rep. Kirsten E. Gillibrand, who in 2008 won a second term to an upstate New York district surrounding Albany. Paterson considered appointing Caroline Kennedy, the daughter of President John F. Kennedy, but she took herself out of the running after initially pursing the appointment. Gillibrand planned to run in a 2010 special election to serve the final two years of Clinton's term. ■

Majority Gains 21 More House Seats

DEMOCRATS SOLIDIFIED control of the House on Nov. 4, the second consecutive election in which the party gained a significant number of House seats. Democrats had a net gain of 21 seats to augment the 30-seat gain in the 2006 midterm elections, when Democrats ended a dozen years of GOP control in the House.

Democrats unseated 14 Republican incumbents and captured 12 other districts where GOP lawmakers were not on the ballot. The party's success was fueled by ever-deepening public disapproval of President Bush and the Republican Party in general and by a surge in Democratic turnout spurred by Barack Obama's winning presidential campaign.

Yet many Democrats fared well in districts that Obama did not carry. Of the 49 districts voting for John McCain for president but for a Democratic House candidate, a dozen elected a Democrat to replace a Republican. Of the 34 Republicans who won districts Obama carried, just two were elected for their first terms, and both won seats Republicans were defending.

The Republicans won just five Democratic seats, defeating incumbents in each. That, though, was a significantly better GOP performance than two years before, when the party did not take a single seat away to partly offset their own losses.

House Speaker Nancy Pelosi of California said Nov. 5 that she was "very pleased with our congressional results" and that "our increased numbers in the House better enable us to work closely with our new president for a vision for America."

Republicans—who had expected to lose seats almost from the start of the campaign cycle two years earlier, given Bush's unpopularity—expressed a measure of relief that they did not suffer even greater losses.

Democrats entered Election Day with effective control of 236 districts—counting a vacant, heavily Democratic district in Ohio that the party easily retained—compared with 199 seats for the Republicans. The 2008 results gave Democrats 257 seats, their largest caucus since early 1994, when they effectively controlled 259 seats.

That was the year when Republicans made a net gain of 52 seats to end a four-decade run by Democrats as the majority party in the House. The Democrats' cumulative gains in 2006 and 2008 matched the GOP House gains in 1994.

REPUBLICANS ROUTED

The 14 House Republicans who lost were Marilyn Musgrave of Colorado, Christopher Shays of Connecticut, Ric Keller and Tom Feeney of Florida, Bill Sali of Idaho, Tim Walberg and Joe Knollenberg of Michigan, Jon Porter of Nevada, John R. "Randy" Kuhl Jr. of New York, Robin Hayes of North Carolina, Steve Chabot of Ohio, Phil English of Pennsylvania, and Virgil H. Goode Jr. and Thelma Drake of Virginia.

Their ideologies ran the gamut of the GOP political spectrum. Shays, a member of the party's shrinking moderate wing, lost his bid

THE HOUSE

110th Congress		111th Congress	
Democrats	235	Democrats	256
Republicans	199	Republicans	178
Vacant on Nov. 4*	1	Vacant on Jan. 3*	1

* Seat had been held by a Democrat.

DEMOCRATS

Net gain	21
Freshmen	33
Incumbents re-elected	224
Incumbents defeated	5

REPUBLICANS

Net loss	21
Freshmen	22
Incumbents re-elected	156
Incumbents defeated**	17

** Three lost in primaries.

for an 11th full term to Democratic investment banker Jim Himes. Musgrave, who was one of the most conservative members of the House, was beaten by Democrat Betsy Markey, a former Senate aide, in a conservative-leaning swath of northern and eastern Colorado.

Some of the losing Republicans were hamstrung by political flaws. Sali, a freshman, had never solidified the GOP base after winning the 2006 primary and general elections by unimpressive margins. Walberg, another strongly conservative freshman, had unseated a moderate Republican in the 2006 primary who was a better ideological match for the district. Feeney, whose 16-point loss was the largest of the 14 House Republicans who were unseated by Democrats, was hampered by his ties to jailed lobbyist Jack Abramoff.

House Democratic officials described the election as an unmitigated success, pointing to the rarity of the same party making ample gains in the House in consecutive election years. The Republicans lost House seats in 1996, two years after their watershed election, and the Democrats also sustained losses in 1984, two years after they made big gains midway through Ronald Reagan's first term.

Not since 1952 had a party gained at least 20 House seats in an election after winning at least as many in the previous election. "As the results show, we not only protected the gains we made in 2006, but we stayed on offense — we won a lot of seats," said Maryland's Chris Van Hollen, chairman of the Democratic Congressional Campaign Committee (DCCC), the campaign arm of House Democrats.

Democrats ran in a political environment that was at least as favorable to their party as in 2006, when voters were angry over Bush's Iraq War policy and over corruption scandals involving House Republicans. Those issues were less of a factor in the 2008 campaign. But they were replaced by the deteriorating economy, an issue that also weighed strongly against the party holding the White House. Throughout the election cycle, voters gave the Bush administration poor marks on handling economic policy, and the GOP bore the lion's share of the blame from voters for the turmoil in the financial markets.

"Obviously, the president has low approval ratings; we've had a tough economy; we've had an unpopular war; and then we had a financial crisis," said Oklahoma's Tom Cole, who chaired the National Republican Congressional Committee (NRCC), the party's House campaign arm, during the 2007-08 campaign cycle.

The public unhappiness with the Republicans allowed Democrats to thrive in candidate recruitment and expand the number of competitive districts. Democrats mounted especially vigorous challenges in many generally Republican-leaning districts that had voted decisively for Bush in 2004. Of the 26 Democratic candidates who prevailed in GOP-held seats, 12 were from districts that voted for McCain, and all but three were from districts that went for Bush in 2004.

The Democratic campaign effort also was aided by a lopsided partisan disparity in the districts where incumbents were not seeking

Departing Members of the 110th Congress

SENATORS DEFEATED IN GENERAL ELECTION (4 R)		
	ELECTED	WINNER
Elizabeth Dole, R-N.C.	2002	Kay Hagan (D)
Gordon H. Smith, R-Ore.	1996	Jeff Merkley (D)
Ted Stevens, R-Alaska	1970	Mark Begich, (D)
John E. Sununu, R-N.H.	2002	Jeanne Shaheen (D)

HOUSE MEMBERS DEFEATED IN GENERAL ELECTION (5 D, 14 R)		
	ELECTED	WINNER
Nancy Boyda, D-Kan. (2nd)	2006	Lynn Jenkins (R)
Don Cazayoux, D-La. (6th)	2008	Bill Cassidy (R)
Steve Chabot, R-Ohio (1st)	1994	Steve Driehaus (D)
Thelma Drake, R-Va. (2nd)	2004	Glenn Nye (D)
Phil English, R-Pa. (3rd)	1994	Kathy Dahlkemper (D)
Tom Feeney, R-Fla. (24th)	2002	Suzanne Kosmas (D)
Virgil H. Goode Jr., R-Va. (5)	1996	Tom Perriello (D)
Robin Hayes, R-N.C. (8th)	1998	Larry Kissell (D)
William J. Jefferson, D-La. (2nd)	1990	Anh "Joseph" Cao (R)
Ric Keller, R-Fla. (8th)	2000	Alan Grayson (D)
Joe Knollenberg, R-Mich. (9th)	1992	Gary Peters (D)
John R. "Randy" Kuhl Jr., R-N.Y. (29th)	2004	Eric Massa (D)
Nick Lampson, D-Texas (22nd)	1996	Pete Olson (R)
Tim Mahoney, D-Fla. (16th)	2006	Tom Rooney (R)
Marilyn Musgrave, R-Colo. (4th)	2002	Betsy Markey (D)
Jon Porter, R-Nev. (3rd)	2002	Dina Titus (D)
Bill Sali, R-Idaho (1st)	2006	Walt Minnick (D)
Christopher Shays, R-Conn. (4th)	1987	Jim Himes (D)
Tim Walberg, R-Mich. (7th)	2006	Mark Schauer (D)

RESIGNED SENATORS (1 R, 1 D)	RESIGNED	SUCCESSOR
Trent Lott, R-Miss.	Dec. 18, 2007	Roger Wicker, R *appointed Dec. 31, 2007*
Barack Obama,D-Ill.	Nov. 16, 2008	Roland W. Burris, D *appointed Dec. 30, 2008*

RESIGNED HOUSE MEMBERS (3 D, 5 R)	RESIGNED	SUCCESSOR
Martin T. Meehan, D-Mass. (5)	July 1, 2007	Niki Tsongas, D *Oct. 16, 2007, special election*
J. Dennis Hastert, R-Ill. (14)	Nov. 26, 2007	Bill Foster, D *March 8, 2008, special election*
Roger Wicker, R-Miss. (1)	Dec. 31, 2007	Travis W. Childers, D *May 13, 2008, special election*
Bobby Jindal, R-La. (1)	Jan. 14, 2008	Steve Scalise, R *May 3, 2008, special election*
Richard H. Baker, R-La. (6)	Feb. 2, 2008	Don Cazayoux, D *May 3, 2008, special election*
Albert R. Wynn, D-Md. (4)	May 31, 2008	Donna Edwards, D *June 17, 2008, special election*
Thomas M. Davis III, R-Va. (11)	Nov. 24, 2008	No successor in the 110th
Rahm Emanuel, D-Ill. (5)	Jan. 2, 2009	No successor in the 110th

MEMBERS WHO LOST HOUSE PRIMARIES (1 D, 3 R)
Chris Cannon, R-Utah (3) (1)
David Davis, R-Tenn. (1)
Wayne T. Gilchrest, R-Md. (1)
Albert R. Wynn, D-Md. (4)

re-election, either because they retired or were seeking other offices, or because they were defeated in primary elections. Of those 35 seats, Republicans were defending 29 and the Democrats just six. (This tally does not include the Cleveland-based district of Ohio Democrat Stephanie Tubbs Jones, who was renominated in the primary election, but died in August and was replaced by Democrat Marcia L. Fudge.)

ADVANTAGES IN FUNDING

For the second consecutive election cycle, Democrats did not lose any of their open seats to Republicans. But they wrested a dozen such districts from GOP control: two each in New Mexico, New York and Ohio and one apiece in Alabama, Arizona, Illinois, Maryland, New Jersey and Virginia. Democrats made a larger net gain in the open-seat races (12) than in contests in which incumbents were seeking re-election (nine).

In this group, perhaps the most groundbreaking Democratic win came in the southeastern corner of Alabama, where Bobby N. Bright, a conservative Democratic mayor of Montgomery, defeated Republican state Rep. Jay Love for the seat left open by Republican Terry Everett, who retired after eight terms. The district was a longtime Republican stronghold that gave Bush two-thirds of its votes in 2004 and McCain 63 percent of its votes in 2008.

"In order to win a lot of these congressional elections, however, not only did you need a boosted turnout among Democratic voters, including Democratic voters who may not have participated in the past, but you also needed many crossover voters," Van Hollen said. "In order for Bobby Bright to win, he also had to pick up voters who also voted for John McCain for president."

Democrats made gains in virtually every region of the nation, although it was especially striking that, with Shays' loss in Connecticut, the Republicans were left without a single House seat in New England for the first time in the party's history.

A Democratic gain of three seats in New York put the party in control of 26 of the state's 29 congressional districts, including all 13 that included parts of New York City. After a one-seat gain in Pennsylvania, Democrats controlled 12 of 19 seats in that state, even though GOP lawmakers had redrawn the congressional map early in the decade.

Democrats also registered major gains in the Mountain West, a fast-growing, generally politically independent region. They came out of the election with control of all three House seats in New Mexico, five of seven in Colorado and five of eight in Arizona, McCain's home state.

A high turnout from strongly Democratic African-American voters — energized by Obama's presence at the top of the ticket — helped Democratic challengers unseat Hayes in southern North Carolina,

RETIRING SENATORS (5 R)	ELECTED	SUCCESSOR
Wayne Allard, R-Colo.	1996	Mark Udall (D)
Larry E. Craig, R-Idaho	1990	Jim Risch (R)
Pete V. Domenici, R-N.M.	1972	Tom Udall (D)
Chuck Hagel, R-Neb.	1996	Mike Johanns (R)
John W. Warner, R-Va.	1978	Mark Warner (D)

RETIRING HOUSE MEMBERS (3 D, 23 R)	ELECTED	SUCCESSOR
Robert E. "Bud" Cramer, D-Ala. (5)	1990	Parker Griffith (D)
Barbara Cubin, R-Wyo. (At large)	1994	Cynthia M. Lummis (R)
Thomas M. Davis III, R-Va. (11)	1994	Gerald E. Connolly (D)
John T. Doolittle, R-Calif. (4)	1990	Tom McClintock (R)
Terry Everett, R-Ala. (2)	1992	Bobby N. Bright (D)
Mike Ferguson, R-N.J. (7)	2000	Leonard Lance (R)
Vito J. Fossella, R-N.Y. (13)	1997	Michael E. McMahon (D)
David L. Hobson, R-Ohio (7)	1990	Steve Austria (R)
Darlene Hooley, D-Ore. (5)	1996	Kurt Schrader (D)
Duncan Hunter, R-Calif. (52)	1980	Duncan Hunter (R)
Ray LaHood, R-Ill. (18)	1994	Aaron Schock (R)
Ron Lewis, R-Ky. (2)	1994	Brett Guthrie (R)
Jim McCrery, R-La. (4)	1988	John Fleming (R)
Michael R. McNulty, D-N.Y. (21)	1988	Paul Tonko (D)
John E. Peterson, R-Pa. (5)	1996	Glenn Thompson (R)
C.W. "Chip" Pickering Jr., R-Miss. (3)	1996	Gregg Harper (R)
Deborah Pryce, R-Ohio (15)	1992	Mary Jo Kilroy (D)
Jim Ramstad, R-Minn. (3)	1990	Erik Paulsen (R)
Ralph Regula, R-Ohio (16)	1972	John Boccieri (D)
Rick Renzi, R-Ariz. (1)	2002	Ann Kirkpatrick (D)
Thomas M. Reynolds, R-N.Y. (26)	1998	Christopher Lee (R)
H. James Saxton, R-N.J. (3)	1984	John Adler (D)
Tom Tancredo, R-Colo. (6)	1998	Mike Coffman (R)
James T. Walsh, R-N.Y. (25)	1988	Dan Maffei (D)
Dave Weldon, R-Fla. (15)	1994	Bill Posey (R)
Jerry Weller, R-Ill. (11)	1994	Debbie Halvorson (D)

MEMBERS WHO SOUGHT OTHER OFFICES (6 D, 4 R)	ELECTED	OFFICE SOUGHT / RESULT
Sen. John McCain, R-Ariz.*	1986	President / lost
Sen. Barack Obama, D-Ill.	2004	President / won
Sen. Joseph R. Biden Jr., D-Del.	1972	Vice President / won
Rep. Tom Allen, D-Maine (1)	1996	Senate / lost
Rep. Kenny Hulshof, R-Mo. (9)	1996	Governor / lost
Rep. Steve Pearce, R-N.M. (2)	2002	Senate / lost
Rep. Mark Udall, D-Colo. (2)	1998	Senate / won
Rep. Tom Udall, D-N.M. (3)	1998	Senate / won
Rep. Heather A. Wilson, R-N.M. (1)	1998	Senate / lost primary
Rep. Robert E. Andrews, D-N.J. (1)**	1998	Senate / lost primary

*Senate term expires in 2010   **won re-election to the House

DECEASED SENATOR (1 R)	DIED	SUCCESSOR
Craig Thomas, R-Wyo.	June 4, 2007	John Barrasso, R appointed June 22, 2007

DECEASED HOUSE MEMBERS (4 D, 3 R)	DIED	SUCCESSOR
Charlie Norwood, R-Ga. (10)	Feb. 13, 2007	Paul Broun, R July 17, 2007, special election
Juanita Millender-McDonald, D-Calif. (37)	April 22, 2007	Laura Richardson Aug. 21, 2007, special election
Paul E. Gillmor, R-Ohio (5)	Sept. 5, 2007	Bob Latta, R Dec. 11, 2007, special election
Jo Ann Davis, R-Va. (1)	Oct. 6, 2007	Rob Wittman, R Dec. 11, 2007, special election
Julia Carson, D-Ind. (7)	Dec. 15, 2007	André Carson, D March 11, 2008 special election
Tom Lantos, D-Calif. (12)	Feb. 11, 2008	Jackie Speier, D April 8 special election
Stephanie Tubbs Jones, D-Ohio (11)	Aug. 20, 2008	Marcia L. Fudge, D Nov. 18 special election

Chabot in Cincinnati, Goode in south-central Virginia and Drake in southeastern Virginia; all four districts were more than one-fifth black. Shays' district was just one-ninth black, but Van Hollen pointed to a heavy black turnout in Bridgeport as a major factor in Himes' win.

The Democrats far outpaced their Republican counterparts in campaign fundraising. The DCCC raised $176.2 million during the 2007-08 campaign cycle, compared with $118.3 million by the NRCC.

Democratic freshmen in particular amassed substantial reserves to prepare for vigorous GOP challenges that in some cases did not materialize. Kirsten Gillibrand of New York raised more than $4.6 million in her first term in office. Pennsylvania's Patrick J. Murphy took in almost $4 million; he was re-elected by 15 percentage points in suburban Philadelphia against an opponent who raised less than one-third as much.

As the campaign entered September, the DCCC had $54.4 million left to spend on races around the nation — nearly four times as much as the NRCC. The DCCC was able to spend lavishly on "independent expenditures," the outlays for television and radio advertisements and mail pieces that could not be made in cooperation with candidates' campaigns but were a preferred vehicle of party committee spending because they were unlimited. According to the Campaign Finance Institute, the DCCC laid out at least $1 million in independent expen-

ditures in each of 38 districts, and the NRCC in just four districts.

The unfavorable political environment for Republicans, Cole said, "was complicated by the fact that we had about 30 open seats and a pretty big financial disadvantage with our opponents."

Republicans held down their net loss by unseating five Democrats, four of them freshmen from districts that normally voted Republican: Nancy Boyda in the Topeka area of Kansas, Don Cazayoux of the Baton Rouge area of Louisiana, Nick Lampson in the Houston suburbs and Tim Mahoney in central Florida. Mahoney was rendered unelectable by a sex scandal that came to light in the waning weeks of the campaign.

The fifth Democrat unseated was William J. Jefferson of Louisiana, although his loss to Republican lawyer Anh "Joseph" Cao in and around New Orleans owed to highly unusual circumstances. Jefferson was indicted in 2007 on federal corruption charges, and he lost to Cao in a low-turnout election that was held in early December. Hurricane Gustav's landfall in early September prompted Republican Gov. Bobby Jindal to delay the election schedule.

That Republicans could unseat only four freshmen was a setback for the GOP, given that many first-term Democrats were elected in 2006 from districts that had backed Bush in 2004. Christopher Carney, whose 2006 victory in a Republican-leaning swath of north-

Special Elections Foretell Democratic Trend

EIGHT SPECIAL ELECTIONS FOR HOUSE SEATS foreshadowed the rough time Republicans would face in November 2008. Democrats picked up three seats from the Republicans, the first time in 30 years that one political party took that many seats away from the opposing party during a single Congress. Democrats also maintained control of four seats, while Republicans held onto one.

DEMOCRATIC GAINS

● **Illinois 14.** Bill Foster, a scientist and first-time candidate, won the first special election since 2004 in which a House seat changed partisan hands. His March 8 triumph with 53 percent was especially sweet for the Democratic Party because the district, stretching from Chicago's far western suburbs almost to the Mississippi River, had been held since 1986 by J. Dennis Hastert, who resigned in November 2007 and served as the Republican Speaker of the House from 1999 through 2006. President Bush won 55 percent of the district's 2004 vote. Foster's campaign against Republican Don Oberweis, who had run for senator in 2002 and 2004 and for governor in 2006, featured advertising testimonials by Sen. Barack Obama, D-Ill.

● **Louisiana 6.** Don Cazayoux won a May 3 special election with 49 percent in a Baton Rouge-centered district the GOP had held since 1975. The Republican candidate was state legislator Woody Jenkins. The seat had been held for 21 years by Richard H. Baker, who resigned in February to lobby for the hedge fund industry. Cazayoux, who had been in the state House since 2000, campaigned with a mix of conservative positions on social issues and conventional Democratic positions on education and health care. (He lost in November to Republican Bill Cassidy, becoming the only special election winner of 2008 to lose a campaign for a full term.)

● **Mississippi 1.** Travis W. Childers, a small-business owner, was elected with 53 percent on May 13 to replace Roger Wicker, who had been appointed in December to the Senate to succeed fellow Republican Trent Lott, who resigned. Childers' victory against Republican Greg Davis, a small-city mayor, was an upset in the state's

northeastern corner. Bush had won 66 percent there in 2004, and the GOP spent more than $1 million trying to hold the seat.

NO PARTISAN SWITCH

● **Indiana 7.** Democrat André Carson, a city-county council member in Indianapolis, the political center of the district, took 54 percent in a March 11 special election to succeed his grandmother, Democrat Julia Carson, an African-American political pioneer in the state who died in December 2007. He became the second Muslim elected to Congress, after Minnesota Democrat Keith Ellison.

● **California 12.** Democratic lawyer Jackie Speier took 78 percent to win an April 8 special election in the district, which lies between San Francisco and Silicon Valley. She succeeded Democrat Tom Lantos, the only Holocaust survivor elected to Congress and the chairman of the Foreign Affairs Committee since the start of 2007, who died Feb. 11 at age 80.

● **Louisiana 1.** Republican Steve Scalise, a state legislator since 1996, took 75 percent in a May 3 special election to succeed Republican Bobby Jindal, who resigned in January to become governor. The district skims the edges of New Orleans and reaches north across Lake Pontchartrain to the Mississippi border.

● **Maryland 4.** Democrat Donna Edwards took 81 percent in a June 17 special election called in the Washington suburbs after Albert R. Wynn resigned. Wynn became a lobbyist after losing his bid for the Democratic nomination to a ninth term in the February primary to Edwards, a community activist and lawyer. She became the first black woman to represent the state in Congress.

● **Ohio 11.** Marcia L. Fudge, the Democratic mayor of the Cleveland suburb of Warrensville Heights, won a Nov. 18 special election to complete the term of Democrat Stephanie Tubbs Jones, who died in August at age 58. First elected in 1998, Tubbs Jones was the first African-American congresswoman from Ohio and had been chairwoman of the Committee on Standards of Official Conduct since the start of 2007. No Republican ran in the special election.

eastern Pennsylvania was aided by a sex scandal involving the GOP incumbent, beat a well-funded Republican challenger by 13 percentage points. Carol Shea-Porter, whose victory in eastern New Hampshire was perhaps the biggest upset of 2006, won a rematch with the previous occupant of the seat, Republican Jeb Bradley. Gillibrand, who represented a historically Republican district in the North Hudson Valley, took 62 percent of the vote against a well-funded Republican.

The Republicans thwarted bigger losses by retaining most of their open districts, including some in which top-flight GOP candidates were victorious in districts that were less Republican-leaning than other districts that Democrats captured from the GOP.

In a district that zigzagged across north-central New Jersey, GOP state Sen. Leonard Lance defeated Democratic state Rep. Linda Stender much more convincingly than Republican Mike Ferguson, who was retiring, had beat Stender two years before.

In a set of politically competitive suburbs near Minneapolis and St. Paul, Republican state Rep. Erik Paulsen defeated Democrat Ashwin Madia, an Iraq War veteran, by 8 percentage points. Lance

and Paulsen were the only two Republicans first elected in 2008 from districts that Obama carried.

It was clear well ahead of the Nov. 4 balloting that Democrats were headed for gains in the House. Throughout the campaign, public-opinion surveys showed that voters preferred a Democratic-run Congress. Bush's poor approval rating was a major hindrance to House Republican campaign efforts and motivated Democrats to air commercials linking GOP candidates to the unpopular president and his policies.

There were warning signs for Republicans in the spring, when the Democrats won three special elections in GOP-leaning districts that Republican incumbents vacated. *(Special elections, this page)*

That string of special election defeats stunned the Republican Party and led the retiring Thomas M. Davis III of Virginia — a former NRCC chairman whose own open seat in the Washington suburbs went Democratic — to issue a memo to the GOP leadership warning that "the political atmosphere facing House Republicans this November was the worst since Watergate and was far more toxic than the fall of 2006 when we lost 30 seats." ∎

New House Members in the 111th Congress

Alabama 2	Bobby Bright, D	Succeeded Terry Everett, R, who retired
Alabama 5	Parker Griffith, D	Succeeded Robert E. "Bud" Cramer, D, who retired
Arizona 1	Ann Kirkpatrick, D	Succeeded Rick Renzi, R, who retired
California 4	Tom McClintock, R	Succeeded John T. Doolittle, R, who retired
California 52	Duncan Hunter, R	Succeeded Duncan Hunter, R, who retired
Colorado 2	Jared Polis, D	Succeeded Mark Udall, D, who was elected to the Senate
Colorado 4	Betsy Markey, D	Defeated Marilyn Musgrave, R
Colorado 6	Mike Coffman, R	Succeeded Tom Tancredo, R, who retired
Connecticut 4	Jim Himes, D	Defeated Christopher Shays, R
Florida 8	Alan Grayson, D	Defeated Ric Keller, R
Florida 15	Bill Posey, R	Succeeded Dave Weldon, R, who retired
Florida 16	Tom Rooney, R	Defeated Tim Mahoney, D
Florida 24	Suzanne M. Kosmas, D	Defeated Tom Feeney, R
Idaho 1	Walt Minnick, D	Defeated Bill Sali, R
Illinois 11	Debbie Halvorson, D	Succeeded Jerry Weller, R, who retired
Illinois 18	Aaron Schock, R	Succeeded Ray LaHood, R, who retired
Kansas 2	Lynn Jenkins, R	Defeated Nancy Boyda, D
Kentucky 2	Brett Guthrie, R	Succeeded Ron Lewis, R, who retired
Louisiana 2	Anh "Joseph" Cao, R	Defeated William J. Jefferson, D
Louisiana 4	John Fleming, R	Succeeded Jim McCrery, R, who retired
Louisiana 6	Bill Cassidy, R	Defeated Don Cazayoux, D
Maine 1	Chellie Pingree, D	Succeeded Tom Allen, D, who ran for Senate
Maryland 1	Frank Kratovil Jr., D	Defeated Andy Harris, R, to succeed Wayne T. Gilchrest, R, who was defeated in the primary
Michigan 7	Mark Schauer, D	Defeated Tim Walberg, R
Michigan 9	Gary Peters, D	Defeated Joe Knollenberg, R
Minnesota 3	Erik Paulsen, R	Succeeded Jim Ramstad, R, who retired
Mississippi 3	Gregg Harper, R	Succeeded Charles W. "Chip" Pickering Jr., R, who retired
Missouri 9	Blaine Luetkemeyer, R	Succeeded Kenny Hulshof, R, who ran for governor
Nevada 3	Dina Titus, D	Defeated Jon Porter, R
New Jersey 3	John Adler, D	Succeeded H. James Saxton, R, who retired
New Jersey 7	Leonard Lance, R	Succeeded Mike Ferguson, R, who retired
New Mexico 1	Martin Heinrich, D	Succeeded Heather A. Wilson, R, who ran for Senate
New Mexico 2	Harry Teague, D	Succeeded Steve Pearce, R, who ran for Senate
New Mexico 3	Ben Ray Luján, D	Succeeded Tom Udall, D, who was elected to the Senate
New York 13	Michael E. McMahon, D	Succeeded Vito J. Fossella, R, who retired
New York 21	Paul Tonko, D	Succeeded Michael R. McNulty, D, who retired
New York 25	Dan Maffei, D	Succeeded James T. Walsh, R, who retired
New York 26	Christopher Lee, R	Succeeded Thomas M. Reynolds, R, who retired
New York 29	Eric Massa, D	Defeated John R. "Randy" Kuhl Jr., R
N. Carolina 8	Larry Kissell, D	Defeated Robin Hayes, R
Ohio 1	Steve Driehaus, D	Defeated Steve Chabot, R
Ohio 7	Steve Austria, R	Succeeded David L. Hobson, R, who retired
Ohio 11	Marcia L. Fudge, D	Succeeded Stephanie Tubbs Jones, D, who died (Fudge also won a Nov. 18 special election)
Ohio 15	Mary Jo Kilroy, D	Succeeded Deborah Pryce, R, who retired
Ohio 16	John Boccieri, D	Succeeded Ralph Regula, R, who retired
Oregon 5	Kurt Schrader, D	Succeeded Darlene Hooley, D, who retired
Pennsylvania 3	Kathy Dahlkemper, D	Defeated Phil English, R
Pennsylvania 5	Glenn Thompson, R	Succeeded John E. Peterson, R, who retired
Tennessee 1	Phil Roe, R	Succeeded David Davis, R, who lost in primary
Texas 22	Pete Olson, R	Defeated Nick Lampson, D
Utah 3	Jason Chaffetz, R	Succeeded Chris Cannon, R, who lost in primary
Virginia 2	Glenn Nye, D	Defeated Thelma Drake, R
Virginia 5	Tom Perriello, D	Defeated Virgil H. Goode Jr., R
Virginia 11	Gerald E. Connolly, D	Succeeded Thomas M. Davis III, R, who retired
Wyoming AL	Cynthia M. Lummis, R	Succeeded Barbara Cubin, R, who retired

Slow and Steady Wins State Races

IN ADDITION TO WINNING back the White House and expanding their majorities in Congress, Democrats continued their slow march to dominance of state-level politics by adding to their majorities among governorships and legislatures on Nov. 4. Their numbers returned to about where they were before the 1994 Republican sweep. But there had been a geographic shift in power since 1994, with Democrats becoming especially strong in the Northeast.

Democrats carried seven of 11 governorships in play in 2008, with only one state switching party control. That was Missouri, where the Democratic attorney general, Jay Nixon, was elected to succeed Republican Matt Blunt, who decided not to seek a second term. So in 2009 Democrats would hold 29 governorships, the party's biggest advantage since 1994.

The party also made gains in state legislatures. As was true of members of Congress, Republican state legislators were the clear minority in the Northeast. Democrats won the New York Senate and the Delaware House on Nov. 4, so in January 2009 they would gain control of every legislative chamber east of Ohio and north of Virginia except one, the Pennsylvania Senate.

Republican victories came primarily in the South, where legislative chambers had been slower than federal offices to switch to the GOP. On Nov. 4, Republicans won the Tennessee House. It was the first time they had won the House since 1970, and the first time they held both chambers simultaneously since Reconstruction. They also carried the Oklahoma Senate for the first time ever.

After a long period of divided control, legislatures were becoming one-sided affairs. Just eight states were split after the 2008 elections. Democrats controlled 27 legislatures outright, for a net gain of four. Republicans held 14 legislatures, exclusively in the Southeast, the Plains states and the Interior West.

"It's the lowest number of split legislatures since 1982," said Tim Storey, an elections expert with the National Conference of State Legislatures. "We may be moving back to a more polarized form of government."

But the GOP could look forward with some hope. In all but two midterm elections since 1902, according to Storey, the party that controlled the White House lost legislative seats. (The exceptions were 1934 and 2002.)

"The last two election cycles have probably been the most difficult for those running on the Republican ticket," said Carrie Cantrell, spokeswoman for the Republican State Leadership Committee, a fundraising group.

And the next election was sure to create more expensive and contentious campaigns at the state level. The parties were expected to jockey for control especially hard because the people elected to run the state capitals and sit in the governors' mansions would be in charge of the once-in-a-decade process of legislative redistricting — the redrawing of congressional and state legislative district maps to accommodate

THE GOVERNORS

	Before 2008 Election		2008 Election
Democrats	28	Democrats	29
Republicans	22	Republicans	21

DEMOCRATS

Net gain	1
Freshmen	3
Incumbents re-elected	4
Incumbents defeated	0

REPUBLICANS

Net loss	1
Freshmen	0
Incumbents re-elected	4
Incumbents defeated	0

population changes that would be reflected in the 2010 census.

"We're heading into the redistricting year," said Bruce E. Cain, a political scientist at the University of California at Berkeley, "and the makeup of governorships and control of the state legislatures becomes the critical factor."

Three dozen governorships were slated to be in play in 2010, half of which were coming vacant because of term limits. Democrats set their hopes on recapturing generally friendly territory such as California, Hawaii and Rhode Island, but the party would have to defend more seats across the country than the GOP — 21, compared with Republicans' 15.

"We know it's going to be a challenging year for us," said Nathan Daschle, executive director of the Democratic Governors Association. "We're going to have a number of seats we need to protect in states like Kansas, Arizona and Oklahoma, where we've had successful two-term governors but which we consider red states."

DEFENDING THEIR TURF

In 2008, Democrats won every competitive election for governor.

Nixon was favored from the start in Missouri, and he raised twice as much money as his Republican opponent, Kenny Hulshof, who had represented the state's northeast corner in the House for a dozen years. Hulshof was unable to heal party wounds after a competitive primary. He also suffered from what some called the "Bush and Blunt effect." Blunt — a son of Roy Blunt, the outgoing House minority whip — was unpopular because of massive Medicaid cuts and changes he made to the state's student loan system. Nixon's central campaign pledge was to restore health coverage. Despite Hulshof's charges that Nixon would be a free spender, the Democrat was able to position himself as a moderate, opposing gay marriage and supporting the death penalty. He won by a lopsided 19 percentage points.

In Washington, incumbent Democratic Gov. Christine Gregoire prevailed by 8 points against Dino Rossi, a former state senator. Gregoire beat him in 2004 by 133 votes after several controversial recounts. But Rossi did not seem armed in the rematch with many fresh arguments for turning Gregoire out, although the state's economy had slowed. Gregoire took credit for increased spending before the downturn on programs such as education, children's health insurance and environmental policy, and she touted her record as a strong manager. The governor also tied her fortunes to the popularity of Barack Obama, who carried the state by a ratio of nearly 3-to-2.

In North Carolina, Democratic Lt. Gov. Bev Perdue, who won a narrow victory, clearly benefited from the presidential candidate's organizational efforts, said Ferrell Guillory, a University of North Carolina journalism professor. Perdue took 50 percent to 47 percent for Mayor Pat McCrory of Charlotte, who sought to borrow a page from the Democratic playbook, presenting himself as a change agent and pointing out that Democrats had held the governorship for 16 years.

"There was some truth to the fact Perdue's a longtime Raleigh figure,"

Guillory said. "But you look at her and she's the first woman governor ever in a state where women make up 55 percent of the vote. She didn't look status quo."

Perdue's campaign was largely negative as well, featuring TV ads that linked McCrory to President Bush and warned of his support for large solid-waste landfills. McCrory said that the latter ad misrepresented his position, complaining to fellow local officials that it "trashes not only me about garbage but you."

Two Republican incumbents, Mitch Daniels of Indiana and Jim Douglas of Vermont, both easily won contests that had at one time looked potentially competitive.

The Indiana General Assembly enacted a property tax relief package that Daniels had crafted earlier in the year. That seemed to ease voter doubts about unpopular moves he'd made earlier in his term, including the leasing of the Indiana Toll Road and statewide adherence to daylight saving time, which was a surprisingly controversial topic. In addition to the passage of time, the governor benefited from the weakness of his opponent, former Rep. Jill Long Thompson, whose campaign was underfunded. Daniels won his second term with 58 percent.

Douglas had been a successful Republican governor in Vermont since 2002, despite the state's Democratic leanings. His only vulnerability was a quirk in state law that threw the governor's race to the state legislature if no candidate won 50 percent of the vote. Because Douglas' Democratic opponent was state House Speaker Gaye Symington, that pointed to potential peril. But Douglas finished with an overwhelming majority, 55 percent of the vote. Symington and independent Anthony Pollina each took about 21 percent.

Montana Democrat Brian Schweitzer won his second term with 65 percent. His opponent, state Sen. Roy Brown, had accused Schweitzer, whose national star rose with a barn-burning speech at the party's national convention, of being a "show horse." But voters credited Schweitzer with good things on his watch, including more energy production.

As expected, the other incumbent governors also coasted to big wins, including Republican John Hoeven of North Dakota, who won a record third four-year term, as well as Democrats Joe Manchin III of West Virginia and John Lynch of New Hampshire.

Republican Jon Huntsman Jr. was so confident of winning a second term in Utah that he raised only about a fourth of what he spent in 2004. He had compiled a record as a moderate Republican by Utah standards, voicing concern about climate change. He was able to point to successes in areas such as a "flatter, fairer" income tax, blocking a nuclear fuel storage proposal and the recent completion of the Legacy Parkway, which offered an alternative route to commuters heading north out of Salt Lake City.

When a late poll suggested that Huntsman would win easily, his foe, Democratic management consultant Bob Springmeyer, told The Salt Lake Tribune, "I'd obviously be tickled to death if we were up in the 40 percent range." In the end, he took 20 percent.

State Treasurer Jack Markell, a Democrat, had no trouble holding Delaware, where Gov. Ruth Ann Minner was term-limited.

LIMITED DEMOCRATIC GAINS

The Republicans' strong showing in 2002 gave them their first majority in state legislative seats since the Eisenhower administration, but Democrats had been whittling down their numbers ever since. In 2006, they won back 665 seats, out of a total of 7,382 nationwide, and

made a net gain of nine legislative chambers to give them the overall majority of seats. After that big win, Democrats consolidated their gains in the 2008 elections, netting about 100 new seats nationwide and expanding narrow majorities in the Indiana and Michigan houses and the Maine Senate.

Democrats managed to add two seats to their one-seat majority in the Pennsylvania House, despite concerns raised by a scandal that had led to the indictment of a dozen legislators and legislative aides. Dan Surra, a member of the chamber's Democratic leadership, was unseated, but Bill DeWeese, the majority leader, survived a challenge.

Democrats also captured the Nevada Senate and Ohio House. But the party failed to make great inroads in targeted states such as Arizona and the Dakotas. Democrats also fell two seats shy of winning the Texas House.

Even their new majority in the New York Senate, which was their first since 1964, was not secure. They won 32 of the chamber's 62 seats. Though at the time of the election four Democrats were threatening to vote with the Republicans for majority leader, a Democratic majority leader was eventually appointed, giving Democrats all of Albany's levers of power for the first time since the Great Depression.

In addition to their victories in Oklahoma and Tennessee, Republicans took back the Montana Senate, though with Schweitzer in the governor's office, the Democrats held control in the evenly divided House. The Republicans surrendered a narrow lead in the Alaska Senate, leaving that chamber tied.

Every election cycle since 1984 had resulted in at least one tied chamber. But in 2008, Democrats built on already-large margins in states such as California, Hawaii and Massachusetts. Minnesota House Democrats added to their large majority but fell three seats short of a veto-proof majority, which Minnesota Senate Democrats already hold. Republican Gov. Tim Pawlenty would have to count on the GOP House minority for support.

In New Hampshire, the Senate became the first state legislative chamber in American history with a majority of women, 13 of 24 total senators. Nationwide, women make up about one-fourth of state legislators.

VOTERS SAY 'NO'

There was no trend in ballot measures, except perhaps that voters were slightly more inclined than usual to vote them down.

Bans on same-sex marriage, which had been a ballot fixture since the Massachusetts Supreme Court legalized gay marriages in 2004, passed in all three states where they were on the ballot: California, Florida and Arizona. The California ban was particularly close-fought and expensive. Supporters and opponents spent a total of $74 million, at least double the combined amount spent in more than a score of other states where gay marriage had been at issue.

Most other social-issue measures failed, however. A Colorado initiative to extend "personhood" rights to fertilized human eggs was defeated, as was a strict ban on abortion in South Dakota, a near-replay of a 2006 fight meant to create a test case to challenge *Roe v. Wade*.

Voters also said no to taxes — both increases and cuts. Massachusetts voters rejected a measure that would have eliminated the state income tax. Colorado voters turned down a proposed amendment to end a tax rebate program. A North Dakota measure to cut corporate and personal income taxes also failed.

But voters in four states approved proposals to create or expand state gambling operations. ∎

Gubernatorial, Senate and House Election Results

SYMBOLS	
Winner's name in bold	
● Unopposed	* New Member
> Runoff race	AL At large district

Alabama

SENATE

Jeff Sessions (R)	**1,305,383**	**63.4**
Vivian Davis Figures (D)	752,391	36.5

HOUSE

1	**Jo Bonner (R)**	**210,652**	**98.3**
	write-ins	3,707	1.7
2	**Bobby Bright (D)***	**144,368**	**50.2**
	Jay Love (R)	142,578	49.6
	write-ins	448	.2
3	**Mike D. Rogers (R)**	**150,819**	**53.4**
	Joshua Segall (D)	131,299	46.5
	write-ins	367	.1
4	**Robert B. Aderholt (R)**	**196,741**	**74.8**
	Nicholas B. Sparks (D)	66,077	25.1
	write-ins	349	.1
5	**Parker Griffith (D)***	**156,642**	**51.3**
	Wayne Parker (R)	147,314	48.2
	write-ins	1,644	.5
6	**Spencer Bachus (R)**	**280,902**	**97.8**
	write-ins	6,335	2.2
7	**Artur Davis (D)**	**228,518**	**98.6**
	write-ins	3,183	1.4

Alaska

SENATE

Mark Begich (D)*	**151,767**	**47.8**
Ted Stevens (R)	147,814	46.5
Bob Bird (AKI)	13,197	4.2
Frederick D. "David" Haase (LIBERT)	2,483	.8
Ted Gianoutsos (X)	1,385	.4

HOUSE

AL	**Don Young (R)**	**158,939**	**50.1**
	Ethan Berkowitz (D)	142,560	45.0
	Don R. Wright (AKI)	14,274	4.5
	write-ins	1,205	.4

Arizona

HOUSE

1	**Ann Kirkpatrick (D)***	**155,791**	**55.9**
	Sydney Hay (R)	109,924	39.4
	Brent Maupin (I)	9,394	3.4
	Thane Eichenauer (LIBERT)	3,678	1.3
2	**Trent Franks (R)**	**200,914**	**59.4**
	John Thrasher (D)	125,611	37.2
	Powell Gammill (LIBERT)	7,882	2.3
	William Crum (GREEN)	3,616	1.1
3	**John Shadegg (R)**	**148,800**	**54.1**
	Bob Lord (D)	115,759	42.1
	Michael Shoen (LIBERT)	10,602	3.8
4	**Ed Pastor (D)**	**89,721**	**72.1**
	Don Karg (R)	26,435	21.2
	Rebecca DeWitt (GREEN)	4,464	3.6
	Joe Cobb (LIBERT)	3,807	3.1
5	**Harry E. Mitchell (D)**	**149,033**	**53.2**
	David Schweikert (R)	122,165	43.6
	Warren Severin (LIBERT)	9,158	3.3
	write-in	9	—
6	**Jeff Flake (R)**	**208,582**	**62.4**
	Rebecca Schneider (D)	115,457	34.6
	Rick Biondi (LIBERT)	10,137	3.0
7	**Raúl M. Grijalva (D)**	**124,304**	**63.3**
	Joseph Sweeney (R)	64,425	32.8
	Raymond Patrick Petrulsky (LIBERT)	7,755	3.9
	write-in	5	—
8	**Gabrielle Giffords (D)**	**179,629**	**54.7**
	Timothy S. Bee (R)	140,553	42.8
	Paul Davis (LIBERT)	8,081	2.5
	write-in	3	—

Arkansas

SENATE

Mark Pryor (D)	**804,678**	**79.5**
Rebekah Kennedy (GREEN)	207,076	20.5

HOUSE

1	**Marion Berry (D)**		●
2	**Vic Snyder (D)**	**212,303**	**76.5**
	Deb McFarland (GREEN)	64,398	23.2
	write-in	665	.2
3	**John Boozman (R)**	**215,196**	**78.5**
	Abel Noah Tomlinson (GREEN)	58,850	21.5
4	**Mike Ross (D)**	**203,178**	**86.2**
	Joshua Drake (GREEN)	32,603	13.8

California

HOUSE

1	**Mike Thompson (D)**	**197,812**	**68.1**
	Zane Starkewolf (R)	67,853	23.4
	Carol Wolman (GREEN)	24,793	8.5
	write-in	14	—
2	**Wally Herger (R)**	**163,459**	**57.9**
	Jeff Morris (D)	118,878	42.1
3	**Dan Lungren (R)**	**155,424**	**49.5**
	Bill Durston (D)	137,971	43.9
	Dina J. Padilla (PFP)	13,378	4.3
	Douglas Arthur Tuma (LIBERT)	7,273	2.3
4	**Tom McClintock (R)***	**185,790**	**50.2**
	Charlie Brown (D)	183,990	49.8
5	**Doris Matsui (D)**	**164,242**	**74.3**
	Paul A Smith (R)	46,002	20.8
	L.R. Roberts (PFP)	10,731	4.8
	write-in	180	.1
6	**Lynn Woolsey (D)**	**229,672**	**71.7**
	Mike Halliwell (R)	77,073	24.1
	Joel R. Smolen (LIBERT)	13,617	4.2
7	**George Miller (D)**	**170,962**	**72.8**
	Roger Allen Petersen (R)	51,166	21.8
	Bill Callison (PFP)	6,695	2.8
	Camden McConnell (LIBERT)	5,950	2.5
8	**Nancy Pelosi (D)**	**204,996**	**71.9**
	Cindy Sheehan (I)	46,118	16.2
	Dana Walsh (R)	27,614	9.7
	Philip Z. Berg (LIBERT)	6,504	2.3
	write-ins	15	—
9	**Barbara Lee (D)**	**238,915**	**86.1**
	Charles Hargrave (R)	26,917	9.7
	James M. Eyer (LIBERT)	11,704	4.2
	write-ins	64	—
10	**Ellen O. Tauscher (D)**	**192,226**	**65.1**
	Nicholas Gerber (R)	91,877	31.1
	Eugene E. Ruyle (PFP)	11,062	3.7

Abbreviation for Party Designations

AC	— American Constitution	GREEN	— Green	PPC	— Poor People's Campaign
ADBP	— All-Day Breakfast Party	HFC	— Hsing for Congress	PRO	— Progressive
AKI	— Alaskan Independence	I	— Independent	PROS	— Prosperity Not War
AMI	— American Independent	IA	— Independent American	PTY	— Term Limits for the U.S. Congress Party
BFS	— Boss for Senate	IGREEN	— Independent Green	R	— Republican
BLU	— Blue Enigma	INDC	— Independence	REF	— Reform
BTB	— Back to Basics	IGWT	— In God We Trust	RTB	— Rock the Boat
C	— Conservative	LFC	— Lindsay for Congress	S	— Socialist
CNSTP	— Constitution	LIBERT	— Libertarian	SW	— Socialist Workers
CS	— Common Sense	LU	— Liberty Union	TI	— Think Independently
CRE	— Cheap Renewable Energy	MOUNT	— Mountain	UNT	— Unity
D	— Democratic	NEB	— Nebraska	USTAX	— U.S. Taxpayers
EINDC	— Energy Independence	NL	— Natural Law	VPC	— Vote People Change
ELIM	— Eliminate the Primary	PACGRN	— Pacific Green	WFM	— Working Families
FTP	— For the People	PFP	— Peace and Freedom	X	— No party affiliation listed

11	Jerry McNerney (D)	164,500	55.3
	Dean Andal (R)	133,104	44.7
	write-in	12	—
12	Jackie Speier (D)	200,442	75.1
	Greg Conlon (R)	49,258	18.5
	Nathalie Hrizi (PFP)	5,793	2.2
	Barry Hermanson (GREEN)	5,776	2.2
	Kevin Dempsey Peterson (LIBERT)	5,584	2.1
13	Pete Stark (D)	166,829	76.4
	Raymond Chui (R)	51,447	23.6
14	Anna G. Eshoo (D)	190,301	69.8
	Ronny Santana (R)	60,610	22.2
	Brian Holtz (LIBERT)	11,929	4.4
	Carol Brouillet (GREEN)	9,926	3.6
15	Michael M. Honda (D)	170,977	71.7
	Joyce Stoer Cordi (R)	55,489	23.3
	Peter Myers (GREEN)	12,123	5.1
16	Zoe Lofgren (D)	146,481	71.3
	Charel Winston (R)	49,399	24.1
	Steven Wells (LIBERT)	9,447	4.6
17	Sam Farr (D)	168,907	73.9
	Jeff Taylor (R)	59,037	25.8
	write-in	682	.3
18	Dennis Cardoza (D)	130,192	100.0
19	George Radanovich (R)	179,245	98.4
	Peter Leinau (D)	2,490	1.4
	write-in	366	.2
20	Jim Costa (D)	93,023	74.3
	Jim Lopez (R)	32,118	25.7
21	Devin Nunes (R)	143,498	68.4
	Larry Johnson (D)	66,317	31.6
22	Kevin McCarthy (R)	224,549	100.0
23	Lois Capps (D)	171,403	68.1
	Matt T. Kokkonen (R)	80,385	31.9
24	Elton Gallegly (R)	174,492	58.2
	Marta Ann Jorgensen (D)	125,560	41.8
25	Howard P. "Buck" McKeon (R)	144,660	57.7
	Jackie Conaway (D)	105,929	42.3
26	David Dreier (R)	140,615	52.6
	Russ Warner (D)	108,039	40.4
	Ted Brown (LIBERT)	18,476	6.9
27	Brad Sherman (D)	145,812	68.5
	Navraj Singh (R)	52,852	24.8
	Tim Denton (LIBERT)	14,171	6.7
28	Howard L. Berman (D)	137,471	99.9
	write-in	150	.1
29	Adam B. Schiff (D)	146,198	68.9
	Charles Hahn (R)	56,727	26.7
	Alan Pyeatt (LIBERT)	9,219	4.3
30	Henry A. Waxman (D)	242,792	100.0
31	Xavier Becerra (D)	110,955	100.0
32	Hilda L. Solis (D)	130,142	100.0
	write-in	8	—
33	Diane Watson (D)	186,924	87.6
	David C. Crowley II (R)	26,536	12.4
34	Lucille Roybal-Allard (D)	98,503	77.1
	Christopher Balding (R)	29,266	22.9
35	Maxine Waters (D)	150,778	82.6
	Ted Hayes (R)	24,169	13.2
	Herb Peters (LIBERT)	7,632	4.2
36	Jane Harman (D)	171,948	68.6
	Brian Gibson (R)	78,543	31.4

37	Laura Richardson (D)	131,342	75.0
	Nicholas "Nick" Dibs (I)	42,774	24.4
	write-ins	1,136	.6
38	Grace F. Napolitano (D)	130,211	81.7
	Christopher M. Agrella (LIBERT)	29,113	18.3
39	Linda T. Sánchez (D)	125,289	69.7
	Diane A. Lenning (R)	54,533	30.3
40	Ed Royce (R)	144,923	62.5
	Christina Avalos (D)	86,772	37.4
41	Jerry Lewis (R)	159,486	61.6
	Tim Prince (D)	99,214	38.4
42	Gary G. Miller (R)	158,404	60.2
	Edwin "Ed" Chau (D)	104,909	39.8
43	Joe Baca (D)	108,259	69.1
	John Roberts (R)	48,312	30.9
44	Ken Calvert (R)	129,937	51.2
	Bill Hedrick (D)	123,890	48.8
45	Mary Bono Mack (R)	155,166	58.3
	Julie Bornstein (D)	111,026	41.7
46	Dana Rohrabacher (R)	149,818	52.5
	Debbie Cook (D)	122,891	43.1
	Tom Lash (GREEN)	8,257	2.9
	Ernst P. Gasteiger (LIBERT)	4,311	1.5
47	Loretta Sanchez (D)	85,878	69.5
	Rosemarie "Rosie" Avila (R)	31,432	25.4
	Robert Lauten (AMI)	6,274	5.1
48	John Campbell (R)	171,658	55.6
	Steve Young (D)	125,537	40.7
	Don Patterson (LIBERT)	11,507	3.7
49	Darrell Issa (R)	140,300	58.3
	Robert Hamilton (D)	90,138	37.4
	Lars R. Grossmith (LIBERT)	10,232	4.2
50	Brian P. Bilbray (R)	157,502	50.2
	Nick Leibham (D)	141,635	45.2
	Wayne Dunlap (LIBERT)	14,365	4.6
51	Bob Filner (D)	148,281	72.7
	David Lee Joy (R)	49,345	24.2
	Dan "Frodo" Litwin (LIBERT)	6,199	3.0
52	Duncan Hunter (R)*	160,724	56.4
	Mike Lumpkin (D)	111,051	38.9
	Michael Benoit (LIBERT)	13,316	4.7
	write-in	47	—
53	Susan A. Davis (D)	161,315	68.5
	Michael Crimmins (R)	64,658	27.4
	Edward M. Teyssier (LIBERT)	9,569	4.1

Colorado

SENATE

Mark Udall (D)*		1,230,994	52.8
Bob Schaffer (R)		990,755	42.5
Douglas "Dayhorse" Campbell (AC)		59,733	2.6
Bob Kinsey (GREEN)		50,004	2.2

HOUSE

1	Diana DeGette (D)	203,755	71.9
	George C. Lilly (R)	67,345	23.8
	Martin L. Buchanan (LIBERT)	12,135	4.3
	write-in	11	—
2	Jared Polis (D)*	215,571	62.6
	Scott Starin (R)	116,591	33.9
	J.A. Calhoun (GREEN)	10,026	2.9
	William Robert Hammons (UNT)	2,176	.6
3	John Salazar (D)	203,455	61.6
	Wayne Wolf (R)	126,762	38.4

4	Betsy Markey (D)*	187,347	56.2
	Marilyn Musgrave (R)	146,028	43.8
5	Doug Lamborn (R)	183,178	60.0
	Hal Bidlack (D)	113,025	37.0
	Brian X. Scott (AC)	8,894	2.9
	write-in	45	—
6	Mike Coffman (R)*	250,877	60.7
	Hank Eng (D)	162,639	39.3
7	Ed Perlmutter (D)	173,931	63.5
	John W. Lerew (R)	100,055	36.5

Connecticut

HOUSE

1	John B. Larson (D)	211,493	71.6
	Joe Visconti (R)	76,860	26.0
	Stephen E. D. Fournier (GREEN)	7,201	2.4
	write-in	3	—
2	Joe Courtney (D)	212,148	65.7
	Sean Sullivan (R)	104,574	32.4
	G. Scott Deshefy (GREEN)	6,300	2.0
	write-in	19	-
3	Rosa DeLauro (D)	230,172	77.4
	Bo Itshaky (R)	58,583	19.7
	Ralph A. Ferrucci (GREEN)	8,613	2.9
4	Jim Himes (D)*	158,475	51.3
	Christopher Shays (R)	146,854	47.6
	Michael Anthony Carrano (LIBERT)	2,049	.7
	Richard Z. Duffee (GREEN)	1,388	.4
	write-in	10	—
5	Christopher S. Murphy (D)	179,327	59.2
	David J. Cappiello (R)	117,914	39.0
	Thomas L. Winn (I)	3,082	1.0
	Harold H. Burbank II (GREEN)	2,324	.8
	write-in	10	—

Delaware

GOVERNOR

Jack Markell (D)		266,861	67.5
William Swain Lee (R)		126,662	32.0
Jeffrey Brown (BLU)		1,681	.4

SENATE

Joseph R. Biden Jr. (D)		257,539	64.7
Christine O'Donnell (R)		140,595	35.3

HOUSE

AL	Michael N. Castle (R)	235,437	61.1
	Karen Hartley-Nagle (D)	146,434	38.0
	Mark Anthony Parks (LIBERT)	3,586	.9

Florida

HOUSE

1	Jeff Miller (R)	232,559	70.2
	James "Jim" Bryan (D)	98,797	29.8
2	Allen Boyd (D)	216,804	61.9
	Mark Mulligan (R)	133,404	38.1
	write-in	159	—
3	Corrine Brown (D)		●
4	Ander Crenshaw (R)	224,112	65.2
	Jay McGovern (D)	119,330	34.7
5	Ginny Brown-Waite (R)	265,186	61.2
	John Russell (D)	168,446	38.8
6	Cliff Stearns (R)	228,302	60.9
	Tim Cunha (D)	146,655	39.1
7	John L. Mica (R)	238,721	62.0
	Faye Armitage (D)	146,292	38.0

District	Candidate	Votes	%
8	**Alan Grayson (D)***	172,854	52.0
	Ric Keller (R)	159,490	48.0
9	**Gus Bilirakis (R)**	216,591	62.2
	Bill Mitchell (D)	126,346	36.3
	John "Johnny K" Kalimnios (X)	3,394	1.0
	Richard O. Emmons (PTY)	2,042	.6
	write-in	5	—
10	**C.W. Bill Young (R)**	182,781	60.7
	Bob Hackworth (D)	118,430	39.3
	write-in	9	—
11	**Kathy Castor (D)**	184,106	71.7
	Eddie Adams Jr. (R)	72,825	28.3
12	**Adam H. Putnam (R)**	185,698	57.5
	Doug Tudor (D)	137,465	42.5
13	**Vern Buchanan (R)**	204,382	55.5
	Christine Jennings (D)	137,967	37.5
	Jan Schneider (X)	20,289	5.5
	Don Baldauf (X)	5,358	1.5
14	**Connie Mack (R)**	224,602	59.4
	Robert M. Neeld (D)	93,590	24.8
	Burt Saunders (X)	54,750	14.5
	Jeff George (X)	4,949	1.3
15	**Bill Posey (R)***	192,151	53.1
	Stephen Blythe (D)	151,951	42.0
	Frank Zilaitis (X)	14,274	3.9
	Trevor Lowing (X)	3,495	1.0
16	**Tom Rooney (R)***	209,874	60.1
	Tim Mahoney (D)	139,373	39.9
17	**Kendrick B. Meek (D)**		●
18	**Ileana Ros-Lehtinen (R)**	140,617	57.9
	Annette Taddeo (D)	102,372	42.1
19	**Robert Wexler (D)**	202,465	66.2
	Edward J. Lynch (R)	83,357	27.2
	Ben Graber (X)	20,214	6.6
20	**Debbie Wasserman Schultz (D)**	202,832	77.5
	Margaret Hostetter (X)	58,958	22.5
	write-in	9	-
21	**Lincoln Diaz-Balart (R)**	137,226	57.9
	Raúl L. Martinez (D)	99,776	42.1
22	**Ron Klein (D)**	169,041	54.7
	Allen West (R)	140,104	45.3
	write-in	6	—
23	**Alcee L. Hastings (D)**	172,835	82.2
	Marion D. Thorpe Jr. (R)	37,431	17.8
	write-in	40	—
24	**Suzanne M. Kosmas (D)***	211,284	57.2
	Tom Feeney (R)	151,863	41.1
	Gaurav Bhola (X)	6,223	1.7
25	**Mario Diaz-Balart (R)**	130,891	53.0
	Joe Garcia (D)	115,820	46.9

Georgia

SENATE

Candidate	Votes	%
Saxby Chambliss (R) >	1,228,033	57.4
Jim Martin (D) >	909,923	42.6

HOUSE

District	Candidate	Votes	%
1	**Jack Kingston (R)**	165,890	66.5
	Bill Gillespie (D)	83,444	33.5
2	**Sanford D. Bishop Jr. (D)**	158,435	68.9
	Lee Ferrell (R)	71,351	31.0
3	**Lynn Westmoreland (R)**	225,055	65.7
	Stephen Camp (D)	117,522	34.3
	write-in	3	—
4	**Hank Johnson (D)**	224,494	99.9
	write-ins	199	.1
5	**John Lewis (D)**	231,368	100.0
	write-ins	106	—
6	**Tom Price (R)**	231,520	68.5
	Bill Jones (D)	106,551	31.5
7	**John Linder (R)**	209,354	62.0
	Doug Heckman (D)	128,159	38.0
8	**Jim Marshall (D)**	157,241	57.2
	Rick Goddard (R)	117,446	42.8
9	**Nathan Deal (R)**	217,493	75.5
	Jeff Scott (D)	70,537	24.5
10	**Paul Broun (R)**	177,265	60.7
	Bobby Saxon (D)	114,638	39.3
11	**Phil Gingrey (R)**	204,082	68.2
	Hugh "Bud" Gammon (D)	95,220	31.8
12	**John Barrow (D)**	164,562	66.0
	John Stone (R)	84,773	34.0
13	**David Scott (D)**	205,919	69.0
	Deborah Honeycutt (R)	92,320	31.0

Hawaii

HOUSE

District	Candidate	Votes	%
1	**Neil Abercrombie (D)**	154,208	77.1
	Steve Tataii (R)	38,115	19.1
	Li Zhao (LIBERT)	7,594	3.8
2	**Mazie K. Hirono (D)**	165,748	76.1
	Roger B. Evans (R)	44,425	20.4
	Shaun Stenshol (I)	4,042	1.8
	Lloyd J. "Jeff" Mallan (LIBERT)	3,699	1.7

Idaho

SENATE

Candidate	Votes	%
Jim Risch (R)*	371,744	57.6
Larry LaRocco (D)	219,903	34.1
Rex Rammell (I)	34,510	5.4
Kent A. Marmon (LIBERT)	9,958	1.5
Pro-Life (I)	8,662	1.3

HOUSE

District	Candidate	Votes	%
1	**Walt Minnick (D)***	175,898	50.6
	Bill Sali (R)	171,687	49.4
2	**Mike Simpson (R)**	205,777	71.0
	Deborah Holmes (D)	83,878	29.0

Illinois

SENATE

Candidate	Votes	%
Richard J. Durbin (D)	3,615,844	67.8
Steve Sauerberg (R)	1,520,621	28.5
Kathy Cummings (GREEN)	119,135	2.2
Larry A. Stafford (LIBERT)	50,224	.9
Chad N. Koppie (CNSTP)	24,059	.4

HOUSE

District	Candidate	Votes	%
1	**Bobby L. Rush (D)**	233,036	85.9
	Antoine Members (R)	38,361	14.1
2	**Jesse L. Jackson Jr. (D)**	251,052	89.4
	Anthony W. Williams (R)	29,721	10.6
3	**Daniel Lipinski (D)**	172,581	73.3
	Michael Hawkins (R)	50,336	21.4
	Jerome Pohlen (GREEN)	12,607	5.4
4	**Luis V. Gutierrez (D)**	112,529	80.6
	Daniel Cunningham (R)	16,024	11.5
	Omar Lopez (GREEN)	11,053	7.9
5	**Rahm Emanuel (D)**	170,728	73.9
	Tom Hanson (R)	50,881	22.0
	Alan Augustson (GREEN)	9,283	4.0
6	**Peter Roskam (R)**	147,906	57.6
	Jill Morgenthaler (D)	109,007	42.4
7	**Danny K. Davis (D)**	235,343	85.0
	Steve Miller (R)	41,474	15.0
8	**Melissa Bean (D)**	179,444	60.7
	Steve Greenberg (R)	116,081	39.3
9	**Jan Schakowsky (D)**	181,948	74.7
	Michael Benjamin Younan (R)	53,593	22.0
	Morris Shanfield (GREEN)	8,140	3.3
	write-in	13	—
10	**Mark Steven Kirk (R)**	153,082	52.6
	Dan Seals (D)	138,176	47.4
11	**Debbie Halvorson (D)***	185,652	58.4
	Marty Ozinga (R)	109,608	34.5
	Jason M. Wallace (GREEN)	22,635	7.1
12	**Jerry F. Costello (D)**	213,270	71.4
	Timmy Jay Richardson Jr. (R)	74,634	25.0
	Roger W. Jennings (GREEN)	10,931	3.7
	write-in	1	—
13	**Judy Biggert (R)**	180,888	53.6
	Scott Harper (D)	147,430	43.6
	Steve Alesch (GREEN)	9,402	2.8
	write-in	51	—
14	**Bill Foster (D)**	185,404	57.7
	Jim Oberweis (R)	135,653	42.2
15	**Timothy V. Johnson (R)**	187,121	64.2
	Steve Cox (D)	104,393	35.8
16	**Donald Manzullo (R)**	190,039	60.9
	Robert G. Abboud (D)	112,648	36.1
	Scott Summers (GREEN)	9,533	3.0
17	**Phil Hare (D)**	220,961	99.8
	write-in	517	.2
18	**Aaron Schock (R)***	182,589	58.9
	Colleen Callahan (D)	117,642	37.9
	Sheldon Schafer (GREEN)	9,857	3.2
19	**John Shimkus (R)**	203,434	64.5
	Daniel Davis (D)	105,338	33.4
	Troy Dennis (GREEN)	6,817	2.2

Indiana

GOVERNOR

Candidate	Votes	%
Mitch Daniels (R)	1,563,885	57.8
Jill Long Thompson (D)	1,082,463	40.0
Andy Horning (LIBERT)	57,376	2.1
Christopher Stried (I)	19	—
Timothy Lee Frye (I)	8	—

HOUSE

District	Candidate	Votes	%
1	**Peter J. Visclosky (D)**	199,954	70.9
	Mark Leyva (R)	76,647	27.2
	Jeff Duensing (LIBERT)	5,421	1.9
2	**Joe Donnelly (D)**	187,416	67.1
	Luke Puckett (R)	84,455	30.2
	Mark Vogel (LIBERT)	7,475	2.7
3	**Mark Souder (R)**	155,693	55.0
	Michael Montagano (D)	112,309	39.7
	William Larsen (LIBERT)	14,877	5.3
4	**Steve Buyer (R)**	192,526	59.9
	Nels Ackerson (D)	129,038	40.1
5	**Dan Burton (R)**	234,705	65.5
	Mary Etta Ruley (D)	123,357	34.4
6	**Mike Pence (R)**	180,608	64.0
	Barry A. Welsh (D)	94,265	33.4
	George Thomas Holland (LIBERT)	7,539	2.7

7	André Carson (D)	172,650	65.1
	Gabrielle Campo (R)	92,645	34.9
	write-in	4	—
8	Brad Ellsworth (D)	188,693	64.7
	Greg Goode (R)	102,769	35.3
9	Baron P. Hill (D)	181,281	57.8
	Mike Sodrel (R)	120,529	38.4
	D. Eric Schansberg (LIBERT)	11,994	3.8

Iowa

SENATE

Tom Harkin (D)		941,665	62.7
Christopher Reed (R)		560,006	37.3

HOUSE

1	Bruce Braley (D)	186,991	64.6
	David Hartsuch (R)	102,439	35.4
	write-ins	199	.1
2	Dave Loebsack (D)	175,218	57.2
	Mariannette Miller-Meeks (R)	118,778	38.8
	Wendy Barth (GREEN)	6,664	2.2
	Brian White (X)	5,437	1.8
	write-ins	261	.1
3	Leonard L. Boswell (D)	176,904	56.3
	Kim Schmett (R)	132,136	42.1
	Frank V. Forrestal (SW)	4,599	1.5
	write-ins	521	.2
4	Tom Latham (R)	185,458	60.5
	Becky Greenwald (D)	120,746	39.4
	write-ins	197	.1
5	Steve King (R)	159,430	59.8
	Rob Hubler (D)	99,601	37.4
	Victor Vara (I)	7,406	2.8
	write-ins	180	.1

Kansas

SENATE

Pat Roberts (R)		727,121	60.1
Jim Slattery (D)		441,399	36.5
Randall L. Hodgkinson (LIBERT)		25,727	2.1
Joseph L. Martin (REF)		16,443	1.4

HOUSE

1	Jerry Moran (R)	214,549	81.9
	James Bordonaro (D)	34,771	13.3
	Kathleen M. Burton (REF)	7,145	2.7
	Jack Warner (LIBERT)	5,562	2.1
2	Lynn Jenkins (R)*	155,532	50.6
	Nancy Boyda (D)	142,013	46.2
	Leslie S. Martin (REF)	5,080	1.6
	Robert Garrard (LIBERT)	4,683	1.5
3	Dennis Moore (D)	202,541	56.4
	Nick Jordan (R)	142,307	39.7
	Joe Bellis (LIBERT)	10,073	2.8
	Roger D. Tucker (REF)	3,937	1.1
4	Todd Tiahrt (R)	177,617	63.4
	Donald Betts Jr. (D)	90,706	32.4
	Susan G. Ducey (REF)	6,441	2.3
	Steven A. Rosile (LIBERT)	5,345	1.9

Kentucky

SENATE

Mitch McConnell (R)		953,816	53.0
Bruce Lunsford (D)		847,005	47.0

HOUSE

1	Ed Whitfield (R)	178,107	64.3
	Heather A. Ryan (D)	98,674	35.6
2	Brett Guthrie (R)*	158,936	52.6
	David E. Boswell (D)	143,379	47.4
3	John Yarmuth (D)	203,843	59.4
	Anne M. Northup (R)	139,527	40.6
	Edward Martin (LIBERT)	0	—
4	Geoff Davis (R)	190,210	63.0
	Michael Kelley (D)	111,549	37.0
5	Harold Rogers (R)	177,024	84.1
	Jim Holbert (I)	33,444	15.9
6	Ben Chandler (D)	203,764	64.7
	Jon Larson (R)	111,378	35.3

Louisiana

SENATE

Mary L. Landrieu (D)		988,298	52.1
John Kennedy (R)		867,177	45.7
Richard Fontanesi (LIBERT)		18,590	1.0
Jay Patel (X)		13,729	.7
Robert Stewart (X)		8,780	.5

HOUSE

1	Steve Scalise (R)	189,168	65.7
	Jim Harlan (D)	98,839	34.3
2	Anh "Joseph" Cao (R)*	33,132	49.5
	William J. Jefferson (D)	31,318	46.8
	Malik Rahim (GREEN)	1,883	2.8
	Gregory W. Kahn (LIBERT)	549	.8
3	Charlie Melancon (D)		●
4	John Fleming (R)*	44,501	48.1
	Paul J. Carmouche (D)	44,151	47.7
	Chester T. Kelley (X)	3,245	3.5
	Gerard J. Bowen (X)	675	.7
5	Rodney Alexander (R)		●
6	Bill Cassidy (R)*	150,332	48.1
	Don Cazayoux (D)	125,886	40.3
	Michael Jackson (X)	36,198	11.6
7	Charles Boustany Jr. (R)	177,173	61.9
	Donald "Don" Cravins Jr. (D)	98,280	34.3
	Peter Vidrine (X)	10,846	3.8

Maine

SENATE

Susan Collins (R)		444,300	61.3
Tom Allen (D)		279,510	38.6

HOUSE

1	Chellie Pingree (D)*	205,629	54.9
	Charlie Summers (R)	168,930	45.1
2	Michael H. Michaud (D)	226,274	67.4
	John N. Frary (R)	109,268	32.6

Maryland

HOUSE

1	Frank Kratovil Jr. (D)*	177,065	49.1
	Andy Harris (R)	174,213	48.3
	Richard James Davis (LIBERT)	8,873	2.5
	write-ins	329	.1
2	C.A. Dutch Ruppersberger (D)	198,542	71.9
	Richard Pryce Matthews (R)	68,561	24.8
	Lorenzo Gaztañaga (LIBERT)	8,786	3.2
	write-ins	408	.1
3	John Sarbanes (D)	203,711	69.7
	Thomas E. "Pinkston" Harris (R)	87,971	30.1
	write-ins	766	.2
4	Donna Edwards (D)	258,704	85.8
	Peter James (R)	38,739	12.8
	Thibeaux Lincecum (LIBERT)	3,384	1.1
	write-ins	604	.2

5	Steny H. Hoyer (D)	253,854	73.6
	Collins Bailey (R)	82,631	24.0
	Darlene H. Nicholas (LIBERT)	7,829	2.3
	write-ins	377	.1
6	Roscoe G. Bartlett (R)	190,926	57.8
	Jennifer P. Dougherty (D)	128,207	38.8
	Gary W. Hoover Sr. (LIBERT)	11,060	3.3
	write-ins	342	.1
7	Elijah E. Cummings (D)	227,379	79.5
	Michael T. Hargadon (R)	53,147	18.6
	Ronald M. Owens-Bey (LIBERT)	5,214	1.8
	write-ins	280	.1
8	Chris Van Hollen (D)	229,740	75.1
	Steve Hudson (R)	66,351	21.7
	Gordon Clark (GREEN)	6,828	2.2
	Ian Thomas (LIBERT)	2,562	.8
	write-ins	533	.2

Massachusetts

SENATE

John Kerry (D)		1,971,974	65.9
Jeffrey K. Beatty (R)		926,044	31.0
Robert J. Underwood (LIBERT)		93,713	3.1

HOUSE

1	John W. Olver (D)	215,696	72.8
	Nathan A. Bech (R)	80,067	27.0
	write-ins	336	.1
2	Richard E. Neal (D)	234,369	98.5
	write-ins	3,631	1.5
3	Jim McGovern (D)	227,619	98.5
	write-ins	3,488	1.5
4	Barney Frank (D)	203,032	68.0
	Earl Henry Sholley (R)	75,571	25.3
	Susan Allen (I)	19,848	6.6
	write-ins	337	.1
5	Niki Tsongas (D)	225,947	98.7
	write-ins	2,960	1.3
6	John F. Tierney (D)	226,216	70.4
	Richard A. Baker (R)	94,845	29.5
	write-ins	251	.1
7	Edward J. Markey (D)	212,304	75.6
	John Cunningham (R)	67,978	24.2
	write-ins	400	.1
8	Michael E. Capuano (D)	185,530	98.6
	write-ins	2,722	1.4
9	Stephen F. Lynch (D)	242,166	98.7
	write-ins	3,128	1.3
10	Bill Delahunt (D)	272,899	98.6
	write-ins	3,774	1.4

Michigan

SENATE

Carl Levin (D)		3,038,386	62.7
Jack Hoogendyk Jr. (R)		1,641,070	33.8
Scotty Boman (LIBERT)		76,347	1.6
Harley G. Mikkelson (GREEN)		43,440	.9
Michael N. Nikitin (USTAX)		30,827	.6
Doug Dern (NL)		18,550	.4

HOUSE

1	Bart Stupak (D)	213,216	65.0
	Tom Casperson (R)	107,340	32.7
	Jean Treacy (GREEN)	2,669	.8
	Daniel W. Grow (LIBERT)	2,533	.8
	Joshua J. Warren (USTAX)	2,070	.6
	write-ins	8	—
2	Peter Hoekstra (R)	214,100	62.4
	Fred Johnson (D)	119,506	34.8

	Dan Johnson (LIBERT)	5,496	1.6
	Ronald E. Graeser (USTAX)	4,200	1.2
	write-ins	7	—
3	**Vernon J. Ehlers (R)**	**203,799**	**61.1**
	Henry Sanchez (D)	117,961	35.4
	Erwin J. Haas (LIBERT)	11,758	3.5
4	**Dave Camp (R)**	**204,259**	**61.9**
	Andrew D. Concannon (D)	117,665	35.7
	John Emerick (USTAX)	4,055	1.2
	Allitta Hren (LIBERT)	3,785	1.1
5	**Dale E. Kildee (D)**	**221,841**	**70.4**
	Matt Sawicki (R)	85,017	27.0
	Leonard Schwartz (LIBERT)	4,293	1.4
	Ken Mathenia (GREEN)	4,144	1.3
6	**Fred Upton (R)**	**188,157**	**58.9**
	Don Cooney (D)	123,257	38.6
	Greg Merle (LIBERT)	4,720	1.5
	Edward Pinkney (GREEN)	3,512	1.1
7	**Mark Schauer (D)***	**157,213**	**48.8**
	Tim Walberg (R)	149,781	46.5
	Lynn Meadows (GREEN)	9,528	3.0
	Ken Proctor (LIBERT)	5,675	1.8
	write-ins	89	—
8	**Mike Rogers (R)**	**204,408**	**56.5**
	Robert D. Alexander (D)	145,491	40.2
	Will Tyler White (LIBERT)	4,373	1.2
	Aaron Stuttman (GREEN)	3,836	1.1
	George M. Zimmer (USTAX)	3,499	1.0
9	**Gary Peters (D)***	**183,311**	**52.1**
	Joe Knollenberg (R)	150,035	42.6
	Jack Kevorkian (X)	8,987	2.6
	Adam Goodman (LIBERT)	4,893	1.4
	Douglas Campbell (GREEN)	4,737	1.3
10	**Candice S. Miller (R)**	**230,471**	**66.3**
	Robert Denison (D)	108,354	31.2
	Neil Kiernan Stephenson (LIBERT)	4,632	1.3
	Candace R. Caveny (GREEN)	4,146	1.2
11	**Thaddeus McCotter (R)**	**177,461**	**51.4**
	Joseph W. Larkin (D)	156,625	45.4
	John Tatar (LIBERT)	6,001	1.7
	Erik Shelley (GREEN)	5,072	1.5
	write-ins	23	—
12	**Sander M. Levin (D)**	**225,094**	**72.1**
	Bert Copple (R)	74,565	23.9
	John Vico (LIBERT)	4,767	1.5
	Les Townsend (USTAX)	4,076	1.3
	William J. Opalicky (GREEN)	3,842	1.2
13	**Carolyn Cheeks Kilpatrick (D)**	**167,481**	**74.1**
	Edward J. Gubics (R)	43,098	19.1
	George L. Corsetti (GREEN)	9,579	4.2
	Gregory Creswell (LIBERT)	5,764	2.6
14	**John Conyers Jr. (D)**	**227,841**	**92.4**
	Richard J. Secula (LIBERT)	10,732	4.4
	Clyde K. Shabazz (GREEN)	8,015	3.2
15	**John D. Dingell (D)**	**231,784**	**70.7**
	John J. Lynch (R)	81,802	25.0
	Aimee Smith (GREEN)	7,082	2.2
	Gregory Scott Stempfle (LIBERT)	4,002	1.2
	James H. Wagner (USTAX)	3,157	1.0

Minnesota

SENATE (UNCALLED)

Al Franken (D)	1,212,431[1]	41.5
Norm Coleman (R)	1,212,206[1]	41.5
others	496,109	17.0

[1]Recount results, certified Jan. 5, 2009.

HOUSE

1	**Tim Walz (D)**	**207,753**	**62.5**
	Brian J. Davis (R)	109,453	32.9
	Gregory Mikkelson (INDC)	14,904	4.5
	write-ins	290	.1
2	**John Kline (R)**	**220,924**	**57.3**
	Steve Sarvi (D)	164,093	42.5
	write-ins	639	.2
3	**Erik Paulsen (R)***	**178,932**	**48.5**
	Ashwin Madia (D)	150,787	40.8
	David Dillon (INDC)	38,970	10.6
	write-ins	406	.1
4	**Betty McCollum (D)**	**216,267**	**68.4**
	Ed Matthews (R)	98,936	31.3
	write-ins	815	.3
5	**Keith Ellison (D)**	**228,776**	**70.9**
	Barb Davis White (R)	71,020	22.0
	Bill McGaughey (INDC)	22,318	6.9
	write-ins	633	.2
6	**Michele Bachmann (R)**	**187,817**	**46.4**
	El Tinklenberg (D)	175,786	43.4
	Bob Anderson (INDC)	40,643	10.0
	write-ins	479	.1
7	**Collin C. Peterson (D)**	**227,187**	**72.2**
	Glen Menze (R)	87,062	27.7
	write-ins	431	.1
8	**James L. Oberstar (D)**	**241,831**	**67.7**
	Michael Cummins (R)	114,871	32.2
	write-ins	582	.2

Mississippi

SENATE

Thad Cochran (R)	**766,111**	**61.4**
Erik Fleming (D)	480,915	38.6
Roger Wicker (R)	**683,409**	**55.0**
Ronnie Musgrove (D)	560,064	45.0

HOUSE

1	**Travis W. Childers (D)**	**185,959**	**54.5**
	Greg Davis (R)	149,818	43.9
	Wally Pang (I)	3,736	1.1
	John M. Wages Jr. (GREEN)	1,876	.6
2	**Bennie Thompson (D)**	**201,606**	**69.0**
	Richard Cook (R)	90,364	31.0
3	**Gregg Harper (R)***	**213,171**	**62.5**
	Joel L. Gill (D)	127,698	37.5
4	**Gene Taylor (D)**	**216,542**	**74.5**
	John McCay III (R)	73,977	25.5

Missouri

GOVERNOR

Jay Nixon (D)	**1,680,611**	**58.4**
Kenny Hulshof (R)	1,136,364	39.5
Andrew W. Finkenstadt (LIBERT)	31,850	1.1
Gregory E. Thompson (CNSTP)	28,941	1.0

HOUSE

1	**William Lacy Clay (D)**	**242,570**	**86.9**
	Robb E. Cunningham (LIBERT)	36,700	13.1
	write-in	7	—
2	**Todd Akin (R)**	**232,276**	**62.3**
	William C. "Bill" Haas (D)	132,068	35.4
	Thomas L. Knapp (LIBERT)	8,628	2.3
3	**Russ Carnahan (D)**	**202,470**	**66.4**
	Chris Sander (R)	92,759	30.4
	Kevin C. Babcock (LIBERT)	5,518	1.8
	Cynthia "Cindy" Redburn (CNSTP)	4,324	1.4
4	**Ike Skelton (D)**	**200,009**	**65.9**
	Jeff Parnell (R)	103,446	34.1
5	**Emanuel Cleaver II (D)**	**197,249**	**64.4**
	Jacob Turk (R)	109,166	35.6
6	**Sam Graves (R)**	**196,526**	**59.4**
	Kay Barnes (D)	121,894	36.9
	Dave Browning (LIBERT)	12,279	3.7
7	**Roy Blunt (R)**	**219,016**	**67.8**
	Richard Monroe (D)	91,010	28.2
	Kevin Craig (LIBERT)	6,971	2.2
	Travis Maddox (CNSTP)	6,166	1.9
	write-in	49	—
8	**Jo Ann Emerson (R)**	**198,798**	**71.4**
	Joe Allen (D)	72,790	26.2
	Branden C. McCullough (LIBERT)	4,443	1.6
	Richard L. Smith (CNSTP)	2,257	.8
9	**Blaine Luetkemeyer (R)***	**161,031**	**50.0**
	Judy Baker (D)	152,956	47.5
	Tamara A. Millay (LIBERT)	8,108	2.5

Montana

GOVERNOR

Brian Schweitzer (D)	**318,670**	**65.5**
Roy Brown (R)	158,268	32.5
Stan Jones (LIBERT)	9,796	2.0

SENATE

Max Baucus (D)	**348,289**	**72.9**
Bob Kelleher (R)	129,369	27.1

HOUSE

AL	**Denny Rehberg (R)**	**308,470**	**64.1**
	John Driscoll (D)	155,930	32.4
	Mike Fellows (LIBERT)	16,500	3.4

Nebraska

SENATE

Mike Johanns (R)*	**455,854**	**57.5**
Scott Kleeb (D)	317,456	40.1
Kelly Renee Rosberg (NEB)	11,438	1.4
Steven R. Larrick (GREEN)	7,763	1.0

HOUSE

1	**Jeff Fortenberry (R)**	**184,923**	**70.4**
	Max Yashirin (D)	77,897	29.6
2	**Lee Terry (R)**	**142,473**	**51.9**
	Jim Esch (D)	131,901	48.1
3	**Adrian Smith (R)**	**183,117**	**76.9**
	Jay C. Stoddard (D)	55,087	23.1

Nevada

HOUSE

1	**Shelley Berkley (D)**	**154,860**	**67.6**
	Kenneth Wegner (R)	64,837	28.3
	Caren Alexander (IA)	4,697	2.0
	Raymond J. Duensing Jr. (LIBERT)	4,528	2.0
2	**Dean Heller (R)**	**170,771**	**51.8**
	Jill Derby (D)	136,548	41.4
	John Everhart (IA)	11,179	3.4
	Sean Patrick Morse (LIBERT)	5,740	1.7
	Craig Bergland (GREEN)	5,282	1.6

	Candidate	Votes	%
3	**Dina Titus (D)***	165,912	47.4
	Jon Porter (R)	147,940	42.3
	Jeffrey C. Reeves (I)	14,922	4.3
	Joseph P. Silvestri (LIBERT)	10,164	2.9
	Floyd Fitzgibbons (IA)	6,937	2.0
	Bob Giaquinta (GREEN)	3,937	1.1

New Hampshire

GOVERNOR

Candidate	Votes	%
John Lynch (D)	479,042	70.2
Joe Kenney (R)	188,555	27.6
Susan M. Newell (LIBERT)	14,987	2.2

SENATE

Candidate	Votes	%
Jeanne Shaheen (D)*	358,438	51.6
John E. Sununu (R)	314,403	45.3
Ken Blevens (LIBERT)	21,516	3.1

HOUSE

	Candidate	Votes	%
1	**Carol Shea-Porter (D)**	176,435	51.7
	Jeb Bradley (R)	156,338	45.8
	Robert Kingsbury (LIBERT)	8,100	2.4
	write-ins	198	.1
2	**Paul W. Hodes (D)**	188,332	56.4
	Jennifer M. Horn (R)	138,222	41.4
	Chester L. Lapointe II (LIBERT)	7,121	2.1
	write-ins	229	.1

New Jersey

SENATE

Candidate	Votes	%
Frank R. Lautenberg (D)	1,951,218	56.0
Dick Zimmer (R)	1,461,025	42.0
Jason Scheurer (LIBERT)	18,810	.5
J.M. Carter (IGWT)	15,935	.5
Daryl Mikell Brooks (PPC)	15,925	.5
Jeffrey Boss (BFS)	10,345	.3
Sara J. Lobman (SW)	9,187	.3

HOUSE

	Candidate	Votes	%
1	**Robert E. Andrews (D)**	206,453	72.4
	Dale M. Glading (R)	74,001	26.0
	Matthew Thieke (GREEN)	1,927	.7
	Margaret M. Chapman (BTB)	1,258	.4
	Everitt M. Williams III (TI)	1,010	.4
	Alvin Lindsay Jr. (LFC)	508	.2
2	**Frank A. LoBiondo (R)**	167,701	59.1
	David Kurkowski (D)	110,990	39.1
	Jason M. Grover (GREEN)	1,763	.6
	Peter F. Boyce (CNSTP)	1,551	.5
	Gary Stein (RTB)	1,312	.5
	Constantino Rozzo (S)	648	.2
3	**John Adler (D)***	166,390	52.1
	Chris Myers (R)	153,122	47.9
4	**Christopher H. Smith (R)**	202,972	66.2
	Joshua M. Zeitz (D)	100,036	32.6
	Steven Welzer (GREEN)	3,543	1.2
5	**Scott Garrett (R)**	172,653	55.9
	Dennis Shulman (D)	131,033	42.4
	Ed Fanning (GREEN)	5,321	1.7
6	**Frank Pallone Jr. (D)**	164,077	66.9
	Robert McLeod (R)	77,469	31.6
	Herb Tarbous (I)	3,531	1.4
7	**Leonard Lance (R)***	148,461	50.2
	Linda Stender (D)	124,818	42.2
	Michael P. Hsing (HFC)	16,419	5.6
	Dean Greco (ADBP)	3,259	1.1
	Thomas D. Abrams (PROS)	2,671	.9
8	**Bill Pascrell Jr. (D)**	159,279	71.1
	Roland Straten (R)	63,107	28.2
	Derek DeMarco (LIBERT)	1,600	.7
9	**Steven R. Rothman (D)**	151,182	67.5
	Vincent Micco (R)	69,503	31.0
	Michael Perrone Jr. (PRO)	3,200	1.4
10	**Donald M. Payne (D)**	169,945	98.9
	Michael Taber (SW)	1,848	1.1
11	**Rodney Frelinghuysen (R)**	189,696	62.4
	Tom Wyka (D)	113,510	37.3
	Chandler Tedholm (FTP)	711	.2
12	**Rush D. Holt (D)**	193,732	63.1
	Alan R. Bateman (R)	108,400	35.3
	David Corsi (CS)	4,802	1.6
13	**Albio Sires (D)**	120,382	75.4
	Joseph Turula (R)	34,735	21.7
	Julio A. Fernandez (X)	3,661	2.3
	Louis Vernotico (ELIM)	975	.6

New Mexico

SENATE

Candidate	Votes	%
Tom Udall (D)*	505,128	61.3
Steve Pearce (R)	318,522	38.7

HOUSE

	Candidate	Votes	%
1	**Martin Heinrich (D)***	166,271	55.6
	Darren White (R)	132,485	44.3
2	**Harry Teague (D)***	129,572	56.0
	Ed Tinsley (R)	101,980	44.0
3	**Ben Ray Luján (D)***	161,292	56.7
	Daniel K. East (R)	86,618	30.5
	Carol Miller (I)	36,348	12.8

New York

HOUSE

	Candidate	Votes	%
1	**Timothy H. Bishop (D, INDC, WFM)**	162,083	58.4
	Lee M. Zeldin (R, C)	115,545	41.6
2	**Steve Israel (D, INDC, WFM)**	161,279	66.9
	Frank J. Stalzer (R, C)	79,641	33.1
3	**Peter T. King (R, INDC, C)**	172,774	63.9
	Graham E. Long (D, WFM)	97,525	36.1
4	**Carolyn McCarthy (D, INDC, WFM)**	164,028	64.0
	Jack M. Martins (R, C)	92,242	36.0
5	**Gary L. Ackerman (D, INDC, WFM)**	112,724	71.0
	Elizabeth Berney (R)	43,039	27.1
	Jun Policarpio (C)	3,010	1.9
6	**Gregory W. Meeks (D)**	141,180	100.0
7	**Joseph Crowley (D, WFM)**	118,459	84.6
	William E. Britt Jr. (R, C)	21,477	15.3
8	**Jerrold Nadler (D, WFM)**	160,730	80.4
	Grace Lin (R, C)	39,047	19.5
9	**Anthony Weiner (D, WFM)**	112,205	93.0
	Alfred F. Donohue (C)	8,378	6.9
10	**Edolphus Towns (D)**	155,090	94.2
	Salvatore Grupico (R, C)	9,565	5.8
11	**Yvette D. Clarke (D, WFM)**	168,562	92.8
	Hugh C. Carr (R)	11,644	6.4
	Cartrell Gore (C)	1,517	.8
12	**Nydia M. Velázquez (D, WFM)**	123,046	90.0
	Allan E. Romaguera (R, C)	13,747	10.0
13	**Michael E. McMahon (D, WFM)***	114,219	60.9
	Robert A. Straniere (R)	62,441	33.3
	Timothy J. Cochrane (C)	5,799	3.1
	Carmine A. Morano (INDC)	4,947	2.6
14	**Carolyn B. Maloney (D, WFM)**	183,190	79.9
	Robert G. Heim (R)	43,365	18.9
	Isiah Matos (LIBERT)	2,659	1.2
15	**Charles B. Rangel (D, WFM)**	177,060	89.2
	Edward Daniels (R)	15,668	7.9
	Craig Schley (VPC)	3,706	1.9
	Martin Koppel (SW)	2,141	1.1
16	**José E. Serrano (D, WFM)**	127,179	96.6
	Ali Mohamed (R, C)	4,488	3.4
17	**Eliot L. Engel (D, INDC, WFM)**	161,594	79.9
	Robert Goodman (R, C)	40,707	20.1
18	**Nita M. Lowey (D, WFM)**	174,791	68.5
	Jim Russell (R, C)	80,498	31.5
19	**John Hall (D, INDC, WFM)**	164,859	58.7
	Kieran Michael Lalor (R, C)	116,120	41.3
20	**Kirsten Gillibrand (D, WFM)**	193,651	62.1
	Sandy Treadwell (R, INDC, C)	118,031	37.9
21	**Paul Tonko (D, WFM)***	171,286	62.1
	James Buhrmaster (R, C)	96,599	35.0
	Phillip G. Steck (INDC)	7,965	2.9
22	**Maurice D. Hinchey (D, INDC, WFM)**	168,558	66.4
	George K. Phillips (R, C)	85,126	33.6
23	**John M. McHugh (R, INDC, C)**	143,029	65.3
	Michael P. Oot (D, WFM)	75,871	34.7
24	**Michael Arcuri (D, WFM)**	130,799	52.0
	Richard Hanna (R, INDC, C)	120,880	48.0
25	**Dan Maffei (D, WFM)***	157,375	54.8
	Dale A. Sweetland (R, C)	120,217	41.9
	Howie Hawkins (GRP)	9,483	3.3
26	**Christopher Lee (R, INDC, C)***	148,607	55.0
	Alice Kryzan (D)	109,615	40.5
	Jonathan P. Powers (WFM)	12,104	4.5
27	**Brian Higgins (D, WFM)**	185,713	74.4
	Daniel J. Humiston (R, INDC)	56,354	22.6
	Harold W. Schroeder (C)	7,478	3.0
28	**Louise M. Slaughter (D, INDC, WFM)**	172,655	78.0
	David W. Crimmen (R, C)	48,690	22.0
29	**Eric Massa (D, WFM)***	140,529	51.0
	John R. "Randy" Kuhl Jr. (R, INDC, C)	135,199	49.0

North Carolina

GOVERNOR

Candidate	Votes	%
Beverly Perdue (D)	2,146,189	50.3
Pat McCrory (R)	2,001,168	46.9
Michael C. Munger (LIBERT)	121,584	2.8

SENATE

Candidate	Votes	%
Kay Hagan (D)*	2,249,311	52.6
Elizabeth Dole (R)	1,887,510	44.2
Christopher Cole (LIBERT)	133,430	3.1

HOUSE

	Candidate	Votes	%
1	**G.K. Butterfield (D)**	192,765	70.3
	Dean Stephens (R)	81,506	29.7
2	**Bob Etheridge (D)**	199,730	66.9
	Dan Mansell (R)	93,323	31.3
	Will Adkins (LIBERT)	5,377	1.8
3	**Walter B. Jones (R)**	201,686	65.9
	Craig Weber (D)	104,364	34.1

4	David E. Price (D)	265,751	63.3
	William "B.J." Lawson (R)	153,947	36.7
5	Virginia Foxx (R)	190,820	58.4
	Roy Carter (D)	136,103	41.6
6	Howard Coble (R)	221,018	67.0
	Teresa Sue Bratton (D)	108,873	33.0
7	Mike McIntyre (D)	215,383	68.8
	Will Breazeale (R)	97,472	31.2
8	Larry Kissell (D)*	157,185	55.4
	Robin Hayes (R)	126,634	44.6
9	Sue Myrick (R)	241,053	62.4
	Harry Taylor (D)	138,719	35.9
	Andy Grum (LIBERT)	6,711	1.7
10	Patrick T. McHenry (R)	171,774	57.6
	Daniel Johnson (D)	126,699	42.4
11	Heath Shuler (D)	211,112	62.0
	Carl Mumpower (R)	122,087	35.8
	Keith Smith (LIBERT)	7,517	2.2
12	Melvin Watt (D)	215,908	71.6
	Ty Cobb Jr. (R)	85,814	28.4
13	Brad Miller (D)	221,379	65.9
	Hugh Webster (R)	114,383	34.1

North Dakota

GOVERNOR

John Hoeven (R)	235,009	74.4
Tim Mathern (D)	74,279	23.5
DuWayne Hendrickson (I)	6,404	2.0

HOUSE

AL	Earl Pomeroy (D)	194,577	62.0
	Duane Sand (R)	119,388	38.0

Ohio

HOUSE

1	Steve Driehaus (D)*	155,455	52.5
	Steve Chabot (R)	140,683	47.5
	write-ins	152	—
2	Jean Schmidt (R)	148,671	44.8
	Victoria Wulsin (D)	124,213	37.5
	David Krikorian (I)	58,710	17.7
	write-in	30	—
3	Michael R. Turner (R)	200,204	63.3
	Jane Mitakides (D)	115,976	36.7
4	Jim Jordan (R)	186,154	65.2
	Mike Carroll (D)	99,499	34.8
5	Bob Latta (R)	188,905	64.1
	George Mays (D)	105,840	35.9
6	Charlie Wilson (D)	176,330	62.3
	Richard Stobbs (R)	92,968	32.8
	Dennis Spisak (GREEN)	13,812	4.9
7	Steve Austria (R)*	174,915	58.2
	Sharen Neuhardt (D)	125,547	41.8
8	John A. Boehner (R)	202,063	67.9
	Nicholas von Stein (D)	95,510	32.1
9	Marcy Kaptur (D)	222,054	74.4
	Bradley Leavitt (R)	76,512	25.6
10	Dennis J. Kucinich (D)	157,268	57.0
	Jim Trakas (R)	107,918	39.1
	Paul Conroy (LIBERT)	10,623	3.8
11	Marcia L. Fudge (D)*	212,667	85.2
	Thomas Pekarek (R)	36,708	14.7
	write-ins	167	.1
12	Pat Tiberi (R)	197,447	54.8
	David Robinson (D)	152,234	42.2
	Steven Linnabary (LIBERT)	10,707	3.0

13	Betty Sutton (D)	192,593	64.7
	David Potter (R)	105,050	35.3
	write-in	37	—
14	Steven C. LaTourette (R)	188,488	58.3
	Bill O'Neill (D)	125,214	38.7
	David Macko (LIBERT)	9,511	2.9
15	Mary Jo Kilroy (D)*	139,584	45.9
	Steve Stivers (R)	137,272	45.2
	Mark Noble (LIBERT)	14,061	4.6
	Don Eckhart (I)	12,915	4.2
	write-in	6	—
16	John Boccieri (D)*	169,044	55.4
	Kirk Schuring (R)	136,293	44.6
17	Tim Ryan (D)	218,896	78.1
	Duane Grassell (R)	61,216	21.8
18	Zack Space (D)	164,187	59.9
	Fred Dailey (R)	110,031	40.1

Oklahoma

SENATE

James M. Inhofe (R)	763,375	56.7
Andrew Rice (D)	527,736	39.2
Stephen P. Wallace (I)	55,708	4.1

HOUSE

1	John Sullivan (R)	193,404	66.2
	Georgianna W. Oliver (D)	98,890	33.8
2	Dan Boren (D)	173,757	70.5
	Raymond J. Wickson (R)	72,815	29.5
3	Frank D. Lucas (R)	184,306	69.7
	Frankie Robbins (D)	62,297	23.6
	Forrest Michael (I)	17,756	6.7
4	Tom Cole (R)	180,080	66.0
	Blake Cummings (D)	79,674	29.2
	David E. Joyce (I)	13,027	4.8
5	Mary Fallin (R)	171,925	65.9
	Steven L. Perry (D)	88,996	34.1

Oregon

SENATE

Jeff Merkley (D)*	864,392	48.9
Gordon H. Smith (R)	805,159	45.6
David Brownlow (CNSTP)	92,565	5.2

HOUSE

1	David Wu (D)	237,567	71.5
	Joel Haugen (I)	58,279	17.5
	Scott Semrau (CNSTP)	14,172	4.3
	H. Joe Tabor (LIBERT)	10,992	3.3
	Chris Henry (PACGRN)	7,128	2.1
	write-ins	4,110	1.2
2	Greg Walden (R)	236,560	69.5
	Noah Lemas (D)	87,649	25.8
	Tristin Mock (PACGRN)	9,668	2.8
	Richard D. Hake (CNSTP)	5,817	1.7
	write-ins	685	.2
3	Earl Blumenauer (D)	254,235	74.5
	Delia Lopez (R)	71,063	20.8
	Michael Meo (PACGRN)	15,063	4.4
	write-ins	701	.2
4	Peter A. DeFazio (D)	275,143	82.3
	Jaynee Germond (CNSTP)	43,133	12.9
	Mike Beilstein (PACGRN)	13,162	3.9
	write-ins	2,708	.8
5	Kurt Schrader (D)*	181,577	54.2
	Mike Erickson (R)	128,297	38.3
	Sean Bates (I)	6,830	2.0

	Douglas Patterson (CNSTP)	6,558	2.0
	Alex Polikoff (PACGRN)	5,272	1.6
	Steve Milligan (LIBERT)	4,814	1.4
	write-ins	1,326	.4

Pennsylvania

HOUSE

1	Robert A. Brady (D)	242,799	90.8
	Mike Muhammad (R)	24,714	9.2
2	Chaka Fattah (D)	276,870	88.9
	Adam A. Lang (R)	34,466	11.1
3	Kathy Dahlkemper (D)*	146,846	51.2
	Phil English (R)	139,757	48.8
4	Jason Altmire (D)	186,536	55.9
	Melissa A. Hart (R)	147,411	44.1
5	Glenn Thompson (R)*	155,513	56.7
	Mark B. McCracken (D)	112,509	41.0
	James Fryman (LIBERT)	6,155	2.2
6	Jim Gerlach (R)	179,423	52.1
	Bob Roggio (D)	164,952	47.9
7	Joe Sestak (D)	209,955	59.6
	W. Craig Williams (R)	142,362	40.4
8	Patrick J. Murphy (D)	197,869	56.8
	Tom Manion (R)	145,103	41.6
	Tom Lingenfelter (I)	5,543	1.6
9	Bill Shuster (R)	174,951	63.9
	Tony Barr (D)	98,735	36.1
10	Christopher Carney (D)	160,837	56.3
	Chris Hackett (R)	124,681	43.7
11	Paul E. Kanjorski (D)	146,379	51.6
	Lou Barletta (R)	137,151	48.4
12	John P. Murtha (D)	155,268	57.8
	William Russell (R)	113,120	42.1
13	Allyson Y. Schwartz (D)	196,868	62.8
	Marina Kats (R)	108,271	34.5
	John P. McDermott (CNSTP)	8,374	2.7
14	Mike Doyle (D)	242,326	91.3
	Titus North (GREEN)	23,214	8.7
15	Charlie Dent (R)	181,433	58.6
	Sam Bennett (D)	128,333	41.4
16	Joe Pitts (R)	170,329	55.8
	Bruce A. Slater (D)	120,193	39.4
	John A. Murphy (I)	11,768	3.9
	Daniel Frank (CNSTP)	2,877	.9
17	Tim Holden (D)	192,699	63.7
	Toni Gilhooley (R)	109,909	36.3
18	Tim Murphy (R)	213,349	64.1
	Steve O'Donnell (D)	119,661	35.9
19	Todd R. Platts (R)	218,862	66.6
	Philip J. Avillo Jr. (D)	109,533	33.4

Rhode Island

SENATE

Jack Reed (D)	320,644	73.4
Robert G. Tingle (R)	116,174	26.6

HOUSE

1	Patrick J. Kennedy (D)	145,254	68.6
	Jonathan P. Scott (R)	51,340	24.2
	Kenneth A. Capalbo (I)	15,108	7.1
2	Jim Langevin (D)	158,416	70.1
	Mark S. Zaccaria (R)	67,433	29.9

South Carolina

SENATE

Lindsey Graham (R)	1,014,396	57.6
Bob Conley (D)	742,362	42.2

HOUSE

1	Henry E. Brown Jr. (R)	177,540	51.9
	Linda Ketner (D)	163,724	47.9
	write-ins	615	.2
2	Joe Wilson (R)	184,583	53.7
	Rob Miller (D)	158,627	46.2
	write-ins	276	.1
3	J. Gresham Barrett (R)	186,799	64.7
	Jane Ballard Dyer (D)	101,724	35.2
	write-ins	218	.1
4	Bob Inglis (R)	184,440	60.1
	Paul Corden (D)	113,291	36.9
	C. Faye Walters (GREEN)	7,332	2.4
	write-ins	1,865	.6
5	John M. Spratt Jr. (D)	188,785	61.6
	Albert F. Spencer (R)	113,282	37.0
	Frank Waggoner (CNSTP)	4,093	1.3
	write-ins	125	—
6	James E. Clyburn (D)	193,378	67.5
	Nancy Harrelson (R)	93,059	32.5
	write-ins	134	—

South Dakota

SENATE

Tim Johnson (D)	237,889	62.5
Joel Dykstra (R)	142,784	37.5

HOUSE

AL	Stephanie Herseth Sandlin (D)	256,041	67.6
	Chris Lien (R)	122,966	32.4

Tennessee

SENATE

Lamar Alexander (R)	1,579,477	65.1
Robert D. Tuke (D)	767,236	31.6
Edward L. Buck (I)	31,631	1.3
Christopher G. Fenner (I)	11,073	.5
Daniel Towers Lewis (I)	9,367	.4
Chris Lugo (I)	9,170	.4
Ed Lawhorn (I)	8,986	.4
David Gatchell (I)	7,645	.3

HOUSE

1	Phil Roe (R)*	168,343	71.8
	Rob Russell (D)	57,525	24.5
	Joel Goodman (I)	3,988	1.7
	James W. Reeves (I)	2,544	1.1
	Thomas "T.K." Owens (I)	1,981	.8
2	John J. "Jimmy" Duncan Jr. (R)	227,120	78.1
	Bob Scott (D)	63,639	21.9
3	Zach Wamp (R)	184,964	69.4
	Doug Vandagriff (D)	73,059	27.4
	Jean Howard-Hill (I)	4,848	1.8
	Ed Choate (I)	3,750	1.4
	write-in	7	—
4	Lincoln Davis (D)	146,776	58.8
	Monty J. Lankford (R)	94,447	37.8
	James Anthony Gray (I)	4,869	1.9
	Kevin Ragsdale (I)	3,713	1.5
5	Jim Cooper (D)	181,467	65.8
	Gerard Donovan (R)	85,471	31.0
	Jon Jackson (I)	5,464	2.0
	John P. Miglietta (I)	3,196	1.2
	write-in	4	—
6	Bart Gordon (D)	194,264	74.4
	Chris Baker (I)	66,764	25.6
7	Marsha Blackburn (R)	217,332	68.6
	Randy G. Morris (D)	99,549	31.4
8	John Tanner (D)	180,465	100.0
	write-in	54	—
9	Steve Cohen (D)	198,798	87.8
	Jake Ford (I)	11,003	4.9
	Dewey Clark (I)	10,047	4.4
	Mary "Taylor Shelby" Wright (I)	6,434	2.8

Texas

SENATE

John Cornyn (R)	4,337,469	54.8
Richard J. "Rick" Noriega (D)	3,389,365	42.8
Yvonne Adams Schick (LIBERT)	185,241	2.3

HOUSE

1	Louie Gohmert (R)	189,012	87.6
	Roger L. Owen (I)	26,814	12.4
2	Ted Poe (R)	175,101	88.9
	Craig Wolfe (LIBERT)	21,813	11.1
3	Sam Johnson (R)	170,742	59.7
	Tom Daley (D)	108,693	38.0
	Christopher J. Claytor (LIBERT)	6,348	2.2
4	Ralph M. Hall (R)	206,906	68.8
	Glenn Melancon (D)	88,067	29.3
	Fred Annett (LIBERT)	5,771	1.9
5	Jeb Hensarling (R)	162,894	83.6
	Ken Ashby (LIBERT)	31,967	16.4
6	Joe L. Barton (R)	174,008	62.0
	Ludwig Otto (D)	99,919	35.6
	Max W. Koch III (LIBERT)	6,655	2.4
7	John Culberson (R)	162,635	55.9
	Michael Skelly (D)	123,242	42.4
	Drew Parks (LIBERT)	5,057	1.7
8	Kevin Brady (R)	207,128	72.6
	Kent Hargett (D)	70,758	24.8
	Brian Stevens (LIBERT)	7,565	2.6
9	Al Green (D)	143,868	93.6
	Brad Walters (LIBERT)	9,760	6.4
10	Michael McCaul (R)	179,493	53.9
	Larry Joe Doherty (D)	143,719	43.1
	Matt Finkel (LIBERT)	9,871	3.0
11	K. Michael Conaway (R)	189,625	88.3
	James R. Strohm (LIBERT)	25,051	11.7
12	Kay Granger (R)	181,662	67.6
	Tracey Smith (D)	82,250	30.6
	Shiloh S. Shambaugh (LIBERT)	4,842	1.8
13	William M. "Mac" Thornberry (R)	180,078	77.6
	Roger James Waun (D)	51,841	22.4
14	Ron Paul (R)	191,293	100.0
15	Rubén Hinojosa (D)	107,578	65.7
	Eddie Zamora (R)	52,303	31.9
	Gricha Raether (LIBERT)	3,827	2.3
16	Silvestre Reyes (D)	130,375	82.1
	Benjamin Eloy "Ben" Mendoza (I)	16,348	10.3
	Mette A. Baker (LIBERT)	12,000	7.6
17	Chet Edwards (D)	134,592	53.0
	Rob Curnock (R)	115,581	45.5
	Gardner C. Osborne (LIBERT)	3,849	1.5
18	Sheila Jackson Lee (D)	148,617	77.3
	John Faulk (R)	39,095	20.3
	Mike Taylor (LIBERT)	4,486	2.3
19	Randy Neugebauer (R)	168,501	72.4
	Dwight Fullingim (D)	58,030	24.9
	Richard "Chip" Peterson (LIBERT)	6,080	2.6
20	Charlie Gonzalez (D)	127,298	71.9
	Robert Litoff (R)	44,585	25.2
	Michael Idrogo (LIBERT)	5,172	2.9
21	Lamar Smith (R)	243,471	80.0
	James Arthur Stohm (LIBERT)	60,879	20.0
22	Pete Olson (R)*	161,996	52.4
	Nick Lampson (D)	140,160	45.4
	John Wieder (LIBERT)	6,839	2.2
23	Ciro D. Rodriguez (D)	134,090	55.8
	Lyle Larson (R)	100,799	41.9
	Lani Connolly (LIBERT)	5,581	2.3
24	Kenny Marchant (R)	151,434	56.0
	Tom Love (D)	111,089	41.1
	David A. Casey (LIBERT)	7,972	2.9
25	Lloyd Doggett (D)	191,755	65.8
	George L. Morovich (R)	88,693	30.4
	Jim Stutsman (LIBERT)	10,848	3.7
26	Michael C. Burgess (R)	195,181	60.2
	Ken Leach (D)	118,167	36.4
	Stephanie B. Weiss (LIBERT)	11,028	3.4
27	Solomon P. Ortiz (D)	104,864	58.0
	William "Willie" Vaden (R)	69,458	38.4
	Robert E. Powell (LIBERT)	6,629	3.7
28	Henry Cuellar (D)	123,494	68.7
	Jim Fish (R)	52,524	29.2
	Ross Lynn Leone (LIBERT)	3,722	2.1
29	Gene Green (D)	79,718	74.6
	Eric Story (R)	25,512	23.9
	Joel Grace (LIBERT)	1,564	1.5
30	Eddie Bernice Johnson (D)	168,249	82.5
	Fred Wood (R)	32,361	15.9
	Jarrett Woods (LIBERT)	3,366	1.6
31	John Carter (R)	175,563	60.3
	Brian P. Ruiz (D)	106,559	36.6
	Barry N. Cooper (LIBERT)	9,182	3.2
32	Pete Sessions (R)	116,283	57.2
	Eric Roberson (D)	82,406	40.6
	Alex Bischoff (LIBERT)	4,421	2.2

Utah

GOVERNOR

Jon Huntsman Jr. (R)	734,049	77.6
Bob Springmeyer (D)	186,503	19.7
Superdell Dell Schanze (LIBERT)	24,820	2.6

HOUSE

1	Rob Bishop (R)	196,799	64.8
	Morgan Bowen (D)	92,469	30.5
	Kirk D. Pearson (CNSTP)	7,397	2.4
	Joseph G. Buchman (LIBERT)	6,780	2.2
2	Jim Matheson (D)	220,666	63.4
	Bill Dew (R)	120,083	34.5
	Matthew Arndt (LIBERT)	4,576	1.3
	Dennis Ray Emery (CNSTP)	3,000	.9
3	Jason Chaffetz (R)*	187,035	65.6
	Bennion L. Spencer (D)	80,626	28.3
	Jim Noorlander (CNSTP)	17,408	6.1

Vermont

GOVERNOR

Jim Douglas (R)	170,492	53.4
Anthony Pollina (I)	69,791	21.9
Gaye Symington (D)	69,534	21.8

	Tony O'Connor (CRE)	3,106	1.0
	Sam Young (I)	2,490	.8
	Peter Diamondstone (LU)	1,710	.5
	Cris Ericson (I)	1,704	.5

HOUSE

AL	Peter Welch (D)	248,203	83.2
	Mike Bethel (I)	14,349	4.8
	Jerry Trudell (EINDC)	10,818	3.6
	Thomas James Hermann (PRO)	9,081	3.0
	Cris Ericson (I)	7,841	2.6
	Jane Newton (LU)	5,307	1.8
	write-ins	2,552	.9

Virginia

SENATE

Mark Warner (D)*	2,369,327	65.0
James S. Gilmore III (R)	1,228,830	33.7
Glenda Gail Parker (IGREEN)	21,690	.6
William B. Redpath (LIBERT)	20,269	.6

HOUSE

1	Rob Wittman (R)	203,839	56.6
	Bill S. Day Jr. (D)	150,432	41.8
	Nathan D. Larson (LIBERT)	5,265	1.5
	write-ins	756	.2
2	Glenn Nye (D)*	141,857	52.4
	Thelma Drake (R)	128,486	47.5
	write-ins	368	.1
3	Robert C. Scott (D)	239,911	97.0
	write-ins	7,377	3.0
4	J. Randy Forbes (R)	199,075	59.5
	Andrea Miller (D)	135,041	40.4
	write-ins	405	.1
5	Tom Perriello (D)*	158,810	50.1
	Virgil H. Goode Jr. (R)	158,083	49.9
	write-ins	183	.1
6	Robert W. Goodlatte (R)	192,350	61.6
	S. "Sam" Rasoul (D)	114,367	36.6
	Janice Lee Allen (I)	5,413	1.7
	write-ins	262	.1
7	Eric Cantor (R)	233,531	62.7
	Anita Hartke (D)	138,123	37.1
	write-ins	683	.2
8	James P. Moran (D)	222,986	67.9
	Mark W. Ellmore (R)	97,425	29.7
	J. Ron Fisher (IGREEN)	6,829	2.1
	write-ins	957	.3

9	Rick Boucher (D)	207,306	97.1
	write-ins	6,264	2.9
10	Frank R. Wolf (R)	223,140	58.8
	Judy M. Feder (D)	147,357	38.8
	Neeraj C. Nigam (I)	8,457	2.2
	write-ins	526	.1
11	Gerald E. Connolly (D)*	196,598	54.7
	Keith Fimian (R)	154,758	43.0
	Joseph P. Oddo (IGREEN)	7,271	2.0
	write-ins	864	.2

Washington

GOVERNOR

Christine Gregoire (D)	1,598,738	53.2
Dino Rossi (R)	1,404,124	46.8

HOUSE

1	Jay Inslee (D)	233,780	67.8
	Larry Ishmael (X)	111,240	32.2
2	Rick Larsen (D)	217,416	62.4
	Rick Bart (R)	131,051	37.6
3	Brian Baird (D)	216,701	64.0
	Michael Delavar (R)	121,828	36.0
4	Doc Hastings (R)	169,940	63.1
	George Fearing (D)	99,430	36.9
5	Cathy McMorris Rodgers (R)	211,305	65.3
	Mark Mays (D)	112,382	34.7
6	Norm Dicks (D)	205,991	66.9
	Doug Cloud (R)	102,081	33.1
7	Jim McDermott (D)	291,963	83.6
	Steve Beren (R)	57,054	16.3
8	Dave Reichert (R)	191,568	52.8
	Darcy Burner (D)	171,358	47.2
9	Adam Smith (D)	176,295	65.4
	James Postma (R)	93,080	34.6

West Virginia

GOVERNOR

Joe Manchin III (D)	492,697	69.8
Russ Weeks (R)	181,612	25.7
Jesse Johnson (MOUNT)	31,486	4.5

SENATE

John D. Rockefeller IV (D)	447,560	63.7
Jay Wolfe (R)	254,629	36.3

HOUSE

1	Alan B. Mollohan (D)	187,734	99.9
	write-ins	130	.1
2	Shelley Moore Capito (R)	147,334	57.1
	Anne Barth (D)	110,819	42.9
	write-in	16	—

3	Nick J. Rahall II (D)	133,522	66.9
	Marty Gearhart (R)	66,005	33.1

Wisconsin

HOUSE

1	Paul D. Ryan (R)	231,009	64.0
	Marge Krupp (D)	125,268	34.7
	Joseph Kexel (LIBERT)	4,606	1.3
	write-ins	224	.1
2	Tammy Baldwin (D)	277,914	69.3
	Peter Theron (R)	122,513	30.6
	write-ins	414	.1
3	Ron Kind (D)	225,208	63.2
	Paul Stark (R)	122,760	34.4
	Kevin Barrett (LIBERT)	8,236	2.3
	write-ins	196	—
4	Gwen Moore (D)	222,728	87.6
	Michael D. LaForest (I)	29,282	11.5
	write-ins	2,169	.8
5	F. James Sensenbrenner Jr. (R)	275,271	79.6
	Robert R. Raymond (I)	69,715	20.2
	write-ins	913	.3
6	Tom Petri (R)	221,875	63.7
	Roger A. Kittelson (D)	126,090	36.2
	write-ins	299	.1
7	David R. Obey (D)	212,666	60.8
	Dan Mielke (R)	136,938	39.1
	write-ins	233	.1
8	Steve Kagen (D)	193,662	54.0
	John Gard (R)	164,621	45.9
	write-ins	364	.1

Wyoming

SENATE

Michael B. Enzi (R)	189,046	75.6
Chris Rothfuss (D)	60,631	24.3
John Barrasso (R)	183,063	73.4
Nick Carter (D)	66,202	26.5

HOUSE

AL	Cynthia M. Lummis (R)*	131,244	52.6
	Gary Trauner (D)	106,758	42.8
	W. David Herbert (LIBERT)	11,030	4.4
	write-ins	363	.1

Appendix A

CONGRESS AND ITS MEMBERS

Glossary of Congressional Terms

Act — The term for legislation once it has passed both chambers of Congress and has been signed by the president or passed over his veto, thus becoming law. Also used in parliamentary terminology for a bill that has been passed by one house and engrossed. *(Also see engrossed bill.)*

Adjournment sine die — Adjournment without a fixed day for reconvening — literally, "adjournment without a day." Usually used to connote the final adjournment of a session of Congress. A session can continue until noon Jan. 3 of the following year, when, under the 20th Amendment to the Constitution, it automatically terminates. Both chambers must agree to a concurrent resolution for either chamber to adjourn for more than three days.

Adjournment to a day certain — Adjournment under a motion or resolution that fixes the next time of meeting. Under the Constitution, neither chamber can adjourn for more than three days without the concurrence of the other. A session of Congress is not ended by adjournment to a day certain.

Amendment — A proposal by a member of Congress to alter the language, provisions or stipulations in a bill or in another amendment. An amendment usually is printed, debated and voted upon in the same manner as a bill.

Amendment in the nature of a substitute — Usually an amendment that seeks to replace the entire text of a bill by striking out everything after the enacting clause and inserting a new version of the bill. An amendment in the nature of a substitute can also refer to an amendment that replaces a large portion of the text of a bill.

Appeal — A member's challenge of a ruling or decision made by the presiding officer of the chamber. A senator can appeal to members of the Senate to override the decision. If carried by a majority vote, the appeal nullifies the chair's ruling. In the House, the decision of the Speaker traditionally has been final; seldom are there appeals to the members to reverse the Speaker's stand. To appeal a ruling is considered an attack on the Speaker.

Appropriations bill — A bill that gives legal authority to spend or obligate money from the Treasury. The Constitution disallows money to be drawn from the Treasury "but in Consequence of Appropriations made by Law."

By congressional custom, an appropriations bill originates in the House. It is not supposed to be considered by the full House or Senate until a related measure authorizing the funding is enacted. An appropriations bill grants the actual budget authority approved by the authorization bill, though not necessarily the full amount permissible under the authorization.

If the 12 regular appropriations bills are not enacted by the start of the fiscal year, Congress must pass a stopgap spending bill or the departments and agencies covered by the unfinished bills must shut down.

About half of all budget authority, notably that for Social Security and interest on the federal debt, does not require annual appropriations; those programs exist under permanent appropriations. *(Also see authorization bill, budget authority, budget process and supplemental appropriations bill.)*

Authorization bill — Basic, substantive legislation that establishes or continues the legal operation of a federal program or agency either indefinitely or for a specific period of time, or which sanctions a particular type of obligation or expenditure. Under the rules of both chambers, appropriations for a program or agency may not be considered until the program has been authorized, although this requirement is often waived.

An authorization sets the maximum amount of funds that can be given to a program or agency, although sometimes it merely authorizes "such sums as may be necessary." *(Also see backdoor spending authority.)*

Backdoor spending authority — Budget authority provided in legislation outside the normal appropriations process. The most common forms of backdoor spending are borrowing authority, contract authority, entitlements and loan guarantees that commit the government to payments of principal and interest on loans — such as guaranteed student loans — made by banks or other private lenders. Loan guarantees result in actual outlays only when there is a default by the borrower.

In some cases, such as interest on the public debt, a permanent appropriation is provided that becomes available without further action by Congress.

Bills — Most legislative proposals before Congress are in the form of bills and are designated according to the chamber in which they originate — HR in the House of Representatives or S in the Senate — and by a number assigned in the order in which they are introduced during the two-year period of a congressional term.

"Public bills" address general questions and become public laws if they are cleared by Congress and signed by the president. "Private bills" deal with individual matters, such as claims against the government, immigration and naturalization cases, or land titles, and become private laws if approved and signed. *(Also see private bill, resolution.)*

Bills introduced — In both the House and Senate, any number of members may join in introducing a single bill or resolution. The first member listed is the sponsor of the bill, and all subsequent members listed are cosponsors.

Many bills are committee bills and are introduced under the name of the chairman of the committee or subcommittee. All appropriations bills fall into this category. A committee frequently holds hearings on a number of related bills and may agree to one of them or to an entirely new bill. *(Also see clean bill.)*

Bills referred — After a bill is introduced, it is referred to the committee or committees that have jurisdiction over the subject with which the bill is concerned. Under the standing rules of the House and Senate, bills are referred by the Speaker in the House and by the presiding officer in the Senate. In practice, the House and Senate parliamentarians act for these officials and refer the vast majority of bills. *(Also see discharge a committee.)*

Borrowing authority — Statutory authority that permits a federal agency to incur obligations and make payments for specified purposes with borrowed money.

Budget — The document sent to Congress by the president early each year estimating government revenue and expenditures for the ensuing fiscal year.

Budget Act — The common name for the Congressional Budget and Impoundment Control Act of 1974, which established the current budget process and created the Congressional Budget Office. The act also put limits on presidential authority to spend appropriated money. It has undergone several major revisions since 1974. *(Also see budget process.)*

Budget authority — Authority for federal agencies to enter into obligations that result in immediate or future outlays. The basic forms of budget authority are appropriations, contract authority and borrowing authority. Budget authority may be classified by (1) the period of availability (one-year, multiple-year or without a time limitation), (2) the timing of congressional action (current or permanent) or (3) the manner of determining the amount available (definite or indefinite). *(Also see appropriations bill, outlays.)*

Budget process — The annual budget process was created by the Congressional Budget and Impoundment Control Act of 1974, with a timetable that was modified in 1990. Under the law, the president must submit his proposed budget by the first Monday in February. Congress is supposed to complete an annual budget resolution by April 15, setting guidelines for congressional action on spending and tax measures. *(Also see pay-as-you-go rules.)*

Budget resolution — A concurrent resolution that is adopted by both chambers of Congress but does not require the president's signature. The measure sets a strict ceiling on discretionary budget authority, along with non-binding recommendations about how the spending should be allocated. The budget resolution may also contain "reconciliation instructions" requiring authorizing and tax-writing committees to propose changes in existing law to meet deficit-reduction goals. If more than one committee is involved, the Budget Committee in each chamber bundles those proposals, without change, into a reconciliation bill and sends it to the floor. *(Also see reconciliation.)*

By request — A phrase used when a senator or representative introduces a bill at the request of an executive agency or private organization but does not necessarily endorse the legislation.

Calendar — An agenda or list of business awaiting possible action by each chamber. The House uses four legislative calendars. They are the Discharge, House, Private and Union calendars. *(Also see individual calendar listings.)*

In the Senate, all legislative matters reported from committee go on one calendar. They are listed there in the order in which committees report them or the Senate places them on the calendar, but they may be called up out of order by the majority leader, either by obtaining unanimous consent of the Senate or by a motion to call up a bill. The Senate also has one non-legislative calendar, which is used for treaties and nominations. *(Also see Executive Calendar.)*

Call of the calendar — Senate bills that are not brought up for debate by a motion, unanimous consent or a unanimous consent agreement are brought before the Senate for action when the calendar listing them is "called." Bills must be called in the order listed. Measures considered by this method usually are non-controversial, and debate on the bill and any proposed amendments is limited to five minutes for each senator.

Chamber — The meeting place for the membership of either the House or the Senate; also the membership of the House or Senate meeting as such.

Chief Administrative Officer — An elected officer of the House who, under House rules, has operational and functional responsibility for matters assigned by the House Administration Committee. The office of the chief administrative officer was established under a 1995 change to House rules and replaced the office of director of non-legislative and financial services.

Clean bill — Frequently after a committee has finished a major revision of a bill, one of the committee members, usually the chairman, will assemble the changes and what is left of the original bill into a new measure and introduce it as a "clean bill." The revised measure, which is given a new number, is referred back to the committee, which reports it to the floor for consideration. This often is a timesaver, as committee-recommended changes in a clean bill do not have to be considered and voted on by the chamber. Reporting a clean bill also protects committee amendments that could be subject to points of order concerning germaneness.

Clerk of the House — An officer of the House of Representatives who supervises its records and legislative business.

Cloture — The process by which a filibuster can be ended in the Senate other than by unanimous consent. A motion for cloture can apply to any measure before the Senate, including a proposal to change the chamber's rules. To end a filibuster, the cloture motion must obtain the votes of three-fifths of the entire Senate membership (60 if there are no vacancies), except when the filibuster is against a proposal to amend the standing rules of the Senate and a two-thirds vote of senators present and voting is required.

The cloture request is put to a roll call vote one hour after the Senate meets on the second day following introduction of the motion. If approved, cloture limits each senator to one hour of debate. The bill or amendment in question comes to a final vote after 30 hours of consideration, including debate time and the time it takes to conduct roll calls, quorum calls and other procedural motions. *(Also see filibuster.)*

Committee — A division of the House or Senate that prepares legislation for action by the parent chamber or makes investigations as directed by the parent chamber.

There are several types of committees. Most standing committees are divided into subcommittees, which study legislation, hold hearings and report bills, with or without amendments, to the full committee. Only the full committee can report legislation for action by the House or Senate. *(Also see standing, oversight, and select or special committees.)*

Committee of the Whole — The working title of what is formally "The Committee of the Whole House [of Representatives] on the State of the Union." The membership is composed of all House members sitting as a committee. Any 100 members who are present on the floor of the chamber to consider legislation comprise a quorum of the committee. Any legislation, however, must first have passed through the regular legislative or appropriations committee and have been placed on the calendar.

Technically, the Committee of the Whole considers only bills directly or indirectly appropriating money, authorizing appropriations, or involving taxes or charges on the public. Because the Committee of the Whole need number only 100 representatives, a quorum is more

readily attained and legislative business is expedited. Before 1971, members' positions were not individually recorded on votes taken in the Committee of the Whole.

When the full House resolves itself into the Committee of the Whole, it replaces the Speaker with a "chairman." A measure is debated and amendments may be proposed, with votes on amendments as needed. (Also see five-minute rule.)

When the committee completes its work on the measure, it dissolves itself by "rising." The Speaker returns, and the chairman of the Committee of the Whole reports to the House that the committee's work has been completed. At this time, members may demand a roll call vote on any amendment adopted in the Committee of the Whole. The final vote is on passage of the legislation. (Also see delegate.)

Committee veto — A requirement added to a few statutes directing that certain policy directives by an executive department or agency be reviewed by certain congressional committees before they are implemented. Under common practice, the government department or agency and the committees involved are expected to reach a consensus before the directives are carried out.

Concurrent resolution — A concurrent resolution, designated H Con Res or S Con Res, must be adopted by both chambers, but it is not sent to the president for approval and, therefore, does not have the force of law. A concurrent resolution, for example, is used to fix the time for adjournment of a Congress. It is also used to express the sense of Congress on a foreign policy or domestic issue. The annual budget resolution is a concurrent resolution.

Conference — A meeting between representatives of the House and the Senate to reconcile differences between the two chambers on provisions of a bill. Members of the conference committee are appointed by the Speaker and the presiding officer of the Senate.

A majority of the conferees for each chamber must agree on a compromise, reflected in a "conference report," before the final bill can go back to both chambers for approval. When the conference report goes to the floor, it is difficult to amend. If it is not approved by both chambers, the bill may go back to conference under certain situations or a new conference may be convened. Many rules and informal practices govern the conduct of conference committees.

Bills that are passed by both chambers with only minor differences need not be sent to conference. Either chamber may "concur" with the other's amendments, completing action on the legislation. Sometimes leaders of the committees of jurisdiction work out an informal compromise instead of having a formal conference. (Also see custody of the papers.)

Confirmations — (See nominations.)

Congressional Record — The daily printed account of proceedings in both the House and Senate chambers, showing substantially verbatim debate and statements and a record of floor action. Highlights of legislative and committee action are given in a Daily Digest section of the Record, and members are entitled to have their extraneous remarks printed in an appendix known as "Extension of Remarks." Members may edit and revise remarks made on the floor during debate.

The Congressional Record provides a way to distinguish remarks spoken on the floor of the House and Senate from undelivered speeches. In the Senate, all speeches, articles and other matter that members insert in the Record without actually reading them on the floor are set off by large black dots, or bullets. However, a loophole

allows a member to avoid the bulleting if he or she delivers any portion of the speech in person. In the House, undelivered speeches and other material are printed in a distinctive typeface. The record is also available in electronic form. (Also see Journal.)

Congressional terms of office — Terms normally begin on Jan. 3 of the year following a general election. Terms are two years for representatives and six years for senators. Representatives elected in special elections are sworn in for the remainder of a term. Under most state laws, a person may be appointed to fill a Senate vacancy and serve until a successor is elected; the successor serves until the end of the term applying to the vacant seat.

Continuing resolution — A joint resolution, cleared by Congress and signed by the president, to provide new budget authority for federal agencies and programs whose regular appropriations bills have not been enacted. Also known as CRs' or continuing appropriations, continuing resolutions are used to keep agencies operating when, as often happens, Congress fails to finish the regular appropriations process by the start of the new fiscal year.

The CR usually specifies a maximum rate at which an agency may incur obligations, based on the rate of the prior year, the president's budget request, or an appropriations bill passed by either or both chambers of Congress but not yet enacted.

A CR can be a short-term measure that funds programs temporarily until the regular appropriations bill is enacted, or it can carry spending for the balance of the fiscal year in lieu of the unfinished appropriations bills.

Contract authority — Budget authority contained in an authorization bill that permits the federal government to enter into contracts or other obligations for future payments from funds not yet appropriated by Congress. The assumption is that funds will be provided in a subsequent appropriations act. (Also see budget authority.)

Correcting recorded votes — Rules prohibit members from changing their votes after the result has been announced. Occasionally, however, a member may announce hours, days or months after a vote has been taken that he or she was "incorrectly recorded." In the Senate, a request to change one's vote almost always receives unanimous consent, as long as it does not change the outcome. In the House, members are prohibited from changing votes if they were tallied by the electronic voting system.

Cosponsor — (See bills introduced.)

Current services estimates — Estimated budget authority and outlays for federal programs and operations for the forthcoming fiscal year based on continuation of existing levels of service without policy changes but with adjustments for inflation and for demographic changes that affect programs. These estimates, accompanied by the underlying economic and policy assumptions upon which they are based, are transmitted by the president to Congress when the budget is submitted.

Custody of the papers — To reconcile differences between the House and Senate versions of a bill, a conference may be arranged. The chamber with "custody of the papers" — the engrossed bill, engrossed amendments, messages of transmittal — is the only body empowered to request the conference. By custom, the chamber that asks for a conference is the last to act on the conference report.

Custody of the papers sometimes is manipulated to ensure that a

particular chamber acts either first or last on the conference report. *(Also see conference.)*

Deferral — Executive branch action to defer, or delay, the spending of appropriated money. The 1974 Congressional Budget and Impoundment Control Act requires a special message from the president to Congress reporting a proposed deferral of spending. Deferrals may not extend beyond the end of the fiscal year in which the message is transmitted. A federal district court in 1986 struck down the president's authority to defer spending for policy reasons; the ruling was upheld by a federal appeals court in 1987. Congress can prohibit proposed deferrals by enacting a law doing so; most often, cancellations of proposed deferrals are included in appropriations bills. *(Also see rescission.)*

Delegate — A non-voting official representing the District of Columbia, Guam, American Samoa, the U.S. Virgin Islands, the Northern Mariana Islands or Puerto Rico in the House. The first five serve two-year terms. Puerto Rico's non-voting representative is known as a resident commissioner and serves a four-year term. The delegates cannot vote in the full House but are permitted to vote in committees and can introduce and cosponsor legislation. Under a House rule in place in 1993 and 1994, and restored in 2007, delegates are permitted to vote in the Committee of the Whole, in which the House considers appropriations, authorization and tax bills for amendment. If the votes of the delegates are decisive on any vote in the Committee of the Whole, the amendment is automatically voted on again in the full House, where the delegates cannot vote.

Dilatory motion — A motion made for the purpose of killing time and preventing action on a bill or amendment. House rules outlaw dilatory motions, but enforcement is largely within the discretion of the Speaker or chairman of the Committee of the Whole. The Senate does not have a rule barring dilatory motions except under cloture.

Discharge a committee — Occasionally, attempts are made to relieve a committee of jurisdiction over a bill that is before it. This is attempted more often in the House than in the Senate, and the procedure rarely is successful.

In the House, if a committee does not report a bill within 30 days after the measure is referred to it, any member may file a discharge motion. Once offered, the motion is treated as a petition needing the signatures of a majority of members (218 if there are no vacancies). After the required signatures have been obtained, there is a delay of seven days.

Thereafter, on the second and fourth Mondays of each month, except during the last six days of a session, any member who has signed the petition must be recognized, if he or she so desires, to move that the committee be discharged. Debate on the motion to discharge is limited to 20 minutes. If the motion is carried, consideration of the bill becomes a matter of high privilege.

If a resolution to consider a bill is held up in the Rules Committee for more than seven legislative days, any member may enter a motion to discharge the committee. The motion is handled like any other discharge petition in the House. Occasionally, to expedite non-controversial legislative business, a committee is discharged by unanimous consent of the House, and a petition is not required. In 1993, the signatures on pending discharge petitions — previously kept secret — were made a matter of public record. *(For Senate procedure, see discharge resolution.)*

Discharge Calendar — The House calendar to which motions to discharge committees are referred when they have the required number of signatures (218) and are awaiting floor action. *(Also see calendar.)*

Discharge petition — *(See discharge a committee.)*

Discharge resolution — In the Senate, a special motion that any senator may introduce to relieve a committee from consideration of a bill before it. The resolution can be called up for Senate approval or disapproval in the same manner as any other Senate business. *(For House procedure, see discharge a committee.)*

Discretionary spending — Budget authority provided through appropriations bills in amounts determined by Congress. *(Also see mandatory spending.)*

Direct spending — *(See mandatory spending.)*

Division of a question for voting — A practice that is more common in the Senate but also used in the House whereby a member may demand a division of an amendment or a motion for purposes of voting. When the amendment or motion lends itself to such a division, the individual parts are voted on separately. This procedure occurs most often during the consideration of conference reports.

Emergency spending — Spending that the president and Congress have designated as an emergency requirement. Emergency spending is not subject to limits on discretionary spending set in the budget resolution or to pay-as-you-go rules. The designation is intended for unanticipated items that are not included in the budget for a fiscal year, such as spending to respond to disasters. However, most of the appropriations for the Iraq War have been designated as emergency spending.

Enacting clause — Key phrase in bills beginning, "Be it enacted by the Senate and House of Representatives." A successful motion to strike it from legislation kills the measure.

Engrossed bill — The final copy of a bill as passed by one chamber, with the text as amended by floor action and certified by the clerk of the House or the secretary of the Senate.

Enrolled bill — The final copy of a bill that has been passed in identical form by both chambers. It is certified by an officer of the chamber of origin (clerk of the House or secretary of the Senate) and then sent on for the signatures of the House Speaker, the Senate president pro tempore and the president of the United States. An enrolled bill is printed on parchment.

Entitlement — A program that guarantees payments to anyone who meets the eligibility criteria set in law. Examples included Social Security, Medicare, Medicaid and food stamps. *(Also see mandatory spending.)*

Executive Calendar — A non-legislative calendar in the Senate that lists presidential documents such as treaties and nominations. *(Also see calendar.)*

Executive document — A document, usually a treaty, sent to the Senate by the president for consideration or approval. Executive documents are referred to committee in the same manner as other measures. Unlike legislative documents, treaties do not die at the end of a Congress but remain "live" proposals until acted on by the Senate or withdrawn by the president.

Executive session — A meeting of a Senate or House committee (or occasionally of either chamber) that only its members may attend. Witnesses regularly appear at committee meetings in executive session — for example, Defense Department officials during presentations of classified Defense information. Other members of Congress may be invited, but the public and news media are not allowed to attend.

Filibuster — A time-delaying tactic associated with the Senate and used by a minority in an effort to prevent a vote on a bill or amendment that probably would pass if voted upon directly. The most common method is to take advantage of the Senate's rules permitting unlimited debate, but other forms of parliamentary maneuvering may be used.

The stricter rules of the House make filibusters more difficult, but delaying tactics are employed occasionally through various procedural devices allowed by House rules. *(Also see cloture.)*

Fiscal year — Financial operations of the government are carried out in a 12-month fiscal year, beginning Oct. 1 and ending Sept. 30. The fiscal year carries the date of the calendar year in which it ends. (From fiscal 1844 to fiscal 1976, the fiscal year began July 1 and ended the following June 30.)

Five-minute rule — A debate-limiting rule of the House that is invoked when the House sits as the Committee of the Whole. Under the rule, a member offering an amendment and a member opposing it are each allowed to speak for five minutes. Debate is then closed. In practice, amendments regularly are debated for more than 10 minutes, with members gaining the floor by offering pro forma amendments or obtaining unanimous consent to speak longer than five minutes. *(Also see Committee of the Whole, hour rule, strike out the last word.)*

Floor manager — A member who has the task of steering legislation through floor debate and amendment to a final vote in the House or the Senate. Floor managers usually are chairmen or ranking members of the committee that reported the bill. Managers are responsible for apportioning the debate time granted to supporters of the bill. The ranking minority member of the committee normally apportions time for the minority party's participation in the debate.

Frank — A member's facsimile signature, which is used on envelopes in lieu of stamps for the member's official outgoing mail. The "franking privilege" is the right to send mail postage-free.

Germane — Pertaining to the subject matter of the measure at hand. All House amendments must be germane to the bill being considered. The Senate requires that amendments be germane when they are proposed to general appropriations bills or to bills being considered once cloture has been adopted or, frequently, when the Senate is proceeding under a unanimous consent agreement placing a time limit on consideration of a bill. The 1974 Budget Act also requires that amendments to concurrent budget resolutions be germane.

In the House, floor debate must be germane, and the first three hours of debate each day in the Senate must be germane to the pending business.

Gramm-Rudman-Hollings Deficit Reduction Act — *(See sequester.)*

Grandfather clause — A provision that exempts people or other entities already engaged in an activity from new rules or legislation affecting that activity.

Hearings — Committee sessions for taking testimony from witnesses. At hearings on legislation, witnesses usually include specialists, government officials, and spokesmen for individuals or entities affected by the bill or bills under study. Hearings related to special investigations bring forth a variety of witnesses. Committees sometimes use their subpoena power to summon reluctant witnesses. The public and news media may attend open hearings but are barred from closed, or "executive," hearings. The vast majority of hearings are open to the public. *(Also see executive session.)*

Hold-harmless clause — A provision added to legislation to ensure that recipients of federal funds do not receive less in a future year than they did in the current year if a new formula for allocating funds authorized in the legislation would result in a reduction to the recipients. This clause has been used most often to soften the impact of sudden reductions in federal grants.

Hopper — Box on House clerk's desk into which members deposit bills and resolutions to introduce them.

Hour rule — A provision in the rules of the House that permits one hour of debate time for each member on amendments debated in the House of Representatives sitting as the House. Therefore, the House normally amends bills while sitting as the Committee of the Whole, where the five-minute rule on amendments operates.

House as in the Committee of the Whole — A procedure that can be used to expedite consideration of certain measures such as continuing resolutions and, when there is debate, private bills. The procedure can be invoked only with the unanimous consent of the House or a rule from the Rules Committee and has procedural elements of both the House sitting as the House of Representatives, such as the Speaker presiding and the previous question motion being in order, and the House sitting as the Committee of the Whole, with the five-minute rule being in order. *(Also see Committee of the Whole.)*

House Calendar — A listing for action by the House of public bills that do not directly or indirectly appropriate money or raise revenue. *(Also see calendar.)*

Immunity — The constitutional privilege of members of Congress to make verbal statements on the floor and in committee for which they cannot be sued or arrested for slander or libel. Also, freedom from arrest while traveling to or from sessions of Congress or on official business. Members in this status may only be arrested for treason, felonies or a breach of the peace, as defined by congressional manuals.

Joint committee — A committee composed of a specified number of members of both the House and Senate. A joint committee may be investigative or research-oriented, an example of the latter being the Joint Economic Committee. Others have housekeeping duties; examples include the joint committees on Printing and the Library of Congress.

Joint resolution — Like a bill, a joint resolution, designated H J Res or S J Res, requires the approval of both chambers and the signature of the president, and has the force of law if approved. There is no practical difference between a bill and a joint resolution. A joint resolution generally is used to address a limited matter such as a single appropriation.

Joint resolutions are also used to propose amendments to the Constitution. In that case, they require a two-thirds majority in both

chambers. They do not require a presidential signature, but they must be ratified by three-fourths of the states to become a part of the Constitution. (*Also see concurrent resolution, resolution.*)

Journal — The official record of the proceedings of the House and Senate. The Journal records the actions taken in each chamber, but, unlike the Congressional Record, it does not include the substantially verbatim report of speeches, debates, statements and the like.

Law — An act of Congress that has been signed by the president or passed, over his veto, by Congress. Public bills, when signed, become public laws and are cited by the letters PL and a hyphenated number. The number before the hyphen corresponds to the Congress, and the one or more digits after the hyphen refer to the numerical sequence in which the president signed the bills during that Congress. Private bills, when signed, become private laws. (*Also see bills, private bill.*)

Legislative day — The "day" extending from the time either chamber meets after an adjournment until the time it next adjourns. Because the House normally adjourns from day to day, legislative days and calendar days usually coincide. But in the Senate, a legislative day may, and frequently does, extend over several calendar days. (*Also see recess.*)

Line-item veto — Presidential authority to strike individual items from appropriations bills, which presidents since Ulysses S. Grant have sought. Congress gave the president a form of the power in 1996 (PL 104-130), but this "enhanced rescission authority" was struck down by the Supreme Court in 1998 as unconstitutional because it allowed the president to change laws on his own.

Loan guarantees — Loans to third parties for which the federal government guarantees the repayment of principal or interest, in whole or in part, to the lender in the event of default.

Lobby — A group seeking to influence the passage or defeat of legislation. Originally the term referred to people frequenting the lobbies or corridors of legislative chambers to speak to lawmakers.

The definition of a lobby and the activity of lobbying is a matter of differing interpretation. By some definitions, lobbying is limited to direct attempts to influence lawmakers through personal interviews and persuasion. Under other definitions, lobbying includes attempts at indirect, or grass-roots, influence, such as persuading members of a group to write or visit their district's representative and state's senators or attempting to create a climate of opinion favorable to a desired legislative goal.

The right to attempt to influence legislation is based on the First Amendment to the Constitution, which says Congress shall make no law abridging the right of the people "to petition the government for a redress of grievances."

Majority leader — Floor leader for the majority party in each chamber. In the Senate, in consultation with the minority leader, the majority leader directs the legislative schedule for the chamber. He or she is also his party's spokesman and chief strategist. In the House, the majority leader is second to the Speaker in the majority party's leadership and serves as the party's legislative strategist. (*Also see Speaker, whip.*)

Mandatory spending — Budget authority and outlays provided under laws other than appropriations acts. Mandatory spending, also known as direct spending, includes entitlement funding and payment of interest on the public debt. (*Also see entitlement.*)

Manual — The official handbook in each chamber prescribing in detail its organization, procedures and operations.

Marking up a bill — Going through the contents of a piece of legislation in committee or subcommittee to, for example, consider the provisions, act on amendments to provisions and proposed revisions to the language, and insert new sections and phraseology. If the bill is extensively amended, the committee's version may be introduced as a separate (or "clean") bill, with a new number, before being considered by the full House or Senate. (*Also see clean bill.*)

Minority leader — Floor leader for the minority party in each chamber.

Morning hour — The time set aside at the beginning of each legislative day for the consideration of regular, routine business. The "hour" is of indefinite duration in the House, where it is rarely used. In the Senate, it is the first two hours of a session following an adjournment, as distinguished from a recess. The morning hour can be terminated earlier if the morning business has been completed.

Business includes such matters as messages from the president, communications from the heads of departments, messages from the House, the presentation of petitions, reports of standing and select committees, and the introduction of bills and resolutions.

During the first hour of the morning hour in the Senate, no motion to proceed to the consideration of any bill on the calendar is in order except by unanimous consent. During the second hour, motions can be made but must be decided without debate. Senate committees may meet while the Senate conducts the morning hour.

Motion — In the House or Senate chamber, a request by a member to institute any one of a wide array of parliamentary actions. He or she "moves" for a certain procedure, such as the consideration of a measure. The precedence of motions, and whether they are debatable, is set forth in the House and Senate manuals.

Nominations — Presidential appointments to office subject to Senate confirmation. Although most nominations win quick Senate approval, some are controversial and become the topic of hearings and debate. Sometimes senators object to appointees for patronage reasons — for example, when a nomination to a local federal job is made without consulting the senators of the state concerned. In some situations a senator may object that the nominee is "personally obnoxious" to him. Usually other senators join in blocking such appointments out of courtesy to their colleagues. (*Also see senatorial courtesy.*)

One-minute speeches — Addresses by House members at the beginning of a legislative day. The speeches may cover any subject but are limited to one minute's duration.

Outlays — Actual spending that flows from the liquidation of budget authority. Outlays associated with appropriations bills and other legislation are estimates of future spending made by the Congressional Budget Office (CBO) and the White House's Office of Management and Budget (OMB). CBO's estimates govern bills for the purpose of congressional floor debate, while OMB's numbers govern when it comes to determining whether legislation exceeds spending caps.

Outlays in a given fiscal year may result from budget authority provided in the current year or in previous years. (*Also see budget authority, budget process.*)

Override a veto — If the president vetoes a bill and sends it back to Congress with his objections, Congress may try to override his veto and enact the bill into law. Neither chamber is required to attempt to override a veto. The override of a veto requires a recorded vote with a two-thirds majority of those present and voting in each chamber. The question put to each chamber is: "Shall the bill pass, the objections of the president to the contrary notwithstanding?" *(Also see pocket veto, veto.)*

Oversight committee — A congressional committee or designated subcommittee that is charged with general oversight of one or more federal agencies' programs and activities. Usually, the oversight panel for a particular agency is also the authorizing committee for that agency's programs and operations.

Pair — A voluntary, informal arrangement that two lawmakers, usually on opposite sides of an issue, make on recorded votes. In many cases, the result is to subtract a vote from each side, with no effect on the outcome.

Pairs are not authorized in the rules of either chamber, are not counted in tabulating the final result and have no official standing. However, paired members are identified in the Congressional Record, along with their positions on such votes, if known. A member who expects to be absent for a vote can pair with a member who plans to vote, with the latter agreeing to withhold his or her vote.

There are three types of pairs:

(1) A live pair involves a member who is present for a vote and another who is absent. The member in attendance votes and then withdraws the vote, announcing that he or she has a live pair with colleague "X" and stating how the two members would have voted, one in favor, the other opposed. A live pair may affect the outcome of a closely contested vote, since it subtracts one "yea" or one "nay" from the final tally. A live pair may cover one or several specific issues.

(2) A general pair, widely used in the House, does not entail any arrangement between two members and does not affect the vote. Members who expect to be absent notify the clerk that they wish to make a general pair. Each member then is paired with another desiring a pair, and their names are listed in the Congressional Record. The member may or may not be paired with another taking the opposite position, and no indication of how the members would have voted is given.

(3) A specific pair is similar to a general pair, except that the opposing stands of the two members are identified and printed in the Congressional Record.

Pay-as-you-go (PAYGO) rules — House rules for the 110th Congress specify that it is out of order to consider any legislation, including conference reports, that contains tax provisions or new or expanded entitlement programs that have the net effect of increasing the deficit or reducing the surplus. The restriction applies to the current year and the following five years, as well as the current year and the following 10 years.

Under the fiscal 2008 budget resolution, any entitlement spending or tax legislation in the Senate that would increase the budget during the current fiscal year or the ensuing four or nine years is subject to a point of order. The point of order is only relevant if the legislation, together with other legislation enacted during the year, increases the deficit compared with a baseline set in the annual budget resolution. *(Also see point of order.)*

Petition — A request or plea sent to one or both chambers from an organization or private citizens' group seeking support for particular legislation or favorable consideration of a matter not yet receiving congressional attention. Petitions are referred to appropriate committees. In the House, a petition signed by a majority of members (218) can discharge a bill from a committee. *(Also see discharge a committee.)*

Pocket veto — The act of the president in withholding his approval of a bill after Congress has adjourned. When Congress is in session, a bill becomes law without the president's signature if he does not act upon it within 10 days, excluding Sundays, from the time he receives it. But if Congress adjourns sine die within that 10-day period, the bill, if unsigned, will die even if the president does not formally veto it.

The Supreme Court in 1986 agreed to decide whether the president could pocket veto a bill during recesses and between sessions of the same Congress or only between Congresses. The justices in 1987 declared the case moot, however, because the bill in question was invalid once the case reached the court. *(Also see adjournment sine die, veto.)*

Point of order — An objection raised by a member that the chamber is departing from rules governing its conduct of business. The objector cites the rule violated, with the chair sustaining his or her objection if correctly made. The chair restores order by suspending proceedings of the chamber until it conforms to the prescribed "order of business."

Both chambers have procedures for overcoming a point of order, either by vote or — what is most common in the House — by including language in the rule for floor consideration that waives a point of order against a given bill. *(Also see rules.)*

President of the Senate — Under the Constitution, the vice president of the United States presides over the Senate. In his absence, the president pro tempore, or a senator designated by the president pro tempore, presides over the chamber.

President pro tempore — The chief officer of the Senate in the absence of the vice president — literally, but loosely, the president for a time. The president pro tempore is elected by his fellow senators. Recent practice has been to elect the senator of the majority party with the longest period of continuous service. The president pro tempore is third in the line of presidential succession, after the vice president and the Speaker of the House.

Previous question — A motion for the previous question, when carried, has the effect of cutting off further debate, preventing the offering of further amendments and forcing a vote on the pending matter. In the House, a motion for the previous question is not permitted in the Committee of the Whole, unless a rule governing debate provides otherwise. The motion for the previous question is not in order in the Senate.

Printed amendment — Some House rules guarantee five minutes of floor debate in support and five minutes in opposition, and no other debate time, on amendments printed in the Congressional Record at least one day prior to the amendment's consideration in the Committee of the Whole.

In the Senate, while amendments may be submitted for printing, they have no parliamentary standing or status. An amendment submitted for printing in the Senate, however, may be called up by any senator.

Private bill — A bill dealing with individual matters, such as claims against the government, immigration or land titles. If two members officially object to consideration of a private bill that is before the chamber, it is recommitted to committee. The backers still have re-

course, however. The measure can be put into an omnibus claims bill — several private bills rolled into one. As with any bill, no part of an omnibus claims bill may be deleted without a vote. When the private bill goes back to the House floor in this form, it can be deleted from the omnibus bill only by majority vote.

Private Calendar — The House calendar for private bills. The Private Calendar must be called on the first Tuesday of each month, and the Speaker may call it on the third Tuesday of each month as well. *(Also see calendar, private bill.)*

Privileged questions — The order in which bills, motions and other legislative measures are considered on the floor of the Senate and House is governed by strict priorities. A motion to table, for instance, is more privileged than a motion to recommit. Thus, if a member moves to recommit a bill to committee for further consideration, another member can supersede the first action by moving to table it, and a vote will occur on the motion to table (or kill) before the motion to recommit. A motion to adjourn is considered "of the highest privilege" and must be considered before virtually any other motion.

Pro forma amendment — *(See strike out the last word.)*

Pro forma session — A meeting of the House and Senate during which no legislative business is conducted. The sessions are held to satisfy a provision of the Constitution that prohibits either chamber from adjourning for more than three days without the permission of the other chamber. When the House or Senate recesses or adjourns for more than three days, both chambers adopt concurrent resolutions providing for the recess or adjournment. Also, the Senate sometimes holds pro-forma sessions during recess periods to prevent the president from making recess appointments.

Public laws — *(See law.)*

Questions of privilege — These are matters affecting members of Congress individually or collectively. Matters affecting the rights, safety, dignity and integrity of proceedings of the House or Senate as a whole are questions of privilege in both chambers.

Questions involving individual members are called questions of "personal privilege." A member rising to ask a question of personal privilege is given precedence over almost all other proceedings. For instance, if a member feels that he or she has been improperly impugned in comments by another member, he or she can immediately demand to be heard on the floor on a question of personal privilege. An annotation in the House rules points out that the privilege rests primarily on the Constitution, which gives members a conditional immunity from arrest and an unconditional freedom to speak in the House.

In 1993, the House changed its rules to allow the Speaker to delay for two legislative days the floor consideration of a resolution raising a question of the privileges of the House unless it is offered by the majority leader or minority leader.

Quorum — The number of members whose presence is necessary for the transaction of business. In the Senate and House, it is a majority of the membership. In the Committee of the Whole House, a quorum is 100. If a point of order is made that a quorum is not present, the only business that is in order is either a motion to adjourn or a motion to direct the sergeant at arms to request the attendance of absentees. In practice, however, both chambers conduct much of their business without a quorum present. *(Also see Committee of the Whole.)*

Quorum call — Procedures used in the House and Senate to establish that a quorum is present. In the House, quorum calls are usually conducted using the electronic voting system, and no roll call is recorded. In the Senate, quorums are usually conducted by calling the roll of senators. The House and Senate conduct annual quorum calls at the beginning of each session of Congress. The Senate also uses quorum calls when no senators are speaking on the floor.

Reading of bills — Traditional parliamentary procedure required bills to be read three times before they were passed. This custom is of little modern significance. Normally a bill is considered to have its first reading when it is introduced and printed, by title, in the Congressional Record. In the House, a bill's second reading comes when floor consideration begins. (The actual reading of a bill is most likely to occur at this point if at all.) The second reading in the Senate is supposed to occur on the legislative day after the measure is introduced, but before it is referred to committee. The third reading (again, usually by title) takes place when floor action has been completed on amendments.

Recess — A recess, as distinguished from adjournment, does not end a legislative day and, therefore, does not interrupt unfinished business. The House usually adjourns from day to day. The Senate often recesses, thus meeting on the same legislative day for several calendar days or even weeks at a time. The rules in each chamber set forth certain matters to be taken up and disposed of at the beginning of each legislative day.

Recognition — The power of recognition of a member is lodged in the Speaker of the House and the presiding officer of the Senate. The presiding officer names the member to speak first when two or more members simultaneously request recognition. The order of recognition is governed by precedents and tradition for many situations. In the Senate, for instance, the majority leader has the right to be recognized first.

Recommit — A motion, made on the floor after a bill has been debated, to return it to the committee that reported it. If agreed to, recommittal usually is considered a death blow to the bill. In the House, the right to offer a motion to recommit is guaranteed to the minority leader or someone he or she designates.

A motion to recommit may include instructions to the committee to report the bill again with specific amendments or by a certain date. Or the instructions may direct that a particular study be made, with no definite deadline for further action.

If the recommittal motion includes instructions to "report the bill back forthwith" and the motion is adopted, floor action on the bill continues and the House votes to approve the revision, usually by voice vote; the committee does not actually reconsider the legislation.

Reconciliation — The 1974 Budget Act created a reconciliation procedure for bringing existing tax and spending laws into conformity with ceilings set in the congressional budget resolution. Under the procedure, the budget resolution sets specific deficit-reduction targets and instructs tax-writing and authorizing committees to propose changes in existing law to meet those targets. If more than one committee is involved, the Budget committees consolidate the recommendations, without change, into an omnibus reconciliation bill, which then must be considered and approved by both chambers of Congress.

Special rules in the Senate limit debate on a reconciliation bill to

20 hours and bar extraneous or non-germane amendments. *(Also see budget resolution, sequester.)*

Reconsider a vote — Until it is disposed of, a motion to reconsider the vote by which an action was taken has the effect of putting the action in abeyance. In the Senate, the motion can be made only by a member who voted on the prevailing side of the original question or by a member who did not vote at all. In the House, it can be made only by a member on the prevailing side.

A common practice in the Senate after close votes on an issue is a motion to reconsider, followed by a motion to table the motion to reconsider. On this motion to table, senators vote as they voted on the original question, which allows the motion to table to prevail, assuming there are no switches. That closes the matter, and further motions to reconsider are not entertained.

In the House, as a routine precaution, a motion to reconsider usually is made every time a measure is passed. Such a motion almost always is tabled immediately, thus shutting off the possibility of future reconsideration except by unanimous consent.

Motions to reconsider must be entered in the Senate within the next two days the Senate is in session after the original vote has been taken. In the House, they must be entered either on the same day or on the next succeeding day the House is in session. Sometimes on a close vote, a member will switch his or her vote to be eligible to offer a motion to reconsider.

Recorded vote — A vote upon which each member's stand is individually made known. In the Senate, this is accomplished through a roll call of the entire membership, to which each senator on the floor must answer "yea," "nay" or "present." Since January 1973, the House has used an electronic voting system for recorded votes, including "yea" and "nay" votes formerly taken by roll calls.

When not required by the Constitution, a recorded vote can be obtained on questions in the House on the demand of one-fifth (44 members) of a quorum or one-fourth (25) of a quorum in the Committee of the Whole. Recorded votes are required in the House for appropriations, budget and tax bills. *(Also see "yeas" and "nays.")*

Report — Both a verb and a noun as a congressional term. A committee that has been examining a bill referred to it by the parent chamber "reports" its findings and recommendations to the chamber when it completes consideration and returns the measure. The process is called "reporting" a bill. In some cases, a bill is reported without a written report.

A "report" is the document setting forth the committee's explanation of its action. Senate and House reports are numbered separately and are designated S Rept or H Rept. When a committee report is not unanimous, the dissenting committee members may file a statement of their views, called minority or dissenting views and referred to as a minority report. Members in disagreement with some provisions of a bill may file additional or supplementary views. Sometimes a bill is reported without a committee recommendation.

Legislative committees occasionally submit adverse reports. However, when a committee is opposed to a bill, it usually does not report the bill at all. Some laws require that committee reports — favorable or adverse — be filed.

Rescission — Cancellation of budget authority that was previously appropriated but has not yet been spent.

Resolution — A "simple" resolution, designated H Res or S Res, deals with matters entirely within the prerogatives of a single chamber. It requires neither passage by the other chamber nor approval by the president, and it does not have the force of law. Most resolutions deal with the rules or procedures of one chamber. They are also used to express the sentiments of a single chamber, such as condolences to the family of a deceased member, or to comment on foreign policy or executive business. A simple resolution is the vehicle for a "rule" from the House Rules Committee. *(Also see concurrent and joint resolutions, rules.)*

Rider — An amendment, usually not germane, that its sponsor hopes to get through more easily by including it in other legislation. A rider becomes law if the bill to which it is attached is enacted. Amendments providing legislative directives in appropriations bills are examples of riders, although technically legislation is banned from appropriations bills.

The House, unlike the Senate, has a strict germaneness rule; thus, riders usually are Senate devices to get legislation enacted quickly or to bypass lengthy House consideration and, possibly, opposition.

Rules — Each chamber has a body of rules and precedents that govern the conduct of business. These rules deal with issues such as duties of officers, the order of business, admission to the floor, parliamentary procedures on handling amendments and voting, and jurisdictions of committees.

The House re-adopts its rules, usually with some changes, at the beginning of each Congress. Senate rules carry over from one Congress to the next.

In the House, a rule may also be a resolution reported by the Rules Committee to govern the handling of a particular bill on the floor. The committee may report a rule, also called a special order, in the form of a simple resolution. If the House adopts the resolution, the temporary rule becomes as valid as any standing rule and lapses only after action has been completed on the measure to which it pertains.

The rule sets the time limit on general debate. It may also waive points of order against provisions of the bill in question such as non-germane language or against certain amendments expected on the floor. It may even forbid all amendments or all amendments except those proposed by the legislative committee that handled the bill. In this instance, it is known as a "closed" rule as opposed to an "open" rule, which puts no limitation on floor amendments, thus leaving the bill completely open to alteration by the adoption of germane amendments. *(Also see point of order.)*

Secretary of the Senate — Chief administrative officer of the Senate, responsible for overseeing the duties of Senate employees, educating Senate pages, administering oaths, overseeing the registration of lobbyists and handling other tasks necessary for the continuing operation of the Senate. *(Also see Clerk of the House.)*

Select or special committee — A committee set up for a special purpose and, usually, for a limited time by resolution of either the House or Senate. Most special committees are investigative and lack legislative authority: Legislation is not referred to them, and they cannot report bills to their parent chambers. Each chamber has a Select Committee on Intelligence.

Senatorial courtesy — A general practice with no written rule — sometimes referred to as "the courtesy of the Senate" — applied to consideration of executive nominations. Generally, it means that nominees from a state are not to be confirmed unless they have been

approved by the senators of the president's party of that state, with other senators following their colleagues' lead in the attitude they take toward consideration of such nominations. *(Also see nominations.)*

Sequester — Automatic, across-the-board spending cuts. Under the 1985 Gramm-Rudman-Hollings anti-deficit law, modified in 1987, a year-end sequester was triggered if the deficit exceeded a pre-set maximum. The Budget Enforcement Act of 1990, updated in 1993 and 1997, effectively replaced that procedure through fiscal 2002.

Sine die — *(See adjournment sine die.)*

Speaker — The presiding officer of the House of Representatives, selected by the majority party's caucus and formally elected by the whole House. While both parties nominate candidates, choice by the majority party is tantamount to election. The Speaker is second in the line of presidential succession, after the vice president.

Special session — A session of Congress after it has adjourned sine die, completing its regular session. Special sessions are convened by the president.

Spending authority — The 1974 Budget Act defines spending authority as borrowing authority, contract authority and entitlement authority for which budget authority is not provided in advance by appropriations acts.

Sponsor — *(See bills introduced.)*

Standing committees — Committees that are permanently established by House and Senate rules. The standing committees of the House were reorganized in 1974, with some changes in jurisdictions and titles made when Republicans took control of the House in 1995. House Democrats changed the names of five committees in 2007. The last major realignment of Senate committees was in 1977. The standing committees are legislative committees: Legislation may be referred to them, and they may report bills and resolutions to their parent chambers.

Standing vote — A non-recorded vote used in both the House and Senate. (A standing vote is also called a division vote.) Members in favor of a proposal stand and are counted by the presiding officer. Then members opposed stand and are counted. There is no record of how individual members voted.

Statutes at large — A chronological arrangement of the laws enacted in each session of Congress. Though indexed, the laws are not arranged by subject matter, and there is no indication of how they changed previously enacted laws. *(Also see law, U.S. Code.)*

Strike from the Record — A member of the House who is offended by remarks made on the House floor may move that the offending words be "taken down" for the Speaker's cognizance and then expunged from the debate as published in the Congressional Record.

Strike out the last word — A motion whereby a House member is entitled to speak for five minutes on an amendment then being debated by the chamber. A member gains recognition from the chair by moving to "strike out the last word" of the amendment or section of the bill under consideration. The motion is pro forma, requires no vote and does not change the amendment being debated. *(Also see five-minute rule.)*

Substitute — A motion, amendment or entire bill introduced in place of the pending legislative business. Passage of the substitute kills the original measure by supplanting it. The substitute may also be amended. *(Also see amendment in the nature of a substitute.)*

Supplemental appropriations bill — Legislation appropriating funds after the regular annual appropriations bill for a federal department or agency has been enacted. In the past, supplemental appropriations bills often arrived about halfway through the fiscal year to pay for urgent needs, such as relief from natural disasters, that Congress and the president did not anticipate (or may not have wanted to fund). President Bush used emergency supplementals to pay for the wars in Iraq and Afghanistan.

Suspend the rules — A time-saving procedure for passing bills in the House. The wording of the motion, which may be made by any member recognized by the Speaker, is "I move to suspend the rules and pass the bill." A favorable vote by two-thirds of those present is required for passage. Debate is limited to 40 minutes, and no amendments from the floor are permitted. If a two-thirds favorable vote is not attained, the bill may be considered later under regular procedures. The suspension procedure is in order every Monday, Tuesday and Wednesday, and it is intended to be reserved for non-controversial bills. It also may be used to concur in Senate amendments and conference reports.

Table a bill — Motions to table, or to "lay on the table," are used to block or kill amendments or other parliamentary questions. When approved, a tabling motion is considered the final disposition of that issue. One of the most widely used parliamentary procedures, the motion to table is not debatable, and adoption requires a simple majority vote.

In the Senate, however, different language sometimes is used. The motion may be worded to let a bill "lie on the table," perhaps for subsequent "picking up." This motion is more flexible, keeping the bill pending for later action, if desired. Tabling motions on amendments are effective debate-ending devices in the Senate.

Treaties — Executive proposals — in the form of resolutions of ratification — that must be submitted to the Senate for approval by two-thirds of the senators present. Treaties are normally sent to the Foreign Relations Committee for scrutiny before the Senate takes action. Foreign Relations has jurisdiction over all treaties, regardless of the subject matter. Treaties are read three times and debated on the floor in much the same manner as legislative proposals. After approval by the Senate, treaties are formally ratified by the president.

Trust funds — Funds collected and used by the federal government for carrying out specific purposes and programs according to terms of a trust agreement or statute such as the Social Security and unemployment compensation trust funds. Such funds are administered by the government in a fiduciary capacity and are not available for the general purposes of the government.

Unanimous consent — A procedure used to expedite floor action. Proceedings of the House or Senate and action on legislation often take place upon the unanimous consent of the chamber, whether or not a rule of the chamber is being violated. It is frequently used in a routine fashion, such as by a senator requesting the unanimous consent of the Senate to have specified members of his or her staff present on the floor during debate on a specific amendment. A single member's objection blocks a unanimous consent request.

Unanimous consent agreement — A device used in the Senate to expedite legislation. Much of the Senate's legislative business, dealing with both minor and controversial issues, is conducted through unanimous consent or unanimous consent agreements. On major legislation, such agreements usually are printed and transmitted to all senators in advance of floor debate. Once agreed to, they are binding on all members unless the Senate, by unanimous consent, agrees to modify them. An agreement may list the order in which various bills are to be considered; specify the length of time for debate on bills and contested amendments and when they are to be voted upon; and, frequently, require that all amendments introduced be germane to the bill under consideration.

In this regard, unanimous consent agreements are similar to the "rules" issued by the House Rules Committee for bills pending in the House. The House rarely sets conditions for floor debate under unanimous consent.

Union Calendar — Bills that directly or indirectly appropriate money or raise revenue are placed on this House calendar according to the date they are reported from committee. *(Also see calendar.)*

U.S. Code — A consolidation and codification of the general and permanent laws of the United States arranged by subject under 50 titles, the first six dealing with general or political subjects, and the other 44 alphabetically arranged from agriculture to war. The U.S. Code is updated annually, and a new set of bound volumes is published every six years. *(Also see law, statutes at large.)*

Veto — Disapproval by the president of a bill or joint resolution (other than one proposing an amendment to the Constitution). When Congress is in session, the president must veto a bill within 10 days, excluding Sundays, after he has received it; otherwise, it becomes law without his signature. When the president vetoes a bill, he returns it to the chamber of origin along with a message stating his objections. *(Also see pocket veto, override a veto.)*

Voice vote — In either the House or Senate, members answer "aye" or "no" in chorus, and the presiding officer decides the result. The term is also used loosely to indicate action by unanimous consent or without objection. *(Also see "yeas" and "nays.")*

Whip — In effect, the assistant majority or minority leader, in either the House or Senate. His or her job is to help marshal votes in support of party strategy and legislation.

Without objection — Used in lieu of a vote on non-controversial motions, amendments or bills that may be passed in either chamber if no member voices an objection.

"Yeas" and "nays" — The Constitution requires that "yea" and "nay" votes be taken and recorded when requested by one-fifth of the members present. In the House, the Speaker determines whether one-fifth of the members present requested a vote. In the Senate, practice requires only 11 members. The Constitution requires the yeas and nays on a veto-override attempt. *(Also see recorded vote.)*

Yielding — When a member has been recognized to speak, no other member may speak unless he or she obtains permission from the member recognized. This permission is called yielding and usually is requested in the form, "Will the gentleman (or gentlelady) yield to me?" While this activity occasionally is seen in the Senate, the Senate has no rule or practice to parcel out time.

In the House, the floor manager of a bill usually apportions debate time by yielding specific amounts of time to members who have requested it. ■

Members of the 110th Congress, 2nd Session . . .

(As of Jan. 3, 2009, when the Senate adjourned sine die.)

REPRESENTATIVES
D 236, R 198
Vacancies 1

— A —

Abercrombie, Neil, D-Hawaii (1)
Ackerman, Gary L., D-N.Y. (5)
Aderholt, Robert B., R-Ala. (4)
Akin, Todd, R-Mo. (2)
Alexander, Rodney, R-La. (5)
Allen, Tom, D-Maine (1)
Altmire, Jason, D-Pa. (4)
Andrews, Robert E., D-N.J. (1)
Arcuri, Michael, D-N.Y. (24)

— B —

Baca, Joe, D-Calif. (43)
Bachmann, Michele, R-Minn. (6)
Bachus, Spencer, R-Ala. (6)
Baird, Brian, D-Wash. (3)
Baldwin, Tammy, D-Wis. (2)
Barrett, J. Gresham, R-S.C. (3)
Barrow, John, D-Ga. (12)
Bartlett, Roscoe G., R-Md. (6)
Barton, Joe L., R-Texas (6)
Bean, Melissa, D-Ill. (8)
Becerra, Xavier, D-Calif. (31)
Berkley, Shelley, D-Nev. (1)
Berman, Howard L., D-Calif. (28)
Berry, Marion, D-Ark. (1)
Biggert, Judy, R-Ill. (13)
Bilbray, Brian P., R-Calif. (50)
Bilirakis, Gus, R-Fla. (9)
Bishop, Rob, R-Utah (1)
Bishop, Sanford D. Jr., D-Ga. (2)
Bishop, Timothy H., D-N.Y. (1)
Blackburn, Marsha, R-Tenn. (7)
Blumenauer, Earl, D-Ore. (3)
Blunt, Roy, R-Mo. (7)
Boehner, John A., R-Ohio (8)
Bonner, Jo, R-Ala. (1)
Bono Mack, Mary, R-Calif. (45)
Boozman, John, R-Ark. (3)
Boren, Dan, D-Okla. (2)
Boswell, Leonard L., D-Iowa (3)
Boucher, Rick, D-Va. (9)
Boustany, Charles Jr., R-La. (7)
Boyd, Allen, D-Fla. (2)
Boyda, Nancy, D-Kan. (2)
Brady, Kevin, R-Texas (8)
Brady, Robert A., D-Pa. (1)
Braley, Bruce, D-Iowa (1)
Broun, Paul, R-Ga. (10)
Brown, Corrine, D-Fla. (3)
Brown, Henry E. Jr., R-S.C. (1)
Brown-Waite, Ginny, R-Fla. (5)
Buchanan, Vern, R-Fla. (13)
Burgess, Michael C., R-Texas (26)
Burton, Dan, R-Ind. (5)
Butterfield, G.K., D-N.C. (1)
Buyer, Steve, R-Ind. (4)

— C —

Calvert, Ken, R-Calif. (44)
Camp, Dave, R-Mich. (4)
Campbell, John, R-Calif. (48)
Cannon, Chris, R-Utah (3)
Cantor, Eric, R-Va. (7)
Capito, Shelley Moore, R-W.Va. (2)
Capps, Lois, D-Calif. (23)
Capuano, Michael E., D-Mass. (8)
Cardoza, Dennis, D-Calif. (18)
Carnahan, Russ, D-Mo. (3)
Carney, Christopher, D-Pa. (10)
Carter, John, R-Texas (31)
Carson, André, D-Ind. (7)
Castle, Michael N., R-Del. (AL)
Castor, Kathy, D-Fla. (11)
Cazayoux, Don, D-La. (6)
Chabot, Steve, R-Ohio
Chandler, Ben, D-Ky. (6)
Clarke, Yvette D., D-N.Y. (11)
Clay, William Lacy, D-Mo. (1)

Childers, Travis W., D-Miss. (1)
Cleaver, Emanuel II, D-Mo. (5)
Clyburn, James E., D-S.C. (6)
Coble, Howard, R-N.C. (6)
Cohen, Steve, D-Tenn. (9)
Cole, Tom, R-Okla. (4)
Conaway, K. Michael, R-Texas (11)
Conyers, John Jr., D-Mich. (14)
Cooper, Jim, D-Tenn. (5)
Costa, Jim, D-Calif. (20)
Costello, Jerry F., D-Ill. (12)
Courtney, Joe, D-Conn. (2)
Cramer, Robert E. "Bud," D-Ala. (5)
Crenshaw, Ander, R-Fla. (4)
Crowley, Joseph, D-N.Y. (7)
Cubin, Barbara, R-Wyo. (AL)
Cuellar, Henry, D-Texas (28)
Culberson, John, R-Texas (7)
Cummings, Elijah E., D-Md. (7)

— D —

Davis, Artur, D-Ala. (7)
Davis, Danny K., D-Ill. (7)
Davis, David, R-Tenn. (1)
Davis, Geoff, R-Ky. (4)
Davis, Lincoln, D-Tenn. (4)
Davis, Susan A., D-Calif. (53)
Deal, Nathan, R-Ga. (9)
DeFazio, Peter A., D-Ore. (4)
DeGette, Diana, D-Colo. (1)
Delahunt, Bill, D-Mass. (10)
DeLauro, Rosa, D-Conn. (3)
Dent, Charlie, R-Pa. (15)
Diaz-Balart, Lincoln, R-Fla. (21)
Diaz-Balart, Mario, R-Fla. (25)
Dicks, Norm, D-Wash. (6)
Dingell, John D., D-Mich. (15)
Doggett, Lloyd, D-Texas (25)
Donnelly, Joe, D-Ind. (2)
Doolittle, John T., R-Calif. (4)
Doyle, Mike, D-Pa. (14)
Drake, Thelma, R-Va. (2)
Dreier, David, R-Calif. (26)
Duncan, John J. "Jimmy" Jr., R-Tenn. (2)

— E —

Edwards, Chet, D-Texas (17)
Edwards, Donna, D-Md. (4)
Ehlers, Vernon J., R-Mich. (3)
Ellison, Keith, D-Minn. (5)
Ellsworth, Brad, D-Ind. (8)
Emanuel, Rahm, D-Ill. (5)
Emerson, Jo Ann, R-Mo. (8)
Engel, Eliot L., D-N.Y. (17)
English, Phil, R-Pa. (3)
Eshoo, Anna G., D-Calif. (14)
Etheridge, Bob, D-N.C. (2)
Everett, Terry, R-Ala. (2)

— F —

Fallin, Mary, R-Okla. (5)
Farr, Sam, D-Calif. (17)
Fattah, Chaka, D-Pa. (2)
Feeney, Tom, R-Fla. (24)
Ferguson, Mike, R-N.J. (7)
Filner, Bob, D-Calif. (51)
Flake, Jeff, R-Ariz. (6)
Forbes, J. Randy, R-Va. (4)
Fortenberry, Jeff, R-Neb. (1)
Fossella, Vito J., R-N.Y. (13)
Foster, Bill, D-Ill. (14)
Foxx, Virginia, R-N.C. (5)
Frank, Barney, D-Mass. (4)
Franks, Trent, R-Ariz. (2)
Frelinghuysen, Rodney, R-N.J. (11)
Fudge, Marcia L., D-Ohio (11)

— G —

Gallegly, Elton, R-Calif. (24)
Garrett, Scott, R-N.J. (5)
Gerlach, Jim, R-Pa. (6)
Giffords, Gabrielle, D-Ariz. (8)
Gilchrest, Wayne T., R-Md. (1)
Gillibrand, Kirsten, D-N.Y. (20)
Gingrey, Phil, R-Ga. (11)
Gohmert, Louie, R-Texas (1)
Gonzalez, Charlie, D-Texas (20)

Goode, Virgil H. Jr., R-Va. (5)
Goodlatte, Robert W., R-Va. (6)
Gordon, Bart, D-Tenn. (6)
Granger, Kay, R-Texas (12)
Graves, Sam, R-Mo. (6)
Green, Al, D-Texas (9)
Green, Gene, D-Texas (29)
Grijalva, Raúl M., D-Ariz. (7)
Gutierrez, Luis V., D-Ill. (4)

— H —

Hall, John, D-N.Y. (19)
Hall, Ralph M., R-Texas (4)
Hare, Phil, D-Ill. (17)
Harman, Jane, D-Calif. (36)
Hastings, Alcee L., D-Fla. (23)
Hastings, Doc, R-Wash. (4)
Hayes, Robin, R-N.C. (8)
Heller, Dean, R-Nev. (2)
Hensarling, Jeb, R-Texas (5)
Herger, Wally, R-Calif. (2)
Herseth Sandlin, Stephanie, D-S.D. (AL)
Higgins, Brian, D-N.Y. (27)
Hill, Baron P., D-Ind. (9)
Hinchey, Maurice D., D-N.Y. (22)
Hinojosa, Rubén, D-Texas (15)
Hirono, Mazie K., D-Hawaii (2)
Hobson, David L., R-Ohio (7)
Hodes, Paul W., D-N.H. (2)
Hoekstra, Peter, R-Mich. (2)
Holden, Tim, D-Pa. (17)
Holt, Rush D., D-N.J. (12)
Honda, Michael M., D-Calif. (15)
Hooley, Darlene, D-Ore. (5)
Hoyer, Steny H., D-Md. (5)
Hulshof, Kenny, R-Mo. (9)
Hunter, Duncan, R-Calif. (52)

— I, J —

Inglis, Bob, R-S.C. (4)
Inslee, Jay, D-Wash. (1)
Israel, Steve, D-N.Y. (2)
Issa, Darrell, R-Calif. (49)
Jackson, Jesse L. Jr., D-Ill. (2)
Jackson Lee, Sheila, D-Texas (18)
Jefferson, William J., D-La. (2)
Johnson, Eddie Bernice, D-Texas (30)
Johnson, Hank, D-Ga. (4)
Johnson, Sam, R-Texas (3)
Johnson, Timothy V., R-Ill. (15)
Jones, Walter B., R-N.C. (3)
Jordan, Jim, R-Ohio (4)

— K —

Kagen, Steve, D-Wis. (8)
Kanjorski, Paul E., D-Pa. (11)
Kaptur, Marcy, D-Ohio (9)
Keller, Ric, R-Fla. (8)
Kennedy, Patrick J., D-R.I. (1)
Kildee, Dale E., D-Mich. (5)
Kilpatrick, Carolyn Cheeks, D-Mich. (13)
Kind, Ron, D-Wis. (3)
King, Peter T., R-N.Y. (3)
King, Steve, R-Iowa (5)
Kingston, Jack, R-Ga. (1)
Kirk, Mark Steven, R-Ill. (10)
Klein, Ron, D-Fla. (22)
Kline, John, R-Minn. (2)
Knollenberg, Joe, R-Mich. (9)
Kucinich, Dennis J., D-Ohio (10)
Kuhl, John R. "Randy" Jr., R-N.Y. (29)

— L —

LaHood, Ray, R-Ill. (18)
Lamborn, Doug, R-Colo. (5)
Lampson, Nick, D-Texas (22)
Langevin, Jim, D-R.I. (2)
Larsen, Rick, D-Wash. (2)
Larson, John B., D-Conn. (1)
Latham, Tom, R-Iowa (4)
LaTourette, Steven C., R-Ohio (14)
Latta, Bob, R-Ohio (5)
Lee, Barbara, D-Calif. (9)
Levin, Sander M., D-Mich. (12)
Lewis, Jerry, R-Calif. (41)
Lewis, John, D-Ga. (5)
Lewis, Ron, R-Ky. (2)

Linder, John, R-Ga. (7)
Lipinski, Daniel, D-Ill. (3)
LoBiondo, Frank A., R-N.J. (2)
Loebsack, Dave, D-Iowa (2)
Lofgren, Zoe, D-Calif. (16)
Lowey, Nita M., D-N.Y. (18)
Lucas, Frank D., R-Okla. (3)
Lungren, Dan, R-Calif. (3)
Lynch, Stephen F., D-Mass. (9)

— M —

Mack, Connie, R-Fla. (14)
Mahoney, Tim, D-Fla. (16)
Maloney, Carolyn B., D-N.Y. (14)
Manzullo, Donald, R-Ill. (16)
Marchant, Kenny, R-Texas (24)
Markey, Edward J., D-Mass. (7)
Marshall, Jim, D-Ga. (8)
Matheson, Jim, D-Utah (2)
Matsui, Doris, D-Calif. (5)
McCarthy, Carolyn, D-N.Y. (4)
McCarthy, Kevin, R-Calif. (22)
McCaul, Michael, R-Texas (10)
McCollum, Betty, D-Minn. (4)
McCotter, Thaddeus, R-Mich. (11)
McCrery, Jim, R-La. (4)
McDermott, Jim, D-Wash. (7)
McGovern, Jim, D-Mass. (3)
McHenry, Patrick T., R-N.C. (10)
McHugh, John M., R-N.Y. (23)
McIntyre, Mike, D-N.C. (7)
McKeon, Howard P. "Buck," R-Calif. (25)
McMorris Rodgers, Cathy, R-Wash. (5)
McNerney, Jerry, D-Calif. (11)
McNulty, Michael R., D-N.Y. (21)
Meek, Kendrick B., D-Fla. (17)
Meeks, Gregory W., D-N.Y. (6)
Melancon, Charlie, D-La. (3)
Mica, John L., R-Fla. (7)
Michaud, Michael H., D-Maine (2)
Miller, Brad, D-N.C. (13)
Miller, Candice S., R-Mich. (10)
Miller, Gary G., R-Calif. (42)
Miller, George, D-Calif. (7)
Miller, Jeff, R-Fla. (1)
Mitchell, Harry E., D-Ariz. (5)
Mollohan, Alan B., D-W.Va. (1)
Moore, Dennis, D-Kan. (3)
Moore, Gwen, D-Wis. (4)
Moran, James P., D-Va. (8)
Moran, Jerry, R-Kan. (1)
Murphy, Christopher S., D-Conn. (5)
Murphy, Patrick J., D-Pa. (8)
Murphy, Tim, R-Pa. (18)
Murtha, John P., D-Pa. (12)
Musgrave, Marilyn, R-Colo. (4)
Myrick, Sue, R-N.C. (9)

— N, O —

Nadler, Jerrold, D-N.Y. (8)
Napolitano, Grace F., D-Calif. (38)
Neal, Richard E., D-Mass. (2)
Neugebauer, Randy, R-Texas (19)
Nunes, Devin, R-Calif. (21)
Oberstar, James L., D-Minn. (8)
Obey, David R., D-Wis. (7)
Olver, John W., D-Mass. (1)
Ortiz, Solomon P., D-Texas (27)

— P —

Pallone, Frank Jr., D-N.J. (6)
Pascrell, Bill Jr., D-N.J. (8)
Pastor, Ed, D-Ariz. (4)
Paul, Ron, R-Texas (14)
Payne, Donald M., D-N.J. (10)
Pearce, Steve, R-N.M. (2)
Pelosi, Nancy, D-Calif. (8)
Pence, Mike, R-Ind. (6)
Perlmutter, Ed, D-Colo. (7)
Peterson, Collin C., D-Minn. (7)
Peterson, John E., R-Pa. (5)
Petri, Tom, R-Wis. (6)
Pickering, Charles W. "Chip" Jr., R-Miss. (3)
Pitts, Joe, R-Pa. (16)
Platts, Todd R., R-Pa. (19)
Poe, Ted, R-Texas (2)
Pomeroy, Earl, D-N.D. (AL)

. . . Governors, Supreme Court, Executive Branch

Porter, Jon, R-Nev. (3)
Price, David E., D-N.C. (4)
Price, Tom, R-Ga. (6)
Pryce, Deborah, R-Ohio (15)
Putnam, Adam H., R-Fla. (12)

— Q, R —

Radanovich, George, R-Calif. (19)
Rahall, Nick J. II, D-W.Va. (3)
Ramstad, Jim, R-Minn. (3)
Rangel, Charles B., D-N.Y. (15)
Regula, Ralph, R-Ohio (16)
Rehberg, Denny, R-Mont. (AL)
Reichert, Dave, R-Wash. (8)
Renzi, Rick, R-Ariz. (1)
Reyes, Silvestre, D-Texas (16)
Reynolds, Thomas M., R-N.Y. (26)
Richardson, Laura, D-Calif. (37)
Rodriguez, Ciro D., D-Texas (23)
Rogers, Harold, R-Ky. (5)
Rogers, Mike D., R-Ala. (3)
Rogers, Mike, R-Mich. (8)
Rohrabacher, Dana, R-Calif. (46)
Ros-Lehtinen, Ileana, R-Fla. (18)
Roskam, Peter, R-Ill. (6)
Ross, Mike, D-Ark. (4)
Rothman, Steven R., D-N.J. (9)
Roybal-Allard, Lucille, D-Calif. (34)
Royce, Ed, R-Calif. (40)
Ruppersberger, C.A. Dutch, D-Md. (2)
Rush, Bobby L., D-Ill. (1)
Ryan, Paul D., R-Wis. (1)
Ryan, Tim, D-Ohio (17)

— S —

Salazar, John, D-Colo. (3)
Sali, Bill, R-Idaho (1)
Sánchez, Linda T., D-Calif. (39)
Sanchez, Loretta, D-Calif. (47)
Sarbanes, John, D-Md. (3)
Saxton, H. James, R-N.J. (3)
Scalise, Steve, R-La. (1)
Schakowsky, Jan, D-Ill. (9)
Schiff, Adam B., D-Calif. (29)
Schmidt, Jean, R-Ohio (2)
Schwartz, Allyson Y., D-Pa. (13)
Scott, David, D-Ga. (13)
Scott, Robert C., D-Va. (3)
Sensenbrenner, F. James Jr., R-Wis. (5)
Serrano, José E., D-N.Y. (16)
Sessions, Pete, R-Texas (32)
Sestak, Joe, D-Pa. (7)
Shadegg, John, R-Ariz. (3)
Shays, Christopher, R-Conn. (4)
Shea-Porter, Carol, D-N.H. (1)
Sherman, Brad, D-Calif. (27)
Shimkus, John, R-Ill. (19)
Shuler, Heath, D-N.C. (11)
Shuster, Bill, R-Pa. (9)
Simpson, Mike, R-Idaho (2)
Sires, Albio, D-N.J. (13)
Skelton, Ike, D-Mo. (4)
Slaughter, Louise M., D-N.Y. (28)
Smith, Adam, D-Wash. (9)
Smith, Adrian, R-Neb. (3)
Smith, Christopher H., R-N.J. (4)
Smith, Lamar, R-Texas (21)
Snyder, Vic, D-Ark. (2)
Solis, Hilda L., D-Calif. (32)
Souder, Mark, R-Ind. (3)
Space, Zack, D-Ohio (18)
Speier, Jackie, D-Calif. (12)
Spratt, John M. Jr., D-S.C. (5)
Stark, Pete, D-Calif. (13)
Stearns, Cliff, R-Fla. (6)
Stupak, Bart, D-Mich. (1)
Sullivan, John, R-Okla. (1)
Sutton, Betty, D-Ohio (13)

— T —

Tancredo, Tom, R-Colo. (6)
Tanner, John, D-Tenn. (8)
Tauscher, Ellen O., D-Calif. (10)
Taylor, Gene, D-Miss. (4)
Terry, Lee, R-Neb. (2)
Thompson, Bennie, D-Miss. (2)
Thompson, Mike, D-Calif. (1)

Thornberry, William M. "Mac," R-Texas (13)
Tiahrt, Todd, R-Kan. (4)
Tiberi, Pat, R-Ohio (12)
Tierney, John F., D-Mass. (6)
Towns, Edolphus, D-N.Y. (10)
Tsongas, Niki, D-Mass. (5)
Turner, Michael R., R-Ohio (3)

— U, V —

Udall, Mark, D-Colo. (2)
Udall, Tom, D-N.M. (3)
Upton, Fred, R-Mich. (6)
Van Hollen, Chris, D-Md. (8)
Velázquez, Nydia M., D-N.Y. (12)
Visclosky, Peter J., D-Ind. (1)

— W —

Walberg, Tim, R-Mich. (7)
Walden, Greg, R-Ore. (2)
Walsh, James T., R-N.Y. (25)
Walz, Tim, D-Minn. (1)
Wamp, Zach, R-Tenn. (3)
Wasserman Schultz, Debbie, D-Fla. (20)
Waters, Maxine, D-Calif. (35)
Watson, Diane, D-Calif. (33)
Watt, Melvin, D-N.C. (12)
Waxman, Henry A., D-Calif. (30)
Weiner, Anthony, D-N.Y. (9)
Welch, Peter, D-Vt. (AL)
Weldon, Dave, R-Fla. (15)
Weller, Jerry, R-Ill. (11)
Westmoreland, Lynn, R-Ga. (3)
Wexler, Robert, D-Fla. (19)
Whitfield, Edward, R-Ky. (1)
Wilson, Charlie, D-Ohio (6)
Wilson, Heather A., R-N.M. (1)
Wilson, Joe, R-S.C. (2)
Wittman, Rob, R-Va. (1)
Wolf, Frank R., R-Va. (10)
Woolsey, Lynn, D-Calif. (6)
Wu, David, D-Ore. (1)

— X, Y, Z —

Yarmuth, John, D-Ky. (3)
Young, C.W. Bill, R-Fla. (10)
Young, Don, R-Alaska (AL)

DELEGATES

Bordallo, Madeleine Z., D-Guam
Christensen, Donna M.C., D-Virgin Is.
Faleomavaega, Eni F.H., D-Am. Samoa
Fortuño, Luis, R-P.R.
Norton, Eleanor Holmes, D-D.C.

SENATORS
D 48, R 49, I 2
Vacancies 1

Akaka, Daniel K., D-Hawaii
Alexander, Lamar, R-Tenn.
Allard, Wayne, R-Colo.
Barrasso, John, R-Wyo.
Baucus, Max, D-Mont.
Bayh, Evan, D-Ind.
Bennett, Robert F., R-Utah
Biden, Joseph R. Jr., D-Del.
Bingaman, Jeff, D-N.M.
Bond, Christopher S., R-Mo.
Boxer, Barbara, D-Calif.
Brown, Sherrod, D-Ohio
Brownback, Sam, R-Kan.
Bunning, Jim, R-Ky.
Burr, Richard M., R-N.C.
Byrd, Robert C., D-W.Va.
Cantwell, Maria, D-Wash.
Cardin, Benjamin L., D-Md.
Carper, Thomas R., D-Del.
Casey, Bob, D-Pa.
Chambliss, Saxby, R-Ga.
Clinton, Hillary Rodham, D-N.Y.
Coburn, Tom, R-Okla.
Cochran, Thad, R-Miss.
Coleman, Norm, R-Minn.
Collins, Susan, R-Maine
Conrad, Kent, D-N.D.
Corker, Bob, R-Tenn.

Cornyn, John, R-Texas
Craig, Larry E., R-Idaho
Crapo, Michael D., R-Idaho
DeMint, Jim, R-S.C.
Dodd, Christopher J., D-Conn.
Dole, Elizabeth, R-N.C.
Domenici, Pete V., R-N.M.
Dorgan, Byron L., D-N.D.
Durbin, Richard J., D-Ill.
Ensign, John, R-Nev.
Enzi, Michael B., R-Wyo.
Feingold, Russ, D-Wis.
Feinstein, Dianne, D-Calif.
Graham, Lindsey, R-S.C.
Grassley, Charles E., R-Iowa
Gregg, Judd, R-N.H.
Hagel, Chuck, R-Neb.
Harkin, Tom, D-Iowa
Hatch, Orrin G., R-Utah
Hutchison, Kay Bailey, R-Texas
Inhofe, James M., R-Okla.
Inouye, Daniel K., D-Hawaii
Isakson, Johnny, R-Ga.
Johnson, Tim, D-S.D.
Kennedy, Edward M., D-Mass.
Kerry, John, D-Mass.
Klobuchar, Amy, D-Minn.
Kohl, Herb, D-Wis.
Kyl, Jon, R-Ariz.
Landrieu, Mary L., D-La.
Lautenberg, Frank R., D-N.J.
Leahy, Patrick J., D-Vt.
Levin, Carl, D-Mich.
Lieberman, Joseph I., I-Conn.
Lincoln, Blanche, D-Ark.
Lugar, Richard G., R-Ind.
Martinez, Mel, R-Fla.
McCain, John, R-Ariz.
McCaskill, Claire, D-Mo.
McConnell, Mitch, R-Ky.
Menendez, Robert, D-N.J.
Mikulski, Barbara A., D-Md.
Murkowski, Lisa, R-Alaska
Murray, Patty, D-Wash.
Nelson, Ben, D-Neb.
Nelson, Bill, D-Fla.
Pryor, Mark, D-Ark.
Reed, Jack, D-R.I.
Reid, Harry, D-Nev.
Roberts, Pat, R-Kan.
Rockefeller, John D. IV, D-W.Va.
Salazar, Ken, D-Colo.
Sanders, Bernard, I-Vt.
Schumer, Charles E., D-N.Y.
Sessions, Jeff, R-Ala.
Shelby, Richard C., R-Ala.
Smith, Gordon H., R-Ore.
Snowe, Olympia J., R-Maine
Specter, Arlen, R-Pa.
Stabenow, Debbie, D-Mich.
Stevens, Ted, R-Alaska
Sununu, John E., R-N.H.
Tester, Jon, D-Mont.
Thune, John, R-S.D.
Vitter, David, R-La.
Voinovich, George V., R-Ohio
Warner, John W., R-Va.
Webb, Jim, D-Va.
Whitehouse, Sheldon, D-R.I.
Wicker, Roger, R-Miss.
Wyden, Ron, D-Ore.

GOVERNORS
D 28, R 22

Ala. — Bob Riley, R
Alaska — Sarah Palin, R
Ariz. — Janet Napolitano, D
Ark. — Mike Beebe, D
Calif. — Arnold Schwarzenegger, R
Colo. — Bill Ritter Jr., D
Conn. — M. Jodi Rell, R
Del. — Ruth Ann Minner, D
Fla. — Charlie Crist, R
Ga. — Sonny Perdue, R
Hawaii — Linda Lingle, R
Idaho — C. L. "Butch" Otter, R
Ill. — Rod R. Blagojevich, D
Ind. — Mitch Daniels, R

Iowa — Chet Culver, D
Kan. — Kathleen Sebelius, D
Ky. — Steven L. Beshear, D
La. — Bobby Jindal, R
Maine — John Baldacci, D
Md. — Martin O'Malley, D
Mass. — Deval Patrick, D
Mich. — Jennifer M. Granholm, D
Minn. — Tim Pawlenty, R
Miss. — Haley Barbour, R
Mo. — Matt Blunt, R
Mont. — Brian Schweitzer, D
Neb. — Dave Heineman, R
Nev. — Jim Gibbons, R
N.H. — John Lynch, D
N.J. — Jon Corzine, D
N.M. — Bill Richardson, D
N.Y. — David A. Paterson, D
N.C. — Michael F. Easley, D
N.D. — John Hoeven, R
Ohio — Ted Strickland, D
Okla. — Brad Henry, D
Ore. — Theodore R. Kulongoski, D
Pa. — Edward G. Rendell, D
R.I. — Donald L. Carcieri, R
S.C. — Mark Sanford, R
S.D. — Michael Rounds, R
Tenn. — Phil Bredesen, D
Texas — Rick Perry, R
Utah — Jon Huntsman Jr., R
Vt. — Jim Douglas, R
Va. — Tim Kaine, D
Wash. — Christine Gregoire, D
W.Va. — Joe Manchin III, D
Wis. — James E. Doyle, D
Wyo. — Dave Freudenthal, D

SUPREME COURT

Roberts, John G. Jr. — Md., Chief Justice
Alito, Samuel A. Jr. — N.J.
Breyer, Stephen G. — Mass.
Ginsburg, Ruth Bader — N.Y.
Kennedy, Anthony M. — Calif.
Scalia, Antonin — Va.
Souter, David H. — N.H.
Stevens, John Paul — Ill.
Thomas, Clarence — Ga.

EXECUTIVE BRANCH

Bush, George W. — President
Cheney, Dick — Vice President

CABINET

Bodman, Samuel W. — Energy
Chao, Elaine L. — Labor
Chertoff, Michael — Homeland Security
Gates, Robert M. — Defense
Gutierrez, Carlos — Commerce
Kempthorne, Dirk — Interior
Leavitt, Michael O. — Health and Human Services
Mukasey, Michael B. — Attorney General
Paulson, Henry M. Jr. — Treasury
Peake, James B. — Veterans Affairs
Peters, Mary E. — Transportation
Preston, Steven C. — Housing & Urban Development
Rice, Condoleezza — State
Schafer, Ed — Agriculture
Spellings, Margaret — Education

OTHER EXECUTIVE BRANCH OFFICERS

Bolten, Joshua B. — Chief of Staff
Hadley, Stephen J. — Assistant to the President for National Security Affairs
Hennessey, Keith — Director, National Economic Council
Johnson, Stephen L. — EPA Administrator
McConnell, Michael — Director of National Intelligence
Nussle, Jim — OMB Director
Schwab, Susan C. — U.S. Trade Representative

Appendix B

VOTE STUDIES

CQ Vote Study Guide

Congressional Quarterly has conducted studies analyzing the voting behavior of members of Congress since 1945. The three principal vote studies currently produced by CQ — presidential support, party unity and voting participation — have been conducted in a consistent manner since 1953. This is how the studies are carried out:

Selecting votes: CQ bases its vote studies on all floor votes on which members were asked to vote "yea" or "nay." In 2008, there were 688 such roll call votes in the House and 215 in the Senate. The House total excludes quorum calls (there were two in 2008) because they require only that members vote "present."

The House total does include votes on procedural matters, including votes to approve the Journal (13 in 2008). The Senate total includes votes to instruct the sergeant at arms to request members' presence in the chamber (three in 2008).

The presidential support and party-unity studies are based on votes selected from the total according to the criteria described on pp. B-7 and B-16.

Individual scores: Members' scores in the accompanying charts are based only on the votes each member actually cast. This makes individual support and opposition scores add up to 100 percent. The same method is used to identify the leading scorers on pp. B-5 and B-14.

Overall scores: For consistency with previous years, calculations of average scores by chamber, party and region are based on all eligible yea or nay votes, whether or not all members participated. As a result, a member's failure to vote reduces the average support and opposition scores. Therefore, chamber, party and regional averages are not strictly comparable with individual member scores. (Methodology, 1987 Almanac, p. 22-C)

Rounding: Scores in the tables for the full House and Senate membership are rounded to the nearest percentage point, although rounding is not used to increase any score to 100 percent or to reduce any score to zero. Scores for party and chamber support and opposition leaders are reported to one decimal point to rank them more precisely.

Compromise, Procedural Clout Help Bush Win on Some Big Issues

GEORGE W. BUSH SPENT the final year of his presidency weighed down by rock-bottom public approval ratings and overshadowed by the race to succeed him, enduring a campaign where "voted with Bush" became an attack-ad punch line.

That shrinking popularity, combined with war and recession, was a prescription for making Bush the ultimate lame duck, a president with no ability to press his agenda in Congress or to prevent members of his party from abandoning White House policies to save their careers.

For the most part, that's exactly what happened, according to Congressional Quarterly's annual study of presidential support and success. Bush prevailed on just 47.8 percent of roll call votes in 2008 where he took a clear position. That was the eighth-lowest score in the 56-year history of the survey, although it was higher than Bush's 38.3 percent success rate in 2007. Congress forced him to accept a farm bill and Medicare doctor-payment changes he didn't want, and lawmakers challenged him repeatedly on issues from tobacco regulation to infrastructure spending.

Moderate Republicans fled from the president as the election neared, and the average House Republican supported Bush just 64 percent of the time. That was down 8 percentage points from a year before and the lowest for a president's party since 1990, midway through Bush's father's term in the White House. His average support score of 70 percent among GOP senators was also the lowest for a president's party since 1990.

As in 2007, Democrats voted with Bush far less often than they had when the Republicans were in charge and could set the agenda. House Democrats voted with Bush just 16 percent of the time on average — above their 2007 support score of 7 percent but still the second-lowest for any president. Democratic senators joined Bush on 34 percent of roll call votes, down from their average support score of 37 percent a year ago.

They also made Bush play on Democratic turf, forcing votes on their tax, energy and health care policies. Meanwhile, faced with political reality, Bush abandoned the domestic policy agenda that he had campaigned on in 2004 and pushed in the first part of his second term. He made no progress on adding private accounts to Social Security, overhauling the tax code, changing immigration laws, extending his tax cuts beyond their expiration date or limiting punitive damages in medical malpractice lawsuits.

At the same time, despite his political weakness, Democratic control of Congress and frequent defeats, Bush got his way on some of the biggest issues of the year.

Playing offense, the administration secured more money for his effort to fight AIDS globally and cemented a nuclear cooperation deal with India. But Bush scored most often with blocking tactics, using threatened vetoes and the Senate filibuster to avoid significant changes to his Iraq policies, major restrictions on intelligence-gathering tactics, and removal of tax breaks for oil and gas companies. He was resilient, losing plenty of votes along the way but remaining the biggest obstacle to the Democrats' ability to turn their campaign agenda into law.

"Clearly, we were playing more defense than anything else," said Sen. John Cornyn, R-Texas, who cited the Bush team's continued success on Iraq policy as "quite an accomplishment." Cornyn, historically one of Bush's steadiest defenders, voted with the president just 73 percent of the time in 2008, down from a cumulative 92 percent support score over eight years. "It was all contingent on our ability to have 41 senators to stop some of the misguided efforts," he said.

Even in the closing days of the Congress, Democrats were forced to negotiate with the White House on a controversial loan package for automakers. "President Bush is still president of the United States," Senate Majority Leader Harry Reid of Nevada said somewhat ruefully. "He has tremendous power, and rightfully so."

Nonetheless, Bush also cooperated with the Democrats, something he avoided in 2007. When the economic crisis struck with full force, Bush made deals with the leadership on an economic stimulus bill, housing legislation and a $700 billion financial bailout package. In those cases, the administration used implicit or explicit veto threats to force Democrats to concede important points.

After a contentious 2007, Bush and Congress settled into a calmer stalemate in 2008, said Gary C. Jacobson, professor of political science at the University of California at San Diego. They avoided the hot-button partisan issues on which neither side would budge, and Bush lowered his aspirations for victories. "He wasn't going to achieve them through Congress, at least not the grander ones," Jacobson said. "And so things that he actually pushed on Congress are things where he had some prospect of winning."

BUSH'S OVERALL SUCCESS

Bush finished out his last year with a legislative scorecard that looked stronger than those of the most recent two-term presidents, Bill Clinton and Ronald Reagan. Over eight years, Bush succeeded on 67.7 percent of roll calls where he decided to weigh in, topping Clinton's 57.4 percent success score and Reagan's 62.2 percent. Then again, neither Clinton nor Reagan had the benefit of a House of Representatives under his party's control for six years. By the end of 2006, Bush appeared on track to achieve one of the highest success rates in the CQ survey's history, with a chance of topping John F. Kennedy's 84.6 percent.

All that changed when Democrats took over in 2007. House Speaker Nancy Pelosi of California and Reid repeatedly challenged Bush, forcing votes in the face of veto threats on such issues as a timetable for withdrawing troops from Iraq. The Democrats tried to fulfill campaign pledges and punch back after years of watching Bush steamroll Congress. That confrontation inevitably led to presidential vetoes and a sharper partisan tone.

"I think we'll look back and say his mode of dealing with Congress came back to haunt him," said Thomas E. Mann, senior fellow at the Brookings Institution. "He had contempt for the institution."

That bitterness lingered into 2008, and Congress continued to confront the White House. But the economic slowdown provided opportunities for Bush and the Democrats to learn how to work together. At the

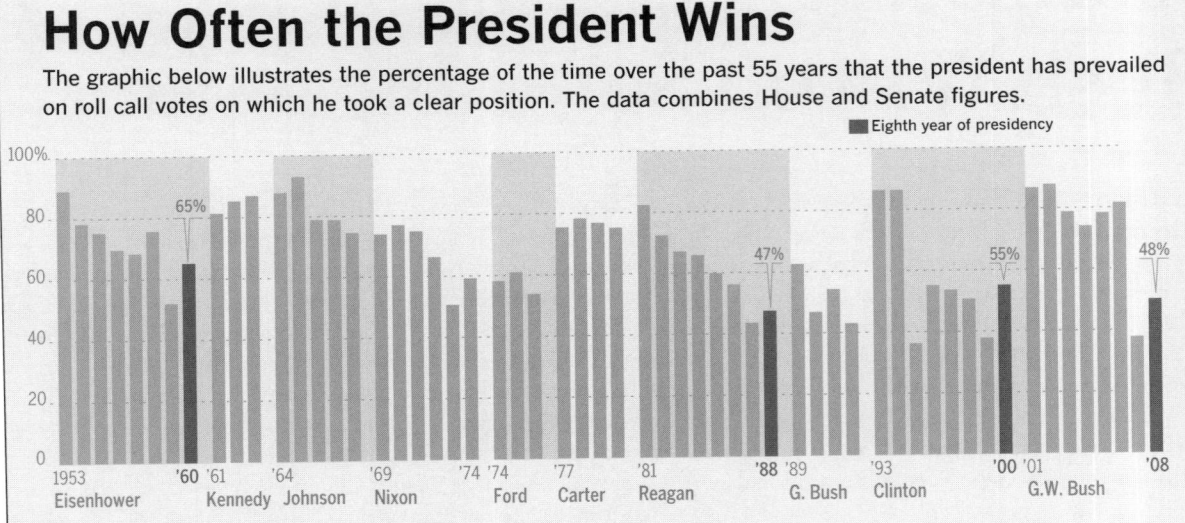

How Often the President Wins

The graphic below illustrates the percentage of the time over the past 55 years that the president has prevailed on roll call votes on which he took a clear position. The data combines House and Senate figures.

■ Eighth year of presidency

100%. 80. 60. 40. 20. 0

1953 Eisenhower '60 '61 Kennedy '64 Johnson '69 Nixon '74 '74 Ford '77 Carter '81 Reagan '88 '89 G. Bush '93 Clinton '00 '01 G.W. Bush '08

65% 47% 55% 48%

2008 DATA
HOUSE TOTALS
Victories
27
53 Defeats

SENATE TOTALS
37 victories, 17 defeats
Nominations
7
Other issues
17 30

BUSH SUCCESS TOTALS CONGRESSWIDE
64 70

FOR MORE INFORMATION

Top scorers	B-5
Background	B-7
Vote lists	B-8
Senators' scores	B-9
House members' scores	B-10

beginning of the year, the administration cut a deal with House leaders from both parties on an economic stimulus bill with tax rebates for individuals and investment incentives for businesses. Bush and House lawmakers from both parties resisted Senate attempts to enlarge the package by adding energy tax breaks, extending unemployment benefits and raising the income phaseout thresholds for the rebates.

While the House bill didn't survive intact, Congress reached a true compromise with the administration. Democrats gave ground by including the business tax breaks, and the administration allowed rebate checks to go to workers who owed Social Security taxes but no income tax. The votes on the stimulus bill were among the few where an overwhelming majority of Democrats voted with Bush. The initial bill passed the House, 385-35, with just 10 Democrats voting against it.

"Congress and the president were quite contentious, but the president did something he hasn't done in the first seven years, and that was consult and compromise," said Stephen J. Wayne, a professor at Georgetown University. "And that helped him achieve."

At the time, Pelosi said she hoped the stimulus agreement she negotiated with Treasury Secretary Henry M. Paulson Jr. and House GOP Leader John A. Boehner of Ohio might serve as a model for future compromises, noting that it was the first time Democrats and the president had worked to reach an upfront agreement on a bill the president wanted to pass. "You have to share common values or you have to be in a position where you can negotiate," Pelosi said. Throughout the year, her cautionary observation proved prescient, as the president and Congress routinely found themselves at odds.

Still, lawmakers turned to compromise again in September, and again it involved Paulson and Pelosi trying to navigate an economic crisis. The administration asked Congress for $700 billion to rescue the financial system, an episode that tested the ability of members to work together. After expressing outrage at Paulson's three-page, no-oversight first draft, Democrats worked closely with the administration to create a consensus measure that would have more congressional input. Nonetheless, the administration proved adept at retaining flexibility in the legislative language, as demonstrated by Paulson's easy shift from using the money to purchase worthless securities to investing directly in banks.

In a sign of the administration's difficulties on Capitol Hill, the first House vote to pass the bailout bill collapsed, not because of a confrontation with Democrats, but because the weakened president couldn't persuade Republicans to vote for it. Bush faced similar trouble on the auto bailout bill at the end of the session, when the White House could not sway Senate Republicans to support a deal Bush struck with Democrats.

PROCEDURAL POWER PLAY

With instances of compromise relatively rare, Republicans gave Bush a lift by exerting the power of procedure, showing repeatedly that the majority could not always get its way. Republicans sustained vetoes, filibustered Democratic initiatives and even used House rules to their advantage. They required Democrats to try to find three-fifths or two-thirds supermajorities to prevail on many votes. Even as some Republicans voted less frequently with the president than they once had, his core supporters had enough clout to block Democratic priorities, including an expansion of children's health insurance and authority for bankruptcy judges to change the terms of home mortgages.

As a result, Bush prevailed on almost 34 percent of the House votes where he took a position — twice his success rate of a year earlier — and on almost 69 percent in the Senate, also better than in 2007.

In the Senate, filibusters remained routine, and the Democrats' slim 51-49 advantage meant leaders either had to water down their bills or run into a consistent roadblock. Moderate Republicans, particularly those up for re-election in 2008, voted often with the Democrats on motions to invoke cloture, thereby limiting debate, but Bush prevailed nonetheless because the Democrats needed 60 votes. An effort to broaden wage discrimination laws came up four votes short. An attempt to consider a House tax bill that proposed to offset tax cuts with other revenue increases was nine short. The more generous stimulus package in February came up two short.

That obstructionism may have hurt the GOP, however. Democrats raised it frequently, especially in Senate campaigns, and some moderate-voting Republicans — Elizabeth Dole of North Carolina, Gordon H.

Leading Scorers: Presidential Support

Support indicates those who voted in 2008 most often for President Bush's position, when it was clearly known. **Opposition** shows those who voted most often against his position. Members who missed half or more of the votes cast are not listed. Scores are reported to one decimal point; those with identical scores are listed alphabetically. *(Complete scores, pp. B-9, B-10)*

SENATE

SUPPORT

Democrats		Republicans		Democrats		Republicans	
Landrieu, La.	52.9%	Lugar, Ind.	86.8%				
Nelson, Neb.	48.1	Coburn, Okla.	85.4				
Bayh, Ind.	47.2	Bennett, Utah	85.2				
Pryor, Ark.	46.3	DeMint, S.C.	84.3				
Inouye, Hawaii	46.0	Kyl, Ariz.	83.3				
Carper, Del.	45.3	Domenici, N.M.	83.0				
McCaskill, Mo.	45.3	Ensign, Nev.	83.0				
Rockefeller, W.Va.	45.3	Gregg, N.H.	82.4				
Johnson, S.D.	44.4	Burr, N.C.	80.8				
Reid, Nev.	42.6	Hatch, Utah	79.6				
Salazar, Colo.	42.6	Hagel, Neb.	79.2				
3 members	41.5	Bunning, Ky.	78.8				
		Sununu, N.H.	78.8				

OPPOSITION

Democrats		Republicans	
Harkin, Iowa	75.0%	Snowe, Maine	51.9%
Bingaman, N.M.	72.2	Smith, Ore.	50.9
Cantwell, Wash.	72.2	Dole, N.C.	42.0
Menendez, N.J.	71.7	Coleman, Minn.	41.5
Murray, Wash.	71.7	Specter, Pa.	41.5
Wyden, Ore.	71.7	Collins, Maine	40.7
Akaka, Hawaii	70.4	Craig, Idaho	35.3
Feingold, Wis.	70.4	Roberts, Kan.	35.2
Lautenberg, N.J.	70.4	Martinez, Fla.	33.3
Leahy, Vt.	70.4	Hutchison, Texas	32.7
Schumer, N.Y.	70.4	Stevens, Alaska	31.4
Tester, Mont.	70.4	Wicker, Miss.	29.6
4 members	69.8	2 members	28.3

HOUSE

SUPPORT

Democrats		Republicans	
Lampson, Texas	38.9%	Campbell, Calif.	88.6%
Boren, Okla.	36.3	McCrery, La.	87.7
Bean, Ill.	32.5	Pence, Ind.	87.7
Marshall, Ga.	32.5	Hensarling, Texas	87.2
Matheson, Utah	32.1	Franks, Ariz.	87.0
Cuellar, Texas	30.0	Tancredo, Colo.	86.8
Cazayoux, La.	29.8	Cannon, Utah	86.4
Cramer, Ala.	28.8	Lungren, Calif.	85.7
Cooper, Tenn.	27.8	Ryan, Wis.	85.7
Kind, Wis.	27.8	Flake, Ariz.	85.3
Barrow, Ga.	27.3	Boehner, Ohio	85.1
Melancon, La.	27.3	Jordan, Ohio	84.8
Ortiz, Texas	27.1	Miller, Fla.	84.6
Childers, Miss.	26.4	Sessions, Texas	84.6
Carney, Penn.	26.3	Weldon, Fla.	84.0
Green, G., Texas	26.3	Foxx, N.C.	83.5
Mahoney, Fla.	26.3	Lamborn, Colo.	83.3

OPPOSITION

Democrats		Republicans	
Kaptur, Ohio	90.8%	Gilchrest, Md.	75.0%
Sanchez, Loretta, Calif.	90.8	Smith, N.J.	67.9
Tubbs Jones, Ohio	90.5	Ros-Lehtinen, Fla.	67.1
Becerra, Calif.	90.0	Shays, Conn.	65.8
Courtney, Conn.	90.0	Jones, N.C.	63.3
Delahunt, Mass.	90.0	Hayes, N.C.	60.8
Sánchez, Linda, Calif.	90.0	LoBiondo, N.J.	60.8
Grijalva, Ariz.	89.9	Castle, Del.	59.5
Napolitano, Calif.	89.9	Diaz-Balart, M., Fla.	58.9
Speier, Calif.	89.8	Diaz-Balart, L., Fla.	58.7
Lynch, Mass.	89.7	Johnson, Ill.	57.0
Watson, Calif.	89.6	Miller, Mich.	56.4
Doggett, Texas	89.3	Gerlach, Pa.	56.0
Clay, Mo.	88.8	Buchanan, Fla.	55.7
Kagen, Wis.	88.8	English, Pa.	55.7
Scott, Va.	88.8	Murphy, Pa.	55.1
2 members	88.6	Ramstad, Minn.	54.4

Smith of Oregon, John E. Sununu of New Hampshire and possibly Norm Coleman of Minnesota — lost their seats as Democrats successfully tied them to the administration.

Even in the House, where the majority could usually do whatever it wanted, Bush and the GOP took advantage of the rules. During the summer, with gasoline prices rising quickly, Democrats brought several energy bills opposed by Bush to the House floor under a procedure known as suspension of the rules that prevented Republicans from offering amendments to lift a ban on offshore drilling but required two-thirds majorities for passage.

On four occasions, Democrats attracted large numbers of GOP votes to supplement their side's strength but still couldn't corral enough support to win. So, as Republicans ran away from him, Bush was able to claim victory. Add in unsuccessful attempts to override vetoes and other rejected motions under suspension of the rules, and 11 of Bush's 27 House successes came on votes where a majority voted against him but a supermajority was needed to defeat him.

THOSE WHO RAN AWAY

Winning despite losing support among his fellow Republicans became more of a pattern as the 2008 election neared and Bush became increasingly toxic on the campaign trail. Intentionally or not, moderate Republicans distanced themselves from the president in a bid to save their careers. For many, tepid support for Bush marked a sharp

Share of Presidential Positions Increases

The House and Senate held 134 roll call votes in 2008 on which the editors of CQ Weekly determined that President Bush took a clear position. While the actual number of so-called presidential support votes declined, the figure rose in 2008 as a share of all House and Senate votes to 14.8 percent. That was the second-highest of the Bush presidency, behind 15.3 percent in 2003.

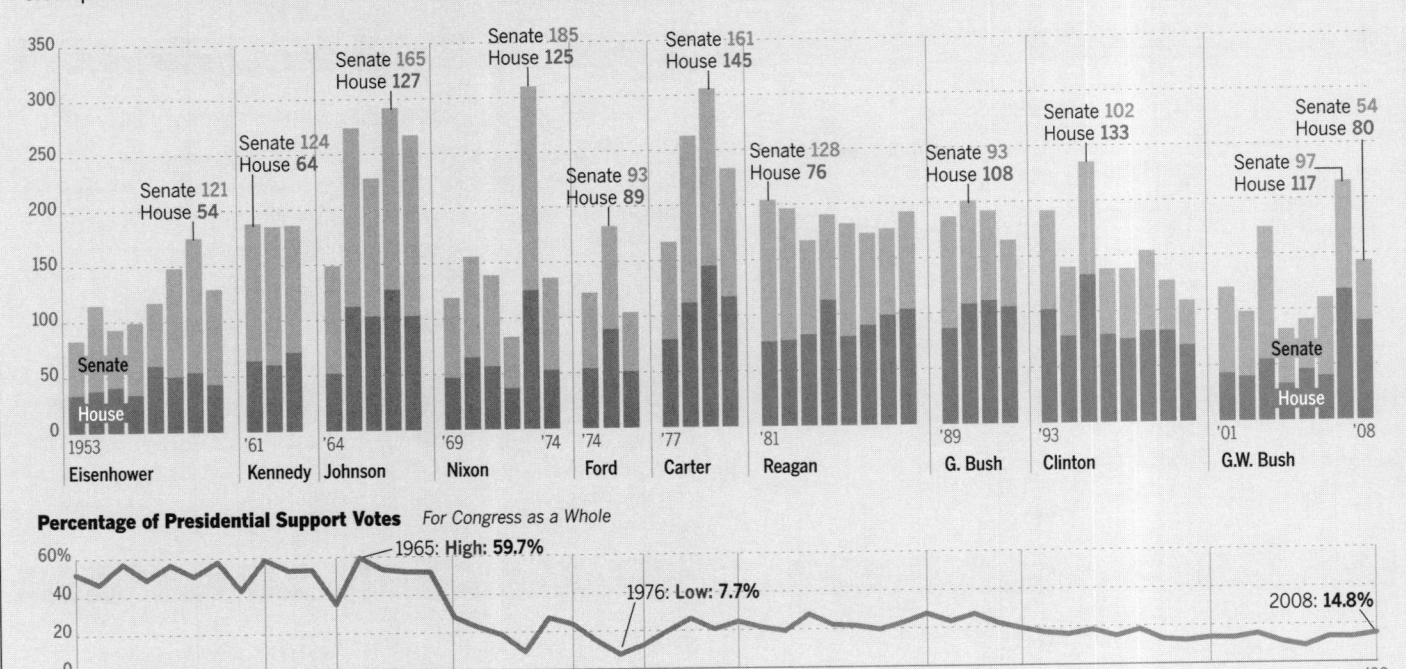

departure from their voting patterns in the previous seven years.

Oregon's Smith, who lost a tough re-election fight, voted with Bush 49 percent of the time in 2008, down from 80 percent for the entire Bush presidency. That was the biggest percentage point drop in support for any senator, and it included votes for an intelligence bill that would have restricted interrogation techniques and for a climate change bill. At one point during the campaign, Smith even ran an ad citing praise he had received from Democrat Barack Obama.

Smith said he was never consciously trying to distinguish himself from the president. "I just try to represent Oregon, and you have an obligation to represent a majority of your constituents without abandoning your principles, and so that was always on my mind," he said after the election. "It wasn't George Bush, though they obviously nationalized the race by making any Republican into George Bush Jr."

Rep. Robin Hayes of North Carolina faced a similar fate, losing at the polls after barely winning a fifth term two years ago. In 2008, Hayes voted with Bush 39 percent of the time, down from 71 percent during the entire presidency. He voted against Bush on both versions of the bailout bill, on a school construction bill and on a bill requiring insurers to provide equal coverage for mental and physical illnesses.

Hayes said he wasn't trying to abandon the president, and he quickly rattled off a list of district-specific accomplishments that he credited to Bush, including restrictions on illegal imported goods that harmed his textile-manufacturing constituents and money for

Customs enforcement. "We're always trying to effectively and correctly represent the district," Hayes said, adding that the array of votes presented by the Democratic leadership may have made a difference. "As the dynamic changed, you could possibly connect our voting pattern to that."

A handful of other House Republicans also voted less frequently with Bush and lost their re-election bids amid the Democratic tide: Joe Knollenberg of Michigan, Phil English of Pennsylvania, Jon Porter of Nevada, Ric Keller of Florida and Steve Chabot of Ohio.

"The tide generated by congressional scandal followed by Iraq followed by the economic meltdown was just too great for Republicans in competitive districts to swim against," said Georgetown's Wayne.

Some moderate Republicans ran away from Bush and survived, including Reps. Don Young of Alaska, Mario Diaz-Balart of Florida and Sam Graves of Missouri. Sen. Susan Collins of Maine easily won a third term, even as Obama carried her state. Collins voted less often with Bush in 2008 than in previous years, supporting him just 59 percent of the time. She had backed Bush just 77 percent of the time throughout his presidency.

"I have taken the same approach in the last two years as I have in my entire career," Collins said. "I've supported the president when I thought he was right, and I haven't supported him when I thought he was wrong." By the end of the Bush presidency, more and more lawmakers were reaching the latter conclusion. ■

Presidential Support Background

Congressional Quarterly's editors select presidential support votes each year based on clear statements by the president or authorized spokesmen. **Support** scores show the percentage of roll calls on which members of Congress voted in agreement with the president's position. **Success** shows the percentage of the selected votes on which the president prevailed.

Presidential Success by Issues

Economic affairs includes votes on tax, trade, omnibus and some supplemental spending bills, which may fund both domestic and defense/foreign policy programs. **Confirmation** votes in the Senate are included only in chamber average scores.

	Defense/Foreign Policy		Domestic		Economic Affairs		Overall	
	2008	2007	2008	2007	2008	2007	2008	2007
House	43%	28%	30%	9%	36%	25%	34%	15%
Senate	71	61	59	39	69	86	69	66
Congress	52	44	41	19	49	43	48	38

House Average Presidential Support Scores

DEMOCRATS | REPUBLICANS

Eisenhower, R

1954	44%	71%
1955	53	60
1956	52	72
1957	49	54
1958	44	67
1959	40	68
1960	44	59

Kennedy, D

1961	73	37
1962	72	42
1963	72	32

Johnson, D

1964	74%	38%
1965	74	41
1966	63	37
1967	69	46
1968	64	51

Nixon, R

1969	48	57
1970	53	66
1971	47	72
1972	47	64
1973	35	62
1974	46	65

Ford, R

1974	41%	51%
1975	38	63
1976	32	63

Carter, D

1977	63	42
1978	60	36
1979	64	34
1980	63	40

Reagan, R

1981	42	68
1982	39	64
1983	28	70
1984	34	60

1985	30%	67%
1986	25	65
1987	24	62
1988	25	57

G. Bush, R

1989	36	69
1990	25	63
1991	34	72
1992	25	71

Clinton, D

1993	77	39
1994	75	47
1995	75	22
1996	74	38

1997	71%	30%
1998	74	26
1999	73	23
2000	73	27

G.W. Bush, R

2001	31	86
2002	32	82
2003	26	89
2004	30	80
2005	24	81
2006	31	85
2007	7	72
2008	16	64

Senate Average Presidential Support Scores

DEMOCRATS | REPUBLICANS

Eisenhower, R

1954	38%	73%
1955	56	72
1956	39	72
1957	51	69
1958	44	67
1959	38	72
1960	43	66

Kennedy, D

1961	65	36
1962	63	39
1963	63	44

Johnson, D

1964	61%	45%
1965	64	48
1966	57	43
1967	61	53
1968	48	47

Nixon, R

1969	47	66
1970	45	60
1971	40	64
1972	44	66
1973	37	61
1974	39	57

Ford, R

1974	39%	55%
1975	47	68
1976	39	62

Carter, D

1977	70	52
1978	66	41
1979	68	47
1980	62	45

Reagan, R

1981	49	80
1982	43	74
1983	42	73
1984	41	76

1985	35%	75%
1986	37	78
1987	36	64
1988	47	68

G. Bush, R

1989	55	82
1990	38	70
1991	41	83
1992	32	73

Clinton, D

1993	87	29
1994	86	42
1995	81	29
1996	83	37

1997	85%	60%
1998	82	41
1999	84	34
2000	89	46

G.W. Bush, R

2001	66	94
2002	71	89
2003	48	94
2004	60	91
2005	38	86
2006	51	85
2007	37	78
2008	34	70

2008 Presidential Position Votes

The following is a list of 80 House and 54 Senate roll call votes in 2008 on which the president took a clear position, based on his statements or those of authorized spokesmen. A victory is a vote on which the president's position prevailed.

HOUSE

Economic Affairs and Trade

VOTE NUMBER · DESCRIPTION

8 Victories

25	Economic stimulus
42	Economic stimulus
403	Unemployment benefits
519	Fannie Mae, Freddie Mac rescue
540	Futures industry regulation
634	Alternative minimum tax
681	Financial industry bailout
690	Automaker assistance

14 Defeats

84	Energy taxes
181	Trade (Colombia)
190	Federal contracting
299	Mortgage relief
332	Energy prices
344	Tax extenders
412	Unemployment benefits
454	Alternative minimum tax
455	Alternative minimum tax
575	Trade (Mexican trucks)

608	Futures market regulation
649	Tax extenders
660	Economic stimulus
674	Financial industry bailout

Defense and Foreign Policy

VOTE NUMBER · DESCRIPTION

6 Victories

117	Intelligence authorization (veto override)
158	Global HIV/AIDS
357	Missile defense
431	Iraq War funding
531	Global HIV/AIDS
662	U.S.-India nuclear pact

8 Defeats

223	Coast Guard reauthorization
328	Iraq War funding
329	Iraq War policy
356	Missile defense
359	Iraq War policy
361	Interrogation policy
362	Interrogation policy
365	Defense authorization

Domestic Policy

VOTE NUMBER · DESCRIPTION

13 Victories

22	Children's health (veto override)
54	Domestic surveillance
188	State election assistance
387	Federal payments
437	Domestic surveillance
448	Energy prices
460	Disability rights
469	Domestic drilling
493	State election assistance
511	Domestic drilling
527	Energy policy
600	Gun restrictions
601	Gun restrictions

31 Defeats

10	Mine safety
13	Public housing
18	Public housing
40	Higher education
60	Executive privilege
101	Mental health parity
145	Domestic surveillance
209	Medicaid rules

217	Small business assistance
229	Highway projects
233	Workplace safety
315	Farm bill
330	Emergency spending
346	Farm bill (veto override)
353	Farm bill
379	School construction
400	Amtrak authorization
417	Farm bill (veto override)
421	NASA authorization
428	Federal labor rules
443	Medicare doctors' pay
459	Child abuse
467	Mass transit grants
477	Executive privilege
478	Labor pay rules
491	Medicare doctors' pay (veto override)
518	Highway funding
530	Bridge safety
542	Tobacco regulation
556	Wage discrimination
599	Domestic drilling

SENATE

Economic Affairs and Trade

VOTE NUMBER · DESCRIPTION

9 Victories

8	Economic stimulus (cloture)
9	Economic stimulus
10	Economic stimulus
117	Flood insurance
146	Energy taxes (cloture)
186	Fannie Mae, Freddie Mac rescue
203	Alternative minimum tax
206	Economic stimulus
213	Financial industry bailout

4 Defeats

96	Mortgage relief
125	Flood insurance
157	Mortgage relief
215	Automaker assistance (cloture)

Defense and Foreign Policy

VOTE NUMBER · DESCRIPTION

5 Victories

138	Iraq War policy
139	Iraq War funding
162	Iraq War funding
182	Global HIV/AIDS
211	U.S.-India nuclear pact

2 Defeats

22	Intelligence authorization
201	Defense authorization

Domestic Policy

VOTE NUMBER · DESCRIPTION

16 Victories

2	Domestic surveillance
4	Domestic surveillance (cloture)
13	Domestic surveillance
15	Domestic surveillance
20	Domestic surveillance

35	Energy policy (cloture)
88	Mortgage relief (bankruptcy)
110	Wage discrimination (cloture)
115	FAA reauthorization (cloture)
145	Climate change (cloture)
149	Medicare doctors' pay (cloture)
160	Medicare doctors' pay (cloture)
164	Domestic surveillance
165	Domestic surveillance
166	Domestic surveillance
168	Domestic surveillance

11 Defeats

41	Product safety
108	Highway projects
123	Domestic drilling
127	Veterans' benefits
130	Farm bill

137	Emergency spending
140	Farm bill (veto override)
144	Farm bill
151	Farm bill (veto override)
169	Medicare doctors' pay (cloture)
177	Medicare doctors' pay (veto override)

Nominations

VOTE NUMBER · DESCRIPTION

7 Victories

102	Brian Stacy Miller
136	G. Steven Agee
148	Mark S. Davis
156	Helene N. White
159	William T. Lawrence
171	David H. Petraeus
172	Raymond T. Odierno

SENATE

1. Presidential Support Score. Percentage of recorded votes cast in 2008 on which President Bush took a position and on which the senator voted "yea" or "nay" in agreement with the president's position. Failure to vote does not lower an individual's score.

2. Presidential Opposition Score. Percentage of recorded votes cast in 2008 on which President Bush took a position and on which the senator voted "yea" or "nay" in disagreement with the president's position. Failure to vote does not lower an individual's score.

3. Participation in Presidential Support Votes. Percentage of the 54 recorded Senate votes in 2008 on which President Bush took a position and for which the senator was eligible and present and voted "yea" or "nay."

State / Senator	1	2	3	State / Senator	1	2	3
ALABAMA				**MONTANA**			
Shelby	74	26	100	Baucus	35	65	100
Sessions	74	26	98	Tester	30	70	100
ALASKA				**NEBRASKA**			
Stevens	69	31	94	**Hagel**	79	21	89
Murkowski	72	28	98	Nelson	48	52	96
ARIZONA				**NEVADA**			
McCain	89	11	17	Reid	43	57	100
Kyl	83	17	100	**Ensign**	83	17	98
ARKANSAS				**NEW HAMPSHIRE**			
Lincoln	41	59	100	**Gregg**	82	18	94
Pryor	46	54	100	**Sununu**	79	21	96
CALIFORNIA				**NEW JERSEY**			
Feinstein	38	62	98	Lautenberg	30	70	100
Boxer	30	70	98	Menendez	28	72	98
COLORADO				**NEW MEXICO**			
Allard	72	28	98	**Domenici**	83	17	98
Salazar	43	57	100	Bingaman	28	72	100
CONNECTICUT				**NEW YORK**			
Dodd	31	69	100	Schumer	30	70	100
Lieberman	52	48	96	Clinton	38	62	54
DELAWARE				**NORTH CAROLINA**			
Biden	33	67	85	**Dole**	58	42	93
Carper	45	55	98	**Burr**	81	19	96
FLORIDA				**NORTH DAKOTA**			
Nelson	42	58	98	Conrad	40	60	98
Martinez	67	33	100	Dorgan	30	70	98
GEORGIA				**OHIO**			
Chambliss	72	28	100	**Voinovich**	74	26	100
Isakson	72	28	100	Brown	30	70	98
HAWAII				**OKLAHOMA**			
Inouye	46	54	93	**Inhofe**	75	25	89
Akaka	30	70	100	**Coburn**	85	15	89
IDAHO				**OREGON**			
Craig	65	35	94	Wyden	28	72	98
Crapo	76	24	100	**Smith**	49	51	98
ILLINOIS				**PENNSYLVANIA**			
Durbin	31	69	100	**Specter**	58	42	98
Obama[1]	28	72	34	Casey	35	65	100
INDIANA				**RHODE ISLAND**			
Lugar	87	13	98	Reed	35	65	100
Bayh	47	53	98	Whitehouse	41	59	100
IOWA				**SOUTH CAROLINA**			
Grassley	72	28	100	**Graham**	72	28	80
Harkin	25	75	96	**DeMint**	84	16	94
KANSAS				**SOUTH DAKOTA**			
Brownback	78	22	100	Johnson	44	56	100
Roberts	65	35	100	**Thune**	76	24	100
KENTUCKY				**TENNESSEE**			
McConnell	76	24	100	**Alexander**	77	23	96
Bunning	79	21	96	**Corker**	72	28	100
LOUISIANA				**TEXAS**			
Landrieu	53	47	94	**Hutchison**	67	33	96
Vitter	76	24	100	**Cornyn**	73	27	96
MAINE				**UTAH**			
Snowe	48	52	100	**Hatch**	80	20	100
Collins	59	41	100	**Bennett**	85	15	100
MARYLAND				**VERMONT**			
Mikulski	42	58	98	Leahy	30	70	100
Cardin	31	69	100	*Sanders*	30	70	98
MASSACHUSETTS				**VIRGINIA**			
Kennedy	18	82	41	**Warner**	72	28	93
Kerry	30	70	98	Webb	42	58	98
MICHIGAN				**WASHINGTON**			
Levin	31	69	100	Murray	28	72	98
Stabenow	31	69	100	Cantwell	28	72	100
MINNESOTA				**WEST VIRGINIA**			
Coleman	58	42	98	Byrd	31	69	83
Klobuchar	31	69	100	Rockefeller	45	55	98
MISSISSIPPI				**WISCONSIN**			
Cochran	74	26	100	Kohl	37	63	100
Wicker	70	30	100	Feingold	30	70	100
MISSOURI				**WYOMING**			
Bond	78	22	94	**Enzi**	78	22	100
McCaskill	45	55	98	**Barrasso**	76	24	100

KEY   **Republicans**   Democrats   *Independents*

[1] Sen. Barack Obama, D-Ill., resigned effective Nov. 16. The last vote for which Obama was eligible was vote 213. He was eligible for all but one presidential support vote in 2008.

HOUSE

1. Presidential Support. Percentage of recorded votes cast in 2008 on which President Bush took a position and on which the member voted "yea" or "nay" in agreement with the president's position. Failure to vote does not lower an individual's score.

2. Presidential Opposition. Percentage of recorded votes cast in 2008 on which President Bush took a position and on which the member voted "yea" or "nay" in disagreement with the president's position. Failure to vote does not lower an individual's score.

3. Participation in Presidential Support Votes. Percentage of the 80 recorded House votes in 2008 on which President Bush took a position and for which the member was eligible and present and voted "yea" or "nay."

[1] The Speaker votes only at her discretion.

[2] Rep. Jackie Speier, D-Calif., was sworn in April 10 to fill the seat vacated by the death of Democrat Tom Lantos on Feb. 11. The first vote for which Speier was eligible was vote 179; the last vote for which Lantos was eligible was vote 42. Lantos did not participate in any presidential support votes in 2008.

[3] Rep. Bill Foster, D-Ill., was sworn in March 11. The first vote for which he was eligible was vote 116.

[4] Rep. André Carson, D-Ind., was sworn in March 13 to fill the seat vacated by the death of Democrat Julia Carson on Dec. 15, 2007. The first vote for which he was eligible was vote 140.

[5] Rep. Steve Scalise, R-La., was sworn in May 7 to fill the seat vacated by Republican Bobby Jindal, who resigned Jan. 14 to become governor. The first vote for which Scalise was eligible was vote 268; Jindal was not eligible for any presidential support votes in 2008.

[6] Rep. Don Cazayoux, D-La., was sworn in May 6 to fill the seat vacated by Republican Richard H. Baker, who resigned Feb. 2. The first vote for which Cazayoux was eligible was vote 247; the last vote for which Baker was eligible was vote 28. Baker did not participate in any presidential support votes in 2008.

[7] Rep. Donna Edwards, D-Md., was sworn in June 19 to replace Democrat Albert R. Wynn, who resigned effective May 31. The first vote for which Edwards was eligible was vote 427. The last vote for which Wynn was eligible was vote 366.

[8] Rep. Travis W. Childers, D-Miss., was sworn in May 20. The first vote for which he was eligible was vote 332.

[9] Rep. Marcia L. Fudge, D-Ohio, was sworn in Nov. 19 to replace Democrat Stephanie Tubbs Jones, who died Aug. 20. The first vote for which Fudge was eligible was vote 684. The last vote for which Tubbs Jones was eligible was vote 566.

[10] Rep. Thomas M. Davis III, R-Va., resigned Nov. 24. The last vote for which he was eligible was vote 683.

	1	2	3			1	2	3
ALABAMA					**COLORADO**			
1 Bonner	76	24	93		1 DeGette	13	87	96
2 Everett	75	25	84		2 Udall	21	79	89
3 Rogers	53	47	98		3 Salazar	19	81	99
4 Aderholt	67	33	95		4 Musgrave	67	33	88
5 Cramer	29	71	91		5 Lamborn	83	17	98
6 Bachus	68	32	95		6 Tancredo	87	13	85
7 Davis	24	76	100		7 Perlmutter	16	84	99
ALASKA					**CONNECTICUT**			
AL Young	54	46	85		1 Larson	13	87	96
ARIZONA					2 Courtney	10	90	100
1 Renzi	61	39	90		3 DeLauro	13	87	100
2 Franks	87	13	96		4 Shays	34	66	99
3 Shadegg	83	17	96		5 Murphy	17	83	100
4 Pastor	13	87	100		**DELAWARE**			
5 Mitchell	25	75	99		AL Castle	41	59	99
6 Flake	85	15	94		**FLORIDA**			
7 Grijalva	10	90	99		1 Miller	85	15	98
8 Giffords	19	81	100		2 Boyd	23	77	98
ARKANSAS					3 Brown	17	83	95
1 Berry	21	79	98		4 Crenshaw	74	26	81
2 Snyder	20	80	93		5 Brown-Waite	60	40	75
3 Boozman	71	29	98		6 Stearns	76	24	99
4 Ross	24	76	100		7 Mica	77	23	96
CALIFORNIA					8 Keller	64	36	95
1 Thompson	15	85	100		9 Bilirakis	63	37	98
2 Herger	78	22	95		10 Young	64	36	98
3 Lungren	86	14	96		11 Castor	14	86	89
4 Doolittle	76	24	90		12 Putnam	75	25	91
5 Matsui	13	87	100		13 Buchanan	44	56	99
6 Woolsey	16	84	93		14 Mack	77	23	91
7 Miller, George	13	87	95		15 Weldon	84	16	94
8 Pelosi[1]	25	75	45		16 Mahoney	26	74	95
9 Lee	14	86	98		17 Meek	18	82	99
10 Tauscher	16	84	99		18 Ros-Lehtinen	33	67	95
11 McNerney	17	83	100		19 Wexler	15	85	81
12 Speier[2]	10	90	89		20 Wasserman Schultz	13	87	99
13 Stark	13	87	89		21 Diaz-Balart, L.	41	59	94
14 Eshoo	14	86	100		22 Klein	17	83	100
15 Honda	15	85	93		23 Hastings	13	87	96
16 Lofgren	14	86	100		24 Feeney	81	19	90
17 Farr	13	87	96		25 Diaz-Balart, M.	41	59	91
18 Cardoza	16	84	99		**GEORGIA**			
19 Radanovich	77	23	93		1 Kingston	68	32	93
20 Costa	26	74	96		2 Bishop	21	79	98
21 Nunes	83	17	94		3 Westmoreland	76	24	98
22 McCarthy	73	27	98		4 Johnson	12	88	98
23 Capps	14	86	100		5 Lewis	15	85	94
24 Gallegly	63	37	98		6 Price	76	24	98
25 McKeon	78	22	98		7 Linder	77	23	94
26 Dreier	78	22	93		8 Marshall	33	67	100
27 Sherman	14	86	96		9 Deal	74	26	95
28 Berman	20	80	93		10 Broun	83	17	95
29 Schiff	14	86	100		11 Gingrey	72	28	98
30 Waxman	16	84	99		12 Barrow	27	73	96
31 Becerra	10	90	100		13 Scott	18	82	99
32 Solis	12	88	96		**HAWAII**			
33 Watson	10	90	96		1 Abercrombie	16	84	100
34 Roybal-Allard	11	89	99		2 Hirono	13	87	100
35 Waters	18	82	98		**IDAHO**			
36 Harman	18	82	98		1 Sali	77	23	98
37 Richardson	16	84	94		2 Simpson	62	38	98
38 Napolitano	10	90	99		**ILLINOIS**			
39 Sánchez, Linda	10	90	100		1 Rush	29	71	26
40 Royce	82	18	96		2 Jackson	14	86	100
41 Lewis	82	18	98		3 Lipinski	16	84	100
42 Miller, Gary	79	21	88		4 Gutierrez	16	84	94
43 Baca	19	81	96		5 Emanuel	16	84	99
44 Calvert	76	24	95		6 Roskam	71	29	98
45 Bono Mack	64	36	94		7 Davis	16	84	93
46 Rohrabacher	74	26	96		8 Bean	33	67	100
47 Sanchez, Loretta	9	91	95		9 Schakowsky	16	84	100
48 Campbell	89	11	88		10 Kirk	53	47	99
49 Issa	79	21	95		11 Weller	67	33	76
50 Bilbray	67	33	98		12 Costello	15	85	98
51 Filner	13	87	98		13 Biggert	69	31	98
52 Hunter	71	29	91		14 Foster[3]	21	79	99
53 Davis	15	85	100		15 Johnson	43	57	99

KEY Republicans Democrats

	1	2	3
16 Manzullo	73	27	98
17 Hare	12	88	98
18 LaHood	53	47	88
19 Shimkus	71	29	94
INDIANA			
1 Visclosky	12	88	95
2 Donnelly	25	75	100
3 Souder	64	36	95
4 Buyer	66	34	91
5 Burton	77	23	99
6 Pence	88	12	91
7 Carson, A.[4]	12	88	100
8 Ellsworth	25	75	100
9 Hill	18	82	98
IOWA			
1 Braley	13	87	94
2 Loebsack	13	87	94
3 Boswell	17	83	88
4 Latham	63	37	99
5 King	77	23	94
KANSAS			
1 Moran	69	31	96
2 Boyda	16	84	100
3 Moore	22	78	99
4 Tiahrt	69	31	90
KENTUCKY			
1 Whitfield	56	44	96
2 Lewis	74	26	88
3 Yarmuth	13	87	94
4 Davis	73	27	96
5 Rogers	69	31	98
6 Chandler	19	81	100
LOUISIANA			
1 Scalise[5]	79	21	98
2 Jefferson	13	87	94
3 Melancon	27	73	96
4 McCrery	88	12	91
5 Alexander	70	30	95
6 Baker[6]	0	0	0
6 Cazayoux[6]	30	70	98
7 Boustany	68	32	95
MAINE			
1 Allen	17	83	100
2 Michaud	13	87	100
MARYLAND			
1 Gilchrest	25	75	85
2 Ruppersberger	21	79	94
3 Sarbanes	16	84	100
4 Wynn[7]	10	90	78
4 Edwards[7]	17	83	100
5 Hoyer	18	82	99
6 Bartlett	65	35	96
7 Cummings	12	88	98
8 Van Hollen	14	86	99
MASSACHUSETTS			
1 Olver	14	86	99
2 Neal	14	86	99
3 McGovern	13	87	100
4 Frank	14	86	100
5 Tsongas	15	85	99
6 Tierney	12	88	96
7 Markey	14	86	100
8 Capuano	22	78	98
9 Lynch	10	90	98
10 Delahunt	10	90	88
MICHIGAN			
1 Stupak	15	85	100
2 Hoekstra	76	24	95
3 Ehlers	64	36	90
4 Camp	72	28	98
5 Kildee	15	85	100
6 Upton	47	53	99
7 Walberg	68	32	95
8 Rogers	68	32	96
9 Knollenberg	60	40	98
10 Miller	44	56	98
11 McCotter	58	42	95
12 Levin	16	84	99
13 Kilpatrick	13	87	98
14 Conyers	12	88	98
15 Dingell	15	85	99
MINNESOTA			
1 Walz	14	86	100
2 Kline	77	23	96
3 Ramstad	46	54	99
4 McCollum	13	87	100

	1	2	3
5 Ellison	13	87	95
6 Bachmann	75	25	96
7 Peterson	21	79	98
8 Oberstar	15	85	98
MISSISSIPPI			
1 Childers[8]	26	74	100
2 Thompson	13	87	96
3 Pickering	70	30	89
4 Taylor	17	83	100
MISSOURI			
1 Clay	11	89	100
2 Akin	81	19	96
3 Carnahan	16	84	99
4 Skelton	20	80	100
5 Cleaver	13	87	99
6 Graves	54	46	99
7 Blunt	80	20	94
8 Emerson	53	47	99
9 Hulshof	72	28	63
MONTANA			
AL Rehberg	65	35	98
NEBRASKA			
1 Fortenberry	56	44	96
2 Terry	68	32	99
3 Smith	74	26	98
NEVADA			
1 Berkley	18	82	96
2 Heller	68	32	99
3 Porter	49	51	95
NEW HAMPSHIRE			
1 Shea-Porter	14	86	100
2 Hodes	15	85	99
NEW JERSEY			
1 Andrews	17	83	79
2 LoBiondo	39	61	99
3 Saxton	63	37	94
4 Smith	32	68	98
5 Garrett	77	23	98
6 Pallone	17	83	98
7 Ferguson	69	31	94
8 Pascrell	13	87	96
9 Rothman	14	86	100
10 Payne	13	87	95
11 Frelinghuysen	73	27	99
12 Holt	15	85	100
13 Sires	16	84	99
NEW MEXICO			
1 Wilson	73	27	93
2 Pearce	70	30	96
3 Udall	14	86	99
NEW YORK			
1 Bishop	16	84	96
2 Israel	15	85	99
3 King	67	33	99
4 McCarthy	16	84	100
5 Ackerman	15	85	99
6 Meeks	19	81	90
7 Crowley	19	81	100
8 Nadler	14	86	89
9 Weiner	15	85	99
10 Towns	13	87	95
11 Clarke	16	84	100
12 Velázquez	14	86	100
13 Fossella	68	32	90
14 Maloney	17	83	98
15 Rangel	16	84	93
16 Serrano	13	87	100
17 Engel	17	83	94
18 Lowey	14	86	95
19 Hall	14	86	100
20 Gillibrand	22	78	79
21 McNulty	13	87	95
22 Hinchey	15	85	100
23 McHugh	51	49	98
24 Arcuri	20	80	100
25 Walsh	54	46	86
26 Reynolds	73	27	93
27 Higgins	20	80	94
28 Slaughter	12	88	98
29 Kuhl	60	40	98
NORTH CAROLINA			
1 Butterfield	11	89	99
2 Etheridge	20	80	99
3 Jones	37	63	99
4 Price	14	86	100

	1	2	3
5 Foxx	84	16	99
6 Coble	65	35	96
7 McIntyre	17	83	100
8 Hayes	39	61	99
9 Myrick	79	21	94
10 McHenry	78	22	99
11 Shuler	18	82	96
12 Watt	15	85	100
13 Miller	15	85	100
NORTH DAKOTA			
AL Pomeroy	20	80	99
OHIO			
1 Chabot	64	36	96
2 Schmidt	72	28	95
3 Turner	58	42	98
4 Jordan	85	15	99
5 Latta	73	27	99
6 Wilson	22	78	99
7 Hobson	69	31	85
8 Boehner	85	15	93
9 Kaptur	9	91	95
10 Kucinich	20	80	100
11 Tubbs Jones[9]	10	90	93
11 Fudge[9]	100	0	100
12 Tiberi	60	40	98
13 Sutton	13	87	100
14 LaTourette	46	54	98
15 Pryce	67	33	71
16 Regula	59	41	95
17 Ryan	20	80	100
18 Space	23	77	100
OKLAHOMA			
1 Sullivan	69	31	94
2 Boren	36	64	100
3 Lucas	66	34	95
4 Cole	73	27	98
5 Fallin	67	33	98
OREGON			
1 Wu	13	87	98
2 Walden	63	37	89
3 Blumenauer	15	85	98
4 DeFazio	13	87	100
5 Hooley	12	88	95
PENNSYLVANIA			
1 Brady	14	86	100
2 Fattah	13	87	99
3 English	44	56	99
4 Altmire	24	76	100
5 Peterson	74	26	76
6 Gerlach	44	56	94
7 Sestak	18	82	99
8 Murphy, P.	20	80	100
9 Shuster	67	33	98
10 Carney	26	74	100
11 Kanjorski	23	77	100
12 Murtha	23	77	98
13 Schwartz	15	85	99
14 Doyle	16	84	91
15 Dent	49	51	98
16 Pitts	76	24	88
17 Holden	20	80	100
18 Murphy, T.	45	55	98
19 Platts	49	51	98
RHODE ISLAND			
1 Kennedy	14	86	95
2 Langevin	15	85	100
SOUTH CAROLINA			
1 Brown	69	31	98
2 Wilson	82	18	98
3 Barrett	83	17	96
4 Inglis	79	21	98
5 Spratt	20	80	100
6 Clyburn	18	82	99
SOUTH DAKOTA			
AL Herseth Sandlin	22	78	99
TENNESSEE			
1 Davis, D.	71	29	99
2 Duncan	67	33	100
3 Wamp	70	30	96
4 Davis, L.	24	76	99
5 Cooper	28	72	99
6 Gordon	21	79	96
7 Blackburn	78	22	96
8 Tanner	22	78	95
9 Cohen	14	86	98

	1	2	3
TEXAS			
1 Gohmert	63	37	91
2 Poe	68	32	95
3 Johnson, S.	81	19	98
4 Hall	65	35	99
5 Hensarling	87	13	98
6 Barton	82	18	96
7 Culberson	77	23	94
8 Brady	77	23	93
9 Green, A.	14	86	99
10 McCaul	68	32	96
11 Conaway	76	24	99
12 Granger	80	20	94
13 Thornberry	82	18	98
14 Paul	70	30	79
15 Hinojosa	22	78	85
16 Reyes	24	76	98
17 Edwards	22	78	99
18 Jackson Lee	14	86	96
19 Neugebauer	80	20	94
20 Gonzalez	23	77	98
21 Smith	70	30	96
22 Lampson	39	61	90
23 Rodriguez	23	77	100
24 Marchant	82	18	91
25 Doggett	11	89	94
26 Burgess	73	27	93
27 Ortiz	27	73	88
28 Cuellar	30	70	100
29 Green, G.	26	74	95
30 Johnson, E.	14	86	96
31 Carter	80	20	86
32 Sessions	85	15	98
UTAH			
1 Bishop	78	22	86
2 Matheson	32	68	99
3 Cannon	86	14	74
VERMONT			
AL Welch	15	85	99
VIRGINIA			
1 Wittman	63	37	100
2 Drake	64	36	98
3 Scott	11	89	100
4 Forbes	60	40	90
5 Goode	60	40	96
6 Goodlatte	64	36	96
7 Cantor	79	21	94
8 Moran	15	85	98
9 Boucher	23	77	94
10 Wolf	66	34	96
11 Davis[10]	65	35	91
WASHINGTON			
1 Inslee	15	85	98
2 Larsen	16	84	100
3 Baird	16	84	99
4 Hastings	70	30	99
5 McMorris Rodgers	64	36	96
6 Dicks	19	81	98
7 McDermott	17	83	100
8 Reichert	53	47	99
9 Smith	20	80	94
WEST VIRGINIA			
1 Mollohan	20	80	100
2 Capito	46	54	98
3 Rahall	18	82	99
WISCONSIN			
1 Ryan	86	14	96
2 Baldwin	14	86	100
3 Kind	28	72	99
4 Moore	19	81	99
5 Sensenbrenner	82	18	96
6 Petri	62	38	99
7 Obey	13	87	98
8 Kagen	11	89	100
WYOMING			
AL Cubin	79	21	70
DELEGATES			
Faleomavaega (A.S.)	17	83	86
Norton (D.C.)	14	86	100
Bordallo (Guam)	20	80	71
Fortuño (P.R.)	100	0	14
Christensen (V.I.)	0	100	43

Polarization Pushed to Limit Again

WHEN GEORGE W. BUSH ARRIVED in Washington, he promised to bring a central claim of his presidential campaign — being "a uniter, not a divider" — to bear in his dealings with Congress. But he prepared to leave office having presided over the most polarized period at the Capitol since Congressional Quarterly began quantifying partisanship in the House and Senate in 1953.

That reality was reflected both in the relatively high percentage of party-unity votes — those that pitted a majority of Republicans against a majority of Democrats — and in the increasing propensity of individual lawmakers to vote with their fellow partisans.

The year fit a recent trend as well. In both the House and Senate, more than half the roll call votes split the parties. Moreover, House Democrats voted on average with the majority of their caucus 92 percent of the time, tying the high-water mark for cohesion they set in 2007. House Republicans, even in the face of public antipathy toward an unpopular president and a tarnished GOP brand, stuck together 87 percent of the time, a figure that was higher than a year before and just below their record of 91 percent, reached three times: in 1995, 2001 and 2003.

The Senate was almost as polarized. The chamber's Democrats voted as a unified caucus 87 percent of the time, a shade below the party's all-time high of 89 percent reached in 1999 and 2001. And Senate Republicans stuck together 83 percent of the time, more than in 2007 and not far below their high mark of 94 percent in 2003.

Whether the sustained deep partisanship on Capitol Hill reflected the ideological attitude of the electorate or the intractable nature of the politicians themselves, almost every lawmaker was eager to declare that polarization ought to come to an end. Some suggested that the newly elected president, Barack Obama, might help make that possible.

"The country must be governed from the middle," House Speaker Nancy Pelosi, D-Calif., said. "You have to bring people together to reach consensus on solutions that are sustainable and acceptable to the American people."

Pelosi's Republican counterpart, Minority Leader John A. Boehner of Ohio, sounded a similar, hopeful tone.

"If President Obama and the Democrats who run Congress choose to keep their promise and govern in a bipartisan way," House Republicans will work with them, Boehner said.

It's exactly the type of rhetoric party leaders had used for years, even as their actions repeatedly belied their claims. There appeared to be good reason for the divide between rhetoric and reality: History showed that polarization, which clarified for voters the differences between the two sides, could yield big election victories, as it did for Re-

publicans in their revolution of 1994 and for Democrats in 2006 and again in November 2008.

DOES PARTISANSHIP PAY?

In the sense that it's hard to argue with what works, it would have been easy for Democrats to conclude that they benefited in an election year marked by extreme partisanship in the House and almost as much in the Senate.

Despite what some might argue was lackluster legislative output in 2008, the Democrats racked up big election gains in no small part by portraying the other side as obstructionists. That could be a tribute to the success of Pelosi in setting an agenda that fed the Democrats' goals. With her power to control the House floor and a deft ability to assuage her party's fiscally conservative Blue Dog Coalition, House Democrats in 2008 posted an all-time-high success rate on party-unity votes, winning more than 93 percent of the time.

In addition, the high percentage of party-unity votes in the House — 367 of 688 roll call votes, at 53 percent the third-highest rate in the previous decade — indicated that Republicans were usually not happy with the agenda set by Pelosi and her leadership team.

But partisanship didn't always lead to success for the Democrats. The Senate often couldn't follow the House's lead because Majority Leader Harry Reid of Nevada had a razor-thin majority of 51-49 in a chamber where procedural rules benefited a minority that could hang together. For Reid, the biggest hurdle was finding 60 votes to invoke cloture and break a filibuster. Time and again that proved impossible.

Democrats Dominate In House, Not Senate

House Democrats won an all-time-high 93 percent of roll call votes that divided the parties this year. Republicans thwarted Democrats in the Senate, however, allowing them victories on just 54 percent of party-unity votes. Congresswide, Republicans voted unanimously more often than Democrats for the first time since 2004 on such unity votes.

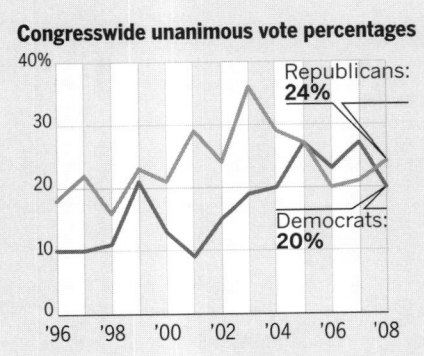

Congresswide unanimous vote percentages

Republicans: **24%**

Democrats: **20%**

Majority party victory percentages

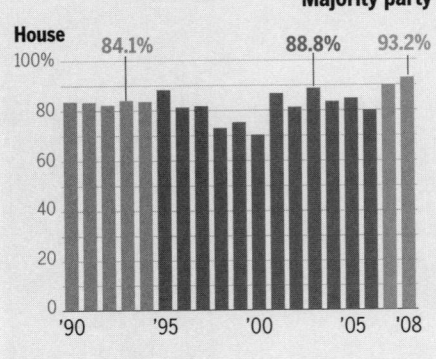

House
84.1%   88.8%   93.2%

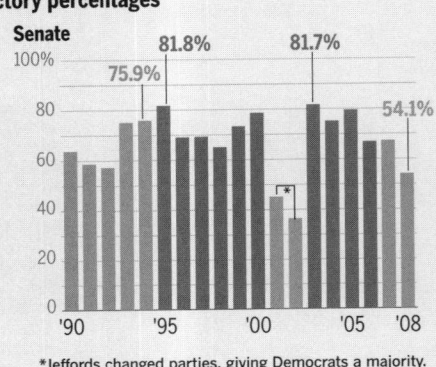

Senate
75.9%   81.8%   81.7%   54.1%

*Jeffords changed parties, giving Democrats a majority.

House Democrats Remain United

Matching the record set a year before, House Democrats voted with their party's majority 92 percent of the time in 2008 on roll call votes where the two parties divided. Senate Democrats, too, held at a high level of party unity. Their average score of 87 percent matched 2007, although it fell below the 89 percent performance of almost a decade ago. House Republicans voted with their party's majority 87 percent of the time, and Senate Republicans had an average 83 percent party-unity score. Average House and Senate GOP scores were higher in 2008 than a year earlier, which was the lowest for both since 1994.

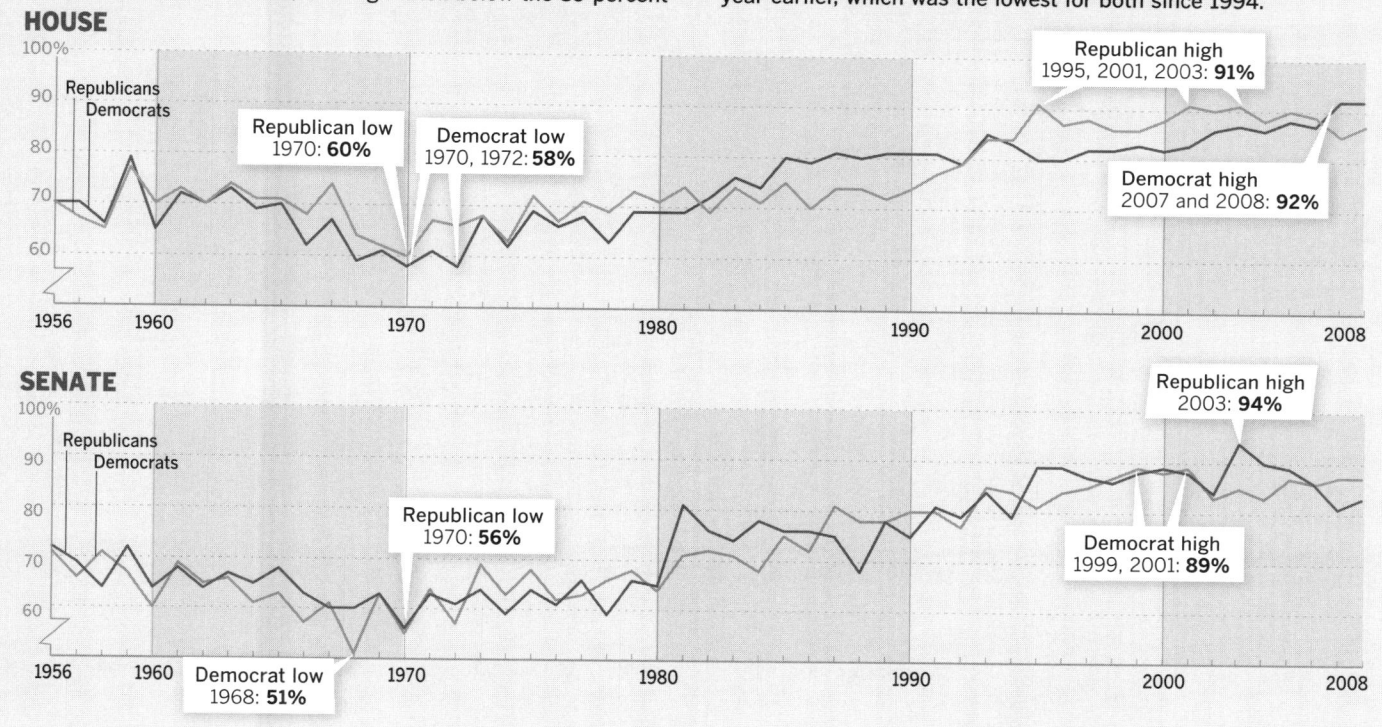

HOUSE

Republican high
1995, 2001, 2003: **91%**

Republican low
1970: **60%**

Democrat low
1970, 1972: **58%**

Democrat high
2007 and 2008: **92%**

Republicans
Democrats

SENATE

Republican high
2003: **94%**

Republican low
1970: **56%**

Democrat high
1999, 2001: **89%**

Democrat low
1968: **51%**

Republicans
Democrats

A typical case arose over a House-passed bill to expand wage discrimination protections for workers. The bill aimed to overturn a Supreme Court decision that had prevented a woman from suing her employer because she had waited too long to file suit. House Democrats were almost entirely unified behind the bill; only six of them defected when the chamber passed it in 2007. Republicans, who objected that the bill would allow lawsuits for unintentional discrimination, were similarly united and voted against it, 2-193. That partisan split was mirrored in the Senate when Reid tried to bring the measure to the floor in April 2008. Only six Republicans joined the Democrats in voting to invoke cloture, and 41 voted "nay", just enough to block action. Reid cast the sole Democratic "nay" vote — a parliamentary maneuver that preserved his right to try again later to revive the legislation, which never happened.

Another instance came in July, when House Democrats moved legislation to permit the Food and Drug Administration to regulate tobacco products. While the Republican caucus split, a narrow majority opposed the bill. And then, stiff GOP resistance in the Senate prevented further consideration.

Even the last vote of the session reflected how partisan splits were more inhibiting to legislative action in the Senate. On a mostly party-line vote, the House passed a bill, brokered between Democrats and the White House, to give emergency loans to U.S. automakers. One day later in the Senate, Reid could not persuade a sufficient number of Republicans to join the effort to advance the measure, and Congress quit for the year, leaving it languishing.

In the face of tough odds, Senate Democrats were victorious on more than 54 percent of party-unity votes in 2008. But in historical terms, that was hardly impressive. Reid had prevailed on more than 67 percent of the votes that divided the parties in 2007, and Senate Republicans posted bigger victory margins every year between 1995 and 2006 — and in two of those years the Democrats had a nominal majority.

Several Republicans who often side with Democrats on critical votes were re-elected, notably Olympia J. Snowe and Susan Collins of Maine, Arlen Specter of Pennsylvania, and George V. Voinovich of Ohio. Snowe voted with the Democrats 61 percent of the time on party-unity votes in 2008, and Collins was a party defector only slightly less often, at 54 percent. Specter and Voinovich both sided with the Democrats more than 30 percent of the time.

ROPING THE STRAYS

Hands down among congressional leaders, Pelosi had the greatest success in win-

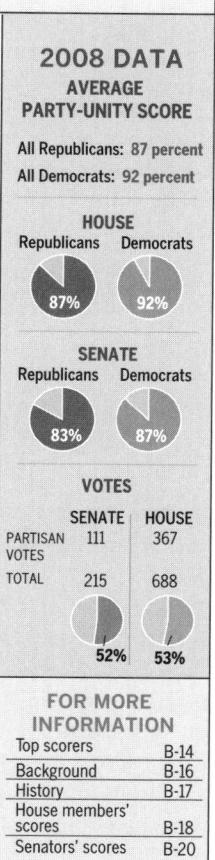

2008 DATA
AVERAGE PARTY-UNITY SCORE

All Republicans: **87 percent**
All Democrats: **92 percent**

HOUSE
Republicans   Democrats
87%   **92%**

SENATE
Republicans   Democrats
83%   **87%**

VOTES

	SENATE	HOUSE
PARTISAN VOTES	111	367
TOTAL	215	688
	52%	**53%**

FOR MORE INFORMATION

Leading Scorers: Party Unity

Support indicates those who voted most often with a majority of their party against a majority of the other party in 2008. **Opposition** shows those who voted most often against their party's majority on party-unity votes. Members who missed half or more of the votes cast are not listed. Scores are reported to one decimal point; those with identical scores are listed alphabetically. *(Complete scores, pp. B-18, B-20)*

SENATE

SUPPORT

Democrats		Republicans	
Akaka, Hawaii	99.1%	Allard, Colo.	100.0%
Bingaman, N.M.	99.1	DeMint, S.C.	100.0
Boxer, Calif.	99.1	Ensign, Nev.	100.0
Lautenberg, N.J.	99.1	Kyl, Ariz.	100.0
Murray, Wash.	99.1	Barrasso, Wyo.	99.1
Reed, R.I.	99.1	Burr, N.C.	99.1
Kennedy, Mass.	98.6	Enzi, Wyo.	99.1
Clinton, N.Y.	98.5	Inhofe, Okla.	99.1
Durbin, Ill.	98.2	Coburn, Okla.	99.0
Leahy, Vt.	98.2	Sessions, Ala.	98.2
Menendez, N.J.	98.2	Vitter, La.	98.2
Schumer, N.Y.	98.2	McConnell, Ky.	97.3
Stabenow, Mich.	98.2	Cornyn, Texas	97.1

OPPOSITION

Democrats		Republicans	
Bayh, Ind.	35.2%	Snowe, Maine	61.3%
Landrieu, La.	30.6	Collins, Maine	54.1
Nelson, Neb.	28.4	Smith, Ore.	45.9
Pryor, Ark.	20.7	Specter, Pa.	37.6
Carper, Del.	20.0	Voinovich, Ohio	33.3
Johnson, S.D.	19.8	Coleman, Minn.	31.5
McCaskill, Mo.	19.4	Murkowski, Alaska	28.2
Lincoln, Ark.	18.9	Dole, N.C.	27.6
Inouye, Hawaii	16.7	Stevens, Alaska	26.9
Reid, Nev.	16.2	Warner, Va.	24.5
Rockefeller, W.Va.	15.7	Hagel, Neb.	22.2
Salazar, Colo.	12.6	Martinez, Fla.	21.8
Mikulski, Md.	11.9	Lugar, Ind.	19.3

HOUSE

SUPPORT

Democrats		Republicans	
Andrews, N.J.	100.0%	Broun, Ga.	100.0%
Honda, Calif.	100.0	Akin, Mo.	99.7
Neal, Mass.	100.0	Blackburn, Tenn.	99.7
Olver, Mass.	100.0	Hensarling, Texas	99.7
Rangel, N.Y.	100.0	Lamborn, Colo.	99.7
Slaughter, N.Y.	100.0	Price, Ga.	99.7
Velázquez, N.Y.	100.0	Miller, Fla.	99.4
22 members	99.7	Franks, Ariz.	99.2
		Johnson, S., Texas	99.2
		Royce, Calif.	99.2
		Boehner, Ohio	99.1
		Burton, Ind.	99.1
		Pence, Ind.	99.1
		Flake, Ariz.	98.9
		Gingrey, Ga.	98.9
		Shadegg, Ariz.	98.9
		Scalise, La.	98.7

OPPOSITION

Democrats		Republicans	
Lampson, Texas	43.1%	Gilchrest, Md.	35.5%
Childers, Miss.	31.6	Ros-Lehtinen, Fla.	32.9
Hill, Ind.	28.0	Smith, N.J.	31.8
Cazayoux, La.	24.7	Shays, Conn.	31.5
Donnelly, Ind.	20.5	Ramstad, Minn.	30.1
Mitchell, Ariz.	20.3	Castle, Del.	29.9
Carney, Pa.	17.4	Johnson, Ill.	28.2
Shuler, N.C.	17.4	Kirk, Ill.	27.5
Marshall, Ga.	16.7	LoBiondo, N.J.	27.2
Barrow, Ga.	16.6	Reichert, Wash.	24.9
Altmire, Pa.	15.5	Gerlach, Pa.	24.7
Ellsworth, Ind.	14.8	Murphy, Pa.	24.3
Matheson, Utah	14.0	Porter, Nev.	23.5
Giffords, Ariz.	13.8	Jones, N.C.	22.6
Bean, Ill.	12.1	LaHood, Ill.	22.2
Taylor, Miss.	11.9	Dent, Pa.	21.9
McIntyre, N.C.	10.7	Diaz-Balart, M., Fla.	20.1

ning partisan votes during the year by exploiting GOP defectors and at the same time holding the sometimes fractious Democratic caucus in line.

In several cases, Republicans who were potentially vulnerable to defeat backed away from their party label and became frequent, if not reliable, Democratic allies. Florida Republican Ileana Ros-Lehtinen, for example, moved steadily away from her party's leaders, and her party-unity score in 2008 was 18 percentage points lower than it was for the entire eight years of the Bush presidency. Two other Florida Republicans similarly abandoned their party more often. Mario Diaz-Balart's party-unity score was 9 percentage points lower in 2008 than it was during the Bush presidency overall, while his brother Lincoln

Diaz-Balart's was 8 points lower. All survived serious challenges in November.

Not all Republican defectors were able to capitalize on their independence. Wayne T. Gilchrest of Maryland long had one of his party's lowest party-unity scores, and his ideological moderation was why he lost his bid for a 10th term — to a much more conservative Republican in the party primary. Christopher Shays of Connecticut, who had voted frequently with Democrats since he arrived in 1987 and had the fourth-lowest party-unity score in the House GOP during the year, lost in November mainly because he stuck with his party on one unpopular top-tier issue, the Iraq War, and broke with it on another, the financial industry bailout.

Frequency of Party-Unity Votes Drops

The number of roll call votes in 2008 in which a majority of Democrats opposed a majority of Republicans declined from 2007 in no small part because there were almost half as many total votes. But the percentage of roll calls that were party-unity votes also fell to the lowest since 2004, although at 53 percent it is close to the 54 percent average for the previous eight years.

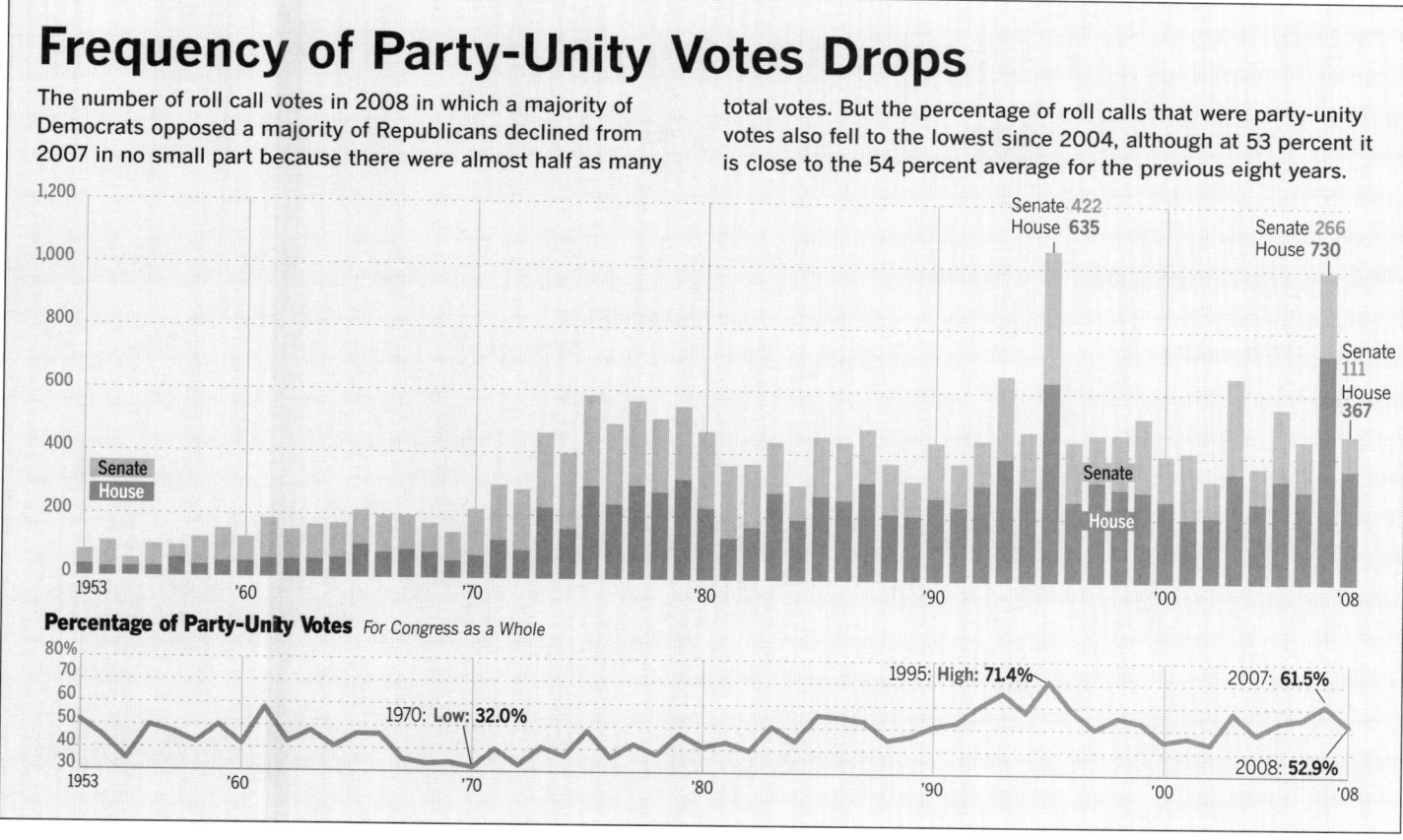

While some Republicans were abandoning their party, Pelosi encouraged partisan discipline from the most fiscally conservative in her ranks by sticking mostly to her pledge to pay for new spending increases or tax cuts with revenue raisers that would prevent the budget deficit from growing.

Blue Dogs Gene Taylor of Mississippi, Robert E. "Bud" Cramer of Alabama, Collin C. Peterson of Minnesota and Dan Boren of Oklahoma all posted unity scores that were higher by 17 percentage points in 2008 than for the Bush era as a whole. Overall, Blue Dogs voted the party line on average 91 percent of the time, barely less often than all House Democrats.

"The leadership allowed us the opportunity to make our case for fiscal responsibility," said Charlie Melancon of Louisiana, who was slated to be co-chairman of the Blue Dog caucus in the 111th Congress.

COMPARATIVE COMITY

The level of partisanship seen in 2008 — and actually during the previous decade or two — had not always been the pattern in the post-World War II period. Votes that divided the parties tended to be less frequent, and regional or other differences often pitted Republicans or Democrats against themselves instead of against each other.

That did occur on rare occasions in 2008. House Republicans were at times internally divided over reauthorizing farm programs, combating AIDS overseas and the Bush administration's request for authority to save faltering financial institutions. House Democrats disagreed among themselves over defense programs and international debt relief. And in the Senate, Republicans couldn't agree on a Democratic bill to expand government-funded health care for children, while their Democratic counterparts struggled for unity on legislation granting Bush more authority to conduct surveillance of foreign intelligence targets communicating with people in the United States.

Such instances were far more common during the early years of CQ's vote studies. In the decades before the Clinton administration, instances of party-unity votes were fewer and average lawmaker unity scores were lower — typically in the 70 percent range and occasionally in the 60s. In a few years, they reached as high as 81 percent.

The period of polarization began roughly in 1993, when Republicans and Democrats alike saw their average party-unity scores jump into the mid-80s. That high level of partisanship accelerated with the GOP takeover of Congress after the 1994 elections and continued unabated since.

The extent of the shift might have been amplified by tighter floor control exercised by leaders of the majority party, said Jon R. Bond, a political scientist at Texas A&M University. "The majority party just won't bring a vote up unless they know they are going to win," he said. More telling, Bond said, the partisanship at the time was a return to traditional American party politics, while the relative comity that existed from the 1950s to the 1980s was the exception.

"Even after all these years of increases in party voting, it's still not nearly as high as it was in the 19th century," he said. ■

Party-Unity Background

Roll call votes used for the party-unity study are those on which a majority of voting Democrats opposed a majority of voting Republicans. **Support** indicates the percentage of the time that members voted in agreement with the majority of their party on such party-unity votes. **Opposition** indicates the percentage of the time that members voted against the majority of their party. In calculations of average scores by party and chamber, a member's failure to vote lowers the score for the group. The tables below also show the number of party-unity votes on which each party was victorious and the number of instances in which either party voted unanimously.

Average Party-Unity Scores by Chamber

		SUPPORT		OPPOSITION	
		2008	**2007**	**2008**	**2007**
HOUSE	Democrats	92%	92%	3%	5%
	Republicans	87	85	8	10
SENATE	Democrats	87	87	8	8
	Republicans	83	81	12	15
CONGRESS	Democrats	92	91	4	5
	Republicans	87	85	8	10

Victories in Party-Unity Votes

YEAR	HOUSE DEMOCRATS	HOUSE REPUBLICANS	SENATE DEMOCRATS	SENATE REPUBLICANS	CONGRESS DEMOCRATS	CONGRESS REPUBLICANS
2008	342	25	60	51	402	76
2007	658	72	179	87	837	159
2006	59	236	53	107	112	343
2005	50	278	47	182	97	460
2004	42	213	28	85	70	298
2003	39	310	56	250	95	560
2002	39	170	42	73	81	243
2001	27	177	95	115	122	292
2000	77	182	31	114	108	296
1999	58	177	77	211	135	388
1998	80	216	61	114	141	330
1997	58	261	46	104	104	365
1996	48	208	59	132	107	340
1995	74	561	77	345	151	906
1994	257	50	129	41	386	91
1993	329	62	199	66	528	128

Unanimous Voting by Parties

YEAR	HOUSE DEMOCRATS	HOUSE REPUBLICANS	SENATE DEMOCRATS	SENATE REPUBLICANS	CONGRESS DEMOCRATS	CONGRESS REPUBLICANS
2008	66	96	30	19	96	115
2007	170	177	102	35	272	212
2006	70	62	34	30	104	92
2005	82	91	69	59	151	150
2004	70	77	3	31	73	108
2003	94	109	32	130	126	239
2002	37	54	12	23	49	77
2001	1	66	37	55	38	121
2000	1	67	52	19	53	86
1999	11	59	100	63	111	122
1998	8	42	46	33	54	75
1997	11	63	35	38	46	101
1996	10	32	35	47	45	79
1995	17	159	63	104	80	263
1994	7	38	37	19	44	57
1993	13	65	29	57	42	122

Party-Unity History

The table below, at left, shows how frequently during roll call votes a majority of Democrats aligned against a majority of Republicans. The tables in the center and at the right show the average party-unity support score for each party in each chamber.

YEAR	Frequency of Unity Votes		House Average Scores		Senate Average Scores	
	HOUSE	SENATE	DEMOCRATS	REPUBLICANS	DEMOCRATS	REPUBLICANS
2008	53.3%	51.6%	92%	87%	87%	83%
2007	62.0	60.2	92	85	87	81
2006	54.5	57.3	86	88	86	86
2005	49.0	62.6	88	90	88	88
2004	47.0	52.3	86	88	83	90
2003	51.7	66.7	87	91	85	94
2002	43.3	45.5	86	90	83	84
2001	40.2	55.3	83	91	89	88
2000	43.2	48.7	82	88	88	89
1999	47.3	62.8	83	86	89	88
1998	55.5	55.7	82	86	87	86
1997	50.4	50.3	82	88	85	87
1996	56.4	62.4	80	87	84	89
1995	73.2	68.8	80	91	81	89
1994	61.8	51.7	83	84	84	79
1993	65.5	67.1	85	84	85	84
1992	64.5	53.0	79	79	77	79
1991	55.1	49.3	81	77	80	81
1990	49.1	54.3	81	74	80	75
1989	56.3	35.3	81	72	78	78
1988	47.0	42.5	80	74	78	68
1987	63.7	40.7	81	74	81	75
1986	56.5	52.3	79	70	72	76
1985	61.0	49.6	80	75	75	76
1984	47.1	40.0	74	71	68	78
1983	55.6	43.7	76	74	71	74
1982	36.4	43.4	72	69	72	76
1981	37.4	47.8	69	74	71	81
1980	37.6	45.8	69	71	64	65
1979	47.3	46.7	69	73	68	66
1978	33.2	45.2	63	69	66	59
1977	42.2	42.4	68	71	63	66
1976	35.9	37.2	66	67	62	61
1975	48.4	47.8	69	72	68	64
1974	29.4	44.3	62	63	63	59
1973	41.8	39.9	68	68	69	64
1972	27.1	36.5	58	66	57	61
1971	37.8	41.6	61	67	64	63
1970	27.1	35.2	58	60	55	56
1969	31.1	36.3	61	62	63	63
1968	35.2	32.0	59	64	51	60
1967	36.3	34.6	67	74	61	60
1966	41.5	50.2	62	68	57	63
1965	52.2	41.9	70	71	63	68
1964	54.9	35.7	69	71	61	65
1963	48.7	47.2	73	74	66	67
1962	46.0	41.1	70	70	65	64
1961	50.0	62.3	72	73	69	68
1960	52.7	36.7	65	70	60	64
1959	55.2	47.9	79	77	67	72
1958	39.8	43.5	66	65	71	64
1957	59.0	35.5	70	67	66	69
1956	43.8	53.1	70	70	71	72
1955	40.8	29.9				
1954	38.2	48.0				
1953	52.1	51.7				

Tallying Party-Unity Votes

In the House in 2008, the two parties aligned against each other on 367 of 688 roll call votes, or 53.3 percent of the time. In the Senate, the parties opposed each other on 111 of 215 roll calls, or 51.6 percent of the time. A list of roll call votes that pitted majorities of the two parties against one another is available upon request from Congressional Quarterly.

Calculations of average scores by chamber, party and region are based on all eligible "yea" or "nay" votes, whether or not all members participated. Under this methodology, average support and opposition scores are reduced when members choose not to vote. Because individual member scores are based on the number of votes cast, party and chamber averages are not strictly comparable with individual member scores. (Complete scores, pp. B-18, B-20)

Also, in the member score tables, independent Sens. Joseph I. Lieberman of Connecticut and Bernard Sanders of Vermont are treated as if they were Democrats when calculating their support and opposition scores. However, Lieberman's and Sanders' votes were not used to determine which roll calls were party-unity votes, and they are not included in the Democratic Party averages for the Senate.

HOUSE

1. Party Unity. Percentage of recorded party-unity votes in 2008 on which a member voted "yea" or "nay" in agreement with a majority of his or her party. (Party-unity votes are those on which a majority of voting Democrats opposed a majority of voting Republicans.) Percentages are based on votes cast; thus, failure to vote does not lower a member's score.

2. Party Opposition. Percentage of recorded party-unity votes in 2008 on which a member voted "yea" or "nay" in disagreement with a majority of his or her party. Percentages are based on votes cast; thus, failure to vote does not lower a member's score.

3. Participation in Party-Unity Votes. Percentage of the 367 recorded House party-unity votes in 2008 for which a member was eligible and present and voted "yea" or "nay."

	1	2	3			1	2	3
ALABAMA					**COLORADO**			
1 **Bonner**	97	3	97		1 DeGette	99	1	97
2 **Everett**	97	3	90		2 Udall	94	6	85
3 **Rogers**	88	12	97		3 Salazar	96	4	99
4 **Aderholt**	96	4	95		4 **Musgrave**	97	3	92
5 Cramer	95	5	89		5 **Lamborn**	99	1	98
6 **Bachus**	94	6	92		6 **Tancredo**	96	4	82
7 Davis	96	4	98		7 Perlmutter	97	3	98
ALASKA					**CONNECTICUT**			
AL **Young**	88	12	82		1 Larson	99	1	95
ARIZONA					2 Courtney	99	1	100
1 **Renzi**	88	12	83		3 DeLauro	99	1	98
2 **Franks**	99	1	99		4 **Shays**	68	32	96
3 **Shadegg**	99	1	99		5 Murphy	98	2	100
4 Pastor	99	1	100		**DELAWARE**			
5 Mitchell	80	20	98		AL **Castle**	70	30	99
6 **Flake**	99	1	95		**FLORIDA**			
7 Grijalva	99	1	96		1 **Miller**	99	1	96
8 Giffords	86	14	99		2 Boyd	92	8	99
ARKANSAS					3 Brown	98	2	95
1 Berry	96	4	95		4 **Crenshaw**	97	3	89
2 Snyder	97	3	94		5 **Brown-Waite**	87	13	80
3 **Boozman**	95	5	99		6 **Stearns**	97	3	98
4 Ross	95	5	99		7 **Mica**	93	7	99
CALIFORNIA					8 **Keller**	94	6	91
1 Thompson	95	5	99		9 **Bilirakis**	89	11	96
2 **Herger**	97	3	96		10 **Young**	92	8	98
3 **Lungren**	95	5	96		11 Castor	99	1	94
4 **Doolittle**	96	4	90		12 **Putnam**	95	5	94
5 Matsui	99	1	99		13 **Buchanan**	80	20	99
6 Woolsey	98	2	85		14 **Mack**	98	2	93
7 Miller, George	99	1	96		15 **Weldon**	96	4	90
8 Pelosi[1]	98	2	12		16 Mahoney	94	6	97
9 Lee	99	1	98		17 Meek	99	1	94
10 Tauscher	98	2	98		18 **Ros-Lehtinen**	67	33	96
11 McNerney	93	7	89		19 Wexler	99	1	82
12 Speier[2]	99	1	79		20 Wasserman Schultz	99	1	98
13 Stark	94	6	90		21 **Diaz-Balart, L.**	80	20	95
14 Eshoo	99	1	100		22 Klein	98	2	99
15 Honda	100	0	93		23 Hastings	99	1	95
16 Lofgren	99	1	99		24 **Feeney**	96	4	93
17 Farr	99	1	97		25 **Diaz-Balart, M.**	80	20	95
18 Cardoza	97	3	96		**GEORGIA**			
19 **Radanovich**	97	3	92		1 **Kingston**	93	7	95
20 Costa	94	6	92		2 Bishop	98	2	96
21 **Nunes**	97	3	96		3 **Westmoreland**	98	2	98
22 **McCarthy**	97	3	99		4 Johnson	99	1	98
23 Capps	99	1	99		5 Lewis	99	1	96
24 **Gallegly**	96	4	98		6 **Price**	99	1	99
25 **McKeon**	97	3	98		7 **Linder**	97	3	94
26 **Dreier**	96	4	95		8 Marshall	83	17	96
27 Sherman	98	2	98		9 **Deal**	99	1	96
28 Berman	98	2	95		10 **Broun**	100	0	98
29 Schiff	98	2	99		11 **Gingrey**	99	1	97
30 Waxman	99	1	95		12 Barrow	83	17	99
31 Becerra	99	1	98		13 Scott	98	2	99
32 Solis	99	1	97		**HAWAII**			
33 Watson	99	1	96		1 Abercrombie	96	4	97
34 Roybal-Allard	99	1	99		2 Hirono	99	1	98
35 Waters	98	2	94		**IDAHO**			
36 Harman	98	2	95		1 **Sali**	95	5	99
37 Richardson	99	1	89		2 **Simpson**	92	8	98
38 Napolitano	99	1	99		**ILLINOIS**			
39 Sánchez, Linda	99	1	99		1 Rush	99	1	24
40 **Royce**	99	1	98		2 Jackson	99	1	100
41 **Lewis**	94	6	98		3 Lipinski	97	3	97
42 **Miller, Gary**	97	3	91		4 Gutierrez	99	1	90
43 Baca	98	2	94		5 Emanuel	99	1	98
44 **Calvert**	96	4	97		6 **Roskam**	95	5	99
45 **Bono Mack**	90	10	96		7 Davis	99	1	95
46 **Rohrabacher**	95	5	96		8 Bean	88	12	97
47 Sanchez, Loretta	96	4	97		9 Schakowsky	99	1	99
48 **Campbell**	97	3	80		10 **Kirk**	73	27	97
49 **Issa**	99	1	95		11 **Weller**	85	15	84
50 **Bilbray**	94	6	96		12 Costello	96	4	96
51 Filner	95	5	96		13 **Biggert**	89	11	98
52 **Hunter**	98	2	87		14 Foster[3]	92	8	99
53 Davis	99	1	99		15 **Johnson**	72	28	96

KEY **Republicans**   Democrats

[1] The Speaker votes only at her discretion.

[2] Rep. Jackie Speier, D-Calif., was sworn in April 10 to fill the seat vacated by the death of Democrat Tom Lantos on Feb. 11. The first vote for which Speier was eligible was vote 179; the last vote for which Lantos was eligible was vote 42. Lantos did not participate in any party-unity votes in 2008.

[3] Rep. Bill Foster, D-Ill., was sworn in March 11. The first vote for which he was eligible was vote 116.

[4] Rep. André Carson, D-Ind., was sworn in March 13 to fill the seat vacated by the death of Democrat Julia Carson on Dec. 15, 2007. The first vote for which he was eligible was vote 140.

[5] Rep. Steve Scalise, R-La., was sworn in May 7 to fill the seat vacated by Republican Bobby Jindal, who resigned Jan. 14 to become governor. The first vote for which Scalise was eligible was vote 268; Jindal was not eligible for any party-unity votes in 2008.

[6] Rep. Don Cazayoux, D-La., was sworn in May 6 to fill the seat vacated by Republican Richard H. Baker, who resigned Feb. 2. The first vote for which Cazayoux was eligible was vote 247; the last vote for which Baker was eligible was vote 28. Baker did not participate in any party-unity votes in 2008.

[7] Rep. Donna Edwards, D-Md., was sworn in June 19 to replace Democrat Albert R. Wynn, who resigned effective May 31. The first vote for which Edwards was eligible was vote 427. The last vote for which Wynn was eligible was vote 366.

[8] Rep. Travis W. Childers, D-Miss., was sworn in May 20. The first vote for which he was eligible was vote 332.

[9] Rep. Marcia L. Fudge, D-Ohio, was sworn in Nov. 19 to replace Democrat Stephanie Tubbs Jones, who died Aug. 20. The first vote for which Fudge was eligible was vote 684. The last vote for which Tubbs Jones was eligible was vote 566.

[10] Rep. Thomas M. Davis III, R-Va., resigned Nov. 24. The last vote for which he was eligible was vote 683.

		1	2	3
16	**Manzullo**	92	8	98
17	**Hare**	99	1	99
18	**LaHood**	78	22	91
19	**Shimkus**	94	6	95
INDIANA				
1	**Visclosky**	99	1	97
2	**Donnelly**	79	21	99
3	**Souder**	92	8	96
4	**Buyer**	93	7	93
5	**Burton**	99	1	92
6	**Pence**	99	1	93
7	**Carson, A.**[4]	99	1	93
8	**Ellsworth**	85	15	99
9	**Hill**	72	28	97
IOWA				
1	**Braley**	98	2	93
2	**Loebsack**	97	3	93
3	**Boswell**	98	2	89
4	**Latham**	90	10	99
5	**King**	97	3	98
KANSAS				
1	**Moran**	90	10	97
2	**Boyda**	92	8	98
3	**Moore**	97	3	99
4	**Tiahrt**	92	8	92
KENTUCKY				
1	**Whitfield**	89	11	97
2	**Lewis**	96	4	92
3	**Yarmuth**	98	2	99
4	**Davis**	95	5	98
5	**Rogers**	96	4	99
6	**Chandler**	93	7	99
LOUISIANA				
1	**Scalise**[5]	99	1	99
2	**Jefferson**	98	2	92
3	**Melancon**	93	7	96
4	**McCrery**	95	5	90
5	**Alexander**	95	5	97
6	**Baker**[6]	0	0	0
6	**Cazayoux**[6]	75	25	98
7	**Boustany**	94	6	95
MAINE				
1	**Allen**	98	2	99
2	**Michaud**	94	6	99
MARYLAND				
1	**Gilchrest**	65	35	81
2	**Ruppersberger**	97	3	92
3	**Sarbanes**	99	1	99
4	**Wynn**[7]	99	1	73
4	**Edwards**[7]	99	1	99
5	**Hoyer**	99	1	99
6	**Bartlett**	94	6	98
7	**Cummings**	99	1	95
8	**Van Hollen**	99	1	98
MASSACHUSETTS				
1	**Olver**	100	0	99
2	**Neal**	100	0	97
3	**McGovern**	99	1	99
4	**Frank**	99	1	97
5	**Tsongas**	99	1	99
6	**Tierney**	98	2	95
7	**Markey**	99	1	98
8	**Capuano**	99	1	98
9	**Lynch**	98	2	99
10	**Delahunt**	99	1	90
MICHIGAN				
1	**Stupak**	94	6	99
2	**Hoekstra**	96	4	98
3	**Ehlers**	81	19	95
4	**Camp**	95	5	99
5	**Kildee**	99	1	100
6	**Upton**	84	16	99
7	**Walberg**	92	8	96
8	**Rogers**	91	9	96
9	**Knollenberg**	90	10	99
10	**Miller**	83	17	99
11	**McCotter**	86	14	98
12	**Levin**	99	1	97
13	**Kilpatrick**	99	1	94
14	**Conyers**	98	2	92
15	**Dingell**	99	1	94
MINNESOTA				
1	**Walz**	96	4	99
2	**Kline**	97	3	98
3	**Ramstad**	70	30	99
4	**McCollum**	99	1	98

		1	2	3
5	**Ellison**	99	1	95
6	**Bachmann**	96	4	99
7	**Peterson**	91	9	96
8	**Oberstar**	99	1	87
MISSISSIPPI				
1	**Childers**[8]	68	32	99
2	**Thompson**	99	1	95
3	**Pickering**	90	10	87
4	**Taylor**	88	12	99
MISSOURI				
1	**Clay**	97	3	98
2	**Akin**	99	1	98
3	**Carnahan**	99	1	98
4	**Skelton**	97	3	99
5	**Cleaver**	99	1	98
6	**Graves**	89	11	98
7	**Blunt**	97	3	93
8	**Emerson**	86	14	98
9	**Hulshof**	89	11	66
MONTANA				
AL	**Rehberg**	93	7	99
NEBRASKA				
1	**Fortenberry**	82	18	95
2	**Terry**	90	10	98
3	**Smith**	98	2	99
NEVADA				
1	**Berkley**	97	3	95
2	**Heller**	92	8	98
3	**Porter**	77	23	98
NEW HAMPSHIRE				
1	**Shea-Porter**	97	3	99
2	**Hodes**	97	3	98
NEW JERSEY				
1	**Andrews**	100	0	77
2	**LoBiondo**	73	27	99
3	**Saxton**	85	15	90
4	**Smith**	68	32	97
5	**Garrett**	97	3	98
6	**Pallone**	99	1	98
7	**Ferguson**	88	12	89
8	**Pascrell**	99	1	96
9	**Rothman**	98	2	97
10	**Payne**	99	1	93
11	**Frelinghuysen**	87	13	98
12	**Holt**	98	2	98
13	**Sires**	99	1	96
NEW MEXICO				
1	**Wilson**	92	8	87
2	**Pearce**	94	6	97
3	**Udall**	96	4	96
NEW YORK				
1	**Bishop**	99	1	93
2	**Israel**	99	1	98
3	**King**	87	13	96
4	**McCarthy**	99	1	99
5	**Ackerman**	99	1	98
6	**Meeks**	99	1	92
7	**Crowley**	98	2	99
8	**Nadler**	99	1	95
9	**Weiner**	99	1	94
10	**Towns**	99	1	95
11	**Clarke**	99	1	99
12	**Velázquez**	100	0	98
13	**Fossella**	89	11	88
14	**Maloney**	99	1	95
15	**Rangel**	100	0	85
16	**Serrano**	99	1	99
17	**Engel**	98	2	94
18	**Lowey**	99	1	96
19	**Hall**	99	1	98
20	**Gillibrand**	91	9	85
21	**McNulty**	99	1	99
22	**Hinchey**	98	2	96
23	**McHugh**	81	19	99
24	**Arcuri**	96	4	99
25	**Walsh**	82	18	94
26	**Reynolds**	94	6	92
27	**Higgins**	99	1	95
28	**Slaughter**	100	0	93
29	**Kuhl**	84	16	97
NORTH CAROLINA				
1	**Butterfield**	98	2	93
2	**Etheridge**	98	2	100
3	**Jones**	77	23	92
4	**Price**	99	1	99

		1	2	3
5	**Foxx**	97	3	99
6	**Coble**	96	4	96
7	**McIntyre**	89	11	99
8	**Hayes**	87	13	99
9	**Myrick**	99	1	96
10	**McHenry**	98	2	93
11	**Shuler**	83	17	94
12	**Watt**	99	1	99
13	**Miller**	99	1	98
NORTH DAKOTA				
AL	**Pomeroy**	97	3	99
OHIO				
1	**Chabot**	94	6	98
2	**Schmidt**	95	5	95
3	**Turner**	85	15	98
4	**Jordan**	95	5	99
5	**Latta**	99	1	99
6	**Wilson**	97	3	98
7	**Hobson**	92	8	94
8	**Boehner**	99	1	93
9	**Kaptur**	95	5	96
10	**Kucinich**	91	9	99
11	**Tubbs Jones**[9]	99	1	82
11	**Fudge**[9]	100	0	100
12	**Tiberi**	92	8	97
13	**Sutton**	99	1	98
14	**LaTourette**	82	18	96
15	**Pryce**	89	11	69
16	**Regula**	88	12	99
17	**Ryan**	98	2	95
18	**Space**	94	6	99
OKLAHOMA				
1	**Sullivan**	97	3	96
2	**Boren**	91	9	99
3	**Lucas**	96	4	95
4	**Cole**	95	5	96
5	**Fallin**	95	5	98
OREGON				
1	**Wu**	97	3	96
2	**Walden**	93	7	94
3	**Blumenauer**	98	2	99
4	**DeFazio**	93	7	97
5	**Hooley**	99	1	89
PENNSYLVANIA				
1	**Brady**	99	1	98
2	**Fattah**	99	1	93
3	**English**	82	18	98
4	**Altmire**	84	16	100
5	**Peterson**	93	7	77
6	**Gerlach**	75	25	95
7	**Sestak**	97	3	96
8	**Murphy, P.**	95	5	99
9	**Shuster**	94	6	99
10	**Carney**	83	17	99
11	**Kanjorski**	96	4	99
12	**Murtha**	97	3	98
13	**Schwartz**	99	1	98
14	**Doyle**	99	1	93
15	**Dent**	78	22	99
16	**Pitts**	98	2	89
17	**Holden**	95	5	99
18	**Murphy, T.**	76	24	98
19	**Platts**	80	20	98
RHODE ISLAND				
1	**Kennedy**	99	1	92
2	**Langevin**	99	1	97
SOUTH CAROLINA				
1	**Brown**	92	8	98
2	**Wilson**	98	2	99
3	**Barrett**	98	2	98
4	**Inglis**	93	7	99
5	**Spratt**	98	2	98
6	**Clyburn**	99	1	98
SOUTH DAKOTA				
AL	**Herseth Sandlin**	91	9	99
TENNESSEE				
1	**Davis, D.**	99	1	99
2	**Duncan**	94	6	99
3	**Wamp**	96	4	98
4	**Davis, L.**	93	7	95
5	**Cooper**	92	8	99
6	**Gordon**	93	7	94
7	**Blackburn**	99	1	96
8	**Tanner**	95	5	95
9	**Cohen**	99	1	97

		1	2	3
TEXAS				
1	**Gohmert**	92	8	88
2	**Poe**	94	6	93
3	**Johnson, S.**	99	1	98
4	**Hall**	96	4	99
5	**Hensarling**	99	1	99
6	**Barton**	98	2	95
7	**Culberson**	97	3	93
8	**Brady**	94	6	93
9	**Green, A.**	99	1	96
10	**McCaul**	95	5	97
11	**Conaway**	97	3	90
12	**Granger**	96	4	92
13	**Thornberry**	98	2	99
14	**Paul**	89	11	81
15	**Hinojosa**	97	3	86
16	**Reyes**	97	3	93
17	Edwards	97	3	96
18	Jackson Lee	98	2	92
19	**Neugebauer**	98	2	95
20	Gonzalez	98	2	95
21	Smith	95	5	97
22	Lampson	57	43	92
23	Rodriguez	95	5	99
24	Marchant	98	2	92
25	Doggett	97	3	95
26	**Burgess**	94	6	95
27	Ortiz	95	5	88
28	Cuellar	94	6	98
29	Green, G.	94	6	95
30	Johnson, E.	99	1	93
31	Carter	99	1	93
32	Sessions	99	1	98
UTAH				
1	Bishop	96	4	91
2	Matheson	86	14	99
3	**Cannon**	97	3	82
VERMONT				
AL	Welch	98	2	99
VIRGINIA				
1	**Wittman**	93	7	99
2	**Drake**	96	4	99
3	Scott	99	1	98
4	**Forbes**	95	5	93
5	**Goode**	94	6	99
6	**Goodlatte**	94	6	98
7	**Cantor**	98	2	97
8	**Moran**	98	2	96
9	**Boucher**	96	4	92
10	**Wolf**	87	13	97
11	**Davis**[10]	86	14	92
WASHINGTON				
1	**Inslee**	99	1	98
2	**Larsen**	98	2	99
3	**Baird**	94	6	96
4	**Hastings**	98	2	97
5	**McMorris Rodgers**	95	5	96
6	**Dicks**	98	2	95
7	**McDermott**	98	2	98
8	**Reichert**	75	25	99
9	**Smith**	97	3	96
WEST VIRGINIA				
1	**Mollohan**	98	2	97
2	**Capito**	82	18	97
3	**Rahall**	97	3	99
WISCONSIN				
1	**Ryan**	97	3	98
2	**Baldwin**	99	1	99
3	**Kind**	95	5	97
4	**Moore**	99	1	98
5	**Sensenbrenner**	98	2	95
6	**Petri**	91	9	99
7	**Obey**	99	1	99
8	**Kagen**	96	4	99
WYOMING				
AL	**Cubin**	95	5	60
DELEGATES				
	Faleomavaega (A.S.)	97	3	73
	Norton (D.C.)	94	6	85
	Bordallo (Guam)	97	3	85
	Fortuño (P.R.)	63	37	39
	Christensen (V.I.)	100	0	71

SENATE

1. Party Unity. Percentage of recorded party-unity votes in 2008 on which a senator voted "yea" or "nay" in agreement with a majority of his or her party. (Party-unity roll calls are those on which a majority of voting Democrats opposed a majority of voting Republicans.) Percentages are based on votes cast; thus, failure to vote does not lower a member's score.

2. Party Opposition. Percentage of recorded party-unity votes in 2008 on which a senator voted "yea" or "nay" in disagreement with a majority of his or her party. Percentages are based on votes cast; thus, failure to vote does not lower a member's score.

3. Participation in Party-Unity Votes. Percentage of the 111 recorded Senate party-unity votes in 2008 for which a senator was eligible and present and voted "yea" or "nay."

	1	2	3		1	2	3
ALABAMA				**MONTANA**			
Shelby	95	5	99	Baucus	89	11	99
Sessions	98	2	99	Tester	92	8	100
ALASKA				**NEBRASKA**			
Stevens	73	27	94	Hagel	78	22	89
Murkowski	72	28	99	Nelson	72	28	98
ARIZONA				**NEVADA**			
McCain	93	7	25	Reid	84	16	100
Kyl	100	0	99	Ensign	100	0	95
ARKANSAS				**NEW HAMPSHIRE**			
Lincoln	81	19	100	Gregg	95	5	97
Pryor	79	21	100	Sununu	87	13	97
CALIFORNIA				**NEW JERSEY**			
Feinstein	91	9	99	Lautenberg	99	1	96
Boxer	99	1	97	Menendez	98	2	99
COLORADO				**NEW MEXICO**			
Allard	100	0	97	Domenici	81	19	89
Salazar	87	13	100	Bingaman	99	1	98
CONNECTICUT				**NEW YORK**			
Dodd	96	4	98	Schumer	98	2	100
Lieberman	81	19	97	Clinton	99	1	61
DELAWARE				**NORTH CAROLINA**			
Biden	97	3	88	Dole	72	28	95
Carper	80	20	99	Burr	99	1	97
FLORIDA				**NORTH DAKOTA**			
Nelson	89	11	97	Conrad	91	9	96
Martinez	78	22	99	Dorgan	92	8	97
GEORGIA				**OHIO**			
Chambliss	95	5	100	Voinovich	67	33	100
Isakson	94	6	98	Brown	97	3	100
HAWAII				**OKLAHOMA**			
Inouye	83	17	92	Inhofe	99	1	95
Akaka	99	1	99	Coburn	99	1	95
IDAHO				**OREGON**			
Craig	94	6	96	Wyden	97	3	98
Crapo	94	6	97	Smith	54	46	98
ILLINOIS				**PENNSYLVANIA**			
Durbin*	98	2	100	Specter	62	38	98
Obama*	95	5	52	Casey	93	7	100
INDIANA				**RHODE ISLAND**			
Lugar	81	19	98	Reed	99	1	100
Bayh	65	35	95	Whitehouse	95	5	99
IOWA				**SOUTH CAROLINA**			
Grassley	93	7	100	Graham	97	3	83
Harkin	97	3	97	DeMint	100	0	97
KANSAS				**SOUTH DAKOTA**			
Brownback	94	6	99	Johnson	80	20	100
Roberts	87	13	99	Thune	95	5	100
KENTUCKY				**TENNESSEE**			
McConnell	97	3	100	Alexander	92	8	91
Bunning	95	5	95	Corker	90	10	95
LOUISIANA				**TEXAS**			
Landrieu	69	31	97	Hutchison	94	6	97
Vitter	98	2	100	Cornyn	97	3	95
MAINE				**UTAH**			
Snowe	39	61	100	Hatch	93	7	99
Collins	46	54	100	Bennett	85	15	99
MARYLAND				**VERMONT**			
Mikulski	88	12	98	Leahy	98	2	100
Cardin	97	3	99	*Sanders*	98	2	100
MASSACHUSETTS				**VIRGINIA**			
Kennedy	99	1	66	Warner	75	25	92
Kerry	98	2	97	Webb	89	11	97
MICHIGAN				**WASHINGTON**			
Levin	97	3	99	Murray	99	1	98
Stabenow	98	2	99	Cantwell	97	3	100
MINNESOTA				**WEST VIRGINIA**			
Coleman	69	31	97	Byrd	95	5	68
Klobuchar	94	6	98	Rockefeller	84	16	97
MISSISSIPPI				**WISCONSIN**			
Cochran	85	15	97	Kohl	94	6	100
Wicker	94	6	98	Feingold	93	7	100
MISSOURI				**WYOMING**			
Bond	92	8	94	Enzi	99	1	100
McCaskill	81	19	97	Barrasso	99	1	100

KEY **Republicans**   Democrats   *Independents*

*Sen. Barack Obama, D-Ill., resigned effective Nov. 16. The last vote for which Obama was eligible was vote 213. He was eligible for all but one presidential support vote in 2008.

Voting Participation Scores Drop

GIVEN MEMBERS' NEED TO CAMPAIGN, congressional leaders didn't try to keep up the record-breaking pace of voting that they established in 2007. The lack of common ground between Democrats and the outgoing president, a campaign-driven drop in the number of legislative days and a derailed appropriations process made for far fewer roll call votes than a year before.

House lawmakers were called to the floor 690 times in 2008, twice for quorum calls and 688 times to cast "yea" or "nay" votes, down 40 percent from 2007. Even so, the number of House roll calls was historically high — the fifth highest since Congressional Quarterly began analyzing members' voting practices. Senate voting dropped more precipitously, with the roll called only 215 times in 2008. That's half as many as in 2007 and the lowest since 1961.

At the same time, fewer lawmakers seemed concerned about perfect attendance. Only 11 lawmakers — nine senators and two House members — made it to the floor for every vote held in 2008 , down from 13 in 2007 and 27 in 2006. Sen. Charles E. Grassley of Iowa held on to the longest-running perfect attendance record; the last roll call he missed was in July 1993. Weekend votes in both the House and the Senate may have cut into the number with perfect attendance. And a Republican walkout in the House over a domestic surveillance bill also may have contributed to the falloff.

On average, House and Senate lawmakers alike showed up to vote slightly less often in 2008 than in most of the previous 20 years. For both chambers, lawmakers on average participated in 94.3 percent of the votes for which they were eligible.

In part, the low scores resulted from a large number of missed votes by some presidential contenders and a few ailing members. In the Senate, presidential candidates had the lowest participation rates in each party. Republican John McCain of Arizona made only 20 percent of roll calls — missing almost six straight months of votes. Democrat Barack Obama of Illinois, with a participation score of 36 percent, and his party rival Hillary Rodham Clinton of New York, with 51 percent, made few more.

The next two lowest participation scorers in the Senate both had health issues and missed more than 25 percent of their votes. Democrat Edward M. Kennedy of Massachusetts underwent extensive treatment for a brain tumor diagnosed in May, and fellow Democrat Robert C. Byrd of West Virginia, the oldest member of Congress, was hospitalized several times. More than half the senators voted about 97 percent of the time.

In the House, half the members voted at least 96 percent of the time. Illness curtailed the participation of Democrat Bobby L. Rush of Illinois, who fought off cancer of the salivary gland and cast a quarter of his eligible votes.

CQ gives lawmakers credit for voting only when they cast a "yea" or a "nay" during a roll call. On rare occasions, members vote "present" either to avoid a perceived conflict of interest or to stage a protest. Often, those votes aren't explained; regardless, CQ doesn't count members who vote present as having participated in the vote. ■

Participation in Floor Votes Falls Off

This year marked a recent low point for lawmaker participation in roll call votes in both chambers. The average House member voted 94.3 percent of the time this year, down from 95.5 percent in 2007, when almost twice as many roll call votes were held. That was the lowest score for the chamber since 2004, when members cast "yea" or "nay" votes 94.1 percent of the time. The average senator also voted 94.3 percent of the time in 2008, the lowest in 21 years. In both chambers, absences for campaigning cut into lawmaker attendance.

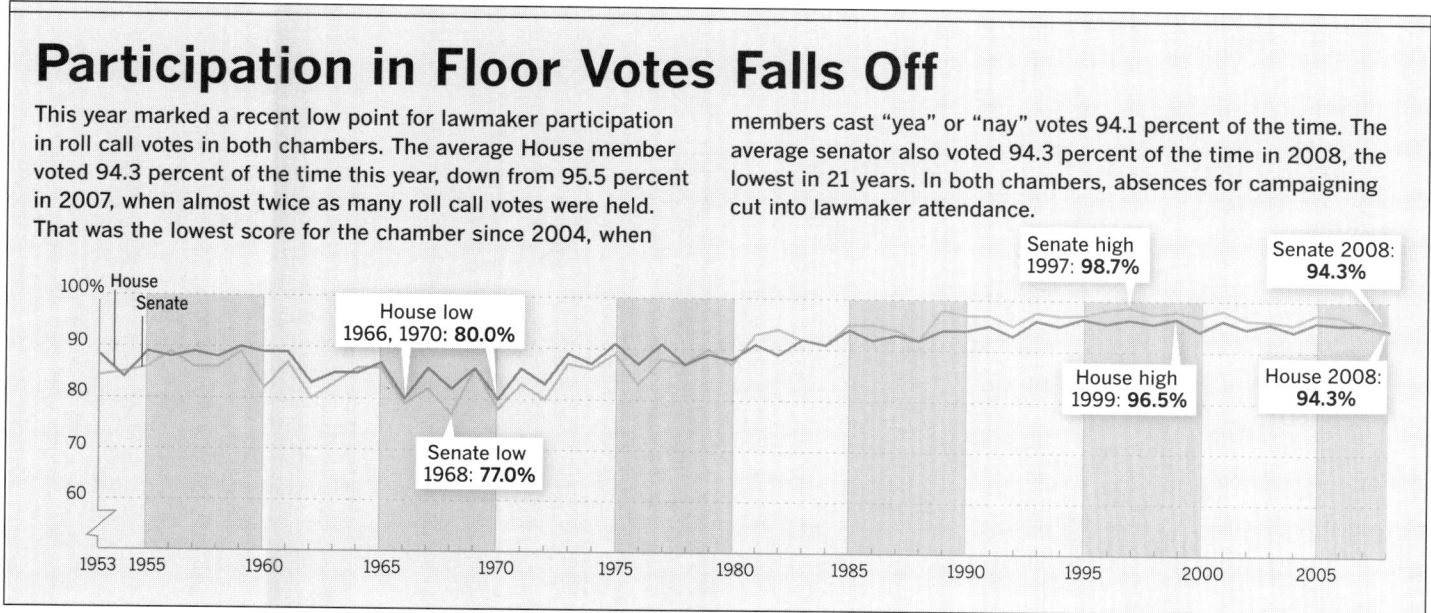

Voting Participation History

These tables show the number of roll call votes in each chamber and in Congress as a whole since 1953 and the frequency with which lawmakers on average cast "yea" or "nay" votes. Participation in floor votes had held close to 95 percent since the mid-1990s.

YEAR	House		Senate		Congress as a Whole	
	ROLL CALLS	RATE	ROLL CALLS	RATE	ROLL CALLS	RATE
2008	688	94.3%	215	94.3%	903	94.3%
2007	1,177	95.5	442	95.0	1,619	95.4
2006	541	95.5	279	97.1	820	95.7
2005	669	95.9	366	97.4	1,035	96.1
2004	543	94.1	216	95.5	759	94.2
2003	675	95.6	459	96.1	1,134	95.7
2002	483	94.6	253	96.3	736	94.8
2001	507	96.2	380	98.2	887	96.5
2000	600	94.1	298	96.9	898	94.4
1999	609	96.5	374	97.9	983	96.6
1998	533	95.5	314	97.4	847	95.7
1997	633	96.3	298	98.7	931	96.5
1996	454	95.5	306	98.2	760	95.8
1995	867	96.4	613	97.1	1,480	96.5
1994	497	95.0	329	97.0	826	95.0
1993	597	96.0	395	97.6	992	96.0
1992	473	93.0	270	95.0	743	93.4
1991	428	95.0	280	97.0	708	95.0
1990	536	94.0	326	97.0	862	95.0
1989	368	94.0	312	98.0	680	95.0
1988	451	92.0	379	92.0	830	92.0
1987	488	93.0	420	94.0	908	93.0
1986	451	92.0	354	95.0	805	93.0
1985	439	94.0	381	95.0	820	94.0
1984	408	91.0	275	91.0	683	91.0
1983	498	92.0	371	92.0	869	92.0
1982	459	89.0	465	94.0	924	90.0
1981	353	91.0	483	93.0	836	92.0
1980	604	88.0	531	87.0	1,135	87.0
1979	672	89.0	497	90.0	1,169	89.0
1978	834	87.0	516	87.0	1,350	87.0
1977	706	91.0	635	88.0	1,341	90.0
1976	661	87.0	688	83.0	1,349	86.0
1975	612	91.0	602	89.0	1,214	91.0
1974	537	87.0	544	86.0	1,081	87.0
1973	541	89.0	594	87.0	1,135	89.0
1972	329	83.0	532	80.0	861	82.0
1971	320	86.0	423	83.0	743	85.0
1970	266	80.0	418	78.0	684	79.0
1969	177	86.0	245	86.0	422	86.0
1968	233	82.0	281	77.0	514	80.0
1967	245	86.0	315	82.0	560	85.0
1966	193	80.0	235	79.0	428	79.0
1965	201	87.0	258	86.0	459	87.0
1964	113	85.0	305	86.0	418	85.0
1963	119	85.0	229	83.0	348	84.0
1962	124	83.0	224	80.0	348	82.0
1961	116	89.0	204	87.0	320	88.0
1960	93	89.0	207	82.0	300	87.0
1959	87	90.0	215	89.0	302	89.0
1958	93	88.0	200	86.0	293	87.0
1957	100	89.0	107	86.0	207	88.0
1956	73	88.0	130	89.0	203	88.0
1955	76	89.0	87	86.0	163	88.0
1954	76	84.0	171	85.0	247	84.0
1953	71	88.2	89	84.3	160	87.4

Perfect Records Of Attendance

Although voting participation slipped a bit in both chambers in 2008, it remained high by historical standards. Still, relatively few lawmakers had perfect attendance on roll call votes. Just two House members — both Democrats — and nine senators — five Democrats and four Republicans — participated in every recorded vote held in 2008.

Perfect Attendance, House

Democrats
Jason Altmire of Pennsylvania
Jesse L. Jackson Jr. of Illinois

Perfect Attendance, Senate

Democrats
Bob Casey of Pennsylvania
Richard J. Durbin of Illinois
Russ Feingold of Wisconsin
Tim Johnson of South Dakota
Herb Kohl of Wisconsin

Republicans
John Barrasso of Wyoming
Susan Collins of Maine
Charles E. Grassley of Iowa
Mitch McConnell of Kentucky

(In the House, 45 Democrats and 34 Republicans participated in 99 percent of all roll call votes for which they were eligible. In addition, new member Marcia L. Fudge, D-Ohio, had a 100 percent score on the seven votes for which she was eligible. In the Senate, 17 Democrats and 10 Republicans had a 99 percent participation score.)

SENATE

1. Voting Participation. Percentage of 215 recorded votes in 2008 on which a senator was eligible and present, and voted "yea" or "nay."

2. Voting Participation (without motions to instruct). Percentage of 212 recorded votes in 2008 on which a senator was eligible and present, and voted "yea" or "nay." In this version of the study, three votes to instruct the sergeant at arms to request the attendance of absent senators were excluded.

Absences because of illness. Congressional Quarterly no longer designates members who missed votes because of illness. In the past, notations to that effect were based on official statements published in the Congressional Record, but these were found to be inconsistently used.

Rounding. Scores are rounded to the nearest percentage point, except that no scores are rounded up to 100 percent. Senators with a 100 percent score participated in all recorded votes for which they were eligible.

	1	2			1	2
ALABAMA				**MONTANA**		
Shelby	99	99		Baucus	99	99
Sessions	99	99		Tester	98	98
ALASKA				**NEBRASKA**		
Stevens	95	96		Hagel	87	87
Murkowski	97	97		Nelson	97	97
ARIZONA				**NEVADA**		
McCain	20	20		Reid	99	99
Kyl	98	99		Ensign	94	95
ARKANSAS				**NEW HAMPSHIRE**		
Lincoln	99	99		Gregg	93	94
Pryor	99	99		Sununu	97	97
CALIFORNIA				**NEW JERSEY**		
Feinstein	99	99		Lautenberg	95	96
Boxer	94	94		Menendez	97	98
COLORADO				**NEW MEXICO**		
Allard	94	95		Domenici	90	91
Salazar	99	99		Bingaman	99	99
CONNECTICUT				**NEW YORK**		
Dodd	98	98		Schumer	99	100
Lieberman	94	95		Clinton	51	51
DELAWARE				**NORTH CAROLINA**		
Biden	83	84		Dole	92	92
Carper	99	99		Burr	96	96
FLORIDA				**NORTH DAKOTA**		
Nelson	98	99		Conrad	97	97
Martinez	98	98		Dorgan	97	97
GEORGIA				**OHIO**		
Chambliss	98	98		Voinovich	99	100
Isakson	98	99		Brown	99	99
HAWAII				**OKLAHOMA**		
Inouye	88	90		Inhofe	92	92
Akaka	99	100		Coburn	94	94
IDAHO				**OREGON**		
Craig	97	97		Wyden	98	99
Crapo	99	99		Smith	99	99
ILLINOIS				**PENNSYLVANIA**		
Durbin	100	100		Specter	98	99
Obama[1]	36	36		Casey	100	100
INDIANA				**RHODE ISLAND**		
Lugar	98	98		Reed	99	99
Bayh	96	97		Whitehouse	99	100
IOWA				**SOUTH CAROLINA**		
Grassley	100	100		Graham	86	86
Harkin	96	96		DeMint	94	94
KANSAS				**SOUTH DAKOTA**		
Brownback	97	98		Johnson	100	100
Roberts	98	99		Thune	99	99
KENTUCKY				**TENNESSEE**		
McConnell	100	100		Alexander	91	91
Bunning	94	95		Corker	96	96
LOUISIANA				**TEXAS**		
Landrieu	94	94		Hutchison	97	97
Vitter	97	97		Cornyn	92	92
MAINE				**UTAH**		
Snowe	99	99		Hatch	99	99
Collins	100	100		Bennett	99	99
MARYLAND				**VERMONT**		
Mikulski	97	97		Leahy	99	99
Cardin	99	99		*Sanders*	99	99
MASSACHUSETTS				**VIRGINIA**		
Kennedy	58	59		Warner	88	88
Kerry	97	97		Webb	98	98
MICHIGAN				**WASHINGTON**		
Levin	99	99		Murray	96	96
Stabenow	98	98		Cantwell	99	99
MINNESOTA				**WEST VIRGINIA**		
Coleman	96	96		Byrd	74	75
Klobuchar	98	98		Rockefeller	97	97
MISSISSIPPI				**WISCONSIN**		
Cochran	98	99		Kohl	100	100
Wicker	95	96		Feingold	100	100
MISSOURI				**WYOMING**		
Bond	93	94		Enzi	99	99
McCaskill	94	94		Barrasso	100	100

KEY   **Republicans**   Democrats   *Independents*

[1] Sen. Barack Obama, D-Ill., resigned effective Nov. 16. The last vote for which Obama was eligible was vote 213.

HOUSE

1. Voting Participation. Percentage of 688 recorded votes in 2008 on which a representative was eligible and present, and voted "yea" or "nay." Quorum calls, although they are included in the House list of recorded roll calls, are not counted as votes because lawmakers are only asked to respond "present."

2. Voting Participation (without Journal votes). Percentage of 675 recorded votes in 2008 on which a representative was eligible and present, and voted "yea" or "nay." In this version of the study, 13 votes on motions to approve the House Journal were excluded.

Absences because of illness. Congressional Quarterly no longer designates members who missed votes because of illness. In the past, notations to that effect were based on official statements published in the Congressional Record, but these were found to be inconsistently used.

Rounding. Scores are rounded to the nearest percentage point, except that no scores are rounded up to 100 percent. Members with a 100 percent score participated in all recorded votes for which they were eligible.

[1] The Speaker votes only at her discretion.

[2] Rep. Jackie Speier, D-Calif., was sworn in April 10 to fill the seat vacated by the death of Democrat Tom Lantos on Feb. 11. The first vote for which Speier was eligible was vote 179; the last vote for which Lantos was eligible was vote 42. Lantos did not participate in any roll call votes in 2008.

[3] Rep. Bill Foster, D-Ill., was sworn in March 11. The first vote for which he was eligible was vote 116.

[4] Rep. André Carson, D-Ind., was sworn in March 13 to fill the seat vacated by the death of Democrat Julia Carson on Dec. 15, 2007. The first vote for which he was eligible was vote 140.

[5] Rep. Steve Scalise, R-La., was sworn in May 7 to fill the seat vacated by Republican Bobby Jindal, who resigned Jan. 14 to become governor. The first vote for which Scalise was eligible was vote 268; Jindal was not eligible for any roll call votes in 2008.

[6] Rep. Don Cazayoux, D-La., was sworn in May 6 to fill the seat vacated by Republican Richard H. Baker, who resigned Feb. 2. The first vote for which Cazayoux was eligible was vote 247; the last vote for which Baker was eligible was vote 28.

[7] Rep. Donna Edwards, D-Md., was sworn in June 19 to replace Democrat Albert R. Wynn, who resigned effective May 31. The first vote for which Edwards was eligible was vote 427. The last vote for which Wynn was eligible was vote 366.

[8] Rep. Travis W. Childers, D-Miss., was sworn in May 20. The first vote for which he was eligible was vote 332.

[9] Rep. Marcia L. Fudge, D-Ohio, was sworn in Nov. 19 to replace Democrat Stephanie Tubbs Jones, who died Aug. 20, 2008. The first vote for which Fudge was eligible was vote 684. The last vote for which Tubbs Jones was eligible was vote 566.

[10] Rep. Thomas M. Davis III, R-Va., resigned Nov. 24. The last vote for which he was eligible was vote 683.

	1	2
ALABAMA		
1 **Bonner**	95	95
2 **Everett**	89	89
3 **Rogers**	97	97
4 **Aderholt**	95	95
5 Cramer	89	89
6 **Bachus**	92	92
7 Davis	98	98
ALASKA		
AL **Young**	84	85
ARIZONA		
1 **Renzi**	83	83
2 **Franks**	98	98
3 **Shadegg**	98	98
4 Pastor	99	99
5 Mitchell	97	97
6 **Flake**	96	96
7 Grijalva	91	91
8 Giffords	98	98
ARKANSAS		
1 Berry	95	95
2 Snyder	95	96
3 **Boozman**	99	99
4 Ross	99	99
CALIFORNIA		
1 Thompson	99	99
2 **Herger**	97	97
3 **Lungren**	97	97
4 **Doolittle**	88	88
5 Matsui	99	100
6 Woolsey	85	85
7 Miller, George	93	93
8 Pelosi[1]	9	9
9 Lee	95	96
10 Tauscher	98	98
11 McNerney	98	98
12 Speier[2]	83	84
13 Stark	87	88
14 Eshoo	99	99
15 Honda	91	91
16 Lofgren	98	98
17 Farr	96	96
18 Cardoza	95	95
19 **Radanovich**	89	89
20 Costa	93	93
21 **Nunes**	96	96
22 **McCarthy**	98	98
23 Capps	99	99
24 **Gallegly**	95	95
25 **McKeon**	98	98
26 **Dreier**	96	96
27 Sherman	97	97
28 Berman	94	94
29 Schiff	99	99
30 Waxman	94	94
31 Becerra	97	97
32 Solis	95	95
33 Watson	96	96
34 Roybal-Allard	98	98
35 Waters	92	92
36 Harman	93	93
37 Richardson	91	91
38 Napolitano	98	98
39 Sánchez, Linda	98	98
40 **Royce**	98	98
41 **Lewis**	98	98
42 **Miller, Gary**	91	91
43 Baca	94	94
44 **Calvert**	97	96
45 **Bono Mack**	95	95
46 **Rohrabacher**	90	90
47 Sanchez, Loretta	94	94
48 **Campbell**	84	84
49 **Issa**	96	96
50 **Bilbray**	97	97
51 Filner	95	95
52 **Hunter**	86	86
53 Davis	99	99

	1	2
COLORADO		
1 DeGette	96	96
2 Udall	78	79
3 Salazar	99	99
4 **Musgrave**	95	95
5 **Lamborn**	99	99
6 **Tancredo**	83	84
7 Perlmutter	98	98
CONNECTICUT		
1 Larson	95	95
2 Courtney	99	99
3 DeLauro	98	98
4 **Shays**	96	96
5 Murphy	99	99
DELAWARE		
AL **Castle**	99	99
FLORIDA		
1 **Miller**	96	97
2 Boyd	99	99
3 Brown	87	87
4 **Crenshaw**	90	90
5 **Brown-Waite**	79	79
6 **Stearns**	99	99
7 **Mica**	99	99
8 Keller	92	92
9 **Bilirakis**	99	99
10 **Young**	94	95
11 Castor	94	94
12 **Putnam**	94	94
13 **Buchanan**	99	99
14 **Mack**	92	92
15 **Weldon**	84	84
16 Mahoney	95	95
17 Meek	93	93
18 **Ros-Lehtinen**	95	95
19 Wexler	85	85
20 Wasserman Schultz	97	96
21 **Diaz-Balart, L.**	93	93
22 Klein	99	99
23 Hastings	95	95
24 **Feeney**	89	89
25 **Diaz-Balart, M.**	94	95
GEORGIA		
1 **Kingston**	93	93
2 Bishop	95	95
3 **Westmoreland**	97	97
4 Johnson	97	97
5 Lewis	95	95
6 **Price**	98	98
7 **Linder**	94	94
8 Marshall	95	96
9 **Deal**	95	95
10 **Broun**	97	97
11 **Gingrey**	95	95
12 Barrow	97	97
13 Scott	98	98
HAWAII		
1 Abercrombie	94	94
2 Hirono	98	98
IDAHO		
1 **Sali**	99	99
2 **Simpson**	96	96
ILLINOIS		
1 Rush	25	25
2 Jackson	100	100
3 Lipinski	96	96
4 Gutierrez	84	84
5 Emanuel	97	97
6 **Roskam**	98	97
7 Davis	93	93
8 Bean	96	96
9 Schakowsky	99	99
10 **Kirk**	97	97
11 **Weller**	79	79
12 Costello	94	94
13 **Biggert**	98	98
14 Foster[3]	99	99
15 **Johnson**	92	92

KEY   **Republicans**   Democrats

Member	1	2
16 Manzullo	97	97
17 Hare	97	97
18 LaHood	90	90
19 Shimkus	93	93
INDIANA		
1 Visclosky	97	97
2 Donnelly	99	99
3 Souder	95	95
4 Buyer	91	91
5 Burton	92	92
6 Pence	91	92
7 Carson, A.[4]	95	95
8 Ellsworth	99	99
9 Hill	97	96
IOWA		
1 Braley	92	92
2 Loebsack	93	93
3 Boswell	88	88
4 Latham	99	99
5 King	98	98
KANSAS		
1 Moran	97	97
2 Boyda	98	98
3 Moore	99	99
4 Tiahrt	93	93
KENTUCKY		
1 Whitfield	96	96
2 Lewis	91	91
3 Yarmuth	99	99
4 Davis	98	98
5 Rogers	99	99
6 Chandler	99	99
LOUISIANA		
1 Scalise[5]	99	99
2 Jefferson	88	88
3 Melancon	95	95
4 McCrery	86	85
5 Alexander	94	94
6 Baker[6]	7	7
6 Cazayoux[6]	96	96
7 Boustany	96	96
MAINE		
1 Allen	97	97
2 Michaud	99	99
MARYLAND		
1 Gilchrest	78	78
2 Ruppersberger	91	91
3 Sarbanes	99	99
4 Wynn[7]	72	72
4 Edwards[7]	98	98
5 Hoyer	99	99
6 Bartlett	99	99
7 Cummings	95	95
8 Van Hollen	99	99
MASSACHUSETTS		
1 Olver	99	99
2 Neal	92	92
3 McGovern	99	99
4 Frank	96	96
5 Tsongas	99	99
6 Tierney	94	94
7 Markey	97	97
8 Capuano	97	97
9 Lynch	98	97
10 Delahunt	90	90
MICHIGAN		
1 Stupak	99	99
2 Hoekstra	97	97
3 Ehlers	96	96
4 Camp	99	99
5 Kildee	99	99
6 Upton	99	99
7 Walberg	97	97
8 Rogers	97	97
9 Knollenberg	97	97
10 Miller	99	99
11 McCotter	98	98
12 Levin	94	94
13 Kilpatrick	93	93
14 Conyers	91	91
15 Dingell	94	94
MINNESOTA		
1 Walz	99	99
2 Kline	99	99
3 Ramstad	99	99
4 McCollum	98	98
5 Ellison	93	93
6 Bachmann	98	98
7 Peterson	94	94
8 Oberstar	89	89
MISSISSIPPI		
1 Childers[8]	99	99
2 Thompson	93	93
3 Pickering	85	85
4 Taylor	96	96
MISSOURI		
1 Clay	97	97
2 Akin	98	98
3 Carnahan	95	95
4 Skelton	99	99
5 Cleaver	98	98
6 Graves	95	95
7 Blunt	93	93
8 Emerson	97	97
9 Hulshof	58	58
MONTANA		
AL Rehberg	99	99
NEBRASKA		
1 Fortenberry	95	95
2 Terry	97	97
3 Smith	99	99
NEVADA		
1 Berkley	95	95
2 Heller	98	98
3 Porter	98	97
NEW HAMPSHIRE		
1 Shea-Porter	98	98
2 Hodes	96	96
NEW JERSEY		
1 Andrews	76	76
2 LoBiondo	99	99
3 Saxton	87	87
4 Smith	97	97
5 Garrett	98	98
6 Pallone	98	98
7 Ferguson	88	89
8 Pascrell	93	93
9 Rothman	95	95
10 Payne	91	91
11 Frelinghuysen	98	98
12 Holt	98	98
13 Sires	94	94
NEW MEXICO		
1 Wilson	86	86
2 Pearce	94	94
3 Udall	92	92
NEW YORK		
1 Bishop	95	96
2 Israel	97	97
3 King	97	97
4 McCarthy	98	98
5 Ackerman	96	96
6 Meeks	90	90
7 Crowley	98	98
8 Nadler	94	94
9 Weiner	90	90
10 Towns	91	91
11 Clarke	99	99
12 Velázquez	96	96
13 Fossella	87	87
14 Maloney	93	93
15 Rangel	84	84
16 Serrano	99	99
17 Engel	90	89
18 Lowey	94	94
19 Hall	98	98
20 Gillibrand	87	87
21 McNulty	96	96
22 Hinchey	94	94
23 McHugh	99	99
24 Arcuri	99	99
25 Walsh	93	93
26 Reynolds	90	90
27 Higgins	95	95
28 Slaughter	94	94
29 Kuhl	97	97
NORTH CAROLINA		
1 Butterfield	93	93
2 Etheridge	99	99
3 Jones	94	95
4 Price	99	99
5 Foxx	99	99
6 Coble	97	97
7 McIntyre	99	99
8 Hayes	98	98
9 Myrick	95	95
10 McHenry	94	94
11 Shuler	91	91
12 Watt	99	99
13 Miller	98	98
NORTH DAKOTA		
AL Pomeroy	98	98
OHIO		
1 Chabot	98	98
2 Schmidt	95	95
3 Turner	96	96
4 Jordan	99	99
5 Latta	99	99
6 Wilson	97	97
7 Hobson	95	95
8 Boehner	92	92
9 Kaptur	95	95
10 Kucinich	99	99
11 Tubbs Jones[9]	81	81
11 Fudge[9]	100	100
12 Tiberi	97	96
13 Sutton	96	96
14 LaTourette	95	95
15 Pryce	65	65
16 Regula	97	97
17 Ryan	95	95
18 Space	96	96
OKLAHOMA		
1 Sullivan	95	95
2 Boren	99	99
3 Lucas	95	95
4 Cole	96	96
5 Fallin	98	98
OREGON		
1 Wu	97	97
2 Walden	95	95
3 Blumenauer	97	97
4 DeFazio	97	97
5 Hooley	89	89
PENNSYLVANIA		
1 Brady	97	97
2 Fattah	94	95
3 English	97	96
4 Altmire	100	100
5 Peterson	72	72
6 Gerlach	94	95
7 Sestak	94	94
8 Murphy, P.	98	98
9 Shuster	98	98
10 Carney	97	97
11 Kanjorski	99	99
12 Murtha	93	93
13 Schwartz	97	97
14 Doyle	93	93
15 Dent	99	99
16 Pitts	90	90
17 Holden	98	98
18 Murphy, T.	97	97
19 Platts	97	97
RHODE ISLAND		
1 Kennedy	92	93
2 Langevin	96	96
SOUTH CAROLINA		
1 Brown	99	99
2 Wilson	97	97
3 Barrett	97	97
4 Inglis	98	98
5 Spratt	97	97
6 Clyburn	98	98
SOUTH DAKOTA		
AL Herseth Sandlin	98	98
TENNESSEE		
1 Davis, D.	98	98
2 Duncan	99	99
3 Wamp	96	96
4 Davis, L.	95	95
5 Cooper	96	96
6 Gordon	94	94
7 Blackburn	94	94
8 Tanner	94	94
9 Cohen	96	96
TEXAS		
1 Gohmert	90	91
2 Poe	92	92
3 Johnson, S.	96	96
4 Hall	97	97
5 Hensarling	99	99
6 Barton	95	95
7 Culberson	92	92
8 Brady	93	93
9 Green, A.	95	95
10 McCaul	97	97
11 Conaway	92	93
12 Granger	90	90
13 Thornberry	99	99
14 Paul	83	83
15 Hinojosa	88	87
16 Reyes	92	92
17 Edwards	96	96
18 Jackson Lee	90	90
19 Neugebauer	95	95
20 Gonzalez	94	94
21 Smith	97	97
22 Lampson	92	92
23 Rodriguez	98	98
24 Marchant	89	89
25 Doggett	93	93
26 Burgess	93	93
27 Ortiz	88	88
28 Cuellar	97	97
29 Green, G.	94	94
30 Johnson, E.	94	94
31 Carter	93	93
32 Sessions	96	96
UTAH		
1 Bishop	89	89
2 Matheson	99	99
3 Cannon	81	81
VERMONT		
AL Welch	98	98
VIRGINIA		
1 Wittman	99	99
2 Drake	97	97
3 Scott	98	98
4 Forbes	92	92
5 Goode	99	99
6 Goodlatte	99	99
7 Cantor	96	96
8 Moran	93	92
9 Boucher	89	89
10 Wolf	98	98
11 Davis[10]	89	89
WASHINGTON		
1 Inslee	98	98
2 Larsen	98	98
3 Baird	96	96
4 Hastings	95	95
5 McMorris Rodgers	96	96
6 Dicks	93	93
7 McDermott	97	97
8 Reichert	99	99
9 Smith	94	93
WEST VIRGINIA		
1 Mollohan	94	95
2 Capito	97	97
3 Rahall	99	99
WISCONSIN		
1 Ryan	97	97
2 Baldwin	99	99
3 Kind	97	95
4 Moore	97	97
5 Sensenbrenner	96	96
6 Petri	99	99
7 Obey	98	98
8 Kagen	97	97
WYOMING		
AL Cubin	60	60
DELEGATES		
Faleomavaega (A.S.)	63	63
Norton (D.C.)	89	89
Bordallo (Guam)	89	89
Fortuño (P.R.)	39	39
Christensen (V.I.)	77	77

Appendix C

KEY VOTES

Financial Rescues, Pivotal Roll Calls: Recession Forces Painful Choices

NOT SINCE THE VOTE in December 1998 to impeach President Bill Clinton had a roll call in Congress drawn as much attention as the initial House rejection of President Bush's plan to save the nation's credit industry. From traders on Wall Street to bankers on Main Street, as well as in Europe and Asia, the world watched House vote 674 with the same intensity usually reserved for celebrity deaths, World Cup finals or highway car chases. There was even a video of it on YouTube.

After the vote was gaveled to a close at 205-228, the Dow Jones industrial average plummeted, losing more points in one day than it had in its 112-year history. At the same time, on radio and television talk shows and on blogs and other Internet forums, average Americans — who had decried the administration's $700 billion asset-buying plan as an unwarranted bailout of big banks — cheered the outcome.

House leaders had scheduled the vote on the hastily written bill (HR 3997) just one day after they reached agreement on its details with their counterparts in the Senate and with Treasury Secretary Henry M. Paulson Jr. and other administration officials. They pleaded their case to the rank and file: Without this bill, leaders insisted, the economy could fall into the deepest recession in 75 years. At the same time, phones and e-mail boxes on the Hill were carrying a different message from very angry constituents: Say "no" to the bailout.

"I don't know that they get much tougher than this," Minority Leader John A. Boehner, R-Ohio, said in his floor speech preceding the vote.

The political, economic and historic consequences of this roll call were enormous, and it easily qualified as one of the 24 key roll call votes of the year for Congress. Indeed, two others also were on the bailout issue: the Senate's vote Oct. 1 to pass a revised version (HR 1424) and the House vote Oct. 3 (four days after the first vote) to clear that measure.

It was a year in which the downturn in the economy dictated the congressional agenda more than any other factor, including party or presidential politics. Nine of the House and Senate roll calls chosen by Congressional Quarterly editors as key votes of the second session of the 110th Congress were on measures intended to boost some sector of the economy.

Two of those — one each in the House and Senate — occurred early in the year on a bill (HR 5140) to give $600 in rebates to most taxpayers. Lawmakers cast their votes for the legislation in the hopes that it would be enough to spur consumer spending and stave off recession. But by summer, the extent of decline in the housing market had become clearer, and Congress agreed — somewhat reluctantly — to give

---

How CQ Picks Key Votes

Since its founding in 1945, Congressional Quarterly has selected a series of key votes for both the House and Senate on major issues of the year.

A vote is judged to be key by the extent to which it represents:

- a matter of major controversy.
- a matter of presidential or political power.
- a matter of potentially great impact on the nation and lives of Americans.

For each group of related votes in each chamber on an issue, one key vote is usually chosen — one that, in the opinion of CQ editors, was the most important in determining the outcome of the issue for the year or best reflected the views of the individual members of that issue.

---

the Treasury Department the authority (HR 3221) to buy the assets and stocks of the two giant mortgage financing companies, Fannie Mae and Freddie Mac. Weeks later, Treasury used that authority and put them into conservatorships despite earlier assertions that it might not need to go to that well.

Then in September, Paulson traveled to the Hill once again, pleading with House and Senate leaders to help him rescue the financial services industry, which was at risk of being choked to the point of collapse by unsalable mortgage-related assets. The rescue plan for which Paulson was seeking congressional authority was unprecedented in size and intent, and lawmakers — especially in the House — found themselves torn between a potential economic crisis and the reality of vocal constituent opposition.

The Senate vote to pass the revised bailout was preceded by a vote to substitute new language into an unrelated shell bill. Senators cast their vote on the substitute from their desks, a formality generally reserved for the most serious of roll calls such as the impeachment of a president. Two days later, the House again voted on the measure. By then, the economic picture had changed so much that 58 members switched their votes from "nay" to "yea." The president signed the bill into law less than two hours after the final House vote.

The final two key votes took place in the December lame-duck session. This time the group in distress was the nation's automakers, and congressional Democrats had negotiated with the White House a measure (HR 7321) that would make available a $14 billion short-term loan, with conditions, for General Motors Corp., Chrysler LLC and Ford Motor Co. The House went along with the deal on a party-line vote, but Senate Republicans could not swallow another bailout package and leaders eventually gave up.

Votes on economic issues were not the only ones that drew attention in 2008. Three of the key votes were chosen because they completed years-long efforts by Democrats to pass legislation on priority issues. With their new majority achieved in 2006, Democratic leaders found the necessary support to clear bills on mental health parity, genetic discrimination and the first reauthorization of Amtrak in a decade.

A handful of key votes represented attempts by lawmakers to separate themselves from Bush as they looked ahead to November. In some cases, they went against the administration. In other instances, particularly those related to foreign affairs and national security issues, Bush won.

Congressional Quarterly's editors selected 14 key votes for the House and 10 for the Senate. What follows are explanations of why these roll-call votes were chosen as the most noteworthy of the year.

HOUSE VOTES

42 Economic Stimulus

Clearing a bill to help stimulate the economy through a tax refund to most taxpayers of up to $600 for individuals and $1,200 for couples.

The vote to clear this bill took place just two weeks after the announcement of the deal, between House leaders and the administration, to create the measure. Senate Democrats had hoped to broaden the legislation to include unemployment benefits and energy tax incentives, and did in fact expand the tax refund to add low-income senior citizens and veterans, but in the end the bill was pretty much as it had been originally designed.

The fact that it moved so quickly through Congress, and that it was a rare example of accord between the two parties and between the legislative and executive branches, was a testament to just how seriously elected officials were starting to take the economic downturn that was becoming more evident. The nation lost jobs in January for the first time in more than four years, and consumer spending slowed sharply in December, according to reports by the Labor and Commerce departments that had been released the week before the final House vote.

By the end of the year, the economy's slump dominated the nation's attention and was a major factor in the election that put Barack Obama in the White House and expanded the Democrats' majorities in the House and Senate.

HOUSE CLEARED HR 5140 (PL 110-185) on Feb. 7, **380-34:** R 165-28; D 215-6. *(House vote 42, p. C-12; Senate vote 10, p. C-20; economic stimulus, p. 7-17)*

181 Colombia Trade Fast-Track Suspension

Adoption of a resolution that suspended "fast-track" requirements for considering a bill that would implement a U.S.-Colombia trade agreement.

This vote allowed House Democrats to sidestep a showdown over trade with the Bush White House after the administration sent Congress a proposed free-trade pact with Colombia. The agreement, opposed by many in the Democratic Caucus, was negotiated under the so-called fast-track procedure, which would have required Congress to cast an up-or-down vote without possibility of amendment.

The fast-track procedure had been used repeatedly over the years for trade agreements both large and small, and Congress had never before rejected a trade pact. The opposition to the Colombia agreement was seen as sufficiently large that House leaders did not want to take the chance on the pact being rejected outright and sending a signal to the world that the United States was backing away from general support for opening trade between countries.

House Speaker Nancy Pelosi, D-Calif., asked President Bush to withhold sending Congress legislation to implement the agreement until changes could be made that would satisfy opponents. Many Democrats were concerned about the violence against labor union officials

in Colombia, and they also wanted an expansion of benefits for U.S. workers who lost their jobs because of increasing international trade.

Bush, however, sent the implementing bill to Capitol Hill on April 8, which started the clock ticking on a potential vote. House Democratic leaders immediately introduced a resolution to change House rules and suspend fast-track procedures for the Colombia deal. That resolution was adopted on a near-party-line vote, putting action on the Colombia agreement on hold. House leaders declined for the rest of the year to say when they might restore the fast-track process or when the Colombia trade pact might be considered.

HOUSE ADOPTED H Res 1092 on April 10, **224-195:** R 6-185; D 218-10. *(House vote 181, p. C-12; trade agreements, p. 6-18)*

329 War Appropriations and Troop Withdrawal

Agreement to amend a war supplemental appropriations bill with language to require a troop withdrawal from Iraq within 30 days of enactment.

Just as they had done on several occasions in 2007, Democratic leaders decided to use a procedure that involved passing the supplemental through a series of votes on motions to concur that would allow lawmakers to tailor their votes on aspects of the measure without having to cast a single up-or-down vote on the bill. They planned votes on three amendments to the underlying measure, which in this case was the Military Construction appropriations bill left over from the previous fall's spending fights. One of the three amendments was for money to operate the wars in Iraq and Afghanistan; the second was to appropriate funds for domestic projects; and the third contained various conditions on U.S. war policy in Iraq, including a requirement that redeployment from Iraq begin within 30 days of enactment, with a "goal" of withdrawing most troops by December 2009. Splitting the measure into these three distinct parts allowed anti-war Democrats to vote against funding for military operations in Iraq and in favor of troop withdrawal. Conversely, it allowed Democrats from typically conservative districts to cast votes that were more in line with their constituents' viewpoints.

At the same time, House leaders and members casting those votes were well aware of the politics in the Senate, where the slim majority held by Democrats meant it would be unlikely that such troop withdrawal requirements could survive in a final bill.

Because efforts to dictate such terms in Iraq had failed repeatedly in the first session of the 110th Congress, and because other issues, such as the economy, were rising in priority, this was the only significant House vote on troop withdrawal in 2008. In fact, several of the Democrats' staunchest anti-war members — such as Maxine Waters and Lynn Woolsey, both of California — voted in favor of the troop withdrawal language, even though it was not as strong as they would have liked. They routinely voted against such language in 2007 because they wanted to see a more definitive deadline for withdrawal.

HOUSE AGREED to a motion to concur with the amendment on HR 2642 (PL 110-252) on May 15, **227-196:** R 8-183; D 219-13. *(House vote 329, p. C-12; war supplemental, p. 2-32)*

346 Farm Bill Reauthorization

Override of President Bush's veto of a bill to reauthorize federal farm and nutrition programs for five years.

With this vote, the second veto override in the Bush presidency, lawmakers showed that the generations-old affinity for financial assistance for farmers continued, despite push-back from the White House. Among other complaints with the legislation, Bush wanted a much lower income cap on eligibility requirements for payments than the final bill provided.

Congress ended up double-stamping this sentiment with a second override less than a month later, after it turned out the first version of the bill Bush had vetoed had been erroneously incomplete. Lawmakers hastily put together a new measure (HR 6124) with all the titles in place; Bush vetoed it June 18, and both chambers voted that same day to override that veto, enacting the bill into law (PL 110-246). This vote on the corrected measure was nearly identical to the first farm bill override: 317-109.

HOUSE PASSED, over President Bush's May 21 veto, HR 2419 (PL 110-234) on May 21, **316-108:** R 100-94; D 216-14. A two-thirds majority of those present and voting (283 in this case) of both chambers is required to override a veto. *(House vote 346, p. C-14; Senate vote 130, p. C-20; farm programs, p. 3-3)*

400 Amtrak Reauthorization

Passage of a bill to authorize $14.4 billion for Amtrak over five years.

House Democrats set the stage with this vote for enactment of the biggest federal intervention in passenger rail since 1997.

To win over enough Republicans to override a possible veto from President Bush, House leaders agreed to insert language to promote private development of a high-speed rail line from New York to Washington — even though Democrats had long resisted such a move. That provision had the potential to stall the bill in the Senate, home to many Amtrak fans but few supporters of privatizing the railroad. However, the rising price of gasoline at the pump during the summer put pressure on lawmakers to reauthorize the only nationwide passenger rail line, and the provisions from the House-passed bill, for the most part, survived House-Senate negotiations. The president chose not to press his earlier veto threat, and a similar Amtrak reauthorization (HR 2095 — PL 110-432), with rail-safety provisions attached to it, cleared Congress on Oct. 1.

HOUSE PASSED HR 6003 on June 11, **311-104:** R 87-104; D 224-0. *(House vote 400, p. C-14; Amtrak reauthorization, p. 3-16)*

437 Foreign Intelligence Surveillance

Passage of a bill to reauthorize the Foreign Intelligence Surveillance Act to include warrantless spying on foreign targets who might be communicating with people in the United States and to provide for the almost-certain dismissal of lawsuits against companies that assisted in President Bush's warrantless surveillance program.

With this vote, House Democrats essentially gave up a long-

running and spirited fight against giving the Bush administration unfettered power to spy on certain groups. Leaders had taken this battle to the brink in February by allowing provisions in a law (PL 110-55) enacted the previous August to expire. However, there were enough safety nets in place in that law to keep it effectively in force until August 2008.

But as that date drew closer — along with that of the November election — Democrats began to feel pressure to yield to the White House and Republicans and to move the legislation. House leaders drew up a new version of the bill that included some concessions to Democrats, such as a provision to strengthen the original law's statement that FISA was the only means by which the executive branch could conduct foreign-intelligence-related surveillance.

Many Democrats, despite their initial opposition, decided to vote for the measure because of the growing political pressures associated with the issue. This was particularly true in the House, where opposition to retroactive legal immunity for the telecommunications companies and expanded spying authority for Bush was stronger than it had been in the Senate. The House had resisted the president on that issue previously (HR 3773).

When a group of House Democrats — members of the fiscally conservative Blue Dog Coalition who favored an earlier Senate bill (S 2248) — began to agitate for an end to the fight, leaders inched toward the administration's position. Some Democrats said privately that they feared election fallout if they did not pass something that the president would sign, because Republicans could use it to attack them as weak on national security. Democratic party leaders, including Speaker Nancy Pelosi of California, voted for the bill.

The Senate cleared the bill July 9, and it became law July 11.

HOUSE PASSED HR 6304 (PL 110-261) on June 20, **293-129:** R 188-1; D 105-128. *(House vote 437, C-14; Senate vote 164, C-21; FISA rewrite, p. 6-12)*

443 Medicare Physicians' Pay

Passage of a bill to prevent a scheduled 10.6 percent cut in pay rates for doctors who participated in Medicare.

With election-year considerations weighing heavily on their minds, two-thirds of the Republicans present for this vote bucked their leadership and supported the bill, giving Democrats more than enough backing to ensure that a threatened veto could be overcome. The lopsided vote in the House suddenly and unexpectedly gave the bill impetus in the Senate, where opposition had been routine and steadfast.

Both parties had offered proposals to block the scheduled July 1 cut in Medicare payments to physicians. But Republicans and the White House objected to the offsetting cuts that House Democrats wanted to keep the legislation revenue-neutral.

House GOP leaders had urged their caucus to vote against the bill. Instead, at least a dozen Republicans changed their votes from "nay" to "yea" as the votes were tallied. The July Fourth recess was scheduled for the next week, and lawmakers wanted to be able to go home and tell physicians and patients that they did something to keep doctors from leaving Medicare.

"The House vote changes the dynamics," said Senate Finance Chairman Max Baucus, D-Mont. "If the House bill passed by such a large margin, there's an argument that it could pass over here, too."

The measure cleared the Senate on July 9, just after lawmakers returned from the recess.

HOUSE PASSED HR 6331 (PL 110-275) on June 24, **355-59:** R 129-59; D 226-0. The bill was considered under suspension of the rules, thereby requiring a two-thirds majority of those present and voting (276 in this case) for passage. *(House vote 443, C-16; Senate vote 169, p. C-21; Medicare doctors' pay, p. 9-3)*

519 Mortgage Relief

Passage of a bill to let the Treasury Department extend new credit to and buy stock in Fannie Mae and Freddie Mac and to help homeowners with loans they cannot afford.

A stalled effort to grant relief to homeowners facing foreclosure came to life in mid-July, when Treasury Secretary Henry M. Paulson Jr. abruptly asked Congress for the tools necessary to bail out Fannie Mae and Freddie Mac. The mortgage giants' share prices were plummeting as investors feared that the entire home loan market would collapse. The Bush administration had strongly objected to elements of the mortgage relief bill. But when the Fannie and Freddie bailout provisions were added to it, the White House reversed course and endorsed enactment. That gave congressional Democrats an opening, and with support from some Republicans, the House passed the measure.

HOUSE PASSED by adopting a motion to concur with the amendment on HR 3221 (PL 110-259) on July 23, **272-152:** R 45-149; D 227-3. *(House vote 519, p. C-16; Senate vote 186, p. C-21; mortgage relief, p. 7-9)*

531 Global AIDS Reauthorization

Clearing a bill to authorize $48 billion over five years for programs to fight AIDS, tuberculosis and malaria overseas.

Congress authorized a significant expansion in the efforts to fight AIDS, tuberculosis and malaria around the world. The bill represented a bipartisan compromise started by Tom Lantos, D-Calif. (1981-2008), and completed in February by Howard L. Berman, also of California, who took over the Foreign Affairs Committee after Lantos died.

Many Republicans, including President Bush and some fiscal conservatives, signed on to the large funding boost ($18 billion more than the administration had sought), and, in exchange, bill writers largely avoided the social-policy debates that had surrounded the program since it was created in 2003 (PL 108-25).

HOUSE CLEARED through a motion to concur on HR 5501 (PL 110-293) on July 24, **303-115:** R 75-114; D 228-1. *(House vote 531, p. C-16; global AIDS reauthorization, p. 6-9)*

542 Regulation of Tobacco Products

Passage of a bill to authorize the Food and Drug Administration to regulate tobacco products.

After more than a decade of trying, supporters of legislation that would give the FDA power to regulate tobacco products not only managed to push a bill through the House but were also able to do so by

a margin large enough to override a threatened veto.

However, the House acted on the measure just before the August recess, and the chances of getting it through the Senate before a planned adjournment in October were slim. So supporters on that side of the Capitol did not bring it up for a vote. With larger majorities in both chambers in the 111th Congress, Democrats were expected to build off their success in the House and try to clear the legislation.

HOUSE PASSED HR 1108 on July 30, **326-102:** R 96-99; D 230-3. *(House vote 542, p. C-16; tobacco regulation, p. 3-13)*

625 Mental Health Parity

Passage of a bill to require insurers to treat mental illness the same as other medical issues.

Passage of this bill in September showed a significant increase in support for mental health parity since a March vote on an earlier version (HR 1424). In that effort, 145 Republicans voted against the measure. After the March vote, supporters — led by Patrick J. Kennedy, D-R.I., and Jim Ramstad, R-Minn., in the House and Pete V. Domenici, R-N.M., and Edward M. Kennedy, D-Mass., in the Senate — spent the summer working out a compromise that could pass in both chambers and be signed by the president. Enactment was a priority for these four, two of whom (Ramstad and Domenici) were retiring, and one of whom (Edward Kennedy, the father of Patrick) was seriously ill. They all had confronted forms of mental illness or addiction themselves or with family members and had fought for such legislation for more than a decade. A 1997 parity law (PL 104-204) that was much more limited was scheduled to expire in December.

The compromise version (HR 6983) was less stringent on insurers than the previous House-passed measure and closer to a bill (S 558) the Senate had passed in 2007. Leaders brought the compromise to the floor as a free-standing bill in late September, and Republican support for it was triple that of the March vote. The degree of support garnered by the compromise encouraged congressional leaders to include the parity language in a broad financial markets bailout bill (PL 110-343) that needed help wherever backers could find it.

HOUSE PASSED HR 6983 on Sept. 23, **376-47:** R 143-47; D 233-0. The bill was considered under suspension of the rules, thereby requiring a two-thirds majority of those present and voting (282 in this case) for passage. *(House vote 625, p. C-18; mental health parity, p. 9-5; financial markets bailout, p. 7-3)*

674 Financial Industry Bailout

Passage of a bill to allow the Treasury to use up to $700 billion to buy certain mortgage-related assets.

With this vote, most House members had to make a difficult choice between the wishes of their party leaders and the demands of their constituents. The election was five weeks away. Constituents, who objected loudly and angrily to the Bush administration's plan to buy up the toxic mortgage-related assets of a financial industry in deep trouble, won. Two-thirds of the Republican caucus and 40 percent of Democrats voted against the measure, despite warnings from the Treasury secretary, the Federal Reserve chairman and House leaders

that the bailout, unprecedented in size and intent, was necessary to prevent the economy from falling into the worst slump since the Great Depression.

Leaders agreed that both parties should produce a majority of "yes" votes, and whip operations went into action. The vote was scheduled for the early afternoon of Sept. 29 — about 36 hours after the deal producing the legislation was worked out between congressional leaders and the administration. While it was assumed that the vote would be close, leaders thought they could eke out passage.

But as the 15-minute clock on the vote wound down, it became clear that the numbers weren't as solid as leaders had thought. Speaker Nancy Pelosi, D-Calif., begged members of the Congressional Black Caucus — who wanted the bill to more directly address the needs of poor people — to switch their votes. Minority Leader John A. Boehner's team had tried to persuade reluctant Republicans to fall in line with leadership, but in the end, most GOP lawmakers voted against the bill. After holding the vote open for about 30 extra minutes, Pelosi conceded defeat and signaled the roll call to a close.

Usually, the effects of a House vote are not felt for months or even years, not until a law is enacted or until voters make known their own opinion of their representative's actions in the polling booth. The repercussions of this vote, however, were immediate. Stunned traders on the floor of the New York Stock Exchange watched the televised vote, and as the bill went down to defeat, the value of shares plummeted. The Dow Jones industrial average fell 777 points, the largest one-day point drop in the 112-year history of the stock index. Pelosi blamed Boehner, R-Ohio, for not coming through with the necessary GOP votes; Boehner said a pre-vote partisan speech by Pelosi riled members of his caucus and led them to allow the bill to fail.

With the seeming dysfunction in the House, Senate leaders stepped up and took control of the issue, quickly producing a new version of the measure that cleared by the end of the week.

A breakdown of the House vote showed broad and varied opposition to the legislation. Most members of the conservative Republican Study Committee voted against the bill and against the president. Members of specific Democratic groups — the fiscally conservative "Blue Dogs," the Hispanic and black caucuses, the Progressives and New Democrats — split their votes almost evenly. Most members who were in highly competitive re-election races — 19 Republicans and 17 Democrats — voted against the bill. Members of the leadership in both parties held together and voted for the measure.

HOUSE REJECTED a motion to concur with amendment on HR 3997 on Sept. 29, **205-228:** R 65-133; D 140-95. (House vote 674, p. C-18; bailout, p. 7-3)

681 Financial Industry Bailout, With Tax Breaks

Clearing a bill that allowed the Treasury to use up to $700 billion to buy troubled mortgage-related assets and included the extension of expiring tax credits, a one-year patch to the alternative minimum tax and a requirement that insurers treat mental health issues the same as other medical issues.

In clearing this bill, four days after rejecting a similar version, the House gave the government unprecedented power to insert itself into the nation's financial markets in order to avert a credit crisis that had the potential to sour the economy for months if not years to come.

For this vote, 33 Democrats and 25 Republicans who had opposed the earlier bill switched positions and voted "yea."

Several vote-switchers cited the new elements in the Senate-revised package and fresh signs that the economy was under stress. Another fluid dynamic was public opinion. While most lawmakers reported hearing overwhelming opposition to the plan before the Sept. 29 vote, the stock market's plunge afterward appeared to rattle constituents worried about the effect the crisis was having on their retirement savings, particularly stock-based mutual funds and 401(k) plans. Business lobbyists also mobilized, warning that they had increasing difficulty getting credit to finance their day-to-day operations.

Four Republicans who voted to clear the bill — Joe Knollenberg of Michigan, John R. "Randy" Kuhl Jr. of New York, Jon Porter of Nevada and Christopher Shays of Connecticut — were defeated Nov. 4. Knollenberg and Kuhl had voted against the original bill and had switched sides for the second vote. One Democratic supporter of the bill, Tim Mahoney of Florida, lost his re-election effort, but he had been embroiled in a sex scandal, which probably contributed more to his loss than the bailout vote did.

HOUSE CLEARED by agreeing to a motion to concur on HR 1424 (PL 110-343) on Oct. 3, **263-171:** R 91-108; D 172-63. (House vote 681, p. C-18; Senate vote 213, p. C-22; bailout, p. 7-3; tax extenders, p. 4-11; mental health parity, p. 9-5)

690 Auto Industry Bailout

Passage of a bill to allow the Treasury to provide up to $14 billion in loans to domestic automakers, which, in return, would be required to submit restructuring plans by March 31, 2009.

For weeks before this vote, Democratic leaders and President Bush were at odds over who would be responsible for a bailout package for the Big Three automakers. Democrats wanted the administration to use money from the $700 billion Troubled Asset Relief Program created in the financial services bailout law (PL 110-343). Bush wanted Congress to use an existing Energy Department loan program (PL 110-140) that had been aimed at helping automakers shift to the production of more fuel-efficient vehicles.

Negotiations seemed at a standstill until Dec. 5, when, hours after the Labor Department announced that the economy had lost 553,000 jobs in November, House Speaker Nancy Pelosi, D-Calif., changed her mind and agreed to the administration's solution. In a scene that had already played out several times over the year, lawmakers and White House officials worked through the weekend to produce a bill, and the House passed it without much trouble Dec. 10.

As with previous votes to help out certain sectors of the U.S. economy, Republicans were reluctant to go along with the plan, despite Bush's support of it. And it was GOP opposition that killed the effort in the Senate. But the fact that the House vote even took place, after Pelosi's earlier adamant refusal to use the Energy Department loan for bailout purposes, showed that in the existing economic climate Democratic leaders in 2009 are going to have a hard time turning away further pleas for federal aid to specific industries.

HOUSE PASSED HR 7321 on Dec. 10, **237-170:** R 32-150; D 205-20. (House vote 690, p. C-18; Senate vote 215, p. C-22; auto bailout, p. 7-20)

SENATE VOTES

🔟 Economic Stimulus

Passage of a bill to help stimulate the economy through a tax refund to most taxpayers up to $600 for individuals and $1,200 for couples.

This vote took place after a four-day standoff in the Senate over how broad the package should be. The week before, the Finance Committee had put together a measure that included not only the rebates that were the core of the House-passed bill but also extended unemployment benefits and tax breaks for renewable-energy initiatives.

The Senate rejected a motion to invoke cloture on an amendment that would have substituted the Finance Committee language into the House measure. Majority Leader Harry Reid, D-Nev., even waited to schedule the cloture vote on Feb. 6 — one day after a crucial multistate primary — so that the Senate's two remaining contenders for the Democratic presidential nomination, Hillary Rodham Clinton and Barack Obama, could participate. Even with their help, though, the Finance package did not get the 60 votes necessary for the cloture motion to succeed, and the Senate, with Clinton and Obama both opting out, moved on to pass a less sweeping measure the next day. Republican presidential candidate John McCain voted for passage, but he did not participate in the earlier cloture vote.

The final measure was a compromise between the two chambers and did include some provisions sought by the Finance panel, such as expanding eligibility for the rebates to include low-income senior citizens, disabled veterans and survivors of veterans. Veterans' groups and the AARP lobbied heavily for those changes, and Finance Chairman Max Baucus, D-Mont., said their efforts made a difference.

In fact, Republicans had initially opposed changing the House bill at all and had urged senators to coalesce behind the original language that Treasury Secretary Henry M. Paulson Jr. negotiated with House Speaker Nancy Pelosi, D-Calif., and House Minority Leader John A. Boehner, R-Ohio. But Senate Minority Leader Mitch McConnell, R-Ky., ultimately pushed for the expanded package.

"We forced McConnell to cry 'uncle,'" Baucus said.

Because the bill did not include the unemployment or renewable-energy provisions, which would have led to opposition in the House and from the White House, passage in the Senate ensured the bill was on a quick path to enactment. The House cleared it the same day, and the president signed it the next week.

SENATE PASSED HR 5140 (PL 110-185) on Feb. 7, **81-16:** R 33-16; D 46-0; I 2-0. *(Senate vote 10, p. C-20; House vote 42, p. C-12; economic stimulus, p. 7-17)*

113 Genetic Discrimination Ban

Passage of a bill to prohibit discrimination on the basis of genetic information.

The House had passed this bill by a wide margin in April 2007, but it languished for a year in the Senate, where leaders could not bring it up because of a hold on the measure by Tom Coburn, R-Okla. When a block of time unexpectedly opened up on the Senate floor in April 2008, leaders and bill sponsors — who had worked for 13 years to ban the use of genetic-screening results in employment or insurance coverage decisions and who would not take "no" for an answer — began intense negotiations with Coburn and the White House.

They worked for a week, revising language on details in the bill that were causing concern, and on April 22, Coburn dropped his hold. Once the deal was reached, the Senate overwhelmingly voted to send the amended version back to the House, where it cleared a week later.

SENATE PASSED HR 493 (PL 110-233) on April 24, **95-0:** R 46-0; D 47-0; I 2-0. *(Senate vote 113, p. C-20; genetic discrimination, p. 9-15)*

130 Farm Bill Reauthorization

Clearing a reauthorization of federal farm and nutrition programs for five years.

This vote completed an 18-month effort to produce a five-year reauthorization of the nation's farm programs, significantly increasing nutrition spending and continuing to preserve crop subsidies. The size of Senate support for the conference report on the bill, along with a similar level of backing in the House, showed a clear split with the White House when it came to the issue of agricultural assistance.

President Bush said the bill did not do enough to trim subsidies, reduce the cost of farm programs or address trade complaints by other nations about unfair U.S. agriculture subsidies. But Senate Republicans, by an almost 3-to-1 ratio, rejected the president's position and voted to clear the measure, and they vowed to vote against him again if he vetoed it.

"I will stand and vote and support overriding that presidential veto," said David Vitter, R-La., who last year supported Bush in 85 percent of votes in which he took a position. "And I would also encourage my colleagues to be firm in that regard." They were: The same 35 Republicans voted to override the president's veto of the bill, thus enacting it into law, a week later.

SENATE CLEARED HR 2419 (PL 110-234) by adopting a conference report on the bill on May 15, **81-15:** R 35-13; D 44-2; I 2-0. *(Senate vote 130, p. C-20; House vote 346, p. C-14; farm programs reauthorization, p. 3-3)*

145 Climate Change

Refusal to invoke cloture on a measure that would have capped greenhouse gas emissions and set up a trading system for companies to buy and sell emissions allowances.

With this vote, the Senate's long-touted debate on global warming fizzled before it got started, as partisan jousting over judicial nominations and other issues overtook the issue at hand.

The vote was on a substitute amendment to a climate change bill by California Democrat Barbara Boxer that was to serve as the base legislation for the climate change debate. Although passage was never

expected, supporters had hoped to get the Senate on the record on several amendments that could help shape a climate change bill in the next Congress. Instead, the Senate never addressed issues that could be critical to any future legislation, such as the role of nuclear power or whether to pre-empt more stringent action at the state level.

The Senate opened the week by voting, 74-14, to bring up the bill. But Majority Leader Harry Reid, D-Nev., and Minority Leader Mitch McConnell, R-Ky., were at odds all week over how to move forward with amendments to the climate bill. Reid had suggested that five amendments should be offered on each side; Republicans wanted dozens more. Also, McConnell said he was protesting the way the majority party had handled confirmation of appellate court nominees.

McConnell's caucus filibustered and would not allow the Senate to proceed to Boxer's amendment. The vote to cut off debate fell so far short of the 60 needed that Reid did not keep open the option of reconsidering it, as he usually did when he intended to try again. The bill never came back to the floor.

SENATE REJECTED a motion to invoke cloture on the Boxer, D-Calif., substitute amendment on S 3036 on June 6, **48-36:** R 7-32; D 39-4; I 2-0. Three-fifths of the total Senate (60) is required to invoke cloture. *(Senate vote 145, p. C-20; climate change, p. 8-6)*

164 Foreign Intelligence Surveillance

Defeat of amendment to the Foreign Intelligence Surveillance Act reauthorization that would have allowed lawsuits against companies that had participated in the National Security Agency's warrantless surveillance program.

The defeat of this amendment, as well as two subsequent efforts to amend the bill, represented the final attempt to confront President Bush over electronic surveillance laws in the 110th Congress. The White House came out of this fight a clear winner, and Democrats decided to drop the issue until a new administration took office.

Democrats voting in favor of the amendment included Barack Obama of Illinois, the party's presumed nominee for president, who earlier pledged to join a filibuster of any bill that provided retroactive legal immunity. But he also voted to clear the measure, saying he was inspired by compromises that had been made on the bill as well as by the need to ensure intelligence gathering. Those opposing the amendment had decided that a commitment to electronic surveillance trumped concern over granting legal immunity to the companies that had helped the government with its controversial spying program.

SENATE REJECTED the Christopher J. Dodd, D-Conn., amendment to HR 6304 (PL 110-261) on July 9, **32-66:** R 0-48; D 31-17; I 1-1. *(Senate vote 164, p. C-21; House vote 437, p. C-14; FISA rewrite, p. 6-12)*

169 Medicare Physicians' Pay

Successful cloture motion that allowed a vote on passage of a bill to prevent a scheduled 10.6 percent cut in pay rates for doctors who participated in Medicare.

This vote cleared the way for a controversial Medicare bill to pass and ensured there would be enough votes in support of it to override an expected veto, sending President Bush one of the strongest rebukes

of his presidency.

The vote was on a motion to invoke cloture to proceed to the measure, the second such effort to move the bill in the Senate in fewer than two weeks. On the first attempt, on June 26, the motion fell just short of the 60 votes needed to succeed. In that instance, 39 Republicans voted against the bill.

Congress left the next day for the July Fourth recess, during which the July 1 deadline for acting on the physician rate cut was due to pass. But the administration announced it would not apply the cut immediately, instead holding doctors' claims for 10 business days — until July 15 — to give Congress more time to pass a bill. In the meantime, Senate Democrats hoped doctors' groups such as the American Medical Association could put enough pressure on vulnerable Republicans that the bill could pass when they returned from recess.

One of the two senators who were absent for the June 26 cloture vote was Democrat Edward M. Kennedy of Massachusetts, the chairman of the Health, Education, Labor and Pensions Committee and a longtime opponent of the Medicare rate cut structure for doctors. Kennedy had been away from the Capitol since mid-May, when he was diagnosed with a brain tumor. Kennedy staff members said June 30 there were no plans for him to return to the Hill for the next vote on the doctors' pay bill, but Majority Leader Harry Reid, D-Nev., did contact Kennedy the week of July 7.

Reid scheduled the next cloture vote on July 9, and, while it appeared to be headed in the same direction as the earlier vote, there was a different atmosphere in the chamber this time. Most senators stayed around after voting, and the Senate gallery was more full than usual. As the votes in favor of cloture drew close to 60, the chamber suddenly erupted in applause and all eyes turned to a door behind the central dais: Kennedy was entering the room, accompanied by his son, Rep. Patrick J. Kennedy, D-R.I., as well as John Kerry, his Democratic colleague from Massachusetts; Barack Obama, the party's presumed nominee for president; and longtime friend Christopher J. Dodd, D-Conn.

Senators and visitors in the gallery, including Kennedy's wife, Vicki, gave Kennedy a standing ovation, complete with whoops and hollers. Kennedy then walked up to the desk and, loud enough for all to hear, shouted out his vote with a resounding "aye."

"Win, lose or draw, I wanted to be here. I wasn't going to take the chance that my vote could make the difference," Kennedy said later in a statement.

His vote did make the difference. Republicans who had not yet voted joined Kennedy in supporting the bill, and others switched from no to yes. The vote to invoke cloture was 69-30, more than enough to override a veto.

Immediately after the cloture motion succeeded, the Senate cleared the bill by voice vote. Six days later, Bush vetoed the bill and both chambers voted to override it. The Senate vote to override was 70-26, with Kennedy absent.

Nine Republicans who had voted against the June 26 cloture motion had changed their minds in the two weeks, including three — Lamar Alexander of Tennessee, Saxby Chambliss of Georgia and John Cornyn of Texas — who were running for re-election.

SENATE AGREED to invoke cloture on a motion to proceed to HR 6331 (PL 110-275) on July 9, **69-30:** R 18-30; D 49-0; I 2-0. Three-fifths of the total Senate (60) is required to invoke cloture. *(Senate vote 169, p. C-21; House vote 443, p. C-16; Medicare doctors' pay, p. 9-3)*

186 Mortgage Relief

Clearing a bill to let the Treasury Department extend new credit to and buy stock in Fannie Mae and Freddie Mac and to help homeowners with loans they could no longer afford.

In what was to be the second of three significant legislative efforts during the year to prevent an economic slowdown from becoming much worse, the Senate overcame objections from conservatives and voted to send President Bush a bill intended to help homeowners facing foreclosure and at the same time to give the administration authority to salvage mortgage giants Fannie Mae and Freddie Mac.

The House and Senate had tried for months to agree on the bill, which would create a $300 billion trust fund in the Federal Housing Administration to help lenders refinance troubled mortgages, give money to local governments to rehabilitate foreclosed properties, and impose a new regulatory structure on Fannie and Freddie. As the two chambers got closer, however, the Bush administration maintained its vigorous opposition to elements of the bill. In addition, for a time some Republican senators tried to use the measure to advance energy tax breaks.

A Senate vote to clear the measure became possible only after Treasury Secretary Henry M. Paulson Jr. decided that the survival of Fannie and Freddie were in doubt, as investors pushed down their share prices to improbably low levels. Paulson asked for authority to inject capital into the two companies and potentially to take them over. He persuaded lawmakers to grant him the authority, and the administration dropped its veto threat over the mortgage relief provisions. After the House voted to pass the revised version of the measure, the Senate overwhelmingly went along during a rare Saturday session.

SENATE CLEARED, through a motion to concur, HR 3221 (PL 110-289) on July 26, **72-13:** R 27-13; D 43-0; I 2-0. *(Senate vote 186, p. C-21; House vote 519, p. C-16; mortgage relief, p. 7-9)*

211 U.S.-India Nuclear Agreement

Clearing a bill to approve the United States' nuclear cooperation agreement with India.

With this vote, Congress gave its approval to a landmark agreement that allowed nuclear trade between India and the United States and brought India's civilian, but not military, reactors under international oversight. The deal was important because, as a country that had tested nuclear weapons but not signed on to the Nuclear Non-Proliferation Treaty, India had been gradually excluded from the global nuclear industry since first testing in 1974.

SENATE CLEARED HR 7081 (PL 110-369) on Oct. 1, **86-13:** R 49-0; D 36-12; I 1-1. *(Senate vote 211, p. C-22; U.S.-India agreement, p. 6-11)*

213 Financial Industry Bailout and Tax Credits

Passage of a bill that allowed the Treasury to use up to $700 billion to buy troubled mortgage-related assets and included the extension of expiring tax credits, a one-year patch to the alternative minimum tax and a requirement that insurers treat mental health issues the same as other medical issues.

After the House unexpectedly voted down the original version of the bill Sept. 29, Senate leaders took control of the debate, combining the core provisions of the bailout with a measure to extend expiring tax credits, create incentives for the use of renewable energy and require parity from insurers in the handling of mental health benefits. They announced their decision Sept. 30 and scheduled the vote for the next evening.

The Senate used as its vehicle for the revised bailout bill a House-passed mental health parity measure. Before voting to pass it, senators first had to amend it with the substitute language that added the bailout provisions and the Senate-passed tax and mental health language. While there was little doubt about the outcome, the vote on the substitute offered a level of drama reserved for the most serious of issues, along the lines of presidential impeachment. Majority Leader Harry Reid, D-Nev., ordered the Senate to remain seated during the roll call on the substitute. One by one, with the chamber otherwise silent, each member shouted out his or her vote. The only senator absent that night — in fact, the only member of Congress to not vote on passage of the bill — was Edward M. Kennedy of Massachusetts, who was recovering from treatment for a brain tumor.

After the bill was amended, Reid allowed the members to cast their votes on passage in the usual manner — by going up to the well, voting nay or yea, and then leaving or staying as they wished. The votes for the substitute and for passage were identical.

Unlike their colleagues in the House, two-thirds of the senators did not have election fights back home, and fewer than a dozen were in highly competitive races — giving them a little more leeway to ignore angry constituents.

Eight Republican senators who were in tight races voted for the bill. Three of those — John E. Sununu of New Hampshire, Gordon H. Smith of Oregon and Ted Stevens of Alaska (who also had been convicted of misrepresenting gifts on disclosure forms the week before the election) — lost their seats. One other — Norm Coleman of Minnesota — faced a recount.

Of the nine Democrats who voted against the bill, only Mary L. Landrieu of Louisiana was in a tough fight back home, and she did win re-election Nov. 4. The others, such as Debbie Stabenow of Michigan, said the measure did not do enough to help homeowners or manufacturers.

SENATE PASSED HR 1424 (PL 110-343) on Oct. 1, **74-25:** R 34-15; D 39-9; I 1-1. By unanimous consent, the Senate agreed to raise the majority requirement for passage of the bill to 60 votes. *(Senate vote 213, p. C-22; House votes 674, 681, p. C-18; bailout, p. 7-3; tax extenders, p. 4-11; mental health parity, p. 9-5)*

215 Auto Industry Bailout

Refusal to invoke cloture to proceed to a bill that would have allowed the Treasury Department to provide up to $14 billion in loans to domestic automakers, who, in return, would have been required to submit restructuring plans by March 31, 2009.

The Senate vote that ended debate on an automaker rescue package showed that Republican lawmakers had reached a point of "bailout fatigue" after a year in which they were asked by the administration and their leaders to approve billions of dollars in aid for the mortgage industry and for financial services companies.

At the same time, negotiations on the legislation, led by Tennessee Republican Bob Corker, set a marker for the 111th Congress, which was expected to return to the issue early in 2009. "He did some wonderful work, and I think the work he did is going to pay dividends next year," Majority Leader Harry Reid, D-Nev., said just before the Senate's vote.

In an odd twist of events, the Senate's rejection of the auto industry bailout ended up giving Democratic leaders the solution they had originally sought. In an effort to calm financial markets before they opened the morning after the vote, the White House announced it would consider using funds from the Troubled Asset Relief Program (PL 110-343) to keep the automakers afloat until the 111th Congress could pass something more concrete in January.

SENATE REJECTED a motion to invoke cloture on HR 7005 (a shell bill intended to be the vehicle for the auto industry bailout) on Dec. 11, **52-35:** R 10-31; D 40-4; I 2-0. *(Senate vote 215, p. C-22; House vote 690, p. C-18; auto bailout, p. 7-20)* ■

IN THE HOUSE | By Vote Number

42. **HR 5140. Economic Stimulus/Motion to Concur.** Rangel, D-N.Y., motion to concur in the Senate amendment to the bill that would provide advance refund of a tax credit for most taxpayers equal to $300 to $600 for individuals and $600 to $1,200 for couples. Families would receive $300 for each child under 17. The benefit would begin phasing out for individuals with adjusted gross incomes above $75,000 ($150,000 for married couples). It would provide businesses with a 50 percent depreciation for certain equipment purchased in 2008 and increase to $250,000 the amount small businesses can expense in the year items are purchased. It would raise the size of mortgage loans the Federal Housing Administration could insure and Fannie Mae and Freddie Mac could purchase. It would expand eligibility for rebate checks to include low-income senior citizens, disabled veterans and widows of veterans. Illegal immigrants would be ineligible. Motion agreed to (thus clearing the bill for the president) 380-34: R 165-28; D 215-6 (ND 165-2, SD 50-4). A "yea" was a vote in support of the president's position. Feb. 7, 2008. *(Story, p. C-4)*

181. **H Res 1092. Colombia Trade 'Fast Track' Requirements/ Adoption.** Adoption of the resolution that would suspend "fast track" requirements for considering a bill (HR 5724) that would implement a U.S.-Colombia free-trade agreement. Adopted 224-195: R 6-185; D 218-10 (ND 169-3, SD 49-7). April 10, 2008. *(Story, p. C-4)*

329. **HR 2642. Supplemental Appropriations/Motion to Concur.** Obey, D-Wis., motion to concur in the Senate amendments with a House amendment. The House amendment would require a troop withdrawal from Iraq within 30 days of the bill's enactment, with a goal of completing the withdrawal of combat troops by December 2009. It would require Congress to authorize any agreement between the U.S. and the Iraqi government committing U.S. forces. It would require the Iraqi government to match U.S. reconstruction aid and to sell fuel to the U.S. military at the same price it is sold to Iraqi consumers. It would prohibit any combat unit not assessed as fully mission-capable from deploying to Iraq and limit deployment time, but it would allow for presidential waivers. It also would prohibit interrogation techniques not authorized in the Army Field Manual on the subject and prohibit establishing a permanent base in Iraq. Motion agreed to 227-196: R 8-183; D 219-13 (ND 168-6, SD 51-7). A "nay" was a vote in support of the president's position. May 15, 2008. *(Story, p. C-4)*

[1] The Speaker votes only at her discretion.

[2] Rep. Jackie Speier, D-Calif., was sworn in April 10, 2008, to fill the seat vacated by the death of Democrat Tom Lantos on Feb. 11. The first vote for which Speier was eligible was vote 179; the last vote for which Lantos was eligible was vote 42.

[3] Rep. Bill Foster, D-Ill., was sworn in March 11, 2008. The first vote for which he was eligible was vote 116.

[4] Rep. André Carson, D-Ind., was sworn in March 13, 2008, to fill the seat vacated by the death of Democrat Julia Carson on Dec. 15, 2007. The first vote for which he was eligible was vote 140.

[5] Rep. Steve Scalise, R-La., was sworn in May 7, 2008, to fill the seat vacated by Republican Bobby Jindal, who resigned Jan. 14 to become governor. The first vote for which Scalise was eligible was vote 268; Jindal was not eligible for any roll call votes in 2008.

[6] Rep. Don Cazayoux, D-La., was sworn in May 6, 2008, to fill the seat vacated by Republican Richard H. Baker, who resigned Feb. 2. The first vote for which Cazayoux was eligible was vote 247; the last vote for which Baker was eligible was vote 28.

ND Northern Democrats, SD Southern Democrats
Southern states: Ala., Ark., Fla., Ga., Ky., La., Miss., N.C., Okla., S.C., Tenn., Texas, Va.

	42	181	329
ALABAMA			
1 **Bonner**	Y	N	N
2 **Everett**	?	N	N
3 **Rogers**	Y	Y	N
4 **Aderholt**	Y	Y	N
5 Cramer	?	N	Y
6 **Bachus**	Y	N	N
7 Davis	Y	Y	Y
ALASKA			
AL **Young**	Y	N	N
ARIZONA			
1 **Renzi**	Y	N	N
2 **Franks**	Y	N	N
3 **Shadegg**	N	N	N
4 Pastor	Y	Y	Y
5 Mitchell	Y	Y	Y
6 **Flake**	N	N	N
7 Grijalva	Y	Y	Y
8 Giffords	Y	Y	Y
ARKANSAS			
1 Berry	N	Y	Y
2 Snyder	Y	Y	N
3 **Boozman**	Y	N	N
4 Ross	Y	Y	Y
CALIFORNIA			
1 Thompson	Y	Y	Y
2 **Herger**	Y	N	N
3 **Lungren**	N	N	N
4 **Doolittle**	Y	N	N
5 Matsui	Y	Y	Y
6 Woolsey	+	Y	Y
7 Miller, George	Y	Y	Y
8 Pelosi[1]	Y	Y	Y
9 Lee	Y	Y	Y
10 Tauscher	Y	Y	Y
11 McNerney	Y	Y	Y
12 Lantos[2]	?		
12 Speier[2]		Y	Y
13 Stark	Y	Y	Y
14 Eshoo	Y	Y	Y
15 Honda	Y	Y	Y
16 Lofgren	Y	Y	Y
17 Farr	?	Y	Y
18 Cardoza	Y	Y	Y
19 **Radanovich**	Y	N	N
20 Costa	Y	Y	N
21 **Nunes**	Y	N	N
22 **McCarthy**	Y	N	N
23 Capps	Y	Y	Y
24 **Gallegly**	Y	N	N
25 **McKeon**	Y	N	N
26 **Dreier**	Y	N	N
27 Sherman	Y	Y	Y
28 Berman	Y	Y	Y
29 Schiff	Y	Y	Y
30 Waxman	Y	Y	Y
31 Becerra	Y	Y	Y
32 Solis	Y	Y	Y
33 Watson	Y	Y	Y
34 Roybal-Allard	Y	Y	Y
35 Waters	Y	Y	Y
36 Harman	Y	Y	Y
37 Richardson	Y	Y	Y
38 Napolitano	Y	Y	Y
39 Sánchez, Linda	Y	Y	Y
40 **Royce**	N	N	N
41 **Lewis**	Y	N	N
42 **Miller, Gary**	Y	N	N
43 Baca	Y	Y	Y
44 **Calvert**	Y	N	N
45 **Bono Mack**	Y	N	?
46 **Rohrabacher**	N	N	N
47 Sanchez, Loretta	–	Y	Y
48 **Campbell**	N	N	?
49 **Issa**	Y	N	N
50 **Bilbray**	Y	N	N
51 Filner	Y	Y	Y
52 **Hunter**	N	N	N
53 Davis	Y	Y	Y

	42	181	329
COLORADO			
1 DeGette	Y	Y	?
2 Udall	Y	Y	Y
3 Salazar	Y	Y	Y
4 **Musgrave**	Y	N	N
5 **Lamborn**	Y	N	N
6 **Tancredo**	N	N	N
7 Perlmutter	Y	Y	Y
CONNECTICUT			
1 Larson	Y	+	Y
2 Courtney	Y	Y	Y
3 DeLauro	Y	Y	Y
4 **Shays**	Y	N	Y
5 Murphy	Y	Y	Y
DELAWARE			
AL **Castle**	Y	N	Y
FLORIDA			
1 **Miller**	Y	N	N
2 Boyd	N	N	Y
3 Brown	Y	Y	Y
4 **Crenshaw**	Y	N	?
5 **Brown-Waite**	Y	N	N
6 **Stearns**	Y	N	N
7 **Mica**	Y	N	N
8 **Keller**	Y	N	N
9 **Bilirakis**	Y	N	N
10 **Young**	Y	N	N
11 Castor	Y	Y	Y
12 **Putnam**	Y	N	N
13 **Buchanan**	Y	N	N
14 **Mack**	Y	N	?
15 **Weldon**	Y	N	N
16 Mahoney	Y	N	Y
17 Meek	Y	Y	Y
18 **Ros-Lehtinen**	Y	N	N
19 Wexler	Y	Y	Y
20 Wasserman Schultz	Y	Y	Y
21 **Diaz-Balart, L.**	Y	N	N
22 Klein	Y	Y	Y
23 Hastings	Y	Y	Y
24 **Feeney**	Y	N	N
25 **Diaz-Balart, M.**	Y	N	N
GEORGIA			
1 **Kingston**	N	N	N
2 Bishop	Y	Y	Y
3 **Westmoreland**	N	N	N
4 Johnson	Y	Y	Y
5 Lewis	Y	Y	Y
6 **Price**	N	N	N
7 **Linder**	N	N	N
8 Marshall	Y	Y	N
9 **Deal**	N	N	N
10 **Broun**	N	N	N
11 **Gingrey**	N	N	N
12 Barrow	Y	Y	N
13 Scott	Y	Y	Y
HAWAII			
1 Abercrombie	Y	Y	Y
2 Hirono	Y	Y	Y
IDAHO			
1 **Sali**	Y	N	N
2 **Simpson**	N	N	N
ILLINOIS			
1 Rush	Y	+	+
2 Jackson	Y	Y	Y
3 Lipinski	Y	Y	Y
4 Gutierrez	Y	Y	Y
5 Emanuel	Y	Y	Y
6 **Roskam**	Y	N	N
7 Davis	Y	Y	Y
8 Bean	Y	N	Y
9 Schakowsky	Y	Y	Y
10 **Kirk**	Y	N	N
11 **Weller**	Y	N	N
12 Costello	Y	Y	Y
13 **Biggert**	Y	N	N
14 Foster[3]		Y	Y
15 **Johnson**	Y	N	N

KEY   **Republicans**   Democrats

Y Voted for (yea)	X Paired against	C Voted "present" to avoid possible conflict of interest
# Paired for	– Announced against	
+ Announced for	P Voted "present"	? Did not vote or otherwise make a position known
N Voted against (nay)		

Member	42	181	329
16 Manzullo	Y	N	N
17 Hare	Y	Y	Y
18 LaHood	Y	N	N
19 Shimkus	Y	N	N
INDIANA			
1 Visclosky	Y	Y	Y
2 Donnelly	Y	Y	Y
3 Souder	Y	N	N
4 Buyer	Y	?	N
5 Burton	Y	N	N
6 Pence	Y	N	N
7 Carson[4]		Y	Y
8 Ellsworth	Y	Y	Y
9 Hill	Y	N	Y
IOWA			
1 Braley	Y	Y	Y
2 Loebsack	Y	Y	Y
3 Boswell	Y	Y	Y
4 Latham	Y	N	N
5 King	Y	N	N
KANSAS			
1 Moran	N	N	N
2 Boyda	Y	Y	Y
3 Moore	Y	Y	Y
4 Tiahrt	Y	N	N
KENTUCKY			
1 Whitfield	Y	N	N
2 Lewis	Y	N	?
3 Yarmuth	Y	Y	Y
4 Davis	Y	N	N
5 Rogers	Y	N	N
6 Chandler	Y	Y	Y
LOUISIANA			
1 Scalise[5]			N
2 Jefferson	Y	Y	Y
3 Melancon	Y	Y	Y
4 McCrery	Y	N	N
5 Alexander	Y	N	N
6 Cazayoux[6]			Y
7 Boustany	Y	N	N
MAINE			
1 Allen	Y	Y	N
2 Michaud	Y	Y	Y
MARYLAND			
1 Gilchrest	Y	N	Y
2 Ruppersberger	?	Y	Y
3 Sarbanes	Y	Y	Y
4 Wynn	Y	Y	Y
5 Hoyer	Y	Y	Y
6 Bartlett	Y	N	N
7 Cummings	Y	Y	Y
8 Van Hollen	Y	Y	Y
MASSACHUSETTS			
1 Olver	Y	Y	Y
2 Neal	Y	Y	Y
3 McGovern	Y	Y	Y
4 Frank	Y	Y	Y
5 Tsongas	Y	Y	Y
6 Tierney	Y	Y	Y
7 Markey	Y	Y	Y
8 Capuano	Y	Y	Y
9 Lynch	Y	Y	Y
10 Delahunt	Y	Y	Y
MICHIGAN			
1 Stupak	Y	Y	Y
2 Hoekstra	Y	N	N
3 Ehlers	Y	N	N
4 Camp	Y	N	N
5 Kildee	Y	Y	Y
6 Upton	Y	N	N
7 Walberg	Y	N	N
8 Rogers	Y	N	N
9 Knollenberg	Y	N	N
10 Miller	Y	N	N
11 McCotter	Y	N	N
12 Levin	Y	Y	Y
13 Kilpatrick	Y	Y	Y
14 Conyers	Y	Y	Y
15 Dingell	Y	Y	Y
MINNESOTA			
1 Walz	Y	Y	Y
2 Kline	Y	N	N
3 Ramstad	Y	?	N
4 McCollum	Y	Y	Y

Member	42	181	329
5 Ellison	Y	Y	Y
6 Bachmann	Y	N	N
7 Peterson	N	Y	N
8 Oberstar	Y	Y	Y
MISSISSIPPI			
1 Vacant			
2 Thompson	Y	Y	Y
3 Pickering	Y	N	N
4 Taylor	N	Y	N
MISSOURI			
1 Clay	Y	Y	Y
2 Akin	Y	N	N
3 Carnahan	Y	Y	Y
4 Skelton	Y	Y	Y
5 Cleaver	Y	Y	Y
6 Graves	Y	N	N
7 Blunt	Y	N	N
8 Emerson	Y	N	N
9 Hulshof	Y	?	?
MONTANA			
AL Rehberg	Y	N	N
NEBRASKA			
1 Fortenberry	+	N	N
2 Terry	Y	N	N
3 Smith	Y	N	N
NEVADA			
1 Berkley	Y	Y	Y
2 Heller	Y	N	N
3 Porter	+	N	N
NEW HAMPSHIRE			
1 Shea-Porter	Y	Y	Y
2 Hodes	Y	Y	Y
NEW JERSEY			
1 Andrews	Y	?	Y
2 LoBiondo	Y	N	N
3 Saxton	Y	N	N
4 Smith	Y	N	N
5 Garrett	N	N	N
6 Pallone	Y	Y	Y
7 Ferguson	Y	?	N
8 Pascrell	Y	Y	Y
9 Rothman	Y	Y	Y
10 Payne	Y	Y	Y
11 Frelinghuysen	Y	N	N
12 Holt	Y	Y	Y
13 Sires	Y	?	Y
NEW MEXICO			
1 Wilson	Y	N	N
2 Pearce	Y	N	N
3 Udall	Y	Y	Y
NEW YORK			
1 Bishop	Y	+	Y
2 Israel	Y	Y	Y
3 King	Y	N	N
4 McCarthy	Y	Y	Y
5 Ackerman	Y	Y	Y
6 Meeks	Y	Y	Y
7 Crowley	Y	Y	Y
8 Nadler	Y	Y	Y
9 Weiner	Y	Y	Y
10 Towns	Y	Y	Y
11 Clarke	Y	Y	Y
12 Velázquez	Y	Y	Y
13 Fossella	Y	N	N
14 Maloney	Y	Y	Y
15 Rangel	Y	Y	Y
16 Serrano	Y	Y	Y
17 Engel	Y	Y	Y
18 Lowey	+	Y	Y
19 Hall	Y	Y	Y
20 Gillibrand	Y	Y	?
21 McNulty	Y	Y	Y
22 Hinchey	Y	Y	Y
23 McHugh	Y	N	N
24 Arcuri	Y	Y	Y
25 Walsh	Y	N	Y
26 Reynolds	Y	N	N
27 Higgins	Y	Y	Y
28 Slaughter	Y	Y	Y
29 Kuhl	Y	N	N
NORTH CAROLINA			
1 Butterfield	Y	Y	Y
2 Etheridge	Y	Y	Y
3 Jones	Y	Y	Y
4 Price	Y	Y	Y

Member	42	181	329
5 Foxx	Y	N	N
6 Coble	N	N	Y
7 McIntyre	Y	Y	Y
8 Hayes	Y	Y	N
9 Myrick	Y	N	?
10 McHenry	Y	N	N
11 Shuler	Y	Y	Y
12 Watt	Y	Y	Y
13 Miller	Y	Y	Y
NORTH DAKOTA			
AL Pomeroy	Y	Y	Y
OHIO			
1 Chabot	Y	N	N
2 Schmidt	Y	N	N
3 Turner	Y	N	N
4 Jordan	Y	N	N
5 Latta	Y	N	N
6 Wilson	Y	Y	Y
7 Hobson	Y	N	N
8 Boehner	Y	N	N
9 Kaptur	Y	Y	Y
10 Kucinich	Y	Y	N
11 Tubbs Jones	Y	Y	Y
12 Tiberi	Y	N	N
13 Sutton	Y	Y	Y
14 LaTourette	Y	N	N
15 Pryce	Y	N	N
16 Regula	Y	N	N
17 Ryan	Y	Y	Y
18 Space	Y	Y	Y
OKLAHOMA			
1 Sullivan	Y	N	N
2 Boren	Y	N	N
3 Lucas	Y	N	N
4 Cole	Y	N	N
5 Fallin	Y	N	N
OREGON			
1 Wu	Y	Y	Y
2 Walden	Y	N	N
3 Blumenauer	Y	Y	Y
4 DeFazio	Y	Y	Y
5 Hooley	Y	Y	Y
PENNSYLVANIA			
1 Brady	Y	Y	Y
2 Fattah	Y	Y	Y
3 English	Y	N	Y
4 Altmire	Y	Y	Y
5 Peterson	Y	N	N
6 Gerlach	Y	N	?
7 Sestak	Y	Y	Y
8 Murphy, P.	Y	Y	Y
9 Shuster	Y	N	N
10 Carney	Y	Y	N
11 Kanjorski	Y	Y	Y
12 Murtha	Y	Y	Y
13 Schwartz	Y	Y	Y
14 Doyle	Y	Y	Y
15 Dent	Y	Y	Y
16 Pitts	?	N	N
17 Holden	Y	Y	Y
18 Murphy, T.	Y	N	N
19 Platts	Y	N	N
RHODE ISLAND			
1 Kennedy	Y	Y	Y
2 Langevin	Y	Y	Y
SOUTH CAROLINA			
1 Brown	Y	N	N
2 Wilson	Y	N	N
3 Barrett	Y	N	N
4 Inglis	Y	N	N
5 Spratt	Y	Y	Y
6 Clyburn	Y	Y	Y
SOUTH DAKOTA			
AL Herseth Sandlin	Y	Y	Y
TENNESSEE			
1 Davis, David	Y	N	N
2 Duncan	N	N	Y
3 Wamp	Y	N	N
4 Davis, L.	Y	Y	N
5 Cooper	N	N	Y
6 Gordon	Y	Y	Y
7 Blackburn	Y	N	N
8 Tanner	?	P	Y
9 Cohen	Y	Y	Y

Member	42	181	329
TEXAS			
1 Gohmert	N	N	N
2 Poe	N	N	N
3 Johnson, S.	Y	N	N
4 Hall	Y	N	N
5 Hensarling	Y	N	N
6 Barton	Y	N	N
7 Culberson	Y	N	N
8 Brady	Y	N	N
9 Green, A.	Y	Y	Y
10 McCaul	Y	N	N
11 Conaway	Y	N	N
12 Granger	Y	–	N
13 Thornberry	Y	N	N
14 Paul	N	Y	N
15 Hinojosa	Y	Y	Y
16 Reyes	Y	Y	Y
17 Edwards	Y	Y	Y
18 Jackson Lee	Y	Y	Y
19 Neugebauer	Y	N	N
20 Gonzalez	Y	Y	Y
21 Smith	Y	N	N
22 Lampson	Y	N	N
23 Rodriguez	Y	N	N
24 Marchant	Y	N	N
25 Doggett	Y	Y	Y
26 Burgess	N	?	N
27 Ortiz	Y	N	Y
28 Cuellar	Y	N	Y
29 Green, G.	Y	Y	Y
30 Johnson, E.	Y	Y	Y
31 Carter	Y	N	N
32 Sessions	Y	N	N
UTAH			
1 Bishop	Y	?	N
2 Matheson	Y	N	N
3 Cannon	Y	N	N
VERMONT			
AL Welch	Y	Y	Y
VIRGINIA			
1 Wittman	Y	N	N
2 Drake	Y	N	N
3 Scott	Y	Y	Y
4 Forbes	N	N	N
5 Goode	N	Y	N
6 Goodlatte	Y	N	N
7 Cantor	Y	N	N
8 Moran	Y	Y	Y
9 Boucher	?	Y	Y
10 Wolf	Y	N	N
11 Davis, T.	?	N	N
WASHINGTON			
1 Inslee	?	Y	Y
2 Larsen	Y	Y	Y
3 Baird	N	Y	N
4 Hastings	Y	N	N
5 McMorris Rodgers	Y	N	N
6 Dicks	Y	Y	Y
7 McDermott	Y	Y	Y
8 Reichert	Y	N	N
9 Smith	–	Y	Y
WEST VIRGINIA			
1 Mollohan	Y	Y	Y
2 Capito	Y	N	N
3 Rahall	Y	Y	Y
WISCONSIN			
1 Ryan	Y	N	N
2 Baldwin	Y	Y	Y
3 Kind	Y	Y	Y
4 Moore	Y	Y	Y
5 Sensenbrenner	N	N	N
6 Petri	Y	N	N
7 Obey	Y	Y	Y
8 Kagen	Y	Y	Y
WYOMING			
AL Cubin	N	N	N
DELEGATES			
Faleomavaega (A.S.)			
Norton (D.C.)			
Bordallo (Guam)			
Fortuño (P.R.)			
Christensen (V.I.)			

IN THE HOUSE | By Vote Number

346. HR 2419. **Farm Bill Reauthorization/Veto Override.** Passage, over President Bush's May 21, 2008, veto, of the bill that would reauthorize federal farm and nutrition programs for five years, including crop subsidies and food stamps, as well as conservation and rural development. It would authorize a $10.4 billion increase for nutrition programs, offset by extending customs user fees. It would cut direct payment subsidies overall by $313 million, in part by reducing the percentage of acres for which a farmer can collect payments. Farmers making more than $750,000 a year in farm-related income and those with more than $500,000 a year in non-farm-related income would be ineligible for federal subsidies. Country-of-origin labels for all meat would be required by September 2008. Passed 316-108: R 100-94; D 216-14 (ND 161-13, SD 55-1). A two-thirds majority of those present and voting (283 in this case for the House) of both chambers is required to override a veto. A "nay" was a vote in support of the president's position. May 21, 2008. *(Story, p. C-5)*

400. HR 6003. **Amtrak Reauthorization/Passage.** Passage of the bill that would authorize $14.4 billion for Amtrak over five years, including $3 billion for operating assistance, $4.2 billion for capital grants and $1.7 billion for Amtrak to pay down its debts. The bill would authorize grants for capital costs in certain high-congestion corridors. It would require changes in Amtrak's management, operations and general policy regarding intercity passenger rail service. The Transportation Department would be directed to solicit bids, including those from private contractors, for construction of a high-speed rail system between Washington, D.C., and New York City. Passed 311-104: R 87-104; D 224-0 (ND 168-0, SD 56-0). A "nay" was a vote in support of the president's position. June 11, 2008. *(Story, p. C-5)*

437. HR 6304. **Foreign Intelligence Surveillance/Passage.** Passage of the bill that would overhaul the Foreign Intelligence Surveillance Act (FISA), which governs electronic surveillance of foreign terrorism suspects. The bill would allow investigations of up to one year that involved surveillance targeting those who are not U.S. persons and who are reasonably believed to be outside the United States. The FISA court would have to approve procedures for conducting the surveillance. Warrantless surveillance would be allowed as long as it does not intentionally target U.S. persons or those located within the United States. It would pave the way for retroactive immunity for telecommunications companies that participated in the National Security Agency's warrantless surveillance program. Passed 293-129: R 188-1; D 105-128 (ND 62-112, SD 43-16). A "yea" was a vote in support of the president's position. June 20, 2008. *(Story, p. C-5)*

[1] The Speaker votes only at her discretion.

[2] Rep. Donna Edwards, D-Md., was sworn in June 19, 2008, to fill the seat vacated by Democrat Albert R. Wynn, who resigned May 31. The first vote for which Edwards was eligible was vote 427; the last vote for which Wynn was eligible was vote 366.

[3] Rep. Travis W. Childers, D-Miss., was sworn in May 20, 2008. The first vote for which he was eligible was vote 332.

ND Northern Democrats, SD Southern Democrats
Southern states: Ala., Ark., Fla., Ga., Ky., La., Miss., N.C., Okla., S.C., Tenn., Texas, Va.

	346	400	437
ALABAMA			
1 Bonner	Y	N	Y
2 Everett	Y	N	Y
3 Rogers	Y	Y	Y
4 Aderholt	Y	N	Y
5 Cramer	Y	Y	Y
6 Bachus	Y	Y	Y
7 Davis	Y	Y	Y
ALASKA			
AL Young	Y	Y	Y
ARIZONA			
1 Renzi	Y	Y	Y
2 Franks	N	N	Y
3 Shadegg	N	N	Y
4 Pastor	Y	Y	N
5 Mitchell	N	Y	Y
6 Flake	N	?	Y
7 Grijalva	Y	Y	N
8 Giffords	Y	Y	Y
ARKANSAS			
1 Berry	Y	Y	Y
2 Snyder	Y	Y	Y
3 Boozman	Y	Y	Y
4 Ross	Y	Y	Y
CALIFORNIA			
1 Thompson	Y	Y	N
2 Herger	Y	N	Y
3 Lungren	N	N	Y
4 Doolittle	Y	N	Y
5 Matsui	Y	Y	N
6 Woolsey	Y	Y	N
7 Miller, George	Y	Y	N
8 Pelosi [1]	Y		Y
9 Lee	Y	Y	N
10 Tauscher	Y	Y	N
11 McNerney	Y	Y	N
12 Speier	Y	Y	N
13 Stark	N	?	?
14 Eshoo	Y	Y	N
15 Honda	Y	Y	N
16 Lofgren	Y	Y	N
17 Farr	Y	Y	N
18 Cardoza	Y	Y	Y
19 Radanovich	Y	N	Y
20 Costa	Y	Y	Y
21 Nunes	N	N	Y
22 McCarthy	N	N	Y
23 Capps	Y	Y	N
24 Gallegly	Y	N	Y
25 McKeon	N	N	Y
26 Dreier	N	N	Y
27 Sherman	Y	Y	Y
28 Berman	Y	Y	Y
29 Schiff	Y	Y	Y
30 Waxman	N	Y	N
31 Becerra	Y	Y	N
32 Solis	Y	Y	N
33 Watson	Y	Y	N
34 Roybal-Allard	Y	Y	N
35 Waters	Y	Y	N
36 Harman	N	Y	Y
37 Richardson	Y	Y	Y
38 Napolitano	Y	Y	N
39 Sánchez, Linda	Y	Y	N
40 Royce	N	N	N
41 Lewis	N	N	Y
42 Miller, Gary	N	N	Y
43 Baca	Y	Y	Y
44 Calvert	N	N	Y
45 Bono Mack	Y	Y	Y
46 Rohrabacher	N	N	Y
47 Sanchez, Loretta	Y	Y	N
48 Campbell	N	N	Y
49 Issa	N	N	Y
50 Bilbray	N	N	Y
51 Filner	Y	Y	N
52 Hunter	N	N	Y
53 Davis	Y	Y	N

	346	400	437
COLORADO			
1 DeGette	Y	Y	N
2 Udall	Y	Y	Y
3 Salazar	Y	Y	Y
4 Musgrave	Y	?	Y
5 Lamborn	N	N	Y
6 Tancredo	N	?	Y
7 Perlmutter	Y	Y	Y
CONNECTICUT			
1 Larson	Y	Y	N
2 Courtney	Y	Y	N
3 DeLauro	Y	Y	N
4 Shays	N	Y	Y
5 Murphy	Y	Y	N
DELAWARE			
AL Castle	N	Y	Y
FLORIDA			
1 Miller	N	N	Y
2 Boyd	Y	Y	Y
3 Brown	?	Y	Y
4 Crenshaw	?	Y	Y
5 Brown-Waite	Y	Y	?
6 Stearns	N	N	Y
7 Mica	N	Y	Y
8 Keller	N	Y	Y
9 Bilirakis	Y	N	Y
10 Young	N	Y	Y
11 Castor	+	Y	Y
12 Putnam	Y	Y	Y
13 Buchanan	Y	Y	Y
14 Mack	N	N	Y
15 Weldon	N	N	Y
16 Mahoney	Y	Y	Y
17 Meek	Y	Y	N
18 Ros-Lehtinen	Y	Y	Y
19 Wexler	?	Y	N
20 Wasserman Schultz	Y	Y	Y
21 Diaz-Balart, L.	Y	Y	Y
22 Klein	Y	Y	Y
23 Hastings	Y	Y	Y
24 Feeney	N	N	Y
25 Diaz-Balart, M.	Y	?	Y
GEORGIA			
1 Kingston	Y	N	Y
2 Bishop	Y	Y	Y
3 Westmoreland	N	Y	Y
4 Johnson	Y	Y	N
5 Lewis	Y	Y	N
6 Price	N	N	Y
7 Linder	N	N	Y
8 Marshall	Y	Y	Y
9 Deal	N	N	Y
10 Broun	N	N	Y
11 Gingrey	Y	N	Y
12 Barrow	Y	Y	Y
13 Scott	Y	Y	Y
HAWAII			
1 Abercrombie	Y	Y	N
2 Hirono	Y	Y	N
IDAHO			
1 Sali	Y	N	Y
2 Simpson	Y	Y	Y
ILLINOIS			
1 Rush	+	+	-
2 Jackson	Y	Y	N
3 Lipinski	Y	Y	Y
4 Gutierrez	Y	?	Y
5 Emanuel	Y	Y	Y
6 Roskam	N	N	Y
7 Davis	Y	Y	N
8 Bean	N	Y	Y
9 Schakowsky	Y	Y	N
10 Kirk	N	Y	Y
11 Weller	Y	Y	+
12 Costello	Y	Y	N
13 Biggert	N	Y	Y
14 Foster	Y	Y	N
15 Johnson	Y	Y	N

KEY	Republicans	Democrats	
Y Voted for (yea)		X Paired against	C Voted "present" to avoid possible conflict of interest
# Paired for		– Announced against	
+ Announced for		P Voted "present"	? Did not vote or otherwise make a position known
N Voted against (nay)			

	346	400	437
16 **Manzullo**	Y	Y	Y
17 Hare	Y	Y	N
18 LaHood	Y	Y	Y
19 **Shimkus**	Y	Y	Y
INDIANA			
1 Visclosky	Y	Y	–
2 Donnelly	Y	Y	Y
3 **Souder**	Y	Y	Y
4 **Buyer**	Y	Y	Y
5 **Burton**	N	N	Y
6 **Pence**	N	N	Y
7 Carson, A.	Y	Y	N
8 Ellsworth	Y	Y	Y
9 Hill	Y	Y	N
IOWA			
1 Braley	Y	+	N
2 Loebsack	Y	?	N
3 Boswell	Y	Y	Y
4 **Latham**	Y	Y	Y
5 **King**	Y	?	Y
KANSAS			
1 **Moran**	N	Y	Y
2 Boyda	Y	Y	Y
3 Moore	Y	Y	Y
4 **Tiahrt**	?	N	?
KENTUCKY			
1 **Whitfield**	Y	Y	Y
2 **Lewis**	Y	N	Y
3 Yarmuth	Y	Y	Y
4 **Davis**	Y	N	Y
5 **Rogers**	Y	N	Y
6 Chandler	Y	Y	Y
LOUISIANA			
1 **Scalise**	N	N	Y
2 Jefferson	Y	Y	N
3 Melancon	Y	Y	Y
4 **McCrery**	N	?	Y
5 **Alexander**	Y	Y	Y
6 Cazayoux	Y	Y	Y
7 Boustany	Y	N	Y
MAINE			
1 Allen	Y	Y	N
2 Michaud	Y	Y	N
MARYLAND			
1 **Gilchrest**	Y	Y	?
2 Ruppersberger	Y	Y	Y
3 Sarbanes	Y	Y	N
4 Wynn[2]	Y		
4 Edwards[2]			N
5 Hoyer	Y	Y	Y
6 **Bartlett**	Y	?	Y
7 Cummings	Y	Y	N
8 Van Hollen	Y	Y	N
MASSACHUSETTS			
1 Olver	Y	Y	N
2 Neal	Y	Y	N
3 McGovern	Y	Y	N
4 Frank	Y	Y	N
5 Tsongas	Y	Y	N
6 Tierney	Y	Y	N
7 Markey	Y	Y	N
8 Capuano	N	Y	N
9 Lynch	Y	Y	N
10 Delahunt	Y	Y	N
MICHIGAN			
1 Stupak	Y	Y	Y
2 **Hoekstra**	Y	N	Y
3 **Ehlers**	N	Y	Y
4 **Camp**	Y	N	Y
5 Kildee	Y	Y	Y
6 **Upton**	Y	Y	Y
7 **Walberg**	Y	N	Y
8 **Rogers**	Y	N	Y
9 **Knollenberg**	N	Y	Y
10 **Miller**	Y	Y	Y
11 **McCotter**	Y	Y	Y
12 Levin	Y	Y	N
13 Kilpatrick	Y	Y	N
14 Conyers	Y	Y	N
15 Dingell	Y	Y	N
MINNESOTA			
1 Walz	Y	Y	N
2 **Kline**	Y	N	Y
3 **Ramstad**	N	N	Y
4 McCollum	Y	Y	N

	346	400	437
5 Ellison	Y	Y	N
6 **Bachmann**	N	N	Y
7 Peterson	Y	Y	Y
8 Oberstar	Y	Y	N
MISSISSIPPI			
1 Childers[3]	Y	Y	Y
2 Thompson	Y	Y	Y
3 **Pickering**	Y	Y	Y
4 Taylor	Y	Y	Y
MISSOURI			
1 Clay	Y	Y	N
2 **Akin**	N	N	Y
3 Carnahan	Y	Y	N
4 Skelton	Y	Y	Y
5 Cleaver	Y	Y	Y
6 **Graves**	Y	Y	Y
7 **Blunt**	Y	N	Y
8 **Emerson**	Y	N	Y
9 **Hulshof**	Y	?	Y
MONTANA			
AL **Rehberg**	Y	Y	Y
NEBRASKA			
1 **Fortenberry**	Y	Y	Y
2 **Terry**	N	N	Y
3 **Smith**	Y	N	Y
NEVADA			
1 Berkley	Y	Y	Y
2 **Heller**	N	N	Y
3 **Porter**	Y	N	Y
NEW HAMPSHIRE			
1 Shea-Porter	Y	Y	N
2 Hodes	Y	Y	N
NEW JERSEY			
1 Andrews	Y	Y	N
2 **LoBiondo**	N	Y	Y
3 **Saxton**	N	Y	Y
4 **Smith**	N	Y	Y
5 **Garrett**	N	Y	Y
6 Pallone	Y	Y	N
7 **Ferguson**	N	Y	Y
8 Pascrell	Y	Y	N
9 Rothman	Y	Y	N
10 Payne	Y	Y	N
11 **Frelinghuysen**	N	Y	Y
12 Holt	Y	Y	N
13 Sires	Y	Y	Y
NEW MEXICO			
1 **Wilson**	N	N	Y
2 **Pearce**	Y	N	Y
3 Udall	Y	Y	N
NEW YORK			
1 Bishop	Y	Y	N
2 Israel	Y	Y	N
3 **King**	N	Y	Y
4 McCarthy	Y	Y	N
5 Ackerman	Y	Y	Y
6 Meeks	Y	Y	Y
7 Crowley	Y	Y	Y
8 Nadler	Y	Y	N
9 Weiner	Y	Y	N
10 Towns	Y	Y	N
11 Clarke	Y	Y	N
12 Velázquez	Y	Y	N
13 **Fossella**	?	Y	Y
14 Maloney	Y	Y	N
15 Rangel	Y	Y	N
16 Serrano	Y	Y	N
17 Engel	Y	Y	N
18 Lowey	Y	Y	Y
19 Hall	Y	Y	N
20 Gillibrand	?	?	Y
21 McNulty	Y	Y	N
22 Hinchey	Y	Y	N
23 **McHugh**	Y	Y	Y
24 Arcuri	Y	Y	Y
25 **Walsh**	Y	Y	Y
26 **Reynolds**	Y	Y	?
27 Higgins	Y	Y	N
28 Slaughter	Y	Y	N
29 **Kuhl**	Y	Y	Y
NORTH CAROLINA			
1 Butterfield	Y	+	Y
2 Etheridge	Y	Y	Y
3 **Jones**	Y	Y	?
4 Price	Y	Y	N

	346	400	437
5 **Foxx**	N	N	Y
6 **Coble**	N	N	Y
7 McIntyre	Y	Y	Y
8 **Hayes**	Y	Y	Y
9 **Myrick**	N	N	Y
10 **McHenry**	N	N	Y
11 Shuler	Y	Y	Y
12 Watt	Y	Y	N
13 Miller	Y	Y	N
NORTH DAKOTA			
AL Pomeroy	Y	Y	Y
OHIO			
1 **Chabot**	N	N	Y
2 **Schmidt**	N	N	Y
3 **Turner**	Y	Y	Y
4 **Jordan**	N	N	Y
5 **Latta**	Y	N	Y
6 Wilson	Y	Y	Y
7 **Hobson**	N	N	Y
8 **Boehner**	N	N	Y
9 Kaptur	Y	+	N
10 Kucinich	Y	Y	N
11 Tubbs Jones	Y	Y	N
12 **Tiberi**	N	Y	N
13 Sutton	Y	Y	N
14 **LaTourette**	Y	Y	Y
15 **Pryce**	N	Y	Y
16 **Regula**	Y	Y	Y
17 Ryan	Y	Y	N
18 Space	Y	Y	Y
OKLAHOMA			
1 **Sullivan**	N	Y	Y
2 Boren	Y	Y	Y
3 **Lucas**	Y	Y	Y
4 **Cole**	Y	Y	Y
5 **Fallin**	Y	Y	Y
OREGON			
1 Wu	Y	Y	N
2 **Walden**	Y	Y	Y
3 Blumenauer	N	Y	N
4 DeFazio	Y	Y	N
5 Hooley	Y	Y	N
PENNSYLVANIA			
1 Brady	Y	Y	N
2 Fattah	Y	Y	N
3 **English**	Y	Y	Y
4 Altmire	Y	Y	Y
5 **Peterson**	Y	N	?
6 **Gerlach**	Y	Y	Y
7 Sestak	Y	Y	Y
8 Murphy, P.	Y	Y	Y
9 **Shuster**	Y	Y	Y
10 Carney	Y	Y	Y
11 Kanjorski	Y	Y	Y
12 Murtha	Y	Y	Y
13 Schwartz	Y	Y	N
14 Doyle	Y	Y	N
15 **Dent**	N	Y	Y
16 **Pitts**	N	N	Y
17 Holden	Y	Y	N
18 **Murphy, T.**	Y	Y	Y
19 **Platts**	Y	Y	Y
RHODE ISLAND			
1 Kennedy	?	Y	N
2 Langevin	Y	Y	Y
SOUTH CAROLINA			
1 **Brown**	Y	Y	Y
2 **Wilson**	N	N	Y
3 **Barrett**	N	N	Y
4 **Inglis**	N	N	Y
5 Spratt	Y	Y	Y
6 Clyburn	Y	Y	Y
SOUTH DAKOTA			
AL Herseth Sandlin	Y	Y	Y
TENNESSEE			
1 **Davis, David**	Y	N	Y
2 **Duncan**	N	N	Y
3 **Wamp**	N	N	Y
4 Davis, L.	Y	Y	Y
5 Cooper	N	Y	Y
6 Gordon	Y	Y	Y
7 **Blackburn**	Y	N	Y
8 Tanner	Y	Y	Y
9 Cohen	Y	Y	Y

	346	400	437
TEXAS			
1 **Gohmert**	Y	Y	?
2 **Poe**	Y	Y	Y
3 **Johnson, S.**	N	N	Y
4 **Hall**	Y	N	Y
5 **Hensarling**	N	N	Y
6 **Barton**	N	N	Y
7 **Culberson**	N	N	Y
8 **Brady**	Y	N	Y
9 Green, A.	Y	+	Y
10 **McCaul**	Y	N	Y
11 **Conaway**	Y	N	Y
12 **Granger**	N	Y	Y
13 **Thornberry**	Y	N	Y
14 **Paul**	N	N	?
15 Hinojosa	Y	Y	Y
16 Reyes	Y	Y	Y
17 Edwards	Y	Y	Y
18 Jackson Lee	Y	Y	N
19 **Neugebauer**	Y	N	Y
20 Gonzalez	Y	Y	N
21 **Smith**	N	N	Y
22 Lampson	Y	Y	Y
23 Rodriguez	Y	Y	Y
24 **Marchant**	N	N	Y
25 Doggett	Y	Y	N
26 **Burgess**	N	N	Y
27 Ortiz	Y	?	Y
28 Cuellar	Y	Y	N
29 Green, G.	Y	Y	N
30 Johnson, E.	Y	Y	N
31 **Carter**	+	N	Y
32 **Sessions**	N	N	Y
UTAH			
1 **Bishop**	?	Y	Y
2 Matheson	N	Y	Y
3 **Cannon**	N	N	?
VERMONT			
AL Welch	Y	Y	N
VIRGINIA			
1 **Wittman**	Y	N	Y
2 **Drake**	Y	Y	Y
3 Scott	Y	Y	N
4 **Forbes**	N	Y	Y
5 **Goode**	N	Y	Y
6 **Goodlatte**	Y	Y	Y
7 **Cantor**	N	Y	Y
8 Moran	Y	Y	N
9 Boucher	Y	Y	Y
10 **Wolf**	N	Y	Y
11 **Davis, T.**	N	Y	Y
WASHINGTON			
1 Inslee	N	Y	N
2 Larsen	Y	Y	N
3 Baird	Y	Y	Y
4 **Hastings**	Y	N	Y
5 **McMorris Rodgers**	Y	N	Y
6 Dicks	Y	Y	Y
7 McDermott	N	Y	N
8 **Reichert**	N	Y	Y
9 Smith	N	Y	Y
WEST VIRGINIA			
1 Mollohan	Y	Y	N
2 **Capito**	Y	Y	Y
3 Rahall	Y	Y	Y
WISCONSIN			
1 **Ryan**	N	N	Y
2 Baldwin	Y	Y	N
3 Kind	N	Y	Y
4 Moore	N	Y	N
5 **Sensenbrenner**	N	N	Y
6 **Petri**	N	Y	Y
7 Obey	Y	Y	N
8 Kagen	Y	Y	N
WYOMING			
AL **Cubin**	Y	N	Y
DELEGATES			
Faleomavaega (A.S.)			
Norton (D.C.)			
Bordallo (Guam)			
Fortuño (P.R.)			
Christensen (V.I.)			

IN THE HOUSE | By Vote Number

443. **HR 6331. Medicare Physician Payments/Passage.** Pallone, D-N.J., motion to suspend the rules and pass the bill that would prevent a 10.6 percent cut in payments to physicians treating Medicare patients, scheduled for July 1; hold payments at current rates for 18 months; and provide a 1.1 percent increase in 2009. The bill would provide an additional $16.6 billion over 10 years for changes to Medicare beneficiary programs. The costs would be partially offset by phasing out bonus payments to Medicare Advantage plans and requiring private "fee for service" plans to form networks with health care providers, thereby slowing the plans' growth. Motion agreed to 355-59: R 129-59; D 226-0 (ND 169-0, SD 57-0). A two-thirds majority of those present and voting (276 in this case) is required for passage under suspension of the rules. A "nay" was a vote in support of the president's position. June 24, 2008. *(Story, p. C-5)*

519. **HR 3221. Mortgage Relief/Motion to Concur.** Frank, D-Mass., motion to concur in the Senate amendment with the House amendment that would grant authority to the Treasury Department to extend new credit to and buy stock in Fannie Mae and Freddie Mac. It also would create an independent regulator for the two mortgage giants and the Federal Home Loan Bank System. It would overhaul the Federal Housing Administration (FHA) and allow it to insure up to $300 billion worth of new, refinanced loans for struggling mortgage borrowers. It also includes a $7,500 tax credit for some first-time homebuyers, higher loan limits for FHA-backed loans, a standard tax deduction for property taxes and revenue-raisers to offset part of the costs. It also would authorize $3.9 billion in grants to states and localities to purchase and rehabilitate foreclosed properties and would increase the federal debt limit to $10.6 trillion. Motion agreed to 272-152: R 45-149; D 227-3 (ND 171-3, SD 56-0). A "yea" was a vote in support of the president's position. July 23, 2008. *(Story, p. C-6)*

531. **HR 5501. Global HIV/AIDS Program Reauthorization/Motion to Concur.** Berman, D-Calif., motion to concur in the Senate amendment to the bill that would authorize $48 billion from fiscal 2009 through 2013 for programs under the President's Emergency Plan for AIDS Relief used to fight AIDS, tuberculosis and malaria overseas. The bill would replace the current requirement that one-third of all HIV prevention funding go to abstinence education with balanced funding for abstinence, fidelity and condom programs. It also would authorize $2 billion for American Indian health, clean water and law enforcement programs. Motion agreed to (thus clearing the bill for the president), 303-115: R 75-114; D 228-1 (ND 172-0, SD 56-1). A "yea" was a vote in support of the president's position. July 24, 2008. *(Story, p. C-6)*

542. **HR 1108. Tobacco Products Regulation/Passage.** Dingell, D-Mich., motion to suspend the rules and pass the bill that would authorize the Food and Drug Administration (FDA) to regulate tobacco products. The FDA could restrict sales and distribution, including advertising and promotion, if it determined that it was necessary to protect public health, although it could not ban a class of tobacco products or reduce the nicotine level to zero. The bill would assess new quarterly user fees on manufacturers and importers of tobacco products to pay for the additional regulations. Motion agreed to 326-102: R 96-99; D 230-3 (ND 173-1, SD 57-2). A two-thirds majority of those present and voting (286 in this case) is required for passage under suspension of the rules. A "nay" was a vote in support of the president's position. July 30, 2008. *(Story, p. C-6)*

[1]The Speaker votes only at her discretion.

ND Northern Democrats, SD Southern Democrats
Southern states: Ala., Ark., Fla., Ga., Ky., La., Miss., N.C., Okla., S.C., Tenn., Texas, Va.

	443	519	531	542
ALABAMA				
1 Bonner	Y	N	Y	Y
2 Everett	Y	N	?	Y
3 Rogers	Y	Y	Y	Y
4 Aderholt	Y	N	Y	N
5 Cramer	Y	Y	Y	Y
6 Bachus	Y	N	Y	N
7 Davis	Y	Y	Y	Y
ALASKA				
AL Young	Y	N	N	Y
ARIZONA				
1 Renzi	N	N	Y	Y
2 Franks	N	N	N	N
3 Shadegg	N	N	N	N
4 Pastor	Y	Y	Y	Y
5 Mitchell	Y	Y	Y	Y
6 Flake	N	N	N	N
7 Grijalva	Y	Y	Y	Y
8 Giffords	Y	Y	Y	Y
ARKANSAS				
1 Berry	Y	Y	Y	Y
2 Snyder	Y	Y	Y	Y
3 Boozman	Y	N	Y	Y
4 Ross	Y	Y	Y	Y
CALIFORNIA				
1 Thompson	Y	Y	Y	Y
2 Herger	N	N	N	N
3 Lungren	N	Y	Y	N
4 Doolittle	N	N	N	N
5 Matsui	Y	Y	Y	Y
6 Woolsey	Y	Y	Y	Y
7 Miller, George	+	Y	Y	Y
8 Pelosi[1]		Y	Y	
9 Lee	Y	Y	Y	Y
10 Tauscher	Y	Y	Y	Y
11 McNerney	Y	Y	Y	Y
12 Speier	?	Y	Y	Y
13 Stark	Y	Y	Y	Y
14 Eshoo	Y	Y	Y	Y
15 Honda	Y	Y	Y	Y
16 Lofgren	Y	Y	Y	Y
17 Farr	Y	Y	Y	Y
18 Cardoza	Y	Y	Y	Y
19 Radanovich	N	N	N	N
20 Costa	Y	Y	Y	Y
21 Nunes	?	N	Y	N
22 McCarthy	N	N	N	Y
23 Capps	Y	Y	Y	Y
24 Gallegly	Y	N	Y	Y
25 McKeon	Y	Y	Y	N
26 Dreier	Y	Y	Y	Y
27 Sherman	Y	Y	Y	Y
28 Berman	Y	Y	Y	Y
29 Schiff	Y	Y	Y	Y
30 Waxman	Y	Y	Y	Y
31 Becerra	Y	Y	Y	Y
32 Solis	Y	Y	Y	Y
33 Watson	Y	Y	Y	Y
34 Roybal-Allard	Y	Y	Y	Y
35 Waters	Y	Y	Y	Y
36 Harman	Y	Y	Y	Y
37 Richardson	Y	Y	Y	Y
38 Napolitano	Y	Y	Y	Y
39 Sánchez, Linda	Y	Y	Y	Y
40 Royce	N	N	N	N
41 Lewis	Y	Y	Y	N
42 Miller, Gary	Y	Y	N	N
43 Baca	Y	Y	Y	Y
44 Calvert	Y	Y	N	N
45 Bono Mack	Y	Y	Y	Y
46 Rohrabacher	N	N	N	N
47 Sanchez, Loretta	Y	Y	Y	Y
48 Campbell	N	Y	N	N
49 Issa	Y	N	Y	N
50 Bilbray	Y	N	Y	Y
51 Filner	Y	Y	Y	Y
52 Hunter	Y	N	N	N
53 Davis	Y	Y	Y	Y

	443	519	531	542
COLORADO				
1 DeGette	Y	Y	Y	Y
2 Udall	Y	Y	Y	Y
3 Salazar	Y	Y	?	Y
4 Musgrave	Y	N	N	N
5 Lamborn	N	N	N	N
6 Tancredo	?	N	N	N
7 Perlmutter	Y	Y	Y	Y
CONNECTICUT				
1 Larson	Y	Y	Y	Y
2 Courtney	Y	Y	Y	Y
3 DeLauro	Y	Y	Y	Y
4 Shays	Y	Y	Y	Y
5 Murphy	Y	Y	Y	Y
DELAWARE				
AL Castle	Y	Y	Y	Y
FLORIDA				
1 Miller	Y	N	N	N
2 Boyd	Y	Y	Y	Y
3 Brown	Y	Y	Y	Y
4 Crenshaw	N	N	N	Y
5 Brown-Waite	Y	?	?	?
6 Stearns	Y	N	N	N
7 Mica	N	N	N	N
8 Keller	Y	N	N	N
9 Bilirakis	Y	N	Y	Y
10 Young	Y	N	Y	Y
11 Castor	Y	Y	Y	Y
12 Putnam	Y	Y	N	Y
13 Buchanan	Y	N	Y	Y
14 Mack	Y	N	N	N
15 Weldon	Y	N	Y	N
16 Mahoney	Y	Y	Y	Y
17 Meek	Y	Y	Y	Y
18 Ros-Lehtinen	Y	Y	Y	Y
19 Wexler	Y	Y	Y	Y
20 Wasserman Schultz	Y	Y	Y	Y
21 Diaz-Balart, L.	Y	Y	N	N
22 Klein	Y	Y	Y	Y
23 Hastings	Y	Y	Y	Y
24 Feeney	Y	N	N	N
25 Diaz-Balart, M.	Y	Y	Y	Y
GEORGIA				
1 Kingston	Y	N	N	N
2 Bishop	Y	+	Y	Y
3 Westmoreland	N	N	N	N
4 Johnson	Y	Y	Y	Y
5 Lewis	Y	Y	Y	Y
6 Price	Y	N	N	N
7 Linder	N	N	N	Y
8 Marshall	Y	Y	Y	Y
9 Deal	Y	N	N	N
10 Broun	N	N	N	N
11 Gingrey	Y	N	N	N
12 Barrow	Y	Y	Y	Y
13 Scott	Y	Y	Y	Y
HAWAII				
1 Abercrombie	Y	Y	Y	Y
2 Hirono	Y	Y	Y	Y
IDAHO				
1 Sali	N	N	N	N
2 Simpson	Y	N	N	Y
ILLINOIS				
1 Rush	+	+	+	Y
2 Jackson	Y	Y	Y	Y
3 Lipinski	Y	Y	Y	Y
4 Gutierrez	Y	Y	Y	Y
5 Emanuel	Y	Y	Y	Y
6 Roskam	N	N	N	Y
7 Davis	?	Y	Y	Y
8 Bean	Y	Y	Y	Y
9 Schakowsky	Y	Y	Y	Y
10 Kirk	Y	N	Y	Y
11 Weller	Y	Y	Y	Y
12 Costello	Y	Y	Y	Y
13 Biggert	Y	Y	Y	Y
14 Foster	Y	Y	Y	Y
15 Johnson	+	N	Y	Y

KEY **Republicans** Democrats

Y Voted for (yea)	X Paired against	C Voted "present" to avoid possible conflict of interest
# Paired for	− Announced against	
+ Announced for	P Voted "present"	? Did not vote or otherwise make a position known
N Voted against (nay)		

Member	443	519	531	542
16 Manzullo	Y	N	N	Y
17 Hare	Y	+	Y	Y
18 LaHood	Y	Y	?	Y
19 Shimkus	N	N	Y	Y
INDIANA				
1 Visclosky	Y	Y	Y	Y
2 Donnelly	Y	Y	Y	Y
3 Souder	Y	N	N	N
4 Buyer	N	N	N	N
5 Burton	Y	N	N	Y
6 Pence	?	N	Y	N
7 Carson, A.	Y	Y	Y	Y
8 Ellsworth	Y	Y	Y	Y
9 Hill	Y	Y	Y	Y
IOWA				
1 Braley	Y	Y	Y	Y
2 Loebsack	Y	Y	Y	Y
3 Boswell	Y	?	?	Y
4 Latham	Y	N	Y	N
5 King	N	N	N	N
KANSAS				
1 Moran	Y	N	Y	Y
2 Boyda	Y	N	Y	Y
3 Moore	Y	Y	Y	Y
4 Tiahrt	Y	N	Y	Y
KENTUCKY				
1 Whitfield	Y	N	N	N
2 Lewis	N	N	N	N
3 Yarmuth	Y	Y	Y	Y
4 Davis	Y	N	N	N
5 Rogers	Y	N	N	N
6 Chandler	Y	Y	Y	Y
LOUISIANA				
1 Scalise	N	N	N	N
2 Jefferson	Y	Y	Y	Y
3 Melancon	N	Y	Y	N
4 McCrery	N	Y	N	N
5 Alexander	Y	N	Y	N
6 Cazayoux	Y	Y	Y	Y
7 Boustany	N	Y	Y	N
MAINE				
1 Allen	Y	Y	Y	Y
2 Michaud	Y	Y	Y	Y
MARYLAND				
1 Gilchrest	Y	Y	Y	Y
2 Ruppersberger	Y	Y	Y	Y
3 Sarbanes	Y	Y	Y	Y
4 Edwards	Y	Y	Y	Y
5 Hoyer	Y	Y	Y	Y
6 Bartlett	N	N	N	Y
7 Cummings	Y	Y	Y	Y
8 Van Hollen	Y	Y	Y	Y
MASSACHUSETTS				
1 Olver	Y	Y	Y	Y
2 Neal	Y	Y	Y	Y
3 McGovern	Y	Y	Y	Y
4 Frank	Y	Y	Y	Y
5 Tsongas	Y	Y	Y	Y
6 Tierney	Y	Y	Y	Y
7 Markey	Y	Y	Y	Y
8 Capuano	Y	Y	Y	Y
9 Lynch	Y	Y	Y	Y
10 Delahunt	Y	Y	Y	Y
MICHIGAN				
1 Stupak	Y	Y	Y	Y
2 Hoekstra	Y	N	Y	Y
3 Ehlers	Y	N	Y	Y
4 Camp	N	N	N	Y
5 Kildee	Y	Y	Y	Y
6 Upton	Y	N	Y	Y
7 Walberg	Y	N	Y	N
8 Rogers	N	N	N	Y
9 Knollenberg	Y	Y	Y	Y
10 Miller	Y	N	N	Y
11 McCotter	Y	N	Y	N
12 Levin	Y	Y	Y	Y
13 Kilpatrick	Y	Y	Y	Y
14 Conyers	Y	Y	Y	Y
15 Dingell	Y	Y	Y	Y
MINNESOTA				
1 Walz	Y	Y	Y	Y
2 Kline	Y	N	Y	N
3 Ramstad	Y	N	Y	Y
4 McCollum	Y	Y	Y	Y

Member	443	519	531	542
5 Ellison	Y	Y	Y	Y
6 Bachmann	N	N	N	N
7 Peterson	Y	Y	Y	Y
8 Oberstar	Y	Y	Y	Y
MISSISSIPPI				
1 Childers	Y	Y	Y	Y
2 Thompson	?	Y	Y	Y
3 Pickering	Y	Y	Y	Y
4 Taylor	Y	Y	Y	Y
MISSOURI				
1 Clay	Y	Y	Y	Y
2 Akin	N	N	N	N
3 Carnahan	Y	Y	Y	Y
4 Skelton	Y	Y	Y	Y
5 Cleaver	Y	Y	Y	Y
6 Graves	Y	N	N	Y
7 Blunt	N	N	N	?
8 Emerson	Y	N	Y	Y
9 Hulshof	N	?	?	?
MONTANA				
AL Rehberg	Y	N	Y	Y
NEBRASKA				
1 Fortenberry	Y	N	Y	Y
2 Terry	Y	N	N	Y
3 Smith	Y	N	N	N
NEVADA				
1 Berkley	Y	Y	Y	Y
2 Heller	Y	Y	N	N
3 Porter	Y	Y	Y	Y
NEW HAMPSHIRE				
1 Shea-Porter	Y	Y	Y	Y
2 Hodes	Y	Y	Y	Y
NEW JERSEY				
1 Andrews	Y	Y	Y	Y
2 LoBiondo	Y	N	N	Y
3 Saxton	?	N	?	Y
4 Smith	N	Y	Y	Y
5 Garrett	N	N	N	N
6 Pallone	Y	Y	Y	Y
7 Ferguson	Y	Y	Y	Y
8 Pascrell	Y	Y	Y	Y
9 Rothman	Y	Y	Y	Y
10 Payne	Y	Y	Y	Y
11 Frelinghuysen	N	N	Y	Y
12 Holt	Y	Y	Y	Y
13 Sires	Y	Y	Y	Y
NEW MEXICO				
1 Wilson	Y	N	Y	Y
2 Pearce	Y	N	Y	N
3 Udall	Y	Y	Y	Y
NEW YORK				
1 Bishop	Y	Y	Y	Y
2 Israel	Y	Y	Y	Y
3 King	Y	Y	Y	Y
4 McCarthy	Y	Y	Y	Y
5 Ackerman	Y	Y	Y	Y
6 Meeks	Y	Y	Y	Y
7 Crowley	Y	Y	Y	Y
8 Nadler	Y	Y	Y	Y
9 Weiner	Y	Y	Y	Y
10 Towns	Y	Y	?	Y
11 Clarke	Y	Y	Y	Y
12 Velázquez	Y	Y	Y	Y
13 Fossella	Y	N	Y	Y
14 Maloney	Y	Y	Y	?
15 Rangel	Y	Y	Y	?
16 Serrano	Y	Y	Y	Y
17 Engel	?	Y	Y	Y
18 Lowey	Y	Y	Y	Y
19 Hall	Y	Y	Y	Y
20 Gillibrand	Y	Y	Y	Y
21 McNulty	?	Y	Y	Y
22 Hinchey	Y	Y	Y	Y
23 McHugh	Y	Y	Y	Y
24 Arcuri	Y	Y	Y	Y
25 Walsh	Y	Y	Y	Y
26 Reynolds	?	Y	Y	N
27 Higgins	?	Y	Y	Y
28 Slaughter	Y	Y	Y	Y
29 Kuhl	Y	N	Y	Y
NORTH CAROLINA				
1 Butterfield	Y	Y	Y	Y
2 Etheridge	Y	Y	Y	Y
3 Jones	Y	N	N	N
4 Price	Y	Y	Y	Y

Member	443	519	531	542
5 Foxx	Y	N	N	N
6 Coble	Y	N	N	N
7 McIntyre	Y	Y	N	Y
8 Hayes	Y	Y	N	N
9 Myrick	Y	N	N	N
10 McHenry	N	N	N	N
11 Shuler	Y	Y	Y	N
12 Watt	Y	Y	Y	Y
13 Miller	Y	Y	Y	Y
NORTH DAKOTA				
AL Pomeroy	Y	Y	Y	Y
OHIO				
1 Chabot	Y	N	N	Y
2 Schmidt	Y	N	Y	N
3 Turner	Y	Y	Y	Y
4 Jordan	N	N	N	N
5 Latta	Y	N	N	N
6 Wilson	Y	Y	Y	Y
7 Hobson	Y	Y	?	Y
8 Boehner	N	N	N	N
9 Kaptur	Y	N	Y	Y
10 Kucinich	Y	Y	Y	Y
11 Tubbs Jones	Y	Y	Y	Y
12 Tiberi	Y	N	Y	Y
13 Sutton	Y	Y	Y	Y
14 LaTourette	Y	Y	Y	Y
15 Pryce	?	Y	Y	Y
16 Regula	Y	N	Y	Y
17 Ryan	Y	Y	Y	Y
18 Space	Y	Y	Y	Y
OKLAHOMA				
1 Sullivan	Y	N	N	N
2 Boren	Y	Y	Y	Y
3 Lucas	Y	N	N	N
4 Cole	N	N	Y	N
5 Fallin	Y	N	?	Y
OREGON				
1 Wu	Y	Y	Y	Y
2 Walden	Y	N	N	Y
3 Blumenauer	Y	Y	Y	Y
4 DeFazio	Y	N	Y	Y
5 Hooley	Y	Y	?	Y
PENNSYLVANIA				
1 Brady	Y	Y	Y	Y
2 Fattah	Y	Y	Y	Y
3 English	Y	Y	Y	Y
4 Altmire	Y	Y	Y	Y
5 Peterson	?	?	N	Y
6 Gerlach	Y	N	Y	Y
7 Sestak	Y	Y	Y	Y
8 Murphy, P.	Y	Y	Y	Y
9 Shuster	Y	N	N	Y
10 Carney	Y	Y	Y	Y
11 Kanjorski	Y	Y	Y	Y
12 Murtha	Y	Y	Y	Y
13 Schwartz	Y	Y	Y	Y
14 Doyle	Y	Y	Y	Y
15 Dent	Y	N	Y	Y
16 Pitts	N	N	N	N
17 Holden	Y	Y	Y	Y
18 Murphy, T.	Y	Y	Y	Y
19 Platts	Y	N	Y	Y
RHODE ISLAND				
1 Kennedy	Y	Y	Y	Y
2 Langevin	Y	Y	Y	Y
SOUTH CAROLINA				
1 Brown	Y	Y	N	Y
2 Wilson	Y	N	Y	N
3 Barrett	N	N	N	N
4 Inglis	Y	N	Y	N
5 Spratt	Y	Y	Y	Y
6 Clyburn	Y	Y	Y	Y
SOUTH DAKOTA				
AL Herseth Sandlin	Y	Y	Y	Y
TENNESSEE				
1 Davis, David	Y	N	N	N
2 Duncan	N	N	N	Y
3 Wamp	Y	N	N	Y
4 Davis, L.	Y	Y	N	Y
5 Cooper	Y	Y	Y	Y
6 Gordon	Y	Y	Y	Y
7 Blackburn	N	N	N	N
8 Tanner	Y	Y	Y	Y
9 Cohen	Y	Y	Y	Y

Member	443	519	531	542
TEXAS				
1 Gohmert	?	?	N	N
2 Poe	Y	N	N	N
3 Johnson, S.	N	N	N	Y
4 Hall	Y	N	N	Y
5 Hensarling	N	N	N	N
6 Barton	N	N	N	N
7 Culberson	N	N	N	N
8 Brady	N	N	N	Y
9 Green, A.	Y	Y	Y	Y
10 McCaul	Y	N	N	Y
11 Conaway	N	N	N	N
12 Granger	N	N	N	Y
13 Thornberry	N	N	N	N
14 Paul	N	N	N	N
15 Hinojosa	Y	Y	?	?
16 Reyes	?	Y	Y	Y
17 Edwards	Y	Y	Y	Y
18 Jackson Lee	Y	Y	Y	Y
19 Neugebauer	N	N	N	N
20 Gonzalez	Y	Y	Y	Y
21 Smith	Y	N	N	Y
22 Lampson	Y	Y	Y	Y
23 Rodriguez	Y	Y	Y	Y
24 Marchant	N	N	N	N
25 Doggett	Y	Y	Y	Y
26 Burgess	Y	N	N	N
27 Ortiz	Y	?	?	Y
28 Cuellar	Y	Y	Y	Y
29 Green, G.	Y	+	Y	Y
30 Johnson, E.	Y	Y	Y	Y
31 Carter	N	N	N	N
32 Sessions	N	N	N	N
UTAH				
1 Bishop	?	?	?	N
2 Matheson	Y	Y	Y	Y
3 Cannon	?	N	?	N
VERMONT				
AL Welch	Y	Y	Y	Y
VIRGINIA				
1 Wittman	Y	N	N	Y
2 Drake	Y	N	N	Y
3 Scott	Y	Y	Y	Y
4 Forbes	Y	N	N	Y
5 Goode	Y	N	N	N
6 Goodlatte	Y	N	N	N
7 Cantor	N	N	N	Y
8 Moran	Y	Y	Y	Y
9 Boucher	Y	Y	Y	Y
10 Wolf	Y	N	Y	Y
11 Davis, T.	Y	N	Y	Y
WASHINGTON				
1 Inslee	Y	Y	Y	Y
2 Larsen	Y	Y	Y	Y
3 Baird	Y	Y	Y	Y
4 Hastings	Y	N	N	Y
5 McMorris Rodgers	Y	N	N	Y
6 Dicks	Y	Y	Y	Y
7 McDermott	Y	Y	Y	Y
8 Reichert	Y	N	Y	Y
9 Smith	Y	Y	Y	Y
WEST VIRGINIA				
1 Mollohan	Y	Y	Y	Y
2 Capito	Y	Y	Y	Y
3 Rahall	Y	Y	Y	Y
WISCONSIN				
1 Ryan	N	N	N	N
2 Baldwin	Y	Y	Y	Y
3 Kind	Y	Y	Y	Y
4 Moore	Y	Y	Y	Y
5 Sensenbrenner	N	N	N	N
6 Petri	Y	N	N	N
7 Obey	Y	Y	Y	Y
8 Kagen	Y	Y	Y	Y
WYOMING				
AL Cubin	Y	N	?	?
DELEGATES				
Faleomavaega (A.S.)				
Norton (D.C.)				
Bordallo (Guam)				
Fortuño (P.R.)				
Christensen (V.I.)				

IN THE HOUSE | By Vote Number

625. HR 6983. Mental Health Parity/Passage. Pallone, D-N.J., motion to suspend the rules and pass the bill that would require health insurers that cover mental illness to do so on a par with physical illness, including equal standards on co-payments, deductibles, number of doctor visits, days in the hospital and financial limits on coverage. The standards would not have to be upheld if they increase coverage costs by more than 2 percent during the first year of enactment and more than 1 percent in subsequent years. Employers with fewer than 50 employees would be exempt. Motion agreed to 376-47: R 143-47; D 233-0 (ND 175-0, SD 58-0). A two-thirds majority of those present and voting (282 in this case) is required for passage under suspension of the rules. Sept. 23, 2008. *(Story, p. C-6)*

674. HR 3997. Mortgage-Backed Securities Buyout/Motion to Concur. Frank, D-Mass., motion to concur in the Senate amendment to the House amendment to the Senate amendment to the bill, with an additional House amendment. The House amendment would allow the Treasury to use up to $700 billion, in installments, to buy certain mortgage assets. It would require the Treasury to insure the assets, would set up systems for congressional oversight and would set compensation limits for executives of companies whose assets the Treasury purchases. Motion rejected 205-228: R 65-133; D 140-95 (ND 106-70, SD 34-25). A "yea" was a vote in support of the president's position. Sept. 29, 2008. *(Story, p. C-6)*

681. HR 1424. Mortgage-Backed Securities Buyout/Motion to Concur. Frank, D-Mass., motion to concur in the Senate amendments to the bill that would allow the Treasury to use up to $700 billion, in installments, to buy certain mortgage assets. The bill would require the Treasury to create a program to insure mortgage assets, would provide for congressional oversight and would limit compensation for executives of companies whose troubled assets are purchased. It would temporarily increase federal deposit insurance to $250,000 per bank account. It would extend dozens of expired or expiring tax provisions, provide a one-year adjustment to the alternative minimum tax and require private insurance plans to put mental health benefits on a par with other medical benefits. Motion agreed to (thus clearing the bill for the president) 263-171: R 91-108; D 172-63 (ND 131-45, SD 41-18). A "yea" was a vote in support of the president's position. Oct. 3, 2008. *(Story, p. C-7)*

690. HR 7321. Automobile Industry Loan Program/Passage. Passage of the bill that would allow up to $14 billion in loans to eligible domestic automakers. One or more presidentially appointed administrators would be empowered to bring together auto companies, unions, creditors and others to negotiate long-term restructuring plans, which companies would have to submit by March 31, 2009. Administrators could recall the loans if they do not approve the plans. Firms getting loans would have to submit any planned investment or transaction of $100 million or more for review. Loan interest rates would be set at 5 percent for the first five years and 9 percent each subsequent year. The bill would give the government warrants for obtaining stock in participating companies. It also would prohibit loan recipients from giving bonuses to its 25 most highly compensated employees while the loan is outstanding. Passed 237-170: R 32-150; D 205-20 (ND 159-11, SD 46-9). A "yea" was a vote in support of the president's position. Dec. 10, 2008. *(Story, p. C-7)*

[1] The Speaker votes only at her discretion.

[2] Rep. Marcia L. Fudge, D-Ohio, was sworn in Nov. 19, 2008, to fill the seat vacated by the death of Democrat Stephanie Tubbs Jones on Aug. 20. The last vote for which Tubbs Jones was eligible was 566. The first vote for which Fudge was eligible was 684.

[3] Rep. Thomas M. Davis III, R-Va., resigned Nov. 24, 2008. The last vote for which he was eligible was 683.

ND Northern Democrats, SD Southern Democrats
Southern states: Ala., Ark., Fla., Ga., Ky., La., Miss., N.C., Okla., S.C., Tenn., Texas, Va.

	625	674	681	690
ALABAMA				
1 Bonner	N	Y	Y	N
2 Everett	Y	Y	Y	?
3 Rogers	Y	Y	Y	N
4 Aderholt	N	N	N	N
5 Cramer	Y	Y	Y	Y
6 Bachus	Y	Y	Y	N
7 Davis	Y	Y	Y	N
ALASKA				
AL Young	Y	N	N	Y
ARIZONA				
1 Renzi	Y	N	N	?
2 Franks	N	N	N	N
3 Shadegg	N	N	Y	N
4 Pastor	Y	N	Y	Y
5 Mitchell	Y	N	Y	N
6 Flake	N	N	N	N
7 Grijalva	Y	N	Y	N
8 Giffords	Y	N	Y	N
ARKANSAS				
1 Berry	Y	Y	Y	Y
2 Snyder	Y	Y	Y	?
3 Boozman	Y	Y	Y	N
4 Ross	Y	Y	Y	Y
CALIFORNIA				
1 Thompson	Y	N	Y	Y
2 Herger	–	Y	Y	N
3 Lungren	Y	Y	Y	N
4 Doolittle	N	N	N	?
5 Matsui	Y	Y	Y	Y
6 Woolsey	Y	N	Y	Y
7 Miller, George	Y	Y	Y	Y
8 Pelosi[1]		Y	Y	Y
9 Lee	Y	N	Y	Y
10 Tauscher	Y	Y	Y	Y
11 McNerney	Y	Y	Y	Y
12 Speier	Y	Y	Y	Y
13 Stark	Y	N	N	Y
14 Eshoo	Y	Y	Y	Y
15 Honda	Y	Y	Y	Y
16 Lofgren	Y	Y	Y	Y
17 Farr	Y	Y	Y	Y
18 Cardoza	Y	Y	Y	N
19 Radanovich	Y	Y	Y	N
20 Costa	Y	Y	Y	?
21 Nunes	Y	N	N	N
22 McCarthy	Y	N	N	N
23 Capps	Y	Y	Y	Y
24 Gallegly	Y	N	N	N
25 McKeon	Y	Y	Y	N
26 Dreier	Y	Y	Y	N
27 Sherman	Y	N	N	Y
28 Berman	Y	Y	Y	Y
29 Schiff	Y	N	Y	Y
30 Waxman	Y	Y	Y	Y
31 Becerra	Y	N	N	Y
32 Solis	Y	N	Y	Y
33 Watson	Y	N	Y	?
34 Roybal-Allard	Y	N	N	Y
35 Waters	Y	Y	Y	Y
36 Harman	Y	Y	Y	Y
37 Richardson	Y	Y	Y	Y
38 Napolitano	Y	N	N	Y
39 Sánchez, Linda	Y	N	N	Y
40 Royce	N	N	N	N
41 Lewis	Y	Y	Y	N
42 Miller, Gary	Y	Y	Y	?
43 Baca	Y	N	Y	Y
44 Calvert	Y	Y	Y	N
45 Bono Mack	Y	Y	Y	N
46 Rohrabacher	N	N	N	?
47 Sanchez, Loretta	Y	N	Y	Y
48 Campbell	N	Y	Y	P
49 Issa	N	N	N	N
50 Bilbray	Y	N	N	N
51 Filner	Y	N	N	N
52 Hunter	?	N	N	Y
53 Davis	Y	Y	Y	Y

	625	674	681	690
COLORADO				
1 DeGette	Y	Y	Y	Y
2 Udall	Y	N	N	Y
3 Salazar	Y	N	N	Y
4 Musgrave	Y	N	N	N
5 Lamborn	N	N	N	N
6 Tancredo	Y	Y	Y	?
7 Perlmutter	Y	Y	Y	Y
CONNECTICUT				
1 Larson	Y	Y	Y	Y
2 Courtney	Y	N	N	Y
3 DeLauro	Y	Y	Y	Y
4 Shays	Y	Y	Y	N
5 Murphy	Y	Y	Y	Y
DELAWARE				
AL Castle	Y	Y	Y	Y
FLORIDA				
1 Miller	N	N	N	N
2 Boyd	Y	Y	Y	N
3 Brown	Y	Y	Y	Y
4 Crenshaw	Y	Y	Y	N
5 Brown-Waite	Y	N	N	N
6 Stearns	Y	N	N	N
7 Mica	Y	N	N	N
8 Keller	Y	N	N	?
9 Bilirakis	Y	N	N	N
10 Young	Y	N	N	N
11 Castor	Y	N	N	Y
12 Putnam	Y	Y	Y	N
13 Buchanan	Y	N	Y	N
14 Mack	N	N	N	N
15 Weldon	N	Y	Y	?
16 Mahoney	Y	Y	Y	N
17 Meek	Y	Y	Y	Y
18 Ros-Lehtinen	Y	N	N	N
19 Wexler	Y	Y	Y	Y
20 Wasserman Schultz	Y	Y	Y	Y
21 Diaz-Balart, L.	Y	N	N	N
22 Klein	Y	Y	Y	Y
23 Hastings	Y	Y	Y	?
24 Feeney	N	N	N	N
25 Diaz-Balart, M.	Y	N	N	N
GEORGIA				
1 Kingston	N	N	N	N
2 Bishop	Y	Y	Y	Y
3 Westmoreland	N	N	N	N
4 Johnson	Y	N	N	Y
5 Lewis	Y	N	Y	Y
6 Price	Y	N	N	N
7 Linder	N	N	N	N
8 Marshall	Y	Y	N	N
9 Deal	Y	N	N	N
10 Broun	N	N	N	N
11 Gingrey	Y	N	N	N
12 Barrow	Y	N	Y	N
13 Scott	Y	N	Y	Y
HAWAII				
1 Abercrombie	Y	N	Y	Y
2 Hirono	Y	N	Y	Y
IDAHO				
1 Sali	N	N	N	N
2 Simpson	Y	Y	Y	N
ILLINOIS				
1 Rush	Y	N	Y	Y
2 Jackson	Y	N	Y	Y
3 Lipinski	Y	N	N	Y
4 Gutierrez	Y	Y	Y	?
5 Emanuel	Y	Y	Y	?
6 Roskam	Y	N	N	N
7 Davis	Y	N	N	N
8 Bean	Y	Y	Y	Y
9 Schakowsky	Y	Y	Y	Y
10 Kirk	Y	Y	Y	N
11 Weller	Y	?	Y	N
12 Costello	Y	N	N	Y
13 Biggert	Y	N	Y	N
14 Foster	Y	Y	Y	Y
15 Johnson	Y	N	N	N

KEY	**Republicans**	Democrats	
Y Voted for (yea)	X Paired against	C Voted "present" to avoid possible conflict of interest
# Paired for	– Announced against	
+ Announced for	P Voted "present"	? Did not vote or otherwise make a position known
N Voted against (nay)		

	625	674	681	690
16 Manzullo	Y	N	N	Y
17 Hare	Y	Y	Y	Y
18 LaHood	Y	Y	Y	Y
19 Shimkus	Y	N	N	N
INDIANA				
1 Visclosky	Y	N	N	Y
2 Donnelly	Y	Y	Y	Y
3 Souder	Y	Y	Y	Y
4 Buyer	Y	N	N	Y
5 Burton	N	N	N	N
6 Pence	N	N	N	N
7 Carson, A.	Y	N	Y	Y
8 Ellsworth	Y	Y	Y	Y
9 Hill	Y	N	N	Y
IOWA				
1 Braley	Y	N	Y	Y
2 Loebsack	Y	Y	Y	Y
3 Boswell	Y	Y	Y	Y
4 Latham	Y	N	N	N
5 King	N	N	N	N
KANSAS				
1 Moran	Y	N	N	N
2 Boyda	Y	N	N	Y
3 Moore	Y	Y	Y	Y
4 Tiahrt	Y	N	N	N
KENTUCKY				
1 Whitfield	Y	N	N	N
2 Lewis	N	Y	Y	Y
3 Yarmuth	Y	N	Y	Y
4 Davis	Y	N	N	N
5 Rogers	Y	Y	Y	N
6 Chandler	Y	N	N	Y
LOUISIANA				
1 Scalise	Y	N	N	Y
2 Jefferson	Y	N	N	Y
3 Melancon	Y	Y	Y	Y
4 McCrery	N	Y	Y	Y
5 Alexander	Y	N	Y	N
6 Cazayoux	Y	N	N	Y
7 Boustany	Y	N	Y	N
MAINE				
1 Allen	Y	Y	Y	Y
2 Michaud	Y	N	N	Y
MARYLAND				
1 Gilchrest	Y	Y	Y	?
2 Ruppersberger	Y	Y	Y	Y
3 Sarbanes	Y	N	Y	Y
4 Edwards	Y	N	Y	Y
5 Hoyer	Y	Y	Y	Y
6 Bartlett	Y	N	N	N
7 Cummings	Y	N	Y	Y
8 Van Hollen	Y	Y	Y	Y
MASSACHUSETTS				
1 Olver	Y	Y	Y	Y
2 Neal	Y	Y	Y	Y
3 McGovern	Y	Y	Y	Y
4 Frank	Y	Y	Y	Y
5 Tsongas	Y	Y	Y	Y
6 Tierney	Y	Y	Y	Y
7 Markey	Y	Y	Y	Y
8 Capuano	Y	Y	Y	Y
9 Lynch	Y	N	Y	Y
10 Delahunt	Y	N	N	?
MICHIGAN				
1 Stupak	Y	N	N	Y
2 Hoekstra	N	N	Y	Y
3 Ehlers	Y	Y	Y	Y
4 Camp	Y	Y	Y	Y
5 Kildee	Y	Y	Y	Y
6 Upton	Y	Y	Y	Y
7 Walberg	Y	N	N	?
8 Rogers	Y	N	N	Y
9 Knollenberg	Y	N	N	Y
10 Miller	Y	N	N	Y
11 McCotter	Y	N	N	Y
12 Levin	Y	Y	Y	Y
13 Kilpatrick	Y	N	Y	Y
14 Conyers	Y	N	Y	Y
15 Dingell	Y	Y	Y	Y
MINNESOTA				
1 Walz	Y	N	N	Y
2 Kline	Y	N	N	N
3 Ramstad	Y	N	Y	Y
4 McCollum	Y	Y	Y	Y

	625	674	681	690
5 Ellison	Y	Y	Y	?
6 Bachmann	N	N	N	N
7 Peterson	Y	N	N	N
8 Oberstar	Y	Y	Y	Y
MISSISSIPPI				
1 Childers	Y	N	N	N
2 Thompson	Y	N	N	Y
3 Pickering	Y	Y	Y	N
4 Taylor	Y	N	N	Y
MISSOURI				
1 Clay	Y	N	N	Y
2 Akin	N	N	N	N
3 Carnahan	Y	Y	Y	Y
4 Skelton	Y	Y	Y	Y
5 Cleaver	Y	N	Y	Y
6 Graves	Y	N	N	N
7 Blunt	?	Y	Y	N
8 Emerson	Y	Y	Y	Y
9 Hulshof	Y	N	N	N
MONTANA				
AL Rehberg	Y	N	N	N
NEBRASKA				
1 Fortenberry	Y	N	N	N
2 Terry	Y	N	Y	N
3 Smith	N	N	N	N
NEVADA				
1 Berkley	Y	N	Y	Y
2 Heller	Y	N	N	N
3 Porter	Y	Y	Y	Y
NEW HAMPSHIRE				
1 Shea-Porter	Y	N	N	Y
2 Hodes	Y	N	N	Y
NEW JERSEY				
1 Andrews	Y	Y	Y	Y
2 LoBiondo	Y	N	N	N
3 Saxton	?	Y	Y	N
4 Smith	Y	N	N	Y
5 Garrett	N	N	N	N
6 Pallone	Y	Y	Y	Y
7 Ferguson	Y	Y	Y	N
8 Pascrell	Y	N	Y	Y
9 Rothman	Y	N	Y	Y
10 Payne	Y	N	N	Y
11 Frelinghuysen	Y	Y	Y	Y
12 Holt	Y	Y	Y	Y
13 Sires	Y	Y	Y	Y
NEW MEXICO				
1 Wilson	Y	Y	Y	N
2 Pearce	Y	N	N	N
3 Udall	Y	N	N	Y
NEW YORK				
1 Bishop	Y	Y	Y	Y
2 Israel	Y	Y	Y	Y
3 King	Y	Y	Y	Y
4 McCarthy	Y	Y	Y	Y
5 Ackerman	Y	Y	Y	Y
6 Meeks	Y	Y	Y	Y
7 Crowley	Y	Y	Y	Y
8 Nadler	Y	Y	Y	Y
9 Weiner	Y	Y	Y	Y
10 Towns	Y	Y	Y	Y
11 Clarke	Y	Y	Y	Y
12 Velázquez	Y	Y	Y	Y
13 Fossella	?	Y	Y	N
14 Maloney	Y	Y	Y	Y
15 Rangel	Y	Y	Y	Y
16 Serrano	Y	N	N	Y
17 Engel	Y	Y	Y	Y
18 Lowey	Y	Y	Y	Y
19 Hall	Y	Y	Y	Y
20 Gillibrand	Y	N	N	Y
21 McNulty	Y	Y	Y	Y
22 Hinchey	Y	N	N	Y
23 McHugh	Y	Y	Y	Y
24 Arcuri	Y	Y	Y	Y
25 Walsh	Y	Y	Y	Y
26 Reynolds	Y	Y	Y	N
27 Higgins	Y	Y	Y	Y
28 Slaughter	Y	Y	Y	Y
29 Kuhl	Y	N	Y	?
NORTH CAROLINA				
1 Butterfield	Y	N	N	Y
2 Etheridge	Y	Y	Y	Y
3 Jones	Y	N	N	N
4 Price	Y	Y	Y	Y

	625	674	681	690
5 Foxx	N	N	N	N
6 Coble	Y	N	Y	N
7 McIntyre	Y	N	N	N
8 Hayes	Y	N	N	N
9 Myrick	Y	N	Y	N
10 McHenry	N	N	N	N
11 Shuler	Y	N	N	N
12 Watt	Y	Y	Y	Y
13 Miller	Y	Y	Y	Y
NORTH DAKOTA				
AL Pomeroy	Y	Y	Y	Y
OHIO				
1 Chabot	Y	N	N	N
2 Schmidt	Y	N	Y	N
3 Turner	Y	N	N	N
4 Jordan	N	N	N	N
5 Latta	N	N	N	N
6 Wilson	Y	Y	Y	Y
7 Hobson	Y	Y	Y	N
8 Boehner	?	Y	Y	N
9 Kaptur	Y	N	N	Y
10 Kucinich	Y	N	N	Y
11 Fudge[2]				Y
12 Tiberi	Y	N	Y	N
13 Sutton	Y	N	Y	Y
14 LaTourette	Y	N	N	Y
15 Pryce	Y	Y	Y	?
16 Regula	Y	Y	Y	Y
17 Ryan	Y	Y	Y	Y
18 Space	Y	Y	Y	Y
OKLAHOMA				
1 Sullivan	Y	N	Y	N
2 Boren	Y	Y	Y	Y
3 Lucas	Y	N	N	N
4 Cole	Y	Y	Y	N
5 Fallin	Y	N	Y	N
OREGON				
1 Wu	Y	N	Y	N
2 Walden	Y	Y	Y	N
3 Blumenauer	Y	N	N	Y
4 DeFazio	Y	N	N	Y
5 Hooley	Y	Y	Y	?
PENNSYLVANIA				
1 Brady	Y	Y	Y	Y
2 Fattah	Y	Y	Y	Y
3 English	Y	N	N	Y
4 Altmire	Y	N	N	Y
5 Peterson	Y	Y	Y	?
6 Gerlach	Y	N	Y	N
7 Sestak	Y	Y	Y	Y
8 Murphy, P.	Y	Y	Y	Y
9 Shuster	Y	N	Y	N
10 Carney	Y	N	N	Y
11 Kanjorski	Y	Y	Y	Y
12 Murtha	Y	Y	Y	Y
13 Schwartz	Y	Y	Y	Y
14 Doyle	Y	Y	Y	Y
15 Dent	Y	N	Y	N
16 Pitts	N	N	N	N
17 Holden	Y	N	N	Y
18 Murphy, T.	Y	N	N	Y
19 Platts	Y	N	Y	N
RHODE ISLAND				
1 Kennedy	Y	Y	Y	Y
2 Langevin	Y	Y	Y	Y
SOUTH CAROLINA				
1 Brown	Y	Y	Y	Y
2 Wilson	Y	Y	Y	N
3 Barrett	N	N	Y	N
4 Inglis	Y	Y	Y	N
5 Spratt	Y	Y	Y	Y
6 Clyburn	Y	Y	Y	Y
SOUTH DAKOTA				
AL Herseth Sandlin	Y	N	N	N
TENNESSEE				
1 Davis, David	Y	N	N	N
2 Duncan	N	N	N	N
3 Wamp	Y	N	Y	N
4 Davis, L.	Y	Y	Y	N
5 Cooper	Y	Y	Y	N
6 Gordon	Y	Y	Y	?
7 Blackburn	N	N	N	N
8 Tanner	Y	Y	Y	Y
9 Cohen	Y	Y	Y	Y

	625	674	681	690
TEXAS				
1 Gohmert	Y	N	N	N
2 Poe	N	N	N	N
3 Johnson, S.	N	N	N	N
4 Hall	Y	N	N	N
5 Hensarling	N	N	N	N
6 Barton	Y	N	N	N
7 Culberson	Y	N	N	N
8 Brady	N	Y	Y	N
9 Green, A.	Y	N	Y	Y
10 McCaul	Y	N	N	N
11 Conaway	N	N	N	N
12 Granger	Y	Y	Y	N
13 Thornberry	N	N	N	N
14 Paul	N	N	N	N
15 Hinojosa	Y	Y	Y	Y
16 Reyes	?	Y	Y	Y
17 Edwards	Y	Y	Y	Y
18 Jackson Lee	Y	N	Y	Y
19 Neugebauer	N	N	N	N
20 Gonzalez	Y	Y	Y	Y
21 Smith	Y	Y	Y	N
22 Lampson	Y	N	N	Y
23 Rodriguez	Y	N	N	N
24 Marchant	N	N	N	N
25 Doggett	Y	N	N	Y
26 Burgess	Y	N	N	N
27 Ortiz	Y	N	Y	Y
28 Cuellar	Y	N	N	Y
29 Green, G.	Y	N	N	Y
30 Johnson, E.	Y	Y	Y	?
31 Carter	N	N	N	N
32 Sessions	Y	Y	Y	N
UTAH				
1 Bishop	?	N	N	N
2 Matheson	Y	N	N	N
3 Cannon	N	Y	Y	N
VERMONT				
AL Welch	Y	N	Y	Y
VIRGINIA				
1 Wittman	Y	N	N	N
2 Drake	Y	N	N	N
3 Scott	Y	N	N	Y
4 Forbes	Y	N	N	N
5 Goode	Y	N	N	N
6 Goodlatte	Y	N	N	N
7 Cantor	?	Y	Y	N
8 Moran	Y	N	N	Y
9 Boucher	Y	Y	Y	Y
10 Wolf	Y	Y	Y	N
11 Davis[3]				
WASHINGTON				
1 Inslee	Y	N	N	Y
2 Larsen	Y	Y	Y	Y
3 Baird	Y	Y	Y	Y
4 Hastings	N	N	N	N
5 McMorris Rodgers	Y	N	N	N
6 Dicks	Y	Y	Y	Y
7 McDermott	Y	N	N	Y
8 Reichert	Y	N	N	N
9 Smith	Y	Y	Y	Y
WEST VIRGINIA				
1 Mollohan	Y	Y	Y	Y
2 Capito	Y	N	N	Y
3 Rahall	Y	Y	Y	N
WISCONSIN				
1 Ryan	Y	Y	Y	Y
2 Baldwin	Y	Y	Y	Y
3 Kind	Y	Y	Y	Y
4 Moore	Y	Y	Y	Y
5 Sensenbrenner	Y	N	N	?
6 Petri	Y	Y	Y	Y
7 Obey	Y	Y	Y	Y
8 Kagen	Y	N	N	N
WYOMING				
AL Cubin	?	Y	Y	?
DELEGATES				
Faleomavaega (A.S.)				
Norton (D.C.)				
Bordallo (Guam)				
Fortuño (P.R.)				
Christensen (V.I.)				

IN THE SENATE | By Vote Number

10. **HR 5140. Economic Stimulus/Passage.** Passage of the bill that would provide advance refund of a tax credit for most taxpayers equal to $300 to $600 for individuals and $600 to $1,200 for couples. Families would receive $300 for each child under 17. The benefit would begin phasing out for individuals with adjusted gross incomes above $75,000 ($150,000 for married couples). It would give businesses a 50 percent depreciation for certain equipment purchased in 2008 and increase to $250,000 the amount small businesses can expense in the year items are purchased. It would raise the size of mortgage loans the Federal Housing Administration could insure and Fannie Mae and Freddie Mac could purchase. As amended, it would expand eligibility for the checks to include low-income senior citizens, disabled veterans and veterans' widows. Illegal immigrants would be ineligible. Passed 81-16: R 33-16; D 46-0 (ND 41-0, SD 5-0); I 2-0. A "yea" was a vote in favor of the president's position. Feb. 7, 2008. *(Story, p. C-8)*

113. **HR 493. Genetic Information Nondiscrimination/Passage.** Passage of the bill that would prohibit insurance companies, employers, employment agencies and labor unions from discriminating on the basis of genetic information. It would bar health plans from requiring genetic testing. Insurers could not adjust premiums or base enrollment decisions on genetic information. Passed 95-0: R 46-0; D 47-0 (ND 42-0, SD 5-0); I 2-0. (Before passage, the Senate adopted the Snowe, R-Maine, substitute by voice vote.) April 24, 2008. *(Story, p. C-8)*

130. **HR 2419. Farm Bill Reauthorization/Conference Report.** Adoption of the conference report on the bill that would reauthorize federal farm and nutrition programs for five years, including crop subsidies and food stamps, as well as conservation, rural development and agricultural trade programs. It would authorize a $10.4 billion increase for nutrition programs, offset by extending customs user fees. It also would cut direct payment subsidies overall by $313 million, in part by reducing the percentage of acres for which a farmer can collect those payments. Farmers making more than $750,000 a year in farm-related income and those with more than $500,000 a year in non-farm-related income would not be eligible for federal subsidies. Country-of-origin labels for all meat would be required by September 2008. Adopted (thus cleared for the president) 81-15: R 35-13; D 44-2 (ND 39-2, SD 5-0); I 2-0. A "nay" was a vote in support of the president's position. May 15, 2008. *(Story, p. C-8)*

145. **S 3036. Climate Change/Cloture.** Motion to invoke cloture (thus limiting debate) on the Boxer, D-Calif., substitute amendment that would cap greenhouse gas emissions nationwide and set up a trading system for companies to buy and sell emission allowances. Motion rejected 48-36: R 7-32; D 39-4 (ND 35-3, SD 4-1); I 2-0. Three-fifths of the total Senate (60) is required to invoke cloture. A "nay" was a vote in support of the president's position. June 6, 2008. *(Story, p. C-8)*

	10	113	130	145
ALABAMA				
Shelby	N	Y	Y	N
Sessions	N	Y	Y	N
ALASKA				
Stevens	Y	Y	Y	?
Murkowski	N	Y	N	?
ARIZONA				
McCain	Y	?	?	+
Kyl	N	Y	N	N
ARKANSAS				
Lincoln	Y	Y	Y	Y
Pryor	Y	Y	Y	Y
CALIFORNIA				
Feinstein	Y	Y	Y	Y
Boxer	Y	Y	Y	Y
COLORADO				
Allard	N	Y	Y	N
Salazar	Y	Y	Y	Y
CONNECTICUT				
Dodd	Y	Y	Y	Y
Lieberman	Y	Y	Y	Y
DELAWARE				
Biden	Y	Y	Y	+
Carper	Y	Y	Y	Y
FLORIDA				
Nelson	Y	Y	Y	Y
Martinez	Y	Y	Y	Y
GEORGIA				
Chambliss	Y	Y	Y	N
Isakson	Y	Y	Y	N
HAWAII				
Inouye	Y	Y	Y	Y
Akaka	Y	Y	Y	Y
IDAHO				
Craig	N	Y	Y	?
Crapo	N	Y	Y	N
ILLINOIS				
Durbin	Y	Y	Y	Y
Obama	?	?	?	+
INDIANA				
Lugar	Y	Y	N	N
Bayh	Y	Y	Y	Y
IOWA				
Grassley	Y	Y	Y	N
Harkin	Y	Y	Y	Y
KANSAS				
Brownback	Y	Y	Y	N
Roberts	Y	Y	Y	N
KENTUCKY				
McConnell	Y	Y	Y	N
Bunning	Y	Y	Y	N
LOUISIANA				
Landrieu	Y	Y	Y	N
Vitter	Y	Y	Y	N
MAINE				
Snowe	Y	Y	Y	Y
Collins	Y	Y	N	Y
MARYLAND				
Mikulski	Y	Y	Y	Y
Cardin	Y	Y	Y	Y
MASSACHUSETTS				
Kennedy	Y	Y	?	+
Kerry	Y	Y	Y	Y
MICHIGAN				
Levin	Y	Y	Y	Y
Stabenow	Y	Y	Y	Y
MINNESOTA				
Coleman	Y	Y	Y	+
Klobuchar	Y	Y	Y	Y
MISSISSIPPI				
Cochran	Y	Y	Y	N
Wicker	Y	Y	Y	N
MISSOURI				
Bond	Y	Y	Y	N
McCaskill	Y	Y	Y	Y

	10	113	130	145
MONTANA				
Baucus	Y	Y	Y	Y
Tester	Y	Y	Y	Y
NEBRASKA				
Hagel	N	Y	N	N
Nelson	+	Y	Y	Y
NEVADA				
Reid	Y	Y	Y	Y
Ensign	N	Y	N	N
NEW HAMPSHIRE				
Gregg	N	?	N	?
Sununu	Y	Y	N	Y
NEW JERSEY				
Lautenberg	Y	Y	Y	Y
Menendez	Y	Y	Y	Y
NEW MEXICO				
Domenici	Y	Y	N	N
Bingaman	Y	Y	Y	Y
NEW YORK				
Schumer	Y	Y	Y	Y
Clinton	?	?	?	+
NORTH CAROLINA				
Dole	Y	Y	Y	N
Burr	Y	Y	Y	N
NORTH DAKOTA				
Conrad	Y	Y	Y	?
Dorgan	Y	Y	N	N
OHIO				
Voinovich	Y	Y	N	N
Brown	Y	Y	Y	Y
OKLAHOMA				
Inhofe	N	Y	Y	N
Coburn	N	Y	N	N
OREGON				
Wyden	Y	Y	Y	Y
Smith	Y	Y	Y	Y
PENNSYLVANIA				
Specter	Y	Y	Y	?
Casey	Y	Y	Y	Y
RHODE ISLAND				
Reed	Y	Y	N	Y
Whitehouse	Y	Y	N	Y
SOUTH CAROLINA				
Graham	Y	Y	Y	?
DeMint	N	?	N	?
SOUTH DAKOTA				
Johnson	Y	Y	Y	N
Thune	Y	Y	Y	N
TENNESSEE				
Alexander	Y	Y	Y	N
Corker	N	Y	Y	N
TEXAS				
Hutchison	Y	Y	Y	N
Cornyn	Y	Y	Y	?
UTAH				
Hatch	Y	Y	Y	N
Bennett	Y	Y	N	N
VERMONT				
Leahy	Y	Y	Y	Y
Sanders	Y	Y	Y	Y
VIRGINIA				
Warner	Y	Y	Y	Y
Webb	Y	Y	Y	Y
WASHINGTON				
Murray	Y	Y	Y	Y
Cantwell	Y	Y	Y	Y
WEST VIRGINIA				
Byrd	Y	Y	Y	?
Rockefeller	Y	Y	Y	Y
WISCONSIN				
Kohl	Y	Y	Y	Y
Feingold	Y	Y	Y	Y
WYOMING				
Enzi	N	Y	Y	N
Barrasso	N	Y	Y	N

KEY   **Republicans**   Democrats   *Independents*

Y Voted for (yea)	X Paired against
# Paired for	– Announced against
+ Announced for	P Voted "present"
N Voted against (nay)	

C Voted "present" to avoid possible conflict of interest

? Did not vote or otherwise make a position known

ND Northern Democrats, SD Southern Democrats
Southern states: Ala., Ark., Fla., Ga., Ky., La., Miss., N.C., Okla., S.C., Tenn., Texas, Va.

IN THE SENATE | By Vote Number

164. HR 6304. **Foreign Intelligence Surveillance/Immunity From Civil Liability.** Dodd, D-Conn., amendment that would strike the provisions providing retroactive immunity from civil liability to telecommunications companies that have participated in the administration's warrantless surveillance program. Rejected 32-66: R 0-48; D 31-17 (ND 31-12, SD 0-5); I 1-1. A "nay" was a vote in support of the president's position. July 9, 2008. *(Story, p. C-9)*

169. HR 6331. **Medicare Physician Payments/Cloture.** Motion to invoke cloture (thus limiting debate) on the motion to proceed to the bill that would prevent a 10.6 percent cut in Medicare physician payments scheduled to take effect July 1, 2008, by holding payments at current rates for 18 months. It would give doctors a 1.1 percent increase in 2009 and provide $16.6 billion over 10 years for changes to Medicare beneficiary programs. The costs would be partially offset by provisions to reduce the cost of Medicare Advantage plans. Motion agreed to 69-30: R 18-30; D 49-0 (ND 44-0, SD 5-0); I 2-0. Three-fifths of the total Senate (60) is required to invoke cloture. (By unanimous consent, the motion to proceed was agreed to, and the bill was passed by voice vote.) A "nay" was a vote in support of the president's position. July 9, 2008. *(Story, p. C-9)*

186. HR 3221. **Mortgage Relief/Motion to Concur.** Reid, D-Nev., motion to concur in the House amendment to the Senate amendment to the House amendments to the Senate amendment. The House amendment would grant authority to the Treasury Department to extend new credit and buy stock in Fannie Mae and Freddie Mac. It would create an independent regulator for the two mortgage giants and the Federal Home Loan Bank System. It would overhaul the Federal Housing Administration (FHA) and allow it to insure up to $300 billion worth of new, refinanced loans for struggling mortgage borrowers. It also includes a $7,500 tax credit for some first-time homebuyers, higher loan limits for FHA-backed loans, a standard tax deduction for property taxes and revenue-raisers to offset part of the costs. It also would authorize $3.9 billion in grants to states and localities to purchase and rehabilitate foreclosed properties and would increase the federal debt limit to $10.6 trillion. Motion agreed to, thus clearing the bill for the president, 72-13: R 27-13; D 43-0 (ND 38-0, SD 5-0); I 2-0. A "yea" was a vote in support of the president's position. July 26, 2008. *(Story, p. C-10)*

ND Northern Democrats, SD Southern Democrats
Southern states: Ala., Ark., Fla., Ga., Ky., La., Miss., N.C., Okla., S.C., Tenn., Texas, Va.

	164	169	186			164	169	186
ALABAMA					**MONTANA**			
Shelby	N	N	Y		Baucus	Y	Y	Y
Sessions	N	N	Y		Tester	Y	Y	Y
ALASKA					**NEBRASKA**			
Stevens	N	Y	Y		Hagel	N	N	Y
Murkowski	N	Y	Y		Nelson	N	Y	Y
ARIZONA					**NEVADA**			
McCain	?	?	?		Reid	Y	Y	Y
Kyl	N	N	N		Ensign	N	N	N
ARKANSAS					**NEW HAMPSHIRE**			
Lincoln	N	Y	Y		Gregg	N	N	Y
Pryor	N	Y	Y		Sununu	N	N	Y
CALIFORNIA					**NEW JERSEY**			
Feinstein	N	Y	Y		Lautenberg	Y	Y	Y
Boxer	Y	Y	Y		Menendez	Y	Y	Y
COLORADO					**NEW MEXICO**			
Allard	N	N	?		Domenici	N	N	Y
Salazar	N	Y	Y		Bingaman	Y	Y	Y
CONNECTICUT					**NEW YORK**			
Dodd	Y	Y	Y		Schumer	Y	Y	Y
Lieberman	N	Y	Y		Clinton	Y	Y	Y
DELAWARE					**NORTH CAROLINA**			
Biden	Y	Y	Y		Dole	N	Y	?
Carper	N	Y	+		Burr	N	N	?
FLORIDA					**NORTH DAKOTA**			
Nelson	N	Y	Y		Conrad	N	Y	Y
Martinez	N	Y	Y		Dorgan	Y	Y	Y
GEORGIA					**OHIO**			
Chambliss	N	Y	Y		Voinovich	N	Y	Y
Isakson	N	Y	Y		Brown	Y	Y	Y
HAWAII					**OKLAHOMA**			
Inouye	N	Y	?		Inhofe	N	N	?
Akaka	Y	Y	Y		Coburn	N	N	N
IDAHO					**OREGON**			
Craig	N	N	Y		Wyden	Y	Y	Y
Crapo	N	N	Y		Smith	N	Y	Y
ILLINOIS					**PENNSYLVANIA**			
Durbin	Y	Y	Y		Specter	N	Y	Y
Obama	Y	Y	?		Casey	Y	Y	Y
INDIANA					**RHODE ISLAND**			
Lugar	N	N	Y		Reed	Y	Y	Y
Bayh	N	Y	Y		Whitehouse	Y	Y	Y
IOWA					**SOUTH CAROLINA**			
Grassley	N	N	N		Graham	N	N	?
Harkin	Y	Y	?		DeMint	N	N	N
KANSAS					**SOUTH DAKOTA**			
Brownback	N	N	Y		Johnson	N	Y	Y
Roberts	N	Y	Y		Thune	N	N	N
KENTUCKY					**TENNESSEE**			
McConnell	N	N	Y		Alexander	N	Y	Y
Bunning	N	N	–		Corker	N	Y	N
LOUISIANA					**TEXAS**			
Landrieu	N	Y	Y		Hutchison	N	Y	N
Vitter	N	N	N		Cornyn	N	Y	N
MAINE					**UTAH**			
Snowe	N	Y	Y		Hatch	N	N	Y
Collins	N	Y	Y		Bennett	N	N	Y
MARYLAND					**VERMONT**			
Mikulski	N	Y	Y		Leahy	Y	Y	Y
Cardin	Y	Y	Y		*Sanders*	Y	Y	Y
MASSACHUSETTS					**VIRGINIA**			
Kennedy	?	Y	?		Warner	N	Y	?
Kerry	Y	Y	Y		Webb	N	Y	Y
MICHIGAN					**WASHINGTON**			
Levin	Y	Y	Y		Murray	Y	Y	?
Stabenow	Y	Y	Y		Cantwell	Y	Y	Y
MINNESOTA					**WEST VIRGINIA**			
Coleman	N	Y	Y		Byrd	Y	Y	Y
Klobuchar	Y	Y	Y		Rockefeller	N	Y	Y
MISSISSIPPI					**WISCONSIN**			
Cochran	N	N	Y		Kohl	N	Y	Y
Wicker	N	N	Y		Feingold	Y	Y	Y
MISSOURI					**WYOMING**			
Bond	N	N	?		Enzi	N	N	N
McCaskill	N	Y	Y		Barrasso	N	N	N

KEY Republicans Democrats *Independents*

Y	Voted for (yea)	X	Paired against	C	Voted "present" to avoid possible conflict of interest
#	Paired for	–	Announced against		
+	Announced for	P	Voted "present"	?	Did not vote or otherwise make a position known
N	Voted against (nay)				

IN THE SENATE | By Vote Number

211. HR 7081. **U.S.-India Nuclear Agreement/Passage.** Passage of
the bill that would grant congressional approval to the U.S.-India nuclear
cooperation agreement. It would require that the president determine
and certify to Congress that certain actions have occurred — including
that India has provided the International Atomic Energy Agency with a
credible plan to separate civilian and military nuclear facilities, materials,
and programs — before the Nuclear Regulatory Commission can issue
licenses for transfers of nuclear-related goods and services. Passed 86-13:
R 49-0; D 36-12 (ND 31-12, SD 5-0); I 1-1. (By unanimous consent, the
Senate agreed to raise the majority requirement for passage of the bill to
60 votes.) A "yea" was a vote in support of the president's position. Oct. 1,
2008. *(Story, p. C-10)*

213. HR 1424. **Mortgage-Backed Securities Buyout/Passage.**
Passage of the bill that would allow the Treasury Department to use up
to $700 billion, in installments, to buy certain mortgage assets. The bill
would require the Treasury to create a program to insure mortgage assets,
would provide for congressional oversight and would limit compensation for executives of companies whose troubled assets are purchased.
It would temporarily increase federal deposit insurance to $250,000 per
bank account. It would extend dozens of expired or expiring tax provisions, provide a one-year adjustment to the alternative minimum tax and
require private insurance plans to put mental health benefits on par with
other medical benefits. Passed 74-25: R 34-15; D 39-9 (ND 36-7, SD 3-2);
I 1-1. (By unanimous consent, the Senate agreed to raise the majority
requirement for passage of the bill to 60 votes.) A "yea" was a vote in support of the president's position. Oct. 1, 2008. *(Story, p. C-10)*

215. HR 7005. **Automobile Industry Loan Program Shell/Cloture.**
Motion to invoke cloture (thus limiting debate) on the motion to proceed
to a bill on the alternative minimum tax, which would serve as the vehicle
for an emergency loan package for domestic automakers. Motion rejected
52-35: R 10-31; D 40-4 (ND 36-3, SD 4-1); I 2-0. Three-fifths of the total
Senate (60) is required to invoke cloture. A "yea" was a vote in support of
the president's position. Dec. 11, 2008. *(Story, p. C-10)*

	211	213	215		211	213	215
ALABAMA				**MONTANA**			
Shelby	Y	N	N	Baucus	Y	Y	N
Sessions	Y	N	N	Tester	Y	N	N
ALASKA				**NEBRASKA**			
Stevens	Y	Y	?	**Hagel**	Y	Y	?
Murkowski	Y	Y	N	Nelson	Y	Y	Y
ARIZONA				**NEVADA**			
McCain	Y	Y	N	Reid	Y	Y	N
Kyl	Y	Y	N	**Ensign**	Y	Y	N
ARKANSAS				**NEW HAMPSHIRE**			
Lincoln	Y	Y	N	**Gregg**	Y	Y	N
Pryor	Y	Y	Y	**Sununu**	Y	Y	?
CALIFORNIA				**NEW JERSEY**			
Feinstein	Y	Y	Y	Lautenberg	Y	Y	Y
Boxer	N	Y	Y	Menendez	Y	Y	Y
COLORADO				**NEW MEXICO**			
Allard	Y	N	N	**Domenici**	Y	Y	Y
Salazar	Y	Y	Y	Bingaman	N	Y	Y
CONNECTICUT				**NEW YORK**			
Dodd	Y	Y	Y	Schumer	Y	Y	Y
Lieberman	Y	Y	Y	Clinton	Y	Y	Y
DELAWARE				**NORTH CAROLINA**			
Biden	Y	Y	?	**Dole**	Y	N	Y
Carper	Y	Y	Y	**Burr**	Y	Y	N
FLORIDA				**NORTH DAKOTA**			
Nelson	Y	N	Y	Conrad	N	Y	Y
Martinez	Y	Y	N	Dorgan	N	N	Y
GEORGIA				**OHIO**			
Chambliss	Y	Y	N	**Voinovich**	Y	Y	Y
Isakson	Y	Y	N	Brown	N	Y	Y
HAWAII				**OKLAHOMA**			
Inouye	Y	Y	Y	**Inhofe**	Y	N	N
Akaka	N	Y	Y	**Coburn**	Y	Y	N
IDAHO				**OREGON**			
Craig	Y	Y	?	Wyden	Y	N	?
Crapo	Y	N	N	**Smith**	Y	Y	?
ILLINOIS				**PENNSYLVANIA**			
Durbin	Y	Y	Y	**Specter**	Y	Y	Y
Obama[1]	Y	Y		Casey	Y	Y	Y
INDIANA				**RHODE ISLAND**			
Lugar	Y	Y	Y	Reed	N	Y	Y
Bayh	Y	Y	Y	Whitehouse	N	Y	Y
IOWA				**SOUTH CAROLINA**			
Grassley	Y	Y	N	**Graham**	Y	Y	?
Harkin	N	Y	Y	**DeMint**	Y	N	N
KANSAS				**SOUTH DAKOTA**			
Brownback	Y	N	Y	Johnson	Y	N	Y
Roberts	Y	N	N	**Thune**	Y	Y	N
KENTUCKY				**TENNESSEE**			
McConnell	Y	Y	N	**Alexander**	Y	Y	–
Bunning	Y	N	N	**Corker**	Y	Y	N
LOUISIANA				**TEXAS**			
Landrieu	Y	N	Y	**Hutchison**	Y	Y	N
Vitter	Y	N	N	**Cornyn**	Y	Y	–
MAINE				**UTAH**			
Snowe	Y	Y	Y	**Hatch**	Y	Y	N
Collins	Y	Y	Y	**Bennett**	Y	Y	N
MARYLAND				**VERMONT**			
Mikulski	Y	Y	Y	Leahy	N	Y	Y
Cardin	Y	Y	Y	*Sanders*	N	N	Y
MASSACHUSETTS				**VIRGINIA**			
Kennedy	?	?	?	Warner	Y	Y	Y
Kerry	Y	Y	+	Webb	Y	Y	Y
MICHIGAN				**WASHINGTON**			
Levin	Y	Y	Y	Murray	Y	Y	Y
Stabenow	Y	N	Y	Cantwell	Y	N	Y
MINNESOTA				**WEST VIRGINIA**			
Coleman	Y	Y	N	Byrd	N	Y	Y
Klobuchar	Y	Y	Y	Rockefeller	Y	Y	Y
MISSISSIPPI				**WISCONSIN**			
Cochran	Y	N	N	Kohl	Y	Y	Y
Wicker	Y	N	N	Feingold	N	N	Y
MISSOURI				**WYOMING**			
Bond	Y	Y	Y	**Enzi**	Y	N	N
McCaskill	Y	Y	Y	**Barrasso**	Y	N	N

KEY	**Republicans**	Democrats	*Independents*
Y Voted for (yea)	X Paired against		C Voted "present" to avoid possible conflict of interest
# Paired for	– Announced against		
+ Announced for	P Voted "present"		? Did not vote or otherwise make a position known
N Voted against (nay)			

[1] Sen. Barack Obama, D-Ill., resigned Nov. 16, 2008, after winning the presidential election. The last
vote for which he was eligible was 213.

ND Northern Democrats, SD Southern Democrats
Southern states: Ala., Ark., Fla., Ga., Ky., La., Miss., N.C., Okla., S.C., Tenn., Texas, Va.

Appendix D

TEXTS

State of the Union Lauds Iraq 'Surge,' Criticizes Congressional Spending

Following is the White House transcript of President Bush's State of the Union address, delivered to a joint session of Congress on Jan. 28.

MADAM SPEAKER, Vice President Cheney, members of Congress, distinguished guests and fellow citizens: Seven years have passed since I first stood before you at this rostrum. In that time, our country has been tested in ways none of us could have imagined. We faced hard decisions about peace and war, rising competition in the world economy, and the health and welfare of our citizens. These issues call for vigorous debate, and I think it's fair to say we've answered the call. Yet history will record that amid our differences, we acted with purpose. And together, we showed the world the power and resilience of American self-government.

All of us were sent to Washington to carry out the people's business. That is the purpose of this body. It is the meaning of our oath. It remains our charge to keep.

The actions of the 110th Congress will affect the security and prosperity of our nation long after this session has ended. In this election year, let us show our fellow Americans that we recognize our responsibilities and are determined to meet them. Let us show them that Republicans and Democrats can compete for votes and cooperate for results at the same time.

From expanding opportunity to protecting our country, we've made good progress. Yet we have unfinished business before us, and the American people expect us to get it done.

In the work ahead, we must be guided by the philosophy that made our nation great. As Americans, we believe in the power of individuals to determine their destiny and shape the course of history. We believe that the most reliable guide for our country is the collective wisdom of ordinary citizens. And so in all we do, we must trust in the ability of free peoples to make wise decisions and empower them to improve their lives for their futures.

ECONOMIC STIMULUS

To build a prosperous future, we must trust people with their own money and empower them to grow our economy. As we meet tonight, our economy is undergoing a period of uncertainty. America has added jobs for a record 52 straight months, but jobs are now growing at a slower pace. Wages are up, but so are prices for food and gas. Exports are rising, but the housing market has declined. At kitchen tables across our country, there is a concern about our economic future.

In the long run, Americans can be confident about our economic growth. But in the short run, we can all see that that growth is slowing. So last week, my administration reached agreement with Speaker Pelosi and Republican Leader Boehner on a robust growth package that includes tax relief for individuals and families and incentives for business investment. The temptation will be to load up the bill. That would delay it or derail it, and neither option is acceptable. This is a good agreement that will keep our economy growing and our people working. And this Congress must pass it as soon as possible.

TAX REFORM

We have other work to do on taxes. Unless Congress acts, most of the tax relief we've delivered over the past seven years will be taken away. Some in Washington argue that letting tax relief expire is not a tax increase. Try explaining that to 116 million American taxpayers who would see their taxes rise by an average of $1,800. Others have said they would personally be happy to pay higher taxes. I welcome their enthusiasm. I'm pleased to report that the IRS accepts both checks and money orders.

Most Americans think their taxes are high enough. With all the other pressures on their finances, American families should not have to worry about their federal government taking a bigger bite out of their paychecks. There's only one way to eliminate this uncertainty: Make the tax relief permanent. And members of Congress should know: If any bill that raises taxes reaches my desk, I will veto it.

Just as we trust Americans with their own money, we need to earn their trust by spending their tax dollars wisely. Next week, I'll send you a budget that terminates or substantially reduces 151 wasteful or bloated programs, totaling more than $18 billion. The budget that I will submit will keep America on track for a surplus in 2012. American families have to balance their budgets; so should their government.

CONGRESSIONAL EARMARKS

The people's trust in their government is undermined by congressional earmarks — special-interest projects that are often snuck in at the last minute, without discussion or debate. Last year, I asked you to voluntarily cut the number and cost of earmarks in half. I also asked you to stop slipping earmarks into committee reports that never even come to a vote. Unfortunately, neither goal was met. So this time, if you send me an appropriations bill that does not cut the number and cost of earmarks in half, I'll send it back to you with my veto.

And tomorrow, I will issue an executive order that directs federal agencies to ignore any future earmark that is not voted on by Congress. If these items are truly worth funding, Congress should debate them in the open and hold a public vote.

HOUSING AND HEALTH CARE

Our shared responsibilities extend beyond matters of taxes and spending. On housing, we must trust Americans with the responsibility of homeownership and empower them to weather turbulent times in the housing market. My administration brought together the HOPE NOW alliance, which is helping many struggling homeowners avoid foreclosure. And Congress can help even more. Tonight I ask you to pass legislation to reform Fannie Mae and Freddie Mac, modernize the Federal Housing Administration, and allow state housing agencies to issue tax-free bonds to help homeowners refinance their mortgages. These are difficult times for many American families, and by taking these steps, we can help more of them keep their homes.

To build a future of quality health care, we must trust patients and doctors to make medical decisions and empower them with better information and better options. We share a

common goal: making health care more affordable and accessible for all Americans. The best way to achieve that goal is by expanding consumer choice, not government control. So I have proposed ending the bias in the tax code against those who do not get their health insurance through their employer. This one reform would put private coverage within reach for millions, and I call on the Congress to pass it this year.

The Congress must also expand health savings accounts, create Association Health Plans for small businesses, promote health information technology and confront the epidemic of junk medical lawsuits. With all these steps, we will help ensure that decisions about your medical care are made in the privacy of your doctor's office — not in the halls of Congress.

EDUCATION

On education, we must trust students to learn if given the chance and empower parents to demand results from our schools. In neighborhoods across our country, there are boys and girls with dreams — and a decent education is their only hope of achieving them.

Six years ago, we came together to pass the No Child Left Behind Act, and today no one can deny its results. Last year, fourth- and eighth-graders achieved the highest math scores on record. Reading scores are on the rise. African-American and Hispanic students posted all-time highs. Now we must work together to increase accountability, add flexibility for states and districts, reduce the number of high school dropouts, and provide extra help for struggling schools.

Members of Congress, the No Child Left Behind Act is a bipartisan achievement. It is succeeding. And we owe it to America's children, their parents and their teachers to strengthen this good law.

We must also do more to help children when their schools do not measure up. Thanks to the D.C. Opportunity Scholarships you approved, more than 2,600 of the poorest children in our nation's capital have found new hope at a faith-based or other non-public school. Sadly, these schools are disappearing at an alarming rate in many of America's inner cities. So I will convene a White House summit aimed at strengthening these lifelines of learning. And to open the doors of these schools to more children, I ask you to support a new $300 million program called Pell Grants for Kids. We have seen how Pell grants help low-income college students realize their full potential. Together, we've expanded the size

and reach of these grants. Now let us apply that same spirit to help liberate poor children trapped in failing public schools.

TRADE AGREEMENTS

On trade, we must trust American workers to compete with anyone in the world and empower them by opening up new markets overseas. Today, our economic growth increasingly depends on our ability to sell American goods and crops and services all over the world. So we're working to break down barriers to trade and investment wherever we can. We're working for a successful Doha round of trade talks, and we must complete a good agreement this year. At the same time, we're pursuing opportunities to open up new markets by passing free-trade agreements.

I thank the Congress for approving a good agreement with Peru. And now I ask you to approve agreements with Colombia and Panama and South Korea. Many products from these nations now enter America duty-free, yet many of our products face steep tariffs in their markets. These agreements will level the playing field. They will give us better access to nearly 100 million customers. They will support good jobs for the finest workers in the world: those whose products say "Made in the USA."

These agreements also promote America's strategic interests. The first agreement that will come before you is with Colombia, a friend of America that is confronting violence and terror and fighting drug traffickers. If we fail to pass this agreement, we will embolden the purveyors of false populism in our hemisphere. So we must come together, pass this agreement and show our neighbors in the region that democracy leads to a better life.

Trade brings better jobs and better choices and better prices. Yet for some Americans, trade can mean losing a job, and the federal government has a responsibility to help. I ask Congress to reauthorize and reform trade adjustment assistance, so we can help these displaced workers learn new skills and find new jobs.

ENERGY POLICY

To build a future of energy security, we must trust in the creative genius of American researchers and entrepreneurs and empower them to pioneer a new generation of clean energy technology. Our security, our prosperity and our environment all require reducing our dependence on oil. Last year, I asked you to pass legislation to reduce oil consumption

over the next decade, and you responded. Together we should take the next steps: Let us fund new technologies that can generate coal power while capturing carbon emissions. Let us increase the use of renewable power and emissions-free nuclear power. Let us continue investing in advanced battery technology and renewable fuels to power the cars and trucks of the future. Let us create a new international clean technology fund, which will help developing nations like India and China make greater use of clean energy sources. And let us complete an international agreement that has the potential to slow, stop and eventually reverse the growth of greenhouse gases.

This agreement will be effective only if it includes commitments by every major economy and gives none a free ride. The United States is committed to strengthening our energy security and confronting global climate change. And the best way to meet these goals is for America to continue leading the way toward the development of cleaner and more energy-efficient technology.

SCIENCE AND ETHICS

To keep America competitive into the future, we must trust in the skill of our scientists and engineers and empower them to pursue the breakthroughs of tomorrow. Last year, Congress passed legislation supporting the American Competitiveness Initiative but never followed through with the funding. This funding is essential to keeping our scientific edge. So I ask Congress to double federal support for critical basic research in the physical sciences and ensure America remains the most dynamic nation on Earth.

On matters of life and science, we must trust in the innovative spirit of medical researchers and empower them to discover new treatments while respecting moral boundaries. In November, we witnessed a landmark achievement when scientists discovered a way to reprogram adult skin cells to act like embryonic stem cells. This breakthrough has the potential to move us beyond the divisive debates of the past by extending the frontiers of medicine without the destruction of human life.

So we're expanding funding for this type of ethical medical research. And as we explore promising avenues of research, we must also ensure that all life is treated with the dignity it deserves. And so I call on Congress to pass legislation that bans unethical practices such as the buying, selling, patenting or cloning of human life.

JUDICIARY AND PUBLIC SERVICE

On matters of justice, we must trust in the wisdom of our founders and empower judges who understand that the Constitution means what it says. I've submitted judicial nominees who will rule by the letter of the law, not the whim of the gavel. Many of these nominees are being unfairly delayed. They are worthy of confirmation, and the Senate should give each of them a prompt up-or-down vote.

In communities across our land, we must trust in the good heart of the American people and empower them to serve their neighbors in need. Over the past seven years, more of our fellow citizens have discovered that the pursuit of happiness leads to the path of service. Americans have volunteered in record numbers. Charitable donations are higher than ever. Faith-based groups are bringing hope to pockets of despair, with newfound support from the federal government. And to help guarantee equal treatment of faith-based organizations when they compete for federal funds, I ask you to permanently extend Charitable Choice.

Tonight the armies of compassion continue the march to a new day in the Gulf Coast. America honors the strength and resilience of the people of this region. We reaffirm our pledge to help them build stronger and better than before. And tonight I'm pleased to announce that in April we will host this year's North American Summit of Canada, Mexico, and the United States in the great city of New Orleans.

SPENDING AND IMMIGRATION

There are two other pressing challenges that I've raised repeatedly before this body and that this body has failed to address: entitlement spending and immigration. Every member in this chamber knows that spending on entitlement programs like Social Security, Medicare and Medicaid is growing faster than we can afford. We all know the painful choices ahead if America stays on this path: massive tax increases, sudden and drastic cuts in benefits, or crippling deficits. I've laid out proposals to reform these programs. Now I ask members of Congress to offer your proposals and come up with a bipartisan solution to save these vital programs for our children and our grandchildren.

The other pressing challenge is immigration. America needs to secure our borders — and with your help, my administration is taking steps to do so. We're increasing work site enforcement, deploying fences and ad-

vanced technologies to stop illegal crossings. We've effectively ended the policy of "catch and release" at the border, and by the end of this year, we will have doubled the number of Border Patrol agents. Yet we also need to acknowledge that we will never fully secure our border until we create a lawful way for foreign workers to come here and support our economy. This will take pressure off the border and allow law enforcement to concentrate on those who mean us harm. We must also find a sensible and humane way to deal with people here illegally. Illegal immigration is complicated, but it can be resolved. And it must be resolved in a way that upholds both our laws and our highest ideals.

This is the business of our nation here at home. Yet building a prosperous future for our citizens also depends on confronting enemies abroad and advancing liberty in troubled regions of the world.

FOREIGN POLICY

Our foreign policy is based on a clear premise: We trust that people, when given the chance, will choose a future of freedom and peace. In the last seven years, we have witnessed stirring moments in the history of liberty. We've seen citizens in Georgia and Ukraine stand up for their right to free and fair elections. We've seen people in Lebanon take to the streets to demand their independence. We've seen Afghans emerge from the tyranny of the Taliban and choose a new president and a new parliament. We've seen jubilant Iraqis holding up ink-stained fingers and celebrating their freedom. These images of liberty have inspired us.

In the past seven years, we've also seen images that have sobered us. We've watched throngs of mourners in Lebanon and Pakistan carrying the caskets of beloved leaders taken by the assassin's hand. We've seen wedding guests in blood-soaked finery staggering from a hotel in Jordan, Afghans and Iraqis blown up in mosques and markets, and trains in London and Madrid ripped apart by bombs. On a clear September day, we saw thousands of our fellow citizens taken from us in an instant. These horrific images serve as a grim reminder: The advance of liberty is opposed by terrorists and extremists — evil men who despise freedom, despise America and aim to subject millions to their violent rule.

Since 9/11, we have taken the fight to these terrorists and extremists. We will stay on the offense, we will keep up the pressure and we will deliver justice to our enemies.

WAR ON TERRORISM

We are engaged in the defining ideological struggle of the 21st century. The terrorists oppose every principle of humanity and decency that we hold dear. Yet in this war on terror, there is one thing we and our enemies agree on: In the long run, men and women who are free to determine their own destinies will reject terror and refuse to live in tyranny. And that is why the terrorists are fighting to deny this choice to the people in Lebanon, Iraq, Afghanistan, Pakistan and the Palestinian territories. And that is why, for the security of America and the peace of the world, we are spreading the hope of freedom.

In Afghanistan, America, our 25 NATO allies and 15 partner nations are helping the Afghan people defend their freedom and rebuild their country. Thanks to the courage of these military and civilian personnel, a nation that was once a safe haven for al Qaeda is now a young democracy where boys and girls are going to school, new roads and hospitals are being built, and people are looking to the future with new hope. These successes must continue, so we're adding 3,200 Marines to our forces in Afghanistan, where they will fight the terrorists and train the Afghan army and police. Defeating the Taliban and al Qaeda is critical to our security, and I thank the Congress for supporting America's vital mission in Afghanistan.

IRAQ WAR

In Iraq, the terrorists and extremists are fighting to deny a proud people their liberty and fighting to establish safe havens for attacks across the world. One year ago, our enemies were succeeding in their efforts to plunge Iraq into chaos. So we reviewed our strategy and changed course. We launched a surge of American forces into Iraq. We gave our troops a new mission: Work with the Iraqi forces to protect the Iraqi people, pursue the enemy in its strongholds and deny the terrorists sanctuary anywhere in the country.

The Iraqi people quickly realized that something dramatic had happened. Those who had worried that America was preparing to abandon them instead saw tens of thousands of American forces flowing into their country. They saw our forces moving into neighborhoods, clearing out the terrorists and staying behind to ensure the enemy did not return. And they saw our troops, along with Provincial Reconstruction Teams that include Foreign Service officers and other skilled public servants, coming in to ensure

that improved security was followed by improvements in daily life. Our military and civilians in Iraq are performing with courage and distinction, and they have the gratitude of our whole nation.

The Iraqis launched a surge of their own. In the fall of 2006, Sunni tribal leaders grew tired of al Qaeda's brutality and started a popular uprising called the Anbar Awakening. Over the past year, similar movements have spread across the country. And today, the grass-roots surge includes more than 80,000 Iraqi citizens who are fighting the terrorists. The government in Baghdad has stepped forward, as well — adding more than 100,000 new Iraqi soldiers and police during the past year.

While the enemy is still dangerous and more work remains, the American and Iraqi surges have achieved results few of us could have imagined just one year ago. When we met last year, many said that containing the violence was impossible. A year later, high-profile terrorist attacks are down, civilian deaths are down, sectarian killings are down.

When we met last year, militia extremists — some armed and trained by Iran — were wreaking havoc in large areas of Iraq. A year later, coalition and Iraqi forces have killed or captured hundreds of militia fighters. And Iraqis of all backgrounds increasingly realize that defeating these militia fighters is critical to the future of their country.

When we met last year, al Qaeda had sanctuaries in many areas of Iraq, and their leaders had just offered American forces safe passage out of the country. Today, it is al Qaeda that is searching for safe passage. They have been driven from many of the strongholds they once held, and over the past year, we've captured or killed thousands of extremists in Iraq, including hundreds of key al Qaeda leaders and operatives.

Last month, Osama bin Laden released a tape in which he railed against Iraqi tribal leaders who have turned on al Qaeda and admitted that coalition forces are growing stronger in Iraq. Ladies and gentlemen, some may deny the surge is working, but among the terrorists there is no doubt. Al Qaeda is on the run in Iraq, and this enemy will be defeated.

TROOP DRAWDOWNS

When we met last year, our troop levels in Iraq were on the rise. Today, because of the progress just described, we are implementing a policy of "return on success," and the surge forces we sent to Iraq are beginning to come home.

This progress is a credit to the valor of our troops and the brilliance of their commanders. This evening, I want to speak directly to our men and women on the front lines. Soldiers and sailors, airmen, Marines, and Coast Guardsmen: In the past year, you have done everything we've asked of you and more. Our nation is grateful for your courage. We are proud of your accomplishments. And tonight in this hallowed chamber, with the American people as our witness, we make you a solemn pledge: In the fight ahead, you will have all you need to protect our nation. And I ask Congress to meet its responsibilities to these brave men and women by fully funding our troops.

Our enemies in Iraq have been hit hard. They are not yet defeated, and we can still expect tough fighting ahead. Our objective in the coming year is to sustain and build on the gains we made in 2007, while transitioning to the next phase of our strategy. American troops are shifting from leading operations to partnering with Iraqi forces and, eventually, to a protective overwatch mission. As part of this transition, one Army brigade combat team and one Marine Expeditionary Unit have already come home and will not be replaced. In the coming months, four additional brigades and two Marine battalions will follow suit. Taken together, this means more than 20,000 of our troops are coming home.

Any further drawdown of U.S. troops will be based on conditions in Iraq and the recommendations of our commanders. Gen. Petraeus has warned that too fast a drawdown could result in the "disintegration of the Iraqi security forces, al Qaeda-Iraq regaining lost ground [and] a marked increase in violence." Members of Congress, having come so far and achieved so much, we must not allow this to happen.

In the coming year, we will work with Iraqi leaders as they build on the progress they're making toward political reconciliation. At the local level, Sunnis, Shia and Kurds are beginning to come together to reclaim their communities and rebuild their lives. Progress in the provinces must be matched by progress in Baghdad. We're seeing some encouraging signs. The national government is sharing oil revenues with the provinces. The parliament recently passed both a pension law and de-Baathification reform. They're now debating a provincial powers law. The Iraqis still have a distance to travel. But after decades of dictatorship and the pain of sectarian violence, reconciliation is taking place — and the Iraqi

people are taking control of their future.

The mission in Iraq has been difficult and trying for our nation. But it is in the vital interest of the United States that we succeed. A free Iraq will deny al Qaeda a safe haven. A free Iraq will show millions across the Middle East that a future of liberty is possible. A free Iraq will be a friend of America, a partner in fighting terror and a source of stability in a dangerous part of the world.

By contrast, a failed Iraq would embolden the extremists, strengthen Iran and give terrorists a base from which to launch new attacks on our friends, our allies and our homeland. The enemy has made its intentions clear. At a time when the momentum seemed to favor them, al Qaeda's top commander in Iraq declared that they will not rest until they have attacked us here in Washington. My fellow Americans, we will not rest either. We will not rest until this enemy has been defeated. We must do the difficult work today, so that years from now people will look back and say that this generation rose to the moment, prevailed in a tough fight, and left behind a more hopeful region and a safer America.

MIDDLE EAST CONFLICT

We're also standing against the forces of extremism in the Holy Land, where we have new cause for hope. Palestinians have elected a president who recognizes that confronting terror is essential to achieving a state where his people can live in dignity and at peace with Israel. Israelis have leaders who recognize that a peaceful, democratic Palestinian state will be a source of lasting security. This month in Ramallah and Jerusalem, I assured leaders from both sides that America will do, and I will do, everything we can to help them achieve a peace agreement that defines a Palestinian state by the end of this year. The time has come for a Holy Land where a democratic Israel and a democratic Palestine live side by side in peace.

We're also standing against the forces of extremism embodied by the regime in Tehran. Iran's rulers oppress a good and talented people. And wherever freedom advances in the Middle East, it seems the Iranian regime is there to oppose it. Iran is funding and training militia groups in Iraq, supporting Hezbollah terrorists in Lebanon, and backing Hamas' efforts to undermine peace in the Holy Land. Tehran is also developing ballistic missiles of increasing range and continues to develop its capability to enrich uranium, which could be used to create a nuclear weapon.

Our message to the people of Iran is clear: We have no quarrel with you. We respect your traditions and your history. We look forward to the day when you have your freedom. Our message to the leaders of Iran is also clear: Verifiably suspend your nuclear enrichment, so negotiations can begin. And to rejoin the community of nations, come clean about your nuclear intentions and past actions, stop your oppression at home, cease your support for terror abroad. But above all, know this: America will confront those who threaten our troops. We will stand by our allies, and we will defend our vital interests in the Persian Gulf.

HOMELAND SECURITY

On the home front, we will continue to take every lawful and effective measure to protect our country. This is our most solemn duty. We are grateful that there has not been another attack on our soil since 9/11. This is not for the lack of desire or effort on the part of the enemy. In the past six years, we've stopped numerous attacks, including a plot to fly a plane into the tallest building in Los Angeles and another to blow up passenger jets bound for America over the Atlantic. Dedicated men and women in our government toil day and night to stop the terrorists from carrying out their plans. These good citizens are saving American lives, and everyone in this chamber owes them our thanks.

And we owe them something more: We owe them the tools they need to keep our people safe. And one of the most important tools we can give them is the ability to monitor terrorist communications. To protect America, we need to know who the terrorists are talking to, what they are saying and what they're planning. Last year, Congress passed legislation to help us do that. Unfortunately, Congress set the legislation to expire on Feb. 1. That means if you don't act by Friday, our ability to track terrorist threats would be weakened and our citizens will be in greater danger. Congress must ensure the flow of vital intelligence is not disrupted. Congress must pass liability protection for companies believed to have assisted in the efforts to defend America. We've had ample time for debate. The time to act is now.

FOREIGN AID

Protecting our nation from the dangers of a new century requires more than good intelligence and a strong military. It also requires changing the conditions that breed resentment and allow extremists to prey on despair. So America is using its influence to build a freer, more hopeful and more compassionate world. This is a reflection of our national interest; it is the calling of our conscience.

America opposes genocide in Sudan. We support freedom in countries from Cuba and Zimbabwe to Belarus and Burma.

America is leading the fight against global poverty with strong education initiatives and humanitarian assistance. We've also changed the way we deliver aid by launching the Millennium Challenge Account. This program strengthens democracy, transparency and the rule of law in developing nations, and I ask you to fully fund this important initiative.

America is leading the fight against global hunger. Today, more than half the world's food aid comes from the United States. And tonight, I ask Congress to support an innovative proposal to provide food assistance by purchasing crops directly from farmers in the developing world, so we can build up local agriculture and help break the cycle of famine.

America is leading the fight against disease. With your help, we're working to cut by half the number of malaria-related deaths in 15 African nations. And our Emergency Plan for AIDS Relief is treating 1.4 million people. We can bring healing and hope to many more. So I ask you to maintain the principles that have changed behavior and made this program a success. And I call on you to double our initial commitment to fighting HIV/AIDS by approving an additional $30 billion over the next five years.

VETERANS' BENEFITS

America is a force for hope in the world because we are a compassionate people, and some of the most compassionate Americans are those who have stepped forward to protect us. We must keep faith with all who have risked life and limb so that we might live in freedom and peace. Over the past seven years,

we've increased funding for veterans by more than 95 percent. And as we increase funding we must also reform our veterans' system to meet the needs of a new war and a new generation. I call on the Congress to enact the reforms recommended by Sen. Bob Dole and Secretary Donna Shalala, so we can improve the system of care for our wounded warriors and help them build lives of hope and promise and dignity.

Our military families also sacrifice for America. They endure sleepless nights and the daily struggle of providing for children while a loved one is serving far from home. We have a responsibility to provide for them. So I ask you to join me in expanding their access to child care, creating new hiring preferences for military spouses across the federal government, and allowing our troops to transfer their unused education benefits to their spouses or children. Our military families serve our nation, they inspire our nation and tonight our nation honors them.

The strength — the secret of our strength, the miracle of America — is that our greatness lies not in our government but in the spirit and determination of our people. When the Federal Convention met in Philadelphia in 1787, our nation was bound by the Articles of Confederation, which began with the words, "We the undersigned delegates." When Gouverneur Morris was asked to draft a preamble to our new Constitution, he offered an important revision and opened with words that changed the course of our nation and the history of the world: "We the people."

By trusting the people, our founders wagered that a great and noble nation could be built on the liberty that resides in the hearts of all men and women. By trusting the people, succeeding generations transformed our fragile young democracy into the most powerful nation on Earth and a beacon of hope for millions. And so long as we continue to trust the people, our nation will prosper, our liberty will be secure and the state of our union will remain strong.

So tonight, with confidence in freedom's power and trust in the people, let us set forth to do their business. God bless America. ■

Democrats' Call: 'Let's Get to Work'

Following is the CQ Transcriptions transcript of the official Democratic response to President Bush's State of the Union address, delivered by Gov. Kathleen Sebelius of Kansas after Bush's speech Jan. 28.

Good evening. I'm Kathleen Sebelius, governor of the state of Kansas. And I'm grateful for the opportunity to speak with you tonight.

I'm a Democrat, but tonight it really doesn't matter whether you think of yourself as a Democrat or a Republican or an independent or none of the above.

Instead, the fact you're tuning in this evening tells me that each of you is, above all, an American first.

You're mothers and fathers, grandparents and grandchildren, working people and business owners — Americans, all.

And the American people — folks like you and me — are not nearly as divided as our rancorous politics might suggest.

In fact, right now, tonight, as the political pundits discuss the president's speech, chances are they'll obsess over reactions of members of Congress: "How many times was the president interrupted by applause? Did Republicans stand? Did the Democrats sit?"

And the rest of us will roll our eyes and think, "What in the world does any of that have to do with me?"

And so I want to take a slight detour from tradition on this State of the Union night.

In this time, normally reserved for a partisan response, I hope to offer something more: an American response, a national call to action on behalf of the struggling families in the heartland and across this great country; a wake-up call to Washington, on behalf of a new American majority, that time is running out on our opportunities to meet our challenges and solve our problems.

ECONOMIC WORRIES

Our struggling economy requires urgent and immediate action and then sustained attention. Families can't pay their bills. They're losing their jobs and now are threatened with losing their homes.

We heard last week and again tonight that Congress and the president are acting quickly on a temporary, targeted stimulus package. That's encouraging. But you and I know that a temporary fix is only the first step toward meeting our challenges and solving our problems.

There's a chance, Mr. President, in the next 357 days, to get real results and give the American people renewed optimism that their challenges are the top priority.

Working together, working hard, committing to results, we can get the job done.

In fact, over the last year, the Democratic majority in Congress has begun to move us in the right direction with bipartisan action to strengthen our national security, raise the minimum wage and reduce the costs of college loans.

These are encouraging first steps. But there's still more to be done.

So we ask you, Mr. President: Will you join us? Let's get to work.

We know that we're stronger as a nation when our people have access to the highest-quality, most affordable health care, when our businesses can compete in the global marketplace without the burden of rising health care costs here at home.

We know that caring for our children so they have a healthy and better start in life is what grown-ups do. Governors in both parties and a large majority of the Congress are ready, right now, to provide health care to 10 million American children, as a first step in overhauling our health care system.

Join us, Mr. President. Sign the bill and let's get to work.

CLIMATE CHANGE AND ENERGY

Sitting with the first lady tonight was Steve Hewitt, the city manager of Greensburg, Kan. Many of you remember Greensburg, our town nearly destroyed by a tornado last year.

Thanks to Steve's efforts, and hundreds of others in our state and across the country, Greensburg will recover. Folks rolled up their sleeves and got to work, and local, state and federal governments assisted in the effort.

But more than just recover, the Kansans who live in Greensburg are building green, rebuilding a better community for their children and grandchildren, making shared sacrifices and investments for the next generation.

Greensburg is not alone. You and I stand ready — ready to protect our environment for future generations and stay economically competitive.

Mayors have committed their cities to going green; governors have joined together, leading efforts for energy security and independence; and the majority in Congress are ready to tackle the challenge of reducing global warming and creating a new energy future for America.

So we ask you, Mr. President: Will you join us? It's time to get to work.

IRAQ WAR

Here in the heartland, we honor and respect military service.

We appreciate the enormous sacrifices made by soldiers and their families.

As governor of Kansas, I'm the commander in chief of our National Guard. Over the past five years, I've seen thousands of soldiers deployed from Kansas. I've visited our troops in Iraq, attended funerals and comforted families, and seen the impact at home of the war being waged.

We stand ready in the heartland and across this country to join forces with peace-loving nations around the globe to fight the war against terrorists, wherever they may strike. But our capable and dedicated soldiers can't solve the political disputes where they are and can't focus on the real enemies elsewhere.

The new Democratic majority of Congress and the vast majority of Americans are ready — ready to chart a new course. If more Republicans in Congress stand with us this year, we won't have to wait for a new president to restore America's role in the world and fight a more effective war on terror.

The last five years have cost us dearly — in lives lost, in thousands of wounded warriors whose futures may never be the same, in challenges not met here at home because our resources were committed elsewhere. America's foreign policy has left us with fewer allies and more enemies.

Join us, Mr. President. In working together with Congress to make tough, smart decisions, we will regain our standing in the world and protect our people and our interests.

I know government can work to benefit the people we serve because I see it every day, not only here in Kansas but in states across the country.

Because I see it every day, not only here in Kansas but in states across the country. I know government can work, Mr. President, because, like you, I grew up in a family committed to public service.

My father and my father-in-law both served in Congress, one a Republican and one a Democrat. They had far more in common than the issues that divided them: a love for their country that led them from military service to public service; a lifetime of working for the common good, making sacrifices so their children and grandchildren could have a better future.

They are called the Greatest Generation. But I believe, like parents across America, that our greatest generations are still to come, that we must chart a new course, at home and abroad, to give our future greatest generations all the opportunities our parents gave us.

These are uncertain times, but, with strength and determination, we can meet the challenges together. If Washington can work quickly together on a short-term fix for families caught in the financial squeeze, then we can work together to transform America.

In these difficult times, the American people aren't afraid to face difficult choices.

But we have no more patience with divisive politics.

Tonight's address begins the final year of this presidency, with new leaders on the horizon and uncertainty throughout our land. Conditions we face, at home and abroad, are results of choices made and challenges unmet.

In spite of the attempts to convince us that we are divided as a people, a new American majority has come together. We're tired of leaders who, rather than asking us what we can do for our country, ask nothing of us at all.

We're Americans sharing a belief in something greater than ourselves, a nation coming together to meet challenges and find solutions, to share sacrifices and share prosperity, and focus, once again, not only on the individual good but on the common good.

On behalf of the new American majority — the majority of elected officials at the national, state and local level, and the majority of Americans — we ask you, Mr. President, to join us.

We're ready to work together to be the America we have been and can be once again.

Thank you for listening.

God bless and sleep well. And, in the morning, let's get to work. ■

Bush Vetoes FY '08 Intelligence Bill

Following is the text of President Bush's veto message on the intelligence authorization for fiscal year 2008 (HR 2082).

TO THE HOUSE OF REPRESENTATIVES:

I am returning herewith without my approval HR 2082, the "Intelligence Authorization Act for Fiscal Year 2008."

The bill would impede the United States government's efforts to protect the American people effectively from terrorist attacks and other threats because it imposes several unnecessary and unacceptable burdens on our intelligence community.

CONFIRMATIONS

Section 444 of the bill would impose additional Senate confirmation requirements on two national security positions — the director of the National Security Agency and the director of the National Reconnaissance Office. The National Commission on Terrorist Attacks Upon the United States (9/11 commission) observed that the effectiveness of the intelligence community suffers due to delays in the confirmation process; Section 444 would only aggravate those serious problems.

Senior intelligence officials need to assume their duties and responsibilities as quickly as possible to address the pressing requirements of national security. Instead of addressing the 9/11 commission's concern, the bill would subject two additional vital positions to a more protracted process of Senate confirmation. Apart from causing such potentially harmful delays, this unwarranted requirement for Senate confirmation would also risk injecting political pressure into these positions of technical expertise and public trust.

INSPECTORS GENERAL

Section 413 would create a new inspector general for the intelligence community. This new office is duplicative and unnecessary. Each intelligence community component already has an inspector general, and the inspector general of the Office of the Director of National Intelligence has been vested with all the legal powers of any inspector general to carry out investigations on matters under the jurisdiction of the director of national intelligence. There is no reason to commit taxpayer resources to an additional inspector general with competing jurisdiction over the same intelligence elements. Creating duplicative inspectors general, who may have inconsistent views on the handling of particular matters, has the potential to create conflicts and impede the intelligence community from efficiently resolving issues and carrying out its core mission. In addition, the creation of a new inspector general would add yet another position in the intelligence community subject to Senate confirmation, contrary to the 9/11 commission's recommendations.

INTERROGATION METHODS

Section 327 of the bill would harm our national security by requiring any element of the intelligence community to use only the interrogation methods authorized in the Army Field Manual on Interrogations. It is vitally important that the Central Intelligence Agency (CIA) be allowed to maintain a separate and classified interrogation program. The Army Field Manual is directed at guiding the actions of nearly 3 million active-duty and reserve military personnel in connection with the detention of lawful combatants during the course of traditional armed conflicts, but terrorists often are trained specifically to resist techniques prescribed in publicly available military regulations such as the manual.

The CIA's ability to conduct a separate and specialized interrogation program for terrorists who possess the most critical information in the war on terror has helped the United States prevent a number of attacks, including plots to fly passenger airplanes into the Library Tower in Los Angeles and into Heathrow Airport or buildings in downtown London.

While details of the current CIA program are classified, the attorney general has reviewed it and determined that it is lawful under existing domestic and international law, including Common Article 3 of the Geneva Conventions. I remain committed to an intelligence-gathering program that complies with our legal obligations and our basic values as a people. The United States opposes torture, and I remain committed to following international and domestic law regarding the humane treatment of people in its custody, including the "Detainee Treatment Act of 2005."

My disagreement over Section 327 is not over any particular interrogation technique; for instance, it is not over waterboarding, which is not part of the current CIA program. Rather, my concern is the need to maintain a separate CIA program that will shield from disclosure to al Qaeda and other terrorists the interrogation techniques they may face upon capture.

In accordance with a clear purpose of the "Military Commissions Act of 2006," my veto is intended to allow the continuation of a separate and classified CIA interrogation program that the Department of Justice has determined is lawful and that operates according to rules distinct from the more general rules applicable to the Department of Defense. While I will continue to work with the Congress on the implementation of laws passed in this area in recent years, I cannot sign into law a bill that would prevent me — and future presidents — from authorizing the CIA to conduct a separate, lawful intelligence program and from taking all lawful actions necessary to protect Americans from attack.

EXECUTIVE POWERS

Other provisions of the bill purport to require the executive branch to submit information to the Congress that may be constitutionally protected from disclosure, including information the disclosure of which could impair foreign relations, the national security, the deliberative processes of the executive, or the performance of the executive's constitutional duties.

Section 326, for example, would require that the executive branch report, on a very short deadline and in accordance with a rigid set of specific statutory requirements, the details of highly classified interrogation techniques and the confidential legal advice concerning them.

The executive branch voluntarily has provided much of this information to appropriate members of Congress, demonstrating that questions concerning access to such information are best addressed through the customary practices and arrangements between the executive and legislative branches on such matters, rather than through the enactment of legislation.

In addition, Section 406 would require a

consolidated inventory of Special Access Programs (SAPs) to be submitted to the Congress. Special Access Programs concern the most sensitive information maintained by the government, and SAP materials are maintained separately precisely to avoid the existence of one document that can serve as a road map to our nation's most vital information. The executive branch must be permitted to present this information in a manner that does not jeopardize national security.

The executive branch will continue to keep the Congress appropriately informed of the matters to which the provisions relate in accordance with the accommodation principles the Constitution contemplates and the executive and legislative branches have long and successfully used to address information sharing on matters of national security.

GEORGE W. BUSH
THE WHITE HOUSE,
March 8, 2008

Spending in Farm Bill Prompts Veto

Following is the text of President Bush's May 21 veto message on HR 2419, a reauthorization of the farm bill.

TO THE HOUSE OF REPRESENTATIVES:

I am returning herewith without my approval HR 2419, the "Food, Conservation and Energy Act of 2008."

For a year and a half, I have consistently asked that the Congress pass a good farm bill that I can sign. Regrettably, the Congress has failed to do so. At a time of high food prices and record farm income, this bill lacks program reform and fiscal discipline. It continues subsidies for the wealthy and increases farm bill spending by more than $20 billion, while using budget gimmicks to hide much of the increase. It is inconsistent with our objectives in international trade negotiations, which include securing greater market access for American farmers and ranchers. It would needlessly expand the size and scope of government. Americans sent us to Washington to achieve results and be good stewards of their hard-earned taxpayer dollars. This bill violates that fundamental commitment.

In January 2007, my administration put forward a fiscally responsible farm bill proposal that would improve the safety net for farmers and move current programs toward more market-oriented policies. The bill before me today fails to achieve these important goals.

At a time when net farm income is projected to increase by more than $28 billion in one year, the American taxpayer should not be forced to subsidize that group of farmers who have adjusted gross incomes of up to $1.5 million. When commodity prices are at record highs, it is irresponsible to increase government subsidy rates for 15 crops, subsidize additional crops and provide payments that further distort markets. Instead of better targeting farm programs, this bill eliminates the existing payment limit on marketing loan subsidies.

Now is also not the time to create a new uncapped revenue guarantee that could cost billions of dollars more than advertised. This is on top of a farm bill that is anticipated to cost more than $600 billion over 10 years. In addition, this bill would force many businesses to prepay their taxes in order to finance the additional spending.

This legislation is also filled with earmarks and other ill-considered provisions. Most notably, HR 2419 provides: $175 million to address water issues for desert lakes; $250 million for a 400,000-acre land purchase from a private owner; funding and authority for the noncompetitive sale of National Forest land to a ski resort; and $382 million earmarked for a specific watershed. These earmarks, and the expansion of Davis-Bacon Act prevailing wage requirements, have no place in the farm bill. Rural and urban Americans alike are frustrated with excessive government spending and the funneling of taxpayer funds for pet projects. This bill will only add to that frustration.

The bill also contains a wide range of other objectionable provisions, including one that restricts our ability to redirect food aid dollars for emergency use at a time of great need globally. The bill does not include the requested authority to buy food in the developing world to save lives. Additionally, provisions in the bill raise serious constitutional concerns. For all the reasons outlined above, I must veto HR 2419, and I urge the Congress to extend current law for a year or more.

I veto this bill fully aware that it is rare for a stand-alone farm bill not to receive the president's signature, but my action today is not without precedent. In 1956, President Eisenhower stood firmly on principle, citing high crop subsidies and too much government control of farm programs among the reasons for his veto. President Eisenhower wrote in his veto message, "Bad as some provisions of this bill are, I would have signed it if in total it could be interpreted as sound and good for farmers and the nation." For similar reasons, I am vetoing the bill before me today.

GEORGE W. BUSH
THE WHITE HOUSE,
May 21, 2008

Bush Also Rejects Revised Farm Bill

Following is the text of President Bush's June 18 veto message on HR 6124, a reauthorization of the farm bill.

TO THE HOUSE OF REPRESENTATIVES:

I am returning herewith without my approval HR 6124, the "Food, Conservation and Energy Act of 2008."

The bill that I vetoed on May 21, 2008, HR 2419, which became Public Law 110-234, did not include the Title III provisions that are in this bill. In passing HR 6124, the Congress had an opportunity to improve on HR 2419 by modifying certain objectionable, onerous and fiscally imprudent provisions. Unfortunately, the Congress chose to send me the same unacceptable farm bill provisions in HR 6124, merely adding Title III. I am returning this bill for the same reasons as stated in my veto message of May 21, 2008, on HR 2419.

For a year and a half, I have consistently asked that the Congress pass a good farm bill that I can sign. Regrettably, the Congress has failed to do so. At a time of high food prices and record farm income, this bill lacks program reform and fiscal discipline. It continues subsidies for the wealthy and increases farm bill spending by more than $20 billion, while using budget gimmicks to hide much of the increase. It is inconsistent with our objectives in international trade negotiations, which include securing greater market access for American farmers and ranchers. It would needlessly expand the size and scope of government. Americans sent us to Washington to achieve results and be good stewards of their hard-earned taxpayer dollars. This bill violates that fundamental commitment.

In January 2007, my administration put forward a fiscally responsible farm bill proposal that would improve the safety net for farmers and move current programs toward more market-oriented policies. The bill before me today fails to achieve these important goals.

At a time when net farm income is projected to increase by more than $28 billion in one year, the American taxpayer should not be forced to subsidize that group of farmers who have adjusted gross incomes of up to $1.5 million. When commodity prices are at record highs, it is irresponsible to increase government subsidy rates for 15 crops, subsidize additional crops and provide payments that further distort markets. Instead of better targeting farm programs, this bill eliminates the existing payment limit on marketing loan subsidies.

Now is also not the time to create a new uncapped revenue guarantee that could cost billions of dollars more than advertised. This is on top of a farm bill that is anticipated to cost more than $600 billion over 10 years. In addition, this bill would force many businesses to prepay their taxes in order to finance the additional spending.

This legislation is also filled with earmarks and other ill-considered provisions. Most notably, HR 6124 provides: $175 million to address water issues for desert lakes; $250 million for a 400,000-acre land purchase from a private owner; funding and authority for the noncompetitive sale of National Forest land to a ski resort; and $382 million earmarked for a specific watershed. These earmarks, and the expansion of Davis-Bacon Act prevailing wage requirements, have no place in the farm bill. Rural and urban Americans alike are frustrated with excessive government spending and the funneling of taxpayer funds for pet projects. This bill will only add to that frustration.

The bill also contains a wide range of other objectionable provisions, including one that restricts our ability to redirect food aid dollars for emergency use at a time of great need globally. The bill does not include the requested authority to buy food in the developing world to save lives. Additionally, provisions in the bill raise serious constitutional concerns. For all the reasons outlined above, I must veto HR 6124.

I veto this bill fully aware that it is rare for a stand-alone farm bill not to receive the president's signature, but my action today is not without precedent. In 1956, President Eisenhower stood firmly on principle, citing high crop subsidies and too much government control of farm programs among the reasons for his veto. President Eisenhower wrote in his veto message, "Bad as some provisions of this bill are, I would have signed it if in total it could be interpreted as sound and good for farmers and the nation." For similar reasons, I am vetoing the bill before me today.

GEORGE W. BUSH
THE WHITE HOUSE,
June 18, 2008

Bush Says Bill Would Harm Seniors

Following is the text of President Bush's July 15 veto message on HR 6331, a bill to forestall a reduction in physician reimbursements for Medicare services.

TO THE HOUSE OF REPRESENTATIVES:

I am returning herewith without my approval HR 6331, the "Medicare Improvements for Patients and Providers Act of 2008." I support the primary objective of this legislation, to forestall reductions in physician payments. Yet taking choices away from seniors to pay physicians is wrong. This bill is objectionable, and I am vetoing it because:

● It would harm beneficiaries by taking private health plan options away from them. Already more than 9.6 million beneficiaries, many of whom are considered lower-income, have chosen to join a Medicare Advantage (MA) plan, and it is estimated that this bill would decrease MA enrollment by about 2.3 million individuals in 2013 relative to the program's current baseline.

● It would undermine the Medicare prescription drug program, which today is effectively providing coverage to 32 million beneficiaries directly through competitive private plans or through Medicare-subsidized retirement plans.

● And it is fiscally irresponsible, and it would imperil the long-term fiscal soundness of Medicare by using short-term budget gimmicks that do not solve the problem. The result would be a steep and unrealistic payment cut for physicians — roughly 20 percent in 2010 — likely leading to yet another expensive temporary fix. And the bill would also perpetuate wasteful overpayments to medical equipment suppliers.

PRIVATE MEDICARE PLANS

In December 2003, when I signed the Medicare Prescription Drug, Improvement and Modernization Act (MMA) into law, I said that "when seniors have the ability to make choices, health care plans within Medicare will have to compete for their business by offering higher-quality service. For the seniors of America, more choices and more control will mean better health care." This is exactly what has happened with drug coverage and with Medicare Advantage.

Today, as a result of the changes in the MMA, 32 million seniors and Americans with disabilities have drug coverage through Medicare prescription drug plans or a Medicare-subsidized retirement plan, while some 9.6 million Medicare beneficiaries — more than 20 percent of all beneficiaries — have chosen to join a private MA plan. To protect the interests of these beneficiaries, I cannot accept the provisions of this legislation that would undermine Medicare Part D, reduce payments for MA plans and restructure the MA program in a way that would lead to limited beneficiary access, benefits and choices and lower-than-expected enrollment in Medicare Advantage.

Medicare beneficiaries need and benefit from having more options than just the one-size-fits-all approach of traditional Medicare fee-for-service. Medicare Advantage plan options include health maintenance organizations, preferred-provider organizations and private fee-for-service (PFFS) plans. Medicare Advantage plans are paid according to a formula established by the Congress in 2003 to ensure that seniors in all parts of the country — including rural areas — have access to private-plan options.

This bill would reduce these options for beneficiaries, particularly those in hard-to-serve rural areas. In particular, HR 6331 would make fundamental changes to the MA PFFS program. The Congressional Budget Office has estimated that HR 6331 would decrease MA enrollment by about 2.3 million individuals in 2013 relative to its current baseline, with the largest effects resulting from these PFFS restrictions.

While the MMA increased the availability of private plan options across the country, it is important to remember that a significant number of beneficiaries who have chosen these options earn lower incomes. The latest data show that 49 percent of beneficiaries enrolled in MA plans report incomes of $20,000 or less. These beneficiaries have made a decision to maximize their Medicare and supplemental benefits through the MA program, in part because of their economic situation. Cuts to MA plan payments required by this legislation would reduce benefits to millions of seniors, including lower-income seniors, who have chosen to join these plans.

PRESCRIPTION DRUG PRICES

The bill would constrain market forces and undermine the success that the Medicare prescription drug program has achieved in providing beneficiaries with robust, high-value coverage — including comprehensive formularies and access to network pharmacies — at lower-than-expected costs. In particular, the provisions that would enable the expansion of "protected classes" of drugs would effectively end meaningful price negotiations between Medicare prescription drug plans and pharmaceutical manufacturers for drugs in those classes. If, as is likely, implementation of this provision results in an increase in the number of protected drug classes, it will lead to increased beneficiary premiums and co-payments, higher drug prices, and lower drug rebates. These new requirements, together with provisions that interfere with the contractual relationships between Part D plans and pharmacies, are expected to increase Medicare spending and have a negative impact on the value and choices that beneficiaries have come to enjoy in the program.

The bill includes budget gimmicks that do not solve the payment problem for physicians, make the problem worse with an abrupt payment cut for physicians of roughly 20 percent in 2010, and add nearly $20 billion to the Medicare Improvement Fund, which would unnecessarily increase Medicare spending and contribute to the unsustainable growth in Medicare. In addition, HR 6331 would delay important reforms like the Durable Medical Equipment, Prosthetics, Orthotics and Supplies competitive bidding program, under which lower payment rates went into effect on July 1, 2008. This program will produce significant savings for Medicare and beneficiaries by obtaining lower prices through competitive bidding. The legislation would leave the Federal Supplementary Medical Insurance Trust Fund vulnerable to litigation because of the revocation of the awarded contracts. Changing policy in midstream is also confusing to beneficiaries who are receiving services from quality suppliers at lower prices. In order to slow the growth in Medicare spending, competition within the program should be expanded, not diminished.

For decades, we promised America's seniors we could do better, and we finally did. We

should not turn the clock back to the days when our Medicare system offered outdated and inefficient benefits and imposed needless costs on its beneficiaries.

Because this bill would severely damage the Medicare program by undermining the Medicare Part D program and by reducing ac-

cess, benefits and choices for all beneficiaries, particularly the approximately 9.6 million beneficiaries in MA, I must veto this bill.

I urge the Congress to send me a bill that reduces the growth in Medicare spending, increases competition and efficiency, implements principles of value-driven health care,

and appropriately offsets increases in physician spending.

GEORGE W. BUSH
THE WHITE HOUSE,
July 15, 2008

Biden Talks of Family, Dignity, Change

Folloiwng is the speech by Democratic vice presidential nominee Sen. Joseph R. Biden Jr. of Delaware to the Democratic National Convention on Aug. 27, 2008.

THANK YOU. Thank you very much. Thank you. Thank you. Thank you. Thank you, John Kerry.

Ladies and gentlemen, thank you. Thank you, thank you. Thanks. Thank you.

I appreciate it. Thank you very much.

You know, folks, my dad used to have an expression. He'd say, "A father knows he's a success when he turns and looks at his son or daughter and knows that they turned out better than he did." I'm a success; I'm a hell of a success.

Beau, I love you. I'm so proud of you. I'm so proud of the son you've become; I'm so proud of the father you are.

And I'm also so proud of my son, Hunter, and my daughter, Ashley.

And my wife, Jill, the only one who leaves me both breathless and speechless at the same time.

It's an honor to share the stage tonight with President Clinton, a man who I think brought this country so far along that I only pray we do it again.

And last night, it was moving to watch Hillary, one of our great leaders, a great leader of this party, a woman who has made history and will continue to make history . . . a colleague, my friend, Sen. Hillary Clinton.

And I am truly honored to live in a country with the bravest warriors in the world.

And I'm honored to represent the first state, my state, the state of Delaware.

Since I've never been called a man of few words, let me say this simply as I can: Yes. Yes, I accept your nomination to run and serve with Barack Obama, the next president of the United States of America.

Let me make this pledge to you right here and now. For every American who is trying to do the right thing, for all those people in government who are honoring the pledge to uphold the law and honor the Constitution, no longer will you hear the eight most-dreaded words in the English language, "The vice president's office is on the phone."

Barack and I took very different journeys to this destination, but we share a common story. Mine began in Scranton, Pennsylvania, and then Wilmington, Delaware.

My dad, who fell on hard times, always told me, though, "Champ, when you get knocked down, get up. Get up." I was taught — I was taught that by my dad. And, God, I wish my dad was here tonight.

But I thank God and I'm grateful that my mom, Catherine Eugenia Finnegan Biden is here tonight.

Mom, I love you.

You know, my mom taught her children — all the children who flocked to our house — that you're defined by your sense of honor and you're redeemed by your loyalty. She believes that bravery lives in every heart, and her expectation is that it will be summoned. Failure — failure at some point in your life is inevitable, but giving up is unforgivable.

As a child, I stuttered, and she lovingly would look at me and tell me, "Joey, it's because you're so bright you can't get the thoughts out quickly enough."

When I was not as well-dressed as the other kids, she'd look at me and say, "Joey, oh, you're so handsome, honey, you're so handsome."

And when I got knocked down by guys bigger than me — and this is the God's truth — she sent me back out and said, "Bloody their nose so you can walk down the street the next day." And that's what I did.

You know — and after the accident, she told me, she said, "Joey, God sends no cross that you cannot bear." And when I triumphed, my mother was quick to remind me it was because of others.

My mother's creed is the American creed: No one is better than you. Everyone is your equal, and everyone is equal to you.

THE AMERICAN DREAM

My parents taught us to live our faith and to treasure our families. We learned the dignity of work, and we were told that anyone can make it if they just try hard enough. That was America's promise.

And for those of us who grew up in middle-class neighborhoods like Scranton and Wilmington, that was the American dream.

Ladies and gentlemen, but today, today that American dream feels like it's slowly slipping away. I don't have to tell you that. You feel it every single day in your own lives. I've never seen a time when Washington has watched so many people get knocked down without doing anything to help them get back up.

Almost every single night, I take the train home to Wilmington, Delaware, sometimes very late. As I sit there in my seat and I look out that window, I see those flickering lights of the homes that pass by, I can almost hear the conversation they're having at their kitchen tables after they put their kids to bed.

Like millions of Americans, they're asking questions as — as ordinary as they are profound, questions they never, ever thought they'd have to ask themselves.

Should Mom move in with us now that Dad's gone? $50, $60, $70 just to fill up the gas tank, how in God's name, with winter coming, how are we going to heat the home? Another year, no raise. Did you hear — did you hear they may be cutting our health care at the company?

Now we owe more money on our home than our home is worth. How in God's name are we going to send the kids to college? How are we going to retire, Joe?

You know, folks, that's the America that George Bush has left us. And that's the America we'll continue to get if George — excuse me, if John McCain is elected president of the United States of America. Freudian slip. Freudian slip.

And, folks, these are not isolated discussions among families down on their luck. These are common stories among middle-class people who worked hard their whole life, played by the rules, on the promise that their tomorrows would be better than their yesterdays.

That promise is the promise of America. It defines who we are as a people. And now — and now it's in jeopardy. I know it. You know it.

But John McCain doesn't seem to get it. Barack Obama gets it, though. Like many of us in this room, like many of us in this hall, Barack Obama has worked his way up. He is the great American story, you know?

I believe the measure of a man is not the road he travels, but the choices he makes along that road.

And, ladies and gentlemen, Barack Obama could have done anything after he graduated from college. With all his talent and promise, he could have written his own ticket to Wall Street. But what did he choose to do?

He chose to go to Chicago, the South Side

of Chicago. There, in the South Side, he met women and men who had lost their jobs. Their neighborhood was devastated when the local steel plant closed. Their dreams had to be deferred; their self-esteem was gone. And, ladies and gentlemen, he made their lives the work of his life.

That's what you do when you're raised by a single mom who worked, went to school and raised two kids on her own. That's how you come to believe to the very core of your being that work is more than a paycheck. It's dignity. It's respect.

It's about whether or not you can look your child in the eye and say, "We're going to be all right."

Because Barack Obama made that choice, 150 more children and parents have health care in Illinois. He fought to make that happen. And because Barack Obama made that choice, working families in Illinois pay less taxes and more people have moved from welfare to the dignity of work. And he got it done.

And when, John [Kerry] and I watched with amazement how he hit the ground running, leading the fight to pass the most sweeping ethics reform in a generation.

He reached across party lines to pass a law that helped keep nuclear weapons out of the hands of terrorists.

And then he moved Congress and the president to give our wonderful wounded warriors the care and dignity they deserve.

You know, you can learn a lot about a man campaigning with him, debating him, seeing how he reacts under pressure. You learn about the strength of his mind. But even more importantly, you learn about the quality of his heart.

I watched how Barack touched people, how he inspired them. And I realized he had tapped into the oldest belief in America: We don't have to accept the situation we cannot bear; we have the power to change it.

And change it — and changing it is exactly what Barack Obama will do. That's what he'll do for this country.

You know, John McCain is my friend. And I know you hear that phrase used all the time in politics. I mean it. John McCain is my friend. We've traveled the world together. It's a friendship that goes beyond politics. And the personal courage and heroism demonstrated by John still amazes me.

But I profoundly — I profoundly disagree with the direction John wants to take this country, from Afghanistan to Iraq, from Am-

trak to veterans.

You know, John thinks that, during the Bush years, quote, "We've made great economic progress." I think it's been abysmal. And in the Senate, John has voted with President Bush 95 percent. And that is very hard to believe.

And when John McCain proposes $200 million in new taxes for corporate America, $1 billion alone for the largest companies in the nation — but no, none, no relief for 100 million American families, that's not change. That's more of the same.

Even today, as oil companies post the biggest profits in history, nearly $500 billion in the last five years, John wants to give them another $4 billion in tax breaks. That's not change. That's the same.

And during the same time, John voted again and again against renewable energy, solar, wind, biofuels. That's not change. That's more of the same.

Millions of Americans have seen their jobs go offshore, yet John continues to support tax breaks for corporations that send them there. That's not change. That's more of the same.

He voted 19 times against the minimum wage for people who are struggling just to make it to the next day. That's not change. That's more of the same.

And when he says he'll continue to spend $10 billion a month, when the Iraqis have a surplus of nearly $80 billion, that's not change. That's more of the same.

'CHANGE WE NEED'

The choice in the election is clear. These times require more than a good soldier. They require a wise leader. A leader who can change, change — the change that everybody knows we need.

Barack Obama's going to deliver that change, because, I want to tell you, Barack Obama will reform our tax code. He will cut taxes for 95 percent of the American people who draw a paycheck. That's the change we need.

Barack Obama — Barack Obama will transform the economy by making alternative energy a national priority and in the process creating 5 million new jobs and finally, finally freeing us from the grip of foreign oil. That's the change we need.

Barack Obama knows that any country that out-teaches us today will out-compete us tomorrow. That's why he'll invest in the next generation of teachers and why he'll make college more affordable. That's the change

we need.

Barack Obama will bring down health care costs by $2,500 for the average family and, at long last, deliver affordable, accessible health care for every American.

That's the change we need.

Barack will put more cops on the street, put security back in Social Security, and he'll never, ever, ever give up until we achieve equal pay for women.

That's the change we need.

And as we gather here tonight, our country is less secure and more isolated than it has been at any time in recent history. The Bush foreign policy has dug us into a very deep hole, with very few friends to help us climb out.

And for the last seven years, the administration has failed to face the biggest — the biggest forces shaping this century: the emergence of Russia, China and India as great powers; the spread of lethal weapons; the shortage of secure supplies of energy, food and water; the challenge of climate change; and the resurgence of fundamentalism in Afghanistan and Pakistan, the real central front in the war on terror.

Ladies and gentlemen, in recent years and in recent days, we've once again seen the consequences of the neglect — of this neglect with Russia challenging the very freedom of a new democratic country of Georgia. Barack and I will end that neglect. We will hold Russia accountable for its actions, and we will help the people of Georgia rebuild.

I've been on the ground in Georgia, Iraq, Pakistan, Afghanistan, and I can tell you in no uncertain terms: This administration's policy has been an abysmal failure.

America cannot afford four more years of this failure. And now, now, despite being complicit in this catastrophic foreign policy, John McCain says Barack Obama is not ready to protect our national security.

Now, let me ask you this: Whose judgment do you trust?

Should you trust the judgment of John McCain, when he said only three years ago, "Afghanistan, we don't read about it anymore in papers because it succeeded"?

Or should you believe Barack Obama who said a year ago, "We need to send two more combat battalions to Afghanistan"?

The fact of the matter is, al Qaeda and the Taliban, the people who actually attacked us on 9/11, they've regrouped in the mountains between Afghanistan and Pakistan and they are plotting new attacks. And the chairman of the Joint Chiefs of Staff has echoed Barack's

call for more troops.

John McCain was wrong, and Barack Obama was right.

Should we trust John McCain's judgment when he rejected talking with Iran and then asked, "What is there to talk about?" Or Barack Obama, who said, "We must talk and make clear to Iran that it must change"?

Now, after seven years of denial, even the Bush administration recognizes that we should talk to Iran because that's the best way to ensure our security.

Again and again, John McCain has been wrong, and Barack Obama is right.

Should we trust John McCain's judgment when he says we can't have timelines to draw down our troops from Iraq, that we must stay indefinitely? Or should we listen to Barack Obama, who says shift the responsibility to the Iraqis and set a time to bring our combat troops home?

Now, after six long years, the administration and the Iraqi government are on the verge of setting a date to bring our troops home. John McCain was wrong, and Barack Obama was right.

Again — again and again, on the most important national security issues of our time, John McCain was wrong, and Barack Obama has been proven right.

Folks, remember when the world used to trust us, when they looked to us for leadership? With Barack Obama as our president, they'll look at us again, they'll trust us again, and we'll be able to lead again.

Folks, Jill and I are truly honored to join Michelle and Barack on this journey. When I look at their young children, when I look at my grandchildren, I know why I'm here.

I'm here for their future. I'm here for everyone I grew up with in Scranton and Wilmington. I'm here for the cops and the firefighters, the teachers and the assembly line workers, the folks whose lives are the very measure of whether the American dream endures.

Our greatest presidents, from Abraham Lincoln to Franklin Roosevelt to John Kennedy, they all challenged us to embrace change. Now it is our responsibility to meet that challenge.

Millions of Americans have been knocked down. And this is the time as Americans together we get back up, back up together.

Our debt to our parents and our grandparents is too great. Our obligation to our children is too sacred. These are extraordinary times; this is an extraordinary election.

The American people are ready. I am ready. Barack is ready. This is his time; this is our time; this is America's time.

God bless America, and may God protect our troops. Thank you very much. Thank you. ■

'We Are a Better Country Than This'

Following is the speech by Democratic presidential nominee Sen. Barack Obama of Illinois to the Democratic National Convention on Aug. 28, 2008.

THANK YOU SO MUCH. Thank you very much. Thank you, everybody.

To Chairman Dean and my great friend Dick Durbin, and to all my fellow citizens of this great nation, with profound gratitude and great humility, I accept your nomination for presidency of the United States.

Let me express my thanks to the historic slate of candidates who accompanied me on this journey, and especially the one who traveled the farthest, a champion for working Americans and an inspiration to my daughters and to yours, Hillary Rodham Clinton.

To President Clinton, to President Bill Clinton, who made last night the case for change as only he can make it — to Ted Kennedy, who embodies the spirit of service — and to the next vice president of the United States, Joe Biden, I thank you.

I am grateful to finish this journey with one of the finest statesmen of our time, a man at ease with everyone from world leaders to the conductors on the Amtrak train he still takes home every night.

To the love of my life, our next first lady, Michelle Obama — and to Malia and Sasha, I love you so much, and I am so proud of you.

Four years ago, I stood before you and told you my story, of the brief union between a young man from Kenya and a young woman from Kansas who weren't well-off or well-known, but shared a belief that in America their son could achieve whatever he put his mind to.

It is that promise that's always set this country apart, that through hard work and sacrifice each of us can pursue our individual dreams, but still come together as one American family, to ensure that the next generation can pursue their dreams, as well.

That's why I stand here tonight. Because for 232 years, at each moment when that promise was in jeopardy, ordinary men and women — students and soldiers, farmers and teachers, nurses and janitors — found the courage to keep it alive.

We meet at one of those defining moments, a moment when our nation is at war, our economy is in turmoil and the American promise has been threatened once more.

Tonight, more Americans are out of work and more are working harder for less. More of you have lost your homes and even more are watching your home values plummet. More of you have cars you can't afford to drive, credit cards, bills you can't afford to pay and tuition that's beyond your reach.

'BROKEN POLITICS'

These challenges are not all of government's making. But the failure to respond is a direct result of a broken politics in Washington and the failed policies of George W. Bush.

America, we are better than these last eight years. We are a better country than this.

This country is more decent than one where a woman in Ohio, on the brink of retirement, finds herself one illness away from disaster after a lifetime of hard work.

We're a better country than one where a man in Indiana has to pack up the equipment that he's worked on for 20 years and watch as it's shipped off to China, and then chokes up as he explains how he felt like a failure when he went home to tell his family the news.

We are more compassionate than a government that lets veterans sleep on our streets and families slide into poverty — that sits on its hands while a major American city drowns before our eyes.

Tonight, tonight, I say to the people of America, to Democrats and Republicans and independents across this great land: Enough.

This moment, this election is our chance to keep, in the 21st century, the American promise alive.

Because next week, in Minnesota, the same party that brought you two terms of George Bush and Dick Cheney will ask this country for a third.

And we are here because we love this country too much to let the next four years look just like the last eight.

On November 4th, we must stand up and say: Eight is enough.

Now, now, let me — let there be no doubt. The Republican nominee, John McCain, has worn the uniform of our country with bravery and distinction, and for that we owe him our gratitude and our respect.

And next week, we'll also hear about those occasions when he's broken with his party as evidence that he can deliver the change that we need. But the record's clear: John McCain has voted with George Bush 90 percent of the time.

Sen. McCain likes to talk about judgment, but, really, what does it say about your judgment when you think George Bush has been right more than 90 percent of the time?

I don't know about you, but I am not ready to take a 10 percent chance on change.

The truth is, on issue after issue that would make a difference in your lives — on health care, and education, and the economy — Sen. McCain has been anything but independent.

He said that our economy has made great progress under this president. He said that the fundamentals of the economy are strong.

And when one of his chief advisers, the man who wrote his economic plan, was talking about the anxieties that Americans are feeling, he said that we were just suffering from a mental recession and that we've become, and I quote, "a nation of whiners."

A nation of whiners? Tell that to the proud autoworkers at a Michigan plant who, after they found out it was closing, kept showing up every day and working as hard as ever, because they knew there were people who counted on the brakes that they made.

Tell that to the military families who shoulder their burdens silently as they watch their loved ones leave for their third, or fourth, or fifth tour of duty.

These are not whiners. They work hard, and they give back, and they keep going without complaint. These are the Americans I know.

Now, I don't believe that Sen. McCain doesn't care what's going on in the lives of Americans; I just think he doesn't know.

Why else would he define "middle class" as someone making under $5 million a year? How else could he propose hundreds of billions in tax breaks for big corporations and oil companies but not one penny of tax relief to more than 100 million Americans?

How else could he offer a health care plan that would actually tax people's benefits, or an education plan that would do nothing to help families pay for college, or a plan that would privatize Social Security and gamble your retirement?

It's not because John McCain doesn't care; it's because John McCain doesn't get it.

For over two decades — for over two decades — he's subscribed to that old, discredited

Republican philosophy: Give more and more to those with the most and hope that prosperity trickles down to everyone else.

In Washington, they call this the "Ownership Society," but what it really means is that you're on your own. Out of work? Tough luck, you're on your own. No health care? The market will fix it. You're on your own. Born into poverty? Pull yourself up by your own bootstraps, even if you don't have boots. You are on your own.

Well, it's time for them to own their failure. It's time for us to change America. And that's why I'm running for president of the United States.

You see, we Democrats have a very different measure of what constitutes progress in this country.

We measure progress by how many people can find a job that pays the mortgage, whether you can put a little extra money away at the end of each month so you can someday watch your child receive her college diploma.

We measure progress in the 23 million new jobs that were created when Bill Clinton was president — when the average American family saw its income go up $7,500 instead of go down $2,000, like it has under George Bush.

We measure the strength of our economy not by the number of billionaires we have or the profits of the Fortune 500, but by whether someone with a good idea can take a risk and start a new business, or whether the waitress who lives on tips can take a day off and look after a sick kid without losing her job, an economy that honors the dignity of work.

The fundamentals we use to measure economic strength are whether we are living up to that fundamental promise that has made this country great, a promise that is the only reason I am standing here tonight.

Because, in the faces of those young veterans who come back from Iraq and Afghanistan, I see my grandfather, who signed up after Pearl Harbor, marched in Patton's army and was rewarded by a grateful nation with the chance to go to college on the G.I. Bill.

In the face of that young student, who sleeps just three hours before working the night shift, I think about my mom, who raised my sister and me on her own while she worked and earned her degree, who once turned to food stamps but was still able to send us to the best schools in the country with the help of student loans and scholarships.

When I listen to another worker tell me that his factory has shut down, I remember all those men and women on the South Side

of Chicago who I stood by and fought for two decades ago after the local steel plant closed.

And when I hear a woman talk about the difficulties of starting her own business or making her way in the world, I think about my grandmother, who worked her way up from the secretarial pool to middle management, despite years of being passed over for promotions because she was a woman.

She's the one who taught me about hard work. She's the one who put off buying a new car or a new dress for herself so that I could have a better life. She poured everything she had into me. And although she can no longer travel, I know that she's watching tonight and that tonight is her night, as well.

Now, I don't know what kind of lives John McCain thinks that celebrities lead, but this has been mine.

These are my heroes; theirs are the stories that shaped my life. And it is on behalf of them that I intend to win this election and keep our promise alive as president of the United States.

THE AMERICAN PROMISE

What — what is that American promise? It's a promise that says each of us has the freedom to make of our own lives what we will, but that we also have obligations to treat each other with dignity and respect.

It's a promise that says the market should reward drive and innovation and generate growth but that businesses should live up to their responsibilities to create American jobs, to look out for American workers, and play by the rules of the road.

Ours is a promise that says government cannot solve all our problems, but what it should do is that which we cannot do for ourselves: protect us from harm and provide every child a decent education; keep our water clean and our toys safe; invest in new schools, and new roads, and science, and technology.

Our government should work for us, not against us. It should help us, not hurt us. It should ensure opportunity not just for those with the most money and influence, but for every American who's willing to work.

That's the promise of America, the idea that we are responsible for ourselves, but that we also rise or fall as one nation, the fundamental belief that I am my brother's keeper, I am my sister's keeper.

That's the promise we need to keep. That's the change we need right now.

So let me spell out exactly what that change would mean if I am president.

TAXES

Change means a tax code that doesn't reward the lobbyists who wrote it, but the American workers and small businesses who deserve it.

You know, unlike John McCain, I will stop giving tax breaks to companies that ship jobs overseas, and I will start giving them to companies that create good jobs right here in America.

I'll eliminate capital gains taxes for the small businesses and start-ups that will create the high-wage, high-tech jobs of tomorrow.

I will — listen now — I will cut taxes — cut taxes — for 95 percent of all working families, because, in an economy like this, the last thing we should do is raise taxes on the middle class.

ENERGY

And for the sake of our economy, our security and the future of our planet, I will set a clear goal as president: In 10 years, we will finally end our dependence on oil from the Middle East.

We will do this. Washington has been talking about our oil addiction for the last 30 years. And, by the way, John McCain has been there for 26 of them.

And in that time, he has said no to higher fuel efficiency standards for cars, no to investments in renewable energy, no to renewable fuels. And today, we import triple the amount of oil than we had on the day that Sen. McCain took office.

Now is the time to end this addiction and to understand that drilling is a stopgap measure, not a long-term solution, not even close. As president, I will tap our natural gas reserves, invest in clean-coal technology and find ways to safely harness nuclear power. I'll help our auto companies re-tool, so that the fuel efficient cars of the future are built right here in America.

I'll make it easier for the American people to afford these new cars.

And I'll invest $150 billion over the next decade in affordable, renewable sources of energy — wind power, and solar power, and the next generation of biofuels — an investment that will lead to new industries and 5 million new jobs that pay well and can't be outsourced.

EDUCATION

America, now is not the time for small plans. Now is the time to finally meet our moral obligation to provide every child a world-class

education, because it will take nothing less to compete in the global economy.

You know, Michelle and I are only here tonight because we were given a chance at an education. And I will not settle for an America where some kids don't have that chance.

I'll invest in early childhood education. I'll recruit an army of new teachers, and pay them higher salaries, and give them more support. And in exchange, I'll ask for higher standards and more accountability.

And we will keep our promise to every young American: If you commit to serving your community or our country, we will make sure you can afford a college education.

HEALTH CARE AND FINANCES

Now is the time to finally keep the promise of affordable, accessible health care for every single American.

If you have health care, my plan will lower your premiums. If you don't, you'll be able to get the same kind of coverage that members of Congress give themselves.

And as someone who watched my mother argue with insurance companies while she lay in bed dying of cancer, I will make certain those companies stop discriminating against those who are sick and need care the most.

Now is the time to help families with paid sick days and better family leave, because nobody in America should have to choose between keeping their job and caring for a sick child or an ailing parent.

Now is the time to change our bankruptcy laws so that your pensions are protected ahead of CEO bonuses, and the time to protect Social Security for future generations.

And now is the time to keep the promise of equal pay for an equal day's work, because I want my daughters to have the exact same opportunities as your sons.

Now, many of these plans will cost money, which is why I've laid out how I'll pay for every dime: by closing corporate loopholes and tax havens that don't help America grow.

But I will also go through the federal budget line by line, eliminating programs that no longer work and making the ones we do need work better and cost less, because we cannot meet 21st century challenges with a 20th-century bureaucracy.

PERSONAL RESPONSIBILITY

And, Democrats, we must also admit that fulfilling America's promise will require more than just money. It will require a renewed sense of responsibility from each of us to recover what John F. Kennedy called our intellectual and moral strength.

Yes, government must lead on energy independence, but each of us must do our part to make our homes and businesses more efficient.

Yes, we must provide more ladders to success for young men who fall into lives of crime and despair. But we must also admit that programs alone can't replace parents, that government can't turn off the television and make a child do her homework, that fathers must take more responsibility to provide love and guidance to their children.

Individual responsibility and mutual responsibility — that's the essence of America's promise. And just as we keep our promise to the next generation here at home, so must we keep America's promise abroad.

If John McCain wants to have a debate about who has the temperament and judgment to serve as the next commander in chief, that's a debate I'm ready to have.

FOREIGN POLICY

For while Sen. McCain was turning his sights to Iraq just days after 9/11, I stood up and opposed this war, knowing that it would distract us from the real threats that we face.

When John McCain said we could just muddle through in Afghanistan, I argued for more resources and more troops to finish the fight against the terrorists who actually attacked us on 9/11, and made clear that we must take out Osama bin Laden and his lieutenants if we have them in our sights.

You know, John McCain likes to say that he'll follow bin Laden to the gates of hell, but he won't even follow him to the cave where he lives.

And today, today, as my call for a time frame to remove our troops from Iraq has been echoed by the Iraqi government and even the Bush administration, even after we learned that Iraq has $79 billion in surplus while we are wallowing in deficit, John McCain stands alone in his stubborn refusal to end a misguided war.

That's not the judgment we need; that won't keep America safe. We need a president who can face the threats of the future, not keep grasping at the ideas of the past.

You don't defeat a terrorist network that operates in 80 countries by occupying Iraq. You don't protect Israel and deter Iran just by talking tough in Washington. You can't truly stand up for Georgia when you've strained our oldest alliances.

If John McCain wants to follow George Bush with more tough talk and bad strategy, that is his choice, but that is not the change that America needs.

We are the party of Roosevelt. We are the party of Kennedy. So don't tell me that Democrats won't defend this country. Don't tell me that Democrats won't keep us safe.

The Bush-McCain foreign policy has squandered the legacy that generations of Americans, Democrats and Republicans, have built, and we are here to restore that legacy.

As commander in chief, I will never hesitate to defend this nation, but I will only send our troops into harm's way with a clear mission and a sacred commitment to give them the equipment they need in battle and the care and benefits they deserve when they come home.

I will end this war in Iraq responsibly and finish the fight against al Qaeda and the Taliban in Afghanistan.

I will rebuild our military to meet future conflicts, but I will also renew the tough, direct diplomacy that can prevent Iran from obtaining nuclear weapons and curb Russian aggression.

I will build new partnerships to defeat the threats of the 21st century: terrorism and nuclear proliferation, poverty and genocide, climate change and disease.

And I will restore our moral standing so that America is once again that last, best hope for all who are called to the cause of freedom, who long for lives of peace, and who yearn for a better future.

These are the policies I will pursue. And in the weeks ahead, I look forward to debating them with John McCain.

But what I will not do is suggest that the senator takes his positions for political purposes, because one of the things that we have to change in our politics is the idea that people cannot disagree without challenging each other's character and each other's patriotism.

The times are too serious, the stakes are too high for this same partisan playbook. So let us agree that patriotism has no party. I love this country, and so do you, and so does John McCain.

The men and women who serve in our battlefields may be Democrats and Republicans and independents, but they have fought together and bled together, and some died together under the same proud flag. They have not served a red America or a blue America; they have served the United States of America.

So I've got news for you, John McCain: We all put our country first.

America, our work will not be easy. The challenges we face require tough choices. And Democrats as well as Republicans will need to cast off the worn-out ideas and politics of the past, for part of what has been lost these past eight years can't just be measured by lost wages or bigger trade deficits. What has also been lost is our sense of common purpose, and that's what we have to restore.

We may not agree on abortion, but surely we can agree on reducing the number of unwanted pregnancies in this country.

The reality of gun ownership may be different for hunters in rural Ohio than they are for those plagued by gang violence in Cleveland, but don't tell me we can't uphold the Second Amendment while keeping AK-47s out of the hands of criminals.

I know there are differences on same-sex marriage, but surely we can agree that our gay and lesbian brothers and sisters deserve to visit the person they love in a hospital and to live lives free of discrimination.

You know, passions may fly on immigration, but I don't know anyone who benefits when a mother is separated from her infant child or an employer undercuts American wages by hiring illegal workers.

But this, too, is part of America's promise, the promise of a democracy where we can find the strength and grace to bridge divides and unite in common effort.

I know there are those who dismiss such beliefs as happy talk. They claim that our insistence on something larger, something firmer and more honest in our public life is just a Trojan horse for higher taxes and the abandonment of traditional values.

And that's to be expected, because if you don't have any fresh ideas, then you use stale tactics to scare voters.

If you don't have a record to run on, then you paint your opponent as someone people should run from. You make a big election about small things.

And you know what? It's worked before, because it feeds into the cynicism we all have about government. When Washington doesn't work, all its promises seem empty. If your hopes have been dashed again and again, then it's best to stop hoping and settle for what you already know.

I get it. I realize that I am not the likeliest candidate for this office. I don't fit the typical pedigree, and I haven't spent my career in the halls of Washington.

But I stand before you tonight because all across America something is stirring. What the naysayers don't understand is that this election has never been about me; it's about you.

It's about you.

For 18 long months, you have stood up, one by one, and said, "Enough," to the politics of the past. You understand that, in this election, the greatest risk we can take is to try the same old politics with the same old players and expect a different result.

'DEFINING MOMENTS'

You have shown what history teaches us, that at defining moments like this one, the change we need doesn't come from Washington. Change comes to Washington.

Change happens because the American people demand it, because they rise up and insist on new ideas and new leadership, a new politics for a new time.

America, this is one of those moments.

I believe that, as hard as it will be, the change we need is coming, because I've seen it, because I've lived it.

Because I've seen it in Illinois, when we provided health care to more children and moved more families from welfare to work.

I've seen it in Washington, where we worked across party lines to open up government and hold lobbyists more accountable, to give better care for our veterans and keep nuclear weapons out of the hands of terrorists.

And I've seen it in this campaign, in the young people who voted for the first time and the young at heart, those who got involved again after a very long time; in the Republicans who never thought they'd pick up a Democratic ballot but did.

I've seen it in the workers who would rather cut their hours back a day, even though they can't afford it, than see their friends lose their jobs; in the soldiers who re-enlist after losing a limb; in the good neighbors who take a stranger in when a hurricane strikes and the floodwaters rise.

You know, this country of ours has more wealth than any nation, but that's not what makes us rich. We have the most powerful military on Earth, but that's not what makes

us strong. Our universities and our culture are the envy of the world, but that's not what keeps the world coming to our shores.

Instead, it is that American spirit, that American promise, that pushes us forward even when the path is uncertain; that binds us together in spite of our differences; that makes us fix our eye not on what is seen but what is unseen, that better place around the bend.

That promise is our greatest inheritance. It's a promise I make to my daughters when I tuck them in at night and a promise that you make to yours, a promise that has led immigrants to cross oceans and pioneers to travel west, a promise that led workers to picket lines and women to reach for the ballot.

And it is that promise that, 45 years ago today, brought Americans from every corner of this land to stand together on a Mall in Washington, before Lincoln's Memorial, and hear a young preacher from Georgia speak of his dream.

The men and women who gathered there could've heard many things. They could've heard words of anger and discord. They could've been told to succumb to the fear and frustrations of so many dreams deferred.

But what the people heard instead — people of every creed and color, from every walk of life — is that, in America, our destiny is inextricably linked, that together our dreams can be one.

"We cannot walk alone," the preacher cried. "And as we walk, we must make the pledge that we shall always march ahead. We cannot turn back."

America, we cannot turn back. Not with so much work to be done; not with so many children to educate, and so many veterans to care for; not with an economy to fix, and cities to rebuild, and farms to save; not with so many families to protect and so many lives to mend.

America, we cannot turn back. We cannot walk alone.

At this moment, in this election, we must pledge once more to march into the future. Let us keep that promise, that American promise, and in the words of Scripture hold firmly, without wavering, to the hope that we confess.

Thank you. God bless you. And God bless the United States of America. ∎

Gov. Palin Defends Her Credentials

Following is the speech by Republican vice presidential nominee Gov. Sarah Palin of Alaska to the Republican National Convention on Sept. 3, 2008.

MR. CHAIRMAN, DELEGATES, and fellow citizens, I will be honored to accept your nomination for vice president of the United States. I accept the call to help our nominee for president to serve and defend America. And I accept the challenge of a tough fight in this election against confident opponents at a crucial hour for our country.

And I accept the privilege of serving with a man who has come through much harder missions and met far graver challenges and knows how tough fights are won, the next president of the United States, John S. McCain.

It was just a year ago when all the experts in Washington counted out our nominee because he refused to hedge his commitment to the security of the country he loves.

With their usual certitude, they told us that all was lost, there was no hope for this candidate, who said that he would rather lose an election than see his country lose a war.

But the pollsters and the pundits, they overlooked just one thing when they wrote him off. They overlooked the caliber of the man himself, the determination, and resolve, and the sheer guts of Sen. John McCain.

The voters knew better, and maybe that's because they realized there's a time for politics and a time for leadership, a time to campaign and a time to put our country first.

Our nominee for president is a true profile in courage, and people like that are hard to come by. He's a man who wore the uniform of his country for 22 years and refused to break faith with those troops in Iraq who now have brought victory within sight.

And as the mother of one of those troops, that is exactly the kind of man I want as commander in chief.

I'm just one of many moms who will say an extra prayer each night for our sons and daughters going into harm's way. Our son, Track, is 19. And one week from tomorrow, Sept. 11, he'll deploy to Iraq with the Army infantry in the service of his country.

My nephew, Casey, also enlisted and serves on a carrier in the Persian Gulf.

My family is so proud of both of them and of all the fine men and women serving the country in uniform.

So Track is the eldest of our five children. In our family, it's two boys and three girls in between, my strong and kind-hearted daughters, Bristol, and Willow, and Piper.

And we were so blessed in April. Todd and I welcomed our littlest one into the world, a perfectly beautiful baby boy named Trig.

You know, from the inside, no family ever seems typical, and that's how it is with us. Our family has the same ups and downs as any other, the same challenges and the same joys.

Sometimes even the greatest joys bring challenge. And children with special needs inspire a very, very special love.

To the families of special-needs children all across this country, I have a message for you: For years, you've sought to make America a more welcoming place for your sons and daughters. And I pledge to you that, if we're elected, you will have a friend and advocate in the White House.

And Todd is a story all by himself. He's a lifelong commercial fisherman and a production operator in the oil fields of Alaska's North Slope, and a proud member of the United Steelworkers union. And Todd is a world champion snow machine racer.

Throw in his Yup'ik Eskimo ancestry, and it all makes for quite a package. And we met in high school. And two decades and five children later, he's still my guy.

My mom and dad both worked at the elementary school in our small town. And among the many things I owe them is a simple lesson that I've learned: that this is America, and every woman can walk through every door of opportunity.

And my parents are here tonight.

I am so proud to be the daughter of Chuck and Sally Heath.

PATH TO THE VICE PRESIDENCY

Long ago, a young farmer and a haberdasher from Missouri, he followed an unlikely path to the vice presidency. And a writer observed, "We grow good people in our small towns, with honesty and sincerity and dignity," and I know just the kind of people that writer had in mind when he praised Harry Truman.

I grew up with those people. They're the ones who do some of the hardest work in America, who grow our food, and run our factories, and fight our wars. They love their country in good times and bad, and they're always proud of America.

I had the privilege of living most of my life in a small town. I was just your average hockey mom and signed up for the PTA.

I love those hockey moms. You know, they say the difference between a hockey mom and a pit bull? Lipstick.

So I signed up for the PTA because I wanted to make my kids' public education even better. And when I ran for city council, I didn't need focus groups and voter profiles because I knew those voters, and I knew their families, too.

Before I became governor of the great state of Alaska, I was mayor of my hometown. And since our opponents in this presidential election seem to look down on that experience, let me explain to them what the job involved.

'ACTUAL RESPONSIBILITIES'

I guess a small-town mayor is sort of like a community organizer, except that you have actual responsibilities.

I might add that, in small towns, we don't quite know what to make of a candidate who lavishes praise on working people when they're listening and then talks about how bitterly they cling to their religion and guns when those people aren't listening.

No, we tend to prefer candidates who don't talk about us one way in Scranton and another way in San Francisco.

As for my running mate, you can be certain that wherever he goes and whoever is listening, John McCain is the same man.

Well, I'm not a member of the permanent political establishment. And I've learned quickly these last few days that, if you're not a member in good standing of the Washington elite, then some in the media consider a candidate unqualified for that reason alone.

But — now, here's a little news flash. Here's a little news flash for those reporters and commentators: I'm not going to Washington to seek their good opinion. I'm going to Washington to serve the people of this great country.

Americans expect us to go to Washington for the right reason and not just to mingle with the right people. Politics isn't just a game of clashing parties and competing interests. The right reason is to challenge the status quo, to serve the common good and to leave this nation better than we found it.

No one expects us all to agree on everything, but we are expected to govern with integrity, and good will, and clear convictions, and a servant's heart.

And I pledge to all Americans that I will carry myself in this spirit as vice president of the United States.

This was the spirit that brought me to the governor's office when I took on the old politics-as-usual in Juneau, when I stood up to the special interests, and the lobbyists, and the Big Oil companies, and the good-old boys.

Suddenly, I realized that sudden and relentless reform never sits well with entrenched interests and power brokers. That's why true reform is so hard to achieve.

But with the support of the citizens of Alaska, we shook things up. And in short order, we put the government of our state back on the side of the people.

I came to office promising major ethics reform to end the culture of self-dealing. And today, that ethics reform is a law.

While I was at it, I got rid of a few things in the governor's office that I didn't believe our citizens should have to pay for. That luxury jet was over the top.

I put it on eBay.

I love to drive myself to work. And I thought we could muddle through without the governor's personal chef, although I got to admit that sometimes my kids sure miss her.

I came to office promising to control spending, by request if possible, but by veto, if necessary.

Sen. McCain also — he promises to use the power of veto in defense of the public interest. And as a chief executive, I can assure you it works.

Our state budget is under control. We have a surplus. And I have protected the taxpayers by vetoing wasteful spending, nearly $500 million in vetoes.

We suspended the state fuel tax and championed reform to end the abuses of earmark spending by Congress. I told the Congress, "Thanks, but no thanks," on that "Bridge to Nowhere."

If our state wanted to build a bridge, we were going to build it ourselves.

When oil and gas prices went up dramatically and filled up the state treasury, I sent a large share of that revenue back where it belonged: directly to the people of Alaska.

And despite fierce opposition from oil company lobbyists, who kind of liked things the way that they were, we broke their monopoly on power and resources. As governor, I insisted on competition and basic fairness to end their control of our state and return it to the people.

ENERGY INDEPENDENCE

I fought to bring about the largest private-sector infrastructure project in North American history. And when that deal was struck, we began a nearly $40 billion natural gas pipeline to help lead America to energy independence.

That pipeline, when the last section is laid and its valves are open, will lead America one step farther away from dependence on dangerous foreign powers that do not have our interests at heart.

The stakes for our nation could not be higher. When a hurricane strikes in the Gulf of Mexico, this country should not be so dependent on imported oil that we're forced to draw from our Strategic Petroleum Reserve. And families cannot throw more and more of their paychecks on gas and heating oil.

With Russia wanting to control a vital pipeline in the Caucasus and to divide and intimidate our European allies by using energy as a weapon, we cannot leave ourselves at the mercy of foreign suppliers.

To confront the threat that Iran might seek to cut off nearly a fifth of the world's energy supplies, or that terrorists might strike again at the Abqaiq facility in Saudi Arabia, or that Venezuela might shut off its oil discoveries and its deliveries of that source, Americans, we need to produce more of our own oil and gas. And take it from a gal who knows the North Slope of Alaska: We've got lots of both.

Our opponents say again and again that drilling will not solve all of America's energy problems, as if we didn't know that already.

But the fact that drilling, though, won't solve every problem is no excuse to do nothing at all.

Starting in January, in a McCain-Palin administration, we're going to lay more pipelines, and build more nuclear plants, and create jobs with clean coal, and move forward on solar, wind, geothermal, and other alternative sources.

We need American sources of resources. We need American energy brought to you by American ingenuity and produced by American workers.

And now, I've noticed a pattern with our opponent, and maybe you have, too. We've all heard his dramatic speeches before devoted followers, and there is much to like and admire about our opponent.

But listening to him speak, it's easy to forget that this is a man who has authored two memoirs but not a single major law or even a reform, not even in the state Senate.

This is a man who can give an entire speech about the wars America is fighting and never use the word "victory," except when he's talking about his own campaign.

But when the cloud of rhetoric has passed, when the roar of the crowd fades away, when the stadium lights go out, and those Styrofoam Greek columns are hauled back to some studio lot — when that happens, what exactly is our opponent's plan? What does he actually seek to accomplish after he's done turning back the waters and healing the planet?

The answer is to make government bigger, and take more of your money, and give you more orders from Washington, and to reduce the strength of America in a dangerous world.

America needs more energy; our opponent is against producing it. Victory in Iraq is finally in sight, and he wants to forfeit. Terrorist states are seeking nuclear weapons without delay; he wants to meet them without preconditions.

Al Qaeda terrorists still plot to inflict catastrophic harm on America, and he's worried that someone won't read them their rights.

TAXES

Government is too big; he wants to grow it. Congress spends too much money; he promises more. Taxes are too high, and he wants to raise them. His tax increases are the fine print in his economic plan.

And let me be specific: The Democratic nominee for president supports plans to raise income taxes, and raise payroll taxes, and raise investment income taxes, and raise the death tax, and raise business taxes, and increase the tax burden on the American people by hundreds of billions of dollars.

My sister, Heather, and her husband, they just built a service station that's now open for business, like millions of others who run small businesses.

How are they going to be better off if taxes go up?

Or maybe you are trying to keep your job at a plant in Michigan or in Ohio, or you're trying to create jobs from clean coal, from Pennsylvania or West Virginia.

You're trying to keep a small farm in the family right here in Minnesota.

How are you — how are you going to be better off if our opponent adds a massive tax

burden to the American economy?

Here's how I look at the choice Americans face in this election: In politics, there are some candidates who use change to promote their careers, and then there are those, like John McCain, who use their careers to promote change.

They are the ones whose names appear on laws and landmark reforms, not just on buttons and banners or on self-designed presidential seals.

Among politicians, there is the idealism of high-flown speechmaking, in which crowds are stirringly summoned to support great things, and then there is the idealism of those leaders, like John McCain, who actually do great things.

They're the ones who are good for more than talk, the ones that we've always been able to count on to serve and to defend America.

Sen. McCain's record of actual achievements and reform helps explain why so many special interests, and lobbyists, and comfortable committee chairmen in Congress have fought the prospect of a McCain presidency from the primary election of 2000 to this very day.

Our nominee doesn't run with the Washington herd. He's a man who's there to serve his country and not just his party, a leader who's not looking for a fight, but sure isn't afraid of one, either.

Harry Reid, the majority [leader] of the current do-nothing Senate, he not long ago summed up his feelings about our nominee.

He said, quote, "I can't stand John McCain."

Ladies and gentlemen, perhaps no accolade we hear this week is better proof that we've chosen the right man.

Clearly, what the majority leader was driving at is that he can't stand up to John McCain, and that is only one more reason to take the maverick out of the Senate, put him in the White House.

My fellow citizens, the American presidency is not supposed to be a journey of personal discovery.

AN AMERICAN HERO

This world of threats and dangers, it's not just a community, and it doesn't just need an organizer. And though both Sen. Obama and Sen. Biden have been going on lately about how they're always, quote, "fighting for you," let us face the matter squarely: There is only one man in this election who has ever really fought for you.

There is only one man in this election who has ever really fought for you in places where winning means survival and defeat means death. And that man is John McCain.

You know, in our day, politicians have readily shared much lesser tales of adversity than the nightmare world, the nightmare world in which this man and others equally brave served and suffered for their country.

And it's a long way from the fear, and pain, and squalor of a 6-by-4 cell in Hanoi to the Oval Office.

But if Sen. McCain is elected president,

that is the journey he will have made. It's the journey of an upright and honorable man, the kind of fellow whose name you will find on war memorials in small towns across this great country, only he was among those who came home.

To the most powerful office on Earth, he would bring the compassion that comes from having once been powerless, the wisdom that comes even to the captives by the grace of God, the special confidence of those who have seen evil and have seen how evil is overcome.

A fellow prisoner of war — a man named Tom Moe of Lancaster, Ohio — Tom Moe recalls looking through a pinhole in his cell door as Lt. Cmdr. John McCain was led down the hallway by the guards, day after day.

And the story is told, when McCain shuffled back from torturous interrogations, he would turn toward Moe's door, and he'd flash a grin and a thumbs up, as if to say, "We're going to pull through this."

My fellow Americans, that is the kind of man America needs to see us through the next four years.

For a season, a gifted speaker can inspire with his words. But for a lifetime, John McCain has inspired with his deeds.

If character is the measure in this election, and hope the theme, and change the goal we share, then I ask you to join our cause. Join our cause and help America elect a great man as the next president of the United States.

Thank you, and God bless America. Thank you. ◼

McCain Embraces the 'Good Fight'

Following is the speech by Republican presidential nominee Sen. John McCain of Arizona to the Republican National Convention on Sept. 4, 2008.

THANK YOU. Thank you all very much. Thank you.

Tonight, I have a privilege given few Americans: the privilege of accepting our party's nomination for president of the United States.

Thank you. Thanks. And I accept it with gratitude, humility and confidence.

In my life, no success has come without a good fight, and this nomination wasn't any different. That's a tribute to the candidates who opposed me and their supporters. They're leaders of great ability who love our country and wish to lead it to better days. Their support is an honor that I won't forget.

I'm grateful to the president of the United States for leading us in these dark days following the worst attack in American history — the worst attack on American soil in our history and keeping us safe from another attack that many thought was inevitable.

And to the first lady, Laura Bush, a model of grace and kindness in public and in private.

And I'm grateful to the 41st president and his bride of 63 years for their outstanding example of honorable service to our country.

As always, I'm indebted to my wife, Cindy, and my seven children. You know, the pleasures of family life can seem like a brief holiday from the crowded calendar of our nation's business. But I have treasured them all the more and can't imagine a life without the happiness that you've given me.

You know, Cindy said a lot of nice things about me tonight. But, in truth, she's more my inspiration than I am hers. Her concern for those less blessed than we are — victims of land mines, children born in poverty, with birth defects — shows the measure of her humanity. And I know that she will make a great first lady.

My friends, when I was growing up, my father was often at sea, and the job of raising my brother, sister and me would fall to my mother alone. Roberta McCain gave us her love of life, her deep interest in the world, her strength and her belief that we're all meant to use our opportunities to make ourselves useful to our country. I wouldn't be here tonight but for the strength of her character.

And she doesn't want me to say this, but she's 96 years young.

My heartfelt thanks to all of you who helped me win this nomination and stood by me when the odds were long. I won't let you down. I won't let you down. I won't let you down.

To Americans who have yet to decide who to vote for, thank you for your consideration and the opportunity to win your trust. I intend to earn it.

And, finally, a word to Sen. Obama and his supporters: We'll go at it over the next two months — you know that's the nature of this business — and there are big differences between us. But you have my respect and my admiration. Despite our differences, much more unites us than divides us. We are fellow Americans, and that's an association that means more to me than any other. We're dedicated to the proposition that all people are created equal and endowed by our creator with inalienable rights. No country ever had a greater cause than that. And I wouldn't be an American worthy of the name if I didn't honor Sen. Obama and his supporters for their achievement.

'WE'RE GOING TO WIN'

But let there be no doubt, my friends: We're going to win this election. And after we've won, we're going to reach out our hand to any willing patriot, make this government start working for you again and get this country back on the road to prosperity and peace.

I know these are tough times for many of you. You're worried about .... [interrupted by crowd noise] Please, please, please. My friends, my dear friends, please. Please don't be diverted by the ground noise and the static. You know, I'm going to talk about it some more. But Americans want us to stop yelling at each other, OK?

These are tough times for many of you. You're worried about keeping your job or finding a new one, and you're struggling to put food on the table and stay in your home.

All you've ever asked of your government is to stand on your side and not in your way. And that's what I intend to do: stand on your side and fight for your future.

And I've found just the right partner to help me shake up Washington, Gov. Sarah Palin of the great state of Alaska.

And I want to thank everyone here and all over America for the tremendous, wonderful, warm reception you gave her last night. Thank you so much. She deserves it. What a great beginning.

You know, she has executive experience and a real record of accomplishment. She's tackled tough problems, like energy independence and corruption. She's balanced a budget, cut taxes, and she's taken on the special interests. She's reached across the aisle and asked Republicans, Democrats and independents to serve in her administration. She's the wonderful mother of five children. She's helped run a small business. She's worked with her hands and knows what it's like to worry about mortgage payments, and health care, and the cost of gasoline and groceries. She knows where she comes from, and she knows who she works for. She stands up for what's right, and she doesn't let anyone tell her to sit down. I'm very proud to have introduced our next vice president to the country, but I can't wait until I introduce her to Washington.

And let me just offer an advance warning to the old, big-spending, do-nothing, me-first, country-second crowd: Change is coming.

I'm not in the habit of breaking my promises to my country, and neither is Gov. Palin. And when we tell you we're going to change Washington and stop leaving our country's problems for some unluckier generation to fix, you can count on it.

And we've got a record of doing just that, and the strength, experience, judgment and backbone to keep our word to you.

THE MAVERICK

You well know I've been called a maverick, someone who marches to the beat of his own drum. Sometimes it's meant as a compliment; sometimes it's not. What it really means is I understand who I work for. I don't work for a party. I don't work for a special interest. I don't work for myself. I work for you.

I've fought corruption, and it didn't matter if the culprits were Democrats or Republicans. They violated their public trust, and they had to be held accountable.

I've fought the big spenders in both parties, who waste your money on things you neither need nor want, and the first big-spending, "pork barrel" earmark bill that comes across my desk, I will veto it. I will make them fa-

mous, and you will know their names. You will know their names.

We're not going to allow that while you struggle to buy groceries, fill your gas tank and make your mortgage payment. I've fought to get million-dollar checks out of our elections. I've fought lobbyists who stole from Indian tribes. I've fought crooked deals in the Pentagon. I've fought tobacco companies and trial lawyers, drug companies and union bosses. I've fought for the right strategy and more troops in Iraq when it wasn't the popular thing to do.

And when the pundits said my campaign was finished, I said I'd rather lose an election than see my country lose a war.

And thanks to the leadership of a brilliant general, David Petraeus, and the brave men and women he has the honor to command, that strategy succeeded, and it rescued us from a defeat that would have demoralized our military, risked a wider war and threatened the security of all Americans.

FIGHTING WORDS

I don't mind a good fight. For reasons known only to God, I've had quite a few tough ones in my life. But I learned an important lesson along the way: In the end, it matters less that you can fight. What you fight for is the real test.

I fight for Americans. I fight for you.

I fight for Bill and Sue Nebe from Farmington Hills, Mich., who lost their real estate investments in the bad housing market. Bill got a temporary job after he was out of work for seven months. Sue works three jobs to help pay the bills.

I fight for Jake and Toni Wimmer of Franklin County, Pa. Jake works on a loading dock, coaches Little League, and raises money for the mentally and physically disabled. Toni is a schoolteacher, working toward her master's degree. They have two sons. The youngest, Luke, has been diagnosed with autism. Their lives should matter to the people they elect to office. And they matter to me. And they matter to you.

I fight for the family of Matthew Stanley of Wolfeboro, N.H. Matthew died serving our country in Iraq. I wear his bracelet and think of him everyday. I intend to honor their sacrifice by making sure the country their son loved so well and never returned to remains safe from its enemies.

I fight to restore the pride and principles of our party. We were elected to change Washington, and we let Washington change us.

We lost the trust of the American people when some Republicans gave in to the temptations of corruption. We lost their trust when rather than reform government, both parties made it bigger. We lost their trust when instead of freeing ourselves from a dangerous dependence on foreign oil, both parties — and Sen. Obama — passed another corporate welfare bill for oil companies. We lost their trust when we valued our power over our principles.

We're going to change that.

We're going to recover the people's trust by standing up again to the values Americans admire. The party of Lincoln, Roosevelt and Reagan is going to get back to basics.

In this country, we believe everyone has something to contribute and deserves the opportunity to reach their God-given potential, from the boy whose descendents arrived on the Mayflower to the Latina daughter of migrant workers. We're all God's children, and we're all Americans.

We believe in low taxes, spending discipline and open markets. We believe in rewarding hard work and risk-takers and letting people keep the fruits of their labor.

We believe in a strong defense, work, faith, service, a culture of life, personal responsibility, the rule of law and judges who dispense justice impartially and don't legislate from the bench.

We believe in the values of families, neighborhoods and communities. We believe in a government that unleashes the creativity and initiative of Americans, government that doesn't make your choices for you but works to make sure you have more choices to make for yourself.

I will keep taxes low and cut them where I can. My opponent will raise them.

I will open new markets to our goods and services. My opponent will close them.

I will cut government spending. He will increase it.

My tax cuts will create jobs; his tax increases will eliminate them.

My health care plan will make it easier for more Americans to find and keep good health care insurance. His plan will force small businesses to cut jobs, reduce wages and force families into a government-run health care system where a bureaucrat stands between you and your doctor.

TAXES AND JOBS

We all know that keeping taxes low helps small businesses grow and create new jobs.

Cutting the second-highest business tax rate in the world will help American companies compete and keep jobs from going overseas.

Doubling the child tax exemption from $3,500 to $7,000 will improve the lives of millions of American families.

Reducing government spending and getting rid of failed programs will let you keep more of your own money to save, spend and invest as you see fit.

Opening new markets and preparing workers to compete in the world economy is essential to our future prosperity.

I know some of you have been left behind in the changing economy, and it often seems that your government hasn't even noticed. Government assistance for the unemployed workers was designed for the economy of the 1950s. That's going to change on my watch.

Now, my opponent promises to bring back old jobs by wishing away the global economy. We're going to help workers who've lost a job that won't come back find a new one that won't go away. We will prepare them for the jobs of today. We will use our community colleges to help train people for new opportunities in their communities.

For workers in industries that have been hard-hit, we'll help make up part of the difference in wages between their old job and a temporary, lower-paid one, while they receive re-training that will help them find secure new employment at a decent wage.

EDUCATION

Education is the civil rights issue of this century. Equal access to public education has been gained, but what is the value of access to a failing school?

We need to shake up failed school bureaucracies with competition, empower parents with choice. Let's remove barriers to qualified instructors, attract and reward good teachers, and help bad teachers find another line of work.

When a public school fails to meet its obligations to students, parents deserve a choice in the education of their children. And I intend to give it to them.

Some may choose a better public school. Some may choose a private one. Many will choose a charter school. But they will have the choice, and their children will have that opportunity.

Sen. Obama wants our schools to answer to unions and entrenched bureaucrats. I want schools to answer to parents and students.

And when I'm president, they will.

ENERGY

My fellow Americans, when I'm president, we're going to embark on the most ambitious national project in decades. We're going to stop sending $700 billion a year to countries that don't like us very much, and some of that money....

We'll attack the problem on every front. We'll produce more energy at home. We will drill new wells offshore, and we'll drill them now. We'll drill them now.

We'll, my friends, we'll build more nuclear power plants. We'll develop clean-coal technology. We'll increase the use of wind, tide, solar and natural gas. We'll encourage the development and use of flex-fuel, hybrid and electric automobiles.

Sen. Obama thinks we can achieve energy independence without more drilling and without more nuclear power. But Americans know better than that.

We must use all resources and develop all technologies necessary to rescue our economy from the damage caused by rising oil prices and restore the health of our planet.

My friends, it's an ambitious plan, but Americans are ambitious by nature, and we've faced greater challenges. It's time for us to show the world again how Americans lead.

This great national cause will create millions of new jobs, many in industries that will be the engine of our future prosperity, jobs that will be there when your children enter the workforce.

FOREIGN POLICY

Today, the prospect of a better world remains within our reach. But we must see the threats to peace and liberty in our time clearly and face them as Americans before us did: with confidence, wisdom and resolve. We have dealt a serious blow to al Qaeda in recent years, but they're not defeated, and they'll strike us again, if they can. Iran remains the chief state sponsor of terrorism and is on the path to acquiring nuclear weapons.

Russia's leaders, rich with oil wealth and corrupt with power, have rejected democratic ideals and the obligations of a responsible power. They invaded a small, democratic neighbor to gain more control over the world's oil supply, intimidate other neighbors and further their ambitions of re-assembling the Russian empire. And the brave people of Georgia need our solidarity and our prayers. As president, I'll work to establish good relations with Russia so that we need not fear a return to the Cold War.

But we can't turn a blind eye to aggression and international lawlessness that threatens the peace and stability of the world and the security of the American people. We face many dangerous threats in this dangerous world, but I'm not afraid of them. I'm prepared for them.

I know how the military works, what it can do, what it can do better and what it shouldn't do. I know how the world works. I know the good and the evil in it. I know how to work with leaders who share our dreams of a freer, safer and more prosperous world, and how to stand up to those who don't. I know how to secure the peace.

My friends, when I was 5 years old, a car pulled up in front of our house. A Navy officer rolled down the window and shouted at my father that the Japanese had bombed Pearl Harbor. I rarely saw my father again for four years.

My grandfather came home from that same war exhausted from the burdens he had borne and died the next day. In Vietnam, where I formed the closest friendships of my life, some of those friends never came home with me. I hate war. It's terrible beyond imagination.

I'm running for president to keep the country I love safe and prevent other families from risking their loved ones in war as my family has. I will draw on all my experience with the world and its leaders, and all the tools at our disposal — diplomatic, economic, military — and the power of our ideals to build the foundations for a stable and enduring peace.

POWER OF CHANGE

In America, we change things that need to be changed. Each generation makes its contribution to our greatness. The work that is ours to do is plainly before us; we don't need to search for it. We need to change the way government does almost everything — from the way we protect our security to the way we compete in the world economy, from the way we respond to disasters to the way we fuel our transportation network, from the way we train our workers to the way we educate our children.

All these functions of government were designed before the rise of the global economy, the information technology revolution and the end of the Cold War. We have to catch up to history, and we have to change the way we do business in Washington.

The constant partisan rancor that stops us from solving these problems isn't a cause. It's

a symptom. It's what happens when people go to Washington to work for themselves and not for you.

Again and again — again and again, I've worked with members of both parties to fix problems that need to be fixed. That's how I will govern as president. I will reach out my hand to anyone to help me get this country moving again.

My friends, I have that record and the scars to prove it. Sen. Obama does not.

Instead of rejecting good ideas because we didn't think of them first, let's use the best ideas from both sides. Instead of fighting over who gets the credit, let's try sharing it.

This amazing country can do anything we put our minds to. I'll ask Democrats and independents to serve with me. And my administration will set a new standard for transparency and accountability.

We're going to finally start getting things done for the people who are counting on us, and I won't care who gets the credit.

My friends, I've been an imperfect servant of my country for many years. But I've been her servant first, last and always. And I've never lived a day, in good times or bad, that I didn't thank God for the privilege.

PRISONER OF WAR

Long ago, something unusual happened to me that taught me the most valuable lesson of my life. I was blessed by misfortune. I mean that sincerely. I was blessed because I served in the company of heroes, and I witnessed a thousand acts of courage and compassion and love.

On an October morning, in the Gulf of Tonkin, I prepared for my 23rd mission over North Vietnam. I hadn't any worry I wouldn't come back safe and sound. I thought I was tougher than anyone. I was pretty independent then, too.

I liked to bend a few rules and pick a few fights for the fun of it. But I did it for my own pleasure, my own pride. I didn't think there was a cause that was more important than me.

Then I found myself falling toward the middle of a small lake in the city of Hanoi, with two broken arms, a broken leg and an angry crowd waiting to greet me.

I was dumped in a dark cell and left to die. I didn't feel so tough anymore. When they discovered my father was an admiral, they took me to a hospital. They couldn't set my bones properly, so they just slapped a cast on me. And when I didn't get better and was down to

about a hundred pounds, they put me in a cell with two other Americans.

I couldn't do anything. I couldn't even feed myself. They did it for me. I was beginning to learn the limits of my selfish independence. Those men saved my life.

I was in solitary confinement when my captors offered to release me. I knew why. If I went home, they would use it as propaganda to demoralize my fellow prisoners.

Our code said we could only go home in the order of our capture, and there were men who had been shot down long before me. I thought about it, though. I wasn't in great shape, and I missed everything about America, but I turned it down.

A lot of prisoners had it much worse. A lot of prisoners had it a lot worse than I did. I'd been mistreated before but not as badly as many others. I always liked to strut a little after I'd been roughed up to show the other guys I was tough enough to take it.

But after I turned down their offer, they worked me over harder than they ever had before — for a long time — and they broke me.

When they brought me back to my cell, I was hurt and ashamed, and I didn't know how I could face my fellow prisoners. The good man in the cell next door to me, my friend, Bob Craner, saved me.

Through taps on a wall, he told me I had fought as hard as I could. No man can always stand alone. And then he told me to get back up and fight again for my country and for the men I had the honor to serve with, because every day they fought for me.

I fell in love with my country when I was a prisoner in someone else's. I loved it not just for the many comforts of life here. I loved it for its decency, for its faith in the wisdom, justice and goodness of its people.

I loved it because it was not just a place but an idea, a cause worth fighting for. I was never the same again; I wasn't my own man anymore; I was my country's.

I'm not running for president because I think I'm blessed with such personal greatness that history has anointed me to save our country in its hour of need.

My country saved me. My country saved me, and I cannot forget it. And I will fight for her for as long as I draw breath, so help me God.

A GREATER CAUSE

My friends, if you find faults with our country, make it a better one. If you're disappointed with the mistakes of government, join its ranks and work to correct them. Enlist in our Armed Forces. Become a teacher. Enter the ministry. Run for public office. Feed a hungry child. Teach an illiterate adult to read. Comfort the afflicted. Defend the rights of the oppressed.

Our country will be the better, and you will be the happier, because nothing brings greater happiness in life than to serve a cause greater than yourself.

I'm going to fight for my cause every day as your president. I'm going to fight to make sure every American has every reason to thank God, as I thank him, that I'm an American, a proud citizen of the greatest country on Earth. And with hard work, strong faith and a little courage, great things are always within our reach.

Fight with me. Fight with me.

Fight for what's right for our country. Fight for the ideals and character of a free people. Fight for our children's future. Fight for justice and opportunity for all.

Stand up to defend our country from its enemies. Stand up for each other, for beautiful, blessed, bountiful America. Stand up, stand up, stand up and fight.

Nothing is inevitable here. We're Americans, and we never give up. We never quit. We never hide from history. We make history.

Thank you, and God bless you, and God bless America. ∎

McCain Concedes Presidential Race

Following is the speech that Sen. John McCain gave to a crowd of supporters at the Biltmore Hotel in Phoenix on Nov. 4, 2008, in which he conceded his defeat in the presidential election.

THANK YOU. THANK YOU, my friends. Thank you for coming here on this beautiful Arizona evening.

My friends, we have — we have come to the end of a long journey. The American people have spoken, and they have spoken clearly. A little while ago, I had the honor of calling Sen. Barack Obama to congratulate him on being elected the next president of the country that we both love.

In a contest as long and difficult as this campaign has been, his success alone commands my respect for his ability and perseverance. But that he managed to do so by inspiring the hopes of so many millions of Americans who had once wrongly believed that they had little at stake or little influence in the election of an American president is something I deeply admire and commend him for achieving.

This is an historic election, and I recognize the special significance it has for African-Americans and for the special pride that must be theirs tonight.

I've always believed that America offers opportunities to all who have the industry and will to seize it. Sen. Obama believes that, too. But we both recognize that though we have come a long way from the old injustices that once stained our nation's reputation and denied some Americans the full blessings of American citizenship, the memory of them still had the power to wound.

A century ago, President Theodore Roosevelt's invitation of Booker T. Washington to visit — to dine at the White House was taken as an outrage in many quarters. America today is a world away from the cruel and prideful bigotry of that time. There is no better evidence of this than the election of an African-American to the presidency of the United States. Let there be no reason now for any American to fail to cherish their citizenship in this, the greatest nation on Earth.

Sen. Obama has achieved a great thing for himself and for his country. I applaud him for it, and offer him my sincere sympathy that his beloved grandmother did not live to see this day, though our faith assures us she is at rest in the presence of her creator and so very proud of the good man she helped raise.

Sen. Obama and I have had and argued our differences, and he has prevailed. No doubt many of those differences remain. These are difficult times for our country, and I pledge to him tonight to do all in my power to help him lead us through the many challenges we face.

I urge all Americans who supported me to join me in not just congratulating him, but offering our next president our good will and earnest effort to find ways to come together, to find the necessary compromises, to bridge our differences, and help restore our prosperity, defend our security in a dangerous world, and leave our children and grandchildren a stronger, better country than we inherited.

Whatever our differences, we are fellow Americans. And please believe me when I say no association has ever meant more to me than that.

'WE MUST MOVE BEYOND'

It is natural — it's natural tonight to feel some disappointment, but tomorrow we must move beyond it and work together to get our country moving again. We fought as hard as we could. And though we fell short, the failure is mine, not yours.

I am so deeply grateful to all of you for the great honor of your support and for all you have done for me. I wish the outcome had been different, my friends. The road was a difficult one from the outset. But your support and friendship never wavered. I cannot adequately express how deeply indebted I am to you.

I am especially grateful to my wife, Cindy, my children, my dear mother and all my family and to the many old and dear friends who have stood by my side through the many ups and downs of this long campaign. I have always been a fortunate man, and never more so for the love and encouragement you have given me.

You know, campaigns are often harder on a candidate's family than on the candidate, and that's been true in this campaign. All I can offer in compensation is my love and gratitude, and the promise of more peaceful years ahead.

I am also, of course, very thankful to Gov. Sarah Palin, one of the best campaigners I have ever seen. One of the best campaigners I have ever seen and an impressive new voice in our party for reform and the principles that have always been our greatest strength. Her husband, Todd, and their five beautiful children, with their tireless dedication to our cause, and the courage and grace they showed in the rough-and-tumble of a presidential campaign. We can all look forward with great interest to her future service to Alaska, the Republican Party and our country.

To all my campaign comrades, from Rick Davis and Steve Schmidt and Mark Salter, to every last volunteer who fought so hard and valiantly month after month in what at times seemed to be the most challenged campaign in modern times, thank you so much. A lost election will never mean more to me than the privilege of your faith and friendship.

I don't know what more we could have done to try to win this election. I'll leave that to others to determine. Every candidate makes mistakes, and I'm sure I made my share of them. But I won't spend a moment of the future regretting what might have been.

This campaign was and will remain the great honor of my life. And my heart is filled with nothing but gratitude for the experience and to the American people for giving me a fair hearing before deciding that Sen. Obama and my old friend Sen. Joe Biden should have the honor of leading us for the next four years.

I would not be an American worthy of the name should I regret a fate that has allowed me the extraordinary privilege of serving this country for a half a century. Today, I was a candidate for the highest office in the country I love so much. And tonight, I remain her servant. That is blessing enough for anyone, and I thank the people of Arizona for it.

Tonight — tonight, more than any night, I hold in my heart nothing but love for this country and for all its citizens, whether they supported me or Sen. Obama. I wish Godspeed to the man who was my former opponent and will be my president.

And I call on all Americans, as I have often in this campaign, to not despair of our present difficulties but to believe always in the promise and greatness of America, because nothing is inevitable here.

Americans never quit. We never surrender. We never hide from history; we make history.

Thank you, and God bless you, and God bless America. Thank you all very much. ■

Obama Cheers 'Yes, We Can' Spirit

The following is a transcript of the speech given by Sen. Barack Obama at a rally Nov. 4, 2008, in Grant Park in Chicago after winning the presidential election.

HELLO, CHICAGO. If there is anyone out there who still doubts that America is a place where all things are possible, who still wonders if the dream of our founders is alive in our time, who still questions the power of our democracy, tonight is your answer.

It's the answer told by lines that stretched around schools and churches in numbers this nation has never seen, by people who waited three hours and four hours, many for the first time in their lives, because they believed that this time must be different, that their voices could be that difference.

It's the answer spoken by young and old, rich and poor, Democrat and Republican, black, white, Hispanic, Asian, Native American, gay, straight, disabled and not disabled. Americans who sent a message to the world that we have never been just a collection of individuals or a collection of red states and blue states.

We are, and always will be, the United States of America.

It's the answer that led those who've been told for so long by so many to be cynical and fearful and doubtful about what we can achieve to put their hands on the arc of history and bend it once more toward the hope of a better day.

It's been a long time coming, but tonight, because of what we did on this date in this election at this defining moment, change has come to America.

A little bit earlier this evening, I received an extraordinarily gracious call from Sen. McCain.

Sen. McCain fought long and hard in this campaign. And he's fought even longer and harder for the country that he loves. He has endured sacrifices for America that most of us cannot begin to imagine. We are better off for the service rendered by this brave and selfless leader.

I congratulate him; I congratulate Gov. Palin for all that they've achieved. And I look forward to working with them to renew this nation's promise in the months ahead.

I want to thank my partner in this journey, a man who campaigned from his heart, and spoke for the men and women he grew up with on the streets of Scranton and rode with on the train home to Delaware, the vice president-elect of the United States, Joe Biden.

And I would not be standing here tonight without the unyielding support of my best friend for the last 16 years, the rock of our family, the love of my life, the nation's next first lady, Michelle Obama.

Sasha and Malia, I love you both more than you can imagine. And you have earned the new puppy that's coming with us to the White House.

And while she's no longer with us, I know my grandmother's watching, along with the family that made me who I am. I miss them tonight. I know that my debt to them is beyond measure.

To my sister Maya, my sister Alma, all my other brothers and sisters, thank you so much for all the support that you've given me. I am grateful to them.

And to my campaign manager, David Plouffe, the unsung hero of this campaign, who built the best — the best political campaign, I think, in the history of the United States of America.

To my chief strategist, David Axelrod, who's been a partner with me every step of the way.

To the best campaign team ever assembled in the history of politics, you made this happen, and I am forever grateful for what you've sacrificed to get it done.

But above all, I will never forget who this victory truly belongs to. It belongs to you. It belongs to you.

'THIS IS YOUR VICTORY'

I was never the likeliest candidate for this office. We didn't start with much money or many endorsements. Our campaign was not hatched in the halls of Washington. It began in the back yards of Des Moines and the living rooms of Concord and the front porches of Charleston. It was built by working men and women who dug into what little savings they had to give $5 and $10 and $20 to the cause.

It grew strength from the young people who rejected the myth of their generation's apathy, who left their homes and their families for jobs that offered little pay and less sleep.

It drew strength from the not-so-young people who braved the bitter cold and scorching heat to knock on doors of perfect strangers, and from the millions of Americans who volunteered and organized and proved that more than two centuries later a government of the people, by the people and for the people has not perished from the Earth.

This is your victory.

And I know you didn't do this just to win an election. And I know you didn't do it for me.

You did it because you understand the enormity of the task that lies ahead. For even as we celebrate tonight, we know the challenges that tomorrow will bring are the greatest of our lifetime — two wars, a planet in peril, the worst financial crisis in a century.

Even as we stand here tonight, we know there are brave Americans waking up in the deserts of Iraq and the mountains of Afghanistan to risk their lives for us.

There are mothers and fathers who will lie awake after the children fall asleep and wonder how they'll make the mortgage or pay their doctors' bills or save enough for their child's college education.

There's new energy to harness, new jobs to be created, new schools to build, and threats to meet, alliances to repair.

The road ahead will be long. Our climb will be steep. We may not get there in one year or even in one term. But, America, I have never been more hopeful than I am tonight that we will get there. I promise you, we as a people will get there.

There will be setbacks and false starts. There are many who won't agree with every decision or policy I make as president. And we know the government can't solve every problem.

But I will always be honest with you about the challenges we face. I will listen to you, especially when we disagree. And, above all, I will ask you to join in the work of remaking this nation, the only way it's been done in America for 221 years — block by block, brick by brick, calloused hand by calloused hand.

What began 21 months ago in the depths of winter cannot end on this autumn night.

This victory alone is not the change we seek. It is only the chance for us to make that change. And that cannot happen if we go back to the way things were.

It can't happen without you, without a new spirit of service, a new spirit of sacrifice.

So let us summon a new spirit of patriotism,

of responsibility, where each of us resolves to pitch in and work harder and look after not only ourselves but each other.

Let us remember that, if this financial crisis taught us anything, it's that we cannot have a thriving Wall Street while Main Street suffers.

In this country, we rise or fall as one nation, as one people. Let's resist the temptation to fall back on the same partisanship and pettiness and immaturity that has poisoned our politics for so long.

Let's remember that it was a man from this state who first carried the banner of the Republican Party to the White House, a party founded on the values of self-reliance and individual liberty and national unity.

Those are values that we all share. And while the Democratic Party has won a great victory tonight, we do so with a measure of humility and determination to heal the divides that have held back our progress.

As Lincoln said to a nation far more divided than ours, we are not enemies but friends. Though passion may have strained, it must not break our bonds of affection.

And to those Americans whose support I have yet to earn, I may not have won your vote tonight, but I hear your voices. I need your help. And I will be your president, too.

And to all those watching tonight from beyond our shores, from parliaments and palaces, to those who are huddled around radios in the forgotten corners of the world, our stories are singular, but our destiny is shared, and a new dawn of American leadership is at hand.

To those — to those who would tear the world down: We will defeat you. To those who seek peace and security: We support you. And to all those who have wondered if Amer-

ica's beacon still burns as bright: Tonight we proved once more that the true strength of our nation comes not from the might of our arms or the scale of our wealth, but from the enduring power of our ideals — democracy, liberty, opportunity and unyielding hope.

That's the true genius of America: that America can change. Our union can be perfected. What we've already achieved gives us hope for what we can and must achieve tomorrow.

'YES, WE CAN'

This election had many firsts and many stories that will be told for generations. But one that's on my mind tonight's about a woman who cast her ballot in Atlanta. She's a lot like the millions of others who stood in line to make their voice heard in this election except for one thing: Ann Nixon Cooper is 106 years old.

She was born just a generation past slavery, a time when there were no cars on the road or planes in the sky, when someone like her couldn't vote for two reasons: because she was a woman and because of the color of her skin.

And tonight, I think about all that she's seen throughout her century in America: the heartache and the hope; the struggle and the progress; the times we were told that we can't, and the people who pressed on with that American creed — yes, we can.

At a time when women's voices were silenced and their hopes dismissed, she lived to see them stand up and speak out and reach for the ballot. Yes, we can.

When there was despair in the Dust Bowl and depression across the land, she saw a nation conquer fear itself with a New Deal, new jobs, a new sense of common purpose.

Yes, we can.

When the bombs fell on our harbor and tyranny threatened the world, she was there to witness a generation rise to greatness, and a democracy was saved. Yes, we can.

She was there for the buses in Montgomery, the hoses in Birmingham, a bridge in Selma, and a preacher from Atlanta who told a people that "we shall overcome." Yes, we can.

A man touched down on the moon, a wall came down in Berlin, a world was connected by our own science and imagination.

And this year, in this election, she touched her finger to a screen and cast her vote, because after 106 years in America, through the best of times and the darkest of hours, she knows how America can change.

Yes, we can.

America, we have come so far. We have seen so much. But there is so much more to do. So tonight, let us ask ourselves: If our children should live to see the next century, if my daughters should be so lucky to live as long as Ann Nixon Cooper, what change will they see? What progress will we have made?

This is our chance to answer that call. This is our moment.

This is our time, to put our people back to work and open doors of opportunity for our kids; to restore prosperity and promote the cause of peace; to reclaim the American dream and reaffirm that fundamental truth, that, out of many, we are one; that while we breathe, we hope. And where we are met with cynicism and doubts and those who tell us that we can't, we will respond with that timeless creed that sums up the spirit of a people: Yes, we can.

Thank you. God bless you. And may God bless the United States of America. ■

Appendix E

PUBLIC LAWS

Laws Enacted in the Second Session Of the 110th Congress

Public Laws 110-1 through 110-175, enacted in the first session of the 110th Congress, were published in the previous edition of the CQ Almanac. (2007 Almanac, p. E-3)

■ **PL 110-176** (S 2436) Amend the Internal Revenue Code of 1986 to clarify the term of the commissioner of Internal Revenue. Introduced by BAUCUS, D-Mont., on Dec. 10, 2007. Senate passed Dec. 19. House passed Dec. 19. President signed Jan. 4, 2008.

■ **PL 110-177** (HR 660) Amend Title 18, U.S. Code, to protect judges, prosecutors, witnesses, victims and their family members. Introduced by CONYERS, D-Mich., on Jan. 24, 2007. House Judiciary reported, amended, July 10 (H Rept 110-218, Part 1). House passed, amended, under suspension of the rules, July 10. Senate Judiciary discharged. Senate passed, amended, Dec. 17. House agreed to Senate amendment, under suspension of the rules, Dec. 19. President signed Jan. 7, 2008.

■ **PL 110-178** (HR 3690) Provide for the transfer of the Library of Congress police to the U.S. Capitol Police. Introduced by BRADY, D-Pa., on Sept. 27, 2007. House Administration reported, amended, Dec. 4 (H Rept 110-470, Part 1). House passed, amended, under suspension of the rules, Dec. 5. Senate passed, amended, Dec. 17. House agreed to Senate amendment, under suspension of the rules, Dec. 18. President signed Jan. 7, 2008.

■ **PL 110-179** (S 863) Amend Title 18, U.S. Code, with respect to fraud in connection with major disaster or emergency funds. Introduced by SESSIONS, R-Ala., on March 13, 2007. Senate Judiciary reported May 22 (S Rept 110-69). Senate passed Dec. 4. House passed, under suspension of the rules, Dec. 19. President signed Jan. 7, 2008.

■ **PL 110-180** (HR 2640) Improve the National Instant Criminal Background Check System. Introduced by McCARTHY, D-N.Y., on June 11, 2007. House passed, under suspension of the rules, June 13. Senate Judiciary discharged. Senate passed, amended, Dec. 19. House agreed to Senate amendment Dec. 19. President signed Jan. 8, 2008.

■ **PL 110-181** (HR 4986) Provide for the enactment of the National Defense Authorization Act for fiscal 2008, as previously enrolled, with certain modifications to address the foreign sovereign immunities provisions of Title 28, U.S. Code, with respect to the attachment of property in certain judgments against Iraq, the lapse of statutory authorities for the payment of bonuses, and special pay and similar benefits for members of the uniformed services. Introduced by SKELTON, D-Mo., on Jan. 16, 2008. House passed, under suspension of the rules, Jan. 16. Senate passed Jan. 22. President signed Jan. 28, 2008.

■ **PL 110-182** (HR 5104) Extend the Protect America Act of 2007 for 15 days. Introduced by CONYERS, D-Mich., on Jan. 23, 2008. House passed, amended, under suspension of the rules, Jan. 29. Senate passed Jan. 29. President signed Jan. 31, 2008.

■ **PL 110-183** (HR 3432) Establish the Commission on the Abolition of the Transatlantic Slave Trade. Introduced by PAYNE, D-N.J. on Aug. 3, 2007. House passed, amended, under suspension of the rules, Oct. 2. Senate Judiciary discharged. Senate passed, amended, Dec. 19. House agreed to Senate amendment, under suspension of the rules, Jan. 22, 2008. President signed Feb. 5, 2008.

■ **PL 110-184** (S 2110) Designate the facility of the U.S. Postal Service located at 427 North St. in Taft, Calif., as the "Larry S. Pierce Post Office." Introduced by FEINSTEIN, D-Calif., on Sept. 27, 2007. Senate Homeland Security and Governmental Affairs reported Nov. 14 (no written report). Senate passed Nov. 16. House passed, under suspension of the rules, Jan. 28, 2008. President signed Feb. 6, 2008.

■ **PL 110-185** (HR 5140) Provide economic stimulus through tax rebates to individuals, incentives for business investment, and an increase in conforming and Federal Housing Administration loan limits. Introduced by PELOSI, D-Calif., on Jan. 28, 2008. House passed, under suspension of the rules, Jan. 29. Senate passed, amended, Feb. 7. House agreed to Senate amendment Feb. 7. President signed Feb. 13, 2008.

■ **PL 110-186** (HR 4253) Improve and expand small-business assistance programs for veterans of the armed forces and military reservists. Introduced by ALTMIRE, D-Pa., on Dec. 4, 2007. House passed, under suspension of the rules, Dec. 6. Senate passed, amended, Dec. 19. House agreed to Senate amendment, with amendment, Jan. 16, 2008. Senate agreed to House amendment to Senate amendment Jan. 31. President signed Feb. 14, 2008.

■ **PL 110-187** (HR 3541) Amend the Do-Not-Call Implementation Act to eliminate the automatic removal of telephone numbers registered on the federal Do Not Call Registry. Introduced by DOYLE, D-Pa., on Sept. 17, 2007. House Energy and Commerce reported, amended, Dec. 11 (H Rept 110-486). House passed, amended, under suspension of the rules, Dec. 11. Senate Commerce, Science and Transportation discharged. Senate passed Feb. 6, 2008. President signed Feb. 15, 2008.

■ **PL 110-188** (S 781) Extend the authority of the Federal Trade Commission to collect Do Not Call Registry fees beyond fiscal 2007. Introduced by PRYOR, D-Ark., on March 6, 2007. Senate Commerce, Science and Transportation reported, amended, Dec. 12 (S Rept 110-244). Senate passed, amended, Dec. 17. House passed, under suspension of the rules, Feb. 6, 2008. President signed Feb. 15, 2008.

■ **PL 110-189** (HR 1216) Direct the secretary of Transportation to issue regulations to reduce the incidence of child injury and death inside or outside light motor vehicles. Introduced by SCHAKOWSKY, D-Ill., on Feb. 27, 2007. House passed, amended, under suspension of the rules, Dec. 19. Senate Commerce, Science and Transportation discharged. Senate passed Feb. 14, 2008. President signed Feb. 28, 2008.

■ **PL 110-190** (HR 5270) Amend the Internal Revenue Code of 1986 to extend the funding and expenditure authority of the Airport and Airway Trust Fund. Introduced by RANGEL, D-N.Y., on Feb. 7, 2008. House passed, under suspension of the rules, Feb. 12. Senate passed Feb. 13. President signed Feb. 28, 2008.

■ **PL 110-191** (HR 5264) Extend the Andean Trade Preference Act. Introduced by RANGEL, D-N.Y., on Feb. 7, 2008. House Ways and Means reported, amended, Feb. 25 (H Rept 110-529). House passed, amended, under suspension of the rules, Feb. 27. Senate passed Feb. 28. President signed Feb. 29, 2008.

■ **PL 110-192** (HR 5478) Provide for the continued minting and issuance of certain $1 coins in 2008. Introduced by GUTIERREZ, D-Ill., on Feb. 25, 2008. House passed, under suspension of the rules, Feb. 25. Senate Banking, Housing and Urban Affairs discharged. Senate passed Feb. 28. President signed Feb. 29, 2008.

■ **PL 110-193** (S 2571) Make technical corrections to the Federal Insecticide, Fungicide and Rodenticide Act. Introduced by HARKIN, D-Iowa, on Jan. 29, 2008. Senate passed Jan. 29. House passed, under suspension of the rules, Feb. 14. President signed March 6, 2008.

■ **PL 110-194** (S 2478) Designate the facility of the U.S. Postal Service located at 59 Colby Corner in E. Hampstead, N.H., the "Capt. Jonathan D. Grassbaugh Post Office." Introduced by SUNUNU, R-N.H., on Dec. 13, 2007. Senate Homeland Security and Governmental Affairs discharged. Senate passed Dec. 19. House passed, under suspension of the rules, Feb. 28, 2008. President signed March 11, 2008.

■ **PL 110-195** (S 2272) Designate the facility of the U.S. Postal Service known as the Southpark Station in Alexandria, La., the "John 'Marty' Thiels Southpark Station," in honor and memory of Thiels, a Louisiana postal worker who was killed in the line of duty on Oct. 4, 2007. Introduced by VITTER, R-La., on Oct. 31, 2007. Senate Homeland Security and Governmental Affairs reported Nov. 15 (no written report). Senate passed Nov. 16. House passed, under suspension of the rules, Feb. 28, 2008. President signed March 12, 2008.

■ **PL 110-196** (S 2745) Extend agricultural programs until April 18, 2008, and suspend permanent price support authorities until that date. Introduced by HARKIN, D-Iowa, on March 12, 2008. Senate passed March 12. House passed, under suspension of the rules, March 12. President signed March 14, 2008.

■ **PL 110-197** (S J Res 25) Provide for the appointment of John W. McCarter as a citizen regent of the Board of Regents of the Smithsonian Institution. Introduced by LEAHY, D-Vt., on Nov. 16, 2007. Senate Rules and Administration discharged. Senate passed Feb. 4,

2008. House passed, under suspension of the rules, March 5. President signed March 14, 2008.

■ **PL 110-198** (S 2733) Temporarily extend the programs under the Higher Education Act of 1965. Introduced by KENNEDY, D-Mass., on March 7, 2008. Senate passed March 7. House passed, under suspension of the rules, March 12. President signed March 24, 2008.

■ **PL 110-199** (HR 1593) Reauthorize the grant program for re-entry of offenders into the community under the Omnibus Crime Control and Safe Streets Act of 1968 and improve re-entry planning and implementation. Introduced by DAVIS, D-Ill., on March 20, 2007. House Judiciary reported May 9 (H Rept 110-140). House passed, amended, under suspension of the rules, Nov. 13. Senate Judiciary discharged. Senate passed March 11, 2008. President signed April 9, 2008.

■ **PL 110-200** (HR 5813) Amend PL 110-196 to temporarily extend programs authorized by the Farm Security and Rural Investment Act of 2002 until April 25, 2008. Introduced by PETERSON, D-Minn., on April 16, 2008. House passed, under suspension of the rules, April 16. Senate passed April 17. President signed April 18, 2008.

■ **PL 110-201** (S 550) Preserve existing judgeships on the Superior Court of the District of Columbia. Introduced by AKAKA, D-Hawaii, on Feb. 12, 2007. Senate Homeland Security and Governmental Affairs reported Jan. 8, 2008 (S Rept 110-256). Senate passed Feb. 4. House passed, under suspension of the rules, April 1. President signed April 18, 2008.

■ **PL 110-202** (S 845) Direct the secretary of Health and Human Services to expand and intensify programs related to research and other activities related to falls by the elderly. Introduced by ENZI, R-Wyo., on March 12, 2007. Senate Health, Education, Labor and Pensions reported, amended, March 29 (S Rept 110-110). Senate passed, amended, Aug. 1. House passed, under suspension of the rules, April 8, 2008. President signed April 23, 2008.

■ **PL 110-203** (H J Res 70) Congratulate the Army Reserve on its centennial, to be formally celebrated on April 23, 2008, and commemorate the historic contributions of its veterans and continuing contributions of its soldiers to the vital national security interests and homeland defense missions of the United States. Introduced by BISHOP, D-Ga., on Dec. 13, 2007. House passed, amended, under suspension of the rules, April 8. Senate passed April 14. President signed April 23, 2008.

■ **PL 110-204** (S 1858) Amend the Public Health Service Act to establish grant programs for education and outreach on newborn screening and coordinated follow-up care once newborn screening has been conducted, and reauthorize programs under Part A of Title XI of the Act. Introduced by DODD, D-Conn., on July 23, 2007. Senate Health, Education, Labor and Pensions reported, amended, Dec. 5 (S Rept 110-280). Senate passed, amended, Dec. 13. House passed, under suspension of the rules, April 8, 2008. President signed April 24, 2008.

■ **PL 110-205** (S 2903) Amend PL 110-196 to provide for a temporary extension of programs authorized by the Farm Security and Rural Investment Act of 2002 until May 2, 2008. Introduced by HARKIN, D-Iowa, on April 24, 2008. Senate passed April 24. House passed April 24. President signed April 25, 2008.

■ **PL 110-206** (S 793) Provide for the expansion and improvement of traumatic brain injury programs. Introduced by HATCH, R-Utah, on March 7, 2007. Senate Health, Education, Labor and Pensions reported, amended, Aug. 1 (S Rept 110-140). Senate passed, amended, Dec. 11. House passed, amended, under suspension of the rules, April 8, 2008. Senate agreed to House amendment April 10. President signed April 28, 2008.

■ **PL 110-207** (HR 1119) Amend Title 36, U.S. Code, to revise the congressional charter of the Military Order of the Purple Heart of the United States of America Inc., to authorize associate membership in the corporation for the spouse and siblings of a recipient of the Purple Heart medal. Introduced by DAVIS, D-Calif., on Feb. 16, 2007. House Judiciary reported, amended, Nov. 6 (H Rept 110-428). House passed, amended, under suspension of the rules, Nov. 6. Senate passed April 14, 2008. President signed April 30, 2008.

■ **PL 110-208** (S 2954) Amend PL 110-196 to provide for a temporary extension of programs authorized by the Farm Security and Rural Investment Act of 2002 until May 16, 2008. Introduced by HARKIN, D-Iowa, on May 1, 2008. Senate passed May 1. House passed, under suspension of the rules, May 1. President signed May 2, 2008.

■ **PL 110-209** (HR 4286) Award a congressional gold medal to Daw Aung San Suu Kyi in recognition of her courageous and unwavering commitment to peace, nonviolence, human rights and democracy in Burma. Introduced by CROWLEY, D-N.Y., on Dec. 5, 2007. House passed, under suspension of the rules, Dec. 17. Senate Banking, Housing and Urban Affairs discharged. Senate passed April 24, 2008. President signed May 6, 2008.

■ **PL 110-210** (HR 3196) Designate the facility of the U.S. Postal Service located at 20 Sussex St. in Port Jervis, N.Y., the "E. Arthur Gray Post Office Building." Introduced by HALL, D-N.Y., on July 26, 2007. House passed, under suspension of the rules, March 10, 2008. Senate Homeland Security and Governmental Affairs reported April 10 (no written report). Senate passed April 22. President signed May 7, 2008.

■ **PL 110-211** (HR 3468) Designate the facility of the U.S. Postal Service located at 1704 Weeksville Road in Elizabeth City, N.C., the "Dr. Clifford Bell Jones Sr. Post Office." Introduced by BUTTERFIELD, D-N.C., on Aug. 4, 2007. House passed, under suspension of the rules, Feb. 12, 2008. Senate Homeland Security and Governmental Affairs reported April 10 (no written report). Senate passed April 22. President signed May 7, 2008.

■ **PL 110-212** (HR 3532) Designate the facility of the U.S. Postal Service located at 5815 McLeod St. in Lula, Ga., the "Pvt. Johnathon Millican Lula Post Office." Introduced by DEAL, R-Ga., on Sept. 14, 2007. House passed, under suspension of the rules, Feb. 12, 2008. Senate Homeland Security and Governmental Affairs reported

April 10 (no written report). Senate passed April 22. President signed May 7, 2008.

■ **PL 110-213** (HR 3720) Designate the facility of the U.S. Postal Service located at 424 Clay Ave. in Waco, Texas, the "Army Pfc. Juan Alonso Covarrubias Post Office Building." Introduced by EDWARDS, D-Texas, on Oct. 2, 2007. House passed, under suspension of the rules, Jan. 22, 2008. Senate Homeland Security and Governmental Affairs reported April 10 (no written report). Senate passed April 22. President signed May 7, 2008.

■ **PL 110-214** (HR 3803) Designate the facility of the U.S. Postal Service located at 3100 Cashwell Drive in Goldsboro, N.C., the "John Henry Wooten Sr. Post Office Building." Introduced by BUTTERFIELD, D-N.C., on Oct. 10, 2007. House passed, under suspension of the rules, Feb. 28, 2008. Senate Homeland Security and Governmental Affairs reported April 10 (no written report). Senate passed April 22. President signed May 7, 2008.

■ **PL 110-215** (HR 3936) Designate the facility of the U.S. Postal Service located at 116 Helen Highway in Cleveland, Ga., the "Sgt. Jason Harkins Post Office Building." Introduced by DEAL, R-Ga., on Oct. 23, 2007. House passed, under suspension of the rules, Feb. 28, 2008. Senate Homeland Security and Governmental Affairs reported April 10 (no written report). Senate passed April 22. President signed May 7, 2008.

■ **PL 110-216** (HR 3988) Designate the facility of the U.S. Postal Service located at 3701 Altamesa Blvd. in Fort Worth, Texas, the "Master Sgt. Kenneth N. Mack Post Office Building." Introduced by GRANGER, R-Texas, on Oct. 29, 2007. House passed, under suspension of the rules, Jan. 22, 2008. Senate Homeland Security and Governmental Affairs reported April 10 (no written report). Senate passed April 22. President signed May 7, 2008.

■ **PL 110-217** (HR 4166) Designate the facility of the U.S. Postal Service located at 701 E. Copeland Drive in Lebanon, Mo., the "Steve W. Allee Carrier Annex." Introduced by SKELTON, D-Mo., on Nov. 13, 2007. House passed, under suspension of the rules, March 10, 2008. Senate Homeland Security and Governmental Affairs reported April 10 (no written report). Senate passed April 22. President signed May 7, 2008.

■ **PL 110-218** (HR 4203) Designate the facility of the U.S. Postal Service located at 3035 Stone Mountain St. in Lithonia, Ga., the "Spc. Jamaal RaShard Addison Post Office Building." Introduced by JOHNSON, D-Ga., on Nov. 15, 2007. House passed, under suspension of the rules, amended, Feb. 12, 2008. Senate Homeland Security and Governmental Affairs reported April 10 (no written report). Senate passed April 22. President signed May 7, 2008.

■ **PL 110-219** (HR 4211) Designate the facility of the U.S. Postal Service located at 725 Roanoke Ave. in Roanoke Rapids, N.C., the "Judge Richard B. Allsbrook Post Office." Introduced by BUTTERFIELD, D-N.C., on Nov. 15, 2007. House passed, under suspension of the rules, Jan. 22, 2008. Senate Homeland Security and Governmental Affairs reported April 10 (no written report). Senate passed April 22. President signed May 7, 2008.

■ **PL 110-220** (HR 4240) Designate the facility of the U.S. Postal Service located at 10799 W. Alameda Ave. in Lakewood, Colo., the "Felix Sparks Post Office Building." Introduced by PERLMUTTER, D-Colo., on Nov. 15, 2007. House passed, under suspension of the rules, Jan. 28, 2008. Senate Homeland Security and Governmental Affairs reported April 10 (no written report). Senate passed April 22. President signed May 7, 2008.

■ **PL 110-221** (HR 4454) Designate the facility of the U.S. Postal Service located at 3050 Hunsinger Lane in Louisville, Ky., the "Iraq and Afghanistan Fallen Military Heroes of Louisville Memorial Post Office Building" in honor of the servicemembers from Louisville who died in service during Operation Enduring Freedom and Operation Iraqi Freedom. Introduced by YARMUTH, D-Ky., on Dec. 11, 2007. House passed, under suspension of the rules, Feb. 28, 2008. Senate Homeland Security and Governmental Affairs reported April 10 (no written report). Senate passed April 22. President signed May 7, 2008.

■ **PL 110-222** (HR 5135) Designate the facility of the U.S. Postal Service located at 201 W. Greenway St. in Derby, Kan., as the "Sgt. Jamie O. Maugans Post Office Building." Introduced by TIAHRT, R-Kan., on Jan. 23, 2008. House passed, under suspension of the rules, Feb. 12. Senate Homeland Security and Governmental Affairs reported April. 10 (no written report). Senate passed April 22. President signed May 7, 2008.

■ **PL 110-223** (HR 5220) Designate the facility of the U.S. Postal Service located at 3800 SW 185th Ave. in Beaverton, Ore., the "Maj. Arthur Chin Post Office Building." Introduced by WU, D-Ore., on Jan. 29, 2008. House passed, under suspension of the rules, March 5. Senate Homeland Security and Governmental Affairs reported April 10 (no written report). Senate passed April 22. President signed May 7, 2008.

■ **PL 110-224** (HR 5400) Designate the facility of the U.S. Postal Service located at 160 E. Washington St. in Chagrin Falls, Ohio, the "Sgt. Michael M. Kashkoush Post Office Building." Introduced by LATOURETTE, R-Ohio, on Feb. 12, 2008. House passed, under suspension of the rules, March 5. Senate Homeland Security and Governmental Affairs reported April 10 (no written report). Senate passed April 22. President signed May 7, 2008.

■ **PL 110-225** (HR 5472) Designate the facility of the U.S. Postal Service located at 2650 Dr. Martin Luther King Jr. St., Indianapolis, Ind., the "Julia M. Carson Post Office Building." Introduced by VISCLOSKY, D-Ind., on Feb. 14, 2008. House passed, under suspension of the rules, April 9. Senate passed April 22. President signed May 7, 2008.

■ **PL 110-226** (HR 5489) Designate the facility of the U.S. Postal Service located at 6892 Main St. in Gloucester, Va., the "Congresswoman Jo Ann S. Davis Post Office." Introduced by WITTMAN, R-Va., on Feb. 26, 2008. House passed, under suspension of the rules, April 9. Senate passed April 22. President signed May 7, 2008.

■ **PL 110-227** (HR 5715) Ensure continued availability of access to the federal student loan program for students and families. Intro-

duced by MILLER, D-Calif., on April 8, 2008. House Education and Labor reported April 14 (H Rept 110-583). House passed, amended, April 17. Senate passed, amended, April 30. House agreed to Senate amendments, under suspension of the rules, May 1. President signed May 7, 2008.

■ **PL 110-228** (S 2457) Provide for extensions of leases of certain land by Mashantucket Pequot (Western) Tribe. Introduced by LIEBERMAN, I-Conn., on Dec. 12, 2007. Senate Indian Affairs discharged. Senate passed, amended, Feb. 5, 2008. House Natural Resources reported April 29 (H Rept 110-611). House passed, under suspension of the rules, April 29. President signed May 8, 2008.

■ **PL 110-229** (S 2739) Authorize certain programs and activities in the Department of the Interior, the Forest Service, and the Department of Energy; further implement the act approving the Covenant to Establish a Commonwealth of the Northern Mariana Islands in Political Union with the United States of America; and amend the Compact of Free Association Amendments Act of 2003. Introduced by BINGAMAN, D-N.M., on March 10, 2008. Senate passed April 10. House passed, under suspension of the rules, April 29. President signed May 8, 2008.

■ **PL 110-230** (S 2929) Temporarily extend the programs under the Higher Education Act of 1965. Introduced by KENNEDY, D-Mass., on April 29, 2008. Senate passed April 29. House passed, amended, under suspension of the rules, May 6. Senate agreed to House amendment May 7. President signed May 13, 2008.

■ **PL 110-231** (HR 6051) Amend PL 110-196 to provide for a temporary extension of programs authorized by the Farm Security and Rural Investment Act of 2002 until May 23, 2008, or the date of the enactment of the Food, Conservation and Energy Act of 2008, , whichever occurs first. Introduced by PETERSON, D-Minn., on May 14, 2008. House passed May 14. Senate passed May 14. President signed May 18, 2008.

■ **PL 110-232** (HR 6022) Suspend the acquisition of petroleum for the Strategic Petroleum Reserve. Introduced by WELCH, D-Vt., on May 12, 2008. House passed, under suspension of the rules, May 13. Senate passed May 14. President signed May 19, 2008.

■ **PL 110-233** (HR 493) Prohibit discrimination on the basis of genetic information with respect to health insurance and employment. Introduced by SLAUGHTER, D-N.Y., on Jan. 16, 2007. House Education and Labor reported, amended, March 5 (H Rept 110-28, Part 1). House Ways and Means reported, amended, March 26 (H Rept 110-28, Part 2). House Energy and Commerce reported, amended, on March 29 (H Rept 110-28, Part 3). House Energy and Commerce filed a supplemental report April 19 (H Rept 110-28, Part 4). House passed, amended, under suspension of the rules, April 25. Senate passed, amended, April 24, 2008. House agreed to Senate amendment May 1. President signed May 21, 2008.

■ **PL 110-234** (HR 2419) Provide for the continuation of agricultural programs through fiscal 2012. Introduced by PETERSON, D-Minn., on May 22, 2007. House Agriculture reported, amended,

July 23 (H Rept 110-256, Part 1). House Foreign Affairs discharged. House passed, amended, July 27. Senate passed, amended, Dec. 14. Conference report filed in the House on May 13, 2008 (H Rept 110-627). House agreed to conference report May 14. Senate agreed to conference report May 15. President vetoed May 21. House passed over president's veto, May 21. Senate passed over president's veto, May 22. Became law without president's signature May 22, 2008.

■ **PL 110-235** (S 3029) Provide for an additional temporary extension of programs under the Small Business Act and the Small Business Investment Act of 1958. Introduced by KERRY, D-Mass., on May 15, 2008. Senate passed May 15. House passed, under suspension of the rules, May 20. President signed May 23, 2008.

■ **PL 110-236** (HR 3522) Ratify a conveyance of a portion of the Jicarilla Apache Reservation to Rio Arriba County, N.M., pursuant to the settlement of litigation between the Jicarilla Apache Nation and Rio Arriba County, authorize issuance of a patent for said lands, and change the exterior boundary of the Jicarilla Apache Reservation accordingly. Introduced by UDALL, D-N.M., on Sept. 10, 2007. House Natural Resources reported April 29, 2008 (H Rept 110-610). House passed, under suspension of the rules, April 29. Senate passed May 1. President signed May 27, 2008.

■ **PL 110-237** (HR 5919) Make technical corrections regarding the Newborn Screening Saves Lives Act of 2007. Introduced by ROYBAL-ALLARD, D-Calif., on April 29, 2008. House passed, under suspension of the rules, April 30. Senate passed May 2. President signed May 27, 2008.

■ **PL 110-238** (S 3035) Temporarily extend the programs under the Higher Education Act of 1965. Introduced by KENNEDY, D-Mass., on May 20, 2008. Senate passed May 20. House passed, under suspension of the rules, May 20. President signed May 30, 2008.

■ **PL 110-239** (HR 2356) Amend Title 4, U.S. Code, to encourage the display of the U.S. flag on Father's Day. Introduced by SCOTT, D-Ga., on May 17, 2007. House passed, under suspension of the rules, June 11. Senate Judiciary discharged. Senate passed May 15, 2008. President signed June 3, 2008.

■ **PL 110-240** (HR 2517) Amend the Missing Children's Assistance Act to authorize appropriations. Introduced by LAMPSON, D-Texas, on May 24, 2007. House passed, amended, under suspension of the rules, Dec. 5. Senate Judiciary discharged. Senate passed May 20, 2008. President signed June 3, 2008.

■ **PL 110-241** (HR 4008) Amend the Fair Credit Reporting Act to make technical corrections to the definition of willful noncompliance with violations involving the printing of an expiration date on certain credit and debit card receipts before the date of enactment of this act. Introduced by MAHONEY, D-Fla., on Oct. 30, 2007. House passed, under suspension of the rules, May 13, 2008. Senate passed May 20. President signed June 3, 2008.

■ **PL 110-242** (S 2829) Make technical corrections to Section 1244 of the fiscal 2008 National Defense Authorization Act, which provides special immigrant status for certain Iraqis. Introduced by

KENNEDY, D-Mass., on April 8, 2008. Senate Judiciary discharged. Senate passed April 28. House passed, under suspension of the rules, May 21. President signed June 3, 2008.

■ **PL 110-243** (S J Res 17) Direct the United States to initiate international discussions and take necessary steps with other nations to negotiate an agreement for managing migratory and transboundary fish stocks in the Arctic Ocean. Introduced by STEVENS, R-Alaska, on Aug. 3, 2007. Senate Foreign Relations discharged. Senate Commerce, Science and Transportation reported Oct. 4 (no written report). Senate passed Oct. 4. House passed, under suspension of the rules, May 21, 2008. President signed June 3, 2008.

■ **PL 110-244** (HR 1195) Amend the Safe, Accountable, Flexible, Efficient Transportation Equity Act: A Legacy for Users to make technical corrections. Introduced by OBERSTAR, D-Minn., on Feb. 27, 2007. House Transportation and Infrastructure reported, amended, March 21 (H Rept 110-62). House passed, amended, under suspension of the rules, March 26. Senate Environment and Public Works reported, amended, March 7, 2008 (no written report). Senate passed, amended, April 17. House agreed to Senate amendment, under suspension of the rules, April 30. President signed June 6, 2008.

■ **PL 110-245** (HR 6081) Amend the Internal Revenue Code of 1986 to provide benefits for military personnel. Introduced by RANGEL, D-N.Y., on May 16, 2008. House passed, amended, under suspension of the rules, May 20. Senate passed May 22. President signed June 17, 2008.

■ **PL 110-246** (HR 6124) Reauthorize agricultural, nutrition, conservation and other programs through fiscal 2012. Introduced by PETERSON, D-Minn., on May 22, 2008. House passed, under suspension of the rules, May 22. Senate passed June 5. President vetoed June 18. House passed over president's veto June 18. Senate passed over president's veto June 18. Became law without president's signature on June 18, 2008.

■ **PL 110-247** (S 2420) Encourage executive contracts to provide for the donation of excess food to nonprofit organizations that provide assistance to needy people. Introduced by SCHUMER, D-N.Y., on Dec. 6, 2007. House Homeland Security and Governmental Affairs reported, amended, May 22, 2008 (S Rept 110-338). Senate passed, amended, May 22. House passed, under suspension of the rules, June 3. President signed June 20, 2008.

■ **PL 110-248** (HR 3179) Amend Title 40, U.S. Code, to authorize the use of federal supply schedules for the acquisition of law enforcement, security, and certain other related items by state and local governments. Introduced by TOWNS, D-N.Y., on July 25, 2007. House Oversight and Government Reform reported Dec. 17 (H Rept 110-494). House passed, under suspension of the rules, Dec. 17. Senate Homeland Security and Governmental Affairs reported June 5, 2008 (S Rept 110-344). Senate passed June 10. President signed June 26, 2008.

■ **PL 110-249** (HR 3913) Amend the International Center Act to authorize the lease or sublease of certain property to an entity other

than a foreign government or international organization if certain conditions are met. Introduced by ROS-LEHTINEN, R-Fla., on Oct. 22, 2007. House Transportation and Infrastructure reported Jan. 28, 2008 (H Rept 110-518). House passed, under suspension of the rules, Jan. 28. Senate Foreign Relations reported June 2 (S Rept 110-343). Senate passed June 5. President signed June 26, 2008.

■ **PL 110-250** (S 1245) Reform mutual aid agreements for the National Capital Region. Introduced by CARDIN, D-Md., on April 26, 2007. Senate Homeland Security and Governmental Affairs reported Dec. 6 (S Rept 110-237). Senate passed Dec. 12. House passed, under suspension of the rules, June 9, 2008. President signed June 26, 2008.

■ **PL 110-251** (S 2516) Assist certain members of the armed forces in obtaining U.S. citizenship. Introduced by MIKULSKI, D-Md., on Dec. 18, 2007. Senate Judiciary discharged. Senate passed, amended, March 11, 2008. House passed, under suspension of the rules, June 9. President signed June 26, 2008.

■ **PL 110-252** (HR 2642) Make emergency supplemental appropriations for U.S. operations in Iraq and Afghanistan and other purposes. Introduced by EDWARDS, D-Texas, on June 11, 2007. House Appropriations reported June 11 (H Rept 110-186). House passed, amended, June 15. Senate passed, amended, Sept. 6. House agreed to Senate amendment, with amendments, May 15, 2008. Senate agreed to House amendment No. 2 to Senate amendment, with amendment, May 22. Senate agreed to House amendment No. 1 to Senate amendment, with amendment, May 22. House agreed to Senate amendment to House amendment No. 1 on June 19. House agreed to Senate amendment to House amendment No. 2, with an amendment, June 19. Senate agreed to House amendment to Senate amendment to House amendment No. 2 on June 26. President signed June 30, 2008.

■ **PL 110-253** (HR 6327) Amend the Internal Revenue Code of 1986 to extend the funding and expenditure authority of the Airport and Airway Trust Fund. Introduced by RANGEL, D-N.Y., on June 20, 2008. House passed, amended, under suspension of the rules, June 24. Senate passed June 26. President signed June 30, 2008.

■ **PL 110-254** (S 1692) Grant a federal charter to the Korean War Veterans Association Inc. Introduced by CARDIN, D-Md., on June 25, 2007. Senate Judiciary reported Sept. 7 (no written report). Senate passed Sept. 12. House passed, under suspension of the rules, June 17, 2008. President signed June 30, 2008.

■ **PL 110-255** (S 2146) Authorize the administrator of the EPA to accept, as part of a settlement, diesel emission reduction supplemental environmental projects. Introduced by CARPER, D-Del., on Oct. 4, 2007. Senate Environment and Public Works reported Feb. 28, 2008 (S Rept 110-266). Senate passed Feb. 29. House passed, amended, under suspension of the rules, June 12. Senate agreed to House amendment June 17. President signed June 30, 2008.

■ **PL 110-256** (S 3180) Temporarily extend the programs under the Higher Education Act of 1965. Introduced by KENNEDY, D-Mass., on June 23, 2008. Senate passed June 23. House passed, under suspension of the rules, June 25. President signed June 30, 2008.

■ **PL 110-257** (HR 5690) Exempt the African National Congress from treatment as a terrorist organization for certain acts or events, and provide relief for certain members of the African National Congress to enter the country without regard to activities undertaken in opposition to apartheid rule in South Africa. Introduced by BERMAN, D-Calif., on April 3, 2008. House Judiciary reported, amended, May 5 (H Rept 110-620, Part 1). House Foreign Affairs discharged. House passed, amended, under suspension of the rules, May 8. Senate Judiciary reported, amended, June 26 (no written report). Senate passed, amended, June 26. House agreed to Senate amendment June 26. President signed July 1, 2008.

■ **PL 110-258** (S 188) Revise the short title of the Fannie Lou Hamer, Rosa Parks, and Coretta Scott King Voting Rights Act Reauthorization and Amendments Act of 2006. Introduced by SALAZAR, D-Colo., on Jan. 4, 2007. Senate Judiciary reported, amended, Feb. 8 (no written report). Senate passed, amended, Feb. 15. Passed House, under suspension of the rules, June 17, 2008. President signed July 1, 2008.

■ **PL 110-259** (S 254) Award a congressional gold medal posthumously to Constantino Brumidi. Introduced by ENZI, R-Wyo., on Jan. 10, 2007. Senate Banking, Housing, and Urban Affairs reported, amended, May 17 (no written report). Senate passed, amended, May 21. House passed, under suspension of the rules, June 10, 2008. President signed July 1, 2008.

■ **PL 110-260** (S 682) Award a congressional gold medal to Edward William Brooke III in recognition of his unprecedented and enduring service to the nation. Introduced by KENNEDY, D-Mass., on Feb. 17, 2007. Senate Banking, Housing, and Urban Affairs discharged. Senate passed March 29. House passed, under suspension of the rules, June 10, 2008. President signed July 1, 2008.

■ **PL 110-261** (HR 6304) Amend the Foreign Intelligence Surveillance Act of 1978 to establish a procedure for authorizing certain acquisitions of foreign intelligence. Introduced by REYES, D-Texas, on June 19, 2008. House passed June 20. Senate passed July 9. President signed July 10, 2008.

■ **PL 110-262** (HR 430) Designate the U.S. bankruptcy courthouse located at 271 Cadman Plaza E., Brooklyn, N.Y., as the "Conrad Duberstein United States Bankruptcy Courthouse." Introduced by TOWNS, D-N.Y., on Jan. 11, 2007. House Transportation and Infrastructure reported, amended, Feb. 16 (H Rept 110-21). House passed, amended, under suspension of the rules, March 13. Senate Environment and Public Works discharged. Senate passed June 24, 2008. President signed July 15, 2008.

■ **PL 110-263** (HR 781) Redesignate Lock and Dam No. 5 of the McClellan-Kerr Arkansas River Navigation System near Redfield, Ark., authorized by the Rivers and Harbors Act of 1946, as the "Col. Charles D. Maynard Lock and Dam." Introduced by ROSS, D-Ark., on Jan 31, 2007. House Transportation and Infrastructure reported July 11 (H Rept 110-229). House passed, under suspension of the rules, July 16. Senate Environment and Public Works reported June 4, 2008 (no written report). Senate passed June 24. President signed July 15, 2008.

■ **PL 110-264** (HR 2728) Designate the station of the U.S. Border Patrol located at 25762 Madison Ave. in Murrieta, Calif., as the "Theodore L. Newton Jr. and George F. Azrak Border Patrol Station." Introduced by ISSA, R-Calif., on June 14, 2007. House Transportation and Infrastructure reported Sept. 14 (H Rept 110–327). House passed, under suspension of the rules, Oct. 29. Senate Environment and Public Works discharged. Senate passed June 24, 2008. President signed July 15, 2008.

■ **PL 110-265** (HR 3721) Designate the facility of the U.S. Postal Service located at 1190 Lorena Road in Lorena, Texas, as the "Marine Gunnery Sgt. John D. Fry Post Office Building." Introduced by EDWARDS, D-Texas, on Oct. 2, 2007. House passed, under suspension of the rules, April 23, 2008. Senate Homeland Security and Governmental Affairs reported June 25 (no written report). Senate passed June 27. President signed July 15, 2008.

■ **PL 110-266** (HR 4140) Designate the Port Angeles Federal Building in Port Angeles, Wash., as the "Richard B. Anderson Federal Building." Introduced by DICKS, D-Wash., on Nov. 9, 2007. House Transportation and Infrastructure reported Jan. 28, 2008 (H Rept 110–515). House passed, under suspension of the rules, Jan. 28. Senate Environment and Public Works reported June 4 (no written report). Senate passed June 24. President signed July 15, 2008.

■ **PL 110-267** (HR 4185) Designate the facility of the U.S. Postal Service located at 11151 Valley Blvd. in El Monte, Calif., as the "Marisol Heredia Post Office Building." Introduced by SOLIS, D-Calif., on Nov. 14, 2007. House passed, under suspension of the rules, April 23, 2008. Senate Homeland Security and Governmental Affairs reported June 25 (no written report). Senate passed June 27. President signed July 15, 2008.

■ **PL 110-268** (HR 5168) Designate the facility of the U.S. Postal Service located at 19101 Cortez Blvd. in Brooksville, Fla., as the "Cody Grater Post Office Building." Introduced by BROWN-WAITE, R-Fla., on Jan 29, 2008. House passed, under suspension of the rules, April 1. Senate Homeland Security and Governmental Affairs reported June 25 (no written report). Senate passed June 27. President signed July 15, 2008.

■ **PL 110-269** (HR 5395) Designate the facility of the U.S. Postal Service located at 11001 Dunklin Drive in St. Louis as the "William 'Bill' Clay Post Office Building." Introduced by CARNAHAN, D-Mo., on Feb. 12, 2008. House passed, under suspension of the rules, April 9. Senate Homeland Security and Governmental Affairs reported June 25 (no written report). Senate passed June 27. President signed July 15, 2008.

■ **PL 110-270** (HR 5479) Designate the facility of the U.S. Postal Service located at 117 N. Kidd St. in Ionia, Mich., as the "Alonzo Woodruff Post Office Building." Introduced by EHLERS, R-Mich., on Feb. 25, 2008. House passed, under suspension of the rules, April 23. Senate Homeland Security and Governmental Affairs reported June 25 (no written report). Senate passed June 27. President signed July 15, 2008.

■ **PL 110-271** (HR 5517) Designate the facility of the U.S. Postal Service located at 7231 FM 1960 in Humble, Texas, as the "Texas Military Veterans Post Office." Introduced by POE, R-Texas, on Feb. 28, 2008. House passed, under suspension of the rules, April 15. Senate Homeland Security and Governmental Affairs reported June 25 (no written report). Senate passed June 27. President signed July 15, 2008.

■ **PL 110-272** (HR 5528) Designate the facility of the U.S. Postal Service located at 120 Commercial St. in Brockton, Mass., as the "Rocky Marciano Post Office Building." Introduced by LYNCH, D-Mass., on March 4, 2008. House passed, under suspension of the rules, April 23. Senate Homeland Security and Governmental Affairs reported June 25 (no written report). Senate passed June 27. President signed July 15, 2008.

■ **PL 110-273** (HR 5778) Preserve the independence of the District of Columbia Water and Sewer Authority. Introduced by VAN HOLLEN, D-Md., on April 10, 2008. House passed, amended, under suspension of the rules, June 9. Senate passed June 16. President signed July 15, 2008.

■ **PL 110-274** (HR 6040) Amend the Water Resources Development Act of 2007 to clarify the authority of the secretary of the Army to provide reimbursement for travel expenses incurred by members of the Committee on Levee Safety. Introduced by MICA, R-Fla., on May 13, 2008. House passed, under suspension of the rules, June 23. Senate passed June 25. President signed July 15, 2008.

■ **PL 110-275** (HR 6331) Amend Titles XVIII and XIX of the Social Security Act to extend expiring provisions under the Medicare Program, improve beneficiary access to preventive and mental health services, enhance low-income benefit programs, and maintain access to care in rural areas, including pharmacy access. Introduced by RANGEL, D-N.Y., on June 20, 2008. House passed, amended, under suspension of the rules, June 24. Senate passed July 9. President vetoed July 15. House passed over president's veto July 15. Senate passed over president's veto July 15. Became law without president's signature July 15, 2008.

■ **PL 110-276** (HR 1019) Designate the U.S. customhouse building located at 31 Gonzalez Clemente Ave. in Mayaguez, P.R., as the "Rafael Martinez Nadal United States Customhouse Building." Introduced by FORTUÑO, R-P.R., on Feb. 13, 2007. House Transportation and Infrastructure reported March 26 (H Rept 110–70). House passed, under suspension of the rules, March 26. Senate Environment and Public Works reported June 4, 2008 (no written report). Senate passed June 24. President signed July 15, 2008.

■ **PL 110-277** (HR 634) Require the secretary of the Treasury to mint coins in commemoration of veterans who became disabled for life while serving in the U.S. armed forces. Introduced by MOORE, D-Kan., on Jan 23, 2007. House passed, amended, under suspension of the rules, May 15, 2007. Senate Banking, Housing, and Urban Affairs reported, amended, June 2, 2008 (no written report). Senate passed, amended, June 10. House agreed to Senate amendment, under suspension of the rules, June 18. President signed July 17, 2008.

■ **PL 110-278** (HR 814) Require the Consumer Product Safety Commission to issue regulations mandating child-resistant closures on all portable gasoline containers. Introduced by MOORE, D-Kan., on Feb. 5, 2007. House Energy and Commerce reported, amended, Oct. 9 (H Rept 110–367). House passed, amended, under suspension of the rules Oct. 9. Senate Commerce, Science and Transportation discharged. Senate passed June 16, 2008. President signed July 17, 2008.

■ **PL 110-279** (S 2967) Provide for the continuation of certain federal employee benefits for certain employees of the Senate Restaurants after operations of the restaurants are contracted out to a private business concern. Introduced by FEINSTEIN, D-Calif., on May 1, 2008. Senate Rules and Administration discharged. Senate passed June 3. House passed July 10. President signed July 17, 2008.

■ **PL 110-280** (HR 802) Amend the Act to Prevent Pollution from Ships to require the Coast Guard and the EPA to prescribe regulations to implement vessel air emission standards outlined under Annex VI to the MARPOL Convention. Introduced by OBERSTAR, D-Minn., on Feb. 5, 2007. House Transportation and Infrastructure reported, amended, March 20 (H Rept 110–54). House passed, amended, under suspension of the rules March 26. Senate Commerce, Science and Transportation reported, amended, June 23, 2008 (S Rept 110–394). Senate passed, amended, June 26. House agreed to Senate amendment, under suspension of the rules, July 8. President signed July 21, 2008.

■ **PL 110-281** (HR 3891) Amend the National Fish and Wildlife Foundation Establishment Act to increase the number of directors on the foundation's board of directors. Introduced by BROWN, R-S.C., on Oct. 18, 2007. House Natural Resources reported March 31, 2008 (H Rept 110–552). House passed, amended, under suspension of the rules, March 31. Senate Environment and Public Works reported June 27 (S Rept 110–405). Senate passed July 7. President signed July 21, 2008.

■ **PL 110-282** (S 3145) Designate a portion of U.S. Route 20A, located in Orchard Park, N.Y., as the "Timothy J. Russert Highway." Introduced by CLINTON, D-N.Y., on June 18, 2008. Senate Homeland Security and Governmental Affairs discharged. Senate Environment and Public Works discharged. Senate passed June 24. House passed, under suspension of the rules, July 15. President signed July 23, 2008.

■ **PL 110-283** (HR 3403) Promote and enhance public safety by facilitating the rapid deployment of IP-enabled 911 and E-911 services, encouraging the nation's transition to a national IP-enabled emergency network and improving 911 and E-911 access to those with disabilities. Introduced by GORDON, D-Tenn., on Aug. 3, 2007. House Energy and Commerce reported, amended, Nov. 13 (H Rept 110–442). House passed, amended, under suspension of the rules, Nov. 13. Senate Commerce, Science and Transportation discharged. Senate passed, amended, June 16, 2008. House agreed to Senate amendment June 23. President signed July 23, 2008.

■ **PL 110-284** (HR 3712) Designate the federal building and U.S. courthouse located at 1716 Spielbusch Ave. in Toledo, Ohio, as the "James M. & Thomas W.L. Ashley Customs Building and United States Courthouse." Introduced by KAPTUR, D-Ohio, on Oct. 1, 2007. House Transportation and Infrastructure reported, amended, Nov. 15 (H Rept 110–455). House passed, amended, under suspension of the rules June 4, 2008. Senate Environment and Public Works discharged. Senate passed June 24. President signed July 23, 2008.

■ **PL 110-285** (HR 1553) Amend the Public Health Service Act to advance medical research and treatments into pediatric cancers, ensure that patients and families have access to the current treatments and information regarding pediatric cancers, establish a population-based national childhood cancer database, and promote public awareness of pediatric cancers. Introduced by PRYCE, R-Ohio, on March 15, 2007. House Energy and Commerce reported, amended, June 10, 2008 (H Rept 110–706). House passed, amended, under suspension of the rules June 12. Senate passed July 16. President signed July 29, 2008.

■ **PL 110-286** (HR 3890) Amend the Burmese Freedom and Democracy Act of 2003 to waive the requirement for annual renewal resolutions on import sanctions, impose import sanctions on Burmese gemstones, expand the number of individuals against whom the visa ban is applicable, and expand the blocking of assets and other prohibited activities. Introduced by LANTOS, D-Calif., on Oct. 18, 2007. House Foreign Affairs reported, amended, Oct. 31 (H Rept 110–418, Part 1). House Judiciary discharged. House passed, amended, under suspension of the rules Dec. 11. Senate Foreign Relations discharged. Senate passed, amended, Dec. 19. House agreed to Senate amendments, with amendments pursuant to H Res 1341, on July 15, 2008. Senate agreed to House amendments to Senate amendments July 22. President signed July 29, 2008.

■ **PL 110-287** (H J Res 93) Approve the renewal of import restrictions in the Burmese Freedom and Democracy Act of 2003. Introduced by CROWLEY, D-N.Y., on June 5, 2008. House passed, amended, under suspension of the rules, July 23. Senate passed July 24. President signed July 29, 2008.

■ **PL 110-288** (S 2766) Amend the Federal Water Pollution Control Act to address certain discharges incidental to the normal operation of a recreational vessel. Introduced by NELSON, D-Fla., on March 13, 2008. Senate Environment and Public Works reported June 23 (S Rept 110–398). Senate passed July 22. House passed, under suspension of the rules, July 22. President signed July 29, 2008.

■ **PL 110-289** (HR 3221) Move the United States toward greater energy independence and security, develop innovative technologies, reduce carbon emissions, create green jobs, protect consumers, increase clean renewable-energy production, and modernize the U.S. energy infrastructure. Introduced by PELOSI, D-Calif., on July 30, 2007. House passed, amended, Aug. 4. Senate passed, amended, April 10, 2008. House agreed to Senate amendments, with amendments, May 8. Senate agreed to House amendments to Senate amendments, with amendments, July 11. House agreed to Senate amendment to House amendments to Senate amendment, with amendments, July 23. Senate agreed to House amendment to Senate amendment to House amendments to Senate amendment July 26. President signed July 30, 2008.

■ **PL 110-290** (HR 3564) Amend Title 5, U.S. Code, to authorize appropriations for the Administrative Conference of the United States through fiscal 2011. Introduced by CANNON, R-Utah, on Sept. 18, 2007. House Judiciary reported Oct. 18 (H Rept 110–390). House passed, under suspension of the rules, Oct. 22. Senate passed, amended, June 27, 2008. House agreed to Senate amendment, under suspension of the rules, July 14. President signed July 30, 2008.

■ **PL 110-291** (HR 3985) Amend Title 49, U.S. Code, to direct the secretary of Transportation to register a person providing transportation by an over-the-road bus as a motor carrier of passengers only if the person is willing and able to comply with certain accessibility requirements in addition to other existing requirements. Introduced by DEFAZIO, D-Ore., on Oct. 29, 2007. House Transportation and Infrastructure reported Nov. 15, 2007 (H Rept 110–456). House passed, under suspension of the rules, Dec. 12. Senate Commerce, Science and Transportation reported June 23, 2008 (S Rept 110–395). Senate passed July 14. President signed July 30, 2008.

■ **PL 110-292** (HR 4289) Name the Department of Veterans Affairs outpatient clinic in Ponce, P.R., as the "Euripides Rubio Department of Veterans Affairs Outpatient Clinic." Introduced by FORTUÑO, R-P.R., on Oct. 29, 2007. House passed, under suspension of the rules, June 24, 2008. Senate Veterans' Affairs discharged. Senate passed July 11. President signed July 30, 2008.

■ **PL 110-293** (HR 5501) Authorize appropriations for fiscal 2009 through 2013 to provide assistance to foreign countries to combat HIV/AIDS, tuberculosis and malaria. Introduced by BERMAN, D-Calif., on Feb. 27, 2008. House Foreign Affairs reported March 10 (H Rept 110–546, Part 1). Financial Services discharged. Foreign Affairs filed supplemental report March 11 (H Rept 110–546, Part 2). House passed, amended, April 2. Senate Foreign Relations discharged. Senate passed, amended, July 16. House agreed to Senate amendment July 24. President signed July 30, 2008.

■ **PL 110-294** (S 231) Authorize the Edward Byrne Memorial Justice Assistance Grant Program at fiscal year 2006 levels through fiscal 2012. Introduced by FEINSTEIN, D-Calif., on Jan. 9, 2007. Senate Judiciary reported May 23 (no written report). Senate passed May 24. House passed, under suspension of the rules, July 14, 2008. President signed July 30, 2008.

■ **PL 110-295** (S 2607) Make a technical correction to Section 3009 of the Deficit Reduction Act of 2005. Introduced by SNOWE, R-Maine, on Feb. 7, 2008. Senate Commerce, Science and Transportation reported June 10 (S Rept 110–348). Senate passed, amended, June 19. House passed, under suspension of the rules, July 9. President signed July 30, 2008.

■ **PL 110-296** (S 3218) Extend the pilot program for volunteer groups to obtain criminal history background checks. Introduced by BIDEN, D-Del., on June 26, 2008. Senate passed June 26. House passed, under suspension of the rules, July 14. President signed July 30, 2008.

■ **PL 110-297** (HR 4841) Approve, ratify and confirm the settlement agreement entered into to resolve claims by the Soboba Band of Luiseño Indians relating to alleged interferences with the water resources of the tribe, and authorize and direct the secretary of the Interior to execute the settlement agreement and related waivers. Introduced by BONO MACK, R-Calif., on Dec. 19, 2007. House Natural Resources reported, amended, May 15, 2008 (H Rept 110-649). House passed, amended, under suspension of the rules, May 21. Senate passed July 23. President signed July 31, 2008.

■ **PL 110-298** (S 2565) Establish an awards mechanism to honor exceptional acts of bravery in the line of duty by federal law enforcement officers. Introduced by BIDEN, D-Del., on Jan. 29, 2008. Judiciary reported, amended, June 24 (no written report). Senate passed, amended, June 26. House passed, under suspension of the rules, July 22. President signed July 31, 2008.

■ **PL 110-299** (S 3298) Clarify the circumstances during which the EPA administrator and applicable states may require permits for discharges from certain vessels, and require the administrator to conduct a study of discharges incidental to the normal operation of vessels. Introduced by MURKOWSKI, R-Alaska, on July 22, 2008. Senate passed July 22. House passed, under suspension of the rules, July 22. President signed July 31, 2008.

■ **PL 110-300** (S 3352) Temporarily extend the programs under the Higher Education Act of 1965. Introduced by KENNEDY, D-Mass., on July 28, 2008. Senate passed July 28. House passed, under suspension of the rules, July 30. President signed July 31, 2008.

■ **PL 110-301** (S 3370) Resolve pending claims against Libya by U.S. nationals. Introduced by BIDEN, D-Del., on July 31, 2008. Senate passed July 31. House passed July 31. President signed Aug. 4, 2008.

■ **PL 110-302** (HR 2245) Designate the Department of Veterans Affairs outpatient clinic in Wenatchee, Wash., as the "Elwood 'Bud' Link Department of Veterans Affairs Outpatient Clinic." Introduced by HASTINGS, R-Wash., on May 9, 2007. House passed, under suspension of the rules, June 26, 2008. Senate Veterans' Affairs discharged. Senate passed Aug. 1. President signed Aug. 12, 2008.

■ **PL 110-303** (HR 4210) Designate the facility of the U.S. Postal Service located at 401 Washington Ave. in Weldon, N.C., as the "Dock M. Brown Post Office Building." Introduced by BUTTERFIELD, D-N.C., on Nov. 15, 2007. House passed, under suspension of the rules, Dec. 17. Senate Homeland Security and Governmental Affairs reported July 30, 2008 (no written report). Senate passed Aug. 1. President signed Aug. 12, 2008.

■ **PL 110-304** (HR 4918) Designate the Department of Veterans Affairs medical center in Miami as the "Bruce W. Carter Department of Veterans Affairs Medical Center." Introduced by ROS-LEHTINEN, R-Fla., on Dec. 19, 2007. House passed, under suspension of the rules, June 26, 2008. Senate Veterans' Affairs discharged. Senate passed Aug. 1. President signed Aug. 12, 2008.

■ **PL 110-305** (HR 5477) Designate the facility of the U.S. Postal Service located at 120 S. Del Mar Ave. in San Gabriel, Calif., as the "Chi Mui Post Office Building." Introduced by SCHIFF, D-Calif., on Feb. 21, 2008. House passed, under suspension of the rules,

June 3. Senate Homeland Security and Governmental Affairs reported July 30 (no written report). Senate passed Aug. 1. President signed Aug. 12, 2008.

■ **PL 110-306** (HR 5483) Designate the facility of the U.S. Postal Service located at 10449 White Granite Drive in Oakton, Va., as the "Pfc. David H. Sharrett II Post Office Building." Introduced by DAVIS, R-Va., on Feb. 25, 2008. House passed, under suspension of the rules, April 23. Senate Homeland Security and Governmental Affairs reported July 30 (no written report). Senate passed Aug. 1. President signed Aug. 12, 2008.

■ **PL 110-307** (HR 5631) Designate the facility of the U.S. Postal Service located at 1155 Seminole Trail in Charlottesville, Va., as the "Cpl. Bradley T. Arms Post Office Building." Introduced by GOODE, R-Va., on March 13, 2008. House passed, under suspension of the rules, April 29. Senate Homeland Security and Governmental Affairs reported July 30 (no written report). Senate passed Aug. 1. President signed Aug. 12, 2008.

■ **PL 110-308** (HR 6061) Designate the facility of the U.S. Postal Service located at 219 E. Main St. in West Frankfort, Ill., as the "Kenneth James Gray Post Office Building." Introduced by COSTELLO, D-Ill., on May 14, 2008. House passed, under suspension of the rules, July 9. Senate Homeland Security and Governmental Affairs reported July 30 (no written report). Senate passed Aug. 1. President signed Aug. 12, 2008.

■ **PL 110-309** (HR 6085) Designate the facility of the U.S. Postal Service located at 42222 Rancho Las Palmas Drive in Rancho Mirage, Calif., as the "Gerald R. Ford Post Office Building." Introduced by BONO MACK, R-Calif., on May 20, 2008. House passed, under suspension of the rules, June 18. Senate Homeland Security and Governmental Affairs reported July 30 (no written report). Senate passed Aug. 1. President signed Aug. 12, 2008.

■ **PL 110-310** (HR 6150) Designate the facility of the U.S. Postal Service located at 14500 Lorain Ave. in Cleveland as the "John P. Gallagher Post Office Building." Introduced by KUCINICH, D-Ohio, on May 22, 2008. House passed, under suspension of the rules, June 18. Senate Homeland Security and Governmental Affairs reported July 30 (no written report). Senate passed Aug. 1. President signed Aug. 12, 2008.

■ **PL 110-311** (HR 6340) Designate the federal building and U.S. courthouse located at 300 Quarropas St. in White Plains, N.Y., as the "Charles L. Brieant Jr. Federal Building and United States Courthouse." Introduced by LOWEY, D-N.Y., on June 20, 2008. House passed, amended, under suspension of the rules, July 29. Senate passed Aug. 1. President signed Aug. 12, 2008.

■ **PL 110-312** (S 3294) Provide for the continued performance of the functions of the U.S. Parole Commission. Introduced by LEAHY, D-Vt., on July 21, 2008. Senate passed July 21. House passed, under suspension of the rules, July 31. President signed Aug. 12, 2008.

■ **PL 110-313** (S 3295) Amend Title 35, U.S. Code, and the Trademark Act of 1946 to provide that the secretary of Commerce, in consultation with the director of the U.S. Patent and Trademark Office, shall appoint administrative patent judges and administrative trademark judges. Introduced by LEAHY, D-Vt., on July 21, 2008. Senate Judiciary discharged. Senate passed July 22. House passed, under suspension of the rules, July 31. President signed Aug. 12, 2008.

■ **PL 110-314** (HR 4040) Establish consumer product safety standards and other safety requirements for children's products and reauthorize and modernize the Consumer Product Safety Commission. Introduced by RUSH, D-Ill., on Nov. 1, 2007. House Energy and Commerce reported, amended, Dec. 19 (H Rept 110-501). House passed, amended, under suspension of the rules, Dec. 19. Senate passed, amended, March 6, 2008. Conference report filed in the House July 29 (H Rept 110-787). House agreed to the conference report, under suspension of the rules, July 30. Senate agreed to the conference report July 31. President signed Aug. 14, 2008.

■ **PL 110-315** (HR 4137) Amend and extend the Higher Education Act of 1965. Introduced by MILLER, D-Calif., on Nov. 9, 2007. House Education and Labor reported, amended, Dec. 19 (H Rept 110-500, Part 1). House Judiciary, Science and Technology, and Financial Services discharged. House passed Feb. 7, 2008. Senate Health, Education, Labor and Pensions discharged. Senate passed, amended, July 29. Conference report filed in the House July 30 (H Rept 110-803). House agreed to the conference report July 31. Senate agreed to the conference report July 31. President signed Aug. 14, 2008.

■ **PL 110-316** (HR 6432) Amend the Federal Food, Drug, and Cosmetic Act to revise and extend the animal drug user fee program. Introduced by PALLONE, D-N.J., on July 8, 2008. House Energy and Commerce reported, amended, July 30 (H Rept 110-804). House passed, under suspension of the rules, July 30. Senate passed Aug. 1. President signed Aug. 14, 2008.

■ **PL 110-317** (HR 6580) Ensure the fair treatment, including continued payment of bonuses and similar benefits, for members of the Armed Forces who receive sole survivorship discharges. Introduced by KIND, D-Wis., on July 23, 2008. House passed, under suspension of the rules, July 29. Senate passed Aug. 1. President signed Aug. 29, 2008.

■ **PL 110-318** (HR 6532) Amend the Internal Revenue Code of 1986 to restore the Highway Trust Fund balance. Introduced by RANGEL, D-N.Y., on July 17, 2008. House passed, under suspension of the rules, July 23. Senate Finance discharged. Senate passed, amended, Sept. 10. House agreed to Senate amendment, under suspension of the rules, Sept. 11. President signed Sept. 15, 2008.

■ **PL 110-319** (S 2837) Designate the U.S. courthouse located at 225 Cadman Plaza E., Brooklyn, N.Y., as the "Theodore Roosevelt United States Courthouse." Introduced by SCHUMER, D-N.Y., on April 9, 2008. Senate Environment and Public Works reported June 4 (no written report). Senate passed June 24. House Transportation and Infrastructure reported Sept. 8 (H Rept 110-823). House passed, under suspension of the rules, Sept. 8. President signed Sept. 17, 2008.

■ **PL 110-320** (S 2403) Designate the new federal courthouse, located in the 700 block of East Broad Street, Richmond, Va., as the "Spottswood W. Robinson III and Robert R. Merhige Jr. Federal Courthouse." Introduced by WARNER, R-Va., on Dec. 3, 2007. Senate Environment and Public Works reported June 4, 2008 (no written report). Senate passed June 24. House Transportation and Infrastructure reported, amended, Sept. 8 (H Rept 110- 824). House passed, amended, under suspension of the rules, Sept. 8. Senate agreed to House amendments Sept. 9. President signed Sept. 18, 2008.

■ **PL 110-321** (HR 6456) Provide for extensions of certain authorities of the Department of State. Introduced by BERMAN, D-Calif., on July 10, 2008. House passed, amended, under suspension of the rules, July 30. Senate Foreign Relations discharged Sept. 8. Senate passed Sept. 8. President signed Sept. 19, 2008.

■ **PL 110-322** (S 2450) Amend the federal rules of evidence to address the waiver of the attorney-client privilege and the work product doctrine. Introduced by LEAHY, D-Vt., on Dec. 11, 2007. Senate Judiciary reported Feb. 25, 2008 (S Rept 110–264). Senate passed Feb. 27. House passed, under suspension of the rules, Sept. 8. President signed Sept. 19, 2008.

■ **PL 110-323** (HR 5683) Make certain reforms with respect to the Government Accountability Office. Introduced by DAVIS, D-Ill., on April 2, 2008. House Oversight and Government Reform reported, amended, May 22 (H Rept 110–671). House passed, amended, under suspension of the rules, June 9. Senate Homeland Security and Governmental Affairs reported, amended, July 26 (no written report). Senate passed, amended, Aug. 1. House agreed to Senate amendment, under suspension of the rules, Sept. 9. President signed Sept. 22, 2008.

■ **PL 110-324** (S 2617) Increase, effective Dec. 1, 2008, the rates of compensation for veterans with service-connected disabilities and the rates of dependency and indemnity compensation for the survivors of certain disabled veterans. Introduced by AKAKA, D-Hawaii, on Feb. 8, 2008. Senate Veterans' Affairs reported, amended, July 24 (S Rept 110–430). Senate passed, amended, July 30. House passed, under suspension of the rules, Sept. 10. President signed Sept. 24, 2008.

■ **PL 110-325** (S 3406) Reauthorize and revise the Americans with Disabilities Act of 1990. Introduced by HARKIN, D-Iowa, on July 31, 2008. Senate passed Sept. 11. House passed, under suspension of the rules, Sept. 17. President signed Sept. 25, 2008.

■ **PL 110-326** (HR 5938) Amend Title 18, U.S. Code, to provide Secret Service protection to former vice presidents. Introduced by CONYERS, D-Mich., on May 1, 2008. House Judiciary reported June 5 (H Rept 110–696). House passed, under suspension of the rules, June 9, 2008. Senate Judiciary discharged. Senate passed, amended, July 30. House agreed to Senate amendments, under suspension of the rules, Sept. 15. President signed Sept. 26, 2008.

■ **PL 110-327** (HR 1777) Amend the Improving America's Schools Act of 1994 to make permanent the favorable treatment of need-based educational aid under antitrust laws. Introduced by DELAHUNT, D-Mass., on March 29, 2007. House Judiciary reported April 10, 2008 (H Rept 110–577). House passed, amended, under suspension of the rules, April 30. Senate Judiciary discharged. Senate passed, amended, Sept. 25. House agreed to Senate amendment, under suspension of the rules, Sept. 27. President signed Sept. 30, 2008.

■ **PL 110-328** (HR 2608) Amend Section 402 of the Personal Responsibility and Work Opportunity Reconciliation Act of 1996 to extend supplemental security income for refugees, asylees and certain other humanitarian immigrants, and amend the Internal Revenue Code to collect unemployment compensation debts resulting from fraud. Introduced by MCDERMOTT, D-Wash., on June 7, 2007. House passed, under suspension of the rules, July 11. Senate Finance discharged. Senate passed, amended, Aug. 1, 2008. House agreed to Senate amendments, under suspension of the rules, Sept. 17. President signed Sept. 30, 2008.

■ **PL 110-329** (HR 2638) Make appropriations for the departments of Homeland Security, Defense and Veterans Affairs and for military construction in fiscal 2009. Provide continuing appropriations for all agencies and activities covered by the remaining nine unfinished fiscal 2009 appropriations bills until March 6, 2009. Introduced by PRICE, D-N.C., on June 8, 2007. House Appropriations reported June 8 (H Rept 110–181). House passed, amended, June 15. Senate passed, amended with the continuing appropriations bill, July 26. House agreed to Senate amendment, with an amendment, Sept. 24, 2008. Senate agreed to House amendment to Senate amendment Sept. 27. President signed Sept. 30, 2008.

■ **PL 110-330** (HR 6984) Amend Title 49, U.S. Code, to extend authorizations for the airport improvement program, and amend the Internal Revenue Code of 1986 to extend the funding and expenditure authority of the Airport and Airway Trust Fund. Introduced by OBERSTAR, D-Minn., on Sept. 22, 2008. House passed, under suspension of the rules, Sept. 23. Senate passed Sept. 23. President signed Sept. 30, 2008.

■ **PL 110-331** (S 171) Designate the facility of the U.S. Postal Service located at 301 Commerce St. in Commerce, Okla., as the "Mickey Mantle Post Office Building." Introduced by INHOFE, R-Okla., on Jan. 4, 2007. Senate Homeland Security and Governmental Affairs discharged. Senate passed Feb. 17. House passed, under suspension of the rules, Sept. 18, 2008. President signed Sept. 30, 2008.

■ **PL 110-332** (S 2339) Designate the Department of Veterans Affairs clinic in Alpena, Mich., as the "Lt. Col. Clement C. Van Wagoner Department of Veterans Affairs Clinic." Introduced by STABENOW, D-Mich., on Nov. 13, 2007. Senate Veterans' Affairs discharged. Senate passed Dec. 13. House passed, under suspension of the rules, Sept. 17, 2008. President signed Sept. 30, 2008.

■ **PL 110-333** (S 3241) Designate the facility of the U.S. Postal Service located at 1717 Orange Ave. in Fort Pierce, Fla., as the "CeeCee Ross Lyles Post Office Building." Introduced by MARTINEZ, R-Fla., on July 10, 2008. Senate Homeland Security and Governmental Affairs reported July 30 (no written report). Senate passed Aug. 1. House

Oversight and Government Reform discharged. House passed Sept. 24. President signed Sept. 30, 2008.

■ **PL 110-334** (S 3009) Designate the FBI building under construction in Omaha, Neb., as the "J. James Exon Federal Bureau of Investigation Building." Introduced by NELSON, D-Neb., on May 12, 2008. Senate Environment and Public Works reported June 4 (no written report). Senate passed June 24. House Transportation reported Sept. 24 (H Rept 110-878). House passed, under suspension of the rules, Sept. 24. President signed Oct. 1, 2008.

■ **PL 110-335** (HR 5551) Amend Title 11, District of Columbia Official Code, to implement the increase provided under the District of Columbia Appropriations Act of 2008, in the amount of funds made available for the compensation of attorneys representing indigent defendants in the District of Columbia courts. Introduced by DAVIS, D-Ill., on March 6, 2008. House Oversight and Government Reform reported March 31 (H Rept 110–560). House passed, under suspension of the rules, April 1. Senate Homeland Security and Governmental Affairs reported July 25 (S Rept 110–432). Senate passed Sept. 16. President signed Oct. 2, 2008.

■ **PL 110-336** (HR 5893) Reauthorize the sound recording and film preservation programs of the Library of Congress. Introduced by BRADY, D-Pa., on April 24, 2008. House Administration reported, amended, June 4 (H Rept 110–683, Part 1). House Judiciary discharged June 4. House passed, amended, under suspension of the rules, June 4. Senate Rules and Administration discharged. Senate passed Sept. 16. President signed Oct. 2, 2008.

■ **PL 110-337** (S 996) Amend Title 49, U.S. Code, to expand passenger facility fee eligibility for certain noise compatibility projects. Introduced by FEINSTEIN, D-Calif., on March 27, 2007. Senate Commerce, Science and Transportation discharged. Senate passed Feb. 28, 2008. House passed, under suspension of the rules, Sept. 17. President signed Oct. 2, 2008.

■ **PL 110-338** (HR 3986) Amend the John F. Kennedy Center Act to authorize appropriations for the John F. Kennedy Center for the Performing Arts. Introduced by OBERSTAR, D-Minn., on Oct. 29, 2007. House Transportation and Infrastructure reported Dec. 10 (H Rept 110–480). House passed, amended, under suspension of the rules, Dec. 11. Senate Environment and Public Works reported, amended, June 4, 2008 (S Rept 110–406). Senate passed, amended, June 26. House agreed to Senate amendment, under suspension of the rules, Sept. 18, 2008. President signed Oct. 3, 2008.

■ **PL 110-339** (S 1760) Amend the Public Health Service Act with respect to the Healthy Start Initiative. Introduced by BROWN, D-Ohio, on July 10, 2007. Senate Health, Education, Labor and Pensions reported, amended, April 29, 2008 (no written report). Senate passed, amended, April 30. House passed, under suspension of the rules, Sept. 23. President signed Oct. 3, 2008.

■ **PL 110-340** (S 2135) Prohibit the recruitment or use of child soldiers, designate persons who recruit or use child soldiers as inadmissible aliens and allow the deportation of those who recruit or use child soldiers. Introduced by DURBIN, D-Ill., on Oct. 3, 2007.

Senate Judiciary reported, amended, Dec. 11 (no written report). Senate passed, amended, Dec. 19. House passed, under suspension of the rules, with amendment, Sept. 8, 2008. Senate agreed to House amendment Sept. 15. President signed Oct. 3, 2008.

■ **PL 110-341** (S J Res 35) Amend Public Law 108-331 to provide for construction and related activities in support of the Very Energetic Radiation Imaging Telescope Array System (VERITAS) project in Arizona. Introduced by LEAHY, D-Vt., on May 22, 2008. Senate Rules and Administration discharged. Senate passed July 17. House Transportation and Infrastructure reported Sept. 15 (H Rept 110–850). House passed, under suspension of the rules, Sept. 18. President signed Oct. 3, 2008.

■ **PL 110-342** (S J Res 45) Express the consent and approval of Congress to an interstate compact regarding water resources in the Great Lakes-St. Lawrence River Basin. Introduced by LEVIN, D-Mich., on July 23, 2008. Senate Judiciary discharged. Senate passed, amended, Aug. 1. House passed, under suspension of the rules, Sept. 23. President signed Oct. 3, 2008.

■ **PL 110-343** (HR 1424) Provide authority for the federal government to purchase and insure certain types of troubled assets for the purposes of providing stability to and preventing disruption in the economy and financial system and protecting taxpayers, to amend the Internal Revenue Code of 1986 to provide incentives for energy production and conservation, extend certain expiring provisions and provide individual income tax relief. Introduced by KENNEDY, D-R.I., on March 9, 2007. House Education and Labor reported, amended, Oct. 15 (H Rept 110–374, Part 1). House Ways and Means reported, amended, Oct. 15 (H Rept 110–374, Part 2). House Energy and Commerce reported, amended, March 4, 2008 (H Rept 110–374, Part 3). House passed, amended, March 5. Senate passed, amended, Oct. 1. House agreed to the Senate amendments Oct. 3. President signed Oct. 3, 2008.

■ **PL 110-344** (HR 923) Designate a deputy chief in the Civil Rights Division of the Department of Justice responsible for unsolved criminal civil rights cases and a supervisory special agent in the Civil Rights Unit of the FBI. Introduced by LEWIS, D-Ga., on Feb. 8, 2007. House Judiciary reported, amended, June 19 (H Rept 110-200). House passed, amended, under suspension of the rules, June 20. Senate passed Sept. 24, 2008. President signed Oct. 7, 2008.

■ **PL 110-345** (HR 1199) Extend a grant program for drug-endangered children. Introduced by CARDOZA, D-Calif., on Feb. 27, 2007. House Judiciary reported Sept. 24 (Rept 110-341, Part 1). House Energy and Commerce discharged. House passed, under suspension of the rules, Sept. 24. Senate Judiciary discharged. Senate passed Sept. 24, 2008. President signed Oct. 7, 2008.

■ **PL 110-346** (HR 5834) Amend the North Korean Human Rights Act of 2004 to promote respect for the fundamental human rights of the people of North Korea. Introduced by ROS-LEHTINEN, R-Fla., on April 17, 2008. House Foreign Affairs reported, amended, May 13 (H Rept 110-628). House passed, amended, under suspension of the rules, May 15. Senate Foreign Relations discharged. Senate passed, amended, Sept. 22. House agreed to Senate

amendments, under suspension of the rules, Sept. 23. President signed Oct. 7, 2008.

■ **PL 110-347** (HR 5975) Designate the facility of the U.S. Postal Service located at 101 W. Main St. in Waterville, N.Y., as the "Cpl. John P. Sigsbee Post Office." Introduced by ARCURI, D-N.Y., on May 6, 2008. House passed, under suspension of the rules, July 8. Senate Homeland Security and Governmental Affairs reported Sept. 24 (no written report). Senate passed Sept. 26. President signed Oct. 7, 2008.

■ **PL 110-348** (HR 6092) Designate the facility of the U.S. Postal Service located at 101 Tallapoosa St. in Bremen, Ga., as the "Sgt. Paul Saylor Post Office Building." Introduced by GINGREY, R-Ga., on May 20, 2008. House passed, under suspension of the rules, July 8. Senate Homeland Security and Governmental Affairs reported Sept. 24 (no written report). Senate passed Sept. 26. President signed Oct. 7, 2008.

■ **PL 110-349** (HR 6437) Designate the facility of the U.S. Postal Service located at 200 N. Texas Ave. in Odessa, Texas, as the "Cpl. Alfred Mac Wilson Post Office." Introduced by CONAWAY, R-Texas, on July 8, 2008. House passed, under suspension of the rules, July 31. Senate Homeland Security and Governmental Affairs reported Sept. 24 (no written report). Senate passed Sept. 26. President signed Oct. 7, 2008.

■ **PL 110-350** (HR 6889) Extend the authority of the secretary of Education to purchase guaranteed student loans for an additional year. Introduced by MILLER, D-Calif., on Sept. 15, 2008. House passed, under suspension of the rules, Sept. 15. Senate passed Sept. 17. President signed Oct. 7, 2008.

■ **PL 110-351** (HR 6893) Amend Parts B and E of Title IV of the Social Security Act to connect and support relative caregivers, improve outcomes for children in foster care, provide for tribal foster care and adoption access, and improve incentives for adoption. Introduced by MCDERMOTT, D-Wash., on Sept. 15, 2008. House passed, under suspension of the rules, Sept. 17. Senate passed Sept. 22. President signed Oct. 7, 2008.

■ **PL 110-352** (S 3015) Designate the facility of the U.S. Postal Service located at 18 S. G St., Lakeview, Ore., as the "Dr. Bernard Daly Post Office Building." Introduced by SMITH, R-Ore., on May 14, 2008. Senate Homeland Security and Governmental Affairs reported June 25 (no written report). Senate passed June 27. House Oversight and Government Reform discharged. House passed Sept. 27. President signed Oct. 7, 2008.

■ **PL 110-353** (S 3082) Designate the facility of the U.S. Postal Service located at 1700 Cleveland Ave. in Kansas City, Mo., as the "Rev. Earl Abel Post Office Building." Introduced by MCCASKILL, on D-Mo., June 4, 2008. Senate Homeland Security and Governmental Affairs reported June 25 (no written report). Senate passed June 27. House Oversight and Government Reform discharged. House passed Sept. 27. President signed Oct. 7, 2008.

■ **PL 110-354** (HR 1157) Amend the Public Health Service Act to authorize the director of the National Institute of Environmental Health Sciences to make grants for the development and operation of research centers regarding environmental factors that may be related to the etiology of breast cancer. Introduced by LOWEY, D-N.Y., on Feb. 16, 2007. House Energy and Commerce reported, amended, Sept. 25, 2008 (H Rept 110-889). House passed, amended, under suspension of the rules, Sept. 25. Senate passed Sept. 27. President signed Oct. 8, 2008.

■ **PL 110-355** (HR 1343) Amend the Public Health Service Act to provide additional authorization of appropriations for the health centers program under Section 330 of the act. Introduced by G. GREEN, D-Texas, on March 6, 2007. House Energy and Commerce reported, amended, June 4, 2008 (H Rept 110-680). House passed, amended, under suspension of the rules, June 4. Senate Health, Education, Labor and Pensions discharged. Senate passed, amended, Sept. 24. House agreed to Senate amendment, under suspension of the rules, Sept. 25. President signed Oct. 8, 2008.

■ **PL 110-356** (HR 3068) Prohibit awarding contracts to provide guard services under the contract security guard program of the Federal Protective Service to a business concern that is owned, controlled or operated by an individual who has been convicted of a felony. Introduced by NORTON, D-D.C., on July 17, 2007. House Transportation and Infrastructure reported, amended, Sept. 14 (H Rept 110-328). House passed, amended, under suspension of the rules, Oct. 2. Senate Homeland Security and Governmental Affairs reported, amended, Sept. 11, 2008 (S Rept 110-455). Senate passed, amended, Sept. 23. House agreed to Senate amendment, under suspension of the rules, Sept. 27. President signed Oct. 8, 2008.

■ **PL 110-357** (HR 3229) Require the secretary of the Treasury to mint coins in commemoration of the legacy of the U.S. Army Infantry and the establishment of the National Infantry Museum and Soldier Center. Introduced by WESTMORELAND, R-Ga., on July 30, 2007. House passed, amended, under suspension of the rules, June 10, 2008. Senate Banking, Housing and Urban Affairs discharged. Senate passed Sept. 27. President signed Oct. 8, 2008.

■ **PL 110-358** (HR 4120) Amend Title 18, U.S Code, to provide for more effective prosecution of cases involving child pornography. Introduced by BOYDA, D-Kan., on Nov. 8, 2007. House passed, under suspension of the rules, Nov. 14. Senate Judiciary discharged. Senate passed, amended, Sept. 23, 2008. House agreed to Senate amendment, under suspension of the rules, Sept. 26. President signed Oct. 8, 2008.

■ **PL 110-359** (HR 5001) Authorize the administrator of General Services to provide for the redevelopment of the Old Post Office Building located in the District of Columbia. Introduced by NORTON, D-D.C., on Jan. 16, 2008. House Transportation and Infrastructure reported, amended, June 19 (H Rept 110-724). House passed, amended, under suspension of the rules, June 23. Senate Environment and Public Works reported Sept. 24 (S Rept 110-501). Senate passed Sept. 26. President signed Oct. 8, 2008.

■ **PL 110-360** (HR 5057) Reauthorize the Debbie Smith DNA Backlog Grant Program. Introduced by MALONEY, D-N.Y., on Jan. 17, 2008. House Judiciary reported, amended, July 14

(H Rept 110-757). House passed, amended, under suspension of the rules, July 14. Senate Health, Education, Labor and Pensions discharged. Senate Judiciary discharged. Senate passed, amended, Sept. 25. House agreed to Senate amendment, under suspension of the rules, Sept. 27. President signed Oct. 8, 2008.

■ **PL 110-361** (HR 5265) Amend the Public Health Service Act to provide for research with respect to various forms of muscular dystrophy, including Becker, congenital, distal, Duchenne, Emery-Dreifuss facioscapulohumeral, limb-girdle, myotonic and oculopharyngeal. Introduced by ENGEL, D-N.Y., on Feb. 7, 2008. House passed, amended, under suspension of the rules, Sept. 24. Senate passed, amended, Sept. 26. House agreed to Senate amendment Sept. 27. President signed Oct. 8, 2008.

■ **PL 110-362** (HR 5571) Extend for five years the program allowing for a waiver of the foreign country residence requirement for international medical graduates. Introduced by LOFGREN, D-Calif., on March 10, 2008. House Judiciary reported May 15 (H Rept 110-646). House passed, amended, under suspension of the rules, May 21. Senate Judiciary discharged. Senate passed, amended, Sept. 26. House agreed to Senate amendment, under suspension of the rules, Sept. 27. President signed Oct. 8, 2008.

■ **PL 110-363** (HR 5872) Require the secretary of the Treasury to mint coins in commemoration of the centennial of the Boy Scouts of America. Introduced by SESSIONS, R-Texas, on April 22, 2008. House passed, amended, under suspension of the rules, May 15. Senate Banking, Housing and Urban Affairs discharged. Senate passed Sept. 27. President signed Oct. 8, 2008.

■ **PL 110-364** (HR 6370) Transfer excess federal property administered by the Coast Guard to the Confederated Tribes of the Coos, Lower Umpqua and Siuslaw Indians. Introduced by DEFAZIO, D-Ore., on June 25, 2008. House Transportation and Infrastructure reported Sept. 22 (H Rept 110-865). House passed, under suspension of the rules, Sept. 22. Senate passed Sept. 24. President signed Oct. 8, 2008.

■ **PL 110-365** (HR 6460) Amend the Federal Water Pollution Control Act to provide for the remediation of sediment contamination in areas of concern. Introduced by EHLERS, R-Mich., on July 10, 2008. House Transportation and Infrastructure reported, amended, Sept. 15 (H Rept 110-849, Part 1). House Science and Technology discharged. House passed, amended, under suspension of the rules, Sept. 18. Senate passed, amended, Sept. 25. House agreed to Senate amendment, under suspension of the rules, Sept. 28. President signed Oct. 8, 2008.

■ **PL 110-366** (HR 6890) Extend the waiver authority for the secretary of Education under Section 105, Subtitle A of Title IV of Division B of PL 109-148, relating to hurricane relief for elementary and secondary schools. Introduced by MELANCON, D-La., on Sept. 15, 2008. House passed, amended, under suspension of the rules, Sept. 22. Senate passed Sept. 25. President signed Oct. 8, 2008.

■ **PL 110-367** (HR 6894) Extend and reauthorize the Defense Production Act of 1950. Introduced by GUTIERREZ, D-Ill., on Sept. 15,

2008. House passed, under suspension of the rules, Sept. 23. Senate passed Sept. 25. President signed Oct. 8, 2008.

■ **PL 110-368** (HR 6946) Make a technical correction in the NET 911 Improvement Act of 2008. Introduced by DINGELL, D-Mich., on Sept. 18, 2008. House Energy and Commerce discharged. House passed Sept. 25. Senate passed Sept. 27. President signed Oct. 8, 2008.

■ **PL 110-369** (HR 7081) Approve the U.S.-India Agreement for Cooperation on Peaceful Uses of Nuclear Energy. Introduced by BERMAN, D-Calif., on Sept. 25, 2008. House passed, under suspension of the rules, Sept. 27. Senate passed Oct. 1. President signed Oct. 8, 2008.

■ **PL 110-370** (H J Res 62) Honor the achievements and contributions to the United States by Native Americans. Introduced by BACA, D-Calif., on Nov. 13, 2007. House passed, under suspension of the rules, Nov. 13. Senate Indian Affairs reported, amended, July 31, 2008 (S Rept 110-435). Senate passed, amended, Sept. 22. House agreed to Senate amendment Sept. 26. President signed Oct. 8, 2008.

■ **PL 110-371** (S 496) Reauthorize and improve the program authorized by the Appalachian Regional Development Act of 1965. Introduced by VOINOVICH, R-Ohio, on Feb. 6, 2007. Senate Environment and Public Works reported, amended, May 7 (S Rept 110-63). Senate passed, amended, Aug. 3. House passed, amended, under suspension of the rules, July 15, 2008. Senate agreed to House amendment Sept. 26. President signed Oct. 8, 2008.

■ **PL 110-372** (S 1046) Modify pay provisions relating to certain senior-level positions in the federal government. Introduced by VOINOVICH, R-Ohio, on March 29, 2007. Senate Homeland Security and Governmental Affairs reported April 22, 2008 (S Rept 110-328). Senate passed, amended, July 11. House passed, under suspension of the rules, Sept. 26. President signed Oct. 8, 2008.

■ **PL 110-373** (S 1382) Amend the Public Health Service Act to provide for the establishment of an Amyotrophic Lateral Sclerosis Registry. Introduced by REID, D-Nev., on May 14, 2007. Senate Health, Education, Labor and Pensions reported, amended, Dec. 4 (no written report). Senate passed, amended, Sept. 23, 2008. House passed, under suspension of the rules, Sept. 26. President signed Oct. 8, 2008.

■ **PL 110-374** (S 1810) Amend the Public Health Service Act to increase the provision of scientifically sound information and support services to patients receiving a positive test diagnosis for Down syndrome or other prenatally and postnatally diagnosed conditions. Introduced by BROWNBACK, R-Kan., on July 18, 2007. Senate Health, Education, Labor and Pensions reported, amended, April 21, 2008 (no written report). Senate passed, amended, Sept. 23. House passed, under suspension of the rules, Sept. 25. President signed Oct. 8, 2008.

■ **PL 110-375** (S 2482) Repeal the provision of Title 46, U.S. Code, requiring a license for employment in the business of salvaging on the coast of Florida. Introduced by NELSON, D-Fla., on Dec. 13, 2007. Senate Commerce, Science and Transportation reported May 22,

2008 (S Rept 110-340). Senate passed June 5. House passed, under suspension of the rules, Sept. 27. President signed Oct. 8, 2008.

■ **PL 110-376** (S 2606) Reauthorize the U.S. Fire Administration. Introduced by DODD, D-Conn., on Feb. 7, 2008. Senate Homeland Security and Governmental Affairs reported, amended, July 10 (S Rept 110-411). Senate passed, amended, Sept. 18. House passed, under suspension of the rules, Sept. 24. President signed Oct. 8, 2008.

■ **PL 110-377** (S 2932) Amend the Public Health Service Act to reauthorize the national poison center toll-free number, national media campaign and grant program to provide assistance for poison prevention, sustain the funding of poison centers and enhance the public health of people of the United States. Introduced by MURRAY, D-Wash., on April 29, 2008. Senate Health, Education, Labor and Pensions discharged. Senate passed, amended, Sept. 23. House passed, under suspension of the rules, Sept. 26. President signed Oct. 8, 2008.

■ **PL 110-378** (S 2982) Amend the Runaway and Homeless Youth Act to authorize appropriations. Introduced by LEAHY, D-Vt., on May 6, 2008. Senate Judiciary reported, amended, May 22 (no written report). Senate passed, amended, Sept. 25. House passed Sept. 26. President signed Oct. 8, 2008.

■ **PL 110-379** (S 3560) Amend Title XIX of the Social Security Act to provide additional funds for the qualifying individual program. Introduced by BAUCUS, D-Mont., on Sept. 24, 2008. Senate Finance discharged. Senate passed Sept. 25. House passed, under suspension of the rules, Sept. 27. President signed Oct. 8, 2008.

■ **PL 110-380** (S 3597) Provide that funds allocated for community food projects for fiscal 2008 remain available until Sept. 30, 2009. Introduced by HARKIN, D-Iowa, on Sept. 25, 2008. Senate passed Sept. 25. House passed, under suspension of the rules, Sept. 27. President signed Oct. 8, 2008.

■ **PL 110-381** (HR 2851) Amend the Employee Retirement Income Security Act of 1974, the Public Health Service Act and the Internal Revenue Code of 1986 to ensure that dependent students who take a medically necessary leave of absence do not lose health insurance coverage. Introduced by HODES, D-N.H., on June 25, 2007. House Energy and Commerce reported, amended, July 30, 2008 (H Rept 110-806, Part 1). House Education and Labor and House Ways and Means discharged. House passed, amended, under suspension of the rules, July 30. Senate Health, Education, Labor and Pensions discharged. Senate passed Sept. 25. President signed Oct. 9, 2008.

■ **PL 110-382** (S 2840) Establish a liaison with the FBI in U.S. Citizenship and Immigration Services to expedite naturalization applications filed by members of the Armed Forces and to establish a deadline for processing such applications. Introduced by SCHUMER, D-N.Y., on April 10, 2008. Senate Judiciary reported, amended, Aug. 1 (S Rept 110-440). Senate passed, amended, Sept. 24. House passed, under suspension of the rules, Sept. 28. President signed Oct. 9, 2008.

■ **PL 110-383** (HR 2963) Transfer certain land in Riverside County, Calif., and San Diego County, Calif., from the Bureau of Land Management to the United States to be held in trust for the Pechanga Band of Luiseño Mission Indians. Introduced by ISSA, R-Calif., on July 10, 2007. House Natural Resources discharged. House passed July 30. Senate Indian Affairs reported, amended, Sept. 25, 2008 (S Rept 110-503). Senate passed, amended, Sept. 26. House agreed to Senate amendments Sept. 29. President signed Oct. 10, 2008.

■ **PL 110-384** (HR 3480) Direct the U.S. Sentencing Commission to assure appropriate punishment enhancements for those involved in receiving stolen property consisting of veterans' grave markers. Introduced by CARNEY, D-Pa., on Sept. 6, 2007. House Judiciary reported, amended, May 15, 2008 (H Rept 110-647). House passed, amended, under suspension of the rules, May 21. Senate Judiciary reported June 12 (no written report). Senate passed Oct. 2. President signed Oct. 10, 2008.

■ **PL 110-385** (S 1492) Improve the quality of federal and state data on the availability and quality of broadband services and promote the deployment of affordable broadband services to all parts of the nation. Introduced by INOUYE, D-Hawaii, on May 24, 2007. Senate Commerce, Science and Transportation reported, amended, Oct. 24 (S Rept 110-204). Senate passed, amended, Sept. 26, 2008. House Energy and Commerce discharged. House passed, amended, Sept. 29. Senate agreed to House amendments Sept. 30. President signed Oct. 10, 2008.

■ **PL 110-386** (S 1582) Reauthorize and amend the Hydrographic Services Improvement Act. Introduced by INOUYE, D-Hawaii, on June 7, 2007. Senate Commerce, Science and Transportation reported, amended, Nov. 2 (S Rept 110-218). Senate passed, amended, Sept. 6, 2008. House passed Sept. 29. President signed Oct. 10, 2008.

■ **PL 110-387** (S 2162) Improve the treatment and services provided by the Department of Veterans Affairs to veterans with post-traumatic stress disorder and substance use disorders. Introduced by AKAKA, D-Hawaii, on Oct. 15, 2007. Senate Veterans' Affairs reported, amended, April 8, 2008 (S Rept 110-281). Senate passed, amended, June 3. House passed, amended, under suspension of the rules, Sept. 24. Senate agreed to House amendment Sept. 27. President signed Oct. 10, 2008.

■ **PL 110-388** (S 2816) Provide for the secretary of Homeland Security to appoint a chief human capital officer for the department. Introduced by VOINOVICH, R-Ohio, on April 3, 2008. Senate Homeland Security and Governmental Affairs reported Sept. 16 (S Rept 110-466). Senate passed Sept. 23. House passed, under suspension of the rules, Sept. 27. President signed Oct. 10, 2008.

■ **PL 110-389** (S 3023) Amend Title 38, U.S. Code, to improve and enhance compensation; pensions; and housing, labor, education and insurance benefits for veterans. Introduced by AKAKA, D-Hawaii, on May 15, 2008. Senate Veterans' Affairs reported, amended, Sept. 9 (S Rept 110-449). Senate passed, amended, Sept. 16. House passed, amended, under suspension of the rules, Sept. 24. Senate agreed to House amendment Sept. 27. President signed Oct. 10, 2008.

■ **PL 110-390** (S 3128) Direct the secretary of the Interior to provide a loan to the White Mountain Apache Tribe for use in planning, engineering and designing a certain water system project. Introduced by KYL, R-Ariz., on June 12, 2008. Senate Indian Affairs reported, amended, Sept. 24 (S Rept 110-502). Senate passed, amended, Sept. 25. House Natural Resources discharged. House passed Sept. 29. President signed Oct. 10, 2008.

■ **PL 110-391** (S 3606) Extend the special immigrant non-minister religious worker program. Introduced by HATCH, R-Utah, on Sept. 26, 2008. Senate passed Sept. 26. House passed, under suspension of the rules, Sept. 27. President signed Oct. 10, 2008.

■ **PL 110-392** (HR 1532) Amend the Public Health Service Act with respect to making progress toward eliminating tuberculosis. Introduced by G. GREEN, D-Texas, on March 15, 2007. House Energy and Commerce reported, amended, Sept. 23, 2008 (H Rept 110-873). House passed, amended, under suspension of the rules, Sept. 24. Senate passed Sept. 27. President signed Oct. 13, 2008.

■ **PL 110-393** (HR 5350) Authorize the secretary of Commerce to sell or exchange certain National Oceanic and Atmospheric Administration property located in Norfolk, Va. Introduced by SCOTT, D-Va., on Feb. 12, 2008. House Natural Resources reported, amended, Aug. 1 (H Rept 110-822, Part 1). House Oversight and Government Reform discharged. House passed, amended, under suspension of the rules, Sept. 17. Senate passed, amended, Sept. 26. House agreed to Senate amendment Sept. 29. President signed Oct. 13, 2008.

■ **PL 110-394** (HR 5618) Reauthorize and amend the National Sea Grant College Program Act. Introduced by BORDALLO, D-Guam, on March 13, 2008. House Natural Resources reported, amended, June 9 (H Rept 110-701, Part 1). House Science and Technology reported, amended, July 11 (H Rept 110-701, Part 2). House passed, amended, under suspension of the rules, July 14. Senate Commerce, Science and Transportation discharged. Senate passed, amended, Sept. 26. House agreed to Senate amendment Sept. 29. President signed Oct. 13, 2008.

■ **PL 110-395** (HR 6199) Designate the facility of the U.S. Postal Service located at 245 N. Main St. in New City, N.Y., as the "Kenneth Peter Zebrowski Post Office Building." Introduced by ENGEL, D-N.Y., on June 5, 2008. House Oversight and Government Reform discharged. House passed Sept. 24. Senate passed Sept. 30. President signed Oct. 13, 2008.

■ **PL 110-396** (HR 6229) Designate the facility of the U.S. Postal Service located at 2523 7th Ave. East in North St. Paul, Minn., as the "Mayor William 'Bill' Sandberg Post Office Building." Introduced by MCCOLLUM, D-Minn., on June 10, 2008. House passed, under suspension of the rules, Sept. 18. Senate passed Sept. 30. President signed Oct. 13, 2008.

■ **PL 110-397** (HR 6338) Designate the facility of the U.S. Postal Service located at 4233 W. Hillsboro Blvd. in Coconut Creek, Fla., as the "Army Spc. Daniel Agami Post Office Building." Introduced by KLEIN, D-Fla., on June 20, 2008. House passed, under suspension of the rules, Sept. 18. Senate passed Sept. 30. President signed Oct. 13, 2008.

■ **PL 110-398** (HR 6849) Amend the commodity provisions of the Food, Conservation and Energy Act of 2008 to permit producers to aggregate base acres and reconstitute farms to avoid the prohibition on receiving direct payments, countercyclical payments or average crop revenue election payments when the sum of the base acres of a farm is 10 acres or less. Introduced by ETHERIDGE, D-N.C., on Sept. 9, 2008. House Agriculture reported, amended, Sept. 24 (H Rept 110-881). House passed, amended, under suspension of the rules, Sept. 24. Senate passed, amended, Sept. 29. House agreed to Senate amendment Sept. 29. President signed Oct. 13, 2008.

■ **PL 110-399** (HR 6874) Designate the facility of the U.S. Postal Service located at 156 Taunton Ave. in Seekonk, Mass., as the "Lance Cpl. Eric Paul Valdepenas Post Office Building." Introduced by MCGOVERN, D-Mass., on Sept. 11, 2008. House Oversight and Government Reform discharged. House passed Sept. 24. Senate passed Sept. 30. President signed Oct. 13, 2008.

■ **PL 110-400** (S 431) Require convicted sex offenders to register online identifiers. Introduced by SCHUMER, D-N.Y., on Jan. 30, 2007. Senate Judiciary reported, amended, April 22, 2008 (S Rept 110-332). Senate passed, amended, May 20. House passed, amended, Sept. 27. Senate agreed to House amendment Sept. 30. President signed Oct. 13, 2008.

■ **PL 110-401** (S 1738) Establish a National Strategy for Child Exploitation Prevention and Interdiction within the Office of the Deputy Attorney General to improve the Internet Crimes Against Children Task Force, to increase resources for regional computer forensic labs and to make other improvements to increase the ability of law enforcement agencies to investigate and prosecute predators. Introduced by BIDEN, D-Del., on June 28, 2007. Senate Judiciary reported, amended, July 7, 2008 (no written report). Senate passed, amended, Sept. 25. House passed, under suspension of the rules, Sept. 27. President signed Oct. 13, 2008.

■ **PL 110-402** (S 3296) Extend the authority of the U.S. Supreme Court Police to protect court officials off the Supreme Court grounds and change the title of the Administrative Assistant to the Chief Justice to Counselor to the Chief Justice. Introduced by LEAHY, D-Vt., on July 21, 2008. Senate Judiciary reported Sept. 11 (no written report). Senate passed, amended, Sept. 25. House passed, under suspension of the rules, Sept. 29. President signed Oct. 13, 2008.

■ **PL 110-403** (S 3325) Enhance remedies for violations of intellectual property laws. Introduced by LEAHY, D-Vt., on July 24, 2008. Senate Judiciary reported, amended, Sept. 15 (no written report). Senate passed, amended, Sept. 28. House passed, under suspension of the rules, Sept. 28. President signed Oct. 13, 2008.

■ **PL 110-404** (S 3477) Amend Title 44, U.S. Code, to authorize grants for Presidential Centers of Historical Excellence. Introduced by WARNER, R-Va., on Sept. 11, 2008. Senate Homeland Security and Governmental Affairs reported, amended, Sept. 25 (no written report). Senate passed, amended, Sept. 26. House passed, under suspension of the rules, Sept. 27. President signed Oct. 13, 2008.

■ **PL 110-405** (S 3536) Amend section 5402 of Title 39, U.S. Code, to modify the authority relating to U.S. Postal Service air transportation contracts. Introduced by CARPER, D-Del., on Sept. 22, 2008. Senate Homeland Security and Governmental Affairs discharged. Senate passed Sept. 26. House passed, under suspension of the rules, Sept. 29. President signed Oct. 13, 2008.

■ **PL 110-406** (S 3569) Make improvements in the operation and administration of the federal courts. Introduced by SCHUMER, D-N.Y., on Sept. 24, 2008. Senate Judiciary discharged. Senate passed Sept. 27. House passed, under suspension of the rules, Sept. 27. President signed Oct. 13, 2008.

■ **PL 110-407** (S 3598) Amend titles 46 and 18, U.S. Code, with respect to the operation of submersible vessels and semi-submersible vessels without nationality. Introduced by INOUYE, D-Hawaii, on Sept. 25, 2008. Senate passed Sept. 25. House passed, under suspension of the rules, Sept. 29. President signed Oct. 13, 2008.

■ **PL 110-408** (S 3605) Extend the pilot program for volunteer groups to obtain criminal-history background checks. Introduced by BIDEN, D-Del., on Sept. 26, 2008. Senate passed Sept. 26. House Judiciary discharged. House passed Sept. 27. President signed Oct. 13, 2008.

■ **PL 110-409** (HR 928) Amend the Inspector General Act of 1978 to enhance the independence of inspectors general and to create a Council of the Inspectors General on Integrity and Efficiency. Introduced by COOPER, D-Tenn., on Feb. 8, 2007. House Oversight and Government Reform reported, amended, Sept. 27 (H Rept 110-354). House passed, amended, Oct. 3. Senate Homeland Security and Governmental Affairs discharged. Senate passed, amended, Sept. 24, 2008. House agreed to Senate amendment, under suspension of the rules, Sept. 27. President signed Oct. 14, 2008.

■ **PL 110-410** (HR 1594) Designate the Department of Veterans Affairs Outpatient Clinic in Hermitage, Pa., as the "Michael A. Marzano Department of Veterans Affairs Outpatient Clinic." Introduced by ENGLISH, R-Pa., on March 20, 2007. House passed, under suspension of the rules, Sept. 17, 2008. Senate passed Sept. 30. President signed Oct. 14, 2008.

■ **PL 110-411** (HR 2786) Reauthorize programs for housing assistance for American Indians. Introduced by KILDEE, D-Mich., on June 20, 2007. House Financial Services reported Aug. 3 (H Rept 110-295). House passed, amended, Sept. 6. Senate Indian Affairs discharged. Senate passed, amended, Sept. 25, 2008. House agreed to Senate amendment, under suspension of the rules, Sept. 27. President signed Oct. 14, 2008.

■ **PL 110-412** (HR 6098) Amend the Homeland Security Act of 2002 to improve the financial assistance provided to state, local and tribal governments for information-sharing activities. Introduced by REICHERT, R-Wash., on May 20, 2008. House Homeland Security reported, amended, July 10 (H Rept 110-752). House passed, amended, under suspension of the rules, July 29. Senate Homeland Security and Governmental Affairs reported, amended, Sept. 24 (no written report). Senate passed, amended, Sept. 27. House agreed to Senate amendment Sept. 29. President signed Oct. 14, 2008.

■ **PL 110-413** (HR 7198) Establish the Stephanie Tubbs Jones Gift of Life Medal for organ donors and the families of organ donors. Introduced by STARK, D-Calif., on Sept. 28, 2008. House Financial Services and House Energy and Commerce discharged. House passed Sept. 29. Senate passed Oct. 1. President signed Oct. 14, 2008.

■ **PL 110-414** (S 906) Prohibit the sale, distribution, transfer and export of elemental mercury. Introduced by OBAMA, D-Ill., on March 15, 2007. Senate Environment and Public Works reported, amended, Sept. 22, 2008 (S Rept 110-477). Senate passed, amended, Sept. 26. House passed, under suspension of the rules, Sept. 29. President signed Oct. 14, 2008.

■ **PL 110-415** (S 1276) Establish a grant program to facilitate the creation of methamphetamine precursor electronic logbook systems. Introduced by DURBIN, D-Ill., on May 3, 2007. Senate Judiciary reported, amended, Sept. 15, 2008 (no written report). Senate passed, amended, Sept. 25. House Energy and Commerce and House Judiciary discharged. House passed Sept. 29. President signed Oct. 14, 2008.

■ **PL 110-416** (S 2304) Amend Title I of the Omnibus Crime Control and Safe Streets Act of 1968 to provide grants for the mental health treatment and services provided to offenders with mental illnesses. Introduced by DOMENICI, R-N.M., on Nov. 5, 2007. Senate Judiciary reported, amended, April 1, 2008 (no written report). Senate passed, amended, Sept. 26. House passed, under suspension of the rules, Sept. 29. President signed Oct. 14, 2008.

■ **PL 110-417** (S 3001) Authorize appropriations for fiscal 2009 for military activities of the Department of Defense, military construction, and defense activities of the Department of Energy and to prescribe military personnel strengths for the fiscal year. Introduced by LEVIN, D-Mich., on May 12, 2008. Senate Armed Services reported May 12 (S Rept 110-335). Senate passed, amended, Sept. 17. House passed, amended, under suspension of the rules, Sept. 24. Senate agreed to House amendment Sept. 27. President signed Oct. 14, 2008.

■ **PL 110-418** (S 3550) Designate a portion of the Rappahannock River in the Commonwealth of Virginia as the "John W. Warner Rapids." Introduced by BOXER, D-Calif., on Sept. 24, 2008. Senate Environment and Public Works reported Sept. 24 (no written report). Senate passed Sept. 24. House Natural Resources discharged. House passed Sept. 29. President signed Oct. 14, 2008.

■ **PL 110-419** (HR 1714) Clarify the boundaries of Coastal Barrier Resources System Clam Pass Unit FL-64P. Introduced by MACK, R-Fla., on March 27, 2007. House passed, under suspension of the rules, July 14, 2008. Senate Environment and Public Works discharged. Senate passed Sept. 30. President signed Oct. 15, 2008.

■ **PL 110-420** (HR 4544) Require the issuance of medals to recognize the dedication and valor of American Indian code talkers. Introduced by BOREN, D-Okla., on Dec. 13, 2007. House passed, amended, Sept. 25, 2008. Senate passed Sept. 30. President signed Oct. 15, 2008.

■ **PL 110-421** (HR 6045) Amend Title I of the Omnibus Crime Control and Safe Streets Act of 1968 to extend the authorization of the Bulletproof Vest Partnership Grant Program through fiscal 2012.

Introduced by VISCLOSKY, D-Ind., on May 13, 2008. House passed, under suspension of the rules, Sept. 26. Senate passed Sept. 30. President signed Oct. 15, 2008.

■ **PL 110-422** (HR 6063) Authorize the programs of the National Aeronautics and Space Administration. Introduced by UDALL, D-Colo., on May 15, 2008. House Science and Technology reported, amended, June 9 (H Rept 110-702). House passed, amended, June 18. Senate Commerce, Science and Transportation discharged. Senate passed, amended, Sept. 25. House agreed to Senate amendment, under suspension of the rules, Sept. 27. President signed Oct. 15, 2008.

■ **PL 110-423** (HR 6073) Provide that federal employees receiving their pay by electronic funds transfer shall be given the option of receiving their pay stubs electronically. Introduced by FOXX, R-N.C., on May 15, 2008. House Oversight and Government Reform reported July 28 (H Rept 110-780). House passed, under suspension of the rules, July 30. Senate Homeland Security and Governmental Affairs reported Sept. 24 (no written report). Senate passed Sept. 30. President signed Oct. 15, 2008.

■ **PL 110-424** (HR 6083) Authorize funding to conduct a national training program for state and local prosecutors. Introduced by SPRATT, D-S.C., on May 19, 2008. House Judiciary reported July 29 (H Rept 110-784). House passed, under suspension of the rules, July 31. Senate Judiciary discharged. Senate passed Sept. 30, 2008. President signed Oct. 15, 2008.

■ **PL 110-425** (HR 6353) Amend the Controlled Substances Act to address online pharmacies. Introduced by STUPAK, D-Mich., on June 24, 2008. House Energy and Commerce reported, amended, Sept. 23. (H Rept 110-869, Part 1). House Judiciary discharged. House passed, amended, under suspension of the rules Sept. 23. Senate passed Sept. 30. President signed Oct. 15, 2008.

■ **PL 110-426** (HR 6469) Amend the Public Health Service Act to authorize increased federal funding for the Organ Procurement and Transplantation Network. Introduced by DEGETTE, D-Colo., on July 10, 2008. House passed, amended, under suspension of the rules Sept. 25. Senate passed, amended, Oct. 2. House agreed to Senate amendment Oct. 3. President signed Oct. 15, 2008.

■ **PL 110-427** (HR 6524) Authorize the Administrator of General Services to take certain actions with respect to parcels of real property located in Eastlake, Ohio, and Koochiching County, Minn. Introduced by LATOURETTE, R-Ohio, on July 16, 2008. House Transportation and Infrastructure reported Sept. 22 (H Rept 110-866, Part 1). House Armed Services discharged. House passed, under suspension of the rules, Sept. 22. Senate passed Sept. 30, 2008. President signed Oct. 15, 2008.

■ **PL 110-428** (HR 7082) Amend the Internal Revenue Code of 1986 to permit the secretary of the Treasury to disclose certain prisoner-return information to the Federal Bureau of Prisons. Introduced by RAMSTAD, R-Minn., on Sept. 25, 2008. House passed, amended, under suspension of the rules, Sept. 27. Senate passed Oct. 2. President signed Oct. 15, 2008.

■ **PL 110-429** (HR 7177) Authorize the transfer of naval vessels to certain foreign recipients. Introduced by BERMAN, D-Calif., on Sept. 27, 2008. House passed, under suspension of the rules, Sept. 27. Senate passed Oct. 1. President signed Oct. 15, 2008.

■ **PL 110-430** (H J Res 100) Appointing the day for the convening of the first session of the 111th Congress and establishing the date for the counting of the electoral votes for president and vice president cast by the electors in December 2008. Introduced by ARCURI, D-N.Y., on Sept. 28, 2008. House passed Sept. 28. Senate passed Oct. 2. President signed Oct. 15, 2008.

■ **PL 110-431** (S 3641) Authorize funding for the National Crime Victim Law Institute to provide support for victims of crime under Crime Victims Legal Assistance Programs as a part of the Victims of Crime Act of 1984. Introduced by KYL, R-Ariz., on Sept. 27, 2008. Senate passed Sept. 27. House passed, under suspension of the rules, Oct. 2. President signed Oct. 15, 2008.

■ **PL 110-432** (HR 2095) Amend Title 49, U.S. Code, to prevent railroad fatalities, injuries and hazardous-materials releases and to authorize the Federal Railroad Safety Administration. Introduced by OBERSTAR, D-Minn., on May 1, 2007. House Transportation reported, amended, Sept. 19 (H Rept 110-336). House passed, amended, Oct. 17. Senate Commerce, Science and Transportation discharged. Senate passed, amended, Aug 1. House agreed to Senate amendment, with an amendment, Sept. 24. Senate agreed to House amendment to Senate amendment Oct. 1. President signed Oct. 16, 2008.

■ **PL 110-433** (HR 6296) Extend through 2013 the authority of the Federal Election Commission to impose civil money penalties on the basis of a schedule of penalties established and published by the commission. Introduced by BRADY, D-Pa., on June 18, 2008. House passed, under suspension of the rules, July 15. Senate Rules and Administration discharged. Senate passed Oct. 2. President signed Oct. 16, 2008.

■ **PL 110-434** (HR 6531) Amend Chapter 13 of Title 17, U.S. Code to clarify the definitions of a vessel hull and a deck. Introduced by BERMAN, D-Calif., on July 17, 2008. House passed, under suspension of the rules, July 22. Senate passed Sept. 30. President signed Oct. 16, 2008.

■ **PL 110-435** (HR 7084) Amend section 114 of Title 17, U.S. Code, to provide for agreements for the reproduction and performance of sound recordings by webcasters. Introduced by INSLEE, D-Wash., on Sept. 25, 2008. House passed, under suspension of the rules, Sept. 27. Senate passed Sept 30. President signed Oct. 16, 2008.

■ **PL 110-436** (HR 7222) Extend the Andean Trade Preference Act. Introduced by RANGEL, D-N.Y., on Sept. 29, 2008. House Ways and Means discharged. House passed Sept. 29. Senate passed, amended, Oct. 2. House agreed to the Senate amendment Oct. 3. President signed Oct. 16, 2008.

■ **PL 110-437** (HR 5159) Establish the Office of the Capitol Visitor Center within the Office of the Architect of the Capitol, headed by the chief executive officer for visitor services, to provide for the

effective management and administration of the Capitol Visitor Center. Introduced by BRADY, D-Pa., on Jan. 29, 2008. House Administration reported, amended, March 3 (H Rept 110-535). House passed, under suspension of the rules, March 5. Senate passed, amended, Sept. 27. House agreed to the Senate amendment Oct. 2. President signed Oct. 20, 2008.

■ **PL 110-438** (S 3197) Amend Title 11, U.S. Code, to make it easier for members of the National Guard and reserve to file for bankruptcy by eliminating the means tests for those who serve for 90 days or more on active duty after Sept. 11, 2001. Introduced by DURBIN, D-Ill., on June 25, 2008. Senate Judiciary reported, amended, Sept. 15 (no written report). Senate passed, amended, Sept. 30. House passed, under suspension of the rules, Oct. 3. President signed Oct. 20, 2008.

■ **PL 110-439** (HR 3511) Designate the facility of the U.S. Postal Service located at 2150 East Hardtner Dr. in Urania, La., as the "Murphy A. Tannehill Post Office Building." Introduced by ALEXANDER, R-La., on Sept. 10, 2007. House Oversight and Government Reform discharged. House passed Sept. 24, 2008. Senate passed Sept. 30. President signed Oct. 21, 2008.

■ **PL 110-440** (HR 4010) Designate the facility of the U.S. Postal Service located at 100 West Percy St. in Indianola, Miss., as the "Minnie Cox Post Office Building." Introduced by THOMPSON, D-Miss., on Oct. 30, 2007. House passed, under suspension of the rules, July 14, 2008. Senate Homeland Security and Governmental Affairs discharged. Senate passed Oct. 2. President signed Oct. 21, 2008.

■ **PL 110-441** (HR 4131) Designate a portion of California State Route 91 located in Los Angeles County, Calif., as the "Juanita Millender-McDonald Highway." Introduced by RICHARDSON, D-Calif., on Nov. 9, 2007. House Transportation and Infrastructure reported Sept. 27, 2008 (H Rept 110-895). House passed, under suspension of the rules, Sept. 29. Senate passed Oct. 2. President signed Oct. 21, 2008.

■ **PL 110-442** (HR 6558) Designate the facility of the U.S. Postal Service located at 1750 Lundy Ave. in San Jose, Calif., as the "Gordon N. Chan Post Office Building." Introduced by HONDA, D-Calif., on July 21, 2008. House Oversight and Government Reform discharged. House passed Sept. 27. Senate passed Oct. 2. President signed Oct. 21, 2008.

■ **PL 110-443** (HR 6681) Designate the facility of the U.S. Postal Service located at 300 Vine St. in New Lenox, Ill., as the "Jacob M. Lowell Post Office Building." Introduced by WELLER, R-Ill., on July 30, 2008. House passed, under suspension of the rules, Sept. 18. Senate passed Sept. 30. President signed Oct. 21, 2008.

■ **PL 110-444** (HR 6834) Designate the facility of the U.S. Postal Service located at 4 South Main St. in Wallingford, Conn., as the "Chief Warrant Officer Richard R. Lee Post Office Building." Introduced by DELAURO, D-Conn., on Sept. 8, 2008. House Oversight and Government Reform discharged. House passed Sept. 27. Senate passed Oct. 2. President signed Oct. 21, 2008.

■ **PL 110-445** (HR 6847) Designate the facility of the U.S. Postal Service located at 801 Industrial Blvd. in Ellijay, Ga., as the "First Lieuten-ant Noah Harris Ellijay Post Office Building." Introduced by DEAL, R-Ga., on Sept. 9, 2008. House passed, under suspension of the rules, Sept. 25. Senate passed Sept. 30. President signed Oct. 21, 2008.

■ **PL 110-446** (HR 6902) Designate the facility of the U.S. Postal Service located at 513 6th Ave. in Dayton, Ky., as the "Staff Sergeant Nicholas Ray Carnes Post Office." Introduced by DAVIS, R-Ky., on Sept. 15, 2008. House Oversight and Government Reform discharged. House passed Sept. 27. Senate passed Oct. 2. President signed Oct. 21, 2008.

■ **PL 110-447** (HR 6982) Designate the facility of the U.S. Postal Service located at 210 South Ellsworth Ave. in San Mateo, Calif., as the "Leo J. Ryan Post Office Building." Introduced by SPEIER, D-Calif., on Sept. 22, 2008. House Oversight and Government Reform discharged. House passed Sept. 27. Senate passed Oct. 2. President signed Oct. 21, 2008.

■ **PL 110-448** (HR 6197) Designate the facility of the U.S. Postal Service located at 7095 Highway 57 in Counce, Tenn., as the "Pickwick Post Office Building." Introduced by BLACKBURN, R-Tenn., on June 5, 2008. House Oversight and Government Reform discharged. House passed Sept. 27. Senate passed Oct. 2. President signed on Oct. 22, 2008.

■ **PL 110-449** (HR 6867) Provide for additional emergency unemployment compensation. Introduced by MCDERMOTT, D-Wash., Sept. 10, 2008. House passed, amended, under suspension of the rules, Oct. 3. Senate passed Nov. 20. President signed Nov. 21, 2008.

■ **PL 110-450** (HR 5714) Require the secretary of the Treasury to mint coins in recognition and celebration of the establishment of the U.S. Army in 1775; to honor the American soldier of today and yesterday, in wartime and in peace; and to commemorate the traditions, history, and heritage of the U.S. Army and its role in American society. Introduced by SKELTON, D-Mo., April 8, 2008. House Financial Services discharged. House passed, amended, Oct. 3. Senate passed Nov. 17. President signed Dec. 1, 2008.

■ **PL 110-451** (HR 2040) Require the secretary of the Treasury to mint coins in commemoration of the semicentennial of the enactment of the Civil Rights Act of 1964. Introduced by LEWIS, D-Ga., April 25, 2007. House passed, amended, under suspension of the rules, April 1, 2008. Senate Banking, Housing and Urban Affairs discharged. Senate passed Nov. 19. President signed Dec. 2, 2008.

■ **PL 110-452** (S 602) Develop the next generation of parental-control technology. Introduced by PRYOR, D-Ark., Feb. 15, 2007. Senate Commerce, Science and Transportation reported, amended, March 3, 2008 (S Rept 110-268). Senate passed, amended, Oct. 1. House Energy and Commerce discharged. House passed, amended, Oct. 3. Senate agreed to House amendment Nov. 17. President signed Dec. 2, 2008.

■ **PL 110-453** (S 1193) Direct the secretary of the Interior to take into trust two parcels of federal land for the benefit of certain Indian Pueblos in the state of New Mexico. Introduced by DOMENICI, R-N.M., April 24, 2007. Senate Indian Affairs reported July 31, 2008

(S Rept 110-434). Senate passed Sept. 22. House Natural Resources discharged. House passed, amended, Sept. 29. Senate agreed to House amendments Nov. 19. President signed Dec. 2, 2008.

■ **PL 110-454** (HR 6859) Designate the facility of the U.S. Postal Service located at 1501 S. Slappey Blvd. in Albany, Ga., as the "Dr. Walter Carl Gordon Jr. Post Office Building." Introduced by BISHOP, D-Ga., Sept. 10, 2008. House Oversight and Government Reform discharged. House passed Sept. 27. Senate passed Nov. 20. President signed Dec. 19, 2008.

■ **PL 110-455** (S J Res 46) Ensure that the compensation and other emoluments attached to the office of secretary of State are those that were in effect on Jan. 1, 2007. Introduced by REID, D-Nev., Dec. 10, 2008. Senate passed Dec. 10. House passed Dec. 10. President signed Dec. 19, 2008.

■ **PL 110-456** (HR 6184) Provide for a program circulating quarter-dollar coins that are emblematic of a national park or other national site in each state, the District of Columbia and each U.S. territory. Introduced by CASTLE, R-Del., June 4, 2008. House Financial Services reported July 8 (H Rept 110-748). House passed, under suspension of the rules, July 9. Senate Banking, Housing and Urban Affairs discharged. Senate passed Dec. 10. President signed Dec. 23, 2008.

■ **PL 110-457** (HR 7311) Authorize appropriations for fiscal years 2008 through 2011 for the Trafficking Victims Protection Act of 2000 and enhance measures to combat trafficking in persons. Introduced by BERMAN, D-Calif., Dec. 9, 2008. House Foreign Affairs, Energy and Commerce, and Judiciary discharged. House passed Dec. 10. Senate passed Dec. 10. President signed Dec. 23, 2008.

■ **PL 110-458** (HR 7327) Make technical corrections related to the Pension Protection Act of 2006. Introduced by RANGEL, D-N.Y., Dec. 10, 2008. House Ways and Means and Education and Labor discharged. House passed Dec. 10. Senate passed Dec. 11. President signed Dec. 23, 2008.

■ **PL 110-459** (S 3663) Require the Federal Communications Commission to provide for a short-term extension of the analog television broadcasting authority so that essential public safety announcements and digital television transition information may be provided for a short time during the transition to digital television broadcasting. Introduced by ROCKEFELLER, D-W.Va., Oct. 1, 2008. Senate Commerce, Science and Transportation discharged. Senate passed, amended, Nov. 20. House Energy and Commerce discharged. House passed Dec. 10. President signed Dec. 23, 2008.

■ **PL 110-460** (S 3712) Make a technical correction in the Paul Wellstone and Pete Domenici Mental Health Parity and Addiction Equity Act of 2008. Introduced by KENNEDY, D-Mass., Nov. 20, 2008. Senate passed Nov. 20. House Energy and Commerce, Education and Labor, and Ways and Means discharged. House passed Dec. 10. President signed Dec. 23, 2008. ■

Appendix H

HOUSE
ROLL CALL
VOTES

House Roll Call Index
By Bill Number

IN THE HOUSE | By Vote Number

1. **Quorum Call.*** 393 members responded (38 members did not respond). Jan. 15, 2008.

2. **HR 2768. Mine Safety Standards/Previous Question.**
Slaughter, D-N.Y., motion to order the previous question (thus ending debate and possibility of amendment) on adoption of the rule (H Res 918) that would provide for House floor consideration of the bill that would authorize the Mine Safety and Health Administration to close mines that fail to address safety violations and increase penalties for mine operators with multiple violations. Motion agreed to 222-191: R 0-190; D 222-1 (ND 169-0, SD 53-1). Subsequently, the rule was adopted by voice vote. Jan. 16, 2008.

3. **H Res 912. Condemn Assassination of Benazir Bhutto/ Adoption.** Ackerman, D-N.Y., motion to suspend the rules and adopt the resolution that would condemn the assassination of former Pakistani Prime Minister Benazir Bhutto and express condolences to her family and the families of other victims of the Dec. 27, 2007, attack. A two-thirds majority of those present and voting (276 in this case) is required for adoption under suspension of the rules. Motion agreed to 413-0: R 189-0; D 224-0 (ND 170-0, SD 54-0). Jan. 16, 2008.

4. **HR 4253. Veterans' Business Assistance/Adoption.**
Velázquez, D-N.Y., motion to suspend the rules and adopt the resolution (H Res 921) to concur with the Senate amendment to the bill with an amendment. The House amendment would strike a provision from the Senate amendment that would require a study to examine obstacles facing veterans who want to start businesses, as well as a provision to eliminate employment loans under the bill's disaster program. Motion agreed to 406-2: R 185-2; D 221-0 (ND 169-0, SD 52-0). A two-thirds majority of those present and voting (272 in this case) is required for adoption under suspension of the rules. Jan. 16, 2008.

5. **HR 2768. Mine Safety Standards/Safety Equipment Requirements.** Miller, D-Calif., amendment that would give the mining industry an additional 90 days to install fire-resistant conveyor belts and authorize $30 million for the Mine Safety and Heath Administration to purchase new dust-monitoring devices. It would establish that requirements in the bill for portable air chambers can be met only by obtaining a chamber, not by placing an order for one. Adopted in Committee of the Whole 234-183: R 8-183; D 226-0 (ND 171-0, SD 55-0). Jan. 16, 2008.

6. **HR 2768. Mine Safety Standards/Mental Health Grants.**
Boucher, D-Va., amendment that would authorize $10 million for grants to provide rehabilitation services to current and former miners suffering from work-related drug dependency. Adopted in Committee of the Whole 364-53: R 138-53; D 226-0 (ND 171-0, SD 55-0). Jan. 16, 2008.

7. **HR 2768. Mine Safety Standards/Safety Program Fund.**
Ellsworth, D-Ind., amendment that would require the Labor secretary to maintain a list of mine operators who fail to pay assessed penalties. An operator would remain on the list until the secretary determines the operator is no longer in arrears or is committed to timely payments of final assessments. The amendment would establish the Mine Safety Program Fund for mine safety inspections and investigations. Adopted in Committee of the Whole 416-0: R 189-0; D 227-0 (ND 172-0, SD 55-0). Jan. 16, 2008.

*CQ does not include quorum calls in its vote charts.

[1]Bobby Jindal, R.-La., resigned Jan. 14, 2008, to become governor. He was not eligible for any votes in 2008.

[2]Roger Wicker, R-Miss., resigned Dec. 31, 2007, to accept appointment to a Senate seat. He was not eligible for any votes in 2008.

ND Northern Democrats, SD Southern Democrats
Southern states: Ala., Ark., Fla., Ga., Ky., La., Miss., N.C., Okla., S.C., Tenn., Texas, Va.Southern states: Ala., Ark., Fla., Ga., Ky., La., Miss., N.C., Okla., S.C., Tenn., Texas, Va.

		2	3	4	5	6	7
ALABAMA							
1	**Bonner**	N	Y	Y	N	N	Y
2	**Everett**	N	Y	Y	N	N	Y
3	**Rogers**	N	Y	Y	N	Y	Y
4	**Aderholt**	N	Y	Y	N	N	Y
5	Cramer	Y	Y	Y	Y	Y	Y
6	**Bachus**	N	Y	Y	N	Y	Y
7	Davis	Y	Y	Y	Y	Y	Y
ALASKA							
AL	**Young**	N	Y	Y	N	Y	Y
ARIZONA							
1	**Renzi**	N	Y	Y	N	Y	Y
2	**Franks**	N	Y	Y	N	N	Y
3	**Shadegg**	N	Y	Y	N	N	Y
4	Pastor	Y	Y	Y	Y	Y	Y
5	Mitchell	Y	Y	Y	Y	Y	Y
6	**Flake**	N	Y	N	N	N	Y
7	Grijalva	Y	Y	Y	Y	Y	Y
8	Giffords	Y	Y	Y	Y	Y	Y
ARKANSAS							
1	Berry	?	?	?	Y	Y	Y
2	Snyder	Y	Y	Y	Y	Y	Y
3	**Boozman**	N	Y	Y	N	Y	Y
4	Ross	Y	Y	Y	Y	Y	Y
CALIFORNIA							
1	Thompson	Y	Y	Y	Y	Y	Y
2	**Herger**	N	Y	Y	N	N	Y
3	**Lungren**	N	Y	Y	N	N	Y
4	**Doolittle**	N	Y	Y	N	Y	Y
5	Matsui	Y	Y	Y	Y	Y	Y
6	Woolsey	Y	Y	Y	Y	Y	Y
7	Miller, George	Y	Y	Y	Y	Y	Y
8	Pelosi		Y				
9	Lee	Y	Y	Y	Y	Y	Y
10	Tauscher	Y	Y	Y	Y	Y	Y
11	McNerney	Y	Y	Y	Y	Y	Y
12	Lantos	?	?	?	?	?	?
13	Stark	Y	Y	Y	Y	Y	Y
14	Eshoo	Y	Y	Y	Y	Y	Y
15	Honda	?	?	?	?	?	?
16	Lofgren	Y	Y	Y	Y	Y	Y
17	Farr	Y	Y	Y	Y	Y	Y
18	Cardoza	Y	Y	Y	Y	Y	Y
19	**Radanovich**	N	Y	Y	N	N	Y
20	Costa	Y	Y	Y	Y	Y	Y
21	**Nunes**	N	Y	Y	N	Y	Y
22	McCarthy	N	Y	Y	N	Y	Y
23	Capps	Y	Y	Y	Y	Y	Y
24	**Gallegly**	N	Y	Y	N	Y	Y
25	**McKeon**	N	Y	Y	N	Y	Y
26	**Dreier**	N	Y	Y	N	Y	Y
27	Sherman	Y	Y	Y	Y	Y	Y
28	Berman	Y	Y	Y	Y	Y	Y
29	Schiff	Y	Y	Y	Y	Y	Y
30	Waxman	Y	Y	Y	Y	Y	Y
31	Becerra	Y	Y	Y	Y	Y	Y
32	Solis	Y	Y	Y	Y	Y	Y
33	Watson	Y	Y	Y	Y	Y	Y
34	Roybal-Allard	Y	Y	Y	Y	Y	Y
35	Waters	Y	Y	Y	Y	Y	Y
36	Harman	Y	Y	Y	Y	Y	Y
37	Richardson	Y	Y	Y	Y	Y	Y
38	Napolitano	Y	Y	Y	Y	Y	Y
39	Sánchez, Linda	Y	Y	Y	Y	Y	Y
40	**Royce**	N	Y	Y	N	N	Y
41	**Lewis**	N	Y	Y	N	Y	?
42	**Miller, Gary**	?	?	?	Y	?	?
43	Baca	?	+	+	?	?	?
44	**Calvert**	N	Y	Y	N	N	Y
45	**Bono Mack**	N	Y	Y	N	Y	Y
46	**Rohrabacher**	N	Y	Y	N	N	Y
47	Sanchez, Loretta	Y	Y	Y	Y	Y	Y
48	**Campbell**	N	Y	Y	N	N	Y
49	**Issa**	N	Y	Y	N	Y	Y
50	**Bilbray**	N	Y	?	N	N	Y
51	Filner	Y	Y	Y	Y	Y	Y
52	**Hunter**	?	?	?	?	?	?
53	Davis	Y	Y	Y	Y	Y	Y

		2	3	4	5	6	7
COLORADO							
1	DeGette	Y	Y	Y	Y	Y	Y
2	Udall	Y	Y	Y	Y	Y	Y
3	Salazar	Y	Y	Y	Y	Y	Y
4	**Musgrave**	N	Y	Y	N	N	Y
5	**Lamborn**	N	Y	Y	N	N	Y
6	**Tancredo**	N	Y	Y	N	N	Y
7	Perlmutter	Y	Y	Y	Y	Y	Y
CONNECTICUT							
1	Larson	Y	Y	Y	Y	Y	Y
2	Courtney	Y	Y	Y	Y	Y	Y
3	DeLauro	Y	Y	Y	Y	Y	Y
4	**Shays**	N	Y	Y	N	Y	Y
5	Murphy	Y	Y	Y	Y	Y	Y
DELAWARE							
AL	**Castle**	N	Y	Y	N	Y	Y
FLORIDA							
1	**Miller**	N	Y	Y	N	N	Y
2	Boyd	Y	Y	Y	Y	Y	Y
3	Brown	Y	Y	Y	Y	Y	Y
4	**Crenshaw**	N	Y	Y	N	Y	Y
5	**Brown-Waite**	N	Y	Y	N	Y	Y
6	**Stearns**	N	Y	Y	N	N	Y
7	**Mica**	N	Y	Y	N	Y	Y
8	**Keller**	N	Y	Y	N	N	Y
9	**Bilirakis**	N	Y	Y	N	Y	Y
10	**Young**	N	Y	Y	N	Y	Y
11	Castor	Y	Y	Y	Y	Y	Y
12	**Putnam**	N	Y	Y	N	Y	Y
13	**Buchanan**	N	Y	Y	N	Y	Y
14	**Mack**	N	Y	Y	N	N	Y
15	**Weldon**	N	Y	Y	N	N	Y
16	Mahoney	Y	Y	Y	Y	Y	Y
17	Meek	Y	Y	Y	Y	Y	Y
18	**Ros-Lehtinen**	N	Y	Y	N	Y	Y
19	Wexler	Y	Y	Y	Y	Y	Y
20	Wasserman Schultz	Y	Y	Y	Y	Y	Y
21	**Diaz-Balart, L.**	N	Y	Y	N	Y	Y
22	Klein	Y	Y	Y	Y	Y	Y
23	Hastings	Y	Y	?	Y	Y	Y
24	**Feeney**	N	Y	Y	N	N	Y
25	**Diaz-Balart, M.**	N	Y	Y	N	Y	Y
GEORGIA							
1	**Kingston**	N	Y	Y	N	N	Y
2	Bishop	Y	Y	Y	Y	Y	Y
3	**Westmoreland**	?	?	?	N	N	Y
4	Johnson	Y	Y	?	Y	Y	Y
5	Lewis	Y	Y	Y	Y	Y	Y
6	**Price**	N	Y	Y	N	N	Y
7	**Linder**	N	Y	Y	N	N	Y
8	Marshall	Y	Y	Y	Y	Y	Y
9	**Deal**	N	Y	Y	N	N	Y
10	**Broun**	N	N	N	N	N	Y
11	**Gingrey**	N	Y	Y	N	N	Y
12	Barrow	N	Y	Y	Y	Y	Y
13	Scott	Y	Y	Y	Y	Y	Y
HAWAII							
1	Abercrombie	Y	Y	Y	Y	Y	Y
2	Hirono	Y	Y	Y	Y	Y	Y
IDAHO							
1	**Sali**	N	Y	Y	N	N	Y
2	**Simpson**	N	Y	Y	N	Y	Y
ILLINOIS							
1	Rush	Y	Y	Y	Y	Y	Y
2	Jackson	Y	Y	Y	Y	Y	Y
3	Lipinski	Y	Y	Y	Y	Y	Y
4	Gutierrez	Y	Y	Y	Y	Y	Y
5	Emanuel	Y	Y	Y	Y	Y	Y
6	**Roskam**	N	Y	Y	N	Y	Y
7	Davis	Y	Y	Y	Y	Y	Y
8	Bean	Y	Y	Y	Y	Y	Y
9	Schakowsky	Y	Y	Y	Y	Y	Y
10	**Kirk**	N	Y	Y	N	Y	Y
11	Weller	Y	Y	Y	Y	Y	Y
12	Costello	Y	Y	Y	Y	Y	Y
13	**Biggert**	N	Y	Y	N	Y	Y
14	Vacant						
15	**Johnson**	N	Y	Y	N	Y	Y

KEY	**Republicans**	Democrats	
Y	Voted for (yea)	X Paired against	C Voted "present" to avoid possible conflict of interest
#	Paired for	– Announced against	
+	Announced for	P Voted "present"	? Did not vote or otherwise make a position known
N	Voted against (nay)		

	2	3	4	5	6	7
16 **Manzullo**	N	Y	Y	N	Y	Y
17 Hare	Y	Y	Y	Y	Y	Y
18 **LaHood**	N	Y	Y	N	Y	Y
19 **Shimkus**	?	?	?	?	?	?
INDIANA						
1 Visclosky	Y	Y	Y	Y	Y	Y
2 Donnelly	Y	Y	Y	Y	Y	Y
3 **Souder**	N	Y	Y	N	Y	Y
4 **Buyer**	N	Y	Y	N	Y	Y
5 **Burton**	N	Y	?	N	N	Y
6 **Pence**	N	Y	Y	N	N	Y
7 Vacant						
8 Ellsworth	Y	Y	Y	Y	Y	Y
9 Hill	Y	Y	Y	Y	Y	Y
IOWA						
1 Braley	Y	Y	Y	Y	Y	Y
2 Loebsack	Y	Y	Y	Y	Y	Y
3 Boswell	Y	Y	Y	Y	Y	Y
4 **Latham**	N	Y	Y	N	Y	Y
5 **King**	N	Y	Y	N	N	Y
KANSAS						
1 **Moran**	N	Y	Y	N	Y	Y
2 Boyda	Y	Y	Y	Y	Y	Y
3 Moore	Y	Y	Y	Y	Y	Y
4 **Tiahrt**	N	Y	Y	N	Y	Y
KENTUCKY						
1 **Whitfield**	N	Y	Y	Y	Y	Y
2 **Lewis**	N	Y	Y	N	Y	Y
3 Yarmuth	Y	Y	Y	Y	Y	Y
4 **Davis**	N	Y	Y	N	Y	Y
5 **Rogers**	N	Y	Y	N	Y	Y
6 Chandler	Y	Y	Y	Y	Y	Y
LOUISIANA						
1 Vacant[1]						
2 Jefferson	?	?	?	?	?	?
3 Melancon	Y	Y	Y	Y	Y	Y
4 **McCrery**	N	Y	Y	N	Y	Y
5 **Alexander**	N	Y	Y	N	Y	Y
6 **Baker**	?	?	?	?	?	?
7 **Boustany**	N	Y	Y	N	Y	Y
MAINE						
1 Allen	Y	Y	Y	Y	Y	Y
2 Michaud	Y	Y	Y	Y	Y	Y
MARYLAND						
1 **Gilchrest**	N	Y	Y	Y	Y	Y
2 Ruppersberger	Y	Y	Y	Y	Y	Y
3 Sarbanes	Y	Y	Y	Y	Y	Y
4 Wynn	Y	Y	Y	Y	Y	Y
5 Hoyer	Y	Y	Y	Y	Y	Y
6 **Bartlett**	N	Y	Y	N	Y	Y
7 Cummings	Y	Y	Y	Y	Y	Y
8 Van Hollen	Y	Y	Y	Y	Y	Y
MASSACHUSETTS						
1 Olver	Y	Y	Y	Y	Y	Y
2 Neal	Y	Y	Y	Y	Y	Y
3 McGovern	Y	Y	Y	Y	Y	Y
4 Frank	Y	Y	Y	Y	Y	Y
5 Tsongas	Y	Y	Y	Y	Y	Y
6 Tierney	Y	Y	Y	Y	Y	Y
7 Markey	Y	Y	Y	Y	Y	Y
8 Capuano	Y	Y	Y	Y	Y	Y
9 Lynch	Y	Y	Y	Y	Y	Y
10 Delahunt	Y	Y	Y	Y	Y	Y
MICHIGAN						
1 Stupak	Y	Y	Y	Y	Y	Y
2 **Hoekstra**	N	Y	Y	N	N	Y
3 **Ehlers**	N	Y	Y	N	Y	Y
4 **Camp**	N	Y	Y	N	Y	Y
5 Kildee	Y	Y	Y	Y	Y	Y
6 **Upton**	N	Y	Y	N	Y	Y
7 **Walberg**	N	Y	Y	N	N	Y
8 **Rogers**	N	Y	Y	N	Y	Y
9 **Knollenberg**	N	Y	Y	N	Y	Y
10 **Miller**	N	Y	Y	N	Y	Y
11 **McCotter**	N	Y	Y	N	Y	Y
12 Levin	Y	Y	Y	Y	Y	Y
13 Kilpatrick	Y	Y	Y	Y	Y	Y
14 Conyers	Y	Y	Y	Y	Y	Y
15 Dingell	Y	Y	Y	Y	Y	Y
MINNESOTA						
1 Walz	Y	Y	Y	Y	Y	Y
2 **Kline**	N	Y	Y	N	Y	Y
3 **Ramstad**	N	Y	Y	N	Y	Y
4 McCollum	Y	Y	Y	Y	Y	Y
5 Ellison	Y	Y	Y	Y	Y	Y
6 **Bachmann**	N	Y	Y	N	Y	Y
7 Peterson	Y	Y	Y	Y	Y	Y
8 Oberstar	Y	Y	Y	Y	Y	Y
MISSISSIPPI						
1 Vacant[2]						
2 Thompson	Y	Y	Y	Y	Y	Y
3 **Pickering**	N	Y	Y	N	Y	Y
4 Taylor	Y	Y	Y	Y	Y	Y
MISSOURI						
1 Clay	Y	Y	Y	Y	Y	Y
2 **Akin**	N	Y	Y	N	N	Y
3 Carnahan	Y	Y	Y	Y	Y	Y
4 Skelton	Y	Y	Y	Y	Y	Y
5 Cleaver	Y	Y	Y	Y	Y	Y
6 **Graves**	N	Y	Y	N	Y	Y
7 **Blunt**	N	Y	Y	N	Y	Y
8 **Emerson**	N	Y	Y	N	Y	Y
9 **Hulshof**	N	Y	Y	N	Y	Y
MONTANA						
AL **Rehberg**	N	Y	Y	N	Y	Y
NEBRASKA						
1 **Fortenberry**	N	Y	Y	N	Y	Y
2 **Terry**	N	Y	Y	N	Y	Y
3 **Smith**	N	Y	Y	N	Y	Y
NEVADA						
1 Berkley	+	+	+	+	+	+
2 **Heller**	N	Y	Y	N	Y	Y
3 **Porter**	N	Y	Y	N	Y	Y
NEW HAMPSHIRE						
1 Shea-Porter	Y	Y	Y	Y	Y	Y
2 Hodes	Y	Y	Y	Y	Y	Y
NEW JERSEY						
1 Andrews	Y	Y	Y	Y	Y	Y
2 **LoBiondo**	N	Y	Y	Y	Y	Y
3 **Saxton**	N	Y	Y	N	Y	Y
4 **Smith**	N	Y	Y	Y	Y	Y
5 **Garrett**	N	Y	Y	N	N	Y
6 Pallone	Y	Y	Y	Y	Y	Y
7 **Ferguson**	N	Y	Y	N	Y	Y
8 Pascrell	Y	Y	Y	Y	Y	Y
9 Rothman	Y	Y	Y	Y	Y	Y
10 Payne	Y	Y	Y	Y	Y	Y
11 **Frelinghuysen**	N	Y	Y	N	Y	Y
12 Holt	Y	Y	Y	Y	Y	Y
13 Sires	Y	Y	Y	Y	Y	Y
NEW MEXICO						
1 **Wilson**	N	Y	Y	N	Y	Y
2 **Pearce**	N	Y	Y	N	Y	Y
3 Udall	Y	Y	Y	Y	Y	Y
NEW YORK						
1 Bishop	Y	Y	Y	Y	Y	Y
2 Israel	Y	Y	Y	Y	Y	Y
3 **King**	N	Y	Y	N	Y	Y
4 McCarthy	Y	Y	Y	Y	Y	Y
5 Ackerman	Y	Y	Y	Y	Y	Y
6 Meeks	?	?	?	?	?	?
7 Crowley	Y	Y	Y	Y	Y	Y
8 Nadler	Y	Y	Y	Y	Y	Y
9 Weiner	Y	Y	Y	Y	Y	Y
10 Towns	Y	Y	Y	Y	Y	Y
11 Clarke	Y	Y	Y	Y	Y	Y
12 Velázquez	Y	Y	Y	Y	Y	Y
13 **Fossella**	?	?	?	?	?	?
14 Maloney	Y	Y	Y	Y	Y	Y
15 Rangel	Y	Y	Y	Y	Y	Y
16 Serrano	Y	Y	Y	Y	Y	Y
17 Engel	Y	Y	Y	Y	Y	Y
18 Lowey	Y	Y	Y	Y	Y	Y
19 Hall	Y	Y	Y	Y	Y	Y
20 Gillibrand	Y	Y	Y	Y	Y	Y
21 McNulty	Y	Y	Y	Y	Y	Y
22 Hinchey	Y	Y	Y	Y	Y	Y
23 **McHugh**	N	Y	Y	N	Y	Y
24 Arcuri	Y	Y	Y	Y	Y	Y
25 **Walsh**	N	Y	Y	N	Y	Y
26 **Reynolds**	N	Y	Y	N	Y	Y
27 Higgins	Y	Y	Y	Y	Y	Y
28 Slaughter	Y	Y	Y	Y	Y	Y
29 **Kuhl**	N	Y	Y	N	Y	Y
NORTH CAROLINA						
1 Butterfield	Y	Y	Y	Y	Y	Y
2 Etheridge	Y	Y	Y	Y	Y	Y
3 **Jones**	N	Y	Y	Y	N	Y
4 Price	Y	Y	Y	Y	Y	Y
5 **Foxx**	N	Y	Y	N	N	Y
6 **Coble**	N	Y	Y	N	N	Y
7 McIntyre	Y	Y	Y	Y	Y	Y
8 **Hayes**	N	Y	Y	N	Y	Y
9 **Myrick**	N	Y	Y	N	Y	Y
10 **McHenry**	N	Y	Y	N	N	Y
11 Shuler	Y	Y	Y	Y	Y	Y
12 Watt	Y	Y	Y	Y	Y	Y
13 Miller	Y	Y	Y	Y	Y	Y
NORTH DAKOTA						
AL Pomeroy	Y	Y	Y	Y	Y	Y
OHIO						
1 **Chabot**	N	Y	Y	N	N	Y
2 **Schmidt**	N	Y	Y	N	Y	Y
3 **Turner**	N	Y	Y	N	Y	Y
4 **Jordan**	N	Y	Y	N	N	Y
5 **Latta**	N	Y	Y	N	Y	Y
6 Wilson	Y	Y	Y	Y	Y	Y
7 **Hobson**	N	Y	Y	N	Y	Y
8 **Boehner**	N	Y	Y	N	Y	Y
9 Kaptur	Y	Y	Y	Y	Y	Y
10 Kucinich	Y	Y	Y	Y	Y	Y
11 Tubbs Jones	Y	Y	Y	Y	Y	Y
12 **Tiberi**	N	Y	Y	N	Y	Y
13 Sutton	Y	Y	Y	Y	Y	Y
14 **LaTourette**	N	Y	Y	N	Y	Y
15 **Pryce**	N	Y	Y	N	Y	Y
16 **Regula**	N	Y	Y	N	Y	Y
17 Ryan	Y	Y	Y	Y	Y	Y
18 Space	Y	Y	Y	Y	Y	Y
OKLAHOMA						
1 **Sullivan**	N	Y	Y	N	Y	Y
2 Boren	Y	Y	Y	Y	Y	Y
3 **Lucas**	N	Y	Y	N	Y	Y
4 **Cole**	N	+	Y	N	Y	Y
5 **Fallin**	N	Y	Y	N	Y	Y
OREGON						
1 Wu	Y	Y	Y	Y	Y	Y
2 **Walden**	N	Y	Y	N	N	Y
3 Blumenauer	Y	Y	Y	Y	Y	Y
4 DeFazio	Y	Y	Y	Y	Y	Y
5 Hooley	Y	Y	Y	Y	Y	Y
PENNSYLVANIA						
1 Brady	Y	Y	Y	Y	Y	Y
2 Fattah	Y	Y	Y	Y	Y	Y
3 **English**	N	Y	Y	N	Y	Y
4 Altmire	Y	Y	Y	Y	Y	Y
5 **Peterson**	N	Y	Y	N	Y	Y
6 **Gerlach**	N	Y	Y	N	Y	Y
7 Sestak	Y	Y	Y	Y	Y	Y
8 Murphy, P.	Y	Y	Y	Y	Y	Y
9 **Shuster**	N	Y	Y	N	Y	Y
10 Carney	Y	Y	Y	Y	Y	Y
11 Kanjorski	Y	Y	Y	Y	Y	Y
12 Murtha	Y	Y	Y	Y	Y	Y
13 Schwartz	Y	Y	Y	Y	Y	Y
14 Doyle	Y	Y	Y	Y	Y	Y
15 **Dent**	N	Y	Y	N	Y	Y
16 **Pitts**	N	Y	Y	N	Y	Y
17 Holden	Y	Y	Y	Y	Y	Y
18 **Murphy, T.**	N	Y	Y	Y	Y	Y
19 **Platts**	N	Y	Y	N	Y	Y
RHODE ISLAND						
1 Kennedy	Y	Y	Y	Y	Y	Y
2 Langevin	Y	Y	Y	Y	Y	Y
SOUTH CAROLINA						
1 **Brown**	N	Y	Y	N	Y	Y
2 **Wilson**	N	Y	Y	N	Y	Y
3 **Barrett**	N	Y	Y	N	N	Y
4 **Inglis**	N	Y	Y	N	Y	Y
5 Spratt	Y	Y	Y	Y	Y	Y
6 Clyburn	Y	Y	Y	Y	Y	Y
SOUTH DAKOTA						
AL Herseth Sandlin	Y	Y	Y	Y	Y	Y
TENNESSEE						
1 **Davis, David**	N	Y	Y	N	Y	Y
2 **Duncan**	N	Y	Y	N	N	Y
3 **Wamp**	N	Y	Y	N	Y	Y
4 Davis, L.	Y	Y	Y	Y	Y	Y
5 Cooper	Y	Y	Y	Y	Y	Y
6 Gordon	Y	Y	Y	Y	Y	Y
7 **Blackburn**	N	Y	Y	N	Y	Y
8 Tanner	?	?	?	?	?	?
9 Cohen	Y	Y	Y	Y	Y	Y
TEXAS						
1 **Gohmert**	N	Y	Y	N	Y	Y
2 **Poe**	N	Y	Y	N	N	Y
3 **Johnson, S.**	N	Y	Y	N	N	Y
4 **Hall**	N	Y	Y	N	N	Y
5 **Hensarling**	N	Y	Y	N	N	Y
6 **Barton**	N	Y	Y	N	Y	Y
7 **Culberson**	?	?	?	?	?	?
8 **Brady**	N	Y	Y	N	Y	Y
9 Green, A.	Y	Y	Y	Y	Y	Y
10 **McCaul**	N	Y	Y	N	Y	Y
11 **Conaway**	N	Y	Y	N	N	Y
12 **Granger**	N	Y	Y	N	Y	Y
13 **Thornberry**	N	Y	Y	N	Y	Y
14 **Paul**	?	?	?	?	?	?
15 Hinojosa	Y	Y	Y	Y	Y	Y
16 Reyes	Y	Y	Y	Y	Y	Y
17 Edwards	Y	Y	Y	Y	Y	Y
18 Jackson Lee	Y	Y	Y	Y	Y	Y
19 **Neugebauer**	N	Y	Y	N	Y	Y
20 Gonzalez	Y	Y	Y	Y	Y	Y
21 **Smith**	N	Y	Y	N	Y	Y
22 Lampson	Y	Y	Y	Y	Y	Y
23 Rodriguez	Y	Y	Y	Y	Y	Y
24 **Marchant**	N	Y	Y	N	N	Y
25 Doggett	Y	Y	Y	Y	Y	Y
26 **Burgess**	N	Y	?	N	Y	Y
27 Ortiz	Y	Y	Y	Y	Y	Y
28 Cuellar	Y	Y	Y	Y	Y	Y
29 Green, G.	Y	Y	Y	Y	Y	Y
30 Johnson, E.	Y	Y	Y	Y	Y	Y
31 **Carter**	N	Y	Y	N	Y	Y
32 **Sessions**	N	Y	Y	N	Y	Y
UTAH						
1 **Bishop**	N	Y	Y	N	Y	Y
2 Matheson	Y	Y	Y	Y	Y	Y
3 **Cannon**	N	Y	Y	N	N	Y
VERMONT						
AL Welch	Y	Y	Y	Y	Y	Y
VIRGINIA						
1 **Wittman**	N	Y	Y	N	Y	Y
2 **Drake**	N	Y	Y	N	Y	Y
3 Scott	Y	Y	Y	Y	Y	Y
4 **Forbes**	?	?	?	?	?	?
5 **Goode**	N	Y	Y	N	Y	Y
6 **Goodlatte**	N	Y	Y	N	Y	Y
7 **Cantor**	N	Y	Y	N	Y	Y
8 Moran	Y	Y	Y	Y	Y	Y
9 Boucher	Y	Y	Y	Y	Y	Y
10 **Wolf**	N	Y	Y	N	Y	Y
11 **Davis, T.**	N	Y	Y	N	Y	Y
WASHINGTON						
1 Inslee	Y	Y	Y	Y	Y	Y
2 Larsen	Y	Y	Y	Y	Y	Y
3 Baird	Y	Y	Y	Y	Y	Y
4 **Hastings**	N	Y	Y	N	Y	Y
5 **McMorris Rodgers**	N	Y	Y	N	Y	Y
6 Dicks	Y	Y	Y	Y	Y	Y
7 McDermott	Y	Y	Y	Y	Y	Y
8 **Reichert**	N	Y	Y	N	Y	?
9 Smith	Y	Y	Y	Y	Y	Y
WEST VIRGINIA						
1 Mollohan	Y	Y	Y	Y	Y	Y
2 **Capito**	N	Y	Y	Y	Y	Y
3 Rahall	Y	Y	Y	Y	Y	Y
WISCONSIN						
1 **Ryan**	N	Y	Y	N	Y	Y
2 Baldwin	Y	Y	Y	Y	Y	Y
3 Kind	Y	Y	Y	Y	Y	Y
4 Moore	Y	Y	Y	Y	Y	Y
5 **Sensenbrenner**	N	Y	Y	N	N	Y
6 **Petri**	N	Y	Y	N	Y	Y
7 Obey	Y	Y	Y	Y	Y	Y
8 Kagen	Y	Y	Y	Y	Y	Y
WYOMING						
AL **Cubin**	N	Y	Y	N	Y	Y
DELEGATES						
Faleomavaega (A.S.)				?	?	?
Norton (D.C.)				Y	Y	Y
Bordallo (Guam)				Y	Y	Y
Fortuño (P.R.)				?	?	?
Christensen (V.I.)				?	?	Y

IN THE HOUSE | By Vote Number

8. HR 2768. Mine Safety Standards/Republican Substitute Amendment. Wilson, R-S.C., substitute amendment that would express the sense of Congress that current laws should be fully implemented, require a "Technical Study Panel" to evaluate the risk-assessment procedures of deep mine conditions, require the Labor Department to promulgate regulations within 180 days of enactment for a drug-testing program for miners and compile a registry of miners who test positive for substance abuse. It also would strike certain enforcement requirements and penalties established in the bill. Rejected in Committee of the Whole 188-229: R 185-5; D 3-224 (ND 2-170, SD 1-54). Jan. 16, 2008.

9. HR 2768. Mine Safety Standards/Motion to Recommit. Souder, R-Ind., motion to recommit the bill to the Education and Labor Committee with instructions to report it back with new language modifying substance-abuse testing requirements for mine workers. Motion rejected 197-217: R 189-1; D 8-216 (ND 4-165, SD 4-51). Jan. 16, 2008.

10. HR 2768. Mine Safety Standards/Passage. Passage of the bill that would shorten deadlines for mine operators to conform to new safety requirements, provide the Mine Safety and Health Administration with subpoena power and increase penalties for multiple safety violations. Mine operators would have to install new communications equipment sooner than previously mandated. Mines would be monitored if their seals are not designed to withstand 240 pounds per square inch. Passed 214-199: R 7-183; D 207-16 (ND 162-6, SD 45-10). A "nay" was a vote in support of the president's position. Jan. 16, 2008.

11. HR 4986. Fiscal 2008 Defense Authorization/Passage. Skelton, D-Mo., motion to suspend the rules and pass the bill that would authorize $696.4 billion for defense programs in fiscal 2008, including $189.5 billion for the wars in Iraq and Afghanistan. It includes $142.8 billion for operations and maintenance, $119.7 billion for military personnel, $23.7 billion for military construction and family housing, and $23.1 billion for the Defense Health Program. It would authorize a 3.5 percent pay increase for military personnel. It would allow the president to waive certain liability provisions as they apply to Iraq. Motion agreed to 369-46: R 187-4; D 182-42 (ND 131-39, SD 51-3). A two-thirds majority of those present and voting (277 in this case) is required for passage under suspension of the rules. Jan. 16, 2008.

12. HR 3524. HOPE VI Housing Reauthorization/Demolition Timelines. Waters, D-Calif., amendment that would require all housing units built as of Jan. 1, 2005, to be replaced at a one-for-one rate if demolished and would extend the timeline for rebuilding replacement housing to 54 months after the grant is enacted. It would clarify that those illegally in the United States would not be eligible for public housing funded by HOPE VI grants. Construction would have to comply with the green building rating system. Adopted in Committee of the Whole 388-20: R 165-20; D 223-0 (ND 169-0, SD 54-0). Jan. 17, 2008.

13. HR 3524. HOPE VI Housing Reauthorization/Housing Replacement. Neugebauer, R-Texas, amendment that would change the bill's requirement for one-to-one replacement of demolished housing units to apply only to units occupied before demolition. Rejected in Committee of the Whole 181-227: R 180-4; D 1-223 (ND 1-168, SD 0-55). A "yea" was a vote in support of the president's position. Jan. 17, 2008.

14. HR 3524. HOPE VI Housing Reauthorization/Demolition-Only Grants. Sessions, R-Texas, amendment that would allow the Department of Housing and Urban Development to continue to issue demolition-only HOPE VI grants. Rejected in Committee of the Whole 186-221: R 185-0; D 1-221 (ND 1-166, SD 0-55). A "nay" was a vote in support of the president's position. Jan. 17, 2008.

ND Northern Democrats, SD Southern Democrats
Southern states: Ala., Ark., Fla., Ga., Ky., La., Miss., N.C., Okla., S.C., Tenn., Texas, Va.

	8	9	10	11	12	13	14
ALABAMA							
1 Bonner	Y	Y	N	Y	Y	Y	Y
2 Everett	Y	Y	N	Y	Y	Y	Y
3 Rogers	Y	Y	N	Y	Y	Y	Y
4 Aderholt	Y	Y	N	Y	Y	Y	Y
5 Cramer	N	N	Y	Y	Y	N	N
6 Bachus	Y	Y	Y	Y	Y	Y	Y
7 Davis	N	N	Y	Y	Y	N	N
ALASKA							
AL Young	Y	Y	N	Y	Y	Y	Y
ARIZONA							
1 Renzi	Y	Y	N	Y	Y	N	Y
2 Franks	Y	Y	N	Y	N	Y	Y
3 Shadegg	Y	Y	N	Y	Y	Y	Y
4 Pastor	N	N	Y	Y	Y	N	N
5 Mitchell	N	N	Y	Y	Y	N	N
6 Flake	Y	Y	N	Y	N	Y	Y
7 Grijalva	N	N	Y	N	Y	N	N
8 Giffords	N	N	Y	Y	Y	N	N
ARKANSAS							
1 Berry	N	N	N	Y	+	-	-
2 Snyder	N	N	Y	Y	Y	N	N
3 Boozman	Y	Y	N	Y	Y	Y	Y
4 Ross	N	N	N	Y	Y	N	N
CALIFORNIA							
1 Thompson	N	N	Y	Y	Y	N	N
2 Herger	Y	Y	N	Y	Y	Y	Y
3 Lungren	Y	Y	N	Y	Y	Y	Y
4 Doolittle	Y	Y	N	Y	Y	Y	Y
5 Matsui	N	N	Y	Y	Y	N	N
6 Woolsey	N	N	Y	N	Y	N	N
7 Miller, George	N	N	Y	N	Y	N	N
8 Pelosi							
9 Lee	N	N	Y	N	Y	N	N
10 Tauscher	N	N	Y	Y	Y	N	N
11 McNerney	N	N	Y	Y	Y	N	N
12 Lantos	?	?	?	?	?	?	?
13 Stark	N	N	Y	N	Y	N	N
14 Eshoo	N	N	Y	Y	Y	N	N
15 Honda	?	?	?	Y	Y	N	N
16 Lofgren	N	N	Y	Y	Y	N	N
17 Farr	N	N	Y	Y	Y	N	N
18 Cardoza	N	N	Y	Y	Y	N	N
19 Radanovich	Y	Y	N	Y	Y	Y	?
20 Costa	N	N	Y	Y	Y	N	N
21 Nunes	Y	Y	N	Y	Y	Y	Y
22 McCarthy	Y	Y	N	Y	Y	Y	Y
23 Capps	N	N	Y	Y	Y	N	N
24 Gallegly	Y	Y	Y	Y	Y	Y	Y
25 McKeon	Y	Y	N	Y	Y	Y	Y
26 Dreier	Y	Y	N	Y	Y	Y	Y
27 Sherman	N	N	Y	Y	?	?	?
28 Berman	N	N	Y	Y	Y	N	N
29 Schiff	N	N	Y	Y	Y	N	N
30 Waxman	N	N	Y	Y	Y	N	N
31 Becerra	N	N	Y	Y	Y	N	N
32 Solis	N	N	Y	Y	Y	N	N
33 Watson	N	N	Y	Y	Y	N	N
34 Roybal-Allard	N	N	Y	Y	Y	N	N
35 Waters	N	N	Y	N	Y	N	N
36 Harman	N	N	Y	Y	Y	N	N
37 Richardson	N	N	Y	Y	Y	N	N
38 Napolitano	N	N	Y	Y	Y	N	N
39 Sánchez, Linda	N	N	Y	Y	Y	N	N
40 Royce	Y	Y	N	Y	N	Y	Y
41 Lewis	Y	Y	N	Y	Y	Y	Y
42 Miller, Gary	?	?	?	?	?	?	?
43 Baca	?	?	+	+	?	?	?
44 Calvert	Y	Y	N	Y	Y	Y	Y
45 Bono Mack	Y	Y	N	Y	Y	Y	Y
46 Rohrabacher	Y	Y	N	Y	Y	Y	Y
47 Sanchez, Loretta	N	N	Y	Y	Y	N	N
48 Campbell	Y	Y	N	Y	N	Y	Y
49 Issa	Y	Y	N	Y	Y	Y	Y
50 Bilbray	Y	Y	N	Y	Y	Y	Y
51 Filner	N	N	Y	N	Y	N	N
52 Hunter	?	?	?	?	?	?	?
53 Davis	N	N	Y	Y	Y	N	N

	8	9	10	11	12	13	14
COLORADO							
1 DeGette	N	N	Y	Y	Y	N	N
2 Udall	N	N	N	Y	Y	N	N
3 Salazar	N	N	N	Y	Y	N	N
4 Musgrave	Y	Y	N	Y	Y	Y	Y
5 Lamborn	Y	Y	N	Y	N	Y	Y
6 Tancredo	Y	N	N	Y	Y	Y	Y
7 Perlmutter	N	N	Y	Y	Y	N	N
CONNECTICUT							
1 Larson	N	N	Y	Y	Y	N	N
2 Courtney	N	N	Y	Y	Y	N	N
3 DeLauro	N	N	Y	Y	Y	N	N
4 Shays	Y	Y	Y	Y	Y	N	Y
5 Murphy	N	N	Y	Y	Y	N	N
DELAWARE							
AL Castle	Y	Y	N	Y	Y	N	Y
FLORIDA							
1 Miller	Y	Y	N	Y	N	Y	Y
2 Boyd	N	N	N	Y	Y	N	N
3 Brown	N	N	Y	Y	Y	N	N
4 Crenshaw	Y	Y	N	Y	Y	Y	Y
5 Brown-Waite	Y	Y	N	Y	N	Y	Y
6 Stearns	Y	Y	N	Y	N	Y	Y
7 Mica	Y	Y	N	Y	Y	Y	Y
8 Keller	Y	Y	N	Y	Y	Y	Y
9 Bilirakis	Y	Y	N	Y	Y	Y	Y
10 Young	Y	Y	N	Y	Y	Y	Y
11 Castor	N	N	Y	Y	Y	N	N
12 Putnam	Y	Y	N	Y	Y	Y	Y
13 Buchanan	Y	Y	N	Y	Y	Y	Y
14 Mack	Y	Y	N	Y	Y	Y	Y
15 Weldon	Y	Y	N	Y	Y	Y	Y
16 Mahoney	N	N	Y	Y	Y	N	N
17 Meek	N	N	Y	Y	Y	N	N
18 Ros-Lehtinen	Y	Y	N	Y	Y	Y	Y
19 Wexler	N	N	Y	Y	Y	N	N
20 Wasserman Schultz	N	N	Y	Y	Y	N	N
21 Diaz-Balart, L.	Y	Y	N	Y	?	?	Y
22 Klein	N	N	Y	Y	Y	N	N
23 Hastings	N	N	Y	Y	Y	N	N
24 Feeney	Y	Y	N	Y	N	Y	Y
25 Diaz-Balart, M.	Y	Y	N	Y	+	+	Y
GEORGIA							
1 Kingston	Y	?	?	?	?	?	?
2 Bishop	N	N	Y	Y	Y	N	N
3 Westmoreland	Y	Y	N	Y	Y	N	N
4 Johnson	N	N	Y	Y	Y	N	N
5 Lewis	N	N	Y	N	Y	N	N
6 Price	Y	Y	N	Y	N	Y	Y
7 Linder	Y	Y	N	Y	N	Y	Y
8 Marshall	N	N	Y	Y	Y	N	N
9 Deal	Y	Y	N	Y	?	?	?
10 Broun	Y	Y	N	Y	N	Y	Y
11 Gingrey	Y	Y	N	Y	N	Y	Y
12 Barrow	N	N	Y	Y	Y	N	N
13 Scott	N	N	Y	Y	Y	N	N
HAWAII							
1 Abercrombie	N	N	Y	Y	Y	N	N
2 Hirono	N	N	Y	Y	Y	N	N
IDAHO							
1 Sali	Y	Y	N	Y	Y	Y	Y
2 Simpson	Y	Y	N	Y	Y	Y	Y
ILLINOIS							
1 Rush	N	N	Y	N	Y	N	N
2 Jackson	N	N	Y	N	Y	N	N
3 Lipinski	N	N	Y	Y	Y	N	N
4 Gutierrez	N	N	Y	Y	Y	N	N
5 Emanuel	N	N	Y	Y	Y	N	N
6 Roskam	Y	Y	N	Y	Y	Y	Y
7 Davis	N	N	Y	N	?	?	?
8 Bean	N	N	Y	Y	Y	N	N
9 Schakowsky	N	N	Y	N	Y	N	N
10 Kirk	Y	Y	N	Y	Y	Y	Y
11 Weller	Y	Y	N	Y	Y	Y	Y
12 Costello	N	N	Y	Y	Y	N	N
13 Biggert	Y	Y	N	Y	Y	Y	Y
14 Vacant							
15 Johnson	Y	Y	N	Y	Y	Y	Y

KEY	Republicans	Democrats		
Y	Voted for (yea)	X	Paired against	C Voted "present" to avoid possible conflict of interest
#	Paired for	-	Announced against	
+	Announced for	P	Voted "present"	? Did not vote or otherwise make a position known
N	Voted against (nay)			

	8	9	10	11	12	13	14
16 **Manzullo**	Y	Y	N	Y	Y	Y	Y
17 Hare	N	N	Y	Y	Y	N	N
18 **LaHood**	Y	Y	N	Y	Y	Y	Y
19 **Shimkus**	?	?	?	?	?	?	?
INDIANA							
1 Visclosky	N	N	Y	Y	?	?	?
2 Donnelly	N	Y	Y	Y	Y	N	N
3 **Souder**	+	Y	N	Y	Y	Y	Y
4 **Buyer**	Y	Y	N	Y	Y	Y	Y
5 **Burton**	Y	Y	N	Y	Y	Y	Y
6 **Pence**	Y	Y	N	Y	N	Y	Y
7 Vacant							
8 Ellsworth	N	N	Y	Y	Y	N	N
9 Hill	N	N	Y	Y	Y	N	N
IOWA							
1 Braley	N	N	Y	Y	Y	N	N
2 Loebsack	N	N	Y	Y	Y	N	N
3 Boswell	N	N	Y	Y	Y	N	N
4 **Latham**	Y	Y	N	Y	Y	Y	Y
5 **King**	Y	Y	N	Y	Y	Y	Y
KANSAS							
1 **Moran**	Y	Y	N	Y	Y	Y	Y
2 Boyda	N	Y	N	Y	Y	N	N
3 Moore	N	N	Y	Y	Y	N	N
4 **Tiahrt**	Y	Y	N	Y	Y	Y	Y
KENTUCKY							
1 **Whitfield**	Y	Y	N	Y	Y	Y	Y
2 **Lewis**	Y	Y	N	Y	?	?	?
3 Yarmuth	N	N	Y	N	Y	N	N
4 **Davis**	Y	Y	N	Y	Y	Y	Y
5 **Rogers**	Y	Y	N	Y	Y	Y	Y
6 Chandler	N	N	Y	Y	Y	N	N
LOUISIANA							
1 Vacant							
2 Jefferson	?	?	?	?	?	?	?
3 Melancon	N	N	N	Y	Y	N	N
4 **McCrery**	Y	Y	N	Y	Y	Y	Y
5 **Alexander**	Y	Y	N	Y	Y	Y	Y
6 **Baker**	?	?	?	Y	?	?	?
7 **Boustany**	Y	Y	N	Y	Y	Y	Y
MAINE							
1 Allen	N	N	Y	Y	Y	N	N
2 Michaud	N	N	Y	Y	Y	N	N
MARYLAND							
1 **Gilchrest**	N	Y	Y	Y	Y	Y	Y
2 Ruppersberger	N	N	Y	Y	Y	N	N
3 Sarbanes	N	N	Y	Y	Y	N	N
4 Wynn	N	N	Y	N	Y	N	?
5 Hoyer	N	N	Y	Y	Y	N	N
6 **Bartlett**	Y	Y	N	Y	N	Y	Y
7 Cummings	N	N	Y	Y	Y	N	N
8 Van Hollen	N	N	Y	Y	Y	N	N
MASSACHUSETTS							
1 Olver	N	N	?	N	Y	N	N
2 Neal	N	N	Y	Y	Y	N	N
3 McGovern	N	N	Y	N	Y	N	N
4 Frank	N	N	Y	N	Y	N	N
5 Tsongas	N	N	Y	Y	Y	N	N
6 Tierney	N	N	Y	N	Y	N	N
7 Markey	N	N	Y	N	Y	N	N
8 Capuano	N	N	Y	N	Y	N	N
9 Lynch	N	N	Y	Y	Y	N	N
10 Delahunt	N	N	Y	N	?	?	?
MICHIGAN							
1 Stupak	N	N	Y	Y	Y	N	N
2 **Hoekstra**	Y	Y	N	Y	Y	Y	Y
3 **Ehlers**	Y	Y	N	Y	Y	Y	Y
4 **Camp**	Y	Y	N	Y	Y	Y	Y
5 Kildee	N	N	Y	Y	Y	N	N
6 **Upton**	Y	Y	N	Y	Y	Y	Y
7 **Walberg**	Y	Y	N	Y	Y	Y	Y
8 **Rogers**	Y	Y	N	Y	Y	Y	Y
9 **Knollenberg**	Y	Y	N	Y	Y	Y	Y
10 **Miller**	Y	Y	N	Y	Y	Y	Y
11 **McCotter**	Y	Y	N	Y	Y	Y	Y
12 Levin	N	N	Y	Y	Y	N	N
13 Kilpatrick	N	N	Y	Y	Y	N	N
14 Conyers	N	N	Y	N	Y	N	N
15 Dingell	N	N	Y	Y	Y	N	N
MINNESOTA							
1 Walz	N	N	Y	Y	Y	N	N
2 **Kline**	Y	Y	N	Y	Y	Y	Y
3 **Ramstad**	Y	Y	N	Y	Y	Y	Y
4 McCollum	N	N	Y	Y	Y	N	N
5 Ellison	N	N	Y	N	Y	N	N
6 **Bachmann**	Y	Y	N	Y	Y	Y	Y
7 Peterson	N	N	N	Y	Y	N	N
8 Oberstar	N	N	Y	N	Y	N	N
MISSISSIPPI							
1 Vacant							
2 Thompson	N	N	Y	Y	Y	N	N
3 **Pickering**	Y	Y	N	Y	Y	Y	Y
4 Taylor	N	Y	Y	Y	Y	N	N
MISSOURI							
1 Clay	N	N	Y	N	Y	N	N
2 **Akin**	Y	Y	N	Y	N	Y	Y
3 Carnahan	N	N	Y	Y	Y	N	N
4 Skelton	N	N	Y	Y	Y	N	N
5 Cleaver	N	N	Y	Y	Y	N	N
6 **Graves**	Y	Y	Y	Y	Y	Y	Y
7 **Blunt**	Y	Y	N	Y	Y	Y	Y
8 **Emerson**	Y	Y	N	Y	Y	Y	Y
9 **Hulshof**	Y	Y	N	Y	Y	Y	Y
MONTANA							
AL **Rehberg**	Y	Y	N	Y	Y	Y	Y
NEBRASKA							
1 **Fortenberry**	Y	Y	N	Y	Y	Y	Y
2 **Terry**	Y	Y	N	Y	Y	Y	Y
3 **Smith**	Y	Y	N	Y	Y	Y	Y
NEVADA							
1 Berkley	–	–	–	+	+	–	–
2 **Heller**	Y	Y	N	Y	Y	Y	Y
3 **Porter**	Y	Y	N	Y	Y	Y	Y
NEW HAMPSHIRE							
1 Shea-Porter	N	N	Y	Y	Y	N	N
2 Hodes	N	N	Y	Y	Y	N	N
NEW JERSEY							
1 Andrews	N	N	Y	Y	Y	N	N
2 **LoBiondo**	N	Y	Y	Y	Y	Y	Y
3 **Saxton**	Y	Y	N	Y	Y	Y	Y
4 **Smith**	N	Y	Y	Y	Y	N	Y
5 **Garrett**	Y	Y	N	Y	N	Y	Y
6 Pallone	N	N	Y	N	Y	N	N
7 **Ferguson**	Y	Y	N	Y	Y	Y	Y
8 Pascrell	N	N	Y	Y	Y	N	N
9 Rothman	N	N	Y	Y	Y	N	N
10 Payne	N	N	Y	N	Y	N	N
11 **Frelinghuysen**	Y	Y	N	Y	Y	Y	Y
12 Holt	N	N	Y	N	Y	N	N
13 Sires	N	N	Y	Y	Y	N	N
NEW MEXICO							
1 **Wilson**	Y	Y	N	Y	Y	Y	Y
2 **Pearce**	Y	Y	N	Y	Y	Y	Y
3 Udall	N	N	Y	Y	Y	N	N
NEW YORK							
1 Bishop	N	N	Y	Y	Y	N	N
2 Israel	N	N	Y	Y	Y	N	N
3 **King**	Y	Y	N	Y	Y	Y	Y
4 McCarthy	N	N	Y	Y	Y	N	N
5 Ackerman	N	N	Y	Y	Y	N	?
6 Meeks	?	?	?	Y	Y	N	N
7 Crowley	N	N	Y	Y	Y	N	N
8 Nadler	N	N	Y	Y	Y	N	N
9 Weiner	N	N	Y	Y	Y	N	N
10 Towns	N	N	Y	N	Y	N	N
11 Clarke	N	N	Y	N	Y	N	N
12 Velázquez	N	N	Y	N	Y	N	N
13 **Fossella**	?	?	?	?	?	?	?
14 Maloney	N	N	Y	Y	Y	N	N
15 Rangel	N	N	Y	Y	Y	N	N
16 Serrano	N	N	Y	N	Y	N	N
17 Engel	N	N	Y	Y	Y	N	N
18 Lowey	N	N	Y	Y	Y	N	N
19 Hall	N	N	Y	Y	Y	N	N
20 Gillibrand	N	N	Y	Y	Y	N	N
21 McNulty	N	N	Y	Y	Y	N	N
22 Hinchey	N	N	Y	Y	Y	N	N
23 **McHugh**	Y	Y	N	Y	Y	Y	Y
24 Arcuri	N	N	Y	Y	Y	N	N
25 **Walsh**	Y	Y	N	Y	Y	Y	Y
26 **Reynolds**	Y	Y	N	Y	Y	Y	Y
27 Higgins	N	N	Y	Y	Y	N	N
28 Slaughter	N	N	Y	Y	Y	N	N
29 **Kuhl**	Y	Y	N	Y	Y	Y	Y
NORTH CAROLINA							
1 Butterfield	N	N	Y	Y	Y	N	N
2 Etheridge	N	N	Y	Y	Y	N	N
3 **Jones**	N	Y	N	Y	Y	Y	Y
4 Price	N	N	Y	Y	Y	N	N
5 **Foxx**	Y	Y	N	Y	Y	Y	Y
6 **Coble**	Y	Y	N	Y	Y	Y	Y
7 McIntyre	N	N	Y	Y	Y	N	N
8 **Hayes**	Y	Y	N	Y	Y	Y	Y
9 **Myrick**	Y	Y	N	Y	Y	Y	Y
10 **McHenry**	Y	Y	N	Y	Y	Y	Y
11 Shuler	N	N	Y	Y	Y	N	N
12 Watt	N	N	Y	Y	Y	N	N
13 Miller	N	N	Y	Y	Y	N	N
NORTH DAKOTA							
AL Pomeroy	N	N	Y	Y	Y	N	N
OHIO							
1 **Chabot**	Y	Y	N	Y	Y	Y	Y
2 **Schmidt**	Y	Y	N	Y	?	?	?
3 **Turner**	Y	Y	N	Y	Y	Y	Y
4 **Jordan**	Y	Y	N	Y	Y	Y	Y
5 **Latta**	Y	Y	N	Y	Y	Y	Y
6 Wilson	N	N	Y	Y	Y	N	N
7 **Hobson**	Y	Y	N	Y	?	?	?
8 **Boehner**	Y	Y	N	Y	Y	?	?
9 Kaptur	N	N	Y	Y	Y	N	N
10 Kucinich	N	N	Y	N	Y	N	N
11 Tubbs Jones	N	N	Y	Y	Y	N	N
12 **Tiberi**	Y	Y	N	Y	Y	Y	Y
13 Sutton	N	N	Y	Y	Y	N	N
14 **LaTourette**	Y	Y	N	Y	Y	Y	Y
15 **Pryce**	Y	Y	N	Y	Y	Y	Y
16 **Regula**	Y	Y	N	Y	Y	Y	Y
17 Ryan	N	N	Y	Y	Y	N	N
18 Space	N	N	Y	Y	Y	N	N
OKLAHOMA							
1 **Sullivan**	Y	Y	N	Y	Y	Y	Y
2 Boren	N	N	N	Y	Y	N	N
3 **Lucas**	Y	Y	N	Y	Y	Y	Y
4 **Cole**	Y	Y	N	Y	Y	Y	Y
5 **Fallin**	Y	Y	N	Y	Y	Y	Y
OREGON							
1 Wu	N	N	Y	N	?	?	?
2 **Walden**	Y	Y	N	Y	Y	Y	Y
3 Blumenauer	N	N	Y	Y	Y	N	N
4 DeFazio	N	N	Y	N	Y	N	N
5 Hooley	N	N	Y	Y	Y	N	N
PENNSYLVANIA							
1 Brady	N	N	Y	Y	Y	N	N
2 Fattah	N	N	Y	N	Y	N	N
3 **English**	Y	Y	N	Y	Y	Y	Y
4 Altmire	N	Y	Y	Y	Y	N	N
5 **Peterson**	Y	Y	N	Y	Y	Y	Y
6 **Gerlach**	Y	Y	N	Y	Y	Y	Y
7 Sestak	N	N	Y	Y	Y	N	N
8 Murphy, P.	N	N	Y	Y	Y	N	N
9 **Shuster**	Y	Y	N	Y	Y	Y	Y
10 Carney	N	Y	Y	Y	Y	Y	Y
11 Kanjorski	N	N	Y	Y	Y	N	N
12 Murtha	N	N	Y	Y	Y	N	N
13 Schwartz	N	N	Y	Y	Y	N	N
14 Doyle	N	N	Y	Y	Y	N	N
15 **Dent**	Y	Y	N	Y	Y	Y	Y
16 **Pitts**	Y	Y	N	Y	Y	Y	Y
17 Holden	N	N	Y	Y	Y	N	N
18 **Murphy, T.**	Y	Y	N	Y	Y	Y	Y
19 **Platts**	Y	Y	N	Y	Y	Y	Y
RHODE ISLAND							
1 Kennedy	N	N	Y	Y	Y	N	N
2 Langevin	N	N	Y	Y	Y	N	N
SOUTH CAROLINA							
1 **Brown**	Y	Y	N	Y	?	?	?
2 **Wilson**	Y	Y	N	Y	N	Y	Y
3 **Barrett**	Y	Y	N	Y	N	Y	Y
4 **Inglis**	Y	Y	N	Y	Y	Y	Y
5 Spratt	N	N	Y	Y	Y	N	N
6 Clyburn	N	N	Y	Y	Y	N	N
SOUTH DAKOTA							
AL Herseth Sandlin	N	N	N	Y	Y	N	N
TENNESSEE							
1 **Davis, David**	Y	Y	N	Y	Y	Y	Y
2 **Duncan**	Y	Y	N	N	Y	Y	Y
3 **Wamp**	Y	Y	N	Y	Y	Y	Y
4 Davis, L.	N	N	N	Y	Y	N	N
5 Cooper	N	N	Y	Y	Y	N	N
6 Gordon	N	N	Y	Y	?	N	N
7 **Blackburn**	Y	Y	N	Y	Y	Y	Y
8 Tanner	?	?	?	?	Y	N	N
9 Cohen	N	N	Y	Y	Y	N	N
TEXAS							
1 **Gohmert**	Y	Y	N	Y	Y	Y	Y
2 **Poe**	Y	Y	N	Y	Y	Y	Y
3 **Johnson, S.**	Y	Y	N	Y	N	Y	Y
4 **Hall**	Y	Y	N	Y	Y	Y	Y
5 **Hensarling**	Y	Y	N	Y	N	Y	Y
6 **Barton**	Y	Y	N	Y	Y	Y	Y
7 **Culberson**	?	?	?	?	Y	Y	Y
8 **Brady**	Y	Y	N	Y	Y	Y	Y
9 Green, A.	N	N	Y	Y	Y	N	N
10 **McCaul**	Y	Y	N	Y	Y	Y	Y
11 **Conaway**	Y	Y	N	Y	Y	Y	Y
12 **Granger**	Y	Y	N	Y	Y	Y	Y
13 **Thornberry**	Y	Y	N	Y	Y	Y	Y
14 **Paul**	?	?	?	?	?	?	?
15 Hinojosa	N	N	Y	Y	Y	N	N
16 Reyes	N	N	Y	Y	Y	N	N
17 Edwards	N	N	Y	Y	Y	N	N
18 Jackson Lee	N	N	Y	+	Y	N	N
19 **Neugebauer**	Y	Y	N	Y	Y	Y	Y
20 Gonzalez	N	N	Y	Y	Y	N	N
21 **Smith**	Y	Y	N	Y	Y	Y	Y
22 Lampson	Y	Y	N	Y	Y	N	N
23 Rodriguez	N	N	Y	Y	Y	N	N
24 **Marchant**	N	Y	N	Y	Y	Y	Y
25 Doggett	N	N	Y	N	Y	N	N
26 **Burgess**	Y	Y	N	Y	Y	Y	Y
27 Ortiz	N	N	Y	Y	Y	N	N
28 Cuellar	N	N	N	Y	Y	N	N
29 Green, G.	N	N	Y	Y	Y	N	N
30 Johnson, E.	N	N	Y	Y	Y	N	N
31 **Carter**	Y	Y	N	Y	Y	Y	Y
32 **Sessions**	Y	Y	N	Y	Y	Y	Y
UTAH							
1 **Bishop**	Y	Y	N	Y	Y	Y	Y
2 Matheson	N	N	Y	Y	Y	N	N
3 **Cannon**	Y	Y	N	Y	N	Y	Y
VERMONT							
AL Welch	N	N	Y	N	Y	N	N
VIRGINIA							
1 **Wittman**	Y	Y	N	Y	Y	Y	Y
2 **Drake**	Y	Y	N	Y	Y	Y	Y
3 Scott	N	N	Y	Y	Y	N	N
4 **Forbes**	?	?	?	?	?	?	?
5 **Goode**	Y	Y	N	N	Y	Y	Y
6 **Goodlatte**	Y	Y	N	Y	Y	Y	Y
7 **Cantor**	Y	Y	N	Y	Y	Y	Y
8 Moran	N	N	Y	Y	Y	N	N
9 Boucher	N	N	Y	Y	Y	N	N
10 **Wolf**	Y	Y	N	Y	Y	Y	Y
11 **Davis, T.**	Y	Y	N	Y	Y	Y	Y
WASHINGTON							
1 Inslee	N	N	Y	Y	Y	N	N
2 Larsen	N	N	Y	Y	Y	N	N
3 Baird	N	N	Y	Y	Y	N	N
4 **Hastings**	Y	Y	N	Y	Y	Y	Y
5 **McMorris Rodgers**	Y	Y	N	Y	Y	Y	Y
6 Dicks	N	N	Y	Y	Y	N	N
7 McDermott	N	N	Y	N	Y	N	N
8 **Reichert**	Y	Y	N	Y	Y	Y	Y
9 Smith	Y	N	Y	Y	Y	N	N
WEST VIRGINIA							
1 Mollohan	N	N	Y	Y	Y	N	N
2 **Capito**	Y	Y	Y	Y	Y	Y	Y
3 Rahall	N	N	Y	Y	Y	N	N
WISCONSIN							
1 **Ryan**	Y	Y	N	Y	Y	Y	Y
2 Baldwin	N	N	Y	N	Y	N	N
3 Kind	Y	N	Y	Y	Y	N	N
4 Moore	N	N	Y	N	Y	N	N
5 **Sensenbrenner**	Y	Y	N	N	Y	Y	Y
6 **Petri**	Y	Y	N	N	Y	Y	Y
7 Obey	N	N	Y	Y	Y	N	N
8 Kagen	N	N	Y	Y	Y	N	N
WYOMING							
AL **Cubin**	Y	Y	N	Y	Y	Y	Y
DELEGATES							
Faleomavaega (A.S.)	?				?	?	?
Norton (D.C.)	N				Y	N	N
Bordallo (Guam)	N				Y	N	N
Fortuño (P.R.)	?				Y	Y	Y
Christensen (V.I.)	N				Y	N	N

IN THE HOUSE | By Vote Number

15. **HR 3524. HOPE VI Housing Reauthorization/Prevailing Wages.** King, R-Iowa, amendment that would bar the use of funds in the bill to pay for local prevailing wage requirements under the Davis-Bacon Act for public housing projects. Rejected in Committee of the Whole 136-268: R 136-48; D 0-220 (ND 0-165, SD 0-55). Jan. 17, 2008.

16. **HR 3524. HOPE VI Housing Reauthorization/Green Building Standards.** Capito, R-W.Va., amendment that would strike the green building standards from the bill and instead require the Housing and Urban Development Department to select a rating system for green buildings. Rejected in Committee of the Whole 169-240: R 165-20; D 4-220 (ND 2-167, SD 2-53). Jan. 17, 2008.

17. **HR 3524. HOPE VI Housing Reauthorization/Recommit.** Graves, R-Mo., motion to recommit the bill to the Financial Services Committee with instructions to include language that would give veterans with at least 90 days of service who were released or discharged honorably increased priority consideration under the housing assistance program. Motion agreed to 372-28: R 182-0; D 190-28 (ND 140-23, SD 50-5). Jan. 17, 2008.

18. **HR 3524. HOPE VI Housing Reauthorization/Passage.** Passage of the bill that would reauthorize $800 million per year in fiscal 2008 through 2015 for the HOPE VI public housing program. It would require one-for-one replacement of housing units demolished under the program, require mixed-income housing on sites of demolished low-income housing and set guidelines for units to be built in areas of lower concentrations of poverty. Passed 271-130: R 53-130; D 218-0 (ND 164-0, SD 54-0). A "nay" was a vote in support of the president's position. Jan. 17, 2008.

19. **HR 4211. Allsbrook Post Office/Passage.** Norton, D-D.C., motion to suspend the rules and pass the bill that would designate a post office in Roanoke Rapids, N.C., as the "Judge Richard B. Allsbrook Post Office." Motion agreed to 391-0: R 186-0; D 205-0 (ND 154-0, SD 51-0). A two-thirds majority of those present and voting (261 in this case) is required for passage under suspension of the rules. Jan. 22, 2008.

20. **H Res 866. Coast Guard Tribute/Adoption.** DeFazio, D-Ore., motion to suspend the rules and adopt the resolution that would honor the U.S. Coast Guard for its 217 years of providing maritime law enforcement and border protection. Motion agreed to 391-0: R 187-0; D 204-0 (ND 153-0, SD 51-0). A two-thirds majority of those present and voting (261 in this case) is required for adoption under suspension of the rules. Jan. 22, 2008.

21. **HR 3963. Children's Health Insurance/Previous Question.** Dingell, D-Mich., motion to order the previous question (thus ending debate) on consideration of a veto override of the bill that would reauthorize the State Children's Health Insurance Program at nearly $60 billion over five years, expanding the program by $35 billion. Motion agreed to 217-195: R 0-194; D 217-1 (ND 162-0, SD 55-1). Jan. 23, 2008.

ND Northern Democrats, SD Southern Democrats
Southern states: Ala., Ark., Fla., Ga., Ky., La., Miss., N.C., Okla., S.C., Tenn., Texas, Va.

	15	16	17	18	19	20	21
ALABAMA							
1 **Bonner**	Y	Y	Y	Y	Y	Y	N
2 **Everett**	Y	Y	Y	N	Y	Y	N
3 **Rogers**	Y	Y	Y	Y	Y	Y	N
4 **Aderholt**	Y	Y	Y	Y	Y	Y	N
5 Cramer	N	N	Y	Y	Y	Y	Y
6 **Bachus**	Y	Y	Y	Y	Y	Y	N
7 Davis	N	N	Y	Y	Y	Y	Y
ALASKA							
AL **Young**	N	Y	Y	N	Y	Y	N
ARIZONA							
1 **Renzi**	N	Y	Y	Y	Y	Y	N
2 **Franks**	Y	Y	Y	N	Y	Y	N
3 **Shadegg**	Y	Y	Y	N	Y	Y	N
4 Pastor	N	N	Y	Y	Y	Y	Y
5 Mitchell	N	N	Y	Y	Y	Y	Y
6 **Flake**	Y	Y	Y	N	Y	Y	N
7 Grijalva	N	N	N	Y	?	?	Y
8 Giffords	N	N	Y	Y	?	?	Y
ARKANSAS							
1 Berry	–	–	+	+	Y	Y	Y
2 Snyder	N	N	Y	Y	?	?	Y
3 **Boozman**	Y	Y	Y	N	Y	Y	N
4 Ross	N	N	Y	Y	+	+	Y
CALIFORNIA							
1 Thompson	N	N	Y	Y	Y	Y	Y
2 **Herger**	Y	Y	Y	N	Y	Y	N
3 **Lungren**	Y	Y	Y	N	Y	Y	N
4 **Doolittle**	Y	Y	Y	N	Y	Y	N
5 Matsui	N	N	Y	Y	Y	Y	Y
6 Woolsey	N	N	N	Y	Y	Y	Y
7 Miller, George	N	N	N	Y	Y	Y	Y
8 Pelosi							
9 Lee	N	N	N	Y	Y	Y	Y
10 Tauscher	N	N	Y	Y	Y	Y	Y
11 McNerney	N	N	Y	Y	Y	Y	Y
12 Lantos	?	?	?	?	?	?	?
13 Stark	N	N	N	Y	Y	Y	Y
14 Eshoo	N	N	Y	Y	Y	Y	Y
15 Honda	N	N	N	Y	Y	Y	Y
16 Lofgren	N	N	Y	Y	Y	Y	Y
17 Farr	N	N	Y	Y	Y	Y	Y
18 Cardoza	?	N	Y	Y	Y	Y	Y
19 **Radanovich**	Y	Y	?	N	?	?	N
20 Costa	N	N	Y	Y	Y	Y	Y
21 **Nunes**	Y	Y	Y	N	Y	Y	N
22 **McCarthy**	Y	Y	Y	N	Y	Y	N
23 Capps	N	N	Y	Y	Y	Y	Y
24 **Gallegly**	Y	Y	Y	N	?	?	N
25 **McKeon**	Y	Y	Y	N	Y	Y	N
26 **Dreier**	Y	Y	Y	N	Y	Y	N
27 Sherman	?	?	?	?	?	?	?
28 Berman	N	N	Y	Y	?	?	Y
29 Schiff	N	N	Y	Y	Y	Y	Y
30 Waxman	N	N	Y	Y	Y	Y	Y
31 Becerra	N	N	N	Y	Y	Y	Y
32 Solis	N	N	N	+	+	+	+
33 Watson	N	N	N	Y	Y	Y	Y
34 Roybal-Allard	N	N	Y	+	+	+	Y
35 Waters	N	N	N	Y	Y	Y	Y
36 Harman	N	N	Y	Y	?	?	Y
37 Richardson	N	N	N	Y	Y	Y	Y
38 Napolitano	N	N	Y	+	+	+	Y
39 Sánchez, Linda	N	N	Y	Y	Y	Y	Y
40 **Royce**	Y	Y	Y	N	Y	Y	N
41 **Lewis**	N	Y	Y	N	Y	Y	N
42 **Miller, Gary**	?	?	?	?	?	?	?
43 Baca	?	?	?	+	Y	Y	Y
44 **Calvert**	Y	Y	Y	Y	Y	Y	N
45 **Bono Mack**	Y	Y	Y	N	Y	Y	N
46 **Rohrabacher**	Y	Y	Y	N	?	?	N
47 Sanchez, Loretta	N	N	Y	+	+	+	+
48 **Campbell**	Y	Y	Y	N	Y	Y	N
49 **Issa**	Y	Y	Y	N	Y	Y	N
50 **Bilbray**	Y	N	Y	N	Y	Y	N
51 Filner	N	N	Y	Y	Y	Y	Y
52 **Hunter**	?	?	?	?	?	?	N
53 Davis	N	N	Y	Y	Y	Y	Y
COLORADO							
1 DeGette	N	N	N	Y	?	?	Y
2 Udall	N	N	Y	Y	Y	Y	Y
3 Salazar	N	N	Y	Y	Y	Y	Y
4 **Musgrave**	Y	Y	Y	Y	Y	Y	N
5 **Lamborn**	Y	Y	Y	N	Y	Y	N
6 **Tancredo**	Y	Y	Y	N	Y	Y	N
7 Perlmutter	N	N	Y	Y	Y	Y	Y
CONNECTICUT							
1 Larson	N	N	Y	Y	Y	Y	Y
2 Courtney	N	N	Y	Y	Y	Y	Y
3 DeLauro	N	N	Y	Y	Y	Y	Y
4 **Shays**	N	Y	Y	Y	Y	Y	N
5 Murphy	N	N	Y	Y	Y	Y	Y
DELAWARE							
AL **Castle**	N	Y	Y	Y	Y	Y	N
FLORIDA							
1 **Miller**	Y	Y	Y	N	Y	Y	N
2 Boyd	N	N	Y	Y	Y	Y	Y
3 Brown	N	N	Y	Y	?	?	Y
4 **Crenshaw**	Y	Y	Y	N	Y	Y	N
5 **Brown-Waite**	N	Y	Y	N	Y	Y	N
6 **Stearns**	Y	Y	Y	N	Y	Y	N
7 **Mica**	Y	Y	Y	N	Y	Y	N
8 **Keller**	Y	Y	Y	N	Y	Y	N
9 **Bilirakis**	Y	Y	Y	N	Y	Y	N
10 **Young**	Y	Y	Y	N	Y	Y	N
11 Castor	N	N	N	Y	Y	Y	Y
12 **Putnam**	Y	Y	Y	N	Y	Y	N
13 **Buchanan**	Y	Y	Y	N	Y	Y	N
14 **Mack**	Y	Y	Y	N	Y	Y	N
15 **Weldon**	Y	N	Y	N	Y	Y	N
16 Mahoney	N	N	Y	Y	Y	Y	Y
17 Meek	N	N	Y	Y	Y	Y	Y
18 **Ros-Lehtinen**	N	N	Y	Y	Y	Y	N
19 Wexler	N	N	Y	Y	Y	Y	Y
20 Wasserman Schultz	N	N	Y	Y	Y	Y	Y
21 **Diaz-Balart, L.**	N	Y	Y	Y	Y	Y	Y
22 Klein	N	N	Y	Y	Y	Y	Y
23 Hastings	N	N	Y	Y	Y	Y	Y
24 Feeney	Y	?	Y	N	Y	Y	N
25 **Diaz-Balart, M.**	N	Y	Y	Y	Y	Y	N
GEORGIA							
1 **Kingston**	?	?	?	?	?	?	N
2 Bishop	N	N	Y	Y	Y	Y	Y
3 **Westmoreland**	Y	Y	Y	N	Y	Y	N
4 Johnson	N	N	Y	Y	Y	Y	Y
5 Lewis	N	N	N	Y	Y	Y	Y
6 **Price**	Y	Y	Y	N	Y	Y	N
7 **Linder**	Y	Y	Y	N	Y	Y	N
8 Marshall	N	N	Y	Y	Y	Y	Y
9 **Deal**	?	?	?	?	Y	Y	N
10 **Broun**	Y	Y	Y	N	Y	Y	N
11 **Gingrey**	Y	Y	Y	N	Y	Y	N
12 Barrow	N	Y	Y	Y	Y	Y	Y
13 Scott	N	N	Y	Y	Y	Y	Y
HAWAII							
1 Abercrombie	N	N	Y	Y	Y	Y	Y
2 Hirono	N	N	Y	Y	Y	Y	Y
IDAHO							
1 **Sali**	Y	Y	Y	N	Y	N	N
2 **Simpson**	Y	Y	Y	N	Y	Y	N
ILLINOIS							
1 Rush	N	N	Y	?	?	?	?
2 Jackson	N	N	Y	Y	Y	Y	Y
3 Lipinski	N	N	Y	Y	Y	Y	Y
4 Gutierrez	N	N	N	Y	Y	Y	Y
5 Emanuel	N	N	Y	Y	Y	Y	Y
6 **Roskam**	N	Y	Y	N	Y	N	N
7 Davis	?	?	N	Y	+	+	+
8 Bean	N	N	Y	Y	Y	Y	Y
9 Schakowsky	N	N	Y	Y	Y	Y	Y
10 **Kirk**	N	N	Y	Y	Y	Y	N
11 **Weller**	N	Y	Y	N	Y	Y	N
12 Costello	N	N	Y	Y	?	?	Y
13 **Biggert**	N	Y	Y	N	Y	Y	N
14 Vacant							
15 **Johnson**	N	N	Y	Y	+	+	N

KEY   **Republicans**   Democrats

Y Voted for (yea)	**X** Paired against	**C** Voted "present" to avoid possible conflict of interest
# Paired for	**–** Announced against	
+ Announced for	**P** Voted "present"	**?** Did not vote or otherwise make a position known
N Voted against (nay)		

	15	16	17	18	19	20	21
16 **Manzullo**	Y	Y	Y	N	Y	Y	N
17 Hare	N	N	Y	Y	+	+	Y
18 **LaHood**	N	Y	Y	Y	?	?	?
19 **Shimkus**	?	?	?	?	Y	Y	N
INDIANA							
1 Visclosky	?	?	?	?	Y	Y	Y
2 Donnelly	N	N	Y	Y	Y	Y	Y
3 **Souder**	Y	Y	Y	N	Y	Y	N
4 **Buyer**	Y	Y	Y	N	Y	Y	N
5 **Burton**	?	Y	Y	N	Y	Y	N
6 **Pence**	Y	Y	Y	N	Y	Y	N
7 Vacant							
8 Ellsworth	N	N	Y	Y	Y	Y	Y
9 Hill	N	N	Y	Y	Y	Y	Y
IOWA							
1 Braley	N	N	Y	Y	Y	Y	Y
2 Loebsack	N	N	Y	Y	Y	Y	Y
3 Boswell	N	N	Y	Y	Y	Y	Y
4 **Latham**	Y	Y	Y	N	Y	Y	N
5 **King**	Y	Y	Y	N	Y	Y	N
KANSAS							
1 **Moran**	Y	Y	Y	N	?	?	?
2 Boyda	N	N	Y	Y	Y	Y	Y
3 Moore	N	N	Y	Y	Y	Y	Y
4 **Tiahrt**	Y	Y	Y	Y	Y	Y	N
KENTUCKY							
1 **Whitfield**	N	Y	Y	Y	Y	Y	N
2 **Lewis**	?	?	?	?	Y	Y	N
3 Yarmuth	N	N	Y	Y	Y	Y	Y
4 **Davis**	Y	Y	Y	N	Y	Y	N
5 **Rogers**	Y	Y	Y	Y	Y	Y	N
6 Chandler	N	N	Y	Y	Y	Y	Y
LOUISIANA							
1 Vacant							
2 Jefferson	?	?	?	?	Y	Y	Y
3 Melancon	N	N	Y	Y	Y	Y	Y
4 **McCrery**	Y	Y	Y	N	Y	Y	N
5 **Alexander**	N	Y	Y	N	Y	Y	N
6 **Baker**	?	?	?	?	?	?	?
7 **Boustany**	Y	Y	Y	Y	Y	Y	N
MAINE							
1 Allen	N	N	Y	Y	Y	Y	Y
2 Michaud	N	Y	Y	Y	Y	Y	Y
MARYLAND							
1 **Gilchrest**	N	N	Y	Y	Y	Y	N
2 Ruppersberger	N	N	Y	Y	Y	Y	Y
3 Sarbanes	N	N	Y	Y	Y	Y	Y
4 Wynn	N	N	N	Y	Y	Y	Y
5 Hoyer	?	N	Y	Y	Y	Y	Y
6 **Bartlett**	Y	N	Y	N	Y	Y	N
7 Cummings	N	N	Y	Y	Y	Y	Y
8 Van Hollen	N	N	Y	Y	Y	Y	Y
MASSACHUSETTS							
1 Olver	N	N	Y	Y	Y	Y	Y
2 Neal	N	N	Y	Y	Y	Y	Y
3 McGovern	N	N	?	Y	Y	Y	Y
4 Frank	N	N	Y	Y	Y	Y	Y
5 Tsongas	N	N	Y	Y	Y	Y	Y
6 Tierney	N	N	Y	Y	Y	Y	Y
7 Markey	N	N	?	Y	Y	Y	Y
8 Capuano	N	N	Y	Y	Y	Y	Y
9 Lynch	N	N	Y	Y	Y	Y	Y
10 Delahunt	?	?	?	?	Y	Y	Y
MICHIGAN							
1 Stupak	N	N	Y	Y	Y	Y	Y
2 **Hoekstra**	Y	Y	Y	N	Y	Y	N
3 **Ehlers**	Y	N	Y	Y	Y	Y	N
4 **Camp**	Y	Y	?	?	Y	Y	N
5 Kildee	N	N	Y	Y	Y	Y	Y
6 **Upton**	N	N	Y	Y	Y	Y	N
7 **Walberg**	Y	Y	Y	N	Y	Y	N
8 **Rogers**	Y	Y	Y	N	Y	Y	N
9 **Knollenberg**	Y	Y	Y	N	Y	Y	N
10 **Miller**	N	Y	Y	N	Y	Y	N
11 **McCotter**	N	Y	Y	Y	Y	Y	N
12 Levin	N	N	Y	Y	Y	Y	Y
13 Kilpatrick	N	N	Y	Y	Y	Y	Y
14 Conyers	N	N	N	Y	Y	Y	Y
15 Dingell	N	N	N	Y	Y	Y	Y
MINNESOTA							
1 Walz	N	N	Y	Y	Y	Y	Y
2 **Kline**	Y	Y	Y	N	Y	Y	N
3 **Ramstad**	Y	N	Y	Y	Y	Y	N
4 McCollum	N	N	Y	Y	Y	Y	Y

	15	16	17	18	19	20	21
5 Ellison	N	N	N	Y	+	+	Y
6 **Bachmann**	Y	Y	Y	N	?	Y	N
7 Peterson	N	N	Y	Y	Y	Y	Y
8 Oberstar	N	N	Y	Y	Y	Y	Y
MISSISSIPPI							
1 Vacant							
2 Thompson	N	N	N	Y	Y	Y	Y
3 **Pickering**	Y	Y	Y	N	Y	Y	N
4 Taylor	N	N	Y	Y	Y	Y	Y
MISSOURI							
1 Clay	N	N	N	Y	Y	Y	Y
2 **Akin**	Y	Y	Y	N	Y	Y	N
3 Carnahan	N	N	Y	Y	Y	Y	Y
4 Skelton	N	N	Y	Y	Y	Y	Y
5 Cleaver	N	N	Y	Y	Y	Y	Y
6 **Graves**	N	Y	Y	N	Y	Y	N
7 **Blunt**	N	Y	Y	N	Y	Y	N
8 **Emerson**	N	Y	Y	N	Y	Y	N
9 **Hulshof**	Y	Y	Y	N	Y	Y	N
MONTANA							
AL **Rehberg**	N	Y	Y	N	Y	Y	N
NEBRASKA							
1 **Fortenberry**	Y	Y	Y	Y	Y	Y	N
2 **Terry**	Y	Y	Y	N	Y	Y	N
3 **Smith**	Y	Y	Y	N	Y	Y	N
NEVADA							
1 Berkley	–	–	+	+	Y	Y	Y
2 **Heller**	?	Y	Y	N	Y	Y	N
3 **Porter**	N	Y	Y	Y	Y	Y	N
NEW HAMPSHIRE							
1 Shea-Porter	N	N	Y	Y	Y	Y	Y
2 Hodes	N	N	Y	Y	Y	Y	Y
NEW JERSEY							
1 Andrews	N	N	Y	Y	Y	Y	Y
2 **LoBiondo**	N	N	Y	Y	Y	Y	N
3 **Saxton**	N	Y	Y	Y	Y	Y	N
4 **Smith**	N	N	Y	Y	Y	Y	N
5 **Garrett**	Y	Y	Y	N	Y	Y	N
6 Pallone	N	N	Y	Y	Y	Y	Y
7 **Ferguson**	N	Y	Y	Y	Y	Y	N
8 Pascrell	N	N	Y	Y	Y	Y	Y
9 Rothman	N	N	Y	Y	Y	Y	Y
10 Payne	?	N	Y	Y	Y	Y	Y
11 **Frelinghuysen**	Y	Y	Y	N	Y	Y	N
12 Holt	N	N	Y	Y	Y	Y	Y
13 Sires	N	N	Y	Y	Y	Y	Y
NEW MEXICO							
1 **Wilson**	Y	Y	Y	N	Y	Y	N
2 **Pearce**	Y	Y	Y	N	Y	Y	N
3 Udall	N	N	Y	Y	Y	Y	Y
NEW YORK							
1 Bishop	N	N	Y	Y	Y	Y	Y
2 Israel	N	N	Y	Y	Y	Y	Y
3 **King**	N	Y	Y	Y	Y	Y	N
4 McCarthy	N	N	Y	Y	Y	Y	Y
5 Ackerman	N	N	Y	Y	Y	Y	Y
6 Meeks	N	N	Y	Y	Y	Y	Y
7 Crowley	N	N	Y	Y	Y	Y	Y
8 Nadler	N	N	Y	Y	Y	Y	Y
9 Weiner	N	N	Y	Y	Y	Y	Y
10 Towns	N	N	Y	Y	Y	Y	Y
11 Clarke	N	N	N	Y	Y	Y	Y
12 Velázquez	N	N	Y	Y	Y	Y	Y
13 **Fossella**	?	?	?	?	Y	Y	N
14 Maloney	N	N	Y	Y	Y	Y	Y
15 Rangel	N	N	Y	Y	Y	Y	Y
16 Serrano	N	N	Y	Y	Y	Y	Y
17 Engel	N	N	Y	Y	Y	Y	Y
18 Lowey	N	N	Y	Y	Y	Y	Y
19 Hall	N	N	Y	Y	Y	Y	Y
20 Gillibrand	N	N	Y	Y	Y	Y	Y
21 McNulty	N	N	Y	Y	Y	Y	Y
22 Hinchey	N	N	Y	Y	Y	Y	Y
23 **McHugh**	N	N	Y	Y	Y	Y	N
24 Arcuri	N	N	Y	Y	Y	Y	Y
25 **Walsh**	N	N	Y	Y	Y	Y	N
26 **Reynolds**	N	Y	Y	N	Y	Y	N
27 Higgins	N	N	Y	Y	Y	Y	Y
28 Slaughter	N	N	N	+	Y	Y	Y
29 **Kuhl**	N	N	Y	N	Y	Y	N
NORTH CAROLINA							
1 Butterfield	N	N	Y	Y	Y	Y	Y
2 Etheridge	N	N	Y	Y	Y	Y	Y
3 **Jones**	Y	Y	Y	N	Y	Y	N
4 Price	N	N	Y	Y	Y	Y	Y

	15	16	17	18	19	20	21
5 **Foxx**	Y	Y	Y	N	Y	Y	N
6 **Coble**	Y	Y	Y	N	Y	Y	N
7 McIntyre	N	N	Y	Y	Y	Y	Y
8 **Hayes**	Y	Y	Y	Y	?	?	N
9 **Myrick**	Y	Y	Y	Y	Y	Y	N
10 **McHenry**	Y	Y	Y	N	Y	Y	N
11 Shuler	N	N	Y	Y	Y	Y	Y
12 Watt	N	N	Y	Y	?	?	Y
13 Miller	N	N	Y	Y	Y	Y	Y
NORTH DAKOTA							
AL Pomeroy	N	N	Y	Y	Y	Y	Y
OHIO							
1 **Chabot**	Y	Y	Y	N	Y	Y	N
2 **Schmidt**	?	?	?	?	Y	Y	N
3 **Turner**	N	Y	Y	Y	Y	Y	N
4 **Jordan**	Y	Y	Y	N	Y	Y	N
5 **Latta**	Y	Y	Y	N	Y	Y	N
6 Wilson	N	N	Y	Y	?	?	+
7 **Hobson**	?	?	?	?	Y	Y	N
8 **Boehner**	?	?	?	?	Y	Y	N
9 Kaptur	N	N	Y	Y	Y	Y	Y
10 Kucinich	N	N	N	Y	Y	Y	Y
11 Tubbs Jones	N	N	Y	Y	Y	Y	Y
12 **Tiberi**	N	Y	Y	Y	Y	Y	N
13 Sutton	N	N	Y	Y	?	?	Y
14 **LaTourette**	N	Y	Y	Y	Y	Y	N
15 **Pryce**	Y	Y	Y	Y	Y	Y	N
16 **Regula**	N	Y	Y	Y	Y	Y	N
17 Ryan	N	N	Y	Y	Y	Y	Y
18 Space	N	N	?	Y	Y	Y	Y
OKLAHOMA							
1 **Sullivan**	Y	Y	Y	?	Y	Y	N
2 Boren	N	N	Y	Y	Y	Y	Y
3 **Lucas**	Y	Y	Y	N	?	?	?
4 **Cole**	Y	Y	Y	N	Y	Y	N
5 **Fallin**	Y	Y	Y	N	Y	Y	N
OREGON							
1 Wu	?	?	?	?	Y	Y	Y
2 **Walden**	N	Y	Y	Y	Y	Y	N
3 Blumenauer	N	N	Y	Y	Y	Y	Y
4 DeFazio	N	N	Y	Y	Y	Y	Y
5 Hooley	N	N	Y	Y	Y	Y	Y
PENNSYLVANIA							
1 Brady	N	N	Y	Y	Y	Y	Y
2 Fattah	?	N	Y	Y	Y	Y	Y
3 **English**	N	Y	Y	N	Y	Y	N
4 Altmire	N	N	Y	Y	Y	Y	Y
5 **Peterson**	Y	Y	Y	N	Y	Y	N
6 **Gerlach**	N	Y	Y	Y	Y	Y	N
7 Sestak	N	N	Y	Y	Y	Y	Y
8 Murphy, P.	N	N	Y	Y	Y	Y	Y
9 **Shuster**	Y	Y	Y	N	Y	Y	N
10 Carney	N	Y	Y	Y	Y	Y	N
11 Kanjorski	N	N	Y	Y	Y	Y	Y
12 Murtha	N	N	Y	Y	Y	Y	Y
13 Schwartz	N	N	Y	Y	Y	Y	Y
14 Doyle	N	N	Y	Y	Y	Y	Y
15 **Dent**	Y	Y	Y	Y	Y	Y	N
16 **Pitts**	Y	Y	Y	N	Y	Y	N
17 Holden	N	N	Y	Y	Y	?	Y
18 **Murphy, T.**	N	Y	Y	Y	Y	Y	N
19 **Platts**	Y	N	Y	Y	Y	Y	N
RHODE ISLAND							
1 Kennedy	N	N	Y	Y	Y	Y	Y
2 Langevin	N	N	Y	Y	Y	Y	Y
SOUTH CAROLINA							
1 **Brown**	?	?	?	?	Y	Y	N
2 **Wilson**	Y	Y	?	N	Y	Y	N
3 **Barrett**	Y	Y	Y	N	Y	Y	N
4 **Inglis**	Y	N	Y	Y	Y	Y	N
5 Spratt	N	N	Y	Y	Y	Y	Y
6 Clyburn	N	N	Y	Y	Y	Y	Y
SOUTH DAKOTA							
AL Herseth Sandlin	N	N	Y	Y	Y	Y	Y
TENNESSEE							
1 **Davis, David**	Y	Y	Y	N	Y	Y	N
2 **Duncan**	Y	Y	Y	N	Y	Y	N
3 **Wamp**	Y	Y	Y	N	Y	Y	N
4 Davis, L.	N	N	Y	Y	Y	Y	Y
5 Cooper	N	N	Y	Y	Y	Y	Y
6 Gordon	N	N	Y	Y	Y	Y	Y
7 **Blackburn**	Y	Y	Y	N	Y	Y	N
8 Tanner	N	N	Y	Y	Y	Y	Y
9 Cohen	N	N	Y	+	Y	Y	Y

	15	16	17	18	19	20	21
TEXAS							
1 **Gohmert**	Y	Y	Y	N	Y	Y	N
2 **Poe**	Y	Y	Y	N	Y	Y	N
3 **Johnson, S.**	Y	Y	Y	N	Y	Y	N
4 **Hall**	Y	Y	Y	N	Y	Y	N
5 **Hensarling**	Y	Y	Y	N	Y	Y	N
6 **Barton**	Y	Y	Y	N	Y	Y	N
7 **Culberson**	Y	Y	Y	N	Y	Y	N
8 **Brady**	Y	Y	Y	N	Y	Y	N
9 Green, A.	N	N	Y	Y	Y	Y	Y
10 **McCaul**	Y	Y	Y	N	Y	Y	N
11 **Conaway**	Y	Y	Y	N	Y	Y	N
12 **Granger**	Y	Y	Y	N	Y	Y	N
13 **Thornberry**	Y	Y	Y	N	Y	Y	N
14 **Paul**	?	?	?	?	Y	Y	N
15 Hinojosa	N	N	Y	Y	?	?	?
16 Reyes	N	N	Y	Y	Y	Y	Y
17 Edwards	N	N	Y	Y	Y	Y	Y
18 Jackson Lee	N	N	Y	Y	Y	Y	Y
19 **Neugebauer**	Y	Y	Y	N	Y	Y	N
20 Gonzalez	N	N	Y	Y	Y	Y	Y
21 **Smith**	Y	Y	Y	N	Y	Y	N
22 Lampson	N	Y	Y	Y	Y	Y	Y
23 Rodriguez	N	N	Y	Y	Y	Y	Y
24 **Marchant**	Y	Y	Y	N	Y	Y	N
25 Doggett	N	N	Y	Y	Y	Y	Y
26 **Burgess**	Y	Y	Y	Y	Y	Y	N
27 Ortiz	N	N	Y	Y	Y	Y	Y
28 Cuellar	N	N	Y	Y	Y	Y	Y
29 Green, G.	N	N	Y	Y	+	+	Y
30 Johnson, E.	N	N	N	Y	Y	Y	Y
31 **Carter**	Y	Y	Y	N	Y	Y	N
32 **Sessions**	Y	Y	Y	N	Y	Y	N
UTAH							
1 **Bishop**	Y	Y	Y	N	Y	Y	N
2 Matheson	N	N	Y	Y	Y	Y	Y
3 **Cannon**	Y	Y	Y	N	Y	Y	N
VERMONT							
AL Welch	N	N	?	Y	Y	Y	Y
VIRGINIA							
1 **Wittman**	Y	Y	Y	N	Y	Y	N
2 **Drake**	Y	Y	Y	N	Y	Y	N
3 Scott	N	N	Y	Y	Y	Y	Y
4 **Forbes**	?	?	?	?	Y	Y	N
5 **Goode**	Y	Y	Y	N	Y	Y	N
6 **Goodlatte**	Y	Y	Y	N	Y	Y	N
7 **Cantor**	Y	Y	Y	N	Y	Y	N
8 Moran	N	N	N	Y	Y	Y	Y
9 Boucher	N	N	Y	Y	Y	Y	Y
10 **Wolf**	Y	Y	Y	Y	Y	Y	N
11 **Davis, T.**	Y	N	Y	Y	Y	Y	N
WASHINGTON							
1 Inslee	N	N	Y	Y	Y	Y	Y
2 Larsen	N	N	Y	Y	Y	Y	Y
3 Baird	N	N	Y	Y	?	+	+
4 **Hastings**	Y	Y	Y	N	Y	Y	N
5 **McMorris Rodgers**	Y	Y	Y	N	Y	Y	N
6 Dicks	N	N	Y	Y	Y	Y	Y
7 McDermott	N	N	N	Y	Y	Y	Y
8 **Reichert**	N	N	Y	Y	Y	Y	N
9 Smith	N	N	Y	Y	Y	Y	Y
WEST VIRGINIA							
1 Mollohan	N	N	Y	Y	Y	Y	Y
2 **Capito**	N	Y	Y	Y	Y	Y	N
3 Rahall	N	Y	Y	Y	?	?	?
WISCONSIN							
1 **Ryan**	N	Y	Y	N	Y	Y	N
2 Baldwin	N	N	Y	Y	Y	Y	Y
3 Kind	N	N	Y	Y	Y	Y	Y
4 Moore	N	N	Y	Y	Y	Y	Y
5 **Sensenbrenner**	Y	Y	Y	N	Y	Y	N
6 **Petri**	N	Y	Y	N	Y	Y	N
7 Obey	N	N	Y	Y	Y	Y	Y
8 Kagen	N	N	Y	Y	Y	Y	Y
WYOMING							
AL **Cubin**	Y	Y	Y	N	Y	Y	N
DELEGATES							
Faleomavaega (A.S.)	?	?					
Norton (D.C.)	N	N					
Bordallo (Guam)	N	N					
Fortuño (P.R.)	N	N					
Christensen (V.I.)	N	N					

IN THE HOUSE | By Vote Number

22. **HR 3963. Children's Health Insurance/Veto Override.** Passage, over President Bush's Dec. 12, 2007, veto, of the bill that would reauthorize the State Children's Health Insurance Program at nearly $60 billion over five years, expanding the program by $35 billion. To offset the cost of the expansion, it would increase the tax on cigarettes by 61 cents, to $1 per pack, and raise taxes on other tobacco products. The bill would limit program eligibility to families earning three times the federal poverty level or less. It would require the Social Security Administration to verify the citizenship of all applicants and require states to phase out coverage of childless adults by the end of 2008. Rejected 260-152: R 42-151; D 218-1 (ND 163-0, SD 55-1). A two-thirds majority of those present and voting (275 in this case) of both chambers is required to override a veto. A "nay" was a vote in support of the president's position. Jan. 23, 2008.

23. **S 2110. Pierce Post Office/Passage.** Davis, D-Ill., motion to suspend the rules and pass the bill that would designate a post office in Taft, Calif., as the "Larry S. Pierce Post Office." Motion agreed to 388-0: R 186-0; D 202-0 (ND 150-0, SD 52-0). A two-thirds majority of those present and voting (259 in this case) is required for passage under suspension of the rules. Jan. 28, 2008.

24. **HR 4140. Anderson Federal Building/Passage.** E. Johnson, D-Texas, motion to suspend the rules and pass the bill that would designate the Port Angeles Federal Building in Port Angeles, Wash., as the "Richard B. Anderson Federal Building." Motion agreed to 388-0: R 186-0; D 202-0 (ND 150-0, SD 52-0). A two-thirds majority of those present and voting (259 in this case) is required for passage under suspension of the rules. Jan. 28, 2008.

25. **HR 5140. Economic Stimulus/Passage.** Rangel, D-N.Y., motion to suspend the rules and pass the bill that would provide advance refunds of a tax credit for most taxpayers equal to $600 for individuals and $1,200 for couples. Families would receive $300 for each child under 17. It would provide businesses with a 50 percent depreciation for certain equipment purchased in 2008 and increase to $250,000 the amount small businesses can expense in the year items are purchased. It would raise the size of mortgage loans the Federal Housing Administration could insure and Fannie Mae and Freddie Mac could purchase. Motion agreed to 385-35: R 169-25; D 216-10 (ND 167-5, SD 49-5). A two-thirds majority of those present and voting (281 in this case) is required for passage under suspension of the rules. A "yea" was a vote in support of the president's position. Jan. 29, 2008.

26. **H Res 933. Louisiana State University Football/Adoption.** Altmire, D-Pa., motion to suspend the rules and adopt the resolution that would commend the Louisiana State University Tigers football team for winning the 2007 Bowl Championship Series national championship game. Motion agreed to 409-1: R 190-0; D 219-1 (ND 165-0, SD 54-1). A two-thirds majority of those present and voting (276 in this case) is required for adoption under suspension of the rules. Jan. 29, 2008.

27. **HR 1528. New England National Scenic Trail/Recommit.** Bishop, R-Utah, motion to recommit the bill to the Natural Resources Committee with instructions that it be immediately reported back with language that would prohibit the use of eminent domain to add lands to the New England National Scenic Trail. Motion rejected 183-205: R 172-0; D 11-205 (ND 6-157, SD 5-48). Jan. 29, 2008.

	22	23	24	25	26	27
ALABAMA						
1 Bonner	N	Y	Y	Y	Y	Y
2 Everett	?	Y	Y	Y	Y	?
3 Rogers	N	Y	Y	Y	Y	Y
4 Aderholt	N	Y	Y	Y	Y	Y
5 Cramer	Y	Y	Y	Y	Y	N
6 Bachus	N	Y	Y	Y	Y	N
7 Davis	Y	Y	Y	Y	N	N
ALASKA						
AL Young	Y	Y	?	Y	Y	Y
ARIZONA						
1 Renzi	Y	?	?	Y	Y	Y
2 Franks	N	Y	Y	Y	Y	Y
3 Shadegg	N	Y	N	N	Y	Y
4 Pastor	Y	Y	Y	Y	Y	N
5 Mitchell	Y	Y	Y	Y	Y	N
6 Flake	N	Y	N	N	Y	Y
7 Grijalva	Y	?	?	Y	Y	N
8 Giffords	Y	Y	Y	Y	Y	N
ARKANSAS						
1 Berry	Y	Y	Y	N	N	?
2 Snyder	Y	Y	Y	Y	Y	N
3 Boozman	N	Y	Y	Y	Y	Y
4 Ross	Y	Y	Y	Y	N	N
CALIFORNIA						
1 Thompson	Y	Y	Y	Y	Y	N
2 Herger	N	Y	Y	Y	Y	Y
3 Lungren	N	Y	Y	Y	Y	Y
4 Doolittle	N	?	?	Y	Y	Y
5 Matsui	Y	Y	Y	Y	Y	N
6 Woolsey	Y	Y	Y	Y	Y	N
7 Miller, George	Y	?	?	Y	Y	N
8 Pelosi	Y			Y		
9 Lee	Y	Y	Y	Y	Y	N
10 Tauscher	Y	Y	Y	Y	Y	N
11 McNerney	Y	Y	Y	Y	Y	N
12 Lantos	?	?	?	?	?	?
13 Stark	Y	?	?	Y	Y	N
14 Eshoo	Y	Y	Y	Y	Y	N
15 Honda	Y	Y	Y	Y	Y	N
16 Lofgren	Y	Y	Y	Y	Y	N
17 Farr	Y	?	?	Y	Y	N
18 Cardoza	Y	?	?	Y	Y	N
19 Radanovich	N	Y	Y	Y	Y	?
20 Costa	Y	?	?	Y	Y	N
21 Nunes	N	Y	Y	Y	Y	Y
22 McCarthy	N	Y	Y	Y	Y	Y
23 Capps	Y	Y	Y	Y	Y	N
24 Gallegly	N	Y	Y	Y	Y	Y
25 McKeon	N	Y	Y	Y	Y	Y
26 Dreier	N	Y	Y	Y	Y	Y
27 Sherman	?	Y	Y	Y	Y	N
28 Berman	?	?	?	Y	Y	N
29 Schiff	Y	Y	Y	Y	Y	N
30 Waxman	Y	Y	Y	Y	Y	N
31 Becerra	Y	Y	Y	Y	Y	N
32 Solis	+	Y	Y	Y	Y	N
33 Watson	Y	Y	Y	Y	Y	N
34 Roybal-Allard	Y	+	+	Y	Y	N
35 Waters	Y	?	?	Y	Y	N
36 Harman	Y	Y	Y	Y	Y	N
37 Richardson	Y	Y	Y	Y	Y	N
38 Napolitano	+	Y	Y	Y	Y	N
39 Sánchez, Linda	Y	Y	Y	Y	Y	N
40 Royce	N	Y	Y	N	Y	Y
41 Lewis	N	Y	Y	Y	Y	Y
42 Miller, Gary	?	?	?	+	?	?
43 Baca	Y	Y	Y	Y	Y	N
44 Calvert	N	Y	Y	Y	Y	?
45 Bono Mack	Y	Y	Y	Y	Y	Y
46 Rohrabacher	N	Y	Y	N	Y	Y
47 Sanchez, Loretta	+	Y	Y	N	Y	N
48 Campbell	N	Y	Y	N	Y	Y
49 Issa	N	Y	Y	Y	Y	Y
50 Bilbray	N	Y	Y	Y	Y	Y
51 Filner	Y	?	+	+	+	–
52 Hunter	N	Y	Y	N	Y	Y
53 Davis	Y	Y	Y	Y	Y	N

	22	23	24	25	26	27
COLORADO						
1 DeGette	Y	Y	Y	Y	Y	N
2 Udall	Y	Y	Y	Y	Y	?
3 Salazar	Y	Y	Y	Y	Y	N
4 Musgrave	N	Y	Y	Y	Y	Y
5 Lamborn	N	Y	Y	Y	Y	Y
6 Tancredo	N	Y	N	N	Y	Y
7 Perlmutter	Y	Y	Y	Y	Y	N
CONNECTICUT						
1 Larson	Y	Y	Y	Y	Y	N
2 Courtney	Y	Y	Y	Y	Y	N
3 DeLauro	Y	Y	Y	Y	Y	N
4 Shays	Y	Y	Y	Y	Y	Y
5 Murphy	Y	Y	Y	Y	Y	N
DELAWARE						
AL Castle	Y	Y	Y	Y	Y	Y
FLORIDA						
1 Miller	N	Y	Y	Y	Y	Y
2 Boyd	Y	Y	Y	N	Y	N
3 Brown	Y	Y	Y	P	Y	N
4 Crenshaw	N	Y	Y	Y	Y	Y
5 Brown-Waite	N	Y	Y	Y	Y	Y
6 Stearns	N	Y	Y	Y	Y	Y
7 Mica	N	Y	Y	Y	Y	Y
8 Keller	N	Y	Y	Y	Y	?
9 Bilirakis	N	Y	Y	Y	Y	Y
10 Young	Y	?	Y	Y	Y	N
11 Castor	Y	Y	Y	Y	Y	N
12 Putnam	N	Y	Y	Y	Y	?
13 Buchanan	Y	Y	Y	Y	Y	Y
14 Mack	N	Y	Y	Y	Y	Y
15 Weldon	N	Y	Y	Y	Y	Y
16 Mahoney	Y	Y	Y	Y	Y	N
17 Meek	Y	?	?	Y	Y	N
18 Ros-Lehtinen	N	?	Y	Y	Y	Y
19 Wexler	Y	Y	Y	N	Y	N
20 Wasserman Schultz	Y	Y	Y	?	?	?
21 Diaz-Balart, L.	N	?	?	Y	Y	?
22 Klein	Y	Y	Y	Y	Y	N
23 Hastings	Y	?	?	?	?	?
24 Feeney	N	+	+	?	?	?
25 Diaz-Balart, M.	N	Y	Y	Y	Y	?
GEORGIA						
1 Kingston	N	Y	Y	N	Y	Y
2 Bishop	Y	Y	Y	Y	Y	N
3 Westmoreland	N	Y	Y	N	Y	?
4 Johnson	Y	Y	Y	Y	Y	N
5 Lewis	Y	Y	Y	Y	Y	N
6 Price	N	Y	Y	N	Y	Y
7 Linder	N	Y	Y	N	Y	Y
8 Marshall	Y	Y	Y	Y	Y	N
9 Deal	N	Y	Y	N	Y	?
10 Broun	N	Y	Y	N	P	Y
11 Gingrey	N	Y	Y	N	P	Y
12 Barrow	Y	Y	Y	Y	Y	N
13 Scott	Y	Y	Y	Y	Y	N
HAWAII						
1 Abercrombie	Y	Y	Y	Y	Y	N
2 Hirono	Y	Y	Y	Y	Y	N
IDAHO						
1 Sali	N	Y	Y	Y	Y	Y
2 Simpson	Y	?	?	?	?	?
ILLINOIS						
1 Rush	?	?	?	Y	Y	N
2 Jackson	Y	Y	Y	Y	Y	N
3 Lipinski	Y	Y	Y	Y	Y	?
4 Gutierrez	Y	?	?	Y	Y	N
5 Emanuel	Y	Y	Y	Y	Y	N
6 Roskam	N	?	?	Y	Y	Y
7 Davis	+	Y	Y	Y	Y	N
8 Bean	Y	Y	Y	Y	Y	N
9 Schakowsky	Y	Y	Y	Y	Y	N
10 Kirk	Y	?	?	Y	Y	N
11 Weller	N	Y	Y	Y	Y	N
12 Costello	?	Y	Y	Y	Y	N
13 Biggert	N	Y	Y	Y	Y	Y
14 Vacant						
15 Johnson	N	Y	Y	N	Y	N

KEY   **Republicans**   Democrats

Y	Voted for (yea)	X	Paired against
#	Paired for	–	Announced against
+	Announced for	P	Voted "present"
N	Voted against (nay)		
		C	Voted "present" to avoid possible conflict of interest
		?	Did not vote or otherwise make a position known

ND Northern Democrats, SD Southern Democrats
Southern states: Ala., Ark., Fla., Ga., Ky., La., Miss., N.C., Okla., S.C., Tenn., Texas, Va.

	22	23	24	25	26	27
16 **Manzullo**	N	Y	Y	Y	Y	Y
17 Hare	Y	Y	Y	Y	Y	N
18 **LaHood**	?	Y	Y	Y	Y	Y
19 **Shimkus**	N	Y	Y	Y	Y	Y
INDIANA						
1 Visclosky	Y	Y	Y	Y	Y	N
2 Donnelly	Y	Y	Y	Y	Y	N
3 **Souder**	N	Y	Y	Y	Y	Y
4 **Buyer**	N	Y	Y	Y	Y	Y
5 **Burton**	N	Y	Y	Y	Y	Y
6 **Pence**	N	Y	Y	Y	Y	Y
7 Vacant						
8 Ellsworth	Y	Y	Y	Y	Y	N
9 Hill	Y	Y	Y	Y	Y	N
IOWA						
1 Braley	Y	Y	Y	Y	Y	N
2 Loebsack	Y	Y	Y	Y	Y	N
3 Boswell	Y	Y	Y	Y	Y	N
4 **Latham**	Y	Y	Y	Y	Y	Y
5 **King**	N	Y	Y	Y	Y	Y
KANSAS						
1 **Moran**	?	Y	Y	Y	Y	Y
2 Boyda	Y	Y	Y	Y	Y	N
3 Moore	Y	Y	Y	Y	Y	N
4 **Tiahrt**	N	Y	Y	Y	Y	Y
KENTUCKY						
1 **Whitfield**	N	Y	Y	Y	Y	Y
2 **Lewis**	N	Y	Y	?	?	?
3 Yarmuth	Y	Y	Y	Y	Y	N
4 **Davis**	N	Y	Y	Y	Y	Y
5 **Rogers**	N	Y	Y	Y	Y	Y
6 Chandler	Y	Y	Y	Y	Y	N
LOUISIANA						
1 Vacant						
2 Jefferson	Y	Y	Y	Y	Y	N
3 Melancon	Y	Y	Y	Y	Y	N
4 **McCrery**	N	Y	Y	Y	Y	?
5 **Alexander**	N	Y	Y	Y	Y	Y
6 **Baker**	?	?	?	?	Y	?
7 **Boustany**	N	Y	Y	Y	Y	Y
MAINE						
1 Allen	Y	Y	Y	Y	Y	N
2 Michaud	Y	Y	Y	Y	Y	N
MARYLAND						
1 **Gilchrest**	Y	Y	Y	Y	Y	?
2 Ruppersberger	Y	Y	Y	Y	Y	N
3 Sarbanes	Y	Y	Y	Y	Y	N
4 Wynn	Y	Y	Y	Y	Y	?
5 Hoyer	Y	Y	Y	Y	Y	N
6 **Bartlett**	N	Y	Y	Y	Y	Y
7 Cummings	Y	Y	Y	Y	Y	N
8 Van Hollen	Y	Y	Y	Y	Y	N
MASSACHUSETTS						
1 Olver	Y	Y	Y	Y	Y	N
2 Neal	Y	?	?	Y	Y	N
3 McGovern	Y	Y	Y	Y	Y	N
4 Frank	Y	?	?	Y	Y	N
5 Tsongas	Y	Y	Y	Y	Y	N
6 Tierney	Y	Y	Y	Y	Y	N
7 Markey	Y	Y	Y	Y	Y	N
8 Capuano	Y	Y	Y	Y	Y	N
9 Lynch	Y	Y	Y	Y	Y	N
10 Delahunt	Y	Y	?	Y	Y	N
MICHIGAN						
1 Stupak	Y	Y	Y	Y	Y	N
2 **Hoekstra**	N	Y	Y	Y	Y	Y
3 **Ehlers**	N	Y	Y	Y	Y	Y
4 **Camp**	N	Y	Y	Y	Y	Y
5 Kildee	Y	Y	Y	Y	Y	N
6 **Upton**	Y	Y	Y	Y	Y	Y
7 **Walberg**	N	Y	Y	Y	Y	Y
8 **Rogers**	N	Y	Y	Y	Y	Y
9 **Knollenberg**	N	Y	Y	Y	Y	Y
10 **Miller**	Y	Y	Y	Y	Y	Y
11 **McCotter**	N	Y	Y	Y	Y	Y
12 Levin	Y	Y	Y	Y	Y	N
13 Kilpatrick	Y	Y	Y	Y	Y	N
14 Conyers	Y	Y	Y	Y	Y	N
15 Dingell	Y	Y	Y	Y	Y	N
MINNESOTA						
1 Walz	Y	Y	Y	Y	Y	N
2 **Kline**	N	Y	Y	Y	Y	Y
3 **Ramstad**	Y	Y	Y	Y	Y	Y
4 McCollum	Y	Y	Y	Y	Y	?
5 Ellison	Y	Y	Y	Y	Y	N
6 **Bachmann**	N	Y	Y	Y	Y	Y
7 Peterson	Y	Y	Y	N	Y	N
8 Oberstar	Y	Y	Y	Y	Y	N
MISSISSIPPI						
1 Vacant						
2 Thompson	Y	Y	Y	Y	Y	N
3 **Pickering**	N	Y	Y	Y	Y	Y
4 Taylor	Y	Y	Y	N	Y	N
MISSOURI						
1 Clay	Y	Y	Y	Y	Y	N
2 **Akin**	N	Y	Y	Y	Y	Y
3 Carnahan	Y	Y	Y	Y	?	N
4 Skelton	Y	Y	Y	Y	Y	N
5 Cleaver	Y	Y	Y	Y	Y	N
6 **Graves**	N	Y	Y	Y	Y	Y
7 **Blunt**	N	Y	Y	Y	Y	Y
8 **Emerson**	Y	Y	Y	Y	Y	Y
9 **Hulshof**	N	?	?	Y	Y	Y
MONTANA						
AL **Rehberg**	Y	Y	Y	Y	Y	Y
NEBRASKA						
1 **Fortenberry**	N	Y	Y	Y	Y	+
2 **Terry**	N	Y	Y	Y	Y	Y
3 **Smith**	N	Y	Y	Y	Y	Y
NEVADA						
1 Berkley	Y	?	?	Y	Y	Y
2 **Heller**	N	Y	Y	Y	Y	Y
3 **Porter**	Y	Y	Y	Y	Y	Y
NEW HAMPSHIRE						
1 Shea-Porter	Y	Y	Y	Y	Y	N
2 Hodes	Y	Y	Y	Y	Y	N
NEW JERSEY						
1 Andrews	Y	Y	Y	Y	Y	?
2 **LoBiondo**	Y	Y	Y	Y	Y	Y
3 **Saxton**	N	Y	Y	Y	Y	?
4 **Smith**	Y	Y	Y	Y	Y	Y
5 **Garrett**	N	Y	Y	Y	Y	Y
6 Pallone	Y	?	?	Y	Y	N
7 **Ferguson**	Y	Y	Y	Y	Y	Y
8 Pascrell	Y	Y	Y	Y	Y	N
9 Rothman	Y	Y	Y	Y	Y	N
10 Payne	Y	Y	Y	Y	Y	N
11 **Frelinghuysen**	N	Y	Y	Y	Y	Y
12 Holt	Y	Y	Y	Y	Y	N
13 Sires	Y	Y	Y	Y	?	N
NEW MEXICO						
1 **Wilson**	Y	Y	Y	Y	Y	?
2 **Pearce**	N	Y	Y	Y	Y	Y
3 Udall	Y	Y	Y	Y	Y	N
NEW YORK						
1 Bishop	Y	Y	Y	Y	Y	N
2 Israel	Y	Y	Y	Y	Y	N
3 **King**	Y	Y	Y	Y	Y	Y
4 McCarthy	Y	Y	Y	Y	Y	N
5 Ackerman	Y	Y	Y	Y	Y	N
6 Meeks	Y	?	?	Y	Y	N
7 Crowley	Y	Y	Y	Y	Y	N
8 Nadler	Y	?	?	Y	Y	N
9 Weiner	Y	Y	Y	Y	Y	N
10 Towns	Y	?	?	Y	Y	N
11 Clarke	Y	Y	Y	Y	Y	N
12 Velázquez	Y	Y	Y	Y	Y	N
13 **Fossella**	Y	Y	Y	Y	Y	Y
14 Maloney	Y	Y	Y	Y	Y	N
15 Rangel	Y	Y	Y	Y	?	N
16 Serrano	Y	Y	Y	Y	Y	N
17 Engel	Y	Y	Y	Y	Y	N
18 Lowey	Y	Y	Y	Y	Y	N
19 Hall	Y	Y	Y	Y	Y	Y
20 Gillibrand	Y	Y	Y	Y	Y	N
21 McNulty	Y	Y	Y	Y	Y	N
22 Hinchey	Y	?	?	Y	Y	N
23 **McHugh**	Y	Y	Y	Y	Y	Y
24 Arcuri	Y	Y	Y	Y	Y	Y
25 **Walsh**	Y	Y	Y	Y	P	Y
26 **Reynolds**	N	Y	Y	Y	Y	Y
27 Higgins	Y	Y	Y	Y	Y	N
28 Slaughter	Y	Y	Y	Y	Y	–
29 **Kuhl**	N	Y	Y	Y	Y	Y
NORTH CAROLINA						
1 Butterfield	Y	Y	Y	Y	Y	N
2 Etheridge	Y	Y	Y	Y	Y	N
3 **Jones**	N	Y	Y	Y	Y	Y
4 Price	Y	?	?	Y	Y	N
5 **Foxx**	N	Y	Y	Y	Y	Y
6 **Coble**	N	Y	Y	N	Y	Y
7 McIntyre	Y	Y	Y	Y	Y	Y
8 **Hayes**	N	Y	Y	Y	Y	Y
9 **Myrick**	N	Y	Y	Y	Y	Y
10 **McHenry**	N	Y	Y	Y	Y	Y
11 Shuler	Y	Y	Y	Y	Y	N
12 Watt	Y	Y	Y	Y	Y	N
13 Miller	Y	Y	Y	Y	Y	N
NORTH DAKOTA						
AL Pomeroy	Y	Y	Y	Y	Y	N
OHIO						
1 **Chabot**	N	Y	Y	Y	Y	Y
2 **Schmidt**	N	Y	Y	Y	Y	Y
3 **Turner**	Y	?	?	Y	Y	Y
4 **Jordan**	N	Y	Y	Y	Y	Y
5 **Latta**	N	Y	Y	Y	Y	Y
6 Wilson	+	Y	Y	Y	Y	N
7 **Hobson**	Y	Y	Y	Y	Y	Y
8 **Boehner**	N	Y	Y	Y	Y	Y
9 Kaptur	Y	Y	Y	N	Y	N
10 Kucinich	Y	Y	Y	Y	Y	N
11 Tubbs Jones	Y	?	Y	+	+	?
12 **Tiberi**	Y	Y	Y	Y	Y	?
13 Sutton	Y	Y	Y	Y	Y	N
14 **LaTourette**	Y	Y	Y	Y	?	?
15 **Pryce**	Y	Y	Y	Y	Y	?
16 **Regula**	Y	Y	Y	Y	Y	Y
17 Ryan	Y	?	Y	Y	Y	N
18 Space	Y	Y	Y	Y	P	N
OKLAHOMA						
1 **Sullivan**	N	Y	Y	Y	Y	Y
2 Boren	Y	Y	Y	Y	Y	N
3 **Lucas**	?	Y	Y	Y	Y	Y
4 **Cole**	N	Y	Y	Y	Y	Y
5 **Fallin**	N	Y	Y	Y	Y	?
OREGON						
1 Wu	Y	Y	Y	Y	Y	N
2 **Walden**	N	Y	Y	Y	Y	Y
3 Blumenauer	Y	Y	Y	Y	Y	N
4 DeFazio	Y	?	?	Y	Y	?
5 Hooley	Y	Y	Y	Y	Y	N
PENNSYLVANIA						
1 Brady	Y	Y	Y	Y	Y	N
2 Fattah	Y	Y	Y	Y	Y	N
3 **English**	Y	Y	Y	Y	Y	Y
4 Altmire	Y	Y	Y	Y	Y	Y
5 **Peterson**	N	Y	Y	Y	Y	Y
6 **Gerlach**	Y	Y	Y	Y	Y	Y
7 Sestak	Y	Y	Y	Y	Y	N
8 Murphy, P.	Y	Y	Y	Y	Y	N
9 **Shuster**	N	Y	Y	Y	Y	Y
10 Carney	Y	Y	Y	Y	Y	Y
11 Kanjorski	Y	Y	Y	Y	Y	N
12 Murtha	Y	Y	Y	Y	Y	N
13 Schwartz	Y	Y	Y	Y	Y	N
14 Doyle	Y	Y	Y	Y	?	?
15 **Dent**	Y	Y	Y	Y	Y	Y
16 **Pitts**	N	Y	Y	Y	Y	Y
17 Holden	Y	Y	Y	Y	Y	N
18 **Murphy, T.**	Y	Y	Y	Y	Y	Y
19 **Platts**	Y	Y	Y	Y	Y	Y
RHODE ISLAND						
1 Kennedy	Y	Y	Y	Y	Y	N
2 Langevin	Y	Y	Y	Y	Y	N
SOUTH CAROLINA						
1 **Brown**	N	Y	Y	Y	Y	Y
2 **Wilson**	N	Y	Y	Y	Y	Y
3 **Barrett**	N	Y	Y	Y	Y	Y
4 **Inglis**	N	Y	Y	Y	Y	Y
5 Spratt	Y	Y	Y	Y	Y	N
6 Clyburn	Y	Y	Y	Y	Y	N
SOUTH DAKOTA						
AL Herseth Sandlin	Y	Y	Y	Y	Y	Y
TENNESSEE						
1 **Davis, David**	N	Y	Y	Y	Y	Y
2 **Duncan**	N	Y	Y	Y	Y	Y
3 **Wamp**	N	Y	Y	Y	Y	Y
4 Davis, L.	Y	Y	Y	Y	Y	N
5 Cooper	Y	Y	Y	N	Y	N
6 Gordon	Y	Y	Y	Y	Y	N
7 **Blackburn**	N	Y	Y	Y	Y	Y
8 Tanner	Y	Y	Y	Y	Y	N
9 Cohen	Y	Y	Y	Y	Y	N
TEXAS						
1 **Gohmert**	N	Y	Y	N	Y	Y
2 **Poe**	N	Y	Y	N	Y	Y
3 **Johnson, S.**	N	Y	Y	Y	Y	Y
4 **Hall**	N	Y	Y	Y	Y	Y
5 **Hensarling**	N	Y	Y	Y	Y	Y
6 **Barton**	N	Y	Y	Y	Y	Y
7 **Culberson**	N	Y	Y	Y	Y	Y
8 **Brady**	N	Y	Y	Y	Y	Y
9 Green, A.	Y	Y	Y	Y	Y	N
10 **McCaul**	N	Y	Y	Y	Y	Y
11 **Conaway**	N	Y	Y	Y	Y	Y
12 **Granger**	N	Y	Y	Y	Y	Y
13 **Thornberry**	N	Y	Y	Y	Y	Y
14 **Paul**	N	Y	Y	N	Y	Y
15 Hinojosa	?	Y	Y	Y	Y	N
16 Reyes	Y	Y	Y	Y	Y	N
17 Edwards	Y	?	?	Y	Y	N
18 Jackson Lee	Y	Y	Y	Y	Y	N
19 **Neugebauer**	N	Y	Y	Y	Y	Y
20 Gonzalez	Y	Y	Y	Y	Y	N
21 **Smith**	N	Y	Y	Y	Y	Y
22 Lampson	Y	Y	Y	Y	Y	Y
23 Rodriguez	Y	Y	Y	Y	Y	N
24 **Marchant**	N	Y	Y	Y	Y	?
25 Doggett	Y	Y	Y	Y	Y	N
26 **Burgess**	N	Y	?	N	Y	Y
27 Ortiz	Y	Y	Y	Y	Y	N
28 Cuellar	Y	Y	Y	Y	Y	N
29 Green, G.	Y	Y	Y	Y	Y	Y
30 Johnson, E.	Y	Y	Y	Y	Y	N
31 **Carter**	N	Y	Y	Y	Y	+
32 **Sessions**	N	Y	Y	Y	Y	Y
UTAH						
1 **Bishop**	N	Y	Y	Y	Y	Y
2 Matheson	Y	Y	Y	Y	Y	N
3 **Cannon**	N	Y	Y	Y	Y	Y
VERMONT						
AL Welch	Y	Y	Y	Y	Y	N
VIRGINIA						
1 **Wittman**	N	Y	Y	Y	Y	Y
2 **Drake**	N	Y	Y	Y	Y	Y
3 Scott	Y	Y	Y	Y	Y	N
4 **Forbes**	N	Y	Y	N	Y	Y
5 **Goode**	N	Y	Y	N	Y	Y
6 **Goodlatte**	N	Y	Y	Y	Y	Y
7 **Cantor**	N	Y	Y	Y	Y	Y
8 Moran	Y	Y	Y	Y	Y	N
9 Boucher	Y	?	?	Y	Y	?
10 **Wolf**	Y	Y	Y	Y	Y	Y
11 **Davis, T.**	Y	Y	Y	N	Y	?
WASHINGTON						
1 Inslee	Y	Y	Y	Y	Y	N
2 Larsen	Y	Y	Y	Y	Y	N
3 Baird	+	Y	Y	N	Y	N
4 **Hastings**	N	Y	Y	Y	?	?
5 **McMorris Rodgers**	Y	Y	Y	Y	Y	Y
6 Dicks	Y	Y	Y	Y	Y	N
7 McDermott	Y	Y	Y	Y	?	N
8 **Reichert**	Y	Y	Y	Y	Y	Y
9 Smith	Y	Y	Y	N	Y	N
WEST VIRGINIA						
1 Mollohan	Y	Y	Y	Y	Y	N
2 **Capito**	Y	Y	Y	Y	Y	Y
3 Rahall	?	Y	Y	Y	Y	N
WISCONSIN						
1 **Ryan**	N	Y	Y	Y	Y	Y
2 Baldwin	Y	Y	Y	Y	Y	N
3 Kind	Y	Y	Y	Y	Y	N
4 Moore	Y	Y	Y	Y	Y	N
5 **Sensenbrenner**	N	Y	Y	N	Y	Y
6 **Petri**	Y	Y	Y	Y	Y	Y
7 Obey	Y	Y	?	Y	Y	N
8 Kagen	Y	Y	Y	Y	Y	N
WYOMING						
AL **Cubin**	N	Y	Y	N	Y	Y
DELEGATES						
Faleomavaega (A.S.)						
Norton (D.C.)						
Bordallo (Guam)						
Fortuño (P.R.)						
Christensen (V.I.)						

IN THE HOUSE | By Vote Number

28. HR 1528. New England National Scenic Trail/Passage. Passage of the bill that would redesignate the Metacomet-Monadnock-Mattabesett trail system as the New England National Scenic Trail. It would expand the trail to 220 miles from Royalston, Mass., to Guilford, Conn. It also would stipulate that the government could acquire private lands for the trail only with the landowners' consent. Passed 261-122: R 48-122; D 213-0 (ND 160-0, SD 53-0). Jan. 29, 2008.

29. H Res 867. Houston Soccer Team Tribute/Adoption. Hodes, D-N.H., motion to suspend the rules and adopt the resolution that would commend the Houston Dynamo Soccer Team for winning the 2007 Major League Soccer Cup. Motion agreed to 373-0: R 170-0; D 203-0 (ND 153-0, SD 50-0). A two-thirds majority of those present and voting (249 in this case) is required for adoption under suspension of the rules. Feb. 6, 2008.

30. H Res 942. Black History Month/Adoption. Hodes, D-N.H., motion to suspend the rules and adopt the resolution that would recognize the significance of Black History Month as an important time to recognize the contributions of African-Americans. Motion agreed to 367-0: R 169-0; D 198-0 (ND 151-0, SD 47-0). A two-thirds majority of those present and voting (245 in this case) is required for adoption under suspension of the rules. Feb. 6, 2008.

31. H Res 943. Space Shuttle Challenger Anniversary/Adoption. Melancon, D-La., motion to suspend the rules and adopt the resolution that would honor the 22nd anniversary of the Jan. 28, 1986, space shuttle Challenger explosion and the seven crew members who died in the accident. Motion agreed to 371-0: R 169-0; D 202-0 (ND 152-0, SD 50-0). A two-thirds majority of those present and voting (248 in this case) is required for adoption under suspension of the rules. Feb. 6, 2008.

32. HR 4137. Higher Education Reauthorization/Previous Question. Sutton, D-Ohio, motion to order the previous question (thus ending debate and possibility of amendment) on adoption of the rule (H Res 956) to provide for House floor consideration of the bill that would reauthorize the Higher Education Act through fiscal 2012. Motion agreed to 204-196: R 0-189; D 204-7 (ND 156-4, SD 48-3). Feb. 7, 2008.

33. HR 4137. Higher Education Reauthorization/Rule. Adoption of the rule (H Res 956) to provide for House floor consideration of the bill that would reauthorize the Higher Education Act through fiscal 2012. Adopted 214-190: R 0-188; D 214-2 (ND 162-1, SD 52-1). Feb. 7, 2008.

34. H Con Res 283. Kenyan Electoral Crisis/Adoption. Payne, D-N.J., motion to suspend the rules and adopt the concurrent resolution that would call for a peaceful resolution to the current electoral crisis in Kenya, commend the Kenyan people for their high voter turnout on election day and condemn the ongoing violence in Kenya. Motion agreed to 405-1: R 188-1; D 217-0 (ND 163-0, SD 54-0). A two-thirds majority of those present and voting (271 in this case) is required for adoption under suspension of the rules. Feb. 7, 2008.

	28	29	30	31	32	33	34
ALABAMA							
1 Bonner	N	Y	Y	Y	N	N	Y
2 Everett	?	Y	Y	Y	?	?	?
3 Rogers	N	Y	Y	Y	N	N	Y
4 Aderholt	N	Y	Y	N	N	N	Y
5 Cramer	Y	Y	Y	Y	?	?	Y
6 Bachus	Y	Y	Y	Y	N	N	Y
7 Davis	Y	Y	Y	Y	Y	Y	Y
ALASKA							
AL Young	N	Y	Y	Y	N	N	Y
ARIZONA							
1 Renzi	N	Y	Y	Y	N	N	Y
2 Franks	N	Y	Y	N	N	N	Y
3 Shadegg	N	Y	Y	Y	N	N	Y
4 Pastor	Y	Y	Y	Y	Y	Y	Y
5 Mitchell	Y	Y	Y	Y	Y	Y	Y
6 Flake	N	Y	Y	Y	N	N	Y
7 Grijalva	Y	?	?	?	Y	Y	Y
8 Giffords	Y	Y	Y	Y	Y	Y	Y
ARKANSAS							
1 Berry	?	?	?	?	Y	Y	Y
2 Snyder	Y	Y	Y	Y	Y	Y	Y
3 Boozman	Y	Y	Y	Y	N	N	Y
4 Ross	Y	+	+	+	Y	Y	Y
CALIFORNIA							
1 Thompson	Y	Y	Y	Y	Y	Y	Y
2 Herger	N	Y	Y	Y	N	N	Y
3 Lungren	N	Y	Y	Y	N	N	Y
4 Doolittle	N	?	?	?	N	N	Y
5 Matsui	Y	Y	Y	Y	Y	Y	Y
6 Woolsey	Y	+	+	+	+	+	+
7 Miller, George	Y	Y	Y	Y	Y	Y	Y
8 Pelosi							
9 Lee	Y	Y	Y	Y	Y	Y	Y
10 Tauscher	Y	Y	Y	Y	Y	Y	Y
11 McNerney	Y	Y	Y	Y	Y	Y	Y
12 Lantos	?	?	?	?	?	?	?
13 Stark	Y	?	?	?	Y	Y	Y
14 Eshoo	Y	Y	Y	Y	Y	Y	Y
15 Honda	Y	Y	Y	Y	Y	Y	Y
16 Lofgren	Y	Y	Y	Y	Y	Y	Y
17 Farr	Y	?	?	?	?	?	?
18 Cardoza	?	Y	Y	Y	Y	Y	Y
19 Radanovich	?	?	?	?	N	N	Y
20 Costa	Y	Y	Y	Y	Y	Y	Y
21 Nunes	N	Y	Y	Y	N	N	Y
22 McCarthy	N	Y	Y	Y	N	N	Y
23 Capps	Y	Y	Y	Y	Y	Y	Y
24 Gallegly	Y	?	?	?	N	N	Y
25 McKeon	N	Y	Y	Y	N	N	Y
26 Dreier	N	Y	Y	Y	N	N	Y
27 Sherman	Y	Y	Y	Y	Y	Y	Y
28 Berman	Y	Y	Y	?	Y	Y	Y
29 Schiff	Y	Y	Y	Y	Y	Y	Y
30 Waxman	Y	Y	Y	Y	Y	Y	Y
31 Becerra	Y	Y	Y	Y	Y	Y	Y
32 Solis	Y	Y	Y	Y	Y	Y	Y
33 Watson	Y	Y	Y	Y	Y	Y	Y
34 Roybal-Allard	Y	Y	Y	Y	Y	Y	Y
35 Waters	Y	Y	Y	Y	Y	Y	Y
36 Harman	Y	?	?	?	Y	Y	Y
37 Richardson	Y	Y	Y	Y	Y	Y	Y
38 Napolitano	Y	Y	Y	Y	Y	Y	Y
39 Sánchez, Linda	Y	Y	Y	Y	Y	Y	Y
40 Royce	N	Y	Y	Y	N	N	Y
41 Lewis	N	Y	Y	Y	N	N	Y
42 Miller, Gary	?	Y	Y	Y	N	N	Y
43 Baca	Y	Y	Y	Y	Y	Y	Y
44 Calvert	?	Y	Y	Y	N	N	Y
45 Bono Mack	N	Y	Y	Y	N	N	Y
46 Rohrabacher	N	?	?	?	N	N	Y
47 Sanchez, Loretta	Y	+	+	+	+	+	+
48 Campbell	N	+	+	+	N	N	Y
49 Issa	N	Y	Y	Y	N	N	Y
50 Bilbray	N	Y	Y	Y	N	N	Y
51 Filner	+	+	+	+	+	+	+
52 Hunter	N	Y	Y	N	N	N	Y
53 Davis	Y	Y	Y	Y	Y	Y	Y
COLORADO							
1 DeGette	Y	Y	Y	Y	Y	Y	Y
2 Udall	?	Y	Y	Y	Y	Y	Y
3 Salazar	Y	Y	Y	Y	Y	Y	Y
4 Musgrave	N	Y	Y	Y	N	N	Y
5 Lamborn	N	Y	Y	N	N	N	Y
6 Tancredo	N	Y	Y	Y	N	N	Y
7 Perlmutter	Y	Y	Y	Y	Y	Y	Y
CONNECTICUT							
1 Larson	Y	Y	Y	Y	Y	Y	Y
2 Courtney	Y	Y	Y	Y	Y	Y	Y
3 DeLauro	Y	Y	Y	Y	Y	Y	Y
4 Shays	Y	Y	Y	Y	N	N	Y
5 Murphy	Y	Y	Y	Y	Y	Y	Y
DELAWARE							
AL Castle	Y	Y	Y	Y	N	N	Y
FLORIDA							
1 Miller	N	Y	Y	Y	N	N	Y
2 Boyd	Y	Y	Y	Y	Y	Y	Y
3 Brown	Y	Y	Y	Y	Y	Y	Y
4 Crenshaw	Y	Y	Y	Y	Y	Y	Y
5 Brown-Waite	N	Y	Y	Y	N	N	Y
6 Stearns	N	Y	Y	Y	N	N	Y
7 Mica	N	Y	Y	Y	N	N	Y
8 Keller	?	Y	Y	Y	N	N	Y
9 Bilirakis	N	Y	Y	Y	N	N	Y
10 Young	N	?	?	?	N	N	Y
11 Castor	Y	Y	Y	Y	Y	Y	Y
12 Putnam	?	Y	Y	Y	N	N	Y
13 Buchanan	N	Y	Y	Y	N	N	Y
14 Mack	N	Y	Y	Y	N	N	Y
15 Weldon	?	Y	?	?	N	N	Y
16 Mahoney	Y	Y	Y	Y	Y	Y	Y
17 Meek	Y	Y	Y	Y	?	Y	Y
18 Ros-Lehtinen	?	Y	Y	Y	N	N	Y
19 Wexler	Y	?	?	?	Y	Y	Y
20 Wasserman Schultz	?	Y	Y	Y	Y	Y	Y
21 Diaz-Balart, L.	N	Y	Y	Y	N	N	Y
22 Klein	Y	Y	Y	Y	Y	Y	Y
23 Hastings	?	Y	Y	Y	Y	Y	Y
24 Feeney	?	Y	Y	Y	N	N	Y
25 Diaz-Balart, M.	?	Y	Y	N	N	N	Y
GEORGIA							
1 Kingston	N	Y	Y	Y	N	N	Y
2 Bishop	Y	Y	?	Y	Y	Y	Y
3 Westmoreland	?	Y	Y	Y	N	N	Y
4 Johnson	Y	Y	Y	Y	Y	Y	Y
5 Lewis	Y	Y	Y	Y	Y	Y	Y
6 Price	N	Y	Y	Y	N	N	Y
7 Linder	N	Y	Y	Y	N	N	Y
8 Marshall	Y	Y	Y	Y	Y	Y	Y
9 Deal	?	Y	Y	Y	N	N	Y
10 Broun	N	Y	Y	Y	N	N	Y
11 Gingrey	N	+	+	+	N	N	Y
12 Barrow	Y	Y	Y	Y	Y	Y	Y
13 Scott	Y	Y	?	Y	Y	Y	Y
HAWAII							
1 Abercrombie	Y	Y	Y	Y	Y	Y	Y
2 Hirono	Y	Y	Y	Y	Y	Y	Y
IDAHO							
1 Sali	N	Y	Y	Y	N	N	Y
2 Simpson	?	Y	Y	Y	N	N	Y
ILLINOIS							
1 Rush	Y	?	?	?	Y	Y	Y
2 Jackson	Y	Y	Y	Y	Y	Y	Y
3 Lipinski	?	?	?	?	?	Y	Y
4 Gutierrez	Y	Y	Y	Y	Y	Y	Y
5 Emanuel	Y	Y	Y	Y	Y	Y	?
6 Roskam	N	Y	Y	Y	N	N	Y
7 Davis	Y	?	?	?	Y	Y	Y
8 Bean	Y	?	?	?	Y	Y	Y
9 Schakowsky	Y	Y	Y	Y	Y	Y	Y
10 Kirk	Y	Y	Y	Y	N	N	Y
11 Weller	Y	+	+	+	N	N	Y
12 Costello	Y	Y	Y	Y	Y	Y	Y
13 Biggert	N	Y	Y	Y	N	N	Y
14 Vacant							
15 Johnson	Y	Y	Y	Y	N	N	Y

KEY	Republicans	Democrats		
Y Voted for (yea)		X Paired against		C Voted "present" to avoid possible conflict of interest
# Paired for		– Announced against		
+ Announced for		P Voted "present"		? Did not vote or otherwise make a position known
N Voted against (nay)				

*Rep. Richard H. Baker, R-La., retired Feb. 2, 2008. The last vote for which he was eligible was vote 28.

ND Northern Democrats, SD Southern Democrats
Southern states: Ala., Ark., Fla., Ga., Ky., La., Miss., N.C., Okla., S.C., Tenn., Texas, Va.

	28	29	30	31	32	33	34
16 **Manzullo**	N	+	+	+	–	–	+
17 Hare	Y	+	+	+	?	Y	Y
18 **LaHood**	Y	Y	Y	Y	N	N	Y
19 **Shimkus**	N	Y	Y	Y	N	N	Y
INDIANA							
1 Visclosky	Y	Y	Y	Y	Y	Y	Y
2 Donnelly	Y	Y	Y	Y	N	Y	Y
3 **Souder**	N	Y	Y	Y	N	N	Y
4 **Buyer**	N	Y	Y	Y	N	N	Y
5 **Burton**	N	Y	Y	Y	N	N	Y
6 **Pence**	N	?	?	?	N	N	Y
7 Vacant							
8 Ellsworth	Y	Y	Y	Y	N	Y	Y
9 Hill	Y	Y	Y	Y	N	N	Y
IOWA							
1 Braley	Y	Y	Y	Y	Y	Y	Y
2 Loebsack	Y	Y	Y	Y	Y	Y	Y
3 Boswell	Y	Y	Y	Y	Y	Y	Y
4 **Latham**	Y	Y	Y	Y	N	N	Y
5 **King**	N	Y	Y	Y	N	N	Y
KANSAS							
1 **Moran**	N	Y	Y	Y	N	N	Y
2 Boyda	?	Y	Y	Y	N	Y	Y
3 Moore	Y	Y	?	Y	Y	Y	Y
4 **Tiahrt**	Y	Y	Y	Y	N	N	Y
KENTUCKY							
1 **Whitfield**	Y	?	?	?	N	N	Y
2 **Lewis**	?	Y	Y	Y	N	N	Y
3 Yarmuth	Y	Y	Y	Y	Y	Y	Y
4 **Davis**	N	Y	Y	Y	N	N	Y
5 **Rogers**	N	Y	Y	Y	N	N	Y
6 Chandler	Y	Y	Y	Y	Y	Y	Y
LOUISIANA							
1 Vacant*							
2 Jefferson	Y	?	?	?	Y	Y	Y
3 Melancon	Y	Y	Y	Y	Y	Y	Y
4 **McCrery**	?	Y	Y	Y	N	N	Y
5 **Alexander**	N	?	?	?	N	N	Y
7 **Boustany**	N	Y	Y	Y	N	N	Y
MAINE							
1 Allen	Y	Y	Y	Y	Y	Y	Y
2 Michaud	Y	Y	Y	Y	Y	Y	Y
MARYLAND							
1 **Gilchrest**	?	Y	Y	Y	N	N	Y
2 Ruppersberger	Y	?	?	?	?	?	?
3 Sarbanes	Y	Y	Y	Y	Y	Y	Y
4 Wynn	?	?	?	?	?	?	?
5 Hoyer	Y	Y	Y	Y	Y	Y	Y
6 **Bartlett**	N	Y	Y	Y	N	N	Y
7 Cummings	Y	Y	Y	Y	Y	Y	Y
8 Van Hollen	Y	Y	Y	Y	Y	Y	Y
MASSACHUSETTS							
1 Olver	Y	Y	Y	Y	Y	Y	Y
2 Neal	Y	Y	Y	Y	Y	Y	Y
3 McGovern	Y	Y	Y	Y	Y	Y	Y
4 Frank	Y	Y	Y	Y	Y	Y	Y
5 Tsongas	Y	Y	Y	Y	Y	Y	Y
6 Tierney	Y	Y	Y	Y	Y	Y	Y
7 Markey	Y	Y	Y	Y	Y	Y	Y
8 Capuano	Y	Y	Y	Y	Y	Y	Y
9 Lynch	Y	Y	Y	Y	Y	Y	Y
10 Delahunt	Y	Y	Y	Y	Y	Y	Y
MICHIGAN							
1 Stupak	Y	Y	Y	Y	Y	Y	Y
2 **Hoekstra**	N	Y	Y	Y	N	N	Y
3 **Ehlers**	Y	Y	Y	Y	N	N	Y
4 **Camp**	N	Y	Y	Y	N	N	Y
5 Kildee	Y	Y	Y	Y	Y	Y	Y
6 **Upton**	Y	Y	Y	Y	N	N	Y
7 **Walberg**	N	Y	Y	Y	N	N	Y
8 **Rogers**	Y	Y	Y	Y	N	N	Y
9 **Knollenberg**	Y	Y	Y	Y	N	N	Y
10 **Miller**	Y	Y	Y	Y	N	N	Y
11 **McCotter**	N	Y	Y	Y	N	N	Y
12 Levin	Y	Y	Y	Y	Y	Y	Y
13 Kilpatrick	Y	Y	Y	Y	Y	Y	Y
14 Conyers	Y	Y	Y	?	Y	Y	Y
15 Dingell	Y	Y	Y	Y	Y	Y	Y
MINNESOTA							
1 Walz	Y	Y	Y	Y	Y	Y	Y
2 **Kline**	N	Y	Y	Y	N	N	Y
3 **Ramstad**	Y	Y	Y	Y	N	N	Y
4 McCollum	?	Y	Y	Y	Y	Y	Y

	28	29	30	31	32	33	34
5 Ellison	Y	Y	Y	Y	Y	Y	Y
6 **Bachmann**	N	Y	Y	Y	N	N	Y
7 Peterson	Y	Y	Y	Y	Y	Y	Y
8 Oberstar	Y	Y	Y	Y	Y	Y	Y
MISSISSIPPI							
1 Vacant							
2 Thompson	Y	Y	Y	Y	Y	Y	Y
3 **Pickering**	Y	Y	Y	Y	N	N	Y
4 Taylor	Y	Y	Y	Y	Y	Y	Y
MISSOURI							
1 Clay	Y	Y	Y	Y	Y	Y	Y
2 **Akin**	N	Y	Y	Y	N	N	Y
3 Carnahan	Y	Y	Y	Y	Y	Y	Y
4 Skelton	Y	Y	Y	Y	Y	Y	Y
5 Cleaver	Y	Y	Y	Y	Y	Y	Y
6 **Graves**	N	+	+	+	–	–	+
7 **Blunt**	Y	Y	Y	Y	N	N	Y
8 **Emerson**	N	Y	Y	Y	N	N	?
9 **Hulshof**	N	+	+	+	N	N	Y
MONTANA							
AL **Rehberg**	N	Y	Y	Y	N	N	Y
NEBRASKA							
1 **Fortenberry**	+	+	+	+	–	–	+
2 **Terry**	Y	?	?	?	N	N	Y
3 **Smith**	N	Y	Y	Y	N	N	Y
NEVADA							
1 Berkley	Y	Y	Y	Y	Y	Y	Y
2 **Heller**	N	Y	Y	Y	N	N	Y
3 **Porter**	N	Y	Y	Y	–	–	+
NEW HAMPSHIRE							
1 Shea-Porter	Y	Y	Y	Y	Y	Y	Y
2 Hodes	Y	Y	Y	Y	Y	Y	Y
NEW JERSEY							
1 Andrews	?	Y	Y	Y	Y	Y	Y
2 **LoBiondo**	Y	Y	Y	Y	N	N	Y
3 **Saxton**	?	Y	Y	Y	N	N	Y
4 **Smith**	Y	Y	Y	Y	N	?	?
5 **Garrett**	N	Y	Y	Y	N	N	Y
6 Pallone	Y	Y	Y	Y	Y	Y	Y
7 **Ferguson**	Y	Y	Y	Y	N	?	Y
8 Pascrell	Y	Y	Y	Y	Y	Y	Y
9 Rothman	Y	Y	Y	Y	Y	Y	Y
10 Payne	Y	Y	Y	Y	Y	Y	Y
11 **Frelinghuysen**	Y	Y	Y	Y	N	N	Y
12 Holt	Y	Y	Y	Y	Y	Y	Y
13 Sires	Y	Y	Y	Y	Y	Y	Y
NEW MEXICO							
1 **Wilson**	?	Y	Y	Y	N	N	Y
2 **Pearce**	N	Y	Y	Y	N	N	Y
3 Udall	Y	Y	Y	Y	Y	Y	Y
NEW YORK							
1 Bishop	Y	Y	Y	Y	Y	Y	Y
2 Israel	Y	Y	Y	Y	Y	Y	Y
3 **King**	Y	Y	Y	Y	N	N	Y
4 McCarthy	Y	Y	Y	Y	Y	Y	Y
5 Ackerman	Y	Y	Y	Y	Y	Y	Y
6 Meeks	Y	Y	Y	Y	Y	Y	Y
7 Crowley	Y	Y	Y	Y	Y	Y	Y
8 Nadler	Y	Y	Y	Y	Y	Y	Y
9 Weiner	Y	Y	Y	Y	Y	Y	Y
10 Towns	Y	Y	Y	Y	?	?	Y
11 Clarke	Y	Y	Y	Y	Y	Y	Y
12 Velázquez	Y	Y	Y	Y	Y	Y	Y
13 **Fossella**	N	Y	Y	Y	N	N	Y
14 Maloney	Y	Y	Y	Y	Y	Y	Y
15 Rangel	Y	Y	?	Y	Y	Y	Y
16 Serrano	Y	Y	Y	Y	Y	Y	Y
17 Engel	Y	Y	Y	Y	Y	Y	Y
18 Lowey	Y	+	+	+	+	+	+
19 Hall	Y	Y	Y	Y	Y	Y	Y
20 Gillibrand	+	Y	Y	Y	Y	Y	Y
21 McNulty	Y	Y	Y	Y	Y	Y	Y
22 Hinchey	Y	Y	Y	Y	Y	Y	Y
23 **McHugh**	N	Y	Y	Y	N	N	Y
24 Arcuri	Y	Y	Y	Y	Y	Y	Y
25 **Walsh**	Y	Y	Y	Y	N	N	Y
26 **Reynolds**	N	Y	?	Y	N	N	Y
27 Higgins	Y	Y	Y	Y	Y	Y	Y
28 Slaughter	Y	Y	Y	Y	Y	Y	Y
29 **Kuhl**	N	?	?	?	N	N	Y
NORTH CAROLINA							
1 Butterfield	Y	Y	Y	Y	Y	Y	Y
2 Etheridge	Y	Y	Y	Y	Y	N	Y
3 **Jones**	N	Y	Y	Y	N	N	Y
4 Price	Y	Y	Y	Y	Y	Y	Y

	28	29	30	31	32	33	34
5 **Foxx**	N	Y	Y	Y	N	N	Y
6 **Coble**	N	Y	Y	Y	N	N	Y
7 McIntyre	Y	Y	Y	Y	Y	Y	Y
8 **Hayes**	N	Y	Y	Y	N	N	Y
9 **Myrick**	N	Y	Y	Y	N	N	Y
10 **McHenry**	N	Y	Y	Y	N	N	Y
11 Shuler	Y	Y	Y	Y	Y	Y	Y
12 Watt	Y	Y	Y	Y	Y	Y	Y
13 Miller	Y	Y	Y	Y	Y	Y	Y
NORTH DAKOTA							
AL Pomeroy	Y	Y	Y	Y	Y	Y	Y
OHIO							
1 **Chabot**	N	Y	Y	Y	N	N	Y
2 **Schmidt**	Y	Y	Y	Y	N	N	Y
3 **Turner**	Y	Y	Y	Y	N	N	Y
4 **Jordan**	N	Y	Y	Y	N	N	Y
5 **Latta**	N	Y	Y	Y	N	N	Y
6 Wilson	Y	Y	Y	Y	Y	Y	Y
7 **Hobson**	Y	Y	Y	Y	N	N	Y
8 **Boehner**	N	Y	Y	Y	N	N	Y
9 Kaptur	Y	Y	Y	Y	Y	Y	Y
10 Kucinich	Y	Y	Y	Y	Y	Y	Y
11 Tubbs Jones	+	Y	Y	Y	Y	Y	Y
12 **Tiberi**	?	Y	Y	Y	N	N	Y
13 Sutton	Y	Y	Y	Y	Y	Y	Y
14 **LaTourette**	?	Y	Y	Y	N	N	Y
15 **Pryce**	?	?	?	?	?	?	?
16 **Regula**	Y	Y	Y	Y	N	N	Y
17 Ryan	Y	Y	Y	Y	Y	Y	Y
18 Space	Y	Y	Y	Y	Y	Y	Y
OKLAHOMA							
1 **Sullivan**	N	Y	Y	Y	N	N	Y
2 Boren	Y	Y	Y	Y	Y	Y	Y
3 **Lucas**	Y	Y	Y	Y	N	N	Y
4 **Cole**	N	Y	Y	Y	N	N	Y
5 **Fallin**	?	Y	Y	Y	N	N	Y
OREGON							
1 Wu	Y	Y	Y	Y	Y	Y	Y
2 **Walden**	N	Y	Y	Y	N	N	Y
3 Blumenauer	Y	?	?	?	Y	Y	Y
4 DeFazio	?	Y	Y	Y	Y	Y	Y
5 Hooley	Y	?	?	Y	Y	Y	Y
PENNSYLVANIA							
1 Brady	Y	Y	Y	Y	Y	Y	Y
2 Fattah	Y	Y	Y	Y	Y	Y	Y
3 **English**	Y	Y	Y	Y	N	N	Y
4 Altmire	Y	Y	Y	Y	Y	Y	Y
5 **Peterson**	Y	Y	Y	Y	N	N	Y
6 **Gerlach**	Y	Y	Y	Y	N	N	Y
7 Sestak	?	Y	Y	Y	Y	Y	Y
8 Murphy, P.	Y	Y	Y	Y	Y	Y	Y
9 **Shuster**	N	Y	Y	Y	N	N	Y
10 Carney	Y	Y	Y	Y	Y	Y	Y
11 Kanjorski	Y	Y	Y	Y	Y	Y	Y
12 Murtha	Y	Y	?	?	Y	Y	Y
13 Schwartz	Y	Y	Y	Y	Y	Y	Y
14 Doyle	?	Y	Y	Y	Y	Y	Y
15 **Dent**	Y	Y	Y	Y	N	N	Y
16 **Pitts**	Y	Y	Y	Y	N	N	Y
17 Holden	Y	Y	Y	Y	Y	Y	Y
18 **Murphy, T.**	Y	Y	Y	Y	N	N	Y
19 **Platts**	Y	Y	Y	?	N	N	Y
RHODE ISLAND							
1 Kennedy	Y	Y	Y	Y	Y	Y	Y
2 Langevin	Y	Y	Y	Y	Y	Y	Y
SOUTH CAROLINA							
1 **Brown**	N	Y	Y	Y	N	N	Y
2 **Wilson**	N	Y	Y	Y	N	N	Y
3 **Barrett**	N	Y	Y	Y	N	N	Y
4 **Inglis**	Y	Y	Y	Y	N	N	Y
5 Spratt	Y	Y	Y	Y	Y	Y	Y
6 Clyburn	Y	Y	Y	Y	Y	Y	Y
SOUTH DAKOTA							
AL Herseth Sandlin	Y	Y	Y	Y	Y	Y	Y
TENNESSEE							
1 **Davis, David**	N	Y	Y	Y	N	N	Y
2 **Duncan**	N	Y	Y	Y	N	N	Y
3 **Wamp**	N	Y	Y	Y	N	N	Y
4 Davis, L.	Y	Y	Y	Y	?	?	Y
5 Cooper	Y	Y	Y	Y	Y	Y	Y
6 Gordon	Y	Y	Y	Y	Y	Y	Y
7 **Blackburn**	N	+	+	+	?	?	?
8 Tanner	Y	?	?	?	?	?	?
9 Cohen	Y	Y	Y	Y	Y	Y	Y

	28	29	30	31	32	33	34
TEXAS							
1 **Gohmert**	N	Y	Y	Y	N	N	Y
2 **Poe**	N	Y	Y	Y	N	N	Y
3 **Johnson, S.**	N	Y	Y	Y	N	N	Y
4 **Hall**	N	Y	Y	Y	N	N	Y
5 **Hensarling**	N	Y	Y	Y	N	N	Y
6 **Barton**	N	Y	Y	Y	N	N	Y
7 **Culberson**	N	Y	Y	Y	N	N	Y
8 **Brady**	Y	Y	Y	Y	N	N	Y
9 Green, A.	Y	Y	Y	Y	Y	Y	Y
10 **McCaul**	N	Y	Y	Y	N	N	Y
11 **Conaway**	N	+	+	+	N	N	Y
12 **Granger**	Y	Y	Y	Y	N	N	Y
13 **Thornberry**	N	Y	Y	Y	N	N	Y
14 **Paul**	N	Y	Y	Y	N	N	N
15 Hinojosa	Y	?	?	?	+	Y	Y
16 Reyes	Y	Y	Y	Y	Y	Y	Y
17 Edwards	Y	Y	Y	Y	Y	Y	Y
18 Jackson Lee	Y	Y	Y	Y	Y	Y	Y
19 **Neugebauer**	N	Y	Y	Y	N	N	Y
20 Gonzalez	Y	Y	Y	Y	Y	Y	Y
21 **Smith**	Y	Y	Y	Y	N	N	Y
22 Lampson	Y	Y	Y	Y	N	Y	Y
23 Rodriguez	+	Y	?	Y	Y	Y	Y
24 **Marchant**	?	Y	Y	Y	N	N	Y
25 Doggett	Y	Y	Y	Y	Y	Y	Y
26 **Burgess**	N	Y	Y	Y	N	N	Y
27 Ortiz	Y	Y	Y	Y	Y	Y	Y
28 Cuellar	Y	Y	Y	Y	Y	Y	Y
29 Green, G.	Y	Y	Y	Y	Y	Y	Y
30 Johnson, E.	Y	Y	Y	Y	Y	Y	Y
31 **Carter**	–	Y	Y	Y	N	N	Y
32 **Sessions**	Y	Y	Y	Y	N	N	Y
UTAH							
1 **Bishop**	N	Y	Y	Y	N	N	Y
2 Matheson	Y	Y	Y	Y	Y	Y	Y
3 **Cannon**	N	?	?	?	N	N	Y
VERMONT							
AL Welch	Y	Y	Y	Y	Y	Y	Y
VIRGINIA							
1 **Wittman**	Y	Y	Y	Y	N	N	Y
2 **Drake**	N	Y	Y	Y	N	N	Y
3 Scott	Y	Y	Y	Y	Y	Y	Y
4 **Forbes**	N	Y	Y	Y	N	N	Y
5 **Goode**	N	Y	Y	Y	N	N	Y
6 **Goodlatte**	N	Y	Y	Y	N	N	Y
7 **Cantor**	N	Y	Y	Y	N	N	Y
8 Moran	Y	Y	Y	Y	Y	Y	Y
9 Boucher	Y	?	?	?	?	?	?
10 **Wolf**	Y	Y	Y	Y	N	N	Y
11 **Davis, T.**	?	?	?	?	N	N	Y
WASHINGTON							
1 Inslee	Y	Y	Y	Y	Y	Y	Y
2 Larsen	Y	Y	Y	Y	Y	Y	Y
3 Baird	Y	Y	Y	Y	Y	Y	Y
4 **Hastings**	?	?	?	?	N	N	Y
5 **McMorris Rodgers**	N	?	?	?	N	N	Y
6 Dicks	Y	Y	Y	Y	Y	Y	Y
7 McDermott	Y	Y	Y	Y	Y	Y	Y
8 **Reichert**	Y	Y	Y	Y	N	N	Y
9 Smith	Y	?	?	?	?	?	?
WEST VIRGINIA							
1 Mollohan	Y	Y	Y	Y	Y	Y	Y
2 **Capito**	N	Y	Y	Y	N	N	Y
3 Rahall	Y	Y	Y	Y	Y	Y	Y
WISCONSIN							
1 **Ryan**	N	+	+	+	?	–	Y
2 Baldwin	Y	+	+	+	?	+	+
3 Kind	Y	Y	Y	Y	Y	Y	Y
4 Moore	Y	+	+	+	?	Y	Y
5 **Sensenbrenner**	N	Y	Y	Y	N	N	Y
6 **Petri**	N	?	?	?	?	N	Y
7 Obey	Y	Y	Y	Y	Y	Y	Y
8 Kagen	Y	Y	Y	Y	Y	Y	Y
WYOMING							
AL **Cubin**	N	?	?	?	N	N	Y
DELEGATES							
Faleomavaega (A.S.)							
Norton (D.C.)							
Bordallo (Guam)							
Fortuño (P.R.)							
Christensen (V.I.)							

IN THE HOUSE | By Vote Number

35. **HR 4848. Mental Health Benefits Parity/Passage.** Pallone, D-N.J., motion to suspend the rules and pass the bill that would extend through 2008 current provisions barring group health plans that offer mental health coverage from imposing different aggregate lifetime or annual dollar limits for such treatment than those imposed for treatment of other illnesses. Motion agreed to 384-23: R 167-23; D 217-0 (ND 164-0, SD 53-0). A two-thirds majority of those present and voting (272 in this case) is required for passage under suspension of the rules. Feb. 7, 2008.

36. **HR 4137. Higher Education Reauthorization/Federal Family Education Loan Program.** Petri, R-Wis., amendment that would require the Education-Treasury Study Group to evaluate the feasibility of a market-based overhaul to the Federal Family Education Loan Program to reduce federal costs to taxpayers and use savings to increase grant aid to low-income students. Adopted in Committee of the Whole 260-153: R 49-143; D 211-10 (ND 163-4, SD 48-6). Feb. 7, 2008.

37. **HR 4137. Higher Education Reauthorization/Audit of Federal Family Education Loan Program.** Petri, R-Wis., amendment that would extend the audit and reporting provisions applied to the Direct Loan program to the Federal Family Education Loan Program. Adopted in Committee of the Whole 222-191: R 25-167; D 197-24 (ND 156-11, SD 41-13). Feb. 7, 2008.

38. **HR 4137. Higher Education Reauthorization/Bankruptcy Options.** Davis, D-Ill., amendment that would allow private student loan borrowers to discharge their loans via bankruptcy. Rejected in Committee of the Whole 179-236: R 9-184; D 170-52 (ND 131-37, SD 39-15). Feb. 7, 2008.

39. **HR 4137. Higher Education Reauthorization/Motion to Recommit.** Ferguson, R-N.J., motion to recommit the bill to the Education and Labor Committee with instructions to include language that would suspend funding for the Fund for the Improvement of Postsecondary Education unless Pell grants and special education programs are fully funded in that fiscal year. Motion rejected 194-216: R 187-4; D 7-212 (ND 4-161, SD 3-51). Feb. 7, 2008.

40. **HR 4137. Higher Education Reauthorization/Passage.** Passage of the bill that would reauthorize the Higher Education Act through fiscal 2012. The measure would raise the maximum Pell grant award from $5,800 to $9,000 and allow the grants to be used year-round. It also would allow the federal government to penalize states that substantially decrease their contributions to public colleges and universities, and increase the amount of information lenders and schools must provide students about loan rates and school costs. The bill would create a "higher education price index" to compare tuition increases and bar lenders from giving schools financial perks in order to get on a "preferred lender list." Passed 354-58: R 135-58; D 219-0 (ND 165-0, SD 54-0). A "nay" was a vote in support of the president's position. Feb. 7, 2008.

41. **H Res 947. Congratulate Lee Myung-Bak/Adoption.** Payne, D-N.J., motion to suspend the rules and adopt the resolution that would congratulate Lee Myung-Bak on his election to the presidency of the Republic of Korea. Motion agreed to 388-0: R 180-0; D 208-0 (ND 157-0, SD 51-0). A two-thirds majority of those present and voting (259 in this case) is required for adoption under suspension of the rules. Feb. 7, 2008.

	35	36	37	38	39	40	41
ALABAMA							
1 Bonner	Y	N	N	N	Y	Y	Y
2 Everett	?	?	?	?	?	?	?
3 Rogers	Y	N	N	N	Y	Y	Y
4 Aderholt	Y	N	N	N	Y	Y	Y
5 Cramer	?	?	?	?	?	?	?
6 Bachus	Y	N	N	N	Y	Y	Y
7 Davis	Y	Y	Y	Y	N	Y	Y
ALASKA							
AL Young	Y	Y	Y	Y	Y	Y	Y
ARIZONA							
1 Renzi	Y	Y	N	N	Y	Y	Y
2 Franks	N	N	N	N	Y	N	Y
3 Shadegg	N	N	N	N	Y	N	Y
4 Pastor	Y	Y	Y	Y	N	Y	Y
5 Mitchell	Y	Y	Y	N	Y	Y	Y
6 Flake	N	N	N	N	Y	N	Y
7 Grijalva	Y	Y	Y	Y	N	Y	Y
8 Giffords	Y	Y	N	N	Y	Y	Y
ARKANSAS							
1 Berry	Y	N	N	N	Y	Y	Y
2 Snyder	Y	Y	Y	N	Y	Y	Y
3 Boozman	Y	N	N	N	Y	Y	Y
4 Ross	Y	N	N	N	Y	Y	Y
CALIFORNIA							
1 Thompson	Y	Y	Y	N	Y	Y	Y
2 Herger	Y	N	N	N	Y	N	Y
3 Lungren	Y	N	N	N	Y	N	Y
4 Doolittle	N	N	N	N	Y	N	Y
5 Matsui	Y	Y	Y	Y	N	Y	Y
6 Woolsey	+	+	+	+	–	+	+
7 Miller, George	Y	Y	Y	Y	N	Y	Y
8 Pelosi							+
9 Lee	Y	Y	Y	Y	N	Y	Y
10 Tauscher	Y	Y	Y	N	Y	Y	Y
11 McNerney	Y	Y	Y	N	Y	Y	Y
12 Lantos	?	?	?	?	?	?	?
13 Stark	Y	Y	Y	Y	N	Y	Y
14 Eshoo	Y	Y	Y	Y	N	Y	Y
15 Honda	Y	Y	Y	Y	N	Y	Y
16 Lofgren	Y	Y	Y	Y	N	Y	Y
17 Farr	?	?	?	?	?	?	?
18 Cardoza	Y	Y	Y	N	Y	Y	Y
19 Radanovich	Y	N	N	N	Y	Y	?
20 Costa	Y	Y	Y	N	Y	Y	Y
21 Nunes	Y	N	N	N	Y	N	Y
22 McCarthy	Y	N	N	N	Y	Y	Y
23 Capps	Y	Y	Y	N	Y	Y	Y
24 Gallegly	Y	N	N	N	Y	Y	Y
25 McKeon	Y	N	N	N	Y	Y	Y
26 Dreier	Y	N	N	N	Y	N	Y
27 Sherman	Y	Y	Y	N	Y	Y	Y
28 Berman	Y	Y	Y	Y	N	Y	Y
29 Schiff	Y	Y	Y	Y	N	Y	Y
30 Waxman	Y	Y	Y	Y	N	Y	Y
31 Becerra	Y	Y	Y	Y	N	Y	Y
32 Solis	Y	Y	Y	Y	N	Y	Y
33 Watson	Y	Y	Y	Y	N	Y	Y
34 Roybal-Allard	Y	Y	Y	Y	N	Y	Y
35 Waters	Y	Y	Y	Y	N	Y	Y
36 Harman	Y	Y	Y	N	Y	Y	Y
37 Richardson	Y	Y	Y	N	Y	Y	Y
38 Napolitano	Y	Y	Y	Y	N	Y	Y
39 Sánchez, Linda	Y	Y	Y	N	Y	Y	Y
40 Royce	N	N	N	N	Y	N	Y
41 Lewis	Y	Y	N	N	Y	Y	?
42 Miller, Gary	Y	N	N	N	Y	Y	Y
43 Baca	Y	Y	Y	N	Y	Y	Y
44 Calvert	Y	N	N	N	Y	Y	Y
45 Bono Mack	Y	N	N	N	Y	Y	Y
46 Rohrabacher	N	Y	N	N	Y	N	Y
47 Sanchez, Loretta	+	–	+	+	–	+	+
48 Campbell	N	N	N	N	Y	N	Y
49 Issa	Y	N	N	N	Y	Y	Y
50 Bilbray	Y	N	N	N	Y	Y	Y
51 Filner	Y	Y	Y	N	Y	Y	Y
52 Hunter	Y	Y	N	N	Y	N	Y
53 Davis	Y	Y	Y	N	Y	Y	Y

	35	36	37	38	39	40	41
COLORADO							
1 DeGette	Y	Y	Y	Y	N	Y	Y
2 Udall	Y	Y	Y	Y	N	Y	Y
3 Salazar	Y	Y	Y	Y	N	Y	Y
4 Musgrave	Y	N	N	N	Y	N	Y
5 Lamborn	N	N	N	N	Y	N	Y
6 Tancredo	Y	N	N	N	N	N	Y
7 Perlmutter	Y	Y	Y	N	Y	Y	Y
CONNECTICUT							
1 Larson	Y	Y	Y	N	Y	Y	Y
2 Courtney	Y	Y	Y	N	Y	Y	Y
3 DeLauro	Y	Y	Y	N	Y	Y	Y
4 Shays	Y	Y	Y	N	Y	Y	Y
5 Murphy	Y	Y	Y	N	Y	Y	?
DELAWARE							
AL Castle	Y	Y	N	N	Y	Y	Y
FLORIDA							
1 Miller	Y	N	N	Y	Y	N	Y
2 Boyd	Y	Y	N	N	Y	N	Y
3 Brown	Y	Y	Y	Y	N	Y	Y
4 Crenshaw	Y	N	N	N	Y	Y	Y
5 Brown-Waite	N	N	N	N	Y	N	Y
6 Stearns	Y	N	N	N	Y	N	Y
7 Mica	Y	Y	N	N	Y	Y	Y
8 Keller	Y	N	N	N	Y	N	Y
9 Bilirakis	Y	N	N	N	Y	Y	Y
10 Young	Y	N	N	N	Y	Y	Y
11 Castor	Y	Y	Y	N	Y	Y	Y
12 Putnam	Y	N	N	N	Y	N	Y
13 Buchanan	Y	N	N	N	Y	Y	Y
14 Mack	N	N	N	N	Y	N	Y
15 Weldon	Y	N	N	N	Y	Y	Y
16 Mahoney	Y	N	N	N	Y	N	?
17 Meek	Y	Y	Y	N	Y	Y	Y
18 Ros-Lehtinen	Y	Y	Y	N	Y	Y	Y
19 Wexler	Y	Y	Y	N	Y	Y	Y
20 Wasserman Schultz	Y	Y	Y	N	Y	Y	Y
21 Diaz-Balart, L.	Y	Y	Y	Y	Y	Y	?
22 Klein	Y	Y	N	N	Y	Y	Y
23 Hastings	Y	Y	Y	N	Y	Y	Y
24 Feeney	Y	N	N	N	Y	N	?
25 Diaz-Balart, M.	Y	Y	Y	Y	Y	Y	Y
GEORGIA							
1 Kingston	Y	N	N	N	Y	N	Y
2 Bishop	Y	Y	Y	N	Y	Y	Y
3 Westmoreland	Y	N	N	N	Y	N	Y
4 Johnson	Y	Y	Y	N	Y	Y	Y
5 Lewis	Y	Y	Y	N	Y	Y	Y
6 Price	Y	N	N	N	Y	N	Y
7 Linder	Y	Y	N	N	Y	N	Y
8 Marshall	Y	Y	Y	N	Y	Y	?
9 Deal	Y	N	N	N	Y	N	Y
10 Broun	N	N	N	N	Y	N	Y
11 Gingrey	Y	N	N	N	Y	N	Y
12 Barrow	Y	Y	Y	N	Y	Y	Y
13 Scott	Y	Y	Y	N	Y	Y	Y
HAWAII							
1 Abercrombie	Y	Y	Y	N	Y	Y	Y
2 Hirono	Y	Y	Y	N	Y	Y	Y
IDAHO							
1 Sali	N	N	N	N	Y	N	Y
2 Simpson	Y	N	N	N	Y	N	Y
ILLINOIS							
1 Rush	Y	Y	Y	N	Y	Y	Y
2 Jackson	Y	Y	Y	N	Y	Y	Y
3 Lipinski	Y	Y	Y	N	Y	Y	Y
4 Gutierrez	Y	Y	Y	N	Y	Y	?
5 Emanuel	Y	Y	Y	N	Y	Y	?
6 Roskam	Y	N	N	N	Y	Y	Y
7 Davis	Y	Y	Y	N	Y	Y	Y
8 Bean	Y	Y	N	N	Y	Y	Y
9 Schakowsky	Y	Y	Y	Y	N	Y	Y
10 Kirk	Y	Y	N	N	Y	Y	Y
11 Weller	Y	N	N	N	Y	Y	Y
12 Costello	Y	Y	Y	N	Y	Y	Y
13 Biggert	Y	Y	N	N	Y	Y	Y
14 Vacant							
15 Johnson	Y	Y	Y	Y	Y	Y	Y

ND Northern Democrats, SD Southern Democrats
Southern states: Ala., Ark., Fla., Ga., Ky., La., Miss., N.C., Okla., S.C., Tenn., Texas, Va.

	35	36	37	38	39	40	41
16 **Manzullo**	+	N	?	N	Y	Y	Y
17 Hare	Y	Y	Y	Y	N	Y	Y
18 **LaHood**	Y	Y	Y	Y	N	Y	Y
19 **Shimkus**	Y	N	N	N	Y	Y	Y
INDIANA							
1 Visclosky	Y	Y	Y	Y	N	Y	Y
2 Donnelly	Y	Y	Y	N	Y	Y	Y
3 **Souder**	Y	N	N	N	Y	Y	Y
4 **Buyer**	Y	N	N	N	Y	Y	Y
5 **Burton**	Y	N	N	N	Y	N	Y
6 **Pence**	N	N	N	N	Y	N	Y
7 Vacant							
8 Ellsworth	Y	Y	Y	N	Y	Y	Y
9 Hill	Y	Y	Y	N	N	Y	Y
IOWA							
1 Braley	Y	Y	N	Y	N	Y	Y
2 Loebsack	Y	Y	N	Y	N	Y	Y
3 Boswell	Y	Y	N	Y	N	Y	Y
4 **Latham**	Y	N	N	N	Y	Y	Y
5 **King**	N	N	N	N	Y	N	Y
KANSAS							
1 **Moran**	Y	N	N	N	Y	N	Y
2 Boyda	Y	N	N	N	N	Y	Y
3 Moore	Y	Y	Y	N	N	Y	Y
4 **Tiahrt**	Y	N	N	N	Y	Y	Y
KENTUCKY							
1 **Whitfield**	Y	N	N	N	Y	Y	Y
2 **Lewis**	Y	Y	N	N	?	Y	Y
3 Yarmuth	?	N	N	Y	N	Y	Y
4 **Davis**	Y	N	N	N	Y	Y	Y
5 **Rogers**	Y	Y	N	N	Y	Y	Y
6 Chandler	Y	Y	Y	N	N	Y	Y
LOUISIANA							
1 Vacant							
2 Jefferson	Y	Y	Y	Y	N	Y	Y
3 Melancon	Y	N	Y	N	N	Y	Y
4 **McCrery**	Y	N	N	N	Y	Y	Y
5 **Alexander**	Y	N	N	N	Y	Y	Y
6 Vacant							
7 **Boustany**	Y	N	N	N	Y	Y	Y
MAINE							
1 Allen	Y	Y	Y	Y	N	Y	Y
2 Michaud	Y	Y	Y	Y	N	Y	Y
MARYLAND							
1 **Gilchrest**	Y	Y	N	N	Y	Y	Y
2 Ruppersberger	?	?	?	?	?	?	?
3 Sarbanes	Y	Y	Y	Y	N	Y	Y
4 Wynn	?	?	?	?	?	?	?
5 Hoyer	Y	Y	Y	Y	N	Y	Y
6 **Bartlett**	Y	Y	N	N	Y	N	Y
7 Cummings	Y	Y	Y	Y	N	Y	Y
8 Van Hollen	Y	Y	Y	Y	N	Y	Y
MASSACHUSETTS							
1 Olver	Y	Y	Y	Y	N	Y	Y
2 Neal	Y	Y	Y	Y	N	Y	?
3 McGovern	Y	Y	Y	Y	N	Y	Y
4 Frank	Y	Y	Y	Y	N	Y	Y
5 Tsongas	Y	Y	Y	Y	N	Y	Y
6 Tierney	Y	Y	Y	Y	N	Y	Y
7 Markey	Y	Y	Y	Y	N	Y	Y
8 Capuano	Y	Y	Y	Y	N	Y	Y
9 Lynch	Y	Y	Y	N	N	Y	?
10 Delahunt	Y	Y	Y	Y	N	Y	Y
MICHIGAN							
1 Stupak	Y	Y	Y	Y	N	Y	Y
2 **Hoekstra**	Y	N	N	N	Y	N	Y
3 **Ehlers**	Y	N	N	N	Y	Y	Y
4 **Camp**	Y	N	N	N	Y	Y	Y
5 Kildee	Y	Y	Y	Y	N	Y	Y
6 **Upton**	Y	N	N	N	Y	Y	Y
7 **Walberg**	Y	N	N	N	Y	Y	Y
8 **Rogers**	Y	Y	N	N	Y	Y	Y
9 **Knollenberg**	Y	N	N	N	Y	Y	Y
10 **Miller**	Y	N	N	N	Y	Y	Y
11 **McCotter**	Y	N	N	N	Y	Y	Y
12 Levin	Y	Y	Y	Y	N	Y	Y
13 Kilpatrick	Y	Y	Y	Y	N	Y	Y
14 Conyers	Y	Y	Y	Y	N	Y	Y
15 Dingell	Y	Y	Y	Y	N	Y	Y
MINNESOTA							
1 Walz	Y	Y	Y	Y	N	Y	Y
2 **Kline**	Y	N	N	N	Y	N	Y
3 **Ramstad**	Y	Y	Y	N	Y	Y	Y
4 McCollum	Y	Y	Y	Y	N	Y	Y

	35	36	37	38	39	40	41
5 Ellison	Y	Y	Y	Y	N	Y	Y
6 **Bachmann**	N	N	N	N	Y	N	?
7 Peterson	Y	Y	Y	N	N	Y	Y
8 Oberstar	Y	Y	Y	Y	N	Y	Y
MISSISSIPPI							
1 Vacant							
2 Thompson	Y	Y	Y	Y	N	Y	Y
3 **Pickering**	Y	Y	Y	N	Y	Y	Y
4 Taylor	Y	Y	Y	N	N	Y	Y
MISSOURI							
1 Clay	Y	Y	Y	Y	N	Y	Y
2 **Akin**	Y	N	N	N	Y	N	Y
3 Carnahan	Y	Y	Y	Y	N	Y	Y
4 Skelton	Y	Y	Y	N	N	Y	Y
5 Cleaver	Y	Y	Y	Y	N	Y	Y
6 **Graves**	Y	Y	Y	N	Y	Y	Y
7 **Blunt**	Y	N	N	N	Y	N	Y
8 **Emerson**	?	Y	N	N	Y	Y	Y
9 **Hulshof**	Y	Y	N	Y	Y	Y	Y
MONTANA							
AL **Rehberg**	Y	N	N	N	Y	Y	Y
NEBRASKA							
1 **Fortenberry**	+	−	−	−	+	+	+
2 **Terry**	Y	N	N	N	Y	Y	Y
3 **Smith**	Y	N	N	N	Y	Y	Y
NEVADA							
1 Berkley	Y	Y	Y	N	N	Y	Y
2 **Heller**	Y	N	N	N	Y	Y	Y
3 **Porter**	+	+	+	−	+	+	?
NEW HAMPSHIRE							
1 Shea-Porter	Y	Y	Y	Y	N	Y	Y
2 Hodes	Y	Y	Y	N	N	Y	Y
NEW JERSEY							
1 Andrews	Y	Y	Y	Y	N	Y	Y
2 **LoBiondo**	Y	Y	Y	N	Y	Y	Y
3 **Saxton**	Y	Y	Y	N	Y	Y	?
4 **Smith**	Y	Y	Y	N	Y	Y	?
5 **Garrett**	N	N	N	N	Y	N	Y
6 Pallone	Y	Y	Y	Y	N	Y	Y
7 **Ferguson**	Y	Y	N	N	Y	Y	Y
8 Pascrell	Y	Y	Y	Y	N	Y	Y
9 Rothman	Y	Y	Y	Y	N	Y	Y
10 Payne	Y	Y	Y	Y	N	Y	Y
11 **Frelinghuysen**	Y	Y	Y	N	Y	Y	Y
12 Holt	Y	Y	Y	Y	N	Y	Y
13 Sires	Y	Y	Y	Y	N	Y	Y
NEW MEXICO							
1 **Wilson**	Y	N	N	N	Y	Y	Y
2 **Pearce**	Y	N	N	N	Y	Y	Y
3 Udall	Y	Y	Y	Y	N	Y	Y
NEW YORK							
1 Bishop	Y	Y	Y	Y	N	Y	Y
2 Israel	Y	Y	Y	Y	N	Y	Y
3 **King**	Y	Y	N	N	Y	Y	Y
4 McCarthy	Y	Y	Y	N	N	Y	?
5 Ackerman	Y	Y	Y	Y	N	Y	Y
6 Meeks	Y	Y	Y	Y	N	Y	Y
7 Crowley	Y	Y	Y	N	N	Y	Y
8 Nadler	Y	Y	Y	Y	N	Y	Y
9 Weiner	Y	?	?	?	N	Y	Y
10 Towns	Y	?	?	Y	N	Y	Y
11 Clarke	Y	Y	Y	Y	N	Y	Y
12 Velázquez	Y	Y	Y	Y	N	Y	Y
13 **Fossella**	Y	Y	N	N	Y	Y	Y
14 Maloney	Y	Y	Y	N	N	Y	Y
15 Rangel	Y	Y	Y	Y	N	Y	Y
16 Serrano	Y	Y	Y	Y	N	Y	Y
17 Engel	Y	Y	Y	Y	N	Y	Y
18 Lowey	+	+	+	+	−	+	+
19 Hall	Y	Y	Y	Y	N	Y	Y
20 Gillibrand	Y	Y	Y	Y	N	Y	Y
21 McNulty	Y	Y	Y	Y	N	Y	Y
22 Hinchey	Y	Y	Y	Y	N	Y	Y
23 **McHugh**	Y	Y	Y	N	Y	Y	Y
24 Arcuri	Y	Y	N	N	N	Y	Y
25 **Walsh**	Y	Y	Y	N	Y	Y	Y
26 **Reynolds**	Y	N	N	N	Y	Y	?
27 Higgins	Y	Y	Y	Y	N	Y	Y
28 Slaughter	Y	Y	Y	Y	N	Y	Y
29 **Kuhl**	Y	Y	Y	N	Y	Y	Y
NORTH CAROLINA							
1 Butterfield	Y	Y	N	Y	N	Y	Y
2 Etheridge	Y	Y	N	Y	N	Y	Y
3 **Jones**	Y	Y	N	N	Y	Y	Y
4 Price	Y	Y	N	Y	N	Y	Y

	35	36	37	38	39	40	41
5 **Foxx**	N	N	N	N	N	N	Y
6 **Coble**	Y	N	N	N	Y	Y	?
7 McIntyre	Y	Y	Y	Y	N	Y	Y
8 **Hayes**	Y	N	N	N	Y	Y	Y
9 **Myrick**	Y	N	N	N	Y	N	Y
10 **McHenry**	Y	N	N	N	Y	N	Y
11 Shuler	Y	N	N	N	N	Y	Y
12 Watt	Y	Y	N	Y	N	Y	Y
13 Miller	Y	Y	Y	Y	N	Y	Y
NORTH DAKOTA							
AL Pomeroy	Y	Y	Y	N	N	Y	Y
OHIO							
1 **Chabot**	Y	N	N	N	Y	Y	Y
2 **Schmidt**	Y	N	N	N	Y	Y	Y
3 **Turner**	Y	N	N	N	+	Y	+
4 **Jordan**	N	N	N	N	Y	N	Y
5 **Latta**	Y	N	N	N	Y	Y	Y
6 Wilson	Y	Y	Y	N	N	Y	Y
7 **Hobson**	Y	N	N	N	Y	Y	Y
8 **Boehner**	Y	?	N	N	Y	N	Y
9 Kaptur	Y	Y	Y	Y	N	Y	Y
10 Kucinich	Y	N	N	Y	N	Y	Y
11 Tubbs Jones	Y	Y	Y	Y	N	Y	Y
12 **Tiberi**	Y	N	N	N	Y	Y	Y
13 Sutton	Y	Y	Y	Y	N	Y	?
14 **LaTourette**	Y	N	N	N	Y	Y	?
15 **Pryce**	?	N	N	N	Y	Y	Y
16 **Regula**	Y	N	N	N	Y	Y	Y
17 Ryan	Y	Y	Y	Y	N	Y	Y
18 Space	Y	Y	Y	N	N	Y	?
OKLAHOMA							
1 **Sullivan**	Y	N	N	N	Y	Y	Y
2 Boren	Y	Y	Y	N	N	Y	Y
3 **Lucas**	Y	N	N	N	Y	Y	Y
4 **Cole**	Y	N	N	N	Y	Y	Y
5 **Fallin**	Y	N	N	N	Y	Y	Y
OREGON							
1 Wu	Y	Y	Y	Y	N	Y	Y
2 **Walden**	Y	N	N	N	Y	Y	Y
3 Blumenauer	?	Y	Y	Y	N	Y	Y
4 DeFazio	Y	Y	Y	Y	N	Y	Y
5 Hooley	Y	Y	Y	Y	N	Y	Y
PENNSYLVANIA							
1 Brady	Y	Y	Y	Y	N	Y	Y
2 Fattah	Y	Y	Y	Y	N	Y	Y
3 **English**	Y	Y	N	N	Y	Y	Y
4 Altmire	Y	N	N	N	N	Y	Y
5 **Peterson**	Y	Y	N	N	Y	Y	Y
6 **Gerlach**	Y	N	N	N	Y	Y	Y
7 Sestak	Y	Y	Y	Y	N	Y	Y
8 Murphy, P.	Y	Y	Y	Y	N	Y	Y
9 **Shuster**	Y	N	N	N	Y	Y	Y
10 Carney	Y	Y	Y	N	Y	Y	Y
11 Kanjorski	Y	Y	N	N	N	Y	Y
12 Murtha	Y	Y	Y	N	N	Y	Y
13 Schwartz	Y	Y	Y	Y	N	Y	Y
14 Doyle	Y	Y	Y	Y	N	Y	Y
15 **Dent**	Y	Y	N	N	Y	Y	Y
16 **Pitts**	Y	?	?	?	?	?	?
17 Holden	Y	Y	Y	N	N	Y	Y
18 **Murphy, T.**	Y	Y	Y	Y	Y	Y	Y
19 **Platts**	Y	Y	N	N	Y	Y	Y
RHODE ISLAND							
1 Kennedy	Y	Y	Y	Y	N	Y	Y
2 Langevin	Y	Y	Y	Y	N	Y	Y
SOUTH CAROLINA							
1 **Brown**	Y	N	N	N	Y	Y	Y
2 **Wilson**	Y	N	N	N	Y	Y	Y
3 **Barrett**	Y	N	N	N	Y	N	Y
4 **Inglis**	Y	N	N	N	Y	Y	Y
5 Spratt	Y	Y	Y	Y	N	Y	Y
6 Clyburn	Y	Y	Y	Y	N	Y	Y
SOUTH DAKOTA							
AL Herseth Sandlin	Y	N	N	N	N	Y	Y
TENNESSEE							
1 **Davis, David**	Y	N	N	N	Y	Y	Y
2 **Duncan**	N	Y	N	N	Y	N	Y
3 **Wamp**	Y	N	N	N	Y	Y	Y
4 Davis, L.	Y	Y	Y	N	N	Y	Y
5 Cooper	Y	Y	Y	Y	N	Y	Y
6 Gordon	Y	Y	N	Y	N	Y	Y
7 **Blackburn**	?	N	N	N	Y	N	Y
8 Tanner	?	?	?	?	?	?	?
9 Cohen	Y	Y	N	Y	N	Y	Y

	35	36	37	38	39	40	41
TEXAS							
1 **Gohmert**	Y	N	N	N	Y	Y	Y
2 **Poe**	N	N	N	N	Y	N	Y
3 **Johnson, S.**	Y	N	N	N	Y	Y	Y
4 **Hall**	Y	N	N	N	Y	Y	Y
5 **Hensarling**	N	N	N	N	Y	N	Y
6 **Barton**	Y	N	N	N	Y	N	Y
7 **Culberson**	Y	N	N	N	Y	N	Y
8 **Brady**	Y	N	N	N	Y	N	Y
9 Green, A.	Y	Y	Y	Y	N	Y	Y
10 **McCaul**	Y	N	N	N	Y	Y	Y
11 **Conaway**	Y	N	N	N	Y	N	Y
12 **Granger**	Y	N	N	N	Y	Y	Y
13 **Thornberry**	Y	N	N	N	Y	Y	Y
14 **Paul**	N	?	?	?	Y	N	Y
15 Hinojosa	Y	Y	Y	Y	N	Y	Y
16 Reyes	Y	Y	Y	Y	N	Y	Y
17 Edwards	Y	Y	Y	N	N	Y	Y
18 Jackson Lee	Y	Y	Y	Y	N	Y	Y
19 **Neugebauer**	Y	N	N	N	Y	Y	Y
20 Gonzalez	Y	Y	Y	Y	N	Y	Y
21 **Smith**	Y	N	N	N	Y	Y	Y
22 Lampson	Y	Y	N	N	Y	Y	?
23 Rodriguez	Y	Y	Y	Y	N	Y	Y
24 **Marchant**	?	N	N	N	Y	Y	?
25 Doggett	Y	Y	Y	Y	N	Y	Y
26 **Burgess**	Y	N	N	N	Y	N	Y
27 Ortiz	Y	Y	Y	Y	N	Y	Y
28 Cuellar	Y	Y	Y	N	N	Y	Y
29 Green, G.	Y	Y	Y	Y	N	Y	Y
30 Johnson, E.	Y	Y	Y	Y	N	Y	Y
31 **Carter**	Y	N	N	N	Y	Y	Y
32 **Sessions**	Y	N	N	N	Y	Y	Y
UTAH							
1 **Bishop**	Y	N	N	N	Y	Y	Y
2 Matheson	Y	Y	Y	N	N	Y	Y
3 **Cannon**	N	Y	N	N	Y	N	Y
VERMONT							
AL Welch	Y	Y	Y	Y	N	Y	Y
VIRGINIA							
1 **Wittman**	Y	N	N	N	Y	Y	Y
2 **Drake**	Y	N	N	N	Y	Y	Y
3 Scott	Y	Y	Y	Y	N	Y	Y
4 **Forbes**	Y	N	N	N	Y	Y	Y
5 **Goode**	Y	N	N	N	Y	Y	Y
6 **Goodlatte**	Y	N	N	N	Y	Y	Y
7 **Cantor**	Y	N	N	N	Y	N	Y
8 Moran	Y	Y	Y	Y	N	Y	Y
9 Boucher	?	?	?	?	?	?	?
10 **Wolf**	Y	Y	Y	N	Y	Y	Y
11 **Davis, T.**	Y	?	?	?	?	?	?
WASHINGTON							
1 Inslee	Y	?	?	?	?	?	?
2 Larsen	Y	Y	Y	N	N	Y	Y
3 Baird	Y	Y	Y	N	N	Y	Y
4 **Hastings**	Y	N	N	N	Y	Y	Y
5 **McMorris Rodgers**	Y	N	N	N	Y	Y	Y
6 Dicks	Y	Y	Y	Y	N	Y	Y
7 McDermott	Y	Y	Y	Y	N	Y	Y
8 **Reichert**	Y	N	Y	N	Y	Y	Y
9 Smith	?	?	?	?	?	?	?
WEST VIRGINIA							
1 Mollohan	Y	Y	Y	Y	N	Y	Y
2 **Capito**	Y	Y	Y	N	Y	Y	Y
3 Rahall	Y	Y	Y	Y	N	Y	Y
WISCONSIN							
1 **Ryan**	Y	N	N	N	Y	N	?
2 Baldwin	+	Y	Y	Y	N	Y	Y
3 Kind	Y	Y	Y	N	N	Y	Y
4 Moore	Y	Y	Y	Y	N	Y	Y
5 **Sensenbrenner**	Y	N	N	N	Y	N	Y
6 **Petri**	Y	Y	Y	Y	Y	Y	Y
7 Obey	Y	Y	Y	Y	N	Y	Y
8 Kagen	Y	Y	Y	Y	N	Y	Y
WYOMING							
AL **Cubin**	Y	N	N	N	Y	N	Y
DELEGATES							
Faleomavaega (A.S.)	Y	Y	Y				
Norton (D.C.)	Y	Y	Y				
Bordallo (Guam)	Y	Y	Y				
Fortuño (P.R.)	N	N	N				
Christensen (V.I.)	Y	Y	Y				

IN THE HOUSE | By Vote Number

42. HR 5140. Economic Stimulus/Motion to Concur. Rangel, D-N.Y., motion to concur in the Senate amendment to the bill that would provide advance refund of a tax credit for most taxpayers equal to $300 to $600 for individuals and $600 to $1,200 for couples. Families would receive $300 for each child under 17. The benefit would begin phasing out for individuals with adjusted gross incomes above $75,000 ($150,000 for married couples). It would provide businesses with a 50 percent depreciation for certain equipment purchased in 2008 and increase to $250,000 the amount small businesses can expense in the year items are purchased. It would raise the size of mortgage loans the Federal Housing Administration could insure and Fannie Mae and Freddie Mac could purchase. It would expand eligibility for rebate checks to include low-income senior citizens, disabled veterans and widows of veterans. Illegal immigrants would be ineligible. Motion agreed to (thus clearing the bill for the president) 380-34: R 165-28; D 215-6 (ND 165-2, SD 50-4). A "yea" was a vote in support of the president's position. Feb. 7, 2008.

43. H Res 954. Fallen Border Patrol Agents Tribute/Adoption. Thompson, D-Miss., motion to suspend the rules and adopt the resolution that would recognize fallen border patrol agents and pay tribute to Luis A. Aguilar, who died in the line of duty. Motion agreed to 357-0: R 161-0; D 196-0 (ND 150-0, SD 46-0). A two-thirds majority of those present and voting (238 in this case) is required for passage under suspension of the rules. Feb. 12, 2008.

44. H Res 909. Haitian Soldiers and U.S. Independence/Adoption. Faleomavaega, D-Am. Samoa, motion to suspend the rules and adopt the resolution that would recognize the role of Haitian soldiers who fought for American independence in the "Siege of Savannah," as well as Haiti's independence and renunciation of slavery. Motion agreed to 361-0: R 164-0; D 197-0 (ND 150-0, SD 47-0). A two-thirds majority of those present and voting (241 in this case) is required for adoption under suspension of the rules. Feb. 12, 2008.

45. H Con Res 281. Abraham Lincoln Birthday Proclamation/Adoption. Butterfield, D-N.C., motion to suspend the rules and adopt the concurrent resolution that would request the president issue a proclamation each year recognizing the anniversary of the birth of President Abraham Lincoln. Motion agreed to 357-0: R 163-0; D 194-0 (ND 148-0, SD 46-0). A two-thirds majority of those present and voting (238 in this case) is required for adoption under suspension of the rules. Feb. 12, 2008.

46. Procedural Motion/Adjourn. Blackburn, R-Tenn., motion to adjourn. Motion rejected 3-366: R 3-167; D 0-199 (ND 0-148, SD 0-51). Feb. 13, 2008.

47. Procedural Motion/Adjourn. Hastings, R-Wash., motion to adjourn. Motion rejected 7-364: R 6-170; D 1-194 (ND 1-147, SD 0-47). Feb. 13, 2008.

48. HR 5349. Foreign Intelligence Surveillance Extension/Previous Question. Arcuri, D-N.Y., motion to order the previous question (thus ending debate and possibility of amendment) on adoption of the rule (H Res 976) to provide for House floor consideration of the bill that would extend the Protect America Act of 2007 (PL 110-55) for 21 days beyond its current extension date of Feb. 16. Motion agreed to 210-195: R 1-190; D 209-5 (ND 157-4, SD 52-1). Feb. 13, 2008.

---

*Rep. Tom Lantos, D-Calif., died Feb. 11, 2008. The last vote for which he was eligible was vote 42.

ND Northern Democrats, SD Southern Democrats
Southern states: Ala., Ark., Fla., Ga., Ky., La., Miss., N.C., Okla., S.C., Tenn., Texas, Va.

	42	43	44	45	46	47	48
ALABAMA							
1 Bonner	Y	Y	Y	Y	N	N	N
2 Everett	?	Y	Y	Y	N	N	N
3 Rogers	Y	Y	Y	Y	N	?	N
4 Aderholt	Y	Y	Y	Y	N	N	N
5 Cramer	?	Y	Y	Y	N	N	Y
6 Bachus	Y	Y	Y	Y	N	?	N
7 Davis	Y	Y	Y	Y	N	N	Y
ALASKA							
AL Young	Y	Y	Y	Y	?	?	N
ARIZONA							
1 Renzi	Y	?	?	?	?	?	?
2 Franks	Y	+	+	+	N	N	N
3 Shadegg	N	Y	Y	Y	N	N	N
4 Pastor	Y	Y	Y	Y	N	N	Y
5 Mitchell	Y	Y	Y	Y	N	N	+
6 Flake	N	+	+	+	N	N	N
7 Grijalva	Y	Y	Y	Y	N	N	Y
8 Giffords	Y	Y	Y	Y	N	N	Y
ARKANSAS							
1 Berry	N	Y	Y	Y	N	N	Y
2 Snyder	Y	Y	Y	Y	N	N	Y
3 Boozman	Y	Y	Y	Y	N	N	N
4 Ross	Y	Y	Y	Y	N	N	Y
CALIFORNIA							
1 Thompson	Y	Y	Y	Y	N	N	Y
2 Herger	Y	Y	Y	Y	N	N	?
3 Lungren	N	Y	Y	Y	N	N	N
4 Doolittle	Y	Y	Y	Y	?	Y	?
5 Matsui	Y	Y	Y	Y	N	N	Y
6 Woolsey	+	Y	Y	Y	N	N	Y
7 Miller, George	Y	Y	Y	Y	?	N	Y
8 Pelosi	Y	?	?	?			
9 Lee	Y	Y	Y	Y	N	N	Y
10 Tauscher	Y	Y	Y	Y	N	N	Y
11 McNerney	Y	Y	Y	Y	N	N	Y
12 Vacant*							
13 Stark	Y	Y	Y	Y	?	N	Y
14 Eshoo	Y	Y	Y	Y	N	N	Y
15 Honda	Y	?	?	?	?	?	?
16 Lofgren	Y	Y	Y	Y	N	N	Y
17 Farr	?	Y	Y	Y	N	?	Y
18 Cardoza	Y	Y	Y	Y	N	N	Y
19 Radanovich	Y	?	?	?	?	?	N
20 Costa	Y	?	?	?	N	?	Y
21 Nunes	Y	Y	Y	Y	N	N	N
22 McCarthy	Y	Y	Y	Y	N	N	N
23 Capps	Y	Y	Y	Y	N	N	Y
24 Gallegly	Y	Y	Y	Y	N	N	N
25 McKeon	Y	Y	Y	Y	N	N	N
26 Dreier	Y	Y	Y	Y	N	N	N
27 Sherman	Y	Y	Y	Y	N	N	Y
28 Berman	Y	Y	Y	Y	N	?	Y
29 Schiff	Y	Y	Y	Y	N	N	Y
30 Waxman	Y	Y	Y	Y	?	?	?
31 Becerra	Y	Y	Y	Y	N	N	Y
32 Solis	Y	Y	Y	Y	N	N	Y
33 Watson	Y	Y	Y	Y	N	N	Y
34 Roybal-Allard	Y	Y	Y	Y	N	N	Y
35 Waters	Y	Y	Y	Y	N	N	Y
36 Harman	Y	Y	Y	Y	N	N	Y
37 Richardson	Y	Y	Y	Y	N	N	Y
38 Napolitano	Y	Y	Y	Y	N	N	Y
39 Sánchez, Linda	Y	Y	Y	Y	N	N	Y
40 Royce	N	Y	Y	Y	N	N	N
41 Lewis	Y	Y	Y	Y	N	N	N
42 Miller, Gary	Y	Y	Y	Y	N	N	N
43 Baca	Y	Y	Y	Y	N	N	Y
44 Calvert	Y	Y	Y	Y	N	N	N
45 Bono Mack	Y	?	?	?	N	N	N
46 Rohrabacher	N	?	?	?	N	N	N
47 Sanchez, Loretta	–	Y	Y	Y	N	N	Y
48 Campbell	N	Y	Y	Y	N	N	N
49 Issa	Y	Y	Y	Y	N	N	N
50 Bilbray	Y	Y	Y	Y	N	N	N
51 Filner	Y	Y	Y	Y	N	N	Y
52 Hunter	N	Y	Y	Y	N	N	N
53 Davis	Y	Y	Y	Y	N	N	Y

	42	43	44	45	46	47	48
COLORADO							
1 DeGette	Y	Y	Y	?	N	N	Y
2 Udall	Y	?	?	?	N	N	Y
3 Salazar	Y	Y	Y	Y	N	N	Y
4 Musgrave	Y	Y	Y	Y	?	N	N
5 Lamborn	Y	Y	Y	Y	N	N	N
6 Tancredo	N	Y	Y	Y	N	N	N
7 Perlmutter	Y	Y	Y	Y	N	N	Y
CONNECTICUT							
1 Larson	Y	Y	Y	Y	N	N	Y
2 Courtney	Y	Y	Y	Y	N	N	Y
3 DeLauro	Y	Y	Y	Y	N	?	Y
4 Shays	Y	Y	Y	Y	N	N	N
5 Murphy	Y	Y	Y	Y	N	N	Y
DELAWARE							
AL Castle	Y	Y	Y	Y	N	N	N
FLORIDA							
1 Miller	Y	Y	Y	Y	N	N	N
2 Boyd	N	Y	Y	Y	N	N	Y
3 Brown	Y	?	?	?	N	?	Y
4 Crenshaw	Y	Y	Y	Y	N	N	N
5 Brown-Waite	Y	Y	Y	Y	N	N	N
6 Stearns	Y	Y	Y	Y	N	N	N
7 Mica	Y	Y	Y	Y	N	N	N
8 Keller	Y	Y	Y	Y	N	N	N
9 Bilirakis	Y	Y	Y	Y	N	N	N
10 Young	Y	Y	Y	Y	N	N	N
11 Castor	Y	Y	Y	Y	N	N	Y
12 Putnam	Y	Y	Y	Y	N	N	N
13 Buchanan	Y	Y	Y	Y	N	N	N
14 Mack	Y	?	?	?	?	N	N
15 Weldon	Y	?	?	?	?	N	N
16 Mahoney	Y	Y	Y	Y	?	N	Y
17 Meek	Y	Y	Y	Y	N	N	Y
18 Ros-Lehtinen	Y	Y	Y	Y	N	N	N
19 Wexler	Y	Y	Y	Y	N	N	Y
20 Wasserman Schultz	Y	Y	Y	Y	N	N	Y
21 Diaz-Balart, L.	Y	Y	Y	Y	N	N	N
22 Klein	Y	Y	Y	Y	N	?	Y
23 Hastings	Y	Y	Y	Y	N	?	Y
24 Feeney	Y	Y	Y	Y	N	N	N
25 Diaz-Balart, M.	Y	Y	Y	Y	N	N	N
GEORGIA							
1 Kingston	N	Y	Y	Y	N	N	N
2 Bishop	Y	Y	Y	Y	N	N	+
3 Westmoreland	N	Y	Y	Y	N	N	N
4 Johnson	Y	Y	Y	Y	N	N	Y
5 Lewis	Y	Y	Y	Y	N	N	Y
6 Price	N	?	?	?	N	N	N
7 Linder	N	?	?	?	N	N	N
8 Marshall	Y	Y	Y	Y	N	N	Y
9 Deal	N	Y	Y	Y	N	N	N
10 Broun	N	Y	Y	Y	N	N	N
11 Gingrey	N	Y	Y	Y	N	N	N
12 Barrow	Y	Y	Y	Y	N	N	Y
13 Scott	Y	Y	Y	Y	N	N	Y
HAWAII							
1 Abercrombie	Y	Y	Y	Y	N	N	Y
2 Hirono	Y	Y	Y	Y	N	N	Y
IDAHO							
1 Sali	Y	Y	Y	Y	N	?	N
2 Simpson	N	Y	Y	Y	N	?	N
ILLINOIS							
1 Rush	Y	Y	Y	Y	N	N	Y
2 Jackson	Y	Y	Y	Y	N	N	Y
3 Lipinski	Y	?	?	?	N	N	Y
4 Gutierrez	Y	+	+	+	N	N	Y
5 Emanuel	Y	Y	Y	Y	N	N	Y
6 Roskam	Y	?	?	?	N	N	N
7 Davis	Y	Y	Y	Y	N	?	Y
8 Bean	Y	?	?	?	N	N	Y
9 Schakowsky	Y	Y	Y	Y	N	N	Y
10 Kirk	Y	Y	Y	Y	N	N	N
11 Weller	Y	Y	Y	Y	N	N	N
12 Costello	Y	Y	Y	Y	N	N	Y
13 Biggert	Y	Y	Y	Y	?	N	N
14 Vacant							
15 Johnson	Y	+	Y	Y	Y	Y	N

KEY | **Republicans** | Democrats

Y Voted for (yea)	X Paired against	C Voted "present" to avoid possible conflict of interest
# Paired for	– Announced against	
+ Announced for	P Voted "present"	? Did not vote or otherwise make a position known
N Voted against (nay)		

	42	43	44	45	46	47	48
16 **Manzullo**	Y	Y	Y	Y	N	N	N
17 Hare	Y	Y	Y	Y	N	N	Y
18 **LaHood**	Y	Y	Y	Y	N	N	N
19 **Shimkus**	Y	Y	Y	Y	N	Y	N
INDIANA							
1 Visclosky	Y	Y	Y	Y	N	N	Y
2 Donnelly	Y	Y	Y	Y	N	N	N
3 **Souder**	Y	Y	Y	Y	?	?	N
4 **Buyer**	Y	?	Y	Y	N	N	N
5 **Burton**	Y	?	?	?	N	N	N
6 **Pence**	Y	Y	Y	Y	N	N	N
7 Vacant							
8 Ellsworth	Y	Y	Y	Y	N	N	Y
9 Hill	Y	Y	Y	Y	N	N	N
IOWA							
1 Braley	Y	Y	Y	Y	?	N	Y
2 Loebsack	Y	Y	Y	Y	N	N	Y
3 Boswell	Y	Y	Y	Y	N	N	Y
4 **Latham**	Y	Y	Y	Y	N	N	N
5 **King**	Y	Y	Y	Y	N	Y	N
KANSAS							
1 **Moran**	N	Y	Y	Y	N	N	N
2 Boyda	Y	Y	Y	?	N	N	Y
3 Moore	Y	Y	Y	Y	N	N	Y
4 **Tiahrt**	Y	Y	Y	Y	Y	Y	N
KENTUCKY							
1 **Whitfield**	Y	Y	Y	Y	?	N	N
2 **Lewis**	Y	?	?	?	N	?	N
3 Yarmuth	Y	Y	Y	Y	N	N	Y
4 **Davis**	Y	+	+	+	N	N	N
5 **Rogers**	Y	?	?	?	N	N	N
6 Chandler	Y	?	?	?	N	N	Y
LOUISIANA							
1 Vacant							
2 Jefferson	Y	?	?	?	N	N	Y
3 Melancon	Y	Y	Y	Y	N	N	Y
4 **McCrery**	Y	?	?	?	?	?	N
5 **Alexander**	Y	Y	Y	Y	N	N	N
6 Vacant							
7 **Boustany**	Y	Y	Y	Y	N	N	N
MAINE							
1 Allen	Y	Y	Y	Y	N	N	Y
2 Michaud	Y	Y	Y	Y	N	N	Y
MARYLAND							
1 **Gilchrest**	Y	?	?	?	?	?	?
2 Ruppersberger	?	?	?	?	?	?	?
3 Sarbanes	Y	Y	Y	Y	N	N	Y
4 Wynn	Y	?	?	?	?	?	?
5 Hoyer	Y	Y	Y	Y	N	N	Y
6 **Bartlett**	Y	?	Y	Y	N	N	N
7 Cummings	Y	+	+	+	?	N	Y
8 Van Hollen	Y	Y	Y	Y	N	N	Y
MASSACHUSETTS							
1 Olver	Y	Y	Y	Y	N	?	Y
2 Neal	Y	Y	Y	Y	N	N	Y
3 McGovern	Y	Y	Y	Y	N	N	Y
4 Frank	Y	Y	Y	Y	N	?	Y
5 Tsongas	Y	Y	Y	Y	N	N	Y
6 Tierney	Y	Y	Y	Y	?	?	Y
7 Markey	Y	Y	Y	Y	N	N	Y
8 Capuano	Y	Y	Y	Y	N	N	Y
9 Lynch	Y	Y	Y	Y	N	N	Y
10 Delahunt	Y	Y	Y	Y	N	?	Y
MICHIGAN							
1 Stupak	Y	Y	Y	?	N	N	Y
2 **Hoekstra**	Y	Y	Y	Y	N	N	N
3 **Ehlers**	Y	Y	Y	Y	N	N	N
4 **Camp**	Y	Y	Y	Y	N	N	N
5 Kildee	Y	Y	Y	Y	N	N	Y
6 **Upton**	Y	Y	Y	Y	N	N	N
7 **Walberg**	Y	Y	Y	Y	N	N	N
8 **Rogers**	Y	Y	Y	Y	N	N	N
9 **Knollenberg**	Y	Y	Y	Y	?	?	N
10 **Miller**	Y	Y	Y	Y	N	N	N
11 **McCotter**	Y	Y	Y	Y	N	N	N
12 Levin	Y	Y	Y	Y	N	N	Y
13 Kilpatrick	Y	Y	Y	Y	N	N	Y
14 Conyers	Y	Y	Y	Y	N	N	Y
15 Dingell	Y	Y	Y	Y	N	N	Y
MINNESOTA							
1 Walz	Y	Y	Y	Y	N	N	Y
2 **Kline**	Y	Y	Y	Y	N	N	N
3 **Ramstad**	Y	Y	Y	Y	N	N	N
4 McCollum	Y	Y	Y	Y	N	N	Y
5 Ellison	Y	Y	Y	Y	N	N	Y
6 **Bachmann**	Y	Y	Y	Y	N	N	N
7 Peterson	N	Y	Y	Y	?	N	Y
8 Oberstar	Y	Y	Y	Y	N	N	Y
MISSISSIPPI							
1 Vacant							
2 Thompson	Y	Y	Y	Y	N	N	Y
3 **Pickering**	Y	?	?	?	?	?	?
4 Taylor	N	Y	Y	Y	?	?	Y
MISSOURI							
1 Clay	Y	?	Y	Y	N	N	?
2 **Akin**	Y	Y	Y	Y	N	N	N
3 Carnahan	Y	Y	Y	Y	N	?	Y
4 Skelton	Y	Y	Y	Y	N	?	Y
5 Cleaver	Y	Y	Y	Y	N	N	Y
6 **Graves**	Y	Y	Y	Y	N	N	N
7 **Blunt**	Y	Y	Y	Y	N	N	N
8 **Emerson**	Y	Y	Y	Y	N	N	N
9 **Hulshof**	Y	+	+	+	N	N	N
MONTANA							
AL **Rehberg**	Y	Y	Y	Y	N	N	N
NEBRASKA							
1 **Fortenberry**	+	Y	Y	Y	N	N	N
2 **Terry**	Y	?	?	?	N	N	N
3 **Smith**	Y	Y	Y	Y	N	N	N
NEVADA							
1 Berkley	Y	Y	Y	?	N	N	Y
2 **Heller**	Y	Y	Y	Y	N	N	N
3 **Porter**	+	Y	Y	Y	N	N	N
NEW HAMPSHIRE							
1 Shea-Porter	Y	Y	Y	Y	N	N	Y
2 Hodes	Y	Y	Y	Y	N	N	Y
NEW JERSEY							
1 Andrews	Y	Y	Y	Y	N	?	Y
2 **LoBiondo**	Y	Y	Y	Y	N	N	N
3 **Saxton**	Y	Y	Y	Y	N	N	N
4 **Smith**	Y	Y	Y	Y	?	N	N
5 **Garrett**	N	Y	Y	Y	?	N	N
6 Pallone	Y	Y	Y	Y	N	N	Y
7 **Ferguson**	Y	Y	Y	Y	N	N	N
8 Pascrell	Y	Y	Y	Y	N	N	Y
9 Rothman	Y	Y	Y	Y	N	N	Y
10 Payne	Y	Y	Y	Y	N	N	Y
11 **Frelinghuysen**	Y	Y	Y	Y	N	N	N
12 Holt	Y	Y	Y	Y	N	N	Y
13 Sires	Y	Y	Y	Y	N	N	Y
NEW MEXICO							
1 **Wilson**	Y	Y	Y	Y	N	N	N
2 **Pearce**	Y	Y	Y	Y	N	N	N
3 Udall	Y	Y	Y	Y	N	N	Y
NEW YORK							
1 Bishop	Y	Y	Y	Y	N	N	Y
2 Israel	Y	Y	Y	Y	N	N	Y
3 **King**	Y	Y	Y	Y	N	N	N
4 McCarthy	Y	Y	Y	Y	N	N	Y
5 Ackerman	Y	?	?	?	?	N	Y
6 Meeks	Y	Y	Y	Y	N	N	Y
7 Crowley	Y	Y	Y	Y	N	N	Y
8 Nadler	Y	Y	Y	Y	N	N	Y
9 Weiner	Y	?	?	?	?	?	Y
10 Towns	Y	?	?	?	?	?	?
11 Clarke	Y	Y	Y	Y	N	N	Y
12 Velázquez	Y	Y	Y	Y	N	N	Y
13 **Fossella**	Y	Y	Y	Y	N	N	N
14 Maloney	Y	Y	Y	Y	N	N	Y
15 Rangel	Y	Y	Y	Y	?	?	Y
16 Serrano	Y	Y	Y	Y	N	N	Y
17 Engel	Y	?	?	?	?	?	?
18 Lowey	+	+	+	+	–	–	+
19 Hall	Y	Y	Y	Y	N	N	Y
20 Gillibrand	Y	Y	Y	Y	N	N	Y
21 McNulty	Y	Y	Y	Y	N	N	Y
22 Hinchey	Y	?	?	?	N	N	Y
23 **McHugh**	Y	Y	Y	Y	N	N	N
24 Arcuri	Y	Y	Y	Y	N	N	Y
25 **Walsh**	Y	Y	Y	Y	N	?	N
26 **Reynolds**	Y	Y	Y	Y	N	N	N
27 Higgins	Y	Y	Y	Y	?	N	Y
28 Slaughter	Y	Y	Y	Y	N	N	Y
29 **Kuhl**	Y	?	?	?	?	N	N
NORTH CAROLINA							
1 Butterfield	Y	Y	Y	Y	N	N	Y
2 Etheridge	Y	Y	Y	Y	N	N	Y
3 **Jones**	Y	Y	Y	Y	N	N	N
4 Price	Y	Y	Y	Y	N	N	Y
5 **Foxx**	Y	Y	Y	Y	N	N	N
6 **Coble**	N	Y	Y	Y	N	N	N
7 McIntyre	Y	Y	Y	Y	N	N	Y
8 **Hayes**	Y	+	+	+	N	N	N
9 **Myrick**	Y	Y	Y	Y	N	N	N
10 **McHenry**	Y	Y	Y	Y	N	N	N
11 Shuler	Y	Y	Y	Y	N	N	Y
12 Watt	Y	Y	Y	Y	N	N	Y
13 Miller	Y	Y	Y	Y	N	?	Y
NORTH DAKOTA							
AL Pomeroy	Y	Y	Y	Y	N	N	Y
OHIO							
1 **Chabot**	Y	Y	Y	Y	N	N	N
2 **Schmidt**	Y	?	?	?	N	N	N
3 **Turner**	Y	Y	Y	Y	N	N	N
4 **Jordan**	Y	Y	Y	Y	N	N	N
5 **Latta**	Y	Y	Y	Y	N	N	N
6 Wilson	Y	?	?	?	N	N	Y
7 **Hobson**	Y	Y	Y	Y	N	N	N
8 **Boehner**	Y	Y	Y	Y	N	N	N
9 Kaptur	Y	Y	Y	Y	N	N	Y
10 Kucinich	Y	Y	Y	Y	N	N	Y
11 Tubbs Jones	Y	Y	Y	Y	N	?	?
12 **Tiberi**	Y	Y	Y	Y	N	N	N
13 Sutton	Y	Y	Y	Y	N	N	Y
14 **LaTourette**	Y	Y	Y	Y	N	N	N
15 **Pryce**	Y	?	?	?	?	?	?
16 **Regula**	Y	?	?	?	N	N	N
17 Ryan	Y	?	?	?	?	?	?
18 Space	Y	?	?	?	N	N	Y
OKLAHOMA							
1 **Sullivan**	Y	?	?	?	?	N	N
2 Boren	Y	Y	Y	Y	N	N	Y
3 **Lucas**	Y	Y	Y	Y	N	N	N
4 **Cole**	Y	Y	Y	Y	–	N	N
5 **Fallin**	Y	Y	Y	Y	N	N	N
OREGON							
1 Wu	Y	Y	Y	Y	N	N	Y
2 **Walden**	Y	Y	Y	Y	N	N	N
3 Blumenauer	Y	?	?	?	N	N	Y
4 DeFazio	Y	Y	Y	Y	?	N	Y
5 Hooley	Y	Y	Y	Y	N	N	Y
PENNSYLVANIA							
1 Brady	Y	Y	Y	Y	N	N	Y
2 Fattah	Y	Y	Y	Y	N	N	Y
3 **English**	Y	Y	Y	Y	N	N	N
4 Altmire	Y	Y	Y	Y	N	N	N
5 **Peterson**	Y	?	?	?	?	N	N
6 **Gerlach**	Y	Y	Y	Y	N	N	N
7 Sestak	Y	Y	Y	Y	N	N	Y
8 Murphy, P.	Y	Y	Y	Y	N	N	Y
9 **Shuster**	Y	Y	Y	Y	N	N	N
10 Carney	Y	Y	Y	Y	N	N	N
11 Kanjorski	Y	Y	Y	Y	N	N	Y
12 Murtha	Y	?	?	?	N	N	Y
13 Schwartz	Y	Y	Y	Y	N	N	Y
14 Doyle	Y	?	?	?	?	?	?
15 **Dent**	Y	Y	Y	Y	N	N	N
16 **Pitts**	?	Y	Y	Y	N	N	N
17 Holden	Y	Y	Y	Y	N	N	Y
18 **Murphy, T.**	Y	Y	Y	Y	N	N	N
19 **Platts**	Y	?	?	?	?	N	N
RHODE ISLAND							
1 Kennedy	Y	Y	Y	Y	N	N	Y
2 Langevin	Y	Y	Y	Y	N	N	Y
SOUTH CAROLINA							
1 **Brown**	Y	Y	Y	Y	N	N	N
2 **Wilson**	Y	Y	Y	Y	N	N	N
3 **Barrett**	Y	Y	Y	Y	N	N	N
4 **Inglis**	Y	?	?	?	N	N	N
5 Spratt	Y	?	Y	Y	?	N	Y
6 Clyburn	Y	Y	Y	Y	N	N	Y
SOUTH DAKOTA							
AL Herseth Sandlin	Y	Y	Y	Y	N	N	Y
TENNESSEE							
1 **Davis, David**	Y	Y	Y	Y	N	N	N
2 **Duncan**	N	Y	Y	Y	N	N	N
3 **Wamp**	Y	Y	Y	Y	N	N	N
4 Davis, L.	Y	Y	Y	Y	N	N	Y
5 Cooper	N	Y	Y	Y	N	N	Y
6 Gordon	Y	Y	Y	Y	N	N	Y
7 **Blackburn**	Y	Y	Y	Y	N	N	N
8 Tanner	?	Y	Y	Y	N	N	Y
9 Cohen	Y	Y	Y	Y	N	N	Y
TEXAS							
1 **Gohmert**	N	Y	Y	Y	?	?	N
2 **Poe**	N	Y	Y	Y	N	N	N
3 **Johnson, S.**	Y	Y	Y	Y	N	?	N
4 **Hall**	Y	Y	Y	Y	N	N	N
5 **Hensarling**	Y	Y	Y	Y	N	N	N
6 **Barton**	Y	Y	Y	Y	?	N	N
7 **Culberson**	Y	Y	Y	Y	?	N	N
8 **Brady**	Y	Y	Y	Y	N	N	N
9 Green, A.	Y	Y	Y	Y	N	N	Y
10 **McCaul**	Y	Y	Y	?	N	N	N
11 **Conaway**	Y	Y	Y	Y	N	N	N
12 **Granger**	Y	Y	Y	Y	N	N	N
13 **Thornberry**	Y	Y	Y	Y	N	N	N
14 **Paul**	N	?	?	?	N	N	N
15 Hinojosa	Y	+	+	+	?	–	+
16 Reyes	Y	?	?	?	?	?	?
17 Edwards	Y	Y	Y	Y	N	?	Y
18 Jackson Lee	Y	Y	Y	Y	N	N	Y
19 **Neugebauer**	Y	Y	Y	Y	N	N	N
20 Gonzalez	Y	Y	Y	Y	N	N	Y
21 **Smith**	Y	Y	Y	Y	N	N	N
22 Lampson	Y	?	?	?	N	N	N
23 Rodriguez	Y	?	?	?	N	N	Y
24 **Marchant**	Y	?	?	?	N	?	?
25 Doggett	Y	Y	Y	Y	N	N	Y
26 **Burgess**	N	Y	Y	Y	N	N	N
27 Ortiz	Y	?	?	?	?	?	?
28 Cuellar	Y	?	?	?	N	N	Y
29 Green, G.	Y	+	+	+	N	N	Y
30 Johnson, E.	Y	Y	Y	Y	N	N	Y
31 **Carter**	Y	Y	Y	Y	N	N	N
32 **Sessions**	Y	Y	Y	Y	N	N	N
UTAH							
1 **Bishop**	Y	Y	Y	Y	N	N	N
2 Matheson	Y	Y	Y	Y	N	N	Y
3 **Cannon**	Y	Y	Y	Y	N	?	N
VERMONT							
AL Welch	Y	Y	Y	Y	N	N	Y
VIRGINIA							
1 **Wittman**	Y	Y	Y	Y	N	N	N
2 **Drake**	Y	Y	Y	Y	N	N	N
3 Scott	Y	Y	Y	Y	N	N	Y
4 **Forbes**	N	Y	Y	Y	N	N	N
5 **Goode**	N	Y	Y	Y	?	N	N
6 **Goodlatte**	Y	Y	Y	Y	N	N	N
7 **Cantor**	Y	?	?	?	N	N	N
8 Moran	Y	Y	Y	?	N	?	Y
9 Boucher	?	Y	Y	Y	N	N	Y
10 **Wolf**	Y	Y	Y	Y	N	N	N
11 **Davis, T.**	?	?	?	?	?	?	N
WASHINGTON							
1 Inslee	?	Y	Y	Y	N	N	Y
2 Larsen	Y	Y	Y	Y	N	N	Y
3 Baird	N	Y	Y	Y	?	N	Y
4 **Hastings**	Y	Y	Y	Y	N	Y	Y
5 **McMorris Rodgers**	Y	Y	Y	Y	N	N	N
6 Dicks	Y	Y	Y	Y	?	Y	Y
7 McDermott	Y	Y	Y	Y	N	N	Y
8 **Reichert**	Y	Y	Y	Y	N	N	N
9 Smith	?	Y	Y	Y	N	N	Y
WEST VIRGINIA							
1 Mollohan	Y	Y	Y	Y	?	N	Y
2 **Capito**	Y	Y	Y	Y	N	N	N
3 Rahall	Y	Y	Y	Y	?	N	Y
WISCONSIN							
1 **Ryan**	Y	+	+	+	N	N	N
2 Baldwin	Y	Y	Y	Y	N	N	Y
3 Kind	Y	Y	Y	Y	N	N	Y
4 Moore	Y	Y	+	Y	–	N	Y
5 **Sensenbrenner**	N	Y	Y	Y	N	N	N
6 **Petri**	Y	Y	Y	Y	N	N	N
7 Obey	Y	Y	Y	Y	N	?	Y
8 Kagen	Y	?	?	?	N	N	Y
WYOMING							
AL **Cubin**	N	Y	Y	Y	?	?	N
DELEGATES							
Faleomavaega (A.S.)							
Norton (D.C.)							
Bordallo (Guam)							
Fortuño (P.R.)							
Christensen (V.I.)							

IN THE HOUSE | By Vote Number

49. **HR 5349. Foreign Intelligence Surveillance Extension/Motion to Reconsider.** Arcuri, D-N.Y., motion to table (kill) the Hastings, R-Wash., motion to reconsider the vote to order the previous question (thus ending debate and possibility of amendment) on adoption of the rule (H Res 976) that would provide for House floor consideration of the bill that would extend the Protect America Act of 2007 (PL 110-55) for 21 days beyond its current extension date of Feb. 16. Motion agreed to 206-194: R 0-189; D 206-5 (ND 156-4, SD 50-1). Feb. 13, 2008.

50. **HR 5349. Foreign Intelligence Surveillance Extension/Rule.** Adoption of the rule (H Res 976) to provide for House floor consideration of the bill that would extend the Protect America Act of 2007 (PL 110-55) for 21 days beyond its current extension date of Feb. 16. Adopted 206-199: R 1-191; D 205-8 (ND 155-6, SD 50-2). Feb. 13, 2008.

51. **HR 5349. Foreign Intelligence Surveillance Extension/ Motion to Reconsider.** Arcuri, D-N.Y., motion to table (kill) the Hastings, R-Wash., motion to reconsider the vote on adoption of the resolution (H Res 976) to provide for House floor consideration of the bill that would extend the Protect America Act of 2007 (PL 110-55) for 21 days beyond its current expiration date of Feb. 16. Motion agreed to 210-195: R 1-192; D 209-3 (ND 158-1, SD 51-2). Feb. 13, 2008.

52. **Procedural Motion/Adjourn.** Hastings, R-Wash., motion to adjourn. Motion rejected 3-395: R 3-186; D 0-209 (ND 0-156, SD 0-53). Feb. 13, 2008.

53. **HR 5349. Foreign Intelligence Surveillance Extension/Motion to Table.** Conyers, D-Mich., motion to table (kill) the Smith, R-Texas, appeal of the ruling of the chair with respect to the Conyers point of order that the Smith motion to recommit the bill to the Judiciary Committee with instructions that it be reported back immediately with language from HR 3773 was not germane. Motion agreed to 222-196: R 0-195; D 222-1 (ND 167-1, SD 55-0). Feb. 13, 2008.

54. **HR 5349. Foreign Intelligence Surveillance Extension/ Passage.** Passage of the bill that would extend the Protect America Act of 2007 (PL 110-55) for 21 days beyond its current expiration date of Feb. 16. The act amended the Foreign Intelligence Surveillance Act of 1978 to expand the authority of the attorney general and the director of national intelligence to conduct surveillance of suspected foreign terrorists without a court warrant. Rejected 191-229: R 0-195; D 191-34 (ND 143-27, SD 48-7). A "nay" was a vote in support of the president's position. Feb. 13, 2008.

55. **H Res 960. New York Giants Tribute/Adoption.** Butterfield, D-N.C., motion to suspend the rules and adopt the resolution that would congratulate the New York Giants of the National Football League on winning Super Bowl XLII. Motion agreed to 412-1: R 194-0; D 218-1 (ND 163-1, SD 55-0). A two-thirds majority of those present and voting (276 in this case) is required for adoption under suspension of the rules. Feb. 13, 2008.

	49	50	51	52	53	54	55
ALABAMA							
1 Bonner	N	N	N	N	N	N	Y
2 Everett	N	N	N	N	N	N	Y
3 Rogers	N	N	N	N	N	N	Y
4 Aderholt	N	N	N	N	N	N	Y
5 Cramer	Y	Y	Y	N	Y	Y	Y
6 Bachus	N	?	N	?	N	N	Y
7 Davis	Y	Y	Y	N	Y	Y	Y
ALASKA							
AL Young	N	N	N	Y	N	N	Y
ARIZONA							
1 Renzi	?	?	?	?	?	?	?
2 Franks	N	N	N	N	N	N	Y
3 Shadegg	N	N	N	N	N	N	Y
4 Pastor	Y	Y	Y	N	Y	Y	Y
5 Mitchell	Y	Y	Y	N	Y	Y	Y
6 Flake	N	N	N	N	N	N	Y
7 Grijalva	Y	Y	Y	N	Y	Y	Y
8 Giffords	Y	Y	Y	N	Y	Y	Y
ARKANSAS							
1 Berry	Y	Y	Y	N	Y	Y	Y
2 Snyder	Y	Y	Y	N	Y	Y	Y
3 Boozman	N	N	N	N	N	N	Y
4 Ross	Y	Y	Y	N	Y	Y	Y
CALIFORNIA							
1 Thompson	Y	Y	Y	N	Y	Y	Y
2 Herger	?	N	N	N	N	N	Y
3 Lungren	N	N	N	N	N	N	Y
4 Doolittle	?	?	?	?	N	N	Y
5 Matsui	Y	Y	Y	N	Y	Y	Y
6 Woolsey	Y	Y	Y	N	Y	N	Y
7 Miller, George	Y	Y	Y	N	Y	Y	Y
8 Pelosi						Y	
9 Lee	Y	Y	Y	N	Y	N	Y
10 Tauscher	Y	Y	Y	N	Y	Y	Y
11 McNerney	Y	Y	Y	N	Y	Y	Y
12 Vacant							
13 Stark	Y	Y	Y	N	Y	Y	?
14 Eshoo	Y	Y	Y	N	Y	Y	Y
15 Honda	?	?	?	?	?	?	?
16 Lofgren	Y	Y	Y	N	Y	Y	Y
17 Farr	Y	Y	Y	N	Y	Y	Y
18 Cardoza	Y	Y	Y	N	Y	Y	Y
19 Radanovich	N	N	N	N	N	N	Y
20 Costa	Y	Y	Y	N	Y	Y	Y
21 Nunes	N	N	N	N	N	N	Y
22 McCarthy	N	N	N	N	N	N	Y
23 Capps	Y	Y	Y	N	Y	Y	Y
24 Gallegly	N	N	N	N	N	N	Y
25 McKeon	N	N	N	N	N	N	Y
26 Dreier	N	N	N	N	N	N	Y
27 Sherman	Y	Y	Y	N	Y	Y	Y
28 Berman	Y	Y	Y	N	Y	Y	Y
29 Schiff	Y	Y	Y	N	Y	Y	Y
30 Waxman	?	?	?	?	Y	Y	Y
31 Becerra	Y	Y	Y	N	Y	Y	Y
32 Solis	Y	Y	Y	N	Y	Y	Y
33 Watson	Y	Y	Y	N	Y	Y	Y
34 Roybal-Allard	Y	Y	Y	N	Y	Y	Y
35 Waters	Y	Y	Y	N	Y	N	?
36 Harman	Y	Y	Y	N	Y	Y	Y
37 Richardson	Y	Y	Y	N	Y	Y	Y
38 Napolitano	Y	Y	Y	?	Y	Y	Y
39 Sánchez, Linda	Y	Y	Y	N	Y	Y	Y
40 Royce	N	N	N	N	N	N	Y
41 Lewis	N	N	N	N	N	N	Y
42 Miller, Gary	N	N	N	N	N	N	Y
43 Baca	Y	Y	Y	N	Y	Y	Y
44 Calvert	N	N	N	N	N	N	Y
45 Bono Mack	N	N	N	N	N	N	Y
46 Rohrabacher	N	N	N	N	N	N	Y
47 Sanchez, Loretta	Y	Y	Y	N	Y	Y	Y
48 Campbell	N	N	N	N	N	N	Y
49 Issa	N	N	N	N	N	N	Y
50 Bilbray	N	N	N	N	N	N	Y
51 Filner	Y	Y	Y	N	Y	N	Y
52 Hunter	N	N	N	N	N	N	Y
53 Davis	Y	Y	Y	N	Y	Y	Y

	49	50	51	52	53	54	55
COLORADO							
1 DeGette	Y	Y	Y	N	Y	Y	Y
2 Udall	Y	Y	Y	?	Y	Y	Y
3 Salazar	Y	Y	Y	N	Y	Y	Y
4 Musgrave	N	N	N	?	N	N	Y
5 Lamborn	N	N	N	N	N	N	Y
6 Tancredo	N	N	N	N	N	N	Y
7 Perlmutter	Y	Y	Y	N	Y	Y	Y
CONNECTICUT							
1 Larson	Y	Y	Y	N	Y	Y	Y
2 Courtney	Y	Y	Y	N	Y	Y	Y
3 DeLauro	Y	Y	Y	N	Y	Y	Y
4 Shays	N	N	N	N	N	N	Y
5 Murphy	Y	Y	Y	N	Y	Y	Y
DELAWARE							
AL Castle	N	N	N	N	N	N	Y
FLORIDA							
1 Miller	N	N	N	N	N	N	Y
2 Boyd	Y	Y	Y	N	Y	Y	Y
3 Brown	Y	Y	Y	N	Y	Y	Y
4 Crenshaw	N	N	N	N	N	N	Y
5 Brown-Waite	N	N	N	N	N	N	Y
6 Stearns	N	N	N	N	N	N	Y
7 Mica	N	N	N	N	N	N	Y
8 Keller	N	N	N	N	N	N	Y
9 Bilirakis	N	N	N	N	N	N	Y
10 Young	N	N	N	N	N	N	Y
11 Castor	Y	Y	Y	N	Y	Y	Y
12 Putnam	N	N	N	N	N	N	Y
13 Buchanan	N	N	N	N	N	N	Y
14 Mack	N	N	N	N	N	N	Y
15 Weldon	N	N	N	N	N	N	Y
16 Mahoney	Y	Y	Y	N	Y	N	Y
17 Meek	?	Y	Y	N	Y	Y	Y
18 Ros-Lehtinen	N	N	N	N	N	N	Y
19 Wexler	Y	Y	Y	N	Y	Y	Y
20 Wasserman Schultz	Y	Y	Y	N	Y	Y	Y
21 Diaz-Balart, L.	N	N	N	N	N	N	Y
22 Klein	Y	Y	Y	N	Y	Y	Y
23 Hastings	Y	Y	Y	N	Y	Y	Y
24 Feeney	N	N	N	N	N	N	Y
25 Diaz-Balart, M.	N	N	N	N	N	N	Y
GEORGIA							
1 Kingston	N	N	N	N	N	N	Y
2 Bishop	?	+	+	−	Y	Y	Y
3 Westmoreland	N	N	N	N	N	N	Y
4 Johnson	Y	Y	Y	N	Y	Y	Y
5 Lewis	Y	Y	Y	N	Y	N	Y
6 Price	N	N	N	N	N	N	Y
7 Linder	N	N	N	N	N	N	Y
8 Marshall	Y	Y	Y	N	Y	Y	Y
9 Deal	N	N	N	N	N	N	Y
10 Broun	N	N	N	N	N	N	Y
11 Gingrey	N	N	N	N	N	N	Y
12 Barrow	Y	Y	Y	N	Y	Y	Y
13 Scott	Y	Y	Y	N	Y	Y	Y
HAWAII							
1 Abercrombie	Y	Y	Y	N	Y	Y	Y
2 Hirono	Y	Y	Y	N	Y	Y	Y
IDAHO							
1 Sali	N	N	N	N	N	N	Y
2 Simpson	N	N	N	N	N	N	Y
ILLINOIS							
1 Rush	Y	Y	Y	?	Y	Y	Y
2 Jackson	Y	Y	Y	N	Y	Y	Y
3 Lipinski	Y	Y	Y	N	Y	Y	Y
4 Gutierrez	Y	Y	Y	?	Y	Y	Y
5 Emanuel	+	Y	Y	N	Y	Y	Y
6 Roskam	N	N	N	N	N	N	Y
7 Davis	Y	Y	Y	N	Y	Y	Y
8 Bean	Y	Y	Y	N	Y	Y	Y
9 Schakowsky	Y	Y	Y	N	Y	N	Y
10 Kirk	N	N	N	N	N	N	Y
11 Weller	N	N	N	N	N	N	Y
12 Costello	Y	Y	Y	N	Y	Y	Y
13 Biggert	N	N	N	N	N	N	Y
14 Vacant							
15 Johnson	N	N	Y	Y	N	N	Y

KEY   **Republicans**   Democrats

Y	Voted for (yea)	X	Paired against	C	Voted "present" to avoid possible conflict of interest
#	Paired for	−	Announced against	
+	Announced for	P	Voted "present"	?	Did not vote or otherwise make a position known
N	Voted against (nay)		

ND Northern Democrats, SD Southern Democrats
Southern states: Ala., Ark., Fla., Ga., Ky., La., Miss., N.C., Okla., S.C., Tenn., Texas, Va.

H-18   2008 CQ ALMANAC | www.cq.com

	49	50	51	52	53	54	55
16 **Manzullo**	N	N	N	N	N	N	Y
17 Hare	Y	Y	Y	N	Y	Y	Y
18 **LaHood**	N	N	N	N	N	N	Y
19 **Shimkus**	N	N	N	N	N	N	Y
INDIANA							
1 Visclosky	Y	Y	Y	N	Y	Y	Y
2 Donnelly	N	Y	Y	N	Y	Y	Y
3 **Souder**	N	N	N	N	N	N	Y
4 **Buyer**	N	N	N	N	N	N	Y
5 **Burton**	N	N	N	N	N	N	Y
6 **Pence**	N	N	N	N	N	N	Y
7 Vacant							
8 Ellsworth	Y	Y	Y	N	Y	Y	Y
9 Hill	N	N	Y	N	Y	Y	Y
IOWA							
1 Braley	Y	Y	Y	N	Y	Y	Y
2 Loebsack	?	Y	Y	N	Y	Y	Y
3 Boswell	Y	Y	Y	N	Y	N	Y
4 **Latham**	N	N	N	N	N	N	Y
5 **King**	N	N	N	N	N	N	Y
KANSAS							
1 **Moran**	N	N	N	N	N	N	Y
2 Boyda	Y	Y	Y	N	Y	Y	Y
3 Moore	Y	Y	Y	N	Y	Y	Y
4 **Tiahrt**	N	N	N	N	N	N	Y
KENTUCKY							
1 **Whitfield**	N	N	N	N	N	N	Y
2 **Lewis**	N	N	N	N	N	N	Y
3 Yarmuth	Y	Y	Y	N	Y	Y	Y
4 **Davis**	N	N	N	N	N	N	Y
5 **Rogers**	N	N	N	N	N	N	Y
6 Chandler	Y	Y	Y	N	Y	Y	Y
LOUISIANA							
1 Vacant							
2 Jefferson	Y	Y	Y	N	Y	Y	Y
3 Melancon	Y	Y	Y	N	Y	Y	Y
4 **McCrery**	N	N	N	?	N	N	Y
5 **Alexander**	N	N	N	N	N	N	Y
6 Vacant							
7 **Boustany**	N	N	N	N	N	N	Y
MAINE							
1 Allen	Y	Y	Y	?	Y	Y	Y
2 Michaud	Y	N	Y	N	Y	Y	Y
MARYLAND							
1 **Gilchrest**	?	?	?	?	?	?	?
2 Ruppersberger	?	?	?	?	?	?	?
3 Sarbanes	Y	Y	Y	N	Y	N	Y
4 Wynn	?	?	?	?	Y	Y	Y
5 Hoyer	Y	Y	Y	N	Y	Y	Y
6 **Bartlett**	N	N	N	N	N	N	Y
7 Cummings	Y	Y	Y	N	Y	Y	Y
8 Van Hollen	Y	Y	Y	N	Y	Y	Y
MASSACHUSETTS							
1 Olver	Y	Y	Y	N	Y	Y	Y
2 Neal	Y	Y	Y	N	Y	Y	Y
3 McGovern	Y	Y	Y	N	?	Y	Y
4 Frank	Y	Y	Y	N	Y	Y	Y
5 Tsongas	Y	Y	Y	N	Y	Y	Y
6 Tierney	Y	Y	Y	N	Y	Y	Y
7 Markey	Y	Y	Y	N	Y	Y	Y
8 Capuano	Y	Y	Y	N	Y	N	Y
9 Lynch	Y	Y	Y	N	Y	Y	Y
10 Delahunt	Y	Y	Y	N	Y	Y	Y
MICHIGAN							
1 Stupak	Y	Y	Y	N	Y	Y	Y
2 **Hoekstra**	N	N	N	N	N	N	Y
3 **Ehlers**	N	N	N	N	N	N	Y
4 **Camp**	N	N	N	N	N	N	Y
5 Kildee	Y	Y	Y	N	Y	Y	Y
6 **Upton**	N	N	N	N	N	N	Y
7 **Walberg**	N	N	N	N	N	N	Y
8 **Rogers**	N	N	N	N	N	N	Y
9 **Knollenberg**	N	N	N	N	N	N	Y
10 **Miller**	N	N	N	N	N	N	Y
11 **McCotter**	N	N	N	N	N	N	Y
12 Levin	Y	Y	Y	N	Y	Y	Y
13 Kilpatrick	Y	Y	Y	N	Y	Y	Y
14 Conyers	Y	Y	Y	N	Y	Y	Y
15 Dingell	Y	Y	?	N	Y	Y	Y
MINNESOTA							
1 Walz	Y	Y	Y	N	Y	N	Y
2 **Kline**	N	N	N	N	N	N	Y
3 **Ramstad**	N	N	N	N	N	N	Y
4 McCollum	Y	Y	Y	N	Y	Y	Y
5 Ellison	Y	Y	Y	N	Y	Y	?
6 **Bachmann**	N	N	N	N	N	N	Y
7 Peterson	Y	Y	?	N	Y	N	Y
8 Oberstar	Y	Y	Y	N	Y	Y	Y
MISSISSIPPI							
1 Vacant							
2 Thompson	Y	Y	Y	N	Y	Y	Y
3 **Pickering**	?	?	?	?	?	?	?
4 Taylor	Y	Y	Y	N	Y	Y	Y
MISSOURI							
1 Clay	Y	Y	Y	N	Y	Y	Y
2 **Akin**	N	N	N	N	N	N	Y
3 Carnahan	Y	Y	Y	N	Y	Y	Y
4 Skelton	Y	Y	Y	N	Y	Y	Y
5 Cleaver	Y	Y	Y	N	Y	Y	Y
6 **Graves**	N	N	N	N	N	N	Y
7 **Blunt**	N	N	N	N	N	N	Y
8 **Emerson**	N	N	N	N	N	N	Y
9 **Hulshof**	N	N	N	N	N	N	Y
MONTANA							
AL **Rehberg**	N	N	N	N	N	N	Y
NEBRASKA							
1 **Fortenberry**	N	N	N	N	N	N	Y
2 **Terry**	N	N	N	N	N	N	Y
3 **Smith**	N	N	N	N	N	N	Y
NEVADA							
1 Berkley	?	Y	Y	N	Y	Y	Y
2 **Heller**	N	N	N	N	N	N	Y
3 **Porter**	N	N	N	N	N	N	Y
NEW HAMPSHIRE							
1 Shea-Porter	Y	Y	Y	N	Y	Y	P
2 Hodes	Y	Y	Y	N	Y	Y	Y
NEW JERSEY							
1 Andrews	Y	Y	Y	N	Y	Y	Y
2 **LoBiondo**	N	N	N	N	N	N	Y
3 **Saxton**	N	N	N	N	N	N	Y
4 **Smith**	N	N	N	N	N	N	Y
5 **Garrett**	N	N	N	N	N	N	Y
6 Pallone	Y	Y	Y	N	Y	N	Y
7 **Ferguson**	N	N	N	N	N	N	Y
8 Pascrell	Y	Y	?	?	Y	N	Y
9 Rothman	Y	Y	Y	N	Y	N	Y
10 Payne	Y	Y	Y	N	Y	N	Y
11 **Frelinghuysen**	N	N	N	N	N	N	Y
12 Holt	Y	N	Y	N	Y	N	Y
13 Sires	Y	Y	Y	N	Y	Y	Y
NEW MEXICO							
1 **Wilson**	N	N	N	N	N	N	Y
2 **Pearce**	N	N	N	N	N	N	Y
3 Udall	Y	Y	Y	N	Y	N	Y
NEW YORK							
1 Bishop	Y	Y	Y	N	Y	Y	Y
2 Israel	Y	Y	Y	N	Y	Y	Y
3 **King**	N	N	N	N	N	N	Y
4 McCarthy	Y	Y	Y	N	Y	Y	Y
5 Ackerman	Y	Y	Y	N	Y	Y	Y
6 Meeks	Y	Y	Y	N	Y	Y	Y
7 Crowley	Y	Y	Y	N	Y	Y	Y
8 Nadler	Y	Y	Y	N	Y	Y	Y
9 Weiner	Y	Y	Y	N	Y	Y	Y
10 Towns	?	?	?	?	?	?	?
11 Clarke	Y	Y	Y	N	Y	Y	Y
12 Velázquez	Y	Y	Y	N	Y	Y	Y
13 **Fossella**	N	N	N	N	N	N	Y
14 Maloney	Y	Y	Y	N	Y	Y	Y
15 Rangel	Y	Y	?	?	Y	Y	Y
16 Serrano	Y	Y	Y	N	Y	N	Y
17 Engel	?	?	?	?	Y	Y	Y
18 Lowey	+	+	+	+	+	+	+
19 Hall	Y	Y	Y	N	Y	N	Y
20 Gillibrand	Y	?	?	N	Y	Y	Y
21 McNulty	Y	Y	Y	N	Y	Y	Y
22 Hinchey	Y	Y	Y	N	Y	N	Y
23 **McHugh**	N	N	N	N	N	N	Y
24 Arcuri	Y	Y	Y	N	Y	Y	Y
25 **Walsh**	?	N	N	N	N	N	Y
26 **Reynolds**	N	N	N	N	N	N	Y
27 Higgins	Y	Y	Y	?	Y	Y	Y
28 Slaughter	Y	Y	Y	N	Y	Y	Y
29 **Kuhl**	N	N	N	N	N	N	Y
NORTH CAROLINA							
1 Butterfield	Y	Y	Y	N	Y	Y	Y
2 Etheridge	Y	Y	Y	N	Y	Y	Y
3 **Jones**	N	N	N	N	N	N	Y
4 Price	Y	Y	Y	N	Y	Y	Y
5 **Foxx**	N	N	N	N	N	N	Y
6 **Coble**	N	N	N	N	N	N	Y
7 McIntyre	Y	?	Y	N	Y	Y	Y
8 **Hayes**	N	N	N	N	N	N	Y
9 **Myrick**	N	N	N	N	N	N	Y
10 **McHenry**	N	N	N	N	N	N	Y
11 Shuler	Y	N	N	N	Y	Y	Y
12 Watt	Y	Y	Y	N	Y	N	Y
13 Miller	Y	Y	Y	N	Y	Y	Y
NORTH DAKOTA							
AL Pomeroy	Y	Y	Y	N	Y	Y	Y
OHIO							
1 **Chabot**	N	N	N	N	N	N	Y
2 **Schmidt**	N	N	N	N	N	N	Y
3 **Turner**	N	N	N	?	N	N	Y
4 **Jordan**	N	N	N	N	N	N	Y
5 **Latta**	N	N	N	N	N	N	Y
6 Wilson	Y	Y	Y	N	Y	Y	Y
7 **Hobson**	N	N	N	N	N	N	Y
8 **Boehner**	N	N	N	N	N	N	Y
9 Kaptur	Y	Y	Y	N	Y	Y	Y
10 Kucinich	Y	N	Y	N	Y	N	Y
11 Tubbs Jones	Y	Y	Y	N	Y	Y	Y
12 **Tiberi**	N	N	N	N	N	N	Y
13 Sutton	Y	Y	Y	N	Y	Y	Y
14 **LaTourette**	N	N	N	N	N	N	Y
15 **Pryce**	?	?	?	?	N	N	Y
16 **Regula**	N	N	N	N	N	N	Y
17 Ryan	?	?	?	?	Y	Y	Y
18 Space	Y	Y	Y	N	Y	Y	Y
OKLAHOMA							
1 **Sullivan**	N	N	N	N	N	N	Y
2 Boren	Y	Y	Y	N	Y	N	Y
3 **Lucas**	N	N	N	N	N	N	Y
4 **Cole**	N	N	N	N	N	N	Y
5 **Fallin**	N	N	N	N	N	N	Y
OREGON							
1 Wu	Y	N	Y	N	Y	N	Y
2 **Walden**	N	N	N	N	N	N	Y
3 Blumenauer	Y	Y	Y	N	Y	Y	Y
4 DeFazio	Y	N	N	N	Y	N	Y
5 Hooley	Y	?	Y	N	Y	Y	Y
PENNSYLVANIA							
1 Brady	Y	Y	Y	N	Y	Y	Y
2 Fattah	Y	Y	Y	N	Y	Y	Y
3 **English**	N	N	N	N	N	N	Y
4 Altmire	N	Y	Y	N	Y	N	Y
5 **Peterson**	N	N	N	N	N	N	Y
6 **Gerlach**	N	N	N	N	N	N	Y
7 Sestak	Y	Y	Y	N	Y	Y	Y
8 Murphy, P.	Y	Y	Y	N	Y	N	N
9 **Shuster**	N	N	N	N	N	N	Y
10 Carney	N	Y	Y	N	N	Y	Y
11 Kanjorski	Y	Y	Y	N	Y	Y	Y
12 Murtha	Y	Y	Y	N	Y	Y	Y
13 Schwartz	Y	Y	Y	N	Y	Y	Y
14 Doyle	?	?	?	?	Y	Y	Y
15 **Dent**	N	N	N	N	N	N	Y
16 **Pitts**	N	N	N	N	N	N	Y
17 Holden	Y	Y	Y	N	Y	Y	Y
18 **Murphy, T.**	N	N	N	N	N	N	Y
19 **Platts**	N	N	N	N	N	N	Y
RHODE ISLAND							
1 Kennedy	Y	Y	Y	N	Y	Y	Y
2 Langevin	Y	Y	Y	N	Y	Y	Y
SOUTH CAROLINA							
1 **Brown**	N	N	N	N	N	N	Y
2 **Wilson**	N	N	N	N	N	N	Y
3 **Barrett**	N	N	N	N	N	N	Y
4 **Inglis**	N	N	N	N	N	N	Y
5 Spratt	Y	Y	Y	N	Y	Y	Y
6 Clyburn	Y	Y	Y	N	Y	Y	Y
SOUTH DAKOTA							
AL Herseth Sandlin	Y	Y	Y	N	Y	Y	Y
TENNESSEE							
1 **Davis, David**	N	N	N	N	N	N	Y
2 **Duncan**	N	N	N	N	N	N	Y
3 **Wamp**	N	N	N	N	N	N	Y
4 Davis, L.	Y	Y	Y	N	Y	N	Y
5 Cooper	Y	Y	Y	N	Y	Y	Y
6 Gordon	Y	Y	Y	N	Y	Y	Y
7 **Blackburn**	N	N	N	N	N	N	?
8 Tanner	Y	Y	Y	N	Y	Y	Y
9 Cohen	Y	Y	Y	N	Y	Y	Y
TEXAS							
1 **Gohmert**	N	N	N	N	N	N	Y
2 **Poe**	N	N	N	N	N	N	Y
3 **Johnson, S.**	N	N	N	N	N	N	Y
4 **Hall**	N	N	N	N	N	N	Y
5 **Hensarling**	N	N	N	N	N	N	Y
6 **Barton**	N	N	N	N	N	N	Y
7 **Culberson**	N	N	N	N	N	N	Y
8 **Brady**	N	N	N	N	N	N	Y
9 Green, A.	Y	Y	Y	N	Y	Y	Y
10 **McCaul**	N	N	N	N	N	N	Y
11 **Conaway**	N	N	N	N	N	N	Y
12 **Granger**	N	N	N	N	N	N	Y
13 **Thornberry**	N	N	N	N	N	N	Y
14 **Paul**	N	N	N	N	N	N	Y
15 Hinojosa	+	+	+	–	+	+	+
16 Reyes	?	?	?	?	Y	Y	Y
17 Edwards	Y	Y	Y	N	Y	Y	Y
18 Jackson Lee	?	Y	Y	N	Y	Y	Y
19 **Neugebauer**	?	N	N	N	N	N	Y
20 Gonzalez	Y	Y	Y	N	Y	Y	Y
21 **Smith**	N	N	N	N	N	N	Y
22 Lampson	N	N	N	N	Y	Y	Y
23 Rodriguez	Y	Y	Y	N	Y	Y	Y
24 **Marchant**	?	N	N	N	N	N	Y
25 Doggett	Y	Y	Y	N	Y	N	Y
26 **Burgess**	N	N	N	N	N	N	Y
27 Ortiz	?	?	?	?	?	?	?
28 Cuellar	Y	Y	Y	N	Y	Y	Y
29 Green, G.	Y	Y	Y	N	Y	Y	Y
30 Johnson, E.	Y	Y	Y	N	Y	Y	Y
31 **Carter**	N	N	N	N	N	N	Y
32 **Sessions**	N	N	N	N	N	N	Y
UTAH							
1 **Bishop**	N	N	N	N	N	N	Y
2 Matheson	Y	Y	Y	N	Y	Y	Y
3 **Cannon**	N	N	N	N	N	N	Y
VERMONT							
AL Welch	Y	?	Y	N	Y	Y	Y
VIRGINIA							
1 **Wittman**	N	N	N	N	N	N	Y
2 **Drake**	N	N	N	N	N	N	Y
3 Scott	Y	Y	Y	N	Y	Y	Y
4 **Forbes**	N	N	N	N	N	N	Y
5 **Goode**	N	N	N	N	N	N	Y
6 **Goodlatte**	N	N	N	N	N	N	Y
7 **Cantor**	N	N	N	N	N	N	Y
8 Moran	Y	Y	Y	N	Y	N	Y
9 Boucher	Y	Y	Y	N	Y	Y	Y
10 **Wolf**	N	N	N	N	N	N	Y
11 **Davis, T.**	N	N	N	N	N	N	Y
WASHINGTON							
1 Inslee	Y	Y	Y	N	Y	Y	Y
2 Larsen	Y	Y	Y	N	Y	Y	Y
3 Baird	Y	Y	Y	N	Y	Y	Y
4 **Hastings**	N	Y	N	Y	N	N	Y
5 **McMorris Rodgers**	N	N	N	N	N	N	Y
6 Dicks	Y	Y	Y	N	Y	Y	Y
7 McDermott	?	Y	Y	N	Y	Y	Y
8 **Reichert**	N	N	N	N	N	N	Y
9 Smith	Y	Y	Y	N	Y	Y	Y
WEST VIRGINIA							
1 Mollohan	Y	Y	Y	N	Y	Y	Y
2 **Capito**	N	N	N	N	N	N	Y
3 Rahall	Y	Y	Y	N	Y	Y	Y
WISCONSIN							
1 **Ryan**	N	N	N	N	N	N	Y
2 Baldwin	Y	Y	Y	N	Y	Y	Y
3 Kind	Y	Y	Y	N	Y	Y	Y
4 Moore	Y	Y	Y	N	Y	Y	Y
5 **Sensenbrenner**	N	N	N	N	N	N	Y
6 **Petri**	N	N	N	N	N	N	Y
7 Obey	Y	Y	Y	N	Y	Y	Y
8 Kagen	Y	Y	Y	N	Y	Y	P
WYOMING							
AL **Cubin**	N	N	N	N	N	N	Y
DELEGATES							
Faleomavaega (A.S.)							
Norton (D.C.)							
Bordallo (Guam)							
Fortuño (P.R.)							
Christensen (V.I.)							

IN THE HOUSE | By Vote Number

56. **H Con Res 293. Adjournment Resolution/Adoption.** Adoption of the concurrent resolution that would provide for adjournment of the House from Thursday, Feb. 14, 2008, until 2 p.m., Friday, Feb. 15, 2008. The resolution also would provide for adjournment of the House until 10 a.m., Tuesday, Feb. 19, 2008, and from Thursday, Feb. 21, 2008, until 2 p.m., Monday, Feb. 25, 2008. Adopted 215-203: R 2-193; D 213-10 (ND 158-10, SD 55-0). Feb. 13, 2008.

57. **H Res 917. National Engineers Week/Adoption.** Lipinski, D-Ill., motion to suspend the rules and adopt the resolution that would support the goals and ideals of National Engineers Week, which runs Feb. 17-23, 2008, in its aim to increase understanding of and interest in engineering and technology careers. Motion agreed to 408-0: R 191-0; D 217-0 (ND 162-0, SD 55-0). A two-thirds majority of those present and voting (272 in this case) is required for adoption under suspension of the rules. Feb. 13, 2008.

58. **Procedural Motion/Adjourn.** L. Diaz-Balart, R-Fla., motion to adjourn. Motion rejected 2-390: R 2-185; D 0-205 (ND 0-152, SD 0-53). Feb. 14, 2008.

59. **Procedural Motion/Adjourn.** L. Diaz-Balart, R-Fla., motion to adjourn. Motion rejected 2-400: R 2-190; D 0-210 (ND 0-157, SD 0-53). Feb. 14, 2008.

60. **H Res 979. H Res 980. Miers and Bolten Contempt Resolutions/ Rule.** Adoption of the self-executing rule (H Res 982) that would provide for the adoption of two privileged resolutions. The first resolution (H Res 979) would recommend that the House of Representatives find former White House counsel Harriet Miers and White House Chief of Staff Joshua Bolten in contempt of Congress for refusing to comply with subpoenas issued by the Judiciary Committee regarding the dismissal of eight U.S. attorneys in December 2006. The second resolution (H Res 980) would authorize the Judiciary Committee to initiate or intervene in judicial proceedings to enforce certain subpoenas. Adopted 223-32: R 3-31; D 220-1 (ND 165-0, SD 55-1). A "nay" was a vote in support of the president's position. Feb. 14, 2008.

61. **H Res 966. Recognize African-American Scientists/Adoption.** Johnson, D-Texas, motion to suspend the rules and adopt the resolution that would recognize the achievements of African-Americans who have contributed to national research in science, technology, engineering and mathematics. Motion agreed to 387-0: R 174-0; D 213-0 (ND 159-0, SD 54-0). A two-thirds majority of those present and voting (258 in this case) is required for adoption under suspension of the rules. Feb. 14, 2008.

62. **HR 1834. Ocean Exploration and Research Programs/Passage.** Lipinski, D-Ill., motion to suspend the rules and pass the bill that would authorize $454 million through fiscal 2014 for two National Oceanic and Atmospheric Administration programs: $289 million over seven years for a national ocean exploration program and $164.5 million over seven years for a national undersea research program. Motion agreed to 352-49: R 139-49; D 213-0 (ND 159-0, SD 54-0). A two-thirds majority of those present and voting (268 in this case) is required for passage under suspension of the rules. Feb. 14, 2008.

	56	57	58	59	60	61	62
ALABAMA							
1 Bonner	N	Y	N	N	?	Y	Y
2 Everett	N	Y	N	N	?	Y	Y
3 Rogers	N	Y	N	N	?	Y	Y
4 Aderholt	N	Y	N	N	N	Y	Y
5 Cramer	Y	Y	N	N	Y	Y	Y
6 Bachus	N	Y	N	N	?	?	Y
7 Davis	Y	Y	N	N	Y	Y	Y
ALASKA							
AL Young	N	Y	N	Y	?	Y	Y
ARIZONA							
1 Renzi	?	?	?	?	?	Y	Y
2 Franks	N	Y	N	N	?	Y	N
3 Shadegg	N	Y	N	N	?	Y	N
4 Pastor	Y	Y	N	N	Y	Y	Y
5 Mitchell	N	Y	N	N	Y	Y	Y
6 Flake	N	Y	N	N	?	Y	N
7 Grijalva	Y	Y	N	N	Y	Y	Y
8 Giffords	N	Y	N	N	Y	Y	Y
ARKANSAS							
1 Berry	Y	Y	N	N	Y	Y	Y
2 Snyder	Y	Y	N	N	Y	Y	Y
3 Boozman	N	Y	N	N	?	Y	Y
4 Ross	Y	Y	N	N	Y	Y	Y
CALIFORNIA							
1 Thompson	Y	Y	N	N	Y	Y	Y
2 Herger	N	Y	N	N	?	Y	Y
3 Lungren	N	Y	N	N	?	Y	Y
4 Doolittle	N	Y	N	N	?	?	N
5 Matsui	Y	Y	N	N	Y	Y	Y
6 Woolsey	Y	Y	N	N	Y	Y	Y
7 Miller, George	Y	Y	N	N	Y	Y	Y
8 Pelosi					Y		
9 Lee	Y	Y	N	N	Y	Y	Y
10 Tauscher	Y	Y	N	N	Y	Y	Y
11 McNerney	Y	Y	N	N	Y	Y	Y
12 Vacant							
13 Stark	Y	Y	N	N	Y	?	Y
14 Eshoo	Y	Y	N	N	Y	Y	Y
15 Honda	?	?	?	?	?	?	?
16 Lofgren	Y	Y	N	N	Y	Y	Y
17 Farr	Y	Y	N	N	Y	Y	Y
18 Cardoza	Y	Y	?	N	Y	Y	Y
19 Radanovich	N	?	N	N	?	Y	N
20 Costa	Y	Y	N	?	Y	Y	Y
21 Nunes	N	Y	N	N	?	Y	N
22 McCarthy	N	Y	N	N	?	Y	Y
23 Capps	Y	Y	N	N	Y	Y	Y
24 Gallegly	N	Y	N	N	N	Y	Y
25 McKeon	N	Y	N	N	?	Y	Y
26 Dreier	N	Y	N	N	?	Y	Y
27 Sherman	Y	?	N	N	Y	Y	Y
28 Berman	Y	?	N	N	Y	Y	Y
29 Schiff	Y	Y	N	N	Y	Y	Y
30 Waxman	Y	?	N	N	Y	Y	Y
31 Becerra	Y	Y	N	N	Y	Y	Y
32 Solis	Y	Y	-	-	+	+	+
33 Watson	Y	Y	?	N	Y	Y	Y
34 Roybal-Allard	Y	Y	N	N	Y	Y	Y
35 Waters	Y	Y	N	N	Y	Y	Y
36 Harman	Y	Y	N	N	Y	Y	Y
37 Richardson	Y	Y	N	N	Y	Y	Y
38 Napolitano	Y	Y	N	N	Y	Y	Y
39 Sánchez, Linda	Y	Y	N	N	Y	Y	Y
40 Royce	N	?	N	N	?	Y	N
41 Lewis	N	Y	N	N	?	Y	Y
42 Miller, Gary	N	Y	N	N	N	Y	Y
43 Baca	Y	Y	N	N	Y	Y	Y
44 Calvert	N	Y	N	N	?	Y	Y
45 Bono Mack	N	Y	N	N	?	?	Y
46 Rohrabacher	N	Y	?	N	N	?	Y
47 Sanchez, Loretta	Y	Y	N	N	Y	Y	Y
48 Campbell	N	Y	N	N	?	Y	N
49 Issa	N	Y	N	N	?	Y	Y
50 Bilbray	N	Y	N	N	?	Y	Y
51 Filner	Y	Y	N	N	Y	Y	Y
52 Hunter	N	Y	N	?	?	Y	Y
53 Davis	Y	Y	N	N	Y	Y	Y

	56	57	58	59	60	61	62
COLORADO							
1 DeGette	Y	Y	N	?	Y	Y	Y
2 Udall	Y	Y	N	N	Y	Y	?
3 Salazar	Y	Y	N	N	Y	Y	Y
4 Musgrave	N	Y	N	N	?	Y	Y
5 Lamborn	N	Y	N	N	?	Y	Y
6 Tancredo	N	Y	N	N	?	Y	N
7 Perlmutter	Y	Y	N	N	Y	Y	Y
CONNECTICUT							
1 Larson	Y	Y	N	N	Y	Y	Y
2 Courtney	Y	Y	N	N	Y	Y	Y
3 DeLauro	Y	Y	N	N	Y	Y	Y
4 Shays	N	Y	?	N	?	Y	Y
5 Murphy	Y	Y	N	N	Y	Y	Y
DELAWARE							
AL Castle	N	Y	N	N	?	Y	Y
FLORIDA							
1 Miller	N	Y	N	N	?	Y	N
2 Boyd	Y	Y	N	N	Y	Y	Y
3 Brown	Y	Y	?	?	?	?	?
4 Crenshaw	N	Y	N	N	?	Y	Y
5 Brown-Waite	N	Y	N	N	?	Y	Y
6 Stearns	N	Y	N	N	?	Y	N
7 Mica	N	Y	N	N	?	Y	Y
8 Keller	N	Y	N	N	?	Y	Y
9 Bilirakis	N	Y	N	N	?	Y	Y
10 Young	N	Y	N	?	?	Y	Y
11 Castor	Y	Y	N	N	Y	Y	Y
12 Putnam	N	Y	N	N	?	Y	Y
13 Buchanan	N	Y	N	N	?	Y	Y
14 Mack	N	Y	N	N	?	?	Y
15 Weldon	N	Y	N	N	?	Y	Y
16 Mahoney	Y	Y	?	?	Y	?	Y
17 Meek	Y	Y	N	N	Y	Y	Y
18 Ros-Lehtinen	N	Y	N	N	?	Y	Y
19 Wexler	Y	Y	N	N	Y	Y	Y
20 Wasserman Schultz	Y	Y	N	N	Y	Y	Y
21 Diaz-Balart, L.	N	Y	N	N	?	Y	Y
22 Klein	Y	Y	N	N	Y	Y	Y
23 Hastings	Y	Y	N	N	Y	Y	Y
24 Feeney	N	Y	N	N	?	?	?
25 Diaz-Balart, M.	N	Y	N	N	?	Y	Y
GEORGIA							
1 Kingston	N	Y	N	N	?	Y	N
2 Bishop	Y	Y	N	N	Y	Y	?
3 Westmoreland	N	Y	N	N	?	?	?
4 Johnson	Y	Y	N	N	Y	Y	Y
5 Lewis	Y	Y	N	N	Y	Y	Y
6 Price	N	Y	N	N	?	Y	Y
7 Linder	N	Y	N	N	?	Y	Y
8 Marshall	Y	Y	N	N	Y	Y	Y
9 Deal	N	Y	N	N	?	?	?
10 Broun	N	Y	N	N	?	Y	N
11 Gingrey	N	Y	N	N	?	Y	N
12 Barrow	Y	Y	N	N	Y	Y	Y
13 Scott	Y	Y	N	N	Y	Y	Y
HAWAII							
1 Abercrombie	Y	Y	N	N	Y	Y	Y
2 Hirono	Y	Y	N	N	Y	Y	Y
IDAHO							
1 Sali	N	Y	N	N	?	Y	N
2 Simpson	N	Y	?	N	N	Y	Y
ILLINOIS							
1 Rush	Y	Y	N	N	Y	Y	Y
2 Jackson	Y	Y	N	N	Y	Y	Y
3 Lipinski	Y	Y	N	N	Y	Y	Y
4 Gutierrez	Y	Y	N	N	Y	Y	Y
5 Emanuel	Y	Y	N	N	Y	Y	Y
6 Roskam	N	Y	N	N	?	Y	Y
7 Davis	Y	Y	?	N	Y	Y	Y
8 Bean	Y	Y	N	N	Y	Y	Y
9 Schakowsky	Y	Y	N	N	Y	Y	Y
10 Kirk	N	Y	N	N	N	Y	Y
11 Weller	N	Y	N	N	?	Y	Y
12 Costello	Y	Y	N	N	Y	Y	Y
13 Biggert	N	Y	N	N	?	Y	Y
14 Vacant							
15 Johnson	N	Y	Y	Y	N	Y	Y

KEY **Republicans** Democrats

Y	Voted for (yea)	X	Paired against	C	Voted "present" to avoid possible conflict of interest
#	Paired for	-	Announced against	
+	Announced for	P	Voted "present"	?	Did not vote or otherwise make a position known
N	Voted against (nay)			

ND Northern Democrats, SD Southern Democrats
Southern states: Ala., Ark., Fla., Ga., Ky., La., Miss., N.C., Okla., S.C., Tenn., Texas, Va.

H-20 2008 CQ ALMANAC | www.cq.com

	56	57	58	59	60	61	62
16 **Manzullo**	N	Y	N	N	?	Y	N
17 Hare	Y	Y	N	N	Y	Y	Y
18 **LaHood**	N	Y	N	N	N	Y	Y
19 **Shimkus**	N	Y	?	N	?	Y	Y
INDIANA							
1 Visclosky	Y	Y	N	N	Y	?	Y
2 Donnelly	N	Y	N	N	Y	Y	Y
3 **Souder**	N	Y	N	N	?	Y	Y
4 **Buyer**	N	Y	N	N	?	Y	Y
5 **Burton**	N	Y	N	N	N	Y	Y
6 **Pence**	N	Y	?	N	?	Y	N
7 Vacant							
8 Ellsworth	N	Y	N	N	Y	Y	Y
9 Hill	Y	Y	N	?	Y	Y	Y
IOWA							
1 Braley	Y	?	N	N	Y	Y	Y
2 Loebsack	Y	Y	N	N	Y	Y	Y
3 Boswell	Y	Y	N	N	Y	Y	Y
4 **Latham**	N	Y	N	N	N	Y	Y
5 **King**	N	Y	N	N	?	?	Y
KANSAS							
1 **Moran**	N	Y	N	N	N	Y	N
2 Boyda	N	Y	N	N	Y	Y	Y
3 Moore	Y	Y	?	N	Y	Y	Y
4 **Tiahrt**	N	Y	N	N	?	Y	N
KENTUCKY							
1 **Whitfield**	N	Y	N	N	?	Y	Y
2 **Lewis**	N	Y	N	N	?	Y	Y
3 Yarmuth	Y	Y	N	N	Y	Y	Y
4 **Davis**	N	Y	N	N	?	Y	Y
5 **Rogers**	N	Y	N	N	?	?	Y
6 Chandler	Y	Y	N	N	Y	Y	Y
LOUISIANA							
1 Vacant							
2 Jefferson	Y	Y	N	N	Y	Y	Y
3 Melancon	Y	Y	N	N	Y	Y	Y
4 **McCrery**	N	?	N	N	?	?	Y
5 **Alexander**	N	Y	N	N	?	?	Y
6 Vacant							
7 **Boustany**	N	Y	N	N	?	?	Y
MAINE							
1 Allen	Y	Y	N	N	Y	Y	Y
2 Michaud	Y	Y	N	N	Y	Y	Y
MARYLAND							
1 **Gilchrest**	?	?	N	N	Y	Y	Y
2 Ruppersberger	?	?	?	?	?	?	?
3 Sarbanes	Y	Y	N	N	Y	Y	Y
4 Wynn	Y	Y	?	N	Y	Y	?
5 Hoyer	Y	Y	N	N	Y	Y	Y
6 **Bartlett**	N	Y	N	N	?	Y	Y
7 Cummings	Y	Y	N	N	Y	Y	Y
8 Van Hollen	Y	Y	N	N	Y	Y	Y
MASSACHUSETTS							
1 Olver	Y	Y	N	N	Y	?	Y
2 Neal	Y	Y	N	N	?	?	?
3 McGovern	Y	Y	N	N	Y	Y	Y
4 Frank	Y	Y	N	N	Y	Y	Y
5 Tsongas	Y	Y	N	N	Y	Y	Y
6 Tierney	Y	Y	?	?	Y	Y	Y
7 Markey	Y	Y	?	?	Y	?	Y
8 Capuano	Y	Y	N	N	Y	Y	?
9 Lynch	Y	Y	N	N	Y	Y	Y
10 Delahunt	Y	Y	N	N	Y	Y	Y
MICHIGAN							
1 Stupak	Y	Y	N	N	Y	Y	Y
2 **Hoekstra**	N	Y	N	N	N	Y	Y
3 **Ehlers**	N	Y	N	N	N	Y	Y
4 **Camp**	N	Y	N	N	N	Y	Y
5 Kildee	Y	Y	N	N	Y	Y	Y
6 **Upton**	N	Y	N	N	?	Y	Y
7 **Walberg**	N	Y	N	N	?	Y	N
8 **Rogers**	N	Y	N	N	?	Y	Y
9 **Knollenberg**	N	Y	N	N	?	Y	Y
10 **Miller**	N	Y	N	N	?	Y	Y
11 **McCotter**	N	Y	N	N	?	Y	Y
12 Levin	Y	Y	N	N	Y	Y	Y
13 Kilpatrick	Y	Y	N	?	Y	Y	Y
14 Conyers	Y	Y	N	N	Y	Y	?
15 Dingell	Y	Y	?	N	Y	Y	Y
MINNESOTA							
1 Walz	Y	Y	N	N	Y	Y	Y
2 **Kline**	N	Y	N	N	?	Y	Y
3 **Ramstad**	N	Y	N	N	N	Y	Y
4 McCollum	Y	Y	N	N	Y	Y	Y

	56	57	58	59	60	61	62
5 Ellison	Y	Y	N	N	Y	Y	Y
6 **Bachmann**	N	Y	N	N	?	Y	Y
7 Peterson	Y	Y	N	N	Y	?	Y
8 Oberstar	Y	Y	N	N	Y	Y	Y
MISSISSIPPI							
1 Vacant							
2 Thompson	Y	Y	N	N	Y	Y	Y
3 **Pickering**	?	?	N	N	?	Y	Y
4 Taylor	Y	Y	N	N	Y	Y	Y
MISSOURI							
1 Clay	Y	Y	N	N	Y	Y	Y
2 **Akin**	N	Y	N	N	?	Y	Y
3 Carnahan	Y	Y	N	N	Y	Y	Y
4 Skelton	Y	Y	N	N	Y	Y	Y
5 Cleaver	Y	Y	N	N	Y	Y	Y
6 **Graves**	N	Y	N	N	?	Y	Y
7 **Blunt**	N	Y	N	N	?	Y	Y
8 **Emerson**	N	Y	N	N	?	?	Y
9 **Hulshof**	N	Y	N	N	?	Y	Y
MONTANA							
AL **Rehberg**	N	Y	N	N	?	Y	Y
NEBRASKA							
1 **Fortenberry**	N	Y	N	N	?	Y	Y
2 **Terry**	N	Y	N	N	?	Y	Y
3 **Smith**	N	Y	N	N	?	Y	Y
NEVADA							
1 Berkley	Y	Y	?	N	Y	Y	Y
2 **Heller**	N	Y	N	N	?	Y	Y
3 **Porter**	N	Y	N	N	P	Y	Y
NEW HAMPSHIRE							
1 Shea-Porter	Y	Y	N	N	Y	Y	Y
2 Hodes	Y	Y	N	N	Y	Y	Y
NEW JERSEY							
1 Andrews	Y	Y	N	N	Y	Y	Y
2 **LoBiondo**	N	Y	N	N	N	Y	Y
3 **Saxton**	N	Y	N	N	?	Y	Y
4 **Smith**	N	Y	N	N	?	Y	Y
5 **Garrett**	N	Y	?	N	?	Y	N
6 Pallone	Y	Y	N	N	Y	Y	Y
7 **Ferguson**	N	Y	N	N	?	Y	Y
8 Pascrell	Y	Y	N	N	Y	Y	Y
9 Rothman	Y	Y	N	N	Y	Y	Y
10 Payne	Y	Y	N	N	Y	Y	Y
11 **Frelinghuysen**	N	Y	N	?	?	Y	Y
12 Holt	Y	Y	N	N	Y	Y	Y
13 Sires	Y	Y	N	N	Y	Y	Y
NEW MEXICO							
1 **Wilson**	N	Y	?	N	?	Y	Y
2 **Pearce**	N	Y	N	N	?	Y	Y
3 Udall	Y	Y	N	N	Y	Y	Y
NEW YORK							
1 Bishop	Y	Y	N	N	Y	Y	Y
2 Israel	Y	Y	N	N	Y	Y	Y
3 **King**	N	Y	N	N	N	Y	Y
4 McCarthy	Y	Y	N	N	Y	Y	Y
5 Ackerman	?	?	?	?	?	?	?
6 Meeks	Y	Y	N	N	Y	Y	Y
7 Crowley	Y	Y	N	N	Y	Y	Y
8 Nadler	Y	Y	N	N	Y	Y	Y
9 Weiner	Y	Y	N	N	Y	Y	Y
10 Towns	?	?	?	?	?	?	?
11 Clarke	Y	?	N	N	Y	Y	Y
12 Velázquez	Y	Y	N	N	Y	Y	Y
13 **Fossella**	N	Y	N	N	N	Y	Y
14 Maloney	Y	Y	N	N	Y	Y	Y
15 Rangel	Y	Y	?	N	Y	Y	Y
16 Serrano	Y	Y	N	N	Y	Y	Y
17 Engel	Y	Y	?	?	?	?	?
18 Lowey	+	+	–	–	+	+	+
19 Hall	Y	Y	N	N	Y	Y	Y
20 Gillibrand	N	Y	N	N	Y	Y	Y
21 McNulty	Y	Y	N	N	Y	Y	Y
22 Hinchey	Y	Y	N	?	Y	Y	Y
23 **McHugh**	N	Y	N	N	N	Y	Y
24 Arcuri	Y	Y	N	N	Y	Y	Y
25 **Walsh**	N	Y	N	N	?	Y	Y
26 **Reynolds**	N	Y	N	N	?	Y	Y
27 Higgins	Y	Y	N	N	Y	Y	Y
28 Slaughter	Y	Y	N	N	Y	Y	+
29 **Kuhl**	N	Y	N	N	N	Y	Y
NORTH CAROLINA							
1 Butterfield	Y	Y	N	N	Y	Y	Y
2 Etheridge	Y	Y	N	N	Y	Y	Y
3 **Jones**	Y	Y	N	N	Y	Y	Y
4 Price	Y	Y	N	N	Y	?	Y

	56	57	58	59	60	61	62
5 **Foxx**	N	Y	N	N	N	Y	N
6 **Coble**	N	Y	N	N	?	Y	Y
7 McIntyre	Y	Y	N	N	Y	Y	Y
8 **Hayes**	N	Y	N	N	–	+	–
9 **Myrick**	N	Y	N	N	?	+	N
10 **McHenry**	N	Y	N	N	?	Y	Y
11 Shuler	Y	Y	N	N	Y	Y	Y
12 Watt	Y	Y	N	N	Y	Y	Y
13 Miller	Y	Y	N	N	Y	Y	?
NORTH DAKOTA							
AL Pomeroy	Y	Y	N	N	Y	Y	Y
OHIO							
1 **Chabot**	N	Y	N	N	?	Y	Y
2 **Schmidt**	N	Y	N	N	?	Y	Y
3 **Turner**	N	Y	N	N	?	Y	Y
4 **Jordan**	N	Y	N	N	?	Y	N
5 **Latta**	N	Y	N	N	?	Y	N
6 Wilson	Y	Y	N	N	Y	Y	Y
7 **Hobson**	N	Y	N	N	?	Y	Y
8 **Boehner**	N	Y	N	N	?	Y	?
9 Kaptur	Y	Y	N	N	Y	Y	Y
10 Kucinich	N	Y	N	N	Y	Y	Y
11 Tubbs Jones	Y	Y	?	?	+	+	+
12 **Tiberi**	N	Y	N	N	?	Y	Y
13 Sutton	Y	Y	N	N	Y	Y	Y
14 **LaTourette**	N	Y	N	N	?	?	Y
15 **Pryce**	N	Y	N	N	?	Y	?
16 **Regula**	N	Y	N	N	?	Y	Y
17 Ryan	Y	Y	?	N	Y	Y	Y
18 Space	Y	Y	N	N	Y	Y	Y
OKLAHOMA							
1 **Sullivan**	N	Y	N	N	?	?	N
2 Boren	Y	Y	N	N	Y	Y	Y
3 **Lucas**	N	Y	?	N	?	Y	Y
4 **Cole**	N	Y	N	N	?	+	Y
5 **Fallin**	N	Y	N	N	?	Y	Y
OREGON							
1 Wu	Y	Y	N	N	Y	Y	Y
2 **Walden**	N	Y	N	N	?	Y	Y
3 Blumenauer	Y	Y	N	N	Y	Y	Y
4 DeFazio	Y	Y	N	N	Y	Y	Y
5 Hooley	Y	Y	N	N	Y	Y	Y
PENNSYLVANIA							
1 Brady	Y	Y	N	N	Y	Y	Y
2 Fattah	Y	Y	N	N	Y	Y	Y
3 **English**	N	?	N	?	?	Y	Y
4 Altmire	Y	Y	N	N	Y	Y	Y
5 **Peterson**	N	Y	?	?	?	?	?
6 **Gerlach**	N	Y	N	N	?	Y	Y
7 Sestak	Y	Y	–	N	Y	Y	Y
8 Murphy, P.	N	Y	N	N	Y	Y	Y
9 **Shuster**	N	Y	N	N	?	Y	N
10 Carney	Y	Y	N	N	Y	Y	Y
11 Kanjorski	Y	Y	N	N	Y	Y	Y
12 Murtha	Y	Y	N	N	Y	Y	Y
13 Schwartz	Y	Y	N	N	Y	Y	Y
14 Doyle	Y	Y	?	N	Y	Y	Y
15 **Dent**	N	Y	N	N	?	Y	Y
16 **Pitts**	N	Y	N	N	?	Y	Y
17 Holden	Y	Y	N	N	Y	Y	Y
18 **Murphy, T.**	N	Y	N	N	?	Y	Y
19 **Platts**	N	Y	N	N	?	Y	Y
RHODE ISLAND							
1 Kennedy	Y	Y	N	N	Y	Y	Y
2 Langevin	Y	Y	N	N	Y	Y	Y
SOUTH CAROLINA							
1 **Brown**	N	Y	N	N	N	Y	Y
2 **Wilson**	N	Y	N	N	?	Y	N
3 **Barrett**	N	Y	N	N	?	Y	N
4 **Inglis**	N	Y	N	N	?	Y	Y
5 Spratt	Y	Y	N	N	Y	Y	Y
6 Clyburn	Y	Y	N	N	Y	Y	Y
SOUTH DAKOTA							
AL Herseth Sandlin	N	Y	N	N	Y	Y	Y
TENNESSEE							
1 **Davis, David**	N	Y	N	N	N	Y	Y
2 **Duncan**	N	Y	N	N	N	Y	N
3 **Wamp**	N	Y	N	N	?	Y	Y
4 Davis, L.	Y	Y	N	N	Y	Y	Y
5 Cooper	Y	Y	N	N	Y	Y	Y
6 Gordon	Y	Y	N	N	Y	Y	Y
7 **Blackburn**	N	Y	N	N	?	Y	N
8 Tanner	Y	Y	N	N	Y	Y	Y
9 Cohen	Y	Y	N	N	Y	Y	Y

	56	57	58	59	60	61	62
TEXAS							
1 **Gohmert**	N	Y	N	N	?	Y	N
2 **Poe**	N	Y	N	N	N	Y	N
3 **Johnson, S.**	N	Y	N	N	?	Y	N
4 **Hall**	N	Y	N	N	N	Y	Y
5 **Hensarling**	N	Y	N	N	?	Y	N
6 **Barton**	N	Y	Y	N	?	Y	Y
7 **Culberson**	N	Y	N	N	?	Y	N
8 **Brady**	N	Y	N	N	?	Y	Y
9 Green, A.	Y	Y	N	N	Y	Y	Y
10 **McCaul**	N	Y	N	N	?	Y	Y
11 **Conaway**	N	Y	N	N	N	Y	N
12 **Granger**	N	Y	N	N	?	Y	Y
13 **Thornberry**	N	Y	N	N	?	Y	N
14 **Paul**	Y	Y	N	N	Y	Y	N
15 Hinojosa	+	+	N	N	Y	Y	Y
16 Reyes	Y	Y	N	N	Y	Y	Y
17 Edwards	Y	Y	N	?	Y	Y	Y
18 Jackson Lee	Y	Y	?	N	Y	Y	Y
19 **Neugebauer**	N	Y	N	N	?	Y	N
20 Gonzalez	Y	Y	N	N	Y	Y	Y
21 **Smith**	N	Y	N	N	?	Y	Y
22 Lampson	Y	Y	N	N	Y	Y	Y
23 Rodriguez	Y	Y	N	N	Y	Y	Y
24 **Marchant**	N	Y	N	N	?	Y	N
25 Doggett	Y	Y	N	N	Y	Y	Y
26 **Burgess**	N	Y	N	N	?	?	?
27 Ortiz	?	?	N	N	Y	Y	Y
28 Cuellar	Y	Y	N	N	N	Y	Y
29 Green, G.	Y	Y	N	–	Y	Y	Y
30 Johnson, E.	Y	Y	N	N	Y	Y	Y
31 **Carter**	N	Y	N	N	?	Y	N
32 **Sessions**	N	Y	N	N	?	Y	N
UTAH							
1 **Bishop**	N	Y	N	N	?	Y	?
2 Matheson	Y	Y	N	N	Y	Y	Y
3 **Cannon**	N	Y	N	N	?	Y	Y
VERMONT							
AL Welch	Y	?	N	N	Y	Y	Y
VIRGINIA							
1 **Wittman**	N	Y	?	N	N	Y	Y
2 **Drake**	N	Y	N	N	?	+	+
3 Scott	Y	Y	N	N	Y	Y	Y
4 **Forbes**	N	Y	N	N	?	Y	Y
5 **Goode**	N	Y	N	N	?	Y	Y
6 **Goodlatte**	N	Y	N	N	?	Y	Y
7 **Cantor**	N	Y	N	N	?	Y	N
8 Moran	Y	Y	?	N	Y	Y	Y
9 Boucher	Y	Y	N	N	Y	Y	Y
10 **Wolf**	N	Y	N	N	?	Y	Y
11 **Davis, T.**	N	Y	N	N	N	Y	Y
WASHINGTON							
1 Inslee	Y	Y	N	N	Y	Y	Y
2 Larsen	Y	Y	N	N	Y	Y	Y
3 Baird	Y	Y	N	N	Y	Y	Y
4 **Hastings**	N	Y	N	N	?	Y	N
5 **McMorris Rodgers**	N	Y	N	N	?	?	Y
6 Dicks	Y	Y	N	?	Y	Y	Y
7 McDermott	Y	Y	N	N	Y	Y	Y
8 **Reichert**	N	Y	N	N	?	?	Y
9 Smith	Y	Y	N	N	Y	Y	Y
WEST VIRGINIA							
1 Mollohan	Y	Y	N	N	Y	Y	Y
2 **Capito**	N	Y	N	N	?	?	Y
3 Rahall	Y	Y	N	N	Y	Y	Y
WISCONSIN							
1 **Ryan**	N	Y	N	N	?	Y	N
2 Baldwin	Y	Y	N	N	Y	Y	Y
3 Kind	Y	Y	N	N	Y	Y	Y
4 Moore	Y	Y	N	N	Y	Y	Y
5 **Sensenbrenner**	N	Y	N	N	N	Y	N
6 **Petri**	N	Y	N	N	?	Y	N
7 Obey	Y	Y	N	N	Y	Y	Y
8 Kagen	Y	Y	N	N	Y	Y	Y
WYOMING							
AL **Cubin**	N	Y	N	N	N	Y	Y
DELEGATES							
Faleomavaega (A.S.)							
Norton (D.C.)							
Bordallo (Guam)							
Fortuño (P.R.)							
Christensen (V.I.)							

IN THE HOUSE | By Vote Number

63. S 2571. Technical Corrections to Pesticides Law/Passage.
Cardoza, D-Calif., motion to suspend the rules and pass the bill that would make technical corrections to the Federal Insecticide, Fungicide and Rodenticide Act and extend the deadline for submitting applications under the program from Sept. 30, 2008, to Sept. 30, 2012. Motion agreed to 400-0: R 190-0; D 210-0 (ND 157-0, SD 53-0). A two-thirds majority of those present and voting (267 in this case) is required for passage under suspension of the rules. Feb. 14, 2008.

64. H Con Res 289. NAACP Tribute/Adoption.
Cohen, D-Tenn., motion to suspend the rules and adopt the concurrent resolution that would honor and recognize the 99th anniversary of the founding of the National Association for the Advancement of Colored People and praise its work in ensuring political, educational, social and economic equality. Motion agreed to 403-0: R 191-0; D 212-0 (ND 158-0, SD 54-0). A two-thirds majority of those present and voting (269 in this case) is required for adoption under suspension of the rules. Feb. 14, 2008.

65. HR 4169. American Braille Flag Memorial/Passage.
Rodriguez, D-Texas, motion to suspend the rules and pass the bill that would authorize the Army to place an American Braille tactile flag in Arlington National Cemetery honoring blind members of the armed forces, blind veterans and other blind Americans. Motion agreed to 396-0: R 190-0; D 206-0 (ND 150-0, SD 56-0). A two-thirds majority of those present and voting (264 in this case) is required for passage under suspension of the rules. Feb. 14, 2008.

66. H Res 790. Washington State Veterans/Adoption.
Rodriguez, D-Texas, motion to suspend the rules and adopt the resolution that would commend the people of Washington state for showing their support for the needs of the state's veterans and encouraging residents of other states to pursue creative ways to show their own support for veterans. Motion agreed to 383-0: R 178-0; D 205-0 (ND 150-0, SD 55-0). A two-thirds majority of those present and voting (256 in this case) is required for adoption under suspension of the rules. Feb. 14, 2008.

67. H Res 963. Salute to Hospitalized Veterans/Adoption.
Rodriguez, D-Texas, motion to suspend the rules and adopt the resolution that would support the goals and ideals of the National Salute to Hospitalized Veterans Week, designated as Feb. 11-15, 2008, and its efforts to pay tribute to and express appreciation for hospitalized veterans. Motion agreed to 384-0: R 179-0; D 205-0 (ND 149-0, SD 56-0). A two-thirds majority of those present and voting (256 in this case) is required for adoption under suspension of the rules. Feb. 14, 2008.

68. H Res 972. American Heart Month and National Wear Red Day/Adoption.
Capps, D-Calif., motion to suspend the rules and adopt the resolution that would support the goals and ideals of American Heart Month and National Wear Red Day and reaffirm a commitment to fighting heart disease and stroke. Motion agreed to 389-0: R 184-0; D 205-0 (ND 151-0, SD 54-0). A two-thirds majority of those present and voting (260 in this case) is required for adoption under suspension of the rules. Feb. 14, 2008.

	63	64	65	66	67	68
ALABAMA						
1 **Bonner**	Y	Y	Y	Y	?	Y
2 **Everett**	Y	Y	Y	Y	Y	Y
3 **Rogers**	Y	Y	Y	Y	Y	Y
4 **Aderholt**	Y	Y	Y	Y	Y	Y
5 Cramer	Y	Y	Y	Y	Y	Y
6 **Bachus**	Y	Y	Y	Y	Y	Y
7 Davis	Y	Y	Y	Y	Y	Y
ALASKA						
AL **Young**	Y	Y	Y	Y	Y	Y
ARIZONA						
1 Renzi	Y	Y	Y	Y	Y	Y
2 **Franks**	Y	Y	Y	Y	Y	Y
3 **Shadegg**	Y	Y	Y	Y	Y	Y
4 Pastor	Y	Y	Y	Y	Y	Y
5 Mitchell	Y	Y	Y	Y	Y	Y
6 **Flake**	Y	Y	Y	Y	Y	Y
7 Grijalva	Y	Y	Y	Y	Y	Y
8 Giffords	Y	Y	Y	Y	Y	Y
ARKANSAS						
1 Berry	Y	Y	Y	Y	Y	Y
2 Snyder	Y	Y	Y	Y	Y	Y
3 **Boozman**	Y	Y	Y	Y	Y	Y
4 Ross	Y	Y	Y	Y	Y	Y
CALIFORNIA						
1 Thompson	Y	Y	?	?	?	?
2 **Herger**	Y	Y	Y	Y	Y	Y
3 **Lungren**	Y	Y	Y	Y	Y	Y
4 **Doolittle**	Y	?	Y	?	Y	Y
5 Matsui	Y	Y	Y	Y	Y	Y
6 Woolsey	Y	Y	Y	Y	Y	?
7 Miller, George	Y	Y	?	?	?	?
8 Pelosi						
9 Lee	Y	Y	Y	Y	Y	Y
10 Tauscher	Y	Y	Y	Y	Y	Y
11 McNerney	Y	Y	?	Y	Y	Y
12 Vacant						
13 Stark	Y	Y	Y	Y	Y	Y
14 Eshoo	?	Y	?	?	?	?
15 Honda	?	?	?	?	?	?
16 Lofgren	Y	Y	?	?	?	?
17 Farr	Y	Y	Y	Y	Y	Y
18 Cardoza	Y	Y	Y	Y	Y	Y
19 **Radanovich**	Y	Y	Y	?	Y	Y
20 Costa	Y	Y	Y	Y	Y	Y
21 **Nunes**	Y	Y	Y	Y	Y	Y
22 **McCarthy**	Y	Y	Y	Y	Y	Y
23 Capps	Y	Y	Y	Y	Y	Y
24 **Gallegly**	Y	Y	Y	Y	Y	Y
25 **McKeon**	Y	Y	Y	Y	Y	Y
26 **Dreier**	Y	Y	Y	Y	Y	Y
27 Sherman	Y	Y	Y	Y	Y	Y
28 Berman	Y	Y	Y	Y	Y	Y
29 Schiff	Y	Y	Y	Y	Y	Y
30 Waxman	Y	Y	Y	Y	Y	Y
31 Becerra	Y	Y	Y	Y	Y	Y
32 Solis	+	+	+	+	+	+
33 Watson	Y	Y	Y	Y	Y	Y
34 Roybal-Allard	Y	Y	Y	Y	Y	Y
35 Waters	Y	Y	Y	Y	Y	Y
36 Harman	Y	Y	Y	Y	Y	Y
37 Richardson	Y	Y	Y	Y	Y	Y
38 Napolitano	Y	Y	Y	Y	Y	Y
39 Sánchez, Linda	Y	Y	Y	Y	Y	Y
40 **Royce**	Y	Y	Y	Y	Y	Y
41 **Lewis**	Y	Y	Y	Y	Y	Y
42 **Miller, Gary**	Y	Y	Y	Y	Y	Y
43 Baca	Y	Y	Y	?	Y	Y
44 **Calvert**	Y	Y	Y	Y	Y	Y
45 **Bono Mack**	Y	Y	Y	Y	Y	Y
46 **Rohrabacher**	Y	Y	Y	Y	Y	Y
47 Sanchez, Loretta	Y	Y	?	Y	Y	Y
48 **Campbell**	Y	Y	Y	Y	Y	Y
49 **Issa**	Y	Y	Y	?	Y	Y
50 **Bilbray**	Y	Y	Y	Y	Y	Y
51 Filner	Y	Y	Y	Y	Y	Y
52 **Hunter**	Y	Y	Y	Y	Y	Y
53 Davis	Y	Y	Y	Y	Y	Y

	63	64	65	66	67	68
COLORADO						
1 DeGette	Y	Y	Y	Y	Y	Y
2 Udall	?	?	?	?	?	?
3 Salazar	Y	Y	Y	Y	Y	Y
4 **Musgrave**	Y	Y	Y	Y	Y	Y
5 **Lamborn**	Y	Y	Y	Y	Y	Y
6 **Tancredo**	Y	Y	Y	Y	Y	Y
7 Perlmutter	Y	Y	Y	Y	Y	Y
CONNECTICUT						
1 Larson	Y	Y	Y	Y	Y	Y
2 Courtney	Y	Y	Y	Y	Y	Y
3 DeLauro	Y	Y	Y	Y	Y	Y
4 **Shays**	Y	Y	Y	Y	Y	Y
5 Murphy	Y	Y	Y	Y	Y	Y
DELAWARE						
AL **Castle**	Y	Y	Y	Y	Y	Y
FLORIDA						
1 **Miller**	Y	Y	Y	Y	Y	Y
2 Boyd	Y	Y	Y	Y	Y	Y
3 Brown	?	?	?	?	?	?
4 **Crenshaw**	Y	Y	Y	Y	Y	Y
5 **Brown-Waite**	Y	Y	Y	Y	Y	Y
6 **Stearns**	Y	Y	Y	Y	Y	Y
7 **Mica**	Y	Y	Y	Y	Y	Y
8 **Keller**	Y	Y	Y	Y	Y	Y
9 **Bilirakis**	Y	Y	Y	Y	Y	Y
10 **Young**	Y	Y	Y	Y	Y	Y
11 Castor	Y	Y	Y	Y	Y	Y
12 **Putnam**	Y	Y	Y	?	Y	Y
13 **Buchanan**	Y	Y	Y	Y	Y	Y
14 **Mack**	Y	Y	Y	Y	Y	Y
15 **Weldon**	Y	Y	Y	Y	?	Y
16 Mahoney	Y	Y	Y	Y	Y	Y
17 Meek	Y	Y	Y	Y	Y	Y
18 **Ros-Lehtinen**	Y	Y	Y	?	Y	Y
19 Wexler	Y	Y	Y	Y	Y	Y
20 Wasserman Schultz	Y	Y	Y	Y	Y	Y
21 **Diaz-Balart, L.**	Y	Y	Y	Y	Y	Y
22 Klein	?	Y	Y	Y	Y	Y
23 Hastings	Y	Y	Y	Y	Y	Y
24 **Feeney**	Y	Y	Y	Y	?	Y
25 **Diaz-Balart, M.**	Y	Y	Y	Y	Y	Y
GEORGIA						
1 **Kingston**	Y	Y	Y	Y	Y	Y
2 Bishop	Y	Y	Y	Y	Y	Y
3 **Westmoreland**	Y	Y	Y	Y	?	Y
4 Johnson	Y	Y	Y	Y	Y	Y
5 Lewis	Y	Y	Y	Y	Y	Y
6 **Price**	Y	Y	Y	Y	Y	Y
7 **Linder**	Y	Y	Y	Y	Y	Y
8 Marshall	Y	Y	Y	Y	Y	Y
9 **Deal**	?	?	?	?	?	?
10 **Broun**	Y	Y	Y	Y	?	Y
11 **Gingrey**	Y	Y	Y	Y	Y	Y
12 Barrow	Y	Y	Y	Y	Y	Y
13 Scott	Y	Y	Y	Y	Y	Y
HAWAII						
1 Abercrombie	Y	Y	Y	Y	?	?
2 Hirono	Y	Y	Y	Y	Y	Y
IDAHO						
1 **Sali**	Y	Y	Y	Y	Y	Y
2 **Simpson**	Y	Y	Y	Y	Y	Y
ILLINOIS						
1 Rush	Y	Y	Y	?	?	Y
2 Jackson	Y	Y	Y	Y	Y	Y
3 Lipinski	Y	Y	Y	Y	Y	Y
4 Gutierrez	Y	Y	Y	Y	Y	Y
5 Emanuel	Y	Y	Y	Y	Y	Y
6 **Roskam**	Y	Y	Y	Y	Y	Y
7 Davis	Y	Y	Y	Y	Y	Y
8 Bean	Y	Y	Y	Y	Y	Y
9 Schakowsky	Y	Y	Y	Y	Y	Y
10 **Kirk**	Y	Y	Y	Y	Y	Y
11 **Weller**	Y	Y	+	Y	Y	Y
12 Costello	Y	Y	Y	Y	Y	Y
13 **Biggert**	Y	Y	Y	Y	Y	Y
14 Vacant						
15 **Johnson**	Y	Y	Y	Y	Y	Y

KEY	**Republicans**	Democrats			
Y	Voted for (yea)		X	Paired against		C	Voted "present" to avoid possible conflict of interest
#	Paired for		–	Announced against		
+	Announced for		P	Voted "present"		?	Did not vote or otherwise make a position known
N	Voted against (nay)					

ND Northern Democrats, SD Southern Democrats
Southern states: Ala., Ark., Fla., Ga., Ky., La., Miss., N.C., Okla., S.C., Tenn., Texas, Va.

H-22 2008 CQ ALMANAC | www.cq.com

	63	64	65	66	67	68
16 **Manzullo**	Y	Y	Y	Y	Y	Y
17 Hare	Y	Y	Y	Y	Y	Y
18 **LaHood**	Y	Y	Y	Y	Y	Y
19 **Shimkus**	Y	Y	Y	Y	Y	Y
INDIANA						
1 Visclosky	Y	Y	Y	Y	Y	Y
2 Donnelly	Y	Y	Y	Y	Y	Y
3 **Souder**	Y	Y	Y	Y	Y	Y
4 **Buyer**	Y	Y	Y	Y	Y	Y
5 **Burton**	Y	Y	Y	Y	Y	Y
6 **Pence**	Y	Y	Y	Y	?	Y
7 Vacant						
8 Ellsworth	Y	Y	Y	Y	Y	Y
9 Hill	Y	Y	Y	Y	Y	Y
IOWA						
1 Braley	Y	Y	Y	Y	Y	Y
2 Loebsack	Y	Y	Y	Y	Y	Y
3 Boswell	Y	Y	Y	?	Y	Y
4 **Latham**	Y	Y	Y	Y	Y	Y
5 **King**	Y	Y	Y	Y	Y	Y
KANSAS						
1 **Moran**	Y	Y	Y	Y	Y	Y
2 Boyda	Y	Y	Y	Y	Y	Y
3 Moore	Y	Y	Y	Y	Y	Y
4 **Tiahrt**	Y	Y	Y	Y	Y	Y
KENTUCKY						
1 **Whitfield**	Y	Y	Y	Y	Y	Y
2 **Lewis**	Y	Y	Y	Y	Y	Y
3 Yarmuth	Y	Y	Y	Y	Y	Y
4 **Davis**	Y	Y	Y	Y	Y	Y
5 **Rogers**	Y	Y	Y	Y	Y	Y
6 Chandler	Y	Y	Y	Y	Y	Y
LOUISIANA						
1 Vacant						
2 Jefferson	Y	Y	Y	Y	Y	Y
3 Melancon	Y	Y	Y	Y	Y	Y
4 **McCrery**	Y	Y	Y	Y	Y	Y
5 **Alexander**	Y	Y	Y	Y	Y	Y
6 Vacant						
7 **Boustany**	Y	Y	Y	Y	Y	Y
MAINE						
1 Allen	Y	Y	Y	Y	Y	Y
2 Michaud	Y	Y	Y	Y	Y	Y
MARYLAND						
1 **Gilchrest**	Y	Y	Y	Y	Y	Y
2 Ruppersberger	?	?	?	?	?	?
3 Sarbanes	Y	Y	Y	Y	Y	Y
4 Wynn	?	?	?	?	?	?
5 Hoyer	Y	Y	Y	Y	Y	Y
6 **Bartlett**	Y	Y	Y	Y	Y	Y
7 Cummings	Y	Y	Y	Y	Y	Y
8 Van Hollen	Y	Y	Y	Y	Y	Y
MASSACHUSETTS						
1 Olver	Y	Y	Y	?	Y	Y
2 Neal	?	?	?	?	?	?
3 McGovern	Y	Y	Y	Y	Y	Y
4 Frank	Y	Y	Y	Y	Y	Y
5 Tsongas	Y	Y	?	Y	Y	Y
6 Tierney	Y	Y	Y	Y	Y	Y
7 Markey	Y	Y	Y	Y	Y	Y
8 Capuano	?	Y	Y	Y	Y	Y
9 Lynch	Y	Y	Y	Y	Y	Y
10 Delahunt	Y	Y	Y	?	?	?
MICHIGAN						
1 Stupak	Y	Y	Y	Y	Y	Y
2 **Hoekstra**	Y	Y	Y	Y	Y	Y
3 **Ehlers**	Y	Y	Y	Y	Y	Y
4 **Camp**	Y	Y	Y	Y	Y	Y
5 Kildee	Y	Y	Y	Y	Y	Y
6 **Upton**	Y	Y	Y	Y	Y	Y
7 **Walberg**	Y	Y	Y	?	Y	Y
8 **Rogers**	Y	Y	Y	Y	Y	Y
9 **Knollenberg**	Y	Y	Y	Y	Y	Y
10 **Miller**	Y	Y	Y	Y	Y	Y
11 **McCotter**	Y	Y	Y	Y	Y	Y
12 Levin	Y	Y	Y	Y	Y	Y
13 Kilpatrick	Y	Y	Y	Y	Y	Y
14 Conyers	?	?	Y	Y	?	Y
15 Dingell	Y	Y	Y	Y	Y	Y
MINNESOTA						
1 Walz	Y	Y	Y	Y	Y	Y
2 **Kline**	Y	Y	Y	Y	Y	Y
3 **Ramstad**	Y	Y	Y	Y	Y	Y
4 McCollum	Y	Y	Y	Y	Y	Y
5 Ellison	Y	Y	Y	Y	Y	+
6 **Bachmann**	Y	Y	Y	Y	Y	Y
7 Peterson	Y	Y	Y	Y	Y	Y
8 Oberstar	Y	Y	Y	Y	Y	Y
MISSISSIPPI						
1 Vacant						
2 Thompson	Y	Y	Y	Y	Y	Y
3 **Pickering**	Y	Y	Y	Y	?	?
4 Taylor	Y	Y	Y	Y	Y	Y
MISSOURI						
1 Clay	Y	Y	Y	Y	Y	Y
2 **Akin**	Y	Y	Y	Y	Y	Y
3 Carnahan	Y	Y	Y	Y	Y	Y
4 Skelton	Y	Y	Y	Y	Y	Y
5 Cleaver	Y	Y	Y	Y	?	Y
6 **Graves**	Y	Y	Y	Y	Y	Y
7 **Blunt**	Y	Y	Y	?	Y	Y
8 **Emerson**	Y	Y	Y	Y	Y	Y
9 **Hulshof**	Y	Y	Y	Y	Y	Y
MONTANA						
AL **Rehberg**	Y	Y	Y	Y	Y	Y
NEBRASKA						
1 **Fortenberry**	Y	Y	Y	Y	Y	Y
2 **Terry**	Y	Y	Y	Y	Y	Y
3 **Smith**	Y	Y	Y	Y	Y	Y
NEVADA						
1 Berkley	Y	Y	Y	Y	Y	Y
2 **Heller**	Y	Y	Y	Y	Y	Y
3 **Porter**	Y	Y	Y	Y	Y	Y
NEW HAMPSHIRE						
1 Shea-Porter	Y	Y	Y	Y	Y	Y
2 Hodes	Y	Y	Y	Y	+	Y
NEW JERSEY						
1 Andrews	Y	Y	Y	+	+	+
2 **LoBiondo**	Y	Y	Y	Y	Y	Y
3 **Saxton**	Y	Y	Y	Y	Y	Y
4 **Smith**	Y	Y	Y	Y	Y	Y
5 **Garrett**	Y	Y	Y	Y	Y	Y
6 Pallone	Y	Y	Y	Y	Y	Y
7 **Ferguson**	Y	Y	Y	Y	Y	Y
8 Pascrell	Y	Y	?	?	?	?
9 Rothman	Y	Y	Y	Y	Y	Y
10 Payne	Y	Y	Y	Y	Y	Y
11 **Frelinghuysen**	Y	Y	Y	Y	Y	Y
12 Holt	Y	Y	Y	Y	Y	Y
13 Sires	Y	Y	Y	Y	Y	Y
NEW MEXICO						
1 **Wilson**	Y	Y	Y	Y	Y	Y
2 **Pearce**	Y	Y	Y	Y	Y	?
3 Udall	Y	Y	Y	Y	Y	Y
NEW YORK						
1 Bishop	Y	Y	Y	Y	Y	Y
2 Israel	Y	Y	Y	Y	Y	Y
3 **King**	Y	Y	Y	Y	Y	Y
4 McCarthy	Y	Y	Y	Y	Y	Y
5 Ackerman	?	?	?	?	?	?
6 Meeks	Y	Y	Y	Y	Y	Y
7 Crowley	Y	?	Y	Y	Y	Y
8 Nadler	Y	Y	Y	Y	Y	Y
9 Weiner	Y	Y	Y	Y	Y	Y
10 Towns	?	?	?	?	?	?
11 Clarke	Y	Y	Y	Y	Y	Y
12 Velázquez	Y	Y	Y	Y	Y	Y
13 **Fossella**	Y	Y	Y	Y	Y	Y
14 Maloney	Y	Y	Y	Y	Y	Y
15 Rangel	Y	Y	Y	Y	Y	Y
16 Serrano	Y	Y	Y	Y	Y	Y
17 Engel	?	?	?	?	?	?
18 Lowey	+	+	+	+	+	+
19 Hall	Y	Y	+	Y	Y	Y
20 Gillibrand	Y	Y	Y	Y	Y	Y
21 McNulty	Y	Y	Y	Y	Y	Y
22 Hinchey	Y	Y	Y	Y	Y	Y
23 **McHugh**	Y	Y	Y	Y	Y	Y
24 Arcuri	Y	Y	Y	Y	Y	Y
25 **Walsh**	Y	Y	Y	Y	?	Y
26 **Reynolds**	Y	Y	Y	Y	Y	Y
27 Higgins	Y	Y	Y	Y	Y	Y
28 Slaughter	+	+	Y	Y	Y	Y
29 **Kuhl**	Y	Y	Y	Y	Y	Y
NORTH CAROLINA						
1 Butterfield	Y	Y	Y	Y	Y	Y
2 Etheridge	Y	Y	Y	Y	Y	Y
3 **Jones**	Y	Y	Y	Y	Y	?
4 Price	Y	Y	Y	Y	Y	Y
5 **Foxx**	Y	Y	Y	Y	Y	Y
6 **Coble**	Y	Y	Y	Y	Y	Y
7 McIntyre	Y	Y	Y	Y	Y	Y
8 **Hayes**	+	+	+	+	+	+
9 **Myrick**	Y	Y	Y	Y	Y	Y
10 **McHenry**	Y	Y	Y	Y	Y	Y
11 Shuler	Y	Y	Y	Y	Y	Y
12 Watt	Y	Y	Y	Y	Y	Y
13 Miller	?	?	Y	Y	Y	Y
NORTH DAKOTA						
AL Pomeroy	Y	Y	Y	Y	Y	Y
OHIO						
1 **Chabot**	Y	Y	Y	Y	Y	Y
2 **Schmidt**	Y	Y	Y	Y	Y	Y
3 **Turner**	Y	Y	Y	?	Y	Y
4 **Jordan**	Y	Y	Y	Y	Y	Y
5 **Latta**	Y	Y	Y	Y	Y	Y
6 Wilson	Y	Y	Y	Y	Y	Y
7 **Hobson**	Y	Y	Y	Y	Y	Y
8 **Boehner**	Y	Y	Y	?	Y	Y
9 Kaptur	Y	Y	Y	Y	Y	Y
10 Kucinich	Y	Y	Y	Y	Y	Y
11 Tubbs Jones	+	+	+	+	+	+
12 **Tiberi**	Y	Y	Y	Y	Y	Y
13 Sutton	Y	Y	Y	Y	Y	Y
14 **LaTourette**	Y	Y	Y	Y	Y	Y
15 **Pryce**	Y	Y	Y	?	?	?
16 **Regula**	Y	Y	Y	Y	Y	Y
17 Ryan	Y	Y	Y	Y	Y	Y
18 Space	Y	Y	Y	Y	Y	Y
OKLAHOMA						
1 **Sullivan**	Y	Y	Y	Y	?	Y
2 Boren	Y	Y	Y	Y	Y	?
3 **Lucas**	Y	Y	Y	Y	Y	Y
4 **Cole**	Y	Y	Y	Y	Y	Y
5 **Fallin**	Y	Y	Y	Y	Y	Y
OREGON						
1 Wu	Y	Y	Y	Y	Y	Y
2 **Walden**	Y	Y	Y	Y	Y	Y
3 Blumenauer	Y	Y	Y	Y	Y	Y
4 DeFazio	Y	Y	Y	Y	Y	Y
5 Hooley	Y	Y	Y	Y	Y	Y
PENNSYLVANIA						
1 Brady	Y	Y	Y	Y	Y	Y
2 Fattah	Y	Y	Y	Y	Y	Y
3 **English**	Y	Y	Y	Y	Y	Y
4 Altmire	Y	Y	Y	Y	Y	Y
5 **Peterson**	?	?	?	?	?	?
6 **Gerlach**	Y	Y	Y	Y	Y	Y
7 Sestak	Y	Y	+	Y	Y	Y
8 Murphy, P.	Y	Y	Y	Y	Y	Y
9 **Shuster**	Y	Y	Y	Y	Y	Y
10 Carney	Y	?	Y	Y	Y	Y
11 Kanjorski	Y	Y	Y	Y	Y	Y
12 Murtha	Y	Y	Y	Y	Y	Y
13 Schwartz	Y	Y	Y	Y	Y	Y
14 Doyle	Y	Y	?	?	?	?
15 **Dent**	Y	Y	Y	Y	Y	Y
16 **Pitts**	Y	Y	Y	Y	Y	Y
17 Holden	Y	Y	Y	Y	Y	Y
18 **Murphy, T.**	Y	Y	+	Y	Y	Y
19 **Platts**	Y	Y	Y	?	?	?
RHODE ISLAND						
1 Kennedy	Y	Y	Y	Y	Y	Y
2 Langevin	Y	Y	Y	Y	Y	Y
SOUTH CAROLINA						
1 **Brown**	Y	Y	Y	Y	Y	Y
2 **Wilson**	Y	Y	Y	Y	Y	Y
3 **Barrett**	Y	Y	Y	Y	?	Y
4 **Inglis**	Y	Y	Y	Y	Y	Y
5 Spratt	Y	Y	Y	Y	Y	Y
6 Clyburn	Y	Y	Y	Y	Y	Y
SOUTH DAKOTA						
AL Herseth Sandlin	Y	Y	Y	Y	Y	Y
TENNESSEE						
1 **Davis, David**	Y	Y	Y	?	Y	Y
2 **Duncan**	Y	Y	Y	Y	Y	Y
3 **Wamp**	Y	Y	Y	Y	Y	Y
4 Davis, L.	Y	Y	Y	Y	Y	Y
5 Cooper	Y	Y	Y	Y	Y	Y
6 Gordon	Y	Y	Y	Y	Y	Y
7 **Blackburn**	Y	Y	Y	Y	Y	Y
8 Tanner	Y	Y	Y	Y	Y	Y
9 Cohen	Y	Y	Y	Y	Y	Y
TEXAS						
1 **Gohmert**	Y	Y	Y	?	?	?
2 **Poe**	Y	Y	Y	Y	Y	Y
3 **Johnson, S.**	Y	Y	Y	Y	Y	Y
4 **Hall**	Y	Y	Y	Y	Y	Y
5 **Hensarling**	Y	Y	Y	Y	Y	Y
6 **Barton**	Y	Y	?	?	?	?
7 **Culberson**	Y	Y	Y	Y	Y	Y
8 **Brady**	Y	Y	Y	Y	Y	Y
9 Green, A.	Y	Y	Y	Y	Y	Y
10 **McCaul**	Y	Y	Y	Y	Y	Y
11 **Conaway**	Y	Y	Y	Y	Y	Y
12 **Granger**	?	Y	Y	Y	Y	Y
13 **Thornberry**	Y	Y	Y	Y	Y	Y
14 **Paul**	Y	Y	Y	Y	Y	Y
15 Hinojosa	?	Y	Y	Y	Y	Y
16 Reyes	Y	Y	Y	Y	Y	Y
17 Edwards	Y	Y	Y	Y	Y	Y
18 Jackson Lee	Y	Y	Y	Y	Y	Y
19 **Neugebauer**	Y	Y	Y	Y	Y	Y
20 Gonzalez	Y	Y	Y	Y	Y	Y
21 **Smith**	Y	Y	Y	Y	Y	?
22 Lampson	Y	Y	Y	Y	Y	Y
23 Rodriguez	Y	Y	Y	Y	Y	Y
24 **Marchant**	Y	Y	Y	Y	Y	Y
25 Doggett	Y	Y	Y	Y	Y	Y
26 **Burgess**	?	?	?	?	?	?
27 Ortiz	Y	Y	Y	Y	Y	Y
28 Cuellar	Y	?	Y	?	Y	Y
29 Green, G.	Y	Y	Y	Y	Y	+
30 Johnson, E.	Y	Y	Y	Y	Y	Y
31 **Carter**	Y	Y	Y	Y	Y	Y
32 **Sessions**	Y	Y	Y	Y	Y	Y
UTAH						
1 **Bishop**	?	?	Y	Y	Y	Y
2 Matheson	Y	Y	Y	Y	Y	Y
3 **Cannon**	Y	Y	Y	Y	Y	Y
VERMONT						
AL Welch	Y	Y	?	Y	Y	Y
VIRGINIA						
1 **Wittman**	Y	Y	Y	Y	Y	Y
2 **Drake**	+	+	+	+	+	+
3 Scott	Y	Y	Y	Y	Y	Y
4 **Forbes**	Y	Y	Y	Y	Y	Y
5 **Goode**	Y	Y	Y	Y	Y	Y
6 **Goodlatte**	Y	Y	Y	Y	Y	Y
7 **Cantor**	Y	Y	Y	?	Y	Y
8 Moran	Y	Y	Y	Y	Y	Y
9 Boucher	Y	Y	Y	Y	Y	Y
10 **Wolf**	Y	Y	Y	Y	Y	Y
11 **Davis, T.**	Y	Y	Y	Y	Y	?
WASHINGTON						
1 Inslee	Y	Y	Y	Y	Y	Y
2 Larsen	Y	Y	Y	Y	Y	Y
3 Baird	Y	Y	Y	Y	Y	Y
4 **Hastings**	Y	Y	Y	Y	Y	Y
5 **McMorris Rodgers**	Y	Y	Y	Y	Y	Y
6 Dicks	Y	Y	Y	Y	Y	Y
7 McDermott	Y	Y	Y	Y	Y	Y
8 **Reichert**	Y	Y	Y	Y	Y	Y
9 Smith	Y	Y	Y	Y	Y	Y
WEST VIRGINIA						
1 Mollohan	Y	Y	Y	Y	Y	Y
2 **Capito**	Y	Y	Y	Y	Y	Y
3 Rahall	Y	Y	Y	Y	Y	Y
WISCONSIN						
1 **Ryan**	Y	Y	Y	Y	Y	Y
2 Baldwin	Y	Y	Y	Y	Y	Y
3 Kind	Y	Y	Y	Y	Y	Y
4 Moore	?	Y	Y	Y	Y	Y
5 **Sensenbrenner**	Y	Y	Y	Y	Y	Y
6 **Petri**	Y	Y	Y	Y	Y	Y
7 Obey	Y	Y	Y	Y	Y	Y
8 Kagen	Y	Y	Y	Y	Y	Y
WYOMING						
AL **Cubin**	Y	Y	Y	Y	Y	Y
DELEGATES						
Faleomavaega (A.S.)						
Norton (D.C.)						
Bordallo (Guam)						
Fortuño (P.R.)						
Christensen (V.I.)						

IN THE HOUSE | By Vote Number

69. **H Res 978. School Social Work Week/Adoption.** Courtney, D-Conn., motion to suspend the rules and adopt the resolution that would recognize the contribution of school social workers and support the designation of March 3-7, 2008, as School Social Work Week. Motion agreed to 379-0: R 170-0; D 209-0 (ND 156-0, SD 53-0). A two-thirds majority of those present and voting (253 in this case) is required for adoption under suspension of the rules. Feb. 25, 2008.

70. **H Res 930. Career and Technical Education Month/Adoption.** Courtney, D-Conn., motion to suspend the rules and adopt the resolution that would support the goals and ideals of Career and Technical Education Month. Motion agreed to 380-0: R 170-0; D 210-0 (ND 157-0, SD 53-0). A two-thirds majority of those present and voting (254 in this case) is required for adoption under suspension of the rules. Feb. 25, 2008.

71. **H Res 944. Lt. Gen. Honore Tribute/Adoption.** Courtney, D-Conn., motion to suspend the rules and adopt the resolution that would honor Lt. Gen. Russel L. Honore for his service and accomplishments during 37 years in the U.S. Army, including his leadership in the post-Hurricane Katrina recovery effort. Motion agreed to 380-0: R 170-0; D 210-0 (ND 157-0, SD 53-0). A two-thirds majority of those present and voting (254 in this case) is required for adoption under suspension of the rules. Feb. 25, 2008.

72. **Procedural Motion/Journal.** Approval of the House Journal of Monday, Feb. 25, 2008. Approved 226-183: R 21-168; D 205-15 (ND 155-10, SD 50-5). Feb. 26, 2008.

73. **HR 3521. Public Housing Asset Management/Previous Question.** Hastings, D-Fla., motion to order the previous question (thus ending debate and possibility of an amendment) on adoption of the rule (H Res 974) to provide for House floor consideration of the bill that would require the Department of Housing and Urban Development (HUD) and public housing agencies to negotiate property and asset fees with stakeholders and would increase the number of public housing agencies that are exempt from asset management. Motion agreed to 212-198: R 0-191; D 212-7 (ND 161-3, SD 51-4). Feb. 26, 2008.

74. **HR 3521. Public Housing Asset Management/Rule.** Hastings, D-Fla., adoption of the rule (H Res 974) to provide for House floor consideration of the bill that would require HUD and public housing agencies to negotiate property and asset fees with stakeholders and would increase the number of public housing agencies that are exempt from asset management. Adopted 218-190: R 0-190; D 218-0 (ND 163-0, SD 55-0). Feb. 26, 2008.

	69	70	71	72	73	74
ALABAMA						
1 Bonner	Y	Y	Y	N	N	N
2 Everett	Y	Y	Y	N	N	N
3 Rogers	Y	Y	Y	N	N	N
4 Aderholt	?	?	?	N	N	N
5 Cramer	Y	Y	Y	Y	N	Y
6 Bachus	?	?	?	N	N	N
7 Davis	Y	Y	Y	Y	Y	Y
ALASKA						
AL Young	?	?	?	N	N	N
ARIZONA						
1 Renzi	Y	Y	Y	N	N	N
2 Franks	Y	Y	Y	N	N	N
3 Shadegg	Y	Y	Y	N	N	N
4 Pastor	Y	Y	Y	Y	Y	Y
5 Mitchell	Y	Y	Y	N	Y	Y
6 Flake	Y	Y	Y	N	N	N
7 Grijalva	?	?	?	Y	Y	Y
8 Giffords	Y	Y	Y	N	Y	Y
ARKANSAS						
1 Berry	Y	Y	Y	Y	Y	Y
2 Snyder	Y	Y	Y	Y	Y	Y
3 Boozman	Y	Y	Y	N	N	N
4 Ross	Y	Y	Y	Y	Y	Y
CALIFORNIA						
1 Thompson	Y	Y	Y	Y	Y	Y
2 Herger	Y	Y	Y	N	N	N
3 Lungren	?	?	?	?	?	?
4 Doolittle	?	?	?	N	N	N
5 Matsui	Y	Y	Y	Y	Y	Y
6 Woolsey	+	+	+	+	+	+
7 Miller, George	Y	Y	Y	Y	Y	Y
8 Pelosi						
9 Lee	Y	Y	Y	Y	Y	Y
10 Tauscher	Y	Y	Y	Y	Y	Y
11 McNerney	Y	Y	Y	Y	Y	Y
12 Vacant						
13 Stark	Y	Y	Y	Y	Y	Y
14 Eshoo	Y	Y	Y	Y	Y	Y
15 Honda	Y	Y	Y	Y	Y	Y
16 Lofgren	Y	Y	Y	Y	Y	Y
17 Farr	?	Y	Y	Y	Y	Y
18 Cardoza	Y	Y	Y	Y	Y	Y
19 Radanovich	Y	Y	Y	N	N	N
20 Costa	Y	Y	Y	Y	Y	Y
21 Nunes	Y	Y	Y	N	N	N
22 McCarthy	Y	Y	Y	N	N	N
23 Capps	Y	Y	Y	Y	Y	Y
24 Gallegly	?	?	?	N	N	N
25 McKeon	Y	Y	Y	N	N	N
26 Dreier	Y	Y	Y	N	N	N
27 Sherman	?	?	?	Y	Y	Y
28 Berman	Y	Y	Y	Y	Y	Y
29 Schiff	Y	Y	Y	Y	Y	Y
30 Waxman	Y	Y	Y	Y	Y	Y
31 Becerra	Y	Y	Y	Y	Y	Y
32 Solis	Y	Y	Y	Y	Y	Y
33 Watson	Y	Y	Y	Y	Y	Y
34 Roybal-Allard	Y	Y	Y	Y	Y	Y
35 Waters	Y	Y	Y	Y	Y	Y
36 Harman	Y	Y	Y	Y	Y	Y
37 Richardson	Y	Y	Y	Y	Y	Y
38 Napolitano	Y	Y	Y	Y	Y	Y
39 Sánchez, Linda	Y	Y	Y	Y	Y	Y
40 Royce	Y	Y	Y	N	N	N
41 Lewis	?	?	?	N	N	N
42 Miller, Gary	Y	Y	Y	N	N	N
43 Baca	Y	Y	Y	Y	Y	Y
44 Calvert	Y	Y	Y	N	N	N
45 Bono Mack	Y	Y	Y	N	N	N
46 Rohrabacher	Y	Y	Y	N	N	N
47 Sanchez, Loretta	Y	Y	Y	N	Y	Y
48 Campbell	Y	Y	Y	N	N	N
49 Issa	Y	Y	Y	N	N	N
50 Bilbray	Y	Y	Y	N	N	N
51 Filner	Y	Y	Y	Y	Y	Y
52 Hunter	?	?	?	Y	N	N
53 Davis	Y	Y	Y	Y	Y	Y

	69	70	71	72	73	74
COLORADO						
1 DeGette	Y	Y	Y	Y	Y	Y
2 Udall	?	?	?	Y	Y	Y
3 Salazar	Y	Y	Y	Y	Y	Y
4 Musgrave	Y	Y	Y	N	N	N
5 Lamborn	Y	Y	Y	N	N	N
6 Tancredo	Y	Y	Y	P	N	N
7 Perlmutter	Y	Y	Y	Y	Y	Y
CONNECTICUT						
1 Larson	Y	Y	Y	Y	Y	Y
2 Courtney	Y	Y	Y	Y	Y	Y
3 DeLauro	Y	Y	Y	Y	Y	Y
4 Shays	Y	Y	Y	N	N	N
5 Murphy	Y	Y	Y	Y	Y	Y
DELAWARE						
AL Castle	Y	Y	Y	N	N	N
FLORIDA						
1 Miller	Y	Y	Y	N	N	N
2 Boyd	Y	Y	Y	Y	Y	Y
3 Brown	Y	Y	Y	Y	Y	Y
4 Crenshaw	Y	Y	Y	N	N	N
5 Brown-Waite	Y	Y	Y	N	N	N
6 Stearns	Y	Y	Y	N	N	N
7 Mica	Y	Y	Y	N	N	N
8 Keller	+	+	+	–	–	–
9 Bilirakis	Y	Y	Y	N	N	N
10 Young	?	?	?	N	N	N
11 Castor	Y	Y	Y	Y	Y	Y
12 Putnam	Y	Y	Y	N	N	N
13 Buchanan	Y	Y	Y	N	N	N
14 Mack	Y	Y	Y	N	N	N
15 Weldon	?	?	?	N	N	N
16 Mahoney	Y	Y	Y	N	Y	Y
17 Meek	Y	Y	Y	Y	Y	Y
18 Ros-Lehtinen	Y	Y	Y	N	N	N
19 Wexler	Y	Y	Y	?	?	?
20 Wasserman Schultz	Y	Y	Y	Y	Y	Y
21 Diaz-Balart, L.	Y	Y	Y	N	N	N
22 Klein	Y	Y	Y	Y	Y	Y
23 Hastings	Y	Y	Y	Y	Y	Y
24 Feeney	Y	Y	Y	N	N	N
25 Diaz-Balart, M.	Y	Y	Y	N	N	N
GEORGIA						
1 Kingston	?	?	?	N	N	N
2 Bishop	+	+	+	Y	Y	Y
3 Westmoreland	Y	Y	Y	N	N	N
4 Johnson	Y	Y	Y	Y	Y	Y
5 Lewis	Y	Y	Y	Y	Y	Y
6 Price	Y	Y	Y	N	N	N
7 Linder	Y	Y	Y	N	N	N
8 Marshall	Y	Y	Y	Y	Y	Y
9 Deal	Y	Y	Y	N	N	N
10 Broun	Y	Y	Y	N	N	N
11 Gingrey	Y	Y	Y	N	N	N
12 Barrow	Y	Y	Y	N	Y	Y
13 Scott	Y	Y	Y	Y	Y	Y
HAWAII						
1 Abercrombie	Y	Y	Y	Y	Y	Y
2 Hirono	Y	Y	Y	Y	Y	Y
IDAHO						
1 Sali	Y	Y	Y	N	N	N
2 Simpson	Y	Y	Y	N	N	N
ILLINOIS						
1 Rush	?	+	+	?	?	?
2 Jackson	Y	Y	Y	Y	Y	Y
3 Lipinski	Y	Y	Y	Y	Y	Y
4 Gutierrez	+	+	+	+	+	+
5 Emanuel	Y	Y	Y	Y	Y	Y
6 Roskam	Y	Y	Y	N	N	N
7 Davis	Y	Y	Y	Y	Y	Y
8 Bean	Y	Y	Y	Y	Y	Y
9 Schakowsky	Y	Y	Y	Y	Y	Y
10 Kirk	Y	Y	Y	N	N	N
11 Weller	Y	Y	Y	N	N	N
12 Costello	Y	Y	Y	Y	Y	Y
13 Biggert	Y	Y	Y	N	N	N
14 Vacant						
15 Johnson	Y	Y	Y	Y	N	N

KEY   **Republicans**   Democrats

Y Voted for (yea)	X Paired against	C Voted "present" to avoid possible conflict of interest
# Paired for	– Announced against	
+ Announced for	P Voted "present"	? Did not vote or otherwise make a position known
N Voted against (nay)		

ND Northern Democrats, SD Southern Democrats
Southern states: Ala., Ark., Fla., Ga., Ky., La., Miss., N.C., Okla., S.C., Tenn., Texas, Va.

	69	70	71	72	73	74
16 **Manzullo**	Y	Y	Y	N	N	N
17 Hare	Y	Y	Y	Y	Y	Y
18 **LaHood**	Y	Y	Y	N	N	N
19 **Shimkus**	Y	Y	Y	N	N	N
INDIANA						
1 Visclosky	Y	Y	Y	Y	Y	Y
2 Donnelly	Y	Y	Y	N	N	Y
3 **Souder**	Y	Y	Y	N	N	N
4 **Buyer**	Y	Y	Y	N	N	N
5 **Burton**	Y	Y	Y	N	N	N
6 **Pence**	Y	Y	Y	N	N	N
7 Vacant						
8 Ellsworth	Y	Y	Y	N	Y	Y
9 Hill	Y	Y	Y	Y	Y	Y
IOWA						
1 Braley	Y	Y	Y	Y	Y	Y
2 Loebsack	Y	Y	Y	Y	Y	Y
3 Boswell	Y	Y	Y	Y	Y	?
4 **Latham**	Y	Y	Y	N	N	N
5 **King**	Y	Y	Y	N	N	N
KANSAS						
1 **Moran**	Y	Y	Y	N	N	N
2 Boyda	Y	Y	Y	Y	Y	Y
3 Moore	Y	Y	Y	Y	Y	Y
4 **Tiahrt**	Y	Y	Y	N	N	N
KENTUCKY						
1 **Whitfield**	Y	Y	Y	Y	N	N
2 **Lewis**	Y	Y	Y	N	N	N
3 Yarmuth	Y	Y	Y	Y	Y	Y
4 **Davis**	Y	Y	Y	N	N	N
5 **Rogers**	Y	Y	Y	N	N	N
6 Chandler	Y	Y	Y	Y	Y	Y
LOUISIANA						
1 Vacant						
2 Jefferson	Y	Y	Y	Y	Y	Y
3 Melancon	Y	Y	Y	Y	Y	Y
4 **McCrery**	Y	Y	Y	N	N	N
5 **Alexander**	Y	Y	Y	N	N	N
6 Vacant						
7 **Boustany**	Y	Y	Y	N	N	N
MAINE						
1 Allen	+	+	+	+	+	+
2 Michaud	Y	Y	Y	Y	Y	Y
MARYLAND						
1 **Gilchrest**	?	?	?	N	N	N
2 Ruppersberger	?	?	?	Y	Y	Y
3 Sarbanes	Y	Y	Y	Y	Y	Y
4 Wynn	Y	Y	Y	Y	Y	Y
5 Hoyer	Y	Y	Y	Y	Y	Y
6 **Bartlett**	Y	Y	Y	N	N	N
7 Cummings	Y	Y	Y	Y	Y	Y
8 Van Hollen	Y	Y	Y	Y	Y	Y
MASSACHUSETTS						
1 Olver	Y	Y	Y	Y	Y	Y
2 Neal	?	?	?	Y	Y	Y
3 McGovern	Y	Y	Y	Y	Y	Y
4 Frank	Y	Y	Y	Y	Y	Y
5 Tsongas	Y	Y	Y	Y	Y	Y
6 Tierney	Y	Y	Y	Y	Y	Y
7 Markey	Y	Y	Y	Y	Y	Y
8 Capuano	?	?	?	Y	Y	Y
9 Lynch	Y	Y	Y	Y	Y	Y
10 Delahunt	Y	Y	Y	Y	Y	Y
MICHIGAN						
1 Stupak	Y	Y	Y	N	Y	Y
2 **Hoekstra**	Y	Y	Y	Y	N	N
3 **Ehlers**	Y	Y	Y	N	N	N
4 **Camp**	Y	Y	Y	N	N	N
5 Kildee	Y	Y	Y	Y	Y	Y
6 **Upton**	Y	Y	Y	N	N	N
7 **Walberg**	Y	Y	Y	N	N	N
8 **Rogers**	Y	Y	Y	N	N	N
9 **Knollenberg**	Y	Y	Y	N	N	N
10 **Miller**	Y	Y	Y	N	N	N
11 **McCotter**	Y	Y	Y	N	N	N
12 Levin	Y	Y	Y	Y	Y	Y
13 Kilpatrick	Y	Y	Y	Y	Y	Y
14 Conyers	Y	Y	Y	Y	Y	Y
15 Dingell	Y	Y	Y	Y	Y	Y
MINNESOTA						
1 Walz	Y	Y	Y	Y	Y	Y
2 **Kline**	Y	Y	Y	N	N	N
3 **Ramstad**	Y	Y	Y	N	N	N
4 McCollum	Y	Y	Y	Y	Y	Y

	69	70	71	72	73	74
5 Ellison	+	+	+	Y	Y	Y
6 **Bachmann**	Y	Y	Y	N	N	N
7 Peterson	Y	Y	Y	N	Y	Y
8 Oberstar	Y	Y	Y	Y	Y	Y
MISSISSIPPI						
1 Vacant						
2 Thompson	Y	Y	Y	Y	Y	Y
3 **Pickering**	Y	Y	Y	Y	N	N
4 Taylor	Y	Y	Y	Y	Y	Y
MISSOURI						
1 Clay	Y	Y	Y	Y	Y	Y
2 **Akin**	Y	Y	Y	N	N	N
3 Carnahan	?	?	?	Y	Y	Y
4 Skelton	Y	Y	Y	Y	Y	Y
5 Cleaver	Y	Y	Y	Y	Y	Y
6 **Graves**	+	+	+	–	–	–
7 **Blunt**	Y	Y	Y	N	N	N
8 **Emerson**	Y	Y	Y	N	N	N
9 **Hulshof**	+	+	?	?	?	?
MONTANA						
AL **Rehberg**	Y	Y	Y	N	N	N
NEBRASKA						
1 **Fortenberry**	Y	Y	Y	N	N	N
2 **Terry**	Y	Y	Y	N	N	N
3 **Smith**	Y	Y	Y	N	N	N
NEVADA						
1 Berkley	Y	Y	Y	Y	Y	Y
2 **Heller**	Y	Y	Y	N	N	N
3 **Porter**	Y	Y	Y	N	N	N
NEW HAMPSHIRE						
1 Shea-Porter	Y	Y	Y	Y	Y	Y
2 Hodes	Y	Y	Y	Y	Y	Y
NEW JERSEY						
1 Andrews	Y	Y	Y	Y	Y	Y
2 **LoBiondo**	Y	Y	Y	N	N	N
3 **Saxton**	Y	Y	Y	Y	N	N
4 **Smith**	Y	Y	Y	Y	N	N
5 **Garrett**	Y	Y	Y	N	N	N
6 Pallone	Y	Y	Y	Y	Y	Y
7 **Ferguson**	?	?	?	N	N	N
8 Pascrell	Y	Y	Y	Y	Y	Y
9 Rothman	Y	Y	Y	Y	Y	Y
10 Payne	Y	Y	Y	Y	Y	Y
11 **Frelinghuysen**	Y	Y	Y	N	N	N
12 Holt	Y	Y	Y	Y	Y	Y
13 Sires	Y	Y	Y	Y	Y	Y
NEW MEXICO						
1 **Wilson**	Y	Y	Y	N	N	N
2 **Pearce**	Y	Y	Y	N	N	N
3 Udall	Y	Y	Y	Y	Y	Y
NEW YORK						
1 Bishop	Y	Y	Y	Y	Y	Y
2 Israel	Y	Y	Y	Y	Y	Y
3 **King**	Y	Y	Y	N	N	N
4 McCarthy	Y	Y	Y	Y	Y	Y
5 Ackerman	Y	Y	Y	Y	Y	Y
6 Meeks	Y	Y	Y	Y	Y	Y
7 Crowley	Y	Y	Y	Y	Y	Y
8 Nadler	Y	Y	Y	Y	Y	Y
9 Weiner	Y	Y	Y	Y	Y	Y
10 Towns	?	?	?	Y	Y	Y
11 Clarke	Y	Y	Y	Y	Y	Y
12 Velázquez	Y	Y	Y	Y	Y	Y
13 **Fossella**	Y	Y	Y	N	N	N
14 Maloney	Y	Y	Y	Y	Y	Y
15 Rangel	Y	Y	Y	Y	?	Y
16 Serrano	Y	Y	Y	Y	Y	Y
17 Engel	Y	Y	Y	Y	Y	Y
18 Lowey	Y	Y	Y	Y	Y	Y
19 Hall	Y	Y	Y	Y	Y	Y
20 Gillibrand	Y	Y	Y	Y	Y	Y
21 McNulty	Y	Y	Y	Y	Y	Y
22 Hinchey	Y	Y	Y	Y	Y	Y
23 **McHugh**	Y	Y	Y	N	N	N
24 Arcuri	Y	Y	Y	Y	Y	Y
25 **Walsh**	Y	Y	Y	N	N	N
26 **Reynolds**	?	?	?	?	?	?
27 Higgins	Y	Y	Y	Y	Y	Y
28 Slaughter	Y	Y	Y	Y	Y	Y
29 **Kuhl**	Y	Y	Y	Y	N	N
NORTH CAROLINA						
1 Butterfield	Y	Y	Y	Y	Y	Y
2 Etheridge	Y	Y	Y	Y	Y	Y
3 **Jones**	Y	Y	Y	Y	N	N
4 Price	Y	Y	Y	Y	Y	Y

	69	70	71	72	73	74
5 **Foxx**	Y	Y	Y	N	N	N
6 **Coble**	Y	Y	Y	N	N	N
7 McIntyre	Y	Y	Y	Y	Y	Y
8 **Hayes**	Y	Y	Y	N	N	N
9 **Myrick**	Y	Y	Y	N	N	N
10 **McHenry**	Y	Y	Y	N	N	N
11 Shuler	Y	Y	Y	N	Y	Y
12 Watt	Y	Y	Y	Y	Y	Y
13 Miller	Y	Y	Y	Y	Y	Y
NORTH DAKOTA						
AL Pomeroy	+	+	+	Y	Y	Y
OHIO						
1 **Chabot**	Y	Y	Y	N	N	N
2 **Schmidt**	Y	Y	Y	N	N	N
3 **Turner**	?	?	?	Y	N	N
4 **Jordan**	Y	Y	Y	N	N	N
5 **Latta**	Y	Y	Y	N	N	N
6 Wilson	Y	Y	Y	Y	Y	Y
7 **Hobson**	Y	Y	Y	N	N	N
8 **Boehner**	Y	Y	Y	N	N	N
9 Kaptur	Y	Y	Y	Y	Y	Y
10 Kucinich	Y	Y	Y	Y	Y	Y
11 Tubbs Jones	Y	Y	Y	?	?	+
12 **Tiberi**	Y	Y	Y	N	N	N
13 Sutton	Y	Y	Y	?	?	?
14 **LaTourette**	?	?	?	N	N	N
15 **Pryce**	?	?	?	?	?	?
16 **Regula**	Y	Y	Y	N	N	N
17 Ryan	Y	Y	Y	?	?	?
18 Space	?	?	?	Y	Y	Y
OKLAHOMA						
1 **Sullivan**	Y	Y	Y	Y	N	N
2 Boren	Y	Y	Y	Y	N	Y
3 **Lucas**	?	?	?	N	N	N
4 **Cole**	Y	Y	Y	N	N	N
5 **Fallin**	Y	Y	Y	N	N	N
OREGON						
1 Wu	Y	Y	Y	Y	Y	Y
2 **Walden**	Y	Y	Y	N	N	N
3 Blumenauer	Y	Y	Y	Y	Y	Y
4 DeFazio	Y	Y	Y	Y	Y	Y
5 Hooley	Y	Y	Y	Y	Y	Y
PENNSYLVANIA						
1 Brady	Y	Y	Y	Y	Y	Y
2 Fattah	Y	Y	Y	Y	Y	Y
3 **English**	Y	Y	Y	N	N	N
4 Altmire	Y	Y	Y	N	Y	Y
5 **Peterson**	?	?	?	Y	N	N
6 **Gerlach**	?	?	?	Y	N	N
7 Sestak	Y	Y	Y	Y	Y	Y
8 Murphy, P.	Y	Y	Y	Y	Y	Y
9 **Shuster**	Y	Y	Y	N	N	N
10 Carney	Y	Y	Y	N	N	Y
11 Kanjorski	Y	Y	Y	Y	Y	Y
12 Murtha	Y	Y	Y	Y	Y	Y
13 Schwartz	Y	Y	Y	Y	Y	Y
14 Doyle	Y	Y	Y	Y	Y	Y
15 **Dent**	Y	Y	Y	Y	N	N
16 **Pitts**	Y	Y	Y	N	N	N
17 Holden	Y	Y	Y	Y	Y	Y
18 **Murphy, T.**	Y	Y	Y	N	N	N
19 **Platts**	?	?	?	N	N	N
RHODE ISLAND						
1 Kennedy	Y	Y	Y	Y	Y	Y
2 Langevin	Y	Y	Y	Y	Y	Y
SOUTH CAROLINA						
1 **Brown**	Y	Y	Y	N	N	N
2 **Wilson**	Y	Y	Y	N	N	N
3 **Barrett**	Y	Y	Y	N	N	N
4 **Inglis**	Y	Y	Y	N	N	N
5 Spratt	?	?	?	Y	Y	Y
6 Clyburn	Y	Y	Y	Y	Y	Y
SOUTH DAKOTA						
AL Herseth Sandlin	?	?	?	Y	Y	Y
TENNESSEE						
1 **Davis, David**	Y	Y	Y	N	N	N
2 **Duncan**	Y	Y	Y	N	N	N
3 **Wamp**	Y	Y	Y	N	N	N
4 Davis, L.	Y	Y	Y	Y	Y	Y
5 Cooper	Y	Y	Y	Y	Y	Y
6 Gordon	Y	Y	Y	N	Y	Y
7 **Blackburn**	Y	Y	Y	N	N	N
8 Tanner	Y	Y	Y	N	Y	Y
9 Cohen	Y	Y	Y	Y	Y	Y

	69	70	71	72	73	74
TEXAS						
1 **Gohmert**	Y	Y	Y	?	N	N
2 **Poe**	Y	Y	Y	N	N	N
3 **Johnson, S.**	Y	Y	Y	N	N	N
4 **Hall**	?	?	?	N	N	N
5 **Hensarling**	Y	Y	Y	N	N	N
6 **Barton**	Y	Y	Y	N	N	N
7 **Culberson**	Y	Y	Y	N	N	N
8 **Brady**	Y	Y	Y	N	N	N
9 Green, A.	Y	Y	Y	Y	Y	Y
10 **McCaul**	Y	Y	Y	N	N	N
11 **Conaway**	Y	Y	Y	N	N	N
12 **Granger**	Y	Y	Y	N	N	N
13 **Thornberry**	Y	Y	Y	N	N	N
14 **Paul**	Y	Y	Y	Y	N	N
15 Hinojosa	?	?	?	Y	+	+
16 Reyes	Y	Y	Y	Y	Y	Y
17 Edwards	?	?	?	Y	Y	Y
18 Jackson Lee	Y	Y	Y	Y	Y	Y
19 **Neugebauer**	Y	Y	Y	N	N	N
20 Gonzalez	Y	Y	Y	?	Y	Y
21 **Smith**	Y	Y	Y	N	N	?
22 Lampson	Y	Y	Y	Y	N	Y
23 Rodriguez	Y	Y	Y	Y	Y	Y
24 **Marchant**	?	?	?	?	?	?
25 Doggett	Y	Y	Y	Y	Y	Y
26 **Burgess**	Y	Y	Y	N	N	N
27 Ortiz	Y	Y	Y	Y	Y	Y
28 Cuellar	Y	Y	Y	N	Y	Y
29 Green, G.	Y	Y	Y	Y	Y	Y
30 Johnson, E.	Y	Y	Y	Y	Y	Y
31 **Carter**	Y	Y	Y	N	N	N
32 **Sessions**	Y	Y	Y	N	N	N
UTAH						
1 **Bishop**	Y	Y	Y	Y	N	N
2 Matheson	Y	Y	Y	N	Y	Y
3 **Cannon**	Y	Y	Y	N	N	N
VERMONT						
AL Welch	Y	Y	Y	Y	Y	Y
VIRGINIA						
1 **Wittman**	Y	Y	Y	N	N	N
2 **Drake**	Y	Y	Y	N	N	N
3 Scott	Y	Y	Y	Y	Y	Y
4 **Forbes**	?	?	?	N	N	N
5 **Goode**	Y	Y	Y	N	N	N
6 **Goodlatte**	Y	Y	Y	N	N	N
7 **Cantor**	Y	Y	Y	N	N	N
8 Moran	Y	Y	Y	Y	Y	Y
9 Boucher	Y	Y	Y	Y	Y	Y
10 **Wolf**	Y	Y	Y	N	N	N
11 **Davis, T.**	Y	Y	Y	N	N	N
WASHINGTON						
1 Inslee	Y	Y	Y	Y	Y	Y
2 Larsen	Y	Y	Y	Y	Y	Y
3 Baird	Y	Y	Y	Y	Y	Y
4 **Hastings**	?	?	?	N	N	N
5 **McMorris Rodgers**	Y	Y	Y	N	N	N
6 Dicks	Y	Y	Y	Y	Y	Y
7 McDermott	Y	Y	Y	Y	Y	Y
8 **Reichert**	Y	Y	Y	N	N	N
9 Smith	Y	Y	Y	Y	Y	Y
WEST VIRGINIA						
1 Mollohan	Y	Y	Y	?	?	?
2 **Capito**	Y	Y	Y	N	N	N
3 Rahall	Y	Y	Y	Y	Y	Y
WISCONSIN						
1 **Ryan**	Y	Y	Y	N	N	N
2 Baldwin	Y	Y	Y	Y	Y	Y
3 Kind	Y	Y	Y	Y	Y	Y
4 Moore	Y	Y	Y	Y	Y	+
5 **Sensenbrenner**	Y	Y	Y	N	N	N
6 **Petri**	Y	Y	Y	N	N	N
7 Obey	Y	Y	Y	Y	Y	Y
8 Kagen	Y	Y	Y	Y	Y	Y
WYOMING						
AL **Cubin**	Y	Y	Y	N	N	N
DELEGATES						
Faleomavaega (A.S.)						
Norton (D.C.)						
Bordallo (Guam)						
Fortuño (P.R.)						
Christensen (V.I.)						

IN THE HOUSE | By Vote Number

75. HR 3521. Public Housing Asset Management/Management Fees. Sires, D-N.J., amendment that would prohibit the Department of Housing and Urban Development (HUD) from considering a public housing agency to be in non-compliance with the bill's asset management requirements solely because the agency's management fees are not reasonable as defined by HUD. Adopted in Committee of the Whole 415-0: R 190-0; D 225-0 (ND 170-0, SD 55-0). Feb. 26, 2008.

76. HR 3521. Public Housing Asset Management/Tenant Agreements. Meek, D-Fla., amendment that would require HUD to recognize any agreements between tenants and public housing agencies in the event of a federal agency takeover. Adopted in Committee of the Whole 337-77: R 114-77; D 223-0 (ND 169-0, SD 54-0). Feb. 26, 2008.

77. HR 3521. Public Housing Asset Management/Motion to Table. Sires, D-N.J., motion to table (kill) the Smith, R-Texas, appeal of the ruling of the chair with respect to the Sires point of order that the Smith motion to recommit the bill to the Financial Services Committee was not germane. The Smith motion would recommit the bill with instructions that it be reported back immediately with an amendment substituting the text of a Senate-passed bill (HR 3773) that would amend the Foreign Intelligence Surveillance Act. Motion agreed to 218-195: R 0-192; D 218-3 (ND 163-2, SD 55-1). Feb. 26, 2008.

78. HR 5351. Energy Tax/Question of Consideration. Question of whether the House should consider the rule (H Res 1001) to provide for House floor consideration of the bill that would provide tax incentives for energy conservation and production of renewable energy, and would eliminate some tax benefits for energy producers. Agreed to consider 224-186: R 1-185; D 223-1 (ND 169-0, SD 54-1). (Conaway, R-Texas, had raised a point of order against the rule on the grounds that it would allow for an unfunded mandate.) Feb. 27, 2008.

79. Procedural Motion/Journal. Approval of the House Journal of Tuesday, Feb. 26, 2008. Approved 217-185: R 12-170; D 205-15 (ND 154-11, SD 51-4). Feb. 27, 2008.

80. HR 5351. Energy Tax/Previous Question. Matsui, D-Calif., motion to order the previous question (thus ending debate and possibility of an amendment) on adoption of the rule (H Res 1001) to provide for House floor consideration of the bill that would provide tax incentives for energy conservation and production of renewable energy, and would eliminate some tax benefits for energy producers. Motion agreed to 214-189: R 0-182; D 214-7 (ND 164-3, SD 50-4). Feb. 27, 2008.

81. HR 5351. Energy Tax/Rule. Adoption of the rule (H Res 1001) to provide for House floor consideration of the bill that would provide tax incentives for energy conservation and production of renewable energy, and would eliminate some tax benefits for energy producers. Adopted 220-188: R 0-187; D 220-1 (ND 166-1, SD 54-0). Feb. 27, 2008.

	75	76	77	78	79	80	81
ALABAMA							
1 Bonner	Y	Y	N	N	N	N	N
2 Everett	Y	Y	N	N	N	N	N
3 Rogers	Y	Y	N	N	N	N	N
4 Aderholt	Y	Y	N	?	?	?	?
5 Cramer	Y	Y	Y	Y	Y	N	Y
6 Bachus	Y	Y	N	N	N	?	N
7 Davis	Y	Y	Y	Y	Y	Y	Y
ALASKA							
AL Young	Y	Y	N	?	N	N	N
ARIZONA							
1 Renzi	Y	Y	N	N	?	?	N
2 Franks	Y	N	N	N	N	N	N
3 Shadegg	Y	N	N	N	N	N	N
4 Pastor	Y	Y	Y	Y	Y	Y	Y
5 Mitchell	Y	Y	Y	Y	N	Y	Y
6 Flake	Y	N	N	N	N	N	N
7 Grijalva	Y	Y	Y	Y	Y	Y	Y
8 Giffords	Y	Y	N	Y	N	Y	Y
ARKANSAS							
1 Berry	Y	Y	Y	Y	Y	Y	?
2 Snyder	Y	Y	Y	Y	Y	Y	Y
3 Boozman	Y	Y	N	N	N	N	N
4 Ross	Y	Y	Y	Y	Y	Y	Y
CALIFORNIA							
1 Thompson	Y	Y	Y	Y	N	Y	Y
2 Herger	Y	N	N	N	N	?	N
3 Lungren	?	?	?	?	?	?	?
4 Doolittle	Y	N	N	?	N	?	N
5 Matsui	Y	Y	Y	Y	Y	Y	Y
6 Woolsey	+	+	+	+	+	+	+
7 Miller, George	Y	Y	Y	?	Y	Y	Y
8 Pelosi							
9 Lee	Y	Y	Y	Y	Y	Y	Y
10 Tauscher	Y	Y	Y	Y	Y	Y	Y
11 McNerney	Y	Y	Y	Y	Y	Y	Y
12 Vacant							
13 Stark	Y	Y	Y	Y	Y	Y	Y
14 Eshoo	Y	Y	Y	Y	Y	Y	Y
15 Honda	Y	Y	Y	Y	Y	Y	Y
16 Lofgren	Y	Y	Y	Y	Y	Y	Y
17 Farr	Y	Y	Y	Y	Y	Y	Y
18 Cardoza	Y	Y	Y	Y	Y	Y	Y
19 Radanovich	Y	N	N	N	N	N	?
20 Costa	Y	Y	Y	Y	Y	Y	Y
21 Nunes	Y	Y	N	N	N	N	N
22 McCarthy	Y	N	N	N	N	N	N
23 Capps	Y	Y	Y	Y	Y	Y	Y
24 Gallegly	Y	Y	N	N	N	N	N
25 McKeon	Y	Y	N	N	N	N	N
26 Dreier	Y	Y	N	N	N	N	N
27 Sherman	Y	Y	Y	Y	Y	Y	Y
28 Berman	Y	Y	Y	Y	Y	Y	Y
29 Schiff	Y	Y	Y	Y	Y	Y	Y
30 Waxman	Y	Y	Y	Y	Y	Y	Y
31 Becerra	Y	Y	Y	Y	Y	Y	Y
32 Solis	Y	Y	Y	Y	Y	Y	Y
33 Watson	Y	Y	Y	Y	Y	Y	Y
34 Roybal-Allard	Y	Y	Y	Y	Y	Y	Y
35 Waters	Y	Y	Y	Y	Y	Y	Y
36 Harman	Y	Y	Y	Y	Y	Y	Y
37 Richardson	Y	Y	Y	Y	Y	Y	Y
38 Napolitano	Y	Y	Y	Y	Y	Y	Y
39 Sánchez, Linda	Y	Y	Y	Y	Y	Y	Y
40 Royce	Y	N	N	N	N	–	N
41 Lewis	Y	Y	N	N	N	N	N
42 Miller, Gary	Y	N	N	N	N	N	N
43 Baca	Y	Y	Y	Y	Y	Y	Y
44 Calvert	Y	Y	N	N	N	N	N
45 Bono Mack	Y	Y	N	N	N	N	N
46 Rohrabacher	Y	N	N	N	N	N	N
47 Sanchez, Loretta	Y	Y	Y	Y	Y	Y	Y
48 Campbell	Y	N	N	N	N	N	N
49 Issa	Y	Y	N	N	N	N	N
50 Bilbray	Y	Y	Y	N	N	?	N
51 Filner	Y	Y	Y	Y	Y	Y	Y
52 Hunter	Y	Y	N	N	?	N	N
53 Davis	Y	Y	Y	Y	Y	Y	+

	75	76	77	78	79	80	81
COLORADO							
1 DeGette	Y	Y	Y	Y	Y	Y	Y
2 Udall	Y	Y	Y	Y	?	?	?
3 Salazar	Y	Y	Y	Y	Y	Y	Y
4 Musgrave	Y	Y	N	N	N	N	N
5 Lamborn	Y	N	N	N	N	N	N
6 Tancredo	Y	N	N	N	N	N	N
7 Perlmutter	Y	Y	Y	Y	Y	Y	Y
CONNECTICUT							
1 Larson	Y	Y	Y	Y	Y	Y	Y
2 Courtney	Y	Y	Y	Y	Y	Y	Y
3 DeLauro	Y	Y	Y	Y	Y	Y	Y
4 Shays	Y	Y	Y	Y	N	N	N
5 Murphy	Y	Y	Y	Y	Y	Y	Y
DELAWARE							
AL Castle	Y	N	N	N	N	N	N
FLORIDA							
1 Miller	Y	N	N	N	N	N	N
2 Boyd	Y	Y	Y	Y	Y	Y	Y
3 Brown	Y	Y	Y	N	N	N	N
4 Crenshaw	Y	N	N	N	N	N	N
5 Brown-Waite	?	?	?	?	?	?	?
6 Stearns	Y	N	N	N	N	N	N
7 Mica	Y	N	N	N	N	N	N
8 Keller	+	+	–	–	–	–	–
9 Bilirakis	Y	N	N	N	N	N	N
10 Young	Y	N	N	N	N	N	N
11 Castor	Y	Y	Y	Y	Y	Y	Y
12 Putnam	Y	Y	Y	Y	Y	Y	Y
13 Buchanan	Y	Y	N	N	N	N	N
14 Mack	Y	N	N	N	N	N	N
15 Weldon	Y	N	N	N	N	N	N
16 Mahoney	Y	Y	Y	Y	Y	Y	Y
17 Meek	Y	Y	Y	Y	Y	Y	Y
18 Ros-Lehtinen	Y	Y	N	N	N	N	N
19 Wexler	?	?	?	Y	Y	Y	Y
20 Wasserman Schultz	Y	Y	Y	Y	Y	Y	Y
21 Diaz-Balart, L.	Y	Y	N	N	N	N	N
22 Klein	Y	Y	Y	Y	Y	Y	Y
23 Hastings	Y	Y	N	N	Y	Y	Y
24 Feeney	Y	N	N	N	N	N	N
25 Diaz-Balart, M.	Y	N	–	–	–	–	–
GEORGIA							
1 Kingston	Y	N	N	N	N	N	N
2 Bishop	Y	Y	Y	Y	Y	Y	Y
3 Westmoreland	Y	N	N	N	N	N	N
4 Johnson	Y	Y	Y	Y	Y	Y	Y
5 Lewis	Y	?	Y	Y	Y	Y	Y
6 Price	Y	N	N	N	N	N	N
7 Linder	Y	N	N	N	N	N	N
8 Marshall	Y	Y	Y	Y	Y	Y	Y
9 Deal	Y	N	N	N	N	N	N
10 Broun	Y	N	N	N	N	N	N
11 Gingrey	Y	N	N	N	?	N	N
12 Barrow	Y	Y	Y	N	N	Y	Y
13 Scott	Y	Y	Y	Y	Y	Y	Y
HAWAII							
1 Abercrombie	Y	Y	Y	Y	Y	Y	Y
2 Hirono	Y	Y	Y	Y	Y	Y	Y
IDAHO							
1 Sali	Y	N	N	N	N	N	N
2 Simpson	Y	Y	N	N	N	N	N
ILLINOIS							
1 Rush	Y	Y	Y	Y	Y	Y	Y
2 Jackson	Y	Y	Y	Y	Y	Y	Y
3 Lipinski	Y	Y	Y	Y	Y	Y	Y
4 Gutierrez	+	+	+	Y	Y	Y	Y
5 Emanuel	Y	Y	Y	Y	Y	Y	Y
6 Roskam	Y	N	N	N	N	N	N
7 Davis	Y	Y	Y	Y	Y	Y	Y
8 Bean	Y	Y	Y	Y	Y	N	Y
9 Schakowsky	Y	Y	Y	Y	Y	Y	Y
10 Kirk	Y	N	N	N	N	N	N
11 Weller	Y	Y	N	N	N	N	N
12 Costello	Y	Y	Y	Y	Y	Y	Y
13 Biggert	Y	Y	N	N	N	N	N
14 Vacant							
15 Johnson	Y	N	N	N	Y	N	N

KEY — Republicans — Democrats

Y Voted for (yea)	X Paired against	C Voted "present" to avoid possible conflict of interest
# Paired for	– Announced against	
+ Announced for	P Voted "present"	? Did not vote or otherwise make a position known
N Voted against (nay)		

ND Northern Democrats, SD Southern Democrats
Southern states: Ala., Ark., Fla., Ga., Ky., La., Miss., N.C., Okla., S.C., Tenn., Texas, Va.

	75	76	77	78	79	80	81
16 **Manzullo**	Y	N	N	N	N	N	N
17 Hare	Y	Y	Y	Y	Y	Y	Y
18 **LaHood**	Y	Y	N	N	N	N	N
19 **Shimkus**	Y	N	N	N	N	N	N
INDIANA							
1 Visclosky	Y	Y	Y	Y	Y	Y	Y
2 Donnelly	Y	Y	Y	Y	N	N	Y
3 **Souder**	Y	Y	N	N	N	N	N
4 **Buyer**	Y	N	N	N	N	N	N
5 **Burton**	Y	Y	N	N	N	N	N
6 **Pence**	Y	N	N	N	N	N	N
7 Vacant							
8 Ellsworth	Y	Y	Y	Y	N	Y	Y
9 Hill	Y	Y	Y	Y	Y	N	N
IOWA							
1 Braley	Y	Y	Y	Y	?	Y	Y
2 Loebsack	Y	Y	Y	Y	Y	Y	Y
3 Boswell	Y	Y	Y	Y	Y	Y	Y
4 **Latham**	Y	Y	N	N	Y	N	N
5 **King**	Y	N	N	N	N	N	N
KANSAS							
1 **Moran**	Y	Y	N	N	N	N	N
2 Boyda	Y	Y	Y	Y	Y	Y	Y
3 Moore	Y	Y	Y	Y	Y	Y	Y
4 **Tiahrt**	Y	N	N	N	N	N	N
KENTUCKY							
1 **Whitfield**	Y	Y	N	N	N	N	N
2 **Lewis**	Y	N	N	N	N	N	N
3 Yarmuth	Y	Y	Y	Y	Y	Y	Y
4 **Davis**	Y	Y	N	N	N	N	N
5 **Rogers**	Y	Y	N	N	N	?	N
6 Chandler	Y	Y	Y	Y	N	Y	Y
LOUISIANA							
1 Vacant							
2 Jefferson	Y	Y	Y	Y	Y	Y	Y
3 Melancon	Y	Y	Y	Y	Y	Y	Y
4 **McCrery**	Y	Y	N	N	N	N	N
5 **Alexander**	Y	Y	N	N	N	N	N
6 Vacant							
7 **Boustany**	Y	Y	N	N	N	N	N
MAINE							
1 Allen	+	+	+	Y	Y	Y	Y
2 Michaud	Y	Y	Y	Y	Y	Y	Y
MARYLAND							
1 **Gilchrest**	Y	Y	N	?	N	N	N
2 Ruppersberger	Y	Y	Y	Y	Y	Y	Y
3 Sarbanes	Y	Y	Y	Y	Y	Y	Y
4 Wynn	Y	Y	Y	Y	Y	Y	Y
5 Hoyer	Y	Y	Y	Y	Y	Y	Y
6 **Bartlett**	Y	Y	N	N	N	N	N
7 Cummings	Y	Y	Y	Y	Y	Y	Y
8 Van Hollen	Y	Y	Y	Y	Y	Y	Y
MASSACHUSETTS							
1 Olver	Y	Y	Y	Y	Y	Y	Y
2 Neal	Y	Y	Y	Y	Y	Y	Y
3 McGovern	Y	Y	Y	Y	Y	Y	Y
4 Frank	Y	Y	?	Y	?	Y	Y
5 Tsongas	Y	Y	Y	Y	Y	Y	Y
6 Tierney	Y	Y	Y	Y	Y	Y	?
7 Markey	Y	Y	Y	Y	Y	Y	Y
8 Capuano	Y	Y	Y	Y	Y	Y	Y
9 Lynch	Y	Y	Y	Y	Y	?	Y
10 Delahunt	Y	Y	Y	Y	Y	Y	Y
MICHIGAN							
1 Stupak	Y	Y	Y	Y	N	Y	Y
2 **Hoekstra**	Y	Y	N	N	N	N	N
3 **Ehlers**	Y	Y	N	N	N	N	N
4 **Camp**	Y	Y	N	N	N	N	N
5 Kildee	Y	Y	Y	Y	Y	Y	Y
6 **Upton**	Y	Y	N	N	N	N	N
7 **Walberg**	Y	Y	N	N	Y	N	N
8 **Rogers**	Y	Y	N	N	N	N	N
9 **Knollenberg**	Y	Y	N	N	N	N	?
10 **Miller**	Y	Y	N	N	N	N	N
11 **McCotter**	Y	Y	N	N	N	N	N
12 Levin	Y	Y	Y	Y	Y	Y	Y
13 Kilpatrick	Y	Y	Y	Y	Y	Y	Y
14 Conyers	Y	Y	Y	Y	Y	?	Y
15 Dingell	Y	Y	Y	Y	Y	Y	Y
MINNESOTA							
1 Walz	Y	Y	Y	Y	Y	Y	Y
2 **Kline**	Y	N	N	N	N	N	N
3 **Ramstad**	Y	Y	N	N	N	N	N
4 McCollum	Y	Y	Y	Y	Y	Y	Y

	75	76	77	78	79	80	81
5 Ellison	Y	Y	Y	Y	Y	Y	Y
6 **Bachmann**	Y	N	N	N	N	N	N
7 Peterson	Y	Y	?	Y	N	Y	Y
8 Oberstar	Y	Y	Y	Y	Y	Y	Y
MISSISSIPPI							
1 Vacant							
2 Thompson	Y	Y	Y	Y	Y	Y	Y
3 **Pickering**	Y	Y	N	N	Y	?	N
4 Taylor	Y	Y	Y	Y	Y	Y	Y
MISSOURI							
1 Clay	Y	Y	Y	Y	?	Y	Y
2 **Akin**	Y	N	N	N	N	N	N
3 Carnahan	Y	Y	Y	Y	Y	Y	Y
4 Skelton	Y	Y	Y	Y	Y	Y	Y
5 Cleaver	Y	Y	Y	Y	Y	Y	Y
6 **Graves**	+	–	–	N	N	N	N
7 **Blunt**	Y	N	N	N	N	N	N
8 **Emerson**	Y	Y	N	N	N	N	N
9 **Hulshof**	?	?	?	N	N	N	N
MONTANA							
AL **Rehberg**	Y	Y	N	N	N	N	N
NEBRASKA							
1 **Fortenberry**	Y	Y	N	N	Y	N	N
2 **Terry**	Y	Y	N	N	N	N	N
3 **Smith**	Y	N	N	N	N	N	N
NEVADA							
1 Berkley	Y	Y	Y	Y	Y	Y	Y
2 **Heller**	Y	N	N	N	N	N	N
3 **Porter**	Y	Y	N	N	N	N	N
NEW HAMPSHIRE							
1 Shea-Porter	Y	Y	Y	Y	Y	Y	Y
2 Hodes	Y	?	Y	Y	Y	Y	Y
NEW JERSEY							
1 Andrews	Y	Y	Y	Y	Y	Y	Y
2 **LoBiondo**	Y	Y	N	N	N	N	N
3 **Saxton**	Y	Y	N	N	N	N	?
4 **Smith**	Y	Y	N	?	N	N	N
5 **Garrett**	Y	N	N	N	?	?	?
6 Pallone	Y	Y	Y	Y	Y	Y	Y
7 **Ferguson**	Y	Y	N	N	N	N	N
8 Pascrell	Y	Y	Y	Y	Y	Y	Y
9 Rothman	Y	Y	Y	Y	Y	Y	Y
10 Payne	Y	Y	Y	Y	Y	Y	Y
11 **Frelinghuysen**	Y	Y	N	N	N	N	N
12 Holt	Y	Y	Y	Y	Y	Y	Y
13 Sires	Y	Y	Y	Y	Y	Y	Y
NEW MEXICO							
1 **Wilson**	Y	Y	N	N	N	N	N
2 **Pearce**	Y	Y	N	N	?	N	N
3 Udall	Y	Y	Y	Y	Y	Y	Y
NEW YORK							
1 Bishop	Y	Y	Y	Y	Y	Y	Y
2 Israel	Y	Y	Y	Y	Y	Y	Y
3 **King**	Y	Y	N	N	N	N	N
4 McCarthy	Y	Y	Y	Y	Y	Y	Y
5 Ackerman	Y	Y	Y	Y	Y	Y	Y
6 Meeks	Y	Y	Y	Y	Y	Y	Y
7 Crowley	Y	Y	Y	Y	Y	Y	Y
8 Nadler	Y	Y	Y	Y	Y	Y	Y
9 Weiner	Y	Y	Y	Y	Y	Y	Y
10 Towns	Y	Y	Y	Y	Y	Y	Y
11 Clarke	Y	Y	Y	Y	Y	Y	Y
12 Velázquez	Y	Y	Y	Y	Y	Y	Y
13 **Fossella**	Y	Y	N	N	N	N	N
14 Maloney	Y	Y	Y	Y	Y	Y	Y
15 Rangel	Y	Y	Y	Y	Y	Y	Y
16 Serrano	Y	Y	Y	Y	Y	Y	Y
17 Engel	Y	Y	Y	Y	Y	Y	Y
18 Lowey	Y	Y	Y	Y	Y	Y	Y
19 Hall	Y	Y	Y	Y	Y	Y	Y
20 Gillibrand	Y	Y	Y	Y	N	Y	Y
21 McNulty	Y	Y	Y	Y	Y	Y	Y
22 Hinchey	Y	Y	Y	Y	Y	Y	Y
23 **McHugh**	Y	Y	N	N	N	N	N
24 Arcuri	Y	Y	Y	Y	Y	Y	Y
25 **Walsh**	Y	Y	N	N	N	N	N
26 **Reynolds**	?	?	N	N	N	N	N
27 Higgins	Y	Y	Y	Y	Y	Y	Y
28 Slaughter	Y	Y	Y	Y	?	Y	Y
29 **Kuhl**	Y	Y	N	N	N	N	N
NORTH CAROLINA							
1 Butterfield	Y	Y	Y	Y	Y	Y	Y
2 Etheridge	Y	Y	Y	Y	Y	Y	Y
3 **Jones**	Y	Y	N	N	N	N	N
4 Price	Y	Y	Y	Y	Y	Y	Y

	75	76	77	78	79	80	81
5 **Foxx**	Y	N	N	N	N	N	N
6 **Coble**	Y	Y	N	N	N	N	N
7 McIntyre	Y	Y	Y	Y	Y	Y	Y
8 **Hayes**	Y	Y	N	N	N	N	N
9 **Myrick**	Y	N	N	N	N	N	N
10 **McHenry**	Y	N	N	N	N	N	N
11 Shuler	Y	Y	Y	Y	N	Y	Y
12 Watt	Y	Y	Y	Y	Y	Y	Y
13 Miller	Y	Y	Y	Y	?	?	?
NORTH DAKOTA							
AL Pomeroy	Y	Y	Y	Y	Y	Y	Y
OHIO							
1 **Chabot**	Y	Y	N	N	N	N	N
2 **Schmidt**	Y	Y	N	N	N	N	N
3 **Turner**	Y	Y	N	N	N	N	N
4 **Jordan**	Y	N	N	N	N	N	N
5 **Latta**	Y	N	N	N	N	N	N
6 Wilson	Y	Y	Y	Y	Y	Y	Y
7 **Hobson**	Y	Y	N	N	N	N	N
8 **Boehner**	Y	Y	N	N	N	N	N
9 Kaptur	Y	Y	Y	Y	Y	Y	Y
10 Kucinich	Y	Y	Y	Y	Y	Y	Y
11 Tubbs Jones	?	?	?	?	?	?	?
12 **Tiberi**	Y	Y	N	N	N	N	N
13 Sutton	?	?	?	Y	Y	Y	Y
14 **LaTourette**	Y	Y	N	?	N	N	N
15 **Pryce**	?	?	?	N	N	N	N
16 **Regula**	Y	Y	N	N	N	N	N
17 Ryan	?	?	?	?	?	?	?
18 Space	Y	Y	Y	Y	Y	Y	Y
OKLAHOMA							
1 **Sullivan**	Y	N	N	N	?	N	N
2 Boren	Y	Y	Y	Y	Y	N	Y
3 **Lucas**	Y	Y	N	N	N	N	N
4 **Cole**	Y	Y	N	N	N	N	N
5 **Fallin**	Y	Y	N	N	N	N	N
OREGON							
1 Wu	Y	Y	Y	Y	Y	Y	Y
2 **Walden**	Y	Y	N	N	N	N	N
3 Blumenauer	Y	Y	Y	Y	Y	Y	Y
4 DeFazio	Y	Y	Y	Y	Y	Y	Y
5 Hooley	Y	Y	Y	Y	Y	Y	Y
PENNSYLVANIA							
1 Brady	Y	Y	Y	Y	Y	Y	Y
2 Fattah	Y	Y	Y	Y	Y	Y	Y
3 **English**	Y	Y	N	N	N	N	N
4 Altmire	Y	Y	Y	Y	N	Y	Y
5 **Peterson**	?	N	N	N	Y	N	N
6 **Gerlach**	Y	Y	N	N	Y	N	N
7 Sestak	Y	Y	Y	Y	Y	Y	Y
8 Murphy, P.	Y	Y	Y	Y	Y	Y	Y
9 **Shuster**	Y	N	N	N	N	N	N
10 Carney	Y	Y	N	Y	N	Y	Y
11 Kanjorski	Y	Y	Y	Y	Y	Y	Y
12 Murtha	Y	Y	Y	Y	Y	Y	Y
13 Schwartz	Y	Y	Y	Y	Y	Y	Y
14 Doyle	Y	Y	Y	Y	Y	Y	Y
15 **Dent**	Y	Y	N	N	Y	N	N
16 **Pitts**	Y	Y	N	N	N	N	N
17 Holden	Y	Y	Y	Y	Y	Y	Y
18 **Murphy, T.**	Y	Y	N	N	N	N	N
19 **Platts**	Y	Y	N	N	N	N	N
RHODE ISLAND							
1 Kennedy	Y	Y	Y	Y	Y	Y	Y
2 Langevin	Y	Y	Y	Y	Y	Y	Y
SOUTH CAROLINA							
1 **Brown**	Y	Y	N	N	N	N	N
2 **Wilson**	Y	N	N	N	N	N	N
3 **Barrett**	Y	N	N	N	N	N	N
4 **Inglis**	Y	N	N	N	N	N	N
5 Spratt	Y	Y	Y	Y	Y	Y	Y
6 Clyburn	Y	Y	Y	Y	Y	Y	Y
SOUTH DAKOTA							
AL Herseth Sandlin	Y	Y	Y	Y	Y	Y	Y
TENNESSEE							
1 **Davis, David**	Y	N	N	N	N	N	N
2 **Duncan**	Y	N	N	N	N	N	N
3 **Wamp**	Y	N	N	N	N	N	N
4 Davis, L.	Y	Y	Y	Y	Y	?	Y
5 Cooper	Y	Y	Y	Y	Y	Y	Y
6 Gordon	Y	Y	Y	Y	N	Y	Y
7 **Blackburn**	Y	N	N	N	N	N	N
8 Tanner	Y	Y	Y	Y	Y	Y	Y
9 Cohen	Y	Y	Y	Y	Y	Y	Y

	75	76	77	78	79	80	81
TEXAS							
1 **Gohmert**	Y	N	N	?	P	N	N
2 **Poe**	Y	N	N	N	N	N	N
3 **Johnson, S.**	Y	N	N	N	N	N	N
4 **Hall**	Y	N	N	N	N	N	N
5 **Hensarling**	Y	N	N	N	N	N	N
6 **Barton**	Y	Y	N	N	?	N	N
7 **Culberson**	Y	N	N	N	N	N	N
8 **Brady**	Y	N	N	N	N	N	N
9 Green, A.	Y	Y	Y	Y	Y	Y	Y
10 **McCaul**	Y	N	N	N	N	N	N
11 **Conaway**	Y	N	N	N	?	N	N
12 **Granger**	Y	N	N	N	N	N	N
13 **Thornberry**	Y	N	N	N	N	N	N
14 **Paul**	Y	Y	N	N	N	N	N
15 Hinojosa	Y	Y	Y	Y	Y	Y	Y
16 Reyes	Y	Y	Y	?	?	?	?
17 Edwards	Y	Y	Y	Y	Y	Y	Y
18 Jackson Lee	Y	Y	Y	Y	Y	Y	Y
19 **Neugebauer**	Y	N	N	N	N	N	N
20 Gonzalez	Y	Y	Y	Y	Y	Y	Y
21 **Smith**	Y	Y	N	N	N	N	N
22 Lampson	Y	Y	N	N	Y	N	Y
23 Rodriguez	Y	Y	Y	Y	Y	Y	Y
24 **Marchant**	Y	N	N	N	N	N	N
25 Doggett	Y	Y	Y	Y	Y	Y	Y
26 **Burgess**	Y	N	N	N	N	N	N
27 Ortiz	Y	Y	Y	Y	Y	Y	Y
28 Cuellar	Y	Y	Y	Y	Y	Y	Y
29 Green, G.	Y	Y	Y	Y	Y	Y	Y
30 Johnson, E.	Y	Y	Y	Y	Y	Y	Y
31 **Carter**	Y	N	N	N	N	N	N
32 **Sessions**	Y	N	N	N	N	N	N
UTAH							
1 **Bishop**	Y	Y	N	N	N	N	N
2 Matheson	Y	Y	Y	Y	N	Y	Y
3 **Cannon**	Y	Y	N	N	N	N	N
VERMONT							
AL Welch	Y	Y	Y	Y	Y	Y	Y
VIRGINIA							
1 **Wittman**	Y	Y	N	N	N	N	N
2 **Drake**	Y	Y	N	N	N	N	N
3 Scott	Y	Y	Y	Y	Y	Y	Y
4 **Forbes**	Y	Y	N	N	N	N	N
5 **Goode**	Y	N	N	N	N	N	N
6 **Goodlatte**	Y	Y	N	N	Y	N	N
7 **Cantor**	Y	Y	N	N	N	N	N
8 Moran	Y	Y	Y	?	Y	Y	Y
9 Boucher	?	?	Y	Y	Y	Y	Y
10 **Wolf**	Y	Y	N	N	N	N	N
11 **Davis, T.**	Y	Y	N	N	N	N	N
WASHINGTON							
1 Inslee	Y	Y	Y	Y	Y	Y	Y
2 Larsen	Y	Y	Y	Y	Y	Y	Y
3 Baird	Y	Y	Y	Y	Y	Y	Y
4 **Hastings**	Y	Y	N	N	N	N	N
5 **McMorris Rodgers**	Y	N	N	N	–	–	–
6 Dicks	Y	Y	Y	Y	Y	Y	Y
7 McDermott	Y	Y	Y	Y	Y	Y	Y
8 **Reichert**	Y	Y	N	N	N	N	N
9 Smith	Y	Y	Y	Y	Y	Y	Y
WEST VIRGINIA							
1 Mollohan	Y	Y	Y	Y	Y	Y	Y
2 **Capito**	Y	Y	N	N	N	N	N
3 Rahall	Y	Y	Y	Y	Y	Y	Y
WISCONSIN							
1 **Ryan**	Y	Y	N	N	N	N	N
2 Baldwin	Y	Y	Y	Y	Y	Y	Y
3 Kind	Y	Y	Y	Y	Y	Y	Y
4 Moore	Y	Y	Y	Y	Y	Y	Y
5 **Sensenbrenner**	Y	Y	N	N	N	N	N
6 **Petri**	Y	Y	N	N	N	N	N
7 Obey	Y	Y	Y	Y	Y	Y	Y
8 Kagen	Y	Y	Y	Y	Y	Y	Y
WYOMING							
AL **Cubin**	Y	N	N	?	?	?	?
DELEGATES							
Faleomavaega (A.S.)	Y	Y					
Norton (D.C.)	Y	Y					
Bordallo (Guam)	Y	Y					
Fortuño (P.R.)	?	?					
Christensen (V.I.)	?	?					

IN THE HOUSE | By Vote Number

82. **HR 5351. Energy Tax/Motion to Table.** Rangel, D-N.Y., motion to table (kill) the Hoekstra, R-Mich., appeal of the ruling of the chair with respect to the Rangel point of order that the Hoekstra motion to recommit the bill to the Ways and Means Committee was not germane. The Hoekstra motion would recommit the bill with instructions that it be reported back immediately with an amendment substituting the text of a Senate-passed bill (HR 3773) that would amend the Foreign Intelligence Surveillance Act. Motion agreed to 222-191: R 0-190; D 222-1 (ND 167-0, SD 55-1). Feb. 27, 2008.

83. **HR 5351. Energy Tax/Motion to Recommit.** English, R-Pa., motion to recommit the bill with instructions that it be reported back to the House promptly with amendments to strike certain revenue-raising provisions, including a manufacturing tax deduction for larger oil and gas companies. The amendments also would eliminate a section of the bill related to energy conservation bonds, strike tax credits for bicycle commuters and add a new title extending so-called marriage penalty tax relief and the child tax credit. Motion rejected 197-222: R 189-3; D 8-219 (ND 4-167, SD 4-52). Feb. 27, 2008.

84. **HR 5351. Energy Tax/Passage.** Passage of the bill that would extend and create several tax incentives for energy conservation and renewable-energy production, including a new tax credit for plug-in hybrid vehicles. It would extend expiring tax credits for wind and solar energy and authorize $5.6 billion in tax-credit bonds to finance renewable energy and energy conservation efforts. To offset the costs, the bill would eliminate or reduce the manufacturing tax deduction for oil and gas companies, and would change the way oil and gas companies calculate foreign oil and gas income. Passed 236-182: R 17-174; D 219-8 (ND 171-0, SD 48-8). A "nay" was a vote in support of the president's position. Feb. 27, 2008.

85. **S 2272. Thiels Post Office/Passage.** Davis, D-Ill., motion to suspend the rules and pass the bill that would designate a post office in Alexandria, La., as the "John 'Marty' Thiels Southpark Station." Motion agreed to 400-0: R 183-0; D 217-0 (ND 163-0, SD 54-0). A two-thirds majority of those present and voting (267 in this case) is required for passage under suspension of the rules. Feb. 28, 2008.

86. **HR 3936. Harkins Post Office/Passage.** Davis, D-Ill., motion to suspend the rules and pass the bill that would designate a post office in Cleveland, Ga., as the "Sgt. Jason Harkins Post Office Building." Motion agreed to 400-0: R 181-0; D 219-0 (ND 165-0, SD 54-0). A two-thirds majority of those present and voting (267 in this case) is required for passage under suspension of the rules. Feb. 28, 2008.

87. **HR 4454. Louisville Military Heroes Post Office/Passage.** Davis, D-Ill., motion to suspend the rules and pass the bill that would designate a post office in Louisville, Ky., as the "Iraq and Afghanistan Fallen Military Heroes of Louisville Memorial Post Office Building." Motion agreed to 404-0: R 181-0; D 223-0 (ND 168-0, SD 55-0). A two-thirds majority of those present and voting (270 in this case) is required for passage under suspension of the rules. Feb. 28, 2008.

	82	83	84	85	86	87
ALABAMA						
1 Bonner	N	Y	N	Y	Y	Y
2 Everett	N	Y	N	?	?	?
3 Rogers	N	Y	Y	Y	Y	Y
4 Aderholt	?	?	?	?	?	?
5 Cramer	Y	N	Y	Y	Y	Y
6 Bachus	N	Y	N	Y	Y	Y
7 Davis	Y	N	Y	Y	Y	Y
ALASKA						
AL Young	N	Y	N	Y	Y	Y
ARIZONA						
1 Renzi	N	Y	N	Y	Y	Y
2 Franks	N	Y	N	Y	Y	Y
3 Shadegg	N	Y	N	Y	Y	Y
4 Pastor	Y	N	Y	Y	Y	Y
5 Mitchell	Y	N	Y	Y	Y	Y
6 Flake	N	Y	N	Y	Y	Y
7 Grijalva	Y	N	Y	Y	Y	Y
8 Giffords	Y	Y	Y	Y	Y	Y
ARKANSAS						
1 Berry	Y	N	Y	Y	Y	Y
2 Snyder	Y	N	Y	Y	Y	Y
3 Boozman	N	Y	N	Y	Y	Y
4 Ross	Y	N	Y	Y	Y	Y
CALIFORNIA						
1 Thompson	Y	N	Y	Y	Y	Y
2 Herger	N	Y	N	Y	Y	Y
3 Lungren	?	?	?	Y	Y	Y
4 Doolittle	N	Y	N	Y	Y	Y
5 Matsui	Y	N	Y	Y	Y	Y
6 Woolsey	+	–	+	+	+	+
7 Miller, George	Y	N	Y	Y	Y	Y
8 Pelosi		Y				
9 Lee	Y	N	Y	Y	Y	Y
10 Tauscher	Y	N	Y	Y	Y	Y
11 McNerney	Y	N	Y	Y	Y	Y
12 Vacant						
13 Stark	?	N	Y	Y	Y	Y
14 Eshoo	Y	N	Y	Y	Y	Y
15 Honda	Y	N	Y	?	Y	Y
16 Lofgren	Y	N	Y	?	Y	Y
17 Farr	Y	N	Y	Y	Y	Y
18 Cardoza	Y	N	Y	Y	Y	Y
19 Radanovich	N	Y	N	Y	Y	Y
20 Costa	Y	N	Y	Y	Y	Y
21 Nunes	N	Y	N	Y	Y	Y
22 McCarthy	N	Y	N	Y	Y	Y
23 Capps	Y	N	Y	Y	Y	Y
24 Gallegly	N	Y	N	?	?	?
25 McKeon	N	Y	N	Y	Y	Y
26 Dreier	N	Y	N	Y	Y	Y
27 Sherman	Y	N	Y	Y	Y	Y
28 Berman	Y	N	Y	Y	Y	Y
29 Schiff	Y	N	Y	Y	Y	Y
30 Waxman	Y	N	Y	Y	Y	Y
31 Becerra	Y	N	Y	Y	Y	Y
32 Solis	Y	N	Y	Y	Y	Y
33 Watson	Y	N	Y	Y	Y	Y
34 Roybal-Allard	Y	N	Y	Y	Y	Y
35 Waters	Y	N	Y	Y	Y	Y
36 Harman	Y	N	Y	Y	Y	Y
37 Richardson	Y	N	Y	Y	Y	Y
38 Napolitano	Y	N	Y	Y	Y	Y
39 Sánchez, Linda	Y	N	Y	Y	Y	Y
40 Royce	N	Y	N	Y	Y	Y
41 Lewis	N	Y	N	Y	Y	Y
42 Miller, Gary	N	Y	N	?	?	?
43 Baca	Y	N	Y	Y	Y	Y
44 Calvert	N	Y	N	Y	Y	Y
45 Bono Mack	N	Y	N	Y	Y	Y
46 Rohrabacher	N	Y	N	Y	Y	Y
47 Sanchez, Loretta	Y	N	Y	Y	Y	Y
48 Campbell	N	Y	N	Y	Y	Y
49 Issa	N	Y	N	Y	Y	Y
50 Bilbray	N	Y	N	Y	?	Y
51 Filner	Y	N	Y	Y	Y	Y
52 Hunter	N	Y	N	?	Y	Y
53 Davis	Y	N	Y	Y	Y	Y

	82	83	84	85	86	87
COLORADO						
1 DeGette	Y	N	Y	Y	Y	Y
2 Udall	?	N	Y	?	?	?
3 Salazar	Y	N	Y	Y	Y	Y
4 Musgrave	N	Y	N	Y	Y	Y
5 Lamborn	N	Y	N	Y	Y	Y
6 Tancredo	N	Y	N	Y	?	?
7 Perlmutter	Y	N	Y	Y	Y	Y
CONNECTICUT						
1 Larson	Y	N	Y	Y	Y	Y
2 Courtney	Y	N	Y	Y	Y	Y
3 DeLauro	Y	N	Y	Y	Y	Y
4 Shays	N	N	Y	Y	Y	Y
5 Murphy	Y	N	Y	Y	Y	Y
DELAWARE						
AL Castle	N	N	Y	Y	Y	Y
FLORIDA						
1 Miller	N	Y	N	Y	Y	Y
2 Boyd	Y	N	Y	Y	Y	Y
3 Brown	Y	N	Y	?	?	?
4 Crenshaw	N	Y	N	Y	Y	Y
5 Brown-Waite	?	?	?	?	?	?
6 Stearns	N	Y	N	Y	Y	Y
7 Mica	N	Y	–	Y	Y	Y
8 Keller	–	–	–	?	?	?
9 Bilirakis	N	Y	N	Y	Y	Y
10 Young	N	Y	N	Y	Y	Y
11 Castor	Y	N	Y	Y	Y	Y
12 Putnam	N	Y	N	Y	Y	Y
13 Buchanan	N	Y	N	Y	Y	Y
14 Mack	N	Y	N	Y	Y	Y
15 Weldon	N	Y	N	Y	Y	Y
16 Mahoney	Y	N	Y	Y	Y	Y
17 Meek	Y	N	Y	Y	Y	Y
18 Ros-Lehtinen	N	Y	N	Y	Y	Y
19 Wexler	Y	N	Y	Y	Y	Y
20 Wasserman Schultz	Y	N	Y	Y	Y	Y
21 Diaz-Balart, L.	N	Y	N	Y	Y	Y
22 Klein	Y	N	Y	Y	Y	Y
23 Hastings	Y	N	Y	Y	Y	Y
24 Feeney	N	Y	N	Y	Y	Y
25 Diaz-Balart, M.	–	–	–	Y	Y	Y
GEORGIA						
1 Kingston	N	Y	N	Y	Y	Y
2 Bishop	Y	N	Y	Y	Y	Y
3 Westmoreland	N	Y	N	Y	Y	Y
4 Johnson	Y	N	Y	Y	Y	Y
5 Lewis	Y	N	Y	Y	Y	Y
6 Price	N	Y	N	Y	Y	Y
7 Linder	N	Y	N	Y	Y	Y
8 Marshall	Y	Y	Y	Y	Y	Y
9 Deal	N	Y	N	Y	Y	Y
10 Broun	N	Y	N	?	Y	Y
11 Gingrey	N	Y	N	+	+	+
12 Barrow	Y	Y	N	Y	Y	Y
13 Scott	Y	N	Y	Y	Y	Y
HAWAII						
1 Abercrombie	Y	N	Y	Y	?	Y
2 Hirono	Y	N	Y	Y	Y	Y
IDAHO						
1 Sali	N	Y	N	Y	Y	Y
2 Simpson	N	Y	N	Y	Y	Y
ILLINOIS						
1 Rush	Y	N	Y	+	+	+
2 Jackson	Y	N	Y	Y	Y	Y
3 Lipinski	Y	N	Y	Y	Y	Y
4 Gutierrez	Y	N	Y	Y	Y	Y
5 Emanuel	Y	N	Y	Y	Y	Y
6 Roskam	N	Y	N	Y	Y	Y
7 Davis	Y	N	Y	Y	Y	Y
8 Bean	Y	N	Y	Y	Y	Y
9 Schakowsky	Y	N	Y	Y	Y	Y
10 Kirk	N	Y	Y	Y	Y	Y
11 Weller	N	Y	N	Y	Y	Y
12 Costello	Y	N	Y	Y	Y	Y
13 Biggert	N	Y	N	Y	Y	Y
14 Vacant						
15 Johnson	N	Y	Y	Y	Y	Y

KEY	**Republicans**	Democrats			
Y Voted for (yea)		X Paired against		C Voted "present" to avoid possible conflict of interest	
# Paired for		– Announced against			
+ Announced for		P Voted "present"		? Did not vote or otherwise make a position known	
N Voted against (nay)					

ND Northern Democrats, SD Southern Democrats
Southern states: Ala., Ark., Fla., Ga., Ky., La., Miss., N.C., Okla., S.C., Tenn., Texas, Va.

	82	83	84	85	86	87
16 **Manzullo**	N	Y	N	?	?	?
17 Hare	Y	N	Y	Y	Y	Y
18 **LaHood**	N	Y	Y	?	?	?
19 **Shimkus**	N	Y	N	Y	Y	Y
INDIANA						
1 Visclosky	Y	N	Y	Y	Y	Y
2 Donnelly	Y	Y	Y	Y	Y	Y
3 **Souder**	N	Y	N	Y	Y	Y
4 **Buyer**	N	Y	N	Y	Y	Y
5 **Burton**	N	Y	N	Y	Y	Y
6 **Pence**	N	Y	N	Y	Y	Y
7 Vacant						
8 Ellsworth	Y	N	Y	Y	Y	Y
9 Hill	Y	N	Y	Y	Y	Y
IOWA						
1 Braley	Y	N	Y	Y	Y	Y
2 Loebsack	Y	N	Y	Y	Y	Y
3 Boswell	Y	N	Y	Y	Y	Y
4 **Latham**	N	Y	N	Y	Y	Y
5 **King**	N	Y	N	Y	Y	Y
KANSAS						
1 **Moran**	N	Y	N	Y	Y	Y
2 Boyda	Y	N	Y	Y	Y	Y
3 Moore	Y	N	Y	Y	Y	Y
4 **Tiahrt**	N	Y	N	Y	Y	Y
KENTUCKY						
1 **Whitfield**	N	Y	N	Y	Y	Y
2 **Lewis**	N	Y	N	?	?	?
3 Yarmuth	Y	N	Y	Y	Y	Y
4 **Davis**	N	Y	N	Y	Y	Y
5 **Rogers**	N	Y	N	Y	Y	Y
6 Chandler	Y	N	Y	Y	Y	Y
LOUISIANA						
1 Vacant						
2 Jefferson	Y	N	Y	Y	Y	Y
3 Melancon	Y	N	N	Y	Y	Y
4 **McCrery**	N	Y	N	Y	Y	Y
5 **Alexander**	N	Y	N	Y	Y	Y
6 Vacant						
7 **Boustany**	N	Y	N	Y	Y	Y
MAINE						
1 Allen	Y	N	Y	Y	Y	Y
2 Michaud	Y	N	Y	Y	Y	Y
MARYLAND						
1 **Gilchrest**	N	Y	Y	Y	Y	?
2 Ruppersberger	Y	N	Y	Y	Y	Y
3 Sarbanes	Y	N	Y	Y	Y	Y
4 Wynn	Y	N	Y	Y	Y	?
5 Hoyer	Y	N	Y	Y	Y	Y
6 **Bartlett**	N	Y	N	Y	Y	Y
7 Cummings	Y	N	Y	Y	Y	Y
8 Van Hollen	Y	N	Y	Y	Y	Y
MASSACHUSETTS						
1 Olver	Y	N	Y	Y	Y	Y
2 Neal	Y	N	Y	Y	Y	Y
3 McGovern	Y	N	Y	?	Y	Y
4 Frank	Y	N	Y	Y	Y	Y
5 Tsongas	Y	N	Y	Y	Y	Y
6 Tierney	?	N	Y	Y	Y	Y
7 Markey	Y	N	Y	Y	Y	Y
8 Capuano	Y	N	Y	Y	Y	Y
9 Lynch	Y	N	Y	Y	Y	Y
10 Delahunt	?	N	Y	Y	?	Y
MICHIGAN						
1 Stupak	Y	N	Y	Y	Y	Y
2 **Hoekstra**	N	Y	N	Y	Y	Y
3 **Ehlers**	N	Y	Y	Y	Y	Y
4 **Camp**	N	Y	N	Y	Y	Y
5 Kildee	Y	N	Y	Y	Y	Y
6 **Upton**	N	Y	N	Y	Y	Y
7 **Walberg**	N	Y	N	Y	Y	Y
8 **Rogers**	N	Y	N	Y	Y	Y
9 **Knollenberg**	N	Y	N	Y	Y	Y
10 **Miller**	N	Y	?	Y	Y	Y
11 **McCotter**	N	Y	N	Y	Y	Y
12 Levin	Y	N	Y	Y	Y	Y
13 Kilpatrick	Y	N	Y	Y	Y	Y
14 Conyers	Y	N	Y	Y	Y	Y
15 Dingell	Y	N	Y	Y	Y	Y
MINNESOTA						
1 Walz	Y	N	Y	Y	Y	Y
2 **Kline**	N	Y	N	Y	Y	Y
3 **Ramstad**	N	N	Y	Y	Y	Y
4 McCollum	Y	N	Y	?	Y	Y

	82	83	84	85	86	87
5 Ellison	Y	N	Y	Y	Y	Y
6 **Bachmann**	N	Y	N	Y	Y	Y
7 Peterson	Y	N	Y	Y	Y	Y
8 Oberstar	Y	N	Y	Y	Y	Y
MISSISSIPPI						
1 Vacant						
2 Thompson	Y	N	Y	Y	Y	Y
3 **Pickering**	N	Y	N	Y	Y	Y
4 Taylor	Y	N	Y	Y	Y	Y
MISSOURI						
1 Clay	Y	N	Y	Y	Y	Y
2 **Akin**	N	Y	N	Y	Y	Y
3 Carnahan	Y	N	Y	Y	Y	Y
4 Skelton	Y	N	Y	Y	Y	Y
5 Cleaver	Y	N	Y	Y	Y	Y
6 **Graves**	N	Y	N	Y	Y	Y
7 **Blunt**	N	Y	N	Y	Y	Y
8 **Emerson**	N	Y	N	Y	Y	Y
9 **Hulshof**	N	Y	N	Y	Y	Y
MONTANA						
AL **Rehberg**	N	Y	N	Y	Y	Y
NEBRASKA						
1 **Fortenberry**	N	Y	Y	Y	Y	Y
2 **Terry**	N	Y	N	Y	Y	Y
3 **Smith**	N	Y	N	Y	Y	Y
NEVADA						
1 Berkley	Y	N	Y	Y	Y	Y
2 **Heller**	N	Y	N	Y	Y	Y
3 **Porter**	N	Y	N	Y	Y	Y
NEW HAMPSHIRE						
1 Shea-Porter	Y	N	Y	Y	Y	Y
2 Hodes	Y	N	Y	Y	Y	Y
NEW JERSEY						
1 Andrews	Y	N	Y	Y	Y	Y
2 **LoBiondo**	N	Y	Y	Y	Y	Y
3 **Saxton**	N	Y	Y	Y	Y	Y
4 **Smith**	N	Y	Y	Y	Y	Y
5 **Garrett**	N	Y	N	Y	Y	Y
6 Pallone	Y	N	Y	Y	Y	Y
7 **Ferguson**	?	?	N	Y	Y	Y
8 Pascrell	Y	N	Y	Y	Y	Y
9 Rothman	Y	N	Y	Y	Y	Y
10 Payne	Y	N	Y	Y	Y	Y
11 **Frelinghuysen**	N	Y	N	Y	Y	Y
12 Holt	Y	N	Y	Y	Y	Y
13 Sires	Y	N	Y	Y	Y	Y
NEW MEXICO						
1 **Wilson**	N	Y	N	Y	Y	Y
2 **Pearce**	N	Y	N	Y	Y	Y
3 Udall	Y	N	Y	Y	Y	Y
NEW YORK						
1 Bishop	Y	N	Y	Y	Y	Y
2 Israel	Y	N	Y	Y	Y	Y
3 **King**	N	Y	N	Y	Y	Y
4 McCarthy	Y	N	Y	Y	Y	Y
5 Ackerman	Y	N	Y	Y	Y	Y
6 Meeks	Y	N	Y	Y	Y	Y
7 Crowley	Y	N	Y	Y	Y	Y
8 Nadler	Y	N	Y	Y	Y	Y
9 Weiner	Y	N	Y	Y	Y	Y
10 Towns	Y	N	Y	Y	Y	Y
11 Clarke	Y	N	Y	Y	Y	Y
12 Velázquez	Y	N	Y	Y	Y	Y
13 **Fossella**	N	Y	N	Y	Y	Y
14 Maloney	Y	N	Y	?	?	Y
15 Rangel	Y	N	Y	Y	Y	Y
16 Serrano	Y	N	Y	Y	Y	Y
17 Engel	Y	N	Y	Y	Y	Y
18 Lowey	Y	N	Y	Y	Y	Y
19 Hall	Y	N	Y	Y	Y	Y
20 Gillibrand	Y	N	Y	Y	Y	Y
21 McNulty	Y	N	Y	Y	Y	Y
22 Hinchey	Y	N	Y	?	?	Y
23 **McHugh**	N	Y	N	Y	Y	Y
24 Arcuri	Y	N	Y	Y	Y	Y
25 **Walsh**	N	Y	N	Y	Y	Y
26 **Reynolds**	N	Y	N	Y	Y	Y
27 Higgins	Y	N	Y	Y	Y	Y
28 Slaughter	Y	N	Y	Y	Y	Y
29 **Kuhl**	N	Y	N	Y	Y	Y
NORTH CAROLINA						
1 Butterfield	Y	N	Y	Y	Y	Y
2 Etheridge	Y	N	Y	Y	Y	Y
3 **Jones**	N	Y	N	Y	Y	Y
4 Price	Y	N	Y	Y	Y	Y

	82	83	84	85	86	87
5 **Foxx**	N	Y	N	Y	Y	Y
6 **Coble**	N	Y	N	Y	Y	Y
7 McIntyre	Y	Y	Y	Y	Y	Y
8 **Hayes**	N	Y	Y	Y	Y	Y
9 **Myrick**	N	Y	N	Y	Y	Y
10 **McHenry**	N	Y	N	Y	Y	Y
11 Shuler	Y	N	Y	Y	Y	Y
12 Watt	Y	N	Y	Y	Y	Y
13 Miller	Y	N	Y	Y	Y	Y
NORTH DAKOTA						
AL Pomeroy	Y	N	Y	Y	Y	Y
OHIO						
1 **Chabot**	N	Y	N	Y	Y	Y
2 **Schmidt**	N	Y	N	Y	Y	Y
3 **Turner**	N	Y	N	Y	Y	Y
4 **Jordan**	N	Y	N	Y	Y	Y
5 **Latta**	N	Y	N	Y	Y	Y
6 Wilson	Y	N	Y	Y	Y	Y
7 **Hobson**	N	Y	N	Y	Y	Y
8 **Boehner**	N	Y	N	Y	Y	Y
9 Kaptur	Y	N	Y	Y	Y	Y
10 Kucinich	Y	N	Y	Y	Y	Y
11 Tubbs Jones	?	?	+	Y	Y	Y
12 **Tiberi**	N	Y	N	Y	Y	Y
13 Sutton	Y	N	Y	Y	Y	Y
14 **LaTourette**	N	Y	N	Y	Y	Y
15 **Pryce**	N	Y	N	Y	Y	Y
16 **Regula**	N	Y	N	Y	Y	Y
17 Ryan	Y	N	Y	Y	Y	Y
18 Space	Y	N	Y	Y	Y	Y
OKLAHOMA						
1 **Sullivan**	N	Y	N	Y	Y	Y
2 Boren	Y	N	N	Y	Y	Y
3 **Lucas**	N	Y	N	Y	Y	Y
4 **Cole**	N	Y	N	Y	Y	Y
5 **Fallin**	N	Y	N	Y	Y	Y
OREGON						
1 Wu	Y	N	Y	Y	Y	Y
2 **Walden**	N	Y	N	Y	Y	Y
3 Blumenauer	Y	N	Y	Y	Y	Y
4 DeFazio	Y	N	Y	Y	Y	Y
5 Hooley	Y	N	Y	Y	Y	Y
PENNSYLVANIA						
1 Brady	Y	N	Y	Y	Y	Y
2 Fattah	Y	N	Y	Y	Y	Y
3 **English**	N	Y	N	Y	Y	Y
4 Altmire	Y	Y	Y	Y	Y	Y
5 **Peterson**	N	Y	N	?	?	?
6 **Gerlach**	N	Y	N	Y	+	Y
7 Sestak	Y	N	Y	Y	Y	Y
8 Murphy, P.	Y	N	Y	Y	Y	Y
9 **Shuster**	N	Y	N	Y	Y	Y
10 Carney	Y	N	Y	Y	Y	Y
11 Kanjorski	Y	N	Y	Y	Y	Y
12 Murtha	Y	N	Y	Y	Y	Y
13 Schwartz	Y	N	Y	Y	Y	Y
14 Doyle	Y	N	Y	Y	Y	Y
15 **Dent**	N	Y	N	Y	Y	Y
16 **Pitts**	N	Y	N	Y	Y	Y
17 Holden	Y	N	Y	Y	Y	Y
18 **Murphy, T.**	N	Y	N	Y	Y	Y
19 **Platts**	N	Y	N	Y	Y	Y
RHODE ISLAND						
1 Kennedy	Y	N	Y	Y	Y	Y
2 Langevin	Y	N	Y	+	+	+
SOUTH CAROLINA						
1 **Brown**	N	Y	N	Y	Y	Y
2 **Wilson**	N	Y	N	Y	Y	Y
3 **Barrett**	N	Y	N	Y	Y	Y
4 **Inglis**	N	Y	N	Y	Y	Y
5 Spratt	Y	N	Y	Y	Y	Y
6 Clyburn	Y	N	Y	Y	Y	Y
SOUTH DAKOTA						
AL Herseth Sandlin	Y	N	Y	Y	Y	Y
TENNESSEE						
1 **Davis, David**	N	Y	N	Y	Y	Y
2 **Duncan**	N	Y	N	Y	Y	Y
3 **Wamp**	N	Y	N	Y	Y	Y
4 Davis, L.	Y	N	Y	Y	Y	Y
5 Cooper	Y	N	Y	Y	Y	Y
6 Gordon	Y	N	Y	Y	Y	Y
7 **Blackburn**	N	Y	N	Y	Y	Y
8 Tanner	Y	N	Y	Y	Y	Y
9 Cohen	Y	N	Y	Y	Y	Y

	82	83	84	85	86	87
TEXAS						
1 **Gohmert**	N	Y	N	Y	Y	Y
2 **Poe**	N	Y	N	Y	Y	Y
3 **Johnson, S.**	N	Y	N	Y	Y	Y
4 **Hall**	N	Y	N	Y	Y	Y
5 **Hensarling**	N	Y	N	Y	Y	Y
6 **Barton**	N	Y	N	Y	Y	Y
7 **Culberson**	N	Y	N	Y	Y	Y
8 **Brady**	N	Y	N	Y	Y	Y
9 Green, A.	Y	N	Y	Y	Y	Y
10 **McCaul**	N	Y	N	Y	Y	Y
11 **Conaway**	N	Y	N	+	+	+
12 **Granger**	N	Y	N	Y	Y	Y
13 **Thornberry**	N	Y	N	Y	Y	Y
14 **Paul**	N	Y	N	Y	Y	Y
15 Hinojosa	Y	N	Y	Y	Y	Y
16 Reyes	?	?	?	Y	Y	Y
17 Edwards	Y	N	Y	Y	Y	Y
18 Jackson Lee	Y	N	Y	?	?	?
19 **Neugebauer**	N	Y	N	Y	Y	Y
20 Gonzalez	Y	N	Y	Y	Y	Y
21 **Smith**	N	Y	N	Y	Y	Y
22 Lampson	N	Y	N	Y	Y	Y
23 Rodriguez	Y	N	N	Y	Y	Y
24 **Marchant**	N	Y	N	Y	Y	Y
25 Doggett	Y	N	Y	?	?	Y
26 **Burgess**	N	Y	N	?	?	?
27 Ortiz	Y	N	N	Y	Y	Y
28 Cuellar	Y	N	N	Y	Y	Y
29 Green, G.	Y	N	N	Y	Y	Y
30 Johnson, E.	Y	N	Y	Y	Y	Y
31 **Carter**	N	Y	N	Y	Y	?
32 **Sessions**	N	Y	N	Y	Y	Y
UTAH						
1 **Bishop**	N	Y	N	Y	Y	Y
2 Matheson	Y	Y	?	Y	Y	Y
3 **Cannon**	N	Y	N	Y	Y	Y
VERMONT						
AL Welch	Y	N	Y	Y	Y	Y
VIRGINIA						
1 **Wittman**	N	Y	N	Y	Y	Y
2 **Drake**	N	Y	N	Y	Y	Y
3 Scott	Y	N	Y	Y	Y	Y
4 **Forbes**	N	Y	N	Y	Y	Y
5 **Goode**	N	Y	N	Y	Y	Y
6 **Goodlatte**	?	Y	N	Y	Y	Y
7 **Cantor**	N	Y	N	Y	Y	Y
8 Moran	Y	N	Y	Y	Y	Y
9 Boucher	Y	N	Y	Y	Y	Y
10 **Wolf**	N	Y	N	Y	Y	Y
11 **Davis, T.**	N	Y	N	Y	Y	Y
WASHINGTON						
1 Inslee	Y	N	Y	Y	Y	Y
2 Larsen	Y	N	Y	Y	Y	Y
3 Baird	Y	N	Y	Y	Y	Y
4 **Hastings**	N	Y	N	Y	Y	Y
5 **McMorris Rodgers**	N	Y	N	Y	Y	Y
6 Dicks	Y	N	Y	Y	Y	Y
7 McDermott	Y	N	Y	Y	Y	Y
8 **Reichert**	N	Y	Y	Y	Y	Y
9 Smith	Y	N	Y	Y	Y	Y
WEST VIRGINIA						
1 Mollohan	Y	N	Y	Y	Y	Y
2 **Capito**	N	Y	N	Y	Y	Y
3 Rahall	Y	N	Y	Y	Y	Y
WISCONSIN						
1 **Ryan**	?	Y	N	Y	Y	Y
2 Baldwin	Y	N	Y	Y	Y	Y
3 Kind	Y	N	Y	Y	Y	Y
4 Moore	Y	N	Y	Y	Y	Y
5 **Sensenbrenner**	N	Y	N	Y	Y	Y
6 **Petri**	N	Y	N	Y	Y	Y
7 Obey	Y	N	Y	Y	Y	Y
8 Kagen	Y	N	Y	Y	Y	Y
WYOMING						
AL **Cubin**	N	Y	N	?	?	?
DELEGATES						
Faleomavaega (A.S.)						
Norton (D.C.)						
Bordallo (Guam)						
Fortuño (P.R.)						
Christensen (V.I.)						

IN THE HOUSE | By Vote Number

88. **HR 1143. Virgin Islands National Park Land Lease/Passage.**
Rahall, D-W.Va., motion to suspend the rules and pass the bill that
would authorize the Interior secretary to lease certain lands in the Virgin
Islands National Park to the current holder of the Caneel Bay Resort, an
estate in the park. The bill would require the resort owners to compensate the federal government for continued private use of park land.
Motion agreed to 378-0: R 171-0; D 207-0 (ND 162-0, SD 45-0). A two-
thirds majority of those present and voting (252 in this case) is required
for passage under suspension of the rules. March 4, 2008.

89. **HR 1311. Nevada Cancer Institute Expansion Act/Passage.**
Rahall, D-W.Va., motion to suspend the rules and pass the bill that would
authorize the Interior Department to give a certain amount of land to
the Nevada Cancer Institute and the city of Las Vegas to develop a new
nonprofit cancer treatment facility and related medical facilities. Motion
agreed to 377-0: R 170-0; D 207-0 (ND 162-0, SD 45-0). A two-thirds majority of those present and voting (252 in this case) is required for passage
under suspension of the rules. March 4, 2008.

90. **HR 816. Orchard Detention Basin Flood Control Act/Passage.**
Rahall, D-W.Va., motion to suspend the rules and pass the bill that would
end wilderness study on 65 acres of the Sunrise Mountain Instant Study
Area in Nevada and require the Interior secretary to provide the county
with a right-of-way to construct and maintain a floodwater retention
basin. Motion agreed to 375-0: R 169-0; D 206-0 (ND 162-0, SD 44-0).
A two-thirds majority of those present and voting (250 in this case) is
required for passage under suspension of the rules. March 4, 2008.

91. **HR 4191. Wright Brothers-Dunbar National Historic Park/
Passage.** Rahall, D-W.Va., motion to suspend the rules and pass the bill
that would rename Dayton Aviation Heritage National Historic Park
in Ohio as "Wright Brothers-Dunbar National Historic Park." Motion
agreed to 407-4: R 189-4; D 218-0 (ND 167-0, SD 51-0). A two-thirds majority of those present and voting (274 in this case) is required for passage
under suspension of the rules. March 5, 2008.

92. **H Con Res 278. Taiwan Democratic Presidential Elections/
Adoption.** Berman, D-Calif., motion to suspend the rules and adopt the
concurrent resolution that would express continuing support for Taiwan's democracy and applaud its fourth direct and democratic presidential elections in March 2008. Motion agreed to 409-1: R 190-1; D 219-0
(ND 168-0, SD 51-0). A two-thirds majority of those present and voting
(274 in this case) is required for adoption under suspension of the rules.
March 5, 2008.

93. **H Res 951. Condemn Rocket Attacks in Israel/Adoption.**
Berman, D-Calif., motion to suspend the rules and adopt the resolution
that would strongly condemn the continuing Palestinian rocket attacks
on Israel and support Israel's right to defend its territory. Motion agreed
to 404-1: R 190-1; D 214-0 (ND 164-0, SD 50-0). A two-thirds majority of
those present and voting (270 in this case) is required for adoption under
suspension of the rules. March 5, 2008.

94. **HR 1424. Mental Health Parity/Question of Consideration.**
Question of whether the House should consider the rule (H Res 1014) to
provide for House floor consideration of the bill that would require health
insurers to offer mental health benefits equal in cost and scope to medical
health benefits and to cover a wide variety of mental health conditions.
Agreed to consider 215-192: R 4-184; D 211-8 (ND 164-3, SD 47-5). (Broun,
R-Ga., had raised a point of order that the rule contained a waiver in violation of the Congressional Budget Act.) March 5, 2008.

ND Northern Democrats, SD Southern Democrats
Southern states: Ala., Ark., Fla., Ga., Ky., La., Miss., N.C., Okla., S.C., Tenn., Texas, Va.

	88	89	90	91	92	93	94
ALABAMA							
1 Bonner	Y	Y	Y	Y	Y	N	N
2 Everett	?	?	?	Y	Y	Y	N
3 Rogers	?	?	?	Y	Y	Y	N
4 Aderholt	Y	Y	Y	Y	Y	Y	N
5 Cramer	Y	Y	Y	Y	Y	Y	Y
6 Bachus	Y	Y	Y	Y	Y	Y	N
7 Davis	Y	Y	Y	Y	Y	Y	Y
ALASKA							
AL Young	Y	Y	Y	Y	Y	Y	N
ARIZONA							
1 Renzi	?	?	?	?	?	?	?
2 Franks	Y	Y	Y	Y	Y	Y	N
3 Shadegg	Y	Y	Y	N	Y	Y	N
4 Pastor	Y	Y	Y	Y	Y	Y	Y
5 Mitchell	Y	Y	Y	Y	Y	Y	Y
6 Flake	Y	Y	Y	N	Y	Y	N
7 Grijalva	Y	Y	Y	Y	Y	Y	Y
8 Giffords	Y	Y	Y	Y	Y	Y	Y
ARKANSAS							
1 Berry	Y	Y	Y	Y	Y	Y	Y
2 Snyder	Y	Y	Y	Y	Y	Y	Y
3 Boozman	Y	Y	Y	Y	Y	Y	N
4 Ross	Y	Y	Y	Y	Y	Y	N
CALIFORNIA							
1 Thompson	Y	Y	Y	Y	Y	Y	Y
2 Herger	Y	Y	Y	Y	+	Y	N
3 Lungren	Y	Y	Y	Y	Y	Y	N
4 Doolittle	Y	Y	Y	Y	Y	Y	N
5 Matsui	Y	Y	Y	Y	Y	Y	Y
6 Woolsey	+	+	+	+	+	+	+
7 Miller, George	Y	Y	Y	Y	Y	Y	Y
8 Pelosi							
9 Lee	Y	Y	Y	Y	Y	Y	Y
10 Tauscher	Y	Y	Y	Y	Y	Y	Y
11 McNerney	Y	Y	Y	Y	Y	Y	Y
12 Vacant							
13 Stark	Y	Y	Y	Y	Y	Y	Y
14 Eshoo	Y	Y	Y	Y	Y	Y	Y
15 Honda	Y	Y	Y	Y	Y	Y	Y
16 Lofgren	Y	Y	Y	Y	Y	Y	Y
17 Farr	Y	Y	Y	Y	Y	Y	Y
18 Cardoza	Y	Y	Y	Y	Y	?	Y
19 Radanovich	?	?	?	Y	Y	Y	N
20 Costa	Y	Y	Y	Y	Y	Y	Y
21 Nunes	Y	Y	Y	Y	Y	Y	N
22 McCarthy	Y	Y	?	Y	Y	Y	N
23 Capps	Y	Y	Y	Y	Y	Y	Y
24 Gallegly	Y	Y	Y	Y	Y	Y	N
25 McKeon	Y	Y	Y	Y	Y	Y	N
26 Dreier	Y	Y	Y	Y	Y	Y	N
27 Sherman	Y	Y	Y	Y	Y	Y	Y
28 Berman	Y	Y	Y	Y	Y	Y	Y
29 Schiff	Y	Y	Y	Y	Y	Y	Y
30 Waxman	Y	Y	Y	Y	Y	Y	Y
31 Becerra	Y	Y	Y	Y	Y	Y	Y
32 Solis	Y	Y	Y	Y	Y	Y	Y
33 Watson	Y	Y	Y	Y	Y	Y	Y
34 Roybal-Allard	Y	Y	Y	Y	Y	Y	Y
35 Waters	Y	Y	Y	Y	Y	Y	Y
36 Harman	Y	Y	Y	Y	Y	Y	Y
37 Richardson	Y	Y	Y	Y	Y	Y	Y
38 Napolitano	Y	Y	Y	Y	Y	Y	Y
39 Sánchez, Linda	Y	Y	Y	Y	Y	Y	Y
40 Royce	Y	Y	Y	Y	Y	Y	N
41 Lewis	Y	Y	Y	Y	Y	Y	N
42 Miller, Gary	Y	Y	Y	Y	Y	Y	N
43 Baca	Y	Y	Y	Y	Y	Y	Y
44 Calvert	Y	Y	?	Y	Y	Y	N
45 Bono Mack	Y	Y	Y	Y	Y	Y	N
46 Rohrabacher	Y	Y	Y	Y	Y	Y	N
47 Sanchez, Loretta	Y	Y	Y	Y	Y	Y	Y
48 Campbell	Y	Y	Y	Y	Y	Y	N
49 Issa	Y	Y	Y	Y	Y	Y	N
50 Bilbray	Y	Y	Y	Y	Y	Y	N
51 Filner	Y	Y	Y	Y	Y	Y	Y
52 Hunter	Y	Y	Y	Y	Y	Y	N
53 Davis	Y	Y	Y	Y	Y	Y	Y

	88	89	90	91	92	93	94
COLORADO							
1 DeGette	Y	Y	Y	Y	Y	Y	Y
2 Udall	Y	Y	Y	Y	Y	Y	?
3 Salazar	Y	Y	Y	Y	Y	Y	N
4 Musgrave	Y	Y	Y	Y	Y	Y	N
5 Lamborn	Y	Y	Y	Y	Y	Y	N
6 Tancredo	Y	Y	Y	Y	Y	Y	N
7 Perlmutter	Y	Y	Y	Y	Y	Y	Y
CONNECTICUT							
1 Larson	Y	Y	Y	Y	Y	Y	Y
2 Courtney	Y	Y	Y	Y	Y	Y	Y
3 DeLauro	Y	Y	Y	Y	Y	Y	Y
4 Shays	Y	Y	Y	Y	Y	Y	N
5 Murphy	Y	Y	Y	Y	Y	Y	Y
DELAWARE							
AL Castle	Y	Y	Y	Y	Y	Y	N
FLORIDA							
1 Miller	+	+	+	Y	Y	Y	N
2 Boyd	Y	Y	Y	Y	Y	Y	Y
3 Brown	Y	Y	Y	Y	Y	Y	Y
4 Crenshaw	Y	Y	Y	Y	Y	Y	N
5 Brown-Waite	?	?	?	?	?	?	?
6 Stearns	Y	Y	Y	Y	Y	Y	N
7 Mica	Y	Y	Y	Y	Y	Y	N
8 Keller	+	+	+	+	+	+	−
9 Bilirakis	Y	Y	Y	Y	Y	Y	N
10 Young	Y	Y	Y	Y	Y	Y	N
11 Castor	Y	Y	Y	Y	Y	Y	Y
12 Putnam	Y	Y	Y	Y	Y	Y	N
13 Buchanan	Y	Y	Y	Y	Y	Y	N
14 Mack	Y	Y	Y	Y	Y	Y	N
15 Weldon	?	?	?	Y	Y	?	N
16 Mahoney	Y	Y	Y	Y	Y	Y	Y
17 Meek	?	?	?	Y	Y	Y	?
18 Ros-Lehtinen	Y	Y	Y	Y	Y	Y	N
19 Wexler	Y	Y	Y	Y	Y	Y	Y
20 Wasserman Schultz	Y	Y	Y	Y	Y	Y	Y
21 Diaz-Balart, L.	Y	Y	Y	Y	Y	Y	N
22 Klein	Y	Y	Y	Y	Y	Y	Y
23 Hastings	Y	Y	Y	Y	Y	Y	Y
24 Feeney	Y	Y	Y	Y	?	Y	N
25 Diaz-Balart, M.	Y	Y	Y	Y	Y	Y	N
GEORGIA							
1 Kingston	Y	Y	Y	Y	Y	Y	N
2 Bishop	Y	Y	Y	Y	Y	Y	Y
3 Westmoreland	Y	Y	Y	Y	Y	Y	N
4 Johnson	Y	Y	Y	Y	Y	Y	Y
5 Lewis	Y	Y	Y	Y	Y	Y	Y
6 Price	Y	Y	?	Y	Y	Y	N
7 Linder	Y	Y	Y	Y	Y	Y	N
8 Marshall	Y	Y	Y	Y	Y	Y	Y
9 Deal	?	?	?	Y	Y	Y	N
10 Broun	Y	Y	N	Y	N	Y	N
11 Gingrey	+	+	+	Y	Y	Y	N
12 Barrow	Y	Y	Y	Y	Y	Y	Y
13 Scott	Y	Y	Y	Y	Y	Y	Y
HAWAII							
1 Abercrombie	Y	Y	Y	Y	Y	P	N
2 Hirono	Y	Y	Y	Y	Y	Y	Y
IDAHO							
1 Sali	Y	Y	Y	Y	Y	N	N
2 Simpson	?	?	?	Y	Y	Y	N
ILLINOIS							
1 Rush	?	?	?	?	?	?	?
2 Jackson	Y	Y	Y	Y	Y	Y	Y
3 Lipinski	Y	Y	Y	Y	Y	Y	Y
4 Gutierrez	+	+	+	Y	Y	Y	Y
5 Emanuel	Y	Y	Y	Y	Y	Y	Y
6 Roskam	Y	Y	Y	Y	Y	Y	N
7 Davis	Y	Y	Y	Y	Y	Y	Y
8 Bean	Y	Y	Y	Y	Y	Y	Y
9 Schakowsky	Y	Y	Y	Y	Y	Y	Y
10 Kirk	Y	Y	Y	Y	Y	Y	Y
11 Weller	?	?	?	Y	Y	Y	N
12 Costello	Y	Y	Y	Y	Y	Y	Y
13 Biggert	Y	Y	Y	Y	Y	Y	N
14 Vacant							
15 Johnson	?	+	+	Y	Y	Y	N

KEY

	Republicans	Democrats	
Y Voted for (yea)		X Paired against	C Voted "present" to avoid possible conflict of interest
# Paired for		− Announced against	
+ Announced for		P Voted "present"	? Did not vote or otherwise make a position known
N Voted against (nay)			

	88	89	90	91	92	93	94
16 **Manzullo**	Y	Y	Y	Y	Y	Y	N
17 Hare	Y	Y	Y	Y	Y	Y	Y
18 **LaHood**	Y	Y	Y	Y	Y	Y	Y
19 **Shimkus**	?	?	?	Y	Y	Y	N
INDIANA							
1 Visclosky	Y	Y	Y	Y	Y	Y	Y
2 Donnelly	Y	Y	Y	Y	Y	Y	Y
3 **Souder**	Y	Y	Y	Y	Y	Y	N
4 **Buyer**	Y	Y	Y	Y	Y	?	N
5 **Burton**	?	?	?	Y	Y	Y	N
6 **Pence**	Y	Y	Y	Y	Y	+	N
7 Vacant							
8 Ellsworth	Y	Y	Y	Y	Y	Y	Y
9 Hill	Y	Y	Y	Y	Y	Y	Y
IOWA							
1 Braley	Y	Y	Y	Y	Y	Y	Y
2 Loebsack	Y	Y	Y	Y	Y	Y	Y
3 Boswell	Y	Y	Y	Y	Y	Y	Y
4 **Latham**	Y	Y	Y	Y	Y	Y	N
5 **King**	Y	Y	Y	Y	Y	Y	N
KANSAS							
1 **Moran**	Y	Y	Y	Y	Y	Y	N
2 Boyda	Y	Y	Y	Y	Y	Y	Y
3 Moore	Y	Y	Y	Y	Y	Y	Y
4 **Tiahrt**	Y	Y	Y	Y	Y	Y	N
KENTUCKY							
1 **Whitfield**	Y	Y	Y	Y	Y	Y	N
2 **Lewis**	Y	Y	Y	Y	Y	Y	N
3 Yarmuth	Y	Y	Y	Y	Y	Y	Y
4 **Davis**	Y	Y	Y	Y	P	Y	N
5 **Rogers**	Y	Y	Y	Y	Y	Y	N
6 Chandler	Y	Y	Y	Y	Y	Y	Y
LOUISIANA							
1 Vacant							
2 Jefferson	Y	Y	Y	Y	Y	Y	Y
3 Melancon	Y	Y	Y	Y	Y	Y	Y
4 **McCrery**	Y	Y	Y	Y	Y	Y	N
5 **Alexander**	Y	Y	Y	Y	Y	Y	N
6 Vacant							
7 **Boustany**	Y	Y	Y	Y	Y	Y	N
MAINE							
1 Allen	Y	Y	Y	Y	Y	Y	Y
2 Michaud	Y	Y	Y	Y	Y	Y	Y
MARYLAND							
1 **Gilchrest**	Y	Y	Y	Y	Y	Y	N
2 Ruppersberger	Y	Y	Y	Y	Y	Y	Y
3 Sarbanes	Y	Y	Y	Y	Y	Y	Y
4 Wynn	Y	Y	Y	Y	Y	Y	Y
5 Hoyer	Y	Y	Y	Y	Y	Y	Y
6 **Bartlett**	Y	Y	Y	Y	Y	Y	N
7 Cummings	Y	Y	Y	Y	Y	Y	Y
8 Van Hollen	Y	Y	Y	Y	Y	Y	Y
MASSACHUSETTS							
1 Olver	Y	Y	Y	Y	Y	Y	Y
2 Neal	Y	Y	Y	Y	Y	Y	Y
3 McGovern	Y	Y	Y	Y	Y	Y	Y
4 Frank	Y	Y	Y	Y	Y	Y	Y
5 Tsongas	Y	Y	Y	Y	Y	Y	Y
6 Tierney	Y	Y	Y	Y	Y	Y	Y
7 Markey	Y	Y	Y	Y	Y	Y	Y
8 Capuano	Y	Y	Y	Y	Y	P	Y
9 Lynch	Y	Y	Y	Y	Y	Y	Y
10 Delahunt	Y	Y	Y	Y	Y	Y	Y
MICHIGAN							
1 Stupak	Y	Y	Y	Y	Y	Y	Y
2 **Hoekstra**	Y	Y	Y	Y	Y	Y	N
3 **Ehlers**	Y	Y	Y	Y	Y	Y	N
4 **Camp**	Y	Y	Y	Y	Y	Y	N
5 Kildee	Y	Y	Y	Y	Y	Y	Y
6 **Upton**	Y	Y	Y	Y	Y	Y	N
7 **Walberg**	Y	Y	Y	Y	Y	Y	N
8 **Rogers**	Y	Y	Y	Y	Y	Y	N
9 **Knollenberg**	Y	Y	Y	Y	Y	Y	N
10 **Miller**	Y	Y	Y	Y	Y	Y	N
11 **McCotter**	Y	Y	Y	Y	Y	Y	N
12 Levin	Y	Y	Y	Y	Y	Y	Y
13 Kilpatrick	Y	Y	Y	Y	Y	Y	Y
14 Conyers	+	+	+	+	+	+	+
15 Dingell	Y	Y	Y	Y	Y	Y	Y
MINNESOTA							
1 Walz	Y	Y	Y	Y	Y	Y	Y
2 **Kline**	Y	Y	Y	Y	Y	Y	N
3 **Ramstad**	Y	Y	Y	Y	Y	Y	Y
4 McCollum	Y	Y	Y	Y	Y	Y	Y
5 Ellison	Y	Y	Y	Y	Y	Y	Y
6 **Bachmann**	Y	Y	Y	Y	Y	Y	P
7 Peterson	Y	Y	Y	Y	Y	Y	Y
8 Oberstar	Y	Y	Y	Y	Y	Y	Y
MISSISSIPPI							
1 Vacant							
2 Thompson	Y	Y	Y	Y	Y	Y	Y
3 **Pickering**	Y	Y	Y	Y	Y	Y	N
4 Taylor	Y	Y	Y	Y	Y	Y	Y
MISSOURI							
1 Clay	Y	Y	Y	Y	Y	Y	Y
2 **Akin**	+	+	+	Y	Y	Y	N
3 Carnahan	?	?	?	Y	Y	Y	Y
4 Skelton	Y	Y	Y	Y	Y	Y	Y
5 Cleaver	Y	Y	Y	Y	Y	Y	Y
6 **Graves**	Y	Y	Y	Y	Y	Y	N
7 **Blunt**	Y	Y	Y	Y	Y	Y	?
8 **Emerson**	Y	Y	Y	Y	Y	Y	N
9 **Hulshof**	?	?	?	Y	Y	Y	N
MONTANA							
AL **Rehberg**	Y	Y	Y	Y	Y	Y	N
NEBRASKA							
1 **Fortenberry**	+	+	+	Y	Y	Y	N
2 **Terry**	Y	Y	Y	Y	Y	Y	N
3 **Smith**	Y	Y	Y	Y	Y	Y	N
NEVADA							
1 Berkley	Y	Y	Y	Y	Y	Y	Y
2 **Heller**	Y	Y	Y	Y	Y	Y	N
3 **Porter**	Y	Y	Y	Y	Y	Y	N
NEW HAMPSHIRE							
1 Shea-Porter	Y	Y	Y	Y	Y	Y	Y
2 Hodes	Y	Y	Y	Y	Y	Y	Y
NEW JERSEY							
1 Andrews	Y	Y	Y	Y	Y	Y	Y
2 **LoBiondo**	Y	Y	Y	Y	Y	Y	N
3 **Saxton**	Y	Y	Y	Y	Y	Y	N
4 **Smith**	Y	Y	Y	Y	Y	Y	N
5 **Garrett**	Y	Y	Y	Y	Y	Y	N
6 Pallone	Y	Y	Y	Y	Y	Y	Y
7 **Ferguson**	Y	Y	Y	Y	Y	Y	N
8 Pascrell	Y	Y	Y	Y	Y	Y	Y
9 Rothman	Y	Y	Y	Y	Y	Y	Y
10 Payne	Y	Y	Y	Y	Y	Y	Y
11 **Frelinghuysen**	Y	Y	Y	Y	Y	Y	N
12 Holt	Y	Y	Y	Y	Y	Y	Y
13 Sires	Y	Y	Y	Y	Y	Y	Y
NEW MEXICO							
1 **Wilson**	Y	Y	Y	Y	Y	Y	N
2 **Pearce**	Y	Y	Y	Y	Y	Y	N
3 Udall	Y	Y	Y	Y	Y	Y	Y
NEW YORK							
1 Bishop	Y	Y	Y	Y	Y	Y	Y
2 Israel	Y	Y	Y	Y	Y	Y	Y
3 **King**	Y	Y	Y	Y	Y	Y	N
4 McCarthy	Y	Y	Y	Y	Y	Y	Y
5 Ackerman	Y	Y	Y	Y	Y	Y	Y
6 Meeks	?	?	?	Y	Y	Y	Y
7 Crowley	Y	Y	Y	Y	Y	Y	Y
8 Nadler	Y	Y	Y	Y	Y	Y	Y
9 Weiner	?	?	?	Y	Y	Y	Y
10 Towns	Y	Y	Y	Y	Y	Y	Y
11 Clarke	Y	Y	Y	Y	Y	Y	Y
12 Velázquez	Y	Y	Y	Y	Y	Y	Y
13 **Fossella**	Y	Y	Y	Y	Y	Y	N
14 Maloney	Y	Y	Y	Y	Y	Y	Y
15 Rangel	?	?	?	?	?	?	?
16 Serrano	Y	Y	Y	Y	Y	Y	Y
17 Engel	Y	Y	Y	Y	Y	Y	Y
18 Lowey	Y	Y	Y	Y	Y	Y	Y
19 Hall	Y	Y	Y	Y	Y	Y	Y
20 Gillibrand	Y	Y	Y	Y	Y	Y	Y
21 McNulty	Y	Y	Y	Y	Y	Y	Y
22 Hinchey	Y	Y	Y	Y	Y	Y	Y
23 **McHugh**	Y	Y	Y	Y	Y	Y	N
24 Arcuri	Y	Y	Y	Y	Y	Y	Y
25 **Walsh**	Y	Y	Y	Y	Y	Y	N
26 **Reynolds**	Y	Y	Y	Y	Y	Y	N
27 Higgins	Y	Y	Y	Y	Y	Y	Y
28 Slaughter	Y	Y	Y	Y	Y	Y	Y
29 **Kuhl**	Y	Y	Y	Y	Y	Y	N
NORTH CAROLINA							
1 Butterfield	?	?	?	Y	Y	Y	Y
2 Etheridge	Y	Y	Y	Y	Y	Y	Y
3 **Jones**	Y	Y	Y	Y	Y	Y	N
4 Price	Y	Y	Y	Y	Y	Y	Y
5 **Foxx**	Y	Y	Y	Y	Y	Y	N
6 **Coble**	Y	Y	Y	Y	Y	Y	N
7 McIntyre	Y	Y	?	Y	Y	Y	Y
8 **Hayes**	Y	Y	Y	Y	Y	Y	N
9 **Myrick**	Y	Y	Y	Y	Y	Y	N
10 **McHenry**	Y	Y	Y	Y	Y	Y	N
11 Shuler	Y	Y	Y	Y	Y	Y	Y
12 Watt	Y	Y	Y	Y	Y	Y	Y
13 Miller	Y	Y	Y	Y	Y	Y	Y
NORTH DAKOTA							
AL Pomeroy	Y	Y	Y	Y	Y	Y	Y
OHIO							
1 **Chabot**	Y	Y	Y	Y	Y	Y	N
2 **Schmidt**	Y	Y	Y	Y	Y	Y	N
3 **Turner**	Y	Y	Y	Y	Y	Y	N
4 **Jordan**	Y	Y	Y	Y	Y	Y	N
5 **Latta**	Y	Y	Y	Y	Y	Y	N
6 Wilson	Y	Y	Y	Y	Y	Y	Y
7 **Hobson**	Y	Y	Y	Y	Y	Y	N
8 **Boehner**	Y	Y	Y	Y	Y	Y	?
9 Kaptur	Y	Y	Y	Y	Y	Y	Y
10 Kucinich	?	?	?	?	?	?	?
11 Tubbs Jones	+	+	+	Y	Y	Y	Y
12 **Tiberi**	Y	Y	Y	Y	Y	Y	N
13 Sutton	Y	Y	Y	Y	Y	Y	Y
14 **LaTourette**	Y	Y	Y	Y	Y	Y	N
15 **Pryce**	Y	Y	Y	Y	Y	Y	N
16 **Regula**	Y	Y	Y	Y	Y	Y	N
17 Ryan	Y	Y	Y	Y	Y	Y	Y
18 Space	Y	Y	Y	Y	Y	Y	Y
OKLAHOMA							
1 **Sullivan**	Y	?	Y	Y	Y	Y	?
2 Boren	Y	Y	Y	Y	Y	Y	Y
3 **Lucas**	Y	Y	Y	Y	Y	Y	N
4 **Cole**	Y	Y	Y	Y	Y	Y	–
5 **Fallin**	?	?	?	Y	Y	Y	N
OREGON							
1 Wu	Y	Y	Y	Y	Y	Y	Y
2 **Walden**	Y	Y	Y	Y	Y	Y	N
3 Blumenauer	Y	Y	Y	Y	Y	Y	Y
4 DeFazio	Y	Y	Y	Y	Y	Y	Y
5 Hooley	Y	Y	Y	Y	Y	Y	Y
PENNSYLVANIA							
1 Brady	Y	Y	Y	Y	Y	Y	Y
2 Fattah	Y	Y	Y	?	Y	Y	Y
3 **English**	Y	Y	Y	Y	Y	Y	N
4 Altmire	Y	Y	Y	Y	Y	Y	Y
5 **Peterson**	?	?	?	Y	Y	Y	N
6 **Gerlach**	Y	Y	Y	Y	Y	Y	N
7 Sestak	Y	Y	Y	Y	Y	Y	Y
8 Murphy, P.	Y	Y	Y	Y	Y	Y	Y
9 **Shuster**	Y	Y	Y	Y	Y	Y	N
10 Carney	?	?	?	Y	Y	Y	Y
11 Kanjorski	Y	Y	Y	Y	Y	Y	Y
12 Murtha	Y	Y	Y	Y	Y	Y	Y
13 Schwartz	Y	Y	Y	Y	Y	Y	Y
14 Doyle	Y	Y	Y	Y	Y	Y	Y
15 **Dent**	Y	Y	Y	Y	Y	Y	N
16 **Pitts**	Y	Y	Y	Y	Y	Y	N
17 Holden	Y	Y	Y	Y	Y	Y	Y
18 **Murphy, T.**	Y	Y	Y	Y	Y	Y	?
19 **Platts**	Y	Y	Y	Y	Y	Y	N
RHODE ISLAND							
1 Kennedy	Y	Y	Y	Y	Y	Y	Y
2 Langevin	Y	Y	Y	Y	Y	Y	Y
SOUTH CAROLINA							
1 **Brown**	Y	Y	Y	Y	Y	Y	N
2 **Wilson**	Y	Y	Y	Y	Y	Y	N
3 **Barrett**	Y	Y	Y	Y	Y	Y	N
4 **Inglis**	Y	Y	Y	Y	Y	Y	N
5 Spratt	Y	Y	Y	Y	Y	Y	Y
6 Clyburn	Y	Y	Y	Y	Y	Y	Y
SOUTH DAKOTA							
AL Herseth Sandlin	Y	Y	Y	Y	Y	Y	Y
TENNESSEE							
1 **Davis, D.**	Y	Y	Y	Y	Y	Y	N
2 **Duncan**	Y	Y	Y	Y	Y	Y	N
3 **Wamp**	Y	Y	Y	Y	Y	Y	N
4 Davis, L.	Y	Y	Y	Y	Y	Y	Y
5 Cooper	Y	Y	Y	Y	Y	Y	Y
6 Gordon	Y	Y	Y	Y	Y	Y	Y
7 **Blackburn**	Y	Y	Y	Y	Y	Y	N
8 Tanner	?	?	?	?	?	?	Y
9 Cohen	Y	Y	Y	Y	Y	Y	Y
TEXAS							
1 **Gohmert**	Y	Y	Y	Y	Y	Y	N
2 **Poe**	Y	Y	Y	Y	Y	Y	?
3 **Johnson, S.**	?	?	?	Y	Y	Y	N
4 **Hall**	?	?	?	Y	Y	Y	N
5 **Hensarling**	?	?	?	Y	Y	Y	N
6 **Barton**	Y	Y	Y	Y	Y	Y	N
7 **Culberson**	Y	Y	Y	Y	Y	Y	N
8 **Brady**	Y	Y	Y	?	Y	Y	N
9 Green, A.	+	+	+	Y	Y	Y	Y
10 **McCaul**	Y	Y	Y	Y	Y	Y	N
11 **Conaway**	Y	Y	Y	Y	Y	Y	N
12 **Granger**	?	?	?	Y	Y	Y	N
13 **Thornberry**	Y	Y	Y	Y	Y	Y	N
14 **Paul**	Y	Y	Y	N	N	N	N
15 Hinojosa	Y	Y	Y	Y	Y	Y	N
16 Reyes	?	?	?	?	?	?	?
17 Edwards	Y	Y	Y	Y	Y	Y	Y
18 Jackson Lee	+	+	+	Y	Y	Y	N
19 **Neugebauer**	Y	Y	Y	Y	Y	Y	N
20 Gonzalez	?	?	?	?	?	?	?
21 **Smith**	Y	Y	Y	Y	Y	Y	N
22 Lampson	Y	Y	Y	Y	Y	Y	N
23 Rodriguez	?	?	?	Y	Y	Y	N
24 **Marchant**	?	?	?	?	?	?	N
25 Doggett	?	?	?	?	?	?	Y
26 **Burgess**	?	?	?	Y	Y	Y	N
27 Ortiz	?	?	?	?	?	?	?
28 Cuellar	Y	Y	Y	Y	Y	Y	Y
29 Green, G.	+	+	+	Y	Y	Y	Y
30 Johnson, E.	+	+	+	+	+	+	+
31 **Carter**	Y	Y	Y	Y	Y	Y	N
32 **Sessions**	?	?	?	Y	Y	Y	N
UTAH							
1 **Bishop**	Y	Y	Y	Y	Y	Y	N
2 Matheson	Y	Y	Y	Y	Y	Y	Y
3 **Cannon**	Y	Y	Y	Y	Y	Y	N
VERMONT							
AL Welch	Y	Y	Y	Y	Y	Y	Y
VIRGINIA							
1 **Wittman**	Y	Y	Y	Y	Y	Y	N
2 **Drake**	Y	Y	Y	Y	Y	Y	N
3 Scott	Y	Y	Y	Y	Y	Y	Y
4 **Forbes**	Y	Y	Y	Y	Y	Y	N
5 **Goode**	Y	Y	Y	Y	Y	Y	N
6 **Goodlatte**	Y	Y	Y	Y	Y	Y	N
7 **Cantor**	Y	Y	Y	Y	Y	Y	N
8 Moran	Y	Y	Y	Y	Y	P	Y
9 Boucher	Y	Y	Y	Y	Y	Y	Y
10 **Wolf**	Y	Y	Y	Y	Y	Y	N
11 **Davis**	Y	Y	Y	Y	Y	Y	N
WASHINGTON							
1 Inslee	Y	Y	Y	Y	Y	Y	Y
2 Larsen	Y	Y	Y	Y	Y	Y	Y
3 Baird	Y	Y	Y	Y	Y	Y	Y
4 **Hastings**	Y	Y	Y	Y	Y	Y	N
5 **McMorris Rodgers**	Y	Y	Y	Y	Y	Y	N
6 Dicks	Y	Y	Y	Y	Y	Y	Y
7 McDermott	Y	Y	Y	Y	Y	P	Y
8 **Reichert**	Y	Y	Y	Y	Y	Y	N
9 Smith	Y	Y	Y	Y	Y	Y	Y
WEST VIRGINIA							
1 Mollohan	Y	Y	Y	Y	Y	Y	Y
2 **Capito**	Y	Y	Y	Y	Y	Y	N
3 Rahall	Y	Y	Y	Y	Y	Y	Y
WISCONSIN							
1 **Ryan**	Y	Y	Y	Y	Y	Y	N
2 Baldwin	Y	Y	Y	Y	Y	Y	Y
3 Kind	Y	Y	Y	Y	Y	Y	Y
4 Moore	Y	Y	Y	Y	Y	Y	Y
5 **Sensenbrenner**	Y	Y	Y	Y	Y	Y	N
6 **Petri**	Y	Y	Y	Y	Y	Y	N
7 Obey	Y	Y	Y	Y	Y	Y	Y
8 Kagen	Y	Y	Y	Y	Y	Y	N
WYOMING							
AL **Cubin**	Y	Y	Y	Y	Y	Y	N
DELEGATES							
Faleomavaega (A.S.)							
Norton (D.C.)							
Bordallo (Guam)							
Fortuño (P.R.)							
Christensen (V.I.)							

IN THE HOUSE | By Vote Number

95. HR 1424. Mental Health Parity/Previous Question. Castor, D-Fla., motion to order the previous question (thus ending debate and possibility of an amendment) on adoption of the rule (H Res 1014) to provide for House floor consideration of the bill that would require health insurers to offer mental health benefits equal in cost and scope to medical health benefits and to cover a wide variety of mental health conditions. Motion agreed to 215-195: R 5-186; D 210-9 (ND 163-4, SD 47-5). March 5, 2008.

96. HR 1424. Mental Health Parity/Rule. Adoption of the rule (H Res 1014) to provide for House floor consideration of the bill that would require health insurers to offer mental health benefits equal in cost and scope to medical health benefits and to cover a wide variety of mental health conditions. Adopted 209-198: R 5-184; D 204-14 (ND 163-3, SD 41-11). March 5, 2008.

97. HR 4774. Krier Post Office/Passage. Davis, D-Ill., motion to suspend the rules and pass the bill that would designate a post office in San Antonio as the "Cyndi Taylor Krier Post Office Building." Motion agreed to 404-0: R 189-0; D 215-0 (ND 164-0, SD 51-0). A two-thirds majority of those present and voting (270 in this case) is required for passage under suspension of the rules. March 5, 2008.

98. H Con Res 286. Earl Lloyd Tribute/Adoption. Davis, D-Ill., motion to suspend the rules and adopt the concurrent resolution that would recognize Earl Lloyd for becoming the first African-American to play in the National Basketball Association 58 years ago. Motion agreed to 412-0: R 192-0; D 220-0 (ND 168-0, SD 52-0). A two-thirds majority of those present and voting (275 in this case) is required for adoption under suspension of the rules. March 5, 2008.

99. HR 1424. Mental Health Parity/Motion to Table. Pallone, D-N.J., motion to table (kill) the Hoekstra, R-Mich., appeal of the ruling of the chair with respect to the Pallone point of order that the Hoekstra motion to recommit the bill to the Energy and Commerce Committee was not germane. The Hoekstra motion would recommit the bill with instructions that it be reported back immediately with an amendment substituting the text of the Senate-passed bill (HR 3773), which would amend the Foreign Intelligence Surveillance Act. Motion agreed to 223-186: R 4-184; D 219-2 (ND 167-0, SD 52-2). March 5, 2008.

100. HR 1424. Mental Health Parity/Motion to Recommit. Kline, R-Minn., motion to recommit the bill to the Energy and Commerce Committee with instructions that it be reported back immediately with language substituting the text of the Senate-passed bill (S 558), which would not specify what conditions insurers must cover. Motion rejected 196-221: R 181-12; D 15-209 (ND 4-165, SD 11-44). March 5, 2008.

101. HR 1424. Mental Health Parity/Passage. Passage of the bill that would require health insurers to offer mental health benefits equal in cost and scope to medical health benefits and to cover a wide variety of mental health conditions. The bill would bar doctors from referring patients to hospitals in which the doctor has an ownership interest and prohibit employers and insurance companies from using genetic information when making employment or insurance premium decisions. Passed 268-148: R 47-145; D 221-3 (ND 169-0, SD 52-3). A "nay" was a vote in support of the president's position. March 5, 2008.

ND Northern Democrats, SD Southern Democrats
Southern states: Ala., Ark., Fla., Ga., Ky., La., Miss., N.C., Okla., S.C., Tenn., Texas, Va.

	95	96	97	98	99	100	101
ALABAMA							
1 Bonner	N	N	Y	Y	N	Y	N
2 Everett	N	N	Y	Y	N	Y	N
3 Rogers	N	N	Y	Y	N	Y	N
4 Aderholt	N	N	Y	Y	N	Y	N
5 Cramer	N	Y	Y	Y	N	Y	Y
6 Bachus	N	N	Y	Y	N	Y	N
7 Davis	Y	Y	Y	Y	Y	N	Y
ALASKA							
AL Young	N	N	Y	Y	N	Y	Y
ARIZONA							
1 Renzi	?	?	?	?	?	?	?
2 Franks	N	N	Y	Y	N	Y	N
3 Shadegg	N	N	Y	Y	N	Y	N
4 Pastor	Y	N	Y	Y	Y	N	Y
5 Mitchell	Y	Y	Y	Y	Y	N	Y
6 Flake	N	N	Y	Y	N	Y	N
7 Grijalva	Y	Y	Y	Y	Y	N	Y
8 Giffords	Y	Y	Y	Y	Y	N	Y
ARKANSAS							
1 Berry	Y	Y	Y	Y	Y	N	Y
2 Snyder	Y	N	Y	Y	Y	N	Y
3 Boozman	N	N	Y	Y	N	Y	N
4 Ross	Y	N	Y	Y	Y	N	Y
CALIFORNIA							
1 Thompson	Y	Y	Y	Y	Y	N	Y
2 Herger	N	N	Y	Y	N	Y	N
3 Lungren	N	N	Y	Y	N	Y	N
4 Doolittle	N	N	Y	Y	N	Y	N
5 Matsui	Y	Y	Y	Y	Y	N	Y
6 Woolsey	+	+	+	+	+	–	+
7 Miller, George	Y	Y	Y	Y	Y	N	Y
8 Pelosi							Y
9 Lee	Y	Y	Y	Y	Y	N	Y
10 Tauscher	Y	Y	Y	Y	Y	N	Y
11 McNerney	Y	Y	Y	Y	Y	N	Y
12 Vacant							
13 Stark	Y	?	Y	Y	Y	N	Y
14 Eshoo	Y	Y	Y	Y	Y	N	Y
15 Honda	Y	Y	Y	Y	Y	N	Y
16 Lofgren	Y	Y	Y	Y	Y	N	Y
17 Farr	Y	Y	Y	Y	Y	N	Y
18 Cardoza	Y	Y	Y	Y	Y	N	Y
19 Radanovich	?	?	?	Y	N	Y	N
20 Costa	?	Y	Y	Y	Y	N	Y
21 Nunes	N	N	Y	Y	N	Y	N
22 McCarthy	N	N	Y	Y	N	Y	N
23 Capps	Y	Y	Y	Y	Y	N	Y
24 Gallegly	N	N	Y	Y	N	Y	N
25 McKeon	N	N	Y	Y	N	Y	N
26 Dreier	N	N	Y	Y	N	Y	N
27 Sherman	Y	Y	Y	Y	Y	N	Y
28 Berman	Y	Y	Y	Y	Y	N	Y
29 Schiff	Y	Y	Y	Y	Y	N	Y
30 Waxman	Y	Y	Y	Y	Y	N	Y
31 Becerra	Y	Y	Y	Y	Y	N	Y
32 Solis	Y	Y	Y	Y	Y	N	Y
33 Watson	Y	Y	Y	Y	Y	N	Y
34 Roybal-Allard	Y	Y	Y	Y	Y	N	Y
35 Waters	Y	Y	Y	Y	Y	N	Y
36 Harman	Y	Y	Y	Y	Y	N	Y
37 Richardson	Y	Y	?	Y	Y	N	Y
38 Napolitano	Y	Y	Y	Y	Y	N	Y
39 Sánchez, Linda	Y	Y	Y	Y	Y	N	Y
40 Royce	N	N	Y	Y	N	Y	N
41 Lewis	N	N	Y	Y	N	Y	N
42 Miller, Gary	N	N	Y	Y	N	Y	N
43 Baca	Y	Y	Y	Y	Y	N	Y
44 Calvert	N	N	Y	Y	N	Y	N
45 Bono Mack	N	N	Y	Y	N	Y	N
46 Rohrabacher	N	N	Y	Y	N	Y	N
47 Sanchez, Loretta	Y	Y	Y	Y	Y	N	Y
48 Campbell	N	N	Y	Y	N	Y	N
49 Issa	N	N	Y	Y	N	Y	N
50 Bilbray	N	N	Y	Y	N	Y	N
51 Filner	Y	Y	Y	Y	Y	N	Y
52 Hunter	N	?	Y	Y	N	Y	N
53 Davis	Y	Y	Y	Y	Y	N	Y

	95	96	97	98	99	100	101
COLORADO							
1 DeGette	Y	Y	Y	Y	Y	N	Y
2 Udall	Y	Y	Y	Y	Y	N	Y
3 Salazar	Y	N	Y	Y	Y	N	Y
4 Musgrave	N	N	Y	Y	N	Y	?
5 Lamborn	N	N	Y	Y	N	Y	N
6 Tancredo	N	N	Y	N	Y	Y	N
7 Perlmutter	Y	Y	Y	Y	Y	N	Y
CONNECTICUT							
1 Larson	Y	Y	Y	Y	Y	N	Y
2 Courtney	Y	Y	Y	Y	Y	N	Y
3 DeLauro	Y	Y	Y	Y	Y	N	Y
4 Shays	N	N	Y	Y	N	N	Y
5 Murphy	Y	Y	Y	Y	Y	N	Y
DELAWARE							
AL Castle	N	N	Y	Y	N	N	Y
FLORIDA							
1 Miller	N	N	Y	Y	N	Y	N
2 Boyd	Y	Y	Y	Y	Y	N	Y
3 Brown	Y	Y	Y	Y	Y	N	Y
4 Crenshaw	N	N	Y	Y	N	Y	N
5 Brown-Waite	?	?	?	?	?	?	?
6 Stearns	N	N	Y	Y	N	Y	N
7 Mica	N	N	Y	Y	N	Y	N
8 Keller	–	–	+	+	–	+	+
9 Bilirakis	N	N	Y	Y	N	Y	N
10 Young	N	N	Y	Y	N	Y	N
11 Castor	Y	Y	Y	Y	Y	N	Y
12 Putnam	N	N	Y	Y	N	Y	N
13 Buchanan	N	N	Y	Y	N	Y	N
14 Mack	N	N	Y	Y	N	Y	N
15 Weldon	N	N	?	Y	N	Y	N
16 Mahoney	Y	Y	Y	Y	Y	N	Y
17 Meek	?	?	?	Y	N	Y	Y
18 Ros-Lehtinen	N	N	Y	Y	N	N	Y
19 Wexler	Y	Y	Y	Y	Y	N	Y
20 Wasserman Schultz	Y	Y	Y	Y	Y	N	Y
21 Diaz-Balart, L.	N	N	Y	Y	?	Y	Y
22 Klein	Y	Y	Y	Y	Y	N	Y
23 Hastings	Y	Y	Y	Y	Y	N	Y
24 Feeney	N	N	Y	Y	N	Y	N
25 Diaz-Balart, M.	N	N	Y	Y	N	Y	Y
GEORGIA							
1 Kingston	N	N	Y	Y	N	Y	N
2 Bishop	Y	Y	?	Y	Y	N	Y
3 Westmoreland	N	N	Y	Y	N	Y	N
4 Johnson	Y	Y	Y	Y	Y	N	Y
5 Lewis	Y	Y	Y	Y	Y	N	Y
6 Price	N	N	Y	Y	N	Y	N
7 Linder	N	N	Y	Y	N	Y	N
8 Marshall	Y	Y	Y	Y	Y	N	Y
9 Deal	N	N	Y	Y	N	Y	N
10 Broun	N	N	Y	Y	N	Y	N
11 Gingrey	N	N	Y	Y	N	Y	N
12 Barrow	N	N	Y	Y	N	Y	Y
13 Scott	Y	Y	Y	Y	Y	N	Y
HAWAII							
1 Abercrombie	N	Y	Y	Y	Y	N	Y
2 Hirono	Y	Y	Y	Y	Y	N	Y
IDAHO							
1 Sali	N	N	Y	Y	N	Y	N
2 Simpson	N	N	Y	Y	N	Y	N
ILLINOIS							
1 Rush	?	?	?	?	?	?	?
2 Jackson	Y	Y	Y	Y	Y	N	Y
3 Lipinski	Y	Y	Y	Y	Y	N	Y
4 Gutierrez	Y	Y	Y	Y	Y	N	Y
5 Emanuel	Y	Y	Y	Y	Y	N	Y
6 Roskam	N	N	Y	Y	N	Y	N
7 Davis	Y	Y	Y	Y	Y	N	Y
8 Bean	N	Y	?	Y	Y	N	Y
9 Schakowsky	Y	Y	Y	Y	Y	N	Y
10 Kirk	Y	Y	Y	Y	N	N	Y
11 Weller	N	N	Y	Y	N	Y	N
12 Costello	Y	Y	Y	Y	Y	N	Y
13 Biggert	N	N	Y	Y	N	Y	Y
14 Vacant							
15 Johnson	N	N	Y	Y	P	Y	Y

KEY   **Republicans**   Democrats

Y Voted for (yea)	X Paired against	C Voted "present" to avoid possible conflict of interest
# Paired for	– Announced against	
+ Announced for	P Voted "present"	? Did not vote or otherwise make a position known
N Voted against (nay)		

	95	96	97	98	99	100	101
16 **Manzullo**	N	N	Y	Y	N	Y	N
17 Hare	Y	Y	Y	Y	Y	N	Y
18 **LaHood**	Y	Y	Y	Y	Y	N	Y
19 **Shimkus**	N	N	Y	Y	N	Y	N
INDIANA							
1 Visclosky	Y	Y	Y	Y	Y	N	Y
2 Donnelly	N	Y	Y	Y	Y	Y	Y
3 **Souder**	N	N	Y	Y	N	Y	N
4 **Buyer**	N	N	Y	Y	N	Y	N
5 **Burton**	N	N	Y	Y	N	Y	N
6 **Pence**	N	N	Y	Y	N	Y	N
7 Vacant							
8 Ellsworth	Y	Y	Y	Y	Y	Y	Y
9 Hill	Y	Y	Y	Y	Y	N	Y
IOWA							
1 Braley	Y	Y	Y	Y	Y	N	Y
2 Loebsack	Y	Y	Y	Y	Y	N	Y
3 Boswell	Y	Y	Y	Y	Y	N	Y
4 **Latham**	N	N	Y	Y	N	Y	N
5 **King**	N	N	Y	Y	N	Y	N
KANSAS							
1 **Moran**	N	N	Y	Y	N	Y	N
2 Boyda	Y	Y	Y	Y	Y	N	Y
3 Moore	Y	Y	Y	Y	Y	N	Y
4 **Tiahrt**	N	N	Y	Y	N	Y	Y
KENTUCKY							
1 **Whitfield**	N	N	Y	Y	N	Y	N
2 **Lewis**	N	N	Y	Y	N	Y	N
3 Yarmuth	Y	Y	Y	Y	Y	N	Y
4 **Davis**	N	N	Y	Y	N	Y	N
5 **Rogers**	N	N	Y	Y	N	Y	N
6 Chandler	Y	Y	Y	Y	Y	N	Y
LOUISIANA							
1 Vacant							
2 Jefferson	Y	Y	Y	Y	Y	N	Y
3 Melancon	Y	Y	Y	Y	Y	N	Y
4 **McCrery**	N	N	Y	Y	N	Y	N
5 **Alexander**	N	N	Y	Y	N	Y	N
6 Vacant							
7 **Boustany**	N	N	Y	Y	N	Y	Y
MAINE							
1 Allen	Y	Y	Y	Y	Y	N	Y
2 Michaud	Y	Y	Y	Y	Y	N	Y
MARYLAND							
1 **Gilchrest**	Y	N	Y	Y	Y	N	Y
2 Ruppersberger	Y	Y	Y	Y	Y	N	Y
3 Sarbanes	Y	Y	Y	Y	Y	N	Y
4 Wynn	Y	?	Y	Y	?	?	?
5 Hoyer	Y	Y	Y	Y	Y	N	Y
6 **Bartlett**	N	N	Y	Y	N	Y	N
7 Cummings	?	Y	Y	Y	Y	N	Y
8 Van Hollen	Y	Y	Y	Y	Y	N	Y
MASSACHUSETTS							
1 Olver	Y	Y	Y	Y	Y	N	Y
2 Neal	Y	Y	Y	Y	Y	N	Y
3 McGovern	Y	Y	Y	Y	Y	N	Y
4 Frank	Y	Y	Y	Y	Y	N	Y
5 Tsongas	Y	Y	Y	Y	Y	N	Y
6 Tierney	Y	Y	Y	Y	Y	N	Y
7 Markey	Y	Y	Y	Y	Y	N	Y
8 Capuano	Y	Y	Y	Y	Y	N	Y
9 Lynch	Y	Y	Y	Y	Y	N	Y
10 Delahunt	Y	Y	Y	Y	Y	N	Y
MICHIGAN							
1 Stupak	Y	Y	Y	Y	Y	N	Y
2 **Hoekstra**	N	N	Y	Y	N	Y	N
3 **Ehlers**	N	N	Y	Y	N	Y	N
4 **Camp**	N	N	Y	Y	N	Y	N
5 Kildee	Y	Y	Y	Y	Y	N	Y
6 **Upton**	N	N	Y	Y	N	Y	Y
7 **Walberg**	N	N	Y	Y	N	Y	?
8 **Rogers**	N	N	Y	Y	N	Y	N
9 **Knollenberg**	N	N	Y	Y	N	Y	Y
10 **Miller**	N	N	Y	Y	N	Y	Y
11 **McCotter**	N	N	Y	Y	N	Y	N
12 Levin	Y	Y	Y	Y	Y	N	Y
13 Kilpatrick	Y	Y	Y	Y	Y	N	Y
14 Conyers	+	+	+	+	?	N	Y
15 Dingell	Y	Y	Y	Y	Y	N	Y
MINNESOTA							
1 Walz	Y	Y	Y	Y	Y	N	Y
2 **Kline**	N	N	Y	Y	N	Y	N
3 **Ramstad**	Y	Y	?	Y	Y	N	Y
4 McCollum	Y	Y	Y	Y	Y	N	Y
5 Ellison	Y	Y	Y	Y	Y	N	Y
6 **Bachmann**	N	N	Y	Y	N	Y	N
7 Peterson	Y	Y	Y	Y	Y	N	Y
8 Oberstar	Y	Y	Y	Y	Y	N	Y
MISSISSIPPI							
1 Vacant							
2 Thompson	Y	Y	Y	Y	Y	N	Y
3 **Pickering**	N	N	?	Y	N	Y	Y
4 Taylor	Y	Y	Y	Y	Y	N	Y
MISSOURI							
1 Clay	Y	Y	Y	Y	Y	N	Y
2 **Akin**	N	N	Y	Y	N	Y	N
3 Carnahan	Y	Y	Y	Y	Y	N	Y
4 Skelton	Y	Y	Y	Y	Y	N	Y
5 Cleaver	Y	Y	Y	Y	Y	N	Y
6 **Graves**	N	N	Y	Y	N	Y	N
7 **Blunt**	N	N	Y	Y	?	Y	N
8 **Emerson**	N	N	Y	Y	N	Y	Y
9 **Hulshof**	N	N	Y	Y	N	Y	N
MONTANA							
AL **Rehberg**	N	N	Y	Y	N	Y	N
NEBRASKA							
1 **Fortenberry**	N	N	Y	Y	N	Y	N
2 **Terry**	N	N	Y	Y	N	Y	N
3 **Smith**	N	N	Y	Y	N	Y	N
NEVADA							
1 Berkley	Y	Y	Y	Y	Y	N	Y
2 **Heller**	N	N	Y	Y	N	Y	N
3 **Porter**	N	N	Y	Y	N	Y	N
NEW HAMPSHIRE							
1 Shea-Porter	Y	?	Y	Y	Y	N	Y
2 Hodes	Y	Y	Y	Y	Y	N	Y
NEW JERSEY							
1 Andrews	Y	Y	Y	Y	Y	N	Y
2 **LoBiondo**	N	N	Y	Y	N	Y	Y
3 **Saxton**	N	N	Y	Y	?	Y	Y
4 **Smith**	N	N	Y	Y	N	Y	N
5 **Garrett**	N	N	Y	Y	N	Y	N
6 Pallone	Y	Y	Y	Y	Y	N	Y
7 **Ferguson**	N	N	Y	Y	N	Y	Y
8 Pascrell	Y	Y	Y	Y	Y	N	Y
9 Rothman	Y	Y	?	Y	Y	N	Y
10 Payne	Y	Y	Y	Y	Y	N	Y
11 **Frelinghuysen**	N	N	Y	Y	N	N	Y
12 Holt	Y	Y	Y	Y	Y	N	Y
13 Sires	Y	Y	Y	+	Y	N	Y
NEW MEXICO							
1 **Wilson**	N	N	Y	Y	N	Y	N
2 **Pearce**	N	N	Y	Y	N	Y	N
3 Udall	Y	Y	Y	Y	Y	N	Y
NEW YORK							
1 Bishop	Y	Y	Y	Y	Y	N	Y
2 Israel	Y	Y	Y	Y	Y	N	Y
3 **King**	N	N	Y	Y	N	Y	Y
4 McCarthy	Y	Y	Y	Y	Y	N	Y
5 Ackerman	Y	Y	Y	Y	Y	N	Y
6 Meeks	Y	Y	Y	Y	Y	N	Y
7 Crowley	Y	Y	Y	Y	Y	N	Y
8 Nadler	Y	Y	Y	Y	Y	N	Y
9 Weiner	Y	Y	Y	Y	Y	N	Y
10 Towns	Y	Y	Y	Y	Y	N	Y
11 Clarke	Y	Y	Y	Y	Y	N	Y
12 Velázquez	Y	Y	Y	Y	Y	N	Y
13 **Fossella**	N	N	Y	Y	N	Y	Y
14 Maloney	Y	Y	Y	Y	Y	N	Y
15 Rangel	?	?	?	?	?	?	?
16 Serrano	Y	Y	Y	Y	Y	N	Y
17 Engel	Y	Y	Y	Y	Y	N	Y
18 Lowey	Y	Y	Y	Y	Y	N	Y
19 Hall	Y	Y	Y	Y	Y	N	Y
20 Gillibrand	Y	Y	Y	Y	Y	N	Y
21 McNulty	Y	Y	Y	Y	Y	N	Y
22 Hinchey	Y	Y	Y	Y	Y	N	Y
23 **McHugh**	N	N	Y	Y	N	Y	Y
24 Arcuri	Y	Y	Y	Y	Y	N	Y
25 **Walsh**	N	Y	Y	Y	N	Y	Y
26 **Reynolds**	N	N	Y	Y	N	Y	N
27 Higgins	Y	Y	?	Y	Y	N	Y
28 Slaughter	Y	Y	Y	Y	Y	N	Y
29 **Kuhl**	N	N	Y	Y	N	Y	N
NORTH CAROLINA							
1 Butterfield	Y	Y	Y	Y	Y	N	Y
2 Etheridge	Y	Y	Y	Y	Y	N	Y
3 **Jones**	N	N	Y	Y	N	Y	N
4 Price	Y	Y	Y	Y	Y	N	Y
5 **Foxx**	N	N	Y	Y	N	Y	N
6 **Coble**	N	N	Y	Y	N	Y	N
7 McIntyre	Y	Y	Y	Y	Y	Y	Y
8 **Hayes**	N	N	Y	Y	N	Y	Y
9 **Myrick**	N	N	Y	Y	N	Y	N
10 **McHenry**	N	N	Y	Y	N	Y	N
11 Shuler	Y	N	Y	Y	Y	Y	Y
12 Watt	Y	Y	Y	Y	Y	N	Y
13 Miller	Y	Y	Y	Y	Y	N	Y
NORTH DAKOTA							
AL Pomeroy	Y	Y	Y	Y	Y	N	Y
OHIO							
1 **Chabot**	N	N	Y	Y	N	Y	N
2 **Schmidt**	N	N	Y	?	N	Y	N
3 **Turner**	N	N	Y	Y	N	Y	N
4 **Jordan**	N	N	Y	Y	N	Y	N
5 **Latta**	N	N	Y	Y	N	Y	N
6 Wilson	Y	Y	Y	Y	Y	N	Y
7 **Hobson**	N	N	Y	Y	N	Y	Y
8 **Boehner**	N	N	Y	Y	?	?	N
9 Kaptur	Y	Y	Y	Y	Y	N	Y
10 Kucinich	Y	Y	Y	Y	Y	N	Y
11 Tubbs Jones	Y	Y	?	Y	Y	N	Y
12 **Tiberi**	N	N	Y	Y	N	Y	N
13 Sutton	Y	Y	Y	Y	Y	N	Y
14 **LaTourette**	N	N	Y	Y	N	Y	Y
15 **Pryce**	N	N	Y	?	N	Y	Y
16 **Regula**	N	N	Y	Y	N	Y	Y
17 Ryan	Y	Y	Y	Y	Y	N	Y
18 Space	Y	Y	Y	Y	Y	N	Y
OKLAHOMA							
1 **Sullivan**	N	N	Y	Y	N	N	Y
2 Boren	Y	N	Y	Y	Y	Y	Y
3 **Lucas**	N	N	Y	Y	N	Y	N
4 **Cole**	–	–	Y	Y	N	Y	N
5 **Fallin**	N	?	Y	Y	N	Y	N
OREGON							
1 Wu	Y	Y	Y	Y	Y	N	Y
2 **Walden**	N	N	Y	Y	N	Y	N
3 Blumenauer	Y	Y	Y	Y	Y	N	Y
4 DeFazio	Y	Y	Y	Y	?	N	Y
5 Hooley	Y	Y	Y	Y	Y	N	Y
PENNSYLVANIA							
1 Brady	Y	Y	Y	Y	Y	N	Y
2 Fattah	Y	Y	Y	Y	Y	N	Y
3 **English**	N	N	Y	Y	N	Y	Y
4 Altmire	Y	Y	Y	Y	Y	Y	Y
5 **Peterson**	?	?	Y	Y	N	Y	N
6 **Gerlach**	N	N	Y	Y	–	Y	Y
7 Sestak	Y	Y	Y	Y	Y	N	Y
8 Murphy, P.	Y	Y	Y	Y	Y	N	Y
9 **Shuster**	N	N	Y	Y	N	Y	N
10 Carney	Y	Y	Y	Y	Y	N	Y
11 Kanjorski	Y	Y	Y	Y	Y	N	Y
12 Murtha	Y	Y	Y	Y	Y	N	Y
13 Schwartz	Y	Y	Y	Y	Y	N	Y
14 Doyle	Y	Y	Y	Y	Y	N	Y
15 **Dent**	N	N	Y	Y	N	Y	Y
16 **Pitts**	N	N	Y	Y	N	Y	N
17 Holden	Y	Y	Y	Y	Y	N	Y
18 **Murphy, T.**	N	N	Y	Y	N	N	Y
19 **Platts**	Y	N	Y	Y	N	N	Y
RHODE ISLAND							
1 Kennedy	Y	Y	Y	Y	Y	N	Y
2 Langevin	Y	Y	Y	Y	Y	N	Y
SOUTH CAROLINA							
1 **Brown**	N	N	Y	Y	N	Y	N
2 **Wilson**	N	N	?	Y	N	Y	N
3 **Barrett**	N	N	Y	Y	N	Y	N
4 **Inglis**	N	N	Y	Y	N	Y	N
5 Spratt	Y	Y	Y	Y	Y	N	Y
6 Clyburn	Y	Y	Y	Y	Y	N	Y
SOUTH DAKOTA							
AL Herseth Sandlin	Y	Y	Y	Y	Y	N	Y
TENNESSEE							
1 **Davis, D.**	N	N	Y	Y	N	Y	N
2 **Duncan**	N	N	Y	Y	N	Y	N
3 **Wamp**	N	N	Y	Y	N	Y	Y
4 Davis, L.	Y	Y	Y	Y	Y	Y	Y
5 Cooper	Y	Y	Y	Y	Y	N	Y
6 Gordon	Y	Y	Y	?	Y	N	Y
7 **Blackburn**	N	N	Y	Y	N	Y	N
8 Tanner	Y	Y	Y	Y	Y	N	Y
9 Cohen	Y	Y	Y	Y	Y	N	Y
TEXAS							
1 **Gohmert**	N	N	Y	Y	N	Y	N
2 **Poe**	?	?	?	?	?	?	?
3 **Johnson, S.**	N	N	Y	Y	N	Y	N
4 **Hall**	N	N	Y	Y	N	Y	N
5 **Hensarling**	N	N	Y	Y	N	Y	N
6 **Barton**	N	N	Y	Y	N	Y	N
7 **Culberson**	N	N	Y	Y	N	Y	N
8 **Brady**	N	N	Y	Y	N	Y	N
9 Green, A.	Y	N	Y	Y	Y	N	Y
10 **McCaul**	N	N	Y	Y	N	Y	N
11 **Conaway**	N	N	Y	Y	N	Y	N
12 **Granger**	N	N	Y	Y	N	Y	N
13 **Thornberry**	N	N	Y	Y	N	Y	N
14 **Paul**	N	N	Y	Y	Y	Y	N
15 Hinojosa	Y	N	Y	Y	Y	Y	N
16 Reyes	?	?	?	Y	Y	Y	Y
17 Edwards	Y	Y	Y	Y	Y	N	Y
18 Jackson Lee	N	N	Y	Y	Y	N	Y
19 **Neugebauer**	N	N	Y	Y	N	Y	N
20 Gonzalez	?	?	?	?	?	?	?
21 **Smith**	N	N	Y	Y	N	Y	Y
22 Lampson	N	N	Y	Y	N	Y	N
23 Rodriguez	N	Y	Y	Y	Y	N	Y
24 **Marchant**	N	N	Y	Y	N	Y	N
25 Doggett	Y	Y	Y	Y	Y	N	Y
26 **Burgess**	N	N	Y	Y	N	Y	N
27 Ortiz	?	?	?	?	Y	Y	Y
28 Cuellar	Y	N	Y	Y	?	Y	Y
29 Green, G.	Y	N	Y	Y	Y	Y	Y
30 Johnson, E.	+	+	+	+	+	–	+
31 **Carter**	N	N	Y	Y	N	Y	N
32 **Sessions**	N	N	Y	Y	N	Y	N
UTAH							
1 **Bishop**	N	N	Y	Y	N	Y	N
2 Matheson	Y	Y	Y	Y	Y	Y	Y
3 **Cannon**	N	Y	Y	Y	N	Y	N
VERMONT							
AL Welch	Y	Y	Y	Y	Y	N	?
VIRGINIA							
1 **Wittman**	N	N	Y	Y	N	Y	N
2 **Drake**	N	N	Y	Y	N	Y	N
3 Scott	Y	Y	Y	Y	Y	N	Y
4 **Forbes**	N	N	Y	Y	N	Y	N
5 **Goode**	N	N	Y	Y	N	Y	N
6 **Goodlatte**	N	N	Y	Y	N	Y	N
7 **Cantor**	N	N	Y	Y	N	Y	N
8 Moran	Y	Y	Y	Y	Y	N	Y
9 Boucher	Y	Y	Y	Y	Y	N	Y
10 **Wolf**	N	N	Y	Y	N	Y	N
11 **Davis**	N	N	Y	Y	N	N	Y
WASHINGTON							
1 Inslee	Y	Y	Y	Y	Y	N	Y
2 Larsen	Y	Y	Y	Y	Y	N	Y
3 Baird	Y	Y	Y	Y	Y	N	Y
4 **Hastings**	N	N	Y	Y	N	Y	N
5 **McMorris Rodgers**	N	N	Y	Y	N	Y	N
6 Dicks	Y	Y	Y	Y	Y	N	Y
7 McDermott	Y	Y	Y	Y	Y	N	Y
8 **Reichert**	N	N	Y	Y	N	Y	N
9 Smith	Y	Y	Y	Y	Y	N	Y
WEST VIRGINIA							
1 Mollohan	Y	Y	Y	Y	Y	N	Y
2 **Capito**	N	N	Y	Y	N	Y	Y
3 Rahall	Y	Y	Y	Y	Y	N	Y
WISCONSIN							
1 **Ryan**	N	N	Y	Y	N	Y	N
2 Baldwin	Y	Y	Y	Y	Y	N	Y
3 Kind	Y	Y	Y	Y	Y	N	Y
4 Moore	Y	Y	Y	Y	Y	N	Y
5 **Sensenbrenner**	N	N	Y	Y	N	Y	Y
6 **Petri**	N	N	Y	Y	N	Y	N
7 Obey	Y	Y	Y	Y	Y	N	Y
8 Kagen	N	N	Y	Y	Y	N	Y
WYOMING							
AL **Cubin**	N	N	Y	Y	N	Y	N
DELEGATES							
Faleomavaega (A.S.)							
Norton (D.C.)							
Bordallo (Guam)							
Fortuño (P.R.)							
Christensen (V.I.)							

IN THE HOUSE | By Vote Number

102. **HR 5400. Kashkoush Post Office/Passage.** Davis, D-Ill., motion to suspend the rules and pass the bill that would designate a post office in Chagrin Falls, Ohio, as the "Sgt. Michael M. Kashkoush Post Office Building." Motion agreed to 402-0: R 192-0; D 210-0 (ND 156-0, SD 54-0). A two-thirds majority of those present and voting (268 in this case) is required for passage under suspension of the rules. March 5, 2008.

103. **HR 2857. Corporation for National and Community Service/ Previous Question.** Matsui, D-Calif., motion to order the previous question (thus ending debate and possibility of an amendment) on adoption of the rule (H Res 1015) to provide for House floor consideration of the bill that would reauthorize the Corporation for National and Community Service for five years and encourage an expansion of AmeriCorps to 100,000 workers. Motion agreed to 217-193: R 0-188; D 217-5 (ND 164-3, SD 53-2). March 6, 2008.

104. **HR 2857. Corporation for National and Community Service/ Rule.** Adoption of the rule (H Res 1015) to provide for House floor consideration of the bill that would reauthorize the Corporation for National and Community Service for five years and encourage an expansion of AmeriCorps to 100,000 workers. Adopted 222-190: R 0-190; D 222-0 (ND 167-0, SD 55-0). March 6, 2008.

105. **HR 2857. Corporation for National and Community Service/ Summer of Service Program.** Flake, R-Ariz., amendment that would strike the "summer of service" grant program and reduce the bill's authorization for the program to $45 million from $65 million for fiscal 2008. Rejected in Committee of the Whole 153-260: R 150-39; D 3-221 (ND 2-168, SD 1-53). March 6, 2008.

106. **HR 2857. Corporation for National and Community Service/ Energy Conservation Corps.** Inslee, D-Wash., amendment that would create an Energy Conservation Corps for projects that support energy conservation, infrastructure and transportation improvement, and emergency operations. Adopted in Committee of the Whole 252-161: R 28-161; D 224-0 (ND 170-0, SD 54-0). March 6, 2008.

107. **HR 2857. Corporation for National and Community Service/ Motion to Table.** Miller, D-Calif., motion to table (kill) the Lungren, R-Calif., appeal of the ruling of the chair with respect to the Miller point of order that the Lungren motion to recommit the bill to the Education and Labor Committee was not germane. The Lungren motion would recommit the bill with instructions that it be reported back immediately with an amendment substituting the text of the Senate-passed bill (HR 3773), which would amend the Foreign Intelligence Surveillance Act. Motion agreed to 221-191: R 2-187; D 219-4 (ND 167-1, SD 52-3). March 6, 2008.

	102	103	104	105	106	107
ALABAMA						
1 Bonner	Y	N	N	Y	N	N
2 Everett	Y	N	N	Y	N	N
3 Rogers	Y	N	N	Y	N	N
4 Aderholt	Y	N	N	Y	N	N
5 Cramer	Y	Y	Y	N	Y	N
6 Bachus	Y	N	N	Y	N	N
7 Davis	Y	Y	Y	N	Y	Y
ALASKA						
AL Young	Y	?	?	Y	N	N
ARIZONA						
1 Renzi	?	?	?	N	Y	N
2 Franks	Y	N	N	Y	N	N
3 Shadegg	Y	N	N	Y	N	N
4 Pastor	Y	Y	Y	N	Y	Y
5 Mitchell	Y	Y	Y	N	Y	Y
6 Flake	Y	N	N	Y	N	N
7 Grijalva	Y	Y	Y	N	Y	Y
8 Giffords	Y	Y	Y	N	Y	Y
ARKANSAS						
1 Berry	Y	Y	Y	N	Y	Y
2 Snyder	Y	Y	Y	N	Y	Y
3 Boozman	Y	N	N	Y	N	N
4 Ross	Y	Y	Y	N	Y	Y
CALIFORNIA						
1 Thompson	Y	Y	Y	N	Y	Y
2 Herger	Y	N	N	Y	N	N
3 Lungren	Y	N	N	Y	N	N
4 Doolittle	Y	N	N	Y	N	N
5 Matsui	Y	Y	Y	N	Y	Y
6 Woolsey	+	?	?	?	?	?
7 Miller, George	Y	Y	Y	N	Y	Y
8 Pelosi						
9 Lee	Y	Y	Y	N	Y	Y
10 Tauscher	Y	Y	Y	N	Y	Y
11 McNerney	Y	Y	Y	N	Y	Y
12 Vacant						
13 Stark	Y	Y	Y	N	Y	Y
14 Eshoo	Y	Y	Y	N	Y	Y
15 Honda	Y	Y	Y	N	Y	Y
16 Lofgren	Y	Y	Y	N	Y	Y
17 Farr	Y	Y	Y	N	Y	Y
18 Cardoza	?	Y	Y	N	Y	Y
19 Radanovich	Y	N	N	Y	N	N
20 Costa	Y	Y	Y	N	Y	Y
21 Nunes	Y	N	N	Y	N	N
22 McCarthy	Y	N	N	Y	N	N
23 Capps	Y	Y	Y	N	Y	Y
24 Gallegly	Y	N	N	N	N	N
25 McKeon	Y	N	N	Y	N	N
26 Dreier	Y	N	N	Y	N	N
27 Sherman	Y	Y	Y	N	Y	Y
28 Berman	Y	Y	Y	N	Y	Y
29 Schiff	Y	Y	Y	-	Y	Y
30 Waxman	Y	Y	Y	N	Y	Y
31 Becerra	Y	Y	Y	N	Y	Y
32 Solis	Y	Y	Y	?	?	?
33 Watson	Y	Y	Y	N	Y	Y
34 Roybal-Allard	Y	Y	Y	N	Y	Y
35 Waters	Y	Y	Y	N	Y	Y
36 Harman	Y	Y	Y	N	Y	Y
37 Richardson	Y	Y	Y	N	Y	Y
38 Napolitano	Y	Y	Y	N	Y	Y
39 Sánchez, Linda	Y	Y	Y	N	Y	Y
40 Royce	Y	N	N	Y	N	N
41 Lewis	Y	N	N	Y	?	N
42 Miller, Gary	Y	N	N	Y	N	N
43 Baca	Y	Y	Y	N	Y	Y
44 Calvert	Y	N	N	Y	N	N
45 Bono Mack	Y	N	N	Y	N	N
46 Rohrabacher	Y	N	N	Y	N	N
47 Sanchez, Loretta	Y	Y	Y	N	Y	Y
48 Campbell	Y	N	N	Y	N	N
49 Issa	Y	N	N	Y	N	N
50 Bilbray	Y	N	N	Y	Y	N
51 Filner	Y	Y	Y	N	Y	Y
52 Hunter	Y	N	N	Y	N	N
53 Davis	Y	Y	Y	N	Y	Y

	102	103	104	105	106	107
COLORADO						
1 DeGette	Y	Y	Y	N	Y	Y
2 Udall	Y	Y	Y	N	Y	Y
3 Salazar	Y	Y	Y	N	Y	Y
4 Musgrave	Y	N	N	Y	N	N
5 Lamborn	Y	N	N	Y	N	N
6 Tancredo	Y	N	N	Y	N	N
7 Perlmutter	Y	Y	Y	N	Y	Y
CONNECTICUT						
1 Larson	Y	Y	Y	N	Y	Y
2 Courtney	Y	Y	Y	N	Y	Y
3 DeLauro	Y	Y	Y	N	Y	Y
4 Shays	Y	N	N	N	N	N
5 Murphy	Y	Y	Y	N	Y	Y
DELAWARE						
AL Castle	Y	N	N	N	Y	N
FLORIDA						
1 Miller	Y	N	N	Y	N	N
2 Boyd	Y	Y	Y	N	Y	Y
3 Brown	Y	Y	Y	N	Y	Y
4 Crenshaw	Y	N	N	Y	N	N
5 Brown-Waite	?	?	?	?	?	?
6 Stearns	Y	N	N	Y	N	N
7 Mica	Y	N	N	N	N	N
8 Keller	+	?	?	?	?	?
9 Bilirakis	Y	N	N	Y	N	N
10 Young	Y	N	N	Y	N	?
11 Castor	Y	Y	Y	N	Y	Y
12 Putnam	Y	N	N	Y	N	N
13 Buchanan	Y	N	N	Y	N	N
14 Mack	Y	N	N	Y	N	N
15 Weldon	Y	N	N	Y	N	N
16 Mahoney	Y	Y	Y	N	Y	Y
17 Meek	Y	Y	Y	?	Y	Y
18 Ros-Lehtinen	Y	N	N	N	Y	N
19 Wexler	Y	Y	Y	N	Y	Y
20 Wasserman Schultz	Y	Y	Y	N	Y	Y
21 Diaz-Balart, L.	?	Y	N	N	Y	N
22 Klein	Y	Y	Y	N	Y	Y
23 Hastings	Y	Y	Y	N	Y	Y
24 Feeney	?	N	N	Y	N	N
25 Diaz-Balart, M.	Y	N	N	N	N	N
GEORGIA						
1 Kingston	Y	N	N	Y	N	N
2 Bishop	Y	Y	Y	N	Y	Y
3 Westmoreland	Y	N	N	Y	N	N
4 Johnson	Y	Y	Y	N	Y	Y
5 Lewis	Y	Y	Y	N	Y	Y
6 Price	Y	N	N	Y	N	N
7 Linder	Y	N	N	?	?	?
8 Marshall	Y	Y	Y	Y	Y	Y
9 Deal	Y	N	N	Y	N	N
10 Broun	Y	N	N	Y	N	N
11 Gingrey	Y	N	N	Y	N	N
12 Barrow	Y	N	N	Y	N	Y
13 Scott	Y	Y	Y	N	Y	Y
HAWAII						
1 Abercrombie	Y	Y	Y	N	Y	Y
2 Hirono	Y	Y	Y	N	Y	Y
IDAHO						
1 Sali	Y	N	N	Y	N	N
2 Simpson	Y	N	N	Y	N	N
ILLINOIS						
1 Rush	?	?	?	?	?	?
2 Jackson	Y	Y	Y	N	Y	Y
3 Lipinski	Y	Y	Y	N	Y	Y
4 Gutierrez	Y	Y	Y	N	Y	Y
5 Emanuel	?	Y	Y	N	Y	Y
6 Roskam	Y	N	N	Y	N	N
7 Davis	Y	Y	Y	N	Y	Y
8 Bean	Y	N	N	Y	N	Y
9 Schakowsky	Y	Y	Y	N	Y	Y
10 Kirk	Y	N	N	N	N	N
11 Weller	Y	N	N	N	N	N
12 Costello	Y	Y	Y	N	Y	Y
13 Biggert	Y	N	N	Y	N	N
14 Vacant						
15 Johnson	Y	P	N	Y	Y	P

KEY

Republicans	Democrats

Y Voted for (yea)	X Paired against	C Voted "present" to avoid possible conflict of interest
# Paired for	– Announced against	
+ Announced for	P Voted "present"	? Did not vote or otherwise make a position known
N Voted against (nay)		

ND Northern Democrats, SD Southern Democrats
Southern states: Ala., Ark., Fla., Ga., Ky., La., Miss., N.C., Okla., S.C., Tenn., Texas, Va.

	102	103	104	105	106	107
16 **Manzullo**	Y	N	N	Y	N	N
17 Hare	Y	Y	Y	N	Y	Y
18 **LaHood**	Y	N	N	N	N	N
19 **Shimkus**	Y	N	N	Y	N	N
INDIANA						
1 Visclosky	Y	Y	Y	N	Y	Y
2 Donnelly	Y	N	Y	N	Y	Y
3 **Souder**	Y	N	N	Y	Y	N
4 **Buyer**	Y	N	N	Y	N	N
5 **Burton**	Y	N	N	Y	N	N
6 **Pence**	Y	N	N	Y	N	N
7 Vacant						
8 Ellsworth	Y	Y	Y	N	Y	Y
9 Hill	Y	Y	Y	N	Y	Y
IOWA						
1 Braley	Y	Y	Y	N	Y	Y
2 Loebsack	Y	Y	Y	N	Y	Y
3 Boswell	Y	Y	Y	N	Y	Y
4 **Latham**	Y	N	N	Y	N	N
5 **King**	Y	N	N	Y	N	N
KANSAS						
1 **Moran**	Y	N	N	Y	N	N
2 Boyda	Y	Y	Y	N	Y	Y
3 Moore	Y	Y	Y	N	Y	Y
4 **Tiahrt**	Y	N	N	+	–	N
KENTUCKY						
1 **Whitfield**	Y	N	N	Y	N	N
2 **Lewis**	Y	N	N	Y	N	N
3 Yarmuth	Y	Y	Y	N	Y	Y
4 **Davis**	Y	N	N	Y	N	N
5 **Rogers**	Y	N	N	Y	N	N
6 Chandler	Y	Y	Y	N	Y	Y
LOUISIANA						
1 Vacant						
2 Jefferson	Y	Y	Y	N	Y	Y
3 Melancon	Y	Y	Y	N	Y	Y
4 **McCrery**	Y	?	?	?	?	?
5 **Alexander**	Y	N	N	Y	N	N
6 Vacant						
7 **Boustany**	Y	N	N	Y	N	N
MAINE						
1 Allen	Y	Y	Y	N	Y	Y
2 Michaud	Y	Y	Y	N	Y	Y
MARYLAND						
1 **Gilchrest**	Y	N	N	N	Y	Y
2 Ruppersberger	Y	Y	Y	N	Y	Y
3 Sarbanes	Y	Y	Y	N	Y	Y
4 Wynn	?	?	?	N	Y	Y
5 Hoyer	Y	Y	Y	N	Y	Y
6 **Bartlett**	Y	N	N	Y	Y	N
7 Cummings	Y	Y	Y	N	Y	Y
8 Van Hollen	Y	Y	Y	N	Y	Y
MASSACHUSETTS						
1 Olver	Y	Y	Y	N	Y	Y
2 Neal	?	Y	Y	N	Y	Y
3 McGovern	Y	Y	Y	N	Y	Y
4 Frank	Y	Y	Y	N	Y	Y
5 Tsongas	Y	Y	Y	N	Y	Y
6 Tierney	Y	Y	Y	N	Y	Y
7 Markey	Y	Y	Y	N	Y	Y
8 Capuano	Y	Y	Y	N	Y	Y
9 Lynch	Y	Y	Y	N	Y	Y
10 Delahunt	Y	Y	Y	N	Y	Y
MICHIGAN						
1 Stupak	Y	Y	Y	N	Y	Y
2 **Hoekstra**	Y	N	N	Y	N	N
3 **Ehlers**	Y	N	N	N	Y	N
4 **Camp**	Y	N	N	Y	N	N
5 Kildee	Y	Y	Y	N	Y	Y
6 **Upton**	Y	N	N	N	Y	N
7 **Walberg**	Y	N	N	Y	N	N
8 **Rogers**	Y	N	N	Y	N	N
9 **Knollenberg**	Y	N	N	Y	N	N
10 **Miller**	Y	N	N	Y	Y	N
11 **McCotter**	Y	N	N	Y	N	N
12 Levin	Y	Y	Y	N	Y	Y
13 Kilpatrick	Y	Y	Y	N	Y	Y
14 Conyers	Y	Y	Y	N	Y	Y
15 Dingell	Y	Y	Y	N	Y	Y
MINNESOTA						
1 Walz	Y	Y	Y	N	Y	Y
2 **Kline**	Y	N	N	Y	N	N
3 **Ramstad**	Y	N	N	N	Y	N
4 McCollum	?	Y	Y	Y	Y	Y
5 Ellison	Y	Y	Y	N	Y	Y
6 **Bachmann**	Y	N	N	N	N	N
7 Peterson	Y	Y	Y	N	Y	Y
8 Oberstar	Y	Y	Y	N	Y	Y
MISSISSIPPI						
1 Vacant						
2 Thompson	Y	Y	Y	N	Y	Y
3 **Pickering**	Y	N	N	N	N	N
4 Taylor	Y	Y	Y	N	Y	Y
MISSOURI						
1 Clay	Y	Y	Y	N	Y	Y
2 **Akin**	Y	N	N	Y	N	N
3 Carnahan	Y	Y	Y	N	Y	Y
4 Skelton	Y	Y	Y	N	Y	Y
5 Cleaver	?	Y	Y	N	Y	Y
6 **Graves**	Y	N	N	Y	N	N
7 **Blunt**	Y	N	N	Y	N	N
8 **Emerson**	Y	N	N	N	N	N
9 **Hulshof**	Y	N	N	?	?	?
MONTANA						
AL **Rehberg**	Y	N	N	Y	N	N
NEBRASKA						
1 **Fortenberry**	Y	N	N	N	Y	N
2 **Terry**	Y	N	N	N	N	N
3 **Smith**	Y	N	N	Y	N	N
NEVADA						
1 Berkley	?	Y	Y	N	Y	Y
2 **Heller**	Y	N	N	Y	N	N
3 **Porter**	Y	N	N	N	Y	N
NEW HAMPSHIRE						
1 Shea-Porter	Y	Y	Y	N	Y	Y
2 Hodes	Y	Y	Y	N	Y	Y
NEW JERSEY						
1 Andrews	Y	Y	Y	N	Y	Y
2 **LoBiondo**	Y	N	N	N	Y	N
3 **Saxton**	Y	N	N	N	Y	N
4 **Smith**	Y	N	N	N	Y	N
5 **Garrett**	Y	N	N	Y	N	N
6 Pallone	Y	Y	Y	N	Y	Y
7 **Ferguson**	Y	N	N	N	Y	N
8 Pascrell	Y	Y	Y	N	Y	Y
9 Rothman	Y	Y	Y	N	Y	Y
10 Payne	Y	Y	Y	N	Y	Y
11 **Frelinghuysen**	Y	N	N	?	Y	N
12 Holt	Y	Y	Y	N	?	Y
13 Sires	Y	Y	Y	N	Y	Y
NEW MEXICO						
1 **Wilson**	Y	N	N	Y	N	N
2 **Pearce**	Y	N	N	Y	N	N
3 Udall	Y	Y	Y	N	Y	Y
NEW YORK						
1 Bishop	Y	Y	Y	N	Y	Y
2 Israel	Y	Y	Y	N	Y	Y
3 **King**	Y	N	N	N	N	N
4 McCarthy	Y	Y	Y	N	Y	Y
5 Ackerman	Y	Y	Y	N	Y	Y
6 Meeks	Y	Y	Y	N	Y	Y
7 Crowley	Y	Y	Y	N	Y	Y
8 Nadler	Y	Y	Y	N	Y	Y
9 Weiner	Y	Y	Y	N	Y	Y
10 Towns	Y	Y	Y	N	Y	Y
11 Clarke	Y	Y	Y	N	Y	Y
12 Velázquez	Y	Y	Y	N	Y	Y
13 **Fossella**	Y	N	N	Y	N	N
14 Maloney	Y	Y	Y	N	Y	Y
15 Rangel	?	?	?	?	?	?
16 Serrano	Y	Y	Y	N	?	Y
17 Engel	Y	Y	Y	N	Y	Y
18 Lowey	Y	Y	Y	N	Y	Y
19 Hall	Y	Y	Y	N	Y	Y
20 Gillibrand	Y	Y	Y	Y	Y	Y
21 McNulty	Y	Y	Y	N	Y	Y
22 Hinchey	Y	Y	Y	N	Y	Y
23 **McHugh**	Y	N	N	N	Y	N
24 Arcuri	?	Y	Y	N	Y	Y
25 **Walsh**	Y	N	N	N	N	N
26 **Reynolds**	Y	?	?	Y	N	N
27 Higgins	Y	Y	Y	N	Y	Y
28 Slaughter	Y	Y	Y	N	Y	Y
29 **Kuhl**	Y	N	N	Y	N	N
NORTH CAROLINA						
1 Butterfield	Y	Y	Y	N	Y	Y
2 Etheridge	Y	Y	Y	N	Y	Y
3 **Jones**	Y	N	N	Y	N	N
4 Price	Y	Y	Y	N	Y	Y
5 **Foxx**	Y	N	N	Y	N	N
6 **Coble**	Y	N	N	Y	N	N
7 McIntyre	Y	Y	Y	N	Y	Y
8 **Hayes**	Y	N	N	Y	N	N
9 **Myrick**	Y	N	N	Y	N	N
10 **McHenry**	Y	N	N	Y	N	N
11 Shuler	Y	Y	Y	N	Y	Y
12 Watt	Y	Y	Y	N	Y	Y
13 Miller	Y	Y	Y	N	Y	Y
NORTH DAKOTA						
AL Pomeroy	Y	Y	Y	N	Y	Y
OHIO						
1 **Chabot**	Y	N	N	Y	N	N
2 **Schmidt**	Y	N	N	Y	N	N
3 **Turner**	Y	N	N	N	N	N
4 **Jordan**	Y	N	N	Y	N	N
5 **Latta**	Y	N	N	N	N	N
6 Wilson	Y	Y	Y	N	Y	Y
7 **Hobson**	Y	N	N	Y	N	N
8 **Boehner**	Y	N	N	Y	N	N
9 Kaptur	Y	Y	Y	N	Y	Y
10 Kucinich	Y	Y	Y	N	Y	Y
11 Tubbs Jones	Y	Y	Y	N	Y	Y
12 **Tiberi**	Y	N	N	Y	N	N
13 Sutton	Y	Y	Y	N	Y	Y
14 **LaTourette**	Y	N	N	N	Y	N
15 **Pryce**	Y	N	N	?	?	?
16 **Regula**	Y	N	N	N	N	N
17 Ryan	Y	Y	Y	N	Y	Y
18 Space	Y	Y	Y	N	Y	Y
OKLAHOMA						
1 **Sullivan**	Y	N	N	Y	N	N
2 Boren	Y	Y	Y	N	Y	Y
3 **Lucas**	Y	N	N	Y	N	N
4 **Cole**	Y	N	N	Y	N	N
5 **Fallin**	Y	N	N	Y	N	N
OREGON						
1 Wu	?	Y	Y	N	Y	Y
2 **Walden**	Y	N	N	N	N	N
3 Blumenauer	Y	Y	Y	N	Y	Y
4 DeFazio	Y	Y	Y	N	Y	Y
5 Hooley	Y	Y	Y	N	Y	Y
PENNSYLVANIA						
1 Brady	Y	Y	Y	N	Y	Y
2 Fattah	Y	?	?	N	Y	Y
3 **English**	Y	N	N	Y	N	N
4 Altmire	Y	Y	Y	N	Y	Y
5 **Peterson**	Y	N	N	Y	Y	N
6 **Gerlach**	Y	N	N	Y	N	N
7 Sestak	Y	Y	Y	?	?	?
8 Murphy, P.	Y	Y	Y	N	Y	Y
9 **Shuster**	Y	N	N	Y	N	N
10 Carney	Y	Y	Y	N	Y	Y
11 Kanjorski	Y	Y	Y	N	Y	Y
12 Murtha	?	Y	Y	N	Y	Y
13 Schwartz	Y	Y	Y	N	Y	Y
14 Doyle	?	Y	Y	N	Y	Y
15 **Dent**	Y	N	N	Y	N	N
16 **Pitts**	Y	N	N	Y	N	N
17 Holden	?	Y	Y	N	Y	Y
18 **Murphy, T.**	Y	?	N	N	N	N
19 **Platts**	Y	N	N	N	N	N
RHODE ISLAND						
1 Kennedy	Y	?	?	N	Y	Y
2 Langevin	Y	Y	Y	N	Y	Y
SOUTH CAROLINA						
1 **Brown**	Y	N	N	Y	N	N
2 **Wilson**	Y	N	N	Y	N	N
3 **Barrett**	Y	N	N	Y	N	N
4 **Inglis**	Y	N	N	Y	N	N
5 Spratt	Y	Y	Y	N	Y	Y
6 Clyburn	Y	Y	Y	N	Y	Y
SOUTH DAKOTA						
AL Herseth Sandlin	Y	Y	Y	N	Y	Y
TENNESSEE						
1 **Davis, D.**	Y	N	N	Y	N	N
2 **Duncan**	Y	N	N	Y	N	N
3 **Wamp**	Y	N	N	Y	N	N
4 Davis, L.	Y	Y	Y	N	Y	N
5 Cooper	Y	Y	Y	N	Y	Y
6 Gordon	Y	Y	Y	N	Y	Y
7 **Blackburn**	Y	N	N	Y	N	N
8 Tanner	Y	Y	Y	N	Y	Y
9 Cohen	Y	Y	Y	N	Y	Y
TEXAS						
1 **Gohmert**	Y	N	N	Y	N	N
2 **Poe**	?	?	?	?	?	?
3 **Johnson, S.**	Y	N	N	Y	N	N
4 **Hall**	Y	N	N	Y	N	N
5 **Hensarling**	Y	N	N	Y	N	N
6 **Barton**	Y	N	N	N	N	N
7 **Culberson**	Y	N	N	Y	N	N
8 **Brady**	Y	N	N	Y	N	N
9 Green, A.	Y	Y	Y	N	Y	Y
10 **McCaul**	Y	N	N	Y	N	N
11 **Conaway**	Y	N	N	Y	N	N
12 **Granger**	Y	N	N	Y	N	N
13 **Thornberry**	Y	N	N	Y	N	N
14 **Paul**	Y	N	N	Y	N	Y
15 Hinojosa	Y	Y	Y	N	Y	Y
16 Reyes	Y	Y	Y	N	Y	Y
17 Edwards	Y	Y	Y	N	Y	Y
18 Jackson Lee	Y	Y	Y	N	+	Y
19 **Neugebauer**	Y	N	N	Y	N	N
20 Gonzalez	?	?	?	?	?	?
21 **Smith**	Y	N	N	Y	N	N
22 Lampson	Y	N	Y	N	Y	N
23 Rodriguez	Y	Y	Y	N	Y	Y
24 **Marchant**	Y	N	N	Y	N	N
25 Doggett	Y	Y	Y	N	Y	Y
26 **Burgess**	Y	N	N	Y	N	N
27 Ortiz	Y	Y	Y	N	Y	Y
28 Cuellar	Y	Y	Y	N	Y	Y
29 Green, G.	Y	Y	Y	N	Y	Y
30 Johnson, E.	+	+	+	–	+	+
31 **Carter**	Y	N	N	Y	N	N
32 **Sessions**	?	N	N	Y	N	N
UTAH						
1 **Bishop**	Y	N	N	Y	N	N
2 Matheson	Y	N	Y	N	Y	N
3 **Cannon**	Y	N	N	Y	N	N
VERMONT						
AL Welch	Y	Y	Y	N	Y	Y
VIRGINIA						
1 **Wittman**	Y	N	N	Y	N	N
2 **Drake**	Y	N	N	Y	N	N
3 Scott	Y	Y	Y	N	Y	Y
4 **Forbes**	Y	N	N	Y	N	N
5 **Goode**	Y	N	N	Y	N	N
6 **Goodlatte**	Y	N	N	Y	N	N
7 **Cantor**	Y	N	N	Y	N	N
8 Moran	Y	Y	Y	N	Y	Y
9 Boucher	Y	Y	Y	N	Y	Y
10 **Wolf**	Y	N	N	Y	N	N
11 **Davis**	Y	N	N	N	N	N
WASHINGTON						
1 Inslee	Y	Y	Y	N	Y	Y
2 Larsen	Y	Y	Y	N	Y	Y
3 Baird	Y	Y	Y	?	Y	Y
4 **Hastings**	Y	N	N	Y	N	N
5 **McMorris Rodgers**	Y	N	N	Y	N	N
6 Dicks	?	Y	Y	N	Y	Y
7 McDermott	?	Y	Y	N	Y	Y
8 **Reichert**	Y	N	N	Y	Y	N
9 Smith	Y	Y	Y	N	Y	Y
WEST VIRGINIA						
1 Mollohan	Y	Y	Y	N	Y	Y
2 **Capito**	Y	N	N	N	Y	N
3 Rahall	Y	Y	Y	N	Y	Y
WISCONSIN						
1 **Ryan**	Y	N	N	Y	N	N
2 Baldwin	Y	Y	Y	N	Y	Y
3 Kind	Y	Y	Y	N	Y	Y
4 Moore	Y	Y	Y	N	Y	Y
5 **Sensenbrenner**	Y	N	N	Y	N	N
6 **Petri**	Y	N	N	N	N	N
7 Obey	Y	Y	Y	N	Y	Y
8 Kagen	Y	Y	Y	N	Y	Y
WYOMING						
AL **Cubin**	Y	?	?	Y	N	N
DELEGATES						
Faleomavaega (A.S.)				N	Y	
Norton (D.C.)				N	Y	
Bordallo (Guam)				N	Y	
Fortuño (P.R.)				?	?	
Christensen (V.I.)				N	Y	

IN THE HOUSE | By Vote Number

108. **H Res 537. 9-1-1 Education Month/Adoption.** Davis, D-Ill., motion to suspend the rules and adopt the resolution that would support designating and observing "National 9-1-1 Education Month." Motion agreed to 381-0: R 176-0; D 205-0 (ND 159-0, SD 46-0). A two-thirds majority of those present and voting (254 in this case) is required for adoption under suspension of the rules. March 10, 2008.

109. **HR 3196. Gray Post Office/Passage.** Davis, D-Ill., motion to suspend the rules and pass the bill that would designate a post office in Port Jervis, N.Y., as the "E. Arthur Gray Post Office Building." Motion agreed to 382-0: R 175-0; D 207-0 (ND 160-0, SD 47-0). A two-thirds majority of those present and voting (255 in this case) is required for passage under suspension of the rules. March 10, 2008.

110. **HR 4166. Allee Post Office/Passage.** Davis, D-Ill., motion to suspend the rules and pass the bill that would designate a post office in Lebanon, Mo., as the "Steve W. Allee Carrier Annex." Motion agreed to 382-0: R 176-0; D 206-0 (ND 158-0, SD 48-0). A two-thirds majority of those present and voting (255 in this case) is required for passage under suspension of the rules. March 10, 2008.

111. **Procedural Motion/Motion to Adjourn.** Gohmert, R-Texas, motion to adjourn. Motion rejected 20-364: R 19-162; D 1-202 (ND 0-152, SD 1-50). March 11, 2008.

112. **Procedural Motion/Motion to Adjourn.** Westmoreland, R-Ga., motion to adjourn. Motion rejected 6-387: R 6-179; D 0-208 (ND 0-156, SD 0-52). March 11, 2008.

113. **Procedural Motion/Motion to Adjourn.** Manzullo, R-Ill., motion to adjourn. Motion rejected 5-388: R 3-183; D 2-205 (ND 2-151, SD 0-54). March 11, 2008.

114. **Procedural Motion/Motion to Adjourn.** Platts, R-Pa., motion to adjourn. Motion rejected 4-396: R 4-183; D 0-213 (ND 0-159, SD 0-54). March 11, 2008.

	108	109	110	111	112	113	114
ALABAMA							
1 Bonner	?	?	?	N	N	N	N
2 Everett	Y	Y	Y	N	N	N	N
3 Rogers	Y	Y	Y	N	N	N	N
4 Aderholt	Y	Y	Y	N	?	N	N
5 Cramer	Y	Y	Y	N	N	N	N
6 Bachus	Y	Y	Y	N	N	N	N
7 Davis	Y	Y	Y	N	N	N	N
ALASKA							
AL Young	Y	Y	Y	Y	Y	Y	Y
ARIZONA							
1 Renzi	Y	Y	Y	Y	?	N	?
2 Franks	Y	Y	Y	N	N	N	N
3 Shadegg	Y	Y	Y	N	N	N	N
4 Pastor	Y	Y	Y	N	N	N	N
5 Mitchell	+	+	+	–	–	–	–
6 Flake	Y	Y	Y	N	N	N	N
7 Grijalva	Y	Y	?	N	N	N	N
8 Giffords	Y	Y	Y	N	N	N	N
ARKANSAS							
1 Berry	?	?	?	N	N	N	N
2 Snyder	Y	Y	Y	N	N	N	N
3 Boozman	Y	Y	Y	N	N	N	N
4 Ross	Y	Y	Y	N	N	N	N
CALIFORNIA							
1 Thompson	Y	Y	Y	N	N	N	N
2 Herger	Y	Y	Y	N	N	N	N
3 Lungren	Y	Y	Y	N	N	N	N
4 Doolittle	?	?	?	Y	N	N	N
5 Matsui	Y	Y	Y	N	N	N	N
6 Woolsey	+	+	+	–	–	–	–
7 Miller, George	Y	Y	Y	N	N	N	N
8 Pelosi							
9 Lee	Y	Y	Y	N	N	N	N
10 Tauscher	Y	Y	Y	N	N	N	N
11 McNerney	Y	Y	Y	N	N	?	?
12 Vacant							
13 Stark	Y	Y	Y	?	N	N	N
14 Eshoo	Y	Y	Y	N	N	N	N
15 Honda	Y	Y	Y	N	N	N	N
16 Lofgren	Y	Y	Y	N	N	N	N
17 Farr	Y	Y	Y	N	N	N	N
18 Cardoza	Y	Y	Y	N	?	N	N
19 Radanovich	Y	Y	Y	Y	N	N	N
20 Costa	Y	Y	Y	N	N	N	N
21 Nunes	Y	Y	Y	N	N	N	N
22 McCarthy	Y	Y	Y	N	N	N	N
23 Capps	Y	Y	Y	N	N	N	N
24 Gallegly	Y	Y	Y	N	N	N	N
25 McKeon	Y	Y	Y	N	N	N	N
26 Dreier	Y	Y	Y	N	N	N	N
27 Sherman	Y	Y	Y	N	N	N	N
28 Berman	Y	Y	Y	N	N	N	?
29 Schiff	Y	Y	Y	?	N	N	N
30 Waxman	Y	Y	Y	N	N	N	N
31 Becerra	Y	Y	Y	N	N	N	N
32 Solis	Y	Y	Y	N	N	N	N
33 Watson	Y	Y	Y	N	N	N	N
34 Roybal-Allard	Y	Y	Y	N	N	N	N
35 Waters	?	?	?	N	N	N	N
36 Harman	Y	Y	Y	N	N	N	N
37 Richardson	Y	Y	Y	N	N	N	N
38 Napolitano	Y	Y	Y	N	N	N	N
39 Sánchez, Linda	Y	Y	Y	N	N	N	N
40 Royce	Y	Y	Y	?	N	N	N
41 Lewis	Y	Y	Y	N	N	N	N
42 Miller, Gary	Y	Y	Y	N	N	N	N
43 Baca	Y	Y	Y	N	N	N	N
44 Calvert	?	?	?	Y	N	N	N
45 Bono Mack	Y	Y	Y	N	N	N	N
46 Rohrabacher	?	?	?	?	N	N	N
47 Sanchez, Loretta	?	?	?	N	N	N	N
48 Campbell	Y	Y	Y	N	N	N	N
49 Issa	Y	Y	Y	N	N	N	N
50 Bilbray	Y	Y	Y	N	N	N	N
51 Filner	Y	Y	Y	N	N	N	N
52 Hunter	Y	Y	Y	N	N	N	N
53 Davis	Y	Y	Y	N	N	N	N

	108	109	110	111	112	113	114
COLORADO							
1 DeGette	Y	Y	Y	N	N	N	N
2 Udall	?	?	?	?	?	?	?
3 Salazar	Y	Y	Y	N	N	N	N
4 Musgrave	Y	Y	Y	N	N	N	N
5 Lamborn	Y	Y	Y	N	N	N	N
6 Tancredo	Y	Y	Y	Y	N	?	?
7 Perlmutter	Y	Y	Y	N	?	N	N
CONNECTICUT							
1 Larson	Y	Y	Y	N	?	N	N
2 Courtney	Y	Y	Y	N	N	N	N
3 DeLauro	Y	Y	Y	N	N	N	N
4 Shays	Y	Y	Y	N	N	N	N
5 Murphy	Y	Y	Y	N	N	N	N
DELAWARE							
AL Castle	Y	Y	Y	N	N	N	N
FLORIDA							
1 Miller	Y	Y	Y	N	N	N	N
2 Boyd	Y	Y	Y	N	N	N	N
3 Brown	?	?	?	N	N	N	N
4 Crenshaw	?	?	?	N	N	N	N
5 Brown-Waite	?	?	?	?	N	N	N
6 Stearns	Y	Y	Y	N	N	N	N
7 Mica	Y	Y	Y	N	N	N	N
8 Keller	Y	Y	Y	N	N	N	N
9 Bilirakis	Y	Y	Y	N	N	N	N
10 Young	?	?	?	?	N	N	N
11 Castor	Y	Y	Y	N	?	N	N
12 Putnam	Y	Y	Y	N	N	N	N
13 Buchanan	Y	Y	Y	N	N	N	N
14 Mack	Y	Y	Y	N	N	N	N
15 Weldon	?	?	?	?	N	?	N
16 Mahoney	Y	Y	Y	?	N	N	N
17 Meek	Y	Y	Y	?	?	N	N
18 Ros-Lehtinen	?	?	?	?	?	?	?
19 Wexler	?	?	?	?	N	N	N
20 Wasserman Schultz	Y	Y	Y	N	N	N	N
21 Diaz-Balart, L.	Y	Y	Y	N	N	N	N
22 Klein	Y	Y	Y	N	N	N	N
23 Hastings	Y	Y	Y	N	N	N	N
24 Feeney	Y	Y	Y	N	N	N	N
25 Diaz-Balart, M.	Y	Y	Y	N	N	N	N
GEORGIA							
1 Kingston	Y	Y	Y	N	N	N	N
2 Bishop	Y	Y	Y	N	N	N	N
3 Westmoreland	Y	Y	Y	N	Y	N	Y
4 Johnson	Y	Y	Y	N	N	N	N
5 Lewis	Y	Y	Y	N	N	N	N
6 Price	Y	Y	Y	N	N	N	N
7 Linder	Y	Y	Y	N	N	N	N
8 Marshall	Y	Y	Y	?	N	N	N
9 Deal	Y	Y	Y	N	N	N	N
10 Broun	Y	Y	Y	N	N	N	N
11 Gingrey	Y	Y	Y	N	N	?	?
12 Barrow	Y	Y	Y	N	N	N	N
13 Scott	Y	Y	Y	N	N	N	?
HAWAII							
1 Abercrombie	Y	Y	Y	N	N	N	N
2 Hirono	Y	Y	Y	N	N	N	N
IDAHO							
1 Sali	Y	Y	Y	N	N	N	N
2 Simpson	Y	Y	Y	N	N	N	N
ILLINOIS							
1 Rush	?	?	?	?	?	?	?
2 Jackson	Y	Y	Y	N	N	N	N
3 Lipinski	Y	Y	Y	N	N	N	N
4 Gutierrez	Y	Y	Y	N	N	N	N
5 Emanuel	Y	Y	Y	N	N	N	N
6 Roskam	Y	Y	Y	N	N	N	N
7 Davis	Y	Y	Y	N	N	?	?
8 Bean	Y	Y	Y	N	?	N	N
9 Schakowsky	Y	Y	Y	N	N	N	N
10 Kirk	Y	Y	Y	N	N	N	N
11 Weller	Y	Y	Y	N	N	N	N
12 Costello	?	?	?	N	N	N	N
13 Biggert	Y	Y	Y	N	N	N	N
14 Vacant[1]							
15 Johnson	Y	Y	Y	Y	Y	Y	Y

KEY   **Republicans**   Democrats

Y Voted for (yea)	X Paired against	C Voted "present" to avoid possible conflict of interest
# Paired for	– Announced against	
+ Announced for	P Voted "present"	? Did not vote or otherwise make a position known
N Voted against (nay)		

ND Northern Democrats, SD Southern Democrats
Southern states: Ala., Ark., Fla., Ga., Ky., La., Miss., N.C., Okla., S.C., Tenn., Texas, Va.

H-36   2008 CQ ALMANAC | www.cq.com

	108	109	110	111	112	113	114
16 **Manzullo**	Y	Y	Y	N	N	N	N
17 Hare	Y	Y	Y	N	N	N	N
18 **LaHood**	Y	Y	Y	?	N	N	N
19 **Shimkus**	Y	Y	Y	N	N	N	N
INDIANA							
1 Visclosky	Y	Y	Y	N	N	N	N
2 Donnelly	Y	Y	Y	N	N	N	N
3 **Souder**	Y	Y	Y	?	?	?	?
4 **Buyer**	?	?	?	N	N	N	N
5 **Burton**	Y	Y	Y	N	N	N	N
6 **Pence**	?	?	?	?	?	?	?
7 Vacant							
8 Ellsworth	Y	Y	Y	N	N	N	N
9 Hill	Y	Y	Y	N	N	N	N
IOWA							
1 Braley	Y	Y	Y	N	N	N	N
2 Loebsack	Y	Y	Y	N	N	N	N
3 Boswell	Y	Y	Y	N	N	N	N
4 **Latham**	Y	Y	Y	N	N	N	N
5 **King**	Y	Y	Y	Y	N	N	N
KANSAS							
1 **Moran**	Y	Y	Y	N	N	N	N
2 Boyda	Y	Y	Y	N	N	N	N
3 Moore	Y	Y	Y	N	N	N	N
4 **Tiahrt**	Y	Y	Y	N	N	N	N
KENTUCKY							
1 **Whitfield**	Y	Y	Y	Y	N	N	N
2 **Lewis**	Y	Y	Y	N	N	N	N
3 Yarmuth	Y	Y	Y	N	N	N	N
4 **Davis**	Y	Y	Y	N	N	N	N
5 **Rogers**	Y	Y	Y	N	N	N	N
6 Chandler	Y	Y	Y	N	N	N	N
LOUISIANA							
1 Vacant							
2 Jefferson	?	?	?	N	N	N	N
3 Melancon	Y	Y	Y	N	N	N	N
4 **McCrery**	?	?	?	N	?	?	N
5 **Alexander**	Y	Y	Y	N	N	N	N
6 Vacant							
7 **Boustany**	Y	Y	Y	?	N	N	N
MAINE							
1 Allen	Y	Y	Y	–	N	N	N
2 Michaud	Y	Y	Y	N	N	N	N
MARYLAND							
1 **Gilchrest**	?	?	?	N	N	?	N
2 Ruppersberger	Y	Y	Y	N	N	N	N
3 Sarbanes	Y	Y	Y	N	N	N	N
4 Wynn	Y	Y	Y	?	?	?	N
5 Hoyer	Y	Y	Y	N	N	N	N
6 **Bartlett**	Y	Y	Y	N	N	N	N
7 Cummings	Y	Y	Y	N	N	N	N
8 Van Hollen	Y	Y	Y	N	N	N	N
MASSACHUSETTS							
1 Olver	Y	Y	Y	N	N	N	N
2 Neal	?	?	?	?	?	N	N
3 McGovern	Y	Y	Y	N	N	N	N
4 Frank	Y	Y	Y	N	N	N	?
5 Tsongas	Y	Y	Y	N	N	N	N
6 Tierney	Y	Y	Y	N	N	N	N
7 Markey	Y	Y	Y	?	?	?	N
8 Capuano	Y	Y	Y	N	N	N	?
9 Lynch	?	?	?	N	N	N	N
10 Delahunt	Y	Y	Y	N	N	N	N
MICHIGAN							
1 Stupak	Y	Y	Y	N	N	N	N
2 **Hoekstra**	Y	Y	Y	N	N	N	N
3 **Ehlers**	Y	Y	Y	N	N	N	N
4 **Camp**	Y	Y	Y	N	N	N	N
5 Kildee	Y	Y	Y	N	N	N	N
6 **Upton**	Y	Y	Y	N	N	N	N
7 **Walberg**	Y	Y	Y	N	N	N	N
8 **Rogers**	Y	Y	Y	N	N	N	N
9 **Knollenberg**	Y	Y	Y	N	N	N	N
10 **Miller**	?	?	?	N	N	N	N
11 **McCotter**	Y	Y	Y	N	N	N	N
12 Levin	Y	Y	Y	N	N	N	N
13 Kilpatrick	+	+	+	?	?	?	?
14 Conyers	Y	Y	Y	N	N	N	N
15 Dingell	Y	Y	Y	N	N	N	N
MINNESOTA							
1 Walz	Y	Y	Y	N	N	N	N
2 **Kline**	Y	Y	Y	?	N	N	N
3 **Ramstad**	Y	Y	Y	N	N	N	N
4 McCollum	Y	Y	Y	N	N	N	N
5 Ellison	Y	Y	Y	N	N	N	N
6 **Bachmann**	Y	Y	Y	N	N	N	N
7 Peterson	Y	Y	Y	N	N	N	N
8 Oberstar	?	?	?	?	?	?	?
MISSISSIPPI							
1 Vacant							
2 Thompson	?	?	?	?	?	?	?
3 **Pickering**	Y	Y	Y	N	N	N	N
4 Taylor	?	?	?	N	N	N	N
MISSOURI							
1 Clay	Y	Y	Y	N	N	N	N
2 **Akin**	Y	Y	Y	N	N	N	N
3 Carnahan	Y	Y	Y	N	N	N	N
4 Skelton	Y	Y	Y	N	N	N	N
5 Cleaver	Y	Y	Y	N	N	Y	N
6 **Graves**	Y	Y	Y	N	N	N	N
7 **Blunt**	Y	Y	Y	N	N	N	?
8 **Emerson**	Y	?	Y	N	N	N	N
9 **Hulshof**	?	?	?	N	N	N	N
MONTANA							
AL **Rehberg**	Y	Y	Y	N	N	N	N
NEBRASKA							
1 **Fortenberry**	Y	Y	Y	N	N	N	N
2 **Terry**	Y	Y	Y	N	N	N	N
3 **Smith**	Y	Y	Y	N	N	N	N
NEVADA							
1 Berkley	Y	Y	Y	N	N	N	N
2 **Heller**	Y	Y	Y	N	N	N	N
3 **Porter**	Y	Y	Y	N	N	N	N
NEW HAMPSHIRE							
1 Shea-Porter	Y	Y	Y	N	N	?	N
2 Hodes	Y	Y	Y	N	N	N	N
NEW JERSEY							
1 Andrews	Y	Y	Y	N	N	N	N
2 **LoBiondo**	Y	Y	Y	N	N	N	N
3 **Saxton**	Y	Y	Y	N	N	N	N
4 **Smith**	Y	Y	Y	N	N	N	N
5 **Garrett**	Y	Y	Y	N	?	?	N
6 Pallone	Y	Y	Y	N	N	N	N
7 **Ferguson**	Y	Y	Y	N	N	N	N
8 Pascrell	Y	Y	Y	N	?	N	N
9 Rothman	Y	Y	Y	N	N	N	N
10 Payne	Y	Y	Y	N	N	N	N
11 **Frelinghuysen**	Y	Y	Y	N	N	N	N
12 Holt	Y	Y	Y	N	N	N	N
13 Sires	Y	Y	Y	N	N	N	N
NEW MEXICO							
1 **Wilson**	+	+	+	N	N	N	N
2 **Pearce**	Y	Y	Y	Y	N	N	N
3 Udall	Y	Y	Y	N	N	N	N
NEW YORK							
1 Bishop	Y	Y	Y	N	N	N	N
2 Israel	Y	Y	Y	N	N	N	N
3 **King**	Y	Y	Y	N	N	N	N
4 McCarthy	Y	Y	Y	N	N	N	N
5 Ackerman	Y	Y	Y	N	N	N	N
6 Meeks	Y	Y	Y	N	N	?	N
7 Crowley	Y	Y	Y	N	N	N	N
8 Nadler	Y	Y	Y	N	N	N	N
9 Weiner	Y	Y	Y	?	N	N	N
10 Towns	Y	Y	Y	N	N	N	N
11 Clarke	Y	Y	Y	N	N	N	N
12 Velázquez	Y	Y	Y	N	N	?	N
13 **Fossella**	Y	Y	Y	N	N	N	N
14 Maloney	Y	Y	Y	N	N	N	N
15 Rangel	?	?	?	?	?	?	?
16 Serrano	Y	Y	Y	N	N	N	N
17 Engel	Y	Y	Y	N	N	N	N
18 Lowey	Y	Y	Y	N	N	N	N
19 Hall	Y	Y	Y	N	N	N	N
20 Gillibrand	Y	Y	Y	N	N	N	N
21 McNulty	Y	Y	Y	N	N	N	N
22 Hinchey	Y	Y	Y	N	?	?	N
23 **McHugh**	Y	Y	Y	N	N	N	N
24 Arcuri	Y	Y	Y	N	N	N	N
25 **Walsh**	?	?	?	N	N	N	N
26 **Reynolds**	Y	Y	Y	N	N	N	N
27 Higgins	Y	Y	Y	?	N	N	N
28 Slaughter	Y	Y	Y	N	N	N	N
29 **Kuhl**	Y	Y	Y	N	N	N	N
NORTH CAROLINA							
1 Butterfield	Y	Y	Y	N	N	N	N
2 Etheridge	Y	Y	Y	N	N	N	N
3 **Jones**	Y	Y	Y	N	N	N	N
4 Price	Y	Y	Y	N	N	N	N
5 **Foxx**	Y	Y	Y	N	N	N	N
6 **Coble**	Y	Y	Y	Y	Y	N	N
7 McIntyre	Y	Y	Y	N	N	N	N
8 **Hayes**	Y	Y	Y	N	N	N	N
9 **Myrick**	Y	Y	Y	–	Y	N	N
10 **McHenry**	Y	Y	Y	N	N	N	N
11 Shuler	Y	Y	Y	N	N	N	N
12 Watt	Y	Y	Y	N	N	N	N
13 Miller	Y	Y	Y	N	N	N	N
NORTH DAKOTA							
AL Pomeroy	Y	Y	Y	N	N	N	N
OHIO							
1 **Chabot**	Y	Y	Y	N	N	N	N
2 **Schmidt**	Y	Y	Y	N	N	N	N
3 **Turner**	Y	?	?	N	N	N	N
4 **Jordan**	Y	Y	Y	N	N	N	N
5 **Latta**	Y	Y	Y	N	N	N	N
6 Wilson	Y	Y	Y	N	N	N	N
7 **Hobson**	Y	Y	Y	N	N	N	N
8 **Boehner**	Y	Y	Y	N	N	N	?
9 Kaptur	Y	Y	Y	N	N	?	N
10 Kucinich	Y	Y	Y	N	N	N	N
11 Tubbs Jones	Y	Y	Y	?	?	N	N
12 **Tiberi**	Y	Y	Y	N	N	N	N
13 Sutton	Y	Y	Y	N	N	N	N
14 **LaTourette**	Y	Y	Y	N	N	N	N
15 **Pryce**	?	?	?	?	?	?	?
16 **Regula**	Y	Y	Y	N	N	N	N
17 Ryan	Y	Y	Y	N	N	N	N
18 Space	Y	Y	Y	N	N	N	N
OKLAHOMA							
1 **Sullivan**	?	Y	Y	N	N	N	N
2 Boren	?	Y	Y	N	N	N	N
3 **Lucas**	Y	Y	Y	N	N	N	N
4 **Cole**	Y	Y	Y	N	N	N	N
5 **Fallin**	Y	Y	Y	N	N	N	N
OREGON							
1 Wu	Y	Y	Y	N	N	N	N
2 **Walden**	Y	Y	Y	N	N	N	N
3 Blumenauer	Y	Y	Y	N	N	N	?
4 DeFazio	Y	Y	Y	N	N	N	N
5 Hooley	?	?	?	?	?	?	?
PENNSYLVANIA							
1 Brady	Y	Y	Y	N	N	N	N
2 Fattah	Y	Y	Y	N	N	N	N
3 **English**	Y	Y	Y	N	N	N	N
4 Altmire	Y	Y	Y	N	N	N	N
5 **Peterson**	?	?	?	?	?	?	N
6 **Gerlach**	Y	Y	Y	N	N	N	N
7 Sestak	Y	Y	Y	N	N	N	N
8 Murphy, P.	Y	Y	Y	N	N	N	N
9 **Shuster**	Y	Y	Y	Y	N	N	N
10 Carney	Y	Y	Y	N	N	N	N
11 Kanjorski	Y	Y	Y	N	N	N	N
12 Murtha	Y	Y	?	N	N	N	N
13 Schwartz	Y	Y	Y	N	N	N	N
14 Doyle	Y	Y	Y	N	N	N	N
15 **Dent**	Y	Y	Y	N	N	N	N
16 **Pitts**	Y	Y	Y	N	N	N	N
17 Holden	Y	Y	Y	N	?	?	N
18 **Murphy, T.**	Y	Y	Y	N	N	N	N
19 **Platts**	Y	Y	Y	N	N	N	N
RHODE ISLAND							
1 Kennedy	Y	Y	Y	N	N	N	N
2 Langevin	?	Y	Y	N	N	N	N
SOUTH CAROLINA							
1 **Brown**	Y	Y	Y	N	N	N	N
2 **Wilson**	Y	Y	Y	Y	N	N	N
3 **Barrett**	Y	Y	Y	N	N	N	N
4 **Inglis**	Y	Y	Y	N	N	N	N
5 Spratt	Y	Y	Y	N	N	N	N
6 Clyburn	Y	Y	Y	N	N	N	N
SOUTH DAKOTA							
AL Herseth Sandlin	Y	Y	Y	N	N	N	N
TENNESSEE							
1 **Davis, D.**	Y	Y	Y	Y	N	N	N
2 **Duncan**	Y	Y	Y	N	N	N	N
3 **Wamp**	Y	Y	Y	N	N	N	N
4 Davis, L.	Y	Y	Y	?	?	?	?
5 Cooper	Y	Y	Y	N	N	?	N
6 Gordon	Y	Y	Y	Y	N	N	N
7 **Blackburn**	Y	Y	Y	?	?	?	?
8 Tanner	Y	Y	Y	N	N	N	N
9 Cohen	+	+	+	N	N	N	N
TEXAS							
1 **Gohmert**	Y	Y	Y	Y	Y	Y	Y
2 **Poe**	Y	Y	Y	?	N	N	N
3 **Johnson, S.**	Y	Y	Y	N	N	N	N
4 **Hall**	Y	Y	Y	N	N	N	N
5 **Hensarling**	Y	Y	Y	N	N	N	N
6 **Barton**	Y	Y	Y	N	?	N	N
7 **Culberson**	Y	Y	Y	N	N	N	N
8 **Brady**	Y	Y	Y	N	N	N	N
9 Green, A.	Y	Y	Y	N	N	N	N
10 **McCaul**	Y	Y	Y	Y	N	N	N
11 **Conaway**	Y	Y	Y	N	N	N	N
12 **Granger**	Y	Y	Y	N	?	N	N
13 **Thornberry**	Y	Y	Y	N	N	N	N
14 **Paul**	Y	Y	Y	N	N	N	N
15 Hinojosa	Y	Y	Y	N	N	N	N
16 Reyes	Y	Y	Y	N	N	N	N
17 Edwards	Y	Y	Y	N	N	N	N
18 Jackson Lee	Y	Y	Y	N	N	N	N
19 **Neugebauer**	Y	Y	Y	N	N	N	N
20 Gonzalez	Y	Y	Y	N	N	N	N
21 **Smith**	Y	Y	Y	N	N	N	N
22 Lampson	Y	Y	Y	N	N	N	N
23 Rodriguez	?	?	Y	N	N	N	N
24 **Marchant**	?	?	?	Y	N	N	N
25 Doggett	Y	Y	Y	N	N	N	N
26 **Burgess**	Y	Y	Y	N	N	N	N
27 Ortiz	Y	Y	Y	N	N	N	N
28 Cuellar	?	?	?	N	N	N	N
29 Green, G.	Y	Y	Y	N	N	N	N
30 Johnson, E.	Y	Y	Y	N	N	N	N
31 **Carter**	Y	Y	Y	N	N	N	N
32 **Sessions**	Y	Y	Y	N	N	N	N
UTAH							
1 **Bishop**	Y	Y	Y	Y	N	N	N
2 Matheson	Y	Y	Y	N	N	N	N
3 **Cannon**	Y	Y	Y	N	N	N	N
VERMONT							
AL Welch	Y	Y	Y	N	N	N	N
VIRGINIA							
1 **Wittman**	Y	Y	Y	N	N	N	N
2 **Drake**	Y	Y	Y	?	N	N	N
3 Scott	Y	Y	Y	N	N	N	N
4 **Forbes**	Y	Y	Y	N	N	N	N
5 **Goode**	Y	Y	Y	N	N	N	N
6 **Goodlatte**	Y	Y	Y	N	N	N	N
7 **Cantor**	Y	Y	Y	N	N	N	N
8 Moran	?	?	?	N	N	N	N
9 Boucher	Y	Y	Y	N	?	N	N
10 **Wolf**	Y	Y	Y	N	N	N	N
11 **Davis**	?	?	?	N	N	N	N
WASHINGTON							
1 Inslee	Y	Y	Y	N	N	N	N
2 Larsen	Y	Y	Y	N	N	N	N
3 Baird	Y	Y	Y	N	N	Y	N
4 **Hastings**	Y	Y	Y	N	N	N	N
5 **McMorris Rodgers**	Y	Y	Y	N	N	N	N
6 Dicks	Y	Y	Y	N	N	N	N
7 McDermott	Y	Y	Y	N	N	N	N
8 **Reichert**	Y	Y	Y	Y	N	N	N
9 Smith	Y	Y	Y	?	N	N	N
WEST VIRGINIA							
1 Mollohan	Y	Y	Y	N	N	N	N
2 **Capito**	Y	Y	Y	N	N	?	?
3 Rahall	Y	Y	Y	?	N	N	N
WISCONSIN							
1 **Ryan**	Y	Y	Y	N	N	N	N
2 Baldwin	Y	Y	Y	N	N	N	N
3 Kind	Y	Y	Y	N	N	N	N
4 Moore	Y	Y	Y	N	N	N	N
5 **Sensenbrenner**	Y	Y	Y	N	N	N	N
6 **Petri**	Y	Y	Y	N	N	N	N
7 Obey	Y	Y	Y	?	N	N	N
8 Kagen	Y	Y	Y	N	N	N	N
WYOMING							
AL **Cubin**	?	?	?	N	?	N	N
DELEGATES							
Faleomavaega (A.S.)							
Norton (D.C.)							
Bordallo (Guam)							
Fortuño (P.R.)							
Christensen (V.I.)							

IN THE HOUSE | By Vote Number

115. **H Res 924. Iowa State University of Science and Technology Tribute/Adoption.** Loebsack, D-Iowa, motion to suspend the rules and adopt the resolution that would congratulate Iowa State University of Science and Technology for 150 years of service as Iowa's land-grant university. Motion agreed to 405-0: R 189-0; D 216-0 (ND 162-0, SD 54-0). A two-thirds majority of those present and voting (270 in this case) is required for adoption under suspension of the rules. March 11, 2008.

116. **HR 3773. Foreign Intelligence Surveillance/Appeal Ruling of the Chair.** Hoyer, D-Md., motion to table (kill) the Price, R-Ga., appeal of the ruling of the chair that the Price draft resolution does not constitute a point of privilege under Rule IX of the House. The draft resolution would express the sense of the House that it should immediately consider a Senate-passed bill (HR 3773) that would amend the Foreign Intelligence Surveillance Act. Motion agreed to 218-192: R 1-188; D 217-4 (ND 165-0, SD 52-4). March 11, 2008.

117. **HR 2082. Fiscal 2008 Intelligence Authorization/Veto Override.** Passage, over President Bush's March 8, 2008, veto, of the bill that would authorize classified amounts in fiscal 2008 for 17 U.S. intelligence agencies and activities, including the CIA, the Office of the Director of National Intelligence and the National Security Agency. It would authorize funds for the intelligence portion of the fiscal 2008 emergency supplemental for the wars in Iraq and Afghanistan. It would prohibit the use of any interrogation treatment not authorized by the U.S. Army Field Manual on Human Intelligence Collector Operations against any individual in the custody of the intelligence community. Rejected 225-188: R 5-185; D 220-3 (ND 165-2, SD 55-1). A two-thirds majority of those present and voting (276 in this case for the House) of both chambers is required to override a veto. A "nay" was a vote in support of the president's position. March 11, 2008.

118. **H Res 948. University of Kansas Football Team Tribute/Adoption.** Loebsack, D-Iowa, motion to suspend the rules and adopt the resolution that would congratulate the University of Kansas football team for winning the 2008 FedEx Orange Bowl and having the most successful year in program history. Motion agreed to 396-0: R 183-0; D 213-0 (ND 161-0, SD 52-0). A two-thirds majority of those present and voting (264 in this case) is required for adoption under suspension of the rules. March 11, 2008.

119. **H Res 493. University of California Women's Water Polo Team Tribute/Adoption.** Loebsack, D-Iowa, motion to suspend the rules and adopt the resolution that would congratulate the University of California, Los Angeles, women's water polo team for winning the 2007 NCAA Division I Women's Water Polo National Championship and the school on its 100th NCAA sports national title. Motion agreed to 400-0: R 187-0; D 213-0 (ND 163-0, SD 50-0). A two-thirds majority of those present and voting (267 in this case) is required for adoption under suspension of the rules. March 11, 2008.

120. **Procedural Motion/Motion to Adjourn.** Abercrombie, D-Hawaii, motion to adjourn. Motion rejected 177-196: R 163-11; D 14-185 (ND 7-144, SD 7-41). March 11, 2008.

121. **H Res 895. House Ethics Panel/Previous Question.** Sutton, D-Ohio, motion to order the previous question (thus ending debate and possibility of amendment) on adoption of the self-executing rule (H Res 1031) to provide for automatic adoption of the resolution that would establish an Office of Congressional Ethics to consider alleged violations by House members and employees. Motion agreed to 207-206: R 4-188; D 203-18 (ND 155-12, SD 48-6). March 11, 2008.

*Rep. Bill Foster, D-Ill., was sworn in March 11, 2008, to fill the seat vacated by Republican J. Dennis Hastert, who resigned Nov. 26, 2007. The first vote for which Foster was eligible was 116.

ND Northern Democrats, SD Southern Democrats
Southern states: Ala., Ark., Fla., Ga., Ky., La., Miss., N.C., Okla., S.C., Tenn., Texas, Va.

	115	116	117	118	119	120	121
ALABAMA							
1 Bonner	Y	N	N	Y	Y	Y	N
2 Everett	Y	N	N	Y	Y	?	N
3 Rogers	Y	N	N	Y	Y	Y	N
4 Aderholt	Y	N	N	Y	Y	Y	N
5 Cramer	Y	Y	Y	Y	Y	N	Y
6 Bachus	Y	N	N	Y	Y	?	N
7 Davis	Y	Y	Y	Y	Y	?	Y
ALASKA							
AL Young	Y	N	N	Y	Y	Y	N
ARIZONA							
1 Renzi	?	N	N	Y	Y	?	?
2 Franks	Y	N	N	Y	Y	?	N
3 Shadegg	Y	N	N	Y	Y	Y	N
4 Pastor	Y	Y	Y	Y	Y	N	Y
5 Mitchell	+	+	+	+	+	−	+
6 Flake	Y	N	N	Y	Y	Y	N
7 Grijalva	Y	Y	Y	Y	Y	?	Y
8 Giffords	Y	Y	Y	Y	Y	N	Y
ARKANSAS							
1 Berry	Y	Y	Y	Y	Y	Y	Y
2 Snyder	Y	Y	Y	Y	Y	N	Y
3 Boozman	Y	N	N	Y	Y	Y	N
4 Ross	Y	Y	Y	Y	Y	Y	Y
CALIFORNIA							
1 Thompson	Y	Y	Y	Y	Y	N	Y
2 Herger	Y	N	N	Y	Y	Y	N
3 Lungren	Y	N	N	Y	Y	Y	N
4 Doolittle	Y	N	N	Y	Y	Y	N
5 Matsui	Y	Y	Y	Y	Y	N	Y
6 Woolsey	+	+	+	+	+	+	+
7 Miller, George	Y	?	Y	Y	Y	?	Y
8 Pelosi			Y				Y
9 Lee	Y	Y	Y	Y	Y	N	Y
10 Tauscher	Y	Y	Y	Y	Y	N	Y
11 McNerney	Y	Y	Y	Y	Y	N	Y
12 Vacant							
13 Stark	Y	Y	Y	Y	Y	?	Y
14 Eshoo	Y	Y	Y	Y	Y	N	Y
15 Honda	Y	Y	Y	Y	Y	N	Y
16 Lofgren	Y	Y	Y	Y	Y	N	Y
17 Farr	Y	Y	Y	Y	Y	N	Y
18 Cardoza	Y	Y	Y	Y	Y	N	Y
19 Radanovich	Y	N	?	?	?	?	?
20 Costa	Y	Y	Y	Y	Y	?	Y
21 Nunes	Y	N	N	Y	Y	Y	N
22 McCarthy	Y	N	N	Y	Y	Y	N
23 Capps	Y	Y	Y	Y	Y	N	Y
24 Gallegly	Y	N	N	Y	Y	Y	N
25 McKeon	Y	N	N	Y	Y	Y	N
26 Dreier	Y	N	N	Y	Y	Y	N
27 Sherman	Y	Y	Y	Y	Y	N	Y
28 Berman	Y	Y	Y	Y	Y	N	Y
29 Schiff	Y	Y	Y	Y	Y	N	Y
30 Waxman	Y	Y	Y	Y	Y	N	Y
31 Becerra	Y	Y	Y	Y	Y	N	Y
32 Solis	Y	Y	Y	Y	Y	−	Y
33 Watson	Y	Y	Y	Y	Y	N	Y
34 Roybal-Allard	Y	Y	Y	Y	Y	N	Y
35 Waters	Y	Y	N	Y	Y	?	N
36 Harman	Y	Y	Y	Y	Y	N	Y
37 Richardson	Y	Y	Y	Y	Y	N	Y
38 Napolitano	Y	Y	Y	Y	Y	N	Y
39 Sánchez, Linda	Y	Y	Y	Y	Y	N	Y
40 Royce	Y	N	N	Y	Y	Y	N
41 Lewis	Y	N	N	Y	Y	Y	N
42 Miller, Gary	Y	N	N	Y	Y	Y	N
43 Baca	Y	Y	Y	Y	Y	N	Y
44 Calvert	Y	N	N	Y	Y	Y	N
45 Bono Mack	Y	N	N	Y	Y	Y	N
46 Rohrabacher	Y	N	N	Y	Y	Y	N
47 Sanchez, Loretta	Y	Y	Y	Y	Y	Y	Y
48 Campbell	Y	N	N	Y	Y	Y	N
49 Issa	Y	N	N	Y	Y	Y	N
50 Bilbray	Y	N	N	Y	Y	Y	N
51 Filner	Y	Y	Y	Y	Y	N	Y
52 Hunter	Y	N	N	Y	Y	Y	N
53 Davis	Y	Y	Y	Y	Y	N	Y

	115	116	117	118	119	120	121
COLORADO							
1 DeGette	Y	Y	Y	Y	Y	N	Y
2 Udall	Y	Y	Y	Y	Y	?	Y
3 Salazar	Y	Y	Y	Y	Y	N	Y
4 Musgrave	Y	N	N	Y	Y	Y	N
5 Lamborn	Y	N	N	Y	Y	Y	N
6 Tancredo	?	?	?	?	?	?	?
7 Perlmutter	Y	Y	Y	Y	Y	N	Y
CONNECTICUT							
1 Larson	Y	Y	Y	Y	Y	N	Y
2 Courtney	Y	Y	Y	Y	Y	N	Y
3 DeLauro	Y	Y	Y	Y	?	?	Y
4 Shays	Y	N	N	Y	Y	N	N
5 Murphy	Y	Y	Y	Y	Y	N	Y
DELAWARE							
AL Castle	Y	N	N	Y	Y	Y	Y
FLORIDA							
1 Miller	Y	N	N	Y	Y	N	N
2 Boyd	Y	Y	Y	Y	Y	N	N
3 Brown	Y	N	Y	Y	Y	N	N
4 Crenshaw	Y	N	N	Y	Y	Y	N
5 Brown-Waite	Y	N	N	Y	Y	Y	N
6 Stearns	Y	N	N	Y	Y	N	N
7 Mica	Y	N	N	Y	Y	Y	N
8 Keller	Y	N	N	Y	Y	N	N
9 Bilirakis	Y	N	N	Y	Y	N	N
10 Young	Y	N	N	Y	Y	Y	N
11 Castor	Y	Y	Y	Y	Y	N	Y
12 Putnam	Y	N	N	Y	Y	Y	N
13 Buchanan	Y	N	N	Y	Y	N	N
14 Mack	Y	N	N	Y	Y	Y	N
15 Weldon	Y	N	N	Y	Y	N	N
16 Mahoney	Y	Y	Y	Y	Y	N	Y
17 Meek	Y	Y	Y	Y	Y	N	Y
18 Ros-Lehtinen	?	?	?	?	?	?	?
19 Wexler	Y	Y	Y	Y	Y	N	Y
20 Wasserman Schultz	Y	Y	Y	Y	?	N	Y
21 Diaz-Balart, L.	Y	N	N	Y	Y	N	N
22 Klein	Y	Y	Y	Y	Y	−	Y
23 Hastings	Y	Y	Y	Y	Y	N	Y
24 Feeney	Y	N	N	Y	Y	?	N
25 Diaz-Balart, M.	Y	N	N	Y	Y	N	N
GEORGIA							
1 Kingston	Y	N	N	Y	Y	Y	N
2 Bishop	Y	Y	Y	Y	Y	N	Y
3 Westmoreland	Y	N	N	Y	Y	Y	N
4 Johnson	Y	Y	Y	Y	Y	N	Y
5 Lewis	Y	Y	Y	Y	?	?	Y
6 Price	Y	N	N	Y	Y	Y	N
7 Linder	Y	N	N	Y	Y	Y	N
8 Marshall	Y	Y	Y	Y	Y	N	Y
9 Deal	Y	N	N	Y	Y	Y	N
10 Broun	Y	N	N	Y	Y	Y	N
11 Gingrey	Y	N	N	Y	Y	?	N
12 Barrow	Y	N	N	Y	Y	N	Y
13 Scott	?	Y	Y	Y	Y	N	Y
HAWAII							
1 Abercrombie	Y	Y	Y	Y	Y	Y	Y
2 Hirono	Y	Y	Y	Y	Y	N	Y
IDAHO							
1 Sali	Y	N	N	Y	Y	Y	N
2 Simpson	Y	N	N	Y	Y	Y	N
ILLINOIS							
1 Rush	?	?	?	?	?	?	?
2 Jackson	Y	Y	Y	Y	Y	N	Y
3 Lipinski	Y	Y	Y	Y	Y	N	Y
4 Gutierrez	Y	Y	Y	Y	Y	?	Y
5 Emanuel	Y	Y	Y	Y	Y	N	Y
6 Roskam	Y	N	N	Y	Y	Y	N
7 Davis	?	Y	Y	Y	Y	N	Y
8 Bean	Y	Y	Y	Y	Y	N	Y
9 Schakowsky	Y	Y	Y	Y	Y	N	Y
10 Kirk	Y	N	N	Y	Y	Y	N
11 Weller	Y	N	N	Y	Y	Y	N
12 Costello	Y	Y	Y	Y	Y	N	Y
13 Biggert	Y	N	N	Y	Y	Y	N
14 Foster*		Y	Y	Y	Y	N	Y
15 Johnson	Y	P	Y	Y	Y	P	Y

	115	116	117	118	119	120	121
16 **Manzullo**	Y	N	N	Y	Y	Y	N
17 Hare	Y	Y	Y	Y	Y	N	Y
18 **LaHood**	Y	N	N	Y	Y	Y	N
19 **Shimkus**	Y	N	N	Y	Y	Y	N
INDIANA							
1 Visclosky	Y	Y	Y	Y	Y	N	Y
2 Donnelly	Y	Y	Y	Y	Y	N	Y
3 **Souder**	?	?	N	Y	Y	Y	N
4 **Buyer**	Y	N	N	Y	Y	Y	N
5 **Burton**	Y	N	N	Y	Y	Y	N
6 **Pence**	?	?	N	Y	Y	Y	N
7 Vacant							
8 Ellsworth	Y	?	Y	Y	Y	N	Y
9 Hill	?	Y	Y	Y	?	N	N
IOWA							
1 Braley	Y	Y	Y	Y	Y	N	Y
2 Loebsack	Y	Y	Y	Y	Y	N	Y
3 Boswell	Y	Y	Y	Y	Y	N	Y
4 **Latham**	Y	N	N	Y	Y	Y	N
5 **King**	Y	N	N	Y	Y	Y	N
KANSAS							
1 **Moran**	Y	N	N	Y	Y	N	N
2 Boyda	Y	Y	Y	Y	Y	N	Y
3 Moore	Y	Y	Y	Y	Y	N	Y
4 **Tiahrt**	Y	N	N	Y	+	Y	N
KENTUCKY							
1 **Whitfield**	Y	N	N	Y	Y	Y	N
2 **Lewis**	Y	N	N	Y	Y	?	N
3 Yarmuth	Y	Y	Y	Y	Y	?	Y
4 **Davis**	Y	N	?	Y	Y	Y	N
5 **Rogers**	Y	N	N	Y	Y	?	N
6 Chandler	Y	Y	Y	Y	Y	Y	N
LOUISIANA							
1 Vacant							
2 Jefferson	Y	Y	Y	Y	Y	Y	Y
3 Melancon	Y	Y	Y	Y	?	N	N
4 **McCrery**	Y	N	N	?	?	?	N
5 **Alexander**	Y	N	N	?	?	?	N
6 Vacant							
7 **Boustany**	Y	N	N	Y	Y	Y	N
MAINE							
1 Allen	Y	Y	Y	Y	Y	N	Y
2 Michaud	Y	Y	Y	Y	Y	Y	Y
MARYLAND							
1 **Gilchrest**	Y	N	Y	Y	Y	Y	N
2 Ruppersberger	Y	Y	Y	Y	Y	N	Y
3 Sarbanes	Y	Y	Y	Y	Y	N	Y
4 Wynn	Y	Y	Y	Y	Y	?	?
5 Hoyer	Y	Y	Y	Y	Y	N	Y
6 **Bartlett**	Y	N	Y	Y	Y	Y	N
7 Cummings	Y	Y	Y	Y	Y	N	Y
8 Van Hollen	Y	Y	Y	Y	Y	N	Y
MASSACHUSETTS							
1 Olver	Y	Y	Y	Y	Y	N	Y
2 Neal	Y	Y	Y	Y	Y	N	Y
3 McGovern	Y	Y	Y	Y	Y	N	Y
4 Frank	?	Y	Y	Y	Y	N	Y
5 Tsongas	Y	Y	Y	Y	Y	N	Y
6 Tierney	Y	Y	Y	Y	Y	N	Y
7 Markey	Y	Y	Y	Y	Y	N	Y
8 Capuano	Y	Y	Y	Y	Y	N	Y
9 Lynch	Y	Y	Y	Y	Y	N	Y
10 Delahunt	Y	Y	Y	Y	Y	N	Y
MICHIGAN							
1 Stupak	Y	Y	Y	Y	Y	Y	Y
2 **Hoekstra**	Y	N	N	Y	Y	?	N
3 **Ehlers**	Y	N	N	Y	Y	Y	N
4 **Camp**	Y	N	N	Y	Y	Y	N
5 Kildee	Y	Y	Y	Y	Y	N	Y
6 **Upton**	Y	N	N	Y	Y	Y	N
7 **Walberg**	Y	N	N	Y	Y	Y	N
8 **Rogers**	Y	N	N	Y	Y	Y	N
9 **Knollenberg**	Y	N	N	Y	Y	Y	N
10 **Miller**	Y	N	N	Y	Y	Y	N
11 **McCotter**	Y	N	N	Y	Y	N	N
12 Levin	Y	Y	Y	Y	Y	N	Y
13 Kilpatrick	?	?	?	?	?	?	?
14 Conyers	Y	Y	Y	Y	Y	N	Y
15 Dingell	Y	Y	Y	?	?	?	N
MINNESOTA							
1 Walz	Y	Y	Y	Y	Y	N	Y
2 **Kline**	Y	N	N	Y	Y	Y	N
3 **Ramstad**	Y	N	N	Y	Y	N	Y
4 McCollum	Y	Y	Y	Y	Y	N	Y

	115	116	117	118	119	120	121
5 Ellison	Y	Y	Y	Y	Y	N	Y
6 **Bachmann**	Y	N	N	Y	?	Y	N
7 Peterson	Y	Y	Y	Y	Y	?	Y
8 Oberstar	?	?	?	?	?	?	?
MISSISSIPPI							
1 Vacant							
2 Thompson	?	?	?	?	?	?	?
3 **Pickering**	Y	N	N	Y	Y	Y	N
4 Taylor	Y	Y	Y	Y	Y	Y	Y
MISSOURI							
1 Clay	Y	Y	Y	P	Y	?	N
2 **Akin**	Y	N	N	P	Y	Y	N
3 Carnahan	Y	Y	Y	P	Y	N	Y
4 Skelton	Y	Y	Y	P	Y	N	N
5 Cleaver	Y	Y	Y	P	Y	N	Y
6 **Graves**	Y	N	N	P	Y	?	N
7 **Blunt**	Y	N	N	P	Y	Y	N
8 **Emerson**	Y	N	N	P	Y	?	N
9 **Hulshof**	Y	N	N	P	Y	Y	N
MONTANA							
AL **Rehberg**	Y	N	N	Y	Y	Y	N
NEBRASKA							
1 **Fortenberry**	Y	N	N	Y	Y	Y	N
2 **Terry**	Y	N	N	Y	Y	Y	N
3 **Smith**	Y	N	N	P	Y	Y	N
NEVADA							
1 Berkley	Y	Y	Y	Y	Y	N	Y
2 **Heller**	Y	N	N	Y	Y	Y	N
3 **Porter**	Y	N	N	Y	Y	Y	N
NEW HAMPSHIRE							
1 Shea-Porter	Y	Y	Y	Y	Y	N	Y
2 Hodes	Y	Y	Y	Y	Y	N	Y
NEW JERSEY							
1 Andrews	Y	Y	Y	Y	Y	N	Y
2 **LoBiondo**	Y	N	N	Y	Y	Y	N
3 **Saxton**	Y	N	N	Y	Y	Y	N
4 **Smith**	Y	N	Y	Y	Y	Y	N
5 **Garrett**	Y	N	N	Y	Y	Y	N
6 Pallone	Y	Y	Y	Y	Y	N	Y
7 **Ferguson**	Y	N	N	Y	Y	Y	N
8 Pascrell	Y	Y	Y	Y	Y	N	Y
9 Rothman	Y	Y	Y	Y	?	N	Y
10 Payne	Y	Y	Y	Y	Y	N	Y
11 **Frelinghuysen**	Y	N	N	Y	Y	Y	N
12 Holt	Y	Y	Y	Y	Y	N	Y
13 Sires	Y	Y	Y	Y	Y	N	Y
NEW MEXICO							
1 **Wilson**	Y	N	N	Y	Y	Y	N
2 **Pearce**	Y	N	N	Y	Y	N	N
3 Udall	Y	Y	Y	Y	Y	N	Y
NEW YORK							
1 Bishop	Y	Y	Y	Y	Y	N	Y
2 Israel	Y	Y	Y	Y	Y	N	Y
3 **King**	Y	N	N	Y	Y	Y	N
4 McCarthy	Y	Y	Y	Y	Y	N	Y
5 Ackerman	Y	Y	Y	Y	Y	N	Y
6 Meeks	Y	Y	Y	Y	Y	N	N
7 Crowley	Y	Y	Y	Y	Y	N	Y
8 Nadler	Y	Y	Y	Y	Y	N	Y
9 Weiner	Y	Y	Y	Y	Y	N	Y
10 Towns	Y	Y	Y	Y	Y	N	Y
11 Clarke	Y	Y	Y	Y	Y	N	Y
12 Velázquez	Y	Y	Y	Y	Y	N	Y
13 **Fossella**	Y	N	N	Y	Y	Y	N
14 Maloney	Y	Y	Y	Y	Y	N	Y
15 Rangel	?	?	?	?	?	?	?
16 Serrano	Y	Y	Y	Y	Y	N	Y
17 Engel	Y	Y	Y	Y	Y	N	Y
18 Lowey	Y	Y	Y	Y	Y	N	Y
19 Hall	?	Y	Y	Y	Y	N	Y
20 Gillibrand	Y	Y	Y	Y	Y	N	Y
21 McNulty	Y	Y	Y	Y	Y	N	Y
22 Hinchey	Y	Y	Y	Y	Y	?	Y
23 **McHugh**	Y	N	N	Y	Y	Y	N
24 Arcuri	Y	Y	Y	Y	Y	N	Y
25 **Walsh**	Y	N	N	Y	Y	?	N
26 **Reynolds**	Y	N	N	Y	Y	Y	N
27 Higgins	Y	Y	Y	Y	Y	N	Y
28 Slaughter	Y	Y	Y	Y	Y	N	Y
29 **Kuhl**	Y	N	N	Y	Y	Y	N
NORTH CAROLINA							
1 Butterfield	Y	Y	Y	?	?	?	Y
2 Etheridge	Y	Y	Y	Y	Y	N	Y
3 **Jones**	Y	N	N	Y	Y	N	Y
4 Price	Y	Y	Y	Y	Y	N	Y

	115	116	117	118	119	120	121
5 **Foxx**	Y	N	N	Y	Y	Y	N
6 **Coble**	Y	N	–	Y	Y	Y	N
7 McIntyre	Y	Y	Y	Y	Y	N	Y
8 **Hayes**	Y	N	N	Y	Y	Y	N
9 **Myrick**	Y	N	N	Y	Y	Y	N
10 **McHenry**	Y	N	N	Y	Y	Y	N
11 Shuler	Y	Y	Y	Y	Y	N	N
12 Watt	Y	Y	Y	Y	Y	?	Y
13 Miller	Y	Y	Y	Y	Y	?	Y
NORTH DAKOTA							
AL Pomeroy	Y	Y	Y	Y	Y	N	Y
OHIO							
1 **Chabot**	Y	N	N	Y	Y	Y	N
2 **Schmidt**	Y	N	N	Y	Y	Y	N
3 **Turner**	Y	N	N	Y	Y	Y	N
4 **Jordan**	Y	N	N	Y	Y	Y	N
5 **Latta**	Y	N	N	Y	Y	Y	N
6 Wilson	Y	Y	Y	Y	Y	?	Y
7 **Hobson**	Y	N	N	Y	Y	Y	N
8 **Boehner**	Y	N	N	Y	Y	Y	N
9 Kaptur	Y	Y	Y	Y	Y	Y	N
10 Kucinich	Y	Y	N	Y	Y	N	N
11 Tubbs Jones	Y	Y	Y	Y	Y	?	Y
12 **Tiberi**	Y	N	N	Y	Y	Y	N
13 Sutton	Y	Y	Y	Y	Y	N	Y
14 **LaTourette**	Y	N	N	Y	Y	Y	N
15 **Pryce**	?	?	?	?	?	?	?
16 **Regula**	Y	N	N	Y	Y	Y	N
17 Ryan	Y	Y	Y	Y	Y	N	Y
18 Space	Y	Y	Y	Y	Y	N	Y
OKLAHOMA							
1 **Sullivan**	Y	N	N	Y	Y	Y	N
2 Boren	Y	Y	Y	Y	?	N	Y
3 **Lucas**	Y	N	N	Y	Y	Y	N
4 **Cole**	Y	N	N	Y	Y	Y	N
5 **Fallin**	Y	N	N	Y	Y	Y	N
OREGON							
1 Wu	Y	Y	Y	Y	Y	Y	Y
2 **Walden**	Y	N	N	Y	Y	Y	N
3 Blumenauer	Y	Y	Y	Y	Y	N	Y
4 DeFazio	Y	Y	Y	Y	Y	N	Y
5 Hooley	?	?	?	?	?	?	?
PENNSYLVANIA							
1 Brady	Y	Y	Y	Y	Y	N	Y
2 Fattah	Y	Y	Y	Y	Y	N	Y
3 **English**	Y	N	N	Y	Y	Y	N
4 Altmire	Y	Y	Y	Y	Y	N	Y
5 **Peterson**	Y	?	N	Y	Y	?	N
6 **Gerlach**	Y	N	N	Y	Y	N	N
7 Sestak	Y	Y	Y	Y	Y	N	Y
8 Murphy, P.	Y	Y	Y	Y	Y	N	Y
9 **Shuster**	Y	N	N	Y	Y	Y	N
10 Carney	Y	Y	Y	Y	Y	N	Y
11 Kanjorski	Y	Y	Y	Y	Y	N	Y
12 Murtha	Y	Y	Y	Y	Y	N	Y
13 Schwartz	Y	Y	+	Y	Y	N	Y
14 Doyle	Y	Y	Y	Y	Y	N	Y
15 **Dent**	Y	N	–	+	+	Y	N
16 **Pitts**	Y	N	N	Y	Y	Y	N
17 Holden	Y	Y	Y	Y	Y	N	Y
18 **Murphy, T.**	Y	N	N	Y	Y	Y	N
19 **Platts**	Y	N	N	Y	Y	N	N
RHODE ISLAND							
1 Kennedy	Y	Y	Y	Y	Y	N	Y
2 Langevin	Y	Y	Y	Y	Y	N	Y
SOUTH CAROLINA							
1 **Brown**	Y	N	N	Y	Y	Y	N
2 **Wilson**	Y	N	N	Y	Y	Y	N
3 **Barrett**	Y	N	N	Y	Y	Y	N
4 **Inglis**	Y	N	N	Y	Y	Y	N
5 Spratt	Y	Y	Y	Y	Y	N	Y
6 Clyburn	Y	Y	Y	Y	Y	N	Y
SOUTH DAKOTA							
AL Herseth Sandlin	Y	Y	Y	Y	Y	N	Y
TENNESSEE							
1 **Davis, D.**	Y	N	N	Y	Y	Y	N
2 **Duncan**	Y	N	N	Y	Y	Y	N
3 **Wamp**	Y	N	N	Y	Y	Y	N
4 Davis, L.	?	N	Y	Y	Y	N	?
5 Cooper	Y	Y	Y	Y	Y	N	Y
6 Gordon	Y	Y	Y	Y	Y	Y	Y
7 **Blackburn**	?	N	N	Y	Y	Y	N
8 Tanner	Y	Y	Y	?	Y	N	N
9 Cohen	Y	Y	Y	Y	Y	Y	Y

	115	116	117	118	119	120	121
TEXAS							
1 **Gohmert**	Y	N	N	Y	Y	?	N
2 **Poe**	Y	N	N	Y	Y	N	N
3 **Johnson, S.**	Y	N	N	Y	Y	Y	N
4 **Hall**	Y	N	N	Y	Y	Y	N
5 **Hensarling**	Y	N	N	Y	Y	Y	N
6 **Barton**	Y	N	N	Y	Y	Y	N
7 **Culberson**	Y	N	N	Y	Y	?	N
8 **Brady**	Y	N	N	Y	Y	Y	N
9 Green, A.	Y	Y	Y	Y	Y	N	Y
10 **McCaul**	Y	N	N	Y	Y	?	N
11 **Conaway**	Y	N	N	Y	Y	Y	N
12 **Granger**	Y	N	N	Y	Y	Y	N
13 **Thornberry**	Y	N	N	Y	Y	Y	N
14 **Paul**	?	Y	Y	Y	Y	N	N
15 Hinojosa	Y	Y	Y	Y	Y	N	Y
16 Reyes	Y	Y	Y	Y	Y	N	Y
17 Edwards	Y	Y	Y	Y	Y	N	Y
18 Jackson Lee	Y	Y	Y	Y	Y	N	Y
19 **Neugebauer**	Y	N	N	Y	Y	Y	N
20 Gonzalez	Y	Y	Y	Y	Y	N	Y
21 **Smith**	Y	N	N	Y	Y	Y	N
22 Lampson	Y	N	Y	Y	Y	N	Y
23 Rodriguez	Y	Y	Y	Y	Y	N	Y
24 **Marchant**	Y	N	N	Y	Y	Y	N
25 Doggett	Y	Y	Y	Y	Y	N	Y
26 **Burgess**	Y	N	N	Y	Y	Y	N
27 Ortiz	Y	Y	Y	Y	Y	N	Y
28 Cuellar	Y	Y	Y	Y	Y	Y	Y
29 Green, G.	Y	Y	Y	Y	Y	N	Y
30 Johnson, E.	Y	Y	Y	Y	Y	N	Y
31 **Carter**	Y	N	N	Y	Y	Y	N
32 **Sessions**	Y	N	N	Y	Y	Y	N
UTAH							
1 **Bishop**	Y	?	N	Y	Y	Y	N
2 Matheson	Y	Y	Y	Y	Y	N	Y
3 **Cannon**	Y	N	N	Y	Y	Y	N
VERMONT							
AL Welch	Y	Y	Y	Y	Y	N	Y
VIRGINIA							
1 **Wittman**	Y	N	N	Y	Y	Y	N
2 **Drake**	Y	N	N	Y	Y	Y	N
3 Scott	Y	Y	Y	Y	Y	N	Y
4 **Forbes**	Y	N	N	Y	Y	Y	N
5 **Goode**	Y	N	N	Y	Y	Y	N
6 **Goodlatte**	Y	N	N	Y	Y	Y	N
7 **Cantor**	Y	N	N	Y	Y	Y	N
8 Moran	Y	Y	Y	?	?	N	Y
9 Boucher	Y	Y	Y	P	Y	?	?
10 **Wolf**	Y	N	N	Y	Y	Y	N
11 **Davis**	Y	N	N	?	?	Y	N
WASHINGTON							
1 Inslee	Y	Y	Y	Y	Y	N	Y
2 Larsen	Y	Y	Y	P	Y	N	Y
3 Baird	Y	Y	Y	Y	Y	N	N
4 **Hastings**	Y	N	N	Y	Y	Y	N
5 **McMorris Rodgers**	Y	N	N	Y	Y	Y	N
6 Dicks	Y	Y	Y	Y	Y	N	Y
7 McDermott	Y	Y	Y	Y	Y	N	Y
8 **Reichert**	Y	N	N	Y	Y	Y	N
9 Smith	Y	Y	Y	Y	Y	N	Y
WEST VIRGINIA							
1 Mollohan	Y	Y	Y	Y	Y	N	Y
2 **Capito**	?	?	?	?	?	?	?
3 Rahall	Y	Y	Y	Y	Y	N	Y
WISCONSIN							
1 **Ryan**	Y	N	N	Y	Y	Y	N
2 Baldwin	Y	Y	Y	Y	Y	N	Y
3 Kind	Y	Y	Y	Y	Y	N	Y
4 Moore	Y	Y	Y	Y	Y	N	Y
5 **Sensenbrenner**	Y	N	N	Y	Y	Y	N
6 **Petri**	Y	N	N	Y	Y	Y	N
7 Obey	Y	Y	Y	Y	Y	N	Y
8 Kagen	Y	Y	Y	Y	Y	N	Y
WYOMING							
AL **Cubin**	Y	N	N	Y	Y	Y	N
DELEGATES							
Faleomavaega (A.S.)							
Norton (D.C.)							
Bordallo (Guam)							
Fortuño (P.R.)							
Christensen (V.I.)							

IN THE HOUSE | By Vote Number

122. **H Res 895. House Ethics Panel/Rule.** Adoption of the self-executing rule (H Res 1031) to provide for automatic adoption of the resolution that would establish an Office of Congressional Ethics to consider alleged violations by House members and employees. Motion adopted 229-182: R 33-159; D 196-23 (ND 148-15, SD 48-8). March 11, 2008.

123. **Procedural Motion/Motion to Adjourn.** Sutton, D-Ohio, motion to adjourn. Motion agreed to 216-186: R 19-170; D 197-16 (ND 148-12, SD 49-4). March 11, 2008.

124. **Procedural Motion/Motion to Adjourn.** Dreier, R-Calif., motion to adjourn. Motion rejected 5-375: R 2-177; D 3-198 (ND 2-150, SD 1-48). March 12, 2008.

125. **H Res 1039. House Ethics Panel Votes/Motion to Table.** McGovern, D-Mass., motion to table (kill) the Boehner, R-Ohio, privileged resolution that would vacate House votes 121 and 122 on the self-executing rule to provide for automatic adoption of the resolution that would establish an Office of Congressional Ethics to consider alleged violations by House members and employees. Motion agreed to 215-193: R 0-192; D 215-1 (ND 163-0, SD 52-1). March 12, 2008.

126. **Procedural Motion/Motion to Adjourn.** Shadegg, R-Ariz., motion to adjourn. Motion rejected 14-384: R 14-176; D 0-208 (ND 0-156, SD 0-52). March 12, 2008.

127. **Procedural Motion/Motion to Adjourn.** LaHood, R-Ill., motion to adjourn. Motion rejected 3-382: R 2-176; D 1-206 (ND 1-156, SD 0-50). March 12, 2008.

128. **H Res 1040. Congressional Earmarks/Motion to Table.** McGovern, D-Mass., motion to table (kill) the Boehner, R-Ohio, privileged resolution that would call for an ethics committee investigation of Rep. David R. Obey, D-Wis., for his actions related to congressional earmarks. Motion agreed to 219-193: R 0-193; D 219-0 (ND 166-0, SD 53-0). March 12, 2008.

	122	123	124	125	126	127	128
ALABAMA							
1 Bonner	N	N	N	N	N	N	N
2 Everett	N	N	N	N	N	N	N
3 Rogers	N	N	N	N	N	N	N
4 Aderholt	N	N	N	N	N	N	N
5 Cramer	Y	?	N	Y	N	N	Y
6 Bachus	N	N	?	N	?	?	?
7 Davis	Y	Y	N	Y	N	N	Y
ALASKA							
AL Young	N	N	?	?	?	?	?
ARIZONA							
1 Renzi	?	?	?	?	?	?	?
2 Franks	N	N	N	N	N	N	N
3 Shadegg	N	N	N	Y	N	N	N
4 Pastor	N	Y	N	Y	N	N	Y
5 Mitchell	+	+	N	Y	N	N	Y
6 Flake	N	N	N	N	N	N	N
7 Grijalva	Y	Y	?	Y	N	N	Y
8 Giffords	Y	N	N	Y	N	N	Y
ARKANSAS							
1 Berry	Y	Y	N	Y	N	N	Y
2 Snyder	Y	Y	N	Y	N	N	Y
3 Boozman	N	N	N	N	N	N	N
4 Ross	Y	Y	N	Y	N	N	Y
CALIFORNIA							
1 Thompson	Y	Y	N	Y	N	N	Y
2 Herger	N	N	N	N	N	?	N
3 Lungren	N	N	N	N	N	N	N
4 Doolittle	N	Y	?	N	N	N	N
5 Matsui	Y	Y	N	Y	N	N	Y
6 Woolsey	–	+	–	–	–	–	+
7 Miller, George	Y	Y	Y	Y	?	N	Y
8 Pelosi	Y						
9 Lee	Y	Y	N	Y	N	N	Y
10 Tauscher	Y	Y	N	Y	N	N	Y
11 McNerney	Y	Y	N	Y	N	Y	Y
12 Vacant							
13 Stark	N	Y	N	Y	N	N	Y
14 Eshoo	Y	Y	N	Y	N	N	Y
15 Honda	Y	Y	Y	Y	N	N	Y
16 Lofgren	Y	Y	N	Y	N	N	Y
17 Farr	Y	Y	N	Y	N	N	Y
18 Cardoza	Y	Y	?	?	?	N	Y
19 Radanovich	?	?	N	N	N	N	N
20 Costa	Y	Y	N	Y	N	N	Y
21 Nunes	N	N	N	N	N	N	N
22 McCarthy	N	N	N	N	N	N	N
23 Capps	Y	Y	N	Y	N	N	Y
24 Gallegly	N	N	N	N	N	N	N
25 McKeon	N	N	N	N	N	N	N
26 Dreier	N	N	N	N	N	N	N
27 Sherman	Y	Y	N	Y	N	N	Y
28 Berman	Y	Y	N	Y	N	N	Y
29 Schiff	Y	Y	N	Y	N	N	Y
30 Waxman	Y	Y	N	Y	N	N	Y
31 Becerra	Y	Y	N	Y	N	N	Y
32 Solis	Y	Y	N	Y	N	N	Y
33 Watson	Y	Y	N	Y	N	N	Y
34 Roybal-Allard	P	Y	N	Y	N	N	Y
35 Waters	N	Y	N	Y	N	N	Y
36 Harman	Y	Y	N	Y	N	N	Y
37 Richardson	Y	Y	N	Y	N	N	Y
38 Napolitano	Y	Y	N	Y	N	N	Y
39 Sánchez, Linda	Y	Y	N	Y	N	N	Y
40 Royce	N	N	N	N	N	N	N
41 Lewis	N	N	N	N	Y	N	N
42 Miller, Gary	N	N	N	N	N	N	N
43 Baca	Y	Y	N	Y	N	N	Y
44 Calvert	N	N	N	N	N	N	N
45 Bono Mack	N	N	N	N	N	N	N
46 Rohrabacher	N	N	N	N	N	N	N
47 Sanchez, Loretta	N	Y	N	Y	N	N	Y
48 Campbell	N	N	N	N	Y	N	N
49 Issa	N	N	N	N	N	?	N
50 Bilbray	N	N	N	N	N	N	N
51 Filner	N	Y	N	Y	N	N	Y
52 Hunter	N	N	N	N	N	?	N
53 Davis	Y	Y	N	Y	N	N	Y

	122	123	124	125	126	127	128
COLORADO							
1 DeGette	Y	Y	N	Y	N	?	Y
2 Udall	Y	Y	?	Y	N	?	Y
3 Salazar	Y	Y	N	Y	N	N	Y
4 Musgrave	N	N	N	N	N	N	N
5 Lamborn	N	N	N	N	N	N	N
6 Tancredo	?	?	?	?	?	?	?
7 Perlmutter	Y	Y	N	Y	N	?	Y
CONNECTICUT							
1 Larson	Y	Y	N	Y	N	N	Y
2 Courtney	Y	Y	N	Y	N	N	Y
3 DeLauro	Y	Y	N	Y	N	N	Y
4 Shays	Y	N	N	N	N	N	N
5 Murphy	Y	Y	N	Y	N	N	Y
DELAWARE							
AL Castle	Y	N	N	N	N	N	N
FLORIDA							
1 Miller	N	N	N	N	N	N	N
2 Boyd	N	Y	N	Y	N	N	Y
3 Brown	N	Y	?	Y	N	?	Y
4 Crenshaw	N	N	N	N	N	N	N
5 Brown-Waite	Y	N	N	N	N	N	N
6 Stearns	N	N	N	N	N	N	N
7 Mica	N	N	N	N	N	N	N
8 Keller	Y	N	N	N	N	N	N
9 Bilirakis	Y	N	N	N	N	N	N
10 Young	N	N	N	N	N	N	N
11 Castor	Y	Y	N	Y	?	N	Y
12 Putnam	N	N	N	N	N	N	N
13 Buchanan	Y	Y	N	N	N	N	N
14 Mack	N	N	N	N	N	N	N
15 Weldon	N	Y	N	N	?	?	N
16 Mahoney	Y	Y	N	Y	N	N	Y
17 Meek	Y	Y	?	Y	N	N	Y
18 Ros-Lehtinen	?	?	N	N	N	N	N
19 Wexler	Y	Y	?	Y	N	N	Y
20 Wasserman Schultz	Y	Y	N	Y	N	N	Y
21 Diaz-Balart, L.	Y	N	N	N	N	N	N
22 Klein	Y	Y	N	Y	N	N	Y
23 Hastings	Y	Y	N	Y	N	N	Y
24 Feeney	N	Y	N	N	N	N	N
25 Diaz-Balart, M.	Y	N	N	N	N	N	N
GEORGIA							
1 Kingston	N	N	Y	N	N	N	N
2 Bishop	N	Y	N	Y	N	N	Y
3 Westmoreland	N	N	N	N	N	?	N
4 Johnson	Y	Y	?	?	?	N	Y
5 Lewis	Y	Y	N	Y	N	N	Y
6 Price	N	N	N	N	N	N	N
7 Linder	N	Y	N	N	Y	N	N
8 Marshall	Y	Y	N	Y	N	N	Y
9 Deal	N	N	N	N	N	?	N
10 Broun	N	N	N	N	N	N	N
11 Gingrey	N	N	?	?	N	N	N
12 Barrow	Y	Y	N	Y	N	N	Y
13 Scott	Y	Y	N	Y	N	N	Y
HAWAII							
1 Abercrombie	N	Y	N	Y	?	N	Y
2 Hirono	Y	Y	N	Y	N	N	Y
IDAHO							
1 Sali	N	N	?	N	N	N	N
2 Simpson	N	N	?	N	N	N	N
ILLINOIS							
1 Rush	?	?	?	?	?	?	?
2 Jackson	Y	Y	N	Y	N	N	Y
3 Lipinski	Y	Y	N	Y	N	N	Y
4 Gutierrez	Y	Y	N	Y	N	N	+
5 Emanuel	Y	Y	N	Y	N	?	Y
6 Roskam	N	N	N	N	N	N	N
7 Davis	Y	Y	N	Y	N	N	Y
8 Bean	Y	Y	N	Y	N	N	Y
9 Schakowsky	Y	Y	N	Y	N	?	Y
10 Kirk	Y	N	N	N	N	N	N
11 Weller	N	?	N	N	N	N	N
12 Costello	N	Y	?	?	?	N	Y
13 Biggert	N	N	N	N	N	N	N
14 Foster	Y	?	Y	Y	N	N	Y
15 Johnson	Y	Y	Y	N	Y	Y	N

ND Northern Democrats, SD Southern Democrats
Southern states: Ala., Ark., Fla., Ga., Ky., La., Miss., N.C., Okla., S.C., Tenn., Texas, Va.

	122	123	124	125	126	127	128
16 **Manzullo**	N	N	N	N	N	?	N
17 Hare	Y	Y	N	Y	N	N	Y
18 **LaHood**	N	N	N	N	N	N	N
19 **Shimkus**	N	N	N	N	N	?	N
INDIANA							
1 Visclosky	Y	Y	N	Y	N	N	Y
2 Donnelly	Y	N	N	Y	N	N	Y
3 **Souder**	Y	N	N	N	N	N	N
4 **Buyer**	N	N	N	N	N	N	N
5 **Burton**	N	N	N	N	N	N	N
6 **Pence**	N	N	N	N	N	N	N
7 Vacant							
8 Ellsworth	Y	N	N	Y	N	N	Y
9 Hill	Y	Y	N	Y	N	N	Y
IOWA							
1 Braley	Y	Y	N	Y	N	N	Y
2 Loebsack	Y	Y	N	Y	N	N	Y
3 Boswell	Y	Y	N	?	N	N	Y
4 **Latham**	N	N	N	N	N	N	N
5 **King**	N	Y	N	N	N	N	N
KANSAS							
1 **Moran**	Y	N	N	N	N	N	N
2 Boyda	Y	Y	N	Y	N	N	Y
3 Moore	Y	Y	N	Y	N	N	Y
4 **Tiahrt**	N	N	N	N	N	N	N
KENTUCKY							
1 **Whitfield**	N	Y	N	N	Y	N	N
2 **Lewis**	N	Y	N	N	Y	N	N
3 Yarmuth	Y	Y	N	Y	N	N	Y
4 **Davis**	N	Y	N	N	N	N	N
5 **Rogers**	N	N	N	N	N	N	N
6 Chandler	N	Y	N	Y	N	N	Y
LOUISIANA							
1 Vacant							
2 Jefferson	Y	Y	?	Y	N	N	Y
3 Melancon	N	?	N	N	N	?	Y
4 **McCrery**	N	N	N	N	N	N	N
5 **Alexander**	N	N	N	N	N	N	N
6 Vacant							
7 **Boustany**	N	N	N	N	N	N	N
MAINE							
1 Allen	Y	Y	N	Y	N	N	Y
2 Michaud	Y	Y	N	Y	N	N	Y
MARYLAND							
1 **Gilchrest**	N	N	?	N	N	N	N
2 Ruppersberger	Y	Y	N	Y	N	N	Y
3 Sarbanes	Y	Y	N	Y	N	N	Y
4 Wynn	?	?	?	Y	N	N	Y
5 Hoyer	Y	Y	N	Y	N	N	Y
6 **Bartlett**	N	Y	N	N	N	N	N
7 Cummings	Y	Y	?	Y	N	N	Y
8 Van Hollen	Y	Y	N	Y	N	N	Y
MASSACHUSETTS							
1 Olver	Y	Y	N	Y	N	N	Y
2 Neal	Y	Y	N	Y	N	N	Y
3 McGovern	Y	Y	N	Y	N	N	Y
4 Frank	Y	Y	N	Y	?	?	Y
5 Tsongas	Y	Y	N	Y	N	N	Y
6 Tierney	Y	Y	N	Y	N	N	Y
7 Markey	Y	Y	?	Y	N	N	Y
8 Capuano	Y	Y	N	Y	N	N	Y
9 Lynch	Y	Y	N	Y	N	N	Y
10 Delahunt	P	Y	N	Y	N	N	Y
MICHIGAN							
1 Stupak	Y	N	N	Y	N	?	Y
2 **Hoekstra**	N	N	N	N	N	N	N
3 **Ehlers**	N	N	N	?	N	N	N
4 **Camp**	N	N	N	N	N	N	N
5 Kildee	Y	Y	N	Y	N	N	Y
6 **Upton**	N	N	N	N	N	N	N
7 **Walberg**	N	N	N	N	N	N	N
8 **Rogers**	N	N	N	N	N	N	N
9 **Knollenberg**	Y	N	N	N	N	N	N
10 **Miller**	Y	N	N	N	N	N	N
11 **McCotter**	N	N	N	N	N	N	N
12 Levin	Y	Y	N	Y	N	N	Y
13 Kilpatrick	?	?	N	Y	N	N	Y
14 Conyers	Y	?	N	Y	N	N	Y
15 Dingell	N	Y	N	Y	N	N	Y
MINNESOTA							
1 Walz	Y	N	N	Y	N	N	Y
2 **Kline**	N	N	N	N	N	N	N
3 **Ramstad**	Y	N	N	N	N	N	N
4 McCollum	Y	Y	N	Y	?	N	Y

	122	123	124	125	126	127	128
5 Ellison	Y	Y	N	Y	N	N	Y
6 **Bachmann**	N	N	N	N	N	N	N
7 Peterson	Y	Y	N	Y	N	N	Y
8 Oberstar	?	?	?	?	?	?	?
MISSISSIPPI							
1 Vacant							
2 Thompson	?	?	?	?	?	?	?
3 **Pickering**	N	Y	N	N	N	?	N
4 Taylor	Y	Y	N	?	N	N	Y
MISSOURI							
1 Clay	N	Y	?	Y	N	?	Y
2 **Akin**	N	N	N	N	N	N	N
3 Carnahan	Y	Y	?	Y	N	N	Y
4 Skelton	N	Y	N	Y	N	N	Y
5 Cleaver	N	Y	N	Y	N	N	Y
6 **Graves**	Y	Y	N	N	N	N	N
7 **Blunt**	N	N	N	N	N	N	N
8 **Emerson**	N	Y	N	N	N	N	N
9 **Hulshof**	Y	N	N	N	Y	N	N
MONTANA							
AL **Rehberg**	N	N	N	N	N	N	N
NEBRASKA							
1 **Fortenberry**	N	N	N	N	N	N	N
2 **Terry**	N	N	N	N	N	N	N
3 **Smith**	N	N	N	N	N	N	N
NEVADA							
1 Berkley	Y	Y	N	Y	N	N	Y
2 **Heller**	Y	N	N	N	N	N	N
3 **Porter**	Y	N	N	N	N	N	N
NEW HAMPSHIRE							
1 Shea-Porter	Y	Y	N	Y	N	N	Y
2 Hodes	Y	Y	N	Y	N	N	Y
NEW JERSEY							
1 Andrews	Y	Y	N	Y	N	N	Y
2 **LoBiondo**	Y	N	N	N	N	N	N
3 **Saxton**	N	?	N	N	N	N	N
4 **Smith**	N	N	N	N	N	?	N
5 **Garrett**	N	N	N	N	N	N	N
6 Pallone	Y	Y	N	Y	N	N	Y
7 **Ferguson**	N	N	N	N	N	N	N
8 Pascrell	Y	?	N	Y	?	N	Y
9 Rothman	Y	Y	N	?	?	N	?
10 Payne	Y	Y	N	Y	N	N	Y
11 **Frelinghuysen**	N	N	N	N	N	N	N
12 Holt	Y	Y	N	Y	N	N	Y
13 Sires	Y	Y	N	Y	N	N	Y
NEW MEXICO							
1 **Wilson**	N	N	N	N	N	N	N
2 **Pearce**	N	N	N	N	N	N	N
3 Udall	Y	N	N	Y	N	N	Y
NEW YORK							
1 Bishop	Y	Y	N	Y	N	N	Y
2 Israel	Y	Y	N	Y	?	N	Y
3 **King**	N	N	N	N	N	N	N
4 McCarthy	Y	?	N	Y	N	N	Y
5 Ackerman	Y	Y	N	Y	N	N	Y
6 Meeks	Y	Y	N	Y	N	N	Y
7 Crowley	Y	Y	N	Y	N	N	Y
8 Nadler	Y	Y	N	Y	N	N	Y
9 Weiner	Y	Y	N	Y	N	N	Y
10 Towns	Y	Y	N	Y	N	?	Y
11 Clarke	Y	Y	N	Y	N	N	Y
12 Velázquez	Y	Y	N	Y	N	N	Y
13 **Fossella**	Y	N	?	N	N	N	N
14 Maloney	Y	Y	N	?	N	N	Y
15 Rangel	?	?	?	?	?	?	?
16 Serrano	Y	Y	N	Y	N	N	Y
17 Engel	Y	Y	N	?	?	N	Y
18 Lowey	Y	Y	N	Y	N	N	Y
19 Hall	Y	Y	N	Y	N	N	Y
20 Gillibrand	Y	Y	N	Y	N	N	Y
21 McNulty	Y	Y	N	Y	N	N	Y
22 Hinchey	N	Y	?	Y	N	?	?
23 **McHugh**	Y	N	N	N	N	N	N
24 Arcuri	Y	Y	N	Y	N	N	Y
25 **Walsh**	N	N	N	N	N	N	N
26 **Reynolds**	Y	N	N	N	N	N	N
27 Higgins	Y	Y	N	Y	N	N	Y
28 Slaughter	Y	Y	N	Y	N	N	Y
29 **Kuhl**	Y	N	N	N	N	N	N
NORTH CAROLINA							
1 Butterfield	Y	Y	N	Y	N	N	Y
2 Etheridge	Y	Y	N	Y	N	N	Y
3 **Jones**	Y	Y	N	N	N	N	N
4 Price	Y	Y	N	Y	N	N	Y

	122	123	124	125	126	127	128
5 **Foxx**	N	N	N	N	N	N	N
6 **Coble**	N	Y	N	N	N	N	N
7 McIntyre	Y	Y	N	Y	N	N	Y
8 **Hayes**	Y	N	N	N	N	N	N
9 **Myrick**	N	N	N	N	N	N	N
10 **McHenry**	N	N	N	N	N	N	N
11 Shuler	N	Y	N	Y	N	N	Y
12 Watt	Y	N	N	Y	N	N	Y
13 Miller	Y	Y	N	Y	N	N	Y
NORTH DAKOTA							
AL Pomeroy	Y	Y	N	Y	N	N	Y
OHIO							
1 **Chabot**	Y	N	N	N	N	N	N
2 **Schmidt**	N	N	N	N	N	N	N
3 **Turner**	N	N	N	N	N	N	N
4 **Jordan**	N	N	N	N	N	N	N
5 **Latta**	N	N	N	N	N	N	N
6 Wilson	Y	Y	N	Y	N	N	Y
7 **Hobson**	N	Y	N	N	N	N	N
8 **Boehner**	N	N	N	N	N	N	N
9 Kaptur	N	Y	?	Y	N	N	Y
10 Kucinich	Y	N	N	Y	N	N	Y
11 Tubbs Jones	P	Y	?	Y	N	N	Y
12 **Tiberi**	N	N	N	N	N	N	N
13 Sutton	Y	Y	?	Y	N	N	Y
14 **LaTourette**	N	N	N	N	N	N	N
15 **Pryce**	?	?	?	N	N	N	N
16 **Regula**	N	N	N	N	Y	N	N
17 Ryan	Y	Y	?	Y	N	N	Y
18 Space	Y	Y	N	Y	N	N	Y
OKLAHOMA							
1 **Sullivan**	N	N	N	N	Y	?	N
2 Boren	Y	Y	N	Y	N	N	Y
3 **Lucas**	N	N	N	N	N	N	N
4 **Cole**	N	N	N	N	Y	?	N
5 **Fallin**	N	N	N	N	N	N	N
OREGON							
1 Wu	Y	Y	N	Y	N	N	Y
2 **Walden**	N	N	N	N	N	N	N
3 Blumenauer	Y	Y	N	Y	?	N	Y
4 DeFazio	Y	Y	N	Y	N	N	Y
5 Hooley	?	?	?	?	?	?	?
PENNSYLVANIA							
1 Brady	Y	Y	N	Y	N	N	Y
2 Fattah	Y	Y	N	Y	N	N	Y
3 **English**	Y	N	N	N	N	N	N
4 Altmire	Y	N	N	Y	N	N	Y
5 **Peterson**	N	N	?	N	?	?	N
6 **Gerlach**	Y	N	N	N	N	N	N
7 Sestak	Y	Y	N	Y	N	N	Y
8 Murphy, P.	Y	Y	N	Y	N	N	Y
9 **Shuster**	N	N	N	N	N	N	N
10 Carney	Y	N	N	Y	N	N	Y
11 Kanjorski	Y	Y	N	Y	N	N	Y
12 Murtha	N	?	?	Y	N	N	Y
13 Schwartz	Y	Y	N	Y	N	N	Y
14 Doyle	P	Y	N	Y	N	?	Y
15 **Dent**	Y	N	N	N	N	N	N
16 **Pitts**	N	N	N	N	N	N	N
17 Holden	Y	?	N	Y	N	N	Y
18 **Murphy, T.**	Y	N	N	N	N	N	N
19 **Platts**	Y	N	N	N	N	N	N
RHODE ISLAND							
1 Kennedy	Y	Y	N	Y	N	N	Y
2 Langevin	Y	Y	N	Y	N	N	Y
SOUTH CAROLINA							
1 **Brown**	N	Y	N	N	N	N	N
2 **Wilson**	N	N	N	N	N	N	N
3 **Barrett**	N	N	N	N	N	N	N
4 **Inglis**	N	N	N	N	N	N	N
5 Spratt	Y	?	N	Y	N	N	?
6 Clyburn	Y	Y	N	Y	N	N	?
SOUTH DAKOTA							
AL Herseth Sandlin	Y	Y	N	Y	N	N	Y
TENNESSEE							
1 **Davis, D.**	N	N	N	N	N	N	N
2 **Duncan**	N	N	N	N	N	N	N
3 **Wamp**	N	N	N	N	N	N	N
4 Davis, L.	Y	Y	Y	Y	N	?	Y
5 Cooper	Y	Y	N	Y	N	N	Y
6 Gordon	Y	Y	?	?	?	N	Y
7 **Blackburn**	N	N	N	N	N	N	N
8 Tanner	N	Y	N	Y	N	N	Y
9 Cohen	Y	Y	N	Y	?	N	Y

	122	123	124	125	126	127	128
TEXAS							
1 **Gohmert**	N	N	N	N	N	N	N
2 **Poe**	N	N	N	N	N	N	N
3 **Johnson, S.**	N	?	N	N	N	N	N
4 **Hall**	N	N	?	N	N	N	?
5 **Hensarling**	N	N	N	N	N	N	N
6 **Barton**	N	N	N	N	N	?	N
7 **Culberson**	N	N	?	N	N	N	N
8 **Brady**	N	N	N	N	N	N	N
9 Green, A.	Y	Y	N	Y	N	N	Y
10 **McCaul**	N	N	?	N	N	N	N
11 **Conaway**	N	N	N	N	N	N	N
12 **Granger**	N	N	N	N	N	N	N
13 **Thornberry**	N	N	N	N	N	N	N
14 **Paul**	N	Y	N	N	N	Y	N
15 Hinojosa	Y	Y	N	Y	N	?	Y
16 Reyes	Y	Y	N	Y	N	N	Y
17 Edwards	Y	Y	N	Y	N	N	Y
18 Jackson Lee	N	Y	N	Y	N	N	Y
19 **Neugebauer**	N	N	N	N	N	N	N
20 Gonzalez	Y	Y	N	Y	N	N	Y
21 **Smith**	N	N	N	N	N	N	N
22 Lampson	Y	N	N	Y	N	N	Y
23 Rodriguez	Y	Y	N	Y	N	N	Y
24 **Marchant**	N	N	?	N	Y	?	N
25 Doggett	Y	Y	N	Y	N	N	Y
26 **Burgess**	N	N	?	N	N	N	N
27 Ortiz	Y	Y	N	Y	N	N	Y
28 Cuellar	Y	Y	N	Y	N	N	Y
29 Green, G.	Y	N	N	Y	N	N	Y
30 Johnson, E.	Y	Y	N	Y	N	N	Y
31 **Carter**	N	N	N	N	Y	N	N
32 **Sessions**	N	N	N	N	Y	N	N
UTAH							
1 **Bishop**	N	N	?	N	N	N	N
2 Matheson	Y	Y	N	Y	N	N	Y
3 **Cannon**	N	N	N	N	N	N	N
VERMONT							
AL Welch	Y	Y	N	Y	N	N	Y
VIRGINIA							
1 **Wittman**	Y	N	N	N	N	N	N
2 **Drake**	N	N	N	N	N	N	N
3 Scott	Y	Y	N	Y	N	N	Y
4 **Forbes**	N	N	N	N	N	N	N
5 **Goode**	N	N	N	N	N	N	N
6 **Goodlatte**	N	N	N	N	N	N	N
7 **Cantor**	N	N	N	N	N	N	N
8 Moran	Y	Y	N	Y	N	?	Y
9 Boucher	Y	N	?	Y	N	?	?
10 **Wolf**	N	N	N	N	N	N	N
11 **Davis**	N	N	N	N	N	N	N
WASHINGTON							
1 Inslee	Y	Y	N	Y	N	N	Y
2 Larsen	Y	Y	N	Y	N	N	Y
3 Baird	N	Y	?	Y	?	N	Y
4 **Hastings**	N	N	N	N	N	N	N
5 **McMorris Rodgers**	N	N	N	N	N	N	N
6 Dicks	Y	Y	?	Y	?	N	Y
7 McDermott	Y	N	N	Y	N	N	Y
8 **Reichert**	N	N	N	N	N	N	N
9 Smith	Y	Y	N	Y	N	N	Y
WEST VIRGINIA							
1 Mollohan	Y	N	N	Y	N	?	Y
2 **Capito**	?	?	N	N	N	N	N
3 Rahall	Y	N	N	Y	N	N	Y
WISCONSIN							
1 **Ryan**	N	N	N	N	N	N	N
2 Baldwin	Y	Y	N	Y	N	N	Y
3 Kind	Y	Y	N	Y	N	N	Y
4 Moore	Y	Y	N	Y	N	N	Y
5 **Sensenbrenner**	N	N	N	N	N	N	N
6 **Petri**	N	N	N	N	N	N	N
7 Obey	Y	Y	N	Y	N	N	Y
8 Kagen	Y	Y	N	Y	N	N	Y
WYOMING							
AL **Cubin**	N	N	?	?	?	?	N
DELEGATES							
Faleomavaega (A.S.)							
Norton (D.C.)							
Bordallo (Guam)							
Fortuño (P.R.)							
Christensen (V.I.)							

IN THE HOUSE | By Vote Number

129. **H Con Res 312. Fiscal 2009 Budget Resolution/Previous Question.** McGovern, D-Mass., motion to order the previous question (thus ending debate and possibility of amendment) on adoption of the rule (H Res 1036) to provide for House floor consideration of the concurrent resolution that would set broad spending and revenue targets for the next five years. Motion agreed to 222-196: R 0-193; D 222-3 (ND 167-1, SD 55-2). March 12, 2008.

130. **H Con Res 312. Fiscal 2009 Budget Resolution/Rule.** Adoption of the rule (H Res 1036) to provide for House floor consideration of the concurrent resolution that would set broad spending and revenue targets for the next five years. Adopted 223-195: R 0-194; D 223-1 (ND 168-0, SD 55-1). March 12, 2008.

131. **HR 5563. National and Community Service Programs/Passage.** Miller, D-Calif., motion to suspend the rules and pass the bill that would authorize $51 million in fiscal 2008 for a number of national service programs, including the AmeriCorps and Volunteers in Service to America programs. Motion rejected 277-140: R 53-140; D 224-0 (ND 167-0, SD 57-0). A two-thirds majority of those present and voting (278 in this case) is required for passage under suspension of the rules. March 12, 2008.

132. **H Con Res 316. Adjournment Resolution/Adoption.** Adoption of the concurrent resolution that would provide for adjournment of the House until 2 p.m., Monday, March 31, 2008, and the Senate until noon, Monday, March 31, 2008. Adopted 211-204: R 2-192; D 209-12 (ND 155-10, SD 54-2). March 12, 2008.

133. **H Res 936. Gallatin Report 200th Anniversary/Adoption.** DeFazio, D-Ore., motion to suspend the rules and adopt the resolution that would commemorate the 200th anniversary of the Gallatin Report, the first national report on transportation infrastructure, and support a new national plan for improving transportation. Motion agreed to 411-0: R 190-0; D 221-0 (ND 164-0, SD 57-0). A two-thirds majority of those present and voting (274 in this case) is required for adoption under suspension of the rules. March 12, 2008.

134. **S 2733. Higher Education Act Extension/Passage.** Miller, D-Calif., motion to suspend the rules and pass the bill that would extend the authorization for Higher Education Act programs through April 30, 2008. Motion agreed to 411-4: R 188-4; D 223-0 (ND 166-0, SD 57-0). A two-thirds majority of those present and voting (277 in this case) is required for passage under suspension of the rules. March 12, 2008.

135. **HR 3773. Foreign Intelligence Surveillance Act/Appeal Ruling of the Chair.** Scott, D-Va., motion to table (kill) the Price, R-Ga., appeal of the ruling of the chair that the Price draft resolution does not constitute a point of privilege under Rule IX of the House. The draft resolution would express the sense of the House that it should immediately consider a Senate-passed bill (HR 3773) that would amend the Foreign Intelligence Surveillance Act, and that the House should not adjourn for its upcoming district work period before considering the bill. Motion agreed to 222-192: R 1-189; D 221-3 (ND 166-1, SD 55-2). March 13, 2008.

ND Northern Democrats, SD Southern Democrats
Southern states: Ala., Ark., Fla., Ga., Ky., La., Miss., N.C., Okla., S.C., Tenn., Texas, Va.

	129	130	131	132	133	134	135
ALABAMA							
1 Bonner	N	N	N	N	Y	Y	N
2 Everett	N	N	N	N	Y	Y	N
3 Rogers	N	N	Y	N	Y	Y	N
4 Aderholt	N	N	N	N	Y	Y	N
5 Cramer	Y	Y	Y	Y	Y	Y	Y
6 Bachus	N	N	Y	N	Y	Y	N
7 Davis	Y	Y	Y	Y	Y	Y	Y
ALASKA							
AL Young	?	?	?	?	?	?	?
ARIZONA							
1 Renzi	?	?	?	?	?	?	?
2 Franks	N	N	N	N	Y	Y	N
3 Shadegg	N	N	N	N	Y	Y	N
4 Pastor	Y	Y	Y	Y	Y	Y	Y
5 Mitchell	Y	Y	Y	N	Y	Y	Y
6 Flake	N	N	N	N	Y	N	N
7 Grijalva	Y	Y	Y	Y	Y	Y	Y
8 Giffords	Y	Y	Y	N	Y	Y	Y
ARKANSAS							
1 Berry	Y	Y	Y	Y	Y	Y	Y
2 Snyder	Y	Y	Y	Y	Y	Y	Y
3 Boozman	N	N	Y	N	Y	Y	N
4 Ross	Y	Y	Y	Y	Y	Y	Y
CALIFORNIA							
1 Thompson	Y	Y	Y	Y	Y	Y	Y
2 Herger	N	N	N	N	Y	Y	N
3 Lungren	N	N	N	N	Y	Y	N
4 Doolittle	N	N	N	N	Y	N	N
5 Matsui	Y	Y	Y	Y	Y	Y	Y
6 Woolsey	+	+	+	+	+	+	?
7 Miller, George	Y	Y	Y	Y	Y	Y	Y
8 Pelosi							
9 Lee	Y	Y	Y	Y	Y	Y	Y
10 Tauscher	Y	Y	Y	Y	Y	Y	Y
11 McNerney	Y	Y	Y	N	Y	Y	Y
12 Vacant							
13 Stark	Y	Y	Y	Y	Y	Y	Y
14 Eshoo	Y	Y	Y	Y	Y	Y	Y
15 Honda	Y	Y	Y	Y	Y	Y	Y
16 Lofgren	Y	Y	Y	Y	Y	Y	Y
17 Farr	Y	Y	Y	Y	Y	Y	Y
18 Cardoza	Y	Y	Y	Y	Y	Y	Y
19 Radanovich	N	N	N	N	Y	Y	N
20 Costa	Y	Y	Y	Y	Y	Y	Y
21 Nunes	N	N	N	N	Y	Y	N
22 McCarthy	N	N	N	N	Y	Y	N
23 Capps	Y	Y	Y	Y	Y	Y	Y
24 Gallegly	N	N	N	N	Y	Y	N
25 McKeon	N	N	?	N	Y	Y	N
26 Dreier	N	N	N	N	Y	Y	N
27 Sherman	Y	Y	Y	Y	Y	Y	Y
28 Berman	Y	Y	Y	Y	Y	Y	Y
29 Schiff	Y	Y	Y	Y	Y	Y	Y
30 Waxman	Y	Y	Y	Y	Y	Y	Y
31 Becerra	Y	Y	Y	Y	?	Y	Y
32 Solis	Y	Y	Y	Y	Y	Y	Y
33 Watson	Y	Y	Y	Y	Y	Y	Y
34 Roybal-Allard	Y	Y	Y	Y	Y	Y	Y
35 Waters	Y	Y	?	Y	Y	Y	Y
36 Harman	Y	Y	Y	Y	Y	Y	Y
37 Richardson	Y	Y	Y	Y	Y	Y	Y
38 Napolitano	Y	Y	Y	Y	Y	Y	Y
39 Sánchez, Linda	Y	Y	Y	Y	Y	Y	Y
40 Royce	N	N	N	N	Y	Y	N
41 Lewis	N	N	N	N	Y	Y	N
42 Miller, Gary	N	N	N	N	Y	Y	N
43 Baca	Y	Y	Y	Y	Y	Y	Y
44 Calvert	N	N	N	N	Y	Y	N
45 Bono Mack	N	N	N	N	?	Y	N
46 Rohrabacher	N	N	N	N	Y	Y	N
47 Sanchez, Loretta	Y	Y	Y	Y	Y	Y	Y
48 Campbell	N	N	N	N	Y	Y	N
49 Issa	N	N	N	?	?	?	?
50 Bilbray	N	N	N	N	Y	Y	N
51 Filner	Y	Y	Y	Y	Y	Y	Y
52 Hunter	N	N	N	N	?	Y	?
53 Davis	Y	Y	Y	Y	Y	Y	Y

	129	130	131	132	133	134	135
COLORADO							
1 DeGette	Y	Y	Y	Y	Y	Y	Y
2 Udall	Y	Y	Y	?	?	?	?
3 Salazar	Y	Y	Y	Y	Y	Y	Y
4 Musgrave	N	N	N	N	Y	Y	N
5 Lamborn	N	N	N	N	Y	Y	N
6 Tancredo	?	?	?	?	?	?	?
7 Perlmutter	Y	Y	Y	Y	Y	Y	Y
CONNECTICUT							
1 Larson	Y	Y	Y	Y	Y	Y	Y
2 Courtney	Y	Y	Y	?	Y	Y	Y
3 DeLauro	Y	Y	Y	Y	Y	Y	Y
4 Shays	N	N	Y	N	Y	Y	N
5 Murphy	Y	Y	Y	Y	Y	Y	Y
DELAWARE							
AL Castle	N	N	N	N	Y	Y	N
FLORIDA							
1 Miller	N	N	N	N	Y	Y	N
2 Boyd	Y	Y	Y	Y	Y	Y	Y
3 Brown	Y	Y	Y	Y	Y	Y	Y
4 Crenshaw	N	N	N	N	Y	Y	N
5 Brown-Waite	N	N	N	N	Y	Y	N
6 Stearns	N	N	N	N	Y	Y	N
7 Mica	N	N	N	N	Y	Y	N
8 Keller	N	N	N	N	Y	Y	N
9 Bilirakis	N	N	N	N	Y	Y	N
10 Young	N	N	N	N	Y	Y	N
11 Castor	Y	Y	Y	Y	Y	Y	Y
12 Putnam	N	N	N	N	Y	Y	N
13 Buchanan	N	N	N	N	Y	Y	N
14 Mack	N	N	N	N	?	Y	N
15 Weldon	N	N	N	N	Y	Y	N
16 Mahoney	Y	Y	Y	Y	Y	Y	Y
17 Meek	Y	Y	Y	Y	Y	Y	Y
18 Ros-Lehtinen	N	N	N	N	Y	Y	N
19 Wexler	Y	Y	Y	Y	Y	Y	Y
20 Wasserman Schultz	Y	Y	Y	Y	Y	Y	Y
21 Diaz-Balart, L.	N	N	N	N	Y	Y	N
22 Klein	Y	Y	Y	Y	Y	Y	Y
23 Hastings	Y	?	Y	Y	Y	Y	Y
24 Feeney	N	N	N	N	Y	Y	N
25 Diaz-Balart, M.	N	N	N	N	Y	Y	N
GEORGIA							
1 Kingston	N	N	N	N	Y	Y	N
2 Bishop	Y	Y	Y	Y	Y	Y	Y
3 Westmoreland	N	N	N	N	Y	Y	N
4 Johnson	Y	Y	Y	Y	Y	Y	Y
5 Lewis	Y	Y	Y	Y	Y	Y	Y
6 Price	N	N	N	N	Y	Y	N
7 Linder	N	?	?	N	Y	N	N
8 Marshall	Y	Y	Y	?	Y	Y	Y
9 Deal	N	N	N	N	Y	Y	N
10 Broun	N	N	N	N	Y	Y	N
11 Gingrey	N	N	N	N	Y	Y	N
12 Barrow	N	Y	N	Y	Y	Y	Y
13 Scott	Y	Y	Y	Y	Y	Y	Y
HAWAII							
1 Abercrombie	Y	Y	Y	Y	Y	Y	Y
2 Hirono	Y	Y	Y	Y	Y	Y	Y
IDAHO							
1 Sali	N	N	N	N	Y	Y	N
2 Simpson	N	N	N	N	Y	Y	N
ILLINOIS							
1 Rush	?	?	?	?	?	?	?
2 Jackson	Y	Y	Y	Y	Y	Y	Y
3 Lipinski	Y	Y	Y	Y	Y	Y	Y
4 Gutierrez	+	+	+	+	+	+	+
5 Emanuel	Y	Y	Y	Y	Y	Y	Y
6 Roskam	N	N	N	N	Y	?	N
7 Davis	Y	Y	Y	Y	Y	Y	Y
8 Bean	Y	Y	Y	Y	Y	Y	Y
9 Schakowsky	Y	Y	Y	Y	Y	Y	Y
10 Kirk	N	N	N	N	Y	Y	N
11 Weller	N	N	N	N	Y	Y	N
12 Costello	Y	Y	Y	Y	Y	Y	Y
13 Biggert	N	N	N	N	Y	Y	N
14 Foster	Y	Y	Y	N	Y	Y	Y
15 Johnson	N	N	Y	N	Y	Y	N

KEY	Republicans		Democrats		
Y Voted for (yea)		X Paired against		C Voted "present" to avoid possible conflict of interest	
# Paired for		– Announced against			
+ Announced for		P Voted "present"		? Did not vote or otherwise make a position known	
N Voted against (nay)					

	129	130	131	132	133	134	135
16 **Manzullo**	N	N	N	N	Y	Y	N
17 Hare	Y	Y	Y	Y	Y	Y	Y
18 **LaHood**	N	N	Y	N	Y	Y	?
19 **Shimkus**	N	N	Y	N	Y	Y	N
INDIANA							
1 Visclosky	Y	Y	Y	Y	Y	Y	Y
2 Donnelly	N	Y	Y	N	Y	Y	Y
3 **Souder**	N	N	N	N	Y	Y	N
4 **Buyer**	N	N	N	N	Y	Y	N
5 **Burton**	N	N	N	N	Y	Y	N
6 **Pence**	N	N	N	N	Y	Y	N
7 Vacant							
8 Ellsworth	Y	Y	Y	N	Y	Y	Y
9 Hill	Y	Y	Y	Y	Y	Y	Y
IOWA							
1 Braley	Y	Y	Y	Y	Y	Y	Y
2 Loebsack	Y	Y	Y	Y	Y	Y	Y
3 Boswell	Y	Y	Y	Y	Y	Y	Y
4 **Latham**	N	N	Y	N	Y	Y	N
5 **King**	N	N	N	N	Y	Y	N
KANSAS							
1 **Moran**	N	N	Y	N	Y	Y	N
2 Boyda	Y	Y	Y	Y	Y	Y	Y
3 Moore	Y	Y	Y	Y	Y	Y	Y
4 **Tiahrt**	N	N	N	N	Y	Y	N
KENTUCKY							
1 **Whitfield**	N	N	N	N	Y	Y	N
2 **Lewis**	N	N	N	N	Y	Y	N
3 Yarmuth	Y	Y	Y	Y	Y	Y	Y
4 **Davis**	N	N	N	N	Y	Y	N
5 **Rogers**	N	N	N	N	Y	Y	N
6 Chandler	Y	Y	Y	Y	Y	Y	Y
LOUISIANA							
1 Vacant							
2 Jefferson	Y	Y	Y	Y	Y	Y	Y
3 Melancon	Y	Y	Y	Y	Y	Y	Y
4 **McCrery**	N	N	N	N	Y	Y	N
5 **Alexander**	N	N	N	N	Y	Y	N
6 Vacant							
7 **Boustany**	N	N	Y	N	Y	Y	?
MAINE							
1 Allen	Y	Y	Y	Y	Y	Y	Y
2 Michaud	Y	Y	Y	Y	Y	Y	Y
MARYLAND							
1 **Gilchrest**	N	N	Y	N	Y	Y	N
2 Ruppersberger	Y	Y	Y	Y	Y	Y	?
3 Sarbanes	Y	Y	Y	Y	Y	Y	Y
4 Wynn	Y	Y	Y	Y	Y	Y	Y
5 Hoyer	Y	Y	Y	Y	Y	Y	Y
6 **Bartlett**	N	N	N	N	Y	Y	N
7 Cummings	Y	Y	Y	Y	Y	Y	Y
8 Van Hollen	Y	Y	Y	Y	Y	Y	Y
MASSACHUSETTS							
1 Olver	Y	Y	Y	Y	Y	Y	Y
2 Neal	Y	Y	Y	Y	Y	Y	Y
3 McGovern	Y	Y	Y	Y	Y	Y	Y
4 Frank	Y	Y	Y	Y	Y	Y	Y
5 Tsongas	Y	Y	Y	Y	Y	Y	Y
6 Tierney	Y	Y	Y	Y	Y	Y	Y
7 Markey	Y	Y	Y	Y	Y	Y	Y
8 Capuano	Y	Y	Y	Y	Y	Y	Y
9 Lynch	Y	Y	Y	Y	Y	Y	Y
10 Delahunt	Y	Y	Y	Y	Y	Y	Y
MICHIGAN							
1 Stupak	Y	Y	Y	Y	Y	Y	Y
2 **Hoekstra**	N	N	N	N	Y	Y	N
3 **Ehlers**	N	N	N	N	Y	Y	N
4 **Camp**	N	N	N	N	Y	Y	N
5 Kildee	Y	Y	Y	Y	Y	Y	Y
6 **Upton**	N	N	Y	N	Y	Y	N
7 **Walberg**	N	N	N	N	Y	Y	N
8 **Rogers**	N	N	N	N	Y	Y	N
9 **Knollenberg**	N	N	Y	N	Y	Y	N
10 **Miller**	N	N	N	N	Y	Y	N
11 **McCotter**	N	N	N	N	Y	Y	N
12 Levin	Y	Y	Y	Y	Y	Y	Y
13 Kilpatrick	Y	Y	Y	Y	Y	Y	Y
14 Conyers	Y	Y	Y	Y	Y	Y	Y
15 Dingell	Y	Y	Y	Y	Y	Y	Y
MINNESOTA							
1 Walz	Y	Y	Y	Y	Y	Y	Y
2 **Kline**	N	N	N	N	Y	Y	N
3 **Ramstad**	N	N	Y	N	Y	Y	N
4 McCollum	Y	Y	Y	Y	Y	Y	Y
5 Ellison	Y	Y	Y	Y	Y	Y	Y
6 **Bachmann**	N	N	N	N	Y	Y	N
7 Peterson	Y	Y	Y	Y	Y	Y	Y
8 Oberstar	?	?	?	?	?	?	?
MISSISSIPPI							
1 Vacant							
2 Thompson	Y	Y	Y	Y	Y	Y	Y
3 **Pickering**	N	N	N	N	Y	Y	N
4 Taylor	Y	Y	Y	Y	Y	Y	Y
MISSOURI							
1 Clay	Y	Y	Y	Y	Y	Y	Y
2 **Akin**	N	N	N	N	Y	Y	N
3 Carnahan	Y	Y	Y	?	Y	Y	N
4 Skelton	Y	Y	Y	Y	Y	Y	Y
5 Cleaver	Y	Y	Y	Y	Y	Y	Y
6 **Graves**	N	N	Y	N	Y	Y	N
7 **Blunt**	N	N	N	N	Y	Y	N
8 **Emerson**	N	N	Y	N	Y	Y	N
9 **Hulshof**	N	N	Y	N	Y	Y	N
MONTANA							
AL **Rehberg**	N	N	N	N	Y	Y	N
NEBRASKA							
1 **Fortenberry**	N	N	Y	N	Y	Y	N
2 **Terry**	?	N	N	N	Y	Y	N
3 **Smith**	N	N	N	N	Y	Y	N
NEVADA							
1 Berkley	Y	Y	Y	Y	Y	Y	Y
2 **Heller**	N	N	N	N	Y	Y	N
3 **Porter**	N	N	Y	N	Y	Y	N
NEW HAMPSHIRE							
1 Shea-Porter	Y	Y	Y	Y	Y	Y	Y
2 Hodes	Y	Y	Y	Y	Y	Y	Y
NEW JERSEY							
1 Andrews	Y	Y	Y	Y	Y	Y	Y
2 **LoBiondo**	N	N	Y	N	Y	Y	N
3 **Saxton**	N	N	Y	N	Y	Y	N
4 **Smith**	N	N	Y	N	Y	Y	N
5 **Garrett**	N	N	N	N	Y	Y	N
6 Pallone	Y	Y	Y	Y	Y	Y	Y
7 **Ferguson**	N	N	Y	N	Y	Y	N
8 Pascrell	Y	Y	Y	Y	Y	Y	Y
9 Rothman	Y	Y	Y	Y	Y	Y	Y
10 Payne	Y	Y	Y	Y	Y	Y	Y
11 **Frelinghuysen**	N	N	Y	N	?	Y	N
12 Holt	Y	Y	Y	Y	Y	Y	Y
13 Sires	Y	Y	Y	Y	Y	Y	Y
NEW MEXICO							
1 **Wilson**	N	N	N	N	Y	Y	N
2 **Pearce**	N	N	N	N	Y	Y	N
3 Udall	Y	Y	Y	Y	Y	Y	Y
NEW YORK							
1 Bishop	Y	Y	Y	Y	Y	Y	Y
2 Israel	Y	Y	Y	Y	Y	Y	Y
3 **King**	N	N	Y	N	Y	Y	N
4 McCarthy	Y	Y	Y	Y	Y	Y	Y
5 Ackerman	Y	Y	Y	Y	Y	Y	Y
6 Meeks	Y	Y	Y	Y	Y	Y	Y
7 Crowley	Y	Y	Y	Y	Y	Y	Y
8 Nadler	Y	Y	Y	Y	Y	Y	Y
9 Weiner	Y	Y	Y	Y	Y	Y	Y
10 Towns	Y	Y	Y	Y	Y	Y	Y
11 Clarke	Y	Y	Y	Y	Y	Y	Y
12 Velázquez	Y	Y	Y	Y	Y	Y	Y
13 **Fossella**	N	N	N	N	Y	Y	N
14 Maloney	Y	Y	Y	Y	Y	Y	Y
15 Rangel	?	?	?	?	?	?	?
16 Serrano	Y	Y	Y	Y	Y	Y	Y
17 Engel	Y	Y	Y	Y	Y	Y	Y
18 Lowey	Y	Y	Y	Y	Y	Y	Y
19 Hall	Y	Y	Y	Y	Y	Y	Y
20 Gillibrand	Y	Y	Y	N	Y	Y	Y
21 McNulty	Y	Y	Y	Y	Y	Y	Y
22 Hinchey	Y	Y	Y	Y	Y	Y	Y
23 **McHugh**	N	N	Y	N	Y	Y	N
24 Arcuri	Y	Y	Y	Y	Y	Y	Y
25 **Walsh**	N	N	Y	N	Y	Y	N
26 **Reynolds**	N	N	N	N	Y	Y	N
27 Higgins	Y	Y	Y	Y	Y	Y	Y
28 Slaughter	Y	Y	Y	Y	Y	Y	Y
29 **Kuhl**	N	N	Y	N	Y	Y	N
NORTH CAROLINA							
1 Butterfield	Y	Y	Y	Y	Y	Y	Y
2 Etheridge	Y	Y	Y	Y	Y	Y	Y
3 **Jones**	N	N	N	Y	Y	Y	N
4 Price	Y	Y	Y	Y	Y	Y	Y
5 **Foxx**	N	N	N	N	Y	Y	N
6 **Coble**	N	N	N	N	Y	Y	N
7 McIntyre	Y	Y	Y	Y	Y	Y	Y
8 **Hayes**	N	N	N	N	Y	Y	N
9 **Myrick**	N	N	N	N	Y	Y	N
10 **McHenry**	N	N	N	N	Y	Y	N
11 Shuler	Y	Y	Y	N	Y	Y	Y
12 Watt	Y	Y	Y	Y	Y	Y	Y
13 Miller	Y	Y	Y	Y	Y	Y	Y
NORTH DAKOTA							
AL Pomeroy	Y	Y	Y	Y	Y	Y	Y
OHIO							
1 **Chabot**	N	N	N	N	Y	Y	N
2 **Schmidt**	N	N	N	N	Y	Y	N
3 **Turner**	N	N	Y	N	Y	Y	N
4 **Jordan**	N	N	N	N	Y	Y	N
5 **Latta**	N	N	N	N	Y	Y	N
6 Wilson	Y	Y	Y	Y	Y	Y	Y
7 **Hobson**	N	N	N	N	Y	Y	N
8 **Boehner**	N	N	N	N	Y	Y	N
9 Kaptur	Y	Y	Y	Y	Y	Y	Y
10 Kucinich	Y	Y	Y	Y	Y	Y	Y
11 Tubbs Jones	Y	Y	Y	Y	Y	Y	Y
12 **Tiberi**	N	N	N	N	Y	Y	N
13 Sutton	Y	Y	Y	Y	Y	Y	Y
14 **LaTourette**	N	N	Y	N	Y	Y	N
15 **Pryce**	N	N	Y	N	Y	Y	N
16 **Regula**	N	N	N	N	Y	Y	N
17 Ryan	Y	Y	Y	Y	Y	Y	Y
18 Space	Y	Y	Y	N	Y	Y	Y
OKLAHOMA							
1 **Sullivan**	N	N	N	N	Y	Y	N
2 Boren	Y	Y	Y	Y	Y	Y	Y
3 **Lucas**	N	N	N	N	Y	Y	N
4 **Cole**	N	N	N	N	Y	Y	N
5 **Fallin**	N	N	N	N	Y	Y	N
OREGON							
1 Wu	Y	Y	Y	Y	Y	Y	Y
2 **Walden**	N	N	N	N	Y	Y	N
3 Blumenauer	Y	Y	Y	Y	Y	Y	Y
4 DeFazio	Y	Y	Y	Y	Y	Y	Y
5 Hooley	?	?	?	?	?	?	?
PENNSYLVANIA							
1 Brady	Y	Y	Y	Y	Y	Y	Y
2 Fattah	Y	Y	Y	Y	Y	Y	Y
3 **English**	N	N	Y	N	Y	Y	N
4 Altmire	Y	Y	Y	Y	Y	Y	Y
5 **Peterson**	N	N	Y	N	Y	Y	N
6 **Gerlach**	N	N	Y	N	Y	Y	N
7 Sestak	Y	Y	Y	Y	Y	?	Y
8 Murphy, P.	Y	Y	Y	Y	Y	Y	Y
9 **Shuster**	N	N	N	N	Y	Y	N
10 Carney	Y	Y	Y	Y	Y	Y	Y
11 Kanjorski	Y	Y	Y	Y	Y	Y	Y
12 Murtha	Y	Y	Y	Y	Y	Y	Y
13 Schwartz	Y	Y	Y	Y	Y	Y	Y
14 Doyle	Y	Y	Y	Y	Y	Y	Y
15 **Dent**	N	N	Y	N	Y	Y	N
16 **Pitts**	N	N	N	N	Y	Y	N
17 Holden	Y	Y	Y	Y	Y	Y	Y
18 **Murphy, T.**	N	N	Y	N	Y	Y	N
19 **Platts**	N	N	Y	N	Y	Y	N
RHODE ISLAND							
1 Kennedy	Y	Y	Y	+	+	Y	Y
2 Langevin	Y	Y	Y	Y	Y	Y	Y
SOUTH CAROLINA							
1 **Brown**	N	N	N	N	Y	Y	N
2 **Wilson**	N	N	N	N	Y	Y	N
3 **Barrett**	N	N	N	N	Y	Y	N
4 **Inglis**	N	N	N	N	Y	Y	N
5 Spratt	Y	Y	Y	Y	Y	Y	Y
6 Clyburn	Y	Y	Y	Y	Y	Y	Y
SOUTH DAKOTA							
AL Herseth Sandlin	Y	Y	Y	N	Y	Y	Y
TENNESSEE							
1 **Davis, D.**	N	N	N	N	Y	Y	N
2 **Duncan**	N	N	N	N	Y	Y	N
3 **Wamp**	N	N	N	N	Y	Y	N
4 Davis, L.	Y	Y	Y	Y	Y	Y	Y
5 Cooper	Y	Y	Y	Y	Y	Y	Y
6 Gordon	Y	Y	Y	Y	Y	Y	Y
7 **Blackburn**	N	N	N	N	Y	Y	N
8 Tanner	Y	Y	Y	Y	Y	Y	Y
9 Cohen	Y	Y	Y	Y	Y	Y	Y
TEXAS							
1 **Gohmert**	N	N	N	N	Y	Y	N
2 **Poe**	N	N	N	N	Y	Y	N
3 **Johnson, S.**	N	N	N	N	Y	Y	N
4 **Hall**	N	N	N	N	Y	Y	N
5 **Hensarling**	N	N	N	N	Y	Y	N
6 **Barton**	N	N	N	N	Y	Y	N
7 **Culberson**	N	N	N	N	Y	Y	N
8 **Brady**	N	N	N	N	Y	Y	N
9 Green, A.	Y	Y	Y	Y	Y	Y	Y
10 **McCaul**	N	N	Y	N	Y	Y	N
11 **Conaway**	N	N	N	N	Y	Y	N
12 **Granger**	N	N	N	N	Y	Y	N
13 **Thornberry**	N	N	N	N	Y	Y	N
14 **Paul**	N	N	N	Y	Y	N	Y
15 Hinojosa	Y	Y	Y	Y	Y	Y	Y
16 Reyes	Y	Y	Y	Y	Y	Y	Y
17 Edwards	Y	Y	Y	Y	Y	Y	Y
18 Jackson Lee	Y	Y	Y	Y	Y	Y	Y
19 **Neugebauer**	N	N	N	N	Y	Y	N
20 Gonzalez	Y	Y	Y	Y	Y	Y	Y
21 **Smith**	N	N	N	N	Y	Y	N
22 Lampson	N	N	Y	Y	Y	Y	N
23 Rodriguez	Y	Y	Y	Y	Y	Y	Y
24 **Marchant**	N	N	N	N	Y	Y	N
25 Doggett	Y	Y	Y	Y	Y	Y	Y
26 **Burgess**	N	N	N	N	Y	Y	N
27 Ortiz	Y	Y	Y	Y	Y	Y	Y
28 Cuellar	Y	Y	Y	Y	Y	Y	Y
29 Green, G.	Y	Y	Y	Y	Y	Y	Y
30 Johnson, E.	Y	Y	Y	Y	Y	Y	Y
31 **Carter**	N	N	N	N	Y	Y	N
32 **Sessions**	N	N	N	N	Y	Y	N
UTAH							
1 **Bishop**	N	N	N	N	Y	Y	N
2 Matheson	Y	Y	Y	N	Y	Y	Y
3 **Cannon**	?	N	N	N	Y	Y	N
VERMONT							
AL Welch	Y	Y	Y	Y	Y	Y	Y
VIRGINIA							
1 **Wittman**	N	N	Y	N	Y	Y	N
2 **Drake**	N	N	N	N	Y	Y	N
3 Scott	Y	Y	Y	Y	Y	Y	Y
4 **Forbes**	N	N	N	N	Y	Y	N
5 **Goode**	N	N	N	N	Y	Y	N
6 **Goodlatte**	N	N	N	N	Y	Y	N
7 **Cantor**	N	N	N	N	Y	Y	N
8 Moran	Y	Y	Y	Y	Y	Y	Y
9 Boucher	Y	Y	Y	Y	Y	Y	Y
10 **Wolf**	N	N	Y	N	Y	Y	N
11 **Davis**	N	N	N	N	Y	?	N
WASHINGTON							
1 Inslee	Y	Y	Y	Y	Y	Y	Y
2 Larsen	Y	Y	Y	Y	Y	Y	Y
3 Baird	Y	Y	Y	Y	Y	Y	Y
4 **Hastings**	N	N	N	N	Y	Y	N
5 **McMorris Rodgers**	N	N	N	N	Y	Y	N
6 Dicks	Y	Y	Y	Y	Y	Y	Y
7 McDermott	Y	Y	Y	Y	Y	Y	Y
8 **Reichert**	N	N	Y	N	Y	Y	N
9 Smith	Y	Y	Y	Y	Y	Y	Y
WEST VIRGINIA							
1 Mollohan	Y	Y	Y	Y	Y	Y	Y
2 **Capito**	N	N	Y	N	Y	Y	N
3 Rahall	Y	Y	Y	Y	Y	Y	Y
WISCONSIN							
1 **Ryan**	N	N	N	N	Y	Y	N
2 Baldwin	Y	Y	Y	Y	Y	Y	Y
3 Kind	Y	Y	Y	Y	Y	Y	Y
4 Moore	Y	Y	Y	Y	Y	Y	Y
5 **Sensenbrenner**	N	N	N	N	Y	Y	N
6 **Petri**	N	N	N	N	Y	Y	N
7 Obey	Y	Y	Y	Y	Y	Y	Y
8 Kagen	Y	Y	Y	Y	Y	Y	Y
WYOMING							
AL **Cubin**	N	N	N	N	Y	Y	?
DELEGATES							
Faleomavaega (A.S.)							
Norton (D.C.)							
Bordallo (Guam)							
Fortuño (P.R.)							
Christensen (V.I.)							

IN THE HOUSE | By Vote Number

136. Procedural Motion/Journal. Approval of the House Journal of Wednesday, March 13, 2008. Approved 222-183: R 15-168; D 207-15 (ND 154-11, SD 53-4). March 13, 2008.

137. H Con Res 312. Fiscal 2009 Budget Resolution/Congressional Black Caucus Substitute. Kilpatrick, D-Mich., substitute amendment that would achieve a budget surplus of $183 billion in fiscal 2012. The amendment would assume increased federal revenue by a repeal of the 2001- and 2003-enacted tax cuts for household income that exceeds $200,000. It also would assume the repeal of certain corporate tax provisions, as well as increase funding for health care, education and job training programs, and veteran benefits and services. Rejected in Committee of the Whole 126-292: R 0-192; D 126-100 (ND 102-68, SD 24-32). March 13, 2008.

138. H Con Res 312. Fiscal 2009 Budget Resolution/Congressional Progressive Caucus Substitute. Lee, D-Calif., substitute amendment that would set non-defense, domestic discretionary spending at $551.7 billion for fiscal 2009. It would project surpluses in fiscal 2012 and 2018. It would assume a redeployment of U.S. military personnel and contractors from Iraq by Sept. 30, 2009, and an extension of tax credits for investment in renewable and alternative energy. It would assume a repeal of the 2001 and 2003 tax cuts for the top 1 percent of U.S. households and the elimination of certain corporate tax provisions. It would call for increased funding for transportation, global warming efforts, education, housing, health care and job training. Rejected in Committee of the Whole 98-322: R 0-191; D 98-131 (ND 79-93, SD 19-38). March 13, 2008.

139. Procedural Matter/Quorum Call.* A quorum was present with 384 members responding (46 members did not respond). March 13, 2008.

140. H Con Res 312. Fiscal 2009 Budget Resolution/Republican Substitute. Ryan, R-Wis., substitute amendment that would set discretionary spending of $973 billion in fiscal 2009 and project budget surpluses in fiscal 2012 and 2013. It would assume an extension of the 2001 and 2003 tax cuts and provide for reconciliation legislation to reduce mandatory spending by $412.4 billion over five years. It would place a moratorium on earmarks and establish procedures for a legislative line-item veto. Rejected in Committee of the Whole 157-263: R 153-38; D 4-225 (ND 0-172, SD 4-53). March 13, 2008.

141. H Con Res 312. Fiscal 2009 Budget Resolution/Adoption. Adoption of the concurrent resolution that would allow up to $1 trillion in discretionary spending in fiscal 2009, plus $70 billion for the wars in Iraq and Afghanistan, and $5.8 billion for hurricane recovery. It would assume a budget surplus in fiscal 2012 and 2013. It would call on the Ways and Means Committee to report two reconciliation bills: a bill to reduce fiscal 2009 revenue by $70 billion, allowing for an AMT patch, offset over five years; and a bill to reduce mandatory spending by $750 million over six years. Adopted 212-207: R 0-191; D 212-16 (ND 160-11, SD 52-5). March 13, 2008.

142. H Res 991. 69th Infantry Regiment Tribute/Adoption. McIntyre, D-N.C., motion to suspend the rules and adopt the resolution that would commend the 69th Infantry Regiment for continually participating in the war on terrorism since the Sept. 11, 2001, attacks. Motion agreed to 406-0: R 187-0; D 219-0 (ND 163-0, SD 56-0). A two-thirds majority (271 in this case) is required for adoption under suspension of the rules. March 13, 2008.

*CQ does not include quorum calls in its vote charts.

[1] Rep. André Carson, D-Ind., was sworn in March 13 to fill the seat vacated by Democrat Julia Carson, who died Dec. 15, 2007. The first vote for which he was eligible was 139.

ND Northern Democrats, SD Southern Democrats
Southern states: Ala., Ark., Fla., Ga., Ky., La., Miss., N.C., Okla., S.C., Tenn., Texas, Va.

	136	137	138	140	141	142
ALABAMA						
1 Bonner	N	N	N	Y	N	Y
2 Everett	N	N	N	Y	N	Y
3 Rogers	N	N	N	N	N	Y
4 Aderholt	N	N	N	Y	N	Y
5 Cramer	Y	N	N	Y	N	?
6 Bachus	Y	N	N	Y	N	Y
7 Davis	Y	Y	N	N	Y	Y
ALASKA						
AL Young	?	?	?	?	?	?
ARIZONA						
1 Renzi	?	?	?	?	?	?
2 Franks	N	N	N	Y	N	Y
3 Shadegg	N	N	N	Y	N	Y
4 Pastor	Y	Y	Y	N	Y	Y
5 Mitchell	N	N	N	N	N	Y
6 Flake	N	N	N	Y	N	Y
7 Grijalva	Y	Y	Y	N	Y	Y
8 Giffords	N	N	N	N	N	Y
ARKANSAS						
1 Berry	Y	N	N	N	Y	Y
2 Snyder	Y	N	N	Y	Y	Y
3 Boozman	N	N	N	N	N	Y
4 Ross	Y	N	N	N	Y	Y
CALIFORNIA						
1 Thompson	N	N	N	N	Y	Y
2 Herger	N	N	N	Y	N	Y
3 Lungren	N	N	N	Y	N	Y
4 Doolittle	N	N	N	Y	N	Y
5 Matsui	Y	Y	N	Y	Y	Y
6 Woolsey	?	?	?	?	?	?
7 Miller, George	Y	Y	Y	N	Y	Y
8 Pelosi					Y	
9 Lee	Y	Y	Y	N	Y	Y
10 Tauscher	Y	N	N	Y	Y	Y
11 McNerney	Y	N	N	Y	Y	Y
12 Vacant						
13 Stark	Y	Y	Y	N	Y	Y
14 Eshoo	Y	N	N	N	Y	Y
15 Honda	Y	Y	Y	N	Y	Y
16 Lofgren	Y	Y	Y	N	Y	Y
17 Farr	Y	Y	Y	N	Y	Y
18 Cardoza	Y	N	N	N	Y	Y
19 Radanovich	N	N	N	Y	N	Y
20 Costa	Y	N	N	N	Y	Y
21 Nunes	N	N	N	Y	N	Y
22 McCarthy	N	N	N	Y	N	Y
23 Capps	Y	Y	N	Y	Y	Y
24 Gallegly	N	N	N	Y	N	Y
25 McKeon	N	N	N	Y	N	Y
26 Dreier	N	N	N	Y	N	Y
27 Sherman	Y	Y	N	N	Y	Y
28 Berman	Y	Y	N	N	Y	?
29 Schiff	Y	N	N	N	Y	Y
30 Waxman	Y	Y	Y	N	Y	Y
31 Becerra	Y	Y	Y	N	Y	Y
32 Solis	Y	Y	Y	N	Y	Y
33 Watson	Y	Y	Y	N	Y	Y
34 Roybal-Allard	Y	Y	N	N	Y	Y
35 Waters	Y	Y	Y	?	Y	?
36 Harman	Y	Y	N	Y	Y	Y
37 Richardson	Y	Y	Y	N	Y	Y
38 Napolitano	Y	Y	Y	N	Y	Y
39 Sánchez, Linda	Y	Y	Y	N	Y	Y
40 Royce	N	N	N	Y	N	Y
41 Lewis	N	N	N	Y	N	?
42 Miller, Gary	N	N	N	Y	N	Y
43 Baca	Y	Y	Y	N	Y	Y
44 Calvert	N	N	N	Y	N	Y
45 Bono Mack	N	N	N	Y	N	Y
46 Rohrabacher	N	N	N	Y	N	Y
47 Sanchez, Loretta	Y	N	N	N	Y	Y
48 Campbell	N	N	N	Y	N	Y
49 Issa	?	N	N	Y	N	Y
50 Bilbray	N	N	N	Y	N	Y
51 Filner	Y	Y	N	Y	Y	Y
52 Hunter	?	?	?	?	?	?
53 Davis	Y	Y	N	Y	Y	Y

	136	137	138	140	141	142
COLORADO						
1 DeGette	?	N	N	N	Y	Y
2 Udall	?	N	N	N	Y	Y
3 Salazar	Y	N	N	N	Y	Y
4 Musgrave	N	N	N	Y	N	Y
5 Lamborn	N	N	N	Y	N	Y
6 Tancredo	?	?	?	?	?	?
7 Perlmutter	N	N	N	N	Y	Y
CONNECTICUT						
1 Larson	Y	Y	Y	N	Y	Y
2 Courtney	Y	N	N	N	Y	Y
3 DeLauro	Y	Y	Y	N	Y	Y
4 Shays	N	N	N	N	N	Y
5 Murphy	Y	N	N	N	Y	Y
DELAWARE						
AL Castle	Y	N	N	N	N	Y
FLORIDA						
1 Miller	N	N	N	Y	N	Y
2 Boyd	Y	N	N	N	Y	Y
3 Brown	Y	N	N	N	Y	Y
4 Crenshaw	N	N	N	Y	N	Y
5 Brown-Waite	Y	N	N	Y	N	Y
6 Stearns	N	N	N	Y	N	Y
7 Mica	N	N	N	Y	N	Y
8 Keller	N	N	N	Y	N	Y
9 Bilirakis	N	N	N	Y	N	Y
10 Young	N	N	N	Y	N	Y
11 Castor	Y	Y	N	Y	Y	Y
12 Putnam	N	N	N	Y	N	Y
13 Buchanan	N	N	N	Y	N	Y
14 Mack	N	N	N	Y	N	Y
15 Weldon	N	N	N	N	N	Y
16 Mahoney	Y	N	N	N	Y	Y
17 Meek	Y	Y	Y	N	Y	Y
18 Ros-Lehtinen	N	N	N	Y	N	Y
19 Wexler	Y	Y	Y	N	Y	Y
20 Wasserman Schultz	Y	Y	Y	N	Y	Y
21 Diaz-Balart, L.	Y	N	N	Y	N	Y
22 Klein	Y	N	N	N	Y	Y
23 Hastings	Y	Y	Y	N	Y	Y
24 Feeney	N	N	N	Y	N	Y
25 Diaz-Balart, M.	Y	N	N	Y	N	Y
GEORGIA						
1 Kingston	N	N	N	Y	N	Y
2 Bishop	Y	Y	N	N	Y	Y
3 Westmoreland	N	N	N	Y	N	Y
4 Johnson	Y	Y	Y	N	Y	Y
5 Lewis	Y	?	Y	N	Y	Y
6 Price	N	N	N	Y	N	Y
7 Linder	?	N	N	Y	N	Y
8 Marshall	Y	N	N	N	Y	Y
9 Deal	N	N	N	Y	N	Y
10 Broun	N	N	N	Y	N	Y
11 Gingrey	N	N	N	Y	N	Y
12 Barrow	Y	N	N	N	Y	Y
13 Scott	Y	Y	Y	N	Y	Y
HAWAII						
1 Abercrombie	Y	Y	Y	N	Y	Y
2 Hirono	Y	Y	Y	N	Y	Y
IDAHO						
1 Sali	N	N	N	Y	N	Y
2 Simpson	N	N	N	Y	N	Y
ILLINOIS						
1 Rush	?	?	?	?	?	?
2 Jackson	Y	Y	Y	N	Y	Y
3 Lipinski	Y	N	N	N	Y	Y
4 Gutierrez	Y	Y	Y	N	Y	?
5 Emanuel	Y	Y	N	N	Y	Y
6 Roskam	N	N	N	Y	N	Y
7 Davis	Y	?	Y	N	Y	Y
8 Bean	Y	N	N	N	Y	Y
9 Schakowsky	Y	Y	Y	N	Y	Y
10 Kirk	Y	N	N	N	N	Y
11 Weller	N	N	?	?	?	?
12 Costello	Y	Y	N	N	Y	Y
13 Biggert	Y	N	N	Y	N	Y
14 Foster	Y	N	N	N	N	Y
15 Johnson	Y	N	N	N	N	Y

	136	137	138	140	141	142
16 **Manzullo**	N	N	N	Y	N	Y
17 Hare	Y	Y	Y	N	Y	Y
18 **LaHood**	?	?	?	?	?	?
19 **Shimkus**	N	N	N	Y	N	Y
INDIANA						
1 Visclosky	Y	N	N	N	Y	Y
2 Donnelly	N	N	N	N	N	Y
3 **Souder**	N	N	N	Y	N	Y
4 **Buyer**	N	N	N	Y	N	Y
5 **Burton**	N	N	N	Y	N	Y
6 **Pence**	N	N	N	Y	N	Y
7 Carson, A.[1]				N	Y	Y
8 Ellsworth	N	N	N	N	N	Y
9 Hill	N	N	N	N	N	Y
IOWA						
1 Braley	Y	Y	N	N	Y	Y
2 Loebsack	Y	Y	N	N	Y	Y
3 Boswell	Y	Y	N	N	Y	Y
4 **Latham**	Y	N	N	Y	N	Y
5 **King**	N	N	N	Y	N	?
KANSAS						
1 **Moran**	N	N	N	N	N	Y
2 Boyda	Y	N	N	N	Y	Y
3 Moore	Y	N	N	N	Y	Y
4 **Tiahrt**	N	N	N	N	N	Y
KENTUCKY						
1 **Whitfield**	N	N	N	Y	N	Y
2 **Lewis**	N	N	N	Y	N	Y
3 Yarmuth	Y	N	N	N	Y	Y
4 **Davis**	N	N	N	Y	N	Y
5 **Rogers**	N	N	N	Y	N	Y
6 Chandler	Y	N	N	N	Y	Y
LOUISIANA						
1 Vacant						
2 Jefferson	Y	Y	Y	N	Y	Y
3 Melancon	Y	N	N	N	Y	Y
4 **McCrery**	N	N	N	Y	N	Y
5 **Alexander**	N	N	N	Y	N	Y
6 Vacant						
7 **Boustany**	?	?	?	?	?	?
MAINE						
1 Allen	Y	N	N	N	Y	Y
2 Michaud	Y	N	N	N	Y	Y
MARYLAND						
1 **Gilchrest**	N	N	N	Y	N	Y
2 Ruppersberger	?	Y	N	N	Y	Y
3 Sarbanes	Y	Y	N	N	Y	Y
4 Wynn	Y	Y	Y	N	Y	Y
5 Hoyer	Y	Y	N	N	Y	Y
6 **Bartlett**	N	N	N	Y	N	Y
7 Cummings	Y	Y	Y	N	Y	Y
8 Van Hollen	Y	Y	N	N	Y	Y
MASSACHUSETTS						
1 Olver	Y	Y	Y	N	Y	Y
2 Neal	Y	Y	Y	N	Y	Y
3 McGovern	Y	Y	Y	N	Y	Y
4 Frank	Y	Y	Y	N	Y	Y
5 Tsongas	Y	Y	Y	N	Y	Y
6 Tierney	Y	Y	Y	N	Y	?
7 Markey	Y	Y	Y	N	Y	Y
8 Capuano	Y	Y	Y	N	Y	Y
9 Lynch	Y	Y	Y	N	Y	Y
10 Delahunt	Y	Y	Y	N	Y	Y
MICHIGAN						
1 Stupak	N	N	N	N	Y	Y
2 **Hoekstra**	N	N	N	Y	N	Y
3 **Ehlers**	N	N	N	Y	N	Y
4 **Camp**	N	N	N	Y	N	Y
5 Kildee	Y	Y	N	N	Y	Y
6 **Upton**	N	N	N	Y	N	Y
7 **Walberg**	Y	N	N	Y	N	Y
8 **Rogers**	N	N	N	Y	N	Y
9 **Knollenberg**	N	N	N	Y	N	Y
10 **Miller**	N	N	N	Y	N	Y
11 **McCotter**	N	N	N	Y	N	?
12 Levin	Y	Y	Y	N	Y	Y
13 Kilpatrick	Y	Y	Y	N	Y	Y
14 Conyers	Y	Y	Y	N	Y	Y
15 Dingell	Y	N	N	N	Y	Y
MINNESOTA						
1 Walz	Y	N	N	N	Y	Y
2 **Kline**	?	N	N	Y	N	Y
3 **Ramstad**	N	N	N	N	N	Y
4 McCollum	?	Y	Y	N	Y	?
5 Ellison	Y	Y	Y	N	Y	Y
6 **Bachmann**	N	N	N	Y	N	Y
7 Peterson	N	N	N	N	Y	Y
8 Oberstar	?	?	?	?	?	?
MISSISSIPPI						
1 Vacant						
2 Thompson	Y	Y	Y	N	Y	Y
3 **Pickering**	N	N	N	Y	N	Y
4 Taylor	Y	N	N	N	Y	Y
MISSOURI						
1 Clay	Y	Y	Y	N	Y	Y
2 **Akin**	N	N	N	Y	N	Y
3 Carnahan	Y	N	N	N	Y	Y
4 Skelton	Y	N	N	N	Y	Y
5 Cleaver	Y	Y	Y	N	Y	Y
6 **Graves**	N	N	N	Y	N	Y
7 **Blunt**	N	N	N	Y	N	Y
8 **Emerson**	N	N	N	N	N	Y
9 **Hulshof**	N	N	N	Y	N	Y
MONTANA						
AL **Rehberg**	N	N	N	Y	N	Y
NEBRASKA						
1 **Fortenberry**	N	N	N	Y	N	Y
2 **Terry**	N	N	N	Y	N	Y
3 **Smith**	N	N	N	Y	N	Y
NEVADA						
1 Berkley	Y	N	N	N	Y	Y
2 **Heller**	N	N	N	N	N	Y
3 **Porter**	N	N	N	N	N	Y
NEW HAMPSHIRE						
1 Shea-Porter	Y	N	N	N	Y	Y
2 Hodes	Y	N	N	N	Y	Y
NEW JERSEY						
1 Andrews	Y	Y	N	N	Y	Y
2 **LoBiondo**	N	N	N	N	N	Y
3 **Saxton**	N	N	N	N	N	Y
4 **Smith**	N	N	N	N	N	Y
5 **Garrett**	N	N	?	Y	N	Y
6 Pallone	Y	Y	Y	N	Y	Y
7 **Ferguso n**	N	N	N	Y	N	Y
8 Pascrell	Y	Y	N	N	Y	Y
9 Rothman	Y	Y	N	N	Y	Y
10 Payne	Y	Y	Y	N	Y	Y
11 **Frelinghuysen**	N	N	N	N	N	Y
12 Holt	Y	Y	Y	N	Y	Y
13 Sires	Y	Y	N	N	Y	Y
NEW MEXICO						
1 **Wilson**	N	N	N	Y	N	Y
2 **Pearce**	N	N	N	Y	N	Y
3 Udall	Y	N	N	N	Y	Y
NEW YORK						
1 Bishop	Y	N	N	N	Y	Y
2 Israel	Y	N	N	N	Y	Y
3 **King**	N	N	N	N	N	Y
4 McCarthy	Y	N	N	N	Y	?
5 Ackerman	Y	Y	Y	N	Y	Y
6 Meeks	Y	Y	Y	N	Y	?
7 Crowley	Y	Y	Y	N	Y	Y
8 Nadler	Y	Y	Y	N	Y	Y
9 Weiner	Y	Y	Y	N	Y	Y
10 Towns	Y	Y	Y	N	Y	Y
11 Clarke	Y	Y	Y	N	Y	Y
12 Velázquez	Y	Y	Y	N	Y	Y
13 **Fossella**	N	N	N	N	N	Y
14 Maloney	Y	Y	Y	N	Y	Y
15 Rangel	?	?	?	?	?	?
16 Serrano	Y	Y	Y	N	Y	Y
17 Engel	Y	Y	Y	N	Y	Y
18 Lowey	Y	Y	N	N	Y	Y
19 Hall	Y	N	N	N	Y	Y
20 Gillibrand	Y	N	N	N	Y	Y
21 McNulty	Y	Y	Y	N	Y	Y
22 Hinchey	Y	Y	Y	N	Y	Y
23 **McHugh**	N	N	N	N	N	Y
24 Arcuri	Y	N	N	N	Y	Y
25 **Walsh**	N	N	N	N	N	Y
26 **Reynolds**	N	N	N	Y	N	Y
27 Higgins	Y	N	N	N	Y	Y
28 Slaughter	Y	Y	Y	N	Y	Y
29 **Kuhl**	Y	N	N	N	N	Y
NORTH CAROLINA						
1 Butterfield	Y	Y	Y	N	Y	Y
2 Etheridge	N	N	N	N	Y	Y
3 **Jones**	N	N	N	Y	N	Y
4 Price	Y	Y	N	N	Y	Y
5 **Foxx**	N	N	N	Y	N	Y
6 **Coble**	N	N	N	Y	N	Y
7 McIntyre	Y	N	N	Y	Y	Y
8 **Hayes**	N	N	N	N	N	Y
9 **Myrick**	N	N	N	Y	N	Y
10 **McHenry**	N	N	N	Y	N	Y
11 Shuler	N	N	N	Y	N	Y
12 Watt	Y	Y	Y	N	Y	Y
13 Miller	Y	Y	N	N	Y	Y
NORTH DAKOTA						
AL Pomeroy	Y	N	N	N	Y	Y
OHIO						
1 **Chabot**	N	N	N	Y	N	Y
2 **Schmidt**	N	N	N	N	N	Y
3 **Turner**	N	N	N	N	N	Y
4 **Jordan**	?	N	N	Y	N	Y
5 **Latta**	N	N	N	Y	N	Y
6 Wilson	Y	N	N	N	Y	Y
7 **Hobson**	N	N	N	N	N	Y
8 **Boehner**	N	N	N	Y	N	Y
9 Kaptur	Y	Y	Y	N	Y	Y
10 Kucinich	Y	Y	Y	N	N	Y
11 Tubbs Jones	Y	Y	Y	N	Y	Y
12 **Tiberi**	N	N	N	Y	N	Y
13 Sutton	Y	Y	N	N	Y	Y
14 **LaTourette**	N	N	N	N	N	Y
15 **Pryce**	N	N	N	Y	N	Y
16 **Regula**	N	N	N	N	N	Y
17 Ryan	Y	Y	Y	N	Y	Y
18 Space	Y	–	N	N	Y	Y
OKLAHOMA						
1 **Sullivan**	?	N	N	Y	N	Y
2 Boren	Y	N	N	N	Y	Y
3 **Lucas**	N	N	N	Y	N	Y
4 **Cole**	N	N	N	Y	N	Y
5 **Fallin**	N	N	N	Y	N	Y
OREGON						
1 Wu	Y	N	N	N	Y	Y
2 **Walden**	N	N	N	N	N	Y
3 Blumenauer	Y	Y	Y	N	Y	Y
4 DeFazio	Y	N	N	N	Y	Y
5 Hooley	?	?	?	?	?	?
PENNSYLVANIA						
1 Brady	Y	Y	Y	N	Y	Y
2 Fattah	Y	Y	Y	N	Y	Y
3 **English**	N	N	N	N	N	Y
4 Altmire	N	N	N	N	Y	Y
5 **Peterson**	N	N	N	Y	N	Y
6 **Gerlach**	N	N	N	N	N	Y
7 Sestak	Y	N	N	N	Y	Y
8 Murphy, P.	Y	N	N	N	N	Y
9 **Shuster**	N	N	N	Y	N	Y
10 Carney	N	N	N	N	Y	Y
11 Kanjorski	Y	N	N	N	Y	Y
12 Murtha	Y	N	N	N	Y	Y
13 Schwartz	Y	N	N	N	Y	Y
14 Doyle	Y	Y	Y	N	Y	Y
15 **Dent**	Y	N	N	N	N	Y
16 **Pitts**	?	N	N	Y	N	Y
17 Holden	Y	N	N	N	Y	Y
18 **Murphy, T.**	N	N	N	N	N	Y
19 **Platts**	N	N	N	Y	N	Y
RHODE ISLAND						
1 Kennedy	Y	Y	N	N	Y	Y
2 Langevin	Y	Y	N	N	Y	Y
SOUTH CAROLINA						
1 **Brown**	N	N	N	Y	N	Y
2 **Wilson**	N	N	N	Y	N	Y
3 **Barrett**	N	N	N	Y	N	Y
4 **Inglis**	N	N	N	Y	N	Y
5 Spratt	Y	N	N	N	Y	Y
6 Clyburn	Y	Y	Y	N	Y	Y
SOUTH DAKOTA						
AL Herseth Sandlin	Y	N	N	N	Y	Y
TENNESSEE						
1 **Davis, David**	N	N	N	Y	N	Y
2 **Duncan**	N	N	N	N	N	Y
3 **Wamp**	N	N	N	Y	N	Y
4 Davis, L.	Y	N	N	N	Y	Y
5 Cooper	Y	N	N	Y	Y	Y
6 Gordon	N	N	Y	N	Y	Y
7 **Blackburn**	?	N	N	Y	N	Y
8 Tanner	Y	N	N	N	Y	Y
9 Cohen	Y	Y	Y	N	Y	Y
TEXAS						
1 **Gohmert**	P	N	N	Y	N	?
2 **Poe**	N	N	N	Y	N	Y
3 **Johnson, S.**	N	N	N	Y	N	Y
4 **Hall**	N	N	N	Y	N	Y
5 **Hensarling**	N	N	N	Y	N	Y
6 **Barton**	N	N	N	Y	N	Y
7 **Culberson**	N	N	N	Y	N	Y
8 **Brady**	N	N	N	Y	N	Y
9 Green, A.	Y	Y	Y	N	Y	Y
10 **McCaul**	N	N	N	Y	N	Y
11 **Conaway**	N	N	N	Y	N	Y
12 **Granger**	N	N	N	Y	N	Y
13 **Thornberry**	N	N	N	Y	N	Y
14 **Paul**	Y	N	N	Y	N	Y
15 Hinojosa	Y	N	N	N	Y	Y
16 Reyes	Y	N	N	N	Y	Y
17 Edwards	Y	N	N	N	Y	Y
18 Jackson Lee	Y	Y	Y	N	Y	Y
19 **Neugebauer**	N	N	N	Y	N	Y
20 Gonzalez	Y	N	N	N	Y	Y
21 **Smith**	Y	N	N	Y	N	Y
22 Lampson	Y	N	N	Y	N	Y
23 Rodriguez	Y	N	N	N	Y	Y
24 **Marchant**	N	N	N	Y	N	Y
25 Doggett	Y	N	N	N	Y	Y
26 **Burgess**	N	N	N	Y	N	Y
27 Ortiz	Y	N	N	N	Y	Y
28 Cuellar	Y	Y	N	N	Y	Y
29 Green, G.	Y	N	Y	N	Y	Y
30 Johnson, E.	Y	Y	Y	N	Y	Y
31 **Carter**	N	N	N	Y	N	Y
32 **Sessions**	N	N	N	Y	N	Y
UTAH						
1 **Bishop**	N	N	N	Y	N	Y
2 Matheson	Y	N	N	N	N	Y
3 **Cannon**	N	N	N	Y	N	Y
VERMONT						
AL Welch	Y	N	Y	N	Y	Y
VIRGINIA						
1 **Wittman**	N	N	N	Y	N	Y
2 **Drake**	N	N	N	Y	N	Y
3 Scott	Y	Y	N	N	Y	Y
4 **Forbes**	N	N	N	Y	N	Y
5 **Goode**	N	N	N	N	N	Y
6 **Goodlatte**	Y	N	N	Y	N	Y
7 **Cantor**	N	N	N	Y	N	Y
8 Moran	Y	Y	N	N	Y	Y
9 Boucher	Y	N	N	N	Y	Y
10 **Wolf**	N	N	N	N	N	Y
11 **Davis, T.**	N	N	N	Y	N	Y
WASHINGTON						
1 Inslee	Y	N	Y	N	Y	Y
2 Larsen	Y	N	N	N	Y	Y
3 Baird	Y	N	N	N	Y	Y
4 **Hastings**	N	N	N	Y	N	Y
5 **McMorris Rodgers**	N	N	N	Y	N	Y
6 Dicks	Y	N	N	N	Y	Y
7 McDermott	Y	Y	Y	N	Y	Y
8 **Reichert**	N	N	N	N	N	Y
9 Smith	Y	N	N	N	Y	Y
WEST VIRGINIA						
1 Mollohan	Y	N	N	N	Y	Y
2 **Capito**	N	N	N	N	N	Y
3 Rahall	Y	N	N	N	Y	Y
WISCONSIN						
1 **Ryan**	N	N	N	Y	N	Y
2 Baldwin	Y	Y	Y	N	Y	Y
3 Kind	Y	N	N	N	Y	Y
4 Moore	Y	Y	Y	N	Y	Y
5 **Sensenbrenner**	N	N	N	Y	N	Y
6 **Petri**	N	N	N	Y	N	Y
7 Obey	Y	Y	N	N	Y	Y
8 Kagen	Y	N	Y	N	Y	Y
WYOMING						
AL **Cubin**	?	?	N	Y	N	Y
DELEGATES						
Faleomavaega (A.S.)		Y	Y	N		
Norton (D.C.)		Y	Y	N		
Bordallo (Guam)		?	?	?		
Fortuño (P.R.)		N	N	?		
Christensen (V.I.)		Y	Y	N		

IN THE HOUSE | By Vote Number

143. **HR 3773. Foreign Intelligence Surveillance/Previous Question.** Arcuri, D-N.Y., motion to order the previous question (thus ending debate and possibility of amendment) on adoption of the rule (H Res 1041) to provide for House floor consideration of the Senate amendment to the bill that would revise the Foreign Intelligence Surveillance Act (FISA), which governs electronic surveillance of terrorism suspects. Motion agreed to 217-190: R 1-182; D 216-8 (ND 165-4, SD 51-4). March 14, 2008.

144. **HR 3773. Foreign Intelligence Surveillance/Rule.** Adoption of the rule (H Res 1041) to provide for House floor consideration of the Senate amendment to the bill that would revise FISA, which governs electronic surveillance of terrorism suspects. Adopted 221-188: R 0-185; D 221-3 (ND 168-1, SD 53-2). March 14, 2008.

145. **HR 3773. Foreign Intelligence Surveillance/Motion to Concur.** Conyers, D-Mich., motion to concur with the Senate amendments to the bill that would revise FISA, which governs electronic surveillance of terrorism suspects, with an additional amendment. The House amendment would strike the retroactive immunity provisions for telecommunications companies on pending civil lawsuits and instead provide immunity for future cooperation with government requests to assist with surveillance. The amendment would create a bipartisan commission to report on conducting surveillance on U.S. persons without obtaining FISA warrants and would allow federal courts to hear classified information in civil suits against telecommunications companies. Motion agreed to 213-197: R 0-185; D 213-12 (ND 163-8, SD 50-4). A "nay" was a vote in support of the president's position. March 14, 2008.

146. **Procedural Motion/Journal.** Approval of the House Journal of Thursday, March 13, 2008. Approved 202-148: R 19-138; D 183-10 (ND 133-9, SD 50-1). March 14, 2008.

	143	144	145	146
ALABAMA				
1 **Bonner**	N	N	N	N
2 **Everett**	N	N	?	?
3 **Rogers**	N	N	N	N
4 **Aderholt**	N	N	N	Y
5 Cramer	?	?	?	?
6 **Bachus**	N	N	N	N
7 Davis	Y	Y	Y	?
ALASKA				
AL **Young**	?	?	?	?
ARIZONA				
1 **Renzi**	N	N	N	Y
2 **Franks**	N	N	N	N
3 **Shadegg**	N	N	N	Y
4 Pastor	Y	Y	Y	Y
5 Mitchell	Y	Y	Y	Y
6 **Flake**	N	N	N	N
7 Grijalva	Y	Y	Y	Y
8 Giffords	Y	Y	Y	Y
ARKANSAS				
1 Berry	Y	Y	Y	Y
2 Snyder	Y	Y	Y	Y
3 **Boozman**	N	N	N	N
4 Ross	Y	Y	Y	Y
CALIFORNIA				
1 Thompson	Y	Y	Y	N
2 **Herger**	N	N	N	N
3 **Lungren**	N	N	N	Y
4 **Doolittle**	N	N	N	N
5 Matsui	Y	Y	Y	?
6 Woolsey	?	?	?	?
7 Miller, George	Y	Y	Y	Y
8 Pelosi		Y		
9 Lee	Y	Y	Y	N
10 Tauscher	Y	Y	Y	?
11 McNerney	Y	Y	Y	Y
12 Vacant				
13 Stark	Y	Y	Y	?
14 Eshoo	Y	Y	Y	Y
15 Honda	Y	Y	Y	Y
16 Lofgren	Y	Y	Y	Y
17 Farr	Y	Y	Y	Y
18 Cardoza	Y	Y	Y	Y
19 **Radanovich**	N	N	N	N
20 Costa	Y	Y	Y	Y
21 **Nunes**	–	–	–	–
22 **McCarthy**	N	N	N	N
23 Capps	Y	Y	Y	Y
24 **Gallegly**	N	N	N	?
25 **McKeon**	N	N	N	N
26 **Dreier**	N	N	N	N
27 Sherman	Y	Y	Y	Y
28 Berman	Y	Y	Y	Y
29 Schiff	Y	Y	Y	Y
30 Waxman	Y	Y	Y	Y
31 Becerra	Y	Y	Y	?
32 Solis	Y	Y	Y	Y
33 Watson	Y	Y	Y	Y
34 Roybal-Allard	Y	Y	Y	Y
35 Waters	Y	Y	Y	Y
36 Harman	Y	Y	Y	?
37 Richardson	Y	Y	Y	Y
38 Napolitano	Y	Y	Y	Y
39 Sánchez, Linda	Y	Y	Y	Y
40 **Royce**	N	N	N	N
41 **Lewis**	N	N	N	N
42 **Miller, Gary**	N	N	N	N
43 Baca	Y	Y	Y	N
44 **Calvert**	N	N	N	N
45 **Bono Mack**	N	N	N	N
46 **Rohrabacher**	N	N	N	N
47 Sanchez, Loretta	Y	Y	Y	Y
48 **Campbell**	N	N	N	N
49 **Issa**	N	N	N	N
50 **Bilbray**	N	N	N	N
51 Filner	Y	Y	N	Y
52 **Hunter**	?	?	?	?
53 Davis	Y	Y	Y	Y

	143	144	145	146
COLORADO				
1 DeGette	Y	Y	Y	Y
2 Udall	Y	Y	Y	N
3 Salazar	Y	Y	Y	Y
4 **Musgrave**	?	?	?	?
5 **Lamborn**	N	N	N	N
6 **Tancredo**	?	?	?	?
7 Perlmutter	Y	Y	Y	N
CONNECTICUT				
1 Larson	Y	Y	Y	?
2 Courtney	Y	Y	Y	Y
3 DeLauro	Y	Y	Y	Y
4 **Shays**	N	N	N	?
5 Murphy	Y	Y	Y	Y
DELAWARE				
AL **Castle**	N	N	N	N
FLORIDA				
1 **Miller**	N	N	N	+
2 Boyd	Y	Y	Y	?
3 Brown	Y	Y	Y	Y
4 **Crenshaw**	N	N	N	N
5 **Brown-Waite**	?	?	?	?
6 **Stearns**	N	N	N	N
7 **Mica**	N	N	N	N
8 **Keller**	N	N	N	N
9 **Bilirakis**	N	N	N	N
10 **Young**	N	N	N	?
11 Castor	Y	Y	Y	Y
12 **Putnam**	N	N	N	N
13 **Buchanan**	N	N	N	Y
14 **Mack**	N	N	N	N
15 **Weldon**	N	N	N	?
16 Mahoney	Y	Y	Y	Y
17 Meek	Y	Y	Y	Y
18 **Ros-Lehtinen**	N	N	N	?
19 Wexler	Y	Y	Y	Y
20 Wasserman Schultz	Y	Y	Y	Y
21 **Diaz-Balart, L.**	N	N	N	N
22 Klein	Y	Y	Y	Y
23 Hastings	Y	Y	Y	Y
24 **Feeney**	N	N	N	N
25 **Diaz-Balart, M.**	N	N	N	N
GEORGIA				
1 **Kingston**	N	N	N	N
2 Bishop	Y	Y	Y	Y
3 **Westmoreland**	N	N	N	N
4 Johnson	Y	Y	Y	Y
5 Lewis	Y	Y	Y	Y
6 **Price**	N	N	N	N
7 **Linder**	N	N	N	N
8 Marshall	Y	Y	Y	Y
9 **Deal**	N	N	N	N
10 **Broun**	N	N	N	N
11 **Gingrey**	N	N	N	?
12 Barrow	N	Y	Y	Y
13 Scott	Y	Y	Y	Y
HAWAII				
1 Abercrombie	Y	Y	Y	?
2 Hirono	Y	Y	Y	?
IDAHO				
1 **Sali**	N	N	N	N
2 **Simpson**	N	N	N	?
ILLINOIS				
1 Rush	?	?	?	?
2 Jackson	Y	Y	Y	Y
3 Lipinski	Y	Y	Y	Y
4 Gutierrez	Y	Y	Y	Y
5 Emanuel	Y	Y	Y	Y
6 **Roskam**	N	N	N	N
7 Davis	Y	Y	Y	Y
8 Bean	Y	Y	Y	Y
9 Schakowsky	Y	Y	Y	Y
10 **Kirk**	N	N	N	Y
11 **Weller**	?	?	?	?
12 Costello	Y	Y	Y	?
13 **Biggert**	N	N	N	Y
14 Foster	Y	Y	Y	Y
15 **Johnson**	N	N	N	Y

KEY	**Republicans**	Democrats		
Y Voted for (yea)		X Paired against		C Voted "present" to avoid possible conflict of interest
# Paired for		– Announced against		
+ Announced for		P Voted "present"		? Did not vote or otherwise make a position known
N Voted against (nay)				

ND Northern Democrats, SD Southern Democrats
Southern states: Ala., Ark., Fla., Ga., Ky., La., Miss., N.C., Okla., S.C., Tenn., Texas, Va.

	143	144	145	146
16 Manzullo	N	N	N	N
17 Hare	Y	Y	Y	Y
18 LaHood	?	?	?	?
19 Shimkus	N	N	N	N
INDIANA				
1 Visclosky	Y	Y	Y	Y
2 Donnelly	N	Y	Y	Y
3 Souder	N	N	N	Y
4 Buyer	N	N	N	?
5 Burton	N	N	N	N
6 Pence	N	N	N	N
7 Carson, A.	Y	Y	Y	Y
8 Ellsworth	Y	Y	Y	N
9 Hill	Y	Y	Y	Y
IOWA				
1 Braley	Y	Y	Y	?
2 Loebsack	Y	Y	Y	Y
3 Boswell	Y	Y	Y	Y
4 Latham	N	N	N	N
5 King	N	N	N	N
KANSAS				
1 Moran	N	N	N	N
2 Boyda	Y	Y	Y	Y
3 Moore	Y	Y	Y	Y
4 Tiahrt	N	N	N	N
KENTUCKY				
1 Whitfield	N	N	N	?
2 Lewis	N	N	N	?
3 Yarmuth	Y	Y	Y	Y
4 Davis	N	N	N	N
5 Rogers	N	N	N	N
6 Chandler	Y	Y	Y	N
LOUISIANA				
1 Vacant				
2 Jefferson	Y	Y	Y	Y
3 Melancon	Y	Y	Y	Y
4 McCrery	N	N	N	Y
5 Alexander	N	N	N	N
6 Vacant				
7 Boustany	?	?	?	?
MAINE				
1 Allen	Y	Y	Y	Y
2 Michaud	Y	Y	Y	Y
MARYLAND				
1 Gilchrest	?	?	N	N
2 Ruppersberger	Y	Y	Y	Y
3 Sarbanes	Y	Y	Y	Y
4 Wynn	Y	Y	Y	Y
5 Hoyer	Y	Y	Y	Y
6 Bartlett	N	N	N	N
7 Cummings	Y	Y	Y	Y
8 Van Hollen	Y	Y	Y	Y
MASSACHUSETTS				
1 Olver	Y	Y	Y	Y
2 Neal	Y	Y	Y	?
3 McGovern	Y	Y	Y	Y
4 Frank	Y	Y	Y	?
5 Tsongas	Y	Y	Y	Y
6 Tierney	Y	Y	Y	Y
7 Markey	Y	Y	Y	Y
8 Capuano	Y	Y	N	Y
9 Lynch	Y	Y	Y	Y
10 Delahunt	Y	Y	Y	?
MICHIGAN				
1 Stupak	Y	Y	Y	?
2 Hoekstra	N	N	N	N
3 Ehlers	N	N	N	N
4 Camp	N	N	N	N
5 Kildee	Y	Y	Y	Y
6 Upton	N	N	N	N
7 Walberg	N	N	N	Y
8 Rogers	N	N	N	N
9 Knollenberg	N	N	N	N
10 Miller	N	N	N	N
11 McCotter	N	N	N	N
12 Levin	Y	Y	Y	Y
13 Kilpatrick	Y	Y	Y	Y
14 Conyers	Y	Y	Y	Y
15 Dingell	Y	Y	Y	?
MINNESOTA				
1 Walz	Y	Y	Y	Y
2 Kline	N	N	N	N
3 Ramstad	N	N	N	N
4 McCollum	Y	Y	Y	Y

	143	144	145	146
5 Ellison	Y	Y	Y	Y
6 Bachmann	N	N	N	N
7 Peterson	Y	Y	Y	N
8 Oberstar	?	?	?	?
MISSISSIPPI				
1 Vacant				
2 Thompson	Y	Y	Y	Y
3 Pickering	?	?	?	?
4 Taylor	Y	Y	Y	Y
MISSOURI				
1 Clay	Y	Y	Y	Y
2 Akin	N	N	N	N
3 Carnahan	Y	Y	Y	Y
4 Skelton	Y	Y	Y	Y
5 Cleaver	Y	Y	Y	Y
6 Graves	N	N	N	N
7 Blunt	N	N	N	N
8 Emerson	N	N	N	Y
9 Hulshof	N	N	N	N
MONTANA				
AL Rehberg	N	N	N	N
NEBRASKA				
1 Fortenberry	N	N	N	N
2 Terry	N	N	N	?
3 Smith	N	N	N	N
NEVADA				
1 Berkley	Y	Y	Y	Y
2 Heller	N	N	N	N
3 Porter	N	N	N	N
NEW HAMPSHIRE				
1 Shea-Porter	Y	Y	Y	Y
2 Hodes	Y	Y	Y	Y
NEW JERSEY				
1 Andrews	Y	Y	Y	Y
2 LoBiondo	N	N	N	N
3 Saxton	N	N	N	?
4 Smith	N	N	N	Y
5 Garrett	N	N	N	N
6 Pallone	Y	Y	Y	Y
7 Ferguson	N	N	N	N
8 Pascrell	Y	Y	Y	?
9 Rothman	Y	Y	Y	Y
10 Payne	Y	Y	Y	Y
11 Frelinghuysen	N	N	N	?
12 Holt	Y	Y	Y	?
13 Sires	Y	Y	Y	Y
NEW MEXICO				
1 Wilson	N	N	N	N
2 Pearce	N	N	N	?
3 Udall	Y	Y	Y	Y
NEW YORK				
1 Bishop	Y	Y	Y	Y
2 Israel	Y	Y	Y	Y
3 King	N	N	N	N
4 McCarthy	Y	Y	Y	Y
5 Ackerman	Y	Y	Y	?
6 Meeks	?	?	Y	Y
7 Crowley	Y	Y	Y	Y
8 Nadler	Y	Y	Y	Y
9 Weiner	Y	Y	Y	Y
10 Towns	Y	Y	Y	Y
11 Clarke	Y	Y	Y	Y
12 Velázquez	Y	Y	Y	Y
13 Fossella	N	N	N	?
14 Maloney	Y	Y	Y	Y
15 Rangel	?	?	?	?
16 Serrano	Y	Y	Y	Y
17 Engel	N	N	Y	Y
18 Lowey	Y	Y	Y	Y
19 Hall	Y	Y	Y	Y
20 Gillibrand	Y	Y	Y	Y
21 McNulty	Y	Y	Y	Y
22 Hinchey	Y	Y	N	Y
23 McHugh	N	N	N	N
24 Arcuri	Y	Y	Y	Y
25 Walsh	N	N	?	?
26 Reynolds	N	N	N	N
27 Higgins	Y	Y	Y	Y
28 Slaughter	Y	Y	Y	?
29 Kuhl	N	N	N	Y
NORTH CAROLINA				
1 Butterfield	Y	Y	Y	Y
2 Etheridge	Y	Y	Y	Y
3 Jones	N	N	N	Y
4 Price	Y	Y	Y	Y

	143	144	145	146
5 Foxx	N	N	N	N
6 Coble	N	N	N	?
7 McIntyre	Y	Y	Y	Y
8 Hayes	N	N	N	?
9 Myrick	N	N	N	N
10 McHenry	N	N	N	N
11 Shuler	Y	Y	N	Y
12 Watt	Y	Y	Y	Y
13 Miller	Y	Y	Y	Y
NORTH DAKOTA				
AL Pomeroy	Y	Y	Y	?
OHIO				
1 Chabot	N	N	N	N
2 Schmidt	N	N	N	?
3 Turner	N	N	N	N
4 Jordan	N	N	N	N
5 Latta	N	N	N	N
6 Wilson	Y	Y	Y	Y
7 Hobson	N	N	N	N
8 Boehner	N	N	N	?
9 Kaptur	Y	Y	Y	Y
10 Kucinich	Y	Y	Y	Y
11 Tubbs Jones	Y	Y	Y	Y
12 Tiberi	N	N	N	N
13 Sutton	Y	Y	Y	Y
14 LaTourette	N	N	N	N
15 Pryce	N	N	N	N
16 Regula	N	N	N	N
17 Ryan	Y	Y	Y	?
18 Space	Y	Y	Y	Y
OKLAHOMA				
1 Sullivan	N	N	N	N
2 Boren	Y	Y	N	Y
3 Lucas	N	N	N	N
4 Cole	N	N	N	N
5 Fallin	N	N	N	N
OREGON				
1 Wu	Y	Y	Y	Y
2 Walden	N	N	N	N
3 Blumenauer	Y	Y	Y	?
4 DeFazio	Y	Y	Y	Y
5 Hooley	?	?	?	?
PENNSYLVANIA				
1 Brady	Y	Y	Y	Y
2 Fattah	Y	Y	Y	Y
3 English	N	N	N	N
4 Altmire	Y	Y	Y	N
5 Peterson	?	?	?	?
6 Gerlach	N	N	N	N
7 Sestak	Y	Y	Y	Y
8 Murphy, P.	Y	Y	Y	Y
9 Shuster	N	N	N	N
10 Carney	N	Y	N	Y
11 Kanjorski	Y	Y	Y	Y
12 Murtha	Y	Y	Y	?
13 Schwartz	Y	Y	Y	Y
14 Doyle	Y	Y	Y	Y
15 Dent	N	N	N	?
16 Pitts	N	N	N	?
17 Holden	Y	Y	N	?
18 Murphy, T.	N	N	N	N
19 Platts	N	N	N	N
RHODE ISLAND				
1 Kennedy	Y	Y	Y	?
2 Langevin	Y	Y	Y	Y
SOUTH CAROLINA				
1 Brown	N	N	N	N
2 Wilson	N	N	N	N
3 Barrett	N	N	N	N
4 Inglis	N	N	N	N
5 Spratt	Y	Y	Y	Y
6 Clyburn	Y	Y	Y	Y
SOUTH DAKOTA				
AL Herseth Sandlin	Y	Y	Y	Y
TENNESSEE				
1 Davis, D.	N	N	N	N
2 Duncan	N	N	N	N
3 Wamp	N	N	N	N
4 Davis, L.	N	Y	P	Y
5 Cooper	N	N	N	Y
6 Gordon	Y	Y	Y	Y
7 Blackburn	N	N	N	N
8 Tanner	Y	Y	Y	Y
9 Cohen	Y	Y	Y	Y

	143	144	145	146
TEXAS				
1 Gohmert	N	N	N	P
2 Poe	N	N	N	N
3 Johnson, S.	N	N	N	N
4 Hall	N	N	N	N
5 Hensarling	N	N	N	N
6 Barton	N	N	N	N
7 Culberson	N	N	N	N
8 Brady	N	N	N	N
9 Green, A.	Y	Y	Y	Y
10 McCaul	N	N	N	N
11 Conaway	N	N	N	N
12 Granger	?	N	N	Y
13 Thornberry	N	N	N	N
14 Paul	Y	N	N	Y
15 Hinojosa	+	+	Y	Y
16 Reyes	Y	Y	Y	Y
17 Edwards	Y	Y	Y	?
18 Jackson Lee	Y	Y	Y	Y
19 Neugebauer	N	N	N	N
20 Gonzalez	Y	Y	Y	Y
21 Smith	N	N	N	N
22 Lampson	N	N	N	Y
23 Rodriguez	Y	Y	Y	Y
24 Marchant	N	N	N	?
25 Doggett	Y	Y	Y	Y
26 Burgess	N	N	N	N
27 Ortiz	Y	Y	Y	Y
28 Cuellar	Y	Y	Y	Y
29 Green, G.	Y	Y	+	+
30 Johnson, E.	Y	Y	Y	?
31 Carter	N	N	N	N
32 Sessions	N	N	N	?
UTAH				
1 Bishop	N	N	N	N
2 Matheson	Y	Y	Y	Y
3 Cannon	N	N	N	N
VERMONT				
AL Welch	Y	Y	N	Y
VIRGINIA				
1 Wittman	N	N	N	N
2 Drake	N	N	N	?
3 Scott	Y	Y	Y	Y
4 Forbes	N	N	N	N
5 Goode	N	N	N	?
6 Goodlatte	N	N	N	N
7 Cantor	N	N	N	N
8 Moran	Y	Y	Y	Y
9 Boucher	Y	Y	Y	Y
10 Wolf	N	N	N	N
11 Davis	N	N	N	N
WASHINGTON				
1 Inslee	Y	Y	Y	Y
2 Larsen	Y	Y	Y	Y
3 Baird	Y	Y	Y	Y
4 Hastings	N	N	N	N
5 McMorris Rodgers	?	N	N	N
6 Dicks	Y	Y	Y	?
7 McDermott	Y	Y	N	Y
8 Reichert	N	N	N	N
9 Smith	Y	Y	Y	Y
WEST VIRGINIA				
1 Mollohan	Y	Y	Y	Y
2 Capito	N	N	N	N
3 Rahall	Y	Y	Y	Y
WISCONSIN				
1 Ryan	N	N	N	N
2 Baldwin	Y	Y	Y	Y
3 Kind	Y	Y	Y	?
4 Moore	Y	Y	Y	Y
5 Sensenbrenner	N	N	N	N
6 Petri	Y	Y	Y	Y
7 Obey	Y	Y	Y	Y
8 Kagen	Y	Y	Y	?
WYOMING				
AL Cubin	?	?	N	N
DELEGATES				
Faleomavaega (A.S.)				
Norton (D.C.)				
Bordallo (Guam)				
Fortuño (P.R.)				
Christensen (V.I.)				

IN THE HOUSE | By Vote Number

147. **HR 3352. NOAA Hydrographic Services Expansion/Passage.** Abercrombie, D-Hawaii, motion to suspend the rules and pass the bill that would authorize the National Oceanic and Atmospheric Administration to expand the use of hydrographic data and hydrographic services to support conservation, protect life and property, support the resumption of commerce after emergencies, and contribute to homeland security and maritime domestic awareness. Motion agreed to 308-60: R 112-60; D 196-0 (ND 147-0, SD 49-0). A two-thirds majority of those present and voting (246 in this case) is required for passage under suspension of the rules. March 31, 2008.

148. **HR 2675. Oklahoma Land Designation for Boy Scouts/ Passage.** Abercrombie, D-Hawaii, motion to suspend the rules and pass the bill that would convey 140 acres of land in the Ouachita National Forest in Oklahoma to the Indian Nations Council Inc. of the Boy Scouts of America. Motion agreed to 370-2: R 176-0; D 194-2 (ND 145-2, SD 49-0). A two-thirds majority of those present and voting (248 in this case) is required for passage under suspension of the rules. March 31, 2008.

149. **H Con Res 302. Colorectal Cancer Awareness Month/ Adoption.** Wynn, D-Md., motion to suspend the rules and adopt the concurrent resolution that would support the observance of Colorectal Cancer Awareness Month. Motion agreed to 371-0: R 176-0; D 195-0 (ND 147-0, SD 48-0). A two-thirds majority of those present and voting (248 in this case) is required for adoption under suspension of the rules. March 31, 2008.

150. **H Con Res 310. Tubman Remembrance/Adoption.** Davis, D-Ill., motion to suspend the rules and adopt the concurrent resolution that would express support for a national day of remembrance for Harriet Ross Tubman, an agent for the Underground Railroad during the Civil War. Motion agreed to 416-0: R 193-0; D 223-0 (ND 168-0, SD 55-0). A two-thirds majority of those present and voting (278 in this case) is required for adoption under suspension of the rules. April 1, 2008.

151. **H Res 1005. Borderline Personality Awareness Month/ Adoption.** Davis, D-Ill., motion to suspend the rules and adopt the resolution that would express support for Borderline Personality Disorder Awareness Month. Motion agreed to 414-0: R 191-0; D 223-0 (ND 168-0, SD 55-0). A two-thirds majority of those present and voting (276 in this case) is required for adoption under suspension of the rules. April 1, 2008.

152. **H Res 1021. Women's History Month/Adoption.** Davis, D-Ill., motion to suspend the rules and adopt the resolution that would express support for National Women's History Month and would honor women and organizations in the United States that have fought for and continue to promote the teaching of women's history. Motion agreed to 413-0: R 190-0; D 223-0 (ND 168-0, SD 55-0). A two-thirds majority of those present and voting (276 in this case) is required for adoption under suspension of the rules. April 1, 2008.

153. **Procedural Motion/Journal.** Approval of the House Journal of Tuesday, April 1, 2008. Approved 232-177: R 19-169; D 213-8 (ND 160-5, SD 53-3). April 2, 2008.

	147	148	149	150	151	152	153
ALABAMA							
1 Bonner	Y	Y	Y	Y	Y	Y	N
2 Everett	N	Y	Y	Y	Y	Y	N
3 Rogers	Y	Y	Y	Y	Y	Y	N
4 Aderholt	N	Y	Y	Y	Y	Y	Y
5 Cramer	Y	Y	Y	Y	Y	Y	Y
6 Bachus	Y	Y	Y	Y	Y	Y	N
7 Davis	Y	Y	Y	Y	Y	Y	Y
ALASKA							
AL Young	Y	Y	Y	Y	Y	Y	N
ARIZONA							
1 Renzi	Y	Y	Y	Y	Y	?	N
2 Franks	N	Y	Y	Y	Y	Y	N
3 Shadegg	?	?	?	Y	Y	Y	N
4 Pastor	Y	Y	Y	Y	Y	Y	Y
5 Mitchell	Y	Y	Y	Y	Y	Y	N
6 Flake	N	Y	Y	Y	Y	Y	N
7 Grijalva	?	?	?	Y	Y	Y	Y
8 Giffords	Y	Y	Y	Y	Y	Y	?
ARKANSAS							
1 Berry	Y	Y	Y	Y	Y	Y	Y
2 Snyder	Y	Y	Y	Y	Y	Y	Y
3 Boozman	Y	Y	Y	Y	Y	Y	N
4 Ross	Y	Y	Y	Y	Y	Y	Y
CALIFORNIA							
1 Thompson	Y	Y	Y	Y	Y	Y	N
2 Herger	Y	Y	Y	Y	Y	Y	N
3 Lungren	Y	Y	Y	Y	Y	Y	Y
4 Doolittle	?	?	?	Y	Y	Y	N
5 Matsui	Y	Y	Y	Y	Y	Y	Y
6 Woolsey	Y	N	Y	Y	Y	Y	Y
7 Miller, George	Y	Y	Y	Y	Y	Y	Y
8 Pelosi							
9 Lee	Y	Y	Y	Y	Y	Y	Y
10 Tauscher	?	?	?	?	?	?	?
11 McNerney	Y	Y	Y	Y	Y	Y	Y
12 Vacant							
13 Stark	?	?	?	Y	Y	Y	Y
14 Eshoo	Y	Y	Y	Y	Y	Y	Y
15 Honda	?	?	?	Y	Y	Y	Y
16 Lofgren	Y	Y	Y	Y	Y	Y	Y
17 Farr	Y	Y	Y	Y	Y	Y	Y
18 Cardoza	Y	Y	Y	Y	Y	Y	Y
19 Radanovich	Y	Y	Y	Y	Y	Y	N
20 Costa	Y	Y	Y	Y	Y	Y	Y
21 Nunes	Y	Y	Y	Y	Y	Y	N
22 McCarthy	Y	Y	Y	Y	Y	Y	N
23 Capps	Y	Y	Y	Y	Y	Y	Y
24 Gallegly	Y	Y	Y	Y	Y	Y	N
25 McKeon	Y	Y	Y	Y	Y	Y	N
26 Dreier	Y	Y	Y	Y	Y	Y	N
27 Sherman	Y	Y	Y	Y	Y	Y	Y
28 Berman	Y	Y	Y	Y	Y	Y	Y
29 Schiff	Y	Y	Y	Y	Y	Y	Y
30 Waxman	?	?	?	?	?	?	Y
31 Becerra	Y	Y	Y	Y	Y	Y	Y
32 Solis	Y	Y	Y	Y	Y	Y	Y
33 Watson	Y	Y	Y	Y	Y	Y	Y
34 Roybal-Allard	Y	Y	Y	Y	Y	Y	Y
35 Waters	Y	Y	?	Y	Y	Y	Y
36 Harman	Y	Y	Y	Y	Y	Y	Y
37 Richardson	Y	Y	Y	Y	Y	Y	Y
38 Napolitano	Y	Y	Y	Y	Y	Y	Y
39 Sánchez, Linda	Y	Y	Y	Y	Y	Y	Y
40 Royce	N	Y	Y	Y	Y	Y	N
41 Lewis	Y	Y	Y	Y	Y	Y	N
42 Miller, Gary	Y	Y	Y	Y	Y	Y	N
43 Baca	Y	Y	Y	Y	Y	Y	Y
44 Calvert	Y	Y	Y	Y	?	?	N
45 Bono Mack	Y	Y	Y	Y	Y	Y	N
46 Rohrabacher	?	?	?	Y	Y	Y	N
47 Sanchez, Loretta	+	+	+	Y	Y	Y	Y
48 Campbell	N	Y	Y	Y	Y	Y	N
49 Issa	N	Y	Y	Y	Y	Y	N
50 Bilbray	Y	Y	Y	Y	Y	Y	N
51 Filner	Y	Y	Y	Y	Y	Y	Y
52 Hunter	Y	Y	Y	Y	Y	Y	N
53 Davis	Y	Y	Y	Y	Y	Y	Y

	147	148	149	150	151	152	153
COLORADO							
1 DeGette	?	?	?	Y	Y	Y	Y
2 Udall	+	+	+	Y	Y	Y	?
3 Salazar	Y	Y	Y	Y	Y	Y	Y
4 Musgrave	Y	Y	Y	Y	Y	Y	N
5 Lamborn	N	Y	Y	Y	Y	Y	N
6 Tancredo	N	Y	Y	Y	Y	Y	P
7 Perlmutter	Y	Y	Y	Y	Y	Y	Y
CONNECTICUT							
1 Larson	Y	Y	Y	Y	Y	Y	Y
2 Courtney	Y	Y	Y	Y	Y	Y	Y
3 DeLauro	Y	Y	Y	Y	Y	Y	?
4 Shays	Y	Y	Y	Y	Y	Y	Y
5 Murphy	Y	Y	Y	Y	Y	Y	Y
DELAWARE							
AL Castle	Y	Y	Y	Y	Y	Y	N
FLORIDA							
1 Miller	N	Y	Y	Y	Y	Y	?
2 Boyd	Y	Y	Y	Y	Y	Y	Y
3 Brown	?	?	?	Y	Y	Y	Y
4 Crenshaw	Y	Y	Y	Y	Y	Y	N
5 Brown-Waite	Y	Y	Y	Y	Y	Y	N
6 Stearns	N	Y	Y	Y	Y	Y	N
7 Mica	Y	Y	Y	Y	Y	Y	N
8 Keller	Y	Y	Y	Y	Y	Y	N
9 Bilirakis	Y	Y	Y	Y	Y	Y	N
10 Young	Y	Y	Y	Y	Y	Y	N
11 Castor	Y	Y	Y	Y	Y	Y	Y
12 Putnam	Y	Y	Y	Y	Y	Y	N
13 Buchanan	Y	Y	Y	Y	Y	Y	N
14 Mack	N	Y	Y	Y	Y	Y	N
15 Weldon	?	?	?	Y	Y	Y	N
16 Mahoney	Y	Y	Y	Y	Y	Y	Y
17 Meek	Y	Y	Y	Y	Y	Y	Y
18 Ros-Lehtinen	Y	Y	Y	Y	Y	Y	N
19 Wexler	Y	Y	Y	Y	Y	Y	Y
20 Wasserman Schultz	Y	Y	Y	Y	Y	Y	Y
21 Diaz-Balart, L.	Y	Y	Y	Y	Y	Y	N
22 Klein	Y	Y	Y	Y	Y	Y	Y
23 Hastings	Y	Y	Y	Y	Y	Y	Y
24 Feeney	?	?	?	Y	Y	Y	N
25 Diaz-Balart, M.	Y	Y	Y	Y	Y	Y	N
GEORGIA							
1 Kingston	?	?	?	Y	Y	Y	N
2 Bishop	Y	Y	Y	Y	Y	Y	Y
3 Westmoreland	N	Y	Y	Y	Y	Y	N
4 Johnson	?	?	?	Y	Y	Y	Y
5 Lewis	Y	Y	?	Y	Y	Y	Y
6 Price	N	Y	Y	Y	Y	Y	N
7 Linder	N	Y	Y	Y	Y	Y	N
8 Marshall	?	?	?	Y	Y	Y	Y
9 Deal	N	Y	Y	Y	Y	Y	N
10 Broun	N	Y	Y	Y	Y	Y	N
11 Gingrey	N	Y	Y	Y	Y	Y	N
12 Barrow	Y	Y	Y	Y	Y	Y	Y
13 Scott	Y	Y	Y	Y	Y	Y	Y
HAWAII							
1 Abercrombie	Y	Y	Y	Y	Y	Y	Y
2 Hirono	Y	+	Y	Y	Y	Y	Y
IDAHO							
1 Sali	N	Y	Y	Y	Y	Y	N
2 Simpson	Y	Y	Y	Y	Y	Y	N
ILLINOIS							
1 Rush	?	?	?	?	?	?	?
2 Jackson	Y	Y	Y	Y	Y	Y	Y
3 Lipinski	Y	Y	Y	Y	Y	Y	Y
4 Gutierrez	?	?	?	Y	Y	Y	Y
5 Emanuel	Y	Y	Y	Y	Y	Y	Y
6 Roskam	Y	Y	Y	Y	Y	Y	N
7 Davis	+	+	+	Y	Y	Y	Y
8 Bean	Y	Y	Y	Y	Y	Y	Y
9 Schakowsky	Y	Y	Y	Y	Y	Y	Y
10 Kirk	Y	Y	Y	Y	Y	Y	N
11 Weller	+	+	+	Y	Y	Y	N
12 Costello	Y	Y	Y	Y	Y	Y	Y
13 Biggert	Y	Y	Y	Y	Y	Y	N
14 Foster	Y	Y	Y	Y	Y	Y	Y
15 Johnson	Y	Y	Y	Y	Y	Y	Y

KEY — **Republicans**, Democrats

Y Voted for (yea)	**X** Paired against	**C** Voted "present" to avoid possible conflict of interest
# Paired for	**–** Announced against	
+ Announced for	**P** Voted "present"	**?** Did not vote or otherwise make a position known
N Voted against (nay)		

ND Northern Democrats, SD Southern Democrats
Southern states: Ala., Ark., Fla., Ga., Ky., La., Miss., N.C., Okla., S.C., Tenn., Texas, Va.

	147	148	149	150	151	152	153
16 **Manzullo**	N	Y	Y	Y	Y	Y	N
17 Hare	+	+	+	Y	Y	Y	Y
18 **LaHood**	Y	Y	Y	Y	Y	Y	N
19 **Shimkus**	Y	Y	Y	Y	Y	Y	N
INDIANA							
1 Visclosky	Y	Y	Y	Y	Y	Y	Y
2 Donnelly	Y	Y	Y	Y	Y	Y	Y
3 **Souder**	Y	Y	Y	Y	Y	Y	?
4 **Buyer**	Y	Y	Y	Y	Y	Y	N
5 **Burton**	N	Y	Y	Y	Y	Y	N
6 **Pence**	N	Y	Y	Y	Y	Y	N
7 Carson, A.	Y	Y	Y	Y	Y	Y	Y
8 Ellsworth	Y	Y	Y	Y	Y	Y	Y
9 Hill	Y	Y	Y	Y	Y	Y	Y
IOWA							
1 Braley	+	+	+	Y	Y	Y	Y
2 Loebsack	Y	Y	Y	Y	Y	Y	Y
3 Boswell	Y	Y	Y	Y	Y	Y	Y
4 **Latham**	Y	Y	Y	Y	Y	Y	Y
5 **King**	N	Y	Y	Y	Y	Y	N
KANSAS							
1 **Moran**	N	Y	Y	Y	Y	Y	N
2 Boyda	Y	Y	Y	Y	Y	Y	Y
3 Moore	Y	Y	Y	Y	Y	Y	Y
4 **Tiahrt**	?	?	?	Y	Y	Y	N
KENTUCKY							
1 **Whitfield**	?	?	?	Y	Y	Y	Y
2 **Lewis**	Y	Y	Y	Y	Y	Y	N
3 Yarmuth	Y	Y	Y	Y	Y	Y	Y
4 **Davis**	Y	Y	Y	Y	Y	Y	N
5 **Rogers**	Y	Y	Y	Y	Y	Y	N
6 Chandler	Y	Y	Y	Y	Y	Y	Y
LOUISIANA							
1 Vacant							
2 Jefferson	?	?	?	?	?	?	?
3 Melancon	Y	Y	Y	Y	Y	Y	Y
4 **McCrery**	Y	Y	Y	Y	Y	Y	N
5 **Alexander**	Y	Y	Y	Y	Y	Y	N
6 Vacant							
7 **Boustany**	Y	Y	Y	Y	Y	Y	N
MAINE							
1 Allen	Y	Y	Y	Y	Y	Y	Y
2 Michaud	Y	Y	Y	Y	Y	Y	Y
MARYLAND							
1 **Gilchrest**	?	?	?	Y	Y	Y	N
2 Ruppersberger	Y	Y	Y	Y	Y	Y	Y
3 Sarbanes	?	?	?	Y	Y	Y	Y
4 Wynn	Y	Y	Y	Y	Y	Y	Y
5 Hoyer	Y	Y	Y	Y	Y	Y	Y
6 **Bartlett**	N	Y	Y	Y	Y	Y	N
7 Cummings	Y	Y	Y	Y	Y	Y	Y
8 Van Hollen	Y	Y	Y	Y	Y	Y	Y
MASSACHUSETTS							
1 Olver	Y	Y	Y	Y	Y	Y	Y
2 Neal	?	?	?	Y	Y	Y	Y
3 McGovern	Y	Y	Y	Y	Y	Y	Y
4 Frank	Y	N	Y	Y	Y	Y	Y
5 Tsongas	Y	Y	Y	Y	Y	Y	Y
6 Tierney	Y	Y	Y	Y	Y	Y	Y
7 Markey	Y	Y	Y	Y	Y	Y	Y
8 Capuano	Y	Y	Y	Y	Y	Y	Y
9 Lynch	Y	Y	Y	Y	Y	Y	Y
10 Delahunt	Y	Y	Y	Y	Y	Y	Y
MICHIGAN							
1 Stupak	Y	Y	Y	Y	Y	Y	N
2 **Hoekstra**	N	Y	Y	Y	Y	Y	N
3 **Ehlers**	Y	Y	Y	Y	Y	Y	N
4 **Camp**	Y	Y	Y	Y	Y	Y	N
5 Kildee	Y	Y	Y	Y	Y	Y	Y
6 **Upton**	?	?	?	Y	Y	Y	N
7 **Walberg**	Y	Y	Y	Y	Y	Y	Y
8 **Rogers**	Y	Y	Y	Y	Y	Y	N
9 **Knollenberg**	Y	Y	Y	Y	Y	Y	N
10 **Miller**	Y	Y	Y	Y	Y	Y	N
11 **McCotter**	Y	Y	Y	Y	Y	Y	N
12 Levin	Y	Y	Y	Y	Y	Y	Y
13 Kilpatrick	Y	Y	Y	Y	Y	Y	Y
14 Conyers	?	Y	Y	Y	Y	Y	Y
15 Dingell	?	?	?	Y	Y	Y	Y
MINNESOTA							
1 Walz	Y	Y	Y	Y	Y	Y	Y
2 **Kline**	N	Y	Y	Y	Y	Y	N
3 **Ramstad**	Y	Y	Y	Y	Y	Y	N
4 McCollum	Y	Y	Y	Y	Y	Y	Y
5 Ellison	Y	Y	Y	Y	Y	Y	Y
6 **Bachmann**	?	?	?	Y	Y	Y	Y
7 Peterson	Y	Y	Y	Y	Y	Y	Y
8 Oberstar	Y	Y	Y	Y	Y	Y	?
MISSISSIPPI							
1 Vacant							
2 Thompson	Y	Y	Y	Y	Y	Y	Y
3 **Pickering**	?	?	?	Y	Y	Y	N
4 Taylor	Y	Y	Y	Y	Y	Y	Y
MISSOURI							
1 Clay	Y	Y	Y	Y	Y	Y	Y
2 **Akin**	N	Y	Y	Y	Y	Y	N
3 Carnahan	Y	Y	Y	Y	Y	Y	Y
4 Skelton	Y	Y	Y	Y	Y	Y	Y
5 Cleaver	Y	Y	Y	Y	Y	Y	Y
6 **Graves**	Y	Y	Y	Y	Y	Y	N
7 **Blunt**	?	Y	Y	Y	Y	Y	N
8 **Emerson**	Y	Y	Y	Y	Y	Y	?
9 **Hulshof**	?	?	?	Y	Y	Y	N
MONTANA							
AL **Rehberg**	Y	Y	Y	Y	Y	Y	N
NEBRASKA							
1 **Fortenberry**	Y	Y	Y	Y	Y	Y	N
2 **Terry**	Y	Y	Y	Y	?	Y	N
3 **Smith**	Y	Y	Y	Y	Y	Y	N
NEVADA							
1 Berkley	Y	Y	Y	Y	Y	Y	Y
2 **Heller**	Y	Y	Y	Y	Y	Y	N
3 **Porter**	Y	Y	Y	Y	Y	Y	N
NEW HAMPSHIRE							
1 Shea-Porter	Y	Y	Y	Y	Y	Y	Y
2 Hodes	Y	Y	Y	Y	Y	Y	Y
NEW JERSEY							
1 Andrews	Y	Y	Y	?	?	?	Y
2 **LoBiondo**	Y	Y	Y	Y	Y	Y	N
3 **Saxton**	Y	Y	Y	Y	Y	Y	?
4 **Smith**	Y	Y	Y	Y	Y	Y	N
5 **Garrett**	N	Y	Y	Y	Y	Y	N
6 Pallone	Y	Y	Y	Y	Y	Y	Y
7 **Ferguson**	Y	Y	Y	Y	Y	Y	N
8 Pascrell	Y	Y	Y	Y	Y	Y	Y
9 Rothman	?	?	?	?	?	?	Y
10 Payne	Y	Y	Y	Y	Y	Y	Y
11 **Frelinghuysen**	Y	Y	Y	Y	Y	Y	N
12 Holt	Y	Y	Y	Y	Y	Y	Y
13 Sires	Y	Y	Y	Y	Y	Y	Y
NEW MEXICO							
1 **Wilson**	Y	Y	Y	Y	Y	Y	Y
2 **Pearce**	Y	Y	Y	Y	Y	Y	N
3 Udall	?	?	?	?	?	?	?
NEW YORK							
1 Bishop	Y	Y	Y	Y	Y	Y	Y
2 Israel	Y	Y	Y	Y	Y	Y	Y
3 **King**	Y	Y	Y	Y	Y	Y	N
4 McCarthy	Y	Y	Y	Y	Y	Y	Y
5 Ackerman	Y	Y	Y	Y	Y	Y	Y
6 Meeks	Y	Y	Y	Y	Y	Y	Y
7 Crowley	Y	Y	Y	Y	Y	Y	Y
8 Nadler	Y	Y	Y	Y	Y	Y	Y
9 Weiner	Y	Y	Y	Y	Y	Y	Y
10 Towns	Y	Y	Y	Y	Y	Y	Y
11 Clarke	Y	Y	Y	Y	Y	Y	Y
12 Velázquez	Y	Y	Y	Y	Y	Y	Y
13 **Fossella**	?	?	?	?	Y	Y	N
14 Maloney	Y	Y	Y	Y	Y	Y	?
15 Rangel	?	?	?	Y	Y	Y	Y
16 Serrano	Y	Y	Y	Y	Y	Y	Y
17 Engel	Y	Y	Y	Y	Y	Y	Y
18 Lowey	Y	Y	Y	Y	Y	Y	Y
19 Hall	Y	Y	Y	Y	Y	Y	Y
20 Gillibrand	Y	Y	Y	Y	Y	Y	Y
21 McNulty	Y	Y	Y	Y	Y	Y	Y
22 Hinchey	?	?	?	Y	Y	Y	?
23 **McHugh**	Y	Y	Y	Y	Y	Y	N
24 Arcuri	Y	Y	Y	Y	Y	Y	Y
25 **Walsh**	Y	Y	Y	Y	Y	Y	Y
26 **Reynolds**	?	?	?	?	?	?	N
27 Higgins	Y	Y	Y	Y	Y	Y	Y
28 Slaughter	Y	Y	Y	Y	Y	Y	Y
29 **Kuhl**	Y	Y	Y	Y	Y	Y	Y
NORTH CAROLINA							
1 Butterfield	Y	Y	Y	Y	Y	Y	Y
2 Etheridge	?	?	?	Y	Y	Y	Y
3 **Jones**	Y	Y	Y	Y	Y	Y	N
4 Price	Y	Y	Y	Y	Y	Y	Y
5 **Foxx**	N	Y	Y	Y	Y	Y	N
6 **Coble**	–	+	+	Y	Y	Y	N
7 McIntyre	Y	Y	Y	Y	Y	Y	Y
8 **Hayes**	Y	Y	Y	Y	Y	Y	N
9 **Myrick**	N	Y	Y	Y	Y	Y	N
10 **McHenry**	N	Y	Y	Y	Y	Y	N
11 Shuler	?	?	?	?	?	?	N
12 Watt	Y	Y	Y	Y	Y	Y	Y
13 Miller	Y	Y	Y	Y	Y	Y	Y
NORTH DAKOTA							
AL Pomeroy	+	+	+	Y	Y	Y	Y
OHIO							
1 **Chabot**	N	Y	Y	Y	Y	Y	N
2 **Schmidt**	Y	Y	Y	Y	Y	Y	N
3 **Turner**	Y	Y	Y	Y	Y	Y	N
4 **Jordan**	N	Y	Y	Y	Y	Y	N
5 **Latta**	Y	Y	Y	Y	Y	Y	N
6 Wilson	Y	Y	Y	Y	Y	Y	Y
7 **Hobson**	?	?	?	Y	Y	Y	N
8 **Boehner**	?	Y	Y	Y	Y	Y	N
9 Kaptur	Y	Y	Y	Y	Y	Y	Y
10 Kucinich	Y	Y	Y	Y	Y	Y	Y
11 Tubbs Jones	Y	Y	Y	Y	Y	Y	Y
12 **Tiberi**	N	Y	Y	Y	Y	Y	N
13 Sutton	?	?	?	Y	Y	Y	Y
14 **LaTourette**	Y	Y	Y	Y	Y	Y	N
15 **Pryce**	?	?	?	?	?	?	N
16 **Regula**	Y	Y	Y	Y	Y	Y	N
17 Ryan	Y	Y	Y	Y	Y	Y	Y
18 Space	Y	Y	Y	Y	Y	Y	Y
OKLAHOMA							
1 **Sullivan**	N	Y	Y	Y	Y	Y	?
2 Boren	Y	Y	Y	Y	Y	Y	Y
3 **Lucas**	Y	Y	Y	Y	Y	Y	N
4 **Cole**	Y	Y	Y	Y	Y	Y	N
5 **Fallin**	Y	Y	Y	Y	Y	Y	N
OREGON							
1 Wu	Y	Y	Y	Y	Y	Y	Y
2 **Walden**	Y	Y	Y	Y	Y	Y	N
3 Blumenauer	Y	Y	Y	Y	Y	Y	Y
4 DeFazio	Y	Y	Y	Y	Y	Y	Y
5 Hooley	Y	Y	Y	Y	Y	Y	Y
PENNSYLVANIA							
1 Brady	Y	Y	Y	Y	Y	Y	Y
2 Fattah	Y	Y	Y	Y	Y	Y	?
3 **English**	Y	Y	Y	Y	Y	Y	Y
4 Altmire	Y	Y	Y	Y	Y	Y	N
5 **Peterson**	?	?	?	Y	Y	Y	N
6 **Gerlach**	Y	Y	Y	Y	Y	Y	N
7 Sestak	Y	Y	Y	Y	Y	Y	Y
8 Murphy, P.	Y	Y	Y	Y	Y	Y	Y
9 **Shuster**	Y	Y	Y	Y	Y	Y	Y
10 Carney	Y	Y	Y	Y	Y	Y	Y
11 Kanjorski	Y	Y	Y	Y	Y	Y	Y
12 Murtha	?	?	?	Y	Y	Y	Y
13 Schwartz	Y	Y	Y	?	?	?	Y
14 Doyle	Y	Y	Y	Y	Y	Y	Y
15 **Dent**	Y	Y	Y	Y	Y	Y	Y
16 **Pitts**	N	Y	Y	Y	Y	Y	N
17 Holden	Y	Y	Y	Y	Y	Y	Y
18 **Murphy, T.**	Y	Y	Y	Y	Y	Y	N
19 **Platts**	Y	Y	Y	Y	Y	Y	N
RHODE ISLAND							
1 Kennedy	Y	Y	Y	Y	Y	Y	Y
2 Langevin	Y	Y	Y	Y	Y	Y	Y
SOUTH CAROLINA							
1 **Brown**	Y	Y	Y	Y	Y	Y	N
2 **Wilson**	N	Y	Y	Y	Y	Y	N
3 **Barrett**	N	Y	Y	Y	Y	Y	N
4 **Inglis**	N	Y	Y	Y	Y	Y	N
5 Spratt	Y	Y	Y	Y	Y	Y	Y
6 Clyburn	Y	Y	Y	Y	Y	Y	Y
SOUTH DAKOTA							
AL Herseth Sandlin	Y	Y	Y	Y	Y	Y	Y
TENNESSEE							
1 **Davis, D.**	Y	Y	Y	Y	Y	Y	N
2 **Duncan**	N	Y	Y	Y	Y	Y	N
3 **Wamp**	N	Y	Y	Y	?	?	N
4 Davis, L.	Y	Y	Y	Y	Y	Y	Y
5 Cooper	Y	Y	Y	Y	Y	Y	Y
6 Gordon	Y	Y	Y	Y	Y	Y	Y
7 **Blackburn**	N	Y	Y	Y	Y	Y	N
8 Tanner	Y	Y	Y	Y	Y	Y	Y
9 Cohen	Y	Y	Y	Y	Y	Y	Y
TEXAS							
1 **Gohmert**	Y	Y	Y	Y	Y	Y	?
2 **Poe**	N	Y	Y	Y	Y	Y	N
3 **Johnson, S.**	N	Y	Y	Y	Y	Y	N
4 **Hall**	Y	Y	Y	Y	Y	Y	N
5 **Hensarling**	N	Y	Y	Y	Y	Y	N
6 **Barton**	N	Y	Y	Y	Y	Y	Y
7 **Culberson**	N	Y	Y	Y	Y	Y	N
8 **Brady**	N	Y	Y	Y	Y	Y	N
9 Green, A.	Y	Y	Y	Y	Y	Y	Y
10 **McCaul**	N	Y	Y	Y	Y	?	N
11 **Conaway**	N	Y	Y	Y	Y	Y	N
12 **Granger**	?	?	?	?	?	?	?
13 **Thornberry**	Y	Y	Y	Y	Y	Y	N
14 **Paul**	N	Y	Y	Y	Y	Y	Y
15 Hinojosa	Y	Y	Y	Y	Y	Y	Y
16 Reyes	Y	Y	Y	Y	Y	Y	Y
17 Edwards	Y	Y	Y	Y	Y	Y	Y
18 Jackson Lee	Y	Y	Y	Y	Y	Y	Y
19 **Neugebauer**	N	Y	Y	Y	Y	Y	N
20 Gonzalez	?	?	?	Y	Y	Y	Y
21 **Smith**	Y	Y	Y	Y	Y	Y	N
22 Lampson	Y	Y	Y	Y	Y	Y	Y
23 Rodriguez	Y	Y	Y	Y	Y	Y	Y
24 **Marchant**	N	Y	Y	Y	Y	Y	N
25 Doggett	Y	Y	Y	Y	Y	Y	Y
26 **Burgess**	Y	Y	Y	Y	Y	Y	N
27 Ortiz	Y	Y	Y	Y	Y	Y	Y
28 Cuellar	Y	Y	Y	Y	Y	Y	Y
29 Green, G.	Y	Y	Y	Y	Y	Y	Y
30 Johnson, E.	Y	Y	Y	Y	Y	Y	Y
31 **Carter**	N	Y	Y	Y	Y	Y	N
32 **Sessions**	N	Y	Y	Y	Y	Y	N
UTAH							
1 **Bishop**	Y	Y	Y	Y	Y	Y	N
2 Matheson	Y	Y	Y	Y	Y	Y	Y
3 **Cannon**	?	?	?	Y	Y	Y	N
VERMONT							
AL Welch	Y	Y	Y	Y	Y	Y	Y
VIRGINIA							
1 **Wittman**	Y	Y	Y	Y	Y	Y	N
2 **Drake**	Y	Y	Y	Y	Y	Y	N
3 Scott	Y	Y	Y	Y	Y	Y	Y
4 **Forbes**	Y	Y	Y	Y	Y	Y	N
5 **Goode**	N	Y	Y	Y	Y	Y	N
6 **Goodlatte**	Y	Y	Y	Y	Y	Y	Y
7 **Cantor**	?	Y	Y	Y	Y	Y	?
8 Moran	?	?	?	Y	Y	Y	Y
9 Boucher	Y	Y	Y	Y	Y	Y	Y
10 **Wolf**	Y	Y	Y	Y	Y	Y	N
11 **Davis**	Y	Y	Y	Y	Y	Y	N
WASHINGTON							
1 Inslee	Y	Y	Y	Y	Y	Y	N
2 Larsen	Y	Y	Y	Y	Y	Y	Y
3 Baird	Y	Y	Y	Y	Y	Y	Y
4 **Hastings**	N	Y	Y	Y	Y	Y	N
5 **McMorris Rodgers**	Y	Y	Y	Y	Y	Y	N
6 Dicks	?	?	?	Y	Y	Y	Y
7 McDermott	Y	Y	Y	Y	Y	Y	Y
8 **Reichert**	Y	Y	Y	Y	Y	Y	N
9 Smith	Y	Y	Y	Y	Y	Y	Y
WEST VIRGINIA							
1 Mollohan	?	?	?	Y	Y	Y	Y
2 **Capito**	Y	Y	Y	Y	Y	Y	Y
3 Rahall	Y	Y	Y	Y	Y	Y	Y
WISCONSIN							
1 **Ryan**	N	Y	Y	Y	Y	Y	N
2 Baldwin	Y	Y	Y	Y	Y	Y	Y
3 Kind	?	?	?	Y	Y	Y	Y
4 Moore	?	?	?	Y	Y	Y	Y
5 **Sensenbrenner**	N	Y	Y	Y	Y	Y	N
6 **Petri**	Y	Y	Y	Y	Y	Y	N
7 Obey	Y	Y	Y	Y	Y	Y	Y
8 Kagen	Y	Y	Y	Y	Y	Y	Y
WYOMING							
AL **Cubin**	?	?	?	?	?	?	?
DELEGATES							
Faleomavaega (A.S.)							
Norton (D.C.)							
Bordallo (Guam)							
Fortuño (P.R.)							
Christensen (V.I.)							

IN THE HOUSE | By Vote Number

154. HR 5501. Global HIV/AIDS Program Reauthorization/Previous Question. Berman, D-Calif., motion to order the previous question (thus ending debate and possibility of amendment) on adoption of the rule (H Res 1065) to provide for House floor consideration of the bill that would authorize $50 billion from fiscal 2009 through 2013 for programs under the President's Emergency Plan for AIDS Relief. Motion agreed to 215-199: R 0-190; D 215-9 (ND 162-6, SD 53-3). April 2, 2008.

155. HR 5501. Global HIV/AIDS Program Reauthorization/Rule. Adoption of the rule (H Res 1065) to provide for House floor consideration of the bill that would authorize $50 billion from fiscal 2009 through 2013 for programs under the President's Emergency Plan for AIDS Relief. Adopted 221-192: R 1-191; D 220-1 (ND 165-1, SD 55-0). April 2, 2008.

156. HR 5501. Global HIV/AIDS Program Reauthorization/ Educational Institutions Collaboration. Carson, D-Ind., amendment that would direct federal agencies to allow African postsecondary educational institutions to collaborate with U.S. postsecondary educational institutions, specifically historically black colleges and universities. Adopted in Committee of the Whole 415-10: R 184-10; D 231-0 (ND 175-0, SD 56-0). April 2, 2008.

157. HR 5501. Global HIV/AIDS Program Reauthorization/Motion to Recommit. Ryan, R-Wis., motion to recommit the bill to the Foreign Affairs Committee with instructions that it be reported back forthwith with language that would reduce the bill's authorization levels from $50 billion for fiscal 2009-2013 to $30 billion. Motion rejected 175-248: R 171-23; D 4-225 (ND 2-171, SD 2-54). April 2, 2008.

158. HR 5501. Global HIV/AIDS Program Reauthorization/ Passage. Passage of the bill that would authorize $50 billion from fiscal 2009 through 2013 for programs under the President's Emergency Plan for AIDS Relief used to fight AIDS, tuberculosis and malaria overseas. The bill would replace the current requirement that one-third of all HIV prevention funding go to abstinence education with balanced funding for abstinence, fidelity and condom programs. It would allow up to $2 billion a year for the Global Fund to Fight AIDS, Tuberculosis and Malaria for fiscal 2009 and 2010 and unspecified sums for fiscal 2011-13. Passed 308-116: R 78-116; D 230-0 (ND 174-0, SD 56-0). A "yea" was a vote in support of the president's position. April 2, 2008.

159. HR 4847. U.S. Fire Administration Reauthorization/Recommit. McMorris Rodgers, R-Wash., motion to recommit the bill to the Science and Technology Committee with instructions that it be reported back with an amendment protecting state and local fire departments from liability regarding child car safety seat advice. Motion rejected 205-209: R 192-0; D 13-209 (ND 6-163, SD 7-46). April 3, 2008.

160. HR 4847. U.S. Fire Administration Reauthorization/Passage. Passage of the bill that would authorize $293 million for the U.S. Fire Administration through fiscal 2012. The bill would provide for training of fire service personnel in dealing with national catastrophes, including incidents from terrorism and weapons of mass destruction. Passed 412-0: R 190-0; D 222-0 (ND 168-0, SD 54-0). April 3, 2008.

	154	155	156	157	158	159	160
ALABAMA							
1 **Bonner**	N	N	Y	Y	Y	Y	Y
2 **Everett**	N	N	Y	Y	N	Y	Y
3 **Rogers**	N	N	Y	Y	Y	Y	Y
4 **Aderholt**	N	N	Y	Y	Y	Y	Y
5 Cramer	Y	?	Y	N	Y	N	Y
6 **Bachus**	N	N	Y	N	Y	Y	Y
7 Davis	Y	Y	Y	N	Y	N	Y
ALASKA							
AL **Young**	N	N	Y	Y	Y	Y	Y
ARIZONA							
1 **Renzi**	N	N	Y	Y	?	Y	Y
2 **Franks**	N	N	Y	Y	N	Y	Y
3 **Shadegg**	N	N	Y	Y	N	Y	Y
4 Pastor	Y	Y	Y	N	Y	N	Y
5 Mitchell	Y	Y	Y	N	Y	N	Y
6 **Flake**	N	N	Y	Y	N	Y	Y
7 Grijalva	Y	Y	Y	N	Y	N	Y
8 Giffords	Y	Y	Y	N	Y	N	Y
ARKANSAS							
1 Berry	Y	Y	Y	N	Y	N	Y
2 Snyder	Y	Y	Y	N	Y	N	Y
3 **Boozman**	N	N	Y	Y	Y	Y	Y
4 Ross	Y	Y	Y	N	Y	N	Y
CALIFORNIA							
1 Thompson	Y	Y	Y	N	Y	N	Y
2 **Herger**	N	N	Y	Y	N	Y	Y
3 **Lungren**	N	N	Y	Y	Y	Y	Y
4 **Doolittle**	N	N	Y	Y	N	Y	Y
5 Matsui	Y	Y	Y	N	Y	N	Y
6 Woolsey	Y	Y	Y	N	Y	N	Y
7 Miller, George	Y	Y	Y	N	Y	N	Y
8 Pelosi					Y		
9 Lee	Y	Y	Y	N	Y	N	Y
10 Tauscher	?	?	?	?	?	N	Y
11 McNerney	Y	Y	Y	N	Y	Y	Y
12 Vacant							
13 Stark	Y	Y	Y	N	Y	N	Y
14 Eshoo	Y	Y	Y	N	Y	N	Y
15 Honda	Y	Y	Y	N	Y	N	Y
16 Lofgren	Y	Y	Y	N	Y	N	Y
17 Farr	Y	Y	Y	N	Y	N	Y
18 Cardoza	Y	Y	Y	N	Y	N	Y
19 **Radanovich**	N	N	Y	Y	N	Y	Y
20 Costa	Y	Y	Y	N	Y	N	Y
21 **Nunes**	N	N	Y	Y	Y	Y	Y
22 **McCarthy**	N	N	Y	Y	N	Y	Y
23 Capps	Y	Y	Y	N	Y	N	Y
24 **Gallegly**	N	N	Y	Y	N	Y	Y
25 **McKeon**	N	N	Y	Y	N	Y	Y
26 **Dreier**	N	N	Y	Y	Y	Y	Y
27 Sherman	Y	Y	Y	N	Y	N	Y
28 Berman	Y	Y	Y	N	Y	N	Y
29 Schiff	Y	Y	Y	N	Y	N	Y
30 Waxman	Y	Y	Y	N	Y	N	Y
31 Becerra	Y	Y	Y	N	Y	N	Y
32 Solis	Y	Y	Y	N	Y	N	Y
33 Watson	Y	Y	Y	N	Y	N	Y
34 Roybal-Allard	Y	Y	Y	N	Y	N	Y
35 Waters	Y	Y	Y	N	Y	N	Y
36 Harman	Y	Y	Y	N	Y	N	Y
37 Richardson	Y	Y	Y	N	Y	N	Y
38 Napolitano	Y	Y	Y	N	Y	N	Y
39 Sánchez, Linda	Y	Y	Y	N	Y	N	Y
40 **Royce**	N	N	Y	Y	N	Y	Y
41 **Lewis**	N	N	Y	Y	Y	Y	Y
42 **Miller, Gary**	N	Y	Y	N	Y	Y	Y
43 Baca	Y	Y	Y	N	Y	N	Y
44 **Calvert**	N	N	Y	N	Y	Y	Y
45 **Bono Mack**	N	N	Y	Y	Y	Y	Y
46 **Rohrabacher**	N	N	Y	Y	N	Y	Y
47 Sanchez, Loretta	Y	Y	Y	N	Y	N	Y
48 **Campbell**	N	N	N	Y	N	Y	Y
49 **Issa**	N	N	Y	Y	Y	Y	Y
50 **Bilbray**	N	N	Y	N	Y	N	Y
51 Filner	Y	Y	Y	N	Y	N	Y
52 **Hunter**	N	N	Y	Y	N	Y	Y
53 Davis	Y	Y	Y	N	Y	N	Y

	154	155	156	157	158	159	160
COLORADO							
1 DeGette	Y	Y	Y	N	Y	N	Y
2 Udall	?	?	Y	N	Y	N	Y
3 Salazar	Y	Y	Y	N	Y	N	Y
4 **Musgrave**	N	N	Y	Y	N	Y	Y
5 **Lamborn**	N	N	Y	N	Y	Y	Y
6 **Tancredo**	N	N	Y	N	N	Y	Y
7 Perlmutter	Y	Y	Y	N	Y	N	Y
CONNECTICUT							
1 Larson	Y	Y	Y	N	Y	N	Y
2 Courtney	Y	Y	Y	N	Y	N	Y
3 DeLauro	Y	Y	Y	N	Y	N	Y
4 **Shays**	N	N	Y	N	Y	Y	Y
5 Murphy	Y	Y	Y	N	Y	N	Y
DELAWARE							
AL **Castle**	N	N	Y	Y	Y	Y	Y
FLORIDA							
1 **Miller**	?	?	?	?	?	?	?
2 Boyd	Y	Y	Y	N	Y	N	Y
3 Brown	Y	Y	Y	N	Y	N	Y
4 **Crenshaw**	N	N	Y	N	Y	Y	Y
5 **Brown-Waite**	N	N	Y	Y	N	Y	Y
6 **Stearns**	N	N	Y	Y	N	Y	Y
7 **Mica**	N	N	Y	Y	N	Y	Y
8 **Keller**	N	N	Y	Y	Y	Y	Y
9 **Bilirakis**	N	N	Y	Y	Y	Y	Y
10 **Young**	N	N	Y	Y	Y	Y	Y
11 Castor	Y	Y	Y	N	Y	?	?
12 **Putnam**	N	N	Y	Y	N	Y	Y
13 **Buchanan**	N	N	Y	Y	Y	Y	Y
14 **Mack**	N	N	Y	N	N	Y	Y
15 **Weldon**	N	N	Y	N	N	Y	Y
16 Mahoney	Y	Y	Y	N	Y	N	Y
17 Meek	Y	Y	Y	N	Y	N	Y
18 **Ros-Lehtinen**	N	N	Y	N	Y	N	Y
19 Wexler	Y	Y	Y	N	Y	N	Y
20 Wasserman Schultz	Y	Y	Y	N	Y	N	Y
21 **Diaz-Balart, L.**	N	N	Y	Y	Y	Y	Y
22 Klein	Y	Y	Y	N	Y	?	Y
23 Hastings	Y	Y	Y	N	Y	N	Y
24 **Feeney**	N	N	Y	Y	N	Y	Y
25 **Diaz-Balart, M.**	N	N	Y	Y	Y	Y	Y
GEORGIA							
1 **Kingston**	N	N	Y	N	Y	Y	Y
2 Bishop	Y	Y	Y	N	Y	N	Y
3 **Westmoreland**	N	N	N	N	N	Y	Y
4 Johnson	Y	Y	Y	N	Y	N	Y
5 Lewis	Y	Y	Y	N	Y	N	Y
6 **Price**	N	N	Y	Y	N	Y	Y
7 **Linder**	N	N	Y	Y	N	Y	Y
8 Marshall	N	Y	Y	N	Y	Y	Y
9 **Deal**	N	N	Y	Y	N	Y	Y
10 **Broun**	N	N	Y	Y	N	Y	Y
11 **Gingrey**	N	N	Y	N	N	Y	Y
12 Barrow	N	Y	Y	N	Y	N	Y
13 Scott	Y	Y	Y	N	Y	N	Y
HAWAII							
1 Abercrombie	Y	Y	Y	N	Y	N	Y
2 Hirono	Y	Y	Y	N	Y	N	Y
IDAHO							
1 **Sali**	N	N	Y	Y	N	Y	Y
2 **Simpson**	N	N	Y	N	Y	Y	Y
ILLINOIS							
1 Rush	?	?	?	?	?	?	?
2 Jackson	Y	Y	Y	N	Y	N	Y
3 Lipinski	Y	Y	Y	N	Y	N	Y
4 Gutierrez	Y	Y	Y	N	Y	N	Y
5 Emanuel	Y	Y	Y	N	Y	N	Y
6 **Roskam**	N	N	Y	N	Y	N	Y
7 Davis	Y	Y	Y	N	Y	N	Y
8 Bean	N	Y	Y	N	Y	N	Y
9 Schakowsky	Y	Y	Y	N	Y	N	Y
10 **Kirk**	N	N	Y	N	Y	Y	Y
11 **Weller**	N	N	Y	N	Y	Y	Y
12 Costello	Y	Y	Y	N	Y	N	Y
13 **Biggert**	N	N	Y	Y	Y	Y	Y
14 Foster	Y	Y	Y	N	Y	N	Y
15 **Johnson**	N	N	Y	Y	Y	Y	Y

KEY   **Republicans**   Democrats

Y Voted for (yea)	X Paired against	C Voted "present" to avoid possible conflict of interest
# Paired for	– Announced against	
+ Announced for	P Voted "present"	? Did not vote or otherwise make a position known
N Voted against (nay)		

ND Northern Democrats, SD Southern Democrats
Southern states: Ala., Ark., Fla., Ga., Ky., La., Miss., N.C., Okla., S.C., Tenn., Texas, Va.

	154	155	156	157	158	159	160
16 **Manzullo**	N	N	Y	N	N	Y	Y
17 Hare	Y	Y	Y	N	Y	N	Y
18 **LaHood**	N	N	Y	Y	Y	Y	Y
19 **Shimkus**	N	N	Y	Y	Y	Y	Y
INDIANA							
1 Visclosky	Y	Y	Y	N	Y	N	Y
2 Donnelly	N	Y	Y	N	Y	Y	Y
3 **Souder**	?	?	?	Y	Y	Y	Y
4 **Buyer**	N	N	Y	Y	N	Y	Y
5 **Burton**	N	N	Y	Y	N	Y	Y
6 **Pence**	N	N	Y	Y	Y	Y	Y
7 Carson, A.	Y	Y	Y	N	Y	N	Y
8 Ellsworth	N	Y	Y	N	Y	N	Y
9 Hill	N	N	Y	N	Y	N	Y
IOWA							
1 Braley	Y	Y	Y	N	Y	N	Y
2 Loebsack	Y	Y	Y	N	Y	N	Y
3 Boswell	Y	Y	?	N	Y	N	Y
4 **Latham**	N	N	Y	Y	Y	Y	Y
5 **King**	N	N	Y	Y	N	Y	Y
KANSAS							
1 **Moran**	N	N	Y	Y	Y	Y	Y
2 Boyda	N	Y	Y	N	Y	Y	Y
3 Moore	Y	Y	Y	N	Y	N	Y
4 **Tiahrt**	N	N	Y	Y	Y	Y	Y
KENTUCKY							
1 **Whitfield**	N	N	Y	Y	N	Y	Y
2 **Lewis**	N	N	Y	Y	Y	Y	Y
3 Yarmuth	Y	Y	Y	N	Y	N	Y
4 **Davis**	N	N	Y	Y	Y	Y	Y
5 **Rogers**	N	N	Y	Y	N	Y	Y
6 Chandler	Y	Y	Y	N	Y	N	Y
LOUISIANA							
1 Vacant							
2 Jefferson	?	?	?	?	?	?	?
3 Melancon	Y	Y	Y	N	Y	N	Y
4 **McCrery**	N	N	Y	Y	N	Y	Y
5 **Alexander**	N	N	Y	Y	N	Y	Y
6 Vacant							
7 **Boustany**	N	N	Y	Y	Y	Y	Y
MAINE							
1 Allen	Y	Y	Y	N	Y	?	?
2 Michaud	Y	Y	Y	N	Y	N	Y
MARYLAND							
1 **Gilchrest**	N	N	Y	N	Y	Y	Y
2 Ruppersberger	Y	Y	Y	N	Y	N	Y
3 Sarbanes	Y	Y	Y	N	Y	N	Y
4 Wynn	Y	Y	Y	N	Y	?	?
5 Hoyer	Y	Y	Y	N	Y	N	Y
6 **Bartlett**	N	N	Y	Y	N	Y	Y
7 Cummings	Y	Y	Y	N	Y	N	Y
8 Van Hollen	Y	Y	Y	N	Y	N	Y
MASSACHUSETTS							
1 Olver	Y	Y	Y	N	Y	N	Y
2 Neal	Y	Y	Y	N	Y	N	Y
3 McGovern	Y	Y	Y	N	Y	N	Y
4 Frank	Y	Y	Y	N	Y	N	Y
5 Tsongas	Y	Y	Y	N	Y	N	Y
6 Tierney	Y	Y	Y	N	Y	N	Y
7 Markey	Y	Y	Y	N	Y	N	Y
8 Capuano	Y	Y	Y	N	Y	N	Y
9 Lynch	Y	Y	Y	N	Y	N	Y
10 Delahunt	Y	Y	Y	N	Y	N	Y
MICHIGAN							
1 Stupak	Y	Y	Y	N	Y	N	Y
2 **Hoekstra**	N	N	Y	Y	N	Y	Y
3 **Ehlers**	N	N	Y	Y	Y	Y	Y
4 **Camp**	N	N	Y	Y	N	Y	Y
5 Kildee	Y	Y	Y	N	Y	N	Y
6 **Upton**	N	N	Y	Y	N	Y	Y
7 **Walberg**	N	N	Y	Y	Y	Y	Y
8 **Rogers**	N	N	Y	Y	Y	Y	Y
9 **Knollenberg**	N	N	Y	Y	Y	?	?
10 **Miller**	N	N	Y	Y	N	Y	Y
11 **McCotter**	N	N	Y	Y	Y	Y	Y
12 Levin	Y	Y	Y	N	Y	N	Y
13 Kilpatrick	Y	Y	Y	N	Y	N	Y
14 Conyers	Y	Y	Y	N	Y	N	Y
15 Dingell	Y	Y	Y	N	Y	N	Y
MINNESOTA							
1 Walz	Y	Y	Y	N	Y	N	Y
2 **Kline**	N	N	Y	Y	Y	Y	Y
3 **Ramstad**	N	N	Y	Y	Y	Y	Y
4 McCollum	Y	Y	Y	N	Y	N	Y

	154	155	156	157	158	159	160
5 Ellison	Y	?	Y	N	Y	N	Y
6 **Bachmann**	N	N	Y	Y	N	Y	Y
7 Peterson	Y	Y	Y	N	Y	N	Y
8 Oberstar	Y	Y	Y	N	Y	N	Y
MISSISSIPPI							
1 Vacant							
2 Thompson	Y	Y	Y	N	Y	N	Y
3 **Pickering**	N	N	Y	Y	Y	Y	Y
4 Taylor	Y	Y	Y	Y	Y	Y	Y
MISSOURI							
1 Clay	Y	Y	Y	N	Y	N	Y
2 **Akin**	N	N	Y	Y	N	Y	Y
3 Carnahan	Y	Y	Y	N	Y	N	Y
4 Skelton	Y	Y	Y	N	Y	N	Y
5 Cleaver	Y	Y	Y	N	Y	N	Y
6 **Graves**	N	N	Y	Y	N	Y	Y
7 **Blunt**	N	N	Y	Y	N	Y	Y
8 **Emerson**	N	N	Y	N	Y	Y	Y
9 **Hulshof**	N	N	Y	Y	Y	Y	Y
MONTANA							
AL **Rehberg**	N	N	Y	Y	Y	Y	Y
NEBRASKA							
1 **Fortenberry**	N	N	Y	N	Y	Y	Y
2 **Terry**	N	N	Y	Y	N	Y	Y
3 **Smith**	N	N	Y	Y	N	Y	Y
NEVADA							
1 Berkley	Y	Y	Y	N	Y	N	Y
2 **Heller**	N	N	Y	Y	N	Y	Y
3 **Porter**	N	N	Y	Y	Y	Y	Y
NEW HAMPSHIRE							
1 Shea-Porter	Y	Y	Y	N	Y	N	Y
2 Hodes	Y	Y	Y	N	Y	N	Y
NEW JERSEY							
1 Andrews	?	?	Y	N	Y	N	Y
2 **LoBiondo**	N	N	Y	Y	N	Y	Y
3 **Saxton**	?	?	Y	Y	N	Y	Y
4 **Smith**	N	Y	Y	N	Y	Y	Y
5 **Garrett**	N	N	N	Y	N	Y	Y
6 Pallone	Y	Y	Y	N	Y	N	Y
7 **Ferguson**	N	N	Y	N	Y	Y	Y
8 Pascrell	Y	Y	Y	N	Y	N	Y
9 Rothman	Y	Y	Y	N	Y	N	Y
10 Payne	Y	Y	Y	N	Y	N	Y
11 **Frelinghuysen**	N	N	Y	Y	Y	Y	Y
12 Holt	Y	Y	Y	N	Y	N	Y
13 Sires	Y	Y	Y	N	Y	?	?
NEW MEXICO							
1 **Wilson**	N	N	Y	Y	Y	Y	Y
2 **Pearce**	N	N	Y	Y	N	Y	Y
3 Udall	Y	Y	Y	N	Y	N	Y
NEW YORK							
1 Bishop	Y	Y	Y	N	Y	N	Y
2 Israel	Y	Y	Y	N	Y	N	Y
3 **King**	N	N	Y	N	Y	Y	Y
4 McCarthy	Y	Y	Y	N	Y	N	Y
5 Ackerman	Y	Y	Y	N	Y	N	Y
6 Meeks	Y	Y	Y	N	Y	N	Y
7 Crowley	Y	Y	Y	N	Y	N	Y
8 Nadler	Y	Y	Y	N	Y	N	Y
9 Weiner	Y	Y	Y	N	Y	N	Y
10 Towns	Y	Y	Y	N	Y	N	Y
11 Clarke	Y	Y	Y	N	Y	N	Y
12 Velázquez	Y	Y	Y	N	Y	N	?
13 **Fossella**	N	N	Y	Y	Y	Y	Y
14 Maloney	?	?	Y	N	Y	N	Y
15 Rangel	Y	?	Y	N	Y	?	?
16 Serrano	Y	Y	Y	N	Y	N	Y
17 Engel	Y	Y	Y	N	Y	N	Y
18 Lowey	Y	Y	Y	N	Y	N	Y
19 Hall	Y	Y	Y	N	Y	N	Y
20 Gillibrand	Y	Y	Y	Y	Y	N	Y
21 McNulty	Y	Y	Y	N	Y	N	Y
22 Hinchey	?	?	Y	N	Y	N	Y
23 **McHugh**	N	N	Y	Y	Y	Y	Y
24 Arcuri	Y	Y	Y	N	Y	N	Y
25 **Walsh**	?	N	Y	N	Y	Y	Y
26 **Reynolds**	N	N	Y	Y	Y	Y	Y
27 Higgins	Y	Y	Y	N	Y	N	Y
28 Slaughter	Y	Y	Y	N	Y	N	Y
29 **Kuhl**	N	N	Y	Y	Y	Y	Y
NORTH CAROLINA							
1 Butterfield	Y	Y	Y	N	Y	N	Y
2 Etheridge	Y	Y	Y	N	Y	N	Y
3 **Jones**	N	N	Y	Y	N	Y	Y
4 Price	Y	Y	Y	N	Y	N	Y

	154	155	156	157	158	159	160
5 **Foxx**	N	N	Y	Y	N	Y	Y
6 **Coble**	N	N	Y	Y	N	Y	Y
7 McIntyre	Y	Y	Y	N	Y	Y	Y
8 **Hayes**	N	N	Y	Y	N	Y	Y
9 **Myrick**	N	N	Y	Y	N	Y	Y
10 **McHenry**	N	N	Y	Y	N	Y	Y
11 Shuler	Y	Y	Y	N	Y	N	Y
12 Watt	Y	Y	Y	N	Y	N	Y
13 Miller	Y	Y	Y	N	Y	N	Y
NORTH DAKOTA							
AL Pomeroy	Y	Y	Y	N	Y	N	Y
OHIO							
1 **Chabot**	N	N	Y	Y	Y	Y	Y
2 **Schmidt**	N	N	Y	Y	Y	Y	Y
3 **Turner**	N	N	Y	Y	Y	Y	Y
4 **Jordan**	N	N	N	N	N	Y	Y
5 **Latta**	N	N	Y	Y	Y	Y	Y
6 Wilson	Y	Y	Y	N	Y	N	Y
7 **Hobson**	N	N	Y	N	Y	Y	Y
8 **Boehner**	N	N	Y	Y	N	Y	?
9 Kaptur	Y	Y	Y	N	Y	N	Y
10 Kucinich	Y	Y	Y	N	Y	N	Y
11 Tubbs Jones	Y	Y	Y	N	Y	N	Y
12 **Tiberi**	N	?	Y	Y	N	Y	Y
13 Sutton	Y	Y	Y	N	Y	N	Y
14 **LaTourette**	N	N	Y	Y	N	Y	Y
15 **Pryce**	N	N	Y	Y	Y	Y	?
16 **Regula**	N	N	Y	Y	Y	Y	Y
17 Ryan	Y	Y	Y	N	Y	N	Y
18 Space	Y	Y	Y	N	Y	Y	Y
OKLAHOMA							
1 **Sullivan**	N	N	Y	Y	N	Y	Y
2 Boren	Y	Y	Y	N	Y	N	Y
3 **Lucas**	N	N	Y	Y	N	Y	Y
4 **Cole**	N	N	Y	Y	Y	Y	Y
5 **Fallin**	N	N	Y	Y	N	Y	Y
OREGON							
1 Wu	Y	Y	Y	N	Y	N	Y
2 **Walden**	N	N	Y	Y	N	Y	Y
3 Blumenauer	Y	Y	Y	N	Y	N	Y
4 DeFazio	Y	Y	Y	N	Y	N	Y
5 Hooley	Y	Y	Y	N	Y	?	?
PENNSYLVANIA							
1 Brady	Y	Y	Y	N	Y	N	Y
2 Fattah	?	?	Y	N	Y	N	Y
3 **English**	N	N	Y	N	Y	Y	Y
4 Altmire	N	Y	Y	Y	Y	Y	Y
5 **Peterson**	N	N	Y	Y	N	Y	Y
6 **Gerlach**	N	N	Y	Y	Y	Y	Y
7 Sestak	Y	Y	Y	N	Y	N	Y
8 Murphy, P.	Y	Y	Y	N	Y	N	Y
9 **Shuster**	N	N	Y	Y	N	Y	Y
10 Carney	Y	Y	Y	N	Y	Y	Y
11 Kanjorski	Y	Y	Y	N	Y	N	Y
12 Murtha	Y	Y	Y	N	Y	N	Y
13 Schwartz	Y	Y	Y	N	Y	N	Y
14 Doyle	Y	Y	Y	N	Y	N	Y
15 **Dent**	N	N	Y	Y	Y	Y	Y
16 **Pitts**	N	N	Y	Y	N	Y	Y
17 Holden	Y	Y	Y	N	Y	N	Y
18 **Murphy, T.**	N	N	Y	Y	Y	Y	Y
19 **Platts**	N	N	Y	Y	Y	Y	Y
RHODE ISLAND							
1 Kennedy	Y	Y	Y	N	Y	N	Y
2 Langevin	Y	Y	Y	N	Y	N	Y
SOUTH CAROLINA							
1 **Brown**	N	N	Y	Y	N	Y	Y
2 **Wilson**	N	N	Y	Y	Y	Y	Y
3 **Barrett**	N	N	Y	Y	N	Y	Y
4 **Inglis**	N	N	Y	Y	Y	Y	Y
5 Spratt	Y	Y	Y	N	Y	N	Y
6 Clyburn	Y	Y	Y	N	Y	N	Y
SOUTH DAKOTA							
AL Herseth Sandlin	Y	Y	Y	N	Y	N	Y
TENNESSEE							
1 **Davis, D.**	N	N	Y	N	N	Y	Y
2 **Duncan**	N	N	Y	N	N	Y	Y
3 **Wamp**	N	N	Y	Y	N	Y	Y
4 Davis, L.	Y	Y	Y	N	Y	N	Y
5 Cooper	Y	Y	Y	N	Y	N	Y
6 Gordon	Y	Y	Y	N	Y	N	Y
7 **Blackburn**	N	N	Y	N	N	Y	Y
8 Tanner	Y	Y	Y	N	Y	N	Y
9 Cohen	Y	Y	Y	N	Y	N	Y

	154	155	156	157	158	159	160
TEXAS							
1 **Gohmert**	?	N	Y	Y	N	Y	Y
2 **Poe**	N	N	N	Y	N	Y	Y
3 **Johnson, S.**	N	N	Y	Y	N	Y	Y
4 **Hall**	N	N	Y	Y	N	Y	Y
5 **Hensarling**	N	N	N	Y	N	Y	Y
6 **Barton**	N	N	Y	Y	N	Y	Y
7 **Culberson**	N	N	Y	?	N	Y	Y
8 **Brady**	N	N	Y	Y	N	Y	Y
9 Green, A.	Y	Y	Y	N	Y	N	Y
10 **McCaul**	N	N	Y	Y	N	Y	Y
11 **Conaway**	N	N	Y	Y	N	Y	Y
12 **Granger**	?	?	?	?	?	?	?
13 **Thornberry**	N	N	Y	Y	Y	Y	Y
14 **Paul**	N	N	Y	Y	N	?	?
15 Hinojosa	Y	Y	Y	N	Y	N	Y
16 Reyes	Y	Y	Y	N	Y	N	Y
17 Edwards	Y	Y	Y	N	Y	Y	Y
18 Jackson Lee	Y	Y	Y	N	Y	N	Y
19 **Neugebauer**	N	N	N	Y	N	Y	Y
20 Gonzalez	Y	Y	Y	N	Y	N	Y
21 **Smith**	N	N	Y	Y	N	Y	Y
22 Lampson	N	Y	Y	Y	Y	Y	Y
23 Rodriguez	Y	Y	Y	N	Y	N	Y
24 **Marchant**	?	N	Y	Y	N	Y	Y
25 Doggett	Y	Y	Y	N	Y	N	Y
26 **Burgess**	N	N	Y	Y	N	Y	Y
27 Ortiz	Y	Y	Y	N	Y	N	Y
28 Cuellar	Y	Y	Y	N	Y	N	Y
29 Green, G.	Y	Y	Y	N	Y	N	Y
30 Johnson, E.	Y	Y	Y	N	Y	N	Y
31 **Carter**	N	N	Y	Y	Y	Y	Y
32 **Sessions**	N	N	N	Y	N	Y	Y
UTAH							
1 **Bishop**	N	N	?	Y	N	Y	Y
2 Matheson	Y	Y	Y	N	Y	N	Y
3 **Cannon**	N	N	N	Y	N	Y	Y
VERMONT							
AL Welch	Y	Y	Y	N	Y	N	Y
VIRGINIA							
1 **Wittman**	N	N	Y	Y	N	?	?
2 **Drake**	N	N	Y	Y	N	Y	Y
3 Scott	Y	Y	Y	N	Y	N	Y
4 **Forbes**	N	N	Y	Y	N	Y	Y
5 **Goode**	N	N	N	Y	N	Y	Y
6 **Goodlatte**	N	N	Y	Y	N	Y	Y
7 **Cantor**	N	N	Y	Y	N	Y	Y
8 Moran	Y	Y	Y	N	Y	N	Y
9 Boucher	Y	Y	Y	N	Y	?	?
10 **Wolf**	N	N	Y	Y	Y	Y	Y
11 **Davis**	N	N	Y	Y	Y	Y	Y
WASHINGTON							
1 Inslee	Y	Y	Y	N	Y	N	Y
2 Larsen	Y	Y	Y	N	Y	N	Y
3 Baird	Y	Y	Y	N	Y	N	Y
4 **Hastings**	N	N	Y	Y	N	Y	Y
5 **McMorris Rodgers**	N	N	Y	Y	N	Y	Y
6 Dicks	Y	Y	Y	N	Y	N	Y
7 McDermott	Y	Y	Y	N	Y	N	Y
8 **Reichert**	N	N	Y	Y	Y	Y	Y
9 Smith	Y	Y	Y	N	Y	N	Y
WEST VIRGINIA							
1 Mollohan	Y	Y	Y	N	Y	N	Y
2 **Capito**	N	N	Y	Y	Y	Y	Y
3 Rahall	Y	Y	Y	N	Y	N	Y
WISCONSIN							
1 **Ryan**	N	N	Y	Y	N	Y	Y
2 Baldwin	Y	Y	Y	N	Y	N	Y
3 Kind	Y	Y	Y	N	Y	N	Y
4 Moore	Y	Y	Y	N	Y	N	Y
5 **Sensenbrenner**	N	N	Y	Y	N	Y	Y
6 **Petri**	N	N	Y	Y	N	Y	Y
7 Obey	Y	Y	Y	N	Y	N	Y
8 Kagen	Y	Y	Y	N	Y	N	Y
WYOMING							
AL **Cubin**	?	?	?	?	?	?	?
DELEGATES							
Faleomavaega (A.S.)			?				
Norton (D.C.)			Y				
Bordallo (Guam)			Y				
Fortuño (P.R.)			Y				
Christensen (V.I.)			Y				

IN THE HOUSE | By Vote Number

161. **H J Res 70. Army Reserve Centennial/Passage.** Bordallo, D-Guam, motion to suspend the rules and pass the joint resolution that would congratulate the Army Reserve on its centennial and commemorate the contributions of its veterans and soldiers. Motion agreed to 393-0: R 182-0; D 211-0 (ND 160-0, SD 51-0). A two-thirds majority of those present and voting (262 in this case) is required for passage under suspension of the rules. April 8, 2008.

162. **HR 2464. Children's Emergency Medical Care/Passage.** Capps, D-Calif., motion to suspend the rules and pass the bill that would extend the length of time for which grants may be awarded for projects that improve children's emergency medical services from three years to four years. It would authorize $25 million in fiscal 2009, gradually increasing to $30 million in fiscal 2013. Motion agreed to 390-1: R 180-1; D 210-0 (ND 158-0, SD 52-0). A two-thirds majority of those present and voting (261 in this case) is required for passage under suspension of the rules. April 8, 2008.

163. **S 793. Traumatic Brain Injury Act Reauthorization/Passage.** Baldwin, D-Wis., motion to suspend the rules and pass the bill that would reauthorize through fiscal 2012 a traumatic brain injury treatment program that provides research and rehabilitation grants to states. Motion agreed to 392-1: R 180-1; D 212-0 (ND 161-0, SD 51-0). A two-thirds majority of those present and voting (262 in this case) is required for passage under suspension of the rules. April 8, 2008.

164. **HR 2016. National Landscape Conservation System/ Previous Question.** Hastings, D-Fla., motion to order the previous question (thus ending debate and possibility of amendment) on adoption of the rule (H Res 1084) to provide for House floor consideration of the bill that would codify the National Landscape Conservation System, comprising approximately 27 million acres of areas considered to have significant historical, cultural, ecological, scientific or scenic value. Motion agreed to 220-190: R 0-187; D 220-3 (ND 167-0, SD 53-3). April 9, 2008.

165. **HR 2016. National Landscape Conservation System/Rule.** Adoption of the rule (H Res 1084) to provide for House floor consideration of the bill that would codify the National Landscape Conservation System, comprising approximately 27 million acres of areas considered to have significant historical, cultural, ecological, scientific or scenic value. Adopted 220-188: R 1-187; D 219-1 (ND 164-1, SD 55-0). April 9, 2008.

	161	162	163	164	165
ALABAMA					
1 Bonner	Y	Y	Y	N	N
2 Everett	Y	Y	Y	N	N
3 Rogers	Y	Y	Y	N	N
4 Aderholt	Y	Y	Y	N	N
5 Cramer	Y	Y	Y	Y	Y
6 Bachus	Y	Y	Y	N	N
7 Davis	Y	Y	Y	Y	Y
ALASKA					
AL Young	Y	Y	Y	N	N
ARIZONA					
1 Renzi	Y	Y	?	N	N
2 Franks	Y	Y	Y	N	N
3 Shadegg	Y	Y	Y	N	N
4 Pastor	Y	Y	Y	Y	Y
5 Mitchell	Y	Y	Y	Y	Y
6 Flake	?	?	?	N	N
7 Grijalva	Y	Y	Y	Y	Y
8 Giffords	Y	Y	Y	Y	Y
ARKANSAS					
1 Berry	Y	Y	Y	Y	Y
2 Snyder	Y	Y	Y	Y	Y
3 Boozman	Y	Y	Y	N	N
4 Ross	Y	Y	Y	Y	Y
CALIFORNIA					
1 Thompson	Y	Y	Y	Y	Y
2 Herger	Y	Y	Y	N	N
3 Lungren	Y	Y	Y	N	N
4 Doolittle	Y	Y	Y	N	N
5 Matsui	Y	Y	Y	Y	Y
6 Woolsey	+	+	+	Y	Y
7 Miller, George	Y	?	Y	Y	Y
8 Pelosi					
9 Lee	Y	Y	Y	Y	Y
10 Tauscher	Y	Y	Y	Y	Y
11 McNerney	Y	Y	Y	Y	Y
12 Vacant					
13 Stark	Y	Y	Y	Y	Y
14 Eshoo	Y	Y	Y	Y	Y
15 Honda	Y	Y	Y	Y	Y
16 Lofgren	Y	Y	Y	Y	Y
17 Farr	Y	Y	Y	Y	Y
18 Cardoza	Y	Y	Y	Y	Y
19 Radanovich	Y	Y	?	N	N
20 Costa	Y	Y	Y	Y	Y
21 Nunes	Y	Y	Y	N	N
22 McCarthy	Y	Y	Y	N	N
23 Capps	Y	Y	Y	Y	Y
24 Gallegly	Y	Y	Y	N	N
25 McKeon	Y	Y	Y	N	N
26 Dreier	Y	Y	Y	N	N
27 Sherman	Y	Y	Y	Y	Y
28 Berman	Y	?	Y	Y	Y
29 Schiff	Y	Y	Y	Y	Y
30 Waxman	Y	Y	Y	Y	?
31 Becerra	Y	Y	Y	Y	Y
32 Solis	Y	Y	Y	Y	Y
33 Watson	Y	Y	Y	Y	Y
34 Roybal-Allard	Y	Y	Y	Y	Y
35 Waters	Y	Y	Y	Y	Y
36 Harman	Y	Y	Y	Y	Y
37 Richardson	Y	Y	Y	Y	Y
38 Napolitano	Y	Y	Y	Y	Y
39 Sánchez, Linda	Y	Y	Y	Y	Y
40 Royce	Y	Y	Y	N	N
41 Lewis	Y	Y	Y	N	N
42 Miller, Gary	Y	Y	Y	N	N
43 Baca	Y	Y	Y	Y	Y
44 Calvert	Y	Y	Y	N	N
45 Bono Mack	Y	Y	Y	N	N
46 Rohrabacher	?	?	?	N	N
47 Sanchez, Loretta	Y	Y	Y	Y	Y
48 Campbell	Y	Y	Y	N	N
49 Issa	Y	Y	Y	N	N
50 Bilbray	Y	Y	Y	N	N
51 Filner	Y	Y	Y	Y	Y
52 Hunter	Y	Y	Y	?	N
53 Davis	Y	Y	Y	Y	Y
COLORADO					
1 DeGette	Y	Y	Y	Y	Y
2 Udall	?	?	?	Y	+
3 Salazar	Y	Y	Y	Y	Y
4 Musgrave	Y	Y	Y	N	N
5 Lamborn	Y	Y	Y	N	N
6 Tancredo	Y	Y	Y	N	N
7 Perlmutter	Y	Y	Y	Y	Y
CONNECTICUT					
1 Larson	Y	Y	Y	+	+
2 Courtney	Y	Y	Y	Y	Y
3 DeLauro	Y	Y	Y	Y	Y
4 Shays	Y	Y	Y	-	+
5 Murphy	Y	Y	Y	Y	Y
DELAWARE					
AL Castle	Y	Y	Y	N	N
FLORIDA					
1 Miller	Y	Y	Y	N	N
2 Boyd	Y	Y	Y	Y	Y
3 Brown	?	?	?	Y	Y
4 Crenshaw	?	?	?	N	N
5 Brown-Waite	Y	Y	Y	N	N
6 Stearns	Y	Y	Y	N	N
7 Mica	Y	Y	Y	N	N
8 Keller	Y	Y	Y	N	N
9 Bilirakis	Y	Y	Y	N	N
10 Young	Y	Y	Y	N	N
11 Castor	Y	Y	Y	Y	Y
12 Putnam	Y	Y	Y	N	N
13 Buchanan	Y	Y	Y	N	N
14 Mack	Y	Y	Y	N	N
15 Weldon	Y	Y	Y	N	N
16 Mahoney	Y	Y	Y	N	Y
17 Meek	Y	Y	Y	Y	Y
18 Ros-Lehtinen	Y	Y	Y	N	N
19 Wexler	Y	Y	Y	Y	Y
20 Wasserman Schultz	Y	Y	Y	Y	Y
21 Diaz-Balart, L.	?	?	?	?	?
22 Klein	Y	Y	Y	Y	Y
23 Hastings	Y	Y	Y	Y	Y
24 Feeney	?	?	?	N	N
25 Diaz-Balart, M.	+	+	+	N	N
GEORGIA					
1 Kingston	Y	Y	Y	N	N
2 Bishop	Y	Y	Y	Y	Y
3 Westmoreland	Y	Y	Y	N	N
4 Johnson	?	?	?	Y	Y
5 Lewis	Y	Y	Y	Y	Y
6 Price	Y	Y	Y	N	N
7 Linder	Y	Y	Y	N	N
8 Marshall	Y	Y	Y	Y	Y
9 Deal	Y	Y	Y	N	N
10 Broun	Y	Y	Y	N	N
11 Gingrey	Y	Y	Y	N	N
12 Barrow	Y	Y	Y	N	Y
13 Scott	Y	Y	Y	Y	Y
HAWAII					
1 Abercrombie	?	?	?	?	?
2 Hirono	Y	Y	Y	Y	Y
IDAHO					
1 Sali	Y	Y	?	N	N
2 Simpson	Y	Y	N	N	N
ILLINOIS					
1 Rush	?	?	?	?	?
2 Jackson	Y	Y	Y	Y	Y
3 Lipinski	Y	Y	Y	Y	Y
4 Gutierrez	Y	Y	Y	Y	Y
5 Emanuel	Y	Y	Y	Y	Y
6 Roskam	Y	Y	Y	N	N
7 Davis	Y	Y	Y	Y	Y
8 Bean	Y	Y	Y	Y	Y
9 Schakowsky	Y	Y	Y	Y	Y
10 Kirk	Y	Y	Y	N	N
11 Weller	Y	Y	Y	N	N
12 Costello	Y	Y	Y	Y	Y
13 Biggert	Y	Y	Y	N	N
14 Foster	Y	Y	Y	Y	Y
15 Johnson	+	Y	Y	N	N

KEY	Republicans	Democrats		
Y	Voted for (yea)	X	Paired against	C Voted "present" to avoid possible conflict of interest
#	Paired for	–	Announced against	
+	Announced for	P	Voted "present"	? Did not vote or otherwise make a position known
N	Voted against (nay)			

ND Northern Democrats, SD Southern Democrats
Southern states: Ala., Ark., Fla., Ga., Ky., La., Miss., N.C., Okla., S.C., Tenn., Texas, Va.

	161	162	163	164	165
16 Manzullo	Y	Y	Y	N	N
17 Hare	Y	Y	Y	Y	Y
18 LaHood	Y	Y	Y	N	N
19 Shimkus	Y	Y	Y	N	N
INDIANA					
1 Visclosky	Y	Y	Y	Y	Y
2 Donnelly	Y	Y	Y	Y	Y
3 Souder	Y	Y	Y	N	N
4 Buyer	?	?	?	?	?
5 Burton	Y	Y	Y	N	N
6 Pence	Y	Y	Y	N	N
7 Carson, A.	Y	Y	Y	Y	Y
8 Ellsworth	Y	Y	Y	Y	Y
9 Hill	Y	Y	Y	?	N
IOWA					
1 Braley	?	+	+	Y	Y
2 Loebsack	Y	Y	Y	Y	Y
3 Boswell	Y	Y	Y	Y	Y
4 Latham	Y	Y	Y	N	N
5 King	Y	Y	Y	N	N
KANSAS					
1 Moran	Y	Y	Y	N	N
2 Boyda	Y	Y	Y	Y	Y
3 Moore	Y	Y	Y	Y	Y
4 Tiahrt	Y	Y	Y	N	N
KENTUCKY					
1 Whitfield	Y	Y	Y	N	N
2 Lewis	Y	Y	Y	N	N
3 Yarmuth	Y	Y	Y	Y	Y
4 Davis	Y	Y	Y	N	N
5 Rogers	Y	Y	Y	N	N
6 Chandler	Y	Y	Y	Y	Y
LOUISIANA					
1 Vacant					
2 Jefferson	Y	Y	Y	Y	Y
3 Melancon	Y	Y	Y	N	N
4 McCrery	Y	Y	Y	N	N
5 Alexander	Y	Y	Y	?	?
6 Vacant					
7 Boustany	Y	Y	Y	N	N
MAINE					
1 Allen	Y	Y	Y	Y	Y
2 Michaud	Y	Y	Y	Y	Y
MARYLAND					
1 Gilchrest	Y	Y	Y	N	N
2 Ruppersberger	Y	Y	Y	Y	Y
3 Sarbanes	Y	Y	Y	Y	Y
4 Wynn	Y	Y	Y	Y	Y
5 Hoyer	Y	Y	Y	Y	Y
6 Bartlett	Y	Y	Y	N	N
7 Cummings	Y	Y	Y	Y	Y
8 Van Hollen	Y	Y	Y	Y	Y
MASSACHUSETTS					
1 Olver	Y	Y	Y	Y	Y
2 Neal	Y	Y	Y	Y	Y
3 McGovern	Y	Y	Y	Y	?
4 Frank	Y	Y	Y	Y	Y
5 Tsongas	Y	Y	Y	Y	Y
6 Tierney	Y	Y	Y	Y	Y
7 Markey	?	?	?	Y	Y
8 Capuano	Y	Y	Y	Y	Y
9 Lynch	Y	Y	Y	Y	Y
10 Delahunt	Y	Y	Y	Y	Y
MICHIGAN					
1 Stupak	Y	Y	Y	Y	Y
2 Hoekstra	Y	Y	Y	N	N
3 Ehlers	Y	Y	Y	N	N
4 Camp	Y	Y	Y	N	N
5 Kildee	Y	Y	Y	Y	Y
6 Upton	Y	Y	Y	N	N
7 Walberg	Y	Y	Y	N	N
8 Rogers	Y	Y	Y	N	N
9 Knollenberg	Y	Y	Y	N	N
10 Miller	Y	Y	Y	N	N
11 McCotter	Y	Y	Y	N	N
12 Levin	Y	Y	Y	Y	Y
13 Kilpatrick	Y	Y	Y	Y	Y
14 Conyers	Y	Y	Y	Y	Y
15 Dingell	Y	Y	Y	Y	Y
MINNESOTA					
1 Walz	Y	Y	Y	Y	Y
2 Kline	Y	Y	Y	N	N
3 Ramstad	Y	Y	Y	N	N
4 McCollum	Y	Y	Y	Y	Y

	161	162	163	164	165
5 Ellison	Y	Y	Y	Y	Y
6 Bachmann	Y	Y	Y	N	N
7 Peterson	Y	Y	Y	Y	Y
8 Oberstar	Y	Y	Y	Y	Y
MISSISSIPPI					
1 Vacant					
2 Thompson	Y	Y	Y	Y	Y
3 Pickering	Y	Y	Y	N	N
4 Taylor	Y	Y	Y	Y	Y
MISSOURI					
1 Clay	Y	Y	Y	Y	Y
2 Akin	Y	Y	Y	N	N
3 Carnahan	?	Y	Y	Y	Y
4 Skelton	Y	Y	Y	Y	Y
5 Cleaver	Y	Y	Y	Y	Y
6 Graves	Y	Y	Y	N	N
7 Blunt	Y	Y	Y	N	N
8 Emerson	?	?	?	N	N
9 Hulshof	Y	Y	Y	N	N
MONTANA					
AL Rehberg	Y	Y	Y	N	N
NEBRASKA					
1 Fortenberry	Y	Y	Y	N	N
2 Terry	Y	Y	Y	N	N
3 Smith	Y	Y	Y	N	N
NEVADA					
1 Berkley	Y	Y	Y	Y	Y
2 Heller	?	?	Y	N	N
3 Porter	Y	Y	Y	N	N
NEW HAMPSHIRE					
1 Shea-Porter	Y	Y	Y	Y	Y
2 Hodes	Y	Y	Y	Y	Y
NEW JERSEY					
1 Andrews	Y	Y	Y	Y	Y
2 LoBiondo	Y	Y	Y	N	N
3 Saxton	Y	Y	Y	N	N
4 Smith	Y	Y	Y	N	N
5 Garrett	Y	Y	Y	N	N
6 Pallone	Y	Y	Y	Y	Y
7 Ferguson	?	?	?	?	?
8 Pascrell	Y	Y	Y	Y	Y
9 Rothman	?	?	?	?	?
10 Payne	?	?	?	Y	Y
11 Frelinghuysen	Y	Y	Y	N	N
12 Holt	Y	Y	Y	Y	Y
13 Sires	?	?	?	?	?
NEW MEXICO					
1 Wilson	?	?	?	N	N
2 Pearce	Y	Y	Y	N	N
3 Udall	Y	Y	Y	Y	Y
NEW YORK					
1 Bishop	Y	Y	Y	Y	Y
2 Israel	Y	Y	Y	Y	Y
3 King	Y	Y	Y	N	N
4 McCarthy	Y	Y	Y	Y	Y
5 Ackerman	Y	Y	Y	Y	Y
6 Meeks	Y	Y	Y	Y	Y
7 Crowley	Y	Y	Y	Y	Y
8 Nadler	Y	Y	Y	Y	Y
9 Weiner	Y	Y	Y	Y	Y
10 Towns	Y	Y	Y	Y	Y
11 Clarke	Y	Y	Y	Y	Y
12 Velázquez	Y	Y	Y	?	?
13 Fossella	Y	Y	Y	N	N
14 Maloney	Y	Y	Y	Y	Y
15 Rangel	Y	Y	Y	Y	Y
16 Serrano	Y	Y	Y	Y	Y
17 Engel	?	?	?	Y	Y
18 Lowey	Y	Y	Y	Y	Y
19 Hall	?	?	?	Y	Y
20 Gillibrand	Y	Y	Y	Y	Y
21 McNulty	Y	Y	Y	Y	Y
22 Hinchey	Y	Y	Y	Y	Y
23 McHugh	Y	Y	Y	N	N
24 Arcuri	Y	Y	Y	Y	Y
25 Walsh	Y	Y	Y	N	N
26 Reynolds	Y	Y	Y	N	N
27 Higgins	Y	Y	Y	Y	Y
28 Slaughter	Y	Y	Y	Y	Y
29 Kuhl	Y	Y	Y	N	N
NORTH CAROLINA					
1 Butterfield	Y	Y	Y	Y	Y
2 Etheridge	Y	Y	Y	Y	Y
3 Jones	Y	Y	Y	?	N
4 Price	Y	Y	Y	Y	Y

	161	162	163	164	165
5 Foxx	Y	Y	Y	N	N
6 Coble	Y	Y	Y	N	N
7 McIntyre	Y	Y	?	Y	Y
8 Hayes	Y	Y	Y	N	N
9 Myrick	Y	Y	Y	N	N
10 McHenry	Y	Y	Y	N	N
11 Shuler	Y	Y	Y	N	N
12 Watt	Y	Y	Y	Y	Y
13 Miller	Y	Y	Y	Y	Y
NORTH DAKOTA					
AL Pomeroy	Y	Y	Y	Y	Y
OHIO					
1 Chabot	Y	Y	Y	N	N
2 Schmidt	Y	Y	Y	N	N
3 Turner	Y	Y	Y	N	N
4 Jordan	Y	Y	Y	N	N
5 Latta	Y	Y	Y	N	N
6 Wilson	Y	Y	Y	Y	Y
7 Hobson	Y	Y	Y	N	N
8 Boehner	Y	Y	Y	N	N
9 Kaptur	Y	Y	Y	?	Y
10 Kucinich	Y	Y	Y	Y	Y
11 Tubbs Jones	Y	Y	Y	Y	Y
12 Tiberi	Y	Y	Y	N	N
13 Sutton	Y	Y	Y	Y	Y
14 LaTourette	Y	Y	Y	N	N
15 Pryce	?	?	?	N	N
16 Regula	Y	Y	Y	N	N
17 Ryan	Y	Y	Y	Y	Y
18 Space	Y	Y	Y	Y	?
OKLAHOMA					
1 Sullivan	Y	?	Y	N	?
2 Boren	Y	Y	Y	Y	Y
3 Lucas	Y	Y	Y	N	N
4 Cole	Y	Y	Y	N	N
5 Fallin	Y	Y	Y	N	N
OREGON					
1 Wu	Y	Y	Y	Y	Y
2 Walden	Y	Y	Y	N	N
3 Blumenauer	Y	Y	Y	Y	Y
4 DeFazio	Y	Y	Y	Y	Y
5 Hooley	Y	Y	Y	Y	Y
PENNSYLVANIA					
1 Brady	Y	Y	Y	Y	Y
2 Fattah	Y	Y	Y	Y	Y
3 English	Y	Y	Y	N	N
4 Altmire	Y	Y	Y	Y	Y
5 Peterson	?	?	?	N	N
6 Gerlach	Y	Y	Y	N	N
7 Sestak	Y	Y	Y	Y	Y
8 Murphy, P.	Y	Y	Y	Y	Y
9 Shuster	Y	Y	Y	N	N
10 Carney	Y	Y	Y	Y	Y
11 Kanjorski	Y	Y	Y	Y	Y
12 Murtha	Y	Y	Y	Y	Y
13 Schwartz	Y	+	Y	Y	Y
14 Doyle	Y	Y	Y	Y	Y
15 Dent	Y	Y	Y	N	N
16 Pitts	Y	Y	Y	N	N
17 Holden	Y	Y	Y	Y	Y
18 Murphy, T.	Y	?	Y	N	N
19 Platts	Y	Y	Y	N	N
RHODE ISLAND					
1 Kennedy	Y	Y	Y	Y	Y
2 Langevin	+	+	+	Y	Y
SOUTH CAROLINA					
1 Brown	Y	Y	Y	N	N
2 Wilson	Y	Y	Y	N	N
3 Barrett	Y	Y	Y	N	N
4 Inglis	Y	Y	Y	N	N
5 Spratt	Y	Y	Y	Y	Y
6 Clyburn	Y	Y	Y	Y	Y
SOUTH DAKOTA					
AL Herseth Sandlin	Y	Y	Y	Y	Y
TENNESSEE					
1 Davis, D.	Y	Y	Y	N	N
2 Duncan	Y	Y	Y	N	N
3 Wamp	Y	Y	Y	N	N
4 Davis, L.	Y	Y	Y	Y	Y
5 Cooper	Y	Y	Y	Y	Y
6 Gordon	?	?	?	Y	Y
7 Blackburn	Y	Y	Y	N	N
8 Tanner	Y	Y	Y	Y	Y
9 Cohen	Y	Y	Y	Y	Y

	161	162	163	164	165
TEXAS					
1 Gohmert	Y	Y	Y	N	N
2 Poe	Y	Y	Y	N	N
3 Johnson, S.	Y	Y	Y	N	N
4 Hall	Y	Y	Y	N	N
5 Hensarling	Y	Y	Y	N	N
6 Barton	Y	Y	Y	N	N
7 Culberson	Y	Y	Y	N	N
8 Brady	Y	Y	Y	N	N
9 Green, A.	Y	Y	Y	Y	+
10 McCaul	Y	Y	Y	N	N
11 Conaway	Y	Y	Y	N	N
12 Granger	?	?	?	?	?
13 Thornberry	Y	Y	Y	N	N
14 Paul	Y	N	N	N	N
15 Hinojosa	Y	Y	Y	Y	Y
16 Reyes	Y	Y	Y	Y	Y
17 Edwards	Y	Y	Y	Y	Y
18 Jackson Lee	Y	Y	Y	Y	Y
19 Neugebauer	Y	Y	Y	–	–
20 Gonzalez	?	?	?	Y	Y
21 Smith	Y	Y	Y	N	N
22 Lampson	Y	Y	Y	N	Y
23 Rodriguez	?	?	Y	Y	Y
24 Marchant	Y	Y	Y	N	N
25 Doggett	Y	Y	Y	Y	Y
26 Burgess	Y	Y	Y	N	N
27 Ortiz	Y	Y	Y	Y	Y
28 Cuellar	Y	Y	Y	Y	Y
29 Green, G.	Y	Y	Y	Y	Y
30 Johnson, E.	Y	Y	Y	Y	Y
31 Carter	Y	Y	Y	N	N
32 Sessions	Y	Y	Y	N	N
UTAH					
1 Bishop	Y	Y	Y	N	N
2 Matheson	Y	Y	Y	Y	Y
3 Cannon	Y	Y	Y	N	N
VERMONT					
AL Welch	Y	Y	Y	Y	Y
VIRGINIA					
1 Wittman	Y	Y	Y	N	N
2 Drake	Y	Y	Y	N	N
3 Scott	Y	Y	Y	Y	Y
4 Forbes	Y	Y	Y	N	N
5 Goode	Y	Y	Y	N	N
6 Goodlatte	Y	Y	Y	N	N
7 Cantor	Y	Y	Y	N	N
8 Moran	Y	Y	Y	Y	Y
9 Boucher	?	?	?	?	?
10 Wolf	Y	Y	Y	N	N
11 Davis	Y	Y	Y	?	?
WASHINGTON					
1 Inslee	Y	Y	Y	Y	Y
2 Larsen	Y	Y	Y	Y	Y
3 Baird	Y	Y	Y	Y	Y
4 Hastings	Y	Y	Y	N	N
5 McMorris Rodgers	Y	Y	Y	N	N
6 Dicks	Y	Y	Y	Y	Y
7 McDermott	+	+	+	Y	Y
8 Reichert	Y	Y	Y	N	N
9 Smith	Y	Y	Y	Y	Y
WEST VIRGINIA					
1 Mollohan	?	?	?	Y	Y
2 Capito	Y	Y	Y	N	N
3 Rahall	Y	Y	Y	Y	Y
WISCONSIN					
1 Ryan	Y	Y	Y	N	N
2 Baldwin	Y	Y	Y	Y	Y
3 Kind	Y	Y	Y	Y	Y
4 Moore	Y	Y	Y	Y	Y
5 Sensenbrenner	Y	Y	Y	N	N
6 Petri	Y	Y	Y	N	N
7 Obey	Y	Y	Y	Y	Y
8 Kagen	Y	Y	Y	Y	Y
WYOMING					
AL Cubin	?	?	?	?	?
DELEGATES					
Faleomavaega (A.S.)					
Norton (D.C.)					
Bordallo (Guam)					
Fortuño (P.R.)					
Christensen (V.I.)					

IN THE HOUSE | By Vote Number

166. **H Res 1077. Tibetan Protection/Adoption.** Berman, D-Calif., motion to suspend the rules and adopt the resolution that would call on the government of China to end the crackdown on non-violent Tibetan protestors, work toward resolution with the Dalai Lama, allow journalists access to Tibetan areas of China and release Tibetans imprisoned for non-violently expressing opposition to the Chinese government. Motion agreed to 413-1: R 189-1; D 224-0 (ND 168-0, SD 56-0). A two-thirds majority of those present and voting (276 in this case) is required for adoption under suspension of the rules. April 9, 2008.

167. **HR 2016. National Landscape Conservation System/Border Security.** Grijalva, D-Ariz., amendment that would clarify that nothing in the bill would impede efforts by the Department of Homeland Security to secure U.S. borders. Adopted in Committee of the Whole 414-0: R 187-0; D 227-0 (ND 170-0, SD 57-0). April 9, 2008.

168. **HR 2016. National Landscape Conservation System/Bureau of Land Management Values.** Bishop, R-Utah, amendment that would strike from the bill language to define the values for establishing the National Landscape Conservation System within the Bureau of Land Management. Rejected in Committee of the Whole 175-246: R 170-23; D 5-223 (ND 5-166, SD 0-57). April 9, 2008.

169. **HR 2016. National Landscape Conservation System/Management.** Bishop, R-Utah, amendment that would strike from the bill language to define the values by which the Interior secretary should manage the National Landscape Conservation System and insert language to require the secretary to manage the system in accordance with each applicable law. Rejected in Committee of the Whole 172-245: R 169-23; D 3-222 (ND 2-166, SD 1-56). April 9, 2008.

170. **HR 2016. National Landscape Conservation System/Energy Development.** Bishop, R-Utah, amendment that would clarify that nothing in the bill is intended to hinder or restrict energy development within the National Landscape Conservation System. Adopted in Committee of the Whole 333-89: R 189-3; D 144-86 (ND 95-78, SD 49-8). April 9, 2008.

	166	167	168	169	170
ALABAMA					
1 **Bonner**	Y	Y	Y	Y	Y
2 **Everett**	Y	Y	Y	Y	Y
3 **Rogers**	Y	Y	Y	Y	Y
4 **Aderholt**	Y	Y	Y	Y	Y
5 Cramer	Y	Y	N	N	Y
6 **Bachus**	Y	Y	Y	Y	Y
7 Davis	Y	Y	N	N	Y
ALASKA					
AL **Young**	Y	Y	Y	Y	Y
ARIZONA					
1 **Renzi**	Y	Y	Y	Y	Y
2 **Franks**	Y	Y	Y	Y	Y
3 **Shadegg**	Y	Y	Y	Y	Y
4 Pastor	Y	Y	N	N	N
5 Mitchell	Y	Y	N	N	Y
6 **Flake**	Y	Y	Y	Y	Y
7 Grijalva	Y	Y	N	N	N
8 Giffords	Y	Y	N	N	Y
ARKANSAS					
1 Berry	Y	Y	N	N	Y
2 Snyder	Y	Y	N	N	Y
3 **Boozman**	Y	Y	Y	Y	Y
4 Ross	Y	Y	N	N	Y
CALIFORNIA					
1 Thompson	Y	Y	N	N	Y
2 **Herger**	Y	+	Y	Y	Y
3 **Lungren**	Y	Y	Y	Y	Y
4 **Doolittle**	Y	Y	Y	Y	Y
5 Matsui	Y	Y	N	N	N
6 Woolsey	Y	Y	N	N	N
7 Miller, George	+	Y	N	N	N
8 Pelosi	Y				
9 Lee	Y	+	–	N	N
10 Tauscher	Y	Y	N	N	N
11 McNerney	Y	Y	N	N	Y
12 Vacant					
13 Stark	Y	Y	N	N	N
14 Eshoo	Y	Y	N	N	N
15 Honda	Y	Y	N	N	N
16 Lofgren	Y	Y	N	N	N
17 Farr	Y	Y	N	N	N
18 Cardoza	Y	Y	N	N	Y
19 **Radanovich**	Y	Y	Y	Y	Y
20 Costa	Y	?	N	N	Y
21 **Nunes**	Y	Y	Y	Y	Y
22 **McCarthy**	Y	Y	Y	Y	Y
23 Capps	Y	Y	N	N	N
24 **Gallegly**	Y	Y	Y	Y	Y
25 **McKeon**	Y	Y	Y	Y	Y
26 **Dreier**	Y	Y	Y	Y	Y
27 Sherman	Y	Y	N	N	N
28 Berman	Y	?	?	N	N
29 Schiff	Y	Y	N	N	Y
30 Waxman	Y	Y	N	N	N
31 Becerra	Y	Y	N	?	?
32 Solis	Y	Y	N	N	N
33 Watson	Y	Y	N	N	N
34 Roybal-Allard	Y	Y	N	N	N
35 Waters	Y	Y	N	N	Y
36 Harman	Y	Y	N	N	Y
37 Richardson	Y	Y	N	N	Y
38 Napolitano	Y	Y	N	N	N
39 Sánchez, Linda	Y	Y	N	N	N
40 **Royce**	Y	Y	Y	Y	Y
41 **Lewis**	Y	Y	Y	Y	Y
42 **Miller, Gary**	Y	Y	Y	Y	Y
43 Baca	Y	Y	N	N	Y
44 **Calvert**	Y	Y	Y	Y	Y
45 **Bono Mack**	Y	Y	N	Y	Y
46 **Rohrabacher**	Y	Y	Y	Y	Y
47 Sanchez, Loretta	Y	Y	N	N	Y
48 **Campbell**	Y	Y	Y	Y	Y
49 **Issa**	Y	Y	Y	Y	Y
50 **Bilbray**	Y	Y	N	Y	Y
51 Filner	Y	Y	N	N	N
52 **Hunter**	Y	Y	Y	Y	?
53 Davis	Y	Y	N	N	Y

	166	167	168	169	170
COLORADO					
1 DeGette	Y	Y	N	N	Y
2 Udall	+	Y	N	N	Y
3 Salazar	Y	Y	N	N	Y
4 **Musgrave**	Y	Y	Y	Y	Y
5 **Lamborn**	Y	Y	Y	Y	Y
6 **Tancredo**	Y	Y	Y	Y	Y
7 Perlmutter	Y	Y	N	?	Y
CONNECTICUT					
1 Larson	+	+	+	–	–
2 Courtney	Y	Y	N	N	N
3 DeLauro	Y	Y	N	N	Y
4 **Shays**	?	+	–	–	+
5 Murphy	Y	Y	N	N	Y
DELAWARE					
AL **Castle**	Y	Y	N	N	Y
FLORIDA					
1 **Miller**	Y	Y	Y	Y	Y
2 Boyd	Y	Y	N	N	Y
3 Brown	Y	Y	N	N	Y
4 **Crenshaw**	Y	Y	Y	Y	Y
5 **Brown-Waite**	Y	Y	Y	Y	Y
6 **Stearns**	Y	Y	Y	Y	Y
7 **Mica**	Y	Y	Y	Y	Y
8 **Keller**	Y	Y	Y	Y	Y
9 **Bilirakis**	Y	Y	Y	Y	Y
10 **Young**	Y	Y	Y	Y	Y
11 Castor	Y	Y	N	N	N
12 **Putnam**	Y	Y	Y	Y	Y
13 **Buchanan**	Y	Y	Y	Y	Y
14 **Mack**	Y	Y	Y	Y	Y
15 **Weldon**	Y	Y	Y	Y	Y
16 Mahoney	Y	Y	N	N	Y
17 Meek	Y	Y	N	N	Y
18 **Ros-Lehtinen**	Y	Y	Y	Y	Y
19 Wexler	Y	Y	N	N	Y
20 Wasserman Schultz	Y	Y	N	N	N
21 **Diaz-Balart, L.**	?	?	?	?	?
22 Klein	Y	Y	N	N	Y
23 Hastings	Y	Y	N	N	N
24 **Feeney**	?	Y	Y	Y	Y
25 **Diaz-Balart, M.**	Y	Y	Y	Y	Y
GEORGIA					
1 **Kingston**	Y	Y	Y	Y	Y
2 Bishop	Y	Y	N	N	Y
3 **Westmoreland**	Y	Y	Y	Y	Y
4 Johnson	Y	Y	N	N	Y
5 Lewis	Y	Y	N	N	Y
6 **Price**	Y	Y	Y	Y	Y
7 **Linder**	Y	Y	Y	Y	Y
8 Marshall	Y	Y	N	N	Y
9 **Deal**	Y	Y	Y	Y	Y
10 **Broun**	Y	Y	Y	Y	Y
11 **Gingrey**	Y	Y	Y	Y	Y
12 Barrow	Y	Y	N	N	Y
13 Scott	Y	Y	N	N	Y
HAWAII					
1 Abercrombie	?	?	?	?	?
2 Hirono	Y	Y	N	N	N
IDAHO					
1 **Sali**	Y	Y	Y	Y	Y
2 **Simpson**	Y	Y	Y	Y	Y
ILLINOIS					
1 Rush	?	?	?	?	?
2 Jackson	Y	Y	N	N	Y
3 Lipinski	Y	Y	N	N	N
4 Gutierrez	Y	Y	N	?	N
5 Emanuel	Y	Y	N	N	Y
6 **Roskam**	Y	Y	Y	Y	Y
7 Davis	Y	Y	N	N	N
8 Bean	Y	Y	N	N	Y
9 Schakowsky	Y	Y	N	N	N
10 **Kirk**	Y	Y	N	N	N
11 **Weller**	Y	Y	Y	Y	Y
12 Costello	Y	Y	N	N	N
13 **Biggert**	Y	Y	N	N	N
14 Foster	Y	Y	N	N	Y
15 **Johnson**	Y	Y	N	N	Y

ND Northern Democrats, SD Southern Democrats
Southern states: Ala., Ark., Fla., Ga., Ky., La., Miss., N.C., Okla., S.C., Tenn., Texas, Va.

	166	167	168	169	170
16 Manzullo	Y	Y	Y	Y	Y
17 Hare	Y	Y	N	N	Y
18 LaHood	Y	Y	N	N	Y
19 Shimkus	Y	Y	N	N	Y
INDIANA					
1 Visclosky	Y	Y	N	N	Y
2 Donnelly	Y	Y	N	N	Y
3 Souder	Y	Y	Y	Y	Y
4 Buyer	?	?	?	?	?
5 Burton	Y	Y	Y	Y	Y
6 Pence	Y	Y	Y	Y	Y
7 Carson, A.	Y	Y	N	N	Y
8 Ellsworth	Y	Y	N	N	Y
9 Hill	Y	Y	N	N	Y
IOWA					
1 Braley	Y	Y	N	N	N
2 Loebsack	Y	Y	N	N	Y
3 Boswell	Y	Y	N	N	Y
4 Latham	Y	Y	Y	Y	Y
5 King	Y	Y	Y	Y	Y
KANSAS					
1 Moran	Y	Y	N	N	Y
2 Boyda	Y	Y	N	Y	Y
3 Moore	Y	Y	N	N	N
4 Tiahrt	Y	Y	Y	Y	Y
KENTUCKY					
1 Whitfield	Y	Y	Y	Y	Y
2 Lewis	Y	Y	Y	Y	Y
3 Yarmuth	Y	Y	N	N	Y
4 Davis	Y	Y	Y	Y	Y
5 Rogers	Y	Y	Y	Y	Y
6 Chandler	Y	Y	N	N	Y
LOUISIANA					
1 Vacant					
2 Jefferson	Y	Y	N	N	Y
3 Melancon	Y	Y	N	N	Y
4 McCrery	Y	?	Y	Y	Y
5 Alexander	Y	Y	Y	Y	Y
6 Vacant					
7 Boustany	Y	Y	Y	Y	Y
MAINE					
1 Allen	Y	Y	N	N	Y
2 Michaud	Y	Y	N	N	Y
MARYLAND					
1 Gilchrest	Y	Y	N	N	Y
2 Ruppersberger	Y	Y	N	N	Y
3 Sarbanes	Y	Y	N	N	Y
4 Wynn	Y	Y	N	N	Y
5 Hoyer	Y	Y	N	N	Y
6 Bartlett	Y	Y	N	N	Y
7 Cummings	Y	Y	N	N	Y
8 Van Hollen	Y	Y	N	N	N
MASSACHUSETTS					
1 Olver	Y	Y	N	N	N
2 Neal	Y	Y	N	N	N
3 McGovern	Y	Y	N	N	N
4 Frank	Y	Y	N	N	N
5 Tsongas	Y	Y	N	N	N
6 Tierney	Y	Y	N	N	N
7 Markey	Y	Y	N	N	N
8 Capuano	Y	Y	N	N	N
9 Lynch	Y	Y	N	N	N
10 Delahunt	Y	Y	N	N	N
MICHIGAN					
1 Stupak	Y	Y	N	N	Y
2 Hoekstra	Y	Y	Y	Y	Y
3 Ehlers	Y	Y	N	N	Y
4 Camp	Y	Y	Y	Y	Y
5 Kildee	Y	Y	N	N	Y
6 Upton	Y	Y	N	N	Y
7 Walberg	Y	Y	Y	Y	Y
8 Rogers	Y	Y	Y	Y	Y
9 Knollenberg	Y	Y	Y	Y	Y
10 Miller	Y	Y	Y	Y	Y
11 McCotter	Y	Y	Y	Y	Y
12 Levin	Y	Y	N	N	Y
13 Kilpatrick	Y	Y	N	N	N
14 Conyers	Y	Y	N	N	Y
15 Dingell	Y	Y	N	N	Y
MINNESOTA					
1 Walz	Y	Y	N	N	Y
2 Kline	Y	Y	Y	Y	Y
3 Ramstad	Y	Y	Y	Y	Y
4 McCollum	Y	Y	N	N	N

	166	167	168	169	170
5 Ellison	Y	Y	N	N	Y
6 Bachmann	Y	Y	Y	Y	Y
7 Peterson	Y	Y	Y	?	Y
8 Oberstar	Y	Y	N	N	Y
MISSISSIPPI					
1 Vacant					
2 Thompson	Y	Y	N	N	N
3 Pickering	Y	Y	Y	Y	Y
4 Taylor	Y	Y	N	N	Y
MISSOURI					
1 Clay	Y	Y	N	N	Y
2 Akin	Y	Y	Y	Y	Y
3 Carnahan	Y	Y	N	N	Y
4 Skelton	Y	Y	N	N	Y
5 Cleaver	Y	Y	N	N	Y
6 Graves	Y	Y	Y	Y	Y
7 Blunt	Y	?	Y	Y	Y
8 Emerson	Y	Y	Y	Y	Y
9 Hulshof	Y	Y	Y	Y	Y
MONTANA					
AL Rehberg	Y	Y	Y	Y	Y
NEBRASKA					
1 Fortenberry	Y	Y	N	N	Y
2 Terry	Y	Y	Y	Y	Y
3 Smith	Y	Y	Y	Y	Y
NEVADA					
1 Berkley	Y	Y	N	N	Y
2 Heller	Y	Y	Y	Y	Y
3 Porter	Y	Y	Y	Y	Y
NEW HAMPSHIRE					
1 Shea-Porter	Y	Y	N	N	Y
2 Hodes	Y	Y	N	N	N
NEW JERSEY					
1 Andrews	Y	Y	N	N	Y
2 LoBiondo	Y	Y	N	N	Y
3 Saxton	Y	Y	N	N	Y
4 Smith	Y	?	?	?	?
5 Garrett	Y	Y	Y	Y	Y
6 Pallone	Y	Y	N	N	N
7 Ferguson	?	?	?	?	?
8 Pascrell	Y	Y	N	N	Y
9 Rothman	?	?	?	?	?
10 Payne	Y	Y	N	N	N
11 Frelinghuysen	Y	Y	N	N	Y
12 Holt	Y	Y	N	N	N
13 Sires	?	?	?	?	?
NEW MEXICO					
1 Wilson	Y	Y	Y	Y	Y
2 Pearce	Y	Y	Y	Y	Y
3 Udall	Y	Y	N	N	Y
NEW YORK					
1 Bishop	Y	Y	N	N	N
2 Israel	Y	Y	N	N	N
3 King	Y	Y	Y	Y	Y
4 McCarthy	Y	Y	N	N	Y
5 Ackerman	Y	Y	N	N	Y
6 Meeks	Y	Y	N	N	Y
7 Crowley	Y	Y	N	N	Y
8 Nadler	Y	Y	N	N	Y
9 Weiner	Y	Y	N	N	Y
10 Towns	Y	Y	N	N	Y
11 Clarke	Y	Y	N	N	N
12 Velázquez	?	Y	N	N	Y
13 Fossella	Y	Y	Y	Y	Y
14 Maloney	Y	Y	N	N	Y
15 Rangel	Y	Y	N	N	Y
16 Serrano	Y	Y	N	N	Y
17 Engel	Y	Y	N	N	Y
18 Lowey	Y	Y	N	N	Y
19 Hall	Y	Y	N	N	Y
20 Gillibrand	Y	Y	N	N	Y
21 McNulty	Y	Y	N	N	N
22 Hinchey	Y	Y	N	N	Y
23 McHugh	Y	Y	Y	Y	Y
24 Arcuri	Y	Y	N	N	Y
25 Walsh	Y	Y	N	N	Y
26 Reynolds	Y	Y	Y	Y	Y
27 Higgins	Y	Y	N	N	Y
28 Slaughter	Y	Y	N	N	N
29 Kuhl	Y	Y	Y	Y	Y
NORTH CAROLINA					
1 Butterfield	Y	Y	N	N	Y
2 Etheridge	Y	Y	N	N	Y
3 Jones	Y	Y	N	N	Y
4 Price	Y	Y	N	N	Y

	166	167	168	169	170
5 Foxx	Y	Y	Y	Y	Y
6 Coble	Y	Y	Y	Y	Y
7 McIntyre	Y	Y	N	N	Y
8 Hayes	Y	Y	Y	Y	Y
9 Myrick	Y	Y	Y	Y	Y
10 McHenry	Y	Y	Y	Y	Y
11 Shuler	Y	Y	N	N	Y
12 Watt	Y	Y	N	N	Y
13 Miller	Y	Y	N	N	Y
NORTH DAKOTA					
AL Pomeroy	Y	Y	N	N	Y
OHIO					
1 Chabot	Y	Y	Y	Y	Y
2 Schmidt	Y	Y	Y	Y	Y
3 Turner	Y	Y	Y	Y	Y
4 Jordan	Y	Y	Y	Y	Y
5 Latta	Y	Y	Y	Y	Y
6 Wilson	Y	Y	N	N	N
7 Hobson	Y	Y	Y	Y	Y
8 Boehner	Y	Y	Y	Y	Y
9 Kaptur	Y	Y	N	N	Y
10 Kucinich	Y	Y	N	N	N
11 Tubbs Jones	Y	Y	N	?	N
12 Tiberi	Y	Y	Y	?	Y
13 Sutton	Y	Y	N	N	Y
14 LaTourette	Y	Y	N	N	Y
15 Pryce	Y	Y	Y	Y	Y
16 Regula	Y	Y	Y	N	Y
17 Ryan	Y	Y	N	N	Y
18 Space	Y	Y	N	N	Y
OKLAHOMA					
1 Sullivan	Y	Y	Y	Y	Y
2 Boren	Y	Y	N	N	Y
3 Lucas	Y	Y	Y	Y	Y
4 Cole	Y	Y	Y	Y	Y
5 Fallin	Y	Y	Y	Y	Y
OREGON					
1 Wu	Y	Y	N	N	N
2 Walden	Y	Y	Y	Y	Y
3 Blumenauer	Y	Y	N	N	N
4 DeFazio	Y	Y	N	N	Y
5 Hooley	Y	Y	N	N	Y
PENNSYLVANIA					
1 Brady	Y	Y	N	N	Y
2 Fattah	Y	Y	N	N	Y
3 English	Y	Y	Y	Y	Y
4 Altmire	Y	Y	N	N	Y
5 Peterson	Y	Y	Y	Y	Y
6 Gerlach	Y	Y	N	N	Y
7 Sestak	Y	Y	N	N	Y
8 Murphy, P.	Y	Y	N	N	Y
9 Shuster	Y	Y	Y	Y	Y
10 Carney	Y	Y	N	N	Y
11 Kanjorski	Y	Y	N	N	Y
12 Murtha	Y	Y	N	N	Y
13 Schwartz	Y	Y	N	N	Y
14 Doyle	Y	Y	N	N	Y
15 Dent	Y	Y	N	N	Y
16 Pitts	Y	Y	Y	Y	Y
17 Holden	Y	Y	N	N	Y
18 Murphy, T.	Y	Y	Y	Y	Y
19 Platts	Y	Y	N	N	Y
RHODE ISLAND					
1 Kennedy	Y	Y	N	N	N
2 Langevin	Y	Y	N	N	N
SOUTH CAROLINA					
1 Brown	Y	Y	Y	Y	Y
2 Wilson	Y	+	Y	Y	Y
3 Barrett	Y	Y	Y	Y	Y
4 Inglis	Y	Y	N	N	Y
5 Spratt	Y	Y	N	N	Y
6 Clyburn	Y	Y	N	N	Y
SOUTH DAKOTA					
AL Herseth Sandlin	Y	Y	Y	Y	Y
TENNESSEE					
1 Davis, D.	Y	Y	Y	Y	Y
2 Duncan	Y	Y	Y	Y	Y
3 Wamp	Y	Y	Y	Y	Y
4 Davis, L.	Y	Y	N	N	Y
5 Cooper	Y	Y	N	N	Y
6 Gordon	Y	Y	N	N	Y
7 Blackburn	Y	Y	Y	Y	Y
8 Tanner	Y	Y	N	N	Y
9 Cohen	Y	Y	N	N	Y

	166	167	168	169	170
TEXAS					
1 Gohmert	Y	Y	Y	Y	Y
2 Poe	Y	Y	Y	Y	Y
3 Johnson, S.	Y	Y	Y	Y	Y
4 Hall	Y	Y	Y	Y	Y
5 Hensarling	Y	Y	Y	Y	Y
6 Barton	Y	Y	Y	Y	Y
7 Culberson	Y	?	Y	Y	Y
8 Brady	Y	?	Y	Y	Y
9 Green, A.	Y	Y	N	N	Y
10 McCaul	Y	Y	Y	Y	Y
11 Conaway	Y	Y	Y	Y	Y
12 Granger	?	?	?	?	?
13 Thornberry	Y	Y	Y	Y	Y
14 Paul	N	Y	Y	Y	Y
15 Hinojosa	Y	Y	N	N	Y
16 Reyes	Y	Y	N	N	N
17 Edwards	Y	Y	N	N	Y
18 Jackson Lee	Y	Y	N	N	Y
19 Neugebauer	+	Y	Y	Y	Y
20 Gonzalez	Y	Y	N	N	Y
21 Smith	Y	Y	Y	Y	Y
22 Lampson	Y	Y	N	N	Y
23 Rodriguez	Y	Y	N	N	Y
24 Marchant	Y	Y	N	N	Y
25 Doggett	Y	Y	N	N	Y
26 Burgess	Y	Y	Y	Y	Y
27 Ortiz	Y	Y	N	N	Y
28 Cuellar	Y	Y	N	N	Y
29 Green, G.	Y	Y	N	N	Y
30 Johnson, E.	Y	Y	N	N	Y
31 Carter	Y	Y	Y	Y	Y
32 Sessions	Y	Y	Y	Y	Y
UTAH					
1 Bishop	Y	Y	Y	Y	Y
2 Matheson	Y	Y	Y	Y	Y
3 Cannon	Y	Y	Y	Y	Y
VERMONT					
AL Welch	Y	Y	N	N	N
VIRGINIA					
1 Wittman	Y	Y	Y	Y	Y
2 Drake	Y	Y	Y	Y	Y
3 Scott	Y	Y	N	N	Y
4 Forbes	Y	Y	Y	Y	Y
5 Goode	Y	Y	Y	Y	Y
6 Goodlatte	Y	Y	Y	Y	Y
7 Cantor	Y	Y	Y	Y	Y
8 Moran	Y	Y	N	N	Y
9 Boucher	?	Y	N	N	Y
10 Wolf	Y	Y	N	N	Y
11 Davis	Y	Y	Y	Y	Y
WASHINGTON					
1 Inslee	Y	Y	N	N	Y
2 Larsen	Y	Y	N	N	Y
3 Baird	Y	Y	N	N	N
4 Hastings	Y	Y	Y	Y	Y
5 McMorris Rodgers	Y	Y	Y	Y	Y
6 Dicks	Y	Y	N	N	Y
7 McDermott	Y	Y	N	N	Y
8 Reichert	Y	Y	N	N	Y
9 Smith	Y	Y	N	N	Y
WEST VIRGINIA					
1 Mollohan	Y	Y	N	N	Y
2 Capito	Y	Y	Y	Y	Y
3 Rahall	Y	Y	N	N	Y
WISCONSIN					
1 Ryan	Y	Y	Y	Y	Y
2 Baldwin	Y	Y	N	N	N
3 Kind	Y	Y	N	N	Y
4 Moore	Y	Y	N	N	Y
5 Sensenbrenner	Y	Y	Y	Y	Y
6 Petri	Y	Y	N	N	Y
7 Obey	Y	Y	N	N	Y
8 Kagen	Y	Y	N	N	Y
WYOMING					
AL Cubin	?	Y	Y	Y	Y
DELEGATES					
Faleomavaega (A.S.)		?	?	?	Y
Norton (D.C.)		Y	N	N	Y
Bordallo (Guam)		Y	N	N	Y
Fortuño (P.R.)		Y	Y	Y	Y
Christensen (V.I.)		Y	N	N	N

IN THE HOUSE | By Vote Number

171. **HR 2016. National Landscape Conservation System/Hunting and Fishing Activities.** Altmire, D-Pa., amendment that would clarify that nothing in the bill should be construed to affect a state's jurisdiction to manage fish and wildlife under state laws, including hunting, fishing, trapping and recreational shooting regulations, on public land managed by the Bureau of Land Management, or to limit access to those activities. Adopted in Committee of the Whole 416-5: R 192-0; D 224-5 (ND 167-5, SD 57-0). April 9, 2008.

172. **HR 2016. National Landscape Conservation System/Grazing Rights.** Pearce, R-N.M., amendment that would stipulate that inclusion of lands in the National Landscape Conservation System would not affect grazing regulations. Adopted in Committee of the Whole 214-207: R 177-14; D 37-193 (ND 26-147, SD 11-46). April 9, 2008.

173. **HR 2016. National Landscape Conservation System/Recommit.** Cannon, R-Utah, motion to recommit the bill to the Committee on Natural Resources with instructions that it be reported back promptly with language that nothing in the bill should affect the right to bear arms under the Second Amendment within the National Landscape Conservation System. Motion rejected 208-212: R 189-3; D 19-209 (ND 12-159, SD 7-50). April 9, 2008.

174. **HR 2016. National Landscape Conservation System/Passage.** Passage of the bill that would codify the National Landscape Conservation System, comprising approximately 27 million acres of areas considered to have significant historical, cultural, ecological, scientific or scenic value. The bill also includes within the system any area that Congress has already designated for preservation. Passed 278-140: R 50-140; D 228-0 (ND 171-0, SD 57-0). April 9, 2008.

175. **HR 2419. Farm Bill Reauthorization/Motion to Instruct.** Goodlatte, R-Va., motion to instruct House conferees to disagree to any provision in the bill that would result in a tax increase. Motion agreed to 400-11: R 190-0; D 210-11 (ND 154-11, SD 56-0). April 9, 2008.

176. **HR 5489. Jo Ann S. Davis Post Office/Passage.** Clay, D-Mo., motion to suspend the rules and pass the bill that would designate a post office in Gloucester, Va., as the "Congresswoman Jo Ann S. Davis Post Office," for the late Virginia Republican who served from 2001 to 2007. Motion agreed to 397-0: R 184-0; D 213-0 (ND 160-0, SD 53-0). A two-thirds majority of those present and voting (265 in this case) is required for passage under suspension of the rules. April 9, 2008.

	171	172	173	174	175	176
ALABAMA						
1 **Bonner**	Y	Y	Y	N	Y	Y
2 **Everett**	Y	Y	Y	N	Y	Y
3 **Rogers**	Y	Y	Y	N	Y	Y
4 **Aderholt**	Y	Y	Y	N	Y	Y
5 Cramer	Y	N	N	Y	Y	Y
6 **Bachus**	Y	Y	Y	N	?	?
7 Davis	Y	N	N	Y	Y	Y
ALASKA						
AL **Young**	Y	Y	Y	N	Y	Y
ARIZONA						
1 **Renzi**	Y	Y	Y	Y	Y	Y
2 **Franks**	Y	Y	Y	N	Y	Y
3 **Shadegg**	Y	Y	Y	N	Y	Y
4 Pastor	Y	N	N	Y	Y	Y
5 Mitchell	Y	N	N	Y	Y	Y
6 **Flake**	Y	Y	Y	N	Y	Y
7 Grijalva	Y	N	N	Y	Y	Y
8 Giffords	Y	Y	Y	Y	?	?
ARKANSAS						
1 Berry	Y	Y	N	Y	Y	Y
2 Snyder	Y	N	N	Y	Y	Y
3 **Boozman**	Y	Y	Y	N	Y	Y
4 Ross	Y	Y	N	Y	Y	Y
CALIFORNIA						
1 Thompson	Y	N	N	Y	Y	Y
2 **Herger**	Y	Y	Y	N	Y	Y
3 **Lungren**	Y	Y	Y	N	Y	Y
4 **Doolittle**	Y	Y	Y	N	Y	Y
5 Matsui	Y	N	N	Y	Y	Y
6 Woolsey	Y	N	N	Y	N	Y
7 Miller, George	Y	N	N	Y	Y	Y
8 Pelosi						
9 Lee	Y	N	N	Y	Y	Y
10 Tauscher	Y	N	N	Y	Y	Y
11 McNerney	Y	Y	Y	Y	Y	Y
12 Vacant						
13 Stark	Y	N	N	Y	?	?
14 Eshoo	Y	N	N	Y	Y	Y
15 Honda	N	N	N	Y	Y	Y
16 Lofgren	N	N	N	Y	Y	Y
17 Farr	Y	N	N	Y	Y	Y
18 Cardoza	Y	N	N	Y	Y	Y
19 **Radanovich**	Y	Y	Y	N	Y	Y
20 Costa	Y	Y	N	Y	Y	Y
21 **Nunes**	Y	Y	Y	N	Y	Y
22 **McCarthy**	Y	Y	Y	N	Y	Y
23 Capps	Y	N	N	Y	Y	Y
24 **Gallegly**	Y	Y	Y	N	Y	Y
25 **McKeon**	Y	Y	Y	N	Y	Y
26 **Dreier**	Y	Y	Y	N	Y	Y
27 Sherman	Y	N	N	Y	Y	Y
28 Berman	Y	N	N	Y	Y	Y
29 Schiff	Y	N	N	Y	Y	Y
30 Waxman	Y	N	N	Y	?	?
31 Becerra	?	?	N	Y	Y	Y
32 Solis	Y	N	N	Y	Y	Y
33 Watson	Y	N	N	Y	Y	Y
34 Roybal-Allard	Y	N	N	Y	Y	Y
35 Waters	Y	N	N	Y	N	Y
36 Harman	Y	N	N	Y	Y	Y
37 Richardson	Y	N	N	Y	Y	Y
38 Napolitano	Y	N	N	Y	Y	Y
39 Sánchez, Linda	Y	N	N	Y	Y	Y
40 **Royce**	Y	Y	Y	N	Y	Y
41 **Lewis**	Y	Y	Y	N	Y	Y
42 **Miller, Gary**	Y	Y	Y	N	Y	Y
43 Baca	Y	N	N	Y	Y	Y
44 **Calvert**	Y	Y	Y	N	Y	Y
45 **Bono Mack**	Y	Y	Y	N	Y	Y
46 **Rohrabacher**	Y	Y	Y	N	Y	Y
47 Sanchez, Loretta	Y	N	N	Y	Y	Y
48 **Campbell**	Y	Y	Y	N	Y	Y
49 **Issa**	Y	Y	Y	N	Y	?
50 **Bilbray**	Y	Y	Y	Y	Y	Y
51 Filner	Y	N	N	Y	Y	Y
52 **Hunter**	Y	Y	Y	N	Y	Y
53 Davis	Y	N	N	Y	Y	Y

	171	172	173	174	175	176
COLORADO						
1 DeGette	Y	Y	N	Y	Y	Y
2 Udall	Y	Y	N	Y	Y	Y
3 Salazar	Y	Y	N	Y	+	Y
4 **Musgrave**	Y	Y	Y	N	Y	Y
5 **Lamborn**	Y	Y	Y	N	Y	Y
6 **Tancredo**	Y	Y	Y	N	Y	Y
7 Perlmutter	Y	Y	N	Y	Y	Y
CONNECTICUT						
1 Larson	–	–	–	–	+	+
2 Courtney	Y	N	N	Y	Y	Y
3 DeLauro	Y	N	N	Y	Y	Y
4 **Shays**	+	+	–	+	+	+
5 Murphy	Y	N	N	Y	Y	Y
DELAWARE						
AL **Castle**	Y	N	Y	Y	Y	Y
FLORIDA						
1 **Miller**	Y	Y	Y	N	Y	Y
2 Boyd	Y	N	N	Y	Y	Y
3 Brown	Y	N	N	Y	Y	Y
4 **Crenshaw**	Y	Y	Y	N	Y	Y
5 **Brown-Waite**	Y	Y	Y	N	Y	Y
6 **Stearns**	Y	Y	Y	N	+	Y
7 **Mica**	Y	Y	Y	N	Y	Y
8 **Keller**	Y	Y	Y	N	Y	Y
9 **Bilirakis**	Y	Y	Y	N	Y	Y
10 **Young**	Y	Y	Y	Y	Y	Y
11 Castor	Y	N	N	Y	Y	Y
12 **Putnam**	Y	Y	Y	N	Y	Y
13 **Buchanan**	Y	Y	Y	Y	Y	Y
14 **Mack**	Y	Y	Y	Y	Y	Y
15 **Weldon**	Y	Y	Y	N	Y	Y
16 Mahoney	Y	N	N	Y	Y	?
17 Meek	Y	N	N	Y	Y	Y
18 **Ros-Lehtinen**	Y	Y	Y	N	Y	Y
19 Wexler	Y	N	N	Y	Y	Y
20 Wasserman Schultz	Y	N	N	Y	Y	Y
21 **Diaz-Balart, L.**	?	?	?	?	Y	Y
22 Klein	Y	N	N	Y	Y	Y
23 Hastings	Y	N	N	Y	Y	Y
24 **Feeney**	Y	Y	Y	?	Y	Y
25 **Diaz-Balart, M.**	Y	Y	Y	Y	Y	Y
GEORGIA						
1 **Kingston**	Y	Y	Y	N	Y	Y
2 Bishop	Y	N	N	Y	Y	Y
3 **Westmoreland**	Y	Y	Y	N	Y	Y
4 Johnson	Y	N	N	Y	Y	Y
5 Lewis	Y	N	N	Y	Y	Y
6 **Price**	Y	Y	Y	N	Y	Y
7 **Linder**	Y	Y	Y	N	Y	Y
8 Marshall	Y	Y	Y	Y	Y	Y
9 **Deal**	Y	Y	Y	N	Y	Y
10 **Broun**	Y	Y	Y	N	Y	Y
11 **Gingrey**	Y	Y	Y	N	Y	Y
12 Barrow	Y	Y	Y	Y	Y	Y
13 Scott	Y	N	N	Y	Y	Y
HAWAII						
1 Abercrombie	?	?	?	?	?	?
2 Hirono	Y	N	N	Y	Y	Y
IDAHO						
1 **Sali**	Y	Y	Y	N	Y	Y
2 **Simpson**	Y	Y	Y	Y	Y	Y
ILLINOIS						
1 Rush	?	?	?	?	?	?
2 Jackson	Y	N	N	Y	Y	Y
3 Lipinski	Y	N	N	Y	Y	Y
4 Gutierrez	Y	N	N	Y	Y	Y
5 Emanuel	Y	N	N	Y	Y	?
6 **Roskam**	Y	Y	Y	Y	Y	Y
7 Davis	Y	N	N	Y	Y	Y
8 Bean	Y	N	Y	Y	Y	Y
9 Schakowsky	Y	N	N	Y	Y	Y
10 **Kirk**	Y	N	Y	Y	Y	Y
11 **Weller**	Y	?	Y	Y	Y	Y
12 Costello	Y	N	N	Y	Y	Y
13 **Biggert**	Y	N	Y	Y	Y	Y
14 Foster	Y	N	Y	Y	Y	Y
15 **Johnson**	Y	N	Y	Y	Y	Y

KEY **Republicans** Democrats

Y Voted for (yea)	X Paired against	C Voted "present" to avoid possible conflict of interest
# Paired for	– Announced against	
+ Announced for	P Voted "present"	? Did not vote or otherwise make a position known
N Voted against (nay)		

ND Northern Democrats, SD Southern Democrats
Southern states: Ala., Ark., Fla., Ga., Ky., La., Miss., N.C., Okla., S.C., Tenn., Texas, Va.

	171	172	173	174	175	176
16 **Manzullo**	Y	Y	Y	N	Y	Y
17 Hare	Y	N	N	Y	Y	Y
18 **LaHood**	Y	Y	Y	Y	Y	Y
19 **Shimkus**	Y	Y	Y	N	Y	Y
INDIANA						
1 Visclosky	Y	N	N	Y	Y	Y
2 Donnelly	Y	Y	Y	Y	Y	Y
3 **Souder**	Y	Y	Y	N	Y	Y
4 **Buyer**	?	?	?	?	?	?
5 **Burton**	Y	Y	Y	N	Y	Y
6 **Pence**	Y	Y	Y	N	Y	Y
7 Carson, A.	Y	N	N	Y	Y	Y
8 Ellsworth	Y	Y	Y	Y	Y	Y
9 Hill	Y	N	Y	Y	Y	Y
IOWA						
1 Braley	Y	N	N	Y	Y	Y
2 Loebsack	Y	Y	N	Y	Y	Y
3 Boswell	Y	Y	N	Y	Y	?
4 **Latham**	Y	Y	Y	N	Y	Y
5 **King**	Y	Y	Y	N	Y	Y
KANSAS						
1 **Moran**	Y	Y	Y	N	Y	Y
2 Boyda	Y	Y	N	Y	Y	Y
3 Moore	Y	N	N	Y	Y	Y
4 **Tiahrt**	Y	Y	Y	N	Y	Y
KENTUCKY						
1 **Whitfield**	Y	N	Y	Y	Y	Y
2 **Lewis**	Y	Y	Y	N	Y	Y
3 Yarmuth	Y	N	N	Y	Y	Y
4 **Davis**	Y	Y	Y	N	Y	Y
5 **Rogers**	Y	Y	Y	N	Y	Y
6 Chandler	Y	N	N	Y	Y	Y
LOUISIANA						
1 Vacant						
2 Jefferson	Y	N	N	Y	Y	Y
3 Melancon	Y	N	N	Y	Y	Y
4 **McCrery**	Y	Y	Y	N	Y	?
5 **Alexander**	?	?	Y	N	Y	Y
6 Vacant						
7 **Boustany**	Y	Y	Y	N	Y	Y
MAINE						
1 Allen	Y	N	N	Y	Y	Y
2 Michaud	Y	N	N	Y	Y	Y
MARYLAND						
1 **Gilchrest**	Y	N	N	Y	Y	Y
2 Ruppersberger	Y	N	N	Y	Y	Y
3 Sarbanes	Y	N	N	Y	Y	Y
4 Wynn	Y	N	N	Y	Y	Y
5 Hoyer	Y	N	N	Y	Y	Y
6 **Bartlett**	Y	Y	Y	N	Y	Y
7 Cummings	Y	N	N	Y	Y	Y
8 Van Hollen	Y	N	N	Y	Y	Y
MASSACHUSETTS						
1 Olver	Y	N	N	Y	N	Y
2 Neal	Y	N	N	Y	Y	Y
3 McGovern	Y	N	N	Y	N	Y
4 Frank	Y	N	N	Y	N	Y
5 Tsongas	Y	N	N	Y	Y	Y
6 Tierney	Y	N	N	Y	Y	Y
7 Markey	Y	N	N	Y	Y	Y
8 Capuano	Y	N	N	Y	N	Y
9 Lynch	Y	N	N	Y	Y	Y
10 Delahunt	Y	N	N	Y	Y	Y
MICHIGAN						
1 Stupak	Y	N	N	Y	Y	Y
2 **Hoekstra**	Y	Y	Y	N	Y	Y
3 **Ehlers**	Y	Y	Y	Y	Y	Y
4 **Camp**	Y	Y	Y	N	Y	Y
5 Kildee	Y	N	N	Y	Y	Y
6 **Upton**	Y	N	Y	Y	Y	Y
7 **Walberg**	Y	Y	Y	N	Y	Y
8 **Rogers**	Y	Y	Y	Y	Y	Y
9 **Knollenberg**	Y	Y	Y	N	Y	Y
10 **Miller**	Y	Y	Y	Y	Y	Y
11 **McCotter**	Y	Y	Y	Y	Y	Y
12 Levin	Y	N	N	Y	Y	Y
13 Kilpatrick	Y	N	N	Y	Y	Y
14 Conyers	Y	N	N	Y	Y	Y
15 Dingell	Y	N	N	Y	Y	Y
MINNESOTA						
1 Walz	Y	Y	N	Y	Y	Y
2 **Kline**	Y	Y	Y	N	Y	Y
3 **Ramstad**	Y	N	Y	Y	Y	Y
4 McCollum	Y	N	N	Y	Y	Y
5 Ellison	Y	N	N	Y	N	Y
6 **Bachmann**	Y	Y	Y	N	Y	Y
7 Peterson	?	Y	N	Y	Y	?
8 Oberstar	Y	N	N	Y	Y	Y
MISSISSIPPI						
1 Vacant						
2 Thompson	Y	N	N	Y	Y	Y
3 **Pickering**	Y	Y	Y	Y	Y	Y
4 Taylor	Y	N	N	Y	Y	Y
MISSOURI						
1 Clay	Y	N	N	Y	Y	Y
2 **Akin**	Y	Y	Y	N	Y	Y
3 Carnahan	Y	N	N	Y	Y	Y
4 Skelton	Y	Y	N	Y	Y	Y
5 Cleaver	Y	N	N	Y	Y	Y
6 **Graves**	Y	Y	Y	N	Y	Y
7 **Blunt**	Y	Y	Y	N	Y	Y
8 **Emerson**	Y	Y	Y	N	Y	Y
9 **Hulshof**	Y	Y	Y	N	Y	?
MONTANA						
AL **Rehberg**	Y	Y	Y	N	Y	Y
NEBRASKA						
1 **Fortenberry**	Y	Y	Y	Y	Y	Y
2 **Terry**	Y	Y	Y	N	Y	Y
3 **Smith**	Y	Y	Y	N	Y	Y
NEVADA						
1 Berkley	Y	N	N	Y	Y	Y
2 **Heller**	Y	Y	Y	N	Y	Y
3 **Porter**	Y	Y	Y	Y	Y	Y
NEW HAMPSHIRE						
1 Shea-Porter	Y	N	N	Y	Y	Y
2 Hodes	Y	N	N	Y	Y	Y
NEW JERSEY						
1 Andrews	Y	N	N	Y	Y	Y
2 **LoBiondo**	Y	N	Y	Y	Y	Y
3 **Saxton**	Y	N	Y	Y	Y	Y
4 **Smith**	?	?	Y	Y	Y	Y
5 **Garrett**	Y	Y	Y	N	Y	Y
6 Pallone	Y	N	N	Y	Y	Y
7 **Ferguson**	?	?	?	?	?	?
8 Pascrell	Y	N	N	Y	Y	Y
9 Rothman	?	?	N	Y	Y	Y
10 Payne	Y	N	N	Y	N	Y
11 **Frelinghuysen**	Y	N	Y	Y	Y	Y
12 Holt	Y	N	N	Y	Y	Y
13 Sires	?	?	?	?	?	?
NEW MEXICO						
1 **Wilson**	Y	Y	Y	Y	Y	Y
2 **Pearce**	Y	Y	Y	N	Y	Y
3 Udall	Y	Y	N	Y	Y	Y
NEW YORK						
1 Bishop	Y	N	N	Y	Y	Y
2 Israel	Y	N	N	Y	Y	Y
3 **King**	Y	Y	Y	N	Y	Y
4 McCarthy	Y	N	N	Y	Y	Y
5 Ackerman	Y	N	N	Y	Y	Y
6 Meeks	Y	N	N	Y	Y	Y
7 Crowley	Y	N	N	Y	Y	Y
8 Nadler	Y	N	N	Y	Y	Y
9 Weiner	Y	N	N	Y	Y	Y
10 Towns	Y	N	N	Y	Y	Y
11 Clarke	Y	N	N	Y	Y	Y
12 Velázquez	Y	N	N	Y	Y	Y
13 **Fossella**	Y	Y	Y	N	Y	?
14 Maloney	Y	N	N	Y	Y	Y
15 Rangel	Y	N	N	Y	?	?
16 Serrano	Y	N	N	Y	Y	Y
17 Engel	Y	N	N	Y	Y	Y
18 Lowey	Y	N	N	Y	Y	Y
19 Hall	Y	N	N	Y	Y	Y
20 Gillibrand	Y	Y	Y	Y	Y	Y
21 McNulty	Y	N	N	Y	Y	Y
22 Hinchey	Y	N	N	Y	Y	Y
23 **McHugh**	Y	Y	Y	N	Y	Y
24 Arcuri	Y	N	N	Y	Y	Y
25 **Walsh**	Y	Y	Y	N	Y	Y
26 **Reynolds**	Y	Y	Y	N	Y	?
27 Higgins	Y	N	N	Y	Y	Y
28 Slaughter	Y	N	N	Y	Y	?
29 **Kuhl**	Y	Y	Y	Y	Y	Y
NORTH CAROLINA						
1 Butterfield	Y	N	N	Y	Y	?
2 Etheridge	Y	N	N	Y	Y	Y
3 **Jones**	Y	Y	Y	N	Y	Y
4 Price	Y	N	N	Y	Y	Y
5 **Foxx**	Y	Y	Y	N	Y	Y
6 **Coble**	Y	Y	Y	N	Y	Y
7 McIntyre	Y	N	Y	Y	Y	Y
8 **Hayes**	Y	Y	Y	N	Y	Y
9 **Myrick**	Y	Y	Y	N	+	Y
10 **McHenry**	Y	Y	Y	N	Y	Y
11 Shuler	Y	Y	Y	Y	Y	Y
12 Watt	Y	N	N	Y	Y	Y
13 Miller	Y	N	N	Y	Y	Y
NORTH DAKOTA						
AL Pomeroy	Y	Y	N	Y	Y	Y
OHIO						
1 **Chabot**	Y	Y	Y	N	Y	Y
2 **Schmidt**	Y	Y	Y	N	Y	Y
3 **Turner**	Y	Y	Y	N	Y	Y
4 **Jordan**	Y	Y	Y	N	Y	Y
5 **Latta**	Y	Y	Y	N	Y	Y
6 Wilson	Y	Y	N	Y	Y	Y
7 **Hobson**	Y	Y	Y	Y	Y	Y
8 **Boehner**	Y	Y	Y	N	Y	?
9 Kaptur	Y	N	N	Y	Y	Y
10 Kucinich	N	N	N	Y	Y	Y
11 Tubbs Jones	Y	N	N	Y	Y	?
12 **Tiberi**	Y	Y	Y	Y	Y	Y
13 Sutton	Y	N	N	Y	Y	Y
14 **LaTourette**	Y	Y	Y	Y	Y	Y
15 **Pryce**	Y	Y	Y	Y	Y	Y
16 **Regula**	Y	Y	Y	Y	Y	Y
17 Ryan	Y	Y	N	Y	Y	Y
18 Space	Y	Y	N	Y	Y	Y
OKLAHOMA						
1 **Sullivan**	Y	Y	Y	N	Y	Y
2 Boren	Y	N	N	Y	Y	Y
3 **Lucas**	Y	Y	Y	N	Y	Y
4 **Cole**	Y	Y	Y	N	Y	?
5 **Fallin**	Y	Y	Y	N	Y	Y
OREGON						
1 Wu	Y	N	N	Y	Y	Y
2 **Walden**	Y	Y	Y	N	Y	Y
3 Blumenauer	Y	N	N	Y	N	Y
4 DeFazio	Y	N	N	Y	N	Y
5 Hooley	Y	N	N	Y	?	?
PENNSYLVANIA						
1 Brady	Y	N	N	Y	Y	Y
2 Fattah	Y	N	N	Y	Y	Y
3 **English**	Y	Y	Y	Y	Y	Y
4 Altmire	Y	Y	Y	Y	Y	Y
5 **Peterson**	Y	Y	Y	N	?	?
6 **Gerlach**	Y	N	Y	Y	Y	Y
7 Sestak	Y	N	N	Y	Y	Y
8 Murphy, P.	Y	N	N	Y	Y	Y
9 **Shuster**	Y	Y	Y	N	Y	Y
10 Carney	Y	Y	Y	Y	Y	Y
11 Kanjorski	Y	N	N	Y	Y	Y
12 Murtha	Y	N	N	Y	Y	?
13 Schwartz	Y	N	N	Y	Y	Y
14 Doyle	Y	N	N	Y	Y	Y
15 **Dent**	Y	Y	Y	Y	Y	Y
16 **Pitts**	Y	Y	Y	N	Y	Y
17 Holden	Y	N	N	Y	Y	Y
18 **Murphy, T.**	Y	Y	Y	Y	Y	Y
19 **Platts**	Y	N	Y	Y	Y	Y
RHODE ISLAND						
1 Kennedy	Y	N	N	Y	Y	Y
2 Langevin	Y	N	N	Y	Y	Y
SOUTH CAROLINA						
1 **Brown**	Y	Y	Y	N	Y	Y
2 **Wilson**	Y	Y	Y	N	Y	Y
3 **Barrett**	Y	Y	Y	N	Y	Y
4 **Inglis**	Y	Y	Y	Y	Y	Y
5 Spratt	Y	N	N	Y	Y	Y
6 Clyburn	Y	N	N	Y	Y	Y
SOUTH DAKOTA						
AL Herseth Sandlin	Y	Y	N	Y	Y	Y
TENNESSEE						
1 **Davis, D.**	Y	Y	Y	N	Y	Y
2 **Duncan**	Y	Y	Y	N	Y	Y
3 **Wamp**	Y	Y	Y	N	Y	Y
4 Davis, L.	Y	Y	N	Y	Y	Y
5 Cooper	Y	N	N	Y	Y	Y
6 Gordon	Y	N	N	Y	Y	Y
7 **Blackburn**	Y	Y	Y	?	Y	Y
8 Tanner	Y	N	N	Y	Y	Y
9 Cohen	Y	N	N	Y	Y	Y
TEXAS						
1 **Gohmert**	Y	Y	Y	N	Y	Y
2 **Poe**	Y	Y	Y	N	Y	Y
3 **Johnson, S.**	Y	Y	Y	N	Y	Y
4 **Hall**	Y	Y	Y	N	Y	Y
5 **Hensarling**	Y	Y	Y	N	Y	Y
6 **Barton**	Y	Y	Y	N	Y	Y
7 **Culberson**	Y	Y	Y	N	Y	Y
8 **Brady**	Y	Y	Y	N	Y	Y
9 Green, A.	Y	N	N	Y	Y	Y
10 **McCaul**	Y	Y	Y	N	Y	Y
11 **Conaway**	Y	Y	Y	N	Y	Y
12 **Granger**	?	?	?	?	?	?
13 **Thornberry**	Y	Y	Y	N	Y	Y
14 **Paul**	Y	Y	?	?	Y	Y
15 Hinojosa	Y	N	N	Y	Y	Y
16 Reyes	Y	N	N	Y	Y	Y
17 Edwards	Y	Y	N	Y	?	?
18 Jackson Lee	Y	N	N	Y	Y	Y
19 **Neugebauer**	Y	Y	Y	N	Y	Y
20 Gonzalez	Y	N	N	Y	Y	Y
21 **Smith**	Y	Y	Y	N	Y	Y
22 Lampson	Y	Y	Y	Y	Y	Y
23 Rodriguez	Y	N	Y	Y	Y	Y
24 **Marchant**	Y	Y	Y	N	Y	?
25 Doggett	Y	N	N	Y	Y	Y
26 **Burgess**	Y	Y	Y	N	Y	Y
27 Ortiz	Y	N	N	Y	Y	Y
28 Cuellar	Y	Y	N	Y	Y	Y
29 Green, G.	Y	N	Y	Y	Y	Y
30 Johnson, E.	Y	N	N	Y	Y	Y
31 **Carter**	Y	Y	Y	N	Y	Y
32 **Sessions**	Y	Y	Y	N	Y	Y
UTAH						
1 **Bishop**	Y	Y	Y	N	Y	Y
2 Matheson	Y	Y	Y	Y	Y	Y
3 **Cannon**	Y	Y	Y	N	Y	Y
VERMONT						
AL Welch	Y	N	N	Y	Y	Y
VIRGINIA						
1 **Wittman**	Y	Y	Y	N	Y	Y
2 **Drake**	Y	Y	Y	N	Y	Y
3 Scott	Y	N	N	Y	Y	Y
4 **Forbes**	Y	Y	Y	N	Y	Y
5 **Goode**	Y	Y	Y	N	Y	Y
6 **Goodlatte**	Y	Y	Y	N	Y	Y
7 **Cantor**	Y	Y	Y	N	Y	Y
8 Moran	Y	N	N	Y	Y	?
9 Boucher	Y	Y	N	Y	Y	Y
10 **Wolf**	Y	Y	Y	N	Y	Y
11 **Davis**	Y	Y	Y	Y	Y	Y
WASHINGTON						
1 Inslee	Y	N	N	Y	Y	Y
2 Larsen	Y	N	N	Y	Y	Y
3 Baird	Y	N	N	Y	Y	Y
4 **Hastings**	Y	Y	Y	N	Y	Y
5 **McMorris Rodgers**	Y	Y	Y	N	Y	Y
6 Dicks	Y	N	N	Y	Y	Y
7 McDermott	N	N	N	Y	N	Y
8 **Reichert**	Y	Y	N	Y	Y	Y
9 Smith	Y	N	N	Y	Y	Y
WEST VIRGINIA						
1 Mollohan	Y	N	N	Y	Y	Y
2 **Capito**	Y	Y	Y	Y	Y	Y
3 Rahall	Y	N	N	Y	Y	Y
WISCONSIN						
1 **Ryan**	Y	Y	Y	N	Y	Y
2 Baldwin	Y	N	N	Y	Y	Y
3 Kind	Y	N	N	Y	Y	Y
4 Moore	N	N	N	Y	Y	Y
5 **Sensenbrenner**	Y	Y	Y	N	Y	Y
6 **Petri**	Y	N	Y	Y	Y	Y
7 Obey	Y	N	N	Y	Y	Y
8 Kagen	Y	N	Y	Y	Y	Y
WYOMING						
AL **Cubin**	Y	Y	Y	N	Y	Y
DELEGATES						
Faleomavaega (A.S.)	Y	N				
Norton (D.C.)	Y	Y				
Bordallo (Guam)	Y	N				
Fortuño (P.R.)	Y	Y				
Christensen (V.I.)	Y	N				

IN THE HOUSE | By Vote Number

177. **HR 5472. Julia M. Carson Post Office/Passage.** Clay, D-Mo., motion to suspend the rules and pass the bill that would designate a post office in Indianapolis as the "Julia M. Carson Post Office Building," for the late Indiana Democrat who served from 1997 to 2007. Motion agreed to 401-0: R 187-0; D 214-0 (ND 159-0, SD 55-0). A two-thirds majority of those present and voting (268 in this case) is required for passage under suspension of the rules. April 9, 2008.

178. **Procedural Motion/Journal.** Approval of the House Journal of Wednesday, April 9, 2008. Approved 228-182: R 13-175; D 215-7 (ND 162-6, SD 53-1). April 10, 2008.

179. **HR 2537. Beach Protection Act/Rule.** Adoption of the rule (H Res 1083) to provide for House floor consideration of the bill that would renew a law requiring the states, assisted by the EPA, to test beach waters for contaminants and would authorize $40 million annually to states for monitoring and notification programs. Adopted 224-192: R 1-189; D 223-3 (ND 166-3, SD 57-0). April 10, 2008.

180. **H Res 1038. Department of Homeland Security Anniversary/ Adoption.** Carney, D-Pa., motion to suspend the rules and adopt the resolution that would recognize the fifth anniversary of the Department of Homeland Security and honor the department's employees for their efforts to protect the United States. Motion agreed to 406-3: R 185-1; D 221-2 (ND 164-2, SD 57-0). A two-thirds majority of those present and voting (273 in this case) is required for adoption under suspension of the rules. April 10, 2008.

181. **H Res 1092. Colombia Trade 'Fast Track' Requirements/ Adoption.** Adoption of the resolution that would suspend "fast track" requirements for considering a bill (HR 5724) that would implement a U.S.-Colombia free-trade agreement. Adopted 224-195: R 6-185; D 218-10 (ND 169-3, SD 49-7). A "nay" was a vote in support of the president's position. April 10, 2008.

182. **HR 2537. Beach Protection Act/Earmark Prohibition.** Flake, R-Ariz., amendment that would bar the use of funds in the bill for congressional earmarks. Adopted in Committee of the Whole 263-117: R 159-14; D 104-103 (ND 79-75, SD 25-28). April 10, 2008.

	177	178	179	180	181	182
ALABAMA						
1 **Bonner**	Y	N	N	Y	N	Y
2 **Everett**	Y	N	N	Y	N	Y
3 **Rogers**	Y	N	N	Y	Y	?
4 **Aderholt**	Y	N	N	Y	Y	Y
5 Cramer	Y	Y	Y	Y	N	N
6 **Bachus**	?	N	?	Y	N	Y
7 Davis	Y	Y	Y	Y	Y	?
ALASKA						
AL **Young**	Y	N	N	Y	N	N
ARIZONA						
1 **Renzi**	Y	N	N	Y	N	Y
2 **Franks**	Y	N	N	Y	N	?
3 **Shadegg**	Y	N	N	Y	N	Y
4 Pastor	Y	Y	Y	Y	Y	N
5 Mitchell	Y	N	Y	Y	Y	Y
6 **Flake**	Y	N	N	Y	N	Y
7 Grijalva	Y	Y	Y	Y	Y	?
8 Giffords	?	Y	Y	Y	Y	Y
ARKANSAS						
1 Berry	Y	Y	Y	Y	Y	N
2 Snyder	Y	Y	Y	Y	Y	N
3 **Boozman**	Y	N	N	Y	N	N
4 Ross	Y	Y	Y	Y	Y	Y
CALIFORNIA						
1 Thompson	Y	N	Y	Y	N	Y
2 **Herger**	Y	N	N	Y	N	Y
3 **Lungren**	Y	N	N	Y	N	Y
4 **Doolittle**	Y	N	N	Y	N	Y
5 Matsui	Y	Y	Y	Y	Y	N
6 Woolsey	Y	Y	Y	Y	Y	Y
7 Miller, George	Y	Y	Y	Y	Y	Y
8 Pelosi				Y		
9 Lee	Y	Y	Y	Y	Y	N
10 Tauscher	Y	Y	Y	Y	Y	Y
11 McNerney	Y	Y	Y	Y	Y	Y
12 Speier*			Y	Y	Y	Y
13 Stark	?	Y	Y	Y	Y	?
14 Eshoo	Y	Y	Y	Y	Y	Y
15 Honda	Y	Y	Y	Y	Y	Y
16 Lofgren	Y	Y	Y	Y	Y	?
17 Farr	Y	Y	Y	Y	Y	N
18 Cardoza	Y	Y	Y	Y	Y	?
19 **Radanovich**	Y	N	N	Y	N	Y
20 Costa	Y	Y	Y	Y	Y	Y
21 **Nunes**	Y	N	N	Y	N	Y
22 **McCarthy**	Y	N	N	Y	N	Y
23 Capps	Y	Y	Y	Y	Y	Y
24 **Gallegly**	Y	N	N	Y	N	?
25 **McKeon**	Y	N	N	Y	N	Y
26 **Dreier**	Y	N	N	Y	N	Y
27 Sherman	Y	Y	Y	Y	Y	N
28 Berman	Y	Y	Y	Y	Y	N
29 Schiff	Y	Y	N	Y	Y	N
30 Waxman	?	Y	Y	Y	Y	Y
31 Becerra	Y	Y	Y	Y	Y	Y
32 Solis	Y	Y	Y	Y	Y	Y
33 Watson	Y	Y	Y	Y	Y	N
34 Roybal-Allard	Y	Y	N	Y	Y	N
35 Waters	Y	Y	Y	Y	Y	?
36 Harman	Y	Y	Y	Y	Y	N
37 Richardson	Y	Y	Y	Y	Y	N
38 Napolitano	Y	Y	Y	Y	Y	N
39 Sánchez, Linda	Y	Y	Y	Y	Y	N
40 **Royce**	Y	N	N	Y	N	Y
41 **Lewis**	Y	N	N	Y	N	Y
42 **Miller, Gary**	Y	N	N	Y	N	Y
43 Baca	Y	Y	Y	Y	Y	?
44 **Calvert**	Y	N	N	Y	N	?
45 **Bono Mack**	Y	N	Y	Y	N	Y
46 **Rohrabacher**	Y	N	Y	Y	N	Y
47 Sanchez, Loretta	Y	Y	Y	Y	Y	?
48 **Campbell**	Y	N	N	Y	N	Y
49 **Issa**	Y	N	N	Y	N	Y
50 **Bilbray**	Y	N	Y	Y	N	N
51 Filner	Y	Y	Y	Y	Y	N
52 **Hunter**	Y	N	N	?	N	N
53 Davis	Y	Y	Y	Y	Y	Y

	177	178	179	180	181	182
COLORADO						
1 DeGette	Y	Y	Y	Y	Y	Y
2 Udall	Y	N	Y	Y	Y	?
3 Salazar	Y	Y	Y	Y	Y	N
4 **Musgrave**	Y	N	N	Y	N	?
5 **Lamborn**	Y	N	N	Y	N	Y
6 **Tancredo**	Y	P	N	Y	N	Y
7 Perlmutter	Y	N	Y	Y	Y	Y
CONNECTICUT						
1 Larson	+	+	+	+	+	?
2 Courtney	Y	Y	Y	Y	Y	Y
3 DeLauro	Y	Y	Y	Y	Y	Y
4 **Shays**	+	N	N	Y	N	Y
5 Murphy	Y	Y	Y	Y	Y	Y
DELAWARE						
AL **Castle**	Y	N	N	Y	N	Y
FLORIDA						
1 **Miller**	Y	N	N	Y	N	Y
2 Boyd	Y	Y	Y	Y	N	N
3 Brown	Y	Y	Y	Y	Y	N
4 **Crenshaw**	Y	N	N	Y	N	Y
5 **Brown-Waite**	Y	Y	N	Y	N	Y
6 **Stearns**	Y	N	N	Y	N	Y
7 **Mica**	Y	N	N	Y	N	N
8 **Keller**	Y	N	N	Y	N	Y
9 **Bilirakis**	Y	N	N	Y	N	Y
10 **Young**	Y	N	N	Y	N	Y
11 Castor	Y	Y	Y	Y	Y	N
12 **Putnam**	Y	N	N	Y	N	Y
13 **Buchanan**	Y	N	N	Y	N	Y
14 **Mack**	Y	N	N	Y	N	Y
15 **Weldon**	Y	N	N	Y	N	Y
16 Mahoney	Y	Y	Y	Y	N	N
17 Meek	Y	Y	Y	Y	Y	Y
18 **Ros-Lehtinen**	Y	N	N	Y	N	N
19 Wexler	Y	?	Y	Y	Y	N
20 Wasserman Schultz	Y	Y	Y	Y	Y	Y
21 **Diaz-Balart, L.**	Y	N	N	Y	N	N
22 Klein	Y	?	Y	Y	Y	N
23 Hastings	Y	Y	Y	Y	Y	N
24 **Feeney**	Y	N	N	Y	N	Y
25 **Diaz-Balart, M.**	Y	N	N	Y	N	N
GEORGIA						
1 **Kingston**	Y	N	N	Y	N	Y
2 Bishop	Y	Y	Y	Y	Y	N
3 **Westmoreland**	Y	N	N	Y	N	Y
4 Johnson	Y	Y	Y	Y	Y	N
5 Lewis	Y	Y	Y	Y	Y	N
6 **Price**	Y	N	N	Y	N	Y
7 **Linder**	Y	N	N	Y	N	Y
8 Marshall	Y	Y	Y	Y	Y	N
9 **Deal**	Y	N	N	Y	N	Y
10 **Broun**	Y	N	N	Y	N	Y
11 **Gingrey**	Y	N	N	Y	N	Y
12 Barrow	Y	Y	Y	Y	Y	Y
13 Scott	Y	Y	Y	Y	Y	?
HAWAII						
1 Abercrombie	?	Y	Y	Y	Y	N
2 Hirono	Y	Y	Y	Y	Y	N
IDAHO						
1 **Sali**	Y	N	N	Y	N	Y
2 **Simpson**	Y	N	N	Y	N	N
ILLINOIS						
1 Rush	?	?	?	?	?	?
2 Jackson	Y	Y	Y	Y	Y	N
3 Lipinski	Y	Y	Y	Y	Y	N
4 Gutierrez	Y	Y	Y	?	Y	Y
5 Emanuel	Y	Y	Y	Y	Y	?
6 **Roskam**	Y	N	N	Y	N	Y
7 Davis	Y	Y	Y	Y	Y	N
8 Bean	Y	Y	Y	Y	Y	Y
9 Schakowsky	Y	Y	Y	Y	Y	N
10 **Kirk**	Y	Y	N	Y	N	Y
11 **Weller**	Y	N	N	Y	N	?
12 Costello	Y	Y	Y	Y	Y	N
13 **Biggert**	Y	N	N	Y	N	Y
14 Foster	Y	Y	Y	Y	Y	N
15 **Johnson**	Y	Y	N	Y	N	Y

KEY

Republicans	Democrats

Y Voted for (yea)	X Paired against	C Voted "present" to avoid possible conflict of interest
# Paired for	– Announced against	
+ Announced for	P Voted "present"	? Did not vote or otherwise make a position known
N Voted against (nay)		

*Rep. Jackie Speier, D-Calif., was sworn in April 10, 2008, to fill the seat vacated by the death of Democratic Rep. Tom Lantos. The first vote for which Speier was eligible was vote 179.

ND Northern Democrats, SD Southern Democrats
Southern states: Ala., Ark., Fla., Ga., Ky., La., Miss., N.C., Okla., S.C., Tenn., Texas, Va.

	177	178	179	180	181	182
16 **Manzullo**	Y	N	N	Y	N	Y
17 Hare	Y	Y	Y	Y	Y	Y
18 **LaHood**	Y	N	N	Y	N	?
19 **Shimkus**	Y	N	N	Y	N	Y
INDIANA						
1 Visclosky	Y	Y	Y	Y	Y	N
2 Donnelly	Y	Y	Y	Y	Y	Y
3 **Souder**	Y	N	N	Y	N	Y
4 **Buyer**	?	?	?	?	?	?
5 **Burton**	Y	N	N	Y	N	Y
6 **Pence**	Y	N	N	Y	N	Y
7 Carson, A.	Y	Y	Y	Y	Y	Y
8 Ellsworth	Y	N	Y	Y	Y	Y
9 Hill	Y	Y	Y	Y	N	Y
IOWA						
1 Braley	Y	Y	Y	Y	Y	Y
2 Loebsack	Y	Y	Y	Y	Y	Y
3 Boswell	?	Y	Y	Y	Y	Y
4 **Latham**	Y	Y	N	Y	N	Y
5 **King**	Y	N	N	Y	N	Y
KANSAS						
1 **Moran**	Y	N	N	Y	N	Y
2 Boyda	Y	Y	Y	Y	Y	Y
3 Moore	Y	Y	Y	Y	Y	Y
4 **Tiahrt**	Y	N	N	Y	N	Y
KENTUCKY						
1 **Whitfield**	Y	Y	N	Y	N	Y
2 **Lewis**	Y	N	N	Y	N	Y
3 Yarmuth	Y	Y	Y	Y	Y	Y
4 **Davis**	Y	N	N	Y	N	Y
5 **Rogers**	Y	N	N	Y	N	Y
6 Chandler	Y	Y	Y	Y	Y	N
LOUISIANA						
1 Vacant						
2 Jefferson	Y	Y	Y	Y	Y	Y
3 Melancon	Y	Y	Y	Y	Y	N
4 **McCrery**	?	N	N	Y	N	Y
5 **Alexander**	Y	N	N	Y	N	Y
6 Vacant						
7 **Boustany**	Y	N	N	Y	N	Y
MAINE						
1 Allen	Y	Y	Y	Y	Y	Y
2 Michaud	Y	Y	Y	Y	Y	Y
MARYLAND						
1 **Gilchrest**	Y	N	N	Y	N	?
2 Ruppersberger	Y	Y	Y	Y	Y	N
3 Sarbanes	Y	Y	Y	Y	Y	N
4 Wynn	Y	Y	Y	Y	Y	N
5 Hoyer	Y	Y	Y	Y	Y	Y
6 **Bartlett**	Y	N	N	Y	N	Y
7 Cummings	Y	Y	Y	Y	Y	N
8 Van Hollen	Y	Y	Y	Y	Y	Y
MASSACHUSETTS						
1 Olver	Y	Y	Y	Y	Y	N
2 Neal	Y	Y	Y	Y	Y	N
3 McGovern	Y	Y	Y	Y	Y	Y
4 Frank	Y	Y	Y	Y	Y	N
5 Tsongas	Y	Y	Y	Y	Y	N
6 Tierney	Y	Y	Y	Y	Y	N
7 Markey	Y	Y	Y	Y	Y	N
8 Capuano	Y	Y	Y	Y	Y	N
9 Lynch	Y	Y	Y	Y	Y	Y
10 Delahunt	Y	Y	Y	Y	Y	N
MICHIGAN						
1 Stupak	Y	N	Y	Y	Y	N
2 **Hoekstra**	Y	N	N	Y	N	Y
3 **Ehlers**	Y	N	N	Y	N	Y
4 **Camp**	Y	N	N	Y	N	Y
5 Kildee	?	Y	Y	Y	Y	Y
6 **Upton**	Y	N	N	Y	N	Y
7 **Walberg**	Y	N	N	Y	N	Y
8 **Rogers**	Y	N	N	Y	N	Y
9 **Knollenberg**	Y	N	N	Y	N	Y
10 **Miller**	Y	N	N	Y	N	Y
11 **McCotter**	Y	N	N	Y	N	Y
12 Levin	Y	Y	Y	Y	Y	Y
13 Kilpatrick	Y	Y	Y	Y	Y	Y
14 Conyers	Y	Y	Y	Y	Y	N
15 Dingell	Y	Y	Y	Y	Y	N
MINNESOTA						
1 Walz	Y	Y	Y	Y	Y	N
2 **Kline**	Y	N	N	Y	N	Y
3 **Ramstad**	Y	?	?	?	?	?
4 McCollum	+	Y	Y	Y	Y	Y

	177	178	179	180	181	182
5 Ellison	Y	Y	Y	Y	Y	N
6 **Bachmann**	Y	N	N	Y	N	Y
7 Peterson	?	Y	Y	Y	Y	Y
8 Oberstar	Y	Y	Y	Y	Y	N
MISSISSIPPI						
1 Vacant						
2 Thompson	Y	Y	Y	Y	Y	N
3 **Pickering**	Y	Y	N	Y	N	Y
4 Taylor	Y	Y	Y	Y	Y	Y
MISSOURI						
1 Clay	Y	Y	Y	Y	Y	Y
2 **Akin**	Y	N	N	Y	N	Y
3 Carnahan	Y	Y	Y	Y	Y	Y
4 Skelton	Y	Y	Y	Y	Y	?
5 Cleaver	Y	Y	Y	Y	Y	N
6 **Graves**	Y	N	N	Y	N	Y
7 **Blunt**	Y	N	N	Y	N	Y
8 **Emerson**	Y	N	N	Y	N	Y
9 **Hulshof**	Y	N	N	Y	?	?
MONTANA						
AL **Rehberg**	Y	N	N	Y	N	Y
NEBRASKA						
1 **Fortenberry**	Y	Y	N	Y	N	Y
2 **Terry**	Y	N	N	Y	N	Y
3 **Smith**	Y	N	N	Y	N	Y
NEVADA						
1 Berkley	Y	Y	Y	Y	Y	N
2 **Heller**	Y	N	N	Y	N	Y
3 **Porter**	Y	N	N	Y	N	Y
NEW HAMPSHIRE						
1 Shea-Porter	Y	Y	Y	Y	Y	Y
2 Hodes	Y	Y	Y	Y	Y	Y
NEW JERSEY						
1 Andrews	Y	?	?	?	?	?
2 **LoBiondo**	Y	N	N	Y	N	Y
3 **Saxton**	Y	N	N	Y	N	Y
4 **Smith**	Y	N	N	Y	N	Y
5 **Garrett**	?	N	N	Y	N	Y
6 Pallone	Y	Y	Y	Y	Y	N
7 **Ferguson**	?	?	?	?	?	?
8 Pascrell	Y	Y	Y	Y	Y	N
9 Rothman	Y	Y	Y	Y	Y	N
10 Payne	Y	Y	Y	Y	Y	?
11 **Frelinghuysen**	Y	N	N	Y	N	Y
12 Holt	Y	Y	Y	Y	Y	N
13 Sires	?	?	?	?	?	?
NEW MEXICO						
1 **Wilson**	Y	N	N	Y	N	?
2 **Pearce**	Y	?	N	Y	N	Y
3 Udall	Y	Y	Y	Y	Y	?
NEW YORK						
1 Bishop	Y	?	?	?	?	?
2 Israel	Y	Y	Y	Y	Y	N
3 **King**	Y	N	N	Y	N	Y
4 McCarthy	Y	Y	Y	Y	Y	Y
5 Ackerman	Y	Y	Y	Y	Y	?
6 Meeks	Y	Y	Y	?	Y	N
7 Crowley	Y	Y	Y	?	Y	N
8 Nadler	Y	Y	Y	N	Y	N
9 Weiner	Y	?	?	Y	Y	N
10 Towns	Y	Y	Y	Y	Y	N
11 Clarke	Y	Y	Y	Y	Y	N
12 Velázquez	Y	Y	Y	Y	Y	N
13 **Fossella**	Y	N	N	Y	N	Y
14 Maloney	Y	Y	Y	Y	Y	Y
15 Rangel	?	Y	Y	?	Y	?
16 Serrano	Y	Y	Y	Y	Y	N
17 Engel	Y	Y	Y	Y	Y	N
18 Lowey	Y	Y	Y	Y	Y	?
19 Hall	Y	Y	Y	Y	Y	Y
20 Gillibrand	Y	Y	Y	Y	Y	Y
21 McNulty	Y	Y	Y	Y	Y	?
22 Hinchey	Y	Y	Y	Y	Y	N
23 **McHugh**	Y	N	N	Y	N	Y
24 Arcuri	Y	Y	Y	Y	Y	Y
25 **Walsh**	Y	N	N	Y	N	N
26 **Reynolds**	Y	N	N	Y	N	Y
27 Higgins	Y	Y	Y	Y	Y	N
28 Slaughter	?	Y	Y	Y	Y	Y
29 **Kuhl**	Y	N	N	Y	N	Y
NORTH CAROLINA						
1 Butterfield	Y	Y	Y	Y	Y	N
2 Etheridge	Y	Y	Y	Y	Y	N
3 **Jones**	Y	N	N	Y	Y	Y
4 Price	Y	Y	Y	Y	Y	N

	177	178	179	180	181	182
5 **Foxx**	Y	N	N	Y	N	Y
6 **Coble**	?	N	N	Y	N	Y
7 McIntyre	Y	Y	Y	Y	Y	Y
8 **Hayes**	Y	N	N	Y	Y	N
9 **Myrick**	Y	N	N	Y	N	Y
10 **McHenry**	Y	N	N	Y	N	Y
11 Shuler	Y	N	Y	Y	Y	Y
12 Watt	Y	Y	Y	Y	Y	N
13 Miller	Y	Y	Y	Y	Y	Y
NORTH DAKOTA						
AL Pomeroy	Y	Y	Y	Y	Y	Y
OHIO						
1 **Chabot**	Y	N	N	Y	N	Y
2 **Schmidt**	Y	N	N	Y	N	Y
3 **Turner**	Y	N	N	Y	N	Y
4 **Jordan**	Y	N	N	Y	N	Y
5 **Latta**	Y	N	N	Y	N	Y
6 Wilson	Y	Y	Y	Y	Y	Y
7 **Hobson**	Y	N	N	Y	N	N
8 **Boehner**	?	N	N	Y	N	?
9 Kaptur	Y	Y	Y	Y	Y	Y
10 Kucinich	Y	Y	Y	N	Y	N
11 Tubbs Jones	Y	+	+	+	Y	–
12 **Tiberi**	Y	N	N	Y	N	Y
13 Sutton	Y	Y	Y	Y	Y	Y
14 **LaTourette**	Y	N	N	Y	N	N
15 **Pryce**	Y	N	N	?	N	?
16 **Regula**	Y	N	N	Y	N	Y
17 Ryan	Y	Y	Y	Y	Y	N
18 Space	Y	Y	Y	Y	Y	Y
OKLAHOMA						
1 **Sullivan**	Y	N	N	Y	N	Y
2 Boren	Y	Y	Y	Y	N	?
3 **Lucas**	Y	N	N	Y	N	Y
4 **Cole**	Y	N	N	Y	N	Y
5 **Fallin**	Y	N	N	?	N	Y
OREGON						
1 Wu	Y	Y	Y	Y	Y	Y
2 **Walden**	Y	N	N	Y	N	?
3 Blumenauer	Y	Y	Y	Y	Y	Y
4 DeFazio	Y	Y	Y	Y	Y	Y
5 Hooley	?	Y	Y	Y	Y	N
PENNSYLVANIA						
1 Brady	Y	Y	Y	Y	Y	N
2 Fattah	Y	Y	Y	Y	Y	N
3 **English**	Y	N	N	Y	N	Y
4 Altmire	Y	Y	Y	Y	Y	Y
5 **Peterson**	?	Y	N	Y	N	Y
6 **Gerlach**	Y	N	N	Y	N	Y
7 Sestak	Y	Y	Y	Y	Y	Y
8 Murphy, P.	Y	Y	Y	Y	Y	Y
9 **Shuster**	Y	N	N	Y	N	Y
10 Carney	Y	Y	Y	Y	Y	Y
11 Kanjorski	Y	Y	Y	Y	Y	Y
12 Murtha	?	Y	Y	Y	Y	N
13 Schwartz	Y	Y	Y	+	Y	Y
14 Doyle	Y	Y	Y	Y	Y	?
15 **Dent**	Y	Y	N	Y	N	Y
16 **Pitts**	Y	N	N	Y	N	Y
17 Holden	Y	Y	Y	Y	Y	?
18 **Murphy, T.**	Y	N	N	Y	N	Y
19 **Platts**	Y	N	N	Y	N	Y
RHODE ISLAND						
1 Kennedy	Y	Y	Y	Y	Y	Y
2 Langevin	Y	Y	Y	Y	Y	Y
SOUTH CAROLINA						
1 **Brown**	Y	N	N	Y	N	Y
2 **Wilson**	Y	N	N	Y	N	Y
3 **Barrett**	Y	N	N	Y	N	Y
4 **Inglis**	Y	N	N	Y	N	Y
5 Spratt	Y	Y	Y	Y	Y	Y
6 Clyburn	Y	Y	Y	Y	Y	N
SOUTH DAKOTA						
AL Herseth Sandlin	Y	Y	Y	Y	Y	Y
TENNESSEE						
1 **Davis, D.**	Y	N	N	Y	N	Y
2 **Duncan**	Y	N	N	Y	N	Y
3 **Wamp**	Y	N	N	Y	N	Y
4 Davis, L.	Y	Y	Y	Y	Y	Y
5 Cooper	Y	Y	Y	Y	N	Y
6 Gordon	Y	?	Y	Y	Y	Y
7 **Blackburn**	Y	N	N	Y	N	Y
8 Tanner	Y	Y	Y	Y	P	N
9 Cohen	Y	Y	Y	Y	Y	Y

	177	178	179	180	181	182
TEXAS						
1 **Gohmert**	Y	?	N	Y	N	Y
2 **Poe**	Y	N	N	Y	N	Y
3 **Johnson, S.**	Y	N	N	Y	N	Y
4 **Hall**	Y	N	N	Y	N	Y
5 **Hensarling**	Y	N	N	Y	N	Y
6 **Barton**	Y	N	N	Y	N	?
7 **Culberson**	Y	N	N	Y	N	Y
8 **Brady**	Y	N	N	Y	N	Y
9 Green, A.	Y	Y	Y	Y	Y	N
10 **McCaul**	Y	N	N	Y	N	Y
11 **Conaway**	Y	N	N	Y	N	Y
12 **Granger**	?	?	?	?	?	?
13 **Thornberry**	Y	N	N	Y	N	Y
14 **Paul**	Y	Y	N	N	Y	N
15 Hinojosa	Y	Y	Y	Y	Y	?
16 Reyes	Y	Y	Y	Y	Y	N
17 Edwards	?	Y	Y	Y	Y	Y
18 Jackson Lee	Y	Y	Y	Y	Y	N
19 **Neugebauer**	Y	N	N	Y	N	Y
20 Gonzalez	Y	Y	Y	Y	Y	N
21 **Smith**	Y	N	N	Y	N	Y
22 Lampson	Y	Y	Y	Y	N	Y
23 Rodriguez	Y	Y	Y	Y	Y	Y
24 **Marchant**	?	N	N	Y	N	?
25 Doggett	Y	Y	Y	Y	Y	Y
26 **Burgess**	Y	N	N	Y	?	?
27 Ortiz	Y	Y	Y	Y	Y	N
28 Cuellar	Y	Y	Y	Y	N	Y
29 Green, G.	Y	Y	Y	Y	Y	Y
30 Johnson, E.	Y	Y	Y	Y	Y	N
31 **Carter**	Y	N	N	Y	N	Y
32 **Sessions**	Y	N	N	Y	N	?
UTAH						
1 **Bishop**	Y	?	?	?	?	?
2 Matheson	Y	Y	Y	Y	N	Y
3 **Cannon**	Y	N	N	Y	N	Y
VERMONT						
AL Welch	Y	Y	Y	Y	Y	Y
VIRGINIA						
1 **Wittman**	Y	N	N	Y	N	Y
2 **Drake**	Y	N	N	Y	N	Y
3 Scott	Y	Y	Y	Y	Y	Y
4 **Forbes**	Y	N	N	?	N	Y
5 **Goode**	Y	N	N	Y	Y	Y
6 **Goodlatte**	Y	Y	N	Y	N	Y
7 **Cantor**	Y	N	N	Y	N	Y
8 Moran	?	Y	Y	Y	Y	N
9 Boucher	Y	Y	Y	Y	Y	Y
10 **Wolf**	Y	N	N	Y	N	Y
11 **Davis**	Y	N	?	?	N	Y
WASHINGTON						
1 Inslee	Y	Y	Y	Y	Y	N
2 Larsen	Y	Y	Y	Y	Y	?
3 Baird	Y	Y	Y	Y	Y	Y
4 **Hastings**	Y	N	N	Y	N	Y
5 **McMorris Rodgers**	Y	N	N	Y	N	Y
6 Dicks	?	Y	Y	Y	Y	Y
7 McDermott	Y	Y	Y	Y	Y	N
8 **Reichert**	Y	N	N	Y	N	Y
9 Smith	Y	Y	Y	Y	Y	N
WEST VIRGINIA						
1 Mollohan	Y	Y	Y	Y	Y	N
2 **Capito**	Y	N	N	Y	N	Y
3 Rahall	Y	Y	Y	Y	Y	N
WISCONSIN						
1 **Ryan**	Y	?	N	Y	N	Y
2 Baldwin	Y	Y	Y	Y	Y	N
3 Kind	Y	Y	Y	Y	Y	Y
4 Moore	Y	Y	Y	Y	Y	N
5 **Sensenbrenner**	Y	N	N	Y	N	Y
6 **Petri**	Y	N	N	?	N	Y
7 Obey	Y	Y	N	Y	Y	P
8 Kagen	Y	Y	Y	Y	Y	Y
WYOMING						
AL **Cubin**	Y	?	?	?	N	?
DELEGATES						
Faleomavaega (A.S.)						N
Norton (D.C.)						Y
Bordallo (Guam)						N
Fortuño (P.R.)						?
Christensen (V.I.)						N

IN THE HOUSE | By Vote Number

183. **H Res 886. Sympathy for Colorado Shooting Victims/ Adoption.** Ellsworth, D-Ind., motion to suspend the rules and adopt the resolution that would express sympathy for the victims and families of the shootings in Colorado Springs, Colo., and Arvada, Colo., and convey gratitude to security officers and city and county officials who responded swiftly. Motion agreed to 380-0: R 176-0; D 204-0 (ND 156-0, SD 48-0). A two-thirds majority of those present and voting (254 in this case) is required for adoption under suspension of the rules. April 14, 2008.

184. **H Res 994. National Glanzmann's Thrombasthenia Awareness Day/Adoption.** Davis, D-Ill., motion to suspend the rules and adopt the resolution that would support the designation of a National Glanz-mann's Thrombasthenia Awareness Day. Motion agreed to 377-0: R 176-0; D 201-0 (ND 153-0, SD 48-0). A two-thirds majority of those present and voting (252 in this case) is required for adoption under suspension of the rules. April 14, 2008.

185. **HR 3548. Plain Language in Government Communications/ Passage.** Braley, D-Iowa, motion to suspend the rules and pass the bill that would require the federal government to use plain language in all communications that explain how to file taxes or obtain government benefits or services. Motion agreed to 376-1: R 174-1; D 202-0 (ND 155-0, SD 47-0). A two-thirds majority of those present and voting (252 in this case) is required for passage under suspension of the rules. April 14, 2008.

186. **HR 5719. Tax-Filing Process Revisions/Previous Question.** Sutton, D-Ohio, motion to order the previous question (thus ending debate and possibility of amendment) on adoption of the rule (H Res 1102) and a Sutton amendment to the rule. The rule would provide for House floor consideration of the bill that would revise certain record-keeping requirements in the tax-filing process and repeal the IRS's authority to outsource federal debt collection to private companies. The Sutton amendment would require a Government Accountability Office study on expenditures from health savings accounts. Motion agreed to 220-196: R 0-191; D 220-5 (ND 167-2, SD 53-3). (Subsequently, the Sutton amendment was adopted by voice vote.) April 15, 2008.

187. **HR 5719. Tax-Filing Process Revisions/Rule.** Adoption of the rule (H Res 1102) to provide for House floor consideration of the bill that would make revisions to certain record-keeping requirements in the tax-filing process and repeal the IRS's authority to outsource federal debt collection to private companies. Adopted 222-195: R 0-192; D 222-3 (ND 166-2, SD 56-1). April 15, 2008.

188. **HR 5036. State Voting Assistance/Passage.** Lofgren, D-Calif., motion to suspend the rules and pass the bill that would authorize reimbursement for states and counties that convert to paper ballot voting machines before the November 2008 elections or need help paying for manual audits afterward. Motion rejected 239-178: R 16-176; D 223-2 (ND 166-2, SD 57-0). A two-thirds majority of those present and voting (278 in this case) is required for passage under suspension of the rules. A "nay" was a vote in support of the president's position. April 15, 2008.

	183	184	185	186	187	188
ALABAMA						
1 **Bonner**	Y	Y	Y	N	N	N
2 **Everett**	Y	Y	Y	N	N	N
3 **Rogers**	Y	Y	Y	N	N	N
4 **Aderholt**	Y	Y	Y	N	N	N
5 Cramer	Y	Y	Y	Y	Y	Y
6 Bachus	Y	Y	Y	N	N	N
7 Davis	Y	Y	Y	Y	Y	Y
ALASKA						
AL **Young**	Y	Y	Y	N	N	N
ARIZONA						
1 **Renzi**	?	?	?	N	N	N
2 **Franks**	Y	Y	Y	N	N	N
3 **Shadegg**	Y	Y	Y	N	N	N
4 Pastor	Y	Y	Y	Y	Y	Y
5 Mitchell	Y	Y	Y	Y	Y	Y
6 **Flake**	Y	Y	N	N	N	N
7 Grijalva	Y	Y	Y	Y	Y	Y
8 Giffords	Y	Y	Y	Y	Y	Y
ARKANSAS						
1 Berry	Y	Y	Y	Y	Y	Y
2 Snyder	Y	Y	Y	Y	Y	Y
3 **Boozman**	Y	Y	Y	N	N	N
4 Ross	Y	Y	Y	Y	Y	Y
CALIFORNIA						
1 Thompson	Y	Y	Y	Y	Y	Y
2 **Herger**	Y	Y	Y	N	N	N
3 **Lungren**	Y	Y	Y	N	N	N
4 **Doolittle**	Y	Y	Y	N	N	N
5 Matsui	Y	Y	Y	Y	Y	Y
6 Woolsey	Y	Y	Y	Y	Y	Y
7 Miller, George	Y	Y	Y	Y	Y	Y
8 Pelosi						
9 Lee	Y	Y	Y	Y	Y	Y
10 Tauscher	Y	Y	Y	Y	Y	Y
11 McNerney	Y	Y	Y	Y	Y	Y
12 Speier	Y	Y	Y	Y	Y	Y
13 Stark	Y	Y	Y	Y	Y	Y
14 Eshoo	Y	Y	Y	Y	Y	Y
15 Honda	?	?	?	?	?	?
16 Lofgren	Y	Y	Y	Y	Y	Y
17 Farr	Y	Y	Y	Y	Y	Y
18 Cardoza	Y	Y	Y	Y	Y	Y
19 **Radanovich**	?	?	?	N	N	N
20 Costa	Y	Y	Y	Y	Y	Y
21 **Nunes**	Y	Y	Y	N	N	N
22 **McCarthy**	Y	Y	Y	N	N	N
23 Capps	Y	Y	Y	Y	Y	Y
24 **Gallegly**	Y	Y	Y	N	N	N
25 **McKeon**	Y	Y	Y	N	N	N
26 **Dreier**	Y	Y	Y	N	N	N
27 Sherman	Y	Y	Y	Y	Y	Y
28 Berman	Y	Y	Y	Y	Y	Y
29 Schiff	Y	Y	Y	Y	Y	Y
30 Waxman	Y	Y	Y	Y	Y	Y
31 Becerra	?	?	Y	Y	Y	Y
32 Solis	?	?	Y	Y	Y	Y
33 Watson	Y	Y	Y	Y	Y	Y
34 Roybal-Allard	Y	Y	Y	Y	Y	Y
35 Waters	Y	Y	Y	Y	Y	Y
36 Harman	Y	Y	Y	Y	Y	Y
37 Richardson	?	?	?	?	?	?
38 Napolitano	Y	Y	Y	Y	Y	Y
39 Sánchez, Linda	Y	Y	Y	Y	Y	Y
40 **Royce**	Y	Y	Y	N	N	N
41 **Lewis**	Y	Y	Y	N	N	N
42 **Miller, Gary**	Y	Y	Y	N	N	N
43 Baca	Y	Y	Y	Y	Y	Y
44 **Calvert**	Y	Y	Y	N	N	N
45 **Bono Mack**	Y	Y	Y	N	N	N
46 **Rohrabacher**	?	?	?	N	N	N
47 Sanchez, Loretta	Y	Y	Y	Y	Y	Y
48 **Campbell**	Y	Y	Y	N	N	N
49 **Issa**	Y	Y	Y	N	N	N
50 **Bilbray**	Y	Y	Y	N	N	N
51 Filner	Y	Y	Y	Y	Y	Y
52 **Hunter**	Y	Y	?	N	N	N
53 Davis	Y	Y	Y	Y	Y	Y

	183	184	185	186	187	188
COLORADO						
1 DeGette	Y	Y	Y	Y	Y	Y
2 Udall	+	+	+	Y	Y	Y
3 Salazar	Y	Y	Y	Y	Y	Y
4 **Musgrave**	Y	Y	Y	N	N	N
5 **Lamborn**	Y	Y	Y	N	N	N
6 **Tancredo**	Y	Y	Y	N	N	N
7 Perlmutter	Y	Y	Y	Y	Y	Y
CONNECTICUT						
1 Larson	Y	Y	Y	Y	Y	Y
2 Courtney	Y	Y	Y	Y	Y	Y
3 DeLauro	Y	Y	Y	Y	Y	Y
4 **Shays**	+	+	+	N	N	Y
5 Murphy	Y	Y	Y	Y	Y	Y
DELAWARE						
AL **Castle**	Y	Y	N	N	N	N
FLORIDA						
1 **Miller**	Y	Y	Y	N	N	N
2 Boyd	Y	Y	Y	Y	Y	Y
3 Brown	?	?	?	Y	Y	Y
4 **Crenshaw**	Y	Y	Y	N	N	N
5 **Brown-Waite**	Y	Y	Y	N	N	N
6 **Stearns**	Y	Y	Y	N	N	N
7 **Mica**	Y	Y	Y	N	N	N
8 **Keller**	Y	Y	Y	N	N	N
9 **Bilirakis**	Y	Y	Y	N	N	N
10 **Young**	?	?	?	N	N	N
11 Castor	Y	Y	Y	Y	Y	Y
12 **Putnam**	Y	Y	Y	N	N	N
13 **Buchanan**	Y	Y	Y	N	N	N
14 **Mack**	?	?	?	?	?	?
15 **Weldon**	?	?	?	N	N	N
16 Mahoney	Y	Y	Y	Y	Y	Y
17 Meek	?	?	?	Y	Y	Y
18 **Ros-Lehtinen**	Y	Y	Y	N	N	N
19 Wexler	Y	Y	Y	Y	Y	Y
20 Wasserman Schultz	Y	Y	Y	Y	Y	Y
21 **Diaz-Balart, L.**	Y	Y	Y	N	N	N
22 Klein	Y	Y	Y	Y	Y	Y
23 Hastings	?	?	?	Y	Y	Y
24 **Feeney**	Y	Y	Y	N	N	N
25 **Diaz-Balart, M.**	Y	Y	Y	N	N	N
GEORGIA						
1 **Kingston**	Y	Y	Y	N	N	N
2 Bishop	+	+	+	Y	Y	Y
3 **Westmoreland**	Y	Y	Y	N	N	N
4 Johnson	Y	Y	Y	Y	Y	Y
5 Lewis	Y	Y	Y	Y	Y	Y
6 **Price**	Y	Y	Y	N	N	N
7 **Linder**	Y	Y	Y	N	N	N
8 Marshall	Y	Y	Y	Y	Y	Y
9 **Deal**	Y	Y	Y	N	N	N
10 **Broun**	Y	Y	Y	N	N	N
11 **Gingrey**	Y	Y	Y	N	N	N
12 Barrow	Y	Y	Y	Y	Y	Y
13 Scott	Y	Y	Y	Y	Y	Y
HAWAII						
1 Abercrombie	Y	Y	Y	Y	Y	Y
2 Hirono	Y	Y	Y	Y	Y	Y
IDAHO						
1 **Sali**	Y	Y	Y	N	N	N
2 **Simpson**	Y	Y	Y	N	N	N
ILLINOIS						
1 Rush	?	?	?	?	?	?
2 Jackson	Y	Y	Y	Y	Y	Y
3 Lipinski	Y	Y	Y	Y	Y	Y
4 Gutierrez	+	+	–	Y	?	Y
5 Emanuel	Y	Y	Y	Y	Y	Y
6 **Roskam**	Y	Y	Y	N	N	N
7 Davis	Y	Y	Y	Y	Y	Y
8 Bean	Y	Y	Y	N	Y	Y
9 Schakowsky	Y	Y	Y	Y	Y	Y
10 **Kirk**	Y	Y	Y	N	N	N
11 **Weller**	Y	Y	Y	N	N	N
12 Costello	Y	Y	Y	Y	Y	Y
13 **Biggert**	Y	Y	Y	N	N	N
14 Foster	Y	Y	Y	Y	Y	Y
15 **Johnson**	Y	Y	Y	N	N	N

KEY	Republicans		Democrats			
Y	Voted for (yea)		X	Paired against	C	Voted "present" to avoid possible conflict of interest
#	Paired for		–	Announced against		
+	Announced for		P	Voted "present"	?	Did not vote or otherwise make a position known
N	Voted against (nay)					

ND Northern Democrats, SD Southern Democrats
Southern states: Ala., Ark., Fla., Ga., Ky., La., Miss., N.C., Okla., S.C., Tenn., Texas, Va.

	183	184	185	186	187	188
16 **Manzullo**	Y	Y	Y	N	N	N
17 Hare	Y	Y	Y	Y	Y	Y
18 **LaHood**	Y	Y	Y	N	N	N
19 **Shimkus**	Y	Y	Y	N	N	N
INDIANA						
1 Visclosky	Y	Y	Y	Y	Y	Y
2 Donnelly	Y	Y	Y	Y	Y	Y
3 **Souder**	Y	Y	Y	N	N	N
4 **Buyer**	?	?	?	N	N	N
5 **Burton**	Y	Y	Y	N	N	N
6 **Pence**	Y	Y	Y	N	N	N
7 Carson, A.	Y	?	Y	Y	Y	Y
8 Ellsworth	Y	Y	Y	Y	Y	Y
9 Hill	Y	Y	Y	N	N	Y
IOWA						
1 Braley	Y	Y	Y	Y	Y	Y
2 Loebsack	Y	Y	Y	Y	Y	Y
3 Boswell	Y	Y	Y	Y	Y	Y
4 **Latham**	Y	Y	Y	N	N	N
5 **King**	Y	Y	Y	N	N	N
KANSAS						
1 **Moran**	Y	Y	Y	N	N	N
2 Boyda	Y	Y	Y	Y	N	Y
3 Moore	Y	Y	Y	Y	Y	Y
4 **Tiahrt**	Y	Y	Y	N	N	N
KENTUCKY						
1 **Whitfield**	Y	Y	Y	N	N	N
2 **Lewis**	Y	Y	Y	N	N	N
3 Yarmuth	Y	Y	Y	Y	Y	Y
4 **Davis**	Y	Y	Y	N	N	N
5 **Rogers**	Y	Y	Y	N	N	N
6 Chandler	Y	Y	?	Y	Y	Y
LOUISIANA						
1 Vacant						
2 Jefferson	?	?	?	Y	Y	Y
3 Melancon	Y	Y	Y	Y	Y	Y
4 **McCrery**	Y	Y	Y	N	N	N
5 **Alexander**	Y	Y	Y	N	N	N
6 Vacant						
7 **Boustany**	Y	Y	Y	N	N	N
MAINE						
1 Allen	+	+	+	Y	Y	Y
2 Michaud	Y	Y	Y	Y	Y	Y
MARYLAND						
1 **Gilchrest**	?	?	?	N	N	N
2 Ruppersberger	Y	Y	Y	Y	Y	Y
3 Sarbanes	Y	Y	Y	Y	Y	Y
4 Wynn	Y	Y	Y	Y	Y	Y
5 Hoyer	Y	Y	Y	Y	Y	Y
6 **Bartlett**	Y	Y	Y	N	N	N
7 Cummings	Y	Y	Y	Y	Y	Y
8 Van Hollen	Y	Y	Y	Y	Y	Y
MASSACHUSETTS						
1 Olver	Y	Y	Y	Y	Y	Y
2 Neal	?	?	?	Y	Y	Y
3 McGovern	Y	Y	Y	Y	Y	Y
4 Frank	Y	Y	Y	Y	Y	Y
5 Tsongas	?	?	?	Y	Y	Y
6 Tierney	Y	Y	Y	Y	Y	Y
7 Markey	Y	Y	Y	Y	Y	Y
8 Capuano	+	+	+	+	+	+
9 Lynch	Y	Y	Y	Y	Y	Y
10 Delahunt	?	?	?	?	?	?
MICHIGAN						
1 Stupak	Y	Y	Y	Y	Y	Y
2 **Hoekstra**	Y	Y	Y	N	N	N
3 **Ehlers**	Y	Y	Y	N	N	N
4 **Camp**	Y	Y	Y	N	N	N
5 Kildee	Y	Y	Y	Y	Y	Y
6 **Upton**	Y	Y	Y	N	N	N
7 **Walberg**	Y	Y	Y	N	N	N
8 **Rogers**	Y	Y	Y	N	N	N
9 **Knollenberg**	Y	Y	Y	N	N	N
10 **Miller**	Y	Y	Y	N	N	N
11 **McCotter**	Y	Y	Y	N	N	N
12 Levin	Y	Y	Y	Y	Y	Y
13 Kilpatrick	Y	Y	Y	Y	Y	Y
14 Conyers	Y	Y	Y	Y	Y	Y
15 Dingell	Y	Y	Y	Y	Y	Y
MINNESOTA						
1 Walz	Y	Y	Y	Y	Y	Y
2 **Kline**	Y	Y	Y	N	N	N
3 **Ramstad**	Y	Y	Y	N	N	Y
4 McCollum	Y	Y	Y	Y	Y	Y
5 Ellison	Y	Y	Y	Y	Y	Y
6 **Bachmann**	Y	Y	Y	N	N	N
7 Peterson	Y	Y	Y	Y	Y	Y
8 Oberstar	Y	Y	Y	Y	Y	Y
MISSISSIPPI						
1 Vacant						
2 Thompson	Y	Y	Y	Y	Y	Y
3 **Pickering**	?	?	?	N	N	N
4 Taylor	Y	Y	Y	Y	Y	Y
MISSOURI						
1 Clay	Y	Y	Y	Y	Y	Y
2 **Akin**	Y	Y	Y	N	N	N
3 Carnahan	Y	Y	Y	Y	Y	Y
4 Skelton	Y	Y	Y	Y	Y	Y
5 Cleaver	Y	Y	Y	Y	Y	Y
6 **Graves**	Y	Y	Y	N	N	N
7 **Blunt**	Y	Y	Y	?	N	N
8 **Emerson**	Y	Y	Y	N	N	N
9 **Hulshof**	?	?	?	N	N	N
MONTANA						
AL **Rehberg**	Y	Y	Y	N	N	N
NEBRASKA						
1 **Fortenberry**	?	Y	Y	N	N	N
2 **Terry**	Y	Y	Y	N	N	N
3 **Smith**	Y	Y	Y	N	N	N
NEVADA						
1 Berkley	Y	Y	Y	Y	Y	Y
2 **Heller**	Y	Y	Y	N	N	Y
3 **Porter**	Y	Y	Y	N	N	Y
NEW HAMPSHIRE						
1 Shea-Porter	Y	Y	Y	Y	Y	Y
2 Hodes	Y	Y	Y	Y	Y	Y
NEW JERSEY						
1 Andrews	+	+	+	Y	Y	Y
2 **LoBiondo**	+	+	+	–	–	+
3 **Saxton**	Y	Y	Y	N	N	N
4 **Smith**	Y	Y	Y	N	N	Y
5 **Garrett**	Y	Y	Y	N	N	N
6 Pallone	Y	Y	Y	?	?	+
7 **Ferguson**	Y	Y	Y	N	N	N
8 Pascrell	?	?	?	+	+	+
9 Rothman	Y	Y	Y	Y	Y	Y
10 Payne	?	?	?	Y	Y	Y
11 **Frelinghuysen**	Y	Y	Y	N	N	N
12 Holt	Y	Y	Y	Y	Y	Y
13 Sires	Y	Y	Y	Y	Y	Y
NEW MEXICO						
1 **Wilson**	?	?	?	?	?	?
2 **Pearce**	Y	Y	Y	N	N	N
3 Udall	Y	Y	Y	Y	Y	Y
NEW YORK						
1 Bishop	Y	Y	Y	Y	Y	Y
2 Israel	Y	Y	Y	Y	Y	Y
3 **King**	Y	Y	Y	N	N	N
4 McCarthy	Y	Y	Y	Y	Y	Y
5 Ackerman	Y	Y	Y	Y	Y	Y
6 Meeks	Y	Y	Y	Y	Y	Y
7 Crowley	Y	Y	Y	Y	Y	Y
8 Nadler	Y	Y	Y	Y	Y	Y
9 Weiner	?	?	?	Y	Y	Y
10 Towns	Y	Y	Y	Y	Y	Y
11 Clarke	Y	Y	Y	Y	Y	Y
12 Velázquez	Y	Y	Y	Y	Y	Y
13 **Fossella**	Y	Y	Y	N	N	N
14 Maloney	Y	Y	Y	Y	Y	Y
15 Rangel	Y	Y	Y	Y	Y	?
16 Serrano	Y	Y	Y	Y	Y	Y
17 Engel	Y	Y	Y	Y	Y	Y
18 Lowey	Y	Y	Y	Y	Y	Y
19 Hall	Y	Y	Y	Y	Y	Y
20 Gillibrand	Y	Y	Y	Y	Y	Y
21 McNulty	Y	Y	Y	Y	Y	Y
22 Hinchey	Y	Y	Y	Y	Y	Y
23 **McHugh**	Y	Y	Y	N	N	N
24 Arcuri	Y	Y	Y	Y	Y	Y
25 **Walsh**	Y	?	Y	N	N	N
26 **Reynolds**	Y	Y	Y	N	N	N
27 Higgins	Y	Y	Y	Y	Y	Y
28 Slaughter	Y	Y	Y	Y	Y	Y
29 **Kuhl**	Y	Y	Y	N	N	N
NORTH CAROLINA						
1 Butterfield	?	?	?	Y	Y	Y
2 Etheridge	Y	Y	Y	Y	Y	Y
3 **Jones**	Y	Y	Y	N	N	N
4 Price	Y	Y	Y	Y	Y	Y
5 **Foxx**	Y	Y	Y	N	N	N
6 **Coble**	Y	Y	Y	N	N	N
7 McIntyre	Y	Y	Y	N	Y	Y
8 **Hayes**	Y	Y	Y	N	N	N
9 **Myrick**	Y	Y	Y	N	N	N
10 **McHenry**	Y	Y	Y	N	N	N
11 Shuler	Y	Y	Y	Y	Y	Y
12 Watt	Y	Y	Y	Y	Y	Y
13 Miller	Y	Y	Y	Y	Y	Y
NORTH DAKOTA						
AL Pomeroy	Y	Y	Y	Y	Y	Y
OHIO						
1 **Chabot**	Y	Y	Y	N	N	Y
2 **Schmidt**	Y	Y	Y	N	N	N
3 **Turner**	?	?	?	N	N	N
4 **Jordan**	Y	Y	Y	N	N	N
5 **Latta**	Y	Y	Y	N	N	N
6 Wilson	Y	Y	Y	Y	Y	Y
7 **Hobson**	Y	Y	Y	N	N	N
8 **Boehner**	Y	Y	Y	N	N	N
9 Kaptur	Y	Y	Y	Y	Y	Y
10 Kucinich	Y	Y	Y	Y	Y	N
11 Tubbs Jones	Y	Y	Y	Y	Y	Y
12 **Tiberi**	Y	Y	Y	N	N	N
13 Sutton	Y	Y	Y	Y	Y	Y
14 **LaTourette**	Y	Y	Y	N	N	N
15 **Pryce**	?	?	?	N	N	N
16 **Regula**	Y	Y	Y	N	N	N
17 Ryan	Y	Y	Y	Y	Y	Y
18 Space	Y	Y	Y	Y	Y	Y
OKLAHOMA						
1 **Sullivan**	Y	Y	Y	N	N	N
2 Boren	Y	Y	Y	Y	Y	Y
3 **Lucas**	Y	Y	Y	N	N	N
4 **Cole**	Y	Y	Y	N	N	Y
5 **Fallin**	Y	Y	Y	N	N	N
OREGON						
1 Wu	Y	Y	Y	Y	Y	Y
2 **Walden**	Y	Y	Y	N	N	N
3 Blumenauer	Y	Y	Y	Y	Y	Y
4 DeFazio	Y	Y	Y	Y	Y	Y
5 Hooley	Y	Y	Y	Y	Y	Y
PENNSYLVANIA						
1 Brady	?	?	?	Y	Y	Y
2 Fattah	?	?	?	Y	Y	Y
3 **English**	+	+	+	N	N	N
4 Altmire	Y	Y	Y	Y	Y	Y
5 **Peterson**	?	?	?	?	?	?
6 **Gerlach**	Y	Y	Y	N	N	Y
7 Sestak	Y	Y	Y	Y	Y	Y
8 Murphy, P.	Y	Y	Y	Y	Y	Y
9 **Shuster**	?	?	?	N	N	N
10 Carney	Y	?	Y	Y	Y	Y
11 Kanjorski	Y	Y	Y	Y	Y	Y
12 Murtha	Y	?	?	Y	Y	Y
13 Schwartz	?	?	?	Y	Y	Y
14 Doyle	Y	Y	Y	Y	Y	Y
15 **Dent**	Y	Y	Y	N	N	Y
16 **Pitts**	Y	Y	Y	N	N	N
17 Holden	Y	Y	Y	Y	Y	Y
18 **Murphy, T.**	Y	Y	Y	N	N	Y
19 **Platts**	Y	Y	Y	N	N	N
RHODE ISLAND						
1 Kennedy	Y	Y	Y	Y	Y	Y
2 Langevin	Y	Y	Y	Y	Y	Y
SOUTH CAROLINA						
1 **Brown**	Y	Y	Y	N	N	N
2 **Wilson**	Y	Y	Y	N	N	N
3 **Barrett**	Y	Y	Y	N	N	N
4 **Inglis**	Y	Y	Y	N	N	N
5 Spratt	Y	Y	Y	Y	Y	Y
6 Clyburn	Y	Y	Y	Y	Y	Y
SOUTH DAKOTA						
AL Herseth Sandlin	Y	Y	Y	Y	Y	Y
TENNESSEE						
1 **Davis, D.**	Y	Y	Y	N	N	N
2 **Duncan**	Y	Y	Y	N	N	N
3 **Wamp**	Y	Y	Y	N	N	N
4 Davis, L.	?	?	?	Y	Y	Y
5 Cooper	Y	Y	Y	Y	Y	Y
6 Gordon	Y	Y	Y	Y	Y	Y
7 **Blackburn**	Y	Y	Y	N	N	N
8 Tanner	Y	Y	Y	Y	Y	Y
9 Cohen	Y	Y	Y	Y	Y	Y
TEXAS						
1 **Gohmert**	?	?	?	?	?	?
2 **Poe**	Y	Y	Y	N	N	N
3 **Johnson, S.**	Y	Y	Y	N	N	N
4 **Hall**	Y	Y	Y	N	N	N
5 **Hensarling**	Y	Y	Y	N	N	N
6 **Barton**	Y	Y	Y	N	N	N
7 **Culberson**	?	?	?	?	?	?
8 **Brady**	Y	Y	Y	N	N	N
9 Green, A.	Y	Y	Y	Y	Y	Y
10 **McCaul**	Y	Y	Y	N	N	N
11 **Conaway**	Y	Y	Y	N	N	N
12 **Granger**	Y	Y	Y	N	N	N
13 **Thornberry**	Y	Y	Y	N	N	N
14 **Paul**	?	?	?	N	N	N
15 Hinojosa	Y	Y	Y	Y	Y	Y
16 Reyes	Y	Y	Y	Y	Y	Y
17 Edwards	Y	Y	Y	Y	Y	Y
18 Jackson Lee	Y	Y	Y	Y	Y	Y
19 **Neugebauer**	Y	Y	Y	N	N	N
20 Gonzalez	Y	Y	Y	Y	Y	Y
21 **Smith**	Y	Y	Y	N	N	N
22 Lampson	?	?	?	N	N	Y
23 Rodriguez	Y	Y	Y	Y	Y	Y
24 **Marchant**	Y	Y	?	N	N	N
25 Doggett	Y	Y	Y	Y	Y	Y
26 **Burgess**	Y	Y	Y	N	N	N
27 Ortiz	Y	Y	Y	Y	Y	Y
28 Cuellar	Y	Y	Y	Y	Y	Y
29 Green, G.	Y	Y	Y	Y	Y	Y
30 Johnson, E.	Y	Y	Y	Y	Y	Y
31 **Carter**	Y	Y	Y	N	N	N
32 **Sessions**	Y	Y	Y	N	N	N
UTAH						
1 **Bishop**	Y	Y	Y	N	N	N
2 Matheson	Y	Y	Y	Y	Y	Y
3 **Cannon**	Y	Y	Y	N	N	N
VERMONT						
AL Welch	Y	Y	Y	Y	Y	Y
VIRGINIA						
1 **Wittman**	Y	Y	Y	N	N	N
2 **Drake**	Y	Y	Y	N	N	N
3 Scott	Y	Y	Y	Y	Y	Y
4 **Forbes**	Y	Y	Y	N	N	N
5 **Goode**	Y	Y	Y	N	N	N
6 **Goodlatte**	Y	Y	Y	N	N	N
7 **Cantor**	Y	Y	Y	N	N	N
8 Moran	?	?	?	Y	Y	Y
9 Boucher	Y	Y	Y	Y	Y	Y
10 **Wolf**	Y	Y	Y	N	N	N
11 **Davis**	Y	Y	Y	N	N	Y
WASHINGTON						
1 Inslee	Y	Y	Y	Y	Y	Y
2 Larsen	Y	Y	Y	Y	Y	Y
3 Baird	Y	Y	Y	Y	Y	Y
4 **Hastings**	Y	Y	Y	N	N	N
5 **McMorris Rodgers**	Y	Y	Y	N	N	N
6 Dicks	Y	Y	Y	Y	Y	Y
7 McDermott	Y	Y	Y	Y	Y	Y
8 **Reichert**	Y	Y	Y	N	N	N
9 Smith	?	?	?	Y	Y	Y
WEST VIRGINIA						
1 Mollohan	Y	Y	Y	Y	Y	Y
2 **Capito**	Y	Y	Y	N	N	N
3 Rahall	Y	Y	Y	Y	Y	N
WISCONSIN						
1 **Ryan**	Y	Y	Y	N	N	N
2 Baldwin	Y	Y	Y	Y	Y	Y
3 Kind	Y	Y	Y	Y	Y	Y
4 Moore	Y	Y	Y	Y	Y	Y
5 **Sensenbrenner**	Y	Y	Y	N	N	N
6 **Petri**	Y	Y	Y	N	N	N
7 Obey	Y	Y	Y	Y	Y	Y
8 Kagen	Y	Y	Y	Y	Y	Y
WYOMING						
AL **Cubin**	Y	Y	Y	N	N	N
DELEGATES						
Faleomavaega (A.S.)						
Norton (D.C.)						
Bordallo (Guam)						
Fortuño (P.R.)						
Christensen (V.I.)						

IN THE HOUSE | By Vote Number

189. HR 5719. Tax-Filing Process Revisions/Recommit. Herger, R-Calif., motion to recommit the bill to the Ways and Means Committee with instructions that it be reported back promptly with language that would require the IRS to increase efforts to ensure that illegal immigrants do not obtain earned-income tax credits and add provisions to bar tax exemptions for interest on bonds issued by state or local governments that do not require their employees to report illegal immigrants to federal officials. Motion rejected 210-210: R 189-3; D 21-207 (ND 14-157, SD 7-50). April 15, 2008.

190. HR 5719. Tax-Filing Process Revisions/Passage. Passage of the bill that would make revisions to certain record-keeping requirements in the tax-filing process and repeal the IRS's authority to outsource federal debt collection to private companies. The bill would require that individuals prove that their tax-free withdrawals from health savings accounts are being used for medical purposes after Dec. 31, 2010. Passed 238-179: R 14-177; D 224-2 (ND 169-1, SD 55-1). A "nay" was a vote in support of the president's position. April 15, 2008.

191. HR 5517. Texas Military Veterans Post Office/Passage. Davis, D-Ill., motion to suspend the rules and pass the bill that would designate a post office in Humble, Texas, as the "Texas Military Veterans Post Office." Motion agreed to 413-0: R 190-0; D 223-0 (ND 167-0, SD 56-0). A two-thirds majority of those present and voting (276 in this case) is required for passage under suspension of the rules. April 15, 2008.

192. HR 2634. International Debt Relief/Previous Question. Welch, D-Vt., motion to order the previous question (thus ending debate and possibility of amendment) on adoption of the rule (H Res 1103) that would provide for House floor consideration of the bill that would allow as many as two dozen poor countries to qualify for new debt relief. Motion agreed to 217-196: R 0-191; D 217-5 (ND 165-2, SD 52-3). April 16, 2008.

193. HR 2634. International Debt Relief/Rule. Adoption of the rule (H Res 1103) that would allow for House floor consideration of the bill that would allow as many as two dozen poor countries to qualify for new debt relief. Adopted 220-190: R 1-189; D 219-1 (ND 166-1, SD 53-0). April 16, 2008.

194. HR 5715. Student Loan Access/Previous Question. Castor, D-Fla., motion to order the previous question (thus ending debate and possibility of amendment) on adoption of the rule (H Res 1107) that would provide for House floor consideration of the bill that would increase annual loan limits on federal college loans and give the Education Department a bigger role in ensuring loan availability. Motion agreed to 218-198: R 0-193; D 218-5 (ND 166-2, SD 52-3). April 16, 2008.

	189	190	191	192	193	194
ALABAMA						
1 Bonner	Y	N	Y	N	N	N
2 Everett	Y	N	Y	N	N	N
3 Rogers	Y	N	Y	N	?	N
4 Aderholt	Y	N	Y	N	?	N
5 Cramer	N	Y	Y	Y	?	Y
6 Bachus	Y	N	Y	N	N	N
7 Davis	N	Y	Y	Y	Y	Y
ALASKA						
AL Young	Y	N	Y	N	N	N
ARIZONA						
1 Renzi	Y	N	Y	N	N	N
2 Franks	Y	N	Y	N	N	N
3 Shadegg	Y	N	Y	N	N	N
4 Pastor	N	Y	Y	Y	Y	Y
5 Mitchell	Y	Y	Y	Y	Y	Y
6 Flake	Y	N	N	N	N	N
7 Grijalva	N	Y	Y	Y	Y	Y
8 Giffords	Y	Y	Y	Y	Y	Y
ARKANSAS						
1 Berry	N	Y	Y	Y	Y	Y
2 Snyder	N	Y	Y	Y	Y	Y
3 Boozman	Y	N	Y	N	N	N
4 Ross	N	Y	Y	Y	Y	Y
CALIFORNIA						
1 Thompson	N	Y	Y	Y	Y	Y
2 Herger	Y	N	Y	N	N	N
3 Lungren	Y	N	Y	N	N	N
4 Doolittle	Y	N	Y	N	N	N
5 Matsui	N	Y	Y	Y	Y	Y
6 Woolsey	N	Y	Y	?	Y	Y
7 Miller, George	N	Y	Y	Y	Y	Y
8 Pelosi	N					
9 Lee	N	Y	Y	Y	Y	Y
10 Tauscher	N	Y	Y	Y	Y	Y
11 McNerney	N	Y	Y	Y	Y	Y
12 Speier	N	Y	Y	Y	Y	Y
13 Stark	N	Y	Y	Y	Y	Y
14 Eshoo	N	Y	Y	Y	Y	Y
15 Honda	?	?	?	Y	Y	Y
16 Lofgren	N	Y	Y	Y	Y	Y
17 Farr	N	Y	Y	Y	Y	Y
18 Cardoza	N	Y	Y	Y	Y	Y
19 Radanovich	?	?	?	N	N	N
20 Costa	N	Y	Y	?	?	Y
21 Nunes	Y	N	Y	–	–	N
22 McCarthy	Y	N	Y	N	N	N
23 Capps	N	Y	Y	Y	Y	Y
24 Gallegly	Y	N	Y	N	N	N
25 McKeon	Y	N	Y	N	N	N
26 Dreier	Y	N	Y	N	N	N
27 Sherman	N	Y	Y	Y	Y	Y
28 Berman	N	Y	Y	Y	Y	Y
29 Schiff	N	Y	Y	Y	Y	Y
30 Waxman	N	Y	Y	Y	Y	Y
31 Becerra	N	Y	Y	Y	Y	Y
32 Solis	N	Y	Y	Y	Y	Y
33 Watson	N	Y	Y	Y	Y	Y
34 Roybal-Allard	N	Y	Y	Y	Y	Y
35 Waters	N	Y	Y	Y	Y	Y
36 Harman	N	Y	Y	?	?	Y
37 Richardson	?	?	?	Y	Y	Y
38 Napolitano	N	Y	Y	Y	Y	Y
39 Sánchez, Linda	N	Y	Y	Y	Y	Y
40 Royce	Y	N	Y	N	N	N
41 Lewis	Y	N	Y	N	N	N
42 Miller, Gary	Y	N	Y	N	N	N
43 Baca	N	Y	Y	Y	Y	Y
44 Calvert	Y	N	Y	N	N	N
45 Bono Mack	Y	N	Y	?	N	N
46 Rohrabacher	Y	N	Y	N	Y	N
47 Sanchez, Loretta	N	Y	Y	Y	Y	Y
48 Campbell	Y	N	Y	N	N	N
49 Issa	Y	N	Y	N	N	N
50 Bilbray	Y	N	Y	N	N	?
51 Filner	N	Y	Y	Y	Y	Y
52 Hunter	Y	N	Y	N	N	N
53 Davis	N	Y	Y	Y	Y	Y

	189	190	191	192	193	194
COLORADO						
1 DeGette	N	Y	Y	Y	Y	Y
2 Udall	N	Y	Y	Y	Y	Y
3 Salazar	N	Y	Y	Y	Y	Y
4 Musgrave	Y	N	N	N	N	N
5 Lamborn	Y	N	Y	N	N	N
6 Tancredo	Y	N	N	N	N	N
7 Perlmutter	N	Y	Y	Y	Y	Y
CONNECTICUT						
1 Larson	N	Y	Y	Y	Y	Y
2 Courtney	N	Y	?	Y	Y	Y
3 DeLauro	N	Y	Y	?	?	?
4 Shays	Y	N	N	N	N	N
5 Murphy	N	Y	Y	Y	Y	Y
DELAWARE						
AL Castle	Y	N	Y	N	N	N
FLORIDA						
1 Miller	Y	N	Y	N	N	N
2 Boyd	N	Y	Y	Y	Y	Y
3 Brown	N	Y	Y	Y	Y	Y
4 Crenshaw	Y	N	Y	N	N	N
5 Brown-Waite	Y	N	Y	N	N	N
6 Stearns	Y	N	Y	N	N	N
7 Mica	Y	N	Y	N	N	N
8 Keller	Y	N	Y	N	N	N
9 Bilirakis	Y	N	Y	N	N	N
10 Young	Y	N	Y	N	N	N
11 Castor	N	Y	Y	Y	Y	Y
12 Putnam	Y	N	Y	N	N	N
13 Buchanan	Y	N	Y	N	N	N
14 Mack	?	?	?	?	?	?
15 Weldon	Y	N	Y	N	N	N
16 Mahoney	Y	Y	Y	Y	Y	Y
17 Meek	N	Y	Y	?	?	?
18 Ros-Lehtinen	N	Y	Y	N	N	N
19 Wexler	N	Y	Y	?	?	?
20 Wasserman Schultz	N	Y	Y	Y	Y	Y
21 Diaz-Balart, L.	N	Y	Y	N	N	N
22 Klein	N	Y	Y	Y	Y	Y
23 Hastings	N	Y	Y	Y	Y	Y
24 Feeney	Y	Y	Y	N	N	N
25 Diaz-Balart, M.	N	Y	Y	N	N	N
GEORGIA						
1 Kingston	Y	N	Y	N	N	N
2 Bishop	N	Y	Y	Y	Y	Y
3 Westmoreland	Y	N	Y	N	N	N
4 Johnson	N	Y	Y	Y	Y	Y
5 Lewis	N	Y	Y	Y	Y	Y
6 Price	Y	N	Y	N	N	N
7 Linder	Y	N	?	N	N	N
8 Marshall	N	Y	Y	N	N	N
9 Deal	Y	N	Y	N	N	N
10 Broun	Y	N	Y	N	N	N
11 Gingrey	Y	N	Y	N	N	N
12 Barrow	Y	Y	Y	Y	Y	Y
13 Scott	N	Y	Y	Y	Y	Y
HAWAII						
1 Abercrombie	N	Y	Y	Y	Y	Y
2 Hirono	N	Y	Y	Y	Y	Y
IDAHO						
1 Sali	Y	N	Y	N	N	N
2 Simpson	Y	N	Y	N	N	N
ILLINOIS						
1 Rush	?	?	?	?	?	?
2 Jackson	N	Y	Y	Y	Y	Y
3 Lipinski	N	Y	Y	Y	Y	Y
4 Gutierrez	N	Y	Y	Y	Y	Y
5 Emanuel	N	Y	Y	Y	Y	Y
6 Roskam	Y	N	Y	?	N	N
7 Davis	N	Y	Y	Y	Y	Y
8 Bean	N	Y	Y	Y	Y	Y
9 Schakowsky	N	Y	Y	Y	Y	Y
10 Kirk	Y	N	Y	N	N	N
11 Weller	N	Y	Y	Y	Y	Y
12 Costello	N	Y	Y	Y	Y	Y
13 Biggert	Y	N	Y	N	N	N
14 Foster	Y	Y	Y	Y	Y	Y
15 Johnson	Y	N	Y	N	N	N

KEY   **Republicans**   Democrats

Y Voted for (yea)	X Paired against	C Voted "present" to avoid possible conflict of interest
# Paired for	– Announced against	
+ Announced for	P Voted "present"	? Did not vote or otherwise make a position known
N Voted against (nay)		

ND Northern Democrats, SD Southern Democrats
Southern states: Ala., Ark., Fla., Ga., Ky., La., Miss., N.C., Okla., S.C., Tenn., Texas, Va.

H-62 2008 CQ ALMANAC | www.cq.com

	189	190	191	192	193	194
16 **Manzullo**	Y	N	Y	N	N	N
17 Hare	N	Y	Y	Y	Y	Y
18 **LaHood**	Y	N	Y	N	N	N
19 **Shimkus**	Y	N	Y	N	N	N
INDIANA						
1 Visclosky	N	Y	Y	Y	Y	Y
2 Donnelly	Y	Y	Y	Y	Y	Y
3 **Souder**	Y	N	Y	N	N	N
4 **Buyer**	Y	N	Y	N	N	N
5 **Burton**	Y	N	Y	N	N	N
6 **Pence**	Y	N	Y	N	N	N
7 Carson, A.	N	Y	Y	Y	Y	Y
8 Ellsworth	Y	Y	Y	Y	Y	Y
9 Hill	Y	Y	Y	N	N	N
IOWA						
1 Braley	N	N	Y	Y	Y	Y
2 Loebsack	N	Y	Y	Y	Y	Y
3 Boswell	N	Y	Y	Y	Y	?
4 **Latham**	Y	N	Y	N	N	N
5 **King**	Y	N	Y	N	N	N
KANSAS						
1 **Moran**	Y	N	Y	N	N	N
2 Boyda	N	Y	Y	Y	Y	Y
3 Moore	N	Y	Y	Y	Y	Y
4 **Tiahrt**	Y	N	Y	N	N	N
KENTUCKY						
1 **Whitfield**	Y	N	Y	N	N	N
2 **Lewis**	Y	N	Y	N	N	N
3 Yarmuth	N	Y	Y	Y	Y	Y
4 **Davis**	Y	N	Y	N	N	N
5 **Rogers**	Y	N	Y	N	N	N
6 Chandler	N	Y	?	Y	Y	Y
LOUISIANA						
1 Vacant						
2 Jefferson	N	Y	Y	Y	Y	Y
3 Melancon	N	Y	Y	Y	Y	Y
4 **McCrery**	Y	N	Y	N	N	N
5 **Alexander**	Y	N	Y	N	N	N
6 Vacant						
7 **Boustany**	Y	N	Y	N	N	N
MAINE						
1 Allen	N	Y	Y	Y	Y	Y
2 Michaud	N	Y	Y	Y	Y	Y
MARYLAND						
1 **Gilchrest**	Y	Y	Y	N	N	N
2 Ruppersberger	N	Y	Y	Y	Y	Y
3 Sarbanes	N	Y	Y	Y	Y	Y
4 Wynn	N	Y	Y	Y	Y	?
5 Hoyer	N	Y	Y	Y	Y	Y
6 **Bartlett**	Y	N	Y	N	N	N
7 Cummings	?	Y	Y	Y	Y	Y
8 Van Hollen	N	Y	Y	Y	Y	Y
MASSACHUSETTS						
1 Olver	N	Y	Y	Y	Y	Y
2 Neal	N	Y	Y	Y	Y	Y
3 McGovern	N	Y	Y	Y	Y	Y
4 Frank	N	Y	Y	Y	Y	Y
5 Tsongas	N	Y	Y	Y	Y	Y
6 Tierney	N	Y	Y	Y	Y	Y
7 Markey	N	Y	Y	?	?	?
8 Capuano	N	Y	Y	Y	Y	Y
9 Lynch	N	Y	Y	Y	Y	Y
10 Delahunt	?	?	?	Y	Y	Y
MICHIGAN						
1 Stupak	N	Y	Y	Y	Y	Y
2 **Hoekstra**	Y	N	Y	N	N	N
3 **Ehlers**	Y	N	Y	N	N	N
4 **Camp**	Y	N	Y	N	N	N
5 Kildee	N	Y	Y	Y	Y	Y
6 **Upton**	Y	N	Y	N	N	N
7 **Walberg**	Y	N	Y	N	N	N
8 **Rogers**	Y	N	Y	N	N	N
9 **Knollenberg**	Y	N	Y	N	N	N
10 **Miller**	Y	Y	Y	N	N	N
11 **McCotter**	Y	N	Y	N	N	N
12 Levin	N	Y	Y	Y	Y	Y
13 Kilpatrick	N	Y	Y	Y	Y	Y
14 Conyers	N	Y	Y	Y	Y	Y
15 Dingell	N	Y	Y	Y	Y	Y
MINNESOTA						
1 Walz	N	Y	Y	Y	Y	Y
2 **Kline**	Y	N	Y	N	N	N
3 **Ramstad**	Y	N	Y	N	N	N
4 McCollum	N	Y	Y	Y	Y	Y

	189	190	191	192	193	194
5 Ellison	N	Y	Y	Y	Y	Y
6 **Bachmann**	Y	N	Y	N	N	N
7 Peterson	N	?	Y	Y	Y	Y
8 Oberstar	N	Y	Y	Y	Y	Y
MISSISSIPPI						
1 Vacant						
2 Thompson	N	Y	Y	Y	Y	Y
3 **Pickering**	Y	N	Y	N	N	N
4 Taylor	N	Y	Y	Y	Y	Y
MISSOURI						
1 Clay	N	Y	Y	Y	Y	Y
2 **Akin**	Y	N	Y	N	N	N
3 Carnahan	N	Y	Y	Y	Y	Y
4 Skelton	N	Y	Y	Y	Y	Y
5 Cleaver	N	Y	Y	Y	Y	Y
6 **Graves**	Y	N	Y	N	N	N
7 **Blunt**	Y	N	Y	N	N	N
8 **Emerson**	Y	N	Y	N	N	N
9 **Hulshof**	Y	N	Y	N	N	N
MONTANA						
AL **Rehberg**	Y	N	Y	N	N	N
NEBRASKA						
1 **Fortenberry**	Y	N	Y	N	N	N
2 **Terry**	Y	N	Y	N	N	N
3 **Smith**	Y	N	Y	N	N	N
NEVADA						
1 Berkley	N	Y	Y	Y	Y	Y
2 **Heller**	Y	N	Y	N	N	N
3 **Porter**	Y	N	Y	N	N	N
NEW HAMPSHIRE						
1 Shea-Porter	N	Y	Y	Y	Y	Y
2 Hodes	N	Y	Y	Y	Y	Y
NEW JERSEY						
1 Andrews	N	Y	Y	Y	Y	Y
2 **LoBiondo**	Y	Y	Y	N	N	N
3 **Saxton**	Y	N	Y	N	N	N
4 **Smith**	Y	Y	Y	N	N	N
5 **Garrett**	Y	N	Y	N	N	N
6 Pallone	–	+	+	Y	Y	Y
7 **Ferguson**	Y	N	Y	?	?	?
8 Pascrell	N	Y	Y	Y	Y	Y
9 Rothman	N	Y	Y	+	+	+
10 Payne	N	Y	Y	Y	Y	Y
11 **Frelinghuysen**	Y	N	Y	N	N	N
12 Holt	N	Y	Y	Y	Y	Y
13 Sires	N	Y	Y	Y	Y	Y
NEW MEXICO						
1 **Wilson**	?	?	?	?	?	?
2 **Pearce**	Y	N	Y	N	N	N
3 Udall	N	Y	Y	Y	Y	Y
NEW YORK						
1 Bishop	N	Y	Y	Y	Y	Y
2 Israel	N	Y	Y	Y	Y	Y
3 **King**	Y	N	Y	N	N	N
4 McCarthy	N	Y	Y	Y	Y	Y
5 Ackerman	N	Y	Y	Y	Y	Y
6 Meeks	N	Y	Y	Y	Y	Y
7 Crowley	N	Y	Y	Y	Y	Y
8 Nadler	N	Y	Y	Y	Y	Y
9 Weiner	N	Y	Y	Y	Y	Y
10 Towns	N	Y	Y	Y	Y	Y
11 Clarke	N	Y	Y	Y	Y	Y
12 Velázquez	N	Y	Y	Y	Y	Y
13 **Fossella**	Y	N	Y	N	N	N
14 Maloney	N	Y	Y	Y	Y	Y
15 Rangel	N	Y	?	Y	Y	Y
16 Serrano	N	Y	Y	Y	Y	Y
17 Engel	N	Y	Y	Y	Y	Y
18 Lowey	N	Y	Y	Y	Y	Y
19 Hall	N	Y	Y	Y	Y	Y
20 Gillibrand	Y	Y	Y	Y	Y	Y
21 McNulty	N	Y	Y	Y	Y	Y
22 Hinchey	N	Y	Y	Y	Y	Y
23 **McHugh**	Y	Y	Y	N	N	N
24 Arcuri	N	Y	Y	Y	Y	Y
25 **Walsh**	Y	N	Y	N	N	N
26 **Reynolds**	Y	N	Y	N	N	N
27 Higgins	N	Y	Y	Y	Y	Y
28 Slaughter	N	Y	Y	+	Y	Y
29 **Kuhl**	Y	N	Y	N	N	N
NORTH CAROLINA						
1 Butterfield	N	Y	Y	Y	Y	Y
2 Etheridge	N	Y	Y	Y	Y	Y
3 **Jones**	Y	N	Y	N	N	N
4 Price	N	Y	Y	Y	Y	Y

	189	190	191	192	193	194
5 **Foxx**	Y	N	Y	N	N	N
6 **Coble**	Y	N	Y	N	N	N
7 McIntyre	Y	Y	Y	N	Y	N
8 **Hayes**	Y	N	Y	N	N	N
9 **Myrick**	Y	N	Y	N	N	N
10 **McHenry**	Y	N	Y	N	N	N
11 Shuler	Y	Y	Y	Y	Y	Y
12 Watt	N	Y	Y	Y	Y	Y
13 Miller	N	Y	Y	Y	Y	Y
NORTH DAKOTA						
AL Pomeroy	N	Y	Y	Y	Y	Y
OHIO						
1 **Chabot**	Y	N	Y	N	N	N
2 **Schmidt**	Y	N	Y	N	N	N
3 **Turner**	Y	N	Y	N	N	N
4 **Jordan**	Y	N	Y	N	N	N
5 **Latta**	Y	N	Y	N	N	N
6 Wilson	N	Y	Y	Y	Y	Y
7 **Hobson**	Y	N	Y	N	N	N
8 **Boehner**	Y	N	Y	N	N	N
9 Kaptur	N	Y	Y	Y	Y	Y
10 Kucinich	N	Y	Y	Y	Y	Y
11 Tubbs Jones	N	Y	Y	Y	Y	Y
12 **Tiberi**	Y	N	Y	N	N	N
13 Sutton	N	Y	Y	Y	Y	Y
14 **LaTourette**	Y	Y	Y	N	N	N
15 **Pryce**	Y	N	Y	N	N	N
16 **Regula**	Y	N	Y	N	N	N
17 Ryan	N	Y	Y	Y	Y	Y
18 Space	Y	Y	Y	Y	Y	Y
OKLAHOMA						
1 **Sullivan**	Y	N	Y	N	N	N
2 Boren	Y	Y	Y	Y	Y	Y
3 **Lucas**	Y	N	Y	N	N	N
4 **Cole**	Y	N	Y	N	N	N
5 **Fallin**	Y	N	Y	N	N	N
OREGON						
1 Wu	N	Y	Y	Y	Y	Y
2 **Walden**	Y	N	Y	N	N	N
3 Blumenauer	N	Y	Y	Y	Y	Y
4 DeFazio	N	Y	Y	Y	Y	Y
5 Hooley	N	Y	Y	Y	Y	Y
PENNSYLVANIA						
1 Brady	N	Y	Y	?	?	?
2 Fattah	N	Y	Y	?	?	?
3 **English**	Y	N	Y	N	N	N
4 Altmire	Y	Y	Y	Y	Y	Y
5 **Peterson**	?	?	?	?	?	?
6 **Gerlach**	Y	N	Y	N	N	N
7 Sestak	N	Y	Y	Y	Y	Y
8 Murphy, P.	Y	Y	Y	Y	Y	Y
9 **Shuster**	Y	N	Y	N	N	N
10 Carney	Y	Y	Y	Y	Y	Y
11 Kanjorski	Y	Y	Y	Y	Y	Y
12 Murtha	N	Y	Y	Y	Y	Y
13 Schwartz	N	Y	Y	Y	Y	Y
14 Doyle	N	Y	Y	Y	Y	Y
15 **Dent**	Y	N	Y	N	N	N
16 **Pitts**	Y	N	Y	N	N	N
17 Holden	N	Y	Y	Y	Y	Y
18 **Murphy, T.**	Y	Y	Y	N	N	N
19 **Platts**	Y	N	Y	N	N	N
RHODE ISLAND						
1 Kennedy	N	Y	Y	Y	Y	Y
2 Langevin	N	Y	Y	Y	Y	Y
SOUTH CAROLINA						
1 **Brown**	Y	N	Y	N	N	N
2 **Wilson**	Y	N	Y	N	N	N
3 **Barrett**	Y	N	Y	N	N	N
4 **Inglis**	Y	N	Y	N	N	N
5 Spratt	N	Y	Y	Y	Y	Y
6 Clyburn	N	Y	Y	Y	Y	Y
SOUTH DAKOTA						
AL Herseth Sandlin	N	Y	Y	Y	Y	Y
TENNESSEE						
1 **Davis, D.**	Y	N	Y	N	N	N
2 **Duncan**	Y	N	Y	N	N	N
3 **Wamp**	Y	N	Y	N	N	N
4 Davis, L.	N	Y	Y	Y	Y	Y
5 Cooper	N	Y	Y	Y	Y	Y
6 Gordon	N	Y	Y	Y	Y	Y
7 **Blackburn**	Y	N	Y	N	N	N
8 Tanner	N	Y	Y	Y	Y	Y
9 Cohen	N	Y	Y	Y	Y	Y

	189	190	191	192	193	194
TEXAS						
1 **Gohmert**	+	?	?	N	N	N
2 **Poe**	Y	N	Y	N	N	N
3 **Johnson, S.**	Y	N	Y	N	N	N
4 **Hall**	Y	N	Y	N	N	N
5 **Hensarling**	Y	N	Y	N	N	N
6 **Barton**	Y	N	Y	N	N	N
7 **Culberson**	?	?	?	N	N	N
8 **Brady**	Y	N	Y	N	N	N
9 Green, A.	N	Y	Y	Y	Y	Y
10 **McCaul**	Y	N	Y	N	N	N
11 **Conaway**	Y	N	Y	N	N	N
12 **Granger**	Y	N	Y	N	N	N
13 **Thornberry**	Y	N	Y	N	N	N
14 **Paul**	Y	?	?	N	N	N
15 Hinojosa	N	Y	Y	Y	Y	Y
16 Reyes	N	Y	Y	Y	?	Y
17 Edwards	N	Y	Y	Y	Y	Y
18 Jackson Lee	N	Y	Y	Y	Y	Y
19 **Neugebauer**	Y	N	Y	N	N	N
20 Gonzalez	N	Y	Y	Y	Y	Y
21 **Smith**	Y	N	Y	N	N	N
22 Lampson	Y	Y	Y	N	Y	N
23 Rodriguez	N	Y	Y	Y	Y	Y
24 **Marchant**	Y	N	Y	N	N	N
25 Doggett	N	Y	Y	Y	Y	Y
26 **Burgess**	Y	N	Y	N	N	N
27 Ortiz	N	Y	Y	Y	Y	Y
28 Cuellar	N	Y	Y	Y	Y	Y
29 Green, G.	N	Y	Y	Y	Y	Y
30 Johnson, E.	N	?	Y	Y	Y	Y
31 **Carter**	Y	N	Y	N	N	N
32 **Sessions**	Y	N	Y	N	N	N
UTAH						
1 **Bishop**	Y	N	Y	N	N	N
2 Matheson	Y	Y	Y	Y	Y	Y
3 **Cannon**	Y	N	Y	N	N	N
VERMONT						
AL Welch	N	Y	Y	Y	Y	Y
VIRGINIA						
1 **Wittman**	Y	N	Y	N	N	N
2 **Drake**	Y	N	Y	N	N	N
3 Scott	N	Y	Y	Y	Y	Y
4 **Forbes**	Y	N	Y	N	N	N
5 **Goode**	Y	N	Y	N	N	N
6 **Goodlatte**	Y	N	Y	N	N	N
7 **Cantor**	Y	N	Y	N	N	N
8 Moran	N	Y	Y	Y	Y	Y
9 Boucher	N	Y	Y	Y	Y	Y
10 **Wolf**	Y	Y	Y	N	N	N
11 **Davis**	Y	Y	Y	N	N	N
WASHINGTON						
1 Inslee	N	Y	Y	Y	Y	Y
2 Larsen	N	Y	Y	Y	Y	Y
3 Baird	N	Y	Y	Y	Y	Y
4 **Hastings**	Y	N	Y	N	N	N
5 **McMorris Rodgers**	Y	N	Y	N	N	N
6 Dicks	N	Y	?	Y	Y	Y
7 McDermott	N	Y	Y	Y	Y	Y
8 **Reichert**	Y	N	Y	N	N	N
9 Smith	N	Y	Y	Y	Y	Y
WEST VIRGINIA						
1 Mollohan	N	Y	Y	Y	Y	Y
2 **Capito**	Y	Y	Y	N	N	N
3 Rahall	N	Y	Y	Y	Y	Y
WISCONSIN						
1 **Ryan**	Y	N	Y	N	N	N
2 Baldwin	N	Y	Y	Y	Y	Y
3 Kind	N	Y	Y	Y	Y	Y
4 Moore	N	Y	Y	Y	Y	Y
5 **Sensenbrenner**	Y	N	Y	N	N	N
6 **Petri**	Y	N	Y	N	N	N
7 Obey	N	Y	Y	Y	Y	Y
8 Kagen	N	Y	Y	Y	Y	Y
WYOMING						
AL **Cubin**	Y	N	Y	N	N	N
DELEGATES						
Faleomavaega (A.S.)						
Norton (D.C.)						
Bordallo (Guam)						
Fortuño (P.R.)						
Christensen (V.I.)						

IN THE HOUSE | By Vote Number

195. **HR 5715. Student Loan Access/Rule.** Adoption of the rule (H Res 1107) that would provide for House floor consideration of the bill that would increase annual loan limits on federal college loans and give the Education Department a bigger role in ensuring loan availability. Adopted 223-192: R 1-191; D 222-1 (ND 167-1, SD 55-0). April 16, 2008.

196. **HR 2634. International Debt Relief/Relief Eligibility.** Frank, D-Mass., amendment that would change the criteria for debt relief eligibility to include requirements that a country comply with minimum standards for eliminating human trafficking, cooperate with U.S. efforts to stop illegal immigration and be committed to free and fair elections. Adopted in Committee of the Whole 424-0: R 195-0; D 229-0 (ND 174-0, SD 55-0). April 16, 2008.

197. **HR 2634. International Debt Relief/Free Elections.** Rohrabacher, R-Calif., amendment that would require countries to have a government chosen by free elections in order to be eligible for debt relief. Adopted in Committee of the Whole 382-41: R 196-0; D 186-41 (ND 142-30, SD 44-11). April 16, 2008.

198. **HR 2634. International Debt Relief/Recommit.** Diaz-Balart, R-Fla., motion to recommit the bill to the Financial Services Committee with instructions that it be reported back forthwith with language that would bar countries that have business relationships with Iran from being eligible for debt relief. Motion agreed to 291-130: R 194-1; D 97-129 (ND 68-103, SD 29-26). April 16, 2008.

199. **HR 2634. International Debt Relief/Passage.** Passage of the bill that would require the Treasury Department to negotiate with the World Bank and the International Monetary Fund, as well as other lending nations, to forgive debt. Congress would have to approve any agreement that came from the negotiations. Eligible countries would be required to have a good human rights record, oppose terrorism and demonstrate a record of fighting drug trafficking. It would exclude countries with excessive military spending and forbid an aid reduction with debt relief. Passed 285-132: R 69-126; D 216-6 (ND 165-4, SD 51-2). April 16, 2008.

200. **HR 5715. Student Loan Access/Motion to Rise.** Miller, D-Calif., motion to rise from the Committee of the Whole. Motion agreed to 395-1: R 181-0; D 214-1 (ND 162-1, SD 52-0). April 16, 2008.

ND Northern Democrats, SD Southern Democrats
Southern states: Ala., Ark., Fla., Ga., Ky., La., Miss., N.C., Okla., S.C., Tenn., Texas, Va.

	195	196	197	198	199	200
ALABAMA						
1 **Bonner**	N	Y	Y	Y	N	Y
2 **Everett**	N	Y	Y	Y	N	Y
3 **Rogers**	N	Y	Y	Y	Y	Y
4 **Aderholt**	N	Y	Y	Y	N	Y
5 Cramer	Y	Y	Y	Y	Y	Y
6 **Bachus**	N	?	Y	Y	Y	?
7 Davis	Y	Y	Y	Y	Y	Y
ALASKA						
AL **Young**	N	Y	Y	Y	Y	Y
ARIZONA						
1 **Renzi**	N	Y	Y	Y	Y	?
2 **Franks**	N	Y	Y	N	N	?
3 **Shadegg**	N	Y	Y	Y	N	Y
4 Pastor	Y	Y	Y	N	Y	Y
5 Mitchell	Y	Y	Y	Y	Y	Y
6 **Flake**	N	Y	Y	N	N	Y
7 Grijalva	Y	Y	Y	N	Y	Y
8 Giffords	Y	Y	Y	Y	Y	Y
ARKANSAS						
1 Berry	Y	Y	Y	N	Y	?
2 Snyder	Y	Y	N	N	Y	Y
3 **Boozman**	N	Y	Y	Y	N	Y
4 Ross	Y	Y	Y	Y	Y	Y
CALIFORNIA						
1 Thompson	Y	Y	Y	Y	Y	Y
2 **Herger**	N	Y	Y	Y	N	Y
3 **Lungren**	N	Y	Y	Y	Y	Y
4 **Doolittle**	N	Y	Y	Y	Y	Y
5 Matsui	Y	Y	Y	Y	Y	Y
6 Woolsey	Y	Y	N	N	Y	Y
7 Miller, George	Y	Y	N	N	Y	Y
8 Pelosi					Y	
9 Lee	Y	Y	N	N	Y	Y
10 Tauscher	Y	Y	Y	Y	Y	Y
11 McNerney	Y	Y	Y	Y	Y	Y
12 Speier	Y	Y	Y	N	Y	Y
13 Stark	Y	Y	Y	N	Y	N
14 Eshoo	Y	Y	Y	N	Y	Y
15 Honda	Y	Y	N	N	Y	Y
16 Lofgren	Y	Y	Y	Y	Y	Y
17 Farr	Y	Y	Y	N	Y	Y
18 Cardoza	Y	Y	Y	Y	Y	Y
19 **Radanovich**	N	Y	Y	N	N	Y
20 Costa	Y	Y	Y	Y	Y	Y
21 **Nunes**	N	Y	Y	N	N	Y
22 **McCarthy**	N	Y	Y	Y	N	Y
23 Capps	Y	Y	Y	N	Y	Y
24 **Gallegly**	N	Y	Y	Y	N	Y
25 **McKeon**	N	Y	Y	Y	N	Y
26 **Dreier**	N	Y	Y	Y	Y	Y
27 Sherman	Y	Y	Y	P	Y	Y
28 Berman	Y	Y	Y	N	Y	?
29 Schiff	Y	Y	Y	Y	Y	Y
30 Waxman	Y	Y	Y	Y	?	Y
31 Becerra	Y	Y	Y	N	Y	Y
32 Solis	Y	Y	Y	N	Y	Y
33 Watson	Y	Y	Y	N	Y	Y
34 Roybal-Allard	Y	Y	Y	N	Y	Y
35 Waters	Y	Y	N	N	Y	Y
36 Harman	Y	Y	?	?	?	?
37 Richardson	Y	Y	N	N	Y	Y
38 Napolitano	Y	Y	Y	N	Y	Y
39 Sánchez, Linda	Y	Y	Y	N	Y	Y
40 **Royce**	N	Y	Y	Y	N	Y
41 **Lewis**	N	Y	Y	Y	Y	Y
42 **Miller, Gary**	N	Y	Y	N	N	Y
43 Baca	Y	Y	Y	Y	Y	Y
44 **Calvert**	N	Y	Y	Y	N	Y
45 **Bono Mack**	N	Y	Y	Y	N	Y
46 **Rohrabacher**	N	Y	Y	N	N	Y
47 Sanchez, Loretta	Y	Y	Y	N	Y	Y
48 **Campbell**	N	Y	Y	Y	N	Y
49 **Issa**	N	Y	Y	Y	N	Y
50 **Bilbray**	?	Y	Y	Y	N	Y
51 Filner	Y	Y	Y	N	Y	Y
52 **Hunter**	N	Y	Y	Y	N	Y
53 Davis	Y	Y	Y	Y	Y	Y

	195	196	197	198	199	200
COLORADO						
1 DeGette	Y	Y	Y	Y	Y	Y
2 Udall	Y	Y	Y	Y	Y	Y
3 Salazar	Y	Y	Y	Y	Y	Y
4 **Musgrave**	N	Y	Y	Y	N	Y
5 **Lamborn**	N	Y	Y	N	N	Y
6 **Tancredo**	N	Y	Y	Y	N	Y
7 Perlmutter	Y	Y	Y	Y	Y	Y
CONNECTICUT						
1 Larson	Y	Y	Y	N	Y	Y
2 Courtney	Y	Y	Y	Y	Y	Y
3 DeLauro	?	Y	Y	Y	Y	Y
4 **Shays**	N	Y	Y	Y	Y	Y
5 Murphy	Y	Y	Y	Y	Y	Y
DELAWARE						
AL **Castle**	Y	Y	Y	Y	Y	Y
FLORIDA						
1 **Miller**	N	Y	Y	Y	N	Y
2 Boyd	Y	Y	Y	Y	Y	Y
3 Brown	Y	?	?	?	?	?
4 **Crenshaw**	N	Y	Y	Y	N	Y
5 **Brown-Waite**	N	Y	Y	Y	N	Y
6 **Stearns**	N	Y	Y	Y	N	Y
7 **Mica**	N	Y	Y	Y	N	Y
8 **Keller**	N	Y	Y	Y	N	Y
9 **Bilirakis**	N	Y	Y	Y	N	Y
10 **Young**	N	Y	Y	Y	N	?
11 Castor	Y	Y	Y	N	Y	Y
12 **Putnam**	N	Y	Y	Y	N	Y
13 **Buchanan**	N	Y	Y	Y	N	Y
14 **Mack**	?	?	?	?	?	?
15 **Weldon**	N	Y	Y	Y	N	Y
16 Mahoney	Y	Y	Y	Y	Y	Y
17 Meek	?	?	?	?	?	?
18 **Ros-Lehtinen**	N	Y	Y	Y	N	Y
19 Wexler	?	Y	Y	Y	Y	Y
20 Wasserman Schultz	Y	Y	Y	Y	Y	Y
21 **Diaz-Balart, L.**	N	Y	Y	Y	Y	Y
22 Klein	Y	Y	Y	Y	Y	Y
23 Hastings	Y	Y	Y	N	Y	Y
24 **Feeney**	N	Y	Y	N	N	?
25 **Diaz-Balart, M.**	N	Y	Y	Y	Y	Y
GEORGIA						
1 **Kingston**	N	Y	Y	N	N	Y
2 Bishop	Y	Y	Y	N	Y	Y
3 **Westmoreland**	N	Y	Y	N	N	Y
4 Johnson	Y	Y	Y	N	Y	Y
5 Lewis	Y	Y	N	N	Y	Y
6 **Price**	N	Y	Y	Y	N	Y
7 **Linder**	N	Y	Y	Y	N	?
8 Marshall	Y	Y	Y	Y	Y	Y
9 **Deal**	N	Y	Y	N	N	Y
10 **Broun**	N	Y	Y	Y	N	Y
11 **Gingrey**	N	Y	Y	Y	N	Y
12 Barrow	Y	Y	Y	Y	Y	Y
13 Scott	Y	Y	N	N	Y	Y
HAWAII						
1 Abercrombie	Y	Y	Y	N	Y	Y
2 Hirono	Y	Y	Y	N	Y	Y
IDAHO						
1 **Sali**	N	Y	Y	Y	N	Y
2 **Simpson**	N	Y	Y	Y	Y	?
ILLINOIS						
1 Rush	?	?	?	?	?	?
2 Jackson	Y	Y	N	N	Y	Y
3 Lipinski	Y	Y	Y	Y	Y	Y
4 Gutierrez	Y	Y	N	N	Y	Y
5 Emanuel	Y	Y	Y	Y	Y	Y
6 **Roskam**	N	Y	Y	Y	N	Y
7 Davis	Y	Y	Y	Y	Y	?
8 Bean	Y	Y	Y	Y	Y	Y
9 Schakowsky	Y	Y	Y	Y	Y	Y
10 **Kirk**	N	Y	Y	Y	Y	Y
11 **Weller**	N	Y	Y	Y	Y	Y
12 Costello	Y	Y	Y	Y	Y	Y
13 **Biggert**	N	Y	Y	Y	Y	Y
14 Foster	Y	Y	Y	Y	Y	Y
15 **Johnson**	N	Y	Y	Y	N	Y

KEY **Republicans** Democrats

Y Voted for (yea)	X Paired against	C Voted "present" to avoid possible conflict of interest
# Paired for	− Announced against	
+ Announced for	P Voted "present"	? Did not vote or otherwise make a position known
N Voted against (nay)		

	195	196	197	198	199	200
16 **Manzullo**	N	Y	Y	Y	N	Y
17 Hare	Y	Y	Y	Y	Y	Y
18 **LaHood**	N	Y	Y	Y	Y	Y
19 **Shimkus**	N	Y	Y	Y	Y	Y
INDIANA						
1 Visclosky	Y	Y	Y	N	Y	Y
2 Donnelly	Y	Y	Y	Y	Y	Y
3 **Souder**	N	Y	Y	Y	N	Y
4 **Buyer**	N	Y	Y	Y	N	Y
5 **Burton**	N	Y	Y	Y	N	Y
6 **Pence**	N	Y	Y	Y	N	Y
7 Carson, A.	Y	Y	Y	Y	?	Y
8 Ellsworth	Y	Y	Y	Y	N	Y
9 Hill	N	Y	Y	Y	Y	Y
IOWA						
1 Braley	Y	Y	Y	N	Y	Y
2 Loebsack	Y	Y	Y	N	Y	Y
3 Boswell	Y	Y	Y	N	Y	Y
4 **Latham**	N	Y	Y	Y	Y	Y
5 **King**	N	Y	Y	Y	N	Y
KANSAS						
1 **Moran**	N	Y	Y	Y	N	Y
2 Boyda	Y	Y	Y	Y	Y	Y
3 Moore	Y	Y	?	Y	Y	Y
4 **Tiahrt**	N	Y	Y	Y	N	Y
KENTUCKY						
1 **Whitfield**	N	Y	Y	Y	N	Y
2 **Lewis**	N	Y	Y	Y	N	Y
3 Yarmuth	Y	Y	Y	Y	Y	Y
4 **Davis**	N	Y	Y	Y	Y	Y
5 **Rogers**	N	Y	Y	Y	N	Y
6 Chandler	Y	Y	Y	Y	Y	Y
LOUISIANA						
1 Vacant						
2 Jefferson	Y	Y	Y	N	Y	Y
3 Melancon	Y	Y	Y	Y	?	Y
4 **McCrery**	N	Y	Y	Y	Y	?
5 **Alexander**	N	Y	Y	Y	Y	Y
6 Vacant						
7 **Boustany**	N	Y	Y	Y	Y	Y
MAINE						
1 Allen	Y	Y	Y	N	Y	Y
2 Michaud	Y	Y	Y	N	Y	Y
MARYLAND						
1 **Gilchrest**	N	Y	Y	N	Y	Y
2 Ruppersberger	Y	Y	Y	Y	Y	Y
3 Sarbanes	Y	Y	Y	N	Y	Y
4 Wynn	?	?	N	N	Y	?
5 Hoyer	Y	Y	Y	N	Y	Y
6 **Bartlett**	N	Y	Y	Y	N	Y
7 Cummings	Y	Y	Y	N	Y	Y
8 Van Hollen	Y	Y	Y	N	Y	Y
MASSACHUSETTS						
1 Olver	Y	Y	N	N	Y	Y
2 Neal	Y	Y	Y	N	Y	Y
3 McGovern	Y	Y	N	N	Y	Y
4 Frank	Y	Y	Y	N	Y	Y
5 Tsongas	Y	Y	N	N	Y	Y
6 Tierney	Y	Y	Y	N	Y	?
7 Markey	Y	Y	Y	N	Y	?
8 Capuano	Y	Y	N	N	Y	Y
9 Lynch	Y	Y	Y	Y	Y	Y
10 Delahunt	Y	Y	Y	N	Y	Y
MICHIGAN						
1 Stupak	Y	Y	Y	N	Y	Y
2 **Hoekstra**	N	Y	Y	Y	N	Y
3 **Ehlers**	N	Y	Y	Y	Y	Y
4 **Camp**	N	Y	Y	Y	Y	Y
5 Kildee	Y	Y	Y	Y	Y	Y
6 **Upton**	N	Y	Y	Y	Y	Y
7 **Walberg**	N	Y	Y	Y	N	Y
8 **Rogers**	N	Y	Y	Y	N	Y
9 **Knollenberg**	N	Y	Y	Y	Y	Y
10 **Miller**	N	Y	Y	Y	Y	Y
11 **McCotter**	N	Y	Y	Y	Y	Y
12 Levin	Y	Y	Y	N	Y	Y
13 Kilpatrick	Y	Y	N	N	Y	Y
14 Conyers	Y	Y	Y	N	Y	+
15 Dingell	Y	Y	Y	N	Y	Y
MINNESOTA						
1 Walz	Y	Y	Y	Y	Y	Y
2 **Kline**	N	Y	Y	Y	N	Y
3 **Ramstad**	N	Y	Y	Y	Y	Y
4 McCollum	Y	Y	Y	N	Y	Y

	195	196	197	198	199	200
5 Ellison	Y	Y	P	N	Y	Y
6 **Bachmann**	N	Y	Y	Y	N	Y
7 Peterson	Y	Y	Y	N	Y	Y
8 Oberstar	Y	Y	Y	N	Y	Y
MISSISSIPPI						
1 Vacant						
2 Thompson	Y	Y	Y	N	Y	Y
3 **Pickering**	N	Y	Y	Y	Y	?
4 Taylor	Y	Y	Y	Y	N	Y
MISSOURI						
1 Clay	Y	Y	Y	N	Y	Y
2 **Akin**	N	Y	Y	Y	N	Y
3 Carnahan	Y	Y	Y	Y	Y	Y
4 Skelton	Y	Y	Y	N	Y	Y
5 Cleaver	Y	Y	N	N	Y	Y
6 **Graves**	N	Y	Y	Y	N	Y
7 **Blunt**	N	Y	Y	Y	N	Y
8 **Emerson**	N	Y	Y	Y	Y	Y
9 **Hulshof**	N	Y	Y	Y	N	?
MONTANA						
AL **Rehberg**	N	Y	Y	Y	Y	Y
NEBRASKA						
1 **Fortenberry**	N	Y	Y	Y	Y	Y
2 **Terry**	N	Y	Y	Y	Y	Y
3 **Smith**	N	Y	Y	Y	N	Y
NEVADA						
1 Berkley	Y	Y	Y	Y	Y	Y
2 **Heller**	N	Y	Y	Y	N	Y
3 **Porter**	N	Y	Y	Y	Y	Y
NEW HAMPSHIRE						
1 Shea-Porter	Y	Y	Y	N	Y	Y
2 Hodes	Y	Y	Y	Y	Y	Y
NEW JERSEY						
1 Andrews	Y	Y	Y	N	Y	Y
2 **LoBiondo**	N	Y	Y	Y	N	Y
3 **Saxton**	N	Y	Y	Y	N	Y
4 **Smith**	N	Y	Y	Y	Y	Y
5 **Garrett**	N	Y	Y	Y	Y	Y
6 Pallone	Y	Y	Y	N	Y	Y
7 **Ferguson**	?	Y	Y	Y	Y	Y
8 Pascrell	Y	Y	Y	N	Y	Y
9 Rothman	+	Y	Y	N	Y	Y
10 Payne	Y	Y	N	N	Y	Y
11 **Frelinghuysen**	N	Y	Y	Y	Y	Y
12 Holt	+	Y	Y	N	Y	Y
13 Sires	Y	Y	Y	N	Y	Y
NEW MEXICO						
1 **Wilson**	?	?	?	?	?	?
2 **Pearce**	N	Y	Y	Y	Y	Y
3 Udall	Y	Y	Y	Y	Y	Y
NEW YORK						
1 Bishop	Y	Y	Y	N	Y	Y
2 Israel	Y	Y	Y	N	Y	Y
3 **King**	N	Y	Y	Y	Y	Y
4 McCarthy	Y	Y	Y	N	Y	Y
5 Ackerman	Y	Y	Y	N	Y	Y
6 Meeks	Y	Y	Y	N	Y	Y
7 Crowley	Y	Y	Y	N	Y	Y
8 Nadler	Y	Y	N	Y	Y	Y
9 Weiner	Y	Y	Y	Y	Y	?
10 Towns	Y	Y	N	Y	Y	Y
11 Clarke	Y	Y	P	N	Y	Y
12 Velázquez	Y	Y	Y	N	Y	Y
13 **Fossella**	N	Y	Y	Y	N	Y
14 Maloney	Y	Y	Y	Y	Y	Y
15 Rangel	Y	Y	Y	N	Y	Y
16 Serrano	Y	Y	N	N	Y	Y
17 Engel	Y	Y	Y	Y	Y	Y
18 Lowey	Y	Y	Y	Y	Y	Y
19 Hall	Y	Y	Y	Y	+	Y
20 Gillibrand	Y	?	Y	Y	N	Y
21 McNulty	Y	Y	N	N	Y	Y
22 Hinchey	Y	Y	N	N	Y	Y
23 **McHugh**	N	Y	Y	Y	Y	Y
24 Arcuri	Y	Y	Y	Y	Y	Y
25 **Walsh**	N	Y	Y	Y	Y	Y
26 **Reynolds**	N	Y	Y	Y	N	Y
27 Higgins	Y	Y	Y	N	Y	Y
28 Slaughter	Y	Y	Y	N	+	?
29 **Kuhl**	N	Y	Y	Y	Y	Y
NORTH CAROLINA						
1 Butterfield	Y	Y	N	N	Y	Y
2 Etheridge	Y	Y	Y	N	Y	Y
3 **Jones**	N	Y	Y	Y	N	Y
4 Price	Y	Y	N	N	Y	Y

	195	196	197	198	199	200
5 **Foxx**	–	Y	Y	Y	N	Y
6 **Coble**	N	Y	Y	Y	N	Y
7 McIntyre	Y	Y	Y	Y	Y	Y
8 **Hayes**	N	Y	Y	Y	N	Y
9 **Myrick**	N	Y	Y	Y	N	Y
10 **McHenry**	N	Y	Y	Y	N	Y
11 Shuler	Y	Y	Y	Y	Y	Y
12 Watt	Y	Y	N	N	Y	?
13 Miller	Y	Y	Y	N	Y	Y
NORTH DAKOTA						
AL Pomeroy	Y	Y	Y	N	Y	Y
OHIO						
1 **Chabot**	N	Y	Y	Y	N	Y
2 **Schmidt**	N	Y	Y	Y	Y	Y
3 **Turner**	N	Y	Y	Y	Y	Y
4 **Jordan**	N	Y	Y	Y	N	Y
5 **Latta**	N	Y	Y	Y	N	Y
6 Wilson	Y	Y	Y	N	Y	Y
7 **Hobson**	N	Y	Y	Y	Y	Y
8 **Boehner**	N	Y	Y	Y	N	Y
9 Kaptur	Y	Y	Y	Y	Y	Y
10 Kucinich	Y	Y	N	N	Y	Y
11 Tubbs Jones	Y	Y	N	N	Y	Y
12 **Tiberi**	N	Y	Y	Y	N	Y
13 Sutton	Y	Y	Y	N	Y	Y
14 **LaTourette**	N	Y	Y	Y	Y	Y
15 **Pryce**	N	Y	Y	Y	Y	Y
16 **Regula**	N	Y	Y	Y	N	Y
17 Ryan	Y	Y	Y	N	Y	Y
18 Space	Y	Y	Y	Y	Y	Y
OKLAHOMA						
1 **Sullivan**	N	Y	Y	Y	N	?
2 Boren	Y	Y	Y	Y	Y	Y
3 **Lucas**	N	Y	Y	Y	Y	Y
4 **Cole**	N	Y	Y	Y	Y	Y
5 **Fallin**	N	Y	Y	Y	Y	Y
OREGON						
1 Wu	Y	Y	Y	N	Y	Y
2 **Walden**	N	Y	Y	Y	Y	Y
3 Blumenauer	Y	Y	N	N	Y	Y
4 DeFazio	Y	Y	Y	Y	Y	Y
5 Hooley	Y	Y	Y	Y	Y	Y
PENNSYLVANIA						
1 Brady	?	?	?	?	?	?
2 Fattah	?	?	?	?	+	?
3 **English**	N	Y	Y	Y	Y	Y
4 Altmire	Y	Y	Y	Y	N	Y
5 **Peterson**	?	?	?	?	?	?
6 **Gerlach**	N	Y	Y	Y	Y	Y
7 Sestak	Y	Y	Y	Y	Y	?
8 Murphy, P.	Y	Y	Y	Y	Y	Y
9 **Shuster**	N	Y	Y	Y	N	Y
10 Carney	Y	Y	Y	Y	N	Y
11 Kanjorski	Y	Y	Y	Y	Y	Y
12 Murtha	Y	Y	Y	N	Y	Y
13 Schwartz	?	Y	Y	Y	Y	Y
14 Doyle	Y	Y	Y	N	Y	Y
15 **Dent**	N	Y	Y	Y	N	Y
16 **Pitts**	N	Y	Y	Y	N	Y
17 Holden	Y	Y	Y	Y	Y	Y
18 **Murphy, T.**	N	Y	Y	Y	Y	Y
19 **Platts**	N	Y	Y	Y	N	?
RHODE ISLAND						
1 Kennedy	Y	Y	Y	Y	Y	Y
2 Langevin	Y	Y	Y	Y	Y	Y
SOUTH CAROLINA						
1 **Brown**	N	Y	Y	Y	Y	Y
2 **Wilson**	N	Y	Y	Y	N	Y
3 **Barrett**	N	Y	Y	Y	N	Y
4 **Inglis**	N	Y	Y	Y	Y	Y
5 Spratt	Y	Y	Y	N	Y	?
6 Clyburn	Y	Y	Y	N	Y	Y
SOUTH DAKOTA						
AL Herseth Sandlin	Y	Y	Y	Y	Y	Y
TENNESSEE						
1 **Davis, D.**	N	Y	Y	Y	N	Y
2 **Duncan**	N	Y	Y	Y	N	Y
3 **Wamp**	N	Y	Y	Y	N	Y
4 Davis, L.	Y	Y	Y	Y	Y	Y
5 Cooper	Y	Y	Y	N	Y	Y
6 Gordon	Y	Y	Y	Y	?	Y
7 **Blackburn**	N	Y	Y	Y	N	Y
8 Tanner	Y	Y	Y	Y	Y	Y
9 Cohen	Y	Y	N	Y	Y	Y

	195	196	197	198	199	200
TEXAS						
1 **Gohmert**	N	Y	Y	Y	N	Y
2 **Poe**	N	Y	Y	Y	N	Y
3 **Johnson, S.**	N	Y	Y	Y	N	Y
4 **Hall**	N	Y	Y	Y	N	Y
5 **Hensarling**	N	Y	Y	Y	N	Y
6 **Barton**	N	Y	Y	Y	N	Y
7 **Culberson**	N	Y	Y	Y	N	Y
8 **Brady**	N	Y	Y	Y	N	Y
9 Green, A.	Y	Y	Y	Y	Y	Y
10 **McCaul**	N	Y	Y	Y	Y	Y
11 **Conaway**	N	Y	Y	Y	N	Y
12 **Granger**	N	Y	Y	Y	N	Y
13 **Thornberry**	N	Y	Y	Y	N	Y
14 **Paul**	N	Y	Y	Y	N	Y
15 Hinojosa	Y	Y	Y	N	Y	Y
16 Reyes	Y	Y	Y	Y	Y	Y
17 Edwards	Y	Y	Y	Y	Y	Y
18 Jackson Lee	Y	Y	N	N	Y	Y
19 **Neugebauer**	N	Y	Y	Y	N	Y
20 Gonzalez	Y	Y	Y	N	Y	Y
21 **Smith**	N	Y	Y	Y	N	Y
22 Lampson	Y	Y	Y	Y	N	Y
23 Rodriguez	Y	Y	Y	Y	Y	Y
24 **Marchant**	N	Y	Y	Y	N	Y
25 Doggett	Y	Y	Y	N	Y	Y
26 **Burgess**	N	Y	Y	Y	N	Y
27 Ortiz	Y	Y	N	Y	Y	Y
28 Cuellar	Y	Y	Y	N	Y	Y
29 Green, G.	Y	Y	Y	Y	Y	Y
30 Johnson, E.	Y	Y	N	N	Y	Y
31 **Carter**	N	Y	Y	Y	N	Y
32 **Sessions**	N	Y	Y	Y	N	Y
UTAH						
1 **Bishop**	N	Y	Y	Y	N	?
2 Matheson	Y	Y	Y	Y	Y	Y
3 **Cannon**	N	Y	Y	Y	N	Y
VERMONT						
AL Welch	Y	Y	Y	N	Y	Y
VIRGINIA						
1 **Wittman**	N	Y	Y	Y	Y	Y
2 **Drake**	N	Y	Y	Y	N	Y
3 Scott	Y	Y	Y	N	Y	Y
4 **Forbes**	N	Y	Y	Y	N	Y
5 **Goode**	N	Y	Y	Y	N	Y
6 **Goodlatte**	N	Y	Y	Y	N	Y
7 **Cantor**	N	Y	Y	Y	N	Y
8 Moran	Y	Y	N	N	Y	Y
9 Boucher	Y	Y	Y	Y	Y	Y
10 **Wolf**	N	Y	Y	Y	Y	Y
11 **Davis**	N	Y	Y	Y	N	Y
WASHINGTON						
1 Inslee	Y	Y	Y	N	Y	Y
2 Larsen	Y	Y	Y	N	Y	Y
3 Baird	Y	Y	Y	N	Y	Y
4 **Hastings**	N	Y	Y	Y	N	Y
5 **McMorris Rodgers**	N	Y	Y	Y	N	Y
6 Dicks	Y	Y	Y	Y	Y	?
7 McDermott	Y	Y	N	N	Y	Y
8 **Reichert**	N	Y	Y	Y	Y	Y
9 Smith	Y	Y	Y	N	Y	Y
WEST VIRGINIA						
1 Mollohan	Y	Y	N	N	Y	Y
2 **Capito**	N	Y	Y	Y	Y	Y
3 Rahall	Y	Y	N	N	Y	?
WISCONSIN						
1 **Ryan**	N	Y	Y	Y	N	Y
2 Baldwin	Y	Y	N	N	Y	Y
3 Kind	Y	Y	Y	N	Y	Y
4 Moore	Y	Y	N	N	Y	Y
5 **Sensenbrenner**	N	Y	Y	Y	N	Y
6 **Petri**	N	Y	Y	Y	N	Y
7 Obey	Y	Y	N	N	Y	Y
8 Kagen	Y	Y	Y	Y	Y	Y
WYOMING						
AL **Cubin**	N	Y	Y	Y	Y	Y
DELEGATES						
Faleomavaega (A.S.)	?	?				?
Norton (D.C.)	Y	Y				Y
Bordallo (Guam)	Y	Y				Y
Fortuño (P.R.)	Y	Y				?
Christensen (V.I.)	Y	Y				?

IN THE HOUSE | By Vote Number

201. **HR 2537. Beach Protection Act/Ruling of the Chair.** Judgment of the House to sustain the ruling of the chair to uphold the Johnson, D-Texas, point of order that the Fossella, R-N.Y., amendment was not germane. The Fossella amendment would add the text of the Senate-passed bill (HR 3773) that would amend the Foreign Intelligence Surveillance Act. Ruling of the chair upheld 216-193: R 1-190; D 215-3 (ND 163-1, SD 52-2). April 16, 2008.

202. **H Res 1097. National Child Abuse Prevention Month/Adoption.** Woolsey, D-Calif., motion to suspend the rules and adopt the resolution that would express support for designating National Child Abuse Prevention Month. Motion agreed to 410-0: R 191-0; D 219-0 (ND 165-0, SD 54-0). A two-thirds majority of those present and voting (274 in this case) is required for adoption under suspension of the rules. April 16, 2008.

203. **HR 5715. Student Loan Access/Loan Qualifications.** Miller, D-Calif., amendment that would target loan limit increases to students in the most need, clarify that the Education secretary can determine whether a school qualifies for loan help and specify that income from loan sales would be used to make new loans, among other provisions. Adopted in Committee of the Whole 413-0: R 189-0; D 224-0 (ND 172-0, SD 52-0). April 17, 2008.

204. **HR 5715. Student Loan Access/Passage.** Passage of the bill that would increase annual loan limits on federal college loans and give the Education Department a bigger role in ensuring loan availability. The bill would increase the amount of federal loans undergraduates can borrow from $23,000 to $31,000. Students who are not dependents could borrow up to $57,500, up from $46,000. It would allow the Education Department to buy up existing loans at a discount and would codify the department's ability to advance funds to guarantee agencies. Passed 383-27: R 161-27; D 222-0 (ND 171-0, SD 51-0). April 17, 2008.

	201	202	203	204
ALABAMA				
1 **Bonner**	N	Y	Y	Y
2 **Everett**	N	Y	Y	Y
3 **Rogers**	N	Y	Y	Y
4 **Aderholt**	N	Y	Y	Y
5 Cramer	Y	Y	Y	Y
6 **Bachus**	N	Y	Y	Y
7 Davis	Y	Y	Y	Y
ALASKA				
AL **Young**	N	Y	?	?
ARIZONA				
1 **Renzi**	N	Y	Y	Y
2 **Franks**	N	Y	Y	N
3 **Shadegg**	N	Y	?	?
4 Pastor	Y	Y	Y	Y
5 Mitchell	Y	Y	Y	Y
6 **Flake**	N	Y	Y	N
7 Grijalva	Y	Y	Y	Y
8 Giffords	Y	Y	Y	Y
ARKANSAS				
1 Berry	?	?	Y	Y
2 Snyder	Y	Y	Y	Y
3 **Boozman**	N	Y	Y	Y
4 Ross	Y	Y	Y	Y
CALIFORNIA				
1 Thompson	Y	Y	Y	Y
2 **Herger**	N	Y	Y	N
3 **Lungren**	N	Y	Y	Y
4 **Doolittle**	N	Y	Y	Y
5 Matsui	Y	Y	Y	Y
6 Woolsey	Y	Y	Y	Y
7 Miller, George	Y	Y	Y	Y
8 Pelosi				
9 Lee	Y	Y	Y	Y
10 Tauscher	Y	Y	Y	Y
11 McNerney	Y	Y	Y	Y
12 Speier	Y	Y	Y	Y
13 Stark	Y	Y	Y	Y
14 Eshoo	Y	Y	Y	Y
15 Honda	Y	Y	Y	Y
16 Lofgren	Y	Y	Y	Y
17 Farr	Y	Y	Y	Y
18 Cardoza	Y	Y	Y	Y
19 **Radanovich**	N	Y	Y	Y
20 Costa	Y	Y	Y	Y
21 **Nunes**	N	Y	Y	Y
22 **McCarthy**	N	Y	Y	Y
23 Capps	Y	Y	Y	Y
24 **Gallegly**	N	Y	Y	Y
25 **McKeon**	N	Y	Y	Y
26 **Dreier**	N	Y	Y	Y
27 Sherman	Y	Y	Y	Y
28 Berman	Y	Y	Y	Y
29 Schiff	Y	Y	Y	Y
30 Waxman	Y	Y	Y	Y
31 Becerra	Y	Y	Y	Y
32 Solis	Y	Y	Y	Y
33 Watson	Y	Y	Y	Y
34 Roybal-Allard	Y	Y	Y	Y
35 Waters	Y	Y	Y	Y
36 Harman	?	Y	Y	Y
37 Richardson	Y	Y	Y	Y
38 Napolitano	+	Y	Y	Y
39 Sánchez, Linda	Y	Y	Y	Y
40 **Royce**	N	Y	Y	Y
41 **Lewis**	N	Y	Y	Y
42 **Miller, Gary**	N	Y	Y	Y
43 Baca	Y	Y	Y	Y
44 **Calvert**	N	Y	Y	Y
45 **Bono Mack**	N	Y	Y	Y
46 **Rohrabacher**	N	Y	Y	Y
47 Sanchez, Loretta	Y	Y	Y	Y
48 **Campbell**	N	Y	N	N
49 **Issa**	N	Y	Y	Y
50 **Bilbray**	N	Y	Y	Y
51 Filner	+	Y	Y	Y
52 **Hunter**	N	Y	Y	Y
53 Davis	Y	Y	Y	Y

	201	202	203	204
COLORADO				
1 DeGette	Y	Y	Y	Y
2 Udall	Y	Y	Y	Y
3 Salazar	Y	Y	Y	Y
4 **Musgrave**	N	Y	Y	Y
5 **Lamborn**	N	Y	Y	N
6 **Tancredo**	N	Y	Y	N
7 Perlmutter	Y	Y	Y	Y
CONNECTICUT				
1 Larson	Y	Y	Y	Y
2 Courtney	Y	Y	Y	Y
3 DeLauro	Y	Y	Y	Y
4 **Shays**	N	Y	Y	Y
5 Murphy	Y	Y	Y	Y
DELAWARE				
AL **Castle**	N	Y	Y	Y
FLORIDA				
1 **Miller**	N	Y	Y	N
2 Boyd	Y	Y	Y	Y
3 Brown	?	?	?	?
4 **Crenshaw**	N	Y	Y	Y
5 **Brown-Waite**	N	Y	?	Y
6 **Stearns**	N	Y	Y	Y
7 **Mica**	N	Y	Y	Y
8 **Keller**	N	Y	Y	Y
9 **Bilirakis**	N	Y	Y	Y
10 **Young**	N	Y	Y	Y
11 Castor	Y	Y	Y	Y
12 **Putnam**	N	Y	Y	Y
13 **Buchanan**	N	Y	Y	Y
14 **Mack**	?	?	?	?
15 **Weldon**	N	Y	Y	Y
16 Mahoney	Y	Y	+	+
17 Meek	?	?	Y	Y
18 **Ros-Lehtinen**	N	Y	Y	Y
19 Wexler	Y	Y	Y	Y
20 Wasserman Schultz	Y	Y	Y	Y
21 **Diaz-Balart, L.**	Y	Y	Y	Y
22 Klein	Y	Y	Y	Y
23 Hastings	Y	Y	Y	Y
24 **Feeney**	?	?	Y	Y
25 **Diaz-Balart, M.**	N	Y	Y	Y
GEORGIA				
1 **Kingston**	N	Y	Y	N
2 Bishop	Y	Y	?	?
3 **Westmoreland**	N	Y	Y	N
4 Johnson	Y	Y	Y	Y
5 Lewis	Y	Y	Y	Y
6 **Price**	N	Y	Y	N
7 **Linder**	N	Y	Y	Y
8 Marshall	Y	Y	Y	?
9 **Deal**	N	Y	Y	N
10 **Broun**	N	Y	Y	–
11 **Gingrey**	N	Y	Y	N
12 Barrow	N	Y	Y	Y
13 Scott	Y	Y	?	Y
HAWAII				
1 Abercrombie	Y	Y	Y	Y
2 Hirono	Y	Y	Y	Y
IDAHO				
1 **Sali**	N	Y	Y	Y
2 **Simpson**	?	?	Y	Y
ILLINOIS				
1 Rush	?	?	?	?
2 Jackson	Y	Y	Y	Y
3 Lipinski	Y	Y	Y	Y
4 Gutierrez	Y	Y	Y	Y
5 Emanuel	Y	Y	Y	Y
6 **Roskam**	N	Y	Y	Y
7 Davis	Y	Y	Y	Y
8 Bean	Y	Y	Y	Y
9 Schakowsky	Y	Y	Y	Y
10 **Kirk**	N	Y	Y	Y
11 **Weller**	N	Y	Y	Y
12 Costello	Y	Y	Y	Y
13 **Biggert**	N	Y	Y	Y
14 Foster	Y	Y	Y	Y
15 **Johnson**	N	Y	Y	Y

KEY **Republicans** Democrats

Y Voted for (yea)	X Paired against
# Paired for	– Announced against
+ Announced for	P Voted "present"
N Voted against (nay)	
C Voted "present" to avoid possible conflict of interest	
? Did not vote or otherwise make a position known	

ND Northern Democrats, SD Southern Democrats
Southern states: Ala., Ark., Fla., Ga., Ky., La., Miss., N.C., Okla., S.C., Tenn., Texas, Va.

	201	202	203	204
16 Manzullo	N	Y	Y	Y
17 Hare	Y	Y	Y	Y
18 LaHood	N	Y	Y	Y
19 Shimkus	N	Y	Y	Y
INDIANA				
1 Visclosky	Y	Y	Y	Y
2 Donnelly	Y	Y	Y	Y
3 Souder	N	Y	Y	Y
4 Buyer	N	Y	Y	Y
5 Burton	N	Y	Y	Y
6 Pence	N	Y	Y	N
7 Carson, A.	Y	Y	Y	Y
8 Ellsworth	Y	Y	Y	Y
9 Hill	Y	Y	Y	Y
IOWA				
1 Braley	Y	Y	Y	Y
2 Loebsack	Y	Y	Y	Y
3 Boswell	Y	Y	Y	Y
4 Latham	Y	Y	Y	Y
5 King	N	Y	Y	N
KANSAS				
1 Moran	N	Y	Y	Y
2 Boyda	Y	Y	Y	Y
3 Moore	Y	Y	Y	Y
4 Tiahrt	N	Y	Y	Y
KENTUCKY				
1 Whitfield	N	Y	Y	Y
2 Lewis	N	Y	Y	Y
3 Yarmuth	Y	Y	Y	Y
4 Davis	N	Y	Y	Y
5 Rogers	N	Y	Y	Y
6 Chandler	Y	Y	Y	Y
LOUISIANA				
1 Vacant				
2 Jefferson	Y	Y	Y	Y
3 Melancon	Y	Y	Y	Y
4 McCrery	N	Y	Y	Y
5 Alexander	N	Y	Y	Y
6 Vacant				
7 Boustany	N	Y	Y	Y
MAINE				
1 Allen	Y	Y	Y	Y
2 Michaud	Y	Y	Y	Y
MARYLAND				
1 Gilchrest	N	Y	Y	Y
2 Ruppersberger	Y	Y	Y	Y
3 Sarbanes	Y	Y	Y	Y
4 Wynn	?	Y	?	?
5 Hoyer	Y	Y	Y	Y
6 Bartlett	N	Y	Y	Y
7 Cummings	Y	Y	Y	Y
8 Van Hollen	Y	Y	Y	Y
MASSACHUSETTS				
1 Olver	Y	Y	Y	Y
2 Neal	Y	Y	Y	Y
3 McGovern	Y	Y	Y	Y
4 Frank	Y	Y	Y	Y
5 Tsongas	Y	Y	Y	Y
6 Tierney	?	?	Y	Y
7 Markey	Y	Y	?	?
8 Capuano	Y	Y	Y	Y
9 Lynch	Y	Y	?	Y
10 Delahunt	Y	Y	Y	Y
MICHIGAN				
1 Stupak	Y	Y	Y	Y
2 Hoekstra	N	Y	Y	Y
3 Ehlers	N	Y	Y	Y
4 Camp	N	Y	Y	Y
5 Kildee	Y	Y	Y	Y
6 Upton	N	Y	Y	Y
7 Walberg	N	Y	Y	Y
8 Rogers	N	Y	Y	Y
9 Knollenberg	N	Y	Y	Y
10 Miller	N	Y	Y	Y
11 McCotter	N	Y	Y	Y
12 Levin	Y	Y	Y	Y
13 Kilpatrick	Y	Y	Y	Y
14 Conyers	Y	Y	Y	Y
15 Dingell	Y	Y	Y	Y
MINNESOTA				
1 Walz	Y	Y	Y	Y
2 Kline	N	Y	Y	Y
3 Ramstad	N	Y	Y	Y
4 McCollum	Y	Y	Y	Y

	201	202	203	204
5 Ellison	Y	Y	Y	Y
6 Bachmann	N	Y	Y	Y
7 Peterson	Y	Y	Y	Y
8 Oberstar	Y	Y	Y	Y
MISSISSIPPI				
1 Vacant				
2 Thompson	Y	Y	Y	Y
3 Pickering	?	?	Y	Y
4 Taylor	Y	Y	Y	Y
MISSOURI				
1 Clay	Y	Y	Y	Y
2 Akin	N	Y	Y	N
3 Carnahan	Y	Y	Y	Y
4 Skelton	Y	Y	Y	Y
5 Cleaver	Y	Y	Y	Y
6 Graves	N	Y	Y	Y
7 Blunt	N	Y	Y	Y
8 Emerson	N	Y	Y	Y
9 Hulshof	N	Y	?	?
MONTANA				
AL Rehberg	N	Y	Y	Y
NEBRASKA				
1 Fortenberry	N	Y	Y	Y
2 Terry	N	Y	Y	Y
3 Smith	N	Y	Y	Y
NEVADA				
1 Berkley	Y	Y	?	?
2 Heller	N	Y	Y	Y
3 Porter	N	Y	Y	Y
NEW HAMPSHIRE				
1 Shea-Porter	Y	Y	Y	Y
2 Hodes	Y	Y	Y	Y
NEW JERSEY				
1 Andrews	Y	Y	Y	Y
2 LoBiondo	N	Y	Y	Y
3 Saxton	N	Y	Y	Y
4 Smith	N	Y	Y	Y
5 Garrett	N	Y	Y	Y
6 Pallone	Y	Y	?	?
7 Ferguson	N	Y	Y	Y
8 Pascrell	Y	Y	Y	Y
9 Rothman	Y	Y	Y	Y
10 Payne	Y	Y	Y	Y
11 Frelinghuysen	N	Y	Y	Y
12 Holt	Y	Y	Y	Y
13 Sires	Y	Y	Y	Y
NEW MEXICO				
1 Wilson	?	?	?	?
2 Pearce	N	Y	Y	Y
3 Udall	Y	Y	Y	Y
NEW YORK				
1 Bishop	Y	Y	Y	Y
2 Israel	Y	Y	Y	Y
3 King	N	Y	Y	Y
4 McCarthy	Y	Y	Y	Y
5 Ackerman	Y	?	Y	Y
6 Meeks	Y	Y	Y	Y
7 Crowley	Y	Y	Y	Y
8 Nadler	Y	Y	Y	Y
9 Weiner	?	?	Y	Y
10 Towns	Y	Y	?	Y
11 Clarke	Y	Y	Y	Y
12 Velázquez	Y	Y	Y	Y
13 Fossella	N	Y	Y	Y
14 Maloney	Y	Y	Y	Y
15 Rangel	?	?	Y	Y
16 Serrano	Y	Y	Y	Y
17 Engel	Y	Y	Y	Y
18 Lowey	Y	Y	Y	Y
19 Hall	Y	Y	Y	Y
20 Gillibrand	Y	Y	Y	Y
21 McNulty	Y	Y	Y	Y
22 Hinchey	Y	Y	Y	Y
23 McHugh	+	Y	Y	+
24 Arcuri	Y	Y	Y	Y
25 Walsh	N	Y	Y	Y
26 Reynolds	N	Y	Y	Y
27 Higgins	Y	Y	Y	Y
28 Slaughter	+	Y	Y	Y
29 Kuhl	N	Y	Y	Y
NORTH CAROLINA				
1 Butterfield	Y	Y	?	?
2 Etheridge	Y	Y	Y	Y
3 Jones	N	Y	Y	Y
4 Price	Y	Y	Y	Y

	201	202	203	204
5 Foxx	N	Y	Y	N
6 Coble	N	Y	Y	Y
7 McIntyre	Y	Y	Y	Y
8 Hayes	N	Y	Y	Y
9 Myrick	N	Y	Y	Y
10 McHenry	N	Y	Y	N
11 Shuler	Y	Y	Y	Y
12 Watt	Y	Y	Y	Y
13 Miller	Y	Y	Y	Y
NORTH DAKOTA				
AL Pomeroy	Y	Y	Y	Y
OHIO				
1 Chabot	N	Y	Y	Y
2 Schmidt	N	Y	Y	Y
3 Turner	N	Y	Y	Y
4 Jordan	N	Y	Y	N
5 Latta	N	Y	Y	Y
6 Wilson	Y	Y	Y	Y
7 Hobson	N	Y	Y	Y
8 Boehner	N	Y	Y	Y
9 Kaptur	Y	Y	Y	Y
10 Kucinich	Y	Y	Y	Y
11 Tubbs Jones	Y	Y	Y	Y
12 Tiberi	N	Y	Y	Y
13 Sutton	Y	Y	Y	Y
14 LaTourette	N	Y	Y	Y
15 Pryce	N	Y	Y	Y
16 Regula	N	Y	Y	Y
17 Ryan	Y	Y	Y	Y
18 Space	Y	Y	Y	Y
OKLAHOMA				
1 Sullivan	N	Y	Y	Y
2 Boren	Y	Y	Y	Y
3 Lucas	N	Y	Y	Y
4 Cole	N	Y	+	Y
5 Fallin	N	Y	Y	Y
OREGON				
1 Wu	Y	Y	Y	Y
2 Walden	N	Y	Y	Y
3 Blumenauer	Y	Y	Y	Y
4 DeFazio	Y	?	Y	Y
5 Hooley	Y	Y	Y	Y
PENNSYLVANIA				
1 Brady	?	?	Y	Y
2 Fattah	?	?	Y	Y
3 English	N	Y	Y	Y
4 Altmire	Y	Y	Y	Y
5 Peterson	?	?	?	?
6 Gerlach	N	Y	Y	Y
7 Sestak	?	?	Y	Y
8 Murphy, P.	Y	Y	Y	Y
9 Shuster	N	Y	Y	Y
10 Carney	Y	Y	Y	Y
11 Kanjorski	Y	Y	Y	Y
12 Murtha	Y	Y	Y	Y
13 Schwartz	?	?	Y	Y
14 Doyle	Y	Y	Y	Y
15 Dent	N	Y	Y	Y
16 Pitts	N	Y	Y	Y
17 Holden	Y	Y	Y	Y
18 Murphy, T.	N	Y	Y	Y
19 Platts	N	Y	Y	Y
RHODE ISLAND				
1 Kennedy	Y	Y	Y	Y
2 Langevin	Y	Y	Y	Y
SOUTH CAROLINA				
1 Brown	N	Y	Y	Y
2 Wilson	N	Y	Y	Y
3 Barrett	N	Y	Y	N
4 Inglis	N	Y	Y	Y
5 Spratt	Y	Y	Y	?
6 Clyburn	Y	Y	Y	Y
SOUTH DAKOTA				
AL Herseth Sandlin	Y	Y	Y	Y
TENNESSEE				
1 Davis, D.	N	Y	Y	Y
2 Duncan	N	Y	Y	N
3 Wamp	N	Y	Y	Y
4 Davis, L.	Y	Y	Y	Y
5 Cooper	Y	Y	Y	Y
6 Gordon	Y	Y	Y	Y
7 Blackburn	N	Y	Y	Y
8 Tanner	Y	Y	Y	Y
9 Cohen	Y	Y	Y	Y

	201	202	203	204
TEXAS				
1 Gohmert	N	Y	Y	Y
2 Poe	N	Y	Y	N
3 Johnson, S.	N	Y	Y	N
4 Hall	N	Y	Y	Y
5 Hensarling	N	Y	Y	N
6 Barton	N	Y	Y	Y
7 Culberson	N	Y	Y	Y
8 Brady	N	Y	Y	N
9 Green, A.	Y	Y	Y	Y
10 McCaul	N	Y	Y	Y
11 Conaway	N	Y	Y	Y
12 Granger	N	Y	Y	Y
13 Thornberry	N	Y	Y	Y
14 Paul	Y	Y	Y	N
15 Hinojosa	Y	Y	Y	Y
16 Reyes	Y	Y	Y	Y
17 Edwards	Y	Y	Y	Y
18 Jackson Lee	Y	Y	Y	Y
19 Neugebauer	N	Y	Y	Y
20 Gonzalez	Y	Y	Y	Y
21 Smith	N	Y	Y	Y
22 Lampson	N	Y	Y	Y
23 Rodriguez	Y	Y	Y	Y
24 Marchant	N	?	?	?
25 Doggett	Y	Y	Y	Y
26 Burgess	N	Y	Y	Y
27 Ortiz	Y	Y	Y	Y
28 Cuellar	Y	Y	Y	Y
29 Green, G.	Y	Y	Y	Y
30 Johnson, E.	Y	Y	Y	Y
31 Carter	N	Y	Y	Y
32 Sessions	N	Y	Y	Y
UTAH				
1 Bishop	N	Y	Y	Y
2 Matheson	Y	Y	Y	Y
3 Cannon	N	Y	Y	N
VERMONT				
AL Welch	Y	Y	Y	Y
VIRGINIA				
1 Wittman	N	Y	Y	Y
2 Drake	N	Y	Y	Y
3 Scott	Y	Y	Y	Y
4 Forbes	N	Y	Y	Y
5 Goode	N	Y	Y	Y
6 Goodlatte	N	Y	Y	Y
7 Cantor	N	Y	Y	Y
8 Moran	Y	Y	Y	Y
9 Boucher	Y	Y	Y	Y
10 Wolf	N	Y	Y	Y
11 Davis	N	Y	Y	Y
WASHINGTON				
1 Inslee	Y	Y	Y	Y
2 Larsen	Y	Y	Y	Y
3 Baird	Y	Y	Y	Y
4 Hastings	N	Y	Y	Y
5 McMorris Rodgers	N	Y	Y	Y
6 Dicks	Y	Y	Y	Y
7 McDermott	Y	Y	Y	Y
8 Reichert	N	Y	Y	Y
9 Smith	Y	Y	Y	Y
WEST VIRGINIA				
1 Mollohan	Y	Y	Y	Y
2 Capito	N	Y	Y	Y
3 Rahall	Y	Y	Y	Y
WISCONSIN				
1 Ryan	N	Y	Y	Y
2 Baldwin	Y	Y	Y	Y
3 Kind	Y	Y	Y	Y
4 Moore	Y	Y	Y	Y
5 Sensenbrenner	N	Y	Y	Y
6 Petri	N	Y	Y	Y
7 Obey	Y	Y	Y	Y
8 Kagen	Y	Y	Y	Y
WYOMING				
AL Cubin	N	Y	Y	N
DELEGATES				
Faleomavaega (A.S.)	?		?	
Norton (D.C.)	?		Y	
Bordallo (Guam)	Y		Y	
Fortuño (P.R.)	?		?	
Christensen (V.I.)	?		Y	

IN THE HOUSE | By Vote Number

205. **H Res 981. World Glaucoma Day/Adoption.** Towns, D-N.Y., motion to suspend the rules and adopt the resolution that would recognize the first ever World Glaucoma Day and congratulate the American Glaucoma Society for its efforts to expand glaucoma awareness. Motion agreed to 387-0: R 179-0; D 208-0 (ND 158-0, SD 50-0). A two-thirds majority of those present and voting (258 in this case) is required for adoption under suspension of the rules. April 22, 2008.

206. **HR 5151. Monongahela National Forest Expansion/Passage.** Rahall, D-W.Va., motion to suspend the rules and pass the bill that would designate three new federal wilderness areas and expand three existing wilderness areas within the Monongahela National Forest in West Virginia. Motion agreed to 368-17: R 161-17; D 207-0 (ND 157-0, SD 50-0). A two-thirds majority of those present and voting (257 in this case) is required for passage under suspension of the rules. April 22, 2008.

207. **HR 831. Coffman Cove Land Conveyance/Passage.** Rahall, D-W.Va., motion to suspend the rules and pass the bill that would direct the Agriculture Department to convey 12 acres of land previously used by the National Forest Service to the city of Coffman Cove, Alaska. Motion agreed to 382-0: R 176-0; D 206-0 (ND 156-0, SD 50-0). A two-thirds majority of those present and voting (255 in this case) is required for passage under suspension of the rules. April 22, 2008.

208. **Procedural Motion/Motion to Adjourn.** Sessions, R-Texas, motion to adjourn. Motion rejected 57-345: R 50-130; D 7-215 (ND 3-168, SD 4-47). April 23, 2008.

209. **HR 5613. Medicaid Rule Postponement/Passage.** Dingell, D-Mich., motion to suspend the rules and pass the bill that would place a one-year moratorium, until April 1, 2009, on the implementation of proposed new rules that would reduce federal Medicaid payments to states. The bill also would authorize $25 million annually for efforts to reduce fraud and abuse in Medicaid. Motion agreed to 349-62: R 128-62; D 221-0 (ND 171-0, SD 50-0). A two-thirds majority of those present and voting (274 in this case) is required for passage under suspension of the rules. A "nay" was a vote in support of the president's position. April 23, 2008.

210. **H Con Res 322. Israel 60th Anniversary Recognition/Adoption.** Berman, D-Calif., motion to suspend the rules and adopt the concurrent resolution that would recognize the 60th anniversary of the re-establishment of Israel and reaffirm the bonds of friendship and cooperation between the United States and Israel. Motion agreed to 417-0: R 192-0; D 225-0 (ND 174-0, SD 51-0). A two-thirds majority of those present and voting (278 in this case) is required for adoption under suspension of the rules. April 23, 2008.

211. **HR 5819. Small-Business Programs Reauthorization/Previous Question.** Welch, D-Vt., motion to order the previous question (thus ending debate and possibility of amendment) on adoption of the rule (H Res 1125) that would provide for House floor consideration of the bill that would reauthorize the Small Business Innovation Research and Small Business Technology Transfer programs through fiscal 2010. Motion agreed to 222-194: R 0-192; D 222-2 (ND 170-1, SD 52-1). April 23, 2008.

	205	206	207	208	209	210	211
ALABAMA							
1 Bonner	Y	Y	Y	N	Y	Y	N
2 Everett	Y	Y	Y	N	Y	Y	N
3 Rogers	Y	Y	Y	N	Y	Y	N
4 Aderholt	Y	Y	Y	N	Y	Y	N
5 Cramer	Y	Y	Y	?	?	?	?
6 Bachus	Y	Y	Y	N	Y	Y	N
7 Davis	Y	Y	Y	N	Y	Y	Y
ALASKA							
AL Young	?	?	?	Y	Y	Y	N
ARIZONA							
1 Renzi	?	?	?	Y	Y	Y	N
2 Franks	Y	N	Y	N	N	Y	N
3 Shadegg	Y	N	N	N	Y	N	
4 Pastor	Y	Y	Y	N	Y	Y	Y
5 Mitchell	Y	Y	Y	N	Y	Y	Y
6 Flake	Y	N	Y	N	N	Y	N
7 Grijalva	?	?	?	N	Y	Y	Y
8 Giffords	Y	Y	Y	N	Y	Y	Y
ARKANSAS							
1 Berry	Y	Y	Y	Y	Y	Y	Y
2 Snyder	Y	Y	Y	N	Y	Y	Y
3 Boozman	Y	Y	Y	N	Y	Y	N
4 Ross	Y	Y	Y	N	Y	Y	Y
CALIFORNIA							
1 Thompson	Y	Y	Y	N	Y	Y	Y
2 Herger	Y	Y	Y	N	N	Y	N
3 Lungren	Y	Y	Y	Y	Y	Y	N
4 Doolittle	Y	Y	Y	Y	N	Y	N
5 Matsui	Y	Y	Y	N	Y	Y	Y
6 Woolsey	Y	Y	Y	N	Y	Y	Y
7 Miller, George	Y	Y	Y	N	Y	Y	Y
8 Pelosi					Y		
9 Lee	Y	Y	Y	N	Y	Y	Y
10 Tauscher	Y	Y	Y	N	Y	Y	Y
11 McNerney	Y	Y	Y	N	Y	Y	Y
12 Speier	Y	Y	Y	N	Y	Y	Y
13 Stark	Y	Y	Y	N	Y	Y	Y
14 Eshoo	Y	Y	Y	N	Y	Y	Y
15 Honda	Y	Y	Y	N	Y	Y	Y
16 Lofgren	Y	Y	Y	N	Y	Y	Y
17 Farr	Y	Y	Y	?	Y	Y	Y
18 Cardoza	Y	Y	Y	N	Y	Y	Y
19 Radanovich	Y	Y	Y	N	Y	Y	N
20 Costa	Y	Y	Y	N	Y	Y	Y
21 Nunes	Y	Y	Y	N	Y	Y	N
22 McCarthy	Y	Y	Y	N	Y	Y	N
23 Capps	Y	Y	Y	N	Y	Y	Y
24 Gallegly	Y	Y	Y	N	Y	Y	N
25 McKeon	Y	Y	Y	N	N	Y	N
26 Dreier	Y	Y	Y	N	Y	Y	N
27 Sherman	Y	Y	Y	N	Y	Y	Y
28 Berman	Y	Y	Y	N	Y	Y	?
29 Schiff	Y	Y	Y	N	Y	Y	Y
30 Waxman	Y	Y	Y	N	Y	Y	Y
31 Becerra	Y	Y	Y	N	Y	Y	Y
32 Solis	Y	Y	Y	N	Y	Y	Y
33 Watson	Y	Y	Y	N	Y	Y	Y
34 Roybal-Allard	Y	Y	Y	N	Y	Y	Y
35 Waters	Y	Y	Y	N	+	Y	Y
36 Harman	Y	Y	Y	N	Y	Y	Y
37 Richardson	Y	Y	Y	N	Y	Y	Y
38 Napolitano	Y	Y	?	N	Y	Y	Y
39 Sánchez, Linda	Y	Y	Y	N	Y	Y	Y
40 Royce	Y	Y	Y	N	?	Y	N
41 Lewis	Y	Y	Y	N	Y	Y	N
42 Miller, Gary	Y	N	Y	Y	Y	Y	N
43 Baca	Y	Y	Y	N	Y	Y	Y
44 Calvert	Y	Y	Y	N	Y	Y	N
45 Bono Mack	Y	Y	Y	N	Y	Y	N
46 Rohrabacher	?	?	?	N	Y	Y	N
47 Sanchez, Loretta	Y	Y	Y	N	Y	Y	Y
48 Campbell	?	?	?	?	?	?	?
49 Issa	Y	Y	Y	N	N	Y	N
50 Bilbray	Y	Y	Y	Y	Y	Y	N
51 Filner	Y	Y	Y	N	Y	Y	Y
52 Hunter	Y	Y	Y	N	Y	Y	N
53 Davis	Y	Y	Y	N	Y	Y	Y

	205	206	207	208	209	210	211
COLORADO							
1 DeGette	Y	Y	Y	N	Y	Y	Y
2 Udall	+	+	?	N	Y	Y	Y
3 Salazar	Y	Y	Y	N	Y	Y	Y
4 Musgrave	Y	Y	Y	N	N	Y	N
5 Lamborn	Y	Y	Y	Y	N	Y	N
6 Tancredo	Y	N	Y	N	Y	Y	N
7 Perlmutter	Y	Y	Y	N	Y	Y	Y
CONNECTICUT							
1 Larson	Y	Y	Y	N	Y	Y	Y
2 Courtney	Y	Y	Y	N	Y	Y	Y
3 DeLauro	Y	Y	Y	N	Y	Y	Y
4 Shays	Y	Y	Y	N	Y	Y	N
5 Murphy	Y	Y	Y	N	Y	Y	Y
DELAWARE							
AL Castle	Y	Y	Y	N	Y	Y	N
FLORIDA							
1 Miller	Y	Y	Y	N	N	Y	N
2 Boyd	Y	Y	Y	N	Y	Y	Y
3 Brown	?	?	?	N	Y	Y	Y
4 Crenshaw	Y	Y	Y	N	Y	Y	N
5 Brown-Waite	?	?	?	?	?	?	?
6 Stearns	Y	N	Y	Y	Y	Y	N
7 Mica	Y	Y	Y	N	Y	Y	N
8 Keller	Y	Y	Y	Y	Y	Y	N
9 Bilirakis	Y	Y	Y	N	Y	Y	N
10 Young	?	?	?	N	Y	Y	N
11 Castor	?	?	?	N	Y	Y	Y
12 Putnam	?	?	?	N	Y	Y	N
13 Buchanan	Y	Y	Y	N	Y	Y	N
14 Mack	Y	Y	Y	N	Y	Y	N
15 Weldon	Y	Y	Y	N	Y	Y	N
16 Mahoney	Y	Y	Y	N	Y	Y	Y
17 Meek	Y	Y	Y	N	Y	Y	Y
18 Ros-Lehtinen	Y	Y	Y	N	Y	Y	N
19 Wexler	Y	Y	Y	N	Y	Y	Y
20 Wasserman Schultz	?	?	?	N	Y	Y	Y
21 Diaz-Balart, L.	Y	Y	Y	N	Y	Y	N
22 Klein	Y	Y	Y	N	Y	Y	Y
23 Hastings	Y	Y	Y	N	Y	Y	Y
24 Feeney	?	?	?	?	?	?	?
25 Diaz-Balart, M.	Y	Y	Y	N	Y	Y	N
GEORGIA							
1 Kingston	?	?	?	N	N	Y	N
2 Bishop	Y	Y	Y	N	Y	Y	Y
3 Westmoreland	Y	Y	Y	N	Y	Y	N
4 Johnson	Y	Y	Y	N	Y	Y	Y
5 Lewis	Y	Y	Y	?	?	Y	Y
6 Price	Y	Y	Y	N	N	Y	N
7 Linder	Y	Y	Y	N	?	Y	N
8 Marshall	Y	Y	Y	N	Y	Y	Y
9 Deal	Y	Y	Y	Y	N	Y	N
10 Broun	Y	N	Y	N	N	Y	N
11 Gingrey	Y	Y	Y	N	N	Y	N
12 Barrow	Y	Y	Y	N	Y	Y	Y
13 Scott	Y	Y	Y	N	Y	Y	Y
HAWAII							
1 Abercrombie	+	+	+	N	Y	Y	Y
2 Hirono	Y	Y	Y	N	Y	Y	Y
IDAHO							
1 Sali	Y	Y	Y	N	N	Y	N
2 Simpson	Y	Y	Y	N	Y	Y	N
ILLINOIS							
1 Rush	?	?	?	?	?	?	?
2 Jackson	Y	Y	Y	N	Y	Y	Y
3 Lipinski	Y	Y	Y	N	Y	Y	Y
4 Gutierrez	+	+	+	N	Y	Y	Y
5 Emanuel	Y	Y	Y	N	Y	Y	Y
6 Roskam	Y	Y	Y	N	N	Y	N
7 Davis	Y	Y	Y	N	Y	Y	Y
8 Bean	Y	Y	Y	N	Y	Y	Y
9 Schakowsky	Y	Y	Y	N	Y	Y	Y
10 Kirk	Y	Y	Y	N	Y	Y	N
11 Weller	?	?	?	?	?	?	?
12 Costello	Y	Y	Y	N	Y	Y	Y
13 Biggert	Y	Y	Y	N	Y	Y	N
14 Foster	Y	Y	Y	N	Y	Y	Y
15 Johnson	Y	Y	Y	Y	Y	Y	N

KEY   **Republicans**   Democrats

Y	Voted for (yea)	X Paired against
#	Paired for	– Announced against
+	Announced for	P Voted "present"
N	Voted against (nay)	

C Voted "present" to avoid possible conflict of interest
? Did not vote or otherwise make a position known

ND Northern Democrats, SD Southern Democrats
Southern states: Ala., Ark., Fla., Ga., Ky., La., Miss., N.C., Okla., S.C., Tenn., Texas, Va.

	205	206	207	208	209	210	211
16 **Manzullo**	Y	Y	Y	N	N	Y	N
17 Hare	Y	Y	Y	N	Y	Y	Y
18 **LaHood**	Y	Y	Y	Y	Y	Y	N
19 **Shimkus**	Y	N	Y	?	Y	Y	N
INDIANA							
1 Visclosky	Y	Y	Y	N	Y	Y	Y
2 Donnelly	Y	Y	Y	N	Y	Y	Y
3 **Souder**	Y	Y	Y	Y	?	Y	N
4 **Buyer**	Y	Y	Y	N	Y	Y	N
5 **Burton**	Y	Y	Y	N	N	Y	N
6 **Pence**	Y	Y	Y	N	N	Y	N
7 Carson, A.	Y	Y	Y	N	Y	Y	Y
8 Ellsworth	Y	Y	Y	N	Y	Y	Y
9 Hill	Y	Y	Y	N	Y	Y	N
IOWA							
1 Braley	Y	Y	Y	N	Y	Y	Y
2 Loebsack	Y	Y	Y	N	Y	Y	Y
3 Boswell	Y	Y	Y	N	Y	Y	Y
4 **Latham**	Y	Y	Y	N	Y	Y	N
5 **King**	Y	N	Y	Y	N	Y	N
KANSAS							
1 **Moran**	Y	Y	Y	N	Y	Y	N
2 Boyda	Y	Y	Y	N	Y	Y	Y
3 Moore	Y	Y	Y	N	Y	Y	Y
4 **Tiahrt**	Y	Y	Y	Y	Y	Y	N
KENTUCKY							
1 **Whitfield**	?	?	?	N	Y	Y	N
2 **Lewis**	Y	Y	Y	N	Y	Y	N
3 Yarmuth	Y	Y	Y	N	Y	Y	Y
4 **Davis**	Y	Y	Y	N	Y	Y	N
5 **Rogers**	Y	Y	Y	N	Y	Y	N
6 Chandler	Y	Y	Y	Y	Y	Y	Y
LOUISIANA							
1 Vacant							
2 Jefferson	?	?	?	N	Y	Y	Y
3 Melancon	Y	Y	Y	N	Y	Y	Y
4 **McCrery**	Y	Y	Y	?	N	Y	N
5 **Alexander**	?	?	?	N	N	?	N
6 Vacant							
7 **Boustany**	Y	Y	Y	N	Y	Y	N
MAINE							
1 Allen	Y	Y	Y	N	Y	Y	Y
2 Michaud	Y	Y	Y	N	Y	Y	Y
MARYLAND							
1 **Gilchrest**	Y	Y	Y	N	Y	Y	N
2 Ruppersberger	Y	Y	Y	N	Y	Y	Y
3 Sarbanes	Y	Y	Y	N	Y	Y	Y
4 Wynn	Y	Y	Y	N	?	Y	Y
5 Hoyer	Y	Y	Y	N	Y	Y	Y
6 **Bartlett**	Y	Y	Y	Y	N	Y	N
7 Cummings	Y	Y	Y	N	Y	Y	Y
8 Van Hollen	Y	Y	Y	N	Y	Y	Y
MASSACHUSETTS							
1 Olver	Y	Y	Y	N	Y	Y	Y
2 Neal	Y	Y	Y	N	Y	Y	Y
3 McGovern	Y	Y	Y	N	Y	Y	Y
4 Frank	Y	Y	Y	N	Y	Y	Y
5 Tsongas	Y	Y	Y	N	Y	Y	Y
6 Tierney	Y	Y	Y	N	Y	Y	Y
7 Markey	Y	Y	Y	N	Y	Y	Y
8 Capuano	Y	Y	Y	N	Y	Y	Y
9 Lynch	Y	Y	Y	N	Y	Y	Y
10 Delahunt	Y	Y	Y	N	Y	Y	Y
MICHIGAN							
1 Stupak	Y	Y	Y	N	Y	Y	Y
2 **Hoekstra**	Y	Y	Y	Y	Y	Y	N
3 **Ehlers**	Y	Y	Y	N	Y	Y	N
4 **Camp**	Y	Y	Y	N	Y	Y	N
5 Kildee	Y	Y	Y	N	Y	Y	Y
6 **Upton**	Y	Y	Y	N	Y	Y	N
7 **Walberg**	Y	Y	Y	Y	Y	Y	N
8 **Rogers**	Y	Y	Y	N	Y	Y	N
9 **Knollenberg**	Y	Y	Y	N	Y	Y	N
10 **Miller**	Y	Y	Y	N	Y	Y	N
11 **McCotter**	Y	Y	Y	?	Y	Y	N
12 Levin	Y	Y	Y	N	Y	Y	Y
13 Kilpatrick	Y	Y	Y	N	Y	Y	Y
14 Conyers	Y	Y	Y	N	Y	Y	Y
15 Dingell	Y	Y	Y	N	Y	Y	Y
MINNESOTA							
1 Walz	Y	Y	Y	N	Y	Y	Y
2 **Kline**	Y	Y	Y	N	Y	Y	N
3 **Ramstad**	Y	Y	Y	N	Y	Y	N
4 McCollum	Y	Y	Y	N	Y	Y	Y

	205	206	207	208	209	210	211
5 Ellison	Y	Y	Y	N	Y	Y	Y
6 **Bachmann**	Y	Y	Y	N	Y	Y	N
7 Peterson	Y	Y	Y	N	Y	Y	Y
8 Oberstar	Y	Y	Y	N	Y	Y	Y
MISSISSIPPI							
1 Vacant							
2 Thompson	Y	Y	Y	N	Y	Y	Y
3 **Pickering**	Y	Y	Y	N	Y	Y	N
4 Taylor	Y	Y	Y	N	Y	Y	Y
MISSOURI							
1 Clay	Y	Y	Y	N	Y	Y	Y
2 **Akin**	Y	Y	Y	Y	N	Y	N
3 Carnahan	Y	Y	Y	N	Y	Y	Y
4 Skelton	Y	Y	Y	N	Y	Y	Y
5 Cleaver	Y	Y	Y	N	Y	Y	Y
6 **Graves**	Y	Y	Y	N	Y	Y	N
7 **Blunt**	Y	N	Y	?	N	Y	N
8 **Emerson**	Y	Y	Y	Y	Y	Y	N
9 **Hulshof**	?	?	?	?	?	?	?
MONTANA							
AL **Rehberg**	Y	Y	Y	Y	Y	Y	N
NEBRASKA							
1 **Fortenberry**	Y	Y	Y	N	Y	Y	N
2 **Terry**	Y	Y	Y	N	Y	Y	N
3 **Smith**	Y	Y	Y	N	N	Y	N
NEVADA							
1 Berkley	Y	Y	Y	N	Y	Y	Y
2 **Heller**	Y	Y	Y	N	Y	Y	N
3 **Porter**	Y	Y	Y	N	Y	Y	N
NEW HAMPSHIRE							
1 Shea-Porter	Y	Y	Y	N	Y	Y	Y
2 Hodes	Y	Y	Y	N	Y	Y	Y
NEW JERSEY							
1 Andrews	+	+	+	?	?	?	?
2 **LoBiondo**	Y	Y	Y	N	Y	Y	N
3 **Saxton**	?	?	?	N	Y	Y	N
4 **Smith**	Y	Y	Y	N	Y	Y	N
5 **Garrett**	Y	Y	Y	N	N	Y	N
6 Pallone	Y	Y	Y	N	Y	Y	Y
7 **Ferguson**	Y	Y	Y	N	Y	Y	N
8 Pascrell	Y	Y	Y	N	Y	Y	Y
9 Rothman	Y	Y	Y	N	Y	Y	Y
10 Payne	Y	Y	Y	N	Y	Y	Y
11 **Frelinghuysen**	Y	Y	Y	N	Y	Y	N
12 Holt	Y	Y	Y	N	Y	Y	Y
13 Sires	Y	Y	Y	N	Y	Y	Y
NEW MEXICO							
1 **Wilson**	Y	Y	Y	N	Y	Y	N
2 **Pearce**	Y	Y	Y	Y	N	Y	N
3 Udall	Y	Y	Y	N	Y	Y	Y
NEW YORK							
1 Bishop	Y	Y	Y	N	Y	Y	Y
2 Israel	Y	Y	Y	N	Y	Y	Y
3 **King**	Y	Y	Y	N	Y	Y	N
4 McCarthy	Y	Y	Y	N	Y	Y	Y
5 Ackerman	Y	Y	Y	N	Y	Y	Y
6 Meeks	Y	Y	Y	N	Y	Y	Y
7 Crowley	Y	Y	Y	N	Y	Y	Y
8 Nadler	?	?	?	?	?	?	?
9 Weiner	?	?	?	N	Y	Y	Y
10 Towns	Y	Y	Y	N	Y	Y	Y
11 Clarke	Y	Y	Y	N	Y	Y	Y
12 Velázquez	Y	Y	Y	N	Y	Y	Y
13 **Fossella**	Y	Y	Y	N	Y	Y	N
14 Maloney	+	+	+	N	Y	Y	Y
15 Rangel	Y	Y	Y	N	Y	Y	Y
16 Serrano	Y	Y	Y	N	Y	Y	Y
17 Engel	?	?	?	N	Y	Y	Y
18 Lowey	Y	Y	Y	N	Y	Y	Y
19 Hall	Y	Y	Y	N	Y	Y	+
20 Gillibrand	Y	Y	Y	N	Y	Y	Y
21 McNulty	Y	Y	Y	N	Y	Y	Y
22 Hinchey	Y	Y	Y	N	Y	Y	Y
23 **McHugh**	Y	Y	Y	N	Y	Y	N
24 Arcuri	Y	Y	Y	N	Y	Y	Y
25 **Walsh**	Y	Y	Y	?	Y	Y	N
26 **Reynolds**	Y	Y	Y	N	Y	Y	N
27 Higgins	Y	Y	Y	N	Y	Y	Y
28 Slaughter	Y	Y	Y	N	Y	Y	Y
29 **Kuhl**	Y	Y	Y	N	Y	Y	N
NORTH CAROLINA							
1 Butterfield	Y	Y	Y	N	Y	Y	Y
2 Etheridge	Y	Y	Y	?	+	+	Y
3 **Jones**	Y	Y	Y	N	Y	Y	N
4 Price	Y	Y	Y	N	Y	Y	Y

	205	206	207	208	209	210	211
5 **Foxx**	Y	Y	Y	N	N	Y	N
6 **Coble**	Y	N	Y	N	Y	Y	N
7 McIntyre	Y	Y	Y	Y	Y	Y	Y
8 **Hayes**	Y	Y	Y	N	Y	Y	N
9 **Myrick**	Y	Y	Y	N	Y	Y	N
10 **McHenry**	Y	Y	Y	?	Y	Y	N
11 Shuler	Y	Y	Y	N	Y	Y	Y
12 Watt	Y	Y	Y	N	Y	Y	Y
13 Miller	Y	Y	Y	N	Y	Y	Y
NORTH DAKOTA							
AL Pomeroy	Y	Y	Y	N	Y	Y	Y
OHIO							
1 **Chabot**	Y	Y	Y	N	N	Y	N
2 **Schmidt**	Y	Y	Y	N	Y	Y	N
3 **Turner**	Y	Y	Y	N	Y	Y	N
4 **Jordan**	Y	Y	Y	N	N	Y	N
5 **Latta**	Y	Y	Y	N	N	Y	N
6 Wilson	Y	Y	Y	N	Y	Y	Y
7 **Hobson**	Y	Y	Y	Y	Y	Y	N
8 **Boehner**	Y	Y	Y	?	N	Y	N
9 Kaptur	Y	Y	Y	N	Y	Y	Y
10 Kucinich	Y	Y	Y	N	Y	Y	Y
11 Tubbs Jones	+	+	+	?	Y	Y	Y
12 **Tiberi**	?	?	?	N	Y	Y	N
13 Sutton	Y	Y	Y	N	Y	Y	Y
14 **LaTourette**	Y	Y	Y	N	Y	Y	N
15 **Pryce**	Y	Y	Y	N	Y	Y	N
16 **Regula**	Y	Y	Y	Y	Y	Y	N
17 Ryan	Y	Y	Y	N	Y	Y	Y
18 Space	Y	?	Y	N	Y	Y	Y
OKLAHOMA							
1 **Sullivan**	Y	Y	?	Y	Y	Y	N
2 Boren	Y	Y	Y	N	Y	Y	Y
3 **Lucas**	Y	Y	Y	N	Y	Y	N
4 **Cole**	Y	Y	?	?	Y	Y	N
5 **Fallin**	Y	Y	Y	Y	Y	Y	N
OREGON							
1 Wu	Y	Y	Y	N	Y	Y	Y
2 **Walden**	Y	Y	Y	N	Y	Y	N
3 Blumenauer	Y	Y	Y	N	Y	Y	Y
4 DeFazio	Y	Y	Y	N	Y	Y	Y
5 Hooley	Y	Y	Y	N	Y	Y	Y
PENNSYLVANIA							
1 Brady	?	?	?	N	Y	Y	Y
2 Fattah	?	?	?	N	Y	Y	Y
3 **English**	?	?	?	N	Y	Y	N
4 Altmire	Y	Y	Y	N	Y	Y	Y
5 **Peterson**	?	?	?	N	Y	Y	N
6 **Gerlach**	Y	Y	Y	N	Y	Y	N
7 Sestak	?	?	?	N	Y	Y	Y
8 Murphy, P.	?	?	?	Y	Y	Y	Y
9 **Shuster**	Y	Y	Y	N	Y	Y	N
10 Carney	?	?	?	N	Y	Y	Y
11 Kanjorski	Y	Y	Y	N	Y	Y	Y
12 Murtha	Y	Y	?	N	Y	Y	Y
13 Schwartz	?	?	?	Y	Y	Y	Y
14 Doyle	Y	Y	Y	N	Y	Y	Y
15 **Dent**	Y	Y	Y	N	Y	Y	N
16 **Pitts**	Y	Y	Y	N	N	Y	N
17 Holden	Y	Y	Y	N	Y	Y	Y
18 **Murphy, T.**	Y	Y	Y	N	Y	Y	N
19 **Platts**	Y	Y	Y	N	Y	Y	N
RHODE ISLAND							
1 Kennedy	Y	Y	Y	N	Y	Y	Y
2 Langevin	Y	Y	Y	N	Y	Y	Y
SOUTH CAROLINA							
1 **Brown**	Y	Y	Y	N	Y	Y	N
2 **Wilson**	Y	Y	Y	N	N	Y	N
3 **Barrett**	Y	Y	Y	N	N	Y	N
4 **Inglis**	Y	Y	Y	N	N	Y	N
5 Spratt	Y	Y	Y	N	Y	Y	Y
6 Clyburn	Y	Y	Y	–	+	+	+
SOUTH DAKOTA							
AL Herseth Sandlin	Y	Y	Y	N	Y	Y	Y
TENNESSEE							
1 **Davis, D.**	Y	Y	Y	Y	N	Y	N
2 **Duncan**	Y	N	Y	Y	N	Y	N
3 **Wamp**	Y	Y	Y	N	N	Y	N
4 Davis, L.	Y	Y	Y	Y	Y	Y	Y
5 Cooper	+	+	+	–	+	+	+
6 Gordon	Y	Y	Y	N	Y	Y	Y
7 **Blackburn**	Y	N	Y	Y	N	Y	N
8 Tanner	Y	Y	Y	N	Y	Y	Y
9 Cohen	Y	Y	Y	N	Y	Y	Y

	205	206	207	208	209	210	211
TEXAS							
1 **Gohmert**	Y	Y	Y	N	Y	Y	N
2 **Poe**	Y	Y	Y	N	N	Y	N
3 **Johnson, S.**	Y	Y	Y	Y	N	Y	N
4 **Hall**	?	?	?	?	Y	Y	N
5 **Hensarling**	Y	Y	Y	N	N	Y	N
6 **Barton**	Y	Y	Y	Y	Y	Y	N
7 **Culberson**	Y	Y	Y	N	Y	Y	N
8 **Brady**	Y	Y	Y	Y	Y	Y	N
9 Green, A.	Y	Y	Y	N	Y	Y	Y
10 **McCaul**	Y	Y	Y	Y	Y	Y	?
11 **Conaway**	Y	Y	Y	Y	N	Y	N
12 **Granger**	Y	?	Y	?	Y	Y	N
13 **Thornberry**	Y	Y	Y	N	N	Y	N
14 **Paul**	Y	N	Y	N	N	Y	N
15 Hinojosa	Y	Y	Y	N	Y	Y	Y
16 Reyes	Y	Y	Y	N	Y	Y	Y
17 Edwards	Y	Y	Y	N	Y	Y	Y
18 Jackson Lee	?	?	?	N	Y	?	Y
19 **Neugebauer**	Y	Y	Y	N	N	Y	N
20 Gonzalez	Y	Y	Y	N	Y	Y	Y
21 **Smith**	Y	Y	Y	N	Y	Y	N
22 Lampson	Y	Y	Y	N	Y	Y	N
23 Rodriguez	Y	Y	Y	N	Y	Y	Y
24 **Marchant**	Y	Y	Y	Y	N	Y	N
25 Doggett	?	?	?	?	?	?	?
26 **Burgess**	Y	Y	Y	N	Y	Y	N
27 Ortiz	Y	Y	Y	N	+	Y	Y
28 Cuellar	Y	Y	Y	N	Y	Y	Y
29 Green, G.	Y	Y	Y	N	Y	Y	Y
30 Johnson, E.	Y	Y	Y	N	Y	Y	Y
31 **Carter**	Y	Y	Y	?	N	Y	N
32 **Sessions**	Y	Y	Y	Y	N	Y	N
UTAH							
1 **Bishop**	Y	Y	Y	Y	Y	Y	N
2 Matheson	Y	Y	Y	N	Y	Y	Y
3 **Cannon**	Y	Y	Y	N	N	Y	N
VERMONT							
AL Welch	Y	Y	Y	N	Y	Y	Y
VIRGINIA							
1 **Wittman**	Y	Y	Y	N	Y	Y	N
2 **Drake**	Y	Y	Y	N	Y	Y	N
3 Scott	Y	Y	Y	N	Y	Y	Y
4 **Forbes**	Y	Y	Y	N	Y	Y	N
5 **Goode**	Y	N	Y	Y	Y	Y	N
6 **Goodlatte**	Y	N	Y	N	Y	Y	N
7 **Cantor**	?	?	?	?	Y	Y	N
8 Moran	Y	Y	Y	N	Y	Y	Y
9 Boucher	Y	Y	Y	N	Y	Y	Y
10 **Wolf**	Y	Y	Y	N	Y	Y	N
11 **Davis**	Y	Y	Y	N	Y	Y	N
WASHINGTON							
1 Inslee	Y	Y	Y	N	Y	Y	Y
2 Larsen	Y	Y	Y	N	Y	Y	Y
3 Baird	Y	Y	Y	N	Y	Y	Y
4 **Hastings**	Y	Y	Y	N	Y	Y	N
5 **McMorris Rodgers**	Y	Y	Y	N	Y	Y	N
6 Dicks	Y	Y	Y	N	Y	Y	Y
7 McDermott	Y	Y	Y	N	Y	Y	Y
8 **Reichert**	Y	Y	Y	N	Y	Y	N
9 Smith	Y	Y	Y	N	Y	Y	Y
WEST VIRGINIA							
1 Mollohan	?	?	?	N	Y	Y	Y
2 **Capito**	Y	Y	Y	N	Y	Y	N
3 Rahall	Y	Y	Y	N	Y	Y	Y
WISCONSIN							
1 **Ryan**	Y	Y	Y	N	N	Y	N
2 Baldwin	Y	Y	Y	N	Y	Y	Y
3 Kind	Y	Y	Y	N	Y	Y	Y
4 Moore	Y	Y	Y	N	Y	Y	Y
5 **Sensenbrenner**	Y	N	Y	Y	N	Y	N
6 **Petri**	Y	Y	Y	Y	N	Y	N
7 Obey	Y	Y	Y	N	Y	Y	Y
8 Kagen	Y	Y	Y	N	Y	Y	Y
WYOMING							
AL **Cubin**	Y	Y	Y	Y	N	Y	N
DELEGATES							
Faleomavaega (A.S.)							
Norton (D.C.)							
Bordallo (Guam)							
Fortuño (P.R.)							
Christensen (V.I.)							

IN THE HOUSE | By Vote Number

212. HR 5819. **Small-Business Programs Reauthorization/Rule.**
Adoption of the rule (H Res 1125) that would provide for House floor consideration of the bill that would reauthorize the Small Business Innovation Research and Small Business Technology Transfer programs through fiscal 2010. Adopted 221-190: R 0-190; D 221-0 (ND 168-0, SD 53-0). April 23, 2008.

213. HR 5819. **Small-Business Programs Reauthorization/Energy Efficiency.** Matheson, D-Utah, amendment that would give priority for federal grants to small businesses that are making significant contributions toward energy efficiency, including those making efforts to reduce their carbon footprints or that are carbon-neutral. Adopted in Committee of the Whole 355-48: R 132-48; D 223-0 (ND 171-0, SD 52-0). April 23, 2008.

214. HR 5819. **Small-Business Programs Reauthorization/Service-Disabled Veterans.** Capito, R-W.Va., amendment that would direct the Small Business Innovation Research advisory board to encourage more grant applications from small-business owners who are service-disabled veterans. Adopted in Committee of the Whole 405-0: R 183-0; D 222-0 (ND 170-0, SD 52-0). April 23, 2008.

215. HR 5819. **Small-Business Programs Reauthorization/Illegal Immigrants.** Foster, D-Ill., amendment that would prohibit businesses owned or partly owned by an illegal immigrant from receiving Small Business Innovation Research grants and would ban any business that knowingly recruited or hired an illegal immigrant from receiving future grants. Adopted in Committee of the Whole 406-0: R 184-0; D 222-0 (ND 170-0, SD 52-0). April 23, 2008.

216. HR 5819. **Small-Business Programs Reauthorization/Recommit.** Heller, R-Nev., motion to recommit the bill to the Small Business Committee with instructions that it be reported back promptly with language that would add projects that could lower gasoline and diesel fuel costs to the energy-related research topics in the bill. Motion rejected 195-215: R 186-0; D 9-215 (ND 5-166, SD 4-49). April 23, 2008.

217. HR 5819. **Small-Business Programs Reauthorization/Passage.**
Passage of the bill that would reauthorize the Small Business Innovation Research and Small Business Technology Transfer programs through fiscal 2010. The bill would give preference in awarding grants to businesses that are owned by veterans, located in areas with high unemployment or that have taken steps to increase energy efficiency and reduce carbon emissions. Passed 368-43: R 149-38; D 219-5 (ND 166-5, SD 53-0). A "nay" was a vote in support of the president's position. April 23, 2008.

218. HR 2830. **Coast Guard Reauthorization/Previous Question.**
Arcuri, D-N.Y., motion to order the previous question (thus ending debate and possibility of amendment) on adoption of the rule (H Res 1126) that would provide for House floor consideration of the bill that would authorize $8.4 billion in fiscal 2008 for the Coast Guard and require several changes in the Deepwater program to replace aging ships and aircraft. Motion agreed to 220-187: R 1-185; D 219-2 (ND 168-1, SD 51-1). April 23, 2008.

	212	213	214	215	216	217	218
ALABAMA							
1 Bonner	N	Y	Y	Y	Y	Y	N
2 Everett	N	?	?	?	?	?	?
3 Rogers	N	Y	Y	Y	Y	Y	N
4 Aderholt	N	N	Y	Y	Y	Y	N
5 Cramer	?	?	?	?	?	?	?
6 Bachus	N	Y	Y	Y	Y	Y	N
7 Davis	Y	Y	Y	Y	N	Y	Y
ALASKA							
AL Young	N	Y	Y	Y	Y	Y	N
ARIZONA							
1 Renzi	N	Y	Y	Y	Y	Y	N
2 Franks	N	N	Y	Y	Y	N	N
3 Shadegg	N	Y	Y	Y	Y	N	N
4 Pastor	Y	Y	Y	Y	N	Y	Y
5 Mitchell	Y	Y	Y	Y	N	Y	Y
6 Flake	N	N	Y	Y	Y	N	N
7 Grijalva	Y	Y	?	Y	N	Y	Y
8 Giffords	Y	Y	Y	Y	N	Y	Y
ARKANSAS							
1 Berry	Y	Y	Y	Y	N	Y	Y
2 Snyder	Y	Y	Y	Y	N	Y	Y
3 Boozman	N	Y	Y	Y	Y	Y	N
4 Ross	Y	Y	Y	Y	N	Y	Y
CALIFORNIA							
1 Thompson	Y	Y	Y	Y	N	Y	Y
2 Herger	N	Y	Y	Y	Y	N	N
3 Lungren	N	N	Y	Y	Y	Y	N
4 Doolittle	N	N	Y	Y	Y	Y	N
5 Matsui	Y	Y	Y	Y	N	Y	Y
6 Woolsey	Y	Y	Y	Y	N	Y	Y
7 Miller, George	Y	Y	Y	Y	N	Y	Y
8 Pelosi							
9 Lee	Y	Y	Y	Y	N	Y	Y
10 Tauscher	Y	Y	Y	Y	N	Y	Y
11 McNerney	Y	Y	Y	Y	Y	Y	Y
12 Speier	Y	Y	Y	Y	N	Y	Y
13 Stark	Y	Y	Y	P	N	Y	Y
14 Eshoo	Y	Y	Y	Y	N	Y	Y
15 Honda	Y	Y	Y	Y	N	Y	Y
16 Lofgren	Y	Y	Y	Y	N	Y	Y
17 Farr	Y	Y	Y	Y	N	Y	Y
18 Cardoza	Y	Y	Y	Y	N	Y	Y
19 Radanovich	N	Y	Y	Y	Y	N	N
20 Costa	Y	Y	Y	Y	N	Y	Y
21 Nunes	N	N	Y	Y	Y	N	N
22 McCarthy	N	Y	Y	Y	Y	Y	N
23 Capps	Y	Y	Y	Y	N	Y	Y
24 Gallegly	N	Y	Y	Y	Y	Y	N
25 McKeon	N	Y	Y	Y	Y	Y	N
26 Dreier	N	Y	Y	Y	Y	Y	N
27 Sherman	Y	Y	Y	Y	N	Y	Y
28 Berman	Y	Y	Y	Y	N	Y	Y
29 Schiff	Y	Y	Y	Y	N	Y	Y
30 Waxman	?	Y	Y	Y	N	Y	Y
31 Becerra	Y	Y	Y	P	N	Y	Y
32 Solis	Y	Y	Y	Y	N	Y	Y
33 Watson	Y	Y	Y	Y	N	Y	Y
34 Roybal-Allard	Y	Y	Y	Y	N	Y	Y
35 Waters	Y	Y	Y	Y	N	Y	Y
36 Harman	Y	Y	Y	Y	N	Y	Y
37 Richardson	Y	Y	Y	Y	N	Y	Y
38 Napolitano	Y	Y	Y	Y	N	Y	Y
39 Sánchez, Linda	Y	Y	Y	Y	N	Y	Y
40 Royce	N	Y	Y	Y	Y	N	N
41 Lewis	N	Y	Y	Y	Y	Y	N
42 Miller, Gary	N	N	Y	Y	Y	N	N
43 Baca	Y	Y	Y	Y	N	Y	Y
44 Calvert	N	Y	Y	Y	Y	Y	N
45 Bono Mack	N	Y	Y	Y	Y	Y	N
46 Rohrabacher	N	N	Y	Y	N	N	N
47 Sanchez, Loretta	Y	Y	Y	Y	N	Y	Y
48 Campbell	?	?	?	?	?	?	?
49 Issa	N	Y	Y	Y	Y	Y	N
50 Bilbray	N	Y	Y	Y	Y	Y	N
51 Filner	Y	Y	Y	Y	N	Y	Y
52 Hunter	N	?	Y	Y	Y	Y	N
53 Davis	Y	Y	Y	Y	N	Y	Y

	212	213	214	215	216	217	218
COLORADO							
1 DeGette	Y	Y	Y	Y	N	Y	Y
2 Udall	Y	Y	Y	Y	N	Y	Y
3 Salazar	Y	Y	Y	Y	N	Y	Y
4 Musgrave	N	N	Y	Y	Y	Y	N
5 Lamborn	N	N	Y	?	Y	Y	N
6 Tancredo	?	N	Y	Y	N	N	N
7 Perlmutter	Y	Y	Y	Y	N	Y	Y
CONNECTICUT							
1 Larson	Y	Y	Y	Y	N	Y	Y
2 Courtney	Y	Y	Y	Y	N	Y	Y
3 DeLauro	Y	Y	Y	Y	N	Y	Y
4 Shays	N	Y	Y	Y	Y	Y	N
5 Murphy	Y	Y	Y	Y	N	Y	Y
DELAWARE							
AL Castle	N	Y	Y	Y	Y	Y	N
FLORIDA							
1 Miller	N	N	Y	Y	Y	N	N
2 Boyd	Y	Y	Y	Y	N	Y	Y
3 Brown	Y	Y	Y	Y	N	Y	Y
4 Crenshaw	N	Y	Y	Y	Y	Y	N
5 Brown-Waite	?	?	?	?	?	?	?
6 Stearns	N	N	Y	Y	Y	N	N
7 Mica	N	Y	Y	Y	Y	Y	N
8 Keller	N	Y	Y	Y	Y	Y	N
9 Bilirakis	N	Y	Y	Y	Y	Y	N
10 Young	N	Y	Y	Y	Y	Y	N
11 Castor	Y	Y	Y	Y	N	Y	Y
12 Putnam	N	Y	Y	Y	Y	Y	N
13 Buchanan	N	Y	Y	Y	Y	Y	N
14 Mack	N	Y	Y	Y	Y	Y	N
15 Weldon	N	Y	Y	Y	Y	Y	N
16 Mahoney	Y	Y	Y	Y	N	Y	Y
17 Meek	Y	Y	Y	Y	N	Y	Y
18 Ros-Lehtinen	N	Y	Y	Y	Y	Y	N
19 Wexler	Y	Y	Y	Y	N	Y	Y
20 Wasserman Schultz	Y	Y	Y	Y	N	Y	Y
21 Diaz-Balart, L.	N	Y	Y	Y	Y	Y	N
22 Klein	Y	Y	Y	Y	N	Y	Y
23 Hastings	Y	Y	Y	Y	N	Y	Y
24 Feeney	?	?	?	?	?	?	?
25 Diaz-Balart, M.	N	Y	Y	Y	Y	Y	N
GEORGIA							
1 Kingston	N	N	Y	Y	Y	Y	N
2 Bishop	Y	Y	Y	Y	N	Y	Y
3 Westmoreland	N	?	Y	Y	Y	N	N
4 Johnson	Y	Y	Y	Y	N	Y	Y
5 Lewis	Y	Y	Y	Y	N	Y	Y
6 Price	N	Y	Y	Y	Y	Y	N
7 Linder	N	N	Y	Y	Y	N	N
8 Marshall	Y	Y	Y	Y	Y	Y	Y
9 Deal	N	Y	Y	Y	Y	Y	N
10 Broun	N	N	Y	Y	Y	N	N
11 Gingrey	N	N	Y	Y	Y	Y	N
12 Barrow	Y	Y	Y	Y	Y	Y	Y
13 Scott	Y	Y	Y	Y	N	Y	Y
HAWAII							
1 Abercrombie	Y	Y	Y	Y	N	Y	Y
2 Hirono	Y	Y	Y	Y	N	Y	Y
IDAHO							
1 Sali	N	N	Y	Y	Y	N	N
2 Simpson	N	Y	Y	Y	Y	Y	N
ILLINOIS							
1 Rush	?	?	?	?	?	?	?
2 Jackson	Y	Y	Y	Y	N	Y	Y
3 Lipinski	Y	Y	Y	Y	N	Y	Y
4 Gutierrez	Y	Y	Y	Y	N	Y	Y
5 Emanuel	Y	Y	Y	Y	N	Y	Y
6 Roskam	N	Y	Y	Y	Y	Y	N
7 Davis	Y	Y	Y	Y	N	Y	Y
8 Bean	Y	Y	Y	Y	N	Y	Y
9 Schakowsky	Y	Y	Y	Y	N	Y	Y
10 Kirk	N	Y	Y	Y	Y	Y	N
11 Weller	?	?	?	?	?	?	?
12 Costello	Y	Y	Y	Y	N	Y	Y
13 Biggert	N	Y	Y	Y	Y	Y	N
14 Foster	Y	Y	Y	Y	N	Y	Y
15 Johnson	N	Y	Y	Y	Y	Y	N

KEY

	Republicans	Democrats	
Y	Voted for (yea)	X Paired against	C Voted "present" to avoid possible conflict of interest
#	Paired for	– Announced against	
+	Announced for	P Voted "present"	? Did not vote or otherwise make a position known
N	Voted against (nay)		

ND Northern Democrats, SD Southern Democrats
Southern states: Ala., Ark., Fla., Ga., Ky., La., Miss., N.C., Okla., S.C., Tenn., Texas, Va.

	212	213	214	215	216	217	218
16 **Manzullo**	N	Y	Y	Y	Y	N	N
17 Hare	Y	Y	Y	Y	N	Y	Y
18 **LaHood**	N	?	?	?	?	?	?
19 **Shimkus**	N	N	Y	Y	Y	Y	N
INDIANA							
1 Visclosky	Y	Y	Y	Y	N	Y	Y
2 Donnelly	Y	Y	Y	Y	Y	Y	Y
3 **Souder**	N	Y	Y	Y	Y	Y	N
4 **Buyer**	N	?	?	?	Y	Y	N
5 **Burton**	N	N	Y	Y	Y	Y	N
6 **Pence**	N	N	Y	Y	Y	Y	N
7 Carson, A.	Y	Y	Y	Y	N	Y	Y
8 Ellsworth	Y	Y	Y	Y	N	Y	Y
9 Hill	Y	Y	Y	Y	Y	Y	Y
IOWA							
1 Braley	?	+	+	Y	N	Y	Y
2 Loebsack	Y	Y	Y	Y	N	Y	Y
3 Boswell	Y	Y	Y	Y	N	Y	Y
4 **Latham**	N	Y	Y	Y	Y	Y	N
5 **King**	N	N	Y	Y	?	Y	N
KANSAS							
1 **Moran**	N	Y	Y	Y	Y	Y	N
2 Boyda	Y	Y	Y	Y	N	Y	Y
3 Moore	Y	Y	Y	Y	N	Y	Y
4 **Tiahrt**	N	Y	Y	Y	Y	Y	N
KENTUCKY							
1 **Whitfield**	N	?	Y	Y	Y	Y	N
2 **Lewis**	N	Y	Y	Y	Y	Y	N
3 Yarmuth	Y	Y	Y	Y	N	Y	Y
4 **Davis**	N	N	Y	Y	Y	N	N
5 **Rogers**	N	Y	Y	Y	Y	Y	N
6 Chandler	Y	Y	Y	Y	N	Y	Y
LOUISIANA							
1 Vacant							
2 Jefferson	Y	Y	Y	Y	N	Y	Y
3 Melancon	Y	Y	Y	Y	N	Y	Y
4 **McCrery**	N	Y	Y	Y	Y	Y	N
5 **Alexander**	N	?	?	?	?	?	?
6 Vacant							
7 **Boustany**	N	Y	Y	Y	Y	Y	N
MAINE							
1 Allen	Y	Y	Y	Y	N	Y	Y
2 Michaud	Y	Y	Y	Y	N	Y	Y
MARYLAND							
1 **Gilchrest**	N	Y	Y	Y	Y	Y	N
2 Ruppersberger	Y	+	+	Y	N	Y	Y
3 Sarbanes	Y	Y	Y	Y	N	Y	Y
4 Wynn	Y	Y	Y	Y	N	Y	Y
5 Hoyer	Y	Y	Y	Y	N	Y	Y
6 **Bartlett**	N	Y	Y	Y	Y	Y	N
7 Cummings	Y	Y	Y	Y	N	Y	Y
8 Van Hollen	Y	Y	Y	Y	N	Y	Y
MASSACHUSETTS							
1 Olver	Y	Y	Y	Y	N	Y	Y
2 Neal	Y	Y	Y	Y	N	Y	Y
3 McGovern	Y	Y	Y	Y	N	Y	Y
4 Frank	Y	Y	Y	Y	N	Y	Y
5 Tsongas	Y	Y	Y	Y	N	N	Y
6 Tierney	Y	Y	Y	Y	N	Y	Y
7 Markey	Y	Y	Y	Y	N	N	Y
8 Capuano	Y	Y	Y	Y	N	Y	Y
9 Lynch	Y	Y	Y	Y	N	Y	Y
10 Delahunt	Y	Y	Y	Y	N	Y	Y
MICHIGAN							
1 Stupak	Y	Y	Y	Y	N	Y	Y
2 **Hoekstra**	N	Y	Y	Y	Y	Y	N
3 **Ehlers**	N	Y	Y	Y	Y	Y	N
4 **Camp**	N	Y	Y	Y	Y	Y	N
5 Kildee	Y	Y	Y	Y	N	Y	Y
6 **Upton**	N	Y	Y	Y	Y	Y	N
7 **Walberg**	N	Y	Y	Y	Y	Y	N
8 **Rogers**	N	N	Y	Y	Y	Y	N
9 **Knollenberg**	N	Y	Y	Y	Y	Y	N
10 **Miller**	N	Y	Y	Y	Y	Y	N
11 **McCotter**	N	Y	Y	Y	Y	Y	N
12 Levin	Y	Y	Y	Y	N	Y	Y
13 Kilpatrick	Y	Y	Y	Y	N	Y	Y
14 Conyers	Y	Y	Y	Y	N	Y	Y
15 Dingell	Y	Y	Y	Y	N	Y	Y
MINNESOTA							
1 Walz	Y	Y	Y	Y	N	Y	Y
2 **Kline**	N	Y	Y	Y	Y	Y	N
3 **Ramstad**	N	Y	Y	Y	Y	Y	N
4 McCollum	Y	Y	Y	Y	N	Y	Y

	212	213	214	215	216	217	218
5 Ellison	Y	Y	Y	Y	N	Y	Y
6 **Bachmann**	N	N	Y	Y	Y	Y	N
7 Peterson	Y	Y	Y	Y	N	Y	Y
8 Oberstar	Y	Y	Y	Y	N	Y	Y
MISSISSIPPI							
1 Vacant							
2 Thompson	Y	Y	Y	Y	N	Y	Y
3 **Pickering**	N	Y	?	Y	Y	Y	N
4 Taylor	Y	Y	Y	Y	N	Y	Y
MISSOURI							
1 Clay	Y	Y	Y	Y	N	Y	N
2 **Akin**	N	N	Y	Y	Y	Y	N
3 Carnahan	Y	Y	Y	Y	N	Y	Y
4 Skelton	Y	Y	Y	Y	N	Y	Y
5 Cleaver	?	Y	Y	Y	N	Y	Y
6 **Graves**	N	Y	Y	Y	Y	Y	N
7 **Blunt**	N	?	?	?	?	?	?
8 **Emerson**	N	Y	Y	Y	Y	Y	N
9 **Hulshof**	?	?	?	?	?	?	?
MONTANA							
AL **Rehberg**	N	Y	Y	Y	Y	Y	N
NEBRASKA							
1 **Fortenberry**	N	Y	Y	Y	Y	Y	N
2 **Terry**	N	Y	Y	Y	Y	Y	N
3 **Smith**	N	Y	Y	Y	Y	Y	N
NEVADA							
1 Berkley	Y	Y	Y	Y	N	Y	Y
2 **Heller**	N	Y	Y	Y	Y	Y	N
3 **Porter**	N	Y	Y	Y	Y	Y	N
NEW HAMPSHIRE							
1 Shea-Porter	Y	Y	Y	Y	N	Y	Y
2 Hodes	Y	Y	Y	Y	N	N	Y
NEW JERSEY							
1 Andrews	?	?	?	?	?	?	?
2 **LoBiondo**	N	Y	Y	Y	Y	Y	N
3 **Saxton**	N	?	?	?	Y	Y	N
4 **Smith**	N	Y	Y	Y	Y	Y	N
5 **Garrett**	N	N	Y	Y	Y	Y	N
6 Pallone	Y	Y	Y	Y	N	Y	Y
7 **Ferguson**	?	Y	Y	Y	Y	Y	?
8 Pascrell	Y	Y	Y	Y	N	Y	Y
9 Rothman	Y	Y	Y	Y	N	Y	Y
10 Payne	Y	Y	Y	Y	N	Y	Y
11 **Frelinghuysen**	N	Y	Y	Y	Y	Y	N
12 Holt	Y	Y	Y	Y	N	Y	Y
13 Sires	Y	Y	Y	Y	N	Y	Y
NEW MEXICO							
1 **Wilson**	N	N	Y	Y	Y	Y	N
2 **Pearce**	N	Y	Y	Y	Y	Y	N
3 Udall	Y	Y	Y	Y	N	Y	Y
NEW YORK							
1 Bishop	Y	Y	Y	Y	N	Y	Y
2 Israel	Y	Y	Y	Y	N	Y	Y
3 **King**	N	Y	Y	Y	Y	Y	N
4 McCarthy	Y	Y	Y	Y	N	Y	Y
5 Ackerman	Y	Y	Y	Y	N	Y	Y
6 Meeks	Y	Y	Y	Y	N	Y	Y
7 Crowley	Y	Y	Y	Y	N	Y	Y
8 Nadler	?	?	?	?	?	?	?
9 Weiner	Y	Y	Y	Y	N	Y	Y
10 Towns	Y	Y	Y	Y	N	Y	Y
11 Clarke	Y	Y	Y	Y	N	Y	Y
12 Velázquez	Y	Y	Y	Y	N	Y	Y
13 **Fossella**	N	Y	Y	Y	Y	Y	N
14 Maloney	Y	Y	Y	Y	N	Y	Y
15 Rangel	Y	Y	Y	Y	N	Y	?
16 Serrano	Y	Y	Y	Y	N	Y	Y
17 Engel	Y	Y	Y	Y	N	Y	Y
18 Lowey	Y	Y	Y	Y	N	Y	Y
19 Hall	Y	Y	Y	Y	N	Y	Y
20 Gillibrand	Y	Y	Y	Y	N	Y	Y
21 McNulty	Y	Y	Y	Y	N	Y	Y
22 Hinchey	Y	Y	Y	Y	N	Y	Y
23 **McHugh**	N	Y	Y	Y	Y	Y	N
24 Arcuri	Y	Y	Y	Y	N	Y	Y
25 **Walsh**	N	?	Y	Y	Y	Y	N
26 **Reynolds**	N	Y	Y	Y	Y	Y	N
27 Higgins	Y	?	?	?	?	?	?
28 Slaughter	Y	Y	Y	?	N	Y	Y
29 **Kuhl**	N	Y	Y	Y	Y	N	N
NORTH CAROLINA							
1 Butterfield	Y	Y	Y	Y	N	Y	Y
2 Etheridge	Y	Y	Y	Y	N	Y	Y
3 **Jones**	?	Y	Y	Y	Y	Y	N
4 Price	Y	Y	Y	Y	N	Y	Y

	212	213	214	215	216	217	218
5 **Foxx**	N	N	Y	Y	Y	N	N
6 **Coble**	N	Y	Y	Y	Y	Y	N
7 McIntyre	Y	Y	Y	Y	Y	Y	Y
8 **Hayes**	N	Y	Y	Y	Y	Y	N
9 **Myrick**	N	Y	Y	Y	Y	N	N
10 **McHenry**	N	Y	Y	Y	Y	Y	N
11 Shuler	Y	Y	Y	Y	N	Y	Y
12 Watt	Y	Y	Y	Y	N	Y	Y
13 Miller	Y	Y	Y	Y	N	Y	Y
NORTH DAKOTA							
AL Pomeroy	Y	Y	Y	Y	N	Y	Y
OHIO							
1 **Chabot**	N	Y	Y	Y	Y	Y	N
2 **Schmidt**	N	Y	Y	Y	Y	Y	N
3 **Turner**	N	Y	Y	Y	Y	Y	N
4 **Jordan**	N	N	Y	Y	Y	N	N
5 **Latta**	N	Y	Y	Y	Y	Y	N
6 Wilson	Y	Y	Y	Y	N	Y	Y
7 **Hobson**	N	Y	Y	Y	Y	Y	N
8 **Boehner**	N	Y	Y	Y	Y	N	N
9 Kaptur	Y	Y	Y	Y	N	Y	Y
10 Kucinich	Y	Y	Y	P	N	N	Y
11 Tubbs Jones	Y	Y	Y	Y	N	Y	Y
12 **Tiberi**	N	Y	Y	Y	Y	Y	N
13 Sutton	Y	Y	Y	Y	N	Y	Y
14 **LaTourette**	N	Y	Y	Y	Y	Y	N
15 **Pryce**	N	Y	Y	Y	Y	Y	N
16 **Regula**	N	Y	?	Y	Y	Y	N
17 Ryan	Y	Y	Y	Y	N	Y	Y
18 Space	Y	Y	Y	Y	Y	Y	Y
OKLAHOMA							
1 **Sullivan**	N	N	Y	Y	Y	Y	N
2 Boren	Y	Y	Y	Y	N	Y	Y
3 **Lucas**	N	Y	Y	Y	Y	Y	N
4 **Cole**	N	Y	Y	Y	Y	Y	N
5 **Fallin**	N	Y	Y	Y	Y	Y	N
OREGON							
1 Wu	Y	Y	?	?	N	Y	Y
2 **Walden**	N	Y	Y	Y	Y	Y	N
3 Blumenauer	Y	?	?	Y	N	Y	Y
4 DeFazio	Y	?	Y	Y	N	Y	Y
5 Hooley	Y	Y	Y	Y	N	Y	Y
PENNSYLVANIA							
1 Brady	Y	Y	Y	Y	N	Y	Y
2 Fattah	Y	Y	Y	Y	N	Y	Y
3 **English**	N	Y	Y	Y	Y	Y	N
4 Altmire	Y	Y	Y	Y	N	Y	Y
5 **Peterson**	N	?	?	?	?	?	?
6 **Gerlach**	N	Y	Y	Y	Y	Y	N
7 Sestak	Y	Y	Y	Y	N	Y	Y
8 Murphy, P.	Y	Y	Y	Y	N	Y	Y
9 **Shuster**	N	Y	Y	Y	Y	Y	N
10 Carney	Y	Y	Y	Y	N	Y	Y
11 Kanjorski	Y	Y	Y	Y	N	Y	Y
12 Murtha	Y	Y	Y	Y	N	Y	Y
13 Schwartz	Y	Y	Y	Y	N	Y	+
14 Doyle	Y	Y	Y	Y	N	Y	Y
15 **Dent**	N	Y	Y	Y	Y	Y	N
16 **Pitts**	N	Y	Y	Y	Y	Y	N
17 Holden	Y	Y	Y	Y	N	Y	Y
18 **Murphy, T.**	N	Y	Y	Y	Y	Y	N
19 **Platts**	N	Y	Y	Y	Y	Y	N
RHODE ISLAND							
1 Kennedy	Y	Y	Y	Y	N	Y	Y
2 Langevin	Y	Y	Y	Y	N	Y	Y
SOUTH CAROLINA							
1 **Brown**	N	Y	Y	Y	Y	Y	N
2 **Wilson**	N	N	Y	Y	Y	Y	N
3 **Barrett**	N	N	Y	Y	Y	Y	N
4 **Inglis**	N	Y	Y	Y	Y	Y	N
5 Spratt	Y	Y	Y	Y	N	Y	Y
6 Clyburn	+	+	+	+	−	+	+
SOUTH DAKOTA							
AL Herseth Sandlin	Y	Y	Y	Y	N	N	Y
TENNESSEE							
1 **Davis, D.**	N	N	Y	Y	Y	Y	N
2 **Duncan**	N	N	Y	Y	Y	N	N
3 **Wamp**	N	Y	Y	Y	Y	Y	N
4 Davis, L.	Y	Y	Y	Y	N	Y	Y
5 Cooper	+	+	+	+	N	Y	Y
6 Gordon	Y	Y	Y	Y	N	Y	Y
7 **Blackburn**	N	Y	Y	Y	Y	Y	N
8 Tanner	Y	Y	Y	Y	N	Y	Y
9 Cohen	Y	Y	Y	Y	N	Y	Y

	212	213	214	215	216	217	218
TEXAS							
1 **Gohmert**	N	Y	Y	Y	Y	Y	N
2 **Poe**	N	N	Y	Y	Y	N	N
3 **Johnson, S.**	N	Y	Y	Y	Y	Y	N
4 **Hall**	N	Y	Y	Y	Y	Y	N
5 **Hensarling**	N	Y	Y	Y	Y	N	N
6 **Barton**	N	N	Y	Y	Y	N	N
7 **Culberson**	N	Y	Y	Y	Y	N	N
8 **Brady**	N	N	Y	Y	Y	Y	N
9 Green, A.	Y	Y	Y	Y	N	Y	Y
10 **McCaul**	N	Y	Y	Y	Y	Y	N
11 **Conaway**	N	N	Y	Y	Y	Y	N
12 **Granger**	N	Y	Y	Y	Y	Y	N
13 **Thornberry**	N	N	Y	Y	Y	N	N
14 **Paul**	N	Y	Y	Y	Y	N	N
15 Hinojosa	Y	Y	Y	Y	N	Y	Y
16 Reyes	Y	Y	Y	Y	N	Y	Y
17 Edwards	Y	Y	Y	Y	N	Y	?
18 Jackson Lee	Y	Y	Y	Y	N	Y	Y
19 **Neugebauer**	N	N	Y	Y	Y	N	N
20 Gonzalez	Y	Y	Y	Y	N	Y	Y
21 **Smith**	N	Y	Y	Y	Y	Y	N
22 Lampson	Y	Y	Y	Y	Y	Y	N
23 Rodriguez	Y	Y	Y	Y	N	Y	Y
24 **Marchant**	N	N	Y	Y	Y	N	N
25 Doggett	?	?	?	?	?	?	?
26 **Burgess**	N	N	Y	Y	Y	N	N
27 Ortiz	Y	Y	Y	Y	N	Y	Y
28 Cuellar	Y	Y	Y	Y	N	Y	Y
29 Green, G.	Y	Y	Y	Y	N	Y	Y
30 Johnson, E.	Y	Y	Y	Y	N	Y	Y
31 **Carter**	N	N	Y	Y	Y	N	N
32 **Sessions**	N	Y	Y	Y	Y	N	N
UTAH							
1 **Bishop**	N	Y	Y	Y	Y	Y	N
2 Matheson	Y	Y	Y	Y	N	Y	Y
3 **Cannon**	N	Y	Y	Y	Y	Y	N
VERMONT							
AL Welch	Y	Y	Y	Y	N	Y	Y
VIRGINIA							
1 **Wittman**	N	Y	Y	Y	Y	Y	N
2 **Drake**	N	Y	Y	Y	Y	Y	N
3 Scott	Y	Y	Y	Y	N	Y	Y
4 **Forbes**	N	Y	Y	Y	Y	Y	N
5 **Goode**	N	Y	Y	Y	Y	Y	N
6 **Goodlatte**	N	+	Y	Y	Y	Y	N
7 **Cantor**	N	Y	Y	Y	Y	Y	N
8 Moran	Y	?	?	?	?	?	?
9 Boucher	Y	Y	Y	Y	N	Y	Y
10 **Wolf**	N	Y	Y	Y	Y	Y	N
11 **Davis**	N	?	?	?	?	?	?
WASHINGTON							
1 Inslee	Y	Y	Y	Y	N	Y	Y
2 Larsen	Y	Y	Y	Y	N	Y	Y
3 Baird	Y	Y	Y	Y	N	Y	Y
4 **Hastings**	N	Y	Y	Y	Y	Y	N
5 **McMorris Rodgers**	N	Y	Y	Y	Y	Y	N
6 Dicks	Y	?	?	?	?	?	?
7 McDermott	Y	Y	Y	Y	N	Y	Y
8 **Reichert**	N	Y	Y	Y	Y	Y	N
9 Smith	Y	Y	Y	Y	N	Y	Y
WEST VIRGINIA							
1 Mollohan	Y	Y	Y	Y	N	Y	Y
2 **Capito**	N	Y	Y	Y	Y	Y	N
3 Rahall	Y	Y	Y	Y	N	Y	Y
WISCONSIN							
1 **Ryan**	N	N	Y	Y	Y	Y	N
2 Baldwin	Y	Y	Y	Y	N	Y	Y
3 Kind	Y	Y	Y	Y	N	Y	Y
4 Moore	Y	Y	Y	Y	N	Y	Y
5 **Sensenbrenner**	N	N	Y	Y	Y	N	N
6 **Petri**	N	N	Y	Y	Y	Y	N
7 Obey	?	Y	Y	Y	N	Y	Y
8 Kagen	?	Y	Y	Y	N	Y	Y
WYOMING							
AL **Cubin**	N	N	Y	Y	Y	N	N
DELEGATES							
Faleomavaega (A.S.)		Y	Y	Y			
Norton (D.C.)		Y	Y	Y			
Bordallo (Guam)		Y	Y	Y			
Fortuño (P.R.)		?	?	?			
Christensen (V.I.)		Y	Y	Y			

IN THE HOUSE | By Vote Number

219. **HR 2830. Coast Guard Reauthorization/Rule.** Adoption of the rule (H Res 1126) that would provide for House floor consideration of the bill that would authorize $8.4 billion in fiscal 2008 for the Coast Guard and require several changes in the Deepwater program to replace aging ships and aircraft. The rule also would add provisions to increase penalties for knowingly bringing an illegal immigrant into the country or harboring an illegal immigrant. Adopted 223-183: R 5-181; D 218-2 (ND 169-1, SD 49-1). April 23, 2008.

220. **HR 2830. Coast Guard Reauthorization/Submersible Vessel.** Poe, R-Texas, amendment that would make the operation of any stateless submersible or semi-submersible vessel a federal crime, subject to fines, imprisonment or both. Adopted in Committee of the Whole 408-1: R 182-1; D 226-0 (ND 171-0, SD 55-0). April 24, 2008.

221. **HR 2830. Coast Guard Reauthorization/Homeland Security.** McNerney, D-Calif., amendment that would clarify that the bill's marine-safety provisions would not harm the Coast Guard's legal authority to carry out its homeland security mission. Adopted in Committee of the Whole 408-0: R 184-0; D 224-0 (ND 171-0, SD 53-0). April 24, 2008.

222. **HR 2830. Coast Guard Reauthorization/Recommit.** Chabot, R-Ohio, motion to recommit the bill to the Transportation and Infrastructure Committee with instructions that it be reported back forthwith with language that would extend an exemption regarding fire-retardant materials on passenger vessels from November 2008 to November 2018. Motion rejected 195-208: R 173-10; D 22-198 (ND 14-152, SD 8-46). April 24, 2008.

223. **HR 2830. Coast Guard Reauthorization/Passage.** Passage of the bill that would authorize $8.4 billion in fiscal 2008 for the Coast Guard, including $6 billion for operations and maintenance, and $1.1 billion for acquisition and construction. It would authorize 47,000 active-duty personnel for the Coast Guard and require several changes in the Deepwater program to replace aging ships and aircraft. The bill also would set requirements for security around vessels that transport liquefied natural gas (LNG) and for LNG-processing facilities. Passed 395-7: R 175-7; D 220-0 (ND 167-0, SD 53-0). A "nay" was a vote in support of the president's position. April 24, 2008.

	219	220	221	222	223
ALABAMA					
1 Bonner	N	Y	Y	Y	Y
2 Everett	?	?	?	?	?
3 Rogers	N	Y	Y	Y	Y
4 Aderholt	N	Y	Y	Y	Y
5 Cramer	?	?	?	?	?
6 Bachus	N	Y	Y	Y	Y
7 Davis	Y	Y	Y	Y	Y
ALASKA					
AL Young	Y	Y	Y	N	Y
ARIZONA					
1 Renzi	N	Y	Y	Y	Y
2 Franks	N	Y	Y	Y	Y
3 Shadegg	N	Y	Y	Y	Y
4 Pastor	Y	Y	Y	N	Y
5 Mitchell	Y	Y	Y	N	Y
6 Flake	N	Y	Y	Y	N
7 Grijalva	Y	Y	Y	N	Y
8 Giffords	Y	Y	Y	N	Y
ARKANSAS					
1 Berry	Y	Y	Y	N	Y
2 Snyder	Y	Y	Y	N	Y
3 Boozman	N	Y	Y	Y	Y
4 Ross	Y	Y	Y	N	Y
CALIFORNIA					
1 Thompson	Y	Y	Y	N	Y
2 Herger	N	Y	Y	Y	Y
3 Lungren	N	?	Y	Y	Y
4 Doolittle	N	Y	Y	Y	Y
5 Matsui	Y	Y	Y	N	Y
6 Woolsey	Y	Y	Y	N	Y
7 Miller, George	Y	Y	Y	N	?
8 Pelosi					
9 Lee	Y	Y	Y	N	Y
10 Tauscher	Y	Y	Y	N	Y
11 McNerney	Y	Y	Y	Y	Y
12 Speier	Y	Y	Y	N	Y
13 Stark	Y	Y	Y	N	Y
14 Eshoo	Y	Y	Y	N	Y
15 Honda	Y	Y	Y	N	Y
16 Lofgren	Y	Y	Y	N	Y
17 Farr	Y	Y	Y	N	Y
18 Cardoza	?	Y	Y	N	Y
19 Radanovich	N	Y	?	?	?
20 Costa	Y	Y	Y	N	Y
21 Nunes	N	Y	Y	Y	N
22 McCarthy	N	Y	Y	Y	Y
23 Capps	Y	Y	Y	N	Y
24 Gallegly	N	Y	Y	Y	Y
25 McKeon	N	Y	Y	Y	Y
26 Dreier	N	Y	Y	Y	Y
27 Sherman	Y	Y	Y	N	Y
28 Berman	Y	Y	Y	N	Y
29 Schiff	Y	Y	Y	N	Y
30 Waxman	Y	?	Y	N	Y
31 Becerra	Y	Y	Y	N	Y
32 Solis	Y	Y	Y	N	Y
33 Watson	Y	Y	Y	N	Y
34 Roybal-Allard	Y	Y	Y	N	Y
35 Waters	Y	Y	Y	N	Y
36 Harman	Y	Y	Y	N	Y
37 Richardson	Y	Y	Y	N	Y
38 Napolitano	Y	Y	Y	N	Y
39 Sánchez, Linda	Y	Y	Y	N	Y
40 Royce	N	Y	Y	Y	Y
41 Lewis	N	Y	Y	Y	Y
42 Miller, Gary	N	Y	Y	Y	Y
43 Baca	Y	Y	Y	N	Y
44 Calvert	N	Y	Y	Y	Y
45 Bono Mack	N	Y	Y	Y	Y
46 Rohrabacher	N	Y	Y	Y	Y
47 Sanchez, Loretta	Y	Y	Y	N	Y
48 Campbell	?	?	?	?	?
49 Issa	N	Y	Y	Y	Y
50 Bilbray	N	Y	Y	Y	Y
51 Filner	Y	Y	Y	N	Y
52 Hunter	N	Y	Y	Y	Y
53 Davis	Y	Y	Y	N	Y

	219	220	221	222	223
COLORADO					
1 DeGette	Y	Y	Y	N	Y
2 Udall	Y	Y	Y	N	Y
3 Salazar	Y	Y	Y	N	Y
4 Musgrave	N	Y	Y	Y	Y
5 Lamborn	N	Y	Y	Y	Y
6 Tancredo	N	Y	Y	Y	N
7 Perlmutter	Y	Y	Y	N	Y
CONNECTICUT					
1 Larson	Y	Y	Y	N	Y
2 Courtney	Y	Y	Y	N	Y
3 DeLauro	Y	Y	Y	N	Y
4 Shays	N	Y	Y	Y	Y
5 Murphy	Y	Y	Y	N	Y
DELAWARE					
AL Castle	N	Y	Y	Y	Y
FLORIDA					
1 Miller	N	Y	Y	Y	Y
2 Boyd	Y	Y	Y	N	?
3 Brown	Y	Y	Y	N	Y
4 Crenshaw	N	Y	Y	Y	Y
5 Brown-Waite	?	?	?	?	?
6 Stearns	N	Y	Y	Y	Y
7 Mica	N	Y	Y	Y	Y
8 Keller	N	Y	Y	Y	Y
9 Bilirakis	N	Y	Y	Y	Y
10 Young	N	Y	Y	Y	Y
11 Castor	Y	Y	Y	N	Y
12 Putnam	N	Y	Y	Y	Y
13 Buchanan	N	Y	Y	Y	Y
14 Mack	N	Y	Y	Y	Y
15 Weldon	N	Y	Y	Y	?
16 Mahoney	Y	Y	Y	N	Y
17 Meek	Y	Y	Y	N	Y
18 Ros-Lehtinen	N	Y	Y	Y	Y
19 Wexler	Y	Y	Y	N	Y
20 Wasserman Schultz	Y	Y	Y	N	Y
21 Diaz-Balart, L.	N	?	Y	N	Y
22 Klein	Y	Y	Y	N	Y
23 Hastings	Y	Y	Y	N	Y
24 Feeney	?	?	?	?	?
25 Diaz-Balart, M.	N	Y	Y	N	Y
GEORGIA					
1 Kingston	N	Y	Y	Y	Y
2 Bishop	Y	Y	Y	N	Y
3 Westmoreland	N	Y	Y	Y	Y
4 Johnson	Y	Y	Y	N	Y
5 Lewis	Y	Y	Y	N	Y
6 Price	N	Y	Y	Y	Y
7 Linder	N	Y	Y	Y	Y
8 Marshall	?	Y	?	Y	Y
9 Deal	N	Y	Y	Y	Y
10 Broun	N	Y	Y	Y	Y
11 Gingrey	N	Y	Y	Y	Y
12 Barrow	Y	Y	Y	N	Y
13 Scott	Y	Y	Y	N	Y
HAWAII					
1 Abercrombie	Y	Y	Y	N	Y
2 Hirono	Y	Y	Y	N	Y
IDAHO					
1 Sali	N	Y	Y	Y	Y
2 Simpson	N	Y	Y	Y	Y
ILLINOIS					
1 Rush	?	?	?	?	?
2 Jackson	Y	Y	Y	N	Y
3 Lipinski	Y	Y	Y	N	Y
4 Gutierrez	Y	Y	Y	N	Y
5 Emanuel	Y	Y	Y	N	Y
6 Roskam	N	Y	Y	Y	Y
7 Davis	Y	Y	Y	N	Y
8 Bean	Y	Y	Y	N	Y
9 Schakowsky	Y	Y	Y	N	Y
10 Kirk	Y	Y	Y	Y	Y
11 Weller	?	?	?	?	?
12 Costello	Y	Y	Y	?	Y
13 Biggert	N	Y	Y	?	Y
14 Foster	Y	Y	Y	Y	Y
15 Johnson	N	Y	Y	Y	Y

KEY	Republicans	Democrats			
Y	Voted for (yea)	X	Paired against	C	Voted "present" to avoid possible conflict of interest
#	Paired for	−	Announced against		
+	Announced for	P	Voted "present"	?	Did not vote or otherwise make a position known
N	Voted against (nay)				

ND Northern Democrats, SD Southern Democrats
Southern states: Ala., Ark., Fla., Ga., Ky., La., Miss., N.C., Okla., S.C., Tenn., Texas, Va.

Member	219	220	221	222	223
16 Manzullo	N	Y	Y	Y	Y
17 Hare	Y	Y	Y	Y	Y
18 LaHood	?	?	?	?	?
19 Shimkus	N	Y	Y	Y	Y
INDIANA					
1 Visclosky	Y	Y	Y	N	Y
2 Donnelly	Y	Y	Y	N	Y
3 Souder	N	Y	Y	Y	Y
4 Buyer	N	Y	Y	Y	?
5 Burton	N	Y	Y	Y	Y
6 Pence	N	Y	Y	Y	Y
7 Carson, A.	Y	Y	Y	N	Y
8 Ellsworth	Y	Y	Y	Y	Y
9 Hill	Y	Y	Y	Y	Y
IOWA					
1 Braley	Y	Y	Y	Y	Y
2 Loebsack	Y	Y	+	Y	Y
3 Boswell	Y	Y	Y	N	Y
4 Latham	N	Y	Y	Y	Y
5 King	N	Y	Y	Y	Y
KANSAS					
1 Moran	N	Y	Y	Y	Y
2 Boyda	Y	Y	Y	Y	Y
3 Moore	Y	Y	Y	N	Y
4 Tiahrt	N	Y	Y	Y	Y
KENTUCKY					
1 Whitfield	N	Y	Y	Y	Y
2 Lewis	N	Y	Y	Y	Y
3 Yarmuth	Y	Y	?	?	?
4 Davis	N	Y	Y	Y	Y
5 Rogers	N	Y	Y	Y	N
6 Chandler	Y	Y	Y	Y	Y
LOUISIANA					
1 Vacant					
2 Jefferson	Y	Y	Y	Y	Y
3 Melancon	Y	Y	Y	Y	Y
4 McCrery	N	?	Y	Y	Y
5 Alexander	?	?	?	?	?
6 Vacant					
7 Boustany	N	Y	Y	Y	Y
MAINE					
1 Allen	Y	Y	Y	N	Y
2 Michaud	Y	Y	Y	N	Y
MARYLAND					
1 Gilchrest	N	Y	Y	Y	Y
2 Ruppersberger	Y	Y	Y	N	Y
3 Sarbanes	Y	Y	Y	N	Y
4 Wynn	Y	Y	Y	?	Y
5 Hoyer	Y	Y	Y	N	Y
6 Bartlett	N	Y	Y	Y	Y
7 Cummings	Y	Y	Y	N	Y
8 Van Hollen	Y	Y	Y	N	Y
MASSACHUSETTS					
1 Olver	Y	Y	Y	N	Y
2 Neal	Y	Y	Y	N	Y
3 McGovern	Y	Y	Y	N	Y
4 Frank	Y	Y	Y	N	Y
5 Tsongas	Y	Y	Y	N	Y
6 Tierney	Y	Y	Y	N	Y
7 Markey	Y	Y	Y	N	Y
8 Capuano	Y	Y	Y	N	Y
9 Lynch	Y	Y	Y	N	Y
10 Delahunt	Y	Y	Y	N	Y
MICHIGAN					
1 Stupak	Y	Y	Y	N	Y
2 Hoekstra	N	Y	Y	Y	Y
3 Ehlers	N	Y	Y	Y	Y
4 Camp	N	Y	Y	Y	Y
5 Kildee	Y	Y	Y	N	Y
6 Upton	N	Y	Y	Y	Y
7 Walberg	N	Y	Y	Y	Y
8 Rogers	N	Y	Y	Y	Y
9 Knollenberg	N	Y	Y	Y	Y
10 Miller	N	Y	Y	Y	N
11 McCotter	N	Y	Y	Y	Y
12 Levin	Y	Y	Y	N	Y
13 Kilpatrick	Y	Y	Y	N	Y
14 Conyers	Y	Y	Y	N	Y
15 Dingell	Y	Y	Y	N	Y
MINNESOTA					
1 Walz	Y	Y	Y	N	Y
2 Kline	N	Y	Y	Y	Y
3 Ramstad	N	Y	Y	Y	Y
4 McCollum	Y	Y	Y	N	Y

Member	219	220	221	222	223
5 Ellison	Y	Y	Y	N	Y
6 Bachmann	N	Y	Y	Y	Y
7 Peterson	Y	Y	Y	N	Y
8 Oberstar	Y	Y	Y	N	Y
MISSISSIPPI					
1 Vacant					
2 Thompson	Y	Y	Y	N	Y
3 Pickering	N	Y	Y	Y	Y
4 Taylor	N	Y	Y	Y	Y
MISSOURI					
1 Clay	N	Y	Y	Y	Y
2 Akin	N	Y	Y	Y	Y
3 Carnahan	Y	Y	Y	N	Y
4 Skelton	Y	Y	Y	N	Y
5 Cleaver	Y	Y	Y	N	Y
6 Graves	N	Y	Y	Y	Y
7 Blunt	?	Y	Y	Y	Y
8 Emerson	N	Y	Y	Y	Y
9 Hulshof	?	?	?	?	?
MONTANA					
AL Rehberg	N	Y	Y	Y	Y
NEBRASKA					
1 Fortenberry	N	Y	Y	Y	Y
2 Terry	N	Y	Y	Y	Y
3 Smith	N	Y	Y	Y	Y
NEVADA					
1 Berkley	Y	Y	Y	N	Y
2 Heller	N	Y	Y	Y	Y
3 Porter	N	?	?	?	?
NEW HAMPSHIRE					
1 Shea-Porter	Y	Y	Y	N	Y
2 Hodes	Y	Y	Y	N	Y
NEW JERSEY					
1 Andrews	?	?	?	?	?
2 LoBiondo	N	Y	Y	N	Y
3 Saxton	Y	Y	Y	Y	Y
4 Smith	N	Y	Y	N	Y
5 Garrett	N	Y	Y	Y	Y
6 Pallone	Y	Y	Y	N	Y
7 Ferguson	?	Y	Y	Y	Y
8 Pascrell	Y	?	?	?	?
9 Rothman	Y	Y	Y	N	Y
10 Payne	Y	Y	Y	N	Y
11 Frelinghuysen	N	Y	Y	Y	Y
12 Holt	Y	Y	Y	N	Y
13 Sires	Y	Y	Y	N	Y
NEW MEXICO					
1 Wilson	N	Y	Y	Y	Y
2 Pearce	N	Y	Y	Y	Y
3 Udall	Y	?	?	?	?
NEW YORK					
1 Bishop	Y	Y	Y	N	Y
2 Israel	Y	Y	Y	N	Y
3 King	N	Y	Y	N	Y
4 McCarthy	Y	Y	Y	N	Y
5 Ackerman	Y	Y	Y	N	Y
6 Meeks	Y	Y	Y	N	Y
7 Crowley	Y	Y	Y	N	Y
8 Nadler	?	?	?	?	?
9 Weiner	Y	Y	Y	N	Y
10 Towns	Y	Y	Y	N	Y
11 Clarke	Y	Y	Y	N	Y
12 Velázquez	Y	Y	Y	N	Y
13 Fossella	N	Y	Y	Y	Y
14 Maloney	Y	Y	Y	N	Y
15 Rangel	Y	Y	Y	N	Y
16 Serrano	Y	Y	Y	N	Y
17 Engel	Y	Y	Y	N	Y
18 Lowey	Y	Y	Y	N	Y
19 Hall	Y	Y	Y	N	Y
20 Gillibrand	Y	Y	Y	N	Y
21 McNulty	Y	Y	Y	?	?
22 Hinchey	Y	Y	Y	N	Y
23 McHugh	N	Y	Y	N	Y
24 Arcuri	Y	Y	Y	N	Y
25 Walsh	N	Y	Y	Y	Y
26 Reynolds	N	Y	?	Y	Y
27 Higgins	?	?	?	?	?
28 Slaughter	Y	Y	Y	?	Y
29 Kuhl	N	Y	Y	Y	Y
NORTH CAROLINA					
1 Butterfield	Y	Y	Y	N	Y
2 Etheridge	Y	Y	Y	N	Y
3 Jones	N	Y	Y	Y	Y
4 Price	Y	Y	Y	N	Y

Member	219	220	221	222	223
5 Foxx	N	Y	Y	Y	Y
6 Coble	N	Y	Y	Y	N
7 McIntyre	Y	Y	Y	N	Y
8 Hayes	N	Y	Y	Y	Y
9 Myrick	N	Y	Y	Y	Y
10 McHenry	N	Y	Y	Y	Y
11 Shuler	Y	Y	Y	N	Y
12 Watt	Y	Y	Y	N	Y
13 Miller	Y	Y	Y	N	Y
NORTH DAKOTA					
AL Pomeroy	Y	Y	Y	N	Y
OHIO					
1 Chabot	N	Y	Y	Y	Y
2 Schmidt	N	Y	Y	Y	Y
3 Turner	N	Y	Y	Y	Y
4 Jordan	N	Y	Y	Y	Y
5 Latta	N	Y	Y	Y	Y
6 Wilson	Y	Y	Y	N	Y
7 Hobson	N	Y	Y	Y	Y
8 Boehner	N	Y	Y	Y	Y
9 Kaptur	Y	Y	Y	N	Y
10 Kucinich	Y	Y	Y	N	Y
11 Tubbs Jones	Y	Y	Y	N	Y
12 Tiberi	N	Y	Y	Y	Y
13 Sutton	Y	Y	Y	N	Y
14 LaTourette	Y	Y	Y	N	Y
15 Pryce	N	?	?	?	?
16 Regula	N	Y	Y	Y	Y
17 Ryan	Y	Y	Y	N	Y
18 Space	Y	Y	Y	N	Y
OKLAHOMA					
1 Sullivan	N	Y	Y	Y	Y
2 Boren	?	Y	Y	N	Y
3 Lucas	N	Y	Y	Y	Y
4 Cole	N	Y	Y	Y	Y
5 Fallin	N	Y	Y	Y	Y
OREGON					
1 Wu	Y	Y	Y	N	Y
2 Walden	N	Y	Y	Y	Y
3 Blumenauer	Y	Y	?	N	Y
4 DeFazio	Y	Y	Y	N	Y
5 Hooley	Y	Y	Y	N	Y
PENNSYLVANIA					
1 Brady	Y	Y	Y	N	Y
2 Fattah	Y	Y	Y	N	Y
3 English	N	Y	Y	Y	Y
4 Altmire	Y	Y	Y	Y	Y
5 Peterson	?	Y	Y	Y	Y
6 Gerlach	N	Y	Y	Y	Y
7 Sestak	Y	Y	Y	N	Y
8 Murphy, P.	Y	Y	Y	N	Y
9 Shuster	N	Y	Y	Y	Y
10 Carney	Y	Y	Y	N	Y
11 Kanjorski	Y	Y	Y	N	Y
12 Murtha	Y	Y	Y	N	Y
13 Schwartz	Y	Y	Y	N	Y
14 Doyle	Y	Y	Y	N	Y
15 Dent	N	Y	Y	Y	Y
16 Pitts	N	Y	Y	Y	Y
17 Holden	Y	Y	Y	N	Y
18 Murphy, T.	N	Y	Y	N	Y
19 Platts	N	Y	Y	Y	Y
RHODE ISLAND					
1 Kennedy	Y	Y	Y	N	Y
2 Langevin	Y	Y	Y	N	Y
SOUTH CAROLINA					
1 Brown	N	Y	Y	Y	Y
2 Wilson	N	Y	Y	Y	Y
3 Barrett	N	Y	Y	Y	Y
4 Inglis	N	Y	Y	Y	Y
5 Spratt	Y	Y	Y	N	Y
6 Clyburn	+	Y	Y	N	Y
SOUTH DAKOTA					
AL Herseth Sandlin	Y	Y	Y	N	Y
TENNESSEE					
1 Davis, D.	N	Y	Y	Y	Y
2 Duncan	N	Y	Y	Y	N
3 Wamp	N	Y	Y	Y	Y
4 Davis, L.	Y	Y	Y	N	Y
5 Cooper	Y	Y	Y	N	Y
6 Gordon	Y	Y	Y	N	Y
7 Blackburn	N	?	?	?	?
8 Tanner	Y	Y	Y	N	Y
9 Cohen	Y	Y	Y	N	Y

Member	219	220	221	222	223
TEXAS					
1 Gohmert	N	Y	Y	Y	Y
2 Poe	N	Y	Y	Y	Y
3 Johnson, S.	N	Y	Y	Y	Y
4 Hall	N	Y	Y	Y	Y
5 Hensarling	N	Y	Y	Y	Y
6 Barton	N	Y	Y	Y	Y
7 Culberson	N	Y	Y	Y	Y
8 Brady	N	Y	Y	Y	Y
9 Green, A.	Y	Y	Y	N	Y
10 McCaul	N	Y	Y	Y	Y
11 Conaway	N	Y	Y	Y	Y
12 Granger	N	Y	Y	Y	Y
13 Thornberry	N	Y	Y	Y	Y
14 Paul	N	N	Y	Y	N
15 Hinojosa	Y	Y	Y	N	Y
16 Reyes	Y	Y	Y	N	Y
17 Edwards	?	Y	Y	N	Y
18 Jackson Lee	Y	Y	Y	N	Y
19 Neugebauer	N	Y	Y	Y	Y
20 Gonzalez	Y	Y	Y	N	Y
21 Smith	N	Y	Y	Y	Y
22 Lampson	Y	Y	Y	N	Y
23 Rodriguez	Y	Y	Y	N	Y
24 Marchant	N	Y	Y	Y	Y
25 Doggett	?	?	?	?	?
26 Burgess	N	?	?	?	?
27 Ortiz	Y	Y	Y	N	Y
28 Cuellar	Y	Y	Y	N	Y
29 Green, G.	Y	Y	Y	N	Y
30 Johnson, E.	Y	Y	Y	N	Y
31 Carter	N	Y	Y	Y	Y
32 Sessions	N	Y	Y	Y	Y
UTAH					
1 Bishop	N	Y	Y	Y	Y
2 Matheson	Y	Y	Y	N	Y
3 Cannon	N	Y	Y	Y	Y
VERMONT					
AL Welch	Y	Y	Y	N	Y
VIRGINIA					
1 Wittman	N	Y	Y	Y	Y
2 Drake	N	Y	Y	Y	Y
3 Scott	Y	Y	Y	N	Y
4 Forbes	N	Y	Y	Y	Y
5 Goode	N	Y	Y	Y	Y
6 Goodlatte	N	Y	Y	Y	Y
7 Cantor	N	Y	Y	Y	Y
8 Moran	?	Y	Y	N	Y
9 Boucher	Y	Y	Y	N	Y
10 Wolf	N	Y	Y	Y	Y
11 Davis	?	Y	Y	Y	Y
WASHINGTON					
1 Inslee	Y	Y	Y	N	Y
2 Larsen	Y	Y	Y	N	Y
3 Baird	Y	Y	Y	N	Y
4 Hastings	N	Y	Y	Y	Y
5 McMorris Rodgers	N	Y	Y	Y	Y
6 Dicks	?	Y	Y	N	Y
7 McDermott	Y	Y	Y	N	Y
8 Reichert	N	Y	Y	Y	Y
9 Smith	Y	Y	Y	N	Y
WEST VIRGINIA					
1 Mollohan	Y	Y	Y	N	Y
2 Capito	N	Y	Y	Y	Y
3 Rahall	Y	Y	Y	N	Y
WISCONSIN					
1 Ryan	N	?	?	?	?
2 Baldwin	Y	Y	Y	N	Y
3 Kind	Y	?	Y	Y	Y
4 Moore	Y	Y	Y	N	Y
5 Sensenbrenner	N	Y	Y	Y	Y
6 Petri	N	Y	Y	Y	Y
7 Obey	Y	Y	Y	N	Y
8 Kagen	Y	Y	Y	N	Y
WYOMING					
AL Cubin	Y	Y	Y	Y	Y
DELEGATES					
Faleomavaega (A.S.)	?	?			
Norton (D.C.)	Y	Y			
Bordallo (Guam)	Y	Y			
Fortuño (P.R.)	Y	Y			
Christensen (V.I.)	Y	Y			

IN THE HOUSE | By Vote Number

224. **H Res 1079. Financial Literacy Month/Adoption.** Hinojosa, D-Texas, motion to suspend the rules and adopt the resolution that would support the goals and ideals of Financial Literacy Month and recognize the importance of managing personal finances. Motion agreed to 402-2: R 186-2; D 216-0 (ND 162-0, SD 54-0). A two-thirds majority of those present and voting (270 in this case) is required for adoption under suspension of the rules. April 29, 2008.

225. **HR 4332. Financial Consumer Hotline/Passage.** Maloney, D-N.Y., motion to suspend the rules and pass the bill that would create a toll-free consumer hotline for complaints and inquiries and would direct consumers to the appropriate banking regulator for assistance. Motion agreed to 408-1: R 186-1; D 222-0 (ND 168-0, SD 54-0). A two-thirds majority of those present and voting (273 in this case) is required for passage under suspension of the rules. April 29, 2008.

226. **S 2739. Omnibus Public Lands/Passage.** Rahall, D-W.Va., motion to suspend the rules and pass the bill that would designate new park, wilderness and scenic areas and would authorize programs and activities in the Forest Service, the departments of Interior and Energy, the Bureau of Reclamation, the U.S. Geological Survey and the Bureau of Land Management. It would add 106,000 acres in Washington state to the National Wilderness Preservation System, which would be known as the "Wild Sky Wilderness." It would also apply federal immigration laws to the Northern Mariana Islands and give the commonwealth a non-voting House delegate. Motion agreed to 291-117: R 70-117; D 221-0 (ND 167-0, SD 54-0). A two-thirds majority of those present and voting (272 in this case) is required for passage under suspension of the rules. April 29, 2008.

227. **HR 5522. Combustible Dust Safety/Previous Question.** McGovern, D-Mass., motion to order the previous question (thus ending debate and possibility of amendment) on adoption of the rule (H Res 1157) that would provide for House floor consideration of the bill that would require regulation of combustible dusts. Motion agreed to 226-194: R 0-193; D 226-1 (ND 171-0, SD 55-1). April 30, 2008.

228. **HR 5522. Combustible Dust Safety/Rule.** Adoption of the rule (H Res 1157) that would provide for House floor consideration of the bill that would require regulation of combustible dusts. Adopted 222-193: R 0-192; D 222-1 (ND 169-0, SD 53-1). April 30, 2008.

229. **HR 1195. Surface Transportation Law Revisions/Passage.** Oberstar, D-Minn., motion to suspend the rules and concur in the Senate amendment to the bill that amends the 2005 surface transportation law to make technical corrections and certain policy changes. The bill would increase the minimum state share of total highway safety formula grants from 0.5 percent to 0.75 percent, allow states to impose certain requirements on repeat intoxicated drivers and authorize $45 million for a high-speed, magnetic levitation rail line from Las Vegas to Anaheim, Calif. It would call for a Justice Department review of allegations of federal criminal law violations regarding the $10 million earmark in the 2005 surface transportation bill that was altered after Congress cleared it. Motion agreed to (thus clearing the bill for the president) 358-51: R 138-51; D 220-0 (ND 167-0, SD 53-0). A two-thirds majority of those present and voting (273 in this case) is required for passage under suspension of the rules. A "nay" was a vote in support of the president's position. April 30, 2008.

	224	225	226	227	228	229
ALABAMA						
1 **Bonner**	Y	Y	N	N	N	P
2 **Everett**	Y	Y	N	N	N	Y
3 **Rogers**	Y	Y	N	N	N	Y
4 **Aderholt**	Y	Y	N	N	N	Y
5 Cramer	Y	Y	Y	Y	Y	Y
6 **Bachus**	Y	Y	N	N	N	Y
7 Davis	Y	Y	Y	Y	Y	Y
ALASKA						
AL **Young**	Y	Y	N	N	N	Y
ARIZONA						
1 **Renzi**	Y	Y	Y	N	N	Y
2 **Franks**	Y	Y	N	N	N	N
3 **Shadegg**	Y	Y	N	N	N	N
4 Pastor	Y	Y	Y	Y	Y	Y
5 Mitchell	Y	Y	Y	Y	Y	Y
6 **Flake**	N	Y	N	N	N	N
7 Grijalva	Y	Y	Y	Y	Y	Y
8 Giffords	Y	Y	Y	Y	Y	Y
ARKANSAS						
1 Berry	Y	Y	Y	Y	Y	Y
2 Snyder	Y	Y	Y	Y	Y	Y
3 **Boozman**	Y	Y	N	N	N	Y
4 Ross	Y	Y	Y	Y	Y	Y
CALIFORNIA						
1 Thompson	Y	Y	Y	Y	Y	Y
2 **Herger**	Y	Y	N	N	N	N
3 **Lungren**	Y	Y	N	N	N	N
4 **Doolittle**	Y	Y	N	N	N	N
5 Matsui	Y	Y	Y	Y	Y	Y
6 Woolsey	Y	Y	Y	Y	Y	Y
7 Miller, George	Y	Y	Y	Y	Y	Y
8 Pelosi						
9 Lee	Y	Y	Y	Y	Y	Y
10 Tauscher	Y	Y	Y	Y	Y	Y
11 McNerney	Y	Y	Y	Y	Y	Y
12 Speier	Y	Y	Y	Y	Y	Y
13 Stark	Y	Y	Y	Y	Y	Y
14 Eshoo	Y	Y	Y	Y	Y	Y
15 Honda	Y	Y	Y	Y	Y	Y
16 Lofgren	Y	Y	Y	Y	Y	Y
17 Farr	Y	Y	Y	Y	Y	Y
18 Cardoza	Y	Y	Y	Y	Y	Y
19 **Radanovich**	Y	Y	Y	N	N	Y
20 Costa	Y	Y	Y	Y	Y	Y
21 **Nunes**	Y	Y	N	N	N	N
22 **McCarthy**	Y	Y	N	N	N	Y
23 Capps	Y	Y	Y	Y	Y	Y
24 **Gallegly**	Y	Y	N	N	N	Y
25 **McKeon**	Y	Y	N	N	?	Y
26 **Dreier**	Y	Y	N	N	N	Y
27 Sherman	Y	Y	Y	Y	Y	Y
28 Berman	Y	Y	Y	Y	?	Y
29 Schiff	Y	Y	Y	Y	Y	Y
30 Waxman	?	Y	Y	Y	Y	Y
31 Becerra	+	Y	Y	Y	Y	Y
32 Solis	?	?	?	Y	Y	Y
33 Watson	Y	Y	Y	Y	Y	Y
34 Roybal-Allard	Y	Y	Y	Y	Y	P
35 Waters	Y	Y	Y	Y	Y	Y
36 Harman	Y	Y	Y	Y	Y	Y
37 Richardson	Y	Y	Y	Y	Y	Y
38 Napolitano	Y	Y	Y	Y	Y	Y
39 Sánchez, Linda	Y	Y	Y	Y	Y	Y
40 **Royce**	Y	Y	N	N	N	N
41 **Lewis**	Y	Y	N	N	N	Y
42 **Miller, Gary**	Y	Y	N	N	N	Y
43 Baca	Y	Y	Y	Y	Y	Y
44 **Calvert**	Y	Y	Y	N	N	Y
45 **Bono Mack**	Y	Y	Y	N	N	Y
46 **Rohrabacher**	?	?	?	N	N	N
47 Sanchez, Loretta	Y	Y	Y	Y	Y	Y
48 **Campbell**	Y	Y	N	N	N	N
49 **Issa**	Y	Y	N	N	N	Y
50 **Bilbray**	Y	Y	N	N	N	Y
51 Filner	Y	Y	Y	Y	Y	Y
52 **Hunter**	Y	Y	N	N	N	Y
53 Davis	Y	Y	Y	Y	Y	Y

	224	225	226	227	228	229
COLORADO						
1 DeGette	?	?	?	Y	Y	Y
2 Udall	Y	Y	Y	Y	Y	Y
3 Salazar	Y	Y	Y	Y	Y	Y
4 **Musgrave**	Y	Y	Y	N	N	N
5 **Lamborn**	Y	Y	N	N	?	N
6 **Tancredo**	Y	Y	N	N	N	N
7 Perlmutter	Y	Y	Y	Y	Y	Y
CONNECTICUT						
1 Larson	Y	Y	Y	Y	Y	Y
2 Courtney	Y	Y	Y	Y	Y	Y
3 DeLauro	Y	Y	Y	Y	Y	Y
4 **Shays**	Y	Y	Y	N	N	Y
5 Murphy	Y	Y	Y	Y	Y	Y
DELAWARE						
AL **Castle**	Y	Y	Y	N	N	Y
FLORIDA						
1 **Miller**	Y	Y	N	–	–	N
2 Boyd	Y	Y	Y	Y	Y	Y
3 Brown	Y	Y	Y	Y	Y	Y
4 **Crenshaw**	Y	Y	N	N	N	Y
5 **Brown-Waite**	Y	Y	N	N	N	Y
6 **Stearns**	Y	Y	N	N	N	Y
7 **Mica**	Y	Y	N	N	N	Y
8 **Keller**	Y	Y	N	N	N	Y
9 **Bilirakis**	Y	?	Y	N	N	Y
10 **Young**	Y	Y	Y	N	N	Y
11 Castor	Y	Y	Y	Y	Y	Y
12 **Putnam**	Y	Y	N	N	N	Y
13 **Buchanan**	Y	Y	N	N	N	Y
14 **Mack**	Y	Y	N	N	N	Y
15 **Weldon**	?	?	?	N	N	Y
16 Mahoney	Y	Y	Y	Y	Y	Y
17 Meek	Y	Y	Y	Y	Y	Y
18 **Ros-Lehtinen**	Y	Y	N	N	N	Y
19 Wexler	Y	Y	Y	Y	?	?
20 Wasserman Schultz	Y	Y	Y	Y	Y	Y
21 **Diaz-Balart, L.**	Y	Y	N	N	N	Y
22 Klein	Y	Y	Y	Y	Y	Y
23 Hastings	Y	Y	Y	Y	Y	Y
24 **Feeney**	?	Y	N	N	N	N
25 **Diaz-Balart, M.**	Y	Y	N	N	N	Y
GEORGIA						
1 **Kingston**	Y	Y	N	N	N	Y
2 Bishop	Y	Y	Y	Y	Y	Y
3 **Westmoreland**	Y	Y	N	N	N	Y
4 Johnson	Y	Y	Y	Y	Y	Y
5 Lewis	Y	Y	Y	Y	Y	Y
6 **Price**	Y	Y	N	N	N	Y
7 **Linder**	Y	?	?	N	N	N
8 Marshall	Y	Y	Y	Y	Y	Y
9 **Deal**	Y	Y	N	N	N	Y
10 **Broun**	Y	Y	N	N	N	N
11 **Gingrey**	Y	Y	N	N	N	Y
12 Barrow	Y	Y	Y	Y	Y	Y
13 Scott	Y	Y	Y	Y	Y	Y
HAWAII						
1 Abercrombie	Y	Y	Y	Y	Y	Y
2 Hirono	Y	Y	Y	Y	Y	Y
IDAHO						
1 **Sali**	Y	Y	Y	N	N	Y
2 **Simpson**	Y	Y	Y	N	N	Y
ILLINOIS						
1 Rush	?	?	?	?	?	?
2 Jackson	Y	Y	Y	Y	Y	Y
3 Lipinski	Y	Y	Y	Y	Y	Y
4 Gutierrez	?	?	?	Y	Y	Y
5 Emanuel	Y	Y	Y	Y	Y	Y
6 **Roskam**	Y	Y	N	N	N	Y
7 Davis	Y	Y	Y	Y	Y	Y
8 Bean	Y	Y	Y	Y	Y	Y
9 Schakowsky	Y	Y	Y	Y	Y	Y
10 **Kirk**	Y	Y	Y	N	N	Y
11 **Weller**	Y	Y	Y	N	P	P
12 Costello	Y	Y	Y	Y	Y	Y
13 **Biggert**	Y	Y	Y	N	N	Y
14 Foster	Y	Y	Y	Y	Y	Y
15 Johnson	Y	Y	N	N	N	Y

KEY   **Republicans**   Democrats

Y Voted for (yea)	**X** Paired against	**C** Voted "present" to avoid possible conflict of interest
# Paired for	**–** Announced against	
+ Announced for	**P** Voted "present"	**?** Did not vote or otherwise make a position known
N Voted against (nay)		

ND Northern Democrats, SD Southern Democrats
Southern states: Ala., Ark., Fla., Ga., Ky., La., Miss., N.C., Okla., S.C., Tenn., Texas, Va.

	224	225	226	227	228	229
16 **Manzullo**	Y	Y	Y	N	N	N
17 Hare	Y	Y	Y	Y	Y	Y
18 **LaHood**	Y	Y	Y	N	N	N
19 **Shimkus**	Y	Y	N	N	N	N
INDIANA						
1 Visclosky	Y	Y	Y	Y	Y	Y
2 Donnelly	Y	Y	Y	Y	Y	Y
3 **Souder**	Y	Y	N	N	N	N
4 **Buyer**	Y	Y	N	N	N	Y
5 **Burton**	Y	Y	N	N	N	N
6 **Pence**	Y	Y	N	?	?	?
7 Carson, A.	Y	Y	Y	Y	Y	Y
8 Ellsworth	Y	Y	Y	Y	Y	Y
9 Hill	Y	Y	Y	?	?	?
IOWA						
1 Braley	+	Y	Y	Y	Y	Y
2 Loebsack	Y	Y	Y	Y	Y	Y
3 Boswell	Y	Y	Y	Y	Y	Y
4 **Latham**	Y	Y	Y	N	N	Y
5 **King**	Y	Y	N	N	N	N
KANSAS						
1 **Moran**	Y	Y	N	N	N	Y
2 Boyda	Y	Y	Y	Y	Y	Y
3 Moore	Y	Y	?	Y	Y	Y
4 **Tiahrt**	Y	Y	Y	N	N	Y
KENTUCKY						
1 **Whitfield**	Y	Y	Y	N	N	Y
2 **Lewis**	Y	Y	N	N	N	Y
3 Yarmuth	Y	Y	Y	Y	Y	Y
4 **Davis**	Y	Y	N	N	N	N
5 **Rogers**	Y	Y	N	N	N	Y
6 Chandler	Y	Y	Y	Y	Y	Y
LOUISIANA						
1 Vacant						
2 Jefferson	Y	Y	Y	Y	Y	Y
3 Melancon	Y	Y	Y	Y	Y	Y
4 **McCrery**	?	?	?	N	N	Y
5 **Alexander**	Y	Y	N	N	N	Y
6 Vacant						
7 **Boustany**	Y	Y	N	N	N	Y
MAINE						
1 Allen	Y	Y	Y	Y	Y	Y
2 Michaud	Y	Y	Y	Y	Y	Y
MARYLAND						
1 **Gilchrest**	Y	Y	Y	N	N	Y
2 Ruppersberger	Y	Y	Y	Y	Y	Y
3 Sarbanes	Y	Y	Y	Y	Y	Y
4 Wynn	Y	Y	Y	Y	Y	Y
5 Hoyer	Y	Y	Y	Y	Y	Y
6 **Bartlett**	Y	Y	N	N	N	Y
7 Cummings	Y	Y	Y	Y	?	Y
8 Van Hollen	Y	Y	Y	Y	Y	Y
MASSACHUSETTS						
1 Olver	Y	Y	Y	Y	Y	Y
2 Neal	?	?	Y	Y	Y	Y
3 McGovern	Y	Y	Y	Y	Y	Y
4 Frank	Y	Y	Y	Y	Y	Y
5 Tsongas	Y	Y	Y	Y	Y	Y
6 Tierney	Y	Y	Y	Y	Y	Y
7 Markey	Y	Y	Y	Y	Y	Y
8 Capuano	Y	Y	Y	Y	Y	Y
9 Lynch	Y	Y	Y	Y	Y	Y
10 Delahunt	Y	Y	Y	Y	Y	P
MICHIGAN						
1 Stupak	Y	Y	Y	Y	Y	Y
2 **Hoekstra**	Y	Y	N	N	N	N
3 **Ehlers**	Y	Y	Y	N	N	N
4 **Camp**	Y	Y	N	N	N	Y
5 Kildee	Y	Y	Y	Y	Y	Y
6 **Upton**	Y	Y	N	N	N	Y
7 **Walberg**	Y	Y	N	N	N	Y
8 **Rogers**	Y	Y	N	N	N	Y
9 **Knollenberg**	Y	Y	Y	N	N	Y
10 **Miller**	Y	Y	N	N	N	Y
11 **McCotter**	Y	Y	N	N	N	Y
12 Levin	Y	Y	Y	Y	Y	Y
13 Kilpatrick	Y	Y	Y	Y	Y	Y
14 Conyers	Y	Y	Y	Y	Y	Y
15 Dingell	Y	Y	Y	Y	Y	Y
MINNESOTA						
1 Walz	Y	Y	Y	Y	Y	Y
2 **Kline**	Y	Y	N	N	N	P
3 **Ramstad**	Y	Y	Y	N	N	Y
4 McCollum	Y	Y	Y	Y	Y	Y
5 Ellison	Y	Y	Y	Y	Y	Y
6 **Bachmann**	Y	Y	N	N	N	Y
7 Peterson	Y	Y	Y	Y	Y	Y
8 Oberstar	Y	Y	Y	Y	Y	Y
MISSISSIPPI						
1 Vacant						
2 Thompson	Y	Y	Y	Y	Y	Y
3 **Pickering**	Y	Y	N	N	N	Y
4 Taylor	?	?	?	Y	Y	Y
MISSOURI						
1 Clay	Y	Y	Y	Y	Y	Y
2 **Akin**	Y	Y	N	N	N	N
3 Carnahan	Y	Y	Y	Y	Y	Y
4 Skelton	Y	Y	Y	Y	Y	Y
5 Cleaver	Y	Y	?	Y	Y	Y
6 **Graves**	Y	Y	N	N	N	Y
7 **Blunt**	?	?	?	N	N	Y
8 **Emerson**	Y	Y	Y	N	N	Y
9 **Hulshof**	?	?	?	N	N	Y
MONTANA						
AL **Rehberg**	Y	Y	Y	N	N	Y
NEBRASKA						
1 **Fortenberry**	Y	Y	Y	N	N	Y
2 **Terry**	Y	Y	Y	N	N	Y
3 **Smith**	Y	Y	Y	N	N	Y
NEVADA						
1 Berkley	Y	Y	Y	Y	Y	Y
2 **Heller**	Y	Y	Y	N	N	Y
3 **Porter**	Y	Y	Y	N	N	Y
NEW HAMPSHIRE						
1 Shea-Porter	Y	Y	Y	Y	Y	Y
2 Hodes	Y	Y	Y	Y	Y	Y
NEW JERSEY						
1 Andrews	+	+	+	?	?	?
2 **LoBiondo**	Y	Y	Y	N	N	Y
3 **Saxton**	Y	Y	Y	N	N	Y
4 **Smith**	Y	Y	Y	N	N	Y
5 **Garrett**	Y	Y	N	N	N	N
6 Pallone	Y	Y	Y	Y	Y	Y
7 **Ferguson**	Y	Y	Y	N	N	Y
8 Pascrell	+	+	+	Y	Y	Y
9 Rothman	Y	Y	Y	Y	Y	Y
10 Payne	Y	Y	Y	?	?	?
11 **Frelinghuysen**	Y	Y	Y	N	N	Y
12 Holt	Y	Y	Y	Y	Y	Y
13 Sires	Y	Y	Y	Y	Y	Y
NEW MEXICO						
1 **Wilson**	Y	Y	Y	N	N	Y
2 **Pearce**	Y	Y	N	?	N	Y
3 Udall	Y	Y	Y	Y	Y	Y
NEW YORK						
1 Bishop	Y	Y	Y	Y	Y	Y
2 Israel	Y	Y	Y	Y	Y	Y
3 **King**	Y	Y	Y	N	N	Y
4 McCarthy	Y	Y	Y	Y	Y	Y
5 Ackerman	Y	Y	Y	Y	Y	Y
6 Meeks	Y	Y	Y	Y	Y	Y
7 Crowley	Y	Y	Y	Y	Y	Y
8 Nadler	Y	Y	Y	Y	Y	Y
9 Weiner	?	Y	Y	Y	Y	Y
10 Towns	Y	Y	Y	Y	Y	Y
11 Clarke	Y	Y	Y	Y	Y	Y
12 Velázquez	Y	Y	Y	Y	Y	Y
13 **Fossella**	Y	Y	N	N	N	Y
14 Maloney	Y	Y	Y	Y	Y	Y
15 Rangel	Y	Y	Y	Y	Y	Y
16 Serrano	Y	Y	Y	Y	Y	Y
17 Engel	?	Y	Y	Y	Y	Y
18 Lowey	Y	Y	Y	Y	Y	Y
19 Hall	Y	Y	Y	Y	Y	Y
20 Gillibrand	Y	Y	Y	Y	Y	Y
21 McNulty	Y	Y	Y	Y	Y	Y
22 Hinchey	Y	Y	Y	Y	Y	Y
23 **McHugh**	Y	Y	Y	N	N	Y
24 Arcuri	Y	Y	Y	Y	Y	Y
25 **Walsh**	Y	Y	Y	N	N	Y
26 **Reynolds**	Y	Y	N	N	N	Y
27 Higgins	?	?	?	?	?	?
28 Slaughter	Y	Y	Y	Y	Y	Y
29 **Kuhl**	Y	Y	Y	N	N	Y
NORTH CAROLINA						
1 Butterfield	Y	Y	Y	Y	Y	Y
2 Etheridge	Y	Y	Y	Y	Y	Y
3 **Jones**	Y	Y	N	N	N	Y
4 Price	Y	Y	Y	Y	Y	Y
5 **Foxx**	Y	Y	N	N	N	N
6 **Coble**	Y	Y	N	N	N	Y
7 McIntyre	Y	Y	Y	Y	Y	Y
8 **Hayes**	Y	Y	N	N	N	Y
9 **Myrick**	Y	Y	N	N	N	Y
10 **McHenry**	Y	Y	N	N	N	Y
11 Shuler	?	?	?	Y	Y	Y
12 Watt	Y	Y	Y	Y	Y	Y
13 Miller	Y	Y	Y	Y	Y	Y
NORTH DAKOTA						
AL Pomeroy	Y	Y	Y	Y	Y	Y
OHIO						
1 **Chabot**	Y	Y	N	N	N	N
2 **Schmidt**	Y	Y	N	N	N	Y
3 **Turner**	Y	Y	Y	N	N	Y
4 **Jordan**	Y	Y	N	N	N	N
5 **Latta**	Y	Y	N	N	N	Y
6 Wilson	Y	Y	Y	Y	Y	Y
7 **Hobson**	Y	Y	Y	N	N	Y
8 **Boehner**	Y	Y	N	N	N	Y
9 Kaptur	?	Y	Y	Y	Y	Y
10 Kucinich	Y	Y	Y	Y	Y	Y
11 Tubbs Jones	Y	Y	Y	Y	Y	P
12 **Tiberi**	Y	Y	Y	N	N	Y
13 Sutton	Y	Y	Y	Y	Y	Y
14 **LaTourette**	Y	Y	Y	N	N	Y
15 **Pryce**	Y	Y	Y	N	N	Y
16 **Regula**	Y	Y	Y	N	N	Y
17 Ryan	Y	Y	Y	Y	Y	Y
18 Space	Y	Y	Y	Y	Y	Y
OKLAHOMA						
1 **Sullivan**	Y	Y	Y	N	N	Y
2 Boren	Y	Y	Y	Y	?	Y
3 **Lucas**	Y	Y	N	N	N	Y
4 **Cole**	Y	Y	N	N	N	Y
5 **Fallin**	?	Y	N	N	N	Y
OREGON						
1 Wu	Y	Y	Y	Y	Y	Y
2 **Walden**	Y	Y	Y	N	N	Y
3 Blumenauer	Y	Y	Y	Y	Y	Y
4 DeFazio	Y	Y	Y	Y	Y	Y
5 Hooley	Y	Y	Y	Y	Y	Y
PENNSYLVANIA						
1 Brady	Y	Y	Y	Y	Y	Y
2 Fattah	Y	Y	Y	Y	Y	Y
3 **English**	Y	Y	Y	N	N	Y
4 Altmire	Y	Y	Y	Y	Y	Y
5 **Peterson**	Y	Y	N	N	N	Y
6 **Gerlach**	Y	Y	Y	N	N	Y
7 Sestak	Y	Y	Y	Y	Y	Y
8 Murphy, P.	Y	Y	Y	Y	Y	Y
9 **Shuster**	Y	Y	Y	N	N	Y
10 Carney	Y	Y	Y	Y	Y	Y
11 Kanjorski	Y	Y	Y	Y	Y	Y
12 Murtha	Y	Y	Y	Y	Y	Y
13 Schwartz	Y	Y	Y	Y	Y	Y
14 Doyle	Y	Y	Y	Y	Y	P
15 **Dent**	Y	Y	Y	N	N	Y
16 **Pitts**	Y	Y	N	N	N	Y
17 Holden	Y	Y	Y	Y	Y	Y
18 **Murphy, T.**	Y	Y	Y	N	N	Y
19 **Platts**	Y	Y	Y	N	N	Y
RHODE ISLAND						
1 Kennedy	Y	Y	Y	Y	Y	Y
2 Langevin	Y	Y	Y	Y	Y	Y
SOUTH CAROLINA						
1 **Brown**	Y	Y	N	N	N	Y
2 **Wilson**	Y	Y	N	N	N	N
3 **Barrett**	Y	Y	N	N	N	P
4 **Inglis**	Y	Y	N	N	N	N
5 Spratt	Y	Y	Y	Y	Y	Y
6 Clyburn	Y	Y	Y	Y	Y	Y
SOUTH DAKOTA						
AL Herseth Sandlin	Y	Y	Y	Y	Y	Y
TENNESSEE						
1 **Davis, D.**	Y	Y	N	N	N	Y
2 **Duncan**	Y	Y	N	N	N	Y
3 **Wamp**	Y	Y	Y	N	N	Y
4 Davis, L.	Y	Y	Y	Y	Y	Y
5 Cooper	Y	Y	Y	Y	Y	Y
6 Gordon	Y	Y	Y	Y	Y	?
7 **Blackburn**	Y	Y	?	N	N	N
8 Tanner	Y	Y	Y	Y	Y	Y
9 Cohen	Y	Y	Y	Y	Y	Y
TEXAS						
1 **Gohmert**	Y	Y	Y	N	N	N
2 **Poe**	Y	Y	N	N	N	Y
3 **Johnson, S.**	Y	Y	N	N	N	N
4 **Hall**	Y	Y	N	N	N	Y
5 **Hensarling**	Y	Y	N	N	N	N
6 **Barton**	Y	Y	N	N	N	N
7 **Culberson**	Y	Y	N	N	N	Y
8 **Brady**	Y	Y	N	N	N	N
9 Green, A.	Y	Y	Y	Y	Y	Y
10 **McCaul**	Y	Y	N	N	N	P
11 **Conaway**	Y	Y	N	N	N	Y
12 **Granger**	?	?	?	?	?	?
13 **Thornberry**	Y	Y	N	N	N	N
14 **Paul**	N	N	N	N	N	N
15 Hinojosa	Y	Y	Y	Y	Y	Y
16 Reyes	Y	Y	Y	Y	Y	Y
17 Edwards	Y	Y	Y	Y	Y	Y
18 Jackson Lee	Y	Y	Y	Y	Y	Y
19 **Neugebauer**	Y	Y	N	N	N	N
20 Gonzalez	Y	Y	Y	Y	Y	Y
21 **Smith**	Y	Y	N	N	N	Y
22 Lampson	Y	Y	Y	N	N	Y
23 Rodriguez	Y	Y	Y	Y	Y	Y
24 **Marchant**	Y	Y	N	N	N	N
25 Doggett	?	?	?	?	?	?
26 **Burgess**	Y	Y	N	N	N	N
27 Ortiz	Y	Y	Y	Y	Y	Y
28 Cuellar	Y	Y	Y	Y	Y	Y
29 Green, G.	Y	Y	Y	Y	Y	P
30 Johnson, E.	Y	Y	Y	Y	Y	Y
31 **Carter**	Y	Y	N	N	N	N
32 **Sessions**	Y	Y	N	N	N	N
UTAH						
1 **Bishop**	Y	Y	N	N	N	Y
2 Matheson	Y	Y	Y	Y	Y	Y
3 **Cannon**	Y	Y	N	N	N	N
VERMONT						
AL Welch	Y	Y	Y	Y	Y	Y
VIRGINIA						
1 **Wittman**	Y	Y	Y	N	N	Y
2 **Drake**	?	?	?	N	N	Y
3 Scott	Y	Y	Y	Y	Y	Y
4 **Forbes**	?	?	?	?	?	?
5 **Goode**	Y	Y	N	N	N	Y
6 **Goodlatte**	Y	Y	N	N	N	Y
7 **Cantor**	Y	Y	N	N	N	Y
8 Moran	Y	Y	Y	Y	Y	Y
9 Boucher	Y	Y	Y	Y	Y	Y
10 **Wolf**	Y	Y	Y	N	N	Y
11 **Davis**	Y	?	?	N	N	Y
WASHINGTON						
1 Inslee	Y	Y	Y	Y	Y	Y
2 Larsen	Y	Y	Y	Y	Y	Y
3 Baird	Y	Y	Y	Y	Y	Y
4 **Hastings**	Y	Y	N	N	N	P
5 **McMorris Rodgers**	Y	Y	N	N	N	Y
6 Dicks	Y	Y	Y	Y	Y	Y
7 McDermott	Y	Y	Y	Y	Y	Y
8 **Reichert**	Y	Y	Y	N	N	Y
9 Smith	Y	Y	Y	Y	Y	Y
WEST VIRGINIA						
1 Mollohan	Y	Y	Y	Y	Y	Y
2 **Capito**	Y	Y	Y	N	N	Y
3 Rahall	Y	Y	Y	Y	Y	Y
WISCONSIN						
1 **Ryan**	Y	Y	N	N	N	N
2 Baldwin	Y	Y	Y	Y	Y	Y
3 Kind	Y	Y	Y	Y	Y	Y
4 Moore	Y	Y	Y	Y	Y	Y
5 **Sensenbrenner**	Y	Y	N	N	N	N
6 **Petri**	Y	Y	N	N	N	Y
7 Obey	Y	Y	Y	Y	Y	Y
8 Kagen	Y	Y	Y	Y	Y	Y
WYOMING						
AL **Cubin**	Y	Y	N	N	N	Y
DELEGATES						
Faleomavaega (A.S.)						
Norton (D.C.)						
Bordallo (Guam)						
Fortuño (P.R.)						
Christensen (V.I.)						

IN THE HOUSE | By Vote Number

230. **HR 5522. Combustible Dust Safety/Engineering Control Standards.** Miller, D-Calif., amendment that would adjust some requirements in the bill's interim safety standard for combustible dust and make the required engineering controls effective six months after the standards were issued, instead of 30 days. Adopted in Committee of the Whole 412-0: R 187-0; D 225-0 (ND 169-0, SD 56-0). April 30, 2008.

231. **HR 5522. Combustible Dust Safety/Substitute.** Wilson, R-S.C., substitute amendment that would direct the Labor Department to wait for the outcome of an investigation into the Imperial Sugar Plant explosion in Port Wentworth, Ga., and findings from the Combustible Dust National Emphasis Program before deciding on new standards for combustible dust. Rejected in Committee of the Whole 178-237: R 175-11; D 3-226 (ND 2-171, SD 1-55). April 30, 2008.

232. **HR 5522. Combustible Dust Safety/Recommit.** Walberg, R-Mich., motion to recommit the bill to the Education and Labor Committee with instructions that it be reported back forthwith with language that would require an exemption for grain from the bill's new standards and regulations, pending determination of any impact on food prices. Motion rejected 187-225: R 184-3; D 3-222 (ND 1-168, SD 2-54). April 30, 2008.

233. **HR 5522. Combustible Dust Safety/Passage.** Passage of the bill that would require the Occupational Safety and Health Administration to regulate combustible dusts. OSHA would be required to issue an interim standard within 90 days of enactment and a final standard within 18 months. The standards would have to include hazard assessments; mandates for dust inspection, testing, ignition control and methods used to minimize dust accumulation on surfaces; and requirements for operating procedures and employee-safety training. The bill's interim engineering controls would become effective six months after the standards were issued. Passed 247-165: R 22-165; D 225-0 (ND 170-0, SD 55-0). A "nay" was a vote in support of the president's position. April 30, 2008.

234. **HR 493. Genetic Information Non-Discrimination/Motion to Concur.** Miller, D-Calif., motion to concur in the Senate amendment to the bill that would prohibit insurance companies, employers, employment agencies and labor unions from discriminating on the basis of genetic information. It would bar health plans from requiring genetic testing. Insurers could not adjust premiums or base enrollment decisions on genetic information. It would also provide legal protection to employers who contract with insurers to provide health insurance from being sued for a violation committed by the insurer. Motion agreed to (thus clearing the bill for the president) 414-1: R 188-1; D 226-0 (ND 171-0, SD 55-0). May 1, 2008.

235. **HR 493, HR 5715, S 2954. Suspension Motions/Previous Question.** Slaughter, D-N.Y., motion to order the previous question (thus ending debate and possibility of amendment) on adoption of the rule (H Res 1167) to provide for House floor consideration of three bills under suspension of the rules on the legislative day of Thursday, May 1, 2008. Motion agreed to 226-190: R 0-189; D 226-1 (ND 171-0, SD 55-1). May 1, 2008.

	230	231	232	233	234	235
ALABAMA						
1 Bonner	Y	Y	Y	N	Y	N
2 Everett	Y	Y	Y	N	Y	N
3 Rogers	Y	Y	Y	N	Y	N
4 Aderholt	Y	Y	Y	N	Y	N
5 Cramer	Y	N	N	Y	Y	Y
6 Bachus	Y	Y	Y	N	Y	N
7 Davis	Y	N	N	Y	Y	Y
ALASKA						
AL Young	Y	Y	Y	Y	Y	N
ARIZONA						
1 Renzi	Y	Y	Y	N	Y	N
2 Franks	Y	Y	Y	N	Y	N
3 Shadegg	Y	Y	Y	N	Y	N
4 Pastor	Y	N	N	Y	Y	Y
5 Mitchell	Y	N	N	Y	Y	Y
6 Flake	Y	Y	Y	N	Y	N
7 Grijalva	Y	N	N	Y	Y	Y
8 Giffords	Y	N	N	Y	Y	Y
ARKANSAS						
1 Berry	Y	N	N	Y	Y	Y
2 Snyder	Y	N	N	Y	Y	Y
3 Boozman	Y	Y	Y	N	Y	N
4 Ross	Y	N	N	Y	Y	Y
CALIFORNIA						
1 Thompson	Y	N	N	Y	Y	Y
2 Herger	Y	Y	Y	N	Y	N
3 Lungren	Y	Y	Y	N	Y	N
4 Doolittle	Y	Y	Y	N	Y	N
5 Matsui	Y	N	N	Y	Y	Y
6 Woolsey	Y	N	N	Y	Y	Y
7 Miller, George	Y	N	N	Y	Y	Y
8 Pelosi						
9 Lee	?	N	N	Y	Y	Y
10 Tauscher	Y	N	N	Y	Y	Y
11 McNerney	Y	N	N	Y	Y	Y
12 Speier	Y	N	N	Y	Y	Y
13 Stark	Y	N	N	Y	Y	Y
14 Eshoo	Y	N	N	Y	Y	Y
15 Honda	Y	N	N	Y	?	?
16 Lofgren	Y	N	N	Y	Y	Y
17 Farr	Y	N	N	Y	Y	Y
18 Cardoza	Y	N	N	Y	Y	Y
19 Radanovich	Y	Y	Y	N	Y	N
20 Costa	Y	N	N	Y	Y	Y
21 Nunes	Y	Y	Y	N	Y	N
22 McCarthy	Y	Y	Y	N	Y	N
23 Capps	Y	N	N	Y	Y	Y
24 Gallegly	Y	Y	Y	N	Y	N
25 McKeon	Y	Y	Y	N	Y	N
26 Dreier	Y	Y	Y	N	Y	N
27 Sherman	Y	N	N	Y	Y	Y
28 Berman	Y	N	N	Y	Y	Y
29 Schiff	Y	N	N	Y	Y	Y
30 Waxman	Y	N	N	Y	Y	Y
31 Becerra	Y	N	N	Y	Y	Y
32 Solis	Y	N	N	Y	Y	Y
33 Watson	Y	N	N	Y	Y	Y
34 Roybal-Allard	Y	N	N	Y	Y	Y
35 Waters	Y	N	N	Y	Y	Y
36 Harman	Y	N	N	Y	Y	Y
37 Richardson	Y	N	N	Y	Y	Y
38 Napolitano	Y	N	N	Y	Y	Y
39 Sánchez, Linda	?	N	N	Y	Y	Y
40 Royce	Y	Y	Y	N	Y	N
41 Lewis	Y	Y	Y	N	Y	N
42 Miller, Gary	Y	Y	Y	N	Y	N
43 Baca	Y	N	N	Y	Y	Y
44 Calvert	Y	Y	Y	N	Y	N
45 Bono Mack	Y	Y	Y	N	Y	N
46 Rohrabacher	Y	Y	Y	N	Y	N
47 Sanchez, Loretta	Y	N	N	Y	Y	Y
48 Campbell	Y	Y	Y	N	Y	N
49 Issa	?	?	?	?	Y	N
50 Bilbray	Y	Y	Y	N	Y	N
51 Filner	Y	N	N	Y	Y	Y
52 Hunter	Y	Y	Y	?	Y	N
53 Davis	Y	N	N	Y	Y	Y

	230	231	232	233	234	235
COLORADO						
1 DeGette	Y	N	N	Y	Y	Y
2 Udall	Y	N	N	Y	Y	Y
3 Salazar	Y	N	N	Y	Y	Y
4 Musgrave	Y	Y	Y	N	Y	N
5 Lamborn	Y	Y	Y	N	Y	N
6 Tancredo	Y	Y	Y	N	Y	N
7 Perlmutter	Y	N	N	Y	Y	Y
CONNECTICUT						
1 Larson	Y	N	N	Y	Y	Y
2 Courtney	Y	N	N	Y	Y	Y
3 DeLauro	Y	N	N	Y	Y	Y
4 Shays	Y	N	Y	Y	Y	N
5 Murphy	Y	N	N	Y	Y	Y
DELAWARE						
AL Castle	Y	Y	Y	Y	Y	N
FLORIDA						
1 Miller	Y	Y	Y	N	Y	N
2 Boyd	Y	N	N	?	Y	Y
3 Brown	Y	N	N	Y	Y	Y
4 Crenshaw	Y	Y	Y	N	Y	N
5 Brown-Waite	Y	Y	Y	N	Y	N
6 Stearns	Y	Y	Y	N	Y	N
7 Mica	Y	Y	Y	N	Y	N
8 Keller	Y	Y	Y	N	Y	N
9 Bilirakis	Y	Y	Y	N	Y	N
10 Young	Y	Y	Y	N	Y	N
11 Castor	Y	N	N	Y	Y	Y
12 Putnam	Y	Y	Y	N	Y	N
13 Buchanan	Y	Y	Y	N	Y	N
14 Mack	Y	Y	Y	N	Y	N
15 Weldon	Y	Y	Y	N	Y	N
16 Mahoney	Y	N	N	Y	Y	Y
17 Meek	Y	N	N	Y	Y	Y
18 Ros-Lehtinen	Y	Y	Y	Y	Y	N
19 Wexler	Y	N	N	Y	Y	Y
20 Wasserman Schultz	Y	N	N	Y	Y	Y
21 Diaz-Balart, L.	Y	N	Y	Y	Y	N
22 Klein	Y	N	N	Y	Y	Y
23 Hastings	Y	N	N	Y	Y	Y
24 Feeney	Y	Y	Y	N	Y	N
25 Diaz-Balart, M.	Y	N	Y	Y	Y	N
GEORGIA						
1 Kingston	Y	N	N	Y	Y	N
2 Bishop	Y	N	N	Y	Y	Y
3 Westmoreland	Y	Y	Y	N	Y	N
4 Johnson	Y	N	N	Y	Y	Y
5 Lewis	Y	N	N	Y	Y	Y
6 Price	Y	Y	Y	N	Y	N
7 Linder	Y	Y	Y	N	Y	N
8 Marshall	Y	N	Y	Y	Y	Y
9 Deal	Y	Y	Y	N	?	?
10 Broun	Y	Y	Y	N	Y	N
11 Gingrey	Y	Y	Y	N	Y	N
12 Barrow	Y	N	Y	?	?	Y
13 Scott	Y	N	N	Y	Y	Y
HAWAII						
1 Abercrombie	Y	N	N	Y	Y	Y
2 Hirono	Y	N	N	Y	Y	Y
IDAHO						
1 Sali	Y	Y	Y	N	Y	N
2 Simpson	Y	Y	Y	N	Y	N
ILLINOIS						
1 Rush	?	?	?	?	?	?
2 Jackson	Y	N	N	Y	Y	Y
3 Lipinski	Y	N	N	Y	Y	Y
4 Gutierrez	Y	N	N	Y	Y	Y
5 Emanuel	Y	N	N	Y	Y	Y
6 Roskam	Y	Y	Y	N	Y	N
7 Davis	Y	N	N	Y	Y	Y
8 Bean	Y	Y	Y	Y	Y	Y
9 Schakowsky	Y	N	N	Y	Y	Y
10 Kirk	Y	Y	Y	N	Y	N
11 Weller	Y	Y	Y	Y	Y	N
12 Costello	Y	N	N	Y	Y	Y
13 Biggert	Y	Y	Y	N	Y	N
14 Foster	Y	N	N	Y	Y	Y
15 Johnson	Y	P	N	Y	N	Y

KEY   **Republicans**   Democrats

Y Voted for (yea)	**X** Paired against	**C** Voted "present" to avoid possible conflict of interest
# Paired for	**–** Announced against	
+ Announced for	**P** Voted "present"	**?** Did not vote or otherwise make a position known
N Voted against (nay)		

ND Northern Democrats, SD Southern Democrats
Southern states: Ala., Ark., Fla., Ga., Ky., La., Miss., N.C., Okla., S.C., Tenn., Texas, Va.

H-76   2008 CQ ALMANAC | www.cq.com

	230	231	232	233	234	235
16 **Manzullo**	Y	Y	Y	N	Y	N
17 Hare	Y	N	N	Y	Y	Y
18 **LaHood**	Y	Y	Y	Y	?	?
19 **Shimkus**	Y	Y	Y	N	Y	N
INDIANA						
1 Visclosky	Y	N	N	Y	Y	Y
2 Donnelly	Y	N	N	Y	Y	Y
3 **Souder**	Y	Y	Y	N	Y	N
4 **Buyer**	Y	Y	Y	N	Y	N
5 **Burton**	Y	Y	Y	N	Y	N
6 **Pence**	?	?	?	?	Y	N
7 Carson, A.	Y	N	N	Y	Y	Y
8 Ellsworth	Y	N	N	Y	Y	Y
9 Hill	?	?	?	?	Y	Y
IOWA						
1 Braley	Y	N	N	Y	Y	Y
2 Loebsack	Y	N	N	Y	Y	Y
3 Boswell	Y	N	N	Y	Y	Y
4 **Latham**	Y	Y	Y	N	Y	N
5 **King**	Y	Y	Y	N	Y	N
KANSAS						
1 **Moran**	Y	Y	Y	N	Y	N
2 Boyda	Y	N	N	Y	Y	Y
3 Moore	Y	N	N	Y	Y	Y
4 **Tiahrt**	Y	Y	Y	N	Y	N
KENTUCKY						
1 **Whitfield**	Y	Y	Y	N	Y	N
2 **Lewis**	Y	Y	Y	N	Y	N
3 Yarmuth	Y	N	N	Y	Y	Y
4 **Davis**	Y	Y	Y	N	Y	N
5 **Rogers**	Y	Y	Y	N	Y	N
6 Chandler	Y	N	N	Y	Y	Y
LOUISIANA						
1 Vacant						
2 Jefferson	Y	N	N	Y	Y	Y
3 Melancon	Y	N	N	Y	Y	Y
4 **McCrery**	Y	Y	Y	N	Y	N
5 **Alexander**	Y	Y	Y	N	Y	N
6 Vacant						
7 **Boustany**	?	?	?	?	Y	N
MAINE						
1 Allen	Y	N	N	Y	Y	Y
2 Michaud	Y	N	N	Y	Y	Y
MARYLAND						
1 **Gilchrest**	Y	N	N	Y	Y	N
2 Ruppersberger	Y	N	N	Y	Y	Y
3 Sarbanes	Y	N	N	Y	Y	Y
4 Wynn	?	?	?	?	Y	?
5 Hoyer	?	N	N	Y	Y	Y
6 **Bartlett**	Y	Y	Y	N	Y	N
7 Cummings	Y	N	N	Y	Y	Y
8 Van Hollen	Y	N	N	Y	Y	Y
MASSACHUSETTS						
1 Olver	Y	N	N	Y	Y	Y
2 Neal	Y	N	N	Y	Y	Y
3 McGovern	Y	N	N	Y	Y	Y
4 Frank	Y	N	N	Y	Y	Y
5 Tsongas	Y	N	N	Y	Y	Y
6 Tierney	Y	N	?	Y	Y	Y
7 Markey	Y	N	N	Y	Y	Y
8 Capuano	Y	N	N	Y	Y	Y
9 Lynch	Y	N	N	Y	Y	Y
10 Delahunt	Y	N	N	Y	Y	Y
MICHIGAN						
1 Stupak	Y	N	N	Y	Y	Y
2 **Hoekstra**	Y	Y	Y	N	Y	N
3 **Ehlers**	Y	Y	Y	N	Y	N
4 **Camp**	Y	Y	Y	N	Y	N
5 Kildee	Y	N	N	Y	Y	Y
6 **Upton**	Y	Y	Y	Y	Y	N
7 **Walberg**	Y	Y	Y	N	Y	N
8 **Rogers**	Y	Y	Y	N	Y	N
9 **Knollenberg**	Y	Y	Y	N	Y	N
10 **Miller**	Y	Y	Y	Y	Y	N
11 **McCotter**	Y	Y	Y	Y	Y	N
12 Levin	Y	N	N	Y	Y	Y
13 Kilpatrick	Y	N	N	Y	Y	Y
14 Conyers	Y	N	N	Y	Y	Y
15 Dingell	Y	N	N	Y	Y	Y
MINNESOTA						
1 Walz	Y	N	N	Y	Y	Y
2 **Kline**	Y	Y	Y	N	Y	N
3 **Ramstad**	Y	Y	Y	N	Y	N
4 McCollum	Y	N	N	Y	Y	Y
5 Ellison	Y	N	N	Y	Y	Y
6 **Bachmann**	Y	Y	Y	N	Y	N
7 Peterson	Y	N	N	Y	Y	Y
8 Oberstar	Y	N	N	Y	Y	Y
MISSISSIPPI						
1 Vacant						
2 Thompson	Y	N	N	Y	Y	Y
3 **Pickering**	Y	Y	Y	N	Y	N
4 Taylor	Y	N	N	Y	Y	Y
MISSOURI						
1 Clay	Y	N	N	Y	Y	Y
2 **Akin**	Y	Y	Y	N	Y	N
3 Carnahan	Y	N	N	Y	Y	Y
4 Skelton	Y	N	N	Y	Y	Y
5 Cleaver	Y	N	N	Y	Y	Y
6 **Graves**	Y	Y	Y	N	Y	N
7 **Blunt**	?	?	?	?	Y	N
8 **Emerson**	Y	Y	Y	N	Y	N
9 **Hulshof**	Y	Y	Y	N	Y	N
MONTANA						
AL **Rehberg**	Y	Y	Y	N	Y	N
NEBRASKA						
1 **Fortenberry**	Y	Y	Y	N	Y	N
2 **Terry**	Y	Y	Y	N	Y	N
3 **Smith**	Y	Y	Y	N	Y	N
NEVADA						
1 Berkley	Y	N	N	Y	Y	Y
2 **Heller**	Y	Y	Y	N	Y	N
3 **Porter**	Y	Y	Y	Y	Y	N
NEW HAMPSHIRE						
1 Shea-Porter	Y	N	N	Y	Y	Y
2 Hodes	Y	N	N	Y	Y	Y
NEW JERSEY						
1 Andrews	?	?	?	?	Y	Y
2 **LoBiondo**	Y	N	Y	Y	Y	N
3 **Saxton**	Y	Y	Y	N	Y	N
4 **Smith**	Y	N	N	Y	Y	N
5 **Garrett**	Y	Y	Y	N	Y	N
6 Pallone	Y	N	N	Y	Y	Y
7 **Ferguson**	Y	Y	Y	N	Y	N
8 Pascrell	Y	N	N	Y	Y	Y
9 Rothman	Y	N	N	Y	Y	Y
10 Payne	?	?	?	?	?	?
11 **Frelinghuysen**	Y	Y	Y	N	Y	N
12 Holt	Y	N	N	Y	Y	Y
13 Sires	Y	N	N	Y	Y	Y
NEW MEXICO						
1 **Wilson**	Y	Y	Y	N	?	?
2 **Pearce**	Y	Y	Y	N	Y	N
3 Udall	Y	N	N	Y	Y	Y
NEW YORK						
1 Bishop	Y	N	N	Y	Y	Y
2 Israel	Y	N	N	Y	?	?
3 **King**	Y	Y	Y	N	Y	N
4 McCarthy	Y	N	N	Y	Y	Y
5 Ackerman	Y	N	N	Y	Y	Y
6 Meeks	Y	N	N	Y	Y	Y
7 Crowley	Y	N	N	Y	Y	Y
8 Nadler	Y	N	N	Y	Y	Y
9 Weiner	Y	N	N	Y	Y	Y
10 Towns	Y	N	N	Y	Y	Y
11 Clarke	Y	N	N	Y	Y	Y
12 Velázquez	Y	N	N	Y	Y	Y
13 **Fossella**	Y	Y	Y	N	?	?
14 Maloney	Y	N	N	Y	Y	Y
15 Rangel	Y	N	N	Y	Y	Y
16 Serrano	Y	N	N	Y	Y	Y
17 Engel	Y	N	N	Y	Y	Y
18 Lowey	Y	N	N	Y	Y	Y
19 Hall	Y	N	N	Y	Y	Y
20 Gillibrand	Y	N	N	Y	Y	Y
21 McNulty	Y	N	N	Y	Y	Y
22 Hinchey	Y	N	N	Y	Y	Y
23 **McHugh**	Y	N	Y	Y	Y	N
24 Arcuri	Y	N	N	Y	Y	Y
25 **Walsh**	Y	Y	Y	Y	Y	N
26 **Reynolds**	Y	Y	Y	N	Y	N
27 Higgins	?	?	N	Y	Y	Y
28 Slaughter	Y	N	–	Y	Y	Y
29 **Kuhl**	Y	Y	Y	N	Y	N
NORTH CAROLINA						
1 Butterfield	Y	N	N	Y	Y	Y
2 Etheridge	Y	N	N	Y	Y	Y
3 **Jones**	Y	Y	Y	N	Y	N
4 Price	Y	N	N	Y	Y	Y
5 **Foxx**	Y	Y	Y	N	Y	N
6 **Coble**	Y	Y	Y	N	Y	N
7 McIntyre	Y	N	Y	Y	Y	Y
8 **Hayes**	Y	Y	Y	N	Y	N
9 **Myrick**	Y	Y	Y	N	Y	N
10 **McHenry**	Y	Y	Y	N	Y	N
11 Shuler	Y	N	N	Y	Y	Y
12 Watt	Y	N	N	Y	Y	Y
13 Miller	Y	N	N	Y	Y	Y
NORTH DAKOTA						
AL Pomeroy	Y	N	N	Y	Y	Y
OHIO						
1 **Chabot**	Y	Y	Y	N	Y	N
2 **Schmidt**	Y	Y	Y	N	Y	N
3 **Turner**	Y	Y	Y	N	Y	N
4 **Jordan**	Y	Y	Y	N	Y	N
5 **Latta**	Y	Y	Y	N	Y	N
6 Wilson	Y	N	N	Y	Y	Y
7 **Hobson**	Y	Y	Y	N	Y	N
8 **Boehner**	?	?	?	?	Y	N
9 Kaptur	Y	N	N	Y	Y	Y
10 Kucinich	Y	N	N	Y	Y	Y
11 Tubbs Jones	?	?	N	Y	?	Y
12 **Tiberi**	Y	Y	Y	N	Y	N
13 Sutton	Y	N	N	Y	Y	Y
14 **LaTourette**	Y	N	Y	Y	Y	N
15 **Pryce**	Y	Y	Y	N	Y	N
16 **Regula**	Y	Y	Y	Y	Y	N
17 Ryan	Y	N	N	Y	Y	Y
18 Space	Y	N	N	Y	Y	Y
OKLAHOMA						
1 **Sullivan**	Y	Y	Y	N	Y	N
2 Boren	Y	Y	N	Y	Y	Y
3 **Lucas**	Y	Y	Y	N	Y	N
4 **Cole**	+	?	?	–	Y	N
5 **Fallin**	Y	Y	Y	N	Y	N
OREGON						
1 Wu	Y	N	N	Y	Y	Y
2 **Walden**	Y	Y	Y	N	Y	N
3 Blumenauer	Y	N	N	Y	Y	Y
4 DeFazio	Y	N	N	Y	Y	Y
5 Hooley	Y	N	N	Y	Y	Y
PENNSYLVANIA						
1 Brady	Y	N	N	Y	Y	Y
2 Fattah	Y	N	N	Y	Y	Y
3 **English**	Y	N	Y	Y	Y	N
4 Altmire	Y	N	N	Y	Y	Y
5 **Peterson**	Y	Y	Y	N	Y	N
6 **Gerlach**	Y	Y	Y	N	Y	N
7 Sestak	Y	N	N	Y	Y	Y
8 Murphy, P.	Y	N	N	Y	Y	Y
9 **Shuster**	Y	Y	?	N	Y	N
10 Carney	Y	N	N	Y	Y	Y
11 Kanjorski	Y	N	N	Y	Y	Y
12 Murtha	Y	N	N	Y	Y	Y
13 Schwartz	Y	N	N	Y	Y	Y
14 Doyle	Y	N	N	Y	Y	Y
15 **Dent**	Y	Y	Y	N	Y	N
16 **Pitts**	Y	Y	Y	N	Y	N
17 Holden	Y	N	N	Y	Y	Y
18 **Murphy, T.**	Y	N	Y	Y	Y	N
19 **Platts**	Y	Y	Y	N	Y	N
RHODE ISLAND						
1 Kennedy	Y	N	N	Y	Y	Y
2 Langevin	Y	N	N	Y	Y	Y
SOUTH CAROLINA						
1 **Brown**	Y	Y	Y	N	Y	N
2 **Wilson**	Y	Y	Y	N	Y	N
3 **Barrett**	Y	Y	Y	N	Y	N
4 **Inglis**	Y	Y	Y	N	Y	N
5 Spratt	Y	N	N	Y	Y	Y
6 Clyburn	Y	N	N	Y	Y	Y
SOUTH DAKOTA						
AL Herseth Sandlin	Y	N	N	Y	Y	Y
TENNESSEE						
1 **Davis, D.**	Y	Y	Y	N	Y	N
2 **Duncan**	?	?	Y	N	Y	N
3 **Wamp**	Y	Y	Y	N	Y	N
4 Davis, L.	Y	N	N	Y	Y	Y
5 Cooper	Y	N	N	Y	Y	Y
6 Gordon	Y	N	N	Y	Y	Y
7 **Blackburn**	Y	Y	Y	N	?	?
8 Tanner	Y	N	N	Y	Y	Y
9 Cohen	Y	N	N	Y	Y	Y
TEXAS						
1 **Gohmert**	Y	Y	Y	N	?	?
2 **Poe**	Y	Y	Y	N	Y	N
3 **Johnson, S.**	Y	Y	Y	N	Y	N
4 **Hall**	Y	Y	Y	N	Y	N
5 **Hensarling**	Y	Y	Y	N	Y	N
6 **Barton**	?	?	?	?	Y	?
7 **Culberson**	Y	Y	Y	N	Y	N
8 **Brady**	Y	Y	Y	N	Y	N
9 Green, A.	Y	N	N	Y	Y	Y
10 **McCaul**	Y	Y	Y	N	Y	N
11 **Conaway**	Y	Y	Y	N	Y	N
12 **Granger**	Y	Y	Y	N	Y	N
13 **Thornberry**	Y	Y	Y	N	Y	N
14 **Paul**	Y	Y	Y	N	N	N
15 Hinojosa	Y	N	N	Y	Y	Y
16 Reyes	Y	N	N	Y	Y	Y
17 Edwards	Y	N	N	Y	Y	Y
18 Jackson Lee	Y	N	N	Y	Y	Y
19 **Neugebauer**	Y	Y	Y	N	Y	N
20 Gonzalez	Y	N	N	Y	Y	Y
21 **Smith**	Y	Y	Y	N	Y	N
22 Lampson	Y	N	N	Y	Y	N
23 Rodriguez	Y	N	N	Y	Y	Y
24 **Marchant**	Y	Y	Y	N	Y	N
25 Doggett	?	?	?	?	?	?
26 **Burgess**	Y	Y	Y	N	?	N
27 Ortiz	Y	N	N	Y	Y	Y
28 Cuellar	Y	N	N	Y	Y	Y
29 Green, G.	Y	N	N	Y	Y	Y
30 Johnson, E.	Y	N	N	Y	Y	Y
31 **Carter**	Y	Y	Y	N	Y	N
32 **Sessions**	Y	Y	Y	N	Y	N
UTAH						
1 **Bishop**	Y	Y	Y	N	Y	N
2 Matheson	Y	N	N	Y	Y	Y
3 **Cannon**	Y	Y	Y	N	Y	N
VERMONT						
AL Welch	Y	N	N	Y	Y	Y
VIRGINIA						
1 **Wittman**	Y	Y	Y	N	Y	N
2 **Drake**	Y	Y	Y	N	Y	N
3 Scott	Y	N	N	Y	Y	Y
4 **Forbes**	?	?	?	?	?	?
5 **Goode**	Y	Y	Y	N	Y	N
6 **Goodlatte**	?	?	?	?	Y	N
7 **Cantor**	Y	Y	Y	N	Y	N
8 Moran	Y	N	N	Y	Y	Y
9 Boucher	Y	N	N	Y	Y	Y
10 **Wolf**	Y	Y	Y	N	Y	N
11 **Davis**	?	?	?	?	Y	N
WASHINGTON						
1 Inslee	Y	N	N	Y	Y	Y
2 Larsen	Y	N	N	Y	Y	Y
3 Baird	Y	N	N	Y	Y	Y
4 **Hastings**	Y	Y	Y	N	Y	N
5 **McMorris Rodgers**	Y	Y	Y	N	Y	N
6 Dicks	Y	N	N	?	Y	Y
7 McDermott	Y	N	N	Y	Y	Y
8 **Reichert**	Y	Y	Y	N	Y	N
9 Smith	Y	N	N	Y	Y	Y
WEST VIRGINIA						
1 Mollohan	Y	N	N	Y	Y	Y
2 **Capito**	Y	Y	Y	N	Y	N
3 Rahall	Y	N	N	Y	Y	Y
WISCONSIN						
1 **Ryan**	Y	Y	Y	N	Y	N
2 Baldwin	Y	N	N	Y	Y	Y
3 Kind	Y	N	N	Y	Y	Y
4 Moore	Y	N	N	Y	Y	Y
5 **Sensenbrenner**	Y	Y	Y	N	Y	N
6 **Petri**	Y	Y	Y	N	Y	N
7 Obey	?	N	N	Y	Y	Y
8 Kagen	Y	N	Y	Y	Y	Y
WYOMING						
AL **Cubin**	Y	Y	Y	N	?	?
DELEGATES						
Faleomavaega (A.S.)	Y	N				
Norton (D.C.)	Y	N				
Bordallo (Guam)	Y	N				
Fortuño (P.R.)	?	?				
Christensen (V.I.)	Y	N				

IN THE HOUSE | By Vote Number

236. **HR 493, HR 5715, S 2954. Suspension Motions/Rule.** Adoption of the rule (H Res 1167) to provide for House floor consideration of three bills under suspension of the rules on the legislative day of Thursday, May 1, 2008. Adopted 228-189: R 2-188; D 226-1 (ND 170-1, SD 56-0). May 1, 2008.

237. **H Con Res 308. National Peace Officers' Memorial Service/Adoption.** Carney, D-Pa., motion to suspend the rules and adopt the concurrent resolution that would authorize the use of the Capitol grounds for the National Peace Officers' Memorial Service. Motion agreed to 412-0: R 188-0; D 224-0 (ND 168-0, SD 56-0). A two-thirds majority of those present and voting (275 in this case) is required for adoption under suspension of the rules. May 1, 2008.

238. **HR 2419. Farm Bill Reauthorization/Motion to Instruct.** Flake, R-Ariz., motion to instruct House conferees to agree to Senate-passed provisions that would set a $40,000 per person limit for annual direct payments to farmers. Motion rejected 157-259: R 104-86; D 53-173 (ND 47-123, SD 6-50). May 1, 2008.

239. **HR 5715. Student Loan Access/Motion to Concur.** Miller, D-Calif., motion to suspend the rules and concur in the Senate amendment to the bill that would increase annual loan limits on federal college loans and give the Education Department a bigger role in ensuring loan availability. The bill would allow the Education Department to buy up existing loans at a discount and codify the department's ability to advance funds to guarantee agencies. It would sunset the Education Department's authority to designate institutions as lenders of last resort at the end of the 2008-09 school year, and require that loans through that program have similar terms and conditions as other federal loans. Motion agreed to 388-21: R 167-21; D 221-0 (ND 166-0, SD 55-0) A two-thirds majority of those present and voting (273 in this case) is required for passage under suspension of the rules. May 1, 2008.

	236	237	238	239
ALABAMA				
1 **Bonner**	N	Y	N	Y
2 **Everett**	N	Y	N	Y
3 **Rogers**	N	Y	N	Y
4 **Aderholt**	N	Y	N	Y
5 Cramer	Y	Y	N	Y
6 **Bachus**	N	Y	Y	Y
7 Davis	Y	Y	N	Y
ALASKA				
AL **Young**	N	Y	Y	Y
ARIZONA				
1 **Renzi**	N	Y	N	Y
2 **Franks**	N	Y	Y	N
3 **Shadegg**	N	Y	Y	Y
4 Pastor	Y	Y	N	Y
5 Mitchell	N	Y	Y	Y
6 **Flake**	N	Y	Y	N
7 Grijalva	Y	Y	N	Y
8 Giffords	Y	Y	Y	Y
ARKANSAS				
1 Berry	Y	Y	N	Y
2 Snyder	Y	Y	N	Y
3 **Boozman**	N	Y	N	Y
4 Ross	Y	Y	N	Y
CALIFORNIA				
1 Thompson	Y	Y	N	Y
2 **Herger**	N	+	N	Y
3 **Lungren**	N	Y	Y	Y
4 **Doolittle**	N	Y	N	Y
5 Matsui	Y	Y	N	Y
6 Woolsey	Y	Y	Y	Y
7 Miller, George	Y	Y	N	Y
8 Pelosi				
9 Lee	Y	Y	N	+
10 Tauscher	Y	Y	N	Y
11 McNerney	Y	Y	N	Y
12 Speier	Y	Y	Y	Y
13 Stark	Y	Y	Y	Y
14 Eshoo	Y	Y	Y	Y
15 Honda	?	?	?	?
16 Lofgren	Y	Y	Y	Y
17 Farr	Y	Y	N	Y
18 Cardoza	Y	Y	N	Y
19 **Radanovich**	N	Y	Y	Y
20 Costa	Y	Y	N	Y
21 **Nunes**	N	Y	N	Y
22 **McCarthy**	N	Y	N	Y
23 Capps	Y	Y	N	Y
24 **Gallegly**	N	Y	Y	Y
25 **McKeon**	N	Y	Y	Y
26 **Dreier**	N	Y	Y	Y
27 Sherman	Y	Y	Y	Y
28 Berman	Y	Y	Y	Y
29 Schiff	Y	Y	Y	Y
30 Waxman	Y	Y	N	Y
31 Becerra	Y	Y	N	Y
32 Solis	Y	Y	N	Y
33 Watson	Y	Y	N	Y
34 Roybal-Allard	Y	Y	N	Y
35 Waters	Y	Y	Y	Y
36 Harman	Y	Y	Y	Y
37 Richardson	Y	Y	N	Y
38 Napolitano	Y	Y	N	Y
39 Sánchez, Linda	Y	Y	Y	Y
40 **Royce**	N	Y	Y	Y
41 **Lewis**	N	Y	Y	Y
42 **Miller, Gary**	N	Y	Y	Y
43 Baca	Y	Y	N	Y
44 **Calvert**	N	Y	Y	Y
45 **Bono Mack**	N	Y	Y	Y
46 **Rohrabacher**	N	Y	Y	Y
47 Sanchez, Loretta	Y	Y	?	?
48 **Campbell**	N	Y	Y	N
49 **Issa**	N	Y	Y	Y
50 **Bilbray**	?	Y	Y	Y
51 Filner	Y	Y	Y	Y
52 **Hunter**	N	Y	Y	Y
53 Davis	Y	Y	Y	Y

	236	237	238	239
COLORADO				
1 DeGette	Y	Y	N	Y
2 Udall	Y	Y	N	Y
3 Salazar	Y	Y	N	Y
4 **Musgrave**	N	Y	N	Y
5 **Lamborn**	N	Y	Y	N
6 **Tancredo**	N	Y	Y	N
7 Perlmutter	Y	Y	N	Y
CONNECTICUT				
1 Larson	Y	Y	N	Y
2 Courtney	Y	Y	N	Y
3 DeLauro	Y	Y	N	Y
4 **Shays**	N	Y	N	Y
5 Murphy	Y	Y	Y	Y
DELAWARE				
AL **Castle**	N	Y	Y	Y
FLORIDA				
1 **Miller**	N	Y	Y	N
2 Boyd	Y	Y	N	Y
3 Brown	Y	Y	N	Y
4 **Crenshaw**	N	Y	N	Y
5 **Brown-Waite**	N	Y	Y	Y
6 **Stearns**	N	Y	Y	Y
7 **Mica**	N	Y	N	Y
8 **Keller**	N	Y	Y	Y
9 **Bilirakis**	N	Y	N	Y
10 **Young**	N	Y	Y	Y
11 Castor	Y	Y	Y	Y
12 **Putnam**	N	Y	N	Y
13 **Buchanan**	N	Y	N	Y
14 **Mack**	N	Y	Y	Y
15 **Weldon**	N	Y	?	Y
16 Mahoney	Y	Y	N	Y
17 Meek	Y	Y	N	Y
18 **Ros-Lehtinen**	N	Y	N	Y
19 Wexler	Y	Y	N	Y
20 Wasserman Schultz	Y	Y	N	Y
21 **Diaz-Balart, L.**	N	Y	N	Y
22 Klein	Y	Y	N	Y
23 Hastings	Y	Y	N	Y
24 **Feeney**	N	Y	Y	Y
25 **Diaz-Balart, M.**	N	Y	N	Y
GEORGIA				
1 **Kingston**	N	Y	N	N
2 Bishop	Y	Y	N	Y
3 **Westmoreland**	N	Y	N	N
4 Johnson	Y	Y	N	Y
5 Lewis	Y	Y	N	Y
6 **Price**	N	Y	N	Y
7 **Linder**	N	Y	Y	Y
8 Marshall	Y	Y	N	Y
9 **Deal**	?	?	?	?
10 **Broun**	N	Y	N	N
11 **Gingrey**	N	Y	N	N
12 Barrow	Y	Y	N	Y
13 Scott	Y	Y	N	Y
HAWAII				
1 Abercrombie	Y	Y	N	Y
2 Hirono	Y	Y	N	Y
IDAHO				
1 **Sali**	N	Y	N	Y
2 **Simpson**	N	Y	N	Y
ILLINOIS				
1 Rush	?	?	?	?
2 Jackson	Y	Y	N	Y
3 Lipinski	Y	Y	Y	Y
4 Gutierrez	Y	Y	N	?
5 Emanuel	Y	Y	N	Y
6 **Roskam**	N	Y	Y	Y
7 Davis	Y	Y	N	Y
8 Bean	Y	Y	Y	Y
9 Schakowsky	Y	Y	N	Y
10 **Kirk**	N	Y	Y	Y
11 **Weller**	N	Y	N	Y
12 Costello	Y	Y	N	Y
13 **Biggert**	N	Y	Y	Y
14 Foster	Y	Y	N	Y
15 **Johnson**	N	Y	N	Y

ND Northern Democrats, SD Southern Democrats
Southern states: Ala., Ark., Fla., Ga., Ky., La., Miss., N.C., Okla., S.C., Tenn., Texas, Va.

	236	237	238	239
16 Manzullo	N	Y	N	Y
17 Hare	Y	Y	N	Y
18 LaHood	?	?	?	?
19 Shimkus	N	Y	N	Y
INDIANA				
1 Visclosky	Y	Y	N	Y
2 Donnelly	Y	Y	N	Y
3 Souder	N	Y	N	+
4 Buyer	N	Y	N	Y
5 Burton	N	Y	N	Y
6 Pence	N	Y	Y	Y
7 Carson, A.	Y	Y	N	Y
8 Ellsworth	Y	Y	N	Y
9 Hill	Y	Y	N	Y
IOWA				
1 Braley	Y	Y	N	Y
2 Loebsack	Y	Y	N	Y
3 Boswell	Y	Y	N	Y
4 Latham	N	Y	N	+
5 King	N	Y	N	N
KANSAS				
1 Moran	N	Y	N	Y
2 Boyda	Y	Y	N	Y
3 Moore	Y	Y	N	Y
4 Tiahrt	N	Y	N	Y
KENTUCKY				
1 Whitfield	N	Y	N	Y
2 Lewis	N	Y	?	?
3 Yarmuth	Y	Y	N	Y
4 Davis	N	Y	N	Y
5 Rogers	N	Y	Y	Y
6 Chandler	Y	Y	Y	Y
LOUISIANA				
1 Vacant				
2 Jefferson	Y	Y	N	Y
3 Melancon	Y	Y	N	Y
4 McCrery	N	Y	N	Y
5 Alexander	N	Y	N	Y
6 Vacant				
7 Boustany	N	Y	N	Y
MAINE				
1 Allen	Y	Y	Y	Y
2 Michaud	Y	Y	Y	Y
MARYLAND				
1 Gilchrest	N	Y	Y	Y
2 Ruppersberger	Y	Y	N	Y
3 Sarbanes	Y	Y	N	Y
4 Wynn	?	?	N	Y
5 Hoyer	Y	Y	N	Y
6 Bartlett	N	Y	Y	Y
7 Cummings	Y	Y	N	Y
8 Van Hollen	Y	Y	Y	Y
MASSACHUSETTS				
1 Olver	Y	Y	N	Y
2 Neal	Y	Y	N	Y
3 McGovern	Y	Y	Y	Y
4 Frank	Y	Y	N	Y
5 Tsongas	Y	Y	N	Y
6 Tierney	Y	Y	Y	Y
7 Markey	Y	Y	Y	Y
8 Capuano	Y	Y	N	Y
9 Lynch	Y	Y	N	Y
10 Delahunt	Y	Y	N	Y
MICHIGAN				
1 Stupak	Y	Y	N	Y
2 Hoekstra	Y	Y	Y	Y
3 Ehlers	N	Y	Y	Y
4 Camp	N	Y	N	Y
5 Kildee	Y	Y	N	Y
6 Upton	N	Y	N	Y
7 Walberg	N	Y	Y	Y
8 Rogers	N	Y	N	Y
9 Knollenberg	N	Y	Y	Y
10 Miller	N	Y	N	Y
11 McCotter	N	Y	N	Y
12 Levin	Y	Y	N	Y
13 Kilpatrick	Y	Y	N	Y
14 Conyers	Y	Y	Y	Y
15 Dingell	Y	Y	N	Y
MINNESOTA				
1 Walz	Y	Y	N	Y
2 Kline	N	Y	Y	Y
3 Ramstad	N	Y	N	Y
4 McCollum	Y	Y	N	Y

	236	237	238	239
5 Ellison	Y	?	Y	Y
6 Bachmann	N	Y	N	Y
7 Peterson	Y	Y	N	Y
8 Oberstar	Y	Y	N	Y
MISSISSIPPI				
1 Vacant				
2 Thompson	Y	Y	N	Y
3 Pickering	N	Y	Y	Y
4 Taylor	Y	Y	N	Y
MISSOURI				
1 Clay	Y	Y	N	Y
2 Akin	N	Y	N	Y
3 Carnahan	Y	Y	N	Y
4 Skelton	Y	Y	N	Y
5 Cleaver	Y	Y	N	Y
6 Graves	N	Y	N	Y
7 Blunt	N	Y	N	Y
8 Emerson	N	Y	N	Y
9 Hulshof	N	?	N	Y
MONTANA				
AL Rehberg	N	Y	N	Y
NEBRASKA				
1 Fortenberry	N	Y	Y	Y
2 Terry	N	Y	Y	Y
3 Smith	N	Y	Y	Y
NEVADA				
1 Berkley	Y	Y	Y	Y
2 Heller	N	Y	Y	Y
3 Porter	N	Y	N	Y
NEW HAMPSHIRE				
1 Shea-Porter	Y	Y	Y	Y
2 Hodes	Y	Y	Y	Y
NEW JERSEY				
1 Andrews	Y	Y	N	Y
2 LoBiondo	N	Y	Y	Y
3 Saxton	N	Y	Y	Y
4 Smith	N	Y	Y	Y
5 Garrett	N	Y	Y	Y
6 Pallone	Y	?	Y	Y
7 Ferguson	N	Y	Y	Y
8 Pascrell	Y	Y	Y	Y
9 Rothman	Y	Y	N	Y
10 Payne	?	?	?	?
11 Frelinghuysen	N	Y	Y	Y
12 Holt	Y	Y	Y	Y
13 Sires	Y	Y	N	Y
NEW MEXICO				
1 Wilson	?	?	?	?
2 Pearce	N	Y	N	Y
3 Udall	Y	Y	N	Y
NEW YORK				
1 Bishop	Y	Y	Y	Y
2 Israel	?	?	?	?
3 King	N	Y	N	Y
4 McCarthy	Y	Y	N	Y
5 Ackerman	Y	Y	N	Y
6 Meeks	Y	Y	N	Y
7 Crowley	Y	Y	N	Y
8 Nadler	Y	Y	N	Y
9 Weiner	Y	Y	N	Y
10 Towns	Y	Y	N	Y
11 Clarke	Y	Y	N	Y
12 Velázquez	Y	Y	N	Y
13 Fossella	?	?	?	?
14 Maloney	Y	Y	N	Y
15 Rangel	Y	Y	N	Y
16 Serrano	Y	Y	N	Y
17 Engel	Y	Y	N	Y
18 Lowey	Y	Y	N	Y
19 Hall	Y	Y	N	Y
20 Gillibrand	Y	Y	N	Y
21 McNulty	Y	Y	N	Y
22 Hinchey	Y	Y	N	Y
23 McHugh	N	Y	N	Y
24 Arcuri	Y	Y	N	Y
25 Walsh	N	Y	N	Y
26 Reynolds	N	Y	N	Y
27 Higgins	Y	Y	N	?
28 Slaughter	Y	?	?	+
29 Kuhl	N	Y	N	Y
NORTH CAROLINA				
1 Butterfield	Y	Y	N	Y
2 Etheridge	Y	Y	N	Y
3 Jones	N	Y	N	Y
4 Price	Y	Y	N	Y

	236	237	238	239
5 Foxx	N	Y	Y	N
6 Coble	N	Y	N	Y
7 McIntyre	Y	Y	N	Y
8 Hayes	N	Y	N	Y
9 Myrick	N	Y	N	Y
10 McHenry	N	Y	N	Y
11 Shuler	Y	Y	N	Y
12 Watt	Y	Y	N	Y
13 Miller	Y	Y	N	Y
NORTH DAKOTA				
AL Pomeroy	Y	Y	N	Y
OHIO				
1 Chabot	N	Y	Y	Y
2 Schmidt	N	Y	Y	Y
3 Turner	N	Y	N	Y
4 Jordan	N	Y	N	Y
5 Latta	N	Y	N	Y
6 Wilson	Y	Y	N	Y
7 Hobson	N	Y	Y	Y
8 Boehner	N	Y	Y	Y
9 Kaptur	Y	Y	N	Y
10 Kucinich	Y	Y	N	Y
11 Tubbs Jones	Y	Y	N	Y
12 Tiberi	N	Y	N	Y
13 Sutton	Y	Y	N	Y
14 LaTourette	N	Y	N	Y
15 Pryce	N	Y	N	Y
16 Regula	N	Y	N	Y
17 Ryan	Y	Y	N	Y
18 Space	Y	Y	N	Y
OKLAHOMA				
1 Sullivan	N	Y	N	Y
2 Boren	Y	Y	N	Y
3 Lucas	N	Y	N	Y
4 Cole	N	Y	N	Y
5 Fallin	N	Y	N	Y
OREGON				
1 Wu	Y	Y	N	Y
2 Walden	N	Y	N	Y
3 Blumenauer	Y	Y	Y	Y
4 DeFazio	Y	Y	Y	Y
5 Hooley	Y	Y	N	Y
PENNSYLVANIA				
1 Brady	Y	Y	N	Y
2 Fattah	Y	Y	N	Y
3 English	N	Y	Y	Y
4 Altmire	Y	Y	N	Y
5 Peterson	N	Y	Y	Y
6 Gerlach	N	Y	Y	Y
7 Sestak	Y	Y	Y	Y
8 Murphy, P.	Y	Y	Y	Y
9 Shuster	N	Y	Y	Y
10 Carney	Y	Y	N	Y
11 Kanjorski	Y	Y	N	Y
12 Murtha	Y	Y	N	Y
13 Schwartz	Y	Y	N	Y
14 Doyle	Y	Y	N	Y
15 Dent	N	Y	Y	Y
16 Pitts	N	Y	Y	Y
17 Holden	Y	Y	N	Y
18 Murphy, T.	Y	Y	N	Y
19 Platts	N	Y	N	Y
RHODE ISLAND				
1 Kennedy	Y	Y	N	Y
2 Langevin	Y	Y	Y	Y
SOUTH CAROLINA				
1 Brown	N	Y	Y	Y
2 Wilson	N	Y	Y	Y
3 Barrett	N	Y	Y	Y
4 Inglis	N	Y	Y	Y
5 Spratt	Y	Y	N	Y
6 Clyburn	Y	Y	N	Y
SOUTH DAKOTA				
AL Herseth Sandlin	Y	Y	N	Y
TENNESSEE				
1 Davis, D.	N	Y	Y	Y
2 Duncan	N	Y	Y	N
3 Wamp	N	Y	Y	Y
4 Davis, L.	Y	Y	N	Y
5 Cooper	Y	Y	Y	Y
6 Gordon	Y	Y	N	Y
7 Blackburn	?	?	?	?
8 Tanner	Y	Y	N	Y
9 Cohen	Y	Y	N	Y

	236	237	238	239
TEXAS				
1 Gohmert	N	Y	N	Y
2 Poe	N	Y	N	N
3 Johnson, S.	N	Y	Y	N
4 Hall	N	Y	Y	Y
5 Hensarling	N	Y	Y	Y
6 Barton	N	Y	Y	Y
7 Culberson	N	Y	Y	Y
8 Brady	N	Y	N	N
9 Green, A.	Y	Y	N	Y
10 McCaul	N	Y	N	Y
11 Conaway	N	Y	N	Y
12 Granger	N	Y	N	Y
13 Thornberry	N	Y	N	Y
14 Paul	N	Y	N	N
15 Hinojosa	Y	Y	N	Y
16 Reyes	Y	Y	N	Y
17 Edwards	Y	Y	N	Y
18 Jackson Lee	Y	Y	N	Y
19 Neugebauer	N	Y	N	Y
20 Gonzalez	Y	Y	N	Y
21 Smith	N	Y	N	Y
22 Lampson	Y	Y	Y	Y
23 Rodriguez	Y	Y	N	Y
24 Marchant	N	Y	N	Y
25 Doggett	?	?	?	?
26 Burgess	N	?	Y	Y
27 Ortiz	Y	Y	N	Y
28 Cuellar	Y	Y	N	Y
29 Green, G.	Y	Y	N	Y
30 Johnson, E.	Y	Y	N	Y
31 Carter	N	Y	N	Y
32 Sessions	N	Y	Y	Y
UTAH				
1 Bishop	N	Y	Y	Y
2 Matheson	Y	Y	Y	Y
3 Cannon	N	Y	Y	Y
VERMONT				
AL Welch	Y	Y	Y	Y
VIRGINIA				
1 Wittman	N	Y	N	Y
2 Drake	N	Y	N	Y
3 Scott	Y	Y	N	Y
4 Forbes	?	?	?	?
5 Goode	N	Y	Y	Y
6 Goodlatte	N	Y	N	Y
7 Cantor	N	Y	Y	Y
8 Moran	Y	Y	Y	Y
9 Boucher	Y	Y	Y	?
10 Wolf	N	Y	Y	Y
11 Davis	N	Y	Y	Y
WASHINGTON				
1 Inslee	Y	Y	N	Y
2 Larsen	Y	Y	N	?
3 Baird	Y	Y	Y	Y
4 Hastings	N	Y	N	Y
5 McMorris Rodgers	N	Y	N	Y
6 Dicks	Y	Y	N	Y
7 McDermott	Y	Y	Y	Y
8 Reichert	N	Y	Y	Y
9 Smith	Y	Y	N	Y
WEST VIRGINIA				
1 Mollohan	Y	Y	N	Y
2 Capito	N	Y	Y	Y
3 Rahall	Y	Y	N	Y
WISCONSIN				
1 Ryan	N	Y	Y	Y
2 Baldwin	Y	Y	N	Y
3 Kind	Y	Y	Y	Y
4 Moore	Y	Y	N	Y
5 Sensenbrenner	N	Y	Y	Y
6 Petri	N	Y	Y	Y
7 Obey	Y	Y	N	Y
8 Kagen	Y	Y	N	Y
WYOMING				
AL Cubin	?	?	Y	Y
DELEGATES				
Faleomavaega (A.S.)				
Norton (D.C.)				
Bordallo (Guam)				
Fortuño (P.R.)				
Christensen (V.I.)				

IN THE HOUSE | By Vote Number

240. **H Res 952. National Teacher Day/Adoption.** Clay, D-Mo., motion to suspend the rules and adopt the resolution that would express the sense of the House of Representatives that a National Teacher Day should be established to honor and celebrate teachers. Motion agreed to 368-0: R 167-0; D 201-0 (ND 154-0, SD 47-0). A two-thirds majority of those present and voting (246 in this case) is required for adoption under suspension of the rules. May 5, 2008.

241. **H Res 952. National Teacher Day/Motion to Reconsider.** Hastings, D-Fla., motion to table (kill) the Lewis, R-Calif., motion to reconsider the vote on the adoption of the resolution that would express the sense of the House of Representatives that a National Teacher Day should be established to honor and celebrate teachers. Motion agreed to 202-168: R 0-168; D 202-0 (ND 155-0, SD 47-0). May 5, 2008.

242. **H Res 1011. Conflict in Chad/Adoption.** Watson, D-Calif., motion to suspend the rules and adopt the resolution that would condemn the Sudanese president's support of the armed rebellion in Chad and call for continued U.S. humanitarian assistance to refugees in Chad and the Central African Republic. It also would urge the governments of Chad and the Central African Republic to engage in dialogue to end the conflict with opposition groups. Motion agreed to 371-0: R 169-0; D 202-0 (ND 155-0, SD 47-0). A two-thirds majority of those present and voting (248 in this case) is required for adoption under suspension of the rules. May 5, 2008.

243. **H Res 1011. Conflict in Chad/Motion to Reconsider.** Hastings, D-Fla., motion to table (kill) the Lewis, R-Calif., motion to reconsider the vote on the adoption of the resolution on the conflict in Chad. Motion agreed to 199-168: R 0-168; D 199-0 (ND 153-0, SD 46-0). May 5, 2008.

244. **Procedural Motion/Motion to Adjourn.** Serrano, D-N.Y., motion to adjourn. Motion agreed to 199-168: R 6-164; D 193-4 (ND 147-4, SD 46-0). May 5, 2008.

245. **Procedural Motion/Motion to Adjourn.** Walsh, R-N.Y., motion to adjourn. Motion rejected 152-255: R 151-37; D 1-218 (ND 1-165, SD 0-53). May 6, 2008.

246. **Procedural Motion/Journal.** Approval of the House Journal of Monday, May 5, 2008. Approved 220-182: R 15-170; D 205-12 (ND 153-11, SD 52-1). May 6, 2008.

	240	241	242	243	244	245	246
ALABAMA							
1 Bonner	Y	N	Y	N	N	Y	N
2 Everett	Y	N	Y	N	N	N	N
3 Rogers	Y	N	Y	N	Y	Y	N
4 Aderholt	Y	N	Y	N	N	Y	N
5 Cramer	?	?	?	?	?	?	?
6 Bachus	Y	N	Y	N	N	Y	N
7 Davis	?	?	?	?	?	N	Y
ALASKA							
AL Young	Y	N	Y	N	Y	Y	N
ARIZONA							
1 Renzi	Y	N	Y	N	N	Y	N
2 Franks	Y	N	Y	N	N	Y	N
3 Shadegg	Y	N	Y	N	N	Y	N
4 Pastor	Y	Y	Y	Y	Y	N	Y
5 Mitchell	Y	Y	Y	Y	Y	N	N
6 Flake	Y	N	Y	N	N	Y	N
7 Grijalva	Y	Y	Y	Y	Y	N	Y
8 Giffords	Y	Y	Y	Y	Y	N	N
ARKANSAS							
1 Berry	Y	Y	Y	Y	Y	N	Y
2 Snyder	Y	Y	Y	Y	Y	N	Y
3 Boozman	Y	N	Y	N	N	Y	N
4 Ross	Y	Y	Y	Y	Y	N	Y
CALIFORNIA							
1 Thompson	Y	Y	Y	Y	Y	N	N
2 Herger	Y	N	Y	N	N	Y	N
3 Lungren	Y	N	Y	N	N	Y	N
4 Doolittle	?	?	?	?	?	Y	?
5 Matsui	Y	Y	Y	Y	Y	N	Y
6 Woolsey	Y	Y	Y	Y	Y	N	Y
7 Miller, George	Y	Y	Y	Y	Y	?	Y
8 Pelosi							
9 Lee	Y	Y	Y	Y	Y	N	Y
10 Tauscher	Y	Y	Y	Y	Y	N	Y
11 McNerney	Y	Y	Y	Y	Y	N	Y
12 Speier	?	?	?	?	?	?	?
13 Stark	?	?	?	?	?	N	Y
14 Eshoo	Y	Y	Y	Y	Y	N	Y
15 Honda	Y	Y	Y	Y	Y	N	Y
16 Lofgren	Y	Y	Y	Y	Y	N	Y
17 Farr	Y	Y	Y	Y	Y	N	Y
18 Cardoza	Y	Y	Y	Y	Y	N	Y
19 Radanovich	?	?	?	?	?	N	N
20 Costa	Y	Y	Y	Y	Y	N	Y
21 Nunes	Y	N	Y	N	N	Y	N
22 McCarthy	Y	N	Y	N	N	Y	N
23 Capps	Y	Y	Y	Y	Y	N	Y
24 Gallegly	Y	N	Y	N	N	Y	N
25 McKeon	Y	N	Y	N	N	Y	N
26 Dreier	Y	N	Y	N	N	N	Y
27 Sherman	Y	Y	Y	Y	Y	N	Y
28 Berman	Y	Y	Y	Y	Y	N	Y
29 Schiff	Y	Y	Y	Y	Y	N	Y
30 Waxman	Y	Y	Y	Y	Y	N	Y
31 Becerra	Y	Y	Y	Y	Y	N	Y
32 Solis	Y	Y	Y	Y	Y	N	Y
33 Watson	Y	Y	Y	Y	Y	N	Y
34 Roybal-Allard	Y	Y	Y	Y	Y	N	Y
35 Waters	Y	Y	Y	Y	Y	N	Y
36 Harman	Y	Y	Y	Y	Y	N	Y
37 Richardson	Y	Y	Y	Y	Y	N	Y
38 Napolitano	Y	Y	Y	Y	Y	N	Y
39 Sánchez, Linda	Y	Y	Y	Y	Y	N	Y
40 Royce	Y	N	Y	N	N	Y	N
41 Lewis	Y	N	Y	N	N	Y	N
42 Miller, Gary	Y	N	Y	N	N	Y	N
43 Baca	Y	Y	Y	Y	Y	N	Y
44 Calvert	Y	N	Y	N	N	Y	N
45 Bono Mack	Y	N	Y	N	N	N	N
46 Rohrabacher	?	?	?	?	?	Y	N
47 Sanchez, Loretta	Y	Y	Y	Y	Y	N	Y
48 Campbell	?	?	?	?	?	?	?
49 Issa	Y	N	Y	N	N	Y	N
50 Bilbray	Y	N	Y	N	N	Y	N
51 Filner	Y	Y	Y	Y	Y	N	Y
52 Hunter	Y	N	Y	N	N	Y	N
53 Davis	Y	Y	Y	Y	Y	N	Y

	240	241	242	243	244	245	246
COLORADO							
1 DeGette	Y	Y	Y	Y	Y	N	Y
2 Udall	Y	Y	Y	Y	Y	N	N
3 Salazar	Y	Y	Y	Y	Y	N	Y
4 Musgrave	Y	N	Y	N	N	Y	N
5 Lamborn	Y	N	Y	N	N	Y	N
6 Tancredo	Y	N	Y	N	N	Y	N
7 Perlmutter	Y	Y	Y	Y	Y	N	N
CONNECTICUT							
1 Larson	Y	Y	Y	Y	Y	N	Y
2 Courtney	Y	Y	Y	Y	Y	N	Y
3 DeLauro	Y	Y	Y	Y	Y	N	Y
4 Shays	Y	N	Y	N	N	N	Y
5 Murphy	Y	Y	Y	Y	Y	N	Y
DELAWARE							
AL Castle	Y	N	Y	N	N	Y	Y
FLORIDA							
1 Miller	Y	N	Y	N	N	Y	?
2 Boyd	Y	Y	Y	Y	Y	N	Y
3 Brown	Y	Y	Y	Y	Y	N	Y
4 Crenshaw	Y	N	Y	N	N	Y	N
5 Brown-Waite	Y	N	Y	N	N	N	N
6 Stearns	Y	N	Y	N	N	N	N
7 Mica	Y	N	Y	N	N	Y	N
8 Keller	Y	N	Y	N	N	Y	N
9 Bilirakis	Y	N	Y	N	N	Y	N
10 Young	Y	N	Y	N	N	Y	N
11 Castor	Y	Y	Y	Y	Y	N	Y
12 Putnam	Y	N	Y	N	N	Y	N
13 Buchanan	?	?	?	?	N	N	Y
14 Mack	Y	N	Y	N	N	Y	N
15 Weldon	?	?	?	?	?	N	Y
16 Mahoney	Y	Y	Y	Y	Y	N	Y
17 Meek	Y	Y	Y	Y	Y	N	Y
18 Ros-Lehtinen	Y	N	Y	N	N	Y	N
19 Wexler	?	?	?	?	?	N	N
20 Wasserman Schultz	Y	Y	Y	Y	Y	N	Y
21 Diaz-Balart, L.	Y	N	Y	N	N	Y	N
22 Klein	Y	Y	Y	Y	Y	N	Y
23 Hastings	Y	Y	Y	Y	Y	N	Y
24 Feeney	Y	N	Y	N	Y	Y	N
25 Diaz-Balart, M.	Y	N	Y	N	N	Y	N
GEORGIA							
1 Kingston	Y	N	Y	N	N	Y	N
2 Bishop	Y	Y	Y	Y	Y	N	Y
3 Westmoreland	Y	N	Y	N	N	Y	N
4 Johnson	Y	Y	Y	Y	Y	N	Y
5 Lewis	Y	Y	Y	Y	Y	N	Y
6 Price	Y	N	Y	N	N	Y	N
7 Linder	Y	N	Y	N	N	N	N
8 Marshall	?	?	?	?	?	?	?
9 Deal	Y	N	Y	N	N	Y	N
10 Broun	Y	N	Y	N	N	Y	N
11 Gingrey	Y	N	Y	N	N	Y	N
12 Barrow	Y	Y	Y	Y	Y	N	Y
13 Scott	Y	Y	Y	Y	Y	N	Y
HAWAII							
1 Abercrombie	Y	Y	Y	Y	Y	N	Y
2 Hirono	Y	Y	Y	Y	Y	N	+
IDAHO							
1 Sali	Y	N	Y	N	N	N	N
2 Simpson	Y	N	Y	N	N	Y	N
ILLINOIS							
1 Rush	?	?	?	?	?	?	?
2 Jackson	Y	Y	Y	Y	Y	N	Y
3 Lipinski	?	?	?	?	?	N	Y
4 Gutierrez	Y	Y	Y	Y	Y	N	Y
5 Emanuel	Y	Y	Y	Y	Y	N	Y
6 Roskam	Y	N	Y	N	N	Y	N
7 Davis	?	?	?	?	?	N	Y
8 Bean	?	?	?	?	?	N	Y
9 Schakowsky	Y	Y	Y	Y	Y	N	Y
10 Kirk	Y	N	Y	N	Y	N	N
11 Weller	Y	N	Y	N	N	Y	N
12 Costello	?	?	?	?	?	N	Y
13 Biggert	Y	N	Y	N	N	Y	N
14 Foster	Y	Y	Y	Y	Y	N	Y
15 Johnson	+	–	+	–	+	Y	Y

KEY | **Republicans** | Democrats

Y Voted for (yea)	X Paired against
# Paired for	– Announced against
+ Announced for	P Voted "present"
N Voted against (nay)	C Voted "present" to avoid possible conflict of interest
	? Did not vote or otherwise make a position known

ND Northern Democrats, SD Southern Democrats
Southern states: Ala., Ark., Fla., Ga., Ky., La., Miss., N.C., Okla., S.C., Tenn., Texas, Va.

H-80 2008 CQ ALMANAC | www.cq.com

	240	241	242	243	244	245	246
16 **Manzullo**	Y	N	Y	N	N	N	N
17 Hare	Y	Y	Y	Y	Y	N	Y
18 **LaHood**	Y	N	Y	N	N	Y	N
19 **Shimkus**	Y	N	Y	N	N	Y	N
INDIANA							
1 Visclosky	Y	Y	Y	Y	Y	N	Y
2 Donnelly	Y	Y	Y	?	?	N	N
3 **Souder**	Y	?	Y	N	N	Y	N
4 **Buyer**	Y	N	Y	N	N	N	N
5 **Burton**	?	?	?	?	?	?	?
6 **Pence**	Y	N	Y	N	N	Y	?
7 Carson, A.	?	?	?	?	?	?	?
8 Ellsworth	Y	Y	Y	Y	N	N	N
9 Hill	Y	Y	Y	Y	Y	N	N
IOWA							
1 Braley	Y	Y	Y	Y	Y	N	Y
2 Loebsack	Y	Y	Y	Y	Y	N	Y
3 Boswell	Y	Y	Y	Y	Y	N	Y
4 **Latham**	Y	N	Y	N	N	Y	N
5 **King**	Y	N	Y	N	N	Y	N
KANSAS							
1 **Moran**	Y	N	Y	N	N	N	N
2 Boyda	Y	Y	Y	Y	Y	N	Y
3 Moore	Y	Y	Y	Y	Y	N	Y
4 **Tiahrt**	Y	N	Y	N	N	Y	N
KENTUCKY							
1 **Whitfield**	Y	N	Y	N	N	Y	Y
2 **Lewis**	Y	N	Y	N	N	Y	N
3 Yarmuth	Y	Y	Y	Y	Y	N	Y
4 **Davis**	Y	N	Y	N	N	Y	N
5 **Rogers**	Y	N	Y	N	N	Y	N
6 Chandler	Y	Y	Y	Y	Y	N	Y
LOUISIANA							
1 Vacant							
2 Jefferson	Y	Y	Y	Y	Y	N	Y
3 Melancon	Y	Y	Y	Y	Y	N	Y
4 **McCrery**	Y	N	Y	N	N	Y	N
5 **Alexander**	Y	N	Y	N	N	Y	N
6 Vacant							
7 **Boustany**	Y	N	Y	N	N	Y	N
MAINE							
1 Allen	Y	Y	Y	Y	Y	N	Y
2 Michaud	Y	Y	Y	Y	Y	N	Y
MARYLAND							
1 **Gilchrest**	?	?	?	?	?	Y	N
2 Ruppersberger	Y	Y	Y	Y	Y	N	Y
3 Sarbanes	Y	Y	Y	Y	Y	N	Y
4 Wynn	Y	Y	Y	Y	Y	?	?
5 Hoyer	Y	Y	Y	Y	Y	N	Y
6 **Bartlett**	Y	N	Y	N	N	Y	N
7 Cummings	Y	Y	Y	Y	Y	N	Y
8 Van Hollen	Y	Y	Y	Y	Y	N	Y
MASSACHUSETTS							
1 Olver	Y	Y	Y	Y	Y	N	Y
2 Neal	?	?	?	?	?	N	Y
3 McGovern	Y	Y	Y	Y	Y	N	Y
4 Frank	Y	Y	Y	Y	Y	N	Y
5 Tsongas	Y	Y	Y	Y	Y	N	Y
6 Tierney	Y	Y	Y	Y	Y	N	Y
7 Markey	Y	Y	Y	Y	?	N	Y
8 Capuano	Y	Y	Y	Y	Y	N	Y
9 Lynch	Y	Y	Y	Y	Y	N	Y
10 Delahunt	Y	Y	Y	Y	Y	N	?
MICHIGAN							
1 Stupak	Y	Y	Y	Y	Y	N	N
2 **Hoekstra**	?	?	?	?	?	Y	N
3 **Ehlers**	?	N	Y	N	N	N	N
4 **Camp**	Y	N	Y	N	N	?	N
5 Kildee	Y	Y	Y	Y	Y	N	Y
6 **Upton**	Y	N	Y	N	N	Y	N
7 **Walberg**	Y	N	Y	N	N	Y	N
8 **Rogers**	?	?	?	?	?	Y	N
9 **Knollenberg**	Y	N	Y	N	N	Y	N
10 **Miller**	Y	N	Y	N	N	Y	N
11 **McCotter**	Y	N	Y	N	N	N	N
12 Levin	Y	Y	Y	Y	Y	N	Y
13 Kilpatrick	+	?	+	?	?	N	Y
14 Conyers	Y	Y	Y	Y	Y	N	Y
15 Dingell	Y	Y	Y	?	?	?	?
MINNESOTA							
1 Walz	Y	Y	Y	Y	Y	N	Y
2 **Kline**	Y	N	Y	N	N	Y	N
3 **Ramstad**	Y	N	Y	N	N	N	N
4 McCollum	Y	Y	Y	Y	Y	N	Y

	240	241	242	243	244	245	246
5 Ellison	Y	Y	Y	Y	Y	N	Y
6 **Bachmann**	Y	N	Y	N	N	Y	N
7 Peterson	Y	Y	Y	Y	Y	N	N
8 Oberstar	?	?	?	?	?	?	?
MISSISSIPPI							
1 Vacant							
2 Thompson	?	?	?	?	?	N	Y
3 **Pickering**	Y	N	Y	N	N	Y	N
4 Taylor	Y	Y	Y	Y	Y	N	Y
MISSOURI							
1 Clay	Y	Y	Y	Y	Y	N	Y
2 **Akin**	Y	N	Y	N	N	Y	N
3 Carnahan	Y	Y	Y	Y	Y	N	Y
4 Skelton	Y	Y	Y	Y	Y	N	Y
5 Cleaver	Y	Y	Y	Y	Y	N	Y
6 **Graves**	Y	N	Y	N	N	Y	Y
7 **Blunt**	Y	N	Y	N	N	Y	N
8 **Emerson**	Y	N	Y	N	N	Y	N
9 **Hulshof**	?	?	?	?	?	?	?
MONTANA							
AL **Rehberg**	Y	N	Y	N	N	Y	N
NEBRASKA							
1 **Fortenberry**	Y	N	Y	N	N	N	N
2 **Terry**	?	N	Y	N	N	N	N
3 **Smith**	Y	N	Y	N	N	Y	N
NEVADA							
1 Berkley	Y	Y	Y	Y	Y	N	Y
2 **Heller**	+	−	+	−	−	Y	N
3 **Porter**	Y	N	Y	N	N	Y	N
NEW HAMPSHIRE							
1 Shea-Porter	Y	Y	Y	Y	Y	Y	Y
2 Hodes	Y	Y	Y	Y	Y	N	Y
NEW JERSEY							
1 Andrews	+	+	+	+	+	?	?
2 **LoBiondo**	Y	N	Y	N	N	N	N
3 **Saxton**	?	?	?	?	?	N	N
4 **Smith**	Y	N	Y	N	N	N	N
5 **Garrett**	Y	N	Y	N	Y	Y	N
6 Pallone	Y	Y	Y	Y	Y	N	Y
7 **Ferguson**	Y	N	Y	N	N	?	?
8 Pascrell	Y	Y	Y	Y	Y	N	Y
9 Rothman	Y	Y	Y	Y	Y	N	Y
10 Payne	?	?	?	?	?	N	?
11 **Frelinghuysen**	Y	N	Y	N	N	Y	N
12 Holt	Y	Y	Y	Y	Y	N	Y
13 Sires	Y	Y	Y	Y	Y	N	Y
NEW MEXICO							
1 **Wilson**	Y	N	Y	N	N	Y	N
2 **Pearce**	Y	N	Y	N	N	Y	N
3 Udall	Y	Y	Y	Y	Y	N	Y
NEW YORK							
1 Bishop	Y	Y	Y	Y	Y	N	Y
2 Israel	Y	Y	Y	Y	Y	N	Y
3 **King**	?	?	?	?	?	Y	Y
4 McCarthy	Y	Y	Y	Y	Y	N	Y
5 Ackerman	Y	Y	Y	Y	Y	N	Y
6 Meeks	Y	Y	Y	Y	Y	N	Y
7 Crowley	Y	Y	Y	Y	Y	N	Y
8 Nadler	Y	Y	Y	Y	Y	N	Y
9 Weiner	?	?	?	?	?	N	Y
10 Towns	Y	Y	Y	Y	Y	N	Y
11 Clarke	Y	Y	Y	Y	Y	N	Y
12 Velázquez	Y	Y	Y	Y	Y	N	Y
13 **Fossella**	?	?	?	?	?	Y	N
14 Maloney	?	?	?	?	?	N	Y
15 Rangel	Y	Y	Y	Y	Y	N	Y
16 Serrano	Y	Y	Y	Y	Y	N	Y
17 Engel	Y	Y	Y	Y	Y	N	Y
18 Lowey	Y	Y	Y	Y	Y	N	Y
19 Hall	Y	Y	Y	Y	Y	N	Y
20 Gillibrand	Y	Y	Y	Y	Y	N	Y
21 McNulty	Y	Y	Y	Y	Y	N	Y
22 Hinchey	Y	Y	Y	Y	Y	N	Y
23 **McHugh**	Y	N	Y	N	N	N	N
24 Arcuri	Y	Y	Y	Y	Y	N	Y
25 **Walsh**	Y	N	Y	N	N	Y	N
26 **Reynolds**	Y	N	Y	N	N	Y	N
27 Higgins	Y	Y	Y	Y	Y	N	Y
28 Slaughter	Y	Y	Y	Y	Y	N	Y
29 **Kuhl**	Y	N	Y	N	N	?	?
NORTH CAROLINA							
1 Butterfield	?	?	?	?	?	?	?
2 Etheridge	Y	Y	Y	Y	Y	N	Y
3 **Jones**	+	−	+	−	−	?	?
4 Price	Y	Y	Y	Y	Y	N	Y

	240	241	242	243	244	245	246
5 **Foxx**	Y	N	Y	N	N	Y	N
6 **Coble**	Y	N	Y	N	N	N	N
7 McIntyre	Y	Y	Y	Y	Y	N	Y
8 **Hayes**	Y	N	Y	N	N	Y	N
9 **Myrick**	Y	N	Y	N	N	Y	N
10 **McHenry**	?	?	?	?	?	?	?
11 Shuler	?	?	?	?	?	?	?
12 Watt	Y	Y	Y	Y	Y	N	Y
13 Miller	Y	Y	Y	Y	Y	N	Y
NORTH DAKOTA							
AL Pomeroy	Y	Y	Y	Y	Y	N	Y
OHIO							
1 **Chabot**	Y	N	Y	N	N	Y	N
2 **Schmidt**	Y	N	Y	N	N	Y	N
3 **Turner**	Y	N	Y	N	N	Y	N
4 **Jordan**	Y	N	Y	N	N	N	N
5 **Latta**	Y	N	Y	N	N	Y	N
6 Wilson	Y	Y	Y	Y	Y	N	Y
7 **Hobson**	Y	N	Y	N	N	Y	N
8 **Boehner**	Y	N	Y	N	N	Y	N
9 Kaptur	Y	Y	Y	Y	Y	N	Y
10 Kucinich	Y	Y	Y	Y	N	N	Y
11 Tubbs Jones	+	?	+	?	?	?	?
12 **Tiberi**	?	?	?	?	?	N	N
13 Sutton	Y	Y	Y	Y	Y	N	Y
14 **LaTourette**	Y	N	Y	N	N	Y	N
15 **Pryce**	?	?	?	?	?	?	?
16 **Regula**	Y	N	Y	N	N	Y	N
17 Ryan	Y	Y	Y	Y	?	N	Y
18 Space	Y	Y	Y	Y	Y	N	Y
OKLAHOMA							
1 **Sullivan**	Y	N	Y	N	N	N	N
2 Boren	Y	Y	Y	Y	Y	N	Y
3 **Lucas**	Y	N	Y	N	N	N	N
4 **Cole**	Y	N	Y	N	N	N	N
5 **Fallin**	Y	N	Y	N	N	Y	N
OREGON							
1 Wu	Y	Y	Y	Y	Y	N	Y
2 **Walden**	Y	N	Y	N	N	Y	N
3 Blumenauer	Y	Y	Y	Y	Y	N	Y
4 DeFazio	Y	Y	Y	Y	Y	N	Y
5 Hooley	Y	Y	Y	Y	Y	N	Y
PENNSYLVANIA							
1 Brady	Y	Y	Y	Y	Y	N	Y
2 Fattah	Y	Y	Y	Y	Y	N	Y
3 **English**	Y	N	Y	N	N	Y	N
4 Altmire	Y	Y	Y	Y	N	N	N
5 **Peterson**	?	?	?	?	?	?	?
6 **Gerlach**	?	?	?	?	?	Y	N
7 Sestak	Y	Y	Y	Y	Y	N	Y
8 Murphy, P.	Y	Y	Y	Y	Y	N	Y
9 **Shuster**	Y	N	Y	N	N	Y	N
10 Carney	Y	Y	Y	Y	Y	N	N
11 Kanjorski	Y	Y	Y	Y	Y	N	Y
12 Murtha	?	?	?	?	?	N	Y
13 Schwartz	Y	Y	Y	Y	Y	N	Y
14 Doyle	Y	Y	Y	Y	Y	N	Y
15 **Dent**	Y	N	Y	N	N	Y	Y
16 **Pitts**	Y	N	Y	N	N	Y	N
17 Holden	Y	Y	Y	Y	Y	N	Y
18 **Murphy, T.**	Y	N	Y	N	N	N	N
19 **Platts**	Y	N	Y	N	N	N	N
RHODE ISLAND							
1 Kennedy	Y	Y	Y	Y	Y	N	Y
2 Langevin	Y	Y	Y	Y	Y	N	Y
SOUTH CAROLINA							
1 **Brown**	Y	N	Y	N	N	N	N
2 **Wilson**	Y	N	Y	N	N	Y	N
3 **Barrett**	Y	N	Y	N	N	Y	N
4 **Inglis**	Y	N	Y	N	N	Y	N
5 Spratt	Y	Y	Y	Y	Y	N	Y
6 Clyburn	Y	Y	Y	Y	Y	N	Y
SOUTH DAKOTA							
AL Herseth Sandlin	Y	Y	Y	Y	Y	N	Y
TENNESSEE							
1 **Davis, D.**	Y	N	Y	N	N	Y	N
2 **Duncan**	Y	N	Y	N	N	Y	N
3 **Wamp**	?	?	?	?	?	Y	N
4 Davis, L.	+	?	?	?	?	N	Y
5 Cooper	Y	Y	Y	Y	Y	N	Y
6 Gordon	?	?	?	?	?	N	N
7 **Blackburn**	Y	N	Y	N	N	Y	N
8 Tanner	Y	Y	Y	Y	Y	N	Y
9 Cohen	Y	Y	Y	Y	Y	N	Y

	240	241	242	243	244	245	246
TEXAS							
1 **Gohmert**	Y	N	Y	?	N	N	P
2 **Poe**	Y	N	Y	N	N	N	N
3 **Johnson, S.**	Y	N	Y	N	N	Y	N
4 **Hall**	Y	N	Y	N	N	Y	N
5 **Hensarling**	Y	N	Y	N	N	Y	N
6 **Barton**	Y	N	Y	N	N	Y	N
7 **Culberson**	?	?	?	?	?	Y	N
8 **Brady**	Y	N	Y	N	N	N	N
9 Green, A.	Y	Y	Y	Y	Y	N	Y
10 **McCaul**	Y	N	Y	N	N	Y	N
11 **Conaway**	Y	N	Y	N	N	N	N
12 **Granger**	Y	N	Y	N	N	Y	N
13 **Thornberry**	Y	N	Y	N	N	Y	N
14 **Paul**	?	?	?	?	?	Y	Y
15 Hinojosa	Y	Y	Y	Y	Y	N	Y
16 Reyes	Y	Y	Y	Y	Y	N	Y
17 Edwards	Y	Y	Y	Y	Y	N	Y
18 Jackson Lee	Y	Y	Y	Y	Y	N	Y
19 **Neugebauer**	Y	N	Y	N	N	Y	N
20 Gonzalez	Y	Y	Y	Y	Y	N	Y
21 **Smith**	Y	N	Y	N	N	Y	N
22 Lampson	Y	Y	Y	Y	Y	N	Y
23 Rodriguez	Y	Y	Y	Y	Y	N	Y
24 **Marchant**	?	?	?	?	?	Y	N
25 Doggett	Y	Y	Y	Y	Y	N	Y
26 **Burgess**	Y	N	Y	N	N	N	N
27 Ortiz	Y	Y	Y	Y	Y	N	Y
28 Cuellar	?	?	?	?	?	N	Y
29 Green, G.	Y	Y	Y	Y	Y	N	Y
30 Johnson, E.	Y	Y	Y	Y	Y	N	Y
31 **Carter**	Y	N	Y	N	N	Y	N
32 **Sessions**	?	?	?	?	?	Y	N
UTAH							
1 **Bishop**	?	?	?	?	?	Y	N
2 Matheson	Y	Y	Y	Y	Y	N	Y
3 **Cannon**	Y	N	Y	N	N	Y	N
VERMONT							
AL Welch	Y	Y	Y	Y	Y	N	Y
VIRGINIA							
1 **Wittman**	Y	N	Y	N	N	Y	N
2 **Drake**	Y	N	Y	N	N	Y	N
3 Scott	Y	Y	Y	Y	Y	N	Y
4 **Forbes**	Y	N	Y	N	N	Y	N
5 **Goode**	Y	N	Y	N	N	Y	N
6 **Goodlatte**	Y	N	Y	N	N	Y	N
7 **Cantor**	Y	N	Y	N	N	Y	N
8 Moran	Y	Y	Y	?	?	N	Y
9 Boucher	Y	Y	Y	Y	Y	N	Y
10 **Wolf**	?	?	?	?	?	Y	N
11 **Davis**	Y	N	Y	N	N	Y	N
WASHINGTON							
1 Inslee	?	?	?	?	?	N	Y
2 Larsen	Y	Y	Y	Y	Y	N	Y
3 Baird	Y	Y	Y	Y	Y	?	Y
4 **Hastings**	Y	N	Y	N	N	Y	N
5 **McMorris Rodgers**	Y	N	Y	N	N	Y	N
6 Dicks	?	?	?	?	?	N	?
7 McDermott	Y	Y	Y	Y	Y	N	Y
8 **Reichert**	Y	N	Y	N	N	Y	Y
9 Smith	?	?	?	?	?	N	Y
WEST VIRGINIA							
1 Mollohan	?	?	?	?	?	N	Y
2 **Capito**	Y	N	Y	N	N	Y	N
3 Rahall	Y	Y	Y	Y	N	N	Y
WISCONSIN							
1 **Ryan**	Y	N	Y	N	N	Y	N
2 Baldwin	Y	Y	Y	Y	Y	N	Y
3 Kind	Y	Y	Y	Y	Y	N	Y
4 Moore	?	Y	Y	Y	Y	N	Y
5 **Sensenbrenner**	Y	N	Y	N	Y	Y	N
6 **Petri**	Y	N	Y	N	N	Y	N
7 Obey	Y	Y	Y	Y	Y	N	Y
8 Kagen	Y	Y	Y	Y	Y	N	Y
WYOMING							
AL **Cubin**	Y	N	Y	N	N	Y	Y
DELEGATES							
Faleomavaega (A.S.)							
Norton (D.C.)							
Bordallo (Guam)							
Fortuño (P.R.)							
Christensen (V.I.)							

IN THE HOUSE | By Vote Number

247. HR 2419. Farm Bill Reauthorization/Motion to Instruct. Ryan, R-Wis., motion to instruct House conferees to use the most recent baseline estimates supplied by the Congressional Budget Office when determining whether the bill complies with House pay-as-you-go rules. Motion rejected 172-241: R 141-49; D 31-192 (ND 27-141, SD 4-51). May 6, 2008.

248. HR 2419. Farm Bill Reauthorization/Motion to Reconsider. Hastings, D-Fla., motion to table (kill) the Walsh, R-N.Y., motion to reconsider the vote on the motion to instruct House conferees on using the Congressional Budget Office baseline. Motion agreed to 203-176: R 2-176; D 201-0 (ND 153-0, SD 48-0). May 6, 2008.

249. HR 3658. Foreign Service Home Leave/Passage. Watson, D-Calif., motion to suspend the rules and pass the bill that would allow rest and recuperation travel and home leave for U.S. Foreign Service personnel to American Samoa, Puerto Rico, Guam, the Commonwealth of the Northern Mariana Islands and the U.S. Virgin Islands. Motion agreed to 416-0: R 191-0; D 225-0 (ND 169-0, SD 56-0). A two-thirds majority of those present and voting (278 in this case) is required for passage under suspension of the rules. May 6, 2008.

250. HR 3658. Foreign Service Home Leave/Motion to Reconsider. Hastings, D-Fla., motion to table (kill) the Rogers, R-Ky., motion to reconsider the vote on passage of the bill on home leave for certain U.S. Foreign Service personnel. Motion agreed to 226-190: R 0-190; D 226-0 (ND 169-0, SD 57-0). May 6, 2008.

251. H Con Res 317. Myanmar Military Regime/Adoption. Watson, D-Calif., motion to suspend the rules and adopt the concurrent resolution that would denounce the military regime's constitution and scheduled referendum in Myanmar, formerly known as Burma; call for the immediate release of Daw Aung San Suu Kyi, detained Buddhist monks and all other political prisoners; and urge the president to call for an arms embargo against the country's military regime. Motion agreed to 413-1: R 189-1; D 224-0 (ND 168-0, SD 56-0). A two-thirds majority of those present and voting (276 in this case) is required for adoption under suspension of the rules. May 6, 2008.

252. H Con Res 317. Myanmar Military Regime/Motion to Reconsider. Hastings, D-Fla., motion to table (kill) the Rogers, R-Ky., motion to reconsider the vote on adoption of the concurrent resolution on Myanmar. Motion agreed to 225-190: R 0-190; D 225-0 (ND 168-0, SD 57-0). May 6, 2008.

253. H Res 1109. Honoring Dith Pran/Adoption. Watson, D-Calif., motion to suspend the rules and adopt the resolution that would honor Dith Pran for his commitment to raising awareness about genocide that took place under the Khmer Rouge in Cambodia and remember his life's work. Motion agreed to 413-1: R 189-1; D 224-0 (ND 167-0, SD 57-0). A two-thirds majority of those present and voting (276 in this case) is required for adoption under suspension of the rules. May 6, 2008.

*Rep. Don Cazayoux, D-La., was sworn in May 6, 2008, to fill the seat vacated by the resignation of Richard H. Baker. The first vote for which Cazayoux was eligible was 247.

ND Northern Democrats, SD Southern Democrats
Southern states: Ala., Ark., Fla., Ga., Ky., La., Miss., N.C., Okla., S.C., Tenn., Texas, Va.Southern states: Ala., Ark., Fla., Ga., Ky., La., Miss., N.C., Okla., S.C., Tenn., Texas, Va.

	247	248	249	250	251	252	253
ALABAMA							
1 Bonner	Y	N	Y	N	Y	N	Y
2 Everett	Y	N	Y	N	Y	N	Y
3 Rogers	Y	?	Y	N	Y	N	Y
4 Aderholt	Y	N	Y	N	Y	N	Y
5 Cramer	?	?	Y	Y	Y	Y	Y
6 Bachus	Y	N	Y	N	Y	N	Y
7 Davis	N	Y	Y	Y	Y	Y	Y
ALASKA							
AL Young	Y	N	Y	N	Y	N	N
ARIZONA							
1 Renzi	Y	N	Y	N	Y	N	Y
2 Franks	Y	N	Y	N	Y	N	Y
3 Shadegg	Y	N	Y	N	Y	N	Y
4 Pastor	N	Y	Y	Y	Y	Y	Y
5 Mitchell	Y	Y	Y	Y	Y	Y	Y
6 Flake	Y	N	Y	N	Y	N	Y
7 Grijalva	N	Y	Y	Y	Y	Y	Y
8 Giffords	N	Y	Y	Y	Y	Y	Y
ARKANSAS							
1 Berry	N	?	Y	Y	Y	Y	Y
2 Snyder	N	Y	Y	Y	Y	Y	Y
3 Boozman	N	N	Y	N	Y	N	Y
4 Ross	N	Y	Y	Y	Y	Y	Y
CALIFORNIA							
1 Thompson	N	Y	Y	Y	Y	Y	Y
2 Herger	N	?	Y	N	Y	N	Y
3 Lungren	Y	N	Y	N	Y	N	Y
4 Doolittle	N	N	Y	N	Y	N	Y
5 Matsui	N	Y	Y	Y	Y	Y	Y
6 Woolsey	Y	Y	Y	Y	Y	Y	+
7 Miller, George	N	Y	Y	Y	?	Y	Y
8 Pelosi							
9 Lee	N	Y	Y	Y	Y	Y	Y
10 Tauscher	N	Y	Y	Y	Y	Y	Y
11 McNerney	N	Y	Y	Y	Y	Y	Y
12 Speier	?	?	?	?	?	?	?
13 Stark	Y	Y	Y	Y	Y	Y	Y
14 Eshoo	N	Y	Y	Y	Y	Y	Y
15 Honda	N	Y	Y	Y	Y	Y	Y
16 Lofgren	N	Y	Y	Y	Y	Y	Y
17 Farr	N	Y	Y	Y	Y	Y	Y
18 Cardoza	N	Y	Y	Y	Y	Y	Y
19 Radanovich	N	?	Y	N	Y	N	Y
20 Costa	N	Y	Y	Y	Y	Y	Y
21 Nunes	Y	N	Y	N	Y	N	Y
22 McCarthy	Y	N	Y	N	Y	N	Y
23 Capps	N	Y	Y	Y	Y	Y	Y
24 Gallegly	Y	?	Y	N	Y	N	Y
25 McKeon	Y	N	Y	N	Y	N	Y
26 Dreier	Y	N	Y	N	Y	N	Y
27 Sherman	Y	Y	Y	Y	Y	Y	Y
28 Berman	Y	?	Y	Y	Y	Y	Y
29 Schiff	Y	Y	Y	Y	Y	Y	Y
30 Waxman	N	Y	Y	Y	Y	Y	Y
31 Becerra	N	Y	Y	Y	Y	Y	Y
32 Solis	N	?	Y	Y	Y	Y	Y
33 Watson	N	Y	Y	Y	Y	Y	Y
34 Roybal-Allard	N	Y	Y	Y	Y	Y	Y
35 Waters	N	Y	Y	Y	Y	Y	Y
36 Harman	Y	Y	Y	Y	Y	Y	Y
37 Richardson	N	?	Y	Y	Y	Y	Y
38 Napolitano	N	Y	Y	Y	Y	Y	Y
39 Sánchez, Linda	N	?	Y	Y	Y	Y	Y
40 Royce	Y	N	Y	N	Y	N	Y
41 Lewis	Y	N	Y	N	Y	N	Y
42 Miller, Gary	Y	N	Y	N	Y	N	Y
43 Baca	N	Y	Y	Y	Y	Y	Y
44 Calvert	Y	N	Y	N	Y	N	Y
45 Bono Mack	Y	N	Y	N	Y	N	Y
46 Rohrabacher	Y	N	Y	N	Y	N	Y
47 Sanchez, Loretta	N	Y	Y	Y	Y	Y	Y
48 Campbell	?	?	?	?	?	?	?
49 Issa	Y	N	Y	N	Y	N	Y
50 Bilbray	Y	N	Y	N	Y	N	?
51 Filner	N	Y	Y	Y	Y	Y	Y
52 Hunter	Y	N	Y	N	Y	N	Y
53 Davis	N	Y	Y	Y	Y	Y	Y
COLORADO							
1 DeGette	N	Y	Y	Y	Y	Y	Y
2 Udall	N	Y	Y	Y	Y	Y	Y
3 Salazar	N	Y	Y	Y	Y	Y	Y
4 Musgrave	N	N	Y	N	Y	N	Y
5 Lamborn	Y	N	Y	N	Y	N	Y
6 Tancredo	Y	N	Y	N	Y	N	Y
7 Perlmutter	N	Y	Y	Y	Y	Y	Y
CONNECTICUT							
1 Larson	Y	?	Y	Y	Y	Y	Y
2 Courtney	N	Y	Y	Y	Y	Y	Y
3 DeLauro	N	Y	Y	Y	Y	Y	Y
4 Shays	Y	N	Y	N	Y	N	Y
5 Murphy	N	Y	Y	Y	Y	Y	Y
DELAWARE							
AL Castle	Y	N	Y	N	Y	N	Y
FLORIDA							
1 Miller	Y	N	Y	N	Y	N	Y
2 Boyd	N	Y	Y	Y	Y	Y	Y
3 Brown	N	Y	Y	Y	Y	Y	Y
4 Crenshaw	Y	N	Y	N	Y	N	Y
5 Brown-Waite	Y	N	Y	N	Y	N	Y
6 Stearns	Y	N	Y	N	Y	N	Y
7 Mica	Y	N	Y	N	Y	N	Y
8 Keller	Y	N	Y	N	Y	N	Y
9 Bilirakis	Y	N	Y	N	Y	N	Y
10 Young	Y	N	Y	N	Y	N	Y
11 Castor	N	Y	Y	Y	Y	Y	Y
12 Putnam	N	N	Y	N	Y	N	Y
13 Buchanan	N	N	Y	N	Y	N	Y
14 Mack	Y	N	Y	N	Y	N	Y
15 Weldon	Y	N	Y	N	Y	N	Y
16 Mahoney	N	Y	Y	Y	Y	Y	Y
17 Meek	N	?	?	Y	Y	Y	Y
18 Ros-Lehtinen	Y	N	Y	N	Y	N	Y
19 Wexler	N	Y	Y	Y	Y	Y	Y
20 Wasserman Schultz	N	Y	Y	Y	Y	Y	Y
21 Diaz-Balart, L.	Y	N	Y	N	Y	N	Y
22 Klein	N	Y	Y	Y	Y	Y	Y
23 Hastings	N	Y	Y	Y	Y	Y	Y
24 Feeney	Y	?	Y	N	Y	N	Y
25 Diaz-Balart, M.	Y	N	Y	N	Y	N	Y
GEORGIA							
1 Kingston	Y	N	Y	N	Y	N	Y
2 Bishop	N	Y	Y	Y	Y	Y	Y
3 Westmoreland	Y	N	Y	N	?	N	Y
4 Johnson	N	Y	Y	Y	Y	Y	Y
5 Lewis	N	Y	Y	Y	Y	Y	Y
6 Price	Y	N	Y	N	Y	N	Y
7 Linder	Y	N	Y	N	Y	N	Y
8 Marshall	?	?	Y	Y	Y	Y	Y
9 Deal	Y	?	Y	N	Y	N	Y
10 Broun	Y	N	Y	N	Y	N	Y
11 Gingrey	Y	N	Y	N	Y	N	Y
12 Barrow	N	Y	Y	Y	Y	Y	Y
13 Scott	Y	Y	Y	Y	Y	Y	Y
HAWAII							
1 Abercrombie	N	Y	Y	Y	Y	Y	Y
2 Hirono	N	Y	Y	Y	Y	Y	Y
IDAHO							
1 Sali	N	N	Y	N	Y	N	Y
2 Simpson	N	N	Y	N	Y	N	Y
ILLINOIS							
1 Rush	?	?	?	?	?	?	?
2 Jackson	N	Y	Y	Y	Y	Y	Y
3 Lipinski	Y	Y	Y	Y	Y	Y	Y
4 Gutierrez	N	Y	Y	Y	Y	Y	Y
5 Emanuel	N	Y	Y	Y	Y	Y	Y
6 Roskam	Y	N	Y	N	Y	N	Y
7 Davis	N	Y	Y	Y	Y	Y	Y
8 Bean	Y	Y	Y	Y	Y	Y	Y
9 Schakowsky	N	Y	Y	Y	Y	Y	Y
10 Kirk	Y	N	Y	N	Y	N	Y
11 Weller	N	N	Y	N	Y	N	Y
12 Costello	N	Y	Y	Y	Y	Y	Y
13 Biggert	Y	N	Y	N	Y	N	Y
14 Foster	Y	Y	Y	Y	Y	Y	Y
15 Johnson	N	Y	N	Y	N	Y	Y

KEY Republicans Democrats

Y Voted for (yea)	**X** Paired against	**C** Voted "present" to avoid possible conflict of interest
# Paired for	**–** Announced against	
+ Announced for	**P** Voted "present"	**?** Did not vote or otherwise make a position known
N Voted against (nay)		

	247	248	249	250	251	252	253
16 **Manzullo**	N	N	Y	N	Y	N	Y
17 Hare	N	Y	Y	Y	Y	Y	Y
18 **LaHood**	N	N	Y	N	Y	N	Y
19 **Shimkus**	N	N	Y	N	Y	N	Y
INDIANA							
1 Visclosky	N	Y	Y	Y	Y	Y	Y
2 Donnelly	N	Y	Y	Y	Y	Y	Y
3 **Souder**	Y	N	Y	N	Y	N	Y
4 **Buyer**	Y	N	Y	N	Y	N	Y
5 **Burton**	?	?	?	?	?	?	?
6 **Pence**	Y	N	Y	N	Y	N	Y
7 Carson, A.	?	?	?	?	?	?	?
8 Ellsworth	N	Y	Y	Y	Y	Y	Y
9 Hill	N	Y	Y	Y	Y	Y	Y
IOWA							
1 Braley	N	Y	Y	Y	Y	Y	Y
2 Loebsack	N	Y	Y	Y	Y	Y	Y
3 Boswell	N	Y	Y	Y	Y	Y	Y
4 **Latham**	Y	N	Y	N	Y	N	Y
5 **King**	N	N	Y	N	Y	N	Y
KANSAS							
1 **Moran**	N	N	Y	N	Y	N	Y
2 Boyda	N	Y	Y	Y	Y	Y	Y
3 Moore	N	Y	Y	Y	Y	Y	Y
4 **Tiahrt**	N	?	Y	N	Y	N	Y
KENTUCKY							
1 **Whitfield**	Y	Y	Y	N	Y	N	Y
2 **Lewis**	N	N	Y	N	Y	N	Y
3 Yarmuth	N	Y	Y	Y	Y	Y	Y
4 **Davis**	N	N	Y	N	Y	N	Y
5 **Rogers**	Y	N	Y	N	Y	N	Y
6 Chandler	N	?	Y	Y	Y	Y	Y
LOUISIANA							
1 Vacant							
2 Jefferson	N	Y	Y	Y	Y	Y	Y
3 Melancon	N	Y	Y	Y	Y	Y	Y
4 **McCrery**	Y	N	Y	N	Y	N	Y
5 **Alexander**	Y	N	Y	N	Y	N	Y
6 Cazayoux*	N	Y	Y	Y	Y	Y	Y
7 **Boustany**	N	?	Y	N	Y	N	Y
MAINE							
1 Allen	N	Y	Y	Y	Y	Y	Y
2 Michaud	N	?	Y	Y	Y	Y	Y
MARYLAND							
1 **Gilchrest**	Y	N	Y	N	Y	N	Y
2 Ruppersberger	N	Y	Y	Y	Y	Y	Y
3 Sarbanes	N	?	Y	Y	Y	Y	Y
4 Wynn	?	?	Y	Y	Y	Y	Y
5 Hoyer	N	Y	Y	Y	Y	Y	Y
6 **Bartlett**	Y	N	Y	N	Y	N	Y
7 Cummings	N	Y	Y	Y	Y	Y	Y
8 Van Hollen	Y	Y	Y	Y	Y	Y	Y
MASSACHUSETTS							
1 Olver	N	Y	Y	Y	Y	Y	Y
2 Neal	N	Y	Y	Y	Y	Y	Y
3 McGovern	N	Y	Y	Y	Y	Y	Y
4 Frank	N	Y	Y	Y	Y	Y	Y
5 Tsongas	N	Y	Y	Y	Y	Y	Y
6 Tierney	Y	Y	Y	Y	Y	Y	Y
7 Markey	N	Y	Y	Y	Y	Y	Y
8 Capuano	N	Y	Y	Y	Y	Y	Y
9 Lynch	N	Y	Y	Y	Y	Y	Y
10 Delahunt	N	Y	Y	Y	Y	Y	Y
MICHIGAN							
1 Stupak	N	Y	Y	Y	Y	Y	Y
2 **Hoekstra**	Y	N	Y	N	Y	N	Y
3 **Ehlers**	Y	N	Y	N	Y	N	Y
4 **Camp**	Y	N	Y	N	Y	N	Y
5 Kildee	N	Y	Y	Y	Y	Y	Y
6 **Upton**	Y	N	Y	N	Y	N	Y
7 **Walberg**	Y	N	Y	N	Y	N	Y
8 **Rogers**	Y	N	Y	N	Y	N	Y
9 **Knollenberg**	Y	N	Y	N	Y	N	Y
10 **Miller**	N	N	Y	N	Y	N	Y
11 **McCotter**	Y	N	Y	N	Y	N	Y
12 Levin	N	Y	Y	Y	Y	Y	Y
13 Kilpatrick	N	Y	Y	Y	Y	Y	Y
14 Conyers	N	Y	Y	Y	Y	Y	Y
15 Dingell	N	Y	Y	Y	Y	Y	Y
MINNESOTA							
1 Walz	N	Y	Y	Y	Y	Y	Y
2 **Kline**	N	N	Y	N	Y	N	Y
3 **Ramstad**	Y	N	Y	N	Y	N	Y
4 McCollum	N	Y	Y	Y	Y	Y	Y

	247	248	249	250	251	252	253
5 Ellison	N	Y	Y	Y	Y	Y	Y
6 **Bachmann**	N	Y	Y	N	Y	N	Y
7 Peterson	N	Y	Y	Y	Y	Y	Y
8 Oberstar	?	?	?	?	?	?	?
MISSISSIPPI							
1 Vacant							
2 Thompson	N	Y	Y	Y	?	Y	Y
3 **Pickering**	Y	N	Y	N	Y	N	Y
4 Taylor	N	Y	Y	Y	Y	Y	Y
MISSOURI							
1 Clay	N	Y	Y	Y	Y	Y	Y
2 **Akin**	Y	N	Y	N	Y	N	Y
3 Carnahan	N	Y	Y	Y	Y	Y	Y
4 Skelton	N	Y	Y	Y	Y	Y	Y
5 Cleaver	N	Y	Y	Y	Y	Y	Y
6 **Graves**	N	N	Y	N	Y	N	Y
7 **Blunt**	Y	N	Y	N	Y	N	Y
8 **Emerson**	N	N	Y	N	Y	N	Y
9 **Hulshof**	?	?	?	?	?	?	+
MONTANA							
AL **Rehberg**	Y	N	Y	N	Y	N	Y
NEBRASKA							
1 **Fortenberry**	N	N	Y	N	Y	N	Y
2 **Terry**	Y	N	Y	N	Y	N	Y
3 **Smith**	N	N	Y	N	Y	N	Y
NEVADA							
1 Berkley	N	Y	Y	Y	Y	Y	Y
2 **Heller**	Y	?	Y	N	Y	N	Y
3 **Porter**	Y	N	Y	N	Y	N	Y
NEW HAMPSHIRE							
1 Shea-Porter	N	Y	Y	Y	Y	Y	Y
2 Hodes	N	+	Y	Y	Y	Y	Y
NEW JERSEY							
1 Andrews	?	?	?	?	?	?	?
2 **LoBiondo**	Y	N	Y	N	Y	N	Y
3 **Saxton**	Y	N	Y	N	Y	N	Y
4 **Smith**	Y	N	Y	N	Y	N	Y
5 **Garrett**	Y	N	Y	N	Y	N	Y
6 Pallone	N	Y	Y	Y	Y	Y	Y
7 **Ferguson**	Y	N	Y	N	Y	N	Y
8 Pascrell	N	Y	Y	Y	Y	Y	Y
9 Rothman	N	Y	Y	Y	Y	Y	Y
10 Payne	N	Y	Y	Y	Y	Y	Y
11 **Frelinghuysen**	Y	N	Y	N	Y	N	Y
12 Holt	Y	Y	Y	Y	Y	Y	Y
13 Sires	N	Y	Y	Y	Y	Y	Y
NEW MEXICO							
1 **Wilson**	Y	N	Y	N	Y	N	Y
2 **Pearce**	N	N	Y	N	Y	N	Y
3 Udall	N	Y	Y	Y	Y	Y	Y
NEW YORK							
1 Bishop	N	Y	Y	Y	Y	Y	Y
2 Israel	Y	Y	Y	Y	Y	Y	Y
3 **King**	Y	N	Y	N	Y	N	Y
4 McCarthy	N	Y	Y	Y	Y	Y	Y
5 Ackerman	N	Y	Y	Y	Y	Y	Y
6 Meeks	Y	Y	Y	Y	Y	Y	Y
7 Crowley	Y	Y	Y	Y	Y	Y	Y
8 Nadler	N	Y	Y	Y	Y	Y	Y
9 Weiner	Y	Y	?	?	?	?	?
10 Towns	N	Y	Y	Y	Y	Y	Y
11 Clarke	N	Y	Y	Y	Y	Y	Y
12 Velázquez	N	Y	Y	Y	Y	Y	Y
13 **Fossella**	Y	N	Y	N	Y	N	Y
14 Maloney	N	Y	Y	Y	Y	Y	Y
15 Rangel	N	Y	Y	Y	Y	?	Y
16 Serrano	N	Y	Y	Y	Y	Y	Y
17 Engel	N	Y	Y	Y	Y	Y	Y
18 Lowey	N	Y	Y	Y	Y	Y	Y
19 Hall	N	Y	Y	Y	Y	Y	Y
20 Gillibrand	N	Y	Y	Y	Y	Y	Y
21 McNulty	N	Y	Y	Y	Y	Y	Y
22 Hinchey	Y	Y	Y	Y	Y	Y	Y
23 **McHugh**	Y	N	Y	N	Y	N	Y
24 Arcuri	N	?	Y	Y	Y	Y	Y
25 **Walsh**	N	N	Y	N	Y	N	Y
26 **Reynolds**	Y	?	Y	N	Y	N	Y
27 Higgins	N	Y	Y	Y	Y	Y	Y
28 Slaughter	N	Y	Y	Y	Y	Y	Y
29 **Kuhl**	Y	N	Y	N	Y	N	Y
NORTH CAROLINA							
1 Butterfield	?	?	?	?	?	?	?
2 Etheridge	N	Y	Y	Y	Y	Y	Y
3 **Jones**	+	−	+	−	+	−	?
4 Price	N	Y	Y	Y	Y	Y	Y

	247	248	249	250	251	252	253
5 **Foxx**	Y	N	Y	N	Y	N	Y
6 **Coble**	Y	N	Y	N	Y	N	Y
7 McIntyre	N	Y	Y	Y	Y	Y	Y
8 **Hayes**	N	N	Y	N	Y	N	Y
9 **Myrick**	Y	N	Y	N	Y	N	Y
10 **McHenry**	?	?	?	?	?	?	?
11 Shuler	N	Y	Y	Y	Y	Y	Y
12 Watt	N	Y	Y	Y	Y	Y	Y
13 Miller	N	Y	Y	Y	Y	Y	Y
NORTH DAKOTA							
AL Pomeroy	N	Y	Y	Y	Y	Y	Y
OHIO							
1 **Chabot**	Y	N	Y	N	Y	N	Y
2 **Schmidt**	Y	?	Y	N	Y	N	Y
3 **Turner**	Y	N	Y	N	Y	N	Y
4 **Jordan**	Y	N	Y	N	Y	N	Y
5 **Latta**	Y	N	Y	N	Y	N	Y
6 Wilson	N	Y	Y	Y	Y	Y	Y
7 **Hobson**	Y	N	Y	N	Y	N	Y
8 **Boehner**	Y	N	Y	N	Y	N	Y
9 Kaptur	N	?	Y	Y	Y	Y	?
10 Kucinich	N	Y	Y	Y	Y	Y	Y
11 Tubbs Jones	−	?	+	?	+	?	+
12 **Tiberi**	Y	N	Y	N	Y	N	Y
13 Sutton	N	Y	Y	Y	Y	Y	Y
14 **LaTourette**	Y	N	Y	N	Y	N	Y
15 **Pryce**	?	?	?	?	?	?	?
16 **Regula**	Y	N	Y	N	Y	N	Y
17 Ryan	N	?	Y	Y	Y	Y	Y
18 Space	N	Y	Y	Y	Y	Y	Y
OKLAHOMA							
1 **Sullivan**	Y	N	Y	N	Y	N	Y
2 Boren	N	?	Y	Y	Y	Y	Y
3 **Lucas**	N	N	Y	N	Y	N	Y
4 **Cole**	N	N	Y	N	Y	N	Y
5 **Fallin**	N	N	Y	N	Y	N	Y
OREGON							
1 Wu	Y	?	Y	Y	Y	Y	Y
2 **Walden**	N	N	Y	N	Y	N	Y
3 Blumenauer	Y	Y	Y	Y	Y	Y	Y
4 DeFazio	N	Y	Y	Y	Y	Y	Y
5 Hooley	N	Y	Y	Y	Y	Y	Y
PENNSYLVANIA							
1 Brady	N	Y	Y	Y	Y	Y	Y
2 Fattah	N	Y	Y	Y	Y	Y	Y
3 **English**	Y	N	Y	N	Y	N	Y
4 Altmire	N	Y	Y	Y	Y	Y	Y
5 **Peterson**	?	?	Y	N	Y	N	Y
6 **Gerlach**	Y	N	Y	N	Y	N	Y
7 Sestak	Y	Y	Y	Y	Y	Y	Y
8 Murphy, P.	Y	Y	Y	Y	Y	Y	Y
9 **Shuster**	N	N	Y	N	Y	N	Y
10 Carney	N	Y	Y	Y	Y	Y	Y
11 Kanjorski	N	Y	Y	Y	Y	Y	Y
12 Murtha	N	?	Y	Y	Y	Y	Y
13 Schwartz	N	Y	Y	Y	Y	Y	Y
14 Doyle	N	?	Y	Y	Y	Y	Y
15 **Dent**	Y	N	Y	N	Y	N	Y
16 **Pitts**	Y	N	Y	N	Y	N	Y
17 Holden	N	Y	Y	Y	Y	Y	Y
18 **Murphy, T.**	N	N	Y	N	Y	N	Y
19 **Platts**	Y	N	Y	N	Y	N	Y
RHODE ISLAND							
1 Kennedy	N	?	Y	Y	Y	Y	Y
2 Langevin	N	Y	Y	Y	Y	Y	Y
SOUTH CAROLINA							
1 **Brown**	Y	N	Y	N	Y	N	Y
2 **Wilson**	Y	N	Y	N	Y	N	Y
3 **Barrett**	Y	N	Y	N	Y	N	Y
4 **Inglis**	Y	N	Y	N	Y	N	Y
5 Spratt	N	Y	Y	Y	Y	Y	Y
6 Clyburn	N	Y	Y	Y	Y	Y	Y
SOUTH DAKOTA							
AL Herseth Sandlin	N	Y	Y	Y	Y	Y	Y
TENNESSEE							
1 **Davis, D.**	Y	N	Y	N	Y	N	Y
2 **Duncan**	Y	N	Y	N	Y	N	Y
3 **Wamp**	Y	?	Y	N	Y	N	Y
4 Davis, L.	N	Y	Y	Y	Y	Y	Y
5 Cooper	Y	?	Y	Y	Y	Y	Y
6 Gordon	N	Y	Y	Y	Y	Y	Y
7 **Blackburn**	?	?	Y	N	Y	N	Y
8 Tanner	N	Y	Y	Y	Y	Y	Y
9 Cohen	N	Y	Y	Y	Y	Y	Y

	247	248	249	250	251	252	253
TEXAS							
1 **Gohmert**	N	N	Y	N	Y	N	Y
2 **Poe**	N	N	Y	N	Y	N	Y
3 **Johnson, S.**	Y	N	Y	N	Y	N	Y
4 **Hall**	Y	N	Y	?	Y	N	Y
5 **Hensarling**	Y	N	Y	N	Y	N	Y
6 **Barton**	Y	N	Y	N	Y	N	Y
7 **Culberson**	Y	N	Y	N	Y	N	Y
8 **Brady**	Y	N	Y	N	Y	N	Y
9 Green, A.	N	Y	Y	Y	Y	Y	Y
10 **McCaul**	Y	N	Y	N	Y	N	Y
11 **Conaway**	N	N	?	?	?	?	?
12 **Granger**	Y	N	Y	N	Y	N	Y
13 **Thornberry**	N	N	Y	N	Y	N	Y
14 **Paul**	Y	N	Y	N	N	N	Y
15 Hinojosa	N	?	Y	Y	Y	Y	Y
16 Reyes	N	Y	Y	Y	Y	Y	Y
17 Edwards	N	Y	Y	Y	Y	Y	Y
18 Jackson Lee	N	Y	Y	Y	Y	Y	Y
19 **Neugebauer**	N	N	Y	N	Y	N	Y
20 Gonzalez	N	?	Y	Y	Y	Y	Y
21 **Smith**	Y	N	Y	N	Y	N	Y
22 Lampson	Y	Y	Y	Y	Y	Y	Y
23 Rodriguez	N	Y	Y	Y	Y	Y	Y
24 **Marchant**	Y	N	Y	N	Y	N	Y
25 Doggett	N	Y	Y	Y	Y	Y	Y
26 **Burgess**	Y	N	Y	N	Y	N	Y
27 Ortiz	N	Y	Y	Y	Y	Y	Y
28 Cuellar	N	Y	Y	Y	Y	Y	Y
29 Green, G.	N	Y	Y	Y	Y	Y	Y
30 Johnson, E.	N	Y	Y	Y	Y	Y	Y
31 **Carter**	N	N	Y	N	Y	N	Y
32 **Sessions**	Y	N	Y	N	Y	N	Y
UTAH							
1 **Bishop**	N	N	Y	N	Y	N	Y
2 Matheson	Y	Y	Y	Y	Y	Y	Y
3 **Cannon**	Y	N	Y	N	Y	?	Y
VERMONT							
AL Welch	N	Y	Y	Y	Y	Y	Y
VIRGINIA							
1 **Wittman**	N	N	Y	N	Y	N	Y
2 **Drake**	N	N	Y	N	Y	N	Y
3 Scott	N	Y	Y	Y	Y	Y	Y
4 **Forbes**	N	N	Y	N	Y	N	Y
5 **Goode**	Y	N	Y	N	Y	N	Y
6 **Goodlatte**	N	N	Y	N	Y	N	Y
7 **Cantor**	Y	N	Y	N	Y	N	Y
8 Moran	N	Y	Y	Y	Y	Y	Y
9 Boucher	Y	Y	Y	Y	Y	Y	Y
10 **Wolf**	Y	N	Y	N	Y	N	Y
11 **Davis**	Y	N	Y	N	Y	N	Y
WASHINGTON							
1 Inslee	N	Y	Y	Y	Y	Y	Y
2 Larsen	N	Y	Y	Y	Y	Y	Y
3 Baird	Y	Y	Y	Y	Y	Y	Y
4 **Hastings**	Y	N	Y	N	Y	N	Y
5 **McMorris Rodgers**	N	N	Y	N	Y	N	Y
6 Dicks	?	Y	Y	Y	Y	Y	Y
7 McDermott	N	Y	Y	Y	Y	Y	Y
8 **Reichert**	Y	N	Y	N	Y	N	Y
9 Smith	Y	Y	Y	Y	Y	Y	Y
WEST VIRGINIA							
1 Mollohan	N	?	Y	Y	Y	Y	Y
2 **Capito**	Y	N	Y	N	Y	N	Y
3 Rahall	N	Y	Y	Y	Y	Y	Y
WISCONSIN							
1 **Ryan**	Y	N	Y	N	Y	N	Y
2 Baldwin	N	Y	Y	Y	Y	Y	Y
3 Kind	Y	Y	Y	Y	Y	Y	Y
4 Moore	Y	Y	Y	Y	Y	Y	Y
5 **Sensenbrenner**	Y	N	Y	N	Y	N	Y
6 **Petri**	Y	N	Y	N	Y	N	Y
7 Obey	N	Y	Y	Y	Y	Y	Y
8 Kagen	N	Y	Y	Y	Y	Y	Y
WYOMING							
AL **Cubin**	N	N	Y	N	Y	N	Y
DELEGATES							
Faleomavaega (A.S.)							
Norton (D.C.)							
Bordallo (Guam)							
Fortuño (P.R.)							
Christensen (V.I.)							

IN THE HOUSE | By Vote Number

254. **H Res 1109. Honoring Dith Pran/Motion to Reconsider.** Hastings, D-Fla., motion to table (kill) the Rogers, R-Ky., motion to reconsider the vote on adoption of the resolution to honor Dith Pran. Motion agreed to 225-186: R 2-186; D 223-0 (ND 167-0, SD 56-0). May 6, 2008.

255. **Procedural Motion/Motion to Adjourn.** Simpson, R-Idaho, motion to adjourn. Motion rejected 145-271: R 143-48; D 2-223 (ND 1-167, SD 1-56). May 6, 2008.

256. **S 2929. Higher Education Act Extension/Passage.** Tierney, D-Mass., motion to suspend the rules and pass the bill that would extend the authorization of Higher Education Act programs through May 31, 2008. Motion agreed to 408-0: R 187-0; D 221-0 (ND 168-0, SD 53-0). A two-thirds majority of those present and voting (272 in this case) is required for passage under suspension of the rules. May 6, 2008.

257. **S 2929. Higher Education Act Extension/Motion to Reconsider.** Hastings, D-Fla., motion to table (kill) the Emerson, R-Mo., motion to reconsider the vote on passage of the bill to extend the authorization of Higher Education Act programs. Motion agreed to 223-189: R 0-189; D 223-0 (ND 167-0, SD 56-0). May 6, 2008.

258. **HR 2419. Farm Bill Reauthorization/Motion to Instruct.** Kind, D-Wis., motion to instruct House conferees to insist on language to maintain the House-passed funding allotment for three conservation programs: the Grassland Reserve Program, the Environmental Quality Incentives Program and the Wetlands Reserve Program. The motion also would instruct conferees to agree to a Senate-passed provision that would eliminate federal payments for crops planted on land with no previous crop history. Motion rejected 140-274: R 39-150; D 101-124 (ND 88-80, SD 13-44). May 6, 2008.

259. **HR 2419. Farm Bill Reauthorization/Motion to Reconsider.** Hastings, D-Fla., motion to table (kill) the Latham, R-Iowa, motion to reconsider the vote on the Kind, D-Wis., motion to instruct House conferees on the farm bill. Motion agreed to 221-192: R 0-191; D 221-1 (ND 164-1, SD 57-0). May 6, 2008.

260. **Procedural Motion/Motion to Adjourn.** Simpson, R-Idaho, motion to adjourn. Motion rejected 149-251: R 147-41; D 2-210 (ND 0-157, SD 2-53). May 6, 2008.

	254	255	256	257	258	259	260
ALABAMA							
1 Bonner	N	Y	Y	N	N	N	Y
2 Everett	N	Y	Y	N	N	N	Y
3 Rogers	N	Y	Y	N	N	N	Y
4 Aderholt	N	Y	?	N	N	N	Y
5 Cramer	Y	N	Y	Y	N	Y	N
6 Bachus	N	Y	Y	N	N	N	Y
7 Davis	Y	N	Y	Y	N	Y	N
ALASKA							
AL Young	N	Y	Y	N	Y	N	Y
ARIZONA							
1 Renzi	N	N	Y	N	Y	N	Y
2 Franks	N	Y	Y	N	N	N	Y
3 Shadegg	N	Y	Y	N	N	N	Y
4 Pastor	Y	N	Y	Y	N	Y	N
5 Mitchell	Y	N	Y	Y	Y	Y	N
6 Flake	N	Y	Y	N	N	N	Y
7 Grijalva	Y	N	Y	Y	N	Y	N
8 Giffords	Y	N	Y	Y	N	Y	N
ARKANSAS							
1 Berry	Y	N	Y	Y	N	Y	N
2 Snyder	Y	N	Y	Y	N	Y	N
3 Boozman	N	Y	Y	N	N	N	Y
4 Ross	Y	N	Y	Y	N	Y	N
CALIFORNIA							
1 Thompson	Y	N	Y	Y	N	Y	N
2 Herger	N	Y	Y	N	N	N	Y
3 Lungren	N	Y	Y	N	N	N	Y
4 Doolittle	N	Y	Y	N	N	N	Y
5 Matsui	Y	N	Y	Y	N	Y	N
6 Woolsey	Y	-	Y	Y	Y	Y	N
7 Miller, George	Y	N	Y	Y	N	Y	N
8 Pelosi							
9 Lee	Y	N	Y	Y	Y	Y	N
10 Tauscher	Y	N	Y	Y	Y	Y	N
11 McNerney	Y	N	Y	Y	Y	Y	N
12 Speier	?	?	?	?	?	?	?
13 Stark	Y	N	Y	Y	Y	Y	N
14 Eshoo	Y	N	Y	Y	N	Y	N
15 Honda	Y	N	Y	Y	Y	Y	N
16 Lofgren	Y	N	Y	Y	Y	Y	?
17 Farr	Y	N	Y	Y	N	Y	N
18 Cardoza	Y	N	Y	Y	N	Y	N
19 Radanovich	N	N	Y	N	N	N	Y
20 Costa	Y	N	Y	Y	Y	Y	N
21 Nunes	N	Y	Y	N	N	N	Y
22 McCarthy	N	Y	Y	N	N	N	Y
23 Capps	Y	N	Y	Y	Y	Y	N
24 Gallegly	N	Y	Y	N	N	N	Y
25 McKeon	N	Y	Y	N	N	N	Y
26 Dreier	N	Y	Y	N	N	N	Y
27 Sherman	Y	N	Y	Y	Y	Y	N
28 Berman	Y	N	Y	Y	Y	Y	N
29 Schiff	Y	N	Y	Y	Y	Y	N
30 Waxman	Y	N	Y	Y	Y	Y	?
31 Becerra	Y	N	Y	Y	Y	Y	N
32 Solis	Y	N	Y	Y	Y	Y	N
33 Watson	Y	N	Y	Y	N	Y	N
34 Roybal-Allard	Y	N	Y	Y	N	Y	N
35 Waters	?	N	Y	Y	Y	Y	?
36 Harman	Y	N	Y	Y	Y	Y	N
37 Richardson	Y	N	Y	Y	N	Y	N
38 Napolitano	Y	N	Y	Y	N	Y	N
39 Sánchez, Linda	Y	N	Y	Y	Y	Y	N
40 Royce	N	Y	Y	N	N	N	Y
41 Lewis	N	Y	Y	N	N	N	Y
42 Miller, Gary	N	Y	Y	N	N	N	Y
43 Baca	Y	N	Y	Y	N	Y	N
44 Calvert	N	Y	Y	N	N	N	Y
45 Bono Mack	N	Y	Y	N	N	N	Y
46 Rohrabacher	N	Y	Y	N	N	N	Y
47 Sanchez, Loretta	Y	N	Y	Y	N	Y	N
48 Campbell	?	?	?	?	?	?	?
49 Issa	N	Y	Y	N	N	N	Y
50 Bilbray	N	Y	Y	N	N	N	Y
51 Filner	Y	N	Y	Y	N	Y	N
52 Hunter	N	Y	Y	?	N	N	Y
53 Davis	Y	N	Y	Y	Y	Y	N
COLORADO							
1 DeGette	Y	N	Y	Y	Y	Y	N
2 Udall	Y	N	Y	Y	Y	Y	N
3 Salazar	Y	N	Y	Y	N	Y	N
4 Musgrave	N	Y	Y	N	N	N	Y
5 Lamborn	N	Y	Y	N	N	N	Y
6 Tancredo	N	Y	Y	N	N	N	N
7 Perlmutter	Y	N	Y	Y	N	Y	N
CONNECTICUT							
1 Larson	Y	N	Y	Y	Y	?	N
2 Courtney	Y	N	Y	Y	Y	Y	N
3 DeLauro	Y	N	Y	Y	N	Y	N
4 Shays	N	Y	Y	N	Y	N	Y
5 Murphy	Y	N	Y	Y	Y	Y	N
DELAWARE							
AL Castle	N	N	Y	N	Y	N	N
FLORIDA							
1 Miller	N	Y	Y	N	N	N	Y
2 Boyd	Y	N	Y	Y	N	Y	?
3 Brown	Y	N	Y	Y	Y	Y	N
4 Crenshaw	N	Y	Y	N	N	N	Y
5 Brown-Waite	N	N	Y	N	N	N	Y
6 Stearns	N	Y	Y	N	N	N	Y
7 Mica	N	Y	Y	N	N	N	Y
8 Keller	N	Y	Y	N	N	N	Y
9 Bilirakis	N	Y	Y	N	N	N	Y
10 Young	N	Y	Y	N	Y	N	Y
11 Castor	Y	N	Y	Y	Y	Y	N
12 Putnam	N	Y	Y	N	N	N	Y
13 Buchanan	N	Y	Y	N	N	N	N
14 Mack	N	Y	Y	N	N	N	Y
15 Weldon	N	Y	Y	N	N	N	Y
16 Mahoney	Y	N	?	Y	N	Y	N
17 Meek	Y	N	Y	Y	N	Y	N
18 Ros-Lehtinen	N	N	Y	N	N	N	Y
19 Wexler	Y	N	Y	Y	N	Y	N
20 Wasserman Schultz	Y	N	Y	Y	N	Y	N
21 Diaz-Balart, L.	N	Y	Y	N	N	N	Y
22 Klein	Y	N	Y	Y	N	Y	N
23 Hastings	Y	N	Y	Y	Y	Y	N
24 Feeney	N	N	?	N	N	N	Y
25 Diaz-Balart, M.	N	Y	Y	N	N	N	Y
GEORGIA							
1 Kingston	N	N	Y	N	N	N	N
2 Bishop	Y	N	Y	Y	N	Y	N
3 Westmoreland	N	Y	Y	N	N	N	Y
4 Johnson	Y	N	Y	Y	N	Y	N
5 Lewis	Y	N	Y	Y	Y	Y	N
6 Price	N	Y	Y	N	N	N	Y
7 Linder	N	Y	Y	N	N	N	?
8 Marshall	N	Y	?	Y	N	Y	N
9 Deal	N	Y	Y	N	N	N	Y
10 Broun	N	Y	Y	?	N	N	Y
11 Gingrey	?	Y	Y	N	N	N	Y
12 Barrow	Y	N	Y	Y	N	Y	N
13 Scott	Y	N	Y	Y	N	Y	N
HAWAII							
1 Abercrombie	Y	N	Y	Y	N	Y	N
2 Hirono	Y	N	Y	Y	Y	Y	N
IDAHO							
1 Sali	N	N	Y	N	N	N	N
2 Simpson	N	Y	Y	N	N	N	Y
ILLINOIS							
1 Rush	?	?	?	?	?	?	?
2 Jackson	Y	N	Y	Y	N	Y	N
3 Lipinski	Y	N	Y	Y	Y	Y	N
4 Gutierrez	Y	N	Y	Y	N	?	N
5 Emanuel	Y	N	Y	Y	N	Y	N
6 Roskam	N	Y	Y	N	N	N	Y
7 Davis	Y	N	Y	Y	Y	Y	N
8 Bean	Y	N	Y	Y	Y	?	N
9 Schakowsky	Y	N	Y	Y	Y	?	?
10 Kirk	N	N	Y	N	Y	N	N
11 Weller	N	Y	Y	N	N	N	Y
12 Costello	Y	N	Y	Y	N	Y	N
13 Biggert	N	Y	Y	N	Y	N	Y
14 Foster	Y	N	Y	Y	N	Y	N
15 Johnson	N	Y	Y	N	N	N	Y

ND Northern Democrats, SD Southern Democrats
Southern states: Ala., Ark., Fla., Ga., Ky., La., Miss., N.C., Okla., S.C., Tenn., Texas, Va.

	254	255	256	257	258	259	260
16 **Manzullo**	N	N	Y	N	N	N	N
17 Hare	Y	N	Y	Y	N	Y	N
18 **LaHood**	N	Y	Y	N	N	N	Y
19 **Shimkus**	N	Y	Y	N	N	N	Y
INDIANA							
1 Visclosky	Y	N	Y	Y	N	Y	N
2 Donnelly	Y	N	Y	Y	N	Y	N
3 **Souder**	N	Y	Y	N	Y	N	Y
4 **Buyer**	N	N	Y	N	N	N	Y
5 **Burton**	?	?	?	?	?	?	?
6 **Pence**	N	Y	Y	N	N	N	Y
7 Carson, A.	?	?	?	?	?	?	?
8 Ellsworth	Y	N	Y	Y	N	Y	N
9 Hill	Y	N	Y	Y	N	Y	N
IOWA							
1 Braley	Y	N	Y	Y	Y	Y	N
2 Loebsack	Y	N	Y	Y	Y	Y	N
3 Boswell	?	N	Y	Y	N	Y	N
4 **Latham**	N	Y	Y	N	N	N	Y
5 **King**	N	Y	Y	N	N	N	Y
KANSAS							
1 **Moran**	N	N	Y	N	N	N	N
2 Boyda	Y	N	Y	Y	N	Y	N
3 Moore	Y	N	Y	Y	N	Y	N
4 **Tiahrt**	N	N	Y	N	N	N	N
KENTUCKY							
1 **Whitfield**	N	Y	Y	N	N	N	Y
2 **Lewis**	N	Y	Y	N	N	N	Y
3 Yarmuth	Y	N	Y	Y	Y	Y	N
4 **Davis**	N	Y	Y	N	N	N	N
5 **Rogers**	N	Y	Y	N	N	N	Y
6 Chandler	Y	N	Y	Y	Y	Y	N
LOUISIANA							
1 Vacant							
2 Jefferson	Y	N	Y	Y	N	Y	N
3 Melancon	Y	N	Y	Y	N	Y	N
4 **McCrery**	N	Y	Y	N	N	N	Y
5 **Alexander**	N	Y	Y	N	N	N	Y
6 Vacant							
6 Cazayoux	Y	N	Y	Y	N	Y	N
7 **Boustany**	N	Y	Y	N	N	N	Y
MAINE							
1 Allen	Y	N	Y	Y	Y	Y	N
2 Michaud	Y	N	Y	Y	Y	Y	N
MARYLAND							
1 **Gilchrest**	N	Y	Y	N	Y	N	N
2 Ruppersberger	Y	N	Y	Y	N	Y	N
3 Sarbanes	Y	N	Y	Y	Y	Y	N
4 Wynn	Y	N	Y	Y	N	Y	N
5 Hoyer	Y	N	Y	Y	N	Y	N
6 **Bartlett**	N	Y	Y	N	N	N	Y
7 Cummings	Y	N	Y	Y	N	Y	N
8 Van Hollen	Y	N	Y	Y	Y	Y	N
MASSACHUSETTS							
1 Olver	Y	N	Y	Y	Y	Y	N
2 Neal	Y	N	Y	Y	Y	Y	N
3 McGovern	Y	N	Y	Y	Y	Y	N
4 Frank	Y	N	Y	Y	Y	Y	N
5 Tsongas	Y	N	Y	Y	Y	Y	N
6 Tierney	Y	N	Y	Y	Y	Y	N
7 Markey	Y	N	Y	Y	Y	Y	N
8 Capuano	Y	N	Y	Y	Y	Y	N
9 Lynch	Y	N	Y	Y	Y	Y	N
10 Delahunt	Y	N	Y	Y	N	Y	N
MICHIGAN							
1 Stupak	Y	N	Y	Y	N	Y	N
2 **Hoekstra**	N	N	Y	N	N	N	Y
3 **Ehlers**	N	N	Y	N	Y	N	N
4 **Camp**	N	Y	Y	N	N	N	Y
5 Kildee	Y	N	Y	Y	N	Y	N
6 **Upton**	N	Y	Y	N	Y	N	Y
7 **Walberg**	N	N	Y	N	N	N	N
8 **Rogers**	N	Y	Y	N	N	N	N
9 **Knollenberg**	N	Y	Y	N	Y	N	Y
10 **Miller**	N	Y	Y	N	N	N	Y
11 **McCotter**	N	N	Y	N	N	N	N
12 Levin	Y	N	Y	Y	N	Y	N
13 Kilpatrick	Y	N	Y	Y	N	Y	N
14 Conyers	Y	Y	Y	Y	N	Y	N
15 Dingell	Y	N	Y	Y	Y	Y	N
MINNESOTA							
1 Walz	Y	N	Y	Y	N	Y	N
2 **Kline**	N	Y	Y	N	N	N	Y
3 **Ramstad**	N	N	Y	N	Y	N	N
4 McCollum	Y	N	Y	Y	Y	Y	N
5 Ellison	Y	N	Y	Y	Y	Y	N
6 **Bachmann**	N	N	Y	N	N	N	Y
7 Peterson	Y	N	Y	Y	N	Y	N
8 Oberstar	?	?	?	?	?	?	?
MISSISSIPPI							
1 Vacant							
2 Thompson	Y	N	Y	Y	N	Y	N
3 **Pickering**	N	N	Y	N	N	N	Y
4 Taylor	Y	N	Y	Y	Y	Y	Y
MISSOURI							
1 Clay	Y	N	Y	Y	N	Y	N
2 **Akin**	N	Y	Y	N	N	N	Y
3 Carnahan	Y	N	Y	Y	N	Y	N
4 Skelton	Y	N	Y	Y	N	Y	N
5 Cleaver	Y	N	Y	Y	N	Y	N
6 **Graves**	N	Y	Y	N	N	N	Y
7 **Blunt**	N	Y	Y	N	N	N	Y
8 **Emerson**	N	Y	Y	N	N	N	Y
9 **Hulshof**	?	?	?	?	?	?	?
MONTANA							
AL **Rehberg**	N	Y	Y	N	N	N	Y
NEBRASKA							
1 **Fortenberry**	N	N	Y	N	Y	N	N
2 **Terry**	N	N	Y	N	N	N	N
3 **Smith**	N	Y	Y	N	N	N	Y
NEVADA							
1 Berkley	Y	N	Y	Y	Y	Y	N
2 **Heller**	N	Y	Y	N	Y	N	Y
3 **Porter**	N	Y	Y	N	Y	N	N
NEW HAMPSHIRE							
1 Shea-Porter	Y	N	Y	Y	Y	Y	N
2 Hodes	Y	N	Y	Y	Y	Y	N
NEW JERSEY							
1 Andrews	?	?	?	?	?	?	?
2 **LoBiondo**	N	N	Y	N	Y	N	N
3 **Saxton**	N	Y	Y	N	Y	N	N
4 **Smith**	Y	N	Y	N	Y	N	Y
5 **Garrett**	N	Y	Y	N	N	N	Y
6 Pallone	Y	N	Y	Y	Y	Y	N
7 **Ferguson**	N	Y	Y	N	Y	N	Y
8 Pascrell	Y	N	Y	Y	Y	Y	N
9 Rothman	Y	N	Y	Y	Y	Y	N
10 Payne	Y	N	Y	Y	Y	Y	N
11 **Frelinghuysen**	N	Y	Y	N	Y	N	Y
12 Holt	Y	N	Y	Y	Y	Y	N
13 Sires	Y	N	Y	Y	Y	Y	N
NEW MEXICO							
1 **Wilson**	N	Y	Y	N	N	N	Y
2 **Pearce**	N	Y	Y	N	N	N	Y
3 Udall	Y	N	Y	Y	Y	Y	N
NEW YORK							
1 Bishop	Y	N	Y	Y	Y	Y	N
2 Israel	Y	N	Y	Y	Y	Y	N
3 **King**	N	Y	Y	N	Y	N	Y
4 McCarthy	Y	N	Y	Y	Y	Y	N
5 Ackerman	Y	N	Y	Y	Y	Y	N
6 Meeks	Y	N	Y	Y	Y	Y	N
7 Crowley	Y	N	Y	Y	Y	Y	N
8 Nadler	Y	N	Y	Y	Y	Y	N
9 Weiner	?	?	?	?	?	?	?
10 Towns	Y	N	Y	Y	N	Y	N
11 Clarke	Y	N	Y	?	N	Y	N
12 Velázquez	Y	N	Y	Y	N	Y	N
13 **Fossella**	N	N	Y	N	Y	N	N
14 Maloney	Y	N	Y	Y	N	Y	N
15 Rangel	Y	N	Y	Y	Y	Y	N
16 Serrano	Y	N	Y	Y	Y	Y	N
17 Engel	Y	N	Y	Y	Y	Y	N
18 Lowey	Y	N	Y	Y	Y	Y	N
19 Hall	Y	N	Y	Y	Y	Y	?
20 Gillibrand	Y	N	Y	Y	N	Y	N
21 McNulty	Y	N	Y	Y	Y	Y	N
22 Hinchey	Y	N	Y	Y	Y	Y	N
23 **McHugh**	N	N	Y	N	N	N	N
24 Arcuri	Y	N	Y	Y	N	Y	N
25 **Walsh**	N	Y	Y	N	N	N	Y
26 **Reynolds**	N	N	Y	N	N	N	Y
27 Higgins	Y	N	Y	Y	Y	Y	N
28 Slaughter	Y	N	Y	Y	Y	Y	N
29 **Kuhl**	N	N	Y	N	N	N	N
NORTH CAROLINA							
1 Butterfield	?	?	?	?	?	?	?
2 Etheridge	Y	N	Y	Y	N	Y	N
3 **Jones**	–	+	+	–	–	–	+
4 Price	Y	N	Y	Y	N	Y	?
5 **Foxx**	N	Y	Y	N	N	N	N
6 **Coble**	N	Y	Y	N	Y	N	N
7 McIntyre	Y	N	Y	Y	N	Y	N
8 **Hayes**	N	Y	Y	N	N	N	Y
9 **Myrick**	N	Y	Y	N	N	N	Y
10 **McHenry**	?	?	?	?	?	?	?
11 Shuler	Y	N	Y	Y	N	Y	N
12 Watt	Y	N	Y	Y	N	Y	N
13 Miller	Y	N	Y	Y	N	Y	N
NORTH DAKOTA							
AL Pomeroy	Y	N	Y	Y	N	Y	N
OHIO							
1 **Chabot**	N	Y	Y	N	N	N	Y
2 **Schmidt**	N	Y	Y	N	N	N	Y
3 **Turner**	N	Y	Y	N	N	N	Y
4 **Jordan**	N	N	Y	N	N	N	N
5 **Latta**	N	Y	Y	N	N	N	Y
6 Wilson	Y	N	Y	Y	N	Y	N
7 **Hobson**	N	Y	Y	N	N	N	Y
8 **Boehner**	?	Y	Y	N	N	N	Y
9 Kaptur	Y	N	?	Y	N	Y	N
10 Kucinich	Y	N	Y	Y	Y	Y	N
11 Tubbs Jones	?	?	+	?	–	?	?
12 **Tiberi**	N	N	Y	N	N	N	Y
13 Sutton	Y	N	Y	Y	N	Y	N
14 **LaTourette**	N	Y	Y	N	N	N	Y
15 **Pryce**	?	?	?	?	?	?	?
16 **Regula**	N	Y	Y	N	N	N	Y
17 Ryan	Y	N	Y	Y	N	Y	N
18 Space	Y	N	Y	Y	N	Y	N
OKLAHOMA							
1 **Sullivan**	N	Y	Y	N	?	N	?
2 Boren	Y	N	Y	Y	N	Y	N
3 **Lucas**	N	Y	Y	N	N	N	Y
4 **Cole**	N	Y	Y	N	N	N	Y
5 **Fallin**	N	N	Y	N	N	N	Y
OREGON							
1 Wu	Y	N	Y	Y	Y	Y	N
2 **Walden**	N	Y	Y	N	N	N	Y
3 Blumenauer	Y	N	Y	Y	Y	Y	N
4 DeFazio	Y	N	Y	Y	Y	Y	N
5 Hooley	Y	N	Y	Y	N	Y	N
PENNSYLVANIA							
1 Brady	Y	N	Y	Y	N	Y	N
2 Fattah	Y	N	Y	Y	Y	Y	N
3 **English**	N	Y	Y	N	N	N	Y
4 Altmire	Y	N	Y	Y	N	Y	N
5 **Peterson**	N	N	Y	N	N	N	Y
6 **Gerlach**	N	N	Y	N	Y	N	N
7 Sestak	Y	N	Y	Y	Y	Y	?
8 Murphy, P.	Y	N	Y	Y	Y	Y	N
9 **Shuster**	N	N	Y	N	N	N	Y
10 Carney	Y	N	Y	Y	N	Y	N
11 Kanjorski	Y	N	Y	Y	N	Y	N
12 Murtha	Y	N	Y	Y	N	Y	N
13 Schwartz	Y	N	Y	Y	Y	Y	N
14 Doyle	Y	N	Y	Y	N	Y	N
15 **Dent**	N	N	Y	N	Y	N	N
16 **Pitts**	N	N	Y	N	N	N	Y
17 Holden	Y	N	Y	Y	N	Y	?
18 **Murphy, T.**	N	N	Y	N	N	N	N
19 **Platts**	N	N	Y	N	Y	N	N
RHODE ISLAND							
1 Kennedy	Y	N	Y	Y	N	Y	N
2 Langevin	Y	N	Y	Y	N	Y	N
SOUTH CAROLINA							
1 **Brown**	N	N	Y	N	N	N	N
2 **Wilson**	N	Y	Y	N	N	N	Y
3 **Barrett**	N	Y	Y	N	N	N	Y
4 **Inglis**	N	Y	Y	N	N	N	Y
5 Spratt	Y	N	Y	Y	N	Y	N
6 Clyburn	Y	N	Y	Y	N	Y	N
SOUTH DAKOTA							
AL Herseth Sandlin	Y	N	Y	Y	N	Y	N
TENNESSEE							
1 **Davis, D.**	N	Y	Y	N	N	N	Y
2 **Duncan**	N	Y	Y	N	N	N	Y
3 **Wamp**	N	Y	Y	N	N	N	N
4 Davis, L.	Y	N	?	?	N	Y	N
5 Cooper	Y	Y	Y	Y	Y	Y	N
6 Gordon	Y	N	Y	Y	N	Y	Y
7 **Blackburn**	N	Y	Y	N	N	N	Y
8 Tanner	Y	N	Y	Y	N	Y	N
9 Cohen	Y	N	Y	Y	Y	Y	N
TEXAS							
1 **Gohmert**	N	N	Y	N	N	N	N
2 **Poe**	N	N	Y	N	N	N	N
3 **Johnson, S.**	N	Y	Y	N	N	N	Y
4 **Hall**	N	Y	Y	N	N	N	Y
5 **Hensarling**	N	Y	Y	N	Y	N	?
6 **Barton**	N	Y	Y	N	N	N	Y
7 **Culberson**	N	Y	Y	N	N	N	Y
8 **Brady**	N	N	Y	N	N	N	Y
9 Green, A.	Y	N	Y	Y	N	Y	N
10 **McCaul**	N	Y	Y	N	N	N	Y
11 **Conaway**	?	?	?	?	?	?	?
12 **Granger**	N	Y	Y	N	?	N	Y
13 **Thornberry**	N	Y	Y	N	N	N	Y
14 **Paul**	N	Y	?	N	N	N	Y
15 Hinojosa	Y	N	Y	Y	N	Y	N
16 Reyes	?	N	Y	Y	N	Y	N
17 Edwards	Y	N	Y	Y	N	Y	N
18 Jackson Lee	Y	N	Y	Y	N	Y	N
19 **Neugebauer**	N	Y	Y	N	N	N	Y
20 Gonzalez	Y	N	Y	Y	N	Y	N
21 **Smith**	N	Y	Y	N	N	N	Y
22 Lampson	Y	N	Y	Y	N	Y	N
23 Rodriguez	Y	N	Y	Y	N	Y	N
24 **Marchant**	N	Y	?	N	N	N	Y
25 Doggett	Y	N	?	Y	Y	Y	N
26 **Burgess**	N	N	Y	N	N	N	N
27 Ortiz	Y	N	Y	Y	N	Y	N
28 Cuellar	Y	N	Y	Y	N	Y	N
29 Green, G.	Y	N	Y	Y	Y	Y	N
30 Johnson, E.	Y	N	Y	Y	N	Y	N
31 **Carter**	N	Y	Y	N	N	N	Y
32 **Sessions**	N	Y	Y	N	N	N	Y
UTAH							
1 **Bishop**	?	Y	Y	N	N	N	Y
2 Matheson	Y	N	Y	Y	Y	Y	N
3 **Cannon**	N	Y	Y	N	N	N	Y
VERMONT							
AL Welch	Y	N	Y	Y	N	Y	?
VIRGINIA							
1 **Wittman**	N	N	Y	N	N	N	Y
2 **Drake**	N	Y	Y	N	N	N	Y
3 Scott	Y	N	Y	Y	Y	Y	N
4 **Forbes**	N	Y	Y	N	N	N	Y
5 **Goode**	N	Y	Y	N	N	N	Y
6 **Goodlatte**	N	Y	Y	N	N	N	Y
7 **Cantor**	N	Y	Y	N	Y	N	Y
8 Moran	Y	N	Y	Y	Y	Y	N
9 Boucher	Y	N	Y	Y	N	Y	N
10 **Wolf**	N	Y	Y	N	Y	N	Y
11 **Davis**	N	Y	Y	N	Y	N	Y
WASHINGTON							
1 Inslee	Y	N	Y	Y	Y	Y	N
2 Larsen	Y	N	Y	Y	N	Y	N
3 Baird	Y	N	Y	Y	Y	Y	N
4 **Hastings**	N	N	Y	N	N	N	Y
5 **McMorris Rodgers**	N	N	Y	N	N	N	Y
6 Dicks	Y	N	Y	Y	N	Y	N
7 McDermott	Y	N	Y	?	?	?	?
8 **Reichert**	Y	Y	Y	N	Y	N	Y
9 Smith	Y	N	Y	Y	Y	Y	?
WEST VIRGINIA							
1 Mollohan	Y	N	Y	Y	N	Y	N
2 **Capito**	N	Y	Y	N	N	N	Y
3 Rahall	Y	N	Y	Y	N	Y	N
WISCONSIN							
1 **Ryan**	N	Y	Y	N	Y	N	Y
2 Baldwin	Y	N	Y	Y	Y	Y	?
3 Kind	Y	N	Y	Y	Y	Y	N
4 Moore	Y	N	Y	Y	Y	Y	N
5 **Sensenbrenner**	N	Y	Y	N	Y	N	Y
6 **Petri**	N	Y	Y	N	Y	N	Y
7 Obey	Y	N	Y	Y	Y	Y	N
8 Kagen	Y	N	Y	Y	N	Y	?
WYOMING							
AL **Cubin**	N	Y	Y	N	N	N	Y
DELEGATES							
Faleomavaega (A.S.)							
Norton (D.C.)							
Bordallo (Guam)							
Fortuño (P.R.)							
Christensen (V.I.)							

IN THE HOUSE | By Vote Number

261. **Procedural Motion/Motion to Adjourn.** Culberson, R-Texas, motion to adjourn. Motion rejected 138-248: R 134-44; D 4-204 (ND 0-153, SD 4-51). May 6, 2008.

262. **Procedural Motion/Motion to Adjourn.** Carter, R-Texas, motion to adjourn. Motion rejected 149-236: R 147-33; D 2-203 (ND 1-155, SD 1-48). May 6, 2008.

263. **H Res 1168. Charter Schools Tribute/Adoption.** Tierney, D-Mass., motion to suspend the rules and adopt the resolution that would commend U.S. charter schools for improving the public school system and support the ninth annual National Charter Schools Week. Motion agreed to 391-2: R 181-0; D 210-2 (ND 158-2, SD 52-0). A two-thirds majority of those present and voting (262 in this case) is required for adoption under suspension of the rules. May 6, 2008.

264. **H Res 1168. Charter Schools Tribute/Motion to Reconsider.** Hastings, D-Fla., motion to table (kill) the Carter, R-Texas, motion to reconsider the vote on adoption of the resolution that would commend U.S. charter schools. Motion agreed to 215-182: R 0-182; D 215-0 (ND 161-0, SD 54-0). May 6, 2008.

265. **H Res 1155. El Dorado Promise Scholarship/Adoption.** Tierney, D-Mass., motion to suspend the rules and adopt the resolution that would honor recipients of the El Dorado Promise scholarship, a college scholarship program funded by Murphy Oil Corp. for high school graduates of the El Dorado Public School District in Arkansas. Motion agreed to 390-1: R 179-1; D 211-0 (ND 158-0, SD 53-0). A two-thirds majority of those present and voting (261 in this case) is required for adoption under suspension of the rules. May 6, 2008.

266. **H Res 1155. El Dorado Promise Scholarship/Motion to Reconsider.** Hastings, D-Fla., motion to table (kill) the Tiahrt, R-Kan., motion to reconsider the vote on adoption of the resolution that would honor recipients of the El Dorado Promise scholarship. Motion agreed to 216-180: R 0-180; D 216-0 (ND 161-0, SD 55-0). May 6, 2008.

267. **Procedural Motion/Motion to Adjourn.** Sessions, R-Texas, motion to adjourn. Motion rejected 132-269: R 130-54; D 2-215 (ND 0-162, SD 2-53). May 7, 2008.

	261	262	263	264	265	266	267
ALABAMA							
1 **Bonner**	Y	Y	Y	N	Y	N	Y
2 **Everett**	Y	Y	Y	N	Y	N	Y
3 **Rogers**	Y	Y	Y	N	Y	N	?
4 **Aderholt**	Y	Y	Y	N	Y	N	Y
5 Cramer	N	N	Y	Y	Y	Y	N
6 **Bachus**	Y	?	?	?	?	?	Y
7 Davis	N	N	Y	Y	Y	Y	N
ALASKA							
AL **Young**	?	Y	Y	N	N	N	?
ARIZONA							
1 **Renzi**	?	Y	Y	N	Y	N	Y
2 **Franks**	Y	Y	Y	N	Y	N	Y
3 **Shadegg**	Y	Y	Y	N	Y	N	Y
4 Pastor	N	N	Y	Y	Y	Y	N
5 Mitchell	N	N	Y	Y	Y	Y	N
6 **Flake**	Y	Y	N	Y	N	Y	Y
7 Grijalva	N	N	Y	Y	Y	Y	N
8 Giffords	N	N	Y	Y	Y	Y	N
ARKANSAS							
1 Berry	N	?	Y	Y	Y	Y	N
2 Snyder	N	?	?	?	Y	Y	N
3 **Boozman**	Y	Y	Y	N	Y	N	Y
4 Ross	N	?	Y	Y	Y	Y	N
CALIFORNIA							
1 Thompson	N	N	Y	Y	Y	Y	N
2 **Herger**	Y	Y	Y	N	Y	?	Y
3 **Lungren**	Y	Y	Y	N	Y	N	Y
4 **Doolittle**	?	?	?	?	?	?	Y
5 Matsui	N	N	Y	Y	Y	Y	N
6 Woolsey	N	N	Y	Y	Y	Y	N
7 Miller, George	N	N	Y	Y	Y	Y	N
8 Pelosi							
9 Lee	N	N	Y	Y	Y	Y	N
10 Tauscher	N	N	Y	Y	Y	Y	N
11 McNerney	N	?	Y	?	Y	Y	N
12 Speier	?	?	?	?	?	?	?
13 Stark	N	N	Y	Y	?	Y	N
14 Eshoo	N	N	Y	Y	Y	Y	N
15 Honda	N	N	Y	Y	Y	Y	N
16 Lofgren	N	N	?	?	Y	Y	N
17 Farr	N	N	Y	Y	Y	Y	N
18 Cardoza	N	N	Y	Y	Y	Y	?
19 **Radanovich**	Y	Y	Y	N	Y	N	Y
20 Costa	N	?	Y	Y	Y	Y	N
21 **Nunes**	Y	Y	Y	N	Y	N	Y
22 **McCarthy**	Y	Y	Y	N	?	N	Y
23 Capps	N	N	Y	Y	Y	Y	N
24 **Gallegly**	Y	Y	Y	N	Y	N	Y
25 **McKeon**	Y	Y	Y	N	Y	N	Y
26 **Dreier**	Y	Y	Y	N	Y	N	Y
27 Sherman	N	N	Y	Y	Y	Y	N
28 Berman	N	N	Y	Y	Y	Y	N
29 Schiff	N	N	Y	Y	Y	Y	N
30 Waxman	N	N	Y	Y	Y	Y	?
31 Becerra	N	N	Y	Y	Y	Y	N
32 Solis	N	N	Y	Y	Y	Y	N
33 Watson	N	N	Y	Y	Y	Y	N
34 Roybal-Allard	N	N	Y	Y	Y	Y	N
35 Waters	N	N	Y	Y	?	Y	N
36 Harman	N	N	Y	Y	Y	Y	N
37 Richardson	N	N	Y	Y	Y	Y	?
38 Napolitano	N	N	Y	Y	Y	Y	N
39 Sánchez, Linda	N	N	Y	Y	Y	Y	N
40 **Royce**	Y	Y	Y	N	Y	N	Y
41 **Lewis**	Y	Y	Y	N	Y	N	Y
42 **Miller, Gary**	Y	Y	Y	N	Y	N	Y
43 Baca	?	N	Y	Y	Y	Y	N
44 **Calvert**	Y	Y	Y	N	Y	N	Y
45 **Bono Mack**	Y	Y	Y	N	Y	N	Y
46 **Rohrabacher**	Y	Y	Y	N	Y	N	Y
47 Sanchez, Loretta	N	N	Y	Y	Y	Y	N
48 **Campbell**	?	?	?	?	?	?	?
49 **Issa**	Y	Y	Y	N	Y	N	Y
50 **Bilbray**	Y	Y	Y	N	Y	N	Y
51 Filner	N	N	Y	Y	Y	Y	N
52 **Hunter**	Y	Y	Y	N	?	?	Y
53 Davis	N	N	Y	Y	Y	Y	N

	261	262	263	264	265	266	267
COLORADO							
1 DeGette	N	N	Y	Y	Y	Y	N
2 Udall	?	N	Y	Y	Y	Y	?
3 Salazar	N	N	Y	Y	Y	Y	N
4 **Musgrave**	Y	Y	Y	N	Y	N	Y
5 **Lamborn**	Y	Y	Y	N	Y	N	Y
6 **Tancredo**	N	Y	Y	N	Y	N	Y
7 Perlmutter	N	N	Y	Y	Y	Y	N
CONNECTICUT							
1 Larson	N	N	Y	Y	Y	Y	N
2 Courtney	N	N	Y	Y	Y	Y	N
3 DeLauro	?	N	Y	Y	Y	Y	N
4 **Shays**	Y	Y	Y	N	Y	N	Y
5 Murphy	N	N	Y	Y	Y	Y	N
DELAWARE							
AL **Castle**	Y	Y	Y	N	Y	N	N
FLORIDA							
1 **Miller**	Y	Y	Y	N	Y	N	Y
2 Boyd	N	N	Y	Y	Y	Y	N
3 Brown	N	N	Y	Y	Y	Y	N
4 **Crenshaw**	Y	Y	Y	N	Y	N	Y
5 **Brown-Waite**	?	Y	Y	N	Y	N	Y
6 **Stearns**	Y	Y	Y	N	Y	N	Y
7 **Mica**	N	N	Y	N	Y	N	Y
8 **Keller**	Y	Y	?	N	Y	N	Y
9 **Bilirakis**	N	N	Y	N	?	N	N
10 **Young**	Y	Y	Y	N	Y	N	N
11 Castor	N	N	Y	Y	Y	Y	N
12 **Putnam**	Y	Y	Y	N	Y	N	Y
13 **Buchanan**	N	Y	Y	N	Y	N	Y
14 **Mack**	Y	Y	Y	N	Y	N	Y
15 **Weldon**	?	?	Y	N	Y	?	?
16 Mahoney	N	N	Y	Y	Y	Y	N
17 Meek	N	N	Y	Y	Y	Y	N
18 **Ros-Lehtinen**	N	N	Y	N	N	N	N
19 Wexler	N	N	Y	Y	Y	Y	?
20 Wasserman Schultz	N	N	Y	Y	Y	Y	N
21 **Diaz-Balart, L.**	Y	Y	Y	N	Y	N	Y
22 Klein	N	N	Y	Y	Y	Y	N
23 Hastings	N	N	Y	Y	Y	Y	N
24 **Feeney**	Y	Y	Y	N	Y	N	Y
25 **Diaz-Balart, M.**	Y	Y	Y	N	Y	N	Y
GEORGIA							
1 **Kingston**	N	N	Y	N	Y	N	N
2 Bishop	N	N	Y	Y	Y	Y	N
3 **Westmoreland**	Y	Y	Y	N	Y	N	Y
4 Johnson	N	N	Y	Y	Y	Y	N
5 Lewis	N	N	Y	Y	Y	Y	N
6 **Price**	Y	Y	Y	N	Y	N	Y
7 **Linder**	?	Y	Y	N	Y	N	Y
8 Marshall	N	N	Y	Y	Y	Y	N
9 **Deal**	Y	Y	Y	N	Y	N	Y
10 **Broun**	Y	Y	Y	N	Y	N	Y
11 **Gingrey**	Y	Y	Y	N	Y	N	Y
12 Barrow	N	N	Y	Y	Y	Y	N
13 Scott	Y	N	Y	Y	Y	Y	N
HAWAII							
1 Abercrombie	N	N	Y	Y	Y	Y	N
2 Hirono	N	N	Y	Y	Y	Y	N
IDAHO							
1 **Sali**	?	N	Y	N	Y	N	N
2 **Simpson**	Y	Y	Y	N	Y	N	Y
ILLINOIS							
1 Rush	?	?	?	?	?	?	?
2 Jackson	N	N	Y	Y	Y	Y	N
3 Lipinski	N	N	Y	Y	Y	Y	N
4 Gutierrez	N	?	Y	Y	Y	Y	N
5 Emanuel	N	N	Y	Y	Y	Y	N
6 **Roskam**	Y	Y	Y	N	Y	N	Y
7 Davis	N	N	Y	Y	Y	Y	N
8 Bean	N	N	Y	Y	Y	Y	N
9 Schakowsky	?	N	Y	Y	Y	Y	N
10 **Kirk**	N	N	Y	N	Y	N	N
11 **Weller**	Y	?	Y	N	Y	N	N
12 Costello	N	N	Y	Y	Y	Y	N
13 **Biggert**	Y	Y	Y	N	Y	N	Y
14 Foster	N	N	Y	Y	Y	Y	N
15 **Johnson**	Y	Y	Y	N	Y	N	Y

KEY **Republicans** Democrats

Y Voted for (yea)	**X** Paired against	**C** Voted "present" to avoid possible conflict of interest
# Paired for	**–** Announced against	
+ Announced for	**P** Voted "present"	**?** Did not vote or otherwise make a position known
N Voted against (nay)		

ND Northern Democrats, SD Southern Democrats
Southern states: Ala., Ark., Fla., Ga., Ky., La., Miss., N.C., Okla., S.C., Tenn., Texas, Va.

	261	262	263	264	265	266	267
16 **Manzullo**	N	N	Y	N	Y	N	N
17 Hare	N	N	Y	Y	Y	Y	N
18 **LaHood**	Y	Y	Y	N	Y	N	Y
19 **Shimkus**	?	Y	Y	N	Y	N	Y
INDIANA							
1 Visclosky	N	N	Y	Y	Y	Y	N
2 Donnelly	N	N	Y	Y	Y	Y	N
3 **Souder**	Y	Y	Y	N	Y	N	Y
4 **Buyer**	N	Y	Y	N	Y	N	N
5 **Burton**	?	?	?	?	?	?	?
6 **Pence**	Y	Y	Y	N	Y	N	N
7 Carson, A.	?	?	?	?	?	?	?
8 Ellsworth	N	N	Y	Y	Y	Y	N
9 Hill	N	N	Y	Y	Y	Y	N
IOWA							
1 Braley	–	?	Y	Y	Y	Y	N
2 Loebsack	N	N	Y	Y	Y	Y	N
3 Boswell	N	N	Y	Y	Y	Y	N
4 **Latham**	Y	Y	Y	N	Y	N	N
5 **King**	Y	Y	Y	N	Y	N	Y
KANSAS							
1 **Moran**	N	N	Y	N	Y	N	N
2 Boyda	N	N	Y	Y	Y	Y	N
3 Moore	N	N	Y	Y	Y	Y	N
4 **Tiahrt**	?	N	Y	N	Y	N	N
KENTUCKY							
1 **Whitfield**	?	Y	Y	N	Y	N	?
2 **Lewis**	Y	Y	Y	N	Y	N	Y
3 Yarmuth	N	N	Y	Y	Y	Y	N
4 **Davis**	Y	Y	Y	N	Y	N	N
5 **Rogers**	Y	Y	Y	N	Y	N	Y
6 Chandler	N	N	Y	Y	Y	Y	N
LOUISIANA							
1 Vacant							
2 Jefferson	N	N	Y	Y	Y	Y	?
3 Melancon	N	N	Y	Y	?	Y	N
4 **McCrery**	Y	Y	Y	N	Y	N	Y
5 **Alexander**	Y	Y	Y	N	Y	N	Y
6 Cazayoux	N	N	Y	Y	Y	Y	N
7 **Boustany**	Y	Y	Y	N	Y	N	N
MAINE							
1 Allen	N	N	Y	Y	Y	Y	N
2 Michaud	N	N	Y	Y	Y	Y	N
MARYLAND							
1 **Gilchrest**	N	?	?	?	?	?	Y
2 Ruppersberger	N	?	Y	Y	Y	Y	N
3 Sarbanes	N	N	Y	Y	Y	Y	N
4 Wynn	?	N	Y	Y	Y	Y	N
5 Hoyer	N	N	Y	Y	Y	Y	N
6 **Bartlett**	Y	Y	Y	N	Y	N	Y
7 Cummings	?	?	?	?	Y	Y	N
8 Van Hollen	N	N	Y	Y	Y	Y	N
MASSACHUSETTS							
1 Olver	N	N	?	Y	Y	Y	N
2 Neal	N	N	Y	Y	Y	Y	N
3 McGovern	N	N	Y	Y	Y	Y	N
4 Frank	N	N	Y	Y	Y	Y	N
5 Tsongas	N	N	Y	Y	Y	Y	N
6 Tierney	N	N	Y	Y	Y	Y	N
7 Markey	N	N	Y	Y	Y	Y	N
8 Capuano	?	N	Y	Y	Y	Y	N
9 Lynch	N	N	Y	Y	Y	Y	N
10 Delahunt	?	N	Y	Y	Y	Y	N
MICHIGAN							
1 Stupak	N	N	Y	Y	Y	Y	N
2 **Hoekstra**	Y	N	Y	N	Y	N	Y
3 **Ehlers**	N	N	Y	N	Y	N	N
4 **Camp**	Y	Y	Y	N	Y	N	Y
5 Kildee	N	N	Y	Y	Y	Y	N
6 **Upton**	Y	Y	Y	N	Y	N	Y
7 **Walberg**	N	N	Y	N	Y	N	N
8 **Rogers**	N	N	Y	N	Y	N	N
9 **Knollenberg**	Y	Y	Y	N	Y	N	Y
10 **Miller**	N	N	Y	N	Y	N	N
11 **McCotter**	N	N	Y	N	Y	N	N
12 Levin	N	N	Y	Y	Y	Y	N
13 Kilpatrick	N	N	Y	Y	Y	Y	N
14 Conyers	?	N	Y	Y	Y	Y	?
15 Dingell	N	N	Y	Y	Y	Y	N
MINNESOTA							
1 Walz	N	N	Y	Y	Y	Y	N
2 **Kline**	Y	Y	Y	N	Y	N	Y
3 **Ramstad**	N	N	Y	N	Y	N	N
4 McCollum	N	N	Y	Y	Y	Y	?
5 Ellison	N	N	Y	Y	Y	Y	N
6 **Bachmann**	N	Y	Y	N	Y	N	N
7 Peterson	N	N	Y	Y	Y	?	N
8 Oberstar	?	?	?	?	?	?	?
MISSISSIPPI							
1 Vacant							
2 Thompson	N	N	Y	Y	Y	Y	N
3 **Pickering**	Y	Y	Y	N	Y	N	Y
4 Taylor	Y	Y	Y	Y	Y	Y	N
MISSOURI							
1 Clay	N	Y	Y	Y	Y	Y	N
2 **Akin**	Y	Y	Y	N	Y	N	Y
3 Carnahan	N	N	Y	Y	Y	Y	N
4 Skelton	N	N	Y	Y	Y	Y	N
5 Cleaver	N	N	Y	Y	Y	Y	N
6 **Graves**	N	N	Y	N	Y	N	N
7 **Blunt**	Y	Y	Y	N	Y	N	Y
8 **Emerson**	Y	Y	Y	N	Y	N	Y
9 **Hulshof**	?	?	?	?	?	?	N
MONTANA							
AL **Rehberg**	Y	Y	Y	N	Y	N	Y
NEBRASKA							
1 **Fortenberry**	N	N	Y	N	Y	N	N
2 **Terry**	N	N	Y	N	Y	N	N
3 **Smith**	Y	Y	Y	N	Y	N	Y
NEVADA							
1 Berkley	N	N	Y	Y	Y	Y	N
2 **Heller**	Y	Y	Y	N	?	N	Y
3 **Porter**	N	N	Y	N	Y	N	Y
NEW HAMPSHIRE							
1 Shea-Porter	N	N	Y	Y	Y	Y	N
2 Hodes	N	N	Y	Y	Y	Y	N
NEW JERSEY							
1 Andrews	?	?	?	?	?	?	?
2 **LoBiondo**	N	N	Y	N	Y	N	N
3 **Saxton**	N	Y	?	?	Y	N	Y
4 **Smith**	N	N	Y	N	Y	N	N
5 **Garrett**	Y	Y	Y	N	Y	?	Y
6 Pallone	N	N	Y	Y	Y	Y	N
7 **Ferguson**	Y	Y	Y	N	Y	N	?
8 Pascrell	N	N	Y	Y	?	Y	N
9 Rothman	N	N	Y	Y	Y	Y	N
10 Payne	N	N	Y	Y	Y	Y	N
11 **Frelinghuysen**	Y	Y	Y	N	Y	N	N
12 Holt	N	N	Y	Y	Y	Y	N
13 Sires	N	N	Y	Y	Y	Y	N
NEW MEXICO							
1 **Wilson**	Y	Y	Y	N	Y	N	N
2 **Pearce**	Y	Y	Y	N	Y	N	N
3 Udall	?	?	?	?	?	?	N
NEW YORK							
1 Bishop	N	N	Y	Y	Y	Y	–
2 Israel	N	N	Y	Y	Y	Y	N
3 **King**	Y	Y	Y	N	Y	N	Y
4 McCarthy	N	N	Y	Y	?	Y	N
5 Ackerman	N	N	Y	Y	Y	Y	N
6 Meeks	N	?	?	?	?	Y	N
7 Crowley	N	N	Y	Y	Y	Y	N
8 Nadler	N	N	Y	Y	Y	Y	N
9 Weiner	?	?	?	?	?	?	N
10 Towns	N	N	Y	Y	Y	Y	N
11 Clarke	N	N	Y	Y	Y	Y	N
12 Velázquez	?	N	Y	Y	Y	Y	N
13 **Fossella**	N	N	Y	N	Y	N	?
14 Maloney	N	N	Y	Y	Y	Y	N
15 Rangel	?	N	Y	Y	Y	?	N
16 Serrano	N	N	Y	Y	Y	Y	N
17 Engel	N	N	Y	Y	Y	Y	N
18 Lowey	N	N	Y	Y	Y	Y	N
19 Hall	N	N	P	Y	?	Y	N
20 Gillibrand	N	N	Y	Y	Y	Y	N
21 McNulty	N	N	Y	Y	Y	Y	N
22 Hinchey	?	N	N	Y	?	Y	N
23 **McHugh**	N	Y	Y	N	Y	N	N
24 Arcuri	N	N	Y	Y	Y	Y	N
25 **Walsh**	Y	Y	Y	N	Y	N	Y
26 **Reynolds**	Y	Y	Y	N	Y	N	Y
27 Higgins	N	N	Y	Y	Y	Y	N
28 Slaughter	N	N	Y	Y	Y	Y	N
29 **Kuhl**	N	N	Y	N	Y	N	N
NORTH CAROLINA							
1 Butterfield	?	?	?	?	?	?	?
2 Etheridge	N	N	Y	Y	Y	Y	N
3 **Jones**	+	+	+	–	+	–	+
4 Price	N	N	Y	Y	Y	Y	N
5 **Foxx**	N	Y	Y	N	Y	N	Y
6 **Coble**	N	Y	?	?	?	?	Y
7 McIntyre	N	N	Y	Y	Y	Y	N
8 **Hayes**	Y	Y	Y	N	Y	N	Y
9 **Myrick**	Y	Y	Y	N	Y	N	Y
10 **McHenry**	?	?	?	?	?	?	?
11 Shuler	N	N	Y	Y	Y	Y	N
12 Watt	N	?	?	?	?	?	N
13 Miller	N	?	?	?	?	?	N
NORTH DAKOTA							
AL Pomeroy	N	N	Y	Y	Y	Y	N
OHIO							
1 **Chabot**	Y	Y	Y	N	Y	N	Y
2 **Schmidt**	Y	Y	Y	N	Y	N	Y
3 **Turner**	Y	Y	Y	N	Y	N	Y
4 **Jordan**	N	N	Y	N	Y	N	N
5 **Latta**	Y	Y	Y	N	Y	N	Y
6 Wilson	N	N	Y	Y	Y	Y	N
7 **Hobson**	Y	Y	Y	N	Y	N	Y
8 **Boehner**	?	Y	Y	N	Y	N	Y
9 Kaptur	N	N	Y	Y	Y	Y	N
10 Kucinich	N	N	N	Y	Y	Y	N
11 Tubbs Jones	?	?	?	?	?	?	?
12 **Tiberi**	Y	N	Y	N	Y	N	Y
13 Sutton	N	N	Y	Y	Y	Y	N
14 **LaTourette**	Y	Y	Y	N	Y	N	Y
15 **Pryce**	?	?	?	?	?	?	Y
16 **Regula**	Y	Y	Y	N	Y	N	Y
17 Ryan	N	N	Y	Y	Y	Y	N
18 Space	N	N	Y	Y	Y	Y	N
OKLAHOMA							
1 **Sullivan**	N	Y	Y	N	Y	N	Y
2 Boren	N	N	Y	Y	Y	Y	N
3 **Lucas**	Y	Y	Y	N	Y	N	Y
4 **Cole**	Y	Y	?	?	?	?	Y
5 **Fallin**	Y	Y	Y	N	Y	N	Y
OREGON							
1 Wu	N	N	Y	Y	Y	?	N
2 **Walden**	Y	Y	Y	N	Y	N	N
3 Blumenauer	N	N	Y	Y	Y	Y	N
4 DeFazio	N	N	Y	Y	Y	?	N
5 Hooley	N	?	?	?	?	?	N
PENNSYLVANIA							
1 Brady	N	N	Y	Y	Y	Y	N
2 Fattah	N	N	Y	Y	Y	Y	N
3 **English**	Y	Y	Y	N	Y	N	N
4 Altmire	N	N	Y	Y	Y	Y	N
5 **Peterson**	?	?	?	?	?	?	?
6 **Gerlach**	N	N	Y	N	Y	N	N
7 Sestak	N	N	Y	Y	Y	Y	N
8 Murphy, P.	N	N	Y	Y	Y	Y	N
9 **Shuster**	?	Y	Y	N	Y	N	Y
10 Carney	N	N	Y	Y	Y	Y	N
11 Kanjorski	N	N	Y	Y	Y	Y	N
12 Murtha	N	N	Y	Y	Y	Y	N
13 Schwartz	N	N	Y	Y	Y	Y	N
14 Doyle	?	N	Y	Y	Y	Y	N
15 **Dent**	N	N	Y	N	Y	N	N
16 **Pitts**	Y	Y	Y	N	Y	N	Y
17 Holden	?	N	Y	Y	Y	Y	N
18 **Murphy, T.**	N	?	Y	N	Y	N	N
19 **Platts**	N	N	Y	N	Y	N	N
RHODE ISLAND							
1 Kennedy	N	N	Y	Y	Y	Y	?
2 Langevin	N	?	Y	Y	Y	Y	N
SOUTH CAROLINA							
1 **Brown**	N	N	Y	N	Y	N	N
2 **Wilson**	N	Y	Y	N	Y	N	Y
3 **Barrett**	Y	Y	Y	N	Y	N	Y
4 **Inglis**	Y	Y	Y	N	Y	N	Y
5 Spratt	N	?	Y	Y	Y	Y	N
6 Clyburn	N	N	Y	Y	Y	Y	N
SOUTH DAKOTA							
AL Herseth Sandlin	N	N	Y	Y	Y	Y	N
TENNESSEE							
1 **Davis, D.**	Y	Y	Y	N	Y	N	Y
2 **Duncan**	Y	Y	Y	N	Y	N	Y
3 **Wamp**	Y	Y	Y	N	Y	N	Y
4 Davis, L.	?	N	Y	Y	Y	Y	N
5 Cooper	N	N	Y	Y	Y	Y	N
6 Gordon	Y	?	Y	Y	Y	Y	Y
7 **Blackburn**	Y	Y	Y	N	Y	N	Y
8 Tanner	N	N	Y	Y	Y	Y	N
9 Cohen	N	N	Y	Y	Y	Y	N
TEXAS							
1 **Gohmert**	N	?	Y	?	Y	N	N
2 **Poe**	N	N	Y	N	Y	N	N
3 **Johnson, S.**	Y	?	?	?	?	?	Y
4 **Hall**	N	Y	Y	N	Y	N	Y
5 **Hensarling**	Y	Y	Y	N	Y	N	Y
6 **Barton**	Y	Y	Y	N	Y	N	Y
7 **Culberson**	Y	Y	Y	N	Y	N	Y
8 **Brady**	N	N	Y	N	Y	N	N
9 Green, A.	N	N	Y	Y	Y	Y	N
10 **McCaul**	Y	?	Y	N	Y	N	Y
11 **Conaway**	?	?	?	?	?	?	?
12 **Granger**	Y	Y	Y	N	Y	N	Y
13 **Thornberry**	Y	Y	Y	N	Y	N	Y
14 **Paul**	Y	Y	Y	N	Y	N	?
15 Hinojosa	N	N	Y	Y	?	Y	N
16 Reyes	?	N	Y	Y	Y	Y	N
17 Edwards	N	?	Y	Y	Y	Y	N
18 Jackson Lee	N	N	Y	Y	Y	Y	N
19 **Neugebauer**	Y	Y	Y	N	Y	N	N
20 Gonzalez	N	N	Y	Y	Y	Y	N
21 **Smith**	Y	Y	Y	N	Y	N	Y
22 Lampson	N	N	?	Y	Y	Y	N
23 Rodriguez	N	N	Y	Y	Y	Y	N
24 **Marchant**	Y	Y	Y	N	Y	N	Y
25 Doggett	Y	N	Y	Y	Y	Y	Y
26 **Burgess**	N	N	Y	N	Y	N	N
27 Ortiz	N	N	?	Y	Y	Y	N
28 Cuellar	N	N	Y	Y	Y	Y	N
29 Green, G.	N	N	Y	Y	Y	Y	N
30 Johnson, E.	N	N	Y	Y	Y	Y	N
31 **Carter**	Y	Y	Y	N	Y	N	Y
32 **Sessions**	Y	Y	Y	N	Y	N	Y
UTAH							
1 **Bishop**	Y	Y	Y	N	Y	N	Y
2 Matheson	N	N	Y	Y	Y	Y	N
3 **Cannon**	Y	Y	Y	N	Y	N	N
VERMONT							
AL Welch	N	N	Y	Y	Y	Y	N
VIRGINIA							
1 **Wittman**	Y	Y	Y	N	Y	N	Y
2 **Drake**	Y	Y	Y	N	Y	N	Y
3 Scott	N	N	Y	Y	Y	Y	N
4 **Forbes**	Y	Y	Y	N	Y	N	Y
5 **Goode**	Y	Y	Y	N	Y	N	Y
6 **Goodlatte**	Y	Y	Y	N	Y	N	Y
7 **Cantor**	Y	Y	Y	N	Y	N	Y
8 Moran	N	N	Y	Y	Y	Y	N
9 Boucher	N	N	Y	Y	Y	Y	N
10 **Wolf**	Y	Y	Y	N	Y	N	N
11 **Davis**	Y	Y	Y	N	Y	N	Y
WASHINGTON							
1 Inslee	N	N	Y	Y	Y	Y	N
2 Larsen	N	N	Y	Y	Y	Y	N
3 Baird	N	?	?	?	?	?	N
4 **Hastings**	Y	Y	Y	N	Y	N	Y
5 **McMorris Rodgers**	Y	Y	?	N	Y	N	Y
6 Dicks	N	?	?	?	?	?	N
7 McDermott	N	?	Y	Y	Y	Y	N
8 **Reichert**	Y	Y	Y	N	Y	N	Y
9 Smith	N	N	Y	Y	Y	Y	N
WEST VIRGINIA							
1 Mollohan	N	N	Y	Y	Y	Y	N
2 **Capito**	N	?	Y	N	Y	N	Y
3 Rahall	N	N	Y	Y	Y	Y	N
WISCONSIN							
1 **Ryan**	Y	Y	Y	N	Y	N	Y
2 Baldwin	N	N	Y	Y	Y	Y	N
3 Kind	N	N	Y	Y	Y	Y	N
4 Moore	N	N	Y	Y	Y	Y	N
5 **Sensenbrenner**	Y	Y	Y	N	Y	N	Y
6 **Petri**	Y	Y	Y	N	Y	N	Y
7 Obey	N	N	Y	Y	Y	Y	N
8 Kagen	N	N	Y	Y	Y	Y	N
WYOMING							
AL **Cubin**	Y	Y	Y	N	Y	N	?
DELEGATES							
Faleomavaega (A.S.)							
Norton (D.C.)							
Bordallo (Guam)							
Fortuño (P.R.)							
Christensen (V.I.)							

IN THE HOUSE | By Vote Number

268. Procedural Motion/Journal. Approval of the House Journal of Tuesday, May 6, 2008. Approved 229-184: R 14-173; D 215-11 (ND 159-9, SD 56-2). May 7, 2008.

269. H Res 1166. Russian Ties With Regions/Adoption. Watson, D-Calif., motion to suspend the rules and adopt the resolution that would call on the Russian government to revoke its decision to establish official ties with the Abkhazia and South Ossetia regions of Georgia. It also would support Georgia's membership in NATO. Motion agreed to 390-23: R 173-15; D 217-8 (ND 160-7, SD 57-1). A two-thirds majority of those present and voting (276 in this case) is required for adoption under suspension of the rules. May 7, 2008.

270. H Res 1166. Russian Ties With Regions/Motion to Reconsider. Castor, D-Fla., motion to table (kill) the Rehberg, R-Mont., motion to reconsider the vote on adoption of the resolution that would call on the Russian government to revoke its decision to establish official ties with the Abkhazia and South Ossetia regions of Georgia. Motion agreed to 218-191: R 0-185; D 218-6 (ND 161-6, SD 57-0). May 7, 2008.

271. Procedural Motion/Motion to Adjourn. Rehberg, R-Mont., motion to adjourn. Motion rejected 140-246: R 138-44; D 2-202 (ND 1-150, SD 1-52). May 7, 2008.

272. Procedural Motion/Motion to Adjourn. Hastings, R-Wash., motion to adjourn. Motion rejected 144-250: R 141-46; D 3-204 (ND 2-152, SD 1-52). May 7, 2008.

273. Procedural Motion/Motion to Adjourn. Culberson, R-Texas, motion to adjourn. Motion rejected 138-272: R 138-47; D 0-225 (ND 0-167, SD 0-58). May 7, 2008.

274. H Res 1113. Support for Mother's Day/Adoption. Clay, D-Mo., motion to suspend the rules and adopt the resolution that would celebrate the role of mothers in the United States and support the goals and ideals of Mother's Day. Motion agreed to 412-0: R 189-0; D 223-0 (ND 165-0, SD 58-0). A two-thirds majority of those present and voting (275 in this case) is required for adoption under suspension of the rules. May 7, 2008.

	268	269	270	271	272	273	274
ALABAMA							
1 **Bonner**	N	Y	N	Y	Y	?	?
2 **Everett**	N	Y	N	Y	Y	Y	Y
3 **Rogers**	N	Y	N	Y	Y	Y	Y
4 **Aderholt**	N	Y	N	Y	Y	Y	Y
5 Cramer	Y	Y	Y	N	N	N	Y
6 **Bachus**	N	Y	N	Y	Y	Y	Y
7 Davis	Y	Y	Y	N	N	N	Y
ALASKA							
AL **Young**	N	N	N	Y	Y	Y	Y
ARIZONA							
1 **Renzi**	N	Y	N	Y	?	Y	Y
2 **Franks**	N	Y	N	Y	Y	Y	Y
3 **Shadegg**	N	Y	N	Y	Y	Y	Y
4 Pastor	Y	Y	Y	N	N	N	Y
5 Mitchell	N	Y	Y	N	N	N	Y
6 **Flake**	N	Y	N	Y	Y	Y	Y
7 Grijalva	Y	Y	Y	N	?	N	Y
8 Giffords	N	Y	Y	N	N	N	Y
ARKANSAS							
1 Berry	Y	Y	Y	N	N	N	Y
2 Snyder	Y	Y	Y	N	N	N	Y
3 **Boozman**	N	Y	N	Y	Y	Y	Y
4 Ross	Y	Y	Y	N	?	N	Y
CALIFORNIA							
1 Thompson	N	Y	Y	N	N	N	Y
2 **Herger**	N	Y	N	Y	Y	Y	Y
3 **Lungren**	N	Y	N	Y	Y	Y	Y
4 **Doolittle**	N	Y	N	Y	Y	Y	Y
5 Matsui	Y	Y	Y	N	N	N	Y
6 Woolsey	Y	Y	Y	N	N	N	Y
7 Miller, George	Y	Y	Y	?	N	N	Y
8 Pelosi							
9 Lee	Y	N	Y	N	N	N	Y
10 Tauscher	Y	Y	Y	N	N	N	Y
11 McNerney	Y	Y	Y	N	N	N	Y
12 Speier	?	?	?	?	?	?	?
13 Stark	Y	Y	Y	N	N	N	Y
14 Eshoo	Y	Y	Y	N	N	N	Y
15 Honda	Y	Y	Y	N	N	N	Y
16 Lofgren	Y	N	Y	N	N	N	Y
17 Farr	Y	Y	Y	N	N	N	?
18 Cardoza	Y	Y	Y	?	N	N	Y
19 **Radanovich**	N	Y	N	Y	Y	Y	Y
20 Costa	Y	Y	N	?	N	?	Y
21 **Nunes**	N	Y	N	Y	N	Y	Y
22 **McCarthy**	N	Y	N	Y	Y	Y	Y
23 Capps	Y	Y	Y	N	N	N	Y
24 **Gallegly**	N	Y	N	Y	Y	Y	Y
25 **McKeon**	N	N	N	Y	Y	Y	Y
26 **Dreier**	N	Y	N	Y	Y	Y	Y
27 Sherman	Y	N	Y	N	N	N	Y
28 Berman	Y	Y	N	?	?	N	Y
29 Schiff	Y	Y	Y	N	N	N	Y
30 Waxman	Y	Y	Y	N	N	N	Y
31 Becerra	Y	Y	Y	N	N	N	Y
32 Solis	Y	Y	Y	N	N	N	Y
33 Watson	Y	Y	Y	N	N	N	?
34 Roybal-Allard	Y	Y	Y	N	N	N	Y
35 Waters	Y	Y	Y	N	N	N	Y
36 Harman	Y	Y	N	N	N	N	Y
37 Richardson	?	?	?	?	?	?	?
38 Napolitano	Y	Y	Y	N	N	N	Y
39 Sánchez, Linda	Y	Y	Y	?	N	N	Y
40 **Royce**	N	N	N	?	Y	Y	Y
41 **Lewis**	N	Y	N	Y	Y	Y	Y
42 **Miller, Gary**	N	Y	N	Y	Y	Y	Y
43 Baca	Y	Y	Y	?	N	N	Y
44 **Calvert**	N	Y	?	Y	Y	Y	Y
45 **Bono Mack**	N	Y	N	Y	Y	Y	Y
46 **Rohrabacher**	N	N	N	?	Y	Y	Y
47 Sanchez, Loretta	Y	Y	Y	N	N	N	Y
48 **Campbell**	?	?	?	?	?	?	?
49 **Issa**	N	Y	N	Y	Y	Y	Y
50 **Bilbray**	Y	Y	N	Y	Y	Y	Y
51 Filner	Y	Y	Y	N	N	N	Y
52 **Hunter**	N	Y	N	Y	?	Y	Y
53 Davis	Y	Y	Y	N	N	N	Y

	268	269	270	271	272	273	274
COLORADO							
1 DeGette	Y	Y	Y	N	Y	N	Y
2 Udall	?	?	?	?	?	?	?
3 Salazar	Y	Y	Y	N	?	N	Y
4 **Musgrave**	N	Y	N	Y	Y	Y	Y
5 **Lamborn**	N	Y	N	?	Y	Y	Y
6 **Tancredo**	N	N	N	Y	Y	Y	Y
7 Perlmutter	Y	Y	Y	?	N	N	Y
CONNECTICUT							
1 Larson	Y	Y	Y	N	N	N	Y
2 Courtney	Y	Y	Y	N	N	N	Y
3 DeLauro	Y	Y	Y	?	?	N	Y
4 **Shays**	N	Y	N	Y	Y	Y	Y
5 Murphy	Y	Y	Y	N	N	N	Y
DELAWARE							
AL **Castle**	N	Y	N	Y	Y	N	Y
FLORIDA							
1 **Miller**	N	Y	N	Y	Y	Y	Y
2 Boyd	Y	Y	Y	N	N	N	Y
3 Brown	Y	Y	Y	N	N	N	Y
4 **Crenshaw**	N	Y	N	Y	Y	Y	Y
5 **Brown-Waite**	N	?	N	N	N	N	Y
6 **Stearns**	N	Y	N	Y	Y	Y	Y
7 **Mica**	N	Y	N	N	N	N	Y
8 **Keller**	N	Y	N	Y	Y	Y	Y
9 **Bilirakis**	N	Y	N	Y	Y	Y	Y
10 **Young**	N	N	N	Y	?	Y	Y
11 Castor	Y	Y	Y	N	N	N	Y
12 **Putnam**	N	Y	N	Y	Y	Y	Y
13 **Buchanan**	N	Y	N	N	N	N	Y
14 **Mack**	N	Y	N	Y	Y	Y	Y
15 **Weldon**	N	Y	?	?	?	?	Y
16 Mahoney	Y	Y	Y	?	N	N	Y
17 Meek	Y	Y	Y	N	N	N	Y
18 **Ros-Lehtinen**	Y	Y	N	N	N	N	Y
19 Wexler	Y	Y	Y	N	?	N	Y
20 Wasserman Schultz	Y	Y	Y	N	N	N	Y
21 **Diaz-Balart, L.**	Y	Y	N	N	N	N	Y
22 Klein	Y	Y	Y	N	N	N	Y
23 Hastings	Y	Y	Y	N	N	N	Y
24 **Feeney**	N	Y	N	Y	Y	Y	Y
25 **Diaz-Balart, M.**	Y	Y	N	N	N	N	Y
GEORGIA							
1 **Kingston**	N	Y	N	Y	Y	N	Y
2 Bishop	Y	Y	Y	N	N	N	Y
3 **Westmoreland**	N	N	N	Y	Y	N	Y
4 Johnson	Y	Y	Y	N	N	N	Y
5 Lewis	Y	Y	Y	N	N	N	Y
6 **Price**	N	Y	N	Y	Y	Y	Y
7 **Linder**	N	Y	?	?	Y	Y	Y
8 Marshall	Y	Y	Y	N	N	N	Y
9 **Deal**	N	Y	N	Y	Y	?	?
10 **Broun**	N	N	N	Y	Y	Y	Y
11 **Gingrey**	N	N	N	Y	Y	Y	Y
12 Barrow	Y	Y	Y	N	N	N	Y
13 Scott	Y	Y	Y	?	N	N	Y
HAWAII							
1 Abercrombie	Y	N	Y	N	N	N	Y
2 Hirono	Y	Y	Y	N	N	N	Y
IDAHO							
1 **Sali**	N	Y	N	N	N	N	Y
2 **Simpson**	N	Y	N	Y	Y	Y	Y
ILLINOIS							
1 Rush	?	?	?	?	?	?	?
2 Jackson	Y	Y	Y	N	N	N	Y
3 Lipinski	Y	Y	Y	N	N	N	Y
4 Gutierrez	Y	Y	Y	N	N	N	Y
5 Emanuel	Y	Y	Y	?	N	N	Y
6 **Roskam**	N	Y	N	Y	Y	Y	Y
7 Davis	Y	Y	Y	N	N	N	Y
8 Bean	Y	P	Y	N	?	N	Y
9 Schakowsky	Y	Y	Y	N	N	N	Y
10 **Kirk**	Y	Y	Y	N	N	N	Y
11 **Weller**	N	Y	N	Y	N	N	Y
12 Costello	Y	Y	Y	N	N	N	Y
13 **Biggert**	Y	Y	N	Y	N	Y	Y
14 Foster	Y	Y	Y	N	N	N	Y
15 **Johnson**	Y	Y	Y	N	Y	Y	Y

*Rep. Steve Scalise, R-La., was sworn in May 7, 2008, to fill the seat vacated by the resignation of Bobby Jindal, who became governor. The first vote for which Scalise was eligible was 268.

ND Northern Democrats, SD Southern Democrats
Southern states: Ala., Ark., Fla., Ga., Ky., La., Miss., N.C., Okla., S.C., Tenn., Texas, Va.

	268	269	270	271	272	273	274
16 **Manzullo**	N	Y	N	N	N	N	Y
17 Hare	Y	Y	Y	N	N	N	Y
18 **LaHood**	N	Y	N	Y	Y	Y	Y
19 **Shimkus**	N	Y	N	Y	Y	Y	Y
INDIANA							
1 Visclosky	Y	Y	Y	N	N	N	Y
2 Donnelly	N	Y	Y	N	N	N	Y
3 **Souder**	N	Y	N	Y	Y	Y	Y
4 **Buyer**	N	Y	N	?	N	Y	Y
5 **Burton**	?	?	?	?	?	?	?
6 **Pence**	N	Y	N	Y	Y	Y	Y
7 Carson, A.	Y	Y	Y	N	N	N	Y
8 Ellsworth	N	Y	Y	N	N	N	Y
9 Hill	Y	Y	Y	N	N	N	Y
IOWA							
1 Braley	Y	Y	Y	–	N	N	Y
2 Loebsack	Y	Y	Y	N	N	N	Y
3 Boswell	Y	Y	Y	N	N	N	Y
4 **Latham**	Y	Y	N	N	Y	Y	Y
5 **King**	N	Y	N	Y	Y	Y	Y
KANSAS							
1 **Moran**	N	Y	N	N	N	N	Y
2 Boyda	Y	Y	Y	N	N	N	Y
3 Moore	Y	Y	Y	N	N	N	Y
4 **Tiahrt**	N	Y	N	N	N	N	Y
KENTUCKY							
1 **Whitfield**	?	Y	N	Y	Y	Y	Y
2 **Lewis**	N	Y	N	Y	Y	Y	Y
3 Yarmuth	Y	Y	Y	N	N	N	Y
4 **Davis**	N	Y	N	?	N	?	Y
5 **Rogers**	N	Y	N	Y	Y	Y	Y
6 Chandler	Y	Y	Y	N	Y	N	Y
LOUISIANA							
1 **Scalise***	N	Y	N	Y	Y	Y	Y
2 Jefferson	Y	Y	Y	N	N	N	Y
3 Melancon	Y	Y	Y	N	N	N	Y
4 **McCrery**	N	Y	N	Y	Y	Y	Y
5 **Alexander**	N	Y	N	Y	Y	Y	Y
6 Cazayoux	Y	Y	Y	N	N	N	Y
7 **Boustany**	N	Y	N	Y	Y	Y	Y
MAINE							
1 Allen	Y	Y	Y	N	N	N	Y
2 Michaud	Y	Y	Y	N	N	N	Y
MARYLAND							
1 **Gilchrest**	N	Y	N	N	?	Y	Y
2 Ruppersberger	Y	Y	Y	N	N	N	Y
3 Sarbanes	Y	Y	Y	N	N	N	Y
4 Wynn	Y	Y	Y	N	?	N	Y
5 Hoyer	Y	Y	Y	?	N	N	Y
6 **Bartlett**	N	N	N	Y	N	Y	Y
7 Cummings	Y	Y	Y	N	N	N	Y
8 Van Hollen	Y	Y	Y	N	N	N	Y
MASSACHUSETTS							
1 Olver	Y	Y	Y	N	?	N	Y
2 Neal	Y	Y	Y	N	N	N	Y
3 McGovern	Y	Y	Y	N	?	N	Y
4 Frank	Y	Y	Y	N	N	N	Y
5 Tsongas	Y	Y	Y	N	N	N	Y
6 Tierney	Y	P	Y	N	N	N	Y
7 Markey	Y	Y	Y	N	N	N	Y
8 Capuano	Y	Y	Y	N	N	N	Y
9 Lynch	Y	Y	Y	N	N	N	Y
10 Delahunt	Y	N	N	N	N	N	Y
MICHIGAN							
1 Stupak	N	Y	Y	N	N	N	Y
2 **Hoekstra**	N	Y	N	Y	Y	Y	Y
3 **Ehlers**	N	Y	N	N	N	N	Y
4 **Camp**	N	Y	N	Y	Y	Y	Y
5 Kildee	Y	Y	Y	N	N	N	Y
6 **Upton**	N	Y	N	Y	Y	Y	Y
7 **Walberg**	N	Y	N	N	N	N	Y
8 **Rogers**	N	Y	N	N	N	N	Y
9 **Knollenberg**	N	Y	N	Y	Y	Y	Y
10 **Miller**	N	Y	N	N	N	N	Y
11 **McCotter**	N	Y	N	N	N	N	Y
12 Levin	Y	Y	Y	N	N	N	Y
13 Kilpatrick	Y	Y	Y	N	N	N	Y
14 Conyers	Y	Y	Y	N	N	?	Y
15 Dingell	Y	Y	Y	N	N	N	Y
MINNESOTA							
1 Walz	Y	Y	Y	?	N	N	Y
2 **Kline**	N	Y	N	Y	Y	Y	Y
3 **Ramstad**	N	Y	N	N	N	N	Y
4 McCollum	Y	Y	Y	N	?	N	Y

	268	269	270	271	272	273	274
5 Ellison	Y	Y	Y	?	N	N	Y
6 **Bachmann**	N	Y	N	Y	N	N	Y
7 Peterson	N	Y	Y	N	N	N	Y
8 Oberstar	?	?	?	?	?	N	Y
MISSISSIPPI							
1 Vacant							
2 Thompson	Y	Y	Y	N	N	N	Y
3 **Pickering**	N	Y	N	N	Y	N	Y
4 Taylor	Y	Y	?	N	N	N	Y
MISSOURI							
1 Clay	Y	Y	Y	N	N	N	Y
2 **Akin**	N	Y	N	Y	Y	Y	Y
3 Carnahan	Y	Y	Y	?	N	N	Y
4 Skelton	Y	Y	Y	N	N	?	?
5 Cleaver	Y	Y	Y	N	N	N	Y
6 **Graves**	N	Y	N	N	N	N	Y
7 **Blunt**	N	Y	N	Y	Y	Y	Y
8 **Emerson**	N	Y	N	Y	Y	Y	Y
9 **Hulshof**	N	Y	N	N	N	N	Y
MONTANA							
AL **Rehberg**	N	Y	N	Y	Y	Y	Y
NEBRASKA							
1 **Fortenberry**	N	Y	N	N	N	–	+
2 **Terry**	N	Y	N	?	N	N	Y
3 **Smith**	N	Y	N	Y	Y	Y	Y
NEVADA							
1 Berkley	Y	Y	N	N	N	N	Y
2 **Heller**	N	Y	N	Y	Y	Y	Y
3 **Porter**	N	Y	N	N	N	N	Y
NEW HAMPSHIRE							
1 Shea-Porter	Y	Y	Y	N	N	N	Y
2 Hodes	Y	Y	Y	N	N	N	Y
NEW JERSEY							
1 Andrews	?	?	?	?	?	?	?
2 **LoBiondo**	N	Y	N	N	N	N	Y
3 **Saxton**	N	Y	N	Y	N	Y	Y
4 **Smith**	N	Y	N	N	N	N	Y
5 **Garrett**	N	Y	N	Y	N	Y	Y
6 Pallone	Y	Y	Y	N	N	N	Y
7 **Ferguson**	?	?	N	Y	Y	Y	Y
8 Pascrell	Y	Y	Y	N	?	N	Y
9 Rothman	Y	Y	Y	N	N	N	Y
10 Payne	Y	Y	Y	N	N	N	Y
11 **Frelinghuysen**	N	Y	N	N	N	N	Y
12 Holt	Y	Y	Y	N	N	N	Y
13 Sires	Y	Y	Y	N	N	N	Y
NEW MEXICO							
1 **Wilson**	N	Y	N	Y	Y	Y	Y
2 **Pearce**	N	Y	N	Y	Y	Y	Y
3 Udall	Y	Y	Y	N	N	N	Y
NEW YORK							
1 Bishop	+	+	+	–	–	–	+
2 Israel	Y	Y	Y	N	N	N	Y
3 **King**	N	Y	N	Y	Y	Y	Y
4 McCarthy	Y	Y	Y	N	?	N	Y
5 Ackerman	Y	Y	Y	N	N	N	Y
6 Meeks	Y	Y	Y	N	N	N	Y
7 Crowley	Y	Y	Y	N	N	N	Y
8 Nadler	Y	Y	Y	N	N	N	Y
9 Weiner	Y	Y	Y	N	N	N	Y
10 Towns	Y	Y	Y	N	N	N	Y
11 Clarke	Y	N	Y	N	N	N	Y
12 Velázquez	Y	Y	Y	N	N	N	Y
13 **Fossella**	?	?	?	?	?	?	?
14 Maloney	Y	Y	Y	N	N	N	Y
15 Rangel	Y	Y	Y	N	N	N	Y
16 Serrano	Y	Y	Y	N	N	N	Y
17 Engel	Y	Y	Y	N	N	N	Y
18 Lowey	Y	Y	Y	N	N	N	Y
19 Hall	Y	Y	Y	N	N	N	Y
20 Gillibrand	Y	Y	Y	N	N	N	Y
21 McNulty	Y	Y	Y	N	N	N	Y
22 Hinchey	Y	Y	Y	?	?	N	?
23 **McHugh**	N	Y	N	N	N	N	Y
24 Arcuri	Y	Y	Y	N	N	N	Y
25 **Walsh**	N	Y	N	Y	Y	Y	Y
26 **Reynolds**	N	Y	N	Y	?	?	Y
27 Higgins	Y	Y	Y	N	N	N	Y
28 Slaughter	Y	Y	?	N	?	N	Y
29 **Kuhl**	Y	Y	N	N	N	N	Y
NORTH CAROLINA							
1 Butterfield	Y	Y	Y	?	N	N	Y
2 Etheridge	Y	Y	Y	N	N	N	Y
3 **Jones**	?	N	N	Y	N	Y	Y
4 Price	Y	Y	Y	N	N	N	Y

	268	269	270	271	272	273	274
5 **Foxx**	N	Y	N	Y	Y	Y	Y
6 **Coble**	N	N	N	Y	Y	Y	Y
7 McIntyre	Y	Y	Y	N	N	N	Y
8 **Hayes**	N	Y	N	Y	Y	Y	Y
9 **Myrick**	N	Y	N	Y	Y	Y	Y
10 **McHenry**	?	?	?	?	Y	Y	Y
11 Shuler	N	Y	Y	N	N	N	Y
12 Watt	Y	Y	Y	N	N	N	Y
13 Miller	Y	Y	Y	N	N	N	Y
NORTH DAKOTA							
AL Pomeroy	Y	Y	Y	N	N	N	Y
OHIO							
1 **Chabot**	N	Y	N	Y	Y	Y	Y
2 **Schmidt**	N	Y	N	Y	Y	Y	Y
3 **Turner**	N	Y	N	Y	Y	Y	Y
4 **Jordan**	N	Y	N	N	N	N	Y
5 **Latta**	N	Y	N	Y	Y	Y	Y
6 Wilson	Y	Y	Y	N	?	N	Y
7 **Hobson**	N	Y	N	Y	Y	Y	Y
8 **Boehner**	N	Y	N	Y	Y	Y	Y
9 Kaptur	Y	Y	Y	N	N	N	Y
10 Kucinich	Y	N	N	N	N	N	Y
11 Tubbs Jones	?	Y	Y	N	N	N	Y
12 **Tiberi**	N	Y	N	Y	Y	N	Y
13 Sutton	Y	Y	Y	N	N	N	Y
14 **LaTourette**	N	Y	N	Y	Y	N	Y
15 **Pryce**	N	Y	N	Y	Y	Y	Y
16 **Regula**	N	Y	N	Y	Y	N	Y
17 Ryan	Y	Y	Y	?	N	N	Y
18 Space	Y	Y	Y	N	N	N	Y
OKLAHOMA							
1 **Sullivan**	N	?	?	Y	Y	Y	Y
2 Boren	Y	Y	Y	N	N	N	Y
3 **Lucas**	N	Y	N	Y	Y	Y	Y
4 **Cole**	N	Y	N	Y	Y	Y	Y
5 **Fallin**	N	Y	N	Y	Y	Y	Y
OREGON							
1 Wu	Y	Y	Y	N	N	N	Y
2 **Walden**	N	Y	N	Y	Y	Y	Y
3 Blumenauer	Y	Y	Y	N	N	N	Y
4 DeFazio	Y	Y	?	N	N	N	Y
5 Hooley	Y	Y	Y	N	N	N	Y
PENNSYLVANIA							
1 Brady	Y	Y	Y	N	N	N	Y
2 Fattah	Y	Y	Y	N	N	N	Y
3 **English**	N	Y	N	Y	Y	Y	Y
4 Altmire	N	Y	Y	N	N	N	Y
5 **Peterson**	?	Y	N	Y	?	?	?
6 **Gerlach**	Y	Y	N	N	Y	N	Y
7 Sestak	Y	Y	Y	N	N	N	Y
8 Murphy, P.	Y	Y	Y	?	N	N	?
9 **Shuster**	Y	Y	N	Y	Y	Y	Y
10 Carney	N	Y	Y	N	N	N	Y
11 Kanjorski	Y	Y	Y	Y	N	N	Y
12 Murtha	Y	Y	Y	N	Y	N	Y
13 Schwartz	Y	Y	Y	N	N	N	Y
14 Doyle	Y	Y	Y	N	?	N	Y
15 **Dent**	Y	Y	N	N	N	N	Y
16 **Pitts**	N	Y	N	N	Y	Y	Y
17 Holden	Y	Y	Y	N	N	N	Y
18 **Murphy, T.**	N	Y	N	N	N	N	Y
19 **Platts**	N	Y	N	N	N	N	Y
RHODE ISLAND							
1 Kennedy	Y	Y	Y	N	N	N	Y
2 Langevin	Y	Y	Y	N	N	N	Y
SOUTH CAROLINA							
1 **Brown**	N	Y	N	N	N	N	Y
2 **Wilson**	N	Y	N	Y	Y	Y	Y
3 **Barrett**	N	Y	?	Y	Y	Y	Y
4 **Inglis**	N	Y	N	Y	Y	Y	Y
5 Spratt	Y	Y	Y	N	N	N	Y
6 Clyburn	Y	Y	Y	N	N	N	Y
SOUTH DAKOTA							
AL Herseth Sandlin	Y	Y	Y	N	N	N	Y
TENNESSEE							
1 **Davis, D.**	N	Y	N	Y	Y	Y	Y
2 **Duncan**	N	N	N	Y	Y	Y	Y
3 **Wamp**	N	Y	N	Y	Y	Y	Y
4 Davis, L.	Y	Y	Y	N	N	N	Y
5 Cooper	Y	Y	Y	N	N	N	Y
6 Gordon	N	Y	Y	Y	N	N	Y
7 **Blackburn**	N	Y	N	Y	Y	Y	Y
8 Tanner	Y	Y	Y	N	N	N	Y
9 Cohen	Y	Y	Y	?	N	N	Y

	268	269	270	271	272	273	274
TEXAS							
1 **Gohmert**	P	Y	?	?	N	N	Y
2 **Poe**	N	N	N	N	N	N	Y
3 **Johnson, S.**	N	Y	N	Y	Y	Y	Y
4 **Hall**	N	Y	N	Y	Y	Y	Y
5 **Hensarling**	N	Y	N	Y	Y	Y	Y
6 **Barton**	N	?	?	Y	Y	Y	Y
7 **Culberson**	N	Y	N	N	Y	Y	Y
8 **Brady**	N	Y	N	N	Y	N	Y
9 Green, A.	Y	Y	Y	N	N	N	Y
10 **McCaul**	Y	Y	N	Y	Y	Y	Y
11 **Conaway**	?	?	?	?	?	?	?
12 **Granger**	N	Y	N	Y	Y	Y	Y
13 **Thornberry**	N	Y	N	Y	Y	Y	Y
14 **Paul**	?	?	?	?	Y	?	?
15 Hinojosa	Y	Y	Y	N	N	N	Y
16 Reyes	Y	Y	Y	N	N	N	Y
17 Edwards	Y	Y	Y	N	N	N	Y
18 Jackson Lee	Y	Y	Y	N	N	N	Y
19 **Neugebauer**	N	Y	N	Y	Y	Y	Y
20 Gonzalez	Y	Y	Y	N	N	N	Y
21 **Smith**	N	Y	N	Y	Y	Y	Y
22 Lampson	Y	Y	Y	N	N	N	Y
23 Rodriguez	Y	Y	Y	N	N	N	Y
24 **Marchant**	N	Y	N	Y	Y	Y	Y
25 Doggett	Y	Y	Y	?	?	N	Y
26 **Burgess**	N	N	N	N	N	N	Y
27 Ortiz	Y	Y	Y	N	N	N	Y
28 Cuellar	Y	Y	Y	N	N	N	Y
29 Green, G.	Y	Y	Y	N	N	N	Y
30 Johnson, E.	Y	N	Y	N	N	N	Y
31 **Carter**	N	Y	N	?	Y	Y	Y
32 **Sessions**	N	Y	N	Y	Y	Y	Y
UTAH							
1 **Bishop**	N	Y	N	Y	?	Y	Y
2 Matheson	Y	Y	Y	N	N	N	Y
3 **Cannon**	N	Y	N	Y	Y	Y	Y
VERMONT							
AL Welch	Y	Y	Y	N	N	N	Y
VIRGINIA							
1 **Wittman**	N	Y	N	Y	Y	Y	Y
2 **Drake**	N	Y	N	Y	Y	Y	Y
3 Scott	Y	Y	Y	N	N	N	Y
4 **Forbes**	N	Y	N	Y	Y	Y	Y
5 **Goode**	Y	Y	N	Y	Y	Y	Y
6 **Goodlatte**	N	Y	N	Y	Y	Y	Y
7 **Cantor**	N	Y	N	Y	Y	Y	Y
8 Moran	Y	Y	Y	N	?	N	Y
9 Boucher	Y	Y	Y	N	?	N	Y
10 **Wolf**	N	Y	N	N	N	N	Y
11 **Davis**	N	N	N	Y	Y	Y	Y
WASHINGTON							
1 Inslee	Y	Y	Y	N	N	N	Y
2 Larsen	Y	Y	Y	N	N	N	Y
3 Baird	Y	Y	Y	N	N	N	Y
4 **Hastings**	N	Y	N	Y	Y	Y	Y
5 **McMorris Rodgers**	N	Y	N	Y	Y	Y	Y
6 Dicks	Y	Y	Y	N	N	N	Y
7 McDermott	Y	Y	Y	N	N	N	Y
8 **Reichert**	N	Y	N	Y	Y	Y	Y
9 Smith	Y	Y	Y	N	N	N	Y
WEST VIRGINIA							
1 Mollohan	Y	Y	Y	N	N	N	Y
2 **Capito**	N	Y	N	Y	Y	N	Y
3 Rahall	Y	Y	Y	N	N	N	Y
WISCONSIN							
1 **Ryan**	N	Y	N	Y	Y	Y	Y
2 Baldwin	Y	Y	Y	N	N	N	Y
3 Kind	Y	Y	Y	N	N	N	Y
4 Moore	Y	Y	Y	N	N	N	Y
5 **Sensenbrenner**	N	Y	N	Y	Y	Y	Y
6 **Petri**	N	Y	N	Y	Y	Y	Y
7 Obey	Y	Y	Y	N	N	N	Y
8 Kagen	Y	Y	Y	N	N	N	Y
WYOMING							
AL **Cubin**	?	?	?	?	?	?	?
DELEGATES							
Faleomavaega (A.S.)							
Norton (D.C.)							
Bordallo (Guam)							
Fortuño (P.R.)							
Christensen (V.I.)							

IN THE HOUSE | By Vote Number

275. H Res 1113. Support for Mother's Day/Motion to Reconsider. Castor, D-Fla., motion to table (kill) the Tiahrt, R-Kan., motion to reconsider the vote on mothers and Mother's Day. Motion agreed to 237-178: R 13-178; D 224-0 (ND 167-0, SD 57-0). May 7, 2008.

276. Procedural Motion/Motion to Adjourn. Tiahrt, R-Kan., motion to adjourn. Motion rejected 146-276: R 143-50; D 3-226 (ND 1-170, SD 2-56). May 7, 2008.

277. HR 5937. Starrett City Housing/Passage. Meeks, D-N.Y., motion to suspend the rules and pass the bill that would allow any new owner of the Starrett City housing project in Brooklyn, N.Y., to request from the Department of Housing and Urban Development that two subsidy contracts be converted into a new housing assistance contract. Motion agreed to 345-73: R 119-73; D 226-0 (ND 168-0, SD 58-0). A two-thirds majority of those present and voting (279 in this case) is required for passage under suspension of the rules. May 7, 2008.

278. HR 5937. Starrett City Housing/Motion to Reconsider. Welch, D-Vt., motion to table (kill) the Simpson, R-Idaho, motion to reconsider the vote on the Starrett City housing project in Brooklyn, N.Y. Motion agreed to 225-190: R 1-188; D 224-2 (ND 168-0, SD 56-2). May 7, 2008.

279. Procedural Motion/Motion to Adjourn. Calvert, R-Calif., motion to adjourn. Motion rejected 137-260: R 132-52; D 5-208 (ND 3-154, SD 2-54). May 7, 2008.

280. Procedural Motion/Motion to Adjourn. Sessions, R-Texas, motion to adjourn. Motion rejected 138-263: R 137-52; D 1-211 (ND 0-158, SD 1-53). May 7, 2008.

281. HR 3221. Mortgage Relief/Previous Question. Welch, D-Vt., motion to order the previous question (thus ending debate and possibility of amendment) on adoption of the rule (H Res 1175) that would provide for House floor consideration of Senate amendments to the bill, with three amendments. Motion agreed to 226-198: R 1-195; D 225-3 (ND 169-1, SD 56-2). May 7, 2008.

	275	276	277	278	279	280	281
ALABAMA							
1 Bonner	N	Y	Y	N	Y	Y	N
2 Everett	N	Y	N	N	Y	Y	N
3 Rogers	N	Y	Y	N	Y	Y	N
4 Aderholt	N	Y	N	N	Y	Y	N
5 Cramer	Y	N	Y	Y	N	N	Y
6 Bachus	N	?	Y	?	?	Y	N
7 Davis	Y	N	Y	N	N	N	Y
ALASKA							
AL Young	N	Y	N	N	Y	Y	N
ARIZONA							
1 Renzi	N	N	Y	N	Y	Y	N
2 Franks	N	Y	N	N	Y	Y	N
3 Shadegg	N	Y	N	N	Y	Y	N
4 Pastor	Y	Y	Y	Y	N	N	Y
5 Mitchell	Y	N	Y	Y	N	N	Y
6 Flake	N	Y	N	N	Y	Y	N
7 Grijalva	Y	N	Y	Y	N	N	Y
8 Giffords	Y	N	Y	Y	N	N	Y
ARKANSAS							
1 Berry	Y	N	Y	Y	N	N	Y
2 Snyder	Y	N	Y	Y	N	N	Y
3 Boozman	N	Y	Y	N	Y	Y	N
4 Ross	Y	N	Y	Y	N	N	Y
CALIFORNIA							
1 Thompson	Y	N	Y	Y	N	N	Y
2 Herger	N	Y	Y	N	Y	Y	N
3 Lungren	N	Y	N	N	Y	Y	N
4 Doolittle	N	Y	Y	N	Y	Y	N
5 Matsui	Y	N	Y	Y	N	N	Y
6 Woolsey	Y	N	Y	Y	N	N	Y
7 Miller, George	Y	N	Y	Y	Y	?	Y
8 Pelosi							
9 Lee	Y	N	Y	Y	N	N	Y
10 Tauscher	Y	N	Y	?	N	N	Y
11 McNerney	Y	N	Y	Y	N	N	Y
12 Speier	?	?	?	?	?	?	?
13 Stark	Y	N	Y	Y	N	N	Y
14 Eshoo	Y	N	Y	Y	N	N	Y
15 Honda	Y	N	Y	Y	N	N	Y
16 Lofgren	Y	N	Y	Y	N	N	Y
17 Farr	?	N	Y	Y	?	N	Y
18 Cardoza	Y	N	Y	Y	N	N	Y
19 Radanovich	N	Y	N	N	Y	Y	N
20 Costa	Y	N	Y	Y	N	N	Y
21 Nunes	N	Y	N	N	Y	Y	N
22 McCarthy	N	Y	Y	N	N	N	N
23 Capps	Y	N	Y	Y	N	N	Y
24 Gallegly	N	Y	Y	N	Y	Y	N
25 McKeon	N	Y	N	N	Y	Y	N
26 Dreier	N	Y	N	N	Y	Y	N
27 Sherman	Y	N	Y	Y	N	N	Y
28 Berman	Y	N	Y	Y	N	N	Y
29 Schiff	Y	N	Y	Y	N	N	Y
30 Waxman	Y	N	Y	Y	?	N	Y
31 Becerra	Y	N	Y	Y	N	N	Y
32 Solis	Y	N	Y	Y	N	N	Y
33 Watson	Y	N	Y	Y	N	?	Y
34 Roybal-Allard	Y	N	Y	Y	N	N	Y
35 Waters	Y	N	Y	Y	N	N	Y
36 Harman	Y	N	Y	Y	N	N	Y
37 Richardson	?	?	?	?	?	?	?
38 Napolitano	Y	N	Y	Y	N	N	Y
39 Sánchez, Linda	Y	N	Y	Y	N	N	Y
40 Royce	N	Y	N	N	Y	Y	N
41 Lewis	N	Y	Y	N	Y	Y	N
42 Miller, Gary	N	Y	Y	N	Y	Y	N
43 Baca	Y	N	Y	Y	N	N	Y
44 Calvert	N	Y	N	N	Y	Y	N
45 Bono Mack	N	Y	Y	N	Y	Y	N
46 Rohrabacher	N	Y	N	N	Y	Y	N
47 Sanchez, Loretta	Y	N	Y	Y	N	N	Y
48 Campbell	?	?	?	?	?	?	?
49 Issa	N	Y	N	N	Y	Y	N
50 Bilbray	N	Y	Y	N	Y	Y	N
51 Filner	Y	N	Y	Y	N	N	Y
52 Hunter	N	Y	Y	N	Y	?	N
53 Davis	Y	N	Y	Y	N	N	Y

	275	276	277	278	279	280	281
COLORADO							
1 DeGette	Y	N	Y	Y	N	?	Y
2 Udall	?	?	?	?	?	N	Y
3 Salazar	Y	N	Y	Y	N	N	Y
4 Musgrave	N	Y	N	N	Y	Y	N
5 Lamborn	N	Y	Y	N	Y	Y	N
6 Tancredo	N	Y	N	N	?	Y	N
7 Perlmutter	Y	N	Y	Y	N	N	Y
CONNECTICUT							
1 Larson	Y	N	Y	Y	N	N	Y
2 Courtney	Y	N	Y	Y	N	N	Y
3 DeLauro	Y	N	Y	Y	N	N	Y
4 Shays	N	Y	N	Y	Y	Y	N
5 Murphy	Y	N	Y	Y	N	N	Y
DELAWARE							
AL Castle	N	N	Y	N	N	N	N
FLORIDA							
1 Miller	N	Y	N	N	Y	Y	N
2 Boyd	Y	Y	Y	Y	Y	Y	Y
3 Brown	Y	N	Y	Y	N	N	Y
4 Crenshaw	N	Y	N	Y	Y	N	N
5 Brown-Waite	N	Y	N	?	N	N	N
6 Stearns	N	N	N	?	N	N	N
7 Mica	N	N	Y	N	N	N	N
8 Keller	N	Y	N	Y	Y	N	N
9 Bilirakis	N	Y	N	Y	Y	N	N
10 Young	N	Y	Y	N	Y	Y	N
11 Castor	Y	N	Y	Y	N	N	Y
12 Putnam	?	N	Y	N	Y	Y	N
13 Buchanan	N	N	N	N	N	N	N
14 Mack	N	Y	N	N	N	N	N
15 Weldon	N	Y	N	Y	Y	N	N
16 Mahoney	Y	N	Y	Y	N	N	Y
17 Meek	Y	N	Y	Y	N	N	Y
18 Ros-Lehtinen	N	N	Y	N	N	N	N
19 Wexler	Y	N	Y	Y	N	N	Y
20 Wasserman Schultz	Y	N	Y	Y	N	N	Y
21 Diaz-Balart, L.	N	N	Y	N	N	N	N
22 Klein	Y	N	Y	Y	N	N	Y
23 Hastings	Y	N	Y	Y	N	N	Y
24 Feeney	N	N	N	N	?	N	N
25 Diaz-Balart, M.	N	N	N	N	N	N	N
GEORGIA							
1 Kingston	N	N	N	N	N	N	N
2 Bishop	Y	N	Y	Y	N	N	Y
3 Westmoreland	N	Y	N	N	Y	Y	N
4 Johnson	Y	N	Y	Y	N	N	Y
5 Lewis	Y	N	Y	Y	N	N	Y
6 Price	N	Y	N	N	Y	Y	N
7 Linder	N	Y	?	?	?	Y	N
8 Marshall	Y	N	Y	Y	N	N	Y
9 Deal	?	Y	N	N	Y	Y	N
10 Broun	N	N	N	Y	Y	N	N
11 Gingrey	N	Y	N	N	Y	Y	N
12 Barrow	Y	N	Y	Y	N	N	Y
13 Scott	Y	N	Y	Y	N	N	Y
HAWAII							
1 Abercrombie	?	N	Y	Y	N	N	Y
2 Hirono	Y	N	Y	Y	N	N	Y
IDAHO							
1 Sali	N	N	Y	N	N	N	N
2 Simpson	N	Y	Y	N	Y	Y	N
ILLINOIS							
1 Rush	?	?	?	?	?	?	?
2 Jackson	Y	N	Y	Y	N	N	Y
3 Lipinski	Y	N	Y	Y	N	N	Y
4 Gutierrez	Y	N	Y	Y	N	?	Y
5 Emanuel	Y	N	Y	Y	N	N	Y
6 Roskam	Y	Y	N	N	N	N	N
7 Davis	Y	N	Y	Y	?	?	Y
8 Bean	Y	N	Y	Y	N	N	Y
9 Schakowsky	Y	N	Y	Y	N	N	Y
10 Kirk	N	N	N	N	?	N	N
11 Weller	N	?	Y	N	N	N	N
12 Costello	Y	N	Y	Y	N	N	Y
13 Biggert	N	Y	N	N	Y	Y	N
14 Foster	N	N	Y	N	N	N	Y
15 Johnson	Y	Y	Y	N	Y	N	N

ND Northern Democrats, SD Southern Democrats
Southern states: Ala., Ark., Fla., Ga., Ky., La., Miss., N.C., Okla., S.C., Tenn., Texas, Va.

	275	276	277	278	279	280	281
16 **Manzullo**	Y	N	Y	N	N	Y	N
17 Hare	Y	N	Y	Y	N	N	Y
18 **LaHood**	N	Y	Y	N	Y	Y	N
19 **Shimkus**	Y	Y	N	N	Y	Y	N
INDIANA							
1 Visclosky	Y	N	Y	Y	N	N	Y
2 Donnelly	Y	N	Y	Y	N	N	Y
3 **Souder**	N	Y	Y	N	Y	Y	N
4 **Buyer**	N	N	Y	N	N	Y	N
5 **Burton**	?	Y	Y	N	Y	Y	N
6 **Pence**	N	Y	Y	N	Y	Y	N
7 Carson, A.	Y	N	Y	Y	N	N	Y
8 Ellsworth	Y	N	Y	Y	N	N	Y
9 Hill	Y	N	Y	Y	N	N	N
IOWA							
1 Braley	Y	N	Y	Y	N	N	Y
2 Loebsack	Y	N	Y	Y	N	N	Y
3 Boswell	Y	N	Y	Y	N	N	Y
4 **Latham**	N	Y	Y	N	Y	Y	N
5 **King**	N	N	N	N	N	Y	N
KANSAS							
1 **Moran**	N	N	N	N	N	N	N
2 Boyda	Y	N	Y	Y	N	N	Y
3 Moore	Y	N	Y	Y	N	N	Y
4 **Tiahrt**	N	Y	Y	N	N	N	N
KENTUCKY							
1 **Whitfield**	N	Y	Y	N	Y	Y	N
2 **Lewis**	N	Y	N	N	Y	Y	N
3 Yarmuth	?	N	Y	Y	N	?	Y
4 **Davis**	N	N	N	N	N	N	N
5 **Rogers**	N	Y	Y	N	Y	Y	N
6 Chandler	Y	N	Y	Y	N	N	Y
LOUISIANA							
1 **Scalise**	N	Y	N	N	Y	Y	N
2 Jefferson	Y	N	Y	Y	N	N	Y
3 Melancon	Y	N	Y	Y	N	N	Y
4 **McCrery**	N	Y	Y	N	Y	Y	N
5 **Alexander**	N	Y	Y	N	Y	Y	N
6 Cazayoux	Y	N	Y	Y	N	N	Y
7 **Boustany**	N	Y	Y	N	Y	Y	N
MAINE							
1 Allen	Y	N	Y	Y	N	N	Y
2 Michaud	Y	N	Y	Y	N	N	Y
MARYLAND							
1 **Gilchrest**	N	Y	Y	N	Y	?	N
2 Ruppersberger	Y	N	Y	Y	N	N	Y
3 Sarbanes	Y	N	Y	Y	N	N	Y
4 Wynn	Y	N	Y	Y	?	?	Y
5 Hoyer	Y	N	Y	Y	?	N	Y
6 **Bartlett**	N	Y	N	N	Y	Y	N
7 Cummings	Y	N	Y	Y	?	N	Y
8 Van Hollen	?	N	Y	Y	N	N	Y
MASSACHUSETTS							
1 Olver	Y	N	Y	Y	N	N	Y
2 Neal	Y	N	Y	Y	?	N	Y
3 McGovern	Y	N	Y	Y	N	N	Y
4 Frank	Y	N	Y	Y	N	N	Y
5 Tsongas	Y	N	Y	Y	N	N	Y
6 Tierney	Y	N	Y	Y	N	N	Y
7 Markey	Y	N	Y	Y	N	N	Y
8 Capuano	Y	N	Y	Y	N	N	Y
9 Lynch	Y	N	Y	Y	N	N	Y
10 Delahunt	Y	N	Y	Y	N	N	Y
MICHIGAN							
1 Stupak	Y	N	Y	Y	N	N	Y
2 **Hoekstra**	N	Y	N	N	Y	Y	N
3 **Ehlers**	N	N	N	N	N	N	N
4 **Camp**	N	Y	Y	N	Y	Y	N
5 Kildee	Y	N	Y	Y	N	N	Y
6 **Upton**	N	Y	Y	N	Y	Y	N
7 **Walberg**	N	N	N	N	N	N	N
8 **Rogers**	N	N	Y	N	N	N	N
9 **Knollenberg**	N	Y	Y	N	Y	Y	N
10 **Miller**	N	N	Y	N	N	N	N
11 **McCotter**	N	N	Y	N	N	N	N
12 Levin	Y	N	Y	Y	N	N	Y
13 Kilpatrick	Y	N	Y	Y	N	N	Y
14 Conyers	Y	N	Y	Y	N	N	Y
15 Dingell	Y	N	Y	Y	N	N	Y
MINNESOTA							
1 Walz	Y	N	Y	Y	N	N	Y
2 **Kline**	N	Y	Y	N	N	N	N
3 **Ramstad**	Y	N	Y	N	N	N	N
4 McCollum	Y	N	Y	Y	N	?	Y

	275	276	277	278	279	280	281
5 Ellison	Y	N	Y	Y	N	N	Y
6 **Bachmann**	N	N	Y	N	N	N	N
7 Peterson	Y	N	?	?	?	N	Y
8 Oberstar	Y	N	Y	Y	N	N	Y
MISSISSIPPI							
1 Vacant							
2 Thompson	Y	N	Y	Y	N	N	Y
3 **Pickering**	N	Y	Y	N	Y	Y	N
4 Taylor	Y	N	Y	Y	N	N	Y
MISSOURI							
1 Clay	Y	N	Y	Y	N	N	Y
2 **Akin**	N	Y	N	N	Y	Y	N
3 Carnahan	Y	N	Y	Y	N	N	Y
4 Skelton	Y	N	Y	Y	N	N	Y
5 Cleaver	Y	N	Y	Y	N	N	Y
6 **Graves**	N	N	Y	N	N	N	N
7 **Blunt**	N	Y	N	N	Y	Y	N
8 **Emerson**	N	Y	Y	N	Y	Y	N
9 **Hulshof**	N	N	Y	N	N	N	N
MONTANA							
AL **Rehberg**	N	Y	Y	N	Y	Y	N
NEBRASKA							
1 **Fortenberry**	N	N	Y	N	N	N	N
2 **Terry**	N	N	?	?	N	N	N
3 **Smith**	N	Y	Y	N	Y	Y	N
NEVADA							
1 Berkley	Y	N	Y	Y	N	N	Y
2 **Heller**	Y	N	Y	N	N	N	N
3 **Porter**	N	N	Y	N	N	N	N
NEW HAMPSHIRE							
1 Shea-Porter	Y	N	Y	Y	N	N	Y
2 Hodes	Y	N	Y	Y	N	N	Y
NEW JERSEY							
1 Andrews	?	N	Y	Y	N	?	Y
2 **LoBiondo**	N	N	Y	N	N	N	N
3 **Saxton**	N	Y	Y	N	Y	Y	?
4 **Smith**	N	N	Y	N	N	?	N
5 **Garrett**	N	Y	N	N	Y	Y	N
6 Pallone	Y	N	Y	Y	N	N	Y
7 **Ferguson**	N	Y	Y	N	Y	?	N
8 Pascrell	Y	N	Y	Y	N	N	Y
9 Rothman	Y	N	Y	Y	Y	N	Y
10 Payne	Y	N	Y	Y	N	N	Y
11 **Frelinghuysen**	N	Y	Y	N	Y	N	N
12 Holt	Y	N	Y	Y	N	N	Y
13 Sires	Y	N	Y	Y	N	N	Y
NEW MEXICO							
1 **Wilson**	N	Y	Y	N	Y	Y	N
2 **Pearce**	N	Y	Y	N	Y	Y	N
3 Udall	Y	N	Y	Y	N	?	Y
NEW YORK							
1 Bishop	+	–	+	+	–	–	+
2 Israel	Y	N	Y	Y	N	N	Y
3 **King**	N	Y	Y	N	Y	Y	N
4 McCarthy	Y	N	Y	Y	N	N	Y
5 Ackerman	Y	N	Y	Y	N	N	Y
6 Meeks	Y	N	Y	Y	N	N	Y
7 Crowley	Y	N	Y	Y	N	N	Y
8 Nadler	Y	N	Y	Y	N	N	Y
9 Weiner	Y	N	Y	Y	N	N	Y
10 Towns	Y	N	Y	Y	N	N	Y
11 Clarke	Y	N	Y	Y	N	?	Y
12 Velázquez	Y	N	Y	Y	N	N	Y
13 **Fossella**	?	?	?	?	?	N	N
14 Maloney	Y	N	Y	Y	N	N	Y
15 Rangel	Y	N	Y	?	?	N	Y
16 Serrano	Y	N	Y	Y	N	N	Y
17 Engel	Y	N	Y	Y	N	N	Y
18 Lowey	Y	N	Y	Y	N	N	Y
19 Hall	Y	N	Y	Y	N	N	Y
20 Gillibrand	Y	N	Y	Y	N	N	Y
21 McNulty	Y	N	Y	Y	N	N	Y
22 Hinchey	Y	N	Y	Y	N	?	Y
23 **McHugh**	N	N	Y	N	N	N	N
24 Arcuri	Y	N	Y	Y	N	N	Y
25 **Walsh**	N	Y	Y	N	?	Y	N
26 **Reynolds**	N	Y	Y	N	Y	?	N
27 Higgins	Y	N	Y	Y	N	N	Y
28 Slaughter	Y	N	Y	Y	?	N	Y
29 **Kuhl**	N	N	Y	?	N	N	N
NORTH CAROLINA							
1 Butterfield	Y	N	Y	Y	N	N	Y
2 Etheridge	Y	N	Y	Y	N	N	Y
3 **Jones**	N	N	N	N	Y	N	N
4 Price	Y	N	Y	Y	N	N	Y

	275	276	277	278	279	280	281
5 **Foxx**	N	Y	N	N	N	N	N
6 **Coble**	N	Y	N	N	Y	Y	N
7 McIntyre	Y	N	Y	Y	N	N	Y
8 **Hayes**	N	Y	Y	N	Y	Y	N
9 **Myrick**	N	Y	N	N	Y	Y	N
10 **McHenry**	Y	Y	Y	N	Y	Y	N
11 Shuler	Y	N	Y	Y	N	N	Y
12 Watt	Y	N	Y	Y	N	N	Y
13 Miller	Y	N	Y	Y	Y	?	Y
NORTH DAKOTA							
AL Pomeroy	Y	N	Y	Y	N	N	Y
OHIO							
1 **Chabot**	N	Y	N	N	Y	Y	N
2 **Schmidt**	N	Y	N	N	Y	Y	N
3 **Turner**	N	N	Y	N	N	N	N
4 **Jordan**	Y	N	N	N	N	N	N
5 **Latta**	Y	Y	Y	N	Y	Y	N
6 Wilson	Y	N	Y	Y	N	N	Y
7 **Hobson**	N	Y	Y	N	Y	Y	N
8 **Boehner**	N	Y	Y	N	Y	Y	N
9 Kaptur	Y	N	?	Y	?	?	Y
10 Kucinich	Y	N	Y	Y	N	N	Y
11 Tubbs Jones	Y	N	Y	Y	N	?	?
12 **Tiberi**	N	Y	Y	N	Y	Y	N
13 Sutton	Y	N	Y	Y	N	N	Y
14 **LaTourette**	N	N	Y	N	Y	Y	N
15 **Pryce**	N	Y	Y	N	Y	Y	N
16 **Regula**	N	Y	N	N	Y	Y	N
17 Ryan	Y	N	Y	Y	N	N	Y
18 Space	Y	N	Y	Y	N	N	Y
OKLAHOMA							
1 **Sullivan**	N	Y	N	N	Y	Y	N
2 Boren	Y	N	Y	Y	N	N	Y
3 **Lucas**	N	Y	Y	N	Y	Y	N
4 **Cole**	N	Y	Y	N	Y	Y	N
5 **Fallin**	N	Y	Y	N	Y	Y	N
OREGON							
1 Wu	Y	N	Y	Y	N	N	Y
2 **Walden**	N	Y	Y	N	Y	Y	N
3 Blumenauer	Y	N	Y	Y	N	N	Y
4 DeFazio	Y	N	Y	Y	N	N	Y
5 Hooley	Y	N	Y	Y	N	N	Y
PENNSYLVANIA							
1 Brady	Y	N	Y	Y	N	N	Y
2 Fattah	Y	N	Y	Y	N	N	Y
3 **English**	N	Y	Y	N	Y	Y	N
4 Altmire	Y	N	Y	Y	N	N	Y
5 **Peterson**	N	Y	Y	N	N	?	N
6 **Gerlach**	N	N	Y	N	N	N	N
7 Sestak	Y	N	Y	Y	?	N	Y
8 Murphy, P.	Y	N	Y	Y	N	N	Y
9 **Shuster**	N	Y	N	N	Y	Y	N
10 Carney	Y	N	Y	Y	N	N	Y
11 Kanjorski	Y	N	Y	Y	N	N	Y
12 Murtha	Y	N	Y	Y	?	N	Y
13 Schwartz	Y	N	Y	Y	N	N	Y
14 Doyle	Y	N	Y	Y	N	?	Y
15 **Dent**	N	N	Y	N	N	N	N
16 **Pitts**	N	Y	Y	N	Y	Y	N
17 Holden	Y	N	Y	Y	N	N	Y
18 **Murphy, T.**	N	N	Y	N	N	N	N
19 **Platts**	N	N	Y	N	N	N	N
RHODE ISLAND							
1 Kennedy	Y	N	Y	Y	N	N	Y
2 Langevin	Y	N	Y	Y	N	N	Y
SOUTH CAROLINA							
1 **Brown**	Y	N	N	N	N	N	N
2 **Wilson**	N	Y	N	N	?	Y	N
3 **Barrett**	N	Y	Y	N	Y	Y	N
4 **Inglis**	N	Y	N	N	Y	Y	N
5 Spratt	Y	N	Y	Y	N	?	Y
6 Clyburn	Y	N	Y	Y	N	N	Y
SOUTH DAKOTA							
AL Herseth Sandlin	Y	N	Y	Y	N	N	Y
TENNESSEE							
1 **Davis, D.**	Y	Y	N	N	Y	Y	N
2 **Duncan**	N	Y	N	N	Y	Y	N
3 **Wamp**	N	Y	N	N	Y	Y	N
4 Davis, L.	Y	N	Y	Y	N	N	Y
5 Cooper	Y	N	Y	Y	?	N	Y
6 Gordon	Y	Y	Y	Y	?	N	Y
7 **Blackburn**	N	Y	N	N	Y	Y	N
8 Tanner	Y	N	Y	Y	N	N	Y
9 Cohen	Y	N	Y	Y	N	N	Y

	275	276	277	278	279	280	281
TEXAS							
1 **Gohmert**	N	N	N	N	N	?	N
2 **Poe**	N	N	N	N	N	N	N
3 **Johnson, S.**	N	Y	Y	N	Y	Y	N
4 **Hall**	N	Y	Y	N	Y	Y	N
5 **Hensarling**	N	Y	Y	N	Y	Y	N
6 **Barton**	N	Y	Y	N	Y	Y	N
7 **Culberson**	N	Y	Y	N	Y	Y	N
8 **Brady**	N	N	Y	N	N	N	N
9 Green, A.	Y	N	Y	Y	N	N	Y
10 **McCaul**	N	Y	Y	N	Y	N	N
11 **Conaway**	?	?	?	?	?	?	?
12 **Granger**	N	Y	N	?	?	Y	N
13 **Thornberry**	N	Y	N	N	Y	Y	N
14 **Paul**	?	?	?	?	?	Y	N
15 Hinojosa	Y	N	Y	Y	N	–	Y
16 Reyes	Y	N	Y	Y	N	N	Y
17 Edwards	Y	N	Y	Y	N	N	Y
18 Jackson Lee	Y	N	Y	Y	N	N	Y
19 **Neugebauer**	N	Y	N	N	Y	Y	N
20 Gonzalez	Y	N	Y	Y	N	N	Y
21 **Smith**	N	Y	Y	N	Y	Y	N
22 Lampson	Y	N	Y	Y	N	N	N
23 Rodriguez	Y	N	Y	Y	N	N	Y
24 **Marchant**	N	Y	N	N	Y	Y	N
25 Doggett	Y	N	Y	N	N	N	Y
26 **Burgess**	N	N	N	N	N	N	N
27 Ortiz	Y	N	Y	Y	N	N	Y
28 Cuellar	Y	N	Y	Y	N	N	Y
29 Green, G.	Y	N	Y	Y	N	N	Y
30 Johnson, E.	Y	N	Y	Y	N	N	Y
31 **Carter**	N	Y	N	N	Y	Y	Y
32 **Sessions**	N	Y	N	N	Y	Y	N
UTAH							
1 **Bishop**	N	Y	Y	N	Y	?	N
2 Matheson	Y	N	?	Y	N	N	Y
3 **Cannon**	N	Y	N	N	?	Y	N
VERMONT							
AL Welch	Y	N	Y	Y	N	N	Y
VIRGINIA							
1 **Wittman**	N	N	Y	N	N	Y	N
2 **Drake**	N	Y	?	N	Y	Y	N
3 Scott	Y	N	Y	Y	N	N	Y
4 **Forbes**	N	Y	N	N	Y	Y	N
5 **Goode**	N	Y	N	Y	Y	Y	N
6 **Goodlatte**	N	Y	Y	N	Y	Y	N
7 **Cantor**	N	Y	N	N	Y	Y	N
8 Moran	Y	N	Y	N	N	N	Y
9 Boucher	Y	N	Y	Y	N	N	Y
10 **Wolf**	N	N	Y	N	N	N	N
11 **Davis**	N	Y	Y	N	Y	Y	N
WASHINGTON							
1 Inslee	Y	N	Y	Y	N	N	Y
2 Larsen	Y	N	Y	Y	?	N	Y
3 Baird	Y	N	Y	Y	N	N	Y
4 **Hastings**	N	Y	Y	N	Y	Y	N
5 **McMorris Rodgers**	N	Y	Y	N	?	Y	N
6 Dicks	Y	N	Y	Y	N	N	Y
7 McDermott	Y	N	Y	Y	N	N	Y
8 **Reichert**	N	Y	Y	N	Y	Y	N
9 Smith	Y	N	Y	Y	N	N	Y
WEST VIRGINIA							
1 Mollohan	Y	N	Y	Y	N	N	Y
2 **Capito**	N	Y	Y	N	Y	Y	N
3 Rahall	Y	N	Y	Y	N	N	Y
WISCONSIN							
1 **Ryan**	N	Y	Y	N	Y	Y	N
2 Baldwin	Y	N	Y	Y	N	N	Y
3 Kind	Y	N	Y	Y	N	N	Y
4 Moore	Y	N	Y	Y	N	N	Y
5 **Sensenbrenner**	Y	Y	N	N	Y	Y	N
6 **Petri**	Y	Y	N	N	Y	Y	N
7 Obey	Y	N	Y	Y	N	N	Y
8 Kagen	Y	N	Y	Y	N	N	Y
WYOMING							
AL **Cubin**	?	Y	Y	N	Y	Y	N
DELEGATES							
Faleomavaega (A.S.)							
Norton (D.C.)							
Bordallo (Guam)							
Fortuño (P.R.)							
Christensen (V.I.)							

IN THE HOUSE | By Vote Number

282. **HR 3221. Mortgage Relief/Motion to Reconsider.** Welch, D-Vt., motion to table (kill) the Carter, R-Texas, motion to reconsider the vote to order the previous question (thus ending debate and possibility of amendment) on adoption of the rule (H Res 1175) that would provide for House floor consideration of Senate amendments to the bill, with three amendments. Motion agreed to 225-192: R 1-192; D 224-0 (ND 168-0, SD 56-0). May 7, 2008.

283. **HR 3221. Mortgage Relief/Rule.** Adoption of the rule (H Res 1175) that would provide for House floor consideration of the Senate amendments to the bill that would provide tax breaks for home-builders and those buying foreclosed homes, expand Federal Housing Administration mortgage insurance programs, and include other provisions to alleviate the housing crisis. The rule would provide for a motion to concur with the Senate amendments, with three amendments that would incorporate provisions from several housing-related bills and clarify that no provision could be construed to pre-empt state laws dealing with residential foreclosures. Adopted 224-198: R 1-196; D 223-2 (ND 166-1, SD 57-1). May 7, 2008.

284. **HR 3221. Mortgage Relief/Motion to Reconsider.** Welch, D-Vt., motion to table (kill) the Aderholt, R-Ala., motion to reconsider the vote on adoption of the rule (H Res 1175) that would provide for House floor consideration of Senate amendments to the bill, with three amendments. Motion agreed to 227-196: R 0-196; D 227-0 (ND 170-0, SD 57-0). May 7, 2008.

285. **Procedural Motion/Motion to Adjourn.** Price, R-Ga., motion to adjourn. Motion rejected 111-311: R 108-87; D 3-224 (ND 0-169, SD 3-55). May 7, 2008.

286. **Procedural Motion/Motion to Adjourn.** Kingston, R-Ga., motion to adjourn. Motion rejected 143-272: R 140-49; D 3-223 (ND 1-168, SD 2-55). May 7, 2008.

287. **HR 5818. Foreclosed Property Grants and Loans/Previous Question.** Castor, D-Fla., motion to order the previous question (thus ending debate and possibility of amendment) on adoption of the rule (H Res 1174) that would provide for House floor consideration of the bill that would establish a loan and grant program, administered by the Department of Housing and Urban Development, for states and localities to buy and rehabilitate foreclosed properties. Motion agreed to 220-187: R 1-186; D 219-1 (ND 163-1, SD 56-0). May 7, 2008.

	282	283	284	285	286	287
ALABAMA						
1 **Bonner**	N	N	N	Y	Y	N
2 **Everett**	N	N	N	Y	Y	N
3 **Rogers**	N	N	N	Y	Y	N
4 **Aderholt**	N	Y	N	N	Y	N
5 **Cramer**	Y	Y	Y	N	N	Y
6 **Bachus**	N	N	N	Y	N	N
7 **Davis**	Y	Y	Y	N	N	Y
ALASKA						
AL **Young**	N	N	N	Y	Y	N
ARIZONA						
1 **Renzi**	?	N	N	Y	N	?
2 **Franks**	N	N	N	N	Y	N
3 **Shadegg**	N	N	N	N	Y	N
4 **Pastor**	Y	Y	Y	N	N	Y
5 **Mitchell**	Y	Y	Y	N	N	Y
6 **Flake**	N	N	N	Y	Y	N
7 **Grijalva**	Y	Y	Y	N	N	Y
8 **Giffords**	Y	Y	Y	N	N	Y
ARKANSAS						
1 **Berry**	Y	Y	Y	N	?	?
2 **Snyder**	Y	Y	Y	N	N	Y
3 **Boozman**	N	N	N	Y	Y	N
4 **Ross**	Y	Y	Y	N	N	Y
CALIFORNIA						
1 Thompson	Y	Y	Y	N	N	Y
2 **Herger**	N	N	N	Y	Y	N
3 **Lungren**	N	N	N	Y	Y	N
4 **Doolittle**	N	N	N	Y	Y	N
5 Matsui	Y	Y	Y	N	N	Y
6 Woolsey	Y	Y	Y	N	N	Y
7 Miller, George	Y	Y	Y	N	N	Y
8 Pelosi						
9 Lee	Y	Y	Y	N	N	Y
10 Tauscher	Y	Y	Y	N	N	Y
11 McNerney	Y	Y	Y	N	N	Y
12 Speier	?	?	?	?	?	?
13 Stark	Y	?	Y	N	N	Y
14 Eshoo	Y	Y	Y	N	N	Y
15 Honda	Y	Y	Y	N	N	Y
16 Lofgren	Y	Y	Y	N	N	Y
17 Farr	Y	Y	Y	N	N	Y
18 Cardoza	Y	Y	Y	N	N	Y
19 **Radanovich**	N	N	N	Y	Y	N
20 Costa	Y	Y	Y	N	N	Y
21 **Nunes**	N	N	N	Y	Y	N
22 **McCarthy**	N	N	N	Y	Y	N
23 Capps	Y	Y	Y	N	N	Y
24 **Gallegly**	N	N	N	Y	Y	N
25 **McKeon**	N	N	N	Y	Y	N
26 **Dreier**	N	N	N	Y	Y	N
27 Sherman	Y	Y	Y	N	N	Y
28 Berman	Y	Y	Y	N	N	Y
29 Schiff	Y	Y	Y	N	N	Y
30 Waxman	Y	Y	Y	N	N	Y
31 Becerra	Y	Y	Y	N	N	Y
32 Solis	Y	Y	Y	N	N	Y
33 Watson	Y	Y	Y	N	N	Y
34 Roybal-Allard	Y	Y	Y	N	N	Y
35 Waters	Y	Y	Y	N	N	Y
36 Harman	?	?	Y	N	N	Y
37 Richardson	?	?	?	?	?	?
38 Napolitano	Y	Y	Y	N	N	Y
39 Sánchez, Linda	Y	?	Y	N	N	Y
40 **Royce**	N	N	N	Y	Y	N
41 **Lewis**	N	N	N	Y	Y	N
42 **Miller, Gary**	N	N	N	Y	Y	N
43 Baca	Y	Y	Y	N	N	Y
44 **Calvert**	N	N	N	Y	Y	N
45 **Bono Mack**	N	N	N	Y	Y	N
46 **Rohrabacher**	N	N	N	Y	Y	N
47 Sanchez, Loretta	Y	Y	Y	N	N	Y
48 **Campbell**	?	?	?	?	?	?
49 **Issa**	N	N	N	Y	Y	N
50 **Bilbray**	N	N	N	Y	Y	N
51 Filner	Y	Y	Y	N	N	Y
52 **Hunter**	N	N	N	Y	?	?
53 Davis	Y	Y	Y	N	N	Y

	282	283	284	285	286	287
COLORADO						
1 DeGette	Y	Y	Y	N	N	Y
2 Udall	Y	Y	Y	N	N	Y
3 Salazar	Y	Y	Y	N	N	Y
4 **Musgrave**	N	N	N	N	Y	N
5 **Lamborn**	N	N	N	Y	Y	N
6 **Tancredo**	N	N	N	N	Y	N
7 Perlmutter	Y	Y	Y	N	N	Y
CONNECTICUT						
1 Larson	Y	Y	Y	N	N	Y
2 Courtney	Y	Y	Y	N	N	Y
3 DeLauro	Y	Y	Y	N	N	Y
4 **Shays**	N	N	N	Y	Y	N
5 Murphy	Y	Y	Y	N	N	Y
DELAWARE						
AL **Castle**	N	N	N	N	N	N
FLORIDA						
1 **Miller**	N	N	N	Y	Y	N
2 Boyd	Y	Y	Y	Y	Y	Y
3 Brown	Y	Y	Y	N	N	Y
4 **Crenshaw**	N	N	N	Y	Y	N
5 **Brown-Waite**	N	N	N	Y	Y	N
6 **Stearns**	N	N	N	Y	Y	N
7 **Mica**	N	N	N	Y	N	N
8 **Keller**	N	N	N	Y	?	N
9 **Bilirakis**	N	N	N	N	Y	N
10 **Young**	N	N	N	Y	Y	N
11 Castor	Y	Y	Y	N	N	Y
12 **Putnam**	N	N	N	Y	Y	N
13 **Buchanan**	N	N	N	Y	Y	N
14 **Mack**	N	N	N	Y	Y	N
15 **Weldon**	N	N	N	Y	?	N
16 Mahoney	Y	Y	Y	N	N	Y
17 Meek	Y	Y	Y	N	N	Y
18 **Ros-Lehtinen**	?	N	N	N	N	N
19 Wexler	Y	Y	Y	N	N	Y
20 Wasserman Schultz	Y	Y	Y	N	N	Y
21 **Diaz-Balart, L.**	N	N	N	N	N	N
22 Klein	Y	Y	Y	N	N	Y
23 Hastings	Y	Y	Y	N	N	Y
24 **Feeney**	N	N	N	Y	Y	N
25 **Diaz-Balart, M.**	N	N	N	N	N	N
GEORGIA						
1 **Kingston**	N	N	N	N	Y	N
2 Bishop	Y	Y	Y	N	N	Y
3 **Westmoreland**	N	N	N	N	Y	N
4 Johnson	Y	Y	Y	N	N	Y
5 Lewis	Y	Y	?	N	N	Y
6 **Price**	N	N	N	Y	Y	N
7 **Linder**	?	N	N	Y	Y	?
8 Marshall	Y	Y	Y	N	N	Y
9 **Deal**	N	N	N	Y	Y	N
10 **Broun**	N	N	N	Y	Y	N
11 **Gingrey**	N	N	N	Y	Y	N
12 Barrow	Y	Y	Y	N	N	Y
13 Scott	Y	Y	Y	N	N	Y
HAWAII						
1 Abercrombie	Y	Y	Y	N	N	Y
2 Hirono	Y	Y	Y	N	N	Y
IDAHO						
1 **Sali**	N	N	N	Y	N	N
2 **Simpson**	N	N	N	N	Y	Y
ILLINOIS						
1 Rush	?	?	?	?	?	?
2 Jackson	Y	Y	Y	N	N	Y
3 Lipinski	Y	Y	Y	N	N	Y
4 Gutierrez	Y	Y	Y	N	N	?
5 Emanuel	Y	Y	Y	N	N	Y
6 **Roskam**	N	N	N	N	N	N
7 Davis	Y	Y	Y	N	N	Y
8 Bean	Y	Y	Y	N	N	Y
9 Schakowsky	Y	Y	Y	N	N	Y
10 **Kirk**	N	N	N	N	Y	N
11 **Weller**	Y	Y	Y	N	N	Y
12 Costello	Y	Y	Y	N	N	Y
13 **Biggert**	N	N	N	Y	Y	N
14 Foster	Y	Y	Y	N	?	Y
15 **Johnson**	N	N	N	Y	Y	N

KEY	**Republicans**	Democrats		
Y Voted for (yea)		X Paired against		C Voted "present" to avoid possible conflict of interest
# Paired for		– Announced against		
+ Announced for		P Voted "present"		? Did not vote or otherwise make a position known
N Voted against (nay)				

ND Northern Democrats, SD Southern Democrats
Southern states: Ala., Ark., Fla., Ga., Ky., La., Miss., N.C., Okla., S.C., Tenn., Texas, Va.

	282	283	284	285	286	287
16 **Manzullo**	N	N	N	N	N	N
17 Hare	Y	Y	Y	N	N	Y
18 **LaHood**	N	N	N	Y	Y	N
19 **Shimkus**	N	N	N	Y	Y	N
INDIANA						
1 Visclosky	Y	Y	Y	N	N	Y
2 Donnelly	Y	Y	Y	N	N	Y
3 **Souder**	N	N	N	Y	Y	N
4 **Buyer**	N	N	N	Y	Y	N
5 **Burton**	N	N	N	Y	Y	N
6 **Pence**	N	N	N	Y	Y	N
7 Carson, A.	Y	Y	Y	N	N	Y
8 Ellsworth	Y	Y	Y	N	N	Y
9 Hill	Y	N	Y	N	N	N
IOWA						
1 Braley	Y	Y	Y	N	N	Y
2 Loebsack	Y	Y	Y	N	N	Y
3 Boswell	Y	Y	Y	N	N	Y
4 **Latham**	N	N	N	N	N	N
5 **King**	N	N	N	Y	Y	N
KANSAS						
1 **Moran**	N	N	N	N	N	N
2 Boyda	Y	Y	Y	N	N	Y
3 Moore	Y	Y	Y	N	N	?
4 **Tiahrt**	N	N	N	N	N	N
KENTUCKY						
1 **Whitfield**	N	N	N	N	Y	N
2 **Lewis**	N	N	N	N	Y	N
3 Yarmuth	Y	Y	Y	N	N	Y
4 **Davis**	N	N	N	N	N	N
5 **Rogers**	N	N	N	N	Y	N
6 Chandler	Y	Y	Y	N	N	Y
LOUISIANA						
1 **Scalise**	N	N	N	Y	Y	N
2 Jefferson	Y	Y	Y	N	N	Y
3 Melancon	?	Y	Y	N	N	Y
4 **McCrery**	N	N	N	Y	Y	N
5 **Alexander**	N	N	N	Y	Y	N
6 Cazayoux	Y	Y	Y	N	N	Y
7 **Boustany**	N	N	N	N	Y	N
MAINE						
1 Allen	Y	Y	Y	N	N	Y
2 Michaud	Y	Y	Y	N	N	Y
MARYLAND						
1 **Gilchrest**	Y	N	N	Y	Y	?
2 Ruppersberger	Y	Y	Y	?	?	?
3 Sarbanes	Y	Y	Y	N	N	Y
4 Wynn	Y	Y	Y	N	N	Y
5 Hoyer	Y	Y	Y	N	N	Y
6 **Bartlett**	N	N	N	Y	Y	N
7 Cummings	Y	Y	Y	N	N	Y
8 Van Hollen	Y	Y	Y	N	N	Y
MASSACHUSETTS						
1 Olver	Y	Y	Y	N	N	Y
2 Neal	Y	Y	Y	N	N	Y
3 McGovern	Y	Y	Y	N	N	Y
4 Frank	Y	Y	Y	N	N	Y
5 Tsongas	Y	Y	Y	N	N	Y
6 Tierney	Y	Y	Y	?	N	Y
7 Markey	Y	Y	Y	N	N	Y
8 Capuano	Y	Y	Y	N	N	Y
9 Lynch	Y	Y	Y	N	N	Y
10 Delahunt	Y	Y	Y	N	N	Y
MICHIGAN						
1 Stupak	Y	Y	Y	N	N	Y
2 **Hoekstra**	N	N	N	N	Y	N
3 **Ehlers**	N	N	N	N	N	N
4 **Camp**	N	N	N	Y	Y	N
5 Kildee	Y	Y	Y	N	N	Y
6 **Upton**	N	N	N	Y	Y	N
7 **Walberg**	N	N	N	N	N	N
8 **Rogers**	N	N	N	N	N	N
9 **Knollenberg**	N	N	N	Y	Y	N
10 **Miller**	N	N	N	N	Y	N
11 **McCotter**	N	N	N	N	N	N
12 Levin	Y	Y	Y	N	N	Y
13 Kilpatrick	Y	Y	Y	N	N	Y
14 Conyers	Y	Y	Y	N	N	Y
15 Dingell	Y	Y	Y	N	N	Y
MINNESOTA						
1 Walz	Y	Y	Y	N	N	Y
2 **Kline**	N	N	N	N	Y	N
3 **Ramstad**	N	N	N	N	N	N
4 McCollum	Y	Y	Y	N	N	Y
5 Ellison	Y	Y	Y	N	N	Y
6 **Bachmann**	N	N	N	Y	Y	N
7 Peterson	Y	Y	Y	N	N	Y
8 Oberstar	Y	Y	Y	N	N	Y
MISSISSIPPI						
1 Vacant						
2 Thompson	Y	Y	Y	N	N	Y
3 **Pickering**	N	N	N	Y	Y	N
4 Taylor	Y	Y	Y	Y	Y	Y
MISSOURI						
1 Clay	Y	Y	Y	N	Y	Y
2 **Akin**	N	N	N	Y	Y	N
3 Carnahan	?	Y	Y	N	N	Y
4 Skelton	Y	Y	Y	N	N	Y
5 Cleaver	Y	Y	Y	N	N	Y
6 **Graves**	N	N	N	N	N	N
7 **Blunt**	N	N	N	Y	Y	N
8 **Emerson**	N	N	N	Y	Y	N
9 **Hulshof**	N	N	N	N	N	N
MONTANA						
AL **Rehberg**	N	N	N	N	Y	N
NEBRASKA						
1 **Fortenberry**	N	N	N	N	N	N
2 **Terry**	N	N	N	N	N	N
3 **Smith**	N	N	N	N	Y	N
NEVADA						
1 Berkley	?	Y	Y	N	N	Y
2 **Heller**	N	N	N	N	N	N
3 **Porter**	N	N	N	N	N	N
NEW HAMPSHIRE						
1 Shea-Porter	Y	Y	Y	N	N	Y
2 Hodes	Y	Y	Y	N	N	Y
NEW JERSEY						
1 Andrews	Y	Y	Y	N	N	Y
2 **LoBiondo**	N	N	N	N	N	N
3 **Saxton**	N	N	N	Y	?	?
4 **Smith**	N	N	N	N	N	N
5 **Garrett**	N	N	N	N	Y	N
6 Pallone	Y	Y	Y	N	N	Y
7 **Ferguson**	N	N	N	N	Y	N
8 Pascrell	Y	Y	Y	N	N	Y
9 Rothman	Y	Y	Y	N	N	Y
10 Payne	Y	Y	Y	N	N	?
11 **Frelinghuysen**	N	N	N	N	Y	N
12 Holt	Y	Y	Y	N	N	Y
13 Sires	Y	Y	?	N	N	Y
NEW MEXICO						
1 **Wilson**	N	N	N	Y	Y	N
2 **Pearce**	N	N	N	Y	Y	N
3 Udall	Y	Y	Y	N	N	Y
NEW YORK						
1 Bishop	+	+	+	–	–	+
2 Israel	Y	Y	Y	N	N	Y
3 **King**	N	N	N	Y	Y	N
4 McCarthy	Y	Y	Y	N	N	Y
5 Ackerman	Y	Y	Y	N	N	Y
6 Meeks	Y	Y	Y	N	N	Y
7 Crowley	Y	Y	Y	N	N	Y
8 Nadler	Y	Y	Y	N	N	Y
9 Weiner	Y	Y	Y	N	N	Y
10 Towns	Y	Y	Y	N	N	Y
11 Clarke	Y	Y	Y	N	N	Y
12 Velázquez	Y	Y	Y	N	N	?
13 **Fossella**	N	N	N	N	N	N
14 Maloney	Y	Y	Y	N	N	?
15 Rangel	Y	Y	Y	N	N	?
16 Serrano	Y	Y	Y	N	N	Y
17 Engel	Y	Y	Y	N	N	Y
18 Lowey	Y	Y	Y	N	N	Y
19 Hall	Y	Y	Y	N	N	Y
20 Gillibrand	Y	Y	Y	N	N	Y
21 McNulty	Y	Y	Y	N	N	Y
22 Hinchey	Y	Y	Y	N	N	Y
23 **McHugh**	N	N	N	Y	Y	N
24 Arcuri	Y	Y	Y	N	N	Y
25 **Walsh**	N	N	N	Y	Y	N
26 **Reynolds**	N	N	N	N	N	N
27 Higgins	Y	Y	Y	N	N	Y
28 Slaughter	Y	Y	Y	N	N	Y
29 **Kuhl**	N	N	N	N	N	N
NORTH CAROLINA						
1 Butterfield	Y	Y	Y	N	N	Y
2 Etheridge	Y	Y	Y	N	N	Y
3 **Jones**	N	N	N	Y	N	N
4 Price	Y	Y	Y	N	N	Y
5 **Foxx**	N	N	N	N	N	N
6 **Coble**	N	N	N	Y	Y	?
7 McIntyre	Y	Y	Y	N	N	Y
8 **Hayes**	N	N	N	N	Y	N
9 **Myrick**	N	N	N	Y	Y	N
10 **McHenry**	N	N	N	Y	Y	N
11 Shuler	Y	Y	Y	N	N	Y
12 Watt	Y	Y	Y	N	N	Y
13 Miller	Y	Y	Y	N	N	Y
NORTH DAKOTA						
AL Pomeroy	Y	Y	Y	N	N	Y
OHIO						
1 **Chabot**	N	N	N	Y	Y	N
2 **Schmidt**	N	N	N	Y	Y	N
3 **Turner**	N	N	N	N	N	N
4 **Jordan**	N	N	N	N	N	N
5 **Latta**	N	N	N	Y	Y	N
6 Wilson	Y	Y	Y	N	N	Y
7 **Hobson**	N	N	N	Y	Y	N
8 **Boehner**	N	N	N	?	Y	N
9 Kaptur	Y	P	Y	N	N	Y
10 Kucinich	Y	Y	Y	N	N	Y
11 Tubbs Jones	?	?	?	?	?	?
12 **Tiberi**	N	N	N	?	Y	N
13 Sutton	Y	Y	Y	N	N	Y
14 **LaTourette**	N	N	N	Y	?	?
15 **Pryce**	N	N	N	Y	Y	?
16 **Regula**	N	N	N	Y	Y	N
17 Ryan	Y	Y	Y	N	N	Y
18 Space	Y	Y	Y	N	N	Y
OKLAHOMA						
1 **Sullivan**	N	N	N	Y	N	N
2 Boren	Y	Y	Y	N	N	Y
3 **Lucas**	N	N	N	Y	Y	N
4 **Cole**	N	N	N	Y	Y	N
5 **Fallin**	N	N	N	N	Y	N
OREGON						
1 Wu	Y	Y	Y	N	N	Y
2 **Walden**	N	N	N	Y	Y	N
3 Blumenauer	Y	Y	Y	N	N	Y
4 DeFazio	Y	Y	Y	N	N	Y
5 Hooley	Y	Y	Y	N	N	Y
PENNSYLVANIA						
1 Brady	Y	Y	Y	N	N	Y
2 Fattah	Y	Y	Y	N	N	Y
3 **English**	N	N	N	Y	Y	N
4 Altmire	Y	Y	Y	N	N	Y
5 **Peterson**	N	N	N	Y	Y	?
6 **Gerlach**	N	N	N	N	N	N
7 Sestak	Y	Y	Y	N	N	Y
8 Murphy, P.	Y	Y	Y	N	N	Y
9 **Shuster**	N	N	N	Y	Y	N
10 Carney	Y	Y	Y	N	N	Y
11 Kanjorski	Y	Y	Y	N	N	Y
12 Murtha	Y	Y	Y	N	N	Y
13 Schwartz	Y	Y	Y	N	N	Y
14 Doyle	Y	Y	Y	N	N	Y
15 **Dent**	N	N	N	N	N	N
16 **Pitts**	N	N	N	Y	Y	N
17 Holden	Y	Y	Y	N	N	Y
18 **Murphy, T.**	N	N	N	N	N	N
19 **Platts**	N	N	N	N	N	N
RHODE ISLAND						
1 Kennedy	Y	Y	Y	N	N	Y
2 Langevin	Y	Y	Y	N	N	Y
SOUTH CAROLINA						
1 **Brown**	N	N	N	N	Y	N
2 **Wilson**	N	N	N	Y	Y	N
3 **Barrett**	N	N	N	N	Y	N
4 **Inglis**	N	N	N	N	Y	N
5 Spratt	Y	Y	Y	N	N	Y
6 Clyburn	Y	Y	Y	N	N	Y
SOUTH DAKOTA						
AL Herseth Sandlin	Y	Y	Y	N	N	Y
TENNESSEE						
1 **Davis, D.**	N	N	N	N	Y	N
2 **Duncan**	N	N	N	Y	Y	N
3 **Wamp**	N	N	N	Y	Y	N
4 Davis, L.	Y	Y	Y	N	N	Y
5 Cooper	Y	Y	Y	N	N	Y
6 Gordon	Y	Y	Y	Y	N	Y
7 **Blackburn**	N	N	N	Y	Y	N
8 Tanner	Y	Y	Y	N	N	Y
9 Cohen	Y	Y	Y	N	N	Y
TEXAS						
1 **Gohmert**	N	N	N	N	N	N
2 **Poe**	N	N	N	N	?	N
3 **Johnson, S.**	N	N	N	Y	Y	N
4 **Hall**	N	N	N	Y	?	N
5 **Hensarling**	N	N	N	N	Y	N
6 **Barton**	N	N	N	N	Y	N
7 **Culberson**	N	N	N	Y	N	N
8 **Brady**	N	N	N	Y	Y	N
9 Green, A.	Y	Y	Y	N	N	Y
10 **McCaul**	N	N	?	Y	N	N
11 **Conaway**	?	?	?	?	?	?
12 **Granger**	N	N	N	Y	Y	?
13 **Thornberry**	N	N	N	Y	Y	N
14 **Paul**	N	N	N	Y	Y	N
15 Hinojosa	Y	Y	Y	N	N	Y
16 Reyes	Y	Y	Y	N	N	Y
17 Edwards	?	Y	Y	N	N	Y
18 Jackson Lee	Y	Y	Y	N	N	Y
19 **Neugebauer**	N	N	N	N	Y	N
20 Gonzalez	Y	Y	Y	N	N	Y
21 **Smith**	N	N	N	Y	Y	N
22 Lampson	Y	N	Y	N	N	Y
23 Rodriguez	Y	Y	Y	N	N	Y
24 **Marchant**	N	N	N	N	N	N
25 Doggett	Y	Y	Y	N	N	Y
26 **Burgess**	?	N	N	N	N	N
27 Ortiz	Y	Y	Y	N	N	Y
28 Cuellar	Y	Y	Y	N	N	Y
29 Green, G.	Y	Y	Y	N	N	Y
30 Johnson, E.	Y	Y	Y	N	N	?
31 **Carter**	N	N	N	Y	Y	N
32 **Sessions**	N	N	N	Y	Y	N
UTAH						
1 **Bishop**	N	N	N	Y	Y	N
2 Matheson	Y	Y	Y	N	N	Y
3 **Cannon**	N	N	N	Y	Y	N
VERMONT						
AL Welch	Y	Y	Y	N	N	Y
VIRGINIA						
1 **Wittman**	N	N	N	N	N	N
2 **Drake**	N	N	N	N	Y	N
3 Scott	Y	Y	Y	N	N	Y
4 **Forbes**	N	N	N	Y	Y	N
5 **Goode**	N	N	N	Y	Y	N
6 **Goodlatte**	N	N	N	Y	Y	N
7 **Cantor**	N	N	N	Y	Y	N
8 Moran	Y	Y	Y	N	N	Y
9 Boucher	Y	Y	Y	N	N	Y
10 **Wolf**	N	N	N	N	N	N
11 **Davis**	N	N	N	Y	Y	N
WASHINGTON						
1 Inslee	Y	Y	Y	N	N	Y
2 Larsen	Y	Y	Y	N	N	Y
3 Baird	Y	Y	Y	N	N	Y
4 **Hastings**	N	N	N	Y	Y	N
5 **McMorris Rodgers**	N	N	N	N	?	N
6 Dicks	Y	Y	Y	N	N	Y
7 McDermott	Y	Y	Y	N	N	Y
8 **Reichert**	N	N	N	Y	Y	N
9 Smith	Y	Y	Y	N	N	Y
WEST VIRGINIA						
1 Mollohan	Y	Y	Y	N	N	Y
2 **Capito**	N	N	N	N	Y	N
3 Rahall	Y	Y	Y	N	N	Y
WISCONSIN						
1 **Ryan**	N	N	N	Y	Y	N
2 Baldwin	Y	Y	Y	N	N	Y
3 Kind	Y	Y	Y	N	N	Y
4 Moore	Y	Y	Y	N	N	Y
5 **Sensenbrenner**	N	N	N	Y	Y	N
6 **Petri**	N	N	N	Y	Y	N
7 Obey	Y	Y	Y	N	N	Y
8 Kagen	Y	Y	Y	N	N	Y
WYOMING						
AL **Cubin**	N	N	N	Y	Y	N
DELEGATES						
Faleomavaega (A.S.)						
Norton (D.C.)						
Bordallo (Guam)						
Fortuño (P.R.)						
Christensen (V.I.)						

IN THE HOUSE | By Vote Number

288. **HR 5818. Foreclosed Property Grants and Loans/Motion to Reconsider.** Hastings, D-Fla., motion to table (kill) the Simpson, R-Idaho, motion to reconsider the vote on ordering the previous question (thus ending debate and possibility of amendment) on adoption of the rule (H Res 1174) that would provide for House floor consideration of the bill that would establish a loan and grant program for states and localities to buy and rehabilitate foreclosed properties. Motion agreed to 226-186: R 4-186; D 222-0 (ND 168-0, SD 54-0). May 7, 2008.

289. **HR 5818. Foreclosed Property Grants and Loans/Rule.** Adoption of the rule (H Res 1174) to provide for House floor consideration of the bill that would establish a loan and grant program, administered by the Department of Housing and Urban Development, for states and localities to buy and rehabilitate foreclosed properties. Motion adopted 223-192: R 1-190; D 222-2 (ND 167-1, SD 55-1). May 7, 2008.

290. **HR 5818. Foreclosed Property Grants and Loans/Motion to Reconsider.** Welch, D-Vt., motion to table (kill) the Emerson, R-Mo., motion to reconsider the vote on adoption of the rule (H Res 1174) that would provide for House floor consideration of the bill that would establish a loan and grant program for states and localities to buy and rehabilitate foreclosed properties. Motion agreed to 212-183: R 1-183; D 211-0 (ND 156-0, SD 55-0). May 7, 2008.

291. **Procedural Motion/Motion to Adjourn.** Walsh, R-N.Y., motion to adjourn. Motion rejected 140-264: R 136-50; D 4-214 (ND 2-160, SD 2-54). May 7, 2008.

292. **HR 5818. Foreclosed Property Grants and Loans/Motion to Rise.** Simpson, R-Idaho, motion to rise from the Committee of the Whole. Motion rejected 184-231: R 182-8; D 2-223 (ND 0-170, SD 2-53). May 7, 2008.

293. **HR 5818. Foreclosed Property Grants and Loans/Property Price Cap.** Waters, D-Calif., amendment that would allow allocations of the bill's grants and loans to qualified cities and counties and would cap the purchase price of a foreclosed property at its current appraised value. Adopted in Committee of the Whole 256-157: R 31-157; D 225-0 (ND 170-0, SD 55-0). May 7, 2008.

294. **HR 5818. Foreclosed Property Grants and Loans/Office of Community Planning.** Capito, R-W.Va., amendment that would direct the loans and grants authorized by the bill to be administered by the Department of Housing and Urban Development's Office of Community Planning and Development. Adopted in Committee of the Whole 425-0: R 194-0; D 231-0 (ND 175-0, SD 56-0). May 7, 2008.

	288	289	290	291	292	293	294
ALABAMA							
1 Bonner	N	N	N	Y	Y	N	Y
2 Everett	N	N	N	Y	Y	N	Y
3 Rogers	N	N	N	Y	Y	N	Y
4 Aderholt	N	N	N	Y	?	?	Y
5 Cramer	Y	Y	Y	N	N	Y	Y
6 Bachus	?	N	N	?	Y	N	Y
7 Davis	Y	Y	Y	N	N	Y	Y
ALASKA							
AL Young	N	N	N	Y	?	?	?
ARIZONA							
1 Renzi	?	?	?	?	Y	N	Y
2 Franks	N	N	N	Y	Y	N	Y
3 Shadegg	N	N	N	Y	Y	N	Y
4 Pastor	Y	Y	Y	N	N	Y	Y
5 Mitchell	Y	Y	Y	N	N	Y	Y
6 Flake	N	N	N	Y	Y	N	Y
7 Grijalva	Y	Y	Y	N	N	Y	Y
8 Giffords	Y	Y	Y	N	N	Y	Y
ARKANSAS							
1 Berry	?	?	?	?	?	?	?
2 Snyder	Y	Y	Y	N	N	Y	Y
3 Boozman	N	N	N	Y	Y	N	Y
4 Ross	Y	Y	Y	N	N	Y	Y
CALIFORNIA							
1 Thompson	Y	Y	Y	N	N	Y	Y
2 Herger	N	N	N	Y	Y	N	Y
3 Lungren	N	N	N	Y	Y	N	Y
4 Doolittle	N	N	N	Y	N	N	Y
5 Matsui	Y	Y	Y	N	N	Y	Y
6 Woolsey	Y	Y	Y	N	N	Y	Y
7 Miller, George	Y	Y	Y	N	N	Y	Y
8 Pelosi							
9 Lee	Y	Y	Y	N	N	Y	Y
10 Tauscher	Y	Y	Y	N	N	Y	Y
11 McNerney	Y	Y	Y	N	N	Y	Y
12 Speier	?	?	?	?	?	?	?
13 Stark	Y	Y	Y	N	N	Y	Y
14 Eshoo	Y	Y	Y	N	N	Y	Y
15 Honda	Y	Y	Y	N	N	Y	Y
16 Lofgren	Y	Y	Y	N	N	Y	Y
17 Farr	Y	Y	?	N	N	Y	Y
18 Cardoza	Y	Y	Y	N	N	Y	Y
19 Radanovich	N	?	?	Y	Y	N	Y
20 Costa	Y	Y	Y	N	?	?	Y
21 Nunes	N	N	N	Y	Y	N	Y
22 McCarthy	N	N	?	Y	Y	N	Y
23 Capps	Y	Y	Y	N	N	Y	Y
24 Gallegly	N	N	N	Y	Y	N	Y
25 McKeon	N	N	N	Y	Y	N	Y
26 Dreier	N	N	N	Y	Y	N	Y
27 Sherman	Y	Y	Y	N	N	Y	Y
28 Berman	Y	Y	Y	N	N	Y	Y
29 Schiff	Y	Y	Y	N	N	Y	Y
30 Waxman	Y	Y	Y	N	N	Y	Y
31 Becerra	?	Y	Y	N	N	Y	Y
32 Solis	Y	Y	Y	N	N	Y	Y
33 Watson	Y	Y	?	N	N	Y	Y
34 Roybal-Allard	Y	Y	Y	N	N	Y	Y
35 Waters	Y	Y	Y	N	N	Y	Y
36 Harman	Y	Y	?	?	N	Y	Y
37 Richardson	?	?	?	?	?	?	?
38 Napolitano	Y	Y	Y	N	N	Y	Y
39 Sánchez, Linda	Y	Y	Y	N	N	Y	Y
40 Royce	N	N	N	Y	+	−	Y
41 Lewis	N	N	N	Y	Y	N	Y
42 Miller, Gary	N	N	N	Y	Y	N	Y
43 Baca	Y	Y	Y	N	N	Y	Y
44 Calvert	N	N	N	Y	Y	N	Y
45 Bono Mack	N	N	N	Y	Y	N	Y
46 Rohrabacher	N	N	N	Y	Y	N	Y
47 Sanchez, Loretta	Y	Y	Y	Y	N	Y	Y
48 Campbell	?	?	?	?	?	?	?
49 Issa	N	N	N	Y	Y	N	Y
50 Bilbray	N	N	N	Y	Y	N	Y
51 Filner	Y	Y	Y	N	N	Y	Y
52 Hunter	N	N	N	Y	Y	N	Y
53 Davis	Y	Y	Y	N	N	Y	Y

	288	289	290	291	292	293	294
COLORADO							
1 DeGette	Y	Y	Y	N	N	Y	Y
2 Udall	Y	Y	Y	N	N	Y	Y
3 Salazar	Y	Y	Y	N	N	Y	Y
4 Musgrave	N	N	N	?	Y	Y	Y
5 Lamborn	N	N	N	Y	Y	N	Y
6 Tancredo	N	N	N	Y	?	?	?
7 Perlmutter	Y	Y	Y	N	N	Y	Y
CONNECTICUT							
1 Larson	Y	Y	Y	N	N	Y	Y
2 Courtney	Y	Y	Y	N	N	Y	Y
3 DeLauro	Y	Y	Y	N	N	Y	Y
4 Shays	N	N	N	Y	Y	Y	Y
5 Murphy	Y	Y	Y	N	N	Y	Y
DELAWARE							
AL Castle	N	N	N	N	Y	N	Y
FLORIDA							
1 Miller	N	N	N	Y	Y	N	Y
2 Boyd	Y	Y	Y	N	N	Y	Y
3 Brown	Y	Y	Y	N	N	Y	Y
4 Crenshaw	N	N	N	Y	Y	N	Y
5 Brown-Waite	N	N	N	Y	Y	N	Y
6 Stearns	N	N	?	Y	Y	N	Y
7 Mica	N	N	N	Y	Y	N	Y
8 Keller	N	N	N	Y	N	N	Y
9 Bilirakis	N	N	N	Y	Y	N	Y
10 Young	N	N	N	Y	Y	N	Y
11 Castor	Y	Y	Y	N	N	Y	Y
12 Putnam	N	N	N	Y	Y	N	Y
13 Buchanan	N	N	N	Y	Y	N	Y
14 Mack	N	N	N	Y	Y	N	Y
15 Weldon	?	N	N	Y	?	?	Y
16 Mahoney	Y	Y	Y	N	N	Y	Y
17 Meek	Y	Y	Y	N	N	Y	Y
18 Ros-Lehtinen	N	N	N	N	Y	N	Y
19 Wexler	Y	Y	Y	N	?	?	Y
20 Wasserman Schultz	Y	Y	Y	N	N	Y	Y
21 Diaz-Balart, L.	N	N	N	N	Y	N	Y
22 Klein	Y	Y	Y	N	N	Y	+
23 Hastings	Y	Y	Y	N	N	Y	Y
24 Feeney	N	N	N	?	Y	N	Y
25 Diaz-Balart, M.	N	N	N	N	Y	N	Y
GEORGIA							
1 Kingston	Y	N	N	N	Y	N	Y
2 Bishop	Y	Y	Y	N	N	Y	Y
3 Westmoreland	N	N	N	Y	Y	N	Y
4 Johnson	Y	Y	Y	N	N	Y	Y
5 Lewis	Y	Y	Y	N	N	Y	Y
6 Price	N	N	N	Y	Y	N	Y
7 Linder	?	?	?	?	Y	N	Y
8 Marshall	Y	Y	Y	N	?	Y	Y
9 Deal	N	N	N	Y	Y	N	Y
10 Broun	N	N	N	Y	Y	N	Y
11 Gingrey	N	N	N	Y	Y	N	Y
12 Barrow	Y	Y	Y	N	N	Y	Y
13 Scott	Y	Y	Y	N	N	Y	Y
HAWAII							
1 Abercrombie	Y	Y	Y	N	N	Y	Y
2 Hirono	Y	Y	Y	N	N	Y	Y
IDAHO							
1 Sali	N	N	N	N	Y	N	Y
2 Simpson	N	N	N	Y	Y	N	Y
ILLINOIS							
1 Rush	?	?	?	?	?	?	?
2 Jackson	Y	Y	Y	N	N	Y	Y
3 Lipinski	Y	Y	Y	N	N	Y	Y
4 Gutierrez	Y	Y	Y	N	N	Y	Y
5 Emanuel	Y	Y	Y	N	N	Y	Y
6 Roskam	N	N	N	N	Y	N	Y
7 Davis	Y	Y	Y	N	N	Y	Y
8 Bean	Y	Y	Y	N	?	Y	Y
9 Schakowsky	Y	Y	Y	N	N	Y	Y
10 Kirk	N	−	N	N	Y	N	Y
11 Weller	N	N	N	Y	Y	?	Y
12 Costello	Y	Y	?	N	N	Y	Y
13 Biggert	N	N	N	Y	Y	Y	Y
14 Foster	Y	Y	?	N	N	?	Y
15 Johnson	Y	N	Y	Y	Y	N	Y

KEY

	Republicans	Democrats				
Y	Voted for (yea)		X	Paired against	C	Voted "present" to avoid possible conflict of interest
#	Paired for		−	Announced against		
+	Announced for		P	Voted "present"	?	Did not vote or otherwise make a position known
N	Voted against (nay)					

ND Northern Democrats, SD Southern Democrats
Southern states: Ala., Ark., Fla., Ga., Ky., La., Miss., N.C., Okla., S.C., Tenn., Texas, Va.

	288	289	290	291	292	293	294
16 **Manzullo**	N	N	N	N	Y	N	Y
17 Hare	Y	Y	Y	N	N	Y	Y
18 **LaHood**	N	N	N	Y	Y	Y	Y
19 **Shimkus**	N	N	N	Y	Y	N	Y
INDIANA							
1 Visclosky	Y	Y	Y	N	N	Y	Y
2 Donnelly	Y	Y	Y	N	N	Y	Y
3 **Souder**	?	N	N	Y	Y	N	Y
4 **Buyer**	N	N	?	Y	Y	N	Y
5 **Burton**	N	N	N	Y	Y	N	Y
6 **Pence**	N	N	N	Y	Y	N	Y
7 Carson, A.	Y	Y	Y	N	N	Y	Y
8 Ellsworth	Y	Y	Y	N	N	Y	Y
9 Hill	Y	N	Y	N	N	Y	Y
IOWA							
1 Braley	Y	Y	Y	N	N	Y	Y
2 Loebsack	Y	Y	Y	N	N	Y	Y
3 Boswell	Y	Y	Y	N	N	Y	Y
4 **Latham**	N	N	N	N	Y	N	Y
5 **King**	N	N	N	Y	Y	N	Y
KANSAS							
1 **Moran**	N	N	N	N	N	N	Y
2 Boyda	Y	Y	Y	N	N	Y	Y
3 Moore	Y	Y	Y	N	N	Y	Y
4 **Tiahrt**	N	N	N	N	Y	N	Y
KENTUCKY							
1 **Whitfield**	N	N	N	Y	Y	N	Y
2 **Lewis**	N	N	N	Y	Y	N	Y
3 Yarmuth	Y	Y	Y	N	N	Y	Y
4 **Davis**	N	N	N	N	Y	?	Y
5 **Rogers**	N	N	N	Y	Y	N	Y
6 Chandler	Y	Y	Y	Y	N	Y	Y
LOUISIANA							
1 **Scalise**	N	N	N	Y	Y	N	Y
2 Jefferson	Y	Y	Y	N	N	Y	Y
3 Melancon	?	Y	Y	N	N	Y	Y
4 **McCrery**	N	N	N	Y	Y	N	Y
5 **Alexander**	N	N	N	Y	Y	N	Y
6 Cazayoux	Y	Y	Y	N	N	Y	Y
7 **Boustany**	N	N	N	Y	Y	N	Y
MAINE							
1 Allen	Y	Y	Y	N	N	Y	Y
2 Michaud	Y	Y	Y	N	N	Y	Y
MARYLAND							
1 **Gilchrest**	N	N	N	Y	Y	N	Y
2 Ruppersberger	?	Y	Y	N	N	Y	Y
3 Sarbanes	Y	Y	Y	N	N	Y	Y
4 Wynn	Y	Y	Y	N	N	Y	Y
5 Hoyer	Y	Y	Y	N	N	Y	Y
6 **Bartlett**	N	N	N	Y	Y	N	Y
7 Cummings	Y	Y	Y	N	N	Y	Y
8 Van Hollen	Y	Y	?	N	N	Y	Y
MASSACHUSETTS							
1 Olver	Y	Y	Y	N	N	Y	Y
2 Neal	Y	Y	Y	N	N	Y	Y
3 McGovern	Y	Y	Y	N	N	Y	Y
4 Frank	Y	Y	Y	N	N	Y	Y
5 Tsongas	Y	Y	Y	N	N	Y	Y
6 Tierney	Y	Y	Y	N	N	Y	Y
7 Markey	Y	Y	Y	N	N	Y	Y
8 Capuano	Y	Y	Y	N	N	Y	Y
9 Lynch	Y	Y	Y	N	N	Y	Y
10 Delahunt	Y	Y	Y	N	N	Y	Y
MICHIGAN							
1 Stupak	Y	Y	Y	N	N	Y	Y
2 **Hoekstra**	N	N	N	Y	Y	N	Y
3 **Ehlers**	N	N	–	N	N	Y	Y
4 **Camp**	N	N	N	Y	Y	N	Y
5 Kildee	Y	Y	Y	N	N	Y	Y
6 **Upton**	N	N	N	Y	Y	N	Y
7 **Walberg**	N	N	N	N	Y	N	Y
8 **Rogers**	N	N	N	Y	Y	N	Y
9 **Knollenberg**	N	N	N	Y	Y	N	Y
10 **Miller**	N	N	N	N	Y	N	Y
11 **McCotter**	N	N	N	N	Y	N	Y
12 Levin	Y	Y	Y	N	N	Y	Y
13 Kilpatrick	Y	Y	Y	N	N	Y	Y
14 Conyers	Y	Y	?	N	?	Y	Y
15 Dingell	Y	Y	Y	N	N	Y	Y
MINNESOTA							
1 Walz	Y	Y	Y	N	N	Y	Y
2 **Kline**	N	N	N	Y	Y	N	Y
3 **Ramstad**	N	N	N	N	N	Y	Y
4 McCollum	Y	Y	Y	N	N	Y	Y
5 Ellison	Y	Y	Y	N	N	Y	Y
6 **Bachmann**	N	N	N	Y	Y	N	Y
7 Peterson	Y	Y	Y	N	N	Y	Y
8 Oberstar	Y	Y	Y	N	N	Y	Y
MISSISSIPPI							
1 Vacant							
2 Thompson	Y	Y	Y	N	N	Y	Y
3 **Pickering**	N	N	N	Y	Y	N	Y
4 Taylor	Y	Y	Y	Y	Y	Y	Y
MISSOURI							
1 Clay	Y	Y	?	Y	N	Y	Y
2 **Akin**	N	N	N	Y	Y	N	Y
3 Carnahan	Y	Y	Y	N	N	Y	Y
4 Skelton	Y	Y	Y	N	N	Y	Y
5 Cleaver	Y	Y	?	?	N	Y	Y
6 **Graves**	N	N	N	N	Y	N	Y
7 **Blunt**	N	N	?	Y	Y	N	Y
8 **Emerson**	N	Y	N	?	Y	N	Y
9 **Hulshof**	N	N	N	N	Y	N	Y
MONTANA							
AL **Rehberg**	N	N	N	Y	Y	N	Y
NEBRASKA							
1 **Fortenberry**	N	N	N	N	?	Y	Y
2 **Terry**	N	N	N	N	N	N	Y
3 **Smith**	N	N	N	Y	Y	N	Y
NEVADA							
1 Berkley	Y	Y	?	?	N	Y	Y
2 **Heller**	N	N	N	N	Y	N	Y
3 **Porter**	N	N	?	N	Y	Y	Y
NEW HAMPSHIRE							
1 Shea-Porter	Y	Y	Y	N	N	Y	Y
2 Hodes	Y	Y	Y	?	N	Y	Y
NEW JERSEY							
1 Andrews	Y	Y	Y	N	N	Y	Y
2 **LoBiondo**	N	N	N	N	Y	N	Y
3 **Saxton**	N	N	N	Y	?	?	?
4 **Smith**	N	N	N	N	Y	Y	Y
5 **Garrett**	N	N	N	Y	Y	N	Y
6 Pallone	Y	Y	Y	N	N	Y	Y
7 **Ferguson**	N	N	N	Y	Y	Y	Y
8 Pascrell	Y	Y	Y	N	N	Y	Y
9 Rothman	Y	Y	Y	N	N	Y	Y
10 Payne	Y	Y	Y	N	N	Y	Y
11 **Frelinghuysen**	N	N	N	N	Y	N	Y
12 Holt	Y	Y	Y	N	N	Y	Y
13 Sires	Y	Y	Y	N	N	Y	Y
NEW MEXICO							
1 **Wilson**	N	N	N	Y	Y	N	Y
2 **Pearce**	N	N	N	Y	Y	N	Y
3 Udall	Y	Y	Y	N	N	Y	Y
NEW YORK							
1 Bishop	+	+	+	–	N	Y	Y
2 Israel	Y	Y	Y	N	N	Y	Y
3 **King**	N	N	N	Y	Y	N	Y
4 McCarthy	Y	Y	Y	N	N	Y	Y
5 Ackerman	Y	Y	Y	N	N	Y	Y
6 Meeks	Y	?	Y	N	N	Y	Y
7 Crowley	Y	Y	Y	N	N	Y	Y
8 Nadler	Y	Y	Y	N	N	Y	Y
9 Weiner	Y	Y	Y	N	N	Y	Y
10 Towns	Y	Y	Y	N	N	Y	Y
11 Clarke	Y	Y	Y	N	N	Y	Y
12 Velázquez	Y	Y	Y	N	N	Y	Y
13 **Fossella**	N	N	N	N	Y	N	Y
14 Maloney	?	?	?	?	N	Y	Y
15 Rangel	Y	Y	Y	N	?	?	Y
16 Serrano	Y	Y	Y	N	N	Y	Y
17 Engel	Y	Y	Y	N	N	Y	Y
18 Lowey	Y	Y	Y	N	N	Y	Y
19 Hall	Y	Y	Y	N	N	Y	Y
20 Gillibrand	Y	Y	Y	N	N	Y	Y
21 McNulty	Y	Y	Y	N	N	Y	Y
22 Hinchey	Y	Y	Y	N	N	Y	Y
23 **McHugh**	N	N	N	Y	Y	N	Y
24 Arcuri	Y	Y	Y	N	N	Y	Y
25 **Walsh**	N	N	N	Y	Y	Y	Y
26 **Reynolds**	N	N	N	Y	?	?	?
27 Higgins	Y	Y	Y	N	N	Y	Y
28 Slaughter	Y	Y	?	?	N	Y	Y
29 **Kuhl**	N	N	N	N	Y	N	Y
NORTH CAROLINA							
1 Butterfield	Y	Y	Y	N	N	Y	Y
2 Etheridge	Y	Y	Y	N	N	Y	Y
3 **Jones**	N	N	N	N	Y	Y	Y
4 Price	Y	Y	Y	N	N	Y	Y
5 **Foxx**	N	N	N	N	Y	N	Y
6 **Coble**	N	N	N	Y	Y	N	Y
7 McIntyre	Y	Y	Y	N	N	Y	Y
8 **Hayes**	N	N	N	Y	Y	Y	Y
9 **Myrick**	N	N	N	Y	Y	N	Y
10 **McHenry**	N	N	N	Y	Y	N	Y
11 Shuler	Y	Y	Y	N	N	Y	Y
12 Watt	Y	Y	Y	N	N	Y	Y
13 Miller	Y	Y	Y	N	N	Y	Y
NORTH DAKOTA							
AL Pomeroy	Y	Y	Y	N	N	Y	Y
OHIO							
1 **Chabot**	N	N	N	Y	Y	Y	Y
2 **Schmidt**	N	N	N	Y	Y	Y	Y
3 **Turner**	N	N	N	N	N	Y	Y
4 **Jordan**	N	N	N	N	Y	N	Y
5 **Latta**	N	N	N	Y	Y	N	Y
6 Wilson	Y	Y	Y	N	N	Y	Y
7 **Hobson**	N	N	N	Y	Y	N	Y
8 **Boehner**	N	N	N	N	Y	N	Y
9 Kaptur	Y	Y	Y	N	N	Y	Y
10 Kucinich	Y	Y	Y	N	N	Y	Y
11 Tubbs Jones	Y	Y	Y	N	N	?	Y
12 **Tiberi**	N	N	N	Y	Y	N	Y
13 Sutton	Y	Y	Y	N	N	Y	Y
14 **LaTourette**	?	?	?	?	Y	N	Y
15 **Pryce**	N	N	N	?	Y	N	Y
16 **Regula**	N	N	N	Y	Y	N	Y
17 Ryan	Y	Y	?	N	N	Y	Y
18 Space	Y	Y	Y	N	N	Y	Y
OKLAHOMA							
1 **Sullivan**	N	N	N	Y	Y	N	Y
2 Boren	Y	Y	Y	N	N	Y	Y
3 **Lucas**	N	N	N	N	Y	N	Y
4 **Cole**	N	N	N	Y	Y	N	Y
5 **Fallin**	N	N	N	Y	Y	N	Y
OREGON							
1 Wu	Y	Y	Y	N	N	Y	Y
2 **Walden**	N	N	N	Y	Y	N	Y
3 Blumenauer	Y	Y	Y	N	N	Y	Y
4 DeFazio	Y	Y	?	?	?	Y	Y
5 Hooley	?	?	?	?	N	Y	Y
PENNSYLVANIA							
1 Brady	Y	Y	Y	N	N	Y	Y
2 Fattah	Y	Y	?	N	N	?	Y
3 **English**	N	N	N	Y	Y	Y	Y
4 Altmire	Y	Y	Y	N	N	Y	Y
5 **Peterson**	?	?	?	?	Y	N	Y
6 **Gerlach**	N	N	N	N	N	Y	Y
7 Sestak	Y	Y	Y	N	N	Y	Y
8 Murphy, P.	Y	Y	Y	N	N	Y	Y
9 **Shuster**	N	N	N	Y	Y	N	Y
10 Carney	Y	Y	Y	N	N	Y	Y
11 Kanjorski	Y	Y	Y	N	N	Y	Y
12 Murtha	Y	Y	Y	N	N	Y	Y
13 Schwartz	Y	Y	Y	N	N	+	Y
14 Doyle	Y	Y	Y	N	N	Y	Y
15 **Dent**	N	N	N	N	Y	Y	Y
16 **Pitts**	N	N	N	Y	Y	N	Y
17 Holden	Y	Y	Y	N	N	Y	Y
18 **Murphy, T.**	N	N	N	N	Y	N	Y
19 **Platts**	N	N	N	N	Y	Y	Y
RHODE ISLAND							
1 Kennedy	Y	Y	Y	N	N	Y	Y
2 Langevin	Y	Y	Y	N	N	Y	Y
SOUTH CAROLINA							
1 **Brown**	N	N	N	Y	Y	N	Y
2 **Wilson**	N	N	N	Y	Y	N	Y
3 **Barrett**	N	N	N	Y	Y	N	Y
4 **Inglis**	N	N	N	Y	Y	N	Y
5 Spratt	?	Y	Y	N	N	Y	Y
6 Clyburn	Y	Y	Y	N	N	Y	Y
SOUTH DAKOTA							
AL Herseth Sandlin	Y	Y	Y	N	N	Y	Y
TENNESSEE							
1 **Davis, D.**	N	N	N	Y	Y	N	Y
2 **Duncan**	N	N	N	Y	Y	N	Y
3 **Wamp**	N	N	N	Y	Y	N	Y
4 Davis, L.	Y	Y	Y	N	N	Y	Y
5 Cooper	Y	Y	Y	N	N	Y	Y
6 Gordon	Y	Y	Y	N	N	Y	Y
7 **Blackburn**	N	N	N	Y	Y	N	Y
8 Tanner	Y	Y	Y	N	N	Y	Y
9 Cohen	Y	Y	Y	N	N	Y	Y
TEXAS							
1 **Gohmert**	N	N	N	N	Y	N	Y
2 **Poe**	N	N	N	Y	Y	N	Y
3 **Johnson, S.**	N	N	N	Y	Y	N	Y
4 **Hall**	N	N	N	Y	Y	N	Y
5 **Hensarling**	N	N	N	Y	Y	N	Y
6 **Barton**	N	N	N	Y	Y	N	Y
7 **Culberson**	N	N	N	N	Y	?	Y
8 **Brady**	N	N	?	N	Y	N	Y
9 Green, A.	Y	Y	Y	N	N	Y	Y
10 **McCaul**	N	N	N	Y	Y	Y	Y
11 **Conaway**	?	?	?	?	Y	N	Y
12 **Granger**	N	N	N	Y	Y	N	Y
13 **Thornberry**	N	N	N	Y	Y	N	Y
14 **Paul**	N	N	N	Y	?	?	?
15 Hinojosa	?	?	?	?	N	Y	Y
16 Reyes	Y	Y	Y	N	N	Y	Y
17 Edwards	Y	Y	Y	N	N	Y	Y
18 Jackson Lee	Y	Y	Y	N	N	Y	Y
19 **Neugebauer**	Y	N	N	Y	Y	N	Y
20 Gonzalez	Y	Y	Y	N	N	Y	Y
21 **Smith**	N	N	N	Y	Y	Y	Y
22 Lampson	Y	N	Y	N	N	Y	Y
23 Rodriguez	Y	Y	Y	N	N	Y	Y
24 **Marchant**	N	N	N	?	Y	N	Y
25 Doggett	Y	Y	Y	N	N	Y	Y
26 **Burgess**	N	N	N	N	Y	N	Y
27 Ortiz	Y	Y	Y	N	N	Y	Y
28 Cuellar	Y	Y	Y	N	N	?	Y
29 Green, G.	Y	Y	Y	N	N	Y	Y
30 Johnson, E.	Y	Y	Y	N	N	Y	Y
31 **Carter**	N	N	N	Y	Y	N	Y
32 **Sessions**	N	N	N	Y	Y	N	Y
UTAH							
1 **Bishop**	N	N	N	Y	Y	N	Y
2 Matheson	Y	Y	Y	N	N	Y	Y
3 **Cannon**	N	N	N	N	Y	N	Y
VERMONT							
AL Welch	Y	Y	Y	N	N	Y	?
VIRGINIA							
1 **Wittman**	N	N	N	Y	Y	N	Y
2 **Drake**	N	N	N	Y	Y	N	Y
3 Scott	Y	Y	Y	N	N	Y	Y
4 **Forbes**	N	N	N	Y	Y	N	Y
5 **Goode**	N	N	N	Y	Y	N	Y
6 **Goodlatte**	N	N	N	Y	Y	N	Y
7 **Cantor**	N	N	N	Y	Y	N	Y
8 Moran	Y	Y	?	N	N	Y	Y
9 Boucher	Y	Y	Y	N	N	Y	Y
10 **Wolf**	N	N	N	N	Y	N	Y
11 **Davis**	N	N	N	?	Y	N	Y
WASHINGTON							
1 Inslee	Y	Y	Y	N	N	Y	Y
2 Larsen	Y	Y	Y	N	N	Y	Y
3 Baird	Y	Y	Y	N	N	Y	Y
4 **Hastings**	N	N	N	Y	Y	N	Y
5 **McMorris Rodgers**	N	N	N	Y	Y	N	Y
6 Dicks	Y	Y	Y	?	?	Y	Y
7 McDermott	Y	Y	Y	N	N	Y	Y
8 **Reichert**	N	N	N	Y	Y	Y	Y
9 Smith	Y	Y	Y	N	N	Y	Y
WEST VIRGINIA							
1 Mollohan	Y	?	Y	N	N	Y	Y
2 **Capito**	N	N	N	N	Y	Y	Y
3 Rahall	Y	Y	Y	N	N	Y	Y
WISCONSIN							
1 **Ryan**	N	N	N	Y	Y	N	Y
2 Baldwin	Y	Y	Y	N	N	Y	Y
3 Kind	Y	Y	Y	N	N	Y	Y
4 Moore	Y	Y	Y	N	N	Y	Y
5 **Sensenbrenner**	N	N	N	Y	Y	N	Y
6 **Petri**	N	N	N	N	Y	N	Y
7 Obey	Y	Y	Y	N	N	Y	Y
8 Kagen	Y	Y	Y	N	N	Y	Y
WYOMING							
AL **Cubin**	N	N	?	Y	Y	Y	Y
DELEGATES							
Faleomavaega (A.S.)					N	Y	Y
Norton (D.C.)					N	Y	Y
Bordallo (Guam)					N	Y	Y
Fortuño (P.R.)					?	Y	Y
Christensen (V.I.)					?	?	?

IN THE HOUSE | By Vote Number

295. **HR 5818. Foreclosed Property Grants and Loans/Redirect Grant Funding.** Hensarling, R-Texas, amendment that would strike language in the bill providing for state grants and redirect the $7.5 billion in grant money to the loan portion of the bill. Rejected in Committee of the Whole, 190-219: R 188-7; D 2-212 (ND 1-165, SD 1-47). May 8, 2008.

296. **HR 5818. Foreclosed Property Grants and Loans/Ruling of the Chair.** Judgment of the House to sustain the ruling of the chair that Westmoreland, R-Ga., should raise a question of privilege rather than a point of order that roll call vote 295 was held open for the sole purpose of changing the outcome of the vote. Ruling of the chair sustained 235-182: R 5-182; D 230-0 (ND 173-0, SD 57-0). May 8, 2008.

297. **HR 5818. Foreclosed Property Grants and Loans/Illegal Immigrants.** Altmire, D-Pa., amendment that would clarify that illegal immigrants would be ineligible for financial assistance under the bill. Adopted in Committee of the Whole 391-33: R 194-3; D 197-30 (ND 144-27, SD 53-3). May 8, 2008.

298. **HR 5818. Foreclosed Property Grants and Loans/Recommit.** Shadegg, R-Ariz., motion to recommit the bill to the Financial Services Committee with instructions that it be reported back promptly with language that would bar anyone convicted of a drug-dealing offense, a sex offense or mortgage fraud from buying homes made available through the bill's funds. It would give priority to loans and grants that would provide housing for veterans, teachers, law enforcement officers, firefighters and other first-responders. Motion rejected 210-216: R 196-1; D 14-215 (ND 9-163, SD 5-52). May 8, 2008.

299. **HR 5818. Foreclosed Property Grants and Loans/Passage.** Passage of the bill that would establish a loan and grant program, administered by the Department of Housing and Urban Development, for states to buy and rehabilitate foreclosed properties. The bill would authorize $7.5 billion for zero-interest loans and $7.5 billion for grants. The bill would direct states to allocate funds to the 100 largest cities with high foreclosure rates and the 50 most populous counties. Properties purchased for rental with the funds could serve only families having incomes at or below the area's median income. Passed 239-188: R 11-187; D 228-1 (ND 171-1, SD 57-0). A "nay" was a vote in support of the president's position. May 8, 2008.

300. **HR 4279. Intellectual Property/Passage.** Conyers, D-Mich., motion to suspend the rules and pass the bill that would consolidate federal efforts to counter piracy and counterfeiting of American-owned intellectual properties. Motion agreed to 410-11: R 186-7; D 224-4 (ND 168-3, SD 56-1). A two-thirds majority of those present and voting (281 in this case) is required for passage under suspension of the rules. May 8, 2008.

	295	296	297	298	299	300
ALABAMA						
1 **Bonner**	Y	N	Y	Y	N	Y
2 **Everett**	Y	N	Y	Y	N	Y
3 **Rogers**	Y	N	Y	Y	N	Y
4 **Aderholt**	Y	N	Y	Y	N	Y
5 Cramer	?	Y	Y	N	Y	Y
6 **Bachus**	Y	?	Y	Y	N	?
7 Davis	N	Y	Y	N	Y	Y
ALASKA						
AL **Young**	?	N	Y	Y	N	N
ARIZONA						
1 **Renzi**	Y	N	Y	Y	N	Y
2 **Franks**	Y	N	Y	Y	N	Y
3 **Shadegg**	Y	N	Y	N	N	Y
4 Pastor	N	Y	N	N	Y	Y
5 Mitchell	N	Y	Y	Y	Y	Y
6 **Flake**	Y	N	Y	Y	N	N
7 Grijalva	N	Y	N	N	Y	Y
8 Giffords	?	Y	Y	Y	Y	Y
ARKANSAS						
1 Berry	N	Y	Y	N	Y	Y
2 Snyder	N	Y	Y	N	Y	Y
3 **Boozman**	Y	N	Y	Y	N	Y
4 Ross	N	Y	Y	N	Y	Y
CALIFORNIA						
1 Thompson	N	Y	Y	N	Y	Y
2 **Herger**	Y	N	Y	Y	N	?
3 **Lungren**	Y	P	Y	Y	N	Y
4 **Doolittle**	Y	N	Y	Y	N	N
5 Matsui	N	Y	Y	N	Y	Y
6 Woolsey	N	Y	N	N	Y	Y
7 Miller, George	N	?	?	N	Y	Y
8 Pelosi						
9 Lee	N	Y	N	N	Y	Y
10 Tauscher	N	Y	Y	N	Y	Y
11 McNerney	N	Y	Y	Y	Y	Y
12 Speier	N	Y	Y	N	Y	Y
13 Stark	N	Y	N	N	Y	Y
14 Eshoo	N	Y	Y	N	Y	Y
15 Honda	N	Y	N	N	Y	Y
16 Lofgren	N	Y	Y	N	Y	N
17 Farr	N	Y	N	N	Y	Y
18 Cardoza	N	Y	Y	N	Y	Y
19 **Radanovich**	Y	N	Y	Y	N	Y
20 Costa	?	Y	Y	N	Y	Y
21 **Nunes**	Y	N	Y	Y	N	Y
22 **McCarthy**	Y	N	Y	Y	N	Y
23 Capps	N	Y	Y	N	Y	Y
24 **Gallegly**	Y	N	Y	Y	N	Y
25 **McKeon**	Y	N	Y	Y	N	Y
26 **Dreier**	Y	N	Y	Y	N	Y
27 Sherman	N	Y	Y	N	Y	Y
28 Berman	N	Y	Y	N	Y	Y
29 Schiff	–	Y	Y	N	Y	Y
30 Waxman	N	Y	Y	N	Y	Y
31 Becerra	N	Y	Y	N	Y	Y
32 Solis	N	Y	N	N	Y	Y
33 Watson	N	Y	Y	N	Y	Y
34 Roybal-Allard	N	Y	Y	N	Y	Y
35 Waters	N	Y	Y	N	Y	Y
36 Harman	N	Y	Y	N	Y	Y
37 Richardson	?	?	?	?	?	?
38 Napolitano	N	Y	N	N	Y	Y
39 Sánchez, Linda	N	Y	N	N	Y	Y
40 **Royce**	Y	N	Y	Y	N	Y
41 **Lewis**	Y	N	Y	Y	N	Y
42 **Miller, Gary**	Y	N	Y	Y	N	Y
43 Baca	N	Y	N	N	Y	Y
44 **Calvert**	Y	N	Y	Y	N	Y
45 **Bono Mack**	Y	N	Y	Y	N	Y
46 **Rohrabacher**	Y	P	Y	Y	N	Y
47 Sanchez, Loretta	N	Y	N	N	Y	Y
48 **Campbell**	?	?	?	?	?	?
49 **Issa**	Y	N	Y	Y	N	Y
50 **Bilbray**	Y	N	Y	Y	N	Y
51 Filner	N	Y	N	N	Y	Y
52 **Hunter**	Y	?	Y	Y	N	Y
53 Davis	N	Y	Y	N	Y	Y

	295	296	297	298	299	300
COLORADO						
1 DeGette	N	Y	Y	N	Y	Y
2 Udall	N	Y	Y	N	Y	Y
3 Salazar	N	Y	Y	N	Y	Y
4 **Musgrave**	Y	N	Y	Y	N	Y
5 **Lamborn**	Y	N	Y	Y	N	Y
6 **Tancredo**	Y	N	Y	Y	N	Y
7 Perlmutter	N	Y	Y	N	Y	Y
CONNECTICUT						
1 Larson	N	Y	Y	N	Y	Y
2 Courtney	N	Y	Y	N	Y	Y
3 DeLauro	N	Y	Y	N	Y	Y
4 **Shays**	Y	N	Y	Y	Y	Y
5 Murphy	N	Y	Y	N	Y	Y
DELAWARE						
AL **Castle**	Y	N	Y	Y	N	Y
FLORIDA						
1 **Miller**	Y	N	Y	Y	N	Y
2 Boyd	N	Y	Y	N	Y	Y
3 Brown	N	Y	Y	N	Y	Y
4 **Crenshaw**	Y	N	Y	Y	N	Y
5 **Brown-Waite**	Y	N	Y	Y	N	Y
6 **Stearns**	Y	N	Y	Y	N	Y
7 **Mica**	Y	N	Y	Y	N	Y
8 **Keller**	Y	N	Y	Y	N	Y
9 **Bilirakis**	Y	N	Y	Y	N	Y
10 **Young**	Y	Y	Y	Y	N	Y
11 Castor	N	Y	Y	N	Y	Y
12 **Putnam**	Y	N	Y	Y	N	Y
13 **Buchanan**	Y	N	Y	Y	N	Y
14 **Mack**	Y	N	Y	Y	N	Y
15 **Weldon**	Y	N	Y	Y	N	Y
16 Mahoney	?	Y	Y	N	Y	Y
17 Meek	N	Y	Y	N	Y	Y
18 **Ros-Lehtinen**	N	N	N	Y	Y	Y
19 Wexler	N	Y	Y	N	Y	Y
20 Wasserman Schultz	N	Y	Y	N	Y	Y
21 **Diaz-Balart, L.**	N	N	N	Y	Y	Y
22 Klein	N	Y	Y	N	Y	Y
23 Hastings	N	Y	Y	N	Y	Y
24 **Feeney**	Y	N	Y	Y	N	Y
25 **Diaz-Balart, M.**	N	N	N	Y	Y	Y
GEORGIA						
1 **Kingston**	Y	N	Y	Y	N	Y
2 Bishop	?	Y	Y	N	Y	Y
3 **Westmoreland**	Y	N	Y	Y	N	N
4 Johnson	N	Y	N	N	Y	Y
5 Lewis	N	Y	N	Y	Y	Y
6 **Price**	Y	N	Y	Y	N	Y
7 **Linder**	Y	N	Y	Y	N	Y
8 Marshall	N	Y	Y	Y	Y	Y
9 **Deal**	Y	N	Y	Y	N	Y
10 **Broun**	Y	N	Y	Y	N	Y
11 **Gingrey**	Y	N	Y	Y	N	Y
12 Barrow	?	Y	Y	Y	Y	Y
13 Scott	N	Y	Y	N	Y	Y
HAWAII						
1 Abercrombie	N	Y	Y	N	Y	Y
2 Hirono	N	Y	N	N	Y	Y
IDAHO						
1 **Sali**	Y	N	Y	Y	N	Y
2 **Simpson**	Y	N	Y	Y	N	Y
ILLINOIS						
1 Rush	?	?	?	?	?	?
2 Jackson	N	Y	Y	N	Y	Y
3 Lipinski	N	Y	Y	N	Y	Y
4 Gutierrez	N	Y	N	–	+	+
5 Emanuel	N	Y	Y	N	Y	Y
6 **Roskam**	Y	N	Y	Y	N	Y
7 Davis	N	Y	Y	N	Y	Y
8 Bean	?	Y	Y	N	Y	Y
9 Schakowsky	N	Y	N	N	Y	Y
10 **Kirk**	Y	N	Y	Y	N	Y
11 **Weller**	N	Y	Y	N	Y	Y
12 Costello	N	Y	Y	N	Y	Y
13 **Biggert**	Y	N	Y	Y	N	Y
14 Foster	N	Y	Y	N	Y	Y
15 **Johnson**	Y	Y	Y	Y	N	Y

ND Northern Democrats, SD Southern Democrats
Southern states: Ala., Ark., Fla., Ga., Ky., La., Miss., N.C., Okla., S.C., Tenn., Texas, Va.

	295	296	297	298	299	300
16 **Manzullo**	Y	N	Y	Y	N	Y
17 Hare	N	Y	Y	N	Y	Y
18 **LaHood**	Y	Y	Y	Y	N	Y
19 **Shimkus**	Y	N	Y	Y	N	Y
INDIANA						
1 Visclosky	N	Y	Y	N	Y	Y
2 Donnelly	N	Y	Y	Y	Y	Y
3 **Souder**	Y	N	Y	Y	N	Y
4 **Buyer**	Y	N	Y	Y	N	Y
5 **Burton**	Y	N	Y	Y	N	Y
6 **Pence**	Y	P	Y	Y	N	Y
7 Carson, A.	N	Y	Y	N	Y	Y
8 Ellsworth	N	Y	N	Y	Y	Y
9 Hill	?	Y	Y	Y	Y	Y
IOWA						
1 Braley	N	Y	Y	N	Y	Y
2 Loebsack	?	?	?	?	?	?
3 Boswell	N	Y	Y	N	Y	Y
4 **Latham**	Y	N	Y	Y	N	Y
5 **King**	Y	N	Y	Y	N	Y
KANSAS						
1 **Moran**	Y	N	Y	Y	N	Y
2 Boyda	N	Y	Y	N	Y	Y
3 Moore	?	Y	Y	N	Y	Y
4 **Tiahrt**	Y	N	Y	Y	N	Y
KENTUCKY						
1 **Whitfield**	Y	N	Y	Y	N	Y
2 **Lewis**	Y	N	Y	Y	N	Y
3 Yarmuth	N	Y	Y	N	Y	Y
4 **Davis**	Y	N	Y	Y	N	Y
5 **Rogers**	Y	N	Y	Y	N	Y
6 Chandler	?	Y	Y	N	Y	Y
LOUISIANA						
1 **Scalise**	Y	N	Y	Y	N	Y
2 Jefferson	N	Y	Y	N	Y	Y
3 Melancon	?	Y	Y	N	Y	Y
4 **McCrery**	Y	N	?	Y	N	Y
5 **Alexander**	Y	N	Y	Y	N	Y
6 Cazayoux	N	Y	Y	Y	Y	Y
7 **Boustany**	Y	N	Y	Y	N	Y
MAINE						
1 Allen	N	Y	Y	N	Y	Y
2 Michaud	N	Y	Y	N	Y	Y
MARYLAND						
1 **Gilchrest**	Y	P	Y	Y	Y	?
2 Ruppersberger	Y	Y	Y	N	Y	Y
3 Sarbanes	N	Y	Y	N	Y	Y
4 Wynn	N	Y	Y	N	Y	Y
5 Hoyer	N	Y	Y	N	Y	Y
6 **Bartlett**	Y	N	Y	Y	N	Y
7 Cummings	N	Y	?	N	Y	Y
8 Van Hollen	N	Y	Y	N	Y	Y
MASSACHUSETTS						
1 Olver	N	Y	N	N	Y	Y
2 Neal	N	Y	Y	N	Y	Y
3 McGovern	N	Y	N	N	Y	Y
4 Frank	N	Y	Y	N	Y	Y
5 Tsongas	N	Y	Y	N	Y	Y
6 Tierney	N	Y	Y	N	Y	Y
7 Markey	N	Y	Y	N	Y	Y
8 Capuano	N	Y	Y	N	Y	Y
9 Lynch	N	Y	Y	N	Y	?
10 Delahunt	N	Y	Y	N	Y	Y
MICHIGAN						
1 Stupak	N	Y	Y	N	Y	Y
2 **Hoekstra**	Y	N	Y	Y	N	Y
3 **Ehlers**	Y	N	Y	Y	N	Y
4 **Camp**	Y	N	Y	Y	N	Y
5 Kildee	N	Y	Y	N	Y	Y
6 **Upton**	Y	N	Y	Y	N	Y
7 **Walberg**	Y	N	Y	Y	N	Y
8 **Rogers**	Y	N	Y	Y	N	Y
9 **Knollenberg**	Y	N	Y	Y	N	Y
10 **Miller**	Y	N	Y	Y	N	Y
11 **McCotter**	Y	N	Y	Y	N	Y
12 Levin	N	Y	Y	N	Y	Y
13 Kilpatrick	N	Y	Y	N	Y	Y
14 Conyers	N	Y	Y	N	Y	Y
15 Dingell	N	Y	Y	N	Y	Y
MINNESOTA						
1 Walz	N	Y	Y	N	Y	Y
2 **Kline**	Y	N	Y	Y	N	Y
3 **Ramstad**	Y	N	Y	Y	Y	Y
4 McCollum	N	Y	Y	N	Y	Y
5 Ellison	N	Y	Y	N	Y	Y
6 **Bachmann**	Y	N	Y	Y	N	Y
7 Peterson	N	Y	Y	N	Y	Y
8 Oberstar	N	Y	Y	N	Y	Y
MISSISSIPPI						
1 Vacant						
2 Thompson	N	Y	Y	N	Y	Y
3 **Pickering**	Y	?	?	Y	N	Y
4 Taylor	N	Y	Y	N	Y	Y
MISSOURI						
1 Clay	?	Y	Y	N	Y	Y
2 **Akin**	Y	N	Y	Y	N	Y
3 Carnahan	N	Y	Y	N	Y	Y
4 Skelton	N	Y	Y	N	Y	Y
5 Cleaver	N	Y	Y	N	Y	Y
6 **Graves**	Y	N	Y	Y	N	Y
7 **Blunt**	Y	N	Y	Y	N	Y
8 **Emerson**	Y	N	Y	Y	N	Y
9 **Hulshof**	Y	P	Y	Y	N	Y
MONTANA						
AL **Rehberg**	Y	N	Y	Y	N	Y
NEBRASKA						
1 **Fortenberry**	Y	N	Y	Y	N	Y
2 **Terry**	Y	N	Y	Y	N	Y
3 **Smith**	Y	N	Y	Y	N	Y
NEVADA						
1 Berkley	N	Y	Y	N	Y	Y
2 **Heller**	Y	N	Y	Y	N	Y
3 **Porter**	Y	N	Y	Y	Y	Y
NEW HAMPSHIRE						
1 Shea-Porter	N	Y	Y	N	Y	Y
2 Hodes	N	Y	Y	N	Y	Y
NEW JERSEY						
1 Andrews	N	Y	Y	N	Y	Y
2 **LoBiondo**	Y	N	Y	Y	N	Y
3 **Saxton**	Y	N	Y	Y	N	Y
4 **Smith**	Y	N	Y	Y	N	Y
5 **Garrett**	Y	N	Y	Y	N	Y
6 Pallone	N	Y	Y	N	Y	Y
7 **Ferguson**	Y	N	Y	Y	N	Y
8 Pascrell	N	Y	Y	N	Y	Y
9 Rothman	N	Y	Y	N	Y	Y
10 Payne	N	Y	Y	N	Y	Y
11 **Frelinghuysen**	Y	N	Y	Y	N	Y
12 Holt	N	Y	Y	N	Y	Y
13 Sires	N	Y	Y	N	Y	Y
NEW MEXICO						
1 **Wilson**	Y	N	Y	Y	N	Y
2 **Pearce**	Y	N	Y	Y	N	Y
3 Udall	N	Y	Y	N	Y	Y
NEW YORK						
1 Bishop	N	Y	Y	N	Y	Y
2 Israel	N	Y	Y	N	Y	Y
3 **King**	Y	N	Y	Y	N	Y
4 McCarthy	N	+	+	N	Y	Y
5 Ackerman	N	Y	Y	N	Y	Y
6 Meeks	N	Y	Y	N	Y	Y
7 Crowley	N	Y	N	N	Y	Y
8 Nadler	N	Y	Y	N	Y	Y
9 Weiner	N	Y	Y	N	Y	Y
10 Towns	N	Y	Y	N	Y	Y
11 Clarke	N	Y	N	N	Y	Y
12 Velázquez	N	Y	Y	N	Y	Y
13 **Fossella**	Y	N	Y	Y	N	Y
14 Maloney	N	Y	Y	N	Y	Y
15 Rangel	N	Y	Y	N	Y	Y
16 Serrano	N	Y	N	N	Y	Y
17 Engel	N	Y	Y	N	Y	Y
18 Lowey	N	Y	Y	N	Y	Y
19 Hall	N	Y	Y	N	Y	Y
20 Gillibrand	N	Y	Y	Y	N	Y
21 McNulty	N	Y	Y	N	Y	Y
22 Hinchey	N	Y	Y	N	Y	Y
23 **McHugh**	Y	N	Y	Y	N	Y
24 Arcuri	?	Y	Y	N	Y	Y
25 **Walsh**	N	N	Y	Y	Y	Y
26 **Reynolds**	Y	N	Y	Y	N	Y
27 Higgins	N	Y	Y	N	Y	Y
28 Slaughter	N	Y	Y	N	Y	Y
29 **Kuhl**	Y	N	Y	Y	N	Y
NORTH CAROLINA						
1 Butterfield	N	Y	Y	N	Y	Y
2 Etheridge	N	Y	Y	N	Y	Y
3 **Jones**	Y	Y	Y	?	N	Y
4 Price	N	Y	Y	N	Y	Y
5 **Foxx**	Y	N	Y	Y	N	Y
6 **Coble**	Y	N	Y	Y	N	Y
7 McIntyre	–	Y	Y	Y	Y	Y
8 **Hayes**	Y	N	Y	Y	N	Y
9 **Myrick**	Y	N	Y	Y	N	Y
10 **McHenry**	?	N	Y	Y	N	Y
11 Shuler	N	Y	Y	N	Y	Y
12 Watt	N	Y	Y	N	Y	Y
13 Miller	N	Y	Y	N	Y	Y
NORTH DAKOTA						
AL Pomeroy	+	Y	Y	N	Y	Y
OHIO						
1 **Chabot**	Y	N	Y	Y	N	Y
2 **Schmidt**	Y	N	Y	Y	N	Y
3 **Turner**	N	N	Y	Y	Y	Y
4 **Jordan**	Y	N	Y	Y	N	Y
5 **Latta**	Y	N	Y	Y	N	Y
6 Wilson	N	Y	Y	N	Y	Y
7 **Hobson**	Y	N	Y	Y	N	Y
8 **Boehner**	Y	?	Y	Y	N	Y
9 Kaptur	N	Y	Y	N	Y	Y
10 Kucinich	N	Y	N	N	Y	N
11 Tubbs Jones	N	Y	Y	N	Y	Y
12 **Tiberi**	Y	N	Y	Y	N	Y
13 Sutton	N	Y	N	N	Y	Y
14 **LaTourette**	Y	P	Y	Y	Y	Y
15 **Pryce**	Y	N	Y	Y	Y	Y
16 **Regula**	Y	N	Y	Y	N	Y
17 Ryan	N	Y	Y	N	Y	Y
18 Space	?	Y	Y	N	Y	Y
OKLAHOMA						
1 **Sullivan**	Y	N	Y	Y	N	Y
2 Boren	?	Y	Y	N	Y	Y
3 **Lucas**	Y	N	Y	Y	N	Y
4 **Cole**	Y	N	Y	Y	N	Y
5 **Fallin**	Y	N	Y	Y	N	Y
OREGON						
1 Wu	N	?	Y	N	Y	Y
2 **Walden**	Y	N	Y	Y	N	Y
3 Blumenauer	N	Y	Y	N	Y	Y
4 DeFazio	N	Y	Y	N	Y	Y
5 Hooley	N	Y	Y	N	Y	Y
PENNSYLVANIA						
1 Brady	N	Y	Y	N	Y	Y
2 Fattah	N	Y	Y	N	Y	Y
3 **English**	Y	N	Y	Y	N	Y
4 Altmire	N	Y	Y	N	Y	Y
5 **Peterson**	Y	N	Y	Y	N	Y
6 **Gerlach**	Y	N	Y	Y	N	Y
7 Sestak	N	Y	Y	N	Y	Y
8 Murphy, P.	N	Y	Y	Y	Y	Y
9 **Shuster**	Y	N	Y	Y	N	Y
10 Carney	?	Y	Y	Y	Y	Y
11 Kanjorski	N	Y	Y	N	Y	Y
12 Murtha	N	Y	Y	N	Y	Y
13 Schwartz	N	Y	Y	N	Y	Y
14 Doyle	N	Y	Y	N	Y	Y
15 **Dent**	Y	N	Y	Y	N	Y
16 **Pitts**	Y	N	Y	Y	N	Y
17 Holden	N	Y	Y	N	Y	Y
18 **Murphy, T.**	N	N	Y	Y	N	Y
19 **Platts**	Y	?	Y	Y	N	Y
RHODE ISLAND						
1 Kennedy	N	Y	Y	N	Y	Y
2 Langevin	N	Y	Y	N	Y	Y
SOUTH CAROLINA						
1 **Brown**	Y	N	Y	Y	N	Y
2 **Wilson**	Y	N	Y	Y	N	Y
3 **Barrett**	Y	N	Y	Y	N	Y
4 **Inglis**	Y	N	Y	Y	N	Y
5 Spratt	N	Y	Y	N	Y	Y
6 Clyburn	N	Y	Y	N	Y	Y
SOUTH DAKOTA						
AL Herseth Sandlin	N	Y	Y	N	Y	Y
TENNESSEE						
1 **Davis, D.**	Y	N	Y	Y	N	Y
2 **Duncan**	Y	N	Y	Y	N	N
3 **Wamp**	Y	N	Y	Y	N	Y
4 Davis, L.	N	Y	Y	N	Y	Y
5 Cooper	?	Y	Y	N	Y	Y
6 Gordon	N	Y	Y	N	Y	Y
7 **Blackburn**	Y	N	Y	Y	N	Y
8 Tanner	N	Y	Y	N	Y	Y
9 Cohen	?	?	?	?	?	?
TEXAS						
1 **Gohmert**	Y	N	Y	Y	N	Y
2 **Poe**	Y	N	Y	Y	N	N
3 **Johnson, S.**	Y	N	Y	Y	N	Y
4 **Hall**	Y	N	Y	Y	N	Y
5 **Hensarling**	Y	N	Y	Y	N	Y
6 **Barton**	Y	N	Y	Y	N	Y
7 **Culberson**	Y	N	Y	Y	N	Y
8 **Brady**	Y	N	Y	Y	N	Y
9 Green, A.	N	Y	Y	N	Y	Y
10 **McCaul**	Y	N	Y	Y	N	Y
11 **Conaway**	Y	N	Y	Y	N	Y
12 **Granger**	Y	N	Y	Y	N	Y
13 **Thornberry**	Y	N	Y	Y	N	Y
14 **Paul**	Y	?	Y	N	N	N
15 Hinojosa	N	Y	Y	N	Y	Y
16 Reyes	N	Y	Y	N	Y	Y
17 Edwards	N	Y	Y	N	Y	Y
18 Jackson Lee	N	Y	?	N	Y	Y
19 **Neugebauer**	Y	N	Y	Y	N	Y
20 Gonzalez	N	Y	N	N	Y	Y
21 **Smith**	Y	N	Y	Y	N	Y
22 Lampson	Y	Y	Y	Y	Y	Y
23 Rodriguez	N	Y	Y	N	Y	Y
24 **Marchant**	Y	N	Y	Y	N	Y
25 Doggett	N	Y	Y	N	Y	Y
26 **Burgess**	Y	N	Y	Y	N	Y
27 Ortiz	N	Y	Y	N	Y	Y
28 Cuellar	N	Y	Y	N	Y	Y
29 Green, G.	N	Y	Y	N	Y	Y
30 Johnson, E.	N	Y	Y	N	Y	Y
31 **Carter**	Y	N	Y	Y	N	Y
32 **Sessions**	Y	N	Y	Y	N	Y
UTAH						
1 **Bishop**	Y	N	Y	Y	N	Y
2 Matheson	N	Y	Y	N	Y	Y
3 **Cannon**	Y	N	Y	Y	N	Y
VERMONT						
AL Welch	N	Y	?	N	Y	Y
VIRGINIA						
1 **Wittman**	Y	N	Y	Y	N	Y
2 **Drake**	Y	N	Y	Y	N	Y
3 Scott	N	Y	Y	N	Y	Y
4 **Forbes**	Y	N	Y	Y	N	Y
5 **Goode**	?	Y	Y	Y	N	Y
6 **Goodlatte**	Y	N	Y	Y	N	Y
7 **Cantor**	Y	N	Y	Y	N	Y
8 Moran	N	Y	N	N	Y	Y
9 Boucher	N	Y	Y	N	Y	N
10 **Wolf**	Y	N	Y	Y	N	Y
11 **Davis**	Y	N	Y	Y	N	Y
WASHINGTON						
1 Inslee	N	Y	Y	N	Y	Y
2 Larsen	N	Y	Y	N	Y	Y
3 Baird	N	Y	?	N	Y	Y
4 **Hastings**	Y	N	Y	Y	N	?
5 **McMorris Rodgers**	Y	N	Y	Y	N	Y
6 Dicks	N	Y	Y	N	Y	Y
7 McDermott	N	Y	N	N	Y	Y
8 **Reichert**	Y	N	Y	Y	N	Y
9 Smith	N	Y	Y	N	Y	Y
WEST VIRGINIA						
1 Mollohan	N	Y	Y	N	Y	Y
2 **Capito**	Y	N	Y	Y	N	?
3 Rahall	N	Y	Y	N	Y	Y
WISCONSIN						
1 **Ryan**	Y	N	Y	Y	N	Y
2 Baldwin	N	Y	N	N	Y	Y
3 Kind	N	Y	Y	N	Y	Y
4 Moore	N	Y	N	N	Y	N
5 **Sensenbrenner**	Y	N	Y	Y	N	Y
6 **Petri**	Y	N	Y	Y	N	Y
7 Obey	N	Y	Y	N	Y	Y
8 Kagen	N	Y	Y	N	Y	Y
WYOMING						
AL **Cubin**	?	N	Y	Y	N	Y
DELEGATES						
Faleomavaega (A.S.)	N	Y	Y			
Norton (D.C.)	N	Y	Y			
Bordallo (Guam)	N	+	+			
Fortuño (P.R.)	N	N	Y			
Christensen (V.I.)	N	Y	Y			

IN THE HOUSE | By Vote Number

301. **HR 3221. Mortgage Relief/Motion to Concur.** Frank, D-Mass., motion to concur in the Senate amendments, with an amendment. The House amendment would incorporate provisions from six housing-related bills. Among its provisions, the amendment would overhaul the Federal Housing Administration and expand its loan guarantee program. It would overhaul the regulation of Fannie Mae and Freddie Mac and establish an affordable-housing trust paid for by a percentage of their portfolios. It would also provide legal protections for mortgage servicers who made certain loan modifications, permit federal savings associations to make investments designed primarily to promote the public welfare and expand access to reverse mortgages. Motion agreed to 266-154: R 39-154; D 227-0 (ND 172-0, SD 55-0). May 8, 2008.

302. **HR 3221. Mortgage Relief/Motion to Concur.** Frank, D-Mass., motion to concur in the Senate amendments, with an amendment. The House amendment would provide a refundable tax credit of up to $7,500 for first-time homebuyers, which would serve as an interest-free loan. It would provide a one-time deduction in 2008 of up to $350 for individuals ($700 for couples) for state and local property taxes. It would also increase temporarily the low-income housing tax credit. Motion agreed to 322-94: R 95-94; D 227-0 (ND 171-0, SD 56-0). May 8, 2008.

303. **HR 3221. Mortgage Relief/Motion to Concur.** Frank, D-Mass., motion to concur in the Senate amendments, with an amendment. The House amendment would clarify that no provision in the underlying bill or two federal banking statutes — the Home Owners' Loan Act or the National Bank Act — could be construed to pre-empt any state law dealing with residential foreclosures. Motion agreed to 256-160: R 31-159; D 225-1 (ND 170-1, SD 55-0). May 8, 2008.

304. **HR 2419. Farm Bill Reauthorization/Motion to Instruct.** Flake, R-Ariz., motion to instruct House conferees not to recede to provisions in the Senate-passed bill related to a permanent agriculture disaster assistance program. Motion rejected 128-274: R 104-79; D 24-195 (ND 21-143, SD 3-52). May 8, 2008.

305. **HR 2419. Farm Bill Reauthorization/Motion to Instruct.** Cantor, R-Va., motion to instruct conferees not to agree to Senate-passed provisions that would create a qualified tax credit forestry conservation bond program. Motion rejected 169-222: R 161-18; D 8-204 (ND 7-152, SD 1-52). May 8, 2008.

	301	302	303	304	305
ALABAMA					
1 Bonner	N	N	N	N	Y
2 Everett	N	N	N	N	Y
3 Rogers	N	N	N	N	N
4 Aderholt	?	?	?	?	?
5 Cramer	Y	Y	Y	N	N
6 Bachus	N	N	N	?	?
7 Davis	Y	Y	Y	N	N
ALASKA					
AL Young	N	Y	N	Y	Y
ARIZONA					
1 Renzi	?	?	?	?	?
2 Franks	N	N	N	Y	Y
3 Shadegg	N	N	N	Y	?
4 Pastor	Y	Y	Y	N	N
5 Mitchell	Y	Y	Y	N	N
6 Flake	N	N	N	Y	Y
7 Grijalva	Y	Y	Y	N	N
8 Giffords	Y	Y	Y	N	N
ARKANSAS					
1 Berry	Y	Y	Y	N	N
2 Snyder	Y	Y	Y	N	N
3 Boozman	N	Y	N	N	Y
4 Ross	Y	Y	Y	N	N
CALIFORNIA					
1 Thompson	Y	Y	Y	N	N
2 Herger	N	N	N	Y	Y
3 Lungren	N	N	N	N	Y
4 Doolittle	N	N	Y	N	Y
5 Matsui	Y	Y	Y	N	N
6 Woolsey	Y	Y	Y	N	N
7 Miller, George	Y	Y	Y	N	N
8 Pelosi					
9 Lee	Y	Y	Y	N	N
10 Tauscher	Y	Y	Y	N	N
11 McNerney	Y	Y	Y	N	N
12 Speier	Y	Y	Y	N	N
13 Stark	Y	Y	Y	Y	Y
14 Eshoo	Y	Y	Y	N	N
15 Honda	Y	Y	Y	N	N
16 Lofgren	Y	Y	Y	N	N
17 Farr	Y	Y	Y	N	N
18 Cardoza	Y	Y	Y	N	N
19 Radanovich	N	N	N	Y	Y
20 Costa	Y	Y	Y	N	N
21 Nunes	N	?	?	?	?
22 McCarthy	N	Y	N	N	Y
23 Capps	Y	Y	Y	N	N
24 Gallegly	N	N	N	N	Y
25 McKeon	N	Y	N	?	?
26 Dreier	N	Y	N	Y	Y
27 Sherman	Y	Y	Y	N	Y
28 Berman	Y	Y	Y	N	N
29 Schiff	Y	Y	Y	N	N
30 Waxman	Y	Y	Y	Y	?
31 Becerra	Y	Y	Y	N	N
32 Solis	Y	Y	Y	N	N
33 Watson	Y	Y	Y	N	N
34 Roybal-Allard	Y	Y	Y	N	N
35 Waters	Y	Y	?	?	?
36 Harman	Y	Y	Y	Y	N
37 Richardson	?	?	?	?	?
38 Napolitano	Y	Y	Y	N	N
39 Sánchez, Linda	Y	Y	Y	N	N
40 Royce	N	N	N	Y	Y
41 Lewis	N	Y	N	N	Y
42 Miller, Gary	Y	Y	N	?	?
43 Baca	Y	Y	Y	N	N
44 Calvert	N	N	N	?	?
45 Bono Mack	N	Y	N	N	Y
46 Rohrabacher	N	N	N	Y	Y
47 Sanchez, Loretta	Y	Y	Y	N	N
48 Campbell	?	?	?	?	?
49 Issa	N	N	N	Y	Y
50 Bilbray	N	Y	N	Y	Y
51 Filner	Y	Y	Y	–	–
52 Hunter	N	Y	N	Y	Y
53 Davis	Y	Y	Y	N	N

	301	302	303	304	305
COLORADO					
1 DeGette	Y	Y	Y	N	N
2 Udall	Y	Y	Y	N	N
3 Salazar	Y	Y	Y	N	N
4 Musgrave	?	?	?	?	?
5 Lamborn	N	N	N	Y	Y
6 Tancredo	?	?	?	?	?
7 Perlmutter	Y	Y	Y	N	N
CONNECTICUT					
1 Larson	Y	Y	Y	N	N
2 Courtney	Y	Y	Y	N	N
3 DeLauro	Y	Y	Y	N	N
4 Shays	Y	Y	Y	Y	N
5 Murphy	Y	Y	Y	N	N
DELAWARE					
AL Castle	Y	Y	Y	N	Y
FLORIDA					
1 Miller	N	N	N	Y	Y
2 Boyd	Y	Y	Y	N	N
3 Brown	Y	Y	Y	N	N
4 Crenshaw	N	N	N	Y	Y
5 Brown-Waite	Y	Y	Y	N	Y
6 Stearns	N	N	N	Y	Y
7 Mica	N	N	N	Y	Y
8 Keller	Y	Y	Y	N	N
9 Bilirakis	N	Y	N	N	Y
10 Young	Y	Y	N	Y	Y
11 Castor	Y	Y	Y	N	N
12 Putnam	N	N	N	N	Y
13 Buchanan	Y	Y	N	N	Y
14 Mack	N	N	N	Y	Y
15 Weldon	N	N	N	Y	Y
16 Mahoney	Y	Y	Y	N	N
17 Meek	Y	Y	Y	N	N
18 Ros-Lehtinen	Y	Y	Y	N	N
19 Wexler	Y	Y	Y	N	N
20 Wasserman Schultz	Y	Y	Y	N	N
21 Diaz-Balart, L.	Y	Y	N	N	Y
22 Klein	Y	Y	Y	N	N
23 Hastings	Y	Y	Y	N	N
24 Feeney	N	N	N	Y	Y
25 Diaz-Balart, M.	Y	Y	N	N	Y
GEORGIA					
1 Kingston	N	Y	N	Y	Y
2 Bishop	Y	Y	Y	N	N
3 Westmoreland	N	Y	N	Y	Y
4 Johnson	Y	Y	Y	N	N
5 Lewis	Y	Y	Y	N	N
6 Price	N	N	N	Y	Y
7 Linder	N	Y	N	Y	Y
8 Marshall	Y	Y	Y	N	N
9 Deal	N	Y	N	Y	Y
10 Broun	N	N	N	Y	Y
11 Gingrey	N	N	N	Y	Y
12 Barrow	Y	Y	Y	N	N
13 Scott	Y	Y	Y	N	N
HAWAII					
1 Abercrombie	Y	Y	Y	N	N
2 Hirono	Y	Y	Y	N	N
IDAHO					
1 Sali	N	N	N	Y	Y
2 Simpson	N	Y	N	N	N
ILLINOIS					
1 Rush	?	?	?	?	?
2 Jackson	Y	Y	Y	N	N
3 Lipinski	Y	Y	Y	N	N
4 Gutierrez	+	+	+	–	–
5 Emanuel	Y	Y	Y	N	N
6 Roskam	N	Y	N	Y	Y
7 Davis	Y	Y	Y	N	N
8 Bean	Y	Y	Y	N	N
9 Schakowsky	Y	Y	Y	N	N
10 Kirk	Y	N	N	Y	N
11 Weller	N	Y	N	Y	N
12 Costello	Y	Y	Y	N	N
13 Biggert	N	N	N	Y	Y
14 Foster	Y	Y	Y	N	N
15 Johnson	N	N	N	N	N

KEY	**Republicans**	Democrats		
Y Voted for (yea)		X Paired against		C Voted "present" to avoid possible conflict of interest
# Paired for		– Announced against		
+ Announced for		P Voted "present"		? Did not vote or otherwise make a position known
N Voted against (nay)				

ND Northern Democrats, SD Southern Democrats
Southern states: Ala., Ark., Fla., Ga., Ky., La., Miss., N.C., Okla., S.C., Tenn., Texas, Va.

H-98   2008 CQ ALMANAC | www.cq.com

	301	302	303	304	305
16 Manzullo	N	N	Y	N	?
17 Hare	Y	Y	Y	N	N
18 LaHood	Y	Y	N	N	N
19 Shimkus	N	Y	N	N	Y
INDIANA					
1 Visclosky	Y	Y	Y	N	N
2 Donnelly	Y	Y	Y	N	N
3 Souder	Y	Y	N	Y	Y
4 Buyer	N	N	N	N	Y
5 Burton	N	N	N	N	Y
6 Pence	N	N	N	Y	Y
7 Carson, A.	Y	Y	Y	N	N
8 Ellsworth	Y	Y	Y	N	N
9 Hill	Y	Y	Y	N	N
IOWA					
1 Braley	Y	Y	Y	?	?
2 Loebsack	Y	Y	Y	N	N
3 Boswell	Y	Y	Y	N	N
4 Latham	N	Y	N	Y	Y
5 King	N	N	N	N	Y
KANSAS					
1 Moran	N	Y	N	Y	Y
2 Boyda	Y	Y	Y	N	N
3 Moore	Y	Y	Y	N	N
4 Tiahrt	N	Y	N	Y	Y
KENTUCKY					
1 Whitfield	N	Y	N	N	Y
2 Lewis	N	Y	N	N	Y
3 Yarmuth	Y	Y	Y	N	N
4 Davis	N	N	N	N	Y
5 Rogers	N	N	N	Y	Y
6 Chandler	Y	Y	Y	Y	N
LOUISIANA					
1 Scalise	N	N	N	Y	Y
2 Jefferson	Y	Y	Y	?	?
3 Melancon	Y	Y	Y	N	N
4 McCrery	N	N	N	Y	Y
5 Alexander	N	N	N	Y	Y
6 Cazayoux	Y	Y	Y	N	N
7 Boustany	N	N	N	Y	Y
MAINE					
1 Allen	Y	Y	Y	N	N
2 Michaud	Y	Y	Y	N	N
MARYLAND					
1 Gilchrest	Y	Y	Y	N	N
2 Ruppersberger	Y	Y	Y	N	N
3 Sarbanes	Y	Y	Y	N	N
4 Wynn	Y	Y	Y	Y	N
5 Hoyer	Y	Y	Y	N	N
6 Bartlett	N	N	Y	N	Y
7 Cummings	Y	Y	Y	N	N
8 Van Hollen	Y	Y	Y	N	N
MASSACHUSETTS					
1 Olver	Y	Y	Y	N	N
2 Neal	Y	Y	Y	N	N
3 McGovern	Y	Y	Y	Y	N
4 Frank	Y	Y	Y	N	N
5 Tsongas	Y	Y	Y	N	N
6 Tierney	Y	Y	Y	N	N
7 Markey	Y	Y	Y	N	N
8 Capuano	Y	Y	Y	Y	?
9 Lynch	Y	Y	Y	N	N
10 Delahunt	Y	Y	Y	N	N
MICHIGAN					
1 Stupak	Y	Y	Y	N	N
2 Hoekstra	N	Y	N	Y	Y
3 Ehlers	Y	Y	N	Y	N
4 Camp	N	Y	N	Y	N
5 Kildee	Y	Y	Y	N	N
6 Upton	Y	Y	Y	Y	Y
7 Walberg	N	Y	N	Y	Y
8 Rogers	N	Y	N	Y	Y
9 Knollenberg	Y	Y	N	Y	Y
10 Miller	N	Y	N	Y	N
11 McCotter	N	Y	N	Y	Y
12 Levin	Y	Y	Y	N	N
13 Kilpatrick	Y	Y	Y	N	N
14 Conyers	Y	Y	Y	?	N
15 Dingell	Y	Y	Y	N	N
MINNESOTA					
1 Walz	Y	Y	Y	N	N
2 Kline	N	N	N	Y	Y
3 Ramstad	Y	Y	N	Y	N
4 McCollum	Y	Y	Y	N	N

	301	302	303	304	305
5 Ellison	Y	Y	Y	N	N
6 Bachmann	N	N	N	Y	Y
7 Peterson	Y	Y	Y	N	N
8 Oberstar	Y	Y	Y	N	N
MISSISSIPPI					
1 Vacant					
2 Thompson	Y	Y	Y	N	N
3 Pickering	N	Y	N	N	?
4 Taylor	Y	Y	Y	N	N
MISSOURI					
1 Clay	Y	Y	Y	N	N
2 Akin	N	N	N	Y	Y
3 Carnahan	Y	Y	Y	N	N
4 Skelton	Y	Y	Y	N	N
5 Cleaver	Y	Y	Y	N	N
6 Graves	Y	Y	N	N	Y
7 Blunt	N	N	N	Y	Y
8 Emerson	N	Y	N	N	Y
9 Hulshof	N	Y	N	N	Y
MONTANA					
AL Rehberg	N	Y	N	N	N
NEBRASKA					
1 Fortenberry	N	Y	N	Y	Y
2 Terry	N	Y	N	N	Y
3 Smith	N	N	N	N	Y
NEVADA					
1 Berkley	Y	Y	Y	N	N
2 Heller	Y	Y	N	N	Y
3 Porter	Y	Y	Y	N	Y
NEW HAMPSHIRE					
1 Shea-Porter	Y	Y	Y	N	N
2 Hodes	Y	Y	Y	N	N
NEW JERSEY					
1 Andrews	Y	Y	Y	N	N
2 LoBiondo	N	Y	Y	N	N
3 Saxton	N	N	N	N	Y
4 Smith	Y	Y	Y	Y	N
5 Garrett	N	N	N	Y	Y
6 Pallone	Y	Y	Y	N	N
7 Ferguson	N	N	N	Y	Y
8 Pascrell	Y	Y	Y	N	?
9 Rothman	Y	Y	Y	Y	N
10 Payne	Y	Y	Y	N	?
11 Frelinghuysen	N	N	N	Y	N
12 Holt	Y	Y	Y	Y	N
13 Sires	Y	Y	Y	N	N
NEW MEXICO					
1 Wilson	N	Y	N	Y	Y
2 Pearce	N	N	N	N	Y
3 Udall	Y	Y	Y	N	N
NEW YORK					
1 Bishop	Y	Y	Y	N	N
2 Israel	Y	Y	Y	N	N
3 King	Y	Y	Y	N	Y
4 McCarthy	Y	Y	Y	N	N
5 Ackerman	Y	Y	Y	?	?
6 Meeks	Y	Y	Y	N	N
7 Crowley	Y	Y	Y	N	N
8 Nadler	Y	Y	Y	N	?
9 Weiner	Y	Y	Y	N	N
10 Towns	Y	Y	Y	N	N
11 Clarke	Y	Y	Y	N	N
12 Velázquez	Y	Y	Y	N	N
13 Fossella	N	Y	N	Y	Y
14 Maloney	Y	Y	Y	N	N
15 Rangel	Y	Y	Y	N	N
16 Serrano	Y	Y	Y	N	N
17 Engel	Y	Y	Y	N	N
18 Lowey	Y	Y	Y	N	N
19 Hall	Y	Y	Y	N	N
20 Gillibrand	Y	Y	Y	N	N
21 McNulty	Y	Y	Y	N	N
22 Hinchey	Y	Y	Y	N	N
23 McHugh	Y	Y	Y	N	Y
24 Arcuri	Y	Y	Y	N	N
25 Walsh	Y	Y	Y	N	N
26 Reynolds	?	?	?	?	?
27 Higgins	Y	Y	Y	N	N
28 Slaughter	Y	Y	Y	N	N
29 Kuhl	N	N	N	N	N
NORTH CAROLINA					
1 Butterfield	Y	Y	Y	N	N
2 Etheridge	Y	Y	Y	N	N
3 Jones	Y	Y	N	N	Y
4 Price	Y	Y	Y	N	N

	301	302	303	304	305
5 Foxx	N	N	N	Y	Y
6 Coble	N	N	N	Y	Y
7 McIntyre	Y	Y	Y	N	N
8 Hayes	Y	Y	Y	N	Y
9 Myrick	N	N	N	Y	Y
10 McHenry	N	N	N	Y	Y
11 Shuler	Y	Y	Y	N	?
12 Watt	Y	Y	Y	N	N
13 Miller	Y	Y	Y	N	N
NORTH DAKOTA					
AL Pomeroy	Y	Y	Y	N	N
OHIO					
1 Chabot	N	Y	N	Y	Y
2 Schmidt	N	N	N	Y	Y
3 Turner	Y	Y	N	Y	Y
4 Jordan	N	N	N	Y	Y
5 Latta	N	N	N	Y	Y
6 Wilson	Y	Y	Y	N	N
7 Hobson	N	N	N	Y	Y
8 Boehner	N	N	N	Y	Y
9 Kaptur	Y	Y	Y	N	?
10 Kucinich	Y	Y	Y	N	N
11 Tubbs Jones	Y	Y	Y	N	N
12 Tiberi	N	N	N	Y	Y
13 Sutton	Y	Y	Y	N	N
14 LaTourette	Y	Y	Y	Y	Y
15 Pryce	N	Y	N	Y	Y
16 Regula	N	Y	N	Y	Y
17 Ryan	Y	Y	Y	N	N
18 Space	Y	Y	Y	N	N
OKLAHOMA					
1 Sullivan	N	N	N	?	?
2 Boren	Y	Y	Y	N	N
3 Lucas	N	N	N	Y	N
4 Cole	N	N	Y	N	Y
5 Fallin	N	N	Y	N	N
OREGON					
1 Wu	Y	Y	Y	?	?
2 Walden	N	?	?	?	?
3 Blumenauer	Y	Y	Y	Y	N
4 DeFazio	Y	Y	Y	?	?
5 Hooley	Y	Y	Y	N	N
PENNSYLVANIA					
1 Brady	Y	Y	Y	N	N
2 Fattah	Y	Y	Y	N	N
3 English	Y	Y	N	Y	Y
4 Altmire	Y	Y	Y	N	N
5 Peterson	N	Y	N	Y	Y
6 Gerlach	Y	Y	Y	N	Y
7 Sestak	Y	Y	Y	N	N
8 Murphy, P.	Y	Y	Y	N	N
9 Shuster	N	N	N	Y	Y
10 Carney	Y	Y	Y	N	N
11 Kanjorski	Y	Y	Y	N	N
12 Murtha	Y	Y	Y	N	N
13 Schwartz	Y	Y	Y	N	N
14 Doyle	Y	Y	Y	N	N
15 Dent	Y	Y	Y	Y	Y
16 Pitts	N	N	N	Y	Y
17 Holden	Y	Y	Y	N	N
18 Murphy, T.	Y	Y	Y	N	Y
19 Platts	N	Y	Y	N	Y
RHODE ISLAND					
1 Kennedy	Y	Y	Y	N	N
2 Langevin	Y	Y	Y	N	N
SOUTH CAROLINA					
1 Brown	N	N	N	?	?
2 Wilson	N	Y	N	Y	Y
3 Barrett	N	N	N	N	Y
4 Inglis	N	N	N	Y	Y
5 Spratt	Y	Y	Y	N	N
6 Clyburn	Y	Y	?	N	N
SOUTH DAKOTA					
AL Herseth Sandlin	Y	Y	Y	N	N
TENNESSEE					
1 Davis, D.	N	Y	N	Y	Y
2 Duncan	N	Y	N	Y	Y
3 Wamp	N	Y	N	Y	Y
4 Davis, L.	Y	Y	Y	N	?
5 Cooper	Y	Y	Y	Y	N
6 Gordon	Y	Y	Y	N	N
7 Blackburn	N	N	N	Y	Y
8 Tanner	?	?	?	?	?
9 Cohen	?	?	?	?	?

	301	302	303	304	305
TEXAS					
1 Gohmert	N	N	N	N	Y
2 Poe	N	N	N	N	Y
3 Johnson, S.	N	Y	N	N	Y
4 Hall	Y	Y	N	N	Y
5 Hensarling	N	N	N	Y	Y
6 Barton	N	Y	N	?	?
7 Culberson	N	N	N	N	Y
8 Brady	N	N	N	N	Y
9 Green, A.	Y	Y	Y	N	N
10 McCaul	N	N	N	N	Y
11 Conaway	N	N	N	N	Y
12 Granger	N	N	N	N	Y
13 Thornberry	N	N	N	N	Y
14 Paul	N	N	Y	Y	?
15 Hinojosa	Y	Y	Y	N	N
16 Reyes	?	Y	Y	N	N
17 Edwards	Y	Y	Y	N	N
18 Jackson Lee	Y	Y	Y	N	N
19 Neugebauer	N	N	N	N	Y
20 Gonzalez	Y	Y	Y	N	N
21 Smith	N	N	N	N	Y
22 Lampson	Y	Y	Y	N	N
23 Rodriguez	Y	Y	Y	N	N
24 Marchant	N	N	N	N	Y
25 Doggett	Y	Y	Y	Y	Y
26 Burgess	N	Y	N	Y	Y
27 Ortiz	Y	Y	Y	N	N
28 Cuellar	Y	Y	Y	N	N
29 Green, G.	Y	Y	Y	N	N
30 Johnson, E.	Y	Y	Y	N	N
31 Carter	N	N	N	N	Y
32 Sessions	N	N	N	N	Y
UTAH					
1 Bishop	N	N	Y	N	Y
2 Matheson	Y	Y	Y	?	?
3 Cannon	N	?	?	?	?
VERMONT					
AL Welch	Y	Y	Y	N	N
VIRGINIA					
1 Wittman	N	Y	N	Y	Y
2 Drake	N	Y	N	Y	Y
3 Scott	Y	Y	Y	N	N
4 Forbes	N	N	N	Y	Y
5 Goode	N	Y	N	N	Y
6 Goodlatte	N	N	N	N	Y
7 Cantor	N	N	N	Y	Y
8 Moran	Y	Y	Y	N	N
9 Boucher	Y	Y	Y	N	N
10 Wolf	N	N	Y	N	N
11 Davis	N	Y	N	Y	Y
WASHINGTON					
1 Inslee	Y	Y	Y	N	N
2 Larsen	?	?	?	N	N
3 Baird	Y	Y	Y	?	?
4 Hastings	N	N	N	Y	Y
5 McMorris Rodgers	N	?	N	Y	Y
6 Dicks	Y	Y	Y	N	N
7 McDermott	Y	Y	Y	N	N
8 Reichert	Y	Y	Y	N	N
9 Smith	Y	Y	Y	N	Y
WEST VIRGINIA					
1 Mollohan	Y	Y	Y	N	N
2 Capito	Y	Y	N	N	Y
3 Rahall	Y	Y	Y	N	N
WISCONSIN					
1 Ryan	N	N	N	Y	Y
2 Baldwin	Y	Y	Y	N	Y
3 Kind	Y	Y	Y	Y	Y
4 Moore	Y	?	Y	Y	Y
5 Sensenbrenner	N	N	N	Y	Y
6 Petri	N	Y	N	Y	Y
7 Obey	Y	Y	Y	N	N
8 Kagen	Y	Y	Y	N	N
WYOMING					
AL Cubin	N	N	N	N	Y
DELEGATES					
Faleomavaega (A.S.)					
Norton (D.C.)					
Bordallo (Guam)					
Fortuño (P.R.)					
Christensen (V.I.)					

IN THE HOUSE | By Vote Number

306. H Res 1181. Support for Victims of Myanmar Cyclone/
Adoption. Faleomavaega, D-Am. Samoa., motion to suspend the rules and adopt the resolution that would express sympathy for the victims of Cyclone Nargis in Myanmar, formerly known as Burma, and reaffirm the U.S. commitment to providing immediate aid to the storm's victims. It also would urge the Myanmar government to accept international aid and call off a referendum on the military regime's constitution. Motion agreed to 410-1: R 186-1; D 224-0 (ND 167-0, SD 57-0). A two-thirds majority of those present and voting (274 in this case) is required for adoption under suspension of the rules. May 13, 2008.

307. HR 6022. Strategic Petroleum Reserve Suspension/Passage.
Dingell, D-Mich., motion to suspend the rules and pass the bill that would require the Interior and Energy departments to halt acquisition of oil for the Strategic Petroleum Reserve until the end of 2008. The departments could resume shipments if the president determined that the average price of oil in the United States for the most recent 90-day period was $75 a barrel or less. Motion agreed to 385-25: R 162-25; D 223-0 (ND 166-0, SD 57-0). A two-thirds majority of those present and voting (274 in this case) is required for passage under suspension of the rules. May 13, 2008.

308. HR 4008. Credit and Debit Card Receipt Clarification/
Passage. Mahoney, D-Fla., motion to suspend the rules and pass the bill that would provide legal protection to any person who printed an expiration date for a credit card on any receipt between Dec. 4, 2004, and the bill's enactment. Motion agreed to 407-0: R 185-0; D 222-0 (ND 165-0, SD 57-0). A two-thirds majority of those present and voting (272 in this case) is required for passage under suspension of the rules. May 13, 2008.

309. HR 2419. Farm Bill Reauthorization/Question of Consideration.
Question of whether the House should consider the rule (H Res 1189) to provide for House floor consideration of the conference report on the bill that would renew federal farm programs for five years. Agreed to consider 228-189: R 2-186; D 226-3 (ND 171-2, SD 55-1). (Flake, R-Ariz., had raised a point of order that the rule contained a provision violating the Budget Act of 1974.) May 14, 2008.

310. HR 2419. Farm Bill Reauthorization/Previous Question.
Cardoza, D-Calif., motion to order the previous question (thus ending debate and possibility of amendment) on adoption of the rule (H Res 1189) that would provide for House floor consideration of the conference report on the bill that would renew federal farm programs for five years. Motion agreed to 232-188: R 5-185; D 227-3 (ND 171-2, SD 56-1). May 14, 2008.

311. HR 2419. Farm Bill Reauthorization/Rule. Adoption of the rule
(H Res 1189) that would provide for House floor consideration of the conference report on the bill that would renew federal farm programs for five years. Adopted 228-193: R 0-189; D 228-4 (ND 172-3, SD 56-1). May 14, 2008.

312. H Res 1134. Support Mental Health Month/Adoption.
Napolitano, D-Calif., motion to suspend the rules and adopt the resolution that would support the goals and ideals of National Mental Health Month. Motion agreed to 421-0: R 189-0; D 232-0 (ND 175-0, SD 57-0). A two-thirds majority of those present and voting (281 in this case) is required for adoption under suspension of the rules. May 14, 2008.

	306	307	308	309	310	311	312
ALABAMA							
1 **Bonner**	?	?	?	?	N	N	Y
2 **Everett**	Y	Y	Y	N	N	N	Y
3 **Rogers**	Y	Y	Y	N	N	N	Y
4 **Aderholt**	Y	Y	Y	N	N	N	Y
5 Cramer	Y	Y	Y	?	?	?	?
6 **Bachus**	Y	Y	Y	N	N	N	Y
7 Davis	Y	Y	Y	Y	Y	Y	Y
ALASKA							
AL **Young**	Y	Y	Y	N	N	N	Y
ARIZONA							
1 **Renzi**	Y	Y	Y	N	N	N	Y
2 **Franks**	Y	N	Y	N	N	N	Y
3 **Shadegg**	Y	Y	Y	N	N	N	Y
4 Pastor	Y	Y	Y	Y	Y	Y	Y
5 Mitchell	Y	Y	Y	Y	Y	N	Y
6 **Flake**	Y	Y	Y	N	N	N	Y
7 Grijalva	Y	Y	Y	Y	Y	Y	Y
8 Giffords	Y	Y	Y	Y	Y	Y	Y
ARKANSAS							
1 Berry	Y	Y	Y	Y	Y	Y	Y
2 Snyder	Y	Y	Y	Y	Y	Y	Y
3 **Boozman**	Y	Y	Y	N	N	N	Y
4 Ross	Y	Y	Y	Y	Y	Y	Y
CALIFORNIA							
1 Thompson	Y	Y	Y	Y	Y	Y	Y
2 **Herger**	Y	N	Y	N	N	N	Y
3 **Lungren**	Y	Y	Y	N	N	N	Y
4 **Doolittle**	Y	N	Y	N	N	N	Y
5 Matsui	Y	Y	Y	Y	Y	Y	Y
6 Woolsey	Y	Y	Y	Y	Y	Y	Y
7 Miller, George	Y	Y	?	Y	Y	Y	Y
8 Pelosi							
9 Lee	Y	Y	Y	Y	Y	Y	Y
10 Tauscher	Y	Y	Y	Y	Y	Y	Y
11 McNerney	Y	Y	Y	Y	Y	Y	Y
12 Speier	Y	Y	Y	Y	Y	Y	Y
13 Stark	Y	Y	?	Y	?	Y	Y
14 Eshoo	Y	Y	Y	Y	Y	Y	Y
15 Honda	Y	Y	Y	Y	Y	Y	Y
16 Lofgren	Y	Y	Y	Y	Y	Y	Y
17 Farr	Y	Y	Y	Y	Y	Y	Y
18 Cardoza	Y	Y	Y	Y	Y	Y	Y
19 **Radanovich**	Y	N	Y	N	N	N	Y
20 Costa	Y	Y	Y	Y	Y	Y	Y
21 **Nunes**	Y	Y	Y	N	N	N	Y
22 **McCarthy**	Y	Y	Y	N	N	N	Y
23 Capps	Y	Y	Y	Y	Y	Y	Y
24 **Gallegly**	Y	Y	Y	N	N	N	Y
25 **McKeon**	Y	Y	Y	N	N	N	Y
26 **Dreier**	Y	Y	Y	Y	Y	N	Y
27 Sherman	Y	Y	Y	Y	Y	Y	Y
28 Berman	Y	Y	Y	Y	Y	Y	Y
29 Schiff	Y	Y	Y	Y	Y	Y	Y
30 Waxman	Y	Y	Y	Y	Y	Y	Y
31 Becerra	Y	Y	Y	Y	Y	Y	Y
32 Solis	Y	Y	Y	Y	Y	Y	Y
33 Watson	?	?	?	Y	Y	Y	Y
34 Roybal-Allard	Y	Y	Y	Y	Y	Y	Y
35 Waters	Y	Y	Y	Y	Y	Y	Y
36 Harman	Y	Y	Y	Y	Y	Y	Y
37 Richardson	?	?	?	Y	Y	Y	Y
38 Napolitano	Y	Y	Y	Y	Y	Y	Y
39 Sánchez, Linda	Y	Y	Y	Y	Y	Y	Y
40 **Royce**	Y	Y	Y	N	N	N	Y
41 **Lewis**	Y	Y	Y	N	N	N	Y
42 **Miller, Gary**	Y	Y	Y	N	N	N	Y
43 Baca	Y	Y	Y	Y	Y	Y	Y
44 **Calvert**	Y	Y	Y	N	N	N	Y
45 **Bono Mack**	?	?	?	?	?	?	?
46 **Rohrabacher**	?	?	?	N	N	N	Y
47 Sanchez, Loretta	Y	Y	Y	Y	Y	Y	Y
48 **Campbell**	Y	N	Y	N	N	N	Y
49 **Issa**	Y	Y	Y	N	N	N	Y
50 **Bilbray**	Y	Y	?	N	N	N	Y
51 Filner	Y	Y	Y	Y	Y	Y	Y
52 **Hunter**	Y	Y	Y	N	N	N	Y
53 Davis	Y	Y	Y	Y	Y	Y	Y

	306	307	308	309	310	311	312
COLORADO							
1 DeGette	Y	Y	Y	Y	Y	Y	Y
2 Udall	Y	Y	Y	Y	Y	Y	Y
3 Salazar	Y	Y	Y	Y	Y	Y	Y
4 **Musgrave**	Y	Y	Y	N	N	N	Y
5 **Lamborn**	Y	N	Y	N	N	N	Y
6 **Tancredo**	Y	Y	Y	N	N	N	Y
7 Perlmutter	Y	Y	Y	Y	Y	Y	Y
CONNECTICUT							
1 Larson	Y	?	Y	Y	Y	Y	Y
2 Courtney	Y	Y	Y	Y	Y	Y	Y
3 DeLauro	Y	Y	Y	Y	Y	Y	Y
4 **Shays**	Y	Y	Y	N	N	N	Y
5 Murphy	Y	Y	Y	Y	Y	Y	Y
DELAWARE							
AL **Castle**	Y	Y	Y	N	N	N	Y
FLORIDA							
1 **Miller**	Y	Y	Y	N	N	N	Y
2 Boyd	Y	Y	Y	Y	Y	Y	Y
3 Brown	Y	Y	Y	Y	Y	Y	Y
4 **Crenshaw**	?	?	?	?	?	?	?
5 **Brown-Waite**	Y	Y	Y	N	N	N	Y
6 **Stearns**	Y	Y	Y	N	N	N	Y
7 **Mica**	Y	N	Y	N	N	N	Y
8 **Keller**	Y	Y	Y	N	N	N	Y
9 **Bilirakis**	Y	Y	Y	N	N	N	Y
10 **Young**	Y	Y	Y	N	N	N	Y
11 Castor	Y	Y	Y	Y	Y	Y	Y
12 **Putnam**	Y	Y	Y	N	N	N	Y
13 **Buchanan**	Y	Y	Y	N	N	N	Y
14 **Mack**	?	?	?	?	?	?	?
15 **Weldon**	Y	N	Y	N	N	N	Y
16 Mahoney	Y	Y	Y	Y	Y	Y	Y
17 Meek	Y	Y	Y	Y	Y	Y	Y
18 **Ros-Lehtinen**	Y	Y	Y	N	N	N	Y
19 Wexler	Y	Y	Y	Y	Y	Y	Y
20 Wasserman Schultz	Y	Y	Y	Y	Y	Y	Y
21 **Diaz-Balart, L.**	Y	Y	?	N	N	N	Y
22 Klein	Y	Y	Y	Y	Y	Y	Y
23 Hastings	Y	Y	Y	Y	Y	Y	Y
24 **Feeney**	Y	Y	Y	N	N	N	Y
25 **Diaz-Balart, M.**	Y	Y	Y	N	N	N	Y
GEORGIA							
1 **Kingston**	Y	Y	Y	N	N	N	Y
2 Bishop	Y	Y	Y	Y	Y	Y	Y
3 **Westmoreland**	Y	N	Y	N	N	N	Y
4 Johnson	Y	Y	Y	Y	Y	Y	Y
5 Lewis	Y	Y	Y	Y	Y	Y	Y
6 **Price**	Y	Y	Y	N	N	N	Y
7 **Linder**	Y	N	Y	N	N	N	Y
8 Marshall	Y	Y	Y	Y	Y	Y	Y
9 **Deal**	Y	Y	Y	N	N	N	Y
10 **Broun**	Y	Y	Y	N	N	N	Y
11 **Gingrey**	Y	Y	Y	N	N	N	Y
12 Barrow	Y	Y	Y	Y	Y	Y	Y
13 Scott	Y	Y	Y	Y	Y	Y	Y
HAWAII							
1 Abercrombie	Y	Y	Y	Y	Y	Y	Y
2 Hirono	Y	Y	Y	Y	Y	Y	Y
IDAHO							
1 **Sali**	Y	Y	Y	?	N	N	Y
2 **Simpson**	Y	Y	Y	N	N	N	Y
ILLINOIS							
1 Rush	?	?	?	?	?	?	?
2 Jackson	Y	Y	Y	Y	Y	Y	Y
3 Lipinski	Y	Y	Y	Y	Y	Y	Y
4 Gutierrez	Y	Y	Y	Y	Y	Y	Y
5 Emanuel	Y	Y	Y	Y	Y	Y	Y
6 **Roskam**	?	+	?	N	N	N	Y
7 Davis	Y	Y	Y	Y	Y	Y	Y
8 Bean	Y	Y	Y	Y	Y	Y	Y
9 Schakowsky	Y	Y	Y	Y	Y	Y	Y
10 **Kirk**	Y	Y	Y	N	Y	N	Y
11 **Weller**	+	+	+	–	–	–	+
12 Costello	Y	Y	Y	Y	Y	Y	Y
13 **Biggert**	Y	Y	Y	N	N	N	Y
14 Foster	Y	Y	Y	Y	Y	Y	Y
15 **Johnson**	Y	Y	Y	Y	Y	N	Y

KEY **Republicans**   Democrats

Y Voted for (yea)	**X** Paired against	**C** Voted "present" to avoid possible conflict of interest
# Paired for	**–** Announced against	
+ Announced for	**P** Voted "present"	**?** Did not vote or otherwise make a position known
N Voted against (nay)		

ND Northern Democrats, SD Southern Democrats
Southern states: Ala., Ark., Fla., Ga., Ky., La., Miss., N.C., Okla., S.C., Tenn., Texas, Va.

	306	307	308	309	310	311	312
16 **Manzullo**	Y	Y	Y	N	N	N	Y
17 Hare	Y	Y	Y	Y	Y	Y	Y
18 **LaHood**	Y	Y	Y	Y	N	N	Y
19 **Shimkus**	Y	Y	Y	N	N	N	Y
INDIANA							
1 Visclosky	Y	Y	Y	Y	Y	Y	Y
2 Donnelly	Y	Y	Y	Y	N	Y	Y
3 **Souder**	Y	Y	Y	N	N	N	Y
4 **Buyer**	Y	Y	Y	N	N	N	Y
5 **Burton**	Y	Y	Y	N	N	N	Y
6 **Pence**	Y	Y	Y	N	N	N	Y
7 Carson, A.	Y	Y	Y	Y	Y	Y	Y
8 Ellsworth	Y	Y	Y	Y	Y	Y	Y
9 Hill	Y	Y	Y	Y	Y	Y	Y
IOWA							
1 Braley	Y	Y	Y	Y	Y	Y	Y
2 Loebsack	Y	Y	Y	Y	Y	Y	Y
3 Boswell	Y	Y	Y	Y	Y	Y	Y
4 **Latham**	Y	Y	Y	Y	N	N	Y
5 **King**	Y	N	Y	N	N	N	Y
KANSAS							
1 **Moran**	Y	Y	Y	N	N	N	Y
2 Boyda	Y	Y	Y	Y	Y	Y	Y
3 Moore	Y	Y	Y	Y	Y	Y	Y
4 **Tiahrt**	Y	Y	Y	N	N	N	Y
KENTUCKY							
1 **Whitfield**	Y	Y	Y	N	N	N	Y
2 **Lewis**	Y	Y	Y	?	?	?	?
3 Yarmuth	Y	Y	Y	Y	Y	Y	Y
4 **Davis**	Y	Y	Y	N	N	N	Y
5 **Rogers**	Y	Y	Y	N	N	N	Y
6 Chandler	Y	Y	Y	Y	Y	Y	Y
LOUISIANA							
1 **Scalise**	Y	N	Y	N	N	N	Y
2 Jefferson	Y	Y	Y	Y	Y	Y	Y
3 Melancon	Y	Y	Y	Y	Y	Y	Y
4 **McCrery**	Y	Y	Y	N	N	N	Y
5 **Alexander**	Y	Y	Y	N	N	N	Y
6 Cazayoux	Y	Y	Y	Y	Y	Y	Y
7 **Boustany**	Y	Y	Y	N	N	N	Y
MAINE							
1 Allen	Y	Y	Y	Y	Y	Y	Y
2 Michaud	Y	Y	Y	Y	Y	Y	Y
MARYLAND							
1 **Gilchrest**	Y	Y	Y	N	N	N	Y
2 Ruppersberger	Y	Y	Y	Y	Y	Y	Y
3 Sarbanes	Y	Y	Y	Y	Y	Y	Y
4 Wynn	?	?	?	Y	Y	Y	Y
5 Hoyer	Y	Y	Y	Y	Y	Y	Y
6 **Bartlett**	Y	Y	Y	N	N	N	Y
7 Cummings	Y	Y	Y	?	Y	Y	Y
8 Van Hollen	Y	Y	Y	Y	Y	Y	Y
MASSACHUSETTS							
1 Olver	Y	Y	Y	Y	Y	Y	Y
2 Neal	Y	Y	Y	Y	Y	Y	Y
3 McGovern	Y	Y	Y	Y	Y	Y	Y
4 Frank	Y	Y	Y	Y	Y	Y	Y
5 Tsongas	Y	Y	Y	Y	Y	Y	Y
6 Tierney	Y	Y	Y	N	Y	Y	Y
7 Markey	Y	Y	Y	Y	Y	Y	Y
8 Capuano	Y	Y	Y	Y	Y	Y	Y
9 Lynch	Y	Y	Y	Y	Y	Y	Y
10 Delahunt	Y	Y	Y	Y	Y	Y	Y
MICHIGAN							
1 Stupak	Y	Y	Y	Y	Y	Y	Y
2 **Hoekstra**	Y	Y	Y	N	N	N	Y
3 **Ehlers**	Y	N	Y	N	N	N	Y
4 **Camp**	Y	Y	Y	N	N	N	Y
5 Kildee	Y	Y	Y	Y	Y	Y	Y
6 **Upton**	Y	Y	Y	N	N	N	Y
7 **Walberg**	Y	Y	Y	N	N	N	Y
8 **Rogers**	Y	Y	Y	N	N	N	Y
9 **Knollenberg**	Y	Y	Y	N	N	N	Y
10 **Miller**	Y	Y	Y	N	N	N	Y
11 **McCotter**	Y	Y	Y	N	N	N	Y
12 Levin	Y	Y	Y	Y	Y	Y	Y
13 Kilpatrick	Y	Y	Y	Y	Y	Y	Y
14 Conyers	Y	Y	Y	Y	Y	Y	Y
15 Dingell	Y	Y	Y	Y	Y	Y	Y
MINNESOTA							
1 Walz	Y	Y	Y	Y	Y	Y	Y
2 **Kline**	Y	Y	Y	N	N	N	Y
3 **Ramstad**	Y	Y	Y	N	N	N	Y
4 McCollum	Y	Y	Y	Y	Y	Y	Y

	306	307	308	309	310	311	312
5 Ellison	Y	Y	Y	Y	Y	Y	Y
6 **Bachmann**	Y	Y	Y	N	N	N	Y
7 Peterson	Y	Y	Y	Y	Y	Y	Y
8 Oberstar	Y	Y	Y	Y	Y	Y	Y
MISSISSIPPI							
1 Vacant							
2 Thompson	Y	Y	Y	Y	Y	Y	Y
3 **Pickering**	Y	N	Y	N	N	N	Y
4 Taylor	Y	Y	Y	Y	Y	Y	Y
MISSOURI							
1 Clay	Y	?	Y	Y	Y	Y	Y
2 **Akin**	Y	N	Y	N	N	N	Y
3 Carnahan	Y	Y	Y	Y	Y	Y	Y
4 Skelton	Y	Y	Y	Y	Y	Y	Y
5 Cleaver	Y	Y	Y	Y	Y	Y	Y
6 **Graves**	Y	Y	Y	N	N	N	Y
7 **Blunt**	Y	Y	Y	N	N	N	Y
8 **Emerson**	Y	Y	Y	N	N	N	Y
9 **Hulshof**	?	?	?	N	N	N	Y
MONTANA							
AL **Rehberg**	Y	Y	Y	N	N	N	Y
NEBRASKA							
1 **Fortenberry**	Y	Y	Y	N	N	N	Y
2 **Terry**	Y	Y	Y	N	N	N	Y
3 **Smith**	Y	Y	Y	N	N	N	Y
NEVADA							
1 Berkley	Y	Y	Y	Y	Y	Y	Y
2 **Heller**	Y	Y	Y	N	N	N	Y
3 **Porter**	Y	Y	Y	N	N	N	Y
NEW HAMPSHIRE							
1 Shea-Porter	Y	Y	Y	Y	Y	Y	Y
2 Hodes	Y	Y	Y	Y	Y	Y	Y
NEW JERSEY							
1 Andrews	?	?	?	Y	Y	Y	Y
2 **LoBiondo**	Y	Y	Y	N	N	N	Y
3 **Saxton**	Y	Y	Y	N	N	N	Y
4 **Smith**	Y	Y	Y	N	N	N	Y
5 **Garrett**	Y	Y	Y	N	N	N	Y
6 Pallone	Y	Y	Y	Y	Y	Y	Y
7 **Ferguson**	?	?	?	N	N	N	Y
8 Pascrell	Y	Y	Y	Y	Y	Y	Y
9 Rothman	Y	Y	Y	Y	Y	Y	Y
10 Payne	Y	Y	Y	Y	Y	Y	Y
11 **Frelinghuysen**	Y	Y	Y	N	N	N	Y
12 Holt	Y	Y	Y	Y	Y	Y	Y
13 Sires	+	Y	Y	Y	Y	Y	Y
NEW MEXICO							
1 **Wilson**	Y	Y	Y	N	N	N	Y
2 **Pearce**	Y	Y	Y	N	N	N	Y
3 Udall	?	?	?	Y	Y	Y	Y
NEW YORK							
1 Bishop	Y	Y	Y	Y	Y	Y	Y
2 Israel	Y	Y	Y	Y	Y	Y	Y
3 **King**	Y	Y	Y	N	N	N	Y
4 McCarthy	Y	Y	Y	Y	Y	Y	Y
5 Ackerman	Y	Y	Y	Y	Y	Y	Y
6 Meeks	Y	Y	Y	Y	Y	Y	Y
7 Crowley	Y	Y	Y	Y	Y	Y	Y
8 Nadler	Y	Y	Y	Y	Y	Y	Y
9 Weiner	Y	Y	Y	Y	Y	Y	Y
10 Towns	Y	Y	Y	Y	Y	Y	Y
11 Clarke	Y	Y	Y	Y	Y	Y	Y
12 Velázquez	Y	Y	Y	Y	Y	Y	Y
13 **Fossella**	Y	Y	Y	N	N	N	Y
14 Maloney	Y	Y	Y	Y	Y	Y	Y
15 Rangel	Y	Y	Y	Y	Y	Y	Y
16 Serrano	Y	Y	Y	Y	Y	Y	Y
17 Engel	Y	Y	Y	Y	Y	Y	Y
18 Lowey	Y	Y	Y	Y	Y	Y	Y
19 Hall	Y	Y	Y	Y	Y	Y	Y
20 Gillibrand	Y	Y	Y	Y	Y	Y	Y
21 McNulty	Y	Y	Y	Y	Y	Y	Y
22 Hinchey	Y	Y	Y	Y	Y	Y	Y
23 **McHugh**	Y	Y	Y	N	N	N	Y
24 Arcuri	Y	Y	Y	Y	Y	Y	Y
25 **Walsh**	Y	Y	Y	N	N	N	Y
26 **Reynolds**	Y	Y	Y	N	N	N	Y
27 Higgins	Y	Y	?	Y	Y	Y	Y
28 Slaughter	Y	Y	Y	Y	Y	Y	Y
29 **Kuhl**	Y	Y	Y	N	N	N	Y
NORTH CAROLINA							
1 Butterfield	Y	Y	Y	Y	Y	Y	Y
2 Etheridge	Y	Y	Y	Y	Y	Y	Y
3 **Jones**	Y	Y	Y	N	N	N	Y
4 Price	Y	Y	Y	Y	Y	Y	Y

	306	307	308	309	310	311	312
5 **Foxx**	Y	N	Y	N	N	N	Y
6 **Coble**	Y	Y	Y	N	N	N	Y
7 McIntyre	Y	Y	Y	Y	Y	Y	Y
8 **Hayes**	Y	Y	Y	N	N	N	Y
9 **Myrick**	?	?	?	?	?	?	?
10 **McHenry**	Y	Y	Y	N	N	N	Y
11 Shuler	Y	Y	Y	Y	Y	Y	Y
12 Watt	Y	Y	Y	Y	Y	Y	Y
13 Miller	Y	Y	Y	Y	Y	Y	Y
NORTH DAKOTA							
AL Pomeroy	Y	Y	Y	Y	Y	Y	Y
OHIO							
1 **Chabot**	Y	Y	Y	N	N	N	Y
2 **Schmidt**	Y	Y	Y	N	?	?	?
3 **Turner**	Y	Y	Y	N	N	N	Y
4 **Jordan**	Y	Y	Y	N	N	N	Y
5 **Latta**	Y	Y	Y	N	N	N	Y
6 Wilson	Y	Y	Y	Y	Y	Y	Y
7 **Hobson**	Y	Y	Y	N	N	N	Y
8 **Boehner**	Y	Y	Y	N	N	N	Y
9 Kaptur	Y	Y	Y	Y	Y	Y	Y
10 Kucinich	Y	Y	Y	Y	Y	Y	Y
11 Tubbs Jones	Y	Y	Y	Y	Y	Y	Y
12 **Tiberi**	Y	Y	Y	N	N	N	Y
13 Sutton	Y	Y	Y	Y	Y	Y	Y
14 **LaTourette**	Y	Y	Y	N	N	N	Y
15 **Pryce**	Y	Y	Y	N	N	N	Y
16 **Regula**	Y	Y	Y	N	N	N	Y
17 Ryan	Y	Y	Y	Y	Y	Y	Y
18 Space	Y	Y	Y	Y	Y	Y	Y
OKLAHOMA							
1 **Sullivan**	Y	Y	Y	?	N	N	Y
2 Boren	Y	Y	Y	Y	Y	Y	Y
3 **Lucas**	Y	N	Y	N	N	N	Y
4 **Cole**	Y	N	Y	N	N	N	Y
5 **Fallin**	Y	Y	Y	N	N	N	Y
OREGON							
1 Wu	Y	Y	Y	Y	Y	Y	Y
2 **Walden**	Y	Y	Y	N	N	N	Y
3 Blumenauer	Y	Y	Y	Y	N	N	Y
4 DeFazio	Y	Y	Y	Y	Y	Y	Y
5 Hooley	Y	Y	Y	Y	Y	Y	Y
PENNSYLVANIA							
1 Brady	Y	Y	Y	Y	Y	Y	Y
2 Fattah	Y	Y	Y	Y	Y	Y	Y
3 **English**	Y	Y	Y	N	N	N	Y
4 Altmire	Y	Y	Y	Y	Y	Y	Y
5 **Peterson**	?	?	?	N	N	N	Y
6 **Gerlach**	?	?	?	?	?	?	?
7 Sestak	Y	Y	Y	Y	Y	Y	Y
8 Murphy, P.	Y	Y	Y	Y	Y	Y	Y
9 **Shuster**	Y	Y	Y	N	N	N	Y
10 Carney	?	?	?	?	Y	Y	Y
11 Kanjorski	Y	Y	Y	Y	Y	Y	Y
12 Murtha	Y	Y	Y	Y	Y	Y	Y
13 Schwartz	Y	Y	Y	Y	Y	Y	Y
14 Doyle	Y	Y	Y	Y	Y	Y	Y
15 **Dent**	Y	Y	Y	N	N	N	Y
16 **Pitts**	Y	Y	Y	N	N	N	Y
17 Holden	Y	Y	Y	Y	Y	Y	Y
18 **Murphy, T.**	Y	Y	Y	N	N	N	Y
19 **Platts**	Y	Y	Y	N	N	N	Y
RHODE ISLAND							
1 Kennedy	Y	Y	Y	Y	Y	Y	Y
2 Langevin	Y	Y	Y	Y	Y	Y	Y
SOUTH CAROLINA							
1 **Brown**	Y	Y	Y	N	N	N	Y
2 **Wilson**	Y	N	Y	N	N	N	Y
3 **Barrett**	Y	Y	Y	N	N	N	Y
4 **Inglis**	Y	N	Y	N	Y	N	Y
5 Spratt	Y	Y	Y	Y	Y	Y	Y
6 Clyburn	Y	Y	Y	Y	Y	Y	Y
SOUTH DAKOTA							
AL Herseth Sandlin	Y	Y	Y	Y	Y	Y	Y
TENNESSEE							
1 **Davis, D.**	Y	Y	Y	N	N	N	Y
2 **Duncan**	Y	Y	Y	N	N	N	Y
3 **Wamp**	Y	Y	Y	N	N	N	Y
4 Davis, L.	Y	Y	Y	Y	Y	Y	Y
5 Cooper	Y	Y	Y	Y	Y	N	Y
6 Gordon	Y	Y	Y	Y	Y	Y	Y
7 **Blackburn**	Y	Y	Y	N	N	N	Y
8 Tanner	Y	Y	Y	Y	Y	Y	Y
9 Cohen	Y	Y	Y	Y	Y	Y	Y

	306	307	308	309	310	311	312
TEXAS							
1 **Gohmert**	Y	Y	Y	N	N	N	Y
2 **Poe**	Y	Y	Y	N	N	N	Y
3 **Johnson, S.**	Y	Y	Y	N	N	N	Y
4 **Hall**	Y	Y	Y	N	N	N	Y
5 **Hensarling**	Y	N	Y	N	N	N	Y
6 **Barton**	Y	N	Y	N	N	N	Y
7 **Culberson**	Y	Y	Y	N	N	N	Y
8 **Brady**	Y	Y	Y	N	N	N	Y
9 Green, A.	Y	Y	Y	Y	Y	Y	Y
10 **McCaul**	Y	Y	Y	N	N	N	Y
11 **Conaway**	Y	N	Y	N	N	N	Y
12 **Granger**	Y	Y	Y	N	N	N	Y
13 **Thornberry**	Y	Y	Y	N	N	N	Y
14 **Paul**	N	Y	Y	N	N	?	?
15 Hinojosa	+	+	+	?	Y	Y	Y
16 Reyes	Y	Y	Y	Y	Y	Y	Y
17 Edwards	Y	Y	Y	Y	Y	Y	Y
18 Jackson Lee	Y	Y	Y	Y	Y	Y	Y
19 **Neugebauer**	Y	N	Y	N	N	N	Y
20 Gonzalez	Y	Y	Y	Y	Y	Y	Y
21 **Smith**	Y	Y	Y	N	N	N	Y
22 Lampson	Y	Y	Y	Y	N	Y	Y
23 Rodriguez	Y	Y	Y	Y	Y	Y	Y
24 **Marchant**	Y	Y	Y	N	N	N	Y
25 Doggett	Y	Y	Y	N	Y	Y	Y
26 **Burgess**	Y	Y	Y	N	N	N	Y
27 Ortiz	Y	Y	Y	Y	Y	Y	Y
28 Cuellar	Y	Y	Y	Y	Y	Y	Y
29 Green, G.	Y	Y	Y	Y	Y	Y	Y
30 Johnson, E.	Y	Y	Y	Y	Y	Y	Y
31 **Carter**	Y	Y	Y	N	N	N	Y
32 **Sessions**	Y	Y	Y	N	N	N	Y
UTAH							
1 **Bishop**	Y	Y	Y	N	N	N	Y
2 Matheson	Y	Y	Y	Y	Y	Y	Y
3 **Cannon**	Y	Y	Y	N	N	N	Y
VERMONT							
AL Welch	Y	Y	Y	Y	Y	Y	Y
VIRGINIA							
1 **Wittman**	Y	Y	Y	N	N	N	Y
2 **Drake**	Y	Y	Y	N	N	N	Y
3 Scott	Y	Y	Y	Y	Y	Y	Y
4 **Forbes**	Y	Y	Y	N	N	N	Y
5 **Goode**	Y	Y	Y	N	N	N	Y
6 **Goodlatte**	Y	Y	Y	N	N	N	Y
7 **Cantor**	Y	Y	Y	N	N	N	Y
8 Moran	Y	Y	Y	Y	Y	Y	Y
9 Boucher	Y	Y	Y	Y	Y	Y	Y
10 **Wolf**	Y	Y	Y	N	N	N	Y
11 **Davis**	Y	Y	Y	N	N	N	Y
WASHINGTON							
1 Inslee	Y	Y	Y	Y	Y	Y	Y
2 Larsen	Y	Y	Y	Y	Y	Y	Y
3 Baird	Y	Y	Y	Y	Y	Y	Y
4 **Hastings**	Y	Y	Y	N	N	N	Y
5 **McMorris Rodgers**	Y	Y	Y	N	N	N	Y
6 Dicks	Y	Y	Y	Y	Y	Y	Y
7 McDermott	Y	Y	Y	Y	+	Y	Y
8 **Reichert**	Y	Y	Y	N	Y	N	Y
9 Smith	Y	Y	Y	N	Y	Y	Y
WEST VIRGINIA							
1 Mollohan	?	?	?	Y	Y	Y	Y
2 **Capito**	Y	Y	Y	N	N	N	Y
3 Rahall	Y	Y	Y	Y	Y	Y	Y
WISCONSIN							
1 **Ryan**	Y	Y	Y	N	N	N	Y
2 Baldwin	Y	Y	Y	Y	Y	Y	Y
3 Kind	Y	Y	Y	Y	Y	Y	Y
4 Moore	Y	Y	Y	Y	Y	Y	Y
5 **Sensenbrenner**	Y	Y	Y	N	N	N	Y
6 **Petri**	Y	Y	Y	N	N	N	Y
7 Obey	Y	Y	Y	Y	Y	Y	Y
8 Kagen	Y	Y	Y	Y	Y	Y	Y
WYOMING							
AL **Cubin**	Y	N	Y	?	?	?	?
DELEGATES							
Faleomavaega (A.S.)							
Norton (D.C.)							
Bordallo (Guam)							
Fortuño (P.R.)							
Christensen (V.I.)							

IN THE HOUSE | By Vote Number

313. **H Res 1176. Support National Train Day/Adoption.** Brown, D-Fla., motion to suspend the rules and adopt the resolution that would support the goals and ideals of National Train Day. Motion agreed to 415-0: R 187-0; D 228-0 (ND 171-0, SD 57-0). A two-thirds majority of those present and voting (277 in this case) is required for adoption under suspension of the rules. May 14, 2008.

314. **HR 2419. Farm Bill Reauthorization/Recommit.** Cantor, R-Va., motion to recommit the bill to the conference committee with instructions that it be reported back promptly with language that would strike three sections of the bill relating to the sale or exchange of National Forest System lands to Vermont; fisheries disaster assistance; and qualified forestry conservation bonds. Motion rejected 193-230: R 184-6; D 9-224 (ND 5-171, SD 4-53). May 14, 2008.

315. **HR 2419. Farm Bill Reauthorization/Conference Report.** Adoption of the conference report on the bill that would reauthorize federal farm and nutrition programs for five years, including crop subsidies and food stamps, as well as conservation, rural development and agricultural trade programs. It would authorize a $10.4 billion increase for nutrition programs, offset by extending customs user fees. It also would cut direct payment subsidies overall by $313 million, in part by reducing the percentage of acres for which a farmer can collect those payments. Farmers making more than $750,000 a year in farm-related income and those with more than $500,000 a year in non-farm-related income would not be eligible for federal subsidies. Country-of-origin labels for all meat would be required by September 2008. Adopted (thus sent to the Senate) 318-106: R 100-91; D 218-15 (ND 162-14, SD 56-1). A "nay" was a vote in support of the president's position. May 14, 2008.

316. **H Res 1133. Congratulate Winona State University/Adoption.** Walz, D-Minn., motion to suspend the rules and adopt the resolution that would congratulate Winona State University on winning the 2008 Division II men's basketball championships. Motion agreed to 413-0: R 187-0; D 226-0 (ND 170-0, SD 56-0). A two-thirds majority of those present and voting (276 in this case) is required for adoption under suspension of the rules. May 14, 2008.

317. **S Con Res 70. Fiscal 2009 Budget Resolution/Previous Question.** McGovern, D-Mass., motion to order the previous question (thus ending debate and possibility of amendment) on adoption of the rule (H Res 1190) that would take up the Senate's fiscal 2009 budget resolution. It would automatically amend it with the text of the House resolution (H Con Res 312), adopt S Con Res 70 as amended and request a conference with the Senate. Motion agreed to 225-187: R 7-179; D 218-8 (ND 167-4, SD 51-4). May 14, 2008.

318. **S Con Res 70. Fiscal 2009 Budget Resolution/Rule.** Adoption of the rule (H Res 1190) that would take up the Senate's fiscal 2009 budget resolution. It would automatically amend it with the text of the House resolution (H Con Res 312), adopt S Con Res 70 as amended and request a conference with the Senate. Adopted 214-203: R 0-189; D 214-14 (ND 162-9, SD 52-5). May 14, 2008.

	313	314	315	316	317	318
ALABAMA						
1 Bonner	Y	Y	Y	Y	N	N
2 Everett	Y	Y	Y	Y	N	N
3 Rogers	Y	Y	Y	Y	N	N
4 Aderholt	Y	Y	Y	Y	N	N
5 Cramer	?	?	?	?	?	?
6 Bachus	Y	Y	Y	Y	N	N
7 Davis	Y	N	Y	Y	Y	Y
ALASKA						
AL Young	Y	N	Y	Y	N	N
ARIZONA						
1 Renzi	Y	Y	Y	Y	N	N
2 Franks	Y	Y	N	Y	N	N
3 Shadegg	Y	Y	N	Y	N	N
4 Pastor	Y	N	Y	Y	Y	N
5 Mitchell	Y	Y	N	Y	Y	N
6 Flake	Y	Y	N	Y	N	N
7 Grijalva	Y	N	Y	Y	Y	Y
8 Giffords	Y	N	Y	Y	Y	N
ARKANSAS						
1 Berry	Y	N	Y	Y	Y	Y
2 Snyder	Y	N	Y	Y	Y	Y
3 Boozman	Y	Y	Y	Y	N	N
4 Ross	Y	N	Y	Y	Y	Y
CALIFORNIA						
1 Thompson	Y	N	Y	Y	Y	Y
2 Herger	Y	Y	Y	Y	N	N
3 Lungren	Y	Y	N	Y	N	N
4 Doolittle	Y	N	Y	Y	N	N
5 Matsui	Y	N	Y	Y	Y	Y
6 Woolsey	Y	N	Y	Y	Y	Y
7 Miller, George	Y	N	Y	Y	Y	Y
8 Pelosi	N	Y				Y
9 Lee	Y	N	Y	Y	Y	Y
10 Tauscher	Y	N	Y	Y	Y	Y
11 McNerney	Y	N	Y	Y	Y	Y
12 Speier	Y	N	Y	Y	Y	Y
13 Stark	Y	Y	N	Y	N	N
14 Eshoo	Y	N	Y	Y	Y	Y
15 Honda	Y	N	Y	Y	Y	?
16 Lofgren	Y	N	Y	Y	Y	Y
17 Farr	Y	N	Y	Y	Y	Y
18 Cardoza	Y	N	Y	Y	Y	Y
19 Radanovich	Y	Y	Y	Y	N	N
20 Costa	Y	N	Y	Y	Y	Y
21 Nunes	Y	Y	N	Y	N	N
22 McCarthy	Y	Y	N	Y	N	N
23 Capps	Y	N	Y	Y	Y	Y
24 Gallegly	Y	Y	Y	Y	N	N
25 McKeon	Y	Y	N	Y	N	N
26 Dreier	Y	Y	N	Y	N	N
27 Sherman	Y	N	Y	Y	Y	Y
28 Berman	Y	N	Y	Y	Y	Y
29 Schiff	Y	N	Y	Y	Y	Y
30 Waxman	Y	N	Y	Y	Y	Y
31 Becerra	Y	N	Y	Y	Y	Y
32 Solis	Y	N	Y	Y	Y	Y
33 Watson	Y	N	Y	Y	Y	Y
34 Roybal-Allard	Y	N	Y	Y	Y	Y
35 Waters	Y	N	Y	Y	Y	Y
36 Harman	Y	N	Y	Y	Y	Y
37 Richardson	Y	N	Y	Y	Y	Y
38 Napolitano	Y	N	Y	Y	Y	Y
39 Sánchez, Linda	Y	N	Y	Y	Y	Y
40 Royce	Y	Y	N	Y	N	N
41 Lewis	Y	Y	N	Y	N	N
42 Miller, Gary	Y	Y	N	Y	N	N
43 Baca	Y	N	Y	Y	Y	Y
44 Calvert	Y	Y	N	Y	N	N
45 Bono Mack	?	?	?	?	?	?
46 Rohrabacher	Y	Y	N	Y	N	N
47 Sanchez, Loretta	Y	N	Y	Y	Y	Y
48 Campbell	Y	Y	N	Y	N	N
49 Issa	Y	Y	N	Y	N	N
50 Bilbray	?	Y	N	Y	N	N
51 Filner	Y	N	Y	Y	Y	Y
52 Hunter	Y	Y	N	Y	N	N
53 Davis	Y	N	Y	Y	Y	Y

	313	314	315	316	317	318
COLORADO						
1 DeGette	Y	N	Y	?	?	?
2 Udall	Y	N	Y	Y	Y	Y
3 Salazar	Y	N	Y	Y	Y	Y
4 Musgrave	Y	Y	Y	Y	?	N
5 Lamborn	Y	Y	N	Y	N	N
6 Tancredo	Y	Y	N	Y	N	N
7 Perlmutter	Y	N	Y	Y	Y	Y
CONNECTICUT						
1 Larson	Y	N	Y	Y	Y	Y
2 Courtney	Y	N	Y	Y	Y	Y
3 DeLauro	Y	N	Y	Y	Y	Y
4 Shays	Y	Y	N	Y	N	N
5 Murphy	Y	N	Y	Y	Y	Y
DELAWARE						
AL Castle	Y	Y	N	Y	Y	N
FLORIDA						
1 Miller	Y	Y	N	Y	N	N
2 Boyd	Y	N	Y	Y	Y	Y
3 Brown	Y	N	Y	Y	Y	Y
4 Crenshaw	?	?	?	?	?	?
5 Brown-Waite	Y	Y	N	Y	N	N
6 Stearns	Y	Y	N	Y	N	N
7 Mica	Y	Y	N	Y	N	N
8 Keller	Y	Y	N	Y	N	N
9 Bilirakis	Y	Y	Y	Y	N	N
10 Young	Y	Y	N	Y	N	N
11 Castor	Y	N	Y	Y	Y	Y
12 Putnam	Y	Y	Y	Y	N	N
13 Buchanan	Y	Y	Y	Y	N	N
14 Mack	?	?	?	?	?	?
15 Weldon	Y	Y	N	Y	N	N
16 Mahoney	Y	N	Y	Y	Y	Y
17 Meek	Y	N	Y	Y	Y	Y
18 Ros-Lehtinen	Y	Y	Y	Y	Y	N
19 Wexler	Y	N	Y	Y	Y	Y
20 Wasserman Schultz	Y	N	Y	Y	Y	Y
21 Diaz-Balart, L.	Y	Y	Y	Y	N	N
22 Klein	Y	N	Y	Y	Y	Y
23 Hastings	Y	N	Y	Y	Y	Y
24 Feeney	Y	Y	N	?	N	N
25 Diaz-Balart, M.	Y	Y	Y	Y	N	N
GEORGIA						
1 Kingston	Y	Y	Y	Y	N	N
2 Bishop	Y	N	Y	Y	Y	Y
3 Westmoreland	Y	Y	N	Y	N	N
4 Johnson	Y	N	Y	Y	Y	Y
5 Lewis	Y	N	Y	Y	Y	Y
6 Price	Y	Y	N	Y	N	N
7 Linder	Y	Y	N	Y	N	N
8 Marshall	Y	N	Y	Y	N	N
9 Deal	Y	Y	N	Y	N	N
10 Broun	Y	Y	N	Y	N	N
11 Gingrey	Y	Y	Y	Y	N	N
12 Barrow	Y	N	Y	Y	N	N
13 Scott	Y	N	Y	Y	Y	Y
HAWAII						
1 Abercrombie	Y	N	Y	Y	Y	Y
2 Hirono	Y	N	Y	Y	Y	Y
IDAHO						
1 Sali	Y	Y	Y	Y	N	N
2 Simpson	Y	Y	Y	Y	N	N
ILLINOIS						
1 Rush	?	?	?	?	?	?
2 Jackson	Y	N	Y	Y	Y	Y
3 Lipinski	Y	N	Y	Y	Y	Y
4 Gutierrez	Y	N	Y	Y	Y	Y
5 Emanuel	Y	N	Y	Y	Y	Y
6 Roskam	Y	Y	N	Y	N	N
7 Davis	Y	N	Y	Y	Y	Y
8 Bean	Y	Y	N	Y	Y	Y
9 Schakowsky	Y	N	Y	Y	Y	Y
10 Kirk	Y	Y	N	Y	Y	N
11 Weller	+	+	+	+	-	N
12 Costello	Y	N	Y	Y	Y	Y
13 Biggert	Y	Y	N	Y	N	N
14 Foster	Y	N	Y	Y	N	N
15 Johnson	Y	Y	Y	Y	N	N

ND Northern Democrats, SD Southern Democrats
Southern states: Ala., Ark., Fla., Ga., Ky., La., Miss., N.C., Okla., S.C., Tenn., Texas, Va.

	313	314	315	316	317	318
16 **Manzullo**	Y	Y	Y	Y	N	N
17 Hare	Y	N	Y	Y	Y	Y
18 **LaHood**	Y	Y	Y	Y	N	N
19 **Shimkus**	Y	Y	Y	Y	N	N
INDIANA						
1 Visclosky	Y	N	Y	Y	Y	Y
2 Donnelly	Y	N	Y	Y	N	N
3 **Souder**	Y	Y	Y	Y	N	N
4 **Buyer**	Y	Y	Y	Y	N	N
5 **Burton**	Y	Y	N	Y	N	N
6 **Pence**	Y	Y	N	Y	N	N
7 Carson, A.	Y	N	Y	Y	Y	Y
8 Ellsworth	Y	N	Y	Y	Y	N
9 Hill	Y	N	Y	Y	Y	Y
IOWA						
1 Braley	?	N	Y	Y	Y	Y
2 Loebsack	Y	N	Y	Y	Y	Y
3 Boswell	Y	N	Y	Y	Y	Y
4 **Latham**	Y	Y	Y	Y	N	N
5 **King**	Y	Y	Y	Y	N	N
KANSAS						
1 **Moran**	Y	Y	N	Y	N	N
2 Boyda	Y	N	Y	Y	Y	Y
3 Moore	Y	N	Y	Y	Y	Y
4 **Tiahrt**	Y	Y	N	Y	N	N
KENTUCKY						
1 **Whitfield**	Y	Y	Y	Y	N	N
2 **Lewis**	?	?	?	?	?	?
3 Yarmuth	Y	N	Y	Y	Y	Y
4 **Davis**	Y	Y	Y	Y	N	N
5 **Rogers**	Y	Y	Y	Y	N	N
6 Chandler	Y	N	Y	Y	Y	Y
LOUISIANA						
1 **Scalise**	Y	Y	N	Y	N	N
2 Jefferson	Y	N	Y	Y	Y	Y
3 Melancon	Y	N	Y	Y	N	Y
4 **McCrery**	Y	Y	N	Y	N	N
5 **Alexander**	Y	Y	Y	Y	N	N
6 Cazayoux	Y	N	Y	Y	Y	Y
7 **Boustany**	Y	Y	Y	Y	N	N
MAINE						
1 Allen	Y	N	Y	Y	Y	Y
2 Michaud	Y	N	Y	Y	Y	Y
MARYLAND						
1 **Gilchrest**	?	N	Y	Y	N	N
2 Ruppersberger	Y	N	Y	Y	Y	Y
3 Sarbanes	Y	N	Y	Y	Y	Y
4 Wynn	Y	N	Y	Y	?	Y
5 Hoyer	Y	N	Y	Y	Y	Y
6 **Bartlett**	Y	Y	Y	Y	N	N
7 Cummings	Y	N	Y	Y	Y	Y
8 Van Hollen	Y	N	Y	Y	Y	Y
MASSACHUSETTS						
1 Olver	Y	N	Y	Y	Y	Y
2 Neal	Y	N	Y	Y	Y	Y
3 McGovern	Y	N	Y	Y	Y	Y
4 Frank	Y	N	Y	Y	Y	Y
5 Tsongas	Y	N	Y	Y	Y	Y
6 Tierney	Y	N	Y	Y	Y	Y
7 Markey	Y	N	Y	Y	Y	Y
8 Capuano	Y	N	N	Y	Y	Y
9 Lynch	Y	N	Y	Y	Y	Y
10 Delahunt	Y	N	Y	Y	Y	Y
MICHIGAN						
1 Stupak	Y	N	Y	Y	Y	Y
2 **Hoekstra**	Y	Y	Y	Y	N	N
3 **Ehlers**	Y	Y	N	Y	N	N
4 **Camp**	Y	Y	Y	Y	N	N
5 Kildee	Y	N	Y	Y	Y	Y
6 **Upton**	Y	Y	Y	Y	N	N
7 **Walberg**	Y	Y	Y	Y	N	N
8 **Rogers**	Y	Y	Y	Y	N	N
9 **Knollenberg**	Y	Y	N	Y	N	N
10 **Miller**	Y	Y	Y	Y	N	N
11 **McCotter**	Y	Y	Y	Y	N	N
12 Levin	Y	N	Y	Y	Y	Y
13 Kilpatrick	Y	N	Y	Y	Y	Y
14 Conyers	Y	N	Y	Y	Y	Y
15 Dingell	Y	N	Y	Y	Y	Y
MINNESOTA						
1 Walz	Y	N	Y	Y	Y	Y
2 **Kline**	Y	Y	Y	Y	N	N
3 **Ramstad**	Y	Y	N	Y	N	N
4 McCollum	Y	N	Y	Y	Y	Y
5 Ellison	Y	N	Y	?	Y	Y
6 **Bachmann**	Y	Y	N	?	N	N
7 Peterson	Y	N	Y	Y	Y	Y
8 Oberstar	Y	N	Y	Y	Y	Y
MISSISSIPPI						
1 Vacant						
2 Thompson	Y	N	Y	Y	Y	Y
3 **Pickering**	Y	?	Y	Y	N	?
4 Taylor	Y	N	Y	Y	Y	Y
MISSOURI						
1 Clay	Y	N	Y	Y	Y	Y
2 **Akin**	Y	Y	N	Y	N	N
3 Carnahan	Y	N	Y	?	Y	Y
4 Skelton	Y	N	Y	Y	Y	Y
5 Cleaver	Y	N	Y	Y	Y	Y
6 **Graves**	Y	Y	Y	Y	N	N
7 **Blunt**	Y	Y	Y	Y	N	N
8 **Emerson**	Y	Y	Y	Y	N	N
9 **Hulshof**	Y	Y	Y	Y	N	N
MONTANA						
AL **Rehberg**	Y	N	Y	Y	N	N
NEBRASKA						
1 **Fortenberry**	Y	Y	Y	Y	N	N
2 **Terry**	Y	N	N	Y	N	N
3 **Smith**	Y	Y	Y	Y	N	N
NEVADA						
1 Berkley	Y	N	Y	Y	Y	Y
2 **Heller**	Y	Y	N	Y	N	N
3 **Porter**	Y	Y	Y	Y	N	N
NEW HAMPSHIRE						
1 Shea-Porter	Y	N	Y	Y	Y	Y
2 Hodes	Y	N	Y	Y	Y	Y
NEW JERSEY						
1 Andrews	?	N	Y	?	?	?
2 **LoBiondo**	Y	Y	N	Y	N	N
3 **Saxton**	Y	Y	N	Y	N	N
4 **Smith**	Y	Y	N	?	N	N
5 **Garrett**	Y	Y	N	Y	N	N
6 Pallone	Y	N	Y	Y	Y	Y
7 **Ferguson**	Y	Y	N	Y	N	N
8 Pascrell	Y	N	Y	Y	Y	Y
9 Rothman	Y	N	Y	Y	Y	Y
10 Payne	Y	N	Y	Y	Y	Y
11 **Frelinghuysen**	Y	Y	N	Y	N	N
12 Holt	Y	N	Y	Y	Y	Y
13 Sires	Y	N	Y	Y	Y	Y
NEW MEXICO						
1 **Wilson**	Y	Y	N	Y	–	–
2 **Pearce**	Y	Y	Y	Y	N	N
3 Udall	Y	N	Y	Y	Y	Y
NEW YORK						
1 Bishop	Y	N	Y	Y	Y	Y
2 Israel	Y	N	Y	Y	Y	Y
3 **King**	Y	Y	N	Y	N	N
4 McCarthy	Y	N	Y	Y	Y	Y
5 Ackerman	Y	N	Y	Y	Y	Y
6 Meeks	Y	N	Y	Y	?	?
7 Crowley	Y	N	Y	Y	Y	Y
8 Nadler	Y	N	Y	Y	Y	Y
9 Weiner	Y	N	Y	Y	Y	Y
10 Towns	Y	N	Y	Y	Y	Y
11 Clarke	Y	N	Y	Y	Y	Y
12 Velázquez	Y	N	Y	Y	Y	Y
13 **Fossella**	Y	Y	N	Y	N	N
14 Maloney	Y	N	Y	Y	Y	Y
15 Rangel	Y	N	Y	Y	Y	Y
16 Serrano	Y	N	Y	Y	Y	Y
17 Engel	Y	N	Y	Y	Y	Y
18 Lowey	Y	N	Y	Y	Y	Y
19 Hall	Y	N	Y	Y	Y	Y
20 Gillibrand	Y	N	Y	Y	Y	Y
21 McNulty	Y	N	Y	Y	Y	Y
22 Hinchey	Y	N	Y	Y	Y	Y
23 **McHugh**	Y	Y	Y	Y	N	N
24 Arcuri	Y	N	Y	Y	Y	Y
25 **Walsh**	Y	Y	Y	Y	N	N
26 **Reynolds**	Y	Y	Y	Y	N	N
27 Higgins	Y	N	Y	Y	Y	Y
28 Slaughter	Y	N	Y	Y	Y	Y
29 **Kuhl**	Y	Y	Y	Y	N	N
NORTH CAROLINA						
1 Butterfield	Y	N	Y	Y	Y	Y
2 Etheridge	Y	N	Y	Y	Y	Y
3 **Jones**	Y	Y	Y	Y	N	N
4 Price	Y	N	Y	Y	Y	Y
5 **Foxx**	Y	Y	N	Y	N	N
6 **Coble**	Y	Y	Y	Y	N	N
7 McIntyre	Y	N	Y	Y	Y	Y
8 **Hayes**	Y	Y	N	Y	N	N
9 **Myrick**	?	?	?	?	?	?
10 **McHenry**	Y	Y	N	Y	N	N
11 Shuler	Y	N	Y	Y	?	N
12 Watt	Y	N	Y	Y	Y	Y
13 Miller	Y	N	Y	Y	Y	Y
NORTH DAKOTA						
AL Pomeroy	Y	N	Y	Y	Y	Y
OHIO						
1 **Chabot**	Y	Y	N	Y	N	N
2 **Schmidt**	?	?	?	?	?	?
3 **Turner**	Y	Y	Y	Y	N	N
4 **Jordan**	Y	Y	N	Y	N	N
5 **Latta**	Y	Y	Y	Y	N	N
6 Wilson	Y	N	Y	Y	Y	Y
7 **Hobson**	Y	Y	N	Y	N	N
8 **Boehner**	Y	Y	N	Y	N	N
9 Kaptur	Y	N	Y	Y	Y	Y
10 Kucinich	Y	N	N	Y	Y	Y
11 Tubbs Jones	Y	N	Y	Y	Y	Y
12 **Tiberi**	Y	Y	N	Y	N	N
13 Sutton	Y	N	Y	Y	Y	Y
14 **LaTourette**	Y	Y	Y	Y	N	N
15 **Pryce**	Y	Y	N	Y	N	N
16 **Regula**	Y	Y	Y	Y	N	N
17 Ryan	Y	N	Y	Y	Y	Y
18 Space	Y	N	Y	Y	Y	Y
OKLAHOMA						
1 **Sullivan**	Y	Y	Y	Y	N	N
2 Boren	Y	N	Y	Y	Y	Y
3 **Lucas**	Y	Y	Y	Y	N	N
4 **Cole**	Y	Y	Y	Y	N	N
5 **Fallin**	Y	Y	Y	Y	N	N
OREGON						
1 Wu	Y	N	Y	?	Y	?
2 **Walden**	Y	N	Y	?	N	N
3 Blumenauer	Y	N	N	Y	Y	Y
4 DeFazio	Y	N	Y	Y	Y	Y
5 Hooley	?	N	Y	Y	Y	Y
PENNSYLVANIA						
1 Brady	Y	N	Y	Y	Y	Y
2 Fattah	Y	N	Y	Y	Y	Y
3 **English**	Y	Y	Y	Y	N	N
4 Altmire	Y	N	Y	Y	Y	Y
5 **Peterson**	Y	Y	Y	Y	N	N
6 **Gerlach**	?	?	?	?	?	?
7 Sestak	Y	N	Y	Y	Y	Y
8 Murphy, P.	Y	N	Y	Y	Y	N
9 **Shuster**	Y	Y	Y	Y	N	N
10 Carney	Y	N	Y	Y	Y	Y
11 Kanjorski	Y	N	Y	Y	Y	Y
12 Murtha	Y	N	Y	Y	Y	Y
13 Schwartz	Y	N	Y	Y	Y	Y
14 Doyle	Y	N	Y	Y	Y	Y
15 **Dent**	Y	Y	N	Y	N	N
16 **Pitts**	Y	Y	N	Y	N	N
17 Holden	Y	N	Y	Y	Y	Y
18 **Murphy, T.**	Y	Y	Y	Y	N	N
19 **Platts**	Y	Y	Y	Y	N	N
RHODE ISLAND						
1 Kennedy	Y	N	Y	Y	Y	Y
2 Langevin	Y	N	Y	Y	Y	Y
SOUTH CAROLINA						
1 **Brown**	Y	Y	Y	Y	N	N
2 **Wilson**	Y	Y	N	Y	N	N
3 **Barrett**	Y	Y	N	Y	N	N
4 **Inglis**	Y	Y	N	Y	N	N
5 Spratt	Y	N	Y	Y	Y	Y
6 Clyburn	Y	N	Y	Y	Y	Y
SOUTH DAKOTA						
AL Herseth Sandlin	Y	N	Y	Y	Y	Y
TENNESSEE						
1 **Davis, D.**	Y	Y	Y	Y	N	N
2 **Duncan**	Y	Y	N	Y	N	N
3 **Wamp**	Y	Y	N	Y	N	N
4 Davis, L.	Y	N	Y	Y	Y	Y
5 Cooper	Y	Y	N	Y	Y	Y
6 Gordon	Y	N	Y	?	Y	Y
7 **Blackburn**	Y	Y	N	Y	N	N
8 Tanner	Y	N	Y	Y	Y	Y
9 Cohen	Y	N	Y	Y	Y	Y
TEXAS						
1 **Gohmert**	Y	Y	Y	Y	?	N
2 **Poe**	Y	Y	Y	Y	N	N
3 **Johnson, S.**	Y	Y	N	Y	N	N
4 **Hall**	Y	Y	Y	Y	N	N
5 **Hensarling**	Y	Y	N	Y	N	N
6 **Barton**	Y	Y	Y	Y	N	N
7 **Culberson**	Y	Y	N	Y	N	N
8 **Brady**	Y	Y	Y	Y	N	N
9 Green, A.	Y	N	Y	Y	Y	Y
10 **McCaul**	Y	Y	Y	Y	N	N
11 **Conaway**	Y	Y	Y	Y	N	N
12 **Granger**	Y	Y	N	Y	N	N
13 **Thornberry**	Y	Y	Y	Y	N	N
14 **Paul**	?	Y	N	Y	N	N
15 Hinojosa	Y	N	Y	Y	+	Y
16 Reyes	Y	N	Y	Y	Y	Y
17 Edwards	Y	N	Y	Y	Y	Y
18 Jackson Lee	Y	N	Y	Y	Y	Y
19 **Neugebauer**	Y	Y	Y	Y	–	N
20 Gonzalez	Y	N	Y	Y	Y	Y
21 **Smith**	Y	Y	Y	Y	N	N
22 Lampson	Y	Y	Y	Y	N	N
23 Rodriguez	Y	N	Y	Y	Y	Y
24 **Marchant**	Y	Y	Y	Y	N	N
25 Doggett	Y	Y	Y	Y	Y	Y
26 **Burgess**	Y	Y	N	Y	N	N
27 Ortiz	Y	N	Y	Y	Y	Y
28 Cuellar	Y	N	Y	Y	Y	Y
29 Green, G.	Y	N	Y	Y	Y	Y
30 Johnson, E.	Y	N	Y	Y	Y	Y
31 **Carter**	Y	Y	Y	Y	N	N
32 **Sessions**	Y	Y	N	Y	N	N
UTAH						
1 **Bishop**	Y	Y	Y	Y	N	N
2 Matheson	Y	Y	N	Y	Y	N
3 **Cannon**	Y	Y	N	Y	N	N
VERMONT						
AL Welch	Y	N	Y	Y	Y	Y
VIRGINIA						
1 **Wittman**	Y	Y	Y	Y	N	N
2 **Drake**	Y	Y	Y	Y	N	N
3 Scott	Y	N	Y	Y	Y	Y
4 **Forbes**	Y	Y	Y	Y	N	N
5 **Goode**	Y	Y	N	Y	N	N
6 **Goodlatte**	Y	Y	Y	Y	N	N
7 **Cantor**	Y	Y	N	Y	N	N
8 Moran	Y	Y	Y	Y	Y	Y
9 Boucher	Y	N	Y	Y	Y	Y
10 **Wolf**	Y	Y	N	Y	N	N
11 **Davis**	Y	Y	N	Y	N	N
WASHINGTON						
1 Inslee	Y	N	N	Y	Y	Y
2 Larsen	Y	N	Y	Y	Y	Y
3 Baird	Y	N	Y	Y	Y	Y
4 **Hastings**	Y	Y	Y	Y	N	N
5 **McMorris Rodgers**	Y	Y	Y	Y	N	N
6 Dicks	Y	N	Y	Y	Y	Y
7 McDermott	Y	N	N	Y	Y	Y
8 **Reichert**	Y	Y	N	Y	Y	N
9 Smith	Y	N	N	Y	Y	Y
WEST VIRGINIA						
1 Mollohan	Y	N	Y	Y	Y	Y
2 **Capito**	Y	Y	Y	Y	N	N
3 Rahall	Y	N	Y	Y	Y	Y
WISCONSIN						
1 **Ryan**	Y	Y	N	Y	N	N
2 Baldwin	Y	N	Y	Y	Y	Y
3 Kind	Y	Y	N	Y	Y	Y
4 Moore	Y	N	N	Y	Y	Y
5 **Sensenbrenner**	Y	Y	N	Y	N	N
6 **Petri**	Y	Y	N	Y	N	N
7 Obey	Y	N	Y	Y	Y	Y
8 Kagen	?	N	Y	Y	Y	Y
WYOMING						
AL **Cubin**	?	Y	Y	Y	?	?
DELEGATES						
Faleomavaega (A.S.)						
Norton (D.C.)						
Bordallo (Guam)						
Fortuño (P.R.)						
Christensen (V.I.)						

IN THE HOUSE | By Vote Number

319. **H Res 1173. Recognize AmeriCorps Week/Adoption.** Davis, D-Ill., motion to suspend the rules and adopt the resolution that would recognize the accomplishments of AmeriCorps members and alumni and encourage citizens to participate in the AmeriCorps program. Motion agreed to 344-69: R 119-69; D 225-0 (ND 169-0, SD 56-0). A two-thirds majority of those present and voting (276 in this case) is required for adoption under suspension of the rules. May 14, 2008.

320. **HR 4040. Consumer Product Safety Modernization/Motion to Instruct.** Whitfield, R-Ky., motion to instruct conferees to insist on the provisions contained in the House-passed bill. Motion agreed to 405-0: R 183-0; D 222-0 (ND 167-0, SD 55-0). May 14, 2008.

321. **S Con Res 70. Fiscal 2009 Budget Resolution/Motion to Instruct.** Ryan, R-Wis., motion to instruct conferees to adjust budget levels to assume $2 billion in increased revenues from expanding federal leases for oil exploration and development in the western federal lands, the outer continental shelf and the Arctic National Wildlife Refuge. Motion rejected 185-229: R 171-17; D 14-212 (ND 1-169, SD 13-43). May 14, 2008.

322. **H Res 789. Child Welfare Agencies Tribute/Adoption.** Davis, D-Ill., motion to suspend the rules and adopt the resolution that would honor the contributions of nonprofit public child welfare agencies. Motion agreed to 414-0: R 188-0; D 226-0 (ND 170-0, SD 56-0). A two-thirds majority of those present and voting (276 in this case) is required for adoption under suspension of the rules. May 14, 2008.

323. **HR 2642. Supplemental Appropriations/Previous Question.** Slaughter, D-N.Y., motion to order the previous question (thus ending debate and possibility of amendment) on adoption of the rule (H Res 1197) that would provide for House floor consideration of the Senate amendments to the bill that would serve as the vehicle for supplemental appropriations for the wars in Iraq and Afghanistan and for various domestic programs. Motion agreed to 224-195: R 0-191; D 224-4 (ND 167-3, SD 57-1). May 15, 2008.

324. **HR 2642. Supplemental Appropriations/Rule.** Adoption of the rule (H Res 1197) that would provide for House floor consideration of the Senate amendments to the bill that would serve as the vehicle for supplemental appropriations for the wars in Iraq and Afghanistan and for various domestic programs. Adopted 221-200: R 0-192; D 221-8 (ND 166-5, SD 55-3). May 15, 2008.

325. **HR 5614. Saint-Gaudens Double Eagle Coins/Passage.** Gutierrez, D-Ill., motion to suspend the rules and pass the bill that would authorize the production of no more than 15,000 $20 Saint-Gaudens Double Eagle ultra-high-relief bullion coins made of palladium. Motion agreed to 415-0: R 189-0; D 226-0 (ND 169-0, SD 57-0). A two-thirds majority of those present and voting (277 in this case) is required for passage under suspension of the rules. May 15, 2008.

	319	320	321	322	323	324	325
ALABAMA							
1 **Bonner**	Y	Y	Y	Y	N	N	Y
2 **Everett**	Y	Y	Y	Y	N	N	Y
3 **Rogers**	Y	Y	Y	Y	N	N	Y
4 **Aderholt**	Y	Y	Y	Y	N	N	Y
5 Cramer	?	?	?	?	Y	Y	Y
6 Bachus	N	Y	Y	Y	N	N	Y
7 Davis	Y	Y	N	Y	Y	Y	Y
ALASKA							
AL **Young**	N	Y	Y	Y	N	N	Y
ARIZONA							
1 **Renzi**	Y	Y	Y	Y	N	N	Y
2 **Franks**	N	Y	Y	Y	N	N	Y
3 **Shadegg**	N	Y	Y	Y	N	N	Y
4 Pastor	Y	Y	N	Y	Y	Y	Y
5 Mitchell	Y	Y	N	Y	N	N	Y
6 **Flake**	N	Y	Y	Y	N	N	Y
7 Grijalva	Y	Y	N	Y	Y	Y	Y
8 Giffords	Y	Y	N	Y	Y	Y	Y
ARKANSAS							
1 Berry	Y	Y	N	Y	Y	Y	Y
2 Snyder	Y	Y	N	Y	Y	Y	Y
3 **Boozman**	Y	Y	Y	Y	N	N	Y
4 Ross	Y	?	Y	Y	Y	Y	Y
CALIFORNIA							
1 Thompson	Y	Y	N	Y	Y	Y	Y
2 **Herger**	N	Y	Y	Y	N	N	Y
3 **Lungren**	Y	Y	Y	Y	N	N	Y
4 **Doolittle**	Y	Y	Y	Y	N	N	Y
5 Matsui	Y	Y	N	Y	Y	Y	Y
6 Woolsey	Y	Y	N	Y	Y	Y	Y
7 Miller, George	Y	?	N	Y	Y	Y	Y
8 Pelosi							
9 Lee	Y	Y	N	Y	Y	Y	Y
10 Tauscher	Y	Y	N	Y	Y	Y	Y
11 McNerney	Y	Y	N	Y	Y	Y	Y
12 Speier	Y	Y	N	Y	Y	Y	Y
13 Stark	?	Y	N	Y	Y	N	Y
14 Eshoo	Y	Y	N	Y	Y	Y	Y
15 Honda	Y	Y	N	Y	Y	Y	Y
16 Lofgren	Y	Y	N	Y	Y	Y	Y
17 Farr	Y	Y	N	Y	Y	Y	Y
18 Cardoza	Y	Y	N	Y	Y	Y	Y
19 **Radanovich**	N	Y	Y	Y	N	N	Y
20 Costa	Y	Y	N	Y	Y	Y	Y
21 **Nunes**	Y	Y	Y	Y	N	N	Y
22 **McCarthy**	Y	Y	Y	Y	N	N	Y
23 Capps	Y	Y	N	Y	Y	Y	Y
24 **Gallegly**	Y	Y	Y	Y	N	N	Y
25 **McKeon**	Y	Y	Y	Y	N	N	Y
26 **Dreier**	Y	Y	Y	Y	N	N	Y
27 Sherman	Y	Y	N	Y	Y	Y	Y
28 Berman	Y	Y	N	?	Y	Y	Y
29 Schiff	Y	Y	N	Y	Y	Y	Y
30 Waxman	Y	Y	N	Y	Y	Y	Y
31 Becerra	Y	Y	N	?	Y	Y	Y
32 Solis	Y	Y	N	Y	Y	Y	Y
33 Watson	Y	Y	N	Y	Y	Y	Y
34 Roybal-Allard	Y	Y	N	Y	Y	Y	Y
35 Waters	Y	Y	N	Y	Y	Y	Y
36 Harman	Y	Y	N	Y	Y	Y	Y
37 Richardson	Y	Y	N	Y	Y	Y	Y
38 Napolitano	Y	Y	N	Y	Y	Y	Y
39 Sánchez, Linda	Y	Y	N	Y	Y	Y	Y
40 **Royce**	N	Y	Y	Y	N	N	Y
41 **Lewis**	Y	Y	Y	Y	N	N	Y
42 **Miller, Gary**	N	Y	Y	Y	N	N	Y
43 Baca	Y	Y	N	Y	Y	Y	Y
44 **Calvert**	Y	Y	Y	Y	N	N	Y
45 **Bono Mack**	?	?	?	?	?	?	?
46 **Rohrabacher**	N	Y	Y	Y	N	N	Y
47 Sanchez, Loretta	Y	Y	N	Y	Y	Y	Y
48 **Campbell**	N	Y	Y	Y	N	N	Y
49 **Issa**	N	?	Y	Y	N	N	Y
50 **Bilbray**	Y	?	?	Y	Y	N	Y
51 Filner	Y	Y	N	Y	Y	Y	Y
52 **Hunter**	N	Y	Y	Y	N	N	Y
53 Davis	Y	Y	N	Y	Y	Y	Y

	319	320	321	322	323	324	325
COLORADO							
1 DeGette	?	?	?	?	?	?	?
2 Udall	Y	Y	N	Y	Y	Y	Y
3 Salazar	Y	Y	N	Y	Y	Y	Y
4 **Musgrave**	N	Y	Y	Y	N	N	Y
5 **Lamborn**	N	Y	Y	Y	N	N	Y
6 **Tancredo**	N	Y	Y	Y	N	N	Y
7 Perlmutter	Y	Y	N	Y	Y	Y	Y
CONNECTICUT							
1 Larson	Y	Y	N	Y	+	+	+
2 Courtney	Y	Y	N	Y	Y	Y	Y
3 DeLauro	Y	Y	N	Y	Y	Y	Y
4 **Shays**	Y	Y	N	Y	N	N	Y
5 Murphy	Y	Y	N	Y	Y	Y	Y
DELAWARE							
AL **Castle**	Y	Y	N	Y	N	N	Y
FLORIDA							
1 **Miller**	N	Y	Y	Y	N	N	Y
2 Boyd	Y	Y	N	Y	Y	Y	Y
3 Brown	Y	Y	N	Y	Y	Y	Y
4 **Crenshaw**	?	?	?	?	?	?	?
5 **Brown-Waite**	Y	Y	Y	Y	N	N	Y
6 **Stearns**	N	Y	Y	Y	N	N	Y
7 **Mica**	N	Y	Y	Y	N	N	Y
8 **Keller**	Y	Y	Y	Y	N	N	Y
9 **Bilirakis**	Y	Y	N	Y	N	N	Y
10 **Young**	Y	Y	Y	Y	N	N	Y
11 Castor	Y	Y	N	Y	Y	Y	Y
12 **Putnam**	Y	Y	Y	Y	N	N	Y
13 **Buchanan**	Y	Y	N	Y	N	N	Y
14 **Mack**	?	?	?	?	?	?	?
15 **Weldon**	Y	Y	Y	Y	N	N	Y
16 Mahoney	Y	Y	N	Y	Y	Y	Y
17 Meek	Y	Y	N	Y	Y	Y	Y
18 **Ros-Lehtinen**	Y	Y	N	Y	N	N	Y
19 Wexler	Y	Y	N	Y	Y	Y	Y
20 Wasserman Schultz	Y	Y	N	Y	Y	Y	Y
21 **Diaz-Balart, L.**	Y	?	Y	Y	N	N	Y
22 Klein	Y	Y	N	Y	Y	Y	Y
23 Hastings	Y	Y	N	Y	Y	Y	Y
24 **Feeney**	N	Y	Y	Y	N	N	Y
25 **Diaz-Balart, M.**	Y	Y	Y	Y	N	N	Y
GEORGIA							
1 **Kingston**	N	Y	Y	Y	N	N	Y
2 Bishop	Y	Y	N	Y	Y	Y	Y
3 **Westmoreland**	N	?	Y	Y	N	N	Y
4 Johnson	Y	Y	N	Y	Y	Y	Y
5 Lewis	Y	Y	N	Y	Y	Y	Y
6 **Price**	Y	Y	Y	Y	N	N	Y
7 **Linder**	Y	Y	N	Y	N	N	Y
8 Marshall	Y	Y	N	Y	Y	Y	Y
9 **Deal**	N	Y	Y	Y	N	N	Y
10 **Broun**	N	Y	N	N	N	N	Y
11 **Gingrey**	N	Y	Y	Y	N	N	Y
12 Barrow	Y	Y	N	Y	Y	Y	Y
13 Scott	Y	Y	N	Y	Y	Y	Y
HAWAII							
1 Abercrombie	Y	Y	N	Y	Y	Y	Y
2 Hirono	Y	+	–	Y	Y	Y	Y
IDAHO							
1 **Sali**	N	Y	Y	Y	N	N	Y
2 **Simpson**	Y	Y	Y	Y	N	N	Y
ILLINOIS							
1 Rush	?	?	?	?	?	?	?
2 Jackson	Y	Y	N	Y	Y	Y	Y
3 Lipinski	Y	Y	N	Y	Y	Y	Y
4 Gutierrez	Y	Y	N	Y	Y	Y	Y
5 Emanuel	Y	+	N	Y	Y	Y	Y
6 **Roskam**	N	Y	Y	Y	N	N	Y
7 Davis	Y	Y	N	Y	Y	Y	Y
8 Bean	Y	Y	N	Y	Y	Y	Y
9 Schakowsky	Y	Y	N	Y	Y	Y	Y
10 **Kirk**	Y	Y	N	Y	N	N	+
11 **Weller**	Y	Y	N	Y	N	N	Y
12 Costello	Y	Y	N	Y	Y	Y	Y
13 **Biggert**	Y	Y	N	Y	N	N	Y
14 Foster	Y	N	N	Y	Y	Y	Y
15 Johnson	Y	Y	N	Y	N	N	Y

KEY | **Republicans** Democrats

Y	Voted for (yea)	X	Paired against	C	Voted "present" to avoid possible conflict of interest
#	Paired for	–	Announced against		
+	Announced for	P	Voted "present"	?	Did not vote or otherwise make a position known
N	Voted against (nay)				

ND Northern Democrats, SD Southern Democrats
Southern states: Ala., Ark., Fla., Ga., Ky., La., Miss., N.C., Okla., S.C., Tenn., Texas, Va.

	319	320	321	322	323	324	325
16 **Manzullo**	Y	Y	Y	Y	N	N	Y
17 Hare	Y	Y	N	Y	Y	Y	Y
18 **LaHood**	Y	Y	Y	Y	N	N	Y
19 **Shimkus**	Y	?	?	?	N	N	Y
INDIANA							
1 Visclosky	Y	Y	N	Y	Y	Y	Y
2 Donnelly	Y	Y	Y	Y	Y	Y	Y
3 **Souder**	Y	Y	Y	Y	N	N	Y
4 **Buyer**	N	Y	Y	Y	N	N	Y
5 **Burton**	N	Y	Y	Y	N	N	Y
6 **Pence**	Y	Y	Y	Y	N	N	Y
7 Carson, A.	Y	Y	N	Y	Y	Y	Y
8 Ellsworth	Y	Y	N	Y	Y	Y	Y
9 Hill	Y	Y	N	Y	N	N	Y
IOWA							
1 Braley	Y	+	–	Y	Y	Y	Y
2 Loebsack	Y	Y	N	Y	Y	Y	?
3 Boswell	Y	Y	N	Y	Y	Y	Y
4 **Latham**	Y	Y	Y	Y	N	N	Y
5 **King**	N	Y	Y	Y	N	N	Y
KANSAS							
1 **Moran**	Y	Y	Y	Y	N	N	Y
2 Boyda	Y	Y	N	Y	Y	Y	Y
3 Moore	Y	Y	N	Y	Y	Y	Y
4 **Tiahrt**	Y	Y	Y	Y	N	N	Y
KENTUCKY							
1 **Whitfield**	Y	Y	Y	Y	N	N	Y
2 **Lewis**	?	?	?	?	?	?	?
3 Yarmuth	Y	Y	N	Y	Y	Y	Y
4 **Davis**	Y	Y	Y	Y	N	N	Y
5 **Rogers**	Y	Y	Y	Y	N	N	Y
6 Chandler	Y	Y	N	Y	Y	Y	Y
LOUISIANA							
1 **Scalise**	Y	Y	Y	Y	N	N	Y
2 Jefferson	Y	Y	N	Y	Y	Y	Y
3 Melancon	Y	Y	Y	Y	Y	Y	Y
4 **McCrery**	Y	Y	Y	Y	N	N	Y
5 **Alexander**	Y	Y	Y	Y	N	N	Y
6 Cazayoux	Y	Y	Y	Y	Y	Y	Y
7 **Boustany**	Y	Y	Y	Y	N	N	Y
MAINE							
1 Allen	Y	Y	N	Y	Y	Y	Y
2 Michaud	Y	Y	N	Y	Y	N	Y
MARYLAND							
1 **Gilchrest**	Y	Y	Y	Y	?	N	Y
2 Ruppersberger	Y	Y	N	Y	Y	Y	Y
3 Sarbanes	Y	Y	N	Y	Y	Y	Y
4 Wynn	?	?	?	?	?	?	?
5 Hoyer	Y	Y	N	Y	Y	Y	Y
6 **Bartlett**	N	Y	Y	Y	N	N	Y
7 Cummings	Y	Y	N	Y	Y	Y	Y
8 Van Hollen	Y	Y	N	Y	Y	Y	Y
MASSACHUSETTS							
1 Olver	Y	Y	N	Y	Y	Y	Y
2 Neal	Y	Y	N	Y	Y	Y	Y
3 McGovern	Y	Y	N	Y	Y	Y	Y
4 Frank	Y	Y	N	Y	Y	Y	Y
5 Tsongas	Y	Y	N	Y	Y	Y	Y
6 Tierney	Y	Y	N	Y	Y	Y	Y
7 Markey	Y	Y	N	Y	Y	Y	Y
8 Capuano	Y	Y	N	Y	Y	Y	Y
9 Lynch	Y	Y	N	Y	Y	Y	Y
10 Delahunt	Y	Y	N	Y	Y	Y	Y
MICHIGAN							
1 Stupak	Y	Y	N	Y	Y	Y	Y
2 **Hoekstra**	Y	Y	Y	Y	N	N	Y
3 **Ehlers**	Y	Y	N	Y	N	N	Y
4 **Camp**	Y	Y	Y	Y	N	N	Y
5 Kildee	Y	Y	N	Y	Y	Y	Y
6 **Upton**	Y	Y	Y	Y	N	N	Y
7 **Walberg**	N	Y	Y	Y	N	N	Y
8 **Rogers**	Y	Y	Y	Y	N	N	Y
9 **Knollenberg**	Y	Y	Y	Y	N	N	Y
10 **Miller**	Y	Y	Y	Y	N	N	Y
11 **McCotter**	Y	Y	Y	Y	N	N	Y
12 Levin	Y	Y	N	Y	Y	Y	Y
13 Kilpatrick	Y	Y	N	Y	Y	Y	Y
14 Conyers	Y	Y	N	Y	Y	Y	Y
15 Dingell	Y	Y	N	Y	Y	Y	?
MINNESOTA							
1 Walz	Y	Y	N	Y	Y	Y	Y
2 **Kline**	N	Y	Y	Y	N	N	Y
3 **Ramstad**	Y	Y	N	Y	N	N	Y
4 McCollum	Y	Y	N	Y	Y	Y	Y
5 Ellison	Y	Y	N	Y	Y	Y	Y
6 **Bachmann**	N	Y	Y	Y	N	N	Y
7 Peterson	Y	Y	N	Y	Y	Y	Y
8 Oberstar	Y	Y	N	Y	Y	Y	Y
MISSISSIPPI							
1 Vacant							
2 Thompson	Y	Y	N	Y	Y	Y	Y
3 **Pickering**	Y	Y	Y	Y	N	N	Y
4 Taylor	Y	Y	Y	Y	Y	Y	Y
MISSOURI							
1 Clay	Y	Y	N	Y	Y	Y	Y
2 **Akin**	N	Y	Y	Y	N	N	Y
3 Carnahan	Y	Y	N	Y	?	Y	Y
4 Skelton	Y	Y	N	Y	Y	Y	Y
5 Cleaver	Y	Y	N	Y	Y	Y	Y
6 **Graves**	Y	Y	Y	Y	N	N	Y
7 **Blunt**	Y	Y	Y	Y	N	N	Y
8 **Emerson**	Y	Y	Y	Y	N	N	Y
9 **Hulshof**	Y	Y	Y	Y	?	?	?
MONTANA							
AL **Rehberg**	Y	Y	Y	Y	N	N	Y
NEBRASKA							
1 **Fortenberry**	Y	Y	Y	Y	N	N	Y
2 **Terry**	Y	Y	Y	Y	N	N	Y
3 **Smith**	Y	Y	Y	Y	N	N	Y
NEVADA							
1 Berkley	Y	Y	N	Y	Y	Y	Y
2 **Heller**	Y	Y	Y	Y	N	N	Y
3 **Porter**	Y	Y	Y	Y	N	N	Y
NEW HAMPSHIRE							
1 Shea-Porter	Y	Y	N	Y	Y	Y	Y
2 Hodes	Y	Y	N	Y	Y	Y	Y
NEW JERSEY							
1 Andrews	?	Y	N	Y	Y	Y	Y
2 **LoBiondo**	Y	Y	N	Y	N	N	Y
3 **Saxton**	Y	Y	N	Y	N	N	Y
4 **Smith**	Y	Y	N	Y	N	N	Y
5 **Garrett**	N	?	Y	Y	N	N	Y
6 Pallone	Y	Y	N	Y	Y	Y	Y
7 **Ferguson**	Y	Y	N	Y	N	N	Y
8 Pascrell	Y	Y	N	Y	Y	Y	Y
9 Rothman	Y	Y	N	Y	Y	Y	Y
10 Payne	Y	Y	N	Y	Y	Y	Y
11 **Frelinghuysen**	Y	Y	N	Y	N	N	Y
12 Holt	Y	Y	N	Y	Y	Y	Y
13 Sires	Y	Y	N	Y	Y	Y	Y
NEW MEXICO							
1 **Wilson**	+	Y	Y	Y	N	N	Y
2 **Pearce**	N	Y	Y	Y	N	N	Y
3 Udall	Y	Y	N	Y	Y	Y	Y
NEW YORK							
1 Bishop	Y	Y	N	Y	Y	Y	Y
2 Israel	Y	Y	N	Y	Y	Y	Y
3 **King**	Y	Y	Y	Y	N	N	Y
4 McCarthy	Y	Y	N	Y	Y	Y	Y
5 Ackerman	Y	Y	N	Y	Y	Y	Y
6 Meeks	?	Y	N	Y	Y	Y	Y
7 Crowley	Y	?	N	Y	Y	Y	Y
8 Nadler	Y	Y	N	Y	Y	Y	Y
9 Weiner	Y	Y	N	Y	Y	Y	Y
10 Towns	Y	Y	N	Y	Y	Y	Y
11 Clarke	Y	Y	N	Y	Y	Y	Y
12 Velázquez	Y	Y	N	Y	Y	Y	Y
13 **Fossella**	Y	Y	Y	Y	N	N	Y
14 Maloney	Y	Y	N	Y	Y	Y	Y
15 Rangel	Y	Y	N	Y	Y	Y	Y
16 Serrano	Y	Y	N	Y	Y	Y	Y
17 Engel	Y	Y	N	Y	Y	Y	Y
18 Lowey	Y	Y	N	Y	Y	Y	Y
19 Hall	Y	+	N	Y	Y	Y	Y
20 Gillibrand	Y	Y	N	Y	?	?	?
21 McNulty	Y	Y	N	Y	Y	Y	Y
22 Hinchey	Y	Y	N	Y	Y	Y	Y
23 **McHugh**	Y	Y	Y	Y	N	N	Y
24 Arcuri	Y	Y	N	Y	Y	Y	Y
25 **Walsh**	Y	Y	N	Y	N	N	Y
26 **Reynolds**	Y	Y	Y	Y	N	N	Y
27 Higgins	Y	Y	N	Y	Y	Y	Y
28 Slaughter	Y	Y	N	Y	Y	Y	Y
29 **Kuhl**	Y	Y	Y	Y	N	N	Y
NORTH CAROLINA							
1 Butterfield	Y	Y	N	Y	Y	Y	Y
2 Etheridge	Y	Y	N	Y	Y	Y	Y
3 **Jones**	N	Y	Y	Y	N	N	Y
4 Price	Y	Y	N	Y	Y	Y	Y
5 **Foxx**	N	Y	Y	Y	N	N	Y
6 **Coble**	Y	Y	Y	Y	N	N	Y
7 McIntyre	Y	Y	N	Y	Y	Y	Y
8 **Hayes**	Y	Y	Y	Y	N	N	Y
9 **Myrick**	?	?	?	?	?	?	?
10 **McHenry**	N	Y	Y	Y	N	N	Y
11 Shuler	Y	Y	N	Y	Y	Y	Y
12 Watt	Y	Y	N	Y	Y	Y	Y
13 Miller	Y	Y	N	Y	Y	Y	Y
NORTH DAKOTA							
AL Pomeroy	Y	Y	N	Y	Y	Y	Y
OHIO							
1 **Chabot**	Y	Y	Y	Y	N	N	Y
2 **Schmidt**	?	?	?	?	N	N	Y
3 **Turner**	Y	Y	Y	Y	N	N	Y
4 **Jordan**	N	Y	Y	Y	N	N	Y
5 **Latta**	N	Y	Y	Y	N	N	Y
6 Wilson	Y	Y	N	Y	Y	Y	Y
7 **Hobson**	Y	Y	Y	Y	N	N	Y
8 **Boehner**	N	?	Y	Y	N	N	?
9 Kaptur	Y	Y	N	Y	Y	Y	Y
10 Kucinich	Y	Y	N	Y	N	N	Y
11 Tubbs Jones	Y	Y	N	Y	Y	Y	Y
12 **Tiberi**	Y	Y	Y	Y	N	N	Y
13 Sutton	Y	Y	N	Y	Y	Y	Y
14 **LaTourette**	Y	Y	Y	Y	N	N	Y
15 **Pryce**	Y	Y	Y	Y	N	N	Y
16 **Regula**	Y	Y	Y	Y	N	N	Y
17 Ryan	Y	Y	?	Y	Y	Y	Y
18 Space	Y	Y	N	Y	Y	Y	Y
OKLAHOMA							
1 **Sullivan**	N	Y	Y	Y	N	N	Y
2 Boren	Y	Y	Y	Y	Y	Y	Y
3 **Lucas**	Y	Y	Y	Y	N	N	Y
4 **Cole**	Y	Y	Y	Y	N	N	?
5 **Fallin**	Y	Y	Y	Y	N	N	Y
OREGON							
1 Wu	?	Y	N	Y	Y	Y	Y
2 **Walden**	Y	Y	Y	Y	N	N	Y
3 Blumenauer	Y	Y	N	Y	Y	Y	Y
4 DeFazio	Y	Y	N	Y	Y	Y	Y
5 Hooley	Y	Y	N	?	Y	Y	Y
PENNSYLVANIA							
1 Brady	Y	Y	N	Y	Y	Y	Y
2 Fattah	Y	Y	N	Y	Y	Y	Y
3 **English**	Y	Y	Y	Y	N	N	Y
4 Altmire	Y	Y	N	Y	Y	Y	Y
5 **Peterson**	Y	Y	Y	Y	N	N	Y
6 **Gerlach**	?	?	?	?	?	?	?
7 Sestak	Y	Y	N	Y	Y	Y	Y
8 Murphy, P.	Y	Y	N	Y	Y	Y	Y
9 **Shuster**	Y	Y	Y	Y	N	N	Y
10 Carney	Y	Y	N	Y	Y	Y	Y
11 Kanjorski	Y	Y	N	Y	Y	Y	Y
12 Murtha	Y	Y	N	Y	Y	Y	Y
13 Schwartz	Y	Y	N	Y	Y	Y	Y
14 Doyle	Y	Y	N	Y	Y	Y	Y
15 **Dent**	Y	Y	Y	Y	N	N	Y
16 **Pitts**	N	Y	Y	Y	N	N	Y
17 Holden	Y	Y	N	Y	Y	Y	Y
18 **Murphy, T.**	Y	Y	Y	Y	N	N	Y
19 **Platts**	Y	Y	Y	Y	N	N	Y
RHODE ISLAND							
1 Kennedy	Y	Y	N	Y	Y	Y	Y
2 Langevin	Y	Y	N	Y	Y	Y	Y
SOUTH CAROLINA							
1 **Brown**	Y	Y	Y	Y	N	N	Y
2 **Wilson**	Y	Y	Y	Y	N	N	Y
3 **Barrett**	N	Y	Y	Y	N	N	Y
4 **Inglis**	N	Y	N	Y	N	N	Y
5 Spratt	Y	Y	N	Y	Y	Y	Y
6 Clyburn	Y	Y	N	Y	Y	Y	Y
SOUTH DAKOTA							
AL Herseth Sandlin	Y	Y	N	Y	Y	Y	Y
TENNESSEE							
1 **Davis, D.**	N	Y	Y	Y	N	N	Y
2 **Duncan**	N	Y	Y	Y	N	N	Y
3 **Wamp**	N	Y	Y	Y	N	N	Y
4 Davis, L.	Y	Y	N	Y	Y	Y	Y
5 Cooper	Y	Y	N	Y	Y	N	Y
6 Gordon	Y	?	?	?	Y	Y	Y
7 **Blackburn**	?	Y	Y	Y	N	N	Y
8 Tanner	Y	Y	Y	Y	Y	Y	Y
9 Cohen	Y	Y	N	Y	Y	Y	Y
TEXAS							
1 **Gohmert**	N	Y	Y	Y	N	N	Y
2 **Poe**	N	Y	Y	Y	N	N	Y
3 **Johnson, S.**	N	Y	Y	Y	N	N	Y
4 **Hall**	Y	Y	Y	Y	N	N	Y
5 **Hensarling**	N	Y	Y	Y	N	N	Y
6 **Barton**	N	Y	Y	Y	N	N	Y
7 **Culberson**	N	Y	Y	Y	N	N	Y
8 **Brady**	N	Y	Y	Y	N	N	Y
9 Green, A.	Y	Y	N	Y	Y	Y	Y
10 **McCaul**	Y	Y	Y	Y	N	N	Y
11 **Conaway**	N	Y	Y	Y	N	N	Y
12 **Granger**	Y	Y	Y	Y	N	N	Y
13 **Thornberry**	N	Y	Y	Y	N	N	Y
14 **Paul**	N	?	?	?	N	N	Y
15 Hinojosa	Y	Y	Y	Y	Y	Y	Y
16 Reyes	Y	Y	N	Y	Y	Y	Y
17 Edwards	Y	Y	Y	Y	Y	Y	?
18 Jackson Lee	Y	Y	N	Y	Y	Y	Y
19 **Neugebauer**	N	Y	Y	Y	N	N	Y
20 Gonzalez	Y	Y	Y	Y	Y	Y	Y
21 **Smith**	Y	Y	Y	Y	N	N	Y
22 Lampson	Y	Y	Y	Y	N	N	Y
23 Rodriguez	Y	Y	Y	Y	Y	Y	Y
24 **Marchant**	N	Y	Y	Y	N	N	Y
25 Doggett	?	Y	N	Y	Y	N	Y
26 **Burgess**	N	Y	Y	Y	N	N	Y
27 Ortiz	Y	Y	Y	Y	Y	Y	Y
28 Cuellar	Y	Y	N	Y	Y	Y	Y
29 Green, G.	Y	Y	Y	Y	Y	Y	Y
30 Johnson, E.	Y	Y	N	Y	Y	Y	Y
31 **Carter**	N	Y	Y	Y	N	N	Y
32 **Sessions**	N	Y	Y	Y	N	N	Y
UTAH							
1 **Bishop**	?	Y	Y	Y	N	N	Y
2 Matheson	Y	Y	N	Y	Y	Y	Y
3 **Cannon**	N	Y	Y	Y	N	N	Y
VERMONT							
AL Welch	Y	Y	N	Y	Y	Y	Y
VIRGINIA							
1 **Wittman**	Y	Y	Y	Y	N	N	Y
2 **Drake**	Y	Y	Y	Y	N	N	Y
3 Scott	Y	Y	N	Y	Y	Y	Y
4 **Forbes**	N	Y	Y	Y	N	N	Y
5 **Goode**	N	Y	Y	Y	N	N	Y
6 **Goodlatte**	N	Y	Y	Y	N	N	Y
7 **Cantor**	Y	Y	Y	Y	N	N	Y
8 Moran	Y	Y	N	Y	Y	Y	Y
9 Boucher	Y	Y	N	Y	Y	Y	Y
10 **Wolf**	Y	Y	Y	Y	N	N	Y
11 **Davis**	Y	Y	Y	?	N	N	Y
WASHINGTON							
1 Inslee	Y	Y	N	Y	Y	Y	Y
2 Larsen	Y	Y	N	Y	Y	Y	Y
3 Baird	Y	Y	N	Y	Y	Y	Y
4 **Hastings**	Y	Y	Y	Y	N	N	Y
5 **McMorris Rodgers**	Y	Y	Y	Y	N	N	Y
6 Dicks	Y	Y	N	Y	Y	Y	Y
7 McDermott	Y	Y	N	Y	Y	Y	Y
8 **Reichert**	Y	Y	N	Y	N	N	Y
9 Smith	Y	Y	N	Y	Y	Y	Y
WEST VIRGINIA							
1 Mollohan	Y	Y	N	Y	Y	Y	Y
2 **Capito**	Y	Y	Y	Y	N	N	Y
3 Rahall	Y	Y	N	Y	Y	Y	Y
WISCONSIN							
1 **Ryan**	Y	Y	Y	Y	N	N	Y
2 Baldwin	Y	Y	N	Y	Y	Y	Y
3 Kind	Y	Y	N	Y	Y	Y	Y
4 Moore	Y	Y	N	Y	Y	Y	Y
5 **Sensenbrenner**	Y	Y	Y	Y	N	N	Y
6 **Petri**	Y	Y	Y	Y	N	N	Y
7 Obey	Y	Y	N	Y	Y	Y	Y
8 Kagen	Y	Y	N	Y	Y	Y	Y
WYOMING							
AL **Cubin**	?	?	?	?	N	N	Y
DELEGATES							
Faleomavaega (A.S.)							
Norton (D.C.)							
Bordallo (Guam)							
Fortuño (P.R.)							
Christensen (V.I.)							

IN THE HOUSE | By Vote Number

326. **HR 406. Alice Paul Gold Medal/Passage.** Baca, D-Calif., motion to suspend the rules and pass the bill that would award a posthumous congressional gold medal in commemoration of Alice Paul and her work in women's suffrage and equal rights. Motion agreed to 412-1: R 187-1; D 225-0 (ND 167-0, SD 58-0). A two-thirds majority of those present and voting (276 in this case) is required for passage under suspension of the rules. May 15, 2008.

327. **HR 5872. Boy Scouts of America Commemorative Coin/Passage.** Gutierrez, D-Ill., motion to suspend the rules and pass the bill that would require the Treasury to mint coins in 2010 commemorating the centennial of the Boy Scouts of America. Motion agreed to 403-8: R 187-0; D 216-8 (ND 159-8, SD 57-0). A two-thirds majority of those present and voting (274 in this case) is required for passage under suspension of the rules. May 15, 2008.

328. **HR 2642. Supplemental Appropriations/Motion to Concur.** Obey, D-Wis., motion to concur in the Senate amendments with a House amendment. The House amendment would provide $162.5 billion for the wars in Iraq and Afghanistan, with $96.6 billion for fiscal 2008 and $65.9 billion for fiscal 2009. Motion rejected 141-149: R 56-2; D 85-147 (ND 48-126, SD 37-21). A "yea" was a vote in support of the president's position. May 15, 2008.

329. **HR 2642. Supplemental Appropriations/Motion to Concur.** Obey, D-Wis., motion to concur in the Senate amendments with a House amendment. The House amendment would require a troop withdrawal from Iraq within 30 days of the bill's enactment, with a goal of completing the withdrawal of combat troops by December 2009. It would require Congress to authorize any agreement between the U.S. and the Iraqi government committing U.S. forces. It would require the Iraqi government to match U.S. reconstruction aid and to sell fuel to the U.S. military at the same price it is sold to Iraqi consumers. It would prohibit any combat unit not assessed as fully mission-capable from deploying to Iraq and limit deployment time, but would allow for presidential waivers. It also would prohibit interrogation techniques not authorized in the Army Field Manual on the subject and prohibit establishing a permanent base in Iraq. Motion agreed to 227-196: R 8-183; D 219-13 (ND 168-6, SD 51-7). A "nay" was a vote in support of the president's position. May 15, 2008.

330. **HR 2642. Supplemental Appropriations/Motion to Concur.** Obey, D-Wis., motion to concur in the Senate amendments with a House amendment. The House amendment would appropriate $21.2 billion for domestic programs, military construction and foreign aid. It would provide $4.6 billion for military construction and $5.8 billion for levee building in Louisiana. The amendment would provide a permanent expansion of education benefits for post-Sept. 11 veterans, offset with a surtax on wealthy taxpayers. It would temporarily extend federal unemployment benefits and place a moratorium through March 2009 on seven Medicaid regulations proposed by the administration. Motion agreed to 256-166: R 32-159; D 224-7 (ND 169-4, SD 55-3). A "nay" was a vote in support of the president's position. May 15, 2008.

	326	327	328	329	330
ALABAMA					
1 **Bonner**	Y	Y	P	N	N
2 **Everett**	Y	Y	P	N	N
3 **Rogers**	Y	Y	P	N	N
4 **Aderholt**	Y	Y	P	N	N
5 Cramer	Y	Y	Y	Y	Y
6 **Bachus**	Y	Y	P	N	N
7 Davis	Y	Y	Y	Y	Y
ALASKA					
AL **Young**	Y	Y	P	N	Y
ARIZONA					
1 **Renzi**	Y	Y	Y	N	Y
2 **Franks**	Y	Y	P	N	N
3 **Shadegg**	Y	Y	P	N	N
4 Pastor	Y	Y	N	Y	Y
5 Mitchell	Y	Y	Y	Y	Y
6 **Flake**	Y	Y	P	N	N
7 Grijalva	Y	Y	N	Y	Y
8 Giffords	Y	Y	Y	Y	Y
ARKANSAS					
1 Berry	Y	Y	Y	Y	Y
2 Snyder	Y	Y	Y	N	Y
3 **Boozman**	Y	Y	P	N	N
4 Ross	Y	Y	Y	Y	Y
CALIFORNIA					
1 Thompson	Y	Y	N	Y	Y
2 **Herger**	Y	Y	P	N	N
3 **Lungren**	Y	Y	P	N	N
4 **Doolittle**	Y	Y	P	N	N
5 Matsui	Y	Y	N	Y	Y
6 Woolsey	Y	N	N	Y	Y
7 Miller, George	Y	Y	N	Y	Y
8 Pelosi			N	Y	Y
9 Lee	Y	N	N	Y	Y
10 Tauscher	Y	Y	N	Y	Y
11 McNerney	Y	Y	N	Y	Y
12 Speier	Y	Y	N	Y	Y
13 Stark	Y	N	N	Y	Y
14 Eshoo	Y	Y	N	Y	Y
15 Honda	Y	Y	N	Y	Y
16 Lofgren	Y	Y	N	Y	Y
17 Farr	Y	Y	N	Y	Y
18 Cardoza	Y	Y	N	Y	Y
19 **Radanovich**	Y	Y	P	N	N
20 Costa	Y	Y	N	N	Y
21 **Nunes**	Y	Y	P	N	N
22 **McCarthy**	Y	Y	P	N	N
23 Capps	Y	Y	N	Y	Y
24 **Gallegly**	Y	Y	?	N	N
25 **McKeon**	Y	Y	P	N	N
26 **Dreier**	Y	Y	P	N	N
27 Sherman	Y	Y	Y	Y	Y
28 Berman	Y	Y	Y	Y	Y
29 Schiff	Y	Y	Y	Y	Y
30 Waxman	Y	Y	N	Y	Y
31 Becerra	Y	Y	N	Y	Y
32 Solis	Y	Y	N	Y	Y
33 Watson	Y	Y	N	Y	Y
34 Roybal-Allard	Y	Y	Y	Y	Y
35 Waters	Y	Y	N	Y	Y
36 Harman	Y	Y	N	Y	Y
37 Richardson	Y	Y	N	Y	Y
38 Napolitano	Y	Y	N	Y	Y
39 Sánchez, Linda	Y	Y	N	Y	Y
40 **Royce**	Y	Y	N	N	N
41 **Lewis**	Y	Y	P	N	N
42 **Miller, Gary**	Y	Y	P	N	N
43 Baca	Y	Y	N	Y	Y
44 **Calvert**	Y	Y	P	N	N
45 **Bono Mack**	?	?	?	?	?
46 **Rohrabacher**	Y	Y	P	N	N
47 Sanchez, Loretta	Y	Y	N	Y	Y
48 **Campbell**	Y	Y	Y	?	?
49 **Issa**	Y	Y	P	N	N
50 **Bilbray**	Y	Y	P	N	N
51 Filner	Y	Y	N	Y	Y
52 **Hunter**	Y	Y	Y	N	N
53 Davis	Y	Y	Y	Y	Y

	326	327	328	329	330
COLORADO					
1 DeGette	?	?	?	?	?
2 Udall	Y	Y	Y	Y	Y
3 Salazar	Y	Y	Y	Y	Y
4 **Musgrave**	Y	Y	Y	N	N
5 **Lamborn**	Y	Y	P	N	N
6 **Tancredo**	Y	Y	P	N	N
7 Perlmutter	Y	Y	N	Y	Y
CONNECTICUT					
1 Larson	+	+	N	Y	Y
2 Courtney	Y	Y	N	Y	Y
3 DeLauro	Y	Y	N	Y	Y
4 **Shays**	Y	Y	Y	Y	Y
5 Murphy	Y	Y	N	Y	Y
DELAWARE					
AL **Castle**	Y	Y	Y	Y	Y
FLORIDA					
1 **Miller**	Y	Y	Y	N	N
2 Boyd	Y	Y	Y	Y	Y
3 Brown	Y	Y	Y	Y	Y
4 **Crenshaw**	?	?	?	?	?
5 **Brown-Waite**	Y	Y	P	N	N
6 **Stearns**	Y	Y	N	N	N
7 **Mica**	Y	Y	P	N	N
8 **Keller**	Y	Y	N	N	N
9 **Bilirakis**	Y	Y	Y	N	N
10 **Young**	Y	Y	P	N	N
11 Castor	Y	Y	N	Y	Y
12 **Putnam**	Y	Y	P	N	N
13 **Buchanan**	Y	Y	N	N	N
14 **Mack**	?	?	?	?	?
15 **Weldon**	Y	Y	P	N	N
16 Mahoney	Y	Y	Y	Y	Y
17 Meek	Y	Y	N	Y	Y
18 **Ros-Lehtinen**	Y	Y	P	N	Y
19 Wexler	Y	Y	N	Y	Y
20 Wasserman Schultz	Y	Y	N	Y	Y
21 **Diaz-Balart, L.**	Y	Y	P	N	N
22 Klein	Y	Y	N	Y	Y
23 Hastings	Y	Y	N	Y	Y
24 **Feeney**	Y	Y	P	N	N
25 **Diaz-Balart, M.**	Y	Y	P	N	N
GEORGIA					
1 **Kingston**	Y	Y	P	N	N
2 Bishop	Y	Y	Y	Y	Y
3 **Westmoreland**	Y	Y	P	N	N
4 Johnson	Y	Y	N	Y	Y
5 Lewis	Y	Y	N	Y	Y
6 **Price**	Y	Y	P	N	N
7 **Linder**	Y	Y	P	N	N
8 Marshall	Y	?	Y	N	Y
9 **Deal**	Y	Y	P	N	N
10 **Broun**	Y	Y	P	N	N
11 **Gingrey**	Y	Y	P	N	N
12 Barrow	Y	Y	Y	N	Y
13 Scott	Y	Y	Y	Y	Y
HAWAII					
1 Abercrombie	Y	Y	N	Y	Y
2 Hirono	Y	Y	N	Y	Y
IDAHO					
1 **Sali**	Y	Y	+	N	N
2 **Simpson**	Y	Y	P	N	N
ILLINOIS					
1 Rush	?	?	?	?	?
2 Jackson	Y	Y	N	Y	Y
3 Lipinski	Y	Y	Y	Y	Y
4 Gutierrez	Y	N	N	Y	Y
5 Emanuel	Y	Y	Y	Y	Y
6 **Roskam**	Y	Y	P	N	N
7 Davis	Y	Y	N	Y	Y
8 Bean	Y	Y	Y	Y	N
9 Schakowsky	Y	Y	N	Y	Y
10 **Kirk**	Y	Y	P	N	Y
11 **Weller**	Y	Y	P	N	N
12 Costello	Y	Y	Y	Y	Y
13 **Biggert**	Y	Y	P	N	N
14 Foster	Y	Y	Y	Y	Y
15 **Johnson**	Y	Y	Y	N	Y

KEY **Republicans** Democrats

Y Voted for (yea)	X Paired against	C Voted "present" to avoid possible conflict of interest
# Paired for	− Announced against	
+ Announced for	P Voted "present"	? Did not vote or otherwise make a position known
N Voted against (nay)		

ND Northern Democrats, SD Southern Democrats
Southern states: Ala., Ark., Fla., Ga., Ky., La., Miss., N.C., Okla., S.C., Tenn., Texas, Va.

	326	327	328	329	330
16 Manzullo	Y	Y	P	N	N
17 Hare	Y	Y	N	Y	Y
18 LaHood	Y	Y	Y	N	Y
19 Shimkus	Y	Y	P	N	N
INDIANA					
1 Visclosky	Y	Y	Y	Y	Y
2 Donnelly	Y	Y	Y	Y	N
3 Souder	Y	Y	P	N	N
4 Buyer	Y	Y	P	N	Y
5 Burton	Y	Y	P	N	N
6 Pence	Y	Y	P	N	N
7 Carson, A.	Y	Y	N	Y	Y
8 Ellsworth	Y	Y	Y	Y	N
9 Hill	Y	Y	Y	Y	Y
IOWA					
1 Braley	Y	?	N	Y	Y
2 Loebsack	?	?	N	Y	Y
3 Boswell	Y	Y	N	Y	Y
4 Latham	Y	Y	P	N	N
5 King	Y	Y	P	N	N
KANSAS					
1 Moran	Y	Y	P	N	N
2 Boyda	Y	Y	Y	Y	Y
3 Moore	Y	Y	Y	Y	Y
4 Tiahrt	Y	Y	P	N	N
KENTUCKY					
1 Whitfield	Y	Y	Y	N	Y
2 Lewis	?	?	?	?	?
3 Yarmuth	Y	Y	N	Y	Y
4 Davis	Y	Y	P	N	N
5 Rogers	Y	Y	P	N	N
6 Chandler	Y	Y	Y	Y	Y
LOUISIANA					
1 Scalise	Y	Y	P	N	N
2 Jefferson	Y	Y	Y	Y	Y
3 Melancon	Y	Y	Y	Y	Y
4 McCrery	Y	Y	P	N	N
5 Alexander	Y	Y	P	N	N
6 Cazayoux	Y	Y	Y	Y	Y
7 Boustany	Y	Y	P	N	N
MAINE					
1 Allen	Y	Y	N	N	Y
2 Michaud	Y	Y	N	Y	Y
MARYLAND					
1 Gilchrest	Y	Y	Y	Y	Y
2 Ruppersberger	Y	Y	Y	Y	Y
3 Sarbanes	Y	Y	N	Y	Y
4 Wynn	?	?	N	Y	Y
5 Hoyer	Y	Y	Y	Y	Y
6 Bartlett	Y	Y	P	N	N
7 Cummings	?	?	N	Y	Y
8 Van Hollen	Y	Y	N	Y	Y
MASSACHUSETTS					
1 Olver	Y	Y	N	Y	Y
2 Neal	Y	Y	N	Y	Y
3 McGovern	Y	N	N	Y	Y
4 Frank	Y	N	N	Y	Y
5 Tsongas	Y	Y	N	Y	Y
6 Tierney	Y	Y	N	Y	Y
7 Markey	Y	Y	N	Y	Y
8 Capuano	Y	Y	N	Y	Y
9 Lynch	Y	Y	N	Y	Y
10 Delahunt	Y	Y	N	Y	Y
MICHIGAN					
1 Stupak	Y	Y	N	Y	Y
2 Hoekstra	Y	Y	P	N	N
3 Ehlers	Y	Y	P	N	N
4 Camp	Y	Y	P	N	N
5 Kildee	Y	Y	N	Y	Y
6 Upton	Y	Y	N	Y	Y
7 Walberg	Y	Y	Y	N	N
8 Rogers	Y	Y	P	N	N
9 Knollenberg	Y	Y	P	N	Y
10 Miller	Y	Y	P	N	N
11 McCotter	Y	Y	P	N	N
12 Levin	Y	Y	Y	Y	Y
13 Kilpatrick	Y	Y	N	Y	Y
14 Conyers	Y	Y	N	Y	Y
15 Dingell	?	?	N	Y	Y
MINNESOTA					
1 Walz	Y	Y	N	Y	Y
2 Kline	Y	Y	P	N	N
3 Ramstad	Y	Y	N	Y	N
4 McCollum	Y	Y	N	Y	Y

	326	327	328	329	330
5 Ellison	Y	Y	N	Y	Y
6 Bachmann	Y	Y	P	N	N
7 Peterson	Y	Y	Y	Y	Y
8 Oberstar	Y	Y	N	Y	Y
MISSISSIPPI					
1 Vacant					
2 Thompson	Y	Y	N	Y	Y
3 Pickering	Y	Y	P	N	N
4 Taylor	Y	Y	Y	N	Y
MISSOURI					
1 Clay	Y	Y	N	Y	Y
2 Akin	Y	Y	P	N	N
3 Carnahan	Y	Y	Y	Y	Y
4 Skelton	Y	Y	Y	Y	Y
5 Cleaver	Y	Y	N	Y	Y
6 Graves	Y	Y	Y	N	N
7 Blunt	Y	Y	P	N	N
8 Emerson	Y	Y	Y	N	Y
9 Hulshof	?	?	?	?	?
MONTANA					
AL Rehberg	Y	Y	P	N	N
NEBRASKA					
1 Fortenberry	Y	Y	Y	N	Y
2 Terry	Y	Y	Y	N	N
3 Smith	Y	Y	P	N	N
NEVADA					
1 Berkley	Y	Y	Y	Y	Y
2 Heller	Y	Y	Y	N	N
3 Porter	Y	Y	Y	N	Y
NEW HAMPSHIRE					
1 Shea-Porter	Y	Y	N	Y	Y
2 Hodes	Y	Y	N	Y	Y
NEW JERSEY					
1 Andrews	Y	Y	N	Y	Y
2 LoBiondo	Y	Y	Y	N	Y
3 Saxton	Y	Y	P	N	N
4 Smith	Y	Y	P	N	Y
5 Garrett	Y	Y	P	N	N
6 Pallone	Y	Y	N	Y	Y
7 Ferguson	Y	Y	P	N	N
8 Pascrell	Y	Y	N	Y	Y
9 Rothman	Y	Y	N	Y	Y
10 Payne	Y	Y	N	Y	Y
11 Frelinghuysen	Y	Y	Y	N	N
12 Holt	Y	Y	N	Y	Y
13 Sires	Y	Y	N	Y	Y
NEW MEXICO					
1 Wilson	Y	Y	P	N	N
2 Pearce	Y	Y	Y	N	N
3 Udall	Y	Y	N	Y	Y
NEW YORK					
1 Bishop	Y	Y	N	Y	Y
2 Israel	Y	Y	N	Y	Y
3 King	Y	Y	Y	N	Y
4 McCarthy	Y	Y	N	Y	Y
5 Ackerman	Y	Y	N	Y	Y
6 Meeks	Y	Y	N	Y	Y
7 Crowley	Y	Y	N	Y	Y
8 Nadler	Y	Y	N	Y	Y
9 Weiner	Y	Y	N	Y	Y
10 Towns	Y	Y	N	Y	Y
11 Clarke	Y	Y	N	Y	Y
12 Velázquez	Y	Y	N	Y	Y
13 Fossella	Y	Y	Y	N	Y
14 Maloney	Y	Y	N	Y	+
15 Rangel	Y	Y	N	Y	Y
16 Serrano	Y	Y	N	Y	Y
17 Engel	Y	Y	N	Y	Y
18 Lowey	Y	Y	N	Y	Y
19 Hall	Y	Y	N	Y	Y
20 Gillibrand	?	?	?	?	?
21 McNulty	Y	Y	N	Y	Y
22 Hinchey	Y	Y	N	Y	Y
23 McHugh	Y	Y	P	N	Y
24 Arcuri	Y	Y	N	Y	Y
25 Walsh	Y	?	P	Y	N
26 Reynolds	Y	Y	N	Y	N
27 Higgins	Y	Y	N	Y	Y
28 Slaughter	Y	Y	N	Y	Y
29 Kuhl	Y	Y	P	N	N
NORTH CAROLINA					
1 Butterfield	Y	Y	N	Y	Y
2 Etheridge	Y	Y	Y	Y	Y
3 Jones	Y	Y	Y	N	N
4 Price	Y	Y	N	Y	Y

	326	327	328	329	330
5 Foxx	Y	Y	P	N	N
6 Coble	Y	Y	Y	Y	N
7 McIntyre	Y	Y	Y	Y	Y
8 Hayes	Y	Y	Y	N	Y
9 Myrick	?	?	?	?	?
10 McHenry	Y	Y	Y	N	N
11 Shuler	Y	Y	Y	Y	N
12 Watt	Y	Y	N	Y	Y
13 Miller	Y	Y	Y	N	Y
NORTH DAKOTA					
AL Pomeroy	Y	Y	Y	Y	Y
OHIO					
1 Chabot	Y	Y	P	N	N
2 Schmidt	Y	Y	Y	N	N
3 Turner	Y	Y	Y	N	N
4 Jordan	Y	Y	Y	N	N
5 Latta	Y	Y	Y	N	N
6 Wilson	Y	Y	N	Y	Y
7 Hobson	Y	Y	P	N	N
8 Boehner	?	?	P	N	N
9 Kaptur	?	Y	N	Y	Y
10 Kucinich	Y	N	N	N	Y
11 Tubbs Jones	Y	Y	N	Y	Y
12 Tiberi	Y	Y	P	N	N
13 Sutton	Y	Y	N	Y	Y
14 LaTourette	Y	Y	P	N	Y
15 Pryce	Y	Y	P	N	N
16 Regula	Y	Y	P	N	N
17 Ryan	Y	Y	Y	Y	Y
18 Space	Y	Y	Y	Y	Y
OKLAHOMA					
1 Sullivan	Y	Y	P	N	N
2 Boren	Y	Y	N	Y	N
3 Lucas	Y	Y	Y	N	N
4 Cole	Y	Y	Y	N	N
5 Fallin	Y	Y	Y	N	N
OREGON					
1 Wu	Y	N	Y	Y	Y
2 Walden	Y	Y	P	N	N
3 Blumenauer	Y	Y	N	Y	Y
4 DeFazio	Y	Y	N	Y	Y
5 Hooley	Y	Y	Y	Y	Y
PENNSYLVANIA					
1 Brady	Y	Y	N	Y	Y
2 Fattah	Y	Y	N	Y	Y
3 English	Y	Y	Y	N	Y
4 Altmire	Y	Y	Y	Y	Y
5 Peterson	Y	Y	P	N	N
6 Gerlach	?	?	?	?	?
7 Sestak	Y	Y	N	Y	Y
8 Murphy, P.	Y	Y	N	Y	Y
9 Shuster	Y	?	P	N	N
10 Carney	Y	Y	N	Y	Y
11 Kanjorski	Y	Y	N	Y	Y
12 Murtha	Y	Y	Y	Y	Y
13 Schwartz	Y	Y	Y	Y	Y
14 Doyle	Y	Y	N	Y	Y
15 Dent	Y	Y	N	Y	Y
16 Pitts	Y	Y	P	N	N
17 Holden	Y	Y	Y	Y	Y
18 Murphy, T.	Y	Y	Y	N	Y
19 Platts	Y	Y	Y	N	Y
RHODE ISLAND					
1 Kennedy	Y	Y	N	Y	Y
2 Langevin	Y	Y	N	Y	Y
SOUTH CAROLINA					
1 Brown	Y	Y	Y	N	N
2 Wilson	Y	Y	P	N	N
3 Barrett	Y	Y	P	N	N
4 Inglis	Y	Y	P	N	N
5 Spratt	Y	Y	Y	Y	Y
6 Clyburn	Y	Y	Y	Y	Y
SOUTH DAKOTA					
AL Herseth Sandlin	Y	Y	Y	Y	Y
TENNESSEE					
1 Davis, D.	Y	Y	P	N	N
2 Duncan	Y	Y	N	Y	N
3 Wamp	Y	Y	P	N	N
4 Davis, L.	Y	Y	Y	N	Y
5 Cooper	Y	Y	Y	Y	Y
6 Gordon	Y	Y	Y	Y	Y
7 Blackburn	Y	Y	P	N	N
8 Tanner	Y	Y	Y	Y	Y
9 Cohen	Y	Y	N	Y	Y

	326	327	328	329	330
TEXAS					
1 Gohmert	?	Y	P	N	N
2 Poe	Y	Y	P	N	N
3 Johnson, S.	Y	Y	P	N	N
4 Hall	Y	Y	P	N	N
5 Hensarling	Y	Y	P	N	N
6 Barton	Y	Y	P	N	N
7 Culberson	Y	Y	P	N	N
8 Brady	Y	Y	P	N	N
9 Green, A.	Y	Y	N	Y	Y
10 McCaul	Y	Y	P	N	N
11 Conaway	Y	Y	P	N	N
12 Granger	Y	Y	P	N	N
13 Thornberry	Y	Y	P	N	N
14 Paul	N	Y	N	N	N
15 Hinojosa	Y	Y	Y	Y	Y
16 Reyes	Y	Y	Y	Y	Y
17 Edwards	Y	Y	Y	Y	Y
18 Jackson Lee	Y	Y	N	Y	Y
19 Neugebauer	Y	Y	P	N	N
20 Gonzalez	Y	Y	Y	Y	Y
21 Smith	Y	Y	P	N	N
22 Lampson	Y	Y	Y	N	N
23 Rodriguez	Y	Y	Y	Y	Y
24 Marchant	?	Y	P	N	N
25 Doggett	Y	Y	N	Y	Y
26 Burgess	Y	Y	N	N	N
27 Ortiz	Y	Y	Y	Y	Y
28 Cuellar	Y	Y	Y	Y	Y
29 Green, G.	Y	Y	Y	Y	Y
30 Johnson, E.	Y	Y	N	Y	Y
31 Carter	Y	Y	P	N	N
32 Sessions	Y	Y	Y	N	N
UTAH					
1 Bishop	Y	Y	Y	N	N
2 Matheson	Y	Y	Y	N	N
3 Cannon	Y	Y	P	N	N
VERMONT					
AL Welch	Y	Y	N	Y	Y
VIRGINIA					
1 Wittman	Y	Y	Y	N	N
2 Drake	Y	Y	P	N	N
3 Scott	Y	Y	N	Y	Y
4 Forbes	Y	Y	Y	N	N
5 Goode	Y	Y	P	N	N
6 Goodlatte	Y	Y	P	N	N
7 Cantor	Y	Y	P	N	N
8 Moran	Y	Y	N	Y	Y
9 Boucher	Y	Y	Y	Y	Y
10 Wolf	Y	Y	P	N	N
11 Davis	Y	Y	P	N	N
WASHINGTON					
1 Inslee	Y	Y	N	Y	Y
2 Larsen	Y	Y	Y	N	Y
3 Baird	Y	Y	N	Y	Y
4 Hastings	?	?	P	N	N
5 McMorris Rodgers	Y	Y	P	N	N
6 Dicks	Y	Y	Y	N	Y
7 McDermott	Y	N	N	Y	Y
8 Reichert	Y	?	Y	N	N
9 Smith	Y	Y	Y	Y	Y
WEST VIRGINIA					
1 Mollohan	Y	Y	Y	Y	Y
2 Capito	Y	Y	Y	N	Y
3 Rahall	Y	Y	N	Y	Y
WISCONSIN					
1 Ryan	Y	Y	P	N	N
2 Baldwin	Y	N	N	Y	Y
3 Kind	Y	Y	Y	Y	Y
4 Moore	Y	Y	N	Y	Y
5 Sensenbrenner	Y	Y	P	N	N
6 Petri	Y	Y	Y	N	Y
7 Obey	Y	Y	N	Y	Y
8 Kagen	Y	Y	N	Y	Y
WYOMING					
AL Cubin	Y	Y	P	N	N
DELEGATES					
Faleomavaega (A.S.)					
Norton (D.C.)					
Bordallo (Guam)					
Fortuño (P.R.)					
Christensen (V.I.)					

IN THE HOUSE | By Vote Number

331. **HR 6081. Military and Public Employees Tax Package/ Passage.** Rangel, D-N.Y., motion to suspend the rules and pass the bill that would provide several new and extended tax benefits for military personnel and veterans. It would allow certain military families, blind veterans and AmeriCorps volunteers not receiving Supplemental Security Income to do so. It also would extend mental health parity provisions through 2008. Motion agreed to 403-0: R 184-0; D 219-0 (ND 162-0, SD 57-0). A two-thirds majority of those present and voting (269 in this case) is required for passage under suspension of the rules. May 20, 2008.

332. **HR 6074. Energy Price Manipulation/Passage.** Scott, D-Va., motion to suspend the rules and pass the bill that would make it illegal for foreign countries to collectively manipulate energy prices or supplies and allow the federal government to sue foreign countries for any such actions that affect the United States. It also would establish a task force to examine anti-competitive activities in the foreign oil market. Motion agreed to 324-84: R 103-82; D 221-2 (ND 164-0, SD 57-2). A two-thirds majority of those present and voting (272 in this case) is required for passage under suspension of the rules. A "nay" was a vote in favor of the president's position. May 20, 2008.

333. **H Res 1144. Frank Sinatra Day/Adoption.** Watson, D-Calif., motion to suspend the rules and adopt the resolution that would express support for the designation of a "Frank Sinatra Day" in honor of the dedication of the Frank Sinatra commemorative stamp. Motion agreed to 402-3: R 180-3; D 222-0 (ND 164-0, SD 58-0). A two-thirds majority of those present and voting (270 in this case) is required for adoption under suspension of the rules. May 20, 2008.

334. **H Con Res 355. Adjournment/Adoption.** Adoption of the concurrent resolution that would provide for adjournment of the Senate until noon Monday, June 2, 2008, and the House until 2 p.m. Tuesday, June 3, 2008. Adopted 239-175: R 19-167; D 220-8 (ND 164-5, SD 56-3). May 20, 2008.

335. **HR 1464. Rare Cat and Dog Conservation Programs/ Passage.** Bordallo, D-Guam, motion to suspend the rules and pass the bill that would authorize $5 million annually in fiscal 2009 through 2013 for a grant program for rare cat and dog conservation activities in other countries. Motion agreed to 294-119: R 67-118; D 227-1 (ND 170-0, SD 57-1). A two-thirds majority of those present and voting (276 in this case) is required for passage under suspension of the rules. May 20, 2008.

336. **HR 2649. San Diego County Water Reclamation Project/ Passage.** Bordallo, D-Guam, motion to suspend the rules and pass the bill that would allow the Interior Department to participate in the planning and provide as much as 25 percent of the funding for the second phase of a water treatment, recycling and reclamation project in the Olivenhain Municipal Water District in San Diego County, Calif. Motion agreed to 374-39: R 146-39; D 228-0 (ND 169-0, SD 59-0). A two-thirds majority of those present and voting (276 in this case) is required for passage under suspension of the rules. May 20, 2008.

*Rep. Travis W. Childers, D-Miss., was sworn in May 20, 2008, to fill the seat vacated in December by the resignation of Republican Roger Wicker, who was appointed to the Senate. The first vote for which Childers was eligible was vote 332.

ND Northern Democrats, SD Southern Democrats
Southern states: Ala., Ark., Fla., Ga., Ky., La., Miss., N.C., Okla., S.C., Tenn., Texas, Va.

	331	332	333	334	335	336
ALABAMA						
1 **Bonner**	Y	N	Y	N	N	Y
2 **Everett**	Y	N	Y	N	N	Y
3 **Rogers**	Y	Y	Y	Y	Y	Y
4 **Aderholt**	Y	Y	Y	N	N	Y
5 Cramer	Y	Y	Y	Y	Y	Y
6 **Bachus**	Y	Y	Y	N	N	Y
7 Davis	Y	Y	Y	Y	Y	Y
ALASKA						
AL **Young**	Y	N	Y	Y	N	Y
ARIZONA						
1 **Renzi**	Y	N	Y	N	N	Y
2 **Franks**	Y	N	Y	N	N	N
3 **Shadegg**	Y	N	Y	N	N	N
4 Pastor	Y	Y	Y	Y	Y	Y
5 Mitchell	Y	Y	Y	N	Y	Y
6 **Flake**	Y	N	Y	N	N	N
7 Grijalva	Y	Y	Y	Y	Y	Y
8 Giffords	Y	Y	Y	N	Y	Y
ARKANSAS						
1 Berry	Y	Y	Y	Y	Y	Y
2 Snyder	Y	Y	Y	Y	Y	Y
3 **Boozman**	Y	Y	Y	N	N	Y
4 Ross	Y	Y	Y	Y	Y	Y
CALIFORNIA						
1 Thompson	Y	Y	Y	Y	Y	Y
2 **Herger**	Y	Y	Y	N	N	Y
3 **Lungren**	Y	N	Y	N	N	Y
4 **Doolittle**	Y	N	Y	N	N	Y
5 Matsui	Y	Y	Y	Y	Y	Y
6 Woolsey	Y	Y	Y	Y	Y	Y
7 Miller, George	Y	Y	Y	Y	Y	Y
8 Pelosi						
9 Lee	Y	Y	Y	Y	Y	Y
10 Tauscher	Y	Y	Y	Y	Y	Y
11 McNerney	Y	Y	Y	Y	Y	Y
12 Speier	Y	Y	Y	Y	Y	Y
13 Stark	Y	Y	Y	?	Y	Y
14 Eshoo	Y	Y	Y	Y	Y	Y
15 Honda	Y	Y	Y	Y	Y	Y
16 Lofgren	Y	Y	Y	Y	Y	Y
17 Farr	Y	Y	Y	Y	Y	Y
18 Cardoza	Y	Y	Y	Y	Y	Y
19 **Radanovich**	Y	N	Y	N	N	Y
20 Costa	Y	Y	Y	Y	Y	Y
21 **Nunes**	Y	N	Y	N	Y	Y
22 **McCarthy**	Y	N	Y	N	N	Y
23 Capps	Y	Y	Y	Y	Y	Y
24 **Gallegly**	Y	Y	Y	N	N	Y
25 **McKeon**	Y	N	Y	N	Y	Y
26 **Dreier**	Y	Y	Y	N	N	Y
27 Sherman	Y	Y	Y	Y	Y	Y
28 Berman	Y	Y	Y	Y	Y	Y
29 Schiff	Y	Y	Y	Y	Y	Y
30 Waxman	Y	Y	Y	Y	Y	Y
31 Becerra	Y	Y	Y	Y	Y	Y
32 Solis	Y	Y	Y	Y	Y	Y
33 Watson	Y	Y	Y	Y	Y	Y
34 Roybal-Allard	Y	Y	Y	Y	Y	Y
35 Waters	Y	Y	Y	Y	Y	Y
36 Harman	Y	Y	Y	Y	Y	Y
37 Richardson	Y	Y	Y	Y	Y	Y
38 Napolitano	Y	Y	Y	Y	Y	Y
39 Sánchez, Linda	Y	Y	Y	Y	Y	Y
40 **Royce**	Y	Y	Y	N	Y	N
41 **Lewis**	Y	N	Y	N	Y	Y
42 **Miller, Gary**	Y	N	Y	N	Y	Y
43 Baca	Y	Y	Y	Y	Y	Y
44 **Calvert**	Y	Y	Y	N	Y	Y
45 **Bono Mack**	Y	Y	Y	N	Y	Y
46 **Rohrabacher**	Y	N	Y	N	Y	Y
47 Sanchez, Loretta	Y	Y	Y	Y	Y	Y
48 **Campbell**	Y	Y	Y	N	N	N
49 **Issa**	Y	N	Y	N	N	Y
50 **Bilbray**	Y	Y	Y	N	Y	Y
51 Filner	Y	Y	Y	Y	Y	Y
52 **Hunter**	Y	Y	Y	N	N	Y
53 Davis	Y	Y	Y	Y	Y	Y
COLORADO						
1 DeGette	Y	Y	Y	Y	Y	Y
2 Udall	?	?	?	Y	Y	Y
3 Salazar	Y	Y	Y	Y	Y	Y
4 **Musgrave**	Y	Y	Y	N	N	Y
5 **Lamborn**	Y	N	N	N	N	N
6 **Tancredo**	N	N	N	N	N	N
7 Perlmutter	Y	Y	Y	Y	Y	Y
CONNECTICUT						
1 Larson	Y	Y	Y	Y	Y	Y
2 Courtney	Y	Y	Y	Y	Y	Y
3 DeLauro	Y	Y	Y	Y	Y	Y
4 **Shays**	Y	Y	Y	N	Y	Y
5 Murphy	Y	Y	Y	Y	Y	Y
DELAWARE						
AL **Castle**	Y	Y	Y	N	Y	Y
FLORIDA						
1 **Miller**	Y	N	Y	N	N	N
2 Boyd	Y	Y	Y	Y	Y	Y
3 Brown	Y	Y	Y	Y	Y	Y
4 **Crenshaw**	?	?	?	?	?	?
5 **Brown-Waite**	Y	N	Y	N	N	Y
6 **Stearns**	Y	Y	Y	N	N	Y
7 **Mica**	Y	Y	Y	Y	Y	Y
8 **Keller**	Y	Y	Y	N	Y	Y
9 **Bilirakis**	Y	Y	Y	N	Y	Y
10 **Young**	Y	Y	Y	Y	Y	Y
11 Castor	Y	Y	Y	Y	Y	Y
12 **Putnam**	?	?	?	?	?	?
13 **Buchanan**	Y	Y	Y	N	Y	Y
14 **Mack**	Y	N	Y	N	Y	Y
15 **Weldon**	Y	N	Y	N	N	Y
16 Mahoney	Y	Y	Y	Y	Y	Y
17 Meek	Y	Y	Y	Y	Y	Y
18 **Ros-Lehtinen**	Y	Y	Y	Y	Y	Y
19 Wexler	Y	Y	Y	Y	Y	Y
20 Wasserman Schultz	Y	Y	Y	Y	?	Y
21 **Diaz-Balart, L.**	?	?	?	?	?	?
22 Klein	Y	Y	Y	Y	Y	Y
23 Hastings	Y	Y	Y	Y	Y	Y
24 **Feeney**	Y	N	Y	N	Y	Y
25 **Diaz-Balart, M.**	+	+	+	−	+	+
GEORGIA						
1 **Kingston**	?	?	?	?	?	?
2 Bishop	Y	Y	Y	Y	Y	Y
3 **Westmoreland**	Y	N	N	N	N	N
4 Johnson	Y	N	Y	Y	Y	Y
5 Lewis	Y	Y	Y	Y	Y	Y
6 **Price**	Y	N	N	N	N	N
7 **Linder**	Y	Y	Y	N	N	N
8 Marshall	Y	Y	Y	Y	Y	Y
9 **Deal**	Y	N	N	N	N	N
10 **Broun**	Y	N	Y	N	N	N
11 **Gingrey**	Y	N	N	N	N	N
12 Barrow	Y	Y	Y	Y	Y	Y
13 Scott	Y	Y	Y	Y	Y	Y
HAWAII						
1 Abercrombie	Y	Y	Y	Y	Y	Y
2 Hirono	Y	Y	Y	Y	Y	Y
IDAHO						
1 **Sali**	Y	Y	Y	N	N	Y
2 **Simpson**	Y	Y	Y	N	Y	Y
ILLINOIS						
1 Rush	?	?	?	?	?	?
2 Jackson	Y	Y	Y	Y	Y	Y
3 Lipinski	Y	Y	Y	Y	Y	Y
4 Gutierrez	?	?	?	Y	Y	Y
5 Emanuel	Y	Y	Y	Y	Y	Y
6 **Roskam**	Y	Y	Y	N	N	Y
7 Davis	?	?	?	Y	Y	Y
8 Bean	Y	Y	Y	Y	Y	Y
9 Schakowsky	Y	Y	Y	Y	Y	Y
10 **Kirk**	Y	Y	Y	N	Y	Y
11 **Weller**	Y	N	Y	N	Y	Y
12 Costello	Y	Y	Y	Y	Y	Y
13 **Biggert**	Y	Y	Y	N	Y	Y
14 Foster	Y	Y	Y	Y	Y	Y
15 Johnson	+	Y	Y	Y	Y	Y

KEY   **Republicans**   Democrats

Y Voted for (yea)	X Paired against	C Voted "present" to avoid possible conflict of interest
# Paired for	− Announced against	
+ Announced for	P Voted "present"	? Did not vote or otherwise make a position known
N Voted against (nay)		

	331	332	333	334	335	336
16 **Manzullo**	Y	Y	Y	N	N	Y
17 Hare	Y	Y	Y	Y	Y	Y
18 **LaHood**	Y	Y	Y	N	N	Y
19 **Shimkus**	Y	N	Y	N	N	Y
INDIANA						
1 Visclosky	Y	Y	Y	Y	Y	Y
2 Donnelly	Y	Y	Y	N	Y	Y
3 **Souder**	Y	Y	Y	N	N	Y
4 **Buyer**	Y	Y	?	N	N	Y
5 **Burton**	Y	Y	Y	N	N	N
6 **Pence**	Y	N	Y	N	N	N
7 Carson, A.	Y	Y	Y	Y	Y	Y
8 Ellsworth	Y	Y	Y	N	Y	Y
9 Hill	Y	Y	Y	Y	Y	Y
IOWA						
1 Braley	Y	Y	Y	Y	Y	Y
2 Loebsack	Y	Y	Y	Y	Y	Y
3 Boswell	Y	Y	Y	Y	Y	Y
4 **Latham**	Y	Y	Y	N	Y	Y
5 **King**	Y	N	Y	N	N	Y
KANSAS						
1 **Moran**	Y	N	Y	N	N	Y
2 Boyda	Y	Y	Y	Y	Y	Y
3 Moore	Y	Y	Y	Y	Y	Y
4 **Tiahrt**	Y	N	Y	N	N	Y
KENTUCKY						
1 **Whitfield**	Y	Y	Y	N	Y	Y
2 **Lewis**	Y	N	Y	N	N	Y
3 Yarmuth	Y	Y	Y	Y	Y	Y
4 **Davis**	Y	N	Y	N	N	Y
5 **Rogers**	Y	Y	Y	N	Y	Y
6 Chandler	Y	Y	Y	Y	Y	Y
LOUISIANA						
1 **Scalise**	Y	N	Y	N	N	N
2 Jefferson	Y	Y	Y	Y	Y	Y
3 Melancon	Y	Y	Y	Y	Y	Y
4 **McCrery**	Y	N	Y	N	N	Y
5 **Alexander**	Y	Y	Y	N	N	Y
6 Cazayoux	Y	Y	Y	Y	Y	Y
7 **Boustany**	Y	N	Y	N	N	Y
MAINE						
1 Allen	Y	Y	Y	Y	Y	Y
2 Michaud	Y	Y	Y	Y	Y	Y
MARYLAND						
1 **Gilchrest**	?	?	?	?	?	?
2 Ruppersberger	Y	Y	Y	Y	Y	Y
3 Sarbanes	Y	Y	Y	Y	Y	Y
4 Wynn	Y	Y	Y	Y	Y	Y
5 Hoyer	Y	Y	Y	Y	Y	Y
6 **Bartlett**	Y	N	Y	N	Y	Y
7 Cummings	Y	Y	Y	Y	Y	Y
8 Van Hollen	Y	Y	Y	Y	Y	Y
MASSACHUSETTS						
1 Olver	Y	Y	Y	Y	Y	Y
2 Neal	Y	Y	Y	Y	Y	Y
3 McGovern	Y	Y	Y	Y	Y	Y
4 Frank	Y	Y	Y	Y	Y	Y
5 Tsongas	Y	Y	Y	Y	Y	Y
6 Tierney	Y	Y	Y	Y	Y	Y
7 Markey	Y	Y	Y	Y	Y	Y
8 Capuano	Y	Y	Y	Y	Y	Y
9 Lynch	?	Y	Y	Y	Y	Y
10 Delahunt	Y	?	?	Y	Y	Y
MICHIGAN						
1 Stupak	Y	Y	Y	Y	Y	Y
2 **Hoekstra**	Y	N	Y	N	N	Y
3 **Ehlers**	Y	Y	Y	Y	Y	Y
4 **Camp**	Y	Y	Y	N	N	Y
5 Kildee	Y	Y	Y	Y	Y	Y
6 **Upton**	Y	Y	Y	N	Y	Y
7 **Walberg**	Y	N	Y	N	N	N
8 **Rogers**	Y	Y	Y	N	Y	Y
9 **Knollenberg**	Y	Y	Y	N	Y	Y
10 **Miller**	Y	Y	Y	N	Y	Y
11 **McCotter**	Y	Y	Y	N	Y	Y
12 Levin	Y	Y	Y	Y	Y	Y
13 Kilpatrick	Y	Y	Y	Y	Y	Y
14 Conyers	Y	Y	Y	Y	Y	Y
15 Dingell	?	?	?	Y	Y	Y
MINNESOTA						
1 Walz	Y	Y	Y	Y	Y	Y
2 **Kline**	Y	N	Y	N	N	Y
3 **Ramstad**	Y	Y	Y	N	Y	Y
4 McCollum	Y	Y	Y	Y	Y	Y

	331	332	333	334	335	336
5 Ellison	Y	Y	Y	Y	Y	Y
6 **Bachmann**	Y	Y	Y	N	N	Y
7 Peterson	Y	Y	Y	Y	Y	Y
8 Oberstar	Y	Y	Y	Y	Y	Y
MISSISSIPPI						
1 Childers*		Y	Y	Y	Y	Y
2 Thompson	Y	Y	Y	Y	Y	Y
3 **Pickering**	Y	Y	Y	N	N	Y
4 Taylor	Y	Y	?	Y	Y	Y
MISSOURI						
1 Clay	Y	Y	Y	Y	Y	Y
2 **Akin**	Y	N	Y	N	N	N
3 Carnahan	Y	Y	Y	Y	Y	Y
4 Skelton	Y	Y	Y	Y	Y	Y
5 Cleaver	Y	Y	Y	Y	Y	Y
6 **Graves**	Y	Y	Y	N	N	Y
7 **Blunt**	Y	N	Y	N	N	N
8 **Emerson**	Y	Y	Y	N	Y	?
9 **Hulshof**	?	?	?	?	?	?
MONTANA						
AL **Rehberg**	Y	Y	Y	Y	N	Y
NEBRASKA						
1 **Fortenberry**	Y	Y	Y	Y	Y	Y
2 **Terry**	Y	Y	Y	N	N	Y
3 **Smith**	Y	N	Y	N	N	Y
NEVADA						
1 Berkley	Y	Y	Y	Y	Y	Y
2 **Heller**	Y	Y	Y	N	N	Y
3 **Porter**	Y	Y	Y	N	Y	Y
NEW HAMPSHIRE						
1 Shea-Porter	Y	Y	Y	Y	Y	Y
2 Hodes	Y	Y	Y	Y	Y	Y
NEW JERSEY						
1 Andrews	+	+	+	+	+	+
2 **LoBiondo**	Y	Y	Y	N	Y	Y
3 **Saxton**	Y	Y	?	N	Y	Y
4 **Smith**	Y	Y	Y	Y	?	Y
5 **Garrett**	Y	N	Y	N	N	Y
6 Pallone	Y	Y	Y	Y	Y	Y
7 **Ferguson**	?	?	?	?	?	?
8 Pascrell	Y	Y	Y	Y	Y	Y
9 Rothman	Y	Y	Y	Y	Y	Y
10 Payne	Y	Y	Y	Y	Y	Y
11 **Frelinghuysen**	Y	N	Y	N	Y	Y
12 Holt	Y	Y	Y	Y	Y	Y
13 Sires	Y	Y	Y	Y	Y	Y
NEW MEXICO						
1 **Wilson**	?	?	?	?	?	?
2 **Pearce**	Y	N	Y	N	Y	Y
3 Udall	Y	Y	Y	Y	Y	Y
NEW YORK						
1 Bishop	Y	Y	Y	Y	Y	Y
2 Israel	?	?	?	?	?	?
3 **King**	Y	Y	Y	N	N	Y
4 McCarthy	Y	Y	Y	Y	Y	Y
5 Ackerman	Y	Y	Y	Y	Y	Y
6 Meeks	Y	Y	Y	Y	Y	Y
7 Crowley	Y	Y	Y	Y	Y	Y
8 Nadler	Y	Y	Y	Y	Y	Y
9 Weiner	Y	Y	Y	Y	Y	Y
10 Towns	Y	Y	Y	Y	Y	Y
11 Clarke	Y	Y	Y	Y	Y	Y
12 Velázquez	Y	Y	Y	Y	Y	Y
13 **Fossella**	Y	Y	Y	N	N	Y
14 Maloney	Y	Y	Y	Y	Y	Y
15 Rangel	Y	Y	Y	Y	Y	?
16 Serrano	Y	Y	Y	Y	Y	Y
17 Engel	?	Y	Y	Y	Y	Y
18 Lowey	Y	Y	Y	Y	Y	Y
19 Hall	Y	Y	Y	Y	Y	Y
20 Gillibrand	?	?	?	?	?	?
21 McNulty	Y	Y	Y	Y	Y	Y
22 Hinchey	Y	Y	Y	Y	Y	Y
23 **McHugh**	Y	Y	Y	N	Y	Y
24 Arcuri	Y	Y	Y	Y	Y	Y
25 **Walsh**	Y	Y	Y	N	Y	Y
26 **Reynolds**	Y	Y	Y	N	Y	Y
27 Higgins	Y	Y	Y	Y	Y	Y
28 Slaughter	Y	Y	Y	Y	Y	Y
29 **Kuhl**	Y	Y	Y	N	Y	Y
NORTH CAROLINA						
1 Butterfield	Y	Y	Y	Y	Y	Y
2 Etheridge	Y	Y	Y	Y	Y	Y
3 **Jones**	Y	Y	Y	Y	N	N

	331	332	333	334	335	336
5 **Foxx**	Y	N	Y	Y	N	N
6 **Coble**	Y	N	Y	N	N	N
7 McIntyre	Y	Y	Y	Y	Y	Y
8 **Hayes**	Y	Y	Y	N	N	Y
9 **Myrick**	Y	N	Y	N	N	N
10 **McHenry**	Y	Y	Y	N	N	Y
11 Shuler	Y	Y	Y	N	Y	Y
12 Watt	Y	Y	Y	Y	Y	Y
13 Miller	Y	Y	Y	Y	Y	Y
NORTH DAKOTA						
AL Pomeroy	Y	Y	Y	Y	Y	Y
OHIO						
1 **Chabot**	Y	Y	Y	N	Y	Y
2 **Schmidt**	Y	N	Y	N	Y	Y
3 **Turner**	Y	Y	Y	N	Y	Y
4 **Jordan**	Y	Y	Y	N	N	N
5 **Latta**	Y	Y	Y	N	N	Y
6 Wilson	Y	Y	Y	Y	Y	Y
7 **Hobson**	Y	Y	Y	N	Y	Y
8 **Boehner**	Y	N	Y	N	N	Y
9 Kaptur	Y	Y	Y	Y	Y	Y
10 Kucinich	Y	Y	Y	Y	Y	Y
11 Tubbs Jones	+	Y	Y	Y	Y	Y
12 **Tiberi**	Y	Y	Y	N	Y	Y
13 Sutton	Y	Y	Y	Y	Y	Y
14 **LaTourette**	Y	Y	Y	N	Y	Y
15 **Pryce**	?	?	?	?	?	?
16 **Regula**	Y	Y	Y	N	Y	Y
17 Ryan	Y	Y	Y	Y	Y	Y
18 Space	Y	Y	Y	Y	Y	Y
OKLAHOMA						
1 **Sullivan**	Y	N	Y	N	N	Y
2 Boren	Y	Y	Y	Y	Y	Y
3 **Lucas**	Y	N	Y	N	N	Y
4 **Cole**	Y	N	Y	N	N	Y
5 **Fallin**	Y	N	Y	N	N	Y
OREGON						
1 Wu	Y	Y	Y	Y	Y	Y
2 **Walden**	Y	Y	Y	N	Y	Y
3 Blumenauer	?	?	?	?	?	?
4 DeFazio	Y	Y	Y	Y	Y	Y
5 Hooley	Y	Y	Y	Y	Y	Y
PENNSYLVANIA						
1 Brady	Y	Y	Y	Y	Y	Y
2 Fattah	Y	Y	Y	Y	Y	Y
3 **English**	Y	Y	Y	N	Y	Y
4 Altmire	Y	Y	Y	Y	Y	Y
5 **Peterson**	Y	N	Y	N	N	Y
6 **Gerlach**	Y	Y	Y	Y	Y	Y
7 Sestak	Y	Y	Y	Y	Y	Y
8 Murphy, P.	Y	Y	Y	N	Y	Y
9 **Shuster**	Y	N	Y	N	N	Y
10 Carney	Y	Y	Y	Y	Y	Y
11 Kanjorski	Y	Y	Y	Y	Y	Y
12 Murtha	Y	Y	Y	Y	Y	Y
13 Schwartz	Y	Y	Y	Y	Y	Y
14 Doyle	Y	Y	Y	Y	Y	Y
15 **Dent**	Y	Y	Y	N	Y	Y
16 **Pitts**	Y	N	Y	Y	N	N
17 Holden	Y	Y	Y	Y	Y	Y
18 **Murphy, T.**	Y	Y	Y	N	Y	Y
19 **Platts**	Y	Y	Y	N	Y	Y
RHODE ISLAND						
1 Kennedy	?	?	?	?	?	?
2 Langevin	Y	Y	Y	Y	Y	Y
SOUTH CAROLINA						
1 **Brown**	Y	Y	Y	N	Y	Y
2 **Wilson**	Y	Y	Y	N	N	Y
3 **Barrett**	Y	N	Y	N	N	Y
4 **Inglis**	Y	N	Y	N	N	Y
5 Spratt	Y	Y	Y	Y	Y	Y
6 Clyburn	Y	Y	Y	Y	Y	Y
SOUTH DAKOTA						
AL Herseth Sandlin	Y	Y	Y	Y	Y	Y
TENNESSEE						
1 **Davis, David**	Y	Y	Y	N	N	N
2 **Duncan**	Y	Y	Y	N	N	N
3 **Wamp**	Y	Y	Y	N	N	N
4 Davis, L.	Y	Y	Y	Y	Y	Y
5 Cooper	Y	Y	Y	N	Y	Y
6 Gordon	?	Y	Y	N	N	Y
7 **Blackburn**	Y	Y	Y	N	N	Y
8 Tanner	Y	Y	Y	Y	Y	Y
9 Cohen	Y	Y	Y	Y	Y	Y

	331	332	333	334	335	336
TEXAS						
1 **Gohmert**	Y	Y	?	N	N	N
2 **Poe**	Y	N	N	N	N	N
3 **Johnson, S.**	Y	N	Y	N	N	Y
4 **Hall**	Y	N	Y	N	N	Y
5 **Hensarling**	Y	N	Y	N	N	N
6 **Barton**	Y	N	Y	N	N	Y
7 **Culberson**	Y	N	Y	N	N	N
8 **Brady**	Y	N	Y	N	N	Y
9 Green, A.	Y	Y	Y	Y	Y	Y
10 **McCaul**	Y	Y	Y	N	Y	Y
11 **Conaway**	Y	N	N	N	N	N
12 **Granger**	Y	N	Y	Y	N	Y
13 **Thornberry**	Y	N	Y	N	N	Y
14 **Paul**	?	?	?	Y	N	N
15 Hinojosa	Y	Y	Y	Y	Y	Y
16 Reyes	Y	Y	Y	Y	Y	Y
17 Edwards	Y	Y	Y	Y	Y	Y
18 Jackson Lee	Y	Y	Y	Y	Y	Y
19 **Neugebauer**	Y	N	N	N	N	N
20 Gonzalez	Y	Y	Y	Y	Y	Y
21 **Smith**	Y	Y	Y	N	Y	Y
22 Lampson	Y	N	Y	Y	Y	Y
23 Rodriguez	Y	Y	Y	Y	Y	Y
24 **Marchant**	Y	N	Y	N	N	Y
25 Doggett	Y	Y	Y	Y	Y	Y
26 **Burgess**	Y	N	Y	N	N	Y
27 Ortiz	Y	Y	Y	Y	Y	Y
28 Cuellar	Y	Y	Y	Y	Y	Y
29 Green, G.	Y	Y	Y	Y	Y	Y
30 Johnson, E.	Y	Y	Y	Y	Y	Y
31 **Carter**	Y	N	Y	N	N	Y
32 **Sessions**	?	?	?	?	?	?
UTAH						
1 **Bishop**	Y	N	Y	?	Y	Y
2 Matheson	?	?	?	Y	Y	Y
3 **Cannon**	Y	N	Y	N	N	N
VERMONT						
AL Welch	Y	Y	Y	Y	Y	Y
VIRGINIA						
1 **Wittman**	Y	Y	Y	N	N	Y
2 **Drake**	Y	Y	Y	N	N	Y
3 Scott	Y	Y	Y	Y	Y	Y
4 **Forbes**	Y	Y	Y	N	N	Y
5 **Goode**	Y	Y	Y	N	N	N
6 **Goodlatte**	Y	Y	Y	N	N	Y
7 **Cantor**	Y	Y	Y	N	N	Y
8 Moran	Y	Y	Y	Y	Y	Y
9 Boucher	Y	Y	Y	Y	Y	Y
10 **Wolf**	Y	Y	Y	N	Y	Y
11 **Davis, T.**	?	?	?	?	?	?
WASHINGTON						
1 Inslee	Y	Y	Y	Y	Y	Y
2 Larsen	Y	Y	Y	Y	Y	Y
3 Baird	Y	Y	Y	Y	Y	Y
4 **Hastings**	Y	N	Y	N	N	Y
5 **McMorris Rodgers**	?	?	Y	N	Y	Y
6 Dicks	Y	Y	Y	Y	Y	Y
7 McDermott	Y	Y	Y	Y	Y	Y
8 **Reichert**	Y	Y	Y	N	Y	Y
9 Smith	Y	Y	Y	Y	Y	Y
WEST VIRGINIA						
1 Mollohan	Y	Y	Y	Y	Y	Y
2 **Capito**	Y	Y	Y	N	Y	Y
3 Rahall	Y	Y	Y	Y	Y	Y
WISCONSIN						
1 **Ryan**	Y	Y	Y	N	N	Y
2 Baldwin	Y	Y	Y	Y	Y	Y
3 Kind	Y	Y	Y	Y	Y	Y
4 Moore	Y	Y	Y	Y	Y	Y
5 **Sensenbrenner**	Y	Y	Y	N	?	?
6 **Petri**	Y	Y	Y	N	Y	Y
7 Obey	Y	Y	Y	Y	Y	Y
8 Kagen	Y	Y	Y	Y	Y	Y
WYOMING						
AL **Cubin**	Y	N	Y	Y	N	Y
DELEGATES						
Faleomavaega (A.S.)						
Norton (D.C.)						
Bordallo (Guam)						
Fortuño (P.R.)						
Christensen (V.I.)						

IN THE HOUSE | By Vote Number

337. **HR 2744. Airline Flight Crew Leave/Passage.** Bishop, D-N.Y., motion to suspend the rules and pass the bill that would amend the Family and Medical Leave Act to make airline crew members eligible to take up to 12 weeks of unpaid leave to care for a newborn, a newly adopted child or a sick family member, or to recover from serious health conditions. Motion agreed to 402-9: R 176-9; D 226-0 (ND 167-0, SD 59-0). A two-thirds majority of those present and voting (274 in this case) is required for passage under suspension of the rules. May 20, 2008.

338. **HR 6049. Tax Provisions Extension/Previous Question.** Arcuri, D-N.Y., motion to order the previous question (thus ending debate and possibility of amendment) on adoption of the rule (H Res 1212) that would allow for House floor consideration of the bill that would extend dozens of expired or expiring tax provisions and create new energy-related tax incentives. Motion agreed to 223-190: R 1-188; D 222-2 (ND 167-1, SD 55-1). May 21, 2008.

339. **HR 6049. Tax Provisions Extension/Rule.** Adoption of the rule (H Res 1212) to provide for House floor consideration of the bill that would extend dozens of expired or expiring tax provisions and create new energy-related tax incentives. Adopted 223-194: R 0-193; D 223-1 (ND 168-1, SD 55-0). May 21, 2008.

340. **HR 5658. Fiscal 2009 Defense Authorization/Previous Question.** Hastings, D-Fla., motion to order the previous question (thus ending debate and possibility of amendment) on adoption of the rule (H Res 1213) to allow for House floor consideration of the bill that would authorize funds for defense programs in fiscal 2009, including emergency funds for operations in Iraq and Afghanistan and the war on terrorism. (Subsequently, the rule was adopted by voice vote.) Motion agreed to 235-186: R 9-185; D 226-1 (ND 171-0, SD 55-1). May 21, 2008.

341. **S Con Res 70. Fiscal 2009 Budget Resolution/Previous Question.** McGovern, D-Mass., motion to order the previous question (thus ending debate and possibility of amendment) on adoption of the rule (H Res 1214) to provide for House floor consideration of the conference report on the concurrent resolution that would set budget levels for fiscal 2009 through fiscal 2013. Motion agreed to 229-186: R 8-183; D 221-3 (ND 169-1, SD 52-2). May 21, 2008.

342. **S Con Res 70. Fiscal 2009 Budget Resolution/Rule.** Adoption of the rule (H Res 1214) to provide for House floor consideration of the conference report on the concurrent resolution that would set forth budget levels for fiscal 2009 through fiscal 2013. Adopted 220-199: R 0-192; D 220-7 (ND 170-2, SD 50-5). May 21, 2008.

343. **HR 6049. Tax Provisions Extension/Recommit.** McCrery, R-La., motion to recommit the bill to the House Ways and Means Committee with instructions that it be reported back promptly with a substitute amendment that would extend the package of expiring tax credits through 2013, remove the bill's offsets and extend alternative minimum tax exemption amounts through 2008. Motion rejected 201-220: R 194-0; D 7-220 (ND 5-166, SD 2-54). May 21, 2008.

	337	338	339	340	341	342	343
ALABAMA							
1 **Bonner**	Y	N	N	N	N	N	Y
2 **Everett**	Y	N	N	N	N	N	Y
3 **Rogers**	Y	N	N	N	N	N	Y
4 **Aderholt**	Y	N	N	N	N	N	Y
5 Cramer	Y	Y	Y	Y	Y	Y	N
6 **Bachus**	Y	N	N	N	N	N	Y
7 Davis	Y	Y	Y	Y	Y	Y	N
ALASKA							
AL **Young**	Y	N	N	N	N	N	Y
ARIZONA							
1 Renzi	Y	N	N	N	N	N	Y
2 **Franks**	Y	N	N	N	N	N	Y
3 **Shadegg**	Y	N	N	N	N	N	Y
4 Pastor	Y	Y	Y	Y	Y	Y	N
5 Mitchell	Y	Y	Y	Y	Y	Y	N
6 **Flake**	N	N	N	N	N	N	Y
7 Grijalva	Y	Y	Y	Y	Y	Y	N
8 Giffords	Y	Y	Y	Y	Y	Y	N
ARKANSAS							
1 Berry	Y	Y	Y	Y	Y	Y	N
2 Snyder	Y	Y	Y	Y	Y	Y	N
3 **Boozman**	Y	N	N	N	N	N	Y
4 Ross	Y	Y	Y	Y	Y	Y	N
CALIFORNIA							
1 Thompson	Y	Y	Y	Y	Y	Y	N
2 **Herger**	Y	N	N	N	N	N	Y
3 **Lungren**	Y	N	N	N	N	N	Y
4 **Doolittle**	Y	N	N	N	N	N	Y
5 Matsui	Y	Y	Y	Y	Y	Y	N
6 Woolsey	Y	Y	Y	Y	Y	Y	N
7 Miller, George	Y	Y	Y	Y	Y	Y	N
8 Pelosi					Y		
9 Lee	Y	Y	Y	Y	Y	Y	N
10 Tauscher	Y	Y	Y	Y	Y	Y	N
11 McNerney	Y	Y	Y	Y	Y	Y	Y
12 Speier	Y	+	Y	Y	Y	Y	N
13 Stark	Y	Y	Y	Y	Y	Y	N
14 Eshoo	Y	Y	Y	Y	Y	Y	N
15 Honda	Y	Y	Y	Y	Y	Y	N
16 Lofgren	Y	Y	Y	Y	Y	Y	N
17 Farr	Y	Y	Y	Y	Y	Y	N
18 Cardoza	Y	Y	Y	Y	Y	Y	N
19 **Radanovich**	Y	N	N	N	N	N	Y
20 Costa	Y	Y	Y	Y	Y	Y	?
21 **Nunes**	Y	N	N	N	N	N	Y
22 **McCarthy**	Y	N	N	N	N	N	Y
23 Capps	Y	Y	Y	Y	Y	Y	N
24 **Gallegly**	Y	N	N	N	N	N	Y
25 **McKeon**	Y	N	N	N	N	N	Y
26 **Dreier**	Y	N	N	N	N	N	Y
27 Sherman	Y	Y	Y	Y	Y	Y	N
28 Berman	Y	Y	Y	Y	Y	Y	N
29 Schiff	Y	Y	Y	Y	Y	Y	N
30 Waxman	Y	Y	Y	Y	Y	Y	N
31 Becerra	Y	Y	Y	Y	?	Y	N
32 Solis	Y	?	Y	Y	Y	Y	N
33 Watson	Y	Y	Y	Y	Y	Y	N
34 Roybal-Allard	Y	Y	Y	Y	Y	Y	N
35 Waters	Y	Y	Y	Y	Y	Y	N
36 Harman	Y	Y	Y	Y	Y	Y	N
37 Richardson	Y	Y	Y	Y	Y	Y	N
38 Napolitano	Y	Y	Y	Y	Y	Y	N
39 Sánchez, Linda	Y	Y	Y	Y	Y	Y	N
40 **Royce**	Y	N	N	N	N	N	Y
41 **Lewis**	Y	N	N	N	N	N	Y
42 **Miller, Gary**	Y	N	N	N	N	N	Y
43 Baca	Y	Y	Y	Y	Y	Y	N
44 **Calvert**	Y	N	N	N	N	N	Y
45 **Bono Mack**	Y	N	N	N	N	N	Y
46 **Rohrabacher**	Y	N	N	N	N	N	Y
47 Sanchez, Loretta	Y	Y	Y	Y	Y	Y	N
48 **Campbell**	N	N	N	N	N	N	Y
49 **Issa**	Y	N	N	N	N	N	Y
50 **Bilbray**	Y	N	N	N	N	N	Y
51 Filner	Y	Y	Y	Y	Y	Y	N
52 **Hunter**	Y	N	N	N	N	N	Y
53 Davis	Y	Y	Y	Y	Y	Y	N

	337	338	339	340	341	342	343
COLORADO							
1 DeGette	Y	Y	Y	Y	Y	Y	N
2 Udall	Y	Y	Y	Y	Y	Y	N
3 Salazar	Y	Y	Y	Y	Y	Y	N
4 **Musgrave**	Y	N	N	N	N	N	Y
5 **Lamborn**	Y	N	N	N	N	N	Y
6 **Tancredo**	Y	N	N	N	N	N	Y
7 Perlmutter	Y	Y	Y	Y	Y	Y	N
CONNECTICUT							
1 Larson	Y	Y	Y	Y	Y	Y	N
2 Courtney	Y	Y	Y	Y	Y	Y	N
3 DeLauro	Y	Y	Y	Y	Y	Y	N
4 **Shays**	Y	N	Y	N	Y	N	Y
5 Murphy	Y	Y	Y	Y	Y	Y	N
DELAWARE							
AL **Castle**	Y	N	N	Y	Y	N	Y
FLORIDA							
1 **Miller**	Y	N	N	N	N	N	Y
2 Boyd	Y	Y	Y	Y	Y	Y	N
3 Brown	Y	?	?	?	?	?	?
4 **Crenshaw**	?	?	?	?	?	?	?
5 **Brown-Waite**	Y	N	N	N	N	N	Y
6 **Stearns**	Y	N	N	N	N	N	Y
7 **Mica**	Y	N	N	N	N	N	Y
8 **Keller**	Y	N	N	N	N	N	Y
9 **Bilirakis**	Y	N	N	N	N	N	Y
10 **Young**	Y	N	N	N	N	N	Y
11 Castor	Y	?	?	?	?	?	?
12 **Putnam**	?	N	N	N	N	N	Y
13 **Buchanan**	Y	N	N	N	N	N	Y
14 **Mack**	Y	N	N	N	N	N	Y
15 **Weldon**	Y	N	N	N	N	N	Y
16 Mahoney	Y	Y	Y	Y	Y	Y	N
17 Meek	Y	Y	Y	Y	Y	Y	N
18 **Ros-Lehtinen**	Y	N	N	Y	N	N	Y
19 Wexler	Y	?	?	?	?	?	?
20 Wasserman Schultz	Y	Y	Y	Y	Y	Y	N
21 **Diaz-Balart, L.**	?	N	N	N	N	N	Y
22 Klein	Y	Y	Y	Y	Y	Y	N
23 Hastings	Y	Y	Y	Y	Y	Y	N
24 **Feeney**	Y	N	N	N	N	N	Y
25 **Diaz-Balart, M.**	+	N	N	N	N	N	Y
GEORGIA							
1 **Kingston**	?	?	?	?	?	?	Y
2 Bishop	Y	Y	Y	Y	Y	Y	N
3 **Westmoreland**	Y	N	N	N	N	N	Y
4 Johnson	Y	Y	Y	Y	Y	Y	N
5 Lewis	Y	Y	Y	Y	Y	Y	N
6 **Price**	Y	N	N	N	N	N	Y
7 **Linder**	?	N	N	N	N	N	Y
8 Marshall	Y	Y	Y	Y	Y	Y	N
9 **Deal**	Y	N	N	N	N	N	Y
10 **Broun**	N	N	N	N	?	N	Y
11 **Gingrey**	Y	N	N	N	N	N	Y
12 Barrow	Y	Y	Y	Y	N	Y	N
13 Scott	Y	Y	Y	Y	Y	Y	N
HAWAII							
1 Abercrombie	Y	Y	Y	Y	Y	Y	N
2 Hirono	Y	Y	Y	Y	Y	Y	N
IDAHO							
1 **Sali**	Y	N	N	N	N	N	Y
2 **Simpson**	Y	N	N	N	N	N	Y
ILLINOIS							
1 Rush	?	?	?	?	?	?	?
2 Jackson	Y	Y	Y	Y	Y	Y	N
3 Lipinski	Y	Y	Y	Y	Y	Y	N
4 Gutierrez	Y	Y	Y	Y	Y	Y	N
5 Emanuel	Y	Y	Y	Y	Y	Y	N
6 **Roskam**	Y	N	N	N	N	N	Y
7 Davis	Y	Y	Y	Y	Y	Y	N
8 Bean	Y	Y	Y	Y	Y	Y	N
9 Schakowsky	Y	Y	Y	Y	Y	Y	N
10 **Kirk**	Y	N	N	Y	N	N	Y
11 **Weller**	Y	N	N	N	N	N	Y
12 Costello	Y	Y	Y	Y	Y	Y	N
13 **Biggert**	Y	N	N	N	?	?	Y
14 Foster	Y	Y	Y	Y	Y	N	N
15 **Johnson**	Y	N	N	Y	N	Y	N

ND Northern Democrats, SD Southern Democrats
Southern states: Ala., Ark., Fla., Ga., Ky., La., Miss., N.C., Okla., S.C., Tenn., Texas, Va.

	337	338	339	340	341	342	343
16 **Manzullo**	Y	N	N	N	N	N	Y
17 Hare	Y	Y	Y	Y	Y	Y	N
18 **LaHood**	Y	N	N	N	N	N	Y
19 **Shimkus**	Y	N	N	N	N	N	Y
INDIANA							
1 Visclosky	Y	Y	Y	Y	Y	Y	N
2 Donnelly	Y	Y	Y	Y	N	Y	Y
3 **Souder**	Y	N	N	N	N	N	Y
4 **Buyer**	Y	N	N	N	N	N	Y
5 **Burton**	Y	N	N	N	N	N	Y
6 **Pence**	Y	N	N	N	N	N	Y
7 Carson, A.	Y	Y	Y	Y	Y	Y	N
8 Ellsworth	Y	Y	Y	Y	Y	Y	Y
9 Hill	Y	N	N	Y	Y	N	N
IOWA							
1 Braley	Y	Y	Y	Y	Y	Y	N
2 Loebsack	Y	Y	Y	Y	Y	Y	N
3 Boswell	Y	Y	Y	Y	Y	Y	N
4 **Latham**	Y	N	N	N	N	N	Y
5 **King**	Y	–	N	N	N	N	Y
KANSAS							
1 **Moran**	Y	N	N	N	N	N	Y
2 Boyda	Y	Y	Y	Y	Y	Y	N
3 Moore	Y	Y	Y	Y	Y	Y	N
4 **Tiahrt**	Y	?	?	?	?	?	?
KENTUCKY							
1 **Whitfield**	Y	N	N	N	N	N	Y
2 **Lewis**	Y	N	N	N	N	N	Y
3 Yarmuth	Y	Y	Y	Y	Y	Y	N
4 **Davis**	Y	N	N	N	N	N	Y
5 **Rogers**	Y	N	N	N	N	N	Y
6 Chandler	Y	Y	Y	Y	Y	Y	N
LOUISIANA							
1 **Scalise**	Y	N	N	N	N	N	Y
2 Jefferson	Y	Y	Y	Y	Y	Y	N
3 Melancon	Y	Y	Y	Y	Y	Y	N
4 **McCrery**	Y	N	N	N	N	N	Y
5 **Alexander**	Y	N	N	N	N	N	Y
6 Cazayoux	Y	Y	Y	Y	Y	N	N
7 **Boustany**	Y	N	?	N	N	N	Y
MAINE							
1 Allen	Y	Y	Y	Y	Y	Y	N
2 Michaud	Y	Y	Y	Y	Y	Y	N
MARYLAND							
1 **Gilchrest**	?	N	N	N	N	N	Y
2 Ruppersberger	Y	Y	Y	Y	Y	Y	N
3 Sarbanes	Y	Y	Y	Y	Y	Y	N
4 Wynn	Y	Y	?	Y	Y	Y	?
5 Hoyer	Y	Y	Y	Y	Y	Y	N
6 **Bartlett**	Y	N	N	N	N	N	Y
7 Cummings	Y	Y	Y	Y	Y	Y	N
8 Van Hollen	Y	Y	Y	Y	Y	Y	N
MASSACHUSETTS							
1 Olver	Y	?	Y	Y	Y	Y	N
2 Neal	Y	Y	Y	Y	Y	Y	N
3 McGovern	Y	Y	Y	Y	Y	Y	N
4 Frank	Y	Y	Y	Y	Y	Y	N
5 Tsongas	Y	Y	Y	Y	Y	Y	N
6 Tierney	Y	Y	Y	Y	Y	Y	N
7 Markey	Y	Y	Y	Y	Y	Y	N
8 Capuano	Y	Y	Y	Y	Y	Y	N
9 Lynch	Y	Y	?	Y	Y	Y	N
10 Delahunt	Y	Y	Y	Y	Y	Y	N
MICHIGAN							
1 Stupak	Y	Y	Y	Y	Y	Y	N
2 **Hoekstra**	Y	N	N	N	N	N	Y
3 **Ehlers**	Y	N	N	N	N	N	Y
4 **Camp**	Y	N	N	N	N	N	Y
5 Kildee	Y	Y	Y	Y	Y	Y	N
6 **Upton**	Y	N	N	N	N	N	Y
7 **Walberg**	Y	N	N	N	N	N	Y
8 **Rogers**	Y	N	N	N	N	N	Y
9 **Knollenberg**	Y	N	N	N	N	N	Y
10 **Miller**	Y	N	N	N	N	N	Y
11 **McCotter**	Y	N	N	N	N	N	Y
12 Levin	Y	Y	Y	Y	Y	Y	N
13 Kilpatrick	Y	Y	Y	Y	Y	Y	N
14 Conyers	Y	Y	Y	Y	Y	Y	N
15 Dingell	Y	Y	Y	Y	Y	Y	N
MINNESOTA							
1 Walz	Y	Y	Y	Y	Y	Y	N
2 **Kline**	Y	N	N	N	N	N	Y
3 **Ramstad**	Y	N	N	N	N	N	Y
4 McCollum	Y	Y	Y	Y	Y	Y	N

	337	338	339	340	341	342	343
5 Ellison	Y	Y	Y	Y	Y	Y	N
6 **Bachmann**	Y	N	N	N	N	N	Y
7 Peterson	Y	Y	Y	Y	Y	Y	N
8 Oberstar	Y	Y	Y	Y	Y	Y	N
MISSISSIPPI							
1 Childers	Y	Y	Y	Y	Y	N	N
2 Thompson	Y	Y	Y	Y	Y	Y	N
3 **Pickering**	Y	N	N	N	?	N	Y
4 Taylor	Y	Y	Y	Y	Y	Y	N
MISSOURI							
1 Clay	Y	Y	Y	Y	Y	Y	N
2 **Akin**	Y	N	N	N	N	N	Y
3 Carnahan	Y	Y	Y	Y	Y	Y	N
4 Skelton	Y	Y	Y	Y	Y	Y	N
5 Cleaver	Y	Y	Y	Y	Y	Y	N
6 **Graves**	Y	N	N	N	N	N	Y
7 **Blunt**	Y	N	N	N	N	N	Y
8 **Emerson**	Y	N	N	N	N	N	Y
9 **Hulshof**	?	N	N	N	N	N	Y
MONTANA							
AL **Rehberg**	Y	N	N	N	N	N	Y
NEBRASKA							
1 **Fortenberry**	Y	?	N	N	N	N	Y
2 **Terry**	Y	N	N	N	N	N	Y
3 **Smith**	Y	N	N	N	N	N	Y
NEVADA							
1 Berkley	Y	Y	Y	Y	Y	Y	N
2 **Heller**	Y	N	N	N	N	N	Y
3 **Porter**	Y	N	N	N	N	N	Y
NEW HAMPSHIRE							
1 Shea-Porter	Y	Y	Y	Y	Y	Y	N
2 Hodes	Y	Y	Y	Y	Y	Y	N
NEW JERSEY							
1 Andrews	+	?	?	?	?	?	N
2 **LoBiondo**	Y	N	N	Y	Y	N	Y
3 **Saxton**	Y	N	N	N	N	N	Y
4 **Smith**	Y	N	N	Y	Y	N	Y
5 **Garrett**	N	N	N	N	N	N	Y
6 Pallone	Y	Y	Y	Y	Y	Y	N
7 **Ferguson**	?	N	N	N	N	N	Y
8 Pascrell	Y	Y	Y	Y	Y	Y	N
9 Rothman	Y	Y	Y	Y	Y	Y	N
10 Payne	Y	Y	Y	Y	Y	Y	N
11 **Frelinghuysen**	Y	N	N	N	N	N	Y
12 Holt	Y	Y	Y	Y	Y	Y	N
13 Sires	Y	Y	Y	Y	Y	Y	N
NEW MEXICO							
1 **Wilson**	?	N	N	N	N	N	Y
2 **Pearce**	Y	N	N	N	N	N	Y
3 Udall	Y	Y	Y	Y	Y	Y	N
NEW YORK							
1 Bishop	Y	Y	Y	Y	Y	Y	N
2 Israel	?	Y	Y	Y	Y	Y	N
3 **King**	Y	N	N	N	N	N	Y
4 McCarthy	Y	Y	Y	Y	Y	Y	N
5 Ackerman	Y	Y	Y	Y	Y	Y	N
6 Meeks	Y	Y	Y	Y	Y	Y	N
7 Crowley	Y	Y	Y	Y	Y	Y	N
8 Nadler	Y	Y	Y	Y	Y	Y	N
9 Weiner	Y	Y	Y	Y	Y	Y	N
10 Towns	Y	Y	Y	Y	Y	Y	N
11 Clarke	Y	Y	Y	Y	Y	Y	N
12 Velázquez	Y	Y	Y	Y	Y	Y	N
13 **Fossella**	Y	N	N	N	N	N	Y
14 Maloney	Y	Y	Y	Y	Y	Y	N
15 Rangel	?	Y	Y	Y	Y	Y	N
16 Serrano	Y	Y	Y	Y	Y	Y	N
17 Engel	Y	Y	Y	Y	Y	Y	N
18 Lowey	Y	Y	Y	Y	Y	Y	N
19 Hall	Y	Y	Y	Y	Y	Y	N
20 Gillibrand	?	?	?	?	?	?	?
21 McNulty	Y	Y	Y	Y	Y	Y	N
22 Hinchey	Y	Y	Y	Y	Y	Y	N
23 **McHugh**	Y	N	N	N	N	N	Y
24 Arcuri	Y	Y	Y	Y	Y	Y	N
25 **Walsh**	Y	N	N	N	N	N	Y
26 **Reynolds**	Y	?	N	N	N	N	Y
27 Higgins	Y	Y	Y	Y	Y	Y	N
28 Slaughter	Y	?	?	?	?	?	N
29 **Kuhl**	Y	N	N	N	N	N	Y
NORTH CAROLINA							
1 Butterfield	Y	Y	Y	Y	?	Y	N
2 Etheridge	Y	Y	Y	Y	Y	Y	N
3 **Jones**	Y	N	N	N	N	N	Y
4 Price	Y	Y	Y	Y	Y	Y	N

	337	338	339	340	341	342	343
5 **Foxx**	Y	N	N	N	N	N	Y
6 **Coble**	Y	–	–	–	–	–	+
7 McIntyre	Y	Y	Y	Y	Y	Y	Y
8 **Hayes**	Y	N	N	N	N	N	Y
9 **Myrick**	Y	N	N	N	N	N	Y
10 **McHenry**	Y	N	N	N	N	N	Y
11 Shuler	Y	Y	Y	Y	Y	N	N
12 Watt	Y	Y	Y	Y	Y	Y	N
13 Miller	Y	Y	Y	Y	Y	Y	N
NORTH DAKOTA							
AL Pomeroy	Y	Y	Y	Y	Y	Y	N
OHIO							
1 **Chabot**	Y	N	N	N	N	N	Y
2 **Schmidt**	Y	N	N	N	N	N	Y
3 **Turner**	Y	N	N	N	N	N	Y
4 **Jordan**	N	N	N	N	N	N	Y
5 **Latta**	N	N	N	N	N	N	Y
6 Wilson	Y	Y	Y	Y	Y	Y	N
7 **Hobson**	Y	N	N	N	N	N	Y
8 **Boehner**	Y	N	N	N	N	N	Y
9 Kaptur	?	Y	Y	Y	Y	Y	N
10 Kucinich	Y	Y	Y	Y	Y	Y	N
11 Tubbs Jones	?	Y	Y	Y	Y	Y	N
12 **Tiberi**	Y	N	N	N	N	N	Y
13 Sutton	Y	Y	Y	Y	Y	Y	N
14 **LaTourette**	Y	N	N	N	N	N	Y
15 **Pryce**	?	N	N	N	N	N	Y
16 **Regula**	Y	N	N	N	N	N	Y
17 Ryan	Y	Y	Y	Y	Y	Y	N
18 Space	Y	Y	Y	Y	Y	Y	N
OKLAHOMA							
1 **Sullivan**	Y	N	N	N	N	N	Y
2 Boren	Y	Y	Y	Y	Y	Y	N
3 **Lucas**	Y	N	N	N	N	N	Y
4 **Cole**	Y	N	N	N	N	N	Y
5 **Fallin**	Y	N	N	N	N	N	Y
OREGON							
1 Wu	Y	Y	Y	Y	Y	Y	N
2 **Walden**	Y	N	N	N	N	N	Y
3 Blumenauer	?	Y	Y	Y	Y	Y	N
4 DeFazio	Y	Y	Y	Y	Y	Y	N
5 Hooley	Y	Y	Y	Y	Y	Y	N
PENNSYLVANIA							
1 Brady	Y	Y	Y	Y	Y	Y	N
2 Fattah	Y	Y	Y	Y	Y	Y	N
3 **English**	Y	N	N	N	N	N	Y
4 Altmire	Y	Y	Y	Y	Y	Y	N
5 **Peterson**	Y	N	N	N	N	N	Y
6 **Gerlach**	Y	N	N	N	Y	N	Y
7 Sestak	Y	Y	Y	Y	Y	Y	N
8 Murphy, P.	Y	Y	Y	Y	Y	Y	N
9 **Shuster**	Y	N	N	N	N	N	Y
10 Carney	Y	Y	Y	Y	Y	Y	N
11 Kanjorski	Y	Y	Y	Y	Y	Y	N
12 Murtha	Y	Y	Y	Y	Y	Y	N
13 Schwartz	Y	Y	Y	Y	Y	Y	N
14 Doyle	Y	Y	Y	Y	Y	Y	N
15 **Dent**	Y	N	N	N	N	N	Y
16 **Pitts**	Y	N	N	N	N	N	Y
17 Holden	Y	Y	Y	Y	Y	Y	N
18 **Murphy, T.**	Y	N	N	N	N	N	Y
19 **Platts**	Y	N	N	N	N	N	Y
RHODE ISLAND							
1 Kennedy	?	?	?	?	?	?	?
2 Langevin	Y	Y	Y	Y	Y	Y	N
SOUTH CAROLINA							
1 **Brown**	Y	N	N	N	N	N	Y
2 **Wilson**	Y	N	N	N	N	N	Y
3 **Barrett**	Y	N	N	N	N	N	Y
4 **Inglis**	Y	N	N	N	Y	N	Y
5 Spratt	Y	Y	Y	Y	Y	Y	N
6 Clyburn	Y	Y	Y	Y	Y	Y	N
SOUTH DAKOTA							
AL Herseth Sandlin	Y	Y	Y	Y	Y	Y	N
TENNESSEE							
1 **Davis, D.**	Y	N	N	N	N	N	Y
2 **Duncan**	N	N	N	N	N	N	Y
3 **Wamp**	Y	N	N	N	N	N	Y
4 Davis, L.	Y	Y	Y	Y	Y	Y	N
5 Cooper	Y	Y	Y	Y	Y	Y	N
6 Gordon	Y	Y	Y	Y	Y	Y	N
7 **Blackburn**	Y	N	N	N	N	N	Y
8 Tanner	Y	Y	Y	Y	Y	Y	N
9 Cohen	Y	Y	Y	Y	Y	Y	N

	337	338	339	340	341	342	343
TEXAS							
1 **Gohmert**	Y	N	N	N	N	N	Y
2 **Poe**	Y	N	N	N	N	N	Y
3 **Johnson, S.**	Y	N	N	N	N	N	Y
4 **Hall**	Y	N	N	N	N	N	Y
5 **Hensarling**	N	N	N	N	N	N	Y
6 **Barton**	Y	N	N	N	N	N	Y
7 **Culberson**	Y	N	N	N	N	N	Y
8 **Brady**	Y	N	N	N	N	N	Y
9 Green, A.	Y	Y	Y	Y	Y	Y	N
10 **McCaul**	Y	N	N	N	N	N	Y
11 **Conaway**	Y	N	N	N	N	N	Y
12 **Granger**	Y	N	N	N	N	N	Y
13 **Thornberry**	Y	N	N	N	N	N	Y
14 **Paul**	N	N	N	N	N	N	Y
15 Hinojosa	Y	Y	Y	Y	Y	Y	N
16 Reyes	Y	Y	Y	Y	Y	Y	N
17 Edwards	Y	Y	?	Y	?	Y	N
18 Jackson Lee	Y	Y	Y	Y	Y	Y	N
19 **Neugebauer**	Y	N	N	N	N	N	Y
20 Gonzalez	Y	Y	Y	Y	Y	Y	N
21 **Smith**	Y	N	N	N	N	N	Y
22 Lampson	Y	N	Y	N	N	N	Y
23 Rodriguez	Y	Y	Y	Y	Y	Y	N
24 **Marchant**	Y	N	N	N	N	N	Y
25 Doggett	Y	Y	Y	Y	Y	Y	N
26 **Burgess**	Y	N	N	N	N	N	Y
27 Ortiz	Y	Y	Y	Y	Y	Y	N
28 Cuellar	Y	Y	Y	Y	Y	Y	N
29 Green, G.	Y	Y	Y	Y	Y	?	N
30 Johnson, E.	Y	Y	Y	Y	Y	Y	N
31 **Carter**	Y	N	N	N	N	N	?
32 **Sessions**	?	?	N	N	N	N	Y
UTAH							
1 **Bishop**	Y	N	N	N	N	N	Y
2 Matheson	Y	Y	Y	Y	Y	Y	N
3 **Cannon**	Y	N	N	N	N	N	Y
VERMONT							
AL Welch	Y	Y	Y	Y	Y	Y	N
VIRGINIA							
1 **Wittman**	Y	N	N	N	N	N	Y
2 **Drake**	Y	N	N	N	N	N	Y
3 Scott	Y	Y	Y	Y	Y	Y	N
4 **Forbes**	Y	N	N	N	N	?	Y
5 **Goode**	Y	N	N	N	N	N	Y
6 **Goodlatte**	Y	N	N	N	N	N	Y
7 **Cantor**	Y	N	N	N	N	N	Y
8 Moran	Y	Y	Y	Y	Y	Y	N
9 Boucher	Y	Y	Y	Y	Y	Y	N
10 **Wolf**	Y	N	N	N	N	N	Y
11 **Davis**	?	N	N	N	N	N	Y
WASHINGTON							
1 Inslee	Y	Y	Y	Y	Y	Y	N
2 Larsen	Y	Y	Y	Y	Y	Y	N
3 Baird	Y	Y	Y	Y	Y	Y	N
4 **Hastings**	Y	N	N	N	N	N	Y
5 **McMorris Rodgers**	Y	N	N	N	N	N	Y
6 Dicks	Y	Y	Y	Y	Y	Y	N
7 McDermott	Y	Y	Y	Y	Y	Y	N
8 **Reichert**	Y	N	N	Y	Y	N	Y
9 Smith	Y	Y	Y	Y	Y	Y	N
WEST VIRGINIA							
1 Mollohan	Y	Y	Y	Y	Y	Y	N
2 **Capito**	Y	N	N	N	N	N	Y
3 Rahall	Y	Y	Y	Y	Y	Y	N
WISCONSIN							
1 **Ryan**	Y	N	N	N	N	N	Y
2 Baldwin	Y	Y	Y	Y	Y	Y	N
3 Kind	Y	Y	Y	Y	Y	Y	N
4 Moore	Y	Y	Y	Y	Y	Y	N
5 **Sensenbrenner**	?	?	?	?	?	?	?
6 **Petri**	Y	N	N	N	N	N	Y
7 Obey	Y	Y	Y	Y	Y	Y	N
8 Kagen	Y	Y	Y	Y	Y	Y	N
WYOMING							
AL **Cubin**	Y	?	N	N	N	N	Y
DELEGATES							
Faleomavaega (A.S.)							
Norton (D.C.)							
Bordallo (Guam)							
Fortuño (P.R.)							
Christensen (V.I.)							

IN THE HOUSE | By Vote Number

344. HR 6049. Tax Provisions Extension/Passage. Passage of the bill that would extend dozens of expired or expiring tax provisions for one year, including the research tax credit, deductions for tuition and education expenses, and deductions for sales taxes in states without income taxes. It would create and extend several energy tax provisions, such as tax credits for wind and renewable-energy production and for the purchase of fuel cell power plants. It would be offset by delaying new interest allocation rules for multinational companies and changing the rules for taxing deferred compensation. Passed 263-160: R 35-159; D 228-1 (ND 173-0, SD 55-1). A "nay" was a vote in favor of the president's position. May 21, 2008.

345. HR 1771. Crane Conservation/Passage. Bordallo, D-Guam, motion to suspend the rules and pass the bill that would establish a grant program to protect crane populations and authorize $5 million annually from fiscal 2009 through 2013 for the program. Motion agreed to 304-118: R 76-118; D 228-0 (ND 172-0, SD 56-0). A two-thirds majority of those present and voting (282 in this case) is required for passage under suspension of the rules. May 21, 2008.

346. HR 2419. Farm Bill Reauthorization/Veto Override. Passage, over President Bush's May 21, 2008, veto, of the bill that would reauthorize federal farm and nutrition programs for five years, including crop subsidies and food stamps, as well as conservation and rural development. It would authorize a $10.4 billion increase for nutrition programs, offset by extending customs user fees. It would cut direct payment subsidies overall by $313 million, in part by reducing the percentage of acres for which a farmer can collect payments. Farmers making more than $750,000 a year in farm-related income and those with more than $500,000 a year in non-farm-related income would not be eligible for federal subsidies. Country-of-origin labels for all meat would be required by September 2008. Passed 316-108: R 100-94; D 216-14 (ND 161-13, SD 55-1). A two-thirds majority of those present and voting (283 in this case for the House) of both chambers is required to override a veto. A "nay" was a vote in support of the president's position. May 21, 2008.

347. HR 3819. Veterans' Emergency Care/Passage. Filner, D-Calif., motion to suspend the rules and pass the bill that would require the Veterans Affairs Department to reimburse veterans who paid out-of-pocket for care at a non-VA hospital while waiting for transfer to a VA facility. Motion agreed to 412-0: R 187-0; D 225-0 (ND 169-0, SD 56-0). A two-thirds majority of those present and voting (275 in this case) is required for passage under suspension of the rules. May 21, 2008.

348. HR 5826. Veterans' Cost-of-Living Adjustment/Passage. Filner, D-Calif., motion to suspend the rules and pass the bill that would increase the rate of compensation for veterans with service-related disabilities and the rates of dependency and indemnity compensation for veterans' families, starting Dec. 1, 2008. The rate increases would be equal to the increase for Social Security benefits. Motion agreed to 417-0: R 195-0; D 222-0 (ND 167-0, SD 55-0). A two-thirds majority of those present and voting (278 in this case) is required for passage under suspension of the rules. May 21, 2008.

		344	345	346	347	348
ALABAMA						
1	Bonner	N	N	Y	Y	Y
2	Everett	N	N	Y	Y	Y
3	Rogers	Y	Y	Y	Y	Y
4	Aderholt	N	N	Y	Y	Y
5	Cramer	Y	Y	Y	Y	?
6	Bachus	N	Y	Y	Y	Y
7	Davis	Y	Y	Y	Y	Y
ALASKA						
AL	Young	N	N	Y	Y	Y
ARIZONA						
1	Renzi	N	Y	Y	Y	Y
2	Franks	N	N	N	Y	Y
3	Shadegg	N	N	N	Y	Y
4	Pastor	Y	Y	Y	Y	Y
5	Mitchell	Y	Y	Y	Y	Y
6	Flake	N	N	N	Y	Y
7	Grijalva	Y	Y	Y	Y	Y
8	Giffords	Y	Y	Y	Y	Y
ARKANSAS						
1	Berry	Y	Y	Y	Y	Y
2	Snyder	Y	Y	Y	Y	Y
3	Boozman	N	N	Y	Y	Y
4	Ross	Y	Y	Y	Y	Y
CALIFORNIA						
1	Thompson	Y	Y	Y	Y	Y
2	Herger	N	N	Y	+	Y
3	Lungren	N	N	N	N	Y
4	Doolittle	N	N	Y	Y	Y
5	Matsui	Y	Y	Y	Y	Y
6	Woolsey	Y	Y	Y	Y	Y
7	Miller, George	Y	Y	Y	Y	Y
8	Pelosi	Y		Y		
9	Lee	Y	Y	Y	Y	Y
10	Tauscher	Y	Y	Y	Y	Y
11	McNerney	Y	Y	Y	Y	Y
12	Speier	Y	Y	Y	Y	?
13	Stark	Y	Y	N	Y	Y
14	Eshoo	Y	Y	Y	Y	Y
15	Honda	Y	Y	Y	Y	Y
16	Lofgren	Y	Y	Y	Y	Y
17	Farr	Y	Y	Y	Y	Y
18	Cardoza	Y	Y	Y	Y	Y
19	Radanovich	N	N	Y	Y	Y
20	Costa	Y	Y	Y	Y	Y
21	Nunes	N	N	N	Y	Y
22	McCarthy	N	N	N	Y	Y
23	Capps	Y	Y	Y	Y	Y
24	Gallegly	N	N	Y	Y	Y
25	McKeon	N	N	N	Y	Y
26	Dreier	N	N	N	Y	Y
27	Sherman	Y	Y	Y	Y	Y
28	Berman	Y	Y	Y	?	Y
29	Schiff	Y	Y	Y	Y	Y
30	Waxman	Y	Y	N	Y	Y
31	Becerra	Y	Y	Y	Y	Y
32	Solis	Y	Y	Y	Y	Y
33	Watson	Y	Y	Y	Y	Y
34	Roybal-Allard	Y	Y	Y	Y	Y
35	Waters	Y	Y	Y	Y	Y
36	Harman	Y	Y	N	Y	Y
37	Richardson	Y	Y	Y	Y	Y
38	Napolitano	Y	Y	Y	Y	Y
39	Sánchez, Linda	Y	Y	Y	Y	Y
40	Royce	N	N	N	Y	Y
41	Lewis	N	N	N	Y	Y
42	Miller, Gary	N	N	N	Y	Y
43	Baca	Y	Y	Y	Y	Y
44	Calvert	N	N	N	Y	Y
45	Bono Mack	N	Y	N	Y	Y
46	Rohrabacher	N	N	N	Y	Y
47	Sanchez, Loretta	Y	Y	Y	Y	Y
48	Campbell	N	N	N	Y	Y
49	Issa	N	N	N	Y	Y
50	Bilbray	N	N	N	Y	Y
51	Filner	Y	Y	Y	Y	Y
52	Hunter	N	N	N	Y	Y
53	Davis	Y	Y	Y	Y	Y

		344	345	346	347	348
COLORADO						
1	DeGette	Y	Y	Y	Y	Y
2	Udall	Y	Y	Y	Y	Y
3	Salazar	Y	Y	Y	Y	Y
4	Musgrave	N	N	Y	Y	Y
5	Lamborn	N	N	N	Y	Y
6	Tancredo	N	N	N	Y	Y
7	Perlmutter	Y	Y	Y	Y	Y
CONNECTICUT						
1	Larson	Y	Y	Y	Y	Y
2	Courtney	Y	Y	Y	Y	Y
3	DeLauro	Y	Y	Y	?	Y
4	Shays	Y	Y	N	Y	Y
5	Murphy	Y	Y	Y	Y	Y
DELAWARE						
AL	Castle	Y	Y	N	Y	Y
FLORIDA						
1	Miller	N	N	N	Y	Y
2	Boyd	Y	Y	Y	Y	Y
3	Brown	?	?	?	?	?
4	Crenshaw	?	?	?	?	?
5	Brown-Waite	Y	Y	Y	Y	Y
6	Stearns	N	N	N	Y	Y
7	Mica	N	N	N	Y	Y
8	Keller	N	N	N	Y	Y
9	Bilirakis	N	Y	Y	Y	Y
10	Young	N	Y	N	Y	Y
11	Castor	?	?	?	?	?
12	Putnam	N	Y	Y	Y	Y
13	Buchanan	Y	Y	Y	Y	Y
14	Mack	N	N	N	Y	Y
15	Weldon	N	N	N	Y	Y
16	Mahoney	Y	Y	Y	Y	Y
17	Meek	Y	Y	Y	Y	Y
18	Ros-Lehtinen	Y	Y	Y	?	Y
19	Wexler	?	?	?	?	?
20	Wasserman Schultz	?	?	?	?	?
21	Diaz-Balart, L.	Y	Y	Y	Y	Y
22	Klein	Y	Y	Y	Y	Y
23	Hastings	Y	Y	Y	Y	Y
24	Feeney	N	N	N	Y	Y
25	Diaz-Balart, M.	Y	Y	Y	?	Y
GEORGIA						
1	Kingston	N	N	Y	Y	Y
2	Bishop	Y	Y	Y	Y	Y
3	Westmoreland	N	N	N	Y	Y
4	Johnson	Y	Y	Y	Y	Y
5	Lewis	Y	Y	Y	Y	Y
6	Price	N	N	N	Y	Y
7	Linder	N	N	N	Y	Y
8	Marshall	Y	Y	Y	Y	Y
9	Deal	N	N	N	Y	Y
10	Broun	N	N	N	Y	Y
11	Gingrey	N	N	Y	Y	Y
12	Barrow	Y	Y	Y	Y	Y
13	Scott	Y	Y	Y	Y	Y
HAWAII						
1	Abercrombie	Y	Y	Y	Y	Y
2	Hirono	Y	Y	Y	Y	Y
IDAHO						
1	Sali	N	N	Y	Y	Y
2	Simpson	N	Y	Y	Y	Y
ILLINOIS						
1	Rush	?	?	?	?	?
2	Jackson	Y	Y	Y	Y	Y
3	Lipinski	Y	Y	Y	Y	Y
4	Gutierrez	Y	Y	Y	Y	Y
5	Emanuel	Y	Y	Y	Y	Y
6	Roskam	N	N	N	Y	Y
7	Davis	Y	Y	Y	Y	Y
8	Bean	Y	Y	N	Y	Y
9	Schakowsky	Y	Y	Y	Y	Y
10	Kirk	N	Y	N	Y	Y
11	Weller	N	Y	N	Y	Y
12	Costello	Y	Y	Y	Y	Y
13	Biggert	N	Y	Y	Y	Y
14	Foster	Y	Y	Y	Y	Y
15	Johnson	N	Y	Y	Y	Y

KEY — Republicans — Democrats

Y Voted for (yea)	X Paired against	C Voted "present" to avoid possible conflict of interest
# Paired for	– Announced against	? Did not vote or otherwise make a position known
+ Announced for	P Voted "present"	
N Voted against (nay)		

ND Northern Democrats, SD Southern Democrats
Southern states: Ala., Ark., Fla., Ga., Ky., La., Miss., N.C., Okla., S.C., Tenn., Texas, Va.

Member	344	345	346	347	348
16 Manzullo	N	N	Y	Y	Y
17 Hare	Y	Y	Y	Y	Y
18 LaHood	Y	N	Y	Y	Y
19 Shimkus	N	N	Y	Y	Y
INDIANA					
1 Visclosky	Y	Y	Y	Y	Y
2 Donnelly	Y	Y	Y	Y	Y
3 Souder	Y	N	Y	Y	Y
4 Buyer	N	N	Y	Y	Y
5 Burton	N	N	N	Y	Y
6 Pence	N	N	N	Y	Y
7 Carson, A.	Y	Y	Y	Y	Y
8 Ellsworth	Y	Y	Y	Y	Y
9 Hill	Y	Y	Y	Y	Y
IOWA					
1 Braley	Y	Y	Y	Y	Y
2 Loebsack	Y	Y	Y	Y	Y
3 Boswell	Y	Y	Y	Y	Y
4 Latham	Y	Y	Y	Y	Y
5 King	N	N	Y	Y	Y
KANSAS					
1 Moran	Y	Y	N	Y	Y
2 Boyda	Y	Y	Y	Y	Y
3 Moore	Y	Y	Y	Y	Y
4 Tiahrt	?	?	?	?	?
KENTUCKY					
1 Whitfield	N	N	Y	Y	Y
2 Lewis	N	N	Y	Y	Y
3 Yarmuth	Y	Y	Y	Y	Y
4 Davis	N	N	Y	Y	Y
5 Rogers	N	N	Y	Y	Y
6 Chandler	Y	Y	Y	Y	Y
LOUISIANA					
1 Scalise	N	N	N	Y	Y
2 Jefferson	Y	Y	Y	Y	Y
3 Melancon	Y	Y	Y	Y	Y
4 McCrery	N	Y	N	Y	Y
5 Alexander	N	N	Y	Y	Y
6 Cazayoux	Y	Y	Y	Y	Y
7 Boustany	N	Y	Y	Y	Y
MAINE					
1 Allen	Y	Y	Y	Y	Y
2 Michaud	Y	Y	Y	Y	Y
MARYLAND					
1 Gilchrest	Y	Y	Y	Y	Y
2 Ruppersberger	Y	Y	Y	Y	Y
3 Sarbanes	Y	Y	Y	Y	Y
4 Wynn	?	?	Y	?	?
5 Hoyer	Y	Y	Y	Y	Y
6 Bartlett	N	Y	Y	Y	Y
7 Cummings	Y	Y	Y	Y	Y
8 Van Hollen	Y	Y	Y	Y	Y
MASSACHUSETTS					
1 Olver	Y	Y	Y	Y	Y
2 Neal	Y	Y	Y	Y	Y
3 McGovern	Y	Y	Y	Y	Y
4 Frank	Y	Y	Y	Y	?
5 Tsongas	Y	Y	Y	Y	Y
6 Tierney	Y	Y	Y	Y	Y
7 Markey	Y	Y	Y	Y	Y
8 Capuano	Y	Y	N	Y	Y
9 Lynch	Y	Y	Y	Y	Y
10 Delahunt	Y	Y	Y	Y	?
MICHIGAN					
1 Stupak	Y	Y	Y	Y	Y
2 Hoekstra	N	N	Y	Y	Y
3 Ehlers	Y	Y	N	Y	Y
4 Camp	N	N	Y	Y	Y
5 Kildee	Y	Y	Y	Y	Y
6 Upton	Y	Y	Y	Y	Y
7 Walberg	N	N	Y	Y	Y
8 Rogers	N	Y	N	Y	Y
9 Knollenberg	N	Y	N	Y	Y
10 Miller	Y	Y	Y	Y	Y
11 McCotter	N	Y	Y	Y	Y
12 Levin	Y	Y	Y	Y	Y
13 Kilpatrick	Y	Y	Y	Y	Y
14 Conyers	Y	Y	Y	Y	Y
15 Dingell	Y	Y	Y	Y	Y
MINNESOTA					
1 Walz	Y	Y	Y	Y	Y
2 Kline	N	N	Y	Y	Y
3 Ramstad	N	Y	Y	Y	Y
4 McCollum	Y	Y	Y	Y	Y
5 Ellison	Y	Y	Y	Y	Y
6 Bachmann	N	N	N	Y	Y
7 Peterson	Y	Y	Y	Y	Y
8 Oberstar	Y	Y	Y	Y	Y
MISSISSIPPI					
1 Childers	Y	Y	Y	Y	Y
2 Thompson	Y	Y	Y	Y	Y
3 Pickering	N	N	Y	Y	Y
4 Taylor	Y	Y	Y	Y	Y
MISSOURI					
1 Clay	Y	Y	Y	Y	Y
2 Akin	N	N	N	Y	Y
3 Carnahan	Y	Y	Y	Y	Y
4 Skelton	Y	Y	Y	Y	Y
5 Cleaver	Y	Y	Y	Y	Y
6 Graves	N	N	Y	Y	Y
7 Blunt	N	N	Y	Y	Y
8 Emerson	N	N	Y	Y	Y
9 Hulshof	N	N	Y	Y	Y
MONTANA					
AL Rehberg	N	Y	Y	Y	Y
NEBRASKA					
1 Fortenberry	N	Y	Y	?	Y
2 Terry	N	Y	N	?	Y
3 Smith	N	Y	Y	Y	Y
NEVADA					
1 Berkley	Y	Y	Y	Y	Y
2 Heller	N	Y	N	Y	Y
3 Porter	Y	Y	Y	Y	Y
NEW HAMPSHIRE					
1 Shea-Porter	Y	Y	Y	Y	Y
2 Hodes	Y	Y	Y	Y	Y
NEW JERSEY					
1 Andrews	Y	Y	Y	Y	Y
2 LoBiondo	Y	Y	N	Y	Y
3 Saxton	N	Y	Y	Y	Y
4 Smith	Y	Y	N	Y	Y
5 Garrett	N	N	Y	Y	Y
6 Pallone	Y	Y	Y	Y	Y
7 Ferguson	N	Y	Y	Y	Y
8 Pascrell	Y	Y	Y	Y	Y
9 Rothman	Y	Y	Y	Y	Y
10 Payne	Y	Y	Y	Y	Y
11 Frelinghuysen	N	Y	N	Y	Y
12 Holt	Y	Y	Y	Y	Y
13 Sires	Y	Y	Y	Y	Y
NEW MEXICO					
1 Wilson	N	Y	N	Y	Y
2 Pearce	N	Y	Y	Y	Y
3 Udall	Y	Y	Y	Y	Y
NEW YORK					
1 Bishop	Y	Y	Y	Y	Y
2 Israel	Y	Y	Y	Y	Y
3 King	N	N	N	Y	Y
4 McCarthy	Y	Y	Y	Y	Y
5 Ackerman	Y	Y	Y	Y	Y
6 Meeks	Y	Y	Y	Y	Y
7 Crowley	Y	Y	Y	Y	Y
8 Nadler	Y	Y	Y	?	Y
9 Weiner	Y	Y	Y	Y	Y
10 Towns	Y	Y	Y	Y	Y
11 Clarke	Y	Y	Y	Y	Y
12 Velázquez	Y	Y	Y	Y	Y
13 Fossella	N	N	?	?	?
14 Maloney	Y	Y	Y	Y	Y
15 Rangel	Y	Y	Y	Y	Y
16 Serrano	Y	Y	Y	Y	Y
17 Engel	Y	Y	Y	Y	Y
18 Lowey	Y	Y	Y	Y	Y
19 Hall	Y	Y	Y	Y	Y
20 Gillibrand	?	?	?	?	?
21 McNulty	Y	Y	Y	Y	Y
22 Hinchey	Y	Y	Y	Y	Y
23 McHugh	Y	Y	Y	+	Y
24 Arcuri	Y	Y	Y	Y	Y
25 Walsh	N	Y	Y	Y	Y
26 Reynolds	N	Y	Y	?	Y
27 Higgins	Y	Y	Y	Y	Y
28 Slaughter	Y	Y	Y	Y	Y
29 Kuhl	N	Y	Y	Y	Y
NORTH CAROLINA					
1 Butterfield	Y	Y	Y	Y	Y
2 Etheridge	Y	Y	Y	Y	Y
3 Jones	Y	Y	Y	Y	Y
4 Price	Y	Y	Y	Y	Y
5 Foxx	N	N	N	Y	Y
6 Coble	-	?	Y	Y	Y
7 McIntyre	Y	Y	Y	Y	Y
8 Hayes	Y	Y	Y	Y	Y
9 Myrick	N	N	N	Y	Y
10 McHenry	N	N	N	Y	Y
11 Shuler	Y	Y	Y	Y	Y
12 Watt	Y	Y	Y	Y	Y
13 Miller	Y	Y	Y	Y	Y
NORTH DAKOTA					
AL Pomeroy	Y	Y	Y	Y	Y
OHIO					
1 Chabot	N	Y	N	Y	Y
2 Schmidt	N	Y	N	Y	Y
3 Turner	N	Y	N	Y	Y
4 Jordan	N	N	N	Y	Y
5 Latta	N	Y	N	Y	Y
6 Wilson	Y	Y	Y	Y	Y
7 Hobson	Y	Y	N	Y	Y
8 Boehner	N	N	N	Y	Y
9 Kaptur	Y	Y	Y	Y	Y
10 Kucinich	Y	Y	Y	Y	Y
11 Tubbs Jones	Y	Y	Y	Y	Y
12 Tiberi	Y	N	N	Y	Y
13 Sutton	Y	Y	Y	Y	Y
14 LaTourette	Y	Y	Y	Y	Y
15 Pryce	Y	Y	N	Y	Y
16 Regula	Y	Y	Y	Y	Y
17 Ryan	Y	Y	Y	Y	Y
18 Space	Y	Y	Y	Y	Y
OKLAHOMA					
1 Sullivan	N	N	N	Y	Y
2 Boren	Y	Y	Y	Y	Y
3 Lucas	N	N	Y	Y	Y
4 Cole	N	Y	Y	Y	Y
5 Fallin	N	N	Y	Y	Y
OREGON					
1 Wu	Y	Y	Y	Y	Y
2 Walden	N	N	Y	Y	Y
3 Blumenauer	Y	Y	N	Y	Y
4 DeFazio	Y	Y	Y	Y	Y
5 Hooley	Y	Y	Y	Y	Y
PENNSYLVANIA					
1 Brady	Y	Y	Y	Y	Y
2 Fattah	Y	Y	Y	Y	Y
3 English	Y	Y	Y	?	Y
4 Altmire	Y	Y	Y	Y	Y
5 Peterson	N	Y	Y	Y	Y
6 Gerlach	Y	Y	Y	Y	Y
7 Sestak	Y	Y	Y	Y	Y
8 Murphy, P.	Y	Y	Y	Y	Y
9 Shuster	N	N	Y	Y	Y
10 Carney	Y	Y	Y	Y	Y
11 Kanjorski	Y	Y	Y	Y	Y
12 Murtha	Y	Y	Y	Y	Y
13 Schwartz	Y	Y	Y	Y	Y
14 Doyle	Y	Y	Y	Y	Y
15 Dent	Y	Y	N	Y	Y
16 Pitts	N	N	N	Y	Y
17 Holden	Y	Y	Y	Y	Y
18 Murphy, T.	Y	Y	Y	Y	Y
19 Platts	Y	Y	Y	Y	Y
RHODE ISLAND					
1 Kennedy	?	?	?	?	?
2 Langevin	Y	Y	Y	Y	Y
SOUTH CAROLINA					
1 Brown	N	N	Y	Y	Y
2 Wilson	N	N	N	Y	Y
3 Barrett	N	N	N	Y	Y
4 Inglis	N	N	N	Y	Y
5 Spratt	Y	Y	Y	Y	Y
6 Clyburn	Y	Y	Y	Y	Y
SOUTH DAKOTA					
AL Herseth Sandlin	Y	Y	Y	Y	Y
TENNESSEE					
1 Davis, D.	N	N	Y	Y	Y
2 Duncan	Y	N	Y	Y	Y
3 Wamp	N	N	N	Y	Y
4 Davis, L.	Y	Y	Y	Y	Y
5 Cooper	Y	Y	Y	Y	Y
6 Gordon	Y	Y	Y	Y	Y
7 Blackburn	N	N	Y	Y	Y
8 Tanner	Y	Y	Y	Y	Y
9 Cohen	Y	Y	Y	Y	Y
TEXAS					
1 Gohmert	N	N	Y	Y	Y
2 Poe	N	N	Y	Y	Y
3 Johnson, S.	Y	N	N	Y	Y
4 Hall	N	N	Y	Y	Y
5 Hensarling	N	N	N	Y	Y
6 Barton	N	N	N	Y	Y
7 Culberson	N	N	N	Y	Y
8 Brady	N	N	Y	Y	Y
9 Green, A.	Y	Y	Y	Y	Y
10 McCaul	N	N	Y	Y	Y
11 Conaway	N	N	N	Y	Y
12 Granger	N	N	N	Y	Y
13 Thornberry	N	N	Y	Y	Y
14 Paul	N	N	N	Y	Y
15 Hinojosa	Y	Y	Y	Y	Y
16 Reyes	Y	Y	Y	Y	Y
17 Edwards	Y	Y	Y	Y	Y
18 Jackson Lee	Y	Y	Y	Y	Y
19 Neugebauer	N	N	Y	Y	Y
20 Gonzalez	Y	Y	Y	Y	Y
21 Smith	N	Y	N	Y	Y
22 Lampson	N	Y	Y	Y	Y
23 Rodriguez	Y	Y	Y	Y	Y
24 Marchant	N	N	N	Y	Y
25 Doggett	Y	Y	Y	Y	Y
26 Burgess	N	N	N	Y	Y
27 Ortiz	Y	Y	Y	Y	Y
28 Cuellar	Y	Y	Y	Y	Y
29 Green, G.	Y	Y	Y	Y	Y
30 Johnson, E.	Y	Y	Y	Y	Y
31 Carter	?	?	?	?	?
32 Sessions	N	N	N	Y	Y
UTAH					
1 Bishop	N	N	?	Y	Y
2 Matheson	Y	Y	N	Y	Y
3 Cannon	N	N	N	Y	Y
VERMONT					
AL Welch	Y	Y	Y	Y	Y
VIRGINIA					
1 Wittman	N	N	Y	Y	Y
2 Drake	N	N	Y	Y	Y
3 Scott	Y	Y	Y	Y	Y
4 Forbes	N	N	Y	Y	Y
5 Goode	N	N	N	Y	Y
6 Goodlatte	N	Y	Y	Y	Y
7 Cantor	N	N	N	Y	Y
8 Moran	Y	Y	Y	Y	Y
9 Boucher	Y	Y	Y	Y	Y
10 Wolf	N	Y	Y	Y	Y
11 Davis	N	Y	N	Y	Y
WASHINGTON					
1 Inslee	Y	Y	N	Y	Y
2 Larsen	Y	Y	Y	Y	Y
3 Baird	Y	Y	Y	Y	Y
4 Hastings	N	N	Y	Y	Y
5 McMorris Rodgers	N	N	Y	Y	Y
6 Dicks	Y	Y	Y	Y	Y
7 McDermott	Y	Y	N	Y	?
8 Reichert	N	Y	N	Y	Y
9 Smith	Y	Y	Y	Y	Y
WEST VIRGINIA					
1 Mollohan	Y	Y	Y	Y	Y
2 Capito	Y	Y	Y	Y	Y
3 Rahall	Y	Y	Y	Y	Y
WISCONSIN					
1 Ryan	N	N	N	Y	Y
2 Baldwin	Y	Y	Y	Y	Y
3 Kind	Y	Y	Y	Y	Y
4 Moore	Y	Y	Y	Y	Y
5 Sensenbrenner	?	?	N	Y	Y
6 Petri	N	Y	N	Y	Y
7 Obey	Y	Y	Y	Y	Y
8 Kagen	Y	Y	Y	Y	?
WYOMING					
AL Cubin	N	N	Y	Y	Y
DELEGATES					
Faleomavaega (A.S.)					
Norton (D.C.)					
Bordallo (Guam)					
Fortuño (P.R.)					
Christensen (V.I.)					

IN THE HOUSE | By Vote Number

349. HR 5856. VA Medical Facility Leases and Projects/Passage.
Filner, D-Calif., motion to suspend the rules and pass the bill that would authorize several medical facility projects and medical facility leases for the Veterans Affairs Department for fiscal 2009. Motion agreed to 416-0: R 191-0; D 225-0 (ND 171-0, SD 54-0). A two-thirds majority of those present and voting (278 in this case) is required for passage under suspension of the rules. May 21, 2008.

350. HR 5658. Fiscal 2009 Defense Authorization/Previous Question.
Cardoza, D-Calif., motion to order the previous question (thus ending debate and possibility of amendment) on adoption of the rule (H Res 1218) that would allow for House floor consideration of the bill that would authorize funds for defense programs in fiscal 2009, including emergency funds for operations in Iraq and Afghanistan and the war on terrorism. Motion agreed to 228-192: R 2-191; D 226-1 (ND 170-1, SD 56-0). May 22, 2008.

351. HR 5658. Fiscal 2009 Defense Authorization/Rule.
Adoption of the rule (H Res 1218) that would allow for House floor consideration of the bill that would authorize funds for defense programs in fiscal 2009, including emergency funds for operations in Iraq and Afghanistan and the war on terrorism. Adopted 223-197: R 0-193; D 223-4 (ND 168-3, SD 55-1). May 22, 2008.

352. H Res 1221. Enrollment of the Farm Bill/Motion to Table.
Cardoza, D-Calif., motion to table (kill) the Boehner, R-Ohio, privileged resolution that would call for an investigation into the Democratic leadership's role in the inaccuracies in the process and enrollment of HR 2419. Motion agreed to 220-188: R 0-188; D 220-0 (ND 164-0, SD 56-0). May 22, 2008.

353. HR 6124. Farm Bill Reauthorization/Passage.
Peterson, D-Minn., motion to suspend the rules and pass the bill that would reauthorize federal farm and nutrition programs for five years, including crop subsidies and food stamps, as well as conservation, rural development and agricultural trade programs. It would authorize a $10.4 billion increase for nutrition programs, offset by extending customs user fees. It would cut direct payment subsidies overall by $313 million, in part by reducing the percentage of acres for which a farmer can collect the payments. Farmers making more than $750,000 a year in farm-related income and those with more than $500,000 a year in non-farm-related income would not be eligible for federal subsidies. Country-of-origin labels for all meat would be required by September 2008. Motion agreed to 306-110: R 90-98; D 216-12 (ND 162-11, SD 54-1). A two-thirds majority of those present and voting (278 in this case) is required for passage under suspension of the rules. A "nay" was a vote in support of the president's position. May 22, 2008.

	349	350	351	352	353
ALABAMA					
1 **Bonner**	Y	N	N	P	Y
2 **Everett**	Y	N	N	N	Y
3 **Rogers**	Y	N	N	N	Y
4 **Aderholt**	Y	N	N	N	Y
5 Cramer	Y	Y	Y	Y	Y
6 **Bachus**	Y	N	N	N	N
7 Davis	Y	Y	Y	Y	Y
ALASKA					
AL **Young**	Y	?	?	?	?
ARIZONA					
1 **Renzi**	Y	N	N	N	Y
2 **Franks**	Y	N	N	N	N
3 **Shadegg**	Y	N	N	N	N
4 Pastor	Y	Y	Y	Y	Y
5 Mitchell	Y	N	N	Y	N
6 **Flake**	Y	N	N	N	N
7 Grijalva	Y	Y	Y	Y	Y
8 Giffords	Y	Y	Y	Y	Y
ARKANSAS					
1 Berry	Y	Y	Y	Y	Y
2 Snyder	Y	Y	Y	Y	Y
3 **Boozman**	Y	N	N	N	Y
4 Ross	Y	Y	Y	Y	Y
CALIFORNIA					
1 Thompson	Y	Y	Y	Y	Y
2 **Herger**	Y	N	N	N	Y
3 **Lungren**	Y	N	N	N	N
4 **Doolittle**	Y	N	N	N	Y
5 Matsui	Y	Y	Y	Y	Y
6 Woolsey	Y	Y	Y	Y	Y
7 Miller, George	Y	Y	Y	Y	Y
8 Pelosi					Y
9 Lee	Y	Y	Y	Y	Y
10 Tauscher	Y	Y	Y	Y	Y
11 McNerney	Y	Y	Y	Y	Y
12 Speier	Y	Y	Y	Y	Y
13 Stark	Y	Y	N	Y	N
14 Eshoo	Y	Y	Y	Y	Y
15 Honda	Y	Y	Y	Y	Y
16 Lofgren	Y	Y	Y	Y	Y
17 Farr	Y	Y	Y	Y	Y
18 Cardoza	Y	Y	Y	Y	Y
19 **Radanovich**	Y	N	N	N	Y
20 Costa	Y	Y	Y	Y	Y
21 **Nunes**	Y	N	N	N	N
22 **McCarthy**	Y	N	N	N	N
23 Capps	Y	Y	Y	Y	Y
24 **Gallegly**	Y	N	N	N	Y
25 **McKeon**	Y	N	N	N	N
26 **Dreier**	Y	N	N	N	N
27 Sherman	Y	Y	Y	Y	Y
28 Berman	Y	Y	Y	Y	Y
29 Schiff	Y	Y	Y	Y	Y
30 Waxman	Y	Y	Y	Y	Y
31 Becerra	Y	Y	Y	Y	Y
32 Solis	Y	Y	Y	Y	Y
33 Watson	Y	Y	Y	Y	Y
34 Roybal-Allard	Y	Y	Y	P	Y
35 Waters	Y	Y	Y	Y	Y
36 Harman	Y	Y	Y	Y	N
37 Richardson	Y	Y	Y	Y	Y
38 Napolitano	Y	Y	Y	Y	Y
39 Sánchez, Linda	Y	Y	Y	Y	Y
40 **Royce**	Y	N	N	N	N
41 **Lewis**	Y	N	N	N	N
42 **Miller, Gary**	Y	N	N	N	N
43 Baca	Y	Y	Y	Y	Y
44 **Calvert**	Y	N	N	N	N
45 **Bono Mack**	Y	N	N	N	Y
46 **Rohrabacher**	Y	N	N	N	N
47 Sanchez, Loretta	Y	Y	Y	Y	Y
48 **Campbell**	Y	N	N	N	N
49 **Issa**	Y	N	N	N	N
50 **Bilbray**	Y	N	N	N	Y
51 Filner	Y	Y	Y	Y	Y
52 **Hunter**	Y	N	N	N	N
53 Davis	Y	Y	Y	Y	Y

	349	350	351	352	353
COLORADO					
1 DeGette	Y	Y	Y	Y	Y
2 Udall	Y	Y	Y	Y	Y
3 Salazar	Y	Y	Y	Y	Y
4 **Musgrave**	Y	N	N	N	Y
5 **Lamborn**	Y	N	N	N	N
6 **Tancredo**	Y	N	N	N	N
7 Perlmutter	Y	Y	Y	Y	Y
CONNECTICUT					
1 Larson	Y	Y	Y	Y	Y
2 Courtney	Y	Y	Y	Y	Y
3 DeLauro	Y	Y	Y	Y	Y
4 **Shays**	Y	N	N	N	N
5 Murphy	Y	Y	Y	Y	Y
DELAWARE					
AL **Castle**	Y	N	N	N	N
FLORIDA					
1 **Miller**	Y	N	N	N	N
2 Boyd	Y	Y	Y	Y	Y
3 Brown	?	Y	Y	Y	Y
4 **Crenshaw**	?	?	?	?	?
5 **Brown-Waite**	Y	N	N	N	Y
6 **Stearns**	Y	N	N	N	N
7 **Mica**	Y	N	N	N	N
8 **Keller**	Y	N	N	N	N
9 **Bilirakis**	Y	Y	N	N	Y
10 **Young**	Y	N	N	N	N
11 Castor	?	?	?	?	?
12 **Putnam**	Y	N	N	N	Y
13 **Buchanan**	Y	N	N	N	Y
14 **Mack**	Y	N	N	N	N
15 **Weldon**	Y	N	N	N	N
16 Mahoney	Y	Y	Y	Y	Y
17 Meek	Y	Y	Y	Y	Y
18 **Ros-Lehtinen**	Y	N	N	N	?
19 Wexler	?	?	?	?	?
20 Wasserman Schultz	Y	Y	Y	Y	Y
21 **Diaz-Balart, L.**	Y	N	N	N	Y
22 Klein	Y	Y	Y	Y	Y
23 Hastings	Y	Y	Y	Y	Y
24 **Feeney**	?	N	N	N	N
25 **Diaz-Balart, M.**	Y	N	N	N	Y
GEORGIA					
1 **Kingston**	Y	N	N	N	Y
2 Bishop	Y	Y	Y	Y	Y
3 **Westmoreland**	Y	N	N	N	N
4 Johnson	Y	Y	Y	Y	Y
5 Lewis	Y	Y	Y	Y	?
6 **Price**	Y	N	N	N	N
7 **Linder**	Y	N	N	N	N
8 Marshall	Y	Y	Y	Y	Y
9 **Deal**	Y	N	N	N	N
10 **Broun**	Y	N	N	N	N
11 **Gingrey**	Y	N	N	N	Y
12 Barrow	Y	Y	Y	Y	Y
13 Scott	Y	Y	Y	Y	?
HAWAII					
1 Abercrombie	Y	Y	Y	Y	Y
2 Hirono	Y	Y	Y	Y	Y
IDAHO					
1 **Sali**	Y	N	N	N	Y
2 **Simpson**	Y	N	N	N	Y
ILLINOIS					
1 Rush	?	?	?	?	?
2 Jackson	Y	Y	Y	Y	Y
3 Lipinski	Y	Y	Y	Y	Y
4 Gutierrez	Y	Y	Y	Y	Y
5 Emanuel	Y	Y	Y	Y	Y
6 **Roskam**	Y	N	N	N	N
7 Davis	Y	Y	Y	Y	Y
8 Bean	Y	Y	Y	Y	N
9 Schakowsky	Y	Y	Y	Y	Y
10 **Kirk**	Y	N	N	N	N
11 **Weller**	Y	N	N	N	Y
12 Costello	Y	Y	Y	Y	Y
13 **Biggert**	Y	N	N	N	N
14 Foster	Y	Y	Y	Y	Y
15 **Johnson**	Y	N	N	N	Y

KEY **Republicans** Democrats

Y Voted for (yea)	X Paired against	C Voted "present" to avoid possible conflict of interest
# Paired for	– Announced against	
+ Announced for	P Voted "present"	? Did not vote or otherwise make a position known
N Voted against (nay)		

ND Northern Democrats, SD Southern Democrats
Southern states: Ala., Ark., Fla., Ga., Ky., La., Miss., N.C., Okla., S.C., Tenn., Texas, Va.

	349	350	351	352	353
16 Manzullo	Y	N	N	N	Y
17 Hare	Y	Y	Y	Y	Y
18 LaHood	Y	N	N	N	Y
19 Shimkus	Y	N	N	N	Y
INDIANA					
1 Visclosky	Y	Y	Y	Y	Y
2 Donnelly	Y	Y	Y	Y	Y
3 Souder	Y	N	N	N	Y
4 Buyer	Y	N	N	N	Y
5 Burton	Y	N	N	N	N
6 Pence	Y	N	N	N	N
7 Carson, A.	Y	Y	Y	Y	Y
8 Ellsworth	Y	Y	Y	Y	Y
9 Hill	Y	Y	Y	Y	Y
IOWA					
1 Braley	Y	Y	Y	Y	Y
2 Loebsack	Y	Y	Y	Y	Y
3 Boswell	Y	Y	Y	Y	Y
4 Latham	Y	N	N	N	Y
5 King	Y	N	N	N	Y
KANSAS					
1 Moran	Y	N	N	N	N
2 Boyda	Y	Y	Y	Y	Y
3 Moore	Y	Y	Y	Y	Y
4 Tiahrt	?	N	N	N	N
KENTUCKY					
1 Whitfield	Y	N	N	N	Y
2 Lewis	Y	N	N	N	Y
3 Yarmuth	?	Y	Y	Y	Y
4 Davis	Y	N	N	N	Y
5 Rogers	Y	N	N	N	Y
6 Chandler	Y	Y	Y	Y	Y
LOUISIANA					
1 Scalise	Y	N	N	N	N
2 Jefferson	Y	Y	Y	Y	Y
3 Melancon	Y	Y	Y	Y	Y
4 McCrery	Y	N	N	N	N
5 Alexander	Y	N	N	N	Y
6 Cazayoux	Y	Y	Y	Y	Y
7 Boustany	Y	N	N	N	Y
MAINE					
1 Allen	Y	Y	Y	Y	Y
2 Michaud	Y	Y	Y	Y	Y
MARYLAND					
1 Gilchrest	Y	N	N	N	Y
2 Ruppersberger	Y	Y	Y	Y	Y
3 Sarbanes	Y	Y	Y	Y	Y
4 Wynn	?	Y	Y	Y	Y
5 Hoyer	Y	Y	Y	Y	Y
6 Bartlett	Y	N	N	N	Y
7 Cummings	Y	Y	Y	Y	Y
8 Van Hollen	Y	Y	Y	Y	Y
MASSACHUSETTS					
1 Olver	Y	Y	Y	Y	Y
2 Neal	Y	Y	Y	Y	Y
3 McGovern	Y	Y	Y	Y	Y
4 Frank	Y	Y	Y	Y	Y
5 Tsongas	Y	Y	Y	Y	Y
6 Tierney	Y	Y	Y	Y	Y
7 Markey	Y	Y	Y	Y	Y
8 Capuano	Y	Y	Y	Y	N
9 Lynch	Y	Y	Y	?	Y
10 Delahunt	Y	Y	Y	P	Y
MICHIGAN					
1 Stupak	Y	Y	Y	Y	Y
2 Hoekstra	Y	N	N	N	?
3 Ehlers	Y	N	N	N	N
4 Camp	Y	N	N	N	Y
5 Kildee	Y	Y	Y	Y	Y
6 Upton	Y	N	N	N	Y
7 Walberg	Y	N	N	N	N
8 Rogers	Y	N	N	N	Y
9 Knollenberg	Y	N	N	N	N
10 Miller	Y	N	N	N	Y
11 McCotter	Y	N	N	N	Y
12 Levin	Y	Y	Y	Y	Y
13 Kilpatrick	Y	Y	Y	?	Y
14 Conyers	Y	Y	Y	Y	Y
15 Dingell	Y	Y	Y	?	Y
MINNESOTA					
1 Walz	Y	Y	Y	Y	Y
2 Kline	Y	N	N	P	Y
3 Ramstad	Y	N	N	N	N
4 McCollum	Y	Y	Y	Y	Y

	349	350	351	352	353
5 Ellison	Y	Y	Y	Y	Y
6 Bachmann	Y	N	N	N	N
7 Peterson	Y	Y	Y	Y	Y
8 Oberstar	Y	Y	Y	Y	Y
MISSISSIPPI					
1 Childers	Y	Y	Y	Y	Y
2 Thompson	Y	Y	Y	Y	Y
3 Pickering	Y	N	N	N	Y
4 Taylor	Y	Y	Y	Y	Y
MISSOURI					
1 Clay	Y	Y	Y	Y	Y
2 Akin	Y	N	N	N	N
3 Carnahan	Y	Y	Y	Y	Y
4 Skelton	Y	Y	Y	Y	Y
5 Cleaver	Y	Y	Y	?	Y
6 Graves	Y	N	N	N	Y
7 Blunt	Y	N	N	N	Y
8 Emerson	Y	N	N	N	Y
9 Hulshof	Y	N	N	N	Y
MONTANA					
AL Rehberg	Y	N	N	N	Y
NEBRASKA					
1 Fortenberry	Y	N	N	N	Y
2 Terry	Y	N	N	N	N
3 Smith	Y	N	N	N	Y
NEVADA					
1 Berkley	Y	Y	Y	Y	Y
2 Heller	Y	N	N	N	N
3 Porter	Y	N	N	N	Y
NEW HAMPSHIRE					
1 Shea-Porter	Y	Y	Y	Y	Y
2 Hodes	Y	Y	Y	Y	Y
NEW JERSEY					
1 Andrews	Y	?	?	?	?
2 LoBiondo	Y	N	N	N	N
3 Saxton	Y	N	N	N	N
4 Smith	Y	N	N	N	N
5 Garrett	Y	N	N	N	N
6 Pallone	Y	Y	Y	Y	Y
7 Ferguson	Y	N	N	N	N
8 Pascrell	Y	Y	Y	Y	Y
9 Rothman	Y	Y	Y	Y	Y
10 Payne	Y	Y	Y	Y	Y
11 Frelinghuysen	Y	N	N	N	N
12 Holt	Y	Y	Y	Y	Y
13 Sires	Y	Y	Y	Y	Y
NEW MEXICO					
1 Wilson	Y	N	N	N	N
2 Pearce	Y	N	N	N	Y
3 Udall	Y	Y	Y	Y	Y
NEW YORK					
1 Bishop	Y	Y	Y	Y	Y
2 Israel	Y	Y	Y	Y	Y
3 King	Y	N	N	N	N
4 McCarthy	Y	Y	Y	Y	Y
5 Ackerman	Y	Y	Y	Y	Y
6 Meeks	Y	Y	Y	Y	Y
7 Crowley	Y	Y	Y	Y	Y
8 Nadler	Y	Y	Y	Y	Y
9 Weiner	Y	Y	Y	Y	Y
10 Towns	Y	Y	Y	Y	Y
11 Clarke	Y	Y	Y	Y	Y
12 Velázquez	Y	Y	Y	Y	Y
13 Fossella	?	?	?	N	N
14 Maloney	Y	Y	Y	Y	Y
15 Rangel	?	Y	Y	Y	Y
16 Serrano	Y	Y	Y	Y	Y
17 Engel	Y	Y	Y	Y	Y
18 Lowey	Y	Y	Y	Y	Y
19 Hall	Y	Y	Y	Y	Y
20 Gillibrand	?	?	?	?	?
21 McNulty	Y	Y	Y	Y	Y
22 Hinchey	Y	Y	Y	Y	Y
23 McHugh	Y	N	N	N	Y
24 Arcuri	Y	Y	Y	Y	Y
25 Walsh	Y	N	N	N	?
26 Reynolds	Y	N	N	N	N
27 Higgins	Y	Y	Y	Y	Y
28 Slaughter	Y	Y	Y	Y	Y
29 Kuhl	Y	N	N	N	Y
NORTH CAROLINA					
1 Butterfield	Y	Y	Y	Y	Y
2 Etheridge	Y	Y	Y	Y	Y
3 Jones	Y	N	N	N	Y
4 Price	Y	Y	Y	Y	Y

	349	350	351	352	353
5 Foxx	Y	N	N	N	N
6 Coble	Y	N	N	N	Y
7 McIntyre	Y	Y	Y	Y	Y
8 Hayes	Y	N	N	N	Y
9 Myrick	Y	N	N	N	N
10 McHenry	Y	N	N	N	N
11 Shuler	Y	Y	Y	Y	Y
12 Watt	Y	Y	Y	Y	Y
13 Miller	Y	Y	Y	Y	Y
NORTH DAKOTA					
AL Pomeroy	Y	Y	Y	Y	Y
OHIO					
1 Chabot	Y	N	N	N	N
2 Schmidt	Y	N	N	N	N
3 Turner	Y	N	N	N	Y
4 Jordan	Y	N	N	N	N
5 Latta	Y	N	N	N	Y
6 Wilson	Y	Y	Y	Y	Y
7 Hobson	Y	N	N	?	?
8 Boehner	Y	N	N	N	N
9 Kaptur	Y	Y	Y	Y	Y
10 Kucinich	Y	Y	N	Y	Y
11 Tubbs Jones	Y	Y	Y	P	Y
12 Tiberi	Y	N	N	N	Y
13 Sutton	Y	Y	Y	Y	Y
14 LaTourette	?	N	N	N	Y
15 Pryce	Y	N	N	N	N
16 Regula	Y	N	N	N	Y
17 Ryan	Y	Y	Y	Y	Y
18 Space	Y	Y	Y	Y	Y
OKLAHOMA					
1 Sullivan	Y	N	N	N	?
2 Boren	Y	Y	Y	Y	Y
3 Lucas	Y	N	N	N	N
4 Cole	Y	N	N	N	Y
5 Fallin	Y	N	N	N	Y
OREGON					
1 Wu	Y	Y	Y	Y	Y
2 Walden	?	?	?	?	?
3 Blumenauer	Y	Y	?	Y	N
4 DeFazio	Y	Y	Y	Y	Y
5 Hooley	Y	Y	Y	Y	Y
PENNSYLVANIA					
1 Brady	Y	Y	Y	Y	Y
2 Fattah	Y	Y	Y	Y	Y
3 English	Y	N	N	N	Y
4 Altmire	Y	N	N	N	N
5 Peterson	Y	N	N	N	N
6 Gerlach	Y	N	N	N	N
7 Sestak	Y	Y	Y	Y	Y
8 Murphy, P.	Y	Y	Y	Y	Y
9 Shuster	Y	N	N	N	Y
10 Carney	Y	Y	Y	Y	Y
11 Kanjorski	Y	Y	Y	Y	Y
12 Murtha	Y	Y	Y	Y	Y
13 Schwartz	Y	Y	Y	Y	Y
14 Doyle	Y	Y	Y	P	Y
15 Dent	Y	N	N	N	N
16 Pitts	Y	N	N	N	N
17 Holden	Y	Y	Y	Y	Y
18 Murphy, T.	Y	N	N	N	Y
19 Platts	Y	N	N	N	Y
RHODE ISLAND					
1 Kennedy	?	?	?	?	?
2 Langevin	Y	Y	Y	Y	?
SOUTH CAROLINA					
1 Brown	Y	N	N	N	Y
2 Wilson	Y	N	N	N	N
3 Barrett	Y	N	N	P	N
4 Inglis	Y	N	N	N	N
5 Spratt	Y	Y	Y	Y	Y
6 Clyburn	Y	Y	Y	Y	Y
SOUTH DAKOTA					
AL Herseth Sandlin	Y	Y	Y	Y	Y
TENNESSEE					
1 Davis, D.	Y	N	N	N	Y
2 Duncan	Y	N	N	N	N
3 Wamp	Y	N	N	N	Y
4 Davis, L.	Y	Y	Y	Y	Y
5 Cooper	Y	Y	Y	Y	N
6 Gordon	Y	Y	Y	Y	Y
7 Blackburn	Y	N	N	N	N
8 Tanner	Y	Y	Y	Y	Y
9 Cohen	Y	Y	Y	Y	Y

	349	350	351	352	353
TEXAS					
1 Gohmert	Y	N	N	N	Y
2 Poe	Y	N	N	N	Y
3 Johnson, S.	Y	N	N	N	N
4 Hall	Y	N	N	N	Y
5 Hensarling	Y	N	N	N	N
6 Barton	Y	N	N	N	N
7 Culberson	Y	N	N	N	N
8 Brady	Y	N	N	N	Y
9 Green, A.	Y	Y	Y	Y	Y
10 McCaul	Y	N	N	P	Y
11 Conaway	Y	N	N	N	Y
12 Granger	Y	N	N	N	N
13 Thornberry	Y	N	N	N	Y
14 Paul	Y	?	?	?	?
15 Hinojosa	Y	+	+	Y	Y
16 Reyes	Y	Y	Y	Y	Y
17 Edwards	Y	Y	Y	Y	Y
18 Jackson Lee	Y	Y	Y	Y	Y
19 Neugebauer	Y	N	N	N	Y
20 Gonzalez	Y	Y	Y	Y	Y
21 Smith	Y	N	N	N	Y
22 Lampson	Y	Y	N	Y	Y
23 Rodriguez	Y	Y	Y	Y	Y
24 Marchant	Y	N	N	N	N
25 Doggett	Y	Y	Y	Y	Y
26 Burgess	Y	N	N	N	Y
27 Ortiz	Y	Y	Y	Y	Y
28 Cuellar	Y	Y	Y	Y	Y
29 Green, G.	?	Y	Y	P	Y
30 Johnson, E.	Y	Y	Y	Y	Y
31 Carter	?	-	-	-	+
32 Sessions	Y	N	N	N	N
UTAH					
1 Bishop	?	N	N	N	N
2 Matheson	Y	Y	Y	Y	N
3 Cannon	Y	N	N	N	N
VERMONT					
AL Welch	Y	Y	Y	Y	Y
VIRGINIA					
1 Wittman	Y	N	N	N	Y
2 Drake	Y	N	N	N	Y
3 Scott	Y	Y	Y	Y	Y
4 Forbes	Y	N	N	N	Y
5 Goode	Y	N	N	N	N
6 Goodlatte	Y	N	N	N	Y
7 Cantor	Y	N	N	N	Y
8 Moran	Y	Y	Y	Y	Y
9 Boucher	Y	Y	Y	Y	Y
10 Wolf	Y	N	N	N	N
11 Davis	Y	N	N	N	N
WASHINGTON					
1 Inslee	Y	Y	Y	Y	Y
2 Larsen	Y	Y	Y	Y	Y
3 Baird	Y	Y	Y	Y	Y
4 Hastings	Y	N	N	P	Y
5 McMorris Rodgers	Y	N	N	N	N
6 Dicks	Y	Y	Y	Y	Y
7 McDermott	Y	Y	Y	Y	N
8 Reichert	Y	N	N	N	N
9 Smith	Y	Y	Y	Y	N
WEST VIRGINIA					
1 Mollohan	Y	Y	Y	Y	Y
2 Capito	Y	N	N	N	Y
3 Rahall	Y	Y	Y	Y	Y
WISCONSIN					
1 Ryan	Y	N	N	N	Y
2 Baldwin	Y	Y	Y	Y	Y
3 Kind	Y	?	Y	Y	N
4 Moore	Y	Y	Y	Y	N
5 Sensenbrenner	Y	N	N	N	N
6 Petri	Y	N	N	N	N
7 Obey	Y	Y	Y	Y	Y
8 Kagen	Y	Y	Y	Y	Y
WYOMING					
AL Cubin	Y	N	N	N	N
DELEGATES					
Faleomavaega (A.S.)					
Norton (D.C.)					
Bordallo (Guam)					
Fortuño (P.R.)					
Christensen (V.I.)					

IN THE HOUSE | By Vote Number

354. H Res 1194. Reaffirm Support for Lebanese Government/ **Adoption.** Ackerman, D-N.Y., motion to suspend the rules and adopt the resolution that would reaffirm strong support for the government of Lebanon under Prime Minister Fouad Siniora and express sympathy to the people of Lebanon for the conflict initiated by Hezbollah. Motion agreed to 401-10: R 187-1; D 214-9 (ND 161-9, SD 53-0). A two-thirds majority of those present and voting (274 in this case) is required for adoption under suspension of the rules. May 22, 2008.

355. HR 5658. Fiscal 2009 Defense Authorization/Future Combat **Systems.** Akin, R-Mo., amendment that would increase by $193 million funding authorized for the Future Combat Systems, to be offset by decreasing authorized funding levels for Navy research, development, testing and evaluation by $30 million; Department of Defense military personnel by $138 million; and the Defense Health Program by $25 million. Rejected in Committee of the Whole 128-287: R 128-60; D 0-227 (ND 0-171, SD 0-56). May 22, 2008.

356. HR 5658. Fiscal 2009 Defense Authorization/Missile Defense **Budget.** Franks, R-Ariz., amendment that would add $719 million to the bill's authorization for the Missile Defense Agency, to be offset by a decrease of the same amount for the Defense Department's research, development, testing and evaluation activities. Rejected in Committee of the Whole 186-229: R 174-14; D 12-215 (ND 7-164, SD 5-51). A "yea" was a vote in support of the president's position. May 22, 2008.

357. HR 5658. Fiscal 2009 Defense Authorization/Missile Defense. Tierney, D-Mass., amendment that would reduce the bill's authorization for the Missile Defense Agency by $966 million and increase authorized levels by $75 million for the Cooperative Threat Reduction program, $592 million for weapons non-proliferation programs; $30 million each for education support to dependents of servicemembers, family support of wounded servicemembers and suicide prevention programs; and a pilot program to retrain wounded servicemembers as military health professionals. Rejected in Committee of the Whole 122-292: R 5-181; D 117-111 (ND 104-68, SD 13-43). A "nay" was a vote in support of the president's position. May 22, 2008.

358. HR 5658. Fiscal 2009 Defense Authorization/Reliable Replacement Warhead Program. Pearce, R-N.M., amendment that would increase the bill's authorization for the National Nuclear Security Administration's Reliable Replacement Warhead program by $10 million, offset by a decrease of the same amount in authorized funds for energy conservation on military installations. Rejected in Committee of the Whole 145-271: R 144-44; D 1-227 (ND 0-172, SD 1-55). May 22, 2008.

359. HR 5658. Fiscal 2009 Defense Authorization/Iraq Defense. Lee, D-Calif., amendment that would provide that any agreement between the United States and the Iraqi government that obligates the United States to defend Iraq would have to be authorized by Congress or come in the form of a treaty requiring the consent of the Senate. Adopted in Committee of the Whole 234-183: R 13-176; D 221-7 (ND 170-2, SD 51-5). A "nay" was a vote in support of the president's position. May 22, 2008.

360. HR 5658. Fiscal 2009 Defense Authorization/Long-Term War Costs Report. Braley, D-Iowa, amendment that would require the president to submit a report within 90 days of the bill's enactment on the long-term costs of the wars in Iraq and Afghanistan, including the costs of operations, reconstruction and health care benefits, through at least fiscal 2068. Adopted in Committee of the Whole 245-168: R 20-167; D 225-1 (ND 172-0, SD 53-1). May 22, 2008.

	354	355	356	357	358	359	360
ALABAMA							
1 Bonner	Y	N	Y	N	Y	N	N
2 Everett	Y	Y	Y	N	Y	N	N
3 Rogers	Y	Y	Y	N	Y	N	N
4 Aderholt	Y	Y	Y	N	Y	N	N
5 Cramer	Y	N	Y	N	N	Y	Y
6 Bachus	Y	Y	Y	?	Y	N	N
7 Davis	Y	N	N	N	N	Y	Y
ALASKA							
AL Young	?	?	?	?	?	?	?
ARIZONA							
1 Renzi	Y	Y	Y	N	?	N	N
2 Franks	Y	Y	Y	N	Y	N	N
3 Shadegg	Y	Y	Y	N	Y	N	N
4 Pastor	Y	N	N	N	N	Y	Y
5 Mitchell	Y	N	N	N	N	Y	Y
6 Flake	Y	Y	Y	N	Y	N	N
7 Grijalva	Y	N	N	Y	N	Y	Y
8 Giffords	Y	N	N	N	N	Y	Y
ARKANSAS							
1 Berry	Y	N	N	N	N	Y	Y
2 Snyder	Y	N	N	N	N	Y	Y
3 Boozman	Y	Y	Y	N	Y	N	N
4 Ross	Y	N	N	N	N	Y	Y
CALIFORNIA							
1 Thompson	Y	N	N	Y	N	Y	Y
2 Herger	+	Y	Y	N	Y	N	N
3 Lungren	Y	Y	Y	N	Y	N	N
4 Doolittle	Y	Y	Y	N	Y	N	N
5 Matsui	Y	N	N	N	Y	Y	Y
6 Woolsey	N	?	N	N	N	Y	Y
7 Miller, George	Y	N	N	Y	N	Y	Y
8 Pelosi							
9 Lee	N	N	N	Y	N	Y	Y
10 Tauscher	Y	N	N	N	N	Y	Y
11 McNerney	Y	N	N	N	Y	Y	Y
12 Speier	Y	N	N	N	Y	Y	Y
13 Stark	N	N	N	Y	N	Y	Y
14 Eshoo	Y	N	N	N	Y	Y	Y
15 Honda	Y	N	N	N	Y	Y	Y
16 Lofgren	Y	N	N	N	Y	Y	Y
17 Farr	Y	N	N	N	N	Y	Y
18 Cardoza	Y	N	N	N	N	Y	Y
19 Radanovich	Y	Y	Y	N	Y	N	N
20 Costa	Y	N	N	N	N	Y	Y
21 Nunes	Y	Y	Y	N	Y	N	N
22 McCarthy	Y	N	N	N	N	N	Y
23 Capps	Y	N	N	N	Y	N	Y
24 Gallegly	Y	Y	Y	N	Y	N	N
25 McKeon	Y	Y	Y	N	Y	N	N
26 Dreier	Y	Y	Y	N	Y	N	N
27 Sherman	Y	N	N	Y	N	Y	Y
28 Berman	Y	N	N	Y	N	Y	Y
29 Schiff	Y	N	N	Y	N	Y	Y
30 Waxman	Y	N	N	Y	N	Y	Y
31 Becerra	Y	N	N	Y	N	Y	Y
32 Solis	Y	N	N	Y	N	Y	Y
33 Watson	Y	N	N	Y	N	Y	Y
34 Roybal-Allard	Y	N	N	N	N	Y	Y
35 Waters	Y	N	N	N	N	Y	Y
36 Harman	Y	N	N	N	N	Y	Y
37 Richardson	Y	N	N	N	N	Y	Y
38 Napolitano	Y	N	N	Y	N	Y	Y
39 Sánchez, Linda	Y	N	N	N	Y	Y	Y
40 Royce	Y	Y	Y	N	Y	N	N
41 Lewis	Y	Y	Y	N	Y	N	N
42 Miller, Gary	Y	Y	Y	N	Y	N	N
43 Baca	Y	N	N	N	N	Y	Y
44 Calvert	Y	Y	Y	N	Y	N	N
45 Bono Mack	Y	Y	Y	N	Y	N	N
46 Rohrabacher	Y	Y	Y	N	Y	Y	Y
47 Sanchez, Loretta	Y	N	N	N	N	Y	Y
48 Campbell	Y	Y	Y	N	Y	N	N
49 Issa	Y	Y	Y	N	Y	N	N
50 Bilbray	Y	Y	Y	N	Y	N	N
51 Filner	Y	N	N	Y	N	Y	Y
52 Hunter	Y	Y	Y	N	Y	N	N
53 Davis	Y	N	N	N	N	Y	Y

	354	355	356	357	358	359	360
COLORADO							
1 DeGette	Y	N	N	Y	N	Y	Y
2 Udall	Y	?	?	?	?	?	?
3 Salazar	Y	N	N	N	N	Y	Y
4 Musgrave	Y	?	?	?	?	?	?
5 Lamborn	Y	Y	Y	N	Y	N	N
6 Tancredo	Y	Y	Y	N	Y	N	N
7 Perlmutter	Y	N	N	N	N	Y	Y
CONNECTICUT							
1 Larson	Y	N	N	Y	N	Y	Y
2 Courtney	Y	N	N	Y	N	Y	Y
3 DeLauro	Y	N	N	Y	N	Y	Y
4 Shays	Y	N	N	Y	N	Y	Y
5 Murphy	Y	N	N	N	N	Y	Y
DELAWARE							
AL Castle	Y	N	N	Y	N	N	N
FLORIDA							
1 Miller	Y	Y	Y	N	Y	N	N
2 Boyd	Y	N	N	N	Y	Y	Y
3 Brown	Y	N	N	N	Y	Y	Y
4 Crenshaw	?	?	?	?	?	?	?
5 Brown-Waite	Y	N	Y	N	Y	N	N
6 Stearns	Y	N	N	Y	N	Y	Y
7 Mica	Y	N	Y	N	Y	N	N
8 Keller	Y	Y	Y	N	Y	N	N
9 Bilirakis	Y	N	Y	N	Y	N	N
10 Young	Y	Y	Y	N	Y	N	N
11 Castor	?	?	?	?	?	?	?
12 Putnam	Y	Y	Y	N	Y	N	N
13 Buchanan	Y	Y	Y	N	Y	N	N
14 Mack	Y	Y	Y	N	Y	N	N
15 Weldon	Y	N	Y	N	Y	N	N
16 Mahoney	Y	N	N	N	N	Y	Y
17 Meek	Y	N	N	N	N	Y	Y
18 Ros-Lehtinen	Y	N	N	N	N	N	N
19 Wexler	?	?	?	?	?	?	?
20 Wasserman Schultz	Y	N	N	Y	N	Y	Y
21 Diaz-Balart, L.	Y	N	N	Y	N	N	N
22 Klein	Y	N	N	N	N	Y	Y
23 Hastings	Y	N	N	N	N	Y	Y
24 Feeney	Y	N	Y	N	Y	Y	Y
25 Diaz-Balart, M.	Y	N	N	Y	N	N	N
GEORGIA							
1 Kingston	Y	N	Y	N	N	N	N
2 Bishop	Y	N	N	N	N	Y	Y
3 Westmoreland	Y	Y	Y	N	N	N	N
4 Johnson	?	N	N	N	Y	Y	Y
5 Lewis	?	N	Y	N	Y	Y	?
6 Price	Y	Y	Y	N	Y	N	N
7 Linder	Y	Y	Y	N	Y	N	N
8 Marshall	Y	N	N	N	N	Y	Y
9 Deal	Y	N	Y	N	Y	N	N
10 Broun	Y	N	Y	N	Y	N	N
11 Gingrey	Y	Y	Y	N	Y	N	N
12 Barrow	Y	N	N	N	N	N	Y
13 Scott	Y	N	N	N	N	Y	Y
HAWAII							
1 Abercrombie	N	N	N	N	N	Y	Y
2 Hirono	Y	N	N	N	N	Y	Y
IDAHO							
1 Sali	Y	Y	Y	N	Y	N	N
2 Simpson	Y	Y	Y	N	Y	N	N
ILLINOIS							
1 Rush	?	?	?	?	?	?	?
2 Jackson	Y	N	N	Y	N	Y	Y
3 Lipinski	Y	N	N	N	N	Y	Y
4 Gutierrez	Y	N	N	N	N	Y	Y
5 Emanuel	Y	N	N	Y	N	Y	Y
6 Roskam	Y	Y	N	N	N	N	N
7 Davis	Y	N	N	N	N	Y	Y
8 Bean	Y	N	Y	N	N	Y	Y
9 Schakowsky	Y	N	N	N	N	Y	Y
10 Kirk	Y	N	Y	N	N	N	N
11 Weller	Y	Y	Y	N	N	N	N
12 Costello	Y	N	N	N	N	Y	Y
13 Biggert	Y	N	N	Y	N	N	N
14 Foster	Y	N	N	N	Y	Y	Y
15 Johnson	Y	N	Y	N	N	N	N

KEY   Republicans   Democrats

Y Voted for (yea)	X Paired against	C Voted "present" to avoid possible conflict of interest
# Paired for	– Announced against	
+ Announced for	P Voted "present"	? Did not vote or otherwise make a position known
N Voted against (nay)		

ND Northern Democrats, SD Southern Democrats
Southern states: Ala., Ark., Fla., Ga., Ky., La., Miss., N.C., Okla., S.C., Tenn., Texas, Va.

	354	355	356	357	358	359	360
16 **Manzullo**	Y	Y	Y	N	N	N	?
17 Hare	Y	N	N	Y	N	Y	Y
18 **LaHood**	Y	Y	N	N	Y	N	N
19 **Shimkus**	Y	Y	Y	N	Y	N	N
INDIANA							
1 Visclosky	Y	N	N	Y	N	Y	Y
2 Donnelly	Y	N	Y	N	N	Y	Y
3 **Souder**	Y	N	Y	N	Y	N	N
4 **Buyer**	Y	N	Y	?	N	N	N
5 **Burton**	Y	Y	Y	N	Y	N	N
6 **Pence**	Y	Y	Y	N	Y	N	N
7 Carson, A.	Y	N	N	N	N	Y	Y
8 Ellsworth	Y	N	N	N	N	N	Y
9 Hill	Y	N	N	N	N	Y	Y
IOWA							
1 Braley	Y	N	N	Y	N	Y	Y
2 Loebsack	Y	N	N	Y	N	Y	Y
3 Boswell	Y	N	N	Y	N	Y	Y
4 **Latham**	Y	N	Y	N	Y	N	Y
5 **King**	Y	Y	Y	N	Y	N	N
KANSAS							
1 **Moran**	Y	N	Y	Y	Y	N	N
2 Boyda	Y	N	N	N	N	Y	Y
3 Moore	Y	N	N	N	N	Y	Y
4 **Tiahrt**	Y	Y	Y	N	Y	N	N
KENTUCKY							
1 **Whitfield**	Y	N	?	N	Y	N	N
2 **Lewis**	Y	Y	Y	N	Y	N	N
3 Yarmuth	Y	N	N	Y	N	Y	Y
4 **Davis**	Y	Y	Y	N	Y	N	N
5 **Rogers**	Y	N	Y	N	Y	N	N
6 Chandler	Y	N	N	N	N	Y	Y
LOUISIANA							
1 **Scalise**	Y	Y	Y	N	Y	N	N
2 Jefferson	Y	N	N	N	N	Y	Y
3 Melancon	Y	N	N	N	N	Y	?
4 **McCrery**	Y	Y	Y	N	Y	N	N
5 **Alexander**	Y	N	Y	N	Y	N	N
6 Cazayoux	Y	N	Y	N	N	N	Y
7 **Boustany**	Y	Y	Y	N	Y	N	N
MAINE							
1 Allen	Y	N	N	Y	N	Y	Y
2 Michaud	Y	N	N	Y	N	Y	Y
MARYLAND							
1 **Gilchrest**	Y	N	N	N	N	Y	Y
2 Ruppersberger	Y	N	Y	N	N	Y	Y
3 Sarbanes	Y	N	N	N	N	Y	Y
4 Wynn	Y	?	?	?	?	?	?
5 Hoyer	Y	N	N	N	N	Y	Y
6 **Bartlett**	Y	Y	Y	N	Y	N	N
7 Cummings	Y	N	N	Y	N	Y	Y
8 Van Hollen	Y	N	N	Y	N	Y	Y
MASSACHUSETTS							
1 Olver	Y	N	N	Y	N	Y	Y
2 Neal	Y	N	N	Y	N	Y	Y
3 McGovern	Y	N	N	Y	N	Y	Y
4 Frank	Y	N	N	Y	N	Y	Y
5 Tsongas	Y	N	N	N	N	Y	Y
6 Tierney	Y	N	N	Y	N	Y	Y
7 Markey	Y	N	N	Y	N	Y	Y
8 Capuano	Y	N	N	Y	N	Y	Y
9 Lynch	Y	N	?	Y	N	Y	Y
10 Delahunt	Y	N	N	Y	N	Y	Y
MICHIGAN							
1 Stupak	Y	N	N	N	N	Y	Y
2 **Hoekstra**	Y	Y	Y	N	N	N	N
3 **Ehlers**	Y	N	N	N	N	N	N
4 **Camp**	Y	Y	Y	N	Y	N	N
5 Kildee	Y	N	N	Y	N	Y	Y
6 **Upton**	Y	Y	N	N	N	Y	Y
7 **Walberg**	Y	N	Y	N	Y	N	N
8 **Rogers**	Y	Y	Y	N	Y	N	N
9 **Knollenberg**	Y	Y	Y	N	N	N	N
10 **Miller**	Y	Y	Y	N	Y	N	N
11 **McCotter**	Y	Y	Y	N	Y	N	N
12 Levin	Y	N	N	Y	N	Y	Y
13 Kilpatrick	Y	N	N	N	N	Y	Y
14 Conyers	Y	N	N	N	N	Y	Y
15 Dingell	Y	N	N	Y	N	Y	Y
MINNESOTA							
1 Walz	Y	N	N	Y	N	Y	Y
2 **Kline**	Y	Y	Y	N	Y	N	N
3 **Ramstad**	Y	N	N	N	N	N	N
4 McCollum	Y	N	N	Y	N	Y	Y

	354	355	356	357	358	359	360
5 Ellison	Y	N	N	Y	N	Y	Y
6 **Bachmann**	Y	Y	Y	N	Y	N	N
7 Peterson	Y	N	N	N	N	Y	Y
8 Oberstar	Y	N	N	Y	N	Y	Y
MISSISSIPPI							
1 Childers	Y	N	Y	N	N	N	N
2 Thompson	Y	N	N	N	N	Y	Y
3 **Pickering**	Y	Y	Y	N	Y	N	N
4 Taylor	Y	N	N	N	N	Y	Y
MISSOURI							
1 Clay	Y	N	N	Y	N	Y	Y
2 **Akin**	Y	Y	Y	N	Y	N	N
3 Carnahan	Y	N	N	N	N	Y	Y
4 Skelton	Y	N	N	N	N	Y	Y
5 Cleaver	Y	N	N	Y	N	Y	Y
6 **Graves**	Y	N	Y	N	Y	N	N
7 **Blunt**	Y	Y	Y	N	Y	N	N
8 **Emerson**	Y	N	N	N	N	Y	Y
9 **Hulshof**	Y	N	Y	N	Y	N	N
MONTANA							
AL **Rehberg**	Y	N	Y	N	Y	N	N
NEBRASKA							
1 **Fortenberry**	Y	N	Y	N	N	N	Y
2 **Terry**	Y	Y	Y	N	N	N	N
3 **Smith**	Y	Y	Y	N	Y	N	N
NEVADA							
1 Berkley	Y	N	N	N	N	Y	Y
2 **Heller**	Y	Y	Y	N	Y	N	N
3 **Porter**	Y	N	Y	N	N	N	N
NEW HAMPSHIRE							
1 Shea-Porter	Y	N	N	N	N	Y	Y
2 Hodes	Y	N	N	Y	N	Y	Y
NEW JERSEY							
1 Andrews	?	?	?	?	?	?	?
2 **LoBiondo**	Y	N	Y	N	N	N	N
3 **Saxton**	Y	Y	Y	N	Y	N	N
4 **Smith**	Y	N	Y	N	N	N	Y
5 **Garrett**	Y	Y	Y	N	Y	N	Y
6 Pallone	Y	N	N	Y	N	Y	Y
7 **Ferguson**	Y	Y	Y	N	Y	N	N
8 Pascrell	Y	N	N	Y	N	Y	Y
9 Rothman	Y	N	N	N	N	Y	Y
10 Payne	Y	N	N	Y	N	Y	Y
11 **Frelinghuysen**	Y	Y	Y	N	Y	N	N
12 Holt	Y	N	N	Y	N	Y	Y
13 Sires	Y	N	N	Y	N	Y	Y
NEW MEXICO							
1 **Wilson**	Y	Y	Y	N	Y	N	N
2 **Pearce**	Y	Y	Y	N	Y	N	N
3 Udall	Y	N	N	Y	N	Y	Y
NEW YORK							
1 Bishop	Y	N	N	Y	N	Y	Y
2 Israel	Y	N	N	N	N	Y	Y
3 **King**	Y	N	Y	N	Y	N	N
4 McCarthy	Y	N	N	N	N	Y	Y
5 Ackerman	Y	N	N	Y	N	Y	Y
6 Meeks	Y	N	N	N	N	Y	Y
7 Crowley	Y	N	N	N	N	Y	Y
8 Nadler	Y	?	?	?	?	?	?
9 Weiner	Y	N	N	Y	N	Y	Y
10 Towns	Y	N	N	Y	N	Y	Y
11 Clarke	Y	N	N	Y	N	Y	Y
12 Velázquez	Y	N	N	Y	N	Y	Y
13 **Fossella**	?	N	Y	N	Y	N	N
14 Maloney	Y	N	N	Y	N	Y	Y
15 Rangel	?	N	N	Y	N	Y	Y
16 Serrano	Y	N	N	Y	N	Y	Y
17 Engel	Y	N	N	N	N	Y	Y
18 Lowey	Y	N	N	Y	N	Y	Y
19 Hall	Y	N	N	Y	N	Y	Y
20 Gillibrand	?	?	?	?	?	?	?
21 McNulty	Y	N	N	Y	N	Y	Y
22 Hinchey	N	N	N	Y	N	Y	Y
23 **McHugh**	Y	Y	Y	N	Y	N	N
24 Arcuri	Y	N	N	N	N	Y	Y
25 **Walsh**	?	?	?	?	?	?	?
26 **Reynolds**	Y	Y	Y	N	Y	N	N
27 Higgins	Y	N	N	N	N	Y	Y
28 Slaughter	Y	N	N	Y	N	Y	Y
29 **Kuhl**	Y	Y	Y	N	Y	N	Y
NORTH CAROLINA							
1 Butterfield	Y	N	N	N	N	Y	Y
2 Etheridge	Y	N	N	N	N	Y	Y
3 **Jones**	N	N	N	N	N	Y	Y
4 Price	Y	N	N	Y	N	Y	Y

	354	355	356	357	358	359	360
5 **Foxx**	Y	Y	Y	N	Y	N	N
6 **Coble**	Y	Y	N	N	N	Y	Y
7 McIntyre	Y	N	N	N	N	Y	Y
8 **Hayes**	Y	N	Y	Y	N	N	N
9 **Myrick**	Y	N	Y	N	Y	N	N
10 **McHenry**	Y	Y	Y	N	Y	N	N
11 Shuler	Y	N	N	Y	N	Y	Y
12 Watt	P	N	N	Y	N	Y	Y
13 Miller	Y	N	N	N	N	Y	Y
NORTH DAKOTA							
AL Pomeroy	Y	N	N	N	N	Y	Y
OHIO							
1 **Chabot**	Y	N	Y	N	Y	N	Y
2 **Schmidt**	Y	N	Y	N	Y	N	N
3 **Turner**	?	Y	Y	N	Y	N	N
4 **Jordan**	Y	Y	Y	N	Y	N	N
5 **Latta**	Y	Y	Y	N	Y	N	N
6 Wilson	Y	N	N	N	N	Y	Y
7 **Hobson**	?	?	?	?	?	?	?
8 **Boehner**	Y	Y	Y	N	Y	N	N
9 Kaptur	Y	N	N	N	N	Y	Y
10 Kucinich	N	N	N	Y	N	Y	Y
11 Tubbs Jones	Y	N	N	N	N	Y	Y
12 **Tiberi**	Y	Y	Y	N	Y	N	N
13 Sutton	Y	N	N	Y	N	Y	Y
14 **LaTourette**	Y	N	Y	N	N	N	N
15 **Pryce**	Y	?	?	?	?	?	?
16 **Regula**	Y	Y	Y	N	N	N	N
17 Ryan	Y	N	N	N	N	Y	Y
18 Space	Y	N	Y	N	N	Y	Y
OKLAHOMA							
1 **Sullivan**	+	Y	Y	N	Y	N	N
2 Boren	Y	N	N	N	N	Y	Y
3 **Lucas**	Y	Y	Y	N	Y	N	N
4 **Cole**	Y	Y	Y	N	Y	N	N
5 **Fallin**	Y	Y	Y	N	Y	N	N
OREGON							
1 Wu	Y	N	N	Y	N	Y	Y
2 **Walden**	?	?	?	?	?	?	?
3 Blumenauer	Y	N	N	Y	N	Y	Y
4 DeFazio	P	N	N	Y	N	Y	Y
5 Hooley	Y	N	N	Y	N	Y	Y
PENNSYLVANIA							
1 Brady	Y	N	N	Y	N	Y	Y
2 Fattah	Y	N	N	Y	N	Y	Y
3 **English**	Y	N	Y	N	N	Y	N
4 Altmire	Y	N	Y	N	N	Y	Y
5 **Peterson**	Y	N	Y	N	Y	N	N
6 **Gerlach**	Y	N	Y	N	N	N	N
7 Sestak	Y	N	N	N	N	Y	Y
8 Murphy, P.	Y	N	N	N	N	Y	Y
9 **Shuster**	Y	Y	Y	N	Y	N	N
10 Carney	Y	N	N	N	N	N	Y
11 Kanjorski	Y	N	N	Y	N	Y	Y
12 Murtha	Y	N	N	N	N	Y	Y
13 Schwartz	Y	N	N	Y	N	Y	Y
14 Doyle	Y	?	?	?	?	?	?
15 **Dent**	Y	N	Y	N	N	N	N
16 **Pitts**	Y	Y	Y	N	Y	N	N
17 Holden	Y	N	N	Y	N	Y	Y
18 **Murphy, T.**	Y	N	Y	N	Y	N	Y
19 **Platts**	Y	Y	Y	N	N	N	N
RHODE ISLAND							
1 Kennedy	?	N	N	N	N	Y	Y
2 Langevin	Y	N	N	N	N	Y	Y
SOUTH CAROLINA							
1 **Brown**	Y	N	Y	N	Y	N	N
2 **Wilson**	Y	Y	Y	N	Y	N	N
3 **Barrett**	Y	Y	Y	N	Y	N	N
4 **Inglis**	Y	Y	Y	N	N	N	Y
5 Spratt	?	N	N	N	N	Y	Y
6 Clyburn	Y	N	N	N	N	Y	Y
SOUTH DAKOTA							
AL Herseth Sandlin	Y	N	Y	N	N	Y	Y
TENNESSEE							
1 **Davis, D.**	Y	Y	Y	N	Y	N	N
2 **Duncan**	Y	N	N	Y	Y	Y	Y
3 **Wamp**	Y	Y	Y	N	N	N	N
4 Davis, L.	Y	N	N	N	N	Y	Y
5 Cooper	Y	N	N	N	N	Y	Y
6 Gordon	Y	N	N	N	N	Y	Y
7 **Blackburn**	Y	Y	Y	N	Y	N	N
8 Tanner	Y	N	N	N	N	Y	Y
9 Cohen	Y	N	N	Y	N	Y	Y

	354	355	356	357	358	359	360
TEXAS							
1 **Gohmert**	Y	N	Y	N	Y	N	N
2 **Poe**	Y	Y	Y	N	Y	Y	N
3 **Johnson, S.**	Y	Y	Y	N	Y	N	N
4 **Hall**	Y	Y	Y	?	Y	N	N
5 **Hensarling**	Y	Y	Y	N	Y	N	N
6 **Barton**	Y	Y	Y	N	Y	N	N
7 **Culberson**	Y	Y	Y	N	Y	N	N
8 **Brady**	Y	Y	Y	N	Y	N	N
9 Green, A.	Y	N	N	Y	N	Y	Y
10 **McCaul**	Y	N	Y	N	Y	N	N
11 **Conaway**	Y	Y	Y	N	Y	N	N
12 **Granger**	Y	N	Y	N	Y	N	N
13 **Thornberry**	Y	Y	Y	N	Y	N	N
14 **Paul**	?	?	?	?	?	?	?
15 Hinojosa	Y	?	?	?	?	?	?
16 Reyes	Y	N	N	N	N	Y	Y
17 Edwards	Y	N	N	N	N	Y	Y
18 Jackson Lee	Y	N	N	Y	N	Y	Y
19 **Neugebauer**	Y	Y	Y	N	Y	N	N
20 Gonzalez	Y	N	N	N	N	Y	Y
21 **Smith**	Y	Y	Y	N	Y	N	N
22 Lampson	Y	N	N	N	N	N	Y
23 Rodriguez	Y	N	N	N	N	Y	Y
24 **Marchant**	Y	Y	Y	N	Y	N	N
25 Doggett	Y	N	N	Y	N	Y	Y
26 **Burgess**	Y	Y	Y	N	Y	N	N
27 Ortiz	Y	N	N	N	N	Y	Y
28 Cuellar	Y	N	N	N	N	Y	Y
29 Green, G.	Y	N	N	N	N	Y	Y
30 Johnson, E.	Y	N	N	N	N	Y	Y
31 **Carter**	+	?	?	?	?	?	?
32 **Sessions**	Y	N	Y	N	Y	N	N
UTAH							
1 **Bishop**	Y	?	Y	N	Y	N	N
2 Matheson	Y	N	N	Y	N	Y	Y
3 **Cannon**	Y	?	?	?	?	?	?
VERMONT							
AL Welch	Y	N	N	Y	N	Y	Y
VIRGINIA							
1 **Wittman**	Y	Y	Y	N	N	N	N
2 **Drake**	Y	Y	Y	N	N	N	N
3 Scott	Y	N	N	N	N	Y	Y
4 **Forbes**	Y	Y	Y	N	N	N	N
5 **Goode**	Y	Y	Y	N	Y	N	N
6 **Goodlatte**	Y	Y	Y	N	Y	N	N
7 **Cantor**	Y	Y	Y	N	Y	N	N
8 Moran	Y	N	N	Y	N	Y	Y
9 Boucher	Y	N	N	N	N	Y	Y
10 **Wolf**	Y	Y	Y	N	N	N	N
11 **Davis**	Y	N	Y	N	Y	N	N
WASHINGTON							
1 Inslee	Y	N	N	N	N	Y	Y
2 Larsen	Y	N	N	N	N	Y	Y
3 Baird	Y	N	N	Y	N	Y	Y
4 **Hastings**	Y	Y	Y	N	Y	N	N
5 **McMorris Rodgers**	Y	Y	Y	N	N	N	N
6 Dicks	Y	N	N	N	N	Y	Y
7 McDermott	N	N	N	Y	N	Y	Y
8 **Reichert**	Y	Y	Y	N	N	N	N
9 Smith	Y	N	N	N	N	Y	Y
WEST VIRGINIA							
1 Mollohan	Y	N	N	N	N	Y	Y
2 **Capito**	Y	N	Y	N	N	N	N
3 Rahall	Y	N	N	Y	N	Y	Y
WISCONSIN							
1 **Ryan**	Y	Y	Y	N	Y	N	N
2 Baldwin	N	N	N	Y	N	Y	Y
3 Kind	Y	N	N	Y	N	Y	Y
4 Moore	N	N	N	Y	N	Y	Y
5 **Sensenbrenner**	Y	Y	N	N	N	N	N
6 **Petri**	Y	Y	N	N	N	N	N
7 Obey	Y	N	N	Y	N	Y	Y
8 Kagen	Y	N	N	Y	N	Y	Y
WYOMING							
AL **Cubin**	Y	Y	Y	N	Y	N	N
DELEGATES							
Faleomavaega (A.S.)		N	N	N	N	Y	Y
Norton (D.C.)		N	N	N	N	Y	Y
Bordallo (Guam)		N	N	N	N	Y	Y
Fortuño (P.R.)		?	?	?	?	?	?
Christensen (V.I.)		?	?	?	?	?	?

IN THE HOUSE | By Vote Number

361. **HR 5658. Fiscal 2009 Defense Authorization/Interrogations by Contractors.** Price, D-N.C., amendment that would prohibit contractors from performing interrogations but would allow contractors to serve as interpreters. Adopted in Committee of the Whole 240-168: R 17-167; D 223-1 (ND 168-0, SD 55-1). A "nay" was a vote in support of the president's position. May 22, 2008.

362. **HR 5658. Fiscal 2009 Defense Authorization/Videotaping Interrogations.** Holt, D-N.J., amendment that would require interrogations of detainees of the Department of Defense to be videotaped or electronically recorded. It also would require the creation of uniform guidelines for such recording. Adopted in Committee of the Whole 218-192: R 15-169; D 203-23 (ND 159-11, SD 44-12). A "nay" was a vote in support of the president's position. May 22, 2008.

363. **HR 5658. Fiscal 2009 Defense Authorization/Student and Instructor Information Requests.** McGovern, D-Mass., amendment that would require the Defense secretary to release to the public, upon request, the names, ranks, countries of origin, and other information about students and instructors of the Western Hemisphere Institute for Security Cooperation, from fiscal 2005 and beyond. Adopted in Committee of the Whole 220-189: R 3-181; D 217-8 (ND 166-3, SD 51-5). May 22, 2008.

364. **HR 5658. Fiscal 2009 Defense Authorization/Recommit.** Conaway, R-Texas, motion to recommit the bill to the Armed Services Committee with instructions that it be reported back promptly with language that would repeal a ban on federal purchases of unconventional fuels that do not meet a minimum standard of greenhouse gas emissions and require a study on using former military installations as locations for oil refineries. The language also would expand education benefits to additional military servicemembers and allow enhanced transferability of benefits to servicemembers' spouses and children. Motion rejected 186-223: R 184-1; D 2-222 (ND 1-167, SD 1-55). May 22, 2008.

365. **HR 5658. Fiscal 2009 Defense Authorization/Passage.** Passage of the bill that would authorize $601.4 billion for defense programs in fiscal 2009, including $70 billion for the wars in Iraq and Afghanistan. It would authorize $154.5 billion for operations and maintenance; $124.7 billion for military personnel; $24.4 billion for military construction and family housing and base closings; $24.7 billion for the Defense Health Program and $10.2 billion for missile defense. It would authorize a 3.9 percent pay raise for military personnel. The bill would block the closing of Walter Reed Army Medical Center unless the Defense Department provides more information about plans to relocate the hospital's services. As amended, the bill would require that if the United States entered into a Status of Forces agreement with Iraq, the Iraqi government would have to pay for certain costs of the U.S. military presence and Congress would have to authorize the agreement. Passed 384-23: R 181-3; D 203-20 (ND 149-18, SD 54-2). A "nay" was a vote in support of the president's position. May 22, 2008.

366. **H Res 986. Honor Vietnam POWs/Adoption.** Davis, D-Calif., motion to suspend the rules and adopt the resolution that would call upon Americans to show gratitude for the courage and sacrifice for the military members held as prisoners of war during the Vietnam War. It would also call for a full account of the 1,729 military members who remain unaccounted for. Motion agreed to 394-0: R 183-0; D 211-0 (ND 159-0, SD 52-0). A two-thirds majority of those present and voting (263 in this case) is required for adoption under suspension of the rules. May 22, 2008.

	361	362	363	364	365	366
ALABAMA						
1 Bonner	N	N	N	Y	Y	Y
2 Everett	N	N	N	Y	Y	Y
3 Rogers	N	N	N	Y	Y	Y
4 Aderholt	N	N	N	Y	Y	Y
5 Cramer	Y	N	Y	N	Y	Y
6 Bachus	N	N	N	Y	Y	Y
7 Davis	Y	Y	Y	N	Y	Y
ALASKA						
AL Young	?	?	?	?	?	?
ARIZONA						
1 Renzi	N	N	N	Y	Y	Y
2 Franks	N	N	N	Y	Y	Y
3 Shadegg	N	N	N	Y	Y	Y
4 Pastor	Y	Y	Y	N	Y	Y
5 Mitchell	Y	Y	Y	N	Y	Y
6 Flake	N	N	Y	N	Y	N
7 Grijalva	Y	Y	Y	N	Y	Y
8 Giffords	Y	Y	Y	N	Y	Y
ARKANSAS						
1 Berry	Y	Y	Y	N	Y	Y
2 Snyder	Y	Y	N	N	Y	Y
3 Boozman	N	N	N	Y	Y	Y
4 Ross	Y	Y	Y	N	Y	Y
CALIFORNIA						
1 Thompson	Y	Y	Y	N	Y	Y
2 Herger	?	N	N	Y	Y	Y
3 Lungren	N	N	N	Y	Y	Y
4 Doolittle	N	N	N	Y	Y	Y
5 Matsui	Y	Y	Y	N	Y	Y
6 Woolsey	Y	Y	Y	N	N	Y
7 Miller, George	?	Y	Y	N	Y	Y
8 Pelosi						
9 Lee	Y	Y	Y	N	N	Y
10 Tauscher	Y	Y	Y	N	Y	Y
11 McNerney	Y	Y	Y	N	Y	Y
12 Speier	Y	Y	Y	N	Y	Y
13 Stark	?	?	?	?	?	?
14 Eshoo	Y	Y	Y	N	Y	Y
15 Honda	Y	Y	Y	N	Y	Y
16 Lofgren	Y	Y	Y	N	Y	Y
17 Farr	Y	Y	Y	N	Y	?
18 Cardoza	Y	Y	Y	N	Y	Y
19 Radanovich	N	N	N	Y	Y	Y
20 Costa	Y	Y	N	N	Y	Y
21 Nunes	N	N	N	Y	Y	Y
22 McCarthy	N	N	N	Y	Y	Y
23 Capps	Y	Y	Y	N	Y	Y
24 Gallegly	N	N	N	Y	Y	Y
25 McKeon	N	N	N	Y	Y	Y
26 Dreier	N	N	N	Y	Y	Y
27 Sherman	Y	Y	Y	N	Y	Y
28 Berman	Y	Y	Y	N	Y	Y
29 Schiff	Y	Y	Y	N	Y	Y
30 Waxman	Y	Y	Y	N	?	Y
31 Becerra	Y	Y	Y	N	Y	Y
32 Solis	Y	Y	Y	N	Y	Y
33 Watson	Y	Y	Y	N	Y	Y
34 Roybal-Allard	Y	Y	Y	N	Y	Y
35 Waters	Y	Y	Y	N	N	?
36 Harman	Y	Y	Y	N	Y	Y
37 Richardson	Y	Y	Y	N	Y	Y
38 Napolitano	Y	Y	Y	N	Y	Y
39 Sánchez, Linda	Y	Y	Y	N	Y	Y
40 Royce	N	N	N	Y	Y	Y
41 Lewis	N	N	N	Y	Y	Y
42 Miller, Gary	N	N	N	Y	Y	Y
43 Baca	Y	Y	Y	N	Y	Y
44 Calvert	N	N	N	Y	Y	Y
45 Bono Mack	N	N	N	Y	Y	Y
46 Rohrabacher	N	Y	N	Y	Y	Y
47 Sanchez, Loretta	Y	Y	Y	N	Y	Y
48 Campbell	N	N	N	Y	Y	Y
49 Issa	N	N	N	Y	Y	Y
50 Bilbray	N	N	N	Y	Y	Y
51 Filner	Y	Y	Y	N	N	Y
52 Hunter	N	N	N	Y	Y	Y
53 Davis	Y	Y	Y	N	Y	Y
COLORADO						
1 DeGette	Y	Y	Y	N	Y	Y
2 Udall	?	?	?	?	?	?
3 Salazar	Y	N	Y	N	Y	Y
4 Musgrave	?	?	?	?	?	?
5 Lamborn	N	N	N	Y	Y	Y
6 Tancredo	N	N	N	Y	Y	Y
7 Perlmutter	Y	Y	Y	N	Y	Y
CONNECTICUT						
1 Larson	Y	Y	Y	N	Y	Y
2 Courtney	Y	Y	Y	N	Y	Y
3 DeLauro	Y	Y	Y	N	Y	Y
4 Shays	Y	N	N	N	Y	Y
5 Murphy	Y	N	Y	N	Y	Y
DELAWARE						
AL Castle	Y	Y	N	Y	Y	Y
FLORIDA						
1 Miller	N	N	N	Y	Y	Y
2 Boyd	Y	Y	Y	N	Y	Y
3 Brown	Y	Y	Y	N	Y	Y
4 Crenshaw	?	?	?	?	?	?
5 Brown-Waite	N	N	N	Y	Y	Y
6 Stearns	N	N	?	Y	Y	Y
7 Mica	N	N	N	Y	Y	Y
8 Keller	N	N	N	Y	Y	Y
9 Bilirakis	N	N	N	Y	Y	Y
10 Young	Y	N	N	Y	Y	Y
11 Castor	?	?	?	?	?	?
12 Putnam	N	N	N	Y	Y	Y
13 Buchanan	N	N	N	Y	Y	Y
14 Mack	N	N	N	Y	Y	Y
15 Weldon	Y	N	Y	N	Y	Y
16 Mahoney	Y	N	Y	N	Y	Y
17 Meek	Y	Y	Y	N	Y	Y
18 Ros-Lehtinen	N	Y	N	Y	Y	Y
19 Wexler	?	?	?	?	?	?
20 Wasserman Schultz	Y	Y	Y	N	Y	Y
21 Diaz-Balart, L.	N	Y	N	Y	Y	Y
22 Klein	Y	Y	Y	N	Y	Y
23 Hastings	Y	Y	Y	N	Y	Y
24 Feeney	N	N	N	Y	?	Y
25 Diaz-Balart, M.	N	Y	N	Y	Y	Y
GEORGIA						
1 Kingston	N	N	N	Y	Y	Y
2 Bishop	Y	Y	Y	N	Y	Y
3 Westmoreland	N	N	N	Y	Y	Y
4 Johnson	Y	Y	Y	N	Y	Y
5 Lewis	Y	Y	Y	N	Y	N
6 Price	N	N	N	Y	Y	Y
7 Linder	N	N	N	Y	Y	Y
8 Marshall	Y	Y	Y	N	Y	Y
9 Deal	N	N	N	Y	Y	Y
10 Broun	N	N	N	Y	Y	Y
11 Gingrey	N	N	N	Y	Y	Y
12 Barrow	Y	Y	Y	N	Y	Y
13 Scott	Y	Y	Y	N	Y	Y
HAWAII						
1 Abercrombie	Y	Y	Y	N	Y	?
2 Hirono	Y	Y	Y	N	Y	Y
IDAHO						
1 Sali	N	N	N	Y	Y	Y
2 Simpson	N	N	N	Y	Y	Y
ILLINOIS						
1 Rush	?	?	?	?	?	?
2 Jackson	Y	Y	Y	N	Y	Y
3 Lipinski	Y	Y	Y	N	Y	Y
4 Gutierrez	Y	Y	?	N	Y	Y
5 Emanuel	Y	Y	Y	N	Y	Y
6 Roskam	N	N	N	Y	Y	Y
7 Davis	Y	Y	Y	N	Y	Y
8 Bean	Y	Y	Y	N	Y	Y
9 Schakowsky	Y	Y	Y	N	Y	Y
10 Kirk	N	N	N	Y	Y	Y
11 Weller	?	?	?	?	?	?
12 Costello	Y	Y	Y	N	Y	Y
13 Biggert	N	N	N	Y	Y	Y
14 Foster	Y	Y	Y	N	Y	Y
15 Johnson	Y	Y	N	Y	Y	Y

KEY	Republicans	Democrats	
Y Voted for (yea)		X Paired against	C Voted "present" to avoid possible conflict of interest
# Paired for		− Announced against	
+ Announced for		P Voted "present"	? Did not vote or otherwise make a position known
N Voted against (nay)			

ND Northern Democrats, SD Southern Democrats
Southern states: Ala., Ark., Fla., Ga., Ky., La., Miss., N.C., Okla., S.C., Tenn., Texas, Va.

	361	362	363	364	365	366
16 **Manzullo**	N	N	N	Y	Y	Y
17 Hare	Y	Y	Y	N	Y	Y
18 **LaHood**	N	N	Y	Y	Y	Y
19 **Shimkus**	N	N	N	Y	Y	Y
INDIANA						
1 Visclosky	Y	Y	Y	N	Y	Y
2 Donnelly	Y	N	Y	Y	Y	Y
3 **Souder**	N	N	N	Y	Y	Y
4 **Buyer**	N	N	N	Y	Y	Y
5 **Burton**	N	N	N	Y	Y	Y
6 **Pence**	N	N	N	Y	Y	Y
7 Carson, A.	Y	Y	Y	N	Y	Y
8 Ellsworth	Y	N	Y	N	Y	Y
9 Hill	Y	Y	Y	N	Y	Y
IOWA						
1 Braley	Y	?	Y	N	Y	Y
2 Loebsack	Y	Y	Y	N	Y	Y
3 Boswell	Y	Y	Y	N	Y	Y
4 **Latham**	N	N	N	Y	Y	Y
5 **King**	N	N	N	Y	Y	Y
KANSAS						
1 **Moran**	N	Y	N	Y	Y	Y
2 Boyda	Y	Y	Y	N	Y	Y
3 Moore	Y	Y	Y	N	Y	Y
4 **Tiahrt**	N	N	N	Y	Y	Y
KENTUCKY						
1 **Whitfield**	N	N	N	Y	Y	?
2 **Lewis**	N	N	N	Y	Y	Y
3 Yarmuth	Y	Y	Y	N	Y	Y
4 **Davis**	N	N	N	Y	Y	Y
5 **Rogers**	N	N	N	Y	Y	Y
6 Chandler	Y	N	Y	N	Y	Y
LOUISIANA						
1 **Scalise**	N	N	N	Y	Y	Y
2 Jefferson	Y	Y	Y	N	Y	Y
3 Melancon	Y	Y	Y	N	Y	?
4 **McCrery**	N	N	N	Y	Y	Y
5 **Alexander**	N	N	N	Y	Y	Y
6 Cazayoux	Y	N	Y	N	Y	Y
7 **Boustany**	N	N	N	Y	Y	Y
MAINE						
1 Allen	Y	Y	Y	N	Y	Y
2 Michaud	Y	Y	Y	N	N	Y
MARYLAND						
1 **Gilchrest**	Y	Y	N	?	Y	Y
2 Ruppersberger	Y	N	Y	N	Y	Y
3 Sarbanes	Y	Y	Y	N	Y	Y
4 Wynn	Y	Y	Y	N	Y	Y
5 Hoyer	Y	Y	Y	N	Y	Y
6 **Bartlett**	Y	Y	N	Y	Y	Y
7 Cummings	Y	Y	Y	N	Y	Y
8 Van Hollen	Y	Y	Y	N	Y	Y
MASSACHUSETTS						
1 Olver	Y	Y	Y	N	N	Y
2 Neal	Y	Y	Y	N	Y	Y
3 McGovern	Y	Y	Y	N	Y	Y
4 Frank	Y	Y	Y	N	Y	Y
5 Tsongas	Y	Y	Y	N	Y	Y
6 Tierney	Y	Y	Y	N	Y	Y
7 Markey	Y	Y	Y	N	Y	Y
8 Capuano	Y	Y	Y	N	Y	Y
9 Lynch	Y	Y	Y	N	Y	Y
10 Delahunt	Y	Y	Y	N	Y	Y
MICHIGAN						
1 Stupak	Y	Y	Y	N	Y	Y
2 **Hoekstra**	N	N	N	Y	Y	Y
3 **Ehlers**	?	?	?	?	?	?
4 **Camp**	N	N	N	Y	Y	Y
5 Kildee	Y	Y	Y	N	Y	Y
6 **Upton**	Y	Y	N	Y	Y	Y
7 **Walberg**	N	N	N	Y	Y	Y
8 **Rogers**	N	N	N	Y	Y	Y
9 **Knollenberg**	N	N	N	Y	Y	Y
10 **Miller**	N	Y	N	Y	Y	Y
11 **McCotter**	N	N	N	Y	Y	Y
12 Levin	Y	Y	Y	N	Y	Y
13 Kilpatrick	Y	Y	Y	N	Y	?
14 Conyers	Y	Y	Y	N	Y	Y
15 Dingell	Y	Y	Y	N	Y	Y
MINNESOTA						
1 Walz	Y	Y	Y	N	Y	Y
2 **Kline**	N	N	N	Y	Y	Y
3 **Ramstad**	N	N	N	Y	Y	Y
4 McCollum	Y	Y	Y	N	Y	Y

	361	362	363	364	365	366
5 Ellison	Y	Y	Y	N	N	Y
6 **Bachmann**	N	N	N	Y	Y	Y
7 Peterson	Y	N	Y	N	Y	Y
8 Oberstar	Y	Y	Y	N	Y	Y
MISSISSIPPI						
1 Childers	Y	N	Y	N	Y	?
2 Thompson	Y	Y	Y	N	Y	Y
3 **Pickering**	N	N	N	Y	Y	Y
4 Taylor	Y	Y	N	N	Y	?
MISSOURI						
1 Clay	Y	Y	Y	N	Y	Y
2 **Akin**	N	N	N	Y	Y	Y
3 Carnahan	Y	Y	?	N	Y	?
4 Skelton	Y	Y	Y	N	Y	Y
5 Cleaver	Y	Y	Y	N	Y	Y
6 **Graves**	N	N	N	Y	Y	Y
7 **Blunt**	N	N	N	Y	Y	Y
8 **Emerson**	Y	Y	N	Y	Y	Y
9 **Hulshof**	N	N	N	Y	Y	Y
MONTANA						
AL **Rehberg**	N	N	N	Y	Y	Y
NEBRASKA						
1 **Fortenberry**	N	N	N	Y	Y	Y
2 **Terry**	N	N	N	Y	Y	Y
3 **Smith**	N	N	N	Y	Y	Y
NEVADA						
1 Berkley	Y	Y	Y	N	Y	Y
2 **Heller**	N	N	N	Y	Y	Y
3 **Porter**	N	N	N	Y	Y	Y
NEW HAMPSHIRE						
1 Shea-Porter	Y	Y	Y	N	Y	Y
2 Hodes	Y	Y	Y	N	Y	Y
NEW JERSEY						
1 Andrews	?	?	?	?	?	?
2 **LoBiondo**	N	N	N	Y	Y	Y
3 **Saxton**	N	N	N	Y	Y	Y
4 **Smith**	Y	Y	Y	Y	Y	Y
5 **Garrett**	Y	N	N	Y	Y	Y
6 Pallone	Y	Y	Y	N	Y	Y
7 **Ferguson**	N	N	N	Y	Y	Y
8 Pascrell	Y	Y	Y	N	Y	Y
9 Rothman	Y	Y	Y	N	Y	Y
10 Payne	Y	Y	Y	N	Y	Y
11 **Frelinghuysen**	N	N	N	Y	Y	Y
12 Holt	Y	Y	Y	N	Y	Y
13 Sires	Y	Y	Y	N	Y	Y
NEW MEXICO						
1 **Wilson**	N	N	N	Y	Y	Y
2 **Pearce**	N	N	N	Y	Y	Y
3 Udall	Y	Y	Y	N	Y	Y
NEW YORK						
1 Bishop	Y	Y	Y	N	Y	Y
2 Israel	Y	Y	Y	N	Y	Y
3 **King**	N	N	N	Y	Y	Y
4 McCarthy	Y	Y	Y	N	Y	Y
5 Ackerman	Y	Y	Y	N	Y	Y
6 Meeks	?	?	?	?	?	?
7 Crowley	Y	Y	Y	N	Y	Y
8 Nadler	?	?	?	?	?	?
9 Weiner	Y	Y	Y	N	Y	Y
10 Towns	Y	Y	Y	N	Y	Y
11 Clarke	Y	Y	Y	N	N	Y
12 Velázquez	Y	Y	Y	N	N	Y
13 **Fossella**	N	N	N	Y	Y	Y
14 Maloney	Y	Y	Y	N	Y	Y
15 Rangel	Y	Y	Y	N	N	?
16 Serrano	Y	Y	Y	N	N	Y
17 Engel	?	Y	Y	N	Y	Y
18 Lowey	Y	Y	Y	N	Y	Y
19 Hall	Y	Y	Y	N	Y	Y
20 Gillibrand	?	?	?	?	?	?
21 McNulty	Y	Y	Y	N	Y	Y
22 Hinchey	Y	Y	Y	N	Y	Y
23 **McHugh**	N	N	N	Y	Y	Y
24 Arcuri	Y	N	Y	N	Y	Y
25 **Walsh**	?	?	?	?	?	?
26 **Reynolds**	?	?	?	Y	Y	Y
27 Higgins	Y	Y	Y	N	Y	Y
28 Slaughter	Y	Y	Y	N	Y	Y
29 **Kuhl**	N	N	N	Y	Y	Y
NORTH CAROLINA						
1 Butterfield	Y	Y	Y	N	Y	Y
2 Etheridge	Y	Y	Y	N	Y	Y
3 **Jones**	Y	N	N	Y	Y	Y
4 Price	Y	Y	Y	N	Y	Y

	361	362	363	364	365	366
5 **Foxx**	N	N	N	Y	Y	Y
6 **Coble**	Y	N	N	Y	Y	Y
7 McIntyre	Y	Y	Y	N	Y	Y
8 **Hayes**	N	N	N	Y	Y	Y
9 **Myrick**	N	N	N	Y	Y	Y
10 **McHenry**	N	N	N	Y	Y	Y
11 Shuler	Y	N	Y	N	Y	Y
12 Watt	Y	Y	Y	N	Y	Y
13 Miller	Y	Y	Y	N	Y	Y
NORTH DAKOTA						
AL Pomeroy	?	Y	Y	N	Y	Y
OHIO						
1 **Chabot**	N	N	N	Y	Y	Y
2 **Schmidt**	N	N	N	Y	Y	Y
3 **Turner**	N	N	N	Y	Y	Y
4 **Jordan**	N	N	N	Y	Y	Y
5 **Latta**	N	N	N	Y	Y	Y
6 Wilson	Y	Y	Y	N	Y	Y
7 **Hobson**	?	?	?	?	?	?
8 **Boehner**	N	N	N	Y	Y	Y
9 Kaptur	Y	Y	Y	N	Y	Y
10 Kucinich	Y	Y	Y	N	N	Y
11 Tubbs Jones	Y	Y	Y	N	Y	Y
12 **Tiberi**	N	N	N	Y	Y	Y
13 Sutton	Y	Y	Y	N	Y	Y
14 **LaTourette**	N	N	N	Y	Y	Y
15 **Pryce**	?	?	?	?	?	?
16 **Regula**	N	N	N	Y	Y	Y
17 Ryan	Y	Y	Y	N	Y	Y
18 Space	Y	N	Y	N	Y	Y
OKLAHOMA						
1 **Sullivan**	N	N	N	Y	Y	Y
2 Boren	Y	N	Y	N	Y	Y
3 **Lucas**	N	N	N	Y	Y	Y
4 **Cole**	N	N	N	Y	Y	Y
5 **Fallin**	N	N	N	Y	Y	Y
OREGON						
1 Wu	Y	Y	Y	N	Y	Y
2 **Walden**	?	?	?	?	?	?
3 Blumenauer	Y	Y	Y	N	Y	Y
4 DeFazio	Y	Y	Y	N	Y	Y
5 Hooley	Y	Y	Y	N	Y	Y
PENNSYLVANIA						
1 Brady	Y	Y	Y	N	Y	Y
2 Fattah	Y	Y	Y	N	Y	Y
3 **English**	N	Y	N	Y	Y	Y
4 Altmire	Y	N	Y	N	Y	Y
5 **Peterson**	N	N	N	Y	Y	Y
6 **Gerlach**	N	N	N	Y	Y	Y
7 Sestak	Y	Y	Y	N	Y	Y
8 Murphy, P.	Y	Y	Y	N	Y	Y
9 **Shuster**	N	N	N	Y	Y	Y
10 Carney	Y	N	Y	N	Y	Y
11 Kanjorski	Y	Y	Y	N	Y	Y
12 Murtha	Y	Y	Y	N	Y	?
13 Schwartz	Y	Y	Y	N	Y	Y
14 Doyle	?	?	?	?	?	?
15 **Dent**	N	N	N	Y	Y	Y
16 **Pitts**	N	N	N	Y	Y	Y
17 Holden	Y	Y	Y	N	Y	Y
18 **Murphy, T.**	Y	N	N	Y	Y	Y
19 **Platts**	N	N	N	Y	?	Y
RHODE ISLAND						
1 Kennedy	Y	Y	Y	N	Y	Y
2 Langevin	Y	Y	Y	N	Y	Y
SOUTH CAROLINA						
1 **Brown**	N	N	N	Y	Y	Y
2 **Wilson**	N	N	N	Y	Y	Y
3 **Barrett**	N	N	N	Y	Y	Y
4 **Inglis**	N	Y	N	Y	Y	Y
5 Spratt	Y	Y	Y	N	Y	Y
6 Clyburn	Y	Y	Y	N	Y	Y
SOUTH DAKOTA						
AL Herseth Sandlin	Y	Y	N	N	Y	Y
TENNESSEE						
1 **Davis, D.**	N	N	N	Y	Y	Y
2 **Duncan**	Y	N	N	Y	N	Y
3 **Wamp**	N	N	N	Y	Y	Y
4 Davis, L.	Y	Y	N	N	Y	Y
5 Cooper	Y	Y	Y	N	Y	Y
6 Gordon	Y	Y	Y	N	Y	Y
7 **Blackburn**	N	N	N	Y	Y	Y
8 Tanner	Y	N	Y	N	Y	Y
9 Cohen	Y	Y	Y	N	Y	?

	361	362	363	364	365	366
TEXAS						
1 **Gohmert**	N	N	N	Y	Y	Y
2 **Poe**	N	N	N	Y	Y	Y
3 **Johnson, S.**	N	N	N	Y	Y	Y
4 **Hall**	N	N	N	Y	Y	Y
5 **Hensarling**	N	N	N	Y	Y	Y
6 **Barton**	N	N	N	Y	Y	Y
7 **Culberson**	N	N	N	Y	Y	Y
8 **Brady**	N	N	N	Y	Y	Y
9 Green, A.	Y	Y	Y	N	Y	Y
10 **McCaul**	N	N	N	Y	Y	Y
11 **Conaway**	N	N	N	Y	Y	Y
12 **Granger**	N	N	N	Y	Y	?
13 **Thornberry**	N	N	N	Y	Y	Y
14 **Paul**	?	?	?	?	?	?
15 Hinojosa	?	?	?	?	?	?
16 Reyes	Y	Y	Y	N	Y	Y
17 Edwards	Y	Y	Y	N	Y	Y
18 Jackson Lee	Y	Y	Y	N	N	Y
19 **Neugebauer**	N	N	N	Y	Y	Y
20 Gonzalez	Y	Y	Y	N	Y	Y
21 **Smith**	N	?	N	Y	Y	Y
22 Lampson	Y	N	N	Y	Y	Y
23 Rodriguez	Y	Y	Y	N	Y	Y
24 **Marchant**	?	?	?	?	?	?
25 Doggett	Y	Y	Y	N	Y	Y
26 **Burgess**	N	N	N	Y	Y	Y
27 Ortiz	Y	Y	Y	N	Y	Y
28 Cuellar	Y	N	Y	N	Y	Y
29 Green, G.	Y	N	Y	N	Y	Y
30 Johnson, E.	Y	Y	Y	N	Y	Y
31 **Carter**	?	?	?	?	?	?
32 **Sessions**	N	N	N	Y	Y	Y
UTAH						
1 **Bishop**	N	N	N	Y	Y	Y
2 Matheson	Y	N	N	N	Y	Y
3 **Cannon**	?	?	?	?	?	?
VERMONT						
AL Welch	Y	Y	Y	N	N	Y
VIRGINIA						
1 **Wittman**	N	N	N	Y	Y	Y
2 **Drake**	N	N	N	Y	Y	Y
3 Scott	Y	Y	Y	N	Y	Y
4 **Forbes**	N	N	N	Y	Y	Y
5 **Goode**	N	N	N	Y	Y	Y
6 **Goodlatte**	N	N	N	Y	Y	Y
7 **Cantor**	N	N	N	Y	Y	Y
8 Moran	Y	Y	Y	N	Y	Y
9 Boucher	Y	Y	Y	N	Y	Y
10 **Wolf**	Y	N	N	Y	Y	Y
11 **Davis**	N	N	N	Y	Y	Y
WASHINGTON						
1 Inslee	Y	Y	Y	N	Y	Y
2 Larsen	Y	Y	Y	N	Y	Y
3 Baird	Y	Y	Y	N	Y	Y
4 **Hastings**	N	N	N	Y	Y	Y
5 **McMorris Rodgers**	N	N	N	Y	Y	Y
6 Dicks	Y	Y	Y	N	Y	?
7 McDermott	Y	Y	Y	N	Y	Y
8 **Reichert**	N	N	N	Y	Y	Y
9 Smith	Y	Y	Y	N	Y	Y
WEST VIRGINIA						
1 Mollohan	Y	Y	Y	N	Y	Y
2 **Capito**	N	N	N	Y	Y	Y
3 Rahall	Y	Y	Y	N	Y	Y
WISCONSIN						
1 **Ryan**	N	N	N	Y	Y	Y
2 Baldwin	Y	Y	Y	N	N	Y
3 Kind	Y	Y	Y	N	Y	Y
4 Moore	Y	Y	Y	N	N	Y
5 **Sensenbrenner**	N	N	N	Y	Y	Y
6 **Petri**	Y	N	N	Y	Y	Y
7 Obey	Y	Y	Y	N	Y	Y
8 Kagen	Y	Y	Y	N	Y	?
WYOMING						
AL **Cubin**	N	N	N	Y	Y	Y
DELEGATES						
Faleomavaega (A.S.)	Y	Y	Y			
Norton (D.C.)	Y	Y	Y			
Bordallo (Guam)	?	?	?			
Fortuño (P.R.)	?	?	?			
Christensen (V.I.)	Y	Y	Y			

IN THE HOUSE | By Vote Number

367. **H Con Res 138. National Men's Health Week/Adoption.** Davis, D-Ill., motion to suspend the rules and adopt the concurrent resolution that would support the annual National Men's Health Week. Motion agreed to 362-0: R 175-0; D 187-0 (ND 137-0, SD 50-0). A two-thirds majority of those present and voting (242 in this case) is required for adoption under suspension of the rules. June 3, 2008.

368. **H Res 923. 150th Anniversary of Minnesota/Adoption.** Davis, D-Ill., motion to suspend the rules and adopt the resolution that would congratulate Minnesota on its 150th anniversary and the contributions it makes to America's economy and heritage. Motion agreed to 363-0: R 175-0; D 188-0 (ND 136-0, SD 52-0). A two-thirds majority of those present and voting (242 in this case) is required for adoption under suspension of the rules. June 3, 2008.

369. **H Res 1114. National Arbor Day/Adoption.** Davis, D-Ill., motion to suspend the rules and adopt the resolution that would support the goals and ideals of the Arbor Day Foundation and the observation of National Arbor Day. Motion agreed to 364-0: R 175-0; D 189-0 (ND 136-0, SD 53-0). A two-thirds majority of those present and voting (243 in this case) is required for adoption under suspension of the rules. June 3, 2008.

370. **HR 3021. School Construction and Modernization/Previous Question.** Sutton, D-Ohio, motion to order the previous question (thus ending debate and possibility of amendment) on adoption of the rule (H Res 1234) to provide for House floor consideration of the bill that would authorize $6.4 billion in fiscal 2009 to modernize and make repairs to public schools, and $100 million per year in fiscal 2009 through 2013 for repairs to public schools damaged by hurricanes Katrina and Rita. Motion agreed to 221-196: R 0-193; D 221-3 (ND 166-2, SD 55-1). June 4, 2008.

371. **HR 3021. School Construction and Modernization/Rule.** Adoption of the rule (H Res 1234) that would allow for House floor consideration of the bill that would authorize $6.4 billion in fiscal 2009 to modernize and make repairs to public schools, and $100 million per year in fiscal 2009 through 2013 for repairs to public schools damaged by hurricanes Katrina and Rita. Adopted 223-193: R 1-192; D 222-1 (ND 167-1, SD 55-0). June 4, 2008.

372. **HR 1343. Community Health Centers/Passage.** Green, D-Texas, motion to suspend the rules and pass the bill that would authorize $14.1 billion in fiscal 2008 through 2012 for the community health centers program. The bill also would authorize $25 million in fiscal 2009 through 2011 for an integrated health systems project to improve access to care in underserved areas. Motion agreed to 393-24: R 169-24; D 224-0 (ND 168-0, SD 56-0). A two-thirds majority of those present and voting (278 in this case) is required for passage under suspension of the rules. June 4, 2008.

	367	368	369	370	371	372
ALABAMA						
1 Bonner	Y	Y	?	N	N	Y
2 Everett	?	?	?	N	N	Y
3 Rogers	Y	Y	Y	N	N	Y
4 Aderholt	Y	Y	Y	N	N	Y
5 Cramer	Y	Y	Y	Y	Y	Y
6 Bachus	Y	Y	Y	N	N	Y
7 Davis	Y	Y	Y	Y	Y	Y
ALASKA						
AL Young	Y	Y	Y	N	N	Y
ARIZONA						
1 Renzi	Y	Y	Y	N	N	Y
2 Franks	Y	Y	Y	N	N	N
3 Shadegg	?	?	?	N	N	Y
4 Pastor	Y	Y	Y	Y	Y	Y
5 Mitchell	Y	Y	Y	Y	Y	Y
6 Flake	Y	Y	Y	N	N	N
7 Grijalva	?	?	?	Y	Y	Y
8 Giffords	Y	Y	Y	Y	Y	Y
ARKANSAS						
1 Berry	Y	Y	Y	?	?	Y
2 Snyder	Y	Y	Y	Y	Y	Y
3 Boozman	Y	Y	Y	N	N	Y
4 Ross	Y	Y	Y	Y	Y	Y
CALIFORNIA						
1 Thompson	Y	Y	Y	Y	Y	Y
2 Herger	Y	Y	Y	N	N	Y
3 Lungren	Y	Y	Y	N	N	Y
4 Doolittle	?	?	?	N	N	Y
5 Matsui	Y	Y	Y	Y	Y	Y
6 Woolsey	Y	Y	Y	Y	Y	Y
7 Miller, George	Y	Y	Y	Y	Y	Y
8 Pelosi						
9 Lee	+	+	+	Y	Y	Y
10 Tauscher	Y	Y	Y	Y	Y	Y
11 McNerney	?	?	?	Y	Y	Y
12 Speier	Y	Y	Y	Y	Y	Y
13 Stark	Y	Y	Y	Y	Y	Y
14 Eshoo	Y	Y	Y	Y	Y	Y
15 Honda	Y	Y	Y	Y	Y	Y
16 Lofgren	Y	Y	Y	Y	Y	Y
17 Farr	Y	Y	Y	Y	Y	Y
18 Cardoza	?	?	?	Y	Y	Y
19 Radanovich	?	?	?	N	N	N
20 Costa	Y	Y	Y	Y	Y	Y
21 Nunes	Y	Y	Y	N	N	Y
22 McCarthy	Y	Y	Y	N	N	Y
23 Capps	Y	Y	Y	Y	Y	Y
24 Gallegly	?	?	?	–	–	+
25 McKeon	Y	Y	Y	N	N	Y
26 Dreier	Y	Y	Y	N	N	Y
27 Sherman	Y	Y	Y	Y	Y	Y
28 Berman	Y	Y	Y	Y	Y	Y
29 Schiff	Y	Y	Y	Y	Y	Y
30 Waxman	Y	Y	Y	Y	Y	Y
31 Becerra	Y	Y	Y	Y	Y	Y
32 Solis	Y	Y	Y	Y	Y	Y
33 Watson	Y	Y	Y	Y	Y	Y
34 Roybal-Allard	Y	Y	Y	Y	Y	Y
35 Waters	?	?	?	Y	Y	Y
36 Harman	Y	Y	Y	Y	Y	Y
37 Richardson	?	?	?	Y	Y	Y
38 Napolitano	Y	Y	Y	Y	Y	Y
39 Sánchez, Linda	Y	Y	Y	Y	Y	Y
40 Royce	Y	Y	Y	N	N	N
41 Lewis	Y	Y	Y	N	N	N
42 Miller, Gary	Y	Y	Y	N	N	N
43 Baca	?	?	?	?	?	?
44 Calvert	Y	Y	Y	N	N	Y
45 Bono Mack	Y	Y	Y	N	N	Y
46 Rohrabacher	?	?	?	N	N	N
47 Sanchez, Loretta	Y	Y	Y	Y	Y	Y
48 Campbell	Y	Y	Y	N	N	N
49 Issa	Y	Y	Y	N	N	Y
50 Bilbray	Y	Y	Y	N	N	Y
51 Filner	+	+	+	+	+	+
52 Hunter	?	?	?	?	?	?
53 Davis	Y	Y	Y	Y	Y	Y
COLORADO						
1 DeGette	Y	Y	Y	Y	Y	Y
2 Udall	?	?	?	Y	Y	Y
3 Salazar	Y	Y	Y	Y	Y	Y
4 Musgrave	?	Y	Y	N	N	N
5 Lamborn	Y	Y	Y	N	N	N
6 Tancredo	Y	Y	Y	N	N	N
7 Perlmutter	Y	Y	Y	Y	Y	Y
CONNECTICUT						
1 Larson	Y	Y	Y	Y	Y	Y
2 Courtney	+	+	+	Y	Y	Y
3 DeLauro	Y	Y	Y	Y	Y	Y
4 Shays	Y	Y	Y	N	N	Y
5 Murphy	Y	Y	Y	Y	Y	Y
DELAWARE						
AL Castle	Y	Y	Y	N	N	Y
FLORIDA						
1 Miller	Y	Y	Y	N	N	N
2 Boyd	Y	Y	Y	Y	Y	Y
3 Brown	?	?	?	Y	Y	Y
4 Crenshaw	Y	Y	Y	N	N	N
5 Brown-Waite	Y	Y	Y	N	N	Y
6 Stearns	Y	Y	Y	N	N	N
7 Mica	Y	Y	Y	N	N	Y
8 Keller	Y	Y	Y	N	N	Y
9 Bilirakis	Y	Y	Y	N	N	Y
10 Young	?	?	?	N	N	Y
11 Castor	+	+	+	Y	Y	Y
12 Putnam	Y	Y	Y	N	N	Y
13 Buchanan	Y	Y	Y	N	N	Y
14 Mack	Y	Y	Y	N	N	N
15 Weldon	?	?	?	N	N	N
16 Mahoney	Y	Y	Y	Y	Y	Y
17 Meek	?	?	?	Y	Y	Y
18 Ros-Lehtinen	Y	Y	Y	N	N	Y
19 Wexler	Y	Y	Y	Y	Y	Y
20 Wasserman Schultz	?	?	?	Y	Y	Y
21 Diaz-Balart, L.	Y	Y	Y	N	N	Y
22 Klein	Y	Y	Y	Y	Y	Y
23 Hastings	Y	Y	Y	Y	Y	Y
24 Feeney	Y	Y	Y	N	N	Y
25 Diaz-Balart, M.	Y	Y	Y	N	N	Y
GEORGIA						
1 Kingston	Y	Y	Y	N	N	Y
2 Bishop	Y	Y	Y	Y	Y	Y
3 Westmoreland	Y	Y	Y	N	N	Y
4 Johnson	Y	Y	Y	Y	Y	Y
5 Lewis	Y	Y	Y	?	?	?
6 Price	Y	Y	Y	N	N	Y
7 Linder	Y	Y	Y	N	N	Y
8 Marshall	Y	Y	Y	Y	Y	Y
9 Deal	Y	Y	Y	N	N	Y
10 Broun	Y	Y	Y	N	N	N
11 Gingrey	Y	Y	Y	N	N	Y
12 Barrow	Y	Y	Y	Y	Y	Y
13 Scott	Y	Y	Y	Y	Y	Y
HAWAII						
1 Abercrombie	Y	Y	?	Y	Y	Y
2 Hirono	Y	Y	Y	Y	Y	Y
IDAHO						
1 Sali	Y	Y	Y	N	N	Y
2 Simpson	Y	Y	Y	N	N	Y
ILLINOIS						
1 Rush	?	?	?	?	?	?
2 Jackson	Y	Y	Y	Y	Y	Y
3 Lipinski	Y	Y	Y	Y	Y	Y
4 Gutierrez	+	+	+	Y	Y	Y
5 Emanuel	+	+	+	Y	Y	Y
6 Roskam	?	?	?	N	N	Y
7 Davis	Y	Y	Y	Y	Y	Y
8 Bean	Y	Y	Y	Y	Y	Y
9 Schakowsky	Y	Y	Y	Y	Y	Y
10 Kirk	Y	Y	Y	N	N	Y
11 Weller	?	?	?	N	N	Y
12 Costello	Y	Y	Y	Y	Y	Y
13 Biggert	Y	Y	Y	N	N	Y
14 Foster	Y	Y	Y	Y	Y	Y
15 Johnson	+	+	+	N	N	Y

KEY   **Republicans**   Democrats

Y Voted for (yea)	**X** Paired against	**C** Voted "present" to avoid possible conflict of interest
# Paired for	**–** Announced against	
+ Announced for	**P** Voted "present"	**?** Did not vote or otherwise make a position known
N Voted against (nay)		

*Rep. Albert R. Wynn, D-Md., resigned May 31, 2008. The last vote for which he was eligible was vote 366.

ND Northern Democrats, SD Southern Democrats
Southern states: Ala., Ark., Fla., Ga., Ky., La., Miss., N.C., Okla., S.C., Tenn., Texas, Va.

	367	368	369	370	371	372
16 **Manzullo**	Y	Y	Y	N	N	Y
17 Hare	Y	Y	Y	Y	Y	Y
18 **LaHood**	Y	Y	Y	N	N	Y
19 **Shimkus**	Y	Y	Y	N	N	Y
INDIANA						
1 Visclosky	Y	Y	Y	Y	Y	Y
2 Donnelly	Y	Y	Y	N	Y	Y
3 **Souder**	Y	Y	Y	N	N	Y
4 **Buyer**	Y	Y	Y	N	N	Y
5 **Burton**	Y	Y	Y	N	N	N
6 **Pence**	Y	Y	Y	N	N	N
7 Carson, A.	Y	Y	Y	Y	Y	Y
8 Ellsworth	Y	Y	Y	Y	Y	Y
9 Hill	Y	Y	Y	N	N	Y
IOWA						
1 Braley	Y	Y	Y	Y	Y	Y
2 Loebsack	Y	Y	Y	Y	Y	Y
3 Boswell	?	?	?	Y	Y	Y
4 **Latham**	Y	Y	Y	N	N	Y
5 **King**	Y	Y	Y	N	N	Y
KANSAS						
1 **Moran**	Y	Y	Y	N	N	Y
2 Boyda	Y	Y	Y	Y	Y	Y
3 Moore	Y	Y	Y	Y	Y	Y
4 **Tiahrt**	Y	Y	Y	N	N	Y
KENTUCKY						
1 **Whitfield**	Y	Y	Y	N	N	Y
2 **Lewis**	Y	Y	Y	N	N	Y
3 Yarmuth	Y	Y	Y	Y	Y	Y
4 **Davis**	Y	Y	Y	N	N	Y
5 **Rogers**	Y	Y	Y	N	N	Y
6 Chandler	Y	Y	Y	Y	Y	Y
LOUISIANA						
1 **Scalise**	Y	Y	Y	N	N	Y
2 Jefferson	Y	Y	Y	Y	Y	Y
3 Melancon	Y	Y	Y	Y	Y	Y
4 **McCrery**	Y	Y	Y	N	N	Y
5 **Alexander**	Y	Y	Y	N	N	Y
6 Cazayoux	+	Y	Y	Y	Y	Y
7 **Boustany**	Y	Y	?	N	N	Y
MAINE						
1 Allen	Y	Y	Y	Y	Y	Y
2 Michaud	Y	Y	Y	Y	Y	Y
MARYLAND						
1 **Gilchrest**	?	?	?	N	N	Y
2 Ruppersberger	Y	Y	Y	Y	Y	Y
3 Sarbanes	Y	Y	Y	Y	Y	Y
4 Vacant						
5 Hoyer	Y	Y	Y	Y	Y	Y
6 **Bartlett**	Y	Y	Y	N	N	N
7 Cummings	Y	Y	Y	Y	Y	Y
8 Van Hollen	Y	Y	Y	Y	Y	Y
MASSACHUSETTS						
1 Olver	Y	Y	Y	Y	Y	Y
2 Neal	Y	Y	Y	Y	Y	Y
3 McGovern	?	?	?	Y	Y	Y
4 Frank	Y	Y	Y	Y	Y	Y
5 Tsongas	Y	Y	Y	Y	Y	Y
6 Tierney	Y	Y	Y	Y	Y	Y
7 Markey	Y	Y	Y	Y	Y	Y
8 Capuano	Y	Y	Y	Y	Y	Y
9 Lynch	Y	Y	Y	Y	Y	Y
10 Delahunt	Y	Y	Y	Y	Y	Y
MICHIGAN						
1 Stupak	Y	Y	Y	Y	Y	Y
2 **Hoekstra**	Y	Y	Y	N	N	Y
3 **Ehlers**	Y	Y	Y	N	N	Y
4 **Camp**	Y	Y	Y	N	N	Y
5 Kildee	Y	Y	Y	Y	Y	Y
6 **Upton**	Y	Y	Y	N	N	Y
7 **Walberg**	Y	Y	Y	N	N	Y
8 **Rogers**	Y	Y	Y	N	N	Y
9 **Knollenberg**	?	?	?	N	N	Y
10 **Miller**	Y	Y	Y	N	N	Y
11 **McCotter**	Y	Y	Y	N	N	Y
12 Levin	Y	Y	Y	Y	Y	Y
13 Kilpatrick	Y	Y	Y	Y	Y	Y
14 Conyers	Y	Y	Y	Y	Y	Y
15 Dingell	Y	Y	Y	Y	Y	Y
MINNESOTA						
1 Walz	Y	Y	Y	Y	Y	Y
2 **Kline**	Y	Y	Y	N	N	Y
3 **Ramstad**	Y	Y	Y	N	N	Y
4 McCollum	?	?	?	Y	Y	Y

	367	368	369	370	371	372
5 Ellison	+	+	+	Y	Y	Y
6 **Bachmann**	Y	Y	Y	N	N	Y
7 Peterson	Y	Y	Y	Y	Y	Y
8 Oberstar	Y	Y	Y	Y	Y	Y
MISSISSIPPI						
1 Childers	Y	Y	Y	Y	Y	Y
2 Thompson	Y	Y	Y	Y	Y	Y
3 **Pickering**	Y	Y	Y	N	N	Y
4 Taylor	Y	Y	Y	Y	Y	Y
MISSOURI						
1 Clay	Y	Y	Y	Y	Y	Y
2 **Akin**	Y	Y	Y	N	N	Y
3 Carnahan	Y	Y	Y	Y	Y	Y
4 Skelton	Y	Y	Y	Y	Y	Y
5 Cleaver	Y	?	Y	Y	Y	Y
6 **Graves**	Y	Y	Y	N	N	Y
7 **Blunt**	Y	Y	Y	N	N	Y
8 **Emerson**	Y	Y	Y	N	N	Y
9 **Hulshof**	?	?	?	N	N	Y
MONTANA						
AL **Rehberg**	Y	Y	Y	N	N	Y
NEBRASKA						
1 **Fortenberry**	Y	Y	Y	N	N	Y
2 **Terry**	Y	?	Y	N	N	Y
3 **Smith**	Y	Y	Y	N	N	Y
NEVADA						
1 Berkley	Y	Y	Y	Y	Y	Y
2 **Heller**	Y	Y	Y	N	N	Y
3 **Porter**	Y	Y	Y	N	N	Y
NEW HAMPSHIRE						
1 Shea-Porter	Y	Y	Y	Y	Y	Y
2 Hodes	Y	Y	Y	Y	Y	Y
NEW JERSEY						
1 Andrews	?	?	?	?	?	?
2 **LoBiondo**	Y	Y	Y	N	N	Y
3 **Saxton**	Y	Y	Y	?	?	?
4 **Smith**	Y	Y	Y	N	N	Y
5 **Garrett**	Y	Y	Y	N	N	Y
6 Pallone	?	?	?	Y	Y	Y
7 **Ferguson**	?	?	?	N	N	Y
8 Pascrell	?	?	?	Y	Y	Y
9 Rothman	+	+	+	Y	Y	Y
10 Payne	?	?	?	Y	Y	Y
11 **Frelinghuysen**	Y	Y	Y	N	N	Y
12 Holt	Y	Y	Y	Y	Y	Y
13 Sires	+	+	+	Y	Y	Y
NEW MEXICO						
1 **Wilson**	?	?	?	?	?	?
2 **Pearce**	?	?	?	N	N	Y
3 Udall	?	?	?	?	?	?
NEW YORK						
1 Bishop	Y	Y	Y	Y	Y	Y
2 Israel	Y	Y	Y	Y	Y	Y
3 **King**	Y	Y	Y	N	N	Y
4 McCarthy	Y	Y	Y	Y	Y	Y
5 Ackerman	Y	Y	Y	Y	Y	Y
6 Meeks	Y	Y	Y	Y	Y	Y
7 Crowley	+	+	+	Y	Y	Y
8 Nadler	?	?	?	Y	Y	Y
9 Weiner	?	?	?	Y	Y	Y
10 Towns	Y	Y	Y	Y	Y	Y
11 Clarke	Y	Y	Y	Y	Y	Y
12 Velázquez	?	?	?	Y	Y	Y
13 **Fossella**	Y	Y	Y	N	N	Y
14 Maloney	?	?	?	Y	Y	Y
15 Rangel	Y	Y	Y	Y	Y	Y
16 Serrano	Y	Y	Y	Y	Y	Y
17 Engel	Y	Y	Y	Y	Y	Y
18 Lowey	Y	Y	Y	Y	Y	Y
19 Hall	Y	Y	Y	Y	Y	Y
20 Gillibrand	?	?	?	?	?	?
21 McNulty	Y	Y	Y	Y	Y	Y
22 Hinchey	?	?	?	Y	Y	Y
23 **McHugh**	Y	Y	Y	N	N	Y
24 Arcuri	Y	Y	Y	Y	Y	Y
25 **Walsh**	Y	?	Y	N	N	Y
26 **Reynolds**	Y	Y	Y	N	N	Y
27 Higgins	Y	Y	Y	Y	Y	Y
28 Slaughter	Y	Y	Y	Y	Y	Y
29 **Kuhl**	Y	Y	Y	N	N	Y
NORTH CAROLINA						
1 Butterfield	Y	Y	Y	Y	Y	Y
2 Etheridge	Y	Y	Y	Y	Y	Y
3 **Jones**	Y	Y	Y	N	N	Y
4 Price	Y	Y	Y	Y	Y	Y

	367	368	369	370	371	372
5 **Foxx**	Y	Y	Y	N	N	Y
6 **Coble**	Y	Y	Y	N	N	Y
7 McIntyre	Y	Y	Y	Y	Y	Y
8 **Hayes**	Y	Y	Y	N	N	Y
9 **Myrick**	Y	Y	Y	N	N	Y
10 **McHenry**	Y	Y	Y	N	N	N
11 Shuler	?	?	?	?	?	?
12 Watt	Y	Y	Y	Y	Y	Y
13 Miller	Y	Y	Y	Y	Y	Y
NORTH DAKOTA						
AL Pomeroy	Y	Y	Y	Y	Y	Y
OHIO						
1 **Chabot**	Y	Y	Y	?	?	?
2 **Schmidt**	Y	Y	Y	N	N	Y
3 **Turner**	Y	Y	Y	N	N	Y
4 **Jordan**	Y	Y	Y	N	N	N
5 **Latta**	Y	Y	Y	N	N	Y
6 Wilson	Y	Y	Y	Y	Y	Y
7 **Hobson**	Y	Y	Y	N	N	Y
8 **Boehner**	?	Y	Y	N	N	Y
9 Kaptur	Y	Y	Y	Y	Y	Y
10 Kucinich	Y	Y	Y	Y	Y	Y
11 Tubbs Jones	+	+	+	Y	Y	Y
12 **Tiberi**	Y	Y	Y	N	N	Y
13 Sutton	Y	Y	Y	Y	Y	Y
14 **LaTourette**	Y	Y	Y	N	N	Y
15 **Pryce**	?	?	?	?	?	?
16 **Regula**	Y	Y	Y	N	N	Y
17 Ryan	Y	Y	Y	Y	Y	Y
18 Space	Y	Y	Y	Y	Y	Y
OKLAHOMA						
1 **Sullivan**	Y	Y	Y	N	N	Y
2 Boren	Y	Y	Y	Y	Y	Y
3 **Lucas**	Y	Y	Y	N	N	Y
4 **Cole**	Y	Y	Y	N	N	Y
5 **Fallin**	Y	Y	Y	N	N	Y
OREGON						
1 Wu	Y	Y	Y	Y	Y	Y
2 **Walden**	Y	Y	Y	N	N	Y
3 Blumenauer	Y	Y	Y	Y	Y	Y
4 DeFazio	Y	Y	Y	Y	Y	Y
5 Hooley	Y	Y	Y	Y	Y	Y
PENNSYLVANIA						
1 Brady	Y	Y	Y	Y	Y	Y
2 Fattah	Y	Y	Y	Y	Y	Y
3 **English**	Y	Y	Y	N	N	Y
4 Altmire	Y	Y	Y	Y	Y	Y
5 **Peterson**	?	?	?	N	N	Y
6 **Gerlach**	Y	Y	Y	N	N	Y
7 Sestak	?	?	?	Y	Y	Y
8 Murphy, P.	Y	Y	Y	Y	Y	Y
9 **Shuster**	Y	Y	Y	N	N	Y
10 Carney	Y	Y	Y	Y	Y	Y
11 Kanjorski	?	?	?	Y	Y	Y
12 Murtha	?	?	?	Y	Y	Y
13 Schwartz	Y	Y	Y	Y	Y	Y
14 Doyle	Y	Y	Y	Y	Y	Y
15 **Dent**	Y	Y	Y	N	N	Y
16 **Pitts**	Y	Y	Y	N	N	Y
17 Holden	Y	Y	Y	Y	Y	Y
18 **Murphy, T.**	Y	Y	Y	N	N	Y
19 **Platts**	Y	Y	Y	N	N	Y
RHODE ISLAND						
1 Kennedy	?	?	?	Y	Y	Y
2 Langevin	Y	Y	Y	Y	Y	Y
SOUTH CAROLINA						
1 **Brown**	Y	Y	Y	N	N	Y
2 **Wilson**	Y	Y	Y	N	N	Y
3 **Barrett**	Y	Y	Y	N	N	N
4 **Inglis**	?	?	?	N	N	Y
5 Spratt	Y	Y	Y	Y	Y	Y
6 Clyburn	Y	Y	Y	Y	Y	Y
SOUTH DAKOTA						
AL Herseth Sandlin	Y	Y	Y	Y	Y	Y
TENNESSEE						
1 **Davis, D.**	Y	Y	Y	N	N	Y
2 **Duncan**	Y	Y	Y	N	N	N
3 **Wamp**	Y	Y	Y	N	N	Y
4 Davis, L.	Y	Y	Y	Y	Y	Y
5 Cooper	Y	Y	Y	Y	Y	Y
6 Gordon	Y	Y	Y	Y	?	Y
7 **Blackburn**	Y	Y	Y	N	N	Y
8 Tanner	Y	Y	Y	Y	Y	Y
9 Cohen	Y	Y	Y	Y	Y	Y

	367	368	369	370	371	372
TEXAS						
1 **Gohmert**	Y	Y	Y	N	N	Y
2 **Poe**	Y	Y	Y	N	N	Y
3 **Johnson, S.**	Y	Y	Y	N	N	Y
4 **Hall**	Y	Y	Y	N	N	Y
5 **Hensarling**	Y	Y	Y	N	N	N
6 **Barton**	Y	Y	Y	N	N	Y
7 **Culberson**	Y	Y	Y	N	N	Y
8 **Brady**	Y	Y	Y	N	N	Y
9 Green, A.	Y	Y	Y	Y	Y	Y
10 **McCaul**	Y	Y	Y	N	N	Y
11 **Conaway**	Y	Y	Y	N	N	Y
12 **Granger**	Y	Y	Y	N	N	Y
13 **Thornberry**	Y	Y	Y	N	N	Y
14 **Paul**	Y	Y	Y	N	N	N
15 Hinojosa	Y	Y	Y	Y	Y	Y
16 Reyes	Y	Y	Y	Y	Y	Y
17 Edwards	?	?	Y	Y	Y	Y
18 Jackson Lee	?	?	?	?	?	?
19 **Neugebauer**	Y	Y	Y	N	N	Y
20 Gonzalez	Y	Y	Y	Y	Y	Y
21 **Smith**	Y	Y	Y	N	N	Y
22 Lampson	Y	Y	Y	N	Y	Y
23 Rodriguez	Y	Y	Y	Y	Y	Y
24 **Marchant**	Y	Y	Y	N	N	N
25 Doggett	Y	Y	Y	Y	Y	Y
26 **Burgess**	Y	Y	Y	N	N	Y
27 Ortiz	Y	Y	Y	Y	Y	Y
28 Cuellar	Y	Y	Y	Y	Y	Y
29 Green, G.	Y	Y	Y	Y	Y	Y
30 Johnson, E.	Y	Y	Y	Y	Y	Y
31 **Carter**	Y	Y	Y	N	N	Y
32 **Sessions**	Y	Y	Y	N	N	Y
UTAH						
1 **Bishop**	Y	Y	Y	N	N	Y
2 Matheson	Y	Y	Y	Y	Y	Y
3 **Cannon**	Y	Y	Y	N	N	Y
VERMONT						
AL Welch	Y	Y	Y	Y	Y	Y
VIRGINIA						
1 **Wittman**	Y	Y	Y	N	N	Y
2 **Drake**	Y	Y	Y	N	N	Y
3 Scott	Y	Y	Y	Y	Y	Y
4 **Forbes**	Y	Y	Y	N	N	Y
5 **Goode**	Y	Y	Y	N	N	Y
6 **Goodlatte**	Y	Y	Y	N	N	Y
7 **Cantor**	Y	Y	Y	N	N	Y
8 Moran	?	Y	Y	Y	Y	Y
9 Boucher	Y	Y	Y	Y	Y	Y
10 **Wolf**	Y	Y	Y	N	N	Y
11 **Davis**	Y	Y	?	N	Y	Y
WASHINGTON						
1 Inslee	Y	Y	Y	Y	Y	Y
2 Larsen	?	?	?	Y	Y	Y
3 Baird	Y	Y	Y	Y	Y	Y
4 **Hastings**	Y	Y	Y	N	N	Y
5 **McMorris Rodgers**	Y	Y	Y	N	N	Y
6 Dicks	Y	Y	Y	Y	Y	Y
7 McDermott	Y	Y	Y	Y	Y	Y
8 **Reichert**	Y	Y	Y	N	N	Y
9 Smith	?	?	?	Y	Y	Y
WEST VIRGINIA						
1 Mollohan	Y	Y	Y	Y	Y	Y
2 **Capito**	Y	Y	Y	N	N	Y
3 Rahall	Y	Y	Y	Y	Y	Y
WISCONSIN						
1 **Ryan**	Y	Y	Y	N	N	Y
2 Baldwin	Y	Y	Y	Y	Y	Y
3 Kind	Y	Y	Y	Y	Y	Y
4 Moore	Y	Y	Y	Y	Y	Y
5 **Sensenbrenner**	Y	Y	Y	N	N	N
6 **Petri**	Y	Y	Y	N	N	Y
7 Obey	Y	Y	Y	Y	Y	Y
8 Kagen	Y	Y	Y	Y	Y	Y
WYOMING						
AL **Cubin**	?	?	?	N	N	Y
DELEGATES						
Faleomavaega (A.S.)						
Norton (D.C.)						
Bordallo (Guam)						
Fortuño (P.R.)						
Christensen (V.I.)						

IN THE HOUSE | By Vote Number

373. **HR 5669. Poison Center Support/Passage.** Green, D-Texas, motion to suspend the rules and pass the bill that would reauthorize the Poison Center's national toll-free number, national media campaign and grant program through fiscal 2014. Motion agreed to 405-10: R 182-10; D 223-0 (ND 167-0, SD 56-0). A two-thirds majority of those present and voting (277 in this case) is required for passage under suspension of the rules. June 4, 2008.

374. **HR 3021. School Construction and Modernization/Manager's Amendment.** Miller, D-Calif., amendment that would make charter schools eligible for funding, bar states from counting the grants against schools when calculating state aid eligibility and bar the use of funds in the bill to employ illegal immigrants. Adopted in Committee of the Whole 260-151: R 41-150; D 219-1 (ND 165-1, SD 54-0). June 4, 2008.

375. **HR 3021. School Construction and Modernization/Carbon Offsets.** Ehlers, R-Mich., amendment that would bar the use of funds in the bill to purchase carbon offsets. Adopted in Committee of the Whole 397-17: R 191-2; D 206-15 (ND 154-13, SD 52-2). June 4, 2008.

376. **HR 3021. School Construction and Modernization/Renewable-Energy Generation and Heating Systems.** Welch, D-Vt., amendment that would allow funding authorized by the bill to be used for renewable-energy generation and heating systems, such as solar, photovoltaic, wind, geothermal, biomass and wood pellet systems. Adopted in Committee of the Whole 409-5: R 187-5; D 222-0 (ND 167-0, SD 55-0). June 4, 2008.

377. **HR 3021. School Construction and Modernization/Flooring Materials.** Matheson, D-Utah, amendment that would require schools that installed new flooring to report whether it was made with low- or no-Volatile Organic Compounds or with sustainable materials and whether it was cost-effective. Adopted in Committee of the Whole 266-153: R 40-153; D 226-0 (ND 171-0, SD 55-0). June 4, 2008.

378. **HR 3021. School Construction and Maintenance/ Recommit.** McMorris Rodgers, R-Wash., motion to recommit the bill to the Education and Labor Committee with instructions that it be reported back promptly with language that would allow schools whose energy costs have risen more than 50 percent since January 2007 to use funds authorized in the bill for maintenance. Motion rejected 187-230: R 187-5; D 0-225 (ND 0-170, SD 0-55). June 4, 2008.

	373	374	375	376	377	378
ALABAMA						
1 **Bonner**	Y	N	Y	Y	N	Y
2 **Everett**	Y	N	Y	Y	N	Y
3 **Rogers**	Y	N	Y	Y	N	Y
4 **Aderholt**	Y	?	Y	Y	N	Y
5 Cramer	Y	Y	Y	Y	Y	N
6 **Bachus**	Y	N	Y	Y	N	Y
7 Davis	Y	Y	Y	Y	Y	N
ALASKA						
AL **Young**	Y	N	Y	N	N	Y
ARIZONA						
1 **Renzi**	Y	N	Y	Y	Y	Y
2 **Franks**	Y	N	Y	Y	N	Y
3 **Shadegg**	N	N	Y	Y	N	Y
4 Pastor	Y	Y	Y	Y	Y	N
5 Mitchell	Y	Y	Y	Y	Y	N
6 **Flake**	N	N	Y	N	N	Y
7 Grijalva	Y	?	Y	?	Y	N
8 Giffords	Y	Y	Y	Y	Y	N
ARKANSAS						
1 Berry	Y	Y	Y	Y	Y	N
2 Snyder	Y	Y	Y	Y	Y	N
3 **Boozman**	Y	N	Y	Y	N	Y
4 Ross	Y	Y	Y	Y	Y	N
CALIFORNIA						
1 Thompson	Y	Y	Y	Y	Y	N
2 **Herger**	Y	N	Y	Y	N	Y
3 **Lungren**	Y	N	Y	Y	N	Y
4 **Doolittle**	Y	N	Y	N	N	?
5 Matsui	Y	Y	Y	Y	Y	N
6 Woolsey	Y	Y	N	Y	Y	N
7 Miller, George	Y	Y	Y	Y	Y	N
8 Pelosi						
9 Lee	Y	Y	Y	Y	Y	N
10 Tauscher	Y	Y	Y	Y	Y	N
11 McNerney	Y	Y	Y	Y	Y	N
12 Speier	Y	Y	N	Y	Y	N
13 Stark	Y	Y	Y	Y	Y	N
14 Eshoo	Y	Y	Y	Y	Y	N
15 Honda	Y	Y	Y	Y	Y	N
16 Lofgren	Y	Y	Y	Y	Y	N
17 Farr	Y	Y	Y	Y	Y	N
18 Cardoza	?	Y	Y	Y	Y	N
19 **Radanovich**	Y	N	Y	N	N	Y
20 Costa	Y	Y	Y	Y	Y	N
21 **Nunes**	Y	N	Y	Y	N	Y
22 **McCarthy**	Y	N	Y	Y	N	Y
23 Capps	Y	Y	Y	Y	Y	N
24 **Gallegly**	+	–	+	+	–	+
25 **McKeon**	Y	N	Y	Y	N	Y
26 **Dreier**	Y	N	Y	Y	N	Y
27 Sherman	Y	Y	Y	Y	Y	N
28 Berman	Y	Y	Y	Y	Y	N
29 Schiff	Y	Y	Y	Y	Y	N
30 Waxman	Y	Y	Y	Y	Y	N
31 Becerra	Y	Y	Y	Y	Y	N
32 Solis	Y	Y	Y	Y	Y	N
33 Watson	Y	Y	Y	Y	Y	N
34 Roybal-Allard	Y	Y	Y	Y	Y	N
35 Waters	Y	Y	Y	?	Y	N
36 Harman	Y	Y	Y	Y	Y	N
37 Richardson	Y	Y	Y	Y	Y	N
38 Napolitano	Y	Y	Y	Y	Y	N
39 Sánchez, Linda	Y	Y	Y	Y	Y	N
40 **Royce**	Y	Y	Y	Y	N	Y
41 **Lewis**	Y	N	Y	Y	N	Y
42 **Miller, Gary**	Y	N	Y	Y	N	Y
43 Baca	?	Y	Y	Y	Y	N
44 **Calvert**	Y	N	Y	Y	N	Y
45 **Bono Mack**	Y	N	Y	Y	N	Y
46 **Rohrabacher**	Y	N	Y	Y	N	Y
47 Sanchez, Loretta	Y	Y	Y	Y	Y	N
48 **Campbell**	?	?	?	?	?	?
49 **Issa**	Y	N	Y	Y	N	Y
50 **Bilbray**	Y	N	Y	Y	N	Y
51 Filner	?	+	+	+	+	–
52 **Hunter**	?	?	?	?	?	Y
53 Davis	Y	Y	Y	Y	Y	N

	373	374	375	376	377	378
COLORADO						
1 DeGette	Y	Y	Y	Y	Y	N
2 Udall	Y	Y	Y	Y	Y	N
3 Salazar	Y	Y	Y	Y	Y	N
4 **Musgrave**	Y	N	Y	Y	Y	Y
5 **Lamborn**	Y	N	Y	Y	N	Y
6 **Tancredo**	N	N	Y	N	Y	Y
7 Perlmutter	Y	Y	Y	Y	Y	N
CONNECTICUT						
1 Larson	Y	?	Y	Y	Y	N
2 Courtney	Y	Y	Y	Y	Y	N
3 DeLauro	Y	Y	Y	Y	Y	N
4 **Shays**	Y	Y	Y	Y	Y	N
5 Murphy	Y	Y	Y	Y	Y	N
DELAWARE						
AL **Castle**	Y	N	Y	Y	Y	Y
FLORIDA						
1 **Miller**	Y	N	Y	Y	N	Y
2 Boyd	Y	Y	Y	Y	Y	N
3 Brown	Y	Y	Y	Y	Y	N
4 **Crenshaw**	Y	N	Y	Y	N	Y
5 **Brown-Waite**	Y	N	Y	Y	N	Y
6 **Stearns**	Y	Y	Y	Y	N	Y
7 **Mica**	Y	N	Y	Y	N	Y
8 **Keller**	Y	N	Y	Y	N	Y
9 **Bilirakis**	Y	N	Y	Y	N	Y
10 **Young**	Y	N	Y	Y	N	Y
11 Castor	Y	Y	Y	Y	Y	N
12 **Putnam**	Y	Y	Y	Y	N	Y
13 **Buchanan**	Y	Y	Y	Y	Y	N
14 **Mack**	Y	N	Y	Y	N	Y
15 **Weldon**	Y	N	Y	Y	N	Y
16 Mahoney	Y	Y	Y	Y	Y	N
17 Meek	Y	Y	Y	Y	Y	N
18 **Ros-Lehtinen**	Y	N	Y	Y	N	Y
19 Wexler	Y	Y	Y	Y	Y	N
20 Wasserman Schultz	Y	Y	Y	Y	Y	N
21 **Diaz-Balart, L.**	Y	Y	Y	Y	N	Y
22 Klein	Y	Y	Y	Y	Y	N
23 Hastings	Y	Y	Y	Y	Y	N
24 **Feeney**	Y	N	Y	Y	N	Y
25 **Diaz-Balart, M.**	Y	Y	Y	Y	N	Y
GEORGIA						
1 **Kingston**	N	N	Y	Y	N	Y
2 Bishop	Y	Y	Y	Y	Y	N
3 **Westmoreland**	Y	N	Y	Y	N	Y
4 Johnson	Y	Y	Y	Y	Y	N
5 Lewis	?	?	?	?	?	?
6 **Price**	Y	N	Y	Y	N	Y
7 **Linder**	Y	N	Y	N	N	Y
8 Marshall	Y	Y	Y	Y	Y	N
9 **Deal**	Y	N	Y	Y	N	Y
10 **Broun**	N	N	Y	Y	N	Y
11 **Gingrey**	Y	N	Y	Y	N	Y
12 Barrow	Y	Y	Y	Y	Y	N
13 Scott	Y	Y	Y	Y	Y	N
HAWAII						
1 Abercrombie	Y	Y	Y	Y	Y	N
2 Hirono	Y	Y	Y	Y	Y	N
IDAHO						
1 **Sali**	Y	N	Y	Y	N	Y
2 **Simpson**	Y	N	Y	Y	N	Y
ILLINOIS						
1 Rush	?	?	?	?	?	?
2 Jackson	Y	Y	N	Y	Y	N
3 Lipinski	Y	Y	N	Y	Y	N
4 Gutierrez	Y	Y	?	Y	Y	N
5 Emanuel	Y	Y	N	Y	Y	N
6 **Roskam**	Y	N	Y	Y	N	Y
7 Davis	Y	Y	Y	Y	Y	N
8 Bean	Y	Y	Y	Y	Y	N
9 Schakowsky	Y	Y	N	Y	Y	N
10 **Kirk**	Y	Y	N	Y	Y	Y
11 **Weller**	Y	Y	Y	Y	Y	Y
12 Costello	Y	Y	N	Y	Y	N
13 **Biggert**	Y	N	Y	Y	Y	Y
14 Foster	Y	Y	Y	Y	Y	N
15 **Johnson**	Y	Y	Y	Y	Y	N

KEY	**Republicans**	Democrats		
Y Voted for (yea)		X Paired against		C Voted "present" to avoid possible conflict of interest
# Paired for		– Announced against		
+ Announced for		P Voted "present"		? Did not vote or otherwise make a position known
N Voted against (nay)				

ND Northern Democrats, SD Southern Democrats
Southern states: Ala., Ark., Fla., Ga., Ky., La., Miss., N.C., Okla., S.C., Tenn., Texas, Va.

	373	374	375	376	377	378
16 **Manzullo**	Y	N	Y	Y	N	Y
17 Hare	Y	Y	Y	Y	Y	N
18 **LaHood**	Y	Y	Y	Y	Y	Y
19 **Shimkus**	Y	Y	Y	Y	N	Y
INDIANA						
1 Visclosky	Y	Y	Y	Y	Y	N
2 Donnelly	Y	Y	Y	Y	Y	N
3 **Souder**	Y	N	Y	Y	N	N
4 **Buyer**	Y	N	Y	Y	N	Y
5 **Burton**	Y	N	Y	Y	N	Y
6 **Pence**	N	N	Y	Y	N	Y
7 Carson, A.	Y	Y	Y	Y	Y	N
8 Ellsworth	Y	Y	Y	Y	Y	N
9 Hill	Y	Y	Y	Y	Y	N
IOWA						
1 Braley	Y	Y	Y	Y	Y	N
2 Loebsack	Y	Y	Y	Y	Y	N
3 Boswell	Y	Y	Y	Y	Y	N
4 **Latham**	Y	N	Y	Y	N	Y
5 **King**	Y	N	Y	Y	N	Y
KANSAS						
1 **Moran**	Y	N	Y	Y	N	Y
2 Boyda	Y	Y	Y	Y	Y	N
3 Moore	Y	Y	Y	Y	Y	N
4 **Tiahrt**	Y	N	Y	Y	N	Y
KENTUCKY						
1 **Whitfield**	Y	Y	Y	Y	N	Y
2 **Lewis**	Y	N	Y	Y	N	Y
3 Yarmuth	Y	Y	Y	Y	Y	N
4 **Davis**	Y	N	Y	Y	N	Y
5 **Rogers**	Y	N	Y	Y	N	Y
6 Chandler	Y	Y	Y	Y	Y	N
LOUISIANA						
1 **Scalise**	Y	N	Y	Y	N	Y
2 Jefferson	Y	Y	Y	Y	Y	N
3 Melancon	Y	Y	Y	Y	Y	N
4 **McCrery**	Y	?	?	?	?	?
5 **Alexander**	Y	N	Y	Y	N	Y
6 Cazayoux	Y	Y	Y	Y	Y	N
7 **Boustany**	Y	N	Y	Y	N	Y
MAINE						
1 Allen	Y	Y	Y	Y	Y	N
2 Michaud	Y	Y	Y	Y	Y	N
MARYLAND						
1 **Gilchrest**	Y	?	?	?	?	?
2 Ruppersberger	Y	Y	Y	Y	Y	N
3 Sarbanes	Y	Y	Y	Y	Y	N
4 Vacant						
5 Hoyer	Y	Y	Y	Y	Y	N
6 **Bartlett**	Y	N	Y	Y	N	Y
7 Cummings	Y	?	Y	Y	Y	N
8 Van Hollen	Y	?	?	?	?	?
MASSACHUSETTS						
1 Olver	Y	Y	Y	Y	Y	N
2 Neal	Y	Y	Y	Y	Y	N
3 McGovern	Y	Y	Y	Y	Y	N
4 Frank	Y	Y	Y	Y	Y	N
5 Tsongas	Y	Y	Y	Y	Y	N
6 Tierney	Y	Y	Y	Y	Y	N
7 Markey	Y	Y	Y	Y	Y	N
8 Capuano	Y	Y	Y	Y	Y	N
9 Lynch	Y	Y	Y	Y	Y	N
10 Delahunt	Y	Y	Y	Y	Y	N
MICHIGAN						
1 Stupak	Y	Y	Y	Y	Y	N
2 **Hoekstra**	Y	N	Y	Y	N	Y
3 **Ehlers**	Y	Y	Y	Y	Y	Y
4 **Camp**	Y	N	Y	Y	N	Y
5 Kildee	Y	Y	Y	Y	Y	N
6 **Upton**	Y	Y	Y	Y	N	Y
7 **Walberg**	Y	N	Y	Y	N	Y
8 **Rogers**	Y	N	Y	Y	N	Y
9 **Knollenberg**	Y	N	Y	Y	N	Y
10 **Miller**	Y	Y	Y	Y	Y	Y
11 **McCotter**	Y	N	Y	Y	N	Y
12 Levin	Y	Y	Y	Y	Y	N
13 Kilpatrick	Y	?	Y	Y	Y	N
14 Conyers	Y	Y	Y	Y	Y	N
15 Dingell	Y	Y	Y	Y	Y	N
MINNESOTA						
1 Walz	Y	Y	Y	Y	Y	N
2 **Kline**	Y	N	Y	Y	N	Y
3 **Ramstad**	Y	Y	Y	Y	Y	Y
4 McCollum	Y	Y	Y	Y	Y	N
5 Ellison	Y	Y	Y	Y	Y	N
6 **Bachmann**	Y	N	Y	Y	N	Y
7 Peterson	Y	Y	Y	Y	Y	N
8 Oberstar	Y	Y	Y	Y	Y	N
MISSISSIPPI						
1 Childers	Y	Y	Y	Y	Y	N
2 Thompson	Y	Y	Y	Y	Y	N
3 **Pickering**	Y	N	Y	Y	N	Y
4 Taylor	Y	Y	Y	Y	Y	N
MISSOURI						
1 Clay	Y	Y	N	Y	Y	N
2 **Akin**	Y	N	Y	Y	N	Y
3 Carnahan	Y	Y	Y	Y	Y	N
4 Skelton	Y	Y	Y	Y	Y	N
5 Cleaver	Y	Y	Y	Y	Y	N
6 **Graves**	Y	N	Y	Y	N	Y
7 **Blunt**	Y	N	Y	Y	N	Y
8 **Emerson**	Y	N	Y	Y	N	Y
9 **Hulshof**	Y	N	Y	Y	N	Y
MONTANA						
AL **Rehberg**	Y	N	Y	Y	N	Y
NEBRASKA						
1 **Fortenberry**	Y	Y	Y	Y	Y	N
2 **Terry**	Y	N	Y	Y	Y	Y
3 **Smith**	Y	N	Y	Y	N	Y
NEVADA						
1 Berkley	Y	Y	Y	Y	Y	N
2 **Heller**	Y	N	Y	Y	N	Y
3 **Porter**	Y	Y	Y	Y	Y	Y
NEW HAMPSHIRE						
1 Shea-Porter	Y	Y	Y	Y	Y	N
2 Hodes	Y	Y	Y	Y	Y	N
NEW JERSEY						
1 Andrews	?	?	?	?	?	?
2 **LoBiondo**	Y	Y	Y	Y	Y	Y
3 **Saxton**	?	N	Y	Y	Y	Y
4 **Smith**	Y	Y	Y	Y	Y	Y
5 **Garrett**	Y	N	Y	Y	N	N
6 Pallone	Y	Y	Y	Y	Y	N
7 **Ferguson**	Y	N	Y	Y	Y	Y
8 Pascrell	Y	Y	Y	Y	Y	N
9 Rothman	Y	Y	Y	Y	Y	N
10 Payne	Y	Y	Y	Y	Y	N
11 **Frelinghuysen**	Y	N	Y	Y	Y	Y
12 Holt	Y	Y	Y	Y	Y	N
13 Sires	Y	Y	Y	Y	Y	N
NEW MEXICO						
1 **Wilson**	?	Y	Y	Y	N	Y
2 **Pearce**	Y	N	Y	Y	Y	Y
3 Udall	?	Y	Y	Y	Y	N
NEW YORK						
1 Bishop	Y	Y	Y	Y	Y	N
2 Israel	Y	Y	Y	Y	Y	N
3 **King**	Y	Y	Y	Y	N	Y
4 McCarthy	Y	Y	Y	?	Y	N
5 Ackerman	Y	Y	Y	Y	Y	N
6 Meeks	?	Y	?	Y	Y	N
7 Crowley	Y	Y	Y	Y	Y	N
8 Nadler	Y	Y	Y	Y	Y	N
9 Weiner	Y	Y	N	Y	Y	N
10 Towns	Y	Y	Y	Y	Y	N
11 Clarke	Y	Y	?	Y	Y	N
12 Velázquez	Y	Y	Y	?	Y	N
13 **Fossella**	Y	Y	Y	Y	N	Y
14 Maloney	Y	Y	Y	Y	Y	N
15 Rangel	Y	Y	?	Y	Y	N
16 Serrano	Y	Y	Y	Y	Y	N
17 Engel	Y	Y	Y	Y	Y	N
18 Lowey	Y	Y	Y	Y	Y	N
19 Hall	Y	Y	Y	Y	Y	N
20 Gillibrand	?	?	?	?	?	?
21 McNulty	Y	Y	Y	Y	Y	N
22 Hinchey	Y	Y	Y	Y	Y	N
23 **McHugh**	Y	Y	Y	Y	N	Y
24 Arcuri	Y	Y	Y	Y	Y	N
25 **Walsh**	Y	Y	Y	Y	N	Y
26 **Reynolds**	Y	N	Y	Y	N	Y
27 Higgins	Y	Y	Y	Y	Y	N
28 Slaughter	Y	Y	Y	Y	Y	N
29 **Kuhl**	Y	Y	Y	Y	Y	Y
NORTH CAROLINA						
1 Butterfield	Y	Y	Y	Y	Y	N
2 Etheridge	Y	Y	Y	Y	Y	N
3 **Jones**	Y	N	Y	Y	N	Y
4 Price	Y	Y	Y	Y	Y	N
5 **Foxx**	Y	N	Y	Y	N	Y
6 **Coble**	Y	N	Y	Y	N	Y
7 McIntyre	Y	Y	Y	Y	Y	N
8 **Hayes**	Y	N	Y	Y	Y	Y
9 **Myrick**	Y	N	Y	Y	N	Y
10 **McHenry**	Y	N	Y	Y	Y	Y
11 Shuler	?	?	?	?	?	?
12 Watt	Y	Y	Y	Y	Y	N
13 Miller	Y	Y	Y	Y	Y	N
NORTH DAKOTA						
AL Pomeroy	Y	+	Y	Y	Y	N
OHIO						
1 **Chabot**	?	?	?	?	?	?
2 **Schmidt**	Y	N	Y	Y	N	Y
3 **Turner**	Y	Y	Y	Y	Y	Y
4 **Jordan**	Y	N	Y	Y	N	Y
5 **Latta**	Y	N	Y	Y	N	Y
6 Wilson	Y	Y	Y	Y	Y	N
7 **Hobson**	Y	Y	Y	Y	N	Y
8 **Boehner**	Y	N	Y	Y	N	Y
9 Kaptur	Y	Y	Y	Y	Y	N
10 Kucinich	Y	N	Y	Y	Y	N
11 Tubbs Jones	Y	Y	Y	Y	Y	N
12 **Tiberi**	Y	N	Y	Y	N	Y
13 Sutton	Y	Y	Y	Y	Y	N
14 **LaTourette**	Y	Y	Y	Y	Y	Y
15 **Pryce**	?	?	?	?	?	?
16 **Regula**	Y	N	Y	Y	N	Y
17 Ryan	Y	Y	Y	Y	Y	N
18 Space	Y	Y	Y	Y	Y	N
OKLAHOMA						
1 **Sullivan**	Y	N	Y	Y	N	Y
2 Boren	Y	Y	Y	Y	Y	N
3 **Lucas**	Y	N	Y	Y	N	Y
4 **Cole**	Y	N	Y	Y	N	Y
5 **Fallin**	Y	N	Y	Y	N	Y
OREGON						
1 Wu	Y	Y	Y	Y	Y	N
2 **Walden**	Y	N	Y	Y	N	Y
3 Blumenauer	Y	Y	N	Y	Y	N
4 DeFazio	Y	Y	Y	Y	Y	N
5 Hooley	Y	Y	Y	Y	Y	N
PENNSYLVANIA						
1 Brady	Y	Y	Y	Y	Y	N
2 Fattah	Y	Y	Y	Y	Y	N
3 **English**	Y	Y	Y	Y	Y	N
4 Altmire	Y	Y	Y	Y	Y	N
5 **Peterson**	Y	Y	Y	Y	N	Y
6 **Gerlach**	Y	Y	Y	Y	Y	Y
7 Sestak	Y	Y	Y	Y	Y	N
8 Murphy, P.	Y	Y	Y	Y	Y	N
9 **Shuster**	Y	N	Y	Y	N	Y
10 Carney	Y	?	?	?	?	N
11 Kanjorski	Y	Y	Y	Y	Y	N
12 Murtha	Y	Y	Y	Y	Y	N
13 Schwartz	Y	Y	Y	Y	Y	N
14 Doyle	Y	Y	Y	Y	Y	N
15 **Dent**	Y	Y	Y	Y	Y	Y
16 **Pitts**	Y	N	Y	Y	N	Y
17 Holden	Y	Y	Y	Y	Y	N
18 **Murphy, T.**	Y	Y	Y	Y	Y	Y
19 **Platts**	Y	Y	Y	Y	Y	N
RHODE ISLAND						
1 Kennedy	Y	Y	Y	Y	Y	N
2 Langevin	Y	Y	Y	Y	Y	N
SOUTH CAROLINA						
1 **Brown**	Y	N	Y	Y	N	Y
2 **Wilson**	Y	N	Y	Y	N	Y
3 **Barrett**	Y	N	Y	Y	N	Y
4 **Inglis**	Y	N	Y	Y	N	Y
5 Spratt	Y	Y	Y	Y	Y	N
6 Clyburn	Y	Y	Y	Y	Y	N
SOUTH DAKOTA						
AL Herseth Sandlin	Y	Y	Y	Y	Y	N
TENNESSEE						
1 **Davis, D.**	Y	N	Y	Y	N	Y
2 **Duncan**	N	N	Y	Y	N	Y
3 **Wamp**	Y	N	Y	Y	N	Y
4 Davis, L.	Y	Y	Y	Y	Y	N
5 Cooper	Y	Y	Y	Y	Y	N
6 Gordon	Y	Y	Y	Y	Y	N
7 **Blackburn**	Y	N	Y	Y	N	Y
8 Tanner	Y	Y	Y	Y	Y	N
9 Cohen	Y	Y	Y	Y	Y	N
TEXAS						
1 **Gohmert**	Y	N	Y	Y	N	Y
2 **Poe**	N	N	Y	Y	N	Y
3 **Johnson, S.**	Y	N	Y	Y	Y	Y
4 **Hall**	Y	N	Y	Y	N	Y
5 **Hensarling**	Y	N	Y	Y	N	Y
6 **Barton**	Y	N	Y	Y	N	Y
7 **Culberson**	Y	N	Y	Y	Y	Y
8 **Brady**	Y	N	Y	Y	N	Y
9 Green, A.	Y	Y	Y	Y	Y	N
10 **McCaul**	Y	Y	Y	Y	Y	Y
11 **Conaway**	Y	N	Y	Y	N	Y
12 **Granger**	Y	N	Y	Y	N	Y
13 **Thornberry**	Y	N	Y	Y	N	Y
14 **Paul**	N	N	Y	N	N	Y
15 Hinojosa	Y	Y	Y	Y	Y	N
16 Reyes	Y	Y	Y	Y	Y	N
17 Edwards	Y	Y	Y	Y	Y	N
18 Jackson Lee	?	?	?	?	?	?
19 **Neugebauer**	Y	N	Y	Y	N	Y
20 Gonzalez	Y	Y	N	Y	Y	N
21 **Smith**	Y	N	Y	Y	N	Y
22 Lampson	Y	Y	Y	Y	Y	N
23 Rodriguez	Y	Y	Y	Y	Y	N
24 **Marchant**	Y	N	Y	N	N	Y
25 Doggett	Y	Y	Y	Y	Y	N
26 **Burgess**	Y	N	Y	Y	N	Y
27 Ortiz	Y	Y	Y	Y	Y	N
28 Cuellar	Y	Y	Y	Y	Y	N
29 Green, G.	Y	Y	Y	Y	Y	N
30 Johnson, E.	Y	Y	N	Y	Y	N
31 **Carter**	Y	N	Y	Y	N	Y
32 **Sessions**	Y	N	Y	Y	N	Y
UTAH						
1 **Bishop**	Y	?	Y	?	Y	Y
2 Matheson	Y	Y	Y	Y	Y	N
3 **Cannon**	Y	N	Y	Y	N	Y
VERMONT						
AL Welch	Y	Y	Y	Y	Y	N
VIRGINIA						
1 **Wittman**	Y	N	Y	Y	N	Y
2 **Drake**	Y	N	Y	Y	N	Y
3 Scott	Y	Y	Y	Y	Y	N
4 **Forbes**	Y	N	Y	Y	N	Y
5 **Goode**	Y	N	Y	Y	N	Y
6 **Goodlatte**	Y	N	Y	Y	N	Y
7 **Cantor**	Y	N	Y	Y	N	Y
8 Moran	Y	?	?	Y	Y	N
9 Boucher	Y	?	?	?	?	?
10 **Wolf**	Y	N	Y	Y	N	Y
11 **Davis**	Y	Y	Y	Y	N	Y
WASHINGTON						
1 Inslee	Y	Y	Y	Y	Y	N
2 Larsen	Y	Y	Y	Y	Y	N
3 Baird	Y	Y	Y	Y	Y	N
4 **Hastings**	Y	N	Y	Y	N	Y
5 **McMorris Rodgers**	Y	N	Y	Y	N	Y
6 Dicks	Y	Y	Y	Y	Y	N
7 McDermott	Y	Y	Y	Y	Y	N
8 **Reichert**	Y	Y	Y	Y	Y	Y
9 Smith	Y	Y	Y	Y	Y	N
WEST VIRGINIA						
1 Mollohan	Y	Y	Y	Y	Y	N
2 **Capito**	Y	Y	Y	Y	Y	Y
3 Rahall	Y	Y	Y	Y	Y	N
WISCONSIN						
1 **Ryan**	Y	N	Y	Y	N	Y
2 Baldwin	Y	Y	N	Y	Y	N
3 Kind	Y	Y	Y	Y	Y	N
4 Moore	Y	Y	N	Y	Y	N
5 **Sensenbrenner**	N	N	Y	Y	N	Y
6 **Petri**	Y	N	Y	Y	N	Y
7 Obey	Y	Y	Y	Y	Y	N
8 Kagen	Y	Y	Y	Y	Y	N
WYOMING						
AL **Cubin**	Y	N	Y	Y	N	Y
DELEGATES						
Faleomavaega (A.S.)		?	?	?	?	
Norton (D.C.)		?	?	?	?	
Bordallo (Guam)		Y	Y	Y	Y	
Fortuño (P.R.)		Y	Y	Y	Y	
Christensen (V.I.)		Y	Y	Y	Y	

IN THE HOUSE | By Vote Number

379. HR 3021. School Construction and Modernization/Passage.
Passage of the bill that would authorize $6.4 billion in fiscal 2009 to modernize and make repairs to public schools, and $100 million per year in fiscal 2009 through 2013 for repairs to public schools damaged by hurricanes Katrina and Rita. It would allow funds to be used for repairs such as eradicating asbestos and lead-based paint, replacing electric wiring and plumbing, and purchasing technology, and require all repairs to be carried out according to "green" building standards, such as those set by the government's Energy Star rating system. Passed 250-164: R 27-164; D 223-0 (ND 168-0, SD 55-0). A "nay" was a vote in support of the president's position. June 4, 2008.

380. HR 5540. Chesapeake Bay Grant Program/Previous Question.
Arcuri, D-N.Y., motion to order the previous question (thus ending debate and possibility of amendment) on adoption of the rule (H Res 1233) to provide for House floor consideration of the bill that would permanently reauthorize a program to award grants to parks, volunteer groups, wildlife refuges, historic sites, museums and water trails throughout the Chesapeake Bay area. Motion agreed to 221-194: R 0-192; D 221-2 (ND 167-1, SD 54-1). June 5, 2008.

381. HR 5540. Chesapeake Bay Grant Program/Rule. Adoption of the rule (H Res 1233) that would provide for House floor consideration of the bill that would permanently reauthorize a program to award grants to parks, volunteer groups, wildlife refuges, historic sites, museums and water trails throughout the Chesapeake Bay area. Adopted 225-195: R 0-195; D 225-0 (ND 170-0, SD 55-0). June 5, 2008.

382. S Con Res 70. Fiscal 2009 Budget Resolution/Adoption.
Adoption of the conference report on the concurrent resolution that would allow up to $1 trillion in discretionary spending for fiscal 2009, plus $70 billion for the wars in Iraq and Afghanistan, and $5.8 billion for hurricane recovery. It would assume $1.9 trillion in mandatory spending and allow for the statutory debt limit to increase by $800 billion to $10.615 trillion. It would create a "trigger" mechanism that would reinforce pay-as-you-go rules in the House. The measure assumes a one-year alternative minimum tax "patch" that would be offset. It also would create a 60-vote point of order in the Senate against legislation that increases the deficit by $10 billion in a year. Adopted 214-210: R 0-196; D 214-14 (ND 164-9, SD 50-5). June 5, 2008.

	379	380	381	382
ALABAMA				
1 **Bonner**	N	N	N	N
2 **Everett**	N	N	?	?
3 **Rogers**	N	N	N	N
4 **Aderholt**	N	N	N	N
5 Cramer	Y	Y	Y	Y
6 **Bachus**	N	?	N	N
7 Davis	Y	Y	Y	Y
ALASKA				
AL **Young**	N	N	N	N
ARIZONA				
1 **Renzi**	Y	?	N	N
2 **Franks**	N	N	N	N
3 **Shadegg**	N	N	N	N
4 Pastor	Y	Y	Y	Y
5 Mitchell	Y	Y	Y	N
6 **Flake**	N	N	N	N
7 Grijalva	Y	Y	Y	Y
8 Giffords	Y	Y	N	Y
ARKANSAS				
1 Berry	Y	Y	Y	Y
2 Snyder	Y	Y	Y	Y
3 **Boozman**	N	N	N	N
4 Ross	Y	Y	Y	Y
CALIFORNIA				
1 Thompson	Y	Y	Y	Y
2 **Herger**	N	N	N	N
3 **Lungren**	N	N	N	N
4 **Doolittle**	?	N	N	N
5 Matsui	Y	Y	Y	Y
6 Woolsey	Y	Y	Y	Y
7 Miller, George	Y	Y	Y	Y
8 Pelosi				Y
9 Lee	Y	Y	Y	Y
10 Tauscher	Y	Y	Y	Y
11 McNerney	Y	Y	Y	Y
12 Speier	Y	Y	Y	Y
13 Stark	Y	Y	Y	Y
14 Eshoo	Y	Y	Y	Y
15 Honda	Y	Y	Y	Y
16 Lofgren	Y	Y	Y	Y
17 Farr	Y	Y	Y	Y
18 Cardoza	Y	?	Y	Y
19 **Radanovich**	N	N	N	N
20 Costa	Y	Y	Y	Y
21 **Nunes**	N	N	N	N
22 **McCarthy**	N	N	N	N
23 Capps	Y	Y	Y	Y
24 **Gallegly**	–	N	N	N
25 **McKeon**	N	N	N	N
26 **Dreier**	N	N	N	N
27 Sherman	Y	Y	Y	Y
28 Berman	Y	Y	Y	Y
29 Schiff	Y	Y	Y	Y
30 Waxman	Y	Y	Y	Y
31 Becerra	Y	Y	Y	Y
32 Solis	Y	Y	Y	Y
33 Watson	Y	Y	Y	Y
34 Roybal-Allard	Y	Y	Y	Y
35 Waters	Y	Y	Y	Y
36 Harman	Y	Y	Y	Y
37 Richardson	Y	Y	Y	Y
38 Napolitano	Y	Y	Y	Y
39 Sánchez, Linda	Y	Y	Y	Y
40 **Royce**	N	N	N	N
41 **Lewis**	N	N	N	N
42 **Miller, Gary**	N	N	N	N
43 Baca	Y	Y	Y	Y
44 **Calvert**	N	N	N	N
45 **Bono Mack**	N	N	N	N
46 **Rohrabacher**	N	N	N	N
47 Sanchez, Loretta	Y	Y	Y	Y
48 **Campbell**	?	?	?	?
49 **Issa**	N	N	N	N
50 **Bilbray**	N	N	N	N
51 Filner	+	Y	Y	Y
52 **Hunter**	N	N	N	N
53 Davis	Y	Y	Y	Y

	379	380	381	382
COLORADO				
1 DeGette	Y	Y	Y	Y
2 Udall	Y	Y	Y	Y
3 Salazar	Y	Y	Y	Y
4 **Musgrave**	N	N	N	N
5 **Lamborn**	N	N	N	N
6 **Tancredo**	N	N	N	N
7 Perlmutter	Y	Y	Y	Y
CONNECTICUT				
1 Larson	Y	Y	Y	Y
2 Courtney	Y	Y	Y	Y
3 DeLauro	Y	Y	Y	Y
4 **Shays**	Y	N	N	N
5 Murphy	Y	Y	Y	Y
DELAWARE				
AL **Castle**	N	N	N	N
FLORIDA				
1 **Miller**	N	N	N	N
2 Boyd	Y	Y	Y	Y
3 Brown	Y	Y	Y	Y
4 **Crenshaw**	N	N	N	N
5 **Brown-Waite**	N	N	N	N
6 **Stearns**	N	N	N	N
7 **Mica**	N	N	N	N
8 **Keller**	Y	N	N	N
9 **Bilirakis**	N	N	N	N
10 **Young**	N	N	N	N
11 Castor	Y	Y	Y	Y
12 **Putnam**	N	N	N	N
13 **Buchanan**	N	N	N	N
14 **Mack**	N	N	N	N
15 **Weldon**	N	N	N	N
16 Mahoney	Y	Y	Y	Y
17 Meek	Y	Y	Y	Y
18 **Ros-Lehtinen**	Y	N	N	N
19 Wexler	Y	Y	Y	Y
20 Wasserman Schultz	Y	Y	Y	Y
21 **Diaz-Balart, L.**	Y	N	N	N
22 Klein	Y	Y	Y	Y
23 Hastings	Y	Y	Y	Y
24 **Feeney**	Y	N	N	N
25 **Diaz-Balart, M.**	Y	N	N	N
GEORGIA				
1 **Kingston**	N	N	N	N
2 Bishop	Y	Y	Y	Y
3 **Westmoreland**	N	N	N	N
4 Johnson	Y	Y	Y	Y
5 Lewis	?	Y	Y	Y
6 **Price**	N	N	N	N
7 **Linder**	N	N	N	N
8 Marshall	Y	?	?	–
9 **Deal**	N	N	N	N
10 **Broun**	N	N	N	N
11 **Gingrey**	N	N	N	N
12 Barrow	Y	Y	Y	N
13 Scott	Y	Y	Y	Y
HAWAII				
1 Abercrombie	Y	Y	Y	Y
2 Hirono	Y	Y	Y	Y
IDAHO				
1 **Sali**	N	N	N	N
2 **Simpson**	N	N	N	N
ILLINOIS				
1 Rush	?	?	?	?
2 Jackson	Y	Y	Y	Y
3 Lipinski	Y	Y	Y	Y
4 Gutierrez	Y	Y	Y	Y
5 Emanuel	Y	Y	Y	Y
6 **Roskam**	N	N	N	N
7 Davis	Y	Y	Y	Y
8 Bean	Y	+	+	–
9 Schakowsky	Y	Y	Y	Y
10 **Kirk**	Y	N	N	N
11 **Weller**	Y	N	N	N
12 Costello	Y	Y	Y	Y
13 **Biggert**	N	N	N	N
14 Foster	Y	Y	Y	N
15 **Johnson**	Y	N	N	N

KEY Republicans Democrats

Y Voted for (yea)	**X** Paired against
# Paired for	**–** Announced against
+ Announced for	**P** Voted "present"
N Voted against (nay)	

C Voted "present" to avoid possible conflict of interest
? Did not vote or otherwise make a position known

ND Northern Democrats, SD Southern Democrats
Southern states: Ala., Ark., Fla., Ga., Ky., La., Miss., N.C., Okla., S.C., Tenn., Texas, Va.

	379	380	381	382
16 Manzullo	N	N	N	N
17 Hare	Y	Y	Y	Y
18 LaHood	N	N	N	N
19 Shimkus	N	N	N	N
INDIANA				
1 Visclosky	Y	Y	Y	Y
2 Donnelly	Y	N	Y	N
3 Souder	N	N	N	N
4 Buyer	N	N	N	N
5 Burton	N	N	N	N
6 Pence	N	N	N	N
7 Carson, A.	Y	Y	Y	Y
8 Ellsworth	Y	Y	Y	N
9 Hill	Y	Y	Y	N
IOWA				
1 Braley	+	Y	Y	Y
2 Loebsack	Y	Y	Y	Y
3 Boswell	Y	Y	Y	Y
4 Latham	N	N	N	N
5 King	N	N	N	N
KANSAS				
1 Moran	N	N	N	N
2 Boyda	Y	Y	Y	Y
3 Moore	Y	Y	Y	Y
4 Tiahrt	N	N	N	N
KENTUCKY				
1 Whitfield	Y	N	N	N
2 Lewis	N	N	N	N
3 Yarmuth	Y	Y	Y	Y
4 Davis	N	N	N	N
5 Rogers	N	N	N	N
6 Chandler	Y	Y	Y	Y
LOUISIANA				
1 Scalise	N	N	N	N
2 Jefferson	Y	Y	Y	Y
3 Melancon	Y	Y	Y	Y
4 McCrery	?	N	N	N
5 Alexander	N	N	N	N
6 Cazayoux	Y	Y	Y	N
7 Boustany	N	N	N	N
MAINE				
1 Allen	Y	Y	Y	Y
2 Michaud	Y	Y	Y	Y
MARYLAND				
1 Gilchrest	?	N	N	N
2 Ruppersberger	Y	Y	Y	Y
3 Sarbanes	Y	Y	Y	Y
4 Vacant				
5 Hoyer	Y	Y	Y	Y
6 Bartlett	N	N	N	N
7 Cummings	Y	Y	Y	Y
8 Van Hollen	?	Y	Y	Y
MASSACHUSETTS				
1 Olver	Y	Y	Y	Y
2 Neal	Y	Y	Y	Y
3 McGovern	Y	Y	Y	Y
4 Frank	Y	Y	?	Y
5 Tsongas	Y	Y	Y	Y
6 Tierney	Y	Y	Y	Y
7 Markey	Y	Y	Y	Y
8 Capuano	Y	Y	Y	Y
9 Lynch	Y	Y	Y	Y
10 Delahunt	Y	Y	Y	Y
MICHIGAN				
1 Stupak	Y	Y	Y	Y
2 Hoekstra	N	N	N	N
3 Ehlers	N	N	N	N
4 Camp	N	N	N	N
5 Kildee	Y	Y	Y	Y
6 Upton	N	N	N	N
7 Walberg	N	N	N	N
8 Rogers	N	N	N	N
9 Knollenberg	N	Y	N	N
10 Miller	Y	N	N	N
11 McCotter	N	N	N	N
12 Levin	Y	Y	Y	Y
13 Kilpatrick	Y	Y	Y	Y
14 Conyers	Y	Y	Y	Y
15 Dingell	Y	?	?	Y
MINNESOTA				
1 Walz	Y	Y	Y	Y
2 Kline	N	N	N	N
3 Ramstad	N	N	N	N
4 McCollum	Y	Y	Y	Y

	379	380	381	382
5 Ellison	+	Y	Y	Y
6 Bachmann	N	N	N	N
7 Peterson	Y	Y	Y	Y
8 Oberstar	Y	Y	Y	Y
MISSISSIPPI				
1 Childers	Y	Y	Y	N
2 Thompson	Y	Y	Y	Y
3 Pickering	N	N	N	N
4 Taylor	Y	Y	Y	Y
MISSOURI				
1 Clay	Y	Y	Y	Y
2 Akin	N	N	N	N
3 Carnahan	Y	Y	Y	Y
4 Skelton	Y	Y	Y	Y
5 Cleaver	Y	Y	Y	Y
6 Graves	N	N	N	N
7 Blunt	N	N	N	N
8 Emerson	N	N	N	N
9 Hulshof	N	N	N	N
MONTANA				
AL Rehberg	N	N	N	N
NEBRASKA				
1 Fortenberry	N	N	N	N
2 Terry	N	N	N	N
3 Smith	N	N	N	N
NEVADA				
1 Berkley	Y	Y	Y	Y
2 Heller	N	N	N	N
3 Porter	Y	N	N	N
NEW HAMPSHIRE				
1 Shea-Porter	Y	Y	Y	Y
2 Hodes	Y	Y	Y	Y
NEW JERSEY				
1 Andrews	?	Y	Y	Y
2 LoBiondo	Y	N	N	N
3 Saxton	Y	N	N	N
4 Smith	Y	N	N	N
5 Garrett	N	?	N	N
6 Pallone	Y	Y	Y	Y
7 Ferguson	N	N	N	N
8 Pascrell	Y	Y	Y	Y
9 Rothman	Y	Y	Y	Y
10 Payne	Y	Y	Y	Y
11 Frelinghuysen	N	N	N	N
12 Holt	Y	Y	Y	Y
13 Sires	Y	Y	Y	Y
NEW MEXICO				
1 Wilson	N	N	N	N
2 Pearce	N	N	N	N
3 Udall	Y	Y	Y	Y
NEW YORK				
1 Bishop	Y	Y	Y	Y
2 Israel	Y	Y	Y	Y
3 King	N	N	N	N
4 McCarthy	Y	Y	Y	Y
5 Ackerman	Y	Y	Y	Y
6 Meeks	Y	Y	Y	Y
7 Crowley	Y	Y	Y	Y
8 Nadler	Y	Y	Y	Y
9 Weiner	Y	Y	Y	Y
10 Towns	Y	Y	Y	Y
11 Clarke	Y	Y	Y	Y
12 Velázquez	Y	Y	Y	Y
13 Fossella	N	N	N	N
14 Maloney	Y	Y	Y	Y
15 Rangel	Y	Y	Y	Y
16 Serrano	Y	Y	Y	Y
17 Engel	Y	Y	Y	Y
18 Lowey	Y	Y	Y	Y
19 Hall	Y	Y	Y	Y
20 Gillibrand	?	?	Y	Y
21 McNulty	Y	Y	Y	Y
22 Hinchey	Y	?	Y	Y
23 McHugh	Y	N	N	N
24 Arcuri	Y	Y	Y	Y
25 Walsh	N	N	N	N
26 Reynolds	N	N	N	N
27 Higgins	Y	Y	Y	Y
28 Slaughter	Y	Y	Y	Y
29 Kuhl	N	N	N	N
NORTH CAROLINA				
1 Butterfield	Y	Y	Y	Y
2 Etheridge	Y	Y	Y	Y
3 Jones	Y	Y	Y	Y
4 Price	Y	Y	Y	Y

	379	380	381	382
5 Foxx	N	N	N	N
6 Coble	N	N	N	N
7 McIntyre	Y	Y	Y	Y
8 Hayes	Y	N	N	N
9 Myrick	N	N	N	N
10 McHenry	N	N	N	N
11 Shuler	?	?	?	?
12 Watt	Y	Y	Y	Y
13 Miller	Y	Y	Y	Y
NORTH DAKOTA				
AL Pomeroy	Y	Y	Y	Y
OHIO				
1 Chabot	?	N	N	N
2 Schmidt	N	N	N	N
3 Turner	N	N	N	N
4 Jordan	N	N	N	N
5 Latta	N	N	N	N
6 Wilson	Y	Y	Y	Y
7 Hobson	N	N	N	N
8 Boehner	N	N	N	N
9 Kaptur	Y	Y	Y	Y
10 Kucinich	Y	Y	Y	Y
11 Tubbs Jones	Y	Y	Y	Y
12 Tiberi	N	N	N	N
13 Sutton	Y	Y	Y	Y
14 LaTourette	Y	N	N	N
15 Pryce	?	?	?	
16 Regula	N	N	N	N
17 Ryan	Y	Y	Y	Y
18 Space	Y	Y	Y	Y
OKLAHOMA				
1 Sullivan	N	N	N	N
2 Boren	Y	Y	Y	N
3 Lucas	N	N	N	N
4 Cole	N	N	N	N
5 Fallin	N	N	N	N
OREGON				
1 Wu	Y	Y	Y	Y
2 Walden	N	N	N	N
3 Blumenauer	Y	Y	Y	Y
4 DeFazio	Y	Y	Y	Y
5 Hooley	Y	Y	Y	Y
PENNSYLVANIA				
1 Brady	Y	Y	Y	Y
2 Fattah	Y	?	?	?
3 English	Y	N	N	N
4 Altmire	Y	Y	Y	Y
5 Peterson	N	N	N	N
6 Gerlach	Y	N	N	N
7 Sestak	Y	Y	Y	Y
8 Murphy, P.	Y	Y	Y	N
9 Shuster	N	N	N	N
10 Carney	Y	Y	Y	Y
11 Kanjorski	Y	Y	Y	Y
12 Murtha	Y	Y	Y	Y
13 Schwartz	Y	Y	Y	Y
14 Doyle	Y	Y	Y	Y
15 Dent	Y	N	N	N
16 Pitts	N	N	N	N
17 Holden	Y	N	N	N
18 Murphy, T.	Y	N	N	N
19 Platts	Y	N	N	N
RHODE ISLAND				
1 Kennedy	Y	Y	Y	Y
2 Langevin	Y	Y	Y	Y
SOUTH CAROLINA				
1 Brown	N	N	N	N
2 Wilson	N	N	N	N
3 Barrett	N	N	N	N
4 Inglis	N	N	N	N
5 Spratt	Y	Y	Y	Y
6 Clyburn	Y	Y	Y	Y
SOUTH DAKOTA				
AL Herseth Sandlin	Y	Y	Y	Y
TENNESSEE				
1 Davis, D.	N	N	N	N
2 Duncan	N	N	N	N
3 Wamp	N	N	N	N
4 Davis, L.	Y	Y	Y	Y
5 Cooper	Y	Y	Y	Y
6 Gordon	Y	Y	Y	Y
7 Blackburn	N	N	N	N
8 Tanner	Y	Y	Y	Y
9 Cohen	Y	Y	Y	Y

	379	380	381	382
TEXAS				
1 Gohmert	N	N	N	N
2 Poe	N	N	N	N
3 Johnson, S.	N	N	N	N
4 Hall	N	N	N	N
5 Hensarling	N	N	N	N
6 Barton	N	N	N	N
7 Culberson	N	N	N	N
8 Brady	N	N	?	N
9 Green, A.	Y	Y	Y	Y
10 McCaul	Y	N	N	N
11 Conaway	N	N	N	N
12 Granger	N	N	N	N
13 Thornberry	N	N	N	N
14 Paul	N	N	N	N
15 Hinojosa	Y	Y	Y	Y
16 Reyes	Y	Y	Y	Y
17 Edwards	Y	Y	Y	Y
18 Jackson Lee	?	?	?	?
19 Neugebauer	N	N	N	N
20 Gonzalez	Y	Y	Y	Y
21 Smith	N	N	N	N
22 Lampson	Y	N	Y	N
23 Rodriguez	Y	Y	Y	Y
24 Marchant	?	N	N	N
25 Doggett	Y	Y	Y	Y
26 Burgess	N	N	N	N
27 Ortiz	Y	Y	Y	Y
28 Cuellar	Y	Y	Y	Y
29 Green, G.	Y	Y	Y	Y
30 Johnson, E.	Y	Y	Y	Y
31 Carter	N	N	N	N
32 Sessions	N	N	N	N
UTAH				
1 Bishop	N	N	N	N
2 Matheson	Y	Y	Y	N
3 Cannon	N	N	N	N
VERMONT				
AL Welch	Y	Y	Y	Y
VIRGINIA				
1 Wittman	N	N	N	N
2 Drake	N	N	N	N
3 Scott	Y	Y	Y	Y
4 Forbes	N	N	N	N
5 Goode	N	N	N	N
6 Goodlatte	N	N	N	N
7 Cantor	N	N	N	N
8 Moran	Y	Y	Y	Y
9 Boucher	?	?	?	?
10 Wolf	N	?	N	N
11 Davis	Y	N	N	N
WASHINGTON				
1 Inslee	Y	Y	Y	Y
2 Larsen	Y	Y	Y	Y
3 Baird	Y	Y	Y	Y
4 Hastings	N	N	N	N
5 McMorris Rodgers	N	N	N	N
6 Dicks	Y	Y	Y	Y
7 McDermott	Y	Y	Y	Y
8 Reichert	Y	N	N	N
9 Smith	Y	Y	Y	Y
WEST VIRGINIA				
1 Mollohan	Y	Y	Y	Y
2 Capito	N	?	N	N
3 Rahall	Y	Y	Y	Y
WISCONSIN				
1 Ryan	N	N	N	N
2 Baldwin	Y	Y	Y	Y
3 Kind	Y	Y	Y	Y
4 Moore	Y	Y	Y	Y
5 Sensenbrenner	N	N	N	N
6 Petri	Y	Y	Y	Y
7 Obey	Y	Y	Y	Y
8 Kagen	Y	Y	Y	Y
WYOMING				
AL Cubin	N	N	N	N
DELEGATES				
Faleomavaega (A.S.)				
Norton (D.C.)				
Bordallo (Guam)				
Fortuño (P.R.)				
Christensen (V.I.)				

IN THE HOUSE | By Vote Number

383. HR 5940. National Nanotechnology Initiative/Passage.
Gordon, D-Tenn., motion to suspend the rules and pass the bill that would authorize $1.5 million for the National Nanotechnology Initiative to coordinate research, development and education in the field of nanotechnology. The funds would come from 13 supporting federal agencies. Motion agreed to 407-6: R 184-6; D 223-0 (ND 168-0, SD 55-0). A two-thirds majority of those present and voting (276 in this case) is required for passage under suspension of the rules. June 5, 2008.

384. HR 5540. Chesapeake Bay Grant Program/Five-Year Authorization. Bishop, R-Utah, amendment that would authorize funding for the Chesapeake Bay Gateways and Watertrails Network in fiscal 2009 through 2013, replacing the bill's permanent authorization. Rejected 178-232: R 172-14; D 6-218 (ND 4-165, SD 2-53). June 5, 2008.

385. HR 5540. Chesapeake Bay Grant Program/Recommit. Sali, R-Idaho, motion to recommit the bill to the Natural Resources Committee with instructions that it be reported back promptly with language that would direct some of the funds authorized in the bill to public education on the effect of high fuel prices on use of the Chesapeake Bay areas included in the program. Motion rejected 181-223: R 179-3; D 2-220 (ND 2-165, SD 0-55). June 5, 2008.

386. HR 5540. Chesapeake Bay Grant Program/Passage. Passage of the bill that would permanently reauthorize a program that awards grants to parks, volunteer groups, wildlife refuges, historic sites, museums and water trails throughout the Chesapeake Bay area. Passed 321-86: R 96-86; D 225-0 (ND 169-0, SD 56-0). June 5, 2008.

387. HR 3058. Public Land Payment Options/Passage. DeFazio, D-Ore., motion to suspend the rules and pass the bill that would allow counties to receive a percentage of revenue from economic activities, such as logging, on National Forest and Bureau of Land Management lands within their boundaries in lieu of taxes. The bill would create a new formula to allocate funds based on historical funding, the county's amount of federal lands and its economic conditions. It would offset the costs of the payments by imposing a fee on producing and non-producing federal oil and gas drilling leases in the Gulf of Mexico. Motion rejected 218-193: R 16-174; D 202-19 (ND 159-8, SD 43-11). A two-thirds majority of those present and voting (274 in this case) is required for passage under suspension of the rules. A "nay" was a vote in support of the president's position. June 5, 2008.

	383	384	385	386	387
ALABAMA					
1 Bonner	Y	Y	?	?	?
2 Everett	?	?	?	?	?
3 Rogers	Y	Y	Y	Y	Y
4 Aderholt	Y	Y	Y	N	N
5 Cramer	Y	N	N	Y	N
6 Bachus	Y	Y	Y	Y	N
7 Davis	Y	N	N	Y	Y
ALASKA					
AL Young	Y	Y	Y	Y	N
ARIZONA					
1 Renzi	Y	Y	Y	Y	N
2 Franks	Y	Y	Y	N	N
3 Shadegg	Y	Y	Y	N	N
4 Pastor	Y	N	N	Y	Y
5 Mitchell	Y	N	N	Y	Y
6 Flake	N	Y	Y	N	N
7 Grijalva	Y	N	N	Y	Y
8 Giffords	Y	Y	N	Y	Y
ARKANSAS					
1 Berry	Y	N	N	Y	Y
2 Snyder	Y	N	N	Y	Y
3 Boozman	Y	Y	Y	N	N
4 Ross	Y	N	N	Y	Y
CALIFORNIA					
1 Thompson	Y	N	N	Y	Y
2 Herger	Y	Y	Y	N	N
3 Lungren	Y	Y	Y	N	Y
4 Doolittle	Y	Y	Y	Y	N
5 Matsui	Y	N	N	Y	Y
6 Woolsey	Y	N	N	Y	Y
7 Miller, George	Y	N	N	Y	Y
8 Pelosi				Y	Y
9 Lee	Y	N	N	Y	Y
10 Tauscher	Y	N	N	Y	Y
11 McNerney	Y	N	Y	Y	Y
12 Speier	Y	N	N	Y	Y
13 Stark	Y	N	N	Y	Y
14 Eshoo	Y	N	N	Y	Y
15 Honda	Y	N	N	Y	Y
16 Lofgren	Y	N	N	Y	Y
17 Farr	Y	N	N	Y	Y
18 Cardoza	Y	N	N	Y	Y
19 Radanovich	Y	Y	Y	N	N
20 Costa	Y	N	N	Y	Y
21 Nunes	Y	Y	Y	N	N
22 McCarthy	Y	Y	Y	N	N
23 Capps	Y	N	N	Y	Y
24 Gallegly	Y	Y	Y	N	N
25 McKeon	Y	?	Y	N	N
26 Dreier	Y	Y	Y	N	N
27 Sherman	Y	N	N	Y	Y
28 Berman	Y	N	N	Y	?
29 Schiff	Y	N	N	Y	Y
30 Waxman	Y	N	N	Y	Y
31 Becerra	Y	N	N	Y	Y
32 Solis	Y	N	N	Y	Y
33 Watson	Y	N	N	Y	Y
34 Roybal-Allard	Y	N	N	Y	Y
35 Waters	Y	N	N	Y	Y
36 Harman	Y	N	N	Y	Y
37 Richardson	Y	N	N	Y	Y
38 Napolitano	Y	N	N	Y	Y
39 Sánchez, Linda	Y	N	N	Y	Y
40 Royce	Y	Y	Y	N	N
41 Lewis	Y	Y	Y	N	N
42 Miller, Gary	Y	Y	Y	N	N
43 Baca	Y	N	N	Y	Y
44 Calvert	Y	Y	Y	N	N
45 Bono Mack	Y	Y	Y	N	N
46 Rohrabacher	Y	Y	Y	Y	N
47 Sanchez, Loretta	Y	N	N	Y	Y
48 Campbell	?	?	?	?	?
49 Issa	Y	Y	Y	N	N
50 Bilbray	Y	Y	Y	N	Y
51 Filner	Y	N	N	Y	Y
52 Hunter	Y	Y	Y	Y	N
53 Davis	Y	N	N	Y	Y

	383	384	385	386	387
COLORADO					
1 DeGette	Y	N	N	Y	Y
2 Udall	Y	N	N	Y	Y
3 Salazar	Y	N	N	Y	Y
4 Musgrave	Y	Y	Y	N	N
5 Lamborn	Y	Y	Y	N	N
6 Tancredo	N	Y	Y	N	N
7 Perlmutter	Y	N	N	Y	Y
CONNECTICUT					
1 Larson	Y	N	N	Y	Y
2 Courtney	Y	N	N	Y	Y
3 DeLauro	Y	N	N	Y	Y
4 Shays	Y	Y	Y	Y	Y
5 Murphy	Y	N	N	Y	Y
DELAWARE					
AL Castle	Y	N	Y	Y	Y
FLORIDA					
1 Miller	Y	Y	Y	N	N
2 Boyd	Y	N	N	Y	Y
3 Brown	Y	N	N	Y	Y
4 Crenshaw	Y	Y	Y	Y	N
5 Brown-Waite	Y	Y	Y	N	N
6 Stearns	Y	Y	Y	N	N
7 Mica	Y	Y	Y	N	N
8 Keller	Y	Y	Y	Y	N
9 Bilirakis	Y	N	N	Y	N
10 Young	Y	Y	Y	Y	N
11 Castor	Y	N	N	Y	Y
12 Putnam	Y	?	?	?	Y
13 Buchanan	Y	Y	Y	Y	Y
14 Mack	Y	Y	Y	N	N
15 Weldon	?	Y	Y	Y	N
16 Mahoney	Y	Y	N	Y	Y
17 Meek	Y	N	N	Y	?
18 Ros-Lehtinen	Y	Y	Y	Y	Y
19 Wexler	Y	N	N	Y	Y
20 Wasserman Schultz	Y	N	?	Y	Y
21 Diaz-Balart, L.	Y	Y	Y	N	N
22 Klein	Y	N	N	Y	Y
23 Hastings	Y	N	N	Y	Y
24 Feeney	Y	Y	Y	N	N
25 Diaz-Balart, M.	Y	Y	Y	N	N
GEORGIA					
1 Kingston	Y	Y	Y	N	N
2 Bishop	Y	N	N	Y	Y
3 Westmoreland	Y	Y	Y	N	N
4 Johnson	Y	N	N	Y	Y
5 Lewis	Y	N	N	Y	Y
6 Price	Y	Y	Y	N	N
7 Linder	Y	Y	Y	?	?
8 Marshall	?	Y	N	Y	Y
9 Deal	Y	Y	Y	N	N
10 Broun	N	Y	Y	N	N
11 Gingrey	Y	Y	Y	Y	N
12 Barrow	Y	N	N	Y	Y
13 Scott	Y	N	N	Y	Y
HAWAII					
1 Abercrombie	Y	N	N	Y	Y
2 Hirono	Y	N	N	Y	Y
IDAHO					
1 Sali	Y	Y	Y	N	N
2 Simpson	Y	Y	Y	N	N
ILLINOIS					
1 Rush	?	?	?	?	?
2 Jackson	Y	N	N	Y	Y
3 Lipinski	Y	N	N	Y	Y
4 Gutierrez	Y	N	N	Y	Y
5 Emanuel	Y	N	N	Y	Y
6 Roskam	Y	Y	Y	N	N
7 Davis	Y	N	N	Y	Y
8 Bean	+	Y	N	Y	Y
9 Schakowsky	Y	N	N	Y	Y
10 Kirk	Y	Y	Y	Y	Y
11 Weller	Y	Y	Y	Y	Y
12 Costello	Y	N	N	Y	N
13 Biggert	Y	Y	Y	Y	N
14 Foster	Y	N	N	Y	Y
15 Johnson	Y	N	Y	Y	Y

KEY	**Republicans**	Democrats
Y	Voted for (yea)	X Paired against	C Voted "present" to avoid possible conflict of interest
#	Paired for	− Announced against	
+	Announced for	P Voted "present"	? Did not vote or otherwise make a position known
N	Voted against (nay)		

ND Northern Democrats, SD Southern Democrats
Southern states: Ala., Ark., Fla., Ga., Ky., La., Miss., N.C., Okla., S.C., Tenn., Texas, Va.

H-126 2008 CQ ALMANAC | www.cq.com

	383	384	385	386	387
16 Manzullo	?	Y	Y	N	N
17 Hare	Y	N	N	Y	Y
18 LaHood	Y	?	?	?	?
19 Shimkus	Y	Y	Y	Y	N
INDIANA					
1 Visclosky	Y	N	N	Y	Y
2 Donnelly	Y	N	N	Y	Y
3 Souder	Y	Y	Y	N	N
4 Buyer	Y	Y	Y	N	N
5 Burton	Y	Y	Y	N	N
6 Pence	Y	Y	Y	N	N
7 Carson, A.	Y	N	N	Y	Y
8 Ellsworth	Y	N	N	Y	Y
9 Hill	Y	N	N	Y	Y
IOWA					
1 Braley	?	N	N	Y	Y
2 Loebsack	Y	N	N	Y	Y
3 Boswell	Y	N	N	Y	Y
4 Latham	Y	Y	Y	Y	N
5 King	Y	Y	Y	N	N
KANSAS					
1 Moran	Y	Y	Y	N	N
2 Boyda	Y	N	N	Y	Y
3 Moore	Y	N	N	Y	Y
4 Tiahrt	Y	?	?	?	?
KENTUCKY					
1 Whitfield	Y	Y	Y	Y	N
2 Lewis	Y	Y	Y	N	N
3 Yarmuth	Y	N	N	Y	Y
4 Davis	Y	Y	Y	N	N
5 Rogers	Y	Y	Y	N	N
6 Chandler	Y	N	N	Y	Y
LOUISIANA					
1 Scalise	Y	Y	Y	N	N
2 Jefferson	Y	N	N	Y	Y
3 Melancon	Y	N	N	Y	P
4 McCrery	Y	Y	?	Y	N
5 Alexander	Y	Y	Y	Y	N
6 Cazayoux	Y	N	N	Y	N
7 Boustany	Y	Y	Y	N	N
MAINE					
1 Allen	Y	N	N	Y	Y
2 Michaud	Y	N	N	Y	Y
MARYLAND					
1 Gilchrest	Y	N	N	Y	N
2 Ruppersberger	?	N	–	Y	Y
3 Sarbanes	Y	N	N	Y	Y
4 Vacant					
5 Hoyer	Y	N	N	Y	Y
6 Bartlett	Y	Y	Y	Y	N
7 Cummings	Y	N	N	Y	Y
8 Van Hollen	Y	N	N	Y	Y
MASSACHUSETTS					
1 Olver	Y	N	N	Y	Y
2 Neal	Y	N	N	Y	Y
3 McGovern	Y	N	N	Y	Y
4 Frank	Y	N	N	Y	N
5 Tsongas	Y	N	N	Y	Y
6 Tierney	Y	N	N	Y	Y
7 Markey	Y	N	N	Y	Y
8 Capuano	Y	N	N	Y	P
9 Lynch	Y	N	N	Y	Y
10 Delahunt	Y	?	?	?	?
MICHIGAN					
1 Stupak	Y	N	N	Y	Y
2 Hoekstra	Y	Y	Y	N	N
3 Ehlers	Y	?	?	?	?
4 Camp	Y	Y	?	Y	N
5 Kildee	Y	N	N	Y	Y
6 Upton	Y	Y	Y	Y	N
7 Walberg	Y	Y	Y	N	N
8 Rogers	Y	Y	Y	Y	Y
9 Knollenberg	Y	Y	Y	Y	N
10 Miller	Y	Y	Y	Y	Y
11 McCotter	Y	?	?	?	N
12 Levin	Y	N	N	Y	Y
13 Kilpatrick	Y	N	N	Y	Y
14 Conyers	?	N	N	Y	Y
15 Dingell	Y	N	N	Y	Y
MINNESOTA					
1 Walz	Y	N	N	Y	Y
2 Kline	Y	Y	Y	N	N
3 Ramstad	Y	Y	Y	Y	N
4 McCollum	Y	N	N	Y	Y

	383	384	385	386	387
5 Ellison	Y	–	–	+	+
6 Bachmann	Y	Y	Y	N	N
7 Peterson	Y	N	N	Y	Y
8 Oberstar	Y	N	N	Y	Y
MISSISSIPPI					
1 Childers	Y	N	N	Y	Y
2 Thompson	Y	N	N	Y	Y
3 Pickering	Y	Y	Y	Y	N
4 Taylor	Y	N	N	Y	Y
MISSOURI					
1 Clay	Y	N	N	Y	Y
2 Akin	Y	Y	Y	N	N
3 Carnahan	Y	N	N	Y	Y
4 Skelton	Y	N	N	Y	Y
5 Cleaver	Y	N	N	Y	Y
6 Graves	Y	Y	Y	N	N
7 Blunt	Y	?	?	?	N
8 Emerson	Y	Y	Y	N	N
9 Hulshof	Y	Y	Y	N	N
MONTANA					
AL Rehberg	Y	Y	Y	Y	N
NEBRASKA					
1 Fortenberry	Y	Y	Y	Y	N
2 Terry	Y	Y	Y	N	N
3 Smith	Y	Y	Y	N	N
NEVADA					
1 Berkley	Y	N	N	Y	Y
2 Heller	Y	Y	Y	N	N
3 Porter	Y	Y	Y	Y	N
NEW HAMPSHIRE					
1 Shea-Porter	Y	N	N	Y	Y
2 Hodes	Y	N	N	Y	Y
NEW JERSEY					
1 Andrews	Y	N	N	Y	Y
2 LoBiondo	Y	Y	Y	Y	N
3 Saxton	Y	N	N	Y	N
4 Smith	Y	Y	Y	Y	Y
5 Garrett	Y	Y	Y	N	N
6 Pallone	Y	N	N	Y	Y
7 Ferguson	Y	Y	Y	Y	N
8 Pascrell	Y	?	?	?	?
9 Rothman	Y	N	N	Y	Y
10 Payne	Y	N	N	Y	Y
11 Frelinghuysen	Y	Y	Y	Y	N
12 Holt	Y	N	N	Y	Y
13 Sires	Y	N	N	Y	Y
NEW MEXICO					
1 Wilson	Y	Y	Y	Y	N
2 Pearce	Y	Y	Y	N	N
3 Udall	Y	N	N	Y	Y
NEW YORK					
1 Bishop	Y	N	N	Y	Y
2 Israel	Y	N	N	Y	Y
3 King	Y	Y	Y	Y	N
4 McCarthy	Y	N	N	Y	Y
5 Ackerman	Y	N	N	Y	Y
6 Meeks	Y	N	N	Y	Y
7 Crowley	Y	N	N	Y	Y
8 Nadler	Y	N	N	Y	Y
9 Weiner	Y	N	N	Y	Y
10 Towns	Y	N	N	Y	Y
11 Clarke	Y	N	N	Y	Y
12 Velázquez	Y	N	N	Y	Y
13 Fossella	Y	Y	Y	Y	N
14 Maloney	Y	N	N	Y	Y
15 Rangel	Y	N	N	?	?
16 Serrano	Y	N	N	Y	Y
17 Engel	Y	N	N	Y	Y
18 Lowey	Y	N	N	Y	Y
19 Hall	Y	N	N	Y	Y
20 Gillibrand	Y	?	?	?	?
21 McNulty	Y	N	N	Y	Y
22 Hinchey	Y	N	N	Y	Y
23 McHugh	Y	Y	Y	Y	N
24 Arcuri	Y	N	N	Y	Y
25 Walsh	Y	Y	Y	Y	N
26 Reynolds	?	Y	Y	Y	N
27 Higgins	Y	N	N	Y	Y
28 Slaughter	Y	N	N	Y	Y
29 Kuhl	Y	Y	Y	Y	N
NORTH CAROLINA					
1 Butterfield	Y	N	N	Y	Y
2 Etheridge	Y	N	N	Y	Y
3 Jones	Y	Y	Y	N	N
4 Price	Y	N	N	Y	Y

	383	384	385	386	387
5 Foxx	Y	Y	Y	N	N
6 Coble	N	Y	Y	N	N
7 McIntyre	Y	N	N	Y	Y
8 Hayes	Y	Y	Y	N	N
9 Myrick	Y	Y	Y	N	N
10 McHenry	Y	Y	Y	N	N
11 Shuler	?	?	?	?	?
12 Watt	Y	N	N	Y	Y
13 Miller	Y	N	N	Y	Y
NORTH DAKOTA					
AL Pomeroy	Y	N	N	Y	Y
OHIO					
1 Chabot	Y	Y	Y	N	N
2 Schmidt	Y	Y	Y	N	N
3 Turner	Y	Y	Y	Y	N
4 Jordan	Y	Y	Y	N	N
5 Latta	Y	Y	Y	N	N
6 Wilson	Y	N	N	Y	Y
7 Hobson	Y	Y	Y	Y	N
8 Boehner	?	?	?	?	N
9 Kaptur	Y	N	N	Y	Y
10 Kucinich	Y	N	N	Y	Y
11 Tubbs Jones	Y	N	N	Y	Y
12 Tiberi	Y	Y	Y	Y	N
13 Sutton	Y	N	N	Y	Y
14 LaTourette	Y	Y	Y	Y	N
15 Pryce	?	?	?	?	?
16 Regula	Y	Y	Y	Y	N
17 Ryan	Y	N	N	Y	Y
18 Space	Y	N	N	Y	Y
OKLAHOMA					
1 Sullivan	Y	Y	Y	N	N
2 Boren	Y	N	N	Y	N
3 Lucas	Y	Y	Y	N	N
4 Cole	Y	Y	Y	N	N
5 Fallin	Y	Y	Y	N	N
OREGON					
1 Wu	Y	N	N	Y	Y
2 Walden	Y	Y	Y	Y	N
3 Blumenauer	Y	N	N	Y	Y
4 DeFazio	Y	N	N	Y	Y
5 Hooley	Y	N	N	Y	Y
PENNSYLVANIA					
1 Brady	Y	N	N	Y	N
2 Fattah	?	?	?	?	?
3 English	Y	Y	Y	Y	N
4 Altmire	Y	Y	Y	Y	N
5 Peterson	Y	Y	Y	Y	N
6 Gerlach	Y	N	N	Y	N
7 Sestak	Y	N	N	Y	Y
8 Murphy, P.	Y	N	N	Y	Y
9 Shuster	Y	Y	Y	N	N
10 Carney	Y	Y	Y	Y	N
11 Kanjorski	Y	N	N	Y	Y
12 Murtha	Y	N	N	Y	Y
13 Schwartz	Y	N	N	Y	Y
14 Doyle	Y	N	N	Y	Y
15 Dent	Y	Y	Y	Y	N
16 Pitts	Y	Y	Y	N	N
17 Holden	Y	N	N	Y	Y
18 Murphy, T.	Y	Y	Y	Y	N
19 Platts	Y	Y	N	Y	N
RHODE ISLAND					
1 Kennedy	Y	N	N	Y	Y
2 Langevin	Y	N	?	Y	Y
SOUTH CAROLINA					
1 Brown	Y	Y	Y	N	N
2 Wilson	Y	Y	Y	N	N
3 Barrett	Y	Y	Y	N	N
4 Inglis	Y	Y	Y	N	N
5 Spratt	Y	N	N	Y	Y
6 Clyburn	Y	N	N	Y	Y
SOUTH DAKOTA					
AL Herseth Sandlin	Y	N	N	Y	Y
TENNESSEE					
1 Davis, D.	Y	Y	Y	N	N
2 Duncan	Y	Y	Y	N	N
3 Wamp	Y	Y	Y	N	N
4 Davis, L.	Y	N	N	Y	Y
5 Cooper	Y	N	N	Y	Y
6 Gordon	Y	N	N	Y	Y
7 Blackburn	Y	Y	Y	N	N
8 Tanner	Y	N	N	Y	Y
9 Cohen	Y	N	N	Y	Y

	383	384	385	386	387
TEXAS					
1 Gohmert	?	Y	Y	N	N
2 Poe	N	Y	Y	N	N
3 Johnson, S.	Y	Y	Y	N	N
4 Hall	?	Y	Y	N	N
5 Hensarling	Y	Y	Y	N	N
6 Barton	Y	Y	?	N	N
7 Culberson	Y	Y	Y	N	N
8 Brady	Y	Y	Y	N	N
9 Green, A.	Y	N	N	Y	Y
10 McCaul	Y	Y	Y	N	N
11 Conaway	Y	Y	Y	N	N
12 Granger	Y	?	?	?	N
13 Thornberry	Y	Y	Y	N	N
14 Paul	N	Y	Y	N	N
15 Hinojosa	Y	N	N	Y	Y
16 Reyes	Y	N	N	Y	Y
17 Edwards	Y	N	N	Y	Y
18 Jackson Lee	?	?	?	?	?
19 Neugebauer	Y	Y	Y	N	N
20 Gonzalez	Y	N	N	Y	Y
21 Smith	Y	Y	Y	N	N
22 Lampson	Y	N	N	Y	Y
23 Rodriguez	Y	?	N	Y	Y
24 Marchant	Y	Y	Y	N	N
25 Doggett	Y	N	N	Y	Y
26 Burgess	Y	Y	Y	N	N
27 Ortiz	Y	N	N	Y	Y
28 Cuellar	Y	N	N	Y	Y
29 Green, G.	Y	N	N	Y	Y
30 Johnson, E.	Y	N	N	Y	Y
31 Carter	Y	?	?	?	N
32 Sessions	Y	Y	Y	N	N
UTAH					
1 Bishop	Y	Y	Y	N	N
2 Matheson	Y	N	N	Y	Y
3 Cannon	Y	Y	Y	N	N
VERMONT					
AL Welch	Y	N	N	Y	Y
VIRGINIA					
1 Wittman	Y	N	N	Y	N
2 Drake	Y	N	Y	Y	N
3 Scott	Y	N	N	Y	Y
4 Forbes	Y	N	Y	Y	N
5 Goode	Y	N	Y	Y	N
6 Goodlatte	Y	N	Y	Y	N
7 Cantor	Y	N	?	?	?
8 Moran	Y	N	N	Y	Y
9 Boucher	?	?	?	?	?
10 Wolf	Y	N	N	Y	Y
11 Davis	Y	N	Y	Y	N
WASHINGTON					
1 Inslee	Y	N	N	Y	Y
2 Larsen	Y	N	N	Y	Y
3 Baird	Y	N	N	Y	Y
4 Hastings	Y	Y	Y	N	N
5 McMorris Rodgers	Y	Y	Y	N	N
6 Dicks	Y	N	N	Y	Y
7 McDermott	Y	N	N	Y	Y
8 Reichert	Y	Y	Y	N	Y
9 Smith	Y	N	N	Y	Y
WEST VIRGINIA					
1 Mollohan	?	N	N	Y	Y
2 Capito	Y	Y	Y	Y	Y
3 Rahall	Y	N	N	Y	Y
WISCONSIN					
1 Ryan	Y	Y	Y	N	N
2 Baldwin	Y	N	N	Y	Y
3 Kind	Y	N	N	Y	Y
4 Moore	Y	N	N	Y	Y
5 Sensenbrenner	Y	Y	Y	N	N
6 Petri	Y	Y	Y	Y	N
7 Obey	Y	N	N	Y	Y
8 Kagen	Y	N	N	Y	Y
WYOMING					
AL Cubin	Y	Y	Y	Y	N
DELEGATES					
Faleomavaega (A.S.)					
Norton (D.C.)					
Bordallo (Guam)					
Fortuño (P.R.)					
Christensen (V.I.)					

IN THE HOUSE | By Vote Number

388. H Res 1225. Support National Safety Month/Adoption.

Yarmuth, D-Ky., motion to suspend the rules and adopt the resolution that would support the designation of National Safety Month and recognize the National Safety Council's contributions to raising awareness about safety in schools and jobs. Motion agreed to 379-0: R 177-0; D 202-0 (ND 150-0, SD 52-0). A two-thirds majority of those present and voting (253 in this case) is required for adoption under suspension of the rules. June 9, 2008.

389. H Res 1243. Father's Day/Adoption.

Yarmuth, D-Ky., motion to suspend the rules and adopt the resolution that would call on fathers to spend Father's Day with their children and encourage their active involvement in the rearing and development of their children. Motion agreed to 373-0: R 174-0; D 199-0 (ND 149-0, SD 50-0). A two-thirds majority of those present and voting (249 in this case) is required for adoption under suspension of the rules. June 9, 2008.

390. H Res 127. 50th Anniversary of Alaska/Adoption.

Davis, D-Ill., motion to suspend the rules and adopt the resolution that would recognize the 50th anniversary of Alaska as a state. Motion agreed to 375-0: R 174-0; D 201-0 (ND 149-0, SD 52-0). A two-thirds majority of those present and voting (250 in this case) is required for adoption under suspension of the rules. June 9, 2008.

391. HR 6003. Amtrak Reauthorization/Previous Question.

Matsui, D-Calif., motion to order the previous question (thus ending debate and possibility of amendment) on adoption of the rule (H Res 1253) to provide for House floor consideration of the bill that would authorize $14.4 billion for Amtrak and other rail services for fiscal 2009 through 2013, and authorize creation of a high-speed rail corridor program. Motion agreed to 227-185: R 5-183; D 222-2 (ND 167-1, SD 55-1). June 10, 2008.

392. HR 6003. Amtrak Reauthorization/Rule.

Adoption of the rule (H Res 1253) to provide for House floor consideration of the bill that would authorize $14.4 billion for Amtrak and other rail services for fiscal 2009 through 2013, and authorize creation of a high-speed rail corridor program. Adopted 227-187: R 5-186; D 222-1 (ND 167-1, SD 55-0). June 10, 2008.

393. HR 6028. Combat Narcotics Trafficking and Crime/Passage.

Berman, D-Calif., motion to suspend the rules and pass the bill that would authorize $1.1 billion in fiscal 2008-10 to help train and equip Mexican armed forces and law enforcement agencies to control drug trafficking and organized crime, and to strengthen Mexico's judicial system. The bill also would authorize $405 million for fiscal 2008-10 for assistance to several countries in Central America. Motion agreed to 311-106: R 108-84; D 203-22 (ND 148-20, SD 55-2). A two-thirds majority of those present and voting (278 in this case) is required for passage under suspension of the rules. June 10, 2008.

	388	389	390	391	392	393
ALABAMA						
1 Bonner	Y	Y	Y	N	N	N
2 Everett	Y	Y	Y	N	N	N
3 Rogers	Y	Y	Y	N	N	N
4 Aderholt	Y	Y	Y	N	N	N
5 Cramer	Y	Y	Y	Y	Y	Y
6 Bachus	Y	Y	Y	N	N	Y
7 Davis	?	?	?	Y	Y	Y
ALASKA						
AL Young	Y	Y	Y	N	Y	N
ARIZONA						
1 Renzi	Y	Y	Y	N	N	Y
2 Franks	Y	Y	Y	N	N	N
3 Shadegg	Y	Y	Y	N	N	N
4 Pastor	Y	Y	Y	Y	Y	Y
5 Mitchell	Y	Y	Y	Y	Y	Y
6 Flake	Y	Y	Y	N	N	N
7 Grijalva	?	?	?	Y	Y	Y
8 Giffords	Y	Y	Y	Y	Y	Y
ARKANSAS						
1 Berry	Y	Y	Y	Y	Y	Y
2 Snyder	Y	Y	Y	Y	Y	Y
3 Boozman	Y	Y	Y	N	N	Y
4 Ross	Y	Y	Y	Y	Y	Y
CALIFORNIA						
1 Thompson	Y	Y	Y	Y	Y	Y
2 Herger	Y	Y	Y	N	Y	Y
3 Lungren	Y	Y	Y	N	Y	Y
4 Doolittle	Y	Y	Y	N	N	N
5 Matsui	Y	Y	Y	Y	Y	Y
6 Woolsey	Y	Y	Y	Y	Y	N
7 Miller, George	?	Y	Y	?	?	Y
8 Pelosi						
9 Lee	Y	Y	Y	Y	Y	N
10 Tauscher	Y	Y	Y	Y	Y	Y
11 McNerney	Y	Y	Y	Y	Y	Y
12 Speier	Y	Y	?	Y	Y	?
13 Stark	Y	Y	Y	Y	Y	N
14 Eshoo	Y	Y	Y	Y	Y	Y
15 Honda	Y	Y	Y	Y	Y	Y
16 Lofgren	Y	Y	Y	Y	Y	Y
17 Farr	Y	Y	Y	Y	Y	Y
18 Cardoza	Y	Y	Y	Y	Y	Y
19 Radanovich	Y	Y	Y	N	N	N
20 Costa	Y	Y	Y	Y	Y	Y
21 Nunes	Y	Y	Y	N	N	Y
22 McCarthy	Y	Y	Y	N	N	Y
23 Capps	Y	Y	Y	Y	Y	Y
24 Gallegly	Y	Y	Y	N	N	Y
25 McKeon	Y	?	Y	N	N	Y
26 Dreier	Y	Y	Y	N	N	Y
27 Sherman	Y	Y	Y	Y	Y	Y
28 Berman	Y	?	Y	Y	Y	Y
29 Schiff	Y	Y	Y	Y	Y	Y
30 Waxman	Y	Y	Y	Y	Y	Y
31 Becerra	Y	Y	Y	Y	Y	Y
32 Solis	Y	Y	Y	Y	Y	Y
33 Watson	Y	Y	Y	Y	Y	Y
34 Roybal-Allard	Y	Y	Y	Y	Y	Y
35 Waters	?	?	?	Y	Y	Y
36 Harman	?	?	?	Y	Y	Y
37 Richardson	Y	Y	Y	Y	Y	Y
38 Napolitano	Y	Y	Y	Y	Y	Y
39 Sánchez, Linda	Y	Y	Y	Y	Y	Y
40 Royce	Y	Y	Y	N	N	N
41 Lewis	Y	Y	Y	N	N	Y
42 Miller, Gary	Y	Y	Y	N	N	N
43 Baca	Y	Y	Y	Y	Y	Y
44 Calvert	Y	Y	Y	N	N	Y
45 Bono Mack	Y	Y	Y	N	N	Y
46 Rohrabacher	?	?	?	N	N	N
47 Sanchez, Loretta	Y	Y	Y	Y	Y	Y
48 Campbell	Y	Y	Y	N	N	N
49 Issa	Y	Y	Y	N	N	Y
50 Bilbray	Y	Y	Y	N	N	Y
51 Filner	?	?	?	Y	Y	N
52 Hunter	Y	Y	Y	N	N	N
53 Davis	Y	Y	Y	Y	Y	Y
COLORADO						
1 DeGette	Y	Y	Y	Y	Y	Y
2 Udall	Y	Y	Y	Y	Y	Y
3 Salazar	Y	Y	Y	Y	Y	Y
4 Musgrave	Y	Y	Y	N	N	N
5 Lamborn	Y	Y	Y	?	N	N
6 Tancredo	?	?	?	?	?	?
7 Perlmutter	Y	Y	Y	Y	Y	Y
CONNECTICUT						
1 Larson	Y	Y	Y	Y	Y	Y
2 Courtney	Y	Y	Y	Y	Y	Y
3 DeLauro	Y	Y	Y	Y	Y	Y
4 Shays	Y	Y	Y	N	N	Y
5 Murphy	Y	Y	Y	Y	Y	Y
DELAWARE						
AL Castle	Y	Y	Y	N	Y	Y
FLORIDA						
1 Miller	Y	Y	Y	N	N	N
2 Boyd	Y	Y	Y	Y	Y	Y
3 Brown	Y	Y	Y	Y	Y	Y
4 Crenshaw	Y	Y	Y	N	N	Y
5 Brown-Waite	Y	Y	Y	N	N	N
6 Stearns	Y	Y	Y	N	N	N
7 Mica	Y	Y	Y	N	N	N
8 Keller	Y	Y	Y	N	N	N
9 Bilirakis	Y	Y	Y	Y	N	N
10 Young	Y	Y	Y	N	N	Y
11 Castor	Y	Y	Y	Y	Y	Y
12 Putnam	Y	Y	Y	N	N	N
13 Buchanan	Y	Y	Y	N	N	Y
14 Mack	Y	Y	Y	N	N	N
15 Weldon	Y	Y	?	N	N	N
16 Mahoney	Y	Y	Y	Y	Y	Y
17 Meek	?	?	?	?	?	?
18 Ros-Lehtinen	Y	Y	Y	Y	Y	Y
19 Wexler	Y	Y	Y	Y	Y	Y
20 Wasserman Schultz	Y	Y	Y	Y	Y	Y
21 Diaz-Balart, L.	Y	Y	Y	?	N	Y
22 Klein	Y	Y	Y	Y	Y	Y
23 Hastings	Y	Y	Y	Y	Y	Y
24 Feeney	Y	Y	Y	N	N	N
25 Diaz-Balart, M.	Y	Y	Y	?	N	Y
GEORGIA						
1 Kingston	Y	Y	Y	N	N	N
2 Bishop	?	?	?	Y	Y	Y
3 Westmoreland	Y	Y	Y	N	N	N
4 Johnson	Y	Y	Y	Y	Y	Y
5 Lewis	Y	Y	Y	Y	Y	N
6 Price	Y	Y	Y	N	N	N
7 Linder	Y	Y	Y	N	N	N
8 Marshall	Y	Y	Y	Y	Y	Y
9 Deal	Y	Y	Y	N	N	N
10 Broun	Y	Y	Y	N	N	N
11 Gingrey	Y	Y	Y	N	N	N
12 Barrow	Y	Y	Y	Y	Y	Y
13 Scott	Y	Y	Y	Y	Y	Y
HAWAII						
1 Abercrombie	Y	Y	Y	Y	Y	Y
2 Hirono	Y	Y	Y	Y	Y	Y
IDAHO						
1 Sali	Y	Y	Y	N	N	N
2 Simpson	Y	Y	Y	N	N	Y
ILLINOIS						
1 Rush	?	?	?	?	?	?
2 Jackson	Y	Y	Y	Y	Y	Y
3 Lipinski	?	?	?	Y	Y	Y
4 Gutierrez	Y	Y	Y	Y	Y	Y
5 Emanuel	Y	Y	Y	Y	Y	Y
6 Roskam	Y	Y	Y	N	N	Y
7 Davis	Y	Y	Y	Y	Y	Y
8 Bean	Y	Y	Y	Y	Y	Y
9 Schakowsky	Y	Y	Y	Y	Y	N
10 Kirk	Y	Y	Y	N	Y	Y
11 Weller	+	+	+	N	N	Y
12 Costello	?	?	?	Y	Y	?
13 Biggert	Y	Y	Y	N	N	Y
14 Foster	Y	Y	Y	Y	Y	Y
15 Johnson	Y	Y	Y	N	N	Y

ND Northern Democrats, SD Southern Democrats
Southern states: Ala., Ark., Fla., Ga., Ky., La., Miss., N.C., Okla., S.C., Tenn., Texas, Va.

	388	389	390	391	392	393
16 **Manzullo**	Y	Y	Y	N	N	N
17 Hare	?	?	?	Y	Y	Y
18 **LaHood**	Y	Y	Y	N	N	Y
19 **Shimkus**	Y	Y	Y	N	N	Y
INDIANA						
1 Visclosky	Y	Y	Y	Y	Y	Y
2 Donnelly	Y	Y	Y	Y	Y	Y
3 **Souder**	?	?	?	N	N	Y
4 **Buyer**	?	?	?	N	N	N
5 **Burton**	Y	Y	Y	N	N	N
6 **Pence**	Y	Y	Y	N	N	Y
7 Carson, A.	Y	Y	Y	Y	Y	N
8 Ellsworth	Y	Y	Y	Y	Y	N
9 Hill	Y	Y	Y	N	N	Y
IOWA						
1 Braley	Y	Y	Y	Y	Y	Y
2 Loebsack	Y	Y	Y	Y	Y	Y
3 Boswell	Y	Y	Y	Y	Y	Y
4 **Latham**	+	+	+	N	N	Y
5 **King**	Y	Y	Y	N	N	N
KANSAS						
1 **Moran**	Y	Y	Y	N	N	Y
2 Boyda	Y	Y	Y	Y	Y	Y
3 Moore	Y	Y	Y	Y	Y	Y
4 **Tiahrt**	Y	Y	?	N	N	Y
KENTUCKY						
1 **Whitfield**	Y	Y	Y	N	N	N
2 **Lewis**	?	?	?	N	N	Y
3 Yarmuth	Y	Y	Y	Y	Y	Y
4 **Davis**	Y	Y	Y	N	N	Y
5 **Rogers**	Y	Y	Y	N	N	Y
6 Chandler	Y	Y	Y	Y	Y	Y
LOUISIANA						
1 **Scalise**	Y	Y	Y	N	N	Y
2 Jefferson	?	?	?	Y	Y	Y
3 Melancon	Y	Y	Y	Y	?	Y
4 **McCrery**	Y	Y	Y	?	?	?
5 **Alexander**	Y	?	?	N	N	Y
6 Cazayoux	Y	Y	Y	Y	Y	Y
7 **Boustany**	Y	Y	Y	N	N	Y
MAINE						
1 Allen	Y	Y	Y	Y	Y	Y
2 Michaud	Y	Y	Y	Y	Y	Y
MARYLAND						
1 **Gilchrest**	?	?	?	N	N	Y
2 Ruppersberger	Y	Y	Y	Y	Y	Y
3 Sarbanes	Y	Y	Y	Y	Y	Y
4 Vacant						
5 Hoyer	Y	Y	Y	Y	Y	Y
6 **Bartlett**	Y	Y	Y	N	N	Y
7 Cummings	Y	Y	Y	?	?	?
8 Van Hollen	Y	Y	Y	Y	Y	Y
MASSACHUSETTS						
1 Olver	Y	Y	Y	Y	Y	Y
2 Neal	Y	Y	Y	Y	Y	Y
3 McGovern	Y	Y	Y	Y	Y	N
4 Frank	Y	Y	Y	Y	Y	Y
5 Tsongas	Y	Y	Y	Y	Y	Y
6 Tierney	Y	Y	Y	Y	Y	Y
7 Markey	Y	Y	Y	Y	Y	Y
8 Capuano	?	?	?	Y	Y	Y
9 Lynch	Y	Y	Y	Y	Y	Y
10 Delahunt	Y	Y	Y	Y	Y	Y
MICHIGAN						
1 Stupak	Y	Y	Y	Y	Y	Y
2 **Hoekstra**	Y	Y	Y	N	N	N
3 **Ehlers**	?	?	?	N	N	Y
4 **Camp**	Y	Y	Y	N	N	Y
5 Kildee	Y	Y	Y	Y	Y	Y
6 **Upton**	Y	Y	Y	N	N	Y
7 **Walberg**	Y	Y	Y	N	N	N
8 **Rogers**	Y	Y	Y	N	N	Y
9 **Knollenberg**	Y	Y	Y	N	N	Y
10 **Miller**	Y	Y	Y	N	N	Y
11 **McCotter**	Y	Y	Y	N	N	N
12 Levin	Y	Y	Y	Y	Y	Y
13 Kilpatrick	Y	Y	Y	Y	Y	Y
14 Conyers	Y	Y	Y	Y	Y	N
15 Dingell	Y	Y	Y	?	?	?
MINNESOTA						
1 Walz	Y	Y	Y	Y	Y	Y
2 **Kline**	Y	Y	Y	N	N	N
3 **Ramstad**	Y	Y	Y	N	N	Y
4 McCollum	Y	Y	Y	Y	Y	Y

	388	389	390	391	392	393
5 Ellison	Y	Y	Y	Y	Y	N
6 **Bachmann**	Y	Y	Y	N	N	N
7 Peterson	Y	Y	Y	Y	Y	Y
8 Oberstar	Y	Y	Y	Y	Y	Y
MISSISSIPPI						
1 Childers	Y	Y	Y	Y	Y	Y
2 Thompson	Y	Y	Y	Y	Y	Y
3 **Pickering**	Y	Y	Y	?	N	Y
4 Taylor	?	?	?	Y	Y	Y
MISSOURI						
1 Clay	Y	Y	Y	Y	Y	Y
2 **Akin**	Y	Y	Y	N	N	N
3 Carnahan	?	?	?	Y	Y	Y
4 Skelton	Y	Y	Y	Y	Y	Y
5 Cleaver	Y	Y	Y	Y	Y	Y
6 **Graves**	Y	Y	Y	N	N	N
7 **Blunt**	Y	Y	Y	N	N	Y
8 **Emerson**	Y	Y	Y	N	N	Y
9 **Hulshof**	?	?	?	?	?	?
MONTANA						
AL **Rehberg**	Y	Y	Y	N	N	Y
NEBRASKA						
1 **Fortenberry**	Y	Y	Y	N	N	Y
2 **Terry**	?	?	?	N	N	Y
3 **Smith**	Y	Y	Y	N	N	Y
NEVADA						
1 Berkley	Y	Y	Y	Y	Y	Y
2 **Heller**	Y	Y	Y	N	N	N
3 **Porter**	Y	Y	Y	N	N	Y
NEW HAMPSHIRE						
1 Shea-Porter	Y	Y	Y	Y	Y	Y
2 Hodes	Y	Y	Y	Y	Y	Y
NEW JERSEY						
1 Andrews	Y	Y	Y	Y	Y	Y
2 **LoBiondo**	Y	Y	Y	N	N	Y
3 **Saxton**	Y	Y	Y	N	N	Y
4 **Smith**	Y	Y	Y	N	N	Y
5 **Garrett**	Y	Y	Y	N	N	Y
6 Pallone	Y	Y	Y	Y	Y	Y
7 **Ferguson**	Y	Y	Y	?	?	?
8 Pascrell	?	?	?	Y	Y	Y
9 Rothman	Y	Y	Y	Y	Y	Y
10 Payne	Y	Y	Y	Y	Y	N
11 **Frelinghuysen**	Y	Y	Y	N	N	Y
12 Holt	+	+	+	+	+	+
13 Sires	Y	Y	Y	Y	Y	Y
NEW MEXICO						
1 **Wilson**	Y	Y	Y	N	N	Y
2 **Pearce**	?	?	?	N	N	Y
3 Udall	?	?	?	Y	Y	Y
NEW YORK						
1 Bishop	Y	Y	Y	Y	Y	Y
2 Israel	Y	Y	Y	Y	Y	Y
3 **King**	Y	Y	Y	N	N	Y
4 McCarthy	Y	Y	Y	Y	Y	Y
5 Ackerman	Y	Y	Y	Y	Y	Y
6 Meeks	Y	Y	Y	Y	Y	Y
7 Crowley	Y	Y	Y	Y	Y	Y
8 Nadler	Y	Y	Y	Y	Y	Y
9 Weiner	?	?	?	Y	Y	Y
10 Towns	Y	Y	Y	Y	Y	Y
11 Clarke	Y	Y	Y	Y	Y	N
12 Velázquez	Y	Y	Y	Y	Y	Y
13 **Fossella**	?	?	?	?	?	?
14 Maloney	+	+	+	Y	Y	Y
15 Rangel	Y	Y	Y	Y	Y	Y
16 Serrano	Y	Y	Y	Y	Y	N
17 Engel	Y	Y	Y	Y	Y	Y
18 Lowey	Y	Y	Y	Y	Y	Y
19 Hall	Y	Y	Y	+	+	Y
20 Gillibrand	?	?	?	?	?	?
21 McNulty	Y	Y	Y	Y	Y	Y
22 Hinchey	Y	Y	Y	Y	Y	Y
23 **McHugh**	Y	Y	Y	N	N	Y
24 Arcuri	Y	Y	Y	Y	Y	Y
25 **Walsh**	Y	Y	Y	N	N	Y
26 **Reynolds**	Y	Y	Y	N	N	Y
27 Higgins	Y	Y	Y	Y	Y	Y
28 Slaughter	Y	Y	Y	Y	Y	Y
29 **Kuhl**	Y	Y	Y	N	N	Y
NORTH CAROLINA						
1 Butterfield	Y	Y	Y	Y	Y	Y
2 Etheridge	Y	Y	Y	Y	Y	Y
3 **Jones**	Y	Y	Y	N	N	N
4 Price	Y	Y	Y	Y	Y	Y

	388	389	390	391	392	393
5 **Foxx**	Y	Y	Y	N	N	N
6 **Coble**	Y	Y	Y	N	N	N
7 McIntyre	Y	Y	Y	Y	Y	N
8 **Hayes**	Y	Y	Y	N	N	Y
9 **Myrick**	+	+	+	N	N	Y
10 **McHenry**	Y	Y	Y	N	N	N
11 Shuler	Y	Y	Y	Y	Y	Y
12 Watt	Y	Y	Y	Y	Y	Y
13 Miller	Y	Y	Y	Y	Y	Y
NORTH DAKOTA						
AL Pomeroy	Y	Y	Y	Y	Y	Y
OHIO						
1 **Chabot**	Y	Y	Y	N	N	N
2 **Schmidt**	Y	Y	Y	N	N	Y
3 **Turner**	Y	Y	Y	N	N	Y
4 **Jordan**	Y	Y	Y	N	N	N
5 **Latta**	Y	Y	Y	N	N	N
6 Wilson	Y	Y	Y	Y	Y	Y
7 **Hobson**	Y	Y	Y	N	N	Y
8 **Boehner**	Y	Y	Y	N	N	Y
9 Kaptur	?	?	?	Y	Y	Y
10 Kucinich	Y	Y	Y	Y	Y	N
11 Tubbs Jones	Y	Y	Y	Y	Y	N
12 **Tiberi**	Y	Y	Y	N	N	Y
13 Sutton	Y	Y	Y	Y	Y	Y
14 **LaTourette**	Y	Y	Y	N	N	Y
15 **Pryce**	Y	Y	Y	N	N	Y
16 **Regula**	?	?	?	N	N	Y
17 Ryan	Y	Y	Y	Y	Y	Y
18 Space	?	?	?	Y	Y	Y
OKLAHOMA						
1 **Sullivan**	Y	Y	Y	N	N	N
2 Boren	Y	Y	Y	Y	Y	Y
3 **Lucas**	?	?	?	N	N	Y
4 **Cole**	Y	Y	Y	N	N	N
5 **Fallin**	Y	Y	Y	N	N	Y
OREGON						
1 Wu	Y	Y	Y	Y	Y	Y
2 **Walden**	Y	Y	Y	N	N	Y
3 Blumenauer	Y	Y	Y	Y	Y	Y
4 DeFazio	Y	Y	Y	Y	Y	Y
5 Hooley	?	?	?	Y	Y	Y
PENNSYLVANIA						
1 Brady	Y	Y	Y	Y	Y	Y
2 Fattah	Y	Y	Y	Y	Y	Y
3 **English**	Y	Y	Y	N	N	Y
4 Altmire	Y	Y	Y	Y	Y	Y
5 **Peterson**	Y	Y	Y	N	N	Y
6 **Gerlach**	Y	Y	Y	N	N	Y
7 Sestak	Y	Y	Y	Y	Y	Y
8 Murphy, P.	Y	Y	Y	Y	Y	Y
9 **Shuster**	Y	Y	Y	N	N	N
10 Carney	Y	Y	Y	Y	Y	N
11 Kanjorski	Y	Y	Y	Y	Y	Y
12 Murtha	Y	?	?	Y	Y	Y
13 Schwartz	Y	Y	Y	Y	Y	Y
14 Doyle	Y	Y	Y	Y	Y	Y
15 **Dent**	Y	Y	Y	N	Y	Y
16 **Pitts**	Y	Y	Y	N	N	Y
17 Holden	?	?	?	Y	Y	Y
18 **Murphy, T.**	Y	Y	Y	N	N	Y
19 **Platts**	Y	Y	Y	N	N	N
RHODE ISLAND						
1 Kennedy	?	?	?	Y	Y	Y
2 Langevin	Y	Y	Y	Y	Y	Y
SOUTH CAROLINA						
1 **Brown**	Y	Y	Y	N	N	Y
2 **Wilson**	?	?	?	?	?	?
3 **Barrett**	+	+	+	N	N	N
4 **Inglis**	Y	Y	Y	N	N	Y
5 Spratt	Y	Y	Y	Y	Y	Y
6 Clyburn	Y	Y	Y	Y	Y	Y
SOUTH DAKOTA						
AL Herseth Sandlin	+	+	+	Y	Y	Y
TENNESSEE						
1 **Davis, D.**	Y	Y	Y	N	N	N
2 **Duncan**	Y	Y	Y	N	N	N
3 **Wamp**	Y	Y	Y	N	N	N
4 Davis, L.	Y	Y	Y	Y	Y	Y
5 Cooper	Y	Y	Y	Y	Y	Y
6 Gordon	Y	Y	Y	Y	Y	Y
7 **Blackburn**	Y	Y	Y	N	N	N
8 Tanner	?	?	?	Y	Y	Y
9 Cohen	Y	Y	Y	Y	Y	Y

	388	389	390	391	392	393
TEXAS						
1 **Gohmert**	Y	Y	Y	N	N	N
2 **Poe**	Y	Y	Y	N	N	N
3 **Johnson, S.**	Y	Y	Y	N	N	N
4 **Hall**	Y	Y	Y	N	N	N
5 **Hensarling**	Y	Y	Y	N	N	N
6 **Barton**	Y	Y	Y	N	N	Y
7 **Culberson**	Y	Y	Y	N	N	N
8 **Brady**	Y	?	Y	N	N	N
9 Green, A.	Y	Y	Y	+	+	Y
10 **McCaul**	Y	Y	Y	N	N	N
11 **Conaway**	Y	Y	Y	N	N	Y
12 **Granger**	Y	Y	Y	N	N	N
13 **Thornberry**	Y	Y	Y	N	N	N
14 **Paul**	Y	Y	Y	N	N	N
15 Hinojosa	Y	Y	Y	Y	Y	Y
16 Reyes	Y	?	Y	Y	Y	Y
17 Edwards	Y	Y	Y	Y	Y	Y
18 Jackson Lee	Y	Y	Y	Y	Y	Y
19 **Neugebauer**	Y	Y	Y	N	N	N
20 Gonzalez	Y	Y	Y	Y	Y	Y
21 **Smith**	Y	Y	Y	N	N	N
22 Lampson	Y	Y	Y	N	Y	Y
23 Rodriguez	Y	Y	Y	Y	Y	Y
24 **Marchant**	?	?	?	N	?	N
25 Doggett	Y	Y	Y	Y	Y	Y
26 **Burgess**	Y	Y	Y	N	N	N
27 Ortiz	?	?	?	?	?	?
28 Cuellar	Y	Y	Y	Y	Y	Y
29 Green, G.	Y	Y	Y	Y	Y	Y
30 Johnson, E.	Y	?	Y	Y	Y	Y
31 **Carter**	Y	Y	Y	N	N	N
32 **Sessions**	Y	Y	Y	N	N	Y
UTAH						
1 **Bishop**	?	?	?	N	N	N
2 Matheson	Y	Y	Y	Y	Y	Y
3 **Cannon**	Y	Y	Y	N	N	Y
VERMONT						
AL Welch	Y	Y	Y	Y	Y	N
VIRGINIA						
1 **Wittman**	Y	Y	Y	N	N	N
2 **Drake**	Y	Y	Y	N	N	Y
3 Scott	Y	Y	Y	Y	Y	Y
4 **Forbes**	Y	Y	Y	N	N	N
5 **Goode**	Y	Y	Y	N	N	N
6 **Goodlatte**	Y	Y	Y	N	N	N
7 **Cantor**	Y	Y	Y	N	N	N
8 Moran	Y	Y	Y	Y	Y	Y
9 Boucher	Y	Y	Y	Y	Y	Y
10 **Wolf**	Y	Y	Y	N	N	Y
11 **Davis**	Y	Y	Y	N	Y	Y
WASHINGTON						
1 Inslee	Y	Y	Y	Y	Y	Y
2 Larsen	Y	Y	Y	Y	Y	Y
3 Baird	Y	Y	Y	Y	Y	Y
4 **Hastings**	?	?	?	N	N	Y
5 **McMorris Rodgers**	Y	Y	Y	N	N	Y
6 Dicks	Y	Y	Y	Y	Y	Y
7 McDermott	+	+	+	Y	Y	N
8 **Reichert**	Y	Y	Y	Y	N	Y
9 Smith	Y	Y	Y	Y	Y	Y
WEST VIRGINIA						
1 Mollohan	?	?	?	Y	Y	Y
2 **Capito**	Y	Y	Y	N	N	Y
3 Rahall	Y	Y	Y	Y	Y	Y
WISCONSIN						
1 **Ryan**	Y	Y	Y	N	N	N
2 Baldwin	Y	Y	Y	Y	Y	N
3 Kind	Y	Y	Y	Y	Y	Y
4 Moore	Y	Y	Y	Y	Y	N
5 **Sensenbrenner**	Y	Y	Y	N	N	N
6 **Petri**	Y	Y	Y	N	N	N
7 Obey	Y	Y	Y	Y	Y	Y
8 Kagen	Y	Y	Y	Y	Y	Y
WYOMING						
AL **Cubin**	?	?	?	?	?	?
DELEGATES						
Faleomavaega (A.S.)						
Norton (D.C.)						
Bordallo (Guam)						
Fortuño (P.R.)						
Christensen (V.I.)						

IN THE HOUSE | By Vote Number

394. H Res 1063. 225th Anniversary of the Treaty of Paris/ **Adoption.** Payne, D-N.J., motion to suspend the rules and adopt the resolution that would recognize the 225th anniversary of relations between the United States and Great Britain and look forward to a continued strong relationship between the countries. Motion agreed to 414-0: R 188-0; D 226-0 (ND 169-0, SD 57-0). A two-thirds majority of those present and voting (276 in this case) is required for adoption under suspension of the rules. June 10, 2008.

395. H Con Res 318. International Year of Sanitation/Adoption. Payne, D-N.J., motion to suspend the rules and adopt the concurrent resolution that would support the goals and ideals of the International Year of Sanitation and recognize the importance of sanitation to public health. Motion agreed to 411-0: R 190-0; D 221-0 (ND 165-0, SD 56-0). A two-thirds majority of those present and voting (274 in this case) is required for adoption under suspension of the rules. June 10, 2008.

396. H Con Res 336. Honor Disabled Veterans/Adoption. Brown, D-Fla., motion to suspend the rules and adopt the concurrent resolution that would support the goals and ideals of Disabled American Veterans Week, and recognize the sacrifices made by disabled veterans and their families. Motion agreed to 417-0: R 192-0; D 225-0 (ND 169-0, SD 56-0). A two-thirds majority of those present and voting (278 in this case) is required for adoption under suspension of the rules. June 10, 2008.

397. HR 6003. Amtrak Reauthorization/Sunset Limited Route. Sessions, R-Texas, amendment that would bar Amtrak from using funds authorized by the bill for the Sunset Limited Route, which runs between Los Angeles and New Orleans. The Transportation Department could waive the restriction if it found the route was critical to homeland security. Rejected in Committee of the Whole 150-275: R 147-47; D 3-228 (ND 2-172, SD 1-56). June 11, 2008.

398. HR 6003. Amtrak Reauthorization/Washington Area Public **Transit.** Davis, R-Va., amendment that would authorize $1.5 billion for grants from fiscal 2009-18 for the Washington Metropolitan Area Transit Authority to help finance maintenance and preventive projects. The transit authority could not receive the grants until it ensures that Metrorail customers have access to wireless services from licensed providers. Local participating governments would have to provide a dedicated funding source to match the federal funding appropriated in a given year. Adopted 295-127: R 67-126; D 228-1 (ND 170-1, SD 58-0). June 11, 2008.

ND Northern Democrats, SD Southern Democrats
Southern states: Ala., Ark., Fla., Ga., Ky., La., Miss., N.C., Okla., S.C., Tenn., Texas, Va.

	394	395	396	397	398
ALABAMA					
1 **Bonner**	Y	Y	Y	Y	N
2 **Everett**	Y	Y	Y	Y	Y
4 **Aderholt**	Y	Y	Y	Y	Y
5 **Cramer**	Y	Y	Y	N	Y
6 **Bachus**	Y	Y	Y	N	N
7 Davis	Y	Y	Y	N	Y
ALASKA					
AL **Young**	?	Y	Y	Y	Y
ARIZONA					
1 **Renzi**	Y	Y	Y	Y	Y
2 **Franks**	Y	Y	Y	Y	N
3 **Shadegg**	Y	Y	Y	Y	N
4 Pastor	Y	Y	Y	N	Y
5 Mitchell	Y	Y	Y	N	Y
6 **Flake**	Y	Y	Y	?	?
7 Grijalva	Y	Y	Y	N	Y
8 Giffords	Y	Y	Y	N	Y
ARKANSAS					
1 Berry	Y	Y	Y	N	Y
2 Snyder	Y	Y	Y	N	Y
3 **Boozman**	Y	Y	Y	N	N
4 Ross	Y	Y	Y	N	Y
CALIFORNIA					
1 Thompson	Y	Y	Y	N	Y
2 **Herger**	Y	Y	Y	Y	N
3 **Lungren**	Y	Y	Y	Y	Y
4 **Doolittle**	Y	Y	Y	?	Y
5 Matsui	Y	Y	Y	N	Y
6 Woolsey	Y	Y	Y	N	Y
7 Miller, George	Y	Y	Y	N	Y
8 Pelosi					
9 Lee	Y	Y	Y	N	Y
10 Tauscher	Y	Y	Y	N	Y
11 McNerney	Y	Y	Y	N	Y
12 Speier	Y	Y	Y	N	Y
13 Stark	Y	Y	Y	N	Y
14 Eshoo	Y	Y	Y	N	Y
15 Honda	Y	Y	Y	N	Y
16 Lofgren	Y	Y	Y	N	Y
17 Farr	Y	Y	Y	N	Y
18 Cardoza	Y	Y	Y	N	Y
19 **Radanovich**	Y	Y	Y	Y	N
20 Costa	Y	Y	Y	N	Y
21 **Nunes**	Y	Y	Y	Y	Y
22 **McCarthy**	Y	Y	Y	Y	N
23 Capps	Y	Y	Y	N	Y
24 **Gallegly**	Y	Y	Y	Y	N
25 **McKeon**	Y	Y	Y	Y	N
26 **Dreier**	Y	Y	Y	Y	N
27 Sherman	Y	Y	Y	N	Y
28 Berman	Y	Y	Y	N	Y
29 Schiff	Y	Y	Y	N	Y
30 Waxman	Y	Y	Y	N	Y
31 Becerra	Y	Y	Y	N	Y
32 Solis	Y	Y	Y	N	Y
33 Watson	Y	Y	Y	N	Y
34 Roybal-Allard	Y	Y	Y	N	Y
35 Waters	Y	Y	Y	N	Y
36 Harman	Y	Y	Y	N	Y
37 Richardson	Y	Y	Y	N	Y
38 Napolitano	Y	Y	Y	N	Y
39 Sánchez, Linda	Y	Y	Y	N	Y
40 **Royce**	Y	Y	Y	Y	N
41 **Lewis**	Y	Y	Y	Y	N
42 **Miller, Gary**	Y	Y	Y	Y	N
43 Baca	Y	?	Y	N	Y
44 **Calvert**	Y	Y	Y	Y	N
45 **Bono Mack**	Y	Y	Y	N	Y
46 **Rohrabacher**	Y	Y	Y	Y	N
47 Sanchez, Loretta	Y	Y	Y	N	Y
48 **Campbell**	Y	Y	Y	Y	N
49 **Issa**	Y	Y	Y	Y	Y
50 **Bilbray**	Y	Y	Y	Y	N
51 Filner	Y	Y	Y	N	Y
52 **Hunter**	Y	Y	Y	Y	N
53 Davis	Y	Y	Y	N	Y

	394	395	396	397	398
COLORADO					
1 DeGette	Y	Y	Y	N	Y
2 Udall	Y	Y	Y	N	Y
3 Salazar	Y	Y	Y	N	Y
4 **Musgrave**	Y	Y	Y	Y	N
5 **Lamborn**	Y	Y	Y	Y	N
6 **Tancredo**	?	?	?	?	?
7 Perlmutter	Y	Y	Y	Y	Y
CONNECTICUT					
1 Larson	Y	Y	Y	N	Y
2 Courtney	Y	Y	Y	N	Y
3 DeLauro	Y	Y	Y	N	Y
4 **Shays**	Y	Y	Y	N	Y
5 Murphy	Y	Y	Y	N	Y
DELAWARE					
AL **Castle**	Y	Y	Y	N	Y
FLORIDA					
1 **Miller**	Y	Y	Y	Y	N
2 Boyd	Y	Y	Y	N	Y
3 Brown	Y	Y	Y	N	Y
4 **Crenshaw**	Y	Y	Y	N	N
5 **Brown-Waite**	Y	Y	Y	Y	Y
6 **Stearns**	Y	Y	Y	Y	N
7 **Mica**	Y	Y	Y	N	Y
8 **Keller**	Y	Y	Y	Y	N
9 **Bilirakis**	Y	Y	Y	Y	N
10 **Young**	Y	Y	Y	Y	N
11 Castor	Y	Y	Y	N	Y
12 **Putnam**	Y	Y	Y	N	N
13 **Buchanan**	Y	Y	Y	N	N
14 **Mack**	Y	Y	Y	Y	N
15 **Weldon**	Y	Y	Y	Y	Y
16 Mahoney	Y	Y	Y	N	Y
17 Meek	?	?	?	N	Y
18 **Ros-Lehtinen**	Y	Y	Y	N	N
19 Wexler	Y	Y	Y	N	Y
20 Wasserman Schultz	Y	Y	Y	N	Y
21 **Diaz-Balart, L.**	Y	Y	Y	N	N
22 Klein	Y	Y	Y	N	Y
23 Hastings	Y	Y	Y	N	Y
24 **Feeney**	Y	Y	Y	Y	N
25 **Diaz-Balart, M.**	Y	Y	Y	N	N
GEORGIA					
1 **Kingston**	Y	Y	Y	Y	N
2 Bishop	Y	Y	Y	N	Y
3 **Westmoreland**	Y	Y	Y	Y	N
4 Johnson	Y	Y	Y	N	Y
5 Lewis	Y	Y	Y	N	Y
6 **Price**	Y	Y	Y	Y	N
7 **Linder**	Y	Y	Y	Y	N
8 Marshall	Y	Y	Y	N	Y
9 **Deal**	Y	Y	Y	Y	N
10 **Broun**	Y	Y	Y	Y	N
11 **Gingrey**	Y	Y	Y	Y	N
12 Barrow	Y	Y	Y	N	Y
13 Scott	Y	Y	Y	N	Y
HAWAII					
1 Abercrombie	Y	Y	Y	N	Y
2 Hirono	Y	Y	Y	N	Y
IDAHO					
1 **Sali**	Y	Y	Y	Y	N
2 **Simpson**	Y	Y	Y	N	N
ILLINOIS					
1 Rush	?	?	?	?	?
2 Jackson	Y	Y	Y	N	Y
3 Lipinski	Y	Y	Y	N	Y
4 Gutierrez	Y	Y	Y	N	Y
5 Emanuel	Y	Y	Y	N	Y
6 **Roskam**	Y	Y	Y	Y	N
7 Davis	Y	Y	Y	N	Y
8 Bean	Y	Y	Y	N	N
9 Schakowsky	Y	Y	Y	N	Y
10 **Kirk**	Y	Y	Y	Y	Y
11 **Weller**	Y	Y	Y	N	Y
12 Costello	Y	Y	Y	N	Y
13 **Biggert**	Y	Y	Y	Y	N
14 Foster	Y	?	Y	N	Y
15 **Johnson**	Y	Y	Y	N	Y

KEY	**Republicans**	Democrats		
Y Voted for (yea)		X Paired against		C Voted "present" to avoid possible conflict of interest
# Paired for		− Announced against		
+ Announced for		P Voted "present"		? Did not vote or otherwise make a position known
N Voted against (nay)				

	394	395	396	397	398
16 Manzullo	Y	Y	Y	Y	N
17 Hare	Y	Y	Y	N	Y
18 LaHood	Y	Y	Y	Y	Y
19 Shimkus	Y	Y	Y	Y	N
INDIANA					
1 Visclosky	Y	Y	Y	N	Y
2 Donnelly	Y	?	Y	N	Y
3 Souder	Y	Y	Y	Y	N
4 Buyer	Y	Y	Y	N	Y
5 Burton	Y	Y	Y	Y	N
6 Pence	?	?	?	Y	N
7 Carson, A.	Y	Y	Y	N	Y
8 Ellsworth	Y	Y	Y	N	Y
9 Hill	Y	Y	Y	N	Y
IOWA					
1 Braley	+	+	+	?	?
2 Loebsack	Y	Y	Y	?	?
3 Boswell	Y	Y	Y	N	Y
4 Latham	Y	Y	Y	Y	N
5 King	Y	Y	Y	Y	N
KANSAS					
1 Moran	Y	Y	Y	Y	N
2 Boyda	Y	Y	Y	N	Y
3 Moore	Y	Y	Y	N	Y
4 Tiahrt	Y	Y	Y	Y	Y
KENTUCKY					
1 Whitfield	Y	Y	Y	N	N
2 Lewis	Y	Y	Y	Y	N
3 Yarmuth	Y	Y	Y	N	Y
4 Davis	Y	Y	Y	N	N
5 Rogers	Y	Y	Y	Y	N
6 Chandler	Y	Y	Y	N	Y
LOUISIANA					
1 Scalise	Y	Y	Y	Y	N
2 Jefferson	Y	Y	Y	N	Y
3 Melancon	Y	Y	Y	N	Y
4 McCrery	?	?	?	?	?
5 Alexander	Y	Y	Y	N	Y
6 Cazayoux	Y	Y	Y	N	Y
7 Boustany	Y	Y	Y	N	Y
MAINE					
1 Allen	Y	Y	Y	N	Y
2 Michaud	Y	Y	Y	N	Y
MARYLAND					
1 Gilchrest	Y	Y	Y	N	Y
2 Ruppersberger	Y	Y	Y	N	Y
3 Sarbanes	Y	Y	Y	N	Y
4 Vacant					
5 Hoyer	Y	Y	Y	N	Y
6 Bartlett	Y	Y	Y	Y	Y
7 Cummings	Y	Y	Y	N	Y
8 Van Hollen	Y	Y	Y	N	Y
MASSACHUSETTS					
1 Olver	Y	Y	Y	N	Y
2 Neal	Y	Y	Y	N	Y
3 McGovern	Y	Y	Y	N	Y
4 Frank	Y	Y	Y	N	Y
5 Tsongas	Y	Y	Y	N	Y
6 Tierney	Y	Y	Y	N	Y
7 Markey	Y	Y	Y	N	Y
8 Capuano	Y	Y	Y	N	Y
9 Lynch	Y	Y	Y	N	Y
10 Delahunt	Y	Y	Y	N	Y
MICHIGAN					
1 Stupak	Y	Y	Y	N	Y
2 Hoekstra	Y	Y	Y	Y	N
3 Ehlers	Y	Y	Y	N	N
4 Camp	Y	Y	Y	Y	N
5 Kildee	Y	Y	Y	N	Y
6 Upton	Y	Y	Y	N	Y
7 Walberg	Y	Y	Y	Y	N
8 Rogers	Y	Y	Y	N	Y
9 Knollenberg	Y	Y	Y	Y	Y
10 Miller	Y	Y	Y	N	N
11 McCotter	Y	Y	Y	Y	N
12 Levin	Y	Y	Y	N	Y
13 Kilpatrick	Y	Y	Y	N	Y
14 Conyers	Y	Y	Y	N	Y
15 Dingell	Y	Y	Y	N	Y
MINNESOTA					
1 Walz	Y	Y	Y	N	Y
2 Kline	Y	Y	Y	Y	N
3 Ramstad	Y	Y	Y	N	Y
4 McCollum	Y	Y	Y	N	Y

	394	395	396	397	398
5 Ellison	Y	?	Y	N	Y
6 Bachmann	Y	Y	Y	Y	N
7 Peterson	Y	Y	Y	N	Y
8 Oberstar	Y	Y	Y	N	Y
MISSISSIPPI					
1 Childers	Y	Y	Y	N	Y
2 Thompson	Y	Y	Y	N	Y
3 Pickering	?	?	Y	N	Y
4 Taylor	Y	Y	Y	N	Y
MISSOURI					
1 Clay	Y	Y	Y	N	Y
2 Akin	Y	Y	Y	Y	N
3 Carnahan	Y	Y	Y	N	Y
4 Skelton	Y	Y	Y	N	Y
5 Cleaver	Y	Y	Y	N	Y
6 Graves	Y	Y	Y	Y	N
7 Blunt	Y	Y	Y	Y	Y
8 Emerson	Y	Y	Y	Y	Y
9 Hulshof	?	?	?	?	?
MONTANA					
AL Rehberg	Y	Y	Y	N	N
NEBRASKA					
1 Fortenberry	Y	Y	Y	N	Y
2 Terry	Y	Y	Y	Y	N
3 Smith	Y	Y	Y	Y	N
NEVADA					
1 Berkley	Y	Y	Y	N	Y
2 Heller	Y	Y	Y	Y	N
3 Porter	Y	Y	Y	N	Y
NEW HAMPSHIRE					
1 Shea-Porter	Y	Y	Y	N	Y
2 Hodes	Y	Y	Y	N	Y
NEW JERSEY					
1 Andrews	Y	Y	Y	N	Y
2 LoBiondo	Y	Y	Y	N	Y
3 Saxton	Y	Y	Y	N	N
4 Smith	Y	Y	Y	N	Y
5 Garrett	Y	Y	Y	Y	N
6 Pallone	Y	Y	Y	N	Y
7 Ferguson	?	?	?	N	Y
8 Pascrell	Y	Y	Y	N	Y
9 Rothman	Y	Y	Y	N	Y
10 Payne	?	?	?	N	Y
11 Frelinghuysen	Y	Y	Y	N	Y
12 Holt	+	+	+	N	Y
13 Sires	Y	Y	Y	N	Y
NEW MEXICO					
1 Wilson	Y	Y	Y	N	N
2 Pearce	Y	Y	Y	Y	N
3 Udall	Y	Y	Y	N	Y
NEW YORK					
1 Bishop	Y	Y	Y	N	Y
2 Israel	Y	Y	Y	N	Y
3 King	Y	Y	Y	N	Y
4 McCarthy	Y	Y	Y	N	Y
5 Ackerman	Y	Y	Y	N	Y
6 Meeks	Y	Y	Y	N	Y
7 Crowley	Y	Y	Y	N	Y
8 Nadler	Y	Y	Y	N	Y
9 Weiner	Y	Y	Y	N	Y
10 Towns	Y	Y	Y	N	Y
11 Clarke	Y	Y	Y	N	Y
12 Velázquez	Y	Y	Y	N	Y
13 Fossella	Y	Y	Y	Y	Y
14 Maloney	Y	Y	Y	N	Y
15 Rangel	Y	Y	Y	N	Y
16 Serrano	Y	Y	Y	N	Y
17 Engel	Y	Y	Y	N	Y
18 Lowey	Y	Y	Y	N	Y
19 Hall	Y	Y	Y	N	Y
20 Gillibrand	?	?	?	?	?
21 McNulty	Y	Y	Y	N	Y
22 Hinchey	?	Y	Y	N	Y
23 McHugh	Y	Y	Y	N	Y
24 Arcuri	Y	Y	Y	N	Y
25 Walsh	Y	Y	Y	N	Y
26 Reynolds	Y	Y	Y	N	N
27 Higgins	Y	Y	Y	N	Y
28 Slaughter	Y	Y	Y	N	Y
29 Kuhl	Y	Y	Y	Y	N
NORTH CAROLINA					
1 Butterfield	Y	?	Y	N	Y
2 Etheridge	Y	Y	Y	N	Y
3 Jones	Y	Y	Y	N	N
4 Price	Y	Y	Y	N	Y

	394	395	396	397	398
5 Foxx	Y	Y	Y	Y	N
6 Coble	Y	Y	Y	Y	N
7 McIntyre	Y	Y	Y	N	Y
8 Hayes	Y	Y	Y	Y	N
9 Myrick	Y	Y	Y	Y	N
10 McHenry	Y	Y	Y	Y	N
11 Shuler	Y	Y	Y	N	Y
12 Watt	Y	Y	Y	N	Y
13 Miller	Y	Y	Y	N	Y
NORTH DAKOTA					
AL Pomeroy	Y	Y	Y	N	Y
OHIO					
1 Chabot	Y	Y	Y	Y	N
2 Schmidt	Y	Y	Y	Y	N
3 Turner	Y	Y	Y	N	Y
4 Jordan	Y	Y	Y	Y	N
5 Latta	Y	Y	Y	Y	N
6 Wilson	Y	Y	Y	N	Y
7 Hobson	Y	Y	Y	N	Y
8 Boehner	Y	Y	Y	Y	N
9 Kaptur	Y	Y	Y	N	Y
10 Kucinich	Y	Y	Y	N	Y
11 Tubbs Jones	Y	Y	Y	N	Y
12 Tiberi	Y	Y	Y	N	Y
13 Sutton	Y	Y	Y	N	Y
14 LaTourette	Y	Y	Y	N	Y
15 Pryce	Y	Y	Y	N	Y
16 Regula	Y	Y	Y	N	Y
17 Ryan	Y	?	Y	N	Y
18 Space	Y	Y	Y	N	Y
OKLAHOMA					
1 Sullivan	Y	Y	Y	Y	Y
2 Boren	Y	Y	Y	N	Y
3 Lucas	Y	Y	Y	Y	Y
4 Cole	Y	Y	Y	Y	N
5 Fallin	Y	Y	Y	Y	Y
OREGON					
1 Wu	Y	Y	Y	N	Y
2 Walden	Y	Y	Y	Y	N
3 Blumenauer	Y	Y	Y	N	Y
4 DeFazio	Y	Y	Y	N	Y
5 Hooley	Y	Y	Y	N	Y
PENNSYLVANIA					
1 Brady	Y	Y	Y	N	Y
2 Fattah	Y	Y	Y	N	Y
3 English	Y	Y	Y	N	Y
4 Altmire	Y	Y	Y	N	Y
5 Peterson	Y	Y	Y	Y	N
6 Gerlach	Y	Y	Y	N	Y
7 Sestak	Y	Y	Y	N	Y
8 Murphy, P.	Y	Y	Y	N	Y
9 Shuster	Y	Y	Y	Y	N
10 Carney	Y	Y	Y	N	Y
11 Kanjorski	Y	Y	Y	N	Y
12 Murtha	Y	Y	Y	N	Y
13 Schwartz	Y	Y	Y	N	Y
14 Doyle	Y	Y	Y	N	Y
15 Dent	Y	Y	Y	N	Y
16 Pitts	Y	Y	Y	Y	N
17 Holden	Y	Y	Y	N	Y
18 Murphy, T.	Y	Y	Y	N	Y
19 Platts	?	Y	Y	N	Y
RHODE ISLAND					
1 Kennedy	Y	Y	Y	N	Y
2 Langevin	Y	Y	Y	N	Y
SOUTH CAROLINA					
1 Brown	Y	Y	Y	Y	N
2 Wilson	?	?	?	Y	N
3 Barrett	Y	Y	Y	Y	N
4 Inglis	Y	Y	Y	Y	N
5 Spratt	Y	Y	Y	?	Y
6 Clyburn	Y	Y	Y	N	Y
SOUTH DAKOTA					
AL Herseth Sandlin	Y	Y	Y	N	Y
TENNESSEE					
1 Davis, D.	Y	Y	Y	N	N
2 Duncan	Y	Y	Y	Y	N
3 Wamp	?	?	?	N	N
4 Davis, L.	Y	Y	Y	N	Y
5 Cooper	Y	Y	Y	?	Y
6 Gordon	Y	Y	Y	N	Y
7 Blackburn	Y	Y	Y	Y	N
8 Tanner	Y	Y	Y	N	Y
9 Cohen	Y	Y	Y	N	Y

	394	395	396	397	398
TEXAS					
1 Gohmert	Y	Y	Y	Y	Y
2 Poe	Y	Y	Y	Y	N
3 Johnson, S.	Y	Y	Y	Y	N
4 Hall	Y	Y	Y	Y	N
5 Hensarling	Y	Y	Y	Y	N
6 Barton	Y	Y	Y	Y	N
7 Culberson	Y	P	Y	Y	N
8 Brady	Y	Y	Y	Y	N
9 Green, A.	Y	Y	Y	N	Y
10 McCaul	Y	Y	Y	Y	N
11 Conaway	Y	Y	Y	Y	N
12 Granger	Y	Y	Y	Y	N
13 Thornberry	Y	Y	Y	Y	N
14 Paul	Y	Y	Y	Y	N
15 Hinojosa	Y	Y	Y	N	Y
16 Reyes	Y	Y	Y	N	Y
17 Edwards	Y	Y	Y	N	Y
18 Jackson Lee	Y	Y	Y	N	Y
19 Neugebauer	Y	Y	Y	Y	N
20 Gonzalez	Y	Y	Y	N	Y
21 Smith	Y	Y	Y	Y	Y
22 Lampson	Y	Y	Y	N	Y
23 Rodriguez	Y	Y	Y	N	Y
24 Marchant	Y	Y	Y	Y	N
25 Doggett	Y	Y	Y	N	Y
26 Burgess	?	Y	Y	Y	N
27 Ortiz	?	?	?	?	?
28 Cuellar	Y	Y	Y	N	Y
29 Green, G.	Y	Y	Y	N	Y
30 Johnson, E.	Y	Y	Y	N	Y
31 Carter	Y	Y	Y	Y	N
32 Sessions	Y	Y	Y	Y	N
UTAH					
1 Bishop	Y	Y	Y	Y	N
2 Matheson	Y	Y	Y	Y	N
3 Cannon	Y	Y	Y	N	N
VERMONT					
AL Welch	Y	Y	Y	N	Y
VIRGINIA					
1 Wittman	Y	Y	Y	N	Y
2 Drake	Y	Y	Y	Y	Y
3 Scott	Y	Y	Y	N	Y
4 Forbes	Y	Y	Y	Y	Y
5 Goode	Y	Y	Y	Y	Y
6 Goodlatte	Y	Y	Y	Y	Y
7 Cantor	Y	Y	Y	Y	N
8 Moran	Y	Y	Y	N	Y
9 Boucher	Y	Y	Y	N	Y
10 Wolf	Y	Y	Y	Y	Y
11 Davis	Y	Y	Y	Y	Y
WASHINGTON					
1 Inslee	Y	Y	Y	N	Y
2 Larsen	Y	Y	Y	N	Y
3 Baird	Y	?	Y	N	Y
4 Hastings	Y	Y	Y	Y	N
5 McMorris Rodgers	Y	Y	Y	N	?
6 Dicks	Y	Y	Y	N	Y
7 McDermott	Y	Y	Y	N	Y
8 Reichert	Y	Y	Y	Y	N
9 Smith	Y	Y	Y	N	Y
WEST VIRGINIA					
1 Mollohan	Y	Y	Y	N	Y
2 Capito	Y	Y	Y	Y	Y
3 Rahall	Y	Y	Y	N	Y
WISCONSIN					
1 Ryan	Y	Y	Y	Y	N
2 Baldwin	Y	Y	Y	N	Y
3 Kind	Y	Y	Y	N	Y
4 Moore	Y	Y	Y	N	Y
5 Sensenbrenner	Y	Y	Y	Y	N
6 Petri	Y	Y	Y	Y	N
7 Obey	Y	Y	Y	N	Y
8 Kagen	Y	Y	Y	N	Y
WYOMING					
AL Cubin	Y	Y	Y	Y	Y
DELEGATES					
Faleomavaega (A.S.)			N		
Norton (D.C.)				?	
Bordallo (Guam)			N		
Fortuño (P.R.)				?	
Christensen (V.I.)					N

IN THE HOUSE | By Vote Number

399. HR 6003. Amtrak Reauthorization/Recommit. Davis, R-Ky., motion to recommit the bill to the Transportation and Infrastructure Committee with instructions that it be reported back promptly with language that would require a study to investigate alternative fuels for locomotives. Motion rejected 194-230: R 187-8; D 7-222 (ND 5-166, SD 2-56). June 11, 2008.

400. HR 6003. Amtrak Reauthorization/Passage. Passage of the bill that would authorize $14.4 billion for Amtrak over five years, including $3 billion for operating assistance, $4.2 billion for capital grants and $1.7 billion for Amtrak to pay down its debts. The bill would authorize grants for capital costs in certain high-congestion corridors. It would require changes in Amtrak's management, operations and general policy regarding intercity passenger rail service. The Transportation Department would be directed to solicit bids, including those from private contractors, for construction of a high-speed rail system between Washington, D.C., and New York City. Passed 311-104: R 87-104; D 224-0 (ND 168-0, SD 56-0). A "nay" was a vote in support of the president's position. June 11, 2008.

401. H Res 1258. Impeachment of President Bush/Motion to Refer. Kucinich, D-Ohio, motion to refer the Kucinich privileged resolution to the Judiciary Committee. The resolution would bring articles of impeachment against President George W. Bush for "high crimes and misdemeanors." Motion agreed to 251-166: R 24-166; D 227-0 (ND 170-0, SD 57-0). June 11, 2008.

402. H Res 1235. National D-Day Remembrance Day/Adoption. Brown, D-Fla., motion to suspend the rules and adopt the resolution that would support the designation of National D-Day Remembrance Day; honor the veterans who served on D-Day; and thank them for their spirit, courage and sacrifice. Motion agreed to 406-0: R 191-0; D 215-0 (ND 160-0, SD 55-0). A two-thirds majority of those present and voting (271 in this case) is required for adoption under suspension of the rules. June 11, 2008.

403. HR 5749. Unemployment Benefits Extension/Passage. Rangel, D-N.Y., motion to suspend the rules and pass the bill that would extend federal unemployment benefits for individuals who have exhausted their current 26 weeks of compensation. The bill would provide an additional 13 weeks in all states, plus another 13 weeks of extended benefits in states with high unemployment rates. Motion rejected 279-144: R 49-144; D 230-0 (ND 172-0, SD 58-0). A two-thirds majority of those present and voting (282 in this case) is required for passage under suspension of the rules. A "nay" was a vote in support of the president's position. June 11, 2008.

	399	400	401	402	403
ALABAMA					
1 **Bonner**	Y	N	N	Y	N
2 **Everett**	Y	N	N	Y	N
3 **Rogers**	Y	Y	N	Y	Y
4 **Aderholt**	Y	N	N	Y	N
5 Cramer	N	Y	Y	Y	Y
6 **Bachus**	Y	Y	N	Y	N
7 Davis	N	Y	Y	Y	Y
ALASKA					
AL **Young**	Y	Y	N	Y	Y
ARIZONA					
1 **Renzi**	Y	Y	N	Y	N
2 **Franks**	Y	N	N	Y	N
3 **Shadegg**	Y	N	N	Y	N
4 Pastor	N	Y	Y	Y	Y
5 Mitchell	N	Y	Y	Y	Y
6 **Flake**	?	?	?	?	?
7 Grijalva	N	Y	Y	Y	Y
8 Giffords	N	Y	Y	Y	Y
ARKANSAS					
1 Berry	N	Y	Y	Y	Y
2 Snyder	N	Y	Y	Y	Y
3 **Boozman**	Y	Y	N	Y	N
4 Ross	N	Y	Y	Y	Y
CALIFORNIA					
1 Thompson	N	Y	Y	Y	Y
2 **Herger**	Y	N	N	Y	N
3 **Lungren**	Y	N	N	Y	N
4 **Doolittle**	Y	N	N	Y	N
5 Matsui	N	Y	Y	Y	Y
6 Woolsey	N	Y	Y	Y	Y
7 Miller, George	N	Y	Y	?	Y
8 Pelosi					Y
9 Lee	N	Y	Y	Y	Y
10 Tauscher	N	Y	Y	Y	Y
11 McNerney	Y	Y	Y	Y	Y
12 Speier	N	Y	Y	Y	Y
13 Stark	N	?	Y	Y	Y
14 Eshoo	N	Y	Y	Y	Y
15 Honda	N	Y	Y	Y	Y
16 Lofgren	N	Y	Y	Y	Y
17 Farr	N	Y	Y	Y	Y
18 Cardoza	N	Y	Y	?	Y
19 **Radanovich**	Y	N	N	Y	N
20 Costa	N	Y	Y	Y	Y
21 **Nunes**	Y	N	N	Y	N
22 **McCarthy**	Y	N	N	Y	N
23 Capps	N	Y	Y	Y	Y
24 **Gallegly**	Y	N	N	Y	N
25 **McKeon**	Y	N	N	Y	N
26 **Dreier**	Y	N	N	Y	N
27 Sherman	N	Y	Y	Y	Y
28 Berman	N	Y	Y	Y	Y
29 Schiff	N	Y	Y	Y	Y
30 Waxman	N	Y	Y	Y	Y
31 Becerra	N	Y	Y	Y	Y
32 Solis	N	Y	Y	Y	Y
33 Watson	N	Y	Y	Y	Y
34 Roybal-Allard	N	Y	Y	Y	Y
35 Waters	N	Y	Y	Y	Y
36 Harman	N	Y	Y	Y	Y
37 Richardson	N	Y	Y	Y	Y
38 Napolitano	N	Y	Y	Y	Y
39 Sánchez, Linda	N	Y	Y	Y	Y
40 **Royce**	Y	N	N	Y	N
41 **Lewis**	Y	N	N	Y	N
42 **Miller, Gary**	Y	N	N	Y	N
43 Baca	N	Y	Y	Y	Y
44 **Calvert**	Y	N	N	Y	N
45 **Bono Mack**	Y	N	N	Y	N
46 **Rohrabacher**	Y	N	N	Y	N
47 Sanchez, Loretta	N	Y	Y	Y	Y
48 **Campbell**	Y	N	N	Y	N
49 **Issa**	Y	N	N	Y	N
50 **Bilbray**	Y	N	N	Y	N
51 Filner	N	Y	Y	Y	Y
52 **Hunter**	Y	N	N	Y	N
53 Davis	N	Y	Y	Y	Y

	399	400	401	402	403
COLORADO					
1 DeGette	N	Y	Y	Y	Y
2 Udall	N	Y	Y	Y	Y
3 Salazar	N	Y	Y	Y	Y
4 **Musgrave**	Y	?	N	Y	N
5 **Lamborn**	Y	N	N	Y	N
6 **Tancredo**	?	?	?	?	?
7 Perlmutter	N	Y	Y	Y	Y
CONNECTICUT					
1 Larson	N	Y	Y	Y	Y
2 Courtney	N	Y	Y	Y	Y
3 DeLauro	N	Y	Y	Y	Y
4 **Shays**	Y	Y	Y	Y	Y
5 Murphy	N	Y	Y	Y	Y
DELAWARE					
AL **Castle**	N	Y	Y	Y	Y
FLORIDA					
1 **Miller**	Y	N	N	Y	N
2 Boyd	N	Y	Y	Y	Y
3 Brown	N	Y	Y	Y	Y
4 **Crenshaw**	Y	N	N	Y	N
5 **Brown-Waite**	Y	N	N	Y	N
6 **Stearns**	Y	N	N	Y	N
7 **Mica**	Y	Y	N	Y	N
8 **Keller**	Y	Y	N	Y	N
9 **Bilirakis**	Y	N	N	Y	N
10 **Young**	Y	Y	N	Y	N
11 Castor	N	Y	Y	Y	Y
12 **Putnam**	Y	Y	N	Y	N
13 **Buchanan**	Y	Y	N	Y	Y
14 **Mack**	Y	N	N	Y	N
15 **Weldon**	Y	N	N	Y	N
16 Mahoney	N	Y	Y	Y	Y
17 Meek	N	Y	Y	Y	Y
18 **Ros-Lehtinen**	Y	Y	N	Y	Y
19 Wexler	N	Y	Y	Y	Y
20 Wasserman Schultz	N	Y	Y	Y	Y
21 **Diaz-Balart, L.**	Y	Y	Y	Y	Y
22 Klein	N	Y	Y	Y	Y
23 Hastings	N	Y	Y	Y	Y
24 **Feeney**	Y	N	N	Y	N
25 **Diaz-Balart, M.**	Y	?	Y	Y	Y
GEORGIA					
1 **Kingston**	Y	N	N	Y	N
2 Bishop	N	Y	Y	Y	Y
3 **Westmoreland**	Y	Y	N	Y	N
4 Johnson	N	Y	Y	Y	Y
5 Lewis	N	Y	Y	Y	Y
6 **Price**	Y	N	N	Y	N
7 **Linder**	Y	N	N	?	N
8 Marshall	Y	Y	Y	?	Y
9 **Deal**	Y	N	N	Y	N
10 **Broun**	Y	N	N	Y	N
11 **Gingrey**	Y	N	N	Y	N
12 Barrow	N	Y	Y	Y	Y
13 Scott	N	Y	Y	Y	Y
HAWAII					
1 Abercrombie	N	Y	Y	Y	Y
2 Hirono	N	Y	Y	Y	Y
IDAHO					
1 **Sali**	Y	N	N	Y	N
2 **Simpson**	Y	Y	N	Y	N
ILLINOIS					
1 Rush	?	?	?	?	?
2 Jackson	N	Y	Y	Y	Y
3 Lipinski	N	Y	Y	Y	Y
4 Gutierrez	N	?	Y	Y	Y
5 Emanuel	N	Y	Y	Y	Y
6 **Roskam**	Y	N	N	Y	N
7 Davis	N	Y	Y	Y	Y
8 Bean	N	Y	Y	Y	Y
9 Schakowsky	N	Y	Y	Y	Y
10 **Kirk**	Y	Y	N	Y	N
11 **Weller**	N	Y	N	Y	N
12 Costello	N	Y	Y	Y	Y
13 **Biggert**	Y	Y	N	Y	N
14 Foster	N	Y	Y	Y	Y
15 Johnson	Y	Y	Y	Y	Y

KEY   Republicans   Democrats

Y Voted for (yea)	X Paired against
# Paired for	– Announced against
+ Announced for	P Voted "present"
N Voted against (nay)	

C Voted "present" to avoid possible conflict of interest

? Did not vote or otherwise make a position known

ND Northern Democrats, SD Southern Democrats
Southern states: Ala., Ark., Fla., Ga., Ky., La., Miss., N.C., Okla., S.C., Tenn., Texas, Va.

	399	400	401	402	403
16 Manzullo	Y	Y	Y	Y	N
17 Hare	N	Y	Y	Y	Y
18 LaHood	N	Y	N	Y	Y
19 Shimkus	Y	Y	Y	Y	N
INDIANA					
1 Visclosky	N	Y	Y	Y	Y
2 Donnelly	Y	Y	Y	Y	Y
3 Souder	Y	Y	N	Y	Y
4 Buyer	Y	Y	N	Y	N
5 Burton	Y	N	N	Y	N
6 Pence	N	N	N	Y	N
7 Carson, A.	N	Y	Y	Y	Y
8 Ellsworth	Y	Y	Y	Y	Y
9 Hill	Y	Y	Y	Y	Y
IOWA					
1 Braley	?	?	?	?	?
2 Loebsack	?	?	?	?	?
3 Boswell	N	Y	Y	Y	Y
4 Latham	Y	Y	?	Y	N
5 King	Y	?	–	Y	N
KANSAS					
1 Moran	Y	Y	N	Y	N
2 Boyda	N	Y	Y	Y	Y
3 Moore	N	Y	Y	Y	Y
4 Tiahrt	Y	N	N	Y	N
KENTUCKY					
1 Whitfield	Y	Y	N	?	N
2 Lewis	Y	N	N	Y	N
3 Yarmuth	N	Y	Y	Y	Y
4 Davis	Y	N	N	Y	N
5 Rogers	Y	N	N	Y	N
6 Chandler	N	Y	Y	Y	Y
LOUISIANA					
1 Scalise	Y	N	N	Y	N
2 Jefferson	N	Y	Y	Y	Y
3 Melancon	N	Y	Y	Y	Y
4 McCrery	?	?	?	?	?
5 Alexander	Y	Y	N	Y	N
6 Cazayoux	N	Y	Y	Y	Y
7 Boustany	Y	N	N	Y	N
MAINE					
1 Allen	N	Y	Y	Y	Y
2 Michaud	N	Y	Y	Y	Y
MARYLAND					
1 Gilchrest	N	Y	Y	Y	Y
2 Ruppersberger	N	Y	Y	?	Y
3 Sarbanes	N	Y	Y	Y	Y
4 Vacant					
5 Hoyer	N	Y	Y	Y	Y
6 Bartlett	Y	?	N	Y	N
7 Cummings	N	Y	Y	Y	Y
8 Van Hollen	N	Y	Y	Y	Y
MASSACHUSETTS					
1 Olver	N	Y	Y	Y	Y
2 Neal	N	Y	Y	Y	Y
3 McGovern	N	Y	Y	Y	Y
4 Frank	N	Y	Y	Y	Y
5 Tsongas	N	Y	Y	Y	Y
6 Tierney	N	Y	Y	Y	Y
7 Markey	N	Y	Y	Y	Y
8 Capuano	N	Y	Y	Y	Y
9 Lynch	N	Y	Y	Y	Y
10 Delahunt	N	Y	Y	Y	Y
MICHIGAN					
1 Stupak	N	Y	Y	Y	Y
2 Hoekstra	Y	N	N	Y	Y
3 Ehlers	Y	Y	N	Y	Y
4 Camp	Y	N	N	Y	Y
5 Kildee	N	Y	Y	Y	Y
6 Upton	Y	N	Y	Y	Y
7 Walberg	Y	N	N	Y	Y
8 Rogers	Y	N	N	Y	Y
9 Knollenberg	Y	Y	N	Y	Y
10 Miller	Y	Y	N	Y	Y
11 McCotter	Y	Y	N	Y	Y
12 Levin	N	Y	Y	Y	Y
13 Kilpatrick	N	Y	Y	Y	Y
14 Conyers	N	Y	Y	Y	Y
15 Dingell	N	Y	Y	Y	Y
MINNESOTA					
1 Walz	N	Y	Y	Y	Y
2 Kline	Y	Y	N	Y	N
3 Ramstad	Y	N	Y	Y	Y
4 McCollum	N	Y	Y	Y	Y

	399	400	401	402	403
5 Ellison	N	Y	Y	Y	Y
6 Bachmann	Y	N	N	Y	N
7 Peterson	N	Y	Y	Y	Y
8 Oberstar	N	Y	Y	Y	Y
MISSISSIPPI					
1 Childers	N	Y	Y	Y	Y
2 Thompson	N	Y	Y	Y	Y
3 Pickering	Y	Y	N	Y	N
4 Taylor	N	Y	Y	Y	Y
MISSOURI					
1 Clay	N	Y	Y	Y	Y
2 Akin	Y	N	N	Y	N
3 Carnahan	N	Y	Y	Y	Y
4 Skelton	N	Y	Y	Y	N
5 Cleaver	N	Y	Y	Y	Y
6 Graves	Y	Y	N	Y	N
7 Blunt	Y	N	N	Y	N
8 Emerson	Y	N	N	Y	Y
9 Hulshof	?	?	?	?	?
MONTANA					
AL Rehberg	Y	Y	N	Y	N
NEBRASKA					
1 Fortenberry	Y	Y	N	Y	N
2 Terry	Y	N	N	Y	N
3 Smith	Y	N	N	Y	N
NEVADA					
1 Berkley	N	Y	Y	Y	Y
2 Heller	Y	N	N	Y	Y
3 Porter	Y	N	N	Y	Y
NEW HAMPSHIRE					
1 Shea-Porter	N	Y	Y	?	Y
2 Hodes	N	Y	Y	Y	Y
NEW JERSEY					
1 Andrews	N	Y	Y	Y	Y
2 LoBiondo	Y	Y	Y	Y	N
3 Saxton	Y	Y	N	Y	N
4 Smith	Y	Y	N	Y	Y
5 Garrett	Y	Y	N	Y	N
6 Pallone	N	Y	Y	Y	Y
7 Ferguson	Y	Y	N	Y	N
8 Pascrell	N	Y	?	Y	Y
9 Rothman	N	Y	Y	Y	Y
10 Payne	N	Y	Y	Y	Y
11 Frelinghuysen	Y	Y	Y	Y	N
12 Holt	N	Y	Y	Y	Y
13 Sires	N	Y	Y	Y	Y
NEW MEXICO					
1 Wilson	Y	N	Y	Y	N
2 Pearce	Y	N	N	?	N
3 Udall	N	Y	Y	Y	Y
NEW YORK					
1 Bishop	N	Y	Y	Y	Y
2 Israel	N	Y	Y	?	Y
3 King	Y	Y	Y	Y	N
4 McCarthy	N	Y	Y	Y	Y
5 Ackerman	N	Y	Y	Y	Y
6 Meeks	N	Y	Y	Y	Y
7 Crowley	N	Y	Y	?	Y
8 Nadler	N	Y	Y	Y	Y
9 Weiner	N	Y	Y	?	Y
10 Towns	N	Y	Y	Y	Y
11 Clarke	N	Y	Y	Y	Y
12 Velázquez	N	Y	Y	Y	Y
13 Fossella	Y	Y	Y	Y	N
14 Maloney	N	Y	Y	?	Y
15 Rangel	N	Y	Y	Y	Y
16 Serrano	N	Y	Y	Y	Y
17 Engel	N	Y	Y	Y	Y
18 Lowey	N	Y	Y	Y	Y
19 Hall	N	Y	Y	Y	Y
20 Gillibrand	?	?	?	?	?
21 McNulty	N	Y	Y	Y	Y
22 Hinchey	N	Y	Y	Y	Y
23 McHugh	Y	Y	N	Y	Y
24 Arcuri	N	Y	Y	Y	Y
25 Walsh	Y	Y	N	Y	Y
26 Reynolds	Y	Y	N	Y	N
27 Higgins	N	Y	Y	Y	Y
28 Slaughter	N	Y	Y	Y	Y
29 Kuhl	Y	Y	N	Y	Y
NORTH CAROLINA					
1 Butterfield	N	+	Y	Y	Y
2 Etheridge	N	Y	Y	Y	Y
3 Jones	Y	Y	Y	?	Y
4 Price	N	Y	Y	Y	Y

	399	400	401	402	403
5 Foxx	Y	N	N	Y	N
6 Coble	Y	N	N	Y	N
7 McIntyre	N	Y	Y	Y	Y
8 Hayes	Y	Y	N	Y	Y
9 Myrick	Y	N	N	Y	N
10 McHenry	Y	N	N	Y	Y
11 Shuler	N	Y	Y	Y	Y
12 Watt	N	Y	Y	Y	Y
13 Miller	N	Y	Y	Y	Y
NORTH DAKOTA					
AL Pomeroy	N	Y	Y	Y	Y
OHIO					
1 Chabot	Y	N	N	Y	Y
2 Schmidt	Y	N	N	Y	Y
3 Turner	Y	Y	Y	Y	Y
4 Jordan	Y	N	N	Y	N
5 Latta	Y	N	N	Y	N
6 Wilson	N	Y	Y	Y	Y
7 Hobson	Y	N	N	Y	N
8 Boehner	Y	N	N	Y	N
9 Kaptur	N	+	Y	Y	Y
10 Kucinich	N	Y	Y	?	Y
11 Tubbs Jones	N	Y	Y	Y	Y
12 Tiberi	Y	Y	N	Y	N
13 Sutton	N	Y	Y	?	Y
14 LaTourette	N	Y	Y	Y	Y
15 Pryce	Y	N	Y	Y	N
16 Regula	Y	Y	N	Y	N
17 Ryan	N	Y	Y	Y	Y
18 Space	N	Y	Y	Y	Y
OKLAHOMA					
1 Sullivan	Y	Y	N	Y	N
2 Boren	N	Y	Y	Y	Y
3 Lucas	Y	Y	N	Y	N
4 Cole	Y	Y	N	Y	N
5 Fallin	Y	Y	N	Y	N
OREGON					
1 Wu	N	Y	Y	Y	Y
2 Walden	Y	Y	N	Y	N
3 Blumenauer	N	Y	Y	Y	Y
4 DeFazio	N	Y	Y	Y	Y
5 Hooley	N	Y	Y	Y	Y
PENNSYLVANIA					
1 Brady	N	Y	Y	Y	Y
2 Fattah	N	Y	Y	Y	Y
3 English	Y	Y	N	Y	Y
4 Altmire	N	Y	Y	Y	Y
5 Peterson	Y	N	N	Y	?
6 Gerlach	Y	Y	N	Y	Y
7 Sestak	N	Y	Y	Y	Y
8 Murphy, P.	N	Y	Y	Y	Y
9 Shuster	Y	Y	N	Y	N
10 Carney	N	Y	Y	Y	Y
11 Kanjorski	N	Y	Y	Y	Y
12 Murtha	N	Y	Y	Y	Y
13 Schwartz	N	Y	Y	Y	Y
14 Doyle	N	Y	Y	Y	Y
15 Dent	Y	N	Y	Y	Y
16 Pitts	Y	N	N	Y	N
17 Holden	Y	N	Y	Y	Y
18 Murphy, T.	Y	Y	Y	Y	Y
19 Platts	N	Y	N	Y	Y
RHODE ISLAND					
1 Kennedy	N	Y	Y	Y	Y
2 Langevin	N	Y	Y	Y	Y
SOUTH CAROLINA					
1 Brown	Y	Y	N	Y	N
2 Wilson	Y	N	N	Y	N
3 Barrett	Y	N	N	Y	N
4 Inglis	Y	N	N	Y	N
5 Spratt	N	Y	Y	Y	Y
6 Clyburn	N	Y	Y	Y	Y
SOUTH DAKOTA					
AL Herseth Sandlin	N	Y	Y	Y	Y
TENNESSEE					
1 Davis, D.	Y	N	N	Y	N
2 Duncan	Y	N	N	Y	N
3 Wamp	Y	N	N	Y	N
4 Davis, L.	N	Y	Y	Y	Y
5 Cooper	N	Y	Y	Y	Y
6 Gordon	N	Y	Y	Y	Y
7 Blackburn	Y	N	N	Y	N
8 Tanner	N	Y	Y	Y	Y
9 Cohen	N	Y	+	+	Y

	399	400	401	402	403
TEXAS					
1 Gohmert	Y	Y	N	Y	N
2 Poe	Y	Y	N	Y	N
3 Johnson, S.	Y	N	N	Y	N
4 Hall	Y	N	Y	Y	N
5 Hensarling	Y	N	N	Y	N
6 Barton	Y	N	N	Y	N
7 Culberson	Y	N	N	Y	N
8 Brady	Y	N	N	Y	N
9 Green, A.	N	+	Y	Y	Y
10 McCaul	Y	N	N	Y	N
11 Conaway	Y	N	N	Y	N
12 Granger	Y	Y	N	Y	N
13 Thornberry	Y	N	N	Y	N
14 Paul	Y	N	Y	Y	?
15 Hinojosa	N	Y	Y	Y	Y
16 Reyes	N	Y	Y	Y	Y
17 Edwards	N	Y	Y	Y	Y
18 Jackson Lee	N	Y	Y	Y	Y
19 Neugebauer	Y	N	–	Y	N
20 Gonzalez	N	Y	Y	Y	Y
21 Smith	Y	N	N	Y	N
22 Lampson	Y	Y	Y	Y	Y
23 Rodriguez	N	Y	Y	Y	Y
24 Marchant	Y	N	N	Y	N
25 Doggett	N	Y	Y	Y	Y
26 Burgess	Y	N	N	Y	N
27 Ortiz	?	?	?	?	?
28 Cuellar	N	Y	Y	Y	Y
29 Green, G.	N	Y	Y	Y	Y
30 Johnson, E.	N	Y	Y	Y	Y
31 Carter	Y	N	N	Y	N
32 Sessions	Y	N	?	Y	N
UTAH					
1 Bishop	Y	Y	N	Y	N
2 Matheson	Y	Y	Y	Y	Y
3 Cannon	Y	N	N	Y	N
VERMONT					
AL Welch	N	Y	Y	Y	Y
VIRGINIA					
1 Wittman	Y	N	N	Y	N
2 Drake	Y	Y	N	Y	N
3 Scott	N	Y	Y	Y	Y
4 Forbes	Y	N	N	Y	N
5 Goode	Y	Y	N	Y	N
6 Goodlatte	Y	Y	?	Y	N
7 Cantor	Y	N	N	Y	N
8 Moran	N	Y	Y	Y	Y
9 Boucher	N	Y	Y	?	Y
10 Wolf	N	Y	Y	Y	Y
11 Davis	N	Y	N	Y	Y
WASHINGTON					
1 Inslee	N	Y	Y	Y	Y
2 Larsen	N	Y	Y	Y	Y
3 Baird	N	Y	Y	Y	Y
4 Hastings	Y	N	N	Y	N
5 McMorris Rodgers	Y	Y	N	Y	N
6 Dicks	N	Y	Y	Y	Y
7 McDermott	N	Y	Y	Y	Y
8 Reichert	Y	Y	Y	Y	Y
9 Smith	N	Y	Y	Y	Y
WEST VIRGINIA					
1 Mollohan	N	Y	Y	Y	Y
2 Capito	Y	Y	N	Y	Y
3 Rahall	N	Y	Y	?	Y
WISCONSIN					
1 Ryan	Y	N	N	Y	Y
2 Baldwin	N	Y	Y	Y	Y
3 Kind	N	Y	Y	Y	Y
4 Moore	N	Y	Y	Y	Y
5 Sensenbrenner	Y	N	N	Y	N
6 Petri	Y	Y	N	Y	Y
7 Obey	N	Y	Y	Y	Y
8 Kagen	N	Y	Y	Y	Y
WYOMING					
AL Cubin	Y	N	N	Y	N
DELEGATES					
Faleomavaega (A.S.)					
Norton (D.C.)					
Bordallo (Guam)					
Fortuño (P.R.)					
Christensen (V.I.)					

IN THE HOUSE | By Vote Number

404. H Res 977. Stimulus Check Spending/Adoption. Butterfield, D-N.C., motion to suspend the rules and adopt the resolution that would encourage Americans to use their rebate checks from the stimulus package to purchase American-made goods and services from American-owned companies. Motion agreed to 404-6: R 178-6; D 226-0 (ND 168-0, SD 58-0). A two-thirds majority of those present and voting (274 in this case) is required for adoption under suspension of the rules. June 11, 2008.

405. HR 6063. NASA Authorization/Previous Question. Hastings, D-Fla., motion to order the previous question (thus ending debate and possibility of amendment) on adoption of the rule (H Res 1257) to provide for House floor consideration of the bill that would authorize $19.2 billion in fiscal 2009 for NASA programs and $1 billion to accelerate research and development of new space exploration vehicles. Motion agreed to 226-183: R 9-180; D 217-3 (ND 162-2, SD 55-1). June 12, 2008.

406. HR 6063. NASA Authorization/Rule. Adoption of the rule (H Res 1257) to provide for House floor consideration of the bill that would authorize $19.2 billion in fiscal 2009 for NASA programs and $1 billion to accelerate research and development of new space exploration vehicles. Adopted 221-188: R 0-187; D 221-1 (ND 164-1, SD 57-0). June 12, 2008.

407. HR 5749. Unemployment Benefits Extension/Previous Question. Arcuri, D-N.Y., motion to order the previous question (thus ending debate and possibility of amendment) on adoption of the rule (H Res 1265) to provide for House floor consideration of the bill that would extend federal unemployment benefits for individuals who have exhausted their current 26 weeks of compensation. The bill would provide an additional 13 weeks in all states, plus another 13 weeks of extended benefits in states with high unemployment rates. Motion agreed to 225-186: R 7-184; D 218-2 (ND 160-2, SD 58-0). June 12, 2008.

408. HR 5749. Unemployment Benefits Extension/Rule. Adoption of the rule (H Res 1265) that would provide for House floor consideration of the bill that would extend federal unemployment benefits for individuals who have exhausted their current 26 weeks of compensation. The bill would provide an additional 13 weeks in all states, plus another 13 weeks of extended benefits in states with high unemployment rates. Adopted 227-192: R 3-190; D 224-2 (ND 166-2, SD 58-0). June 12, 2008.

	404	405	406	407	408
ALABAMA					
1 Bonner	Y	N	N	N	N
2 Everett	Y	N	N	N	N
3 Rogers	Y	N	N	N	N
4 Aderholt	Y	N	N	N	N
5 Cramer	Y	Y	Y	Y	Y
6 Bachus	Y	N	N	N	N
7 Davis	Y	?	Y	Y	Y
ALASKA					
AL Young	N	N	N	N	N
ARIZONA					
1 Renzi	Y	N	N	N	N
2 Franks	Y	N	N	N	N
3 Shadegg	Y	N	N	N	N
4 Pastor	Y	Y	Y	Y	Y
5 Mitchell	Y	Y	Y	Y	Y
6 Flake	?	?	?	?	?
7 Grijalva	Y	Y	Y	Y	Y
8 Giffords	Y	Y	Y	Y	N
ARKANSAS					
1 Berry	Y	Y	Y	Y	Y
2 Snyder	Y	Y	Y	Y	Y
3 Boozman	Y	N	N	N	N
4 Ross	Y	Y	Y	Y	Y
CALIFORNIA					
1 Thompson	Y	Y	Y	Y	Y
2 Herger	N	N	N	N	N
3 Lungren	Y	N	N	N	N
4 Doolittle	Y	N	N	N	N
5 Matsui	Y	Y	Y	Y	Y
6 Woolsey	Y	Y	Y	Y	Y
7 Miller, George	Y	Y	Y	?	Y
8 Pelosi					
9 Lee	Y	Y	Y	Y	Y
10 Tauscher	Y	Y	Y	Y	Y
11 McNerney	Y	Y	Y	Y	Y
12 Speier	Y	Y	Y	Y	Y
13 Stark	Y	?	?	?	?
14 Eshoo	Y	Y	Y	Y	Y
15 Honda	Y	?	Y	Y	Y
16 Lofgren	Y	Y	Y	Y	Y
17 Farr	Y	Y	Y	Y	Y
18 Cardoza	Y	Y	Y	Y	Y
19 Radanovich	Y	N	N	N	N
20 Costa	Y	Y	Y	Y	Y
21 Nunes	Y	N	N	N	N
22 McCarthy	Y	N	N	N	N
23 Capps	Y	Y	Y	Y	Y
24 Gallegly	Y	N	N	N	N
25 McKeon	Y	N	N	N	N
26 Dreier	Y	N	N	N	N
27 Sherman	Y	Y	Y	Y	Y
28 Berman	Y	Y	Y	Y	Y
29 Schiff	Y	Y	Y	Y	Y
30 Waxman	Y	Y	Y	Y	Y
31 Becerra	Y	Y	Y	Y	Y
32 Solis	Y	Y	Y	Y	Y
33 Watson	Y	Y	Y	Y	Y
34 Roybal-Allard	Y	Y	Y	Y	Y
35 Waters	Y	Y	Y	?	Y
36 Harman	Y	Y	Y	Y	Y
37 Richardson	Y	Y	Y	Y	Y
38 Napolitano	Y	Y	Y	Y	Y
39 Sánchez, Linda	Y	Y	Y	Y	Y
40 Royce	Y	N	N	N	N
41 Lewis	Y	?	N	N	N
42 Miller, Gary	Y	N	N	N	N
43 Baca	Y	Y	Y	Y	Y
44 Calvert	Y	N	N	N	N
45 Bono Mack	Y	N	N	N	N
46 Rohrabacher	Y	N	N	N	N
47 Sanchez, Loretta	Y	Y	Y	Y	Y
48 Campbell	N	N	N	N	N
49 Issa	Y	N	N	N	N
50 Bilbray	Y	N	N	N	N
51 Filner	Y	Y	Y	Y	Y
52 Hunter	Y	N	N	N	N
53 Davis	Y	Y	Y	Y	Y

	404	405	406	407	408
COLORADO					
1 DeGette	Y	Y	Y	Y	Y
2 Udall	Y	Y	Y	Y	Y
3 Salazar	Y	Y	Y	Y	Y
4 Musgrave	Y	N	N	N	N
5 Lamborn	Y	N	N	N	N
6 Tancredo	?	?	?	?	?
7 Perlmutter	Y	Y	Y	Y	Y
CONNECTICUT					
1 Larson	Y	Y	Y	Y	Y
2 Courtney	Y	Y	Y	Y	Y
3 DeLauro	Y	Y	Y	Y	Y
4 Shays	Y	N	N	N	Y
5 Murphy	Y	Y	Y	Y	Y
DELAWARE					
AL Castle	Y	N	N	N	N
FLORIDA					
1 Miller	Y	N	N	N	N
2 Boyd	Y	Y	Y	Y	Y
3 Brown	Y	Y	Y	Y	Y
4 Crenshaw	Y	N	N	N	N
5 Brown-Waite	Y	N	N	N	N
6 Stearns	Y	N	N	N	N
7 Mica	Y	N	N	N	N
8 Keller	Y	N	N	N	N
9 Bilirakis	Y	N	N	N	Y
10 Young	Y	N	N	N	N
11 Castor	Y	Y	Y	Y	Y
12 Putnam	Y	N	N	N	N
13 Buchanan	Y	N	N	N	N
14 Mack	Y	N	N	N	N
15 Weldon	P	N	N	N	N
16 Mahoney	Y	Y	Y	Y	Y
17 Meek	Y	?	Y	Y	Y
18 Ros-Lehtinen	Y	N	Y	N	N
19 Wexler	Y	Y	Y	Y	Y
20 Wasserman Schultz	Y	Y	Y	Y	Y
21 Diaz-Balart, L.	Y	N	N	N	N
22 Klein	Y	Y	Y	Y	Y
23 Hastings	Y	Y	Y	Y	Y
24 Feeney	Y	N	N	N	N
25 Diaz-Balart, M.	Y	N	N	N	N
GEORGIA					
1 Kingston	Y	N	N	N	N
2 Bishop	Y	Y	Y	Y	Y
3 Westmoreland	Y	N	N	N	N
4 Johnson	Y	Y	Y	Y	Y
5 Lewis	Y	Y	Y	Y	Y
6 Price	P	N	N	N	N
7 Linder	Y	N	N	N	N
8 Marshall	Y	Y	Y	Y	Y
9 Deal	Y	N	N	N	N
10 Broun	Y	N	N	N	N
11 Gingrey	Y	N	N	N	N
12 Barrow	Y	Y	Y	Y	Y
13 Scott	Y	Y	Y	Y	Y
HAWAII					
1 Abercrombie	Y	Y	Y	Y	Y
2 Hirono	Y	Y	Y	Y	Y
IDAHO					
1 Sali	Y	N	N	N	N
2 Simpson	Y	N	?	N	N
ILLINOIS					
1 Rush	?	?	?	?	?
2 Jackson	Y	Y	Y	Y	Y
3 Lipinski	Y	Y	Y	Y	Y
4 Gutierrez	?	Y	Y	?	Y
5 Emanuel	Y	Y	Y	Y	Y
6 Roskam	Y	N	N	N	N
7 Davis	Y	Y	Y	Y	Y
8 Bean	Y	Y	Y	Y	Y
9 Schakowsky	Y	Y	Y	Y	Y
10 Kirk	Y	Y	?	N	N
11 Weller	Y	N	N	N	N
12 Costello	Y	Y	Y	Y	Y
13 Biggert	Y	N	N	N	N
14 Foster	Y	Y	Y	Y	Y
15 Johnson	Y	Y	N	Y	N

KEY   **Republicans**   Democrats

Y Voted for (yea)	X Paired against	C Voted "present" to avoid possible conflict of interest
# Paired for	– Announced against	
+ Announced for	P Voted "present"	? Did not vote or otherwise make a position known
N Voted against (nay)		

ND Northern Democrats, SD Southern Democrats
Southern states: Ala., Ark., Fla., Ga., Ky., La., Miss., N.C., Okla., S.C., Tenn., Texas, Va.

	404	405	406	407	408
16 Manzullo	Y	N	N	N	N
17 Hare	Y	Y	Y	Y	Y
18 LaHood	Y	N	N	N	N
19 Shimkus	Y	N	N	N	N
INDIANA					
1 Visclosky	Y	Y	Y	Y	Y
2 Donnelly	Y	N	Y	N	Y
3 Souder	Y	N	N	N	N
4 Buyer	Y	N	N	N	N
5 Burton	?	N	N	N	N
6 Pence	Y	N	N	N	N
7 Carson, A.	Y	Y	Y	Y	Y
8 Ellsworth	Y	Y	Y	Y	Y
9 Hill	Y	N	N	N	N
IOWA					
1 Braley	?	?	?	?	?
2 Loebsack	?	?	?	?	?
3 Boswell	Y	Y	Y	Y	Y
4 Latham	Y	N	N	N	N
5 King	N	N	N	N	N
KANSAS					
1 Moran	Y	?	?	?	?
2 Boyda	Y	+	+	+	+
3 Moore	Y	Y	Y	Y	Y
4 Tiahrt	Y	N	N	N	N
KENTUCKY					
1 Whitfield	Y	N	N	N	N
2 Lewis	Y	N	N	N	N
3 Yarmuth	Y	Y	Y	Y	Y
4 Davis	Y	N	N	N	N
5 Rogers	Y	N	N	N	N
6 Chandler	Y	Y	Y	Y	Y
LOUISIANA					
1 Scalise	Y	N	N	N	N
2 Jefferson	Y	Y	Y	Y	Y
3 Melancon	Y	Y	Y	Y	Y
4 McCrery	?	?	?	?	?
5 Alexander	Y	N	N	N	N
6 Cazayoux	Y	Y	Y	Y	Y
7 Boustany	Y	N	N	N	N
MAINE					
1 Allen	Y	Y	Y	Y	Y
2 Michaud	Y	Y	Y	Y	Y
MARYLAND					
1 Gilchrest	Y	Y	N	N	N
2 Ruppersberger	Y	?	Y	Y	Y
3 Sarbanes	Y	Y	Y	Y	Y
4 Vacant					
5 Hoyer	Y	Y	Y	Y	Y
6 Bartlett	Y	N	N	N	N
7 Cummings	Y	Y	Y	Y	Y
8 Van Hollen	Y	Y	Y	Y	Y
MASSACHUSETTS					
1 Olver	Y	Y	Y	Y	Y
2 Neal	Y	Y	Y	Y	Y
3 McGovern	Y	Y	Y	Y	Y
4 Frank	Y	Y	Y	Y	Y
5 Tsongas	Y	Y	Y	Y	Y
6 Tierney	Y	Y	Y	Y	Y
7 Markey	Y	Y	Y	Y	Y
8 Capuano	Y	Y	Y	Y	Y
9 Lynch	Y	Y	Y	Y	Y
10 Delahunt	Y	Y	Y	Y	Y
MICHIGAN					
1 Stupak	Y	Y	Y	Y	Y
2 Hoekstra	Y	N	N	N	N
3 Ehlers	Y	N	N	N	N
4 Camp	?	N	N	N	N
5 Kildee	Y	Y	Y	Y	Y
6 Upton	Y	N	N	N	N
7 Walberg	Y	N	N	N	N
8 Rogers	?	?	?	?	?
9 Knollenberg	Y	N	N	N	N
10 Miller	Y	N	N	N	N
11 McCotter	Y	N	N	N	N
12 Levin	Y	Y	Y	Y	Y
13 Kilpatrick	Y	Y	Y	Y	Y
14 Conyers	Y	Y	Y	Y	Y
15 Dingell	Y	Y	Y	Y	Y
MINNESOTA					
1 Walz	Y	Y	Y	Y	Y
2 Kline	Y	N	N	N	N
3 Ramstad	Y	N	N	N	N
4 McCollum	Y	Y	Y	Y	Y

	404	405	406	407	408
5 Ellison	Y	Y	Y	Y	Y
6 Bachmann	Y	N	N	N	N
7 Peterson	Y	Y	Y	Y	Y
8 Oberstar	Y	Y	Y	Y	Y
MISSISSIPPI					
1 Childers	Y	N	Y	Y	Y
2 Thompson	Y	Y	Y	Y	Y
3 Pickering	Y	N	N	N	N
4 Taylor	Y	Y	Y	Y	Y
MISSOURI					
1 Clay	Y	Y	Y	Y	Y
2 Akin	Y	N	?	N	N
3 Carnahan	Y	Y	Y	Y	Y
4 Skelton	Y	Y	Y	Y	Y
5 Cleaver	Y	Y	Y	Y	Y
6 Graves	Y	N	N	N	N
7 Blunt	Y	N	N	N	N
8 Emerson	Y	N	N	N	N
9 Hulshof	?	?	?	?	?
MONTANA					
AL Rehberg	Y	N	N	N	N
NEBRASKA					
1 Fortenberry	Y	N	N	N	N
2 Terry	Y	N	N	N	N
3 Smith	Y	N	N	N	N
NEVADA					
1 Berkley	Y	Y	?	Y	Y
2 Heller	Y	N	N	N	N
3 Porter	Y	N	N	N	N
NEW HAMPSHIRE					
1 Shea-Porter	Y	Y	Y	Y	Y
2 Hodes	Y	Y	Y	Y	Y
NEW JERSEY					
1 Andrews	Y	Y	Y	Y	Y
2 LoBiondo	Y	Y	N	N	N
3 Saxton	Y	N	N	N	N
4 Smith	Y	N	N	Y	N
5 Garrett	Y	N	N	N	N
6 Pallone	Y	Y	Y	Y	Y
7 Ferguson	Y	N	N	N	N
8 Pascrell	Y	Y	Y	Y	Y
9 Rothman	Y	Y	Y	Y	Y
10 Payne	Y	Y	Y	Y	Y
11 Frelinghuysen	Y	?	N	N	N
12 Holt	Y	Y	Y	Y	Y
13 Sires	Y	Y	Y	Y	Y
NEW MEXICO					
1 Wilson	Y	N	?	N	N
2 Pearce	Y	N	N	N	N
3 Udall	Y	Y	Y	Y	Y
NEW YORK					
1 Bishop	Y	Y	Y	Y	Y
2 Israel	Y	Y	Y	Y	Y
3 King	Y	N	N	N	N
4 McCarthy	Y	Y	Y	+	Y
5 Ackerman	Y	Y	Y	Y	Y
6 Meeks	Y	Y	Y	Y	Y
7 Crowley	Y	Y	Y	Y	Y
8 Nadler	Y	Y	Y	Y	Y
9 Weiner	Y	Y	Y	Y	Y
10 Towns	Y	Y	Y	Y	Y
11 Clarke	Y	Y	Y	Y	Y
12 Velázquez	Y	Y	Y	?	Y
13 Fossella	Y	N	N	N	N
14 Maloney	Y	Y	Y	Y	Y
15 Rangel	Y	Y	?	Y	Y
16 Serrano	Y	Y	Y	Y	Y
17 Engel	Y	Y	Y	Y	Y
18 Lowey	Y	Y	Y	Y	Y
19 Hall	Y	Y	Y	Y	Y
20 Gillibrand	?	Y	Y	Y	Y
21 McNulty	Y	Y	Y	Y	Y
22 Hinchey	Y	Y	Y	Y	Y
23 McHugh	Y	N	N	N	N
24 Arcuri	Y	Y	Y	Y	Y
25 Walsh	Y	N	N	N	N
26 Reynolds	Y	N	Y	?	N
27 Higgins	Y	?	?	?	?
28 Slaughter	Y	Y	Y	Y	Y
29 Kuhl	Y	N	N	N	N
NORTH CAROLINA					
1 Butterfield	Y	Y	Y	Y	Y
2 Etheridge	Y	Y	Y	Y	Y
3 Jones	Y	N	N	N	N
4 Price	Y	Y	Y	Y	Y

	404	405	406	407	408
5 Foxx	Y	N	N	N	N
6 Coble	Y	N	N	N	N
7 McIntyre	Y	Y	Y	Y	Y
8 Hayes	Y	N	N	N	N
9 Myrick	Y	N	N	N	N
10 McHenry	Y	N	N	N	N
11 Shuler	Y	Y	Y	Y	Y
12 Watt	Y	Y	Y	Y	Y
13 Miller	Y	Y	Y	Y	Y
NORTH DAKOTA					
AL Pomeroy	Y	Y	Y	Y	Y
OHIO					
1 Chabot	Y	N	N	N	N
2 Schmidt	Y	N	N	N	N
3 Turner	Y	N	N	N	N
4 Jordan	Y	N	N	N	N
5 Latta	Y	N	N	N	N
6 Wilson	Y	Y	Y	Y	Y
7 Hobson	Y	N	N	N	N
8 Boehner	Y	N	N	N	N
9 Kaptur	Y	Y	Y	Y	Y
10 Kucinich	Y	Y	Y	Y	Y
11 Tubbs Jones	Y	Y	Y	Y	Y
12 Tiberi	Y	N	N	N	N
13 Sutton	?	Y	Y	Y	Y
14 LaTourette	Y	N	N	N	N
15 Pryce	Y	N	N	N	N
16 Regula	Y	N	N	N	N
17 Ryan	Y	Y	Y	Y	Y
18 Space	Y	Y	Y	Y	Y
OKLAHOMA					
1 Sullivan	Y	N	N	N	N
2 Boren	Y	Y	Y	Y	Y
3 Lucas	Y	N	N	N	N
4 Cole	Y	N	N	N	N
5 Fallin	Y	N	N	N	N
OREGON					
1 Wu	Y	Y	Y	Y	Y
2 Walden	Y	N	N	N	N
3 Blumenauer	Y	Y	Y	Y	Y
4 DeFazio	Y	Y	Y	Y	Y
5 Hooley	Y	Y	Y	Y	Y
PENNSYLVANIA					
1 Brady	Y	Y	Y	Y	Y
2 Fattah	Y	Y	Y	Y	Y
3 English	Y	N	N	Y	N
4 Altmire	Y	Y	Y	Y	Y
5 Peterson	?	?	?	N	N
6 Gerlach	Y	N	N	N	N
7 Sestak	Y	Y	Y	Y	Y
8 Murphy, P.	Y	Y	Y	Y	Y
9 Shuster	Y	N	N	N	N
10 Carney	Y	Y	Y	Y	Y
11 Kanjorski	Y	Y	?	Y	Y
12 Murtha	Y	Y	Y	Y	Y
13 Schwartz	Y	Y	Y	Y	Y
14 Doyle	Y	Y	Y	Y	Y
15 Dent	Y	N	N	N	N
16 Pitts	Y	N	N	N	N
17 Holden	Y	Y	Y	Y	Y
18 Murphy, T.	Y	N	N	N	N
19 Platts	Y	N	N	N	N
RHODE ISLAND					
1 Kennedy	Y	Y	Y	Y	Y
2 Langevin	Y	Y	Y	Y	Y
SOUTH CAROLINA					
1 Brown	Y	N	N	N	N
2 Wilson	Y	N	N	N	N
3 Barrett	Y	N	N	N	N
4 Inglis	Y	N	N	N	N
5 Spratt	Y	Y	Y	Y	Y
6 Clyburn	Y	Y	Y	Y	Y
SOUTH DAKOTA					
AL Herseth Sandlin	Y	Y	Y	Y	Y
TENNESSEE					
1 Davis, D.	Y	N	N	N	N
2 Duncan	Y	N	N	N	N
3 Wamp	Y	N	N	N	N
4 Davis, L.	Y	Y	Y	Y	Y
5 Cooper	Y	Y	Y	Y	Y
6 Gordon	Y	Y	Y	Y	Y
7 Blackburn	Y	N	N	N	N
8 Tanner	Y	Y	Y	Y	Y
9 Cohen	Y	Y	Y	Y	Y

	404	405	406	407	408
TEXAS					
1 Gohmert	Y	Y	N	N	N
2 Poe	Y	N	N	N	N
3 Johnson, S.	Y	N	N	N	N
4 Hall	Y	Y	N	N	N
5 Hensarling	Y	N	N	N	N
6 Barton	Y	N	N	N	N
7 Culberson	Y	N	N	N	N
8 Brady	P	N	?	N	N
9 Green, A.	Y	Y	Y	Y	Y
10 McCaul	Y	N	N	N	N
11 Conaway	N	N	N	N	N
12 Granger	Y	?	N	N	N
13 Thornberry	Y	N	N	N	N
14 Paul	?	N	N	N	N
15 Hinojosa	Y	Y	Y	Y	Y
16 Reyes	Y	Y	Y	Y	Y
17 Edwards	Y	Y	Y	Y	Y
18 Jackson Lee	Y	Y	Y	Y	Y
19 Neugebauer	Y	N	N	N	N
20 Gonzalez	Y	Y	Y	Y	Y
21 Smith	Y	N	N	N	N
22 Lampson	Y	Y	Y	Y	Y
23 Rodriguez	Y	Y	Y	Y	Y
24 Marchant	Y	N	N	N	N
25 Doggett	Y	Y	Y	Y	Y
26 Burgess	Y	N	N	N	N
27 Ortiz	?	?	?	?	?
28 Cuellar	Y	Y	Y	Y	Y
29 Green, G.	Y	Y	Y	Y	Y
30 Johnson, E.	Y	Y	Y	Y	Y
31 Carter	Y	N	N	N	N
32 Sessions	N	N	N	N	N
UTAH					
1 Bishop	P	N	N	N	N
2 Matheson	Y	Y	Y	Y	Y
3 Cannon	P	N	N	N	N
VERMONT					
AL Welch	Y	Y	Y	Y	Y
VIRGINIA					
1 Wittman	Y	N	N	?	N
2 Drake	Y	N	N	N	N
3 Scott	Y	Y	Y	Y	Y
4 Forbes	Y	N	N	N	N
5 Goode	Y	N	N	N	N
6 Goodlatte	Y	N	N	N	N
7 Cantor	Y	N	N	N	N
8 Moran	Y	Y	Y	Y	Y
9 Boucher	Y	Y	Y	Y	Y
10 Wolf	Y	N	N	N	N
11 Davis	P	N	N	N	N
WASHINGTON					
1 Inslee	Y	Y	Y	Y	Y
2 Larsen	Y	Y	Y	Y	Y
3 Baird	Y	Y	Y	Y	Y
4 Hastings	Y	N	N	N	N
5 McMorris Rodgers	Y	N	N	N	N
6 Dicks	Y	Y	Y	Y	Y
7 McDermott	Y	Y	Y	Y	Y
8 Reichert	Y	N	Y	N	N
9 Smith	Y	Y	Y	Y	Y
WEST VIRGINIA					
1 Mollohan	Y	?	Y	Y	Y
2 Capito	Y	N	N	N	N
3 Rahall	Y	Y	Y	Y	Y
WISCONSIN					
1 Ryan	Y	N	N	N	N
2 Baldwin	Y	Y	Y	Y	Y
3 Kind	?	?	?	?	?
4 Moore	Y	Y	Y	Y	Y
5 Sensenbrenner	Y	N	N	N	N
6 Petri	Y	N	N	N	N
7 Obey	Y	?	Y	Y	Y
8 Kagen	Y	Y	Y	Y	Y
WYOMING					
AL Cubin	Y	N	N	N	N
DELEGATES					
Faleomavaega (A.S.)					
Norton (D.C.)					
Bordallo (Guam)					
Fortuño (P.R.)					
Christensen (V.I.)					

IN THE HOUSE | By Vote Number

409. **HR 1553. Pediatric Cancer Research/Passage.** Pallone, D-N.J., motion to suspend the rules and pass the bill that would authorize $30 million a year in fiscal 2009 through 2013 for pediatric cancer research and awareness initiatives. Motion agreed to 416-0: R 191-0; D 225-0 (ND 168-0, SD 57-0). A two-thirds majority of those present and voting (278 in this case) is required for passage under suspension of the rules. June 12, 2008.

410. **HR 5749. Unemployment Benefits Extension/Motion to Table.** Rangel, D-N.Y., motion to table (kill) the Weller, R-Ill., appeal of the ruling of the chair with respect to the Weller point of order that the bill does not comply with House pay-as-you-go rules. Motion agreed to 217-185: R 1-184; D 216-1 (ND 161-1, SD 55-0). June 12, 2008.

411. **HR 5749. Unemployment Benefits Extension/Recommit.** Weller, R-Ill., motion to recommit the bill to the Ways and Means Committee with instructions that it be reported back forthwith with language that would require individuals to work 20 weeks to qualify for the extended benefits, allow for additional money to the newly hired to help with gasoline prices, and target the extended benefits to states with high unemployment rates. Motion rejected 170-243: R 167-19; D 3-224 (ND 2-169, SD 1-55). June 12, 2008.

412. **HR 5749. Unemployment Benefits Extension/Passage.** Passage of the bill that would extend federal unemployment benefits for individuals who have exhausted their current 26 weeks of compensation. The bill would provide an additional 13 weeks in all states, plus another 13 weeks of extended benefits in states with high unemployment rates. The extended benefit program would expire March 31, 2009. Passed 274-137: R 49-137; D 225-0 (ND 169-0, SD 56-0). A "nay" was a vote in support of the president's position. June 12, 2008.

413. **S 2146. Diesel Emission Reduction Projects/Passage.** Boucher, D-Va., motion to suspend the rules and pass the bill that would authorize the EPA to accept diesel emission reduction supplemental environmental projects as part of a settlement of an alleged violation of an environmental law or regulation. Motion agreed to 406-0: R 184-0; D 222-0 (ND 169-0, SD 53-0). A two-thirds majority of those present and voting (271 in this case) is required for passage under suspension of the rules. June 12, 2008.

	409	410	411	412	413
ALABAMA					
1 **Bonner**	Y	N	Y	N	Y
2 **Everett**	Y	N	Y	N	Y
3 **Rogers**	Y	N	Y	Y	Y
4 **Aderholt**	Y	N	Y	N	Y
5 Cramer	Y	Y	N	Y	Y
6 **Bachus**	Y	N	Y	N	Y
7 Davis	Y	Y	N	Y	Y
ALASKA					
AL **Young**	Y	N	Y	Y	Y
ARIZONA					
1 **Renzi**	Y	N	Y	N	Y
2 **Franks**	Y	N	Y	N	Y
3 **Shadegg**	Y	N	Y	N	Y
4 Pastor	Y	Y	N	Y	Y
5 Mitchell	Y	Y	N	Y	Y
6 **Flake**	?	?	?	?	?
7 Grijalva	Y	Y	N	Y	Y
8 Giffords	Y	N	Y	Y	Y
ARKANSAS					
1 Berry	Y	Y	N	Y	Y
2 Snyder	Y	Y	N	Y	Y
3 **Boozman**	Y	N	Y	N	Y
4 Ross	Y	Y	N	Y	Y
CALIFORNIA					
1 Thompson	Y	Y	N	Y	Y
2 **Herger**	Y	N	Y	N	Y
3 **Lungren**	Y	N	Y	N	Y
4 **Doolittle**	Y	N	Y	N	Y
5 Matsui	Y	Y	N	Y	Y
6 Woolsey	Y	Y	N	Y	Y
7 Miller, George	Y	Y	N	Y	Y
8 Pelosi			N	Y	
9 Lee	Y	Y	N	Y	Y
10 Tauscher	Y	Y	N	Y	Y
11 McNerney	Y	Y	Y	Y	Y
12 Speier	Y	Y	N	+	Y
13 Stark	?	?	N	Y	Y
14 Eshoo	Y	Y	N	Y	Y
15 Honda	Y	Y	N	Y	Y
16 Lofgren	Y	Y	N	Y	Y
17 Farr	Y	Y	N	Y	Y
18 Cardoza	Y	Y	N	Y	Y
19 **Radanovich**	Y	?	Y	N	Y
20 Costa	Y	Y	N	Y	Y
21 **Nunes**	Y	N	Y	N	Y
22 **McCarthy**	Y	N	Y	N	Y
23 Capps	Y	Y	N	Y	Y
24 **Gallegly**	Y	N	Y	N	Y
25 **McKeon**	Y	N	Y	N	Y
26 **Dreier**	Y	N	Y	N	Y
27 Sherman	Y	Y	N	Y	Y
28 Berman	Y	Y	N	?	Y
29 Schiff	Y	Y	N	Y	Y
30 Waxman	Y	Y	N	Y	Y
31 Becerra	Y	Y	N	Y	Y
32 Solis	Y	Y	N	Y	Y
33 Watson	Y	Y	N	Y	Y
34 Roybal-Allard	Y	Y	N	Y	Y
35 Waters	Y	Y	N	Y	Y
36 Harman	Y	Y	N	Y	Y
37 Richardson	Y	Y	N	Y	Y
38 Napolitano	Y	Y	N	Y	Y
39 Sánchez, Linda	Y	Y	N	Y	Y
40 **Royce**	Y	N	Y	N	Y
41 **Lewis**	Y	N	Y	N	Y
42 **Miller, Gary**	Y	N	Y	N	Y
43 Baca	Y	?	N	Y	Y
44 **Calvert**	Y	N	Y	N	Y
45 **Bono Mack**	Y	N	Y	N	Y
46 **Rohrabacher**	Y	N	Y	N	Y
47 Sanchez, Loretta	Y	Y	N	Y	Y
48 **Campbell**	Y	N	Y	N	Y
49 **Issa**	Y	N	Y	N	Y
50 **Bilbray**	Y	N	Y	N	Y
51 Filner	Y	Y	N	Y	Y
52 **Hunter**	Y	N	Y	N	Y
53 Davis	Y	Y	N	Y	Y

	409	410	411	412	413
COLORADO					
1 DeGette	Y	Y	N	Y	Y
2 Udall	Y	Y	N	Y	Y
3 Salazar	Y	Y	N	Y	Y
4 **Musgrave**	Y	N	Y	N	Y
5 **Lamborn**	Y	N	Y	N	Y
6 **Tancredo**	?	?	?	?	?
7 Perlmutter	Y	Y	N	Y	Y
CONNECTICUT					
1 Larson	Y	Y	N	Y	Y
2 Courtney	Y	Y	N	Y	Y
3 DeLauro	Y	Y	N	Y	Y
4 Shays	Y	N	Y	Y	Y
5 Murphy	Y	Y	N	Y	Y
DELAWARE					
AL **Castle**	Y	N	N	Y	Y
FLORIDA					
1 **Miller**	Y	?	Y	N	Y
2 Boyd	Y	Y	N	Y	Y
3 Brown	Y	Y	N	Y	Y
4 **Crenshaw**	Y	N	Y	N	Y
5 **Brown-Waite**	Y	N	Y	N	Y
6 **Stearns**	Y	N	Y	N	Y
7 **Mica**	Y	N	Y	N	Y
8 **Keller**	Y	N	Y	N	Y
9 **Bilirakis**	Y	N	Y	N	Y
10 **Young**	Y	N	Y	N	Y
11 Castor	Y	Y	N	Y	Y
12 **Putnam**	Y	N	Y	N	Y
13 **Buchanan**	Y	N	Y	N	Y
14 **Mack**	Y	N	Y	N	Y
15 **Weldon**	Y	N	Y	N	Y
16 Mahoney	Y	Y	N	Y	?
17 Meek	Y	Y	N	Y	Y
18 **Ros-Lehtinen**	Y	N	Y	Y	Y
19 Wexler	Y	Y	N	Y	Y
20 Wasserman Schultz	Y	Y	N	Y	Y
21 **Diaz-Balart, L.**	Y	N	Y	Y	Y
22 Klein	Y	Y	N	Y	?
23 Hastings	Y	Y	N	Y	Y
24 **Feeney**	Y	N	Y	N	Y
25 **Diaz-Balart, M.**	Y	N	Y	Y	Y
GEORGIA					
1 **Kingston**	Y	N	Y	N	Y
2 Bishop	Y	Y	N	Y	Y
3 **Westmoreland**	Y	N	Y	N	Y
4 Johnson	Y	Y	N	Y	Y
5 Lewis	Y	Y	N	Y	Y
6 **Price**	Y	N	Y	N	Y
7 **Linder**	Y	N	Y	N	Y
8 Marshall	Y	Y	N	Y	Y
9 **Deal**	Y	N	Y	N	Y
10 **Broun**	?	N	Y	N	Y
11 **Gingrey**	Y	N	Y	N	Y
12 Barrow	Y	Y	N	Y	Y
13 Scott	Y	Y	N	Y	Y
HAWAII					
1 Abercrombie	Y	Y	N	Y	Y
2 Hirono	Y	Y	N	Y	Y
IDAHO					
1 **Sali**	Y	N	Y	N	Y
2 **Simpson**	Y	N	Y	N	Y
ILLINOIS					
1 Rush	?	?	?	?	?
2 Jackson	Y	Y	N	Y	Y
3 Lipinski	Y	Y	N	Y	Y
4 Gutierrez	Y	Y	N	Y	Y
5 Emanuel	Y	Y	N	Y	Y
6 **Roskam**	Y	N	Y	N	Y
7 Davis	Y	?	N	Y	Y
8 Bean	Y	Y	N	Y	Y
9 Schakowsky	Y	Y	N	Y	Y
10 **Kirk**	Y	N	Y	N	Y
11 **Weller**	Y	N	Y	N	Y
12 Costello	Y	Y	N	Y	Y
13 **Biggert**	Y	N	Y	N	Y
14 Foster	Y	Y	N	Y	Y
15 **Johnson**	Y	Y	N	Y	Y

KEY	Republicans	Democrats		
Y	Voted for (yea)	X	Paired against	C	Voted "present" to avoid possible conflict of interest
#	Paired for	–	Announced against	
+	Announced for	P	Voted "present"	?	Did not vote or otherwise make a position known
N	Voted against (nay)			

ND Northern Democrats, SD Southern Democrats
Southern states: Ala., Ark., Fla., Ga., Ky., La., Miss., N.C., Okla., S.C., Tenn., Texas, Va.

	409	410	411	412	413
16 Manzullo	Y	N	Y	N	Y
17 Hare	Y	Y	N	Y	Y
18 LaHood	Y	N	?	?	?
19 Shimkus	Y	N	Y	N	?
INDIANA					
1 Visclosky	Y	Y	N	Y	Y
2 Donnelly	Y	Y	N	Y	Y
3 Souder	Y	N	Y	Y	Y
4 Buyer	Y	N	?	?	?
5 Burton	Y	N	Y	N	Y
6 Pence	Y	?	Y	N	Y
7 Carson, A.	Y	Y	N	Y	Y
8 Ellsworth	Y	Y	N	Y	Y
9 Hill	Y	Y	N	Y	Y
IOWA					
1 Braley	?	?	?	?	?
2 Loebsack	?	?	?	?	?
3 Boswell	Y	Y	N	Y	Y
4 Latham	Y	N	Y	N	Y
5 King	Y	N	N	N	Y
KANSAS					
1 Moran	?	?	?	?	?
2 Boyda	Y	Y	N	Y	Y
3 Moore	Y	Y	N	Y	Y
4 Tiahrt	Y	N	Y	N	Y
KENTUCKY					
1 Whitfield	Y	N	Y	N	Y
2 Lewis	Y	N	Y	N	Y
3 Yarmuth	Y	Y	N	Y	Y
4 Davis	Y	N	Y	N	Y
5 Rogers	Y	N	Y	N	Y
6 Chandler	Y	Y	N	Y	Y
LOUISIANA					
1 Scalise	Y	N	Y	N	Y
2 Jefferson	Y	Y	N	Y	Y
3 Melancon	Y	Y	N	Y	Y
4 McCrery	?	?	?	?	?
5 Alexander	Y	N	Y	N	Y
6 Cazayoux	Y	Y	N	Y	Y
7 Boustany	Y	N	Y	N	Y
MAINE					
1 Allen	Y	Y	N	Y	Y
2 Michaud	Y	Y	N	Y	Y
MARYLAND					
1 Gilchrest	Y	N	N	Y	Y
2 Ruppersberger	Y	Y	N	Y	Y
3 Sarbanes	Y	Y	N	Y	Y
4 Vacant					
5 Hoyer	Y	Y	N	Y	Y
6 Bartlett	Y	N	Y	N	Y
7 Cummings	Y	Y	N	Y	Y
8 Van Hollen	Y	Y	N	Y	Y
MASSACHUSETTS					
1 Olver	Y	Y	N	Y	Y
2 Neal	Y	Y	N	Y	Y
3 McGovern	Y	Y	N	Y	Y
4 Frank	Y	Y	N	Y	Y
5 Tsongas	Y	Y	N	Y	Y
6 Tierney	Y	Y	N	Y	Y
7 Markey	Y	Y	N	Y	Y
8 Capuano	Y	Y	N	Y	Y
9 Lynch	Y	Y	N	Y	Y
10 Delahunt	Y	Y	N	Y	Y
MICHIGAN					
1 Stupak	Y	Y	N	Y	Y
2 Hoekstra	Y	N	Y	Y	Y
3 Ehlers	Y	N	Y	Y	Y
4 Camp	Y	N	Y	N	Y
5 Kildee	Y	Y	N	Y	Y
6 Upton	Y	N	Y	Y	Y
7 Walberg	Y	N	Y	N	Y
8 Rogers	?	?	?	+	?
9 Knollenberg	Y	N	Y	Y	Y
10 Miller	Y	N	Y	Y	Y
11 McCotter	Y	N	Y	Y	Y
12 Levin	Y	N	N	Y	Y
13 Kilpatrick	Y	?	N	Y	Y
14 Conyers	Y	Y	N	Y	Y
15 Dingell	Y	Y	N	Y	Y
MINNESOTA					
1 Walz	Y	Y	N	Y	Y
2 Kline	Y	N	Y	N	Y
3 Ramstad	Y	N	Y	N	Y
4 McCollum	Y	Y	N	Y	Y

	409	410	411	412	413
5 Ellison	Y	Y	N	Y	Y
6 Bachmann	Y	N	Y	N	Y
7 Peterson	Y	Y	N	Y	Y
8 Oberstar	Y	Y	N	Y	Y
MISSISSIPPI					
1 Childers	Y	Y	N	Y	Y
2 Thompson	Y	Y	N	Y	Y
3 Pickering	Y	N	Y	N	Y
4 Taylor	Y	Y	N	Y	Y
MISSOURI					
1 Clay	Y	Y	N	Y	Y
2 Akin	Y	N	Y	N	Y
3 Carnahan	Y	Y	N	Y	Y
4 Skelton	Y	Y	N	Y	Y
5 Cleaver	Y	Y	N	Y	Y
6 Graves	Y	N	Y	Y	Y
7 Blunt	Y	N	Y	N	Y
8 Emerson	Y	N	Y	Y	Y
9 Hulshof	?	?	?	?	?
MONTANA					
AL Rehberg	Y	N	Y	N	Y
NEBRASKA					
1 Fortenberry	Y	N	Y	N	Y
2 Terry	Y	N	Y	N	Y
3 Smith	Y	N	Y	N	Y
NEVADA					
1 Berkley	Y	Y	N	Y	Y
2 Heller	Y	N	Y	Y	Y
3 Porter	Y	N	Y	Y	Y
NEW HAMPSHIRE					
1 Shea-Porter	Y	Y	N	Y	Y
2 Hodes	Y	Y	N	Y	Y
NEW JERSEY					
1 Andrews	Y	Y	N	Y	Y
2 LoBiondo	Y	N	N	Y	Y
3 Saxton	Y	N	Y	N	Y
4 Smith	Y	?	N	Y	Y
5 Garrett	Y	N	Y	N	Y
6 Pallone	Y	Y	N	Y	Y
7 Ferguson	Y	N	?	?	?
8 Pascrell	Y	Y	N	Y	Y
9 Rothman	Y	Y	N	Y	Y
10 Payne	Y	Y	N	Y	Y
11 Frelinghuysen	Y	N	Y	N	Y
12 Holt	Y	Y	N	Y	Y
13 Sires	Y	Y	N	Y	Y
NEW MEXICO					
1 Wilson	Y	N	Y	N	Y
2 Pearce	Y	N	N	N	Y
3 Udall	Y	Y	N	Y	Y
NEW YORK					
1 Bishop	Y	Y	N	Y	Y
2 Israel	Y	Y	N	Y	Y
3 King	Y	N	Y	Y	Y
4 McCarthy	Y	Y	N	Y	Y
5 Ackerman	Y	Y	N	Y	?
6 Meeks	?	Y	N	Y	Y
7 Crowley	Y	Y	N	Y	Y
8 Nadler	Y	Y	N	Y	Y
9 Weiner	Y	Y	N	Y	Y
10 Towns	Y	Y	N	Y	Y
11 Clarke	Y	Y	N	Y	Y
12 Velázquez	Y	Y	N	Y	Y
13 Fossella	Y	N	Y	Y	Y
14 Maloney	Y	?	N	Y	Y
15 Rangel	Y	Y	N	Y	Y
16 Serrano	Y	Y	N	Y	Y
17 Engel	Y	Y	N	Y	Y
18 Lowey	Y	Y	N	Y	Y
19 Hall	Y	Y	N	Y	Y
20 Gillibrand	Y	Y	N	Y	Y
21 McNulty	Y	Y	N	Y	Y
22 Hinchey	Y	Y	N	Y	Y
23 McHugh	Y	N	Y	Y	Y
24 Arcuri	Y	Y	N	Y	Y
25 Walsh	Y	?	N	Y	Y
26 Reynolds	Y	N	Y	N	Y
27 Higgins	?	?	?	?	?
28 Slaughter	Y	Y	N	Y	Y
29 Kuhl	Y	N	Y	Y	Y
NORTH CAROLINA					
1 Butterfield	Y	Y	N	Y	Y
2 Etheridge	Y	Y	N	Y	Y
3 Jones	Y	N	Y	Y	Y
4 Price	Y	Y	N	Y	Y

	409	410	411	412	413
5 Foxx	Y	N	Y	N	Y
6 Coble	Y	N	Y	N	Y
7 McIntyre	Y	Y	Y	Y	Y
8 Hayes	Y	N	Y	N	Y
9 Myrick	Y	N	Y	N	Y
10 McHenry	Y	N	Y	Y	Y
11 Shuler	Y	Y	N	Y	Y
12 Watt	Y	Y	N	Y	Y
13 Miller	Y	Y	N	Y	Y
NORTH DAKOTA					
AL Pomeroy	Y	Y	N	Y	Y
OHIO					
1 Chabot	Y	N	Y	Y	Y
2 Schmidt	Y	N	Y	Y	Y
3 Turner	Y	N	Y	Y	Y
4 Jordan	Y	N	Y	N	Y
5 Latta	Y	N	Y	N	Y
6 Wilson	Y	Y	N	Y	Y
7 Hobson	Y	N	Y	N	Y
8 Boehner	Y	N	Y	N	Y
9 Kaptur	Y	Y	N	Y	Y
10 Kucinich	Y	Y	N	Y	Y
11 Tubbs Jones	Y	Y	N	Y	Y
12 Tiberi	Y	N	Y	Y	Y
13 Sutton	Y	Y	N	Y	Y
14 LaTourette	Y	N	Y	Y	Y
15 Pryce	Y	?	?	?	?
16 Regula	Y	N	Y	Y	Y
17 Ryan	Y	Y	N	Y	Y
18 Space	Y	Y	N	Y	Y
OKLAHOMA					
1 Sullivan	Y	N	Y	N	Y
2 Boren	Y	Y	N	Y	Y
3 Lucas	Y	N	Y	N	Y
4 Cole	Y	N	Y	N	Y
5 Fallin	Y	N	Y	N	Y
OREGON					
1 Wu	Y	Y	N	Y	Y
2 Walden	Y	N	Y	N	Y
3 Blumenauer	Y	Y	N	Y	Y
4 DeFazio	Y	Y	N	Y	Y
5 Hooley	Y	Y	N	Y	Y
PENNSYLVANIA					
1 Brady	Y	Y	N	Y	Y
2 Fattah	Y	Y	N	Y	Y
3 English	Y	N	N	Y	Y
4 Altmire	Y	Y	N	Y	Y
5 Peterson	Y	N	Y	N	Y
6 Gerlach	Y	Y	N	Y	Y
7 Sestak	Y	Y	N	Y	Y
8 Murphy, P.	Y	Y	N	Y	Y
9 Shuster	Y	N	N	N	Y
10 Carney	Y	Y	N	Y	Y
11 Kanjorski	Y	Y	N	Y	Y
12 Murtha	Y	Y	N	Y	Y
13 Schwartz	Y	Y	N	Y	Y
14 Doyle	Y	Y	N	Y	Y
15 Dent	Y	N	Y	N	Y
16 Pitts	Y	N	Y	N	Y
17 Holden	Y	Y	N	Y	Y
18 Murphy, T.	Y	?	N	Y	Y
19 Platts	Y	N	N	Y	Y
RHODE ISLAND					
1 Kennedy	Y	Y	N	Y	Y
2 Langevin	Y	Y	N	Y	Y
SOUTH CAROLINA					
1 Brown	Y	N	Y	N	Y
2 Wilson	Y	N	Y	N	Y
3 Barrett	Y	N	Y	N	Y
4 Inglis	Y	N	Y	N	Y
5 Spratt	Y	Y	N	Y	Y
6 Clyburn	Y	Y	N	Y	Y
SOUTH DAKOTA					
AL Herseth Sandlin	Y	Y	N	Y	Y
TENNESSEE					
1 Davis, D.	Y	N	Y	N	Y
2 Duncan	Y	N	Y	N	Y
3 Wamp	Y	N	Y	N	Y
4 Davis, L.	Y	Y	N	Y	Y
5 Cooper	Y	Y	N	Y	Y
6 Gordon	Y	Y	N	Y	Y
7 Blackburn	Y	N	Y	N	Y
8 Tanner	Y	Y	N	Y	Y
9 Cohen	Y	Y	N	Y	Y

	409	410	411	412	413
TEXAS					
1 Gohmert	Y	N	Y	N	Y
2 Poe	Y	N	Y	N	Y
3 Johnson, S.	Y	N	Y	N	Y
4 Hall	Y	N	Y	N	Y
5 Hensarling	Y	N	Y	N	Y
6 Barton	Y	N	Y	N	Y
7 Culberson	Y	N	Y	N	Y
8 Brady	Y	N	Y	N	Y
9 Green, A.	Y	Y	N	Y	Y
10 McCaul	Y	N	Y	N	Y
11 Conaway	Y	N	Y	N	Y
12 Granger	Y	N	Y	N	Y
13 Thornberry	Y	N	Y	N	Y
14 Paul	?	N	?	?	?
15 Hinojosa	Y	?	?	?	?
16 Reyes	Y	?	N	Y	Y
17 Edwards	Y	Y	N	Y	Y
18 Jackson Lee	Y	Y	N	Y	Y
19 Neugebauer	Y	N	Y	N	Y
20 Gonzalez	Y	?	?	?	?
21 Smith	Y	N	Y	N	Y
22 Lampson	Y	Y	N	Y	Y
23 Rodriguez	Y	Y	N	Y	Y
24 Marchant	Y	N	Y	N	Y
25 Doggett	?	Y	N	Y	Y
26 Burgess	Y	N	?	?	?
27 Ortiz	?	?	?	?	?
28 Cuellar	Y	Y	N	Y	Y
29 Green, G.	Y	Y	N	Y	Y
30 Johnson, E.	Y	Y	N	Y	Y
31 Carter	Y	N	Y	N	Y
32 Sessions	Y	N	Y	N	Y
UTAH					
1 Bishop	Y	N	Y	N	Y
2 Matheson	Y	Y	N	Y	Y
3 Cannon	Y	N	Y	N	Y
VERMONT					
AL Welch	Y	Y	N	Y	Y
VIRGINIA					
1 Wittman	Y	N	Y	N	Y
2 Drake	Y	N	Y	N	Y
3 Scott	Y	Y	N	Y	Y
4 Forbes	Y	N	Y	N	Y
5 Goode	Y	N	Y	N	Y
6 Goodlatte	Y	N	Y	N	Y
7 Cantor	Y	N	Y	N	Y
8 Moran	Y	Y	N	Y	Y
9 Boucher	Y	Y	N	Y	Y
10 Wolf	Y	?	Y	N	Y
11 Davis	Y	N	?	?	?
WASHINGTON					
1 Inslee	Y	Y	N	Y	Y
2 Larsen	Y	Y	N	Y	Y
3 Baird	Y	Y	N	Y	Y
4 Hastings	Y	N	Y	N	Y
5 McMorris Rodgers	Y	N	Y	N	Y
6 Dicks	Y	?	N	Y	Y
7 McDermott	Y	Y	N	Y	Y
8 Reichert	Y	N	Y	N	Y
9 Smith	Y	N	Y	N	Y
WEST VIRGINIA					
1 Mollohan	Y	Y	N	Y	Y
2 Capito	Y	N	Y	N	Y
3 Rahall	Y	Y	N	Y	Y
WISCONSIN					
1 Ryan	Y	N	Y	Y	Y
2 Baldwin	Y	Y	N	Y	Y
3 Kind	?	?	?	?	?
4 Moore	Y	Y	N	Y	Y
5 Sensenbrenner	Y	N	Y	N	Y
6 Petri	Y	N	Y	Y	Y
7 Obey	Y	Y	N	Y	Y
8 Kagen	Y	?	N	Y	Y
WYOMING					
AL Cubin	Y	N	Y	N	?
DELEGATES					
Faleomavaega (A.S.)					
Norton (D.C.)					
Bordallo (Guam)					
Fortuño (P.R.)					
Christensen (V.I.)					

IN THE HOUSE | By Vote Number

414. **HR 2964. Captive Primate Sale and Importation/Passage.**
Bordallo, D-Guam, motion to suspend the rules and pass the bill that would amend the Lacey Act Amendments of 1981 to treat non-human primates as a prohibited wildlife species, banning their interstate sale or importation. Motion agreed to 302-96: R 82-96; D 220-0 (ND 165-0, SD 55-0). A two-thirds majority of those present and voting (266 in this case) is required for passage under suspension of the rules. June 17, 2008.

415. **HR 3702. Montana Land Conveyance/Passage.** Bordallo, D-Guam, motion to suspend the rules and pass the bill that would require the Agriculture Department to convey 9.67 acres of National Forest System land to Jefferson County, Mont. Motion agreed to 396-0: R 177-0; D 219-0 (ND 164-0, SD 55-0). A two-thirds majority of those present and voting (264 in this case) is required for passage under suspension of the rules. June 17, 2008.

416. **H Res 1275. Tim Russert Tribute/Adoption.** Higgins, D-N.Y., motion to suspend the rules and adopt the resolution that would honor the life and accomplishments of journalist Timothy J. Russert Jr., who died June 13, 2008, and express condolences to his family members and friends. Motion agreed to 395-0: R 176-0; D 219-0 (ND 164-0, SD 55-0). A two-thirds majority of those present and voting (264 in this case) is required for adoption under suspension of the rules. June 17, 2008.

417. **HR 6124. Farm Bill Reauthorization/Veto Override.** Passage, over President Bush's June 18, 2008, veto, of the bill that would reauthorize federal farm and nutrition programs for five years, including crop subsidies and food stamps, as well as conservation, rural development and agricultural trade programs. It would authorize a $10.4 billion increase for nutrition programs, offset by extending customs user fees. It would cut direct payment subsidies overall by $313 million, in part by reducing the percentage of acres for which a farmer can collect those payments. Farmers making more than $750,000 a year in farm-related income and those with more than $500,000 a year in non-farm-related income would not be eligible for federal subsidies. Country-of-origin labels for all meat would be required by September 2008. Passed 317-109: R 99-96; D 218-13 (ND 160-12, SD 58-1). A two-thirds majority of those present and voting (284 in this case for the House) of both chambers is required to override a veto. A "nay" was a vote in support of the president's position. June 18, 2008.

418. **HR 6063. NASA Authorization/Conventional Fuels.** Lampson, D-Texas, amendment that would allow NASA to procure conventional fuels that contain incidental amounts of unconventional fuels. Adopted in Committee of the Whole 429-1: R 197-0; D 232-1 (ND 173-1, SD 59-0). June 18, 2008.

419. **HR 6063. NASA Authorization/Scholarship Program.** Hodes, D-N.H., amendment that would establish a scholarship program for women pursuing higher education degrees in fields related to NASA's missions, in memory of teacher Christa McAuliffe, who died in the *Challenger* disaster. Recipients of the scholarship would receive $10,000 per year. Adopted in Committee of the Whole 423-3: R 191-3; D 232-0 (ND 173-0, SD 59-0). June 18, 2008.

	414	415	416	417	418	419
ALABAMA						
1 Bonner	N	Y	Y	Y	Y	Y
2 Everett	N	Y	Y	Y	Y	Y
3 Rogers	Y	Y	Y	Y	Y	Y
4 Aderholt	N	Y	Y	Y	Y	Y
5 Cramer	Y	Y	Y	Y	Y	Y
6 Bachus	Y	Y	Y	Y	Y	Y
7 Davis	Y	Y	Y	Y	Y	Y
ALASKA						
AL Young	Y	Y	Y	Y	Y	Y
ARIZONA						
1 Renzi	N	Y	Y	Y	Y	Y
2 Franks	N	Y	Y	N	Y	Y
3 Shadegg	?	?	?	N	Y	Y
4 Pastor	Y	Y	Y	Y	Y	Y
5 Mitchell	Y	Y	Y	N	Y	Y
6 Flake	N	Y	Y	N	Y	N
7 Grijalva	Y	Y	Y	Y	Y	Y
8 Giffords	Y	Y	Y	Y	Y	Y
ARKANSAS						
1 Berry	Y	Y	Y	Y	Y	Y
2 Snyder	Y	Y	Y	Y	Y	Y
3 Boozman	Y	Y	Y	Y	Y	Y
4 Ross	Y	Y	Y	Y	Y	Y
CALIFORNIA						
1 Thompson	Y	Y	Y	Y	Y	Y
2 Herger	N	Y	Y	Y	Y	Y
3 Lungren	N	Y	Y	N	Y	Y
4 Doolittle	Y	Y	Y	Y	Y	Y
5 Matsui	Y	Y	Y	Y	Y	Y
6 Woolsey	Y	Y	Y	Y	Y	Y
7 Miller, George	Y	Y	Y	Y	Y	Y
8 Pelosi				Y		
9 Lee	Y	Y	Y	Y	Y	Y
10 Tauscher	Y	Y	Y	Y	Y	Y
11 McNerney	Y	Y	Y	Y	Y	Y
12 Speier	Y	Y	Y	Y	Y	Y
13 Stark	?	?	?	?	?	?
14 Eshoo	Y	Y	Y	Y	Y	Y
15 Honda	Y	Y	Y	Y	Y	Y
16 Lofgren	Y	Y	Y	Y	Y	Y
17 Farr	Y	Y	Y	Y	Y	Y
18 Cardoza	Y	Y	Y	Y	Y	Y
19 Radanovich	?	?	?	Y	Y	Y
20 Costa	Y	Y	Y	Y	Y	Y
21 Nunes	Y	Y	Y	N	Y	Y
22 McCarthy	N	Y	Y	N	Y	Y
23 Capps	Y	Y	Y	Y	Y	Y
24 Gallegly	Y	Y	Y	Y	Y	Y
25 McKeon	N	Y	Y	N	Y	Y
26 Dreier	N	Y	Y	N	Y	Y
27 Sherman	Y	Y	Y	Y	Y	Y
28 Berman	Y	Y	Y	N	Y	Y
29 Schiff	Y	Y	Y	Y	Y	Y
30 Waxman	Y	Y	Y	Y	Y	Y
31 Becerra	Y	Y	Y	Y	Y	Y
32 Solis	Y	Y	Y	Y	Y	Y
33 Watson	Y	Y	Y	Y	Y	Y
34 Roybal-Allard	Y	Y	Y	Y	Y	Y
35 Waters	Y	Y	Y	Y	Y	Y
36 Harman	Y	Y	Y	?	?	?
37 Richardson	Y	Y	Y	Y	Y	Y
38 Napolitano	+	+	+	Y	Y	Y
39 Sánchez, Linda	Y	Y	Y	Y	Y	Y
40 Royce	Y	Y	Y	N	Y	Y
41 Lewis	N	Y	Y	N	Y	Y
42 Miller, Gary	N	Y	Y	N	Y	Y
43 Baca	Y	Y	Y	Y	Y	Y
44 Calvert	Y	Y	Y	N	Y	Y
45 Bono Mack	Y	Y	Y	Y	Y	Y
46 Rohrabacher	?	?	?	N	Y	Y
47 Sanchez, Loretta	Y	Y	Y	Y	Y	Y
48 Campbell	Y	Y	Y	N	Y	Y
49 Issa	Y	Y	Y	N	Y	?
50 Bilbray	Y	Y	Y	N	Y	Y
51 Filner	Y	Y	Y	Y	Y	Y
52 Hunter	?	?	?	N	Y	Y
53 Davis	Y	Y	Y	Y	Y	Y

	414	415	416	417	418	419
COLORADO						
1 DeGette	Y	Y	Y	Y	Y	Y
2 Udall	?	?	?	Y	Y	Y
3 Salazar	Y	Y	Y	Y	Y	Y
4 Musgrave	N	Y	Y	Y	Y	Y
5 Lamborn	N	Y	Y	N	Y	Y
6 Tancredo	N	Y	Y	N	Y	Y
7 Perlmutter	Y	Y	Y	Y	Y	Y
CONNECTICUT						
1 Larson	Y	Y	Y	Y	Y	Y
2 Courtney	Y	Y	Y	Y	Y	Y
3 DeLauro	Y	Y	Y	Y	Y	Y
4 Shays	Y	Y	Y	N	Y	Y
5 Murphy	Y	Y	Y	Y	Y	Y
DELAWARE						
AL Castle	Y	Y	Y	N	Y	Y
FLORIDA						
1 Miller	N	Y	Y	N	Y	Y
2 Boyd	Y	Y	Y	Y	Y	Y
3 Brown	Y	Y	Y	Y	Y	Y
4 Crenshaw	?	Y	Y	Y	Y	Y
5 Brown-Waite	N	Y	Y	Y	Y	Y
6 Stearns	N	Y	Y	N	Y	Y
7 Mica	N	Y	Y	N	Y	Y
8 Keller	Y	Y	Y	Y	Y	Y
9 Bilirakis	Y	Y	Y	Y	Y	Y
10 Young	Y	Y	Y	N	Y	Y
11 Castor	Y	Y	Y	Y	Y	Y
12 Putnam	N	Y	Y	Y	Y	Y
13 Buchanan	Y	Y	Y	Y	Y	Y
14 Mack	N	Y	Y	N	Y	Y
15 Weldon	?	?	?	N	Y	Y
16 Mahoney	Y	Y	Y	Y	Y	Y
17 Meek	Y	Y	Y	Y	Y	Y
18 Ros-Lehtinen	?	?	?	N	Y	Y
19 Wexler	?	?	?	Y	Y	Y
20 Wasserman Schultz	Y	Y	Y	Y	Y	Y
21 Diaz-Balart, L.	Y	Y	Y	Y	Y	Y
22 Klein	Y	Y	Y	Y	Y	Y
23 Hastings	Y	Y	Y	Y	Y	Y
24 Feeney	Y	Y	Y	N	Y	Y
25 Diaz-Balart, M.	Y	Y	Y	Y	Y	Y
GEORGIA						
1 Kingston	N	Y	Y	Y	Y	Y
2 Bishop	Y	Y	Y	Y	Y	Y
3 Westmoreland	N	Y	Y	N	Y	Y
4 Johnson	Y	Y	Y	Y	Y	Y
5 Lewis	Y	Y	Y	Y	Y	Y
6 Price	N	Y	Y	N	Y	Y
7 Linder	Y	Y	Y	N	Y	Y
8 Marshall	Y	Y	Y	Y	Y	Y
9 Deal	N	Y	Y	N	Y	Y
10 Broun	N	Y	Y	N	Y	N
11 Gingrey	N	Y	Y	Y	Y	Y
12 Barrow	Y	Y	Y	Y	Y	Y
13 Scott	Y	Y	Y	Y	Y	Y
HAWAII						
1 Abercrombie	Y	Y	Y	Y	Y	Y
2 Hirono	Y	Y	Y	Y	Y	Y
IDAHO						
1 Sali	N	Y	Y	Y	Y	Y
2 Simpson	Y	Y	Y	Y	Y	Y
ILLINOIS						
1 Rush	?	?	?	?	?	?
2 Jackson	Y	Y	Y	Y	Y	Y
3 Lipinski	Y	Y	Y	Y	Y	Y
4 Gutierrez	Y	Y	Y	Y	Y	Y
5 Emanuel	Y	Y	Y	Y	Y	Y
6 Roskam	N	Y	Y	N	Y	Y
7 Davis	Y	Y	Y	Y	Y	Y
8 Bean	Y	Y	Y	N	Y	Y
9 Schakowsky	Y	Y	Y	Y	Y	Y
10 Kirk	Y	Y	Y	N	Y	Y
11 Weller	Y	Y	Y	Y	Y	Y
12 Costello	Y	Y	Y	Y	Y	Y
13 Biggert	Y	Y	Y	N	Y	Y
14 Foster	Y	Y	Y	Y	Y	?
15 Johnson	+	+	+	Y	Y	Y

KEY   **Republicans**   Democrats

Y Voted for (yea)	X Paired against	C Voted "present" to avoid possible conflict of interest
# Paired for	– Announced against	
+ Announced for	P Voted "present"	? Did not vote or otherwise make a position known
N Voted against (nay)		

ND Northern Democrats, SD Southern Democrats
Southern states: Ala., Ark., Fla., Ga., Ky., La., Miss., N.C., Okla., S.C., Tenn., Texas, Va.

	414	415	416	417	418	419
16 **Manzullo**	N	Y	Y	Y	Y	Y
17 Hare	Y	Y	Y	Y	Y	Y
18 **LaHood**	N	Y	Y	Y	Y	Y
19 **Shimkus**	?	?	?	Y	Y	Y
INDIANA						
1 Visclosky	Y	Y	Y	Y	Y	Y
2 Donnelly	Y	Y	Y	Y	Y	Y
3 **Souder**	N	Y	Y	Y	Y	Y
4 **Buyer**	N	Y	Y	Y	Y	Y
5 **Burton**	N	Y	Y	N	Y	Y
6 **Pence**	?	?	?	N	Y	Y
7 Carson, A.	Y	Y	Y	Y	Y	Y
8 Ellsworth	Y	Y	Y	Y	Y	Y
9 Hill	Y	Y	Y	Y	Y	Y
IOWA						
1 Braley	Y	Y	Y	Y	Y	Y
2 Loebsack	?	?	?	Y	Y	Y
3 Boswell	Y	Y	Y	Y	Y	Y
4 **Latham**	Y	Y	Y	Y	Y	Y
5 **King**	N	?	Y	Y	Y	Y
KANSAS						
1 **Moran**	N	Y	Y	N	Y	Y
2 Boyda	Y	Y	Y	Y	Y	Y
3 Moore	Y	Y	Y	Y	Y	Y
4 **Tiahrt**	N	Y	Y	N	Y	Y
KENTUCKY						
1 **Whitfield**	Y	Y	Y	Y	Y	Y
2 **Lewis**	N	Y	Y	Y	Y	Y
3 Yarmuth	Y	Y	Y	Y	Y	Y
4 **Davis**	N	?	Y	Y	Y	Y
5 **Rogers**	Y	Y	Y	Y	Y	Y
6 Chandler	Y	Y	Y	Y	Y	Y
LOUISIANA						
1 **Scalise**	N	Y	Y	N	Y	Y
2 Jefferson	Y	Y	Y	Y	Y	Y
3 Melancon	Y	Y	Y	Y	Y	Y
4 **McCrery**	Y	Y	Y	N	Y	Y
5 **Alexander**	Y	Y	Y	Y	Y	Y
6 Cazayoux	Y	Y	Y	Y	Y	Y
7 **Boustany**	N	Y	Y	Y	Y	Y
MAINE						
1 Allen	Y	Y	Y	Y	Y	Y
2 Michaud	Y	Y	Y	Y	Y	Y
MARYLAND						
1 **Gilchrest**	?	?	?	?	?	?
2 Ruppersberger	Y	Y	Y	Y	Y	Y
3 Sarbanes	Y	Y	Y	Y	Y	Y
4 Vacant*						
5 Hoyer	Y	Y	Y	Y	Y	Y
6 **Bartlett**	Y	Y	Y	Y	Y	Y
7 Cummings	Y	Y	Y	Y	Y	Y
8 Van Hollen	Y	Y	Y	Y	Y	Y
MASSACHUSETTS						
1 Olver	Y	Y	Y	Y	Y	Y
2 Neal	Y	Y	Y	Y	Y	Y
3 McGovern	Y	Y	Y	Y	Y	Y
4 Frank	Y	Y	Y	Y	Y	Y
5 Tsongas	Y	Y	Y	Y	Y	Y
6 Tierney	Y	Y	Y	Y	Y	Y
7 Markey	Y	Y	Y	Y	Y	Y
8 Capuano	Y	Y	Y	N	Y	Y
9 Lynch	Y	Y	Y	Y	Y	Y
10 Delahunt	Y	Y	Y	Y	Y	Y
MICHIGAN						
1 Stupak	Y	Y	Y	Y	Y	Y
2 **Hoekstra**	Y	Y	Y	Y	Y	Y
3 **Ehlers**	Y	Y	Y	N	Y	Y
4 **Camp**	Y	Y	Y	Y	Y	Y
5 Kildee	Y	Y	Y	Y	Y	Y
6 **Upton**	Y	Y	Y	Y	Y	Y
7 **Walberg**	N	Y	Y	Y	Y	Y
8 **Rogers**	Y	Y	Y	Y	Y	Y
9 **Knollenberg**	Y	Y	Y	N	Y	Y
10 **Miller**	Y	Y	Y	Y	Y	Y
11 **McCotter**	Y	Y	Y	Y	Y	Y
12 Levin	Y	Y	Y	Y	Y	Y
13 Kilpatrick	Y	Y	Y	Y	Y	Y
14 Conyers	+	+	+	Y	Y	Y
15 Dingell	Y	Y	Y	Y	Y	Y
MINNESOTA						
1 Walz	Y	Y	Y	Y	Y	Y
2 **Kline**	N	Y	Y	Y	Y	Y
3 **Ramstad**	Y	Y	Y	N	Y	Y
4 McCollum	Y	Y	Y	Y	Y	Y
5 Ellison	Y	Y	Y	Y	Y	Y
6 **Bachmann**	N	Y	Y	N	Y	Y
7 Peterson	Y	Y	Y	Y	Y	Y
8 Oberstar	Y	Y	Y	Y	Y	Y
MISSISSIPPI						
1 Childers	Y	Y	Y	Y	Y	Y
2 Thompson	Y	Y	Y	Y	Y	Y
3 **Pickering**	Y	Y	Y	Y	Y	Y
4 Taylor	?	?	?	Y	Y	Y
MISSOURI						
1 Clay	Y	Y	Y	Y	Y	Y
2 **Akin**	–	+	+	Y	Y	Y
3 Carnahan	Y	Y	Y	Y	Y	Y
4 Skelton	Y	Y	Y	Y	Y	Y
5 Cleaver	Y	Y	Y	Y	Y	Y
6 **Graves**	N	Y	Y	Y	Y	Y
7 **Blunt**	N	Y	Y	Y	Y	Y
8 **Emerson**	N	Y	Y	Y	Y	Y
9 **Hulshof**	?	?	?	?	?	?
MONTANA						
AL **Rehberg**	Y	Y	Y	Y	Y	Y
NEBRASKA						
1 **Fortenberry**	Y	Y	?	Y	Y	Y
2 **Terry**	N	Y	Y	N	Y	Y
3 **Smith**	N	Y	Y	Y	Y	Y
NEVADA						
1 Berkley	Y	Y	Y	Y	Y	Y
2 **Heller**	Y	Y	Y	N	Y	Y
3 **Porter**	Y	Y	Y	Y	Y	Y
NEW HAMPSHIRE						
1 Shea-Porter	Y	Y	Y	Y	Y	Y
2 Hodes	Y	Y	Y	Y	Y	Y
NEW JERSEY						
1 Andrews	Y	Y	Y	Y	Y	Y
2 **LoBiondo**	Y	Y	Y	N	Y	Y
3 **Saxton**	?	?	?	N	Y	Y
4 **Smith**	Y	Y	Y	N	Y	Y
5 **Garrett**	N	Y	Y	N	Y	Y
6 Pallone	Y	Y	Y	Y	Y	Y
7 **Ferguson**	Y	Y	?	N	Y	Y
8 Pascrell	Y	Y	Y	Y	Y	Y
9 Rothman	?	?	?	Y	Y	Y
10 Payne	Y	Y	Y	Y	Y	Y
11 **Frelinghuysen**	+	+	+	N	Y	Y
12 Holt	Y	Y	Y	Y	Y	Y
13 Sires	Y	Y	Y	Y	Y	Y
NEW MEXICO						
1 **Wilson**	Y	Y	Y	N	Y	Y
2 **Pearce**	Y	Y	Y	Y	Y	Y
3 Udall	Y	Y	Y	Y	Y	Y
NEW YORK						
1 Bishop	Y	Y	Y	Y	Y	Y
2 Israel	Y	Y	Y	Y	Y	Y
3 **King**	N	Y	Y	N	Y	Y
4 McCarthy	Y	Y	Y	Y	Y	Y
5 Ackerman	Y	Y	Y	Y	Y	Y
6 Meeks	?	?	?	?	?	?
7 Crowley	Y	Y	Y	Y	Y	Y
8 Nadler	Y	Y	Y	Y	Y	Y
9 Weiner	Y	Y	Y	Y	Y	Y
10 Towns	Y	Y	Y	Y	Y	Y
11 Clarke	Y	Y	Y	Y	Y	Y
12 Velázquez	Y	Y	Y	Y	Y	Y
13 **Fossella**	?	?	?	N	Y	Y
14 Maloney	Y	Y	Y	Y	Y	Y
15 Rangel	Y	Y	Y	Y	Y	Y
16 Serrano	Y	Y	Y	Y	Y	Y
17 Engel	?	?	?	Y	Y	Y
18 Lowey	Y	Y	Y	Y	Y	Y
19 Hall	Y	Y	Y	Y	Y	Y
20 Gillibrand	Y	Y	Y	Y	Y	Y
21 McNulty	Y	Y	Y	Y	Y	Y
22 Hinchey	Y	Y	Y	Y	Y	Y
23 **McHugh**	Y	Y	Y	Y	Y	Y
24 Arcuri	Y	Y	Y	Y	Y	Y
25 **Walsh**	Y	Y	Y	Y	Y	Y
26 **Reynolds**	Y	Y	Y	Y	Y	Y
27 Higgins	Y	Y	Y	Y	Y	Y
28 Slaughter	Y	Y	Y	Y	Y	Y
29 **Kuhl**	N	Y	?	Y	Y	Y
NORTH CAROLINA						
1 Butterfield	Y	Y	Y	Y	Y	Y
2 Etheridge	Y	Y	Y	Y	Y	Y
3 **Jones**	Y	Y	Y	Y	Y	Y
4 Price	Y	Y	Y	Y	Y	Y
5 **Foxx**	N	Y	Y	N	Y	Y
6 **Coble**	N	Y	Y	Y	Y	Y
7 McIntyre	Y	Y	Y	Y	Y	Y
8 **Hayes**	Y	Y	Y	Y	Y	Y
9 **Myrick**	N	Y	Y	N	Y	Y
10 **McHenry**	?	?	?	N	Y	Y
11 Shuler	Y	Y	Y	Y	Y	Y
12 Watt	Y	Y	Y	Y	Y	Y
13 Miller	Y	Y	Y	Y	Y	Y
NORTH DAKOTA						
AL Pomeroy	Y	Y	Y	Y	Y	Y
OHIO						
1 **Chabot**	Y	Y	Y	N	Y	Y
2 **Schmidt**	?	?	?	N	Y	Y
3 **Turner**	Y	Y	Y	Y	Y	Y
4 **Jordan**	N	Y	Y	N	Y	Y
5 **Latta**	N	Y	Y	Y	Y	Y
6 Wilson	Y	Y	Y	Y	Y	Y
7 **Hobson**	Y	Y	Y	N	Y	Y
8 **Boehner**	N	Y	Y	N	Y	?
9 Kaptur	Y	Y	Y	Y	Y	Y
10 Kucinich	Y	Y	Y	Y	Y	Y
11 Tubbs Jones	Y	Y	Y	Y	Y	Y
12 **Tiberi**	Y	Y	Y	N	Y	Y
13 Sutton	Y	Y	Y	Y	Y	Y
14 **LaTourette**	Y	Y	Y	Y	Y	Y
15 **Pryce**	?	?	?	N	Y	Y
16 **Regula**	Y	Y	Y	Y	Y	Y
17 Ryan	Y	Y	Y	Y	Y	Y
18 Space	Y	Y	Y	Y	Y	Y
OKLAHOMA						
1 **Sullivan**	N	Y	Y	Y	Y	Y
2 Boren	Y	Y	Y	Y	Y	Y
3 **Lucas**	Y	Y	Y	Y	Y	Y
4 **Cole**	Y	Y	Y	Y	Y	Y
5 **Fallin**	N	Y	Y	Y	Y	Y
OREGON						
1 Wu	Y	Y	Y	Y	Y	Y
2 **Walden**	N	Y	Y	Y	Y	Y
3 Blumenauer	Y	Y	Y	N	N	Y
4 DeFazio	Y	Y	Y	Y	Y	Y
5 Hooley	Y	Y	Y	Y	Y	Y
PENNSYLVANIA						
1 Brady	Y	Y	Y	Y	Y	Y
2 Fattah	Y	Y	Y	Y	Y	Y
3 **English**	?	?	?	Y	Y	Y
4 Altmire	Y	Y	Y	Y	Y	Y
5 **Peterson**	N	Y	Y	?	?	?
6 **Gerlach**	Y	Y	Y	Y	Y	Y
7 Sestak	Y	Y	Y	Y	Y	Y
8 Murphy, P.	Y	Y	Y	Y	Y	Y
9 **Shuster**	Y	Y	Y	Y	Y	Y
10 Carney	Y	Y	Y	Y	Y	Y
11 Kanjorski	Y	Y	Y	Y	Y	Y
12 Murtha	Y	?	?	Y	Y	Y
13 Schwartz	Y	Y	Y	Y	Y	Y
14 Doyle	Y	Y	Y	Y	Y	Y
15 **Dent**	Y	Y	Y	N	Y	Y
16 **Pitts**	N	Y	Y	N	Y	Y
17 Holden	Y	Y	Y	Y	Y	Y
18 **Murphy, T.**	N	Y	Y	Y	Y	Y
19 **Platts**	Y	Y	Y	Y	Y	Y
RHODE ISLAND						
1 Kennedy	Y	Y	Y	Y	Y	Y
2 Langevin	Y	Y	Y	Y	Y	Y
SOUTH CAROLINA						
1 **Brown**	Y	Y	Y	Y	Y	Y
2 **Wilson**	N	Y	Y	N	Y	Y
3 **Barrett**	N	Y	Y	N	Y	Y
4 **Inglis**	N	Y	Y	N	Y	Y
5 Spratt	Y	Y	Y	Y	Y	Y
6 Clyburn	Y	Y	Y	Y	Y	Y
SOUTH DAKOTA						
AL Herseth Sandlin	Y	Y	Y	Y	Y	Y
TENNESSEE						
1 **Davis, D.**	N	Y	Y	Y	Y	Y
2 **Duncan**	Y	Y	Y	N	Y	Y
3 **Wamp**	N	Y	Y	N	Y	Y
4 Davis, L.	Y	Y	Y	Y	Y	Y
5 Cooper	Y	Y	Y	N	Y	Y
6 Gordon	Y	Y	Y	Y	Y	Y
7 **Blackburn**	N	Y	Y	Y	Y	Y
8 Tanner	?	?	?	Y	Y	Y
9 Cohen	Y	Y	Y	Y	Y	Y
TEXAS						
1 **Gohmert**	N	Y	Y	Y	Y	Y
2 **Poe**	N	Y	Y	Y	Y	+
3 **Johnson, S.**	N	Y	Y	N	Y	Y
4 **Hall**	N	Y	Y	Y	Y	Y
5 **Hensarling**	N	Y	Y	N	Y	Y
6 **Barton**	N	Y	Y	N	Y	Y
7 **Culberson**	N	Y	Y	N	Y	Y
8 **Brady**	N	Y	Y	Y	Y	Y
9 Green, A.	Y	Y	Y	Y	Y	Y
10 **McCaul**	N	Y	Y	Y	Y	Y
11 **Conaway**	N	Y	Y	Y	Y	Y
12 **Granger**	Y	Y	Y	N	Y	Y
13 **Thornberry**	N	Y	Y	Y	Y	Y
14 **Paul**	N	Y	Y	N	Y	N
15 Hinojosa	Y	Y	Y	Y	Y	Y
16 Reyes	Y	Y	Y	Y	Y	Y
17 Edwards	Y	Y	Y	Y	Y	Y
18 Jackson Lee	Y	Y	Y	Y	Y	Y
19 **Neugebauer**	N	Y	Y	Y	Y	Y
20 Gonzalez	Y	Y	Y	Y	Y	Y
21 **Smith**	N	Y	Y	N	Y	Y
22 Lampson	Y	Y	Y	Y	Y	Y
23 Rodriguez	Y	Y	Y	Y	Y	Y
24 **Marchant**	N	Y	Y	N	Y	Y
25 Doggett	Y	Y	Y	Y	Y	Y
26 **Burgess**	N	Y	Y	N	Y	Y
27 Ortiz	Y	Y	Y	Y	Y	Y
28 Cuellar	Y	Y	Y	Y	Y	Y
29 Green, G.	+	+	+	Y	Y	Y
30 Johnson, E.	Y	Y	Y	Y	Y	Y
31 **Carter**	N	Y	Y	Y	Y	Y
32 **Sessions**	N	Y	Y	N	Y	Y
UTAH						
1 **Bishop**	N	Y	Y	?	Y	Y
2 Matheson	Y	Y	Y	N	Y	Y
3 **Cannon**	?	?	?	N	Y	Y
VERMONT						
AL Welch	Y	Y	Y	Y	Y	Y
VIRGINIA						
1 **Wittman**	Y	Y	Y	Y	Y	Y
2 **Drake**	Y	Y	Y	Y	Y	Y
3 Scott	Y	Y	Y	Y	Y	Y
4 **Forbes**	Y	Y	Y	Y	Y	Y
5 **Goode**	N	Y	Y	N	Y	Y
6 **Goodlatte**	N	Y	Y	Y	Y	Y
7 **Cantor**	N	Y	Y	N	Y	Y
8 Moran	Y	Y	Y	Y	Y	Y
9 Boucher	Y	Y	Y	Y	Y	Y
10 **Wolf**	Y	Y	Y	N	Y	Y
11 **Davis**	Y	Y	Y	N	Y	Y
WASHINGTON						
1 Inslee	Y	Y	Y	N	Y	Y
2 Larsen	Y	Y	Y	Y	Y	Y
3 Baird	Y	Y	Y	Y	Y	Y
4 **Hastings**	N	Y	Y	Y	Y	Y
5 **McMorris Rodgers**	Y	Y	Y	Y	Y	Y
6 Dicks	Y	Y	Y	Y	Y	Y
7 McDermott	Y	Y	Y	N	Y	Y
8 **Reichert**	Y	Y	Y	N	Y	Y
9 Smith	Y	Y	Y	N	Y	Y
WEST VIRGINIA						
1 Mollohan	Y	Y	Y	Y	Y	Y
2 **Capito**	Y	Y	Y	Y	Y	Y
3 Rahall	Y	Y	Y	Y	Y	Y
WISCONSIN						
1 **Ryan**	N	Y	Y	N	Y	Y
2 Baldwin	Y	Y	Y	Y	Y	Y
3 Kind	+	+	+	N	Y	Y
4 Moore	Y	Y	Y	N	Y	Y
5 **Sensenbrenner**	Y	Y	Y	N	Y	Y
6 **Petri**	Y	Y	Y	N	Y	Y
7 Obey	Y	Y	Y	Y	Y	Y
8 Kagen	Y	Y	Y	Y	Y	Y
WYOMING						
AL **Cubin**	N	Y	Y	N	Y	Y
DELEGATES						
Faleomavaega (A.S.)					?	?
Norton (D.C.)					Y	Y
Bordallo (Guam)					Y	Y
Fortuño (P.R.)					Y	Y
Christensen (V.I.)					Y	Y

IN THE HOUSE | By Vote Number

420. **HR 6063. NASA Authorization/Recommit.** Gingrey, R-Ga., motion to recommit the bill to the Science and Technology Committee with instructions to report it back promptly with language that would create competition within the private sector for energy efficiency and waive greenhouse gas emission restrictions on fuel used by NASA. Motion rejected 196-225: R 191-2; D 5-223 (ND 5-165, SD 0-58). June 18, 2008.

421. **HR 6063. NASA Authorization/Passage.** Passage of the bill that would authorize $20.2 billion for NASA in fiscal 2009, including $6.1 billion for space operations and $1 billion to accelerate research and development of new space exploration vehicles. It would direct NASA to conduct safety reviews, monitor near-Earth objects, plan to return Americans to the moon and review the causes of increasing costs related to spacecraft missions. The bill would reaffirm congressional support for continued exploration of Mars and require NASA to complete planned space shuttle missions before retiring the shuttle. Passed 409-15: R 181-15; D 228-0 (ND 169-0, SD 59-0). A "nay" was a vote in support of the president's position. June 18, 2008.

422. **H Res 1002. Public Radio Recognition Month/Adoption.** Davis, D-Ill., motion to suspend the rules and adopt the resolution that would support the designation of a Public Radio Recognition Month and encourage the celebration of America's public radio stations. Motion agreed to 414-0: R 191-0; D 223-0 (ND 167-0, SD 56-0). A two-thirds majority of those present and voting (276 in this case) is required for adoption under suspension of the rules. June 18, 2008.

423. **HR 5781. Federal Employees Paid Parental Leave/Previous Question.** McGovern, D-Mass., motion to order the previous question (thus ending debate and possibility of amendment) on adoption of the rule (H Res 1277) to provide for House floor consideration of the bill that would allow federal and congressional employees to take four weeks of paid leave for the birth or adoption of a child. Motion agreed to 222-197: R 0-195; D 222-2 (ND 165-1, SD 57-1). June 19, 2008.

424. **HR 5781. Federal Employees Paid Parental Leave/Rule.** Adoption of the rule (H Res 1277) that would provide for House floor consideration of the bill that would allow federal and congressional employees to take four weeks of paid leave for the birth or adoption of a child. Adopted 230-194: R 2-193; D 228-1 (ND 169-1, SD 59-0). June 19, 2008.

425. **HR 5710. Eastern New Mexico Rural Water System/Passage.** Bordallo, D-Guam, motion to suspend the rules and pass the bill that would authorize $327 million for the construction of the Eastern New Mexico Rural Water System. Motion agreed to 301-124: R 71-124; D 230-0 (ND 171-0, SD 59-0). A two-thirds majority of those present and voting (284 in this case) is required for passage under suspension of the rules. June 19, 2008.

	420	421	422	423	424	425
ALABAMA						
1 Bonner	Y	Y	Y	N	N	N
2 Everett	Y	Y	Y	N	N	N
3 Rogers	Y	Y	Y	N	N	N
4 Aderholt	Y	Y	Y	N	N	N
5 Cramer	N	Y	Y	Y	Y	Y
6 Bachus	Y	Y	Y	N	N	N
7 Davis	N	Y	Y	Y	Y	Y
ALASKA						
AL Young	Y	Y	Y	N	N	Y
ARIZONA						
1 Renzi	Y	Y	Y	N	N	Y
2 Franks	Y	N	Y	N	N	N
3 Shadegg	Y	Y	Y	N	N	N
4 Pastor	N	Y	Y	Y	Y	Y
5 Mitchell	N	Y	Y	Y	Y	Y
6 Flake	Y	N	Y	N	N	N
7 Grijalva	N	Y	Y	Y	Y	Y
8 Giffords	N	Y	Y	Y	Y	Y
ARKANSAS						
1 Berry	N	Y	Y	Y	Y	Y
2 Snyder	N	Y	Y	Y	Y	Y
3 Boozman	Y	Y	Y	N	N	N
4 Ross	N	Y	Y	Y	Y	Y
CALIFORNIA						
1 Thompson	N	Y	Y	Y	Y	Y
2 Herger	Y	Y	Y	N	N	Y
3 Lungren	Y	Y	Y	N	N	N
4 Doolittle	Y	Y	Y	N	N	Y
5 Matsui	N	Y	Y	Y	Y	Y
6 Woolsey	N	Y	Y	Y	Y	Y
7 Miller, George	N	Y	Y	Y	Y	Y
8 Pelosi						
9 Lee	N	Y	Y	Y	Y	Y
10 Tauscher	N	Y	Y	Y	Y	Y
11 McNerney	N	Y	Y	Y	Y	Y
12 Speier	N	Y	Y	Y	Y	Y
13 Stark	?	?	?	?	?	?
14 Eshoo	N	Y	Y	Y	Y	Y
15 Honda	N	Y	Y	Y	Y	Y
16 Lofgren	N	Y	Y	Y	Y	Y
17 Farr	N	Y	Y	Y	Y	Y
18 Cardoza	N	Y	Y	Y	Y	Y
19 Radanovich	Y	Y	Y	N	N	N
20 Costa	N	Y	Y	Y	Y	Y
21 Nunes	Y	Y	Y	N	N	N
22 McCarthy	Y	Y	Y	N	N	N
23 Capps	N	Y	Y	Y	Y	Y
24 Gallegly	Y	Y	Y	N	N	N
25 McKeon	Y	Y	?	N	N	Y
26 Dreier	Y	Y	Y	N	N	N
27 Sherman	N	Y	Y	Y	Y	Y
28 Berman	N	?	Y	Y	Y	Y
29 Schiff	N	Y	Y	Y	Y	Y
30 Waxman	N	Y	Y	Y	Y	Y
31 Becerra	N	Y	Y	Y	Y	Y
32 Solis	N	Y	Y	Y	Y	Y
33 Watson	N	Y	Y	Y	Y	Y
34 Roybal-Allard	N	Y	Y	Y	Y	Y
35 Waters	N	Y	Y	Y	Y	Y
36 Harman	?	?	?	Y	Y	Y
37 Richardson	N	Y	Y	Y	Y	Y
38 Napolitano	N	Y	Y	Y	Y	Y
39 Sánchez, Linda	N	Y	Y	Y	Y	Y
40 Royce	Y	Y	Y	N	N	N
41 Lewis	Y	Y	Y	N	N	Y
42 Miller, Gary	Y	Y	Y	N	N	N
43 Baca	N	Y	Y	Y	Y	Y
44 Calvert	Y	Y	Y	N	N	N
45 Bono Mack	Y	Y	Y	N	N	Y
46 Rohrabacher	Y	Y	Y	N	N	Y
47 Sanchez, Loretta	N	Y	Y	Y	Y	Y
48 Campbell	Y	Y	Y	N	N	N
49 Issa	Y	Y	Y	N	N	N
50 Bilbray	N	Y	Y	N	N	Y
51 Filner	N	Y	Y	Y	Y	Y
52 Hunter	Y	Y	?	N	N	N
53 Davis	N	Y	Y	Y	Y	Y

	420	421	422	423	424	425
COLORADO						
1 DeGette	N	Y	Y	Y	Y	Y
2 Udall	N	Y	Y	Y	Y	Y
3 Salazar	N	Y	Y	Y	Y	Y
4 Musgrave	Y	Y	Y	N	N	N
5 Lamborn	Y	Y	Y	N	N	N
6 Tancredo	Y	N	Y	N	N	N
7 Perlmutter	N	Y	Y	Y	Y	Y
CONNECTICUT						
1 Larson	N	Y	Y	Y	Y	Y
2 Courtney	N	Y	Y	Y	Y	Y
3 DeLauro	N	Y	Y	Y	Y	Y
4 Shays	Y	Y	Y	N	N	Y
5 Murphy	N	Y	Y	Y	Y	Y
DELAWARE						
AL Castle	Y	Y	Y	N	N	N
FLORIDA						
1 Miller	Y	Y	Y	N	N	N
2 Boyd	N	Y	Y	Y	Y	Y
3 Brown	N	Y	Y	Y	Y	Y
4 Crenshaw	Y	Y	Y	N	N	N
5 Brown-Waite	Y	Y	?	N	N	Y
6 Stearns	Y	Y	Y	N	N	N
7 Mica	Y	Y	Y	N	N	N
8 Keller	Y	Y	Y	N	N	Y
9 Bilirakis	Y	Y	Y	N	N	N
10 Young	Y	Y	Y	N	N	N
11 Castor	N	Y	Y	Y	Y	Y
12 Putnam	Y	Y	Y	N	N	Y
13 Buchanan	Y	Y	Y	N	N	N
14 Mack	Y	Y	Y	N	N	N
15 Weldon	Y	Y	Y	N	N	N
16 Mahoney	N	Y	Y	Y	Y	Y
17 Meek	N	Y	Y	Y	Y	Y
18 Ros-Lehtinen	Y	Y	Y	N	N	Y
19 Wexler	N	Y	Y	Y	Y	Y
20 Wasserman Schultz	N	Y	Y	?	Y	Y
21 Diaz-Balart, L.	Y	Y	Y	N	N	Y
22 Klein	N	Y	Y	Y	Y	Y
23 Hastings	N	Y	Y	Y	Y	Y
24 Feeney	Y	Y	Y	N	N	N
25 Diaz-Balart, M.	Y	Y	Y	N	N	Y
GEORGIA						
1 Kingston	Y	Y	Y	N	N	N
2 Bishop	N	Y	Y	Y	Y	Y
3 Westmoreland	Y	Y	Y	N	N	N
4 Johnson	N	Y	Y	Y	Y	Y
5 Lewis	N	Y	Y	Y	Y	Y
6 Price	Y	Y	Y	N	N	N
7 Linder	Y	Y	Y	N	N	N
8 Marshall	N	Y	?	Y	Y	Y
9 Deal	Y	Y	Y	N	N	N
10 Broun	Y	N	N	N	N	N
11 Gingrey	Y	Y	Y	N	N	N
12 Barrow	N	Y	Y	Y	Y	Y
13 Scott	N	Y	Y	Y	Y	Y
HAWAII						
1 Abercrombie	N	Y	Y	Y	Y	Y
2 Hirono	N	Y	Y	Y	Y	Y
IDAHO						
1 Sali	Y	Y	Y	N	N	Y
2 Simpson	Y	Y	N	N	N	N
ILLINOIS						
1 Rush	?	?	?	?	?	?
2 Jackson	N	Y	Y	Y	Y	Y
3 Lipinski	N	Y	Y	Y	Y	Y
4 Gutierrez	N	Y	Y	Y	Y	Y
5 Emanuel	N	Y	Y	Y	Y	Y
6 Roskam	Y	Y	Y	N	N	N
7 Davis	N	Y	Y	Y	Y	Y
8 Bean	N	Y	Y	Y	Y	Y
9 Schakowsky	N	Y	Y	Y	Y	Y
10 Kirk	Y	Y	Y	N	N	Y
11 Weller	Y	Y	Y	N	N	Y
12 Costello	N	Y	Y	Y	Y	Y
13 Biggert	Y	Y	Y	N	N	N
14 Foster	N	Y	Y	Y	Y	Y
15 Johnson	Y	Y	Y	N	N	Y

KEY | **Republicans** | Democrats

Y Voted for (yea)	X Paired against	C Voted "present" to avoid possible conflict of interest
# Paired for	– Announced against	
+ Announced for	P Voted "present"	? Did not vote or otherwise make a position known
N Voted against (nay)		

ND Northern Democrats, SD Southern Democrats
Southern states: Ala., Ark., Fla., Ga., Ky., La., Miss., N.C., Okla., S.C., Tenn., Texas, Va.

	420	421	422	423	424	425
16 **Manzullo**	Y	Y	Y	N	N	N
17 Hare	N	Y	Y	Y	Y	Y
18 **LaHood**	Y	Y	Y	N	N	Y
19 **Shimkus**	Y	Y	Y	N	N	Y
INDIANA						
1 Visclosky	N	Y	Y	Y	Y	Y
2 Donnelly	N	Y	Y	Y	Y	Y
3 **Souder**	Y	Y	Y	N	N	Y
4 **Buyer**	Y	Y	Y	N	N	Y
5 **Burton**	Y	Y	Y	N	N	N
6 **Pence**	Y	Y	?	N	N	N
7 Carson, A.	N	Y	Y	Y	Y	Y
8 Ellsworth	Y	Y	Y	Y	Y	Y
9 Hill	N	Y	Y	N	N	Y
IOWA						
1 Braley	N	Y	Y	Y	Y	Y
2 Loebsack	N	Y	Y	?	?	?
3 Boswell	N	Y	Y	Y	Y	Y
4 **Latham**	Y	Y	Y	N	N	Y
5 **King**	Y	Y	Y	N	N	Y
KANSAS						
1 **Moran**	Y	Y	Y	N	N	N
2 Boyda	N	Y	Y	Y	Y	Y
3 Moore	N	Y	Y	Y	Y	Y
4 **Tiahrt**	Y	Y	Y	?	?	?
KENTUCKY						
1 **Whitfield**	Y	Y	Y	N	N	Y
2 **Lewis**	Y	Y	Y	N	N	N
3 Yarmuth	N	Y	Y	Y	Y	Y
4 **Davis**	Y	Y	Y	N	N	N
5 **Rogers**	Y	Y	Y	N	N	N
6 Chandler	N	Y	Y	Y	Y	Y
LOUISIANA						
1 **Scalise**	Y	Y	Y	N	N	N
2 Jefferson	N	Y	Y	Y	Y	Y
3 Melancon	N	Y	Y	Y	Y	Y
4 **McCrery**	Y	Y	Y	N	N	N
5 **Alexander**	Y	Y	Y	N	N	Y
6 Cazayoux	N	Y	Y	Y	Y	Y
7 **Boustany**	Y	Y	Y	N	N	N
MAINE						
1 Allen	N	Y	Y	Y	Y	Y
2 Michaud	N	Y	Y	Y	Y	Y
MARYLAND						
1 **Gilchrest**	?	?	?	?	?	?
2 Ruppersberger	N	Y	Y	Y	Y	Y
3 Sarbanes	N	Y	Y	Y	Y	Y
4 Vacant*						
5 Hoyer	N	Y	Y	Y	Y	Y
6 **Bartlett**	Y	Y	Y	N	N	N
7 Cummings	N	Y	Y	Y	Y	Y
8 Van Hollen	N	Y	Y	Y	Y	Y
MASSACHUSETTS						
1 Olver	N	Y	Y	Y	Y	Y
2 Neal	N	Y	Y	Y	Y	Y
3 McGovern	N	Y	Y	Y	Y	Y
4 Frank	N	Y	Y	Y	Y	Y
5 Tsongas	N	Y	Y	Y	Y	Y
6 Tierney	N	Y	Y	Y	Y	Y
7 Markey	N	Y	Y	Y	Y	Y
8 Capuano	N	Y	Y	Y	Y	Y
9 Lynch	N	Y	Y	Y	Y	Y
10 Delahunt	N	Y	Y	Y	Y	Y
MICHIGAN						
1 Stupak	N	Y	Y	Y	Y	Y
2 **Hoekstra**	Y	N	Y	N	N	N
3 **Ehlers**	Y	Y	Y	N	N	N
4 **Camp**	Y	Y	Y	N	N	N
5 Kildee	N	Y	Y	Y	Y	Y
6 **Upton**	Y	Y	Y	N	N	N
7 **Walberg**	Y	Y	Y	N	N	N
8 **Rogers**	Y	Y	Y	N	N	N
9 **Knollenberg**	Y	Y	Y	N	N	Y
10 **Miller**	Y	Y	Y	N	N	Y
11 **McCotter**	Y	Y	Y	N	N	N
12 Levin	N	Y	Y	Y	Y	Y
13 Kilpatrick	N	Y	Y	Y	Y	Y
14 Conyers	N	Y	Y	Y	Y	Y
15 Dingell	N	Y	Y	Y	Y	Y
MINNESOTA						
1 Walz	N	Y	Y	Y	Y	Y
2 **Kline**	Y	Y	Y	N	N	N
3 **Ramstad**	Y	Y	Y	N	N	Y
4 McCollum	N	Y	Y	Y	Y	Y

	420	421	422	423	424	425
5 Ellison	N	Y	?	Y	Y	Y
6 **Bachmann**	Y	Y	Y	N	N	N
7 Peterson	N	Y	Y	Y	Y	Y
8 Oberstar	N	Y	Y	Y	Y	Y
MISSISSIPPI						
1 Childers	N	Y	Y	Y	Y	Y
2 Thompson	N	Y	Y	Y	Y	Y
3 **Pickering**	+	Y	Y	N	N	N
4 Taylor	N	Y	Y	Y	Y	Y
MISSOURI						
1 Clay	N	Y	Y	Y	Y	Y
2 **Akin**	Y	Y	Y	N	N	N
3 Carnahan	N	Y	Y	Y	Y	Y
4 Skelton	N	Y	Y	Y	Y	Y
5 Cleaver	N	Y	Y	Y	Y	Y
6 **Graves**	Y	Y	Y	N	N	Y
7 **Blunt**	Y	N	Y	N	N	Y
8 **Emerson**	Y	Y	Y	N	N	Y
9 **Hulshof**	?	?	?	?	?	?
MONTANA						
AL **Rehberg**	Y	Y	Y	N	N	Y
NEBRASKA						
1 **Fortenberry**	Y	Y	Y	N	N	Y
2 **Terry**	Y	Y	Y	N	N	Y
3 **Smith**	Y	Y	Y	N	N	N
NEVADA						
1 Berkley	N	Y	Y	Y	Y	Y
2 **Heller**	Y	Y	Y	N	N	N
3 **Porter**	Y	Y	Y	N	N	Y
NEW HAMPSHIRE						
1 Shea-Porter	N	Y	Y	Y	Y	Y
2 Hodes	N	Y	Y	Y	Y	Y
NEW JERSEY						
1 Andrews	N	Y	Y	?	Y	Y
2 **LoBiondo**	Y	N	Y	N	N	N
3 **Saxton**	Y	Y	Y	N	N	Y
4 **Smith**	Y	Y	Y	N	Y	Y
5 **Garrett**	Y	Y	Y	N	N	N
6 Pallone	N	Y	Y	Y	Y	Y
7 **Ferguson**	Y	Y	Y	N	N	Y
8 Pascrell	N	Y	Y	Y	Y	Y
9 Rothman	N	Y	Y	Y	Y	Y
10 Payne	N	Y	Y	Y	Y	Y
11 **Frelinghuysen**	Y	Y	Y	N	N	Y
12 Holt	N	Y	Y	Y	Y	Y
13 Sires	N	Y	Y	Y	Y	Y
NEW MEXICO						
1 **Wilson**	Y	Y	Y	N	N	Y
2 **Pearce**	Y	Y	Y	N	N	Y
3 Udall	N	Y	Y	Y	Y	Y
NEW YORK						
1 Bishop	N	Y	Y	Y	Y	Y
2 Israel	N	Y	Y	Y	Y	Y
3 **King**	Y	Y	Y	N	N	Y
4 McCarthy	N	Y	Y	Y	Y	Y
5 Ackerman	N	Y	Y	Y	Y	Y
6 Meeks	?	?	?	?	?	?
7 Crowley	N	Y	Y	Y	Y	Y
8 Nadler	N	Y	Y	Y	Y	Y
9 Weiner	N	Y	Y	Y	Y	Y
10 Towns	N	Y	Y	Y	Y	Y
11 Clarke	N	Y	Y	Y	Y	Y
12 Velázquez	N	Y	Y	Y	Y	Y
13 **Fossella**	Y	Y	Y	N	N	N
14 Maloney	N	Y	Y	Y	Y	Y
15 Rangel	?	Y	Y	Y	Y	Y
16 Serrano	N	Y	Y	Y	Y	Y
17 Engel	N	Y	Y	?	?	Y
18 Lowey	N	Y	Y	Y	Y	Y
19 Hall	N	Y	Y	Y	Y	Y
20 Gillibrand	N	Y	Y	?	Y	Y
21 McNulty	N	Y	Y	Y	Y	Y
22 Hinchey	N	Y	Y	Y	Y	Y
23 **McHugh**	Y	Y	Y	N	N	Y
24 Arcuri	N	Y	Y	Y	Y	Y
25 **Walsh**	Y	Y	Y	N	N	Y
26 **Reynolds**	Y	Y	Y	N	N	N
27 Higgins	N	Y	Y	?	Y	Y
28 Slaughter	N	Y	Y	Y	Y	Y
29 **Kuhl**	Y	Y	Y	N	N	N
NORTH CAROLINA						
1 Butterfield	N	Y	Y	Y	Y	Y
2 Etheridge	N	Y	Y	Y	Y	Y
3 **Jones**	Y	Y	Y	N	N	Y
4 Price	N	Y	Y	Y	Y	Y

	420	421	422	423	424	425
5 **Foxx**	Y	Y	Y	N	N	N
6 **Coble**	Y	Y	Y	N	N	N
7 McIntyre	N	Y	Y	Y	Y	Y
8 **Hayes**	Y	Y	Y	N	N	N
9 **Myrick**	Y	N	Y	N	N	N
10 **McHenry**	Y	N	Y	N	N	N
11 Shuler	N	Y	Y	Y	Y	Y
12 Watt	N	Y	Y	Y	Y	Y
13 Miller	N	Y	Y	Y	Y	Y
NORTH DAKOTA						
AL Pomeroy	N	Y	Y	Y	Y	Y
OHIO						
1 **Chabot**	Y	Y	Y	N	N	N
2 **Schmidt**	Y	Y	Y	N	N	N
3 **Turner**	Y	Y	Y	N	N	Y
4 **Jordan**	Y	Y	Y	N	N	N
5 **Latta**	Y	Y	Y	N	N	N
6 Wilson	Y	Y	Y	Y	Y	Y
7 **Hobson**	Y	Y	Y	N	N	N
8 **Boehner**	Y	Y	Y	N	N	N
9 Kaptur	N	Y	Y	Y	Y	Y
10 Kucinich	N	Y	Y	Y	Y	Y
11 Tubbs Jones	N	Y	Y	Y	Y	Y
12 **Tiberi**	Y	Y	Y	N	N	N
13 Sutton	N	Y	Y	Y	Y	Y
14 **LaTourette**	Y	Y	Y	N	N	Y
15 **Pryce**	Y	Y	Y	N	N	Y
16 **Regula**	Y	Y	?	N	N	Y
17 Ryan	N	Y	Y	Y	Y	Y
18 Space	N	Y	Y	Y	Y	Y
OKLAHOMA						
1 **Sullivan**	Y	Y	Y	N	N	N
2 Boren	N	Y	Y	Y	Y	Y
3 **Lucas**	Y	Y	Y	N	N	N
4 **Cole**	Y	Y	Y	N	N	N
5 **Fallin**	Y	Y	Y	N	N	N
OREGON						
1 Wu	N	Y	Y	Y	Y	Y
2 **Walden**	Y	Y	Y	N	N	Y
3 Blumenauer	N	Y	Y	Y	Y	Y
4 DeFazio	N	Y	Y	Y	Y	Y
5 Hooley	N	Y	Y	Y	Y	Y
PENNSYLVANIA						
1 Brady	N	Y	Y	Y	Y	Y
2 Fattah	N	Y	Y	Y	Y	Y
3 **English**	Y	Y	Y	N	N	Y
4 Altmire	N	Y	Y	Y	Y	Y
5 **Peterson**	Y	Y	Y	N	N	N
6 **Gerlach**	Y	Y	Y	N	N	Y
7 Sestak	N	Y	Y	Y	Y	Y
8 Murphy, P.	N	Y	Y	Y	Y	Y
9 **Shuster**	Y	Y	Y	N	N	Y
10 Carney	Y	Y	?	Y	Y	Y
11 Kanjorski	N	Y	Y	Y	Y	Y
12 Murtha	N	?	?	Y	Y	Y
13 Schwartz	N	Y	Y	Y	Y	Y
14 Doyle	N	Y	Y	Y	Y	Y
15 **Dent**	Y	Y	Y	N	N	Y
16 **Pitts**	Y	Y	Y	N	N	N
17 Holden	Y	Y	Y	Y	Y	Y
18 **Murphy, T.**	Y	Y	Y	N	N	Y
19 **Platts**	Y	Y	Y	N	N	N
RHODE ISLAND						
1 Kennedy	N	Y	Y	Y	Y	Y
2 Langevin	N	Y	Y	Y	Y	Y
SOUTH CAROLINA						
1 **Brown**	Y	Y	Y	N	N	N
2 **Wilson**	Y	Y	Y	N	N	N
3 **Barrett**	Y	Y	Y	N	N	N
4 **Inglis**	Y	Y	Y	N	N	N
5 Spratt	N	Y	Y	Y	Y	Y
6 Clyburn	N	Y	?	Y	Y	Y
SOUTH DAKOTA						
AL Herseth Sandlin	N	Y	Y	Y	Y	Y
TENNESSEE						
1 **Davis, D.**	Y	Y	Y	N	N	N
2 **Duncan**	Y	N	Y	N	N	N
3 **Wamp**	Y	Y	Y	N	N	N
4 Davis, L.	N	Y	Y	Y	Y	Y
5 Cooper	N	Y	Y	Y	Y	Y
6 Gordon	N	Y	Y	Y	Y	Y
7 **Blackburn**	Y	Y	Y	N	N	N
8 Tanner	N	Y	Y	Y	Y	Y
9 Cohen	N	Y	?	Y	Y	Y

	420	421	422	423	424	425
TEXAS						
1 **Gohmert**	Y	Y	Y	N	N	N
2 **Poe**	+	+	+	N	N	N
3 **Johnson, S.**	Y	Y	Y	N	N	N
4 **Hall**	Y	Y	Y	N	N	N
5 **Hensarling**	Y	Y	Y	N	N	N
6 **Barton**	Y	Y	Y	N	N	N
7 **Culberson**	Y	Y	Y	N	N	N
8 **Brady**	Y	Y	Y	N	N	N
9 Green, A.	N	Y	Y	Y	Y	Y
10 **McCaul**	Y	Y	Y	N	N	Y
11 **Conaway**	Y	Y	Y	N	N	N
12 **Granger**	Y	Y	Y	N	N	N
13 **Thornberry**	Y	Y	Y	N	N	N
14 **Paul**	Y	N	Y	N	N	N
15 Hinojosa	N	Y	Y	Y	Y	Y
16 Reyes	N	Y	Y	Y	Y	Y
17 Edwards	N	Y	Y	Y	Y	Y
18 Jackson Lee	–	Y	Y	Y	Y	Y
19 **Neugebauer**	Y	Y	Y	N	N	N
20 Gonzalez	N	Y	Y	Y	Y	Y
21 **Smith**	Y	Y	Y	N	N	N
22 Lampson	N	Y	Y	N	Y	Y
23 Rodriguez	N	Y	Y	Y	Y	Y
24 **Marchant**	Y	Y	Y	N	N	N
25 Doggett	N	Y	Y	Y	Y	Y
26 **Burgess**	Y	Y	Y	N	N	N
27 Ortiz	N	Y	Y	Y	Y	Y
28 Cuellar	N	Y	Y	Y	Y	Y
29 Green, G.	N	Y	Y	Y	Y	Y
30 Johnson, E.	N	Y	Y	Y	Y	Y
31 **Carter**	Y	Y	Y	N	N	N
32 **Sessions**	Y	Y	Y	N	N	N
UTAH						
1 **Bishop**	Y	Y	Y	N	N	Y
2 Matheson	N	Y	Y	Y	Y	Y
3 **Cannon**	Y	Y	Y	N	N	N
VERMONT						
AL Welch	N	Y	Y	Y	Y	Y
VIRGINIA						
1 **Wittman**	Y	Y	Y	N	N	N
2 **Drake**	Y	Y	Y	N	N	N
3 Scott	N	Y	Y	Y	Y	Y
4 **Forbes**	Y	Y	Y	N	N	N
5 **Goode**	Y	Y	Y	N	N	N
6 **Goodlatte**	Y	Y	Y	N	N	N
7 **Cantor**	?	Y	Y	N	N	N
8 Moran	N	Y	Y	Y	Y	Y
9 Boucher	N	Y	Y	Y	Y	Y
10 **Wolf**	Y	Y	Y	N	Y	N
11 **Davis**	Y	Y	Y	N	N	Y
WASHINGTON						
1 Inslee	N	Y	Y	Y	Y	Y
2 Larsen	N	Y	Y	Y	Y	Y
3 Baird	N	Y	Y	Y	Y	Y
4 **Hastings**	Y	Y	Y	N	N	Y
5 **McMorris Rodgers**	?	Y	Y	N	N	Y
6 Dicks	N	Y	Y	?	Y	Y
7 McDermott	N	Y	Y	Y	Y	Y
8 **Reichert**	N	Y	Y	N	N	Y
9 Smith	N	Y	Y	Y	Y	Y
WEST VIRGINIA						
1 Mollohan	N	Y	Y	Y	Y	Y
2 **Capito**	Y	Y	Y	N	N	Y
3 Rahall	N	Y	Y	Y	Y	Y
WISCONSIN						
1 **Ryan**	Y	N	Y	N	N	Y
2 Baldwin	N	Y	Y	Y	Y	Y
3 Kind	N	Y	Y	Y	Y	Y
4 Moore	N	Y	Y	Y	Y	Y
5 **Sensenbrenner**	Y	N	Y	N	N	N
6 **Petri**	Y	N	Y	N	N	N
7 Obey	N	Y	Y	Y	Y	Y
8 Kagen	N	Y	?	Y	Y	Y
WYOMING						
AL **Cubin**	Y	N	Y	?	?	?
DELEGATES						
Faleomavaega (A.S.)						
Norton (D.C.)						
Bordallo (Guam)						
Fortuño (P.R.)						
Christensen (V.I.)						

IN THE HOUSE | By Vote Number

426. HR 5781. Federal Employees Paid Parental Leave/Eliminate Study Requirement.
Davis, D-Ill., manager's amendment that, among other things, would eliminate a requirement for a study of the feasibility and desirability of offering an insurance benefit to federal employees that would provide wage replacement during absences related to a health condition. It also would provide that the bill's requirements not apply to births occurring within six months of the bill's enactment. Adopted 422-0: R 193-0; D 229-0 (ND 170-0, SD 59-0). June 19, 2008.

427. HR 5781. Federal Employees Paid Parental Leave/Recommit.
Jordan, R-Ohio, motion to recommit the bill to the Oversight and Government Reform Committee with instructions that it be reported back promptly with language that would bar employees who do not comply with court-ordered child support arrangements from being eligible for the paid leave provisions. Motion rejected 206-220: R 194-1; D 12-219 (ND 7-165, SD 5-54). June 19, 2008.

428. HR 5781. Federal Employees Paid Parental Leave/Passage.
Passage of the bill that would provide that four of the 12 weeks of parental leave given to federal and congressional employees be paid leave. Employees could also use accrued annual or sick leave for parental leave, and would not be required to demonstrate a medical need for using their sick time for that purpose. The bill would also authorize the Office of Personnel Management to extend the parental leave period for up to eight weeks. Passed 278-146: R 50-145; D 228-1 (ND 170-1, SD 58-0). A "nay" was a vote in support of the president's position. June 19, 2008.

429. HR 2642. Supplemental Appropriations/Rule.
Adoption of the rule (H Res 1284) that would provide for House floor consideration of the Senate amendments to the House amendments to the Senate amendment to the bill that would provide supplemental appropriations for the wars in Iraq and Afghanistan, and for various domestic programs. Adopted 342-83: R 150-43; D 192-40 (ND 147-26, SD 45-14). June 19, 2008.

430. H Res 1230. Condemn Violence in Zimbabwe/Adoption.
Payne, D-N.J., motion to suspend the rules and adopt the resolution that would call on Zimbabwean security forces, informal militias and individuals to immediately cease their attacks and condemn the orchestrated campaign of violence conducted by the ruling party. It would urge the United Nations to send an envoy to monitor the runoff elections. Motion agreed to 412-1: R 184-1; D 228-0 (ND 172-0, SD 56-0). A two-thirds majority of those present and voting (276 in this case) is required for adoption under suspension of the rules. June 19, 2008.

*Rep. Donna Edwards, D-Md., was sworn in June 19, 2008, to fill the seat vacated by Albert R. Wynn. The first vote for which Edwards was eligible was vote 427.

ND Northern Democrats, SD Southern Democrats
Southern states: Ala., Ark., Fla., Ga., Ky., La., Miss., N.C., Okla., S.C., Tenn., Texas, Va.

	426	427	428	429	430
ALABAMA					
1 **Bonner**	Y	Y	N	Y	Y
2 **Everett**	Y	Y	N	Y	Y
3 **Rogers**	Y	Y	Y	Y	Y
4 **Aderholt**	Y	Y	N	Y	Y
5 Cramer	Y	N	Y	Y	?
6 Bachus	Y	Y	N	Y	Y
7 Davis	Y	N	Y	Y	Y
ALASKA					
AL **Young**	Y	Y	Y	Y	Y
ARIZONA					
1 **Renzi**	Y	Y	N	Y	Y
2 **Franks**	Y	Y	N	N	Y
3 **Shadegg**	Y	Y	N	N	Y
4 Pastor	Y	N	Y	Y	Y
5 Mitchell	Y	N	Y	Y	Y
6 **Flake**	Y	Y	N	N	Y
7 Grijalva	Y	N	Y	Y	Y
8 Giffords	Y	Y	Y	N	Y
ARKANSAS					
1 Berry	Y	N	Y	Y	Y
2 Snyder	Y	N	Y	Y	Y
3 **Boozman**	Y	Y	N	Y	Y
4 Ross	Y	N	Y	N	Y
CALIFORNIA					
1 Thompson	Y	N	Y	Y	Y
2 **Herger**	Y	Y	N	Y	Y
3 **Lungren**	Y	Y	N	Y	Y
4 **Doolittle**	Y	Y	N	Y	Y
5 Matsui	Y	N	Y	Y	Y
6 Woolsey	Y	N	Y	Y	Y
7 Miller, George	Y	N	Y	Y	Y
8 Pelosi					
9 Lee	Y	N	Y	Y	Y
10 Tauscher	Y	N	Y	Y	Y
11 McNerney	Y	Y	Y	Y	Y
12 Speier	Y	N	Y	Y	Y
13 Stark	?	?	?	?	?
14 Eshoo	Y	N	Y	Y	Y
15 Honda	Y	N	?	Y	Y
16 Lofgren	Y	N	Y	Y	Y
17 Farr	Y	N	Y	Y	Y
18 Cardoza	Y	N	Y	Y	Y
19 **Radanovich**	Y	Y	N	Y	Y
20 Costa	Y	N	Y	N	Y
21 **Nunes**	Y	Y	N	Y	Y
22 **McCarthy**	Y	Y	N	Y	Y
23 Capps	Y	N	Y	Y	Y
24 **Gallegly**	Y	Y	N	Y	Y
25 **McKeon**	Y	Y	N	Y	Y
26 **Dreier**	Y	Y	N	Y	Y
27 Sherman	Y	N	Y	Y	Y
28 Berman	Y	N	Y	Y	Y
29 Schiff	Y	N	Y	Y	Y
30 Waxman	Y	N	Y	Y	Y
31 Becerra	Y	N	Y	Y	Y
32 Solis	Y	N	Y	Y	Y
33 Watson	Y	N	Y	Y	Y
34 Roybal-Allard	Y	N	Y	Y	Y
35 Waters	Y	N	Y	Y	Y
36 Harman	Y	N	Y	N	Y
37 Richardson	Y	N	Y	Y	Y
38 Napolitano	Y	N	Y	Y	Y
39 Sánchez, Linda	Y	N	Y	Y	Y
40 **Royce**	Y	Y	N	N	Y
41 **Lewis**	Y	Y	N	Y	Y
42 **Miller, Gary**	Y	Y	N	Y	Y
43 Baca	Y	N	Y	N	Y
44 **Calvert**	Y	Y	N	Y	Y
45 **Bono Mack**	Y	Y	N	Y	Y
46 **Rohrabacher**	Y	Y	N	N	Y
47 Sanchez, Loretta	Y	N	Y	N	Y
48 **Campbell**	Y	Y	N	N	Y
49 **Issa**	Y	Y	N	Y	Y
50 **Bilbray**	Y	Y	Y	Y	Y
51 Filner	Y	N	Y	N	Y
52 **Hunter**	Y	Y	N	Y	Y
53 Davis	Y	N	Y	Y	Y

	426	427	428	429	430
COLORADO					
1 DeGette	Y	N	Y	Y	Y
2 Udall	Y	N	Y	Y	Y
3 Salazar	Y	N	Y	Y	Y
4 **Musgrave**	Y	Y	N	Y	Y
5 **Lamborn**	Y	Y	N	N	Y
6 **Tancredo**	Y	Y	N	Y	Y
7 Perlmutter	Y	N	Y	Y	Y
CONNECTICUT					
1 Larson	Y	N	Y	Y	Y
2 Courtney	Y	N	Y	Y	Y
3 DeLauro	Y	N	Y	Y	Y
4 **Shays**	Y	Y	Y	Y	Y
5 Murphy	Y	N	Y	Y	Y
DELAWARE					
AL **Castle**	Y	Y	N	Y	Y
FLORIDA					
1 **Miller**	Y	Y	N	N	Y
2 Boyd	Y	N	Y	N	?
3 Brown	Y	N	Y	Y	Y
4 **Crenshaw**	Y	Y	N	Y	Y
5 **Brown-Waite**	Y	Y	N	Y	Y
6 **Stearns**	Y	Y	N	Y	Y
7 **Mica**	Y	Y	N	Y	Y
8 **Keller**	Y	Y	N	Y	?
9 **Bilirakis**	Y	Y	N	Y	Y
10 **Young**	Y	Y	Y	Y	Y
11 Castor	Y	N	Y	Y	Y
12 **Putnam**	Y	Y	N	Y	Y
13 **Buchanan**	Y	Y	N	Y	Y
14 **Mack**	Y	Y	N	Y	Y
15 **Weldon**	Y	Y	N	Y	Y
16 Mahoney	Y	N	Y	N	Y
17 Meek	Y	N	Y	Y	Y
18 **Ros-Lehtinen**	Y	Y	Y	Y	Y
19 Wexler	Y	N	Y	Y	Y
20 Wasserman Schultz	Y	N	Y	Y	Y
21 **Diaz-Balart, L.**	Y	Y	Y	Y	?
22 Klein	Y	N	Y	Y	Y
23 Hastings	Y	N	Y	Y	Y
24 **Feeney**	Y	Y	N	Y	Y
25 **Diaz-Balart, M.**	Y	Y	Y	Y	?
GEORGIA					
1 **Kingston**	Y	Y	N	N	Y
2 Bishop	Y	N	Y	Y	Y
3 **Westmoreland**	Y	Y	N	N	Y
4 Johnson	Y	N	Y	Y	Y
5 Lewis	Y	N	Y	Y	Y
6 **Price**	Y	Y	N	N	?
7 **Linder**	Y	Y	N	N	Y
8 Marshall	Y	Y	N	Y	Y
9 **Deal**	Y	Y	N	N	Y
10 **Broun**	Y	Y	N	N	Y
11 **Gingrey**	?	Y	N	N	Y
12 Barrow	Y	N	Y	Y	Y
13 Scott	Y	N	Y	N	Y
HAWAII					
1 Abercrombie	Y	N	Y	Y	Y
2 Hirono	Y	N	Y	Y	Y
IDAHO					
1 **Sali**	Y	Y	N	N	Y
2 **Simpson**	Y	Y	Y	Y	Y
ILLINOIS					
1 Rush	?	?	?	?	?
2 Jackson	Y	N	Y	Y	Y
3 Lipinski	Y	N	Y	Y	Y
4 Gutierrez	Y	N	Y	Y	Y
5 Emanuel	Y	N	Y	Y	Y
6 **Roskam**	Y	Y	N	Y	Y
7 Davis	Y	N	Y	Y	Y
8 Bean	Y	N	Y	N	Y
9 Schakowsky	Y	N	Y	Y	Y
10 **Kirk**	Y	Y	Y	Y	Y
11 **Weller**	Y	Y	N	N	Y
12 Costello	Y	N	Y	Y	Y
13 **Biggert**	Y	Y	N	Y	Y
14 Foster	Y	N	Y	Y	Y
15 **Johnson**	Y	Y	Y	Y	Y

KEY	Republicans	Democrats		
Y Voted for (yea)		X Paired against		C Voted "present" to avoid possible conflict of interest
# Paired for		– Announced against		
+ Announced for		P Voted "present"		? Did not vote or otherwise make a position known
N Voted against (nay)				

	426	427	428	429	430
16 **Manzullo**	Y	Y	N	Y	Y
17 Hare	Y	N	Y	Y	Y
18 **LaHood**	Y	Y	Y	Y	?
19 **Shimkus**	Y	Y	N	Y	Y
INDIANA					
1 Visclosky	Y	N	Y	Y	?
2 Donnelly	Y	Y	Y	N	Y
3 **Souder**	Y	Y	N	Y	Y
4 **Buyer**	Y	Y	Y	N	Y
5 **Burton**	Y	Y	N	N	Y
6 **Pence**	Y	Y	N	N	Y
7 Carson, A.	Y	N	Y	Y	Y
8 Ellsworth	Y	Y	Y	N	Y
9 Hill	Y	N	Y	N	Y
IOWA					
1 Braley	Y	N	Y	Y	Y
2 Loebsack	?	?	?	Y	Y
3 Boswell	Y	N	Y	Y	Y
4 **Latham**	Y	Y	N	Y	Y
5 **King**	Y	Y	N	N	Y
KANSAS					
1 **Moran**	Y	Y	N	N	Y
2 Boyda	Y	N	Y	N	Y
3 Moore	Y	N	Y	N	Y
4 **Tiahrt**	?	?	?	?	?
KENTUCKY					
1 **Whitfield**	Y	Y	N	Y	Y
2 **Lewis**	Y	Y	N	Y	Y
3 Yarmuth	Y	N	Y	Y	Y
4 **Davis**	Y	Y	N	Y	Y
5 **Rogers**	Y	Y	N	Y	Y
6 Chandler	Y	N	Y	N	Y
LOUISIANA					
1 **Scalise**	Y	Y	N	Y	Y
2 Jefferson	Y	N	Y	Y	Y
3 Melancon	Y	N	Y	Y	Y
4 **McCrery**	Y	Y	N	?	?
5 **Alexander**	Y	Y	Y	Y	Y
6 Cazayoux	Y	N	Y	Y	Y
7 **Boustany**	Y	Y	N	Y	Y
MAINE					
1 Allen	Y	N	Y	Y	Y
2 Michaud	Y	N	Y	N	Y
MARYLAND					
1 **Gilchrest**	?	?	?	?	?
2 Ruppersberger	Y	N	Y	Y	Y
3 Sarbanes	Y	N	Y	Y	Y
4 Edwards*		N	Y	Y	Y
5 Hoyer	Y	N	Y	Y	Y
6 **Bartlett**	Y	Y	N	Y	Y
7 Cummings	Y	N	Y	Y	Y
8 Van Hollen	Y	N	Y	Y	Y
MASSACHUSETTS					
1 Olver	Y	N	Y	Y	Y
2 Neal	Y	N	Y	Y	Y
3 McGovern	Y	N	Y	Y	Y
4 Frank	Y	N	Y	Y	Y
5 Tsongas	Y	N	Y	Y	Y
6 Tierney	Y	N	Y	Y	Y
7 Markey	Y	N	Y	Y	Y
8 Capuano	Y	N	Y	Y	Y
9 Lynch	Y	N	Y	Y	Y
10 Delahunt	Y	N	Y	Y	Y
MICHIGAN					
1 Stupak	Y	N	Y	Y	Y
2 **Hoekstra**	Y	Y	N	Y	Y
3 **Ehlers**	Y	Y	N	Y	Y
4 **Camp**	Y	Y	N	Y	Y
5 Kildee	Y	N	Y	Y	Y
6 **Upton**	Y	Y	Y	Y	Y
7 **Walberg**	Y	Y	N	Y	Y
8 **Rogers**	Y	Y	N	Y	Y
9 **Knollenberg**	Y	Y	N	Y	Y
10 **Miller**	Y	Y	Y	Y	Y
11 **McCotter**	Y	Y	Y	Y	Y
12 Levin	Y	N	Y	Y	Y
13 Kilpatrick	Y	N	Y	Y	Y
14 Conyers	Y	N	Y	Y	Y
15 Dingell	Y	N	Y	Y	Y
MINNESOTA					
1 Walz	Y	N	Y	Y	Y
2 **Kline**	Y	Y	N	Y	Y
3 **Ramstad**	Y	Y	Y	Y	Y
4 McCollum	Y	N	Y	Y	Y
5 Ellison	Y	N	Y	Y	Y
6 **Bachmann**	Y	Y	N	N	Y
7 Peterson	Y	N	Y	N	Y
8 Oberstar	Y	N	Y	Y	Y
MISSISSIPPI					
1 Childers	Y	Y	Y	Y	Y
2 Thompson	Y	N	Y	Y	Y
3 **Pickering**	Y	Y	N	Y	Y
4 Taylor	Y	N	Y	Y	Y
MISSOURI					
1 Clay	?	N	Y	N	Y
2 **Akin**	Y	Y	N	Y	Y
3 Carnahan	Y	N	Y	Y	Y
4 Skelton	Y	N	Y	?	Y
5 Cleaver	Y	N	Y	Y	Y
6 **Graves**	Y	Y	N	Y	Y
7 **Blunt**	Y	Y	N	Y	Y
8 **Emerson**	Y	Y	Y	Y	Y
9 **Hulshof**	?	?	?	?	?
MONTANA					
AL **Rehberg**	Y	Y	Y	Y	Y
NEBRASKA					
1 **Fortenberry**	Y	Y	Y	Y	Y
2 **Terry**	Y	Y	N	Y	Y
3 **Smith**	Y	Y	N	Y	Y
NEVADA					
1 Berkley	Y	N	Y	Y	Y
2 **Heller**	Y	Y	N	Y	Y
3 **Porter**	Y	Y	Y	Y	Y
NEW HAMPSHIRE					
1 Shea-Porter	Y	N	Y	Y	Y
2 Hodes	Y	N	Y	Y	Y
NEW JERSEY					
1 Andrews	Y	N	Y	Y	Y
2 **LoBiondo**	Y	Y	Y	Y	Y
3 **Saxton**	Y	Y	Y	?	Y
4 **Smith**	Y	Y	Y	Y	Y
5 **Garrett**	Y	Y	N	N	Y
6 Pallone	Y	N	Y	Y	Y
7 **Ferguson**	Y	Y	Y	Y	Y
8 Pascrell	Y	N	Y	Y	Y
9 Rothman	Y	N	Y	Y	Y
10 Payne	Y	N	Y	Y	Y
11 **Frelinghuysen**	Y	Y	N	Y	Y
12 Holt	Y	N	Y	N	Y
13 Sires	Y	N	Y	Y	Y
NEW MEXICO					
1 **Wilson**	Y	Y	N	Y	Y
2 **Pearce**	Y	Y	Y	Y	Y
3 Udall	Y	N	Y	Y	Y
NEW YORK					
1 Bishop	Y	N	Y	Y	Y
2 Israel	Y	N	Y	Y	Y
3 **King**	Y	Y	N	Y	Y
4 McCarthy	Y	N	Y	Y	Y
5 Ackerman	Y	N	Y	Y	Y
6 Meeks	?	?	?	Y	Y
7 Crowley	Y	N	Y	Y	Y
8 Nadler	Y	N	Y	Y	Y
9 Weiner	Y	N	Y	Y	Y
10 Towns	Y	N	Y	Y	Y
11 Clarke	Y	N	Y	N	Y
12 Velázquez	Y	N	Y	Y	Y
13 **Fossella**	Y	Y	N	Y	Y
14 Maloney	Y	N	Y	Y	Y
15 Rangel	Y	N	Y	Y	Y
16 Serrano	Y	N	Y	Y	Y
17 Engel	Y	N	Y	Y	Y
18 Lowey	Y	N	Y	Y	Y
19 Hall	Y	N	Y	Y	Y
20 Gillibrand	Y	N	Y	N	Y
21 McNulty	Y	N	Y	Y	Y
22 Hinchey	Y	N	Y	Y	Y
23 **McHugh**	Y	Y	Y	Y	Y
24 Arcuri	Y	N	Y	Y	Y
25 **Walsh**	Y	Y	N	Y	Y
26 **Reynolds**	?	Y	N	Y	Y
27 Higgins	Y	N	Y	Y	Y
28 Slaughter	Y	N	Y	Y	Y
29 **Kuhl**	Y	Y	N	Y	Y
NORTH CAROLINA					
1 Butterfield	Y	N	Y	Y	Y
2 Etheridge	Y	N	Y	Y	Y
3 **Jones**	Y	Y	Y	Y	Y
4 Price	Y	N	Y	Y	Y
5 **Foxx**	Y	Y	N	Y	Y
6 **Coble**	Y	Y	N	N	?
7 McIntyre	Y	Y	Y	N	Y
8 **Hayes**	Y	Y	Y	Y	Y
9 **Myrick**	Y	Y	N	Y	Y
10 **McHenry**	Y	Y	N	N	Y
11 Shuler	Y	Y	Y	N	Y
12 Watt	Y	N	Y	Y	Y
13 Miller	Y	N	Y	Y	Y
NORTH DAKOTA					
AL Pomeroy	Y	N	Y	Y	Y
OHIO					
1 **Chabot**	Y	Y	N	Y	Y
2 **Schmidt**	Y	Y	N	Y	Y
3 **Turner**	Y	Y	Y	Y	?
4 **Jordan**	Y	Y	N	Y	Y
5 **Latta**	Y	Y	N	Y	Y
6 Wilson	Y	N	Y	N	Y
7 **Hobson**	Y	Y	Y	Y	Y
8 **Boehner**	Y	Y	N	Y	Y
9 Kaptur	Y	N	Y	Y	Y
10 Kucinich	Y	N	Y	N	Y
11 Tubbs Jones	Y	N	Y	Y	Y
12 **Tiberi**	Y	Y	Y	Y	Y
13 Sutton	Y	N	Y	Y	Y
14 **LaTourette**	Y	Y	Y	Y	Y
15 **Pryce**	Y	Y	Y	Y	?
16 **Regula**	Y	Y	Y	Y	Y
17 Ryan	Y	N	Y	Y	Y
18 Space	Y	Y	Y	N	Y
OKLAHOMA					
1 **Sullivan**	Y	Y	N	N	?
2 Boren	Y	N	Y	N	Y
3 **Lucas**	Y	Y	N	Y	Y
4 **Cole**	Y	Y	N	Y	Y
5 **Fallin**	Y	Y	N	Y	Y
OREGON					
1 Wu	Y	N	Y	Y	Y
2 **Walden**	Y	Y	N	Y	Y
3 Blumenauer	Y	N	Y	Y	Y
4 DeFazio	Y	N	Y	N	Y
5 Hooley	Y	N	Y	Y	Y
PENNSYLVANIA					
1 Brady	Y	N	Y	Y	Y
2 Fattah	Y	N	Y	Y	Y
3 **English**	Y	Y	Y	Y	Y
4 Altmire	Y	Y	Y	Y	Y
5 **Peterson**	Y	Y	Y	Y	Y
6 **Gerlach**	Y	Y	Y	Y	Y
7 Sestak	Y	N	Y	Y	Y
8 Murphy, P.	Y	N	Y	Y	Y
9 **Shuster**	Y	Y	N	Y	Y
10 Carney	Y	Y	Y	N	Y
11 Kanjorski	Y	N	N	Y	Y
12 Murtha	Y	N	Y	Y	Y
13 Schwartz	Y	N	Y	Y	Y
14 Doyle	Y	N	Y	Y	Y
15 **Dent**	Y	Y	Y	Y	Y
16 **Pitts**	Y	Y	N	N	Y
17 Holden	Y	N	Y	Y	Y
18 **Murphy, T.**	Y	Y	Y	Y	Y
19 **Platts**	Y	Y	Y	Y	Y
RHODE ISLAND					
1 Kennedy	Y	N	Y	Y	Y
2 Langevin	Y	N	Y	Y	Y
SOUTH CAROLINA					
1 **Brown**	Y	Y	N	Y	Y
2 **Wilson**	Y	Y	N	Y	Y
3 **Barrett**	Y	Y	N	N	Y
4 **Inglis**	Y	Y	N	N	Y
5 Spratt	Y	N	Y	Y	Y
6 Clyburn	Y	N	Y	Y	Y
SOUTH DAKOTA					
AL Herseth Sandlin	Y	N	Y	N	Y
TENNESSEE					
1 **Davis, D.**	Y	Y	N	Y	Y
2 **Duncan**	Y	Y	N	N	Y
3 **Wamp**	Y	Y	N	Y	Y
4 Davis, L.	Y	N	Y	N	Y
5 Cooper	Y	N	Y	N	?
6 Gordon	Y	N	Y	Y	Y
7 **Blackburn**	Y	Y	N	Y	Y
8 Tanner	Y	N	Y	N	Y
9 Cohen	Y	N	Y	Y	Y
TEXAS					
1 **Gohmert**	Y	Y	N	Y	Y
2 **Poe**	Y	Y	N	N	Y
3 **Johnson, S.**	Y	Y	N	Y	Y
4 **Hall**	Y	Y	Y	Y	Y
5 **Hensarling**	Y	Y	N	N	Y
6 **Barton**	Y	Y	N	Y	Y
7 **Culberson**	Y	Y	N	N	Y
8 **Brady**	Y	Y	N	Y	Y
9 Green, A.	Y	N	Y	Y	Y
10 **McCaul**	Y	Y	N	Y	Y
11 **Conaway**	Y	Y	N	N	Y
12 **Granger**	Y	Y	N	Y	Y
13 **Thornberry**	Y	Y	N	Y	Y
14 **Paul**	Y	Y	N	N	N
15 Hinojosa	Y	N	Y	Y	Y
16 Reyes	Y	N	Y	Y	Y
17 Edwards	Y	N	+	Y	Y
18 Jackson Lee	Y	N	Y	Y	Y
19 **Neugebauer**	Y	Y	N	N	Y
20 Gonzalez	Y	N	Y	Y	Y
21 **Smith**	Y	Y	Y	Y	Y
22 Lampson	Y	Y	Y	Y	Y
23 Rodriguez	Y	N	Y	Y	Y
24 **Marchant**	Y	Y	N	Y	Y
25 Doggett	Y	N	Y	N	Y
26 **Burgess**	Y	Y	N	Y	Y
27 Ortiz	Y	N	Y	Y	Y
28 Cuellar	Y	N	Y	N	Y
29 Green, G.	Y	N	Y	Y	Y
30 Johnson, E.	Y	N	Y	Y	Y
31 **Carter**	Y	Y	N	Y	Y
32 **Sessions**	Y	Y	N	Y	Y
UTAH					
1 **Bishop**	Y	Y	N	Y	Y
2 Matheson	Y	N	Y	N	Y
3 **Cannon**	Y	Y	N	?	?
VERMONT					
AL Welch	Y	N	Y	Y	Y
VIRGINIA					
1 **Wittman**	Y	Y	Y	Y	Y
2 **Drake**	Y	Y	Y	Y	Y
3 Scott	Y	N	Y	Y	Y
4 **Forbes**	Y	Y	Y	Y	Y
5 **Goode**	Y	Y	N	N	Y
6 **Goodlatte**	Y	Y	N	Y	Y
7 **Cantor**	Y	Y	N	Y	Y
8 Moran	Y	N	Y	Y	Y
9 Boucher	Y	N	Y	Y	Y
10 **Wolf**	?	?	+	Y	Y
11 **Davis**	Y	N	Y	N	Y
WASHINGTON					
1 Inslee	Y	N	Y	Y	Y
2 Larsen	Y	N	Y	Y	?
3 Baird	Y	N	Y	N	Y
4 **Hastings**	Y	Y	N	Y	Y
5 **McMorris Rodgers**	Y	Y	N	Y	Y
6 Dicks	Y	N	Y	Y	Y
7 McDermott	Y	N	Y	Y	Y
8 **Reichert**	Y	Y	Y	Y	Y
9 Smith	Y	N	Y	Y	Y
WEST VIRGINIA					
1 Mollohan	Y	N	Y	Y	Y
2 **Capito**	Y	Y	Y	Y	Y
3 Rahall	Y	N	Y	Y	Y
WISCONSIN					
1 **Ryan**	Y	Y	N	N	Y
2 Baldwin	Y	N	Y	Y	Y
3 Kind	Y	N	Y	Y	Y
4 Moore	Y	N	Y	Y	Y
5 **Sensenbrenner**	Y	Y	N	N	Y
6 **Petri**	Y	Y	N	N	Y
7 Obey	Y	N	Y	Y	Y
8 Kagen	Y	N	Y	Y	Y
WYOMING					
AL **Cubin**	Y	Y	N	Y	Y
DELEGATES					
Faleomavaega (A.S.)					
Norton (D.C.)					
Bordallo (Guam)					
Fortuño (P.R.)					
Christensen (V.I.)					

IN THE HOUSE | By Vote Number

431. HR 2642. Supplemental Appropriations/Motion to Concur.
Obey, D-Wis., motion to concur in the Senate amendment to the House amendment that would appropriate $165.4 billion for the wars in Iraq and Afghanistan — $99.5 billion for military operations for fiscal 2008 and $65.9 billion for fiscal 2009. Motion agreed to 268-155: R 188-4; D 80-151 (ND 43-129, SD 37-22). A "yea" was a vote in support of the president's position. June 19, 2008.

432. HR 2642. Supplemental Appropriations/Motion to Concur.
Obey, D-Wis., motion to concur in the Senate amendment to the House amendment with an additional amendment. The House amendment would appropriate $21.1 billion for domestic programs, including $2.7 billion for disaster relief in the Midwest and $5.8 billion to rebuild levees in Louisiana. It would provide for a permanent expansion of education benefits for post-Sept. 11 veterans and cut $3.6 billion from funding for the wars in Iraq and Afghanistan to fund domestic programs. It also would temporarily extend unemployment insurance benefits and place a moratorium through March 2009 on six Medicaid regulations proposed by the administration. Motion agreed to 416-12: R 186-9; D 230-3 (ND 172-2, SD 58-1). June 19, 2008.

433. H Res 1029. Chi-Chi Rodriguez Tribute/Adoption. Davis, D-Ill., motion to suspend the rules and adopt the resolution that would congratulate Juan Antonio "Chi-Chi" Rodriguez for his successes in golf, commend him for exemplary conduct as a private citizen and for a life devoted to service of others, and express gratitude for his service as a role model. Motion agreed to 415-0: R 193-0; D 222-0 (ND 164-0, SD 58-0). A two-thirds majority of those present and voting (277 in this case) is required for adoption under suspension of the rules. June 19, 2008.

434. Procedural Motion/Journal. Approval of the House Journal of Thursday, June 19, 2008. Approved 230-168: R 18-157; D 212-11 (ND 156-10, SD 56-1). June 20, 2008.

435. HR 5876. Child Abuse in Residential Programs/Previous
Question. Cardoza, D-Calif., motion to order the previous question (thus ending debate and possibility of amendment) on adoption of the rule (H Res 1276) to provide for House floor consideration of the bill that would establish new federal regulations for private residential programs that focus on serving children with emotional, behavioral or mental health problems, or problems with alcohol and substance abuse. Motion agreed to 220-179: R 1-177; D 219-2 (ND 163-1, SD 56-1). June 20, 2008.

	431	432	433	434	435
ALABAMA					
1 **Bonner**	Y	Y	Y	N	N
2 **Everett**	Y	Y	Y	N	Y
3 **Rogers**	Y	Y	Y	N	N
4 **Aderholt**	Y	Y	Y	N	N
5 Cramer	Y	Y	Y	Y	Y
6 **Bachus**	+	Y	Y	N	N
7 Davis	Y	Y	Y	Y	Y
ALASKA					
AL **Young**	Y	Y	Y	?	?
ARIZONA					
1 **Renzi**	Y	Y	Y	N	N
2 **Franks**	Y	N	Y	N	N
3 **Shadegg**	Y	Y	Y	N	N
4 Pastor	N	Y	Y	Y	Y
5 Mitchell	Y	Y	Y	N	Y
6 **Flake**	N	N	Y	N	N
7 Grijalva	N	Y	Y	Y	Y
8 Giffords	Y	Y	Y	Y	Y
ARKANSAS					
1 Berry	Y	Y	Y	Y	Y
2 Snyder	Y	Y	Y	Y	Y
3 **Boozman**	Y	Y	Y	N	N
4 Ross	Y	Y	Y	Y	Y
CALIFORNIA					
1 Thompson	N	Y	Y	N	Y
2 **Herger**	Y	Y	Y	N	N
3 **Lungren**	Y	Y	Y	N	N
4 **Doolittle**	Y	Y	Y	N	N
5 Matsui	N	Y	Y	Y	Y
6 Woolsey	N	Y	Y	Y	Y
7 Miller, George	N	Y	Y	Y	Y
8 Pelosi	N	Y			
9 Lee	N	Y	Y	Y	Y
10 Tauscher	N	Y	Y	Y	Y
11 McNerney	N	Y	Y	Y	Y
12 Speier	N	Y	Y	Y	Y
13 Stark	?	?	?	?	?
14 Eshoo	N	Y	Y	Y	Y
15 Honda	N	Y	Y	Y	Y
16 Lofgren	N	Y	Y	Y	Y
17 Farr	–	Y	Y	Y	Y
18 Cardoza	N	Y	Y	Y	Y
19 **Radanovich**	Y	Y	Y	?	?
20 Costa	Y	Y	Y	Y	Y
21 **Nunes**	+	Y	Y	N	N
22 **McCarthy**	Y	Y	Y	N	N
23 Capps	N	Y	Y	Y	Y
24 **Gallegly**	Y	Y	Y	N	N
25 **McKeon**	Y	Y	Y	N	N
26 **Dreier**	Y	Y	Y	N	N
27 Sherman	N	Y	Y	Y	Y
28 Berman	Y	Y	Y	Y	Y
29 Schiff	N	Y	Y	Y	Y
30 Waxman	N	Y	Y	Y	Y
31 Becerra	N	Y	Y	Y	Y
32 Solis	N	Y	Y	Y	Y
33 Watson	N	Y	Y	Y	Y
34 Roybal-Allard	N	Y	Y	Y	Y
35 Waters	N	Y	?	Y	Y
36 Harman	N	Y	Y	Y	Y
37 Richardson	N	Y	Y	Y	Y
38 Napolitano	N	Y	?	Y	Y
39 Sánchez, Linda	N	Y	Y	Y	Y
40 **Royce**	Y	N	Y	N	N
41 **Lewis**	Y	Y	Y	N	N
42 **Miller, Gary**	Y	Y	Y	N	N
43 Baca	N	Y	Y	Y	Y
44 **Calvert**	Y	Y	Y	N	N
45 **Bono Mack**	Y	Y	Y	N	N
46 **Rohrabacher**	Y	Y	Y	N	N
47 Sanchez, Loretta	N	Y	Y	Y	Y
48 **Campbell**	N	N	Y	N	N
49 **Issa**	Y	Y	Y	N	N
50 **Bilbray**	Y	Y	Y	?	?
51 Filner	N	Y	Y	Y	Y
52 **Hunter**	Y	Y	N	N	N
53 Davis	Y	Y	Y	Y	Y

	431	432	433	434	435
COLORADO					
1 DeGette	N	Y	Y	Y	Y
2 Udall	Y	Y	Y	N	Y
3 Salazar	Y	Y	Y	Y	Y
4 **Musgrave**	Y	Y	Y	N	N
5 **Lamborn**	Y	Y	Y	N	N
6 **Tancredo**	Y	Y	Y	N	N
7 Perlmutter	–	Y	Y	Y	Y
CONNECTICUT					
1 Larson	N	Y	Y	Y	Y
2 Courtney	N	Y	Y	Y	Y
3 DeLauro	N	Y	?	Y	Y
4 **Shays**	Y	Y	Y	N	N
5 Murphy	N	Y	Y	Y	Y
DELAWARE					
AL **Castle**	Y	Y	Y	N	N
FLORIDA					
1 **Miller**	Y	Y	Y	Y	N
2 Boyd	Y	Y	Y	Y	Y
3 Brown	Y	Y	Y	Y	Y
4 **Crenshaw**	Y	Y	Y	N	N
5 **Brown-Waite**	Y	Y	Y	?	?
6 **Stearns**	Y	Y	Y	N	N
7 **Mica**	Y	Y	Y	N	N
8 **Keller**	Y	Y	Y	N	N
9 **Bilirakis**	Y	Y	Y	N	N
10 **Young**	Y	Y	Y	N	N
11 Castor	N	Y	Y	Y	Y
12 **Putnam**	Y	Y	Y	N	N
13 **Buchanan**	Y	Y	Y	N	N
14 **Mack**	Y	Y	N	N	N
15 **Weldon**	Y	N	Y	N	N
16 Mahoney	Y	Y	Y	Y	Y
17 Meek	Y	Y	Y	Y	Y
18 **Ros-Lehtinen**	Y	Y	Y	N	N
19 Wexler	N	Y	Y	Y	Y
20 Wasserman Schultz	N	Y	Y	Y	Y
21 **Diaz-Balart, L.**	Y	Y	Y	N	N
22 Klein	N	Y	Y	Y	Y
23 Hastings	N	Y	Y	Y	Y
24 **Feeney**	Y	Y	Y	N	N
25 **Diaz-Balart, M.**	Y	Y	Y	N	N
GEORGIA					
1 **Kingston**	Y	Y	Y	N	N
2 Bishop	Y	Y	Y	Y	Y
3 **Westmoreland**	Y	Y	Y	N	N
4 Johnson	N	Y	Y	Y	Y
5 Lewis	N	Y	Y	Y	Y
6 **Price**	Y	Y	Y	N	N
7 **Linder**	Y	Y	Y	N	N
8 Marshall	Y	Y	Y	Y	Y
9 **Deal**	Y	Y	Y	N	N
10 **Broun**	Y	Y	Y	N	N
11 **Gingrey**	Y	Y	Y	?	N
12 Barrow	Y	Y	Y	Y	Y
13 Scott	Y	Y	Y	Y	Y
HAWAII					
1 Abercrombie	N	Y	Y	Y	Y
2 Hirono	N	Y	?	Y	Y
IDAHO					
1 **Sali**	Y	Y	Y	N	N
2 **Simpson**	Y	Y	Y	N	N
ILLINOIS					
1 Rush	–	+	+	+	+
2 Jackson	N	Y	Y	Y	Y
3 Lipinski	Y	Y	Y	Y	Y
4 Gutierrez	N	Y	Y	Y	Y
5 Emanuel	Y	Y	Y	Y	Y
6 **Roskam**	Y	Y	Y	N	N
7 Davis	Y	Y	Y	Y	Y
8 Bean	Y	Y	Y	Y	Y
9 Schakowsky	N	Y	Y	Y	Y
10 **Kirk**	Y	Y	Y	Y	N
11 **Weller**	Y	Y	–	–	+
12 Costello	N	Y	Y	Y	Y
13 **Biggert**	Y	Y	Y	N	N
14 Foster	Y	Y	Y	Y	Y
15 **Johnson**	Y	Y	Y	Y	N

ND Northern Democrats, SD Southern Democrats
Southern states: Ala., Ark., Fla., Ga., Ky., La., Miss., N.C., Okla., S.C., Tenn., Texas, Va.

	431	432	433	434	435
16 Manzullo	Y	Y	Y	N	N
17 Hare	N	Y	Y	Y	Y
18 LaHood	Y	Y	Y	N	N
19 Shimkus	Y	Y	Y	N	N
INDIANA					
1 Visclosky	+	+	+	+	+
2 Donnelly	Y	Y	Y	Y	Y
3 Souder	Y	Y	Y	N	N
4 Buyer	Y	Y	Y	N	N
5 Burton	Y	Y	Y	N	N
6 Pence	Y	Y	Y	N	N
7 Carson, A.	N	Y	Y	Y	Y
8 Ellsworth	Y	Y	Y	N	Y
9 Hill	Y	Y	Y	N	N
IOWA					
1 Braley	N	Y	Y	Y	Y
2 Loebsack	N	Y	Y	Y	Y
3 Boswell	N	Y	Y	Y	Y
4 Latham	Y	Y	Y	N	N
5 King	Y	Y	Y	N	N
KANSAS					
1 Moran	Y	Y	Y	N	N
2 Boyda	Y	Y	Y	Y	Y
3 Moore	Y	Y	Y	Y	Y
4 Tiahrt	?	?	?	?	?
KENTUCKY					
1 Whitfield	Y	Y	Y	Y	?
2 Lewis	Y	Y	Y	N	N
3 Yarmuth	N	Y	Y	Y	Y
4 Davis	Y	Y	Y	N	N
5 Rogers	Y	Y	Y	N	N
6 Chandler	Y	Y	Y	Y	Y
LOUISIANA					
1 Scalise	Y	Y	Y	N	N
2 Jefferson	N	Y	Y	Y	Y
3 Melancon	Y	Y	Y	N	N
4 McCrery	Y	Y	Y	N	N
5 Alexander	Y	Y	Y	N	N
6 Cazayoux	Y	Y	Y	Y	N
7 Boustany	Y	Y	Y	?	N
MAINE					
1 Allen	N	Y	Y	Y	Y
2 Michaud	N	Y	Y	Y	Y
MARYLAND					
1 Gilchrest	?	?	?	?	?
2 Ruppersberger	Y	Y	Y	+	+
3 Sarbanes	N	Y	Y	Y	Y
4 Edwards	N	Y	Y	Y	Y
5 Hoyer	Y	Y	Y	Y	Y
6 Bartlett	Y	Y	Y	?	?
7 Cummings	N	Y	Y	Y	Y
8 Van Hollen	N	Y	Y	Y	Y
MASSACHUSETTS					
1 Olver	N	Y	Y	Y	Y
2 Neal	N	Y	Y	Y	Y
3 McGovern	N	Y	Y	Y	Y
4 Frank	N	Y	Y	Y	Y
5 Tsongas	N	Y	Y	Y	Y
6 Tierney	N	Y	Y	Y	Y
7 Markey	N	Y	Y	Y	Y
8 Capuano	N	Y	Y	Y	Y
9 Lynch	N	Y	Y	Y	Y
10 Delahunt	N	Y	Y	Y	Y
MICHIGAN					
1 Stupak	N	Y	Y	N	Y
2 Hoekstra	Y	Y	Y	N	N
3 Ehlers	Y	Y	Y	N	N
4 Camp	Y	Y	Y	N	N
5 Kildee	Y	Y	Y	Y	Y
6 Upton	Y	Y	Y	N	N
7 Walberg	Y	Y	Y	N	N
8 Rogers	Y	Y	Y	N	N
9 Knollenberg	Y	Y	Y	N	N
10 Miller	Y	Y	Y	N	N
11 McCotter	Y	Y	Y	N	N
12 Levin	Y	Y	Y	Y	Y
13 Kilpatrick	N	Y	Y	Y	Y
14 Conyers	N	Y	Y	Y	Y
15 Dingell	N	Y	Y	Y	Y
MINNESOTA					
1 Walz	Y	Y	Y	N	N
2 Kline	Y	Y	Y	N	N
3 Ramstad	Y	Y	Y	N	N
4 McCollum	N	Y	Y	Y	Y

	431	432	433	434	435
5 Ellison	N	Y	Y	Y	Y
6 Bachmann	Y	Y	Y	Y	N
7 Peterson	Y	Y	Y	N	Y
8 Oberstar	N	Y	Y	?	?
MISSISSIPPI					
1 Childers	Y	Y	Y	Y	Y
2 Thompson	N	Y	Y	Y	Y
3 Pickering	Y	Y	?	N	N
4 Taylor	Y	Y	Y	Y	Y
MISSOURI					
1 Clay	N	Y	Y	Y	Y
2 Akin	Y	Y	Y	N	N
3 Carnahan	N	Y	Y	Y	Y
4 Skelton	Y	Y	Y	Y	Y
5 Cleaver	N	Y	Y	Y	Y
6 Graves	Y	Y	Y	N	N
7 Blunt	Y	Y	Y	?	N
8 Emerson	Y	Y	Y	N	N
9 Hulshof	?	?	?	Y	N
MONTANA					
AL Rehberg	Y	Y	Y	N	N
NEBRASKA					
1 Fortenberry	Y	Y	Y	?	?
2 Terry	Y	Y	Y	N	N
3 Smith	Y	Y	Y	N	N
NEVADA					
1 Berkley	Y	Y	Y	Y	Y
2 Heller	Y	Y	Y	N	N
3 Porter	Y	Y	Y	N	N
NEW HAMPSHIRE					
1 Shea-Porter	N	Y	Y	Y	Y
2 Hodes	N	Y	Y	Y	Y
NEW JERSEY					
1 Andrews	N	Y	?	Y	Y
2 LoBiondo	Y	Y	Y	N	N
3 Saxton	Y	Y	Y	N	N
4 Smith	Y	Y	Y	N	N
5 Garrett	Y	Y	N	N	N
6 Pallone	N	Y	Y	Y	Y
7 Ferguson	Y	Y	Y	?	?
8 Pascrell	N	Y	Y	Y	Y
9 Rothman	N	Y	Y	Y	Y
10 Payne	N	Y	Y	Y	Y
11 Frelinghuysen	Y	Y	Y	N	N
12 Holt	N	Y	Y	Y	Y
13 Sires	N	Y	Y	Y	Y
NEW MEXICO					
1 Wilson	Y	Y	Y	?	?
2 Pearce	Y	Y	Y	N	N
3 Udall	N	Y	Y	Y	Y
NEW YORK					
1 Bishop	N	Y	Y	Y	Y
2 Israel	N	Y	Y	Y	Y
3 King	Y	Y	Y	N	N
4 McCarthy	N	Y	Y	Y	Y
5 Ackerman	N	Y	Y	Y	Y
6 Meeks	N	Y	Y	?	?
7 Crowley	N	Y	Y	Y	Y
8 Nadler	N	Y	Y	Y	Y
9 Weiner	N	Y	Y	Y	Y
10 Towns	N	Y	Y	?	?
11 Clarke	N	Y	Y	Y	Y
12 Velázquez	N	Y	Y	Y	Y
13 Fossella	Y	Y	Y	N	N
14 Maloney	N	Y	Y	Y	Y
15 Rangel	N	Y	?	Y	Y
16 Serrano	N	Y	Y	Y	Y
17 Engel	N	Y	Y	Y	Y
18 Lowey	N	Y	Y	Y	Y
19 Hall	N	Y	Y	Y	+
20 Gillibrand	Y	Y	Y	Y	Y
21 McNulty	N	Y	Y	Y	Y
22 Hinchey	N	Y	Y	Y	Y
23 McHugh	Y	Y	Y	N	N
24 Arcuri	N	Y	Y	Y	Y
25 Walsh	Y	Y	Y	N	N
26 Reynolds	Y	Y	Y	?	?
27 Higgins	N	Y	Y	Y	Y
28 Slaughter	N	Y	Y	Y	Y
29 Kuhl	Y	Y	Y	Y	N
NORTH CAROLINA					
1 Butterfield	N	Y	Y	Y	Y
2 Etheridge	Y	Y	Y	Y	Y
3 Jones	Y	Y	Y	?	?
4 Price	N	Y	Y	Y	Y

	431	432	433	434	435
5 Foxx	Y	Y	Y	N	N
6 Coble	Y	Y	Y	N	N
7 McIntyre	Y	Y	Y	Y	Y
8 Hayes	Y	Y	Y	N	N
9 Myrick	Y	Y	Y	N	N
10 McHenry	Y	Y	Y	N	N
11 Shuler	Y	Y	Y	N	Y
12 Watt	N	Y	Y	Y	Y
13 Miller	N	Y	Y	Y	Y
NORTH DAKOTA					
AL Pomeroy	Y	Y	Y	Y	Y
OHIO					
1 Chabot	Y	Y	Y	N	N
2 Schmidt	Y	Y	Y	N	N
3 Turner	Y	Y	Y	N	N
4 Jordan	Y	Y	Y	N	N
5 Latta	Y	Y	Y	N	N
6 Wilson	Y	Y	Y	Y	Y
7 Hobson	Y	Y	Y	N	N
8 Boehner	Y	Y	Y	N	N
9 Kaptur	N	Y	Y	Y	Y
10 Kucinich	N	Y	Y	N	N
11 Tubbs Jones	N	Y	Y	Y	Y
12 Tiberi	Y	Y	Y	N	N
13 Sutton	N	Y	Y	Y	Y
14 LaTourette	Y	Y	Y	N	N
15 Pryce	Y	Y	Y	N	N
16 Regula	Y	Y	Y	N	N
17 Ryan	N	Y	Y	Y	Y
18 Space	Y	Y	Y	Y	Y
OKLAHOMA					
1 Sullivan	+	Y	Y	N	N
2 Boren	Y	Y	Y	Y	Y
3 Lucas	Y	Y	Y	N	N
4 Cole	Y	Y	Y	N	N
5 Fallin	Y	Y	Y	N	N
OREGON					
1 Wu	N	Y	Y	Y	Y
2 Walden	Y	Y	Y	N	N
3 Blumenauer	N	Y	Y	Y	Y
4 DeFazio	N	N	Y	Y	Y
5 Hooley	N	Y	Y	Y	Y
PENNSYLVANIA					
1 Brady	N	Y	Y	Y	Y
2 Fattah	N	Y	Y	?	?
3 English	Y	Y	Y	Y	N
4 Altmire	Y	Y	Y	N	Y
5 Peterson	Y	Y	Y	?	?
6 Gerlach	Y	Y	Y	?	?
7 Sestak	Y	Y	Y	Y	Y
8 Murphy, P.	N	Y	Y	Y	Y
9 Shuster	Y	Y	Y	N	N
10 Carney	Y	Y	Y	N	Y
11 Kanjorski	Y	Y	Y	Y	Y
12 Murtha	Y	Y	?	Y	Y
13 Schwartz	N	Y	Y	Y	Y
14 Doyle	N	Y	Y	Y	Y
15 Dent	Y	Y	Y	N	N
16 Pitts	Y	Y	Y	N	N
17 Holden	Y	Y	Y	Y	Y
18 Murphy, T.	Y	Y	Y	N	N
19 Platts	Y	Y	Y	N	N
RHODE ISLAND					
1 Kennedy	N	Y	Y	?	Y
2 Langevin	N	Y	Y	+	+
SOUTH CAROLINA					
1 Brown	Y	Y	Y	N	N
2 Wilson	Y	Y	Y	N	N
3 Barrett	Y	Y	Y	N	N
4 Inglis	Y	Y	Y	N	N
5 Spratt	Y	Y	Y	Y	Y
6 Clyburn	Y	Y	Y	Y	Y
SOUTH DAKOTA					
AL Herseth Sandlin	Y	Y	?	Y	?
TENNESSEE					
1 Davis, David	Y	Y	Y	N	N
2 Duncan	N	N	Y	N	N
3 Wamp	Y	Y	Y	N	N
4 Davis, L.	Y	Y	?	?	?
5 Cooper	Y	N	Y	Y	Y
6 Gordon	Y	Y	Y	?	?
7 Blackburn	Y	Y	Y	N	N
8 Tanner	Y	Y	Y	N	Y
9 Cohen	N	Y	Y	Y	Y

	431	432	433	434	435
TEXAS					
1 Gohmert	Y	Y	Y	?	?
2 Poe	Y	Y	Y	N	N
3 Johnson, S.	Y	Y	Y	N	N
4 Hall	Y	Y	Y	N	N
5 Hensarling	Y	Y	Y	N	N
6 Barton	Y	Y	Y	?	?
7 Culberson	Y	Y	Y	?	N
8 Brady	Y	N	Y	N	N
9 Green, A.	N	Y	Y	Y	Y
10 McCaul	Y	Y	Y	N	N
11 Conaway	Y	Y	Y	N	N
12 Granger	Y	Y	Y	N	N
13 Thornberry	Y	Y	Y	N	N
14 Paul	N	N	Y	?	?
15 Hinojosa	Y	Y	Y	Y	Y
16 Reyes	Y	Y	Y	Y	Y
17 Edwards	Y	Y	Y	Y	Y
18 Jackson Lee	N	Y	Y	Y	Y
19 Neugebauer	Y	Y	Y	N	N
20 Gonzalez	Y	Y	Y	Y	Y
21 Smith	Y	Y	Y	N	N
22 Lampson	Y	Y	Y	Y	Y
23 Rodriguez	Y	Y	Y	Y	Y
24 Marchant	Y	Y	Y	N	N
25 Doggett	N	Y	Y	Y	Y
26 Burgess	Y	Y	Y	N	N
27 Ortiz	Y	Y	Y	Y	Y
28 Cuellar	Y	Y	Y	Y	Y
29 Green, G.	Y	Y	Y	Y	Y
30 Johnson, E.	N	Y	Y	Y	Y
31 Carter	Y	Y	Y	N	N
32 Sessions	Y	Y	Y	N	N
UTAH					
1 Bishop	Y	Y	Y	Y	N
2 Matheson	Y	Y	Y	Y	Y
3 Cannon	?	?	?	?	?
VERMONT					
AL Welch	N	Y	Y	Y	Y
VIRGINIA					
1 Wittman	Y	Y	Y	N	N
2 Drake	Y	Y	Y	N	N
3 Scott	N	Y	Y	Y	Y
4 Forbes	Y	Y	Y	N	N
5 Goode	Y	Y	Y	N	N
6 Goodlatte	Y	Y	Y	N	N
7 Cantor	Y	Y	Y	N	N
8 Moran	N	Y	Y	Y	Y
9 Boucher	Y	Y	Y	Y	Y
10 Wolf	Y	Y	Y	N	N
11 Davis, T.	Y	Y	Y	N	N
WASHINGTON					
1 Inslee	N	Y	Y	Y	Y
2 Larsen	Y	Y	Y	Y	Y
3 Baird	Y	Y	Y	Y	Y
4 Hastings	Y	Y	Y	N	N
5 McMorris Rodgers	Y	Y	Y	N	N
6 Dicks	Y	Y	?	Y	Y
7 McDermott	N	Y	Y	Y	Y
8 Reichert	Y	Y	Y	N	N
9 Smith	N	N	Y	Y	Y
WEST VIRGINIA					
1 Mollohan	Y	Y	Y	Y	Y
2 Capito	Y	Y	Y	N	N
3 Rahall	N	Y	Y	Y	Y
WISCONSIN					
1 Ryan	Y	Y	Y	N	N
2 Baldwin	N	Y	Y	Y	Y
3 Kind	Y	Y	Y	Y	Y
4 Moore	N	Y	Y	Y	Y
5 Sensenbrenner	Y	Y	Y	N	N
6 Petri	Y	Y	Y	N	N
7 Obey	N	Y	Y	Y	Y
8 Kagen	N	Y	Y	Y	?
WYOMING					
AL Cubin	Y	Y	Y	?	?
DELEGATES					
Faleomavaega (A.S.)					
Norton (D.C.)					
Bordallo (Guam)					
Fortuño (P.R.)					
Christensen (V.I.)					

IN THE HOUSE | By Vote Number

436. HR 5876. **Child Abuse in Residential Programs/Rule.** Adoption of the rule (H Res 1276) to provide for House floor consideration of the bill that would establish new federal regulations for private residential programs that focus on serving children with emotional, behavioral or mental health problems, or problems with alcohol and substance abuse. Adopted 223-185: R 0-183; D 223-2 (ND 167-1, SD 56-1). June 20, 2008.

437. HR 6304. **Foreign Intelligence Surveillance/Passage.** Passage of the bill that would overhaul the Foreign Intelligence Surveillance Act (FISA), which governs electronic surveillance of foreign terrorism suspects. The bill would allow investigations of up to one year that involved surveillance targeting those who are not U.S. persons and who are reasonably believed to be outside the United States. The FISA court would have to approve procedures for conducting the surveillance. Warrantless surveillance would be allowed as long as it does not intentionally target U.S. persons or those located within the United States. It would pave the way for retroactive immunity for telecommunications companies that participated in the National Security Agency's warrantless surveillance program. Passed 293-129: R 188-1; D 105-128 (ND 62-112, SD 43-16). A "yea" was a vote in support of the president's position. June 20, 2008.

438. H Res 1242. **Louis Jordan 100th Anniversary/Adoption.** Sarbanes, D-Md., motion to suspend the rules and adopt the resolution that would honor the 100th anniversary of Louis Jordan's birth and recognize his contributions to American music. Motion agreed to 348-0: R 164-0; D 184-0 (ND 129-0, SD 55-0). A two-thirds majority of those present and voting (232 in this case) is required for adoption under suspension of the rules. June 23, 2008.

439. H Con Res 372. **Support Black Music Month/Adoption.** Sarbanes, D-Md., motion to suspend the rules and adopt the concurrent resolution that would support the goals and ideals of Black Music Month and honor the contributions of African-American singers and musicians. Motion agreed to 353-0: R 167-0; D 186-0 (ND 131-0, SD 55-0). A two-thirds majority of those present and voting (236 in this case) is required for adoption under suspension of the rules. June 23, 2008.

440. H Res 1051. **James Madison University Tribute/Adoption.** Sarbanes, D-Md., motion to suspend the rules and adopt the resolution that would congratulate James Madison University for 100 years of leadership and service to Virginia and the United States. Motion agreed to 354-0: R 163-0; D 191-0 (ND 135-0, SD 56-0). A two-thirds majority of those present and voting (236 in this case) is required for adoption under suspension of the rules. June 23, 2008.

		436	437	438	439	440
ALABAMA						
1	Bonner	N	Y	Y	Y	Y
2	Everett	N	Y	Y	Y	Y
3	Rogers	N	Y	Y	Y	Y
4	Aderholt	N	Y	Y	Y	Y
5	Cramer	Y	Y	Y	Y	Y
6	Bachus	N	Y	Y	Y	Y
7	Davis	Y	Y	Y	Y	Y
ALASKA						
AL	Young	?	Y	Y	Y	Y
ARIZONA						
1	Renzi	N	Y	Y	Y	Y
2	Franks	N	Y	Y	Y	Y
3	Shadegg	N	Y	Y	Y	Y
4	Pastor	Y	N	Y	Y	Y
5	Mitchell	Y	Y	Y	Y	Y
6	Flake	N	Y	Y	Y	Y
7	Grijalva	Y	N	?	?	?
8	Giffords	Y	Y	Y	Y	Y
ARKANSAS						
1	Berry	Y	Y	Y	Y	Y
2	Snyder	Y	Y	Y	Y	Y
3	Boozman	N	Y	Y	Y	Y
4	Ross	Y	Y	Y	Y	Y
CALIFORNIA						
1	Thompson	Y	N	Y	Y	Y
2	Herger	N	Y	Y	Y	Y
3	Lungren	N	Y	Y	Y	Y
4	Doolittle	N	Y	Y	Y	Y
5	Matsui	Y	N	Y	Y	Y
6	Woolsey	Y	N	Y	Y	Y
7	Miller, George	Y	N	Y	Y	?
8	Pelosi		Y			
9	Lee	Y	N	Y	Y	Y
10	Tauscher	Y	Y	Y	Y	Y
11	McNerney	Y	N	Y	Y	Y
12	Speier	Y	N	Y	Y	Y
13	Stark	?	?	Y	Y	Y
14	Eshoo	Y	N	Y	Y	Y
15	Honda	Y	N	Y	Y	Y
16	Lofgren	Y	N	Y	Y	Y
17	Farr	Y	N	Y	Y	Y
18	Cardoza	Y	Y	Y	Y	Y
19	Radanovich	N	Y	?	?	?
20	Costa	Y	Y	?	?	?
21	Nunes	N	Y	+	+	+
22	McCarthy	N	Y	Y	Y	Y
23	Capps	Y	N	Y	Y	Y
24	Gallegly	N	Y	?	?	?
25	McKeon	N	Y	Y	Y	Y
26	Dreier	N	Y	Y	Y	Y
27	Sherman	Y	Y	Y	Y	Y
28	Berman	Y	Y	?	?	?
29	Schiff	Y	Y	+	+	+
30	Waxman	Y	N	Y	Y	Y
31	Becerra	Y	N	+	Y	Y
32	Solis	Y	N	?	?	?
33	Watson	Y	N	Y	Y	Y
34	Roybal-Allard	Y	N	?	?	?
35	Waters	Y	N	?	?	?
36	Harman	Y	Y	Y	Y	Y
37	Richardson	Y	Y	Y	Y	Y
38	Napolitano	Y	N	Y	Y	Y
39	Sánchez, Linda	Y	N	+	+	+
40	Royce	N	Y	Y	Y	Y
41	Lewis	N	Y	Y	Y	Y
42	Miller, Gary	N	Y	?	?	?
43	Baca	Y	Y	Y	Y	Y
44	Calvert	N	Y	Y	Y	Y
45	Bono Mack	N	Y	Y	Y	Y
46	Rohrabacher	N	Y	Y	Y	Y
47	Sanchez, Loretta	Y	N	Y	Y	Y
48	Campbell	N	Y	Y	Y	Y
49	Issa	N	Y	Y	Y	Y
50	Bilbray	?	Y	Y	Y	Y
51	Filner	Y	N	Y	Y	Y
52	Hunter	N	Y	?	?	?
53	Davis	Y	N	Y	Y	Y

		436	437	438	439	440
COLORADO						
1	DeGette	Y	N	Y	Y	Y
2	Udall	Y	Y	?	?	?
3	Salazar	Y	Y	Y	Y	Y
4	Musgrave	N	Y	Y	Y	Y
5	Lamborn	N	Y	Y	Y	Y
6	Tancredo	N	Y	?	?	?
7	Perlmutter	Y	Y	Y	Y	Y
CONNECTICUT						
1	Larson	Y	N	Y	Y	Y
2	Courtney	Y	N	?	?	?
3	DeLauro	Y	N	Y	Y	Y
4	Shays	N	Y	Y	Y	Y
5	Murphy	Y	N	?	?	?
DELAWARE						
AL	Castle	N	Y	Y	Y	Y
FLORIDA						
1	Miller	N	Y	Y	Y	Y
2	Boyd	Y	Y	Y	Y	Y
3	Brown	Y	Y	Y	Y	Y
4	Crenshaw	N	Y	Y	Y	Y
5	Brown-Waite	?	?	Y	Y	Y
6	Stearns	N	Y	Y	Y	Y
7	Mica	N	Y	Y	Y	Y
8	Keller	N	Y	Y	Y	Y
9	Bilirakis	N	Y	Y	Y	Y
10	Young	N	Y	?	?	?
11	Castor	Y	Y	Y	Y	Y
12	Putnam	N	Y	Y	Y	Y
13	Buchanan	N	Y	Y	Y	Y
14	Mack	N	Y	Y	Y	Y
15	Weldon	N	Y	?	?	?
16	Mahoney	Y	Y	Y	Y	Y
17	Meek	Y	N	Y	Y	Y
18	Ros-Lehtinen	Y	N	Y	Y	Y
19	Wexler	Y	N	Y	Y	Y
20	Wasserman Schultz	Y	N	Y	Y	Y
21	Diaz-Balart, L.	Y	Y	Y	Y	Y
22	Klein	Y	Y	Y	Y	Y
23	Hastings	Y	Y	Y	Y	Y
24	Feeney	Y	Y	Y	Y	Y
25	Diaz-Balart, M.	N	Y	Y	Y	Y
GEORGIA						
1	Kingston	N	Y	?	?	?
2	Bishop	Y	Y	Y	Y	Y
3	Westmoreland	N	Y	Y	Y	Y
4	Johnson	Y	N	Y	Y	Y
5	Lewis	Y	N	Y	Y	Y
6	Price	N	Y	Y	Y	Y
7	Linder	N	Y	Y	Y	Y
8	Marshall	Y	Y	Y	Y	Y
9	Deal	N	Y	Y	Y	Y
10	Broun	N	Y	Y	Y	Y
11	Gingrey	N	Y	Y	Y	Y
12	Barrow	Y	Y	Y	Y	Y
13	Scott	?	Y	Y	Y	Y
HAWAII						
1	Abercrombie	Y	N	Y	Y	Y
2	Hirono	Y	N	Y	Y	Y
IDAHO						
1	Sali	N	Y	Y	Y	Y
2	Simpson	N	Y	Y	Y	Y
ILLINOIS						
1	Rush	+	-	?	?	?
2	Jackson	Y	N	Y	Y	Y
3	Lipinski	Y	Y	Y	Y	Y
4	Gutierrez	Y	Y	?	?	?
5	Emanuel	Y	Y	Y	Y	Y
6	Roskam	N	Y	Y	Y	Y
7	Davis	Y	N	?	?	?
8	Bean	Y	Y	Y	Y	Y
9	Schakowsky	Y	N	Y	Y	Y
10	Kirk	N	Y	Y	Y	Y
11	Weller	-	+	+	+	+
12	Costello	Y	N	?	?	?
13	Biggert	N	Y	Y	Y	Y
14	Foster	Y	N	Y	Y	Y
15	Johnson	N	N	+	+	+

KEY	**Republicans**	Democrats		
Y	Voted for (yea)	X	Paired against	C	Voted "present" to avoid possible conflict of interest
#	Paired for	–	Announced against	
+	Announced for	P	Voted "present"	?	Did not vote or otherwise make a position known
N	Voted against (nay)			

ND Northern Democrats, SD Southern Democrats
Southern states: Ala., Ark., Fla., Ga., Ky., La., Miss., N.C., Okla., S.C., Tenn., Texas, Va.

	436	437	438	439	440
16 **Manzullo**	N	Y	Y	Y	Y
17 Hare	Y	N	Y	Y	Y
18 **LaHood**	N	Y	Y	Y	Y
19 **Shimkus**	N	Y	?	?	?
INDIANA					
1 Visclosky	+	–	Y	Y	Y
2 Donnelly	Y	Y	Y	Y	Y
3 **Souder**	N	Y	?	?	?
4 **Buyer**	N	Y	?	?	?
5 **Burton**	N	Y	+	+	+
6 **Pence**	N	Y	Y	Y	Y
7 Carson, A.	Y	N	Y	Y	Y
8 Ellsworth	Y	Y	Y	Y	Y
9 Hill	N	N	?	?	?
IOWA					
1 Braley	Y	N	Y	Y	Y
2 Loebsack	Y	N	?	?	?
3 Boswell	Y	Y	Y	Y	Y
4 **Latham**	N	Y	Y	Y	Y
5 **King**	N	Y	Y	Y	Y
KANSAS					
1 **Moran**	N	Y	?	?	?
2 Boyda	Y	Y	?	?	?
3 Moore	Y	Y	Y	Y	Y
4 **Tiahrt**	?	?	Y	Y	Y
KENTUCKY					
1 **Whitfield**	N	Y	Y	Y	Y
2 **Lewis**	N	Y	Y	Y	Y
3 Yarmuth	Y	Y	Y	Y	Y
4 **Davis**	N	Y	Y	Y	Y
5 **Rogers**	N	Y	Y	Y	Y
6 Chandler	Y	Y	Y	Y	Y
LOUISIANA					
1 **Scalise**	N	Y	Y	Y	Y
2 Jefferson	Y	N	Y	Y	Y
3 Melancon	Y	Y	Y	?	Y
4 **McCrery**	N	Y	Y	Y	Y
5 **Alexander**	N	Y	?	?	?
6 Cazayoux	N	Y	Y	Y	Y
7 **Boustany**	N	Y	Y	Y	Y
MAINE					
1 Allen	Y	N	+	+	+
2 Michaud	Y	N	Y	Y	Y
MARYLAND					
1 **Gilchrest**	?	?	?	?	?
2 Ruppersberger	+	Y	Y	Y	Y
3 Sarbanes	Y	N	Y	Y	Y
4 Edwards	Y	N	Y	Y	Y
5 Hoyer	Y	Y	Y	Y	Y
6 **Bartlett**	?	Y	Y	Y	Y
7 Cummings	Y	N	Y	Y	Y
8 Van Hollen	Y	N	Y	Y	Y
MASSACHUSETTS					
1 Olver	Y	N	Y	Y	Y
2 Neal	Y	N	Y	Y	Y
3 McGovern	Y	N	Y	Y	Y
4 Frank	Y	N	?	?	?
5 Tsongas	Y	N	Y	Y	Y
6 Tierney	Y	N	Y	Y	Y
7 Markey	Y	N	Y	Y	Y
8 Capuano	Y	N	Y	Y	Y
9 Lynch	Y	N	Y	Y	Y
10 Delahunt	Y	N	Y	?	Y
MICHIGAN					
1 Stupak	Y	Y	Y	Y	Y
2 **Hoekstra**	N	Y	?	?	?
3 **Ehlers**	N	Y	Y	Y	Y
4 **Camp**	N	Y	Y	Y	Y
5 Kildee	Y	Y	Y	Y	Y
6 **Upton**	N	Y	Y	Y	Y
7 **Walberg**	N	Y	Y	Y	Y
8 **Rogers**	N	Y	Y	Y	Y
9 **Knollenberg**	N	Y	?	?	?
10 **Miller**	N	Y	Y	Y	Y
11 **McCotter**	N	Y	Y	Y	Y
12 Levin	Y	N	Y	Y	Y
13 Kilpatrick	Y	N	+	+	+
14 Conyers	Y	N	Y	Y	Y
15 Dingell	Y	Y	Y	Y	Y
MINNESOTA					
1 Walz	Y	N	Y	+	Y
2 **Kline**	N	Y	Y	Y	Y
3 **Ramstad**	N	Y	Y	Y	Y
4 McCollum	Y	N	Y	Y	Y

	436	437	438	439	440
5 Ellison	Y	N	Y	Y	Y
6 **Bachmann**	N	Y	Y	Y	Y
7 Peterson	Y	Y	Y	Y	Y
8 Oberstar	?	N	Y	Y	Y
MISSISSIPPI					
1 Childers	Y	Y	Y	Y	Y
2 Thompson	Y	Y	?	?	?
3 **Pickering**	N	Y	?	?	?
4 Taylor	Y	Y	Y	Y	Y
MISSOURI					
1 Clay	Y	N	Y	Y	Y
2 **Akin**	N	Y	Y	Y	Y
3 Carnahan	Y	N	?	?	?
4 Skelton	Y	Y	Y	Y	Y
5 Cleaver	Y	Y	Y	Y	Y
6 **Graves**	N	Y	Y	Y	Y
7 **Blunt**	N	Y	Y	Y	Y
8 **Emerson**	N	Y	Y	Y	Y
9 **Hulshof**	N	Y	?	?	?
MONTANA					
AL **Rehberg**	N	Y	Y	Y	Y
NEBRASKA					
1 **Fortenberry**	N	Y	Y	Y	Y
2 **Terry**	N	Y	Y	Y	Y
3 **Smith**	N	Y	Y	Y	Y
NEVADA					
1 Berkley	Y	Y	Y	Y	Y
2 **Heller**	N	Y	Y	Y	?
3 **Porter**	N	Y	Y	Y	Y
NEW HAMPSHIRE					
1 Shea-Porter	Y	N	?	?	?
2 Hodes	Y	N	Y	Y	Y
NEW JERSEY					
1 Andrews	Y	N	Y	Y	Y
2 **LoBiondo**	N	Y	Y	Y	Y
3 **Saxton**	N	Y	Y	Y	Y
4 **Smith**	N	Y	Y	Y	Y
5 **Garrett**	N	Y	Y	Y	Y
6 Pallone	Y	N	Y	Y	Y
7 **Ferguson**	?	Y	?	?	?
8 Pascrell	Y	N	?	?	?
9 Rothman	Y	N	Y	Y	Y
10 Payne	Y	N	?	?	?
11 **Frelinghuysen**	N	Y	Y	Y	Y
12 Holt	Y	N	Y	Y	Y
13 Sires	Y	Y	+	+	+
NEW MEXICO					
1 **Wilson**	?	Y	Y	Y	Y
2 **Pearce**	N	Y	+	+	+
3 Udall	Y	N	?	?	?
NEW YORK					
1 Bishop	Y	Y	Y	Y	Y
2 Israel	Y	N	?	?	?
3 **King**	N	Y	Y	Y	Y
4 McCarthy	Y	Y	Y	Y	Y
5 Ackerman	Y	Y	Y	Y	Y
6 Meeks	?	Y	Y	Y	Y
7 Crowley	Y	Y	Y	Y	Y
8 Nadler	Y	N	Y	Y	Y
9 Weiner	Y	N	?	?	?
10 Towns	?	N	Y	Y	Y
11 Clarke	Y	N	Y	Y	Y
12 Velázquez	Y	N	Y	Y	Y
13 **Fossella**	N	Y	Y	Y	Y
14 Maloney	Y	N	+	+	+
15 Rangel	Y	N	Y	Y	Y
16 Serrano	Y	N	Y	Y	Y
17 Engel	Y	Y	?	Y	Y
18 Lowey	Y	Y	Y	Y	Y
19 Hall	Y	N	Y	Y	Y
20 Gillibrand	Y	Y	Y	Y	Y
21 McNulty	Y	N	?	?	?
22 Hinchey	Y	N	Y	Y	Y
23 **McHugh**	N	Y	Y	Y	Y
24 Arcuri	Y	Y	Y	Y	Y
25 **Walsh**	N	Y	Y	Y	Y
26 **Reynolds**	?	?	?	?	?
27 Higgins	Y	Y	Y	Y	Y
28 Slaughter	Y	N	Y	Y	Y
29 **Kuhl**	N	Y	Y	Y	Y
NORTH CAROLINA					
1 Butterfield	Y	Y	Y	Y	Y
2 Etheridge	Y	Y	Y	Y	Y
3 **Jones**	?	?	Y	Y	Y
4 Price	Y	N	Y	Y	Y

	436	437	438	439	440
5 **Foxx**	N	Y	Y	Y	Y
6 **Coble**	N	Y	Y	Y	Y
7 McIntyre	Y	Y	Y	Y	Y
8 Hayes	N	Y	Y	Y	Y
9 **Myrick**	N	Y	Y	Y	Y
10 **McHenry**	N	Y	Y	Y	Y
11 Shuler	Y	Y	Y	Y	Y
12 Watt	Y	N	Y	Y	Y
13 Miller	Y	N	Y	Y	Y
NORTH DAKOTA					
AL Pomeroy	Y	Y	Y	Y	Y
OHIO					
1 **Chabot**	N	Y	Y	Y	Y
2 **Schmidt**	N	Y	Y	Y	Y
3 **Turner**	N	Y	Y	Y	Y
4 **Jordan**	N	Y	Y	Y	Y
5 **Latta**	N	Y	Y	Y	Y
6 Wilson	Y	Y	?	?	?
7 **Hobson**	N	Y	Y	Y	Y
8 **Boehner**	N	Y	Y	Y	Y
9 Kaptur	Y	N	?	?	Y
10 Kucinich	Y	N	Y	Y	Y
11 Tubbs Jones	N	Y	?	Y	Y
12 **Tiberi**	N	Y	Y	Y	Y
13 Sutton	Y	N	Y	Y	Y
14 **LaTourette**	N	Y	Y	Y	Y
15 **Pryce**	N	Y	?	?	?
16 **Regula**	N	Y	Y	Y	Y
17 Ryan	Y	N	?	?	?
18 Space	Y	Y	Y	Y	Y
OKLAHOMA					
1 **Sullivan**	N	Y	Y	Y	Y
2 Boren	Y	Y	Y	Y	Y
3 **Lucas**	N	Y	Y	Y	Y
4 **Cole**	N	Y	Y	Y	Y
5 **Fallin**	N	Y	Y	Y	Y
OREGON					
1 Wu	Y	N	Y	Y	Y
2 **Walden**	N	Y	?	Y	Y
3 Blumenauer	Y	N	Y	Y	Y
4 DeFazio	Y	N	Y	Y	Y
5 Hooley	Y	N	Y	Y	Y
PENNSYLVANIA					
1 Brady	Y	N	Y	Y	Y
2 Fattah	Y	N	Y	Y	Y
3 **English**	N	Y	Y	Y	Y
4 Altmire	Y	Y	Y	Y	Y
5 **Peterson**	?	?	?	?	?
6 **Gerlach**	N	Y	Y	Y	Y
7 Sestak	Y	Y	?	?	?
8 Murphy, P.	Y	Y	Y	Y	Y
9 **Shuster**	N	Y	Y	Y	Y
10 Carney	Y	Y	?	?	?
11 Kanjorski	Y	Y	?	?	?
12 Murtha	Y	Y	Y	Y	Y
13 Schwartz	Y	N	?	?	?
14 Doyle	Y	N	?	?	?
15 **Dent**	N	Y	Y	Y	Y
16 **Pitts**	N	Y	Y	Y	Y
17 Holden	Y	Y	Y	Y	Y
18 **Murphy, T.**	N	Y	+	+	+
19 **Platts**	N	Y	Y	Y	Y
RHODE ISLAND					
1 Kennedy	Y	N	Y	Y	Y
2 Langevin	+	Y	+	+	Y
SOUTH CAROLINA					
1 **Brown**	N	Y	Y	Y	Y
2 **Wilson**	N	Y	Y	Y	Y
3 **Barrett**	N	Y	Y	Y	Y
4 **Inglis**	N	Y	Y	Y	Y
5 Spratt	Y	Y	Y	Y	Y
6 Clyburn	Y	Y	Y	Y	Y
SOUTH DAKOTA					
AL Herseth Sandlin	Y	Y	Y	Y	Y
TENNESSEE					
1 **Davis, David**	N	Y	Y	Y	Y
2 **Duncan**	N	Y	Y	Y	Y
3 **Wamp**	N	Y	Y	Y	Y
4 Davis, L.	?	Y	Y	Y	Y
5 Cooper	Y	Y	Y	Y	Y
6 Gordon	Y	Y	Y	Y	Y
7 **Blackburn**	N	Y	?	?	?
8 Tanner	Y	Y	Y	Y	Y
9 Cohen	Y	N	+	+	+

	436	437	438	439	440
TEXAS					
1 **Gohmert**	?	?	?	?	?
2 **Poe**	?	?	?	?	?
3 **Johnson, S.**	N	Y	?	?	?
4 **Hall**	N	Y	Y	Y	Y
5 **Hensarling**	N	Y	Y	Y	Y
6 **Barton**	N	Y	Y	Y	Y
7 **Culberson**	N	Y	Y	Y	Y
8 **Brady**	N	Y	Y	Y	Y
9 Green, A.	N	Y	Y	Y	Y
10 **McCaul**	N	Y	Y	Y	Y
11 **Conaway**	N	Y	Y	Y	Y
12 **Granger**	?	Y	Y	Y	Y
13 **Thornberry**	N	Y	Y	Y	Y
14 **Paul**	?	?	Y	Y	Y
15 Hinojosa	Y	Y	Y	Y	Y
16 Reyes	Y	Y	?	?	?
17 Edwards	Y	Y	Y	Y	Y
18 Jackson Lee	Y	N	Y	Y	Y
19 **Neugebauer**	N	Y	Y	Y	Y
20 Gonzalez	Y	N	Y	Y	Y
21 **Smith**	N	Y	Y	Y	Y
22 Lampson	Y	Y	Y	Y	Y
23 Rodriguez	Y	Y	Y	Y	Y
24 **Marchant**	N	Y	Y	Y	Y
25 Doggett	Y	N	Y	Y	Y
26 **Burgess**	N	Y	Y	Y	Y
27 Ortiz	Y	Y	Y	Y	Y
28 Cuellar	Y	Y	Y	Y	Y
29 Green, G.	Y	Y	Y	Y	Y
30 Johnson, E.	Y	N	Y	Y	Y
31 **Carter**	N	Y	Y	Y	Y
32 **Sessions**	N	Y	Y	Y	Y
UTAH					
1 **Bishop**	N	Y	Y	Y	Y
2 Matheson	Y	Y	Y	Y	Y
3 **Cannon**	?	?	?	?	?
VERMONT					
AL Welch	Y	N	Y	Y	Y
VIRGINIA					
1 **Wittman**	N	Y	Y	Y	Y
2 **Drake**	N	Y	?	Y	Y
3 Scott	Y	N	Y	Y	Y
4 **Forbes**	N	Y	Y	Y	Y
5 **Goode**	N	Y	Y	Y	Y
6 **Goodlatte**	N	Y	Y	Y	Y
7 **Cantor**	N	Y	?	Y	Y
8 Moran	Y	N	Y	Y	Y
9 Boucher	Y	N	Y	Y	Y
10 **Wolf**	N	Y	Y	Y	Y
11 **Davis, T.**	N	Y	Y	Y	Y
WASHINGTON					
1 Inslee	Y	N	Y	Y	Y
2 Larsen	Y	N	Y	Y	Y
3 Baird	Y	Y	Y	Y	Y
4 **Hastings**	N	Y	Y	Y	Y
5 **McMorris Rodgers**	N	Y	Y	Y	?
6 Dicks	Y	Y	Y	Y	Y
7 McDermott	Y	N	Y	Y	Y
8 **Reichert**	N	Y	Y	Y	Y
9 Smith	Y	Y	Y	Y	Y
WEST VIRGINIA					
1 Mollohan	Y	N	?	?	?
2 **Capito**	N	Y	Y	Y	Y
3 Rahall	Y	Y	Y	Y	Y
WISCONSIN					
1 **Ryan**	N	Y	Y	Y	Y
2 Baldwin	Y	N	Y	Y	Y
3 Kind	Y	Y	+	+	Y
4 Moore	Y	N	Y	Y	Y
5 **Sensenbrenner**	N	Y	Y	Y	Y
6 **Petri**	N	Y	Y	Y	Y
7 Obey	Y	N	Y	Y	Y
8 Kagen	Y	N	Y	Y	Y
WYOMING					
AL **Cubin**	N	Y	Y	Y	Y
DELEGATES					
Faleomavaega (A.S.)					
Norton (D.C.)					
Bordallo (Guam)					
Fortuño (P.R.)					
Christensen (V.I.)					

IN THE HOUSE | By Vote Number

441. **Procedural Motion/Motion to Adjourn.** Sullivan, R-Okla., motion to adjourn. Motion rejected 87-299: R 82-99; D 5-200 (ND 4-149, SD 1-51). June 24, 2008.

442. **Procedural Motion/Motion to Adjourn.** Culberson, R-Texas, motion to adjourn. Motion rejected 75-309: R 72-112; D 3-197 (ND 1-151, SD 2-46). June 24, 2008.

443. **HR 6331. Medicare Physician Payments/Passage.** Pallone, D-N.J., motion to suspend the rules and pass the bill that would prevent a 10.6 percent cut in payments to physicians treating Medicare patients, scheduled for July 1; hold payments at current rates for 18 months; and provide a 1.1 percent increase in 2009. The bill would provide an additional $16.6 billion over 10 years for changes to Medicare beneficiary programs. The costs would be partially offset by phasing out bonus payments to Medicare Advantage plans and requiring private "fee for service" plans to form networks with health care providers, thereby slowing the plans' growth. Motion agreed to 355-59: R 129-59; D 226-0 (ND 169-0, SD 57-0). A two-thirds majority of those present and voting (276 in this case) is required for passage under suspension of the rules. A "nay" was a vote in support of the president's position. June 24, 2008.

444. **HR 5876. Child Abuse in Residential Programs/Eliminate Site Inspection Requirement.** Miller, D-Calif., amendment that would strike the exclusion of psychiatric residential treatment facilities and the exclusion of foster care group homes from the bill's definition of residential treatment programs. The amendment also would eliminate required unannounced site inspections of covered programs at least once every two years. Adopted in Committee of the Whole 422-0: R 193-0; D 229-0 (ND 173-0, SD 56-0). June 24, 2008.

445. **H Con Res 379. Adjournment Resolution/Adoption.** Adoption of the concurrent resolution that would provide for adjournment of the Senate until noon, Monday, July 7, 2008, and the House until 2 p.m., Tuesday, July 8, 2008. Adopted 225-197: R 3-191; D 222-6 (ND 169-3, SD 53-3). June 24, 2008.

446. **Procedural Motion/Journal.** Approval of the House Journal of Monday, June 23, 2008. Approved 239-181: R 25-168; D 214-13 (ND 161-10, SD 53-3). June 24, 2008.

447. **HR 6327. Federal Aviation Administration Extension/Passage.** Neal, D-Mass., motion to suspend the rules and pass the bill that would extend through Sept. 30 the authority of the Federal Aviation Administration (FAA) to collect certain aviation-related taxes deposited in the Airport and Airway Trust Fund and the authority to spend those funds on certain FAA programs. It also would provide contract authority for the Airport Improvement Program for the rest of fiscal 2008. Motion agreed to 422-0: R 196-0; D 226-0 (ND 170-0, SD 56-0). A two-thirds majority of those present and voting (282 in this case) is required for passage under suspension of the rules. June 24, 2008.

	441	442	443	444	445	446	447
ALABAMA							
1 **Bonner**	Y	N	Y	Y	N	N	Y
2 **Everett**	Y	Y	Y	Y	N	N	Y
3 **Rogers**	Y	Y	Y	Y	N	N	Y
4 **Aderholt**	N	N	Y	Y	N	N	Y
5 Cramer	N	N	Y	Y	Y	Y	Y
6 **Bachus**	Y	Y	Y	Y	?	N	Y
7 Davis	N	N	Y	Y	Y	Y	Y
ALASKA							
AL **Young**	?	Y	Y	Y	N	Y	Y
ARIZONA							
1 **Renzi**	Y	Y	N	Y	N	N	Y
2 **Franks**	Y	Y	N	Y	N	N	Y
3 **Shadegg**	Y	Y	N	Y	N	N	Y
4 Pastor	N	N	Y	Y	Y	Y	Y
5 Mitchell	N	N	Y	Y	N	N	Y
6 **Flake**	Y	Y	N	Y	N	N	Y
7 Grijalva	N	N	Y	Y	Y	Y	Y
8 Giffords	N	N	Y	Y	N	N	Y
ARKANSAS							
1 Berry	N	N	Y	Y	Y	Y	Y
2 Snyder	N	N	Y	?	?	?	?
3 **Boozman**	N	N	Y	Y	N	N	Y
4 Ross	?	?	Y	Y	Y	Y	Y
CALIFORNIA							
1 Thompson	N	N	Y	Y	Y	N	Y
2 **Herger**	Y	Y	N	Y	N	N	Y
3 **Lungren**	Y	Y	N	Y	N	Y	Y
4 **Doolittle**	Y	Y	N	Y	N	N	Y
5 Matsui	N	N	Y	Y	Y	Y	Y
6 Woolsey	N	–	Y	Y	Y	Y	Y
7 Miller, George	Y	?	+	Y	Y	Y	Y
8 Pelosi							
9 Lee	N	N	Y	Y	Y	Y	Y
10 Tauscher	N	N	Y	Y	Y	Y	Y
11 McNerney	N	N	Y	Y	Y	Y	Y
12 Speier	N	?	?	?	?	?	?
13 Stark	N	N	Y	Y	Y	Y	Y
14 Eshoo	?	?	Y	Y	Y	Y	Y
15 Honda	N	N	Y	Y	Y	Y	Y
16 Lofgren	N	N	Y	Y	Y	Y	Y
17 Farr	N	N	Y	Y	Y	Y	Y
18 Cardoza	?	?	Y	Y	Y	Y	Y
19 **Radanovich**	?	?	N	Y	N	N	Y
20 Costa	?	?	Y	Y	Y	Y	Y
21 **Nunes**	?	?	?	Y	N	N	Y
22 **McCarthy**	N	N	Y	Y	N	N	Y
23 Capps	N	N	Y	Y	–	Y	Y
24 **Gallegly**	Y	N	Y	Y	N	N	Y
25 **McKeon**	Y	Y	Y	Y	N	N	Y
26 **Dreier**	N	N	Y	Y	N	N	Y
27 Sherman	N	N	Y	Y	Y	Y	Y
28 Berman	N	N	Y	Y	Y	Y	Y
29 Schiff	N	N	Y	Y	Y	Y	Y
30 Waxman	?	N	Y	Y	Y	Y	Y
31 Becerra	N	N	Y	Y	Y	Y	Y
32 Solis	N	N	Y	Y	Y	Y	Y
33 Watson	N	N	Y	Y	Y	Y	Y
34 Roybal-Allard	N	N	Y	Y	Y	Y	Y
35 Waters	N	N	Y	Y	Y	Y	?
36 Harman	N	N	Y	Y	Y	Y	Y
37 Richardson	N	N	Y	Y	Y	Y	Y
38 Napolitano	N	N	Y	Y	Y	Y	Y
39 Sánchez, Linda	N	N	Y	Y	Y	Y	Y
40 **Royce**	N	N	N	Y	N	N	Y
41 **Lewis**	N	N	Y	Y	N	N	Y
42 **Miller, Gary**	Y	Y	Y	Y	N	N	Y
43 Baca	N	N	Y	Y	Y	Y	Y
44 **Calvert**	N	N	Y	Y	N	N	Y
45 **Bono Mack**	N	N	Y	Y	N	N	Y
46 **Rohrabacher**	N	N	Y	Y	N	N	Y
47 Sanchez, Loretta	N	N	Y	?	Y	Y	Y
48 **Campbell**	Y	Y	N	Y	N	N	Y
49 **Issa**	N	N	Y	Y	N	N	Y
50 **Bilbray**	Y	N	Y	?	N	Y	Y
51 Filner	N	N	Y	Y	Y	Y	Y
52 **Hunter**	Y	Y	Y	?	N	N	Y
53 Davis	N	N	Y	Y	Y	Y	Y

	441	442	443	444	445	446	447
COLORADO							
1 DeGette	N	N	Y	Y	Y	Y	Y
2 Udall	?	?	Y	Y	Y	Y	Y
3 Salazar	N	N	Y	Y	Y	Y	Y
4 **Musgrave**	Y	Y	Y	Y	N	N	Y
5 **Lamborn**	Y	Y	N	Y	N	N	Y
6 **Tancredo**	?	?	?	Y	N	P	Y
7 Perlmutter	N	N	Y	Y	Y	Y	Y
CONNECTICUT							
1 Larson	N	N	Y	Y	Y	Y	Y
2 Courtney	N	?	Y	Y	Y	Y	Y
3 DeLauro	N	?	Y	Y	Y	Y	Y
4 **Shays**	N	N	Y	Y	N	N	Y
5 Murphy	N	N	Y	Y	Y	Y	Y
DELAWARE							
AL **Castle**	N	N	Y	Y	N	N	Y
FLORIDA							
1 **Miller**	N	N	Y	Y	N	N	Y
2 Boyd	N	N	Y	Y	Y	Y	Y
3 Brown	N	N	Y	Y	Y	Y	Y
4 **Crenshaw**	Y	N	N	Y	N	N	Y
5 **Brown-Waite**	N	N	Y	Y	N	N	Y
6 **Stearns**	N	N	Y	Y	N	N	Y
7 **Mica**	N	N	Y	Y	N	N	Y
8 **Keller**	Y	Y	Y	Y	N	N	Y
9 **Bilirakis**	Y	Y	Y	Y	N	N	Y
10 **Young**	N	N	Y	Y	N	N	Y
11 Castor	N	N	Y	Y	Y	Y	Y
12 **Putnam**	N	N	Y	Y	N	N	Y
13 **Buchanan**	N	N	Y	Y	N	N	Y
14 **Mack**	N	N	Y	Y	N	N	Y
15 **Weldon**	N	N	Y	?	N	N	Y
16 **Mahoney**	?	?	Y	Y	Y	Y	Y
17 Meek	N	N	Y	Y	Y	Y	Y
18 **Ros-Lehtinen**	N	N	Y	Y	N	N	Y
19 Wexler	N	?	Y	?	?	?	?
20 Wasserman Schultz	N	N	Y	Y	Y	Y	Y
21 **Diaz-Balart, L.**	N	N	Y	Y	N	N	Y
22 Klein	N	N	Y	Y	Y	Y	Y
23 Hastings	?	Y	Y	Y	Y	Y	Y
24 **Feeney**	Y	Y	Y	N	Y	N	Y
25 **Diaz-Balart, M.**	N	N	Y	Y	N	N	Y
GEORGIA							
1 **Kingston**	N	N	Y	N	N	N	Y
2 Bishop	N	N	Y	Y	Y	Y	Y
3 **Westmoreland**	Y	N	N	Y	N	N	Y
4 Johnson	N	N	Y	Y	Y	Y	Y
5 Lewis	N	N	Y	Y	Y	Y	Y
6 **Price**	N	N	Y	Y	N	N	Y
7 **Linder**	N	N	Y	N	N	N	Y
8 Marshall	N	N	Y	Y	Y	Y	Y
9 **Deal**	N	Y	Y	Y	N	N	Y
10 **Broun**	Y	Y	N	Y	N	N	Y
11 **Gingrey**	N	N	Y	Y	N	N	Y
12 Barrow	N	N	Y	Y	Y	Y	Y
13 Scott	N	N	Y	Y	Y	Y	Y
HAWAII							
1 Abercrombie	–	N	Y	Y	Y	Y	Y
2 Hirono	N	N	Y	Y	Y	?	Y
IDAHO							
1 **Sali**	N	N	N	Y	N	N	Y
2 **Simpson**	N	N	Y	N	N	N	Y
ILLINOIS							
1 Rush	?	?	?	?	?	?	?
2 Jackson	N	N	Y	Y	Y	Y	Y
3 Lipinski	N	N	Y	Y	Y	Y	Y
4 Gutierrez	N	N	Y	Y	Y	Y	Y
5 Emanuel	N	N	Y	Y	Y	Y	Y
6 **Roskam**	Y	Y	N	Y	N	N	Y
7 Davis	?	?	?	?	?	?	?
8 Bean	N	N	Y	Y	Y	Y	Y
9 Schakowsky	N	N	Y	Y	Y	Y	Y
10 **Kirk**	N	N	Y	Y	N	Y	Y
11 **Weller**	N	N	Y	Y	N	N	Y
12 Costello	N	N	Y	Y	Y	Y	Y
13 **Biggert**	Y	N	Y	Y	N	N	Y
14 Foster	N	N	Y	Y	Y	Y	Y
15 **Johnson**	+	+	+	Y	Y	Y	Y

ND Northern Democrats, SD Southern Democrats
Southern states: Ala., Ark., Fla., Ga., Ky., La., Miss., N.C., Okla., S.C., Tenn., Texas, Va.

	441	442	443	444	445	446	447
16 **Manzullo**	Y	Y	Y	Y	N	N	Y
17 Hare	N	N	Y	Y	Y	Y	Y
18 **LaHood**	Y	N	Y	Y	N	N	Y
19 **Shimkus**	Y	Y	N	Y	N	N	Y
INDIANA							
1 Visclosky	N	N	Y	Y	Y	Y	Y
2 Donnelly	N	N	Y	Y	Y	N	Y
3 **Souder**	?	?	Y	Y	N	N	Y
4 **Buyer**	N	N	N	Y	N	N	Y
5 **Burton**	?	Y	Y	Y	N	N	Y
6 **Pence**	?	?	?	?	?	?	?
7 Carson, A.	N	N	Y	Y	Y	Y	Y
8 Ellsworth	N	N	Y	Y	N	N	Y
9 Hill	N	N	Y	Y	Y	Y	Y
IOWA							
1 Braley	Y	N	Y	Y	Y	Y	Y
2 Loebsack	N	N	Y	Y	Y	Y	Y
3 Boswell	?	?	Y	Y	Y	Y	Y
4 **Latham**	N	N	Y	Y	N	Y	Y
5 **King**	Y	Y	N	Y	N	N	Y
KANSAS							
1 **Moran**	N	N	Y	Y	N	N	Y
2 Boyda	N	N	Y	Y	Y	Y	Y
3 Moore	N	N	Y	Y	Y	Y	Y
4 **Tiahrt**	N	N	Y	Y	N	N	Y
KENTUCKY							
1 **Whitfield**	Y	Y	Y	Y	N	N	Y
2 **Lewis**	Y	Y	N	Y	N	Y	Y
3 Yarmuth	N	?	Y	Y	Y	Y	Y
4 **Davis**	N	N	Y	Y	N	N	Y
5 **Rogers**	N	N	Y	Y	N	N	Y
6 Chandler	N	N	Y	Y	Y	Y	Y
LOUISIANA							
1 **Scalise**	N	N	N	Y	N	N	Y
2 Jefferson	?	?	Y	Y	Y	Y	Y
3 Melancon	?	N	Y	Y	Y	Y	Y
4 **McCrery**	?	Y	N	Y	N	N	Y
5 **Alexander**	Y	Y	Y	Y	N	N	Y
6 Cazayoux	N	N	Y	Y	N	N	Y
7 **Boustany**	N	N	N	Y	N	N	Y
MAINE							
1 Allen	N	N	Y	Y	Y	Y	Y
2 Michaud	N	N	Y	Y	Y	Y	Y
MARYLAND							
1 **Gilchrest**	N	Y	Y	Y	Y	N	Y
2 Ruppersberger	N	N	Y	Y	Y	Y	Y
3 Sarbanes	N	N	Y	Y	Y	Y	Y
4 Edwards	N	N	Y	Y	Y	Y	Y
5 Hoyer	N	N	Y	Y	Y	Y	Y
6 **Bartlett**	Y	Y	N	Y	N	N	Y
7 Cummings	N	N	Y	Y	Y	Y	Y
8 Van Hollen	N	N	Y	Y	Y	Y	Y
MASSACHUSETTS							
1 Olver	N	N	Y	Y	Y	Y	Y
2 Neal	N	N	Y	Y	Y	Y	Y
3 McGovern	N	N	Y	Y	Y	Y	Y
4 Frank	N	N	Y	Y	Y	Y	Y
5 Tsongas	N	N	Y	Y	Y	Y	Y
6 Tierney	N	?	Y	Y	Y	Y	Y
7 Markey	N	N	Y	?	Y	Y	Y
8 Capuano	N	N	Y	Y	Y	Y	Y
9 Lynch	N	N	Y	Y	Y	Y	Y
10 Delahunt	?	?	Y	Y	Y	Y	Y
MICHIGAN							
1 Stupak	N	N	Y	Y	Y	N	Y
2 **Hoekstra**	Y	Y	Y	Y	N	N	Y
3 **Ehlers**	N	N	Y	Y	N	Y	Y
4 **Camp**	Y	Y	N	Y	N	N	Y
5 Kildee	N	N	Y	Y	Y	Y	Y
6 **Upton**	Y	N	Y	Y	N	N	Y
7 **Walberg**	N	N	Y	Y	N	N	Y
8 **Rogers**	N	N	N	Y	N	N	Y
9 **Knollenberg**	N	N	Y	Y	N	N	Y
10 **Miller**	Y	N	Y	Y	N	N	Y
11 **McCotter**	N	N	Y	Y	N	N	Y
12 Levin	N	N	Y	Y	Y	Y	Y
13 Kilpatrick	N	N	Y	Y	Y	Y	Y
14 Conyers	Y	N	Y	Y	Y	Y	Y
15 Dingell	N	N	Y	Y	Y	Y	Y
MINNESOTA							
1 Walz	N	N	Y	Y	Y	Y	Y
2 **Kline**	N	N	Y	Y	N	N	Y
3 **Ramstad**	N	N	Y	Y	N	N	Y
4 McCollum	N	N	Y	Y	Y	Y	Y

	441	442	443	444	445	446	447
5 Ellison	N	N	Y	Y	Y	Y	Y
6 **Bachmann**	N	N	N	Y	N	N	Y
7 Peterson	N	N	Y	Y	Y	N	?
8 Oberstar	N	?	Y	Y	Y	Y	Y
MISSISSIPPI							
1 Childers	N	N	Y	Y	N	N	Y
2 Thompson	?	?	?	Y	Y	Y	Y
3 **Pickering**	Y	Y	Y	Y	N	?	Y
4 Taylor	N	N	Y	Y	Y	Y	Y
MISSOURI							
1 Clay	N	Y	Y	Y	Y	Y	Y
2 **Akin**	Y	Y	N	Y	N	N	Y
3 Carnahan	N	N	Y	Y	Y	Y	Y
4 Skelton	N	N	Y	Y	Y	Y	Y
5 Cleaver	N	N	Y	Y	Y	Y	Y
6 **Graves**	N	N	Y	Y	N	N	Y
7 **Blunt**	Y	Y	N	Y	N	N	Y
8 **Emerson**	Y	Y	Y	Y	N	N	Y
9 **Hulshof**	N	N	N	Y	N	Y	Y
MONTANA							
AL **Rehberg**	Y	Y	Y	Y	N	N	Y
NEBRASKA							
1 **Fortenberry**	N	N	Y	Y	N	Y	Y
2 **Terry**	N	N	Y	Y	N	N	Y
3 **Smith**	N	N	Y	Y	N	N	Y
NEVADA							
1 Berkley	N	N	Y	Y	Y	Y	Y
2 **Heller**	N	N	Y	Y	N	Y	Y
3 **Porter**	N	N	Y	Y	N	N	Y
NEW HAMPSHIRE							
1 Shea-Porter	?	?	Y	Y	Y	Y	Y
2 Hodes	N	N	Y	Y	Y	Y	Y
NEW JERSEY							
1 Andrews	N	N	Y	Y	Y	Y	Y
2 **LoBiondo**	N	N	Y	Y	N	N	Y
3 **Saxton**	?	?	?	Y	N	N	Y
4 **Smith**	N	N	N	Y	N	N	Y
5 **Garrett**	Y	Y	N	Y	N	N	Y
6 Pallone	N	N	Y	Y	Y	Y	Y
7 **Ferguson**	N	N	Y	Y	N	Y	Y
8 Pascrell	?	?	Y	Y	Y	Y	Y
9 Rothman	N	N	Y	Y	Y	Y	Y
10 Payne	?	N	Y	Y	Y	Y	Y
11 **Frelinghuysen**	N	N	N	Y	N	N	Y
12 Holt	N	N	Y	Y	Y	Y	Y
13 Sires	N	N	Y	Y	Y	Y	Y
NEW MEXICO							
1 **Wilson**	N	N	Y	Y	N	N	Y
2 **Pearce**	N	N	Y	Y	N	Y	Y
3 Udall	N	N	Y	Y	Y	Y	Y
NEW YORK							
1 Bishop	N	N	Y	Y	Y	Y	Y
2 Israel	N	N	Y	Y	Y	Y	Y
3 **King**	N	N	Y	Y	N	N	Y
4 McCarthy	N	N	Y	Y	Y	Y	+
5 Ackerman	N	N	Y	Y	Y	Y	Y
6 Meeks	N	N	Y	Y	Y	Y	Y
7 Crowley	N	N	Y	Y	Y	Y	Y
8 Nadler	N	N	Y	Y	Y	Y	Y
9 Weiner	?	?	Y	Y	Y	Y	Y
10 Towns	N	N	Y	Y	Y	Y	Y
11 Clarke	N	N	Y	Y	Y	Y	Y
12 Velázquez	N	N	Y	?	Y	Y	Y
13 **Fossella**	N	N	Y	Y	N	N	Y
14 Maloney	N	N	Y	Y	Y	Y	Y
15 Rangel	N	N	Y	Y	Y	Y	Y
16 Serrano	N	N	Y	Y	Y	Y	Y
17 Engel	?	?	?	Y	Y	Y	Y
18 Lowey	N	N	Y	Y	Y	Y	Y
19 Hall	N	N	Y	Y	Y	Y	Y
20 Gillibrand	?	?	Y	Y	Y	Y	Y
21 McNulty	?	?	?	Y	Y	Y	Y
22 Hinchey	N	N	Y	Y	Y	Y	Y
23 **McHugh**	Y	Y	Y	Y	N	N	Y
24 Arcuri	N	N	Y	Y	Y	Y	Y
25 **Walsh**	N	N	Y	Y	N	N	Y
26 **Reynolds**	?	?	?	Y	N	N	Y
27 Higgins	N	N	?	Y	Y	Y	Y
28 Slaughter	?	N	Y	Y	Y	Y	Y
29 **Kuhl**	N	N	Y	Y	N	N	Y
NORTH CAROLINA							
1 Butterfield	N	N	Y	Y	Y	Y	Y
2 Etheridge	N	N	Y	Y	Y	Y	Y
3 **Jones**	N	N	Y	Y	Y	Y	Y
4 Price	N	N	Y	Y	Y	Y	Y

	441	442	443	444	445	446	447
5 **Foxx**	Y	Y	Y	Y	N	N	Y
6 **Coble**	Y	Y	Y	Y	N	N	Y
7 McIntyre	N	N	Y	Y	Y	Y	Y
8 **Hayes**	N	N	Y	Y	N	Y	Y
9 **Myrick**	Y	Y	Y	Y	N	N	Y
10 **McHenry**	Y	Y	N	Y	N	N	Y
11 Shuler	N	N	Y	Y	N	N	Y
12 Watt	N	N	Y	Y	Y	Y	Y
13 Miller	N	N	Y	Y	Y	Y	Y
NORTH DAKOTA							
AL Pomeroy	N	N	Y	Y	Y	Y	Y
OHIO							
1 **Chabot**	N	N	Y	Y	N	N	Y
2 **Schmidt**	N	N	Y	Y	N	N	Y
3 **Turner**	?	?	Y	Y	N	N	Y
4 **Jordan**	N	N	N	Y	N	N	Y
5 **Latta**	N	N	Y	Y	N	N	Y
6 Wilson	N	N	Y	Y	Y	Y	Y
7 **Hobson**	Y	Y	Y	Y	N	N	Y
8 **Boehner**	Y	Y	N	Y	N	N	Y
9 Kaptur	N	N	Y	Y	Y	Y	Y
10 Kucinich	N	N	Y	Y	Y	Y	Y
11 Tubbs Jones	N	N	Y	Y	Y	Y	Y
12 **Tiberi**	N	N	Y	Y	N	N	Y
13 Sutton	?	N	Y	Y	Y	Y	Y
14 **LaTourette**	Y	N	Y	Y	N	N	Y
15 **Pryce**	?	?	?	?	?	?	?
16 **Regula**	N	N	Y	Y	N	N	Y
17 Ryan	N	N	Y	Y	Y	Y	Y
18 Space	N	N	Y	Y	Y	Y	Y
OKLAHOMA							
1 **Sullivan**	Y	Y	Y	Y	N	N	Y
2 Boren	N	N	Y	Y	Y	Y	Y
3 **Lucas**	Y	Y	Y	Y	N	N	Y
4 **Cole**	N	N	N	Y	N	N	Y
5 **Fallin**	Y	N	Y	Y	N	N	Y
OREGON							
1 Wu	N	N	Y	Y	Y	Y	Y
2 **Walden**	Y	N	Y	Y	N	N	Y
3 Blumenauer	N	N	Y	Y	Y	Y	Y
4 DeFazio	N	N	Y	Y	Y	Y	Y
5 Hooley	N	N	Y	Y	Y	Y	Y
PENNSYLVANIA							
1 Brady	Y	N	Y	Y	Y	Y	Y
2 Fattah	N	N	Y	Y	Y	Y	Y
3 **English**	Y	Y	Y	Y	N	N	Y
4 Altmire	N	N	Y	Y	Y	N	Y
5 **Peterson**	?	?	?	Y	N	N	Y
6 **Gerlach**	N	N	Y	Y	N	Y	Y
7 Sestak	N	N	Y	Y	Y	Y	Y
8 Murphy, P.	N	N	Y	Y	Y	Y	Y
9 **Shuster**	Y	N	Y	Y	N	N	Y
10 Carney	N	N	Y	Y	N	N	Y
11 Kanjorski	N	N	Y	Y	Y	Y	Y
12 Murtha	N	N	Y	Y	Y	Y	Y
13 Schwartz	N	N	Y	Y	Y	Y	Y
14 Doyle	N	N	Y	Y	Y	Y	Y
15 **Dent**	N	N	Y	Y	N	Y	Y
16 **Pitts**	Y	N	N	Y	N	N	Y
17 Holden	N	N	Y	Y	Y	Y	Y
18 **Murphy, T.**	N	N	Y	Y	N	N	Y
19 **Platts**	N	N	Y	Y	N	N	Y
RHODE ISLAND							
1 Kennedy	N	N	Y	Y	Y	Y	Y
2 Langevin	N	N	Y	Y	Y	Y	Y
SOUTH CAROLINA							
1 **Brown**	N	N	Y	Y	N	N	Y
2 **Wilson**	Y	?	Y	Y	N	N	Y
3 **Barrett**	Y	Y	N	Y	N	N	Y
4 **Inglis**	Y	Y	Y	Y	N	N	Y
5 Spratt	N	?	Y	Y	Y	Y	Y
6 Clyburn	N	N	Y	Y	Y	Y	Y
SOUTH DAKOTA							
AL Herseth Sandlin	?	N	Y	Y	Y	Y	Y
TENNESSEE							
1 **Davis, D.**	N	N	Y	Y	N	N	Y
2 **Duncan**	Y	Y	N	Y	N	N	Y
3 **Wamp**	N	?	Y	Y	N	N	Y
4 Davis, L.	N	?	Y	Y	Y	Y	Y
5 Cooper	N	N	Y	Y	Y	Y	Y
6 Gordon	Y	Y	Y	Y	Y	Y	Y
7 **Blackburn**	Y	Y	N	Y	N	N	Y
8 Tanner	N	N	Y	Y	Y	Y	Y
9 Cohen	N	N	Y	Y	Y	Y	Y

	441	442	443	444	445	446	447
TEXAS							
1 **Gohmert**	?	?	?	Y	N	P	Y
2 **Poe**	N	N	Y	Y	N	N	Y
3 **Johnson, S.**	?	Y	N	Y	N	N	Y
4 **Hall**	N	N	Y	Y	N	N	Y
5 **Hensarling**	Y	Y	N	Y	N	N	Y
6 **Barton**	N	Y	N	Y	N	N	Y
7 **Culberson**	N	N	N	Y	N	N	Y
8 **Brady**	N	N	N	Y	N	N	Y
9 Green, A.	N	N	Y	Y	Y	Y	Y
10 **McCaul**	Y	Y	Y	Y	N	N	Y
11 **Conaway**	N	N	N	Y	N	N	Y
12 **Granger**	Y	Y	N	Y	N	N	Y
13 **Thornberry**	N	N	N	Y	N	N	Y
14 **Paul**	N	N	N	Y	N	N	Y
15 Hinojosa	N	N	Y	Y	Y	Y	Y
16 Reyes	?	?	?	Y	Y	Y	Y
17 Edwards	N	N	Y	Y	Y	?	Y
18 Jackson Lee	N	N	Y	Y	Y	Y	Y
19 **Neugebauer**	Y	N	N	Y	N	N	Y
20 Gonzalez	N	N	Y	Y	Y	Y	Y
21 **Smith**	N	N	Y	Y	N	N	Y
22 Lampson	N	N	Y	Y	Y	Y	Y
23 Rodriguez	N	N	Y	Y	Y	Y	Y
24 **Marchant**	N	Y	N	Y	N	N	Y
25 Doggett	N	N	Y	Y	Y	Y	Y
26 **Burgess**	?	N	Y	Y	N	N	Y
27 Ortiz	N	N	Y	Y	Y	Y	Y
28 Cuellar	N	N	Y	Y	+	Y	Y
29 Green, G.	N	N	Y	Y	Y	Y	Y
30 Johnson, E.	N	N	Y	?	Y	Y	Y
31 **Carter**	Y	Y	N	Y	N	N	Y
32 **Sessions**	Y	Y	N	Y	N	N	Y
UTAH							
1 **Bishop**	Y	Y	?	Y	N	Y	Y
2 Matheson	N	N	Y	Y	Y	N	Y
3 **Cannon**	?	?	?	?	?	?	?
VERMONT							
AL Welch	?	N	Y	Y	Y	Y	Y
VIRGINIA							
1 **Wittman**	N	N	Y	Y	N	N	Y
2 **Drake**	N	N	Y	Y	N	N	Y
3 Scott	N	?	Y	Y	Y	Y	?
4 **Forbes**	N	N	Y	Y	N	N	Y
5 **Goode**	N	N	Y	Y	N	Y	Y
6 **Goodlatte**	N	N	Y	Y	N	Y	Y
7 **Cantor**	Y	Y	N	Y	N	N	Y
8 Moran	N	N	Y	Y	Y	Y	Y
9 Boucher	N	?	Y	Y	Y	Y	Y
10 **Wolf**	N	N	Y	Y	N	N	Y
11 **Davis**	Y	Y	Y	Y	N	N	Y
WASHINGTON							
1 Inslee	N	N	Y	Y	Y	Y	Y
2 Larsen	?	?	Y	Y	Y	Y	Y
3 Baird	N	N	Y	Y	Y	Y	Y
4 **Hastings**	Y	Y	Y	Y	N	N	Y
5 **McMorris Rodgers**	Y	Y	Y	Y	N	Y	Y
6 Dicks	N	N	Y	Y	Y	Y	Y
7 McDermott	N	N	Y	Y	Y	Y	Y
8 **Reichert**	Y	Y	Y	Y	N	N	Y
9 Smith	N	N	Y	Y	Y	Y	Y
WEST VIRGINIA							
1 Mollohan	?	?	Y	Y	Y	Y	Y
2 **Capito**	N	N	Y	Y	N	N	Y
3 Rahall	N	?	Y	Y	Y	Y	Y
WISCONSIN							
1 **Ryan**	Y	Y	N	Y	N	N	Y
2 Baldwin	N	N	Y	Y	Y	Y	Y
3 Kind	N	N	Y	Y	Y	Y	Y
4 Moore	N	N	Y	Y	Y	?	Y
5 **Sensenbrenner**	Y	Y	N	Y	N	N	Y
6 **Petri**	Y	Y	Y	Y	N	N	Y
7 Obey	N	N	Y	Y	Y	Y	Y
8 Kagen	N	N	Y	Y	Y	Y	Y
WYOMING							
AL **Cubin**	Y	Y	Y	Y	N	N	Y
DELEGATES							
Faleomavaega (A.S.)				Y			
Norton (D.C.)				Y			
Bordallo (Guam)				Y			
Fortuño (P.R.)				?			
Christensen (V.I.)				?			

IN THE HOUSE | By Vote Number

448. **HR 6346. Energy Price Gouging/Passage.** Stupak, D-Mich., motion to suspend the rules and pass the bill that would prohibit price gouging for fuels in areas experiencing an energy emergency, set civil and criminal penalties for such price gouging, and permit states to bring lawsuits against retailers for price gouging. Motion rejected 276-146: R 51-145; D 225-1 (ND 169-1, SD 56-0). A two-thirds majority of those present and voting (282 in this case) is required for passage under suspension of the rules. A "nay" was a vote in support of the president's position. June 24, 2008.

449. **HR 2176. American Indian Land Agreement/Previous Question.** Hastings, D-Fla., motion to order the previous question (thus ending debate and possibility of amendment) on adoption of the rule (H Res 1298) to provide for House floor consideration of the bill that would ratify a land claims settlement between the state of Michigan and the Bay Mills Indian Community and add the text of a separate bill. Motion agreed to 226-194: R 3-191; D 223-3 (ND 169-2, SD 54-1). June 25, 2008.

450. **HR 2176. American Indian Land Agreement/Rule.** Adoption of the rule (H Res 1298) to provide for House floor consideration of the bill that would ratify a land claims settlement between the state of Michigan and the Bay Mills Indian Community. It also would add the text of a bill (HR 4115) that would ratify a land claims settlement between Michigan and the Sault Ste. Marie Tribe of Chippewa Indians. Adopted 207-204: R 4-184; D 203-20 (ND 152-16, SD 51-4). June 25, 2008.

451. **HR 6275. Alternative Minimum Tax Adjustment/Previous Question.** Welch, D-Vt., motion to order the previous question (thus ending debate and possibility of amendment) on adoption of the rule (H Res 1297) to provide for House floor consideration of the bill that would provide a one-year adjustment to prevent an additional 21 million taxpayers from paying the alternative minimum tax (AMT) on 2008 income. Motion agreed to 225-194: R 1-192; D 224-2 (ND 169-2, SD 55-0). June 25, 2008.

452. **HR 6275. Alternative Minimum Tax Adjustment/Rule.** Adoption of the rule (H Res 1297) to provide for House floor consideration of the bill that would provide a one-year adjustment to prevent an additional 21 million taxpayers from paying the AMT on 2008 income. Adopted 224-193: R 0-192; D 224-1 (ND 170-1, SD 54-0). June 25, 2008.

453. HR 3195. Disabilities Act Definitions/Previous Question. Sutton, D-Ohio, motion to order the previous question (thus ending debate and possibility of amendment) on adoption of the rule (H Res 1299) to provide for House floor consideration of the bill that would amend the Americans With Disabilities Act to redefine a disability as a physical or mental impairment that materially restricts one or more major life activities. Motion agreed to 221-194: R 1-191; D 220-3 (ND 165-3, SD 55-0). June 25, 2008.

454. **HR 6275. Alternative Minimum Tax Adjustment/Recommit.** McCrery, R-La., motion to recommit the bill to the Ways and Means Committee with instructions that it be reported back promptly with language that would eliminate tax increases providing offsets in the bill and provide that deductions in mileage rates for vehicles used for charitable purposes are treated the same as medical travel and moving rates. Motion rejected 199-222: R 194-1; D 5-221 (ND 2-168, SD 3-53). A "yea" was a vote in support of the president's position. June 25, 2008.

ND Northern Democrats, SD Southern Democrats
Southern states: Ala., Ark., Fla., Ga., Ky., La., Miss., N.C., Okla., S.C., Tenn., Texas, Va.

	448	449	450	451	452	453	454
ALABAMA							
1 **Bonner**	N	N	N	N	N	N	Y
2 **Everett**	N	N	N	N	N	N	Y
3 **Rogers**	N	N	?	N	N	N	Y
4 **Aderholt**	N	N	N	N	N	N	Y
5 Cramer	Y	Y	Y	Y	Y	Y	N
6 **Bachus**	N	N	N	N	N	N	Y
7 Davis	Y	Y	Y	Y	Y	Y	N
ALASKA							
AL **Young**	N	Y	Y	N	N	N	Y
ARIZONA							
1 **Renzi**	Y	N	N	N	N	N	Y
2 **Franks**	N	N	N	N	N	N	Y
3 **Shadegg**	N	N	N	N	N	N	Y
4 Pastor	Y	Y	Y	Y	Y	Y	N
5 Mitchell	Y	Y	Y	Y	Y	Y	Y
6 **Flake**	N	N	N	N	N	N	Y
7 Grijalva	Y	Y	Y	Y	Y	Y	N
8 Giffords	Y	Y	Y	Y	Y	Y	N
ARKANSAS							
1 Berry	Y	Y	Y	Y	Y	Y	N
2 Snyder	?	?	?	?	?	?	?
3 **Boozman**	N	N	N	N	N	N	Y
4 Ross	Y	Y	Y	Y	Y	Y	N
CALIFORNIA							
1 Thompson	Y	Y	N	Y	Y	Y	N
2 **Herger**	N	N	N	N	N	N	Y
3 **Lungren**	N	N	N	N	N	N	Y
4 **Doolittle**	N	N	N	N	N	N	Y
5 Matsui	Y	Y	Y	Y	Y	Y	N
6 Woolsey	Y	Y	Y	Y	Y	Y	N
7 Miller, George	?	Y	Y	Y	Y	?	N
8 Pelosi	Y						
9 Lee	Y	Y	Y	Y	Y	Y	N
10 Tauscher	Y	Y	Y	Y	Y	Y	N
11 McNerney	Y	Y	Y	Y	?	Y	N
12 Speier	?	?	?	?	?	?	?
13 Stark	Y	Y	N	Y	Y	Y	N
14 Eshoo	Y	Y	N	Y	Y	Y	N
15 Honda	Y	Y	?	Y	Y	Y	N
16 Lofgren	Y	Y	Y	Y	Y	Y	N
17 Farr	Y	Y	Y	Y	Y	Y	N
18 Cardoza	Y	Y	Y	Y	Y	Y	N
19 **Radanovich**	N	N	N	N	N	N	Y
20 Costa	Y	Y	Y	Y	Y	Y	N
21 **Nunes**	N	N	N	N	N	N	Y
22 **McCarthy**	N	N	N	N	N	N	Y
23 Capps	Y	Y	Y	Y	Y	Y	N
24 **Gallegly**	N	N	N	N	N	N	Y
25 **McKeon**	N	N	N	N	N	N	Y
26 **Dreier**	N	N	N	N	N	N	Y
27 Sherman	Y	Y	Y	Y	Y	Y	N
28 Berman	?	Y	Y	Y	Y	Y	N
29 Schiff	Y	Y	Y	Y	Y	Y	N
30 Waxman	Y	Y	Y	Y	Y	Y	N
31 Becerra	Y	Y	Y	Y	Y	Y	N
32 Solis	Y	Y	Y	Y	Y	Y	N
33 Watson	Y	?	?	?	?	?	?
34 Roybal-Allard	Y	Y	Y	Y	Y	Y	N
35 Waters	Y	Y	N	Y	Y	Y	N
36 Harman	Y	Y	Y	Y	Y	Y	N
37 Richardson	Y	Y	N	Y	Y	Y	N
38 Napolitano	Y	Y	Y	Y	Y	Y	N
39 Sánchez, Linda	Y	Y	Y	Y	Y	Y	N
40 **Royce**	N	N	N	N	N	N	Y
41 **Lewis**	N	N	N	N	N	N	Y
42 **Miller, Gary**	N	N	N	N	N	N	Y
43 Baca	Y	?	?	?	?	?	N
44 **Calvert**	N	N	N	N	N	N	Y
45 **Bono Mack**	N	N	N	N	N	N	Y
46 **Rohrabacher**	N	N	N	N	N	N	Y
47 Sanchez, Loretta	Y	Y	Y	Y	Y	Y	N
48 **Campbell**	N	N	N	N	N	N	Y
49 **Issa**	N	N	N	N	N	N	Y
50 **Bilbray**	Y	Y	?	N	?	N	Y
51 Filner	Y	Y	Y	Y	Y	Y	N
52 **Hunter**	N	N	N	N	N	N	Y
53 Davis	Y	Y	Y	Y	Y	Y	N

	448	449	450	451	452	453	454
COLORADO							
1 DeGette	Y	Y	Y	Y	Y	Y	N
2 Udall	Y	Y	Y	Y	Y	Y	N
3 Salazar	Y	Y	Y	Y	Y	Y	N
4 **Musgrave**	N	N	N	N	N	N	Y
5 **Lamborn**	N	N	N	N	N	N	Y
6 **Tancredo**	N	N	N	N	N	N	Y
7 Perlmutter	Y	Y	Y	Y	Y	Y	N
CONNECTICUT							
1 Larson	Y	Y	Y	Y	Y	Y	N
2 Courtney	Y	Y	Y	Y	Y	Y	N
3 DeLauro	Y	Y	Y	Y	Y	Y	N
4 **Shays**	Y	N	N	N	N	N	Y
5 Murphy	Y	Y	Y	Y	Y	Y	N
DELAWARE							
AL **Castle**	Y	N	N	N	N	N	Y
FLORIDA							
1 **Miller**	N	N	N	N	N	N	Y
2 Boyd	Y	Y	Y	Y	Y	Y	N
3 Brown	Y	Y	Y	Y	Y	Y	N
4 **Crenshaw**	N	N	N	N	N	N	Y
5 **Brown-Waite**	Y	N	N	N	N	N	Y
6 **Stearns**	N	N	N	N	N	N	Y
7 **Mica**	N	N	N	N	N	N	Y
8 **Keller**	Y	N	N	N	N	N	Y
9 **Bilirakis**	N	N	N	N	N	N	Y
10 **Young**	Y	N	N	N	N	N	Y
11 Castor	Y	Y	Y	Y	Y	Y	N
12 **Putnam**	N	–	–	–	–	–	+
13 **Buchanan**	Y	N	N	N	N	N	Y
14 **Mack**	N	N	N	N	N	N	Y
15 **Weldon**	N	N	N	N	N	N	Y
16 Mahoney	Y	+	+	+	+	+	–
17 Meek	Y	Y	Y	Y	Y	Y	N
18 **Ros-Lehtinen**	Y	N	?	N	N	N	Y
19 Wexler	?	?	?	?	?	?	N
20 Wasserman Schultz	Y	Y	Y	Y	Y	Y	N
21 **Diaz-Balart, L.**	N	N	N	N	N	N	Y
22 Klein	Y	Y	Y	Y	Y	Y	N
23 Hastings	Y	Y	Y	Y	Y	Y	N
24 **Feeney**	N	N	N	N	N	N	Y
25 **Diaz-Balart, M.**	N	N	N	N	N	N	Y
GEORGIA							
1 **Kingston**	N	N	N	N	N	N	Y
2 Bishop	Y	Y	Y	Y	?	Y	N
3 **Westmoreland**	N	N	N	N	N	N	Y
4 Johnson	Y	Y	Y	Y	Y	Y	N
5 Lewis	Y	Y	Y	Y	Y	Y	N
6 **Price**	N	N	N	N	N	N	Y
7 **Linder**	N	N	N	N	N	N	Y
8 Marshall	Y	Y	Y	Y	Y	Y	N
9 **Deal**	N	N	N	N	N	N	Y
10 **Broun**	N	N	N	N	N	N	Y
11 **Gingrey**	N	N	N	N	N	N	Y
12 Barrow	Y	Y	Y	Y	Y	Y	N
13 Scott	Y	Y	Y	Y	Y	Y	N
HAWAII							
1 Abercrombie	Y	Y	Y	Y	Y	Y	N
2 Hirono	Y	Y	Y	Y	Y	Y	N
IDAHO							
1 **Sali**	N	N	N	N	N	N	Y
2 **Simpson**	N	N	N	N	N	N	Y
ILLINOIS							
1 Rush	?	?	?	?	?	?	?
2 Jackson	Y	Y	Y	Y	Y	Y	N
3 Lipinski	Y	Y	Y	Y	Y	Y	N
4 Gutierrez	Y	Y	Y	Y	Y	Y	N
5 Emanuel	Y	Y	Y	Y	Y	Y	N
6 **Roskam**	N	N	N	N	N	N	Y
7 Davis	?	Y	Y	Y	Y	Y	N
8 Bean	Y	Y	Y	Y	Y	Y	Y
9 Schakowsky	Y	Y	Y	Y	Y	Y	N
10 **Kirk**	Y	N	N	N	N	N	Y
11 **Weller**	N	N	N	N	N	N	Y
12 Costello	Y	Y	Y	Y	Y	Y	N
13 **Biggert**	Y	N	N	N	N	N	Y
14 Foster	Y	Y	Y	Y	Y	Y	N
15 **Johnson**	Y	N	N	N	N	N	Y

	448	449	450	451	452	453	454
16 **Manzullo**	N	N	N	?	N	N	Y
17 Hare	Y	Y	Y	Y	Y	Y	N
18 **LaHood**	N	N	N	N	N	N	Y
19 **Shimkus**	N	N	N	N	N	N	Y
INDIANA							
1 Visclosky	Y	Y	Y	Y	Y	Y	N
2 Donnelly	Y	N	Y	N	Y	N	N
3 **Souder**	N	N	N	N	N	N	Y
4 **Buyer**	N	N	N	N	N	N	Y
5 **Burton**	N	N	N	N	N	?	Y
6 **Pence**	?	N	N	N	N	N	Y
7 Carson, A.	Y	Y	Y	Y	Y	Y	N
8 Ellsworth	Y	Y	Y	Y	Y	Y	N
9 Hill	Y	N	Y	N	N	N	N
IOWA							
1 Braley	Y	Y	Y	Y	Y	Y	N
2 Loebsack	Y	Y	Y	Y	Y	Y	N
3 Boswell	Y	Y	Y	Y	Y	Y	N
4 **Latham**	N	N	N	N	N	N	Y
5 **King**	N	N	N	N	N	N	Y
KANSAS							
1 **Moran**	N	N	N	N	N	N	Y
2 Boyda	Y	Y	N	Y	Y	Y	N
3 Moore	?	Y	Y	Y	Y	Y	N
4 **Tiahrt**	N	N	N	N	N	N	Y
KENTUCKY							
1 **Whitfield**	Y	N	?	N	N	N	Y
2 **Lewis**	N	N	N	N	N	N	Y
3 Yarmuth	Y	Y	Y	Y	Y	Y	N
4 **Davis**	N	N	N	N	N	N	Y
5 **Rogers**	N	N	N	N	N	N	Y
6 Chandler	Y	Y	Y	Y	Y	Y	N
LOUISIANA							
1 **Scalise**	N	N	N	N	N	N	Y
2 Jefferson	Y	Y	Y	Y	Y	Y	N
3 Melancon	?	Y	Y	Y	Y	Y	N
4 **McCrery**	N	N	N	N	N	N	Y
5 **Alexander**	N	N	N	N	N	N	Y
6 Cazayoux	Y	Y	Y	Y	Y	Y	N
7 **Boustany**	N	N	N	N	N	N	Y
MAINE							
1 Allen	Y	Y	Y	Y	Y	Y	N
2 Michaud	Y	Y	Y	Y	Y	Y	N
MARYLAND							
1 **Gilchrest**	Y	N	N	N	N	N	Y
2 Ruppersberger	Y	Y	N	Y	Y	?	N
3 Sarbanes	Y	Y	Y	Y	Y	Y	N
4 Edwards	Y	Y	Y	Y	Y	Y	N
5 Hoyer	Y	Y	Y	Y	Y	Y	N
6 **Bartlett**	N	N	N	N	N	N	Y
7 Cummings	Y	Y	Y	Y	Y	Y	?
8 Van Hollen	Y	Y	Y	Y	Y	Y	N
MASSACHUSETTS							
1 Olver	Y	Y	Y	Y	Y	Y	N
2 Neal	Y	Y	?	Y	Y	Y	N
3 McGovern	Y	Y	Y	Y	Y	Y	N
4 Frank	Y	Y	Y	Y	Y	Y	N
5 Tsongas	Y	Y	Y	Y	Y	Y	?
6 Tierney	Y	Y	Y	Y	Y	Y	N
7 Markey	Y	Y	Y	Y	Y	Y	N
8 Capuano	Y	Y	Y	Y	Y	Y	N
9 Lynch	Y	Y	Y	Y	Y	Y	N
10 Delahunt	Y	Y	Y	Y	Y	Y	N
MICHIGAN							
1 Stupak	Y	Y	Y	Y	Y	Y	N
2 **Hoekstra**	N	N	N	N	N	N	Y
3 **Ehlers**	N	N	N	N	N	N	Y
4 **Camp**	N	N	N	N	N	N	Y
5 Kildee	Y	Y	Y	Y	Y	Y	N
6 **Upton**	N	N	N	N	N	N	Y
7 **Walberg**	N	N	N	N	N	?	Y
8 **Rogers**	N	N	N	N	N	N	Y
9 **Knollenberg**	N	N	N	N	N	N	Y
10 **Miller**	Y	N	Y	N	N	N	Y
11 **McCotter**	Y	N	N	N	N	N	Y
12 Levin	Y	Y	Y	Y	Y	Y	N
13 Kilpatrick	Y	Y	N	Y	Y	Y	N
14 Conyers	Y	Y	Y	Y	Y	Y	N
15 Dingell	Y	Y	Y	Y	?	Y	N
MINNESOTA							
1 Walz	Y	Y	Y	Y	Y	Y	N
2 **Kline**	N	N	N	N	N	N	Y
3 **Ramstad**	Y	N	N	N	N	N	Y
4 McCollum	Y	Y	Y	Y	Y	Y	N

	448	449	450	451	452	453	454
5 Ellison	Y	Y	Y	Y	Y	Y	N
6 **Bachmann**	N	N	N	N	N	N	Y
7 Peterson	N	Y	N	Y	Y	Y	N
8 Oberstar	Y	Y	Y	Y	Y	Y	N
MISSISSIPPI							
1 Childers	Y	N	N	Y	Y	Y	N
2 Thompson	Y	Y	Y	Y	Y	Y	N
3 **Pickering**	N	N	N	N	N	N	Y
4 Taylor	Y	Y	N	Y	Y	Y	N
MISSOURI							
1 Clay	Y	Y	Y	Y	Y	Y	N
2 **Akin**	N	N	N	N	N	N	Y
3 Carnahan	Y	Y	Y	Y	Y	Y	N
4 Skelton	Y	Y	Y	Y	Y	Y	N
5 Cleaver	Y	Y	Y	Y	Y	Y	N
6 **Graves**	Y	Y	N	N	N	N	Y
7 **Blunt**	N	N	N	N	?	?	Y
8 **Emerson**	Y	N	N	N	N	N	Y
9 **Hulshof**	Y	N	N	N	N	N	Y
MONTANA							
AL **Rehberg**	N	N	N	N	N	N	Y
NEBRASKA							
1 **Fortenberry**	Y	N	N	N	N	N	Y
2 **Terry**	N	N	N	N	N	N	Y
3 **Smith**	N	N	N	N	N	N	Y
NEVADA							
1 Berkley	Y	Y	Y	Y	Y	Y	N
2 **Heller**	Y	N	N	N	N	N	Y
3 **Porter**	N	N	N	N	N	N	Y
NEW HAMPSHIRE							
1 Shea-Porter	Y	Y	Y	Y	Y	Y	N
2 Hodes	Y	Y	Y	Y	Y	Y	N
NEW JERSEY							
1 Andrews	Y	Y	Y	Y	Y	?	N
2 **LoBiondo**	Y	N	N	N	N	N	Y
3 **Saxton**	N	N	?	N	N	N	Y
4 **Smith**	Y	N	N	N	N	N	Y
5 **Garrett**	N	N	N	N	N	N	Y
6 Pallone	Y	Y	Y	Y	Y	Y	N
7 **Ferguson**	N	N	N	N	N	N	Y
8 Pascrell	Y	Y	N	Y	Y	Y	N
9 Rothman	Y	Y	Y	Y	Y	Y	N
10 Payne	Y	Y	Y	Y	Y	Y	N
11 **Frelinghuysen**	N	N	N	N	N	N	Y
12 Holt	Y	Y	Y	Y	Y	Y	N
13 Sires	Y	Y	Y	Y	Y	Y	N
NEW MEXICO							
1 **Wilson**	Y	N	N	N	N	N	Y
2 **Pearce**	N	N	N	N	N	N	Y
3 Udall	Y	Y	?	Y	Y	Y	N
NEW YORK							
1 Bishop	Y	Y	Y	Y	Y	Y	N
2 Israel	Y	Y	Y	Y	Y	Y	N
3 **King**	N	N	N	N	?	N	Y
4 McCarthy	Y	Y	Y	Y	Y	Y	N
5 Ackerman	Y	Y	Y	Y	Y	Y	N
6 Meeks	Y	Y	Y	Y	Y	Y	N
7 Crowley	Y	Y	Y	Y	Y	Y	N
8 Nadler	Y	Y	Y	Y	Y	Y	N
9 Weiner	Y	Y	Y	Y	Y	Y	N
10 Towns	Y	Y	Y	Y	Y	Y	N
11 Clarke	Y	Y	Y	Y	Y	Y	N
12 Velázquez	Y	Y	Y	Y	Y	Y	N
13 **Fossella**	N	N	N	N	N	N	Y
14 Maloney	Y	Y	Y	Y	Y	Y	N
15 Rangel	Y	Y	Y	Y	Y	Y	N
16 Serrano	Y	Y	Y	Y	Y	Y	N
17 Engel	Y	Y	Y	Y	Y	Y	N
18 Lowey	Y	Y	Y	Y	Y	Y	N
19 Hall	Y	Y	Y	Y	Y	Y	N
20 Gillibrand	Y	?	?	?	Y	Y	N
21 McNulty	Y	Y	Y	Y	Y	Y	N
22 Hinchey	Y	Y	Y	Y	Y	Y	N
23 **McHugh**	Y	N	N	N	N	N	Y
24 Arcuri	Y	Y	Y	Y	Y	Y	N
25 **Walsh**	N	N	?	N	N	N	Y
26 **Reynolds**	N	N	N	N	N	N	Y
27 Higgins	Y	Y	Y	Y	Y	Y	N
28 Slaughter	Y	Y	Y	Y	Y	Y	N
29 **Kuhl**	Y	?	?	N	N	N	Y
NORTH CAROLINA							
1 Butterfield	Y	Y	Y	Y	Y	Y	N
2 Etheridge	Y	Y	Y	Y	Y	Y	N
3 **Jones**	Y	N	N	N	N	N	Y
4 Price	Y	Y	Y	Y	Y	Y	N

	448	449	450	451	452	453	454
5 **Foxx**	N	N	N	N	N	N	Y
6 **Coble**	N	N	N	N	N	N	Y
7 McIntyre	Y	Y	Y	Y	Y	Y	Y
8 **Hayes**	Y	N	N	N	N	N	Y
9 **Myrick**	N	N	N	N	N	N	Y
10 **McHenry**	N	N	N	N	N	N	Y
11 Shuler	Y	Y	N	Y	Y	Y	N
12 Watt	Y	Y	Y	Y	Y	Y	N
13 Miller	Y	Y	Y	Y	Y	Y	N
NORTH DAKOTA							
AL Pomeroy	Y	Y	Y	Y	Y	Y	N
OHIO							
1 **Chabot**	Y	N	N	N	N	N	Y
2 **Schmidt**	Y	N	N	N	N	N	Y
3 **Turner**	Y	N	N	N	N	N	Y
4 **Jordan**	N	N	N	N	N	N	Y
5 **Latta**	N	N	N	N	N	N	Y
6 Wilson	Y	Y	Y	Y	Y	Y	N
7 **Hobson**	N	N	N	N	N	N	Y
8 **Boehner**	N	N	N	N	N	N	Y
9 Kaptur	Y	Y	Y	Y	Y	Y	N
10 Kucinich	Y	Y	N	Y	Y	Y	N
11 Tubbs Jones	Y	Y	N	Y	Y	Y	N
12 **Tiberi**	Y	N	N	N	N	N	Y
13 Sutton	Y	Y	Y	Y	Y	Y	N
14 **LaTourette**	Y	N	N	N	N	N	Y
15 **Pryce**	?	?	?	?	?	?	?
16 **Regula**	N	N	N	N	N	N	Y
17 Ryan	Y	Y	Y	Y	Y	Y	N
18 Space	Y	Y	Y	Y	Y	Y	N
OKLAHOMA							
1 **Sullivan**	N	N	N	N	N	N	Y
2 Boren	Y	Y	Y	Y	Y	Y	N
3 **Lucas**	N	N	N	N	N	N	Y
4 **Cole**	N	N	Y	N	N	N	Y
5 **Fallin**	N	N	N	N	N	N	Y
OREGON							
1 Wu	Y	Y	Y	Y	Y	Y	N
2 **Walden**	Y	N	N	N	N	N	Y
3 Blumenauer	?	Y	N	Y	Y	Y	N
4 DeFazio	Y	Y	Y	Y	Y	Y	N
5 Hooley	Y	Y	Y	Y	Y	Y	N
PENNSYLVANIA							
1 Brady	Y	Y	Y	Y	Y	Y	N
2 Fattah	Y	Y	Y	Y	Y	Y	N
3 **English**	Y	N	N	N	N	N	Y
4 Altmire	Y	Y	Y	Y	Y	Y	N
5 **Peterson**	N	N	N	N	N	N	Y
6 **Gerlach**	Y	N	N	N	N	N	Y
7 Sestak	Y	Y	Y	Y	Y	Y	N
8 Murphy, P.	Y	Y	Y	Y	Y	Y	N
9 **Shuster**	N	N	N	N	N	N	Y
10 Carney	Y	Y	Y	Y	Y	Y	N
11 Kanjorski	Y	Y	Y	Y	Y	Y	N
12 Murtha	Y	Y	N	Y	Y	Y	N
13 Schwartz	Y	Y	Y	Y	Y	Y	N
14 Doyle	Y	Y	Y	Y	Y	Y	N
15 **Dent**	Y	N	N	N	N	N	Y
16 **Pitts**	N	N	N	N	N	N	Y
17 Holden	Y	Y	Y	Y	Y	N	N
18 **Murphy, T.**	N	N	N	N	N	N	Y
19 **Platts**	Y	N	N	N	N	N	Y
RHODE ISLAND							
1 Kennedy	Y	Y	Y	Y	Y	Y	N
2 Langevin	Y	Y	N	Y	Y	Y	N
SOUTH CAROLINA							
1 **Brown**	N	N	N	N	N	N	Y
2 **Wilson**	N	N	N	N	N	N	Y
3 **Barrett**	N	N	N	N	N	N	Y
4 **Inglis**	N	N	N	N	N	N	Y
5 Spratt	Y	Y	Y	Y	Y	Y	N
6 Clyburn	Y	Y	Y	Y	Y	Y	N
SOUTH DAKOTA							
AL Herseth Sandlin	Y	Y	Y	Y	Y	Y	N
TENNESSEE							
1 **Davis, D.**	N	N	N	N	N	N	Y
2 **Duncan**	N	N	N	N	N	N	Y
3 **Wamp**	N	N	N	N	N	N	Y
4 Davis, L.	Y	Y	Y	Y	Y	Y	N
5 Cooper	Y	Y	Y	Y	Y	Y	N
6 Gordon	Y	Y	Y	Y	Y	Y	N
7 **Blackburn**	N	N	N	N	N	N	Y
8 Tanner	Y	Y	Y	Y	Y	Y	N
9 Cohen	Y	Y	Y	Y	Y	Y	N

	448	449	450	451	452	453	454
TEXAS							
1 **Gohmert**	N	N	N	N	N	N	Y
2 **Poe**	N	N	N	N	N	N	Y
3 **Johnson, S.**	N	N	N	N	N	N	Y
4 **Hall**	Y	N	N	N	N	N	Y
5 **Hensarling**	N	N	N	N	N	N	Y
6 **Barton**	N	N	N	?	N	N	Y
7 **Culberson**	N	N	N	N	N	N	Y
8 **Brady**	N	N	N	N	N	N	Y
9 Green, A.	Y	Y	Y	Y	Y	Y	N
10 **McCaul**	N	N	N	N	N	N	Y
11 **Conaway**	N	N	N	N	N	N	Y
12 **Granger**	N	N	N	N	N	N	Y
13 **Thornberry**	N	N	N	N	N	N	Y
14 **Paul**	N	N	N	N	N	N	Y
15 Hinojosa	Y	Y	Y	Y	Y	Y	N
16 Reyes	Y	Y	Y	Y	Y	Y	N
17 Edwards	Y	Y	Y	Y	Y	Y	N
18 Jackson Lee	Y	Y	Y	Y	Y	Y	N
19 **Neugebauer**	N	N	N	N	N	N	Y
20 Gonzalez	Y	Y	Y	Y	Y	Y	N
21 **Smith**	N	N	N	N	N	N	Y
22 Lampson	Y	?	?	?	?	?	?
23 Rodriguez	Y	Y	N	Y	Y	Y	N
24 **Marchant**	N	N	N	N	N	N	Y
25 Doggett	Y	Y	Y	Y	Y	Y	N
26 **Burgess**	N	N	N	N	N	N	Y
27 Ortiz	Y	Y	Y	Y	Y	Y	N
28 Cuellar	Y	Y	Y	Y	Y	Y	N
29 Green, G.	Y	Y	Y	Y	Y	Y	N
30 Johnson, E.	Y	Y	Y	Y	Y	Y	N
31 **Carter**	N	N	N	N	N	N	Y
32 **Sessions**	N	N	N	N	N	N	Y
UTAH							
1 **Bishop**	N	N	N	N	N	N	Y
2 Matheson	Y	Y	Y	Y	Y	Y	N
3 **Cannon**	?	?	?	?	?	?	?
VERMONT							
AL Welch	Y	Y	Y	Y	Y	Y	N
VIRGINIA							
1 **Wittman**	Y	N	N	N	N	N	Y
2 **Drake**	N	N	N	N	N	N	Y
3 Scott	Y	Y	Y	Y	Y	Y	N
4 **Forbes**	Y	N	N	N	N	N	Y
5 **Goode**	Y	N	N	N	N	N	Y
6 **Goodlatte**	Y	N	N	N	N	N	Y
7 **Cantor**	N	N	N	N	N	N	Y
8 Moran	Y	Y	Y	Y	Y	Y	N
9 Boucher	Y	Y	Y	Y	Y	Y	N
10 **Wolf**	Y	N	N	N	N	N	Y
11 **Davis**	N	N	N	N	N	N	Y
WASHINGTON							
1 Inslee	Y	Y	Y	Y	Y	Y	N
2 Larsen	Y	Y	Y	Y	Y	Y	N
3 Baird	Y	Y	Y	Y	Y	Y	N
4 **Hastings**	N	N	N	N	N	N	Y
5 **McMorris Rodgers**	N	N	N	N	N	N	Y
6 Dicks	Y	Y	Y	Y	Y	Y	N
7 McDermott	Y	Y	Y	Y	Y	Y	N
8 **Reichert**	Y	N	N	Y	N	Y	Y
9 Smith	Y	Y	Y	Y	Y	Y	N
WEST VIRGINIA							
1 Mollohan	Y	Y	Y	Y	Y	Y	N
2 **Capito**	Y	N	N	N	N	N	Y
3 Rahall	Y	Y	Y	Y	Y	Y	N
WISCONSIN							
1 **Ryan**	N	N	N	N	N	N	Y
2 Baldwin	Y	Y	Y	Y	Y	Y	N
3 Kind	Y	Y	Y	Y	Y	Y	N
4 Moore	Y	Y	Y	Y	Y	Y	?
5 **Sensenbrenner**	Y	N	N	N	N	N	Y
6 **Petri**	Y	N	N	N	N	N	Y
7 Obey	Y	Y	Y	Y	Y	Y	N
8 Kagen	Y	Y	Y	Y	Y	Y	N
WYOMING							
AL **Cubin**	N	?	?	?	?	?	?
DELEGATES							
Faleomavaega (A.S.)							
Norton (D.C.)							
Bordallo (Guam)							
Fortuño (P.R.)							
Christensen (V.I.)							

IN THE HOUSE | By Vote Number

455. HR 6275. Alternative Minimum Tax Adjustment/Passage.
Passage of the bill that would provide a one-year adjustment to prevent an additional 21 million taxpayers from paying the alternative minimum tax (AMT) on 2008 income. It would increase the exemption amounts used in calculating the AMT and extend a provision that allows certain non-refundable credits to be claimed against the tax. To offset the costs, the bill would tax the profit-sharing income of private-equity managers at rates for ordinary income, repeal a manufacturing deduction for major oil and gas companies, tighten rules on foreign-owned companies that use tax treaties to reduce their tax burdens, and require credit card issuers to report more information to the IRS about purchases at merchants. Passed 233-189: R 10-183; D 223-6 (ND 171-2, SD 52-4). A "nay" was a vote in support of the president's position. June 25, 2008.

456. HR 3546. Law Enforcement Grants/Passage.
Conyers, D-Mich., motion to suspend the rules and pass the bill that would authorize $1.1 billion annually in fiscal 2008 through 2012 for the Edward Byrne Memorial Justice Assistance Grant Program, which awards grants to states for criminal justice programs. Motion agreed to 406-11: R 182-11; D 224-0 (ND 170-0, SD 54-0). A two-thirds majority of those present and voting (278 in this case) is required for passage under suspension of the rules. June 25, 2008.

457. HR 2176. American Indian Land Agreement/Motion to Table.
Rahall, D-W.Va., motion to table (kill) the Hensarling, R-Texas, appeal of the ruling of the chair with respect to the Rahall point of order that the Hensarling motion to recommit the bill to the Natural Resources Committee was not germane. The Hensarling motion would recommit the bill with instructions that it be reported back forthwith with language that would repeal alternative fuel procurement requirements for federal agencies. Motion agreed to 226-189: R 1-189; D 225-0 (ND 170-0, SD 55-0). June 25, 2008.

458. HR 2176. American Indian Land Agreement/Passage.
Passage of the bill that would ratify a land claims settlement between the state of Michigan and two Michigan Indian tribes, the Bay Mills Indian Community and the Sault Ste. Marie Tribe of Chippewa Indians. The bill would allow the tribes to operate a gambling facility on the new parcel of land in Port Huron, Mich., in exchange for the tribes relinquishing their claim to a 110-acre parcel of land in Charlotte Beach, Mich. Rejected 121-298: R 25-167; D 96-131 (ND 76-95, SD 20-36). June 25, 2008.

459. HR 6358. Child Abuse in Residential Programs/Passage.
Miller, D-Calif., motion to suspend the rules and pass the bill that would establish new federal regulations for private residential programs that focus on serving children with emotional, behavioral or mental health problems, or problems with alcohol and substance abuse. It would require the Health and Human Services Department to enforce health and safety standards for children in such programs, including a ban on specific abusive practices. Motion agreed to 318-103: R 89-103; D 229-0 (ND 174-0, SD 55-0). A two-thirds majority of those present and voting (281 in this case) is required for passage under suspension of the rules. A "nay" was a vote in support of the president's position. June 25, 2008.

	455	456	457	458	459
ALABAMA					
1 Bonner	N	Y	N	N	N
2 Everett	N	Y	N	N	N
3 Rogers	Y	Y	N	N	N
4 Aderholt	N	Y	N	N	N
5 Cramer	Y	Y	Y	Y	Y
6 Bachus	N	Y	N	N	Y
7 Davis	Y	Y	Y	N	Y
ALASKA					
AL Young	N	Y	N	Y	Y
ARIZONA					
1 Renzi	N	Y	N	Y	Y
2 Franks	N	N	N	N	N
3 Shadegg	N	Y	N	N	N
4 Pastor	Y	Y	Y	Y	Y
5 Mitchell	N	Y	Y	N	Y
6 Flake	N	N	N	N	N
7 Grijalva	Y	Y	Y	Y	Y
8 Giffords	Y	Y	Y	Y	Y
ARKANSAS					
1 Berry	Y	Y	Y	Y	Y
2 Snyder	?	?	?	?	?
3 Boozman	N	Y	N	N	N
4 Ross	Y	Y	Y	Y	Y
CALIFORNIA					
1 Thompson	Y	Y	Y	N	Y
2 Herger	N	Y	N	N	N
3 Lungren	N	Y	N	Y	N
4 Doolittle	N	Y	N	N	N
5 Matsui	Y	Y	Y	Y	Y
6 Woolsey	Y	Y	Y	N	Y
7 Miller, George	Y	Y	Y	Y	Y
8 Pelosi					
9 Lee	Y	Y	Y	N	Y
10 Tauscher	Y	Y	Y	N	Y
11 McNerney	Y	Y	Y	N	Y
12 Speier	?	?	?	?	?
13 Stark	Y	Y	Y	N	Y
14 Eshoo	Y	Y	Y	N	Y
15 Honda	Y	Y	Y	N	Y
16 Lofgren	Y	Y	Y	N	Y
17 Farr	Y	Y	Y	N	Y
18 Cardoza	Y	Y	Y	N	Y
19 Radanovich	?	Y	N	N	N
20 Costa	Y	Y	Y	N	Y
21 Nunes	N	Y	N	N	Y
22 McCarthy	N	Y	N	N	Y
23 Capps	Y	Y	Y	Y	Y
24 Gallegly	N	Y	N	N	Y
25 McKeon	N	Y	N	Y	Y
26 Dreier	N	Y	N	N	Y
27 Sherman	Y	Y	Y	N	Y
28 Berman	Y	Y	Y	Y	Y
29 Schiff	Y	Y	Y	N	Y
30 Waxman	Y	Y	Y	N	Y
31 Becerra	Y	Y	Y	N	Y
32 Solis	Y	Y	Y	Y	Y
33 Watson	?	?	Y	Y	Y
34 Roybal-Allard	Y	Y	Y	N	Y
35 Waters	Y	Y	Y	N	Y
36 Harman	Y	Y	Y	Y	Y
37 Richardson	Y	Y	Y	N	Y
38 Napolitano	Y	Y	Y	N	Y
39 Sánchez, Linda	Y	Y	Y	N	Y
40 Royce	N	Y	N	N	N
41 Lewis	N	Y	N	N	Y
42 Miller, Gary	N	Y	N	N	Y
43 Baca	Y	Y	Y	N	Y
44 Calvert	N	Y	N	N	Y
45 Bono Mack	N	Y	N	N	Y
46 Rohrabacher	N	Y	N	Y	N
47 Sanchez, Loretta	Y	Y	Y	N	Y
48 Campbell	N	N	N	N	N
49 Issa	N	Y	N	N	Y
50 Bilbray	Y	Y	N	Y	N
51 Filner	Y	Y	Y	N	Y
52 Hunter	N	Y	N	N	N
53 Davis	Y	Y	Y	N	Y

	455	456	457	458	459
COLORADO					
1 DeGette	Y	Y	Y	Y	Y
2 Udall	Y	Y	Y	N	Y
3 Salazar	Y	Y	?	N	Y
4 Musgrave	N	Y	N	N	N
5 Lamborn	N	Y	N	N	N
6 Tancredo	N	N	N	N	N
7 Perlmutter	Y	Y	Y	N	Y
CONNECTICUT					
1 Larson	Y	Y	Y	N	Y
2 Courtney	Y	Y	Y	N	Y
3 DeLauro	Y	Y	Y	N	Y
4 Shays	N	Y	N	N	Y
5 Murphy	Y	Y	Y	Y	Y
DELAWARE					
AL Castle	N	Y	N	N	Y
FLORIDA					
1 Miller	N	Y	N	N	N
2 Boyd	Y	Y	Y	N	Y
3 Brown	Y	Y	Y	N	Y
4 Crenshaw	N	Y	N	N	N
5 Brown-Waite	N	Y	N	N	N
6 Stearns	N	Y	N	N	N
7 Mica	N	Y	N	N	N
8 Keller	N	Y	N	N	Y
9 Bilirakis	N	Y	N	N	Y
10 Young	N	Y	N	N	Y
11 Castor	Y	Y	Y	Y	Y
12 Putnam	–	+	–	–	–
13 Buchanan	N	Y	N	N	Y
14 Mack	N	Y	N	N	N
15 Weldon	N	Y	N	N	N
16 Mahoney	–	+	+	–	+
17 Meek	Y	Y	Y	N	Y
18 Ros-Lehtinen	Y	Y	N	?	Y
19 Wexler	N	Y	Y	N	Y
20 Wasserman Schultz	Y	Y	Y	Y	Y
21 Diaz-Balart, L.	N	Y	N	Y	Y
22 Klein	N	?	Y	N	Y
23 Hastings	Y	Y	Y	Y	Y
24 Feeney	N	Y	N	N	N
25 Diaz-Balart, M.	N	Y	N	Y	Y
GEORGIA					
1 Kingston	N	Y	N	N	N
2 Bishop	Y	Y	Y	N	Y
3 Westmoreland	N	Y	N	N	N
4 Johnson	Y	Y	Y	N	?
5 Lewis	Y	Y	Y	N	Y
6 Price	N	Y	N	N	N
7 Linder	N	Y	N	N	N
8 Marshall	Y	Y	Y	N	Y
9 Deal	N	Y	N	N	N
10 Broun	N	N	N	N	N
11 Gingrey	N	Y	N	N	N
12 Barrow	Y	Y	Y	Y	Y
13 Scott	Y	Y	Y	N	Y
HAWAII					
1 Abercrombie	Y	Y	Y	Y	Y
2 Hirono	Y	Y	Y	Y	Y
IDAHO					
1 Sali	N	Y	N	N	N
2 Simpson	N	Y	N	N	Y
ILLINOIS					
1 Rush	?	?	?	?	?
2 Jackson	Y	Y	Y	Y	Y
3 Lipinski	Y	Y	Y	Y	Y
4 Gutierrez	Y	Y	Y	N	Y
5 Emanuel	Y	Y	Y	N	Y
6 Roskam	N	Y	N	N	Y
7 Davis	Y	Y	Y	N	Y
8 Bean	N	Y	Y	Y	Y
9 Schakowsky	Y	Y	Y	N	Y
10 Kirk	Y	Y	N	N	Y
11 Weller	N	Y	N	N	+
12 Costello	Y	Y	Y	N	Y
13 Biggert	N	Y	N	N	Y
14 Foster	Y	Y	Y	Y	Y
15 Johnson	Y	Y	N	N	Y

KEY

ND Northern Democrats, SD Southern Democrats
Southern states: Ala., Ark., Fla., Ga., Ky., La., Miss., N.C., Okla., S.C., Tenn., Texas, Va.

	455	456	457	458	459
16 Manzullo	N	Y	N	N	N
17 Hare	Y	Y	Y	N	Y
18 LaHood	Y	Y	Y	N	Y
19 Shimkus	N	Y	N	N	N
INDIANA					
1 Visclosky	Y	Y	Y	N	Y
2 Donnelly	Y	Y	Y	N	Y
3 Souder	N	Y	N	N	N
4 Buyer	N	Y	N	N	Y
5 Burton	N	Y	N	N	N
6 Pence	N	Y	N	N	N
7 Carson, A.	Y	Y	Y	N	Y
8 Ellsworth	Y	Y	Y	Y	Y
9 Hill	Y	Y	Y	Y	Y
IOWA					
1 Braley	Y	Y	Y	Y	Y
2 Loebsack	Y	Y	Y	Y	Y
3 Boswell	Y	Y	Y	Y	Y
4 Latham	N	Y	N	N	Y
5 King	?	Y	N	N	N
KANSAS					
1 Moran	N	Y	N	N	Y
2 Boyda	Y	?	Y	N	Y
3 Moore	Y	Y	Y	Y	Y
4 Tiahrt	N	Y	N	N	Y
KENTUCKY					
1 Whitfield	N	Y	N	N	Y
2 Lewis	N	Y	N	N	N
3 Yarmuth	Y	Y	?	N	Y
4 Davis	N	Y	N	N	N
5 Rogers	N	Y	N	N	Y
6 Chandler	Y	Y	Y	N	Y
LOUISIANA					
1 Scalise	N	Y	N	N	Y
2 Jefferson	Y	?	Y	N	Y
3 Melancon	Y	Y	Y	Y	Y
4 McCrery	N	Y	N	Y	N
5 Alexander	N	Y	N	N	Y
6 Cazayoux	Y	Y	Y	N	Y
7 Boustany	N	Y	N	N	Y
MAINE					
1 Allen	Y	Y	Y	Y	Y
2 Michaud	Y	Y	Y	Y	Y
MARYLAND					
1 Gilchrest	Y	Y	N	Y	?
2 Ruppersberger	Y	Y	Y	N	Y
3 Sarbanes	Y	Y	Y	N	Y
4 Edwards	Y	Y	Y	N	Y
5 Hoyer	Y	Y	Y	N	Y
6 Bartlett	N	Y	N	N	Y
7 Cummings	Y	Y	?	?	Y
8 Van Hollen	Y	Y	Y	N	Y
MASSACHUSETTS					
1 Olver	Y	Y	Y	Y	Y
2 Neal	Y	Y	Y	N	Y
3 McGovern	Y	Y	Y	N	Y
4 Frank	Y	Y	Y	Y	Y
5 Tsongas	Y	Y	Y	N	Y
6 Tierney	Y	Y	Y	N	Y
7 Markey	Y	Y	Y	Y	Y
8 Capuano	Y	Y	Y	Y	Y
9 Lynch	Y	Y	Y	Y	Y
10 Delahunt	Y	Y	?	?	Y
MICHIGAN					
1 Stupak	Y	Y	Y	Y	Y
2 Hoekstra	N	Y	N	N	N
3 Ehlers	N	Y	N	N	N
4 Camp	N	Y	N	N	Y
5 Kildee	Y	Y	Y	Y	Y
6 Upton	N	Y	N	N	Y
7 Walberg	N	Y	N	N	Y
8 Rogers	N	Y	N	N	N
9 Knollenberg	N	Y	N	N	Y
10 Miller	N	Y	N	N	Y
11 McCotter	N	?	?	?	?
12 Levin	Y	Y	Y	N	Y
13 Kilpatrick	Y	Y	Y	N	Y
14 Conyers	Y	Y	Y	N	Y
15 Dingell	Y	Y	Y	N	Y
MINNESOTA					
1 Walz	Y	Y	Y	N	Y
2 Kline	N	Y	N	N	N
3 Ramstad	N	Y	N	N	Y
4 McCollum	Y	Y	Y	N	Y

	455	456	457	458	459
5 Ellison	Y	Y	Y	N	Y
6 Bachmann	N	Y	N	N	N
7 Peterson	Y	Y	Y	N	Y
8 Oberstar	Y	Y	Y	N	Y
MISSISSIPPI					
1 Childers	Y	Y	Y	N	Y
2 Thompson	Y	Y	Y	N	Y
3 Pickering	N	Y	N	N	Y
4 Taylor	Y	Y	Y	N	Y
MISSOURI					
1 Clay	Y	Y	Y	Y	Y
2 Akin	N	Y	N	N	N
3 Carnahan	Y	Y	Y	N	Y
4 Skelton	Y	Y	Y	N	Y
5 Cleaver	Y	Y	Y	N	Y
6 Graves	N	Y	N	N	Y
7 Blunt	N	Y	N	N	N
8 Emerson	N	Y	N	N	Y
9 Hulshof	N	Y	N	N	N
MONTANA					
AL Rehberg	N	Y	N	N	Y
NEBRASKA					
1 Fortenberry	N	Y	N	N	Y
2 Terry	N	Y	N	N	Y
3 Smith	N	Y	N	N	N
NEVADA					
1 Berkley	Y	Y	Y	N	Y
2 Heller	N	Y	N	N	Y
3 Porter	N	Y	N	N	Y
NEW HAMPSHIRE					
1 Shea-Porter	Y	Y	Y	N	Y
2 Hodes	Y	Y	Y	Y	Y
NEW JERSEY					
1 Andrews	Y	Y	Y	Y	Y
2 LoBiondo	N	Y	N	N	Y
3 Saxton	N	Y	N	N	Y
4 Smith	Y	Y	N	N	Y
5 Garrett	N	Y	N	N	N
6 Pallone	Y	Y	Y	N	Y
7 Ferguson	N	Y	N	N	Y
8 Pascrell	Y	Y	Y	N	Y
9 Rothman	Y	Y	Y	N	Y
10 Payne	Y	Y	Y	N	Y
11 Frelinghuysen	N	Y	N	N	Y
12 Holt	Y	?	Y	N	Y
13 Sires	Y	Y	Y	Y	Y
NEW MEXICO					
1 Wilson	N	Y	N	N	N
2 Pearce	N	Y	N	N	Y
3 Udall	Y	Y	Y	N	Y
NEW YORK					
1 Bishop	Y	Y	Y	N	Y
2 Israel	Y	Y	Y	N	Y
3 King	N	Y	N	Y	Y
4 McCarthy	Y	Y	Y	N	Y
5 Ackerman	Y	Y	Y	N	Y
6 Meeks	Y	Y	Y	N	Y
7 Crowley	Y	Y	Y	N	Y
8 Nadler	Y	Y	Y	N	Y
9 Weiner	Y	Y	Y	N	Y
10 Towns	Y	Y	Y	Y	Y
11 Clarke	Y	Y	Y	N	Y
12 Velázquez	Y	Y	Y	Y	Y
13 Fossella	N	Y	?	?	?
14 Maloney	Y	Y	Y	N	Y
15 Rangel	Y	Y	Y	N	Y
16 Serrano	Y	Y	Y	N	Y
17 Engel	Y	Y	Y	N	Y
18 Lowey	Y	Y	Y	N	Y
19 Hall	Y	Y	Y	N	Y
20 Gillibrand	Y	Y	Y	N	Y
21 McNulty	Y	Y	Y	N	Y
22 Hinchey	Y	Y	Y	N	Y
23 McHugh	N	Y	N	Y	Y
24 Arcuri	Y	Y	Y	N	Y
25 Walsh	N	Y	N	Y	Y
26 Reynolds	N	Y	N	Y	Y
27 Higgins	Y	Y	Y	N	Y
28 Slaughter	Y	Y	Y	N	Y
29 Kuhl	N	Y	N	Y	Y
NORTH CAROLINA					
1 Butterfield	Y	Y	Y	N	Y
2 Etheridge	Y	Y	Y	N	Y
3 Jones	Y	Y	Y	N	Y
4 Price	Y	Y	Y	N	Y

	455	456	457	458	459
5 Foxx	N	Y	N	N	N
6 Coble	N	Y	N	N	N
7 McIntyre	Y	Y	Y	N	Y
8 Hayes	Y	Y	N	N	Y
9 Myrick	N	Y	N	N	N
10 McHenry	N	Y	N	N	N
11 Shuler	Y	Y	Y	N	Y
12 Watt	Y	Y	Y	N	Y
13 Miller	Y	Y	Y	N	Y
NORTH DAKOTA					
AL Pomeroy	Y	Y	Y	Y	Y
OHIO					
1 Chabot	N	Y	N	N	N
2 Schmidt	N	Y	N	N	N
3 Turner	N	Y	N	N	N
4 Jordan	N	Y	N	N	N
5 Latta	N	Y	N	N	N
6 Wilson	Y	Y	Y	Y	Y
7 Hobson	N	Y	N	N	Y
8 Boehner	N	Y	N	N	N
9 Kaptur	Y	Y	Y	N	Y
10 Kucinich	Y	Y	Y	N	Y
11 Tubbs Jones	Y	Y	Y	N	Y
12 Tiberi	N	Y	N	N	Y
13 Sutton	Y	Y	?	?	Y
14 LaTourette	N	Y	N	Y	Y
15 Pryce	?	?	N	N	Y
16 Regula	N	Y	N	N	Y
17 Ryan	Y	Y	Y	N	Y
18 Space	Y	Y	Y	N	Y
OKLAHOMA					
1 Sullivan	N	Y	?	N	Y
2 Boren	N	Y	Y	N	Y
3 Lucas	N	Y	N	N	Y
4 Cole	N	Y	N	Y	N
5 Fallin	N	Y	N	N	Y
OREGON					
1 Wu	Y	Y	Y	N	Y
2 Walden	N	Y	N	N	Y
3 Blumenauer	Y	Y	Y	N	Y
4 DeFazio	Y	Y	Y	N	Y
5 Hooley	Y	Y	Y	N	Y
PENNSYLVANIA					
1 Brady	Y	Y	Y	Y	Y
2 Fattah	Y	Y	Y	N	Y
3 English	N	Y	N	N	Y
4 Altmire	Y	Y	Y	N	Y
5 Peterson	N	Y	?	?	N
6 Gerlach	N	Y	N	N	Y
7 Sestak	Y	Y	Y	N	Y
8 Murphy, P.	Y	Y	Y	N	Y
9 Shuster	N	Y	N	N	N
10 Carney	Y	Y	Y	N	Y
11 Kanjorski	Y	Y	Y	N	Y
12 Murtha	Y	Y	Y	N	Y
13 Schwartz	Y	Y	Y	N	Y
14 Doyle	Y	Y	Y	N	Y
15 Dent	N	Y	N	N	Y
16 Pitts	N	Y	N	N	N
17 Holden	Y	Y	Y	N	Y
18 Murphy, T.	N	Y	N	N	Y
19 Platts	N	Y	N	N	Y
RHODE ISLAND					
1 Kennedy	Y	Y	Y	Y	Y
2 Langevin	Y	Y	Y	N	Y
SOUTH CAROLINA					
1 Brown	N	Y	N	N	Y
2 Wilson	N	Y	N	N	N
3 Barrett	N	Y	N	N	N
4 Inglis	N	N	N	N	N
5 Spratt	Y	Y	Y	N	Y
6 Clyburn	Y	Y	Y	Y	Y
SOUTH DAKOTA					
AL Herseth Sandlin	Y	Y	Y	Y	Y
TENNESSEE					
1 Davis, D.	N	Y	N	N	N
2 Duncan	N	Y	N	N	N
3 Wamp	N	Y	N	N	N
4 Davis, L.	Y	Y	Y	N	Y
5 Cooper	Y	Y	Y	N	Y
6 Gordon	Y	Y	Y	N	Y
7 Blackburn	N	Y	N	N	N
8 Tanner	Y	Y	Y	N	Y
9 Cohen	Y	Y	Y	N	Y

	455	456	457	458	459
TEXAS					
1 Gohmert	N	Y	?	N	N
2 Poe	N	N	N	N	N
3 Johnson, S.	N	Y	N	N	N
4 Hall	N	?	N	Y	N
5 Hensarling	N	N	N	N	N
6 Barton	N	Y	N	Y	N
7 Culberson	N	Y	N	N	Y
8 Brady	N	Y	N	N	N
9 Green, A.	Y	Y	Y	N	Y
10 McCaul	N	Y	N	N	N
11 Conaway	N	Y	N	N	N
12 Granger	N	Y	N	N	N
13 Thornberry	N	Y	N	N	N
14 Paul	N	N	N	N	N
15 Hinojosa	Y	Y	Y	N	Y
16 Reyes	Y	Y	Y	Y	Y
17 Edwards	Y	Y	Y	N	Y
18 Jackson Lee	Y	Y	Y	N	Y
19 Neugebauer	N	N	N	N	N
20 Gonzalez	Y	Y	Y	Y	Y
21 Smith	N	Y	N	N	N
22 Lampson	?	?	?	?	?
23 Rodriguez	Y	Y	Y	Y	Y
24 Marchant	N	N	N	N	N
25 Doggett	Y	Y	Y	N	Y
26 Burgess	N	Y	N	N	N
27 Ortiz	Y	Y	Y	Y	Y
28 Cuellar	Y	Y	Y	Y	Y
29 Green, G.	N	Y	Y	N	Y
30 Johnson, E.	Y	Y	Y	N	Y
31 Carter	N	Y	N	N	N
32 Sessions	N	Y	N	N	N
UTAH					
1 Bishop	N	Y	N	Y	N
2 Matheson	Y	Y	Y	N	Y
3 Cannon	?	?	?	?	?
VERMONT					
AL Welch	Y	Y	Y	Y	Y
VIRGINIA					
1 Wittman	N	Y	N	N	N
2 Drake	N	Y	N	N	N
3 Scott	Y	Y	Y	N	Y
4 Forbes	N	Y	N	N	N
5 Goode	N	Y	N	N	Y
6 Goodlatte	N	Y	N	N	N
7 Cantor	N	Y	?	N	Y
8 Moran	Y	Y	Y	N	Y
9 Boucher	Y	Y	Y	Y	Y
10 Wolf	N	Y	N	N	N
11 Davis	N	Y	N	Y	Y
WASHINGTON					
1 Inslee	Y	Y	Y	N	Y
2 Larsen	Y	Y	Y	N	Y
3 Baird	Y	Y	Y	N	Y
4 Hastings	N	Y	N	N	Y
5 McMorris Rodgers	N	Y	N	N	Y
6 Dicks	Y	Y	Y	N	Y
7 McDermott	Y	Y	Y	N	Y
8 Reichert	N	Y	N	Y	Y
9 Smith	Y	Y	Y	N	Y
WEST VIRGINIA					
1 Mollohan	Y	Y	Y	Y	Y
2 Capito	N	Y	N	N	Y
3 Rahall	Y	Y	Y	N	Y
WISCONSIN					
1 Ryan	N	Y	N	N	N
2 Baldwin	Y	Y	Y	Y	Y
3 Kind	Y	?	Y	N	Y
4 Moore	Y	Y	Y	N	Y
5 Sensenbrenner	N	Y	N	N	N
6 Petri	N	Y	N	N	Y
7 Obey	Y	Y	Y	N	Y
8 Kagen	Y	Y	Y	Y	Y
WYOMING					
AL Cubin	?	?	?	?	?
DELEGATES					
Faleomavaega (A.S.)					
Norton (D.C.)					
Bordallo (Guam)					
Fortuño (P.R.)					
Christensen (V.I.)					

HOUSE VOTES

IN THE HOUSE | By Vote Number

460. **HR 3195. Disabilities Act Definitions/Passage.** Passage of the bill that would amend the Americans with Disabilities Act to redefine a disability as a physical or mental impairment that materially restricts one or more major life activities. It would extend protections to people with disabilities not immediately evident, such as those of the immune, digestive and neurological systems. It would clarify that the effects of "mitigating measures," such as hearing aids and prosthetics, could not be used in weighing how a person's disability affects life activities. Passed 402-17: R 174-17; D 228-0 (ND 173-0, SD 55-0). A "yea" was a vote in support of the president's position. June 25, 2008.

461. **HR 4040. Consumer Product Safety Commission Overhaul/ Motion to Instruct.** Kirk, R-Ill., motion to instruct conferees to insist on the provisions contained in the House-passed bill regarding the definition of "children's product." Motion agreed to 415-0: R 189-0; D 226-0 (ND 172-0, SD 54-0). June 25, 2008.

462. **HR 6052. Public Transportation Grants/Previous Question.** Castor, D-Fla., motion to order the previous question (thus ending debate and possibility of amendment) on adoption of the rule (H Res 1304) to provide for House floor consideration of the bill that would authorize $1.7 billion for grants in fiscal 2008 and fiscal 2009 for transit agencies that reduce fares or expand public transportation services. Motion agreed to 228-198: R 2-194; D 226-4 (ND 170-2, SD 56-2). June 26, 2008.

463. **HR 6052. Public Transportation Grants/Rule.** Adoption of the rule (H Res 1304) to provide for House floor consideration of the bill that would authorize $1.7 billion for grants in fiscal 2008 and fiscal 2009 for transit agencies that reduce fares or expand public transportation services. Adopted 230-196: R 1-195; D 229-1 (ND 171-1, SD 58-0). June 26, 2008.

464. **H Res 1291. American GI Forum Anniversary/Adoption.** Filner, D-Calif., motion to suspend the rules and adopt the resolution that would support the goals, ideals and deeds of the American GI Forum, recognize the forum's 60th anniversary, and recognize the need for equal access to veterans' benefits for all who have served. Motion agreed to 421-0: R 195-0; D 226-0 (ND 170-0, SD 56-0). A two-thirds majority of those present and voting (281 in this case) is required for adoption under suspension of the rules. June 26, 2008.

465. **HR 6052. Public Transportation Grants/Conventional Fuel Purchases.** Mahoney, D-Fla., amendment that would allow federal agencies to contract to purchase a generally available fuel that is not alternative or synthetic or produced from a non-conventional source if the contract does not require providing alternative fuels, the contract's purpose is not to obtain alternative fuels and the contract does not provide incentives for a refinery upgrade or expansion. Adopted in Committee of the Whole 421-0: R 191-0; D 230-0 (ND 172-0, SD 58-0). June 26, 2008.

	460	461	462	463	464	465
ALABAMA						
1 Bonner	Y	Y	N	N	Y	Y
2 Everett	Y	Y	N	N	Y	Y
3 Rogers	Y	Y	N	N	Y	Y
4 Aderholt	Y	Y	N	N	Y	Y
5 Cramer	Y	Y	Y	Y	?	Y
6 Bachus	Y	Y	N	N	Y	Y
7 Davis	Y	Y	Y	Y	Y	Y
ALASKA						
AL Young	Y	Y	N	N	Y	Y
ARIZONA						
1 Renzi	Y	Y	N	N	Y	Y
2 Franks	Y	Y	N	N	Y	Y
3 Shadegg	Y	Y	N	N	Y	Y
4 Pastor	Y	Y	Y	Y	Y	Y
5 Mitchell	Y	Y	Y	Y	Y	Y
6 Flake	N	Y	N	N	Y	Y
7 Grijalva	Y	Y	Y	Y	Y	Y
8 Giffords	Y	Y	Y	Y	Y	Y
ARKANSAS						
1 Berry	Y	Y	Y	Y	Y	Y
2 Snyder	?	?	Y	Y	Y	Y
3 Boozman	Y	Y	N	N	Y	Y
4 Ross	Y	Y	Y	Y	Y	Y
CALIFORNIA						
1 Thompson	Y	Y	Y	Y	Y	Y
2 Herger	Y	Y	N	N	Y	Y
3 Lungren	Y	Y	N	N	Y	Y
4 Doolittle	N	Y	N	N	Y	?
5 Matsui	Y	Y	Y	Y	Y	Y
6 Woolsey	Y	Y	Y	Y	Y	Y
7 Miller, George	Y	Y	Y	Y	Y	Y
8 Pelosi						
9 Lee	Y	Y	Y	Y	Y	Y
10 Tauscher	Y	Y	Y	Y	Y	Y
11 McNerney	Y	Y	Y	Y	Y	Y
12 Speier	?	?	Y	Y	Y	Y
13 Stark	Y	Y	Y	Y	Y	Y
14 Eshoo	Y	Y	Y	Y	Y	Y
15 Honda	Y	Y	Y	Y	Y	Y
16 Lofgren	Y	Y	Y	Y	Y	Y
17 Farr	Y	Y	Y	Y	Y	Y
18 Cardoza	Y	Y	Y	Y	Y	Y
19 Radanovich	Y	Y	N	N	Y	Y
20 Costa	Y	Y	Y	Y	Y	Y
21 Nunes	Y	Y	N	N	Y	Y
22 McCarthy	Y	Y	N	N	Y	Y
23 Capps	Y	Y	Y	Y	Y	Y
24 Gallegly	Y	Y	N	N	Y	Y
25 McKeon	Y	Y	N	N	Y	Y
26 Dreier	Y	Y	N	N	Y	Y
27 Sherman	Y	Y	Y	Y	Y	Y
28 Berman	Y	Y	Y	Y	Y	Y
29 Schiff	Y	Y	Y	Y	Y	Y
30 Waxman	Y	Y	Y	Y	Y	Y
31 Becerra	Y	Y	Y	Y	Y	Y
32 Solis	Y	Y	Y	Y	?	Y
33 Watson	Y	Y	Y	Y	Y	Y
34 Roybal-Allard	Y	Y	Y	Y	Y	Y
35 Waters	Y	Y	Y	Y	Y	Y
36 Harman	Y	Y	Y	Y	Y	Y
37 Richardson	Y	Y	Y	Y	Y	Y
38 Napolitano	Y	Y	Y	Y	Y	Y
39 Sánchez, Linda	Y	Y	Y	Y	Y	Y
40 Royce	Y	Y	N	N	Y	Y
41 Lewis	Y	Y	N	N	Y	Y
42 Miller, Gary	Y	Y	N	N	Y	Y
43 Baca	Y	Y	Y	Y	Y	Y
44 Calvert	Y	Y	N	N	Y	?
45 Bono Mack	Y	Y	N	N	Y	Y
46 Rohrabacher	Y	Y	N	N	Y	Y
47 Sanchez, Loretta	Y	Y	Y	Y	Y	Y
48 Campbell	N	Y	N	N	Y	Y
49 Issa	Y	Y	N	N	Y	Y
50 Bilbray	Y	Y	N	N	Y	Y
51 Filner	Y	Y	Y	Y	Y	Y
52 Hunter	Y	Y	N	N	Y	Y
53 Davis	Y	Y	Y	Y	Y	Y

	460	461	462	463	464	465
COLORADO						
1 DeGette	Y	Y	Y	Y	Y	Y
2 Udall	Y	Y	Y	Y	Y	Y
3 Salazar	Y	Y	Y	Y	Y	Y
4 Musgrave	Y	Y	N	N	Y	Y
5 Lamborn	Y	Y	N	N	Y	Y
6 Tancredo	N	Y	N	N	Y	?
7 Perlmutter	Y	Y	Y	Y	Y	Y
CONNECTICUT						
1 Larson	Y	Y	Y	Y	Y	Y
2 Courtney	Y	Y	Y	Y	Y	Y
3 DeLauro	Y	Y	Y	Y	Y	?
4 Shays	Y	Y	N	N	Y	Y
5 Murphy	Y	Y	Y	Y	Y	Y
DELAWARE						
AL Castle	Y	Y	Y	N	Y	Y
FLORIDA						
1 Miller	Y	Y	N	N	Y	Y
2 Boyd	Y	Y	Y	Y	Y	Y
3 Brown	Y	Y	Y	Y	Y	Y
4 Crenshaw	Y	Y	N	N	Y	Y
5 Brown-Waite	Y	Y	N	N	Y	Y
6 Stearns	Y	Y	N	N	Y	Y
7 Mica	Y	Y	N	N	Y	Y
8 Keller	Y	Y	N	N	Y	?
9 Bilirakis	Y	Y	N	N	Y	Y
10 Young	Y	Y	Y	Y	Y	Y
11 Castor	Y	Y	Y	Y	Y	Y
12 Putnam	+	+	N	N	Y	Y
13 Buchanan	Y	Y	N	N	Y	Y
14 Mack	Y	Y	N	N	Y	Y
15 Weldon	N	Y	N	N	Y	Y
16 Mahoney	+	+	Y	Y	Y	Y
17 Meek	Y	Y	Y	Y	Y	Y
18 Ros-Lehtinen	Y	Y	N	N	Y	Y
19 Wexler	Y	Y	Y	Y	Y	?
20 Wasserman Schultz	Y	Y	Y	Y	Y	Y
21 Diaz-Balart, L.	Y	Y	N	N	Y	Y
22 Klein	Y	Y	Y	Y	Y	Y
23 Hastings	Y	Y	Y	Y	Y	Y
24 Feeney	Y	Y	N	N	Y	Y
25 Diaz-Balart, M.	Y	Y	N	N	Y	Y
GEORGIA						
1 Kingston	N	Y	N	N	Y	Y
2 Bishop	Y	Y	Y	Y	Y	Y
3 Westmoreland	N	Y	N	N	Y	Y
4 Johnson	+	?	Y	Y	Y	Y
5 Lewis	Y	Y	Y	Y	Y	Y
6 Price	N	Y	N	?	?	Y
7 Linder	N	Y	N	N	Y	Y
8 Marshall	Y	Y	N	Y	Y	Y
9 Deal	Y	Y	N	N	Y	Y
10 Broun	N	Y	N	N	Y	Y
11 Gingrey	Y	Y	N	N	Y	Y
12 Barrow	Y	Y	Y	Y	Y	Y
13 Scott	Y	Y	Y	Y	Y	Y
HAWAII						
1 Abercrombie	Y	Y	Y	Y	Y	Y
2 Hirono	Y	Y	Y	Y	Y	Y
IDAHO						
1 Sali	Y	Y	N	N	Y	Y
2 Simpson	Y	?	N	N	Y	Y
ILLINOIS						
1 Rush	?	?	?	?	?	?
2 Jackson	Y	Y	Y	Y	Y	Y
3 Lipinski	Y	Y	Y	Y	Y	Y
4 Gutierrez	Y	Y	Y	Y	?	Y
5 Emanuel	Y	Y	Y	Y	Y	Y
6 Roskam	Y	Y	N	N	Y	Y
7 Davis	Y	Y	Y	Y	Y	Y
8 Bean	Y	Y	Y	Y	Y	Y
9 Schakowsky	Y	Y	Y	Y	Y	Y
10 Kirk	Y	Y	N	N	Y	Y
11 Weller	+	Y	N	N	Y	?
12 Costello	Y	Y	Y	Y	Y	Y
13 Biggert	Y	Y	N	N	Y	Y
14 Foster	Y	Y	Y	Y	Y	Y
15 Johnson	Y	Y	N	N	Y	Y

KEY	**Republicans**	Democrats			
Y	Voted for (yea)		X Paired against		C Voted "present" to avoid possible conflict of interest
#	Paired for		– Announced against		
+	Announced for		P Voted "present"		? Did not vote or otherwise make a position known
N	Voted against (nay)				

ND Northern Democrats, SD Southern Democrats
Southern states: Ala., Ark., Fla., Ga., Ky., La., Miss., N.C., Okla., S.C., Tenn., Texas, Va.

	460	461	462	463	464	465
16 **Manzullo**	Y	Y	N	N	Y	Y
17 Hare	Y	Y	Y	Y	Y	Y
18 **LaHood**	Y	Y	N	N	Y	Y
19 **Shimkus**	Y	Y	N	N	Y	Y
INDIANA						
1 Visclosky	Y	Y	Y	Y	Y	Y
2 Donnelly	Y	Y	N	Y	Y	Y
3 **Souder**	?	Y	N	N	Y	Y
4 **Buyer**	Y	Y	N	N	Y	Y
5 **Burton**	Y	Y	N	N	Y	Y
6 **Pence**	Y	Y	N	N	Y	Y
7 Carson, A.	Y	Y	Y	Y	Y	Y
8 Ellsworth	Y	Y	Y	Y	Y	Y
9 Hill	Y	Y	N	N	Y	Y
IOWA						
1 Braley	Y	Y	Y	Y	Y	Y
2 Loebsack	Y	?	Y	Y	Y	Y
3 Boswell	Y	Y	Y	Y	Y	Y
4 **Latham**	Y	Y	N	N	Y	Y
5 **King**	Y	Y	N	N	Y	Y
KANSAS						
1 **Moran**	Y	Y	N	N	Y	Y
2 Boyda	Y	Y	Y	Y	Y	Y
3 Moore	Y	Y	Y	Y	Y	Y
4 **Tiahrt**	Y	Y	N	N	Y	Y
KENTUCKY						
1 **Whitfield**	Y	Y	N	N	Y	Y
2 **Lewis**	Y	Y	N	N	Y	?
3 Yarmuth	Y	Y	Y	Y	Y	Y
4 **Davis**	Y	Y	N	N	Y	Y
5 **Rogers**	Y	Y	N	N	Y	Y
6 Chandler	Y	Y	Y	Y	Y	Y
LOUISIANA						
1 **Scalise**	Y	Y	N	N	Y	Y
2 Jefferson	Y	?	Y	Y	Y	Y
3 Melancon	Y	Y	Y	Y	Y	Y
4 **McCrery**	Y	Y	N	N	Y	Y
5 **Alexander**	Y	Y	N	N	Y	Y
6 Cazayoux	Y	Y	Y	Y	Y	Y
7 **Boustany**	Y	Y	N	N	Y	Y
MAINE						
1 Allen	Y	Y	Y	Y	Y	Y
2 Michaud	Y	Y	Y	Y	Y	Y
MARYLAND						
1 **Gilchrest**	?	?	N	N	Y	Y
2 Ruppersberger	Y	Y	Y	Y	Y	Y
3 Sarbanes	Y	Y	Y	Y	Y	Y
4 Edwards	Y	Y	Y	Y	Y	Y
5 Hoyer	Y	Y	Y	Y	Y	Y
6 **Bartlett**	Y	Y	N	N	Y	Y
7 Cummings	Y	Y	Y	Y	Y	Y
8 Van Hollen	Y	Y	Y	Y	Y	Y
MASSACHUSETTS						
1 Olver	Y	Y	Y	Y	Y	Y
2 Neal	Y	Y	Y	Y	Y	Y
3 McGovern	Y	Y	Y	Y	Y	Y
4 Frank	Y	Y	Y	Y	Y	Y
5 Tsongas	Y	Y	Y	Y	Y	Y
6 Tierney	Y	Y	Y	Y	Y	Y
7 Markey	Y	Y	Y	Y	Y	Y
8 Capuano	Y	Y	Y	Y	Y	Y
9 Lynch	Y	Y	Y	Y	Y	Y
10 Delahunt	Y	Y	Y	Y	Y	Y
MICHIGAN						
1 Stupak	Y	Y	?	Y	Y	Y
2 **Hoekstra**	Y	Y	N	N	Y	Y
3 **Ehlers**	Y	Y	N	N	Y	Y
4 **Camp**	Y	Y	N	N	Y	Y
5 Kildee	Y	Y	Y	Y	Y	Y
6 **Upton**	Y	Y	N	N	Y	Y
7 **Walberg**	Y	Y	N	N	Y	Y
8 **Rogers**	Y	Y	N	N	Y	Y
9 **Knollenberg**	Y	Y	N	N	Y	Y
10 **Miller**	Y	Y	N	N	Y	Y
11 **McCotter**	?	?	N	N	Y	Y
12 Levin	Y	Y	Y	Y	Y	Y
13 Kilpatrick	Y	Y	Y	Y	Y	Y
14 Conyers	Y	Y	Y	Y	Y	Y
15 Dingell	Y	Y	Y	Y	Y	Y
MINNESOTA						
1 Walz	Y	Y	Y	Y	Y	Y
2 **Kline**	Y	Y	N	N	Y	Y
3 **Ramstad**	Y	Y	N	N	Y	Y
4 McCollum	Y	Y	Y	Y	Y	Y

	460	461	462	463	464	465
5 Ellison	Y	Y	Y	Y	Y	+
6 **Bachmann**	Y	Y	N	N	Y	Y
7 Peterson	Y	Y	Y	Y	Y	Y
8 Oberstar	Y	Y	Y	Y	Y	Y
MISSISSIPPI						
1 Childers	Y	Y	N	Y	Y	Y
2 Thompson	Y	Y	Y	Y	Y	Y
3 **Pickering**	Y	Y	N	N	Y	Y
4 Taylor	Y	Y	Y	?	?	Y
MISSOURI						
1 Clay	Y	Y	Y	Y	Y	Y
2 **Akin**	Y	Y	N	N	Y	Y
3 Carnahan	Y	Y	Y	Y	Y	Y
4 Skelton	Y	Y	Y	Y	Y	Y
5 Cleaver	Y	Y	Y	Y	Y	Y
6 **Graves**	Y	Y	N	N	Y	Y
7 **Blunt**	Y	Y	N	N	Y	Y
8 **Emerson**	Y	Y	N	N	Y	Y
9 **Hulshof**	Y	Y	N	N	Y	Y
MONTANA						
AL **Rehberg**	Y	Y	N	N	Y	Y
NEBRASKA						
1 **Fortenberry**	Y	Y	N	N	Y	Y
2 **Terry**	Y	Y	N	N	Y	Y
3 **Smith**	Y	Y	N	N	Y	Y
NEVADA						
1 Berkley	Y	Y	Y	Y	Y	Y
2 **Heller**	Y	Y	N	N	Y	Y
3 **Porter**	Y	Y	N	N	Y	Y
NEW HAMPSHIRE						
1 Shea-Porter	Y	Y	Y	Y	Y	Y
2 Hodes	Y	Y	Y	Y	Y	Y
NEW JERSEY						
1 Andrews	Y	Y	Y	Y	Y	Y
2 **LoBiondo**	Y	Y	N	N	Y	Y
3 **Saxton**	Y	Y	N	N	Y	Y
4 **Smith**	Y	Y	N	N	Y	Y
5 **Garrett**	N	Y	N	N	Y	Y
6 Pallone	Y	Y	Y	Y	Y	Y
7 **Ferguson**	Y	Y	N	N	Y	Y
8 Pascrell	Y	Y	Y	Y	Y	Y
9 Rothman	Y	Y	Y	Y	Y	Y
10 Payne	Y	Y	Y	Y	Y	Y
11 **Frelinghuysen**	Y	Y	N	N	?	Y
12 Holt	Y	Y	Y	Y	Y	Y
13 Sires	Y	Y	Y	Y	Y	Y
NEW MEXICO						
1 **Wilson**	Y	Y	N	N	Y	Y
2 **Pearce**	Y	Y	N	N	Y	Y
3 Udall	Y	Y	Y	Y	Y	Y
NEW YORK						
1 Bishop	Y	Y	Y	Y	Y	Y
2 Israel	Y	Y	Y	Y	Y	Y
3 **King**	Y	Y	N	N	Y	Y
4 McCarthy	Y	Y	Y	Y	Y	Y
5 Ackerman	Y	Y	Y	Y	Y	Y
6 Meeks	Y	Y	Y	Y	Y	Y
7 Crowley	Y	Y	Y	Y	Y	Y
8 Nadler	Y	Y	Y	Y	Y	Y
9 Weiner	Y	Y	Y	Y	Y	Y
10 Towns	Y	Y	Y	Y	Y	Y
11 Clarke	Y	Y	Y	Y	Y	Y
12 Velázquez	Y	Y	Y	Y	?	Y
13 **Fossella**	+	?	N	N	Y	Y
14 Maloney	Y	Y	Y	Y	Y	Y
15 Rangel	Y	Y	Y	?	Y	Y
16 Serrano	Y	Y	Y	Y	Y	Y
17 Engel	Y	Y	Y	Y	Y	Y
18 Lowey	Y	Y	Y	Y	Y	Y
19 Hall	Y	Y	Y	Y	Y	Y
20 Gillibrand	Y	Y	Y	Y	Y	Y
21 McNulty	Y	Y	Y	Y	Y	Y
22 Hinchey	Y	Y	Y	Y	Y	Y
23 **McHugh**	Y	Y	N	N	Y	Y
24 Arcuri	Y	Y	Y	Y	Y	Y
25 **Walsh**	Y	?	N	N	Y	Y
26 **Reynolds**	Y	Y	N	N	Y	Y
27 Higgins	Y	Y	Y	Y	Y	Y
28 Slaughter	?	Y	Y	Y	Y	Y
29 **Kuhl**	Y	Y	N	N	Y	Y
NORTH CAROLINA						
1 Butterfield	Y	Y	Y	Y	Y	Y
2 Etheridge	Y	Y	Y	Y	Y	Y
3 **Jones**	Y	Y	N	N	Y	Y
4 Price	Y	Y	Y	Y	Y	Y

	460	461	462	463	464	465
5 **Foxx**	Y	Y	N	N	Y	Y
6 **Coble**	Y	Y	N	N	Y	Y
7 McIntyre	Y	Y	Y	Y	Y	Y
8 **Hayes**	Y	Y	N	N	Y	Y
9 **Myrick**	Y	Y	N	N	Y	Y
10 **McHenry**	Y	Y	N	N	Y	Y
11 Shuler	Y	Y	Y	Y	Y	Y
12 Watt	Y	Y	Y	Y	Y	Y
13 Miller	Y	Y	Y	Y	Y	Y
NORTH DAKOTA						
AL Pomeroy	Y	Y	Y	Y	Y	Y
OHIO						
1 **Chabot**	Y	Y	N	N	Y	Y
2 **Schmidt**	Y	Y	N	N	Y	Y
3 **Turner**	Y	Y	N	N	Y	Y
4 **Jordan**	Y	Y	N	N	Y	Y
5 **Latta**	Y	Y	N	N	Y	Y
6 Wilson	Y	Y	Y	Y	Y	Y
7 **Hobson**	Y	Y	N	N	Y	Y
8 **Boehner**	Y	Y	N	N	Y	Y
9 Kaptur	Y	?	Y	Y	Y	Y
10 Kucinich	Y	Y	Y	Y	Y	Y
11 Tubbs Jones	Y	Y	Y	Y	Y	?
12 **Tiberi**	Y	Y	N	N	Y	Y
13 Sutton	Y	Y	Y	Y	Y	Y
14 **LaTourette**	Y	Y	N	N	Y	Y
15 **Pryce**	Y	Y	N	N	Y	Y
16 **Regula**	Y	Y	N	N	Y	Y
17 Ryan	Y	Y	Y	Y	Y	Y
18 Space	Y	Y	?	?	?	Y
OKLAHOMA						
1 **Sullivan**	Y	Y	N	N	Y	Y
2 Boren	Y	Y	Y	Y	Y	Y
3 **Lucas**	Y	Y	N	N	Y	Y
4 **Cole**	Y	Y	N	N	Y	Y
5 **Fallin**	Y	Y	N	N	Y	Y
OREGON						
1 Wu	Y	Y	Y	Y	Y	Y
2 **Walden**	Y	Y	N	N	Y	Y
3 Blumenauer	Y	Y	Y	Y	Y	Y
4 DeFazio	Y	Y	Y	Y	Y	Y
5 Hooley	Y	Y	Y	Y	Y	Y
PENNSYLVANIA						
1 Brady	Y	Y	Y	Y	Y	Y
2 Fattah	Y	Y	Y	Y	Y	Y
3 **English**	Y	Y	N	N	Y	Y
4 Altmire	Y	Y	Y	Y	Y	Y
5 **Peterson**	Y	Y	N	N	Y	Y
6 **Gerlach**	Y	Y	N	N	Y	Y
7 Sestak	Y	Y	Y	Y	Y	Y
8 Murphy, P.	Y	Y	Y	Y	Y	Y
9 **Shuster**	Y	Y	N	N	Y	Y
10 Carney	Y	Y	Y	Y	Y	Y
11 Kanjorski	Y	Y	Y	Y	Y	Y
12 Murtha	Y	Y	Y	Y	?	Y
13 Schwartz	Y	Y	Y	Y	Y	Y
14 Doyle	Y	Y	Y	Y	Y	Y
15 **Dent**	Y	Y	N	N	Y	Y
16 **Pitts**	Y	Y	N	N	Y	Y
17 Holden	Y	Y	Y	Y	Y	Y
18 **Murphy, T.**	Y	Y	N	N	Y	Y
19 **Platts**	Y	Y	N	N	Y	Y
RHODE ISLAND						
1 Kennedy	Y	Y	Y	Y	Y	Y
2 Langevin	Y	Y	Y	Y	Y	Y
SOUTH CAROLINA						
1 **Brown**	Y	Y	N	N	Y	Y
2 **Wilson**	Y	Y	N	N	Y	Y
3 **Barrett**	Y	Y	N	N	Y	Y
4 **Inglis**	Y	Y	N	N	Y	Y
5 Spratt	Y	Y	Y	Y	Y	Y
6 Clyburn	Y	Y	Y	Y	Y	Y
SOUTH DAKOTA						
AL Herseth Sandlin	Y	Y	Y	Y	Y	Y
TENNESSEE						
1 **Davis, D.**	Y	Y	N	N	Y	Y
2 **Duncan**	N	Y	N	N	Y	Y
3 **Wamp**	Y	Y	N	N	Y	Y
4 Davis, L.	Y	Y	?	Y	Y	Y
5 Cooper	Y	Y	Y	Y	Y	Y
6 Gordon	Y	Y	Y	Y	Y	Y
7 **Blackburn**	Y	Y	N	N	Y	Y
8 Tanner	Y	Y	Y	Y	Y	Y
9 Cohen	Y	Y	Y	Y	Y	Y

	460	461	462	463	464	465
TEXAS						
1 **Gohmert**	N	Y	N	N	Y	Y
2 **Poe**	N	Y	N	N	Y	Y
3 **Johnson, S.**	Y	Y	N	N	Y	Y
4 **Hall**	Y	Y	N	N	Y	Y
5 **Hensarling**	N	Y	N	N	Y	Y
6 **Barton**	Y	Y	N	N	Y	Y
7 **Culberson**	Y	Y	N	N	Y	Y
8 **Brady**	Y	Y	N	N	Y	Y
9 Green, A.	Y	Y	Y	Y	Y	Y
10 **McCaul**	Y	Y	N	N	Y	Y
11 **Conaway**	Y	Y	N	N	Y	Y
12 **Granger**	Y	Y	N	N	Y	Y
13 **Thornberry**	Y	Y	N	N	Y	Y
14 **Paul**	N	Y	N	N	Y	Y
15 Hinojosa	Y	Y	Y	Y	Y	Y
16 Reyes	Y	Y	Y	Y	Y	Y
17 Edwards	Y	Y	Y	Y	Y	Y
18 Jackson Lee	Y	Y	Y	Y	Y	Y
19 **Neugebauer**	Y	Y	N	N	Y	Y
20 Gonzalez	Y	Y	Y	Y	Y	Y
21 **Smith**	Y	Y	N	N	Y	Y
22 Lampson	?	?	N	Y	Y	Y
23 Rodriguez	Y	Y	Y	Y	Y	Y
24 **Marchant**	N	?	N	N	Y	Y
25 Doggett	Y	Y	Y	Y	Y	Y
26 **Burgess**	Y	Y	?	N	Y	Y
27 Ortiz	Y	Y	Y	Y	Y	Y
28 Cuellar	Y	Y	Y	Y	Y	Y
29 Green, G.	Y	Y	Y	Y	Y	Y
30 Johnson, E.	Y	Y	Y	Y	Y	Y
31 **Carter**	Y	Y	N	N	Y	Y
32 **Sessions**	Y	Y	N	N	Y	Y
UTAH						
1 **Bishop**	Y	Y	N	N	Y	Y
2 Matheson	Y	Y	Y	Y	Y	Y
3 **Cannon**	?	?	?	?	?	?
VERMONT						
AL Welch	Y	Y	Y	Y	Y	Y
VIRGINIA						
1 **Wittman**	Y	Y	N	N	Y	Y
2 **Drake**	Y	Y	N	N	Y	Y
3 Scott	Y	Y	Y	Y	Y	Y
4 **Forbes**	Y	Y	?	?	?	?
5 **Goode**	Y	Y	N	N	Y	Y
6 **Goodlatte**	Y	Y	N	N	Y	Y
7 **Cantor**	Y	Y	N	N	Y	Y
8 Moran	Y	Y	Y	Y	Y	Y
9 Boucher	Y	Y	Y	Y	?	Y
10 **Wolf**	Y	Y	N	N	Y	Y
11 **Davis**	Y	Y	N	Y	Y	Y
WASHINGTON						
1 Inslee	Y	Y	Y	Y	Y	Y
2 Larsen	Y	Y	Y	Y	Y	Y
3 Baird	Y	Y	Y	Y	Y	Y
4 **Hastings**	Y	Y	N	N	Y	Y
5 **McMorris Rodgers**	Y	Y	N	N	Y	Y
6 Dicks	Y	Y	Y	Y	Y	Y
7 McDermott	Y	Y	+	+	Y	Y
8 **Reichert**	Y	Y	Y	N	Y	Y
9 Smith	Y	Y	Y	Y	Y	+
WEST VIRGINIA						
1 Mollohan	Y	Y	Y	Y	Y	Y
2 **Capito**	Y	Y	N	N	Y	Y
3 Rahall	Y	Y	Y	Y	Y	Y
WISCONSIN						
1 **Ryan**	Y	Y	N	N	Y	Y
2 Baldwin	Y	Y	Y	Y	Y	Y
3 Kind	Y	Y	Y	Y	Y	Y
4 Moore	Y	Y	Y	Y	Y	Y
5 **Sensenbrenner**	Y	Y	N	N	Y	Y
6 **Petri**	Y	Y	N	N	Y	Y
7 Obey	Y	Y	Y	Y	Y	Y
8 Kagen	Y	Y	Y	Y	Y	Y
WYOMING						
AL **Cubin**	?	?	N	N	Y	Y
DELEGATES						
Faleomavaega (A.S.)						?
Norton (D.C.)						+
Bordallo (Guam)						Y
Fortuño (P.R.)						?
Christensen (V.I.)						Y

IN THE HOUSE | By Vote Number

466. **HR 6052. Public Transportation Grants/Recommit.** Walden, R-Ore., motion to recommit the bill to the Transportation and Infrastructure Committee with instructions that it be reported back promptly with language that would direct funds from the bill's grants to be used for school bus transportation with preference to rural areas where the buses travel greater distances and are adversely affected by high fuel prices. Motion rejected 199-221: R 185-4; D 14-217 (ND 8-165, SD 6-52). June 26, 2008.

467. **HR 6052. Public Transportation Grants/Passage.** Passage of the bill that would authorize $1.7 billion for grants in fiscal 2008 and 2009 for transit agencies that reduce fares or expand public transportation services, as well as an additional $750 million each year for urbanized area formula grants and $100 million per year for formula grants to rural areas. Transit agencies could use the grants to offset the increased cost of fuel and educate commuters on transportation alternatives. The bill would allow federal funds to be used to cover a greater portion of the cost of certain projects and expenses, such as expanding parking facilities and providing grants for clean- or alternative-fuel facilities and equipment for transit buses, ferries or locomotives. It also would extend a transportation benefits program for federal employees across the nation and establish a pilot program for vanpool projects. Passed 322-98: R 91-98; D 231-0 (ND 173-0, SD 58-0). A "nay" was a vote in support of the president's position. June 26, 2008.

468. **HR 6377. Curb Oil Speculation/Passage.** Peterson, D-Minn., motion to suspend the rules and pass the bill that would direct the Commodity Futures Trading Commission to immediately curb the role of "excessive" speculation in oil futures trading. Motion agreed to 402-19: R 170-19; D 232-0 (ND 174-0, SD 58-0). A two-thirds majority of those present and voting (281 in this case) is required for passage under suspension of the rules. June 26, 2008.

469. **HR 6251. Oil and Natural Gas Exploration Leases/Passage.** Rahall, D-W.Va., motion to suspend the rules and pass the bill that would require current holders of oil or natural gas exploration leases to develop or relinquish their existing leases before they could receive new ones. Leaseholders who do not comply could be subject to fines ranging from $500 to $25,000 a day. Motion rejected 223-195: R 11-176; D 212-19 (ND 171-2, SD 41-17). A two-thirds majority of those present and voting (279 in this case) is required for passage under suspension of the rules. A "nay" was a vote in support of the president's position. June 26, 2008.

470. **H Res 1098. Year of the American Veteran/Adoption.** Filner, D-Calif., motion to suspend the rules and adopt the resolution that would support the goals and ideals of the Year of the American Veteran and encourage Americans to acknowledge the sacrifices and contributions of veterans. Motion agreed to 409-0: R 182-0; D 227-0 (ND 169-0, SD 58-0). A two-thirds majority of those present and voting (273 in this case) is required for adoption under suspension of the rules. June 26, 2008.

	466	467	468	469	470
ALABAMA					
1 **Bonner**	Y	N	Y	N	Y
2 **Everett**	Y	?	?	?	?
3 **Rogers**	Y	Y	Y	Y	?
4 **Aderholt**	Y	?	Y	N	Y
5 Cramer	N	Y	Y	N	Y
6 **Bachus**	Y	Y	Y	N	Y
7 Davis	N	Y	Y	Y	Y
ALASKA					
AL **Young**	Y	Y	N	N	Y
ARIZONA					
1 **Renzi**	Y	Y	Y	N	Y
2 **Franks**	Y	N	N	N	Y
3 **Shadegg**	Y	N	Y	–	Y
4 Pastor	N	Y	Y	Y	Y
5 Mitchell	Y	Y	Y	Y	Y
6 **Flake**	Y	N	N	N	Y
7 Grijalva	N	Y	Y	Y	Y
8 Giffords	Y	Y	Y	Y	Y
ARKANSAS					
1 Berry	N	Y	Y	N	Y
2 Snyder	N	Y	Y	N	Y
3 **Boozman**	Y	Y	Y	N	Y
4 Ross	N	Y	Y	N	Y
CALIFORNIA					
1 Thompson	N	Y	Y	Y	Y
2 **Herger**	Y	N	Y	N	Y
3 **Lungren**	Y	N	Y	N	Y
4 **Doolittle**	?	?	?	?	?
5 Matsui	N	Y	Y	Y	Y
6 Woolsey	N	Y	Y	Y	Y
7 Miller, George	N	Y	Y	Y	Y
8 Pelosi					
9 Lee	N	Y	Y	Y	Y
10 Tauscher	N	Y	Y	Y	Y
11 McNerney	Y	Y	Y	Y	Y
12 Speier	N	Y	Y	Y	Y
13 Stark	N	Y	Y	Y	Y
14 Eshoo	N	Y	Y	Y	Y
15 Honda	N	Y	Y	Y	Y
16 Lofgren	N	Y	Y	Y	Y
17 Farr	N	Y	Y	Y	Y
18 Cardoza	N	Y	Y	Y	Y
19 **Radanovich**	Y	N	Y	N	Y
20 Costa	N	Y	Y	Y	Y
21 **Nunes**	Y	N	Y	N	Y
22 **McCarthy**	Y	N	Y	N	Y
23 Capps	N	Y	Y	Y	Y
24 **Gallegly**	Y	N	Y	N	Y
25 **McKeon**	Y	N	Y	N	Y
26 **Dreier**	Y	N	Y	N	Y
27 Sherman	N	Y	Y	Y	Y
28 Berman	N	Y	Y	Y	Y
29 Schiff	N	Y	Y	Y	Y
30 Waxman	N	Y	Y	Y	Y
31 Becerra	N	Y	Y	Y	Y
32 Solis	N	Y	Y	Y	Y
33 Watson	N	Y	Y	Y	Y
34 Roybal-Allard	N	Y	Y	Y	Y
35 Waters	N	Y	Y	Y	Y
36 Harman	N	Y	Y	Y	Y
37 Richardson	N	Y	Y	Y	Y
38 Napolitano	N	Y	Y	Y	Y
39 Sánchez, Linda	N	Y	Y	Y	Y
40 **Royce**	Y	N	Y	N	Y
41 **Lewis**	Y	N	N	N	Y
42 **Miller, Gary**	?	?	?	?	?
43 Baca	N	Y	Y	Y	Y
44 **Calvert**	?	?	?	?	?
45 **Bono Mack**	Y	Y	Y	N	Y
46 **Rohrabacher**	N	N	N	N	Y
47 Sanchez, Loretta	N	Y	Y	Y	Y
48 **Campbell**	Y	N	Y	N	Y
49 **Issa**	Y	N	Y	N	Y
50 **Bilbray**	Y	Y	Y	N	?
51 Filner	N	Y	Y	Y	Y
52 **Hunter**	Y	N	Y	Y	Y
53 Davis	N	Y	Y	Y	Y
COLORADO					
1 DeGette	N	Y	Y	Y	Y
2 Udall	N	Y	Y	Y	Y
3 Salazar	N	Y	Y	Y	Y
4 **Musgrave**	Y	Y	Y	N	Y
5 **Lamborn**	Y	N	Y	N	Y
6 **Tancredo**	?	?	?	?	?
7 Perlmutter	N	Y	Y	Y	Y
CONNECTICUT					
1 Larson	N	Y	Y	Y	Y
2 Courtney	N	Y	Y	Y	Y
3 DeLauro	N	Y	Y	Y	Y
4 **Shays**	Y	Y	Y	Y	Y
5 Murphy	N	Y	Y	Y	Y
DELAWARE					
AL **Castle**	Y	Y	Y	Y	Y
FLORIDA					
1 **Miller**	Y	N	Y	N	Y
2 Boyd	N	Y	Y	Y	Y
3 Brown	N	Y	Y	Y	Y
4 **Crenshaw**	Y	N	Y	N	Y
5 **Brown-Waite**	Y	N	Y	N	Y
6 **Stearns**	Y	N	Y	N	Y
7 **Mica**	Y	Y	Y	N	Y
8 **Keller**	Y	Y	Y	N	Y
9 **Bilirakis**	Y	Y	Y	N	Y
10 **Young**	Y	Y	Y	N	Y
11 Castor	N	Y	Y	Y	Y
12 **Putnam**	Y	N	Y	N	Y
13 **Buchanan**	Y	N	Y	N	Y
14 **Mack**	Y	N	N	N	Y
15 **Weldon**	?	N	Y	N	Y
16 Mahoney	N	Y	Y	Y	Y
17 Meek	N	Y	Y	Y	Y
18 **Ros-Lehtinen**	Y	Y	Y	N	Y
19 Wexler	?	?	?	?	?
20 Wasserman Schultz	N	Y	Y	Y	Y
21 **Diaz-Balart, L.**	Y	Y	Y	Y	Y
22 Klein	N	Y	Y	Y	Y
23 Hastings	N	Y	Y	Y	Y
24 **Feeney**	Y	Y	Y	Y	Y
25 **Diaz-Balart, M.**	Y	Y	Y	Y	Y
GEORGIA					
1 **Kingston**	Y	N	Y	N	Y
2 Bishop	N	Y	Y	Y	Y
3 **Westmoreland**	Y	Y	Y	N	Y
4 Johnson	N	Y	Y	Y	Y
5 Lewis	N	Y	Y	Y	Y
6 **Price**	Y	N	Y	N	Y
7 **Linder**	Y	N	N	N	Y
8 Marshall	Y	Y	Y	Y	Y
9 **Deal**	Y	Y	Y	N	Y
10 **Broun**	Y	N	Y	N	Y
11 **Gingrey**	Y	N	Y	N	Y
12 Barrow	Y	Y	Y	Y	Y
13 Scott	N	Y	Y	Y	Y
HAWAII					
1 Abercrombie	N	Y	Y	Y	Y
2 Hirono	N	Y	Y	Y	Y
IDAHO					
1 **Sali**	Y	N	N	N	Y
2 **Simpson**	Y	Y	N	N	Y
ILLINOIS					
1 Rush	?	?	?	?	?
2 Jackson	N	Y	Y	Y	Y
3 Lipinski	N	Y	Y	Y	Y
4 Gutierrez	?	Y	Y	Y	Y
5 Emanuel	N	Y	Y	Y	Y
6 **Roskam**	Y	Y	Y	N	Y
7 Davis	N	Y	Y	Y	Y
8 Bean	N	Y	Y	Y	Y
9 Schakowsky	N	Y	Y	Y	Y
10 **Kirk**	Y	Y	Y	N	Y
11 **Weller**	?	?	?	?	?
12 Costello	N	Y	Y	Y	Y
13 **Biggert**	Y	Y	Y	N	Y
14 Foster	Y	Y	Y	Y	Y
15 **Johnson**	Y	Y	Y	N	Y

ND Northern Democrats, SD Southern Democrats
Southern states: Ala., Ark., Fla., Ga., Ky., La., Miss., N.C., Okla., S.C., Tenn., Texas, Va.

	466	467	468	469	470
16 Manzullo	Y	N	Y	N	Y
17 Hare	N	Y	Y	Y	Y
18 LaHood	Y	Y	Y	N	Y
19 Shimkus	Y	N	Y	N	Y
INDIANA					
1 Visclosky	N	Y	Y	Y	Y
2 Donnelly	Y	Y	Y	Y	Y
3 Souder	Y	Y	N	N	Y
4 Buyer	Y	Y	Y	N	Y
5 Burton	Y	N	Y	N	Y
6 Pence	Y	N	N	N	Y
7 Carson, A.	N	Y	Y	Y	Y
8 Ellsworth	Y	Y	Y	Y	Y
9 Hill	N	Y	Y	Y	Y
IOWA					
1 Braley	N	Y	Y	Y	Y
2 Loebsack	N	Y	Y	Y	Y
3 Boswell	Y	Y	Y	Y	Y
4 Latham	Y	N	Y	N	Y
5 King	Y	N	N	N	Y
KANSAS					
1 Moran	Y	Y	Y	N	Y
2 Boyda	N	Y	Y	Y	Y
3 Moore	N	Y	Y	Y	Y
4 Tiahrt	Y	Y	Y	N	Y
KENTUCKY					
1 Whitfield	Y	Y	Y	N	Y
2 Lewis	?	?	?	?	?
3 Yarmuth	N	Y	Y	Y	Y
4 Davis	Y	Y	Y	N	Y
5 Rogers	Y	N	Y	N	Y
6 Chandler	N	Y	Y	Y	Y
LOUISIANA					
1 Scalise	Y	N	Y	N	Y
2 Jefferson	N	Y	Y	N	Y
3 Melancon	N	Y	Y	N	Y
4 McCrery	Y	N	Y	N	Y
5 Alexander	Y	N	Y	N	Y
6 Cazayoux	N	Y	Y	Y	Y
7 Boustany	Y	Y	Y	N	Y
MAINE					
1 Allen	N	Y	Y	Y	Y
2 Michaud	N	Y	Y	Y	Y
MARYLAND					
1 Gilchrest	?	Y	Y	Y	Y
2 Ruppersberger	N	Y	Y	Y	Y
3 Sarbanes	N	Y	Y	Y	Y
4 Edwards	N	Y	Y	Y	Y
5 Hoyer	N	Y	Y	Y	Y
6 Bartlett	Y	Y	Y	N	Y
7 Cummings	N	Y	Y	Y	Y
8 Van Hollen	N	Y	Y	Y	?
MASSACHUSETTS					
1 Olver	N	Y	Y	Y	Y
2 Neal	N	Y	Y	Y	?
3 McGovern	N	Y	Y	Y	Y
4 Frank	N	Y	Y	Y	Y
5 Tsongas	N	Y	Y	Y	Y
6 Tierney	N	Y	Y	Y	Y
7 Markey	N	Y	Y	Y	Y
8 Capuano	N	Y	Y	Y	?
9 Lynch	N	Y	Y	Y	Y
10 Delahunt	N	Y	Y	Y	Y
MICHIGAN					
1 Stupak	N	Y	Y	Y	Y
2 Hoekstra	Y	N	Y	N	Y
3 Ehlers	Y	Y	Y	N	Y
4 Camp	Y	N	Y	N	Y
5 Kildee	N	Y	Y	Y	Y
6 Upton	Y	Y	Y	N	Y
7 Walberg	Y	N	Y	N	Y
8 Rogers	Y	Y	Y	N	Y
9 Knollenberg	Y	Y	Y	N	Y
10 Miller	Y	Y	Y	N	?
11 McCotter	Y	Y	Y	N	Y
12 Levin	N	Y	Y	Y	Y
13 Kilpatrick	N	Y	Y	Y	Y
14 Conyers	N	Y	Y	Y	Y
15 Dingell	N	Y	Y	Y	Y
MINNESOTA					
1 Walz	N	Y	Y	Y	Y
2 Kline	Y	Y	Y	N	Y
3 Ramstad	Y	N	Y	N	Y
4 McCollum	N	Y	Y	Y	Y

	466	467	468	469	470
5 Ellison	N	Y	Y	Y	Y
6 Bachmann	Y	Y	Y	N	Y
7 Peterson	N	Y	Y	Y	Y
8 Oberstar	N	Y	Y	Y	Y
MISSISSIPPI					
1 Childers	Y	Y	Y	N	Y
2 Thompson	N	Y	Y	Y	Y
3 Pickering	Y	N	Y	N	Y
4 Taylor	N	Y	Y	Y	Y
MISSOURI					
1 Clay	N	Y	Y	Y	Y
2 Akin	Y	N	Y	?	Y
3 Carnahan	N	Y	Y	Y	Y
4 Skelton	N	Y	Y	Y	Y
5 Cleaver	N	Y	Y	Y	Y
6 Graves	Y	N	Y	N	Y
7 Blunt	Y	N	Y	N	Y
8 Emerson	Y	Y	Y	N	Y
9 Hulshof	Y	Y	Y	N	Y
MONTANA					
AL Rehberg	Y	N	Y	N	Y
NEBRASKA					
1 Fortenberry	Y	Y	Y	N	Y
2 Terry	Y	N	Y	N	Y
3 Smith	Y	N	Y	N	Y
NEVADA					
1 Berkley	N	Y	Y	Y	Y
2 Heller	Y	N	Y	N	Y
3 Porter	Y	Y	Y	N	Y
NEW HAMPSHIRE					
1 Shea-Porter	N	Y	Y	Y	Y
2 Hodes	N	Y	Y	Y	Y
NEW JERSEY					
1 Andrews	N	Y	Y	Y	Y
2 LoBiondo	Y	Y	Y	Y	Y
3 Saxton	Y	Y	Y	N	?
4 Smith	Y	Y	Y	Y	Y
5 Garrett	Y	Y	Y	N	Y
6 Pallone	N	Y	Y	Y	Y
7 Ferguson	Y	Y	Y	N	Y
8 Pascrell	N	Y	Y	Y	Y
9 Rothman	N	Y	Y	Y	?
10 Payne	N	Y	Y	Y	Y
11 Frelinghuysen	Y	Y	Y	N	Y
12 Holt	N	Y	Y	Y	Y
13 Sires	N	Y	Y	Y	Y
NEW MEXICO					
1 Wilson	Y	Y	Y	N	?
2 Pearce	Y	Y	Y	N	Y
3 Udall	N	Y	Y	Y	Y
NEW YORK					
1 Bishop	N	Y	Y	Y	Y
2 Israel	N	Y	Y	Y	Y
3 King	Y	Y	Y	N	Y
4 McCarthy	N	Y	Y	Y	Y
5 Ackerman	N	Y	Y	Y	Y
6 Meeks	N	Y	Y	Y	Y
7 Crowley	N	Y	Y	Y	Y
8 Nadler	N	Y	Y	Y	Y
9 Weiner	N	Y	Y	Y	Y
10 Towns	N	Y	Y	Y	Y
11 Clarke	N	Y	Y	Y	Y
12 Velázquez	N	Y	Y	Y	Y
13 Fossella	Y	Y	Y	N	Y
14 Maloney	N	Y	Y	Y	Y
15 Rangel	N	Y	Y	Y	Y
16 Serrano	N	Y	Y	Y	Y
17 Engel	N	Y	Y	Y	Y
18 Lowey	N	Y	Y	Y	Y
19 Hall	N	Y	Y	Y	Y
20 Gillibrand	Y	Y	Y	Y	Y
21 McNulty	N	Y	Y	Y	Y
22 Hinchey	N	Y	Y	Y	Y
23 McHugh	Y	Y	Y	N	Y
24 Arcuri	N	Y	Y	Y	Y
25 Walsh	Y	Y	Y	N	Y
26 Reynolds	Y	Y	Y	N	Y
27 Higgins	N	Y	Y	Y	Y
28 Slaughter	N	Y	Y	Y	Y
29 Kuhl	Y	Y	Y	N	Y
NORTH CAROLINA					
1 Butterfield	N	Y	Y	Y	Y
2 Etheridge	N	Y	Y	Y	Y
3 Jones	Y	N	Y	N	Y
4 Price	N	Y	Y	Y	Y

	466	467	468	469	470
5 Foxx	Y	N	Y	N	Y
6 Coble	Y	Y	Y	N	Y
7 McIntyre	Y	Y	Y	Y	Y
8 Hayes	Y	Y	Y	Y	Y
9 Myrick	Y	N	Y	N	Y
10 McHenry	Y	N	Y	N	Y
11 Shuler	Y	Y	Y	Y	Y
12 Watt	N	Y	Y	Y	Y
13 Miller	N	Y	Y	Y	Y
NORTH DAKOTA					
AL Pomeroy	N	Y	Y	Y	Y
OHIO					
1 Chabot	Y	Y	Y	N	Y
2 Schmidt	Y	N	Y	N	Y
3 Turner	Y	Y	Y	N	Y
4 Jordan	Y	N	N	N	Y
5 Latta	Y	N	Y	N	Y
6 Wilson	N	+	Y	Y	Y
7 Hobson	Y	Y	Y	N	Y
8 Boehner	Y	N	Y	N	Y
9 Kaptur	N	Y	Y	?	Y
10 Kucinich	N	Y	Y	Y	Y
11 Tubbs Jones	N	Y	Y	Y	Y
12 Tiberi	Y	Y	Y	N	Y
13 Sutton	N	Y	Y	Y	Y
14 LaTourette	Y	Y	Y	N	Y
15 Pryce	Y	Y	Y	N	Y
16 Regula	Y	Y	Y	N	Y
17 Ryan	N	Y	Y	Y	Y
18 Space	N	Y	Y	Y	Y
OKLAHOMA					
1 Sullivan	Y	N	Y	N	Y
2 Boren	N	Y	Y	N	Y
3 Lucas	Y	N	Y	N	Y
4 Cole	Y	Y	Y	N	Y
5 Fallin	Y	Y	Y	N	Y
OREGON					
1 Wu	N	Y	Y	Y	Y
2 Walden	Y	N	Y	N	Y
3 Blumenauer	N	Y	Y	Y	Y
4 DeFazio	N	Y	Y	Y	Y
5 Hooley	N	Y	Y	Y	Y
PENNSYLVANIA					
1 Brady	N	Y	Y	Y	Y
2 Fattah	N	Y	Y	Y	Y
3 English	Y	Y	Y	N	Y
4 Altmire	N	Y	Y	Y	Y
5 Peterson	Y	N	?	?	?
6 Gerlach	Y	Y	Y	N	Y
7 Sestak	N	Y	Y	Y	Y
8 Murphy, P.	N	Y	Y	Y	Y
9 Shuster	Y	Y	Y	N	?
10 Carney	N	Y	Y	Y	Y
11 Kanjorski	N	Y	Y	Y	Y
12 Murtha	N	Y	Y	Y	Y
13 Schwartz	N	Y	Y	Y	Y
14 Doyle	N	Y	Y	Y	?
15 Dent	Y	Y	Y	N	Y
16 Pitts	Y	Y	Y	N	Y
17 Holden	N	Y	Y	Y	Y
18 Murphy, T.	Y	Y	Y	N	?
19 Platts	Y	Y	Y	N	Y
RHODE ISLAND					
1 Kennedy	N	Y	Y	Y	Y
2 Langevin	N	Y	Y	Y	Y
SOUTH CAROLINA					
1 Brown	Y	Y	Y	N	Y
2 Wilson	Y	N	Y	N	Y
3 Barrett	Y	N	Y	N	Y
4 Inglis	N	Y	Y	N	Y
5 Spratt	N	Y	Y	Y	Y
6 Clyburn	N	Y	Y	Y	Y
SOUTH DAKOTA					
AL Herseth Sandlin	N	Y	Y	Y	Y
TENNESSEE					
1 Davis, D.	Y	N	Y	N	Y
2 Duncan	Y	N	N	N	Y
3 Wamp	Y	N	Y	N	Y
4 Davis, L.	N	Y	Y	Y	Y
5 Cooper	N	Y	Y	Y	Y
6 Gordon	N	Y	Y	Y	Y
7 Blackburn	Y	N	N	N	Y
8 Tanner	N	Y	Y	Y	Y
9 Cohen	N	Y	Y	Y	Y

	466	467	468	469	470
TEXAS					
1 Gohmert	Y	N	Y	N	Y
2 Poe	Y	N	Y	N	Y
3 Johnson, S.	Y	N	N	N	Y
4 Hall	Y	N	Y	N	Y
5 Hensarling	Y	N	N	N	Y
6 Barton	Y	N	Y	N	Y
7 Culberson	Y	N	Y	N	Y
8 Brady	Y	N	Y	N	Y
9 Green, A.	N	Y	Y	Y	Y
10 McCaul	Y	N	Y	N	Y
11 Conaway	Y	N	Y	N	Y
12 Granger	Y	N	Y	N	Y
13 Thornberry	Y	N	Y	N	Y
14 Paul	Y	N	N	N	Y
15 Hinojosa	N	Y	Y	N	Y
16 Reyes	N	Y	Y	Y	Y
17 Edwards	N	Y	Y	Y	Y
18 Jackson Lee	N	Y	Y	Y	Y
19 Neugebauer	Y	N	Y	N	Y
20 Gonzalez	N	Y	Y	Y	Y
21 Smith	Y	N	Y	N	Y
22 Lampson	Y	N	Y	N	Y
23 Rodriguez	N	Y	Y	Y	Y
24 Marchant	Y	N	N	N	Y
25 Doggett	N	Y	Y	Y	Y
26 Burgess	Y	N	Y	N	Y
27 Ortiz	N	Y	Y	Y	Y
28 Cuellar	N	Y	Y	Y	Y
29 Green, G.	N	Y	Y	Y	Y
30 Johnson, E.	N	Y	Y	Y	Y
31 Carter	Y	N	Y	N	Y
32 Sessions	Y	N	N	N	Y
UTAH					
1 Bishop	Y	N	Y	N	Y
2 Matheson	Y	Y	Y	N	Y
3 Cannon	?	?	?	?	?
VERMONT					
AL Welch	N	Y	Y	Y	Y
VIRGINIA					
1 Wittman	Y	Y	Y	N	Y
2 Drake	Y	Y	Y	N	Y
3 Scott	N	Y	Y	Y	Y
4 Forbes	?	?	?	?	?
5 Goode	Y	N	Y	N	Y
6 Goodlatte	Y	N	Y	N	Y
7 Cantor	Y	N	Y	N	Y
8 Moran	N	Y	Y	Y	Y
9 Boucher	N	Y	Y	Y	Y
10 Wolf	N	Y	Y	N	Y
11 Davis	N	Y	Y	N	Y
WASHINGTON					
1 Inslee	N	Y	Y	Y	Y
2 Larsen	N	Y	Y	Y	Y
3 Baird	N	Y	Y	Y	Y
4 Hastings	Y	N	Y	N	Y
5 McMorris Rodgers	Y	N	Y	N	Y
6 Dicks	N	Y	Y	Y	Y
7 McDermott	N	Y	Y	Y	Y
8 Reichert	Y	Y	Y	N	Y
9 Smith	—	+	+	+	+
WEST VIRGINIA					
1 Mollohan	N	Y	Y	Y	Y
2 Capito	Y	Y	Y	N	Y
3 Rahall	N	Y	Y	Y	Y
WISCONSIN					
1 Ryan	Y	N	Y	N	Y
2 Baldwin	N	Y	Y	Y	Y
3 Kind	N	Y	Y	Y	Y
4 Moore	N	Y	Y	Y	Y
5 Sensenbrenner	Y	N	Y	N	Y
6 Petri	Y	Y	Y	N	Y
7 Obey	N	Y	Y	Y	Y
8 Kagen	N	Y	Y	Y	Y
WYOMING					
AL Cubin	Y	N	N	N	Y
DELEGATES					
Faleomavaega (A.S.)					
Norton (D.C.)					
Bordallo (Guam)					
Fortuño (P.R.)					
Christensen (V.I.)					

IN THE HOUSE | By Vote Number

471. HR 3981. Preserve America and Save America's Treasures Grants/Passage.
Bordallo, D-Guam, motion to suspend the rules and pass the bill that would authorize $25 million annually in fiscal 2009 through 2013 for the Preserve America Program, which provides grants to support historic preservation, education and tourism. It also would authorize $50 million annually for the Save America's Treasures Program, which awards grants to projects designed to stop the destruction or deterioration of historic properties and collections of writings or art. Motion agreed to 360-23: R 145-23; D 215-0 (ND 161-0, SD 54-0). A two-thirds majority of those present and voting (256 in this case) is required for passage under suspension of the rules. July 8, 2008.

472. HR 1423. Dorothy Buell Memorial Visitor Center/Passage.
Bordallo, D-Guam, motion to suspend the rules and pass the bill that would authorize the use of a portion of the Dorothy Buell Memorial Visitor Center as a visitor center for the Indiana Dunes National Lakeshore and allow the agency to create exhibits at a cost that does not exceed $1.5 million. Motion agreed to 376-11: R 156-11; D 220-0 (ND 163-0, SD 57-0). A two-thirds majority of those present and voting (258 in this case) is required for passage under suspension of the rules. July 8, 2008.

473. HR 4199. Wright Brothers-Dunbar National Historic Park/Passage.
Bordallo, D-Guam, motion to suspend the rules and pass the bill that would add sites to the Dayton Aviation Heritage National Historical Park and redesignate the area as the "Wright Brothers-Dunbar National Historical Park." Motion agreed to 368-18: R 149-18; D 219-0 (ND 163-0, SD 56-0). A two-thirds majority of those present and voting (258 in this case) is required for passage under suspension of the rules. July 8, 2008.

474. HR 5811. Electronic Communications Preservation/Previous Question.
Welch, D-Vt., motion to order the previous question (thus ending debate and possibility of amendment) on adoption of the rule (H Res 1318) to provide for House floor consideration of the bill that would set new standards for managing and preserving presidential records and require federal agencies to electronically preserve messages and documents. Motion agreed to 228-193: R 3-189; D 225-4 (ND 169-2, SD 56-2). July 9, 2008.

475. HR 5811. Electronic Communications Preservation/Rule.
Adoption of the rule (H Res 1318) to provide for House floor consideration of the bill that would set new standards for managing and preserving presidential records and require federal agencies to electronically preserve messages and documents. Adopted 229-193: R 0-192; D 229-1 (ND 171-1, SD 58-0). July 9, 2008.

476. HR 5811. Electronic Communications Preservation/Recommit.
Davis, R-Va., motion to recommit the bill to the Oversight and Government Reform Committee with instructions that it be reported back forthwith with language that would prevent unauthorized removal, damage or destruction of classified records from the National Archives and restrict the viewing of classified materials by non-National Archives and Records Administration personnel. Motion agreed to 419-1: R 192-0; D 227-1 (ND 169-1, SD 58-0). July 9, 2008.

	471	472	473	474	475	476
ALABAMA						
1 Bonner	Y	Y	Y	N	N	Y
2 Everett	Y	Y	Y	N	N	Y
3 Rogers	Y	Y	Y	N	N	Y
4 Aderholt	Y	Y	Y	N	N	Y
5 Cramer	Y	Y	Y	Y	Y	Y
6 Bachus	?	Y	Y	N	N	Y
7 Davis	Y	Y	Y	Y	Y	Y
ALASKA						
AL Young	Y	Y	Y	N	N	Y
ARIZONA						
1 Renzi	Y	Y	Y	?	?	?
2 Franks	N	Y	N	N	N	Y
3 Shadegg	N	Y	N	N	N	Y
4 Pastor	Y	Y	Y	Y	Y	Y
5 Mitchell	Y	Y	Y	Y	Y	Y
6 Flake	N	N	N	N	N	Y
7 Grijalva	Y	Y	Y	Y	Y	Y
8 Giffords	Y	Y	Y	Y	Y	Y
ARKANSAS						
1 Berry	Y	Y	Y	Y	Y	Y
2 Snyder	Y	Y	Y	Y	Y	Y
3 Boozman	Y	Y	Y	N	N	Y
4 Ross	Y	Y	Y	Y	Y	Y
CALIFORNIA						
1 Thompson	Y	Y	Y	Y	Y	Y
2 Herger	Y	Y	Y	N	N	Y
3 Lungren	Y	Y	Y	N	N	Y
4 Doolittle	?	?	?	N	N	Y
5 Matsui	Y	Y	Y	Y	Y	Y
6 Woolsey	Y	Y	Y	Y	Y	Y
7 Miller, George	Y	Y	Y	Y	Y	Y
8 Pelosi						
9 Lee	Y	Y	Y	Y	Y	Y
10 Tauscher	Y	Y	Y	Y	Y	Y
11 McNerney	Y	Y	Y	Y	Y	Y
12 Speier	Y	Y	Y	Y	Y	Y
13 Stark	Y	Y	Y	Y	Y	Y
14 Eshoo	Y	Y	Y	Y	Y	Y
15 Honda	Y	Y	Y	Y	Y	Y
16 Lofgren	Y	Y	Y	Y	Y	Y
17 Farr	Y	Y	Y	Y	Y	Y
18 Cardoza	Y	Y	Y	Y	Y	Y
19 Radanovich	Y	Y	Y	N	N	Y
20 Costa	Y	Y	Y	Y	Y	Y
21 Nunes	Y	Y	Y	N	N	Y
22 McCarthy	Y	Y	Y	N	N	Y
23 Capps	Y	Y	Y	Y	Y	Y
24 Gallegly	Y	Y	Y	N	N	Y
25 McKeon	Y	Y	Y	N	N	Y
26 Dreier	Y	Y	Y	N	N	Y
27 Sherman	Y	Y	Y	Y	Y	Y
28 Berman	Y	Y	Y	Y	Y	Y
29 Schiff	+	+	+	Y	Y	Y
30 Waxman	Y	Y	Y	Y	Y	Y
31 Becerra	Y	Y	Y	Y	Y	Y
32 Solis	Y	Y	Y	Y	Y	Y
33 Watson	Y	Y	Y	Y	Y	Y
34 Roybal-Allard	Y	Y	Y	Y	Y	Y
35 Waters	Y	Y	Y	Y	Y	P
36 Harman	Y	Y	Y	Y	Y	Y
37 Richardson	Y	Y	Y	Y	Y	?
38 Napolitano	Y	Y	Y	Y	Y	Y
39 Sánchez, Linda	+	+	Y	Y	Y	Y
40 Royce	N	N	N	N	N	Y
41 Lewis	Y	Y	Y	N	N	Y
42 Miller, Gary	Y	Y	Y	N	N	Y
43 Baca	Y	Y	Y	Y	Y	Y
44 Calvert	?	?	?	N	N	Y
45 Bono Mack	Y	Y	Y	N	N	Y
46 Rohrabacher	?	?	?	N	N	Y
47 Sanchez, Loretta	Y	Y	Y	Y	Y	Y
48 Campbell	N	N	N	N	N	Y
49 Issa	Y	Y	Y	N	N	Y
50 Bilbray	Y	Y	Y	N	N	Y
51 Filner	Y	Y	Y	Y	Y	Y
52 Hunter	Y	Y	Y	N	N	Y
53 Davis	Y	Y	Y	Y	Y	Y

	471	472	473	474	475	476
COLORADO						
1 DeGette	Y	Y	Y	Y	Y	Y
2 Udall	?	?	?	?	?	?
3 Salazar	Y	Y	Y	Y	Y	Y
4 Musgrave	Y	Y	Y	N	N	Y
5 Lamborn	N	Y	N	N	N	Y
6 Tancredo	N	N	N	N	N	Y
7 Perlmutter	Y	Y	Y	Y	Y	Y
CONNECTICUT						
1 Larson	Y	Y	Y	Y	Y	Y
2 Courtney	Y	Y	Y	Y	Y	Y
3 DeLauro	Y	Y	Y	Y	Y	Y
4 Shays	Y	Y	Y	Y	N	Y
5 Murphy	Y	Y	Y	Y	Y	Y
DELAWARE						
AL Castle	Y	Y	Y	Y	N	Y
FLORIDA						
1 Miller	Y	Y	Y	N	N	Y
2 Boyd	Y	Y	Y	Y	Y	Y
3 Brown	Y	Y	Y	Y	Y	Y
4 Crenshaw	Y	Y	Y	N	N	Y
5 Brown-Waite	?	?	?	?	?	?
6 Stearns	Y	N	N	N	N	Y
7 Mica	Y	Y	Y	N	N	Y
8 Keller	Y	Y	Y	N	N	Y
9 Bilirakis	?	?	Y	N	N	Y
10 Young	?	?	?	N	N	Y
11 Castor	Y	Y	Y	Y	Y	Y
12 Putnam	Y	Y	Y	N	N	Y
13 Buchanan	Y	Y	Y	N	N	Y
14 Mack	Y	Y	Y	N	N	Y
15 Weldon	?	?	?	N	N	Y
16 Mahoney	Y	Y	Y	Y	Y	Y
17 Meek	Y	Y	Y	Y	Y	Y
18 Ros-Lehtinen	Y	?	?	N	N	Y
19 Wexler	Y	Y	Y	Y	Y	Y
20 Wasserman Schultz	Y	Y	Y	Y	Y	Y
21 Diaz-Balart, L.	Y	Y	Y	N	N	Y
22 Klein	Y	Y	Y	Y	Y	Y
23 Hastings	Y	Y	Y	Y	Y	Y
24 Feeney	Y	Y	Y	N	N	Y
25 Diaz-Balart, M.	Y	Y	Y	N	N	Y
GEORGIA						
1 Kingston	N	Y	N	N	N	Y
2 Bishop	Y	Y	Y	Y	Y	Y
3 Westmoreland	N	Y	N	N	N	Y
4 Johnson	Y	Y	Y	Y	Y	Y
5 Lewis	Y	Y	Y	Y	Y	Y
6 Price	Y	Y	Y	N	N	Y
7 Linder	Y	Y	Y	N	N	Y
8 Marshall	Y	Y	Y	Y	Y	Y
9 Deal	Y	Y	Y	N	N	Y
10 Broun	N	N	?	N	N	Y
11 Gingrey	N	N	Y	N	N	Y
12 Barrow	Y	Y	Y	Y	Y	Y
13 Scott	Y	Y	Y	Y	Y	Y
HAWAII						
1 Abercrombie	?	Y	Y	Y	Y	Y
2 Hirono	Y	Y	Y	Y	Y	Y
IDAHO						
1 Sali	N	N	Y	N	N	Y
2 Simpson	?	?	?	N	N	Y
ILLINOIS						
1 Rush	?	?	?	?	?	?
2 Jackson	Y	Y	Y	Y	Y	Y
3 Lipinski	Y	Y	Y	Y	Y	Y
4 Gutierrez	Y	Y	Y	Y	Y	Y
5 Emanuel	Y	Y	Y	Y	Y	Y
6 Roskam	Y	Y	Y	N	N	Y
7 Davis	Y	Y	Y	Y	Y	Y
8 Bean	Y	Y	Y	Y	Y	Y
9 Schakowsky	Y	Y	Y	Y	Y	Y
10 Kirk	Y	Y	Y	N	N	Y
11 Weller	+	+	+	N	N	Y
12 Costello	Y	Y	Y	Y	Y	Y
13 Biggert	Y	Y	Y	N	N	Y
14 Foster	Y	Y	Y	Y	Y	Y
15 Johnson	+	+	+	N	N	Y

KEY	Republicans	Democrats		
Y Voted for (yea)		X Paired against		C Voted "present" to avoid possible conflict of interest
# Paired for		– Announced against		
+ Announced for		P Voted "present"		? Did not vote or otherwise make a position known
N Voted against (nay)				

ND Northern Democrats, SD Southern Democrats
Southern states: Ala., Ark., Fla., Ga., Ky., La., Miss., N.C., Okla., S.C., Tenn., Texas, Va.

H-158 2008 CQ ALMANAC | www.cq.com

	471	472	473	474	475	476
16 **Manzullo**	N	Y	N	N	N	Y
17 Hare	Y	Y	Y	Y	Y	Y
18 **LaHood**	Y	Y	Y	N	N	Y
19 **Shimkus**	Y	Y	Y	N	N	Y
INDIANA						
1 Visclosky	Y	Y	Y	Y	Y	Y
2 Donnelly	Y	Y	Y	Y	Y	Y
3 **Souder**	?	?	?	N	N	Y
4 **Buyer**	Y	Y	Y	N	N	Y
5 **Burton**	Y	Y	Y	N	N	Y
6 **Pence**	Y	Y	Y	N	N	Y
7 Carson, A.	Y	Y	Y	Y	Y	Y
8 Ellsworth	Y	Y	Y	Y	Y	Y
9 Hill	Y	Y	Y	N	N	Y
IOWA						
1 Braley	Y	Y	Y	Y	Y	Y
2 Loebsack	Y	Y	Y	Y	Y	Y
3 Boswell	Y	Y	Y	?	?	?
4 **Latham**	Y	Y	Y	N	N	Y
5 **King**	N	?	N	N	N	Y
KANSAS						
1 **Moran**	Y	Y	N	N	N	Y
2 Boyda	Y	Y	Y	Y	Y	Y
3 Moore	Y	Y	Y	Y	Y	Y
4 **Tiahrt**	Y	Y	Y	N	N	Y
KENTUCKY						
1 **Whitfield**	Y	Y	Y	N	N	Y
2 **Lewis**	Y	Y	Y	N	N	Y
3 Yarmuth	Y	Y	Y	Y	Y	Y
4 **Davis**	Y	Y	Y	N	N	Y
5 **Rogers**	Y	Y	Y	N	N	Y
6 Chandler	Y	Y	Y	Y	Y	Y
LOUISIANA						
1 **Scalise**	Y	Y	Y	N	N	Y
2 Jefferson	Y	Y	Y	Y	Y	Y
3 Melancon	?	?	?	?	?	Y
4 **McCrery**	Y	Y	Y	N	N	Y
5 **Alexander**	?	?	?	N	N	Y
6 Cazayoux	Y	Y	Y	Y	Y	Y
7 **Boustany**	Y	Y	Y	N	N	Y
MAINE						
1 Allen	Y	Y	Y	Y	Y	Y
2 Michaud	Y	Y	Y	Y	Y	Y
MARYLAND						
1 **Gilchrest**	?	?	?	N	N	Y
2 Ruppersberger	Y	Y	Y	Y	Y	Y
3 Sarbanes	Y	Y	Y	Y	Y	Y
4 Edwards	Y	Y	Y	Y	Y	Y
5 Hoyer	Y	Y	Y	Y	Y	Y
6 **Bartlett**	Y	Y	Y	N	N	Y
7 Cummings	Y	Y	Y	Y	Y	Y
8 Van Hollen	Y	Y	Y	Y	Y	Y
MASSACHUSETTS						
1 Olver	Y	Y	Y	Y	Y	Y
2 Neal	Y	Y	Y	Y	Y	Y
3 McGovern	Y	Y	Y	Y	Y	Y
4 Frank	Y	Y	Y	Y	Y	Y
5 Tsongas	Y	Y	Y	Y	Y	Y
6 Tierney	Y	Y	Y	Y	Y	Y
7 Markey	Y	Y	Y	Y	Y	Y
8 Capuano	Y	Y	Y	Y	Y	Y
9 Lynch	Y	Y	Y	Y	Y	Y
10 Delahunt	?	?	?	Y	Y	Y
MICHIGAN						
1 Stupak	Y	Y	Y	Y	Y	Y
2 **Hoekstra**	N	Y	Y	N	N	Y
3 **Ehlers**	Y	Y	Y	N	N	Y
4 **Camp**	Y	Y	Y	N	N	Y
5 Kildee	Y	Y	Y	Y	Y	Y
6 **Upton**	Y	Y	Y	N	N	Y
7 **Walberg**	Y	Y	Y	N	N	Y
8 **Rogers**	Y	Y	Y	N	N	Y
9 **Knollenberg**	Y	Y	Y	N	N	Y
10 **Miller**	Y	Y	Y	N	N	Y
11 **McCotter**	Y	Y	Y	N	N	Y
12 Levin	+	+	+	Y	Y	Y
13 Kilpatrick	Y	Y	Y	Y	Y	Y
14 Conyers	Y	Y	?	Y	Y	Y
15 Dingell	?	Y	Y	Y	Y	Y
MINNESOTA						
1 Walz	Y	Y	Y	Y	Y	Y
2 **Kline**	Y	Y	Y	N	N	Y
3 **Ramstad**	Y	Y	Y	N	N	Y
4 McCollum	Y	Y	Y	Y	Y	Y

	471	472	473	474	475	476
5 Ellison	Y	Y	Y	Y	Y	Y
6 **Bachmann**	Y	Y	Y	N	N	Y
7 Peterson	Y	Y	Y	Y	Y	Y
8 Oberstar	Y	Y	Y	Y	Y	Y
MISSISSIPPI						
1 Childers	Y	Y	Y	N	Y	Y
2 Thompson	Y	Y	Y	Y	Y	Y
3 **Pickering**	?	?	?	?	?	?
4 Taylor	?	Y	Y	Y	Y	Y
MISSOURI						
1 Clay	Y	Y	Y	Y	Y	Y
2 **Akin**	Y	Y	Y	N	N	Y
3 Carnahan	Y	Y	Y	Y	Y	Y
4 Skelton	Y	Y	Y	Y	Y	Y
5 Cleaver	Y	Y	Y	Y	Y	Y
6 **Graves**	Y	Y	Y	N	N	Y
7 **Blunt**	Y	Y	Y	N	N	Y
8 **Emerson**	Y	Y	Y	N	N	Y
9 **Hulshof**	?	?	?	?	?	?
MONTANA						
AL **Rehberg**	Y	Y	Y	N	N	Y
NEBRASKA						
1 **Fortenberry**	Y	Y	Y	N	N	Y
2 **Terry**	Y	Y	Y	N	N	Y
3 **Smith**	Y	Y	Y	N	N	Y
NEVADA						
1 Berkley	Y	Y	Y	Y	Y	Y
2 **Heller**	Y	Y	Y	N	N	Y
3 **Porter**	Y	Y	Y	N	N	Y
NEW HAMPSHIRE						
1 Shea-Porter	Y	Y	Y	Y	Y	Y
2 Hodes	Y	Y	Y	?	Y	Y
NEW JERSEY						
1 Andrews	+	+	+	Y	Y	?
2 **LoBiondo**	Y	Y	Y	N	N	Y
3 **Saxton**	?	?	?	N	N	Y
4 **Smith**	Y	Y	Y	N	N	Y
5 **Garrett**	Y	Y	Y	N	N	Y
6 Pallone	Y	Y	Y	Y	Y	Y
7 **Ferguson**	?	?	?	N	N	Y
8 Pascrell	Y	Y	Y	Y	Y	Y
9 Rothman	Y	Y	Y	Y	Y	Y
10 Payne	Y	Y	Y	Y	Y	Y
11 **Frelinghuysen**	Y	Y	Y	N	N	Y
12 Holt	Y	Y	Y	Y	Y	Y
13 Sires	Y	Y	Y	Y	Y	Y
NEW MEXICO						
1 **Wilson**	Y	Y	Y	N	N	+
2 **Pearce**	?	?	?	N	N	Y
3 Udall	?	?	?	Y	Y	Y
NEW YORK						
1 Bishop	Y	Y	Y	Y	Y	Y
2 Israel	Y	Y	Y	Y	Y	Y
3 **King**	Y	Y	Y	N	N	Y
4 McCarthy	Y	Y	Y	Y	Y	Y
5 Ackerman	Y	Y	Y	Y	Y	Y
6 Meeks	?	?	?	Y	Y	Y
7 Crowley	Y	Y	Y	Y	Y	Y
8 Nadler	Y	Y	Y	Y	Y	Y
9 Weiner	Y	Y	Y	Y	Y	Y
10 Towns	?	?	?	Y	Y	Y
11 Clarke	Y	Y	Y	Y	Y	Y
12 Velázquez	Y	Y	Y	Y	Y	Y
13 **Fossella**	?	?	?	?	?	?
14 Maloney	Y	Y	Y	Y	Y	Y
15 Rangel	Y	Y	Y	Y	Y	Y
16 Serrano	Y	Y	Y	Y	Y	Y
17 Engel	Y	Y	Y	Y	Y	Y
18 Lowey	Y	Y	Y	Y	Y	Y
19 Hall	Y	Y	Y	Y	Y	Y
20 Gillibrand	Y	Y	Y	Y	Y	Y
21 McNulty	Y	Y	Y	Y	Y	Y
22 Hinchey	Y	Y	Y	Y	Y	Y
23 **McHugh**	Y	Y	Y	N	N	Y
24 Arcuri	Y	Y	Y	Y	Y	Y
25 **Walsh**	Y	Y	Y	N	N	Y
26 **Reynolds**	?	?	?	N	N	Y
27 Higgins	Y	Y	Y	Y	Y	Y
28 Slaughter	Y	Y	Y	Y	Y	Y
29 **Kuhl**	Y	Y	Y	N	N	Y
NORTH CAROLINA						
1 Butterfield	Y	Y	Y	Y	Y	Y
2 Etheridge	Y	Y	Y	Y	Y	Y
3 **Jones**	Y	Y	Y	N	N	Y
4 Price	Y	Y	Y	Y	Y	Y

	471	472	473	474	475	476
5 **Foxx**	N	N	Y	N	N	Y
6 **Coble**	Y	?	?	N	N	Y
7 McIntyre	Y	Y	Y	Y	Y	Y
8 **Hayes**	Y	Y	Y	N	N	Y
9 **Myrick**	Y	Y	Y	N	N	Y
10 **McHenry**	Y	Y	Y	N	N	Y
11 Shuler	?	?	?	Y	Y	Y
12 Watt	Y	Y	Y	Y	Y	Y
13 Miller	Y	Y	?	Y	Y	Y
NORTH DAKOTA						
AL Pomeroy	Y	Y	Y	Y	Y	Y
OHIO						
1 **Chabot**	Y	Y	Y	N	N	Y
2 **Schmidt**	Y	Y	Y	N	N	Y
3 **Turner**	Y	Y	Y	N	N	Y
4 **Jordan**	Y	Y	Y	N	N	Y
5 **Latta**	Y	Y	Y	N	N	Y
6 Wilson	?	?	?	Y	Y	Y
7 **Hobson**	Y	Y	Y	N	N	Y
8 **Boehner**	Y	Y	Y	N	N	Y
9 Kaptur	?	?	Y	Y	Y	Y
10 Kucinich	Y	Y	Y	Y	Y	Y
11 Tubbs Jones	Y	Y	Y	Y	Y	Y
12 **Tiberi**	Y	Y	Y	N	N	Y
13 Sutton	Y	Y	Y	Y	Y	Y
14 **LaTourette**	Y	Y	Y	N	N	Y
15 **Pryce**	?	?	?	?	?	?
16 **Regula**	Y	Y	Y	N	N	Y
17 Ryan	Y	Y	Y	Y	Y	Y
18 Space	Y	Y	Y	Y	Y	Y
OKLAHOMA						
1 **Sullivan**	Y	Y	Y	N	N	Y
2 Boren	Y	Y	Y	Y	Y	Y
3 **Lucas**	Y	Y	Y	N	N	Y
4 **Cole**	Y	Y	Y	N	N	Y
5 **Fallin**	Y	Y	Y	N	N	Y
OREGON						
1 Wu	Y	Y	Y	Y	Y	Y
2 **Walden**	Y	Y	Y	N	N	Y
3 Blumenauer	Y	Y	Y	Y	Y	Y
4 DeFazio	Y	Y	Y	Y	Y	Y
5 Hooley	Y	Y	Y	Y	Y	Y
PENNSYLVANIA						
1 Brady	Y	Y	Y	Y	Y	Y
2 Fattah	Y	Y	Y	Y	Y	Y
3 **English**	?	Y	Y	N	N	Y
4 Altmire	Y	Y	Y	Y	Y	Y
5 **Peterson**	?	?	?	N	N	Y
6 **Gerlach**	Y	Y	Y	N	N	Y
7 Sestak	Y	Y	Y	Y	Y	Y
8 Murphy, P.	Y	Y	Y	Y	Y	Y
9 **Shuster**	Y	Y	Y	N	N	Y
10 Carney	Y	Y	Y	Y	Y	Y
11 Kanjorski	Y	Y	Y	Y	Y	Y
12 Murtha	?	?	?	Y	Y	Y
13 Schwartz	Y	Y	Y	Y	Y	Y
14 Doyle	Y	Y	Y	Y	Y	Y
15 **Dent**	Y	Y	Y	N	N	Y
16 **Pitts**	Y	Y	Y	N	N	Y
17 Holden	Y	Y	Y	N	Y	Y
18 **Murphy, T.**	Y	Y	Y	N	N	Y
19 **Platts**	Y	Y	Y	N	N	Y
RHODE ISLAND						
1 Kennedy	Y	Y	Y	Y	Y	Y
2 Langevin	Y	Y	Y	Y	Y	Y
SOUTH CAROLINA						
1 **Brown**	Y	Y	Y	N	N	Y
2 **Wilson**	Y	Y	Y	N	N	Y
3 **Barrett**	Y	Y	Y	N	N	Y
4 **Inglis**	Y	Y	Y	N	N	Y
5 Spratt	Y	Y	Y	Y	Y	Y
6 Clyburn	Y	Y	Y	Y	Y	Y
SOUTH DAKOTA						
AL Herseth Sandlin	Y	Y	Y	Y	Y	Y
TENNESSEE						
1 **Davis, D.**	Y	Y	Y	N	N	Y
2 **Duncan**	N	Y	N	N	N	Y
3 **Wamp**	Y	Y	Y	N	N	Y
4 Davis, L.	Y	Y	Y	Y	Y	Y
5 Cooper	Y	Y	Y	Y	Y	Y
6 Gordon	Y	Y	Y	Y	Y	Y
7 **Blackburn**	Y	Y	Y	N	N	Y
8 Tanner	Y	Y	Y	Y	Y	Y
9 Cohen	+	Y	Y	Y	Y	Y

	471	472	473	474	475	476
TEXAS						
1 **Gohmert**	Y	N	Y	N	N	Y
2 **Poe**	+	+	+	N	N	Y
3 **Johnson, S.**	Y	Y	N	N	N	Y
4 **Hall**	Y	Y	Y	N	N	Y
5 **Hensarling**	N	N	N	N	N	Y
6 **Barton**	N	Y	Y	N	N	Y
7 **Culberson**	Y	Y	Y	N	N	Y
8 **Brady**	Y	Y	Y	N	N	Y
9 Green, A.	Y	Y	Y	Y	Y	Y
10 **McCaul**	Y	Y	Y	N	N	Y
11 **Conaway**	Y	Y	Y	N	N	Y
12 **Granger**	Y	Y	Y	N	N	Y
13 **Thornberry**	Y	Y	Y	N	N	Y
14 **Paul**	N	N	N	N	N	Y
15 Hinojosa	Y	Y	Y	Y	Y	Y
16 Reyes	Y	Y	Y	Y	Y	Y
17 Edwards	Y	Y	Y	Y	Y	Y
18 Jackson Lee	Y	Y	Y	Y	Y	P
19 **Neugebauer**	Y	N	N	N	N	Y
20 Gonzalez	Y	Y	Y	Y	Y	Y
21 **Smith**	?	?	?	?	N	Y
22 Lampson	?	Y	Y	N	Y	Y
23 Rodriguez	Y	Y	Y	Y	Y	Y
24 **Marchant**	N	Y	N	N	N	Y
25 Doggett	Y	Y	Y	Y	Y	Y
26 **Burgess**	N	Y	Y	N	N	Y
27 Ortiz	Y	Y	Y	Y	Y	Y
28 Cuellar	Y	Y	Y	Y	Y	Y
29 Green, G.	Y	Y	Y	Y	Y	Y
30 Johnson, E.	Y	Y	Y	Y	Y	Y
31 **Carter**	+	+	+	N	N	Y
32 **Sessions**	Y	Y	Y	N	N	Y
UTAH						
1 **Bishop**	N	Y	Y	N	N	Y
2 Matheson	Y	Y	Y	Y	Y	Y
3 **Cannon**	?	?	?	N	N	Y
VERMONT						
AL Welch	Y	Y	Y	Y	Y	Y
VIRGINIA						
1 **Wittman**	Y	Y	Y	N	N	Y
2 **Drake**	Y	Y	Y	N	N	Y
3 Scott	Y	Y	Y	Y	Y	Y
4 **Forbes**	?	?	?	N	N	Y
5 **Goode**	Y	Y	Y	N	N	Y
6 **Goodlatte**	Y	Y	N	N	N	Y
7 **Cantor**	Y	Y	Y	N	N	Y
8 Moran	Y	Y	Y	Y	Y	Y
9 Boucher	Y	Y	Y	Y	Y	Y
10 **Wolf**	Y	Y	Y	N	N	Y
11 **Davis**	Y	Y	Y	N	N	Y
WASHINGTON						
1 Inslee	Y	Y	Y	Y	Y	Y
2 Larsen	Y	Y	Y	Y	Y	Y
3 Baird	Y	Y	Y	?	?	Y
4 **Hastings**	Y	Y	Y	N	N	Y
5 **McMorris Rodgers**	+	+	+	N	?	Y
6 Dicks	Y	Y	Y	Y	Y	N
7 McDermott	Y	Y	Y	Y	Y	Y
8 **Reichert**	Y	Y	Y	Y	N	Y
9 Smith	Y	Y	Y	Y	Y	Y
WEST VIRGINIA						
1 Mollohan	Y	Y	Y	Y	Y	Y
2 **Capito**	Y	Y	Y	N	N	Y
3 Rahall	Y	Y	Y	Y	Y	Y
WISCONSIN						
1 **Ryan**	Y	Y	Y	N	N	Y
2 Baldwin	Y	Y	Y	Y	Y	Y
3 Kind	Y	Y	Y	Y	Y	Y
4 Moore	Y	Y	Y	Y	Y	Y
5 **Sensenbrenner**	Y	Y	Y	N	N	Y
6 **Petri**	Y	Y	Y	N	N	Y
7 Obey	Y	Y	Y	Y	Y	Y
8 Kagen	Y	Y	Y	Y	Y	Y
WYOMING						
AL **Cubin**	?	?	?	N	N	Y
DELEGATES						
Faleomavaega (A.S.)						
Norton (D.C.)						
Bordallo (Guam)						
Fortuño (P.R.)						
Christensen (V.I.)						

IN THE HOUSE | By Vote Number

477. HR 5811. Electronic Communications Preservation/Passage.
Passage of the bill that would direct the National Archives and Records Administration to create regulations on the capture, management and preservation of electronic messages that would be electronically searchable. All federal agencies would be required to comply with the regulations within four years of the bill's enactment. The bill also would require the archivist to set standards for the management of presidential records and to certify annually that the president's records management controls meet those standards. Passed 286-137: R 56-137; D 230-0 (ND 171-0, SD 59-0). A "nay" was a vote in support of the president's position. July 9, 2008.

478. HR 3329. Veterans Housing Assistance/Passage.
A. Green, D-Texas, motion to suspend the rules and pass the bill that would provide at least 20,000 rental home vouchers for homeless veterans. It would authorize $200 million in fiscal 2008 and such sums as may be necessary for each subsequent fiscal year for housing programs for veterans. Motion agreed to 412-9: R 181-9; D 231-0 (ND 172-0, SD 59-0). A two-thirds majority of those present and voting (281 in this case) is required for passage under suspension of the rules. A "nay" was a vote in support of the president's position. July 9, 2008.

479. HR 6184. National Parks Quarter Dollar Coins/Passage.
Maloney, D-N.Y., motion to suspend the rules and pass the bill that would authorize the issuance of quarter dollars with designs of national parks or other national sites starting in 2010. Motion agreed to 419-0: R 190-0; D 229-0 (ND 171-0, SD 58-0). A two-thirds majority of those present and voting (280 in this case) is required for passage under suspension of the rules. July 9, 2008.

480. HR 1286. Washington-Rochambeau Historic Trail/Previous Question.
Cardoza, D-Calif., motion to order the previous question (thus ending debate and possibility of amendment) on adoption of the rule (H Res 1317) to provide for House floor consideration of the bill that would designate the 600-mile route traveled by Revolutionary War Gen. George Washington and French Lt. Gen. Count de Rochambeau as a national historic trail. Motion agreed to 226-185: R 4-184; D 222-1 (ND 166-0, SD 56-1). July 10, 2008.

481. HR 1286. Washington-Rochambeau Historic Trail/Rule.
Adoption of the rule (H Res 1317) to provide for House floor consideration of the bill that would designate the 600-mile route traveled by Washington and Rochambeau as a national historic trail. Adopted 224-182: R 0-182; D 224-0 (ND 166-0, SD 58-0). July 10, 2008.

	477	478	479	480	481
ALABAMA					
1 Bonner	N	Y	Y	N	N
2 Everett	N	Y	Y	N	N
3 Rogers	N	Y	Y	N	N
4 Aderholt	N	Y	Y	N	N
5 Cramer	Y	Y	Y	Y	Y
6 Bachus	N	Y	Y	N	N
7 Davis	Y	Y	Y	Y	Y
ALASKA					
AL Young	N	Y	Y	N	N
ARIZONA					
1 Renzi	?	?	?	N	N
2 Franks	N	Y	Y	N	N
3 Shadegg	N	Y	Y	N	N
4 Pastor	Y	Y	Y	Y	Y
5 Mitchell	Y	Y	Y	Y	Y
6 Flake	N	N	Y	N	N
7 Grijalva	Y	Y	Y	Y	Y
8 Giffords	Y	Y	Y	Y	Y
ARKANSAS					
1 Berry	Y	Y	Y	Y	Y
2 Snyder	Y	Y	Y	Y	Y
3 Boozman	N	Y	Y	N	N
4 Ross	Y	Y	Y	Y	Y
CALIFORNIA					
1 Thompson	Y	Y	Y	Y	Y
2 Herger	N	Y	Y	N	N
3 Lungren	N	Y	Y	Y	?
4 Doolittle	N	Y	Y	N	N
5 Matsui	Y	Y	Y	Y	Y
6 Woolsey	Y	Y	Y	Y	Y
7 Miller, George	Y	Y	?	Y	Y
8 Pelosi					
9 Lee	Y	Y	Y	Y	Y
10 Tauscher	Y	Y	Y	Y	Y
11 McNerney	Y	Y	Y	Y	Y
12 Speier	Y	Y	Y	?	Y
13 Stark	Y	Y	Y	Y	Y
14 Eshoo	Y	Y	Y	Y	Y
15 Honda	Y	Y	Y	Y	Y
16 Lofgren	Y	Y	Y	Y	Y
17 Farr	Y	Y	Y	Y	Y
18 Cardoza	?	Y	Y	Y	Y
19 Radanovich	N	Y	Y	N	N
20 Costa	Y	Y	Y	Y	Y
21 Nunes	N	Y	Y	N	N
22 McCarthy	N	Y	Y	N	N
23 Capps	Y	Y	Y	Y	Y
24 Gallegly	Y	Y	Y	N	N
25 McKeon	N	Y	Y	N	N
26 Dreier	N	Y	Y	N	N
27 Sherman	Y	Y	Y	Y	Y
28 Berman	Y	Y	Y	Y	Y
29 Schiff	Y	Y	Y	Y	Y
30 Waxman	Y	Y	Y	?	?
31 Becerra	Y	Y	Y	Y	Y
32 Solis	Y	Y	Y	Y	Y
33 Watson	Y	Y	Y	Y	Y
34 Roybal-Allard	Y	Y	Y	Y	Y
35 Waters	Y	Y	Y	Y	Y
36 Harman	Y	Y	Y	?	?
37 Richardson	?	?	Y	Y	Y
38 Napolitano	Y	Y	Y	Y	Y
39 Sánchez, Linda	Y	Y	Y	Y	Y
40 Royce	N	Y	Y	N	N
41 Lewis	N	Y	Y	N	N
42 Miller, Gary	N	Y	Y	N	N
43 Baca	Y	Y	Y	Y	Y
44 Calvert	N	Y	Y	N	N
45 Bono Mack	N	Y	Y	N	N
46 Rohrabacher	Y	Y	Y	N	N
47 Sanchez, Loretta	Y	Y	Y	Y	Y
48 Campbell	N	N	Y	N	N
49 Issa	N	Y	Y	N	?
50 Bilbray	N	Y	Y	N	N
51 Filner	Y	Y	Y	Y	Y
52 Hunter	N	Y	Y	N	N
53 Davis	Y	Y	Y	Y	Y

	477	478	479	480	481
COLORADO					
1 DeGette	Y	Y	Y	Y	Y
2 Udall	?	?	?	Y	Y
3 Salazar	Y	Y	Y	Y	Y
4 Musgrave	N	Y	Y	N	N
5 Lamborn	N	Y	Y	N	N
6 Tancredo	N	N	Y	N	N
7 Perlmutter	Y	Y	Y	Y	Y
CONNECTICUT					
1 Larson	Y	Y	Y	Y	Y
2 Courtney	Y	Y	Y	Y	Y
3 DeLauro	Y	Y	Y	Y	Y
4 Shays	Y	Y	Y	Y	N
5 Murphy	Y	Y	Y	Y	Y
DELAWARE					
AL Castle	Y	Y	Y	Y	N
FLORIDA					
1 Miller	N	Y	Y	N	N
2 Boyd	Y	Y	Y	Y	Y
3 Brown	Y	Y	Y	Y	Y
4 Crenshaw	N	Y	Y	N	N
5 Brown-Waite	?	?	?	?	?
6 Stearns	N	Y	Y	N	N
7 Mica	N	Y	Y	N	N
8 Keller	Y	Y	Y	N	N
9 Bilirakis	Y	Y	Y	N	N
10 Young	Y	Y	Y	N	N
11 Castor	Y	Y	Y	Y	Y
12 Putnam	N	Y	Y	N	N
13 Buchanan	Y	Y	Y	N	N
14 Mack	N	Y	Y	N	N
15 Weldon	N	Y	Y	N	N
16 Mahoney	Y	Y	Y	Y	Y
17 Meek	Y	Y	Y	Y	Y
18 Ros-Lehtinen	Y	Y	Y	N	N
19 Wexler	Y	Y	Y	Y	Y
20 Wasserman Schultz	Y	Y	Y	Y	Y
21 Diaz-Balart, L.	Y	Y	Y	N	N
22 Klein	Y	Y	Y	Y	Y
23 Hastings	Y	Y	Y	Y	Y
24 Feeney	N	Y	Y	N	N
25 Diaz-Balart, M.	Y	Y	Y	N	N
GEORGIA					
1 Kingston	N	Y	Y	N	N
2 Bishop	Y	Y	Y	Y	Y
3 Westmoreland	N	Y	Y	N	N
4 Johnson	Y	Y	?	Y	Y
5 Lewis	Y	Y	Y	Y	Y
6 Price	N	Y	Y	N	N
7 Linder	N	?	Y	N	N
8 Marshall	Y	Y	Y	Y	Y
9 Deal	N	Y	Y	N	N
10 Broun	N	Y	Y	N	N
11 Gingrey	N	Y	Y	N	N
12 Barrow	Y	Y	Y	Y	Y
13 Scott	Y	Y	Y	Y	Y
HAWAII					
1 Abercrombie	Y	Y	Y	Y	Y
2 Hirono	Y	Y	Y	Y	Y
IDAHO					
1 Sali	N	Y	Y	N	N
2 Simpson	Y	Y	Y	N	N
ILLINOIS					
1 Rush	?	?	?	?	?
2 Jackson	Y	Y	Y	Y	Y
3 Lipinski	Y	Y	Y	Y	Y
4 Gutierrez	Y	Y	Y	Y	Y
5 Emanuel	Y	Y	Y	Y	Y
6 Roskam	Y	Y	Y	N	N
7 Davis	Y	Y	Y	Y	Y
8 Bean	Y	Y	Y	Y	Y
9 Schakowsky	Y	Y	Y	Y	Y
10 Kirk	Y	Y	Y	N	N
11 Weller	Y	Y	Y	N	N
12 Costello	Y	Y	Y	Y	Y
13 Biggert	N	Y	Y	N	N
14 Foster	Y	Y	Y	Y	Y
15 Johnson	Y	Y	Y	N	N

KEY	Republicans	Democrats		
Y	Voted for (yea)	X	Paired against	C Voted "present" to avoid possible conflict of interest
#	Paired for	–	Announced against	
+	Announced for	P	Voted "present"	? Did not vote or otherwise make a position known
N	Voted against (nay)			

ND Northern Democrats, SD Southern Democrats
Southern states: Ala., Ark., Fla., Ga., Ky., La., Miss., N.C., Okla., S.C., Tenn., Texas, Va.

	477	478	479	480	481
16 Manzullo	N	Y	Y	N	N
17 Hare	Y	Y	Y	Y	Y
18 LaHood	Y	Y	Y	N	N
19 Shimkus	N	Y	Y	N	N
INDIANA					
1 Visclosky	Y	Y	Y	Y	Y
2 Donnelly	Y	Y	Y	Y	Y
3 Souder	N	Y	Y	N	N
4 Buyer	N	Y	Y	N	N
5 Burton	N	Y	Y	N	N
6 Pence	N	Y	Y	N	N
7 Carson, A.	Y	Y	Y	Y	Y
8 Ellsworth	Y	Y	Y	Y	Y
9 Hill	Y	Y	Y	?	?
IOWA					
1 Braley	Y	Y	Y	Y	Y
2 Loebsack	Y	Y	Y	Y	Y
3 Boswell	?	?	?	?	?
4 Latham	Y	Y	Y	N	N
5 King	N	Y	Y	N	N
KANSAS					
1 Moran	Y	Y	Y	N	N
2 Boyda	Y	Y	Y	Y	Y
3 Moore	Y	Y	Y	Y	Y
4 Tiahrt	Y	Y	Y	N	N
KENTUCKY					
1 Whitfield	N	Y	Y	N	N
2 Lewis	N	Y	Y	N	N
3 Yarmuth	Y	Y	Y	Y	Y
4 Davis	N	Y	Y	N	N
5 Rogers	N	Y	Y	N	N
6 Chandler	Y	Y	Y	Y	Y
LOUISIANA					
1 Scalise	N	Y	Y	N	N
2 Jefferson	Y	Y	Y	Y	Y
3 Melancon	Y	Y	Y	Y	Y
4 McCrery	N	Y	Y	N	N
5 Alexander	N	Y	Y	N	N
6 Cazayoux	Y	Y	Y	Y	Y
7 Boustany	Y	Y	Y	N	N
MAINE					
1 Allen	Y	Y	Y	Y	Y
2 Michaud	Y	Y	Y	Y	Y
MARYLAND					
1 Gilchrest	Y	Y	Y	N	N
2 Ruppersberger	Y	Y	Y	Y	Y
3 Sarbanes	Y	Y	Y	Y	Y
4 Edwards	Y	Y	Y	Y	Y
5 Hoyer	Y	Y	Y	Y	Y
6 Bartlett	N	Y	Y	N	N
7 Cummings	Y	Y	Y	Y	Y
8 Van Hollen	Y	Y	Y	Y	Y
MASSACHUSETTS					
1 Olver	Y	Y	Y	Y	Y
2 Neal	Y	Y	Y	Y	Y
3 McGovern	Y	Y	Y	Y	Y
4 Frank	Y	Y	Y	?	?
5 Tsongas	Y	Y	Y	Y	Y
6 Tierney	Y	Y	Y	Y	Y
7 Markey	Y	Y	Y	Y	Y
8 Capuano	Y	Y	Y	Y	?
9 Lynch	Y	Y	Y	Y	Y
10 Delahunt	Y	Y	Y	Y	Y
MICHIGAN					
1 Stupak	Y	Y	Y	Y	Y
2 Hoekstra	N	Y	Y	N	?
3 Ehlers	N	Y	Y	N	N
4 Camp	N	Y	Y	N	N
5 Kildee	Y	Y	Y	Y	Y
6 Upton	Y	Y	Y	N	N
7 Walberg	Y	Y	Y	N	N
8 Rogers	N	Y	Y	N	?
9 Knollenberg	N	Y	Y	N	N
10 Miller	N	Y	Y	N	N
11 McCotter	N	Y	Y	N	N
12 Levin	Y	Y	Y	Y	Y
13 Kilpatrick	Y	Y	Y	Y	Y
14 Conyers	Y	Y	Y	Y	Y
15 Dingell	Y	Y	Y	?	?
MINNESOTA					
1 Walz	Y	Y	Y	Y	Y
2 Kline	N	Y	Y	N	N
3 Ramstad	Y	Y	Y	N	N
4 McCollum	Y	Y	Y	Y	Y

	477	478	479	480	481
5 Ellison	Y	Y	Y	Y	Y
6 Bachmann	N	Y	Y	N	N
7 Peterson	Y	Y	Y	Y	Y
8 Oberstar	Y	Y	Y	Y	Y
MISSISSIPPI					
1 Childers	Y	Y	Y	N	N
2 Thompson	Y	Y	Y	Y	Y
3 Pickering	?	?	?	?	?
4 Taylor	Y	Y	Y	Y	Y
MISSOURI					
1 Clay	Y	Y	Y	Y	Y
2 Akin	N	Y	Y	N	N
3 Carnahan	Y	Y	Y	Y	Y
4 Skelton	Y	Y	Y	Y	Y
5 Cleaver	Y	Y	Y	Y	Y
6 Graves	Y	Y	Y	N	N
7 Blunt	N	Y	Y	N	?
8 Emerson	N	Y	Y	N	N
9 Hulshof	?	?	?	?	?
MONTANA					
AL Rehberg	N	Y	Y	N	N
NEBRASKA					
1 Fortenberry	Y	Y	Y	?	?
2 Terry	Y	Y	Y	N	N
3 Smith	N	Y	Y	N	N
NEVADA					
1 Berkley	Y	Y	Y	Y	Y
2 Heller	Y	Y	Y	N	?
3 Porter	Y	Y	Y	N	N
NEW HAMPSHIRE					
1 Shea-Porter	Y	Y	Y	Y	Y
2 Hodes	Y	Y	Y	Y	Y
NEW JERSEY					
1 Andrews	Y	Y	Y	?	?
2 LoBiondo	Y	Y	Y	N	N
3 Saxton	Y	Y	Y	N	N
4 Smith	Y	Y	Y	N	N
5 Garrett	N	Y	Y	N	N
6 Pallone	Y	Y	Y	Y	Y
7 Ferguson	N	Y	Y	N	N
8 Pascrell	Y	Y	Y	Y	Y
9 Rothman	Y	Y	Y	Y	Y
10 Payne	Y	Y	Y	Y	Y
11 Frelinghuysen	Y	Y	Y	?	?
12 Holt	Y	Y	Y	Y	Y
13 Sires	Y	Y	Y	Y	Y
NEW MEXICO					
1 Wilson	Y	Y	Y	?	?
2 Pearce	N	Y	Y	N	N
3 Udall	Y	Y	Y	Y	Y
NEW YORK					
1 Bishop	Y	Y	Y	Y	Y
2 Israel	Y	Y	Y	Y	Y
3 King	N	Y	Y	N	N
4 McCarthy	Y	Y	Y	Y	Y
5 Ackerman	Y	Y	Y	Y	Y
6 Meeks	Y	Y	Y	Y	Y
7 Crowley	Y	Y	Y	Y	Y
8 Nadler	Y	Y	Y	Y	Y
9 Weiner	Y	Y	Y	Y	Y
10 Towns	Y	Y	Y	Y	Y
11 Clarke	Y	Y	Y	Y	Y
12 Velázquez	Y	Y	Y	Y	Y
13 Fossella	?	?	?	N	N
14 Maloney	Y	Y	Y	Y	Y
15 Rangel	Y	Y	Y	Y	Y
16 Serrano	Y	Y	Y	Y	Y
17 Engel	Y	Y	Y	Y	Y
18 Lowey	Y	Y	Y	Y	Y
19 Hall	Y	Y	Y	Y	Y
20 Gillibrand	Y	Y	Y	Y	Y
21 McNulty	Y	Y	Y	Y	Y
22 Hinchey	Y	Y	Y	Y	Y
23 McHugh	Y	?	Y	N	N
24 Arcuri	Y	Y	Y	Y	Y
25 Walsh	Y	Y	Y	N	N
26 Reynolds	N	Y	Y	N	N
27 Higgins	Y	Y	Y	Y	Y
28 Slaughter	Y	Y	Y	Y	Y
29 Kuhl	Y	Y	Y	N	N
NORTH CAROLINA					
1 Butterfield	Y	Y	Y	Y	Y
2 Etheridge	Y	Y	Y	Y	Y
3 Jones	Y	Y	Y	N	N
4 Price	Y	Y	Y	Y	Y

	477	478	479	480	481
5 Foxx	N	Y	Y	N	N
6 Coble	N	Y	Y	N	N
7 McIntyre	Y	Y	Y	Y	Y
8 Hayes	N	Y	Y	N	N
9 Myrick	N	Y	Y	N	N
10 McHenry	N	Y	Y	N	N
11 Shuler	Y	Y	Y	Y	Y
12 Watt	Y	Y	Y	Y	Y
13 Miller	Y	Y	Y	Y	Y
NORTH DAKOTA					
AL Pomeroy	Y	Y	Y	Y	Y
OHIO					
1 Chabot	Y	Y	Y	N	N
2 Schmidt	Y	Y	Y	N	N
3 Turner	Y	Y	Y	N	N
4 Jordan	N	Y	Y	N	N
5 Latta	N	Y	Y	N	N
6 Wilson	Y	Y	Y	Y	Y
7 Hobson	Y	Y	Y	N	N
8 Boehner	N	Y	Y	N	?
9 Kaptur	Y	Y	Y	Y	Y
10 Kucinich	Y	Y	Y	Y	Y
11 Tubbs Jones	Y	Y	Y	Y	Y
12 Tiberi	Y	Y	Y	N	N
13 Sutton	Y	Y	Y	Y	Y
14 LaTourette	Y	Y	Y	N	N
15 Pryce	?	?	?	?	?
16 Regula	Y	Y	Y	N	N
17 Ryan	Y	Y	Y	Y	Y
18 Space	Y	Y	Y	Y	Y
OKLAHOMA					
1 Sullivan	N	Y	Y	N	N
2 Boren	Y	Y	Y	Y	Y
3 Lucas	N	Y	Y	N	N
4 Cole	N	Y	Y	N	N
5 Fallin	N	Y	Y	N	N
OREGON					
1 Wu	Y	Y	Y	Y	Y
2 Walden	Y	Y	Y	N	N
3 Blumenauer	Y	Y	Y	Y	Y
4 DeFazio	Y	Y	Y	Y	Y
5 Hooley	Y	Y	Y	Y	Y
PENNSYLVANIA					
1 Brady	Y	Y	Y	Y	Y
2 Fattah	Y	Y	Y	Y	Y
3 English	Y	Y	Y	N	N
4 Altmire	Y	Y	Y	Y	Y
5 Peterson	N	?	Y	N	N
6 Gerlach	Y	Y	Y	N	N
7 Sestak	Y	Y	Y	Y	Y
8 Murphy, P.	Y	Y	Y	Y	?
9 Shuster	Y	Y	Y	N	N
10 Carney	Y	Y	Y	Y	Y
11 Kanjorski	Y	Y	Y	Y	Y
12 Murtha	Y	Y	Y	Y	Y
13 Schwartz	Y	Y	Y	Y	Y
14 Doyle	Y	Y	Y	Y	Y
15 Dent	Y	Y	Y	N	N
16 Pitts	N	Y	Y	N	N
17 Holden	Y	Y	Y	Y	Y
18 Murphy, T.	Y	Y	Y	N	N
19 Platts	Y	Y	Y	N	N
RHODE ISLAND					
1 Kennedy	Y	Y	?	?	Y
2 Langevin	Y	Y	Y	Y	Y
SOUTH CAROLINA					
1 Brown	N	Y	Y	N	N
2 Wilson	N	Y	Y	N	N
3 Barrett	N	Y	Y	N	N
4 Inglis	N	Y	Y	N	N
5 Spratt	Y	Y	Y	Y	Y
6 Clyburn	Y	Y	Y	Y	Y
SOUTH DAKOTA					
AL Herseth Sandlin	Y	Y	Y	Y	Y
TENNESSEE					
1 Davis, D.	N	Y	Y	N	N
2 Duncan	N	N	Y	N	N
3 Wamp	N	Y	Y	N	N
4 Davis, L.	Y	Y	Y	Y	Y
5 Cooper	Y	Y	Y	Y	Y
6 Gordon	Y	Y	Y	Y	Y
7 Blackburn	N	Y	Y	N	N
8 Tanner	Y	Y	Y	Y	Y
9 Cohen	Y	Y	Y	Y	Y

	477	478	479	480	481
TEXAS					
1 Gohmert	N	Y	Y	?	?
2 Poe	N	Y	Y	N	N
3 Johnson, S.	N	Y	Y	N	N
4 Hall	N	Y	Y	N	N
5 Hensarling	N	N	Y	N	N
6 Barton	N	Y	Y	N	N
7 Culberson	Y	Y	Y	N	N
8 Brady	N	Y	Y	N	N
9 Green, A.	Y	Y	Y	Y	Y
10 McCaul	N	Y	Y	N	N
11 Conaway	N	Y	Y	N	N
12 Granger	N	Y	Y	?	N
13 Thornberry	N	Y	Y	N	N
14 Paul	N	N	Y	N	N
15 Hinojosa	Y	Y	Y	Y	Y
16 Reyes	Y	Y	Y	?	?
17 Edwards	Y	Y	Y	?	?
18 Jackson Lee	Y	Y	Y	Y	Y
19 Neugebauer	N	Y	?	N	N
20 Gonzalez	Y	Y	Y	Y	Y
21 Smith	N	Y	Y	?	?
22 Lampson	Y	Y	Y	Y	Y
23 Rodriguez	Y	Y	Y	Y	Y
24 Marchant	N	N	?	N	N
25 Doggett	Y	Y	Y	Y	Y
26 Burgess	N	Y	Y	N	N
27 Ortiz	Y	Y	Y	Y	Y
28 Cuellar	Y	Y	Y	Y	Y
29 Green, G.	Y	Y	Y	Y	Y
30 Johnson, E.	Y	Y	Y	Y	Y
31 Carter	N	Y	Y	?	N
32 Sessions	N	Y	Y	N	N
UTAH					
1 Bishop	N	Y	Y	N	N
2 Matheson	Y	Y	Y	Y	Y
3 Cannon	N	N	Y	N	?
VERMONT					
AL Welch	Y	Y	Y	Y	Y
VIRGINIA					
1 Wittman	N	Y	Y	N	N
2 Drake	N	Y	Y	N	N
3 Scott	Y	Y	Y	Y	Y
4 Forbes	N	Y	Y	N	N
5 Goode	N	Y	Y	N	N
6 Goodlatte	N	Y	Y	N	N
7 Cantor	N	Y	Y	N	N
8 Moran	Y	Y	Y	Y	Y
9 Boucher	Y	Y	Y	Y	Y
10 Wolf	N	Y	Y	N	N
11 Davis	N	Y	Y	N	N
WASHINGTON					
1 Inslee	Y	Y	Y	Y	Y
2 Larsen	Y	Y	Y	Y	Y
3 Baird	Y	Y	Y	Y	Y
4 Hastings	N	Y	Y	N	N
5 McMorris Rodgers	N	Y	Y	N	N
6 Dicks	Y	Y	Y	Y	Y
7 McDermott	Y	Y	Y	Y	Y
8 Reichert	Y	Y	Y	Y	Y
9 Smith	Y	Y	Y	Y	Y
WEST VIRGINIA					
1 Mollohan	Y	Y	Y	Y	Y
2 Capito	Y	Y	Y	N	N
3 Rahall	Y	Y	Y	Y	Y
WISCONSIN					
1 Ryan	N	Y	Y	N	N
2 Baldwin	Y	Y	Y	Y	Y
3 Kind	Y	Y	Y	Y	Y
4 Moore	Y	Y	Y	Y	?
5 Sensenbrenner	N	N	N	N	N
6 Petri	N	Y	Y	N	N
7 Obey	Y	Y	Y	Y	Y
8 Kagen	Y	Y	Y	Y	Y
WYOMING					
AL Cubin	N	Y	Y	N	N
DELEGATES					
Faleomavaega (A.S.)					
Norton (D.C.)					
Bordallo (Guam)					
Fortuño (P.R.)					
Christensen (V.I.)					

IN THE HOUSE | By Vote Number

482. HR 1286. Washington-Rochambeau Historic Trail/Energy
Resources. Pearce, R-N.M., amendment that would require the Interior secretary to report to Congress on potential energy resources included within the trail. Adopted in Committee of the Whole 424-0: R 192-0; D 232-0 (ND 173-0, SD 59-0). July 10, 2008.

483. HR 1286. Washington-Rochambeau Historic Trail/Recommit.
Fallin, R-Okla., motion to recommit the bill to the Natural Resources Committee with instructions that it be reported back promptly with language that would require the land within the trail to be governed by state and local gun laws. Motion rejected 202-211: R 185-5; D 17-206 (ND 11-156, SD 6-50). July 10, 2008.

484. HR 1286. Washington-Rochambeau Historic Trail/Passage.
Passage of the bill that would designate the 600-mile route from Rhode Island to Virginia traveled by Revolutionary War Gen. George Washington and French Lt. Gen. Count de Rochambeau as a national historic trail. As amended, it would clarify that the bill would not limit access to hunting, fishing or shooting, nor limit a state's right to regulate those activities. It also would bar the use of eminent domain to acquire lands for the trail. Passed 345-69: R 122-69; D 223-0 (ND 166-0, SD 57-0). July 10, 2008.

485. HR 3121. National Flood Insurance Program/Motion to
Instruct. Neugebauer, R-Texas, motion to instruct conferees to include in the conference report a section of the Senate-passed bill that phases out premium subsidies more quickly and for more types of properties. It also would require that some premium subsidies be eliminated 90 days after enactment. Motion agreed to 385-26: R 177-12; D 208-14 (ND 152-13, SD 56-1). July 10, 2008.

	482	483	484	485
ALABAMA				
1 Bonner	Y	Y	Y	Y
2 Everett	Y	Y	Y	Y
3 Rogers	Y	Y	Y	Y
4 Aderholt	Y	Y	Y	Y
5 Cramer	Y	N	Y	Y
6 Bachus	Y	Y	Y	Y
7 Davis	Y	N	Y	Y
ALASKA				
AL Young	Y	?	N	Y
ARIZONA				
1 Renzi	Y	Y	Y	Y
2 Franks	Y	Y	N	Y
3 Shadegg	Y	Y	N	Y
4 Pastor	Y	N	Y	Y
5 Mitchell	Y	Y	Y	Y
6 Flake	Y	Y	N	Y
7 Grijalva	Y	N	Y	Y
8 Giffords	Y	N	Y	N
ARKANSAS				
1 Berry	Y	N	Y	Y
2 Snyder	Y	N	Y	Y
3 Boozman	Y	Y	Y	Y
4 Ross	Y	N	Y	Y
CALIFORNIA				
1 Thompson	Y	N	Y	Y
2 Herger	Y	Y	N	Y
3 Lungren	Y	Y	Y	Y
4 Doolittle	Y	Y	N	Y
5 Matsui	Y	N	Y	Y
6 Woolsey	Y	N	Y	Y
7 Miller, George	Y	N	Y	Y
8 Pelosi				
9 Lee	Y	N	Y	Y
10 Tauscher	Y	N	Y	Y
11 McNerney	Y	Y	Y	Y
12 Speier	Y	N	Y	Y
13 Stark	Y	N	Y	Y
14 Eshoo	Y	N	Y	Y
15 Honda	Y	N	Y	Y
16 Lofgren	Y	N	Y	Y
17 Farr	Y	N	Y	Y
18 Cardoza	Y	N	Y	Y
19 Radanovich	Y	Y	Y	Y
20 Costa	Y	N	Y	Y
21 Nunes	Y	Y	N	Y
22 McCarthy	Y	Y	Y	Y
23 Capps	Y	N	Y	Y
24 Gallegly	Y	Y	Y	Y
25 McKeon	Y	Y	Y	Y
26 Dreier	Y	Y	Y	Y
27 Sherman	Y	N	?	Y
28 Berman	Y	N	Y	Y
29 Schiff	Y	N	Y	Y
30 Waxman	?	?	?	?
31 Becerra	Y	N	Y	Y
32 Solis	Y	N	Y	Y
33 Watson	Y	N	Y	Y
34 Roybal-Allard	Y	N	Y	N
35 Waters	Y	N	Y	Y
36 Harman	Y	N	Y	Y
37 Richardson	Y	N	Y	Y
38 Napolitano	Y	N	Y	Y
39 Sánchez, Linda	Y	N	Y	Y
40 Royce	Y	Y	N	Y
41 Lewis	Y	Y	Y	Y
42 Miller, Gary	Y	Y	Y	Y
43 Baca	Y	N	Y	Y
44 Calvert	Y	Y	Y	Y
45 Bono Mack	Y	Y	Y	Y
46 Rohrabacher	Y	Y	Y	Y
47 Sanchez, Loretta	Y	N	Y	Y
48 Campbell	Y	Y	N	Y
49 Issa	Y	Y	N	Y
50 Bilbray	Y	Y	Y	Y
51 Filner	Y	N	Y	Y
52 Hunter	Y	Y	N	Y
53 Davis	Y	N	Y	Y

	482	483	484	485
COLORADO				
1 DeGette	Y	N	Y	Y
2 Udall	Y	N	Y	Y
3 Salazar	Y	N	Y	Y
4 Musgrave	Y	Y	N	Y
5 Lamborn	Y	Y	N	Y
6 Tancredo	Y	Y	N	Y
7 Perlmutter	Y	N	Y	Y
CONNECTICUT				
1 Larson	Y	N	Y	Y
2 Courtney	Y	N	Y	Y
3 DeLauro	Y	N	Y	Y
4 Shays	Y	N	Y	Y
5 Murphy	Y	N	Y	Y
DELAWARE				
AL Castle	Y	N	Y	Y
FLORIDA				
1 Miller	Y	Y	N	Y
2 Boyd	Y	N	Y	Y
3 Brown	Y	N	Y	Y
4 Crenshaw	Y	Y	Y	Y
5 Brown-Waite	?	?	?	?
6 Stearns	Y	Y	N	Y
7 Mica	Y	Y	Y	?
8 Keller	Y	Y	Y	Y
9 Bilirakis	Y	Y	Y	Y
10 Young	Y	Y	Y	Y
11 Castor	Y	N	Y	Y
12 Putnam	Y	Y	Y	Y
13 Buchanan	Y	Y	Y	Y
14 Mack	Y	Y	N	Y
15 Weldon	Y	Y	N	Y
16 Mahoney	Y	N	Y	Y
17 Meek	Y	N	Y	Y
18 Ros-Lehtinen	Y	Y	Y	Y
19 Wexler	Y	N	Y	Y
20 Wasserman Schultz	Y	N	Y	Y
21 Diaz-Balart, L.	Y	Y	Y	Y
22 Klein	Y	N	Y	N
23 Hastings	Y	N	Y	Y
24 Feeney	Y	Y	N	Y
25 Diaz-Balart, M.	Y	Y	Y	Y
GEORGIA				
1 Kingston	Y	Y	N	Y
2 Bishop	Y	N	Y	Y
3 Westmoreland	Y	Y	N	Y
4 Johnson	Y	N	Y	Y
5 Lewis	Y	N	Y	Y
6 Price	Y	Y	N	Y
7 Linder	Y	Y	N	Y
8 Marshall	Y	Y	Y	Y
9 Deal	Y	?	?	?
10 Broun	Y	Y	N	N
11 Gingrey	Y	Y	N	Y
12 Barrow	Y	Y	Y	Y
13 Scott	Y	N	Y	Y
HAWAII				
1 Abercrombie	Y	N	Y	Y
2 Hirono	Y	N	Y	Y
IDAHO				
1 Sali	Y	Y	N	Y
2 Simpson	Y	Y	Y	Y
ILLINOIS				
1 Rush	?	?	?	?
2 Jackson	Y	N	Y	Y
3 Lipinski	Y	N	Y	Y
4 Gutierrez	Y	N	Y	Y
5 Emanuel	Y	N	Y	Y
6 Roskam	Y	Y	Y	Y
7 Davis	Y	N	Y	Y
8 Bean	Y	N	Y	Y
9 Schakowsky	Y	N	Y	Y
10 Kirk	Y	N	Y	N
11 Weller	Y	Y	Y	Y
12 Costello	Y	N	Y	Y
13 Biggert	Y	Y	Y	Y
14 Foster	Y	Y	Y	Y
15 Johnson	Y	Y	Y	Y

ND Northern Democrats, SD Southern Democrats
Southern states: Ala., Ark., Fla., Ga., Ky., La., Miss., N.C., Okla., S.C., Tenn., Texas, Va.

Member	482	483	484	485
16 Manzullo	Y	Y	N	Y
17 Hare	Y	N	Y	Y
18 LaHood	Y	Y	Y	Y
19 Shimkus	Y	Y	Y	Y
INDIANA				
1 Visclosky	Y	N	Y	Y
2 Donnelly	Y	Y	Y	Y
3 Souder	Y	Y	Y	Y
4 Buyer	Y	Y	Y	N
5 Burton	Y	Y	N	N
6 Pence	Y	Y	N	Y
7 Carson, A.	Y	N	Y	Y
8 Ellsworth	Y	Y	Y	Y
9 Hill	?	?	?	?
IOWA				
1 Braley	Y	N	Y	N
2 Loebsack	Y	N	Y	N
3 Boswell	?	?	?	?
4 Latham	Y	Y	Y	N
5 King	Y	Y	N	N
KANSAS				
1 Moran	Y	Y	N	Y
2 Boyda	Y	N	Y	Y
3 Moore	Y	N	Y	Y
4 Tiahrt	Y	Y	N	Y
KENTUCKY				
1 Whitfield	Y	Y	Y	Y
2 Lewis	Y	Y	N	Y
3 Yarmuth	Y	N	Y	Y
4 Davis	Y	Y	N	Y
5 Rogers	Y	Y	Y	Y
6 Chandler	Y	N	Y	Y
LOUISIANA				
1 Scalise	Y	Y	N	N
2 Jefferson	Y	N	Y	Y
3 Melancon	Y	Y	Y	Y
4 McCrery	Y	Y	Y	Y
5 Alexander	Y	Y	Y	Y
6 Cazayoux	Y	Y	Y	Y
7 Boustany	Y	Y	Y	N
MAINE				
1 Allen	Y	N	Y	Y
2 Michaud	Y	N	Y	Y
MARYLAND				
1 Gilchrest	Y	N	Y	N
2 Ruppersberger	Y	N	Y	Y
3 Sarbanes	Y	N	Y	Y
4 Edwards	Y	N	Y	Y
5 Hoyer	Y	N	Y	Y
6 Bartlett	Y	Y	Y	Y
7 Cummings	Y	N	Y	Y
8 Van Hollen	Y	N	Y	Y
MASSACHUSETTS				
1 Olver	Y	N	Y	Y
2 Neal	Y	?	?	?
3 McGovern	Y	N	Y	Y
4 Frank	Y	N	Y	Y
5 Tsongas	Y	N	Y	Y
6 Tierney	Y	N	Y	Y
7 Markey	Y	?	Y	Y
8 Capuano	Y	N	Y	Y
9 Lynch	Y	N	Y	Y
10 Delahunt	Y	N	Y	Y
MICHIGAN				
1 Stupak	Y	N	Y	Y
2 Hoekstra	Y	Y	N	Y
3 Ehlers	Y	Y	Y	Y
4 Camp	Y	Y	Y	Y
5 Kildee	Y	N	Y	Y
6 Upton	Y	Y	Y	Y
7 Walberg	Y	Y	N	Y
8 Rogers	Y	Y	Y	Y
9 Knollenberg	Y	Y	Y	Y
10 Miller	Y	Y	Y	Y
11 McCotter	Y	Y	Y	Y
12 Levin	Y	N	Y	Y
13 Kilpatrick	Y	N	Y	Y
14 Conyers	+	+	+	+
15 Dingell	Y	N	Y	Y
MINNESOTA				
1 Walz	Y	N	Y	Y
2 Kline	Y	Y	Y	Y
3 Ramstad	Y	Y	Y	Y
4 McCollum	Y	N	Y	Y
5 Ellison	Y	N	Y	Y
6 Bachmann	Y	Y	Y	Y
7 Peterson	Y	N	Y	Y
8 Oberstar	Y	N	Y	Y
MISSISSIPPI				
1 Childers	Y	Y	Y	Y
2 Thompson	Y	N	Y	Y
3 Pickering	?	?	?	?
4 Taylor	Y	N	Y	Y
MISSOURI				
1 Clay	Y	N	Y	Y
2 Akin	Y	Y	Y	Y
3 Carnahan	Y	N	Y	Y
4 Skelton	Y	N	Y	Y
5 Cleaver	Y	N	Y	?
6 Graves	Y	Y	Y	Y
7 Blunt	Y	Y	Y	Y
8 Emerson	Y	Y	Y	Y
9 Hulshof	?	?	?	?
MONTANA				
AL Rehberg	Y	Y	Y	Y
NEBRASKA				
1 Fortenberry	?	?	?	?
2 Terry	Y	Y	Y	Y
3 Smith	Y	Y	N	Y
NEVADA				
1 Berkley	Y	N	Y	Y
2 Heller	Y	Y	N	Y
3 Porter	Y	Y	Y	Y
NEW HAMPSHIRE				
1 Shea-Porter	Y	Y	Y	Y
2 Hodes	Y	Y	Y	Y
NEW JERSEY				
1 Andrews	?	?	?	?
2 LoBiondo	Y	Y	Y	Y
3 Saxton	Y	Y	Y	Y
4 Smith	Y	Y	Y	Y
5 Garrett	Y	Y	N	Y
6 Pallone	Y	N	Y	N
7 Ferguson	Y	N	Y	Y
8 Pascrell	Y	N	Y	Y
9 Rothman	Y	N	Y	Y
10 Payne	Y	N	Y	Y
11 Frelinghuysen	?	?	?	?
12 Holt	Y	N	Y	Y
13 Sires	Y	N	Y	Y
NEW MEXICO				
1 Wilson	Y	N	Y	Y
2 Pearce	Y	Y	Y	Y
3 Udall	Y	N	Y	Y
NEW YORK				
1 Bishop	Y	N	Y	N
2 Israel	Y	N	Y	N
3 King	Y	N	Y	N
4 McCarthy	Y	N	Y	Y
5 Ackerman	Y	N	Y	Y
6 Meeks	Y	N	Y	Y
7 Crowley	Y	N	Y	Y
8 Nadler	Y	N	Y	Y
9 Weiner	Y	N	Y	N
10 Towns	Y	N	Y	Y
11 Clarke	Y	N	Y	Y
12 Velázquez	Y	N	Y	Y
13 Fossella	Y	Y	Y	Y
14 Maloney	Y	N	Y	Y
15 Rangel	Y	N	Y	Y
16 Serrano	Y	N	Y	Y
17 Engel	Y	N	Y	Y
18 Lowey	Y	N	Y	Y
19 Hall	Y	N	Y	Y
20 Gillibrand	Y	Y	Y	Y
21 McNulty	Y	N	Y	?
22 Hinchey	Y	N	Y	Y
23 McHugh	Y	Y	Y	Y
24 Arcuri	Y	N	Y	Y
25 Walsh	Y	Y	Y	Y
26 Reynolds	Y	Y	Y	Y
27 Higgins	Y	N	Y	N
28 Slaughter	Y	?	?	?
29 Kuhl	Y	Y	Y	Y
NORTH CAROLINA				
1 Butterfield	Y	N	Y	Y
2 Etheridge	Y	N	Y	Y
3 Jones	Y	Y	Y	Y
4 Price	Y	N	Y	Y
5 Foxx	Y	Y	N	Y
6 Coble	Y	Y	N	Y
7 McIntyre	Y	Y	Y	Y
8 Hayes	Y	Y	Y	Y
9 Myrick	Y	Y	Y	Y
10 McHenry	Y	Y	N	Y
11 Shuler	Y	N	Y	Y
12 Watt	Y	N	Y	Y
13 Miller	Y	N	Y	Y
NORTH DAKOTA				
AL Pomeroy	Y	N	Y	Y
OHIO				
1 Chabot	Y	Y	Y	Y
2 Schmidt	Y	Y	Y	Y
3 Turner	Y	Y	Y	Y
4 Jordan	Y	Y	N	Y
5 Latta	Y	Y	Y	Y
6 Wilson	Y	N	Y	Y
7 Hobson	Y	Y	Y	Y
8 Boehner	Y	Y	N	Y
9 Kaptur	Y	N	Y	Y
10 Kucinich	Y	N	Y	Y
11 Tubbs Jones	Y	N	Y	Y
12 Tiberi	Y	Y	Y	Y
13 Sutton	Y	N	Y	Y
14 LaTourette	Y	Y	Y	Y
15 Pryce	?	?	?	?
16 Regula	Y	N	Y	Y
17 Ryan	Y	N	Y	Y
18 Space	Y	Y	Y	Y
OKLAHOMA				
1 Sullivan	Y	Y	Y	Y
2 Boren	Y	?	Y	Y
3 Lucas	Y	Y	Y	Y
4 Cole	Y	Y	Y	Y
5 Fallin	Y	Y	Y	Y
OREGON				
1 Wu	Y	N	Y	Y
2 Walden	Y	Y	Y	Y
3 Blumenauer	Y	N	Y	N
4 DeFazio	Y	N	Y	Y
5 Hooley	Y	N	Y	Y
PENNSYLVANIA				
1 Brady	Y	N	Y	Y
2 Fattah	Y	N	Y	Y
3 English	Y	Y	Y	Y
4 Altmire	Y	Y	Y	Y
5 Peterson	Y	Y	Y	?
6 Gerlach	Y	Y	Y	Y
7 Sestak	Y	N	Y	Y
8 Murphy, P.	Y	Y	Y	N
9 Shuster	Y	Y	Y	Y
10 Carney	Y	N	Y	Y
11 Kanjorski	Y	N	Y	Y
12 Murtha	Y	N	Y	Y
13 Schwartz	Y	N	Y	Y
14 Doyle	Y	N	?	Y
15 Dent	Y	Y	Y	Y
16 Pitts	Y	Y	N	Y
17 Holden	Y	N	Y	Y
18 Murphy, T.	Y	Y	Y	Y
19 Platts	Y	Y	Y	Y
RHODE ISLAND				
1 Kennedy	Y	N	Y	Y
2 Langevin	Y	N	Y	Y
SOUTH CAROLINA				
1 Brown	Y	Y	Y	Y
2 Wilson	Y	Y	N	Y
3 Barrett	Y	Y	Y	Y
4 Inglis	Y	Y	Y	Y
5 Spratt	Y	N	Y	Y
6 Clyburn	Y	N	Y	Y
SOUTH DAKOTA				
AL Herseth Sandlin	Y	N	Y	Y
TENNESSEE				
1 Davis, D.	Y	Y	N	Y
2 Duncan	Y	Y	N	Y
3 Wamp	Y	Y	Y	Y
4 Davis, L.	Y	N	Y	Y
5 Cooper	Y	N	Y	Y
6 Gordon	Y	?	?	?
7 Blackburn	Y	Y	Y	Y
8 Tanner	Y	N	Y	Y
9 Cohen	Y	N	Y	Y
TEXAS				
1 Gohmert	Y	Y	N	Y
2 Poe	Y	Y	N	Y
3 Johnson, S.	Y	Y	N	Y
4 Hall	Y	Y	N	Y
5 Hensarling	Y	Y	N	Y
6 Barton	Y	Y	N	Y
7 Culberson	Y	Y	N	Y
8 Brady	Y	Y	N	Y
9 Green, A.	Y	N	Y	Y
10 McCaul	Y	Y	Y	Y
11 Conaway	Y	Y	N	Y
12 Granger	Y	Y	Y	Y
13 Thornberry	Y	Y	N	Y
14 Paul	Y	Y	N	Y
15 Hinojosa	Y	N	Y	Y
16 Reyes	Y	N	Y	Y
17 Edwards	Y	N	Y	Y
18 Jackson Lee	Y	N	Y	Y
19 Neugebauer	Y	Y	N	Y
20 Gonzalez	Y	N	Y	Y
21 Smith	Y	Y	N	Y
22 Lampson	Y	Y	Y	Y
23 Rodriguez	Y	N	Y	Y
24 Marchant	?	?	?	?
25 Doggett	Y	N	Y	Y
26 Burgess	Y	Y	N	Y
27 Ortiz	Y	N	Y	Y
28 Cuellar	Y	N	Y	Y
29 Green, G.	Y	N	Y	Y
30 Johnson, E.	Y	N	Y	Y
31 Carter	Y	Y	N	Y
32 Sessions	Y	Y	N	Y
UTAH				
1 Bishop	Y	N	Y	Y
2 Matheson	Y	N	Y	Y
3 Cannon	Y	N	Y	Y
VERMONT				
AL Welch	Y	N	Y	Y
VIRGINIA				
1 Wittman	Y	Y	Y	Y
2 Drake	Y	Y	Y	Y
3 Scott	Y	N	Y	Y
4 Forbes	Y	Y	Y	N
5 Goode	Y	Y	N	Y
6 Goodlatte	Y	Y	N	Y
7 Cantor	Y	Y	N	Y
8 Moran	Y	N	Y	Y
9 Boucher	Y	?	?	?
10 Wolf	Y	Y	Y	Y
11 Davis	Y	Y	N	Y
WASHINGTON				
1 Inslee	Y	N	Y	Y
2 Larsen	Y	N	Y	Y
3 Baird	Y	N	Y	Y
4 Hastings	Y	Y	N	Y
5 McMorris Rodgers	Y	Y	Y	Y
6 Dicks	Y	N	Y	Y
7 McDermott	Y	N	Y	Y
8 Reichert	Y	Y	Y	Y
9 Smith	Y	N	Y	Y
WEST VIRGINIA				
1 Mollohan	Y	N	Y	Y
2 Capito	Y	Y	Y	Y
3 Rahall	Y	N	Y	Y
WISCONSIN				
1 Ryan	Y	Y	Y	Y
2 Baldwin	Y	N	Y	Y
3 Kind	Y	N	Y	Y
4 Moore	Y	N	Y	Y
5 Sensenbrenner	Y	Y	N	Y
6 Petri	Y	Y	Y	Y
7 Obey	Y	N	Y	Y
8 Kagen	Y	N	Y	Y
WYOMING				
AL Cubin	Y	Y	N	N
DELEGATES				
Faleomavaega (A.S.)	?			
Norton (D.C.)	Y			
Bordallo (Guam)	Y			
Fortuño (P.R.)	?			
Christensen (V.I.)	?			

IN THE HOUSE | By Vote Number

486. H Res 1067. *USS Nautilus* 50th Anniversary/Adoption.
Courtney, D-Conn., motion to suspend the rules and adopt the resolution that would recognize the 50th anniversary of the crossing of the North Pole by the *USS Nautilus* and commend the submarine's officers and crew. Motion agreed to 375-0: R 175-0; D 200-0 (ND 151-0, SD 49-0). A two-thirds majority of those present and voting (250 in this case) is required for adoption under suspension of the rules. July 14, 2008.

487. H Res 1080. Honor 101st Airborne Division/Adoption.
Courtney, D-Conn., motion to suspend the rules and adopt the resolution that would recognize the service, sacrifice and patriotism of the 101st Airborne Division, also known as the Screaming Eagles. Motion agreed to 378-0: R 176-0; D 202-0 (ND 153-0, SD 49-0). A two-thirds majority of those present and voting (252 in this case) is required for adoption under suspension of the rules. July 14, 2008.

488. H Con Res 297. Equality in the Armed Services/Adoption.
Courtney, D-Conn., motion to suspend the rules and adopt the concurrent resolution that would express the sense of Congress honoring the 60th anniversary of President Harry S Truman's declaration on July 26, 1948, that there should be equality of treatment for members of the armed services. Motion agreed to 378-0: R 174-0; D 204-0 (ND 155-0, SD 49-0). A two-thirds majority of those present and voting (252 in this case) is required for adoption under suspension of the rules. July 14, 2008.

489. H Res 1259. Congratulate Hamilton College Women's Lacrosse/Adoption.
Bishop, D-N.Y., motion to suspend the rules and adopt the resolution that would congratulate the Hamilton College Continentals on winning the National Collegiate Athletic Association Division III women's lacrosse championship. Motion agreed to 423-0: R 192-0; D 231-0 (ND 174-0, SD 57-0). A two-thirds majority of those present and voting (282 in this case) is required for adoption under suspension of the rules. July 15, 2008.

490. H Res 1323. Congratulate Arizona State University Softball/Adoption.
Bishop, D-N.Y., motion to suspend the rules and adopt the resolution that would commend the Arizona State University softball team for its victory in the 2008 Women's College World Series. Motion agreed to 425-0: R 194-0; D 231-0 (ND 174-0, SD 57-0). A two-thirds majority of those present and voting (284 in this case) is required for adoption under suspension of the rules. July 15, 2008.

491. HR 6331. Medicare Physician Payments/Veto Override.
Passage, over President Bush's July 15, 2008, veto, of the bill that would prevent a 10.6 percent cut in Medicare physician payments scheduled to take effect July 1, 2008, by holding payments at current rates for 18 months. It would give doctors a 1.1 percent increase in payments in 2009 and provide $16.6 billion over 10 years for changes to Medicare beneficiary programs. The costs would be partially offset by provisions to reduce the cost of Medicare Advantage plans. Passed 383-41: R 153-41; D 230-0 (ND 173-0, SD 57-0). A two-thirds majority of those present and voting (283 in this case for the House) of both chambers is required to override a veto. A "nay" was a vote in support of the president's position. July 15, 2008.

	486	487	488	489	490	491
ALABAMA						
1 **Bonner**	?	?	?	?	?	?
2 **Everett**	Y	Y	Y	Y	Y	Y
3 **Rogers**	Y	Y	Y	Y	Y	Y
4 **Aderholt**	Y	Y	Y	Y	Y	Y
5 Cramer	?	?	?	Y	Y	Y
6 **Bachus**	Y	Y	Y	Y	Y	Y
7 Davis	Y	Y	Y	Y	Y	Y
ALASKA						
AL **Young**	Y	Y	Y	Y	Y	Y
ARIZONA						
1 **Renzi**	Y	Y	Y	Y	Y	N
2 **Franks**	?	Y	Y	Y	Y	N
3 **Shadegg**	Y	Y	Y	Y	Y	Y
4 Pastor	Y	Y	Y	Y	Y	Y
5 Mitchell	Y	Y	Y	Y	Y	Y
6 **Flake**	Y	Y	Y	Y	Y	N
7 Grijalva	?	Y	Y	Y	Y	Y
8 Giffords	Y	Y	Y	Y	Y	Y
ARKANSAS						
1 Berry	Y	Y	Y	Y	Y	Y
2 Snyder	Y	Y	Y	Y	Y	Y
3 **Boozman**	Y	Y	Y	Y	Y	Y
4 Ross	Y	Y	Y	Y	Y	Y
CALIFORNIA						
1 Thompson	Y	Y	Y	Y	Y	Y
2 **Herger**	Y	Y	Y	Y	Y	Y
3 **Lungren**	Y	Y	Y	Y	Y	Y
4 **Doolittle**	?	?	?	Y	Y	N
5 Matsui	Y	Y	Y	Y	Y	Y
6 Woolsey	+	Y	Y	Y	Y	Y
7 Miller, George	?	?	?	Y	Y	Y
8 Pelosi						Y
9 Lee	Y	Y	Y	Y	Y	Y
10 Tauscher	Y	Y	Y	Y	Y	Y
11 McNerney	Y	Y	Y	Y	Y	Y
12 Speier	Y	?	Y	Y	Y	Y
13 Stark	Y	Y	Y	Y	Y	Y
14 Eshoo	Y	Y	Y	Y	Y	Y
15 Honda	Y	Y	Y	Y	Y	Y
16 Lofgren	Y	Y	Y	Y	Y	Y
17 Farr	Y	Y	Y	Y	Y	Y
18 Cardoza	Y	Y	Y	Y	Y	Y
19 **Radanovich**	?	?	?	Y	Y	Y
20 Costa	?	?	?	Y	Y	Y
21 **Nunes**	Y	Y	Y	Y	Y	Y
22 **McCarthy**	Y	Y	Y	Y	Y	Y
23 Capps	Y	Y	Y	Y	Y	Y
24 **Gallegly**	Y	Y	Y	Y	Y	Y
25 **McKeon**	Y	Y	Y	Y	Y	Y
26 **Dreier**	Y	Y	Y	Y	Y	Y
27 Sherman	Y	Y	Y	Y	Y	Y
28 Berman	Y	Y	Y	Y	Y	Y
29 Schiff	Y	Y	Y	Y	Y	Y
30 Waxman	Y	Y	Y	Y	Y	Y
31 Becerra	Y	Y	Y	Y	Y	Y
32 Solis	Y	Y	Y	Y	Y	Y
33 Watson	Y	Y	Y	Y	Y	Y
34 Roybal-Allard	Y	Y	Y	Y	Y	Y
35 Waters	Y	Y	Y	Y	Y	Y
36 Harman	Y	Y	Y	Y	Y	Y
37 Richardson	Y	Y	Y	Y	Y	Y
38 Napolitano	Y	Y	Y	Y	Y	Y
39 Sánchez, Linda	Y	Y	Y	Y	Y	Y
40 **Royce**	Y	Y	Y	Y	Y	N
41 **Lewis**	Y	Y	Y	Y	Y	Y
42 **Miller, Gary**	Y	Y	Y	Y	Y	Y
43 Baca	Y	Y	Y	Y	Y	Y
44 **Calvert**	Y	Y	Y	Y	Y	Y
45 **Bono Mack**	Y	Y	Y	Y	Y	Y
46 **Rohrabacher**	?	?	?	Y	Y	Y
47 Sanchez, Loretta	Y	Y	Y	Y	Y	Y
48 **Campbell**	Y	Y	Y	Y	Y	N
49 **Issa**	Y	Y	Y	Y	Y	Y
50 **Bilbray**	Y	Y	Y	Y	Y	Y
51 Filner	Y	Y	Y	Y	Y	Y
52 **Hunter**	Y	Y	Y	Y	Y	Y
53 Davis	+	+	+	Y	Y	Y

	486	487	488	489	490	491
COLORADO						
1 DeGette	Y	Y	Y	Y	Y	Y
2 Udall	?	?	?	Y	Y	Y
3 Salazar	Y	Y	Y	Y	Y	Y
4 **Musgrave**	Y	Y	Y	Y	Y	Y
5 **Lamborn**	Y	Y	Y	Y	Y	Y
6 **Tancredo**	?	?	?	?	Y	N
7 Perlmutter	Y	Y	Y	Y	Y	Y
CONNECTICUT						
1 Larson	Y	Y	Y	Y	Y	Y
2 Courtney	Y	Y	Y	Y	Y	Y
3 DeLauro	Y	Y	Y	Y	Y	Y
4 **Shays**	+	+	+	Y	Y	Y
5 Murphy	Y	Y	Y	Y	Y	Y
DELAWARE						
AL **Castle**	Y	Y	Y	Y	Y	Y
FLORIDA						
1 **Miller**	Y	Y	Y	Y	Y	Y
2 Boyd	Y	Y	Y	Y	Y	Y
3 Brown	?	?	?	Y	Y	Y
4 **Crenshaw**	Y	Y	Y	Y	Y	Y
5 **Brown-Waite**	Y	Y	Y	Y	Y	Y
6 **Stearns**	Y	Y	Y	Y	Y	Y
7 **Mica**	Y	Y	Y	Y	Y	N
8 **Keller**	Y	Y	Y	Y	Y	Y
9 **Bilirakis**	Y	Y	Y	Y	Y	Y
10 **Young**	Y	Y	Y	Y	Y	Y
11 Castor	Y	Y	Y	Y	Y	Y
12 **Putnam**	Y	Y	Y	Y	Y	Y
13 **Buchanan**	Y	Y	Y	Y	Y	Y
14 **Mack**	Y	Y	Y	Y	Y	Y
15 **Weldon**	Y	Y	Y	Y	Y	N
16 Mahoney	Y	Y	Y	Y	Y	Y
17 Meek	Y	Y	Y	Y	Y	Y
18 **Ros-Lehtinen**	Y	Y	Y	Y	Y	Y
19 Wexler	Y	Y	Y	Y	Y	Y
20 Wasserman Schultz	?	?	?	Y	Y	Y
21 **Diaz-Balart, L.**	Y	Y	Y	Y	Y	Y
22 Klein	Y	Y	Y	Y	Y	Y
23 Hastings	Y	Y	Y	Y	Y	Y
24 **Feeney**	Y	Y	Y	Y	Y	Y
25 **Diaz-Balart, M.**	Y	Y	Y	Y	Y	Y
GEORGIA						
1 **Kingston**	Y	Y	Y	Y	Y	Y
2 Bishop	Y	Y	Y	Y	Y	Y
3 **Westmoreland**	Y	Y	Y	Y	Y	N
4 Johnson	Y	Y	Y	Y	Y	Y
5 Lewis	?	?	?	?	?	?
6 **Price**	Y	Y	Y	Y	Y	Y
7 **Linder**	Y	Y	Y	Y	Y	N
8 Marshall	Y	Y	Y	Y	Y	Y
9 **Deal**	Y	Y	Y	Y	Y	Y
10 **Broun**	?	?	?	?	?	?
11 **Gingrey**	Y	Y	Y	Y	Y	Y
12 Barrow	+	+	+	+	+	+
13 Scott	Y	Y	Y	Y	Y	Y
HAWAII						
1 Abercrombie	Y	Y	Y	Y	Y	Y
2 Hirono	Y	+	Y	Y	Y	Y
IDAHO						
1 **Sali**	Y	Y	Y	Y	Y	N
2 **Simpson**	Y	Y	Y	Y	Y	Y
ILLINOIS						
1 Rush	?	?	?	?	?	?
2 Jackson	Y	Y	Y	Y	Y	Y
3 Lipinski	?	?	?	Y	Y	Y
4 Gutierrez	?	?	?	Y	Y	Y
5 Emanuel	Y	Y	Y	Y	Y	Y
6 **Roskam**	Y	Y	Y	Y	Y	Y
7 Davis	Y	Y	Y	Y	Y	?
8 Bean	Y	Y	Y	Y	Y	Y
9 Schakowsky	Y	Y	Y	Y	Y	Y
10 **Kirk**	Y	Y	Y	Y	Y	Y
11 **Weller**	+	+	+	Y	Y	Y
12 Costello	?	?	?	Y	Y	Y
13 **Biggert**	Y	Y	Y	Y	Y	Y
14 Foster	Y	Y	Y	Y	Y	Y
15 **Johnson**	+	+	+	Y	Y	Y

KEY	**Republicans**	Democrats		
Y	Voted for (yea)	X	Paired against	C	Voted "present" to avoid possible conflict of interest
#	Paired for	–	Announced against	
+	Announced for	P	Voted "present"	?	Did not vote or otherwise make a position known
N	Voted against (nay)			

ND Northern Democrats, SD Southern Democrats
Southern states: Ala., Ark., Fla., Ga., Ky., La., Miss., N.C., Okla., S.C., Tenn., Texas, Va.

	486	487	488	489	490	491
16 **Manzullo**	Y	Y	?	Y	Y	Y
17 Hare	Y	Y	Y	Y	Y	Y
18 **LaHood**	Y	Y	Y	Y	Y	Y
19 **Shimkus**	Y	Y	Y	Y	Y	Y
INDIANA						
1 Visclosky	Y	Y	Y	Y	Y	Y
2 Donnelly	Y	Y	Y	Y	Y	Y
3 **Souder**	Y	Y	Y	Y	Y	Y
4 **Buyer**	Y	Y	Y	Y	Y	N
5 **Burton**	Y	Y	Y	Y	Y	Y
6 **Pence**	Y	Y	Y	Y	Y	N
7 Carson, A.	Y	Y	Y	Y	Y	Y
8 Ellsworth	Y	Y	Y	Y	Y	Y
9 Hill	Y	Y	Y	Y	Y	Y
IOWA						
1 Braley	?	?	?	Y	Y	Y
2 Loebsack	Y	Y	Y	Y	Y	Y
3 Boswell	?	?	?	?	?	?
4 **Latham**	Y	Y	Y	Y	Y	Y
5 **King**	Y	Y	Y	Y	Y	N
KANSAS						
1 **Moran**	Y	Y	Y	Y	Y	Y
2 Boyda	Y	Y	Y	Y	Y	Y
3 Moore	+	Y	Y	Y	Y	Y
4 **Tiahrt**	Y	Y	Y	Y	Y	Y
KENTUCKY						
1 **Whitfield**	Y	Y	Y	Y	Y	Y
2 **Lewis**	Y	Y	Y	Y	Y	N
3 Yarmuth	Y	Y	Y	Y	Y	Y
4 **Davis**	Y	Y	Y	Y	Y	Y
5 **Rogers**	Y	Y	Y	Y	Y	Y
6 Chandler	Y	Y	Y	Y	Y	Y
LOUISIANA						
1 **Scalise**	Y	Y	Y	Y	Y	N
2 Jefferson	?	?	?	Y	Y	Y
3 Melancon	Y	Y	Y	Y	Y	Y
4 **McCrery**	Y	Y	Y	Y	Y	N
5 **Alexander**	Y	Y	Y	Y	Y	Y
6 Cazayoux	Y	Y	Y	Y	Y	Y
7 **Boustany**	Y	Y	Y	Y	Y	Y
MAINE						
1 Allen	Y	Y	Y	Y	Y	Y
2 Michaud	Y	Y	Y	Y	Y	Y
MARYLAND						
1 **Gilchrest**	Y	Y	Y	Y	Y	Y
2 Ruppersberger	Y	Y	Y	Y	Y	Y
3 Sarbanes	Y	Y	Y	Y	Y	Y
4 Edwards	Y	Y	Y	Y	Y	Y
5 Hoyer	Y	Y	Y	Y	Y	Y
6 **Bartlett**	Y	Y	Y	Y	Y	Y
7 Cummings	Y	Y	Y	Y	Y	Y
8 Van Hollen	Y	Y	Y	Y	Y	Y
MASSACHUSETTS						
1 Olver	Y	Y	Y	Y	Y	Y
2 Neal	?	?	?	Y	Y	Y
3 McGovern	Y	Y	Y	Y	Y	Y
4 Frank	Y	Y	Y	Y	Y	Y
5 Tsongas	Y	Y	Y	Y	Y	Y
6 Tierney	Y	Y	Y	Y	Y	Y
7 Markey	Y	Y	Y	Y	Y	Y
8 Capuano	Y	Y	Y	Y	Y	Y
9 Lynch	Y	Y	Y	Y	Y	Y
10 Delahunt	Y	Y	Y	Y	Y	+
MICHIGAN						
1 Stupak	Y	Y	Y	Y	Y	Y
2 **Hoekstra**	Y	Y	Y	Y	Y	Y
3 **Ehlers**	Y	Y	Y	Y	Y	Y
4 **Camp**	Y	Y	Y	Y	Y	N
5 Kildee	Y	Y	Y	Y	Y	Y
6 **Upton**	Y	Y	Y	Y	Y	Y
7 **Walberg**	Y	Y	Y	Y	Y	Y
8 **Rogers**	Y	Y	Y	Y	Y	N
9 **Knollenberg**	Y	Y	Y	Y	Y	Y
10 **Miller**	Y	Y	Y	Y	Y	Y
11 **McCotter**	Y	Y	Y	Y	Y	Y
12 Levin	Y	Y	Y	Y	Y	Y
13 Kilpatrick	+	+	+	Y	Y	Y
14 Conyers	Y	Y	Y	Y	Y	Y
15 Dingell	Y	Y	Y	Y	Y	Y
MINNESOTA						
1 Walz	Y	Y	Y	Y	Y	Y
2 **Kline**	Y	Y	Y	Y	Y	Y
3 **Ramstad**	Y	Y	Y	Y	Y	Y
4 McCollum	Y	Y	Y	Y	Y	Y

	486	487	488	489	490	491
5 Ellison	?	?	?	Y	Y	Y
6 **Bachmann**	?	?	?	Y	Y	Y
7 Peterson	Y	Y	Y	Y	Y	Y
8 Oberstar	Y	Y	Y	Y	Y	Y
MISSISSIPPI						
1 Childers	Y	Y	Y	Y	Y	Y
2 Thompson	Y	Y	Y	Y	Y	Y
3 **Pickering**	Y	Y	Y	Y	Y	Y
4 Taylor	?	?	?	Y	Y	Y
MISSOURI						
1 Clay	Y	Y	Y	Y	Y	Y
2 **Akin**	Y	Y	Y	Y	Y	N
3 Carnahan	Y	Y	Y	Y	Y	Y
4 Skelton	Y	Y	Y	Y	Y	Y
5 Cleaver	Y	Y	Y	Y	Y	Y
6 **Graves**	+	+	+	Y	Y	Y
7 **Blunt**	Y	Y	Y	Y	Y	N
8 **Emerson**	Y	Y	Y	Y	Y	Y
9 **Hulshof**	?	?	?	Y	Y	Y
MONTANA						
AL **Rehberg**	Y	Y	Y	Y	Y	Y
NEBRASKA						
1 **Fortenberry**	Y	Y	Y	Y	Y	Y
2 **Terry**	Y	Y	Y	Y	Y	Y
3 **Smith**	Y	Y	Y	Y	Y	N
NEVADA						
1 Berkley	Y	Y	Y	Y	Y	Y
2 **Heller**	Y	Y	Y	Y	Y	Y
3 **Porter**	Y	Y	Y	Y	Y	Y
NEW HAMPSHIRE						
1 Shea-Porter	Y	Y	Y	Y	Y	Y
2 Hodes	Y	Y	Y	Y	Y	Y
NEW JERSEY						
1 Andrews	+	+	+	Y	Y	Y
2 **LoBiondo**	Y	Y	Y	Y	Y	Y
3 **Saxton**	?	?	?	Y	Y	Y
4 **Smith**	Y	Y	Y	Y	Y	Y
5 **Garrett**	Y	Y	Y	Y	Y	Y
6 Pallone	Y	Y	Y	Y	Y	Y
7 **Ferguson**	Y	Y	Y	Y	Y	Y
8 Pascrell	Y	Y	Y	Y	Y	Y
9 Rothman	Y	Y	Y	Y	Y	Y
10 Payne	Y	Y	Y	Y	Y	Y
11 **Frelinghuysen**	Y	Y	Y	Y	Y	Y
12 Holt	Y	Y	Y	Y	Y	Y
13 Sires	+	+	+	Y	Y	Y
NEW MEXICO						
1 **Wilson**	?	?	?	Y	Y	Y
2 **Pearce**	?	?	?	?	?	?
3 Udall	?	?	?	Y	Y	Y
NEW YORK						
1 Bishop	Y	Y	Y	Y	Y	Y
2 Israel	Y	Y	Y	Y	Y	Y
3 **King**	Y	Y	Y	Y	Y	Y
4 McCarthy	Y	Y	Y	Y	Y	Y
5 Ackerman	Y	Y	Y	Y	Y	Y
6 Meeks	Y	Y	Y	Y	Y	Y
7 Crowley	Y	Y	Y	Y	Y	Y
8 Nadler	Y	Y	Y	Y	Y	Y
9 Weiner	Y	Y	Y	Y	Y	Y
10 Towns	?	?	?	Y	Y	Y
11 Clarke	Y	Y	Y	Y	Y	Y
12 Velázquez	Y	Y	Y	Y	Y	Y
13 **Fossella**	?	?	?	Y	Y	Y
14 Maloney	+	+	+	Y	Y	Y
15 Rangel	Y	Y	Y	Y	Y	Y
16 Serrano	Y	Y	Y	Y	Y	Y
17 Engel	Y	Y	Y	Y	Y	Y
18 Lowey	Y	Y	Y	Y	Y	Y
19 Hall	Y	Y	Y	Y	Y	Y
20 Gillibrand	Y	Y	Y	Y	Y	Y
21 McNulty	Y	Y	Y	Y	Y	Y
22 Hinchey	Y	Y	Y	Y	Y	Y
23 **McHugh**	Y	Y	Y	Y	Y	Y
24 Arcuri	Y	Y	Y	Y	Y	Y
25 **Walsh**	Y	Y	Y	Y	Y	Y
26 **Reynolds**	Y	Y	Y	Y	Y	Y
27 Higgins	Y	Y	Y	Y	Y	Y
28 Slaughter	Y	Y	Y	Y	Y	Y
29 **Kuhl**	Y	Y	Y	Y	Y	Y
NORTH CAROLINA						
1 Butterfield	Y	Y	Y	Y	Y	Y
2 Etheridge	Y	Y	Y	Y	Y	Y
3 **Jones**	Y	Y	Y	Y	Y	Y
4 Price	Y	Y	Y	Y	Y	Y

	486	487	488	489	490	491
5 **Foxx**	Y	Y	Y	Y	Y	Y
6 **Coble**	Y	Y	Y	Y	Y	Y
7 McIntyre	Y	Y	Y	Y	Y	Y
8 **Hayes**	Y	Y	Y	Y	Y	Y
9 **Myrick**	Y	Y	Y	Y	Y	Y
10 **McHenry**	Y	Y	Y	Y	Y	Y
11 Shuler	Y	Y	Y	Y	Y	Y
12 Watt	Y	Y	Y	Y	Y	Y
13 Miller	Y	Y	Y	Y	Y	Y
NORTH DAKOTA						
AL Pomeroy	Y	Y	Y	Y	Y	Y
OHIO						
1 **Chabot**	Y	Y	Y	Y	Y	Y
2 **Schmidt**	Y	Y	Y	Y	Y	Y
3 **Turner**	Y	Y	Y	Y	Y	Y
4 **Jordan**	Y	Y	Y	Y	Y	N
5 **Latta**	Y	Y	Y	Y	Y	Y
6 Wilson	Y	Y	Y	Y	Y	Y
7 **Hobson**	Y	Y	Y	Y	Y	Y
8 **Boehner**	Y	Y	Y	Y	Y	N
9 Kaptur	Y	Y	Y	Y	Y	Y
10 Kucinich	Y	Y	Y	Y	Y	Y
11 Tubbs Jones	?	?	?	Y	Y	Y
12 **Tiberi**	?	?	?	Y	Y	Y
13 Sutton	Y	Y	Y	Y	Y	Y
14 **LaTourette**	?	?	?	Y	Y	Y
15 **Pryce**	?	?	?	?	Y	Y
16 **Regula**	Y	Y	Y	Y	Y	Y
17 Ryan	Y	Y	Y	Y	Y	Y
18 Space	Y	Y	Y	Y	Y	Y
OKLAHOMA						
1 **Sullivan**	Y	Y	Y	Y	Y	Y
2 Boren	Y	Y	Y	Y	Y	Y
3 **Lucas**	Y	Y	Y	Y	Y	Y
4 **Cole**	Y	Y	Y	Y	Y	N
5 **Fallin**	Y	Y	Y	Y	Y	Y
OREGON						
1 Wu	Y	Y	Y	Y	Y	Y
2 **Walden**	Y	Y	Y	Y	Y	Y
3 Blumenauer	Y	Y	Y	Y	Y	Y
4 DeFazio	Y	Y	Y	Y	Y	Y
5 Hooley	Y	Y	Y	Y	Y	Y
PENNSYLVANIA						
1 Brady	Y	Y	Y	Y	Y	Y
2 Fattah	Y	Y	Y	Y	Y	Y
3 **English**	Y	Y	Y	Y	Y	Y
4 Altmire	Y	Y	Y	Y	Y	Y
5 **Peterson**	Y	Y	Y	Y	Y	Y
6 **Gerlach**	Y	Y	Y	Y	Y	Y
7 Sestak	Y	Y	Y	Y	Y	Y
8 Murphy, P.	Y	Y	Y	Y	Y	Y
9 **Shuster**	Y	Y	Y	Y	Y	Y
10 Carney	Y	Y	Y	Y	Y	Y
11 Kanjorski	Y	Y	Y	Y	Y	Y
12 Murtha	?	?	?	Y	Y	Y
13 Schwartz	Y	Y	Y	Y	Y	Y
14 Doyle	Y	Y	Y	Y	Y	Y
15 **Dent**	Y	Y	Y	Y	Y	Y
16 **Pitts**	Y	Y	Y	Y	Y	Y
17 Holden	Y	Y	Y	Y	Y	Y
18 **Murphy, T.**	Y	Y	Y	Y	Y	Y
19 **Platts**	?	?	?	Y	Y	Y
RHODE ISLAND						
1 Kennedy	Y	Y	Y	Y	Y	Y
2 Langevin	Y	Y	Y	Y	Y	Y
SOUTH CAROLINA						
1 **Brown**	Y	Y	Y	Y	Y	Y
2 **Wilson**	Y	Y	Y	Y	Y	Y
3 **Barrett**	Y	Y	Y	Y	Y	N
4 **Inglis**	Y	Y	Y	Y	Y	Y
5 Spratt	Y	Y	Y	Y	Y	Y
6 Clyburn	Y	Y	Y	Y	Y	Y
SOUTH DAKOTA						
AL Herseth Sandlin	Y	Y	Y	Y	Y	Y
TENNESSEE						
1 **Davis, D.**	Y	Y	Y	Y	Y	Y
2 **Duncan**	Y	Y	Y	Y	Y	N
3 **Wamp**	Y	Y	Y	?	?	?
4 Davis, L.	Y	Y	Y	Y	Y	Y
5 Cooper	Y	Y	Y	Y	Y	Y
6 Gordon	Y	Y	Y	Y	Y	Y
7 **Blackburn**	Y	Y	Y	Y	Y	Y
8 Tanner	Y	Y	Y	Y	Y	Y
9 Cohen	Y	Y	Y	Y	Y	Y

	486	487	488	489	490	491
TEXAS						
1 **Gohmert**	Y	Y	Y	Y	Y	Y
2 **Poe**	Y	Y	Y	Y	Y	Y
3 **Johnson, S.**	Y	Y	Y	Y	Y	N
4 **Hall**	Y	Y	Y	Y	Y	Y
5 **Hensarling**	Y	Y	Y	Y	Y	N
6 **Barton**	Y	Y	Y	Y	Y	N
7 **Culberson**	Y	Y	Y	Y	Y	Y
8 **Brady**	Y	Y	Y	Y	Y	N
9 Green, A.	+	+	+	Y	Y	Y
10 **McCaul**	Y	Y	Y	Y	Y	Y
11 **Conaway**	Y	Y	Y	Y	Y	N
12 **Granger**	?	?	?	Y	Y	Y
13 **Thornberry**	Y	Y	Y	Y	Y	Y
14 **Paul**	Y	Y	Y	Y	Y	N
15 Hinojosa	Y	Y	Y	Y	Y	Y
16 Reyes	Y	Y	Y	Y	Y	Y
17 Edwards	Y	Y	Y	Y	Y	Y
18 Jackson Lee	Y	Y	Y	Y	Y	Y
19 **Neugebauer**	Y	Y	Y	Y	Y	N
20 Gonzalez	Y	Y	Y	Y	Y	Y
21 **Smith**	Y	Y	Y	Y	Y	Y
22 Lampson	Y	Y	Y	Y	Y	Y
23 Rodriguez	Y	Y	Y	Y	Y	Y
24 **Marchant**	Y	Y	Y	Y	Y	N
25 Doggett	Y	Y	Y	Y	Y	Y
26 **Burgess**	Y	Y	Y	Y	Y	Y
27 Ortiz	Y	Y	Y	Y	Y	Y
28 Cuellar	Y	Y	Y	Y	Y	Y
29 Green, G.	Y	Y	Y	Y	Y	Y
30 Johnson, E.	Y	Y	Y	Y	Y	Y
31 **Carter**	Y	Y	?	Y	Y	N
32 **Sessions**	Y	Y	Y	Y	Y	Y
UTAH						
1 **Bishop**	Y	Y	Y	Y	Y	N
2 Matheson	Y	Y	Y	Y	Y	Y
3 **Cannon**	Y	Y	Y	Y	Y	N
VERMONT						
AL Welch	?	Y	Y	Y	Y	Y
VIRGINIA						
1 **Wittman**	Y	Y	Y	Y	Y	Y
2 **Drake**	Y	Y	Y	Y	Y	Y
3 Scott	?	?	?	Y	Y	Y
4 **Forbes**	Y	Y	Y	Y	Y	Y
5 **Goode**	Y	Y	Y	Y	Y	Y
6 **Goodlatte**	Y	Y	Y	Y	Y	Y
7 **Cantor**	Y	Y	Y	Y	Y	N
8 Moran	?	?	?	Y	Y	Y
9 Boucher	Y	Y	Y	Y	Y	Y
10 **Wolf**	Y	Y	Y	Y	Y	Y
11 **Davis**	?	?	?	Y	Y	Y
WASHINGTON						
1 Inslee	Y	Y	Y	Y	Y	Y
2 Larsen	Y	Y	Y	Y	Y	Y
3 Baird	Y	Y	Y	Y	Y	Y
4 **Hastings**	Y	Y	Y	Y	Y	Y
5 **McMorris Rodgers**	Y	Y	Y	Y	Y	Y
6 Dicks	Y	Y	Y	Y	Y	Y
7 McDermott	Y	Y	Y	Y	Y	Y
8 **Reichert**	Y	Y	Y	Y	Y	Y
9 Smith	Y	Y	Y	Y	Y	Y
WEST VIRGINIA						
1 Mollohan	Y	Y	Y	Y	Y	Y
2 **Capito**	Y	Y	Y	Y	Y	Y
3 Rahall	Y	Y	Y	Y	Y	Y
WISCONSIN						
1 **Ryan**	Y	Y	Y	Y	Y	Y
2 Baldwin	Y	Y	Y	Y	Y	Y
3 Kind	?	?	?	Y	Y	Y
4 Moore	Y	Y	Y	Y	Y	Y
5 **Sensenbrenner**	Y	Y	Y	Y	Y	N
6 **Petri**	Y	Y	Y	Y	Y	Y
7 Obey	Y	Y	Y	Y	Y	Y
8 Kagen	Y	Y	Y	Y	Y	Y
WYOMING						
AL **Cubin**	?	?	?	?	?	?
DELEGATES						
Faleomavaega (A.S.)						
Norton (D.C.)						
Bordallo (Guam)						
Fortuño (P.R.)						
Christensen (V.I.)						

IN THE HOUSE | By Vote Number

492. **H Res 1345. Impeachment of President Bush/Motion to Refer.** Kucinich, D-Ohio, motion to refer the Kucinich, D-Ohio, privileged resolution to the Judiciary Committee. The Kucinich resolution would bring articles of impeachment against President George W. Bush for "high crimes and misdemeanors." Motion agreed to 238-180: R 9-180; D 229-0 (ND 172-0, SD 57-0). July 15, 2008.

493. **HR 5803. Paper Ballot Grants/Passage.** Lofgren, D-Calif., motion to suspend the rules and pass the bill that would establish a program to provide grants to states and local governments to reimburse them for costs associated with making available backup paper ballots in the November 2008 general election and authorize $75 million for the grants. Motion rejected 248-170: R 20-170; D 228-0 (ND 171-0, SD 57-0). A two-thirds majority of those present and voting (279 in this case) is required for passage under suspension of the rules. A "nay" was a vote in support of the president's position. July 15, 2008.

494. **H Res 1090. Honor Former President Nelson Mandela/Adoption.** Payne, D-N.J., motion to suspend the rules and adopt the resolution that would honor former South Africa President Nelson Rolihlahla Mandela on his 90th birthday. Motion agreed to 411-0: R 188-0; D 223-0 (ND 166-0, SD 57-0). A two-thirds majority of those present and voting (274 in this case) is required for adoption under suspension of the rules. July 15, 2008.

495. **HR 5959. Fiscal 2009 Intelligence Authorization/Previous Question.** Hastings, D-Fla., motion to order the previous question (thus ending debate and possibility of amendment) on adoption of the rule (H Res 1343) to provide for House floor consideration of the bill that would authorize classified amounts in fiscal 2009 for 16 spy agencies and the Office of the Director of National Intelligence. Motion agreed to 226-192: R 0-191; D 226-1 (ND 168-1, SD 58-0). July 16, 2008.

496. **HR 5959. Fiscal 2009 Intelligence Authorization/Rule.** Adoption of the rule (H Res 1343) to provide for House floor consideration of the bill that would authorize classified amounts in fiscal 2009 for 16 spy agencies and the Office of the Director of National Intelligence. Adopted 226-193: R 2-191; D 224-2 (ND 166-2, SD 58-0). July 16, 2008.

497. **HR 415. Taunton Wild and Scenic River/Previous Question.** McGovern, D-Mass., motion to order the previous question (thus ending debate and possibility of amendment) on adoption of the rule (H Res 1339) to provide for House floor consideration of the bill that would designate a 40-mile segment of the Taunton River in Massachusetts part of the National Wild and Scenic Rivers System. Motion agreed to 223-198: R 0-194; D 223-4 (ND 169-1, SD 54-3). July 16, 2008.

498. **HR 415. Taunton Wild and Scenic River/Rule.** Adoption of the rule (H Res 1339) to provide for House consideration of the bill that would designate a 40-mile segment of the Taunton River in Massachusetts part of the National Wild and Scenic Rivers System. Adopted 224-195: R 0-192; D 224-3 (ND 170-1, SD 54-2). July 16, 2008.

	492	493	494	495	496	497	498
ALABAMA							
1 Bonner	?	?	?	N	N	N	N
2 Everett	N	N	Y	N	N	N	N
3 Rogers	N	N	Y	N	N	N	N
4 Aderholt	N	Y	Y	N	N	N	N
5 Cramer	Y	Y	Y	Y	Y	Y	Y
6 Bachus	N	N	Y	N	N	N	N
7 Davis	Y	Y	Y	Y	Y	Y	Y
ALASKA							
AL Young	N	N	Y	N	N	N	N
ARIZONA							
1 Renzi	N	N	Y	N	N	N	N
2 Franks	N	N	Y	N	N	N	N
3 Shadegg	N	N	Y	N	N	N	N
4 Pastor	Y	Y	Y	Y	Y	Y	Y
5 Mitchell	Y	Y	Y	Y	Y	Y	Y
6 Flake	N	N	Y	N	N	N	N
7 Grijalva	Y	Y	Y	Y	Y	Y	Y
8 Giffords	Y	Y	Y	Y	Y	Y	Y
ARKANSAS							
1 Berry	Y	Y	Y	Y	Y	Y	Y
2 Snyder	Y	Y	Y	Y	Y	Y	Y
3 Boozman	N	N	Y	N	N	N	N
4 Ross	Y	Y	Y	Y	Y	Y	Y
CALIFORNIA							
1 Thompson	Y	Y	Y	Y	Y	?	Y
2 Herger	N	N	Y	N	N	N	N
3 Lungren	N	N	Y	N	N	N	N
4 Doolittle	?	N	Y	N	N	N	N
5 Matsui	Y	Y	Y	Y	Y	Y	Y
6 Woolsey	Y	Y	Y	Y	Y	Y	Y
7 Miller, George	Y	Y	Y	Y	Y	Y	Y
8 Pelosi							
9 Lee	Y	Y	Y	Y	Y	Y	Y
10 Tauscher	Y	Y	Y	Y	Y	Y	Y
11 McNerney	Y	Y	Y	Y	Y	Y	Y
12 Speier	Y	Y	Y	Y	Y	Y	Y
13 Stark	Y	Y	Y	Y	N	Y	Y
14 Eshoo	Y	Y	Y	Y	Y	Y	Y
15 Honda	Y	Y	Y	Y	Y	Y	Y
16 Lofgren	Y	Y	Y	Y	Y	Y	Y
17 Farr	Y	Y	Y	Y	Y	Y	Y
18 Cardoza	Y	Y	Y	Y	Y	Y	Y
19 Radanovich	N	N	Y	N	N	N	N
20 Costa	Y	Y	Y	Y	Y	Y	Y
21 Nunes	N	N	Y	N	N	N	N
22 McCarthy	N	N	Y	N	N	N	N
23 Capps	Y	Y	Y	Y	Y	Y	Y
24 Gallegly	N	N	Y	N	N	N	N
25 McKeon	N	N	Y	N	N	N	N
26 Dreier	N	N	Y	N	N	N	N
27 Sherman	Y	Y	Y	Y	Y	Y	Y
28 Berman	Y	Y	Y	Y	?	Y	Y
29 Schiff	Y	Y	Y	Y	Y	Y	Y
30 Waxman	Y	Y	Y	Y	Y	Y	Y
31 Becerra	Y	Y	Y	Y	Y	Y	Y
32 Solis	Y	Y	Y	Y	Y	Y	Y
33 Watson	Y	Y	Y	Y	Y	Y	Y
34 Roybal-Allard	Y	Y	Y	Y	Y	Y	Y
35 Waters	Y	Y	Y	Y	Y	Y	Y
36 Harman	Y	Y	Y	Y	Y	Y	Y
37 Richardson	Y	Y	Y	Y	Y	Y	Y
38 Napolitano	Y	Y	Y	Y	Y	Y	Y
39 Sánchez, Linda	Y	Y	Y	Y	Y	Y	Y
40 Royce	N	N	Y	N	N	N	N
41 Lewis	N	N	Y	N	N	N	N
42 Miller, Gary	N	N	Y	N	N	N	N
43 Baca	Y	Y	Y	Y	Y	Y	Y
44 Calvert	N	N	Y	N	N	N	N
45 Bono Mack	N	N	Y	N	N	N	N
46 Rohrabacher	N	N	Y	N	N	N	N
47 Sanchez, Loretta	Y	Y	Y	Y	Y	Y	Y
48 Campbell	N	N	Y	N	N	N	N
49 Issa	N	N	Y	N	N	N	N
50 Bilbray	N	N	Y	N	N	N	N
51 Filner	Y	Y	Y	Y	Y	Y	Y
52 Hunter	N	N	Y	N	N	N	N
53 Davis	Y	Y	Y	Y	Y	Y	Y

	492	493	494	495	496	497	498
COLORADO							
1 DeGette	Y	Y	Y	Y	Y	Y	Y
2 Udall	Y	Y	Y	Y	Y	Y	Y
3 Salazar	Y	Y	Y	Y	Y	Y	Y
4 Musgrave	N	N	Y	?	N	N	N
5 Lamborn	N	N	Y	N	N	N	N
6 Tancredo	N	N	Y	N	N	N	N
7 Perlmutter	Y	Y	Y	?	?	Y	Y
CONNECTICUT							
1 Larson	Y	Y	Y	Y	Y	Y	Y
2 Courtney	Y	Y	Y	Y	Y	Y	Y
3 DeLauro	Y	Y	Y	Y	Y	Y	Y
4 Shays	Y	Y	Y	N	–	N	N
5 Murphy	Y	Y	Y	Y	Y	Y	Y
DELAWARE							
AL Castle	N	N	Y	N	N	N	N
FLORIDA							
1 Miller	N	N	Y	N	N	N	N
2 Boyd	Y	Y	Y	Y	Y	Y	Y
3 Brown	Y	Y	Y	Y	Y	Y	Y
4 Crenshaw	N	N	Y	N	N	N	N
5 Brown-Waite	N	N	Y	N	N	N	N
6 Stearns	N	N	Y	N	N	N	N
7 Mica	N	N	Y	N	N	N	N
8 Keller	N	N	Y	N	N	N	N
9 Bilirakis	N	N	Y	N	N	N	N
10 Young	N	N	Y	N	N	N	N
11 Castor	Y	Y	Y	Y	Y	Y	Y
12 Putnam	N	N	Y	N	N	N	N
13 Buchanan	N	N	Y	N	N	N	N
14 Mack	N	N	Y	N	N	N	N
15 Weldon	N	N	Y	N	N	N	N
16 Mahoney	Y	Y	Y	Y	Y	Y	Y
17 Meek	Y	Y	Y	Y	Y	Y	Y
18 Ros-Lehtinen	Y	Y	Y	N	N	N	N
19 Wexler	Y	Y	Y	Y	Y	Y	?
20 Wasserman Schultz	Y	Y	Y	Y	Y	Y	Y
21 Diaz-Balart, L.	?	?	?	N	N	N	N
22 Klein	Y	Y	Y	Y	Y	Y	Y
23 Hastings	Y	Y	Y	Y	Y	Y	Y
24 Feeney	N	N	Y	N	N	N	?
25 Diaz-Balart, M.	?	?	?	N	N	N	N
GEORGIA							
1 Kingston	N	N	Y	N	N	N	N
2 Bishop	Y	Y	Y	Y	Y	Y	Y
3 Westmoreland	N	N	Y	N	N	N	N
4 Johnson	Y	Y	Y	Y	Y	Y	Y
5 Lewis	?	?	Y	Y	Y	Y	Y
6 Price	N	N	Y	N	N	N	N
7 Linder	N	N	Y	N	N	N	N
8 Marshall	Y	Y	Y	Y	Y	Y	Y
9 Deal	N	N	Y	N	N	N	N
10 Broun	?	?	?	N	N	N	N
11 Gingrey	N	N	Y	N	N	N	N
12 Barrow	+	+	+	Y	Y	Y	Y
13 Scott	Y	Y	Y	Y	Y	Y	Y
HAWAII							
1 Abercrombie	Y	Y	Y	Y	Y	Y	Y
2 Hirono	Y	Y	Y	Y	Y	Y	Y
IDAHO							
1 Sali	N	N	Y	N	N	N	N
2 Simpson	N	N	Y	N	N	N	N
ILLINOIS							
1 Rush	?	?	?	?	?	?	?
2 Jackson	Y	Y	Y	Y	Y	Y	Y
3 Lipinski	Y	Y	Y	Y	Y	Y	Y
4 Gutierrez	Y	Y	Y	Y	Y	Y	Y
5 Emanuel	Y	Y	Y	Y	Y	Y	Y
6 Roskam	N	N	Y	N	N	N	N
7 Davis	Y	Y	Y	Y	Y	Y	Y
8 Bean	Y	Y	Y	?	Y	Y	Y
9 Schakowsky	Y	Y	Y	Y	Y	Y	Y
10 Kirk	N	N	Y	N	N	N	N
11 Weller	N	N	Y	N	N	N	N
12 Costello	Y	Y	Y	Y	Y	Y	Y
13 Biggert	N	N	Y	N	N	N	N
14 Foster	Y	Y	Y	Y	Y	Y	Y
15 Johnson	N	N	Y	N	N	N	N

KEY **Republicans** Democrats

Y Voted for (yea)	X Paired against	C Voted "present" to avoid possible conflict of interest
# Paired for	– Announced against	
+ Announced for	P Voted "present"	? Did not vote or otherwise make a position known
N Voted against (nay)		

ND Northern Democrats, SD Southern Democrats
Southern states: Ala., Ark., Fla., Ga., Ky., La., Miss., N.C., Okla., S.C., Tenn., Texas, Va.

	492	493	494	495	496	497	498
16 **Manzullo**	Y	N	Y	N	N	N	N
17 Hare	Y	Y	Y	Y	Y	Y	Y
18 **LaHood**	N	N	Y	N	N	N	N
19 **Shimkus**	N	N	Y	N	N	N	N
INDIANA							
1 Visclosky	Y	Y	Y	Y	Y	Y	Y
2 Donnelly	Y	Y	Y	Y	Y	Y	Y
3 **Souder**	N	N	Y	N	N	N	N
4 **Buyer**	N	N	Y	?	?	?	?
5 **Burton**	N	N	Y	N	N	N	N
6 **Pence**	N	N	Y	N	N	N	N
7 Carson, A.	Y	Y	Y	Y	Y	Y	Y
8 Ellsworth	Y	Y	Y	Y	Y	Y	Y
9 Hill	Y	Y	Y	N	N	N	N
IOWA							
1 Braley	Y	Y	Y	Y	Y	Y	Y
2 Loebsack	Y	Y	Y	Y	Y	Y	Y
3 Boswell	?	?	?	?	?	?	?
4 **Latham**	N	N	Y	N	N	N	N
5 **King**	N	N	Y	N	N	N	N
KANSAS							
1 **Moran**	N	N	Y	N	N	N	N
2 Boyda	Y	Y	Y	Y	Y	Y	Y
3 Moore	Y	Y	Y	Y	Y	Y	Y
4 **Tiahrt**	N	N	Y	N	N	N	N
KENTUCKY							
1 **Whitfield**	N	N	Y	N	N	N	?
2 **Lewis**	N	N	Y	N	N	N	N
3 Yarmuth	Y	Y	Y	Y	Y	Y	Y
4 **Davis**	N	N	Y	N	N	N	N
5 **Rogers**	N	N	Y	N	N	N	N
6 Chandler	Y	Y	Y	Y	Y	Y	Y
LOUISIANA							
1 **Scalise**	N	N	Y	N	N	N	N
2 Jefferson	Y	Y	Y	Y	Y	Y	Y
3 Melancon	Y	Y	Y	Y	Y	?	?
4 **McCrery**	N	N	Y	N	N	N	N
5 **Alexander**	N	N	Y	N	N	N	N
6 Cazayoux	Y	Y	Y	Y	Y	N	N
7 **Boustany**	N	N	Y	N	N	N	N
MAINE							
1 Allen	Y	Y	Y	Y	Y	Y	Y
2 Michaud	Y	Y	Y	Y	Y	Y	Y
MARYLAND							
1 **Gilchrest**	Y	Y	Y	?	?	?	?
2 Ruppersberger	Y	Y	Y	Y	Y	Y	Y
3 Sarbanes	Y	Y	Y	Y	Y	Y	Y
4 Edwards	Y	Y	Y	Y	Y	Y	Y
5 Hoyer	Y	Y	Y	Y	Y	Y	Y
6 **Bartlett**	N	Y	Y	N	N	N	N
7 Cummings	Y	Y	Y	Y	Y	Y	Y
8 Van Hollen	Y	Y	Y	Y	Y	Y	Y
MASSACHUSETTS							
1 Olver	Y	Y	Y	Y	Y	Y	Y
2 Neal	Y	Y	Y	Y	Y	Y	Y
3 McGovern	Y	Y	Y	Y	Y	Y	Y
4 Frank	Y	Y	?	?	?	Y	Y
5 Tsongas	Y	Y	Y	Y	Y	Y	Y
6 Tierney	Y	Y	Y	Y	Y	Y	Y
7 Markey	Y	Y	Y	Y	Y	Y	Y
8 Capuano	Y	Y	Y	Y	Y	Y	Y
9 Lynch	Y	Y	Y	Y	Y	Y	Y
10 Delahunt	Y	Y	?	?	?	?	?
MICHIGAN							
1 Stupak	Y	Y	Y	Y	Y	Y	Y
2 **Hoekstra**	N	N	Y	N	Y	N	N
3 **Ehlers**	N	N	Y	N	N	N	N
4 **Camp**	N	N	Y	N	N	N	N
5 Kildee	Y	Y	Y	Y	Y	Y	Y
6 **Upton**	N	N	Y	N	N	N	N
7 **Walberg**	N	N	Y	N	N	N	N
8 **Rogers**	N	N	Y	N	N	N	N
9 **Knollenberg**	N	N	Y	N	N	N	N
10 **Miller**	N	N	Y	N	N	N	N
11 **McCotter**	N	N	Y	N	N	N	N
12 Levin	Y	Y	Y	Y	Y	Y	Y
13 Kilpatrick	Y	Y	Y	Y	Y	Y	Y
14 Conyers	+	+	+	Y	Y	Y	Y
15 Dingell	Y	Y	Y	Y	Y	Y	Y
MINNESOTA							
1 Walz	Y	Y	Y	Y	Y	Y	Y
2 **Kline**	N	N	Y	N	N	N	N
3 **Ramstad**	N	Y	Y	N	N	N	N
4 McCollum	Y	Y	Y	Y	Y	Y	Y

	492	493	494	495	496	497	498
5 Ellison	Y	Y	Y	Y	Y	Y	Y
6 **Bachmann**	N	N	Y	N	N	N	N
7 Peterson	Y	Y	?	Y	Y	Y	Y
8 Oberstar	Y	Y	Y	Y	Y	Y	Y
MISSISSIPPI							
1 Childers	Y	Y	Y	Y	Y	N	N
2 Thompson	Y	Y	Y	Y	Y	Y	Y
3 **Pickering**	N	N	Y	N	N	N	N
4 Taylor	Y	Y	Y	Y	Y	Y	Y
MISSOURI							
1 Clay	Y	Y	Y	Y	Y	Y	Y
2 **Akin**	N	N	Y	N	N	N	N
3 Carnahan	Y	Y	Y	Y	Y	Y	Y
4 Skelton	Y	Y	Y	Y	Y	Y	Y
5 Cleaver	Y	Y	Y	Y	Y	Y	Y
6 **Graves**	N	N	Y	N	N	N	N
7 **Blunt**	N	N	Y	N	N	N	N
8 **Emerson**	N	N	Y	N	N	N	N
9 **Hulshof**	N	N	Y	N	N	N	N
MONTANA							
AL **Rehberg**	N	N	Y	N	N	N	N
NEBRASKA							
1 **Fortenberry**	N	N	Y	N	N	N	N
2 **Terry**	N	N	Y	N	N	N	N
3 **Smith**	N	N	Y	N	N	N	N
NEVADA							
1 Berkley	Y	Y	Y	Y	Y	Y	Y
2 **Heller**	N	N	Y	N	N	N	N
3 **Porter**	N	N	Y	N	N	N	N
NEW HAMPSHIRE							
1 Shea-Porter	Y	Y	Y	Y	Y	Y	Y
2 Hodes	Y	Y	Y	Y	Y	Y	Y
NEW JERSEY							
1 Andrews	Y	Y	?	Y	Y	Y	Y
2 **LoBiondo**	N	Y	Y	N	N	N	N
3 **Saxton**	N	Y	Y	N	N	N	N
4 **Smith**	N	Y	Y	N	N	N	N
5 **Garrett**	N	N	Y	?	N	N	N
6 Pallone	Y	Y	Y	Y	Y	Y	Y
7 **Ferguson**	N	N	Y	N	N	N	N
8 Pascrell	Y	Y	Y	Y	Y	Y	Y
9 Rothman	Y	Y	Y	Y	Y	Y	Y
10 Payne	Y	Y	Y	Y	Y	Y	Y
11 **Frelinghuysen**	N	N	Y	N	N	N	N
12 Holt	Y	Y	Y	Y	Y	Y	Y
13 Sires	Y	Y	Y	Y	Y	Y	Y
NEW MEXICO							
1 **Wilson**	N	N	Y	N	N	N	N
2 **Pearce**	?	?	?	N	N	N	N
3 Udall	Y	Y	Y	Y	Y	Y	Y
NEW YORK							
1 Bishop	Y	Y	Y	Y	Y	Y	Y
2 Israel	Y	Y	Y	Y	Y	Y	Y
3 **King**	N	N	Y	N	N	N	N
4 McCarthy	Y	Y	Y	Y	Y	Y	Y
5 Ackerman	Y	Y	Y	Y	Y	Y	Y
6 Meeks	Y	Y	Y	Y	Y	Y	Y
7 Crowley	Y	Y	Y	Y	Y	Y	Y
8 Nadler	Y	Y	Y	Y	Y	Y	Y
9 Weiner	Y	Y	Y	Y	Y	Y	Y
10 Towns	Y	Y	?	Y	Y	Y	Y
11 Clarke	Y	Y	Y	Y	Y	Y	Y
12 Velázquez	Y	Y	Y	Y	Y	Y	Y
13 **Fossella**	N	N	Y	N	N	N	N
14 Maloney	Y	Y	Y	Y	Y	Y	Y
15 Rangel	Y	Y	Y	Y	Y	Y	Y
16 Serrano	Y	Y	Y	Y	Y	Y	Y
17 Engel	?	?	?	?	?	?	?
18 Lowey	Y	Y	Y	Y	Y	Y	Y
19 Hall	Y	Y	Y	Y	Y	Y	Y
20 Gillibrand	Y	Y	Y	Y	Y	Y	Y
21 McNulty	Y	Y	Y	Y	Y	Y	Y
22 Hinchey	Y	Y	Y	Y	Y	Y	Y
23 **McHugh**	N	N	Y	N	N	N	N
24 Arcuri	Y	Y	Y	Y	Y	Y	Y
25 **Walsh**	N	N	Y	N	N	N	N
26 **Reynolds**	N	N	Y	N	N	N	N
27 Higgins	Y	Y	Y	Y	Y	Y	Y
28 Slaughter	Y	Y	Y	Y	Y	Y	Y
29 **Kuhl**	N	N	Y	N	N	N	N
NORTH CAROLINA							
1 Butterfield	Y	Y	Y	Y	Y	Y	Y
2 Etheridge	Y	Y	Y	Y	Y	Y	Y
3 **Jones**	Y	Y	Y	N	N	N	N
4 Price	Y	Y	Y	Y	Y	Y	Y

	492	493	494	495	496	497	498
5 **Foxx**	N	N	Y	N	N	N	N
6 **Coble**	N	N	Y	N	N	N	N
7 McIntyre	Y	Y	Y	Y	Y	Y	Y
8 **Hayes**	N	N	Y	N	N	N	N
9 **Myrick**	N	N	Y	N	N	N	N
10 **McHenry**	N	N	Y	N	N	N	N
11 Shuler	Y	Y	Y	Y	Y	Y	Y
12 Watt	Y	Y	Y	Y	Y	Y	Y
13 Miller	Y	Y	Y	Y	Y	Y	Y
NORTH DAKOTA							
AL Pomeroy	Y	Y	Y	Y	Y	Y	Y
OHIO							
1 **Chabot**	N	Y	Y	N	N	N	N
2 **Schmidt**	N	N	Y	N	N	N	N
3 **Turner**	Y	N	Y	N	N	N	N
4 **Jordan**	N	N	Y	N	N	N	N
5 **Latta**	N	N	Y	N	N	N	N
6 Wilson	Y	Y	Y	Y	Y	Y	Y
7 **Hobson**	N	N	Y	N	N	N	N
8 **Boehner**	N	N	Y	N	N	N	N
9 Kaptur	Y	Y	Y	Y	Y	Y	Y
10 Kucinich	Y	Y	Y	Y	Y	Y	Y
11 Tubbs Jones	Y	Y	Y	Y	Y	Y	Y
12 **Tiberi**	N	N	Y	N	N	N	N
13 Sutton	Y	Y	Y	Y	Y	Y	Y
14 **LaTourette**	N	N	?	N	N	N	N
15 **Pryce**	N	N	Y	N	N	N	N
16 **Regula**	N	N	Y	N	N	N	N
17 Ryan	Y	Y	Y	Y	Y	Y	Y
18 Space	Y	Y	Y	Y	Y	Y	Y
OKLAHOMA							
1 **Sullivan**	N	N	Y	N	N	N	N
2 Boren	Y	Y	Y	Y	Y	Y	Y
3 **Lucas**	?	?	?	?	?	?	?
4 **Cole**	N	Y	Y	N	N	N	N
5 **Fallin**	N	N	Y	N	N	N	N
OREGON							
1 Wu	Y	Y	Y	Y	Y	Y	?
2 **Walden**	N	N	Y	N	N	N	N
3 Blumenauer	Y	Y	Y	Y	Y	Y	Y
4 DeFazio	Y	Y	Y	Y	Y	Y	Y
5 Hooley	Y	Y	Y	Y	?	Y	Y
PENNSYLVANIA							
1 Brady	Y	Y	Y	Y	Y	Y	Y
2 Fattah	Y	Y	Y	Y	Y	Y	Y
3 **English**	N	Y	Y	N	N	N	N
4 Altmire	Y	Y	Y	Y	Y	Y	Y
5 **Peterson**	N	N	Y	N	N	N	N
6 **Gerlach**	N	Y	Y	N	N	N	N
7 Sestak	Y	Y	Y	Y	Y	Y	Y
8 Murphy, P.	Y	Y	Y	Y	Y	Y	Y
9 **Shuster**	N	N	Y	N	N	N	N
10 Carney	Y	Y	Y	Y	Y	Y	Y
11 Kanjorski	Y	Y	Y	Y	Y	Y	Y
12 Murtha	Y	?	?	Y	Y	Y	Y
13 Schwartz	Y	Y	Y	Y	Y	Y	Y
14 Doyle	Y	Y	Y	Y	Y	Y	Y
15 **Dent**	N	Y	Y	N	N	N	N
16 **Pitts**	?	?	?	N	N	N	N
17 Holden	Y	Y	Y	Y	Y	Y	Y
18 **Murphy, T.**	Y	Y	Y	N	Y	N	N
19 **Platts**	N	N	Y	?	?	?	?
RHODE ISLAND							
1 Kennedy	Y	Y	Y	Y	Y	Y	Y
2 Langevin	Y	Y	Y	Y	Y	Y	Y
SOUTH CAROLINA							
1 **Brown**	N	N	Y	N	N	N	N
2 **Wilson**	N	N	Y	N	N	N	N
3 **Barrett**	N	N	Y	N	N	N	N
4 **Inglis**	N	N	Y	N	N	N	N
5 Spratt	Y	Y	Y	Y	Y	Y	Y
6 Clyburn	Y	Y	Y	Y	Y	Y	Y
SOUTH DAKOTA							
AL Herseth Sandlin	Y	Y	Y	Y	Y	Y	Y
TENNESSEE							
1 **Davis, D.**	N	N	Y	N	N	N	N
2 **Duncan**	N	N	Y	N	N	N	N
3 **Wamp**	N	N	Y	N	N	N	N
4 Davis, L.	Y	Y	Y	Y	Y	Y	Y
5 Cooper	Y	Y	Y	Y	Y	Y	Y
6 Gordon	Y	Y	Y	Y	Y	Y	Y
7 **Blackburn**	N	N	Y	N	N	N	N
8 Tanner	Y	Y	Y	Y	Y	Y	Y
9 Cohen	Y	Y	Y	Y	Y	Y	Y

	492	493	494	495	496	497	498
TEXAS							
1 **Gohmert**	N	N	Y	N	N	N	N
2 **Poe**	N	N	Y	N	N	N	N
3 **Johnson, S.**	N	N	Y	N	N	N	N
4 **Hall**	N	N	Y	N	N	N	N
5 **Hensarling**	N	N	Y	N	N	N	N
6 **Barton**	N	N	Y	?	N	N	N
7 **Culberson**	N	N	Y	N	N	N	N
8 **Brady**	N	N	Y	N	N	N	N
9 Green, A.	Y	Y	Y	?	?	?	?
10 **McCaul**	N	N	Y	N	N	N	N
11 **Conaway**	N	N	Y	N	N	N	N
12 **Granger**	N	N	Y	N	N	N	N
13 **Thornberry**	N	N	Y	N	N	N	N
14 **Paul**	Y	Y	Y	N	N	N	N
15 Hinojosa	Y	Y	Y	Y	Y	Y	Y
16 Reyes	Y	Y	Y	Y	Y	Y	Y
17 Edwards	Y	Y	Y	Y	Y	Y	Y
18 Jackson Lee	Y	Y	Y	Y	Y	Y	Y
19 **Neugebauer**	N	N	Y	N	N	N	N
20 Gonzalez	Y	Y	Y	Y	Y	Y	Y
21 **Smith**	N	N	Y	N	N	N	N
22 Lampson	Y	Y	Y	Y	Y	N	Y
23 Rodriguez	Y	Y	Y	Y	Y	Y	Y
24 **Marchant**	N	N	Y	N	N	N	N
25 Doggett	Y	Y	Y	Y	Y	Y	Y
26 **Burgess**	?	?	?	N	N	N	N
27 Ortiz	Y	Y	Y	Y	Y	Y	Y
28 Cuellar	Y	Y	Y	Y	Y	Y	Y
29 Green, G.	Y	Y	Y	Y	Y	Y	Y
30 Johnson, E.	Y	Y	Y	Y	Y	Y	Y
31 **Carter**	N	N	Y	N	N	N	N
32 **Sessions**	N	N	Y	N	N	N	N
UTAH							
1 **Bishop**	N	N	Y	N	N	N	N
2 Matheson	Y	Y	Y	Y	Y	Y	Y
3 **Cannon**	N	N	?	N	N	N	N
VERMONT							
AL Welch	Y	Y	Y	Y	Y	Y	Y
VIRGINIA							
1 **Wittman**	N	N	Y	N	N	N	N
2 **Drake**	N	N	Y	N	N	N	N
3 Scott	Y	Y	Y	Y	Y	Y	Y
4 **Forbes**	N	N	Y	N	N	N	N
5 **Goode**	N	N	Y	N	N	N	N
6 **Goodlatte**	N	N	Y	N	N	N	N
7 **Cantor**	N	N	Y	N	N	N	N
8 Moran	Y	Y	Y	Y	Y	Y	Y
9 Boucher	Y	Y	Y	Y	Y	Y	Y
10 **Wolf**	N	N	Y	N	N	N	N
11 **Davis**	N	Y	Y	N	N	N	N
WASHINGTON							
1 Inslee	Y	Y	Y	Y	Y	Y	Y
2 Larsen	Y	Y	Y	Y	Y	Y	Y
3 Baird	Y	Y	Y	Y	Y	Y	Y
4 **Hastings**	N	N	Y	N	N	N	N
5 **McMorris Rodgers**	N	N	Y	N	N	N	N
6 Dicks	Y	Y	Y	Y	Y	?	Y
7 McDermott	Y	Y	Y	Y	Y	Y	Y
8 **Reichert**	Y	N	Y	N	N	N	N
9 Smith	Y	Y	Y	Y	Y	Y	Y
WEST VIRGINIA							
1 Mollohan	Y	Y	Y	Y	Y	Y	Y
2 **Capito**	N	N	Y	N	N	N	N
3 Rahall	Y	Y	Y	Y	Y	Y	Y
WISCONSIN							
1 **Ryan**	N	N	Y	N	N	N	N
2 Baldwin	Y	Y	Y	Y	Y	Y	Y
3 Kind	Y	Y	Y	Y	Y	Y	Y
4 Moore	Y	Y	Y	Y	Y	Y	Y
5 **Sensenbrenner**	N	N	Y	N	N	N	N
6 **Petri**	N	N	Y	N	N	N	N
7 Obey	Y	Y	Y	Y	Y	Y	Y
8 Kagen	Y	Y	Y	Y	Y	Y	Y
WYOMING							
AL **Cubin**	?	?	?	?	?	?	?
DELEGATES							
Faleomavaega (A.S.)							
Norton (D.C.)							
Bordallo (Guam)							
Fortuño (P.R.)							
Christensen (V.I.)							

IN THE HOUSE | By Vote Number

499. HR 5959. Fiscal 2009 Intelligence Authorization/Colombian **Intelligence.** Hoekstra, R-Mich., amendment that would express the sense of Congress that the permanent defeat of Colombian paramilitary organizations is in the best interest of the United States and that it is critical that the United States continue to support the government of Colombia in protecting against terrorist groups. It would state that the July 2 release of hostages held by the Revolutionary Armed Forces of Colombia demonstrates the professionalism of the Colombian security forces and intelligence operatives, and that U.S. intelligence has played a key role in developing the capabilities of the Colombian government. Adopted in Committee of the Whole 414-10: R 196-1; D 218-9 (ND 161-9, SD 57-0). July 16, 2008.

500. HR 5959. Fiscal 2009 Intelligence Authorization/Terrorism **Phrases.** Hoekstra, R-Mich., amendment that would bar the use of funds to prohibit or discourage the use of the phrases "jihadist," "jihad," "Islamo-fascism," "caliphate," "Islamist" or "Islamic terrorist" within the intelligence community or the federal government. Adopted in Committee of the Whole 249-180: R 194-2; D 55-178 (ND 37-139, SD 18-39). July 16, 2008.

501. HR 5959. Fiscal 2009 Intelligence Authorization/Narcotics **Report.** Kirk, R-Ill., amendment that would require the director of national intelligence to submit a National Intelligence Estimate on the production and sale of narcotics in support of international terrorism, including support to the Taliban and al Qaeda. Adopted in Committee of the Whole 426-2: R 196-1; D 230-1 (ND 173-1, SD 57-0). July 16, 2008.

502. HR 5959. Fiscal 2009 Intelligence Authorization/ **Recommit.** Hoekstra, R-Mich., motion to recommit the bill to the permanent Select Committee on Intelligence with instructions that it be reported back promptly with language that would require the director of national intelligence to submit a National Intelligence Estimate assessment on national security and energy security issues related to rising energy costs, including an outlook for prices and supply of key forms of energy, the national security implications of energy costs and the risk of U.S. adversaries using energy sources as leverage against the United States. Motion rejected 200-225: R 192-3; D 8-222 (ND 3-170, SD 5-52). July 16, 2008.

503. HR 415. Taunton Wild and Scenic River/Remove Portion of **River.** Bishop, R-Utah, amendment that would remove the lower 9-mile portion of the river from designation under the Wild and Scenic Rivers Act. Rejected in Committee of the Whole 189-235: R 188-3; D 1-232 (ND 0-176, SD 1-56). July 16, 2008.

504. HR 415. Taunton Wild and Scenic River/Hunting and Fishing **Activities.** Shuler, D-N.C., amendment that would clarify that nothing in the bill should be construed to affect Massachusetts' jurisdiction to manage fish and wildlife under state laws, including hunting, fishing, trapping and recreational shooting regulations, or to limit access to those activities. Adopted in Committee of the Whole 425-0: R 191-0; D 234-0 (ND 177-0, SD 57-0). July 16, 2008.

505. HR 415. Taunton Wild and Scenic River/Domestic Energy. Boyda, D-Kan., amendment that would require that nothing in the bill have an impact on the supply of domestically produced energy resources. Adopted in Committee of the Whole 421-0: R 188-0; D 233-0 (ND 177-0, SD 56-0). July 16, 2008.

	499	500	501	502	503	504	505
ALABAMA							
1 Bonner	Y	Y	Y	Y	Y	Y	Y
2 Everett	Y	Y	Y	Y	Y	Y	Y
3 Rogers	Y	Y	Y	Y	Y	Y	Y
4 Aderholt	Y	Y	Y	Y	Y	Y	Y
5 Cramer	Y	N	Y	N	N	Y	Y
6 Bachus	Y	Y	Y	Y	Y	Y	Y
7 Davis	Y	Y	Y	N	N	Y	Y
ALASKA							
AL Young	Y	Y	Y	Y	Y	Y	Y
ARIZONA							
1 Renzi	Y	Y	Y	Y	Y	Y	Y
2 Franks	Y	Y	Y	Y	Y	Y	Y
3 Shadegg	Y	Y	Y	Y	Y	Y	Y
4 Pastor	Y	N	Y	N	N	Y	Y
5 Mitchell	Y	Y	Y	N	Y	Y	Y
6 Flake	Y	Y	Y	Y	Y	Y	Y
7 Grijalva	Y	N	Y	N	N	Y	Y
8 Giffords	Y	Y	Y	N	Y	Y	Y
ARKANSAS							
1 Berry	Y	N	Y	N	N	Y	Y
2 Snyder	Y	N	Y	N	N	Y	Y
3 Boozman	Y	Y	Y	Y	Y	Y	Y
4 Ross	Y	N	Y	N	N	Y	Y
CALIFORNIA							
1 Thompson	Y	N	Y	N	N	Y	Y
2 Herger	Y	Y	Y	Y	Y	Y	Y
3 Lungren	Y	Y	Y	Y	Y	Y	Y
4 Doolittle	Y	Y	Y	Y	Y	Y	Y
5 Matsui	Y	N	Y	N	N	Y	Y
6 Woolsey	Y	N	Y	N	N	Y	Y
7 Miller, George	Y	N	Y	N	N	Y	Y
8 Pelosi							
9 Lee	Y	N	Y	N	N	Y	Y
10 Tauscher	Y	N	Y	N	N	Y	Y
11 McNerney	Y	Y	Y	N	N	Y	Y
12 Speier	Y	N	Y	N	N	Y	Y
13 Stark	N	N	N	N	N	Y	Y
14 Eshoo	Y	N	Y	N	N	Y	Y
15 Honda	Y	N	Y	N	N	Y	Y
16 Lofgren	P	N	Y	N	N	Y	Y
17 Farr	Y	N	Y	N	N	Y	Y
18 Cardoza	Y	Y	Y	N	N	Y	Y
19 Radanovich	Y	Y	Y	Y	Y	Y	Y
20 Costa	Y	Y	Y	N	N	Y	Y
21 Nunes	Y	Y	Y	Y	Y	Y	Y
22 McCarthy	Y	Y	Y	Y	Y	Y	Y
23 Capps	Y	N	Y	N	N	Y	Y
24 Gallegly	Y	Y	Y	Y	Y	Y	Y
25 McKeon	Y	Y	Y	Y	Y	Y	Y
26 Dreier	Y	Y	Y	Y	Y	Y	Y
27 Sherman	Y	Y	Y	N	Y	Y	Y
28 Berman	Y	N	?	N	N	Y	Y
29 Schiff	Y	N	Y	N	N	Y	Y
30 Waxman	Y	N	Y	N	N	Y	Y
31 Becerra	Y	N	Y	N	N	Y	Y
32 Solis	Y	N	Y	N	–	+	Y
33 Watson	Y	Y	?	N	N	Y	Y
34 Roybal-Allard	Y	N	Y	N	N	Y	Y
35 Waters	Y	N	Y	N	N	Y	Y
36 Harman	Y	N	Y	N	N	Y	Y
37 Richardson	Y	N	Y	N	N	Y	Y
38 Napolitano	Y	N	Y	N	N	Y	Y
39 Sánchez, Linda	Y	N	Y	N	N	Y	Y
40 Royce	Y	Y	Y	Y	Y	Y	Y
41 Lewis	Y	Y	Y	Y	Y	Y	Y
42 Miller, Gary	Y	Y	Y	Y	?	?	?
43 Baca	Y	N	Y	N	N	Y	Y
44 Calvert	Y	Y	Y	Y	Y	Y	Y
45 Bono Mack	Y	Y	Y	Y	Y	Y	Y
46 Rohrabacher	Y	Y	Y	N	Y	Y	Y
47 Sanchez, Loretta	Y	N	Y	N	N	Y	Y
48 Campbell	Y	Y	Y	Y	Y	Y	Y
49 Issa	Y	Y	Y	Y	Y	Y	Y
50 Bilbray	Y	Y	Y	Y	Y	Y	Y
51 Filner	N	N	N	N	N	Y	Y
52 Hunter	Y	Y	Y	Y	?	?	Y
53 Davis	Y	N	Y	N	N	Y	Y
COLORADO							
1 DeGette	Y	N	Y	N	N	Y	Y
2 Udall	Y	Y	Y	N	N	Y	Y
3 Salazar	Y	N	Y	N	N	Y	Y
4 Musgrave	Y	Y	Y	Y	Y	Y	Y
5 Lamborn	Y	Y	Y	Y	Y	Y	Y
6 Tancredo	Y	Y	Y	Y	Y	Y	Y
7 Perlmutter	Y	Y	Y	N	N	Y	Y
CONNECTICUT							
1 Larson	Y	N	Y	N	N	Y	Y
2 Courtney	Y	N	Y	N	N	Y	Y
3 DeLauro	Y	N	Y	N	N	Y	Y
4 Shays	Y	Y	Y	N	Y	Y	Y
5 Murphy	Y	N	Y	N	N	Y	Y
DELAWARE							
AL Castle	Y	Y	Y	Y	Y	Y	Y
FLORIDA							
1 Miller	Y	Y	Y	Y	Y	Y	Y
2 Boyd	Y	N	Y	N	N	Y	Y
3 Brown	Y	N	Y	N	N	Y	Y
4 Crenshaw	Y	Y	Y	Y	Y	Y	Y
5 Brown-Waite	Y	Y	Y	Y	Y	Y	+
6 Stearns	Y	Y	Y	Y	Y	Y	Y
7 Mica	Y	Y	Y	Y	Y	Y	Y
8 Keller	Y	Y	Y	Y	Y	Y	Y
9 Bilirakis	Y	Y	Y	Y	Y	Y	Y
10 Young	Y	Y	Y	Y	Y	Y	Y
11 Castor	Y	N	Y	N	N	Y	Y
12 Putnam	Y	Y	Y	Y	Y	Y	Y
13 Buchanan	Y	Y	Y	Y	Y	Y	Y
14 Mack	Y	Y	Y	Y	Y	Y	Y
15 Weldon	Y	Y	Y	Y	Y	Y	Y
16 Mahoney	Y	Y	Y	N	Y	Y	Y
17 Meek	Y	N	Y	N	N	Y	Y
18 Ros-Lehtinen	Y	Y	Y	Y	Y	Y	Y
19 Wexler	Y	N	Y	N	N	Y	Y
20 Wasserman Schultz	Y	N	Y	N	N	Y	Y
21 Diaz-Balart, L.	Y	Y	Y	Y	Y	Y	Y
22 Klein	Y	Y	Y	N	Y	Y	Y
23 Hastings	Y	N	Y	N	N	Y	Y
24 Feeney	Y	Y	Y	Y	Y	Y	Y
25 Diaz-Balart, M.	Y	Y	Y	Y	Y	Y	Y
GEORGIA							
1 Kingston	Y	Y	Y	Y	Y	Y	Y
2 Bishop	Y	N	Y	N	N	Y	Y
3 Westmoreland	Y	Y	Y	Y	Y	Y	Y
4 Johnson	Y	N	Y	N	N	Y	Y
5 Lewis	Y	N	Y	N	N	Y	Y
6 Price	Y	Y	Y	Y	Y	Y	Y
7 Linder	Y	Y	Y	Y	Y	Y	Y
8 Marshall	Y	Y	Y	Y	Y	Y	Y
9 Deal	Y	Y	Y	Y	Y	Y	Y
10 Broun	Y	Y	Y	Y	Y	Y	Y
11 Gingrey	Y	Y	Y	Y	Y	Y	Y
12 Barrow	Y	N	Y	N	Y	Y	Y
13 Scott	Y	N	Y	N	N	Y	?
HAWAII							
1 Abercrombie	P	N	Y	N	N	Y	Y
2 Hirono	P	N	Y	N	N	Y	Y
IDAHO							
1 Sali	Y	Y	Y	Y	Y	Y	Y
2 Simpson	Y	Y	Y	Y	Y	Y	Y
ILLINOIS							
1 Rush	?	?	?	?	?	?	?
2 Jackson	Y	N	Y	N	N	Y	Y
3 Lipinski	Y	N	Y	N	N	Y	Y
4 Gutierrez	Y	N	Y	N	N	Y	Y
5 Emanuel	Y	N	Y	N	N	Y	Y
6 Roskam	Y	Y	Y	Y	Y	Y	Y
7 Davis	Y	N	Y	N	N	Y	Y
8 Bean	Y	N	Y	N	N	Y	Y
9 Schakowsky	Y	N	Y	N	N	Y	Y
10 Kirk	Y	Y	Y	Y	Y	Y	Y
11 Weller	Y	Y	Y	Y	Y	Y	Y
12 Costello	Y	Y	Y	N	N	Y	Y
13 Biggert	Y	Y	Y	Y	Y	Y	Y
14 Foster	Y	Y	Y	N	N	Y	Y
15 Johnson	Y	Y	Y	Y	Y	Y	Y

KEY	Republicans	Democrats		
Y Voted for (yea)		X Paired against		C Voted "present" to avoid possible conflict of interest
# Paired for		– Announced against		
+ Announced for		P Voted "present"		? Did not vote or otherwise make a position known
N Voted against (nay)				

ND Northern Democrats, SD Southern Democrats
Southern states: Ala., Ark., Fla., Ga., Ky., La., Miss., N.C., Okla., S.C., Tenn., Texas, Va.

H-168   2008 CQ ALMANAC | www.cq.com

	499	500	501	502	503	504	505
16 **Manzullo**	Y	Y	Y	Y	Y	Y	Y
17 Hare	Y	N	Y	N	N	Y	Y
18 **LaHood**	Y	N	Y	N	Y	Y	Y
19 **Shimkus**	Y	Y	Y	Y	?	?	?
INDIANA							
1 Visclosky	Y	N	Y	N	N	Y	Y
2 Donnelly	Y	Y	Y	N	N	Y	Y
3 **Souder**	Y	Y	Y	Y	Y	Y	Y
4 **Buyer**	Y	Y	Y	Y	Y	Y	Y
5 **Burton**	Y	Y	Y	Y	Y	Y	Y
6 **Pence**	Y	Y	Y	Y	Y	Y	Y
7 Carson, A.	Y	N	Y	N	N	Y	Y
8 Ellsworth	Y	Y	Y	N	N	Y	Y
9 Hill	Y	Y	Y	N	N	Y	Y
IOWA							
1 Braley	Y	N	Y	N	N	Y	Y
2 Loebsack	Y	N	Y	N	N	Y	Y
3 Boswell	?	?	?	?	?	?	?
4 **Latham**	Y	Y	Y	Y	Y	Y	Y
5 **King**	Y	Y	Y	Y	Y	Y	Y
KANSAS							
1 **Moran**	Y	Y	Y	Y	Y	Y	Y
2 Boyda	Y	N	Y	N	N	Y	Y
3 Moore	Y	N	Y	N	N	Y	Y
4 **Tiahrt**	Y	Y	Y	Y	Y	Y	Y
KENTUCKY							
1 **Whitfield**	Y	Y	Y	Y	Y	Y	Y
2 **Lewis**	Y	Y	Y	Y	Y	Y	Y
3 Yarmuth	Y	N	Y	N	N	Y	Y
4 **Davis**	Y	Y	Y	Y	Y	Y	Y
5 **Rogers**	Y	Y	Y	Y	Y	Y	Y
6 Chandler	Y	Y	Y	N	N	Y	Y
LOUISIANA							
1 **Scalise**	Y	Y	Y	Y	Y	Y	Y
2 Jefferson	Y	N	Y	N	N	Y	Y
3 Melancon	Y	Y	Y	N	N	Y	Y
4 **McCrery**	Y	Y	Y	Y	Y	Y	Y
5 **Alexander**	Y	Y	Y	Y	Y	Y	Y
6 Cazayoux	Y	Y	Y	Y	N	Y	Y
7 **Boustany**	Y	Y	Y	Y	Y	Y	Y
MAINE							
1 Allen	Y	Y	Y	N	N	Y	Y
2 Michaud	Y	Y	Y	N	N	Y	Y
MARYLAND							
1 **Gilchrest**	?	?	?	?	?	?	?
2 Ruppersberger	Y	N	Y	N	N	Y	Y
3 Sarbanes	Y	N	Y	N	N	Y	Y
4 Edwards	P	N	Y	N	N	Y	Y
5 Hoyer	Y	N	Y	N	N	Y	Y
6 **Bartlett**	Y	Y	Y	Y	Y	Y	Y
7 Cummings	Y	Y	Y	N	N	Y	Y
8 Van Hollen	Y	N	Y	N	N	Y	Y
MASSACHUSETTS							
1 Olver	Y	N	Y	N	N	Y	Y
2 Neal	Y	N	Y	N	N	Y	Y
3 McGovern	Y	N	Y	N	N	Y	Y
4 Frank	Y	N	Y	N	N	Y	Y
5 Tsongas	Y	N	Y	N	N	Y	Y
6 Tierney	Y	N	Y	N	N	Y	Y
7 Markey	Y	N	Y	N	N	Y	Y
8 Capuano	Y	N	Y	N	N	Y	Y
9 Lynch	Y	Y	Y	N	N	Y	Y
10 Delahunt	?	?	?	?	N	Y	Y
MICHIGAN							
1 Stupak	Y	Y	Y	N	N	Y	Y
2 **Hoekstra**	Y	Y	Y	Y	Y	Y	Y
3 **Ehlers**	Y	Y	Y	Y	Y	Y	Y
4 **Camp**	Y	Y	Y	Y	Y	Y	Y
5 Kildee	Y	N	Y	N	N	Y	Y
6 **Upton**	Y	Y	Y	Y	Y	Y	Y
7 **Walberg**	Y	Y	Y	Y	Y	Y	Y
8 **Rogers**	Y	Y	Y	Y	Y	Y	Y
9 **Knollenberg**	Y	Y	Y	Y	Y	Y	Y
10 **Miller**	Y	Y	Y	Y	Y	Y	Y
11 **McCotter**	Y	Y	Y	Y	Y	Y	Y
12 Levin	Y	N	Y	N	N	Y	Y
13 Kilpatrick	Y	N	Y	N	N	Y	Y
14 Conyers	Y	N	Y	N	N	Y	Y
15 Dingell	Y	N	Y	N	N	Y	Y
MINNESOTA							
1 Walz	Y	N	Y	N	N	Y	Y
2 **Kline**	Y	Y	Y	Y	Y	Y	Y
3 **Ramstad**	Y	Y	Y	Y	Y	Y	Y
4 McCollum	Y	N	Y	N	N	Y	Y

	499	500	501	502	503	504	505
5 Ellison	N	N	Y	N	N	Y	Y
6 **Bachmann**	Y	Y	Y	Y	Y	Y	Y
7 Peterson	Y	N	Y	N	N	Y	Y
8 Oberstar	Y	N	Y	N	N	Y	Y
MISSISSIPPI							
1 Childers	Y	Y	Y	N	N	Y	Y
2 Thompson	Y	N	Y	N	N	Y	Y
3 **Pickering**	Y	Y	Y	?	Y	Y	Y
4 Taylor	Y	Y	Y	N	N	Y	Y
MISSOURI							
1 Clay	Y	N	Y	N	N	Y	Y
2 **Akin**	Y	Y	Y	Y	Y	Y	Y
3 Carnahan	Y	N	Y	N	N	Y	Y
4 Skelton	Y	N	Y	N	N	Y	Y
5 Cleaver	Y	N	Y	N	N	Y	Y
6 **Graves**	Y	Y	Y	Y	Y	Y	?
7 **Blunt**	Y	Y	Y	Y	?	?	?
8 **Emerson**	Y	?	Y	Y	Y	Y	Y
9 **Hulshof**	Y	Y	Y	Y	Y	Y	Y
MONTANA							
AL **Rehberg**	Y	Y	Y	Y	Y	Y	Y
NEBRASKA							
1 **Fortenberry**	Y	Y	Y	Y	Y	Y	Y
2 **Terry**	Y	Y	Y	Y	Y	Y	Y
3 **Smith**	Y	Y	Y	Y	Y	Y	+
NEVADA							
1 Berkley	Y	Y	Y	N	N	Y	Y
2 **Heller**	Y	Y	Y	Y	Y	Y	Y
3 **Porter**	Y	Y	Y	Y	Y	Y	Y
NEW HAMPSHIRE							
1 Shea-Porter	Y	Y	Y	N	N	Y	Y
2 Hodes	Y	N	Y	N	N	Y	Y
NEW JERSEY							
1 Andrews	Y	N	Y	N	N	Y	Y
2 **LoBiondo**	Y	Y	Y	Y	Y	Y	Y
3 **Saxton**	Y	Y	Y	Y	Y	Y	Y
4 **Smith**	Y	Y	Y	Y	Y	Y	Y
5 **Garrett**	Y	Y	Y	Y	Y	Y	Y
6 Pallone	Y	N	Y	N	N	Y	Y
7 **Ferguson**	Y	Y	Y	Y	Y	Y	Y
8 Pascrell	Y	N	Y	N	N	Y	Y
9 Rothman	Y	N	Y	N	N	Y	Y
10 Payne	N	N	Y	N	N	Y	Y
11 **Frelinghuysen**	Y	Y	Y	Y	Y	Y	Y
12 Holt	Y	N	Y	N	N	Y	Y
13 Sires	Y	N	Y	N	N	Y	Y
NEW MEXICO							
1 **Wilson**	Y	Y	Y	Y	Y	Y	Y
2 **Pearce**	Y	Y	Y	Y	Y	Y	Y
3 Udall	Y	N	Y	N	N	Y	Y
NEW YORK							
1 Bishop	Y	N	Y	N	N	Y	Y
2 Israel	Y	Y	Y	N	N	Y	Y
3 **King**	Y	Y	Y	Y	Y	Y	Y
4 McCarthy	Y	N	Y	N	N	Y	Y
5 Ackerman	Y	Y	Y	N	N	Y	Y
6 Meeks	Y	N	Y	N	N	Y	Y
7 Crowley	Y	N	Y	N	N	Y	Y
8 Nadler	Y	N	Y	N	N	Y	Y
9 Weiner	Y	Y	Y	N	?	Y	Y
10 Towns	Y	N	Y	N	N	Y	Y
11 Clarke	P	N	Y	N	N	Y	Y
12 Velázquez	Y	N	Y	N	N	Y	Y
13 **Fossella**	Y	Y	Y	Y	Y	Y	Y
14 Maloney	Y	N	Y	N	N	Y	Y
15 Rangel	Y	N	Y	N	N	Y	Y
16 Serrano	Y	N	Y	N	N	Y	Y
17 Engel	Y	Y	Y	N	N	Y	Y
18 Lowey	Y	N	Y	N	N	Y	Y
19 Hall	Y	N	Y	N	N	Y	Y
20 Gillibrand	Y	Y	Y	N	N	Y	Y
21 McNulty	Y	Y	Y	N	N	Y	Y
22 Hinchey	N	N	Y	N	N	Y	Y
23 **McHugh**	Y	Y	Y	Y	Y	Y	Y
24 Arcuri	Y	Y	Y	N	N	Y	Y
25 **Walsh**	Y	Y	Y	Y	Y	Y	Y
26 **Reynolds**	Y	Y	Y	Y	Y	Y	Y
27 Higgins	Y	N	Y	N	N	Y	Y
28 Slaughter	Y	N	Y	N	N	Y	Y
29 **Kuhl**	Y	Y	Y	Y	Y	Y	Y
NORTH CAROLINA							
1 Butterfield	Y	N	Y	N	N	Y	Y
2 Etheridge	Y	N	Y	N	N	Y	Y
3 **Jones**	Y	Y	Y	Y	N	Y	Y
4 Price	Y	N	Y	N	N	Y	Y

	499	500	501	502	503	504	505
5 **Foxx**	Y	Y	Y	Y	Y	Y	Y
6 **Coble**	Y	Y	Y	Y	Y	Y	Y
7 McIntyre	Y	Y	Y	Y	N	Y	Y
8 **Hayes**	Y	Y	Y	Y	Y	Y	Y
9 **Myrick**	Y	Y	Y	Y	Y	Y	Y
10 **McHenry**	Y	Y	Y	Y	Y	Y	Y
11 Shuler	Y	Y	Y	N	N	Y	Y
12 Watt	Y	N	Y	N	N	Y	Y
13 Miller	Y	N	Y	N	N	Y	Y
NORTH DAKOTA							
AL Pomeroy	Y	N	Y	N	N	Y	Y
OHIO							
1 **Chabot**	Y	Y	Y	Y	Y	Y	Y
2 **Schmidt**	Y	Y	Y	Y	Y	Y	Y
3 **Turner**	Y	Y	Y	Y	Y	Y	Y
4 **Jordan**	Y	Y	Y	Y	Y	Y	Y
5 **Latta**	Y	Y	Y	Y	Y	Y	Y
6 Wilson	Y	Y	Y	N	N	Y	Y
7 **Hobson**	Y	Y	Y	Y	Y	Y	Y
8 **Boehner**	Y	Y	Y	Y	Y	Y	Y
9 Kaptur	Y	N	Y	N	N	Y	Y
10 Kucinich	N	N	Y	N	N	Y	Y
11 Tubbs Jones	Y	N	Y	N	N	Y	Y
12 **Tiberi**	Y	Y	Y	Y	Y	Y	Y
13 Sutton	P	N	Y	N	N	Y	Y
14 **LaTourette**	Y	Y	Y	Y	Y	Y	Y
15 **Pryce**	Y	Y	Y	Y	Y	Y	Y
16 **Regula**	Y	Y	Y	Y	Y	Y	Y
17 Ryan	Y	N	Y	N	N	Y	Y
18 Space	Y	Y	Y	N	N	Y	Y
OKLAHOMA							
1 **Sullivan**	Y	Y	Y	Y	Y	Y	Y
2 Boren	Y	Y	Y	N	N	Y	Y
3 **Lucas**	?	?	?	?	?	?	?
4 **Cole**	Y	Y	Y	Y	Y	Y	Y
5 **Fallin**	Y	Y	Y	Y	Y	Y	Y
OREGON							
1 Wu	Y	N	Y	N	N	Y	Y
2 **Walden**	Y	Y	Y	Y	Y	Y	Y
3 Blumenauer	Y	N	Y	N	N	Y	Y
4 DeFazio	Y	N	Y	N	N	Y	Y
5 Hooley	Y	N	Y	N	N	Y	Y
PENNSYLVANIA							
1 Brady	Y	N	Y	N	N	Y	Y
2 Fattah	Y	Y	Y	N	N	Y	Y
3 **English**	Y	Y	Y	Y	Y	Y	Y
4 Altmire	Y	N	Y	Y	N	Y	Y
5 **Peterson**	Y	Y	Y	Y	Y	Y	?
6 **Gerlach**	Y	Y	Y	Y	Y	Y	Y
7 Sestak	Y	N	Y	N	N	Y	Y
8 Murphy, P.	Y	N	Y	N	N	Y	Y
9 **Shuster**	Y	Y	Y	Y	Y	Y	Y
10 Carney	Y	Y	Y	N	N	Y	Y
11 Kanjorski	Y	N	Y	N	N	Y	Y
12 Murtha	Y	N	Y	N	N	Y	Y
13 Schwartz	Y	N	Y	N	N	Y	Y
14 Doyle	Y	N	Y	N	N	Y	Y
15 **Dent**	Y	Y	Y	Y	Y	Y	Y
16 **Pitts**	Y	Y	Y	Y	Y	Y	Y
17 Holden	Y	Y	Y	N	N	Y	Y
18 **Murphy, T.**	Y	Y	Y	Y	Y	Y	Y
19 **Platts**	Y	Y	Y	N	Y	Y	Y
RHODE ISLAND							
1 Kennedy	Y	N	Y	N	N	Y	Y
2 Langevin	Y	N	Y	N	N	Y	Y
SOUTH CAROLINA							
1 **Brown**	Y	Y	Y	Y	Y	Y	Y
2 **Wilson**	Y	Y	Y	Y	Y	Y	Y
3 **Barrett**	Y	Y	Y	Y	Y	Y	Y
4 **Inglis**	Y	Y	Y	?	Y	Y	Y
5 Spratt	Y	N	Y	N	N	Y	Y
6 Clyburn	Y	N	Y	N	N	Y	Y
SOUTH DAKOTA							
AL Herseth Sandlin	Y	Y	Y	N	N	Y	Y
TENNESSEE							
1 **Davis, D.**	Y	Y	Y	Y	Y	Y	Y
2 **Duncan**	Y	Y	Y	Y	Y	Y	Y
3 **Wamp**	Y	Y	Y	Y	Y	Y	Y
4 Davis, L.	Y	Y	Y	N	N	Y	Y
5 Cooper	Y	N	Y	N	N	Y	Y
6 Gordon	Y	Y	Y	N	N	Y	Y
7 **Blackburn**	Y	Y	Y	Y	Y	Y	Y
8 Tanner	Y	Y	Y	N	N	Y	Y
9 Cohen	P	N	Y	N	N	Y	Y

	499	500	501	502	503	504	505
TEXAS							
1 **Gohmert**	Y	Y	Y	Y	Y	Y	Y
2 **Poe**	Y	Y	Y	Y	Y	Y	Y
3 **Johnson, S.**	Y	Y	Y	Y	Y	Y	Y
4 **Hall**	Y	Y	Y	Y	Y	Y	Y
5 **Hensarling**	Y	Y	Y	Y	Y	Y	Y
6 **Barton**	Y	Y	Y	Y	Y	?	?
7 **Culberson**	Y	Y	Y	Y	Y	Y	Y
8 **Brady**	Y	Y	Y	Y	Y	Y	Y
9 Green, A.	?	?	?	?	?	?	?
10 **McCaul**	Y	Y	Y	Y	Y	Y	Y
11 **Conaway**	Y	Y	Y	Y	Y	Y	Y
12 **Granger**	Y	Y	Y	Y	Y	Y	Y
13 **Thornberry**	Y	Y	Y	Y	Y	Y	Y
14 **Paul**	N	N	N	Y	Y	Y	Y
15 Hinojosa	Y	N	Y	N	N	Y	Y
16 Reyes	Y	N	Y	N	N	Y	Y
17 Edwards	Y	N	Y	N	N	Y	Y
18 Jackson Lee	Y	N	Y	N	N	Y	Y
19 **Neugebauer**	Y	Y	Y	Y	Y	Y	Y
20 Gonzalez	Y	N	Y	N	N	Y	Y
21 **Smith**	Y	Y	Y	Y	?	Y	Y
22 Lampson	Y	Y	Y	Y	Y	Y	Y
23 Rodriguez	Y	N	Y	N	N	Y	Y
24 **Marchant**	Y	Y	Y	Y	Y	Y	Y
25 Doggett	Y	N	Y	N	N	Y	Y
26 **Burgess**	Y	Y	Y	Y	Y	Y	Y
27 Ortiz	Y	N	Y	N	N	Y	Y
28 Cuellar	Y	Y	Y	N	N	Y	Y
29 Green, G.	Y	N	Y	N	N	Y	Y
30 Johnson, E.	Y	+	+	–	–	+	+
31 **Carter**	Y	Y	Y	Y	Y	Y	Y
32 **Sessions**	Y	Y	Y	Y	Y	Y	Y
UTAH							
1 **Bishop**	Y	Y	Y	Y	Y	Y	Y
2 Matheson	Y	Y	Y	N	N	Y	Y
3 **Cannon**	Y	Y	Y	Y	Y	Y	Y
VERMONT							
AL Welch	Y	N	Y	N	N	Y	Y
VIRGINIA							
1 **Wittman**	Y	Y	Y	Y	Y	Y	Y
2 **Drake**	Y	Y	Y	Y	Y	Y	Y
3 Scott	Y	N	Y	N	N	Y	Y
4 **Forbes**	Y	Y	Y	Y	Y	Y	Y
5 **Goode**	Y	Y	Y	Y	Y	Y	Y
6 **Goodlatte**	Y	Y	Y	Y	Y	Y	Y
7 **Cantor**	Y	Y	Y	Y	Y	Y	Y
8 Moran	Y	N	Y	N	N	Y	Y
9 Boucher	Y	Y	Y	N	N	Y	Y
10 **Wolf**	Y	Y	Y	Y	Y	Y	Y
11 **Davis**	Y	Y	Y	Y	Y	Y	Y
WASHINGTON							
1 Inslee	Y	N	Y	N	N	Y	Y
2 Larsen	Y	N	Y	N	N	Y	Y
3 Baird	Y	N	Y	N	N	Y	Y
4 **Hastings**	Y	Y	Y	Y	Y	Y	Y
5 **McMorris Rodgers**	Y	Y	Y	Y	Y	Y	Y
6 Dicks	Y	N	Y	N	N	Y	Y
7 McDermott	N	N	Y	N	N	Y	?
8 **Reichert**	Y	Y	Y	Y	Y	Y	Y
9 Smith	Y	N	Y	N	N	Y	Y
WEST VIRGINIA							
1 Mollohan	Y	N	Y	N	N	Y	Y
2 **Capito**	Y	Y	Y	Y	Y	Y	Y
3 Rahall	Y	N	Y	N	N	Y	Y
WISCONSIN							
1 **Ryan**	Y	Y	Y	Y	Y	Y	Y
2 Baldwin	Y	N	Y	N	N	Y	Y
3 Kind	Y	N	Y	N	N	Y	Y
4 Moore	N	N	Y	N	N	Y	Y
5 **Sensenbrenner**	Y	Y	Y	Y	Y	Y	Y
6 **Petri**	Y	Y	Y	Y	Y	Y	Y
7 Obey	N	N	Y	N	N	Y	Y
8 Kagen	Y	Y	Y	N	N	Y	Y
WYOMING							
AL **Cubin**	Y	Y	Y	Y	?	?	?
DELEGATES							
Faleomavaega (A.S.)	Y	N	?		N	Y	Y
Norton (D.C.)	Y	?	Y		N	Y	Y
Bordallo (Guam)	+	N	Y		N	Y	Y
Fortuño (P.R.)	?	?	?		?	?	?
Christensen (V.I.)	Y	N	Y		N	Y	Y

HOUSE VOTES

IN THE HOUSE | By Vote Number

506. **HR 415. Taunton Wild and Scenic River/Recommit.** Wittman, R-Va., motion to recommit the bill to the Natural Resources Committee with instructions that it be reported back promptly with language that would ensure that it would not restrict development of energy infrastructure, easements and environmental mitigation related to energy, business or economic activities. Motion rejected 188-227: R 184-3; D 4-224 (ND 1-171, SD 3-53). July 16, 2008.

507. **HR 415. Taunton Wild and Scenic River/Passage.** Passage of the bill that would designate a 40-mile segment of the Taunton River in Massachusetts as part of the National Wild and Scenic Rivers System. It would allow the Interior Department to acquire land only through purchase from a willing seller or through a land donation. The bill would require the Interior secretary to report on the energy resources available on the lands and waters included in the segment of the river. Passed 242-175: R 11-175; D 231-0 (ND 175-0, SD 56-0). July 16, 2008.

508. **H Con Res 295. Appreciation for Armed Forces Families/ Adoption.** Courtney, D-Conn., motion to suspend the rules and adopt the concurrent resolution that would express congressional appreciation for the families of members of the U.S. armed forces. Motion agreed to 415-0: R 190-0; D 225-0 (ND 172-0, SD 53-0). A two-thirds majority of those present and voting (277 in this case) is required for adoption under suspension of the rules. July 16, 2008.

509. **HR 6515. Oil and Natural Gas Exploration/Previous Question.** Welch, D-Vt., motion to order the previous question (thus ending debate and possibility of amendment) on adoption of the rule (H Res 1350) to provide for House floor consideration of a bill concerning domestic production of oil and natural gas, under suspension of the rules on the legislative day of Thursday, July 17, 2008. Motion agreed to 228-188: R 2-186; D 226-2 (ND 170-0, SD 56-2). July 17, 2008.

510. **HR 6515. Oil and Natural Gas Exploration/Rule.** Adoption of the rule (H Res 1350) to provide for House floor consideration of a bill concerning domestic production of oil and natural gas, under suspension of the rules on the legislative day of Thursday, July 17, 2008. Adopted 222-194: R 0-190; D 222-4 (ND 168-0, SD 54-4). July 17, 2008.

511. **HR 6515. Oil and Natural Gas Exploration/Passage.** Rahall, D-W.Va., motion to suspend the rules and pass the bill that would require the Interior Department to offer oil and gas lease sales on an annual basis. It would require current holders of oil or natural gas exploration leases to develop or relinquish their existing leases before they could receive new ones. It would seek to expedite construction of oil and natural gas pipelines in Alaska and ban the export of oil from Alaska. Motion rejected 244-173: R 26-162; D 218-11 (ND 168-2, SD 50-9). A two-thirds majority of those present and voting (278 in this case) is required for passage under suspension of the rules. A "nay" was a vote in support of the president's position. July 17, 2008.

	506	507	508	509	510	511
ALABAMA						
1 Bonner	Y	N	Y	N	N	N
2 Everett	Y	N	Y	N	N	N
3 Rogers	Y	N	Y	N	N	Y
4 Aderholt	Y	N	Y	N	N	N
5 Cramer	N	Y	Y	Y	Y	Y
6 Bachus	Y	N	Y	N	N	N
7 Davis	N	Y	Y	Y	Y	Y
ALASKA						
AL Young	Y	N	Y	?	?	?
ARIZONA						
1 Renzi	Y	N	Y	N	N	N
2 Franks	Y	N	Y	N	N	N
3 Shadegg	Y	N	Y	N	N	N
4 Pastor	N	Y	Y	Y	Y	Y
5 Mitchell	N	Y	Y	Y	Y	Y
6 Flake	Y	N	Y	N	N	N
7 Grijalva	N	Y	Y	Y	Y	Y
8 Giffords	N	Y	Y	Y	Y	Y
ARKANSAS						
1 Berry	N	Y	Y	Y	Y	Y
2 Snyder	N	Y	Y	Y	Y	Y
3 Boozman	Y	N	Y	N	N	N
4 Ross	N	Y	Y	Y	Y	Y
CALIFORNIA						
1 Thompson	N	Y	Y	Y	Y	Y
2 Herger	Y	N	Y	-	-	-
3 Lungren	Y	N	Y	N	N	N
4 Doolittle	Y	N	Y	?	?	?
5 Matsui	N	Y	Y	Y	Y	Y
6 Woolsey	N	Y	Y	Y	Y	Y
7 Miller, George	N	Y	Y	Y	Y	Y
8 Pelosi		Y				Y
9 Lee	N	Y	Y	Y	Y	Y
10 Tauscher	N	Y	Y	Y	Y	Y
11 McNerney	N	Y	Y	Y	Y	Y
12 Speier	N	Y	Y	Y	Y	Y
13 Stark	N	Y	Y	Y	Y	Y
14 Eshoo	N	Y	Y	Y	Y	Y
15 Honda	N	Y	Y	Y	Y	Y
16 Lofgren	N	Y	Y	Y	Y	Y
17 Farr	N	Y	Y	Y	Y	Y
18 Cardoza	N	Y	Y	Y	Y	Y
19 Radanovich	Y	N	Y	N	N	N
20 Costa	N	Y	Y	Y	Y	N
21 Nunes	Y	N	Y	N	N	N
22 McCarthy	Y	N	Y	N	N	N
23 Capps	-	Y	Y	Y	Y	Y
24 Gallegly	Y	N	Y	N	N	N
25 McKeon	Y	N	Y	N	N	N
26 Dreier	Y	N	Y	N	N	N
27 Sherman	N	Y	Y	Y	Y	Y
28 Berman	N	Y	Y	Y	Y	Y
29 Schiff	N	Y	Y	Y	Y	Y
30 Waxman	N	Y	Y	Y	Y	Y
31 Becerra	N	Y	Y	Y	Y	Y
32 Solis	N	Y	Y	Y	Y	Y
33 Watson	N	Y	Y	Y	Y	Y
34 Roybal-Allard	N	Y	Y	Y	Y	Y
35 Waters	N	Y	Y	Y	Y	Y
36 Harman	N	Y	Y	Y	Y	Y
37 Richardson	N	Y	Y	Y	Y	Y
38 Napolitano	N	Y	Y	Y	Y	Y
39 Sánchez, Linda	N	Y	Y	Y	Y	Y
40 Royce	Y	?	Y	N	N	N
41 Lewis	Y	N	Y	N	N	N
42 Miller, Gary	?	?	?	?	?	?
43 Baca	N	Y	Y	Y	Y	Y
44 Calvert	Y	N	Y	N	N	N
45 Bono Mack	Y	N	Y	N	N	N
46 Rohrabacher	Y	N	Y	N	N	N
47 Sanchez, Loretta	N	Y	Y	Y	Y	?
48 Campbell	Y	N	Y	N	N	N
49 Issa	?	N	Y	N	N	N
50 Bilbray	Y	N	Y	N	N	N
51 Filner	N	Y	Y	Y	Y	Y
52 Hunter	Y	N	Y	?	?	?
53 Davis	N	Y	Y	Y	Y	Y
COLORADO						
1 DeGette	N	Y	Y	Y	Y	Y
2 Udall	N	Y	Y	Y	Y	Y
3 Salazar	N	Y	Y	Y	Y	Y
4 Musgrave	Y	N	Y	N	N	N
5 Lamborn	Y	N	Y	N	N	N
6 Tancredo	Y	N	Y	N	N	N
7 Perlmutter	N	Y	Y	Y	Y	Y
CONNECTICUT						
1 Larson	N	Y	Y	Y	?	Y
2 Courtney	N	Y	Y	Y	Y	Y
3 DeLauro	N	Y	Y	Y	Y	Y
4 Shays	N	Y	Y	N	N	Y
5 Murphy	N	Y	Y	Y	Y	Y
DELAWARE						
AL Castle	Y	Y	Y	N	N	Y
FLORIDA						
1 Miller	Y	N	Y	N	N	N
2 Boyd	N	Y	Y	Y	Y	Y
3 Brown	N	Y	Y	Y	Y	Y
4 Crenshaw	Y	N	Y	N	N	N
5 Brown-Waite	Y	N	Y	N	N	?
6 Stearns	?	-	Y	N	N	N
7 Mica	Y	N	Y	N	N	N
8 Keller	Y	N	Y	N	N	N
9 Bilirakis	Y	N	Y	N	N	N
10 Young	Y	N	Y	N	N	N
11 Castor	N	Y	Y	Y	Y	Y
12 Putnam	Y	N	Y	N	N	N
13 Buchanan	Y	N	Y	N	N	N
14 Mack	Y	N	Y	N	N	N
15 Weldon	Y	N	Y	N	N	N
16 Mahoney	N	Y	Y	Y	Y	Y
17 Meek	N	Y	Y	Y	Y	Y
18 Ros-Lehtinen	Y	Y	Y	Y	Y	Y
19 Wexler	N	Y	Y	Y	Y	Y
20 Wasserman Schultz	N	Y	Y	Y	Y	Y
21 Diaz-Balart, L.	Y	N	Y	N	N	N
22 Klein	N	Y	Y	Y	Y	Y
23 Hastings	N	Y	Y	Y	Y	Y
24 Feeney	Y	N	Y	N	N	N
25 Diaz-Balart, M.	Y	N	Y	N	N	N
GEORGIA						
1 Kingston	Y	N	Y	N	N	N
2 Bishop	N	Y	Y	Y	Y	Y
3 Westmoreland	Y	N	Y	N	N	N
4 Johnson	N	Y	Y	Y	Y	Y
5 Lewis	N	Y	?	Y	Y	Y
6 Price	Y	N	Y	N	N	N
7 Linder	Y	N	Y	N	N	N
8 Marshall	N	Y	?	Y	Y	Y
9 Deal	Y	N	Y	N	N	N
10 Broun	Y	N	Y	N	N	N
11 Gingrey	Y	N	Y	N	N	N
12 Barrow	Y	Y	Y	Y	Y	Y
13 Scott	?	?	?	Y	Y	Y
HAWAII						
1 Abercrombie	N	Y	Y	Y	Y	N
2 Hirono	N	Y	Y	Y	Y	Y
IDAHO						
1 Sali	Y	N	Y	N	N	N
2 Simpson	Y	N	Y	N	N	N
ILLINOIS						
1 Rush	?	?	?	?	?	?
2 Jackson	N	Y	Y	Y	Y	Y
3 Lipinski	N	Y	Y	Y	Y	Y
4 Gutierrez	N	Y	Y	Y	Y	Y
5 Emanuel	N	Y	Y	Y	Y	Y
6 Roskam	Y	N	Y	N	N	N
7 Davis	N	Y	Y	Y	Y	Y
8 Bean	N	Y	Y	Y	Y	Y
9 Schakowsky	N	Y	Y	Y	Y	Y
10 Kirk	Y	N	Y	N	N	N
11 Weller	Y	N	Y	N	N	N
12 Costello	N	Y	Y	Y	Y	Y
13 Biggert	Y	N	Y	N	N	Y
14 Foster	N	Y	Y	Y	Y	Y
15 Johnson	Y	N	Y	N	N	N

KEY   **Republicans**   Democrats

Y Voted for (yea)	X Paired against	C Voted "present" to avoid possible conflict of interest
# Paired for	– Announced against	
+ Announced for	P Voted "present"	? Did not vote or otherwise make a position known
N Voted against (nay)		

ND Northern Democrats, SD Southern Democrats
Southern states: Ala., Ark., Fla., Ga., Ky., La., Miss., N.C., Okla., S.C., Tenn., Texas, Va.

	506	507	508	509	510	511
16 **Manzullo**	Y	N	Y	N	N	N
17 Hare	N	Y	Y	Y	Y	Y
18 **LaHood**	Y	N	Y	N	N	N
19 **Shimkus**	?	?	?	N	N	N
INDIANA						
1 Visclosky	N	Y	Y	Y	Y	Y
2 Donnelly	N	Y	Y	Y	Y	Y
3 **Souder**	Y	?	Y	N	N	N
4 **Buyer**	Y	N	Y	N	N	N
5 **Burton**	Y	N	Y	N	N	N
6 **Pence**	Y	N	Y	N	N	N
7 Carson, A.	N	Y	Y	Y	Y	Y
8 Ellsworth	N	Y	Y	Y	Y	Y
9 Hill	N	Y	Y	Y	Y	Y
IOWA						
1 Braley	N	Y	Y	Y	Y	Y
2 Loebsack	N	Y	Y	Y	?	Y
3 Boswell	?	?	?	?	?	?
4 **Latham**	Y	N	Y	N	N	N
5 **King**	Y	N	Y	N	N	N
KANSAS						
1 **Moran**	Y	N	Y	N	N	N
2 Boyda	N	Y	Y	Y	Y	Y
3 Moore	N	Y	Y	Y	Y	Y
4 **Tiahrt**	Y	N	Y	N	N	N
KENTUCKY						
1 **Whitfield**	Y	N	Y	N	N	N
2 **Lewis**	Y	N	Y	N	N	N
3 Yarmuth	N	Y	Y	Y	Y	Y
4 **Davis**	Y	N	Y	N	N	N
5 **Rogers**	Y	N	Y	N	N	N
6 Chandler	N	Y	Y	Y	Y	Y
LOUISIANA						
1 **Scalise**	Y	N	Y	N	N	N
2 Jefferson	N	Y	Y	Y	Y	Y
3 Melancon	N	Y	Y	Y	Y	Y
4 **McCrery**	Y	N	Y	N	N	N
5 **Alexander**	Y	N	Y	N	N	N
6 Cazayoux	N	Y	Y	N	N	Y
7 **Boustany**	Y	N	Y	N	N	N
MAINE						
1 Allen	N	Y	Y	Y	Y	Y
2 Michaud	N	Y	Y	Y	Y	Y
MARYLAND						
1 **Gilchrest**	?	?	?	?	?	?
2 Ruppersberger	N	Y	Y	+	+	+
3 Sarbanes	N	Y	Y	Y	Y	Y
4 Edwards	N	Y	Y	Y	Y	Y
5 Hoyer	N	Y	Y	Y	Y	Y
6 **Bartlett**	Y	N	Y	N	N	N
7 Cummings	N	Y	Y	Y	Y	Y
8 Van Hollen	N	Y	Y	Y	Y	Y
MASSACHUSETTS						
1 Olver	N	Y	Y	Y	Y	Y
2 Neal	N	Y	Y	Y	Y	Y
3 McGovern	N	Y	Y	Y	Y	Y
4 Frank	N	Y	Y	?	Y	Y
5 Tsongas	N	Y	Y	Y	Y	Y
6 Tierney	N	Y	Y	Y	?	Y
7 Markey	N	Y	Y	Y	Y	Y
8 Capuano	N	Y	Y	Y	Y	Y
9 Lynch	N	Y	Y	Y	Y	Y
10 Delahunt	N	Y	Y	Y	Y	Y
MICHIGAN						
1 Stupak	N	Y	Y	Y	Y	Y
2 **Hoekstra**	Y	Y	Y	N	N	N
3 **Ehlers**	Y	Y	Y	N	N	N
4 **Camp**	Y	N	Y	N	N	N
5 Kildee	N	Y	Y	Y	Y	Y
6 **Upton**	Y	N	Y	N	N	N
7 **Walberg**	Y	N	Y	N	N	N
8 **Rogers**	Y	N	Y	N	N	N
9 **Knollenberg**	Y	N	Y	N	N	Y
10 **Miller**	Y	N	Y	N	N	N
11 **McCotter**	Y	N	Y	N	N	N
12 Levin	N	Y	Y	Y	Y	Y
13 Kilpatrick	N	Y	Y	Y	Y	Y
14 Conyers	N	Y	Y	Y	Y	Y
15 Dingell	N	Y	Y	Y	Y	Y
MINNESOTA						
1 Walz	N	Y	Y	Y	Y	Y
2 **Kline**	Y	N	Y	N	N	N
3 **Ramstad**	Y	Y	Y	N	N	Y
4 McCollum	N	Y	Y	Y	Y	Y

	506	507	508	509	510	511
5 Ellison	N	Y	Y	Y	Y	Y
6 **Bachmann**	Y	N	Y	N	N	N
7 Peterson	N	Y	Y	Y	Y	Y
8 Oberstar	N	Y	Y	Y	Y	Y
MISSISSIPPI						
1 Childers	N	Y	Y	N	N	Y
2 Thompson	N	Y	Y	Y	Y	Y
3 **Pickering**	Y	N	Y	?	N	N
4 Taylor	N	Y	Y	Y	Y	Y
MISSOURI						
1 Clay	N	Y	Y	Y	Y	Y
2 **Akin**	Y	N	Y	N	N	N
3 Carnahan	N	Y	Y	Y	Y	Y
4 Skelton	N	Y	Y	Y	Y	Y
5 Cleaver	N	Y	Y	Y	Y	Y
6 **Graves**	Y	N	Y	N	N	Y
7 **Blunt**	Y	N	Y	N	N	N
8 **Emerson**	Y	N	Y	N	N	N
9 **Hulshof**	Y	N	Y	N	N	N
MONTANA						
AL **Rehberg**	Y	N	Y	N	N	N
NEBRASKA						
1 **Fortenberry**	Y	N	Y	N	N	N
2 **Terry**	Y	N	Y	?	N	N
3 **Smith**	Y	N	Y	N	N	N
NEVADA						
1 Berkley	N	Y	Y	Y	Y	Y
2 **Heller**	Y	N	Y	N	N	N
3 **Porter**	Y	N	Y	N	N	Y
NEW HAMPSHIRE						
1 Shea-Porter	N	Y	Y	Y	Y	Y
2 Hodes	N	Y	Y	Y	Y	Y
NEW JERSEY						
1 Andrews	N	Y	Y	?	?	?
2 **LoBiondo**	Y	N	Y	N	N	Y
3 **Saxton**	?	?	?	N	N	N
4 **Smith**	Y	N	Y	N	N	Y
5 **Garrett**	Y	N	Y	N	N	N
6 Pallone	N	Y	Y	Y	Y	Y
7 **Ferguson**	Y	N	Y	N	N	N
8 Pascrell	N	Y	Y	Y	Y	Y
9 Rothman	N	Y	Y	Y	Y	Y
10 Payne	N	Y	Y	Y	Y	Y
11 **Frelinghuysen**	Y	Y	Y	N	N	N
12 Holt	N	Y	Y	Y	Y	Y
13 Sires	N	Y	Y	Y	Y	Y
NEW MEXICO						
1 **Wilson**	Y	N	Y	N	N	N
2 **Pearce**	Y	N	Y	N	N	N
3 Udall	N	Y	Y	Y	Y	Y
NEW YORK						
1 Bishop	N	Y	Y	Y	Y	Y
2 Israel	N	Y	Y	Y	Y	Y
3 **King**	Y	N	Y	N	N	N
4 McCarthy	N	Y	Y	Y	Y	Y
5 Ackerman	N	Y	Y	Y	Y	Y
6 Meeks	N	Y	Y	Y	Y	Y
7 Crowley	N	Y	Y	Y	Y	Y
8 Nadler	N	Y	Y	Y	Y	Y
9 Weiner	N	Y	Y	Y	Y	Y
10 Towns	N	Y	Y	Y	Y	Y
11 Clarke	N	Y	Y	Y	Y	Y
12 Velázquez	N	Y	Y	Y	Y	Y
13 **Fossella**	Y	Y	Y	N	N	N
14 Maloney	N	Y	Y	Y	Y	Y
15 Rangel	N	Y	Y	Y	Y	Y
16 Serrano	N	Y	Y	Y	Y	Y
17 Engel	N	Y	Y	Y	Y	Y
18 Lowey	N	Y	Y	Y	Y	Y
19 Hall	N	Y	Y	Y	Y	Y
20 Gillibrand	N	Y	Y	Y	Y	Y
21 McNulty	N	Y	Y	Y	Y	?
22 Hinchey	N	Y	Y	Y	Y	Y
23 **McHugh**	Y	N	Y	N	N	N
24 Arcuri	N	Y	Y	Y	Y	Y
25 **Walsh**	Y	N	Y	N	N	N
26 **Reynolds**	Y	N	Y	N	N	N
27 Higgins	N	Y	Y	Y	Y	Y
28 Slaughter	N	Y	Y	Y	Y	Y
29 **Kuhl**	Y	N	Y	N	N	Y
NORTH CAROLINA						
1 Butterfield	N	Y	Y	Y	Y	Y
2 Etheridge	N	Y	Y	Y	Y	Y
3 **Jones**	N	Y	Y	N	N	Y
4 Price	N	Y	Y	Y	Y	Y

	506	507	508	509	510	511
5 **Foxx**	Y	N	Y	N	N	N
6 **Coble**	Y	N	Y	N	N	N
7 McIntyre	Y	Y	Y	Y	Y	Y
8 **Hayes**	Y	N	Y	N	N	Y
9 **Myrick**	Y	N	Y	N	N	N
10 **McHenry**	Y	N	Y	N	N	N
11 Shuler	N	Y	Y	Y	N	Y
12 Watt	N	Y	Y	Y	Y	Y
13 Miller	N	Y	Y	Y	Y	Y
NORTH DAKOTA						
AL Pomeroy	N	Y	Y	Y	Y	Y
OHIO						
1 **Chabot**	Y	N	Y	N	N	Y
2 **Schmidt**	Y	N	Y	N	N	N
3 **Turner**	Y	N	Y	N	N	N
4 **Jordan**	Y	N	Y	N	N	N
5 **Latta**	Y	N	Y	N	N	N
6 Wilson	?	Y	Y	Y	Y	Y
7 **Hobson**	Y	N	Y	N	N	N
8 **Boehner**	Y	N	Y	N	N	N
9 Kaptur	N	Y	Y	Y	Y	?
10 Kucinich	N	Y	Y	Y	Y	Y
11 Tubbs Jones	N	Y	Y	Y	Y	Y
12 **Tiberi**	Y	N	Y	N	N	N
13 Sutton	N	Y	Y	Y	Y	Y
14 **LaTourette**	Y	N	Y	N	N	N
15 **Pryce**	Y	Y	Y	N	N	N
16 **Regula**	Y	N	Y	N	N	N
17 Ryan	N	Y	Y	Y	Y	Y
18 Space	N	Y	Y	Y	Y	Y
OKLAHOMA						
1 **Sullivan**	Y	N	Y	N	N	N
2 Boren	N	Y	Y	Y	Y	N
3 **Lucas**	?	?	?	?	?	?
4 **Cole**	Y	–	Y	N	N	N
5 **Fallin**	Y	N	Y	N	N	N
OREGON						
1 Wu	N	Y	Y	Y	Y	Y
2 **Walden**	Y	N	Y	N	N	N
3 Blumenauer	N	Y	Y	Y	Y	Y
4 DeFazio	N	Y	Y	Y	Y	Y
5 Hooley	N	Y	Y	Y	Y	Y
PENNSYLVANIA						
1 Brady	N	Y	Y	Y	Y	Y
2 Fattah	N	Y	Y	Y	Y	Y
3 **English**	Y	N	Y	N	N	Y
4 Altmire	Y	Y	Y	Y	Y	Y
5 **Peterson**	?	?	?	N	N	N
6 **Gerlach**	Y	N	Y	N	N	Y
7 Sestak	N	Y	Y	Y	Y	Y
8 Murphy, P.	N	Y	Y	Y	Y	Y
9 **Shuster**	Y	N	Y	N	N	N
10 Carney	N	Y	Y	Y	Y	Y
11 Kanjorski	N	Y	Y	Y	Y	Y
12 Murtha	N	Y	?	Y	Y	Y
13 Schwartz	N	Y	Y	Y	Y	Y
14 Doyle	N	Y	Y	Y	Y	Y
15 **Dent**	Y	N	Y	N	N	Y
16 **Pitts**	Y	N	Y	N	N	N
17 Holden	N	Y	Y	Y	Y	Y
18 **Murphy, T.**	+	N	Y	N	N	Y
19 **Platts**	Y	N	Y	N	N	N
RHODE ISLAND						
1 Kennedy	N	Y	Y	Y	Y	Y
2 Langevin	N	Y	Y	Y	Y	Y
SOUTH CAROLINA						
1 **Brown**	Y	N	Y	N	N	N
2 **Wilson**	Y	N	Y	N	N	N
3 **Barrett**	Y	N	Y	N	N	N
4 **Inglis**	Y	N	Y	N	N	N
5 Spratt	N	Y	Y	Y	Y	Y
6 Clyburn	N	Y	Y	Y	Y	Y
SOUTH DAKOTA						
AL Herseth Sandlin	N	Y	Y	Y	Y	Y
TENNESSEE						
1 **Davis, D.**	Y	N	Y	N	N	N
2 **Duncan**	Y	N	Y	N	N	N
3 **Wamp**	Y	N	Y	N	N	Y
4 Davis, L.	N	Y	Y	Y	Y	Y
5 Cooper	N	Y	Y	?	?	Y
6 Gordon	N	Y	Y	Y	Y	Y
7 **Blackburn**	Y	N	Y	N	N	N
8 Tanner	N	Y	Y	Y	Y	Y
9 Cohen	N	Y	Y	Y	Y	Y

	506	507	508	509	510	511
TEXAS						
1 **Gohmert**	Y	N	Y	N	N	N
2 **Poe**	Y	N	Y	N	N	N
3 **Johnson, S.**	Y	N	Y	N	N	N
4 **Hall**	Y	N	Y	N	N	N
5 **Hensarling**	Y	N	Y	N	N	N
6 **Barton**	?	?	?	N	N	N
7 **Culberson**	Y	N	Y	N	N	N
8 **Brady**	Y	N	Y	N	N	N
9 Green, A.	?	?	?	Y	Y	Y
10 **McCaul**	Y	N	Y	N	N	N
11 **Conaway**	Y	N	Y	N	N	N
12 **Granger**	Y	N	Y	N	N	N
13 **Thornberry**	Y	N	Y	N	N	N
14 **Paul**	Y	N	Y	?	?	?
15 Hinojosa	N	Y	Y	Y	Y	N
16 Reyes	N	Y	Y	Y	Y	N
17 Edwards	N	Y	Y	Y	Y	Y
18 Jackson Lee	N	Y	Y	Y	Y	Y
19 **Neugebauer**	Y	N	Y	N	N	N
20 Gonzalez	N	Y	Y	Y	Y	N
21 **Smith**	?	?	Y	N	N	N
22 Lampson	Y	Y	Y	Y	N	N
23 Rodriguez	N	Y	Y	Y	Y	N
24 **Marchant**	Y	N	Y	N	N	?
25 Doggett	N	Y	Y	Y	Y	Y
26 **Burgess**	Y	N	Y	N	N	N
27 Ortiz	N	Y	Y	Y	Y	N
28 Cuellar	N	Y	?	Y	Y	N
29 Green, G.	N	Y	Y	Y	Y	N
30 Johnson, E.	–	+	+	Y	Y	Y
31 **Carter**	Y	N	Y	N	N	N
32 **Sessions**	Y	N	Y	N	N	N
UTAH						
1 **Bishop**	Y	N	Y	N	N	N
2 Matheson	N	Y	Y	Y	Y	Y
3 **Cannon**	Y	N	Y	N	N	N
VERMONT						
AL Welch	N	Y	Y	Y	Y	Y
VIRGINIA						
1 **Wittman**	Y	N	+	N	N	N
2 **Drake**	Y	N	Y	N	N	N
3 Scott	N	Y	Y	Y	Y	Y
4 **Forbes**	Y	N	Y	N	N	Y
5 **Goode**	Y	N	Y	N	N	Y
6 **Goodlatte**	Y	N	Y	N	N	N
7 **Cantor**	Y	N	Y	N	N	N
8 Moran	N	Y	Y	Y	Y	Y
9 Boucher	N	Y	Y	Y	Y	Y
10 **Wolf**	Y	N	Y	N	N	N
11 **Davis**	Y	N	Y	N	N	N
WASHINGTON						
1 Inslee	N	Y	Y	?	Y	Y
2 Larsen	N	Y	Y	Y	Y	Y
3 Baird	N	Y	Y	Y	Y	Y
4 **Hastings**	Y	N	Y	N	N	N
5 **McMorris Rodgers**	Y	N	Y	N	N	N
6 Dicks	N	Y	?	Y	Y	Y
7 McDermott	N	Y	Y	Y	Y	Y
8 **Reichert**	N	Y	Y	Y	N	Y
9 Smith	N	Y	Y	Y	?	Y
WEST VIRGINIA						
1 Mollohan	N	Y	Y	Y	Y	Y
2 **Capito**	Y	N	Y	N	N	N
3 Rahall	N	Y	Y	Y	Y	Y
WISCONSIN						
1 **Ryan**	Y	N	Y	N	N	N
2 Baldwin	N	Y	Y	Y	Y	Y
3 Kind	N	Y	Y	Y	Y	Y
4 Moore	N	Y	Y	Y	Y	Y
5 **Sensenbrenner**	Y	N	Y	N	N	N
6 **Petri**	Y	N	Y	N	N	N
7 Obey	N	Y	Y	Y	Y	Y
8 Kagen	N	Y	Y	Y	Y	Y
WYOMING						
AL **Cubin**	?	?	?	?	?	?
DELEGATES						
Faleomavaega (A.S.)						
Norton (D.C.)						
Bordallo (Guam)						
Fortuño (P.R.)						
Christensen (V.I.)						

IN THE HOUSE | By Vote Number

512. **HR 6493. Aviation Safety/Passage.** Oberstar, D-Minn., motion to suspend the rules and pass the bill that would create an Aviation Safety Whistleblower Investigation Office within the Federal Aviation Administration; create rules for flight standard inspectors who leave the agency; and bar maintenance inspectors from overseeing an airline for more than five continuous years. Motion agreed to 392-0: R 178-0; D 214-0 (ND 163-0, SD 51-0). A two-thirds majority of those present and voting (262 in this case) is required for passage under suspension of the rules. July 22, 2008.

513. **H Res 1311. National GEAR UP Day/Adoption.** Higgins, D-N.Y., motion to suspend the rules and adopt the resolution that would express support of National GEAR UP Day to recognize the GEAR UP program, which provides college preparatory services to 640,000 students in more than 46 states. Motion agreed to 385-1: R 171-1; D 214-0 (ND 163-0, SD 51-0). A two-thirds majority of those present and voting (258 in this case) is required for adoption under suspension of the rules. July 22, 2008.

514. **H Res 1202. National Guard Youth Challenge Day/Adoption.** Higgins, D-N.Y., motion to suspend the rules and adopt the resolution that would support the goals and ideals of a National Guard Youth Challenge Day. Motion agreed to 388-0: R 174-0; D 214-0 (ND 163-0, SD 51-0). A two-thirds majority of those present and voting (259 in this case) is required for adoption under suspension of the rules. July 22, 2008.

515. **Procedural Motion/Motion to Adjourn.** Sessions, R-Texas, motion to adjourn. Motion rejected 20-400: R 19-174; D 1-226 (ND 1-170, SD 0-56). July 23, 2008.

516. **HR 3221. Mortgage Relief/Previous Question.** Castor, D-Fla., motion to order the previous question (thus ending debate and possibility of amendment) on adoption of the rule (H Res 1363) to provide for House floor consideration of the Senate amendment to the House amendments to the Senate amendment to the bill that would provide tax breaks for homebuilders and those buying foreclosed homes, expand Federal Housing Administration mortgage insurance programs and include other provisions to alleviate the housing crisis. Motion agreed to 226-183: R 4-181; D 222-2 (ND 167-1, SD 55-1). July 23, 2008.

517. **HR 3221. Mortgage Relief/Rule.** Adoption of the rule (H Res 1363) that would provide for House floor consideration of the Senate amendment to the House amendments to the Senate amendment to the bill that would provide tax breaks for homebuilders and those buying foreclosed homes, expand Federal Housing Administration mortgage insurance programs and include other provisions to alleviate the housing crisis. The rule would provide for a motion to concur with the Senate amendments with an additional amendment that would provide government backing to Fannie Mae and Freddie Mac. Adopted 223-201: R 0-195; D 223-6 (ND 169-4, SD 54-2). July 23, 2008.

	512	513	514	515	516	517
ALABAMA						
1 Bonner	Y	Y	Y	N	N	N
2 Everett	?	?	?	N	N	N
3 Rogers	Y	Y	Y	N	N	N
4 Aderholt	Y	Y	Y	N	N	N
5 Cramer	Y	Y	Y	N	Y	Y
6 Bachus	Y	Y	Y	N	N	N
7 Davis	Y	Y	Y	N	Y	Y
ALASKA						
AL Young	?	?	?	Y	N	N
ARIZONA						
1 Renzi	?	?	?	N	N	N
2 Franks	Y	Y	Y	N	N	N
3 Shadegg	Y	Y	Y	N	N	N
4 Pastor	Y	Y	Y	N	Y	Y
5 Mitchell	Y	Y	Y	N	N	N
6 Flake	Y	N	N	N	N	N
7 Grijalva	?	?	?	N	Y	Y
8 Giffords	Y	Y	Y	N	Y	Y
ARKANSAS						
1 Berry	Y	Y	Y	N	Y	Y
2 Snyder	Y	Y	Y	N	Y	Y
3 Boozman	Y	Y	Y	N	N	N
4 Ross	Y	Y	Y	N	Y	Y
CALIFORNIA						
1 Thompson	Y	Y	Y	N	Y	Y
2 Herger	Y	Y	Y	N	N	N
3 Lungren	Y	Y	Y	N	N	N
4 Doolittle	?	?	?	N	N	N
5 Matsui	Y	Y	Y	N	Y	Y
6 Woolsey	Y	Y	Y	N	Y	Y
7 Miller, George	Y	Y	Y	N	Y	Y
8 Pelosi						
9 Lee	Y	Y	Y	N	Y	Y
10 Tauscher	Y	Y	Y	N	Y	Y
11 McNerney	Y	Y	Y	N	Y	Y
12 Speier	Y	Y	Y	N	?	Y
13 Stark	Y	?	Y	N	Y	Y
14 Eshoo	Y	Y	Y	N	Y	Y
15 Honda	Y	Y	Y	N	Y	Y
16 Lofgren	Y	Y	Y	N	Y	Y
17 Farr	Y	Y	Y	N	Y	Y
18 Cardoza	Y	Y	Y	N	Y	Y
19 Radanovich	Y	Y	Y	N	?	N
20 Costa	Y	Y	Y	N	Y	Y
21 Nunes	Y	Y	Y	N	N	N
22 McCarthy	Y	Y	Y	N	N	N
23 Capps	Y	Y	Y	N	Y	Y
24 Gallegly	Y	Y	Y	N	N	N
25 McKeon	Y	Y	Y	N	N	N
26 Dreier	Y	Y	Y	N	?	N
27 Sherman	Y	Y	Y	N	Y	Y
28 Berman	Y	Y	Y	N	?	Y
29 Schiff	Y	Y	Y	N	Y	Y
30 Waxman	Y	Y	Y	N	Y	Y
31 Becerra	Y	Y	Y	N	Y	Y
32 Solis	+	Y	Y	N	Y	Y
33 Watson	Y	Y	Y	N	Y	Y
34 Roybal-Allard	Y	Y	Y	N	Y	Y
35 Waters	Y	Y	Y	N	Y	Y
36 Harman	?	?	?	N	Y	Y
37 Richardson	Y	Y	Y	N	Y	Y
38 Napolitano	Y	Y	Y	N	Y	Y
39 Sánchez, Linda	Y	Y	Y	N	Y	Y
40 Royce	Y	Y	Y	N	N	N
41 Lewis	Y	Y	Y	N	N	N
42 Miller, Gary	Y	Y	Y	N	N	N
43 Baca	Y	Y	Y	N	Y	Y
44 Calvert	Y	Y	Y	N	N	N
45 Bono Mack	Y	Y	Y	N	N	N
46 Rohrabacher	Y	Y	Y	N	N	N
47 Sanchez, Loretta	+	+	+	N	Y	Y
48 Campbell	Y	Y	Y	N	N	N
49 Issa	Y	Y	Y	N	N	N
50 Bilbray	Y	Y	Y	N	N	N
51 Filner	Y	Y	Y	N	Y	Y
52 Hunter	?	?	?	N	N	N
53 Davis	Y	Y	Y	N	Y	Y

	512	513	514	515	516	517
COLORADO						
1 DeGette	Y	Y	Y	N	Y	Y
2 Udall	Y	Y	Y	N	Y	Y
3 Salazar	Y	Y	Y	N	Y	Y
4 Musgrave	Y	Y	Y	N	N	?
5 Lamborn	Y	Y	Y	N	N	N
6 Tancredo	Y	?	Y	Y	N	N
7 Perlmutter	Y	Y	Y	N	Y	Y
CONNECTICUT						
1 Larson	Y	Y	Y	N	Y	Y
2 Courtney	Y	Y	Y	N	Y	Y
3 DeLauro	Y	Y	Y	N	Y	Y
4 Shays	Y	Y	+	N	Y	N
5 Murphy	Y	?	Y	N	Y	Y
DELAWARE						
AL Castle	Y	Y	Y	N	?	N
FLORIDA						
1 Miller	Y	Y	Y	N	N	N
2 Boyd	Y	Y	Y	N	Y	Y
3 Brown	Y	Y	Y	N	Y	Y
4 Crenshaw	Y	Y	Y	N	N	N
5 Brown-Waite	?	?	?	?	?	?
6 Stearns	Y	Y	Y	N	N	N
7 Mica	Y	Y	Y	N	N	N
8 Keller	Y	Y	Y	N	N	N
9 Bilirakis	Y	Y	Y	N	N	N
10 Young	?	?	?	N	N	N
11 Castor	Y	Y	Y	N	Y	Y
12 Putnam	Y	Y	Y	N	?	N
13 Buchanan	Y	Y	Y	N	N	N
14 Mack	Y	Y	Y	N	N	N
15 Weldon	?	?	?	N	N	N
16 Mahoney	Y	Y	Y	N	Y	Y
17 Meek	Y	Y	Y	N	Y	Y
18 Ros-Lehtinen	Y	Y	Y	N	Y	N
19 Wexler	Y	Y	Y	N	Y	Y
20 Wasserman Schultz	Y	Y	Y	N	Y	Y
21 Diaz-Balart, L.	Y	Y	Y	N	N	N
22 Klein	Y	Y	Y	N	Y	Y
23 Hastings	Y	Y	Y	N	Y	Y
24 Feeney	Y	Y	Y	N	N	N
25 Diaz-Balart, M.	Y	Y	?	N	N	N
GEORGIA						
1 Kingston	Y	Y	Y	N	N	N
2 Bishop	+	+	+	-	+	+
3 Westmoreland	?	Y	Y	N	N	N
4 Johnson	Y	Y	Y	N	Y	Y
5 Lewis	Y	Y	Y	N	Y	Y
6 Price	Y	Y	?	N	N	N
7 Linder	Y	Y	Y	N	N	N
8 Marshall	Y	Y	Y	N	Y	Y
9 Deal	Y	Y	Y	N	N	N
10 Broun	Y	Y	Y	N	N	N
11 Gingrey	Y	Y	Y	N	N	N
12 Barrow	Y	Y	Y	N	Y	Y
13 Scott	Y	Y	Y	N	Y	Y
HAWAII						
1 Abercrombie	Y	Y	Y	N	Y	Y
2 Hirono	Y	Y	Y	N	Y	Y
IDAHO						
1 Sali	Y	Y	Y	N	N	N
2 Simpson	?	?	?	N	N	N
ILLINOIS						
1 Rush	?	?	?	?	?	?
2 Jackson	Y	Y	Y	N	Y	Y
3 Lipinski	Y	Y	Y	N	Y	Y
4 Gutierrez	+	+	+	N	Y	Y
5 Emanuel	Y	Y	Y	N	Y	Y
6 Roskam	Y	Y	Y	N	N	N
7 Davis	Y	Y	Y	N	Y	Y
8 Bean	?	?	?	N	?	Y
9 Schakowsky	Y	Y	Y	N	Y	Y
10 Kirk	Y	Y	Y	N	Y	Y
11 Weller	Y	Y	Y	N	N	N
12 Costello	Y	Y	Y	N	Y	Y
13 Biggert	Y	Y	Y	N	N	N
14 Foster	Y	Y	Y	N	Y	Y
15 Johnson	Y	Y	Y	N	Y	N

KEY	**Republicans**	Democrats			
Y Voted for (yea)		X Paired against		C Voted "present" to avoid possible conflict of interest	
# Paired for		− Announced against			
+ Announced for		P Voted "present"		? Did not vote or otherwise make a position known	
N Voted against (nay)					

ND Northern Democrats, SD Southern Democrats
Southern states: Ala., Ark., Fla., Ga., Ky., La., Miss., N.C., Okla., S.C., Tenn., Texas, Va.

H-172   2008 CQ ALMANAC | www.cq.com

	512	513	514	515	516	517
16 **Manzullo**	Y	Y	Y	N	N	N
17 Hare	+	+	+	–	+	+
18 **LaHood**	Y	?	?	N	N	N
19 **Shimkus**	Y	Y	Y	Y	N	N
INDIANA						
1 Visclosky	Y	Y	Y	N	Y	Y
2 Donnelly	Y	Y	Y	N	Y	Y
3 **Souder**	Y	Y	Y	Y	N	N
4 **Buyer**	Y	Y	Y	N	N	N
5 **Burton**	Y	Y	Y	N	N	N
6 **Pence**	Y	Y	Y	N	N	N
7 Carson, A.	Y	Y	Y	N	Y	Y
8 Ellsworth	Y	Y	Y	N	Y	Y
9 Hill	?	?	?	N	Y	Y
IOWA						
1 Braley	Y	Y	Y	N	Y	Y
2 Loebsack	Y	Y	Y	N	Y	Y
3 Boswell	?	?	?	?	?	?
4 **Latham**	Y	Y	Y	N	N	N
5 **King**	Y	Y	Y	Y	N	N
KANSAS						
1 **Moran**	Y	Y	Y	N	N	N
2 Boyda	Y	Y	Y	N	Y	N
3 Moore	Y	Y	Y	N	Y	Y
4 **Tiahrt**	?	?	?	N	N	N
KENTUCKY						
1 **Whitfield**	Y	Y	Y	N	N	N
2 **Lewis**	Y	Y	Y	N	N	N
3 Yarmuth	Y	Y	Y	N	Y	Y
4 **Davis**	Y	Y	Y	N	N	N
5 **Rogers**	Y	Y	Y	N	N	N
6 Chandler	Y	Y	Y	N	Y	Y
LOUISIANA						
1 **Scalise**	Y	Y	Y	N	N	N
2 Jefferson	Y	Y	Y	N	Y	Y
3 Melancon	Y	Y	Y	N	Y	Y
4 **McCrery**	Y	?	?	N	N	N
5 **Alexander**	Y	Y	Y	N	N	N
6 Cazayoux	Y	Y	Y	N	Y	Y
7 **Boustany**	Y	Y	Y	N	N	N
MAINE						
1 Allen	Y	Y	Y	N	Y	Y
2 Michaud	Y	Y	Y	N	Y	N
MARYLAND						
1 **Gilchrest**	Y	Y	Y	N	N	N
2 Ruppersberger	Y	Y	Y	N	Y	Y
3 Sarbanes	Y	Y	Y	N	Y	Y
4 Edwards	Y	Y	Y	N	Y	Y
5 Hoyer	Y	Y	Y	N	Y	Y
6 **Bartlett**	Y	Y	Y	Y	N	N
7 Cummings	Y	Y	Y	N	Y	Y
8 Van Hollen	Y	Y	Y	N	?	Y
MASSACHUSETTS						
1 Olver	Y	Y	Y	N	Y	Y
2 Neal	Y	Y	Y	N	Y	Y
3 McGovern	Y	Y	Y	N	Y	Y
4 Frank	Y	Y	Y	N	Y	Y
5 Tsongas	Y	Y	Y	N	Y	Y
6 Tierney	Y	Y	Y	N	Y	Y
7 Markey	Y	Y	Y	N	Y	Y
8 Capuano	Y	Y	Y	N	Y	Y
9 Lynch	Y	Y	Y	N	Y	Y
10 Delahunt	Y	Y	Y	Y	Y	Y
MICHIGAN						
1 Stupak	Y	Y	Y	N	Y	Y
2 **Hoekstra**	Y	Y	Y	N	N	N
3 **Ehlers**	Y	Y	Y	N	N	N
4 **Camp**	Y	?	Y	N	N	N
5 Kildee	Y	Y	Y	N	Y	Y
6 **Upton**	Y	Y	Y	N	N	N
7 **Walberg**	Y	Y	Y	N	N	N
8 **Rogers**	Y	Y	Y	N	N	N
9 **Knollenberg**	Y	Y	Y	N	N	N
10 **Miller**	Y	Y	Y	N	N	N
11 **McCotter**	Y	Y	Y	N	N	N
12 Levin	Y	Y	Y	N	Y	Y
13 Kilpatrick	Y	Y	?	N	Y	Y
14 Conyers	Y	Y	Y	N	Y	Y
15 Dingell	Y	Y	Y	N	Y	Y
MINNESOTA						
1 Walz	Y	Y	Y	N	Y	Y
2 **Kline**	Y	Y	Y	N	N	N
3 **Ramstad**	Y	Y	Y	N	N	N
4 McCollum	Y	Y	Y	N	Y	Y
5 Ellison	Y	Y	Y	N	Y	Y
6 **Bachmann**	Y	Y	Y	N	N	N
7 Peterson	Y	Y	Y	N	Y	Y
8 Oberstar	Y	Y	Y	N	Y	Y
MISSISSIPPI						
1 Childers	Y	Y	Y	N	Y	Y
2 Thompson	Y	Y	Y	N	Y	Y
3 **Pickering**	Y	Y	Y	N	N	N
4 Taylor	Y	Y	Y	N	Y	Y
MISSOURI						
1 Clay	Y	Y	Y	N	Y	Y
2 **Akin**	Y	Y	Y	N	N	N
3 Carnahan	Y	Y	Y	N	Y	Y
4 Skelton	Y	Y	Y	N	Y	Y
5 Cleaver	Y	Y	Y	N	Y	Y
6 **Graves**	Y	Y	Y	N	N	N
7 **Blunt**	Y	Y	Y	N	?	N
8 **Emerson**	Y	Y	Y	Y	N	N
9 **Hulshof**	?	?	?	?	?	?
MONTANA						
AL **Rehberg**	Y	Y	Y	N	N	N
NEBRASKA						
1 **Fortenberry**	Y	Y	Y	N	N	N
2 **Terry**	Y	Y	Y	N	N	N
3 **Smith**	Y	Y	Y	N	N	N
NEVADA						
1 Berkley	Y	Y	Y	N	Y	Y
2 **Heller**	Y	Y	Y	N	N	N
3 **Porter**	Y	Y	Y	N	N	N
NEW HAMPSHIRE						
1 Shea-Porter	Y	Y	Y	N	Y	Y
2 Hodes	Y	Y	Y	N	Y	Y
NEW JERSEY						
1 Andrews	Y	Y	Y	N	Y	Y
2 **LoBiondo**	Y	Y	Y	N	N	N
3 **Saxton**	?	?	?	N	N	N
4 **Smith**	Y	Y	Y	N	N	N
5 **Garrett**	Y	Y	Y	N	N	N
6 Pallone	Y	Y	Y	N	Y	Y
7 **Ferguson**	Y	Y	Y	N	N	N
8 Pascrell	Y	Y	Y	N	Y	Y
9 Rothman	Y	Y	Y	N	Y	Y
10 Payne	Y	Y	Y	N	Y	Y
11 **Frelinghuysen**	Y	Y	Y	N	N	N
12 Holt	Y	Y	Y	N	Y	Y
13 Sires	Y	Y	Y	N	Y	Y
NEW MEXICO						
1 **Wilson**	Y	Y	Y	N	N	N
2 **Pearce**	?	?	?	N	N	N
3 Udall	Y	Y	Y	N	Y	Y
NEW YORK						
1 Bishop	Y	Y	Y	N	Y	Y
2 Israel	Y	Y	Y	N	Y	Y
3 **King**	Y	Y	Y	N	N	N
4 McCarthy	Y	Y	Y	N	Y	Y
5 Ackerman	Y	Y	Y	N	Y	Y
6 Meeks	Y	Y	Y	N	Y	Y
7 Crowley	Y	Y	Y	N	Y	Y
8 Nadler	Y	Y	Y	N	Y	Y
9 Weiner	Y	Y	Y	N	Y	Y
10 Towns	Y	Y	Y	N	Y	Y
11 Clarke	Y	Y	Y	N	Y	Y
12 Velázquez	Y	Y	Y	N	Y	Y
13 **Fossella**	Y	Y	Y	N	N	N
14 Maloney	Y	Y	Y	N	Y	Y
15 Rangel	Y	Y	Y	N	Y	Y
16 Serrano	Y	Y	Y	N	Y	Y
17 Engel	Y	Y	Y	N	Y	Y
18 Lowey	Y	Y	Y	N	Y	Y
19 Hall	Y	Y	Y	N	Y	Y
20 Gillibrand	Y	Y	Y	N	Y	Y
21 McNulty	Y	Y	Y	N	Y	Y
22 Hinchey	?	?	?	N	Y	Y
23 **McHugh**	Y	Y	Y	N	N	N
24 Arcuri	Y	Y	Y	N	Y	Y
25 **Walsh**	Y	Y	Y	N	N	N
26 **Reynolds**	Y	?	Y	N	N	N
27 Higgins	Y	Y	Y	N	Y	Y
28 Slaughter	Y	Y	Y	N	Y	Y
29 **Kuhl**	Y	Y	Y	N	N	N
NORTH CAROLINA						
1 Butterfield	Y	Y	Y	N	Y	Y
2 Etheridge	Y	Y	Y	N	Y	Y
3 **Jones**	Y	Y	Y	N	N	N
4 Price	Y	Y	Y	N	Y	Y
5 **Foxx**	Y	Y	Y	N	N	N
6 **Coble**	Y	Y	Y	N	N	N
7 McIntyre	Y	Y	Y	N	Y	Y
8 **Hayes**	Y	Y	Y	N	N	N
9 **Myrick**	Y	Y	Y	Y	N	N
10 **McHenry**	Y	Y	Y	N	N	N
11 Shuler	?	?	Y	N	Y	N
12 Watt	Y	Y	Y	N	Y	Y
13 Miller	Y	Y	Y	N	Y	Y
NORTH DAKOTA						
AL Pomeroy	Y	Y	Y	N	Y	Y
OHIO						
1 **Chabot**	Y	Y	Y	N	N	N
2 **Schmidt**	Y	Y	Y	N	N	N
3 **Turner**	Y	Y	Y	N	?	N
4 **Jordan**	Y	Y	Y	N	N	N
5 **Latta**	Y	Y	Y	N	N	N
6 Wilson	Y	Y	Y	N	Y	Y
7 **Hobson**	Y	Y	Y	N	N	N
8 **Boehner**	Y	Y	Y	N	?	N
9 Kaptur	Y	Y	Y	N	Y	N
10 Kucinich	Y	Y	Y	N	Y	Y
11 Tubbs Jones	Y	Y	Y	N	Y	Y
12 **Tiberi**	Y	Y	Y	N	N	N
13 Sutton	Y	Y	Y	N	Y	Y
14 **LaTourette**	Y	Y	Y	N	N	N
15 **Pryce**	Y	Y	Y	N	N	N
16 **Regula**	Y	Y	Y	N	N	N
17 Ryan	Y	Y	Y	N	Y	Y
18 Space	Y	Y	Y	N	Y	Y
OKLAHOMA						
1 **Sullivan**	Y	?	Y	?	N	N
2 Boren	Y	Y	Y	N	Y	Y
3 **Lucas**	Y	Y	Y	N	N	N
4 **Cole**	Y	Y	?	N	?	N
5 **Fallin**	Y	Y	Y	N	N	N
OREGON						
1 Wu	Y	Y	Y	N	Y	Y
2 **Walden**	Y	Y	Y	N	N	N
3 Blumenauer	Y	Y	Y	N	Y	Y
4 DeFazio	Y	Y	Y	N	Y	Y
5 Hooley	Y	Y	Y	N	Y	Y
PENNSYLVANIA						
1 Brady	Y	Y	Y	N	Y	Y
2 Fattah	Y	Y	Y	N	Y	Y
3 **English**	Y	Y	Y	Y	N	N
4 Altmire	Y	Y	Y	N	Y	Y
5 **Peterson**	?	?	?	N	N	N
6 **Gerlach**	Y	Y	Y	N	N	N
7 Sestak	?	?	?	N	Y	Y
8 Murphy, P.	Y	Y	Y	N	Y	Y
9 **Shuster**	Y	Y	Y	N	N	N
10 Carney	Y	Y	Y	N	Y	Y
11 Kanjorski	Y	Y	Y	N	Y	Y
12 Murtha	Y	Y	Y	N	Y	Y
13 Schwartz	Y	Y	Y	N	Y	Y
14 Doyle	Y	Y	Y	N	Y	Y
15 **Dent**	Y	Y	Y	N	N	N
16 **Pitts**	Y	Y	Y	N	N	N
17 Holden	Y	Y	Y	N	Y	Y
18 **Murphy, T.**	Y	Y	Y	N	N	N
19 **Platts**	Y	Y	Y	N	N	N
RHODE ISLAND						
1 Kennedy	Y	Y	Y	N	?	Y
2 Langevin	?	Y	Y	N	Y	Y
SOUTH CAROLINA						
1 **Brown**	Y	Y	Y	N	N	N
2 **Wilson**	Y	Y	Y	?	N	N
3 **Barrett**	Y	Y	Y	N	N	N
4 **Inglis**	Y	Y	Y	N	N	N
5 Spratt	Y	Y	Y	N	Y	Y
6 Clyburn	Y	Y	Y	N	Y	Y
SOUTH DAKOTA						
AL Herseth Sandlin	Y	Y	Y	N	Y	Y
TENNESSEE						
1 **Davis, D.**	Y	Y	Y	N	N	N
2 **Duncan**	Y	Y	Y	N	N	N
3 **Wamp**	Y	Y	Y	N	N	N
4 Davis, L.	Y	Y	Y	N	Y	Y
5 Cooper	Y	Y	Y	N	Y	Y
6 Gordon	Y	Y	Y	N	Y	Y
7 **Blackburn**	Y	Y	Y	Y	N	N
8 Tanner	Y	Y	Y	N	Y	Y
9 Cohen	Y	Y	Y	N	Y	Y
TEXAS						
1 **Gohmert**	Y	Y	Y	N	N	N
2 **Poe**	?	?	?	N	N	N
3 **Johnson, S.**	Y	?	Y	Y	N	N
4 **Hall**	Y	Y	Y	N	N	N
5 **Hensarling**	Y	Y	Y	N	N	N
6 **Barton**	Y	Y	Y	?	N	N
7 **Culberson**	Y	?	Y	N	N	N
8 **Brady**	Y	Y	Y	N	N	N
9 Green, A.	Y	Y	Y	N	Y	Y
10 **McCaul**	Y	Y	Y	N	N	N
11 **Conaway**	Y	Y	Y	N	N	N
12 **Granger**	Y	Y	Y	N	?	N
13 **Thornberry**	Y	Y	Y	Y	N	N
14 **Paul**	?	?	?	N	N	N
15 Hinojosa	Y	Y	Y	N	Y	Y
16 Reyes	Y	Y	Y	N	Y	Y
17 Edwards	Y	Y	Y	N	Y	Y
18 Jackson Lee	Y	Y	Y	N	Y	Y
19 **Neugebauer**	Y	Y	Y	N	N	N
20 Gonzalez	Y	Y	Y	N	Y	Y
21 **Smith**	Y	Y	Y	N	N	N
22 Lampson	?	?	?	N	N	N
23 Rodriguez	?	?	?	N	Y	Y
24 **Marchant**	Y	Y	Y	Y	N	N
25 Doggett	Y	Y	?	N	Y	Y
26 **Burgess**	Y	Y	Y	N	N	N
27 Ortiz	?	?	?	?	?	?
28 Cuellar	?	?	?	N	Y	Y
29 Green, G.	+	+	+	–	+	+
30 Johnson, E.	Y	Y	Y	N	Y	Y
31 **Carter**	+	+	+	N	?	N
32 **Sessions**	?	?	?	Y	N	N
UTAH						
1 **Bishop**	?	?	?	?	?	?
2 Matheson	Y	Y	Y	N	Y	Y
3 **Cannon**	?	?	?	Y	N	N
VERMONT						
AL Welch	Y	Y	Y	N	Y	Y
VIRGINIA						
1 **Wittman**	Y	Y	Y	N	N	N
2 **Drake**	Y	Y	Y	N	N	N
3 Scott	Y	Y	Y	N	Y	Y
4 **Forbes**	Y	Y	Y	N	N	N
5 **Goode**	Y	Y	Y	N	N	N
6 **Goodlatte**	Y	Y	Y	N	N	N
7 **Cantor**	Y	Y	Y	N	?	N
8 Moran	Y	Y	Y	N	Y	Y
9 Boucher	?	?	?	N	Y	Y
10 **Wolf**	Y	Y	Y	N	N	N
11 **Davis**	Y	Y	Y	N	N	N
WASHINGTON						
1 Inslee	Y	Y	Y	N	Y	Y
2 Larsen	Y	Y	Y	N	Y	Y
3 Baird	Y	Y	Y	N	Y	Y
4 **Hastings**	Y	Y	Y	N	N	N
5 **McMorris Rodgers**	Y	Y	Y	N	N	N
6 Dicks	Y	Y	Y	N	Y	Y
7 McDermott	Y	Y	Y	N	Y	Y
8 **Reichert**	Y	Y	Y	N	Y	N
9 Smith	Y	Y	Y	N	Y	Y
WEST VIRGINIA						
1 Mollohan	Y	Y	Y	N	Y	Y
2 **Capito**	Y	Y	Y	N	N	N
3 Rahall	Y	Y	Y	N	Y	Y
WISCONSIN						
1 **Ryan**	Y	Y	Y	N	N	N
2 Baldwin	Y	Y	Y	N	Y	Y
3 Kind	Y	Y	Y	?	Y	Y
4 Moore	Y	Y	Y	N	Y	Y
5 **Sensenbrenner**	Y	Y	Y	N	N	N
6 **Petri**	Y	Y	Y	Y	N	N
7 Obey	Y	Y	Y	?	Y	Y
8 Kagen	Y	Y	Y	N	Y	Y
WYOMING						
AL **Cubin**	Y	Y	Y	N	N	N
DELEGATES						
Faleomavaega (A.S.)						
Norton (D.C.)						
Bordallo (Guam)						
Fortuño (P.R.)						
Christensen (V.I.)						

IN THE HOUSE | By Vote Number

518. HR 6532. Highway Trust Fund Money Transfer/Passage. Lewis, D-Ga., motion to suspend the rules and pass the bill that would appropriate $8 billion to the Highway Trust Fund, which would be drawn out of money in the Treasury not otherwise appropriated. Motion agreed to 387-37: R 159-37; D 228-0 (ND 172-0, SD 56-0). A two-thirds majority of those present and voting (283 in this case) is required for passage under suspension of the rules. A "nay" was a vote in support of the president's position. July 23, 2008.

519. HR 3221. Mortgage Relief/Motion to Concur. Frank, D-Mass., motion to concur in the Senate amendment with the House amendment that would grant authority to the Treasury Department to extend new credit to and buy stock in Fannie Mae and Freddie Mac. It also would create an independent regulator for the two mortgage giants and the Federal Home Loan Bank System. It would overhaul the Federal Housing Administration (FHA) and allow it to insure up to $300 billion worth of new, refinanced loans for struggling mortgage borrowers. It also includes a $7,500 tax credit for some first-time homebuyers, higher loan limits for FHA-backed loans, a standard tax deduction for property taxes and revenue-raisers to offset part of the costs. It also would authorize $3.9 billion in grants to states and localities to purchase and rehabilitate foreclosed properties, and increase the federal debt limit to $10.6 trillion. Motion agreed to 272-152: R 45-149; D 227-3 (ND 171-3, SD 56-0). A "yea" was a vote in support of the president's position. July 23, 2008.

520. HR 6545. Energy Security Intelligence Assessment/Passage. Ruppersberger, D-Md., motion to suspend the rules and pass the bill that would require the director of national intelligence to submit a national intelligence assessment to Congress on security and energy security issues related to energy costs. Motion agreed to 414-0: R 190-0; D 224-0 (ND 169-0, SD 55-0). A two-thirds majority of those present and voting (276 in this case) is required for passage under suspension of the rules. July 23, 2008.

521. HR 6545. Energy Security Intelligence Assessment/Motion to Reconsider. Hastings, D-Fla., motion to table (kill) the Price, R-Ga., motion to reconsider the vote on the Ruppersberger, D-Md., motion to suspend the rules and pass the bill that would require the national intelligence director to submit a national intelligence assessment to Congress on security and energy security issues related to energy costs. Motion agreed to 242-179: R 15-179; D 227-0 (ND 172-0, SD 55-0). July 23, 2008.

522. HR 3999. Highway Bridge Safety/Previous Question. Arcuri, D-N.Y., motion to order the previous question (thus ending debate and possibility of amendment) on adoption of the rule (H Res 1344) to provide for House floor consideration of the bill that would authorize additional funds for bridge inspection and reconstruction. Motion agreed to 228-192: R 4-188; D 224-4 (ND 170-2, SD 54-2). July 23, 2008.

523. HR 3999. Highway Bridge Safety/Rule. Adoption of the rule (H Res 1344) that would provide for House floor consideration of the bill that would authorize additional funds for bridge inspection and reconstruction. Adopted 228-193: R 2-192; D 226-1 (ND 170-1, SD 56-0). July 23, 2008.

	518	519	520	521	522	523
ALABAMA						
1 Bonner	Y	N	Y	N	N	N
2 Everett	Y	N	Y	N	N	N
3 Rogers	Y	Y	Y	N	N	N
4 Aderholt	Y	N	Y	N	N	N
5 Cramer	Y	Y	Y	Y	Y	Y
6 Bachus	Y	N	Y	N	N	N
7 Davis	Y	Y	Y	Y	Y	Y
ALASKA						
AL Young	Y	N	Y	N	N	N
ARIZONA						
1 Renzi	Y	N	Y	N	N	N
2 Franks	N	N	Y	N	N	N
3 Shadegg	N	N	Y	N	N	N
4 Pastor	Y	Y	Y	Y	Y	Y
5 Mitchell	Y	Y	Y	Y	Y	Y
6 Flake	N	N	Y	N	N	N
7 Grijalva	Y	Y	Y	Y	Y	Y
8 Giffords	Y	Y	Y	Y	Y	Y
ARKANSAS						
1 Berry	Y	Y	Y	Y	Y	Y
2 Snyder	Y	Y	Y	Y	Y	Y
3 Boozman	Y	N	Y	N	N	N
4 Ross	Y	Y	Y	Y	Y	Y
CALIFORNIA						
1 Thompson	Y	Y	Y	Y	Y	Y
2 Herger	Y	N	Y	N	N	N
3 Lungren	N	Y	?	N	N	N
4 Doolittle	Y	N	Y	N	N	N
5 Matsui	Y	Y	Y	Y	Y	Y
6 Woolsey	Y	Y	Y	Y	Y	Y
7 Miller, George	Y	Y	Y	Y	Y	Y
8 Pelosi		Y				
9 Lee	Y	Y	Y	Y	Y	Y
10 Tauscher	Y	Y	Y	Y	Y	Y
11 McNerney	Y	Y	Y	Y	Y	Y
12 Speier	Y	Y	Y	Y	Y	Y
13 Stark	Y	Y	Y	Y	Y	Y
14 Eshoo	Y	Y	Y	Y	Y	Y
15 Honda	Y	Y	Y	Y	Y	Y
16 Lofgren	Y	Y	Y	Y	Y	Y
17 Farr	Y	Y	Y	Y	Y	Y
18 Cardoza	Y	Y	Y	Y	Y	Y
19 Radanovich	N	N	Y	N	N	N
20 Costa	Y	Y	?	Y	Y	Y
21 Nunes	N	N	P	N	N	N
22 McCarthy	Y	N	Y	N	N	N
23 Capps	Y	Y	Y	Y	Y	Y
24 Gallegly	Y	Y	Y	N	N	N
25 McKeon	Y	Y	Y	N	N	N
26 Dreier	Y	Y	Y	N	N	N
27 Sherman	Y	Y	Y	Y	Y	Y
28 Berman	Y	Y	Y	Y	Y	Y
29 Schiff	Y	Y	Y	Y	Y	Y
30 Waxman	Y	Y	Y	Y	Y	Y
31 Becerra	Y	Y	Y	Y	Y	Y
32 Solis	Y	Y	Y	Y	Y	Y
33 Watson	Y	Y	Y	Y	Y	Y
34 Roybal-Allard	Y	Y	Y	Y	Y	Y
35 Waters	Y	Y	Y	Y	Y	Y
36 Harman	Y	Y	Y	Y	Y	Y
37 Richardson	Y	Y	Y	Y	Y	Y
38 Napolitano	Y	Y	Y	Y	Y	Y
39 Sánchez, Linda	Y	Y	Y	Y	Y	Y
40 Royce	N	N	Y	N	N	N
41 Lewis	N	Y	Y	N	N	N
42 Miller, Gary	Y	Y	N	N	N	N
43 Baca	Y	Y	Y	Y	Y	Y
44 Calvert	Y	Y	Y	N	N	N
45 Bono Mack	Y	Y	Y	N	N	N
46 Rohrabacher	Y	N	Y	N	N	N
47 Sanchez, Loretta	Y	Y	Y	Y	Y	Y
48 Campbell	N	Y	Y	N	N	N
49 Issa	Y	N	Y	N	N	N
50 Bilbray	Y	N	Y	N	N	N
51 Filner	Y	Y	Y	Y	Y	?
52 Hunter	Y	Y	Y	N	N	N
53 Davis	Y	Y	Y	Y	Y	Y
COLORADO						
1 DeGette	Y	Y	Y	Y	Y	Y
2 Udall	Y	Y	Y	Y	Y	Y
3 Salazar	Y	Y	Y	Y	Y	Y
4 Musgrave	N	N	Y	N	N	N
5 Lamborn	N	N	Y	N	N	N
6 Tancredo	N	N	Y	N	N	N
7 Perlmutter	Y	Y	Y	Y	Y	Y
CONNECTICUT						
1 Larson	+	Y	Y	Y	Y	Y
2 Courtney	Y	Y	Y	Y	Y	Y
3 DeLauro	Y	Y	Y	Y	Y	Y
4 Shays	Y	Y	Y	N	Y	Y
5 Murphy	Y	Y	Y	Y	Y	Y
DELAWARE						
AL Castle	Y	Y	N	N	N	N
FLORIDA						
1 Miller	N	N	Y	N	N	N
2 Boyd	Y	Y	Y	Y	Y	Y
3 Brown	Y	Y	Y	Y	Y	Y
4 Crenshaw	Y	N	Y	N	N	N
5 Brown-Waite	?	?	?	?	?	?
6 Stearns	N	N	Y	N	N	N
7 Mica	Y	N	Y	N	N	N
8 Keller	Y	Y	Y	N	N	N
9 Bilirakis	Y	N	Y	N	N	N
10 Young	N	N	Y	N	N	N
11 Castor	Y	Y	Y	Y	Y	Y
12 Putnam	Y	Y	Y	N	-	N
13 Buchanan	Y	Y	Y	N	N	N
14 Mack	Y	N	Y	N	N	N
15 Weldon	Y	N	Y	N	N	N
16 Mahoney	Y	Y	Y	Y	Y	Y
17 Meek	Y	Y	Y	Y	Y	Y
18 Ros-Lehtinen	Y	Y	Y	Y	Y	N
19 Wexler	Y	Y	Y	Y	Y	Y
20 Wasserman Schultz	Y	Y	Y	Y	Y	Y
21 Diaz-Balart, L.	Y	Y	Y	N	N	N
22 Klein	Y	Y	Y	Y	Y	Y
23 Hastings	Y	Y	Y	Y	Y	Y
24 Feeney	Y	N	Y	?	N	N
25 Diaz-Balart, M.	Y	Y	Y	N	N	N
GEORGIA						
1 Kingston	N	N	Y	N	N	N
2 Bishop	+	+	+	+	+	+
3 Westmoreland	Y	N	Y	N	N	N
4 Johnson	Y	Y	Y	Y	Y	Y
5 Lewis	Y	Y	Y	Y	Y	Y
6 Price	Y	N	Y	N	N	N
7 Linder	Y	N	Y	N	N	N
8 Marshall	Y	Y	Y	?	Y	Y
9 Deal	Y	N	Y	N	N	N
10 Broun	N	N	Y	N	N	N
11 Gingrey	Y	N	Y	N	N	N
12 Barrow	Y	Y	Y	Y	Y	Y
13 Scott	Y	Y	Y	Y	Y	Y
HAWAII						
1 Abercrombie	Y	Y	Y	Y	Y	Y
2 Hirono	Y	Y	Y	Y	Y	Y
IDAHO						
1 Sali	Y	N	Y	N	N	N
2 Simpson	Y	N	Y	N	N	N
ILLINOIS						
1 Rush	?	?	?	?	?	?
2 Jackson	Y	Y	Y	Y	Y	Y
3 Lipinski	Y	Y	Y	Y	Y	Y
4 Gutierrez	Y	Y	?	Y	Y	Y
5 Emanuel	Y	Y	Y	Y	Y	Y
6 Roskam	Y	N	Y	N	N	N
7 Davis	Y	Y	Y	Y	Y	Y
8 Bean	Y	Y	Y	Y	Y	Y
9 Schakowsky	Y	Y	Y	Y	Y	Y
10 Kirk	Y	N	Y	N	N	N
11 Weller	Y	Y	Y	N	N	N
12 Costello	Y	Y	Y	Y	Y	Y
13 Biggert	Y	Y	Y	N	N	N
14 Foster	Y	Y	Y	Y	Y	Y
15 Johnson	Y	N	Y	N	N	N

KEY **Republicans** Democrats

Y Voted for (yea)	X Paired against
# Paired for	– Announced against
+ Announced for	P Voted "present"
N Voted against (nay)	C Voted "present" to avoid possible conflict of interest
	? Did not vote or otherwise make a position known

ND Northern Democrats, SD Southern Democrats
Southern states: Ala., Ark., Fla., Ga., Ky., La., Miss., N.C., Okla., S.C., Tenn., Texas, Va.

H-174 2008 CQ ALMANAC | www.cq.com

	518	519	520	521	522	523
16 **Manzullo**	N	N	Y	N	N	N
17 Hare	+	+	+	Y	Y	Y
18 **LaHood**	Y	Y	Y	N	N	N
19 **Shimkus**	Y	N	Y	Y	N	N
INDIANA						
1 Visclosky	Y	Y	Y	Y	Y	Y
2 Donnelly	Y	Y	Y	Y	N	Y
3 **Souder**	Y	N	Y	N	N	N
4 **Buyer**	Y	N	Y	N	N	N
5 **Burton**	Y	N	Y	N	N	N
6 **Pence**	N	N	Y	N	N	N
7 Carson, A.	Y	Y	Y	Y	Y	Y
8 Ellsworth	Y	Y	Y	Y	Y	Y
9 Hill	Y	Y	Y	Y	N	N
IOWA						
1 Braley	Y	Y	Y	Y	Y	Y
2 Loebsack	Y	Y	Y	Y	Y	Y
3 Boswell	?	?	?	?	?	?
4 **Latham**	Y	N	Y	Y	N	N
5 **King**	Y	N	Y	N	N	N
KANSAS						
1 **Moran**	Y	N	Y	N	N	N
2 Boyda	Y	N	Y	Y	Y	Y
3 Moore	Y	Y	Y	Y	Y	Y
4 **Tiahrt**	Y	N	Y	N	N	N
KENTUCKY						
1 **Whitfield**	Y	N	Y	N	N	N
2 **Lewis**	Y	N	Y	N	N	N
3 Yarmuth	Y	Y	Y	Y	Y	Y
4 **Davis**	Y	N	Y	N	N	N
5 **Rogers**	Y	N	Y	N	N	N
6 Chandler	Y	Y	Y	Y	Y	Y
LOUISIANA						
1 **Scalise**	Y	N	Y	N	N	N
2 Jefferson	Y	Y	Y	Y	Y	Y
3 Melancon	Y	Y	Y	Y	Y	Y
4 **McCrery**	N	Y	Y	N	N	N
5 **Alexander**	Y	N	Y	N	N	N
6 Cazayoux	Y	Y	Y	Y	Y	Y
7 **Boustany**	Y	Y	Y	N	N	N
MAINE						
1 Allen	Y	Y	Y	Y	Y	Y
2 Michaud	Y	Y	Y	Y	Y	Y
MARYLAND						
1 **Gilchrest**	Y	Y	?	?	?	?
2 Ruppersberger	Y	Y	Y	Y	Y	Y
3 Sarbanes	Y	Y	Y	Y	Y	Y
4 Edwards	Y	Y	Y	Y	Y	Y
5 Hoyer	Y	Y	Y	Y	Y	Y
6 **Bartlett**	Y	N	Y	N	N	N
7 Cummings	Y	Y	Y	Y	Y	Y
8 Van Hollen	Y	Y	Y	Y	Y	Y
MASSACHUSETTS						
1 Olver	Y	Y	Y	Y	Y	Y
2 Neal	Y	Y	Y	Y	Y	Y
3 McGovern	Y	Y	Y	Y	Y	Y
4 Frank	Y	Y	Y	Y	Y	Y
5 Tsongas	Y	Y	Y	Y	Y	Y
6 Tierney	Y	Y	Y	Y	Y	Y
7 Markey	Y	Y	Y	Y	Y	Y
8 Capuano	Y	Y	Y	Y	Y	Y
9 Lynch	Y	Y	Y	Y	Y	Y
10 Delahunt	Y	Y	Y	Y	Y	Y
MICHIGAN						
1 Stupak	Y	Y	Y	Y	Y	Y
2 **Hoekstra**	Y	N	P	N	N	N
3 **Ehlers**	Y	N	Y	N	N	Y
4 **Camp**	Y	N	Y	N	N	N
5 Kildee	Y	Y	Y	Y	Y	Y
6 **Upton**	Y	N	Y	Y	N	N
7 **Walberg**	Y	N	Y	Y	N	N
8 **Rogers**	Y	N	Y	N	N	N
9 **Knollenberg**	Y	Y	Y	N	N	N
10 **Miller**	Y	N	Y	Y	N	N
11 **McCotter**	Y	N	Y	N	N	N
12 Levin	Y	Y	Y	Y	Y	Y
13 Kilpatrick	Y	Y	Y	Y	Y	Y
14 Conyers	Y	Y	Y	Y	Y	Y
15 Dingell	Y	Y	Y	Y	Y	Y
MINNESOTA						
1 Walz	Y	Y	Y	Y	Y	Y
2 **Kline**	Y	N	Y	N	N	N
3 **Ramstad**	Y	N	Y	Y	Y	N
4 McCollum	Y	Y	Y	Y	Y	Y

	518	519	520	521	522	523
5 Ellison	Y	Y	Y	Y	Y	Y
6 **Bachmann**	Y	N	Y	N	N	N
7 Peterson	Y	Y	Y	?	Y	Y
8 Oberstar	Y	Y	Y	Y	Y	Y
MISSISSIPPI						
1 Childers	Y	Y	Y	Y	N	Y
2 Thompson	Y	Y	Y	Y	Y	Y
3 **Pickering**	Y	Y	Y	N	N	N
4 Taylor	Y	Y	Y	Y	Y	Y
MISSOURI						
1 Clay	Y	Y	Y	Y	Y	Y
2 **Akin**	Y	N	Y	N	N	N
3 Carnahan	Y	Y	Y	Y	Y	Y
4 Skelton	Y	Y	Y	Y	Y	Y
5 Cleaver	Y	Y	Y	Y	Y	Y
6 **Graves**	Y	N	Y	N	N	N
7 **Blunt**	Y	N	Y	N	N	N
8 **Emerson**	Y	N	Y	N	N	N
9 **Hulshof**	?	?	?	?	?	?
MONTANA						
AL **Rehberg**	Y	N	Y	N	N	N
NEBRASKA						
1 **Fortenberry**	Y	N	Y	N	N	N
2 **Terry**	Y	N	Y	N	N	N
3 **Smith**	Y	N	Y	N	N	N
NEVADA						
1 Berkley	Y	Y	Y	Y	Y	Y
2 **Heller**	Y	Y	Y	N	N	N
3 **Porter**	Y	Y	Y	N	N	N
NEW HAMPSHIRE						
1 Shea-Porter	Y	Y	Y	Y	Y	Y
2 Hodes	Y	Y	Y	Y	Y	Y
NEW JERSEY						
1 Andrews	Y	Y	Y	Y	Y	Y
2 **LoBiondo**	Y	N	Y	N	N	N
3 **Saxton**	Y	N	Y	N	N	N
4 **Smith**	Y	Y	Y	N	N	N
5 **Garrett**	N	N	Y	N	N	N
6 Pallone	Y	Y	Y	Y	Y	Y
7 **Ferguson**	Y	Y	Y	N	N	N
8 Pascrell	Y	Y	Y	Y	Y	Y
9 Rothman	Y	Y	Y	Y	Y	Y
10 Payne	Y	Y	Y	Y	Y	Y
11 **Frelinghuysen**	N	N	Y	N	N	N
12 Holt	Y	Y	Y	Y	Y	Y
13 Sires	Y	Y	?	Y	Y	Y
NEW MEXICO						
1 **Wilson**	Y	N	Y	Y	N	N
2 **Pearce**	Y	N	Y	N	N	N
3 Udall	Y	Y	Y	Y	Y	Y
NEW YORK						
1 Bishop	Y	Y	Y	Y	Y	Y
2 Israel	Y	Y	Y	Y	Y	Y
3 **King**	Y	Y	Y	N	N	N
4 McCarthy	Y	Y	Y	Y	Y	Y
5 Ackerman	Y	Y	Y	Y	Y	Y
6 Meeks	Y	Y	Y	Y	Y	Y
7 Crowley	Y	Y	Y	Y	Y	Y
8 Nadler	Y	Y	Y	Y	Y	Y
9 Weiner	Y	Y	Y	Y	Y	Y
10 Towns	Y	Y	Y	Y	Y	Y
11 Clarke	Y	Y	Y	Y	Y	Y
12 Velázquez	Y	Y	Y	Y	Y	Y
13 **Fossella**	Y	N	Y	Y	N	N
14 Maloney	Y	Y	Y	Y	Y	Y
15 Rangel	Y	Y	Y	Y	Y	Y
16 Serrano	Y	Y	Y	Y	Y	Y
17 Engel	Y	Y	Y	Y	Y	Y
18 Lowey	Y	Y	Y	Y	Y	Y
19 Hall	Y	Y	Y	Y	Y	Y
20 Gillibrand	Y	Y	Y	Y	Y	Y
21 McNulty	Y	Y	Y	Y	Y	Y
22 Hinchey	Y	Y	Y	Y	Y	Y
23 **McHugh**	Y	Y	Y	Y	N	N
24 Arcuri	Y	Y	Y	Y	Y	Y
25 **Walsh**	Y	Y	Y	N	N	N
26 **Reynolds**	Y	Y	Y	N	N	N
27 Higgins	Y	Y	Y	Y	Y	Y
28 Slaughter	Y	Y	?	?	Y	Y
29 **Kuhl**	Y	N	Y	Y	N	N
NORTH CAROLINA						
1 Butterfield	Y	Y	Y	Y	Y	Y
2 Etheridge	Y	Y	Y	Y	Y	Y
3 **Jones**	Y	N	Y	N	N	N
4 Price	Y	Y	Y	Y	Y	Y

	518	519	520	521	522	523
5 **Foxx**	N	N	Y	Y	N	N
6 **Coble**	Y	N	Y	N	N	N
7 McIntyre	Y	Y	Y	Y	Y	Y
8 **Hayes**	Y	Y	Y	N	–	N
9 **Myrick**	Y	N	Y	N	N	N
10 **McHenry**	N	N	Y	N	N	N
11 Shuler	Y	Y	Y	Y	Y	Y
12 Watt	Y	Y	Y	Y	Y	Y
13 Miller	Y	Y	Y	Y	Y	Y
NORTH DAKOTA						
AL Pomeroy	Y	Y	Y	Y	Y	Y
OHIO						
1 **Chabot**	N	N	Y	N	N	N
2 **Schmidt**	Y	N	Y	N	N	N
3 **Turner**	Y	Y	Y	N	N	N
4 **Jordan**	N	N	Y	Y	N	N
5 **Latta**	Y	N	Y	N	N	N
6 Wilson	Y	Y	Y	Y	Y	Y
7 **Hobson**	N	Y	Y	N	N	N
8 **Boehner**	Y	N	Y	N	N	N
9 Kaptur	Y	N	Y	Y	Y	Y
10 Kucinich	Y	Y	Y	Y	Y	Y
11 Tubbs Jones	Y	Y	Y	Y	?	?
12 **Tiberi**	Y	Y	Y	N	N	N
13 Sutton	Y	Y	Y	Y	Y	Y
14 **LaTourette**	Y	Y	Y	N	N	N
15 **Pryce**	Y	Y	Y	N	N	N
16 **Regula**	N	N	Y	N	N	N
17 Ryan	Y	Y	Y	Y	Y	Y
18 Space	Y	Y	Y	Y	Y	Y
OKLAHOMA						
1 **Sullivan**	Y	N	Y	N	N	N
2 Boren	Y	Y	Y	Y	Y	Y
3 **Lucas**	Y	N	Y	N	N	N
4 **Cole**	Y	N	Y	N	N	N
5 **Fallin**	Y	N	+	N	N	N
OREGON						
1 Wu	Y	Y	Y	Y	Y	Y
2 **Walden**	Y	N	Y	N	N	N
3 Blumenauer	Y	Y	Y	Y	Y	Y
4 DeFazio	Y	N	Y	Y	Y	Y
5 Hooley	Y	Y	Y	Y	Y	Y
PENNSYLVANIA						
1 Brady	Y	Y	Y	Y	Y	Y
2 Fattah	Y	Y	Y	Y	Y	Y
3 **English**	Y	Y	Y	N	N	N
4 Altmire	Y	Y	Y	Y	Y	Y
5 **Peterson**	Y	?	Y	N	N	N
6 **Gerlach**	Y	N	Y	N	N	N
7 Sestak	Y	Y	Y	Y	Y	Y
8 Murphy, P.	Y	Y	Y	Y	Y	Y
9 **Shuster**	Y	N	Y	N	N	N
10 Carney	Y	Y	Y	Y	Y	Y
11 Kanjorski	Y	Y	Y	Y	Y	Y
12 Murtha	Y	Y	Y	Y	Y	Y
13 Schwartz	Y	Y	Y	Y	Y	Y
14 Doyle	Y	Y	Y	Y	Y	Y
15 **Dent**	Y	N	Y	N	N	N
16 **Pitts**	Y	N	Y	N	N	N
17 Holden	Y	Y	Y	Y	Y	Y
18 **Murphy, T.**	Y	Y	Y	N	N	N
19 **Platts**	Y	N	Y	N	N	N
RHODE ISLAND						
1 Kennedy	Y	Y	Y	Y	?	?
2 Langevin	Y	Y	Y	Y	Y	Y
SOUTH CAROLINA						
1 **Brown**	Y	Y	Y	N	N	N
2 **Wilson**	Y	N	?	N	N	N
3 **Barrett**	Y	N	Y	N	N	N
4 **Inglis**	N	N	Y	N	N	N
5 Spratt	Y	Y	Y	Y	Y	Y
6 Clyburn	Y	Y	Y	Y	Y	Y
SOUTH DAKOTA						
AL Herseth Sandlin	Y	Y	Y	Y	Y	Y
TENNESSEE						
1 **Davis, D.**	Y	N	Y	N	N	N
2 **Duncan**	Y	N	Y	N	N	N
3 **Wamp**	Y	N	Y	N	N	N
4 Davis, L.	Y	Y	Y	Y	Y	Y
5 Cooper	Y	Y	Y	Y	Y	Y
6 Gordon	Y	Y	Y	Y	Y	Y
7 **Blackburn**	Y	N	Y	N	N	N
8 Tanner	Y	Y	Y	Y	Y	Y
9 Cohen	Y	Y	Y	Y	Y	Y

	518	519	520	521	522	523
TEXAS						
1 **Gohmert**	Y	?	Y	N	N	N
2 **Poe**	Y	N	Y	N	N	N
3 **Johnson, S.**	N	N	Y	N	N	N
4 **Hall**	Y	N	Y	N	N	N
5 **Hensarling**	N	N	Y	N	N	N
6 **Barton**	Y	N	Y	N	N	N
7 **Culberson**	Y	N	Y	N	N	N
8 **Brady**	Y	N	Y	N	N	N
9 Green, A.	Y	Y	Y	Y	Y	Y
10 **McCaul**	Y	N	Y	N	N	N
11 **Conaway**	Y	N	Y	N	N	N
12 **Granger**	N	N	Y	N	N	N
13 **Thornberry**	N	N	Y	N	N	N
14 **Paul**	Y	N	Y	N	N	N
15 Hinojosa	Y	Y	Y	Y	Y	Y
16 Reyes	Y	Y	Y	Y	Y	Y
17 Edwards	Y	Y	Y	Y	Y	Y
18 Jackson Lee	Y	Y	Y	Y	Y	Y
19 **Neugebauer**	N	N	Y	N	N	N
20 Gonzalez	Y	Y	Y	Y	Y	Y
21 **Smith**	Y	N	Y	N	N	N
22 Lampson	Y	Y	Y	Y	N	Y
23 Rodriguez	Y	Y	Y	Y	Y	Y
24 **Marchant**	N	N	Y	N	N	N
25 Doggett	Y	Y	Y	Y	Y	Y
26 **Burgess**	Y	N	Y	N	N	N
27 Ortiz	?	?	?	?	?	?
28 Cuellar	Y	Y	?	Y	Y	Y
29 Green, G.	+	+	+	+	+	+
30 Johnson, E.	Y	Y	Y	Y	Y	Y
31 **Carter**	Y	N	Y	N	N	N
32 **Sessions**	Y	N	Y	N	N	N
UTAH						
1 **Bishop**	?	?	?	?	?	?
2 Matheson	Y	Y	Y	Y	Y	Y
3 **Cannon**	Y	N	Y	N	N	N
VERMONT						
AL Welch	Y	Y	Y	Y	Y	Y
VIRGINIA						
1 **Wittman**	Y	N	Y	N	N	N
2 **Drake**	Y	N	Y	N	N	N
3 Scott	Y	Y	Y	Y	Y	Y
4 **Forbes**	Y	N	Y	N	N	N
5 **Goode**	Y	N	Y	N	N	N
6 **Goodlatte**	Y	N	Y	N	N	N
7 **Cantor**	Y	N	Y	N	N	N
8 Moran	Y	Y	Y	Y	Y	Y
9 Boucher	Y	Y	Y	Y	Y	Y
10 **Wolf**	Y	N	Y	N	N	N
11 **Davis**	Y	N	Y	Y	?	?
WASHINGTON						
1 Inslee	Y	Y	Y	Y	Y	Y
2 Larsen	Y	Y	Y	Y	Y	Y
3 Baird	Y	Y	Y	Y	Y	Y
4 **Hastings**	Y	N	Y	N	N	N
5 **McMorris Rodgers**	Y	N	Y	N	N	N
6 Dicks	Y	Y	Y	Y	Y	Y
7 McDermott	Y	Y	Y	Y	Y	Y
8 **Reichert**	Y	N	Y	N	Y	N
9 Smith	Y	Y	Y	Y	Y	Y
WEST VIRGINIA						
1 Mollohan	Y	Y	Y	Y	Y	Y
2 **Capito**	Y	Y	Y	N	N	N
3 Rahall	Y	Y	Y	Y	Y	Y
WISCONSIN						
1 **Ryan**	N	N	Y	N	N	N
2 Baldwin	Y	Y	Y	Y	Y	Y
3 Kind	Y	Y	Y	Y	Y	Y
4 Moore	Y	Y	Y	Y	Y	Y
5 **Sensenbrenner**	N	N	Y	N	N	N
6 **Petri**	Y	N	Y	N	N	N
7 Obey	Y	Y	Y	Y	Y	Y
8 Kagen	Y	Y	Y	Y	Y	Y
WYOMING						
AL **Cubin**	Y	N	Y	N	N	N
DELEGATES						
Faleomavaega (A.S.)						
Norton (D.C.)						
Bordallo (Guam)						
Fortuño (P.R.)						
Christensen (V.I.)						

HOUSE VOTES

IN THE HOUSE | By Vote Number

524. HR 6578. **Strategic Petroleum Reserve Exchange/Previous Question.** Welch, D-Vt., motion to order the previous question (thus ending debate and possibility of amendment) on adoption of the rule (H Res 1367) to provide for House floor consideration of a bill that would release oil from the nation's Strategic Petroleum Reserve under suspension of the rules on the legislative day of Thursday, July 24, 2008. Motion agreed to 232-184: R 7-183; D 225-1 (ND 170-0, SD 55-1). July 24, 2008.

525. HR 6578. **Strategic Petroleum Reserve Exchange/Rule.** Adoption of the rule (H Res 1367) to provide for House floor consideration of a bill that would release oil from the nation's Strategic Petroleum Reserve under suspension of the rules on the legislative day of Thursday, July 24, 2008. Adopted 226-190: R 0-188; D 226-2 (ND 171-0, SD 55-2). July 24, 2008.

526. HR 5501. **Global HIV/AIDS Program Reauthorization/Previous Question.** Hastings, D-Fla., motion to order the previous question (thus ending debate and possibility of amendment) on adoption of the rule (H Res 1362) to provide for House floor consideration of the Senate amendment to the bill that would authorize $48 billion from fiscal 2009 through 2013 for programs under the President's Emergency Plan for AIDS Relief. Motion agreed to 231-185: R 8-182; D 223-3 (ND 169-0, SD 54-3). (Subsequently, the rule was adopted by voice vote.) July 24, 2008.

527. HR 6578. **Strategic Petroleum Reserve Exchange/Passage.** Barrow, D-Ga., motion to suspend the rules and pass the bill that would require the Energy Department to release 70 million barrels of light, sweet crude oil from the Strategic Petroleum Reserve in exchange for the same amount of heavier-grade crude oil. Motion rejected 268-157: R 37-157; D 231-0 (ND 174-0, SD 57-0). A two-thirds majority of those present and voting (284 in this case) is required for passage under suspension of the rules. A "nay" was a vote in support of the president's position. July 24, 2008.

528. HR 3999. **Highway Bridge Safety/Illegal Immigrant Employment.** Childers, D-Miss., amendment that would bar the use of funds to employ workers in violation of a law that prohibits the hiring or continued employment of illegal immigrants. Adopted in Committee of the Whole 416-1: R 192-0; D 224-1 (ND 167-1, SD 57-0). July 24, 2008.

529. HR 3999. **Highway Bridge Safety/Recommit.** Poe, R-Texas, motion to recommit the bill to the Transportation and Infrastructure Committee with instructions that it be reported back forthwith with language that would require removal of structurally deficient federal bridges on federal highways once replacement bridges had been constructed. Motion rejected 151-268: R 151-37; D 0-231 (ND 0-174, SD 0-57). July 24, 2008.

	524	525	526	527	528	529
ALABAMA						
1 Bonner	N	N	N	N	Y	P
2 Everett	N	N	N	N	Y	P
3 Rogers	N	N	N	Y	Y	P
4 Aderholt	N	N	N	Y	Y	P
5 Cramer	Y	Y	Y	Y	Y	N
6 Bachus	N	N	N	N	Y	Y
7 Davis	Y	Y	Y	Y	Y	N
ALASKA						
AL Young	N	N	?	N	?	Y
ARIZONA						
1 Renzi	?	N	N	N	Y	Y
2 Franks	N	N	N	N	Y	Y
3 Shadegg	N	N	N	N	Y	Y
4 Pastor	Y	Y	Y	Y	Y	N
5 Mitchell	Y	Y	Y	Y	Y	N
6 Flake	N	N	N	N	Y	Y
7 Grijalva	Y	Y	Y	Y	P	N
8 Giffords	Y	Y	Y	Y	Y	N
ARKANSAS						
1 Berry	Y	Y	Y	Y	Y	N
2 Snyder	Y	Y	Y	Y	Y	N
3 Boozman	?	?	?	N	Y	Y
4 Ross	Y	Y	Y	Y	Y	N
CALIFORNIA						
1 Thompson	Y	Y	Y	Y	Y	N
2 Herger	N	N	N	N	Y	Y
3 Lungren	N	N	N	N	Y	N
4 Doolittle	N	N	N	N	Y	Y
5 Matsui	Y	Y	Y	Y	Y	N
6 Woolsey	Y	Y	Y	Y	Y	N
7 Miller, George	Y	?	Y	Y	Y	N
8 Pelosi				Y		
9 Lee	Y	Y	Y	Y	Y	N
10 Tauscher	Y	Y	Y	Y	Y	N
11 McNerney	?	Y	Y	Y	Y	N
12 Speier	Y	Y	Y	Y	Y	N
13 Stark	Y	Y	Y	Y	Y	N
14 Eshoo	Y	Y	Y	Y	Y	N
15 Honda	Y	Y	Y	Y	P	N
16 Lofgren	Y	Y	Y	Y	Y	N
17 Farr	Y	Y	Y	Y	Y	N
18 Cardoza	Y	Y	Y	Y	Y	N
19 Radanovich	N	N	N	N	Y	Y
20 Costa	Y	Y	Y	Y	Y	N
21 Nunes	N	N	N	N	Y	Y
22 McCarthy	N	N	N	N	Y	Y
23 Capps	Y	Y	Y	Y	Y	N
24 Gallegly	N	N	N	N	Y	Y
25 McKeon	N	N	N	N	Y	Y
26 Dreier	N	N	N	N	Y	Y
27 Sherman	Y	Y	Y	Y	Y	N
28 Berman	Y	Y	Y	Y	Y	N
29 Schiff	Y	Y	Y	Y	Y	N
30 Waxman	Y	Y	Y	Y	Y	N
31 Becerra	Y	Y	Y	Y	Y	N
32 Solis	Y	Y	Y	Y	Y	N
33 Watson	Y	Y	Y	Y	Y	N
34 Roybal-Allard	Y	Y	Y	Y	Y	N
35 Waters	?	Y	Y	Y	Y	N
36 Harman	Y	Y	Y	Y	Y	N
37 Richardson	Y	Y	Y	Y	Y	N
38 Napolitano	Y	Y	Y	Y	Y	N
39 Sánchez, Linda	Y	Y	Y	Y	Y	N
40 Royce	N	N	N	N	Y	Y
41 Lewis	N	N	N	N	Y	Y
42 Miller, Gary	N	N	N	N	Y	Y
43 Baca	Y	Y	Y	Y	Y	N
44 Calvert	N	N	N	N	Y	Y
45 Bono Mack	N	N	N	N	Y	Y
46 Rohrabacher	N	N	N	Y	Y	N
47 Sanchez, Loretta	Y	Y	Y	Y	Y	N
48 Campbell	N	N	N	N	Y	Y
49 Issa	N	N	N	N	Y	Y
50 Bilbray	N	N	N	Y	Y	Y
51 Filner	Y	Y	Y	Y	Y	N
52 Hunter	N	N	N	N	Y	Y
53 Davis	Y	Y	Y	Y	Y	N

	524	525	526	527	528	529
COLORADO						
1 DeGette	Y	Y	Y	Y	Y	N
2 Udall	Y	Y	Y	Y	Y	N
3 Salazar	Y	Y	Y	Y	Y	N
4 Musgrave	N	N	N	N	Y	Y
5 Lamborn	N	?	N	N	Y	Y
6 Tancredo	N	N	N	N	Y	Y
7 Perlmutter	Y	Y	Y	Y	Y	N
CONNECTICUT						
1 Larson	Y	Y	Y	Y	Y	N
2 Courtney	Y	Y	Y	Y	Y	N
3 DeLauro	Y	Y	Y	?	Y	N
4 Shays	Y	N	Y	Y	Y	N
5 Murphy	Y	Y	Y	Y	Y	N
DELAWARE						
AL Castle	Y	N	Y	Y	Y	Y
FLORIDA						
1 Miller	N	N	N	N	Y	Y
2 Boyd	Y	Y	Y	Y	Y	N
3 Brown	Y	Y	Y	Y	Y	N
4 Crenshaw	N	N	N	N	Y	Y
5 Brown-Waite	?	?	?	?	?	?
6 Stearns	N	N	N	N	Y	Y
7 Mica	N	N	N	N	Y	Y
8 Keller	N	N	N	N	Y	Y
9 Bilirakis	N	N	N	N	Y	Y
10 Young	N	N	N	N	Y	Y
11 Castor	Y	Y	Y	Y	Y	N
12 Putnam	N	N	N	N	Y	Y
13 Buchanan	N	N	N	N	Y	Y
14 Mack	N	N	N	N	Y	Y
15 Weldon	N	N	N	N	Y	Y
16 Mahoney	Y	Y	Y	Y	Y	N
17 Meek	Y	Y	Y	Y	Y	N
18 Ros-Lehtinen	Y	Y	Y	Y	Y	N
19 Wexler	Y	Y	Y	Y	Y	N
20 Wasserman Schultz	Y	Y	Y	Y	Y	N
21 Diaz-Balart, L.	N	N	N	Y	Y	Y
22 Klein	Y	Y	Y	Y	Y	N
23 Hastings	Y	Y	Y	Y	Y	N
24 Feeney	N	N	N	N	Y	Y
25 Diaz-Balart, M.	N	N	N	Y	Y	Y
GEORGIA						
1 Kingston	N	N	N	Y	Y	Y
2 Bishop	Y	Y	Y	Y	Y	N
3 Westmoreland	N	N	N	N	Y	Y
4 Johnson	Y	Y	Y	Y	Y	N
5 Lewis	Y	Y	Y	Y	Y	N
6 Price	N	N	N	N	Y	Y
7 Linder	N	N	N	N	Y	Y
8 Marshall	Y	Y	Y	Y	Y	N
9 Deal	N	N	N	N	Y	Y
10 Broun	N	N	N	N	Y	Y
11 Gingrey	N	N	N	N	Y	Y
12 Barrow	Y	Y	Y	Y	Y	N
13 Scott	Y	Y	Y	Y	Y	N
HAWAII						
1 Abercrombie	Y	Y	Y	Y	Y	N
2 Hirono	+	+	+	Y	Y	N
IDAHO						
1 Sali	N	N	N	N	Y	Y
2 Simpson	N	N	N	N	Y	N
ILLINOIS						
1 Rush	?	?	?	?	?	?
2 Jackson	Y	Y	Y	Y	Y	N
3 Lipinski	Y	Y	Y	Y	Y	N
4 Gutierrez	Y	Y	Y	Y	Y	N
5 Emanuel	Y	Y	Y	Y	Y	N
6 Roskam	N	N	N	N	Y	Y
7 Davis	Y	Y	Y	Y	Y	N
8 Bean	Y	Y	Y	Y	Y	N
9 Schakowsky	Y	Y	Y	Y	Y	N
10 Kirk	N	?	N	N	Y	N
11 Weller	N	N	N	N	Y	P
12 Costello	Y	Y	Y	Y	Y	N
13 Biggert	N	N	N	N	Y	Y
14 Foster	Y	Y	Y	Y	Y	N
15 Johnson	N	N	N	Y	Y	Y

KEY   **Republicans**   Democrats

Y Voted for (yea)	X Paired against	C Voted "present" to avoid possible conflict of interest
# Paired for	– Announced against	
+ Announced for	P Voted "present"	? Did not vote or otherwise make a position known
N Voted against (nay)		

ND Northern Democrats, SD Southern Democrats
Southern states: Ala., Ark., Fla., Ga., Ky., La., Miss., N.C., Okla., S.C., Tenn., Texas, Va.

ND Northern Democrats, SD Southern Democrats
Southern states: Ala., Ark., Fla., Ga., Ky., La., Miss., N.C., Okla., S.C., Tenn., Texas, Va.

	524	525	526	527	528	529
16 **Manzullo**	N	N	N	N	Y	N
17 Hare	Y	Y	Y	Y	Y	N
18 **LaHood**	?	?	?	?	?	?
19 **Shimkus**	N	N	N	N	Y	Y
INDIANA						
1 Visclosky	Y	Y	Y	Y	Y	N
2 Donnelly	Y	Y	Y	Y	Y	N
3 **Souder**	N	N	N	Y	Y	Y
4 **Buyer**	N	N	N	N	Y	Y
5 **Burton**	N	N	N	N	Y	Y
6 **Pence**	N	N	N	N	Y	Y
7 Carson, A.	Y	Y	Y	Y	Y	N
8 Ellsworth	Y	Y	Y	Y	Y	N
9 Hill	Y	Y	Y	Y	Y	N
IOWA						
1 Braley	Y	Y	+	Y	Y	N
2 Loebsack	Y	Y	Y	Y	Y	N
3 Boswell	?	?	?	?	?	?
4 **Latham**	N	N	N	N	Y	Y
5 **King**	N	N	N	N	Y	Y
KANSAS						
1 **Moran**	N	N	N	N	Y	N
2 Boyda	Y	Y	Y	Y	Y	N
3 Moore	Y	Y	Y	Y	Y	N
4 **Tiahrt**	N	–	N	N	Y	Y
KENTUCKY						
1 **Whitfield**	N	N	N	Y	Y	N
2 **Lewis**	N	N	N	N	Y	Y
3 Yarmuth	Y	Y	Y	Y	Y	N
4 **Davis**	N	N	N	N	Y	Y
5 **Rogers**	N	N	N	N	Y	Y
6 Chandler	Y	Y	Y	Y	Y	N
LOUISIANA						
1 **Scalise**	N	N	N	N	Y	Y
2 Jefferson	Y	Y	Y	Y	Y	N
3 Melancon	Y	Y	Y	Y	Y	N
4 **McCrery**	N	N	N	N	Y	Y
5 **Alexander**	N	N	N	N	Y	Y
6 Cazayoux	Y	Y	N	Y	Y	N
7 **Boustany**	N	N	N	N	Y	Y
MAINE						
1 Allen	Y	Y	Y	Y	Y	N
2 Michaud	Y	Y	Y	Y	Y	N
MARYLAND						
1 **Gilchrest**	N	N	N	Y	Y	N
2 Ruppersberger	Y	Y	Y	Y	Y	N
3 Sarbanes	Y	Y	Y	Y	Y	N
4 Edwards	Y	Y	Y	Y	P	N
5 Hoyer	Y	Y	Y	Y	Y	N
6 **Bartlett**	N	N	N	N	Y	Y
7 Cummings	Y	Y	Y	Y	Y	N
8 Van Hollen	Y	Y	Y	Y	Y	N
MASSACHUSETTS						
1 Olver	Y	Y	Y	Y	Y	N
2 Neal	Y	Y	Y	Y	Y	N
3 McGovern	Y	Y	Y	Y	Y	N
4 Frank	Y	Y	Y	Y	Y	N
5 Tsongas	Y	Y	Y	Y	Y	N
6 Tierney	Y	Y	Y	Y	Y	N
7 Markey	Y	Y	Y	Y	Y	N
8 Capuano	Y	Y	Y	Y	Y	N
9 Lynch	Y	Y	Y	Y	Y	N
10 Delahunt	Y	Y	Y	Y	Y	N
MICHIGAN						
1 Stupak	Y	Y	Y	Y	Y	N
2 **Hoekstra**	N	N	N	N	Y	Y
3 **Ehlers**	N	N	N	N	Y	Y
4 **Camp**	N	N	N	N	Y	Y
5 Kildee	Y	Y	Y	Y	Y	N
6 **Upton**	N	N	N	N	Y	Y
7 **Walberg**	N	N	N	N	Y	Y
8 **Rogers**	?	N	N	N	Y	Y
9 **Knollenberg**	N	N	N	Y	Y	Y
10 **Miller**	N	N	N	N	Y	Y
11 **McCotter**	N	N	N	N	Y	N
12 Levin	Y	Y	Y	Y	Y	N
13 Kilpatrick	Y	Y	Y	Y	Y	N
14 Conyers	Y	Y	Y	Y	Y	N
15 Dingell	?	?	?	Y	Y	N
MINNESOTA						
1 Walz	Y	Y	Y	Y	Y	N
2 **Kline**	N	N	N	N	Y	Y
3 **Ramstad**	Y	N	Y	Y	Y	N
4 McCollum	Y	Y	Y	Y	Y	N

	524	525	526	527	528	529
5 Ellison	Y	Y	?	Y	P	N
6 **Bachmann**	N	N	N	N	Y	Y
7 Peterson	Y	Y	Y	Y	Y	N
8 Oberstar	Y	Y	Y	Y	Y	N
MISSISSIPPI						
1 Childers	Y	Y	N	Y	Y	N
2 Thompson	Y	Y	Y	Y	Y	N
3 **Pickering**	N	N	N	N	Y	N
4 Taylor	Y	Y	Y	Y	Y	N
MISSOURI						
1 Clay	Y	Y	Y	Y	Y	N
2 **Akin**	N	N	N	N	Y	Y
3 Carnahan	Y	Y	Y	Y	Y	N
4 Skelton	Y	Y	Y	Y	Y	N
5 Cleaver	Y	Y	Y	Y	Y	N
6 **Graves**	N	N	N	N	Y	Y
7 **Blunt**	N	N	N	N	Y	Y
8 **Emerson**	N	N	N	Y	Y	N
9 **Hulshof**	?	?	?	?	?	?
MONTANA						
AL **Rehberg**	N	N	N	N	Y	Y
NEBRASKA						
1 **Fortenberry**	N	N	N	N	Y	Y
2 **Terry**	N	N	N	N	Y	Y
3 **Smith**	N	N	N	N	Y	Y
NEVADA						
1 Berkley	Y	Y	Y	Y	Y	N
2 **Heller**	N	N	N	N	Y	N
3 **Porter**	N	N	N	Y	Y	N
NEW HAMPSHIRE						
1 Shea-Porter	Y	Y	Y	Y	Y	N
2 Hodes	Y	Y	Y	Y	Y	N
NEW JERSEY						
1 Andrews	Y	Y	Y	Y	Y	N
2 **LoBiondo**	Y	N	Y	Y	Y	N
3 **Saxton**	N	N	N	N	Y	Y
4 **Smith**	N	N	Y	Y	Y	N
5 **Garrett**	N	N	N	N	Y	Y
6 Pallone	Y	Y	Y	Y	Y	N
7 **Ferguson**	N	N	N	N	Y	N
8 Pascrell	Y	Y	Y	Y	Y	N
9 Rothman	Y	Y	Y	Y	Y	N
10 Payne	Y	Y	Y	Y	Y	N
11 **Frelinghuysen**	N	N	N	N	Y	N
12 Holt	Y	Y	Y	Y	Y	N
13 Sires	Y	Y	Y	Y	Y	N
NEW MEXICO						
1 **Wilson**	N	N	N	N	Y	Y
2 **Pearce**	N	N	N	N	Y	Y
3 Udall	Y	Y	Y	Y	Y	N
NEW YORK						
1 Bishop	Y	Y	Y	Y	Y	N
2 Israel	Y	Y	Y	Y	Y	N
3 **King**	N	N	N	N	Y	N
4 McCarthy	Y	Y	Y	Y	Y	N
5 Ackerman	Y	Y	Y	Y	Y	N
6 Meeks	Y	Y	?	Y	Y	N
7 Crowley	Y	Y	Y	Y	Y	N
8 Nadler	Y	Y	Y	Y	Y	N
9 Weiner	Y	Y	Y	Y	Y	N
10 Towns	Y	Y	Y	Y	P	N
11 Clarke	Y	Y	Y	Y	P	N
12 Velázquez	Y	Y	Y	Y	Y	N
13 **Fossella**	N	N	N	Y	Y	N
14 Maloney	Y	Y	Y	Y	Y	N
15 Rangel	Y	Y	Y	Y	Y	N
16 Serrano	Y	Y	Y	Y	Y	N
17 Engel	Y	Y	Y	Y	Y	N
18 Lowey	Y	Y	Y	Y	Y	N
19 Hall	Y	Y	Y	Y	Y	N
20 Gillibrand	Y	Y	Y	Y	Y	N
21 McNulty	Y	Y	Y	Y	Y	N
22 Hinchey	Y	Y	Y	Y	Y	N
23 **McHugh**	N	N	N	N	Y	Y
24 Arcuri	Y	Y	Y	Y	Y	N
25 **Walsh**	N	N	N	N	Y	Y
26 **Reynolds**	N	N	N	N	Y	Y
27 Higgins	Y	Y	Y	Y	Y	N
28 Slaughter	Y	Y	Y	Y	?	N
29 **Kuhl**	N	N	N	N	Y	Y
NORTH CAROLINA						
1 Butterfield	Y	Y	Y	Y	Y	N
2 Etheridge	Y	Y	Y	Y	Y	N
3 **Jones**	N	N	N	Y	Y	N
4 Price	Y	Y	Y	Y	Y	N

	524	525	526	527	528	529
5 **Foxx**	N	N	N	N	Y	Y
6 **Coble**	N	N	N	N	Y	Y
7 McIntyre	Y	Y	Y	Y	Y	N
8 **Hayes**	N	N	N	Y	Y	Y
9 **Myrick**	N	N	N	N	Y	Y
10 **McHenry**	N	N	N	N	Y	Y
11 Shuler	Y	N	Y	Y	Y	N
12 Watt	Y	Y	Y	Y	Y	N
13 Miller	Y	Y	Y	Y	Y	N
NORTH DAKOTA						
AL Pomeroy	Y	Y	Y	Y	Y	N
OHIO						
1 **Chabot**	N	N	N	Y	Y	Y
2 **Schmidt**	N	N	N	N	Y	Y
3 **Turner**	N	N	N	N	Y	Y
4 **Jordan**	N	N	N	N	Y	Y
5 **Latta**	N	N	N	N	Y	Y
6 Wilson	Y	Y	Y	Y	Y	N
7 **Hobson**	N	N	N	N	Y	N
8 **Boehner**	N	N	N	N	Y	Y
9 Kaptur	Y	Y	Y	Y	Y	N
10 Kucinich	Y	Y	Y	Y	Y	N
11 Tubbs Jones	Y	Y	Y	+	Y	N
12 **Tiberi**	N	N	N	Y	Y	Y
13 Sutton	Y	Y	Y	Y	?	N
14 **LaTourette**	N	N	N	N	Y	N
15 **Pryce**	N	N	N	N	Y	N
16 **Regula**	N	N	N	N	Y	Y
17 Ryan	Y	Y	Y	Y	Y	N
18 Space	Y	Y	Y	Y	Y	N
OKLAHOMA						
1 **Sullivan**	N	N	N	N	Y	Y
2 Boren	Y	Y	Y	Y	Y	N
3 **Lucas**	N	N	N	N	Y	Y
4 **Cole**	N	–	–	N	Y	Y
5 **Fallin**	N	N	N	N	Y	Y
OREGON						
1 Wu	Y	Y	Y	Y	Y	N
2 **Walden**	N	N	N	N	Y	Y
3 Blumenauer	Y	Y	Y	Y	Y	N
4 DeFazio	Y	Y	Y	Y	Y	N
5 Hooley	Y	Y	Y	Y	Y	N
PENNSYLVANIA						
1 Brady	Y	Y	Y	Y	Y	N
2 Fattah	Y	Y	Y	Y	Y	N
3 **English**	N	N	N	N	Y	Y
4 Altmire	Y	Y	Y	Y	Y	N
5 **Peterson**	N	N	N	N	Y	Y
6 **Gerlach**	Y	N	Y	Y	Y	N
7 Sestak	Y	Y	Y	Y	Y	N
8 Murphy, P.	Y	Y	Y	Y	Y	N
9 **Shuster**	N	N	N	N	Y	Y
10 Carney	Y	Y	Y	Y	Y	N
11 Kanjorski	Y	Y	Y	Y	Y	N
12 Murtha	Y	Y	Y	Y	Y	N
13 Schwartz	Y	Y	Y	Y	Y	N
14 Doyle	Y	Y	Y	Y	Y	N
15 **Dent**	N	N	N	N	Y	Y
16 **Pitts**	N	N	N	N	Y	Y
17 Holden	Y	Y	Y	Y	Y	N
18 **Murphy, T.**	N	N	N	N	Y	N
19 **Platts**	N	N	N	N	Y	N
RHODE ISLAND						
1 Kennedy	Y	Y	Y	Y	Y	N
2 Langevin	Y	Y	Y	Y	Y	N
SOUTH CAROLINA						
1 **Brown**	N	N	N	N	Y	Y
2 **Wilson**	N	N	N	N	Y	Y
3 **Barrett**	N	N	N	N	Y	Y
4 **Inglis**	N	N	N	N	Y	Y
5 Spratt	Y	Y	Y	Y	Y	N
6 Clyburn	Y	Y	Y	Y	Y	N
SOUTH DAKOTA						
AL Herseth Sandlin	Y	Y	Y	Y	Y	N
TENNESSEE						
1 **Davis, D.**	N	N	N	N	Y	Y
2 **Duncan**	N	N	N	Y	Y	Y
3 **Wamp**	N	N	N	Y	Y	Y
4 Davis, L.	Y	Y	Y	Y	Y	N
5 Cooper	Y	Y	Y	Y	Y	N
6 Gordon	Y	Y	Y	Y	Y	N
7 **Blackburn**	N	N	N	N	Y	Y
8 Tanner	Y	Y	Y	Y	Y	N
9 Cohen	Y	Y	Y	Y	Y	N

	524	525	526	527	528	529
TEXAS						
1 **Gohmert**	?	?	?	N	Y	Y
2 **Poe**	N	N	N	N	Y	Y
3 **Johnson, S.**	N	N	N	N	?	Y
4 **Hall**	N	N	N	N	Y	Y
5 **Hensarling**	N	N	N	N	Y	Y
6 **Barton**	N	N	N	N	Y	Y
7 **Culberson**	N	N	N	N	Y	Y
8 **Brady**	N	N	N	N	Y	Y
9 Green, A.	Y	Y	Y	Y	Y	N
10 **McCaul**	N	N	N	N	Y	Y
11 **Conaway**	N	N	N	N	Y	Y
12 **Granger**	N	N	N	N	Y	Y
13 **Thornberry**	N	N	N	N	Y	Y
14 **Paul**	N	N	N	Y	Y	N
15 Hinojosa	?	?	?	?	?	?
16 Reyes	Y	Y	Y	Y	Y	N
17 Edwards	Y	Y	Y	Y	Y	N
18 Jackson Lee	Y	Y	Y	Y	Y	N
19 **Neugebauer**	N	N	N	N	Y	Y
20 Gonzalez	Y	Y	Y	Y	Y	N
21 **Smith**	N	N	N	N	Y	N
22 Lampson	N	N	N	Y	Y	N
23 Rodriguez	Y	Y	Y	Y	Y	N
24 **Marchant**	N	N	N	N	Y	Y
25 Doggett	Y	Y	Y	Y	Y	N
26 **Burgess**	N	N	N	N	Y	Y
27 Ortiz	?	?	?	?	?	?
28 Cuellar	Y	Y	Y	Y	Y	N
29 Green, G.	Y	Y	Y	Y	Y	N
30 Johnson, E.	Y	Y	Y	Y	Y	N
31 **Carter**	N	N	N	N	Y	Y
32 **Sessions**	N	N	N	N	Y	Y
UTAH						
1 **Bishop**	?	?	?	?	?	?
2 Matheson	Y	Y	Y	Y	Y	N
3 **Cannon**	N	N	N	N	Y	?
VERMONT						
AL Welch	Y	Y	Y	Y	Y	N
VIRGINIA						
1 **Wittman**	N	N	N	N	Y	N
2 **Drake**	N	N	N	N	Y	Y
3 Scott	Y	Y	Y	Y	Y	N
4 **Forbes**	N	N	N	N	Y	Y
5 **Goode**	N	N	N	Y	Y	Y
6 **Goodlatte**	N	N	N	N	Y	Y
7 **Cantor**	N	N	N	N	Y	Y
8 Moran	?	Y	Y	Y	Y	N
9 Boucher	Y	Y	Y	Y	Y	N
10 **Wolf**	N	N	N	N	Y	Y
11 **Davis**	N	N	N	N	Y	N
WASHINGTON						
1 Inslee	Y	Y	Y	Y	Y	N
2 Larsen	Y	Y	Y	Y	Y	N
3 Baird	Y	Y	Y	Y	Y	N
4 **Hastings**	N	N	N	N	Y	Y
5 **McMorris Rodgers**	N	N	N	N	Y	Y
6 Dicks	Y	Y	Y	Y	Y	N
7 McDermott	Y	Y	Y	Y	Y	N
8 **Reichert**	Y	N	Y	N	Y	Y
9 Smith	Y	Y	Y	Y	Y	N
WEST VIRGINIA						
1 Mollohan	Y	Y	Y	Y	Y	N
2 **Capito**	N	N	N	Y	Y	Y
3 Rahall	Y	Y	Y	Y	Y	N
WISCONSIN						
1 **Ryan**	N	N	N	N	Y	Y
2 Baldwin	Y	Y	Y	Y	Y	N
3 Kind	Y	Y	Y	Y	Y	N
4 Moore	Y	Y	Y	Y	N	N
5 **Sensenbrenner**	N	N	N	Y	Y	Y
6 **Petri**	N	N	N	Y	Y	Y
7 Obey	Y	Y	Y	Y	Y	N
8 Kagen	Y	Y	Y	Y	Y	N
WYOMING						
AL **Cubin**	?	?	?	?	?	?
DELEGATES						
Faleomavaega (A.S.)				?		
Norton (D.C.)				Y		
Bordallo (Guam)				Y		
Fortuño (P.R.)				?		
Christensen (V.I.)				Y		

IN THE HOUSE | By Vote Number

530. HR 3999. Highway Bridge Safety/Passage. Passage of the bill that would authorize $1 billion for fiscal 2009 for the Federal Highway Administration's Highway Bridge Program. The bill would require annual inspections of "structurally deficient" bridges and improve uniformity in state bridge inspections and evaluations. It also would require a risk-based prioritization of bridges and an independent review of the FHWA's risk-determination process. The bill would create a National Tunnel Inspection Program; require a Government Accountability Office study of FHWA's bridge rating system and one on bridge construction delays; and require reports on the impact of bridge closings and a study on the cost benefits of using carbon fiber composite materials in bridge projects. Passed 367-55: R 137-55; D 230-0 (ND 173-0, SD 57-0). A "nay" was a vote in support of the president's position. July 24, 2008.

531. HR 5501. Global HIV/AIDS Program Reauthorization/Motion to Concur. Berman, D-Calif., motion to concur in the Senate amendment to the bill that would authorize $48 billion from fiscal 2009 through 2013 for programs under the President's Emergency Plan for AIDS Relief used to fight AIDS, tuberculosis and malaria overseas. The bill would replace the current requirement that one-third of all HIV prevention funding go to abstinence education with balanced funding for abstinence, fidelity and condom programs. It also would authorize $2 billion for American Indian health, clean water and law enforcement programs. Motion agreed to (thus clearing the bill for the president), 303-115: R 75-114; D 228-1 (ND 172-0, SD 56-1). A "yea" was a vote in support of the president's position. July 24, 2008.

532. H Res 1368. Suspend Medicare Trigger/Adoption. Adoption of the resolution that would suspend a requirement for expedited floor consideration of legislation to reduce Medicare spending triggered by a provision in the 2003 Medicare law. The exemption would apply for the remainder of the 110th Congress. Adopted 231-184: R 15-174; D 216-10 (ND 163-6, SD 53-4). July 24, 2008.

533. H Res 1296. National Child Awareness Month/Adoption.
Davis, D-Ill., motion to suspend the rules and adopt the resolution that would support the designation of September as National Child Awareness Month to promote awareness of children's charities and youth-serving organizations. Motion agreed to 404-0: R 182-0; D 222-0 (ND 166-0, SD 56-0). A two-thirds majority of those present and voting (270 in this case) is required for adoption under suspension of the rules. July 24, 2008.

	530	531	532	533
ALABAMA				
1 Bonner	N	Y	N	Y
2 Everett	N	?	?	?
3 Rogers	N	Y	Y	Y
4 Aderholt	N	Y	N	Y
5 Cramer	Y	Y	Y	Y
6 Bachus	Y	Y	N	Y
7 Davis	Y	Y	Y	Y
ALASKA				
AL Young	Y	N	N	Y
ARIZONA				
1 Renzi	Y	Y	N	Y
2 Franks	N	N	N	Y
3 Shadegg	N	N	N	Y
4 Pastor	Y	Y	Y	Y
5 Mitchell	Y	Y	Y	Y
6 Flake	N	N	N	Y
7 Grijalva	Y	Y	Y	Y
8 Giffords	Y	Y	Y	Y
ARKANSAS				
1 Berry	Y	Y	Y	Y
2 Snyder	Y	Y	Y	Y
3 Boozman	Y	Y	N	Y
4 Ross	Y	Y	Y	Y
CALIFORNIA				
1 Thompson	Y	Y	Y	Y
2 Herger	Y	N	N	Y
3 Lungren	Y	Y	N	Y
4 Doolittle	N	N	N	Y
5 Matsui	Y	Y	Y	Y
6 Woolsey	Y	Y	Y	Y
7 Miller, George	Y	Y	Y	?
8 Pelosi		Y		
9 Lee	Y	Y	Y	Y
10 Tauscher	Y	Y	Y	Y
11 McNerney	Y	Y	Y	Y
12 Speier	Y	Y	Y	Y
13 Stark	Y	Y	Y	Y
14 Eshoo	Y	Y	Y	Y
15 Honda	Y	Y	Y	Y
16 Lofgren	Y	Y	Y	Y
17 Farr	Y	Y	Y	Y
18 Cardoza	Y	Y	Y	Y
19 Radanovich	Y	N	N	Y
20 Costa	Y	Y	Y	Y
21 Nunes	Y	Y	N	Y
22 McCarthy	Y	N	N	Y
23 Capps	Y	Y	Y	Y
24 Gallegly	Y	N	N	Y
25 McKeon	Y	N	N	Y
26 Dreier	Y	Y	N	Y
27 Sherman	Y	Y	Y	Y
28 Berman	Y	Y	Y	Y
29 Schiff	Y	Y	Y	Y
30 Waxman	Y	Y	Y	Y
31 Becerra	Y	Y	Y	Y
32 Solis	Y	Y	Y	Y
33 Watson	Y	Y	Y	Y
34 Roybal-Allard	Y	Y	Y	Y
35 Waters	Y	Y	Y	Y
36 Harman	Y	Y	Y	Y
37 Richardson	Y	Y	Y	Y
38 Napolitano	Y	Y	Y	Y
39 Sánchez, Linda	Y	Y	Y	Y
40 Royce	N	N	N	Y
41 Lewis	Y	N	N	Y
42 Miller, Gary	Y	N	N	Y
43 Baca	Y	Y	Y	Y
44 Calvert	Y	N	N	Y
45 Bono Mack	Y	Y	N	Y
46 Rohrabacher	N	N	N	Y
47 Sanchez, Loretta	Y	Y	Y	Y
48 Campbell	N	N	N	Y
49 Issa	Y	Y	N	Y
50 Bilbray	N	N	N	Y
51 Filner	Y	Y	Y	Y
52 Hunter	N	N	N	Y
53 Davis	Y	Y	Y	Y

	530	531	532	533
COLORADO				
1 DeGette	Y	Y	Y	Y
2 Udall	Y	Y	Y	Y
3 Salazar	Y	?	?	?
4 Musgrave	Y	N	N	Y
5 Lamborn	N	N	N	Y
6 Tancredo	N	N	N	Y
7 Perlmutter	Y	Y	Y	Y
CONNECTICUT				
1 Larson	Y	Y	Y	Y
2 Courtney	Y	Y	Y	Y
3 DeLauro	Y	Y	Y	Y
4 Shays	Y	Y	N	Y
5 Murphy	Y	Y	Y	Y
DELAWARE				
AL Castle	Y	Y	N	Y
FLORIDA				
1 Miller	N	N	N	Y
2 Boyd	Y	Y	N	Y
3 Brown	Y	Y	Y	Y
4 Crenshaw	N	N	N	Y
5 Brown-Waite	?	?	?	?
6 Stearns	N	N	N	Y
7 Mica	N	N	N	Y
8 Keller	Y	N	N	Y
9 Bilirakis	Y	Y	N	Y
10 Young	Y	Y	N	Y
11 Castor	Y	Y	Y	Y
12 Putnam	N	N	N	Y
13 Buchanan	Y	N	N	Y
14 Mack	N	N	N	Y
15 Weldon	N	Y	N	Y
16 Mahoney	Y	Y	Y	Y
17 Meek	Y	Y	Y	Y
18 Ros-Lehtinen	Y	Y	Y	Y
19 Wexler	Y	Y	Y	?
20 Wasserman Schultz	Y	Y	Y	Y
21 Diaz-Balart, L.	Y	Y	N	Y
22 Klein	Y	Y	Y	Y
23 Hastings	Y	Y	Y	Y
24 Feeney	Y	Y	N	?
25 Diaz-Balart, M.	Y	Y	N	Y
GEORGIA				
1 Kingston	N	N	N	Y
2 Bishop	Y	Y	Y	Y
3 Westmoreland	Y	N	N	Y
4 Johnson	Y	Y	Y	Y
5 Lewis	Y	Y	Y	Y
6 Price	N	N	N	Y
7 Linder	Y	N	N	Y
8 Marshall	Y	Y	Y	Y
9 Deal	N	N	N	Y
10 Broun	N	N	N	Y
11 Gingrey	N	N	N	Y
12 Barrow	Y	Y	Y	Y
13 Scott	Y	Y	Y	Y
HAWAII				
1 Abercrombie	Y	Y	Y	Y
2 Hirono	Y	Y	Y	Y
IDAHO				
1 Sali	N	N	N	Y
2 Simpson	Y	N	N	Y
ILLINOIS				
1 Rush	?	?	?	?
2 Jackson	Y	Y	Y	Y
3 Lipinski	Y	Y	Y	Y
4 Gutierrez	Y	Y	Y	Y
5 Emanuel	Y	Y	Y	Y
6 Roskam	Y	N	N	Y
7 Davis	Y	Y	Y	Y
8 Bean	Y	Y	Y	Y
9 Schakowsky	Y	Y	Y	Y
10 Kirk	Y	Y	Y	Y
11 Weller	Y	Y	N	Y
12 Costello	Y	Y	?	?
13 Biggert	Y	Y	N	Y
14 Foster	Y	Y	Y	Y
15 Johnson	Y	Y	N	Y

KEY	Republicans	Democrats	
Y Voted for (yea)	X Paired against	C Voted "present" to avoid possible conflict of interest
# Paired for	− Announced against	
+ Announced for	P Voted "present"	? Did not vote or otherwise make a position known
N Voted against (nay)		

ND Northern Democrats, SD Southern Democrats
Southern states: Ala., Ark., Fla., Ga., Ky., La., Miss., N.C., Okla., S.C., Tenn., Texas, Va.

	530	531	532	533
16 Manzullo	Y	N	N	Y
17 Hare	Y	Y	Y	Y
18 LaHood	?	?	?	?
19 Shimkus	Y	Y	N	Y
INDIANA				
1 Visclosky	Y	Y	Y	Y
2 Donnelly	Y	Y	Y	Y
3 Souder	Y	N	N	Y
4 Buyer	Y	N	N	Y
5 Burton	Y	N	N	Y
6 Pence	N	Y	N	Y
7 Carson, A.	Y	Y	Y	Y
8 Ellsworth	Y	Y	Y	Y
9 Hill	Y	Y	Y	Y
IOWA				
1 Braley	Y	Y	Y	Y
2 Loebsack	Y	Y	Y	Y
3 Boswell	?	?	?	?
4 Latham	Y	Y	N	Y
5 King	N	N	N	Y
KANSAS				
1 Moran	N	Y	N	Y
2 Boyda	Y	Y	Y	Y
3 Moore	Y	Y	Y	Y
4 Tiahrt	N	Y	N	Y
KENTUCKY				
1 Whitfield	Y	N	N	Y
2 Lewis	Y	N	N	Y
3 Yarmuth	Y	Y	Y	Y
4 Davis	Y	N	N	Y
5 Rogers	Y	N	N	Y
6 Chandler	Y	Y	Y	Y
LOUISIANA				
1 Scalise	Y	N	N	Y
2 Jefferson	Y	Y	Y	Y
3 Melancon	Y	Y	Y	Y
4 McCrery	Y	Y	N	Y
5 Alexander	Y	Y	N	Y
6 Cazayoux	Y	Y	Y	Y
7 Boustany	Y	Y	N	Y
MAINE				
1 Allen	Y	Y	Y	Y
2 Michaud	Y	Y	N	Y
MARYLAND				
1 Gilchrest	Y	Y	Y	Y
2 Ruppersberger	Y	Y	Y	Y
3 Sarbanes	Y	Y	Y	Y
4 Edwards	Y	Y	Y	Y
5 Hoyer	?	Y	Y	Y
6 Bartlett	Y	N	N	Y
7 Cummings	Y	Y	Y	Y
8 Van Hollen	Y	Y	Y	Y
MASSACHUSETTS				
1 Olver	Y	Y	Y	Y
2 Neal	Y	Y	Y	Y
3 McGovern	Y	Y	Y	Y
4 Frank	Y	Y	Y	Y
5 Tsongas	Y	Y	Y	Y
6 Tierney	Y	Y	Y	Y
7 Markey	Y	Y	Y	Y
8 Capuano	Y	Y	Y	Y
9 Lynch	Y	Y	Y	Y
10 Delahunt	Y	Y	Y	Y
MICHIGAN				
1 Stupak	Y	Y	Y	Y
2 Hoekstra	N	Y	N	Y
3 Ehlers	Y	Y	N	Y
4 Camp	Y	N	N	Y
5 Kildee	Y	Y	Y	Y
6 Upton	Y	Y	N	Y
7 Walberg	Y	Y	N	Y
8 Rogers	Y	N	N	Y
9 Knollenberg	Y	Y	N	Y
10 Miller	Y	N	N	Y
11 McCotter	Y	Y	N	Y
12 Levin	Y	Y	Y	Y
13 Kilpatrick	Y	Y	Y	?
14 Conyers	Y	Y	Y	Y
15 Dingell	Y	Y	Y	Y
MINNESOTA				
1 Walz	Y	Y	Y	Y
2 Kline	Y	Y	N	Y
3 Ramstad	Y	Y	Y	Y
4 McCollum	Y	Y	Y	Y

	530	531	532	533
5 Ellison	Y	Y	Y	Y
6 Bachmann	Y	N	N	Y
7 Peterson	Y	Y	Y	Y
8 Oberstar	Y	Y	Y	Y
MISSISSIPPI				
1 Childers	Y	Y	Y	Y
2 Thompson	Y	Y	Y	Y
3 Pickering	N	Y	N	Y
4 Taylor	Y	Y	Y	Y
MISSOURI				
1 Clay	Y	Y	Y	Y
2 Akin	Y	N	N	?
3 Carnahan	Y	Y	Y	Y
4 Skelton	Y	Y	Y	Y
5 Cleaver	Y	Y	Y	Y
6 Graves	Y	N	N	?
7 Blunt	Y	N	N	Y
8 Emerson	Y	Y	N	Y
9 Hulshof	?	?	?	?
MONTANA				
AL Rehberg	Y	Y	N	Y
NEBRASKA				
1 Fortenberry	Y	Y	N	Y
2 Terry	Y	N	N	Y
3 Smith	N	N	N	Y
NEVADA				
1 Berkley	Y	Y	Y	Y
2 Heller	N	N	N	Y
3 Porter	Y	Y	Y	Y
NEW HAMPSHIRE				
1 Shea-Porter	Y	Y	Y	Y
2 Hodes	Y	Y	Y	Y
NEW JERSEY				
1 Andrews	Y	Y	Y	Y
2 LoBiondo	Y	N	Y	Y
3 Saxton	Y	?	?	?
4 Smith	Y	Y	Y	Y
5 Garrett	N	N	N	Y
6 Pallone	Y	Y	Y	Y
7 Ferguson	Y	Y	N	Y
8 Pascrell	Y	Y	+	+
9 Rothman	Y	Y	Y	Y
10 Payne	Y	Y	Y	Y
11 Frelinghuysen	Y	Y	N	Y
12 Holt	Y	Y	?	Y
13 Sires	Y	Y	Y	Y
NEW MEXICO				
1 Wilson	Y	Y	N	Y
2 Pearce	Y	Y	N	Y
3 Udall	Y	Y	Y	Y
NEW YORK				
1 Bishop	Y	Y	Y	Y
2 Israel	Y	Y	Y	Y
3 King	Y	Y	N	Y
4 McCarthy	Y	Y	Y	Y
5 Ackerman	Y	Y	Y	Y
6 Meeks	Y	Y	Y	Y
7 Crowley	Y	Y	Y	Y
8 Nadler	Y	Y	Y	Y
9 Weiner	Y	Y	Y	Y
10 Towns	Y	?	?	?
11 Clarke	Y	Y	Y	Y
12 Velázquez	Y	Y	Y	Y
13 Fossella	Y	Y	N	Y
14 Maloney	Y	Y	Y	Y
15 Rangel	Y	Y	Y	Y
16 Serrano	Y	Y	Y	Y
17 Engel	Y	Y	Y	Y
18 Lowey	Y	Y	Y	Y
19 Hall	Y	Y	Y	Y
20 Gillibrand	Y	Y	Y	Y
21 McNulty	Y	Y	Y	Y
22 Hinchey	Y	Y	Y	Y
23 McHugh	Y	Y	N	Y
24 Arcuri	Y	Y	Y	Y
25 Walsh	Y	Y	N	Y
26 Reynolds	N	Y	N	Y
27 Higgins	Y	Y	Y	Y
28 Slaughter	Y	Y	Y	Y
29 Kuhl	Y	Y	N	Y
NORTH CAROLINA				
1 Butterfield	Y	Y	Y	Y
2 Etheridge	Y	Y	Y	Y
3 Jones	Y	N	Y	Y
4 Price	Y	Y	Y	Y

	530	531	532	533
5 Foxx	N	N	N	Y
6 Coble	N	N	N	Y
7 McIntyre	Y	N	Y	Y
8 Hayes	Y	N	N	Y
9 Myrick	Y	N	N	Y
10 McHenry	N	N	N	Y
11 Shuler	Y	Y	Y	Y
12 Watt	Y	Y	Y	Y
13 Miller	Y	Y	Y	Y
NORTH DAKOTA				
AL Pomeroy	Y	Y	Y	Y
OHIO				
1 Chabot	Y	N	N	Y
2 Schmidt	Y	Y	N	Y
3 Turner	Y	Y	N	Y
4 Jordan	N	N	N	Y
5 Latta	N	N	N	Y
6 Wilson	Y	Y	Y	Y
7 Hobson	Y	?	?	?
8 Boehner	?	N	N	Y
9 Kaptur	Y	Y	Y	Y
10 Kucinich	Y	Y	Y	Y
11 Tubbs Jones	Y	Y	Y	Y
12 Tiberi	Y	N	N	Y
13 Sutton	Y	Y	Y	Y
14 LaTourette	Y	Y	N	?
15 Pryce	Y	Y	N	?
16 Regula	Y	Y	N	Y
17 Ryan	Y	Y	Y	Y
18 Space	Y	Y	Y	Y
OKLAHOMA				
1 Sullivan	Y	N	N	Y
2 Boren	Y	Y	Y	Y
3 Lucas	Y	Y	N	Y
4 Cole	Y	Y	N	Y
5 Fallin	Y	?	?	?
OREGON				
1 Wu	Y	Y	Y	Y
2 Walden	Y	N	N	Y
3 Blumenauer	Y	Y	Y	Y
4 DeFazio	Y	Y	Y	?
5 Hooley	Y	?	Y	Y
PENNSYLVANIA				
1 Brady	Y	Y	Y	Y
2 Fattah	Y	Y	Y	Y
3 English	Y	Y	N	Y
4 Altmire	Y	Y	Y	Y
5 Peterson	Y	N	N	Y
6 Gerlach	Y	Y	Y	Y
7 Sestak	Y	Y	Y	Y
8 Murphy, P.	Y	Y	Y	Y
9 Shuster	Y	Y	N	Y
10 Carney	Y	Y	Y	Y
11 Kanjorski	Y	Y	Y	Y
12 Murtha	Y	Y	Y	Y
13 Schwartz	Y	Y	Y	Y
14 Doyle	Y	Y	Y	Y
15 Dent	Y	Y	Y	Y
16 Pitts	Y	N	N	Y
17 Holden	Y	Y	Y	Y
18 Murphy, T.	Y	Y	Y	Y
19 Platts	Y	Y	Y	Y
RHODE ISLAND				
1 Kennedy	Y	Y	Y	Y
2 Langevin	Y	Y	Y	Y
SOUTH CAROLINA				
1 Brown	N	N	N	Y
2 Wilson	Y	Y	N	Y
3 Barrett	Y	N	N	Y
4 Inglis	Y	Y	N	Y
5 Spratt	Y	Y	Y	Y
6 Clyburn	Y	Y	Y	Y
SOUTH DAKOTA				
AL Herseth Sandlin	Y	Y	Y	Y
TENNESSEE				
1 Davis, D.	Y	N	N	Y
2 Duncan	Y	N	N	Y
3 Wamp	Y	N	N	Y
4 Davis, L.	Y	Y	Y	Y
5 Cooper	Y	Y	Y	Y
6 Gordon	Y	Y	Y	Y
7 Blackburn	Y	N	N	Y
8 Tanner	Y	Y	Y	Y
9 Cohen	Y	Y	Y	Y

	530	531	532	533
TEXAS				
1 Gohmert	Y	N	N	Y
2 Poe	N	N	N	Y
3 Johnson, S.	N	N	N	Y
4 Hall	Y	N	N	Y
5 Hensarling	N	N	N	Y
6 Barton	Y	N	N	Y
7 Culberson	N	N	N	Y
8 Brady	Y	N	N	?
9 Green, A.	Y	Y	Y	Y
10 McCaul	Y	N	N	Y
11 Conaway	Y	N	N	Y
12 Granger	Y	N	N	Y
13 Thornberry	N	N	N	Y
14 Paul	N	N	N	Y
15 Hinojosa	?	?	?	?
16 Reyes	Y	Y	Y	Y
17 Edwards	Y	Y	Y	Y
18 Jackson Lee	Y	Y	Y	Y
19 Neugebauer	N	N	N	Y
20 Gonzalez	Y	Y	Y	Y
21 Smith	Y	N	N	Y
22 Lampson	Y	Y	N	Y
23 Rodriguez	Y	Y	N	Y
24 Marchant	N	N	N	Y
25 Doggett	Y	Y	Y	Y
26 Burgess	Y	N	N	Y
27 Ortiz	?	?	?	?
28 Cuellar	Y	Y	Y	Y
29 Green, G.	Y	Y	Y	Y
30 Johnson, E.	Y	Y	Y	Y
31 Carter	Y	N	N	Y
32 Sessions	N	N	N	Y
UTAH				
1 Bishop	?	?	?	?
2 Matheson	Y	Y	N	Y
3 Cannon	?	?	?	?
VERMONT				
AL Welch	Y	Y	Y	Y
VIRGINIA				
1 Wittman	Y	N	N	Y
2 Drake	Y	N	N	Y
3 Scott	Y	Y	Y	Y
4 Forbes	Y	Y	N	Y
5 Goode	Y	Y	N	Y
6 Goodlatte	Y	N	N	Y
7 Cantor	Y	N	N	Y
8 Moran	Y	Y	N	Y
9 Boucher	Y	Y	Y	Y
10 Wolf	Y	Y	N	Y
11 Davis	Y	Y	N	Y
WASHINGTON				
1 Inslee	Y	Y	Y	Y
2 Larsen	Y	Y	N	Y
3 Baird	Y	Y	N	Y
4 Hastings	Y	N	N	Y
5 McMorris Rodgers	Y	N	N	Y
6 Dicks	Y	Y	Y	?
7 McDermott	Y	Y	Y	Y
8 Reichert	Y	Y	Y	Y
9 Smith	Y	Y	N	Y
WEST VIRGINIA				
1 Mollohan	Y	Y	Y	Y
2 Capito	Y	Y	N	Y
3 Rahall	Y	Y	Y	Y
WISCONSIN				
1 Ryan	N	N	N	?
2 Baldwin	Y	Y	Y	Y
3 Kind	Y	Y	Y	Y
4 Moore	Y	Y	Y	Y
5 Sensenbrenner	N	N	N	Y
6 Petri	Y	N	N	Y
7 Obey	Y	Y	Y	Y
8 Kagen	Y	Y	Y	Y
WYOMING				
AL Cubin	?	?	?	?
DELEGATES				
Faleomavaega (A.S.)				
Norton (D.C.)				
Bordallo (Guam)				
Fortuño (P.R.)				
Christensen (V.I.)				

IN THE HOUSE | By Vote Number

534. HR 2490. Mobile Biometric Identification Program/Passage.
Thompson, D-Miss., motion to suspend the rules and pass the bill that would require the Coast Guard to conduct a mobile biometric identification program of suspected individuals, including terrorists. Motion agreed to 394-3: R 178-1; D 216-2 (ND 160-2, SD 56-0). A two-thirds majority of those present and voting (265 in this case) is required for passage under suspension of the rules. July 29, 2008.

535. HR 6113. Federal Agency Information Collection/Passage.
Davis, D-Ill., motion to suspend the rules and pass the bill that would require each agency to include a contact telephone number in its collection of information. Motion agreed to 394-0: R 175-0; D 219-0 (ND 163-0, SD 56-0). A two-thirds majority of those present and voting (263 in this case) is required for passage under suspension of the rules. July 29, 2008.

536. HR 2192. Veterans Health Administration Ombudsman/ Passage. Hare, D-Ill., motion to suspend the rules and pass the bill that would establish an Office of the Ombudsman within the Veterans Health Administration. Motion agreed to 398-0: R 178-0; D 220-0 (ND 164-0, SD 56-0). A two-thirds majority of those present and voting (266 in this case) is required for passage under suspension of the rules. July 29, 2008.

537. H Con Res 398. Adjournment/Adoption. Adoption of the concurrent resolution that would provide for adjournment of the Senate until 12 p.m., Monday, Sept. 8, 2008, and the House until 2 p.m., Monday, Sept. 8, 2008. Adopted 213-212: R 0-195; D 213-17 (ND 158-14, SD 55-3). July 30, 2008.

538. HR 5892. Veterans Disability Benefits Claims/Passage. Filner, D-Calif., motion to suspend the rules and pass the bill that would revise the disability benefits claims processing system for veterans. Motion agreed to 429-0: R 196-0; D 233-0 (ND 175-0, SD 58-0). A two-thirds majority of those present and voting (286 in this case) is required for passage under suspension of the rules. July 30, 2008.

539. H Res 1370. Human Rights in China/Adoption. Berman, D-Calif., motion to suspend the rules and adopt the resolution that would call on the Chinese government to end human rights abuses, cease repression of its Tibetan and Uighur citizens, and end its support for the Burmese and Sudanese governments before the 2008 Beijing Olympics. Motion agreed to 419-1: R 190-1; D 229-0 (ND 171-0, SD 58-0). A two-thirds majority of those present and voting (280 in this case) is required for adoption under suspension of the rules. July 30, 2008.

540. HR 6604. Commodity Markets Transparency/Passage.
Peterson, D-Minn., motion to suspend the rules and pass the bill that would direct foreign exchanges trading U.S. commodities to impose limits on the number of futures contracts an investor can own. Investors trading on such overseas exchanges would have to reduce positions, if they exceed the limits or their activity threatens to distort prices. The Commodity Futures Trading Commission would be authorized to set position limits on over-the-counter trading. Motion rejected 276-151: R 61-135; D 215-16 (ND 162-11, SD 53-5). A two-thirds majority of those present and voting (285 in this case) is required for passage under suspension of the rules. A "nay" was a vote of support for the president. July 30, 2008.

	534	535	536	537	538	539	540
ALABAMA							
1 Bonner	Y	Y	Y	N	Y	Y	N
2 Everett	Y	Y	Y	N	Y	Y	N
3 Rogers	Y	?	Y	N	Y	Y	Y
4 Aderholt	Y	Y	Y	N	Y	Y	N
5 Cramer	Y	Y	Y	Y	Y	Y	Y
6 Bachus	Y	Y	Y	N	Y	Y	N
7 Davis	Y	Y	Y	Y	Y	Y	N
ALASKA							
AL Young	Y	Y	Y	N	Y	Y	N
ARIZONA							
1 Renzi	Y	Y	Y	N	Y	Y	N
2 Franks	Y	Y	Y	N	Y	Y	N
3 Shadegg	Y	Y	Y	N	Y	Y	N
4 Pastor	Y	Y	Y	Y	Y	Y	Y
5 Mitchell	Y	Y	Y	N	Y	Y	Y
6 Flake	Y	Y	Y	N	Y	N	N
7 Grijalva	Y	Y	Y	Y	Y	Y	Y
8 Giffords	Y	Y	Y	Y	Y	Y	Y
ARKANSAS							
1 Berry	Y	Y	Y	Y	Y	Y	Y
2 Snyder	Y	Y	Y	Y	Y	Y	Y
3 Boozman	Y	Y	Y	N	Y	Y	N
4 Ross	Y	Y	Y	Y	Y	Y	Y
CALIFORNIA							
1 Thompson	Y	Y	Y	Y	Y	Y	Y
2 Herger	Y	Y	Y	N	Y	Y	N
3 Lungren	Y	Y	Y	N	Y	Y	N
4 Doolittle	?	?	?	N	Y	Y	N
5 Matsui	Y	Y	Y	Y	Y	Y	Y
6 Woolsey	Y	Y	Y	Y	Y	Y	Y
7 Miller, George	Y	Y	Y	Y	Y	Y	Y
8 Pelosi				Y	Y	Y	Y
9 Lee	Y	Y	Y	Y	Y	Y	?
10 Tauscher	Y	Y	Y	Y	Y	Y	N
11 McNerney	Y	Y	Y	Y	Y	Y	Y
12 Speier	Y	Y	Y	Y	Y	Y	Y
13 Stark	N	Y	Y	Y	Y	Y	Y
14 Eshoo	Y	Y	Y	Y	Y	Y	Y
15 Honda	Y	Y	Y	Y	Y	Y	Y
16 Lofgren	?	?	Y	Y	Y	Y	Y
17 Farr	Y	Y	Y	Y	Y	Y	Y
18 Cardoza	Y	Y	Y	Y	Y	Y	Y
19 Radanovich	Y	Y	Y	N	Y	Y	N
20 Costa	Y	Y	Y	Y	Y	Y	N
21 Nunes	Y	Y	Y	N	Y	Y	N
22 McCarthy	?	?	?	N	Y	Y	N
23 Capps	Y	Y	Y	Y	Y	Y	Y
24 Gallegly	Y	Y	Y	N	Y	Y	Y
25 McKeon	Y	?	Y	N	Y	Y	Y
26 Dreier	Y	Y	Y	N	Y	Y	N
27 Sherman	Y	Y	Y	Y	Y	Y	Y
28 Berman	Y	Y	Y	Y	Y	Y	?
29 Schiff	Y	Y	Y	Y	Y	Y	Y
30 Waxman	Y	Y	Y	Y	Y	Y	Y
31 Becerra	Y	Y	Y	Y	Y	Y	Y
32 Solis	Y	Y	Y	Y	Y	Y	Y
33 Watson	Y	Y	Y	Y	Y	Y	Y
34 Roybal-Allard	Y	Y	Y	Y	Y	Y	Y
35 Waters	Y	Y	Y	?	Y	Y	Y
36 Harman	Y	Y	Y	Y	Y	Y	Y
37 Richardson	Y	Y	Y	Y	Y	Y	Y
38 Napolitano	Y	Y	Y	Y	Y	Y	Y
39 Sánchez, Linda	Y	Y	Y	Y	Y	Y	Y
40 Royce	Y	Y	Y	N	Y	N	N
41 Lewis	Y	Y	Y	N	Y	Y	N
42 Miller, Gary	Y	Y	Y	N	Y	Y	N
43 Baca	Y	Y	Y	Y	Y	Y	Y
44 Calvert	Y	Y	Y	N	Y	Y	N
45 Bono Mack	Y	Y	Y	N	Y	Y	Y
46 Rohrabacher	Y	Y	Y	N	Y	Y	N
47 Sanchez, Loretta	Y	Y	Y	Y	Y	Y	Y
48 Campbell	Y	Y	Y	N	Y	Y	N
49 Issa	Y	Y	Y	N	Y	Y	N
50 Bilbray	Y	Y	Y	N	Y	Y	N
51 Filner	Y	Y	Y	Y	Y	Y	Y
52 Hunter	Y	Y	Y	N	Y	Y	N
53 Davis	Y	Y	Y	Y	Y	Y	Y

	534	535	536	537	538	539	540
COLORADO							
1 DeGette	Y	Y	Y	Y	Y	Y	Y
2 Udall	?	?	?	–	Y	Y	Y
3 Salazar	Y	Y	Y	Y	Y	Y	Y
4 Musgrave	Y	Y	Y	N	Y	Y	N
5 Lamborn	Y	Y	Y	N	Y	Y	N
6 Tancredo	Y	Y	Y	N	Y	Y	N
7 Perlmutter	Y	Y	Y	Y	Y	Y	Y
CONNECTICUT							
1 Larson	Y	Y	Y	Y	Y	Y	Y
2 Courtney	Y	Y	Y	Y	Y	Y	Y
3 DeLauro	Y	Y	Y	Y	Y	Y	Y
4 Shays	Y	Y	Y	N	Y	Y	Y
5 Murphy	Y	Y	Y	Y	Y	Y	Y
DELAWARE							
AL Castle	Y	Y	Y	N	Y	Y	Y
FLORIDA							
1 Miller	Y	Y	Y	N	Y	Y	N
2 Boyd	Y	Y	Y	Y	Y	Y	N
3 Brown	?	?	?	Y	Y	Y	Y
4 Crenshaw	Y	Y	Y	N	Y	Y	N
5 Brown-Waite	?	?	?	?	?	?	?
6 Stearns	Y	Y	Y	N	Y	Y	N
7 Mica	Y	Y	Y	N	Y	Y	N
8 Keller	Y	Y	Y	N	Y	Y	Y
9 Bilirakis	Y	Y	Y	N	Y	Y	N
10 Young	Y	Y	Y	N	Y	Y	N
11 Castor	Y	Y	Y	Y	Y	Y	Y
12 Putnam	Y	Y	Y	N	Y	Y	N
13 Buchanan	Y	Y	Y	N	Y	Y	N
14 Mack	Y	Y	Y	N	Y	Y	N
15 Weldon	?	?	Y	N	Y	Y	N
16 Mahoney	Y	Y	Y	Y	Y	Y	Y
17 Meek	Y	Y	Y	Y	Y	Y	Y
18 Ros-Lehtinen	?	?	?	N	Y	Y	N
19 Wexler	Y	Y	Y	Y	Y	Y	Y
20 Wasserman Schultz	Y	Y	Y	Y	Y	Y	Y
21 Diaz-Balart, L.	Y	Y	Y	N	Y	Y	Y
22 Klein	Y	Y	Y	Y	Y	Y	Y
23 Hastings	Y	Y	Y	Y	Y	Y	Y
24 Feeney	Y	?	Y	N	Y	Y	N
25 Diaz-Balart, M.	Y	Y	Y	N	Y	Y	N
GEORGIA							
1 Kingston	Y	Y	Y	N	Y	Y	N
2 Bishop	Y	Y	Y	Y	Y	Y	Y
3 Westmoreland	Y	Y	Y	N	Y	Y	N
4 Johnson	Y	Y	Y	Y	Y	Y	Y
5 Lewis	Y	Y	Y	Y	Y	Y	Y
6 Price	Y	Y	Y	N	Y	Y	N
7 Linder	Y	Y	Y	N	Y	Y	N
8 Marshall	Y	Y	Y	N	Y	Y	Y
9 Deal	Y	Y	Y	N	Y	Y	N
10 Broun	Y	Y	Y	N	Y	Y	N
11 Gingrey	Y	Y	?	N	Y	Y	N
12 Barrow	?	?	?	?	?	?	?
13 Scott	Y	Y	Y	Y	Y	Y	Y
HAWAII							
1 Abercrombie	Y	Y	Y	Y	Y	Y	Y
2 Hirono	Y	Y	Y	Y	Y	Y	Y
IDAHO							
1 Sali	Y	Y	Y	N	Y	Y	N
2 Simpson	Y	Y	Y	N	Y	Y	N
ILLINOIS							
1 Rush	?	?	?	?	?	?	?
2 Jackson	Y	Y	Y	Y	Y	Y	Y
3 Lipinski	Y	Y	Y	Y	Y	Y	Y
4 Gutierrez	?	?	?	Y	Y	Y	Y
5 Emanuel	Y	Y	Y	Y	Y	Y	Y
6 Roskam	Y	Y	Y	N	Y	?	N
7 Davis	Y	Y	Y	Y	Y	Y	Y
8 Bean	Y	Y	Y	Y	Y	Y	N
9 Schakowsky	Y	Y	Y	Y	Y	Y	Y
10 Kirk	Y	Y	Y	N	Y	Y	Y
11 Weller	?	?	?	N	Y	Y	Y
12 Costello	?	?	?	Y	Y	Y	Y
13 Biggert	Y	Y	Y	N	Y	Y	N
14 Foster	Y	Y	Y	Y	Y	N	Y
15 Johnson	?	?	?	N	Y	Y	Y

KEY Republicans Democrats

Y Voted for (yea)	X Paired against
# Paired for	– Announced against
+ Announced for	P Voted "present"
N Voted against (nay)	

C Voted "present" to avoid possible conflict of interest	
? Did not vote or otherwise make a position known	

ND Northern Democrats, SD Southern Democrats
Southern states: Ala., Ark., Fla., Ga., Ky., La., Miss., N.C., Okla., S.C., Tenn., Texas, Va.

	534	535	536	537	538	539	540
16 **Manzullo**	Y	Y	Y	N	Y	Y	N
17 Hare	Y	Y	Y	Y	Y	Y	Y
18 **LaHood**	Y	Y	Y	N	Y	Y	Y
19 **Shimkus**	Y	Y	Y	N	Y	Y	N
INDIANA							
1 Visclosky	Y	Y	Y	Y	Y	Y	Y
2 Donnelly	Y	Y	Y	N	Y	Y	Y
3 **Souder**	Y	Y	Y	N	Y	Y	Y
4 **Buyer**	Y	Y	Y	N	Y	Y	N
5 **Burton**	Y	Y	Y	N	Y	Y	N
6 **Pence**	Y	Y	Y	N	Y	Y	N
7 Carson, A.	Y	Y	Y	Y	Y	Y	Y
8 Ellsworth	Y	Y	Y	N	Y	Y	Y
9 Hill	Y	Y	Y	Y	Y	Y	Y
IOWA							
1 Braley	Y	Y	Y	N	Y	Y	Y
2 Loebsack	Y	Y	Y	N	Y	Y	Y
3 Boswell	Y	Y	Y	N	Y	Y	Y
4 **Latham**	Y	Y	Y	N	Y	Y	Y
5 **King**	Y	Y	Y	N	Y	Y	N
KANSAS							
1 **Moran**	Y	Y	Y	N	Y	Y	N
2 Boyda	Y	Y	Y	Y	Y	Y	Y
3 Moore	Y	Y	Y	Y	Y	Y	Y
4 **Tiahrt**	Y	?	Y	N	Y	Y	N
KENTUCKY							
1 **Whitfield**	Y	Y	Y	N	Y	Y	N
2 **Lewis**	Y	Y	Y	N	Y	Y	Y
3 Yarmuth	Y	Y	Y	Y	Y	Y	Y
4 **Davis**	Y	Y	Y	N	Y	Y	N
5 **Rogers**	Y	Y	Y	N	Y	Y	N
6 Chandler	Y	Y	Y	Y	Y	Y	Y
LOUISIANA							
1 **Scalise**	Y	Y	Y	N	Y	Y	N
2 Jefferson	Y	Y	Y	Y	Y	Y	Y
3 Melancon	Y	Y	Y	Y	Y	Y	N
4 **McCrery**	?	?	?	N	Y	Y	N
5 **Alexander**	Y	Y	Y	N	Y	Y	N
6 Cazayoux	Y	Y	Y	Y	Y	Y	Y
7 **Boustany**	Y	Y	Y	N	Y	Y	Y
MAINE							
1 Allen	+	+	+	Y	Y	Y	Y
2 Michaud	Y	Y	Y	Y	Y	Y	Y
MARYLAND							
1 **Gilchrest**	?	?	?	N	Y	Y	Y
2 Ruppersberger	Y	Y	Y	Y	Y	Y	Y
3 Sarbanes	Y	Y	Y	Y	Y	Y	Y
4 Edwards	Y	Y	Y	Y	Y	Y	Y
5 Hoyer	Y	Y	Y	Y	Y	Y	Y
6 **Bartlett**	Y	Y	Y	N	Y	Y	N
7 Cummings	Y	Y	Y	Y	Y	Y	Y
8 Van Hollen	Y	Y	Y	Y	Y	Y	Y
MASSACHUSETTS							
1 Olver	Y	Y	Y	Y	Y	Y	Y
2 Neal	Y	Y	Y	Y	Y	Y	Y
3 McGovern	Y	Y	Y	Y	Y	Y	Y
4 Frank	Y	Y	Y	Y	Y	Y	Y
5 Tsongas	Y	Y	Y	Y	Y	Y	Y
6 Tierney	Y	Y	Y	Y	Y	Y	Y
7 Markey	Y	Y	Y	Y	Y	Y	Y
8 Capuano	Y	Y	Y	Y	Y	Y	Y
9 Lynch	?	?	?	Y	Y	Y	Y
10 Delahunt	Y	Y	Y	Y	Y	?	Y
MICHIGAN							
1 Stupak	Y	Y	Y	Y	Y	Y	Y
2 **Hoekstra**	Y	Y	Y	N	Y	Y	N
3 **Ehlers**	Y	Y	Y	N	Y	Y	Y
4 **Camp**	Y	Y	Y	N	Y	Y	N
5 Kildee	Y	Y	Y	Y	Y	Y	Y
6 **Upton**	Y	Y	Y	N	Y	Y	Y
7 **Walberg**	Y	Y	Y	N	Y	Y	N
8 **Rogers**	Y	Y	Y	N	Y	?	N
9 **Knollenberg**	Y	Y	Y	N	Y	Y	Y
10 **Miller**	Y	Y	Y	N	Y	Y	Y
11 **McCotter**	Y	Y	Y	N	Y	Y	Y
12 Levin	+	+	+	+	+	+	Y
13 Kilpatrick	Y	Y	Y	Y	Y	Y	Y
14 Conyers	Y	Y	Y	Y	Y	Y	Y
15 Dingell	Y	Y	Y	Y	Y	Y	Y
MINNESOTA							
1 Walz	Y	Y	Y	Y	Y	Y	Y
2 **Kline**	Y	Y	Y	N	Y	Y	N
3 **Ramstad**	Y	Y	Y	N	Y	Y	Y
4 McCollum	Y	Y	Y	Y	Y	Y	Y

	534	535	536	537	538	539	540
5 Ellison	Y	Y	Y	Y	Y	Y	Y
6 **Bachmann**	Y	Y	Y	N	Y	Y	N
7 Peterson	Y	Y	Y	Y	Y	Y	Y
8 Oberstar	Y	Y	Y	Y	Y	Y	Y
MISSISSIPPI							
1 Childers	Y	Y	Y	N	Y	Y	Y
2 Thompson	Y	Y	Y	Y	Y	Y	Y
3 **Pickering**	Y	Y	Y	N	Y	Y	N
4 Taylor	Y	Y	Y	Y	Y	Y	Y
MISSOURI							
1 Clay	Y	Y	Y	Y	Y	Y	Y
2 **Akin**	Y	Y	Y	N	Y	Y	N
3 Carnahan	Y	Y	Y	Y	Y	Y	Y
4 Skelton	Y	Y	Y	Y	Y	Y	Y
5 Cleaver	Y	Y	Y	Y	Y	Y	Y
6 **Graves**	+	+	+	N	Y	Y	Y
7 **Blunt**	Y	Y	Y	?	Y	Y	N
8 **Emerson**	Y	Y	Y	N	Y	Y	Y
9 **Hulshof**	?	?	?	?	?	?	?
MONTANA							
AL **Rehberg**	Y	Y	Y	N	Y	Y	N
NEBRASKA							
1 **Fortenberry**	Y	Y	Y	N	Y	Y	Y
2 **Terry**	Y	Y	Y	N	Y	Y	Y
3 **Smith**	Y	Y	Y	N	Y	Y	N
NEVADA							
1 Berkley	Y	Y	Y	Y	Y	Y	Y
2 **Heller**	Y	Y	Y	N	Y	Y	N
3 **Porter**	Y	Y	Y	N	Y	Y	Y
NEW HAMPSHIRE							
1 Shea-Porter	Y	Y	Y	Y	Y	Y	Y
2 Hodes	Y	Y	Y	Y	Y	Y	Y
NEW JERSEY							
1 Andrews	?	?	?	Y	Y	Y	Y
2 **LoBiondo**	Y	Y	Y	N	Y	Y	Y
3 **Saxton**	?	?	?	N	Y	Y	N
4 **Smith**	Y	Y	Y	N	Y	Y	Y
5 **Garrett**	Y	Y	Y	N	Y	Y	N
6 Pallone	Y	Y	Y	Y	Y	Y	Y
7 **Ferguson**	Y	Y	Y	N	Y	Y	N
8 Pascrell	Y	Y	Y	Y	Y	Y	Y
9 Rothman	Y	Y	Y	Y	Y	Y	Y
10 Payne	Y	Y	Y	Y	Y	Y	?
11 **Frelinghuysen**	Y	Y	Y	N	Y	Y	Y
12 Holt	Y	Y	Y	Y	Y	Y	Y
13 Sires	Y	Y	Y	Y	Y	Y	Y
NEW MEXICO							
1 **Wilson**	Y	Y	Y	N	Y	Y	N
2 **Pearce**	?	?	?	N	Y	Y	N
3 Udall	?	?	?	N	Y	Y	Y
NEW YORK							
1 Bishop	Y	Y	Y	Y	Y	Y	Y
2 Israel	Y	Y	Y	Y	Y	Y	Y
3 **King**	Y	Y	Y	N	Y	Y	N
4 McCarthy	Y	Y	Y	Y	Y	Y	Y
5 Ackerman	Y	Y	Y	Y	Y	Y	Y
6 Meeks	Y	Y	Y	?	Y	Y	N
7 Crowley	Y	Y	Y	Y	Y	Y	N
8 Nadler	Y	Y	Y	Y	Y	Y	Y
9 Weiner	Y	Y	Y	Y	Y	Y	N
10 Towns	Y	Y	Y	Y	Y	Y	Y
11 Clarke	P	Y	Y	Y	Y	Y	N
12 Velázquez	Y	Y	Y	Y	Y	Y	Y
13 **Fossella**	Y	Y	Y	N	Y	Y	N
14 Maloney	Y	Y	Y	Y	Y	Y	N
15 Rangel	Y	Y	Y	Y	Y	?	Y
16 Serrano	Y	Y	Y	Y	Y	Y	Y
17 Engel	?	?	?	Y	Y	Y	Y
18 Lowey	Y	Y	Y	Y	Y	Y	Y
19 Hall	Y	Y	Y	Y	Y	Y	Y
20 Gillibrand	Y	Y	Y	N	Y	Y	Y
21 McNulty	Y	Y	Y	Y	Y	Y	Y
22 Hinchey	Y	Y	Y	Y	Y	Y	Y
23 **McHugh**	?	?	?	N	Y	Y	Y
24 Arcuri	Y	Y	Y	N	Y	Y	Y
25 **Walsh**	Y	Y	Y	N	Y	Y	Y
26 **Reynolds**	Y	Y	Y	N	Y	Y	N
27 Higgins	Y	Y	Y	Y	Y	Y	Y
28 Slaughter	Y	Y	Y	Y	Y	Y	Y
29 **Kuhl**	Y	Y	Y	N	Y	Y	Y
NORTH CAROLINA							
1 Butterfield	Y	Y	Y	Y	Y	Y	Y
2 Etheridge	Y	Y	Y	Y	Y	Y	Y
3 **Jones**	Y	Y	Y	N	Y	Y	Y
4 Price	Y	Y	Y	Y	Y	Y	Y

	534	535	536	537	538	539	540
5 **Foxx**	Y	Y	Y	N	Y	Y	N
6 **Coble**	Y	Y	Y	N	Y	Y	N
7 McIntyre	Y	Y	Y	Y	Y	Y	Y
8 **Hayes**	Y	Y	Y	N	Y	Y	Y
9 **Myrick**	Y	Y	Y	N	Y	Y	N
10 **McHenry**	Y	Y	Y	N	Y	Y	N
11 Shuler	Y	Y	Y	Y	Y	Y	Y
12 Watt	Y	Y	Y	Y	Y	Y	Y
13 Miller	Y	Y	Y	Y	Y	Y	Y
NORTH DAKOTA							
AL Pomeroy	Y	Y	Y	Y	Y	Y	Y
OHIO							
1 **Chabot**	Y	Y	Y	N	Y	Y	Y
2 **Schmidt**	Y	Y	Y	N	Y	Y	N
3 **Turner**	Y	Y	Y	N	Y	Y	N
4 **Jordan**	Y	Y	Y	N	Y	Y	N
5 **Latta**	Y	Y	Y	N	Y	Y	N
6 Wilson	Y	Y	Y	Y	Y	Y	Y
7 **Hobson**	Y	Y	Y	N	Y	Y	N
8 **Boehner**	?	?	?	N	Y	Y	N
9 Kaptur	Y	Y	Y	Y	Y	Y	Y
10 Kucinich	N	Y	Y	Y	Y	P	Y
11 Tubbs Jones	Y	Y	Y	Y	Y	Y	Y
12 **Tiberi**	?	?	?	N	Y	Y	N
13 Sutton	?	?	?	Y	Y	Y	Y
14 **LaTourette**	?	?	?	N	Y	Y	Y
15 **Pryce**	Y	Y	Y	N	Y	Y	N
16 **Regula**	?	?	?	N	Y	Y	N
17 Ryan	Y	Y	Y	Y	Y	Y	Y
18 Space	Y	Y	Y	Y	Y	Y	Y
OKLAHOMA							
1 **Sullivan**	Y	Y	Y	N	Y	?	N
2 Boren	Y	Y	Y	Y	Y	Y	Y
3 **Lucas**	Y	Y	Y	N	Y	Y	N
4 **Cole**	Y	Y	Y	N	Y	Y	N
5 **Fallin**	Y	Y	Y	N	Y	Y	N
OREGON							
1 Wu	Y	Y	Y	Y	Y	Y	Y
2 **Walden**	Y	Y	Y	N	Y	Y	N
3 Blumenauer	Y	Y	Y	Y	Y	Y	Y
4 DeFazio	Y	Y	Y	Y	Y	Y	Y
5 Hooley	Y	Y	Y	Y	Y	Y	Y
PENNSYLVANIA							
1 Brady	Y	Y	Y	Y	Y	Y	Y
2 Fattah	Y	Y	Y	Y	Y	Y	Y
3 **English**	Y	Y	Y	N	Y	Y	Y
4 Altmire	Y	Y	Y	N	Y	Y	Y
5 **Peterson**	Y	Y	Y	N	Y	Y	N
6 **Gerlach**	Y	Y	Y	N	Y	Y	Y
7 Sestak	Y	Y	Y	N	Y	Y	Y
8 Murphy, P.	Y	Y	Y	N	Y	Y	Y
9 **Shuster**	Y	Y	Y	N	Y	Y	Y
10 Carney	Y	Y	Y	N	Y	Y	Y
11 Kanjorski	Y	Y	Y	Y	Y	Y	Y
12 Murtha	Y	Y	Y	Y	Y	Y	Y
13 Schwartz	Y	Y	Y	Y	Y	Y	Y
14 Doyle	Y	Y	Y	Y	Y	Y	Y
15 **Dent**	Y	Y	Y	N	Y	Y	Y
16 **Pitts**	Y	Y	Y	N	Y	Y	N
17 Holden	Y	Y	Y	Y	Y	Y	Y
18 **Murphy, T.**	Y	Y	Y	N	Y	Y	Y
19 **Platts**	Y	Y	Y	N	Y	Y	Y
RHODE ISLAND							
1 Kennedy	Y	Y	Y	Y	Y	Y	Y
2 Langevin	Y	Y	Y	Y	Y	Y	Y
SOUTH CAROLINA							
1 **Brown**	Y	Y	Y	N	Y	Y	N
2 **Wilson**	Y	Y	Y	N	Y	Y	N
3 **Barrett**	Y	Y	Y	N	Y	Y	N
4 **Inglis**	?	?	?	N	Y	Y	N
5 Spratt	Y	Y	Y	Y	Y	Y	Y
6 Clyburn	Y	Y	Y	Y	Y	Y	Y
SOUTH DAKOTA							
AL Herseth Sandlin	Y	Y	Y	N	Y	Y	Y
TENNESSEE							
1 **Davis, D.**	Y	Y	Y	N	Y	Y	N
2 **Duncan**	Y	Y	Y	N	Y	Y	Y
3 **Wamp**	Y	Y	Y	N	Y	Y	Y
4 Davis, L.	Y	Y	Y	Y	Y	Y	Y
5 Cooper	Y	Y	Y	Y	Y	Y	N
6 Gordon	Y	Y	Y	Y	Y	Y	Y
7 **Blackburn**	Y	Y	Y	N	Y	Y	N
8 Tanner	Y	Y	Y	Y	Y	Y	Y
9 Cohen	Y	Y	Y	Y	Y	Y	Y

	534	535	536	537	538	539	540
TEXAS							
1 **Gohmert**	Y	Y	Y	N	Y	Y	Y
2 **Poe**	Y	Y	Y	N	Y	Y	N
3 **Johnson, S.**	Y	Y	Y	N	Y	Y	N
4 **Hall**	Y	Y	Y	N	Y	Y	N
5 **Hensarling**	Y	Y	Y	N	Y	?	N
6 **Barton**	Y	Y	Y	N	Y	Y	N
7 **Culberson**	Y	Y	Y	N	Y	Y	N
8 **Brady**	Y	Y	Y	N	Y	?	N
9 Green, A.	Y	Y	Y	Y	Y	Y	Y
10 **McCaul**	Y	Y	Y	N	Y	Y	N
11 **Conaway**	Y	Y	Y	N	Y	Y	Y
12 **Granger**	Y	Y	Y	N	Y	Y	N
13 **Thornberry**	Y	Y	Y	N	Y	Y	N
14 **Paul**	N	Y	Y	N	Y	N	N
15 Hinojosa	Y	Y	Y	Y	Y	Y	Y
16 Reyes	?	?	?	Y	Y	Y	Y
17 Edwards	Y	Y	Y	Y	Y	Y	Y
18 Jackson Lee	Y	Y	Y	Y	Y	Y	Y
19 **Neugebauer**	Y	Y	Y	N	Y	Y	N
20 Gonzalez	Y	Y	Y	Y	Y	Y	Y
21 **Smith**	Y	Y	Y	N	Y	Y	N
22 Lampson	Y	Y	Y	N	Y	Y	N
23 Rodriguez	Y	Y	Y	Y	Y	Y	Y
24 **Marchant**	Y	Y	Y	N	Y	Y	N
25 Doggett	Y	Y	Y	Y	Y	Y	Y
26 **Burgess**	Y	Y	Y	N	Y	Y	N
27 Ortiz	Y	Y	Y	Y	Y	Y	Y
28 Cuellar	Y	Y	Y	Y	Y	Y	Y
29 Green, G.	Y	Y	Y	Y	Y	Y	Y
30 Johnson, E.	Y	Y	Y	Y	Y	Y	Y
31 **Carter**	Y	Y	Y	N	Y	Y	N
32 **Sessions**	Y	Y	Y	N	Y	Y	N
UTAH							
1 **Bishop**	Y	Y	Y	N	Y	Y	N
2 Matheson	Y	Y	Y	Y	Y	Y	N
3 **Cannon**	Y	Y	Y	N	Y	Y	N
VERMONT							
AL Welch	Y	Y	Y	Y	Y	Y	Y
VIRGINIA							
1 **Wittman**	Y	Y	Y	N	Y	Y	Y
2 **Drake**	Y	Y	Y	N	Y	Y	N
3 Scott	Y	Y	Y	Y	Y	Y	Y
4 **Forbes**	Y	Y	Y	N	Y	Y	Y
5 **Goode**	Y	Y	Y	N	Y	Y	Y
6 **Goodlatte**	Y	Y	Y	N	Y	Y	Y
7 **Cantor**	Y	Y	Y	N	Y	Y	N
8 Moran	Y	Y	Y	Y	Y	Y	Y
9 Boucher	Y	Y	Y	Y	Y	Y	Y
10 **Wolf**	Y	Y	Y	N	Y	Y	Y
11 **Davis**	Y	Y	Y	N	Y	Y	N
WASHINGTON							
1 Inslee	Y	Y	Y	Y	Y	Y	Y
2 Larsen	Y	Y	Y	Y	Y	Y	Y
3 Baird	Y	Y	Y	Y	Y	Y	Y
4 **Hastings**	Y	Y	Y	N	Y	Y	N
5 **McMorris Rodgers**	Y	Y	Y	N	Y	Y	N
6 Dicks	Y	Y	Y	Y	Y	Y	Y
7 McDermott	Y	Y	Y	Y	Y	Y	Y
8 **Reichert**	Y	Y	Y	N	Y	Y	N
9 Smith	Y	Y	Y	Y	Y	?	Y
WEST VIRGINIA							
1 Mollohan	Y	Y	Y	Y	Y	Y	Y
2 **Capito**	Y	Y	Y	N	Y	Y	Y
3 Rahall	Y	Y	Y	Y	Y	Y	Y
WISCONSIN							
1 **Ryan**	Y	Y	Y	N	Y	Y	N
2 Baldwin	Y	Y	Y	Y	Y	Y	Y
3 Kind	Y	Y	Y	Y	Y	Y	N
4 Moore	Y	Y	Y	Y	Y	Y	Y
5 **Sensenbrenner**	Y	Y	Y	N	Y	Y	N
6 **Petri**	Y	Y	Y	N	Y	Y	N
7 Obey	Y	Y	Y	Y	Y	Y	Y
8 Kagen	?	?	?	Y	Y	Y	Y
WYOMING							
AL **Cubin**	?	?	?	?	?	?	?
DELEGATES							
Faleomavaega (A.S.)							
Norton (D.C.)							
Bordallo (Guam)							
Fortuño (P.R.)							
Christensen (V.I.)							

IN THE HOUSE | By Vote Number

541. **HR 6445. Bar Co-Payments for Catastrophically Disabled Veterans/Passage.** Filner, D-Calif., motion to suspend the rules and pass the bill that would bar the collection of co-payments from veterans for hospital and nursing home care if the veterans are considered catastrophically disabled. The measure also incorporates the text of four other veterans' bills. Motion agreed to 421-0: R 193-0; D 228-0 (ND 171-0, SD 57-0). A two-thirds majority of those present and voting (281 in this case) is required for passage under suspension of the rules. July 30, 2008.

542. **HR 1108. Tobacco Products Regulation/Passage.** Dingell, D-Mich., motion to suspend the rules and pass the bill that would authorize the Food and Drug Administration to regulate tobacco products. The FDA could restrict sales and distribution, including advertising and promotion, if it determines that it is necessary to protect public health, although it could not ban a class of tobacco products or reduce the nicotine level to zero. The bill would assess new quarterly user fees on manufacturers and importers of tobacco products to pay for the additional regulations. Motion agreed to 326-102: R 96-99; D 230-3 (ND 173-1, SD 57-2). A two-thirds majority of those present and voting (286 in this case) is required for passage under suspension of the rules. A "nay" was a vote in support of the president's position. July 30, 2008.

543. **HR 4040. Consumer Product Safety Commission Overhaul/ Conference Report.** Dingell, D-Mich., motion to suspend the rules and adopt the conference report on the bill that would authorize $626 million for the Consumer Product Safety Commission in fiscal 2010-14. The bill would set lower thresholds for lead in toys and ban certain phthalates, or plastic softeners, in products for children. It would require an online database of product-related injuries and risks, ban the sale of All-Terrain Vehicles that do not meet certain standards and provide whistleblower protections to certain employees. It also would provide states with increased consumer protection authority. Motion agreed to (thus sent to the Senate) 424-1: R 193-1; D 231-0 (ND 172-0, SD 59-0). A two-thirds majority of those present and voting (284 in this case) is required for adoption under suspension of the rules. July 30, 2008.

544. **HR 4137. Higher Education Reauthorization/Conference Report.** Adoption of the conference report on the bill that would reauthorize the Higher Education Act through fiscal 2012. The bill would increase the maximum Pell grant to $8,000 per year by the 2014-15 academic year. It would bar lenders from giving schools financial perks in order to get on a "preferred lender list." It also would penalize states that cut funding for institutions of higher education by withholding some federal funds if the state's funding for such institutions falls below the average amount allocated by the state over the last five academic years. It would establish a new loan-forgiveness program, providing up to $2,000 a year for five years for individuals such as nurses, early childhood educators and librarians serving in high-need areas. Adopted (thus sent to the Senate) 380-49: R 146-49; D 234-0 (ND 175-0, SD 59-0). July 31, 2008.

	541	542	543	544
ALABAMA				
1 **Bonner**	Y	Y	Y	Y
2 **Everett**	Y	Y	Y	Y
3 **Rogers**	Y	Y	Y	Y
4 **Aderholt**	Y	N	Y	Y
5 Cramer	Y	Y	Y	Y
6 **Bachus**	Y	N	Y	Y
7 Davis	Y	Y	Y	Y
ALASKA				
AL **Young**	Y	Y	Y	?
ARIZONA				
1 **Renzi**	Y	Y	Y	Y
2 **Franks**	Y	N	Y	N
3 **Shadegg**	Y	N	Y	N
4 Pastor	Y	Y	Y	Y
5 Mitchell	Y	Y	Y	Y
6 **Flake**	Y	N	Y	N
7 Grijalva	Y	Y	Y	Y
8 Giffords	Y	Y	Y	Y
ARKANSAS				
1 Berry	Y	Y	Y	Y
2 Snyder	Y	Y	Y	Y
3 **Boozman**	Y	Y	Y	Y
4 Ross	Y	Y	Y	Y
CALIFORNIA				
1 Thompson	Y	Y	Y	Y
2 **Herger**	Y	N	Y	N
3 **Lungren**	Y	N	Y	N
4 **Doolittle**	Y	N	Y	N
5 Matsui	Y	Y	Y	Y
6 Woolsey	Y	Y	Y	Y
7 Miller, George	Y	Y	Y	Y
8 Pelosi				
9 Lee	?	Y	Y	Y
10 Tauscher	Y	Y	Y	Y
11 McNerney	Y	Y	Y	Y
12 Speier	Y	Y	Y	Y
13 Stark	Y	Y	Y	Y
14 Eshoo	Y	Y	Y	Y
15 Honda	Y	Y	Y	Y
16 Lofgren	Y	Y	Y	Y
17 Farr	Y	Y	Y	Y
18 Cardoza	?	Y	Y	Y
19 **Radanovich**	Y	N	Y	Y
20 Costa	Y	Y	Y	Y
21 **Nunes**	Y	N	Y	Y
22 **McCarthy**	Y	Y	Y	Y
23 Capps	Y	Y	Y	Y
24 **Gallegly**	Y	Y	Y	Y
25 **McKeon**	Y	Y	Y	Y
26 **Dreier**	Y	Y	Y	Y
27 Sherman	Y	Y	Y	Y
28 Berman	?	Y	Y	Y
29 Schiff	Y	Y	Y	Y
30 Waxman	Y	Y	Y	Y
31 Becerra	Y	Y	Y	Y
32 Solis	Y	Y	Y	Y
33 Watson	Y	Y	Y	Y
34 Roybal-Allard	Y	Y	Y	Y
35 Waters	Y	Y	Y	Y
36 Harman	Y	Y	Y	Y
37 Richardson	Y	Y	Y	Y
38 Napolitano	Y	Y	Y	Y
39 Sánchez, Linda	Y	Y	Y	Y
40 **Royce**	Y	N	Y	Y
41 **Lewis**	Y	N	Y	Y
42 **Miller, Gary**	Y	N	Y	Y
43 Baca	Y	N	Y	Y
44 **Calvert**	Y	N	Y	Y
45 **Bono Mack**	Y	Y	Y	Y
46 **Rohrabacher**	Y	N	Y	N
47 Sanchez, Loretta	Y	Y	Y	Y
48 **Campbell**	Y	N	Y	N
49 **Issa**	Y	N	Y	Y
50 **Bilbray**	Y	Y	Y	Y
51 Filner	Y	Y	Y	Y
52 **Hunter**	Y	N	Y	Y
53 Davis	Y	Y	Y	Y

	541	542	543	544
COLORADO				
1 DeGette	Y	Y	Y	Y
2 Udall	Y	Y	Y	Y
3 Salazar	Y	Y	Y	Y
4 **Musgrave**	Y	N	Y	Y
5 **Lamborn**	Y	N	Y	N
6 **Tancredo**	Y	N	Y	N
7 Perlmutter	Y	Y	Y	Y
CONNECTICUT				
1 Larson	Y	Y	Y	Y
2 Courtney	Y	Y	Y	Y
3 DeLauro	Y	Y	Y	Y
4 **Shays**	Y	Y	Y	Y
5 Murphy	Y	Y	Y	Y
DELAWARE				
AL **Castle**	Y	Y	Y	Y
FLORIDA				
1 **Miller**	Y	N	Y	N
2 Boyd	Y	Y	Y	Y
3 Brown	Y	Y	Y	Y
4 **Crenshaw**	Y	Y	Y	Y
5 **Brown-Waite**	?	?	?	?
6 **Stearns**	Y	N	Y	Y
7 **Mica**	Y	N	Y	Y
8 **Keller**	Y	N	Y	Y
9 **Bilirakis**	Y	Y	Y	Y
10 **Young**	Y	Y	Y	Y
11 Castor	Y	Y	Y	Y
12 **Putnam**	Y	Y	Y	Y
13 **Buchanan**	Y	Y	Y	Y
14 **Mack**	Y	N	Y	N
15 **Weldon**	Y	N	Y	N
16 Mahoney	Y	Y	Y	Y
17 Meek	Y	Y	Y	Y
18 **Ros-Lehtinen**	Y	Y	Y	Y
19 Wexler	Y	Y	Y	Y
20 Wasserman Schultz	Y	Y	Y	Y
21 **Diaz-Balart, L.**	Y	N	Y	Y
22 Klein	Y	Y	Y	Y
23 Hastings	Y	Y	Y	Y
24 **Feeney**	Y	N	Y	Y
25 **Diaz-Balart, M.**	Y	N	Y	Y
GEORGIA				
1 **Kingston**	Y	N	Y	N
2 Bishop	Y	Y	Y	Y
3 **Westmoreland**	Y	N	Y	N
4 Johnson	?	Y	Y	Y
5 Lewis	Y	Y	Y	Y
6 **Price**	Y	N	Y	N
7 **Linder**	Y	Y	Y	N
8 Marshall	Y	Y	Y	Y
9 **Deal**	Y	N	Y	N
10 **Broun**	Y	N	?	N
11 **Gingrey**	Y	N	Y	N
12 Barrow	?	Y	Y	Y
13 Scott	Y	Y	Y	Y
HAWAII				
1 Abercrombie	Y	Y	Y	Y
2 Hirono	Y	Y	Y	Y
IDAHO				
1 **Sali**	Y	N	Y	N
2 **Simpson**	Y	Y	Y	Y
ILLINOIS				
1 Rush	?	Y	Y	Y
2 Jackson	Y	Y	Y	Y
3 Lipinski	Y	Y	Y	?
4 Gutierrez	Y	Y	Y	Y
5 Emanuel	Y	Y	Y	Y
6 **Roskam**	Y	Y	Y	Y
7 Davis	Y	Y	Y	Y
8 Bean	Y	Y	Y	Y
9 Schakowsky	Y	Y	Y	Y
10 **Kirk**	Y	Y	Y	Y
11 **Weller**	Y	Y	Y	Y
12 Costello	Y	Y	Y	Y
13 **Biggert**	Y	Y	Y	Y
14 Foster	Y	Y	Y	Y
15 **Johnson**	Y	Y	Y	Y

KEY	Republicans		Democrats			
Y	Voted for (yea)		X	Paired against	C	Voted "present" to avoid possible conflict of interest
#	Paired for		–	Announced against		
+	Announced for		P	Voted "present"	?	Did not vote or otherwise make a position known
N	Voted against (nay)					

ND Northern Democrats, SD Southern Democrats
Southern states: Ala., Ark., Fla., Ga., Ky., La., Miss., N.C., Okla., S.C., Tenn., Texas, Va.

	541	542	543	544
16 Manzullo	Y	Y	Y	Y
17 Hare	Y	Y	Y	Y
18 LaHood	Y	Y	Y	Y
19 Shimkus	Y	Y	Y	Y
INDIANA				
1 Visclosky	Y	Y	Y	Y
2 Donnelly	Y	N	Y	Y
3 Souder	Y	N	Y	Y
4 Buyer	Y	N	?	Y
5 Burton	Y	Y	Y	N
6 Pence	?	N	Y	N
7 Carson, A.	Y	Y	Y	Y
8 Ellsworth	Y	Y	Y	Y
9 Hill	Y	Y	Y	Y
IOWA				
1 Braley	Y	Y	Y	Y
2 Loebsack	Y	Y	Y	Y
3 Boswell	Y	Y	Y	Y
4 Latham	Y	N	Y	Y
5 King	Y	N	Y	N
KANSAS				
1 Moran	Y	Y	Y	N
2 Boyda	Y	Y	Y	Y
3 Moore	Y	Y	Y	Y
4 Tiahrt	Y	Y	Y	Y
KENTUCKY				
1 Whitfield	Y	N	Y	Y
2 Lewis	Y	N	Y	Y
3 Yarmuth	Y	Y	Y	Y
4 Davis	Y	N	Y	Y
5 Rogers	Y	N	Y	Y
6 Chandler	Y	Y	Y	Y
LOUISIANA				
1 Scalise	Y	N	Y	Y
2 Jefferson	Y	Y	Y	Y
3 Melancon	Y	Y	Y	Y
4 McCrery	Y	N	Y	Y
5 Alexander	Y	Y	Y	Y
6 Cazayoux	Y	Y	Y	Y
7 Boustany	Y	N	Y	Y
MAINE				
1 Allen	Y	Y	Y	Y
2 Michaud	Y	Y	Y	Y
MARYLAND				
1 Gilchrest	Y	Y	Y	Y
2 Ruppersberger	Y	Y	Y	Y
3 Sarbanes	Y	Y	Y	Y
4 Edwards	Y	Y	Y	Y
5 Hoyer	Y	Y	Y	Y
6 Bartlett	Y	Y	Y	N
7 Cummings	Y	Y	Y	Y
8 Van Hollen	Y	Y	Y	Y
MASSACHUSETTS				
1 Olver	Y	Y	Y	Y
2 Neal	Y	Y	Y	Y
3 McGovern	Y	Y	Y	Y
4 Frank	Y	Y	Y	Y
5 Tsongas	Y	Y	Y	Y
6 Tierney	Y	Y	Y	Y
7 Markey	Y	Y	Y	Y
8 Capuano	Y	Y	Y	Y
9 Lynch	Y	Y	Y	Y
10 Delahunt	Y	Y	Y	Y
MICHIGAN				
1 Stupak	Y	Y	Y	Y
2 Hoekstra	Y	Y	Y	N
3 Ehlers	Y	Y	Y	Y
4 Camp	Y	Y	Y	Y
5 Kildee	Y	Y	Y	Y
6 Upton	Y	Y	Y	Y
7 Walberg	Y	N	Y	Y
8 Rogers	Y	Y	Y	Y
9 Knollenberg	Y	Y	Y	Y
10 Miller	Y	Y	Y	Y
11 McCotter	Y	N	Y	Y
12 Levin	Y	Y	Y	Y
13 Kilpatrick	Y	Y	Y	Y
14 Conyers	Y	Y	?	Y
15 Dingell	Y	Y	Y	Y
MINNESOTA				
1 Walz	Y	Y	Y	Y
2 Kline	Y	N	Y	Y
3 Ramstad	Y	Y	Y	Y
4 McCollum	Y	Y	Y	Y

	541	542	543	544
5 Ellison	Y	Y	Y	Y
6 Bachmann	Y	N	Y	Y
7 Peterson	Y	Y	Y	Y
8 Oberstar	Y	Y	Y	Y
MISSISSIPPI				
1 Childers	Y	Y	Y	Y
2 Thompson	Y	Y	Y	Y
3 Pickering	Y	Y	Y	Y
4 Taylor	Y	Y	Y	Y
MISSOURI				
1 Clay	Y	Y	Y	Y
2 Akin	Y	N	Y	N
3 Carnahan	Y	Y	Y	Y
4 Skelton	Y	Y	Y	Y
5 Cleaver	Y	Y	Y	Y
6 Graves	Y	Y	Y	Y
7 Blunt	Y	?	Y	N
8 Emerson	Y	Y	Y	Y
9 Hulshof	?	?	?	?
MONTANA				
AL Rehberg	Y	Y	Y	Y
NEBRASKA				
1 Fortenberry	Y	Y	Y	Y
2 Terry	Y	Y	Y	Y
3 Smith	Y	N	Y	Y
NEVADA				
1 Berkley	Y	Y	Y	Y
2 Heller	Y	N	Y	Y
3 Porter	Y	Y	Y	Y
NEW HAMPSHIRE				
1 Shea-Porter	Y	Y	Y	Y
2 Hodes	Y	Y	Y	Y
NEW JERSEY				
1 Andrews	Y	Y	Y	Y
2 LoBiondo	Y	Y	Y	Y
3 Saxton	Y	Y	Y	Y
4 Smith	Y	Y	Y	Y
5 Garrett	Y	N	Y	N
6 Pallone	Y	Y	Y	Y
7 Ferguson	Y	Y	Y	Y
8 Pascrell	Y	Y	Y	Y
9 Rothman	Y	Y	Y	Y
10 Payne	?	Y	Y	Y
11 Frelinghuysen	Y	Y	Y	Y
12 Holt	Y	Y	Y	Y
13 Sires	Y	Y	Y	Y
NEW MEXICO				
1 Wilson	Y	Y	Y	Y
2 Pearce	Y	N	Y	Y
3 Udall	Y	Y	Y	Y
NEW YORK				
1 Bishop	Y	Y	Y	Y
2 Israel	Y	Y	Y	Y
3 King	Y	Y	Y	Y
4 McCarthy	Y	Y	Y	Y
5 Ackerman	Y	Y	Y	Y
6 Meeks	Y	Y	Y	Y
7 Crowley	Y	Y	Y	Y
8 Nadler	Y	Y	Y	Y
9 Weiner	Y	Y	Y	Y
10 Towns	Y	Y	Y	Y
11 Clarke	Y	Y	Y	Y
12 Velázquez	Y	Y	Y	Y
13 Fossella	Y	Y	Y	Y
14 Maloney	Y	?	?	Y
15 Rangel	Y	?	?	Y
16 Serrano	Y	Y	Y	Y
17 Engel	Y	Y	Y	Y
18 Lowey	Y	Y	Y	Y
19 Hall	Y	Y	Y	Y
20 Gillibrand	Y	Y	Y	Y
21 McNulty	Y	Y	Y	Y
22 Hinchey	Y	Y	Y	Y
23 McHugh	Y	Y	Y	Y
24 Arcuri	Y	Y	Y	Y
25 Walsh	Y	Y	Y	Y
26 Reynolds	Y	N	Y	Y
27 Higgins	Y	Y	Y	Y
28 Slaughter	Y	Y	Y	Y
29 Kuhl	Y	Y	Y	Y
NORTH CAROLINA				
1 Butterfield	Y	Y	Y	Y
2 Etheridge	Y	Y	Y	Y
3 Jones	Y	N	Y	Y
4 Price	Y	Y	Y	Y

	541	542	543	544
5 Foxx	Y	N	Y	N
6 Coble	Y	N	Y	Y
7 McIntyre	Y	Y	Y	Y
8 Hayes	Y	N	Y	Y
9 Myrick	Y	N	Y	Y
10 McHenry	Y	N	Y	N
11 Shuler	Y	N	Y	Y
12 Watt	Y	Y	Y	Y
13 Miller	Y	Y	Y	Y
NORTH DAKOTA				
AL Pomeroy	Y	Y	Y	Y
OHIO				
1 Chabot	Y	Y	Y	Y
2 Schmidt	Y	N	Y	Y
3 Turner	Y	Y	Y	Y
4 Jordan	Y	N	Y	N
5 Latta	Y	N	Y	Y
6 Wilson	Y	Y	Y	Y
7 Hobson	Y	Y	Y	Y
8 Boehner	Y	N	Y	N
9 Kaptur	Y	Y	Y	Y
10 Kucinich	Y	Y	Y	Y
11 Tubbs Jones	Y	Y	Y	Y
12 Tiberi	Y	Y	Y	Y
13 Sutton	Y	Y	Y	Y
14 LaTourette	Y	Y	Y	Y
15 Pryce	Y	Y	Y	Y
16 Regula	Y	Y	Y	Y
17 Ryan	Y	Y	Y	Y
18 Space	Y	Y	Y	Y
OKLAHOMA				
1 Sullivan	Y	N	Y	Y
2 Boren	Y	Y	Y	Y
3 Lucas	Y	N	Y	Y
4 Cole	Y	N	Y	Y
5 Fallin	Y	Y	Y	Y
OREGON				
1 Wu	Y	Y	Y	Y
2 Walden	Y	Y	Y	Y
3 Blumenauer	Y	Y	Y	Y
4 DeFazio	Y	Y	Y	Y
5 Hooley	Y	Y	Y	Y
PENNSYLVANIA				
1 Brady	Y	Y	Y	Y
2 Fattah	Y	Y	Y	Y
3 English	Y	Y	Y	Y
4 Altmire	Y	Y	Y	Y
5 Peterson	Y	Y	Y	Y
6 Gerlach	Y	Y	Y	Y
7 Sestak	Y	Y	Y	Y
8 Murphy, P.	Y	Y	Y	Y
9 Shuster	Y	Y	Y	Y
10 Carney	Y	Y	Y	Y
11 Kanjorski	Y	Y	Y	Y
12 Murtha	Y	Y	Y	Y
13 Schwartz	Y	Y	Y	Y
14 Doyle	Y	Y	Y	Y
15 Dent	Y	Y	Y	Y
16 Pitts	Y	N	Y	Y
17 Holden	Y	Y	Y	Y
18 Murphy, T.	Y	Y	Y	Y
19 Platts	Y	Y	Y	Y
RHODE ISLAND				
1 Kennedy	Y	Y	Y	Y
2 Langevin	Y	Y	Y	Y
SOUTH CAROLINA				
1 Brown	Y	Y	Y	Y
2 Wilson	Y	N	Y	Y
3 Barrett	Y	N	Y	N
4 Inglis	Y	N	Y	Y
5 Spratt	Y	Y	Y	Y
6 Clyburn	Y	Y	Y	Y
SOUTH DAKOTA				
AL Herseth Sandlin	Y	Y	Y	Y
TENNESSEE				
1 Davis, D.	Y	N	Y	Y
2 Duncan	Y	Y	Y	N
3 Wamp	Y	Y	Y	Y
4 Davis, L.	Y	N	Y	Y
5 Cooper	Y	Y	Y	Y
6 Gordon	Y	Y	Y	Y
7 Blackburn	Y	N	Y	N
8 Tanner	Y	Y	Y	Y
9 Cohen	Y	Y	Y	Y

	541	542	543	544
TEXAS				
1 Gohmert	Y	N	Y	Y
2 Poe	Y	N	Y	N
3 Johnson, S.	Y	Y	Y	N
4 Hall	Y	Y	Y	Y
5 Hensarling	Y	N	Y	N
6 Barton	Y	N	Y	Y
7 Culberson	Y	N	Y	Y
8 Brady	Y	Y	Y	N
9 Green, A.	Y	Y	Y	Y
10 McCaul	Y	Y	Y	Y
11 Conaway	Y	N	Y	Y
12 Granger	Y	Y	Y	Y
13 Thornberry	Y	N	Y	Y
14 Paul	Y	N	N	N
15 Hinojosa	Y	Y	Y	Y
16 Reyes	Y	Y	Y	Y
17 Edwards	Y	Y	Y	Y
18 Jackson Lee	Y	Y	Y	Y
19 Neugebauer	Y	N	Y	Y
20 Gonzalez	Y	Y	Y	Y
21 Smith	?	Y	Y	Y
22 Lampson	Y	Y	Y	Y
23 Rodriguez	Y	Y	Y	Y
24 Marchant	Y	N	Y	Y
25 Doggett	Y	Y	Y	Y
26 Burgess	Y	N	Y	N
27 Ortiz	Y	Y	Y	Y
28 Cuellar	Y	Y	Y	Y
29 Green, G.	Y	Y	Y	Y
30 Johnson, E.	Y	Y	Y	Y
31 Carter	Y	N	Y	Y
32 Sessions	Y	N	Y	Y
UTAH				
1 Bishop	Y	N	Y	N
2 Matheson	Y	Y	Y	Y
3 Cannon	Y	N	Y	N
VERMONT				
AL Welch	Y	Y	Y	Y
VIRGINIA				
1 Wittman	Y	Y	Y	Y
2 Drake	Y	Y	Y	Y
3 Scott	Y	Y	Y	Y
4 Forbes	Y	N	Y	Y
5 Goode	Y	N	Y	Y
6 Goodlatte	Y	N	Y	Y
7 Cantor	Y	Y	Y	N
8 Moran	Y	Y	Y	Y
9 Boucher	Y	Y	Y	Y
10 Wolf	Y	Y	Y	Y
11 Davis	Y	Y	Y	Y
WASHINGTON				
1 Inslee	Y	Y	Y	Y
2 Larsen	Y	Y	Y	Y
3 Baird	Y	Y	Y	Y
4 Hastings	Y	Y	Y	Y
5 McMorris Rodgers	Y	Y	Y	Y
6 Dicks	Y	Y	?	Y
7 McDermott	Y	Y	Y	Y
8 Reichert	Y	Y	Y	Y
9 Smith	Y	Y	Y	Y
WEST VIRGINIA				
1 Mollohan	Y	Y	Y	Y
2 Capito	?	Y	Y	Y
3 Rahall	Y	Y	Y	Y
WISCONSIN				
1 Ryan	Y	N	Y	N
2 Baldwin	Y	Y	Y	Y
3 Kind	Y	Y	Y	Y
4 Moore	Y	Y	Y	Y
5 Sensenbrenner	Y	N	Y	N
6 Petri	Y	Y	Y	Y
7 Obey	Y	Y	Y	Y
8 Kagen	Y	Y	Y	Y
WYOMING				
AL Cubin	?	?	?	?
DELEGATES				
Faleomavaega (A.S.)				
Norton (D.C.)				
Bordallo (Guam)				
Fortuño (P.R.)				
Christensen (V.I.)				

IN THE HOUSE | By Vote Number

545. **Procedural Motion/Journal.** Approval of the House Journal of Wednesday, July 30, 2008. Approved 223-203: R 0-194; D 223-9 (ND 167-7, SD 56-2). July 31, 2008.

546. **H Res 1396. Censure of Rep. Charles B. Rangel/Motion to Table.** Hastings, D-Fla., motion to table (kill) the Boehner, R-Ohio, privileged resolution that would censure Rep. Charles B. Rangel, D-N.Y., for violating clause 5 of Rule XXV of the House in the renting of three rent-stabilized Manhattan apartments and one rent-stabilized apartment used for a campaign office. Motion agreed to 254-138: R 25-138; D 229-0 (ND 171-0, SD 58-0). July 31, 2008.

547. **HR 1338. Paycheck Equality/Previous Question.** Slaughter, D-N.Y., motion to order the previous question (thus ending debate and possibility of amendment) on adoption of the rule (H Res 1388) to provide for House floor consideration of the bill that would make it easier for women who are paid less than their male counterparts to bring suits against their employers and receive compensation. Motion agreed to 232-191: R 5-187; D 227-4 (ND 171-2, SD 56-2). July 31, 2008.

548. **HR 1338. Paycheck Equality/Rule.** Adoption of the rule (H Res 1388) that would provide for House floor consideration of the bill that would make it easier for women who are paid less than their male counterparts to bring suits against their employers and receive compensation. Adopted 229-194: R 0-193; D 229-1 (ND 173-1, SD 56-0). July 31, 2008.

549. **HR 6599. Fiscal 2009 Military Construction-VA Appropriations/Previous Question.** Castor, D-Fla., motion to order the previous question (thus ending debate and possibility of amendment) on adoption of the rule (H Res 1384) to provide for House floor consideration of the bill that would provide $118.7 billion in fiscal 2009 for the Department of Veterans Affairs, military construction and military housing. Motion agreed to 243-181: R 11-181; D 232-0 (ND 173-0, SD 59-0). July 31, 2008.

550. **HR 6599. Fiscal 2009 Military Construction-VA Appropriations/Rule.** Adoption of the rule (H Res 1384) to provide for House floor consideration of the bill that would provide $118.7 billion in fiscal 2009 for the Department of Veterans Affairs, military construction and military housing. Adopted 230-186: R 4-186; D 226-0 (ND 169-0, SD 57-0). July 31, 2008.

	545	546	547	548	549	550
ALABAMA						
1 Bonner	N	P	N	N	N	N
2 Everett	N	N	N	N	N	N
3 Rogers	N	P	N	N	N	N
4 Aderholt	N	P	N	N	N	N
5 Cramer	Y	Y	Y	Y	Y	?
6 Bachus	N	P	N	N	N	N
7 Davis	Y	Y	Y	Y	Y	Y
ALASKA						
AL Young	?	?	?	?	?	?
ARIZONA						
1 Renzi	N	Y	N	N	N	N
2 Franks	N	N	N	N	N	N
3 Shadegg	N	N	N	N	N	N
4 Pastor	Y	Y	Y	Y	Y	Y
5 Mitchell	N	Y	Y	Y	Y	Y
6 Flake	N	Y	N	N	N	N
7 Grijalva	Y	Y	Y	Y	Y	Y
8 Giffords	Y	Y	Y	Y	Y	Y
ARKANSAS						
1 Berry	Y	Y	Y	Y	Y	Y
2 Snyder	Y	Y	Y	Y	Y	Y
3 Boozman	N	N	N	N	N	N
4 Ross	Y	Y	Y	Y	Y	Y
CALIFORNIA						
1 Thompson	N	Y	Y	Y	Y	Y
2 Herger	N	Y	N	N	N	N
3 Lungren	N	N	N	N	N	N
4 Doolittle	N	N	N	N	N	N
5 Matsui	Y	Y	Y	Y	Y	Y
6 Woolsey	Y	Y	Y	Y	Y	Y
7 Miller, George	Y	Y	Y	Y	Y	Y
8 Pelosi		Y				
9 Lee	Y	Y	Y	Y	Y	Y
10 Tauscher	Y	Y	Y	Y	Y	Y
11 McNerney	Y	Y	Y	Y	Y	Y
12 Speier	Y	Y	Y	Y	Y	?
13 Stark	Y	Y	Y	Y	Y	Y
14 Eshoo	Y	Y	Y	Y	Y	Y
15 Honda	?	Y	Y	Y	Y	Y
16 Lofgren	Y	Y	Y	Y	Y	Y
17 Farr	Y	Y	Y	Y	Y	Y
18 Cardoza	Y	Y	Y	Y	Y	Y
19 Radanovich	N	N	N	N	N	N
20 Costa	Y	Y	Y	Y	Y	Y
21 Nunes	N	N	N	N	N	N
22 McCarthy	N	N	N	N	N	N
23 Capps	Y	Y	Y	Y	Y	Y
24 Gallegly	N	N	N	N	N	N
25 McKeon	N	N	N	N	N	N
26 Dreier	N	N	N	N	N	N
27 Sherman	Y	Y	Y	Y	Y	Y
28 Berman	Y	Y	Y	Y	Y	Y
29 Schiff	Y	Y	Y	Y	Y	Y
30 Waxman	Y	Y	Y	Y	Y	Y
31 Becerra	Y	Y	Y	Y	Y	Y
32 Solis	Y	Y	Y	Y	Y	Y
33 Watson	Y	Y	Y	Y	Y	Y
34 Roybal-Allard	Y	P	Y	Y	Y	Y
35 Waters	Y	Y	Y	Y	Y	Y
36 Harman	Y	Y	Y	Y	Y	Y
37 Richardson	Y	Y	Y	Y	Y	Y
38 Napolitano	Y	Y	Y	Y	Y	Y
39 Sánchez, Linda	Y	Y	Y	Y	Y	Y
40 Royce	N	N	N	N	N	?
41 Lewis	N	?	N	N	N	N
42 Miller, Gary	N	Y	N	N	N	N
43 Baca	Y	Y	Y	Y	Y	Y
44 Calvert	N	N	N	N	N	N
45 Bono Mack	N	N	N	N	N	N
46 Rohrabacher	N	Y	N	N	N	N
47 Sanchez, Loretta	Y	Y	Y	Y	Y	Y
48 Campbell	N	N	N	N	N	N
49 Issa	N	N	N	N	N	N
50 Bilbray	N	N	N	N	N	N
51 Filner	Y	Y	Y	Y	Y	Y
52 Hunter	N	P	N	N	N	N
53 Davis	Y	Y	Y	Y	Y	Y

	545	546	547	548	549	550
COLORADO						
1 DeGette	Y	Y	Y	Y	Y	Y
2 Udall	Y	Y	Y	Y	Y	Y
3 Salazar	Y	Y	Y	Y	Y	Y
4 Musgrave	N	N	N	N	N	N
5 Lamborn	N	N	N	N	N	N
6 Tancredo	N	N	N	N	N	N
7 Perlmutter	Y	Y	Y	Y	Y	Y
CONNECTICUT						
1 Larson	Y	Y	Y	Y	Y	Y
2 Courtney	Y	Y	Y	Y	Y	Y
3 DeLauro	Y	Y	Y	Y	Y	Y
4 Shays	N	N	N	N	Y	Y
5 Murphy	Y	Y	Y	Y	Y	Y
DELAWARE						
AL Castle	N	Y	N	N	Y	Y
FLORIDA						
1 Miller	N	N	N	N	N	N
2 Boyd	Y	Y	Y	Y	Y	Y
3 Brown	Y	Y	Y	Y	Y	Y
4 Crenshaw	N	N	N	N	N	N
5 Brown-Waite	?	?	?	?	?	?
6 Stearns	N	N	N	N	N	N
7 Mica	N	N	N	N	N	N
8 Keller	N	N	N	N	N	N
9 Bilirakis	N	N	N	N	N	N
10 Young	N	P	N	N	N	Y
11 Castor	Y	Y	Y	Y	Y	Y
12 Putnam	N	N	N	N	N	N
13 Buchanan	N	Y	N	N	N	N
14 Mack	N	N	N	N	N	N
15 Weldon	N	P	?	N	N	?
16 Mahoney	Y	Y	Y	Y	Y	Y
17 Meek	Y	Y	Y	Y	Y	Y
18 Ros-Lehtinen	N	Y	N	Y	N	Y
19 Wexler	Y	Y	Y	Y	Y	Y
20 Wasserman Schultz	Y	Y	Y	Y	Y	Y
21 Diaz-Balart, L.	N	N	N	N	N	N
22 Klein	Y	Y	Y	Y	Y	Y
23 Hastings	Y	Y	Y	Y	Y	Y
24 Feeney	N	N	N	N	N	N
25 Diaz-Balart, M.	N	N	N	N	N	N
GEORGIA						
1 Kingston	N	N	N	N	N	N
2 Bishop	Y	Y	Y	Y	Y	Y
3 Westmoreland	N	N	N	N	N	N
4 Johnson	Y	Y	Y	Y	Y	Y
5 Lewis	Y	Y	Y	Y	Y	Y
6 Price	N	N	N	N	N	N
7 Linder	N	N	N	N	N	N
8 Marshall	Y	Y	Y	Y	Y	Y
9 Deal	N	N	N	N	N	N
10 Broun	N	N	N	N	N	N
11 Gingrey	N	N	N	N	N	N
12 Barrow	Y	Y	Y	Y	Y	Y
13 Scott	Y	Y	Y	Y	Y	Y
HAWAII						
1 Abercrombie	Y	Y	Y	Y	Y	Y
2 Hirono	Y	Y	Y	Y	Y	Y
IDAHO						
1 Sali	N	N	N	N	N	N
2 Simpson	N	N	N	N	N	N
ILLINOIS						
1 Rush	Y	Y	?	?	?	?
2 Jackson	Y	Y	Y	Y	Y	Y
3 Lipinski	?	?	?	?	?	?
4 Gutierrez	Y	Y	Y	Y	Y	Y
5 Emanuel	Y	Y	Y	Y	Y	Y
6 Roskam	N	N	N	N	N	N
7 Davis	Y	Y	Y	Y	Y	Y
8 Bean	Y	Y	Y	Y	Y	Y
9 Schakowsky	Y	Y	Y	Y	Y	Y
10 Kirk	N	N	N	N	Y	N
11 Weller	N	P	N	N	N	N
12 Costello	Y	Y	Y	Y	Y	Y
13 Biggert	N	N	N	N	N	N
14 Foster	Y	Y	Y	Y	Y	Y
15 Johnson	N	N	N	N	?	N

KEY	**Republicans**	Democrats	
Y Voted for (yea)	X Paired against	C Voted "present" to avoid possible conflict of interest
# Paired for	– Announced against	
+ Announced for	P Voted "present"	? Did not vote or otherwise make a position known
N Voted against (nay)		

ND Northern Democrats, SD Southern Democrats
Southern states: Ala., Ark., Fla., Ga., Ky., La., Miss., N.C., Okla., S.C., Tenn., Texas, Va.

	545	546	547	548	549	550
16 **Manzullo**	N	N	N	N	N	N
17 Hare	Y	Y	Y	Y	Y	Y
18 **LaHood**	N	N	N	N	N	Y
19 **Shimkus**	N	N	N	N	N	N
INDIANA						
1 Visclosky	Y	Y	Y	Y	Y	Y
2 Donnelly	Y	Y	N	Y	Y	Y
3 **Souder**	N	N	N	N	N	N
4 **Buyer**	N	N	N	N	N	N
5 **Burton**	N	P	N	N	N	N
6 **Pence**	N	P	N	N	N	N
7 Carson, A.	Y	Y	Y	Y	Y	Y
8 Ellsworth	Y	Y	Y	Y	Y	Y
9 Hill	Y	Y	N	N	Y	Y
IOWA						
1 Braley	Y	Y	Y	Y	Y	Y
2 Loebsack	Y	Y	Y	Y	Y	Y
3 Boswell	Y	Y	Y	Y	Y	Y
4 **Latham**	N	N	N	N	N	N
5 **King**	N	N	N	N	N	N
KANSAS						
1 **Moran**	N	Y	N	N	N	N
2 Boyda	Y	Y	Y	Y	Y	Y
3 Moore	Y	Y	Y	Y	Y	Y
4 **Tiahrt**	N	N	N	N	N	N
KENTUCKY						
1 **Whitfield**	N	N	N	N	N	N
2 **Lewis**	N	P	N	N	N	?
3 Yarmuth	Y	Y	Y	Y	Y	Y
4 **Davis**	N	N	N	N	N	N
5 **Rogers**	N	P	N	N	N	N
6 Chandler	Y	Y	Y	Y	Y	Y
LOUISIANA						
1 **Scalise**	N	N	N	N	N	N
2 Jefferson	Y	Y	Y	Y	Y	Y
3 Melancon	Y	Y	Y	Y	Y	Y
4 **McCrery**	N	Y	N	N	N	N
5 **Alexander**	N	Y	N	N	N	N
6 Cazayoux	N	Y	Y	Y	Y	Y
7 **Boustany**	N	Y	N	N	N	N
MAINE						
1 Allen	Y	Y	Y	Y	Y	Y
2 Michaud	Y	Y	Y	Y	Y	Y
MARYLAND						
1 **Gilchrest**	N	Y	N	N	N	N
2 Ruppersberger	Y	Y	Y	Y	Y	Y
3 Sarbanes	Y	Y	Y	Y	Y	Y
4 Edwards	Y	Y	Y	Y	Y	Y
5 Hoyer	Y	Y	Y	Y	Y	Y
6 **Bartlett**	N	P	N	N	N	N
7 Cummings	Y	Y	Y	Y	Y	Y
8 Van Hollen	Y	Y	Y	Y	Y	Y
MASSACHUSETTS						
1 Olver	Y	Y	Y	Y	Y	Y
2 Neal	Y	Y	Y	Y	Y	Y
3 McGovern	Y	Y	Y	Y	Y	Y
4 Frank	Y	Y	Y	Y	Y	Y
5 Tsongas	Y	Y	Y	Y	Y	Y
6 Tierney	Y	Y	Y	Y	Y	Y
7 Markey	Y	Y	Y	Y	Y	Y
8 Capuano	Y	Y	Y	Y	Y	Y
9 Lynch	Y	Y	Y	Y	Y	Y
10 Delahunt	Y	P	Y	Y	Y	?
MICHIGAN						
1 Stupak	N	Y	Y	Y	Y	Y
2 **Hoekstra**	N	N	N	N	N	N
3 **Ehlers**	N	N	N	N	N	N
4 **Camp**	N	P	N	N	N	N
5 Kildee	Y	Y	Y	Y	Y	Y
6 **Upton**	N	N	N	N	N	N
7 **Walberg**	N	N	N	N	N	N
8 **Rogers**	N	N	N	N	N	N
9 **Knollenberg**	N	N	N	N	N	N
10 **Miller**	N	N	N	N	N	N
11 **McCotter**	N	N	N	N	N	N
12 Levin	Y	Y	Y	Y	Y	Y
13 Kilpatrick	Y	?	Y	Y	Y	Y
14 Conyers	Y	Y	Y	Y	Y	Y
15 Dingell	Y	Y	Y	Y	Y	Y
MINNESOTA						
1 Walz	Y	Y	Y	Y	Y	Y
2 **Kline**	N	P	N	N	N	N
3 **Ramstad**	N	Y	N	N	Y	Y
4 McCollum	Y	Y	Y	Y	Y	Y

	545	546	547	548	549	550
5 Ellison	Y	Y	Y	Y	Y	Y
6 **Bachmann**	N	N	N	N	N	N
7 Peterson	N	Y	Y	Y	Y	Y
8 Oberstar	Y	Y	Y	Y	Y	Y
MISSISSIPPI						
1 Childers	Y	Y	N	?	Y	Y
2 Thompson	Y	Y	Y	?	Y	Y
3 **Pickering**	N	Y	N	N	N	N
4 Taylor	Y	Y	Y	Y	Y	Y
MISSOURI						
1 Clay	Y	Y	Y	Y	Y	Y
2 **Akin**	N	P	N	N	N	N
3 Carnahan	Y	Y	Y	Y	Y	Y
4 Skelton	Y	Y	Y	Y	Y	Y
5 Cleaver	Y	Y	?	Y	Y	?
6 **Graves**	N	N	N	N	N	N
7 **Blunt**	N	N	N	N	N	N
8 **Emerson**	N	P	N	N	N	N
9 **Hulshof**	?	?	?	?	?	?
MONTANA						
AL **Rehberg**	N	N	N	N	N	N
NEBRASKA						
1 **Fortenberry**	N	P	N	N	N	N
2 **Terry**	N	N	N	N	N	N
3 **Smith**	N	N	N	N	N	N
NEVADA						
1 Berkley	Y	Y	Y	Y	Y	Y
2 **Heller**	N	N	N	N	N	N
3 **Porter**	N	Y	N	N	N	N
NEW HAMPSHIRE						
1 Shea-Porter	Y	Y	Y	Y	Y	Y
2 Hodes	Y	Y	Y	Y	Y	Y
NEW JERSEY						
1 Andrews	Y	Y	Y	Y	Y	Y
2 **LoBiondo**	N	N	Y	N	Y	N
3 **Saxton**	N	?	Y	N	Y	N
4 **Smith**	N	P	Y	N	Y	N
5 **Garrett**	N	N	N	N	N	N
6 Pallone	Y	Y	Y	Y	Y	Y
7 **Ferguson**	N	P	N	N	N	N
8 Pascrell	Y	Y	Y	Y	Y	Y
9 Rothman	Y	Y	Y	Y	Y	Y
10 Payne	Y	Y	Y	Y	Y	?
11 **Frelinghuysen**	N	N	N	N	N	N
12 Holt	Y	Y	Y	Y	Y	Y
13 Sires	Y	Y	Y	Y	Y	Y
NEW MEXICO						
1 **Wilson**	N	N	?	?	?	?
2 **Pearce**	N	N	N	N	N	N
3 Udall	Y	Y	Y	Y	Y	Y
NEW YORK						
1 Bishop	Y	Y	Y	Y	Y	Y
2 Israel	Y	Y	Y	Y	Y	Y
3 **King**	N	Y	N	N	N	N
4 McCarthy	Y	Y	Y	Y	Y	Y
5 Ackerman	Y	Y	Y	Y	Y	Y
6 Meeks	Y	Y	Y	Y	Y	Y
7 Crowley	Y	Y	Y	Y	Y	Y
8 Nadler	Y	Y	Y	Y	Y	Y
9 Weiner	Y	Y	Y	Y	Y	Y
10 Towns	Y	Y	Y	Y	Y	Y
11 Clarke	Y	Y	Y	Y	Y	Y
12 Velázquez	Y	Y	Y	Y	Y	Y
13 **Fossella**	N	Y	N	N	N	N
14 Maloney	Y	Y	Y	Y	Y	Y
15 Rangel	Y	Y	Y	Y	Y	Y
16 Serrano	Y	Y	Y	Y	Y	Y
17 Engel	Y	Y	Y	Y	Y	Y
18 Lowey	Y	Y	Y	Y	Y	Y
19 Hall	Y	Y	Y	Y	Y	Y
20 Gillibrand	Y	Y	Y	Y	Y	Y
21 McNulty	Y	Y	Y	Y	Y	Y
22 Hinchey	Y	Y	Y	Y	Y	Y
23 **McHugh**	N	N	N	N	N	N
24 Arcuri	Y	Y	Y	Y	Y	Y
25 **Walsh**	N	N	N	N	N	N
26 **Reynolds**	N	N	N	N	N	N
27 Higgins	Y	Y	Y	Y	Y	Y
28 Slaughter	Y	Y	Y	Y	Y	Y
29 **Kuhl**	N	N	N	N	N	N
NORTH CAROLINA						
1 Butterfield	Y	Y	Y	Y	Y	Y
2 Etheridge	Y	Y	Y	Y	Y	Y
3 **Jones**	N	Y	N	N	N	N
4 Price	Y	Y	Y	Y	Y	Y

	545	546	547	548	549	550
5 **Foxx**	N	N	N	N	N	N
6 **Coble**	N	N	N	N	N	N
7 McIntyre	Y	Y	Y	Y	Y	Y
8 **Hayes**	N	N	N	N	N	N
9 **Myrick**	N	N	N	N	N	N
10 **McHenry**	N	N	N	N	N	N
11 Shuler	Y	Y	Y	Y	Y	Y
12 Watt	Y	Y	Y	Y	Y	Y
13 Miller	Y	Y	Y	Y	Y	Y
NORTH DAKOTA						
AL Pomeroy	Y	Y	Y	Y	Y	Y
OHIO						
1 **Chabot**	N	N	N	N	N	N
2 **Schmidt**	N	N	N	N	N	N
3 **Turner**	N	N	N	N	N	N
4 **Jordan**	N	N	N	N	N	N
5 **Latta**	N	N	N	N	N	N
6 Wilson	Y	Y	Y	Y	?	Y
7 **Hobson**	N	N	N	N	N	N
8 **Boehner**	N	N	N	N	N	N
9 Kaptur	Y	Y	Y	Y	Y	Y
10 Kucinich	Y	Y	Y	Y	Y	Y
11 Tubbs Jones	Y	P	Y	Y	Y	Y
12 **Tiberi**	N	N	N	N	N	N
13 Sutton	Y	Y	Y	Y	Y	Y
14 **LaTourette**	N	N	N	N	N	N
15 **Pryce**	N	N	N	N	N	N
16 **Regula**	N	Y	N	N	N	N
17 Ryan	Y	Y	Y	Y	Y	Y
18 Space	Y	Y	Y	Y	Y	Y
OKLAHOMA						
1 **Sullivan**	N	N	N	N	N	N
2 Boren	Y	Y	Y	Y	Y	Y
3 **Lucas**	N	N	N	N	N	N
4 **Cole**	N	N	N	N	N	N
5 **Fallin**	N	N	N	N	N	N
OREGON						
1 Wu	Y	Y	Y	Y	Y	Y
2 **Walden**	N	N	N	N	N	N
3 Blumenauer	Y	Y	Y	Y	Y	Y
4 DeFazio	Y	Y	Y	Y	Y	Y
5 Hooley	Y	Y	Y	Y	Y	Y
PENNSYLVANIA						
1 Brady	Y	Y	Y	Y	Y	Y
2 Fattah	Y	Y	Y	Y	Y	Y
3 **English**	N	Y	N	N	N	N
4 Altmire	N	Y	Y	Y	Y	Y
5 **Peterson**	N	P	N	N	N	N
6 **Gerlach**	N	N	N	N	Y	N
7 Sestak	Y	Y	Y	Y	Y	Y
8 Murphy, P.	N	Y	Y	Y	Y	Y
9 **Shuster**	N	N	N	N	N	N
10 Carney	N	Y	Y	Y	Y	Y
11 Kanjorski	Y	Y	Y	Y	Y	Y
12 Murtha	Y	Y	Y	Y	Y	Y
13 Schwartz	Y	Y	Y	Y	Y	Y
14 Doyle	Y	P	Y	Y	Y	Y
15 **Dent**	N	N	N	N	N	N
16 **Pitts**	N	N	N	N	N	N
17 Holden	Y	Y	Y	Y	Y	Y
18 **Murphy, T.**	N	Y	N	N	N	N
19 **Platts**	N	N	N	N	N	N
RHODE ISLAND						
1 Kennedy	Y	Y	Y	Y	Y	Y
2 Langevin	Y	Y	Y	Y	Y	Y
SOUTH CAROLINA						
1 **Brown**	N	N	N	N	N	N
2 **Wilson**	N	N	N	N	N	N
3 **Barrett**	N	P	N	N	N	N
4 **Inglis**	N	N	N	N	N	N
5 Spratt	Y	Y	Y	Y	Y	Y
6 Clyburn	Y	Y	Y	Y	Y	Y
SOUTH DAKOTA						
AL Herseth Sandlin	Y	Y	Y	Y	Y	Y
TENNESSEE						
1 **Davis, D.**	N	N	N	N	N	N
2 **Duncan**	N	Y	N	N	N	N
3 **Wamp**	N	Y	N	N	N	N
4 Davis, L.	Y	Y	Y	Y	Y	Y
5 Cooper	Y	Y	Y	Y	Y	Y
6 Gordon	Y	Y	Y	Y	Y	Y
7 **Blackburn**	N	N	N	N	N	N
8 Tanner	Y	Y	Y	Y	Y	Y
9 Cohen	Y	Y	Y	Y	Y	Y

	545	546	547	548	549	550
TEXAS						
1 **Gohmert**	N	N	N	N	N	N
2 **Poe**	N	P	N	N	N	N
3 **Johnson, S.**	N	N	N	N	N	N
4 **Hall**	N	N	N	N	N	N
5 **Hensarling**	N	N	N	N	N	N
6 **Barton**	N	N	N	N	N	N
7 **Culberson**	N	N	N	N	N	N
8 **Brady**	N	N	N	N	N	N
9 Green, A.	Y	Y	Y	Y	Y	Y
10 **McCaul**	N	P	N	N	N	N
11 **Conaway**	N	N	N	N	N	N
12 **Granger**	N	N	N	N	N	N
13 **Thornberry**	N	N	N	N	N	N
14 **Paul**	N	Y	N	N	N	N
15 Hinojosa	Y	Y	Y	Y	Y	Y
16 Reyes	Y	Y	Y	Y	Y	Y
17 Edwards	?	Y	Y	?	Y	Y
18 Jackson Lee	Y	Y	Y	Y	Y	Y
19 **Neugebauer**	N	N	N	N	N	N
20 Gonzalez	Y	Y	Y	Y	Y	Y
21 **Smith**	?	N	N	N	N	N
22 Lampson	N	Y	N	Y	Y	Y
23 Rodriguez	Y	Y	Y	Y	Y	Y
24 **Marchant**	N	N	N	N	N	N
25 Doggett	Y	Y	Y	Y	Y	Y
26 **Burgess**	N	N	N	N	N	N
27 Ortiz	Y	Y	Y	Y	Y	Y
28 Cuellar	Y	Y	Y	Y	Y	Y
29 Green, G.	Y	P	Y	Y	Y	Y
30 Johnson, E.	Y	Y	?	Y	Y	Y
31 **Carter**	N	N	N	N	N	N
32 **Sessions**	N	N	N	N	N	N
UTAH						
1 **Bishop**	N	N	N	N	N	N
2 Matheson	Y	Y	Y	Y	Y	Y
3 **Cannon**	N	?	?	?	?	?
VERMONT						
AL Welch	Y	Y	Y	Y	Y	Y
VIRGINIA						
1 **Wittman**	N	P	N	N	N	N
2 **Drake**	N	N	N	N	N	N
3 Scott	Y	Y	Y	Y	Y	?
4 **Forbes**	N	P	N	N	N	N
5 **Goode**	N	N	N	N	N	N
6 **Goodlatte**	N	N	N	N	N	N
7 **Cantor**	N	N	N	N	N	N
8 Moran	Y	Y	Y	Y	Y	Y
9 Boucher	Y	Y	Y	Y	Y	Y
10 **Wolf**	N	P	N	N	N	N
11 **Davis**	N	P	N	N	N	N
WASHINGTON						
1 Inslee	Y	Y	Y	Y	Y	Y
2 Larsen	Y	Y	Y	Y	Y	Y
3 Baird	Y	Y	Y	Y	Y	Y
4 **Hastings**	N	P	N	N	N	N
5 **McMorris Rodgers**	N	N	N	N	N	N
6 Dicks	Y	Y	Y	Y	Y	Y
7 McDermott	Y	Y	Y	Y	Y	Y
8 **Reichert**	N	N	Y	N	Y	N
9 Smith	Y	Y	Y	Y	Y	Y
WEST VIRGINIA						
1 Mollohan	Y	Y	Y	Y	Y	Y
2 **Capito**	N	N	N	N	N	N
3 Rahall	Y	Y	Y	Y	Y	Y
WISCONSIN						
1 **Ryan**	N	Y	N	N	N	N
2 Baldwin	Y	Y	Y	Y	Y	Y
3 Kind	Y	Y	Y	Y	Y	Y
4 Moore	Y	Y	Y	Y	Y	?
5 **Sensenbrenner**	N	N	N	N	N	N
6 **Petri**	N	N	N	N	N	N
7 Obey	Y	Y	Y	Y	Y	Y
8 Kagen	Y	Y	Y	Y	Y	Y
WYOMING						
AL **Cubin**	?	?	?	?	?	?
DELEGATES						
Faleomavaega (A.S.)						
Norton (D.C.)						
Bordallo (Guam)						
Fortuño (P.R.)						
Christensen (V.I.)						

IN THE HOUSE | By Vote Number

551. HR 1338. Paycheck Equality/Labor Department Study. Price, R-Ga., amendment that would direct the Labor Department to report to Congress within 90 days on the effect of the bill's provisions related to employers' ability to recruit and hire employees regardless of gender. Enactment of the provisions would be delayed pending the department's report. If the agency finds that the provisions are likely to significantly hinder an employer's ability to hire and recruit regardless of gender, they would not go into effect. Rejected in Committee of the Whole 188-240: R 188-2; D 0-238 (ND 0-179, SD 0-59). July 31, 2008.

552. HR 1338. Paycheck Equality/Small Businesses. Altmire, D-Pa., amendment that would delay the bill's effective date by six months from enactment and require the Labor Department to educate small businesses about the bill's requirements and assist them with compliance. Adopted in Committee of the Whole 426-1: R 191-0; D 235-1 (ND 177-0, SD 58-1). July 31, 2008.

553. HR 1338. Paycheck Equality/Intent for Punitive Damages. Giffords, D-Ariz., amendment that would clarify that a plaintiff would be required to show intent (malice or reckless indifference) to recover punitive damages. Adopted in Committee of the Whole 397-29: R 190-0; D 207-29 (ND 154-24, SD 53-5). July 31, 2008.

554. HR 1338. Paycheck Equality/Immigration Compliance. Cazayoux, D-La., amendment that would clarify that nothing in the bill would affect the obligation of employers and employees to comply with applicable immigration laws. Adopted in Committee of the Whole 410-16: R 191-0; D 219-16 (ND 163-15, SD 56-1). July 31, 2008.

555. HR 1338. Paycheck Equality/Recommit. Price, R-Ga., motion to recommit the bill to the Education and Labor Committee with instructions that it be reported back promptly with language that would add a finding stating that gas prices are high and Congress has not enacted measures to lower the price. The language also would cap attorney fees at $1,000 per hour. Motion rejected 189-236: R 188-4; D 1-232 (ND 0-174, SD 1-58). July 31, 2008.

556. HR 1338. Paycheck Equality/Passage. Passage of the bill that would make it easier for women who are paid less than their male counterparts to bring suits against their employers. Employers seeking to justify unequal pay would have to prove that disparities are job-related and required by a business necessity. Workers who won wage discrimination cases could collect compensatory and punitive damages. As amended, it would specify that punitive damages could only be awarded to plaintiffs who prove intentional discrimination. Passed 247-178: R 14-178; D 233-0 (ND 174-0, SD 59-0). A "nay" was a vote in support of the president's position. July 31, 2008.

ND Northern Democrats, SD Southern Democrats
Southern states: Ala., Ark., Fla., Ga., Ky., La., Miss., N.C., Okla., S.C., Tenn., Texas, Va.

	551	552	553	554	555	556
ALABAMA						
1 **Bonner**	Y	Y	Y	Y	Y	N
2 **Everett**	Y	Y	Y	Y	Y	N
3 **Rogers**	Y	Y	Y	Y	Y	N
4 **Aderholt**	Y	Y	Y	Y	Y	N
5 Cramer	N	Y	Y	Y	N	Y
6 **Bachus**	Y	Y	Y	Y	Y	N
7 Davis	N	Y	Y	Y	N	Y
ALASKA						
AL **Young**	?	?	?	?	?	?
ARIZONA						
1 **Renzi**	Y	Y	Y	Y	Y	N
2 **Franks**	Y	Y	Y	Y	Y	N
3 **Shadegg**	Y	Y	Y	Y	Y	N
4 Pastor	N	Y	N	Y	N	Y
5 Mitchell	N	Y	Y	Y	N	Y
6 **Flake**	Y	Y	Y	Y	Y	N
7 Grijalva	N	Y	N	N	N	Y
8 Giffords	N	Y	Y	Y	N	Y
ARKANSAS						
1 Berry	N	Y	Y	Y	N	Y
2 Snyder	N	Y	Y	Y	N	Y
3 **Boozman**	Y	Y	Y	Y	Y	N
4 Ross	N	Y	Y	Y	N	Y
CALIFORNIA						
1 Thompson	N	Y	Y	Y	N	Y
2 **Herger**	Y	Y	Y	Y	Y	N
3 **Lungren**	Y	Y	Y	Y	Y	N
4 **Doolittle**	Y	Y	Y	Y	N	N
5 Matsui	N	Y	Y	Y	N	Y
6 Woolsey	N	Y	Y	Y	N	Y
7 Miller, George	N	Y	Y	Y	N	Y
8 Pelosi						
9 Lee	N	Y	N	N	N	Y
10 Tauscher	N	Y	Y	Y	N	Y
11 McNerney	N	Y	Y	Y	N	Y
12 Speier	N	Y	Y	Y	N	Y
13 Stark	N	Y	N	N	N	Y
14 Eshoo	N	Y	Y	Y	N	Y
15 Honda	N	Y	N	N	N	Y
16 Lofgren	N	Y	Y	Y	N	Y
17 Farr	N	Y	Y	Y	N	Y
18 Cardoza	N	Y	Y	Y	N	Y
19 **Radanovich**	Y	Y	Y	Y	Y	N
20 Costa	N	Y	Y	Y	N	Y
21 **Nunes**	Y	Y	Y	Y	Y	N
22 **McCarthy**	Y	Y	Y	Y	Y	N
23 Capps	N	Y	Y	Y	N	Y
24 **Gallegly**	Y	Y	Y	Y	Y	N
25 **McKeon**	Y	Y	Y	Y	Y	N
26 **Dreier**	Y	Y	Y	Y	Y	N
27 Sherman	N	Y	Y	Y	N	Y
28 Berman	N	Y	Y	Y	N	Y
29 Schiff	N	Y	Y	Y	N	Y
30 Waxman	N	Y	Y	Y	N	Y
31 Becerra	N	Y	Y	Y	N	Y
32 Solis	N	Y	N	N	N	Y
33 Watson	N	Y	Y	Y	N	Y
34 Roybal-Allard	N	Y	Y	Y	N	Y
35 Waters	N	Y	N	N	N	Y
36 Harman	N	?	Y	Y	N	Y
37 Richardson	N	Y	Y	Y	N	Y
38 Napolitano	N	Y	N	N	N	Y
39 Sánchez, Linda	N	Y	Y	Y	N	Y
40 **Royce**	Y	Y	Y	Y	Y	N
41 **Lewis**	Y	Y	Y	Y	Y	N
42 **Miller, Gary**	Y	Y	Y	Y	Y	N
43 Baca	N	Y	Y	Y	N	Y
44 **Calvert**	Y	Y	Y	Y	Y	N
45 **Bono Mack**	Y	Y	Y	Y	Y	N
46 **Rohrabacher**	Y	Y	Y	Y	Y	N
47 Sanchez, Loretta	N	Y	Y	Y	N	Y
48 **Campbell**	Y	Y	Y	Y	Y	N
49 **Issa**	Y	Y	Y	Y	Y	N
50 **Bilbray**	Y	Y	Y	Y	Y	N
51 Filner	N	Y	N	N	N	Y
52 **Hunter**	Y	Y	Y	Y	Y	N
53 Davis	N	Y	Y	Y	N	Y

	551	552	553	554	555	556
COLORADO						
1 DeGette	N	Y	Y	Y	N	Y
2 Udall	N	Y	Y	Y	N	Y
3 Salazar	N	Y	Y	Y	N	Y
4 **Musgrave**	Y	Y	Y	Y	Y	N
5 **Lamborn**	Y	Y	Y	Y	Y	N
6 **Tancredo**	Y	Y	Y	Y	Y	N
7 Perlmutter	N	Y	Y	Y	N	Y
CONNECTICUT						
1 Larson	N	Y	Y	Y	N	Y
2 Courtney	N	Y	Y	Y	N	Y
3 DeLauro	N	Y	Y	Y	N	Y
4 **Shays**	N	Y	Y	Y	N	Y
5 Murphy	N	Y	Y	Y	N	Y
DELAWARE						
AL **Castle**	Y	Y	Y	Y	Y	Y
FLORIDA						
1 **Miller**	Y	Y	Y	Y	Y	N
2 Boyd	N	Y	Y	Y	N	Y
3 Brown	N	Y	Y	Y	N	Y
4 **Crenshaw**	Y	Y	Y	Y	Y	N
5 **Brown-Waite**	?	?	?	?	?	?
6 **Stearns**	Y	Y	Y	Y	Y	N
7 **Mica**	Y	Y	Y	Y	Y	N
8 **Keller**	Y	Y	Y	Y	Y	N
9 **Bilirakis**	Y	Y	Y	Y	Y	N
10 **Young**	Y	Y	Y	Y	Y	N
11 Castor	N	Y	?	?	N	Y
12 **Putnam**	Y	Y	Y	Y	Y	N
13 **Buchanan**	Y	Y	Y	Y	Y	N
14 **Mack**	Y	Y	Y	Y	Y	N
15 **Weldon**	Y	Y	Y	Y	Y	N
16 Mahoney	N	Y	Y	Y	N	Y
17 Meek	N	Y	Y	Y	N	Y
18 **Ros-Lehtinen**	Y	Y	Y	Y	Y	Y
19 Wexler	N	Y	Y	Y	N	Y
20 Wasserman Schultz	N	Y	Y	Y	N	Y
21 **Diaz-Balart, L.**	?	Y	Y	Y	Y	Y
22 Klein	N	Y	Y	Y	N	Y
23 Hastings	N	Y	Y	Y	N	Y
24 **Feeney**	Y	Y	Y	Y	Y	N
25 **Diaz-Balart, M.**	Y	Y	Y	Y	Y	Y
GEORGIA						
1 **Kingston**	Y	Y	Y	Y	Y	N
2 Bishop	N	Y	Y	Y	N	Y
3 **Westmoreland**	Y	Y	Y	Y	Y	N
4 Johnson	N	N	Y	N	N	Y
5 Lewis	N	Y	N	N	N	Y
6 **Price**	Y	Y	Y	Y	Y	N
7 **Linder**	Y	Y	Y	Y	Y	N
8 Marshall	N	Y	Y	Y	N	Y
9 **Deal**	Y	Y	Y	Y	Y	N
10 **Broun**	Y	Y	Y	Y	Y	N
11 **Gingrey**	Y	Y	Y	Y	Y	N
12 Barrow	N	Y	Y	?	N	Y
13 Scott	N	Y	Y	Y	N	Y
HAWAII						
1 Abercrombie	N	Y	N	N	N	Y
2 Hirono	N	Y	Y	N	N	Y
IDAHO						
1 **Sali**	Y	Y	Y	Y	Y	N
2 **Simpson**	Y	Y	Y	Y	Y	N
ILLINOIS						
1 Rush	?	?	?	?	?	?
2 Jackson	N	Y	Y	Y	N	Y
3 Lipinski	N	Y	Y	Y	N	Y
4 Gutierrez	N	Y	N	N	N	Y
5 Emanuel	N	Y	Y	Y	N	Y
6 **Roskam**	Y	Y	Y	Y	Y	N
7 Davis	N	Y	N	N	N	Y
8 Bean	N	Y	Y	Y	N	Y
9 Schakowsky	N	Y	Y	Y	N	Y
10 **Kirk**	Y	Y	Y	Y	Y	Y
11 **Weller**	Y	Y	Y	Y	Y	N
12 Costello	N	Y	Y	Y	N	Y
13 **Biggert**	Y	Y	Y	Y	Y	Y
14 Foster	N	Y	Y	Y	N	Y
15 **Johnson**	Y	Y	Y	Y	N	N

	551	552	553	554	555	556
16 **Manzullo**	Y	Y	Y	Y	Y	N
17 Hare	N	Y	Y	Y	N	Y
18 **LaHood**	Y	Y	Y	Y	Y	N
19 **Shimkus**	Y	Y	Y	Y	Y	N
INDIANA						
1 Visclosky	N	Y	Y	Y	N	Y
2 Donnelly	N	Y	Y	Y	N	Y
3 **Souder**	Y	Y	Y	Y	Y	N
4 **Buyer**	Y	Y	Y	Y	Y	N
5 **Burton**	Y	Y	Y	Y	Y	N
6 **Pence**	Y	Y	Y	Y	Y	N
7 Carson, A.	N	Y	Y	Y	N	Y
8 Ellsworth	N	Y	Y	Y	N	Y
9 Hill	N	Y	Y	Y	N	Y
IOWA						
1 Braley	N	Y	Y	Y	N	Y
2 Loebsack	N	Y	Y	Y	N	Y
3 Boswell	N	Y	Y	Y	N	Y
4 **Latham**	Y	Y	Y	Y	Y	N
5 **King**	Y	Y	Y	Y	Y	N
KANSAS						
1 **Moran**	Y	Y	Y	Y	Y	N
2 Boyda	N	Y	Y	Y	N	Y
3 Moore	N	Y	Y	Y	N	Y
4 **Tiahrt**	Y	Y	Y	Y	Y	N
KENTUCKY						
1 **Whitfield**	Y	Y	Y	Y	Y	N
2 **Lewis**	Y	Y	Y	Y	Y	N
3 Yarmuth	N	Y	Y	Y	N	Y
4 **Davis**	Y	Y	Y	Y	Y	N
5 **Rogers**	Y	Y	Y	Y	Y	N
6 Chandler	N	Y	Y	Y	N	Y
LOUISIANA						
1 **Scalise**	Y	Y	Y	Y	Y	N
2 Jefferson	N	Y	N	Y	N	Y
3 Melancon	N	Y	Y	Y	N	Y
4 **McCrery**	Y	Y	Y	Y	Y	N
5 **Alexander**	Y	Y	Y	Y	Y	N
6 Cazayoux	N	Y	Y	Y	Y	Y
7 **Boustany**	Y	Y	Y	Y	Y	N
MAINE						
1 Allen	N	Y	Y	Y	N	Y
2 Michaud	N	Y	Y	Y	N	Y
MARYLAND						
1 **Gilchrest**	N	Y	Y	Y	Y	Y
2 Ruppersberger	N	Y	Y	Y	N	Y
3 Sarbanes	N	Y	Y	Y	N	Y
4 Edwards	N	Y	Y	P	N	Y
5 Hoyer	N	Y	Y	Y	N	Y
6 **Bartlett**	Y	Y	Y	Y	Y	N
7 Cummings	N	Y	N	Y	N	Y
8 Van Hollen	N	Y	Y	Y	N	Y
MASSACHUSETTS						
1 Olver	N	Y	Y	Y	N	Y
2 Neal	N	Y	Y	Y	N	Y
3 McGovern	N	Y	N	Y	N	Y
4 Frank	N	Y	Y	Y	N	Y
5 Tsongas	N	Y	Y	Y	N	Y
6 Tierney	N	Y	Y	Y	N	Y
7 Markey	N	Y	Y	Y	N	Y
8 Capuano	N	Y	Y	Y	N	Y
9 Lynch	N	Y	Y	Y	N	Y
10 Delahunt	N	Y	Y	Y	N	Y
MICHIGAN						
1 Stupak	N	Y	Y	Y	N	Y
2 **Hoekstra**	Y	Y	Y	Y	Y	N
3 **Ehlers**	Y	Y	Y	Y	Y	N
4 **Camp**	Y	Y	Y	Y	Y	N
5 Kildee	N	Y	Y	Y	N	Y
6 **Upton**	Y	Y	Y	Y	Y	N
7 **Walberg**	Y	Y	Y	Y	Y	N
8 **Rogers**	Y	Y	Y	Y	Y	N
9 **Knollenberg**	Y	Y	Y	Y	Y	N
10 **Miller**	Y	Y	Y	Y	Y	N
11 **McCotter**	Y	Y	Y	Y	Y	N
12 Levin	N	Y	Y	Y	N	Y
13 Kilpatrick	N	Y	N	Y	–	+
14 Conyers	N	Y	Y	Y	N	Y
15 Dingell	N	Y	Y	Y	N	Y
MINNESOTA						
1 Walz	N	Y	Y	Y	N	Y
2 **Kline**	Y	Y	Y	Y	Y	N
3 **Ramstad**	Y	Y	Y	Y	Y	Y
4 McCollum	N	Y	Y	Y	N	Y

	551	552	553	554	555	556
5 Ellison	N	Y	Y	Y	N	Y
6 **Bachmann**	Y	Y	Y	Y	Y	N
7 Peterson	N	Y	Y	Y	N	Y
8 Oberstar	N	Y	Y	Y	N	Y
MISSISSIPPI						
1 Childers	N	Y	Y	Y	N	Y
2 Thompson	N	Y	N	Y	N	Y
3 **Pickering**	Y	Y	Y	Y	Y	N
4 Taylor	N	Y	Y	Y	N	Y
MISSOURI						
1 Clay	N	Y	N	Y	N	Y
2 **Akin**	Y	Y	Y	Y	Y	N
3 Carnahan	N	Y	Y	Y	N	Y
4 Skelton	N	Y	Y	Y	N	Y
5 Cleaver	N	Y	Y	Y	N	Y
6 **Graves**	Y	Y	Y	Y	Y	N
7 **Blunt**	Y	Y	Y	Y	Y	N
8 **Emerson**	Y	Y	Y	Y	Y	N
9 **Hulshof**	?	?	?	?	?	?
MONTANA						
AL **Rehberg**	Y	Y	Y	Y	Y	N
NEBRASKA						
1 **Fortenberry**	Y	Y	Y	Y	Y	N
2 **Terry**	Y	Y	Y	Y	Y	N
3 **Smith**	Y	Y	Y	Y	Y	N
NEVADA						
1 Berkley	N	Y	Y	Y	N	Y
2 **Heller**	Y	Y	Y	Y	Y	N
3 **Porter**	Y	Y	Y	Y	Y	Y
NEW HAMPSHIRE						
1 Shea-Porter	N	Y	Y	Y	N	Y
2 Hodes	N	Y	Y	Y	N	Y
NEW JERSEY						
1 Andrews	N	Y	Y	Y	N	Y
2 **LoBiondo**	Y	Y	Y	Y	Y	N
3 **Saxton**	Y	Y	Y	Y	Y	N
4 **Smith**	Y	Y	Y	Y	Y	Y
5 **Garrett**	Y	Y	Y	Y	Y	N
6 Pallone	N	Y	Y	Y	N	Y
7 **Ferguson**	Y	Y	Y	Y	Y	N
8 Pascrell	N	Y	Y	Y	N	Y
9 Rothman	N	Y	Y	Y	N	Y
10 Payne	N	Y	N	Y	N	Y
11 **Frelinghuysen**	Y	Y	Y	Y	Y	N
12 Holt	N	Y	Y	Y	N	Y
13 Sires	N	Y	Y	Y	N	Y
NEW MEXICO						
1 **Wilson**	?	?	?	?	?	?
2 **Pearce**	Y	Y	Y	Y	Y	N
3 Udall	N	Y	Y	Y	N	Y
NEW YORK						
1 Bishop	N	Y	Y	Y	N	Y
2 Israel	N	Y	Y	Y	N	Y
3 **King**	Y	Y	Y	Y	Y	N
4 McCarthy	N	Y	Y	Y	N	Y
5 Ackerman	N	Y	Y	Y	N	Y
6 Meeks	N	Y	Y	Y	N	Y
7 Crowley	N	Y	Y	Y	N	Y
8 Nadler	N	Y	Y	Y	N	Y
9 Weiner	N	Y	Y	Y	N	Y
10 Towns	N	Y	Y	Y	N	Y
11 Clarke	N	Y	Y	N	N	Y
12 Velázquez	N	Y	N	Y	N	Y
13 **Fossella**	Y	Y	Y	Y	Y	N
14 Maloney	N	Y	Y	Y	N	Y
15 Rangel	N	?	Y	Y	N	Y
16 Serrano	N	Y	N	N	N	Y
17 Engel	N	Y	Y	Y	N	Y
18 Lowey	N	Y	Y	Y	N	Y
19 Hall	N	Y	Y	Y	N	Y
20 Gillibrand	N	Y	Y	Y	N	Y
21 McNulty	N	Y	Y	Y	N	Y
22 Hinchey	N	Y	Y	Y	N	Y
23 **McHugh**	Y	Y	Y	Y	Y	N
24 Arcuri	N	Y	Y	Y	N	Y
25 **Walsh**	Y	Y	Y	Y	Y	N
26 **Reynolds**	Y	Y	Y	Y	Y	N
27 Higgins	N	Y	Y	Y	N	Y
28 Slaughter	N	Y	N	Y	N	Y
29 **Kuhl**	Y	Y	Y	Y	Y	N
NORTH CAROLINA						
1 Butterfield	N	Y	Y	Y	N	Y
2 Etheridge	N	Y	Y	Y	N	Y
3 **Jones**	Y	Y	Y	Y	Y	N
4 Price	N	Y	Y	Y	N	Y

	551	552	553	554	555	556
5 **Foxx**	Y	Y	Y	Y	Y	N
6 **Coble**	Y	Y	Y	Y	Y	N
7 McIntyre	N	Y	Y	Y	N	Y
8 **Hayes**	Y	Y	Y	Y	Y	Y
9 **Myrick**	Y	Y	Y	Y	Y	N
10 **McHenry**	Y	Y	Y	Y	Y	N
11 Shuler	N	Y	Y	Y	N	Y
12 Watt	N	Y	Y	Y	N	Y
13 Miller	N	Y	Y	Y	N	Y
NORTH DAKOTA						
AL Pomeroy	N	Y	Y	Y	N	Y
OHIO						
1 **Chabot**	Y	Y	Y	Y	Y	N
2 **Schmidt**	Y	Y	Y	Y	Y	N
3 **Turner**	?	?	?	?	?	?
4 **Jordan**	Y	Y	Y	Y	Y	N
5 **Latta**	Y	Y	Y	Y	Y	N
6 Wilson	N	Y	Y	Y	N	Y
7 **Hobson**	Y	Y	Y	Y	Y	N
8 **Boehner**	Y	Y	Y	Y	Y	N
9 Kaptur	N	Y	Y	Y	N	Y
10 Kucinich	N	Y	N	N	N	Y
11 Tubbs Jones	N	Y	Y	Y	N	Y
12 **Tiberi**	Y	Y	Y	Y	Y	N
13 Sutton	N	Y	Y	Y	N	Y
14 **LaTourette**	Y	Y	?	Y	Y	N
15 **Pryce**	Y	Y	Y	Y	Y	N
16 **Regula**	Y	Y	Y	Y	Y	N
17 Ryan	N	Y	Y	Y	N	Y
18 Space	N	Y	Y	Y	N	Y
OKLAHOMA						
1 **Sullivan**	Y	Y	Y	Y	Y	N
2 Boren	N	Y	Y	Y	N	Y
3 **Lucas**	Y	Y	Y	Y	Y	N
4 **Cole**	Y	?	Y	Y	Y	N
5 **Fallin**	Y	Y	Y	Y	Y	N
OREGON						
1 Wu	N	Y	Y	Y	N	Y
2 **Walden**	Y	Y	Y	Y	Y	N
3 Blumenauer	N	Y	Y	Y	N	Y
4 DeFazio	N	Y	Y	Y	N	Y
5 Hooley	N	Y	Y	Y	N	Y
PENNSYLVANIA						
1 Brady	N	Y	Y	Y	N	Y
2 Fattah	N	Y	?	Y	N	Y
3 **English**	Y	Y	Y	Y	Y	Y
4 Altmire	N	Y	Y	Y	N	Y
5 **Peterson**	Y	Y	Y	?	Y	N
6 **Gerlach**	Y	Y	Y	Y	Y	Y
7 Sestak	N	Y	Y	Y	N	Y
8 Murphy, P.	N	Y	Y	Y	N	Y
9 **Shuster**	Y	Y	Y	Y	Y	N
10 Carney	N	Y	Y	Y	N	Y
11 Kanjorski	N	Y	Y	Y	N	Y
12 Murtha	N	Y	Y	Y	N	Y
13 Schwartz	N	Y	Y	Y	N	Y
14 Doyle	N	Y	Y	Y	N	Y
15 **Dent**	Y	Y	Y	Y	Y	Y
16 **Pitts**	Y	Y	Y	Y	Y	N
17 Holden	N	Y	Y	Y	N	Y
18 **Murphy, T.**	Y	Y	Y	Y	Y	N
19 **Platts**	Y	Y	Y	Y	Y	N
RHODE ISLAND						
1 Kennedy	N	Y	Y	Y	N	Y
2 Langevin	N	Y	Y	Y	N	Y
SOUTH CAROLINA						
1 **Brown**	Y	Y	Y	Y	Y	N
2 **Wilson**	Y	Y	Y	Y	Y	N
3 **Barrett**	Y	Y	Y	Y	Y	N
4 **Inglis**	Y	Y	Y	Y	Y	N
5 Spratt	N	Y	Y	Y	N	Y
6 Clyburn	N	Y	N	N	N	Y
SOUTH DAKOTA						
AL Herseth Sandlin	N	Y	Y	Y	N	Y
TENNESSEE						
1 **Davis, D.**	Y	Y	Y	Y	Y	N
2 **Duncan**	Y	Y	Y	Y	Y	N
3 **Wamp**	Y	Y	?	Y	Y	N
4 Davis, L.	N	Y	Y	Y	N	Y
5 Cooper	N	Y	Y	Y	N	Y
6 Gordon	N	Y	Y	Y	N	Y
7 **Blackburn**	Y	Y	Y	Y	Y	N
8 Tanner	N	Y	Y	Y	N	Y
9 Cohen	N	Y	Y	Y	N	Y

	551	552	553	554	555	556
TEXAS						
1 **Gohmert**	Y	Y	Y	Y	Y	N
2 **Poe**	Y	Y	Y	Y	N	N
3 **Johnson, S.**	Y	Y	Y	Y	Y	N
4 **Hall**	Y	Y	Y	Y	Y	N
5 **Hensarling**	Y	Y	Y	Y	Y	N
6 **Barton**	Y	Y	Y	Y	Y	N
7 **Culberson**	?	Y	Y	Y	Y	N
8 **Brady**	Y	Y	Y	Y	Y	N
9 Green, A.	N	Y	Y	Y	N	Y
10 **McCaul**	Y	Y	Y	Y	Y	N
11 **Conaway**	Y	Y	Y	Y	Y	N
12 **Granger**	Y	Y	Y	Y	Y	N
13 **Thornberry**	Y	Y	Y	Y	Y	N
14 **Paul**	Y	Y	Y	Y	Y	N
15 Hinojosa	N	Y	Y	Y	N	Y
16 Reyes	N	Y	Y	Y	N	Y
17 Edwards	N	Y	Y	Y	N	Y
18 Jackson Lee	N	Y	Y	Y	N	Y
19 **Neugebauer**	Y	Y	Y	Y	Y	N
20 Gonzalez	N	Y	Y	Y	N	Y
21 **Smith**	Y	Y	Y	Y	Y	N
22 Lampson	N	Y	Y	Y	N	Y
23 Rodriguez	N	Y	Y	Y	N	Y
24 **Marchant**	Y	Y	Y	Y	Y	N
25 Doggett	N	Y	Y	Y	N	Y
26 **Burgess**	Y	Y	Y	Y	Y	N
27 Ortiz	N	Y	Y	Y	N	Y
28 Cuellar	N	Y	Y	Y	N	Y
29 Green, G.	N	Y	Y	Y	N	Y
30 Johnson, E.	N	Y	N	Y	N	Y
31 **Carter**	Y	Y	Y	Y	Y	N
32 **Sessions**	Y	Y	Y	Y	Y	N
UTAH						
1 **Bishop**	Y	Y	Y	Y	Y	N
2 Matheson	N	Y	Y	Y	N	Y
3 **Cannon**	?	?	?	?	?	?
VERMONT						
AL Welch	N	Y	Y	Y	N	Y
VIRGINIA						
1 **Wittman**	Y	Y	Y	Y	Y	N
2 **Drake**	Y	Y	Y	Y	Y	N
3 Scott	N	Y	Y	Y	N	Y
4 **Forbes**	Y	Y	Y	Y	Y	N
5 **Goode**	Y	Y	Y	Y	Y	N
6 **Goodlatte**	Y	Y	Y	Y	Y	N
7 **Cantor**	Y	Y	Y	Y	Y	N
8 Moran	N	Y	Y	Y	N	Y
9 Boucher	N	Y	Y	Y	N	Y
10 **Wolf**	Y	Y	Y	Y	Y	N
11 **Davis**	Y	Y	Y	Y	Y	N
WASHINGTON						
1 Inslee	N	Y	Y	Y	N	Y
2 Larsen	N	Y	Y	Y	N	Y
3 Baird	N	Y	Y	Y	N	Y
4 **Hastings**	Y	Y	Y	Y	Y	N
5 **McMorris Rodgers**	Y	Y	Y	Y	Y	N
6 Dicks	N	Y	Y	Y	N	Y
7 McDermott	N	Y	Y	N	N	Y
8 **Reichert**	Y	Y	Y	Y	Y	Y
9 Smith	N	Y	Y	Y	N	Y
WEST VIRGINIA						
1 Mollohan	N	Y	Y	Y	N	Y
2 **Capito**	Y	Y	Y	Y	Y	N
3 Rahall	N	Y	Y	Y	N	Y
WISCONSIN						
1 **Ryan**	Y	Y	Y	Y	Y	N
2 Baldwin	N	Y	Y	N	N	Y
3 Kind	N	Y	Y	Y	N	Y
4 Moore	N	Y	N	N	N	Y
5 **Sensenbrenner**	Y	Y	Y	Y	Y	N
6 **Petri**	Y	Y	Y	Y	Y	N
7 Obey	N	Y	Y	Y	N	Y
8 Kagen	N	Y	Y	Y	N	Y
WYOMING						
AL **Cubin**	?	?	?	?	?	?
DELEGATES						
Faleomavaega (A.S.)	N	Y	Y	Y		
Norton (D.C.)	N	Y	N	Y		
Bordallo (Guam)	N	Y	Y	Y		
Fortuño (P.R.)	?	?	?	?		
Christensen (V.I.)	N	Y	Y	Y		

IN THE HOUSE | By Vote Number

557. **HR 6633. Employee Verification/Passage.** Lofgren, D-Calif., motion to suspend the rules and pass the bill that would reauthorize through fiscal 2013 the E-Verify pilot employment eligibility verification program, an Internet-based program that allows employers to verify the employment eligibility of their hires. It would require the Homeland Security Department, which administers the program, to provide funding to the Social Security Administration for checking employee Social Security numbers submitted under the program. Motion agreed to 407-2: R 183-1; D 224-1 (ND 166-1, SD 58-0). A two-thirds majority of those present and voting (273 in this case) is required for passage under suspension of the rules. July 31, 2008.

558. **HR 6599. Fiscal 2009 Military Construction-VA Appropriations/State Extended Care Facilities.** Garrett, R-N.J., amendment that would increase grants for construction of state extended-care facilities by $18 million, offset by a reduction of the same amount for the VA departmental administration general operating expenses account. Rejected in Committee of the Whole 185-227: R 174-13; D 11-214 (ND 9-160, SD 2-54). Aug. 1, 2008.

559. **HR 6599. Fiscal 2009 Military Construction-VA Appropriations/Naming of Projects or Programs.** McCaul, R-Texas, amendment that would bar the use of the funds in the bill for a project or program named for an individual currently serving as a House member, delegate, resident commissioner or senator. Adopted in Committee of the Whole 329-86: R 186-2; D 143-84 (ND 105-64, SD 38-20). Aug. 1, 2008.

560. **HR 6599. Fiscal 2009 Military Construction-VA Appropriations/Earmark Elimination.** Flake, R-Ariz., amendment that would eliminate 103 earmarks from the bill related to military construction. Rejected in Committee of the Whole 63-350: R 61-126; D 2-224 (ND 0-169, SD 2-55). Aug. 1, 2008.

561. **HR 6599. Fiscal 2009 Military Construction-VA Appropriations/Davis-Bacon Requirements.** King, R-Iowa, amendment that would bar the use of the funds in the bill for the enforcement of the Davis-Bacon Act, which requires government contractors to pay employees the prevailing wage. Rejected in Committee of the Whole 143-275: R 143-44; D 0-231 (ND 0-173, SD 0-58). Aug. 1, 2008.

	557	558	559	560	561
ALABAMA					
1 Bonner	Y	Y	Y	N	Y
2 Everett	Y	Y	Y	N	Y
3 Rogers	Y	?	?	?	?
4 Aderholt	Y	Y	Y	N	Y
5 Cramer	Y	N	Y	?	N
6 Bachus	?	Y	Y	N	Y
7 Davis	Y	N	Y	N	N
ALASKA					
AL Young	?	?	?	?	?
ARIZONA					
1 Renzi	Y	Y	Y	N	N
2 Franks	Y	Y	Y	Y	Y
3 Shadegg	Y	Y	Y	Y	Y
4 Pastor	P	N	N	N	N
5 Mitchell	Y	Y	Y	N	N
6 Flake	Y	Y	Y	Y	Y
7 Grijalva	P	N	N	N	N
8 Giffords	Y	Y	Y	N	N
ARKANSAS					
1 Berry	Y	N	Y	N	N
2 Snyder	Y	N	Y	N	N
3 Boozman	Y	Y	Y	N	Y
4 Ross	Y	N	Y	N	N
CALIFORNIA					
1 Thompson	Y	N	N	N	N
2 Herger	Y	Y	Y	Y	Y
3 Lungren	Y	Y	Y	N	Y
4 Doolittle	Y	N	Y	N	Y
5 Matsui	Y	N	N	N	N
6 Woolsey	Y	N	N	N	N
7 Miller, George	?	N	Y	N	N
8 Pelosi					
9 Lee	Y	N	N	N	N
10 Tauscher	Y	N	Y	N	N
11 McNerney	Y	N	Y	N	N
12 Speier	Y	N	Y	N	N
13 Stark	Y	N	N	N	N
14 Eshoo	Y	N	Y	N	N
15 Honda	Y	N	Y	?	N
16 Lofgren	Y	N	Y	N	N
17 Farr	Y	N	N	N	N
18 Cardoza	Y	N	N	N	N
19 Radanovich	Y	Y	Y	N	Y
20 Costa	Y	N	Y	N	N
21 Nunes	Y	Y	Y	Y	Y
22 McCarthy	Y	Y	Y	Y	Y
23 Capps	Y	N	N	N	N
24 Gallegly	Y	Y	Y	N	Y
25 McKeon	Y	Y	Y	N	Y
26 Dreier	Y	Y	Y	N	Y
27 Sherman	Y	N	Y	N	N
28 Berman	Y	N	N	N	N
29 Schiff	Y	N	Y	N	N
30 Waxman	Y	N	Y	N	N
31 Becerra	Y	N	Y	N	N
32 Solis	Y	N	N	N	N
33 Watson	Y	N	N	N	N
34 Roybal-Allard	P	N	N	N	N
35 Waters	Y	N	N	N	N
36 Harman	Y	?	?	?	?
37 Richardson	Y	N	Y	N	N
38 Napolitano	Y	N	N	N	N
39 Sánchez, Linda	Y	N	N	N	N
40 Royce	Y	Y	Y	Y	Y
41 Lewis	Y	Y	Y	N	N
42 Miller, Gary	Y	Y	Y	N	Y
43 Baca	Y	N	Y	N	N
44 Calvert	Y	Y	Y	N	Y
45 Bono Mack	Y	Y	Y	N	Y
46 Rohrabacher	Y	Y	Y	Y	Y
47 Sanchez, Loretta	Y	N	Y	N	N
48 Campbell	Y	Y	Y	Y	Y
49 Issa	Y	Y	Y	Y	Y
50 Bilbray	Y	Y	Y	N	Y
51 Filner	N	N	Y	N	N
52 Hunter	Y	Y	Y	N	Y
53 Davis	Y	N	Y	N	N
COLORADO					
1 DeGette	Y	N	Y	N	N
2 Udall	Y	N	Y	N	N
3 Salazar	Y	N	Y	N	N
4 Musgrave	Y	Y	Y	Y	Y
5 Lamborn	Y	Y	Y	Y	Y
6 Tancredo	Y	Y	Y	Y	Y
7 Perlmutter	Y	N	Y	N	N
CONNECTICUT					
1 Larson	Y	N	Y	N	N
2 Courtney	Y	N	Y	N	N
3 DeLauro	Y	N	Y	N	N
4 Shays	Y	Y	Y	N	N
5 Murphy	Y	N	Y	N	N
DELAWARE					
AL Castle	Y	Y	Y	N	N
FLORIDA					
1 Miller	Y	Y	Y	N	Y
2 Boyd	Y	N	Y	N	N
3 Brown	Y	?	?	?	?
4 Crenshaw	Y	Y	Y	N	Y
5 Brown-Waite	?	?	?	?	?
6 Stearns	Y	Y	Y	Y	Y
7 Mica	Y	Y	Y	N	Y
8 Keller	Y	Y	Y	N	Y
9 Bilirakis	Y	Y	Y	N	Y
10 Young	Y	Y	Y	N	N
11 Castor	Y	N	Y	N	N
12 Putnam	Y	Y	Y	N	Y
13 Buchanan	Y	Y	Y	N	Y
14 Mack	Y	Y	Y	Y	Y
15 Weldon	?	Y	Y	Y	Y
16 Mahoney	Y	N	Y	N	N
17 Meek	Y	?	N	N	N
18 Ros-Lehtinen	Y	Y	Y	N	N
19 Wexler	Y	N	N	N	N
20 Wasserman Schultz	Y	N	N	N	N
21 Diaz-Balart, L.	Y	Y	Y	N	N
22 Klein	Y	?	Y	N	N
23 Hastings	Y	N	N	N	N
24 Feeney	Y	Y	Y	Y	Y
25 Diaz-Balart, M.	Y	Y	Y	Y	N
GEORGIA					
1 Kingston	Y	Y	Y	N	Y
2 Bishop	Y	N	Y	N	N
3 Westmoreland	Y	Y	Y	N	Y
4 Johnson	Y	N	N	N	N
5 Lewis	Y	N	N	N	N
6 Price	Y	Y	Y	Y	Y
7 Linder	Y	Y	Y	Y	Y
8 Marshall	?	N	Y	N	Y
9 Deal	Y	Y	Y	N	Y
10 Broun	Y	Y	Y	Y	Y
11 Gingrey	Y	Y	Y	Y	Y
12 Barrow	Y	N	Y	N	N
13 Scott	Y	N	N	N	N
HAWAII					
1 Abercrombie	Y	N	Y	N	N
2 Hirono	Y	N	Y	?	N
IDAHO					
1 Sali	Y	Y	Y	Y	Y
2 Simpson	Y	Y	Y	N	Y
ILLINOIS					
1 Rush	?	?	?	?	?
2 Jackson	Y	N	Y	N	N
3 Lipinski	Y	N	N	N	N
4 Gutierrez	Y	N	N	N	N
5 Emanuel	Y	N	Y	N	N
6 Roskam	Y	Y	Y	N	N
7 Davis	Y	N	N	N	N
8 Bean	Y	N	Y	N	N
9 Schakowsky	Y	N	N	N	N
10 Kirk	Y	N	Y	N	N
11 Weller	Y	?	?	?	?
12 Costello	Y	N	N	N	N
13 Biggert	Y	Y	Y	N	N
14 Foster	Y	N	Y	N	N
15 Johnson	Y	Y	Y	Y	N

KEY	Republicans	Democrats		
Y	Voted for (yea)	X	Paired against	C Voted "present" to avoid possible conflict of interest
#	Paired for	–	Announced against	
+	Announced for	P	Voted "present"	? Did not vote or otherwise make a position known
N	Voted against (nay)			

ND Northern Democrats, SD Southern Democrats
Southern states: Ala., Ark., Fla., Ga., Ky., La., Miss., N.C., Okla., S.C., Tenn., Texas, Va.

	557	558	559	560	561
16 **Manzullo**	Y	Y	Y	N	Y
17 Hare	Y	N	Y	N	N
18 **LaHood**	Y	Y	Y	N	N
19 **Shimkus**	Y	Y	Y	N	N
INDIANA					
1 Visclosky	Y	N	N	N	N
2 Donnelly	Y	N	Y	N	N
3 **Souder**	Y	N	Y	N	Y
4 **Buyer**	Y	Y	Y	N	Y
5 **Burton**	Y	Y	Y	Y	Y
6 **Pence**	Y	Y	Y	Y	Y
7 Carson, A.	Y	N	Y	N	N
8 Ellsworth	Y	N	Y	N	N
9 Hill	Y	N	Y	N	N
IOWA					
1 Braley	Y	N	Y	N	N
2 Loebsack	Y	N	Y	N	N
3 Boswell	Y	?	?	?	?
4 **Latham**	Y	Y	Y	N	Y
5 **King**	Y	Y	Y	N	Y
KANSAS					
1 **Moran**	Y	Y	Y	Y	Y
2 Boyda	Y	N	Y	N	N
3 Moore	Y	N	Y	N	N
4 **Tiahrt**	Y	Y	Y	N	Y
KENTUCKY					
1 **Whitfield**	Y	N	Y	N	N
2 **Lewis**	Y	Y	Y	N	Y
3 Yarmuth	Y	N	Y	N	N
4 **Davis**	Y	Y	Y	N	Y
5 **Rogers**	Y	Y	Y	N	Y
6 Chandler	Y	N	Y	N	N
LOUISIANA					
1 **Scalise**	Y	Y	Y	Y	Y
2 Jefferson	Y	N	N	N	N
3 Melancon	Y	N	Y	N	N
4 **McCrery**	Y	Y	Y	N	Y
5 **Alexander**	Y	Y	Y	N	N
6 Cazayoux	Y	N	Y	N	N
7 **Boustany**	Y	Y	Y	N	Y
MAINE					
1 Allen	Y	N	Y	N	N
2 Michaud	Y	N	Y	N	N
MARYLAND					
1 **Gilchrest**	Y	N	Y	N	N
2 Ruppersberger	Y	N	Y	N	N
3 Sarbanes	Y	N	Y	N	N
4 Edwards	Y	N	N	N	N
5 Hoyer	Y	N	N	N	N
6 **Bartlett**	Y	Y	Y	N	Y
7 Cummings	Y	?	?	?	?
8 Van Hollen	Y	N	N	N	N
MASSACHUSETTS					
1 Olver	Y	N	N	N	N
2 Neal	Y	N	N	N	N
3 McGovern	Y	N	N	N	N
4 Frank	Y	N	N	N	N
5 Tsongas	Y	N	Y	N	N
6 Tierney	Y	N	Y	N	N
7 Markey	Y	N	N	N	N
8 Capuano	Y	N	N	N	N
9 Lynch	Y	N	N	N	N
10 Delahunt	Y	N	N	N	N
MICHIGAN					
1 Stupak	Y	N	Y	N	N
2 **Hoekstra**	Y	Y	Y	Y	Y
3 **Ehlers**	Y	Y	Y	Y	Y
4 **Camp**	Y	Y	Y	N	Y
5 Kildee	Y	N	Y	N	N
6 **Upton**	Y	Y	Y	N	N
7 **Walberg**	Y	Y	Y	Y	Y
8 **Rogers**	Y	Y	Y	Y	Y
9 **Knollenberg**	Y	Y	Y	N	Y
10 **Miller**	Y	Y	Y	N	N
11 **McCotter**	Y	Y	Y	Y	N
12 Levin	Y	?	?	?	?
13 Kilpatrick	+	?	?	?	?
14 Conyers	Y	N	N	N	N
15 Dingell	Y	N	N	N	N
MINNESOTA					
1 Walz	Y	N	Y	N	N
2 **Kline**	Y	Y	Y	Y	Y
3 **Ramstad**	Y	Y	Y	N	Y
4 McCollum	Y	N	N	N	N

	557	558	559	560	561
5 Ellison	Y	N	N	N	N
6 **Bachmann**	Y	Y	Y	Y	Y
7 Peterson	Y	N	Y	N	N
8 Oberstar	Y	N	N	N	N
MISSISSIPPI					
1 Childers	Y	N	Y	N	N
2 Thompson	Y	N	N	N	N
3 **Pickering**	Y	Y	Y	N	?
4 Taylor	Y	N	N	N	N
MISSOURI					
1 Clay	Y	N	N	N	N
2 **Akin**	Y	Y	Y	N	Y
3 Carnahan	Y	N	Y	N	N
4 Skelton	Y	N	Y	N	N
5 Cleaver	Y	N	Y	N	N
6 **Graves**	?	Y	Y	N	Y
7 **Blunt**	Y	Y	Y	N	Y
8 **Emerson**	Y	N	Y	N	N
9 **Hulshof**	?	?	?	?	?
MONTANA					
AL **Rehberg**	Y	Y	Y	N	N
NEBRASKA					
1 **Fortenberry**	Y	Y	Y	N	Y
2 **Terry**	Y	Y	Y	Y	Y
3 **Smith**	Y	Y	Y	N	Y
NEVADA					
1 Berkley	Y	N	Y	N	N
2 **Heller**	Y	Y	Y	Y	Y
3 **Porter**	Y	N	Y	N	N
NEW HAMPSHIRE					
1 Shea-Porter	Y	N	Y	N	N
2 Hodes	Y	N	Y	N	N
NEW JERSEY					
1 Andrews	Y	?	?	?	?
2 **LoBiondo**	Y	Y	Y	N	N
3 **Saxton**	Y	?	?	?	?
4 **Smith**	Y	Y	Y	N	N
5 **Garrett**	Y	Y	Y	Y	Y
6 Pallone	Y	Y	Y	N	N
7 **Ferguson**	Y	Y	Y	N	N
8 Pascrell	Y	Y	N	N	N
9 Rothman	Y	Y	Y	N	N
10 Payne	Y	N	N	N	N
11 **Frelinghuysen**	Y	Y	Y	N	Y
12 Holt	Y	Y	Y	N	N
13 Sires	Y	Y	N	N	N
NEW MEXICO					
1 **Wilson**	?	?	?	?	?
2 **Pearce**	Y	Y	Y	N	Y
3 Udall	Y	N	Y	N	N
NEW YORK					
1 Bishop	Y	N	Y	N	N
2 Israel	Y	N	Y	N	N
3 **King**	Y	Y	Y	Y	N
4 McCarthy	Y	N	Y	N	N
5 Ackerman	Y	N	N	N	N
6 Meeks	Y	N	N	N	N
7 Crowley	Y	N	N	N	N
8 Nadler	Y	N	N	N	N
9 Weiner	Y	N	N	N	N
10 Towns	Y	N	Y	N	N
11 Clarke	Y	N	N	N	N
12 Velázquez	P	N	N	N	N
13 **Fossella**	Y	Y	Y	Y	N
14 Maloney	Y	?	?	?	N
15 Rangel	Y	N	N	N	N
16 Serrano	Y	N	N	N	N
17 Engel	Y	?	?	N	N
18 Lowey	Y	N	Y	N	N
19 Hall	Y	N	Y	N	N
20 Gillibrand	Y	N	Y	N	N
21 McNulty	Y	N	Y	N	N
22 Hinchey	Y	N	Y	N	N
23 **McHugh**	Y	Y	Y	N	N
24 Arcuri	Y	N	Y	N	N
25 **Walsh**	Y	Y	Y	N	N
26 **Reynolds**	Y	Y	Y	N	Y
27 Higgins	Y	N	Y	N	N
28 Slaughter	Y	N	N	N	N
29 **Kuhl**	Y	N	Y	N	N
NORTH CAROLINA					
1 Butterfield	Y	N	N	N	N
2 Etheridge	Y	N	Y	N	N
3 **Jones**	Y	N	Y	N	Y
4 Price	Y	N	Y	N	N

	557	558	559	560	561
5 **Foxx**	Y	Y	Y	Y	Y
6 **Coble**	Y	Y	Y	N	Y
7 McIntyre	Y	N	Y	N	N
8 **Hayes**	Y	Y	Y	N	Y
9 **Myrick**	Y	N	Y	N	Y
10 **McHenry**	Y	Y	Y	N	Y
11 Shuler	Y	Y	Y	N	N
12 Watt	Y	N	N	N	N
13 Miller	Y	N	Y	N	N
NORTH DAKOTA					
AL Pomeroy	Y	Y	Y	N	N
OHIO					
1 **Chabot**	Y	Y	Y	Y	Y
2 **Schmidt**	Y	Y	Y	N	N
3 **Turner**	?	Y	Y	N	N
4 **Jordan**	Y	Y	Y	N	Y
5 **Latta**	Y	Y	Y	N	Y
6 Wilson	Y	N	Y	N	N
7 **Hobson**	Y	Y	N	N	N
8 **Boehner**	Y	Y	Y	Y	Y
9 Kaptur	Y	?	?	N	N
10 Kucinich	Y	N	N	N	N
11 Tubbs Jones	Y	N	N	N	N
12 **Tiberi**	Y	Y	Y	Y	N
13 Sutton	Y	N	Y	N	N
14 **LaTourette**	?	Y	Y	N	N
15 **Pryce**	Y	?	?	?	?
16 **Regula**	Y	Y	Y	N	N
17 Ryan	Y	N	Y	N	N
18 Space	Y	Y	Y	N	N
OKLAHOMA					
1 **Sullivan**	Y	Y	Y	N	Y
2 Boren	Y	N	Y	N	N
3 **Lucas**	Y	Y	Y	N	Y
4 **Cole**	Y	Y	Y	N	Y
5 **Fallin**	Y	Y	Y	N	Y
OREGON					
1 Wu	Y	N	N	N	N
2 **Walden**	Y	Y	Y	N	N
3 Blumenauer	Y	N	Y	N	N
4 DeFazio	Y	N	Y	N	N
5 Hooley	Y	N	Y	N	N
PENNSYLVANIA					
1 Brady	Y	N	N	N	N
2 Fattah	Y	N	N	N	N
3 **English**	Y	Y	Y	Y	N
4 Altmire	Y	N	Y	N	N
5 **Peterson**	?	?	Y	N	Y
6 **Gerlach**	Y	Y	Y	N	N
7 Sestak	Y	N	Y	N	N
8 Murphy, P.	Y	N	Y	N	N
9 **Shuster**	Y	Y	Y	N	Y
10 Carney	Y	N	Y	N	N
11 Kanjorski	Y	N	Y	N	N
12 Murtha	Y	N	N	N	N
13 Schwartz	Y	N	Y	N	N
14 Doyle	Y	N	N	N	N
15 **Dent**	Y	Y	Y	N	Y
16 **Pitts**	Y	?	?	?	?
17 Holden	Y	N	Y	N	N
18 **Murphy, T.**	?	Y	Y	N	N
19 **Platts**	Y	Y	Y	Y	Y
RHODE ISLAND					
1 Kennedy	Y	?	Y	N	N
2 Langevin	Y	N	Y	N	N
SOUTH CAROLINA					
1 **Brown**	Y	Y	Y	N	Y
2 **Wilson**	Y	Y	Y	N	Y
3 **Barrett**	Y	Y	Y	N	Y
4 **Inglis**	Y	Y	Y	N	Y
5 Spratt	Y	N	Y	N	N
6 Clyburn	Y	N	N	N	N
SOUTH DAKOTA					
AL Herseth Sandlin	Y	N	Y	N	N
TENNESSEE					
1 **Davis, D.**	Y	Y	Y	N	Y
2 **Duncan**	Y	Y	Y	Y	Y
3 **Wamp**	Y	Y	Y	N	Y
4 Davis, L.	Y	N	Y	N	N
5 Cooper	Y	N	Y	Y	N
6 Gordon	Y	N	Y	Y	N
7 **Blackburn**	Y	Y	Y	N	Y
8 Tanner	Y	Y	Y	N	N
9 Cohen	Y	N	Y	N	N

	557	558	559	560	561
TEXAS					
1 **Gohmert**	Y	N	Y	Y	Y
2 **Poe**	Y	Y	Y	N	Y
3 **Johnson, S.**	Y	Y	Y	N	Y
4 **Hall**	Y	N	N	N	Y
5 **Hensarling**	Y	Y	Y	Y	Y
6 **Barton**	Y	Y	Y	Y	Y
7 **Culberson**	Y	Y	Y	N	Y
8 **Brady**	Y	Y	Y	N	Y
9 Green, A.	Y	N	N	N	N
10 **McCaul**	Y	Y	Y	Y	Y
11 **Conaway**	Y	Y	Y	N	Y
12 **Granger**	Y	Y	Y	N	Y
13 **Thornberry**	Y	Y	Y	N	Y
14 **Paul**	N	Y	Y	N	Y
15 Hinojosa	Y	N	N	N	N
16 Reyes	Y	N	N	N	N
17 Edwards	Y	N	Y	N	N
18 Jackson Lee	Y	N	N	N	N
19 **Neugebauer**	Y	Y	Y	N	Y
20 Gonzalez	Y	N	N	N	N
21 **Smith**	Y	Y	Y	N	Y
22 Lampson	Y	N	Y	N	N
23 Rodriguez	Y	N	Y	N	N
24 **Marchant**	Y	Y	Y	Y	Y
25 Doggett	Y	N	N	N	N
26 **Burgess**	Y	N	Y	Y	Y
27 Ortiz	Y	N	Y	N	N
28 Cuellar	Y	N	Y	N	N
29 Green, G.	Y	N	Y	N	N
30 Johnson, E.	Y	N	N	N	N
31 **Carter**	?	Y	Y	N	Y
32 **Sessions**	?	Y	Y	N	Y
UTAH					
1 **Bishop**	Y	Y	Y	?	Y
2 Matheson	Y	N	Y	N	N
3 **Cannon**	?	?	?	?	?
VERMONT					
AL Welch	Y	N	Y	N	N
VIRGINIA					
1 **Wittman**	Y	Y	Y	N	Y
2 **Drake**	Y	Y	Y	N	Y
3 Scott	Y	N	Y	N	N
4 **Forbes**	Y	Y	Y	N	Y
5 **Goode**	Y	Y	Y	Y	Y
6 **Goodlatte**	Y	Y	Y	Y	Y
7 **Cantor**	Y	Y	Y	Y	Y
8 Moran	Y	N	N	N	N
9 Boucher	Y	N	Y	N	N
10 **Wolf**	Y	Y	Y	N	Y
11 **Davis**	Y	Y	Y	N	Y
WASHINGTON					
1 Inslee	Y	N	Y	N	N
2 Larsen	Y	N	Y	N	N
3 Baird	Y	N	Y	N	N
4 **Hastings**	Y	Y	Y	N	Y
5 **McMorris Rodgers**	Y	Y	Y	Y	Y
6 Dicks	?	N	Y	N	N
7 McDermott	Y	N	N	N	N
8 **Reichert**	Y	Y	Y	N	N
9 Smith	Y	N	Y	N	N
WEST VIRGINIA					
1 Mollohan	?	N	N	N	N
2 **Capito**	Y	Y	Y	N	N
3 Rahall	Y	N	N	N	N
WISCONSIN					
1 **Ryan**	Y	Y	Y	Y	N
2 Baldwin	Y	N	N	N	N
3 Kind	Y	N	Y	P	N
4 Moore	Y	N	N	N	N
5 **Sensenbrenner**	Y	Y	Y	Y	Y
6 **Petri**	Y	Y	Y	Y	N
7 Obey	Y	N	?	N	N
8 Kagen	Y	N	Y	N	N
WYOMING					
AL **Cubin**	?	?	?	?	?
DELEGATES					
Faleomavaega (A.S.)		N	Y	N	N
Norton (D.C.)		N	Y	N	N
Bordallo (Guam)		N	Y	N	N
Fortuño (P.R.)		?	?	?	?
Christensen (V.I.)		N	N	N	N

IN THE HOUSE | By Vote Number

562. HR 6599. Fiscal 2009 Military Construction-VA Appropriations/Motion to Table. Edwards, D-Texas, motion to table (kill) the Peterson, R-Pa., appeal of the ruling of the chair with respect to the Edwards point of order that the Lewis, R-Calif., motion to recommit constituted legislating on an appropriations bill. The motion would recommit the bill to the Appropriations Committee with instructions that it be reported back forthwith with language adding the text of a bill (HR 6566) to allow offshore drilling in areas where it is currently prohibited, provide tax breaks for individuals and businesses who buy fuel-efficient vehicles, and extend tax credits for alternative sources of energy. Motion agreed to 230-184: R 10-179; D 220-5 (ND 169-1, SD 51-4). Aug. 1, 2008.

563. HR 6599. Fiscal 2009 Military Construction-VA Appropriations/Passage. Passage of the bill that would provide $118.7 billion in fiscal 2009 for the Department of Veterans Affairs, military construction and military housing. The total includes $93.7 billion for the Department of Veterans Affairs, $40.8 billion of which would go to veterans' health programs. The bill would provide $46 billion in mandatory spending for veterans' service-connected compensation benefits and pensions. The total also includes $11.7 billion for military construction, $3.2 billion for military family housing and $9.1 billion for the latest round of base closures. Passed 409-4: R 180-4; D 229-0 (ND 171-0, SD 58-0). Aug. 1, 2008.

564. H Res 1008. Persecution of Baha'is in Iran/Adoption. Berman, D-Calif., motion to suspend the rules and adopt the resolution that would condemn the Iranian government for the state-sponsored persecution of Baha'is and call on Iran to immediately cease activities aimed at the repression of the Iranian Baha'i community. Motion agreed to 408-3: R 181-3; D 227-0 (ND 170-0, SD 57-0). A two-thirds majority of those present and voting (274 in this case) is required for adoption under suspension of the rules. Aug. 1, 2008.

565. H Res 1316. Tribute to LST Veterans/Adoption. Ellsworth, D-Ind., motion to suspend the rules and adopt the resolution that would recognize the essential role played by landing ship tanks (LSTs) during World War II, the Korean War, the Vietnam War, Operation Desert Shield, Operation Desert Storm and other missions, and honor the sailors who served on them. Motion agreed to 415-0: R 186-0; D 229-0 (ND 171-0, SD 58-0). A two-thirds majority of those present and voting (277 in this case) is required for adoption under suspension of the rules. Aug. 1, 2008.

566. Procedural Motion/Adjourn. Hoyer, D-Md., motion to adjourn. Motion agreed to 213-197: R 2-182; D 211-15 (ND 157-12, SD 54-3). Aug. 1, 2008.

	562	563	564	565	566
ALABAMA					
1 Bonner	N	Y	Y	Y	N
2 Everett	N	Y	Y	Y	N
3 Rogers	?	?	Y	Y	N
4 Aderholt	N	Y	Y	Y	N
5 Cramer	Y	Y	Y	Y	Y
6 Bachus	N	Y	?	?	?
7 Davis	Y	Y	Y	Y	?
ALASKA					
AL Young	?	?	?	?	?
ARIZONA					
1 Renzi	N	Y	Y	Y	N
2 Franks	N	Y	Y	Y	N
3 Shadegg	N	Y	Y	Y	N
4 Pastor	Y	Y	Y	Y	Y
5 Mitchell	Y	Y	Y	Y	N
6 Flake	N	N	Y	Y	N
7 Grijalva	Y	Y	Y	Y	Y
8 Giffords	Y	Y	Y	Y	Y
ARKANSAS					
1 Berry	Y	Y	Y	Y	Y
2 Snyder	Y	Y	Y	Y	Y
3 Boozman	N	Y	Y	Y	N
4 Ross	Y	Y	Y	Y	Y
CALIFORNIA					
1 Thompson	Y	Y	Y	Y	Y
2 Herger	N	Y	Y	Y	N
3 Lungren	N	Y	?	Y	N
4 Doolittle	N	Y	Y	Y	N
5 Matsui	Y	Y	Y	Y	Y
6 Woolsey	Y	Y	Y	Y	Y
7 Miller, George	Y	Y	?	?	?
8 Pelosi					
9 Lee	Y	Y	Y	Y	Y
10 Tauscher	Y	Y	Y	Y	Y
11 McNerney	Y	Y	Y	Y	Y
12 Speier	Y	Y	Y	Y	Y
13 Stark	Y	Y	Y	Y	Y
14 Eshoo	Y	Y	Y	Y	Y
15 Honda	Y	Y	Y	Y	Y
16 Lofgren	Y	Y	Y	Y	Y
17 Farr	Y	Y	Y	Y	Y
18 Cardoza	Y	Y	Y	Y	Y
19 Radanovich	N	?	Y	Y	N
20 Costa	Y	Y	Y	Y	Y
21 Nunes	N	Y	Y	Y	N
22 McCarthy	N	Y	Y	Y	N
23 Capps	Y	Y	Y	Y	Y
24 Gallegly	N	Y	Y	Y	N
25 McKeon	N	Y	Y	Y	N
26 Dreier	N	Y	Y	Y	N
27 Sherman	Y	Y	?	Y	Y
28 Berman	Y	Y	Y	Y	Y
29 Schiff	Y	Y	Y	Y	Y
30 Waxman	Y	Y	Y	Y	Y
31 Becerra	Y	Y	Y	Y	Y
32 Solis	Y	Y	Y	Y	Y
33 Watson	Y	Y	Y	Y	Y
34 Roybal-Allard	Y	Y	Y	Y	Y
35 Waters	Y	Y	Y	Y	Y
36 Harman	?	?	?	?	?
37 Richardson	Y	Y	Y	Y	Y
38 Napolitano	Y	Y	Y	Y	Y
39 Sánchez, Linda	Y	Y	Y	Y	Y
40 Royce	N	Y	Y	Y	N
41 Lewis	N	Y	Y	Y	N
42 Miller, Gary	N	Y	Y	Y	N
43 Baca	Y	Y	Y	Y	Y
44 Calvert	N	Y	Y	Y	N
45 Bono Mack	N	Y	Y	Y	N
46 Rohrabacher	N	Y	Y	Y	N
47 Sanchez, Loretta	Y	Y	Y	Y	Y
48 Campbell	N	N	Y	Y	N
49 Issa	N	Y	Y	Y	N
50 Bilbray	N	Y	Y	Y	N
51 Filner	Y	Y	Y	Y	Y
52 Hunter	N	Y	Y	Y	N
53 Davis	Y	Y	Y	Y	Y
COLORADO					
1 DeGette	Y	Y	Y	Y	Y
2 Udall	Y	Y	Y	Y	N
3 Salazar	Y	Y	Y	Y	Y
4 Musgrave	N	Y	Y	Y	N
5 Lamborn	N	Y	Y	Y	N
6 Tancredo	N	?	?	?	?
7 Perlmutter	Y	Y	Y	Y	Y
CONNECTICUT					
1 Larson	Y	Y	Y	Y	Y
2 Courtney	Y	Y	Y	Y	Y
3 DeLauro	Y	Y	Y	Y	Y
4 Shays	Y	Y	Y	Y	N
5 Murphy	Y	Y	Y	Y	Y
DELAWARE					
AL Castle	N	Y	Y	Y	N
FLORIDA					
1 Miller	N	Y	Y	Y	N
2 Boyd	Y	Y	Y	Y	Y
3 Brown	?	?	?	?	?
4 Crenshaw	N	Y	Y	Y	N
5 Brown-Waite	?	?	?	?	?
6 Stearns	N	Y	Y	Y	N
7 Mica	N	Y	Y	Y	N
8 Keller	N	Y	Y	Y	N
9 Bilirakis	N	Y	Y	Y	N
10 Young	N	Y	Y	Y	N
11 Castor	Y	Y	Y	Y	Y
12 Putnam	N	Y	Y	Y	N
13 Buchanan	N	Y	Y	Y	N
14 Mack	N	Y	Y	Y	N
15 Weldon	N	Y	?	?	N
16 Mahoney	Y	Y	Y	Y	Y
17 Meek	Y	Y	Y	Y	Y
18 Ros-Lehtinen	Y	Y	Y	Y	N
19 Wexler	Y	Y	Y	Y	Y
20 Wasserman Schultz	Y	Y	Y	Y	Y
21 Diaz-Balart, L.	N	Y	Y	Y	N
22 Klein	Y	Y	Y	Y	Y
23 Hastings	Y	Y	Y	Y	Y
24 Feeney	N	Y	?	Y	N
25 Diaz-Balart, M.	N	Y	Y	Y	N
GEORGIA					
1 Kingston	N	Y	Y	Y	N
2 Bishop	Y	Y	Y	Y	Y
3 Westmoreland	N	Y	Y	Y	N
4 Johnson	Y	Y	Y	Y	Y
5 Lewis	Y	Y	Y	Y	Y
6 Price	N	Y	Y	Y	N
7 Linder	N	Y	Y	Y	N
8 Marshall	Y	Y	Y	Y	Y
9 Deal	N	Y	Y	Y	N
10 Broun	N	Y	Y	Y	N
11 Gingrey	N	Y	Y	Y	N
12 Barrow	Y	Y	Y	Y	Y
13 Scott	Y	Y	Y	Y	Y
HAWAII					
1 Abercrombie	Y	Y	Y	Y	Y
2 Hirono	Y	Y	Y	Y	Y
IDAHO					
1 Sali	N	Y	Y	Y	N
2 Simpson	N	Y	Y	Y	N
ILLINOIS					
1 Rush	?	?	?	?	?
2 Jackson	Y	Y	Y	Y	Y
3 Lipinski	Y	Y	Y	Y	Y
4 Gutierrez	Y	Y	Y	Y	Y
5 Emanuel	Y	Y	Y	Y	Y
6 Roskam	N	Y	Y	Y	N
7 Davis	Y	Y	Y	Y	Y
8 Bean	Y	Y	Y	Y	Y
9 Schakowsky	Y	Y	Y	Y	N
10 Kirk	N	Y	Y	Y	N
11 Weller	?	?	?	?	?
12 Costello	Y	Y	Y	Y	Y
13 Biggert	N	Y	Y	Y	N
14 Foster	Y	Y	Y	Y	Y
15 Johnson	N	Y	Y	Y	N

KEY	Republicans	Democrats		
Y Voted for (yea)		X Paired against		C Voted "present" to avoid possible conflict of interest
# Paired for		− Announced against		
+ Announced for		P Voted "present"		? Did not vote or otherwise make a position known
N Voted against (nay)				

ND Northern Democrats, SD Southern Democrats
Southern states: Ala., Ark., Fla., Ga., Ky., La., Miss., N.C., Okla., S.C., Tenn., Texas, Va.

	562	563	564	565	566
16 **Manzullo**	N	Y	Y	Y	N
17 Hare	Y	Y	Y	Y	Y
18 **LaHood**	N	Y	Y	Y	N
19 **Shimkus**	N	Y	Y	Y	N
INDIANA					
1 Visclosky	Y	Y	Y	Y	Y
2 Donnelly	N	Y	Y	Y	N
3 **Souder**	N	Y	Y	Y	N
4 **Buyer**	N	Y	Y	Y	N
5 **Burton**	N	Y	Y	Y	N
6 **Pence**	N	Y	Y	Y	N
7 Carson, A.	Y	Y	Y	Y	Y
8 Ellsworth	Y	Y	Y	Y	N
9 Hill	Y	Y	Y	Y	Y
IOWA					
1 Braley	Y	Y	Y	Y	N
2 Loebsack	Y	Y	Y	Y	N
3 Boswell	Y	Y	Y	Y	Y
4 **Latham**	N	Y	Y	Y	N
5 **King**	N	?	Y	Y	N
KANSAS					
1 **Moran**	N	Y	Y	Y	N
2 Boyda	Y	Y	Y	Y	Y
3 Moore	Y	Y	Y	Y	Y
4 **Tiahrt**	N	Y	Y	Y	N
KENTUCKY					
1 **Whitfield**	N	Y	Y	Y	N
2 **Lewis**	N	Y	Y	Y	N
3 Yarmuth	Y	Y	Y	Y	Y
4 **Davis**	N	Y	Y	Y	N
5 **Rogers**	N	Y	Y	Y	N
6 Chandler	Y	Y	Y	Y	Y
LOUISIANA					
1 **Scalise**	N	Y	Y	Y	N
2 Jefferson	Y	Y	Y	Y	Y
3 Melancon	Y	Y	Y	Y	Y
4 **McCrery**	N	Y	Y	Y	N
5 **Alexander**	N	Y	Y	Y	N
6 Cazayoux	N	Y	Y	Y	Y
7 **Boustany**	N	Y	Y	Y	N
MAINE					
1 Allen	Y	Y	Y	Y	Y
2 Michaud	Y	Y	Y	Y	Y
MARYLAND					
1 **Gilchrest**	Y	Y	N	Y	Y
2 Ruppersberger	Y	Y	Y	Y	Y
3 Sarbanes	Y	Y	Y	Y	Y
4 Edwards	Y	Y	Y	Y	Y
5 Hoyer	Y	Y	Y	Y	Y
6 **Bartlett**	N	Y	Y	Y	N
7 Cummings	Y	Y	Y	Y	Y
8 Van Hollen	Y	Y	Y	Y	Y
MASSACHUSETTS					
1 Olver	Y	Y	Y	Y	Y
2 Neal	Y	Y	Y	Y	Y
3 McGovern	Y	Y	Y	Y	Y
4 Frank	Y	Y	Y	Y	Y
5 Tsongas	Y	Y	Y	Y	Y
6 Tierney	Y	Y	Y	Y	Y
7 Markey	Y	Y	Y	Y	Y
8 Capuano	Y	Y	Y	Y	Y
9 Lynch	Y	Y	Y	Y	Y
10 Delahunt	Y	Y	Y	Y	Y
MICHIGAN					
1 Stupak	Y	Y	Y	Y	Y
2 **Hoekstra**	N	Y	Y	Y	N
3 **Ehlers**	N	Y	Y	Y	N
4 **Camp**	N	Y	Y	Y	N
5 Kildee	Y	Y	Y	Y	Y
6 **Upton**	N	Y	Y	Y	N
7 **Walberg**	N	Y	Y	Y	N
8 **Rogers**	N	Y	Y	Y	N
9 **Knollenberg**	N	Y	Y	Y	N
10 **Miller**	N	Y	Y	Y	N
11 **McCotter**	N	Y	Y	Y	N
12 Levin	?	?	?	?	?
13 Kilpatrick	?	?	?	?	?
14 Conyers	Y	Y	Y	Y	Y
15 Dingell	Y	Y	Y	Y	Y
MINNESOTA					
1 Walz	Y	Y	Y	Y	Y
2 **Kline**	N	Y	Y	Y	N
3 **Ramstad**	Y	Y	Y	Y	N
4 McCollum	Y	Y	Y	Y	Y
5 Ellison	Y	Y	Y	Y	Y
6 **Bachmann**	N	Y	Y	Y	N
7 Peterson	Y	Y	Y	Y	Y
8 Oberstar	Y	Y	Y	Y	Y
MISSISSIPPI					
1 Childers	N	Y	Y	Y	N
2 Thompson	Y	Y	Y	Y	Y
3 **Pickering**	N	Y	Y	Y	N
4 Taylor	Y	Y	Y	Y	Y
MISSOURI					
1 Clay	Y	Y	Y	Y	Y
2 **Akin**	N	Y	Y	Y	N
3 Carnahan	Y	Y	Y	Y	Y
4 Skelton	Y	Y	Y	Y	Y
5 Cleaver	Y	Y	Y	Y	Y
6 **Graves**	N	Y	Y	Y	N
7 **Blunt**	N	Y	Y	Y	N
8 **Emerson**	N	Y	Y	Y	N
9 **Hulshof**	?	?	?	?	?
MONTANA					
AL **Rehberg**	N	Y	Y	Y	N
NEBRASKA					
1 **Fortenberry**	N	Y	Y	Y	N
2 **Terry**	N	Y	Y	Y	N
3 **Smith**	N	Y	Y	Y	N
NEVADA					
1 Berkley	Y	Y	Y	Y	Y
2 **Heller**	Y	Y	Y	Y	N
3 **Porter**	Y	Y	Y	Y	N
NEW HAMPSHIRE					
1 Shea-Porter	Y	Y	Y	Y	Y
2 Hodes	Y	Y	Y	Y	Y
NEW JERSEY					
1 Andrews	?	Y	Y	Y	Y
2 **LoBiondo**	Y	Y	Y	Y	N
3 **Saxton**	?	?	?	?	?
4 **Smith**	Y	Y	Y	Y	N
5 **Garrett**	N	Y	Y	Y	N
6 Pallone	Y	Y	Y	Y	Y
7 **Ferguson**	N	Y	Y	Y	N
8 Pascrell	Y	Y	Y	Y	Y
9 Rothman	Y	Y	Y	Y	Y
10 Payne	Y	Y	Y	Y	Y
11 **Frelinghuysen**	N	Y	Y	Y	N
12 Holt	Y	Y	Y	Y	Y
13 Sires	Y	Y	Y	Y	Y
NEW MEXICO					
1 **Wilson**	?	?	?	?	?
2 **Pearce**	N	Y	Y	Y	N
3 Udall	Y	Y	Y	Y	N
NEW YORK					
1 Bishop	Y	Y	Y	Y	Y
2 Israel	Y	Y	Y	Y	Y
3 **King**	N	Y	Y	Y	N
4 McCarthy	Y	Y	Y	Y	Y
5 Ackerman	Y	Y	Y	Y	?
6 Meeks	Y	Y	Y	Y	Y
7 Crowley	Y	Y	Y	Y	Y
8 Nadler	Y	Y	Y	Y	Y
9 Weiner	Y	Y	Y	Y	Y
10 Towns	Y	Y	Y	Y	?
11 Clarke	Y	Y	Y	Y	Y
12 Velázquez	?	Y	Y	Y	Y
13 **Fossella**	N	Y	Y	Y	N
14 Maloney	Y	Y	Y	Y	Y
15 Rangel	Y	Y	Y	Y	Y
16 Serrano	Y	Y	Y	Y	Y
17 Engel	Y	Y	Y	Y	Y
18 Lowey	Y	Y	Y	Y	Y
19 Hall	Y	Y	Y	Y	Y
20 Gillibrand	Y	Y	Y	Y	N
21 McNulty	Y	Y	Y	Y	Y
22 Hinchey	Y	Y	Y	Y	Y
23 **McHugh**	N	Y	Y	Y	N
24 Arcuri	Y	Y	Y	Y	Y
25 **Walsh**	N	Y	Y	Y	N
26 **Reynolds**	N	Y	Y	Y	N
27 Higgins	Y	Y	Y	Y	Y
28 Slaughter	Y	Y	Y	Y	Y
29 **Kuhl**	N	Y	Y	Y	N
NORTH CAROLINA					
1 Butterfield	Y	Y	Y	Y	Y
2 Etheridge	Y	Y	Y	Y	Y
3 **Jones**	Y	Y	N	Y	Y
4 Price	Y	Y	Y	Y	Y
5 **Foxx**	N	Y	Y	Y	N
6 **Coble**	N	Y	Y	Y	N
7 McIntyre	Y	Y	Y	Y	Y
8 **Hayes**	N	Y	Y	Y	?
9 **Myrick**	N	Y	Y	Y	N
10 **McHenry**	N	Y	Y	Y	N
11 Shuler	Y	Y	Y	Y	Y
12 Watt	Y	Y	Y	Y	Y
13 Miller	Y	Y	Y	Y	Y
NORTH DAKOTA					
AL Pomeroy	Y	Y	Y	Y	Y
OHIO					
1 **Chabot**	N	Y	Y	Y	N
2 **Schmidt**	N	Y	Y	Y	?
3 **Turner**	N	Y	Y	Y	N
4 **Jordan**	N	Y	Y	Y	N
5 **Latta**	N	Y	Y	Y	N
6 Wilson	Y	Y	Y	Y	Y
7 **Hobson**	N	Y	Y	Y	N
8 **Boehner**	N	Y	Y	Y	N
9 Kaptur	Y	Y	Y	Y	Y
10 Kucinich	Y	Y	Y	Y	Y
11 Tubbs Jones	Y	Y	Y	Y	Y
12 **Tiberi**	N	Y	Y	Y	N
13 Sutton	Y	Y	Y	Y	Y
14 **LaTourette**	N	Y	Y	Y	N
15 **Pryce**	?	?	?	?	?
16 **Regula**	N	Y	Y	Y	N
17 Ryan	Y	Y	Y	Y	Y
18 Space	Y	Y	Y	Y	Y
OKLAHOMA					
1 **Sullivan**	N	Y	Y	Y	N
2 Boren	Y	Y	Y	Y	Y
3 **Lucas**	N	Y	Y	Y	N
4 **Cole**	N	Y	Y	Y	N
5 **Fallin**	N	Y	Y	Y	N
OREGON					
1 Wu	Y	Y	Y	Y	Y
2 **Walden**	N	Y	Y	Y	N
3 Blumenauer	Y	Y	Y	Y	Y
4 DeFazio	Y	Y	Y	Y	Y
5 Hooley	Y	Y	Y	Y	Y
PENNSYLVANIA					
1 Brady	Y	Y	Y	Y	Y
2 Fattah	Y	Y	Y	Y	Y
3 **English**	N	Y	Y	Y	N
4 Altmire	Y	Y	Y	Y	N
5 **Peterson**	N	Y	Y	Y	N
6 **Gerlach**	N	Y	Y	Y	N
7 Sestak	Y	Y	Y	Y	Y
8 Murphy, P.	Y	Y	Y	Y	N
9 **Shuster**	N	Y	Y	Y	N
10 Carney	Y	Y	Y	Y	N
11 Kanjorski	Y	Y	Y	Y	Y
12 Murtha	Y	Y	Y	Y	Y
13 Schwartz	Y	Y	Y	Y	Y
14 Doyle	Y	Y	Y	Y	Y
15 **Dent**	N	Y	Y	Y	N
16 **Pitts**	N	Y	Y	Y	?
17 Holden	Y	Y	Y	Y	Y
18 **Murphy, T.**	N	Y	Y	Y	N
19 **Platts**	N	Y	Y	Y	N
RHODE ISLAND					
1 Kennedy	Y	Y	Y	Y	Y
2 Langevin	Y	Y	Y	Y	Y
SOUTH CAROLINA					
1 **Brown**	N	Y	Y	Y	N
2 **Wilson**	N	Y	Y	Y	N
3 **Barrett**	N	Y	Y	Y	N
4 **Inglis**	N	Y	Y	Y	N
5 Spratt	Y	Y	Y	Y	Y
6 Clyburn	Y	Y	Y	Y	Y
SOUTH DAKOTA					
AL Herseth Sandlin	Y	Y	Y	Y	Y
TENNESSEE					
1 **Davis, D.**	N	Y	Y	Y	N
2 **Duncan**	N	N	Y	Y	N
3 **Wamp**	N	Y	Y	Y	N
4 Davis, L.	Y	Y	Y	Y	Y
5 Cooper	Y	Y	Y	Y	Y
6 Gordon	Y	Y	Y	Y	Y
7 **Blackburn**	N	Y	Y	Y	N
8 Tanner	Y	Y	Y	Y	Y
9 Cohen	Y	Y	Y	Y	Y
TEXAS					
1 **Gohmert**	N	Y	Y	Y	N
2 **Poe**	N	Y	Y	Y	N
3 **Johnson, S.**	N	Y	Y	Y	N
4 **Hall**	N	Y	Y	Y	N
5 **Hensarling**	N	Y	Y	Y	N
6 **Barton**	N	Y	Y	Y	N
7 **Culberson**	N	Y	Y	Y	N
8 **Brady**	N	Y	Y	Y	N
9 Green, A.	Y	Y	Y	Y	Y
10 **McCaul**	N	Y	Y	Y	N
11 **Conaway**	N	Y	Y	Y	N
12 **Granger**	N	Y	Y	Y	N
13 **Thornberry**	N	Y	Y	Y	N
14 **Paul**	N	N	N	Y	N
15 Hinojosa	Y	Y	?	Y	Y
16 Reyes	?	Y	Y	Y	Y
17 Edwards	Y	Y	Y	Y	Y
18 Jackson Lee	Y	Y	Y	Y	Y
19 **Neugebauer**	N	Y	Y	Y	N
20 Gonzalez	Y	Y	Y	Y	Y
21 **Smith**	N	Y	Y	Y	N
22 Lampson	N	Y	Y	Y	N
23 Rodriguez	Y	Y	Y	Y	Y
24 **Marchant**	N	Y	?	?	?
25 Doggett	Y	Y	Y	Y	Y
26 **Burgess**	N	Y	Y	Y	N
27 Ortiz	?	Y	Y	Y	Y
28 Cuellar	N	Y	Y	Y	Y
29 Green, G.	?	Y	Y	Y	Y
30 Johnson, E.	Y	Y	Y	Y	Y
31 **Carter**	N	Y	Y	Y	N
32 **Sessions**	N	Y	Y	Y	N
UTAH					
1 **Bishop**	N	Y	Y	Y	N
2 Matheson	Y	Y	Y	Y	Y
3 **Cannon**	?	?	?	?	?
VERMONT					
AL Welch	Y	Y	Y	Y	Y
VIRGINIA					
1 **Wittman**	N	Y	Y	Y	N
2 **Drake**	N	?	Y	Y	N
3 Scott	Y	Y	Y	Y	Y
4 **Forbes**	N	Y	Y	Y	N
5 **Goode**	N	Y	Y	Y	N
6 **Goodlatte**	N	Y	Y	Y	N
7 **Cantor**	N	Y	Y	Y	N
8 Moran	Y	Y	Y	Y	Y
9 Boucher	Y	Y	Y	Y	Y
10 **Wolf**	N	Y	Y	Y	N
11 **Davis**	N	Y	Y	Y	N
WASHINGTON					
1 Inslee	Y	Y	Y	Y	Y
2 Larsen	Y	Y	Y	Y	Y
3 Baird	Y	Y	Y	Y	Y
4 **Hastings**	N	?	Y	Y	N
5 **McMorris Rodgers**	N	Y	Y	Y	N
6 Dicks	Y	Y	Y	Y	Y
7 McDermott	Y	Y	Y	Y	Y
8 **Reichert**	Y	Y	Y	Y	N
9 Smith	Y	Y	Y	Y	Y
WEST VIRGINIA					
1 Mollohan	Y	Y	Y	Y	Y
2 **Capito**	N	Y	Y	Y	N
3 Rahall	Y	Y	Y	Y	Y
WISCONSIN					
1 **Ryan**	N	Y	Y	Y	N
2 Baldwin	Y	Y	Y	Y	Y
3 Kind	Y	Y	Y	Y	Y
4 Moore	Y	?	Y	Y	Y
5 **Sensenbrenner**	N	Y	Y	Y	N
6 **Petri**	N	Y	Y	Y	N
7 Obey	Y	Y	Y	Y	Y
8 Kagen	Y	Y	Y	Y	Y
WYOMING					
AL **Cubin**	?	?	?	?	?
DELEGATES					
Faleomavaega (A.S.)					
Norton (D.C.)					
Bordallo (Guam)					
Fortuño (P.R.)					
Christensen (V.I.)					

IN THE HOUSE | By Vote Number

567. **S 2403. Robinson and Merhige Courthouse/Passage.** Carney, D-Pa., motion to suspend the rules and pass the bill that would name a federal courthouse in Richmond, Va., after the late Robert R. Merhige Jr. and Spottswood W. Robinson III. Merhige was a federal judge known for his 1970s desegregation rulings, and Robinson represented some of the plaintiffs in the civil rights case *Brown v. Board of Education* in 1954. Motion agreed to 376-0: R 180-0; D 196-0 (ND 146-0, SD 50-0). A two-thirds majority of those present and voting (251 in this case) is required for passage under suspension of the rules. Sept. 8, 2008.

568. **S 2837. Theodore Roosevelt Courthouse/Passage.** Carney, D-Pa., motion to suspend the rules and pass the bill that would name a federal courthouse in Brooklyn, N.Y., after Theodore Roosevelt, the 26th president of the United States. Motion agreed to 375-1: R 179-1; D 196-0 (ND 145-0, SD 51-0). A two-thirds majority of those present and voting (251 in this case) is required for passage under suspension of the rules. Sept. 8, 2008.

569. **S 2135. Child Soldier Prevention/Passage.** Jackson Lee, D-Texas, motion to suspend the rules and pass the bill that would make it a federal crime to knowingly recruit or enlist a child under age 15 into an army, militia or other military organization. Violators would be subject to fines or sentences of up to 20 years in prison, or both. If death of a person results, the bill would allow for a sentence of life in prison. It would set a statute of limitations of 10 years for such offenses. Motion agreed to 371-0: R 177-0; D 194-0 (ND 143-0, SD 51-0). A two-thirds majority of those present and voting (248 in this case) is required for passage under suspension of the rules. Sept. 8, 2008.

570. **H Con Res 344. Global Food Crisis/Adoption.** Jackson Lee, D-Texas, motion to suspend the rules and adopt the concurrent resolution that would express the sense of Congress that there is a global food crisis and that children are affected disproportionately. It would call for the United States and other G-8 countries to work to alleviate the crisis. Motion agreed to 404-1: R 190-1; D 214-0 (ND 159-0, SD 55-0). A two-thirds majority of those present and voting (270 in this case) is required for adoption under suspension of the rules. Sept. 9, 2008.

571. **H Res 937. Red Cross Emergency Military Communication/Adoption.** Jackson Lee, D-Texas, motion to suspend the rules and adopt the resolution that would express the sense of the House of Representatives that emergency communication services of the American Red Cross are vital to maintain contact between military members and their families during emergencies. Motion agreed to 411-0: R 193-0; D 218-0 (ND 162-0, SD 56-0). A two-thirds majority of those present and voting (274 in this case) is required for adoption under suspension of the rules. Sept. 9, 2008.

572. **H Res 1069. Condemnation of Incitement to Violence/Adoption.** Jackson Lee, D-Texas, motion to suspend the rules and adopt the resolution that would condemn the broadcasting of incitement to violence against Americans, Israelis and the West in media based in the Middle East. It would also condemn Hamas for using children's TV programming to incite hatred, violence and anti-Semitism and call on the president to designate Hamas-owned al-Aqsa TV as a global terrorist entity. Motion agreed to 409-1: R 192-1; D 217-0 (ND 161-0, SD 56-0). A two-thirds majority of those present and voting (274 in this case) is required for adoption under suspension of the rules. Sept. 9, 2008.

*Rep. Stephanie Tubbs Jones, D-Ohio, died Aug. 20, 2008. The last vote for which she was eligible was vote 566.

ND Northern Democrats, SD Southern Democrats
Southern states: Ala., Ark., Fla., Ga., Ky., La., Miss., N.C., Okla., S.C., Tenn., Texas, Va.

	567	568	569	570	571	572
ALABAMA						
1 Bonner	Y	Y	Y	Y	Y	Y
2 Everett	Y	Y	Y	Y	Y	Y
3 Rogers	Y	Y	Y	Y	Y	Y
4 Aderholt	Y	Y	Y	Y	Y	Y
5 Cramer	Y	Y	Y	Y	Y	Y
6 Bachus	Y	Y	Y	Y	Y	Y
7 Davis	Y	Y	Y	Y	Y	Y
ALASKA						
AL Young	Y	Y	Y	Y	Y	?
ARIZONA						
1 Renzi	Y	Y	Y	Y	Y	Y
2 Franks	Y	Y	Y	Y	Y	Y
3 Shadegg	Y	Y	Y	Y	Y	Y
4 Pastor	Y	Y	Y	Y	Y	Y
5 Mitchell	Y	Y	Y	Y	Y	Y
6 Flake	Y	Y	Y	Y	Y	Y
7 Grijalva	?	?	?	Y	Y	Y
8 Giffords	Y	Y	Y	Y	Y	Y
ARKANSAS						
1 Berry	?	?	?	Y	Y	Y
2 Snyder	Y	Y	Y	Y	Y	Y
3 Boozman	Y	Y	Y	Y	Y	Y
4 Ross	Y	Y	Y	Y	Y	Y
CALIFORNIA						
1 Thompson	Y	Y	Y	Y	Y	Y
2 Herger	Y	Y	Y	Y	Y	Y
3 Lungren	Y	Y	Y	Y	Y	Y
4 Doolittle	Y	Y	Y	Y	Y	Y
5 Matsui	Y	Y	Y	Y	Y	Y
6 Woolsey	Y	Y	Y	Y	Y	Y
7 Miller, George	Y	Y	Y	Y	Y	Y
8 Pelosi						
9 Lee	+	+	+	+	+	+
10 Tauscher	Y	Y	Y	Y	Y	Y
11 McNerney	Y	Y	Y	Y	Y	Y
12 Speier	Y	Y	Y	Y	Y	Y
13 Stark	Y	Y	Y	Y	Y	Y
14 Eshoo	Y	Y	Y	Y	Y	Y
15 Honda	Y	Y	Y	Y	Y	Y
16 Lofgren	Y	Y	Y	Y	Y	Y
17 Farr	Y	Y	Y	Y	Y	Y
18 Cardoza	Y	Y	Y	Y	Y	Y
19 Radanovich	Y	Y	Y	Y	Y	Y
20 Costa	Y	Y	Y	Y	Y	Y
21 Nunes	Y	Y	Y	Y	Y	Y
22 McCarthy	Y	Y	Y	Y	Y	Y
23 Capps	Y	Y	Y	Y	Y	Y
24 Gallegly	Y	Y	Y	Y	Y	Y
25 McKeon	Y	Y	Y	Y	Y	Y
26 Dreier	Y	Y	Y	Y	Y	Y
27 Sherman	Y	Y	Y	Y	Y	Y
28 Berman	Y	Y	?	Y	Y	Y
29 Schiff	Y	Y	Y	Y	Y	Y
30 Waxman	Y	Y	Y	Y	Y	Y
31 Becerra	Y	Y	?	Y	Y	Y
32 Solis	Y	Y	Y	Y	Y	Y
33 Watson	Y	Y	Y	Y	Y	Y
34 Roybal-Allard	Y	Y	Y	Y	Y	Y
35 Waters	Y	Y	Y	?	Y	Y
36 Harman	Y	Y	Y	Y	Y	Y
37 Richardson	Y	Y	Y	Y	Y	Y
38 Napolitano	Y	Y	Y	Y	Y	Y
39 Sánchez, Linda	Y	Y	Y	Y	Y	Y
40 Royce	Y	Y	Y	Y	Y	Y
41 Lewis	Y	Y	Y	Y	Y	Y
42 Miller, Gary	Y	Y	Y	Y	Y	Y
43 Baca	Y	Y	Y	Y	Y	Y
44 Calvert	Y	Y	Y	Y	Y	Y
45 Bono Mack	Y	Y	Y	Y	Y	Y
46 Rohrabacher	?	?	?	Y	Y	Y
47 Sanchez, Loretta	Y	Y	Y	Y	Y	Y
48 Campbell	Y	Y	Y	Y	Y	Y
49 Issa	Y	Y	Y	Y	Y	Y
50 Bilbray	Y	Y	Y	Y	Y	Y
51 Filner	Y	Y	Y	Y	Y	Y
52 Hunter	Y	Y	Y	Y	Y	Y
53 Davis	Y	Y	Y	Y	Y	Y

	567	568	569	570	571	572
COLORADO						
1 DeGette	Y	?	?	Y	Y	Y
2 Udall	?	?	?	Y	Y	Y
3 Salazar	Y	Y	Y	Y	Y	Y
4 Musgrave	Y	Y	Y	Y	Y	Y
5 Lamborn	Y	Y	Y	Y	Y	Y
6 Tancredo	Y	Y	Y	Y	Y	Y
7 Perlmutter	Y	Y	Y	Y	Y	Y
CONNECTICUT						
1 Larson	Y	Y	Y	Y	Y	Y
2 Courtney	Y	Y	Y	Y	Y	Y
3 DeLauro	Y	Y	Y	Y	Y	Y
4 Shays	Y	Y	Y	Y	Y	Y
5 Murphy	Y	Y	Y	Y	Y	Y
DELAWARE						
AL Castle	Y	Y	Y	Y	Y	Y
FLORIDA						
1 Miller	Y	Y	Y	Y	Y	Y
2 Boyd	Y	Y	Y	Y	Y	Y
3 Brown	?	?	?	Y	Y	Y
4 Crenshaw	Y	Y	Y	Y	Y	Y
5 Brown-Waite	Y	Y	Y	Y	Y	Y
6 Stearns	Y	Y	Y	Y	Y	Y
7 Mica	Y	Y	Y	Y	Y	Y
8 Keller	Y	Y	Y	Y	Y	Y
9 Bilirakis	Y	Y	Y	Y	Y	Y
10 Young	Y	Y	Y	Y	Y	Y
11 Castor	Y	Y	Y	Y	Y	Y
12 Putnam	Y	Y	Y	Y	Y	Y
13 Buchanan	Y	Y	Y	Y	Y	Y
14 Mack	Y	Y	Y	Y	Y	Y
15 Weldon	Y	Y	Y	Y	Y	Y
16 Mahoney	Y	Y	Y	Y	Y	Y
17 Meek	Y	Y	Y	Y	Y	Y
18 Ros-Lehtinen	Y	Y	Y	Y	Y	Y
19 Wexler	Y	Y	Y	Y	Y	Y
20 Wasserman Schultz	Y	Y	Y	Y	Y	Y
21 Diaz-Balart, L.	?	?	?	Y	Y	Y
22 Klein	Y	Y	Y	Y	Y	Y
23 Hastings	Y	Y	Y	Y	Y	Y
24 Feeney	Y	Y	Y	Y	Y	Y
25 Diaz-Balart, M.	?	?	?	Y	Y	Y
GEORGIA						
1 Kingston	Y	Y	Y	Y	Y	Y
2 Bishop	Y	Y	Y	Y	Y	Y
3 Westmoreland	Y	Y	Y	Y	Y	Y
4 Johnson	Y	Y	Y	Y	Y	Y
5 Lewis	Y	Y	Y	Y	Y	Y
6 Price	Y	Y	Y	Y	Y	Y
7 Linder	Y	Y	?	Y	Y	Y
8 Marshall	Y	Y	Y	Y	Y	Y
9 Deal	Y	Y	Y	Y	Y	Y
10 Broun	Y	Y	Y	Y	Y	Y
11 Gingrey	Y	Y	Y	Y	Y	Y
12 Barrow	Y	Y	Y	Y	Y	Y
13 Scott	Y	Y	Y	Y	Y	Y
HAWAII						
1 Abercrombie	Y	Y	Y	Y	Y	Y
2 Hirono	Y	Y	Y	Y	Y	Y
IDAHO						
1 Sali	Y	Y	Y	Y	Y	Y
2 Simpson	Y	Y	Y	Y	Y	Y
ILLINOIS						
1 Rush	+	+	+	Y	Y	Y
2 Jackson	Y	Y	Y	Y	Y	Y
3 Lipinski	Y	Y	Y	Y	Y	Y
4 Gutierrez	Y	Y	Y	Y	?	Y
5 Emanuel	Y	Y	Y	Y	Y	Y
6 Roskam	Y	Y	Y	Y	Y	Y
7 Davis	Y	Y	Y	Y	Y	Y
8 Bean	Y	Y	Y	Y	Y	Y
9 Schakowsky	Y	Y	Y	Y	Y	Y
10 Kirk	?	?	?	Y	Y	Y
11 Weller	+	+	+	Y	Y	Y
12 Costello	Y	Y	Y	Y	Y	Y
13 Biggert	Y	Y	Y	Y	Y	Y
14 Foster	Y	Y	Y	Y	Y	Y
15 Johnson	Y	Y	Y	Y	Y	Y

KEY **Republicans** Democrats

Y Voted for (yea)	X Paired against	C Voted "present" to avoid possible conflict of interest
# Paired for	− Announced against	
+ Announced for	P Voted "present"	? Did not vote or otherwise make a position known
N Voted against (nay)		

	567	568	569	570	571	572
16 **Manzullo**	Y	Y	Y	Y	Y	Y
17 Hare	Y	Y	Y	Y	Y	Y
18 **LaHood**	Y	Y	Y	Y	Y	Y
19 **Shimkus**	Y	Y	Y	Y	Y	Y
INDIANA						
1 Visclosky	Y	Y	Y	Y	Y	Y
2 Donnelly	Y	Y	Y	Y	Y	Y
3 **Souder**	Y	Y	Y	Y	Y	Y
4 **Buyer**	Y	Y	Y	Y	Y	Y
5 **Burton**	Y	Y	Y	Y	Y	Y
6 **Pence**	Y	Y	Y	Y	Y	Y
7 Carson, A.	Y	Y	Y	Y	Y	Y
8 Ellsworth	Y	Y	Y	Y	Y	Y
9 Hill	Y	Y	Y	Y	Y	Y
IOWA						
1 Braley	+	+	+	Y	Y	Y
2 Loebsack	?	?	?	Y	Y	Y
3 Boswell	?	?	?	Y	Y	Y
4 **Latham**	Y	Y	Y	Y	Y	Y
5 **King**	Y	Y	Y	Y	Y	Y
KANSAS						
1 **Moran**	Y	Y	Y	Y	Y	Y
2 Boyda	Y	Y	Y	Y	Y	Y
3 Moore	Y	Y	Y	Y	Y	Y
4 **Tiahrt**	Y	Y	Y	Y	Y	Y
KENTUCKY						
1 **Whitfield**	Y	Y	Y	Y	Y	Y
2 **Lewis**	Y	Y	Y	Y	Y	Y
3 Yarmuth	Y	Y	Y	Y	Y	Y
4 **Davis**	Y	Y	Y	Y	Y	Y
5 **Rogers**	Y	Y	Y	Y	Y	Y
6 Chandler	?	?	?	Y	Y	Y
LOUISIANA						
1 **Scalise**	Y	Y	Y	Y	Y	Y
2 Jefferson	Y	Y	Y	Y	Y	Y
3 Melancon	?	?	?	?	?	?
4 **McCrery**	?	?	?	Y	Y	Y
5 **Alexander**	Y	Y	Y	Y	Y	Y
6 Cazayoux	?	?	?	?	?	?
7 **Boustany**	Y	Y	Y	Y	Y	Y
MAINE						
1 Allen	Y	Y	Y	Y	Y	Y
2 Michaud	Y	Y	Y	Y	Y	Y
MARYLAND						
1 **Gilchrest**	?	?	?	Y	Y	Y
2 Ruppersberger	Y	Y	Y	Y	Y	Y
3 Sarbanes	Y	Y	Y	Y	Y	Y
4 Edwards	Y	Y	Y	Y	Y	Y
5 Hoyer	Y	Y	Y	Y	Y	Y
6 **Bartlett**	Y	Y	Y	Y	Y	Y
7 Cummings	?	?	?	Y	Y	Y
8 Van Hollen	Y	Y	Y	Y	Y	Y
MASSACHUSETTS						
1 Olver	Y	?	Y	Y	Y	Y
2 Neal	?	?	?	Y	Y	Y
3 McGovern	Y	Y	Y	Y	Y	Y
4 Frank	Y	Y	Y	Y	Y	Y
5 Tsongas	Y	Y	Y	Y	Y	Y
6 Tierney	Y	Y	Y	Y	Y	Y
7 Markey	Y	Y	Y	Y	Y	Y
8 Capuano	Y	Y	Y	Y	Y	Y
9 Lynch	Y	Y	Y	Y	Y	Y
10 Delahunt	Y	Y	Y	Y	Y	Y
MICHIGAN						
1 Stupak	?	?	?	Y	Y	Y
2 **Hoekstra**	?	?	?	Y	Y	Y
3 **Ehlers**	Y	Y	Y	Y	Y	Y
4 **Camp**	Y	Y	Y	Y	Y	Y
5 Kildee	Y	Y	Y	Y	Y	Y
6 **Upton**	Y	Y	Y	Y	Y	Y
7 **Walberg**	Y	Y	Y	Y	Y	Y
8 **Rogers**	Y	Y	Y	Y	Y	Y
9 **Knollenberg**	Y	Y	Y	Y	Y	Y
10 **Miller**	Y	Y	Y	Y	Y	Y
11 **McCotter**	Y	Y	Y	Y	Y	Y
12 Levin	?	?	?	?	?	?
13 Kilpatrick	Y	Y	Y	Y	Y	Y
14 Conyers	+	+	+	Y	Y	Y
15 Dingell	Y	Y	Y	Y	Y	Y
MINNESOTA						
1 Walz	Y	Y	Y	Y	Y	Y
2 **Kline**	Y	Y	Y	Y	Y	Y
3 **Ramstad**	Y	Y	Y	Y	Y	Y
4 McCollum	Y	Y	Y	Y	Y	Y
5 Ellison	?	?	?	?	?	?
6 **Bachmann**	Y	Y	Y	Y	Y	Y
7 Peterson	?	?	?	?	?	?
8 Oberstar	Y	Y	Y	Y	Y	Y
MISSISSIPPI						
1 Childers	Y	Y	Y	Y	Y	Y
2 Thompson	Y	Y	Y	Y	Y	Y
3 **Pickering**	?	?	?	Y	Y	Y
4 Taylor	Y	Y	Y	Y	Y	Y
MISSOURI						
1 Clay	?	?	?	Y	Y	Y
2 **Akin**	Y	Y	Y	Y	Y	Y
3 Carnahan	?	?	?	?	?	?
4 Skelton	Y	Y	Y	?	Y	Y
5 Cleaver	Y	Y	Y	Y	Y	Y
6 **Graves**	Y	Y	Y	Y	Y	Y
7 **Blunt**	Y	Y	Y	Y	Y	Y
8 **Emerson**	?	?	?	Y	Y	Y
9 **Hulshof**	?	?	?	?	?	?
MONTANA						
AL **Rehberg**	Y	Y	Y	Y	Y	Y
NEBRASKA						
1 **Fortenberry**	Y	Y	Y	Y	Y	Y
2 **Terry**	?	?	?	Y	Y	Y
3 **Smith**	?	?	?	Y	Y	Y
NEVADA						
1 Berkley	Y	Y	Y	Y	Y	Y
2 **Heller**	Y	Y	Y	Y	Y	Y
3 **Porter**	Y	Y	Y	Y	Y	Y
NEW HAMPSHIRE						
1 Shea-Porter	Y	Y	Y	Y	Y	Y
2 Hodes	?	?	?	?	?	?
NEW JERSEY						
1 Andrews	?	?	?	Y	Y	Y
2 **LoBiondo**	Y	Y	Y	Y	Y	Y
3 **Saxton**	?	?	?	Y	Y	Y
4 **Smith**	Y	Y	Y	Y	Y	Y
5 **Garrett**	Y	Y	Y	Y	Y	Y
6 Pallone	Y	Y	Y	Y	Y	Y
7 **Ferguson**	Y	Y	Y	Y	Y	Y
8 Pascrell	Y	Y	Y	Y	Y	Y
9 Rothman	Y	Y	Y	Y	Y	Y
10 Payne	Y	Y	Y	Y	Y	Y
11 **Frelinghuysen**	Y	Y	Y	Y	Y	Y
12 Holt	Y	Y	Y	Y	Y	Y
13 Sires	Y	Y	Y	Y	Y	Y
NEW MEXICO						
1 **Wilson**	Y	Y	Y	Y	?	Y
2 **Pearce**	Y	Y	Y	Y	Y	Y
3 Udall	?	?	?	Y	Y	Y
NEW YORK						
1 Bishop	Y	Y	Y	Y	Y	Y
2 Israel	Y	Y	Y	Y	Y	?
3 **King**	Y	Y	Y	Y	Y	Y
4 McCarthy	Y	Y	Y	Y	Y	Y
5 Ackerman	Y	Y	Y	Y	Y	Y
6 Meeks	?	?	?	?	?	?
7 Crowley	Y	Y	Y	Y	Y	Y
8 Nadler	Y	Y	Y	Y	?	Y
9 Weiner	Y	Y	Y	Y	Y	Y
10 Towns	?	?	?	?	?	?
11 Clarke	Y	Y	Y	Y	Y	Y
12 Velázquez	?	?	?	Y	Y	Y
13 **Fossella**	Y	Y	Y	Y	Y	Y
14 Maloney	?	?	?	Y	Y	Y
15 Rangel	Y	Y	Y	Y	Y	Y
16 Serrano	Y	Y	Y	Y	Y	Y
17 Engel	?	?	?	?	?	?
18 Lowey	Y	Y	Y	Y	Y	Y
19 Hall	Y	Y	Y	Y	Y	Y
20 Gillibrand	Y	Y	Y	Y	Y	Y
21 McNulty	?	?	?	?	?	?
22 Hinchey	Y	Y	Y	Y	Y	Y
23 **McHugh**	Y	Y	Y	Y	Y	Y
24 Arcuri	Y	Y	Y	Y	Y	Y
25 **Walsh**	Y	Y	Y	Y	Y	Y
26 **Reynolds**	Y	Y	Y	Y	Y	Y
27 Higgins	Y	Y	Y	Y	Y	Y
28 Slaughter	Y	Y	Y	+	Y	Y
29 **Kuhl**	Y	Y	Y	Y	Y	Y
NORTH CAROLINA						
1 Butterfield	?	?	?	Y	Y	Y
2 Etheridge	Y	Y	Y	P	Y	Y
3 **Jones**	Y	Y	Y	Y	Y	Y
4 Price	Y	Y	Y	Y	Y	Y
5 **Foxx**	Y	Y	Y	P	Y	Y
6 **Coble**	Y	Y	Y	Y	Y	Y
7 McIntyre	Y	Y	Y	Y	Y	Y
8 **Hayes**	Y	Y	Y	Y	Y	Y
9 **Myrick**	Y	Y	Y	Y	Y	Y
10 **McHenry**	Y	Y	Y	Y	Y	Y
11 Shuler	?	?	?	Y	Y	Y
12 Watt	Y	Y	Y	Y	Y	Y
13 Miller	Y	Y	Y	Y	Y	Y
NORTH DAKOTA						
AL Pomeroy	Y	Y	Y	P	Y	Y
OHIO						
1 **Chabot**	Y	Y	Y	Y	Y	Y
2 **Schmidt**	Y	Y	Y	Y	Y	Y
3 **Turner**	Y	Y	Y	Y	Y	Y
4 **Jordan**	Y	Y	Y	Y	Y	Y
5 **Latta**	Y	Y	Y	Y	Y	?
6 Wilson	Y	Y	Y	Y	Y	Y
7 **Hobson**	Y	Y	Y	Y	Y	Y
8 **Boehner**	Y	Y	Y	Y	Y	Y
9 Kaptur	Y	Y	Y	Y	Y	Y
10 Kucinich	Y	Y	Y	Y	Y	Y
11 Vacant*						
12 **Tiberi**	Y	Y	Y	Y	Y	Y
13 Sutton	Y	Y	Y	Y	Y	Y
14 **LaTourette**	Y	Y	Y	Y	Y	Y
15 **Pryce**	Y	Y	Y	Y	Y	Y
16 **Regula**	Y	Y	Y	Y	Y	Y
17 Ryan	Y	Y	Y	Y	Y	Y
18 Space	Y	Y	Y	Y	Y	Y
OKLAHOMA						
1 **Sullivan**	Y	Y	Y	Y	Y	Y
2 Boren	Y	Y	Y	Y	Y	Y
3 **Lucas**	Y	Y	Y	Y	Y	Y
4 **Cole**	Y	Y	Y	Y	Y	Y
5 **Fallin**	Y	Y	Y	Y	Y	Y
OREGON						
1 Wu	Y	Y	Y	Y	Y	Y
2 **Walden**	Y	Y	Y	Y	Y	Y
3 Blumenauer	Y	Y	Y	Y	Y	Y
4 DeFazio	Y	Y	Y	Y	Y	Y
5 Hooley	Y	Y	Y	Y	Y	Y
PENNSYLVANIA						
1 Brady	Y	Y	Y	Y	Y	Y
2 Fattah	Y	Y	Y	Y	Y	Y
3 **English**	Y	Y	Y	Y	Y	Y
4 Altmire	Y	Y	Y	Y	Y	Y
5 **Peterson**	?	?	?	Y	?	Y
6 **Gerlach**	Y	Y	Y	Y	Y	Y
7 Sestak	Y	Y	?	Y	Y	?
8 Murphy, P.	Y	Y	Y	Y	Y	Y
9 **Shuster**	Y	Y	Y	Y	Y	Y
10 Carney	Y	Y	Y	Y	Y	Y
11 Kanjorski	Y	Y	Y	Y	Y	Y
12 Murtha	Y	Y	Y	Y	Y	Y
13 Schwartz	Y	Y	Y	Y	Y	Y
14 Doyle	Y	Y	Y	Y	Y	Y
15 **Dent**	Y	Y	Y	Y	Y	Y
16 **Pitts**	?	?	?	?	?	?
17 Holden	?	?	?	Y	Y	Y
18 **Murphy, T.**	Y	Y	Y	Y	Y	Y
19 **Platts**	Y	Y	Y	Y	Y	Y
RHODE ISLAND						
1 Kennedy	?	Y	Y	Y	Y	?
2 Langevin	Y	Y	Y	Y	Y	Y
SOUTH CAROLINA						
1 **Brown**	Y	Y	Y	Y	Y	Y
2 **Wilson**	Y	Y	Y	Y	Y	Y
3 **Barrett**	Y	Y	Y	Y	Y	Y
4 **Inglis**	Y	Y	Y	Y	Y	Y
5 Spratt	Y	Y	Y	Y	Y	Y
6 Clyburn	Y	Y	Y	Y	Y	Y
SOUTH DAKOTA						
AL Herseth Sandlin	Y	Y	Y	P	Y	Y
TENNESSEE						
1 **Davis, David**	Y	Y	Y	Y	Y	Y
2 **Duncan**	Y	Y	Y	Y	Y	Y
3 **Wamp**	Y	Y	Y	Y	Y	Y
4 Davis, L.	Y	Y	Y	Y	Y	Y
5 Cooper	Y	Y	Y	Y	Y	Y
6 Gordon	Y	Y	Y	Y	Y	Y
7 **Blackburn**	Y	Y	?	Y	Y	Y
8 Tanner	Y	Y	Y	Y	Y	Y
9 Cohen	Y	Y	Y	Y	Y	Y
TEXAS						
1 **Gohmert**	Y	Y	Y	?	Y	Y
2 **Poe**	Y	Y	Y	Y	Y	Y
3 **Johnson, S.**	Y	Y	Y	Y	Y	Y
4 **Hall**	Y	Y	Y	Y	Y	Y
5 **Hensarling**	Y	Y	Y	Y	Y	Y
6 **Barton**	Y	Y	Y	Y	Y	Y
7 **Culberson**	Y	Y	Y	Y	Y	Y
8 **Brady**	Y	Y	Y	Y	Y	Y
9 Green, A.	Y	Y	Y	Y	Y	Y
10 **McCaul**	Y	Y	Y	Y	Y	Y
11 **Conaway**	Y	Y	Y	Y	Y	Y
12 **Granger**	Y	Y	Y	Y	Y	Y
13 **Thornberry**	Y	Y	Y	Y	Y	Y
14 **Paul**	Y	N	?	N	Y	N
15 Hinojosa	Y	Y	Y	Y	Y	Y
16 Reyes	Y	Y	Y	Y	Y	Y
17 Edwards	Y	Y	Y	Y	Y	Y
18 Jackson Lee	Y	Y	Y	Y	Y	Y
19 **Neugebauer**	Y	Y	Y	Y	Y	Y
20 Gonzalez	Y	Y	Y	Y	Y	Y
21 **Smith**	Y	Y	Y	Y	Y	Y
22 Lampson	Y	Y	Y	Y	Y	Y
23 Rodriguez	Y	Y	Y	Y	Y	Y
24 **Marchant**	Y	Y	Y	Y	Y	Y
25 Doggett	Y	Y	Y	Y	Y	Y
26 **Burgess**	Y	Y	Y	Y	Y	Y
27 Ortiz	Y	Y	Y	Y	Y	Y
28 Cuellar	Y	Y	Y	Y	Y	Y
29 Green, G.	Y	Y	Y	Y	Y	Y
30 Johnson, E.	Y	Y	Y	Y	Y	Y
31 **Carter**	Y	Y	Y	?	Y	Y
32 **Sessions**	Y	Y	Y	Y	Y	Y
UTAH						
1 **Bishop**	Y	Y	Y	Y	Y	Y
2 Matheson	Y	Y	Y	Y	Y	Y
3 **Cannon**	?	?	?	?	?	?
VERMONT						
AL Welch	Y	Y	Y	Y	Y	Y
VIRGINIA						
1 **Wittman**	Y	Y	Y	Y	Y	Y
2 **Drake**	Y	Y	Y	Y	Y	Y
3 Scott	+	Y	Y	Y	Y	Y
4 **Forbes**	Y	Y	Y	Y	Y	Y
5 **Goode**	Y	Y	Y	Y	Y	Y
6 **Goodlatte**	Y	Y	Y	Y	Y	Y
7 **Cantor**	Y	Y	Y	Y	Y	Y
8 Moran	Y	Y	Y	Y	Y	Y
9 Boucher	?	?	?	?	?	?
10 **Wolf**	Y	Y	Y	Y	Y	Y
11 **Davis, T.**	?	?	?	Y	Y	Y
WASHINGTON						
1 Inslee	Y	Y	Y	Y	Y	Y
2 Larsen	Y	Y	Y	Y	Y	Y
3 Baird	Y	Y	Y	Y	Y	Y
4 **Hastings**	Y	Y	Y	Y	Y	Y
5 **McMorris Rodgers**	Y	Y	Y	Y	Y	Y
6 Dicks	?	?	?	Y	Y	Y
7 McDermott	Y	Y	Y	Y	Y	Y
8 **Reichert**	Y	Y	Y	Y	Y	Y
9 Smith	?	?	?	?	?	?
WEST VIRGINIA						
1 Mollohan	Y	Y	Y	Y	Y	Y
2 **Capito**	Y	Y	Y	Y	Y	Y
3 Rahall	Y	Y	Y	Y	Y	Y
WISCONSIN						
1 **Ryan**	Y	Y	Y	Y	Y	Y
2 Baldwin	Y	Y	Y	Y	Y	Y
3 Kind	Y	Y	Y	Y	Y	Y
4 Moore	Y	Y	Y	Y	Y	Y
5 **Sensenbrenner**	Y	Y	Y	?	?	?
6 **Petri**	Y	Y	Y	Y	Y	Y
7 Obey	Y	Y	Y	Y	Y	Y
8 Kagen	Y	Y	Y	Y	Y	Y
WYOMING						
AL **Cubin**	?	?	?	?	Y	Y
DELEGATES						
Faleomavaega (A.S.)						
Norton (D.C.)						
Bordallo (Guam)						
Fortuño (P.R.)						
Christensen (V.I.)						

IN THE HOUSE | By Vote Number

573. **H Res 1307. Kingdom of Bhutan Tribute/Adoption.** Baird, D-Wash., motion to suspend the rules and adopt the resolution that would commend the Kingdom of Bhutan for participating in the 2008 Smithsonian Folklife Festival, recognize the achievements of the Bhutanese people and commend the government for transitioning to a parliamentary democracy. Motion agreed to 395-15: R 179-15; D 216-0 (ND 160-0, SD 56-0). A two-thirds majority of those present and voting (274 in this case) is required for adoption under suspension of the rules. Sept. 9, 2008.

574. **HR 6168. Weaver Post Office/Passage.** Davis, D-Ill., motion to suspend the rules and pass the bill that would designate a post office in St. Charles, Mo., as the "Lance Cpl. Drew W. Weaver Post Office Building." Motion agreed to 403-0: R 192-0; D 211-0 (ND 156-0, SD 55-0). A two-thirds majority of those present and voting (269 in this case) is required for passage under suspension of the rules. Sept. 9, 2008.

575. **HR 6630. Mexican Motor Carrier Restrictions/Passage.** DeFazio, D-Ore., motion to suspend the rules and pass the bill that would bar the Transportation secretary from granting authority to motor carriers domiciled in Mexico to operate beyond U.S. municipalities and commercial zones on the U.S.-Mexican border unless authorized by Congress. It also would require the secretary to end a one-year cross-border demonstration project that began in September 2007. Motion agreed to 395-18: R 180-15; D 215-3 (ND 163-0, SD 52-3). A two-thirds majority of those present and voting (276 in this case) is required for passage under suspension of the rules. A "nay" was a vote in support of the president's position. Sept. 9, 2008.

576. **HR 3667. Wild and Scenic River Study/Previous Question.** Welch, D-Vt., motion to order the previous question (thus ending debate and possibility of amendment) on adoption of the rule (H Res 1419) to provide for House floor consideration of the bill that would direct the Interior Department to study portions of the Missisquoi River and a tributary, the Trout River, in Vermont as wild and scenic rivers. Motion agreed to 224-189: R 5-185; D 219-4 (ND 166-2, SD 53-2). Sept. 10, 2008.

577. **HR 3667. Wild and Scenic River Study/Rule.** Adoption of the rule (H Res 1419) that would provide for House floor consideration of the bill that would direct the Interior Department to study portions of the Missisquoi River and a tributary, the Trout River, in Vermont as wild and scenic rivers. Adopted 223-190: R 1-189; D 222-1 (ND 167-1, SD 55-0). Sept. 10, 2008.

578. **HR 1527. Rural Veterans' Health Care Access/Passage.** Filner, D-Calif., motion to suspend the rules and pass the bill that would require the Department of Veterans Affairs to conduct a three-year pilot program to permit veterans in rural areas to receive eligible health care from non-VA providers. Veterans who live more than 60 miles from a primary care VA facility or 120 miles from a facility providing acute hospital care would be eligible for the program. Motion agreed to 417-0: R 191-0; D 226-0 (ND 169-0, SD 57-0). A two-thirds majority of those present and voting (278 in this case) is required for passage under suspension of the rules. Sept. 10, 2008.

	573	574	575	576	577	578
ALABAMA						
1 Bonner	Y	Y	Y	N	N	Y
2 Everett	Y	Y	Y	N	N	Y
3 Rogers	Y	Y	Y	N	N	Y
4 Aderholt	Y	Y	Y	N	N	Y
5 Cramer	Y	Y	Y	Y	Y	Y
6 Bachus	Y	Y	Y	N	N	Y
7 Davis	Y	Y	Y	Y	Y	Y
ALASKA						
AL Young	Y	Y	Y	N	N	Y
ARIZONA						
1 Renzi	Y	Y	Y	N	N	Y
2 Franks	Y	Y	Y	N	N	Y
3 Shadegg	Y	Y	Y	N	N	Y
4 Pastor	Y	Y	Y	Y	Y	Y
5 Mitchell	Y	Y	Y	Y	Y	Y
6 Flake	Y	N	Y	N	N	Y
7 Grijalva	Y	?	Y	Y	Y	Y
8 Giffords	Y	Y	Y	Y	Y	Y
ARKANSAS						
1 Berry	Y	Y	Y	Y	Y	Y
2 Snyder	Y	Y	Y	Y	Y	Y
3 Boozman	Y	Y	Y	N	N	Y
4 Ross	Y	Y	Y	Y	Y	Y
CALIFORNIA						
1 Thompson	Y	Y	Y	Y	Y	Y
2 Herger	Y	Y	Y	N	N	Y
3 Lungren	Y	Y	N	N	N	Y
4 Doolittle	N	Y	Y	N	N	Y
5 Matsui	Y	Y	Y	Y	Y	Y
6 Woolsey	Y	Y	Y	Y	Y	Y
7 Miller, George	?	Y	Y	Y	Y	Y
8 Pelosi						
9 Lee	+	+	+	+	+	+
10 Tauscher	Y	Y	Y	Y	Y	Y
11 McNerney	Y	Y	Y	Y	Y	Y
12 Speier	Y	Y	Y	Y	Y	Y
13 Stark	Y	?	Y	Y	Y	Y
14 Eshoo	Y	Y	Y	Y	Y	Y
15 Honda	Y	Y	Y	Y	Y	Y
16 Lofgren	Y	Y	Y	Y	Y	Y
17 Farr	Y	Y	Y	Y	Y	Y
18 Cardoza	Y	Y	Y	Y	Y	Y
19 Radanovich	Y	Y	Y	N	N	Y
20 Costa	Y	Y	Y	Y	Y	Y
21 Nunes	Y	Y	Y	N	N	Y
22 McCarthy	Y	Y	Y	N	N	Y
23 Capps	Y	Y	Y	Y	Y	Y
24 Gallegly	Y	Y	Y	N	N	Y
25 McKeon	Y	Y	Y	N	N	Y
26 Dreier	Y	Y	Y	N	N	Y
27 Sherman	Y	Y	Y	Y	Y	Y
28 Berman	Y	Y	Y	Y	Y	Y
29 Schiff	Y	Y	Y	Y	Y	Y
30 Waxman	Y	Y	Y	Y	Y	Y
31 Becerra	Y	Y	Y	Y	Y	Y
32 Solis	Y	Y	Y	Y	Y	Y
33 Watson	Y	Y	Y	Y	Y	Y
34 Roybal-Allard	Y	Y	Y	Y	Y	Y
35 Waters	Y	Y	Y	Y	Y	Y
36 Harman	Y	Y	Y	Y	Y	Y
37 Richardson	Y	Y	Y	Y	Y	Y
38 Napolitano	Y	Y	Y	Y	Y	Y
39 Sánchez, Linda	Y	Y	Y	Y	Y	Y
40 Royce	Y	Y	Y	N	N	Y
41 Lewis	Y	?	Y	N	N	Y
42 Miller, Gary	Y	Y	Y	N	N	Y
43 Baca	Y	Y	Y	Y	Y	Y
44 Calvert	Y	Y	Y	N	N	Y
45 Bono Mack	Y	Y	Y	N	N	Y
46 Rohrabacher	Y	Y	Y	N	N	Y
47 Sanchez, Loretta	Y	Y	Y	Y	Y	Y
48 Campbell	Y	Y	N	N	N	Y
49 Issa	Y	Y	N	N	N	Y
50 Bilbray	Y	Y	Y	N	N	Y
51 Filner	Y	Y	Y	Y	Y	Y
52 Hunter	Y	Y	Y	N	?	?
53 Davis	Y	Y	Y	Y	Y	Y
COLORADO						
1 DeGette	Y	Y	Y	Y	Y	Y
2 Udall	Y	Y	Y	Y	Y	Y
3 Salazar	Y	Y	Y	Y	Y	Y
4 Musgrave	Y	Y	Y	N	N	Y
5 Lamborn	Y	Y	Y	N	N	Y
6 Tancredo	N	Y	N	N	N	Y
7 Perlmutter	Y	Y	Y	Y	Y	Y
CONNECTICUT						
1 Larson	Y	Y	Y	Y	Y	Y
2 Courtney	Y	Y	Y	Y	Y	Y
3 DeLauro	Y	Y	Y	Y	Y	Y
4 Shays	Y	Y	Y	Y	Y	Y
5 Murphy	Y	Y	Y	Y	Y	Y
DELAWARE						
AL Castle	Y	Y	Y	N	N	Y
FLORIDA						
1 Miller	N	Y	Y	N	N	Y
2 Boyd	Y	Y	Y	Y	Y	Y
3 Brown	Y	Y	Y	Y	Y	Y
4 Crenshaw	Y	Y	Y	N	N	Y
5 Brown-Waite	Y	Y	Y	N	N	Y
6 Stearns	Y	Y	Y	N	N	Y
7 Mica	Y	Y	Y	N	N	Y
8 Keller	Y	Y	Y	N	N	Y
9 Bilirakis	Y	Y	Y	N	N	Y
10 Young	Y	Y	Y	N	N	Y
11 Castor	Y	Y	Y	Y	Y	Y
12 Putnam	Y	Y	Y	N	N	Y
13 Buchanan	Y	Y	Y	N	N	Y
14 Mack	Y	Y	Y	N	N	Y
15 Weldon	Y	Y	Y	N	N	Y
16 Mahoney	Y	Y	Y	Y	Y	Y
17 Meek	Y	Y	Y	Y	Y	Y
18 Ros-Lehtinen	Y	Y	Y	N	Y	Y
19 Wexler	Y	Y	Y	Y	Y	Y
20 Wasserman Schultz	Y	Y	Y	Y	Y	Y
21 Diaz-Balart, L.	Y	Y	Y	N	N	Y
22 Klein	Y	Y	Y	Y	Y	Y
23 Hastings	Y	Y	Y	Y	Y	Y
24 Feeney	Y	Y	Y	Y	Y	Y
25 Diaz-Balart, M.	Y	Y	Y	N	N	Y
GEORGIA						
1 Kingston	N	Y	Y	N	N	Y
2 Bishop	Y	Y	Y	Y	Y	Y
3 Westmoreland	Y	Y	Y	N	N	Y
4 Johnson	Y	Y	Y	Y	Y	Y
5 Lewis	Y	Y	Y	Y	Y	Y
6 Price	Y	Y	Y	N	N	Y
7 Linder	Y	Y	Y	N	N	Y
8 Marshall	Y	Y	Y	Y	Y	Y
9 Deal	Y	Y	Y	N	N	Y
10 Broun	Y	Y	Y	N	N	Y
11 Gingrey	Y	Y	Y	N	N	Y
12 Barrow	Y	Y	Y	Y	Y	Y
13 Scott	Y	Y	Y	Y	Y	Y
HAWAII						
1 Abercrombie	Y	Y	Y	Y	Y	Y
2 Hirono	Y	Y	Y	Y	Y	Y
IDAHO						
1 Sali	Y	Y	Y	N	N	Y
2 Simpson	Y	Y	Y	N	N	Y
ILLINOIS						
1 Rush	Y	Y	Y	Y	Y	Y
2 Jackson	Y	Y	Y	Y	Y	Y
3 Lipinski	Y	Y	Y	Y	Y	Y
4 Gutierrez	Y	Y	Y	Y	Y	Y
5 Emanuel	Y	Y	Y	Y	Y	Y
6 Roskam	Y	Y	Y	N	N	Y
7 Davis	Y	Y	Y	Y	Y	Y
8 Bean	Y	Y	Y	Y	Y	Y
9 Schakowsky	Y	Y	Y	Y	Y	Y
10 Kirk	Y	Y	Y	N	Y	Y
11 Weller	Y	Y	N	N	N	Y
12 Costello	Y	Y	Y	Y	Y	Y
13 Biggert	Y	Y	Y	N	N	Y
14 Foster	Y	Y	Y	Y	Y	Y
15 Johnson	Y	Y	Y	N	N	Y

KEY	**Republicans**	Democrats		
Y	Voted for (yea)	X	Paired against	C Voted "present" to avoid possible conflict of interest
#	Paired for	–	Announced against	
+	Announced for	P	Voted "present"	? Did not vote or otherwise make a position known
N	Voted against (nay)			

ND Northern Democrats, SD Southern Democrats
Southern states: Ala., Ark., Fla., Ga., Ky., La., Miss., N.C., Okla., S.C., Tenn., Texas, Va.

	573	574	575	576	577	578
16 **Manzullo**	Y	Y	Y	N	N	Y
17 Hare	Y	Y	Y	Y	Y	Y
18 **LaHood**	Y	Y	Y	N	N	Y
19 **Shimkus**	Y	Y	Y	N	N	Y
INDIANA						
1 Visclosky	Y	Y	Y	Y	Y	Y
2 Donnelly	Y	Y	Y	N	Y	Y
3 **Souder**	Y	Y	Y	N	N	Y
4 **Buyer**	Y	Y	Y	N	N	Y
5 **Burton**	N	Y	Y	N	N	Y
6 **Pence**	Y	Y	N	N	N	Y
7 Carson, A.	Y	Y	Y	Y	Y	Y
8 Ellsworth	Y	Y	Y	Y	Y	Y
9 Hill	Y	Y	Y	N	N	Y
IOWA						
1 Braley	Y	Y	Y	Y	Y	Y
2 Loebsack	Y	Y	Y	Y	Y	Y
3 Boswell	Y	Y	Y	Y	Y	Y
4 **Latham**	Y	Y	Y	N	N	Y
5 **King**	Y	Y	Y	N	N	Y
KANSAS						
1 **Moran**	Y	Y	Y	N	N	Y
2 Boyda	Y	Y	Y	Y	Y	Y
3 Moore	Y	Y	Y	Y	Y	Y
4 **Tiahrt**	Y	Y	Y	N	N	Y
KENTUCKY						
1 **Whitfield**	Y	?	Y	N	N	Y
2 **Lewis**	Y	Y	Y	N	N	Y
3 Yarmuth	Y	Y	Y	Y	Y	Y
4 **Davis**	Y	Y	Y	N	N	Y
5 **Rogers**	Y	Y	Y	N	N	Y
6 Chandler	Y	Y	Y	Y	Y	Y
LOUISIANA						
1 **Scalise**	Y	Y	Y	N	N	Y
2 Jefferson	Y	Y	Y	Y	Y	Y
3 Melancon	?	?	?	Y	Y	Y
4 **McCrery**	?	?	?	N	N	Y
5 **Alexander**	Y	Y	Y	N	N	Y
6 Cazayoux	?	?	?	?	?	?
7 **Boustany**	Y	Y	Y	N	N	Y
MAINE						
1 Allen	Y	Y	Y	Y	Y	Y
2 Michaud	Y	Y	Y	Y	Y	Y
MARYLAND						
1 **Gilchrest**	Y	Y	Y	N	N	Y
2 Ruppersberger	Y	Y	Y	Y	Y	Y
3 Sarbanes	Y	Y	Y	Y	Y	Y
4 Edwards	Y	Y	Y	Y	Y	Y
5 Hoyer	Y	Y	Y	Y	Y	Y
6 **Bartlett**	Y	Y	Y	N	N	Y
7 Cummings	Y	Y	Y	Y	Y	Y
8 Van Hollen	Y	Y	Y	Y	Y	Y
MASSACHUSETTS						
1 Olver	?	Y	Y	Y	Y	Y
2 Neal	Y	Y	Y	Y	Y	Y
3 McGovern	Y	Y	Y	Y	Y	Y
4 Frank	Y	?	Y	Y	Y	Y
5 Tsongas	Y	Y	Y	Y	Y	Y
6 Tierney	Y	Y	Y	Y	Y	Y
7 Markey	Y	Y	Y	Y	Y	Y
8 Capuano	Y	Y	Y	Y	Y	Y
9 Lynch	Y	Y	Y	Y	Y	Y
10 Delahunt	Y	?	Y	Y	Y	Y
MICHIGAN						
1 Stupak	Y	Y	Y	Y	Y	Y
2 **Hoekstra**	Y	Y	Y	N	N	Y
3 **Ehlers**	Y	Y	Y	N	N	Y
4 **Camp**	Y	Y	Y	N	N	Y
5 Kildee	Y	Y	Y	Y	Y	Y
6 **Upton**	Y	Y	Y	N	N	Y
7 **Walberg**	Y	Y	Y	N	N	Y
8 **Rogers**	Y	Y	Y	N	N	Y
9 **Knollenberg**	Y	Y	Y	N	N	Y
10 **Miller**	Y	Y	Y	N	N	Y
11 **McCotter**	Y	Y	Y	N	N	Y
12 Levin	?	?	?	?	?	?
13 Kilpatrick	Y	Y	Y	Y	Y	Y
14 Conyers	Y	Y	Y	Y	Y	Y
15 Dingell	Y	Y	Y	Y	Y	Y
MINNESOTA						
1 Walz	Y	Y	Y	Y	Y	Y
2 **Kline**	Y	Y	Y	N	N	Y
3 **Ramstad**	Y	Y	Y	?	?	Y
4 McCollum	Y	Y	Y	Y	Y	Y
5 Ellison	?	?	?	Y	Y	Y
6 **Bachmann**	Y	Y	Y	N	N	Y
7 Peterson	?	?	?	?	?	?
8 Oberstar	Y	Y	Y	Y	Y	Y
MISSISSIPPI						
1 Childers	Y	Y	Y	N	Y	Y
2 Thompson	Y	Y	Y	Y	Y	Y
3 **Pickering**	Y	Y	Y	N	N	Y
4 Taylor	Y	Y	Y	Y	Y	Y
MISSOURI						
1 Clay	Y	Y	Y	Y	Y	Y
2 **Akin**	Y	Y	Y	N	N	Y
3 Carnahan	?	?	?	Y	Y	Y
4 Skelton	Y	Y	Y	Y	Y	Y
5 Cleaver	Y	Y	Y	Y	Y	Y
6 **Graves**	Y	Y	Y	N	N	Y
7 **Blunt**	Y	Y	Y	N	N	Y
8 **Emerson**	Y	Y	Y	N	N	+
9 **Hulshof**	?	?	?	?	?	?
MONTANA						
AL **Rehberg**	Y	Y	Y	N	N	Y
NEBRASKA						
1 **Fortenberry**	Y	Y	Y	N	N	Y
2 **Terry**	Y	Y	Y	N	N	Y
3 **Smith**	Y	Y	Y	N	N	Y
NEVADA						
1 Berkley	Y	Y	Y	Y	Y	Y
2 **Heller**	Y	Y	Y	Y	N	Y
3 **Porter**	Y	Y	Y	Y	N	Y
NEW HAMPSHIRE						
1 Shea-Porter	Y	Y	Y	Y	Y	Y
2 Hodes	?	?	?	?	?	?
NEW JERSEY						
1 Andrews	Y	?	?	Y	Y	Y
2 **LoBiondo**	Y	Y	Y	N	N	Y
3 **Saxton**	Y	Y	Y	N	N	Y
4 **Smith**	Y	Y	Y	N	N	Y
5 **Garrett**	Y	Y	Y	N	N	Y
6 Pallone	Y	Y	Y	Y	Y	Y
7 **Ferguson**	Y	Y	Y	?	N	Y
8 Pascrell	Y	Y	Y	Y	Y	Y
9 Rothman	Y	Y	Y	Y	Y	Y
10 Payne	Y	Y	Y	Y	Y	Y
11 **Frelinghuysen**	Y	Y	Y	N	N	Y
12 Holt	Y	Y	Y	Y	Y	Y
13 Sires	Y	Y	Y	Y	Y	Y
NEW MEXICO						
1 **Wilson**	Y	Y	Y	N	N	Y
2 **Pearce**	Y	Y	Y	N	N	Y
3 Udall	Y	Y	Y	Y	Y	Y
NEW YORK						
1 Bishop	Y	Y	Y	Y	Y	Y
2 Israel	Y	Y	Y	Y	Y	Y
3 **King**	Y	Y	Y	N	N	Y
4 McCarthy	?	?	Y	Y	Y	Y
5 Ackerman	Y	Y	Y	Y	Y	Y
6 Meeks	?	?	?	Y	Y	Y
7 Crowley	Y	Y	Y	Y	Y	Y
8 Nadler	Y	Y	Y	Y	Y	Y
9 Weiner	Y	Y	Y	Y	Y	Y
10 Towns	?	?	?	Y	Y	Y
11 Clarke	Y	Y	Y	Y	Y	Y
12 Velázquez	Y	Y	Y	Y	Y	Y
13 **Fossella**	Y	Y	Y	N	N	Y
14 Maloney	Y	Y	Y	Y	Y	Y
15 Rangel	Y	Y	Y	Y	Y	Y
16 Serrano	Y	Y	Y	Y	Y	Y
17 Engel	?	?	?	Y	Y	Y
18 Lowey	Y	Y	Y	Y	Y	Y
19 Hall	Y	Y	Y	Y	Y	Y
20 Gillibrand	Y	Y	Y	Y	Y	Y
21 McNulty	?	?	?	?	?	?
22 Hinchey	Y	Y	Y	Y	Y	Y
23 **McHugh**	Y	Y	Y	N	N	Y
24 Arcuri	Y	Y	Y	Y	Y	Y
25 **Walsh**	Y	Y	Y	N	N	Y
26 **Reynolds**	?	Y	Y	N	N	Y
27 Higgins	Y	Y	Y	Y	Y	Y
28 Slaughter	Y	Y	Y	Y	Y	Y
29 **Kuhl**	Y	Y	Y	N	N	Y
NORTH CAROLINA						
1 Butterfield	Y	Y	Y	Y	Y	Y
2 Etheridge	Y	Y	Y	Y	Y	Y
3 **Jones**	Y	Y	Y	N	N	Y
4 Price	Y	Y	Y	Y	Y	Y
5 **Foxx**	Y	Y	Y	N	N	Y
6 **Coble**	Y	Y	Y	N	N	Y
7 McIntyre	Y	Y	Y	Y	Y	Y
8 **Hayes**	Y	Y	Y	N	N	Y
9 **Myrick**	Y	Y	Y	N	N	Y
10 **McHenry**	Y	Y	Y	N	N	Y
11 Shuler	Y	Y	Y	Y	Y	Y
12 Watt	Y	Y	Y	Y	Y	Y
13 Miller	Y	Y	Y	Y	Y	Y
NORTH DAKOTA						
AL Pomeroy	Y	Y	Y	Y	Y	Y
OHIO						
1 **Chabot**	Y	Y	Y	N	N	Y
2 **Schmidt**	Y	Y	Y	N	N	Y
3 **Turner**	Y	Y	Y	N	N	Y
4 **Jordan**	Y	Y	Y	N	N	Y
5 **Latta**	Y	Y	Y	N	N	Y
6 Wilson	Y	Y	Y	Y	Y	Y
7 **Hobson**	Y	Y	Y	N	N	Y
8 **Boehner**	Y	Y	Y	N	N	Y
9 Kaptur	Y	Y	Y	Y	Y	Y
10 Kucinich	Y	Y	Y	Y	Y	Y
11 Vacant						
12 **Tiberi**	Y	Y	Y	N	N	Y
13 Sutton	Y	?	Y	Y	Y	Y
14 **LaTourette**	Y	Y	Y	N	N	Y
15 **Pryce**	Y	Y	Y	N	N	Y
16 **Regula**	Y	Y	Y	N	N	Y
17 Ryan	Y	Y	Y	Y	Y	Y
18 Space	Y	Y	Y	Y	Y	Y
OKLAHOMA						
1 **Sullivan**	N	Y	Y	N	N	Y
2 Boren	Y	Y	Y	Y	Y	Y
3 **Lucas**	N	Y	Y	N	N	Y
4 **Cole**	Y	?	Y	N	N	Y
5 **Fallin**	Y	Y	Y	N	N	Y
OREGON						
1 Wu	Y	Y	Y	Y	Y	Y
2 **Walden**	Y	Y	Y	N	N	Y
3 Blumenauer	Y	Y	Y	Y	Y	Y
4 DeFazio	Y	Y	Y	Y	Y	Y
5 Hooley	Y	Y	Y	Y	Y	Y
PENNSYLVANIA						
1 Brady	Y	Y	Y	Y	Y	Y
2 Fattah	Y	Y	Y	Y	Y	Y
3 **English**	Y	Y	Y	N	N	Y
4 Altmire	Y	Y	Y	Y	Y	Y
5 **Peterson**	Y	Y	Y	N	?	Y
6 **Gerlach**	Y	Y	Y	N	N	Y
7 Sestak	Y	Y	Y	Y	Y	Y
8 Murphy, P.	Y	Y	Y	Y	Y	Y
9 **Shuster**	Y	Y	Y	N	N	Y
10 Carney	Y	Y	Y	Y	Y	Y
11 Kanjorski	Y	Y	Y	Y	Y	Y
12 Murtha	Y	Y	Y	Y	Y	Y
13 Schwartz	Y	Y	Y	Y	Y	Y
14 Doyle	Y	Y	Y	Y	Y	Y
15 **Dent**	Y	Y	Y	N	N	Y
16 **Pitts**	?	?	?	?	?	?
17 Holden	Y	Y	Y	Y	Y	Y
18 **Murphy, T.**	Y	Y	Y	N	N	Y
19 **Platts**	Y	Y	Y	N	N	Y
RHODE ISLAND						
1 Kennedy	Y	Y	Y	?	?	Y
2 Langevin	Y	Y	Y	Y	Y	Y
SOUTH CAROLINA						
1 **Brown**	Y	Y	Y	N	N	Y
2 **Wilson**	Y	Y	Y	N	N	Y
3 **Barrett**	Y	Y	Y	N	N	Y
4 **Inglis**	Y	Y	Y	N	N	Y
5 Spratt	Y	Y	Y	Y	Y	Y
6 Clyburn	Y	Y	Y	Y	Y	Y
SOUTH DAKOTA						
AL Herseth Sandlin	Y	Y	Y	Y	Y	Y
TENNESSEE						
1 **Davis, David**	Y	Y	Y	N	N	Y
2 **Duncan**	Y	Y	Y	N	N	Y
3 **Wamp**	Y	Y	Y	N	N	Y
4 Davis, L.	Y	Y	Y	Y	Y	Y
5 Cooper	Y	Y	Y	Y	Y	Y
6 Gordon	Y	?	?	?	?	Y
7 **Blackburn**	N	Y	Y	N	N	?
8 Tanner	Y	Y	Y	Y	Y	Y
9 Cohen	Y	Y	Y	Y	Y	Y
TEXAS						
1 **Gohmert**	Y	Y	Y	N	N	Y
2 **Poe**	N	Y	Y	N	N	Y
3 **Johnson, S.**	N	Y	Y	N	N	Y
4 **Hall**	Y	Y	Y	N	N	Y
5 **Hensarling**	Y	Y	N	N	N	Y
6 **Barton**	N	Y	Y	N	N	Y
7 **Culberson**	N	Y	Y	N	N	Y
8 **Brady**	Y	Y	N	N	N	Y
9 Green, A.	Y	Y	Y	Y	Y	Y
10 **McCaul**	Y	Y	Y	N	N	Y
11 **Conaway**	Y	Y	N	N	N	Y
12 **Granger**	Y	Y	Y	N	N	Y
13 **Thornberry**	Y	Y	N	?	?	?
14 **Paul**	Y	Y	Y	N	N	Y
15 Hinojosa	Y	Y	Y	+	+	Y
16 Reyes	Y	Y	Y	Y	Y	Y
17 Edwards	Y	Y	Y	Y	Y	Y
18 Jackson Lee	Y	Y	Y	Y	Y	Y
19 **Neugebauer**	N	Y	N	N	N	Y
20 Gonzalez	Y	Y	N	Y	Y	Y
21 **Smith**	Y	Y	Y	N	N	Y
22 Lampson	Y	Y	Y	N	Y	Y
23 Rodriguez	Y	Y	Y	Y	Y	Y
24 **Marchant**	Y	Y	Y	N	N	Y
25 Doggett	Y	Y	Y	Y	Y	Y
26 **Burgess**	Y	Y	Y	?	?	Y
27 Ortiz	Y	Y	N	Y	Y	Y
28 Cuellar	Y	Y	N	Y	Y	Y
29 Green, G.	Y	Y	Y	Y	Y	Y
30 Johnson, E.	Y	Y	Y	Y	Y	Y
31 **Carter**	N	Y	Y	N	N	Y
32 **Sessions**	Y	Y	Y	N	N	Y
UTAH						
1 **Bishop**	Y	Y	Y	N	N	Y
2 Matheson	Y	Y	Y	Y	Y	Y
3 **Cannon**	Y	Y	Y	?	?	?
VERMONT						
AL Welch	Y	Y	Y	Y	Y	Y
VIRGINIA						
1 **Wittman**	Y	Y	Y	N	N	Y
2 **Drake**	Y	Y	Y	N	N	Y
3 Scott	Y	Y	Y	+	+	+
4 **Forbes**	Y	Y	Y	N	N	Y
5 **Goode**	N	Y	Y	N	N	Y
6 **Goodlatte**	Y	Y	Y	N	N	Y
7 **Cantor**	Y	Y	N	N	N	Y
8 Moran	Y	Y	Y	Y	Y	Y
9 Boucher	?	?	?	Y	Y	Y
10 **Wolf**	Y	Y	Y	N	N	Y
11 **Davis, T.**	Y	Y	N	?	N	Y
WASHINGTON						
1 Inslee	Y	Y	Y	Y	Y	Y
2 Larsen	Y	Y	Y	Y	Y	Y
3 Baird	Y	Y	Y	?	?	?
4 **Hastings**	Y	Y	Y	N	N	Y
5 **McMorris Rodgers**	Y	Y	Y	N	N	Y
6 Dicks	Y	Y	Y	Y	Y	Y
7 McDermott	Y	Y	Y	Y	Y	Y
8 **Reichert**	Y	Y	Y	Y	N	Y
9 Smith	?	?	?	Y	Y	Y
WEST VIRGINIA						
1 Mollohan	Y	Y	Y	Y	Y	Y
2 **Capito**	Y	Y	Y	N	N	Y
3 Rahall	Y	Y	Y	Y	Y	Y
WISCONSIN						
1 **Ryan**	Y	Y	Y	N	N	Y
2 Baldwin	Y	Y	Y	Y	Y	Y
3 Kind	Y	Y	Y	Y	Y	Y
4 Moore	Y	Y	Y	Y	Y	Y
5 **Sensenbrenner**	?	?	?	?	?	?
6 **Petri**	Y	Y	Y	N	N	Y
7 Obey	Y	Y	Y	Y	Y	Y
8 Kagen	?	?	Y	Y	Y	Y
WYOMING						
AL **Cubin**	Y	Y	Y	N	N	Y
DELEGATES						
Faleomavaega (A.S.)						
Norton (D.C.)						
Bordallo (Guam)						
Fortuño (P.R.)						
Christensen (V.I.)						

IN THE HOUSE | By Vote Number

579. **S 2617. Veterans' Cost-of-Living Adjustment/Passage.** Filner, D-Calif., motion to suspend the rules and pass the bill that would increase the rate of compensation for veterans with service-connected disabilities and the rates of dependency and indemnity compensation for survivors of certain disabled veterans. The rate would be linked to the cost-of-living increase for Social Security recipients. Motion agreed to 418-0: R 193-0; D 225-0 (ND 169-0, SD 56-0). A two-thirds majority of those present and voting (279 in this case) is required for passage under suspension of the rules. Sept. 10, 2008.

580. **HR 3667. Wild and Scenic River Study/Motion to Rise.** Grijalva, D-Ariz., motion to rise from Committee of the Whole. Motion agreed to 221-193: R 1-188; D 220-5 (ND 166-3, SD 54-2). Sept. 10, 2008.

581. **HR 3667. Wild and Scenic River Study/Weapon Impacts.** Grijalva, D-Ariz., amendment that would require the study under the bill to analyze any potential impacts on the possession or use of a weapon, trap or net, including a concealed weapon. Adopted in Committee of the Whole 418-0: R 193-0; D 225-0 (ND 169-0, SD 56-0). Sept. 10, 2008.

582. **HR 3667. Wild and Scenic River Study/Motion to Table.** Grijalva, D-Ariz., motion to table (kill) the Sali, R-Idaho, appeal of the ruling of the chair with respect to the Grijalva point of order that the Sali motion to recommit the bill to the Natural Resources Committee was not germane. The Sali motion would recommit the bill with instructions that it be reported back forthwith with language that would add the text of a bill (HR 6566) to provide for offshore drilling in areas where it is currently prohibited, provide tax breaks for individuals and businesses who buy fuel-efficient vehicles, and extend tax credits for alternative sources of energy. Motion agreed to 228-187: R 8-185; D 220-2 (ND 167-0, SD 53-2). Sept. 10, 2008.

583. **HR 3667. Wild and Scenic River Study/Passage.** Passage of the bill that would direct the Interior Department to study portions of the Missisquoi River and a tributary, the Trout River, in Vermont as wild and scenic rivers. Passed 299-118: R 77-118; D 222-0 (ND 166-0, SD 56-0). Sept. 10, 2008.

584. **HR 4081. Cigarette-Trafficking Prevention/Passage.** Scott, D-Va., motion to suspend the rules and pass the bill that would require sellers that mail or ship tobacco products to use a shipping method that includes verification that recipients are of legal age in their states or localities. It also would prohibit consumer shipment of tobacco-product packages that weigh more than 10 pounds. Motion agreed to 379-12: R 176-10; D 203-2 (ND 151-2, SD 52-0). A two-thirds majority of those present and voting (261 in this case) is required for passage under suspension of the rules. Sept. 10, 2008.

	579	580	581	582	583	584
ALABAMA						
1 Bonner	Y	N	Y	N	Y	Y
2 Everett	Y	N	Y	N	N	Y
3 Rogers	Y	N	Y	N	Y	Y
4 Aderholt	Y	N	Y	N	N	Y
5 Cramer	Y	Y	Y	Y	Y	?
6 Bachus	Y	N	Y	N	N	Y
7 Davis	Y	Y	Y	?	Y	Y
ALASKA						
AL Young	Y	N	Y	N	N	N
ARIZONA						
1 Renzi	Y	N	Y	N	Y	?
2 Franks	Y	N	Y	N	N	Y
3 Shadegg	Y	N	Y	N	N	Y
4 Pastor	Y	Y	Y	Y	Y	?
5 Mitchell	Y	Y	Y	Y	Y	Y
6 Flake	Y	N	Y	N	N	N
7 Grijalva	Y	Y	Y	Y	Y	?
8 Giffords	Y	Y	Y	Y	Y	Y
ARKANSAS						
1 Berry	Y	Y	Y	Y	Y	Y
2 Snyder	Y	Y	Y	Y	Y	Y
3 Boozman	Y	N	Y	N	N	Y
4 Ross	Y	Y	Y	Y	Y	Y
CALIFORNIA						
1 Thompson	Y	Y	Y	Y	Y	Y
2 Herger	Y	N	Y	N	N	Y
3 Lungren	Y	N	Y	N	N	Y
4 Doolittle	Y	N	Y	N	N	Y
5 Matsui	Y	Y	Y	Y	Y	Y
6 Woolsey	Y	Y	Y	Y	Y	Y
7 Miller, George	Y	Y	Y	Y	Y	Y
8 Pelosi						
9 Lee	+	+	?	?	+	+
10 Tauscher	Y	Y	Y	Y	Y	Y
11 McNerney	Y	Y	Y	Y	Y	Y
12 Speier	Y	Y	Y	Y	Y	Y
13 Stark	Y	N	Y	Y	Y	Y
14 Eshoo	Y	Y	Y	Y	Y	Y
15 Honda	Y	Y	Y	Y	Y	Y
16 Lofgren	Y	Y	Y	Y	Y	?
17 Farr	Y	Y	Y	Y	Y	Y
18 Cardoza	Y	Y	?	?	?	?
19 Radanovich	Y	N	Y	N	N	Y
20 Costa	Y	Y	Y	Y	Y	Y
21 Nunes	Y	N	Y	N	N	Y
22 McCarthy	Y	N	Y	N	N	Y
23 Capps	Y	Y	Y	Y	Y	Y
24 Gallegly	Y	N	Y	N	N	Y
25 McKeon	Y	N	Y	N	N	Y
26 Dreier	Y	N	Y	N	N	Y
27 Sherman	Y	Y	Y	Y	Y	Y
28 Berman	Y	Y	Y	Y	?	Y
29 Schiff	Y	Y	Y	Y	Y	Y
30 Waxman	Y	Y	Y	Y	Y	Y
31 Becerra	Y	Y	Y	Y	Y	?
32 Solis	Y	Y	Y	Y	Y	?
33 Watson	Y	Y	Y	Y	Y	?
34 Roybal-Allard	Y	Y	Y	Y	Y	?
35 Waters	Y	Y	Y	Y	Y	Y
36 Harman	Y	Y	?	?	?	?
37 Richardson	Y	Y	Y	Y	Y	Y
38 Napolitano	Y	Y	Y	Y	Y	Y
39 Sánchez, Linda	Y	Y	Y	Y	Y	Y
40 Royce	Y	N	Y	N	N	Y
41 Lewis	Y	N	Y	N	Y	Y
42 Miller, Gary	Y	N	Y	N	Y	Y
43 Baca	Y	Y	?	?	?	?
44 Calvert	Y	N	Y	N	N	Y
45 Bono Mack	Y	N	Y	N	N	Y
46 Rohrabacher	Y	N	Y	N	N	Y
47 Sanchez, Loretta	Y	Y	Y	Y	Y	Y
48 Campbell	Y	N	Y	N	N	N
49 Issa	Y	N	Y	N	N	Y
50 Bilbray	Y	?	Y	N	N	?
51 Filner	Y	Y	Y	Y	Y	Y
52 Hunter	Y	N	Y	N	N	Y
53 Davis	Y	Y	Y	Y	Y	Y

	579	580	581	582	583	584
COLORADO						
1 DeGette	Y	Y	Y	Y	Y	Y
2 Udall	Y	?	Y	Y	Y	Y
3 Salazar	Y	Y	Y	Y	Y	?
4 Musgrave	Y	N	Y	N	N	Y
5 Lamborn	Y	N	Y	N	N	Y
6 Tancredo	Y	N	Y	N	N	Y
7 Perlmutter	Y	Y	Y	Y	Y	Y
CONNECTICUT						
1 Larson	Y	Y	Y	Y	Y	Y
2 Courtney	Y	Y	Y	Y	Y	Y
3 DeLauro	Y	Y	Y	Y	Y	Y
4 Shays	Y	N	Y	Y	Y	Y
5 Murphy	Y	Y	Y	Y	Y	Y
DELAWARE						
AL Castle	Y	N	Y	N	Y	Y
FLORIDA						
1 Miller	Y	N	Y	N	N	Y
2 Boyd	Y	Y	Y	Y	Y	Y
3 Brown	Y	Y	Y	Y	Y	Y
4 Crenshaw	Y	N	Y	N	N	Y
5 Brown-Waite	Y	N	Y	N	Y	Y
6 Stearns	Y	N	Y	N	N	Y
7 Mica	Y	N	Y	N	N	Y
8 Keller	Y	N	?	N	N	Y
9 Bilirakis	Y	N	Y	N	Y	Y
10 Young	Y	N	Y	N	Y	Y
11 Castor	Y	Y	Y	Y	Y	Y
12 Putnam	Y	N	Y	N	N	Y
13 Buchanan	Y	N	Y	N	Y	Y
14 Mack	Y	N	Y	N	N	Y
15 Weldon	Y	?	Y	N	N	Y
16 Mahoney	Y	Y	Y	Y	Y	Y
17 Meek	Y	Y	Y	Y	Y	Y
18 Ros-Lehtinen	Y	N	Y	Y	Y	Y
19 Wexler	Y	Y	Y	Y	Y	Y
20 Wasserman Schultz	Y	Y	Y	Y	Y	?
21 Diaz-Balart, L.	Y	N	Y	N	Y	Y
22 Klein	Y	Y	Y	Y	Y	Y
23 Hastings	Y	Y	Y	Y	Y	Y
24 Feeney	Y	N	?	?	?	?
25 Diaz-Balart, M.	Y	N	Y	N	Y	Y
GEORGIA						
1 Kingston	Y	N	Y	N	N	N
2 Bishop	Y	Y	Y	Y	Y	Y
3 Westmoreland	Y	N	Y	N	N	?
4 Johnson	Y	Y	Y	Y	Y	Y
5 Lewis	Y	Y	Y	Y	Y	Y
6 Price	Y	N	Y	N	N	Y
7 Linder	Y	N	Y	N	N	?
8 Marshall	Y	Y	Y	Y	Y	Y
9 Deal	Y	N	Y	N	N	Y
10 Broun	Y	N	Y	N	N	N
11 Gingrey	Y	N	Y	N	N	Y
12 Barrow	Y	Y	Y	Y	Y	Y
13 Scott	Y	Y	Y	Y	Y	Y
HAWAII						
1 Abercrombie	Y	N	+	Y	Y	Y
2 Hirono	Y	Y	Y	Y	Y	Y
IDAHO						
1 Sali	Y	N	Y	N	N	Y
2 Simpson	Y	N	Y	N	N	Y
ILLINOIS						
1 Rush	Y	?	Y	Y	Y	?
2 Jackson	Y	Y	Y	Y	Y	Y
3 Lipinski	Y	Y	Y	Y	Y	Y
4 Gutierrez	Y	Y	Y	Y	Y	?
5 Emanuel	Y	Y	Y	Y	Y	Y
6 Roskam	Y	N	Y	N	N	Y
7 Davis	Y	Y	Y	Y	Y	Y
8 Bean	Y	Y	Y	Y	Y	Y
9 Schakowsky	Y	Y	Y	Y	Y	Y
10 Kirk	Y	N	Y	N	Y	Y
11 Weller	?	N	Y	N	Y	Y
12 Costello	Y	Y	Y	Y	Y	Y
13 Biggert	Y	N	Y	N	Y	Y
14 Foster	Y	Y	Y	Y	Y	Y
15 Johnson	Y	N	Y	N	Y	Y

KEY   **Republicans**   Democrats

Y	Voted for (yea)
#	Paired for
+	Announced for
N	Voted against (nay)
X	Paired against
–	Announced against
P	Voted "present"
C	Voted "present" to avoid possible conflict of interest
?	Did not vote or otherwise make a position known

ND Northern Democrats, SD Southern Democrats
Southern states: Ala., Ark., Fla., Ga., Ky., La., Miss., N.C., Okla., S.C., Tenn., Texas, Va.

	579	580	581	582	583	584
16 **Manzullo**	Y	N	Y	N	Y	Y
17 Hare	Y	Y	Y	Y	Y	Y
18 **LaHood**	Y	N	Y	Y	Y	Y
19 **Shimkus**	Y	N	Y	N	Y	Y
INDIANA						
1 Visclosky	Y	Y	Y	Y	Y	Y
2 Donnelly	Y	Y	Y	Y	Y	Y
3 **Souder**	Y	N	Y	N	N	Y
4 **Buyer**	Y	N	Y	N	N	?
5 **Burton**	Y	N	Y	N	N	Y
6 **Pence**	Y	N	Y	N	N	?
7 Carson, A.	Y	Y	Y	Y	Y	Y
8 Ellsworth	Y	Y	Y	Y	Y	N
9 Hill	Y	Y	Y	Y	Y	Y
IOWA						
1 Braley	Y	Y	Y	Y	Y	Y
2 Loebsack	Y	Y	Y	Y	Y	Y
3 Boswell	Y	Y	Y	Y	Y	Y
4 **Latham**	Y	N	Y	N	N	Y
5 **King**	Y	N	Y	N	N	Y
KANSAS						
1 **Moran**	Y	?	Y	N	N	Y
2 Boyda	Y	Y	Y	Y	Y	Y
3 Moore	Y	Y	Y	Y	Y	Y
4 **Tiahrt**	Y	N	Y	N	N	Y
KENTUCKY						
1 **Whitfield**	Y	N	Y	N	Y	Y
2 **Lewis**	Y	N	Y	N	N	Y
3 Yarmuth	Y	Y	Y	Y	Y	Y
4 **Davis**	Y	N	Y	N	N	Y
5 **Rogers**	Y	N	Y	N	N	Y
6 Chandler	Y	Y	Y	Y	Y	Y
LOUISIANA						
1 **Scalise**	Y	N	Y	N	N	Y
2 Jefferson	Y	Y	Y	Y	Y	Y
3 Melancon	?	Y	Y	Y	Y	Y
4 **McCrery**	Y	N	Y	?	?	?
5 **Alexander**	Y	N	Y	N	Y	Y
6 Cazayoux	?	?	?	?	?	?
7 **Boustany**	Y	?	Y	N	N	Y
MAINE						
1 Allen	Y	Y	Y	Y	Y	Y
2 Michaud	Y	Y	Y	Y	Y	Y
MARYLAND						
1 **Gilchrest**	Y	N	Y	Y	Y	Y
2 Ruppersberger	Y	Y	Y	Y	Y	Y
3 Sarbanes	Y	Y	Y	Y	Y	Y
4 Edwards	Y	Y	Y	Y	Y	Y
5 Hoyer	Y	Y	Y	Y	Y	Y
6 **Bartlett**	Y	N	Y	N	Y	Y
7 Cummings	Y	Y	Y	Y	Y	Y
8 Van Hollen	Y	Y	Y	Y	Y	Y
MASSACHUSETTS						
1 Olver	Y	Y	?	Y	Y	Y
2 Neal	Y	Y	Y	?	Y	Y
3 McGovern	Y	Y	Y	Y	Y	Y
4 Frank	Y	Y	Y	Y	Y	Y
5 Tsongas	Y	Y	Y	Y	Y	Y
6 Tierney	Y	Y	Y	Y	Y	Y
7 Markey	Y	Y	Y	Y	Y	Y
8 Capuano	Y	Y	Y	Y	Y	Y
9 Lynch	Y	Y	Y	Y	Y	Y
10 Delahunt	Y	Y	Y	Y	Y	Y
MICHIGAN						
1 Stupak	Y	Y	Y	Y	Y	Y
2 **Hoekstra**	Y	N	Y	N	N	Y
3 **Ehlers**	Y	N	Y	N	Y	Y
4 **Camp**	Y	N	Y	N	Y	Y
5 Kildee	Y	Y	Y	Y	Y	Y
6 **Upton**	Y	N	Y	N	Y	Y
7 **Walberg**	Y	N	Y	N	N	Y
8 **Rogers**	Y	N	Y	N	Y	Y
9 **Knollenberg**	Y	N	Y	N	Y	Y
10 **Miller**	Y	N	Y	N	Y	Y
11 **McCotter**	Y	N	Y	N	Y	Y
12 Levin	?	?	?	?	?	?
13 Kilpatrick	Y	Y	Y	Y	Y	Y
14 Conyers	Y	Y	Y	Y	Y	Y
15 Dingell	Y	Y	Y	Y	Y	Y
MINNESOTA						
1 Walz	Y	Y	Y	Y	Y	Y
2 **Kline**	Y	N	Y	N	N	Y
3 **Ramstad**	Y	N	Y	Y	Y	Y
4 McCollum	Y	Y	Y	Y	Y	Y
5 Ellison	Y	Y	Y	Y	Y	Y
6 **Bachmann**	Y	N	Y	N	N	Y
7 Peterson	?	?	?	?	?	?
8 Oberstar	Y	Y	Y	Y	Y	N
MISSISSIPPI						
1 Childers	Y	Y	Y	N	Y	Y
2 Thompson	Y	Y	Y	Y	Y	Y
3 **Pickering**	Y	N	Y	N	N	Y
4 Taylor	Y	Y	Y	Y	Y	Y
MISSOURI						
1 Clay	Y	Y	Y	Y	Y	Y
2 **Akin**	Y	N	Y	N	N	Y
3 Carnahan	Y	Y	Y	Y	Y	Y
4 Skelton	Y	Y	Y	Y	Y	Y
5 Cleaver	Y	Y	Y	Y	Y	Y
6 **Graves**	Y	N	Y	N	N	Y
7 **Blunt**	Y	N	Y	N	N	Y
8 **Emerson**	Y	N	Y	N	N	Y
9 **Hulshof**	?	?	?	?	?	?
MONTANA						
AL **Rehberg**	Y	N	Y	N	Y	Y
NEBRASKA						
1 **Fortenberry**	Y	N	Y	N	Y	Y
2 **Terry**	Y	N	Y	N	Y	Y
3 **Smith**	Y	N	Y	N	N	Y
NEVADA						
1 Berkley	Y	Y	Y	Y	Y	Y
2 **Heller**	Y	N	Y	Y	N	Y
3 **Porter**	Y	N	Y	Y	Y	Y
NEW HAMPSHIRE						
1 Shea-Porter	Y	Y	Y	Y	Y	Y
2 Hodes	?	?	?	?	?	?
NEW JERSEY						
1 Andrews	Y	Y	Y	Y	Y	Y
2 **LoBiondo**	Y	N	Y	N	Y	Y
3 **Saxton**	Y	N	Y	N	Y	?
4 **Smith**	Y	N	Y	N	Y	Y
5 **Garrett**	Y	N	Y	N	Y	Y
6 Pallone	Y	Y	Y	Y	Y	Y
7 **Ferguson**	Y	N	Y	N	Y	Y
8 Pascrell	Y	Y	Y	Y	Y	Y
9 Rothman	Y	Y	Y	Y	Y	Y
10 Payne	Y	?	Y	Y	Y	Y
11 **Frelinghuysen**	Y	N	Y	N	Y	Y
12 Holt	Y	Y	Y	Y	Y	Y
13 Sires	Y	Y	Y	Y	Y	Y
NEW MEXICO						
1 **Wilson**	Y	N	Y	N	N	Y
2 **Pearce**	Y	N	Y	?	N	Y
3 Udall	Y	?	Y	Y	Y	Y
NEW YORK						
1 Bishop	Y	Y	Y	Y	Y	Y
2 Israel	Y	Y	Y	Y	Y	Y
3 **King**	Y	N	Y	N	Y	Y
4 McCarthy	Y	Y	Y	Y	Y	Y
5 Ackerman	Y	Y	Y	Y	Y	Y
6 Meeks	Y	Y	Y	Y	Y	Y
7 Crowley	Y	Y	Y	Y	Y	Y
8 Nadler	Y	Y	Y	Y	Y	Y
9 Weiner	Y	Y	Y	Y	Y	Y
10 Towns	Y	Y	Y	Y	Y	Y
11 Clarke	Y	Y	Y	Y	Y	Y
12 Velázquez	Y	Y	Y	Y	?	?
13 **Fossella**	Y	N	Y	?	Y	Y
14 Maloney	Y	Y	Y	Y	Y	Y
15 Rangel	Y	Y	Y	Y	Y	?
16 Serrano	Y	Y	Y	Y	Y	?
17 Engel	Y	Y	Y	Y	Y	Y
18 Lowey	Y	Y	Y	Y	Y	Y
19 Hall	Y	Y	Y	Y	Y	Y
20 Gillibrand	Y	Y	Y	Y	Y	Y
21 McNulty	?	Y	Y	Y	Y	Y
22 Hinchey	Y	Y	Y	Y	Y	Y
23 **McHugh**	Y	N	Y	N	Y	Y
24 Arcuri	Y	Y	Y	Y	Y	Y
25 **Walsh**	Y	N	Y	N	Y	Y
26 **Reynolds**	Y	?	Y	N	N	Y
27 Higgins	Y	Y	Y	Y	Y	Y
28 Slaughter	Y	Y	Y	Y	Y	Y
29 **Kuhl**	Y	N	Y	N	Y	Y
NORTH CAROLINA						
1 Butterfield	Y	Y	Y	Y	Y	Y
2 Etheridge	Y	Y	Y	Y	Y	Y
3 **Jones**	Y	N	Y	N	Y	Y
4 Price	Y	Y	Y	Y	Y	Y
5 **Foxx**	Y	N	Y	N	N	Y
6 **Coble**	Y	N	Y	N	N	N
7 McIntyre	Y	Y	Y	Y	Y	Y
8 **Hayes**	Y	N	Y	N	Y	Y
9 **Myrick**	Y	N	Y	N	N	Y
10 **McHenry**	Y	N	Y	N	Y	N
11 Shuler	Y	Y	Y	Y	Y	Y
12 Watt	Y	Y	Y	Y	Y	Y
13 Miller	Y	Y	Y	Y	Y	Y
NORTH DAKOTA						
AL Pomeroy	Y	Y	Y	Y	Y	Y
OHIO						
1 **Chabot**	Y	N	Y	N	N	Y
2 **Schmidt**	Y	N	Y	N	Y	Y
3 **Turner**	Y	N	Y	N	Y	Y
4 **Jordan**	Y	N	Y	N	N	Y
5 **Latta**	Y	N	Y	N	N	Y
6 Wilson	Y	Y	Y	Y	Y	Y
7 **Hobson**	Y	N	Y	N	N	Y
8 **Boehner**	Y	N	Y	N	N	Y
9 Kaptur	Y	Y	Y	Y	Y	Y
10 Kucinich	Y	Y	Y	Y	Y	Y
11 Vacant						
12 **Tiberi**	Y	N	Y	N	Y	Y
13 Sutton	Y	Y	Y	Y	Y	Y
14 **LaTourette**	Y	Y	Y	N	Y	Y
15 **Pryce**	Y	N	Y	N	Y	Y
16 **Regula**	Y	N	Y	N	N	Y
17 Ryan	Y	Y	Y	Y	Y	Y
18 Space	Y	Y	Y	Y	Y	Y
OKLAHOMA						
1 **Sullivan**	Y	N	Y	N	N	N
2 Boren	Y	Y	Y	Y	Y	Y
3 **Lucas**	Y	N	Y	N	N	Y
4 **Cole**	Y	N	Y	N	N	Y
5 **Fallin**	Y	N	Y	N	N	Y
OREGON						
1 Wu	Y	Y	Y	Y	Y	Y
2 **Walden**	Y	N	Y	N	Y	Y
3 Blumenauer	Y	Y	Y	Y	Y	Y
4 DeFazio	Y	Y	Y	Y	Y	Y
5 Hooley	Y	Y	Y	Y	Y	Y
PENNSYLVANIA						
1 Brady	Y	Y	Y	Y	Y	Y
2 Fattah	Y	Y	Y	Y	Y	Y
3 **English**	Y	?	Y	N	Y	Y
4 Altmire	Y	Y	Y	Y	Y	Y
5 **Peterson**	Y	N	?	N	Y	Y
6 **Gerlach**	Y	N	Y	N	Y	Y
7 Sestak	Y	Y	Y	Y	Y	Y
8 Murphy, P.	Y	Y	Y	Y	Y	Y
9 **Shuster**	Y	N	Y	N	N	Y
10 Carney	Y	Y	Y	Y	Y	Y
11 Kanjorski	Y	Y	Y	Y	Y	Y
12 Murtha	Y	Y	Y	Y	Y	?
13 Schwartz	Y	Y	Y	Y	Y	Y
14 Doyle	Y	Y	Y	Y	Y	Y
15 **Dent**	Y	N	Y	N	Y	Y
16 **Pitts**	?	?	?	?	?	?
17 Holden	Y	Y	Y	Y	Y	Y
18 **Murphy, T.**	Y	N	Y	N	Y	Y
19 **Platts**	Y	N	Y	N	Y	Y
RHODE ISLAND						
1 Kennedy	Y	Y	Y	Y	Y	Y
2 Langevin	Y	Y	Y	Y	Y	Y
SOUTH CAROLINA						
1 **Brown**	Y	N	Y	N	N	Y
2 **Wilson**	Y	N	Y	N	N	Y
3 **Barrett**	Y	N	Y	N	Y	Y
4 **Inglis**	Y	N	Y	N	Y	Y
5 Spratt	Y	Y	Y	Y	Y	Y
6 Clyburn	Y	Y	Y	Y	Y	Y
SOUTH DAKOTA						
AL Herseth Sandlin	Y	Y	Y	Y	Y	Y
TENNESSEE						
1 **Davis, David**	Y	N	Y	N	N	Y
2 **Duncan**	Y	N	Y	N	N	Y
3 **Wamp**	Y	N	Y	N	N	Y
4 Davis, L.	Y	Y	Y	Y	Y	Y
5 Cooper	Y	Y	Y	Y	Y	Y
6 Gordon	Y	Y	Y	Y	Y	Y
7 **Blackburn**	Y	N	Y	N	N	?
8 Tanner	Y	Y	Y	Y	Y	Y
9 Cohen	Y	Y	Y	Y	Y	Y
TEXAS						
1 **Gohmert**	Y	N	Y	N	N	Y
2 **Poe**	Y	N	Y	N	N	Y
3 **Johnson, S.**	Y	N	Y	N	N	?
4 **Hall**	Y	N	Y	N	N	Y
5 **Hensarling**	Y	N	Y	N	N	Y
6 **Barton**	Y	N	Y	N	N	N
7 **Culberson**	Y	N	?	N	N	Y
8 **Brady**	Y	N	Y	N	N	Y
9 Green, A.	Y	Y	Y	Y	Y	Y
10 **McCaul**	Y	N	Y	N	Y	Y
11 **Conaway**	Y	N	Y	N	N	Y
12 **Granger**	Y	N	Y	N	N	Y
13 **Thornberry**	?	N	Y	N	N	Y
14 **Paul**	Y	?	Y	N	N	N
15 Hinojosa	Y	Y	?	?	?	?
16 Reyes	Y	Y	Y	Y	Y	?
17 Edwards	Y	?	Y	Y	Y	Y
18 Jackson Lee	Y	N	Y	Y	Y	Y
19 **Neugebauer**	Y	N	Y	N	N	Y
20 Gonzalez	Y	?	Y	Y	Y	?
21 **Smith**	Y	N	Y	N	Y	Y
22 Lampson	Y	Y	Y	N	Y	Y
23 Rodriguez	Y	Y	Y	Y	Y	Y
24 **Marchant**	Y	N	Y	N	N	Y
25 Doggett	Y	Y	Y	Y	Y	Y
26 **Burgess**	Y	N	Y	N	N	Y
27 Ortiz	Y	Y	?	?	?	?
28 Cuellar	Y	Y	Y	Y	Y	Y
29 Green, G.	Y	Y	Y	Y	Y	Y
30 Johnson, E.	Y	Y	Y	Y	Y	Y
31 **Carter**	Y	N	Y	N	N	Y
32 **Sessions**	Y	N	Y	N	N	Y
UTAH						
1 **Bishop**	Y	N	Y	N	Y	Y
2 Matheson	Y	Y	Y	Y	Y	Y
3 **Cannon**	?	?	Y	N	Y	Y
VERMONT						
AL Welch	Y	Y	Y	Y	Y	Y
VIRGINIA						
1 **Wittman**	Y	N	Y	N	N	Y
2 **Drake**	Y	N	Y	N	N	Y
3 Scott	+	Y	Y	Y	Y	Y
4 **Forbes**	Y	N	Y	N	N	Y
5 **Goode**	Y	N	Y	N	N	Y
6 **Goodlatte**	Y	N	Y	N	N	Y
7 **Cantor**	Y	N	Y	N	N	Y
8 Moran	Y	N	Y	Y	Y	Y
9 Boucher	Y	Y	Y	Y	Y	Y
10 **Wolf**	Y	N	Y	N	Y	Y
11 **Davis, T.**	Y	N	Y	N	Y	Y
WASHINGTON						
1 Inslee	Y	Y	Y	Y	Y	Y
2 Larsen	Y	Y	Y	Y	Y	Y
3 Baird	?	Y	Y	Y	Y	Y
4 **Hastings**	Y	N	Y	N	N	Y
5 **McMorris Rodgers**	Y	N	Y	N	N	Y
6 Dicks	Y	Y	Y	Y	Y	?
7 McDermott	Y	Y	Y	Y	Y	Y
8 **Reichert**	Y	N	Y	Y	Y	Y
9 Smith	Y	Y	Y	Y	Y	Y
WEST VIRGINIA						
1 Mollohan	Y	Y	Y	Y	Y	Y
2 **Capito**	Y	N	Y	N	Y	Y
3 Rahall	Y	N	Y	Y	Y	Y
WISCONSIN						
1 **Ryan**	Y	N	Y	N	N	Y
2 Baldwin	Y	Y	Y	Y	Y	Y
3 Kind	Y	Y	Y	Y	Y	Y
4 Moore	Y	Y	Y	Y	Y	Y
5 **Sensenbrenner**	?	N	Y	N	N	Y
6 **Petri**	Y	N	Y	N	Y	Y
7 Obey	Y	Y	Y	Y	Y	Y
8 Kagen	Y	Y	Y	Y	Y	Y
WYOMING						
AL **Cubin**	Y	N	Y	N	N	Y
DELEGATES						
Faleomavaega (A.S.)		Y	Y			
Norton (D.C.)		?	Y			
Bordallo (Guam)		Y	Y			
Fortuño (P.R.)		?	?			
Christensen (V.I.)		?	?			

IN THE HOUSE | By Vote Number

585. **Procedural Motion/Journal.** Approval of the House Journal of Wednesday, Sept. 10, 2008. Approved 215-190: R 0-183; D 215-7 (ND 164-3, SD 51-4). Sept. 11, 2008.

586. **H Res 1420. Sept. 11 Commemoration/Adoption.** Hoyer, D-Md., motion to suspend the rules and adopt the resolution that would recognize Sept. 11 as a day of commemoration, extend sympathies to the loved ones of those who lost their lives in the 2001 terrorist attacks, honor the actions of first-responders and armed forces, and express gratitude to the nations that have helped the United States combat terrorism. Motion agreed to 402-0: R 180-0; D 222-0 (ND 168-0, SD 54-0). A two-thirds majority of those present and voting (268 in this case) is required for adoption under suspension of the rules. Sept. 11, 2008.

587. **HR 6532. Highway Trust Fund Money Transfer/Passage.** Lewis, D-Ga., motion to suspend the rules and concur in the Senate amendment to the bill that would appropriate $8.02 billion to the Highway Trust Fund, which would be drawn out of money in the Treasury not otherwise appropriated. The transfer would take effect upon enactment. Motion agreed to (thus clearing the bill for the president) 376-29: R 152-29; D 224-0 (ND 169-0, SD 55-0). A two-thirds majority of those present and voting (270 in this case) is required for passage under suspension of the rules. Sept. 11, 2008.

588. **Procedural Motion/Adjourn.** Hoyer, D-Md., motion to adjourn. Motion agreed to 208-190: R 0-177; D 208-13 (ND 155-12, SD 53-1). Sept. 11, 2008.

	585	586	587	588
ALABAMA				
1 Bonner	N	Y	Y	N
2 Everett	N	Y	Y	N
3 Rogers	N	Y	Y	N
4 Aderholt	N	Y	Y	N
5 Cramer	Y	Y	Y	Y
6 Bachus	N	Y	Y	N
7 Davis	Y	Y	Y	Y
ALASKA				
AL Young	N	Y	Y	N
ARIZONA				
1 Renzi	N	Y	Y	N
2 Franks	N	Y	N	N
3 Shadegg	N	Y	N	N
4 Pastor	Y	Y	Y	Y
5 Mitchell	N	Y	Y	N
6 Flake	N	Y	N	N
7 Grijalva	Y	Y	Y	Y
8 Giffords	Y	Y	Y	Y
ARKANSAS				
1 Berry	Y	Y	Y	Y
2 Snyder	Y	Y	Y	Y
3 Boozman	N	Y	Y	N
4 Ross	Y	Y	Y	Y
CALIFORNIA				
1 Thompson	N	Y	Y	Y
2 Herger	N	Y	Y	N
3 Lungren	N	Y	Y	N
4 Doolittle	N	Y	Y	N
5 Matsui	Y	Y	Y	Y
6 Woolsey	Y	Y	Y	Y
7 Miller, George	Y	Y	Y	Y
8 Pelosi				
9 Lee	?	?	?	?
10 Tauscher	Y	Y	Y	Y
11 McNerney	Y	Y	Y	Y
12 Speier	Y	Y	Y	Y
13 Stark	?	?	Y	Y
14 Eshoo	Y	Y	Y	Y
15 Honda	Y	Y	Y	Y
16 Lofgren	Y	Y	Y	Y
17 Farr	Y	Y	Y	Y
18 Cardoza	Y	Y	Y	Y
19 Radanovich	?	?	?	?
20 Costa	Y	Y	Y	Y
21 Nunes	N	Y	Y	N
22 McCarthy	N	Y	Y	N
23 Capps	Y	Y	Y	Y
24 Gallegly	N	Y	Y	N
25 McKeon	N	Y	Y	N
26 Dreier	N	Y	Y	N
27 Sherman	Y	Y	Y	Y
28 Berman	Y	Y	Y	Y
29 Schiff	Y	Y	Y	Y
30 Waxman	Y	Y	Y	Y
31 Becerra	Y	Y	Y	Y
32 Solis	Y	Y	Y	Y
33 Watson	Y	Y	Y	Y
34 Roybal-Allard	Y	Y	Y	Y
35 Waters	Y	Y	Y	Y
36 Harman	Y	Y	Y	Y
37 Richardson	Y	Y	Y	Y
38 Napolitano	Y	Y	Y	Y
39 Sánchez, Linda	Y	Y	Y	Y
40 Royce	N	Y	N	N
41 Lewis	N	Y	Y	N
42 Miller, Gary	N	Y	Y	N
43 Baca	Y	Y	Y	Y
44 Calvert	N	Y	Y	N
45 Bono Mack	N	Y	Y	N
46 Rohrabacher	N	Y	Y	N
47 Sanchez, Loretta	Y	Y	Y	Y
48 Campbell	N	Y	N	?
49 Issa	N	Y	?	N
50 Bilbray	N	Y	Y	N
51 Filner	Y	Y	Y	Y
52 Hunter	N	?	Y	N
53 Davis	Y	Y	Y	Y

	585	586	587	588
COLORADO				
1 DeGette	Y	Y	Y	Y
2 Udall	Y	Y	Y	N
3 Salazar	Y	Y	Y	Y
4 Musgrave	N	Y	Y	N
5 Lamborn	N	Y	N	N
6 Tancredo	P	Y	N	N
7 Perlmutter	?	?	?	?
CONNECTICUT				
1 Larson	Y	Y	Y	Y
2 Courtney	Y	Y	Y	Y
3 DeLauro	Y	Y	Y	Y
4 Shays	N	Y	Y	N
5 Murphy	Y	Y	Y	Y
DELAWARE				
AL Castle	N	Y	Y	N
FLORIDA				
1 Miller	N	Y	Y	N
2 Boyd	Y	Y	Y	Y
3 Brown	Y	Y	Y	Y
4 Crenshaw	N	Y	Y	N
5 Brown-Waite	N	Y	N	N
6 Stearns	N	Y	N	N
7 Mica	N	Y	Y	N
8 Keller	N	Y	Y	N
9 Bilirakis	N	Y	Y	N
10 Young	N	Y	N	N
11 Castor	Y	Y	Y	Y
12 Putnam	N	Y	Y	N
13 Buchanan	N	Y	Y	N
14 Mack	N	Y	Y	N
15 Weldon	N	Y	Y	N
16 Mahoney	Y	Y	Y	Y
17 Meek	Y	Y	Y	Y
18 Ros-Lehtinen	N	Y	Y	N
19 Wexler	Y	Y	Y	Y
20 Wasserman Schultz	Y	?	Y	Y
21 Diaz-Balart, L.	N	Y	Y	N
22 Klein	Y	Y	Y	Y
23 Hastings	Y	Y	Y	Y
24 Feeney	?	?	?	?
25 Diaz-Balart, M.	N	Y	Y	N
GEORGIA				
1 Kingston	N	Y	N	N
2 Bishop	Y	Y	Y	Y
3 Westmoreland	N	Y	N	N
4 Johnson	Y	Y	Y	Y
5 Lewis	Y	Y	Y	Y
6 Price	N	Y	N	N
7 Linder	N	Y	N	N
8 Marshall	Y	Y	Y	Y
9 Deal	N	Y	N	N
10 Broun	N	Y	N	N
11 Gingrey	N	Y	N	N
12 Barrow	Y	Y	Y	Y
13 Scott	Y	Y	Y	Y
HAWAII				
1 Abercrombie	N	Y	Y	Y
2 Hirono	Y	Y	Y	Y
IDAHO				
1 Sali	N	Y	Y	N
2 Simpson	N	Y	Y	N
ILLINOIS				
1 Rush	?	?	?	?
2 Jackson	Y	Y	Y	Y
3 Lipinski	Y	Y	Y	Y
4 Gutierrez	Y	Y	Y	?
5 Emanuel	Y	Y	Y	Y
6 Roskam	N	Y	Y	N
7 Davis	Y	Y	Y	Y
8 Bean	Y	Y	Y	Y
9 Schakowsky	Y	Y	Y	Y
10 Kirk	N	Y	Y	N
11 Weller	N	Y	Y	N
12 Costello	Y	Y	Y	Y
13 Biggert	N	Y	Y	N
14 Foster	Y	Y	Y	Y
15 Johnson	N	Y	Y	N

KEY	Republicans	Democrats		
Y Voted for (yea)		X Paired against		C Voted "present" to avoid possible conflict of interest
# Paired for		− Announced against		? Did not vote or otherwise make a position known
+ Announced for		P Voted "present"		
N Voted against (nay)				

ND Northern Democrats, SD Southern Democrats
Southern states: Ala., Ark., Fla., Ga., Ky., La., Miss., N.C., Okla., S.C., Tenn., Texas, Va.

	585	586	587	588
16 **Manzullo**	N	Y	N	N
17 Hare	Y	Y	Y	Y
18 **LaHood**	?	?	?	?
19 **Shimkus**	?	?	?	?
INDIANA				
1 Visclosky	Y	Y	Y	Y
2 Donnelly	Y	Y	Y	N
3 **Souder**	N	Y	Y	N
4 **Buyer**	N	Y	Y	N
5 **Burton**	N	Y	N	N
6 **Pence**	N	Y	N	N
7 Carson, A.	Y	Y	Y	Y
8 Ellsworth	Y	Y	Y	Y
9 Hill	Y	Y	Y	Y
IOWA				
1 Braley	Y	Y	Y	Y
2 Loebsack	Y	Y	Y	N
3 Boswell	Y	Y	Y	Y
4 Latham	N	Y	Y	N
5 King	N	Y	Y	N
KANSAS				
1 **Moran**	N	Y	Y	N
2 Boyda	Y	Y	Y	Y
3 Moore	Y	Y	Y	Y
4 **Tiahrt**	N	Y	Y	N
KENTUCKY				
1 **Whitfield**	N	Y	Y	N
2 Lewis	N	Y	Y	N
3 Yarmuth	Y	Y	Y	Y
4 Davis	N	Y	Y	N
5 **Rogers**	N	Y	Y	N
6 Chandler	Y	Y	Y	Y
LOUISIANA				
1 **Scalise**	N	Y	Y	N
2 Jefferson	Y	Y	Y	Y
3 Melancon	N	Y	Y	Y
4 **McCrery**	N	Y	N	N
5 **Alexander**	N	Y	Y	?
6 Cazayoux	N	Y	Y	Y
7 **Boustany**	N	Y	Y	N
MAINE				
1 Allen	Y	Y	Y	Y
2 Michaud	Y	Y	Y	Y
MARYLAND				
1 **Gilchrest**	N	Y	N	N
2 Ruppersberger	Y	Y	Y	Y
3 Sarbanes	Y	Y	Y	Y
4 Edwards	Y	Y	Y	Y
5 Hoyer	Y	Y	Y	Y
6 **Bartlett**	N	Y	Y	N
7 Cummings	Y	Y	Y	Y
8 Van Hollen	Y	Y	Y	Y
MASSACHUSETTS				
1 Olver	Y	Y	Y	Y
2 Neal	Y	Y	Y	Y
3 McGovern	Y	Y	Y	Y
4 Frank	Y	Y	Y	Y
5 Tsongas	Y	Y	Y	Y
6 Tierney	Y	Y	Y	Y
7 Markey	Y	Y	Y	Y
8 Capuano	Y	Y	Y	Y
9 Lynch	Y	Y	Y	Y
10 Delahunt	Y	Y	Y	Y
MICHIGAN				
1 Stupak	Y	Y	Y	Y
2 **Hoekstra**	N	Y	Y	N
3 **Ehlers**	N	Y	Y	N
4 **Camp**	N	Y	Y	N
5 Kildee	Y	Y	Y	Y
6 **Upton**	N	Y	Y	N
7 **Walberg**	N	Y	Y	N
8 **Rogers**	N	Y	Y	N
9 **Knollenberg**	N	Y	Y	N
10 **Miller**	N	Y	Y	N
11 **McCotter**	N	Y	Y	N
12 Levin	?	?	?	?
13 Kilpatrick	Y	Y	Y	Y
14 Conyers	Y	Y	Y	Y
15 Dingell	Y	Y	Y	Y
MINNESOTA				
1 Walz	Y	Y	Y	Y
2 Kline	N	Y	Y	N
3 **Ramstad**	N	Y	N	N
4 McCollum	Y	Y	Y	Y

	585	586	587	588
5 Ellison	Y	Y	Y	Y
6 **Bachmann**	N	Y	Y	N
7 Peterson	?	?	?	?
8 Oberstar	Y	Y	Y	Y
MISSISSIPPI				
1 Childers	N	Y	Y	N
2 Thompson	Y	Y	Y	Y
3 **Pickering**	N	Y	Y	N
4 Taylor	Y	Y	Y	Y
MISSOURI				
1 Clay	Y	Y	Y	Y
2 **Akin**	N	Y	N	N
3 Carnahan	Y	Y	Y	Y
4 Skelton	Y	Y	Y	Y
5 Cleaver	Y	Y	Y	Y
6 **Graves**	N	Y	Y	N
7 **Blunt**	N	Y	Y	N
8 **Emerson**	N	Y	Y	N
9 **Hulshof**	?	?	?	?
MONTANA				
AL **Rehberg**	N	Y	Y	N
NEBRASKA				
1 **Fortenberry**	N	Y	Y	N
2 **Terry**	N	Y	Y	N
3 **Smith**	N	Y	Y	N
NEVADA				
1 Berkley	Y	Y	Y	Y
2 **Heller**	N	Y	Y	N
3 **Porter**	N	Y	Y	N
NEW HAMPSHIRE				
1 Shea-Porter	Y	Y	Y	Y
2 Hodes	Y	Y	Y	Y
NEW JERSEY				
1 Andrews	Y	Y	Y	Y
2 **LoBiondo**	N	Y	Y	N
3 **Saxton**	N	Y	Y	N
4 **Smith**	N	Y	Y	N
5 **Garrett**	N	Y	N	N
6 Pallone	Y	Y	Y	Y
7 **Ferguson**	N	Y	Y	N
8 Pascrell	Y	Y	Y	Y
9 Rothman	Y	Y	Y	Y
10 Payne	Y	Y	Y	Y
11 **Frelinghuysen**	N	Y	Y	N
12 Holt	Y	Y	Y	Y
13 Sires	Y	Y	Y	Y
NEW MEXICO				
1 **Wilson**	N	?	?	?
2 **Pearce**	N	Y	Y	N
3 Udall	Y	Y	Y	N
NEW YORK				
1 Bishop	Y	Y	Y	Y
2 Israel	Y	Y	Y	Y
3 **King**	N	Y	?	?
4 McCarthy	Y	Y	Y	Y
5 Ackerman	Y	Y	Y	Y
6 Meeks	Y	Y	Y	Y
7 Crowley	Y	Y	Y	Y
8 Nadler	?	?	?	?
9 Weiner	Y	Y	Y	Y
10 Towns	Y	Y	Y	Y
11 Clarke	Y	Y	Y	Y
12 Velázquez	Y	Y	Y	Y
13 **Fossella**	N	Y	Y	N
14 Maloney	Y	Y	Y	Y
15 Rangel	Y	Y	Y	Y
16 Serrano	Y	Y	Y	Y
17 Engel	Y	Y	Y	Y
18 Lowey	Y	Y	Y	Y
19 Hall	Y	Y	Y	Y
20 Gillibrand	Y	Y	Y	N
21 McNulty	Y	Y	Y	Y
22 Hinchey	Y	Y	Y	Y
23 **McHugh**	N	Y	Y	N
24 Arcuri	Y	Y	Y	Y
25 **Walsh**	N	Y	Y	N
26 **Reynolds**	N	Y	Y	N
27 Higgins	Y	Y	Y	Y
28 Slaughter	Y	Y	Y	Y
29 **Kuhl**	N	Y	Y	N
NORTH CAROLINA				
1 Butterfield	Y	Y	Y	Y
2 Etheridge	Y	Y	Y	Y
3 **Jones**	N	Y	Y	N
4 Price	Y	Y	Y	Y

	585	586	587	588
5 **Foxx**	N	Y	N	N
6 **Coble**	N	Y	Y	N
7 McIntyre	Y	Y	Y	Y
8 **Hayes**	N	Y	Y	N
9 **Myrick**	N	Y	Y	N
10 **McHenry**	N	Y	N	N
11 Shuler	N	Y	Y	N
12 Watt	Y	Y	Y	Y
13 Miller	Y	Y	Y	Y
NORTH DAKOTA				
AL Pomeroy	Y	Y	Y	Y
OHIO				
1 **Chabot**	N	Y	N	N
2 **Schmidt**	?	?	?	?
3 **Turner**	N	Y	Y	N
4 **Jordan**	N	Y	N	N
5 **Latta**	N	Y	Y	N
6 Wilson	Y	Y	Y	Y
7 **Hobson**	N	Y	N	N
8 **Boehner**	N	Y	Y	N
9 Kaptur	Y	Y	Y	Y
10 Kucinich	Y	Y	Y	N
11 Vacant*				
12 **Tiberi**	N	Y	Y	N
13 Sutton	Y	Y	Y	Y
14 **LaTourette**	N	Y	Y	N
15 **Pryce**	N	Y	?	?
16 **Regula**	N	Y	Y	N
17 Ryan	Y	Y	Y	Y
18 Space	Y	Y	Y	Y
OKLAHOMA				
1 **Sullivan**	N	?	Y	N
2 Boren	Y	Y	Y	Y
3 **Lucas**	N	Y	Y	N
4 **Cole**	N	Y	Y	N
5 **Fallin**	N	Y	Y	N
OREGON				
1 Wu	Y	Y	Y	Y
2 **Walden**	N	Y	Y	N
3 Blumenauer	Y	Y	Y	Y
4 DeFazio	Y	Y	Y	?
5 Hooley	Y	Y	Y	Y
PENNSYLVANIA				
1 Brady	Y	Y	Y	Y
2 Fattah	Y	Y	Y	Y
3 **English**	N	Y	Y	N
4 Altmire	Y	Y	Y	N
5 **Peterson**	?	?	?	?
6 **Gerlach**	N	Y	Y	N
7 Sestak	Y	Y	Y	Y
8 Murphy, P.	Y	Y	Y	Y
9 **Shuster**	N	Y	Y	N
10 Carney	Y	Y	Y	Y
11 Kanjorski	Y	Y	Y	Y
12 Murtha	Y	Y	Y	Y
13 Schwartz	Y	Y	Y	Y
14 Doyle	Y	Y	Y	Y
15 **Dent**	N	Y	Y	N
16 **Pitts**	?	?	?	?
17 Holden	Y	Y	Y	Y
18 **Murphy, T.**	?	?	?	?
19 **Platts**	N	Y	Y	N
RHODE ISLAND				
1 Kennedy	?	Y	Y	Y
2 Langevin	Y	Y	Y	Y
SOUTH CAROLINA				
1 **Brown**	N	Y	Y	N
2 **Wilson**	N	Y	Y	N
3 **Barrett**	N	Y	Y	N
4 **Inglis**	N	Y	Y	N
5 Spratt	Y	Y	Y	Y
6 Clyburn	Y	Y	Y	Y
SOUTH DAKOTA				
AL Herseth Sandlin	Y	Y	Y	Y
TENNESSEE				
1 **Davis, David**	N	Y	Y	N
2 **Duncan**	N	Y	Y	N
3 **Wamp**	N	Y	Y	N
4 Davis, L.	Y	Y	Y	Y
5 Cooper	Y	Y	Y	Y
6 Gordon	Y	Y	Y	?
7 **Blackburn**	N	Y	N	N
8 Tanner	Y	Y	Y	Y
9 Cohen	Y	Y	Y	Y

	585	586	587	588
TEXAS				
1 **Gohmert**	?	?	Y	N
2 **Poe**	?	?	?	?
3 **Johnson, S.**	N	Y	N	N
4 **Hall**	N	Y	Y	?
5 **Hensarling**	N	Y	N	N
6 **Barton**	N	Y	Y	?
7 **Culberson**	?	?	?	?
8 **Brady**	?	?	?	?
9 Green, A.	Y	Y	Y	Y
10 **McCaul**	N	Y	Y	N
11 **Conaway**	N	Y	Y	N
12 **Granger**	N	Y	Y	N
13 **Thornberry**	N	Y	N	N
14 **Paul**	?	?	?	?
15 Hinojosa	Y	Y	Y	Y
16 Reyes	Y	Y	Y	Y
17 Edwards	Y	Y	Y	Y
18 Jackson Lee	?	?	?	?
19 **Neugebauer**	N	Y	N	N
20 Gonzalez	Y	Y	Y	Y
21 **Smith**	N	Y	Y	N
22 Lampson	?	?	?	?
23 Rodriguez	Y	Y	Y	Y
24 **Marchant**	N	?	Y	N
25 Doggett	Y	Y	Y	Y
26 **Burgess**	N	Y	Y	N
27 Ortiz	?	?	?	?
28 Cuellar	Y	Y	Y	Y
29 Green, G.	?	?	?	?
30 Johnson, E.	Y	Y	Y	Y
31 **Carter**	N	Y	Y	N
32 **Sessions**	N	Y	Y	N
UTAH				
1 **Bishop**	N	Y	Y	N
2 Matheson	Y	Y	Y	Y
3 **Cannon**	N	Y	N	N
VERMONT				
AL Welch	Y	Y	Y	Y
VIRGINIA				
1 **Wittman**	N	Y	Y	N
2 **Drake**	N	Y	Y	N
3 Scott	Y	Y	Y	Y
4 **Forbes**	N	Y	Y	N
5 **Goode**	N	Y	Y	N
6 **Goodlatte**	N	Y	Y	N
7 **Cantor**	N	Y	Y	N
8 Moran	Y	Y	Y	Y
9 Boucher	Y	Y	Y	Y
10 **Wolf**	N	Y	Y	N
11 **Davis, T.**	N	Y	Y	N
WASHINGTON				
1 Inslee	Y	Y	Y	Y
2 Larsen	Y	Y	Y	Y
3 Baird	Y	Y	Y	Y
4 **Hastings**	?	?	?	?
5 **McMorris Rodgers**	N	Y	Y	N
6 Dicks	Y	Y	Y	Y
7 McDermott	Y	Y	Y	Y
8 **Reichert**	N	Y	Y	N
9 Smith	Y	Y	Y	Y
WEST VIRGINIA				
1 Mollohan	Y	Y	Y	Y
2 **Capito**	N	Y	Y	?
3 Rahall	Y	Y	Y	Y
WISCONSIN				
1 **Ryan**	N	Y	N	N
2 Baldwin	Y	Y	Y	Y
3 Kind	Y	Y	Y	Y
4 Moore	Y	Y	Y	Y
5 **Sensenbrenner**	N	Y	N	N
6 **Petri**	N	Y	Y	N
7 Obey	Y	Y	Y	Y
8 Kagen	Y	Y	Y	Y
WYOMING				
AL **Cubin**	N	Y	Y	N
DELEGATES				
Faleomavaega (A.S.)				
Norton (D.C.)				
Bordallo (Guam)				
Fortuño (P.R.)				
Christensen (V.I.)				

IN THE HOUSE | By Vote Number

589. H Res 1200. Honoring Military Support Groups/Adoption. Bordallo, D-Guam, motion to suspend the rules and adopt the resolution that would honor the dedication and work of military support groups in the United States in supporting members of the armed forces and their families. Motion agreed to 374-0: R 170-0; D 204-0 (ND 153-0, SD 51-0). A two-thirds majority of those present and voting (250 in this case) is required for adoption under suspension of the rules. Sept. 15, 2008.

590. H Con Res 390. Honoring the 28th Infantry Division/Adoption. Bordallo, D-Guam, motion to suspend the rules and adopt the resolution that would honor the 28th Infantry Division for protecting the United States. Motion agreed to 374-0: R 169-0; D 205-0 (ND 154-0, SD 51-0). A two-thirds majority of those present and voting (250 in this case) is required for adoption under suspension of the rules. Sept. 15, 2008.

591. HR 6889. Student Loan Access Renewal/Passage. Hinojosa, D-Texas, motion to suspend the rules and pass the bill that would extend the authority of the Education secretary to purchase guaranteed student loans for an additional year. Motion agreed to 368-4: R 165-4; D 203-0 (ND 153-0, SD 50-0). A two-thirds majority of those present and voting (248 in this case) is required for passage under suspension of the rules. Sept. 15, 2008.

592. Procedural Motion/Adjourn. Pence, R-Ind., motion to adjourn. Motion rejected 11-393: R 11-170; D 0-223 (ND 0-168, SD 0-55); Sept. 16, 2008.

593. HR 6899. Energy Policy/Question of Consideration. Question of whether the House should consider the rule (H Res 1433) to provide for House floor consideration of the bill that would open new areas in U.S. waters to oil and gas drilling and provide incentives for renewable energy and energy-efficient buildings. Agreed to consider 230-180: R 2-179; D 228-1 (ND 172-1, SD 56-0). (Cantor, R-Va., had raised a point of order that the rule contained a waiver in violation of the Congressional Budget Act.) Sept. 16, 2008.

594. Procedural Motion/Adjourn. Price, R-Ga., motion to adjourn. Motion rejected 9-386: R 8-165; D 1-221 (ND 1-167, SD 0-54). Sept. 16, 2008.

595. HR 6899. Energy Policy/Previous Question. Slaughter, D-N.Y., motion to order the previous question (thus ending debate and possibility of amendment) on adoption of the rule (H Res 1433) to provide for House floor consideration of the bill that would open new areas in U.S. waters to oil and gas drilling and provide incentives for renewable energy and energy-efficient buildings. Motion agreed to 238-185: R 8-183; D 230-2 (ND 174-1, SD 56-1). Sept. 16, 2008.

	589	590	591	592	593	594	595
ALABAMA							
1 Bonner	?	?	?	N	N	N	N
2 Everett	Y	Y	Y	N	N	?	N
3 Rogers	Y	Y	Y	N	N	N	N
4 Aderholt	Y	Y	Y	?	?	?	N
5 Cramer	Y	Y	Y	N	Y	N	Y
6 Bachus	Y	Y	Y	N	N	N	N
7 Davis	Y	Y	Y	N	Y	N	Y
ALASKA							
AL Young	Y	Y	Y	N	N	?	N
ARIZONA							
1 Renzi	Y	Y	Y	?	N	?	N
2 Franks	Y	Y	Y	N	N	N	N
3 Shadegg	Y	Y	Y	N	N	N	N
4 Pastor	Y	Y	Y	N	Y	N	Y
5 Mitchell	Y	Y	Y	N	Y	N	Y
6 Flake	Y	Y	N	N	N	N	N
7 Grijalva	Y	Y	Y	N	Y	N	Y
8 Giffords	Y	Y	Y	N	Y	N	Y
ARKANSAS							
1 Berry	Y	Y	Y	N	Y	N	Y
2 Snyder	Y	Y	Y	N	Y	N	Y
3 Boozman	Y	Y	Y	N	N	N	N
4 Ross	Y	Y	Y	N	Y	N	Y
CALIFORNIA							
1 Thompson	Y	Y	Y	N	Y	N	Y
2 Herger	Y	Y	Y	N	N	N	N
3 Lungren	Y	Y	Y	N	N	N	N
4 Doolittle	Y	Y	Y	Y	N	Y	N
5 Matsui	Y	Y	Y	N	Y	N	Y
6 Woolsey	Y	Y	Y	N	Y	N	Y
7 Miller, George	?	?	?	N	Y	N	Y
8 Pelosi							
9 Lee	Y	Y	Y	N	Y	N	Y
10 Tauscher	Y	Y	Y	N	Y	N	Y
11 McNerney	?	?	?	N	Y	N	Y
12 Speier	Y	Y	Y	N	Y	N	Y
13 Stark	Y	Y	Y	N	Y	N	Y
14 Eshoo	Y	Y	Y	N	Y	N	Y
15 Honda	Y	Y	Y	N	Y	N	Y
16 Lofgren	Y	Y	Y	N	Y	N	Y
17 Farr	Y	Y	Y	N	Y	N	Y
18 Cardoza	Y	Y	Y	N	Y	N	Y
19 Radanovich	Y	Y	Y	N	N	N	N
20 Costa	Y	Y	Y	N	Y	N	Y
21 Nunes	Y	Y	Y	N	N	N	N
22 McCarthy	?	?	?	N	N	N	N
23 Capps	Y	Y	Y	N	Y	N	Y
24 Gallegly	Y	Y	Y	N	N	N	N
25 McKeon	Y	Y	Y	N	N	Y	N
26 Dreier	?	?	?	?	?	?	?
27 Sherman	Y	Y	Y	N	Y	N	Y
28 Berman	Y	Y	Y	N	Y	N	Y
29 Schiff	Y	Y	Y	N	Y	N	Y
30 Waxman	Y	Y	Y	?	Y	Y	Y
31 Becerra	Y	Y	Y	N	Y	N	Y
32 Solis	Y	Y	Y	N	Y	N	Y
33 Watson	?	Y	Y	N	Y	N	Y
34 Roybal-Allard	Y	Y	Y	N	Y	N	Y
35 Waters	Y	Y	Y	N	Y	N	Y
36 Harman	?	?	?	N	Y	N	Y
37 Richardson	Y	Y	Y	N	Y	N	Y
38 Napolitano	Y	Y	Y	N	Y	N	Y
39 Sánchez, Linda	+	+	+	N	Y	N	Y
40 Royce	Y	Y	Y	N	N	N	N
41 Lewis	Y	Y	Y	N	N	N	N
42 Miller, Gary	Y	Y	Y	N	N	Y	N
43 Baca	Y	Y	Y	N	Y	N	Y
44 Calvert	Y	Y	Y	N	N	N	N
45 Bono Mack	Y	Y	Y	N	N	N	N
46 Rohrabacher	?	?	?	N	N	N	N
47 Sanchez, Loretta	?	?	?	N	Y	N	Y
48 Campbell	Y	Y	Y	N	N	N	N
49 Issa	Y	Y	Y	N	N	N	N
50 Bilbray	Y	Y	Y	N	N	N	N
51 Filner	Y	Y	Y	N	Y	N	Y
52 Hunter	Y	Y	Y	N	?	?	N
53 Davis	Y	Y	Y	N	Y	N	Y

	589	590	591	592	593	594	595
COLORADO							
1 DeGette	Y	Y	Y	N	Y	N	Y
2 Udall	?	?	?	?	?	?	Y
3 Salazar	Y	Y	Y	N	Y	N	Y
4 Musgrave	Y	Y	Y	N	N	N	N
5 Lamborn	Y	Y	Y	N	N	N	N
6 Tancredo	Y	Y	Y	N	N	?	N
7 Perlmutter	Y	Y	Y	N	Y	N	Y
CONNECTICUT							
1 Larson	Y	Y	Y	N	Y	N	Y
2 Courtney	Y	Y	Y	N	Y	N	Y
3 DeLauro	Y	Y	Y	N	Y	N	Y
4 Shays	Y	Y	Y	N	N	N	Y
5 Murphy	Y	Y	Y	N	Y	N	Y
DELAWARE							
AL Castle	Y	Y	Y	N	N	N	N
FLORIDA							
1 Miller	Y	Y	Y	N	N	N	N
2 Boyd	Y	Y	Y	N	Y	N	Y
3 Brown	?	?	?	N	Y	N	Y
4 Crenshaw	Y	Y	Y	N	N	N	N
5 Brown-Waite	Y	Y	N	N	?	N	N
6 Stearns	Y	Y	Y	N	N	N	N
7 Mica	Y	Y	Y	N	N	N	N
8 Keller	Y	Y	Y	N	N	?	N
9 Bilirakis	Y	Y	Y	N	N	N	N
10 Young	Y	Y	Y	N	N	N	N
11 Castor	Y	Y	Y	N	Y	N	Y
12 Putnam	Y	Y	Y	N	N	N	N
13 Buchanan	Y	Y	Y	N	N	N	N
14 Mack	Y	Y	Y	N	N	N	N
15 Weldon	Y	Y	Y	N	Y	N	N
16 Mahoney	Y	Y	Y	–	Y	–	Y
17 Meek	Y	Y	Y	N	Y	N	Y
18 Ros-Lehtinen	Y	Y	Y	N	N	N	N
19 Wexler	Y	Y	Y	N	Y	N	Y
20 Wasserman Schultz	Y	Y	Y	N	Y	?	Y
21 Diaz-Balart, L.	?	?	?	N	N	N	N
22 Klein	Y	Y	Y	N	Y	N	Y
23 Hastings	Y	Y	Y	N	Y	N	Y
24 Feeney	Y	Y	Y	N	N	N	N
25 Diaz-Balart, M.	+	+	+	N	N	N	N
GEORGIA							
1 Kingston	Y	Y	Y	N	N	N	N
2 Bishop	Y	Y	Y	N	Y	N	Y
3 Westmoreland	Y	Y	Y	N	?	?	N
4 Johnson	Y	Y	Y	N	Y	N	Y
5 Lewis	Y	Y	Y	N	Y	N	Y
6 Price	Y	Y	N	N	N	N	N
7 Linder	Y	Y	Y	N	Y	N	N
8 Marshall	Y	Y	Y	N	Y	N	Y
9 Deal	Y	Y	Y	N	N	N	N
10 Broun	Y	Y	N	N	N	N	N
11 Gingrey	Y	Y	Y	N	N	N	N
12 Barrow	Y	Y	Y	N	Y	N	Y
13 Scott	Y	Y	Y	N	Y	N	Y
HAWAII							
1 Abercrombie	Y	Y	Y	N	N	N	Y
2 Hirono	Y	Y	Y	N	Y	N	Y
IDAHO							
1 Sali	Y	Y	Y	N	N	N	N
2 Simpson	Y	Y	Y	N	N	N	N
ILLINOIS							
1 Rush	Y	Y	Y	N	Y	N	Y
2 Jackson	Y	Y	Y	N	Y	N	Y
3 Lipinski	?	?	?	N	Y	N	Y
4 Gutierrez	?	?	?	N	Y	N	Y
5 Emanuel	Y	Y	Y	N	Y	N	Y
6 Roskam	Y	Y	Y	N	N	N	N
7 Davis	Y	Y	Y	N	Y	N	Y
8 Bean	Y	Y	Y	N	Y	N	Y
9 Schakowsky	Y	Y	Y	N	Y	N	Y
10 Kirk	Y	Y	Y	N	N	N	N
11 Weller	Y	Y	Y	N	N	N	N
12 Costello	?	?	?	N	Y	N	Y
13 Biggert	Y	Y	Y	N	N	N	N
14 Foster	Y	Y	Y	N	Y	N	Y
15 Johnson	+	+	+	–	N	Y	N

ND Northern Democrats, SD Southern Democrats
Southern states: Ala., Ark., Fla., Ga., Ky., La., Miss., N.C., Okla., S.C., Tenn., Texas, Va.

	589	590	591	592	593	594	595
16 **Manzullo**	Y	Y	Y	N	N	N	N
17 Hare	Y	Y	Y	N	Y	N	Y
18 **LaHood**	?	?	?	N	N	N	N
19 **Shimkus**	Y	Y	Y	Y	N	Y	N
INDIANA							
1 Visclosky	Y	Y	Y	N	Y	?	Y
2 Donnelly	Y	Y	Y	N	Y	N	Y
3 **Souder**	Y	Y	Y	N	N	N	N
4 **Buyer**	Y	Y	Y	N	N	N	N
5 **Burton**	Y	Y	Y	N	N	N	N
6 **Pence**	Y	Y	Y	N	N	?	N
7 Carson, A.	Y	Y	Y	N	Y	N	Y
8 Ellsworth	Y	Y	Y	N	Y	N	Y
9 Hill	Y	Y	Y	N	Y	N	Y
IOWA							
1 Braley	Y	Y	Y	N	Y	N	Y
2 Loebsack	Y	Y	Y	N	Y	N	Y
3 Boswell	Y	Y	Y	N	Y	?	Y
4 **Latham**	Y	Y	Y	N	N	N	N
5 **King**	Y	Y	Y	N	N	N	N
KANSAS							
1 **Moran**	Y	Y	Y	N	N	N	N
2 Boyda	Y	Y	Y	N	Y	N	Y
3 Moore	Y	Y	Y	N	Y	N	Y
4 **Tiahrt**	Y	Y	Y	N	N	N	N
KENTUCKY							
1 **Whitfield**	Y	Y	Y	N	N	?	N
2 **Lewis**	?	?	?	N	N	N	N
3 Yarmuth	Y	Y	Y	N	Y	N	Y
4 **Davis**	Y	Y	Y	N	N	N	N
5 **Rogers**	Y	Y	Y	N	N	N	N
6 Chandler	Y	Y	Y	N	Y	N	Y
LOUISIANA							
1 **Scalise**	Y	Y	Y	N	N	N	N
2 Jefferson	?	?	?	N	Y	N	Y
3 Melancon	Y	Y	Y	N	Y	N	Y
4 **McCrery**	Y	Y	Y	N	N	N	N
5 **Alexander**	Y	Y	Y	N	N	N	N
6 Cazayoux	Y	Y	Y	N	Y	N	N
7 **Boustany**	?	?	?	N	N	N	N
MAINE							
1 Allen	Y	Y	+	N	Y	N	Y
2 Michaud	Y	Y	Y	N	N	N	N
MARYLAND							
1 **Gilchrest**	Y	Y	Y	N	N	N	N
2 Ruppersberger	Y	Y	Y	N	Y	N	Y
3 Sarbanes	Y	Y	Y	N	Y	N	Y
4 Edwards	Y	Y	Y	N	Y	N	Y
5 Hoyer	Y	Y	Y	N	Y	N	Y
6 **Bartlett**	Y	Y	Y	Y	N	N	N
7 Cummings	Y	Y	Y	N	Y	N	Y
8 Van Hollen	Y	Y	Y	N	Y	N	Y
MASSACHUSETTS							
1 Olver	Y	Y	Y	N	Y	N	Y
2 Neal	?	?	?	N	Y	N	Y
3 McGovern	Y	Y	Y	N	Y	N	Y
4 Frank	Y	Y	Y	N	Y	N	Y
5 Tsongas	Y	Y	Y	N	Y	N	Y
6 Tierney	Y	Y	Y	N	Y	N	Y
7 Markey	Y	Y	Y	N	Y	N	Y
8 Capuano	Y	Y	Y	N	Y	N	Y
9 Lynch	Y	Y	Y	N	Y	N	Y
10 Delahunt	Y	Y	Y	?	Y	N	Y
MICHIGAN							
1 Stupak	Y	Y	Y	N	Y	N	Y
2 **Hoekstra**	Y	Y	Y	N	N	N	N
3 **Ehlers**	?	?	?	?	?	?	?
4 **Camp**	Y	Y	Y	N	N	N	N
5 Kildee	Y	Y	Y	N	Y	N	Y
6 **Upton**	Y	Y	Y	N	N	N	N
7 **Walberg**	+	+	+	–	–	–	–
8 **Rogers**	Y	Y	Y	N	N	N	N
9 **Knollenberg**	Y	Y	Y	N	N	N	N
10 **Miller**	Y	Y	Y	N	N	N	N
11 **McCotter**	Y	Y	Y	N	N	N	N
12 Levin	Y	Y	Y	N	Y	N	Y
13 Kilpatrick	Y	Y	Y	N	Y	N	Y
14 Conyers	Y	Y	Y	N	Y	N	Y
15 Dingell	Y	Y	Y	?	?	?	Y
MINNESOTA							
1 Walz	Y	Y	Y	N	Y	N	Y
2 **Kline**	Y	Y	Y	N	N	N	N
3 **Ramstad**	Y	Y	Y	N	N	N	Y
4 McCollum	Y	Y	Y	N	Y	N	Y
5 Ellison	?	?	?	N	Y	N	Y
6 **Bachmann**	Y	Y	Y	N	N	N	N
7 Peterson	Y	Y	Y	N	Y	N	Y
8 Oberstar	Y	Y	Y	N	Y	N	Y
MISSISSIPPI							
1 Childers	Y	Y	Y	N	Y	N	Y
2 Thompson	Y	Y	?	N	Y	N	Y
3 **Pickering**	Y	Y	Y	N	N	N	N
4 Taylor	?	?	?	N	Y	N	Y
MISSOURI							
1 Clay	Y	Y	Y	N	Y	N	Y
2 **Akin**	Y	Y	Y	N	N	N	N
3 Carnahan	Y	Y	Y	N	Y	N	Y
4 Skelton	Y	Y	Y	N	Y	N	Y
5 Cleaver	Y	Y	Y	N	Y	N	Y
6 **Graves**	Y	Y	Y	N	N	N	N
7 **Blunt**	Y	Y	Y	N	N	N	N
8 **Emerson**	Y	Y	Y	N	N	N	N
9 **Hulshof**	?	?	?	N	N	N	N
MONTANA							
AL **Rehberg**	Y	Y	Y	N	N	N	N
NEBRASKA							
1 **Fortenberry**	Y	Y	Y	N	N	N	N
2 **Terry**	Y	Y	Y	N	N	N	N
3 **Smith**	Y	Y	Y	N	N	N	N
NEVADA							
1 Berkley	Y	Y	Y	N	Y	N	Y
2 **Heller**	Y	Y	Y	N	N	N	Y
3 **Porter**	Y	Y	Y	N	N	N	Y
NEW HAMPSHIRE							
1 Shea-Porter	Y	Y	Y	N	Y	N	Y
2 Hodes	+	+	+	N	Y	N	Y
NEW JERSEY							
1 Andrews	Y	Y	Y	N	Y	N	Y
2 **LoBiondo**	Y	Y	Y	N	N	N	Y
3 **Saxton**	?	?	?	N	N	Y	N
4 **Smith**	Y	Y	Y	N	N	N	Y
5 **Garrett**	Y	Y	Y	N	N	N	N
6 Pallone	Y	Y	Y	N	Y	N	Y
7 **Ferguson**	Y	Y	Y	N	N	N	N
8 Pascrell	Y	Y	Y	N	Y	N	Y
9 Rothman	Y	Y	Y	N	Y	N	Y
10 Payne	?	?	?	N	Y	N	Y
11 **Frelinghuysen**	Y	Y	Y	N	N	N	N
12 Holt	Y	Y	Y	N	Y	N	Y
13 Sires	Y	Y	Y	N	Y	N	Y
NEW MEXICO							
1 **Wilson**	Y	Y	Y	N	N	N	N
2 **Pearce**	Y	Y	?	N	N	N	N
3 Udall	?	?	?	N	Y	N	Y
NEW YORK							
1 Bishop	Y	Y	Y	N	Y	N	Y
2 Israel	Y	Y	Y	N	Y	N	Y
3 **King**	Y	Y	Y	N	Y	N	N
4 McCarthy	Y	Y	Y	N	Y	N	Y
5 Ackerman	Y	Y	Y	N	Y	N	Y
6 Meeks	Y	Y	Y	N	Y	N	Y
7 Crowley	Y	Y	Y	N	Y	N	Y
8 Nadler	Y	Y	Y	N	Y	N	Y
9 Weiner	Y	Y	Y	N	Y	N	Y
10 Towns	Y	Y	Y	N	Y	N	Y
11 Clarke	Y	Y	Y	N	Y	N	Y
12 Velázquez	Y	Y	Y	?	Y	N	Y
13 **Fossella**	Y	Y	Y	N	Y	N	N
14 Maloney	+	+	+	N	Y	N	Y
15 Rangel	Y	Y	Y	N	Y	N	Y
16 Serrano	Y	Y	Y	N	Y	N	Y
17 Engel	Y	Y	Y	N	Y	N	Y
18 Lowey	Y	Y	Y	N	Y	N	Y
19 Hall	Y	Y	Y	N	Y	N	Y
20 Gillibrand	Y	Y	Y	N	Y	N	Y
21 McNulty	Y	Y	Y	N	Y	N	Y
22 Hinchey	Y	Y	Y	N	Y	N	Y
23 **McHugh**	Y	Y	Y	N	N	N	N
24 Arcuri	?	?	?	N	Y	N	Y
25 **Walsh**	Y	Y	Y	N	N	?	N
26 **Reynolds**	?	?	?	N	N	N	N
27 Higgins	Y	Y	Y	N	Y	N	Y
28 Slaughter	Y	Y	Y	N	Y	N	Y
29 **Kuhl**	Y	Y	Y	N	N	N	N
NORTH CAROLINA							
1 Butterfield	Y	Y	Y	N	Y	N	Y
2 Etheridge	Y	Y	Y	N	Y	N	Y
3 **Jones**	Y	Y	Y	N	N	N	N
4 Price	Y	Y	Y	N	Y	N	Y
5 **Foxx**	Y	Y	N	N	N	N	N
6 **Coble**	Y	Y	Y	N	N	N	N
7 McIntyre	Y	Y	Y	N	Y	N	Y
8 **Hayes**	Y	Y	Y	N	N	N	N
9 **Myrick**	Y	Y	Y	N	N	N	N
10 **McHenry**	Y	Y	Y	N	N	N	N
11 Shuler	?	?	?	N	Y	N	Y
12 Watt	Y	Y	Y	N	Y	N	Y
13 Miller	Y	Y	Y	N	Y	N	Y
NORTH DAKOTA							
AL Pomeroy	Y	Y	Y	N	Y	N	Y
OHIO							
1 **Chabot**	Y	Y	Y	N	N	N	N
2 **Schmidt**	Y	Y	Y	N	N	N	N
3 **Turner**	Y	Y	Y	N	N	N	N
4 **Jordan**	Y	Y	Y	N	N	N	N
5 **Latta**	Y	Y	Y	N	N	N	N
6 Wilson	Y	Y	Y	N	Y	N	Y
7 **Hobson**	Y	Y	Y	N	N	N	N
8 **Boehner**	Y	Y	Y	N	N	N	N
9 Kaptur	Y	Y	Y	N	Y	N	Y
10 Kucinich	Y	Y	Y	N	Y	N	Y
11 Vacant							
12 **Tiberi**	Y	Y	Y	N	N	N	N
13 Sutton	Y	Y	Y	?	Y	?	Y
14 **LaTourette**	Y	Y	Y	N	N	N	N
15 **Pryce**	?	?	?	?	N	N	N
16 **Regula**	?	?	?	N	N	N	N
17 Ryan	Y	Y	Y	N	Y	N	Y
18 Space	?	?	?	N	Y	N	Y
OKLAHOMA							
1 **Sullivan**	Y	Y	Y	N	N	N	N
2 Boren	Y	Y	Y	N	Y	N	Y
3 **Lucas**	Y	Y	Y	N	N	N	N
4 **Cole**	Y	Y	Y	N	N	N	N
5 **Fallin**	Y	Y	Y	N	N	N	N
OREGON							
1 Wu	Y	Y	Y	N	Y	N	Y
2 **Walden**	Y	Y	Y	N	N	N	N
3 Blumenauer	Y	Y	Y	N	Y	N	Y
4 DeFazio	Y	Y	Y	N	Y	N	Y
5 Hooley	?	?	?	N	Y	N	Y
PENNSYLVANIA							
1 Brady	?	?	?	N	Y	N	Y
2 Fattah	Y	Y	Y	N	Y	N	Y
3 **English**	Y	Y	Y	Y	N	?	N
4 Altmire	Y	Y	Y	N	Y	N	Y
5 **Peterson**	Y	Y	Y	?	N	N	N
6 **Gerlach**	Y	Y	Y	N	N	N	N
7 Sestak	Y	Y	Y	N	Y	N	Y
8 Murphy, P.	?	?	?	N	Y	N	Y
9 **Shuster**	+	+	+	N	N	N	N
10 Carney	Y	Y	Y	N	Y	N	Y
11 Kanjorski	Y	Y	Y	N	Y	N	Y
12 Murtha	Y	Y	Y	N	Y	N	Y
13 Schwartz	Y	Y	Y	N	Y	N	Y
14 Doyle	Y	Y	Y	N	Y	N	Y
15 **Dent**	Y	Y	Y	N	N	N	N
16 **Pitts**	?	?	?	?	?	?	?
17 Holden	Y	Y	Y	N	Y	?	Y
18 **Murphy, T.**	Y	Y	Y	N	N	N	N
19 **Platts**	Y	Y	Y	N	N	N	N
RHODE ISLAND							
1 Kennedy	Y	Y	Y	N	Y	N	Y
2 Langevin	Y	Y	Y	N	Y	N	Y
SOUTH CAROLINA							
1 **Brown**	Y	Y	Y	N	N	N	N
2 **Wilson**	Y	Y	Y	N	N	N	N
3 **Barrett**	+	+	+	–	–	–	N
4 **Inglis**	Y	Y	Y	N	N	N	N
5 Spratt	Y	Y	Y	N	?	N	Y
6 Clyburn	Y	Y	Y	N	Y	N	Y
SOUTH DAKOTA							
AL Herseth Sandlin	Y	Y	Y	N	Y	N	Y
TENNESSEE							
1 **Davis, D.**	Y	Y	Y	N	N	N	N
2 **Duncan**	Y	Y	Y	N	N	N	N
3 **Wamp**	Y	Y	Y	N	N	N	N
4 Davis, L.	Y	Y	Y	N	Y	N	Y
5 Cooper	Y	Y	Y	N	Y	N	Y
6 Gordon	Y	Y	Y	N	Y	N	Y
7 **Blackburn**	Y	Y	Y	N	N	N	N
8 Tanner	Y	Y	Y	N	Y	N	Y
9 Cohen	Y	Y	Y	N	Y	N	Y
TEXAS							
1 **Gohmert**	Y	Y	Y	N	N	N	N
2 **Poe**	+	+	+	?	?	?	N
3 **Johnson, S.**	Y	Y	Y	Y	?	?	N
4 **Hall**	Y	Y	Y	N	N	N	N
5 **Hensarling**	Y	Y	Y	N	N	N	N
6 **Barton**	Y	Y	Y	N	N	N	N
7 **Culberson**	?	?	?	?	?	?	N
8 **Brady**	?	?	?	?	?	?	?
9 Green, A.	+	+	+	N	Y	N	Y
10 **McCaul**	?	?	?	?	?	N	N
11 **Conaway**	Y	Y	Y	N	N	N	N
12 **Granger**	Y	Y	Y	N	N	N	N
13 **Thornberry**	Y	Y	Y	N	N	N	N
14 **Paul**	?	?	?	?	?	?	?
15 Hinojosa	Y	Y	Y	N	Y	N	Y
16 Reyes	Y	Y	Y	N	Y	N	Y
17 Edwards	Y	Y	Y	N	Y	?	Y
18 Jackson Lee	?	?	?	?	?	?	?
19 **Neugebauer**	+	+	+	–	–	–	–
20 Gonzalez	Y	Y	Y	N	Y	N	Y
21 **Smith**	Y	Y	Y	?	N	N	N
22 Lampson	?	?	?	?	?	?	?
23 Rodriguez	Y	Y	Y	N	Y	N	Y
24 **Marchant**	Y	Y	Y	N	N	N	N
25 Doggett	Y	Y	Y	N	Y	N	Y
26 **Burgess**	Y	Y	Y	N	N	N	N
27 Ortiz	Y	Y	Y	N	Y	N	Y
28 Cuellar	Y	Y	Y	N	Y	N	Y
29 Green, G.	?	?	?	N	Y	N	Y
30 Johnson, E.	Y	Y	Y	N	Y	N	Y
31 **Carter**	Y	Y	Y	Y	N	N	N
32 **Sessions**	Y	Y	Y	Y	N	N	N
UTAH							
1 **Bishop**	Y	Y	Y	N	N	N	N
2 Matheson	Y	Y	Y	N	Y	N	Y
3 **Cannon**	Y	?	Y	Y	N	N	N
VERMONT							
AL Welch	Y	Y	Y	?	Y	N	Y
VIRGINIA							
1 **Wittman**	Y	Y	Y	N	N	N	N
2 **Drake**	Y	Y	Y	N	N	N	N
3 Scott	Y	Y	Y	N	Y	N	Y
4 **Forbes**	Y	Y	Y	N	N	N	N
5 **Goode**	Y	Y	Y	N	N	N	N
6 **Goodlatte**	Y	Y	Y	N	N	N	N
7 **Cantor**	Y	Y	Y	N	N	?	N
8 Moran	Y	Y	Y	N	Y	N	Y
9 Boucher	Y	Y	Y	?	Y	N	Y
10 **Wolf**	Y	Y	Y	N	N	N	N
11 **Davis**	?	?	?	N	?	?	N
WASHINGTON							
1 Inslee	Y	Y	Y	N	Y	N	Y
2 Larsen	Y	Y	Y	N	Y	?	Y
3 Baird	Y	Y	Y	N	Y	N	Y
4 **Hastings**	Y	Y	Y	N	N	N	N
5 **McMorris Rodgers**	Y	Y	Y	N	N	N	N
6 Dicks	Y	Y	Y	N	Y	N	Y
7 McDermott	Y	Y	Y	N	Y	N	Y
8 **Reichert**	+	+	+	N	N	N	Y
9 Smith	Y	Y	Y	N	Y	N	Y
WEST VIRGINIA							
1 Mollohan	Y	Y	Y	N	Y	N	Y
2 **Capito**	Y	Y	Y	N	N	N	N
3 Rahall	Y	Y	Y	N	Y	N	Y
WISCONSIN							
1 **Ryan**	Y	Y	Y	N	N	N	N
2 Baldwin	Y	Y	Y	N	Y	N	Y
3 Kind	?	?	?	N	Y	N	Y
4 Moore	Y	Y	Y	N	Y	N	Y
5 **Sensenbrenner**	Y	Y	Y	N	N	N	N
6 **Petri**	Y	Y	Y	Y	N	N	N
7 Obey	Y	Y	Y	N	Y	N	Y
8 Kagen	Y	Y	Y	N	Y	N	Y
WYOMING							
AL **Cubin**	?	?	?	?	?	?	?
DELEGATES							
Faleomavaega (A.S.)							
Norton (D.C.)							
Bordallo (Guam)							
Fortuño (P.R.)							
Christensen (V.I.)							

IN THE HOUSE | By Vote Number

596. **HR 6899. Energy Policy/Rule.** Adoption of the rule
(H Res 1433) to provide for House floor consideration of the bill that
would open new areas in U.S. waters to oil and gas drilling and provide
incentives for renewable energy and energy-efficient buildings. Adopted
229-194: R 0-190; D 229-4 (ND 174-1, SD 55-3). Sept. 16, 2008.

597. **HR 6842. District of Columbia Gun Laws/Previous
Question.** McGovern, D-Mass., motion to order the previous question
(thus ending debate and possibility of amendment) on adoption of the
rule (H Res 1434) to provide for House floor consideration of the bill
that would require the District of Columbia to enact new regulations
that comply with a Supreme Court ruling that struck down the city's ban
on handguns. Motion agreed to 241-183: R 10-181; D 231-2 (ND 173-2,
SD 58-0). (Subsequently, the rule was adopted by voice vote.)
Sept. 16, 2008.

598. **HR 6899. Energy Policy/Recommit.** Peterson, R-Pa., motion to
recommit the bill to the Natural Resources Committee with instructions
that it be reported back forthwith with a substitute amendment that
would repeal the existing 125-mile moratorium on oil and gas exploration and production in the eastern Gulf of Mexico and allow coastal
states to opt out of oil and gas production from 25 miles to 50 miles
offshore within one year of enactment. Motion rejected 191-226:
R 178-10; D 13-216 (ND 7-165, SD 6-51). Sept. 16, 2008.

599. **HR 6899. Energy Policy/Passage.** Passage of the bill that
would give states the option to allow oil and gas offshore drilling between
50 miles and 100 miles off their Pacific and Atlantic coasts, except for waters in the Gulf of Mexico off the Florida coast. The federal government
could permit drilling from 100 miles to 200 miles offshore and would
collect all royalties from new oil and gas leases permitted under the bill.
The bill would require utilities to obtain 15 percent of their power from
renewable sources by 2020 and includes $19 billion in new tax incentives
for renewable energy, new coal technologies and alternative-fuel vehicles.
Passed 236-189: R 15-176; D 221-13 (ND 167-9, SD 54-4). A "nay" was a
vote in support of the president's position. Sept. 16, 2008.

600. **HR 6842. District of Columbia Gun Laws/Substitute.** Childers,
D-Miss., substitute amendment that would repeal District of Columbia
laws prohibiting firearm possession, remove criminal penalties for possessing firearms in the home, and allow District residents to purchase
firearms in Maryland and Virginia. Adopted in Committee of the Whole
260-160: R 178-9; D 82-151 (ND 52-123, SD 30-28). A "yea" was a vote in
support of the president's position. Sept. 17, 2008.

601. **HR 6842. District of Columbia Gun Laws/Passage.** Passage of
the bill that would repeal District of Columbia laws prohibiting firearm
possession, including the possession of semiautomatic firearms. It would
repeal the District's requirements for firearm registration and the requirement that firearms be disassembled or secured with a trigger lock in the
home. It would remove criminal penalties for possessing firearms in the
home and allow the District's residents to purchase firearms in Maryland
and Virginia. Passed 266-152: R 181-7; D 85-145 (ND 54-118, SD 31-27).
A "yea" was a vote in support of the president's position. Sept. 17, 2008.

602. **H Res 1335. State Veterans Homes Association Tribute/
Adoption.** Filner, D-Calif., motion to suspend the rules and adopt the
resolution that would commend the contributions of the U.S. armed
forces and the efforts of the National Association of State Veterans
Homes for the past 120 years. Motion agreed to 411-0: R 188-0; D 223-0
(ND 168-0, SD 55-0). A two-thirds majority of those present and voting
(274 in this case) is required for adoption under suspension of the rules.
Sept. 17, 2008.

ND Northern Democrats, SD Southern Democrats
Southern states: Ala., Ark., Fla., Ga., Ky., La., Miss., N.C., Okla., S.C., Tenn., Texas, Va.

	596	597	598	599	600	601	602
ALABAMA							
1 **Bonner**	N	N	Y	N	Y	Y	Y
2 **Everett**	N	N	Y	N	Y	Y	Y
3 **Rogers**	N	N	Y	N	Y	Y	Y
4 **Aderholt**	N	N	Y	N	Y	Y	Y
5 Cramer	Y	Y	N	Y	Y	Y	Y
6 Bachus	N	N	Y	N	Y	Y	Y
7 Davis	Y	Y	N	Y	Y	Y	Y
ALASKA							
AL **Young**	N	N	Y	N	Y	Y	Y
ARIZONA							
1 **Renzi**	N	N	Y	N	Y	Y	Y
2 **Franks**	N	N	Y	N	Y	Y	Y
3 **Shadegg**	N	N	Y	N	Y	Y	Y
4 Pastor	Y	Y	N	Y	N	N	Y
5 Mitchell	Y	Y	Y	Y	Y	Y	Y
6 **Flake**	N	N	Y	N	Y	Y	Y
7 Grijalva	Y	Y	N	Y	N	N	?
8 Giffords	Y	Y	N	Y	Y	Y	Y
ARKANSAS							
1 Berry	Y	Y	N	Y	Y	Y	Y
2 Snyder	Y	Y	N	Y	N	N	Y
3 Boozman	N	N	Y	N	Y	Y	Y
4 Ross	Y	Y	N	Y	Y	Y	Y
CALIFORNIA							
1 Thompson	Y	Y	N	Y	Y	Y	Y
2 **Herger**	N	N	Y	N	Y	Y	Y
3 **Lungren**	N	N	Y	N	Y	Y	Y
4 **Doolittle**	N	N	Y	N	Y	Y	Y
5 Matsui	Y	Y	N	Y	N	N	Y
6 Woolsey	Y	Y	N	Y	N	N	Y
7 Miller, George	Y	Y	N	Y	N	N	Y
8 Pelosi			N	Y			
9 Lee	Y	Y	N	Y	N	N	Y
10 Tauscher	Y	Y	N	Y	N	N	Y
11 McNerney	Y	Y	–	Y	Y	Y	Y
12 Speier	Y	Y	N	Y	N	N	Y
13 Stark	Y	N	N	Y	N	N	?
14 Eshoo	Y	Y	N	Y	N	N	Y
15 Honda	Y	Y	N	Y	N	N	Y
16 Lofgren	Y	Y	N	Y	N	N	Y
17 Farr	Y	Y	N	N	N	N	Y
18 Cardoza	Y	Y	N	Y	Y	Y	Y
19 **Radanovich**	N	N	Y	N	Y	Y	Y
20 Costa	Y	Y	N	Y	Y	Y	Y
21 **Nunes**	N	N	Y	N	Y	Y	Y
22 **McCarthy**	N	N	Y	N	Y	Y	Y
23 Capps	Y	Y	N	Y	N	N	Y
24 **Gallegly**	N	N	Y	N	Y	Y	Y
25 **McKeon**	N	N	Y	N	Y	Y	Y
26 **Dreier**	?	?	?	?	?	?	?
27 Sherman	Y	Y	N	Y	N	N	Y
28 Berman	Y	Y	N	Y	N	N	Y
29 Schiff	Y	Y	N	Y	N	N	Y
30 Waxman	Y	Y	N	Y	N	N	?
31 Becerra	Y	Y	N	Y	N	N	Y
32 Solis	Y	Y	N	Y	N	N	Y
33 Watson	Y	Y	N	Y	N	N	Y
34 Roybal-Allard	Y	Y	N	Y	N	N	Y
35 Waters	Y	Y	N	Y	N	N	Y
36 Harman	Y	Y	N	Y	N	N	Y
37 Richardson	Y	Y	N	Y	N	N	Y
38 Napolitano	Y	Y	N	Y	N	N	Y
39 Sánchez, Linda	Y	Y	N	Y	N	N	Y
40 **Royce**	N	N	Y	N	Y	Y	Y
41 **Lewis**	N	N	Y	N	Y	Y	Y
42 **Miller, Gary**	N	N	Y	N	Y	Y	Y
43 Baca	Y	Y	N	Y	Y	Y	?
44 **Calvert**	N	N	Y	N	Y	Y	Y
45 **Bono Mack**	N	N	Y	N	Y	Y	Y
46 **Rohrabacher**	N	N	Y	N	Y	Y	Y
47 Sanchez, Loretta	Y	N	N	Y	N	N	Y
48 **Campbell**	N	N	Y	N	Y	Y	Y
49 **Issa**	N	N	Y	N	Y	Y	Y
50 **Bilbray**	N	N	Y	N	Y	Y	Y
51 Filner	Y	Y	N	N	N	N	Y
52 **Hunter**	N	N	Y	N	Y	Y	?
53 Davis	Y	Y	N	Y	N	N	Y

	596	597	598	599	600	601	602
COLORADO							
1 DeGette	Y	Y	N	Y	N	N	Y
2 Udall	Y	Y	N	Y	Y	Y	?
3 Salazar	Y	Y	N	Y	Y	Y	Y
4 **Musgrave**	N	N	Y	N	Y	Y	Y
5 **Lamborn**	N	N	Y	N	Y	Y	Y
6 **Tancredo**	N	N	Y	N	Y	Y	Y
7 Perlmutter	Y	Y	N	Y	N	N	Y
CONNECTICUT							
1 Larson	Y	Y	N	?	N	N	Y
2 Courtney	Y	Y	N	Y	N	N	Y
3 DeLauro	Y	Y	N	Y	N	N	Y
4 **Shays**	N	Y	Y	Y	N	N	Y
5 Murphy	Y	Y	N	Y	N	N	Y
DELAWARE							
AL **Castle**	N	Y	Y	Y	N	N	Y
FLORIDA							
1 **Miller**	N	N	Y	N	Y	Y	Y
2 Boyd	Y	Y	Y	Y	Y	Y	Y
3 Brown	Y	Y	N	Y	Y	Y	Y
4 **Crenshaw**	N	N	Y	N	Y	Y	Y
5 **Brown-Waite**	N	N	Y	N	Y	Y	Y
6 **Stearns**	N	N	Y	N	Y	Y	Y
7 **Mica**	N	N	Y	N	Y	Y	Y
8 **Keller**	N	N	Y	N	Y	Y	Y
9 **Bilirakis**	N	N	Y	N	Y	Y	Y
10 **Young**	N	N	Y	N	Y	Y	Y
11 Castor	Y	Y	N	Y	N	N	Y
12 **Putnam**	N	N	Y	N	Y	Y	Y
13 **Buchanan**	N	N	Y	N	Y	Y	Y
14 **Mack**	N	N	Y	N	Y	Y	Y
15 **Weldon**	N	N	Y	N	Y	Y	Y
16 Mahoney	Y	Y	N	Y	Y	Y	Y
17 Meek	Y	Y	N	Y	N	N	Y
18 **Ros-Lehtinen**	N	N	Y	N	Y	Y	Y
19 Wexler	Y	Y	N	Y	N	N	Y
20 Wasserman Schultz	Y	Y	N	Y	N	N	Y
21 **Diaz-Balart, L.**	N	N	Y	N	Y	Y	Y
22 Klein	Y	Y	N	Y	N	N	Y
23 Hastings	Y	Y	N	Y	N	N	?
24 **Feeney**	N	N	Y	N	Y	Y	Y
25 **Diaz-Balart, M.**	N	N	Y	N	Y	Y	Y
GEORGIA							
1 **Kingston**	N	N	Y	N	Y	Y	Y
2 Bishop	Y	Y	N	Y	Y	Y	Y
3 **Westmoreland**	N	N	Y	N	Y	Y	Y
4 Johnson	Y	Y	N	Y	N	N	Y
5 Lewis	Y	Y	N	Y	N	N	Y
6 **Price**	N	N	Y	N	Y	Y	Y
7 **Linder**	N	N	Y	N	Y	Y	Y
8 Marshall	Y	Y	N	Y	Y	Y	Y
9 **Deal**	N	N	Y	N	Y	Y	Y
10 **Broun**	N	N	Y	N	Y	Y	Y
11 **Gingrey**	N	N	Y	N	Y	Y	Y
12 Barrow	Y	Y	Y	Y	Y	Y	?
13 Scott	Y	Y	N	Y	N	N	Y
HAWAII							
1 Abercrombie	Y	Y	N	Y	Y	Y	Y
2 Hirono	Y	Y	N	Y	N	N	Y
IDAHO							
1 **Sali**	N	N	Y	N	Y	Y	Y
2 **Simpson**	N	N	Y	N	Y	Y	Y
ILLINOIS							
1 Rush	Y	Y	N	Y	N	N	Y
2 Jackson	Y	Y	N	Y	N	N	Y
3 Lipinski	Y	Y	N	Y	N	N	Y
4 Gutierrez	Y	Y	N	Y	N	N	Y
5 Emanuel	Y	Y	N	Y	N	N	Y
6 **Roskam**	N	N	Y	N	Y	Y	Y
7 Davis	Y	Y	N	Y	N	N	Y
8 Bean	Y	Y	N	Y	Y	Y	Y
9 Schakowsky	Y	Y	N	Y	N	N	Y
10 **Kirk**	N	N	Y	N	Y	Y	Y
11 **Weller**	N	N	Y	N	Y	Y	Y
12 Costello	Y	Y	N	Y	Y	Y	Y
13 **Biggert**	N	N	Y	N	Y	Y	Y
14 Foster	Y	Y	Y	Y	Y	Y	Y
15 **Johnson**	N	N	Y	N	Y	Y	Y

KEY **Republicans**   Democrats

Y	Voted for (yea)	X	Paired against
#	Paired for	–	Announced against
+	Announced for	P	Voted "present"
N	Voted against (nay)		

C	Voted "present" to avoid possible conflict of interest
?	Did not vote or otherwise make a position known

	596	597	598	599	600	601	602
16 **Manzullo**	N	N	Y	N	Y	Y	Y
17 Hare	Y	Y	N	Y	N	N	Y
18 **LaHood**	N	N	Y	Y	Y	Y	Y
19 **Shimkus**	N	N	Y	N	Y	Y	Y
INDIANA							
1 Visclosky	Y	Y	N	Y	N	N	Y
2 Donnelly	Y	Y	Y	Y	Y	Y	Y
3 **Souder**	N	N	Y	N	Y	Y	Y
4 **Buyer**	N	N	Y	N	Y	Y	Y
5 **Burton**	N	N	Y	N	Y	Y	Y
6 **Pence**	N	N	Y	N	Y	Y	Y
7 Carson, A.	Y	Y	N	Y	N	N	Y
8 Ellsworth	Y	Y	N	Y	Y	Y	Y
9 Hill	Y	Y	N	Y	Y	Y	Y
IOWA							
1 Braley	Y	Y	N	Y	N	N	Y
2 Loebsack	Y	Y	N	Y	N	N	Y
3 Boswell	Y	Y	N	Y	Y	Y	Y
4 **Latham**	N	N	Y	N	Y	Y	Y
5 **King**	N	N	Y	N	Y	?	Y
KANSAS							
1 **Moran**	N	N	Y	N	Y	Y	Y
2 Boyda	Y	Y	N	Y	Y	Y	Y
3 Moore	Y	Y	N	Y	Y	Y	Y
4 **Tiahrt**	?	N	Y	N	Y	Y	Y
KENTUCKY							
1 **Whitfield**	N	N	Y	N	Y	Y	Y
2 **Lewis**	N	N	Y	N	Y	Y	Y
3 Yarmuth	Y	Y	N	Y	N	N	Y
4 **Davis**	N	N	Y	N	Y	Y	Y
5 **Rogers**	N	N	Y	N	Y	Y	Y
6 Chandler	Y	Y	N	Y	Y	Y	Y
LOUISIANA							
1 **Scalise**	N	N	Y	N	Y	Y	Y
2 Jefferson	Y	Y	N	Y	N	N	Y
3 Melancon	Y	Y	N	Y	Y	Y	Y
4 **McCrery**	N	N	Y	N	Y	Y	?
5 **Alexander**	N	N	Y	N	Y	Y	Y
6 Cazayoux	N	Y	Y	N	Y	Y	Y
7 **Boustany**	N	N	Y	N	Y	Y	Y
MAINE							
1 Allen	Y	Y	N	Y	Y	Y	Y
2 Michaud	N	Y	N	Y	Y	Y	Y
MARYLAND							
1 **Gilchrest**	N	N	N	Y	N	N	Y
2 Ruppersberger	Y	Y	N	Y	N	N	Y
3 Sarbanes	Y	Y	N	Y	N	N	Y
4 Edwards	Y	Y	N	Y	N	N	Y
5 Hoyer	Y	Y	N	Y	N	N	Y
6 **Bartlett**	N	N	Y	N	Y	Y	Y
7 Cummings	Y	Y	N	Y	N	N	Y
8 Van Hollen	Y	Y	N	Y	N	N	Y
MASSACHUSETTS							
1 Olver	Y	Y	N	Y	N	N	Y
2 Neal	Y	Y	N	Y	N	N	Y
3 McGovern	Y	Y	N	Y	N	N	Y
4 Frank	Y	Y	N	Y	N	N	Y
5 Tsongas	Y	Y	N	Y	N	N	Y
6 Tierney	Y	Y	N	Y	N	N	Y
7 Markey	Y	Y	N	Y	N	N	Y
8 Capuano	Y	Y	N	Y	N	N	Y
9 Lynch	Y	Y	N	Y	N	N	Y
10 Delahunt	Y	Y	N	Y	N	N	Y
MICHIGAN							
1 Stupak	Y	Y	N	Y	Y	Y	Y
2 **Hoekstra**	N	N	Y	N	?	?	?
3 **Ehlers**	?	?	?	?	+	+	Y
4 **Camp**	N	N	Y	N	Y	Y	Y
5 Kildee	Y	Y	N	Y	N	N	Y
6 **Upton**	N	N	Y	N	Y	Y	Y
7 **Walberg**	–	–	+	–	Y	Y	Y
8 **Rogers**	N	N	Y	N	Y	Y	Y
9 **Knollenberg**	N	N	Y	Y	Y	Y	Y
10 **Miller**	N	N	+	N	Y	Y	Y
11 **McCotter**	N	N	Y	N	Y	Y	Y
12 Levin	Y	Y	N	Y	N	N	Y
13 Kilpatrick	Y	Y	N	Y	N	N	Y
14 Conyers	Y	Y	?	Y	N	N	+
15 Dingell	Y	Y	N	Y	Y	Y	Y
MINNESOTA							
1 Walz	Y	Y	Y	Y	Y	Y	Y
2 **Kline**	N	N	Y	N	Y	Y	Y
3 **Ramstad**	N	Y	Y	Y	N	N	Y
4 McCollum	Y	Y	N	Y	N	N	Y
5 Ellison	Y	Y	N	Y	N	N	Y
6 **Bachmann**	N	N	Y	N	+	Y	Y
7 Peterson	Y	Y	N	Y	Y	Y	Y
8 Oberstar	Y	Y	N	Y	Y	Y	Y
MISSISSIPPI							
1 Childers	Y	Y	Y	Y	Y	Y	Y
2 Thompson	Y	Y	N	Y	N	N	Y
3 **Pickering**	N	N	Y	N	Y	Y	Y
4 Taylor	N	Y	Y	N	Y	Y	Y
MISSOURI							
1 Clay	Y	Y	N	Y	N	N	Y
2 **Akin**	N	N	Y	N	Y	Y	Y
3 Carnahan	Y	Y	N	Y	N	Y	Y
4 Skelton	Y	Y	N	Y	Y	Y	Y
5 Cleaver	Y	Y	N	Y	N	?	Y
6 **Graves**	N	N	Y	N	Y	Y	Y
7 **Blunt**	N	N	Y	N	Y	Y	Y
8 **Emerson**	N	N	Y	N	Y	Y	Y
9 **Hulshof**	N	N	Y	N	?	?	?
MONTANA							
AL **Rehberg**	N	N	Y	N	Y	Y	Y
NEBRASKA							
1 **Fortenberry**	N	N	Y	N	Y	Y	Y
2 **Terry**	N	N	Y	N	Y	Y	Y
3 **Smith**	N	N	Y	N	Y	Y	Y
NEVADA							
1 Berkley	Y	Y	N	Y	N	N	Y
2 **Heller**	N	Y	N	N	Y	Y	Y
3 **Porter**	N	Y	N	Y	Y	Y	Y
NEW HAMPSHIRE							
1 Shea-Porter	Y	Y	N	Y	Y	Y	Y
2 Hodes	Y	Y	N	Y	Y	Y	Y
NEW JERSEY							
1 Andrews	Y	Y	N	Y	N	N	Y
2 **LoBiondo**	N	Y	N	Y	Y	Y	Y
3 **Saxton**	N	N	Y	N	Y	Y	Y
4 **Smith**	N	Y	N	Y	N	N	Y
5 **Garrett**	N	N	Y	N	Y	Y	Y
6 Pallone	Y	Y	N	N	N	N	Y
7 **Ferguson**	N	N	Y	N	N	Y	Y
8 Pascrell	Y	Y	N	Y	N	N	Y
9 Rothman	Y	Y	N	N	N	N	Y
10 Payne	Y	Y	N	N	N	N	Y
11 **Frelinghuysen**	N	N	N	N	Y	Y	Y
12 Holt	Y	Y	N	N	N	N	Y
13 Sires	Y	Y	N	Y	N	Y	Y
NEW MEXICO							
1 **Wilson**	N	N	Y	N	Y	Y	Y
2 **Pearce**	N	N	Y	N	Y	Y	Y
3 Udall	Y	Y	N	Y	Y	Y	Y
NEW YORK							
1 Bishop	Y	Y	N	Y	–	–	Y
2 Israel	Y	Y	N	Y	N	N	Y
3 **King**	N	N	Y	N	N	N	Y
4 McCarthy	Y	Y	N	Y	N	N	+
5 Ackerman	Y	Y	N	Y	N	N	Y
6 Meeks	Y	Y	N	Y	N	N	Y
7 Crowley	Y	Y	N	Y	N	N	Y
8 Nadler	Y	Y	N	Y	N	N	Y
9 Weiner	Y	Y	N	Y	N	N	Y
10 Towns	Y	Y	N	Y	N	N	Y
11 Clarke	Y	Y	N	Y	N	N	Y
12 Velázquez	Y	Y	N	Y	N	N	Y
13 **Fossella**	N	N	Y	N	Y	Y	Y
14 Maloney	Y	Y	N	Y	N	N	Y
15 Rangel	Y	Y	N	Y	N	N	Y
16 Serrano	Y	Y	N	Y	N	N	Y
17 Engel	Y	Y	N	Y	N	N	Y
18 Lowey	Y	Y	N	Y	N	N	Y
19 Hall	Y	Y	N	Y	N	N	Y
20 Gillibrand	Y	Y	N	Y	Y	Y	Y
21 McNulty	Y	Y	N	Y	N	N	Y
22 Hinchey	Y	Y	N	Y	Y	Y	Y
23 **McHugh**	N	N	Y	N	Y	Y	Y
24 Arcuri	Y	Y	N	Y	Y	Y	Y
25 **Walsh**	N	N	Y	N	Y	Y	Y
26 **Reynolds**	N	N	Y	N	Y	Y	?
27 Higgins	Y	Y	?	Y	Y	Y	Y
28 Slaughter	Y	Y	+	Y	N	N	Y
29 **Kuhl**	N	N	Y	N	Y	Y	Y
NORTH CAROLINA							
1 Butterfield	Y	Y	N	Y	N	N	Y
2 Etheridge	Y	Y	N	Y	N	Y	Y
3 **Jones**	N	N	Y	Y	Y	Y	Y
4 Price	Y	Y	N	Y	N	N	Y
5 **Foxx**	N	N	Y	N	Y	Y	Y
6 **Coble**	N	N	Y	N	Y	Y	Y
7 McIntyre	Y	Y	Y	Y	Y	Y	Y
8 **Hayes**	N	N	Y	Y	Y	Y	Y
9 **Myrick**	N	N	Y	N	Y	Y	Y
10 **McHenry**	N	N	Y	N	Y	Y	Y
11 Shuler	N	Y	N	Y	Y	Y	Y
12 Watt	Y	Y	N	Y	N	N	Y
13 Miller	Y	Y	N	Y	N	N	Y
NORTH DAKOTA							
AL Pomeroy	Y	Y	N	Y	Y	Y	Y
OHIO							
1 **Chabot**	N	N	Y	N	Y	Y	Y
2 **Schmidt**	N	N	Y	N	Y	Y	Y
3 **Turner**	N	N	Y	N	Y	Y	Y
4 **Jordan**	N	N	Y	N	Y	Y	Y
5 **Latta**	N	N	Y	N	Y	Y	Y
6 Wilson	Y	Y	N	Y	Y	Y	Y
7 **Hobson**	N	N	Y	N	Y	Y	Y
8 **Boehner**	N	N	Y	N	Y	Y	Y
9 Kaptur	Y	Y	N	Y	N	N	Y
10 Kucinich	Y	Y	N	Y	N	N	Y
11 Vacant							
12 **Tiberi**	N	N	Y	N	Y	Y	Y
13 Sutton	Y	Y	N	Y	N	N	Y
14 **LaTourette**	N	N	Y	N	Y	Y	Y
15 **Pryce**	N	N	?	N	Y	Y	Y
16 **Regula**	N	N	Y	N	?	?	Y
17 Ryan	Y	Y	N	Y	Y	Y	Y
18 Space	Y	Y	N	Y	Y	Y	Y
OKLAHOMA							
1 **Sullivan**	N	N	Y	N	Y	Y	Y
2 Boren	Y	Y	N	Y	Y	Y	Y
3 **Lucas**	N	N	Y	N	Y	Y	Y
4 **Cole**	N	N	Y	N	Y	Y	Y
5 **Fallin**	N	N	Y	N	Y	Y	Y
OREGON							
1 Wu	Y	Y	N	Y	N	N	Y
2 **Walden**	N	N	Y	N	Y	Y	Y
3 Blumenauer	Y	Y	N	Y	N	N	Y
4 DeFazio	Y	Y	N	Y	Y	Y	Y
5 Hooley	Y	Y	N	Y	N	N	Y
PENNSYLVANIA							
1 Brady	Y	Y	N	Y	N	N	Y
2 Fattah	Y	Y	N	Y	N	N	Y
3 **English**	N	N	Y	N	Y	Y	Y
4 Altmire	Y	Y	Y	Y	Y	Y	Y
5 **Peterson**	N	N	Y	N	?	Y	Y
6 **Gerlach**	N	Y	Y	N	Y	Y	Y
7 Sestak	Y	Y	N	Y	N	N	Y
8 Murphy, P.	Y	Y	N	Y	Y	Y	Y
9 **Shuster**	N	N	Y	N	Y	Y	Y
10 Carney	Y	Y	N	Y	Y	Y	Y
11 Kanjorski	Y	Y	N	Y	Y	Y	Y
12 Murtha	Y	Y	N	Y	Y	Y	Y
13 Schwartz	Y	Y	N	Y	N	N	Y
14 Doyle	Y	Y	N	Y	N	N	Y
15 **Dent**	N	N	Y	N	Y	Y	Y
16 **Pitts**	?	?	?	?	?	?	?
17 Holden	Y	Y	Y	Y	Y	Y	Y
18 **Murphy, T.**	N	N	Y	N	Y	Y	Y
19 **Platts**	N	N	Y	N	Y	Y	Y
RHODE ISLAND							
1 Kennedy	Y	Y	N	Y	N	N	Y
2 Langevin	Y	Y	N	Y	N	N	Y
SOUTH CAROLINA							
1 **Brown**	N	N	Y	N	Y	Y	Y
2 **Wilson**	N	N	Y	N	Y	Y	Y
3 **Barrett**	N	N	Y	N	Y	Y	Y
4 **Inglis**	N	N	Y	Y	Y	Y	Y
5 Spratt	Y	Y	N	Y	Y	Y	Y
6 Clyburn	Y	Y	N	Y	N	N	Y
SOUTH DAKOTA							
AL Herseth Sandlin	Y	Y	Y	Y	Y	Y	Y
TENNESSEE							
1 **Davis, D.**	N	N	Y	N	Y	Y	Y
2 **Duncan**	N	N	Y	N	Y	Y	Y
3 **Wamp**	N	N	Y	N	Y	Y	Y
4 Davis, L.	Y	Y	N	Y	Y	Y	Y
5 Cooper	Y	Y	N	Y	Y	Y	Y
6 Gordon	Y	Y	N	Y	Y	Y	Y
7 **Blackburn**	N	N	Y	N	Y	Y	Y
8 Tanner	Y	Y	N	Y	Y	Y	Y
9 Cohen	Y	Y	N	Y	N	N	Y
TEXAS							
1 **Gohmert**	N	N	Y	N	Y	Y	Y
2 **Poe**	N	N	Y	N	Y	Y	?
3 **Johnson, S.**	N	N	Y	N	Y	Y	Y
4 **Hall**	N	N	Y	N	Y	Y	Y
5 **Hensarling**	N	N	Y	N	Y	Y	Y
6 **Barton**	N	N	Y	N	Y	Y	Y
7 **Culberson**	N	N	Y	N	Y	Y	Y
8 **Brady**	?	?	?	?	?	?	?
9 Green, A.	Y	Y	–	Y	N	N	Y
10 **McCaul**	N	N	+	N	Y	Y	Y
11 **Conaway**	N	N	Y	N	Y	Y	Y
12 **Granger**	N	N	Y	N	Y	Y	Y
13 **Thornberry**	N	N	Y	N	Y	Y	Y
14 **Paul**	?	?	?	?	Y	Y	Y
15 Hinojosa	Y	Y	N	Y	N	N	Y
16 Reyes	Y	Y	N	Y	Y	Y	Y
17 Edwards	Y	Y	N	Y	Y	Y	Y
18 Jackson Lee	Y	Y	N	Y	N	N	?
19 **Neugebauer**	–	–	+	–	+	+	Y
20 Gonzalez	Y	Y	N	Y	N	N	Y
21 **Smith**	N	N	Y	N	Y	Y	Y
22 Lampson	?	?	?	?	?	?	?
23 Rodriguez	Y	Y	N	Y	Y	Y	Y
24 **Marchant**	N	N	Y	N	Y	Y	Y
25 Doggett	Y	Y	N	Y	N	N	Y
26 **Burgess**	N	N	Y	N	Y	Y	Y
27 Ortiz	Y	Y	N	Y	Y	Y	Y
28 Cuellar	Y	Y	N	Y	Y	Y	Y
29 Green, G.	Y	Y	N	Y	Y	Y	Y
30 Johnson, E.	Y	Y	N	Y	N	N	Y
31 **Carter**	N	N	Y	N	Y	Y	Y
32 **Sessions**	N	N	Y	N	Y	Y	Y
UTAH							
1 **Bishop**	N	N	Y	N	Y	Y	Y
2 Matheson	Y	Y	N	Y	Y	Y	Y
3 **Cannon**	N	N	Y	N	Y	Y	?
VERMONT							
AL Welch	Y	Y	N	Y	Y	Y	Y
VIRGINIA							
1 **Wittman**	N	N	Y	N	Y	Y	Y
2 **Drake**	N	N	Y	N	Y	Y	Y
3 Scott	Y	Y	N	Y	N	N	Y
4 **Forbes**	N	N	Y	N	Y	Y	Y
5 **Goode**	N	N	Y	N	Y	Y	Y
6 **Goodlatte**	N	N	Y	N	Y	Y	Y
7 **Cantor**	N	N	Y	N	?	?	Y
8 Moran	Y	Y	N	Y	N	N	?
9 Boucher	Y	Y	N	Y	Y	Y	Y
10 **Wolf**	N	N	Y	N	Y	Y	Y
11 **Davis**	N	N	Y	N	N	Y	Y
WASHINGTON							
1 Inslee	Y	Y	N	Y	N	N	Y
2 Larsen	Y	Y	N	Y	N	N	Y
3 Baird	Y	Y	N	Y	Y	Y	Y
4 **Hastings**	N	N	Y	N	Y	Y	Y
5 **McMorris Rodgers**	N	N	Y	N	Y	Y	Y
6 Dicks	Y	Y	N	Y	N	N	Y
7 McDermott	Y	Y	N	Y	N	N	Y
8 **Reichert**	N	Y	N	Y	Y	Y	Y
9 Smith	Y	Y	N	Y	N	N	Y
WEST VIRGINIA							
1 Mollohan	Y	Y	N	Y	Y	Y	Y
2 **Capito**	N	N	Y	N	Y	Y	Y
3 Rahall	Y	Y	N	Y	Y	Y	Y
WISCONSIN							
1 **Ryan**	N	N	Y	N	Y	Y	Y
2 Baldwin	Y	Y	N	Y	N	N	Y
3 Kind	Y	Y	N	Y	Y	Y	Y
4 Moore	Y	Y	N	Y	N	N	Y
5 **Sensenbrenner**	N	N	Y	N	Y	Y	Y
6 **Petri**	N	N	Y	N	Y	Y	Y
7 Obey	Y	Y	N	Y	P	P	Y
8 Kagen	Y	Y	N	Y	Y	Y	Y
WYOMING							
AL **Cubin**	?	?	?	?	?	?	?
DELEGATES							
Faleomavaega (A.S.)					N		
Norton (D.C.)					N		
Bordallo (Guam)					N		
Fortuño (P.R.)					?		
Christensen (V.I.)					?		

IN THE HOUSE | By Vote Number

603. S 2339. Van Wagoner Veterans Affairs Clinic/Passage. Filner, D-Calif., motion to suspend the rules and pass the bill that would designate the Department of Veterans Affairs clinic in Alpena, Mich., as the "Lt. Col. Clement C. Van Wagoner Department of Veterans Affairs Clinic." Motion agreed to 412-0: R 188-0; D 224-0 (ND 168-0, SD 56-0). A two-thirds majority of those present and voting (275 in this case) is required for passage under suspension of the rules. Sept. 17, 2008.

604. HR 1594. Marzano Veterans Affairs Clinic/Passage. Filner, D-Calif., motion to suspend the rules and pass the bill that would designate the Department of Veterans Affairs clinic in Hermitage, Pa., as the "Michael A. Marzano Department of Veterans Affairs Outpatient Clinic." Motion agreed to 410-0: R 187-0; D 223-0 (ND 167-0, SD 56-0). A two-thirds majority of those present and voting (274 in this case) is required for passage under suspension of the rules. Sept. 17, 2008.

605. HR 6604. Commodity Markets Transparency/Previous Question. Sutton, D-Ohio, motion to order the previous question (thus ending debate and possibility of amendment) on adoption of the rule (H Res 1449) to provide for House floor consideration of the bill that would authorize federal regulators to set limits on over-the-counter trading to ensure that energy futures prices reflect supply and demand. Foreign exchanges trading U.S. commodities would have to impose limits on the number of futures contracts an investor can own, if investor activity threatens to distort prices. Motion agreed to 224-187: R 3-184; D 221-3 (ND 169-2, SD 52-1). Sept. 18, 2008.

606. HR 6604. Commodity Markets Transparency/Rule. Adoption of the rule (H Res 1449) to provide for House floor consideration of the bill that would authorize federal regulators to set limits on over-the-counter trading to ensure that energy futures prices reflect supply and demand. Foreign exchanges trading U.S. commodities would have to impose limits on the number of futures contracts an investor can own, if investor activity threatens to distort prices. Adopted 218-190: R 0-186; D 218-4 (ND 165-3, SD 53-1). Sept. 18, 2008.

607. HR 6604. Commodity Markets Transparency/Recommit. Moran, R-Kan., motion to recommit the bill to the Agriculture Committee with instructions that it be reported back promptly with language that would bar the provisions from taking effect until the Commodity Futures Trading Commission determines that the bill's energy market regulatory actions would not result in any equity loss for individuals' pension funds. Motion rejected 196-221: R 189-0; D 7-221 (ND 6-166, SD 1-55). Sept. 18, 2008.

608. HR 6604. Commodity Markets Transparency/Passage. Passage of the bill that would authorize federal regulators to set limits on over-the-counter trading to ensure that energy futures prices reflect supply and demand. Foreign exchanges trading U.S. commodities would have to impose limits on the number of futures contracts an investor can own, if investor activity threatens to distort prices. Passed 283-133: R 69-119; D 214-14 (ND 162-10, SD 52-4). A "nay" was a vote in support of the president's position. Sept. 18, 2008.

609. H Res 1460. Rep. Rangel Tax Investigation/Motion to Table. Hoyer, D-Md., motion to table (kill) the Boehner, R-Ohio, privileged resolution that would remove Rep. Charles B. Rangel, D-N.Y., from his chairmanship of the House Ways and Means Committee and establish a subcommittee in the House Committee on Standards of Official Conduct within 10 days of the resolution's adoption to investigate whether Rangel violated the U.S. tax code in his failure to report rental income for property he has owned in the Dominican Republic since 1988. Motion agreed to 226-176: R 5-176; D 221-0 (ND 168-0, SD 53-0). Sept. 18, 2008.

ND Northern Democrats, SD Southern Democrats
Southern states: Ala., Ark., Fla., Ga., Ky., La., Miss., N.C., Okla., S.C., Tenn., Texas, Va.

	603	604	605	606	607	608	609
ALABAMA							
1 **Bonner**	Y	Y	N	N	Y	N	P
2 **Everett**	Y	Y	N	N	Y	N	N
3 **Rogers**	Y	Y	N	N	Y	Y	N
4 **Aderholt**	Y	Y	N	N	Y	N	N
5 Cramer	Y	Y	Y	Y	N	Y	Y
6 **Bachus**	Y	Y	N	?	Y	N	N
7 Davis	Y	Y	Y	Y	N	N	Y
ALASKA							
AL **Young**	Y	Y	N	N	Y	N	N
ARIZONA							
1 **Renzi**	Y	Y	?	?	Y	N	?
2 **Franks**	Y	Y	N	N	Y	N	N
3 **Shadegg**	Y	Y	N	N	Y	N	N
4 Pastor	Y	Y	Y	Y	N	Y	Y
5 Mitchell	Y	Y	Y	Y	Y	Y	Y
6 **Flake**	Y	Y	N	N	Y	N	N
7 Grijalva	?	?	?	?	?	?	?
8 Giffords	Y	Y	Y	Y	N	Y	Y
ARKANSAS							
1 Berry	Y	Y	Y	Y	N	Y	Y
2 Snyder	Y	Y	Y	N	Y	Y	?
3 **Boozman**	Y	Y	N	N	Y	N	N
4 Ross	Y	Y	Y	Y	N	Y	Y
CALIFORNIA							
1 Thompson	Y	Y	Y	Y	N	Y	Y
2 **Herger**	Y	Y	N	N	Y	N	N
3 **Lungren**	Y	Y	N	N	Y	N	N
4 **Doolittle**	Y	Y	N	N	Y	N	N
5 Matsui	Y	Y	Y	Y	N	Y	Y
6 Woolsey	Y	Y	Y	?	N	Y	Y
7 Miller, George	Y	Y	Y	Y	N	Y	Y
8 Pelosi	Y	Y	Y	Y			
9 Lee	Y	Y	Y	Y	N	Y	Y
10 Tauscher	Y	Y	Y	Y	N	Y	Y
11 McNerney	Y	Y	Y	Y	Y	Y	Y
12 Speier	Y	Y	Y	Y	N	Y	Y
13 Stark	?	?	Y	Y	N	Y	Y
14 Eshoo	Y	Y	Y	Y	N	Y	Y
15 Honda	Y	Y	Y	Y	N	Y	Y
16 Lofgren	Y	Y	Y	Y	N	Y	Y
17 Farr	Y	Y	Y	Y	N	Y	Y
18 Cardoza	Y	Y	Y	Y	N	Y	Y
19 **Radanovich**	Y	Y	N	N	Y	N	N
20 Costa	Y	Y	Y	Y	N	Y	Y
21 **Nunes**	Y	Y	N	N	Y	N	N
22 **McCarthy**	Y	Y	N	N	Y	N	N
23 Capps	Y	Y	Y	Y	N	Y	Y
24 **Gallegly**	Y	Y	N	N	Y	N	N
25 **McKeon**	Y	Y	N	N	Y	N	N
26 **Dreier**	?	?	?	?	?	?	?
27 Sherman	Y	Y	Y	Y	N	Y	Y
28 Berman	Y	Y	Y	Y	N	Y	Y
29 Schiff	Y	Y	Y	Y	N	Y	Y
30 Waxman	Y	Y	Y	Y	N	Y	Y
31 Becerra	Y	Y	Y	Y	N	Y	Y
32 Solis	Y	Y	Y	Y	N	Y	Y
33 Watson	Y	Y	Y	Y	N	Y	Y
34 Roybal-Allard	Y	Y	Y	Y	N	Y	P
35 Waters	?	Y	Y	Y	N	Y	Y
36 Harman	Y	Y	Y	Y	N	Y	Y
37 Richardson	Y	Y	Y	Y	N	Y	Y
38 Napolitano	Y	Y	Y	Y	N	Y	Y
39 Sánchez, Linda	Y	Y	Y	Y	N	Y	Y
40 **Royce**	Y	Y	N	N	Y	N	N
41 **Lewis**	Y	Y	N	N	Y	N	N
42 **Miller, Gary**	Y	Y	N	N	Y	N	N
43 Baca	?	?	Y	Y	N	Y	Y
44 **Calvert**	Y	Y	N	N	Y	N	N
45 **Bono Mack**	Y	Y	N	N	Y	N	Y
46 **Rohrabacher**	Y	Y	N	N	Y	N	Y
47 Sanchez, Loretta	Y	Y	Y	Y	N	Y	Y
48 **Campbell**	Y	Y	N	N	Y	N	N
49 **Issa**	Y	Y	?	?	?	?	?
50 **Bilbray**	Y	Y	N	N	Y	N	N
51 Filner	Y	Y	Y	Y	N	Y	Y
52 **Hunter**	Y	Y	N	N	Y	N	N
53 Davis	Y	Y	Y	N	Y	Y	Y

	603	604	605	606	607	608	609
COLORADO							
1 DeGette	Y	Y	Y	Y	N	Y	Y
2 Udall	?	?	?	?	N	Y	Y
3 Salazar	Y	Y	Y	Y	N	Y	Y
4 **Musgrave**	Y	Y	N	N	Y	N	N
5 **Lamborn**	Y	Y	N	N	Y	N	N
6 **Tancredo**	Y	Y	N	N	Y	N	N
7 Perlmutter	Y	Y	Y	Y	N	Y	Y
CONNECTICUT							
1 Larson	Y	Y	Y	Y	N	Y	Y
2 Courtney	Y	Y	Y	Y	N	Y	Y
3 DeLauro	Y	Y	Y	Y	N	Y	Y
4 **Shays**	Y	Y	N	Y	Y	Y	N
5 Murphy	Y	Y	Y	Y	N	Y	Y
DELAWARE							
AL **Castle**	Y	Y	N	N	Y	Y	N
FLORIDA							
1 **Miller**	Y	Y	N	N	Y	N	N
2 Boyd	Y	Y	Y	Y	N	Y	Y
3 Brown	Y	Y	?	?	N	Y	Y
4 **Crenshaw**	Y	Y	N	N	Y	N	N
5 **Brown-Waite**	Y	Y	N	N	Y	N	N
6 **Stearns**	Y	Y	N	N	Y	N	N
7 **Mica**	Y	Y	N	N	Y	N	N
8 **Keller**	Y	Y	N	N	Y	N	N
9 **Bilirakis**	Y	Y	N	N	Y	N	N
10 **Young**	Y	Y	N	N	Y	N	N
11 Castor	Y	Y	Y	Y	N	Y	Y
12 **Putnam**	Y	Y	N	N	Y	N	N
13 **Buchanan**	Y	?	N	N	Y	N	N
14 **Mack**	Y	Y	N	N	Y	N	N
15 **Weldon**	Y	Y	N	N	Y	N	N
16 Mahoney	Y	Y	Y	Y	Y	Y	Y
17 Meek	Y	Y	Y	Y	N	Y	Y
18 **Ros-Lehtinen**	Y	Y	N	Y	Y	N	N
19 Wexler	Y	Y	Y	Y	N	Y	Y
20 Wasserman Schultz	Y	Y	Y	Y	N	Y	Y
21 **Diaz-Balart, L.**	Y	Y	N	N	Y	N	N
22 Klein	Y	Y	Y	Y	N	Y	Y
23 Hastings	?	?	?	?	?	?	?
24 **Feeney**	Y	Y	N	N	Y	N	N
25 **Diaz-Balart, M.**	Y	Y	N	N	Y	N	N
GEORGIA							
1 **Kingston**	Y	Y	N	N	Y	N	N
2 Bishop	Y	Y	Y	Y	N	Y	Y
3 **Westmoreland**	Y	Y	N	N	Y	N	N
4 Johnson	Y	Y	Y	Y	N	Y	Y
5 Lewis	Y	Y	Y	Y	N	Y	Y
6 **Price**	Y	Y	N	N	Y	N	N
7 **Linder**	Y	?	N	N	Y	N	N
8 Marshall	Y	Y	Y	Y	Y	Y	Y
9 **Deal**	Y	Y	N	N	Y	N	N
10 **Broun**	Y	Y	N	N	Y	N	N
11 **Gingrey**	Y	Y	N	N	Y	N	N
12 Barrow	Y	Y	Y	Y	N	Y	Y
13 Scott	Y	Y	Y	Y	N	Y	Y
HAWAII							
1 Abercrombie	Y	?	Y	Y	N	Y	Y
2 Hirono	Y	Y	Y	Y	N	Y	Y
IDAHO							
1 **Sali**	Y	Y	N	N	Y	N	N
2 **Simpson**	Y	Y	N	N	Y	N	N
ILLINOIS							
1 Rush	Y	Y	Y	Y	N	Y	Y
2 Jackson	Y	Y	Y	Y	N	Y	Y
3 Lipinski	Y	Y	Y	Y	N	Y	Y
4 Gutierrez	Y	Y	Y	Y	N	Y	Y
5 Emanuel	Y	Y	Y	Y	N	Y	Y
6 **Roskam**	Y	Y	N	N	Y	N	N
7 Davis	Y	Y	Y	Y	N	Y	Y
8 Bean	Y	Y	Y	N	Y	N	Y
9 Schakowsky	Y	Y	Y	Y	N	Y	Y
10 **Kirk**	Y	Y	N	Y	Y	N	N
11 **Weller**	Y	Y	Y	Y	N	Y	Y
12 Costello	Y	Y	Y	Y	N	Y	Y
13 **Biggert**	Y	Y	N	N	Y	N	N
14 Foster	Y	Y	Y	Y	N	Y	N
15 **Johnson**	Y	Y	N	Y	Y	N	N

KEY	Republicans	Democrats		
Y	Voted for (yea)	X	Paired against	C Voted "present" to avoid possible conflict of interest
#	Paired for	–	Announced against	
+	Announced for	P	Voted "present"	? Did not vote or otherwise make a position known
N	Voted against (nay)			

	603	604	605	606	607	608	609
16 **Manzullo**	Y	Y	N	N	Y	N	N
17 Hare	Y	Y	Y	Y	N	Y	Y
18 **LaHood**	Y	Y	N	N	Y	Y	N
19 **Shimkus**	Y	Y	N	N	Y	N	N
INDIANA							
1 Visclosky	Y	Y	Y	Y	N	Y	Y
2 Donnelly	Y	Y	Y	Y	N	Y	Y
3 **Souder**	Y	Y	?	?	Y	Y	N
4 **Buyer**	Y	Y	N	N	Y	N	N
5 **Burton**	Y	Y	N	N	Y	N	P
6 **Pence**	Y	Y	?	?	?	?	?
7 Carson, A.	Y	Y	Y	Y	N	Y	Y
8 Ellsworth	Y	Y	Y	Y	N	Y	Y
9 Hill	Y	Y	N	N	Y	Y	Y
IOWA							
1 Braley	Y	Y	Y	Y	N	Y	Y
2 Loebsack	Y	Y	Y	Y	N	Y	Y
3 Boswell	Y	Y	Y	Y	N	Y	Y
4 **Latham**	Y	Y	N	N	Y	Y	N
5 **King**	Y	Y	N	N	Y	N	N
KANSAS							
1 **Moran**	Y	Y	N	N	Y	N	N
2 Boyda	Y	Y	Y	Y	N	Y	Y
3 Moore	Y	Y	Y	N	N	Y	Y
4 **Tiahrt**	Y	Y	N	N	Y	N	N
KENTUCKY							
1 **Whitfield**	Y	Y	N	N	Y	Y	N
2 **Lewis**	Y	Y	N	N	Y	Y	N
3 Yarmuth	Y	Y	Y	Y	N	Y	Y
4 **Davis**	Y	Y	N	N	Y	N	N
5 **Rogers**	Y	Y	N	N	Y	Y	N
6 Chandler	Y	Y	Y	Y	N	Y	Y
LOUISIANA							
1 **Scalise**	Y	Y	N	N	Y	N	N
2 Jefferson	Y	Y	Y	Y	N	Y	Y
3 Melancon	Y	Y	Y	Y	N	N	Y
4 **McCrery**	?	?	N	N	Y	N	N
5 **Alexander**	Y	Y	N	N	Y	N	N
6 Cazayoux	Y	Y	N	N	N	Y	Y
7 **Boustany**	Y	Y	N	N	Y	N	N
MAINE							
1 Allen	Y	Y	Y	Y	N	Y	Y
2 Michaud	Y	Y	Y	Y	N	Y	Y
MARYLAND							
1 **Gilchrest**	Y	Y	N	N	Y	Y	Y
2 Ruppersberger	Y	Y	Y	Y	N	Y	Y
3 Sarbanes	Y	Y	Y	Y	N	Y	Y
4 Edwards	Y	Y	Y	Y	N	Y	Y
5 Hoyer	Y	Y	Y	Y	N	Y	Y
6 **Bartlett**	Y	Y	N	N	Y	N	N
7 Cummings	Y	Y	Y	Y	N	Y	Y
8 Van Hollen	Y	Y	Y	Y	N	Y	Y
MASSACHUSETTS							
1 Olver	Y	Y	Y	Y	N	Y	Y
2 Neal	Y	Y	Y	Y	N	Y	Y
3 McGovern	Y	Y	Y	Y	N	Y	Y
4 Frank	Y	Y	Y	Y	N	Y	Y
5 Tsongas	?	?	Y	Y	N	Y	Y
6 Tierney	Y	Y	Y	Y	N	Y	Y
7 Markey	Y	Y	Y	Y	N	Y	Y
8 Capuano	Y	Y	?	?	N	Y	Y
9 Lynch	Y	Y	Y	Y	N	Y	Y
10 Delahunt	Y	Y	Y	Y	N	Y	P
MICHIGAN							
1 Stupak	Y	Y	Y	Y	N	Y	Y
2 **Hoekstra**	?	?	N	N	Y	N	N
3 **Ehlers**	Y	Y	N	N	Y	Y	N
4 **Camp**	Y	Y	N	N	Y	N	N
5 Kildee	Y	Y	Y	Y	N	Y	Y
6 **Upton**	Y	Y	N	N	Y	Y	N
7 **Walberg**	Y	Y	N	N	Y	N	N
8 **Rogers**	Y	Y	N	N	Y	N	N
9 **Knollenberg**	Y	Y	N	N	Y	Y	N
10 **Miller**	Y	Y	N	N	Y	Y	N
11 **McCotter**	Y	Y	N	N	Y	Y	N
12 Levin	Y	Y	Y	Y	N	Y	Y
13 Kilpatrick	Y	Y	Y	Y	N	Y	Y
14 Conyers	Y	Y	?	+	–	+	+
15 Dingell	Y	Y	Y	Y	N	Y	Y
MINNESOTA							
1 Walz	Y	Y	Y	Y	N	Y	Y
2 **Kline**	Y	Y	N	N	Y	N	P
3 **Ramstad**	Y	Y	N	N	Y	Y	Y
4 McCollum	Y	Y	Y	Y	N	Y	Y
5 Ellison	Y	Y	Y	Y	N	Y	Y
6 **Bachmann**	Y	Y	N	N	Y	N	N
7 Peterson	Y	Y	Y	Y	N	Y	Y
8 Oberstar	Y	Y	Y	Y	N	Y	Y
MISSISSIPPI							
1 Childers	Y	Y	Y	Y	N	Y	Y
2 Thompson	Y	Y	Y	Y	N	Y	Y
3 **Pickering**	Y	Y	N	N	Y	N	N
4 Taylor	Y	Y	Y	Y	N	Y	Y
MISSOURI							
1 Clay	Y	Y	Y	Y	N	Y	Y
2 **Akin**	Y	Y	N	N	Y	N	N
3 Carnahan	Y	Y	Y	Y	N	Y	Y
4 Skelton	Y	Y	Y	Y	N	Y	Y
5 Cleaver	Y	Y	Y	?	N	Y	Y
6 **Graves**	Y	Y	N	N	Y	Y	N
7 **Blunt**	Y	Y	N	N	Y	N	N
8 **Emerson**	Y	Y	N	N	Y	Y	N
9 **Hulshof**	?	?	?	?	?	?	?
MONTANA							
AL **Rehberg**	Y	Y	N	N	Y	N	N
NEBRASKA							
1 **Fortenberry**	Y	Y	N	N	Y	Y	N
2 **Terry**	Y	Y	N	N	Y	Y	N
3 **Smith**	Y	Y	N	N	Y	N	N
NEVADA							
1 Berkley	Y	Y	Y	Y	N	Y	Y
2 **Heller**	Y	Y	N	N	Y	N	N
3 **Porter**	Y	Y	N	N	Y	Y	N
NEW HAMPSHIRE							
1 Shea-Porter	Y	Y	Y	Y	N	Y	Y
2 Hodes	Y	Y	Y	Y	N	Y	Y
NEW JERSEY							
1 Andrews	Y	Y	Y	Y	N	Y	Y
2 **LoBiondo**	Y	Y	N	N	Y	Y	N
3 **Saxton**	Y	Y	N	N	Y	Y	N
4 **Smith**	Y	Y	N	N	Y	Y	N
5 **Garrett**	Y	Y	N	N	Y	N	N
6 Pallone	Y	Y	Y	Y	N	Y	Y
7 **Ferguson**	Y	Y	N	N	Y	N	N
8 Pascrell	Y	Y	Y	Y	N	Y	Y
9 Rothman	Y	Y	Y	Y	N	Y	Y
10 Payne	Y	Y	Y	Y	N	Y	Y
11 **Frelinghuysen**	Y	Y	N	N	Y	Y	N
12 Holt	Y	Y	Y	Y	N	Y	Y
13 Sires	Y	Y	Y	Y	N	Y	Y
NEW MEXICO							
1 **Wilson**	Y	Y	N	N	Y	N	N
2 **Pearce**	Y	Y	N	N	Y	N	N
3 Udall	Y	Y	Y	Y	N	Y	Y
NEW YORK							
1 Bishop	Y	Y	Y	Y	N	Y	Y
2 Israel	Y	Y	Y	Y	N	Y	Y
3 **King**	Y	Y	?	?	?	?	?
4 McCarthy	+	+	Y	Y	N	Y	Y
5 Ackerman	Y	Y	Y	Y	N	Y	Y
6 Meeks	Y	Y	Y	Y	N	Y	Y
7 Crowley	Y	Y	Y	Y	N	N	Y
8 Nadler	Y	Y	Y	Y	N	Y	Y
9 Weiner	Y	Y	Y	Y	N	N	Y
10 Towns	Y	Y	Y	Y	N	Y	Y
11 Clarke	Y	Y	Y	Y	N	N	Y
12 Velázquez	Y	Y	Y	Y	N	Y	Y
13 **Fossella**	Y	Y	N	N	Y	N	?
14 Maloney	Y	Y	Y	Y	N	N	Y
15 Rangel	Y	Y	Y	?	N	Y	Y
16 Serrano	Y	Y	Y	Y	N	Y	Y
17 Engel	Y	Y	Y	Y	N	Y	Y
18 Lowey	Y	Y	Y	Y	N	Y	Y
19 Hall	Y	Y	Y	Y	N	Y	Y
20 Gillibrand	Y	Y	Y	Y	N	Y	Y
21 McNulty	Y	Y	Y	Y	N	Y	Y
22 Hinchey	Y	Y	Y	Y	N	Y	Y
23 **McHugh**	Y	Y	N	N	Y	Y	N
24 Arcuri	Y	Y	Y	Y	N	Y	Y
25 **Walsh**	Y	Y	N	N	Y	Y	N
26 **Reynolds**	?	?	N	N	Y	N	N
27 Higgins	Y	Y	Y	Y	N	Y	Y
28 Slaughter	Y	Y	Y	Y	N	Y	Y
29 **Kuhl**	Y	Y	N	N	Y	Y	N
NORTH CAROLINA							
1 Butterfield	Y	Y	Y	Y	N	Y	Y
2 Etheridge	Y	Y	Y	Y	N	Y	Y
3 **Jones**	Y	Y	N	N	Y	Y	Y
4 Price	Y	Y	Y	Y	N	Y	Y
5 **Foxx**	Y	Y	N	N	Y	N	N
6 **Coble**	Y	Y	N	N	Y	N	N
7 McIntyre	Y	Y	Y	Y	N	Y	Y
8 **Hayes**	Y	Y	N	N	Y	Y	N
9 **Myrick**	Y	Y	N	N	Y	N	N
10 **McHenry**	Y	Y	N	N	Y	N	N
11 Shuler	Y	Y	Y	Y	N	Y	Y
12 Watt	Y	Y	Y	Y	N	Y	Y
13 Miller	Y	Y	Y	Y	N	Y	Y
NORTH DAKOTA							
AL Pomeroy	Y	Y	Y	Y	N	Y	Y
OHIO							
1 **Chabot**	Y	Y	N	N	Y	Y	N
2 **Schmidt**	Y	Y	N	N	Y	Y	N
3 **Turner**	Y	Y	N	N	Y	N	N
4 **Jordan**	Y	Y	N	N	Y	N	N
5 **Latta**	Y	Y	N	N	Y	N	N
6 Wilson	Y	Y	Y	Y	N	Y	Y
7 **Hobson**	Y	Y	N	N	Y	N	N
8 **Boehner**	Y	Y	N	N	Y	N	N
9 Kaptur	Y	Y	Y	Y	N	Y	Y
10 Kucinich	Y	Y	Y	Y	N	Y	Y
11 Vacant							
12 **Tiberi**	Y	Y	N	N	Y	N	N
13 Sutton	Y	Y	Y	Y	N	Y	Y
14 **LaTourette**	Y	Y	N	N	Y	Y	N
15 **Pryce**	Y	Y	N	N	Y	N	N
16 **Regula**	Y	Y	N	N	Y	Y	N
17 Ryan	Y	Y	Y	Y	N	Y	Y
18 Space	Y	Y	Y	Y	N	Y	Y
OKLAHOMA							
1 **Sullivan**	Y	Y	N	N	Y	N	N
2 Boren	Y	Y	Y	Y	N	Y	Y
3 **Lucas**	Y	Y	N	N	Y	Y	N
4 **Cole**	Y	Y	N	N	Y	N	N
5 **Fallin**	Y	Y	N	N	Y	Y	N
OREGON							
1 Wu	Y	Y	Y	Y	N	Y	Y
2 **Walden**	Y	Y	N	N	Y	N	N
3 Blumenauer	Y	Y	Y	Y	N	Y	Y
4 DeFazio	Y	Y	Y	Y	N	Y	Y
5 Hooley	Y	Y	Y	Y	N	Y	Y
PENNSYLVANIA							
1 Brady	Y	Y	Y	Y	N	Y	Y
2 Fattah	Y	Y	Y	Y	N	Y	Y
3 **English**	Y	Y	N	N	Y	Y	N
4 Altmire	Y	Y	Y	Y	Y	Y	Y
5 **Peterson**	Y	Y	N	N	Y	?	N
6 **Gerlach**	Y	Y	N	N	Y	Y	N
7 Sestak	Y	Y	Y	Y	?	?	?
8 Murphy, P.	Y	Y	Y	Y	N	Y	Y
9 **Shuster**	Y	Y	N	N	Y	N	N
10 Carney	Y	Y	Y	Y	N	Y	Y
11 Kanjorski	Y	Y	Y	Y	N	Y	Y
12 Murtha	Y	Y	Y	Y	N	Y	Y
13 Schwartz	Y	Y	Y	Y	N	Y	Y
14 Doyle	Y	Y	Y	Y	N	Y	P
15 **Dent**	Y	Y	N	N	Y	Y	N
16 **Pitts**	?	?	?	?	?	?	?
17 Holden	Y	Y	Y	Y	N	Y	Y
18 **Murphy, T.**	Y	Y	N	N	Y	Y	N
19 **Platts**	Y	Y	N	N	Y	Y	N
RHODE ISLAND							
1 Kennedy	Y	Y	Y	Y	N	Y	?
2 Langevin	Y	Y	Y	Y	N	Y	Y
SOUTH CAROLINA							
1 **Brown**	Y	Y	N	N	Y	N	N
2 **Wilson**	Y	Y	N	N	Y	N	N
3 **Barrett**	Y	Y	N	N	Y	N	P
4 **Inglis**	Y	Y	N	N	Y	N	N
5 Spratt	Y	Y	Y	Y	N	Y	Y
6 Clyburn	Y	Y	Y	Y	N	Y	Y
SOUTH DAKOTA							
AL Herseth Sandlin	Y	Y	Y	Y	N	Y	Y
TENNESSEE							
1 **Davis, D.**	Y	Y	N	N	Y	N	N
2 **Duncan**	Y	Y	N	N	Y	Y	N
3 **Wamp**	Y	Y	N	N	Y	Y	N
4 Davis, L.	Y	Y	Y	Y	N	Y	Y
5 Cooper	Y	Y	Y	Y	N	N	Y
6 Gordon	Y	Y	Y	Y	N	Y	Y
7 **Blackburn**	Y	Y	N	N	Y	N	N
8 Tanner	Y	Y	Y	Y	N	Y	Y
9 Cohen	Y	Y	Y	Y	N	Y	Y
TEXAS							
1 **Gohmert**	Y	Y	N	N	Y	Y	N
2 **Poe**	?	?	?	?	?	?	?
3 **Johnson, S.**	Y	Y	N	N	Y	N	N
4 **Hall**	Y	Y	N	N	Y	Y	N
5 **Hensarling**	Y	Y	N	N	Y	N	N
6 **Barton**	Y	Y	N	N	Y	N	N
7 **Culberson**	Y	Y	N	N	Y	N	N
8 **Brady**	?	?	?	?	?	?	?
9 Green, A.	Y	Y	Y	Y	N	Y	Y
10 **McCaul**	Y	Y	N	N	Y	N	P
11 **Conaway**	Y	Y	N	N	Y	N	N
12 **Granger**	Y	?	N	N	Y	N	N
13 **Thornberry**	Y	Y	N	N	Y	N	N
14 **Paul**	Y	Y	N	N	Y	N	Y
15 Hinojosa	Y	Y	Y	Y	N	Y	Y
16 Reyes	Y	Y	Y	Y	N	Y	Y
17 Edwards	Y	Y	Y	Y	N	Y	Y
18 Jackson Lee	?	?	?	?	?	?	?
19 **Neugebauer**	Y	Y	N	N	Y	N	N
20 Gonzalez	Y	Y	Y	Y	N	Y	Y
21 **Smith**	?	Y	N	N	Y	N	N
22 Lampson	?	?	?	?	?	?	?
23 Rodriguez	Y	Y	Y	Y	N	Y	Y
24 **Marchant**	Y	Y	N	N	Y	Y	N
25 Doggett	Y	Y	Y	Y	N	Y	Y
26 **Burgess**	Y	Y	?	?	?	?	?
27 Ortiz	Y	Y	Y	Y	N	Y	Y
28 Cuellar	Y	Y	Y	Y	N	Y	Y
29 Green, G.	Y	Y	Y	Y	N	Y	P
30 Johnson, E.	Y	Y	Y	Y	N	Y	Y
31 **Carter**	Y	Y	N	N	Y	N	N
32 **Sessions**	Y	Y	N	N	Y	N	N
UTAH							
1 **Bishop**	?	Y	N	N	Y	N	N
2 Matheson	Y	?	Y	Y	N	N	Y
3 **Cannon**	Y	Y	N	N	Y	N	N
VERMONT							
AL Welch	Y	Y	Y	Y	N	Y	Y
VIRGINIA							
1 **Wittman**	Y	Y	N	N	Y	Y	N
2 **Drake**	Y	Y	N	N	Y	N	N
3 Scott	Y	Y	Y	Y	N	Y	P
4 **Forbes**	Y	Y	N	N	Y	Y	N
5 **Goode**	Y	Y	N	N	Y	Y	N
6 **Goodlatte**	Y	Y	N	N	Y	Y	N
7 **Cantor**	Y	Y	N	N	Y	N	N
8 Moran	Y	Y	?	?	N	Y	Y
9 Boucher	Y	Y	?	Y	N	Y	Y
10 **Wolf**	Y	Y	N	N	Y	Y	N
11 **Davis**	Y	Y	N	N	Y	N	N
WASHINGTON							
1 Inslee	Y	Y	Y	Y	N	Y	Y
2 Larsen	Y	Y	Y	Y	N	Y	Y
3 Baird	Y	Y	Y	Y	N	Y	Y
4 **Hastings**	Y	Y	N	N	Y	N	P
5 **McMorris Rodgers**	Y	Y	N	N	Y	Y	N
6 Dicks	Y	Y	Y	Y	N	Y	Y
7 McDermott	Y	Y	Y	Y	N	Y	Y
8 **Reichert**	Y	Y	Y	N	Y	N	N
9 Smith	Y	Y	Y	Y	N	Y	Y
WEST VIRGINIA							
1 Mollohan	Y	Y	Y	Y	N	Y	Y
2 **Capito**	Y	Y	N	N	Y	Y	N
3 Rahall	Y	Y	Y	Y	N	Y	Y
WISCONSIN							
1 **Ryan**	Y	Y	N	N	Y	N	N
2 Baldwin	Y	Y	Y	Y	N	Y	Y
3 Kind	Y	Y	Y	Y	N	N	Y
4 Moore	Y	Y	Y	Y	N	Y	Y
5 **Sensenbrenner**	Y	Y	N	N	Y	N	N
6 **Petri**	Y	Y	N	N	Y	N	N
7 Obey	Y	Y	Y	Y	N	Y	Y
8 Kagen	Y	Y	Y	Y	N	Y	Y
WYOMING							
AL **Cubin**	?	?	?	?	?	?	?
DELEGATES							
Faleomavaega (A.S.)							
Norton (D.C.)							
Bordallo (Guam)							
Fortuño (P.R.)							
Christensen (V.I.)							

IN THE HOUSE | By Vote Number

610. HR 3036. Environmental Education Grant Program/Previous Question. Castor, D-Fla., motion to order the previous question (thus ending debate and possibility of amendment) on adoption of the rule (H Res 1441) to provide for House floor consideration of the bill that would establish a competitive grant program to develop environmental education curricula and reauthorize the Environmental Education and Training Program in fiscal 2009. Motion agreed to 227-188: R 3-185; D 224-3 (ND 170-1, SD 54-2). Sept. 18, 2008.

611. HR 3036. Environmental Education Grant Program/Rule. Adoption of the rule (H Res 1441) to provide House floor consideration of the bill that would establish a competitive grant program to develop environmental education curricula and reauthorize the Environmental Education and Training Program in fiscal 2009. Adopted 221-182: R 2-181; D 219-1 (ND 165-1, SD 54-0). Sept. 18, 2008.

612. HR 3036. Environmental Education Grant Program/ Environmental Justice. Sarbanes, D-Md., amendment that would allow grant funds under the bill to be used to address environmental justice issues in low-income communities and to develop policy approaches to environmental education. Adopted in Committee of the Whole 383-23: R 158-22; D 225-1 (ND 172-1, SD 53-0). Sept. 18, 2008.

613. HR 3036. Environmental Education Grant Program/ Recommit. Price, R-Ga., motion to recommit the bill to the Education and Labor Committee with instructions that it be reported back forthwith with language that would require that priority be given to local education agencies before funds are awarded to other eligible applicants and bar the use of funds in the bill for lobbyists or lobbying organizations that advocate against energy production, as well as organizations that do not address a full spectrum of environmental issues. Motion rejected 172-230: R 172-8; D 0-222 (ND 0-168, SD 0-54). Sept. 18, 2008.

614. HR 3036. Environmental Education Grant Program/Passage. Passage of the bill that would establish a competitive grant program for nonprofit organizations, institutions of higher education, and state and local governments to develop environmental education curricula. It also would reauthorize $14 million for the Environmental Education and Training Program in fiscal 2009 and make changes to the program, requiring the EPA to consult with the Education Department when making program grants. It would require the program to encourage traditionally underrepresented individuals to pursue degrees in environmental fields. Passed 293-109: R 68-108; D 225-1 (ND 170-1, SD 55-0). Sept. 18, 2008.

615. HR 6460. Great Lakes Legacy Programs/Passage. Johnson, D-Texas, motion to suspend the rules and pass the bill that would reauthorize the Great Lakes Legacy programs through fiscal 2013. The measure would authorize $750 million to remediate sediment contamination and restore aquatic habitats in the Great Lakes region and $25 million for development of technologies for the programs. Motion agreed to 371-20: R 151-20; D 220-0 (ND 166-0, SD 54-0). A two-thirds majority of those present and voting (261 in this case) is required for passage under suspension of the rules. Sept. 18, 2008.

	610	611	612	613	614	615
ALABAMA						
1 **Bonner**	N	N	Y	Y	N	Y
2 **Everett**	N	N	Y	Y	?	?
3 **Rogers**	N	N	Y	Y	Y	Y
4 **Aderholt**	N	N	N	Y	N	Y
5 **Cramer**	Y	Y	Y	?	?	?
6 **Bachus**	N	?	Y	Y	Y	Y
7 Davis	Y	Y	Y	N	Y	Y
ALASKA						
AL **Young**	?	?	Y	Y	N	Y
ARIZONA						
1 **Renzi**	N	N	Y	Y	Y	Y
2 **Franks**	N	N	Y	Y	N	N
3 **Shadegg**	N	N	Y	Y	N	?
4 **Pastor**	Y	Y	Y	N	Y	Y
5 **Mitchell**	Y	Y	Y	N	Y	Y
6 **Flake**	N	N	Y	?	?	?
7 **Grijalva**	?	?	?	?	?	?
8 **Giffords**	Y	Y	Y	N	Y	Y
ARKANSAS						
1 **Berry**	Y	Y	Y	N	Y	Y
2 **Snyder**	Y	Y	Y	N	Y	Y
3 **Boozman**	N	N	Y	Y	N	Y
4 **Ross**	Y	Y	Y	N	Y	Y
CALIFORNIA						
1 Thompson	Y	Y	Y	N	Y	Y
2 **Herger**	N	N	Y	Y	N	Y
3 **Lungren**	N	N	Y	Y	N	N
4 **Doolittle**	N	N	N	Y	N	Y
5 Matsui	Y	Y	Y	N	Y	Y
6 Woolsey	Y	Y	Y	N	Y	Y
7 Miller, George	Y	Y	Y	N	Y	Y
8 Pelosi						
9 Lee	Y	Y	Y	N	Y	Y
10 Tauscher	Y	Y	Y	N	Y	Y
11 McNerney	Y	Y	Y	N	Y	?
12 Speier	Y	Y	Y	N	Y	Y
13 Stark	Y	Y	Y	N	Y	Y
14 Eshoo	Y	Y	Y	N	Y	Y
15 Honda	Y	Y	Y	N	Y	Y
16 Lofgren	Y	Y	Y	N	Y	Y
17 Farr	Y	Y	Y	N	Y	Y
18 Cardoza	Y	Y	Y	N	Y	Y
19 **Radanovich**	N	N	Y	Y	N	Y
20 Costa	Y	Y	Y	N	Y	Y
21 **Nunes**	N	N	–	–	–	+
22 **McCarthy**	N	N	Y	Y	N	Y
23 Capps	Y	Y	Y	N	Y	Y
24 **Gallegly**	N	N	Y	Y	N	Y
25 **McKeon**	N	N	Y	Y	N	Y
26 **Dreier**	?	?	?	?	?	?
27 Sherman	Y	Y	Y	N	Y	Y
28 Berman	?	?	Y	Y	N	Y
29 Schiff	Y	Y	Y	N	Y	Y
30 Waxman	Y	Y	Y	N	Y	Y
31 Becerra	Y	Y	Y	N	Y	Y
32 Solis	Y	Y	Y	N	Y	Y
33 Watson	Y	Y	Y	N	Y	Y
34 Roybal-Allard	Y	Y	Y	N	Y	+
35 Waters	Y	?	Y	N	Y	Y
36 Harman	Y	Y	Y	N	Y	Y
37 Richardson	Y	Y	Y	N	?	Y
38 Napolitano	Y	Y	Y	N	Y	?
39 Sánchez, Linda	Y	Y	Y	N	Y	Y
40 **Royce**	N	N	Y	Y	N	Y
41 **Lewis**	N	N	Y	Y	N	Y
42 **Miller, Gary**	N	N	N	Y	N	Y
43 **Baca**	Y	Y	Y	N	Y	Y
44 **Calvert**	N	N	Y	Y	N	Y
45 **Bono Mack**	N	N	Y	Y	Y	Y
46 **Rohrabacher**	N	N	Y	Y	N	Y
47 Sanchez, Loretta	Y	Y	Y	N	Y	Y
48 **Campbell**	N	N	Y	Y	N	N
49 **Issa**	?	?	?	?	?	?
50 **Bilbray**	N	N	Y	Y	Y	Y
51 Filner	Y	Y	Y	N	Y	Y
52 **Hunter**	N	N	Y	Y	?	?
53 Davis	Y	Y	Y	N	Y	Y

	610	611	612	613	614	615
COLORADO						
1 DeGette	Y	Y	Y	N	Y	Y
2 Udall	Y	Y	?	N	Y	Y
3 Salazar	Y	Y	Y	N	Y	Y
4 **Musgrave**	N	N	Y	Y	N	Y
5 **Lamborn**	N	N	Y	Y	N	N
6 **Tancredo**	N	N	N	Y	N	N
7 Perlmutter	Y	Y	Y	N	Y	Y
CONNECTICUT						
1 Larson	Y	Y	Y	N	Y	Y
2 Courtney	Y	Y	Y	N	Y	Y
3 DeLauro	Y	Y	Y	N	Y	Y
4 **Shays**	N	N	Y	–	Y	Y
5 Murphy	Y	Y	Y	N	Y	Y
DELAWARE						
AL **Castle**	N	Y	Y	N	Y	Y
FLORIDA						
1 **Miller**	N	N	N	Y	N	Y
2 Boyd	Y	Y	Y	N	Y	Y
3 Brown	Y	Y	Y	N	Y	Y
4 **Crenshaw**	N	N	Y	Y	Y	Y
5 **Brown-Waite**	N	N	Y	Y	Y	Y
6 **Stearns**	N	N	Y	Y	N	Y
7 **Mica**	N	N	Y	Y	N	Y
8 **Keller**	N	N	Y	Y	N	Y
9 **Bilirakis**	N	N	Y	Y	Y	Y
10 **Young**	N	N	Y	Y	N	Y
11 Castor	Y	Y	?	N	Y	Y
12 **Putnam**	N	N	Y	Y	N	Y
13 **Buchanan**	N	N	Y	Y	N	Y
14 **Mack**	N	N	Y	Y	N	N
15 **Weldon**	N	N	N	Y	N	?
16 Mahoney	Y	Y	?	N	Y	Y
17 Meek	Y	Y	Y	N	Y	Y
18 **Ros-Lehtinen**	N	N	Y	Y	N	Y
19 Wexler	Y	Y	Y	N	Y	Y
20 Wasserman Schultz	Y	Y	Y	N	Y	Y
21 **Diaz-Balart, L.**	N	N	Y	Y	N	Y
22 Klein	Y	Y	Y	N	Y	Y
23 Hastings	?	?	?	?	?	?
24 **Feeney**	N	N	?	Y	N	Y
25 **Diaz-Balart, M.**	N	N	Y	Y	Y	Y
GEORGIA						
1 **Kingston**	N	N	?	?	?	?
2 Bishop	Y	Y	Y	N	Y	?
3 **Westmoreland**	N	N	Y	Y	N	N
4 Johnson	Y	Y	Y	N	Y	Y
5 Lewis	Y	Y	Y	N	Y	Y
6 **Price**	N	N	Y	Y	N	Y
7 **Linder**	N	N	Y	Y	N	Y
8 Marshall	Y	Y	Y	N	Y	Y
9 **Deal**	N	N	Y	N	N	Y
10 **Broun**	N	N	Y	Y	N	N
11 **Gingrey**	N	N	N	Y	N	?
12 Barrow	Y	Y	Y	N	Y	Y
13 Scott	Y	Y	Y	N	Y	Y
HAWAII						
1 Abercrombie	Y	Y	Y	N	Y	Y
2 Hirono	Y	Y	Y	N	Y	Y
IDAHO						
1 **Sali**	N	N	Y	Y	N	N
2 **Simpson**	N	N	Y	Y	N	Y
ILLINOIS						
1 Rush	Y	Y	Y	N	Y	Y
2 Jackson	Y	Y	Y	N	Y	Y
3 Lipinski	Y	Y	Y	N	Y	Y
4 Gutierrez	Y	Y	Y	N	Y	Y
5 Emanuel	Y	Y	Y	N	Y	Y
6 **Roskam**	N	N	Y	Y	Y	Y
7 Davis	Y	Y	Y	N	Y	Y
8 Bean	Y	Y	Y	N	Y	Y
9 Schakowsky	Y	Y	Y	N	Y	Y
10 **Kirk**	N	N	Y	Y	Y	Y
11 **Weller**	N	N	Y	Y	Y	Y
12 Costello	Y	Y	Y	N	Y	Y
13 **Biggert**	N	?	?	?	?	?
14 Foster	Y	Y	Y	N	Y	Y
15 **Johnson**	N	Y	N	Y	Y	Y

KEY	**Republicans**	Democrats		
Y Voted for (yea)		X Paired against		C Voted "present" to avoid possible conflict of interest
# Paired for		– Announced against		
+ Announced for		P Voted "present"		? Did not vote or otherwise make a position known
N Voted against (nay)				

ND Northern Democrats, SD Southern Democrats
Southern states: Ala., Ark., Fla., Ga., Ky., La., Miss., N.C., Okla., S.C., Tenn., Texas, Va.

	610	611	612	613	614	615
16 **Manzullo**	N	N	N	Y	N	Y
17 Hare	Y	Y	Y	N	Y	Y
18 **LaHood**	N	N	Y	Y	Y	Y
19 **Shimkus**	N	N	Y	Y	Y	Y
INDIANA						
1 Visclosky	Y	Y	Y	N	Y	Y
2 Donnelly	Y	Y	Y	N	Y	Y
3 **Souder**	N	N	Y	Y	Y	Y
4 **Buyer**	N	?	Y	Y	Y	Y
5 **Burton**	N	N	N	Y	N	Y
6 **Pence**	?	?	?	?	?	?
7 Carson, A.	Y	Y	Y	N	Y	Y
8 Ellsworth	Y	Y	Y	N	N	Y
9 Hill	N	N	Y	N	Y	Y
IOWA						
1 Braley	Y	Y	Y	N	Y	Y
2 Loebsack	Y	Y	Y	N	Y	Y
3 Boswell	Y	Y	Y	N	Y	Y
4 **Latham**	N	N	Y	Y	Y	Y
5 **King**	N	N	Y	Y	N	Y
KANSAS						
1 **Moran**	N	N	N	Y	N	Y
2 Boyda	Y	Y	N	N	Y	Y
3 Moore	Y	Y	Y	N	Y	Y
4 **Tiahrt**	N	N	Y	Y	N	Y
KENTUCKY						
1 **Whitfield**	N	N	Y	Y	Y	Y
2 **Lewis**	N	N	N	Y	N	Y
3 Yarmuth	Y	Y	Y	N	Y	Y
4 **Davis**	N	N	Y	Y	N	Y
5 **Rogers**	N	N	Y	Y	Y	Y
6 Chandler	Y	Y	Y	N	Y	Y
LOUISIANA						
1 **Scalise**	N	N	Y	Y	N	Y
2 Jefferson	Y	Y	Y	N	Y	Y
3 Melancon	Y	?	Y	N	Y	Y
4 **McCrery**	N	?	Y	Y	?	?
5 **Alexander**	N	N	Y	Y	N	Y
6 Cazayoux	N	Y	Y	N	Y	Y
7 **Boustany**	N	N	Y	Y	N	Y
MAINE						
1 Allen	Y	Y	Y	N	Y	Y
2 Michaud	Y	Y	Y	N	Y	Y
MARYLAND						
1 **Gilchrest**	N	N	Y	N	Y	Y
2 Ruppersberger	Y	Y	Y	N	Y	Y
3 Sarbanes	Y	Y	Y	N	Y	Y
4 Edwards	Y	Y	Y	N	Y	Y
5 Hoyer	Y	Y	Y	N	Y	Y
6 **Bartlett**	N	N	Y	Y	N	Y
7 Cummings	Y	Y	Y	N	Y	Y
8 Van Hollen	Y	Y	Y	N	Y	Y
MASSACHUSETTS						
1 Olver	Y	Y	Y	N	Y	Y
2 Neal	Y	?	Y	N	Y	Y
3 McGovern	Y	Y	Y	N	Y	Y
4 Frank	Y	Y	Y	N	Y	Y
5 Tsongas	Y	Y	Y	N	Y	Y
6 Tierney	Y	Y	Y	N	Y	Y
7 Markey	Y	Y	Y	?	Y	Y
8 Capuano	Y	Y	Y	N	Y	Y
9 Lynch	Y	Y	Y	N	Y	Y
10 Delahunt	Y	Y	Y	N	Y	Y
MICHIGAN						
1 Stupak	Y	Y	Y	N	Y	Y
2 **Hoekstra**	N	N	N	Y	N	Y
3 **Ehlers**	N	N	Y	Y	Y	Y
4 **Camp**	N	N	Y	Y	N	Y
5 Kildee	Y	Y	Y	N	Y	Y
6 **Upton**	N	N	Y	Y	Y	Y
7 **Walberg**	N	N	Y	Y	N	Y
8 **Rogers**	N	N	Y	Y	N	Y
9 **Knollenberg**	N	N	Y	Y	Y	Y
10 **Miller**	N	N	Y	Y	Y	Y
11 **McCotter**	N	N	Y	Y	N	Y
12 Levin	Y	Y	Y	N	Y	Y
13 Kilpatrick	Y	Y	Y	N	Y	Y
14 Conyers	+	+	Y	N	Y	?
15 Dingell	Y	Y	Y	?	Y	Y
MINNESOTA						
1 Walz	Y	Y	Y	N	Y	Y
2 **Kline**	N	N	Y	Y	N	Y
3 **Ramstad**	N	Y	Y	N	Y	Y
4 McCollum	Y	Y	Y	N	Y	Y

	610	611	612	613	614	615
5 Ellison	Y	?	Y	N	Y	Y
6 **Bachmann**	N	N	Y	Y	N	Y
7 Peterson	Y	Y	Y	N	Y	Y
8 Oberstar	Y	Y	Y	N	Y	Y
MISSISSIPPI						
1 Childers	N	Y	Y	N	Y	Y
2 Thompson	Y	Y	Y	N	Y	Y
3 **Pickering**	N	N	Y	Y	N	Y
4 Taylor	Y	Y	Y	N	Y	Y
MISSOURI						
1 Clay	Y	Y	Y	N	Y	Y
2 **Akin**	N	N	N	Y	N	Y
3 Carnahan	Y	Y	Y	N	Y	Y
4 Skelton	Y	Y	Y	N	Y	Y
5 Cleaver	Y	Y	Y	N	Y	Y
6 **Graves**	N	N	Y	Y	Y	Y
7 **Blunt**	N	N	Y	Y	N	Y
8 **Emerson**	N	N	Y	Y	N	Y
9 **Hulshof**	?	?	?	?	?	?
MONTANA						
AL **Rehberg**	N	N	Y	Y	N	Y
NEBRASKA						
1 **Fortenberry**	N	N	Y	Y	Y	Y
2 **Terry**	N	N	Y	Y	Y	Y
3 **Smith**	N	N	Y	Y	N	Y
NEVADA						
1 Berkley	Y	?	Y	N	Y	Y
2 **Heller**	N	N	Y	Y	N	Y
3 **Porter**	N	N	Y	Y	Y	Y
NEW HAMPSHIRE						
1 Shea-Porter	Y	Y	Y	N	Y	?
2 Hodes	Y	Y	Y	N	Y	Y
NEW JERSEY						
1 Andrews	Y	Y	Y	N	Y	Y
2 **LoBiondo**	N	N	Y	N	Y	Y
3 **Saxton**	N	N	Y	Y	N	Y
4 **Smith**	N	N	Y	N	Y	Y
5 **Garrett**	N	N	Y	Y	N	N
6 Pallone	Y	Y	Y	N	Y	Y
7 **Ferguson**	N	N	Y	Y	Y	Y
8 Pascrell	Y	Y	Y	N	Y	Y
9 Rothman	Y	Y	Y	N	Y	Y
10 Payne	Y	Y	Y	N	Y	Y
11 **Frelinghuysen**	N	N	Y	Y	Y	?
12 Holt	Y	Y	Y	N	Y	Y
13 Sires	Y	Y	Y	N	Y	Y
NEW MEXICO						
1 **Wilson**	N	N	Y	Y	N	Y
2 **Pearce**	N	N	Y	Y	Y	Y
3 Udall	Y	Y	Y	N	Y	Y
NEW YORK						
1 Bishop	Y	Y	Y	N	Y	Y
2 Israel	Y	Y	Y	N	Y	Y
3 **King**	?	?	?	?	?	?
4 McCarthy	Y	Y	Y	N	Y	Y
5 Ackerman	Y	Y	Y	N	Y	Y
6 Meeks	Y	Y	Y	N	Y	Y
7 Crowley	Y	Y	?	?	?	?
8 Nadler	Y	Y	Y	N	Y	Y
9 Weiner	Y	Y	Y	N	Y	Y
10 Towns	Y	Y	Y	N	Y	Y
11 Clarke	Y	Y	Y	N	Y	Y
12 Velázquez	Y	Y	Y	N	Y	?
13 **Fossella**	N	N	Y	Y	Y	Y
14 Maloney	Y	Y	Y	N	Y	Y
15 Rangel	Y	Y	Y	N	Y	Y
16 Serrano	Y	Y	Y	N	Y	Y
17 Engel	Y	Y	Y	N	Y	Y
18 Lowey	Y	Y	Y	N	Y	Y
19 Hall	Y	Y	Y	N	Y	Y
20 Gillibrand	Y	Y	Y	N	Y	Y
21 McNulty	Y	Y	Y	N	Y	Y
22 Hinchey	Y	Y	Y	N	Y	Y
23 **McHugh**	N	N	Y	Y	Y	Y
24 Arcuri	Y	Y	Y	N	Y	Y
25 **Walsh**	N	N	Y	N	Y	Y
26 **Reynolds**	N	N	Y	Y	Y	+
27 Higgins	Y	Y	Y	N	Y	Y
28 Slaughter	Y	Y	Y	?	Y	Y
29 **Kuhl**	N	N	Y	Y	Y	Y
NORTH CAROLINA						
1 Butterfield	Y	Y	Y	N	Y	Y
2 Etheridge	Y	Y	Y	N	Y	Y
3 **Jones**	N	N	Y	Y	N	Y
4 Price	Y	Y	Y	N	Y	Y

	610	611	612	613	614	615
5 **Foxx**	N	N	N	Y	N	N
6 **Coble**	N	N	Y	Y	N	N
7 McIntyre	Y	Y	Y	N	Y	Y
8 **Hayes**	N	N	Y	Y	Y	Y
9 **Myrick**	N	N	Y	Y	N	Y
10 **McHenry**	N	N	Y	Y	N	Y
11 Shuler	Y	Y	Y	N	Y	Y
12 Watt	Y	Y	Y	N	Y	Y
13 Miller	Y	Y	Y	N	Y	Y
NORTH DAKOTA						
AL Pomeroy	Y	Y	Y	N	Y	Y
OHIO						
1 **Chabot**	N	N	Y	Y	N	Y
2 **Schmidt**	N	N	Y	Y	Y	Y
3 **Turner**	N	N	Y	Y	Y	Y
4 **Jordan**	N	N	Y	Y	N	Y
5 **Latta**	N	N	Y	Y	N	Y
6 Wilson	Y	Y	Y	N	Y	Y
7 **Hobson**	N	N	Y	Y	Y	Y
8 **Boehner**	N	N	Y	Y	N	Y
9 Kaptur	Y	Y	Y	N	Y	Y
10 Kucinich	Y	Y	Y	N	Y	Y
11 Vacant						
12 **Tiberi**	N	N	Y	Y	Y	Y
13 Sutton	Y	Y	Y	N	Y	Y
14 **LaTourette**	N	N	Y	Y	Y	Y
15 **Pryce**	N	N	?	?	?	?
16 **Regula**	N	N	Y	Y	Y	Y
17 Ryan	Y	Y	Y	?	Y	Y
18 Space	Y	Y	Y	N	Y	Y
OKLAHOMA						
1 **Sullivan**	N	N	Y	Y	N	Y
2 Boren	Y	Y	Y	N	Y	Y
3 **Lucas**	N	N	Y	Y	N	Y
4 **Cole**	N	N	Y	Y	N	Y
5 **Fallin**	N	N	Y	Y	N	Y
OREGON						
1 Wu	Y	Y	?	N	Y	Y
2 **Walden**	N	N	Y	Y	?	?
3 Blumenauer	Y	Y	Y	N	Y	Y
4 DeFazio	Y	Y	Y	N	Y	Y
5 Hooley	Y	Y	Y	N	Y	Y
PENNSYLVANIA						
1 Brady	Y	Y	Y	N	Y	Y
2 Fattah	Y	Y	Y	N	Y	Y
3 **English**	N	N	Y	Y	Y	Y
4 Altmire	Y	Y	Y	N	Y	Y
5 **Peterson**	N	?	?	Y	N	Y
6 **Gerlach**	N	N	Y	Y	Y	Y
7 Sestak	?	?	?	?	?	?
8 Murphy, P.	Y	Y	Y	N	Y	Y
9 **Shuster**	N	N	Y	Y	N	Y
10 Carney	Y	Y	Y	N	Y	Y
11 Kanjorski	Y	Y	Y	N	Y	Y
12 Murtha	Y	Y	Y	N	Y	Y
13 Schwartz	Y	Y	Y	N	Y	Y
14 Doyle	Y	Y	Y	N	Y	Y
15 **Dent**	N	N	Y	Y	Y	Y
16 **Pitts**	?	?	?	?	?	?
17 Holden	Y	Y	Y	N	Y	Y
18 **Murphy, T.**	N	N	Y	Y	N	Y
19 **Platts**	N	N	Y	Y	Y	Y
RHODE ISLAND						
1 Kennedy	Y	?	Y	N	Y	Y
2 Langevin	Y	Y	Y	N	Y	Y
SOUTH CAROLINA						
1 **Brown**	N	N	Y	Y	N	Y
2 **Wilson**	N	N	Y	Y	N	Y
3 **Barrett**	N	N	Y	Y	N	N
4 **Inglis**	N	N	Y	Y	N	Y
5 Spratt	Y	Y	Y	N	Y	Y
6 Clyburn	Y	Y	Y	N	Y	Y
SOUTH DAKOTA						
AL Herseth Sandlin	Y	Y	Y	N	Y	Y
TENNESSEE						
1 **Davis, D.**	N	N	Y	Y	N	Y
2 **Duncan**	N	N	N	Y	N	Y
3 **Wamp**	N	N	Y	Y	Y	Y
4 Davis, L.	Y	Y	Y	N	Y	Y
5 Cooper	Y	Y	Y	N	Y	Y
6 Gordon	Y	Y	Y	N	Y	Y
7 **Blackburn**	N	N	Y	Y	N	Y
8 Tanner	Y	Y	Y	N	Y	Y
9 Cohen	Y	Y	Y	N	Y	Y

	610	611	612	613	614	615
TEXAS						
1 **Gohmert**	N	N	Y	Y	N	Y
2 **Poe**	?	?	?	?	?	?
3 **Johnson, S.**	N	N	N	Y	N	N
4 **Hall**	N	N	Y	Y	N	Y
5 **Hensarling**	N	N	Y	Y	N	Y
6 **Barton**	N	N	Y	Y	N	Y
7 **Culberson**	N	N	Y	Y	N	Y
8 **Brady**	?	?	?	?	?	?
9 Green, A.	Y	Y	Y	N	Y	Y
10 **McCaul**	N	N	Y	Y	Y	Y
11 **Conaway**	N	N	N	Y	N	N
12 **Granger**	N	N	Y	Y	N	Y
13 **Thornberry**	N	N	Y	Y	N	Y
14 **Paul**	N	N	N	Y	N	N
15 Hinojosa	Y	Y	Y	–	Y	Y
16 Reyes	Y	Y	Y	N	Y	Y
17 Edwards	Y	Y	Y	N	Y	Y
18 Jackson Lee	?	?	?	?	?	?
19 **Neugebauer**	N	N	Y	Y	N	N
20 Gonzalez	Y	Y	Y	N	Y	Y
21 **Smith**	N	N	Y	Y	N	Y
22 Lampson	?	?	?	?	?	?
23 Rodriguez	Y	Y	Y	N	Y	Y
24 **Marchant**	N	N	?	?	?	?
25 Doggett	Y	Y	Y	N	Y	Y
26 **Burgess**	?	?	?	?	?	?
27 Ortiz	Y	Y	Y	N	Y	Y
28 Cuellar	Y	Y	Y	N	Y	Y
29 Green, G.	Y	?	Y	N	Y	Y
30 Johnson, E.	Y	Y	Y	N	Y	Y
31 **Carter**	N	N	Y	Y	N	N
32 **Sessions**	N	N	Y	Y	N	Y
UTAH						
1 **Bishop**	N	N	?	?	?	?
2 Matheson	Y	Y	Y	N	Y	Y
3 **Cannon**	N	N	N	Y	N	N
VERMONT						
AL Welch	Y	Y	Y	N	Y	Y
VIRGINIA						
1 **Wittman**	N	N	Y	Y	Y	Y
2 **Drake**	N	N	Y	Y	N	Y
3 Scott	Y	Y	Y	N	Y	Y
4 **Forbes**	N	N	Y	Y	N	Y
5 **Goode**	N	N	Y	Y	N	Y
6 **Goodlatte**	N	N	Y	Y	N	Y
7 **Cantor**	N	N	N	Y	N	Y
8 Moran	Y	Y	Y	N	Y	Y
9 Boucher	Y	Y	Y	N	Y	Y
10 **Wolf**	N	N	Y	Y	Y	Y
11 **Davis**	N	N	Y	Y	Y	Y
WASHINGTON						
1 Inslee	Y	Y	Y	N	Y	Y
2 Larsen	Y	Y	Y	N	Y	Y
3 Baird	Y	Y	Y	N	Y	Y
4 **Hastings**	N	N	?	?	?	?
5 **McMorris Rodgers**	N	N	Y	Y	?	?
6 Dicks	Y	Y	Y	N	Y	Y
7 McDermott	Y	Y	Y	N	Y	Y
8 **Reichert**	Y	N	Y	N	Y	Y
9 Smith	Y	Y	Y	N	Y	Y
WEST VIRGINIA						
1 Mollohan	Y	Y	Y	N	Y	Y
2 **Capito**	N	N	Y	Y	Y	Y
3 Rahall	Y	Y	Y	N	Y	Y
WISCONSIN						
1 **Ryan**	N	N	Y	Y	N	Y
2 Baldwin	Y	Y	Y	N	Y	Y
3 Kind	Y	Y	Y	N	Y	Y
4 Moore	Y	Y	Y	N	Y	Y
5 **Sensenbrenner**	N	N	Y	Y	N	Y
6 **Petri**	N	N	Y	Y	Y	Y
7 Obey	Y	Y	Y	N	Y	Y
8 Kagen	Y	Y	Y	N	Y	Y
WYOMING						
AL **Cubin**	?	?	?	?	?	?
DELEGATES						
Faleomavaega (A.S.)			?			
Norton (D.C.)			Y			
Bordallo (Guam)			Y			
Fortuño (P.R.)			?			
Christensen (V.I.)			Y			

IN THE HOUSE | By Vote Number

616. **HR 6685. Indian Tribe Training/Passage.** Bordallo, D-Guam, motion to suspend the rules and pass the bill that would establish a grant program in the Interior Department's Bureau of Indian Affairs to provide training in iron-working skills to adults in federally recognized Indian tribes and facilitate job placement for those who complete the program. Motion agreed to 302-72: R 94-72; D 208-0 (ND 155-0, SD 53-0). A two-thirds majority of those present and voting (250 in this case) is required for passage under suspension of the rules. Sept. 22, 2008.

617. **HR 1907. Coastal Land Conservation/Passage.** Bordallo, D-Guam, motion to suspend the rules and pass the bill that would authorize $60 million a year for five years for the Coastal and Estuarine Land Conservation Program within the National Oceanic and Atmospheric Administration to protect areas threatened by potential development. Motion agreed to 313-59: R 105-59; D 208-0 (ND 155-0, SD 53-0). A two-thirds majority of those present and voting (248 in this case) is required for passage under suspension of the rules. Sept. 22, 2008.

618. **HR 6853. Mortgage Fraud Coordinator/Passage.** Sutton, D-Ohio, motion to suspend the rules and pass the bill that would establish an FBI national mortgage fraud coordinator with regional task forces that include federal, state and local participation. The coordinator would provide training, collect data and recommend efforts to combat mortgage fraud. Motion agreed to 350-23: R 142-23; D 208-0 (ND 155-0, SD 53-0). A two-thirds majority of those present and voting (249 in this case) is required for passage under suspension of the rules. Sept. 22, 2008.

619. **HR 5244. Credit Card Billing Practices/Previous Question.** Welch, D-Vt., motion to order the previous question (thus ending debate and possibility of amendment) on adoption of the rule (H Res 1476) to provide for House floor consideration of the bill that would prohibit credit card companies from retroactively increasing interest rates on existing credit card balances in most instances. Motion agreed to 221-192: R 3-189; D 218-3 (ND 168-1, SD 50-2). Sept. 23, 2008.

620. **HR 5244. Credit Card Billing Practices/Rule.** Adoption of the rule (H Res 1476) to provide for House floor consideration of the bill that would prohibit credit card companies from retroactively increasing interest rates on existing credit card balances in most instances. Adopted 220-194: R 0-192; D 220-2 (ND 169-1, SD 51-1). Sept. 23, 2008.

621. **S J Res 45. Great Lakes-St. Lawrence River Compact/Passage.** Sutton, D-Ohio, motion to suspend the rules and pass the joint resolution that would grant congressional approval to the Great Lakes-St. Lawrence River Basin Compact, an agreement on the rights between the states of Illinois, Indiana, Michigan, Minnesota, New York, Ohio, Pennsylvania and Wisconsin, regarding use of the waters and maintenance of the watershed of the Great Lakes and St. Lawrence Seaway and River. Motion agreed to 390-25: R 185-6; D 205-19 (ND 160-12, SD 45-7). A two-thirds majority of those present and voting (277 in this case) is required for passage under suspension of the rules. Sept. 23, 2008.

	616	617	618	619	620	621
ALABAMA						
1 Bonner	N	Y	Y	N	N	Y
2 Everett	N	Y	N	N	N	Y
3 Rogers	Y	Y	Y	N	N	Y
4 Aderholt	Y	Y	Y	N	N	Y
5 Cramer	Y	Y	Y	Y	Y	Y
6 Bachus	Y	Y	Y	N	N	Y
7 Davis	Y	Y	Y	Y	Y	Y
ALASKA						
AL Young	Y	Y	Y	N	N	Y
ARIZONA						
1 Renzi	Y	Y	Y	N	N	Y
2 Franks	N	N	Y	N	N	Y
3 Shadegg	N	N	Y	N	N	Y
4 Pastor	Y	Y	Y	Y	Y	Y
5 Mitchell	Y	Y	Y	Y	Y	Y
6 Flake	N	N	N	N	N	Y
7 Grijalva	Y	Y	Y	Y	Y	Y
8 Giffords	?	?	?	?	?	?
ARKANSAS						
1 Berry	Y	Y	Y	Y	Y	N
2 Snyder	Y	Y	Y	Y	Y	Y
3 Boozman	N	Y	Y	N	N	Y
4 Ross	Y	Y	Y	Y	Y	Y
CALIFORNIA						
1 Thompson	Y	Y	Y	Y	Y	Y
2 Herger	N	N	Y	N	N	Y
3 Lungren	Y	Y	Y	N	N	Y
4 Doolittle	?	?	?	N	N	N
5 Matsui	Y	Y	Y	Y	Y	Y
6 Woolsey	Y	Y	Y	Y	Y	Y
7 Miller, George	Y	Y	Y	Y	Y	Y
8 Pelosi						
9 Lee	Y	Y	Y	Y	Y	Y
10 Tauscher	Y	Y	Y	Y	Y	Y
11 McNerney	Y	Y	Y	Y	Y	Y
12 Speier	Y	Y	Y	Y	Y	Y
13 Stark	Y	Y	Y	Y	Y	Y
14 Eshoo	Y	Y	Y	Y	Y	Y
15 Honda	Y	Y	Y	Y	Y	Y
16 Lofgren	Y	Y	Y	Y	Y	Y
17 Farr	Y	Y	Y	Y	Y	Y
18 Cardoza	Y	Y	Y	Y	Y	Y
19 Radanovich	N	N	Y	N	N	Y
20 Costa	Y	Y	Y	Y	Y	Y
21 Nunes	N	N	Y	N	N	Y
22 McCarthy	N	Y	Y	N	N	Y
23 Capps	Y	Y	Y	Y	Y	Y
24 Gallegly	Y	Y	Y	N	N	Y
25 McKeon	?	?	?	N	N	Y
26 Dreier	Y	Y	Y	N	N	Y
27 Sherman	Y	Y	Y	Y	Y	Y
28 Berman	Y	Y	Y	Y	Y	Y
29 Schiff	Y	Y	Y	Y	Y	Y
30 Waxman	Y	Y	Y	Y	Y	Y
31 Becerra	Y	+	+	Y	Y	Y
32 Solis	Y	Y	Y	Y	Y	Y
33 Watson	Y	Y	Y	Y	Y	Y
34 Roybal-Allard	Y	Y	Y	Y	Y	Y
35 Waters	Y	Y	Y	Y	Y	Y
36 Harman	Y	Y	Y	Y	Y	Y
37 Richardson	Y	Y	Y	Y	Y	Y
38 Napolitano	Y	Y	Y	Y	Y	Y
39 Sánchez, Linda	Y	Y	Y	Y	Y	Y
40 Royce	N	Y	Y	N	N	Y
41 Lewis	Y	N	Y	N	N	Y
42 Miller, Gary	Y	N	Y	N	N	Y
43 Baca	Y	Y	Y	Y	Y	Y
44 Calvert	Y	N	Y	N	N	Y
45 Bono Mack	Y	Y	Y	N	N	Y
46 Rohrabacher	?	?	?	N	N	Y
47 Sanchez, Loretta	Y	Y	Y	Y	Y	Y
48 Campbell	N	Y	Y	N	N	Y
49 Issa	Y	N	Y	N	N	Y
50 Bilbray	Y	Y	Y	N	N	Y
51 Filner	Y	Y	Y	Y	Y	Y
52 Hunter	Y	N	Y	N	N	Y
53 Davis	Y	Y	Y	Y	Y	Y

	616	617	618	619	620	621
COLORADO						
1 DeGette	Y	Y	Y	Y	Y	Y
2 Udall	?	?	?	Y	Y	Y
3 Salazar	Y	Y	Y	?	Y	Y
4 Musgrave	Y	Y	Y	N	N	?
5 Lamborn	N	N	N	N	N	Y
6 Tancredo	?	?	?	N	N	N
7 Perlmutter	Y	Y	Y	Y	Y	Y
CONNECTICUT						
1 Larson	Y	?	?	Y	Y	Y
2 Courtney	Y	Y	Y	Y	Y	Y
3 DeLauro	Y	Y	Y	Y	Y	Y
4 Shays	Y	Y	Y	N	Y	Y
5 Murphy	Y	Y	Y	Y	Y	Y
DELAWARE						
AL Castle	Y	Y	Y	N	N	Y
FLORIDA						
1 Miller	N	Y	N	N	N	Y
2 Boyd	Y	Y	Y	Y	Y	Y
3 Brown	Y	Y	Y	Y	Y	Y
4 Crenshaw	Y	Y	?	N	N	Y
5 Brown-Waite	Y	Y	Y	N	N	Y
6 Stearns	N	N	Y	N	N	Y
7 Mica	Y	Y	Y	N	N	Y
8 Keller	Y	Y	Y	N	N	Y
9 Bilirakis	N	Y	Y	N	N	Y
10 Young	Y	Y	Y	N	N	Y
11 Castor	Y	Y	Y	Y	Y	Y
12 Putnam	Y	Y	Y	N	N	Y
13 Buchanan	Y	Y	Y	N	N	Y
14 Mack	N	Y	N	N	N	Y
15 Weldon	?	?	?	N	N	Y
16 Mahoney	Y	Y	Y	Y	Y	Y
17 Meek	Y	Y	Y	Y	Y	Y
18 Ros-Lehtinen	Y	Y	Y	Y	Y	Y
19 Wexler	Y	Y	Y	Y	Y	Y
20 Wasserman Schultz	Y	Y	Y	Y	Y	Y
21 Diaz-Balart, L.	Y	Y	Y	N	N	Y
22 Klein	Y	Y	Y	Y	Y	Y
23 Hastings	Y	Y	Y	Y	Y	Y
24 Feeney	?	?	?	N	N	Y
25 Diaz-Balart, M.	Y	Y	Y	N	N	Y
GEORGIA						
1 Kingston	N	N	N	N	N	Y
2 Bishop	Y	Y	Y	Y	Y	Y
3 Westmoreland	?	?	?	N	N	Y
4 Johnson	Y	Y	Y	Y	Y	Y
5 Lewis	Y	Y	Y	Y	Y	N
6 Price	N	N	Y	N	N	Y
7 Linder	N	N	N	N	N	?
8 Marshall	Y	Y	Y	Y	Y	Y
9 Deal	N	N	Y	N	N	Y
10 Broun	N	N	N	N	N	N
11 Gingrey	N	N	N	N	N	Y
12 Barrow	Y	Y	Y	Y	Y	Y
13 Scott	Y	Y	Y	Y	Y	Y
HAWAII						
1 Abercrombie	Y	?	Y	Y	Y	Y
2 Hirono	Y	Y	Y	Y	Y	Y
IDAHO						
1 Sali	Y	N	Y	N	N	Y
2 Simpson	Y	Y	Y	N	N	Y
ILLINOIS						
1 Rush	?	?	?	?	?	?
2 Jackson	Y	Y	Y	Y	Y	Y
3 Lipinski	Y	Y	Y	Y	Y	Y
4 Gutierrez	+	+	+	Y	Y	Y
5 Emanuel	Y	Y	Y	Y	Y	Y
6 Roskam	N	Y	Y	N	N	Y
7 Davis	Y	Y	Y	Y	Y	Y
8 Bean	Y	Y	Y	Y	?	Y
9 Schakowsky	Y	Y	Y	Y	Y	Y
10 Kirk	Y	?	Y	N	N	Y
11 Weller	+	+	?	N	N	Y
12 Costello	Y	Y	Y	Y	Y	Y
13 Biggert	Y	Y	Y	N	N	Y
14 Foster	Y	Y	Y	Y	Y	Y
15 Johnson	+	?	+	?	?	?

KEY	**Republicans**	Democrats		
Y	Voted for (yea)		X	Paired against	C	Voted "present" to avoid possible conflict of interest
#	Paired for		–	Announced against	
+	Announced for		P	Voted "present"	?	Did not vote or otherwise make a position known
N	Voted against (nay)			

ND Northern Democrats, SD Southern Democrats
Southern states: Ala., Ark., Fla., Ga., Ky., La., Miss., N.C., Okla., S.C., Tenn., Texas, Va.

H-208   2008 CQ ALMANAC | www.cq.com

	616	617	618	619	620	621
16 **Manzullo**	N	N	N	N	N	Y
17 Hare	Y	Y	Y	Y	Y	Y
18 **LaHood**	Y	Y	Y	N	N	Y
19 **Shimkus**	Y	N	Y	N	N	Y
INDIANA						
1 Visclosky	Y	Y	Y	Y	Y	Y
2 Donnelly	Y	Y	Y	Y	Y	Y
3 **Souder**	Y	Y	Y	N	N	Y
4 **Buyer**	N	N	Y	N	N	Y
5 **Burton**	N	N	Y	N	N	N
6 **Pence**	N	N	Y	N	N	Y
7 Carson, A.	Y	Y	Y	Y	Y	Y
8 Ellsworth	Y	Y	Y	Y	Y	Y
9 Hill	Y	Y	Y	N	N	Y
IOWA						
1 Braley	Y	Y	Y	Y	Y	N
2 Loebsack	Y	Y	Y	Y	Y	Y
3 Boswell	Y	Y	Y	Y	Y	Y
4 **Latham**	?	?	?	N	N	Y
5 **King**	N	N	N	N	N	Y
KANSAS						
1 **Moran**	N	N	Y	N	N	Y
2 Boyda	Y	Y	Y	Y	Y	Y
3 Moore	Y	Y	Y	Y	Y	Y
4 **Tiahrt**	Y	N	Y	N	N	Y
KENTUCKY						
1 **Whitfield**	N	Y	N	N	N	N
2 **Lewis**	N	Y	N	N	N	Y
3 Yarmuth	Y	Y	Y	Y	Y	Y
4 **Davis**	Y	Y	Y	N	N	Y
5 **Rogers**	N	Y	Y	N	N	Y
6 Chandler	Y	Y	Y	Y	Y	N
LOUISIANA						
1 **Scalise**	N	Y	Y	N	N	Y
2 Jefferson	?	?	?	Y	Y	Y
3 Melancon	Y	Y	Y	Y	Y	N
4 **McCrery**	?	?	?	N	N	Y
5 **Alexander**	?	?	?	N	N	Y
6 Cazayoux	Y	Y	Y	N	Y	N
7 **Boustany**	Y	Y	Y	N	N	Y
MAINE						
1 Allen	Y	Y	Y	Y	Y	Y
2 Michaud	Y	Y	Y	Y	Y	Y
MARYLAND						
1 **Gilchrest**	?	?	?	N	N	Y
2 Ruppersberger	Y	Y	Y	Y	Y	Y
3 Sarbanes	Y	Y	Y	Y	Y	Y
4 Edwards	Y	Y	Y	Y	Y	Y
5 Hoyer	Y	Y	Y	Y	Y	Y
6 **Bartlett**	Y	Y	Y	N	N	Y
7 Cummings	Y	Y	Y	Y	Y	Y
8 Van Hollen	Y	Y	Y	Y	Y	Y
MASSACHUSETTS						
1 Olver	Y	Y	Y	Y	Y	Y
2 Neal	?	?	?	Y	Y	Y
3 McGovern	Y	Y	Y	Y	Y	Y
4 Frank	Y	Y	?	Y	Y	Y
5 Tsongas	Y	Y	Y	Y	Y	Y
6 Tierney	?	?	?	?	?	?
7 Markey	Y	Y	Y	Y	Y	Y
8 Capuano	Y	Y	Y	Y	Y	N
9 Lynch	Y	Y	Y	Y	Y	Y
10 Delahunt	Y	Y	Y	Y	Y	Y
MICHIGAN						
1 Stupak	Y	Y	Y	Y	Y	N
2 **Hoekstra**	N	N	Y	N	N	Y
3 **Ehlers**	Y	N	Y	N	N	Y
4 **Camp**	Y	Y	Y	N	N	Y
5 Kildee	Y	Y	Y	Y	Y	Y
6 **Upton**	Y	Y	Y	N	N	Y
7 **Walberg**	N	Y	Y	N	N	Y
8 **Rogers**	Y	Y	Y	N	N	Y
9 **Knollenberg**	?	?	?	N	N	Y
10 **Miller**	Y	Y	Y	N	N	Y
11 **McCotter**	Y	Y	Y	N	N	Y
12 Levin	Y	Y	Y	Y	Y	Y
13 Kilpatrick	Y	Y	Y	Y	Y	Y
14 Conyers	Y	Y	Y	Y	Y	Y
15 Dingell	Y	Y	Y	Y	Y	Y
MINNESOTA						
1 Walz	Y	Y	Y	Y	Y	Y
2 **Kline**	Y	N	Y	N	N	Y
3 **Ramstad**	Y	?	Y	N	N	Y
4 McCollum	Y	Y	Y	Y	Y	N

	616	617	618	619	620	621
5 Ellison	Y	Y	Y	Y	Y	N
6 **Bachmann**	N	N	Y	N	N	Y
7 Peterson	Y	Y	Y	Y	Y	Y
8 Oberstar	Y	Y	Y	Y	Y	Y
MISSISSIPPI						
1 Childers	Y	Y	Y	N	Y	N
2 Thompson	Y	Y	Y	Y	Y	Y
3 **Pickering**	?	?	?	N	N	Y
4 Taylor	Y	Y	Y	Y	Y	Y
MISSOURI						
1 Clay	Y	Y	Y	Y	Y	Y
2 **Akin**	N	N	Y	N	N	Y
3 Carnahan	Y	Y	Y	Y	Y	Y
4 Skelton	Y	Y	Y	Y	Y	Y
5 Cleaver	Y	Y	Y	Y	Y	Y
6 **Graves**	–	–	+	?	N	Y
7 **Blunt**	N	N	Y	N	N	Y
8 **Emerson**	Y	Y	Y	N	N	Y
9 **Hulshof**	?	?	?	?	?	?
MONTANA						
AL **Rehberg**	Y	Y	Y	N	N	Y
NEBRASKA						
1 **Fortenberry**	Y	Y	Y	N	N	Y
2 **Terry**	Y	Y	Y	N	N	Y
3 **Smith**	Y	N	Y	N	N	Y
NEVADA						
1 Berkley	Y	Y	Y	Y	Y	Y
2 **Heller**	Y	Y	Y	N	N	Y
3 **Porter**	Y	Y	Y	N	N	Y
NEW HAMPSHIRE						
1 Shea-Porter	Y	Y	Y	Y	Y	Y
2 Hodes	Y	Y	Y	Y	Y	Y
NEW JERSEY						
1 Andrews	Y	Y	Y	Y	Y	Y
2 **LoBiondo**	Y	Y	Y	N	N	Y
3 **Saxton**	Y	Y	Y	N	N	Y
4 **Smith**	Y	Y	Y	N	N	Y
5 **Garrett**	N	N	N	N	N	Y
6 Pallone	Y	Y	Y	Y	Y	Y
7 **Ferguson**	Y	Y	Y	N	N	Y
8 Pascrell	?	?	?	Y	Y	Y
9 Rothman	Y	Y	Y	Y	Y	Y
10 Payne	?	?	?	Y	Y	Y
11 **Frelinghuysen**	Y	Y	Y	N	N	Y
12 Holt	Y	Y	Y	Y	Y	Y
13 Sires	+	+	+	Y	Y	Y
NEW MEXICO						
1 **Wilson**	Y	N	Y	N	N	Y
2 **Pearce**	?	?	?	?	?	?
3 Udall	?	?	?	?	?	?
NEW YORK						
1 Bishop	Y	Y	Y	Y	Y	Y
2 Israel	Y	Y	Y	Y	Y	Y
3 **King**	N	Y	Y	N	N	Y
4 McCarthy	Y	Y	Y	Y	Y	Y
5 Ackerman	Y	Y	Y	Y	Y	Y
6 Meeks	?	?	?	Y	Y	Y
7 Crowley	Y	Y	Y	Y	Y	Y
8 Nadler	Y	Y	Y	Y	Y	Y
9 Weiner	?	?	?	Y	Y	Y
10 Towns	Y	Y	Y	Y	Y	Y
11 Clarke	Y	Y	Y	Y	Y	Y
12 Velázquez	Y	Y	Y	Y	Y	Y
13 **Fossella**	N	Y	Y	N	N	Y
14 Maloney	Y	Y	Y	Y	Y	Y
15 Rangel	Y	Y	Y	Y	Y	Y
16 Serrano	Y	Y	Y	Y	Y	Y
17 Engel	Y	Y	Y	Y	Y	Y
18 Lowey	Y	Y	Y	Y	Y	Y
19 Hall	Y	Y	Y	Y	Y	Y
20 Gillibrand	Y	Y	Y	Y	Y	Y
21 McNulty	Y	Y	Y	Y	Y	Y
22 Hinchey	?	Y	Y	Y	Y	Y
23 **McHugh**	Y	Y	Y	N	N	Y
24 Arcuri	Y	Y	Y	Y	Y	Y
25 **Walsh**	Y	Y	Y	N	N	Y
26 **Reynolds**	Y	Y	Y	N	N	Y
27 Higgins	Y	Y	Y	Y	Y	Y
28 Slaughter	Y	Y	Y	Y	Y	Y
29 **Kuhl**	Y	Y	Y	N	N	Y
NORTH CAROLINA						
1 Butterfield	Y	Y	Y	Y	Y	Y
2 Etheridge	+	–	+	Y	Y	Y
3 **Jones**	Y	Y	Y	N	N	Y
4 Price	Y	Y	Y	Y	Y	Y

	616	617	618	619	620	621
5 **Foxx**	N	N	N	N	N	Y
6 **Coble**	N	Y	N	N	N	Y
7 McIntyre	Y	Y	Y	Y	Y	Y
8 **Hayes**	Y	Y	Y	N	N	Y
9 **Myrick**	N	Y	Y	N	N	Y
10 **McHenry**	?	?	?	N	N	Y
11 Shuler	Y	Y	Y	Y	Y	N
12 Watt	Y	Y	Y	Y	Y	Y
13 Miller	Y	Y	Y	Y	Y	Y
NORTH DAKOTA						
AL Pomeroy	Y	Y	Y	Y	Y	Y
OHIO						
1 **Chabot**	Y	Y	Y	N	N	Y
2 **Schmidt**	Y	Y	Y	N	N	Y
3 **Turner**	Y	Y	Y	N	N	Y
4 **Jordan**	N	N	Y	N	N	Y
5 **Latta**	N	Y	Y	N	N	Y
6 Wilson	Y	Y	Y	Y	Y	Y
7 **Hobson**	Y	Y	Y	N	N	Y
8 **Boehner**	Y	Y	Y	N	N	Y
9 Kaptur	Y	Y	Y	Y	Y	N
10 Kucinich	Y	Y	Y	Y	Y	N
11 Vacant						
12 **Tiberi**	?	?	?	N	N	Y
13 Sutton	Y	Y	Y	Y	Y	Y
14 **LaTourette**	Y	Y	Y	N	?	Y
15 **Pryce**	?	?	?	?	?	?
16 **Regula**	Y	Y	Y	N	N	Y
17 Ryan	Y	Y	Y	Y	Y	Y
18 Space	Y	Y	Y	Y	Y	Y
OKLAHOMA						
1 **Sullivan**	Y	N	Y	N	N	Y
2 Boren	Y	Y	Y	Y	Y	Y
3 **Lucas**	Y	Y	Y	N	N	Y
4 **Cole**	Y	Y	Y	N	N	Y
5 **Fallin**	?	?	?	N	N	Y
OREGON						
1 Wu	Y	Y	Y	Y	Y	Y
2 **Walden**	Y	Y	Y	N	N	Y
3 Blumenauer	Y	Y	Y	Y	Y	Y
4 DeFazio	Y	Y	Y	Y	Y	N
5 Hooley	Y	Y	Y	Y	Y	Y
PENNSYLVANIA						
1 Brady	?	?	?	Y	Y	Y
2 Fattah	Y	Y	Y	Y	Y	Y
3 **English**	?	?	?	N	N	Y
4 Altmire	Y	Y	Y	Y	Y	N
5 **Peterson**	Y	Y	Y	N	N	Y
6 **Gerlach**	Y	Y	Y	N	N	Y
7 Sestak	?	?	?	Y	Y	Y
8 Murphy, P.	Y	Y	Y	Y	Y	Y
9 **Shuster**	+	+	?	N	N	Y
10 Carney	Y	Y	Y	Y	Y	Y
11 Kanjorski	Y	Y	Y	Y	Y	Y
12 Murtha	Y	Y	Y	Y	Y	Y
13 Schwartz	Y	Y	Y	Y	Y	Y
14 Doyle	Y	Y	Y	Y	Y	Y
15 **Dent**	Y	Y	Y	N	N	Y
16 **Pitts**	Y	Y	Y	N	N	Y
17 Holden	Y	Y	Y	Y	Y	Y
18 **Murphy, T.**	Y	Y	Y	N	N	Y
19 **Platts**	Y	Y	Y	N	N	Y
RHODE ISLAND						
1 Kennedy	?	Y	Y	Y	Y	Y
2 Langevin	+	Y	Y	Y	Y	Y
SOUTH CAROLINA						
1 **Brown**	Y	Y	Y	N	N	Y
2 **Wilson**	Y	Y	Y	N	N	Y
3 **Barrett**	N	N	Y	N	N	Y
4 **Inglis**	Y	Y	N	N	N	Y
5 Spratt	Y	Y	Y	Y	Y	Y
6 Clyburn	Y	Y	Y	Y	Y	Y
SOUTH DAKOTA						
AL Herseth Sandlin	Y	Y	Y	?	Y	Y
TENNESSEE						
1 **Davis, D.**	N	N	Y	N	N	Y
2 **Duncan**	N	N	N	N	N	Y
3 **Wamp**	Y	N	N	N	N	Y
4 Davis, L.	Y	Y	Y	?	?	?
5 Cooper	Y	Y	Y	?	?	?
6 Gordon	Y	Y	Y	?	?	?
7 **Blackburn**	N	N	?	N	N	Y
8 Tanner	Y	Y	Y	Y	Y	Y
9 Cohen	Y	Y	Y	Y	Y	Y

	616	617	618	619	620	621
TEXAS						
1 **Gohmert**	N	?	Y	N	N	Y
2 **Poe**	–	+	+	N	N	N
3 **Johnson, S.**	N	N	N	N	N	Y
4 **Hall**	Y	Y	Y	N	N	Y
5 **Hensarling**	N	N	Y	N	N	Y
6 **Barton**	N	N	Y	N	N	Y
7 **Culberson**	?	?	?	N	N	Y
8 **Brady**	?	?	?	N	N	Y
9 Green, A.	Y	Y	Y	Y	Y	Y
10 **McCaul**	Y	Y	Y	N	N	Y
11 **Conaway**	N	N	N	N	N	Y
12 **Granger**	?	?	?	N	N	Y
13 **Thornberry**	N	N	Y	N	N	Y
14 **Paul**	N	N	N	N	N	Y
15 Hinojosa	Y	Y	Y	Y	Y	Y
16 Reyes	?	?	?	?	?	?
17 Edwards	Y	Y	Y	Y	Y	Y
18 Jackson Lee	?	?	?	?	?	?
19 **Neugebauer**	–	–	+	–	–	+
20 Gonzalez	?	?	?	?	?	?
21 **Smith**	Y	Y	Y	N	N	Y
22 Lampson	Y	Y	Y	Y	N	?
23 Rodriguez	Y	Y	Y	Y	Y	Y
24 **Marchant**	N	N	Y	N	N	Y
25 Doggett	Y	Y	Y	Y	Y	Y
26 **Burgess**	N	N	Y	N	N	Y
27 Ortiz	Y	Y	Y	Y	Y	Y
28 Cuellar	Y	Y	Y	Y	Y	Y
29 Green, G.	Y	Y	Y	Y	Y	Y
30 Johnson, E.	Y	Y	Y	Y	Y	Y
31 **Carter**	N	N	Y	N	N	Y
32 **Sessions**	N	Y	Y	N	N	Y
UTAH						
1 **Bishop**	?	Y	Y	N	N	Y
2 Matheson	Y	Y	Y	Y	Y	Y
3 **Cannon**	N	N	N	N	N	Y
VERMONT						
AL Welch	Y	Y	Y	Y	Y	N
VIRGINIA						
1 **Wittman**	Y	Y	Y	N	N	Y
2 **Drake**	Y	Y	Y	N	N	Y
3 Scott	Y	Y	Y	Y	Y	Y
4 **Forbes**	Y	Y	Y	N	N	Y
5 **Goode**	N	N	Y	N	N	Y
6 **Goodlatte**	N	N	Y	N	N	Y
7 **Cantor**	N	N	Y	N	N	Y
8 Moran	?	?	?	?	?	Y
9 Boucher	Y	Y	Y	Y	Y	Y
10 **Wolf**	Y	Y	Y	N	N	Y
11 **Davis**	?	?	?	N	N	Y
WASHINGTON						
1 Inslee	Y	Y	Y	Y	Y	Y
2 Larsen	Y	Y	Y	Y	Y	Y
3 Baird	Y	Y	Y	Y	Y	Y
4 **Hastings**	N	N	Y	N	N	Y
5 **McMorris Rodgers**	?	?	?	N	N	Y
6 Dicks	?	?	?	Y	Y	Y
7 McDermott	Y	Y	Y	Y	Y	N
8 **Reichert**	Y	Y	Y	Y	N	Y
9 Smith	Y	Y	Y	Y	Y	Y
WEST VIRGINIA						
1 Mollohan	Y	Y	Y	Y	Y	N
2 **Capito**	Y	Y	Y	N	N	Y
3 Rahall	Y	Y	Y	Y	Y	Y
WISCONSIN						
1 **Ryan**	N	Y	Y	N	N	Y
2 Baldwin	Y	Y	Y	Y	Y	Y
3 Kind	Y	Y	Y	Y	Y	Y
4 Moore	?	?	?	Y	Y	Y
5 **Sensenbrenner**	N	Y	Y	N	N	Y
6 **Petri**	N	Y	Y	N	N	Y
7 Obey	Y	Y	Y	Y	Y	Y
8 Kagen	?	?	?	Y	Y	Y
WYOMING						
AL **Cubin**	?	?	?	?	?	?
DELEGATES						
Faleomavaega (A.S.)						
Norton (D.C.)						
Bordallo (Guam)						
Fortuño (P.R.)						
Christensen (V.I.)						

IN THE HOUSE | By Vote Number

622. **HR 5244. Credit Card Billing Practices/Recommit.** Castle, R-Del., motion to recommit the bill to the Financial Services Committee with instructions that it be reported back promptly with an amendment stipulating that no provisions of the bill would take effect until the Federal Reserve's Board of Governors conducted a study determining that the bill would not result in a reduction of the availability of credit to small businesses, veterans or minorities. Motion rejected 198-219: R 189-0; D 9-219 (ND 4-170, SD 5-49). Sept. 23, 2008.

623. **HR 5244. Credit Card Billing Practices/Passage.** Passage of the bill that would prohibit credit card companies from retroactively increasing interest rates on existing balances in most cases, issuing finance charges on balances for days not included in the most recent billing cycle, and charging fees on outstanding balances created only from interest accrued in the previous billing period until the end of the current bill period. The measure also would require companies to send statements at least 25 days before payment is due and give at least 45 days notice before increasing rates. Passed 312-112: R 84-111; D 228-1 (ND 173-1, SD 55-0). A "nay" was a vote in support of the president's position. Sept. 23, 2008.

624. **HR 6897. Filipino Veterans' Compensation/Passage.** Filner, D-Calif., motion to suspend the rules and pass the bill that would require the Veterans Affairs Department to compensate Filipino veterans who fought for the United States in Word War II between July 26, 1941, and July 1, 1946, including those who served in the Philippines' commonwealth armed forces and certain guerrilla units. Motion agreed to 392-23: R 172-22; D 220-1 (ND 168-0, SD 52-1). A two-thirds majority of those present and voting (277 in this case) is required for passage under suspension of the rules. Sept. 23, 2008.

625. **HR 6983. Mental Health Parity/Passage.** Pallone, D-N.J., motion to suspend the rules and pass the bill that would require health insurers that cover mental illness to do so on a par with physical illness, including equal standards on co-payments, deductibles, number of doctor visits, days in the hospital and financial limits on coverage. The standards would not have to be upheld if they increase coverage costs by more than 2 percent during the first year of enactment and more than 1 percent in subsequent years. Employers with fewer than 50 employees would be exempt. Motion agreed to 376-47: R 143-47; D 233-0 (ND 175-0, SD 58-0). A two-thirds majority of those present and voting (282 in this case) is required for passage under suspension of the rules. Sept. 23, 2008.

626. **HR 5352. Elder Abuse Prevention/Passage.** Sutton, D-Ohio, motion to suspend the rules and pass the bill that would establish Justice Department grant programs for states and localities for law enforcement and prosecutorial training on enforcing laws regarding abuse of the elderly. Motion agreed to 387-28: R 161-28; D 226-0 (ND 168-0, SD 58-0). A two-thirds majority of those present and voting (277 in this case) is required for passage under suspension of the rules. Sept. 23, 2008.

	622	623	624	625	626
ALABAMA					
1 Bonner	Y	N	Y	N	Y
2 Everett	Y	N	N	Y	Y
3 Rogers	Y	Y	Y	Y	Y
4 Aderholt	Y	Y	Y	Y	Y
5 Cramer	N	Y	Y	Y	Y
6 Bachus	Y	N	Y	Y	Y
7 Davis	N	Y	Y	Y	Y
ALASKA					
AL Young	Y	Y	Y	Y	Y
ARIZONA					
1 Renzi	Y	Y	Y	Y	Y
2 Franks	Y	N	Y	N	N
3 Shadegg	Y	N	Y	N	N
4 Pastor	N	Y	Y	Y	Y
5 Mitchell	Y	Y	Y	Y	Y
6 Flake	Y	N	N	N	N
7 Grijalva	N	Y	Y	Y	Y
8 Giffords	Y	Y	Y	Y	Y
ARKANSAS					
1 Berry	N	Y	Y	Y	Y
2 Snyder	N	Y	Y	Y	Y
3 Boozman	Y	Y	Y	Y	Y
4 Ross	N	Y	Y	Y	Y
CALIFORNIA					
1 Thompson	N	Y	Y	Y	Y
2 Herger	Y	N	Y	–	Y
3 Lungren	Y	N	Y	Y	Y
4 Doolittle	Y	N	Y	N	N
5 Matsui	N	Y	Y	Y	Y
6 Woolsey	N	Y	Y	Y	+
7 Miller, George	N	Y	Y	Y	Y
8 Pelosi					
9 Lee	N	Y	Y	Y	Y
10 Tauscher	N	Y	Y	Y	Y
11 McNerney	Y	Y	Y	Y	Y
12 Speier	N	Y	Y	Y	Y
13 Stark	N	Y	?	Y	Y
14 Eshoo	N	Y	Y	Y	Y
15 Honda	N	Y	Y	Y	Y
16 Lofgren	N	Y	Y	Y	Y
17 Farr	N	Y	Y	Y	Y
18 Cardoza	N	Y	Y	Y	Y
19 Radanovich	Y	Y	?	Y	Y
20 Costa	N	Y	Y	Y	Y
21 Nunes	Y	N	Y	Y	Y
22 McCarthy	Y	N	Y	Y	Y
23 Capps	N	Y	Y	Y	Y
24 Gallegly	Y	Y	Y	Y	Y
25 McKeon	Y	N	Y	Y	Y
26 Dreier	Y	N	Y	Y	Y
27 Sherman	N	Y	Y	Y	Y
28 Berman	N	Y	Y	Y	Y
29 Schiff	N	Y	Y	Y	Y
30 Waxman	N	Y	Y	Y	Y
31 Becerra	N	Y	Y	Y	Y
32 Solis	N	Y	Y	Y	Y
33 Watson	N	Y	Y	Y	Y
34 Roybal-Allard	N	Y	Y	Y	Y
35 Waters	N	Y	Y	Y	Y
36 Harman	N	Y	Y	Y	Y
37 Richardson	N	Y	Y	Y	Y
38 Napolitano	N	Y	Y	Y	Y
39 Sánchez, Linda	N	Y	Y	Y	Y
40 Royce	Y	N	Y	N	Y
41 Lewis	Y	N	Y	Y	Y
42 Miller, Gary	Y	N	Y	Y	Y
43 Baca	N	Y	Y	Y	Y
44 Calvert	Y	N	Y	Y	Y
45 Bono Mack	Y	Y	Y	Y	Y
46 Rohrabacher	Y	N	Y	N	Y
47 Sanchez, Loretta	N	Y	Y	Y	Y
48 Campbell	Y	N	N	N	N
49 Issa	Y	N	Y	N	Y
50 Bilbray	Y	N	Y	Y	Y
51 Filner	N	Y	Y	Y	Y
52 Hunter	?	Y	Y	?	?
53 Davis	N	Y	Y	Y	Y

	622	623	624	625	626
COLORADO					
1 DeGette	N	Y	Y	Y	Y
2 Udall	N	Y	Y	Y	Y
3 Salazar	N	Y	Y	Y	Y
4 Musgrave	?	N	Y	Y	Y
5 Lamborn	Y	N	N	N	N
6 Tancredo	Y	N	Y	Y	N
7 Perlmutter	N	Y	Y	Y	Y
CONNECTICUT					
1 Larson	N	Y	Y	Y	+
2 Courtney	N	Y	Y	Y	Y
3 DeLauro	N	Y	Y	Y	Y
4 Shays	Y	Y	Y	Y	Y
5 Murphy	N	Y	Y	Y	Y
DELAWARE					
AL Castle	Y	N	Y	Y	Y
FLORIDA					
1 Miller	Y	N	Y	N	Y
2 Boyd	N	Y	Y	Y	Y
3 Brown	N	Y	Y	Y	Y
4 Crenshaw	Y	Y	Y	Y	Y
5 Brown-Waite	Y	Y	Y	Y	Y
6 Stearns	Y	Y	N	Y	Y
7 Mica	Y	Y	N	Y	Y
8 Keller	Y	Y	Y	Y	Y
9 Bilirakis	Y	Y	Y	Y	Y
10 Young	Y	Y	Y	Y	Y
11 Castor	N	Y	Y	Y	Y
12 Putnam	Y	N	Y	Y	+
13 Buchanan	Y	Y	Y	Y	Y
14 Mack	Y	N	Y	N	Y
15 Weldon	Y	N	N	N	?
16 Mahoney	N	Y	Y	Y	Y
17 Meek	N	Y	Y	Y	Y
18 Ros-Lehtinen	Y	Y	Y	Y	Y
19 Wexler	N	Y	Y	Y	Y
20 Wasserman Schultz	N	Y	Y	Y	Y
21 Diaz-Balart, L.	Y	Y	Y	Y	Y
22 Klein	N	Y	Y	Y	Y
23 Hastings	N	Y	Y	Y	Y
24 Feeney	?	N	Y	N	Y
25 Diaz-Balart, M.	Y	Y	Y	Y	Y
GEORGIA					
1 Kingston	Y	N	N	N	N
2 Bishop	N	Y	Y	Y	Y
3 Westmoreland	Y	N	N	N	N
4 Johnson	?	Y	Y	Y	Y
5 Lewis	N	Y	Y	Y	Y
6 Price	Y	N	N	N	N
7 Linder	Y	N	Y	N	N
8 Marshall	Y	Y	Y	Y	Y
9 Deal	Y	N	N	Y	N
10 Broun	Y	N	N	N	N
11 Gingrey	Y	N	N	N	Y
12 Barrow	N	Y	Y	Y	Y
13 Scott	N	Y	Y	Y	Y
HAWAII					
1 Abercrombie	N	Y	Y	Y	Y
2 Hirono	N	Y	Y	Y	Y
IDAHO					
1 Sali	Y	N	Y	N	N
2 Simpson	Y	Y	Y	Y	Y
ILLINOIS					
1 Rush	N	Y	?	Y	Y
2 Jackson	N	Y	Y	Y	Y
3 Lipinski	N	Y	Y	Y	Y
4 Gutierrez	N	Y	Y	Y	Y
5 Emanuel	N	Y	Y	Y	Y
6 Roskam	Y	N	Y	Y	Y
7 Davis	N	Y	Y	Y	Y
8 Bean	N	Y	Y	Y	Y
9 Schakowsky	N	Y	Y	Y	Y
10 Kirk	Y	Y	Y	Y	Y
11 Weller	+	Y	Y	Y	Y
12 Costello	N	Y	Y	Y	Y
13 Biggert	Y	Y	Y	Y	Y
14 Foster	N	Y	Y	Y	Y
15 Johnson	Y	Y	Y	Y	Y

KEY	**Republicans**	Democrats		
Y Voted for (yea)		X Paired against		C Voted "present" to avoid possible conflict of interest
# Paired for		– Announced against		
+ Announced for		P Voted "present"		? Did not vote or otherwise make a position known
N Voted against (nay)				

ND Northern Democrats, SD Southern Democrats
Southern states: Ala., Ark., Fla., Ga., Ky., La., Miss., N.C., Okla., S.C., Tenn., Texas, Va.

H-210 2008 CQ ALMANAC | www.cq.com

	622	623	624	625	626
16 Manzullo	Y	N	Y	Y	Y
17 Hare	N	Y	Y	Y	Y
18 LaHood	Y	Y	Y	Y	Y
19 Shimkus	Y	Y	Y	Y	Y
INDIANA					
1 Visclosky	N	Y	Y	Y	Y
2 Donnelly	N	Y	Y	Y	Y
3 Souder	Y	N	Y	Y	Y
4 Buyer	Y	Y	N	Y	Y
5 Burton	Y	N	Y	Y	Y
6 Pence	Y	N	Y	N	Y
7 Carson, A.	N	Y	Y	Y	Y
8 Ellsworth	N	Y	Y	Y	Y
9 Hill	N	Y	Y	Y	Y
IOWA					
1 Braley	–	+	+	Y	Y
2 Loebsack	N	Y	Y	Y	Y
3 Boswell	N	Y	Y	Y	Y
4 Latham	Y	N	Y	Y	Y
5 King	Y	N	Y	N	N
KANSAS					
1 Moran	Y	N	Y	Y	Y
2 Boyda	N	Y	Y	Y	Y
3 Moore	N	Y	Y	Y	Y
4 Tiahrt	Y	N	Y	Y	Y
KENTUCKY					
1 Whitfield	Y	Y	Y	Y	Y
2 Lewis	Y	Y	Y	N	Y
3 Yarmuth	N	Y	Y	Y	Y
4 Davis	Y	N	Y	Y	Y
5 Rogers	Y	Y	Y	Y	Y
6 Chandler	N	Y	Y	Y	Y
LOUISIANA					
1 Scalise	Y	N	N	Y	Y
2 Jefferson	N	Y	Y	Y	Y
3 Melancon	N	Y	Y	Y	Y
4 McCrery	Y	Y	Y	N	Y
5 Alexander	Y	N	Y	Y	Y
6 Cazayoux	N	Y	Y	Y	Y
7 Boustany	Y	Y	Y	Y	Y
MAINE					
1 Allen	N	Y	Y	Y	Y
2 Michaud	N	Y	Y	Y	Y
MARYLAND					
1 Gilchrest	Y	Y	Y	Y	Y
2 Ruppersberger	N	Y	Y	Y	Y
3 Sarbanes	N	Y	Y	Y	Y
4 Edwards	N	Y	Y	Y	Y
5 Hoyer	N	Y	Y	Y	Y
6 Bartlett	Y	Y	Y	Y	Y
7 Cummings	N	Y	?	Y	Y
8 Van Hollen	N	Y	Y	Y	Y
MASSACHUSETTS					
1 Olver	N	Y	Y	Y	Y
2 Neal	N	Y	Y	Y	?
3 McGovern	N	Y	Y	Y	Y
4 Frank	N	Y	Y	Y	Y
5 Tsongas	N	Y	Y	Y	Y
6 Tierney	N	Y	Y	Y	Y
7 Markey	N	Y	Y	Y	Y
8 Capuano	N	Y	Y	Y	Y
9 Lynch	N	Y	Y	Y	Y
10 Delahunt	N	Y	Y	Y	Y
MICHIGAN					
1 Stupak	N	Y	Y	Y	Y
2 Hoekstra	Y	N	Y	N	Y
3 Ehlers	Y	Y	Y	Y	Y
4 Camp	Y	Y	Y	Y	Y
5 Kildee	N	Y	Y	Y	Y
6 Upton	Y	Y	Y	Y	Y
7 Walberg	Y	N	Y	Y	Y
8 Rogers	Y	Y	Y	Y	Y
9 Knollenberg	Y	Y	Y	Y	Y
10 Miller	Y	Y	Y	Y	Y
11 McCotter	Y	Y	Y	Y	Y
12 Levin	N	Y	Y	Y	Y
13 Kilpatrick	N	Y	Y	Y	Y
14 Conyers	N	Y	Y	Y	Y
15 Dingell	N	Y	?	Y	Y
MINNESOTA					
1 Walz	N	Y	Y	Y	Y
2 Kline	Y	N	Y	Y	Y
3 Ramstad	Y	Y	Y	Y	Y
4 McCollum	N	Y	Y	Y	Y

	622	623	624	625	626
5 Ellison	N	Y	Y	Y	Y
6 Bachmann	?	N	Y	N	Y
7 Peterson	N	Y	Y	Y	Y
8 Oberstar	N	Y	Y	Y	Y
MISSISSIPPI					
1 Childers	Y	Y	Y	Y	Y
2 Thompson	N	Y	Y	Y	Y
3 Pickering	Y	Y	Y	Y	Y
4 Taylor	N	Y	N	Y	Y
MISSOURI					
1 Clay	N	Y	Y	Y	Y
2 Akin	Y	N	N	N	N
3 Carnahan	N	Y	Y	Y	Y
4 Skelton	N	Y	Y	Y	Y
5 Cleaver	N	Y	Y	Y	Y
6 Graves	Y	Y	Y	Y	Y
7 Blunt	Y	N	Y	?	?
8 Emerson	Y	Y	Y	Y	Y
9 Hulshof	?	?	?	Y	Y
MONTANA					
AL Rehberg	Y	Y	Y	Y	Y
NEBRASKA					
1 Fortenberry	N	Y	Y	Y	Y
2 Terry	Y	N	Y	Y	Y
3 Smith	Y	N	Y	N	Y
NEVADA					
1 Berkley	N	Y	Y	Y	Y
2 Heller	Y	N	Y	Y	Y
3 Porter	Y	Y	Y	Y	Y
NEW HAMPSHIRE					
1 Shea-Porter	N	Y	Y	Y	Y
2 Hodes	N	Y	Y	Y	Y
NEW JERSEY					
1 Andrews	N	Y	Y	Y	Y
2 LoBiondo	Y	Y	Y	Y	Y
3 Saxton	Y	Y	Y	?	?
4 Smith	Y	Y	Y	Y	Y
5 Garrett	Y	N	Y	N	N
6 Pallone	N	Y	Y	Y	Y
7 Ferguson	Y	N	Y	Y	Y
8 Pascrell	N	Y	Y	Y	Y
9 Rothman	N	Y	Y	Y	Y
10 Payne	N	Y	Y	Y	?
11 Frelinghuysen	Y	N	Y	Y	Y
12 Holt	N	Y	Y	Y	Y
13 Sires	N	Y	Y	Y	Y
NEW MEXICO					
1 Wilson	Y	Y	Y	Y	Y
2 Pearce	Y	N	Y	Y	Y
3 Udall	N	Y	Y	Y	Y
NEW YORK					
1 Bishop	N	Y	Y	Y	Y
2 Israel	N	Y	Y	Y	Y
3 King	Y	N	Y	Y	Y
4 McCarthy	N	Y	Y	Y	Y
5 Ackerman	N	Y	Y	Y	Y
6 Meeks	N	Y	Y	Y	Y
7 Crowley	N	Y	Y	Y	Y
8 Nadler	N	Y	Y	Y	Y
9 Weiner	N	Y	Y	Y	Y
10 Towns	N	Y	Y	Y	Y
11 Clarke	N	Y	Y	Y	Y
12 Velázquez	N	Y	?	Y	?
13 Fossella	Y	N	?	?	?
14 Maloney	N	Y	Y	Y	Y
15 Rangel	N	Y	Y	Y	Y
16 Serrano	N	Y	Y	Y	Y
17 Engel	N	Y	Y	Y	Y
18 Lowey	N	Y	Y	Y	Y
19 Hall	N	Y	Y	Y	Y
20 Gillibrand	N	Y	Y	Y	Y
21 McNulty	N	Y	Y	Y	Y
22 Hinchey	N	Y	Y	Y	Y
23 McHugh	Y	Y	Y	Y	Y
24 Arcuri	N	Y	Y	Y	Y
25 Walsh	Y	Y	Y	Y	Y
26 Reynolds	Y	N	Y	Y	Y
27 Higgins	N	Y	Y	Y	Y
28 Slaughter	N	Y	Y	Y	Y
29 Kuhl	Y	N	Y	Y	Y
NORTH CAROLINA					
1 Butterfield	N	Y	Y	Y	Y
2 Etheridge	N	Y	Y	Y	Y
3 Jones	Y	N	Y	Y	Y
4 Price	N	Y	Y	Y	Y

	622	623	624	625	626
5 Foxx	Y	N	N	N	N
6 Coble	Y	N	N	N	Y
7 McIntyre	Y	Y	Y	Y	Y
8 Hayes	Y	Y	Y	Y	Y
9 Myrick	Y	N	Y	Y	Y
10 McHenry	Y	N	N	Y	Y
11 Shuler	Y	Y	Y	Y	Y
12 Watt	N	Y	Y	Y	Y
13 Miller	N	Y	Y	Y	Y
NORTH DAKOTA					
AL Pomeroy	N	Y	Y	Y	Y
OHIO					
1 Chabot	Y	N	Y	Y	Y
2 Schmidt	Y	N	Y	Y	Y
3 Turner	Y	Y	Y	Y	Y
4 Jordan	Y	N	N	N	N
5 Latta	Y	N	N	Y	Y
6 Wilson	N	Y	Y	Y	Y
7 Hobson	Y	N	Y	Y	Y
8 Boehner	Y	N	Y	?	?
9 Kaptur	N	Y	Y	Y	Y
10 Kucinich	N	Y	Y	Y	Y
11 Vacant					
12 Tiberi	Y	N	Y	Y	Y
13 Sutton	N	Y	Y	Y	Y
14 LaTourette	Y	Y	Y	Y	Y
15 Pryce	?	?	?	Y	Y
16 Regula	Y	N	Y	Y	Y
17 Ryan	N	Y	Y	Y	Y
18 Space	N	Y	Y	Y	Y
OKLAHOMA					
1 Sullivan	Y	N	Y	Y	Y
2 Boren	N	Y	Y	Y	Y
3 Lucas	Y	N	Y	Y	Y
4 Cole	Y	N	Y	Y	Y
5 Fallin	Y	N	Y	Y	Y
OREGON					
1 Wu	N	Y	Y	Y	Y
2 Walden	Y	Y	Y	Y	Y
3 Blumenauer	N	Y	Y	Y	Y
4 DeFazio	N	Y	Y	Y	?
5 Hooley	N	Y	Y	Y	Y
PENNSYLVANIA					
1 Brady	N	Y	Y	Y	Y
2 Fattah	N	Y	Y	Y	Y
3 English	Y	Y	Y	Y	Y
4 Altmire	Y	Y	Y	Y	Y
5 Peterson	Y	Y	Y	Y	Y
6 Gerlach	Y	Y	Y	Y	Y
7 Sestak	N	Y	Y	Y	Y
8 Murphy, P.	N	Y	Y	Y	Y
9 Shuster	Y	N	Y	Y	Y
10 Carney	N	Y	Y	Y	Y
11 Kanjorski	N	Y	Y	Y	?
12 Murtha	N	Y	Y	Y	Y
13 Schwartz	N	Y	Y	Y	Y
14 Doyle	N	Y	Y	Y	Y
15 Dent	Y	Y	Y	Y	Y
16 Pitts	Y	N	Y	N	Y
17 Holden	N	Y	Y	Y	Y
18 Murphy, T.	Y	Y	Y	Y	Y
19 Platts	Y	Y	Y	Y	Y
RHODE ISLAND					
1 Kennedy	N	Y	Y	Y	Y
2 Langevin	N	Y	Y	Y	Y
SOUTH CAROLINA					
1 Brown	Y	Y	Y	Y	Y
2 Wilson	Y	N	Y	Y	Y
3 Barrett	Y	N	Y	N	N
4 Inglis	Y	N	N	N	N
5 Spratt	N	Y	Y	Y	Y
6 Clyburn	N	Y	Y	Y	Y
SOUTH DAKOTA					
AL Herseth Sandlin	N	N	Y	Y	Y
TENNESSEE					
1 Davis, D.	Y	Y	N	Y	Y
2 Duncan	Y	Y	N	N	Y
3 Wamp	Y	Y	Y	Y	Y
4 Davis, L.	?	?	?	Y	Y
5 Cooper	?	?	?	Y	Y
6 Gordon	?	?	?	Y	Y
7 Blackburn	Y	N	Y	Y	Y
8 Tanner	N	Y	Y	Y	Y
9 Cohen	N	Y	Y	Y	Y

	622	623	624	625	626
TEXAS					
1 Gohmert	Y	N	Y	Y	Y
2 Poe	Y	N	Y	Y	Y
3 Johnson, S.	?	N	Y	N	N
4 Hall	Y	Y	Y	Y	Y
5 Hensarling	Y	N	N	N	N
6 Barton	Y	Y	Y	N	Y
7 Culberson	Y	Y	Y	Y	Y
8 Brady	Y	N	Y	N	Y
9 Green, A.	N	Y	Y	Y	Y
10 McCaul	Y	Y	Y	Y	Y
11 Conaway	Y	N	N	N	N
12 Granger	Y	N	Y	Y	Y
13 Thornberry	Y	N	Y	N	N
14 Paul	Y	N	Y	N	N
15 Hinojosa	N	Y	Y	Y	Y
16 Reyes	?	?	?	?	?
17 Edwards	N	Y	Y	Y	Y
18 Jackson Lee	N	Y	Y	Y	Y
19 Neugebauer	+	–	+	N	N
20 Gonzalez	N	Y	?	Y	Y
21 Smith	Y	N	Y	Y	Y
22 Lampson	Y	Y	Y	Y	Y
23 Rodriguez	N	Y	Y	Y	Y
24 Marchant	Y	N	Y	N	Y
25 Doggett	N	Y	?	Y	Y
26 Burgess	Y	N	Y	Y	Y
27 Ortiz	N	Y	Y	Y	Y
28 Cuellar	N	Y	Y	Y	Y
29 Green, G.	N	Y	Y	Y	Y
30 Johnson, E.	N	Y	Y	Y	Y
31 Carter	Y	N	Y	N	Y
32 Sessions	Y	N	Y	Y	Y
UTAH					
1 Bishop	Y	N	Y	?	?
2 Matheson	N	Y	Y	Y	Y
3 Cannon	Y	N	Y	N	N
VERMONT					
AL Welch	N	Y	Y	Y	Y
VIRGINIA					
1 Wittman	Y	Y	Y	Y	Y
2 Drake	Y	Y	Y	Y	Y
3 Scott	N	Y	Y	Y	Y
4 Forbes	Y	Y	Y	Y	Y
5 Goode	Y	Y	N	Y	Y
6 Goodlatte	Y	N	N	Y	Y
7 Cantor	Y	N	Y	?	?
8 Moran	N	Y	Y	Y	Y
9 Boucher	N	Y	Y	Y	Y
10 Wolf	Y	Y	Y	Y	Y
11 Davis	Y	Y	Y	Y	Y
WASHINGTON					
1 Inslee	N	Y	Y	Y	Y
2 Larsen	N	Y	Y	Y	Y
3 Baird	N	Y	Y	Y	Y
4 Hastings	Y	N	Y	N	Y
5 McMorris Rodgers	Y	N	Y	Y	Y
6 Dicks	N	Y	Y	Y	Y
7 McDermott	N	Y	Y	Y	Y
8 Reichert	Y	Y	Y	Y	Y
9 Smith	N	Y	Y	Y	Y
WEST VIRGINIA					
1 Mollohan	N	Y	Y	Y	Y
2 Capito	Y	Y	Y	Y	Y
3 Rahall	N	Y	Y	Y	Y
WISCONSIN					
1 Ryan	Y	N	Y	Y	Y
2 Baldwin	N	Y	Y	Y	Y
3 Kind	N	Y	Y	Y	Y
4 Moore	N	Y	Y	Y	Y
5 Sensenbrenner	Y	N	Y	N	Y
6 Petri	Y	N	Y	Y	Y
7 Obey	N	Y	?	Y	Y
8 Kagen	N	Y	Y	Y	Y
WYOMING					
AL Cubin	?	?	?	?	?
DELEGATES					
Faleomavaega (A.S.)					
Norton (D.C.)					
Bordallo (Guam)					
Fortuño (P.R.)					
Christensen (V.I.)					

IN THE HOUSE | By Vote Number

627. **HR 642. Fire Sprinkler Grants/Passage.** Davis, D-Calif., motion to suspend the rules and pass the bill that would direct the Education Department to establish a program to award competitive grants to colleges, universities, fraternities and sororities for up to half the cost of installing fire sprinkler systems or other fire prevention devices. Motion agreed to 365-51: R 138-51; D 227-0 (ND 170-0, SD 57-0). A two-thirds majority of those present and voting (278 in this case) is required for passage under suspension of the rules. Sept. 23, 2008.

628. **HR 2638. Continuing Appropriations/Question of Consideration.** Question of whether the House should consider the rule (H Res 1488) to provide for floor consideration of the House amendment to the Senate amendment to the bill. The House amendment would provide fiscal 2009 appropriations through March 6, 2009. Agreed to consider 242-168: R 22-167; D 220-1 (ND 166-0, SD 54-1). (Flake, R-Ariz., had raised a point of order that the rule contained a provision in violation of the Congressional Budget Act.) Sept. 24, 2008.

629. **HR 2638. Continuing Appropriations/Previous Question.** Mc-Govern, D-Mass., motion to order the previous question (thus ending debate and possibility of amendment) on adoption of the rule (H Res 1488) to provide for floor consideration of the House amendment to the Senate amendment to the bill. The House amendment would provide fiscal 2009 appropriations through March 6, 2009. Motion agreed to 231-198: R 4-193; D 227-5 (ND 170-3, SD 57-2). Sept. 24, 2008.

630. **HR 2638. Continuing Appropriations/Rule.** Adoption of the rule (H Res 1488) to provide for House floor consideration of the House amendment to the Senate amendment to the bill. The House amendment would provide fiscal 2009 appropriations through March 6, 2009. Adopted 228-202: R 0-197; D 228-5 (ND 170-4, SD 58-1). Sept. 24, 2008.

631. **S 3001. Fiscal 2009 Defense Authorization/Passage.** Skelton, D-Mo., motion to suspend the rules and pass the bill, as amended. The bill would authorize $611.1 billion for defense programs in fiscal 2009, including $68.6 billion for the wars in Iraq and Afghanistan. It would authorize a 3.9 percent pay increase for military personnel. It also contains provisions to govern oversight of contracts, including one to set up a database of defense contractors found to have violated the law. Motion agreed to 392-39: R 192-5; D 200-34 (ND 143-32, SD 57-2). A two-thirds majority of those present and voting (288 in this case) is required for passage under suspension of the rules. Sept. 24, 2008.

632. **HR 2638. Continuing Appropriations/Motion to Concur.** Obey, D-Wis., motion to concur in the Senate amendment to the bill with a House amendment that would provide $41.2 billion in fiscal 2009 for the Homeland Security Department, $487.7 billion for the Defense Department, $119.6 billion for military construction and veterans' programs, and $22.9 billion for disaster relief. The amendment would appropriate funding through March 6, 2009, for programs covered by the nine unfunded fiscal 2009 appropriations bills. It also would provide extra funding, including $7.5 billion for an Energy Department auto company loan program and $2.5 billion above fiscal 2008 levels for Pell grants. Motion agreed to 370-58: R 146-51; D 224-7 (ND 167-7, SD 57-0). Sept. 24, 2008.

	627	628	629	630	631	632
ALABAMA						
1 Bonner	Y	N	N	Y	Y	Y
2 Everett	Y	Y	N	N	Y	Y
3 Rogers	Y	Y	N	N	Y	Y
4 Aderholt	N	Y	N	N	Y	Y
5 Cramer	Y	Y	Y	Y	Y	Y
6 Bachus	Y	N	N	N	Y	Y
7 Davis	Y	Y	Y	Y	Y	Y
ALASKA						
AL Young	Y	Y	N	N	Y	Y
ARIZONA						
1 Renzi	Y	N	N	N	Y	Y
2 Franks	N	N	N	N	Y	N
3 Shadegg	N	N	N	N	Y	N
4 Pastor	Y	Y	Y	Y	Y	Y
5 Mitchell	Y	Y	Y	N	Y	Y
6 Flake	N	N	N	N	N	N
7 Grijalva	Y	Y	Y	Y	Y	Y
8 Giffords	Y	Y	Y	Y	Y	Y
ARKANSAS						
1 Berry	Y	Y	Y	Y	Y	Y
2 Snyder	Y	Y	Y	Y	Y	Y
3 Boozman	Y	N	N	N	Y	Y
4 Ross	Y	Y	Y	Y	Y	Y
CALIFORNIA						
1 Thompson	Y	Y	Y	Y	Y	Y
2 Herger	N	N	N	N	Y	N
3 Lungren	N	N	N	N	Y	Y
4 Doolittle	N	N	N	N	Y	Y
5 Matsui	Y	Y	Y	Y	Y	Y
6 Woolsey	Y	Y	Y	Y	N	N
7 Miller, George	Y	Y	Y	Y	Y	Y
8 Pelosi						
9 Lee	Y	Y	Y	Y	N	N
10 Tauscher	Y	Y	Y	Y	Y	Y
11 McNerney	Y	Y	Y	Y	Y	Y
12 Speier	Y	Y	Y	N	Y	Y
13 Stark	Y	Y	Y	Y	N	N
14 Eshoo	Y	Y	Y	Y	Y	Y
15 Honda	Y	Y	Y	Y	Y	Y
16 Lofgren	Y	Y	Y	Y	Y	Y
17 Farr	Y	?	Y	Y	Y	Y
18 Cardoza	Y	Y	Y	Y	Y	Y
19 Radanovich	Y	N	N	N	Y	Y
20 Costa	Y	Y	Y	Y	Y	Y
21 Nunes	Y	N	N	N	Y	Y
22 McCarthy	Y	N	N	N	Y	Y
23 Capps	Y	Y	Y	Y	Y	Y
24 Gallegly	Y	N	N	N	Y	Y
25 McKeon	Y	N	N	N	Y	Y
26 Dreier	Y	N	N	N	Y	Y
27 Sherman	Y	Y	Y	Y	Y	Y
28 Berman	Y	Y	Y	Y	Y	Y
29 Schiff	Y	Y	Y	Y	Y	Y
30 Waxman	Y	Y	Y	Y	Y	Y
31 Becerra	Y	Y	Y	Y	Y	Y
32 Solis	Y	Y	Y	Y	Y	Y
33 Watson	Y	Y	Y	Y	N	?
34 Roybal-Allard	Y	Y	Y	Y	Y	Y
35 Waters	Y	Y	Y	Y	N	Y
36 Harman	Y	Y	Y	Y	Y	Y
37 Richardson	Y	Y	Y	Y	Y	Y
38 Napolitano	Y	Y	Y	Y	Y	Y
39 Sánchez, Linda	Y	Y	Y	Y	Y	Y
40 Royce	N	N	N	N	Y	Y
41 Lewis	Y	Y	N	N	Y	Y
42 Miller, Gary	Y	N	N	N	Y	Y
43 Baca	Y	Y	Y	Y	Y	Y
44 Calvert	Y	N	N	N	Y	Y
45 Bono Mack	Y	N	N	N	Y	Y
46 Rohrabacher	N	N	N	N	Y	Y
47 Sanchez, Loretta	Y	Y	Y	Y	Y	Y
48 Campbell	N	N	N	N	N	C
49 Issa	N	N	N	N	Y	N
50 Bilbray	Y	N	N	Y	Y	Y
51 Filner	Y	Y	Y	Y	Y	Y
52 Hunter	?	N	N	N	Y	Y
53 Davis	Y	Y	Y	Y	Y	Y

	627	628	629	630	631	632
COLORADO						
1 DeGette	Y	Y	Y	Y	Y	Y
2 Udall	Y	?	Y	Y	Y	Y
3 Salazar	?	Y	Y	Y	Y	Y
4 Musgrave	Y	?	N	N	Y	Y
5 Lamborn	N	N	N	N	Y	N
6 Tancredo	N	N	N	N	Y	N
7 Perlmutter	Y	Y	Y	Y	Y	Y
CONNECTICUT						
1 Larson	Y	?	Y	Y	Y	Y
2 Courtney	Y	Y	Y	Y	Y	Y
3 DeLauro	Y	Y	Y	Y	Y	Y
4 Shays	Y	N	Y	N	Y	Y
5 Murphy	?	Y	Y	Y	Y	Y
DELAWARE						
AL Castle	Y	N	N	N	Y	Y
FLORIDA						
1 Miller	Y	N	N	N	Y	Y
2 Boyd	Y	?	Y	Y	Y	Y
3 Brown	Y	?	Y	Y	Y	Y
4 Crenshaw	Y	N	N	N	Y	Y
5 Brown-Waite	N	N	N	N	Y	Y
6 Stearns	Y	N	N	N	Y	N
7 Mica	Y	N	N	N	Y	N
8 Keller	?	N	N	N	Y	Y
9 Bilirakis	Y	N	N	N	Y	Y
10 Young	Y	N	N	N	Y	Y
11 Castor	Y	Y	Y	Y	Y	Y
12 Putnam	+	N	N	N	Y	Y
13 Buchanan	Y	N	N	N	Y	Y
14 Mack	Y	N	N	N	Y	N
15 Weldon	N	N	N	N	Y	Y
16 Mahoney	Y	Y	Y	Y	Y	Y
17 Meek	Y	Y	Y	Y	Y	Y
18 Ros-Lehtinen	Y	Y	Y	N	Y	Y
19 Wexler	Y	Y	Y	Y	Y	Y
20 Wasserman Schultz	Y	Y	Y	Y	Y	Y
21 Diaz-Balart, L.	N	N	N	N	Y	Y
22 Klein	Y	Y	Y	Y	Y	Y
23 Hastings	Y	Y	Y	Y	Y	Y
24 Feeney	N	N	N	N	Y	N
25 Diaz-Balart, M.	Y	N	N	N	Y	Y
GEORGIA						
1 Kingston	N	N	N	N	Y	Y
2 Bishop	Y	Y	Y	Y	Y	Y
3 Westmoreland	N	N	N	N	Y	N
4 Johnson	Y	?	Y	Y	Y	Y
5 Lewis	Y	Y	Y	N	Y	Y
6 Price	N	N	N	N	Y	N
7 Linder	N	N	N	N	Y	N
8 Marshall	Y	N	Y	Y	Y	Y
9 Deal	N	N	N	N	Y	N
10 Broun	N	N	N	N	Y	N
11 Gingrey	N	N	N	N	Y	N
12 Barrow	Y	Y	Y	Y	Y	Y
13 Scott	Y	Y	Y	Y	Y	Y
HAWAII						
1 Abercrombie	Y	Y	Y	Y	Y	Y
2 Hirono	Y	Y	Y	+	Y	Y
IDAHO						
1 Sali	Y	N	N	N	Y	N
2 Simpson	Y	Y	N	N	Y	Y
ILLINOIS						
1 Rush	Y	Y	?	Y	Y	Y
2 Jackson	Y	Y	Y	Y	N	Y
3 Lipinski	Y	Y	Y	Y	Y	Y
4 Gutierrez	Y	Y	Y	N	Y	Y
5 Emanuel	Y	Y	Y	Y	Y	Y
6 Roskam	Y	N	N	N	Y	N
7 Davis	Y	Y	Y	N	Y	Y
8 Bean	Y	Y	Y	Y	Y	Y
9 Schakowsky	Y	Y	Y	Y	Y	Y
10 Kirk	Y	N	N	N	Y	Y
11 Weller	Y	N	N	N	Y	Y
12 Costello	Y	Y	Y	Y	Y	Y
13 Biggert	Y	N	N	N	Y	Y
14 Foster	Y	Y	Y	Y	Y	Y
15 Johnson	Y	N	Y	N	Y	N

ND Northern Democrats, SD Southern Democrats
Southern states: Ala., Ark., Fla., Ga., Ky., La., Miss., N.C., Okla., S.C., Tenn., Texas, Va.

	627	628	629	630	631	632
16 **Manzullo**	N	N	N	N	Y	Y
17 Hare	Y	Y	Y	Y	Y	Y
18 **LaHood**	Y	Y	N	N	Y	Y
19 **Shimkus**	Y	N	N	N	Y	N
INDIANA						
1 Visclosky	Y	Y	Y	Y	Y	Y
2 Donnelly	Y	Y	Y	Y	Y	Y
3 **Souder**	N	N	N	N	Y	Y
4 **Buyer**	N	N	N	N	Y	Y
5 **Burton**	Y	N	N	N	Y	N
6 **Pence**	N	N	N	N	Y	N
7 Carson, A.	Y	Y	Y	Y	Y	Y
8 Ellsworth	Y	Y	Y	Y	Y	Y
9 Hill	Y	Y	Y	Y	Y	Y
IOWA						
1 Braley	Y	Y	Y	Y	Y	Y
2 Loebsack	Y	Y	Y	Y	Y	Y
3 Boswell	Y	Y	Y	Y	Y	Y
4 **Latham**	Y	N	N	N	Y	Y
5 **King**	N	N	N	N	Y	N
KANSAS						
1 **Moran**	Y	N	N	N	Y	N
2 Boyda	Y	Y	?	Y	Y	Y
3 Moore	Y	Y	Y	Y	Y	Y
4 **Tiahrt**	Y	N	N	N	Y	N
KENTUCKY						
1 **Whitfield**	Y	?	N	N	Y	Y
2 **Lewis**	Y	N	N	N	Y	Y
3 Yarmuth	Y	Y	Y	Y	Y	Y
4 **Davis**	Y	?	N	N	Y	N
5 **Rogers**	Y	N	N	N	Y	Y
6 Chandler	Y	Y	Y	Y	Y	Y
LOUISIANA						
1 **Scalise**	Y	N	N	N	Y	Y
2 Jefferson	Y	Y	Y	Y	Y	?
3 Melancon	Y	Y	Y	Y	Y	Y
4 **McCrery**	Y	N	N	N	Y	Y
5 **Alexander**	Y	N	N	N	Y	Y
6 Cazayoux	Y	Y	N	Y	Y	Y
7 **Boustany**	Y	N	N	N	Y	Y
MAINE						
1 Allen	Y	Y	Y	Y	Y	Y
2 Michaud	Y	Y	Y	Y	N	Y
MARYLAND						
1 **Gilchrest**	Y	Y	N	N	N	Y
2 Ruppersberger	Y	Y	Y	Y	Y	Y
3 Sarbanes	Y	Y	Y	Y	Y	Y
4 Edwards	Y	Y	Y	Y	N	Y
5 Hoyer	Y	Y	Y	Y	Y	Y
6 **Bartlett**	Y	N	N	N	Y	Y
7 Cummings	?	Y	Y	Y	Y	Y
8 Van Hollen	Y	Y	Y	Y	Y	Y
MASSACHUSETTS						
1 Olver	Y	Y	Y	Y	N	Y
2 Neal	Y	Y	Y	Y	Y	Y
3 McGovern	Y	Y	Y	Y	Y	Y
4 Frank	Y	Y	Y	Y	N	Y
5 Tsongas	Y	Y	Y	Y	Y	Y
6 Tierney	Y	Y	N	Y	N	Y
7 Markey	Y	Y	Y	Y	N	Y
8 Capuano	Y	Y	Y	Y	N	Y
9 Lynch	Y	Y	Y	Y	Y	Y
10 Delahunt	Y	Y	Y	Y	N	Y
MICHIGAN						
1 Stupak	Y	Y	Y	Y	Y	Y
2 **Hoekstra**	N	N	N	N	Y	Y
3 **Ehlers**	Y	N	N	N	Y	Y
4 **Camp**	Y	N	N	N	Y	Y
5 Kildee	Y	Y	Y	Y	Y	Y
6 **Upton**	Y	N	N	N	Y	Y
7 **Walberg**	N	N	N	N	Y	Y
8 **Rogers**	Y	N	N	N	Y	Y
9 **Knollenberg**	Y	N	N	N	Y	Y
10 **Miller**	Y	N	N	N	Y	Y
11 **McCotter**	Y	N	N	N	Y	Y
12 Levin	Y	Y	Y	Y	Y	Y
13 Kilpatrick	Y	Y	Y	Y	Y	Y
14 Conyers	Y	Y	Y	Y	N	Y
15 Dingell	Y	Y	Y	Y	Y	Y
MINNESOTA						
1 Walz	Y	Y	Y	Y	Y	Y
2 **Kline**	Y	N	N	N	Y	Y
3 **Ramstad**	Y	N	N	N	Y	Y
4 McCollum	Y	Y	Y	Y	Y	Y

	627	628	629	630	631	632
5 Ellison	Y	+	Y	Y	N	Y
6 **Bachmann**	N	N	N	N	Y	Y
7 Peterson	Y	Y	Y	Y	Y	Y
8 Oberstar	Y	Y	Y	Y	Y	Y
MISSISSIPPI						
1 Childers	Y	Y	N	Y	Y	Y
2 Thompson	Y	Y	Y	Y	Y	Y
3 **Pickering**	Y	N	N	N	Y	Y
4 Taylor	Y	Y	Y	Y	Y	Y
MISSOURI						
1 Clay	Y	Y	Y	Y	Y	Y
2 **Akin**	N	N	N	N	Y	Y
3 Carnahan	Y	Y	Y	Y	Y	Y
4 Skelton	Y	Y	Y	Y	Y	Y
5 Cleaver	Y	Y	Y	Y	Y	Y
6 **Graves**	Y	N	N	N	Y	Y
7 **Blunt**	?	N	N	N	Y	N
8 **Emerson**	Y	N	N	N	Y	Y
9 **Hulshof**	Y	N	N	N	Y	Y
MONTANA						
AL **Rehberg**	Y	N	N	N	Y	Y
NEBRASKA						
1 **Fortenberry**	Y	N	N	N	Y	Y
2 **Terry**	Y	N	N	N	Y	Y
3 **Smith**	N	N	N	N	Y	Y
NEVADA						
1 Berkley	Y	Y	Y	Y	Y	Y
2 **Heller**	Y	N	N	N	Y	Y
3 **Porter**	Y	N	N	N	Y	Y
NEW HAMPSHIRE						
1 Shea-Porter	Y	Y	Y	Y	Y	Y
2 Hodes	Y	Y	Y	Y	Y	Y
NEW JERSEY						
1 Andrews	Y	Y	Y	Y	Y	Y
2 **LoBiondo**	Y	N	N	N	Y	Y
3 **Saxton**	?	Y	N	N	Y	Y
4 **Smith**	Y	N	N	N	Y	Y
5 **Garrett**	N	Y	N	N	Y	N
6 Pallone	Y	Y	Y	Y	Y	Y
7 **Ferguson**	Y	N	N	N	Y	Y
8 Pascrell	Y	Y	Y	Y	Y	Y
9 Rothman	Y	Y	Y	Y	Y	Y
10 Payne	?	Y	Y	Y	N	Y
11 **Frelinghuysen**	Y	N	N	N	Y	Y
12 Holt	Y	Y	Y	Y	Y	Y
13 Sires	Y	Y	Y	Y	Y	Y
NEW MEXICO						
1 **Wilson**	Y	Y	N	N	Y	Y
2 **Pearce**	Y	Y	N	N	Y	Y
3 Udall	Y	Y	Y	Y	Y	Y
NEW YORK						
1 Bishop	Y	Y	Y	Y	Y	Y
2 Israel	Y	Y	Y	Y	Y	Y
3 **King**	Y	N	N	N	Y	Y
4 McCarthy	Y	Y	Y	Y	Y	Y
5 Ackerman	Y	Y	Y	Y	Y	Y
6 Meeks	Y	Y	Y	Y	N	Y
7 Crowley	Y	Y	Y	Y	Y	Y
8 Nadler	Y	Y	Y	Y	Y	Y
9 Weiner	Y	Y	Y	Y	Y	Y
10 Towns	Y	Y	Y	Y	N	Y
11 Clarke	Y	Y	Y	Y	Y	Y
12 Velázquez	Y	Y	Y	Y	N	Y
13 **Fossella**	?	?	N	N	Y	N
14 Maloney	Y	Y	Y	Y	Y	Y
15 Rangel	Y	Y	Y	Y	Y	Y
16 Serrano	?	Y	Y	Y	N	Y
17 Engel	Y	?	Y	Y	Y	Y
18 Lowey	Y	Y	Y	Y	Y	Y
19 Hall	Y	Y	Y	Y	Y	Y
20 Gillibrand	Y	Y	Y	Y	Y	Y
21 McNulty	Y	Y	Y	Y	Y	Y
22 Hinchey	Y	?	Y	Y	N	Y
23 **McHugh**	Y	N	N	N	Y	Y
24 Arcuri	Y	Y	Y	Y	Y	Y
25 **Walsh**	Y	Y	N	N	Y	Y
26 **Reynolds**	Y	?	N	N	Y	Y
27 Higgins	Y	Y	Y	Y	Y	Y
28 Slaughter	Y	Y	Y	Y	Y	Y
29 **Kuhl**	Y	N	N	N	Y	Y
NORTH CAROLINA						
1 Butterfield	Y	Y	Y	Y	Y	Y
2 Etheridge	Y	Y	Y	Y	Y	Y
3 **Jones**	Y	Y	N	N	Y	N
4 Price	Y	Y	Y	Y	Y	Y

	627	628	629	630	631	632
5 **Foxx**	N	N	N	N	Y	N
6 **Coble**	Y	N	N	N	Y	Y
7 McIntyre	Y	Y	Y	Y	Y	Y
8 **Hayes**	Y	N	N	N	Y	Y
9 **Myrick**	Y	N	N	N	Y	Y
10 **McHenry**	Y	N	N	N	Y	Y
11 Shuler	Y	Y	Y	N	Y	?
12 Watt	Y	Y	Y	Y	Y	Y
13 Miller	Y	Y	Y	Y	Y	Y
NORTH DAKOTA						
AL Pomeroy	Y	Y	Y	Y	Y	Y
OHIO						
1 **Chabot**	Y	N	N	N	Y	Y
2 **Schmidt**	Y	N	N	N	Y	Y
3 **Turner**	Y	Y	N	N	Y	Y
4 **Jordan**	N	N	N	N	Y	N
5 **Latta**	N	N	N	N	Y	Y
6 Wilson	Y	Y	Y	Y	Y	Y
7 **Hobson**	Y	Y	N	N	Y	Y
8 **Boehner**	?	N	N	N	Y	N
9 Kaptur	Y	?	Y	Y	Y	Y
10 Kucinich	Y	Y	N	N	N	N
11 Vacant						
12 **Tiberi**	Y	N	N	N	Y	Y
13 Sutton	Y	Y	Y	Y	Y	Y
14 **LaTourette**	Y	N	N	N	Y	Y
15 **Pryce**	Y	Y	N	N	Y	Y
16 **Regula**	Y	Y	N	N	Y	Y
17 Ryan	Y	Y	Y	Y	Y	Y
18 Space	Y	Y	Y	Y	Y	Y
OKLAHOMA						
1 **Sullivan**	Y	N	N	N	Y	N
2 Boren	Y	Y	Y	Y	Y	Y
3 **Lucas**	Y	N	N	N	Y	Y
4 **Cole**	Y	N	N	N	Y	Y
5 **Fallin**	Y	N	N	N	Y	Y
OREGON						
1 Wu	Y	Y	Y	Y	Y	Y
2 **Walden**	Y	N	N	N	Y	Y
3 Blumenauer	Y	Y	Y	Y	N	N
4 DeFazio	Y	?	Y	N	N	N
5 Hooley	Y	Y	Y	Y	Y	Y
PENNSYLVANIA						
1 Brady	Y	Y	Y	Y	Y	Y
2 Fattah	Y	Y	Y	Y	Y	Y
3 **English**	Y	?	N	N	Y	Y
4 Altmire	Y	Y	Y	Y	Y	Y
5 **Peterson**	Y	N	N	N	Y	Y
6 **Gerlach**	Y	N	N	N	Y	Y
7 Sestak	Y	Y	Y	Y	Y	Y
8 Murphy, P.	Y	Y	Y	Y	Y	Y
9 **Shuster**	Y	N	N	N	Y	Y
10 Carney	Y	Y	Y	Y	Y	Y
11 Kanjorski	Y	Y	Y	Y	Y	Y
12 Murtha	Y	Y	Y	Y	Y	Y
13 Schwartz	Y	Y	Y	Y	Y	Y
14 Doyle	Y	Y	Y	Y	Y	Y
15 **Dent**	Y	N	N	N	Y	Y
16 **Pitts**	Y	N	N	N	Y	N
17 Holden	Y	Y	Y	Y	Y	Y
18 **Murphy, T.**	Y	N	N	N	Y	Y
19 **Platts**	Y	N	N	N	Y	Y
RHODE ISLAND						
1 Kennedy	Y	Y	Y	Y	Y	Y
2 Langevin	Y	Y	Y	Y	Y	Y
SOUTH CAROLINA						
1 **Brown**	Y	N	N	N	Y	Y
2 **Wilson**	Y	N	N	N	Y	Y
3 **Barrett**	Y	N	N	N	Y	N
4 **Inglis**	N	N	N	N	Y	N
5 Spratt	Y	?	Y	Y	Y	Y
6 Clyburn	Y	Y	Y	Y	Y	Y
SOUTH DAKOTA						
AL Herseth Sandlin	Y	Y	Y	Y	Y	Y
TENNESSEE						
1 **Davis, D.**	N	N	N	N	Y	N
2 **Duncan**	N	N	N	N	N	N
3 **Wamp**	Y	N	N	N	Y	Y
4 Davis, L.	Y	Y	Y	Y	Y	Y
5 Cooper	Y	Y	Y	Y	Y	Y
6 Gordon	Y	Y	Y	Y	Y	Y
7 **Blackburn**	Y	N	N	N	Y	N
8 Tanner	Y	Y	Y	Y	Y	Y
9 Cohen	Y	Y	Y	Y	Y	Y

	627	628	629	630	631	632
TEXAS						
1 **Gohmert**	Y	N	N	N	Y	Y
2 **Poe**	N	N	N	N	Y	Y
3 **Johnson, S.**	N	N	N	N	Y	Y
4 **Hall**	Y	N	N	N	Y	Y
5 **Hensarling**	N	N	N	N	Y	N
6 **Barton**	N	N	N	N	Y	Y
7 **Culberson**	N	N	N	N	Y	Y
8 **Brady**	Y	N	N	N	Y	Y
9 Green, A.	Y	Y	Y	Y	Y	Y
10 **McCaul**	Y	N	N	N	Y	Y
11 **Conaway**	N	N	N	N	Y	Y
12 **Granger**	Y	N	N	N	Y	Y
13 **Thornberry**	N	N	N	N	Y	Y
14 **Paul**	N	?	N	N	N	N
15 Hinojosa	Y	Y	Y	Y	Y	Y
16 Reyes	?	Y	Y	Y	Y	Y
17 Edwards	Y	Y	Y	Y	Y	Y
18 Jackson Lee	Y	Y	Y	Y	N	Y
19 **Neugebauer**	N	N	N	N	Y	Y
20 Gonzalez	Y	Y	Y	Y	Y	Y
21 **Smith**	Y	N	N	N	Y	Y
22 Lampson	Y	Y	Y	Y	Y	Y
23 Rodriguez	?	Y	Y	Y	Y	Y
24 **Marchant**	Y	N	N	N	Y	Y
25 Doggett	Y	Y	Y	Y	Y	Y
26 **Burgess**	Y	N	N	N	Y	Y
27 Ortiz	Y	Y	Y	Y	Y	Y
28 Cuellar	Y	Y	Y	Y	Y	Y
29 Green, G.	Y	Y	Y	Y	Y	Y
30 Johnson, E.	Y	Y	Y	Y	Y	Y
31 **Carter**	N	N	N	N	Y	Y
32 **Sessions**	Y	N	N	N	Y	Y
UTAH						
1 **Bishop**	?	?	?	?	?	?
2 Matheson	Y	Y	N	Y	Y	Y
3 **Cannon**	N	N	N	N	Y	N
VERMONT						
AL Welch	Y	Y	Y	Y	N	Y
VIRGINIA						
1 **Wittman**	Y	N	N	N	Y	Y
2 **Drake**	Y	N	N	N	Y	Y
3 Scott	Y	Y	Y	Y	Y	Y
4 **Forbes**	Y	N	N	N	Y	Y
5 **Goode**	Y	N	N	N	Y	N
6 **Goodlatte**	Y	N	N	N	Y	N
7 **Cantor**	?	N	N	N	Y	N
8 Moran	Y	Y	Y	Y	Y	Y
9 Boucher	Y	Y	Y	Y	Y	Y
10 **Wolf**	Y	Y	N	N	Y	Y
11 **Davis**	Y	Y	N	N	Y	Y
WASHINGTON						
1 Inslee	Y	Y	Y	Y	Y	Y
2 Larsen	Y	Y	Y	Y	Y	Y
3 Baird	Y	?	Y	N	Y	Y
4 **Hastings**	Y	N	N	N	Y	N
5 **McMorris Rodgers**	Y	?	N	N	Y	Y
6 Dicks	Y	Y	Y	Y	Y	Y
7 McDermott	Y	Y	Y	Y	Y	N
8 **Reichert**	Y	N	Y	N	Y	Y
9 Smith	Y	Y	Y	Y	Y	Y
WEST VIRGINIA						
1 Mollohan	Y	Y	Y	Y	Y	Y
2 **Capito**	Y	N	N	N	Y	Y
3 Rahall	Y	Y	Y	Y	Y	Y
WISCONSIN						
1 **Ryan**	Y	N	N	N	Y	N
2 Baldwin	Y	Y	Y	Y	N	Y
3 Kind	Y	Y	Y	Y	Y	Y
4 Moore	Y	Y	Y	Y	N	Y
5 **Sensenbrenner**	Y	N	N	N	Y	N
6 **Petri**	Y	N	N	N	Y	N
7 Obey	Y	Y	Y	Y	Y	Y
8 Kagen	Y	Y	Y	Y	Y	Y
WYOMING						
AL **Cubin**	?	?	?	?	?	N
DELEGATES						
Faleomavaega (A.S.)						
Norton (D.C.)						
Bordallo (Guam)						
Fortuño (P.R.)						
Christensen (V.I.)						

IN THE HOUSE | By Vote Number

633. **HR 5265. Muscular Dystrophy Research/Passage.** Pallone, D-N.J., motion to suspend the rules and pass the bill that would direct the Centers for Disease Control and Prevention to partner with leaders in the muscular dystrophy patient community to disseminate care options. It would direct the Health and Human Services Department to update patient condition data. Motion agreed to 418-2: R 193-2; D 225-0 (ND 171-0, SD 54-0). A two-thirds majority of those present and voting (280 in this case) is required for passage under suspension of the rules. Sept. 24, 2008.

634. **HR 7005. Alternative Minimum Tax Adjustment/Passage.** Neal, D-Mass., motion to suspend the rules and pass the bill that would provide a one-year adjustment to prevent more than 20 million taxpayers from paying the alternative minimum tax on 2008 income. It also would increase the refundable credit amount for individuals with long-term unused credits. Motion agreed to 393-30: R 193-0; D 200-30 (ND 154-19, SD 46-11). A two-thirds majority of those present and voting (282 in this case) is required for passage under suspension of the rules. A "yea" was a vote in support of the president's position. Sept. 24, 2008.

635. **HR 7006. Disaster Tax Relief/Passage.** Rangel, D-N.Y., motion to suspend the rules and pass the bill that would provide tax relief to people affected by any federally declared disaster after Jan. 1, 2007, and before Jan. 1, 2012. The bill would provide low-income housing tax credits to areas affected by federally declared disasters. Motion agreed to 419-4: R 193-0; D 226-4 (ND 173-1, SD 53-3). A two-thirds majority of those present and voting (282 in this case) is required for passage under suspension of the rules. Sept. 24, 2008.

636. **S 2606. Fire Administration Reauthorization/Passage.** Edwards, D-Md., motion to suspend the rules and pass the bill that would authorize $293 million from fiscal 2009 through 2012 for the U.S. Fire Administration. The agency could contract with certain nationally recognized organizations to provide training to fire-service personnel and increase authorized amounts available for such training. Motion agreed to 418-2: R 189-2; D 229-0 (ND 172-0, SD 57-0). A two-thirds majority of those present and voting (280 in this case) is required for passage under suspension of the rules. Sept. 24, 2008.

637. **H Res 1490. Tax Extensions/Previous Question.** Arcuri, D-N.Y., motion to order the previous question (thus ending debate and possibility of amendment) on adoption of the resolution that would waive through Sept. 27, 2008, the two-thirds majority vote requirement for same-day consideration of a rule for a bill that would extend expiring tax provisions and provide tax incentives for investment in renewable energy and energy conservation. Motion agreed to 227-198: R 4-191; D 223-7 (ND 168-4, SD 55-3). Sept. 25, 2008.

638. **H Res 1490. Tax Extensions/Same-Day Consideration.** Adoption of the resolution that would waive through Sept. 27, 2008, the two-thirds majority vote requirement for same-day consideration of a rule for a bill that would extend expiring tax provisions and provide tax incentives for investment in renewable energy and energy conservation. Adopted 222-198: R 0-193; D 222-5 (ND 168-3, SD 54-2). Sept. 25, 2008.

	633	634	635	636	637	638
ALABAMA						
1 Bonner	Y	Y	Y	Y	N	N
2 Everett	Y	Y	Y	Y	N	N
3 Rogers	Y	Y	Y	Y	N	N
4 Aderholt	Y	Y	Y	Y	N	N
5 Cramer	Y	Y	Y	Y	Y	Y
6 Bachus	Y	Y	Y	Y	N	?
7 Davis	Y	Y	Y	Y	Y	Y
ALASKA						
AL Young	Y	Y	Y	Y	N	N
ARIZONA						
1 Renzi	Y	?	?	?	N	N
2 Franks	Y	Y	Y	Y	N	N
3 Shadegg	Y	Y	Y	Y	N	N
4 Pastor	Y	Y	Y	Y	Y	Y
5 Mitchell	Y	Y	Y	Y	Y	N
6 Flake	N	Y	Y	N	N	N
7 Grijalva	Y	Y	Y	Y	Y	Y
8 Giffords	Y	Y	Y	Y	Y	Y
ARKANSAS						
1 Berry	Y	N	N	Y	Y	Y
2 Snyder	Y	Y	Y	Y	Y	Y
3 Boozman	Y	Y	Y	Y	N	N
4 Ross	Y	Y	Y	Y	Y	Y
CALIFORNIA						
1 Thompson	Y	Y	Y	Y	Y	Y
2 Herger	Y	Y	Y	Y	N	N
3 Lungren	Y	Y	Y	Y	N	N
4 Doolittle	Y	Y	Y	Y	N	N
5 Matsui	Y	Y	Y	Y	Y	Y
6 Woolsey	Y	Y	Y	Y	Y	Y
7 Miller, George	Y	Y	Y	Y	Y	Y
8 Pelosi						
9 Lee	Y	Y	Y	Y	Y	Y
10 Tauscher	Y	Y	Y	Y	Y	Y
11 McNerney	Y	Y	Y	Y	Y	Y
12 Speier	Y	Y	Y	Y	Y	Y
13 Stark	Y	N	Y	Y	Y	Y
14 Eshoo	Y	Y	Y	Y	Y	Y
15 Honda	Y	Y	Y	Y	Y	Y
16 Lofgren	Y	Y	Y	Y	Y	Y
17 Farr	Y	Y	Y	Y	Y	Y
18 Cardoza	Y	N	Y	Y	Y	Y
19 Radanovich	Y	Y	Y	Y	N	N
20 Costa	Y	N	Y	Y	Y	Y
21 Nunes	Y	Y	Y	Y	N	N
22 McCarthy	Y	Y	Y	Y	N	N
23 Capps	Y	Y	Y	Y	Y	Y
24 Gallegly	Y	Y	Y	Y	N	N
25 McKeon	Y	Y	Y	Y	N	N
26 Dreier	Y	Y	Y	Y	N	N
27 Sherman	Y	Y	Y	Y	Y	Y
28 Berman	Y	Y	Y	Y	Y	Y
29 Schiff	Y	Y	Y	Y	Y	Y
30 Waxman	Y	Y	Y	Y	Y	Y
31 Becerra	Y	N	Y	Y	Y	Y
32 Solis	Y	Y	Y	Y	Y	Y
33 Watson	?	Y	Y	Y	Y	Y
34 Roybal-Allard	Y	Y	Y	Y	Y	Y
35 Waters	Y	Y	Y	Y	Y	Y
36 Harman	Y	N	Y	Y	Y	Y
37 Richardson	Y	Y	Y	Y	Y	Y
38 Napolitano	Y	Y	Y	Y	Y	Y
39 Sánchez, Linda	Y	Y	Y	Y	Y	Y
40 Royce	Y	Y	Y	Y	N	N
41 Lewis	Y	Y	Y	Y	N	?
42 Miller, Gary	Y	Y	Y	Y	N	N
43 Baca	Y	Y	Y	Y	Y	Y
44 Calvert	Y	Y	Y	Y	N	N
45 Bono Mack	Y	Y	Y	Y	N	N
46 Rohrabacher	Y	Y	Y	Y	N	N
47 Sanchez, Loretta	Y	N	Y	Y	Y	Y
48 Campbell	Y	Y	Y	Y	N	N
49 Issa	Y	Y	Y	Y	N	N
50 Bilbray	Y	Y	Y	Y	N	N
51 Filner	Y	Y	Y	Y	Y	Y
52 Hunter	Y	Y	Y	Y	N	N
53 Davis	Y	Y	Y	Y	Y	Y

	633	634	635	636	637	638
COLORADO						
1 DeGette	Y	Y	Y	Y	Y	Y
2 Udall	Y	Y	Y	Y	?	?
3 Salazar	Y	N	Y	Y	Y	Y
4 Musgrave	Y	Y	Y	Y	N	N
5 Lamborn	Y	Y	Y	Y	N	N
6 Tancredo	Y	?	?	?	N	N
7 Perlmutter	Y	Y	Y	Y	Y	Y
CONNECTICUT						
1 Larson	Y	N	Y	Y	Y	Y
2 Courtney	Y	Y	Y	Y	Y	Y
3 DeLauro	Y	Y	Y	Y	Y	Y
4 Shays	Y	Y	Y	Y	Y	N
5 Murphy	Y	Y	Y	Y	Y	Y
DELAWARE						
AL Castle	Y	Y	Y	Y	N	N
FLORIDA						
1 Miller	Y	Y	Y	Y	?	?
2 Boyd	Y	N	N	Y	Y	Y
3 Brown	Y	Y	Y	Y	Y	Y
4 Crenshaw	Y	Y	Y	Y	N	N
5 Brown-Waite	Y	Y	Y	Y	N	N
6 Stearns	Y	Y	Y	Y	N	N
7 Mica	Y	Y	Y	Y	N	N
8 Keller	Y	Y	Y	Y	N	N
9 Bilirakis	Y	Y	Y	Y	N	N
10 Young	Y	Y	Y	Y	N	N
11 Castor	Y	Y	Y	Y	Y	Y
12 Putnam	Y	Y	Y	Y	N	N
13 Buchanan	Y	Y	Y	Y	N	N
14 Mack	Y	Y	Y	Y	N	N
15 Weldon	Y	?	?	?	N	N
16 Mahoney	?	Y	Y	Y	Y	Y
17 Meek	Y	Y	Y	Y	Y	Y
18 Ros-Lehtinen	Y	Y	Y	Y	Y	Y
19 Wexler	Y	Y	Y	Y	Y	Y
20 Wasserman Schultz	Y	Y	Y	Y	Y	Y
21 Diaz-Balart, L.	Y	Y	Y	Y	N	N
22 Klein	Y	Y	Y	Y	Y	Y
23 Hastings	Y	Y	Y	Y	Y	Y
24 Feeney	Y	Y	Y	Y	N	N
25 Diaz-Balart, M.	Y	Y	Y	Y	N	N
GEORGIA						
1 Kingston	Y	Y	Y	Y	N	N
2 Bishop	Y	Y	Y	Y	Y	Y
3 Westmoreland	Y	Y	Y	Y	N	N
4 Johnson	Y	Y	Y	Y	Y	Y
5 Lewis	Y	Y	Y	Y	Y	?
6 Price	Y	Y	Y	Y	N	N
7 Linder	Y	Y	Y	Y	N	N
8 Marshall	?	Y	Y	Y	Y	Y
9 Deal	Y	Y	Y	Y	N	N
10 Broun	?	Y	Y	Y	N	N
11 Gingrey	Y	Y	Y	Y	N	N
12 Barrow	Y	Y	Y	Y	Y	Y
13 Scott	Y	Y	Y	Y	Y	Y
HAWAII						
1 Abercrombie	Y	Y	Y	Y	Y	Y
2 Hirono	Y	Y	Y	Y	Y	Y
IDAHO						
1 Sali	Y	Y	Y	Y	N	N
2 Simpson	Y	Y	Y	Y	N	N
ILLINOIS						
1 Rush	Y	Y	Y	Y	Y	Y
2 Jackson	Y	Y	Y	Y	Y	Y
3 Lipinski	Y	Y	Y	Y	Y	Y
4 Gutierrez	Y	Y	Y	?	Y	Y
5 Emanuel	Y	Y	Y	Y	Y	Y
6 Roskam	Y	Y	Y	Y	N	N
7 Davis	Y	Y	Y	Y	?	Y
8 Bean	Y	Y	Y	Y	Y	Y
9 Schakowsky	+	Y	Y	Y	Y	Y
10 Kirk	Y	Y	Y	Y	N	N
11 Weller	Y	Y	Y	Y	N	N
12 Costello	Y	N	Y	Y	Y	Y
13 Biggert	Y	Y	Y	Y	N	N
14 Foster	Y	Y	Y	Y	Y	Y
15 Johnson	Y	Y	Y	Y	Y	N

KEY	Republicans	Democrats

Y Voted for (yea)	X Paired against	C Voted "present" to avoid possible conflict of interest
# Paired for	– Announced against	
+ Announced for	P Voted "present"	? Did not vote or otherwise make a position known
N Voted against (nay)		

ND Northern Democrats, SD Southern Democrats
Southern states: Ala., Ark., Fla., Ga., Ky., La., Miss., N.C., Okla., S.C., Tenn., Texas, Va.

H-214 2008 CQ ALMANAC | www.cq.com

	633	634	635	636	637	638
16 **Manzullo**	Y	Y	Y	Y	N	N
17 Hare	Y	Y	Y	Y	Y	Y
18 **LaHood**	Y	Y	Y	Y	N	N
19 **Shimkus**	Y	Y	Y	Y	N	N
INDIANA						
1 Visclosky	Y	Y	Y	Y	Y	Y
2 Donnelly	Y	Y	Y	Y	Y	Y
3 **Souder**	Y	Y	Y	Y	N	N
4 **Buyer**	Y	Y	Y	Y	N	N
5 **Burton**	Y	Y	Y	Y	N	N
6 **Pence**	Y	Y	Y	Y	N	N
7 Carson, A.	Y	Y	Y	Y	Y	Y
8 Ellsworth	Y	Y	Y	Y	Y	Y
9 Hill	Y	N	Y	Y	N	N
IOWA						
1 Braley	Y	Y	Y	Y	Y	Y
2 Loebsack	Y	Y	Y	Y	Y	Y
3 Boswell	Y	Y	Y	Y	Y	Y
4 **Latham**	Y	Y	Y	Y	N	N
5 **King**	Y	Y	Y	Y	N	N
KANSAS						
1 **Moran**	Y	Y	Y	Y	N	N
2 Boyda	Y	N	Y	Y	Y	Y
3 Moore	Y	Y	Y	Y	Y	Y
4 **Tiahrt**	Y	Y	Y	Y	N	–
KENTUCKY						
1 **Whitfield**	Y	Y	Y	?	N	N
2 **Lewis**	Y	Y	Y	Y	N	N
3 Yarmuth	Y	Y	Y	Y	Y	Y
4 **Davis**	Y	Y	Y	Y	N	N
5 **Rogers**	Y	Y	Y	Y	N	N
6 Chandler	Y	N	Y	Y	Y	Y
LOUISIANA						
1 **Scalise**	Y	Y	Y	Y	N	N
2 Jefferson	Y	Y	Y	Y	Y	Y
3 Melancon	Y	N	Y	Y	Y	Y
4 **McCrery**	Y	Y	Y	Y	?	N
5 **Alexander**	Y	Y	Y	Y	N	N
6 Cazayoux	Y	Y	Y	Y	N	N
7 **Boustany**	Y	Y	Y	Y	N	N
MAINE						
1 Allen	Y	Y	Y	Y	Y	Y
2 Michaud	Y	N	Y	Y	Y	Y
MARYLAND						
1 **Gilchrest**	Y	Y	Y	Y	N	N
2 Ruppersberger	Y	Y	Y	Y	Y	Y
3 Sarbanes	Y	Y	Y	Y	Y	Y
4 Edwards	Y	Y	Y	Y	Y	Y
5 Hoyer	Y	N	Y	Y	Y	Y
6 **Bartlett**	Y	Y	Y	Y	N	N
7 Cummings	Y	Y	Y	Y	Y	Y
8 Van Hollen	Y	Y	Y	Y	Y	Y
MASSACHUSETTS						
1 Olver	Y	Y	Y	Y	Y	Y
2 Neal	Y	Y	Y	Y	Y	Y
3 McGovern	Y	Y	Y	Y	Y	Y
4 Frank	?	Y	Y	Y	Y	Y
5 Tsongas	Y	Y	Y	Y	Y	Y
6 Tierney	Y	Y	Y	Y	Y	Y
7 Markey	Y	Y	Y	Y	Y	Y
8 Capuano	Y	Y	Y	Y	Y	Y
9 Lynch	Y	Y	Y	Y	Y	Y
10 Delahunt	Y	?	Y	Y	Y	Y
MICHIGAN						
1 Stupak	Y	Y	Y	Y	Y	Y
2 **Hoekstra**	Y	Y	Y	Y	N	N
3 **Ehlers**	Y	Y	Y	Y	N	N
4 **Camp**	Y	Y	Y	Y	N	N
5 Kildee	Y	Y	Y	Y	Y	Y
6 **Upton**	Y	Y	Y	Y	N	N
7 **Walberg**	Y	Y	Y	Y	N	N
8 **Rogers**	Y	Y	Y	Y	N	N
9 **Knollenberg**	Y	Y	Y	Y	N	N
10 **Miller**	Y	Y	Y	Y	N	N
11 **McCotter**	Y	Y	Y	Y	N	N
12 Levin	Y	Y	Y	Y	Y	Y
13 Kilpatrick	Y	Y	Y	Y	Y	Y
14 Conyers	Y	Y	Y	Y	Y	Y
15 Dingell	Y	Y	?	?	Y	Y
MINNESOTA						
1 Walz	Y	N	Y	Y	Y	Y
2 **Kline**	Y	Y	Y	Y	N	N
3 **Ramstad**	Y	Y	Y	Y	N	N
4 McCollum	Y	Y	Y	Y	Y	Y

	633	634	635	636	637	638
5 Ellison	Y	Y	Y	Y	Y	Y
6 **Bachmann**	Y	Y	Y	Y	N	N
7 Peterson	Y	N	Y	Y	Y	Y
8 Oberstar	Y	Y	Y	Y	Y	Y
MISSISSIPPI						
1 Childers	Y	Y	Y	Y	N	N
2 Thompson	Y	Y	Y	Y	Y	?
3 **Pickering**	Y	Y	Y	Y	N	N
4 Taylor	Y	N	Y	Y	Y	Y
MISSOURI						
1 Clay	Y	Y	Y	Y	Y	Y
2 **Akin**	Y	Y	Y	Y	N	N
3 Carnahan	Y	Y	Y	Y	Y	Y
4 Skelton	Y	Y	Y	Y	Y	Y
5 Cleaver	Y	Y	Y	Y	Y	Y
6 **Graves**	Y	Y	Y	Y	N	N
7 **Blunt**	Y	Y	Y	Y	N	N
8 **Emerson**	Y	Y	Y	Y	N	N
9 **Hulshof**	Y	Y	Y	Y	N	N
MONTANA						
AL **Rehberg**	Y	Y	Y	Y	N	N
NEBRASKA						
1 **Fortenberry**	Y	Y	Y	Y	N	N
2 **Terry**	Y	Y	Y	Y	N	N
3 **Smith**	Y	Y	Y	Y	N	N
NEVADA						
1 Berkley	Y	Y	Y	Y	Y	Y
2 **Heller**	Y	Y	Y	Y	N	N
3 **Porter**	Y	Y	Y	Y	N	N
NEW HAMPSHIRE						
1 Shea-Porter	Y	Y	Y	Y	Y	Y
2 Hodes	Y	Y	Y	Y	Y	Y
NEW JERSEY						
1 Andrews	Y	Y	Y	Y	Y	Y
2 **LoBiondo**	Y	Y	Y	Y	N	N
3 **Saxton**	Y	Y	Y	Y	N	N
4 **Smith**	Y	Y	Y	Y	N	N
5 **Garrett**	Y	Y	Y	Y	N	N
6 Pallone	Y	Y	Y	Y	Y	Y
7 **Ferguson**	Y	Y	Y	Y	N	N
8 Pascrell	Y	Y	Y	Y	Y	Y
9 Rothman	Y	Y	Y	Y	Y	Y
10 Payne	Y	Y	Y	Y	Y	Y
11 **Frelinghuysen**	Y	Y	Y	Y	N	N
12 Holt	Y	Y	Y	Y	Y	Y
13 Sires	Y	Y	Y	Y	Y	Y
NEW MEXICO						
1 **Wilson**	Y	Y	Y	Y	N	N
2 **Pearce**	Y	Y	Y	Y	N	N
3 Udall	Y	Y	Y	Y	Y	Y
NEW YORK						
1 Bishop	Y	Y	Y	Y	Y	Y
2 Israel	Y	Y	Y	Y	Y	Y
3 **King**	Y	Y	Y	Y	N	N
4 McCarthy	Y	Y	Y	Y	Y	Y
5 Ackerman	Y	Y	Y	Y	Y	Y
6 Meeks	Y	Y	Y	Y	Y	Y
7 Crowley	Y	Y	Y	Y	Y	Y
8 Nadler	Y	Y	Y	Y	Y	Y
9 Weiner	Y	Y	Y	Y	Y	Y
10 Towns	Y	Y	Y	Y	Y	Y
11 Clarke	Y	Y	Y	Y	Y	Y
12 Velázquez	Y	Y	Y	Y	Y	?
13 **Fossella**	Y	Y	Y	Y	N	N
14 Maloney	Y	Y	Y	Y	Y	Y
15 Rangel	Y	Y	Y	Y	Y	Y
16 Serrano	Y	Y	Y	Y	Y	Y
17 Engel	Y	Y	Y	Y	Y	Y
18 Lowey	Y	Y	Y	Y	Y	Y
19 Hall	Y	Y	Y	Y	Y	Y
20 Gillibrand	Y	Y	Y	Y	Y	Y
21 McNulty	Y	Y	Y	Y	Y	Y
22 Hinchey	Y	Y	Y	Y	Y	Y
23 **McHugh**	Y	Y	Y	Y	N	N
24 Arcuri	Y	Y	Y	Y	Y	Y
25 **Walsh**	?	Y	Y	Y	N	N
26 **Reynolds**	Y	Y	Y	Y	N	N
27 Higgins	Y	Y	Y	Y	Y	Y
28 Slaughter	Y	Y	Y	Y	Y	Y
29 **Kuhl**	Y	Y	Y	Y	N	N
NORTH CAROLINA						
1 Butterfield	Y	Y	?	Y	Y	Y
2 Etheridge	Y	Y	Y	Y	Y	Y
3 **Jones**	Y	Y	Y	Y	N	N
4 Price	Y	Y	Y	Y	Y	Y

	633	634	635	636	637	638
5 **Foxx**	Y	Y	Y	Y	N	N
6 **Coble**	Y	Y	Y	Y	N	N
7 McIntyre	Y	Y	Y	Y	Y	Y
8 **Hayes**	Y	Y	Y	Y	N	N
9 **Myrick**	Y	Y	Y	Y	N	N
10 **McHenry**	Y	Y	Y	Y	N	N
11 Shuler	?	?	?	?	?	?
12 Watt	Y	Y	Y	Y	Y	Y
13 Miller	?	Y	Y	Y	Y	Y
NORTH DAKOTA						
AL Pomeroy	Y	Y	Y	Y	Y	Y
OHIO						
1 **Chabot**	Y	Y	Y	Y	N	N
2 **Schmidt**	Y	Y	Y	Y	N	N
3 **Turner**	Y	Y	Y	Y	N	N
4 **Jordan**	Y	Y	Y	Y	N	N
5 **Latta**	Y	Y	Y	Y	N	N
6 Wilson	Y	Y	Y	Y	Y	Y
7 **Hobson**	Y	Y	Y	Y	N	N
8 **Boehner**	Y	Y	Y	Y	N	N
9 Kaptur	Y	Y	Y	Y	N	?
10 Kucinich	Y	Y	Y	Y	N	Y
11 Vacant						
12 **Tiberi**	Y	Y	Y	Y	N	N
13 Sutton	Y	Y	Y	Y	Y	Y
14 **LaTourette**	Y	Y	Y	Y	N	N
15 **Pryce**	Y	?	?	?	N	N
16 **Regula**	Y	Y	Y	Y	N	N
17 Ryan	Y	Y	Y	Y	Y	Y
18 Space	Y	Y	Y	Y	Y	Y
OKLAHOMA						
1 **Sullivan**	Y	Y	Y	Y	N	N
2 Boren	Y	Y	Y	Y	Y	Y
3 **Lucas**	Y	Y	Y	Y	N	N
4 **Cole**	Y	Y	Y	Y	N	N
5 **Fallin**	Y	Y	Y	Y	N	N
OREGON						
1 Wu	Y	Y	Y	Y	Y	Y
2 **Walden**	Y	Y	Y	Y	N	N
3 Blumenauer	Y	Y	Y	Y	Y	Y
4 DeFazio	Y	N	Y	?	N	N
5 Hooley	Y	Y	Y	Y	Y	?
PENNSYLVANIA						
1 Brady	Y	Y	Y	Y	Y	Y
2 Fattah	Y	Y	Y	Y	Y	Y
3 **English**	Y	Y	Y	Y	N	N
4 Altmire	Y	Y	Y	Y	Y	Y
5 **Peterson**	Y	Y	Y	Y	N	N
6 **Gerlach**	Y	Y	Y	Y	N	N
7 Sestak	Y	Y	Y	Y	Y	Y
8 Murphy, P.	Y	Y	Y	Y	Y	Y
9 **Shuster**	Y	Y	Y	Y	N	N
10 Carney	Y	Y	Y	Y	Y	Y
11 Kanjorski	Y	Y	Y	Y	Y	Y
12 Murtha	Y	Y	Y	Y	Y	Y
13 Schwartz	Y	Y	Y	Y	Y	Y
14 Doyle	Y	Y	Y	Y	Y	Y
15 **Dent**	Y	Y	Y	Y	N	N
16 **Pitts**	Y	Y	Y	Y	N	N
17 Holden	Y	Y	Y	Y	Y	Y
18 **Murphy, T.**	Y	Y	Y	Y	N	N
19 **Platts**	Y	Y	Y	Y	N	N
RHODE ISLAND						
1 Kennedy	Y	Y	Y	Y	Y	Y
2 Langevin	Y	Y	Y	Y	Y	Y
SOUTH CAROLINA						
1 **Brown**	Y	Y	Y	Y	N	N
2 **Wilson**	Y	Y	Y	Y	N	N
3 **Barrett**	Y	Y	Y	Y	N	N
4 **Inglis**	Y	Y	Y	Y	N	N
5 Spratt	Y	Y	Y	Y	Y	Y
6 Clyburn	Y	Y	Y	Y	Y	Y
SOUTH DAKOTA						
AL Herseth Sandlin	Y	?	Y	Y	Y	Y
TENNESSEE						
1 **Davis, D.**	Y	Y	Y	Y	?	?
2 **Duncan**	Y	Y	Y	Y	N	N
3 **Wamp**	Y	Y	Y	Y	N	N
4 Davis, L.	Y	N	Y	Y	Y	Y
5 Cooper	Y	N	N	Y	Y	Y
6 Gordon	Y	Y	Y	Y	Y	Y
7 **Blackburn**	Y	Y	Y	Y	N	N
8 Tanner	Y	N	Y	Y	Y	Y
9 Cohen	Y	Y	Y	Y	Y	Y

	633	634	635	636	637	638
TEXAS						
1 **Gohmert**	Y	Y	Y	Y	N	N
2 **Poe**	Y	Y	Y	Y	N	N
3 **Johnson, S.**	Y	Y	Y	Y	N	N
4 **Hall**	Y	Y	Y	Y	N	N
5 **Hensarling**	Y	Y	Y	Y	N	N
6 **Barton**	Y	Y	Y	Y	N	N
7 **Culberson**	Y	Y	Y	Y	N	N
8 **Brady**	Y	Y	Y	Y	N	N
9 Green, A.	Y	Y	Y	Y	Y	Y
10 **McCaul**	Y	Y	Y	Y	N	N
11 **Conaway**	Y	Y	Y	Y	N	N
12 **Granger**	Y	Y	Y	Y	N	N
13 **Thornberry**	Y	Y	Y	Y	N	N
14 **Paul**	N	Y	Y	N	N	N
15 Hinojosa	Y	Y	Y	Y	Y	Y
16 Reyes	Y	Y	Y	Y	Y	Y
17 Edwards	Y	Y	Y	Y	Y	Y
18 Jackson Lee	Y	Y	Y	Y	Y	Y
19 **Neugebauer**	Y	Y	Y	Y	N	N
20 Gonzalez	Y	Y	Y	Y	Y	Y
21 **Smith**	Y	Y	Y	Y	N	N
22 Lampson	Y	Y	Y	Y	N	Y
23 Rodriguez	Y	Y	Y	Y	Y	Y
24 **Marchant**	Y	Y	Y	?	N	N
25 Doggett	Y	N	Y	Y	Y	Y
26 **Burgess**	Y	Y	Y	Y	N	N
27 Ortiz	Y	Y	Y	Y	Y	Y
28 Cuellar	Y	N	Y	Y	Y	Y
29 Green, G.	Y	Y	Y	Y	Y	Y
30 Johnson, E.	?	Y	Y	Y	Y	Y
31 **Carter**	Y	Y	Y	Y	N	N
32 **Sessions**	Y	Y	Y	Y	N	N
UTAH						
1 **Bishop**	?	?	?	?	N	N
2 Matheson	Y	Y	Y	Y	Y	Y
3 **Cannon**	Y	Y	Y	Y	N	N
VERMONT						
AL Welch	Y	N	Y	Y	Y	Y
VIRGINIA						
1 **Wittman**	Y	Y	Y	Y	N	N
2 **Drake**	Y	Y	Y	Y	N	N
3 Scott	Y	N	Y	Y	Y	Y
4 **Forbes**	Y	Y	Y	Y	N	N
5 **Goode**	Y	Y	Y	Y	N	N
6 **Goodlatte**	Y	Y	Y	Y	N	N
7 **Cantor**	Y	Y	Y	Y	N	N
8 Moran	Y	?	?	?	Y	Y
9 Boucher	Y	Y	Y	Y	Y	Y
10 **Wolf**	Y	Y	Y	Y	N	N
11 **Davis**	Y	Y	Y	Y	N	N
WASHINGTON						
1 Inslee	Y	Y	Y	Y	Y	Y
2 Larsen	?	Y	Y	Y	Y	Y
3 Baird	Y	N	Y	Y	Y	Y
4 **Hastings**	Y	Y	Y	Y	N	N
5 **McMorris Rodgers**	Y	Y	Y	Y	N	N
6 Dicks	Y	Y	Y	Y	Y	Y
7 McDermott	Y	Y	Y	Y	Y	Y
8 **Reichert**	Y	Y	Y	Y	Y	N
9 Smith	Y	N	N	Y	Y	Y
WEST VIRGINIA						
1 Mollohan	Y	Y	Y	Y	Y	Y
2 **Capito**	Y	Y	Y	Y	N	N
3 Rahall	Y	Y	Y	Y	Y	Y
WISCONSIN						
1 **Ryan**	Y	Y	Y	Y	N	N
2 Baldwin	Y	Y	Y	Y	Y	Y
3 Kind	Y	Y	Y	Y	Y	Y
4 Moore	Y	Y	Y	Y	+	Y
5 **Sensenbrenner**	Y	Y	Y	Y	N	N
6 **Petri**	Y	Y	Y	Y	N	N
7 Obey	Y	Y	Y	Y	Y	Y
8 Kagen	Y	Y	Y	Y	Y	Y
WYOMING						
AL **Cubin**	?	?	?	?	?	?
DELEGATES						
Faleomavaega (A.S.)						
Norton (D.C.)						
Bordallo (Guam)						
Fortuño (P.R.)						
Christensen (V.I.)						

IN THE HOUSE | By Vote Number

639. **HR 758. Breast Surgery Insurance Coverage/Passage.** Pallone, D-N.J., motion to suspend the rules and pass the bill that would bar insurance companies from limiting hospital stays to fewer than 48 hours for a patient undergoing a mastectomy or breast surgery such as a lumpectomy and fewer than 24 hours for those undergoing a lymph node dissection. The bill would prohibit insurers from providing incentives to physicians for limiting a patient's stay or not referring the patient to secondary consultation after surgery. Motion agreed to 421-2: R 190-2; D 231-0 (ND 173-0, SD 58-0). A two-thirds majority of those present and voting (282 in this case) is required for passage under suspension of the rules. Sept. 25, 2008.

640. **HR 7060. Tax Extensions/Previous Question.** Arcuri, D-N.Y., motion to order the previous question (thus ending debate and possibility of amendment) on adoption of the rule (H Res 1501) to provide for House floor consideration of the bill that would extend dozens of expiring tax provisions and provide tax incentives for investment in renewable energy and energy conservation. Motion agreed to 223-200: R 0-194; D 223-6 (ND 167-4, SD 56-2). (Subsequently, proceedings on roll call vote 640 were vacated by unanimous consent.) Sept. 25, 2008.

641. **H Con Res 255. Preservation of Sites/Adoption.** Crowley, D-N.Y., motion to suspend the rules and adopt the concurrent resolution that would express support for the U.S. Commission for the Preservation of America's Heritage Abroad and the European countries that work to preserve sacred historical sites and declare that the Lithuanian government must guarantee the permanent preservation of the Jewish cemetery in the Snipiskes area of Vilnius to strengthen its relationship with the United States. Motion agreed to 414-1: R 189-1; D 225-0 (ND 169-0, SD 56-0). A two-thirds majority of those present and voting (277 in this case) is required for adoption under suspension of the rules. Sept. 25, 2008.

642. **HR 1014. New Drug Application Data/Passage.** Pallone, D-N.J., motion to suspend the rules and pass the bill that would require pharmaceutical companies that submit a new drug application to include data on the drug's safety and effectiveness with respect to age, gender and "racial subgroup." Motion agreed to 418-4: R 189-4; D 229-0 (ND 172-0, SD 57-0). A two-thirds majority of those present and voting (282 in this case) is required for passage under suspension of the rules. Sept. 25, 2008.

643. **HR 6950. Organ Donation Medal/Passage.** Moore, D-Wis., motion to suspend the rules and pass the bill that would direct the Treasury Department to design and produce a congressional commemorative medal for the Health and Human Services Department to award to organ donors or to a surviving family member. Motion agreed to 420-1: R 190-1; D 230-0 (ND 173-0, SD 57-0). A two-thirds majority of those present and voting (281 in this case) is required for passage under suspension of the rules. Sept. 25, 2008.

644. **H Res 1421. Beirut Bombing Victims/Adoption.** Boyda, D-Kan., motion to suspend the rules and adopt the resolution that would honor the service and sacrifice of the victims of the October 1983 terrorist bombing of the U.S. Marine Corps Barracks in Beirut, Lebanon, and of the U.S. troops who died in Beirut from 1982 to 1984. Motion agreed to 414-0: R 189-0; D 225-0 (ND 168-0, SD 57-0). A two-thirds majority of those present and voting (276 in this case) is required for adoption under suspension of the rules. Sept. 25, 2008.

	639	640	641	642	643	644
ALABAMA						
1 Bonner	Y	N	Y	Y	Y	Y
2 Everett	Y	N	?	Y	Y	Y
3 Rogers	Y	N	Y	Y	Y	Y
4 Aderholt	Y	N	Y	Y	Y	Y
5 Cramer	Y	Y	?	Y	Y	Y
6 Bachus	Y	?	+	Y	Y	Y
7 Davis	Y	Y	Y	Y	Y	Y
ALASKA						
AL Young	Y	N	Y	Y	Y	Y
ARIZONA						
1 Renzi	Y	N	Y	Y	Y	Y
2 Franks	Y	N	Y	Y	Y	Y
3 Shadegg	Y	N	Y	Y	Y	Y
4 Pastor	Y	Y	Y	Y	Y	Y
5 Mitchell	Y	Y	Y	Y	Y	Y
6 Flake	N	N	Y	N	Y	Y
7 Grijalva	Y	Y	Y	Y	Y	Y
8 Giffords	Y	Y	Y	Y	Y	Y
ARKANSAS						
1 Berry	Y	Y	Y	Y	Y	Y
2 Snyder	Y	Y	Y	Y	Y	Y
3 Boozman	Y	N	Y	Y	Y	Y
4 Ross	Y	Y	Y	Y	Y	Y
CALIFORNIA						
1 Thompson	Y	Y	Y	Y	Y	Y
2 Herger	Y	N	Y	Y	Y	Y
3 Lungren	Y	N	Y	Y	Y	Y
4 Doolittle	Y	N	Y	Y	Y	Y
5 Matsui	Y	Y	Y	Y	Y	Y
6 Woolsey	Y	Y	Y	Y	Y	Y
7 Miller, George	Y	Y	Y	Y	Y	Y
8 Pelosi						
9 Lee	Y	Y	Y	Y	Y	Y
10 Tauscher	Y	Y	Y	Y	Y	Y
11 McNerney	Y	Y	Y	Y	Y	Y
12 Speier	Y	Y	Y	Y	Y	?
13 Stark	Y	Y	Y	Y	Y	?
14 Eshoo	Y	Y	Y	Y	Y	Y
15 Honda	Y	Y	Y	Y	Y	Y
16 Lofgren	Y	Y	Y	Y	Y	Y
17 Farr	Y	Y	Y	Y	Y	Y
18 Cardoza	Y	Y	Y	Y	Y	Y
19 Radanovich	Y	N	Y	Y	Y	Y
20 Costa	Y	Y	Y	Y	Y	Y
21 Nunes	Y	N	Y	Y	Y	Y
22 McCarthy	Y	N	Y	Y	Y	Y
23 Capps	Y	Y	Y	Y	Y	?
24 Gallegly	Y	N	Y	Y	Y	Y
25 McKeon	Y	N	Y	Y	Y	Y
26 Dreier	Y	N	Y	Y	Y	Y
27 Sherman	Y	Y	Y	Y	Y	Y
28 Berman	Y	Y	Y	Y	Y	Y
29 Schiff	Y	Y	Y	Y	Y	Y
30 Waxman	Y	Y	Y	Y	Y	Y
31 Becerra	Y	Y	Y	Y	Y	Y
32 Solis	Y	Y	Y	Y	Y	Y
33 Watson	Y	Y	Y	Y	Y	Y
34 Roybal-Allard	Y	Y	Y	Y	Y	Y
35 Waters	Y	?	Y	Y	Y	Y
36 Harman	Y	Y	Y	Y	Y	Y
37 Richardson	Y	Y	Y	Y	Y	Y
38 Napolitano	Y	Y	?	Y	Y	Y
39 Sánchez, Linda	Y	Y	Y	Y	Y	Y
40 Royce	Y	N	Y	Y	Y	Y
41 Lewis	Y	N	Y	Y	Y	Y
42 Miller, Gary	Y	N	Y	Y	Y	Y
43 Baca	Y	Y	Y	Y	Y	Y
44 Calvert	Y	N	Y	Y	Y	Y
45 Bono Mack	Y	N	Y	Y	Y	Y
46 Rohrabacher	Y	N	Y	Y	Y	Y
47 Sanchez, Loretta	Y	Y	Y	Y	Y	Y
48 Campbell	?	N	Y	Y	Y	Y
49 Issa	Y	N	Y	Y	Y	Y
50 Bilbray	Y	N	Y	Y	Y	Y
51 Filner	Y	Y	Y	Y	Y	Y
52 Hunter	?	N	Y	Y	Y	Y
53 Davis	Y	Y	Y	Y	Y	Y

	639	640	641	642	643	644
COLORADO						
1 DeGette	Y	Y	Y	Y	Y	Y
2 Udall	?	?	?	Y	Y	Y
3 Salazar	Y	Y	Y	Y	Y	Y
4 Musgrave	Y	N	Y	Y	Y	Y
5 Lamborn	Y	N	Y	Y	Y	Y
6 Tancredo	Y	N	Y	Y	Y	Y
7 Perlmutter	Y	Y	Y	Y	Y	Y
CONNECTICUT						
1 Larson	Y	Y	Y	Y	Y	Y
2 Courtney	Y	Y	Y	Y	Y	Y
3 DeLauro	Y	Y	Y	Y	Y	Y
4 Shays	Y	N	Y	Y	Y	Y
5 Murphy	Y	Y	Y	Y	Y	Y
DELAWARE						
AL Castle	Y	N	Y	Y	Y	Y
FLORIDA						
1 Miller	?	?	?	?	?	?
2 Boyd	Y	Y	Y	Y	Y	Y
3 Brown	Y	Y	Y	+	+	Y
4 Crenshaw	Y	N	Y	Y	Y	Y
5 Brown-Waite	Y	N	Y	Y	Y	Y
6 Stearns	Y	N	Y	Y	Y	Y
7 Mica	Y	N	Y	Y	Y	Y
8 Keller	Y	N	Y	Y	Y	Y
9 Bilirakis	Y	N	Y	Y	Y	Y
10 Young	Y	N	Y	Y	Y	Y
11 Castor	Y	Y	Y	Y	Y	Y
12 Putnam	Y	N	Y	Y	Y	Y
13 Buchanan	Y	N	Y	Y	Y	Y
14 Mack	Y	N	Y	Y	Y	Y
15 Weldon	Y	?	Y	Y	Y	Y
16 Mahoney	Y	Y	Y	Y	Y	Y
17 Meek	Y	Y	Y	Y	Y	Y
18 Ros-Lehtinen	Y	N	Y	Y	Y	Y
19 Wexler	Y	Y	Y	Y	Y	Y
20 Wasserman Schultz	Y	Y	Y	Y	Y	Y
21 Diaz-Balart, L.	Y	N	Y	Y	Y	Y
22 Klein	Y	Y	Y	Y	Y	?
23 Hastings	Y	Y	?	Y	Y	Y
24 Feeney	Y	N	Y	Y	Y	Y
25 Diaz-Balart, M.	Y	N	Y	Y	Y	Y
GEORGIA						
1 Kingston	Y	N	Y	Y	Y	Y
2 Bishop	Y	Y	Y	Y	Y	Y
3 Westmoreland	Y	N	Y	Y	Y	Y
4 Johnson	Y	Y	Y	Y	Y	Y
5 Lewis	Y	Y	Y	Y	Y	Y
6 Price	Y	N	Y	Y	Y	Y
7 Linder	Y	N	Y	Y	Y	Y
8 Marshall	Y	Y	Y	Y	Y	Y
9 Deal	Y	N	Y	Y	Y	Y
10 Broun	?	N	Y	N	Y	Y
11 Gingrey	Y	N	Y	N	Y	?
12 Barrow	Y	Y	Y	Y	Y	Y
13 Scott	Y	Y	Y	Y	Y	Y
HAWAII						
1 Abercrombie	Y	Y	Y	?	Y	Y
2 Hirono	Y	Y	Y	Y	Y	Y
IDAHO						
1 Sali	Y	N	Y	Y	Y	Y
2 Simpson	Y	N	Y	?	?	?
ILLINOIS						
1 Rush	Y	Y	Y	Y	Y	Y
2 Jackson	Y	Y	Y	Y	Y	Y
3 Lipinski	Y	Y	Y	Y	Y	Y
4 Gutierrez	Y	Y	Y	Y	Y	?
5 Emanuel	Y	Y	Y	Y	Y	Y
6 Roskam	Y	N	Y	Y	Y	Y
7 Davis	Y	Y	Y	Y	Y	Y
8 Bean	Y	Y	Y	Y	Y	Y
9 Schakowsky	Y	Y	Y	Y	Y	Y
10 Kirk	?	N	Y	Y	Y	Y
11 Weller	Y	N	Y	Y	Y	Y
12 Costello	Y	Y	Y	Y	Y	Y
13 Biggert	Y	N	Y	Y	Y	Y
14 Foster	Y	Y	Y	Y	Y	Y
15 Johnson	Y	N	Y	Y	Y	Y

KEY	Republicans	Democrats		
Y	Voted for (yea)	X Paired against		C Voted "present" to avoid possible conflict of interest
#	Paired for	– Announced against		
+	Announced for	P Voted "present"		? Did not vote or otherwise make a position known
N	Voted against (nay)			

ND Northern Democrats, SD Southern Democrats
Southern states: Ala., Ark., Fla., Ga., Ky., La., Miss., N.C., Okla., S.C., Tenn., Texas, Va.

	639	640	641	642	643	644
16 **Manzullo**	Y	N	Y	Y	Y	Y
17 Hare	Y	Y	Y	Y	Y	Y
18 **LaHood**	Y	N	Y	Y	Y	Y
19 **Shimkus**	Y	N	Y	Y	Y	Y
INDIANA						
1 Visclosky	Y	Y	Y	Y	Y	Y
2 Donnelly	Y	Y	Y	Y	Y	Y
3 **Souder**	Y	N	?	Y	Y	Y
4 **Buyer**	Y	N	Y	Y	?	Y
5 **Burton**	Y	N	Y	Y	Y	Y
6 **Pence**	Y	N	Y	Y	Y	Y
7 Carson, A.	Y	Y	Y	Y	Y	Y
8 Ellsworth	Y	Y	Y	Y	Y	Y
9 Hill	Y	N	Y	Y	Y	Y
IOWA						
1 Braley	Y	Y	Y	Y	Y	Y
2 Loebsack	Y	Y	Y	Y	Y	Y
3 Boswell	Y	Y	Y	Y	Y	Y
4 **Latham**	Y	N	Y	Y	Y	Y
5 **King**	Y	N	Y	Y	Y	Y
KANSAS						
1 **Moran**	Y	N	Y	Y	Y	Y
2 Boyda	Y	Y	Y	Y	Y	Y
3 Moore	Y	Y	Y	Y	Y	Y
4 **Tiahrt**	Y	N	Y	Y	Y	Y
KENTUCKY						
1 **Whitfield**	Y	N	?	Y	Y	Y
2 **Lewis**	Y	N	Y	?	?	?
3 Yarmuth	Y	Y	Y	Y	Y	Y
4 **Davis**	Y	N	Y	Y	Y	Y
5 **Rogers**	Y	N	Y	Y	Y	Y
6 Chandler	Y	Y	Y	Y	Y	Y
LOUISIANA						
1 **Scalise**	Y	N	Y	Y	Y	Y
2 Jefferson	Y	Y	Y	Y	Y	Y
3 Melancon	Y	Y	Y	Y	Y	Y
4 **McCrery**	Y	N	Y	Y	Y	Y
5 **Alexander**	Y	N	Y	Y	Y	Y
6 Cazayoux	Y	N	Y	Y	Y	Y
7 **Boustany**	Y	N	Y	Y	Y	Y
MAINE						
1 Allen	Y	Y	Y	Y	Y	Y
2 Michaud	Y	Y	Y	Y	Y	Y
MARYLAND						
1 **Gilchrest**	Y	N	Y	Y	Y	Y
2 Ruppersberger	Y	Y	Y	Y	Y	Y
3 Sarbanes	Y	Y	Y	Y	Y	Y
4 Edwards	Y	Y	Y	+	+	Y
5 Hoyer	Y	Y	?	Y	Y	Y
6 **Bartlett**	Y	N	Y	Y	Y	Y
7 Cummings	Y	Y	Y	Y	Y	Y
8 Van Hollen	Y	Y	Y	Y	Y	Y
MASSACHUSETTS						
1 Olver	Y	Y	Y	Y	Y	Y
2 Neal	Y	Y	Y	Y	Y	Y
3 McGovern	Y	Y	Y	Y	Y	Y
4 Frank	Y	Y	?	?	?	Y
5 Tsongas	Y	Y	Y	Y	Y	Y
6 Tierney	Y	Y	Y	Y	Y	?
7 Markey	Y	Y	Y	Y	Y	Y
8 Capuano	Y	Y	Y	Y	Y	Y
9 Lynch	Y	Y	Y	Y	Y	Y
10 Delahunt	Y	Y	Y	Y	Y	Y
MICHIGAN						
1 Stupak	Y	Y	Y	Y	Y	Y
2 **Hoekstra**	Y	N	Y	Y	Y	Y
3 **Ehlers**	Y	N	Y	Y	Y	Y
4 **Camp**	Y	N	Y	Y	Y	Y
5 Kildee	Y	Y	Y	Y	Y	Y
6 **Upton**	Y	N	Y	Y	Y	Y
7 **Walberg**	Y	N	Y	Y	Y	Y
8 **Rogers**	Y	N	Y	Y	Y	Y
9 **Knollenberg**	Y	N	Y	Y	Y	Y
10 **Miller**	Y	N	Y	Y	Y	Y
11 **McCotter**	Y	N	Y	Y	Y	Y
12 Levin	Y	Y	Y	Y	Y	Y
13 Kilpatrick	Y	Y	Y	Y	Y	Y
14 Conyers	Y	?	?	Y	Y	Y
15 Dingell	Y	Y	Y	Y	Y	Y
MINNESOTA						
1 Walz	Y	Y	Y	Y	Y	Y
2 **Kline**	Y	N	Y	Y	Y	Y
3 **Ramstad**	Y	N	Y	Y	Y	Y
4 McCollum	Y	Y	Y	Y	Y	Y

	639	640	641	642	643	644
5 Ellison	Y	Y	Y	Y	Y	Y
6 **Bachmann**	Y	N	Y	Y	Y	Y
7 Peterson	Y	Y	Y	Y	Y	Y
8 Oberstar	Y	Y	Y	Y	Y	Y
MISSISSIPPI						
1 Childers	Y	N	Y	Y	Y	Y
2 Thompson	Y	Y	Y	Y	Y	Y
3 **Pickering**	Y	N	Y	Y	Y	Y
4 Taylor	Y	Y	Y	Y	Y	Y
MISSOURI						
1 Clay	Y	Y	Y	Y	Y	Y
2 **Akin**	Y	N	Y	Y	Y	Y
3 Carnahan	Y	Y	Y	Y	Y	Y
4 Skelton	Y	Y	Y	Y	Y	Y
5 Cleaver	Y	Y	Y	Y	Y	Y
6 **Graves**	Y	N	Y	Y	Y	Y
7 **Blunt**	Y	N	Y	Y	Y	Y
8 **Emerson**	Y	N	Y	Y	Y	Y
9 **Hulshof**	Y	N	Y	Y	Y	Y
MONTANA						
AL **Rehberg**	Y	N	Y	Y	Y	Y
NEBRASKA						
1 **Fortenberry**	Y	N	Y	Y	Y	Y
2 **Terry**	Y	N	Y	Y	Y	Y
3 **Smith**	Y	N	Y	Y	Y	Y
NEVADA						
1 Berkley	Y	Y	Y	Y	Y	Y
2 **Heller**	Y	N	Y	Y	Y	Y
3 **Porter**	Y	N	Y	Y	Y	Y
NEW HAMPSHIRE						
1 Shea-Porter	Y	Y	Y	Y	Y	Y
2 Hodes	Y	Y	Y	Y	Y	Y
NEW JERSEY						
1 Andrews	Y	Y	Y	Y	Y	Y
2 **LoBiondo**	Y	N	Y	Y	Y	Y
3 **Saxton**	Y	N	Y	Y	Y	Y
4 **Smith**	Y	N	Y	Y	Y	Y
5 **Garrett**	Y	N	Y	Y	Y	Y
6 Pallone	Y	Y	Y	Y	Y	Y
7 **Ferguson**	Y	N	Y	Y	Y	Y
8 Pascrell	Y	Y	Y	Y	Y	Y
9 Rothman	Y	Y	Y	Y	Y	Y
10 Payne	Y	Y	Y	Y	Y	Y
11 **Frelinghuysen**	Y	N	Y	Y	Y	Y
12 Holt	Y	Y	Y	Y	Y	Y
13 Sires	Y	Y	Y	Y	Y	Y
NEW MEXICO						
1 **Wilson**	Y	N	Y	Y	Y	Y
2 **Pearce**	Y	N	Y	Y	Y	Y
3 Udall	Y	Y	Y	Y	Y	Y
NEW YORK						
1 Bishop	Y	Y	Y	Y	Y	Y
2 Israel	Y	?	?	Y	Y	Y
3 **King**	Y	N	Y	Y	Y	Y
4 McCarthy	Y	Y	Y	Y	Y	Y
5 Ackerman	Y	Y	Y	Y	Y	Y
6 Meeks	Y	Y	Y	Y	Y	Y
7 Crowley	Y	Y	Y	Y	Y	Y
8 Nadler	Y	Y	Y	Y	Y	Y
9 Weiner	Y	Y	Y	Y	Y	Y
10 Towns	Y	Y	Y	Y	Y	Y
11 Clarke	Y	Y	Y	Y	Y	Y
12 Velázquez	Y	Y	Y	Y	Y	?
13 **Fossella**	Y	N	Y	Y	Y	Y
14 Maloney	Y	Y	Y	Y	Y	Y
15 Rangel	?	Y	Y	Y	Y	Y
16 Serrano	Y	Y	Y	Y	Y	Y
17 Engel	Y	Y	Y	Y	Y	Y
18 Lowey	Y	Y	Y	Y	Y	Y
19 Hall	Y	Y	Y	Y	Y	Y
20 Gillibrand	Y	Y	Y	Y	Y	Y
21 McNulty	Y	Y	Y	Y	Y	Y
22 Hinchey	Y	Y	Y	Y	Y	Y
23 **McHugh**	Y	N	Y	Y	Y	Y
24 Arcuri	Y	Y	Y	Y	Y	Y
25 **Walsh**	Y	N	Y	Y	?	?
26 **Reynolds**	Y	N	Y	Y	Y	Y
27 Higgins	Y	Y	Y	Y	Y	Y
28 Slaughter	Y	Y	Y	Y	Y	Y
29 **Kuhl**	Y	N	Y	Y	Y	Y
NORTH CAROLINA						
1 Butterfield	Y	Y	Y	Y	Y	Y
2 Etheridge	Y	Y	Y	Y	Y	Y
3 **Jones**	Y	N	Y	Y	Y	Y
4 Price	Y	Y	Y	Y	Y	Y

	639	640	641	642	643	644
5 **Foxx**	Y	N	Y	Y	Y	Y
6 **Coble**	Y	N	Y	Y	Y	Y
7 McIntyre	Y	Y	Y	Y	Y	Y
8 **Hayes**	Y	N	Y	Y	Y	Y
9 **Myrick**	Y	N	Y	Y	Y	Y
10 **McHenry**	Y	N	Y	Y	Y	Y
11 Shuler	?	?	?	?	?	?
12 Watt	Y	Y	Y	Y	Y	Y
13 Miller	Y	Y	Y	Y	Y	Y
NORTH DAKOTA						
AL Pomeroy	Y	Y	Y	Y	Y	Y
OHIO						
1 **Chabot**	Y	N	Y	Y	Y	Y
2 **Schmidt**	Y	N	Y	Y	Y	Y
3 **Turner**	Y	N	Y	Y	Y	Y
4 **Jordan**	Y	N	Y	Y	Y	Y
5 **Latta**	Y	N	Y	Y	Y	Y
6 Wilson	Y	Y	Y	Y	Y	Y
7 **Hobson**	Y	N	Y	Y	Y	?
8 **Boehner**	Y	N	?	Y	Y	Y
9 Kaptur	Y	Y	Y	Y	Y	Y
10 Kucinich	Y	Y	Y	Y	Y	Y
11 Vacant						
12 **Tiberi**	Y	N	Y	Y	Y	Y
13 Sutton	Y	Y	Y	Y	Y	Y
14 **LaTourette**	Y	N	Y	Y	Y	Y
15 **Pryce**	Y	N	Y	Y	Y	Y
16 **Regula**	Y	N	Y	Y	Y	Y
17 Ryan	Y	Y	Y	Y	Y	Y
18 Space	Y	Y	Y	Y	Y	Y
OKLAHOMA						
1 **Sullivan**	Y	N	Y	Y	Y	Y
2 Boren	Y	Y	Y	Y	Y	Y
3 **Lucas**	Y	N	Y	Y	Y	Y
4 **Cole**	Y	N	Y	Y	Y	Y
5 **Fallin**	Y	N	Y	Y	Y	Y
OREGON						
1 Wu	Y	N	Y	Y	Y	Y
2 **Walden**	Y	N	?	Y	Y	Y
3 Blumenauer	Y	Y	Y	Y	Y	Y
4 DeFazio	Y	N	Y	Y	Y	Y
5 Hooley	Y	Y	Y	Y	Y	Y
PENNSYLVANIA						
1 Brady	Y	Y	Y	Y	Y	Y
2 Fattah	Y	Y	Y	Y	Y	Y
3 **English**	Y	N	Y	Y	Y	Y
4 Altmire	Y	Y	Y	Y	Y	Y
5 **Peterson**	Y	N	Y	Y	Y	Y
6 **Gerlach**	Y	N	Y	Y	Y	Y
7 Sestak	Y	Y	Y	Y	Y	Y
8 Murphy, P.	Y	Y	Y	Y	Y	Y
9 **Shuster**	Y	N	Y	Y	Y	Y
10 Carney	Y	Y	Y	Y	Y	Y
11 Kanjorski	Y	Y	Y	Y	Y	Y
12 Murtha	Y	Y	Y	Y	Y	Y
13 Schwartz	Y	Y	Y	Y	Y	Y
14 Doyle	Y	Y	Y	Y	Y	Y
15 **Dent**	Y	N	Y	Y	Y	Y
16 **Pitts**	Y	N	Y	Y	Y	Y
17 Holden	Y	Y	Y	Y	Y	Y
18 **Murphy, T.**	Y	N	Y	Y	Y	Y
19 **Platts**	Y	N	Y	Y	Y	Y
RHODE ISLAND						
1 Kennedy	Y	Y	Y	Y	Y	Y
2 Langevin	Y	Y	Y	Y	Y	Y
SOUTH CAROLINA						
1 **Brown**	Y	N	Y	Y	Y	Y
2 **Wilson**	Y	N	Y	Y	Y	Y
3 **Barrett**	Y	N	Y	Y	Y	Y
4 **Inglis**	Y	N	Y	Y	Y	Y
5 Spratt	Y	Y	Y	Y	Y	Y
6 Clyburn	Y	Y	Y	Y	Y	Y
SOUTH DAKOTA						
AL Herseth Sandlin	Y	Y	Y	Y	Y	Y
TENNESSEE						
1 **Davis, D.**	?	?	?	?	?	?
2 **Duncan**	Y	N	Y	Y	Y	Y
3 **Wamp**	Y	N	Y	Y	Y	Y
4 Davis, L.	Y	Y	Y	Y	Y	Y
5 Cooper	Y	Y	Y	Y	Y	Y
6 Gordon	Y	Y	Y	Y	Y	Y
7 **Blackburn**	Y	N	Y	Y	Y	Y
8 Tanner	Y	Y	Y	Y	Y	Y
9 Cohen	Y	Y	Y	Y	Y	Y

	639	640	641	642	643	644
TEXAS						
1 **Gohmert**	Y	N	Y	Y	Y	Y
2 **Poe**	Y	N	Y	Y	Y	Y
3 **Johnson, S.**	Y	N	Y	Y	Y	Y
4 **Hall**	Y	N	Y	Y	Y	Y
5 **Hensarling**	Y	N	Y	Y	Y	?
6 **Barton**	Y	N	Y	Y	Y	Y
7 **Culberson**	Y	N	Y	Y	Y	Y
8 **Brady**	Y	N	Y	Y	Y	Y
9 Green, A.	Y	Y	Y	Y	Y	Y
10 **McCaul**	Y	N	Y	Y	Y	Y
11 **Conaway**	Y	N	Y	Y	Y	Y
12 **Granger**	Y	N	Y	Y	Y	Y
13 **Thornberry**	Y	N	Y	Y	Y	Y
14 **Paul**	N	N	N	N	N	Y
15 Hinojosa	Y	Y	Y	Y	Y	Y
16 Reyes	Y	Y	Y	Y	Y	Y
17 Edwards	Y	Y	Y	Y	Y	Y
18 Jackson Lee	Y	Y	Y	Y	Y	Y
19 **Neugebauer**	Y	N	Y	Y	Y	Y
20 Gonzalez	Y	Y	Y	Y	Y	Y
21 **Smith**	Y	N	Y	Y	Y	Y
22 Lampson	Y	Y	Y	Y	Y	Y
23 Rodriguez	Y	Y	Y	Y	Y	Y
24 **Marchant**	Y	N	Y	Y	Y	Y
25 Doggett	Y	Y	Y	Y	Y	Y
26 **Burgess**	Y	N	Y	Y	Y	Y
27 Ortiz	Y	Y	Y	Y	Y	Y
28 Cuellar	Y	Y	Y	Y	Y	Y
29 Green, G.	Y	Y	Y	Y	Y	Y
30 Johnson, E.	Y	Y	Y	Y	Y	Y
31 **Carter**	Y	N	Y	Y	Y	Y
32 **Sessions**	Y	N	Y	Y	Y	Y
UTAH						
1 **Bishop**	Y	N	Y	Y	Y	Y
2 Matheson	Y	Y	Y	Y	Y	Y
3 **Cannon**	Y	N	Y	?	?	?
VERMONT						
AL Welch	Y	Y	Y	Y	Y	Y
VIRGINIA						
1 **Wittman**	Y	N	Y	Y	Y	Y
2 **Drake**	Y	N	Y	Y	Y	Y
3 Scott	Y	Y	Y	Y	Y	Y
4 **Forbes**	Y	N	Y	Y	Y	Y
5 **Goode**	Y	N	Y	Y	Y	Y
6 **Goodlatte**	Y	N	Y	Y	Y	Y
7 **Cantor**	Y	N	Y	Y	Y	Y
8 Moran	Y	Y	Y	Y	Y	Y
9 Boucher	Y	Y	Y	Y	Y	Y
10 **Wolf**	Y	N	Y	Y	Y	Y
11 **Davis**	Y	N	Y	Y	Y	Y
WASHINGTON						
1 Inslee	Y	Y	Y	Y	Y	Y
2 Larsen	Y	Y	Y	Y	Y	Y
3 Baird	Y	N	Y	Y	Y	Y
4 **Hastings**	Y	N	Y	Y	Y	Y
5 **McMorris Rodgers**	Y	N	Y	Y	Y	Y
6 Dicks	Y	Y	Y	Y	Y	?
7 McDermott	Y	Y	Y	Y	Y	Y
8 **Reichert**	Y	N	Y	Y	Y	Y
9 Smith	Y	Y	Y	Y	Y	Y
WEST VIRGINIA						
1 Mollohan	Y	Y	Y	Y	Y	Y
2 **Capito**	Y	N	Y	Y	Y	Y
3 Rahall	Y	Y	Y	Y	Y	Y
WISCONSIN						
1 **Ryan**	Y	N	Y	Y	Y	Y
2 Baldwin	Y	Y	Y	Y	Y	Y
3 Kind	Y	Y	Y	Y	Y	Y
4 Moore	Y	Y	Y	Y	Y	Y
5 **Sensenbrenner**	Y	N	Y	Y	Y	Y
6 **Petri**	Y	N	Y	Y	Y	Y
7 Obey	Y	Y	Y	Y	Y	Y
8 Kagen	Y	Y	Y	Y	Y	Y
WYOMING						
AL **Cubin**	?	?	?	?	?	?
DELEGATES						
Faleomavaega (A.S.)						
Norton (D.C.)						
Bordallo (Guam)						
Fortuño (P.R.)						
Christensen (V.I.)						

IN THE HOUSE | By Vote Number

645. HR 7060. Tax Extensions/Previous Question. Arcuri, D-N.Y., motion to order the previous question (thus ending debate and possibility of amendment) on adoption of the rule (H Res 1502) to provide for House floor consideration of the bill that would extend certain expiring tax provisions and provide tax incentives for investment in renewable energy and energy conservation. Motion agreed to 206-186: R 0-181; D 206-5 (ND 155-3, SD 51-2). Sept. 26, 2008.

646. HR 7060. Tax Extensions/Rule. Adoption of the rule (H Res 1502) to provide for House floor consideration of the bill that would extend expiring tax provisions and provide tax incentives for investment in renewable energy and energy conservation. Adopted 215-188: R 0-184; D 215-4 (ND 160-3, SD 55-1). Sept. 26, 2008.

647. HR 6045. Bulletproof Vest Partnership/Passage. Conyers, D-Mich., motion to suspend the rules and pass the bill that would re-authorize $25 million a year through fiscal 2012 for the Justice Department's Bulletproof Vest Partnership program, which awards matching-funds grants to state, local and tribal governments for bulletproof vests. Motion agreed to 404-2: R 183-2; D 221-0 (ND 164-0, SD 57-0). A two-thirds majority of those present and voting (271 in this case) is required for passage under suspension of the rules. Sept. 26, 2008.

648. HR 7060. Tax Extensions/Motion to Table. Neal, D-Mass., motion to table (kill) the Camp, R-Mich., appeal of the ruling of the chair with respect to the Neal point of order that the Camp motion to recommit the bill to the Ways and Means Committee was not germane. The Camp motion would recommit the bill with instructions that it be reported back forthwith with language that would replace the current text with the text of a bill (HR 6049) that would extend dozens of expired or expiring tax provisions, including the research tax credit, deductions for tuition and education expenses, and deductions for sales taxes in states without income taxes. Motion agreed to 220-198: R 0-192; D 220-6 (ND 163-4, SD 57-2). Sept. 26, 2008.

649. HR 7060. Tax Extensions/Passage. Passage of the bill that would extend expiring tax provisions through 2009, including the tax credit for research and development, rules for active financing income, state and local sales tax deductions, expenses for teachers, and deductions for tuition expenses, as well as increase the child tax credit. The measure would also provide tax incentives for carbon capture and sequestration demonstration projects and renewable energy production. It would be offset by several provisions, including curtailing an offshore deferred-compensation technique often used by hedge fund executives to reduce their taxes and freezing the deduction amount for oil and gas companies. Passed 257-166: R 30-165; D 227-1 (ND 168-1, SD 59-0). A "nay" was a vote in support of the president's position. Sept. 26, 2008.

650. S 1382. Amyotrophic Lateral Sclerosis Directory/Passage. Pallone, D-N.J., motion to suspend the rules and pass the bill that would direct the Centers for Disease Control and Prevention to develop a system to collect data on Amyotrophic Lateral Sclerosis and direct the Health and Human Services Department to submit a report to Congress within 18 months of the measure's enactment on the data registries for the disease. Motion agreed to 415-2: R 189-2; D 226-0 (ND 167-0, SD 59-0). A two-thirds majority of those present and voting (278 in this case) is required for passage under suspension of the rules. Sept. 26, 2008.

	645	646	647	648	649	650
ALABAMA						
1 Bonner	N	N	Y	N	N	Y
2 Everett	N	N	Y	N	N	Y
3 Rogers	N	N	Y	N	Y	Y
4 Aderholt	N	N	Y	N	N	Y
5 Cramer	?	?	Y	Y	Y	Y
6 Bachus	N	?	Y	N	N	Y
7 Davis	Y	Y	Y	Y	Y	Y
ALASKA						
AL Young	?	?	?	N	N	Y
ARIZONA						
1 Renzi	?	?	?	N	N	Y
2 Franks	N	N	+	N	N	Y
3 Shadegg	N	N	Y	N	N	Y
4 Pastor	Y	Y	Y	Y	Y	Y
5 Mitchell	Y	Y	Y	Y	Y	+
6 Flake	N	N	N	N	N	N
7 Grijalva	Y	Y	Y	Y	Y	Y
8 Giffords	Y	Y	Y	N	Y	Y
ARKANSAS						
1 Berry	Y	Y	Y	Y	Y	Y
2 Snyder	Y	Y	Y	Y	Y	Y
3 Boozman	N	N	Y	N	N	Y
4 Ross	Y	Y	Y	Y	Y	Y
CALIFORNIA						
1 Thompson	Y	Y	Y	Y	Y	Y
2 Herger	-	N	Y	N	N	Y
3 Lungren	N	N	?	N	N	Y
4 Doolittle	?	?	Y	N	N	Y
5 Matsui	Y	Y	Y	Y	Y	Y
6 Woolsey	Y	Y	Y	Y	Y	Y
7 Miller, George	Y	Y	Y	Y	Y	Y
8 Pelosi						
9 Lee	Y	Y	Y	Y	Y	Y
10 Tauscher	Y	Y	Y	Y	Y	Y
11 McNerney	Y	Y	Y	Y	Y	Y
12 Speier	Y	Y	Y	Y	Y	Y
13 Stark	Y	Y	Y	Y	Y	Y
14 Eshoo	Y	Y	Y	Y	Y	Y
15 Honda	Y	Y	Y	Y	Y	Y
16 Lofgren	Y	Y	Y	?	Y	Y
17 Farr	Y	Y	Y	Y	Y	Y
18 Cardoza	Y	Y	Y	Y	Y	Y
19 Radanovich	N	N	Y	N	N	Y
20 Costa	?	?	?	?	?	?
21 Nunes	N	N	Y	N	N	Y
22 McCarthy	N	N	Y	N	N	Y
23 Capps	Y	Y	Y	Y	Y	Y
24 Gallegly	N	N	Y	N	N	Y
25 McKeon	N	N	Y	N	N	Y
26 Dreier	N	N	Y	N	N	Y
27 Sherman	Y	Y	Y	Y	Y	Y
28 Berman	Y	Y	Y	Y	Y	Y
29 Schiff	Y	Y	Y	Y	Y	Y
30 Waxman	Y	Y	Y	Y	Y	Y
31 Becerra	Y	Y	Y	Y	Y	Y
32 Solis	Y	Y	Y	Y	Y	Y
33 Watson	Y	Y	Y	Y	Y	Y
34 Roybal-Allard	Y	Y	Y	Y	Y	Y
35 Waters	?	?	?	?	?	?
36 Harman	Y	Y	Y	Y	Y	Y
37 Richardson	Y	Y	Y	Y	Y	Y
38 Napolitano	Y	Y	Y	Y	Y	?
39 Sánchez, Linda	Y	Y	Y	Y	Y	Y
40 Royce	N	N	Y	N	N	Y
41 Lewis	N	N	Y	N	N	Y
42 Miller, Gary	N	N	Y	N	N	Y
43 Baca	Y	Y	Y	Y	Y	Y
44 Calvert	N	N	Y	N	N	?
45 Bono Mack	N	N	Y	N	N	Y
46 Rohrabacher	N	N	Y	N	N	Y
47 Sanchez, Loretta	?	?	?	Y	Y	Y
48 Campbell	N	N	Y	N	N	Y
49 Issa	N	N	Y	N	N	Y
50 Bilbray	N	N	Y	N	N	Y
51 Filner	Y	Y	Y	Y	N	Y
52 Hunter	N	N	Y	N	N	Y
53 Davis	Y	Y	Y	Y	Y	Y

	645	646	647	648	649	650
COLORADO						
1 DeGette	Y	Y	Y	Y	Y	Y
2 Udall	Y	Y	Y	Y	Y	Y
3 Salazar	Y	Y	Y	Y	Y	Y
4 Musgrave	N	N	Y	N	N	Y
5 Lamborn	N	N	Y	N	N	Y
6 Tancredo	N	N	Y	N	N	Y
7 Perlmutter	Y	Y	Y	Y	Y	Y
CONNECTICUT						
1 Larson	Y	Y	Y	Y	Y	Y
2 Courtney	Y	Y	Y	Y	Y	Y
3 DeLauro	Y	Y	Y	Y	Y	Y
4 Shays	N	N	Y	N	Y	Y
5 Murphy	Y	Y	Y	Y	Y	Y
DELAWARE						
AL Castle	N	N	Y	N	Y	Y
FLORIDA						
1 Miller	N	N	Y	N	N	Y
2 Boyd	Y	Y	Y	Y	Y	Y
3 Brown	?	Y	Y	Y	Y	Y
4 Crenshaw	N	N	Y	N	N	Y
5 Brown-Waite	N	N	Y	N	N	Y
6 Stearns	N	N	?	N	N	Y
7 Mica	N	N	Y	N	N	Y
8 Keller	N	N	Y	N	N	Y
9 Bilirakis	N	N	Y	N	N	Y
10 Young	N	N	Y	N	N	Y
11 Castor	Y	Y	Y	Y	Y	Y
12 Putnam	N	?	Y	N	N	Y
13 Buchanan	N	N	Y	N	N	Y
14 Mack	N	N	Y	N	N	Y
15 Weldon	N	N	?	N	N	Y
16 Mahoney	Y	Y	Y	Y	Y	Y
17 Meek	Y	Y	Y	Y	Y	Y
18 Ros-Lehtinen	N	N	Y	N	N	Y
19 Wexler	Y	Y	Y	Y	Y	Y
20 Wasserman Schultz	Y	Y	Y	Y	Y	Y
21 Diaz-Balart, L.	N	N	Y	N	N	Y
22 Klein	Y	Y	Y	Y	Y	Y
23 Hastings	Y	Y	Y	Y	Y	Y
24 Feeney	N	N	Y	N	N	Y
25 Diaz-Balart, M.	N	N	Y	N	N	Y
GEORGIA						
1 Kingston	N	N	Y	N	N	Y
2 Bishop	?	Y	Y	Y	Y	Y
3 Westmoreland	N	N	Y	N	N	Y
4 Johnson	?	?	?	Y	Y	Y
5 Lewis	Y	Y	Y	Y	Y	Y
6 Price	N	N	Y	N	N	Y
7 Linder	N	N	Y	N	N	Y
8 Marshall	Y	Y	Y	Y	Y	Y
9 Deal	N	N	Y	N	N	Y
10 Broun	N	N	Y	N	N	Y
11 Gingrey	N	N	Y	N	N	Y
12 Barrow	Y	Y	Y	Y	Y	Y
13 Scott	Y	Y	Y	Y	Y	Y
HAWAII						
1 Abercrombie	+	+	+	Y	Y	Y
2 Hirono	Y	Y	Y	Y	Y	Y
IDAHO						
1 Sali	-	N	Y	N	N	Y
2 Simpson	N	N	Y	N	N	Y
ILLINOIS						
1 Rush	?	?	?	?	Y	Y
2 Jackson	Y	Y	Y	Y	Y	Y
3 Lipinski	Y	Y	Y	Y	Y	Y
4 Gutierrez	Y	Y	Y	Y	?	Y
5 Emanuel	Y	Y	Y	Y	Y	Y
6 Roskam	N	N	Y	N	N	?
7 Davis	?	?	?	Y	Y	Y
8 Bean	Y	Y	Y	Y	Y	Y
9 Schakowsky	Y	Y	Y	Y	Y	Y
10 Kirk	N	N	Y	N	Y	Y
11 Weller	?	?	?	?	?	?
12 Costello	Y	Y	Y	Y	Y	Y
13 Biggert	N	N	Y	N	N	Y
14 Foster	Y	Y	Y	Y	Y	Y
15 Johnson	N	N	Y	N	N	Y

KEY   Republicans   Democrats

Y Voted for (yea)	X Paired against
# Paired for	- Announced against
+ Announced for	P Voted "present"
N Voted against (nay)	C Voted "present" to avoid possible conflict of interest
	? Did not vote or otherwise make a position known

ND Northern Democrats, SD Southern Democrats
Southern states: Ala., Ark., Fla., Ga., Ky., La., Miss., N.C., Okla., S.C., Tenn., Texas, Va.

H-218   2008 CQ ALMANAC | www.cq.com

	645	646	647	648	649	650
16 **Manzullo**	N	N	Y	N	N	Y
17 Hare	Y	Y	Y	Y	Y	Y
18 **LaHood**	N	N	Y	N	Y	Y
19 **Shimkus**	N	N	Y	N	N	?
INDIANA						
1 Visclosky	Y	Y	Y	Y	Y	Y
2 Donnelly	Y	Y	Y	Y	Y	Y
3 **Souder**	?	N	Y	N	Y	Y
4 **Buyer**	N	N	Y	N	N	Y
5 **Burton**	?	N	Y	N	N	Y
6 **Pence**	N	N	Y	N	N	Y
7 Carson, A.	Y	Y	Y	Y	Y	Y
8 Ellsworth	Y	N	Y	Y	Y	Y
9 Hill	N	N	Y	Y	Y	Y
IOWA						
1 Braley	Y	Y	Y	N	Y	Y
2 Loebsack	Y	Y	Y	N	Y	Y
3 Boswell	Y	Y	Y	Y	Y	Y
4 **Latham**	N	N	Y	N	N	Y
5 **King**	N	N	Y	N	N	Y
KANSAS						
1 **Moran**	N	N	Y	N	N	Y
2 Boyda	Y	Y	Y	Y	Y	Y
3 Moore	Y	Y	Y	Y	Y	Y
4 **Tiahrt**	–	N	Y	N	N	Y
KENTUCKY						
1 **Whitfield**	N	N	Y	N	Y	Y
2 **Lewis**	N	N	Y	N	N	Y
3 Yarmuth	Y	Y	Y	Y	Y	Y
4 **Davis**	N	N	Y	N	N	Y
5 **Rogers**	N	N	Y	N	N	Y
6 Chandler	Y	Y	Y	Y	Y	Y
LOUISIANA						
1 **Scalise**	N	N	Y	N	N	Y
2 Jefferson	Y	Y	Y	Y	Y	Y
3 Melancon	Y	Y	Y	Y	Y	Y
4 **McCrery**	N	N	Y	N	N	Y
5 **Alexander**	N	N	Y	N	N	Y
6 Cazayoux	N	Y	Y	Y	Y	Y
7 **Boustany**	N	N	Y	N	N	Y
MAINE						
1 Allen	Y	Y	Y	Y	Y	Y
2 Michaud	Y	Y	Y	Y	Y	Y
MARYLAND						
1 **Gilchrest**	N	N	Y	N	Y	Y
2 Ruppersberger	Y	Y	Y	Y	Y	Y
3 Sarbanes	?	Y	Y	Y	Y	Y
4 Edwards	Y	Y	Y	Y	Y	Y
5 Hoyer	Y	Y	Y	Y	Y	Y
6 **Bartlett**	N	N	Y	N	N	Y
7 Cummings	Y	Y	Y	?	?	Y
8 Van Hollen	Y	Y	Y	Y	Y	Y
MASSACHUSETTS						
1 Olver	Y	Y	Y	Y	Y	Y
2 Neal	Y	Y	Y	Y	Y	Y
3 McGovern	Y	Y	Y	Y	Y	Y
4 Frank	Y	Y	Y	Y	Y	Y
5 Tsongas	Y	Y	Y	Y	Y	Y
6 Tierney	Y	Y	Y	?	?	?
7 Markey	Y	Y	Y	Y	Y	Y
8 Capuano	Y	Y	Y	Y	Y	Y
9 Lynch	Y	Y	Y	Y	Y	Y
10 Delahunt	Y	Y	Y	Y	Y	Y
MICHIGAN						
1 Stupak	Y	Y	Y	Y	Y	Y
2 **Hoekstra**	N	N	Y	N	N	Y
3 **Ehlers**	N	N	Y	N	Y	Y
4 **Camp**	N	N	Y	N	N	Y
5 Kildee	Y	Y	Y	Y	Y	Y
6 **Upton**	N	N	Y	N	Y	Y
7 **Walberg**	N	N	Y	N	N	Y
8 **Rogers**	N	N	Y	N	N	Y
9 **Knollenberg**	N	N	Y	N	Y	Y
10 **Miller**	N	N	Y	N	Y	Y
11 **McCotter**	N	N	Y	N	N	Y
12 Levin	Y	Y	Y	Y	Y	Y
13 Kilpatrick	Y	Y	Y	Y	Y	Y
14 Conyers	Y	Y	Y	Y	Y	Y
15 Dingell	?	?	?	Y	Y	Y
MINNESOTA						
1 Walz	Y	Y	Y	Y	Y	Y
2 **Kline**	N	N	Y	N	N	Y
3 **Ramstad**	N	N	Y	N	N	Y
4 McCollum	Y	Y	Y	Y	Y	Y
5 Ellison	Y	Y	Y	?	Y	Y
6 **Bachmann**	N	N	Y	N	N	Y
7 Peterson	Y	Y	Y	Y	Y	Y
8 Oberstar	Y	Y	Y	Y	Y	Y
MISSISSIPPI						
1 Childers	N	N	Y	N	Y	Y
2 Thompson	Y	Y	Y	Y	Y	Y
3 **Pickering**	?	?	?	?	?	?
4 Taylor	Y	Y	Y	Y	Y	Y
MISSOURI						
1 Clay	?	?	?	Y	Y	Y
2 **Akin**	N	N	Y	N	N	Y
3 Carnahan	Y	Y	Y	Y	Y	Y
4 Skelton	Y	Y	Y	Y	Y	Y
5 Cleaver	Y	Y	Y	Y	Y	Y
6 **Graves**	N	N	Y	N	N	Y
7 **Blunt**	N	?	?	N	N	Y
8 **Emerson**	N	N	Y	N	N	Y
9 **Hulshof**	N	N	Y	N	N	Y
MONTANA						
AL **Rehberg**	N	N	Y	N	N	Y
NEBRASKA						
1 **Fortenberry**	N	N	Y	N	N	Y
2 **Terry**	N	N	Y	N	Y	Y
3 **Smith**	N	N	Y	N	N	Y
NEVADA						
1 Berkley	Y	Y	Y	Y	Y	Y
2 **Heller**	N	N	Y	N	N	Y
3 **Porter**	N	N	Y	N	Y	Y
NEW HAMPSHIRE						
1 Shea-Porter	Y	Y	Y	Y	Y	Y
2 Hodes	Y	Y	Y	Y	Y	Y
NEW JERSEY						
1 Andrews	Y	Y	Y	Y	Y	Y
2 **LoBiondo**	N	N	Y	N	Y	Y
3 **Saxton**	N	N	Y	N	N	Y
4 **Smith**	?	N	Y	N	Y	Y
5 **Garrett**	N	N	Y	N	N	Y
6 Pallone	Y	Y	Y	Y	Y	Y
7 **Ferguson**	N	N	Y	N	N	Y
8 Pascrell	Y	Y	Y	Y	Y	Y
9 Rothman	Y	Y	Y	Y	Y	Y
10 Payne	?	?	?	?	?	?
11 **Frelinghuysen**	N	N	Y	N	N	Y
12 Holt	?	?	?	Y	Y	Y
13 Sires	?	?	Y	Y	Y	Y
NEW MEXICO						
1 **Wilson**	N	N	Y	N	N	Y
2 **Pearce**	N	N	Y	N	N	Y
3 Udall	Y	Y	Y	Y	Y	Y
NEW YORK						
1 Bishop	Y	Y	Y	Y	Y	Y
2 Israel	Y	Y	Y	Y	Y	Y
3 **King**	N	N	Y	N	N	Y
4 McCarthy	Y	Y	Y	Y	Y	?
5 Ackerman	Y	Y	Y	Y	Y	Y
6 Meeks	Y	Y	Y	Y	Y	Y
7 Crowley	Y	Y	Y	Y	Y	Y
8 Nadler	Y	Y	Y	Y	Y	Y
9 Weiner	Y	Y	Y	Y	Y	Y
10 Towns	?	Y	Y	Y	Y	Y
11 Clarke	Y	Y	Y	Y	Y	Y
12 Velázquez	Y	Y	Y	Y	Y	Y
13 **Fossella**	N	N	Y	?	N	Y
14 Maloney	Y	Y	Y	Y	Y	Y
15 Rangel	Y	Y	Y	Y	Y	Y
16 Serrano	Y	Y	Y	Y	Y	Y
17 Engel	?	?	?	Y	Y	Y
18 Lowey	Y	Y	Y	Y	Y	Y
19 Hall	Y	Y	Y	Y	Y	Y
20 Gillibrand	Y	Y	Y	Y	Y	Y
21 McNulty	Y	Y	Y	Y	Y	Y
22 Hinchey	Y	Y	Y	Y	Y	Y
23 **McHugh**	N	N	Y	N	Y	Y
24 Arcuri	Y	Y	Y	Y	Y	Y
25 **Walsh**	N	N	Y	N	N	Y
26 **Reynolds**	?	N	Y	N	N	Y
27 Higgins	Y	Y	Y	Y	Y	Y
28 Slaughter	Y	Y	Y	Y	Y	Y
29 **Kuhl**	N	N	Y	N	N	Y
NORTH CAROLINA						
1 Butterfield	Y	Y	Y	Y	Y	Y
2 Etheridge	Y	Y	Y	Y	Y	Y
3 **Jones**	N	N	Y	N	Y	Y
4 Price	Y	Y	Y	Y	Y	Y
5 **Foxx**	N	N	Y	N	N	Y
6 **Coble**	N	N	Y	N	N	Y
7 McIntyre	Y	Y	Y	Y	Y	Y
8 **Hayes**	N	N	Y	N	Y	Y
9 **Myrick**	N	N	Y	N	N	Y
10 **McHenry**	N	N	Y	N	N	Y
11 Shuler	Y	Y	Y	Y	Y	Y
12 Watt	Y	Y	Y	Y	Y	Y
13 Miller	Y	Y	Y	Y	Y	Y
NORTH DAKOTA						
AL Pomeroy	Y	Y	Y	Y	Y	Y
OHIO						
1 **Chabot**	N	N	Y	N	N	Y
2 **Schmidt**	N	N	Y	N	N	Y
3 **Turner**	N	N	Y	N	N	Y
4 **Jordan**	N	N	Y	N	N	Y
5 **Latta**	N	N	Y	N	N	Y
6 Wilson	Y	Y	Y	Y	Y	Y
7 **Hobson**	N	N	Y	N	N	Y
8 **Boehner**	?	?	?	N	N	Y
9 Kaptur	Y	Y	Y	Y	Y	Y
10 Kucinich	Y	Y	Y	Y	Y	Y
11 Vacant						
12 **Tiberi**	N	N	Y	N	N	Y
13 Sutton	Y	Y	Y	Y	Y	Y
14 **LaTourette**	?	N	Y	N	N	Y
15 **Pryce**	N	N	Y	N	N	Y
16 **Regula**	N	N	Y	N	N	Y
17 Ryan	Y	Y	Y	Y	Y	Y
18 Space	Y	Y	Y	Y	Y	Y
OKLAHOMA						
1 **Sullivan**	N	N	Y	N	N	Y
2 Boren	Y	Y	Y	Y	Y	Y
3 **Lucas**	N	N	Y	N	N	Y
4 **Cole**	N	?	Y	N	N	Y
5 **Fallin**	N	N	Y	N	N	Y
OREGON						
1 Wu	Y	Y	Y	Y	Y	Y
2 **Walden**	N	N	Y	N	N	Y
3 Blumenauer	Y	Y	Y	Y	Y	Y
4 DeFazio	N	N	Y	N	N	Y
5 Hooley	Y	Y	Y	Y	Y	Y
PENNSYLVANIA						
1 Brady	Y	Y	Y	Y	Y	Y
2 Fattah	?	Y	Y	Y	Y	Y
3 **English**	N	N	Y	N	N	Y
4 Altmire	Y	Y	Y	Y	Y	Y
5 **Peterson**	?	?	?	?	?	?
6 **Gerlach**	N	N	Y	N	Y	Y
7 Sestak	Y	Y	Y	Y	Y	Y
8 Murphy, P.	Y	Y	Y	Y	Y	Y
9 **Shuster**	N	N	Y	N	N	Y
10 Carney	Y	Y	Y	Y	Y	Y
11 Kanjorski	Y	Y	Y	Y	Y	Y
12 Murtha	Y	Y	Y	Y	Y	Y
13 Schwartz	Y	Y	Y	Y	Y	Y
14 Doyle	Y	Y	Y	Y	Y	Y
15 **Dent**	N	N	Y	N	Y	Y
16 **Pitts**	?	?	?	N	N	Y
17 Holden	Y	Y	Y	Y	Y	Y
18 **Murphy, T.**	N	N	Y	N	Y	Y
19 **Platts**	N	N	Y	N	Y	Y
RHODE ISLAND						
1 Kennedy	Y	Y	Y	Y	Y	Y
2 Langevin	+	Y	Y	Y	Y	Y
SOUTH CAROLINA						
1 **Brown**	N	N	Y	N	N	Y
2 **Wilson**	N	N	Y	N	N	Y
3 **Barrett**	N	N	Y	N	N	Y
4 **Inglis**	N	N	Y	N	N	Y
5 Spratt	Y	Y	Y	Y	Y	Y
6 Clyburn	Y	Y	Y	Y	Y	Y
SOUTH DAKOTA						
AL Herseth Sandlin	Y	Y	Y	Y	Y	Y
TENNESSEE						
1 **Davis, D.**	N	N	Y	N	N	Y
2 **Duncan**	N	N	Y	N	Y	Y
3 **Wamp**	N	N	Y	N	N	Y
4 Davis, L.	Y	Y	Y	Y	Y	Y
5 Cooper	Y	Y	Y	Y	Y	Y
6 Gordon	Y	Y	Y	Y	Y	Y
7 **Blackburn**	N	N	Y	N	N	Y
8 Tanner	Y	Y	Y	Y	Y	Y
9 Cohen	Y	Y	Y	Y	Y	Y
TEXAS						
1 **Gohmert**	N	N	Y	?	N	Y
2 **Poe**	N	N	Y	N	N	Y
3 **Johnson, S.**	N	N	Y	N	N	Y
4 **Hall**	N	N	Y	N	N	Y
5 **Hensarling**	N	N	Y	N	N	Y
6 **Barton**	N	N	Y	N	N	?
7 **Culberson**	N	N	Y	N	N	Y
8 **Brady**	N	N	Y	N	N	Y
9 Green, A.	?	?	?	Y	Y	Y
10 **McCaul**	N	N	Y	N	N	Y
11 **Conaway**	N	N	Y	N	N	Y
12 **Granger**	N	N	Y	N	N	Y
13 **Thornberry**	N	N	Y	N	N	Y
14 **Paul**	N	N	N	N	N	N
15 Hinojosa	Y	Y	Y	Y	Y	Y
16 Reyes	Y	Y	Y	Y	Y	Y
17 Edwards	Y	Y	Y	Y	Y	Y
18 Jackson Lee	Y	Y	Y	Y	Y	Y
19 **Neugebauer**	N	N	Y	N	N	Y
20 Gonzalez	Y	Y	Y	Y	Y	Y
21 **Smith**	N	N	Y	N	N	Y
22 Lampson	Y	Y	Y	N	Y	Y
23 Rodriguez	Y	Y	Y	Y	Y	Y
24 **Marchant**	?	?	?	N	N	Y
25 Doggett	Y	Y	Y	Y	Y	Y
26 **Burgess**	N	N	Y	N	N	Y
27 Ortiz	Y	Y	Y	Y	Y	Y
28 Cuellar	Y	Y	Y	Y	Y	Y
29 Green, G.	Y	Y	Y	Y	Y	Y
30 Johnson, E.	Y	Y	Y	Y	Y	Y
31 **Carter**	N	N	Y	N	N	Y
32 **Sessions**	N	N	Y	N	N	Y
UTAH						
1 **Bishop**	N	N	Y	N	N	Y
2 Matheson	Y	Y	Y	Y	Y	Y
3 **Cannon**	N	N	Y	?	N	Y
VERMONT						
AL Welch	Y	Y	Y	Y	Y	Y
VIRGINIA						
1 **Wittman**	N	N	Y	N	N	Y
2 **Drake**	N	N	Y	N	N	Y
3 Scott	Y	Y	Y	Y	Y	Y
4 **Forbes**	N	N	Y	N	N	Y
5 **Goode**	N	N	Y	N	N	Y
6 **Goodlatte**	N	N	Y	N	N	Y
7 **Cantor**	N	?	Y	N	N	Y
8 Moran	?	Y	Y	Y	Y	Y
9 Boucher	Y	Y	Y	Y	Y	Y
10 **Wolf**	N	N	Y	N	N	Y
11 **Davis**	N	N	Y	N	N	Y
WASHINGTON						
1 Inslee	Y	Y	Y	Y	Y	Y
2 Larsen	Y	Y	Y	Y	Y	Y
3 Baird	N	Y	Y	Y	Y	Y
4 **Hastings**	N	N	Y	N	N	Y
5 **McMorris Rodgers**	N	N	Y	N	N	Y
6 Dicks	Y	Y	Y	Y	Y	Y
7 McDermott	Y	Y	Y	Y	Y	Y
8 **Reichert**	N	N	Y	N	N	Y
9 Smith	Y	Y	Y	Y	Y	Y
WEST VIRGINIA						
1 Mollohan	?	Y	Y	Y	Y	Y
2 **Capito**	N	N	Y	N	Y	Y
3 Rahall	Y	Y	Y	Y	Y	Y
WISCONSIN						
1 **Ryan**	N	N	Y	N	N	Y
2 Baldwin	Y	Y	Y	Y	Y	Y
3 Kind	Y	Y	Y	Y	Y	Y
4 Moore	Y	Y	Y	Y	Y	Y
5 **Sensenbrenner**	N	N	Y	N	N	Y
6 **Petri**	N	N	Y	N	Y	Y
7 Obey	Y	Y	Y	Y	Y	Y
8 Kagen	Y	Y	Y	Y	Y	?
WYOMING						
AL **Cubin**	?	?	?	?	?	?
DELEGATES						
Faleomavaega (A.S.)						
Norton (D.C.)						
Bordallo (Guam)						
Fortuño (P.R.)						
Christensen (V.I.)						

IN THE HOUSE | By Vote Number

651. **H Res 1500. Suspension Motions/Previous Question.** Welch, D-Vt., motion to order the previous question (thus ending debate and possibility of amendment) on adoption of the rule to provide for House floor consideration of bills under suspension of the rules through the calendar day of Sunday, Sept. 28, 2008. Motion agreed to 225-192: R 4-189; D 221-3 (ND 166-0, SD 55-3). Sept. 26, 2008.

652. **H Res 1500. Suspension Motions/Rule.** Adoption of the rule to provide for House floor consideration of bills under suspension of the rules through the calendar day of Sunday, Sept. 28, 2008. Adopted 222-196: R 0-193; D 222-3 (ND 166-1, SD 56-2). Sept. 26, 2008.

653. **S 2932. Poison Center Awareness/Passage.** Pallone, D-N.J., motion to suspend the rules and pass the bill that would reauthorize the Poison Centers grant program, national toll-free number and national media campaign through fiscal 2014 and authorize funds for the program. Motion agreed to 403-6: R 184-6; D 219-0 (ND 161-0, SD 58-0). A two-thirds majority of those present and voting (273 in this case) is required for passage under suspension of the rules. Sept. 26, 2008.

654. **HR 7110. Supplemental Appropriations/Previous Question.** Castor, D-Fla., motion to order the previous question (thus ending debate and possibility of amendment) on adoption of the resolution (H Res 1503) that would waive the two-thirds majority vote requirement for same-day consideration of a rule for a bill to extend unemployment benefits and provide additional fiscal 2009 funds for food assistance programs, infrastructure projects, energy development, public housing, state Medicaid plans and other programs. Motion agreed to 222-198: R 2-190; D 220-8 (ND 165-5, SD 55-3). Sept. 26, 2008.

655. **HR 7110. Supplemental Appropriations/Same-Day Consideration.** Adoption of the resolution (H Res 1503) that would waive the two-thirds majority vote requirement for same-day consideration of a rule for a bill that would extend unemployment benefits and provide additional fiscal 2009 funds for food assistance programs, infrastructure projects, energy development, public housing, state Medicaid plans and other programs. Adopted 216-203: R 0-192; D 216-11 (ND 166-5, SD 50-6). Sept. 26, 2008.

656. **HR 4120. Child Pornography and Interstate Commerce/Passage.** Lofgren, D-Calif., motion to suspend the rules and concur in the Senate amendment to the bill that would clarify that it is a federal felony to reproduce or distribute child pornography, including transmission over the Internet, in any way that constitutes or affects interstate commerce. Motion agreed to 418-0: R 192-0; D 226-0 (ND 169-0, SD 57-0). A two-thirds majority of those present and voting (279 in this case) is required for passage under suspension of the rules. Sept. 26, 2008.

657. **HR 7110. Supplemental Appropriations/Previous Question.** McGovern, D-Mass., motion to order the previous question (thus ending debate and possibility of amendment) on adoption of the rule (H Res 1507) to provide for House floor consideration of the bill that would extend unemployment benefits and provide additional fiscal 2009 funds for food assistance programs, infrastructure projects, energy development, public housing, state Medicaid plans and other programs. Motion agreed to 218-204: R 0-193; D 218-11 (ND 165-7, SD 53-4). Sept. 26, 2008.

	651	652	653	654	655	656	657
ALABAMA							
1 **Bonner**	N	N	Y	N	N	Y	N
2 **Everett**	N	N	Y	N	N	Y	N
3 **Rogers**	N	N	Y	N	N	Y	N
4 **Aderholt**	N	N	Y	N	N	Y	N
5 Cramer	Y	Y	Y	Y	Y	Y	Y
6 Bachus	–	–	+	N	N	Y	N
7 Davis	Y	Y	Y	Y	Y	Y	Y
ALASKA							
AL **Young**	N	N	Y	N	N	Y	N
ARIZONA							
1 **Renzi**	N	N	Y	N	N	Y	N
2 **Franks**	N	N	Y	N	N	Y	N
3 **Shadegg**	N	N	Y	N	N	Y	N
4 Pastor	Y	Y	Y	Y	Y	Y	Y
5 Mitchell	Y	N	Y	+	N	Y	Y
6 **Flake**	N	N	N	N	N	Y	N
7 Grijalva	Y	Y	Y	Y	Y	Y	Y
8 Giffords	Y	Y	Y	Y	Y	Y	Y
ARKANSAS							
1 Berry	Y	Y	Y	Y	Y	Y	Y
2 Snyder	Y	Y	Y	Y	Y	Y	Y
3 **Boozman**	N	N	Y	N	N	Y	N
4 Ross	Y	Y	Y	Y	Y	Y	Y
CALIFORNIA							
1 Thompson	Y	Y	Y	N	Y	Y	N
2 **Herger**	N	N	Y	N	N	Y	N
3 **Lungren**	N	N	Y	N	N	Y	N
4 **Doolittle**	N	N	Y	N	N	Y	N
5 Matsui	Y	Y	Y	Y	Y	Y	Y
6 Woolsey	Y	Y	Y	Y	Y	Y	Y
7 Miller, George	Y	Y	?	Y	Y	Y	Y
8 Pelosi							
9 Lee	Y	Y	Y	Y	Y	Y	Y
10 Tauscher	Y	Y	Y	Y	Y	Y	Y
11 McNerney	Y	Y	Y	Y	Y	Y	Y
12 Speier	Y	Y	Y	Y	Y	Y	Y
13 Stark	Y	Y	Y	Y	Y	Y	Y
14 Eshoo	Y	Y	Y	Y	Y	Y	Y
15 Honda	Y	Y	Y	Y	Y	Y	Y
16 Lofgren	?	Y	Y	Y	Y	Y	Y
17 Farr	Y	Y	Y	Y	Y	Y	Y
18 Cardoza	Y	Y	Y	Y	Y	Y	Y
19 **Radanovich**	N	N	Y	N	N	Y	N
20 Costa	?	?	?	?	?	?	?
21 **Nunes**	N	N	Y	N	N	Y	N
22 **McCarthy**	N	N	Y	N	N	Y	N
23 Capps	Y	Y	?	Y	Y	Y	Y
24 **Gallegly**	N	N	Y	N	N	Y	N
25 **McKeon**	N	N	Y	N	N	Y	N
26 **Dreier**	N	N	Y	N	N	Y	N
27 Sherman	Y	Y	Y	Y	Y	Y	Y
28 Berman	Y	Y	?	Y	Y	Y	Y
29 Schiff	Y	Y	Y	Y	Y	Y	Y
30 Waxman	Y	Y	Y	Y	Y	Y	Y
31 Becerra	Y	Y	Y	Y	Y	Y	Y
32 Solis	Y	Y	Y	Y	Y	Y	Y
33 Watson	?	Y	Y	Y	Y	Y	Y
34 Roybal-Allard	Y	Y	Y	Y	Y	Y	Y
35 Waters	?	?	?	?	?	Y	Y
36 Harman	Y	Y	Y	Y	Y	Y	Y
37 Richardson	Y	Y	Y	?	?	Y	Y
38 Napolitano	Y	Y	Y	Y	Y	Y	Y
39 Sánchez, Linda	Y	Y	Y	Y	Y	Y	Y
40 **Royce**	N	N	+	N	N	Y	N
41 **Lewis**	N	N	Y	N	N	Y	N
42 **Miller, Gary**	N	N	Y	N	N	Y	N
43 Baca	Y	Y	Y	Y	Y	Y	Y
44 **Calvert**	N	N	Y	N	N	Y	N
45 **Bono Mack**	N	N	Y	N	N	Y	N
46 **Rohrabacher**	N	N	Y	N	N	Y	N
47 Sanchez, Loretta	Y	Y	Y	Y	Y	Y	Y
48 **Campbell**	N	N	N	N	N	Y	N
49 **Issa**	N	N	Y	N	N	Y	N
50 **Bilbray**	N	N	Y	N	N	Y	N
51 Filner	Y	Y	Y	Y	Y	Y	Y
52 **Hunter**	N	N	Y	N	N	Y	N
53 Davis	Y	Y	Y	Y	Y	Y	Y

	651	652	653	654	655	656	657
COLORADO							
1 DeGette	Y	Y	Y	Y	Y	Y	Y
2 Udall	?	?	?	Y	Y	Y	?
3 Salazar	Y	Y	Y	Y	Y	Y	Y
4 **Musgrave**	N	N	Y	N	N	Y	N
5 **Lamborn**	N	N	Y	N	N	Y	N
6 **Tancredo**	N	N	Y	N	N	Y	N
7 Perlmutter	Y	Y	Y	Y	Y	Y	Y
CONNECTICUT							
1 Larson	Y	Y	Y	Y	Y	Y	Y
2 Courtney	Y	Y	Y	Y	Y	Y	Y
3 DeLauro	Y	Y	Y	Y	Y	Y	Y
4 **Shays**	Y	N	Y	Y	N	Y	N
5 Murphy	Y	Y	Y	Y	Y	Y	Y
DELAWARE							
AL **Castle**	N	N	Y	N	N	Y	N
FLORIDA							
1 **Miller**	N	N	Y	N	N	Y	N
2 Boyd	Y	Y	Y	Y	N	Y	Y
3 Brown	Y	Y	Y	Y	Y	Y	Y
4 **Crenshaw**	N	N	Y	N	N	Y	N
5 **Brown-Waite**	N	N	Y	N	N	Y	N
6 **Stearns**	N	N	Y	N	N	Y	N
7 **Mica**	N	N	Y	N	N	Y	N
8 **Keller**	N	N	Y	N	N	Y	N
9 **Bilirakis**	N	N	Y	N	N	Y	N
10 **Young**	N	N	Y	N	N	Y	N
11 Castor	Y	Y	Y	Y	Y	Y	Y
12 **Putnam**	N	N	Y	N	N	Y	N
13 **Buchanan**	N	N	Y	N	N	Y	N
14 **Mack**	N	N	Y	N	N	Y	N
15 **Weldon**	N	N	Y	N	N	Y	N
16 Mahoney	Y	Y	Y	Y	Y	Y	Y
17 Meek	Y	Y	Y	Y	Y	Y	Y
18 **Ros-Lehtinen**	Y	N	Y	N	N	Y	N
19 Wexler	?	?	?	?	?	?	?
20 Wasserman Schultz	Y	Y	Y	Y	Y	Y	Y
21 **Diaz-Balart, L.**	N	N	Y	N	N	Y	N
22 Klein	Y	Y	Y	Y	Y	Y	Y
23 Hastings	Y	Y	Y	Y	Y	Y	Y
24 **Feeney**	N	N	Y	N	N	Y	N
25 **Diaz-Balart, M.**	N	N	Y	N	N	Y	N
GEORGIA							
1 **Kingston**	N	N	Y	N	N	Y	N
2 Bishop	Y	Y	Y	Y	Y	Y	Y
3 **Westmoreland**	N	N	Y	N	N	Y	N
4 Johnson	Y	Y	Y	Y	Y	Y	Y
5 Lewis	Y	Y	Y	Y	Y	Y	Y
6 **Price**	N	N	Y	N	N	Y	N
7 **Linder**	N	N	Y	N	N	Y	N
8 Marshall	Y	Y	Y	Y	Y	Y	Y
9 **Deal**	N	N	Y	N	N	Y	N
10 **Broun**	N	N	?	N	N	Y	N
11 **Gingrey**	N	N	Y	–	–	+	–
12 Barrow	Y	Y	Y	Y	Y	Y	Y
13 Scott	Y	Y	Y	Y	Y	Y	Y
HAWAII							
1 Abercrombie	Y	Y	Y	Y	Y	Y	Y
2 Hirono	Y	Y	Y	Y	Y	Y	Y
IDAHO							
1 **Sali**	N	N	Y	N	N	Y	N
2 **Simpson**	N	N	Y	N	N	Y	N
ILLINOIS							
1 Rush	Y	Y	Y	Y	Y	Y	Y
2 Jackson	Y	Y	Y	Y	Y	Y	Y
3 Lipinski	Y	Y	Y	Y	Y	Y	Y
4 Gutierrez	Y	Y	Y	Y	Y	Y	Y
5 Emanuel	Y	Y	Y	Y	Y	+	Y
6 **Roskam**	N	N	Y	N	N	Y	N
7 Davis	Y	Y	Y	Y	Y	Y	Y
8 Bean	Y	Y	Y	Y	Y	Y	Y
9 Schakowsky	Y	Y	Y	Y	Y	Y	Y
10 **Kirk**	N	N	Y	N	N	Y	N
11 **Weller**	?	?	?	?	?	?	?
12 Costello	Y	Y	Y	Y	Y	Y	Y
13 **Biggert**	N	N	Y	N	N	Y	N
14 Foster	Y	Y	Y	Y	Y	Y	Y
15 **Johnson**	Y	N	Y	N	N	Y	N

ND Northern Democrats, SD Southern Democrats
Southern states: Ala., Ark., Fla., Ga., Ky., La., Miss., N.C., Okla., S.C., Tenn., Texas, Va.

	651	652	653	654	655	656	657
16 **Manzullo**	N	N	Y	N	N	Y	N
17 Hare	Y	Y	Y	Y	Y	Y	Y
18 **LaHood**	N	N	Y	N	N	Y	N
19 **Shimkus**	N	N	Y	N	N	Y	N
INDIANA							
1 Visclosky	Y	Y	Y	Y	Y	Y	Y
2 Donnelly	Y	Y	Y	Y	Y	Y	Y
3 **Souder**	N	N	Y	N	N	Y	N
4 **Buyer**	N	N	Y	N	N	Y	N
5 **Burton**	N	N	Y	N	N	Y	N
6 **Pence**	N	N	Y	N	?	?	N
7 Carson, A.	Y	Y	Y	Y	Y	Y	Y
8 Ellsworth	Y	Y	Y	Y	Y	Y	Y
9 Hill	Y	Y	Y	N	N	Y	N
IOWA							
1 Braley	Y	Y	Y	Y	Y	Y	Y
2 Loebsack	Y	Y	Y	Y	Y	Y	Y
3 Boswell	Y	Y	Y	Y	Y	Y	Y
4 **Latham**	N	N	Y	N	N	Y	N
5 **King**	N	N	Y	N	N	Y	N
KANSAS							
1 **Moran**	N	N	Y	N	N	Y	N
2 Boyda	Y	Y	Y	Y	Y	Y	Y
3 Moore	Y	Y	Y	Y	Y	Y	Y
4 **Tiahrt**	N	N	Y	N	N	Y	N
KENTUCKY							
1 **Whitfield**	N	N	Y	N	N	Y	N
2 **Lewis**	N	N	Y	N	N	Y	N
3 Yarmuth	Y	Y	Y	Y	Y	Y	Y
4 **Davis**	N	N	Y	N	N	Y	N
5 **Rogers**	N	N	Y	N	N	Y	N
6 Chandler	Y	Y	Y	Y	Y	Y	Y
LOUISIANA							
1 **Scalise**	N	N	Y	N	N	Y	N
2 Jefferson	Y	Y	Y	Y	Y	Y	Y
3 Melancon	Y	Y	Y	Y	Y	Y	Y
4 **McCrery**	N	N	Y	N	N	Y	?
5 **Alexander**	N	N	Y	N	N	Y	N
6 Cazayoux	N	N	Y	N	N	Y	N
7 **Boustany**	N	N	Y	N	N	Y	N
MAINE							
1 Allen	Y	Y	Y	Y	Y	Y	Y
2 Michaud	Y	Y	Y	Y	Y	Y	Y
MARYLAND							
1 **Gilchrest**	N	N	Y	N	N	Y	N
2 Ruppersberger	Y	Y	Y	Y	Y	Y	Y
3 Sarbanes	Y	Y	Y	Y	Y	Y	Y
4 Edwards	Y	Y	Y	Y	Y	Y	Y
5 Hoyer	Y	Y	Y	Y	Y	Y	Y
6 **Bartlett**	N	N	Y	N	N	Y	N
7 Cummings	Y	Y	Y	Y	Y	Y	Y
8 Van Hollen	Y	Y	Y	Y	Y	Y	Y
MASSACHUSETTS							
1 Olver	Y	Y	Y	Y	Y	Y	Y
2 Neal	Y	Y	Y	Y	Y	Y	Y
3 McGovern	Y	Y	Y	Y	Y	Y	Y
4 Frank	Y	?	Y	Y	Y	Y	Y
5 Tsongas	Y	Y	Y	Y	Y	Y	Y
6 Tierney	?	?	?	?	?	?	?
7 Markey	Y	Y	Y	Y	Y	Y	Y
8 Capuano	Y	Y	Y	Y	Y	Y	Y
9 Lynch	Y	Y	Y	Y	Y	Y	Y
10 Delahunt	Y	Y	Y	Y	Y	Y	Y
MICHIGAN							
1 Stupak	Y	Y	Y	Y	Y	Y	Y
2 **Hoekstra**	N	N	Y	N	N	Y	N
3 **Ehlers**	N	N	Y	N	N	Y	N
4 **Camp**	N	N	Y	N	N	Y	N
5 Kildee	Y	Y	Y	Y	Y	Y	Y
6 **Upton**	N	N	Y	N	N	Y	N
7 **Walberg**	N	N	Y	N	N	Y	N
8 **Rogers**	N	N	Y	N	N	Y	N
9 **Knollenberg**	N	N	Y	N	N	Y	N
10 **Miller**	N	N	Y	N	N	Y	N
11 **McCotter**	N	N	Y	N	N	Y	N
12 Levin	Y	Y	Y	Y	Y	Y	Y
13 Kilpatrick	Y	Y	Y	Y	Y	Y	Y
14 Conyers	?	?	?	Y	Y	Y	Y
15 Dingell	Y	Y	Y	Y	Y	Y	Y
MINNESOTA							
1 Walz	Y	Y	Y	Y	Y	Y	Y
2 **Kline**	N	N	Y	N	N	Y	N
3 **Ramstad**	N	N	Y	N	N	Y	N
4 McCollum	Y	Y	Y	Y	Y	?	Y

	651	652	653	654	655	656	657
5 Ellison	Y	Y	Y	Y	Y	Y	Y
6 **Bachmann**	N	N	Y	N	N	Y	N
7 Peterson	Y	Y	Y	Y	Y	Y	Y
8 Oberstar	Y	Y	Y	Y	Y	Y	Y
MISSISSIPPI							
1 Childers	N	N	Y	N	N	Y	N
2 Thompson	Y	Y	Y	Y	?	?	?
3 **Pickering**	?	?	?	?	?	?	?
4 Taylor	Y	Y	Y	Y	Y	Y	N
MISSOURI							
1 Clay	Y	Y	Y	Y	Y	Y	Y
2 **Akin**	N	N	Y	N	N	Y	N
3 Carnahan	Y	Y	Y	Y	Y	Y	Y
4 Skelton	Y	Y	Y	Y	Y	Y	Y
5 Cleaver	Y	Y	Y	Y	Y	Y	Y
6 **Graves**	N	N	Y	N	N	Y	N
7 **Blunt**	N	N	?	N	N	Y	N
8 **Emerson**	N	N	Y	N	N	Y	N
9 **Hulshof**	N	N	Y	N	N	Y	N
MONTANA							
AL **Rehberg**	N	N	Y	N	N	Y	N
NEBRASKA							
1 **Fortenberry**	N	N	Y	N	N	Y	N
2 **Terry**	N	N	Y	N	N	Y	N
3 **Smith**	N	N	Y	N	N	Y	N
NEVADA							
1 Berkley	Y	Y	Y	Y	Y	Y	Y
2 **Heller**	N	N	Y	N	N	Y	N
3 **Porter**	N	N	Y	N	N	Y	N
NEW HAMPSHIRE							
1 Shea-Porter	Y	Y	?	Y	Y	Y	Y
2 Hodes	Y	Y	Y	Y	Y	Y	Y
NEW JERSEY							
1 Andrews	Y	Y	Y	Y	Y	Y	Y
2 **LoBiondo**	N	N	Y	N	N	Y	N
3 **Saxton**	N	N	Y	N	N	Y	N
4 **Smith**	N	N	Y	N	N	Y	N
5 **Garrett**	N	N	Y	N	N	Y	N
6 Pallone	Y	Y	Y	Y	Y	Y	Y
7 **Ferguson**	N	N	Y	N	N	Y	N
8 Pascrell	Y	Y	Y	Y	Y	Y	Y
9 Rothman	Y	Y	Y	Y	Y	Y	Y
10 Payne	?	?	?	Y	Y	Y	Y
11 **Frelinghuysen**	N	N	Y	N	N	Y	N
12 Holt	Y	Y	Y	Y	Y	Y	Y
13 Sires	Y	Y	Y	Y	Y	Y	Y
NEW MEXICO							
1 **Wilson**	N	N	Y	N	N	Y	N
2 **Pearce**	N	N	Y	N	N	Y	N
3 Udall	Y	Y	Y	Y	Y	Y	Y
NEW YORK							
1 Bishop	Y	Y	Y	Y	Y	Y	Y
2 Israel	Y	Y	Y	Y	Y	Y	Y
3 **King**	N	N	Y	N	N	Y	N
4 McCarthy	Y	Y	Y	Y	Y	Y	Y
5 Ackerman	Y	Y	Y	Y	Y	Y	Y
6 Meeks	Y	Y	Y	Y	Y	Y	Y
7 Crowley	Y	Y	Y	Y	Y	Y	Y
8 Nadler	Y	Y	Y	Y	Y	Y	Y
9 Weiner	Y	Y	Y	Y	Y	Y	Y
10 Towns	Y	Y	Y	Y	Y	Y	Y
11 Clarke	Y	Y	Y	Y	Y	Y	Y
12 Velázquez	Y	Y	Y	Y	Y	Y	Y
13 **Fossella**	N	N	Y	N	N	Y	N
14 Maloney	Y	Y	Y	Y	Y	Y	Y
15 Rangel	?	Y	Y	Y	Y	Y	Y
16 Serrano	Y	Y	Y	Y	Y	Y	Y
17 Engel	Y	Y	Y	Y	Y	Y	Y
18 Lowey	Y	?	Y	Y	Y	Y	Y
19 Hall	Y	Y	Y	Y	Y	Y	Y
20 Gillibrand	Y	Y	Y	Y	Y	Y	Y
21 McNulty	Y	Y	Y	Y	Y	Y	Y
22 Hinchey	Y	Y	Y	Y	Y	Y	Y
23 **McHugh**	N	N	Y	N	N	Y	N
24 Arcuri	Y	Y	Y	Y	Y	Y	Y
25 **Walsh**	N	N	Y	N	N	Y	N
26 **Reynolds**	N	N	Y	N	N	Y	N
27 Higgins	Y	Y	Y	Y	Y	Y	Y
28 Slaughter	Y	Y	?	Y	Y	Y	Y
29 **Kuhl**	N	N	Y	N	N	Y	N
NORTH CAROLINA							
1 Butterfield	Y	Y	Y	Y	Y	Y	Y
2 Etheridge	Y	Y	Y	Y	Y	Y	Y
3 **Jones**	N	N	Y	N	N	Y	N
4 Price	Y	Y	Y	Y	Y	Y	Y

	651	652	653	654	655	656	657
5 **Foxx**	N	N	N	N	N	Y	N
6 **Coble**	N	N	Y	N	N	Y	N
7 McIntyre	Y	Y	Y	Y	Y	Y	Y
8 **Hayes**	N	N	Y	N	N	Y	N
9 **Myrick**	N	N	Y	N	N	Y	N
10 **McHenry**	N	N	Y	N	N	Y	N
11 Shuler	Y	Y	Y	Y	N	Y	Y
12 Watt	Y	Y	Y	Y	Y	Y	Y
13 Miller	Y	Y	Y	Y	Y	Y	Y
NORTH DAKOTA							
AL Pomeroy	Y	Y	Y	Y	Y	Y	Y
OHIO							
1 **Chabot**	N	N	Y	N	N	Y	N
2 **Schmidt**	N	N	Y	N	N	Y	N
3 **Turner**	N	N	Y	N	N	Y	N
4 **Jordan**	N	N	Y	N	N	Y	N
5 **Latta**	N	N	Y	N	N	Y	N
6 Wilson	Y	Y	Y	Y	Y	Y	Y
7 **Hobson**	N	N	Y	N	N	Y	N
8 **Boehner**	N	N	Y	N	N	Y	N
9 Kaptur	Y	Y	Y	Y	Y	Y	Y
10 Kucinich	Y	Y	Y	N	N	Y	Y
11 Vacant							
12 **Tiberi**	N	N	Y	N	N	Y	N
13 Sutton	Y	Y	Y	Y	Y	Y	Y
14 **LaTourette**	N	N	Y	N	N	Y	N
15 **Pryce**	N	N	Y	N	N	Y	N
16 **Regula**	N	N	Y	N	N	Y	N
17 Ryan	Y	Y	Y	Y	Y	Y	Y
18 Space	Y	Y	Y	Y	Y	Y	Y
OKLAHOMA							
1 **Sullivan**	N	N	Y	N	N	Y	N
2 Boren	Y	Y	Y	Y	Y	Y	Y
3 **Lucas**	N	N	Y	N	N	Y	N
4 **Cole**	N	N	Y	N	N	Y	N
5 **Fallin**	N	N	Y	N	N	Y	N
OREGON							
1 Wu	Y	Y	Y	N	Y	Y	N
2 **Walden**	N	N	Y	?	N	Y	N
3 Blumenauer	Y	Y	Y	Y	Y	Y	Y
4 DeFazio	Y	Y	?	N	Y	Y	N
5 Hooley	Y	Y	?	Y	Y	Y	N
PENNSYLVANIA							
1 Brady	Y	Y	Y	Y	Y	Y	Y
2 Fattah	Y	Y	Y	Y	Y	Y	Y
3 **English**	?	?	?	N	N	Y	N
4 Altmire	Y	Y	Y	Y	Y	Y	Y
5 **Peterson**	?	?	?	?	?	?	?
6 **Gerlach**	N	N	Y	N	N	Y	N
7 Sestak	Y	Y	Y	Y	Y	Y	Y
8 Murphy, P.	Y	Y	Y	Y	Y	Y	Y
9 **Shuster**	N	N	Y	N	N	Y	N
10 Carney	Y	Y	Y	Y	Y	Y	Y
11 Kanjorski	Y	Y	Y	Y	Y	Y	Y
12 Murtha	Y	Y	Y	Y	Y	Y	Y
13 Schwartz	Y	Y	Y	Y	Y	Y	Y
14 Doyle	Y	Y	Y	Y	Y	Y	Y
15 **Dent**	N	N	Y	N	N	Y	N
16 **Pitts**	N	N	Y	N	N	Y	N
17 Holden	Y	Y	Y	Y	Y	Y	Y
18 **Murphy, T.**	N	N	Y	N	N	Y	N
19 **Platts**	N	N	Y	N	N	Y	N
RHODE ISLAND							
1 Kennedy	Y	Y	Y	Y	Y	Y	Y
2 Langevin	Y	Y	Y	Y	Y	Y	Y
SOUTH CAROLINA							
1 **Brown**	N	N	Y	N	N	Y	N
2 **Wilson**	N	N	Y	N	N	Y	N
3 **Barrett**	N	N	Y	N	N	Y	N
4 **Inglis**	N	N	Y	N	N	Y	N
5 Spratt	Y	Y	Y	Y	Y	Y	Y
6 Clyburn	Y	Y	Y	Y	Y	Y	Y
SOUTH DAKOTA							
AL Herseth Sandlin	Y	Y	Y	Y	N	Y	Y
TENNESSEE							
1 **Davis, D.**	N	N	Y	N	N	Y	N
2 **Duncan**	N	N	N	N	N	Y	N
3 **Wamp**	N	N	Y	N	N	Y	N
4 Davis, L.	Y	Y	Y	Y	Y	Y	Y
5 Cooper	Y	Y	Y	Y	N	Y	Y
6 Gordon	Y	Y	Y	Y	Y	Y	Y
7 **Blackburn**	N	N	Y	N	N	Y	N
8 Tanner	Y	Y	Y	Y	Y	Y	Y
9 Cohen	Y	Y	Y	Y	Y	Y	Y

	651	652	653	654	655	656	657
TEXAS							
1 **Gohmert**	N	N	Y	N	N	Y	N
2 **Poe**	N	N	N	N	N	Y	N
3 **Johnson, S.**	N	N	Y	N	N	Y	N
4 **Hall**	N	N	Y	N	N	Y	N
5 **Hensarling**	N	N	Y	N	N	Y	N
6 **Barton**	N	N	Y	N	N	Y	N
7 **Culberson**	N	N	Y	N	N	Y	N
8 **Brady**	N	N	Y	N	N	Y	N
9 Green, A.	Y	Y	Y	Y	Y	Y	Y
10 **McCaul**	N	N	Y	N	N	Y	N
11 **Conaway**	N	N	Y	N	N	Y	N
12 **Granger**	N	N	Y	N	N	Y	N
13 **Thornberry**	N	N	Y	N	N	Y	N
14 **Paul**	N	N	N	N	N	?	N
15 Hinojosa	Y	Y	Y	Y	Y	Y	Y
16 Reyes	Y	Y	Y	Y	Y	Y	Y
17 Edwards	Y	Y	Y	Y	Y	Y	Y
18 Jackson Lee	Y	Y	Y	Y	Y	Y	Y
19 **Neugebauer**	N	N	Y	N	N	Y	N
20 Gonzalez	Y	Y	Y	Y	Y	Y	Y
21 **Smith**	N	N	Y	N	N	Y	N
22 Lampson	N	Y	Y	N	N	Y	N
23 Rodriguez	Y	Y	Y	Y	Y	Y	Y
24 **Marchant**	N	N	Y	N	N	Y	N
25 Doggett	Y	Y	Y	Y	Y	Y	Y
26 **Burgess**	N	N	Y	N	N	Y	N
27 Ortiz	Y	Y	Y	Y	Y	Y	Y
28 Cuellar	Y	Y	Y	Y	Y	Y	Y
29 Green, G.	Y	Y	Y	Y	Y	Y	Y
30 Johnson, E.	Y	Y	Y	Y	Y	Y	Y
31 **Carter**	N	N	Y	N	N	Y	N
32 **Sessions**	N	N	Y	N	N	Y	N
UTAH							
1 **Bishop**	N	N	Y	N	N	Y	N
2 Matheson	Y	Y	Y	Y	Y	Y	N
3 **Cannon**	N	N	Y	N	?	Y	N
VERMONT							
AL Welch	Y	Y	Y	Y	Y	Y	Y
VIRGINIA							
1 **Wittman**	N	N	Y	N	N	Y	N
2 **Drake**	N	N	Y	N	N	Y	N
3 Scott	Y	Y	Y	Y	?	Y	Y
4 **Forbes**	N	N	Y	N	N	Y	N
5 **Goode**	N	N	Y	N	N	Y	N
6 **Goodlatte**	N	N	Y	N	N	Y	N
7 **Cantor**	N	N	Y	?	N	Y	N
8 Moran	Y	Y	Y	Y	Y	Y	Y
9 Boucher	Y	Y	Y	Y	Y	Y	Y
10 **Wolf**	N	N	Y	N	N	Y	N
11 **Davis**	N	N	Y	N	N	Y	N
WASHINGTON							
1 Inslee	Y	Y	Y	Y	Y	Y	Y
2 Larsen	Y	Y	Y	Y	Y	Y	Y
3 Baird	Y	Y	Y	Y	N	Y	N
4 **Hastings**	N	N	Y	N	N	Y	N
5 **McMorris Rodgers**	N	N	Y	N	N	Y	N
6 Dicks	Y	Y	Y	Y	Y	Y	Y
7 McDermott	Y	Y	Y	Y	Y	Y	Y
8 **Reichert**	Y	N	Y	Y	N	Y	N
9 Smith	Y	Y	Y	Y	Y	Y	Y
WEST VIRGINIA							
1 Mollohan	Y	Y	Y	Y	Y	Y	Y
2 **Capito**	N	N	Y	N	N	Y	N
3 Rahall	Y	Y	Y	Y	Y	Y	Y
WISCONSIN							
1 **Ryan**	N	N	Y	N	N	Y	N
2 Baldwin	Y	Y	Y	Y	Y	Y	Y
3 Kind	Y	Y	?	Y	Y	Y	Y
4 Moore	Y	Y	Y	Y	Y	Y	Y
5 **Sensenbrenner**	N	N	Y	N	N	Y	N
6 **Petri**	N	N	Y	N	N	Y	N
7 Obey	Y	Y	Y	Y	Y	Y	Y
8 Kagen	Y	Y	Y	Y	Y	Y	Y
WYOMING							
AL **Cubin**	?	?	?	?	?	?	?
DELEGATES							
Faleomavaega (A.S.)							
Norton (D.C.)							
Bordallo (Guam)							
Fortuño (P.R.)							
Christensen (V.I.)							

IN THE HOUSE | By Vote Number

658. HR 7110. **Supplemental Appropriations/Rule.** Adoption of the rule (H Res 1507) to provide for House floor consideration of the bill that would extend unemployment benefits and provide additional fiscal 2009 funds for food assistance programs, infrastructure projects, energy development, public housing, state Medicaid plans and other programs. Adopted 213-208: R 0-192; D 213-16 (ND 164-8, SD 49-8). Sept. 26, 2008.

659. S 1046. **Federal Employee Pay/Passage.** Towns, D-N.Y., motion to suspend the rules and pass the bill that would raise the cap on base pay for certain senior level positions and scientific and professional positions in the federal government to be equal to the current pay for senior executive service positions. The pay change would take effect the first pay period 180 days after the bill's enactment. Motion agreed to 419-0: R 192-0; D 227-0 (ND 170-0, SD 57-0). A two-thirds majority of those present and voting (280 in this case) is required for passage under suspension of the rules. Sept. 26, 2008.

660. HR 7110. **Supplemental Appropriations/Passage.** Passage of the bill that would appropriate $60.8 billion to extend unemployment benefits and provide additional fiscal 2009 funds for food assistance programs, infrastructure projects, energy development, public housing, state Medicaid plans and other programs. The bill includes $12.8 billion for highway infrastructure investment; $5 billion for the Army Corps of Engineers; $7.5 billion for grants for drinking water and sewer projects; $3 billion to modernize and repair schools; $3.6 billion for grants to expand public transportation; and $2.6 billion for food assistance for seniors, people with disabilities and low-income families. Passed 264-158: R 41-150; D 223-8 (ND 171-3, SD 52-5). A "nay" was a vote in support of the president's position. Sept. 26, 2008.

661. HR 928. **Inspector General System/Passage.** Towns, D-N.Y., motion to suspend the rules and concur in the Senate amendment to the bill that would limit the reasons for which inspectors general could be fired. It would provide for direct submission of inspectors' general budgets to Congress. It would create a new panel that would be required to review allegations of misconduct by inspectors general. Motion agreed to 414-0: R 189-0; D 225-0 (ND 168-0, SD 57-0). A two-thirds majority of those present and voting (276 in this case) is required for passage under suspension of the rules. Sept. 27, 2008.

662. HR 7081. **U.S.-India Nuclear Agreement/Passage.** Berman, D-Calif., motion to suspend the rules and pass the bill that would grant congressional approval to the U.S.-India nuclear cooperation agreement. It would require that the president determine and certify to Congress that certain actions have occurred before the Nuclear Regulatory Commission could issue licenses for transfers of nuclear-related goods and services, including that India has provided the International Atomic Energy Agency with a credible plan to separate civilian and military nuclear facilities, materials and programs. Motion agreed to 298-117: R 178-10; D 120-107 (ND 76-94, SD 44-13). A two-thirds majority of those present and voting (277 in this case) is required for passage under suspension of the rules. A "yea" was a vote in support of the president's position. Sept. 27, 2008.

	658	659	660	661	662
ALABAMA					
1 **Bonner**	N	Y	N	Y	Y
2 **Everett**	N	Y	N	Y	N
3 **Rogers**	N	Y	Y	Y	Y
4 **Aderholt**	N	Y	N	Y	?
5 Cramer	Y	Y	Y	Y	Y
6 **Bachus**	N	Y	N	Y	Y
7 Davis	Y	Y	Y	Y	Y
ALASKA					
AL **Young**	N	Y	Y	Y	Y
ARIZONA					
1 **Renzi**	N	Y	Y	Y	Y
2 **Franks**	N	Y	N	Y	+
3 **Shadegg**	N	Y	N	Y	Y
4 Pastor	Y	Y	Y	Y	N
5 Mitchell	Y	Y	Y	Y	N
6 **Flake**	N	Y	N	Y	Y
7 Grijalva	Y	Y	Y	Y	N
8 Giffords	Y	Y	Y	Y	N
ARKANSAS					
1 Berry	Y	Y	N	Y	N
2 Snyder	Y	Y	Y	Y	Y
3 **Boozman**	N	Y	N	Y	Y
4 Ross	Y	Y	Y	Y	Y
CALIFORNIA					
1 Thompson	Y	Y	Y	Y	N
2 **Herger**	N	Y	N	Y	Y
3 **Lungren**	N	Y	N	Y	Y
4 **Doolittle**	N	Y	N	?	?
5 Matsui	Y	Y	Y	Y	N
6 Woolsey	Y	Y	Y	Y	N
7 Miller, George	Y	Y	Y	Y	N
8 Pelosi			Y		
9 Lee	Y	Y	Y	Y	N
10 Tauscher	Y	Y	Y	Y	N
11 McNerney	Y	Y	Y	Y	N
12 Speier	Y	Y	Y	Y	N
13 Stark	Y	Y	Y	Y	N
14 Eshoo	Y	Y	Y	Y	Y
15 Honda	Y	Y	Y	Y	Y
16 Lofgren	Y	Y	Y	Y	Y
17 Farr	Y	Y	Y	Y	N
18 Cardoza	Y	Y	Y	Y	Y
19 **Radanovich**	N	Y	N	Y	Y
20 Costa	?	?	?	Y	Y
21 **Nunes**	N	Y	N	Y	Y
22 **McCarthy**	N	Y	N	Y	Y
23 Capps	Y	Y	Y	Y	N
24 **Gallegly**	N	Y	N	Y	Y
25 **McKeon**	N	Y	N	Y	Y
26 **Dreier**	N	Y	N	Y	Y
27 Sherman	Y	Y	Y	Y	Y
28 Berman	Y	Y	Y	Y	Y
29 Schiff	Y	Y	Y	Y	N
30 Waxman	Y	?	Y	Y	N
31 Becerra	Y	Y	Y	Y	N
32 Solis	Y	Y	Y	Y	N
33 Watson	Y	Y	Y	Y	N
34 Roybal-Allard	Y	Y	Y	Y	N
35 Waters	Y	Y	Y	Y	Y
36 Harman	Y	Y	Y	Y	N
37 Richardson	Y	Y	Y	Y	N
38 Napolitano	Y	Y	Y	Y	N
39 Sánchez, Linda	Y	Y	Y	Y	N
40 **Royce**	N	Y	N	Y	Y
41 **Lewis**	N	Y	N	Y	Y
42 **Miller, Gary**	N	Y	N	Y	Y
43 Baca	Y	Y	Y	Y	Y
44 **Calvert**	N	Y	N	Y	Y
45 **Bono Mack**	N	Y	Y	Y	Y
46 **Rohrabacher**	N	Y	N	Y	Y
47 Sanchez, Loretta	N	Y	Y	Y	N
48 **Campbell**	N	Y	N	Y	Y
49 **Issa**	N	Y	N	Y	Y
50 **Bilbray**	N	Y	N	Y	Y
51 Filner	Y	Y	Y	Y	N
52 **Hunter**	N	Y	N	Y	Y
53 Davis	Y	Y	Y	Y	N

	658	659	660	661	662
COLORADO					
1 DeGette	Y	Y	Y	Y	N
2 Udall	?	?	Y	Y	Y
3 Salazar	Y	Y	Y	Y	Y
4 **Musgrave**	N	Y	Y	Y	Y
5 **Lamborn**	N	Y	N	Y	Y
6 **Tancredo**	N	Y	N	Y	Y
7 Perlmutter	Y	Y	Y	Y	N
CONNECTICUT					
1 Larson	Y	Y	Y	Y	Y
2 Courtney	Y	Y	Y	Y	N
3 DeLauro	Y	Y	Y	Y	N
4 **Shays**	N	Y	Y	Y	Y
5 Murphy	Y	Y	Y	Y	Y
DELAWARE					
AL **Castle**	N	Y	Y	Y	Y
FLORIDA					
1 **Miller**	N	Y	N	Y	Y
2 Boyd	N	Y	N	Y	Y
3 Brown	Y	Y	Y	Y	Y
4 **Crenshaw**	N	Y	N	Y	Y
5 **Brown-Waite**	N	Y	N	Y	Y
6 **Stearns**	N	Y	N	Y	Y
7 **Mica**	N	Y	N	Y	Y
8 **Keller**	N	Y	N	Y	Y
9 **Bilirakis**	N	Y	N	Y	Y
10 **Young**	N	Y	N	Y	Y
11 Castor	Y	Y	Y	Y	N
12 **Putnam**	N	Y	N	Y	Y
13 **Buchanan**	N	Y	N	Y	Y
14 **Mack**	N	Y	N	Y	Y
15 **Weldon**	N	?	N	Y	Y
16 Mahoney	Y	Y	Y	Y	Y
17 Meek	Y	Y	Y	Y	N
18 **Ros-Lehtinen**	N	Y	Y	Y	Y
19 Wexler	?	?	?	?	?
20 Wasserman Schultz	Y	Y	Y	Y	N
21 **Diaz-Balart, L.**	N	Y	Y	Y	Y
22 Klein	Y	Y	Y	Y	Y
23 Hastings	Y	Y	Y	Y	N
24 **Feeney**	N	Y	–	Y	Y
25 **Diaz-Balart, M.**	N	Y	Y	Y	Y
GEORGIA					
1 **Kingston**	N	Y	N	Y	Y
2 Bishop	Y	Y	Y	Y	Y
3 **Westmoreland**	N	Y	N	Y	Y
4 Johnson	Y	Y	Y	Y	N
5 Lewis	Y	Y	Y	Y	N
6 **Price**	N	Y	N	Y	Y
7 **Linder**	N	Y	N	Y	Y
8 Marshall	Y	Y	Y	Y	N
9 **Deal**	N	Y	N	Y	Y
10 **Broun**	N	Y	N	Y	Y
11 **Gingrey**	–	+	N	Y	Y
12 Barrow	Y	Y	Y	Y	Y
13 Scott	Y	Y	Y	Y	Y
HAWAII					
1 Abercrombie	Y	Y	Y	Y	N
2 Hirono	Y	Y	Y	Y	N
IDAHO					
1 **Sali**	N	Y	N	Y	Y
2 **Simpson**	N	Y	N	Y	Y
ILLINOIS					
1 Rush	Y	Y	Y	Y	Y
2 Jackson	Y	Y	Y	Y	Y
3 Lipinski	Y	Y	Y	Y	Y
4 Gutierrez	Y	Y	Y	Y	Y
5 Emanuel	Y	Y	Y	?	Y
6 **Roskam**	N	Y	N	Y	Y
7 Davis	Y	Y	Y	Y	Y
8 Bean	Y	Y	Y	Y	Y
9 Schakowsky	Y	Y	Y	Y	Y
10 **Kirk**	N	Y	N	Y	Y
11 **Weller**	?	?	?	?	?
12 Costello	Y	Y	Y	Y	N
13 **Biggert**	N	Y	N	Y	Y
14 Foster	Y	Y	Y	Y	P
15 **Johnson**	N	Y	N	Y	Y

KEY	**Republicans**	Democrats		
Y Voted for (yea)		X Paired against		C Voted "present" to avoid possible conflict of interest
# Paired for		– Announced against		
+ Announced for		P Voted "present"		? Did not vote or otherwise make a position known
N Voted against (nay)				

ND Northern Democrats, SD Southern Democrats
Southern states: Ala., Ark., Fla., Ga., Ky., La., Miss., N.C., Okla., S.C., Tenn., Texas, Va.

H-222 2008 CQ ALMANAC | www.cq.com

	658	659	660	661	662
16 Manzullo	N	Y	N	Y	Y
17 Hare	Y	Y	Y	Y	N
18 LaHood	N	Y	?	Y	Y
19 Shimkus	N	Y	N	Y	Y
INDIANA					
1 Visclosky	Y	Y	Y	Y	N
2 Donnelly	Y	Y	Y	Y	Y
3 Souder	N	Y	N	Y	Y
4 Buyer	N	Y	N	Y	?
5 Burton	N	Y	N	Y	Y
6 Pence	N	Y	N	Y	Y
7 Carson, A.	Y	Y	Y	Y	N
8 Ellsworth	Y	Y	Y	Y	Y
9 Hill	N	Y	Y	Y	Y
IOWA					
1 Braley	Y	Y	Y	Y	N
2 Loebsack	Y	Y	Y	Y	N
3 Boswell	Y	Y	Y	Y	N
4 Latham	N	Y	N	Y	Y
5 King	N	Y	N	Y	Y
KANSAS					
1 Moran	N	Y	N	Y	Y
2 Boyda	Y	?	Y	Y	N
3 Moore	Y	Y	Y	Y	Y
4 Tiahrt	N	Y	N	Y	Y
KENTUCKY					
1 Whitfield	N	Y	?	Y	Y
2 Lewis	N	Y	N	Y	Y
3 Yarmuth	Y	Y	Y	Y	N
4 Davis	N	Y	N	Y	Y
5 Rogers	N	Y	N	Y	Y
6 Chandler	Y	Y	Y	Y	Y
LOUISIANA					
1 Scalise	N	Y	N	Y	Y
2 Jefferson	Y	Y	Y	?	?
3 Melancon	Y	Y	Y	Y	Y
4 McCrery	?	?	N	Y	Y
5 Alexander	N	Y	N	Y	Y
6 Cazayoux	N	Y	Y	Y	Y
7 Boustany	N	Y	N	Y	Y
MAINE					
1 Allen	Y	Y	Y	Y	Y
2 Michaud	N	Y	Y	Y	N
MARYLAND					
1 Gilchrest	N	Y	Y	Y	Y
2 Ruppersberger	Y	Y	Y	Y	Y
3 Sarbanes	Y	Y	Y	Y	Y
4 Edwards	Y	Y	Y	Y	N
5 Hoyer	Y	Y	Y	Y	Y
6 Bartlett	N	Y	N	Y	Y
7 Cummings	Y	Y	Y	Y	N
8 Van Hollen	Y	Y	Y	Y	Y
MASSACHUSETTS					
1 Olver	Y	Y	Y	Y	N
2 Neal	Y	Y	Y	Y	Y
3 McGovern	Y	Y	Y	Y	N
4 Frank	Y	Y	Y	?	Y
5 Tsongas	Y	Y	Y	Y	N
6 Tierney	?	?	?	?	?
7 Markey	Y	Y	Y	Y	N
8 Capuano	Y	Y	Y	Y	Y
9 Lynch	Y	Y	Y	?	?
10 Delahunt	Y	Y	Y	Y	Y
MICHIGAN					
1 Stupak	Y	Y	Y	Y	N
2 Hoekstra	N	Y	N	Y	Y
3 Ehlers	N	Y	N	Y	Y
4 Camp	N	Y	N	Y	Y
5 Kildee	Y	Y	Y	Y	N
6 Upton	N	Y	N	Y	Y
7 Walberg	N	Y	N	Y	Y
8 Rogers	N	Y	N	Y	Y
9 Knollenberg	N	Y	N	Y	Y
10 Miller	N	Y	Y	Y	Y
11 McCotter	N	Y	N	Y	Y
12 Levin	Y	Y	Y	Y	N
13 Kilpatrick	Y	Y	Y	Y	N
14 Conyers	Y	Y	Y	Y	N
15 Dingell	Y	Y	Y	Y	N
MINNESOTA					
1 Walz	Y	Y	Y	Y	N
2 Kline	N	Y	N	Y	Y
3 Ramstad	N	Y	N	Y	Y
4 McCollum	Y	Y	Y	Y	N

	658	659	660	661	662
5 Ellison	Y	Y	Y	Y	N
6 Bachmann	N	Y	N	Y	Y
7 Peterson	Y	Y	N	Y	Y
8 Oberstar	Y	Y	Y	Y	N
MISSISSIPPI					
1 Childers	N	Y	Y	Y	Y
2 Thompson	?	?	?	Y	N
3 Pickering	?	?	?	?	?
4 Taylor	N	Y	N	Y	Y
MISSOURI					
1 Clay	Y	Y	Y	Y	Y
2 Akin	N	Y	N	Y	Y
3 Carnahan	Y	Y	Y	Y	Y
4 Skelton	Y	Y	Y	Y	N
5 Cleaver	Y	Y	Y	Y	N
6 Graves	N	Y	N	Y	Y
7 Blunt	N	Y	N	?	Y
8 Emerson	N	Y	Y	Y	Y
9 Hulshof	N	Y	N	Y	Y
MONTANA					
AL Rehberg	N	Y	N	Y	Y
NEBRASKA					
1 Fortenberry	N	Y	N	Y	Y
2 Terry	N	Y	N	Y	Y
3 Smith	N	Y	N	Y	Y
NEVADA					
1 Berkley	Y	Y	Y	Y	N
2 Heller	N	Y	Y	Y	Y
3 Porter	N	Y	Y	Y	Y
NEW HAMPSHIRE					
1 Shea-Porter	Y	Y	Y	Y	N
2 Hodes	Y	Y	Y	Y	Y
NEW JERSEY					
1 Andrews	Y	Y	Y	Y	Y
2 LoBiondo	N	Y	Y	Y	Y
3 Saxton	N	Y	?	Y	Y
4 Smith	N	Y	Y	Y	N
5 Garrett	N	Y	N	Y	Y
6 Pallone	Y	Y	Y	Y	Y
7 Ferguson	N	Y	Y	Y	Y
8 Pascrell	Y	Y	Y	Y	N
9 Rothman	Y	Y	Y	Y	N
10 Payne	Y	Y	Y	Y	N
11 Frelinghuysen	N	Y	N	Y	Y
12 Holt	Y	Y	Y	Y	N
13 Sires	Y	Y	Y	Y	Y
NEW MEXICO					
1 Wilson	N	Y	N	Y	Y
2 Pearce	N	Y	N	Y	Y
3 Udall	Y	Y	Y	Y	N
NEW YORK					
1 Bishop	Y	Y	Y	Y	Y
2 Israel	Y	Y	Y	Y	Y
3 King	N	Y	N	Y	Y
4 McCarthy	Y	Y	Y	Y	Y
5 Ackerman	Y	Y	Y	Y	Y
6 Meeks	Y	Y	Y	Y	Y
7 Crowley	Y	Y	Y	Y	Y
8 Nadler	Y	Y	Y	Y	N
9 Weiner	Y	Y	Y	?	?
10 Towns	Y	Y	Y	Y	N
11 Clarke	Y	Y	Y	Y	N
12 Velázquez	Y	Y	Y	Y	N
13 Fossella	N	Y	N	Y	Y
14 Maloney	Y	Y	Y	Y	Y
15 Rangel	Y	Y	Y	?	Y
16 Serrano	Y	Y	Y	Y	N
17 Engel	Y	Y	Y	Y	Y
18 Lowey	Y	Y	Y	Y	Y
19 Hall	Y	Y	Y	Y	N
20 Gillibrand	N	Y	Y	Y	Y
21 McNulty	Y	Y	Y	Y	Y
22 Hinchey	Y	Y	Y	Y	N
23 McHugh	N	Y	Y	Y	Y
24 Arcuri	Y	Y	Y	Y	Y
25 Walsh	N	Y	Y	?	?
26 Reynolds	N	Y	N	Y	Y
27 Higgins	Y	Y	Y	Y	Y
28 Slaughter	Y	Y	Y	Y	N
29 Kuhl	N	Y	Y	Y	Y
NORTH CAROLINA					
1 Butterfield	Y	Y	Y	Y	N
2 Etheridge	Y	Y	Y	Y	Y
3 Jones	N	Y	Y	Y	N
4 Price	Y	Y	Y	Y	N

	658	659	660	661	662
5 Foxx	N	Y	N	Y	Y
6 Coble	N	Y	N	Y	Y
7 McIntyre	Y	Y	Y	Y	Y
8 Hayes	N	Y	Y	Y	N
9 Myrick	N	Y	N	Y	Y
10 McHenry	N	Y	N	Y	Y
11 Shuler	N	Y	Y	Y	N
12 Watt	Y	Y	Y	Y	Y
13 Miller	Y	Y	Y	Y	Y
NORTH DAKOTA					
AL Pomeroy	Y	Y	Y	Y	N
OHIO					
1 Chabot	N	Y	N	Y	Y
2 Schmidt	N	Y	N	Y	Y
3 Turner	N	Y	N	Y	Y
4 Jordan	N	Y	N	Y	Y
5 Latta	N	Y	N	Y	Y
6 Wilson	Y	Y	Y	Y	N
7 Hobson	N	Y	N	Y	Y
8 Boehner	N	Y	N	Y	Y
9 Kaptur	Y	Y	Y	?	?
10 Kucinich	Y	Y	Y	Y	N
11 Vacant					
12 Tiberi	N	Y	N	Y	Y
13 Sutton	Y	Y	Y	Y	N
14 LaTourette	N	Y	Y	Y	Y
15 Pryce	N	Y	N	?	?
16 Regula	N	Y	N	Y	Y
17 Ryan	Y	Y	Y	Y	Y
18 Space	Y	Y	Y	Y	N
OKLAHOMA					
1 Sullivan	N	Y	N	Y	Y
2 Boren	Y	Y	Y	Y	Y
3 Lucas	N	Y	N	Y	Y
4 Cole	N	Y	N	Y	Y
5 Fallin	N	Y	N	Y	Y
OREGON					
1 Wu	Y	Y	Y	Y	Y
2 Walden	N	Y	N	Y	Y
3 Blumenauer	Y	Y	Y	Y	N
4 DeFazio	N	Y	Y	Y	N
5 Hooley	N	Y	Y	Y	Y
PENNSYLVANIA					
1 Brady	Y	Y	Y	Y	N
2 Fattah	Y	Y	Y	Y	N
3 English	N	Y	Y	Y	Y
4 Altmire	Y	Y	Y	Y	Y
5 Peterson	?	?	?	?	?
6 Gerlach	N	Y	Y	Y	Y
7 Sestak	Y	Y	Y	Y	N
8 Murphy, P.	Y	Y	Y	Y	Y
9 Shuster	N	Y	N	Y	Y
10 Carney	Y	Y	Y	Y	Y
11 Kanjorski	Y	Y	Y	Y	Y
12 Murtha	Y	Y	Y	Y	Y
13 Schwartz	Y	Y	Y	Y	Y
14 Doyle	Y	Y	Y	Y	Y
15 Dent	N	Y	Y	Y	Y
16 Pitts	N	Y	N	Y	Y
17 Holden	Y	Y	Y	Y	Y
18 Murphy, T.	N	Y	Y	?	+
19 Platts	N	Y	Y	Y	Y
RHODE ISLAND					
1 Kennedy	Y	Y	Y	Y	N
2 Langevin	Y	Y	Y	Y	N
SOUTH CAROLINA					
1 Brown	N	Y	N	Y	Y
2 Wilson	N	Y	N	Y	Y
3 Barrett	N	Y	N	Y	Y
4 Inglis	N	Y	N	Y	Y
5 Spratt	Y	Y	Y	Y	Y
6 Clyburn	Y	Y	Y	Y	N
SOUTH DAKOTA					
AL Herseth Sandlin	N	Y	N	Y	Y
TENNESSEE					
1 Davis, D.	N	Y	N	Y	Y
2 Duncan	N	Y	N	Y	Y
3 Wamp	N	Y	N	Y	Y
4 Davis, L.	Y	Y	Y	Y	Y
5 Cooper	N	Y	N	Y	Y
6 Gordon	Y	Y	Y	Y	Y
7 Blackburn	N	Y	N	Y	Y
8 Tanner	Y	Y	Y	Y	Y
9 Cohen	Y	Y	Y	Y	N

	658	659	660	661	662
TEXAS					
1 Gohmert	N	Y	N	Y	Y
2 Poe	N	Y	N	Y	Y
3 Johnson, S.	N	Y	N	Y	Y
4 Hall	N	Y	Y	Y	Y
5 Hensarling	N	Y	N	Y	Y
6 Barton	N	Y	N	Y	Y
7 Culberson	N	Y	N	Y	Y
8 Brady	N	Y	N	Y	Y
9 Green, A.	Y	Y	Y	Y	Y
10 McCaul	N	Y	N	Y	Y
11 Conaway	N	Y	N	Y	Y
12 Granger	N	Y	N	Y	Y
13 Thornberry	N	Y	N	Y	Y
14 Paul	N	Y	N	Y	N
15 Hinojosa	Y	Y	Y	Y	N
16 Reyes	Y	Y	Y	Y	Y
17 Edwards	Y	Y	Y	Y	Y
18 Jackson Lee	Y	Y	Y	Y	Y
19 Neugebauer	N	Y	N	Y	Y
20 Gonzalez	Y	Y	Y	Y	Y
21 Smith	N	Y	N	Y	Y
22 Lampson	Y	Y	N	Y	Y
23 Rodriguez	Y	Y	Y	Y	Y
24 Marchant	N	Y	N	Y	Y
25 Doggett	Y	Y	Y	Y	N
26 Burgess	N	Y	N	Y	Y
27 Ortiz	Y	Y	Y	Y	Y
28 Cuellar	Y	Y	Y	Y	Y
29 Green, G.	Y	Y	Y	Y	Y
30 Johnson, E.	Y	Y	Y	Y	Y
31 Carter	N	Y	N	Y	Y
32 Sessions	N	Y	N	Y	Y
UTAH					
1 Bishop	N	Y	N	Y	Y
2 Matheson	Y	Y	Y	Y	Y
3 Cannon	?	Y	N	Y	Y
VERMONT					
AL Welch	Y	Y	Y	Y	N
VIRGINIA					
1 Wittman	N	Y	N	Y	Y
2 Drake	N	Y	N	Y	Y
3 Scott	Y	Y	Y	Y	Y
4 Forbes	N	Y	N	Y	Y
5 Goode	N	Y	N	Y	Y
6 Goodlatte	N	Y	N	Y	Y
7 Cantor	N	Y	N	Y	Y
8 Moran	Y	Y	Y	Y	Y
9 Boucher	Y	Y	Y	Y	Y
10 Wolf	N	Y	N	Y	Y
11 Davis	N	Y	N	Y	Y
WASHINGTON					
1 Inslee	Y	Y	Y	Y	Y
2 Larsen	Y	Y	Y	Y	N
3 Baird	N	Y	Y	Y	Y
4 Hastings	N	Y	N	?	Y
5 McMorris Rodgers	N	Y	N	Y	Y
6 Dicks	Y	Y	Y	Y	Y
7 McDermott	Y	Y	Y	Y	N
8 Reichert	N	Y	Y	Y	Y
9 Smith	Y	Y	Y	Y	Y
WEST VIRGINIA					
1 Mollohan	Y	Y	Y	Y	Y
2 Capito	N	Y	Y	Y	Y
3 Rahall	Y	Y	Y	Y	Y
WISCONSIN					
1 Ryan	N	Y	N	Y	Y
2 Baldwin	Y	Y	Y	Y	N
3 Kind	Y	Y	Y	Y	N
4 Moore	Y	Y	Y	Y	N
5 Sensenbrenner	N	Y	N	Y	Y
6 Petri	N	Y	N	Y	Y
7 Obey	Y	Y	Y	Y	N
8 Kagen	Y	Y	Y	Y	N
WYOMING					
AL Cubin	?	?	?	?	?
DELEGATES					
Faleomavaega (A.S.)					
Norton (D.C.)					
Bordallo (Guam)					
Fortuño (P.R.)					
Christensen (V.I.)					

IN THE HOUSE | By Vote Number

663. **HR 6707. Community Safety and Rail Acquisitions/Passage.**
Oberstar, D-Minn., motion to suspend the rules and pass the bill that would require the Surface Transportation Board to consider the impact on safety, the environment and inner-city passenger rail when weighing proposed railroad mergers. Motion rejected 243-175: R 37-153; D 206-22 (ND 158-13, SD 48-9). A two-thirds majority of those present and voting (279 in this case) is required for passage under suspension of the rules. Sept. 27, 2008.

664. **S 3325. Intellectual Property Laws/Passage.** Conyers, D-Mich., motion to suspend the rules and pass the bill that would stipulate that copyright registrations apply to civil rather than criminal action and establish an intellectual property enforcement coordinator to advise the president. The measure would authorize, from fiscal 2009 to 2013, $125 million for local law enforcement grants to combat intellectual property crimes, $50 million for investigative and forensic resources for the FBI and the attorney general to investigate the crimes, and $50 million each for the FBI and the Justice Department to investigate computer-related intellectual property crimes. Motion agreed to 381-41: R 176-19; D 205-22 (ND 149-21, SD 56-1). A two-thirds majority of those present and voting (282 in this case) is required for passage under suspension of the rules. Sept. 28, 2008.

665. **HR 6460. Great Lakes Legacy Programs/Passage.** Oberstar, D-Minn., motion to suspend the rules and concur in the Senate amendment to the bill that would reauthorize the Great Lakes Legacy programs from fiscal 2004 to fiscal 2010. The bill would authorize $50 million a year to remediate sediment contamination and restore aquatic habitats in the Great Lakes region and $3 million a year for development of program technologies. Motion agreed to 411-9: R 185-9; D 226-0 (ND 169-0, SD 57-0). A two-thirds majority of those present and voting (280 in this case) is required for passage under suspension of the rules. Sept. 28, 2008.

666. **H Res 1514. Same-Day Consideration/Previous Question.**
Slaughter, D-N.Y., motion to order the previous question (thus ending debate and possibility of amendment) on adoption of the resolution (H Res 1514) that would waive the two-thirds majority vote requirement for same-day consideration of certain rules reported from the Rules Committee on the legislative days of Sept. 28 or Sept. 29. Motion agreed to 211-201: R 0-193; D 211-8 (ND 159-5, SD 52-3). Sept. 28, 2008.

667. **H Res 1514. Same-Day Consideration/Adoption.** Adoption of the resolution (H Res 1514) that would waive the two-thirds majority vote requirement for same-day consideration of certain rules reported from the Rules Committee on the legislative days of Sept. 28 or Sept. 29. Adopted 216-200: R 0-192; D 216-8 (ND 163-4, SD 53-4). Sept. 28, 2008.

668. **S 2840. Military Members' Naturalization/Passage.** Conyers, D-Mich., motion to suspend the rules and pass the bill that would authorize establishment of an FBI liaison office within the Homeland Security Department to help expedite naturalization applications for certain current and former members of the U.S. armed forces, their spouses and children. Applications would have to be processed within six months. The bill's provisions would sunset five years after enactment. Motion agreed to 416-0: R 192-0; D 224-0 (ND 167-0, SD 57-0). A two-thirds majority of those present and voting (278 in this case) is required for passage under suspension of the rules. Sept. 28, 2008.

ND Northern Democrats, SD Southern Democrats
Southern states: Ala., Ark., Fla., Ga., Ky., La., Miss., N.C., Okla., S.C., Tenn., Texas, Va.

	663	664	665	666	667	668
ALABAMA						
1 Bonner	N	Y	Y	N	N	Y
2 Everett	N	Y	?	N	N	Y
3 Rogers	Y	Y	Y	N	N	Y
4 Aderholt	N	Y	Y	N	N	Y
5 Cramer	Y	Y	Y	Y	Y	Y
6 Bachus	N	Y	Y	N	N	Y
7 Davis	Y	Y	Y	Y	Y	Y
ALASKA						
AL Young	N	N	Y	N	N	Y
ARIZONA						
1 Renzi	N	Y	Y	N	N	Y
2 Franks	N	Y	N	N	N	Y
3 Shadegg	N	Y	N	N	N	Y
4 Pastor	Y	Y	Y	Y	Y	Y
5 Mitchell	Y	Y	Y	N	N	Y
6 Flake	N	N	N	N	N	Y
7 Grijalva	Y	Y	Y	Y	Y	Y
8 Giffords	Y	Y	Y	Y	Y	Y
ARKANSAS						
1 Berry	Y	Y	Y	Y	Y	Y
2 Snyder	Y	Y	Y	Y	Y	Y
3 Boozman	N	Y	Y	N	N	Y
4 Ross	Y	Y	Y	Y	Y	Y
CALIFORNIA						
1 Thompson	Y	N	Y	Y	Y	Y
2 Herger	N	Y	Y	N	N	Y
3 Lungren	Y	Y	Y	N	N	Y
4 Doolittle	?	N	Y	N	N	Y
5 Matsui	Y	Y	Y	Y	Y	Y
6 Woolsey	Y	N	Y	Y	Y	Y
7 Miller, George	Y	N	Y	Y	Y	Y
8 Pelosi						
9 Lee	Y	N	Y	Y	Y	Y
10 Tauscher	Y	Y	Y	Y	Y	Y
11 McNerney	Y	Y	Y	Y	Y	Y
12 Speier	Y	N	Y	Y	Y	Y
13 Stark	Y	Y	Y	?	?	Y
14 Eshoo	Y	Y	Y	Y	Y	Y
15 Honda	Y	N	Y	Y	Y	Y
16 Lofgren	Y	N	Y	Y	Y	Y
17 Farr	Y	Y	Y	Y	Y	Y
18 Cardoza	Y	?	Y	Y	Y	Y
19 Radanovich	N	Y	Y	N	N	Y
20 Costa	Y	Y	Y	Y	Y	Y
21 Nunes	N	Y	Y	N	N	Y
22 McCarthy	N	Y	Y	N	N	Y
23 Capps	Y	Y	Y	Y	Y	Y
24 Gallegly	N	Y	Y	N	N	Y
25 McKeon	N	Y	Y	N	N	Y
26 Dreier	N	Y	Y	N	N	Y
27 Sherman	Y	Y	Y	?	Y	Y
28 Berman	Y	Y	Y	Y	Y	Y
29 Schiff	Y	Y	Y	Y	Y	Y
30 Waxman	Y	Y	Y	Y	Y	Y
31 Becerra	Y	Y	Y	?	Y	Y
32 Solis	Y	Y	Y	Y	Y	Y
33 Watson	N	Y	Y	Y	Y	Y
34 Roybal-Allard	Y	Y	Y	Y	Y	Y
35 Waters	Y	N	Y	?	?	Y
36 Harman	Y	Y	Y	Y	Y	Y
37 Richardson	Y	Y	Y	Y	Y	Y
38 Napolitano	Y	Y	Y	Y	Y	Y
39 Sánchez, Linda	Y	Y	Y	Y	Y	Y
40 Royce	N	Y	Y	N	N	Y
41 Lewis	N	Y	Y	N	N	Y
42 Miller, Gary	N	Y	Y	N	N	Y
43 Baca	Y	Y	Y	Y	Y	Y
44 Calvert	N	Y	Y	N	N	Y
45 Bono Mack	N	Y	Y	N	N	Y
46 Rohrabacher	N	Y	Y	N	N	Y
47 Sanchez, Loretta	Y	?	Y	Y	Y	Y
48 Campbell	Y	Y	Y	N	N	Y
49 Issa	N	Y	Y	N	N	Y
50 Bilbray	Y	Y	Y	N	N	Y
51 Filner	Y	Y	Y	N	N	Y
52 Hunter	N	Y	Y	N	N	Y
53 Davis	Y	Y	Y	?	Y	Y

	663	664	665	666	667	668
COLORADO						
1 DeGette	Y	Y	Y	Y	Y	Y
2 Udall	Y	Y	Y	Y	Y	Y
3 Salazar	Y	Y	Y	N	Y	Y
4 Musgrave	N	Y	Y	N	N	Y
5 Lamborn	N	Y	Y	N	N	Y
6 Tancredo	Y	Y	Y	N	N	Y
7 Perlmutter	Y	Y	Y	Y	Y	Y
CONNECTICUT						
1 Larson	Y	Y	Y	Y	Y	Y
2 Courtney	Y	Y	Y	Y	Y	Y
3 DeLauro	Y	Y	Y	Y	Y	Y
4 Shays	N	Y	Y	N	N	Y
5 Murphy	Y	Y	Y	Y	Y	Y
DELAWARE						
AL Castle	Y	Y	Y	N	N	Y
FLORIDA						
1 Miller	N	Y	Y	N	N	Y
2 Boyd	Y	Y	Y	Y	Y	Y
3 Brown	N	Y	Y	N	N	Y
4 Crenshaw	N	Y	Y	N	N	Y
5 Brown-Waite	Y	Y	Y	N	N	Y
6 Stearns	N	Y	Y	N	N	Y
7 Mica	Y	Y	Y	N	N	Y
8 Keller	N	Y	Y	N	N	Y
9 Bilirakis	N	Y	Y	N	N	Y
10 Young	N	Y	Y	N	N	Y
11 Castor	Y	Y	Y	Y	Y	Y
12 Putnam	N	Y	Y	N	N	Y
13 Buchanan	N	Y	Y	N	N	Y
14 Mack	N	Y	Y	N	N	Y
15 Weldon	N	Y	Y	N	N	Y
16 Mahoney	Y	Y	Y	Y	Y	Y
17 Meek	N	Y	Y	Y	Y	Y
18 Ros-Lehtinen	N	Y	Y	N	N	Y
19 Wexler	?	?	?	?	?	?
20 Wasserman Schultz	Y	Y	Y	Y	Y	Y
21 Diaz-Balart, L.	N	Y	Y	N	N	Y
22 Klein	Y	Y	Y	Y	Y	Y
23 Hastings	Y	Y	Y	Y	Y	Y
24 Feeney	N	Y	Y	N	N	Y
25 Diaz-Balart, M.	N	Y	Y	N	N	Y
GEORGIA						
1 Kingston	N	N	Y	N	N	Y
2 Bishop	Y	Y	Y	Y	Y	Y
3 Westmoreland	N	N	Y	N	N	Y
4 Johnson	Y	Y	Y	Y	Y	Y
5 Lewis	Y	Y	Y	Y	Y	Y
6 Price	N	N	Y	N	N	Y
7 Linder	N	Y	Y	N	N	Y
8 Marshall	Y	Y	Y	Y	Y	Y
9 Deal	N	Y	Y	N	N	Y
10 Broun	N	N	N	N	N	Y
11 Gingrey	N	Y	Y	N	N	Y
12 Barrow	Y	Y	Y	Y	Y	Y
13 Scott	Y	Y	Y	Y	Y	Y
HAWAII						
1 Abercrombie	Y	Y	Y	Y	Y	Y
2 Hirono	Y	Y	Y	Y	Y	Y
IDAHO						
1 Sali	N	Y	N	N	N	Y
2 Simpson	N	Y	Y	N	N	Y
ILLINOIS						
1 Rush	Y	N	Y	Y	Y	Y
2 Jackson	Y	Y	Y	Y	Y	Y
3 Lipinski	Y	Y	Y	Y	Y	Y
4 Gutierrez	N	N	Y	Y	Y	Y
5 Emanuel	N	Y	Y	Y	Y	Y
6 Roskam	Y	Y	Y	N	N	Y
7 Davis	Y	Y	Y	Y	Y	Y
8 Bean	Y	Y	Y	Y	Y	Y
9 Schakowsky	N	Y	Y	Y	Y	Y
10 Kirk	N	Y	Y	N	N	Y
11 Weller	?	?	?	?	?	?
12 Costello	Y	Y	Y	Y	Y	Y
13 Biggert	Y	Y	Y	N	N	Y
14 Foster	Y	Y	Y	Y	Y	Y
15 Johnson	N	Y	Y	N	N	Y

	663	664	665	666	667	668
16 **Manzullo**	Y	Y	Y	N	N	Y
17 Hare	Y	Y	Y	Y	Y	Y
18 **LaHood**	Y	Y	Y	N	N	Y
19 **Shimkus**	Y	Y	Y	N	N	Y
INDIANA						
1 Visclosky	Y	Y	Y	Y	Y	Y
2 Donnelly	Y	Y	Y	Y	Y	Y
3 **Souder**	N	Y	Y	N	N	Y
4 **Buyer**	N	Y	Y	N	?	Y
5 **Burton**	N	Y	Y	N	N	Y
6 **Pence**	N	Y	Y	N	N	Y
7 Carson, A.	Y	Y	Y	Y	Y	Y
8 Ellsworth	Y	Y	Y	Y	Y	Y
9 Hill	Y	Y	Y	Y	Y	Y
IOWA						
1 Braley	Y	Y	Y	Y	Y	Y
2 Loebsack	Y	Y	Y	N	Y	Y
3 Boswell	Y	Y	Y	Y	Y	Y
4 **Latham**	N	Y	Y	N	N	Y
5 **King**	N	Y	Y	N	N	Y
KANSAS						
1 **Moran**	N	Y	Y	N	N	Y
2 Boyda	N	Y	Y	Y	Y	Y
3 Moore	Y	Y	Y	Y	Y	Y
4 **Tiahrt**	N	Y	Y	N	N	Y
KENTUCKY						
1 **Whitfield**	N	N	Y	N	N	Y
2 **Lewis**	N	Y	Y	N	N	Y
3 Yarmuth	Y	Y	Y	Y	Y	Y
4 **Davis**	N	Y	Y	N	N	Y
5 **Rogers**	N	Y	Y	N	N	Y
6 Chandler	N	Y	Y	Y	Y	Y
LOUISIANA						
1 **Scalise**	Y	Y	Y	N	N	Y
2 Jefferson	?	?	?	?	?	?
3 Melancon	Y	Y	Y	Y	Y	Y
4 **McCrery**	Y	Y	Y	N	N	Y
5 **Alexander**	N	Y	Y	N	N	Y
6 Cazayoux	Y	Y	Y	N	N	Y
7 **Boustany**	N	Y	Y	N	N	Y
MAINE						
1 Allen	Y	Y	Y	Y	Y	Y
2 Michaud	Y	Y	Y	Y	Y	Y
MARYLAND						
1 **Gilchrest**	Y	Y	Y	N	N	Y
2 Ruppersberger	Y	Y	Y	Y	Y	Y
3 Sarbanes	Y	Y	Y	Y	Y	Y
4 Edwards	Y	Y	Y	Y	Y	Y
5 Hoyer	Y	Y	Y	Y	Y	Y
6 **Bartlett**	N	N	Y	N	N	Y
7 Cummings	Y	Y	Y	Y	Y	Y
8 Van Hollen	Y	Y	Y	Y	Y	Y
MASSACHUSETTS						
1 Olver	Y	Y	Y	Y	Y	Y
2 Neal	Y	Y	?	Y	Y	Y
3 McGovern	Y	Y	Y	Y	Y	Y
4 Frank	Y	Y	Y	Y	Y	Y
5 Tsongas	Y	Y	?	Y	Y	Y
6 Tierney	?	Y	Y	Y	Y	Y
7 Markey	Y	Y	Y	Y	Y	Y
8 Capuano	Y	Y	Y	Y	Y	Y
9 Lynch	?	Y	Y	Y	Y	Y
10 Delahunt	Y	Y	Y	Y	Y	Y
MICHIGAN						
1 Stupak	N	Y	Y	Y	Y	Y
2 **Hoekstra**	N	Y	Y	N	N	Y
3 **Ehlers**	N	Y	Y	N	N	Y
4 **Camp**	N	Y	Y	N	N	Y
5 Kildee	Y	Y	Y	Y	Y	Y
6 **Upton**	N	Y	Y	N	N	Y
7 **Walberg**	N	Y	Y	N	N	Y
8 **Rogers**	N	Y	Y	N	N	Y
9 **Knollenberg**	Y	Y	Y	N	N	Y
10 **Miller**	N	Y	Y	N	N	Y
11 **McCotter**	Y	Y	Y	N	N	Y
12 Levin	Y	Y	Y	Y	Y	Y
13 Kilpatrick	Y	Y	Y	?	?	?
14 Conyers	Y	Y	Y	Y	Y	Y
15 Dingell	Y	Y	Y	Y	Y	Y
MINNESOTA						
1 Walz	Y	Y	Y	Y	Y	Y
2 **Kline**	N	Y	Y	N	N	Y
3 **Ramstad**	Y	Y	Y	N	N	Y
4 McCollum	Y	Y	Y	Y	Y	Y

	663	664	665	666	667	668
5 Ellison	Y	Y	Y	Y	Y	Y
6 **Bachmann**	Y	Y	Y	N	N	Y
7 Peterson	N	N	Y	Y	Y	Y
8 Oberstar	Y	Y	Y	Y	Y	Y
MISSISSIPPI						
1 Childers	Y	Y	Y	Y	Y	Y
2 Thompson	Y	Y	Y	Y	Y	Y
3 **Pickering**	?	Y	Y	N	N	Y
4 Taylor	Y	Y	Y	N	N	Y
MISSOURI						
1 Clay	Y	?	?	Y	Y	Y
2 **Akin**	N	Y	Y	N	N	Y
3 Carnahan	Y	Y	Y	Y	Y	Y
4 Skelton	Y	Y	Y	Y	Y	Y
5 Cleaver	Y	Y	Y	Y	Y	Y
6 **Graves**	N	Y	Y	N	N	Y
7 **Blunt**	?	Y	Y	N	N	Y
8 **Emerson**	Y	Y	Y	N	N	Y
9 **Hulshof**	Y	Y	Y	N	N	Y
MONTANA						
AL **Rehberg**	N	Y	Y	N	N	Y
NEBRASKA						
1 **Fortenberry**	Y	Y	Y	N	N	Y
2 **Terry**	N	Y	Y	N	N	Y
3 **Smith**	N	Y	Y	N	N	Y
NEVADA						
1 Berkley	Y	Y	Y	Y	Y	Y
2 **Heller**	N	Y	Y	N	N	Y
3 **Porter**	Y	Y	Y	N	N	Y
NEW HAMPSHIRE						
1 Shea-Porter	Y	Y	Y	Y	Y	Y
2 Hodes	Y	Y	Y	Y	Y	Y
NEW JERSEY						
1 Andrews	Y	Y	Y	Y	Y	Y
2 **LoBiondo**	Y	Y	Y	N	N	Y
3 **Saxton**	Y	Y	Y	N	N	Y
4 **Smith**	Y	Y	Y	N	N	Y
5 **Garrett**	N	Y	Y	N	N	Y
6 Pallone	Y	Y	Y	Y	Y	Y
7 **Ferguson**	Y	Y	Y	N	N	Y
8 Pascrell	Y	Y	Y	Y	Y	Y
9 Rothman	Y	Y	Y	Y	Y	Y
10 Payne	Y	?	?	?	?	?
11 **Frelinghuysen**	N	Y	Y	N	N	Y
12 Holt	Y	Y	Y	Y	Y	Y
13 Sires	Y	Y	Y	Y	Y	Y
NEW MEXICO						
1 **Wilson**	Y	Y	Y	N	N	Y
2 **Pearce**	N	Y	Y	N	N	Y
3 Udall	Y	Y	Y	Y	Y	Y
NEW YORK						
1 Bishop	Y	Y	Y	Y	Y	Y
2 Israel	Y	Y	Y	Y	?	Y
3 **King**	N	Y	Y	N	N	Y
4 McCarthy	Y	Y	Y	Y	Y	Y
5 Ackerman	Y	Y	Y	Y	Y	Y
6 Meeks	Y	Y	Y	Y	Y	Y
7 Crowley	Y	Y	Y	Y	Y	Y
8 Nadler	Y	Y	Y	Y	Y	Y
9 Weiner	?	Y	Y	Y	Y	Y
10 Towns	Y	N	Y	Y	Y	Y
11 Clarke	Y	Y	Y	Y	Y	Y
12 Velázquez	Y	Y	Y	Y	Y	?
13 **Fossella**	N	Y	Y	N	N	Y
14 Maloney	Y	Y	Y	Y	Y	Y
15 Rangel	Y	Y	Y	Y	Y	?
16 Serrano	Y	N	Y	Y	Y	Y
17 Engel	Y	?	?	?	?	?
18 Lowey	Y	Y	Y	Y	Y	Y
19 Hall	Y	Y	Y	Y	Y	Y
20 Gillibrand	Y	Y	Y	Y	Y	Y
21 McNulty	Y	Y	Y	Y	Y	Y
22 Hinchey	Y	Y	Y	Y	Y	Y
23 **McHugh**	Y	Y	Y	N	N	Y
24 Arcuri	Y	Y	Y	Y	Y	Y
25 **Walsh**	?	N	Y	N	N	Y
26 **Reynolds**	N	Y	Y	N	N	Y
27 Higgins	Y	Y	Y	Y	Y	Y
28 Slaughter	Y	Y	Y	Y	Y	Y
29 **Kuhl**	N	Y	Y	N	N	Y
NORTH CAROLINA						
1 Butterfield	Y	Y	Y	Y	Y	Y
2 Etheridge	Y	Y	Y	Y	Y	Y
3 **Jones**	Y	Y	Y	N	N	Y
4 Price	Y	Y	Y	Y	Y	Y

	663	664	665	666	667	668
5 **Foxx**	N	N	N	N	N	Y
6 **Coble**	N	Y	Y	N	N	Y
7 McIntyre	Y	Y	Y	Y	Y	Y
8 **Hayes**	N	Y	Y	N	N	Y
9 **Myrick**	N	Y	Y	N	N	Y
10 **McHenry**	N	Y	Y	N	N	Y
11 Shuler	N	Y	Y	Y	N	Y
12 Watt	Y	Y	Y	Y	Y	Y
13 Miller	Y	Y	Y	Y	Y	Y
NORTH DAKOTA						
AL Pomeroy	Y	Y	Y	Y	Y	Y
OHIO						
1 **Chabot**	N	Y	Y	N	N	Y
2 **Schmidt**	N	Y	Y	N	N	Y
3 **Turner**	N	Y	Y	N	N	Y
4 **Jordan**	N	Y	Y	N	N	Y
5 **Latta**	N	Y	Y	N	N	Y
6 Wilson	Y	Y	Y	Y	Y	Y
7 **Hobson**	N	Y	Y	N	N	Y
8 **Boehner**	N	Y	Y	N	N	Y
9 Kaptur	?	Y	?	N	N	Y
10 Kucinich	Y	N	Y	Y	Y	Y
11 Vacant						
12 **Tiberi**	N	Y	Y	N	N	Y
13 Sutton	Y	Y	Y	Y	Y	Y
14 **LaTourette**	N	Y	Y	N	N	Y
15 **Pryce**	?	Y	Y	?	?	?
16 **Regula**	Y	Y	Y	N	N	Y
17 Ryan	Y	Y	Y	Y	Y	Y
18 Space	Y	Y	Y	Y	Y	Y
OKLAHOMA						
1 **Sullivan**	N	Y	Y	N	N	Y
2 Boren	N	Y	Y	Y	Y	Y
3 **Lucas**	N	Y	Y	N	N	Y
4 **Cole**	N	Y	Y	N	N	Y
5 **Fallin**	N	Y	Y	N	N	Y
OREGON						
1 Wu	Y	N	Y	?	?	?
2 **Walden**	N	Y	Y	N	N	Y
3 Blumenauer	Y	N	Y	Y	Y	Y
4 DeFazio	Y	Y	Y	Y	Y	Y
5 Hooley	Y	Y	Y	Y	Y	Y
PENNSYLVANIA						
1 Brady	Y	Y	Y	Y	Y	Y
2 Fattah	Y	Y	Y	Y	Y	Y
3 **English**	N	Y	Y	N	?	Y
4 Altmire	N	Y	Y	Y	Y	Y
5 **Peterson**	?	Y	Y	N	N	Y
6 **Gerlach**	N	Y	Y	N	N	Y
7 Sestak	Y	Y	Y	Y	Y	Y
8 Murphy, P.	Y	Y	Y	Y	Y	Y
9 **Shuster**	N	Y	Y	N	N	Y
10 Carney	Y	Y	Y	N	N	Y
11 Kanjorski	Y	Y	Y	Y	Y	Y
12 Murtha	Y	Y	Y	Y	Y	Y
13 Schwartz	Y	Y	Y	Y	Y	Y
14 Doyle	Y	N	Y	Y	Y	Y
15 **Dent**	N	Y	Y	N	N	Y
16 **Pitts**	N	Y	Y	N	N	Y
17 Holden	Y	Y	Y	Y	Y	Y
18 **Murphy, T.**	–	Y	Y	N	N	Y
19 **Platts**	N	Y	Y	N	N	Y
RHODE ISLAND						
1 Kennedy	Y	Y	Y	Y	Y	Y
2 Langevin	Y	Y	Y	+	+	+
SOUTH CAROLINA						
1 **Brown**	N	Y	Y	N	N	Y
2 **Wilson**	N	Y	Y	N	N	Y
3 **Barrett**	N	Y	Y	N	N	?
4 **Inglis**	N	Y	Y	N	N	Y
5 Spratt	Y	Y	Y	Y	Y	Y
6 Clyburn	N	Y	Y	Y	Y	Y
SOUTH DAKOTA						
AL Herseth Sandlin	Y	N	Y	Y	Y	Y
TENNESSEE						
1 **Davis, D.**	N	Y	Y	N	N	Y
2 **Duncan**	N	N	Y	N	N	Y
3 **Wamp**	N	?	?	?	?	?
4 Davis, L.	N	Y	Y	Y	Y	Y
5 Cooper	Y	Y	Y	Y	Y	Y
6 Gordon	Y	Y	Y	Y	Y	Y
7 **Blackburn**	N	Y	Y	N	N	Y
8 Tanner	Y	Y	Y	Y	Y	Y
9 Cohen	Y	Y	Y	Y	Y	Y

	663	664	665	666	667	668
TEXAS						
1 **Gohmert**	Y	?	?	?	?	?
2 **Poe**	N	N	N	N	N	Y
3 **Johnson, S.**	N	Y	Y	N	N	Y
4 **Hall**	N	Y	Y	N	N	Y
5 **Hensarling**	N	Y	Y	N	N	Y
6 **Barton**	N	Y	Y	N	N	Y
7 **Culberson**	N	N	Y	N	N	Y
8 **Brady**	N	Y	Y	N	N	Y
9 Green, A.	Y	Y	Y	Y	Y	Y
10 **McCaul**	N	Y	Y	N	N	Y
11 **Conaway**	N	N	Y	N	N	Y
12 **Granger**	N	Y	Y	N	N	Y
13 **Thornberry**	N	Y	Y	N	N	Y
14 **Paul**	N	N	N	N	N	Y
15 Hinojosa	Y	Y	Y	Y	Y	Y
16 Reyes	Y	Y	Y	Y	Y	Y
17 Edwards	Y	Y	Y	Y	Y	Y
18 Jackson Lee	Y	Y	Y	?	Y	Y
19 **Neugebauer**	N	Y	Y	N	N	Y
20 Gonzalez	Y	Y	Y	Y	Y	Y
21 **Smith**	N	Y	Y	N	N	Y
22 Lampson	Y	Y	Y	N	N	Y
23 Rodriguez	Y	Y	Y	Y	Y	Y
24 **Marchant**	N	Y	Y	N	N	Y
25 Doggett	Y	Y	Y	Y	Y	Y
26 **Burgess**	N	Y	Y	N	N	Y
27 Ortiz	Y	Y	Y	Y	Y	Y
28 Cuellar	Y	Y	Y	Y	Y	Y
29 Green, G.	Y	Y	Y	Y	Y	Y
30 Johnson, E.	N	Y	Y	Y	Y	Y
31 **Carter**	N	Y	Y	N	N	Y
32 **Sessions**	N	Y	Y	N	N	Y
UTAH						
1 **Bishop**	N	N	Y	N	N	Y
2 Matheson	N	Y	Y	N	N	Y
3 **Cannon**	N	N	Y	N	N	Y
VERMONT						
AL Welch	Y	Y	Y	Y	Y	Y
VIRGINIA						
1 **Wittman**	N	Y	Y	N	N	Y
2 **Drake**	N	Y	Y	N	N	Y
3 Scott	Y	Y	Y	?	Y	Y
4 **Forbes**	Y	Y	Y	N	N	Y
5 **Goode**	N	N	Y	N	N	?
6 **Goodlatte**	N	Y	Y	N	N	Y
7 **Cantor**	N	Y	Y	N	N	Y
8 Moran	Y	Y	Y	Y	Y	Y
9 Boucher	Y	N	Y	Y	Y	Y
10 **Wolf**	Y	Y	Y	N	N	Y
11 **Davis**	Y	Y	Y	?	N	Y
WASHINGTON						
1 Inslee	Y	Y	Y	Y	Y	Y
2 Larsen	Y	Y	Y	Y	Y	Y
3 Baird	Y	N	Y	Y	Y	Y
4 **Hastings**	N	Y	Y	N	N	Y
5 **McMorris Rodgers**	N	Y	Y	N	N	Y
6 Dicks	Y	Y	Y	Y	Y	Y
7 McDermott	Y	N	Y	Y	Y	Y
8 **Reichert**	N	Y	Y	N	N	Y
9 Smith	N	Y	Y	Y	Y	Y
WEST VIRGINIA						
1 Mollohan	N	Y	Y	Y	Y	Y
2 **Capito**	Y	Y	Y	N	N	Y
3 Rahall	N	Y	Y	Y	Y	Y
WISCONSIN						
1 **Ryan**	N	Y	Y	N	N	Y
2 Baldwin	Y	Y	Y	Y	Y	Y
3 Kind	Y	Y	Y	Y	Y	Y
4 Moore	Y	N	Y	+	Y	Y
5 **Sensenbrenner**	N	Y	Y	N	N	Y
6 **Petri**	N	N	Y	N	N	Y
7 Obey	Y	Y	Y	Y	Y	Y
8 Kagen	Y	Y	Y	Y	Y	Y
WYOMING						
AL **Cubin**	?	?	?	?	?	?
DELEGATES						
Faleomavaega (A.S.)						
Norton (D.C.)						
Bordallo (Guam)						
Fortuño (P.R.)						
Christensen (V.I.)						

IN THE HOUSE | By Vote Number

669. **S 906. Elemental Mercury Ban/Passage.** Allen, D-Maine, motion to suspend the rules and pass the bill that would ban the export of elemental mercury beginning in 2013 and require the Energy Department to provide permanent storage for domestic mercury stocks. Motion agreed to 393-5: R 170-5; D 223-0 (ND 168-0, SD 55-0). A two-thirds majority of those present and voting (266 in this case) is required for passage under suspension of the rules. Sept. 29, 2008.

670. **HR 3997. Mortgage-Backed Securities Buyout/Previous Question.** Slaughter, D-N.Y., motion to order the previous question (thus ending debate and possibility of amendment) on adoption of the rule (H Res 1517) to provide for House floor consideration of the Senate amendment to the House amendment to the Senate amendment to the bill, with an additional amendment that would allow the Treasury to use up to $700 billion, in installments, to buy certain mortgage assets. Motion agreed to 217-196: R 3-188; D 214-8 (ND 163-4, SD 51-4). Sept. 29, 2008.

671. **HR 3997. Mortgage-Backed Securities Buyout/Rule.** Adoption of the rule (H Res 1517) to provide for House floor consideration of the Senate amendment to the House amendment to the Senate amendment to the bill, with an additional amendment that would allow the Treasury to use up to $700 billion, in installments, to buy certain mortgage assets. Adopted 220-198: R 11-181; D 209-17 (ND 160-10, SD 49-7). Sept. 29, 2008.

672. **H Con Res 440. Adjournment/Adoption.** Adoption of the concurrent resolution that would provide for adjournment of the House and Senate until 11 a.m., Saturday, Jan. 3, 2009. Adopted 213-211: R 0-194; D 213-17 (ND 160-13, SD 53-4). Sept. 29, 2008.

673. **Procedural Motion/Motion to Adjourn.** Gohmert, R-Texas, motion to adjourn. Motion rejected 8-394: R 7-173; D 1-221 (ND 1-166, SD 0-55). Sept. 29, 2008.

674. **HR 3997. Mortgage-Backed Securities Buyout/Motion to Concur.** Frank, D-Mass., motion to concur in the Senate amendment to the House amendment to the Senate amendment to the bill, with an additional House amendment. The House amendment would allow the Treasury to use up to $700 billion, in installments, to buy certain mortgage assets. It would require the Treasury to insure the assets, would set up systems for congressional oversight and would set compensation limits for executives of companies whose assets the Treasury purchases. Motion rejected 205-228: R 65-133; D 140-95 (ND 106-70, SD 34-25). A "yea" was a vote in support of the president's position. Sept. 29, 2008.

675. **HR 7175. Small Business Administration Lending/Passage.** Velázquez, D-N.Y., motion to suspend the rules and pass the bill that would revise certain Small Business Administration lending programs, including the 7(a) loan program, in order to accelerate the flow of investment capital and encourage lending from commercial banks. Motion agreed to 374-6: R 168-6; D 206-0 (ND 153-0, SD 53-0). A two-thirds majority of those present and voting (254 in this case) is required for passage under suspension of the rules. A "yea" was a vote in support of the president's position. Sept. 29, 2008.

	669	670	671	672	673	674	675
ALABAMA							
1 Bonner	P	N	N	N	N	Y	Y
2 Everett	P	N	N	N	N	Y	?
3 Rogers	Y	N	N	N	N	Y	Y
4 Aderholt	?	N	N	N	N	Y	Y
5 Cramer	Y	Y	Y	Y	N	Y	?
6 Bachus	Y	N	N	N	N	Y	Y
7 Davis	Y	Y	Y	Y	N	Y	Y
ALASKA							
AL Young	?	?	?	N	Y	N	Y
ARIZONA							
1 Renzi	Y	N	N	N	N	N	Y
2 Franks	P	Y	N	N	N	N	Y
3 Shadegg	Y	N	N	N	N	N	Y
4 Pastor	Y	Y	Y	N	N	N	Y
5 Mitchell	Y	Y	N	N	N	N	Y
6 Flake	N	N	N	N	N	N	N
7 Grijalva	Y	Y	Y	Y	?	N	?
8 Giffords	Y	Y	Y	N	N	N	Y
ARKANSAS							
1 Berry	Y	Y	Y	Y	N	Y	?
2 Snyder	Y	Y	Y	Y	N	Y	?
3 Boozman	Y	N	N	N	N	Y	Y
4 Ross	Y	Y	Y	Y	N	Y	Y
CALIFORNIA							
1 Thompson	Y	Y	Y	Y	N	N	Y
2 Herger	Y	N	N	N	N	Y	Y
3 Lungren	Y	N	Y	N	N	N	Y
4 Doolittle	Y	N	N	N	?	N	Y
5 Matsui	Y	Y	Y	Y	N	Y	Y
6 Woolsey	Y	Y	Y	Y	N	N	Y
7 Miller, George	Y	Y	Y	N	Y	?	
8 Pelosi			Y		Y		
9 Lee	Y	Y	Y	Y	N	N	Y
10 Tauscher	Y	Y	Y	Y	N	N	Y
11 McNerney	Y	Y	Y	Y	N	Y	Y
12 Speier	Y	Y	Y	Y	N	N	Y
13 Stark	Y	Y	Y	Y	?	N	?
14 Eshoo	Y	Y	Y	Y	N	Y	Y
15 Honda	Y	Y	Y	Y	N	Y	Y
16 Lofgren	Y	Y	Y	Y	N	Y	Y
17 Farr	Y	Y	Y	Y	N	Y	Y
18 Cardoza	Y	Y	Y	Y	N	Y	Y
19 Radanovich	Y	N	Y	N	N	Y	Y
20 Costa	Y	Y	Y	Y	N	Y	Y
21 Nunes	Y	N	N	N	N	N	Y
22 McCarthy	Y	N	N	N	N	N	Y
23 Capps	Y	Y	Y	Y	N	Y	Y
24 Gallegly	Y	N	N	N	N	N	?
25 McKeon	Y	N	N	N	N	Y	Y
26 Dreier	Y	N	Y	N	N	Y	Y
27 Sherman	Y	Y	Y	Y	N	N	Y
28 Berman	Y	Y	Y	Y	N	Y	?
29 Schiff	Y	Y	Y	Y	N	N	Y
30 Waxman	?	?	?	?	?	Y	Y
31 Becerra	Y	Y	Y	Y	N	N	Y
32 Solis	Y	Y	Y	Y	N	N	Y
33 Watson	Y	Y	Y	Y	N	N	Y
34 Roybal-Allard	Y	?	Y	Y	N	N	Y
35 Waters	Y	Y	Y	Y	N	Y	Y
36 Harman	Y	Y	Y	Y	N	Y	Y
37 Richardson	Y	Y	Y	Y	N	Y	Y
38 Napolitano	Y	Y	Y	Y	N	N	Y
39 Sánchez, Linda	Y	Y	Y	Y	N	N	Y
40 Royce	Y	N	N	N	N	N	Y
41 Lewis	Y	N	Y	N	N	Y	Y
42 Miller, Gary	Y	?	N	N	Y	N	?
43 Baca	Y	Y	Y	Y	N	N	?
44 Calvert	Y	N	N	N	N	Y	?
45 Bono Mack	Y	N	N	N	N	N	Y
46 Rohrabacher	Y	N	N	N	N	N	Y
47 Sanchez, Loretta	Y	Y	Y	Y	N	N	?
48 Campbell	Y	N	N	N	N	N	Y
49 Issa	Y	N	N	N	N	N	Y
50 Bilbray	Y	N	N	N	N	N	Y
51 Filner	Y	N	N	N	Y	N	Y
52 Hunter	Y	N	N	N	N	N	Y
53 Davis	Y	Y	Y	Y	N	Y	Y

	669	670	671	672	673	674	675
COLORADO							
1 DeGette	Y	Y	Y	Y	N	Y	Y
2 Udall	Y	Y	Y	N	N	N	?
3 Salazar	Y	Y	Y	Y	N	N	Y
4 Musgrave	Y	N	N	N	N	N	Y
5 Lamborn	Y	N	N	N	N	N	Y
6 Tancredo	?	?	?	?	?	Y	?
7 Perlmutter	Y	Y	?	Y	N	Y	Y
CONNECTICUT							
1 Larson	Y	Y	Y	Y	N	Y	Y
2 Courtney	Y	Y	Y	Y	N	N	Y
3 DeLauro	Y	Y	Y	Y	N	N	Y
4 Shays	Y	N	N	N	N	Y	Y
5 Murphy	Y	Y	Y	Y	N	Y	Y
DELAWARE							
AL Castle	Y	N	N	N	N	Y	Y
FLORIDA							
1 Miller	Y	N	N	N	N	N	Y
2 Boyd	Y	Y	Y	Y	N	Y	Y
3 Brown	Y	Y	Y	Y	N	Y	Y
4 Crenshaw	Y	N	N	N	N	Y	?
5 Brown-Waite	Y	N	N	N	N	N	Y
6 Stearns	+	N	N	N	N	N	Y
7 Mica	Y	N	N	N	Y	N	Y
8 Keller	Y	N	N	N	N	Y	?
9 Bilirakis	Y	N	N	N	N	N	Y
10 Young	Y	N	N	N	N	N	Y
11 Castor	Y	N	Y	Y	?	N	Y
12 Putnam	Y	N	N	N	N	Y	Y
13 Buchanan	Y	N	N	N	N	N	Y
14 Mack	Y	N	N	N	N	N	Y
15 Weldon	Y	N	N	N	?	N	Y
16 Mahoney	Y	Y	Y	Y	N	Y	Y
17 Meek	Y	Y	Y	Y	N	Y	Y
18 Ros-Lehtinen	Y	N	N	N	N	N	Y
19 Wexler	?	?	?	?	?	?	Y
20 Wasserman Schultz	Y	Y	Y	Y	N	N	Y
21 Diaz-Balart, L.	Y	N	N	N	N	N	Y
22 Klein	Y	Y	Y	Y	N	Y	Y
23 Hastings	Y	Y	Y	Y	N	Y	Y
24 Feeney	Y	N	N	N	?	N	Y
25 Diaz-Balart, M.	Y	N	N	N	?	N	Y
GEORGIA							
1 Kingston	Y	N	N	N	N	N	Y
2 Bishop	Y	Y	Y	Y	N	Y	Y
3 Westmoreland	N	N	N	N	N	N	Y
4 Johnson	Y	Y	Y	Y	N	N	Y
5 Lewis	Y	?	Y	Y	N	Y	Y
6 Price	Y	N	N	N	N	N	Y
7 Linder	Y	N	N	N	?	N	?
8 Marshall	Y	Y	Y	Y	N	N	Y
9 Deal	Y	N	N	N	N	N	Y
10 Broun	N	N	N	N	N	N	N
11 Gingrey	P	N	N	N	N	N	Y
12 Barrow	Y	Y	Y	Y	N	N	Y
13 Scott	Y	Y	Y	Y	N	N	Y
HAWAII							
1 Abercrombie	Y	Y	Y	Y	N	N	Y
2 Hirono	Y	Y	Y	Y	N	N	Y
IDAHO							
1 Sali	N	N	N	N	N	N	Y
2 Simpson	Y	N	N	N	?	Y	?
ILLINOIS							
1 Rush	?	?	?	Y	N	N	Y
2 Jackson	Y	Y	Y	Y	N	N	Y
3 Lipinski	Y	Y	Y	Y	N	N	Y
4 Gutierrez	Y	Y	Y	Y	?	Y	?
5 Emanuel	Y	Y	Y	Y	N	N	Y
6 Roskam	Y	N	N	N	N	N	Y
7 Davis	Y	Y	Y	Y	N	N	Y
8 Bean	Y	Y	Y	Y	N	Y	Y
9 Schakowsky	Y	Y	Y	Y	N	Y	Y
10 Kirk	Y	N	N	N	N	Y	Y
11 Weller	?	?	?	?	?	?	?
12 Costello	Y	Y	Y	Y	N	N	Y
13 Biggert	Y	N	N	N	N	N	Y
14 Foster	Y	Y	Y	N	Y	Y	Y
15 Johnson	Y	N	N	N	N	N	Y

KEY **Republicans** Democrats

Y Voted for (yea)	X Paired against	C Voted "present" to avoid possible conflict of interest
# Paired for	- Announced against	
+ Announced for	P Voted "present"	? Did not vote or otherwise make a position known
N Voted against (nay)		

ND Northern Democrats, SD Southern Democrats
Southern states: Ala., Ark., Fla., Ga., Ky., La., Miss., N.C., Okla., S.C., Tenn., Texas, Va.

H-226 2008 CQ ALMANAC | www.cq.com

	669	670	671	672	673	674	675
16 **Manzullo**	Y	N	N	N	N	N	Y
17 Hare	Y	Y	Y	Y	N	Y	Y
18 **LaHood**	Y	Y	Y	N	N	Y	?
19 **Shimkus**	Y	N	N	N	Y	N	?
INDIANA							
1 Visclosky	?	Y	Y	Y	N	N	Y
2 Donnelly	Y	Y	Y	N	N	Y	Y
3 **Souder**	?	N	N	N	N	Y	Y
4 **Buyer**	Y	N	N	N	N	N	?
5 **Burton**	Y	N	N	N	N	N	Y
6 **Pence**	Y	N	N	N	N	N	Y
7 Carson, A.	Y	Y	Y	Y	N	N	Y
8 Ellsworth	Y	Y	Y	N	N	Y	Y
9 Hill	Y	Y	N	Y	N	N	Y
IOWA							
1 Braley	Y	Y	Y	Y	N	N	Y
2 Loebsack	Y	Y	Y	N	N	Y	Y
3 Boswell	Y	Y	Y	Y	N	Y	Y
4 **Latham**	Y	N	N	N	N	N	Y
5 **King**	Y	N	N	N	N	N	Y
KANSAS							
1 **Moran**	Y	N	N	N	N	N	Y
2 Boyda	Y	Y	Y	N	N	N	Y
3 Moore	Y	Y	Y	Y	N	Y	Y
4 **Tiahrt**	+	N	N	N	N	N	Y
KENTUCKY							
1 **Whitfield**	Y	N	N	N	N	N	Y
2 **Lewis**	Y	N	N	N	N	Y	Y
3 Yarmuth	Y	Y	Y	Y	N	N	Y
4 **Davis**	Y	N	N	N	N	N	Y
5 **Rogers**	Y	N	N	N	N	Y	Y
6 Chandler	Y	Y	Y	Y	N	N	Y
LOUISIANA							
1 **Scalise**	Y	N	N	N	N	N	Y
2 Jefferson	?	?	?	?	?	N	Y
3 Melancon	Y	Y	Y	Y	N	Y	Y
4 **McCrery**	Y	N	N	N	?	Y	Y
5 **Alexander**	Y	N	N	N	N	N	Y
6 Cazayoux	Y	N	N	N	N	N	Y
7 **Boustany**	Y	N	N	N	N	N	Y
MAINE							
1 Allen	Y	Y	Y	Y	N	Y	Y
2 Michaud	Y	Y	N	Y	N	N	Y
MARYLAND							
1 **Gilchrest**	Y	N	N	N	?	Y	Y
2 Ruppersberger	Y	Y	Y	Y	N	Y	Y
3 Sarbanes	Y	Y	Y	Y	N	Y	Y
4 Edwards	Y	Y	Y	Y	N	N	Y
5 Hoyer	Y	Y	Y	Y	N	Y	Y
6 **Bartlett**	Y	N	N	N	N	N	Y
7 Cummings	Y	Y	Y	Y	N	N	Y
8 Van Hollen	Y	Y	Y	Y	N	Y	Y
MASSACHUSETTS							
1 Olver	Y	Y	Y	Y	N	Y	Y
2 Neal	Y	Y	Y	Y	N	Y	Y
3 McGovern	Y	Y	Y	Y	N	Y	Y
4 Frank	Y	Y	Y	Y	N	Y	Y
5 Tsongas	Y	Y	Y	Y	N	Y	Y
6 Tierney	Y	Y	Y	Y	N	N	Y
7 Markey	Y	Y	Y	Y	N	Y	Y
8 Capuano	Y	Y	Y	Y	N	Y	Y
9 Lynch	Y	Y	Y	Y	N	N	Y
10 Delahunt	Y	Y	Y	Y	N	N	?
MICHIGAN							
1 Stupak	Y	Y	Y	Y	N	N	?
2 **Hoekstra**	Y	N	N	N	N	N	Y
3 **Ehlers**	Y	N	N	N	N	Y	Y
4 **Camp**	Y	N	N	N	N	Y	?
5 Kildee	Y	Y	Y	Y	N	Y	Y
6 **Upton**	Y	N	N	N	N	Y	Y
7 **Walberg**	Y	N	N	N	N	N	Y
8 **Rogers**	Y	N	N	N	N	N	Y
9 **Knollenberg**	Y	N	N	N	?	N	?
10 **Miller**	Y	N	N	N	N	N	Y
11 **McCotter**	Y	N	N	N	N	N	Y
12 Levin	Y	Y	Y	Y	N	Y	Y
13 Kilpatrick	Y	Y	Y	Y	N	N	Y
14 Conyers	Y	Y	N	N	N	N	?
15 Dingell	Y	Y	Y	Y	N	Y	Y
MINNESOTA							
1 Walz	Y	Y	Y	Y	N	N	Y
2 **Kline**	Y	N	N	N	N	Y	Y
3 **Ramstad**	Y	N	N	N	N	N	Y
4 McCollum	Y	Y	Y	Y	N	Y	?

	669	670	671	672	673	674	675
5 Ellison	Y	?	Y	Y	N	Y	Y
6 **Bachmann**	Y	N	N	N	N	N	Y
7 Peterson	Y	Y	Y	Y	N	N	Y
8 Oberstar	Y	Y	Y	Y	N	Y	Y
MISSISSIPPI							
1 Childers	Y	Y	N	N	N	N	Y
2 Thompson	Y	Y	Y	Y	N	N	Y
3 **Pickering**	?	N	N	N	?	Y	Y
4 Taylor	Y	N	N	N	N	N	Y
MISSOURI							
1 Clay	Y	Y	Y	Y	N	N	?
2 **Akin**	Y	?	?	N	N	N	Y
3 Carnahan	Y	Y	Y	Y	N	Y	Y
4 Skelton	?	Y	Y	Y	N	Y	Y
5 Cleaver	Y	Y	Y	Y	N	N	?
6 **Graves**	Y	N	N	N	N	N	Y
7 **Blunt**	Y	N	N	N	N	Y	Y
8 **Emerson**	Y	N	N	N	N	Y	Y
9 **Hulshof**	Y	N	N	N	N	N	?
MONTANA							
AL **Rehberg**	Y	N	N	N	N	N	Y
NEBRASKA							
1 **Fortenberry**	?	N	N	N	N	N	Y
2 **Terry**	Y	N	N	N	N	N	Y
3 **Smith**	Y	N	N	N	N	N	Y
NEVADA							
1 Berkley	?	?	Y	Y	N	N	?
2 **Heller**	Y	N	N	N	Y	N	Y
3 **Porter**	Y	N	N	N	N	Y	Y
NEW HAMPSHIRE							
1 Shea-Porter	Y	Y	Y	N	N	N	Y
2 Hodes	Y	Y	Y	?	N	N	Y
NEW JERSEY							
1 Andrews	Y	Y	Y	Y	N	Y	Y
2 **LoBiondo**	Y	N	N	N	N	N	Y
3 **Saxton**	Y	N	N	N	N	Y	Y
4 **Smith**	Y	N	N	N	N	N	Y
5 **Garrett**	Y	N	N	N	Y	N	Y
6 Pallone	Y	Y	Y	Y	N	Y	Y
7 **Ferguson**	Y	N	N	N	N	Y	Y
8 Pascrell	Y	Y	Y	Y	N	N	Y
9 Rothman	Y	Y	Y	Y	N	N	Y
10 Payne	Y	Y	Y	Y	N	N	Y
11 **Frelinghuysen**	Y	N	N	N	N	N	Y
12 Holt	Y	Y	Y	Y	N	Y	Y
13 Sires	Y	Y	Y	Y	N	Y	Y
NEW MEXICO							
1 **Wilson**	Y	N	N	N	N	Y	Y
2 **Pearce**	Y	N	N	N	N	N	Y
3 Udall	Y	Y	Y	Y	N	N	Y
NEW YORK							
1 Bishop	Y	Y	Y	Y	N	Y	Y
2 Israel	Y	Y	Y	Y	N	Y	Y
3 **King**	Y	N	N	N	N	Y	Y
4 McCarthy	Y	Y	Y	Y	N	Y	Y
5 Ackerman	Y	Y	Y	Y	N	Y	?
6 Meeks	Y	Y	Y	Y	N	Y	Y
7 Crowley	Y	Y	Y	Y	N	Y	Y
8 Nadler	Y	Y	Y	Y	N	Y	?
9 Weiner	Y	Y	Y	Y	N	Y	Y
10 Towns	Y	Y	Y	Y	N	Y	Y
11 Clarke	Y	Y	Y	Y	N	Y	Y
12 Velázquez	Y	Y	Y	Y	N	Y	Y
13 **Fossella**	Y	N	N	N	?	Y	Y
14 Maloney	Y	Y	Y	Y	N	Y	Y
15 Rangel	Y	Y	Y	Y	N	Y	?
16 Serrano	Y	Y	Y	Y	N	N	Y
17 Engel	Y	Y	Y	Y	N	Y	Y
18 Lowey	Y	Y	Y	Y	N	Y	Y
19 Hall	Y	Y	Y	Y	N	Y	Y
20 Gillibrand	Y	Y	Y	N	N	N	Y
21 McNulty	Y	Y	Y	Y	N	Y	?
22 Hinchey	?	?	?	Y	N	N	Y
23 **McHugh**	Y	N	N	N	N	Y	Y
24 Arcuri	Y	Y	Y	Y	N	Y	Y
25 **Walsh**	?	N	N	N	?	Y	Y
26 **Reynolds**	Y	N	N	N	N	Y	Y
27 Higgins	Y	Y	Y	Y	N	Y	Y
28 Slaughter	Y	Y	Y	Y	N	Y	Y
29 **Kuhl**	Y	N	N	N	N	N	Y
NORTH CAROLINA							
1 Butterfield	Y	Y	Y	Y	N	N	Y
2 Etheridge	Y	Y	Y	Y	N	Y	Y
3 **Jones**	Y	N	N	N	N	N	Y
4 Price	Y	Y	Y	Y	N	Y	Y

	669	670	671	672	673	674	675
5 **Foxx**	Y	N	N	N	Y	N	Y
6 **Coble**	Y	N	N	N	N	N	Y
7 McIntyre	Y	Y	N	Y	N	N	Y
8 **Hayes**	Y	N	N	N	N	N	Y
9 **Myrick**	Y	N	N	N	N	N	Y
10 **McHenry**	Y	N	N	N	N	N	Y
11 Shuler	Y	Y	N	Y	N	N	Y
12 Watt	Y	Y	Y	Y	N	Y	Y
13 Miller	Y	Y	Y	Y	N	Y	Y
NORTH DAKOTA							
AL Pomeroy	Y	Y	Y	Y	?	Y	Y
OHIO							
1 **Chabot**	Y	N	N	N	N	N	Y
2 **Schmidt**	Y	N	N	N	N	N	Y
3 **Turner**	Y	N	N	N	N	N	Y
4 **Jordan**	Y	N	N	N	N	N	Y
5 **Latta**	Y	N	N	N	N	N	Y
6 Wilson	Y	Y	Y	Y	N	Y	Y
7 **Hobson**	Y	N	N	N	N	Y	?
8 **Boehner**	Y	N	N	N	N	Y	Y
9 Kaptur	Y	N	N	Y	N	N	Y
10 Kucinich	Y	Y	N	Y	N	N	Y
11 Vacant							
12 **Tiberi**	Y	N	N	N	N	N	Y
13 Sutton	Y	Y	Y	Y	N	N	Y
14 **LaTourette**	Y	N	N	N	N	N	Y
15 **Pryce**	?	?	?	?	?	Y	Y
16 **Regula**	Y	N	N	N	N	Y	Y
17 Ryan	Y	Y	Y	Y	N	Y	Y
18 Space	Y	Y	Y	Y	N	Y	Y
OKLAHOMA							
1 **Sullivan**	Y	N	N	N	N	N	Y
2 Boren	Y	Y	Y	Y	N	Y	Y
3 **Lucas**	Y	N	N	N	N	N	?
4 **Cole**	Y	N	N	N	N	Y	Y
5 **Fallin**	Y	N	N	N	N	N	Y
OREGON							
1 Wu	Y	Y	Y	Y	N	N	Y
2 **Walden**	Y	N	N	N	N	Y	Y
3 Blumenauer	Y	Y	Y	Y	N	N	Y
4 DeFazio	Y	N	N	Y	?	N	Y
5 Hooley	Y	Y	Y	Y	N	Y	Y
PENNSYLVANIA							
1 Brady	Y	Y	Y	Y	N	Y	Y
2 Fattah	Y	Y	Y	Y	?	Y	Y
3 **English**	Y	N	N	N	N	N	Y
4 Altmire	Y	Y	Y	Y	N	N	Y
5 **Peterson**	Y	N	N	N	N	Y	Y
6 **Gerlach**	Y	N	N	N	N	N	Y
7 Sestak	Y	Y	Y	Y	N	Y	Y
8 Murphy, P.	Y	Y	Y	Y	N	Y	Y
9 **Shuster**	Y	N	N	N	N	N	Y
10 Carney	Y	N	N	N	N	N	Y
11 Kanjorski	Y	Y	Y	Y	N	Y	Y
12 Murtha	Y	Y	Y	Y	N	Y	Y
13 Schwartz	Y	Y	Y	Y	N	Y	Y
14 Doyle	Y	Y	Y	Y	N	Y	Y
15 **Dent**	Y	N	N	N	N	Y	Y
16 **Pitts**	Y	N	N	N	N	N	Y
17 Holden	Y	Y	Y	Y	N	N	?
18 **Murphy, T.**	Y	N	N	N	N	N	Y
19 **Platts**	Y	N	N	N	N	N	Y
RHODE ISLAND							
1 Kennedy	Y	Y	Y	Y	N	Y	Y
2 Langevin	?	?	?	?	?	Y	Y
SOUTH CAROLINA							
1 **Brown**	Y	N	N	N	N	Y	Y
2 **Wilson**	Y	N	N	N	N	Y	Y
3 **Barrett**	Y	N	N	N	N	N	Y
4 **Inglis**	Y	N	N	N	N	Y	Y
5 Spratt	Y	Y	Y	Y	N	Y	Y
6 Clyburn	Y	Y	Y	Y	N	Y	Y
SOUTH DAKOTA							
AL Herseth Sandlin	Y	Y	Y	Y	N	N	Y
TENNESSEE							
1 **Davis, D.**	Y	N	N	?	N	N	Y
2 **Duncan**	Y	N	N	N	N	N	Y
3 **Wamp**	Y	N	N	N	N	N	?
4 Davis, L.	Y	Y	Y	Y	N	N	Y
5 Cooper	Y	Y	Y	Y	N	Y	Y
6 Gordon	?	Y	Y	Y	N	Y	Y
7 **Blackburn**	P	N	N	N	?	N	Y
8 Tanner	Y	Y	Y	Y	N	Y	Y
9 Cohen	Y	Y	N	Y	N	Y	Y

	669	670	671	672	673	674	675
TEXAS							
1 **Gohmert**	Y	N	N	N	Y	N	Y
2 **Poe**	P	N	N	N	N	N	N
3 **Johnson, S.**	?	N	N	N	?	N	Y
4 **Hall**	Y	N	Y	N	N	N	Y
5 **Hensarling**	Y	N	N	N	N	N	Y
6 **Barton**	?	N	N	N	N	N	Y
7 **Culberson**	?	?	?	N	N	N	Y
8 **Brady**	Y	N	N	N	N	Y	Y
9 Green, A.	Y	Y	Y	Y	N	N	Y
10 **McCaul**	Y	N	N	N	N	N	Y
11 **Conaway**	Y	N	N	N	?	N	Y
12 **Granger**	Y	N	Y	N	N	Y	Y
13 **Thornberry**	Y	N	N	N	N	N	?
14 **Paul**	N	N	N	N	N	N	N
15 Hinojosa	+	+	+	Y	N	Y	?
16 Reyes	Y	Y	Y	Y	N	Y	Y
17 Edwards	Y	Y	Y	Y	N	Y	Y
18 Jackson Lee	Y	Y	Y	Y	N	N	Y
19 **Neugebauer**	Y	N	N	N	N	N	Y
20 Gonzalez	Y	Y	Y	Y	N	Y	Y
21 **Smith**	Y	N	N	N	N	Y	Y
22 Lampson	Y	N	N	N	N	N	Y
23 Rodriguez	Y	Y	Y	Y	N	N	Y
24 **Marchant**	Y	N	N	N	N	N	?
25 Doggett	Y	Y	Y	Y	N	N	Y
26 **Burgess**	Y	N	N	N	N	N	?
27 Ortiz	Y	Y	Y	Y	N	N	Y
28 Cuellar	Y	Y	Y	Y	N	N	Y
29 Green, G.	Y	Y	Y	Y	N	N	?
30 Johnson, E.	Y	Y	Y	Y	N	Y	Y
31 **Carter**	Y	N	N	N	N	N	Y
32 **Sessions**	Y	N	N	N	N	Y	Y
UTAH							
1 **Bishop**	?	N	N	N	N	N	N
2 Matheson	Y	Y	Y	Y	N	N	Y
3 **Cannon**	Y	N	N	N	N	Y	Y
VERMONT							
AL Welch	Y	Y	Y	Y	N	N	?
VIRGINIA							
1 **Wittman**	Y	N	N	N	N	N	Y
2 **Drake**	Y	N	N	N	N	N	Y
3 Scott	Y	Y	Y	Y	?	N	Y
4 **Forbes**	Y	N	N	N	N	N	Y
5 **Goode**	Y	N	N	N	N	N	N
6 **Goodlatte**	Y	N	N	N	N	N	Y
7 **Cantor**	Y	N	N	N	N	Y	Y
8 Moran	Y	Y	Y	Y	N	Y	Y
9 Boucher	Y	Y	Y	Y	N	Y	Y
10 **Wolf**	?	N	N	N	N	Y	Y
11 **Davis**	Y	Y	Y	N	N	Y	Y
WASHINGTON							
1 Inslee	Y	Y	Y	Y	N	N	Y
2 Larsen	Y	Y	Y	Y	N	Y	Y
3 Baird	Y	Y	Y	Y	N	Y	Y
4 **Hastings**	Y	N	N	N	N	N	?
5 **McMorris Rodgers**	?	N	N	N	N	N	Y
6 Dicks	Y	Y	Y	Y	N	Y	Y
7 McDermott	Y	Y	Y	Y	N	Y	Y
8 **Reichert**	Y	N	N	N	N	N	Y
9 Smith	Y	Y	Y	Y	N	Y	Y
WEST VIRGINIA							
1 Mollohan	Y	?	Y	Y	N	Y	Y
2 **Capito**	Y	N	N	N	N	N	?
3 Rahall	Y	Y	Y	Y	N	Y	Y
WISCONSIN							
1 **Ryan**	Y	N	N	N	N	Y	Y
2 Baldwin	Y	Y	Y	Y	N	Y	Y
3 Kind	Y	Y	Y	Y	N	Y	Y
4 Moore	Y	Y	Y	Y	N	Y	Y
5 **Sensenbrenner**	Y	N	N	N	N	N	Y
6 **Petri**	Y	N	N	N	N	N	Y
7 Obey	Y	Y	Y	Y	N	Y	Y
8 Kagen	Y	Y	Y	Y	N	N	Y
WYOMING							
AL **Cubin**	?	?	?	?	?	Y	Y
DELEGATES							
Faleomavaega (A.S.)							
Norton (D.C.)							
Bordallo (Guam)							
Fortuño (P.R.)							
Christensen (V.I.)							

IN THE HOUSE | By Vote Number

676. S 3641. Crime Victim Programs Reauthorization/Passage.

Conyers, D-Mich., motion to suspend the rules and pass the bill that would reauthorize five Justice Department grant programs through fiscal 2013 that provide legal assistance and services to crime victims. Motion agreed to 410-2: R 188-2; D 222-0 (ND 165-0, SD 57-0). A two-thirds majority of those present and voting (275 in this case) is required for passage under suspension of the rules. Oct. 2, 2008.

677. S 3641. Crime Victim Programs Reauthorization/Motion to Reconsider.

Hastings, D-Fla., motion to table (kill) the Cannon, R-Utah, motion to reconsider the Conyers, D-Mich., motion to suspend the rules and pass the bill that would reauthorize five Justice Department grant programs through fiscal 2013 that provide legal assistance and services to crime victims. Motion agreed to 295-115: R 75-115; D 220-0 (ND 163-0, SD 57-0). Oct. 2, 2008.

678. HR 7221. Homeless Assistance Reauthorization/Passage.

Moore, D-Wis., motion to suspend the rules and pass the bill that would consolidate the Housing and Urban Development Department's homeless assistance competitive grant programs into a single program and authorize $2.2 billion in fiscal 2009 for grants for emergency shelter needs of the homeless. Motion agreed to 355-61: R 131-61; D 224-0 (ND 167-0, SD 57-0). A two-thirds majority of those present and voting (278 in this case) is required for passage under suspension of the rules. Oct. 2, 2008.

679. HR 1424. Mortgage-Backed Securities Buyout/Previous Question.

Slaughter, D-N.Y., motion to order the previous question (thus ending debate and possibility of amendment) on adoption of the rule (H Res 1525) to provide for House floor consideration of the Senate amendment to the bill that would allow the Treasury to use up to $700 billion, in installments, to buy certain mortgage assets. Motion agreed to 235-190: R 19-176; D 216-14 (ND 162-11, SD 54-3). Oct. 3, 2008.

	676	677	678	679
ALABAMA				
1 Bonner	Y	N	Y	N
2 Everett	Y	N	N	N
3 Rogers	Y	N	Y	N
4 Aderholt	Y	N	Y	N
5 Cramer	Y	Y	Y	Y
6 Bachus	Y	N	Y	N
7 Davis	Y	Y	Y	Y
ALASKA				
AL Young	Y	N	Y	N
ARIZONA				
1 Renzi	Y	N	Y	N
2 Franks	Y	Y	N	N
3 Shadegg	Y	Y	N	N
4 Pastor	Y	Y	Y	Y
5 Mitchell	Y	Y	Y	Y
6 Flake	N	N	N	N
7 Grijalva	Y	?	Y	Y
8 Giffords	Y	Y	Y	Y
ARKANSAS				
1 Berry	Y	Y	Y	Y
2 Snyder	Y	Y	Y	Y
3 Boozman	Y	N	Y	N
4 Ross	Y	Y	Y	Y
CALIFORNIA				
1 Thompson	Y	Y	Y	Y
2 Herger	Y	N	Y	N
3 Lungren	Y	Y	Y	N
4 Doolittle	Y	Y	N	N
5 Matsui	Y	Y	Y	Y
6 Woolsey	Y	Y	Y	Y
7 Miller, George	Y	Y	Y	Y
8 Pelosi				
9 Lee	Y	Y	Y	Y
10 Tauscher	Y	Y	Y	Y
11 McNerney	Y	Y	Y	Y
12 Speier	Y	Y	Y	Y
13 Stark	?	?	?	N
14 Eshoo	Y	Y	Y	Y
15 Honda	Y	Y	Y	Y
16 Lofgren	Y	Y	Y	Y
17 Farr	Y	Y	Y	Y
18 Cardoza	Y	Y	Y	Y
19 Radanovich	Y	N	N	N
20 Costa	Y	Y	Y	Y
21 Nunes	Y	Y	N	N
22 McCarthy	Y	Y	Y	Y
23 Capps	Y	Y	Y	Y
24 Gallegly	Y	N	Y	N
25 McKeon	Y	N	Y	N
26 Dreier	Y	N	Y	Y
27 Sherman	Y	Y	Y	Y
28 Berman	Y	Y	Y	Y
29 Schiff	Y	Y	Y	Y
30 Waxman	Y	Y	Y	Y
31 Becerra	Y	Y	Y	Y
32 Solis	Y	Y	Y	Y
33 Watson	Y	Y	Y	Y
34 Roybal-Allard	Y	Y	Y	Y
35 Waters	Y	Y	Y	Y
36 Harman	Y	Y	Y	Y
37 Richardson	Y	Y	Y	Y
38 Napolitano	Y	Y	Y	Y
39 Sánchez, Linda	Y	Y	Y	Y
40 Royce	Y	N	N	N
41 Lewis	Y	N	Y	Y
42 Miller, Gary	Y	N	Y	N
43 Baca	Y	Y	Y	Y
44 Calvert	Y	N	Y	N
45 Bono Mack	Y	Y	Y	Y
46 Rohrabacher	Y	N	N	N
47 Sanchez, Loretta	Y	Y	Y	Y
48 Campbell	Y	Y	N	Y
49 Issa	Y	N	Y	N
50 Bilbray	Y	N	Y	N
51 Filner	Y	Y	Y	N
52 Hunter	?	?	?	N
53 Davis	Y	Y	Y	Y

	676	677	678	679
COLORADO				
1 DeGette	Y	Y	Y	Y
2 Udall	?	?	?	Y
3 Salazar	Y	Y	Y	Y
4 Musgrave	Y	N	N	?
5 Lamborn	Y	N	N	N
6 Tancredo	Y	N	N	?
7 Perlmutter	Y	Y	Y	Y
CONNECTICUT				
1 Larson	Y	Y	Y	Y
2 Courtney	Y	Y	Y	Y
3 DeLauro	Y	Y	Y	Y
4 Shays	Y	?	Y	N
5 Murphy	Y	Y	Y	Y
DELAWARE				
AL Castle	Y	Y	Y	N
FLORIDA				
1 Miller	Y	Y	N	N
2 Boyd	Y	Y	Y	Y
3 Brown	Y	Y	Y	Y
4 Crenshaw	Y	N	Y	N
5 Brown-Waite	Y	N	Y	N
6 Stearns	Y	N	N	N
7 Mica	Y	N	Y	N
8 Keller	Y	N	Y	N
9 Bilirakis	Y	N	Y	N
10 Young	Y	Y	Y	N
11 Castor	Y	Y	Y	Y
12 Putnam	Y	Y	Y	N
13 Buchanan	Y	Y	Y	N
14 Mack	Y	N	Y	N
15 Weldon	Y	Y	Y	N
16 Mahoney	Y	Y	Y	Y
17 Meek	Y	Y	Y	Y
18 Ros-Lehtinen	Y	N	Y	N
19 Wexler	Y	Y	Y	Y
20 Wasserman Schultz	?	?	?	Y
21 Diaz-Balart, L.	Y	N	Y	N
22 Klein	Y	Y	Y	Y
23 Hastings	Y	Y	Y	Y
24 Feeney	Y	N	Y	N
25 Diaz-Balart, M.	Y	N	Y	N
GEORGIA				
1 Kingston	?	?	?	N
2 Bishop	Y	Y	Y	Y
3 Westmoreland	Y	N	N	N
4 Johnson	Y	Y	Y	Y
5 Lewis	Y	Y	Y	Y
6 Price	Y	N	N	N
7 Linder	Y	Y	N	N
8 Marshall	Y	Y	Y	Y
9 Deal	Y	N	N	N
10 Broun	Y	N	N	N
11 Gingrey	Y	N	N	N
12 Barrow	Y	Y	Y	Y
13 Scott	Y	Y	Y	Y
HAWAII				
1 Abercrombie	Y	Y	Y	N
2 Hirono	Y	Y	Y	N
IDAHO				
1 Sali	Y	N	N	N
2 Simpson	Y	Y	Y	Y
ILLINOIS				
1 Rush	Y	Y	Y	Y
2 Jackson	Y	Y	Y	Y
3 Lipinski	Y	Y	Y	Y
4 Gutierrez	+	+	+	Y
5 Emanuel	Y	Y	Y	Y
6 Roskam	Y	Y	N	N
7 Davis	Y	Y	Y	Y
8 Bean	Y	Y	Y	Y
9 Schakowsky	Y	Y	Y	Y
10 Kirk	Y	N	Y	N
11 Weller	Y	Y	Y	N
12 Costello	Y	Y	Y	Y
13 Biggert	Y	N	Y	N
14 Foster	Y	Y	Y	Y
15 Johnson	Y	N	Y	N

ND Northern Democrats, SD Southern Democrats
Southern states: Ala., Ark., Fla., Ga., Ky., La., Miss., N.C., Okla., S.C., Tenn., Texas, Va.

	676	677	678	679
16 Manzullo	Y	Y	Y	N
17 Hare	Y	Y	Y	Y
18 LaHood	Y	Y	Y	Y
19 Shimkus	Y	N	Y	N
INDIANA				
1 Visclosky	Y	Y	Y	Y
2 Donnelly	Y	Y	Y	N
3 Souder	Y	Y	Y	N
4 Buyer	Y	N	N	N
5 Burton	Y	N	N	N
6 Pence	Y	N	N	N
7 Carson, A.	Y	Y	Y	Y
8 Ellsworth	Y	Y	Y	Y
9 Hill	Y	Y	Y	Y
IOWA				
1 Braley	Y	Y	Y	Y
2 Loebsack	Y	Y	Y	Y
3 Boswell	Y	Y	Y	Y
4 Latham	Y	N	Y	N
5 King	Y	Y	N	N
KANSAS				
1 Moran	+	+	Y	N
2 Boyda	Y	Y	Y	Y
3 Moore	Y	Y	Y	Y
4 Tiahrt	Y	Y	Y	N
KENTUCKY				
1 Whitfield	Y	N	Y	N
2 Lewis	Y	N	N	N
3 Yarmuth	Y	Y	Y	Y
4 Davis	Y	N	Y	N
5 Rogers	Y	N	Y	N
6 Chandler	Y	Y	Y	Y
LOUISIANA				
1 Scalise	Y	N	N	N
2 Jefferson	Y	Y	Y	Y
3 Melancon	Y	N	Y	Y
4 McCrery	Y	N	Y	Y
5 Alexander	Y	N	Y	N
6 Cazayoux	Y	Y	Y	N
7 Boustany	Y	N	Y	N
MAINE				
1 Allen	Y	Y	Y	Y
2 Michaud	Y	Y	Y	Y
MARYLAND				
1 Gilchrest	?	?	?	?
2 Ruppersberger	Y	Y	Y	Y
3 Sarbanes	Y	Y	Y	Y
4 Edwards	Y	Y	Y	Y
5 Hoyer	Y	Y	Y	Y
6 Bartlett	Y	N	Y	N
7 Cummings	Y	Y	Y	Y
8 Van Hollen	Y	Y	Y	Y
MASSACHUSETTS				
1 Olver	Y	Y	Y	Y
2 Neal	Y	Y	Y	Y
3 McGovern	Y	Y	Y	Y
4 Frank	Y	?	Y	Y
5 Tsongas	Y	Y	Y	Y
6 Tierney	Y	Y	Y	Y
7 Markey	Y	Y	Y	Y
8 Capuano	Y	Y	Y	Y
9 Lynch	Y	Y	Y	N
10 Delahunt	Y	Y	Y	Y
MICHIGAN				
1 Stupak	Y	Y	Y	Y
2 Hoekstra	Y	Y	Y	N
3 Ehlers	Y	Y	Y	N
4 Camp	Y	Y	Y	N
5 Kildee	Y	Y	Y	Y
6 Upton	Y	N	Y	N
7 Walberg	Y	N	Y	N
8 Rogers	Y	N	Y	N
9 Knollenberg	Y	N	Y	N
10 Miller	Y	N	Y	N
11 McCotter	Y	N	Y	N
12 Levin	Y	Y	Y	Y
13 Kilpatrick	Y	Y	Y	Y
14 Conyers	?	Y	Y	Y
15 Dingell	Y	Y	Y	Y
MINNESOTA				
1 Walz	Y	Y	Y	Y
2 Kline	Y	Y	Y	N
3 Ramstad	Y	Y	Y	Y
4 McCollum	Y	Y	Y	Y

	676	677	678	679
5 Ellison	Y	Y	Y	Y
6 Bachmann	Y	N	Y	N
7 Peterson	Y	Y	Y	Y
8 Oberstar	Y	Y	Y	?
MISSISSIPPI				
1 Childers	Y	Y	Y	Y
2 Thompson	?	?	?	?
3 Pickering	Y	Y	Y	Y
4 Taylor	Y	Y	Y	N
MISSOURI				
1 Clay	?	?	?	Y
2 Akin	Y	N	N	N
3 Carnahan	?	?	?	Y
4 Skelton	Y	Y	Y	Y
5 Cleaver	Y	Y	Y	Y
6 Graves	?	N	Y	N
7 Blunt	Y	Y	Y	N
8 Emerson	Y	Y	Y	N
9 Hulshof	?	?	?	N
MONTANA				
AL Rehberg	Y	N	Y	N
NEBRASKA				
1 Fortenberry	Y	Y	Y	N
2 Terry	Y	Y	Y	N
3 Smith	Y	Y	Y	N
NEVADA				
1 Berkley	Y	Y	Y	Y
2 Heller	Y	N	Y	N
3 Porter	Y	Y	Y	Y
NEW HAMPSHIRE				
1 Shea-Porter	Y	Y	Y	Y
2 Hodes	Y	Y	Y	Y
NEW JERSEY				
1 Andrews	Y	Y	Y	Y
2 LoBiondo	Y	Y	Y	N
3 Saxton	Y	N	Y	N
4 Smith	Y	N	Y	N
5 Garrett	Y	N	N	N
6 Pallone	Y	Y	Y	Y
7 Ferguson	?	?	?	Y
8 Pascrell	Y	Y	Y	Y
9 Rothman	Y	Y	Y	Y
10 Payne	Y	Y	Y	Y
11 Frelinghuysen	Y	Y	Y	N
12 Holt	Y	Y	Y	Y
13 Sires	Y	Y	Y	Y
NEW MEXICO				
1 Wilson	Y	Y	Y	Y
2 Pearce	Y	Y	Y	N
3 Udall	Y	Y	Y	Y
NEW YORK				
1 Bishop	Y	Y	Y	Y
2 Israel	Y	Y	Y	Y
3 King	Y	N	Y	Y
4 McCarthy	Y	Y	Y	Y
5 Ackerman	Y	Y	Y	Y
6 Meeks	Y	Y	Y	Y
7 Crowley	?	?	?	Y
8 Nadler	Y	Y	Y	Y
9 Weiner	Y	Y	Y	Y
10 Towns	Y	Y	Y	Y
11 Clarke	Y	Y	Y	Y
12 Velázquez	Y	Y	Y	Y
13 Fossella	Y	N	Y	N
14 Maloney	?	?	Y	Y
15 Rangel	Y	Y	Y	Y
16 Serrano	Y	Y	Y	Y
17 Engel	Y	Y	Y	Y
18 Lowey	Y	Y	Y	Y
19 Hall	Y	Y	Y	Y
20 Gillibrand	Y	Y	Y	Y
21 McNulty	Y	Y	Y	Y
22 Hinchey	Y	Y	Y	Y
23 McHugh	Y	Y	Y	N
24 Arcuri	Y	Y	Y	Y
25 Walsh	Y	N	Y	N
26 Reynolds	Y	N	Y	N
27 Higgins	Y	Y	Y	Y
28 Slaughter	Y	Y	Y	Y
29 Kuhl	Y	N	Y	N
NORTH CAROLINA				
1 Butterfield	Y	Y	Y	Y
2 Etheridge	Y	Y	Y	Y
3 Jones	Y	Y	Y	N
4 Price	Y	Y	Y	Y

	676	677	678	679
5 Foxx	Y	N	N	N
6 Coble	Y	N	N	N
7 McIntyre	Y	Y	Y	Y
8 Hayes	Y	Y	Y	N
9 Myrick	Y	N	N	N
10 McHenry	Y	N	N	N
11 Shuler	Y	Y	Y	Y
12 Watt	Y	Y	Y	Y
13 Miller	Y	Y	Y	Y
NORTH DAKOTA				
AL Pomeroy	Y	Y	Y	Y
OHIO				
1 Chabot	Y	Y	Y	N
2 Schmidt	Y	Y	Y	N
3 Turner	Y	Y	Y	N
4 Jordan	Y	N	N	N
5 Latta	Y	Y	Y	N
6 Wilson	Y	Y	Y	Y
7 Hobson	Y	N	Y	N
8 Boehner	Y	N	Y	N
9 Kaptur	Y	Y	Y	Y
10 Kucinich	Y	Y	Y	N
11 Vacant				
12 Tiberi	Y	Y	Y	N
13 Sutton	Y	Y	Y	Y
14 LaTourette	Y	N	Y	N
15 Pryce	?	?	?	?
16 Regula	Y	Y	Y	N
17 Ryan	Y	Y	Y	Y
18 Space	?	?	?	Y
OKLAHOMA				
1 Sullivan	Y	N	N	N
2 Boren	Y	Y	Y	Y
3 Lucas	Y	N	Y	N
4 Cole	Y	N	Y	N
5 Fallin	Y	Y	Y	N
OREGON				
1 Wu	Y	Y	Y	Y
2 Walden	Y	Y	Y	N
3 Blumenauer	Y	Y	Y	Y
4 DeFazio	Y	Y	Y	N
5 Hooley	Y	Y	Y	Y
PENNSYLVANIA				
1 Brady	Y	Y	Y	Y
2 Fattah	Y	Y	Y	Y
3 English	Y	Y	Y	N
4 Altmire	Y	N	Y	N
5 Peterson	Y	N	N	N
6 Gerlach	Y	Y	Y	N
7 Sestak	Y	Y	Y	Y
8 Murphy, P.	?	?	?	Y
9 Shuster	Y	N	N	N
10 Carney	Y	Y	Y	Y
11 Kanjorski	Y	Y	Y	Y
12 Murtha	Y	Y	Y	Y
13 Schwartz	Y	Y	Y	Y
14 Doyle	Y	Y	Y	Y
15 Dent	Y	Y	Y	N
16 Pitts	Y	N	N	N
17 Holden	Y	Y	Y	Y
18 Murphy, T.	Y	Y	Y	N
19 Platts	Y	N	Y	N
RHODE ISLAND				
1 Kennedy	Y	Y	Y	Y
2 Langevin	Y	Y	Y	?
SOUTH CAROLINA				
1 Brown	Y	Y	Y	N
2 Wilson	Y	Y	Y	N
3 Barrett	Y	N	N	N
4 Inglis	Y	N	N	Y
5 Spratt	Y	Y	Y	Y
6 Clyburn	Y	Y	Y	Y
SOUTH DAKOTA				
AL Herseth Sandlin	Y	Y	Y	Y
TENNESSEE				
1 Davis, David	Y	N	N	N
2 Duncan	Y	N	N	N
3 Wamp	Y	N	Y	N
4 Davis, L.	Y	Y	Y	Y
5 Cooper	Y	Y	Y	Y
6 Gordon	Y	Y	Y	Y
7 Blackburn	Y	N	N	N
8 Tanner	Y	Y	Y	N
9 Cohen	Y	Y	Y	Y

	676	677	678	679
TEXAS				
1 Gohmert	Y	N	N	N
2 Poe	Y	N	N	N
3 Johnson, S.	Y	N	N	N
4 Hall	Y	N	N	N
5 Hensarling	Y	N	N	N
6 Barton	Y	N	N	N
7 Culberson	Y	N	N	N
8 Brady	Y	N	N	N
9 Green, A.	Y	Y	Y	Y
10 McCaul	Y	N	Y	N
11 Conaway	Y	N	N	N
12 Granger	Y	N	Y	N
13 Thornberry	Y	N	Y	N
14 Paul	N	N	N	N
15 Hinojosa	Y	Y	Y	Y
16 Reyes	Y	Y	Y	Y
17 Edwards	Y	Y	Y	Y
18 Jackson Lee	Y	Y	Y	Y
19 Neugebauer	Y	N	N	N
20 Gonzalez	Y	Y	Y	Y
21 Smith	Y	N	N	N
22 Lampson	Y	Y	Y	Y
23 Rodriguez	Y	Y	Y	Y
24 Marchant	Y	N	N	N
25 Doggett	Y	Y	Y	Y
26 Burgess	Y	Y	Y	N
27 Ortiz	Y	Y	Y	Y
28 Cuellar	Y	Y	Y	Y
29 Green, G.	Y	Y	Y	Y
30 Johnson, E.	Y	Y	Y	Y
31 Carter	Y	N	N	N
32 Sessions	Y	N	N	N
UTAH				
1 Bishop	Y	Y	Y	N
2 Matheson	Y	Y	Y	Y
3 Cannon	Y	N	Y	N
VERMONT				
AL Welch	Y	Y	Y	Y
VIRGINIA				
1 Wittman	Y	N	Y	N
2 Drake	Y	Y	Y	N
3 Scott	Y	Y	Y	Y
4 Forbes	Y	Y	Y	N
5 Goode	Y	N	N	N
6 Goodlatte	Y	N	N	N
7 Cantor	Y	N	N	N
8 Moran	Y	Y	Y	?
9 Boucher	Y	Y	Y	Y
10 Wolf	Y	Y	Y	N
11 Davis, T.	Y	Y	Y	N
WASHINGTON				
1 Inslee	Y	Y	Y	Y
2 Larsen	Y	Y	Y	Y
3 Baird	Y	Y	Y	Y
4 Hastings	Y	N	N	N
5 McMorris Rodgers	Y	N	Y	N
6 Dicks	Y	Y	Y	Y
7 McDermott	Y	Y	Y	Y
8 Reichert	Y	Y	Y	N
9 Smith	Y	Y	Y	Y
WEST VIRGINIA				
1 Mollohan	Y	?	Y	Y
2 Capito	Y	Y	Y	N
3 Rahall	Y	Y	Y	Y
WISCONSIN				
1 Ryan	Y	N	Y	N
2 Baldwin	Y	Y	Y	Y
3 Kind	Y	Y	Y	Y
4 Moore	Y	Y	Y	Y
5 Sensenbrenner	Y	N	N	N
6 Petri	Y	Y	Y	N
7 Obey	Y	Y	Y	Y
8 Kagen	Y	Y	Y	Y
WYOMING				
AL Cubin	?	?	?	?
DELEGATES				
Faleomavaega (A.S.)				
Norton (D.C.)				
Bordallo (Guam)				
Fortuño (P.R.)				
Christensen (V.I.)				

IN THE HOUSE | By Vote Number

680. **HR 1424. Mortgage-Backed Securities Buyout/Rule.** Adoption of the rule (H Res 1525) to provide for House floor consideration of the Senate amendment to the bill that would allow the Treasury to use up to $700 billion, in installments, to buy certain mortgage assets. Adopted 223-205: R 20-176; D 203-29 (ND 155-19, SD 48-10). Oct. 3, 2008.

681. **HR 1424. Mortgage-Backed Securities Buyout/Motion to Concur.** Frank, D-Mass., motion to concur in the Senate amendments to the bill that would allow the Treasury to use up to $700 billion, in installments, to buy certain mortgage assets. The bill would require the Treasury to create a program to insure mortgage assets, would provide for congressional oversight and would limit compensation for executives of companies whose troubled assets are purchased. It would temporarily increase federal deposit insurance to $250,000 per bank account. It would extend dozens of expired or expiring tax provisions, provide a one-year adjustment to the alternative minimum tax and require private insurance plans to put mental health benefits on par with other medical benefits. Motion agreed to (thus clearing the bill for the president) 263-171: R 91-108; D 172-63 (ND 131-45, SD 41-18). A "yea" was a vote in support of the president's position. Oct. 3, 2008.

682. **S 3197. National Guard Bankruptcy Exceptions/Passage.** Conyers, D-Mich., motion to suspend the rules and pass the bill that would exempt National Guard members who served 90 days or more on active duty since Sept. 11, 2001, from the current means-test requirement before filing for bankruptcy. Members would have to file for bankruptcy within 540 days after release from active duty to qualify. Motion agreed to 411-0: R 184-0; D 227-0 (ND 169-0, SD 58-0). A two-thirds majority of those present and voting (274 in this case) is required for passage under suspension of the rules. Oct. 3, 2008.

683. **HR 6867. Unemployment Benefits Extension/Passage.** Rangel, D-N.Y., motion to suspend the rules and pass the bill that would provide an additional seven weeks of unemployment benefits for workers who have exhausted their current compensation by March 31, 2009. The bill also would extend benefits for an additional 13 weeks, or half the duration of regular unemployment compensation, for workers in states with unemployment rates of 6 percent or higher. Motion agreed to 368-28: R 142-28; D 226-0 (ND 171-0, SD 55-0). A two-thirds majority of those present and voting (264 in this case) is required for passage under suspension of the rules. Oct. 3, 2008.

	680	681	682	683
ALABAMA				
1 Bonner	N	Y	Y	Y
2 Everett	N	Y	?	?
3 Rogers	N	Y	Y	Y
4 Aderholt	N	N	Y	Y
5 Cramer	Y	Y	Y	Y
6 Bachus	N	Y	Y	Y
7 Davis	Y	Y	Y	Y
ALASKA				
AL Young	N	N	Y	Y
ARIZONA				
1 Renzi	N	N	Y	?
2 Franks	N	N	Y	N
3 Shadegg	N	Y	Y	N
4 Pastor	Y	Y	Y	Y
5 Mitchell	N	Y	Y	Y
6 Flake	N	N	Y	N
7 Grijalva	Y	N	Y	Y
8 Giffords	Y	Y	Y	Y
ARKANSAS				
1 Berry	Y	Y	Y	Y
2 Snyder	Y	Y	Y	Y
3 Boozman	N	Y	Y	Y
4 Ross	N	Y	Y	Y
CALIFORNIA				
1 Thompson	Y	Y	Y	Y
2 Herger	Y	Y	Y	Y
3 Lungren	N	Y	Y	Y
4 Doolittle	N	N	Y	N
5 Matsui	Y	Y	Y	Y
6 Woolsey	Y	Y	Y	Y
7 Miller, George	Y	Y	?	Y
8 Pelosi		Y		Y
9 Lee	Y	Y	Y	Y
10 Tauscher	Y	Y	Y	Y
11 McNerney	Y	Y	Y	Y
12 Speier	Y	Y	Y	?
13 Stark	N	N	?	Y
14 Eshoo	Y	Y	Y	Y
15 Honda	Y	Y	Y	Y
16 Lofgren	Y	Y	Y	Y
17 Farr	Y	Y	Y	Y
18 Cardoza	Y	Y	Y	Y
19 Radanovich	Y	Y	Y	Y
20 Costa	Y	Y	Y	Y
21 Nunes	N	N	Y	N
22 McCarthy	N	N	Y	Y
23 Capps	Y	Y	Y	Y
24 Gallegly	N	N	?	?
25 McKeon	N	Y	Y	?
26 Dreier	N	Y	Y	Y
27 Sherman	Y	N	Y	Y
28 Berman	Y	Y	Y	Y
29 Schiff	Y	Y	Y	Y
30 Waxman	Y	Y	Y	Y
31 Becerra	Y	N	Y	Y
32 Solis	Y	Y	Y	Y
33 Watson	Y	Y	Y	Y
34 Roybal-Allard	Y	N	Y	Y
35 Waters	Y	Y	Y	Y
36 Harman	N	Y	?	Y
37 Richardson	Y	Y	Y	Y
38 Napolitano	Y	N	Y	Y
39 Sánchez, Linda	Y	N	Y	Y
40 Royce	N	N	Y	?
41 Lewis	Y	Y	Y	Y
42 Miller, Gary	N	Y	Y	?
43 Baca	Y	Y	Y	Y
44 Calvert	Y	Y	Y	Y
45 Bono Mack	Y	Y	Y	Y
46 Rohrabacher	N	N	Y	Y
47 Sanchez, Loretta	Y	N	?	?
48 Campbell	Y	Y	Y	Y
49 Issa	N	N	Y	Y
50 Bilbray	N	N	?	Y
51 Filner	N	N	Y	Y
52 Hunter	N	N	Y	Y
53 Davis	Y	Y	Y	Y

	680	681	682	683
COLORADO				
1 DeGette	Y	Y	Y	Y
2 Udall	Y	N	Y	Y
3 Salazar	Y	N	Y	Y
4 Musgrave	N	N	Y	Y
5 Lamborn	N	N	Y	N
6 Tancredo	?	Y	Y	Y
7 Perlmutter	Y	Y	Y	Y
CONNECTICUT				
1 Larson	Y	Y	Y	Y
2 Courtney	Y	N	Y	Y
3 DeLauro	Y	Y	Y	Y
4 Shays	N	Y	Y	Y
5 Murphy	Y	Y	Y	Y
DELAWARE				
AL Castle	N	Y	Y	Y
FLORIDA				
1 Miller	N	N	Y	N
2 Boyd	N	Y	Y	Y
3 Brown	Y	Y	Y	Y
4 Crenshaw	N	Y	Y	Y
5 Brown-Waite	N	N	Y	Y
6 Stearns	N	N	Y	Y
7 Mica	N	N	Y	Y
8 Keller	N	N	Y	Y
9 Bilirakis	N	N	Y	Y
10 Young	N	N	Y	?
11 Castor	Y	N	Y	Y
12 Putnam	N	Y	Y	Y
13 Buchanan	N	Y	Y	Y
14 Mack	N	N	Y	Y
15 Weldon	N	Y	Y	?
16 Mahoney	Y	Y	Y	Y
17 Meek	Y	Y	Y	Y
18 Ros-Lehtinen	N	N	Y	Y
19 Wexler	Y	Y	Y	Y
20 Wasserman Schultz	Y	Y	Y	Y
21 Diaz-Balart, L.	N	N	Y	Y
22 Klein	Y	Y	Y	Y
23 Hastings	Y	Y	?	?
24 Feeney	N	N	Y	?
25 Diaz-Balart, M.	N	N	Y	Y
GEORGIA				
1 Kingston	N	N	?	?
2 Bishop	N	Y	Y	Y
3 Westmoreland	N	N	Y	?
4 Johnson	Y	N	Y	Y
5 Lewis	Y	Y	Y	Y
6 Price	N	N	Y	Y
7 Linder	N	N	Y	N
8 Marshall	Y	Y	Y	Y
9 Deal	N	N	Y	?
10 Broun	N	N	Y	Y
11 Gingrey	N	N	?	N
12 Barrow	Y	N	Y	Y
13 Scott	Y	Y	Y	Y
HAWAII				
1 Abercrombie	N	Y	Y	Y
2 Hirono	N	Y	Y	Y
IDAHO				
1 Sali	N	N	Y	N
2 Simpson	N	Y	Y	Y
ILLINOIS				
1 Rush	Y	Y	Y	Y
2 Jackson	Y	Y	Y	Y
3 Lipinski	Y	N	Y	Y
4 Gutierrez	Y	Y	Y	Y
5 Emanuel	Y	Y	Y	Y
6 Roskam	N	N	Y	Y
7 Davis	Y	Y	Y	Y
8 Bean	Y	Y	Y	Y
9 Schakowsky	Y	Y	Y	Y
10 Kirk	N	Y	Y	Y
11 Weller	N	Y	Y	Y
12 Costello	N	N	Y	Y
13 Biggert	N	Y	Y	Y
14 Foster	Y	Y	Y	Y
15 Johnson	N	N	Y	?

ND Northern Democrats, SD Southern Democrats
Southern states: Ala., Ark., Fla., Ga., Ky., La., Miss., N.C., Okla., S.C., Tenn., Texas, Va.

	680	681	682	683
16 Manzullo	N	N	Y	Y
17 Hare	Y	Y	Y	Y
18 LaHood	Y	Y	?	?
19 Shimkus	N	N	Y	Y
INDIANA				
1 Visclosky	Y	N	Y	?
2 Donnelly	N	Y	Y	Y
3 Souder	N	Y	Y	Y
4 Buyer	N	N	Y	Y
5 Burton	N	N	Y	Y
6 Pence	N	N	Y	Y
7 Carson, A.	Y	Y	Y	Y
8 Ellsworth	Y	Y	Y	Y
9 Hill	Y	N	Y	Y
IOWA				
1 Braley	Y	Y	Y	Y
2 Loebsack	Y	Y	Y	Y
3 Boswell	Y	Y	Y	Y
4 Latham	N	N	Y	Y
5 King	N	N	Y	N
KANSAS				
1 Moran	N	N	Y	Y
2 Boyda	N	N	Y	Y
3 Moore	Y	Y	Y	Y
4 Tiahrt	N	N	Y	Y
KENTUCKY				
1 Whitfield	N	N	Y	Y
2 Lewis	N	Y	Y	?
3 Yarmuth	Y	Y	Y	Y
4 Davis	N	N	Y	Y
5 Rogers	N	Y	Y	Y
6 Chandler	Y	N	Y	Y
LOUISIANA				
1 Scalise	N	N	Y	Y
2 Jefferson	Y	N	Y	Y
3 Melancon	N	Y	Y	Y
4 McCrery	Y	Y	?	?
5 Alexander	N	Y	Y	Y
6 Cazayoux	N	N	Y	Y
7 Boustany	N	Y	Y	Y
MAINE				
1 Allen	Y	Y	Y	Y
2 Michaud	N	N	Y	Y
MARYLAND				
1 Gilchrest	?	Y	?	?
2 Ruppersberger	Y	Y	Y	Y
3 Sarbanes	Y	Y	Y	Y
4 Edwards	Y	Y	Y	Y
5 Hoyer	Y	Y	Y	Y
6 Bartlett	N	N	Y	Y
7 Cummings	Y	Y	Y	Y
8 Van Hollen	Y	Y	Y	Y
MASSACHUSETTS				
1 Olver	Y	Y	Y	Y
2 Neal	Y	Y	Y	Y
3 McGovern	Y	Y	Y	Y
4 Frank	Y	Y	Y	Y
5 Tsongas	Y	Y	Y	Y
6 Tierney	Y	Y	Y	Y
7 Markey	Y	Y	Y	Y
8 Capuano	Y	Y	Y	Y
9 Lynch	N	Y	Y	Y
10 Delahunt	Y	N	Y	Y
MICHIGAN				
1 Stupak	Y	N	Y	Y
2 Hoekstra	N	Y	Y	Y
3 Ehlers	Y	Y	Y	Y
4 Camp	N	Y	Y	Y
5 Kildee	Y	Y	Y	Y
6 Upton	N	Y	Y	Y
7 Walberg	N	N	Y	Y
8 Rogers	N	N	Y	Y
9 Knollenberg	N	Y	Y	Y
10 Miller	N	N	Y	Y
11 McCotter	N	N	Y	Y
12 Levin	Y	Y	Y	Y
13 Kilpatrick	Y	Y	Y	Y
14 Conyers	Y	N	Y	Y
15 Dingell	Y	Y	Y	Y
MINNESOTA				
1 Walz	Y	N	Y	Y
2 Kline	N	Y	Y	Y
3 Ramstad	Y	Y	Y	Y
4 McCollum	Y	Y	Y	Y

	680	681	682	683
5 Ellison	Y	Y	Y	Y
6 Bachmann	N	N	Y	N
7 Peterson	Y	N	Y	Y
8 Oberstar	Y	Y	Y	Y
MISSISSIPPI				
1 Childers	Y	N	Y	Y
2 Thompson	?	N	Y	Y
3 Pickering	Y	Y	?	?
4 Taylor	N	N	Y	Y
MISSOURI				
1 Clay	Y	N	Y	Y
2 Akin	N	N	Y	Y
3 Carnahan	Y	Y	Y	Y
4 Skelton	Y	Y	Y	Y
5 Cleaver	Y	Y	Y	Y
6 Graves	N	N	Y	Y
7 Blunt	N	Y	Y	Y
8 Emerson	N	Y	Y	Y
9 Hulshof	N	N	Y	?
MONTANA				
AL Rehberg	N	N	Y	Y
NEBRASKA				
1 Fortenberry	N	N	Y	Y
2 Terry	N	Y	Y	Y
3 Smith	N	N	Y	N
NEVADA				
1 Berkley	Y	Y	Y	Y
2 Heller	N	N	Y	Y
3 Porter	N	Y	Y	Y
NEW HAMPSHIRE				
1 Shea-Porter	Y	N	Y	Y
2 Hodes	Y	N	Y	Y
NEW JERSEY				
1 Andrews	Y	Y	Y	Y
2 LoBiondo	N	N	Y	Y
3 Saxton	Y	Y	Y	?
4 Smith	N	N	Y	Y
5 Garrett	N	N	Y	Y
6 Pallone	Y	Y	Y	Y
7 Ferguson	Y	Y	Y	?
8 Pascrell	Y	Y	Y	Y
9 Rothman	Y	N	Y	Y
10 Payne	Y	N	Y	Y
11 Frelinghuysen	N	Y	Y	Y
12 Holt	Y	Y	Y	Y
13 Sires	Y	Y	?	Y
NEW MEXICO				
1 Wilson	Y	Y	Y	Y
2 Pearce	N	N	Y	Y
3 Udall	Y	N	Y	Y
NEW YORK				
1 Bishop	Y	Y	Y	Y
2 Israel	Y	Y	Y	Y
3 King	Y	Y	Y	Y
4 McCarthy	Y	Y	Y	Y
5 Ackerman	Y	Y	Y	Y
6 Meeks	Y	Y	Y	Y
7 Crowley	Y	Y	Y	Y
8 Nadler	Y	Y	Y	Y
9 Weiner	Y	Y	Y	Y
10 Towns	Y	Y	Y	Y
11 Clarke	Y	Y	Y	Y
12 Velázquez	Y	Y	Y	Y
13 Fossella	Y	Y	Y	Y
14 Maloney	Y	Y	Y	Y
15 Rangel	Y	Y	Y	Y
16 Serrano	Y	N	Y	Y
17 Engel	Y	Y	Y	Y
18 Lowey	Y	Y	Y	Y
19 Hall	Y	Y	Y	Y
20 Gillibrand	Y	N	Y	Y
21 McNulty	Y	Y	Y	Y
22 Hinchey	Y	N	Y	Y
23 McHugh	N	Y	Y	Y
24 Arcuri	Y	Y	Y	Y
25 Walsh	Y	Y	Y	Y
26 Reynolds	N	Y	Y	Y
27 Higgins	Y	Y	Y	Y
28 Slaughter	Y	Y	Y	?
29 Kuhl	N	Y	Y	Y
NORTH CAROLINA				
1 Butterfield	Y	N	Y	Y
2 Etheridge	Y	Y	Y	Y
3 Jones	N	N	Y	Y
4 Price	Y	Y	Y	Y

	680	681	682	683
5 Foxx	N	N	Y	N
6 Coble	N	Y	Y	Y
7 McIntyre	N	N	Y	Y
8 Hayes	N	N	Y	Y
9 Myrick	N	Y	Y	Y
10 McHenry	N	N	Y	Y
11 Shuler	N	N	Y	Y
12 Watt	N	Y	Y	Y
13 Miller	Y	Y	Y	Y
NORTH DAKOTA				
AL Pomeroy	Y	Y	Y	Y
OHIO				
1 Chabot	N	N	Y	Y
2 Schmidt	N	Y	Y	Y
3 Turner	N	N	Y	Y
4 Jordan	N	N	Y	N
5 Latta	N	N	Y	Y
6 Wilson	Y	Y	Y	Y
7 Hobson	N	Y	?	?
8 Boehner	N	Y	?	?
9 Kaptur	N	N	Y	Y
10 Kucinich	N	N	Y	Y
11 Vacant				
12 Tiberi	N	Y	Y	Y
13 Sutton	Y	Y	?	Y
14 LaTourette	N	N	Y	Y
15 Pryce	N	Y	Y	Y
16 Regula	Y	Y	Y	Y
17 Ryan	Y	Y	Y	Y
18 Space	N	Y	Y	Y
OKLAHOMA				
1 Sullivan	N	Y	Y	Y
2 Boren	Y	Y	Y	Y
3 Lucas	N	Y	Y	Y
4 Cole	N	Y	Y	Y
5 Fallin	N	Y	Y	N
OREGON				
1 Wu	Y	Y	Y	Y
2 Walden	N	Y	Y	Y
3 Blumenauer	Y	N	Y	Y
4 DeFazio	N	N	Y	Y
5 Hooley	Y	Y	Y	Y
PENNSYLVANIA				
1 Brady	Y	Y	Y	Y
2 Fattah	Y	Y	Y	Y
3 English	N	N	Y	Y
4 Altmire	Y	N	Y	Y
5 Peterson	Y	Y	Y	Y
6 Gerlach	N	Y	Y	Y
7 Sestak	Y	Y	Y	Y
8 Murphy, P.	Y	Y	Y	Y
9 Shuster	N	Y	Y	Y
10 Carney	N	N	Y	Y
11 Kanjorski	Y	Y	Y	Y
12 Murtha	Y	Y	Y	Y
13 Schwartz	Y	Y	Y	Y
14 Doyle	N	Y	Y	Y
15 Dent	N	Y	Y	Y
16 Pitts	N	N	Y	Y
17 Holden	Y	N	Y	Y
18 Murphy, T.	N	N	Y	Y
19 Platts	N	N	Y	Y
RHODE ISLAND				
1 Kennedy	Y	Y	Y	Y
2 Langevin	Y	Y	Y	Y
SOUTH CAROLINA				
1 Brown	N	N	Y	Y
2 Wilson	N	Y	Y	Y
3 Barrett	N	N	Y	N
4 Inglis	N	Y	Y	N
5 Spratt	Y	Y	Y	Y
6 Clyburn	Y	Y	Y	Y
SOUTH DAKOTA				
AL Herseth Sandlin	N	N	Y	Y
TENNESSEE				
1 Davis, David	N	N	Y	?
2 Duncan	N	N	Y	N
3 Wamp	Y	Y	?	?
4 Davis, L.	Y	N	Y	Y
5 Cooper	Y	Y	Y	?
6 Gordon	Y	Y	Y	Y
7 Blackburn	N	N	Y	N
8 Tanner	N	Y	Y	Y
9 Cohen	Y	Y	Y	Y

	680	681	682	683
TEXAS				
1 Gohmert	N	N	?	N
2 Poe	N	N	Y	N
3 Johnson, S.	N	N	Y	?
4 Hall	N	N	Y	Y
5 Hensarling	N	N	Y	Y
6 Barton	N	N	Y	Y
7 Culberson	N	N	Y	N
8 Brady	N	Y	Y	Y
9 Green, A.	Y	Y	Y	Y
10 McCaul	N	N	Y	Y
11 Conaway	N	N	Y	N
12 Granger	N	Y	Y	Y
13 Thornberry	N	Y	Y	?
14 Paul	N	N	Y	N
15 Hinojosa	Y	Y	Y	Y
16 Reyes	Y	Y	Y	Y
17 Edwards	Y	Y	Y	Y
18 Jackson Lee	Y	Y	Y	Y
19 Neugebauer	N	N	Y	N
20 Gonzalez	Y	Y	Y	Y
21 Smith	N	Y	Y	Y
22 Lampson	Y	N	Y	Y
23 Rodriguez	Y	Y	Y	Y
24 Marchant	N	N	?	Y
25 Doggett	Y	N	Y	Y
26 Burgess	N	N	Y	N
27 Ortiz	Y	Y	Y	Y
28 Cuellar	Y	Y	Y	Y
29 Green, G.	Y	Y	Y	Y
30 Johnson, E.	Y	Y	Y	Y
31 Carter	N	N	?	N
32 Sessions	N	Y	Y	Y
UTAH				
1 Bishop	N	N	Y	?
2 Matheson	Y	N	Y	Y
3 Cannon	N	Y	Y	N
VERMONT				
AL Welch	Y	Y	Y	Y
VIRGINIA				
1 Wittman	N	N	Y	Y
2 Drake	N	N	Y	Y
3 Scott	Y	N	Y	Y
4 Forbes	N	N	Y	Y
5 Goode	N	N	Y	Y
6 Goodlatte	N	N	Y	Y
7 Cantor	N	Y	Y	Y
8 Moran	Y	Y	Y	?
9 Boucher	Y	Y	Y	?
10 Wolf	N	N	Y	Y
11 Davis, T.	N	N	Y	Y
WASHINGTON				
1 Inslee	Y	N	Y	Y
2 Larsen	Y	Y	Y	Y
3 Baird	Y	Y	Y	Y
4 Hastings	N	N	Y	Y
5 McMorris Rodgers	N	N	Y	Y
6 Dicks	Y	Y	Y	Y
7 McDermott	Y	Y	Y	Y
8 Reichert	N	N	Y	Y
9 Smith	Y	Y	Y	Y
WEST VIRGINIA				
1 Mollohan	Y	Y	Y	Y
2 Capito	N	N	Y	Y
3 Rahall	Y	Y	Y	Y
WISCONSIN				
1 Ryan	N	Y	Y	Y
2 Baldwin	Y	Y	Y	Y
3 Kind	N	Y	Y	Y
4 Moore	Y	Y	Y	Y
5 Sensenbrenner	N	N	Y	Y
6 Petri	N	N	Y	Y
7 Obey	?	Y	Y	Y
8 Kagen	Y	N	Y	Y
WYOMING				
AL Cubin	?	Y	?	?
DELEGATES				
Faleomavaega (A.S.)				
Norton (D.C.)				
Bordallo (Guam)				
Fortuño (P.R.)				
Christensen (V.I.)				

IN THE HOUSE | By Vote Number

684. **HR 7321. Automobile Industry Loan Program/Previous Question.** Slaughter, D-N.Y., motion to order the previous question (thus ending debate and possibility of amendment) on adoption of the rule (H Res 1533) that would waive through Dec. 13, 2008, the two-thirds majority vote requirement for same-day consideration of a rule for a bill that would authorize financial assistance for automakers. Motion agreed to 224-174: R 6-170; D 218-4 (ND 165-3, SD 53-1). Dec. 10, 2008.

685. **HR 7321. Automobile Industry Loan Program/Same-Day Consideration.** Adoption of the rule that would waive through Dec. 13, 2008, the two-thirds majority vote requirement for same-day consideration of a rule for a bill that would authorize financial assistance for automakers. Adopted 226-169: R 10-164; D 216-5 (ND 163-4, SD 53-1). Dec. 10, 2008.

686. **Procedural Motion/Journal.** Approval of the House Journal of Tuesday, Dec. 9, 2008. Approved 215-170: R 8-163; D 207-7 (ND 155-7, SD 52-0). Dec. 10, 2008.

687. **HR 7321. Automobile Industry Loan Program/Previous Question.** Slaughter, D-N.Y., motion to order the previous question (thus ending debate and possibility of amendment) on adoption of the rule (H Res 1534) to provide for House floor consideration of the bill that would allow for $14 billion for loans to eligible automobile manufacturers. Motion agreed to 225-180: R 5-176; D 220-4 (ND 165-4, SD 55-0). Dec. 10, 2008.

688. **HR 7321. Automobile Industry Loan Program/Rule.** Adoption of the rule (H Res 1534) to provide for House floor consideration of the bill that would allow for $14 billion for loans to eligible automobile manufacturers. Adopted 225-179: R 10-170; D 215-9 (ND 162-7, SD 53-2). Dec. 10, 2008.

689. **HR 7321. Automobile Industry Loan Program/New Lending Reporting.** LaTourette, R-Ohio, amendment that would require institutions that receive assistance under the Treasury Department's Troubled Asset Relief Program or the Energy Department's future vehicle loan program to report any change in new lending attributed to the assistance from the two programs. Adopted 403-0: R 180-0; D 223-0 (ND 168-0, SD 55-0). Dec. 10, 2008.

690. **HR 7321. Automobile Industry Loan Program/Passage.** Passage of the bill that would allow up to $14 billion in loans to eligible domestic automakers. One or more presidentially appointed administrators would be empowered to bring together auto companies, unions, creditors and others to negotiate long-term restructuring plans, which companies would have to submit by March 31, 2009. Administrators could recall the loans if they did not approve the plans. Companies getting loans would have to submit any planned investment or transaction of $100 million or more for review. Loan interest rates would be set at 5 percent for the first five years and 9 percent each subsequent year. The bill would give the government warrants for obtaining stock in participating companies. It would also prohibit loan recipients from giving bonuses to its 25 most highly compensated employees while the loan was outstanding. Passed 237-170: R 32-150; D 205-20 (ND 159-11, SD 46-9). A "yea" was a vote in support of the president's position. Dec. 10, 2008.

---

[1] Rep. Marcia L. Fudge, D-Ohio, was sworn in Nov. 19, 2008, to fill the seat vacated by the death of Democrat Stephanie Tubbs Jones on Aug. 20. The first vote for which Fudge was eligible was vote 684.

[2] Rep. Thomas M. Davis III, R-Va., resigned Nov. 24, 2008. The last vote for which he was eligible was vote 683.

ND Northern Democrats, SD Southern Democrats
Southern states: Ala., Ark., Fla., Ga., Ky., La., Miss., N.C., Okla., S.C., Tenn., Texas, Va.

	684	685	686	687	688	689	690
ALABAMA							
1 Bonner	N	N	N	N	N	Y	N
2 Everett	?	?	?	?	?	?	?
3 Rogers	N	N	N	N	N	Y	N
4 Aderholt	N	N	N	N	N	Y	N
5 Cramer	Y	Y	Y	Y	Y	Y	Y
6 Bachus	N	N	N	N	N	Y	N
7 Davis	Y	Y	Y	Y	Y	Y	Y
ALASKA							
AL Young	Y	Y	N	N	N	Y	Y
ARIZONA							
1 Renzi	?	?	?	?	?	?	?
2 Franks	N	N	N	N	N	Y	N
3 Shadegg	N	N	N	N	N	Y	N
4 Pastor	Y	Y	Y	Y	Y	Y	Y
5 Mitchell	N	N	N	N	N	Y	N
6 Flake	N	N	N	N	N	Y	N
7 Grijalva	Y	Y	Y	Y	Y	Y	Y
8 Giffords	N	N	Y	N	N	Y	Y
ARKANSAS							
1 Berry	Y	Y	Y	Y	Y	Y	Y
2 Snyder	?	?	?	?	?	?	?
3 Boozman	N	N	N	N	N	Y	N
4 Ross	Y	Y	Y	Y	Y	Y	Y
CALIFORNIA							
1 Thompson	Y	Y	Y	Y	Y	Y	Y
2 Herger	N	?	N	N	N	Y	N
3 Lungren	N	N	N	N	N	Y	N
4 Doolittle	?	?	?	?	?	?	?
5 Matsui	Y	Y	Y	Y	Y	Y	Y
6 Woolsey	Y	Y	?	Y	Y	Y	Y
7 Miller, George	Y	Y	Y	Y	Y	Y	Y
8 Pelosi							Y
9 Lee	Y	Y	Y	Y	Y	Y	Y
10 Tauscher	Y	Y	Y	Y	Y	Y	Y
11 McNerney	Y	Y	Y	Y	Y	Y	Y
12 Speier	Y	Y	Y	Y	Y	Y	Y
13 Stark	Y	Y	Y	Y	Y	Y	N
14 Eshoo	Y	Y	Y	Y	Y	Y	Y
15 Honda	Y	Y	Y	Y	Y	Y	Y
16 Lofgren	Y	Y	Y	Y	Y	Y	Y
17 Farr	Y	Y	Y	Y	Y	Y	Y
18 Cardoza	Y	Y	?	Y	Y	Y	N
19 Radanovich	N	N	?	N	N	Y	N
20 Costa	?	?	?	?	?	?	?
21 Nunes	N	N	N	N	N	?	N
22 McCarthy	N	N	N	N	N	Y	N
23 Capps	Y	Y	Y	Y	Y	Y	Y
24 Gallegly	N	N	N	N	N	Y	N
25 McKeon	N	N	N	N	N	Y	N
26 Dreier	N	N	N	N	N	Y	N
27 Sherman	Y	Y	Y	Y	Y	Y	Y
28 Berman	Y	Y	Y	Y	Y	Y	Y
29 Schiff	Y	Y	Y	Y	Y	Y	Y
30 Waxman	Y	Y	Y	Y	Y	Y	Y
31 Becerra	Y	Y	Y	Y	Y	Y	Y
32 Solis	Y	Y	Y	Y	Y	Y	Y
33 Watson	?	?	?	?	?	?	?
34 Roybal-Allard	Y	Y	Y	Y	Y	Y	Y
35 Waters	Y	Y	Y	Y	Y	Y	Y
36 Harman	Y	Y	Y	Y	Y	Y	Y
37 Richardson	Y	Y	Y	Y	Y	Y	Y
38 Napolitano	Y	Y	Y	Y	Y	Y	Y
39 Sánchez, Linda	Y	Y	Y	Y	Y	Y	Y
40 Royce	N	N	N	N	N	Y	N
41 Lewis	N	N	Y	N	N	Y	N
42 Miller, Gary	?	?	?	?	?	?	?
43 Baca	Y	Y	Y	Y	Y	Y	Y
44 Calvert	N	N	N	N	N	Y	N
45 Bono Mack	N	N	N	N	N	Y	N
46 Rohrabacher	?	?	?	?	?	?	?
47 Sanchez, Loretta	Y	Y	Y	Y	Y	Y	Y
48 Campbell	N	N	N	P	P	P	P
49 Issa	N	N	N	N	N	Y	N
50 Bilbray	N	N	N	N	N	Y	N
51 Filner	Y	Y	Y	Y	Y	Y	Y
52 Hunter	N	N	N	N	N	Y	N
53 Davis	Y	Y	Y	Y	Y	Y	Y

	684	685	686	687	688	689	690
COLORADO							
1 DeGette	Y	Y	Y	Y	Y	Y	Y
2 Udall	Y	Y	Y	Y	Y	Y	Y
3 Salazar	Y	Y	Y	Y	Y	Y	Y
4 Musgrave	N	N	N	N	N	Y	N
5 Lamborn	N	N	N	N	N	Y	N
6 Tancredo	?	?	?	?	?	?	?
7 Perlmutter	Y	Y	Y	Y	Y	Y	Y
CONNECTICUT							
1 Larson	Y	Y	Y	Y	Y	Y	Y
2 Courtney	Y	Y	Y	Y	Y	Y	Y
3 DeLauro	Y	Y	Y	Y	Y	Y	Y
4 Shays	?	?	?	N	N	Y	N
5 Murphy	Y	Y	Y	Y	Y	Y	Y
DELAWARE							
AL Castle	N	N	N	N	N	Y	Y
FLORIDA							
1 Miller	N	N	N	N	N	Y	N
2 Boyd	Y	Y	Y	Y	Y	Y	Y
3 Brown	Y	Y	Y	Y	Y	Y	Y
4 Crenshaw	N	N	N	N	N	Y	N
5 Brown-Waite	N	N	N	N	N	Y	N
6 Stearns	N	N	N	N	N	Y	N
7 Mica	N	N	N	N	N	Y	N
8 Keller	?	?	?	?	?	?	?
9 Bilirakis	N	N	N	N	N	Y	N
10 Young	N	Y	N	N	N	Y	N
11 Castor	Y	Y	Y	Y	Y	Y	Y
12 Putnam	N	N	N	N	N	Y	N
13 Buchanan	N	N	N	N	N	Y	N
14 Mack	N	N	N	N	N	Y	N
15 Weldon	?	?	?	?	?	?	?
16 Mahoney	Y	Y	Y	Y	Y	Y	Y
17 Meek	Y	Y	Y	Y	Y	Y	Y
18 Ros-Lehtinen	N	N	N	N	N	Y	N
19 Wexler	Y	Y	Y	Y	Y	Y	Y
20 Wasserman Schultz	Y	Y	Y	Y	Y	Y	Y
21 Diaz-Balart, L.	N	N	N	N	N	Y	N
22 Klein	Y	Y	Y	Y	Y	Y	Y
23 Hastings	?	?	?	?	?	?	?
24 Feeney	N	N	Y	N	N	Y	N
25 Diaz-Balart, M.	N	N	N	N	N	Y	N
GEORGIA							
1 Kingston	N	N	N	N	N	Y	N
2 Bishop	Y	Y	Y	Y	Y	Y	Y
3 Westmoreland	N	N	N	N	N	Y	N
4 Johnson	Y	Y	Y	Y	Y	Y	Y
5 Lewis	Y	Y	Y	Y	Y	Y	Y
6 Price	N	N	N	N	N	Y	N
7 Linder	N	N	N	N	N	Y	N
8 Marshall	Y	Y	Y	Y	Y	Y	Y
9 Deal	N	N	N	N	N	Y	N
10 Broun	N	N	N	N	N	Y	N
11 Gingrey	N	N	N	N	N	Y	N
12 Barrow	Y	Y	Y	Y	Y	Y	Y
13 Scott	Y	Y	Y	Y	Y	Y	Y
HAWAII							
1 Abercrombie	Y	Y	Y	Y	Y	Y	Y
2 Hirono	Y	Y	Y	Y	Y	Y	Y
IDAHO							
1 Sali	N	N	N	N	N	Y	N
2 Simpson	N	N	N	N	N	Y	N
ILLINOIS							
1 Rush	Y	Y	Y	Y	Y	Y	Y
2 Jackson	Y	Y	Y	Y	Y	Y	Y
3 Lipinski	Y	Y	Y	Y	Y	Y	Y
4 Gutierrez	?	?	?	?	?	?	?
5 Emanuel	?	?	?	?	?	?	?
6 Roskam	N	N	N	N	N	Y	N
7 Davis	Y	Y	?	Y	Y	Y	Y
8 Bean	Y	Y	Y	Y	Y	Y	Y
9 Schakowsky	Y	Y	Y	Y	Y	Y	Y
10 Kirk	?	N	?	?	?	Y	Y
11 Weller	Y	Y	?	Y	Y	Y	Y
12 Costello	Y	Y	Y	Y	Y	Y	Y
13 Biggert	N	N	N	N	N	Y	N
14 Foster	Y	Y	Y	Y	Y	Y	Y
15 Johnson	N	N	Y	N	N	Y	N

KEY **Republicans** Democrats

Y Voted for (yea)	X Paired against
# Paired for	− Announced against
+ Announced for	P Voted "present"
N Voted against (nay)	

C Voted "present" to avoid possible conflict of interest
? Did not vote or otherwise make a position known

	684	685	686	687	688	689	690
16 **Manzullo**	N	N	N	N	N	Y	Y
17 Hare	Y	Y	Y	Y	Y	Y	Y
18 **LaHood**	N	Y	N	N	Y	Y	Y
19 **Shimkus**	N	N	N	N	N	Y	N
INDIANA							
1 Visclosky	Y	Y	Y	Y	Y	Y	Y
2 Donnelly	Y	Y	Y	Y	Y	Y	Y
3 **Souder**	Y	Y	N	Y	Y	Y	Y
4 **Buyer**	N	N	N	N	N	Y	Y
5 **Burton**	N	N	N	N	N	Y	N
6 **Pence**	N	N	N	N	N	Y	N
7 Carson, A.	Y	Y	Y	Y	Y	Y	Y
8 Ellsworth	Y	Y	N	Y	Y	Y	Y
9 Hill	Y	Y	N	N	N	Y	Y
IOWA							
1 Braley	Y	Y	Y	Y	Y	Y	Y
2 Loebsack	Y	Y	Y	Y	Y	Y	Y
3 Boswell	Y	Y	Y	Y	Y	Y	Y
4 **Latham**	N	N	N	N	N	Y	N
5 **King**	N	N	N	N	N	Y	N
KANSAS							
1 **Moran**	N	N	N	N	N	Y	N
2 Boyda	Y	Y	Y	Y	Y	Y	Y
3 Moore	Y	Y	Y	Y	Y	Y	Y
4 **Tiahrt**	N	N	N	N	N	Y	N
KENTUCKY							
1 **Whitfield**	N	N	?	N	N	Y	N
2 **Lewis**	N	N	N	N	N	Y	Y
3 Yarmuth	Y	Y	Y	Y	Y	Y	Y
4 **Davis**	N	N	N	N	N	Y	N
5 **Rogers**	N	N	N	N	N	Y	N
6 Chandler	Y	Y	Y	Y	Y	Y	Y
LOUISIANA							
1 **Scalise**	N	N	N	N	N	Y	N
2 Jefferson	?	?	?	?	?	Y	Y
3 Melancon	N	Y	Y	Y	Y	Y	Y
4 **McCrery**	N	N	N	N	N	Y	Y
5 **Alexander**	N	N	N	N	N	Y	N
6 Cazayoux	Y	Y	Y	Y	Y	Y	Y
7 **Boustany**	N	N	N	N	N	Y	N
MAINE							
1 Allen	Y	Y	Y	Y	Y	Y	Y
2 Michaud	Y	N	Y	Y	N	Y	Y
MARYLAND							
1 **Gilchrest**	?	?	?	?	?	?	?
2 Ruppersberger	Y	Y	Y	Y	Y	Y	Y
3 Sarbanes	Y	Y	Y	Y	Y	Y	Y
4 Edwards	Y	?	Y	Y	Y	Y	Y
5 Hoyer	Y	Y	Y	Y	Y	Y	Y
6 **Bartlett**	N	N	N	N	N	Y	N
7 Cummings	Y	Y	Y	Y	Y	Y	Y
8 Van Hollen	Y	Y	Y	Y	Y	Y	Y
MASSACHUSETTS							
1 Olver	Y	Y	Y	Y	Y	Y	Y
2 Neal	Y	Y	Y	Y	Y	Y	Y
3 McGovern	Y	Y	Y	Y	Y	Y	Y
4 Frank	Y	Y	Y	Y	Y	Y	Y
5 Tsongas	Y	Y	Y	Y	Y	Y	Y
6 Tierney	Y	Y	Y	Y	Y	Y	Y
7 Markey	Y	Y	Y	Y	Y	Y	Y
8 Capuano	Y	Y	Y	Y	Y	Y	Y
9 Lynch	Y	Y	Y	Y	Y	Y	Y
10 Delahunt	?	?	?	?	?	?	?
MICHIGAN							
1 Stupak	Y	Y	N	Y	Y	Y	Y
2 **Hoekstra**	N	N	N	N	N	Y	Y
3 **Ehlers**	N	N	N	N	N	Y	Y
4 **Camp**	Y	Y	N	N	Y	Y	Y
5 Kildee	Y	Y	Y	Y	Y	Y	Y
6 **Upton**	Y	Y	N	Y	Y	Y	Y
7 **Walberg**	?	?	?	?	?	?	?
8 **Rogers**	N	N	N	N	N	Y	Y
9 **Knollenberg**	N	Y	N	N	Y	Y	Y
10 **Miller**	Y	Y	N	Y	Y	Y	Y
11 **McCotter**	Y	Y	N	Y	Y	Y	Y
12 Levin	Y	Y	Y	Y	Y	Y	Y
13 Kilpatrick	Y	Y	Y	Y	Y	Y	Y
14 Conyers	Y	Y	Y	Y	Y	Y	Y
15 Dingell	Y	Y	Y	Y	Y	Y	Y
MINNESOTA							
1 Walz	Y	Y	Y	Y	Y	Y	N
2 **Kline**	N	N	N	N	N	Y	N
3 **Ramstad**	N	Y	N	Y	Y	Y	Y
4 McCollum	Y	Y	Y	Y	Y	Y	Y

	684	685	686	687	688	689	690
5 Ellison	?	?	?	?	?	?	?
6 **Bachmann**	N	N	N	N	N	Y	N
7 Peterson	Y	Y	N	Y	Y	Y	N
8 Oberstar	Y	Y	Y	Y	Y	Y	Y
MISSISSIPPI							
1 Childers	Y	Y	Y	Y	Y	Y	N
2 Thompson	Y	Y	Y	Y	Y	Y	Y
3 **Pickering**	?	?	?	N	N	Y	N
4 Taylor	Y	Y	Y	Y	Y	Y	Y
MISSOURI							
1 Clay	Y	Y	Y	Y	Y	Y	Y
2 **Akin**	N	N	N	N	N	Y	N
3 Carnahan	Y	Y	Y	Y	Y	Y	Y
4 Skelton	Y	Y	Y	Y	Y	Y	Y
5 Cleaver	Y	Y	Y	Y	Y	?	Y
6 **Graves**	N	N	N	N	N	Y	N
7 **Blunt**	N	N	N	N	N	Y	N
8 **Emerson**	N	N	N	N	N	Y	Y
9 **Hulshof**	N	N	N	N	N	Y	N
MONTANA							
AL **Rehberg**	N	N	N	N	N	Y	N
NEBRASKA							
1 **Fortenberry**	N	N	N	N	N	Y	N
2 **Terry**	N	N	N	N	N	Y	N
3 **Smith**	N	N	N	N	N	Y	N
NEVADA							
1 Berkley	Y	Y	Y	Y	Y	Y	Y
2 **Heller**	N	N	N	N	N	Y	N
3 **Porter**	N	N	N	N	N	Y	Y
NEW HAMPSHIRE							
1 Shea-Porter	Y	Y	Y	Y	Y	Y	Y
2 Hodes	Y	Y	Y	Y	Y	Y	Y
NEW JERSEY							
1 Andrews	Y	Y	Y	Y	Y	Y	Y
2 **LoBiondo**	N	N	N	N	N	Y	N
3 **Saxton**	N	N	Y	N	?	?	N
4 **Smith**	N	N	N	N	N	Y	Y
5 **Garrett**	N	N	N	N	N	Y	N
6 Pallone	?	?	?	Y	Y	Y	Y
7 **Ferguson**	N	N	N	N	N	Y	N
8 Pascrell	Y	Y	Y	Y	Y	Y	Y
9 Rothman	Y	Y	Y	Y	Y	Y	Y
10 Payne	Y	Y	Y	Y	Y	Y	Y
11 **Frelinghuysen**	N	N	N	N	N	Y	Y
12 Holt	Y	Y	Y	Y	Y	Y	Y
13 Sires	Y	Y	Y	Y	Y	Y	Y
NEW MEXICO							
1 **Wilson**	?	?	?	N	N	Y	N
2 **Pearce**	N	N	N	N	N	Y	N
3 Udall	Y	Y	Y	Y	Y	Y	Y
NEW YORK							
1 Bishop	Y	Y	Y	Y	Y	Y	Y
2 Israel	Y	Y	Y	Y	Y	Y	Y
3 **King**	N	N	N	N	N	Y	Y
4 McCarthy	Y	Y	Y	Y	Y	Y	Y
5 Ackerman	Y	Y	Y	Y	Y	Y	Y
6 Meeks	Y	Y	Y	Y	Y	Y	Y
7 Crowley	Y	Y	Y	Y	Y	Y	Y
8 Nadler	Y	Y	Y	Y	Y	Y	Y
9 Weiner	Y	Y	Y	Y	Y	Y	Y
10 Towns	Y	Y	Y	Y	Y	Y	Y
11 Clarke	Y	Y	Y	Y	Y	Y	Y
12 Velázquez	Y	Y	Y	Y	Y	Y	Y
13 **Fossella**	?	?	?	N	N	Y	N
14 Maloney	Y	Y	Y	Y	Y	Y	Y
15 Rangel	Y	Y	Y	Y	Y	Y	Y
16 Serrano	Y	Y	?	Y	Y	Y	Y
17 Engel	Y	Y	Y	Y	Y	Y	Y
18 Lowey	Y	Y	Y	Y	Y	Y	Y
19 Hall	Y	Y	Y	Y	Y	Y	Y
20 Gillibrand	Y	Y	Y	Y	Y	Y	Y
21 McNulty	Y	Y	Y	Y	Y	Y	Y
22 Hinchey	Y	Y	Y	Y	Y	Y	Y
23 **McHugh**	N	N	N	N	N	Y	Y
24 Arcuri	Y	Y	N	Y	Y	Y	Y
25 **Walsh**	N	N	Y	N	N	Y	Y
26 **Reynolds**	N	N	N	N	N	Y	N
27 Higgins	Y	Y	Y	Y	Y	Y	Y
28 Slaughter	Y	Y	Y	Y	Y	Y	Y
29 **Kuhl**	?	?	?	?	?	?	?
NORTH CAROLINA							
1 Butterfield	Y	Y	?	Y	Y	Y	N
2 Etheridge	Y	Y	Y	Y	Y	Y	Y
3 **Jones**	?	?	?	N	N	Y	N
4 Price	Y	Y	Y	Y	Y	Y	Y

	684	685	686	687	688	689	690
5 **Foxx**	N	N	N	N	N	Y	N
6 **Coble**	N	N	N	N	N	Y	N
7 McIntyre	Y	Y	Y	Y	N	Y	N
8 **Hayes**	N	N	N	N	N	Y	N
9 **Myrick**	N	N	N	N	N	Y	N
10 **McHenry**	N	N	N	N	N	Y	N
11 Shuler	Y	N	Y	Y	N	Y	N
12 Watt	Y	Y	Y	Y	Y	Y	Y
13 Miller	Y	Y	Y	Y	Y	Y	Y
NORTH DAKOTA							
AL Pomeroy	Y	Y	Y	Y	Y	Y	Y
OHIO							
1 **Chabot**	N	N	N	N	N	Y	N
2 **Schmidt**	N	N	N	N	N	Y	N
3 **Turner**	N	N	N	N	N	Y	N
4 **Jordan**	N	N	N	N	N	Y	N
5 **Latta**	N	N	N	N	N	Y	N
6 Wilson	Y	Y	Y	Y	Y	Y	Y
7 **Hobson**	N	N	N	N	N	Y	N
8 **Boehner**	N	N	N	N	N	Y	N
9 Kaptur	Y	Y	Y	Y	Y	Y	Y
10 Kucinich	Y	Y	Y	Y	Y	Y	Y
11 Fudge[1]	Y	Y	Y	Y	Y	Y	Y
12 **Tiberi**	N	N	N	N	N	Y	N
13 Sutton	Y	Y	Y	Y	Y	Y	Y
14 **LaTourette**	N	N	N	N	Y	Y	Y
15 **Pryce**	?	?	?	?	?	?	?
16 **Regula**	N	N	N	N	N	Y	Y
17 Ryan	Y	Y	Y	Y	Y	Y	Y
18 Space	Y	Y	Y	Y	Y	Y	Y
OKLAHOMA							
1 **Sullivan**	N	N	N	N	N	Y	N
2 Boren	Y	Y	Y	Y	Y	Y	Y
3 **Lucas**	N	N	?	N	N	Y	N
4 **Cole**	N	N	N	N	N	Y	N
5 **Fallin**	N	N	N	N	N	Y	N
OREGON							
1 Wu	Y	Y	Y	Y	Y	Y	Y
2 **Walden**	N	N	N	N	N	Y	N
3 Blumenauer	Y	Y	Y	Y	Y	Y	Y
4 DeFazio	Y	Y	Y	Y	Y	Y	Y
5 Hooley	?	?	?	?	?	?	?
PENNSYLVANIA							
1 Brady	Y	Y	Y	Y	Y	Y	Y
2 Fattah	Y	Y	Y	Y	Y	Y	Y
3 **English**	N	N	N	N	N	Y	Y
4 Altmire	Y	Y	Y	Y	Y	Y	Y
5 **Peterson**	?	?	?	?	?	?	?
6 **Gerlach**	N	N	Y	N	N	Y	N
7 Sestak	Y	Y	Y	Y	Y	Y	Y
8 Murphy, P.	Y	Y	Y	Y	Y	Y	Y
9 **Shuster**	N	N	N	N	N	Y	N
10 Carney	N	N	N	N	N	Y	Y
11 Kanjorski	Y	Y	Y	Y	Y	Y	Y
12 Murtha	Y	Y	Y	Y	Y	Y	Y
13 Schwartz	Y	Y	?	Y	Y	Y	Y
14 Doyle	Y	Y	Y	Y	Y	Y	Y
15 **Dent**	N	N	Y	N	N	Y	N
16 **Pitts**	N	N	N	N	N	Y	N
17 Holden	Y	Y	Y	Y	Y	Y	Y
18 **Murphy, T.**	N	N	N	N	N	Y	Y
19 **Platts**	N	N	N	N	N	Y	N
RHODE ISLAND							
1 Kennedy	Y	Y	Y	Y	Y	Y	Y
2 Langevin	Y	Y	Y	Y	Y	Y	Y
SOUTH CAROLINA							
1 **Brown**	N	N	N	N	N	Y	N
2 **Wilson**	N	N	N	N	N	Y	N
3 **Barrett**	N	N	N	N	N	Y	N
4 **Inglis**	N	N	N	N	N	Y	N
5 Spratt	Y	Y	?	Y	Y	Y	Y
6 Clyburn	Y	Y	Y	Y	Y	Y	Y
SOUTH DAKOTA							
AL Herseth Sandlin	Y	Y	Y	Y	N	Y	N
TENNESSEE							
1 **Davis, D.**	N	N	N	N	N	Y	N
2 **Duncan**	N	N	N	N	N	Y	N
3 **Wamp**	N	N	N	N	N	Y	N
4 Davis, L.	Y	Y	Y	Y	Y	Y	Y
5 Cooper	Y	Y	Y	Y	Y	Y	N
6 Gordon	Y	Y	Y	Y	Y	?	?
7 **Blackburn**	N	N	N	N	N	Y	N
8 Tanner	Y	Y	Y	Y	Y	Y	Y
9 Cohen	Y	Y	Y	Y	Y	Y	Y

	684	685	686	687	688	689	690
TEXAS							
1 **Gohmert**	N	?	P	N	N	Y	N
2 **Poe**	N	N	N	N	N	Y	N
3 **Johnson, S.**	N	N	N	N	N	Y	N
4 **Hall**	N	N	N	N	N	Y	N
5 **Hensarling**	N	N	N	N	N	Y	N
6 **Barton**	N	N	N	N	N	Y	Y
7 **Culberson**	N	N	N	N	N	Y	N
8 **Brady**	N	N	N	N	N	Y	N
9 Green, A.	Y	Y	Y	Y	Y	Y	Y
10 **McCaul**	N	N	N	N	N	Y	N
11 **Conaway**	N	N	N	N	N	Y	N
12 **Granger**	N	N	N	N	N	Y	N
13 **Thornberry**	N	N	N	N	N	Y	N
14 **Paul**	N	N	N	N	N	Y	N
15 Hinojosa	Y	Y	Y	Y	Y	Y	Y
16 Reyes	Y	Y	Y	Y	Y	Y	Y
17 Edwards	Y	Y	Y	Y	Y	Y	Y
18 Jackson Lee	Y	Y	Y	Y	Y	Y	Y
19 **Neugebauer**	N	N	N	N	N	Y	N
20 Gonzalez	Y	Y	Y	Y	Y	Y	Y
21 **Smith**	N	N	N	N	N	Y	N
22 Lampson	Y	Y	Y	Y	Y	Y	Y
23 Rodriguez	Y	Y	Y	Y	Y	Y	N
24 **Marchant**	N	N	N	N	N	Y	N
25 Doggett	Y	Y	Y	Y	Y	Y	Y
26 **Burgess**	N	N	N	N	N	Y	N
27 Ortiz	Y	Y	Y	Y	Y	Y	Y
28 Cuellar	Y	Y	Y	Y	Y	Y	Y
29 Green, G.	Y	Y	Y	Y	Y	Y	Y
30 Johnson, E.	?	?	?	?	?	?	?
31 **Carter**	N	N	N	N	N	Y	N
32 **Sessions**	N	N	N	N	N	Y	N
UTAH							
1 **Bishop**	N	N	N	N	N	Y	N
2 Matheson	Y	Y	Y	Y	N	Y	N
3 **Cannon**	?	?	?	N	N	Y	N
VERMONT							
AL Welch	Y	Y	Y	Y	Y	Y	Y
VIRGINIA							
1 **Wittman**	N	N	N	N	N	Y	N
2 **Drake**	N	N	N	N	N	Y	N
3 Scott	Y	Y	Y	Y	Y	Y	Y
4 **Forbes**	N	N	N	N	N	Y	N
5 **Goode**	N	N	N	N	N	Y	N
6 **Goodlatte**	N	N	N	N	N	Y	N
7 **Cantor**	N	N	N	N	N	Y	N
8 Moran	Y	Y	Y	Y	Y	Y	Y
9 Boucher	?	?	?	Y	Y	Y	Y
10 **Wolf**	N	N	N	N	N	Y	N
11 Vacant[2]							
WASHINGTON							
1 Inslee	Y	Y	Y	Y	Y	Y	Y
2 Larsen	Y	Y	Y	Y	Y	Y	Y
3 Baird	Y	Y	Y	Y	Y	Y	Y
4 **Hastings**	N	N	N	N	N	Y	N
5 **McMorris Rodgers**	N	N	N	N	N	Y	N
6 Dicks	Y	Y	Y	Y	Y	Y	Y
7 McDermott	Y	Y	Y	Y	Y	Y	Y
8 **Reichert**	N	N	N	N	N	Y	N
9 Smith	Y	Y	Y	Y	Y	Y	Y
WEST VIRGINIA							
1 Mollohan	Y	Y	Y	Y	Y	Y	Y
2 **Capito**	N	N	N	N	N	Y	Y
3 Rahall	Y	Y	Y	Y	Y	Y	N
WISCONSIN							
1 **Ryan**	N	N	?	N	N	Y	Y
2 Baldwin	Y	Y	Y	Y	Y	Y	Y
3 Kind	Y	Y	Y	Y	Y	Y	Y
4 Moore	Y	Y	Y	Y	Y	Y	Y
5 **Sensenbrenner**	?	?	?	?	?	?	?
6 **Petri**	N	N	N	N	N	Y	N
7 Obey	Y	Y	Y	Y	Y	Y	Y
8 Kagen	Y	Y	Y	Y	Y	Y	N
WYOMING							
AL **Cubin**	?	?	?	?	?	?	?
DELEGATES							
Faleomavaega (A.S.)							
Norton (D.C.)							
Bordallo (Guam)							
Fortuño (P.R.)							
Christensen (V.I.)							

House Roll Call Index by Subject

Appendix S

SENATE ROLL CALL VOTES

Senate Roll Call Index By Bill Number

IN THE SENATE | By Vote Number

1. HR 4986. Fiscal 2008 Defense Authorization/Passage. Passage of the bill that would authorize $696.4 billion for defense programs in fiscal 2008, including $189.5 billion for the wars in Iraq and Afghanistan. It would authorize $142.8 billion for operations and maintenance; $119.7 billion for military personnel; $23.7 billion for military construction and family housing; and $23.1 billion for the Defense Health Program. It would authorize a 3.5 percent pay increase for military personnel. It also would allow the president to waive certain liability provisions as they apply to Iraq. Passed (thus cleared for the president) 91-3: R 46-0; D 44-2 (ND 39-2, SD 5-0); I 1-1. Jan. 22, 2008.

2. S 2248. Foreign Intelligence Surveillance Revisions/Judiciary Committee Substitute. Bond, R-Mo., motion to table (kill) the Leahy, D-Vt., substitute amendment that would amend the 1978 Foreign Intelligence Surveillance Act (FISA) to allow warrantless surveillance of international calls that may involve U.S. citizens. The substitute would clarify that the government could conduct such electronic surveillance only through the FISA court and through FISA court-approved procedures. It also would strike provisions in the bill that would grant retroactive legal immunity to telecommunications companies alleged to have participated in the National Security Agency's warrantless surveillance program. The substitute would sunset in four years. Motion agreed to 60-36: R 47-0; D 12-35 (ND 9-33, SD 3-2); I 1-1. A "yea" was a vote in support of the president's position. Jan. 24, 2008.

3. S 2248. Foreign Intelligence Surveillance Revisions/Cloture. Motion to invoke cloture (thus limiting debate) on the Rockefeller, D-W.Va., substitute amendment that would amend the 1978 Foreign Intelligence Surveillance Act (FISA) to authorize warrantless surveillance of foreign targets, even if they are communicating with someone in the United States. It would give the FISA court authority to approve several aspects of how such surveillance is conducted. It also would grant retroactive legal immunity to telecommunications companies alleged to have participated in the National Security Agency's warrantless surveillance program. Motion rejected 48-45: R 44-1; D 4-43 (ND 1-42, SD 3-1); I 0-1. Three-fifths of the total Senate (60) is required to invoke cloture. Jan. 28, 2008.

4. S 2248. Foreign Intelligence Surveillance Revisions/Cloture. Motion to invoke cloture (thus limiting debate) on the Reid, D-Nev., amendment that would strike the text of the bill and replace it with language that would extend for 30 days a law set to expire on Feb. 1, 2008, which expands the authority of the attorney general and the director of National Intelligence to conduct surveillance of suspected foreign terrorists without a court warrant. Motion rejected 48-45: R 0-45; D 47-0 (ND 43-0, SD 4-0); I 1-0. Three-fifths of the total Senate (60) is required to invoke cloture. A "nay" was a vote in support of the president's position. Jan. 28, 2008.

5. HR 5140. Economic Stimulus/Cloture. Motion to invoke cloture (thus limiting debate) on the motion to proceed to the bill that would provide advance refund of a tax credit for most taxpayers equal to $300 to $600 for individuals, and $600 to $1,200 for married couples. Motion agreed to 80-4: R 37-4; D 42-0 (ND 37-0, SD 5-0); I 1-0. Three-fifths of the total Senate (60) is required to invoke cloture. Feb. 4, 2008.

6. Procedural Motion/Require Attendance. Reid, D-Nev., motion to instruct the sergeant at arms to request the attendance of absent senators. Motion agreed to 73-12: R 31-12; D 41-0 (ND 36-0, SD 5-0); I 1-0. Feb. 5, 2008.

*Roger Wicker, R-Miss., was sworn in Dec. 31, 2007, to fill the seat vacated by the resignation of Republican Trent Lott on Dec. 17, 2007.

ND Northern Democrats, SD Southern Democrats
Southern states: Ala., Ark., Fla., Ga., Ky., La., Miss., N.C., Okla., S.C., Tenn., Texas, Va.

	1	2	3	4	5	6		1	2	3	4	5	6
ALABAMA							**MONTANA**						
Shelby	Y	Y	Y	N	N	Y	Baucus	Y	N	N	Y	Y	Y
Sessions	Y	Y	Y	N	Y	Y	Tester	Y	N	N	Y	Y	Y
ALASKA							**NEBRASKA**						
Stevens	Y	Y	Y	N	Y	Y	**Hagel**	Y	Y	Y	N	N	Y
Murkowski	Y	Y	Y	N	Y	Y	Nelson	Y	Y	Y	Y	Y	Y
ARIZONA							**NEVADA**						
McCain	?	?	?	?	?	?	Reid	Y	N	N	Y	Y	Y
Kyl	Y	Y	Y	N	Y	N	**Ensign**	Y	Y	?	?	Y	N
ARKANSAS							**NEW HAMPSHIRE**						
Lincoln	Y	N	Y	Y	Y	Y	**Gregg**	Y	Y	Y	N	?	Y
Pryor	Y	Y	Y	Y	Y	Y	**Sununu**	Y	Y	Y	N	Y	Y
CALIFORNIA							**NEW JERSEY**						
Feinstein	Y	N	N	Y	Y	Y	Lautenberg	Y	N	N	Y	Y	Y
Boxer	Y	N	N	Y	Y	Y	Menendez	+	N	N	Y	Y	Y
COLORADO							**NEW MEXICO**						
Allard	Y	Y	Y	N	Y	N	**Domenici**	Y	Y	Y	N	?	?
Salazar	Y	Y	N	Y	Y	Y	Bingaman	Y	N	N	Y	Y	Y
CONNECTICUT							**NEW YORK**						
Dodd	Y	N	N	Y	Y	Y	Schumer	Y	N	N	Y	Y	?
Lieberman	Y	Y	?	?	?	?	Clinton	?	?	N	Y	?	?
DELAWARE							**NORTH CAROLINA**						
Biden	Y	N	N	Y	?	?	**Dole**	Y	Y	+	–	Y	Y
Carper	Y	Y	N	Y	Y	Y	**Burr**	Y	Y	Y	N	Y	?
FLORIDA							**NORTH DAKOTA**						
Nelson	Y	Y	–	+	Y	Y	Conrad	Y	N	N	Y	Y	Y
Martinez	Y	Y	Y	N	Y	Y	Dorgan	Y	N	N	Y	+	Y
GEORGIA							**OHIO**						
Chambliss	Y	Y	Y	N	?	Y	**Voinovich**	Y	Y	Y	N	Y	Y
Isakson	Y	Y	Y	N	Y	Y	Brown	Y	N	N	Y	Y	Y
HAWAII							**OKLAHOMA**						
Inouye	Y	Y	N	Y	Y	?	**Inhofe**	Y	Y	Y	N	Y	N
Akaka	Y	N	N	Y	Y	Y	**Coburn**	Y	Y	?	?	N	N
IDAHO							**OREGON**						
Craig	Y	Y	Y	N	Y	N	Wyden	Y	N	N	Y	Y	Y
Crapo	Y	Y	Y	N	Y	Y	**Smith**	Y	Y	Y	N	Y	Y
ILLINOIS							**PENNSYLVANIA**						
Durbin	Y	N	N	Y	Y	Y	**Specter**	Y	Y	N	N	Y	Y
Obama	?	?	N	Y	?	?	Casey	Y	N	N	Y	Y	Y
INDIANA							**RHODE ISLAND**						
Lugar	Y	Y	Y	N	Y	Y	Reed	Y	N	N	Y	Y	Y
Bayh	Y	Y	N	Y	Y	?	Whitehouse	Y	N	N	Y	Y	Y
IOWA							**SOUTH CAROLINA**						
Grassley	Y	Y	Y	N	Y	N	**Graham**	Y	?	Y	N	?	?
Harkin	Y	N	–	+	Y	Y	**DeMint**	Y	Y	Y	N	?	Y
KANSAS							**SOUTH DAKOTA**						
Brownback	Y	Y	Y	N	Y	?	Johnson	Y	Y	Y	N	Y	Y
Roberts	Y	Y	Y	N	Y	Y	**Thune**	+	Y	Y	N	Y	Y
KENTUCKY							**TENNESSEE**						
McConnell	Y	Y	Y	N	Y	Y	**Alexander**	Y	Y	Y	N	Y	N
Bunning	Y	Y	Y	N	Y	Y	**Corker**	Y	Y	Y	N	N	Y
LOUISIANA							**TEXAS**						
Landrieu	Y	Y	Y	Y	Y	Y	**Hutchison**	Y	Y	Y	N	Y	Y
Vitter	Y	Y	Y	N	?	Y	**Cornyn**	Y	Y	Y	N	Y	Y
MAINE							**UTAH**						
Snowe	Y	Y	Y	N	Y	Y	**Hatch**	Y	Y	Y	N	Y	Y
Collins	Y	Y	Y	N	Y	Y	**Bennett**	Y	Y	Y	N	Y	Y
MARYLAND							**VERMONT**						
Mikulski	Y	Y	N	Y	Y	Y	Leahy	Y	N	N	Y	Y	Y
Cardin	Y	N	N	Y	Y	Y	*Sanders*	N	N	N	Y	Y	Y
MASSACHUSETTS							**VIRGINIA**						
Kennedy	Y	N	N	Y	?	?	**Warner**	?	Y	Y	Y	Y	Y
Kerry	Y	N	N	Y	+	?	Webb	Y	N	N	Y	Y	Y
MICHIGAN							**WASHINGTON**						
Levin	Y	N	N	Y	Y	Y	Murray	Y	N	N	Y	Y	Y
Stabenow	Y	N	N	Y	Y	Y	Cantwell	Y	N	N	Y	Y	Y
MINNESOTA							**WEST VIRGINIA**						
Coleman	Y	Y	Y	N	Y	Y	Byrd	N	N	N	Y	?	?
Klobuchar	Y	N	N	Y	Y	Y	Rockefeller	Y	Y	Y	N	Y	Y
MISSISSIPPI							**WISCONSIN**						
Cochran	Y	Y	Y	N	Y	Y	Kohl	Y	N	N	Y	Y	Y
Wicker*	Y	Y	Y	N	?	?	Feingold	N	N	N	Y	Y	Y
MISSOURI							**WYOMING**						
Bond	Y	Y	Y	N	Y	N	**Enzi**	Y	Y	Y	N	Y	Y
McCaskill	Y	N	Y	Y	Y	Y	**Barrasso**	Y	Y	Y	N	Y	Y

KEY	**Republicans**	Democrats	*Independents*		
Y	Voted for (yea)	X	Paired against	C	Voted "present" to avoid possible conflict of interest
#	Paired for	–	Announced against		
+	Announced for	P	Voted "present"	?	Did not vote or otherwise make a position known
N	Voted against (nay)				

IN THE SENATE | By Vote Number

7. S 2248. Foreign Intelligence Surveillance Revisions/Sunset.
Cardin, D-Md., amendment to the Rockefeller, D-W.Va., substitute. The Cardin amendment would modify the sunset provision in the underlying substitute amendment from six to four years. The substitute would amend the 1978 Foreign Intelligence Surveillance Act (FISA) to authorize warrantless surveillance of foreign targets, even if they are communicating with someone in the United States. It would give the FISA court authority to approve several aspects of how such surveillance is conducted. It also would grant retroactive legal immunity to telecommunications companies alleged to have participated in the National Security Agency's warrantless surveillance program. Rejected 49-46: R 0-46; D 48-0 (ND 43-0, SD 5-0); I 1-0. (By unanimous consent, the Senate agreed to raise the majority requirement for adoption of the Cardin amendment to 60 votes. Subsequently, the Cardin amendment was withdrawn.) Feb. 6, 2008.

8. HR 5140. Economic Stimulus/Cloture. Motion to invoke cloture (thus limiting debate) on the Reid, D-Nev., amendment that would provide advance refunds of a tax credit for most taxpayers equal to $500 for individuals and $1,000 for couples. Families would receive an additional $300 for each child under 17. The amendment would expand eligibility for rebate checks to include low-income seniors and disabled veterans. It also would begin phasing out the benefit for individuals with adjusted gross incomes above $150,000 and married couples with incomes above $300,000. Motion rejected 58-41: R 8-40; D 48-1 (ND 43-1, SD 5-0); I 2-0. Three-fifths of the total Senate (60) is required to invoke cloture. A "nay" was a vote in support of the president's position. Feb. 6, 2008.

9. HR 5140. Economic Stimulus/Substitute. Reid, D-Nev., substitute amendment that would provide advance refund of a tax credit for most taxpayers equal to $300 to $600 for individuals and $600 to $1,200 for married couples. Families would receive $300 for each child under 17. The amendment would expand eligibility for rebate checks to include low-income seniors, disabled veterans and widows of veterans. It also includes more restrictive language than the underlying bill to prevent illegal immigrants from obtaining checks. It would provide businesses with a 50 percent depreciation for certain equipment purchased in 2008 and increase to $250,000 the amount small businesses can expense in the year items are purchased. It would raise the size of mortgage loans the Federal Housing Administration could insure and Fannie Mae and Freddie Mac could purchase. Adopted 91-6: R 43-6; D 46-0 (ND 41-0, SD 5-0); I 2-0. A "yea" was a vote for the president's position. Feb. 7, 2008.

10. HR 5140. Economic Stimulus/Passage. Passage of the bill that would provide advance refund of a tax credit for most taxpayers equal to $300 to $600 for individuals and $600 to $1,200 for couples. Families would receive $300 for each child under 17. The benefit would begin phasing out for individuals with adjusted gross incomes above $75,000 ($150,000 for married couples). It would give businesses a 50 percent depreciation for certain equipment purchased in 2008 and increase to $250,000 the amount small businesses can expense in the year items are purchased. It would raise the size of mortgage loans the Federal Housing Administration could insure and Fannie Mae and Freddie Mac could purchase. As amended, it would expand eligibility for the checks to include low-income senior citizens, disabled veterans and veterans' widows. Illegal immigrants would be ineligible. Passed 81-16: R 33-16; D 46-0 (ND 41-0, SD 5-0); I 2-0. A "yea" was a vote in favor of the president's position. Feb. 7, 2008.

	7	8	9	10			7	8	9	10
ALABAMA						**MONTANA**				
Shelby	N	N	Y	N		Baucus	Y	Y	Y	Y
Sessions	N	N	Y	N		Tester	Y	Y	Y	Y
ALASKA						**NEBRASKA**				
Stevens	N	N	Y	Y		Hagel	N	N	N	N
Murkowski	N	N	Y	N		Nelson	Y	Y	+	+
ARIZONA						**NEVADA**				
McCain	?	?	Y	Y		Reid	Y	N	Y	Y
Kyl	N	N	Y	N		Ensign	N	N	Y	N
ARKANSAS						**NEW HAMPSHIRE**				
Lincoln	Y	Y	Y	Y		Gregg	N	N	N	N
Pryor	Y	Y	Y	Y		Sununu	N	N	Y	N
CALIFORNIA						**NEW JERSEY**				
Feinstein	Y	Y	Y	Y		Lautenberg	Y	Y	Y	Y
Boxer	Y	Y	Y	Y		Menendez	Y	Y	Y	Y
COLORADO						**NEW MEXICO**				
Allard	N	N	N	N		Domenici	N	Y	Y	Y
Salazar	Y	Y	Y	Y		Bingaman	Y	Y	Y	Y
CONNECTICUT						**NEW YORK**				
Dodd	Y	Y	Y	Y		Schumer	Y	Y	Y	Y
Lieberman	?	Y	Y	Y		Clinton	?	Y	?	?
DELAWARE						**NORTH CAROLINA**				
Biden	Y	Y	Y	Y		Dole	N	Y	Y	Y
Carper	Y	Y	Y	Y		Burr	?	N	Y	Y
FLORIDA						**NORTH DAKOTA**				
Nelson	Y	Y	Y	Y		Conrad	Y	Y	Y	Y
Martinez	N	N	Y	Y		Dorgan	Y	Y	Y	Y
GEORGIA						**OHIO**				
Chambliss	N	N	Y	Y		Voinovich	N	N	Y	Y
Isakson	N	N	Y	Y		Brown	Y	Y	Y	Y
HAWAII						**OKLAHOMA**				
Inouye	Y	Y	Y	Y		Inhofe	N	N	Y	N
Akaka	Y	Y	Y	Y		Coburn	N	N	N	N
IDAHO						**OREGON**				
Craig	N	N	N	N		Wyden	Y	Y	Y	Y
Crapo	N	N	Y	N		Smith	N	Y	Y	Y
ILLINOIS						**PENNSYLVANIA**				
Durbin	Y	Y	Y	Y		Specter	N	Y	Y	Y
Obama	Y	Y	?	?		Casey	Y	Y	Y	Y
INDIANA						**RHODE ISLAND**				
Lugar	N	N	Y	Y		Reed	Y	Y	Y	Y
Bayh	Y	Y	Y	Y		Whitehouse	Y	Y	Y	Y
IOWA						**SOUTH CAROLINA**				
Grassley	N	Y	Y	Y		Graham	?	N	Y	Y
Harkin	Y	Y	Y	Y		DeMint	N	N	Y	N
KANSAS						**SOUTH DAKOTA**				
Brownback	N	N	Y	Y		Johnson	Y	Y	Y	Y
Roberts	N	N	Y	Y		Thune	N	N	Y	Y
KENTUCKY						**TENNESSEE**				
McConnell	N	N	Y	Y		Alexander	N	N	Y	Y
Bunning	N	N	Y	Y		Corker	N	N	N	N
LOUISIANA						**TEXAS**				
Landrieu	Y	Y	Y	Y		Hutchison	N	N	Y	Y
Vitter	N	N	Y	Y		Cornyn	N	N	Y	Y
MAINE						**UTAH**				
Snowe	N	Y	Y	Y		Hatch	N	N	Y	Y
Collins	N	Y	Y	Y		Bennett	N	N	Y	Y
MARYLAND						**VERMONT**				
Mikulski	Y	Y	Y	Y		Leahy	Y	Y	Y	Y
Cardin	Y	Y	Y	Y		Sanders	Y	Y	Y	Y
MASSACHUSETTS						**VIRGINIA**				
Kennedy	Y	Y	Y	Y		Warner	N	N	Y	Y
Kerry	Y	Y	Y	Y		Webb	Y	Y	Y	Y
MICHIGAN						**WASHINGTON**				
Levin	Y	Y	Y	Y		Murray	Y	Y	Y	Y
Stabenow	Y	Y	Y	Y		Cantwell	Y	Y	Y	Y
MINNESOTA						**WEST VIRGINIA**				
Coleman	N	Y	Y	Y		Byrd	Y	Y	Y	Y
Klobuchar	Y	Y	Y	Y		Rockefeller	Y	Y	Y	Y
MISSISSIPPI						**WISCONSIN**				
Cochran	N	N	Y	Y		Kohl	Y	Y	Y	Y
Wicker	N	N	Y	Y		Feingold	Y	Y	Y	Y
MISSOURI						**WYOMING**				
Bond	N	N	Y	Y		Enzi	N	N	Y	N
McCaskill	Y	Y	Y	Y		Barrasso	N	N	Y	N

KEY   **Republicans**   Democrats   *Independents*

Y Voted for (yea)	X Paired against	C Voted "present" to avoid possible conflict of interest
# Paired for	– Announced against	
+ Announced for	P Voted "present"	? Did not vote or otherwise make a position known
N Voted against (nay)		

ND Northern Democrats, SD Southern Democrats
Southern states: Ala., Ark., Fla., Ga., Ky., La., Miss., N.C., Okla., S.C., Tenn., Texas, Va.

IN THE SENATE | By Vote Number

11. **S 2248. Foreign Intelligence Surveillance Revisions/ Surveillance Targeting Procedures.** Feingold, D-Wis., amendment to the Rockefeller, D-W.Va., substitute. The Feingold amendment would allow limits on the use of information about U.S. individuals obtained by the government using foreign intelligence targeting procedures found to be deficient. It also would require the government to correct any deficiencies identified no later than 30 days after a court order. The substitute would amend the 1978 Foreign Intelligence Surveillance Act (FISA) to authorize warrantless surveillance of foreign targets, even if they are communicating with someone in the United States. It would give the FISA court authority to approve several aspects of how such surveillance is conducted. It also would grant retroactive legal immunity to telecommunications companies alleged to have participated in the National Security Agency's warrantless surveillance program. Rejected 40-56: R 0-48; D 39-7 (ND 36-5, SD 3-2); I 1-1. Feb. 7, 2008.

12. **S 2248. Foreign Intelligence Surveillance Revisions/Surveillance Targeting Procedures.** Feingold, D-Wis., amendment to the Rockefeller, D-W.Va., substitute. The Feingold amendment would prohibit the government from wiretapping an individual overseas in order to target a person in the United States with whom the foreign individual is communicating, also known as "reverse targeting." Rejected 38-57: R 0-48; D 37-8 (ND 35-5, SD 2-3); I 1-1. Feb. 7, 2008.

13. **S 2248. Foreign Intelligence Surveillance Revisions/Statement of Exclusivity.** Feinstein, D-Calif., amendment to the Rockefeller, D-W.Va., substitute. The Feinstein amendment would provide a statement that FISA is the "exclusive means" of authorizing the conduct of electronic surveillance. Rejected 57-41: R 9-39; D 47-1 (ND 42-1, SD 5-0); I 1-1. (By unanimous consent, the Senate agreed to raise the majority requirement for adoption of the Feinstein amendment to 60 votes. Subsequently, the Feinstein amendment was withdrawn.) A "nay" was a vote in support of the president's position. Feb. 12, 2008.

14. **S 2248. Foreign Intelligence Surveillance Revisions/Targeting Procedures.** Feingold, D-Wis., amendment to the Rockefeller, D-W.Va., substitute. The Feingold amendment would prohibit the government from acquiring any communication that is to or from a person reasonably believed to be located in the United States unless there is reason to believe that the communication concerns international terrorist activities directed against the United States or there is reason to believe that the acquisition is necessary to prevent death or serious bodily harm. Rejected 35-63: R 0-48; D 34-14 (ND 33-10, SD 1-4); I 1-1. Feb. 12, 2008.

15. **S 2248. Foreign Intelligence Surveillance Revisions/Immunity from Civil Liability.** Dodd, D-Conn., amendment to the Rockefeller, D-W.Va., substitute. The Dodd amendment would strike the provisions providing retroactive immunity from civil liability to telecommunications companies alleged to have participated in the National Security Agency's warrantless surveillance program. Rejected 31-67: R 0-48; D 30-18 (ND 30-13, SD 0-5); I 1-1. A "nay" was a vote in support of the president's position. Feb. 12, 2008.

	11	12	13	14	15			11	12	13	14	15
ALABAMA							**MONTANA**					
Shelby	N	N	N	N	N		Baucus	Y	Y	Y	Y	Y
Sessions	N	N	N	N	N		Tester	Y	Y	Y	Y	Y
ALASKA							**NEBRASKA**					
Stevens	N	N	N	N	N		Hagel	N	N	Y	N	N
Murkowski	N	N	Y	N	N		Nelson	–	–	N	N	N
ARIZONA							**NEVADA**					
McCain	?	?	N	N	N		Reid	Y	Y	Y	Y	Y
Kyl	N	N	N	N	N		Ensign	N	N	N	N	N
ARKANSAS							**NEW HAMPSHIRE**					
Lincoln	Y	N	Y	N	N		Gregg	N	N	N	N	N
Pryor	N	N	Y	N	N		Sununu	N	N	Y	N	N
CALIFORNIA							**NEW JERSEY**					
Feinstein	Y	N	Y	N	N		Lautenberg	Y	Y	Y	Y	Y
Boxer	Y	Y	Y	Y	Y		Menendez	Y	Y	Y	Y	Y
COLORADO							**NEW MEXICO**					
Allard	N	N	N	N	N		Domenici	N	N	N	N	N
Salazar	Y	N	Y	N	N		Bingaman	Y	Y	Y	Y	Y
CONNECTICUT							**NEW YORK**					
Dodd	Y	Y	Y	Y	Y		Schumer	Y	Y	Y	Y	Y
Lieberman	N	N	N	N	N		Clinton	?	?	?	?	?
DELAWARE							**NORTH CAROLINA**					
Biden	Y	Y	Y	Y	Y		Dole	N	N	N	N	N
Carper	N	Y	Y	N	N		Burr	N	N	N	N	N
FLORIDA							**NORTH DAKOTA**					
Nelson	Y	Y	Y	N	N		Conrad	Y	Y	Y	N	N
Martinez	N	N	N	N	N		Dorgan	Y	?	Y	Y	Y
GEORGIA							**OHIO**					
Chambliss	N	N	N	N	N		Voinovich	N	N	Y	N	N
Isakson	N	N	N	N	N		Brown	Y	Y	Y	Y	Y
HAWAII							**OKLAHOMA**					
Inouye	N	N	Y	N	N		Inhofe	N	N	N	N	N
Akaka	Y	Y	Y	Y	Y		Coburn	N	N	N	N	N
IDAHO							**OREGON**					
Craig	N	N	Y	N	N		Wyden	Y	Y	Y	Y	Y
Crapo	N	N	N	N	N		Smith	N	N	Y	N	N
ILLINOIS							**PENNSYLVANIA**					
Durbin	Y	Y	Y	Y	Y		Specter	N	N	Y	N	N
Obama	?	?	Y	Y	Y		Casey	Y	Y	Y	Y	Y
INDIANA							**RHODE ISLAND**					
Lugar	N	N	N	N	N		Reed	Y	Y	Y	Y	Y
Bayh	N	Y	Y	N	N		Whitehouse	Y	Y	Y	Y	Y
IOWA							**SOUTH CAROLINA**					
Grassley	N	N	N	N	N		Graham	N	N	–	–	–
Harkin	Y	Y	Y	Y	Y		DeMint	N	N	N	N	N
KANSAS							**SOUTH DAKOTA**					
Brownback	N	N	N	N	N		Johnson	N	N	Y	N	N
Roberts	N	N	N	N	N		Thune	N	N	N	N	N
KENTUCKY							**TENNESSEE**					
McConnell	N	N	N	N	N		Alexander	N	N	N	N	N
Bunning	N	N	N	N	N		Corker	N	N	N	N	N
LOUISIANA							**TEXAS**					
Landrieu	N	N	Y	N	N		Hutchison	N	N	N	N	N
Vitter	N	N	N	N	N		Cornyn	N	N	N	N	N
MAINE							**UTAH**					
Snowe	N	N	Y	N	N		Hatch	N	N	N	N	N
Collins	N	N	Y	N	N		Bennett	N	N	N	N	N
MARYLAND							**VERMONT**					
Mikulski	Y	Y	Y	N	N		Leahy	Y	Y	Y	Y	Y
Cardin	Y	Y	Y	Y	Y		*Sanders*	Y	Y	Y	Y	Y
MASSACHUSETTS							**VIRGINIA**					
Kennedy	Y	Y	Y	Y	Y		Warner	N	N	N	N	N
Kerry	Y	Y	Y	Y	Y		Webb	Y	Y	Y	Y	Y
MICHIGAN							**WASHINGTON**					
Levin	Y	Y	Y	N	Y		Murray	Y	Y	Y	Y	Y
Stabenow	Y	Y	Y	Y	N		Cantwell	Y	Y	Y	Y	Y
MINNESOTA							**WEST VIRGINIA**					
Coleman	N	N	N	N	N		Byrd	Y	Y	Y	Y	Y
Klobuchar	Y	Y	Y	Y	Y		Rockefeller	N	N	Y	N	N
MISSISSIPPI							**WISCONSIN**					
Cochran	N	N	N	N	N		Kohl	Y	Y	Y	Y	N
Wicker	N	N	N	N	N		Feingold	Y	Y	Y	Y	Y
MISSOURI							**WYOMING**					
Bond	N	N	N	N	N		Enzi	N	N	N	N	N
McCaskill	Y	Y	Y	Y	N		Barrasso	N	N	N	N	N

KEY	**Republicans**	Democrats	*Independents*		
Y Voted for (yea)		X Paired against		C Voted "present" to avoid possible conflict of interest	
# Paired for		– Announced against			
+ Announced for		P Voted "present"		? Did not vote or otherwise make a position known	
N Voted against (nay)					

ND Northern Democrats, SD Southern Democrats
Southern states: Ala., Ark., Fla., Ga., Ky., La., Miss., N.C., Okla., S.C., Tenn., Texas, Va.

IN THE SENATE | By Vote Number

16. **S 2248. Foreign Intelligence Surveillance Revisions/Targeting Procedures.** Feingold, D-Wis., amendment to the Rockefeller, D-W.Va., substitute. The Feingold amendment would limit the acquisition of foreign communications to those in which any party is an individual target who is reasonably believed to be located outside of the United States. It also would require that a significant purpose of the acquisition be to obtain foreign intelligence information. The substitute would amend the 1978 Foreign Intelligence Surveillance Act (FISA) to authorize warrantless surveillance of foreign targets, even if they are communicating with someone in the United States. It would give the FISA court authority to approve several aspects of how such surveillance is conducted. It also would grant retroactive legal immunity to telecommunications companies alleged to have participated in the National Security Agency's warrantless surveillance program. Rejected 37-60: R 0-47; D 36-12 (ND 36-7, SD 0-5); I 1-1. Feb. 12, 2008.

17. **S 2248. Foreign Intelligence Surveillance Revisions/Substitute U.S. Government in Lawsuits.** Specter, R-Pa., amendment to the Rockefeller, D-W.Va., substitute. The Specter amendment would substitute the federal government as the defendant in lawsuits against telecommunications companies alleged to have participated in the National Security Agency's warrantless surveillance program. Rejected 30-68: R 1-47; D 28-20 (ND 26-17, SD 2-3); I 1-1. Feb. 12, 2008.

18. **S 2248. Foreign Intelligence Surveillance Revisions/Immunity from Civil Liability.** Feinstein, D-Calif., amendment to the Rockefeller, D-W.Va., substitute. The Feinstein amendment would grant immunity case by-case basis to companies alleged to have participated in the National Security Agency's warrantless surveillance program, after the court determines whether the companies acted with a reasonable belief that their assistance was legal. Rejected 41-57: R 1-47; D 39-9 (ND 36-7, SD 3-2); I 1-1. (By unanimous consent, the Senate agreed to raise the majority requirement for adoption of the Feinstein amendment to 60 votes. Subsequently, the Feinstein amendment was withdrawn.) Feb. 12, 2008.

19. **S 2248. Foreign Intelligence Surveillance Revisions/Cloture.** Motion to invoke cloture (thus limiting debate) on the bill that would amend FISA to authorize warrantless surveillance of foreign targets, even if they are communicating with someone in the United States. It would give the FISA court authority to approve several aspects of how such surveillance is conducted. It also would grant retroactive legal immunity to telecommunications companies alleged to have participated in the National Security Agency's warrantless surveillance program. Motion agreed to 69-29: R 48-0; D 20-28 (ND 15-28, SD 5-0); I 1-1. Three-fifths of the total Senate (60) is required to invoke cloture. Feb. 12, 2008.

20. **S 2248. Foreign Intelligence Surveillance Revisions/Passage.** Passage of the bill that would amend FISA to authorize warrantless surveillance of foreign targets, even if they are communicating with someone in the United States. It would give the FISA court authority to approve several aspects of how such surveillance is conducted. It also would grant retroactive legal immunity to telecommunications companies alleged to have participated in the National Security Agency's warrantless surveillance program. It would sunset in six years. Passed 68-29: R 48-0; D 19-28 (ND 14-28, SD 5-0); I 1-1. A "yea" was a vote in support of the president's position. Feb. 12, 2008.

	16	17	18	19	20			16	17	18	19	20
ALABAMA							**MONTANA**					
Shelby	N	N	N	Y	Y		Baucus	Y	N	Y	Y	Y
Sessions	N	N	N	Y	Y		Tester	Y	N	Y	N	N
ALASKA							**NEBRASKA**					
Stevens	N	N	N	Y	Y		Hagel	N	N	N	Y	Y
Murkowski	N	N	N	Y	Y		Nelson	N	N	N	Y	Y
ARIZONA							**NEVADA**					
McCain	N	N	N	Y	Y		Reid	Y	Y	Y	N	N
Kyl	N	N	N	Y	Y		Ensign	N	N	N	Y	Y
ARKANSAS							**NEW HAMPSHIRE**					
Lincoln	N	N	Y	Y	Y		Gregg	N	N	N	Y	Y
Pryor	N	N	N	Y	Y		Sununu	N	N	N	Y	Y
CALIFORNIA							**NEW JERSEY**					
Feinstein	Y	N	Y	Y	N		Lautenberg	Y	Y	Y	N	N
Boxer	Y	Y	Y	N	N		Menendez	Y	Y	Y	N	N
COLORADO							**NEW MEXICO**					
Allard	N	N	N	Y	Y		Domenici	N	N	N	Y	Y
Salazar	Y	N	Y	Y	Y		Bingaman	Y	Y	Y	N	N
CONNECTICUT							**NEW YORK**					
Dodd	Y	N	N	N	N		Schumer	Y	Y	Y	N	N
Lieberman	N	N	N	Y	Y		Clinton	?	?	?	?	?
DELAWARE							**NORTH CAROLINA**					
Biden	Y	N	Y	N	N		Dole	N	N	N	Y	Y
Carper	N	N	N	Y	Y		Burr	N	N	N	Y	Y
FLORIDA							**NORTH DAKOTA**					
Nelson	N	Y	Y	Y	Y		Conrad	Y	N	Y	Y	Y
Martinez	N	N	N	Y	Y		Dorgan	Y	N	Y	N	N
GEORGIA							**OHIO**					
Chambliss	N	N	N	Y	Y		Voinovich	N	N	N	Y	Y
Isakson	N	N	N	Y	Y		Brown	Y	Y	Y	N	N
HAWAII							**OKLAHOMA**					
Inouye	N	N	Y	Y	Y		Inhofe	N	N	N	Y	Y
Akaka	Y	Y	Y	N	N		Coburn	N	N	N	Y	Y
IDAHO							**OREGON**					
Craig	?	N	N	Y	Y		Wyden	Y	Y	Y	N	N
Crapo	N	N	N	Y	Y		Smith	N	N	N	Y	Y
ILLINOIS							**PENNSYLVANIA**					
Durbin	Y	Y	Y	N	N		Specter	N	Y	Y	Y	Y
Obama	Y	Y	Y	N	?		Casey	Y	Y	Y	Y	Y
INDIANA							**RHODE ISLAND**					
Lugar	N	N	N	Y	Y		Reed	Y	Y	Y	N	N
Bayh	N	N	N	Y	Y		Whitehouse	Y	Y	Y	Y	Y
IOWA							**SOUTH CAROLINA**					
Grassley	N	N	N	Y	Y		Graham	–	–	–	+	+
Harkin	Y	Y	Y	N	N		DeMint	N	N	N	Y	Y
KANSAS							**SOUTH DAKOTA**					
Brownback	N	N	N	Y	Y		Johnson	N	N	N	Y	Y
Roberts	N	N	N	Y	Y		Thune	N	N	N	Y	Y
KENTUCKY							**TENNESSEE**					
McConnell	N	N	N	Y	Y		Alexander	N	N	N	Y	Y
Bunning	N	N	N	Y	Y		Corker	N	N	N	Y	Y
LOUISIANA							**TEXAS**					
Landrieu	N	N	N	Y	Y		Hutchison	N	N	N	Y	Y
Vitter	N	N	N	Y	Y		Cornyn	N	N	N	Y	Y
MAINE							**UTAH**					
Snowe	N	N	N	Y	Y		Hatch	N	N	Y	Y	Y
Collins	N	N	N	Y	Y		Bennett	N	N	N	Y	Y
MARYLAND							**VERMONT**					
Mikulski	N	N	Y	Y	Y		Leahy	Y	Y	Y	N	N
Cardin	Y	Y	Y	N	N		Sanders	Y	Y	Y	N	N
MASSACHUSETTS							**VIRGINIA**					
Kennedy	Y	Y	Y	N	N		Warner	N	N	N	Y	Y
Kerry	Y	Y	Y	N	N		Webb	N	Y	Y	Y	Y
MICHIGAN							**WASHINGTON**					
Levin	Y	Y	Y	N	N		Murray	Y	N	Y	N	N
Stabenow	Y	Y	Y	N	N		Cantwell	Y	Y	Y	N	N
MINNESOTA							**WEST VIRGINIA**					
Coleman	N	N	N	Y	Y		Byrd	Y	Y	Y	N	N
Klobuchar	Y	N	Y	N	N		Rockefeller	N	N	N	Y	Y
MISSISSIPPI							**WISCONSIN**					
Cochran	N	N	N	Y	Y		Kohl	Y	Y	Y	N	N
Wicker	N	N	N	Y	Y		Feingold	Y	Y	Y	N	N
MISSOURI							**WYOMING**					
Bond	N	N	N	Y	Y		Enzi	N	N	N	Y	Y
McCaskill	Y	Y	Y	Y	Y		Barrasso	N	N	N	Y	Y

KEY   **Republicans**   Democrats   *Independents*

Y Voted for (yea)	**X** Paired against	**C** Voted "present" to avoid possible conflict of interest
# Paired for	**–** Announced against	
+ Announced for	**P** Voted "present"	**?** Did not vote or otherwise make a position known
N Voted against (nay)		

ND Northern Democrats, SD Southern Democrats

Southern states: Ala., Ark., Fla., Ga., Ky., La., Miss., N.C., Okla., S.C., Tenn., Texas, Va.

IN THE SENATE | By Vote Number

21. **HR 2082. Fiscal 2008 Intelligence Authorization/Cloture.**
Motion to invoke cloture (thus limiting debate) on the conference report on the bill that would authorize classified amounts in fiscal 2008 for 17 U.S. intelligence agencies, including the CIA, the Office of the Director of National Intelligence and the National Security Agency. Motion agreed to 92-4: R 44-4; D 46-0 (ND 41-0, SD 5-0). I 2-0. Three-fifths of the total Senate (60) is required to invoke cloture. Feb. 13, 2008.

22. **HR 2082. Fiscal 2008 Intelligence Authorization/Conference Report.** Adoption of the conference report on the bill that would authorize classified amounts in fiscal 2008 for 17 U.S. intelligence activities and agencies, including the CIA, the Office of the Director of National Intelligence and the National Security Agency. It would authorize funds for the intelligence portion of the fiscal 2008 emergency supplemental for the wars in Iraq and Afghanistan. It would prohibit the use of any interrogation treatment not authorized by the U.S. Army Field Manual on Human Intelligence Collection Operations against any individual in the custody of the intelligence community. Adopted (thus cleared for the president) 51-45: R 5-43; D 45-1 (ND 40-1, SD 5-0). I 1-1. A "nay" was a vote in support of the president's position. Feb. 13, 2008.

23. **S 1200. Indian Health Care Reauthorization/Law Enforcement, Methamphetamine.** Tester, D-Mont., amendment to the Dorgan, D-N.D., substitute. The Tester amendment would express the sense of Congress that state, local and tribal law enforcement should enter into an agreement to improve law enforcement services to American Indian communities and improve the effectiveness of measures relating to methamphetamine use in Indian country. The substitute would revise and extend through fiscal 2017 the central law directing federal delivery of health services to American Indians and Alaska Natives. Adopted 95-0: R 47-0; D 46-0 (ND 41-0, SD 5-0). I 2-0. Feb. 13, 2008.

24. **S 1200. Indian Health Care Reauthorization/Manager's Amendment.** Dorgan, D-N.D., amendment to the Dorgan, D-N.D., substitute. The Dorgan amendment would clarify provisions related to Davis-Bacon Act prevailing wage requirements and construction projects, the ability of a tribal health program to charge for services, the terminology of "urban Indian organizations" and the definition of "urban Indian," and citizenship-documentation requirements. It also would make several technical changes to the bill. Adopted 95-0: R 47-0; D 46-0 (ND 41-0, SD 5-0); I 2-0. Feb. 14, 2008.

25. **S 1200. Indian Health Care Reauthorization/Health Care Subsidy Pilot Program.** Coburn, R-Okla., amendment to the Dorgan, D-N.D., substitute. The Coburn amendment would create a program in geographically feasible areas to provide American Indians with a risk-adjusted subsidy for the purchase of qualified health insurance. American Indians would be allowed to voluntarily enroll in the program for a minimum of 12 months. The Health and Human Services secretary would ensure that expenditures made under the amendment are budget neutral and would periodically submit reports to Congress regarding the progress of the program. Rejected 28-67: R 28-19; D 0-46 (ND 0-41, SD 0-5); I 0-2. Feb. 14, 2008.

	21	22	23	24	25
ALABAMA					
Shelby	Y	N	Y	Y	Y
Sessions	Y	N	Y	Y	Y
ALASKA					
Stevens	Y	N	Y	Y	N
Murkowski	Y	N	Y	Y	N
ARIZONA					
McCain	Y	N	Y	?	?
Kyl	Y	N	Y	Y	Y
ARKANSAS					
Lincoln	Y	Y	Y	Y	N
Pryor	Y	Y	Y	Y	N
CALIFORNIA					
Feinstein	Y	Y	Y	Y	N
Boxer	Y	Y	Y	Y	N
COLORADO					
Allard	Y	N	Y	Y	Y
Salazar	Y	Y	Y	Y	N
CONNECTICUT					
Dodd	Y	Y	Y	Y	N
Lieberman	Y	N	Y	Y	N
DELAWARE					
Biden	Y	Y	Y	Y	N
Carper	Y	Y	Y	Y	N
FLORIDA					
Nelson	Y	Y	Y	Y	N
Martinez	Y	N	Y	Y	Y
GEORGIA					
Chambliss	N	N	Y	Y	Y
Isakson	Y	N	Y	Y	Y
HAWAII					
Inouye	Y	Y	Y	?	?
Akaka	Y	Y	Y	Y	N
IDAHO					
Craig	Y	N	Y	Y	N
Crapo	Y	N	Y	Y	N
ILLINOIS					
Durbin	Y	Y	Y	Y	N
Obama	?	?	?	?	?
INDIANA					
Lugar	Y	Y	Y	Y	N
Bayh	Y	Y	Y	Y	N
IOWA					
Grassley	Y	N	Y	Y	Y
Harkin	Y	Y	Y	Y	N
KANSAS					
Brownback	Y	N	Y	Y	N
Roberts	Y	N	Y	Y	N
KENTUCKY					
McConnell	Y	N	Y	Y	Y
Bunning	Y	N	Y	Y	Y
LOUISIANA					
Landrieu	Y	Y	Y	Y	N
Vitter	N	N	Y	Y	Y
MAINE					
Snowe	Y	Y	Y	Y	N
Collins	Y	Y	Y	Y	N
MARYLAND					
Mikulski	Y	Y	Y	Y	N
Cardin	Y	Y	Y	Y	N
MASSACHUSETTS					
Kennedy	Y	Y	Y	Y	N
Kerry	Y	Y	Y	Y	N
MICHIGAN					
Levin	Y	Y	Y	Y	N
Stabenow	Y	Y	Y	Y	N
MINNESOTA					
Coleman	Y	N	Y	Y	N
Klobuchar	Y	Y	Y	Y	N
MISSISSIPPI					
Cochran	Y	N	Y	Y	N
Wicker	Y	N	Y	Y	N
MISSOURI					
Bond	Y	N	Y	Y	Y
McCaskill	+	+	?	Y	N

	21	22	23	24	25
MONTANA					
Baucus	Y	Y	Y	Y	N
Tester	Y	Y	Y	Y	N
NEBRASKA					
Hagel	Y	Y	Y	Y	N
Nelson	Y	N	Y	Y	N
NEVADA					
Reid	Y	Y	Y	Y	N
Ensign	Y	N	Y	Y	Y
NEW HAMPSHIRE					
Gregg	Y	N	Y	Y	Y
Sununu	Y	N	Y	Y	Y
NEW JERSEY					
Lautenberg	Y	Y	Y	Y	N
Menendez	Y	Y	Y	Y	N
NEW MEXICO					
Domenici	Y	N	Y	Y	N
Bingaman	Y	Y	Y	Y	N
NEW YORK					
Schumer	Y	Y	Y	Y	N
Clinton	?	?	?	?	?
NORTH CAROLINA					
Dole	Y	N	Y	Y	N
Burr	N	N	Y	Y	Y
NORTH DAKOTA					
Conrad	Y	Y	Y	Y	N
Dorgan	Y	Y	Y	Y	N
OHIO					
Voinovich	Y	N	Y	Y	N
Brown	Y	Y	Y	Y	N
OKLAHOMA					
Inhofe	Y	N	Y	Y	Y
Coburn	Y	N	Y	Y	Y
OREGON					
Wyden	Y	Y	Y	Y	N
Smith	Y	Y	Y	Y	N
PENNSYLVANIA					
Specter	Y	N	Y	Y	Y
Casey	Y	Y	Y	Y	N
RHODE ISLAND					
Reed	Y	Y	Y	Y	N
Whitehouse	Y	Y	Y	Y	N
SOUTH CAROLINA					
Graham	?	–	?	?	?
DeMint	N	N	Y	Y	Y
SOUTH DAKOTA					
Johnson	Y	Y	Y	Y	N
Thune	Y	N	Y	Y	N
TENNESSEE					
Alexander	Y	N	Y	Y	Y
Corker	Y	N	Y	Y	Y
TEXAS					
Hutchison	Y	N	?	Y	Y
Cornyn	Y	N	Y	Y	Y
UTAH					
Hatch	Y	N	Y	Y	N
Bennett	Y	N	Y	Y	N
VERMONT					
Leahy	Y	Y	Y	Y	N
Sanders	Y	Y	Y	Y	N
VIRGINIA					
Warner	Y	N	Y	Y	Y
Webb	Y	Y	Y	Y	N
WASHINGTON					
Murray	Y	Y	Y	Y	N
Cantwell	Y	Y	Y	Y	N
WEST VIRGINIA					
Byrd	Y	Y	Y	Y	N
Rockefeller	Y	Y	Y	Y	N
WISCONSIN					
Kohl	Y	Y	Y	Y	N
Feingold	Y	Y	Y	Y	N
WYOMING					
Enzi	Y	N	Y	Y	Y
Barrasso	Y	N	Y	Y	Y

KEY	**Republicans**	Democrats	*Independents*	
Y	Voted for (yea)	X Paired against	C	Voted "present" to avoid possible conflict of interest
#	Paired for	– Announced against		
+	Announced for	P Voted "present"	?	Did not vote or otherwise make a position known
N	Voted against (nay)			

ND Northern Democrats, SD Southern Democrats
Southern states: Ala., Ark., Fla., Ga., Ky., La., Miss., N.C., Okla., S.C., Tenn., Texas, Va.

IN THE SENATE | By Vote Number

26. **S 1200. Indian Health Care Reauthorization/Medical Service Priorities.** Coburn, R-Okla., amendment to the Dorgan, D-N.D., substitute. The Coburn amendment would require that before providing any hospice care, assisted-living service, long-term-care service, or home- or community-based services, which are expanded under the bill, the Health and Human Services secretary give priority to providing basic medical services to American Indians. The substitute would revise and extend through fiscal 2017 the central law directing federal delivery of health services to American Indians and Alaska Natives. Rejected 21-73: R 21-26; D 0-45 (ND 0-40, SD 0-5); I 0-2. Feb. 14, 2008.

27. **S 1200. Indian Health Care Reauthorization/Rape and Sexual Assault Victims.** Coburn, R-Okla., amendment to the Dorgan, D-N.D., substitute. The Coburn amendment would require the attorney general to ensure that, at the request of an American Indian victim of sexual assault, rape or sexual violence, a defendant would be tested for HIV and other sexually transmitted diseases. Adopted 94-0: R 47-0; D 45-0 (ND 40-0, SD 5-0); I 2-0. Feb. 14, 2008.

28. **S 1200. Indian Health Care Reauthorization/Cloture.** Motion to invoke cloture (thus limiting debate) on the Dorgan, D-N.D., substitute amendment that would revise and extend through fiscal 2017 the central law directing federal delivery of health services to American Indians and Alaska Natives. Motion agreed to 85-2: R 41-2; D 42-0 (ND 38-0, SD 4-0); I 2-0. Three-fifths of the total Senate (60) is required to invoke cloture. Feb. 25, 2008.

29. **S 1200. Indian Health Care Reauthorization/Firearms.** DeMint, R-S.C., amendment to the Dorgan, D-N.D., substitute. The DeMint amendment would bar the use of funds in the bill to carry out anti-firearm or gun buy-back programs, or any program to discourage or stigmatize the private ownership of firearms for collecting, hunting or self-defense purposes. Adopted 78-11: R 44-0; D 32-11 (ND 28-11, SD 4-0); I 2-0. Feb. 25, 2008.

30. **S 1200. Indian Health Care Reauthorization/Abortion Limitation.** , R-La., amendment to the Dorgan, D-N.D., substitute. The Vitter amendment would bar the use of funds or facilities of the Indian Health Service to provide any abortion or to pay the administrative cost of any health benefits plan that includes coverage of an abortion, except in the case of rape, incest or danger to the life of the woman. Adopted 52-42: R 43-3; D 9-37 (ND 7-34, SD 2-3); I 0-2. Feb. 26, 2008.

	26	27	28	29	30
ALABAMA					
Shelby	Y	Y	Y	Y	Y
Sessions	Y	Y	Y	Y	Y
ALASKA					
Stevens	N	Y	Y	Y	Y
Murkowski	N	Y	Y	Y	Y
ARIZONA					
McCain	?	?	?	?	?
Kyl	N	Y	Y	Y	Y
ARKANSAS					
Lincoln	N	Y	Y	Y	N
Pryor	N	Y	Y	Y	Y
CALIFORNIA					
Feinstein	N	Y	Y	N	N
Boxer	?	?	Y	N	N
COLORADO					
Allard	Y	Y	Y	Y	Y
Salazar	N	Y	Y	Y	Y
CONNECTICUT					
Dodd	N	Y	Y	Y	?
Lieberman	N	Y	Y	N	N
DELAWARE					
Biden	N	Y	Y	N	N
Carper	N	Y	Y	N	N
FLORIDA					
Nelson	N	Y	Y	N	N
Martinez	N	Y	Y	Y	Y
GEORGIA					
Chambliss	Y	Y	Y	Y	Y
Isakson	Y	Y	Y	Y	Y
HAWAII					
Inouye	?	?	?	?	N
Akaka	N	Y	Y	Y	N
IDAHO					
Craig	N	Y	Y	Y	Y
Crapo	N	Y	Y	Y	Y
ILLINOIS					
Durbin	N	Y	Y	N	N
Obama	?	?	?	?	?
INDIANA					
Lugar	N	Y	Y	Y	Y
Bayh	N	Y	Y	Y	Y
IOWA					
Grassley	Y	Y	Y	Y	Y
Harkin	N	Y	Y	Y	N
KANSAS					
Brownback	Y	Y	Y	Y	Y
Roberts	N	Y	Y	Y	Y
KENTUCKY					
McConnell	Y	Y	Y	Y	Y
Bunning	N	Y	Y	Y	Y
LOUISIANA					
Landrieu	N	Y	?	?	Y
Vitter	Y	Y	N	Y	Y
MAINE					
Snowe	N	Y	Y	Y	N
Collins	N	Y	Y	Y	N
MARYLAND					
Mikulski	N	Y	Y	N	N
Cardin	N	Y	+	?	N
MASSACHUSETTS					
Kennedy	N	Y	Y	N	N
Kerry	N	Y	?	Y	N
MICHIGAN					
Levin	N	Y	Y	Y	N
Stabenow	N	Y	?	?	N
MINNESOTA					
Coleman	N	Y	Y	Y	Y
Klobuchar	N	Y	Y	Y	N
MISSISSIPPI					
Cochran	N	Y	Y	Y	Y
Wicker	N	Y	?	?	Y
MISSOURI					
Bond	N	Y	Y	Y	Y
McCaskill	N	Y	Y	Y	N

	26	27	28	29	30
MONTANA					
Baucus	N	Y	Y	Y	N
Tester	N	Y	Y	Y	N
NEBRASKA					
Hagel	N	Y	Y	Y	Y
Nelson	N	Y	Y	Y	Y
NEVADA					
Reid	N	Y	Y	Y	Y
Ensign	Y	Y	Y	Y	Y
NEW HAMPSHIRE					
Gregg	Y	Y	Y	Y	Y
Sununu	Y	Y	Y	Y	Y
NEW JERSEY					
Lautenberg	N	Y	Y	N	N
Menendez	N	Y	Y	N	N
NEW MEXICO					
Domenici	N	Y	Y	Y	Y
Bingaman	N	Y	Y	Y	N
NEW YORK					
Schumer	N	Y	Y	N	N
Clinton	?	?	?	?	?
NORTH CAROLINA					
Dole	N	Y	Y	Y	Y
Burr	Y	Y	?	Y	Y
NORTH DAKOTA					
Conrad	N	Y	Y	Y	N
Dorgan	N	Y	Y	Y	N
OHIO					
Voinovich	N	Y	Y	Y	Y
Brown	N	Y	Y	Y	N
OKLAHOMA					
Inhofe	Y	Y	Y	Y	Y
Coburn	Y	Y	Y	Y	Y
OREGON					
Wyden	N	Y	Y	Y	N
Smith	N	Y	Y	Y	Y
PENNSYLVANIA					
Specter	N	Y	Y	Y	N
Casey	N	Y	Y	Y	Y
RHODE ISLAND					
Reed	N	Y	Y	N	N
Whitehouse	N	Y	Y	N	N
SOUTH CAROLINA					
Graham	?	?	Y	Y	Y
DeMint	Y	Y	N	Y	Y
SOUTH DAKOTA					
Johnson	N	Y	Y	Y	Y
Thune	N	Y	Y	Y	Y
TENNESSEE					
Alexander	Y	Y	+	+	Y
Corker	N	Y	Y	Y	Y
TEXAS					
Hutchison	N	Y	Y	Y	Y
Cornyn	Y	Y	+	+	+
UTAH					
Hatch	N	Y	Y	Y	Y
Bennett	N	Y	Y	Y	Y
VERMONT					
Leahy	N	Y	Y	Y	N
Sanders	N	Y	Y	Y	N
VIRGINIA					
Warner	Y	Y	?	?	?
Webb	N	Y	Y	Y	N
WASHINGTON					
Murray	N	Y	Y	Y	N
Cantwell	N	Y	Y	Y	N
WEST VIRGINIA					
Byrd	N	Y	Y	Y	Y
Rockefeller	N	Y	Y	Y	N
WISCONSIN					
Kohl	N	Y	Y	Y	N
Feingold	N	Y	Y	N	N
WYOMING					
Enzi	Y	Y	Y	Y	Y
Barrasso	Y	Y	Y	Y	Y

KEY Republicans Democrats *Independents*

Y Voted for (yea)	X Paired against	C Voted "present" to avoid possible conflict of interest
# Paired for	– Announced against	? Did not vote or otherwise make a position known
+ Announced for	P Voted "present"	
N Voted against (nay)		

ND Northern Democrats, SD Southern Democrats
Southern states: Ala., Ark., Fla., Ga., Ky., La., Miss., N.C., Okla., S.C., Tenn., Texas, Va.

IN THE SENATE | By Vote Number

31. **S 1200. Indian Health Care Reauthorization/Construction of Health Facilities.** Smith, R-Ore., amendment to the Dorgan, D-N.D., substitute. The Smith amendment would require the Health and Human Services secretary to consult and cooperate with American Indian tribes and tribal organizations in developing innovative approaches to address all or part of the unmet needs for construction of health facilities. The substitute would revise and extend through fiscal 2017 the central law directing federal delivery of health services to American Indians and Alaska Natives. Adopted 56-38: R 30-16; D 26-20 (ND 23-18, SD 3-2); I 0-2. Feb. 26, 2008.

32. **S 1200. Indian Health Care Reauthorization/Passage.** Passage of the bill that would revise and extend through fiscal 2017 the central law directing federal delivery of health services to American Indians and Alaska Natives. It would expand American Indian health organizations' access to the State Children's Health Insurance Program (SCHIP) and expand tribal access to Medicaid. The bill would authorize programs to support the recruitment and retention of American Indians entering the health professions and providing health services. Passed 83-10: R 36-10; D 46-0 (ND 41-0, SD 5-0); I 1-0. (Before passage, the Senate adopted the Dorgan, D-N.D., substitute, as amended, by voice vote.) Feb. 26, 2008.

33. **S 2633. U.S. Troop Redeployment From Iraq/Cloture.** Motion to invoke cloture (thus limiting debate) on the motion to proceed to the bill that would bar the use of funds for U.S. troop deployments in Iraq, with limited exceptions, 120 days after enactment. Motion agreed to 70-24: R 43-3; D 26-20 (ND 26-15, SD 0-5); I 1-1. Three-fifths of the total Senate (60) is required to invoke cloture. Feb. 26, 2008.

34. **S 2634. Al Qaeda Report/Cloture.** Motion to invoke cloture (thus limiting debate) on the motion to proceed to the bill that would require within 60 days of enactment the secretaries of Defense, State and Homeland Security, in coordination with the chairman of the Joint Chiefs of Staff and the director of national intelligence, to jointly submit to Congress a report on the U.S. global strategy to combat and defeat al Qaeda and its affiliates. Motion agreed to 89-3: R 42-3; D 45-0 (ND 40-0, SD 5-0); I 2-0. Three-fifths of the total Senate (60) is required to invoke cloture. Feb. 27, 2008.

35. **HR 3221. Renewable Energy/Cloture.** Motion to invoke cloture (thus limiting debate) on the motion to proceed to the bill that would set new efficiency standards for appliances, lighting and buildings, and create new programs to research infrastructure and the delivery of alternative fuels. Motion rejected 48-46: R 1-45; D 45-1 (ND 40-1, SD 5-0); I 2-0. Three-fifths of the total Senate (60) is required to invoke cloture. (The bill was intended to serve as the vehicle for a housing stimulus measure, S 2636.) A "nay" was a vote in support of the president's position. Feb. 28, 2008.

	31	32	33	34	35
ALABAMA					
Shelby	Y	Y	Y	Y	N
Sessions	N	N	Y	Y	N
ALASKA					
Stevens	Y	Y	Y	Y	N
Murkowski	Y	Y	Y	Y	N
ARIZONA					
McCain	?	?	?	?	?
Kyl	N	Y	Y	Y	N
ARKANSAS					
Lincoln	Y	Y	N	Y	Y
Pryor	Y	Y	N	Y	Y
CALIFORNIA					
Feinstein	Y	Y	Y	Y	Y
Boxer	Y	Y	Y	Y	Y
COLORADO					
Allard	N	N	Y	Y	N
Salazar	N	Y	N	Y	Y
CONNECTICUT					
Dodd	?	?	Y	Y	Y
Lieberman	N	+	N	Y	Y
DELAWARE					
Biden	Y	Y	N	Y	Y
Carper	N	Y	N	Y	Y
FLORIDA					
Nelson	N	Y	N	Y	Y
Martinez	N	Y	Y	Y	N
GEORGIA					
Chambliss	Y	Y	Y	Y	N
Isakson	Y	Y	Y	Y	N
HAWAII					
Inouye	N	Y	Y	Y	Y
Akaka	Y	Y	Y	Y	Y
IDAHO					
Craig	Y	Y	Y	Y	N
Crapo	Y	Y	Y	Y	N
ILLINOIS					
Durbin	Y	Y	Y	Y	Y
Obama	?	?	?	?	?
INDIANA					
Lugar	Y	Y	Y	Y	N
Bayh	N	Y	N	Y	Y
IOWA					
Grassley	N	Y	Y	Y	N
Harkin	N	Y	Y	Y	Y
KANSAS					
Brownback	Y	Y	Y	Y	N
Roberts	Y	Y	Y	Y	N
KENTUCKY					
McConnell	Y	Y	Y	Y	N
Bunning	N	Y	Y	Y	N
LOUISIANA					
Landrieu	Y	Y	N	Y	Y
Vitter	Y	N	Y	Y	N
MAINE					
Snowe	Y	Y	Y	Y	N
Collins	Y	Y	Y	Y	N
MARYLAND					
Mikulski	N	Y	Y	Y	Y
Cardin	N	Y	Y	Y	Y
MASSACHUSETTS					
Kennedy	Y	Y	Y	?	Y
Kerry	Y	Y	Y	Y	Y
MICHIGAN					
Levin	Y	Y	N	Y	Y
Stabenow	Y	Y	Y	Y	Y
MINNESOTA					
Coleman	Y	Y	Y	+	Y
Klobuchar	Y	Y	Y	Y	Y
MISSISSIPPI					
Cochran	Y	Y	Y	Y	N
Wicker	Y	Y	Y	Y	N
MISSOURI					
Bond	Y	Y	Y	?	N
McCaskill	N	Y	N	Y	Y
MONTANA					
Baucus	N	Y	N	Y	Y
Tester	N	Y	N	Y	Y
NEBRASKA					
Hagel	N	Y	N	N	N
Nelson	N	Y	N	Y	Y
NEVADA					
Reid	Y	Y	Y	Y	N
Ensign	Y	Y	Y	Y	N
NEW HAMPSHIRE					
Gregg	Y	N	Y	Y	N
Sununu	Y	N	Y	Y	N
NEW JERSEY					
Lautenberg	Y	Y	Y	Y	Y
Menendez	Y	Y	Y	Y	Y
NEW MEXICO					
Domenici	N	Y	Y	Y	N
Bingaman	N	Y	N	Y	Y
NEW YORK					
Schumer	Y	Y	Y	Y	Y
Clinton	?	?	?	?	?
NORTH CAROLINA					
Dole	Y	Y	Y	Y	N
Burr	N	Y	Y	Y	N
NORTH DAKOTA					
Conrad	N	Y	N	Y	Y
Dorgan	N	Y	N	Y	Y
OHIO					
Voinovich	Y	Y	Y	Y	N
Brown	N	Y	Y	Y	Y
OKLAHOMA					
Inhofe	N	N	Y	Y	N
Coburn	N	N	Y	Y	?
OREGON					
Wyden	Y	Y	Y	Y	Y
Smith	Y	Y	Y	Y	Y
PENNSYLVANIA					
Specter	Y	Y	Y	Y	N
Casey	Y	Y	N	Y	Y
RHODE ISLAND					
Reed	Y	Y	N	Y	Y
Whitehouse	Y	Y	Y	Y	Y
SOUTH CAROLINA					
Graham	N	N	Y	Y	N
DeMint	N	N	Y	Y	N
SOUTH DAKOTA					
Johnson	N	Y	N	Y	Y
Thune	N	Y	Y	Y	N
TENNESSEE					
Alexander	Y	Y	Y	Y	N
Corker	Y	N	Y	Y	N
TEXAS					
Hutchison	Y	Y	Y	Y	?
Cornyn	+	+	+	+	N
UTAH					
Hatch	Y	Y	Y	Y	N
Bennett	Y	Y	Y	Y	N
VERMONT					
Leahy	N	Y	Y	Y	Y
Sanders	N	Y	Y	Y	Y
VIRGINIA					
Warner	?	?	?	Y	N
Webb	N	Y	N	Y	Y
WASHINGTON					
Murray	Y	Y	Y	Y	Y
Cantwell	Y	Y	Y	Y	Y
WEST VIRGINIA					
Byrd	Y	Y	?	?	?
Rockefeller	N	Y	Y	Y	Y
WISCONSIN					
Kohl	Y	Y	Y	Y	Y
Feingold	Y	Y	Y	Y	Y
WYOMING					
Enzi	N	Y	N	N	N
Barrasso	N	Y	N	N	N

KEY	**Republicans**	Democrats	*Independents*	
Y Voted for (yea)		X Paired against		C Voted "present" to avoid possible conflict of interest
# Paired for		– Announced against		
+ Announced for		P Voted "present"		? Did not vote or otherwise make a position known
N Voted against (nay)				

ND Northern Democrats, SD Southern Democrats
Southern states: Ala., Ark., Fla., Ga., Ky., La., Miss., N.C., Okla., S.C., Tenn., Texas, Va.

IN THE SENATE | By Vote Number

36. S 2663. Consumer Product Safety Commission Overhaul/ **Cloture.** Motion to invoke cloture (thus limiting debate) on the motion to proceed to the bill that would overhaul the Consumer Product Safety Commission (CPSC), strengthen toy safety standards and authorize funding increases at a rate of 10 percent per year through fiscal 2015. Motion agreed to 86-1: R 41-1; D 43-0 (ND 38-0, SD 5-0); I 2-0. Three-fifths of the total Senate (60) is required to invoke cloture. March 3, 2008.

37. S 2663. Consumer Product Safety Commission Overhaul/ **Substitute.** Pryor, D-Ark., motion to table (kill) the DeMint, R-S.C., substitute that would overhaul the CPSC and authorize $80 million in fiscal 2009, $90 million in fiscal 2010 and $100 million in fiscal 2011. It would set tougher lead standards for children's products, require third-party testing of toys by accredited labs and require manufacturers to apply tracking labels to all toys for children age 12 or younger to help find faulty products in the event of a recall. Motion agreed to 57-39: R 9-39; D 46-0 (ND 41-0, SD 5-0); I 2-0. March 4, 2008.

38. S 2663. Consumer Product Safety Commission Overhaul/ **Travel Expenses.** Klobuchar, D-Minn., amendment that would prohibit any CPSC employee or commissioner from accepting payment or reimbursement for travel or lodging from any person with interests before the commission. It would authorize up to $1.2 million annually for fiscal 2009-2015 for travel, subsistence and related expenses for attendance at meetings or functions. Adopted 96-0: R 48-0; D 46-0 (ND 41-0, SD 5-0); I 2-0. March 5, 2008.

39. S 2663. Consumer Product Safety Commission Overhaul/ **Contingency Fee Agreements.** Pryor, D-Ark., motion to table (kill) the Cornyn, R-Texas, amendment that would prohibit state attorneys general from entering into contingency fee agreements for legal or expert witness services in certain civil actions relating to federal consumer product safety rules and regulations. Motion agreed to 51-45: R 3-45; D 46-0 (ND 41-0, SD 5-0); I 2-0. March 5, 2008.

40. S 2663. Consumer Product Safety Commission Overhaul/ **Attorney Fees.** Pryor, D-Ark., motion to table (kill) the Vitter, R-La., amendment that would permit the prevailing party in certain civil actions related to consumer product safety rules to recover reasonable costs and attorney fees. Motion agreed to 56-39: R 8-39; D 46-0 (ND 41-0, SD 5-0); I 2-0. March 6, 2008.

41. HR 4040. Consumer Product Safety Commission Overhaul/ **Passage.** Passage of the bill that would overhaul the CPSC, strengthen toy safety standards and authorize funding for the commission starting at $88.5 million in fiscal 2009 and increasing by 10 percent per year through 2015. It would increase civil penalties on companies for manufacturing faulty products, create a public database of consumer safety incidents and permit state attorneys general to obtain injunctive relief on behalf of residents to enforce product safety laws. Passed 79-13: R 33-13; D 44-0 (ND 39-0, SD 5-0); I 2-0. (Before passage, the Senate struck all after the enacting clause and inserted the text of S 2663, as amended, into HR 4040.) A "nay" was a vote in support of the president's position. March 6, 2008.

	36	37	38	39	40	41
ALABAMA						
Shelby	Y	N	Y	N	N	Y
Sessions	Y	N	Y	N	N	Y
ALASKA						
Stevens	Y	Y	Y	N	Y	Y
Murkowski	?	Y	Y	N	Y	Y
ARIZONA						
McCain	?	?	?	?	?	?
Kyl	Y	N	Y	N	N	N
ARKANSAS						
Lincoln	Y	Y	Y	Y	Y	Y
Pryor	Y	Y	Y	Y	Y	Y
CALIFORNIA						
Feinstein	Y	Y	Y	Y	Y	Y
Boxer	Y	Y	Y	Y	Y	Y
COLORADO						
Allard	Y	N	Y	N	N	N
Salazar	Y	Y	Y	Y	Y	Y
CONNECTICUT						
Dodd	Y	Y	Y	Y	Y	Y
Lieberman	Y	Y	Y	Y	Y	Y
DELAWARE						
Biden	?	Y	Y	Y	Y	Y
Carper	Y	Y	Y	Y	Y	Y
FLORIDA						
Nelson	Y	Y	Y	Y	Y	Y
Martinez	Y	N	Y	N	Y	Y
GEORGIA						
Chambliss	Y	N	Y	N	N	Y
Isakson	?	N	Y	N	N	Y
HAWAII						
Inouye	Y	Y	Y	Y	Y	Y
Akaka	Y	Y	Y	Y	Y	Y
IDAHO						
Craig	Y	N	Y	N	N	Y
Crapo	Y	N	Y	N	N	Y
ILLINOIS						
Durbin	Y	Y	Y	Y	Y	Y
Obama	?	?	?	?	?	?
INDIANA						
Lugar	Y	N	Y	N	N	Y
Bayh	Y	Y	Y	Y	Y	Y
IOWA						
Grassley	Y	Y	Y	N	N	Y
Harkin	Y	Y	Y	Y	Y	Y
KANSAS						
Brownback	Y	N	Y	N	N	Y
Roberts	Y	N	Y	N	N	Y
KENTUCKY						
McConnell	Y	N	Y	N	N	Y
Bunning	Y	N	Y	N	N	N
LOUISIANA						
Landrieu	Y	Y	Y	Y	Y	Y
Vitter	Y	N	Y	N	N	N
MAINE						
Snowe	Y	Y	Y	N	Y	Y
Collins	Y	Y	Y	N	N	Y
MARYLAND						
Mikulski	Y	Y	Y	Y	Y	Y
Cardin	Y	Y	Y	Y	Y	Y
MASSACHUSETTS						
Kennedy	Y	Y	Y	Y	Y	Y
Kerry	Y	Y	Y	Y	Y	Y
MICHIGAN						
Levin	Y	Y	Y	Y	Y	Y
Stabenow	Y	Y	Y	Y	Y	Y
MINNESOTA						
Coleman	Y	N	Y	N	N	Y
Klobuchar	Y	Y	Y	Y	Y	Y
MISSISSIPPI						
Cochran	Y	N	Y	N	Y	N
Wicker	?	N	Y	N	N	N
MISSOURI						
Bond	Y	N	Y	N	N	Y
McCaskill	?	Y	Y	Y	Y	Y
MONTANA						
Baucus	Y	Y	Y	Y	Y	Y
Tester	Y	Y	Y	Y	Y	Y
NEBRASKA						
Hagel	Y	Y	Y	N	?	?
Nelson	Y	Y	Y	Y	Y	Y
NEVADA						
Reid	Y	Y	Y	Y	Y	Y
Ensign	?	N	Y	N	N	Y
NEW HAMPSHIRE						
Gregg	Y	N	Y	N	N	Y
Sununu	Y	N	Y	N	N	Y
NEW JERSEY						
Lautenberg	Y	Y	Y	Y	Y	Y
Menendez	+	Y	Y	Y	Y	Y
NEW MEXICO						
Domenici	Y	N	Y	N	N	Y
Bingaman	Y	Y	Y	Y	Y	Y
NEW YORK						
Schumer	Y	Y	Y	Y	Y	Y
Clinton	?	?	?	?	?	?
NORTH CAROLINA						
Dole	Y	N	Y	N	N	Y
Burr	Y	N	Y	N	N	N
NORTH DAKOTA						
Conrad	Y	Y	Y	Y	Y	Y
Dorgan	Y	Y	Y	Y	Y	?
OHIO						
Voinovich	Y	N	Y	N	N	Y
Brown	Y	Y	Y	Y	Y	Y
OKLAHOMA						
Inhofe	?	N	Y	N	N	?
Coburn	N	N	Y	N	N	Y
OREGON						
Wyden	Y	Y	Y	Y	Y	Y
Smith	Y	Y	Y	Y	Y	Y
PENNSYLVANIA						
Specter	Y	Y	Y	Y	Y	Y
Casey	Y	Y	Y	Y	Y	Y
RHODE ISLAND						
Reed	Y	Y	Y	Y	Y	Y
Whitehouse	Y	Y	Y	Y	Y	Y
SOUTH CAROLINA						
Graham	Y	N	Y	N	N	Y
DeMint	Y	N	Y	N	N	N
SOUTH DAKOTA						
Johnson	Y	Y	Y	Y	Y	Y
Thune	Y	N	Y	N	N	Y
TENNESSEE						
Alexander	Y	N	Y	N	N	Y
Corker	Y	N	Y	N	N	N
TEXAS						
Hutchison	Y	N	Y	N	N	Y
Cornyn	Y	N	Y	N	N	Y
UTAH						
Hatch	Y	N	Y	N	N	Y
Bennett	Y	N	Y	N	N	Y
VERMONT						
Leahy	Y	Y	Y	Y	Y	Y
Sanders	Y	Y	Y	Y	Y	Y
VIRGINIA						
Warner	Y	Y	Y	N	Y	Y
Webb	Y	Y	Y	Y	Y	Y
WASHINGTON						
Murray	Y	Y	Y	Y	Y	Y
Cantwell	Y	Y	Y	Y	Y	Y
WEST VIRGINIA						
Byrd	?	?	?	?	?	?
Rockefeller	Y	Y	Y	Y	Y	?
WISCONSIN						
Kohl	Y	Y	Y	Y	Y	Y
Feingold	Y	Y	Y	Y	Y	Y
WYOMING						
Enzi	?	N	Y	N	N	Y
Barrasso	Y	N	Y	N	N	N

KEY   **Republicans**   Democrats   *Independents*

Y Voted for (yea)	X Paired against	C Voted "present" to avoid possible conflict of interest
# Paired for	− Announced against	
+ Announced for	P Voted "present"	? Did not vote or otherwise make a position known
N Voted against (nay)		

ND Northern Democrats, SD Southern Democrats
Southern states: Ala., Ark., Fla., Ga., Ky., La., Miss., N.C., Okla., S.C., Tenn., Texas, Va.

IN THE SENATE | By Vote Number

42. S Con Res 70. Fiscal 2009 Budget Resolution/Tax Cuts.
Baucus, D-Mont., amendment that would adjust the resolution to allow
for the extension of certain tax cuts, including the 10 percent tax bracket;
the child tax credit and small-business provisions; and the elimination
of the so-called marriage penalty. The extensions would eliminate most
of the $336 billion in surpluses projected for fiscal 2012 and 2013 in the
resolution. Adopted 99-1: R 49-0; D 48-1 (ND 43-1, SD 5-0); I 2-0.
March 13, 2008.

43. S Con Res 70. Fiscal 2009 Budget Resolution/Tax Cuts.
Graham, R-S.C., amendment that would adjust the resolution to allow
for the extension of certain 2001 and 2003 tax cuts, including the college
tuition deduction, as well as the income tax rate structure. It would adjust the resolution to allow the estate tax exemption to be raised to
$5 million and the maximum estate tax rate to be set at 35 percent.
Rejected 47-52: R 47-2; D 0-48 (ND 0-43, SD 0-5); I 0-2. March 13, 2008.

44. S Con Res 70. Fiscal 2009 Budget Resolution/Alternative
Minimum Tax Fund. Conrad, D-N.D., amendment that would create a
deficit-neutral reserve fund to adjust the budget and allow for the impact
of any legislation to return the alternative minimum tax to its rate before
the 1993 increases. Adopted 53-46: R 3-46; D 48-0 (ND 43-0, SD 5-0);
I 2-0. March 13, 2008.

45. S Con Res 70. Fiscal 2009 Budget Resolution/Alternative
Minimum Tax. Specter, R-Pa., amendment that would adjust the resolution to allow for a reduction in the individual alternative minimum tax
from its current two-rate structure of 26 percent and 28 percent to the
24 percent rate that was in effect before 1993. The revenue loss would not
be offset. Rejected 49-50: R 47-1; D 2-47 (ND 2-42, SD 0-5); I 0-2.
March 13, 2008.

46. S Con Res 70. Fiscal 2009 Budget Resolution/Alternative
Minimum Tax. Conrad, D-N.D., motion to table (kill) the Menendez,
D-N.J., motion to reconsider the vote on the Specter, R-Pa., amend-
ment. Motion rejected 49-51: R 0-49; D 47-2 (ND 42-2, SD 5-0); I 2-0.
March 13, 2008.

47. S Con Res 70. Fiscal 2009 Budget Resolution/Alternative
Minimum Tax. Menendez, D-N.J., motion to reconsider the vote on the
Specter, R-Pa., amendment. Motion agreed to, with Vice President Cheney
casting a "yea" vote to break the tie, 50-50: R 49-0; D 1-48 (ND 1-43,
SD 0-5); I 0-2. March 13, 2008.

48. S Con Res 70. Fiscal 2009 Budget Resolution/Alternative Minimum Tax. Specter, R-Pa., amendment that would adjust the resolution to
allow for a reduction in the individual alternative minimum tax from its
current two-rate structure of 26 percent and 28 percent to the
24 percent rate that was in effect prior to 1993. The revenue loss would
not be offset. Rejected 49-51: R 48-1; D 1-48 (ND 1-43, SD 0-5); I 0-2.
March 13, 2008.

	42	43	44	45	46	47	48
ALABAMA							
Shelby	Y	Y	N	Y	N	Y	Y
Sessions	Y	Y	N	Y	N	Y	Y
ALASKA							
Stevens	Y	Y	N	Y	N	Y	Y
Murkowski	Y	Y	N	Y	N	Y	Y
ARIZONA							
McCain	Y	Y	N	Y	N	Y	Y
Kyl	Y	Y	N	Y	N	Y	Y
ARKANSAS							
Lincoln	Y	N	Y	N	Y	N	N
Pryor	Y	N	Y	N	Y	N	N
CALIFORNIA							
Feinstein	Y	N	Y	N	Y	N	N
Boxer	Y	N	Y	N	Y	N	N
COLORADO							
Allard	Y	Y	N	Y	N	Y	Y
Salazar	Y	N	Y	N	Y	N	N
CONNECTICUT							
Dodd	Y	N	Y	N	Y	N	N
Lieberman	Y	N	Y	N	Y	N	N
DELAWARE							
Biden	Y	N	?	N	Y	N	N
Carper	Y	N	Y	N	Y	N	N
FLORIDA							
Nelson	Y	N	Y	N	Y	N	N
Martinez	Y	Y	N	Y	N	Y	Y
GEORGIA							
Chambliss	Y	Y	N	Y	N	Y	Y
Isakson	Y	Y	N	Y	N	Y	Y
HAWAII							
Inouye	Y	N	Y	N	Y	N	N
Akaka	Y	N	Y	N	Y	N	N
IDAHO							
Craig	Y	Y	N	Y	N	Y	Y
Crapo	Y	Y	N	Y	N	Y	Y
ILLINOIS							
Durbin	Y	N	Y	N	Y	N	N
Obama	Y	N	Y	N	Y	N	N
INDIANA							
Lugar	Y	Y	N	Y	N	Y	Y
Bayh	Y	N	Y	Y	N	Y	Y
IOWA							
Grassley	Y	Y	N	Y	N	Y	Y
Harkin	Y	N	Y	N	Y	N	N
KANSAS							
Brownback	Y	Y	N	Y	N	Y	Y
Roberts	Y	Y	N	Y	N	Y	Y
KENTUCKY							
McConnell	Y	Y	N	Y	N	Y	Y
Bunning	Y	Y	N	Y	N	Y	Y
LOUISIANA							
Landrieu	Y	N	Y	N	Y	N	N
Vitter	Y	Y	N	Y	N	Y	Y
MAINE							
Snowe	Y	N	Y	Y	N	Y	Y
Collins	Y	Y	Y	Y	N	Y	Y
MARYLAND							
Mikulski	Y	N	Y	N	Y	N	N
Cardin	Y	N	Y	N	Y	N	N
MASSACHUSETTS							
Kennedy	Y	N	Y	N	Y	N	N
Kerry	Y	?	Y	N	Y	N	N
MICHIGAN							
Levin	Y	N	Y	N	Y	N	N
Stabenow	Y	N	Y	N	Y	N	N
MINNESOTA							
Coleman	Y	Y	N	Y	N	Y	Y
Klobuchar	Y	N	Y	N	Y	N	N
MISSISSIPPI							
Cochran	Y	Y	N	Y	N	Y	Y
Wicker	Y	Y	N	Y	N	Y	Y
MISSOURI							
Bond	Y	Y	N	Y	N	Y	Y
McCaskill	Y	N	Y	N	Y	N	N
MONTANA							
Baucus	Y	N	Y	N	Y	N	N
Tester	Y	N	Y	N	Y	N	N
NEBRASKA							
Hagel	Y	Y	N	Y	N	Y	Y
Nelson	Y	N	Y	Y	N	N	N
NEVADA							
Reid	Y	N	Y	N	Y	N	N
Ensign	Y	Y	N	Y	N	Y	Y
NEW HAMPSHIRE							
Gregg	Y	Y	N	Y	N	Y	Y
Sununu	Y	Y	N	Y	N	Y	Y
NEW JERSEY							
Lautenberg	Y	N	Y	N	Y	N	N
Menendez	Y	N	Y	N	Y	N	N
NEW MEXICO							
Domenici	Y	Y	N	Y	N	Y	Y
Bingaman	Y	N	Y	N	Y	N	N
NEW YORK							
Schumer	Y	N	Y	N	Y	N	N
Clinton	Y	N	Y	N	Y	N	N
NORTH CAROLINA							
Dole	Y	Y	N	Y	N	Y	Y
Burr	Y	Y	N	Y	N	Y	Y
NORTH DAKOTA							
Conrad	Y	N	Y	N	Y	N	N
Dorgan	Y	N	Y	N	Y	N	N
OHIO							
Voinovich	Y	N	N	N	N	Y	N
Brown	Y	N	Y	N	Y	N	N
OKLAHOMA							
Inhofe	Y	Y	N	Y	N	Y	Y
Coburn	Y	Y	N	Y	N	Y	Y
OREGON							
Wyden	Y	N	Y	N	Y	N	N
Smith	Y	Y	Y	Y	N	Y	Y
PENNSYLVANIA							
Specter	Y	Y	N	Y	N	Y	Y
Casey	Y	N	Y	N	Y	N	N
RHODE ISLAND							
Reed	Y	N	Y	N	Y	N	N
Whitehouse	Y	N	Y	N	Y	N	N
SOUTH CAROLINA							
Graham	Y	Y	N	Y	N	Y	Y
DeMint	Y	Y	N	Y	N	Y	Y
SOUTH DAKOTA							
Johnson	Y	N	Y	N	Y	N	N
Thune	Y	Y	N	Y	N	Y	Y
TENNESSEE							
Alexander	Y	Y	N	Y	N	Y	Y
Corker	Y	Y	N	Y	N	Y	Y
TEXAS							
Hutchison	Y	Y	N	Y	N	Y	Y
Cornyn	Y	Y	N	?	N	Y	Y
UTAH							
Hatch	Y	Y	N	Y	N	Y	Y
Bennett	Y	Y	N	Y	N	Y	Y
VERMONT							
Leahy	Y	N	Y	N	Y	N	N
Sanders	Y	N	Y	N	Y	N	N
VIRGINIA							
Warner	Y	Y	N	Y	N	Y	Y
Webb	Y	N	Y	N	Y	N	N
WASHINGTON							
Murray	Y	N	Y	N	Y	N	N
Cantwell	Y	N	Y	N	Y	N	N
WEST VIRGINIA							
Byrd	Y	N	Y	N	Y	N	N
Rockefeller	Y	N	Y	N	Y	N	N
WISCONSIN							
Kohl	Y	N	Y	N	Y	N	N
Feingold	N	N	Y	N	Y	N	N
WYOMING							
Enzi	Y	Y	N	Y	N	Y	Y
Barrasso	Y	Y	N	Y	N	Y	Y

KEY Republicans   Democrats   *Independents*

Y Voted for (yea)	X Paired against	C Voted "present" to avoid possible conflict of interest
# Paired for	– Announced against	
+ Announced for	P Voted "present"	? Did not vote or otherwise make a position known
N Voted against (nay)		

ND Northern Democrats, SD Southern Democrats
Southern states: Ala., Ark., Fla., Ga., Ky., La., Miss., N.C., Okla., S.C., Tenn., Texas, Va.

IN THE SENATE | By Vote Number

49. S Con Res 70. Fiscal 2009 Budget Resolution/Estate Tax.
Salazar, D-Colo., amendment that would adjust the resolution to allow up to $45 billion for estate tax relief over six years, providing it does not increase the deficit. Rejected 38-62: R 3-46; D 34-15 (ND 29-15, SD 5-0); I 1-1. March 13, 2008.

50. S Con Res 70. Fiscal 2009 Budget Resolution/Estate Tax.
Kyl, R-Ariz., amendment that would adjust the resolution to allow for a $5 million estate tax exemption and a maximum estate tax rate of 35 percent. Rejected 50-50: R 48-1; D 2-47 (ND 0-44, SD 2-3); I 0-2. March 13, 2008.

51. S Con Res 70. Fiscal 2009 Budget Resolution/Social Security.
Conrad, D-N.D., amendment that would create a deficit-neutral reserve fund to allow for the impact of any legislation to repeal the 1993 increase in income tax on Social Security benefits. Adopted 53-46: R 3-46; D 48-0 (ND 43-0, SD 5-0); I 2-0. March 13, 2008.

52. S Con Res 70. Fiscal 2009 Budget Resolution/Social Security.
Bunning, R-Ky., amendment that would adjust the resolution to allow for the repeal of the 1993 tax increase on Social Security benefits, offset by an across-the-board cut in discretionary spending. Rejected 47-53: R 47-2; D 0-49 (ND 0-44, SD 0-5); I 0-2. March 13, 2008.

53. S Con Res 70. Fiscal 2009 Budget Resolution/Health and Energy Assistance Funding.
Specter, R-Pa., amendment that would adjust the resolution to allow for funding increases of $2.1 billion for the National Institutes of Health and $1 billion for the Low Income Home Energy Assistance Program, offset by cuts in discretionary spending. Adopted 95-4: R 45-3; D 48-1 (ND 43-1, SD 5-0); I 2-0. March 13, 2008.

54. S Con Res 70. Fiscal 2009 Budget Resolution/Indian Health Service.
Dorgan, D-N.D., amendment that would shift funding in the budget resolution to allow for an increase of $1 billion for the Indian Health Service. Adopted 69-30: R 20-29; D 47-1 (ND 42-1, SD 5-0); I 2-0. March 13, 2008.

55. S Con Res 70. Fiscal 2009 Budget Resolution/Energy Efficiency and Production.
Nelson, D-Fla., amendment that would create a deficit-neutral reserve fund to allow for the impact of any legislation to encourage consumers to replace conventional wood stoves with EPA-approved stoves and install electricity meters in their homes, and to encourage the capture and storage of carbon dioxide emissions from coal projects and the development of oil and natural gas resources beneath the outer continental shelf area not covered by current moratoria. Adopted 56-43: R 6-42; D 48-1 (ND 44-0, SD 4-1); I 2-0. March 13, 2008.

	49	50	51	52	53	54	55
ALABAMA							
Shelby	N	Y	N	Y	Y	N	N
Sessions	N	Y	N	Y	Y	N	N
ALASKA							
Stevens	N	Y	N	Y	Y	Y	N
Murkowski	N	Y	Y	Y	Y	Y	N
ARIZONA							
McCain	N	Y	N	Y	Y	Y	?
Kyl	N	Y	N	Y	N	N	N
ARKANSAS							
Lincoln	Y	Y	Y	N	Y	Y	Y
Pryor	Y	Y	Y	N	Y	Y	Y
CALIFORNIA							
Feinstein	Y	N	Y	N	Y	Y	Y
Boxer	Y	N	Y	N	Y	Y	Y
COLORADO							
Allard	N	Y	N	Y	Y	N	N
Salazar	Y	N	Y	N	Y	Y	Y
CONNECTICUT							
Dodd	Y	N	Y	N	Y	Y	Y
Lieberman	Y	N	Y	N	Y	Y	Y
DELAWARE							
Biden	Y	N	Y	N	Y	Y	Y
Carper	N	N	Y	N	N	N	Y
FLORIDA							
Nelson	Y	N	Y	N	Y	Y	Y
Martinez	N	Y	N	Y	Y	N	Y
GEORGIA							
Chambliss	N	Y	N	Y	Y	Y	N
Isakson	N	Y	N	Y	Y	N	N
HAWAII							
Inouye	Y	N	Y	N	Y	Y	Y
Akaka	Y	N	Y	N	Y	Y	Y
IDAHO							
Craig	N	Y	N	Y	Y	Y	N
Crapo	N	Y	N	Y	Y	Y	N
ILLINOIS							
Durbin	N	N	Y	N	Y	Y	Y
Obama	Y	N	Y	N	Y	Y	Y
INDIANA							
Lugar	N	Y	N	Y	Y	N	N
Bayh	Y	N	Y	N	Y	Y	Y
IOWA							
Grassley	N	Y	N	Y	Y	Y	N
Harkin	N	N	Y	N	Y	Y	Y
KANSAS							
Brownback	N	Y	N	Y	Y	Y	N
Roberts	N	Y	N	Y	N	N	N
KENTUCKY							
McConnell	N	Y	N	Y	Y	N	N
Bunning	N	Y	N	Y	Y	N	N
LOUISIANA							
Landrieu	Y	Y	Y	N	Y	Y	N
Vitter	N	Y	N	Y	?	N	N
MAINE							
Snowe	Y	Y	Y	N	Y	N	Y
Collins	Y	Y	Y	N	Y	Y	Y
MARYLAND							
Mikulski	Y	N	Y	N	Y	Y	Y
Cardin	N	N	Y	N	Y	Y	Y
MASSACHUSETTS							
Kennedy	N	N	Y	N	Y	Y	Y
Kerry	N	N	Y	N	Y	Y	Y
MICHIGAN							
Levin	N	N	Y	N	Y	Y	Y
Stabenow	Y	N	Y	N	Y	Y	Y
MINNESOTA							
Coleman	N	Y	N	Y	Y	Y	Y
Klobuchar	Y	N	Y	N	Y	Y	Y
MISSISSIPPI							
Cochran	N	Y	N	Y	Y	Y	N
Wicker	N	Y	N	Y	Y	Y	N
MISSOURI							
Bond	N	Y	N	Y	Y	N	N
McCaskill	Y	N	Y	N	Y	Y	Y

	49	50	51	52	53	54	55
MONTANA							
Baucus	Y	N	Y	N	Y	?	Y
Tester	Y	N	Y	N	Y	Y	Y
NEBRASKA							
Hagel	N	Y	N	Y	Y	N	N
Nelson	Y	N	Y	N	Y	Y	Y
NEVADA							
Reid	N	N	Y	N	Y	Y	Y
Ensign	N	Y	N	Y	N	N	N
NEW HAMPSHIRE							
Gregg	N	Y	N	Y	Y	N	N
Sununu	N	Y	N	Y	Y	N	N
NEW JERSEY							
Lautenberg	Y	N	Y	N	Y	Y	Y
Menendez	Y	N	Y	N	Y	Y	Y
NEW MEXICO							
Domenici	N	Y	N	Y	Y	Y	N
Bingaman	N	N	Y	N	Y	Y	Y
NEW YORK							
Schumer	N	N	Y	N	Y	Y	Y
Clinton	Y	N	Y	N	Y	Y	Y
NORTH CAROLINA							
Dole	N	Y	N	Y	Y	Y	Y
Burr	N	Y	N	Y	Y	N	N
NORTH DAKOTA							
Conrad	Y	N	Y	N	Y	Y	Y
Dorgan	N	N	Y	N	Y	Y	Y
OHIO							
Voinovich	Y	N	Y	Y	Y	N	N
Brown	N	N	Y	N	Y	Y	Y
OKLAHOMA							
Inhofe	N	Y	N	Y	N	Y	N
Coburn	N	Y	N	Y	N	N	N
OREGON							
Wyden	Y	N	Y	N	Y	Y	Y
Smith	N	Y	N	Y	Y	Y	Y
PENNSYLVANIA							
Specter	N	Y	N	Y	Y	N	Y
Casey	Y	N	Y	N	Y	Y	Y
RHODE ISLAND							
Reed	N	N	Y	N	Y	Y	Y
Whitehouse	N	N	Y	N	Y	Y	Y
SOUTH CAROLINA							
Graham	N	Y	N	Y	Y	Y	N
DeMint	N	Y	N	Y	N	N	N
SOUTH DAKOTA							
Johnson	Y	N	Y	N	Y	Y	Y
Thune	N	Y	N	Y	Y	Y	Y
TENNESSEE							
Alexander	N	Y	N	Y	Y	N	N
Corker	N	Y	N	Y	Y	N	N
TEXAS							
Hutchison	N	Y	N	Y	Y	N	N
Cornyn	N	Y	N	Y	Y	N	N
UTAH							
Hatch	N	Y	N	Y	Y	N	N
Bennett	N	Y	N	Y	Y	Y	N
VERMONT							
Leahy	Y	N	Y	N	Y	Y	?
Sanders	N	N	Y	N	Y	Y	Y
VIRGINIA							
Warner	N	Y	N	Y	Y	N	N
Webb	Y	N	Y	N	Y	Y	Y
WASHINGTON							
Murray	Y	N	Y	N	Y	Y	Y
Cantwell	Y	N	Y	N	Y	Y	Y
WEST VIRGINIA							
Byrd	Y	N	?	N	Y	Y	Y
Rockefeller	N	N	Y	N	Y	Y	Y
WISCONSIN							
Kohl	Y	N	Y	N	Y	Y	Y
Feingold	Y	N	Y	N	Y	Y	Y
WYOMING							
Enzi	N	Y	N	Y	Y	N	N
Barrasso	N	Y	N	Y	Y	N	N

KEY — **Republicans** — Democrats — *Independents*

Y Voted for (yea)	**X** Paired against	**C** Voted "present" to avoid possible conflict of interest
# Paired for	**–** Announced against	
+ Announced for	**P** Voted "present"	**?** Did not vote or otherwise make a position known
N Voted against (nay)		

ND Northern Democrats, SD Southern Democrats
Southern states: Ala., Ark., Fla., Ga., Ky., La., Miss., N.C., Okla., S.C., Tenn., Texas, Va.

IN THE SENATE | By Vote Number

56. **S Con Res 70. Fiscal 2009 Budget Resolution/Energy Efficiency and Production.** Alexander, R-Tenn., amendment that would create a deficit-neutral reserve fund to allow for the impact of any legislation to encourage consumers to replace conventional wood stoves with EPA-approved stoves and install electricity meters in their homes, and to encourage the capture and storage of carbon dioxide emissions from coal projects and the development of oil and natural gas resources beneath the outer continental shelf off the coast of Virginia. Changes would have to be deficit-neutral. Rejected 47-51: R 43-5; D 4-44 (ND 3-40, SD 1-4); I 0-2. March 13, 2008.

57. **S Con Res 70. Fiscal 2009 Budget Resolution/Adult Literacy.** Kennedy, D-Mass., amendment that would allow for a $2 million increase in funding for the Department of Education's English Literacy-Civics Education State Grant program, with offsets. Adopted 95-2: R 46-2; D 47-0 (ND 42-0, SD 5-0); I 2-0. March 13, 2008.

58. **S Con Res 70. Fiscal 2009 Budget Resolution/English Literacy.** Alexander, R-Tenn., amendment that would assume a shift of $670,000 from the Equal Employment Opportunity Commission to the Department of Education's English Literacy-Civics Education State Grant program. Adopted 54-44: R 47-1; D 7-41 (ND 4-39, SD 3-2); I 0-2. March 13, 2008.

59. **S Con Res 70. Fiscal 2009 Budget Resolution/Immigration Enforcement.** Menendez, D-N.J., amendment that would allow an adjustment to the resolution for increased border security and immigration enforcement, including an increase in criminal and civil penalties against employers who hire undocumented immigrants, and the deployment of National Guard troops to the northern or southern border, as long as the programs do not increase the deficit. Adopted 53-45: R 5-43; D 46-2 (ND 41-2, SD 4-1); I 2-0. March 13, 2008.

60. **S Con Res 70. Fiscal 2009 Budget Resolution/Immigration Enforcement.** Sessions, R-Ala., amendment that would allow an adjustment to the resolution for increased border security and immigration enforcement, including programs that expand the zero-tolerance prosecution policy for illegal entry, completion of 700 miles of border fencing and deployment of up to 6,000 National Guard members to the U.S. southern border, as long as the programs do not increase the deficit. Adopted 61-37: R 48-0; D 13-35 (ND 9-34, SD 4-1); I 0-2. March 13, 2008.

61. **S Con Res 70. Fiscal 2009 Budget Resolution/Income Tax Rates.** Cornyn, R-Texas, motion to waive the Budget Act with respect to the Conrad, D-N.D., point of order against the Cornyn amendment that would create a 60-vote point of order against any legislation that would raise income tax rates. Motion rejected 58-40: R 48-0; D 10-38 (ND 8-35, SD 2-3); I 0-2. A three-fifths majority (60) of the total Senate is required to waive the Budget Act. (Subsequently, the chair upheld the point of order, and the amendment fell.) March 13, 2008.

62. **S Con Res 70. Fiscal 2009 Budget Resolution/Tax Increase.** Allard, R-Colo., amendment that would adjust the resolution to allow for a $1.4 trillion tax increase over five years. Rejected 0-97: R 0-48; D 0-47 (ND 0-43, SD 0-4); I 0-2. March 13, 2008.

	56	57	58	59	60	61	62
ALABAMA							
Shelby	Y	Y	Y	N	Y	Y	N
Sessions	Y	Y	Y	N	Y	Y	N
ALASKA							
Stevens	Y	Y	Y	N	Y	Y	N
Murkowski	Y	Y	Y	N	Y	Y	N
ARIZONA							
McCain	?	?	?	?	?	?	?
Kyl	Y	Y	Y	N	Y	Y	N
ARKANSAS							
Lincoln	N	Y	Y	Y	Y	Y	-
Pryor	N	Y	Y	N	Y	Y	N
CALIFORNIA							
Feinstein	N	Y	N	N	N	N	N
Boxer	N	Y	N	Y	N	N	N
COLORADO							
Allard	Y	Y	Y	N	Y	Y	N
Salazar	N	Y	N	Y	N	Y	N
CONNECTICUT							
Dodd	N	Y	N	Y	N	N	N
Lieberman	N	Y	N	Y	N	N	N
DELAWARE							
Biden	N	Y	N	Y	N	N	N
Carper	N	Y	N	Y	Y	N	N
FLORIDA							
Nelson	N	Y	N	Y	N	N	N
Martinez	N	Y	N	Y	Y	Y	N
GEORGIA							
Chambliss	Y	Y	Y	N	Y	Y	N
Isakson	Y	Y	Y	N	Y	Y	N
HAWAII							
Inouye	N	Y	N	Y	N	N	N
Akaka	N	Y	N	Y	N	N	N
IDAHO							
Craig	Y	Y	Y	N	Y	Y	N
Crapo	Y	Y	Y	N	Y	Y	N
ILLINOIS							
Durbin	N	Y	N	Y	N	N	N
Obama	N	?	N	Y	N	N	N
INDIANA							
Lugar	Y	Y	Y	N	Y	Y	N
Bayh	N	Y	Y	Y	Y	Y	N
IOWA							
Grassley	Y	Y	Y	N	Y	Y	N
Harkin	N	Y	N	Y	N	N	N
KANSAS							
Brownback	Y	Y	Y	N	Y	Y	N
Roberts	Y	Y	Y	N	Y	Y	N
KENTUCKY							
McConnell	Y	Y	Y	N	Y	Y	N
Bunning	Y	Y	Y	N	Y	Y	N
LOUISIANA							
Landrieu	Y	Y	Y	Y	Y	N	N
Vitter	Y	Y	Y	N	Y	Y	N
MAINE							
Snowe	N	Y	Y	Y	Y	Y	N
Collins	N	Y	Y	Y	Y	Y	N
MARYLAND							
Mikulski	N	Y	N	Y	N	N	N
Cardin	N	Y	N	Y	N	N	N
MASSACHUSETTS							
Kennedy	N	Y	N	Y	N	N	N
Kerry	N	Y	N	Y	N	N	N
MICHIGAN							
Levin	N	Y	N	Y	N	N	N
Stabenow	N	Y	N	Y	N	N	N
MINNESOTA							
Coleman	Y	Y	Y	Y	Y	Y	N
Klobuchar	N	Y	N	Y	N	N	N
MISSISSIPPI							
Cochran	Y	Y	Y	N	Y	Y	N
Wicker	Y	Y	Y	N	Y	Y	N
MISSOURI							
Bond	Y	Y	Y	N	Y	Y	N
McCaskill	N	Y	N	Y	Y	Y	N

	56	57	58	59	60	61	62
MONTANA							
Baucus	N	Y	Y	Y	Y	Y	N
Tester	N	Y	Y	Y	Y	Y	N
NEBRASKA							
Hagel	Y	Y	Y	N	Y	Y	N
Nelson	Y	Y	Y	Y	Y	Y	N
NEVADA							
Reid	N	Y	N	Y	N	N	N
Ensign	Y	Y	Y	N	Y	Y	N
NEW HAMPSHIRE							
Gregg	Y	Y	Y	N	Y	Y	N
Sununu	Y	Y	Y	Y	Y	Y	N
NEW JERSEY							
Lautenberg	N	Y	N	N	N	N	N
Menendez	N	Y	N	Y	N	N	N
NEW MEXICO							
Domenici	Y	Y	Y	N	Y	Y	N
Bingaman	N	Y	N	N	N	N	N
NEW YORK							
Schumer	N	Y	N	Y	N	N	N
Clinton	N	Y	N	Y	N	N	N
NORTH CAROLINA							
Dole	N	Y	Y	N	Y	Y	N
Burr	Y	Y	Y	N	Y	Y	N
NORTH DAKOTA							
Conrad	N	Y	N	Y	N	N	N
Dorgan	Y	Y	N	Y	N	Y	N
OHIO							
Voinovich	Y	Y	Y	N	Y	Y	N
Brown	N	Y	N	Y	N	N	N
OKLAHOMA							
Inhofe	Y	N	Y	N	Y	Y	N
Coburn	Y	N	Y	N	Y	Y	N
OREGON							
Wyden	N	Y	N	Y	N	N	N
Smith	N	Y	Y	N	Y	Y	N
PENNSYLVANIA							
Specter	Y	Y	Y	N	Y	Y	N
Casey	N	Y	N	Y	N	N	N
RHODE ISLAND							
Reed	N	Y	N	Y	N	N	N
Whitehouse	N	Y	N	Y	N	N	N
SOUTH CAROLINA							
Graham	Y	Y	Y	N	Y	Y	N
DeMint	Y	Y	Y	N	Y	Y	N
SOUTH DAKOTA							
Johnson	Y	Y	Y	N	N	N	N
Thune	Y	Y	Y	N	Y	Y	N
TENNESSEE							
Alexander	Y	Y	Y	N	Y	Y	N
Corker	Y	Y	Y	N	Y	Y	N
TEXAS							
Hutchison	Y	Y	Y	N	Y	Y	N
Cornyn	Y	Y	Y	N	Y	Y	N
UTAH							
Hatch	Y	Y	Y	N	Y	Y	N
Bennett	Y	Y	Y	N	Y	Y	N
VERMONT							
Leahy	N	Y	N	Y	N	N	N
Sanders	N	Y	N	Y	N	N	N
VIRGINIA							
Warner	Y	Y	Y	N	Y	Y	N
Webb	N	Y	N	Y	N	N	N
WASHINGTON							
Murray	N	Y	N	Y	N	N	N
Cantwell	N	Y	N	Y	N	N	N
WEST VIRGINIA							
Byrd	?	?	?	?	?	?	?
Rockefeller	N	Y	N	Y	N	N	N
WISCONSIN							
Kohl	N	Y	N	Y	N	Y	N
Feingold	N	Y	N	Y	N	N	N
WYOMING							
Enzi	Y	Y	Y	N	Y	Y	N
Barrasso	Y	Y	Y	N	Y	Y	N

KEY	**Republicans**	Democrats	*Independents*	
Y Voted for (yea)		X Paired against		C Voted "present" to avoid possible conflict of interest
# Paired for		– Announced against		
+ Announced for		P Voted "present"		? Did not vote or otherwise make a position known
N Voted against (nay)				

ND Northern Democrats, SD Southern Democrats
Southern states: Ala., Ark., Fla., Ga., Ky., La., Miss., N.C., Okla., S.C., Tenn., Texas, Va.

IN THE SENATE | By Vote Number

63. **S Con Res 70. Fiscal 2009 Budget Resolution/Means Test.**
Ensign, R-Nev., amendment that would adjust the resolution to allow for a requirement that Medicare prescription drug beneficiaries with annual incomes of more than $82,000 for individuals and $164,000 for couples pay a larger share of their Medicare Part D premium. Rejected 42-56: R 40-8; D 2-46 (ND 2-41, SD 0-5); I 0-2. March 13, 2008.

64. **S Con Res 70. Fiscal 2009 Budget Resolution/Tax Cuts.**
Sanders, I-Vt., amendment that would adjust the resolution to assume a repeal of enacted tax cuts for individuals with incomes of more than $1 million, with an increase in funding for programs such as special education. Rejected 43-55: R 1-47; D 40-8 (ND 36-7, SD 4-1); I 2-0. March 13, 2008.

65. **S Con Res 70. Fiscal 2009 Budget Resolution/Social Security Reserve Fund.** DeMint, R-S.C., amendment that would allow an adjustment to the resolution if the Finance Committee reports legislation that would bar Congress from borrowing from the Social Security trust fund to finance other government programs. The change would have to be deficit-neutral. Rejected 41-57: R 40-8; D 1-47 (ND 1-42, SD 0-5); I 0-2. March 13, 2008.

66. **S Con Res 70. Fiscal 2009 Budget Resolution/Spending Reductions.** Allard, R-Colo., amendment that would reduce fiscal 2009 funding by $750 million on programs rated ineffective by the Office of Management and Budget. The savings would go to paying down the debt. Rejected 29-68: R 29-18; D 0-48 (ND 0-43, SD 0-5); I 0-2. March 13, 2008.

67. **S Con Res 70. Fiscal 2009 Budget Resolution/Budget Accountability.** Brownback, R-Kan., amendment that would adjust the resolution to allow for about $25 million over five years for the creation of a Commission on Budgetary Accountability and Review of Federal Agencies. Adopted 49-48: R 38-9; D 11-37 (ND 10-33, SD 1-4); I 0-2. March 13, 2008.

68. **S Con Res 70. Fiscal 2009 Budget Resolution/Provider Background Checks.** Kohl, D-Wis., amendment that would establish a reserve fund to allow up to $160 million for a three-year extension of the pilot program for national and state background checks on direct patient access employees of long-term care facilities or providers, as long as it does not increase the deficit. Adopted 89-7: R 40-7; D 47-0 (ND 42-0, SD 5-0); I 2-0. March 13, 2008.

69. **S Con Res 70. Fiscal 2009 Budget Resolution/COPS Program.**
Conrad, D-N.D., motion to table (kill) the Vitter, R-La., amendment that would allow an adjustment to the resolution for legislation to restrict Community Oriented Policing Services funds from going to jurisdictions that prohibit local law enforcement from cooperating with federal agencies looking for illegal immigrants. Motion agreed to 58-40: R 9-39; D 47-1 (ND 43-0, SD 4-1); I 2-0. March 13, 2008.

	63	64	65	66	67	68	69
ALABAMA							
Shelby	Y	N	N	Y	Y	Y	N
Sessions	Y	N	Y	Y	Y	N	N
ALASKA							
Stevens	Y	N	Y	N	N	Y	Y
Murkowski	Y	N	Y	N	N	Y	Y
ARIZONA							
McCain	?	?	?	?	?	?	?
Kyl	Y	N	Y	Y	Y	N	N
ARKANSAS							
Lincoln	N	N	N	N	N	Y	Y
Pryor	N	Y	N	N	N	Y	Y
CALIFORNIA							
Feinstein	N	Y	N	N	N	Y	Y
Boxer	N	Y	N	N	N	Y	Y
COLORADO							
Allard	Y	N	Y	Y	Y	N	N
Salazar	N	N	N	N	N	Y	Y
CONNECTICUT							
Dodd	N	Y	N	N	Y	Y	Y
Lieberman	N	Y	N	N	N	Y	Y
DELAWARE							
Biden	N	Y	N	N	N	Y	Y
Carper	Y	N	N	N	N	Y	Y
FLORIDA							
Nelson	N	Y	N	N	N	Y	Y
Martinez	N	N	Y	Y	Y	Y	N
GEORGIA							
Chambliss	Y	N	Y	Y	Y	Y	N
Isakson	Y	N	Y	Y	Y	Y	N
HAWAII							
Inouye	N	Y	N	N	Y	Y	Y
Akaka	N	Y	N	N	N	Y	Y
IDAHO							
Craig	Y	N	Y	Y	Y	Y	N
Crapo	Y	N	Y	Y	Y	N	N
ILLINOIS							
Durbin	N	Y	N	N	N	Y	Y
Obama	N	Y	N	N	N	Y	Y
INDIANA							
Lugar	Y	N	Y	N	Y	Y	Y
Bayh	N	Y	N	N	Y	Y	Y
IOWA							
Grassley	Y	N	Y	N	Y	Y	N
Harkin	N	Y	N	N	Y	Y	Y
KANSAS							
Brownback	Y	N	Y	Y	Y	Y	N
Roberts	Y	N	Y	N	Y	Y	N
KENTUCKY							
McConnell	Y	N	Y	Y	Y	Y	N
Bunning	Y	N	Y	Y	Y	N	N
LOUISIANA							
Landrieu	N	Y	N	N	N	Y	Y
Vitter	Y	N	Y	Y	Y	N	N
MAINE							
Snowe	N	N	N	N	N	Y	Y
Collins	Y	Y	N	N	N	Y	Y
MARYLAND							
Mikulski	N	Y	N	N	Y	Y	Y
Cardin	N	Y	N	N	N	Y	Y
MASSACHUSETTS							
Kennedy	N	Y	N	N	N	Y	Y
Kerry	N	Y	N	N	N	Y	Y
MICHIGAN							
Levin	N	Y	N	N	N	Y	Y
Stabenow	N	Y	N	N	N	Y	Y
MINNESOTA							
Coleman	Y	N	Y	N	Y	Y	N
Klobuchar	N	Y	N	N	Y	Y	Y
MISSISSIPPI							
Cochran	N	N	N	N	Y	Y	N
Wicker	N	N	Y	Y	Y	Y	N
MISSOURI							
Bond	Y	N	Y	Y	N	Y	N
McCaskill	Y	Y	Y	N	Y	Y	Y

	63	64	65	66	67	68	69
MONTANA							
Baucus	N	N	N	N	N	Y	Y
Tester	N	N	N	N	N	Y	Y
NEBRASKA							
Hagel	Y	N	Y	?	?	?	Y
Nelson	N	N	N	N	N	Y	Y
NEVADA							
Reid	N	Y	N	N	N	Y	Y
Ensign	Y	N	Y	Y	Y	N	N
NEW HAMPSHIRE							
Gregg	Y	N	Y	Y	Y	Y	N
Sununu	Y	N	Y	Y	Y	Y	N
NEW JERSEY							
Lautenberg	N	Y	N	N	N	Y	Y
Menendez	N	Y	N	N	N	Y	Y
NEW MEXICO							
Domenici	N	N	N	N	Y	Y	N
Bingaman	N	Y	N	N	N	Y	Y
NEW YORK							
Schumer	N	Y	N	N	N	Y	Y
Clinton	N	Y	N	N	N	Y	Y
NORTH CAROLINA							
Dole	Y	N	Y	N	Y	N	Y
Burr	Y	N	Y	N	Y	Y	N
NORTH DAKOTA							
Conrad	N	Y	N	N	N	Y	Y
Dorgan	N	Y	N	N	N	Y	Y
OHIO							
Voinovich	Y	N	N	N	Y	Y	Y
Brown	N	Y	N	N	N	Y	Y
OKLAHOMA							
Inhofe	Y	N	Y	Y	Y	N	N
Coburn	Y	N	Y	Y	Y	N	N
OREGON							
Wyden	N	N	N	N	N	Y	Y
Smith	N	N	N	N	Y	Y	N
PENNSYLVANIA							
Specter	N	N	N	Y	Y	Y	Y
Casey	N	Y	N	N	N	Y	Y
RHODE ISLAND							
Reed	N	Y	N	N	N	Y	Y
Whitehouse	N	Y	N	N	Y	Y	Y
SOUTH CAROLINA							
Graham	Y	N	Y	Y	Y	Y	N
DeMint	Y	N	Y	Y	Y	N	N
SOUTH DAKOTA							
Johnson	N	Y	N	N	Y	Y	Y
Thune	Y	N	Y	Y	Y	Y	N
TENNESSEE							
Alexander	Y	N	Y	N	Y	Y	N
Corker	Y	N	Y	Y	Y	Y	N
TEXAS							
Hutchison	N	N	Y	Y	Y	Y	N
Cornyn	Y	N	Y	Y	Y	Y	N
UTAH							
Hatch	Y	N	Y	Y	Y	Y	N
Bennett	Y	N	N	N	N	Y	N
VERMONT							
Leahy	N	Y	N	N	Y	Y	Y
Sanders	N	Y	N	N	N	Y	Y
VIRGINIA							
Warner	Y	N	Y	N	N	Y	N
Webb	N	Y	N	N	N	Y	Y
WASHINGTON							
Murray	N	Y	N	N	N	?	Y
Cantwell	N	N	N	N	N	Y	Y
WEST VIRGINIA							
Byrd	?	?	?	?	?	?	?
Rockefeller	N	Y	N	N	N	Y	Y
WISCONSIN							
Kohl	N	Y	N	N	N	Y	Y
Feingold	N	Y	N	N	Y	Y	Y
WYOMING							
Enzi	Y	N	Y	Y	Y	Y	N
Barrasso	Y	N	Y	Y	Y	Y	N

KEY **Republicans** Democrats *Independents*

Y Voted for (yea)	**X** Paired against	**C** Voted "present" to avoid possible conflict of interest
# Paired for	**–** Announced against	
+ Announced for	**P** Voted "present"	**?** Did not vote or otherwise make a position known
N Voted against (nay)		

ND Northern Democrats, SD Southern Democrats
Southern states: Ala., Ark., Fla., Ga., Ky., La., Miss., N.C., Okla., S.C., Tenn., Texas, Va.

IN THE SENATE | By Vote Number

70. S Con Res 70. Fiscal 2009 Budget Resolution/Child-Protection Enforcement. Boxer, D-Calif., amendment that would adjust the resolution to allow for a $50 million increase in funding for the Department of Justice to enforce various child protection laws, with assumed corresponding offsets. Adopted 90-5: R 43-5; D 45-0 (ND 40-0, SD 5-0); I 2-0. March 13, 2008.

71. S Con Res 70. Fiscal 2009 Budget Resolution/Parental Notification. Ensign, R-Nev., amendment that would adjust the resolution to allow for a $50 million increase in Justice Department funding for parental notification law enforcement, with assumed corresponding offsets. Rejected 49-49: R 44-4; D 5-43 (ND 4-39, SD 1-4); I 0-2. March 13, 2008.

72. S Con Res 70. Fiscal 2009 Budget Resolution/Gasoline Prices. DeMint, R-S.C., motion to waive the Budget Act with respect to the Conrad, D-N.D., point of order against the DeMint amendment that would create a 60-vote point of order against any legislation that would cause the price of gasoline to increase. Motion rejected 39-59: R 37-11; D 2-46 (ND 2-41, SD 0-5); I 0-2. A three-fifths majority (60) of the total Senate is required to waive the Budget Act. (Subsequently, the chair upheld the point of order, and the amendment fell.) March 13, 2008.

73. S Con Res 70. Fiscal 2009 Budget Resolution/PAYGO Waiver. Cornyn, R-Texas, motion to waive the Budget Act with respect to the Conrad, D-N.D., point of order against the Cornyn amendment that would require the consent of all senators to increase the deficit through tax cuts or increased spending without offsetting the costs. Motion rejected 27-71: R 27-21; D 0-48 (ND 0-43, SD 0-5); I 0-2. A three-fifths majority (60) of the total Senate is required to waive the Budget Act. (Subsequently, the chair upheld the point of order, and the amendment fell.) March 13, 2008.

74. S Con Res 70. Fiscal 2009 Budget Resolution/Tax Credit Extension. Kyl, R-Ariz., amendment that would adjust the resolution to allow for the extension of recently expired tax credits through fiscal 2009, including those for research and development, combat pay, education, and alternative energy. Rejected 49-50: R 48-1; D 1-47 (ND 1-42, SD 0-5); I 0-2. March 13, 2008.

75. S Con Res 70. Fiscal 2009 Budget Resolution/Earmark Moratorium. DeMint, R-S.C., motion to waive the Budget Act with respect to the Conrad, D-N.D., point of order against the DeMint amendment that would allow for a one-year moratorium on earmarks and create a point of order against bills with earmarks for fiscal 2009. Motion rejected 29-71: R 23-26; D 5-44 (ND 5-39, SD 0-5); I 1-1. A three-fifths majority (60) of the total Senate is required to waive the Budget Act. (Subsequently, the chair upheld the point of order, and the amendment fell.) March 13, 2008.

76. S Con Res 70. Fiscal 2009 Budget Resolution/Estate Tax. Landrieu, D-La., amendment that would adjust the resolution to allow for the estate tax rate to be set at 35 percent and the exemption amount at $5 million. It would be offset by assuming the elimination of certain corporate tax provisions. Rejected 23-77: R 3-46; D 19-30 (ND 15-29, SD 4-1); I 1-1. March 13, 2008.

	70	71	72	73	74	75	76
ALABAMA							
Shelby	Y	Y	Y	Y	Y	N	N
Sessions	Y	Y	Y	Y	Y	Y	N
ALASKA							
Stevens	N	Y	N	N	Y	N	N
Murkowski	Y	Y	N	N	Y	N	N
ARIZONA							
McCain	?	?	?	Y	Y	Y	N
Kyl	Y	Y	Y	Y	Y	Y	N
ARKANSAS							
Lincoln	Y	N	N	N	N	N	Y
Pryor	Y	N	N	N	N	N	Y
CALIFORNIA							
Feinstein	Y	N	N	N	N	N	N
Boxer	Y	N	N	N	N	N	N
COLORADO							
Allard	Y	Y	Y	Y	Y	Y	N
Salazar	Y	N	N	N	N	N	N
CONNECTICUT							
Dodd	Y	N	N	N	N	N	N
Lieberman	Y	N	N	N	N	Y	Y
DELAWARE							
Biden	Y	N	N	N	N	N	N
Carper	Y	N	N	N	N	N	N
FLORIDA							
Nelson	Y	N	N	N	N	N	Y
Martinez	Y	Y	N	N	Y	Y	N
GEORGIA							
Chambliss	N	Y	Y	Y	Y	Y	N
Isakson	Y	Y	Y	Y	Y	Y	N
HAWAII							
Inouye	?	N	N	N	N	N	N
Akaka	Y	N	N	N	N	N	N
IDAHO							
Craig	Y	Y	Y	Y	Y	N	N
Crapo	Y	Y	Y	Y	Y	N	N
ILLINOIS							
Durbin	Y	N	N	N	N	N	N
Obama	Y	N	N	N	N	N	N
INDIANA							
Lugar	Y	Y	N	N	Y	N	N
Bayh	Y	N	Y	N	Y	Y	Y
IOWA							
Grassley	Y	Y	Y	Y	Y	Y	N
Harkin	Y	N	N	N	N	N	N
KANSAS							
Brownback	Y	Y	Y	Y	Y	N	N
Roberts	Y	Y	Y	N	Y	N	N
KENTUCKY							
McConnell	Y	Y	Y	Y	Y	Y	N
Bunning	Y	Y	N	N	Y	N	N
LOUISIANA							
Landrieu	Y	Y	N	N	N	N	Y
Vitter	Y	Y	Y	N	Y	N	N
MAINE							
Snowe	Y	N	Y	N	Y	N	Y
Collins	Y	N	Y	N	Y	N	Y
MARYLAND							
Mikulski	Y	N	N	N	N	N	N
Cardin	Y	N	N	N	N	N	N
MASSACHUSETTS							
Kennedy	Y	N	N	N	N	N	N
Kerry	Y	N	N	N	N	N	N
MICHIGAN							
Levin	Y	N	N	N	N	N	Y
Stabenow	Y	N	N	N	N	N	Y
MINNESOTA							
Coleman	Y	Y	Y	N	Y	N	N
Klobuchar	Y	N	N	N	N	N	Y
MISSISSIPPI							
Cochran	Y	N	N	?	Y	N	N
Wicker	Y	Y	Y	N	Y	N	N
MISSOURI							
Bond	Y	Y	Y	Y	Y	N	N
McCaskill	Y	N	N	N	N	Y	N
MONTANA							
Baucus	Y	N	N	N	N	N	Y
Tester	Y	N	N	N	N	N	Y
NEBRASKA							
Hagel	Y	Y	N	Y	Y	N	N
Nelson	Y	Y	Y	N	N	N	Y
NEVADA							
Reid	Y	Y	N	N	N	N	N
Ensign	Y	Y	Y	Y	Y	Y	N
NEW HAMPSHIRE							
Gregg	N	N	N	N	N	N	N
Sununu	Y	Y	Y	Y	Y	Y	N
NEW JERSEY							
Lautenberg	Y	N	N	N	N	N	N
Menendez	Y	N	N	N	N	N	N
NEW MEXICO							
Domenici	Y	Y	N	N	Y	N	N
Bingaman	Y	N	N	N	N	N	N
NEW YORK							
Schumer	Y	N	N	N	N	N	N
Clinton	Y	N	N	N	N	N	Y
NORTH CAROLINA							
Dole	Y	Y	Y	Y	Y	Y	N
Burr	Y	Y	Y	Y	Y	Y	N
NORTH DAKOTA							
Conrad	Y	N	N	N	N	N	Y
Dorgan	Y	N	N	N	N	N	N
OHIO							
Voinovich	Y	Y	N	Y	N	N	N
Brown	Y	N	N	N	N	N	N
OKLAHOMA							
Inhofe	N	Y	Y	Y	Y	Y	N
Coburn	N	Y	Y	Y	Y	Y	N
OREGON							
Wyden	Y	N	N	N	N	N	Y
Smith	Y	Y	Y	Y	Y	N	N
PENNSYLVANIA							
Specter	Y	N	N	N	N	N	N
Casey	Y	Y	N	N	N	N	N
RHODE ISLAND							
Reed	Y	N	N	N	N	N	N
Whitehouse	Y	N	N	N	N	N	N
SOUTH CAROLINA							
Graham	Y	Y	Y	Y	Y	Y	N
DeMint	Y	Y	Y	Y	Y	Y	N
SOUTH DAKOTA							
Johnson	Y	Y	N	N	N	N	N
Thune	Y	Y	Y	N	Y	Y	N
TENNESSEE							
Alexander	Y	Y	N	Y	Y	Y	N
Corker	Y	Y	N	Y	Y	Y	N
TEXAS							
Hutchison	Y	Y	N	Y	N	Y	N
Cornyn	Y	Y	Y	Y	Y	Y	N
UTAH							
Hatch	Y	Y	Y	Y	Y	N	N
Bennett	Y	Y	N	Y	N	N	N
VERMONT							
Leahy	?	N	N	N	N	N	N
Sanders	Y	N	N	N	N	N	N
VIRGINIA							
Warner	Y	Y	Y	N	N	N	N
Webb	Y	N	N	N	N	N	N
WASHINGTON							
Murray	Y	N	N	N	N	N	N
Cantwell	?	N	N	N	N	N	N
WEST VIRGINIA							
Byrd	?	?	?	?	?	N	N
Rockefeller	Y	N	N	N	N	N	N
WISCONSIN							
Kohl	Y	N	N	N	N	N	Y
Feingold	Y	N	N	N	N	Y	N
WYOMING							
Enzi	Y	Y	Y	N	Y	Y	N
Barrasso	Y	Y	Y	N	Y	Y	N

KEY — **Republicans** — Democrats — *Independents*

Y Voted for (yea)	X Paired against
# Paired for	− Announced against
+ Announced for	P Voted "present"
N Voted against (nay)	C Voted "present" to avoid possible conflict of interest
	? Did not vote or otherwise make a position known

ND Northern Democrats, SD Southern Democrats
Southern states: Ala., Ark., Fla., Ga., Ky., La., Miss., N.C., Okla., S.C., Tenn., Texas, Va.

S-16 2008 CQ ALMANAC | www.cq.com

IN THE SENATE | By Vote Number

77. S Con Res 70. Fiscal 2009 Budget Resolution/Estate Tax.
Kyl, R-Ariz., amendment that would adjust the resolution to allow for the estate tax rate to be set at 35 percent and the exemption amount at $5 million. Rejected 48-50: R 47-1; D 1-47 (ND 0-43, SD 1-4); I 0-2. March 13, 2008.

78. S Con Res 70. Fiscal 2009 Budget Resolution/Alternative Minimum Tax Exemption.
Grassley, R-Iowa, amendment that would adjust the resolution to allow for the exemption of the alternative minimum tax from pay-as-you-go rules, which require any tax cuts or new entitlement spending to be offset. Rejected 47-51: R 46-2; D 1-47 (ND 1-42, SD 0-5); I 0-2. March 13, 2008.

79. S Con Res 70. Fiscal 2009 Budget Resolution/Berkeley Funding.
DeMint, R-S.C., amendment that would adjust the resolution to allow for legislation that would rescind any earmarks for the city of Berkeley, Calif., and any entities located there and assume the transfer of those funds to the Marine Corps. Rejected 41-57: R 39-9; D 2-46 (ND 1-42, SD 1-4); I 0-2. March 14, 2008 (in the session that began and the Congressional Record dated March 13, 2008).

80. S Con Res 70. Fiscal 2009 Budget Resolution/SCHIP Coverage.
Boxer, D-Calif., amendment that would adjust the resolution to allow for legislation that would allow pregnant women to be eligible for coverage under the State Children's Health Insurance Program (SCHIP). Adopted 70-27: R 21-27; D 47-0 (ND 42-0, SD 5-0); I 2-0. March 14, 2008 (in the session that began and the Congressional Record dated March 13, 2008).

81. S Con Res 70. Fiscal 2009 Budget Resolution/SCHIP Coverage.
Allard, R-Colo., amendment would amend the definition of "targeted low-income child" in the Social Security Act to include the period from conception to birth and allow for eligibility under the State Children's Health Insurance Program (SCHIP). Rejected 46-52: R 44-4; D 2-46 (ND 2-41, SD 0-5); I 0-2. March 14, 2008 (in the session that began and the Congressional Record dated March 13, 2008).

82. S Con Res 70. Fiscal 2009 Budget Resolution/Health Insurance Tax Deduction.
DeMint, R-S.C., amendment that would create a deficit-neutral reserve fund to pay for the impact of any legislation that would provide an above-the-line federal income tax deduction for individuals who do not receive health insurance through employers and who purchase insurance. Rejected 45-51: R 45-1; D 0-48 (ND 0-43, SD 0-5); I 0-2. March 14, 2008 (in the session that began and the Congressional Record dated March 13, 2008).

83. S Con Res 70. Fiscal 2009 Budget Resolution/International Affairs Funding.
Biden, D-Del., amendment that would adjust the resolution to allow for the full funding of the president's international affairs budget proposal, with assumed offsets to various programs. Adopted 73-23: R 24-22; D 47-1 (ND 42-1, SD 5-0); I 2-0. March 14, 2008 (in the session that began and the Congressional Record dated March 13, 2008).

	77	78	79	80	81	82	83
ALABAMA							
Shelby	Y	Y	Y	N	Y	Y	N
Sessions	Y	Y	Y	N	Y	Y	N
ALASKA							
Stevens	Y	Y	N	Y	Y	Y	N
Murkowski	Y	Y	N	Y	N	Y	Y
ARIZONA							
McCain	Y	Y	Y	Y	?	?	
Kyl	Y	Y	Y	N	Y	Y	N
ARKANSAS							
Lincoln	Y	N	N	Y	N	N	Y
Pryor	N	N	N	Y	N	N	Y
CALIFORNIA							
Feinstein	N	N	N	Y	N	N	Y
Boxer	N	N	N	Y	N	N	Y
COLORADO							
Allard	Y	Y	Y	N	Y	Y	N
Salazar	N	N	N	Y	N	N	Y
CONNECTICUT							
Dodd	N	N	N	Y	N	N	Y
Lieberman	N	N	N	Y	N	N	Y
DELAWARE							
Biden	N	N	N	Y	N	N	Y
Carper	N	N	N	Y	N	N	Y
FLORIDA							
Nelson	N	N	N	Y	N	N	Y
Martinez	Y	Y	Y	N	Y	Y	Y
GEORGIA							
Chambliss	Y	Y	Y	Y	Y	Y	Y
Isakson	Y	Y	Y	Y	Y	Y	Y
HAWAII							
Inouye	N	N	N	Y	N	N	Y
Akaka	N	N	N	Y	N	N	Y
IDAHO							
Craig	Y	Y	Y	N	Y	Y	N
Crapo	Y	Y	Y	N	Y	Y	N
ILLINOIS							
Durbin	N	N	N	Y	N	N	Y
Obama	N	N	N	Y	N	N	Y
INDIANA							
Lugar	Y	Y	N	Y	Y	Y	Y
Bayh	N	Y	Y	Y	N	N	Y
IOWA							
Grassley	Y	Y	Y	Y	Y	Y	N
Harkin	N	N	N	Y	N	N	Y
KANSAS							
Brownback	Y	Y	Y	N	Y	Y	Y
Roberts	Y	Y	Y	N	Y	Y	Y
KENTUCKY							
McConnell	Y	Y	Y	Y	Y	Y	Y
Bunning	Y	Y	Y	N	Y	Y	N
LOUISIANA							
Landrieu	N	Y	Y	Y	N	N	Y
Vitter	Y	Y	Y	N	Y	Y	N
MAINE							
Snowe	Y	N	Y	Y	N	N	Y
Collins	Y	Y	Y	Y	N	Y	Y
MARYLAND							
Mikulski	N	N	N	?	N	N	Y
Cardin	N	N	N	Y	N	N	Y
MASSACHUSETTS							
Kennedy	N	N	N	Y	N	N	Y
Kerry	N	N	N	Y	N	N	Y
MICHIGAN							
Levin	N	N	N	Y	N	N	Y
Stabenow	N	N	N	Y	N	N	Y
MINNESOTA							
Coleman	Y	Y	Y	Y	Y	Y	Y
Klobuchar	N	N	N	Y	N	N	Y
MISSISSIPPI							
Cochran	Y	Y	N	N	Y	Y	N
Wicker	Y	Y	Y	N	Y	Y	N
MISSOURI							
Bond	Y	Y	Y	Y	Y	?	?
McCaskill	N	N	N	Y	N	N	Y

	77	78	79	80	81	82	83
MONTANA							
Baucus	N	N	N	Y	N	N	Y
Tester	N	N	N	Y	N	N	Y
NEBRASKA							
Hagel	Y	Y	N	N	Y	Y	Y
Nelson	N	N	N	Y	N	Y	Y
NEVADA							
Reid	N	N	N	Y	N	N	Y
Ensign	?	Y	Y	N	Y	Y	N
NEW HAMPSHIRE							
Gregg	Y	Y	Y	N	Y	Y	Y
Sununu	Y	Y	Y	N	Y	Y	Y
NEW JERSEY							
Lautenberg	N	N	N	Y	N	N	Y
Menendez	N	N	N	Y	N	N	Y
NEW MEXICO							
Domenici	Y	?	?	?	?	?	?
Bingaman	N	N	N	Y	N	N	Y
NEW YORK							
Schumer	N	N	N	Y	N	N	Y
Clinton	N	N	N	Y	N	N	Y
NORTH CAROLINA							
Dole	Y	Y	Y	Y	Y	Y	Y
Burr	Y	Y	Y	N	Y	Y	Y
NORTH DAKOTA							
Conrad	N	N	N	Y	N	N	Y
Dorgan	N	N	N	Y	N	N	Y
OHIO							
Voinovich	N	N	N	Y	Y	Y	Y
Brown	N	N	N	Y	N	N	Y
OKLAHOMA							
Inhofe	Y	Y	Y	N	Y	Y	N
Coburn	Y	Y	Y	N	Y	Y	N
OREGON							
Wyden	N	N	N	Y	N	N	Y
Smith	Y	Y	Y	Y	Y	Y	Y
PENNSYLVANIA							
Specter	Y	Y	N	Y	Y	N	Y
Casey	N	N	N	Y	Y	N	Y
RHODE ISLAND							
Reed	N	N	N	Y	N	N	Y
Whitehouse	N	N	N	Y	N	N	Y
SOUTH CAROLINA							
Graham	Y	Y	Y	N	Y	Y	N
DeMint	Y	Y	Y	N	Y	Y	N
SOUTH DAKOTA							
Johnson	N	N	N	Y	N	N	Y
Thune	Y	Y	Y	N	Y	Y	N
TENNESSEE							
Alexander	Y	Y	Y	Y	Y	Y	Y
Corker	Y	Y	Y	Y	Y	Y	Y
TEXAS							
Hutchison	Y	Y	Y	Y	Y	Y	N
Cornyn	Y	Y	Y	Y	Y	Y	N
UTAH							
Hatch	Y	Y	Y	N	Y	Y	N
Bennett	Y	Y	N	Y	Y	Y	N
VERMONT							
Leahy	N	N	N	Y	N	N	Y
Sanders	N	N	N	Y	N	N	Y
VIRGINIA							
Warner	Y	Y	N	Y	Y	N	Y
Webb	N	N	N	Y	N	N	Y
WASHINGTON							
Murray	N	N	N	Y	N	N	Y
Cantwell	N	N	N	Y	N	N	Y
WEST VIRGINIA							
Byrd	?	?	?	?	?	?	?
Rockefeller	N	N	N	Y	N	N	Y
WISCONSIN							
Kohl	N	N	N	Y	N	N	Y
Feingold	N	N	N	Y	N	N	Y
WYOMING							
Enzi	Y	Y	Y	N	Y	Y	N
Barrasso	Y	Y	Y	N	Y	Y	N

KEY   **Republicans**   Democrats   *Independents*

Y Voted for (yea)	X Paired against	C Voted "present" to avoid possible conflict of interest
# Paired for	– Announced against	
+ Announced for	P Voted "present"	? Did not vote or otherwise make a position known
N Voted against (nay)		

ND Northern Democrats, SD Southern Democrats
Southern states: Ala., Ark., Fla., Ga., Ky., La., Miss., N.C., Okla., S.C., Tenn., Texas, Va.

IN THE SENATE | By Vote Number

84. **S Con Res 70. Fiscal 2009 Budget Resolution/Prescription Drug Importation.** Vitter, R-La., amendment that would express the sense of the Senate that leaders should bring to the floor for debate legislation that would legalize the importation of prescription drugs from highly industrialized countries. Adopted 73-23: R 26-20; D 45-3 (ND 40-3, SD 5-0); I 2-0. March 14, 2008 (in the session that began and the Congressional Record dated March 13, 2008).

85. **S Con Res 70. Fiscal 2009 Budget Resolution/Adoption.** Adoption of the concurrent resolution that would set broad spending and revenue targets over the next five years. The resolution would allow up to $1 trillion in discretionary spending for 2009. It would allow for a $35 billion economic stimulus package and would assume a one-year adjustment to prevent additional taxpayers from paying the alternative minimum tax. As amended, the resolution would allow for the extension of certain 2001 and 2003 tax cuts, including the 10 percent tax bracket and the child tax credit. Adopted 51-44: R 2-43; D 47-1 (ND 42-1, SD 5-0); I 2-0. March 14, 2008 (in the session that began and the Congressional Record dated March 13, 2008).

86. **HR 3221. Renewable Energy/Cloture.** Motion to invoke cloture (thus limiting debate) on the motion to proceed to the bill that would set new energy efficiency standards and create alternative fuel programs. The bill is intended to serve as the vehicle for a foreclosure relief measure, which would change bankruptcy law to allow judges to alter some mortgage terms. It also would include provisions intended to alleviate the housing crisis. Motion agreed to 94-1: R 47-1; D 45-0 (ND 40-0, SD 5-0); I 2-0. Three-fifths of the total Senate (60) is required to invoke cloture. April 1, 2008.

87. **S Res 501. Honor Troops in Iraq and Afghanistan/Adoption.** Adoption of the resolution that would honor the sacrifice of the members of the U.S. armed forces who have been killed in Iraq and Afghanistan. Adopted 95-0: R 47-0; D 46-0 (ND 41-0, SD 5-0); I 2-0. April 3, 2008.

	84	85	86	87		84	85	86	87
ALABAMA					**MONTANA**				
Shelby	Y	N	Y	Y	Baucus	Y	Y	Y	Y
Sessions	Y	N	Y	Y	Tester	Y	Y	Y	Y
ALASKA					**NEBRASKA**				
Stevens	N	X	Y	Y	Hagel	Y	N	Y	Y
Murkowski	N	N	Y	Y	Nelson	Y	Y	Y	Y
ARIZONA					**NEVADA**				
McCain	?	?	?	?	Reid	Y	Y	Y	Y
Kyl	N	N	Y	Y	Ensign	N	N	Y	Y
ARKANSAS					**NEW HAMPSHIRE**				
Lincoln	Y	Y	Y	Y	Gregg	N	N	Y	Y
Pryor	Y	Y	Y	Y	Sununu	N	N	Y	Y
CALIFORNIA					**NEW JERSEY**				
Feinstein	Y	Y	Y	Y	Lautenberg	N	Y	?	Y
Boxer	Y	Y	Y	Y	Menendez	N	Y	Y	Y
COLORADO					**NEW MEXICO**				
Allard	Y	N	Y	Y	Domenici	?	?	Y	Y
Salazar	Y	Y	Y	Y	Bingaman	Y	Y	Y	Y
CONNECTICUT					**NEW YORK**				
Dodd	Y	Y	Y	Y	Schumer	Y	Y	Y	Y
Lieberman	Y	Y	Y	Y	Clinton	Y	Y	?	?
DELAWARE					**NORTH CAROLINA**				
Biden	Y	Y	Y	Y	Dole	N	N	Y	Y
Carper	N	Y	Y	Y	Burr	N	N	Y	Y
FLORIDA					**NORTH DAKOTA**				
Nelson	Y	Y	Y	Y	Conrad	Y	Y	Y	Y
Martinez	Y	N	Y	Y	Dorgan	Y	Y	Y	Y
GEORGIA					**OHIO**				
Chambliss	Y	N	Y	+	Voinovich	Y	N	Y	Y
Isakson	N	N	Y	Y	Brown	Y	Y	Y	Y
HAWAII					**OKLAHOMA**				
Inouye	Y	Y	?	?	Inhofe	Y	N	Y	Y
Akaka	Y	Y	Y	Y	Coburn	Y	N	Y	Y
IDAHO					**OREGON**				
Craig	Y	N	Y	Y	Wyden	Y	Y	Y	Y
Crapo	N	N	Y	Y	Smith	Y	N	Y	Y
ILLINOIS					**PENNSYLVANIA**				
Durbin	Y	Y	Y	Y	Specter	Y	N	Y	Y
Obama	Y	Y	?	?	Casey	Y	Y	Y	Y
INDIANA					**RHODE ISLAND**				
Lugar	Y	N	Y	Y	Reed	Y	Y	Y	Y
Bayh	Y	N	Y	Y	Whitehouse	Y	Y	Y	Y
IOWA					**SOUTH CAROLINA**				
Grassley	Y	N	Y	Y	Graham	Y	N	Y	Y
Harkin	Y	Y	Y	Y	DeMint	Y	N	Y	Y
KANSAS					**SOUTH DAKOTA**				
Brownback	Y	N	Y	Y	Johnson	Y	Y	Y	Y
Roberts	Y	N	Y	Y	Thune	Y	N	Y	Y
KENTUCKY					**TENNESSEE**				
McConnell	N	N	Y	Y	Alexander	Y	N	Y	Y
Bunning	N	N	N	Y	Corker	Y	N	Y	Y
LOUISIANA					**TEXAS**				
Landrieu	Y	Y	Y	Y	Hutchison	N	N	Y	Y
Vitter	Y	N	Y	Y	Cornyn	N	N	Y	Y
MAINE					**UTAH**				
Snowe	Y	Y	Y	Y	Hatch	N	N	Y	Y
Collins	Y	Y	Y	Y	Bennett	N	N	Y	Y
MARYLAND					**VERMONT**				
Mikulski	Y	Y	Y	Y	Leahy	Y	Y	Y	Y
Cardin	Y	Y	Y	Y	*Sanders*	Y	Y	Y	Y
MASSACHUSETTS					**VIRGINIA**				
Kennedy	Y	Y	Y	Y	Warner	N	N	Y	Y
Kerry	Y	Y	Y	Y	Webb	Y	Y	Y	Y
MICHIGAN					**WASHINGTON**				
Levin	Y	Y	Y	Y	Murray	Y	Y	Y	Y
Stabenow	Y	Y	Y	Y	Cantwell	Y	Y	Y	Y
MINNESOTA					**WEST VIRGINIA**				
Coleman	Y	N	Y	Y	Byrd	?	#	Y	Y
Klobuchar	Y	Y	Y	Y	Rockefeller	Y	Y	Y	Y
MISSISSIPPI					**WISCONSIN**				
Cochran	N	N	Y	Y	Kohl	Y	Y	Y	Y
Wicker	Y	N	Y	Y	Feingold	Y	Y	Y	Y
MISSOURI					**WYOMING**				
Bond	?	?	Y	Y	Enzi	N	N	Y	Y
McCaskill	Y	Y	Y	Y	Barrasso	N	N	Y	Y

KEY	**Republicans**	Democrats	*Independents*	
Y	Voted for (yea)	X Paired against	C Voted "present" to avoid possible conflict of interest
#	Paired for	– Announced against	
+	Announced for	P Voted "present"	? Did not vote or otherwise make a position known
N	Voted against (nay)		

ND Northern Democrats, SD Southern Democrats
Southern states: Ala., Ark., Fla., Ga., Ky., La., Miss., N.C., Okla., S.C., Tenn., Texas, Va.

IN THE SENATE | By Vote Number

88. **HR 3221. Renewable Energy/Mortgage Relief.** Durbin, D-Ill., motion to table (kill) the Durbin amendment to the Dodd, D-Conn., substitute. The Durbin amendment would allow bankruptcy judges to modify the terms of subprime and non-traditional mortgages, including reducing the outstanding principal, during bankruptcy proceedings. The Dodd amendment would substitute mortgage relief provisions, including tax breaks for those buying foreclosed homes and for homebuilders, an overhaul of the Federal Housing Administration's mortgage insurance program, $4 billion in Community Development Block Grants to purchase and rehabilitate foreclosed properties, and other provisions to alleviate the housing crisis. Motion agreed to 58-36: R 47-0; D 10-35 (ND 7-33, SD 3-2); I 1-1. A "yea" was a vote in support of the president's position. April 3, 2008.

89. **HR 3221. Renewable Energy/Mortgage Relief.** Murray, D-Wash., motion to waive the Budget Act with respect to the Kyl, R-Ariz., point of order against the Murray amendment to the Dodd, D-Conn., substitute. The Murray amendment would increase by $100 million the amount provided for housing counseling. Motion rejected 44-40: R 7-38; D 36-1 (ND 32-1, SD 4-0); I 1-1. A three-fifths majority (60) of the total Senate is required to waive the Budget Act. (Subsequently, the chair upheld the point of order, and the amendment fell.) April 3, 2008.

90. **HR 3221. Renewable Energy/Mortgage Relief.** Kyl, R-Ariz., motion to waive the Budget Act with respect to the Baucus, D-Mont., point of order against the Kyl amendment to the Dodd, D-Conn., substitute. The Kyl amendment would index for inflation the capital gains tax exclusion, which is $250,000 for an individual and $500,000 for married couples filing jointly, for selling a primary residence. Motion rejected 41-44: R 40-5; D 1-37 (ND 1-33, SD 0-4); I 0-2. A three-fifths majority (60) of the total Senate is required to waive the Budget Act. (Subsequently, the chair upheld the point of order, and the amendment fell.) April 3, 2008.

	88	89	90			88	89	90
ALABAMA					**MONTANA**			
Shelby	Y	N	Y		Baucus	Y	Y	N
Sessions	Y	N	Y		Tester	Y	Y	N
ALASKA					**NEBRASKA**			
Stevens	Y	N	Y		Hagel	Y	N	Y
Murkowski	Y	N	Y		Nelson	Y	Y	N
ARIZONA					**NEVADA**			
McCain	?	?	?		Reid	N	Y	N
Kyl	Y	N	Y		**Ensign**	Y	N	Y
ARKANSAS					**NEW HAMPSHIRE**			
Lincoln	Y	Y	N		**Gregg**	Y	N	Y
Pryor	Y	Y	N		**Sununu**	Y	N	Y
CALIFORNIA					**NEW JERSEY**			
Feinstein	N	Y	N		Lautenberg	N	?	?
Boxer	?	?	?		Menendez	N	Y	N
COLORADO					**NEW MEXICO**			
Allard	Y	N	Y		**Domenici**	Y	?	?
Salazar	N	Y	N		Bingaman	N	?	N
CONNECTICUT					**NEW YORK**			
Dodd	N	N	N		Schumer	N	Y	N
Lieberman	Y	N	N		Clinton	?	?	?
DELAWARE					**NORTH CAROLINA**			
Biden	N	?	?		**Dole**	Y	N	Y
Carper	Y	Y	N		**Burr**	Y	N	Y
FLORIDA					**NORTH DAKOTA**			
Nelson	N	Y	N		Conrad	N	?	?
Martinez	Y	N	Y		Dorgan	N	?	?
GEORGIA					**OHIO**			
Chambliss	Y	N	Y		**Voinovich**	Y	Y	N
Isakson	Y	N	Y		Brown	N	Y	N
HAWAII					**OKLAHOMA**			
Inouye	?	?	?		**Inhofe**	Y	N	Y
Akaka	N	Y	N		**Coburn**	Y	N	Y
IDAHO					**OREGON**			
Craig	Y	N	Y		Wyden	N	Y	N
Crapo	Y	?	?		**Smith**	Y	Y	Y
ILLINOIS					**PENNSYLVANIA**			
Durbin	N	Y	N		**Specter**	Y	Y	Y
Obama	?	?	?		Casey	N	Y	N
INDIANA					**RHODE ISLAND**			
Lugar	Y	N	Y		Reed	N	Y	N
Bayh	N	Y	Y		Whitehouse	N	Y	N
IOWA					**SOUTH CAROLINA**			
Grassley	Y	N	Y		**Graham**	Y	N	Y
Harkin	N	Y	N		**DeMint**	Y	N	Y
KANSAS					**SOUTH DAKOTA**			
Brownback	Y	N	Y		Johnson	Y	Y	N
Roberts	Y	N	Y		**Thune**	Y	N	Y
KENTUCKY					**TENNESSEE**			
McConnell	Y	N	Y		**Alexander**	Y	N	Y
Bunning	Y	–	+		**Corker**	Y	N	N
LOUISIANA					**TEXAS**			
Landrieu	Y	Y	N		**Hutchison**	Y	N	Y
Vitter	Y	N	Y		**Cornyn**	Y	N	Y
MAINE					**UTAH**			
Snowe	Y	Y	N		**Hatch**	Y	N	Y
Collins	Y	Y	N		**Bennett**	Y	N	Y
MARYLAND					**VERMONT**			
Mikulski	N	Y	N		Leahy	N	Y	N
Cardin	N	Y	N		*Sanders*	N	Y	N
MASSACHUSETTS					**VIRGINIA**			
Kennedy	N	?	?		**Warner**	Y	N	N
Kerry	N	Y	N		Webb	N	?	?
MICHIGAN					**WASHINGTON**			
Levin	N	Y	N		Murray	N	Y	N
Stabenow	N	Y	N		Cantwell	N	Y	N
MINNESOTA					**WEST VIRGINIA**			
Coleman	Y	Y	Y		Byrd	Y	?	?
Klobuchar	N	Y	N		Rockefeller	N	Y	N
MISSISSIPPI					**WISCONSIN**			
Cochran	Y	N	Y		Kohl	N	Y	N
Wicker	Y	N	Y		Feingold	N	Y	N
MISSOURI					**WYOMING**			
Bond	?	Y	Y		**Enzi**	Y	N	Y
McCaskill	Y	Y	N		**Barrasso**	Y	N	Y

KEY **Republicans** Democrats *Independents*

Y Voted for (yea)	**X** Paired against	**C** Voted "present" to avoid possible conflict of interest
# Paired for	**–** Announced against	
+ Announced for	**P** Voted "present"	**?** Did not vote or otherwise make a position known
N Voted against (nay)		

ND Northern Democrats, SD Southern Democrats
Southern states: Ala., Ark., Fla., Ga., Ky., La., Miss., N.C., Okla., S.C., Tenn., Texas, Va.

IN THE SENATE | By Vote Number

91. **HR 3221. Renewable Energy–Mortgage Relief/Bonus Depreciation.** Voinovich, R-Ohio, amendment to the Dodd, D-Conn., substitute amendment. The Voinovich amendment would allow companies operating in the red to use accumulated alternative minimum tax and research and development credits, instead of bonus depreciation deductions, if they use the money to expand their U.S operations. The bonus depreciation included in the bill would not be available for companies that have no income against which to deduct their expenses. The Dodd amendment would substitute mortgage relief provisions, including tax breaks for homebuilders and those buying foreclosed homes, an overhaul of the Federal Housing Administration (FHA) mortgage insurance program, and $4 billion in Community Development Block Grants to purchase and rehabilitate foreclosed properties. Adopted 76-2: R 37-2; D 38-0 (ND 33-0, SD 5-0); I 1-0. April 4, 2008.

92. **HR 3221. Renewable Energy–Mortgage Relief/Casualty Loss Deduction.** Landrieu, D-La., motion to waive the 2008 budget resolution with respect to the Corker, R-Tenn., point of order against the Landrieu amendment to the Dodd, D-Conn., substitute. The Landrieu amendment would allow taxpayers in Louisiana and Mississippi who took a hurricane-related casualty loss deduction in 2005 and received a grant to cover uninsured property losses in 2007 to amend their 2005 tax returns to disallow the casualty loss deduction without penalties. Motion agreed to 74-5: R 35-5; D 38-0 (ND 33-0, SD 5-0); I 1-0. A three-fifths majority (60) of the total Senate is required to waive the budget resolution. (Subsequently, the Landrieu amendment was adopted by voice vote.) April 4, 2008.

93. **HR 3221. Renewable Energy–Mortgage Relief/Cloture.** Motion to invoke cloture (thus limiting debate) on the Dodd, D-Conn., substitute amendment that would provide tax breaks for homebuilders and those buying foreclosed homes, an overhaul of the FHA mortgage insurance program, and $4 billion in Community Development Block Grants to purchase and rehabilitate foreclosed properties. Motion agreed to 92-6: R 41-6; D 49-0 (ND 44-0, SD 5-0); I 2-0. Three-fifths of the total Senate (60) is required to invoke cloture. April 8, 2008.

94. **HR 3221. Renewable Energy–Mortgage Relief/Energy Tax Credits.** Alexander, R-Tenn., amendment to the Ensign, R-Nev., amendment to the Dodd, D-Conn., substitute. The Alexander amendment would extend from one year to two years the renewable-energy production tax credit included in the Ensign amendment, which would extend existing renewable-energy tax breaks totaling $6 billion for producing energy from wind, sunlight and other renewable sources. The Alexander amendment would be offset by reducing the credit rate for wind energy. Rejected 15-79: R 14-33; D 1-44 (ND 1-39, SD 0-5); I 0-2. April 10, 2008.

	91	92	93	94
ALABAMA				
Shelby	Y	Y	Y	Y
Sessions	Y	Y	Y	Y
ALASKA				
Stevens	Y	Y	Y	N
Murkowski	Y	Y	Y	N
ARIZONA				
McCain	?	?	Y	?
Kyl	Y	N	N	Y
ARKANSAS				
Lincoln	Y	Y	Y	N
Pryor	Y	Y	Y	N
CALIFORNIA				
Feinstein	Y	Y	Y	N
Boxer	?	?	Y	N
COLORADO				
Allard	?	?	?	N
Salazar	Y	Y	Y	N
CONNECTICUT				
Dodd	Y	Y	Y	N
Lieberman	?	?	Y	N
DELAWARE				
Biden	Y	Y	Y	N
Carper	Y	Y	Y	N
FLORIDA				
Nelson	Y	Y	Y	N
Martinez	Y	Y	Y	N
GEORGIA				
Chambliss	Y	Y	Y	Y
Isakson	Y	Y	Y	Y
HAWAII				
Inouye	?	?	Y	N
Akaka	Y	Y	Y	N
IDAHO				
Craig	Y	Y	Y	N
Crapo	Y	Y	Y	N
ILLINOIS				
Durbin	Y	Y	Y	N
Obama	?	?	Y	?
INDIANA				
Lugar	Y	Y	Y	N
Bayh	Y	Y	Y	N
IOWA				
Grassley	Y	Y	Y	N
Harkin	Y	Y	Y	?
KANSAS				
Brownback	Y	Y	Y	N
Roberts	Y	Y	Y	N
KENTUCKY				
McConnell	Y	Y	Y	Y
Bunning	–	–	N	Y
LOUISIANA				
Landrieu	Y	Y	Y	N
Vitter	Y	Y	Y	N
MAINE				
Snowe	Y	Y	Y	N
Collins	Y	Y	Y	N
MARYLAND				
Mikulski	Y	Y	Y	N
Cardin	Y	Y	Y	N
MASSACHUSETTS				
Kennedy	?	?	Y	N
Kerry	Y	Y	Y	N
MICHIGAN				
Levin	Y	Y	Y	N
Stabenow	Y	Y	Y	N
MINNESOTA				
Coleman	Y	Y	Y	N
Klobuchar	Y	Y	Y	N
MISSISSIPPI				
Cochran	?	?	Y	N
Wicker	Y	Y	Y	Y
MISSOURI				
Bond	Y	Y	Y	N
McCaskill	Y	Y	Y	N
MONTANA				
Baucus	Y	Y	Y	N
Tester	?	?	Y	N
NEBRASKA				
Hagel	Y	Y	Y	N
Nelson	Y	Y	Y	N
NEVADA				
Reid	Y	Y	Y	N
Ensign	Y	Y	Y	N
NEW HAMPSHIRE				
Gregg	N	N	Y	Y
Sununu	Y	Y	Y	N
NEW JERSEY				
Lautenberg	?	?	Y	N
Menendez	Y	Y	Y	–
NEW MEXICO				
Domenici	Y	Y	Y	N
Bingaman	Y	Y	Y	N
NEW YORK				
Schumer	Y	Y	Y	N
Clinton	?	?	Y	?
NORTH CAROLINA				
Dole	Y	Y	?	?
Burr	Y	Y	Y	N
NORTH DAKOTA				
Conrad	?	?	Y	N
Dorgan	?	?	Y	N
OHIO				
Voinovich	Y	Y	Y	Y
Brown	Y	Y	Y	N
OKLAHOMA				
Inhofe	?	?	N	N
Coburn	Y	Y	N	N
OREGON				
Wyden	Y	Y	Y	N
Smith	Y	Y	Y	N
PENNSYLVANIA				
Specter	?	?	N	N
Casey	Y	Y	Y	N
RHODE ISLAND				
Reed	Y	Y	Y	N
Whitehouse	Y	Y	Y	N
SOUTH CAROLINA				
Graham	Y	Y	Y	N
DeMint	Y	N	N	N
SOUTH DAKOTA				
Johnson	Y	Y	Y	N
Thune	Y	Y	Y	N
TENNESSEE				
Alexander	Y	Y	Y	N
Corker	N	N	Y	N
TEXAS				
Hutchison	Y	Y	Y	N
Cornyn	+	?	Y	N
UTAH				
Hatch	+	+	Y	N
Bennett	?	?	Y	Y
VERMONT				
Leahy	Y	Y	Y	N
Sanders	Y	Y	Y	N
VIRGINIA				
Warner	Y	Y	Y	N
Webb	Y	Y	Y	N
WASHINGTON				
Murray	Y	Y	Y	N
Cantwell	Y	Y	Y	N
WEST VIRGINIA				
Byrd	?	?	Y	Y
Rockefeller	?	?	Y	N
WISCONSIN				
Kohl	Y	Y	Y	N
Feingold	Y	Y	Y	N
WYOMING				
Enzi	?	?	Y	N
Barrasso	Y	N	Y	N

KEY   **Republicans**   Democrats   *Independents*

Y Voted for (yea)	X Paired against	C Voted "present" to avoid possible conflict of interest
# Paired for	– Announced against	
+ Announced for	P Voted "present"	? Did not vote or otherwise make a position known
N Voted against (nay)		

ND Northern Democrats, SD Southern Democrats
Southern states: Ala., Ark., Fla., Ga., Ky., La., Miss., N.C., Okla., S.C., Tenn., Texas, Va.

IN THE SENATE | By Vote Number

95. HR 3221. Renewable Energy-Mortgage Relief/Energy Tax Credits.
Ensign, R-Nev., amendment to the Dodd, D-Conn., substitute. The Ensign amendment would extend existing renewable energy tax breaks totaling $6 billion for producing energy from wind, sunlight and other renewable sources, including a one-year extension of the renewable energy production tax credit. The Dodd amendment would substitute mortgage relief provisions, including tax breaks for homebuilders and those buying foreclosed homes, an overhaul of the Federal Housing Administration (FHA) mortgage insurance program, and $4 billion in Community Development Block Grants to purchase and rehabilitate foreclosed properties. Adopted 88-8: R 42-5; D 44-3 (ND 39-3, SD 5-0); I 2-0. April 10, 2008.

96. HR 3221. Mortgage Relief/Passage.
Passage of the bill that would provide tax breaks for homebuilders and those buying foreclosed homes, overhaul the FHA mortgage insurance program, and authorize $4 billion in Community Development Block Grants to purchase and rehabilitate foreclosed properties. The bill would authorize $100 million for expanded counseling for mortgage borrowers at risk of default. As amended, the bill would extend existing renewable energy tax breaks totaling $6 billion for producing energy from wind, sunlight and other renewable sources, including a one-year extension of the renewable energy production tax credit. Passed 84-12: R 35-12; D 47-0 (ND 42-0, SD 5-0); I 2-0. (Before passage, the Senate adopted by voice vote the Dodd, D-Conn., substitute, which replaced the text of the energy bill with the mortgage relief provisions.) A "nay" was a vote in support of the president's position. April 10, 2008.

97. S 2739. Omnibus Public Lands/Report on Land Ownership.
Coburn, R-Okla., amendment that would require the director of the Office of Management and Budget to post on a public Web site an annual report on the amount of land owned by the federal government; the per-agency maintenance costs; a detailed summary of the number, operating cost, and replacement value of unused or vacant assets; and the estimated costs of the maintenance backlog of each agency. Rejected 30-63: R 28-19; D 2-42 (ND 2-37, SD 0-5); I 0-2. April 10, 2008.

98. S 2739. Omnibus Public Lands/State Property.
Coburn, R-Okla., amendment that would prohibit the assumption of control by the Energy and Interior departments, and the Forest Service of any state property unless local citizens approve the assumption by referendum. The referendum would not apply if the president declares a national emergency or if an exchange is between a private landowner and the government. The approval would expire after 10 years and could be renewed. Rejected 19-76: R 19-28; D 0-46 (ND 0-41, SD 0-5); I 0-2. April 10, 2008.

	95	96	97	98			95	96	97	98
ALABAMA						**MONTANA**				
Shelby	Y	Y	Y	Y		Baucus	Y	Y	N	N
Sessions	N	Y	Y	N		Tester	Y	Y	N	N
ALASKA						**NEBRASKA**				
Stevens	Y	Y	N	N		Hagel	Y	N	N	N
Murkowski	Y	Y	N	N		Nelson	Y	Y	N	N
ARIZONA						**NEVADA**				
McCain	?	?	?	?		Reid	Y	Y	N	N
Kyl	N	N	Y	N		Ensign	Y	Y	Y	Y
ARKANSAS						**NEW HAMPSHIRE**				
Lincoln	Y	Y	N	N		Gregg	Y	N	N	N
Pryor	Y	Y	N	N		Sununu	Y	Y	Y	N
CALIFORNIA						**NEW JERSEY**				
Feinstein	Y	Y	N	N		Lautenberg	Y	Y	N	N
Boxer	Y	Y	N	N		Menendez	Y	Y	N	N
COLORADO						**NEW MEXICO**				
Allard	Y	Y	Y	N		Domenici	Y	Y	N	N
Salazar	Y	Y	N	N		Bingaman	Y	Y	N	N
CONNECTICUT						**NEW YORK**				
Dodd	N	Y	?	N		Schumer	Y	Y	N	N
Lieberman	Y	Y	N	N		Clinton	?	?	?	?
DELAWARE						**NORTH CAROLINA**				
Biden	Y	Y	N	N		Dole	+	+	?	?
Carper	N	Y	N	N		Burr	Y	Y	Y	Y
FLORIDA						**NORTH DAKOTA**				
Nelson	Y	Y	N	N		Conrad	Y	Y	N	N
Martinez	Y	Y	N	N		Dorgan	Y	Y	N	N
GEORGIA						**OHIO**				
Chambliss	Y	Y	Y	Y		Voinovich	N	Y	N	N
Isakson	Y	Y	Y	Y		Brown	Y	Y	N	N
HAWAII						**OKLAHOMA**				
Inouye	Y	Y	N	N		Inhofe	Y	N	Y	Y
Akaka	Y	Y	N	N		Coburn	Y	N	Y	Y
IDAHO						**OREGON**				
Craig	Y	Y	N	N		Wyden	Y	Y	N	N
Crapo	Y	N	N	N		Smith	Y	Y	N	N
ILLINOIS						**PENNSYLVANIA**				
Durbin	Y	Y	N	N		Specter	Y	Y	Y	N
Obama	?	?	?	?		Casey	Y	Y	N	N
INDIANA						**RHODE ISLAND**				
Lugar	Y	Y	Y	N		Reed	Y	Y	N	N
Bayh	Y	Y	Y	N		Whitehouse	Y	Y	N	N
IOWA						**SOUTH CAROLINA**				
Grassley	Y	Y	Y	Y		Graham	Y	Y	Y	Y
Harkin	Y	Y	N	N		DeMint	Y	N	Y	Y
KANSAS						**SOUTH DAKOTA**				
Brownback	Y	Y	Y	Y		Johnson	Y	Y	N	N
Roberts	Y	Y	N	Y		Thune	Y	Y	Y	Y
KENTUCKY						**TENNESSEE**				
McConnell	Y	Y	Y	Y		Alexander	N	Y	N	N
Bunning	N	N	N	N		Corker	Y	N	N	N
LOUISIANA						**TEXAS**				
Landrieu	Y	Y	N	N		Hutchison	Y	Y	Y	N
Vitter	Y	Y	Y	N		Cornyn	Y	Y	Y	N
MAINE						**UTAH**				
Snowe	Y	Y	N	N		Hatch	Y	Y	N	N
Collins	Y	Y	Y	N		Bennett	Y	Y	N	N
MARYLAND						**VERMONT**				
Mikulski	Y	Y	N	N		Leahy	Y	Y	N	N
Cardin	Y	Y	N	N		Sanders	Y	Y	N	N
MASSACHUSETTS						**VIRGINIA**				
Kennedy	Y	Y	?	?		Warner	Y	N	N	N
Kerry	Y	Y	N	N		Webb	Y	Y	N	N
MICHIGAN						**WASHINGTON**				
Levin	Y	Y	?	N		Murray	Y	Y	N	N
Stabenow	Y	Y	N	N		Cantwell	Y	Y	N	N
MINNESOTA						**WEST VIRGINIA**				
Coleman	Y	Y	Y	Y		Byrd	N	Y	N	N
Klobuchar	Y	Y	N	N		Rockefeller	Y	Y	N	N
MISSISSIPPI						**WISCONSIN**				
Cochran	Y	Y	Y	Y		Kohl	Y	Y	N	N
Wicker	Y	Y	Y	Y		Feingold	Y	Y	N	N
MISSOURI						**WYOMING**				
Bond	Y	Y	N	N		Enzi	Y	N	Y	Y
McCaskill	Y	Y	N	N		Barrasso	Y	N	Y	Y

KEY	**Republicans**	Democrats	*Independents*		
Y Voted for (yea)		X Paired against		C Voted "present" to avoid possible conflict of interest
# Paired for		– Announced against		
+ Announced for		P Voted "present"		? Did not vote or otherwise make a position known
N Voted against (nay)				

ND Northern Democrats, SD Southern Democrats
Southern states: Ala., Ark., Fla., Ga., Ky., La., Miss., N.C., Okla., S.C., Tenn., Texas, Va.

IN THE SENATE | By Vote Number

99. **S 2739. Omnibus Public Lands/National Heritage Areas.** Coburn, R-Okla., amendment that would require employees of the National Park Service and members of a local coordinating entity of the National Heritage Area to obtain written consent prior to entering a parcel of private property located in the proposed National Heritage Area. Rejected 27-67: R 27-18; D 0-47 (ND 0-42, SD 0-5); I 0-2. April 10, 2008.

100. **S 2739. Omnibus Public Lands/National Park Service.** Coburn, R-Okla., amendment that would require that an amount equal to 1 percent of the funds made available to the Interior secretary under the bill be used by the director of the National Park Service for asset disposal. Rejected 22-73: R 21-25; D 1-46 (ND 1-41, SD 0-5); I 0-2. April 10, 2008.

101. **S 2739. Omnibus Public Lands/Passage.** Passage of the bill that would designate new park, wilderness and scenic areas and authorize programs and activities in the Forest Service, the departments of Interior and Energy, the Bureau of Reclamation, the U.S. Geological Survey, and the Bureau of Land Management. It would add 107,000 acres in Washington state to the National Wilderness Preservation System, which would be known as the "Wild Sky Wilderness." It would also apply federal immigration laws to the Northern Mariana Islands and give the commonwealth a non-voting House delegate. Passed 91-4: R 42-4; D 47-0 (ND 42-0, SD 5-0); I 2-0. April 10, 2008.

102. **Miller Nomination/Confirmation.** Confirmation of President Bush's nomination of Brian Stacy Miller of Arkansas to be a judge for the U.S. District Court for the Eastern District of Arkansas. Confirmed 88-0: R 43-0; D 44-0 (ND 39-0, SD 5-0); I 1-0. A "yea" was a vote in support of the president's position. April 10, 2008.

	99	100	101	102		99	100	101	102
ALABAMA					**MONTANA**				
Shelby	Y	N	Y	Y	Baucus	N	N	Y	Y
Sessions	Y	Y	Y	Y	Tester	N	N	Y	Y
ALASKA					**NEBRASKA**				
Stevens	N	N	Y	Y	**Hagel**	N	N	Y	Y
Murkowski	N	N	Y	Y	Nelson	N	N	Y	Y
ARIZONA					**NEVADA**				
McCain	?	?	?	?	Reid	N	N	Y	Y
Kyl	Y	Y	Y	Y	Ensign	Y	Y	Y	Y
ARKANSAS					**NEW HAMPSHIRE**				
Lincoln	N	N	Y	Y	**Gregg**	?	?	?	?
Pryor	N	N	Y	Y	**Sununu**	Y	Y	Y	Y
CALIFORNIA					**NEW JERSEY**				
Feinstein	N	N	Y	?	Lautenberg	N	N	Y	Y
Boxer	N	N	Y	Y	Menendez	N	N	Y	+
COLORADO					**NEW MEXICO**				
Allard	Y	N	Y	Y	**Domenici**	N	N	Y	Y
Salazar	N	N	Y	Y	Bingaman	N	N	Y	Y
CONNECTICUT					**NEW YORK**				
Dodd	N	N	Y	Y	Schumer	N	N	Y	Y
Lieberman	N	N	Y	?	Clinton	?	?	?	?
DELAWARE					**NORTH CAROLINA**				
Biden	N	N	Y	Y	**Dole**	?	?	+	+
Carper	N	N	Y	Y	**Burr**	Y	Y	Y	Y
FLORIDA					**NORTH DAKOTA**				
Nelson	N	N	Y	Y	Conrad	N	N	Y	Y
Martinez	N	N	Y	Y	Dorgan	N	N	Y	Y
GEORGIA					**OHIO**				
Chambliss	Y	Y	Y	Y	**Voinovich**	N	N	Y	Y
Isakson	Y	Y	Y	Y	Brown	N	N	Y	?
HAWAII					**OKLAHOMA**				
Inouye	N	N	Y	Y	**Inhofe**	Y	Y	N	?
Akaka	N	N	Y	Y	**Coburn**	Y	Y	N	Y
IDAHO					**OREGON**				
Craig	N	N	Y	Y	Wyden	N	N	Y	Y
Crapo	N	N	Y	Y	**Smith**	N	N	Y	Y
ILLINOIS					**PENNSYLVANIA**				
Durbin	N	N	Y	Y	**Specter**	N	N	Y	Y
Obama	?	?	?	?	Casey	N	N	Y	Y
INDIANA					**RHODE ISLAND**				
Lugar	N	N	Y	Y	Reed	N	N	Y	Y
Bayh	N	N	Y	Y	Whitehouse	N	N	Y	Y
IOWA					**SOUTH CAROLINA**				
Grassley	Y	Y	Y	Y	**Graham**	Y	Y	Y	Y
Harkin	N	N	Y	Y	**DeMint**	Y	Y	N	Y
KANSAS					**SOUTH DAKOTA**				
Brownback	Y	Y	Y	Y	Johnson	N	N	Y	Y
Roberts	Y	N	Y	Y	**Thune**	Y	Y	Y	Y
KENTUCKY					**TENNESSEE**				
McConnell	Y	Y	Y	Y	**Alexander**	N	N	Y	Y
Bunning	N	N	Y	+	**Corker**	N	N	Y	Y
LOUISIANA					**TEXAS**				
Landrieu	N	N	Y	Y	**Hutchison**	Y	N	Y	?
Vitter	Y	Y	N	Y	**Cornyn**	Y	Y	Y	Y
MAINE					**UTAH**				
Snowe	Y	N	Y	Y	**Hatch**	N	Y	Y	Y
Collins	Y	N	Y	Y	**Bennett**	N	N	Y	Y
MARYLAND					**VERMONT**				
Mikulski	N	N	Y	Y	Leahy	N	N	Y	Y
Cardin	N	N	Y	Y	*Sanders*	N	N	Y	Y
MASSACHUSETTS					**VIRGINIA**				
Kennedy	N	N	Y	Y	**Warner**	N	Y	Y	Y
Kerry	N	N	Y	Y	Webb	N	N	Y	Y
MICHIGAN					**WASHINGTON**				
Levin	N	N	Y	Y	Murray	N	N	Y	Y
Stabenow	N	N	Y	Y	Cantwell	N	N	Y	Y
MINNESOTA					**WEST VIRGINIA**				
Coleman	Y	Y	Y	Y	Byrd	N	N	Y	Y
Klobuchar	N	N	Y	Y	Rockefeller	N	N	Y	Y
MISSISSIPPI					**WISCONSIN**				
Cochran	?	N	Y	Y	Kohl	N	N	Y	Y
Wicker	Y	Y	Y	Y	Feingold	N	N	Y	Y
MISSOURI					**WYOMING**				
Bond	N	N	Y	Y	**Enzi**	Y	N	Y	Y
McCaskill	N	N	Y	Y	**Barrasso**	Y	N	Y	Y

KEY	**Republicans**	Democrats	*Independents*		
Y	Voted for (yea)	X	Paired against	C	Voted "present" to avoid possible conflict of interest
#	Paired for	–	Announced against		
+	Announced for	P	Voted "present"	?	Did not vote or otherwise make a position known
N	Voted against (nay)				

ND Northern Democrats, SD Southern Democrats
Southern states: Ala., Ark., Fla., Ga., Ky., La., Miss., N.C., Okla., S.C., Tenn., Texas, Va.

S-22 2008 CQ ALMANAC | www.cq.com

IN THE SENATE | By Vote Number

103. **HR 1195. Technical Corrections to Surface Transportation Law/Cloture.** Motion to invoke cloture (thus limiting debate) on the motion to proceed to the bill that would amend the 2005 surface transportation law to make technical corrections and other minor changes. Motion agreed to 93-1: R 47-1; D 44-0 (ND 39-0, SD 5-0); I 2-0. Three-fifths of the total Senate (60) is required to invoke cloture. April 14, 2008.

104. **HR 1195. Technical Corrections to Surface Transportation Law/Recommit.** Boxer, D-Calif., motion to table (kill) the DeMint, R-S.C., motion to recommit the bill to the Senate Environment and Public Works Committee with instructions that it be reported back with an amendment striking all new earmarks and spending increases for existing earmarks. Motion agreed to 78-18: R 32-15; D 44-3 (ND 39-3, SD 5-0); I 2-0. April 16, 2008.

105. **HR 1195. Technical Corrections to Surface Transportation Law/Earmark Investigation.** Boxer, D-Calif., amendment to the Boxer substitute. The Boxer amendment would call for a Justice Department review of allegations of federal criminal law violations regarding a $10 million earmark in the 2005 surface transportation bill that was altered after the bill was cleared. The substitute would amend the 2005 surface transportation law to make technical corrections and some policy changes, such as adding earmarks and increasing the minimum state share of total highway safety formula grants from 0.5 percent to 0.75 percent. Adopted 64-28: R 20-25; D 42-3 (ND 37-3, SD 5-0); I 2-0. (By unanimous consent, the Senate agreed to raise the majority requirement for adoption of the Boxer amendment to 60 votes.) April 17, 2008.

106. **HR 1195. Technical Corrections to Surface Transportation Law/Earmark Investigation.** Coburn, R-Okla., amendment to the Boxer, D-Calif., substitute. The Coburn amendment would create a special congressional committee to investigate the $10 million earmark in the 2005 surface transportation bill that was altered after the bill was cleared. Rejected 49-43: R 43-2; D 6-39 (ND 5-35, SD 1-4); I 0-2. (By unanimous consent, the Senate agreed to raise the majority requirement for adoption of the Coburn amendment to 60 votes. Subsequently, the Coburn amendment was withdrawn.) April 17, 2008.

107. **HR 1195. Technical Corrections to Surface Transportation Law/Cloture.** Motion to invoke cloture (thus limiting debate) on the Boxer, D-Calif., substitute, as amended. Motion agreed to 90-2: R 43-2; D 45-0 (ND 40-0, SD 5-0); I 2-0. Three-fifths of the total Senate (60) is required to invoke cloture. April 17, 2008.

108. **HR 1195. Surface Transportation Law Revisions/Passage.** Passage of the bill that would amend the 2005 surface transportation law to make technical corrections and certain policy changes. The bill would increase the minimum state share of total highway safety formula grants from 0.5 percent to 0.75 percent, allow states to impose certain requirements on repeat intoxicated drivers and authorize $45 million for a high-speed, magnetic levitation rail line from Las Vegas to Anaheim, Calif. As amended, it would call for a Justice Department review of allegations of federal criminal law violations regarding the $10 million earmark in the 2005 surface transportation bill that was altered after the bill was cleared. Passed 88-2: R 43-2; D 44-0 (ND 40-0, SD 4-0); I 1-0. (Before passage, the Senate adopted the Boxer, D-Calif., substitute amendment, as amended, by voice vote.) A "nay" was a vote in support of the president's position. April 17, 2008.

	103	104	105	106	107	108
ALABAMA						
Shelby	Y	Y	N	Y	Y	Y
Sessions	Y	N	N	Y	Y	Y
ALASKA						
Stevens	Y	Y	N	Y	Y	Y
Murkowski	Y	Y	N	Y	Y	Y
ARIZONA						
McCain	?	?	?	?	?	?
Kyl	Y	N	N	Y	Y	Y
ARKANSAS						
Lincoln	Y	Y	Y	N	Y	Y
Pryor	Y	Y	Y	N	Y	Y
CALIFORNIA						
Feinstein	Y	Y	Y	N	Y	Y
Boxer	Y	Y	Y	N	Y	Y
COLORADO						
Allard	Y	N	N	Y	Y	Y
Salazar	Y	Y	Y	N	Y	Y
CONNECTICUT						
Dodd	Y	Y	Y	N	Y	Y
Lieberman	Y	Y	Y	N	Y	Y
DELAWARE						
Biden	Y	Y	?	?	?	?
Carper	Y	Y	Y	N	Y	Y
FLORIDA						
Nelson	Y	Y	Y	N	Y	Y
Martinez	Y	N	Y	Y	Y	Y
GEORGIA						
Chambliss	Y	Y	Y	Y	Y	Y
Isakson	Y	Y	Y	Y	Y	Y
HAWAII						
Inouye	Y	Y	?	?	?	?
Akaka	Y	Y	Y	N	Y	Y
IDAHO						
Craig	Y	Y	N	Y	Y	Y
Crapo	Y	Y	N	Y	Y	Y
ILLINOIS						
Durbin	Y	Y	Y	N	Y	Y
Obama	?	?	?	?	?	?
INDIANA						
Lugar	Y	Y	?	?	?	?
Bayh	Y	N	Y	Y	Y	Y
IOWA						
Grassley	Y	Y	N	Y	Y	Y
Harkin	Y	Y	Y	N	Y	Y
KANSAS						
Brownback	Y	N	N	Y	Y	Y
Roberts	Y	Y	Y	Y	Y	Y
KENTUCKY						
McConnell	Y	Y	Y	Y	Y	Y
Bunning	Y	Y	Y	Y	Y	Y
LOUISIANA						
Landrieu	Y	Y	Y	N	Y	+
Vitter	Y	Y	Y	Y	Y	Y
MAINE						
Snowe	Y	Y	Y	N	Y	Y
Collins	Y	Y	Y	Y	Y	Y
MARYLAND						
Mikulski	Y	Y	Y	N	Y	Y
Cardin	Y	Y	Y	Y	Y	Y
MASSACHUSETTS						
Kennedy	?	Y	Y	N	Y	Y
Kerry	Y	Y	Y	N	Y	Y
MICHIGAN						
Levin	Y	Y	Y	N	Y	Y
Stabenow	Y	Y	Y	N	Y	Y
MINNESOTA						
Coleman	Y	Y	Y	Y	Y	Y
Klobuchar	Y	Y	Y	Y	Y	Y
MISSISSIPPI						
Cochran	Y	Y	N	Y	Y	Y
Wicker	Y	Y	N	Y	Y	Y
MISSOURI						
Bond	N	Y	Y	Y	Y	Y
McCaskill	Y	N	N	Y	Y	Y
MONTANA						
Baucus	Y	Y	Y	N	Y	Y
Tester	Y	Y	Y	N	Y	Y
NEBRASKA						
Hagel	Y	?	?	?	?	?
Nelson	Y	Y	Y	N	Y	Y
NEVADA						
Reid	Y	Y	Y	N	Y	Y
Ensign	Y	Y	N	Y	Y	Y
NEW HAMPSHIRE						
Gregg	Y	N	N	Y	N	N
Sununu	Y	N	Y	Y	Y	Y
NEW JERSEY						
Lautenberg	?	Y	Y	N	Y	Y
Menendez	+	Y	Y	N	Y	Y
NEW MEXICO						
Domenici	Y	Y	N	Y	Y	Y
Bingaman	Y	Y	Y	N	Y	Y
NEW YORK						
Schumer	Y	Y	Y	N	Y	Y
Clinton	?	?	?	?	?	?
NORTH CAROLINA						
Dole	Y	Y	Y	Y	Y	Y
Burr	Y	N	N	Y	Y	Y
NORTH DAKOTA						
Conrad	Y	Y	Y	N	Y	Y
Dorgan	Y	Y	Y	N	Y	Y
OHIO						
Voinovich	Y	Y	Y	Y	Y	Y
Brown	Y	Y	Y	N	Y	Y
OKLAHOMA						
Inhofe	Y	Y	N	Y	Y	Y
Coburn	Y	N	N	Y	Y	Y
OREGON						
Wyden	Y	Y	Y	N	Y	Y
Smith	Y	Y	Y	Y	Y	Y
PENNSYLVANIA						
Specter	Y	Y	Y	Y	Y	Y
Casey	Y	Y	Y	N	Y	Y
RHODE ISLAND						
Reed	Y	Y	Y	N	Y	Y
Whitehouse	Y	Y	Y	N	Y	Y
SOUTH CAROLINA						
Graham	Y	N	N	Y	Y	Y
DeMint	Y	N	N	Y	N	N
SOUTH DAKOTA						
Johnson	Y	Y	Y	Y	Y	Y
Thune	Y	Y	Y	Y	Y	Y
TENNESSEE						
Alexander	Y	Y	+	+	+	+
Corker	Y	N	Y	Y	Y	Y
TEXAS						
Hutchison	Y	Y	N	Y	Y	Y
Cornyn	Y	N	N	Y	Y	Y
UTAH						
Hatch	Y	Y	N	Y	Y	Y
Bennett	Y	Y	N	Y	Y	Y
VERMONT						
Leahy	Y	Y	Y	N	Y	Y
Sanders	Y	Y	Y	N	Y	?
VIRGINIA						
Warner	Y	Y	Y	Y	Y	Y
Webb	Y	Y	Y	N	Y	Y
WASHINGTON						
Murray	Y	Y	Y	N	Y	Y
Cantwell	Y	Y	Y	N	Y	Y
WEST VIRGINIA						
Byrd	Y	Y	N	Y	Y	Y
Rockefeller	Y	Y	Y	N	Y	Y
WISCONSIN						
Kohl	Y	Y	Y	N	Y	Y
Feingold	Y	N	N	Y	Y	Y
WYOMING						
Enzi	Y	N	N	Y	Y	Y
Barrasso	Y	N	N	Y	Y	Y

KEY   **Republicans**   Democrats   *Independents*

Y Voted for (yea)	**X** Paired against	**C** Voted "present" to avoid possible conflict of interest
# Paired for	**–** Announced against	
+ Announced for	**P** Voted "present"	**?** Did not vote or otherwise make a position known
N Voted against (nay)		

ND Northern Democrats, SD Southern Democrats

Southern states: Ala., Ark., Fla., Ga., Ky., La., Miss., N.C., Okla., S.C., Tenn., Texas, Va.

IN THE SENATE | By Vote Number

109. **S 1315. Veterans' Benefits/Cloture.** Motion to invoke cloture (thus limiting debate) on the motion to proceed to the bill that would expand a wide range of veterans' benefits, including life insurance, housing assistance and education. Motion agreed to 94-0: R 46-0; D 46-0 (ND 42-0, SD 4-0); I 2-0. Three-fifths of the total Senate (60) is required to invoke cloture. April 22, 2008.

110. **HR 2831. Wage Discrimination/Cloture.** Motion to invoke cloture (thus limiting debate) on the motion to proceed to the bill that would amend the 1964 Civil Rights Act to allow employees to file charges of pay discrimination within 180 days of the last received paycheck affected by the alleged discriminatory decision. Motion rejected 56-42: R 6-41; D 48-1 (ND 43-1, SD 5-0); I 2-0. Three-fifths of the total Senate (60) is required to invoke cloture. A "nay" was a vote in support of the president's position. April 23, 2008.

111. **S 1315. Veterans' Benefits/Filipino Veterans.** Burr, R-N.C., amendment that would strike a provision that would require $221 million in new pension benefits for Filipino veterans residing in the Philippines who served in the U.S. armed forces during World War II and were not injured during their time in service. It would redirect the funds toward additional housing, vehicle, education and burial assistance for U.S. veterans. Rejected 41-56: R 40-7; D 1-47 (ND 1-42, SD 0-5); I 0-2. April 24, 2008.

112. **S 1315. Veterans' Benefits/Passage.** Passage of the bill that would expand a wide range of veterans' benefits, including life insurance, housing grants, burial allowances and education. It would require $221 million in new pension benefits for Filipino veterans who served in the U.S. armed forces during World War II. It would establish a new level-premium term life insurance program for certain veterans and increase the maximum amount of supplemental Service-Disabled Veterans Insurance from $20,000 to $30,000. Passed 96-1: R 46-1; D 48-0 (ND 43-0, SD 5-0); I 2-0. April 24, 2008.

113. **HR 493. Genetic Information Nondiscrimination/Passage.** Passage of the bill that would prohibit insurance companies, employers, employment agencies and labor unions from discriminating on the basis of genetic information. It would bar health plans from requiring genetic testing. Insurers could not adjust premiums or base enrollment decisions on genetic information. Passed 95-0: R 46-0; D 47-0 (ND 42-0, SD 5-0); I 2-0. (Before passage, the Senate adopted the Snowe, R-Maine, substitute by voice vote.) April 24, 2008.

114. **HR 2881. FAA Reauthorization/Cloture.** Motion to invoke cloture (thus limiting debate) on the motion to proceed to the bill that would reauthorize the Federal Aviation Administration through fiscal 2011. Motion agreed to 88-0: R 44-0; D 42-0 (ND 37-0, SD 5-0); I 2-0. Three-fifths of the total Senate (60) is required to invoke cloture. April 28, 2008.

	109	110	111	112	113	114
ALABAMA						
Shelby	Y	N	Y	Y	Y	Y
Sessions	Y	N	Y	Y	Y	Y
ALASKA						
Stevens	Y	N	N	Y	Y	Y
Murkowski	Y	N	N	Y	Y	Y
ARIZONA						
McCain	?	?	?	?	?	?
Kyl	Y	N	Y	Y	Y	Y
ARKANSAS						
Lincoln	Y	Y	N	Y	Y	Y
Pryor	Y	Y	N	Y	Y	Y
CALIFORNIA						
Feinstein	Y	Y	N	Y	Y	Y
Boxer	Y	Y	N	Y	Y	Y
COLORADO						
Allard	Y	N	Y	Y	Y	Y
Salazar	Y	Y	N	Y	Y	Y
CONNECTICUT						
Dodd	Y	Y	N	Y	Y	?
Lieberman	Y	Y	N	Y	Y	Y
DELAWARE						
Biden	Y	Y	N	Y	Y	?
Carper	Y	Y	N	Y	Y	Y
FLORIDA						
Nelson	Y	Y	N	Y	Y	Y
Martinez	Y	N	Y	Y	Y	?
GEORGIA						
Chambliss	Y	N	Y	Y	Y	Y
Isakson	Y	N	Y	Y	Y	Y
HAWAII						
Inouye	Y	Y	N	Y	Y	Y
Akaka	Y	Y	N	Y	Y	Y
IDAHO						
Craig	Y	N	Y	Y	Y	Y
Crapo	Y	N	Y	Y	Y	Y
ILLINOIS						
Durbin	Y	Y	N	Y	Y	Y
Obama	?	Y	?	?	?	?
INDIANA						
Lugar	Y	N	N	Y	Y	Y
Bayh	Y	Y	Y	Y	Y	Y
IOWA						
Grassley	Y	N	Y	Y	Y	Y
Harkin	Y	Y	N	Y	Y	Y
KANSAS						
Brownback	Y	N	Y	Y	Y	Y
Roberts	Y	N	Y	Y	Y	Y
KENTUCKY						
McConnell	Y	N	Y	Y	Y	Y
Bunning	Y	N	Y	Y	Y	Y
LOUISIANA						
Landrieu	?	Y	N	Y	Y	Y
Vitter	?	N	Y	N	Y	Y
MAINE						
Snowe	Y	Y	Y	Y	Y	Y
Collins	Y	Y	Y	Y	Y	Y
MARYLAND						
Mikulski	Y	Y	N	Y	Y	Y
Cardin	Y	Y	N	Y	Y	Y
MASSACHUSETTS						
Kennedy	Y	Y	N	Y	Y	?
Kerry	Y	Y	N	Y	Y	+
MICHIGAN						
Levin	Y	Y	N	Y	Y	Y
Stabenow	Y	Y	N	Y	Y	Y
MINNESOTA						
Coleman	Y	Y	Y	Y	Y	Y
Klobuchar	Y	Y	N	Y	Y	Y
MISSISSIPPI						
Cochran	Y	N	Y	Y	Y	Y
Wicker	Y	N	Y	Y	Y	Y
MISSOURI						
Bond	Y	N	Y	Y	Y	Y
McCaskill	Y	Y	N	Y	Y	Y
MONTANA						
Baucus	Y	Y	N	Y	Y	Y
Tester	Y	Y	N	Y	Y	Y
NEBRASKA						
Hagel	Y	?	N	Y	Y	?
Nelson	Y	Y	N	Y	Y	Y
NEVADA						
Reid	Y	N	N	Y	Y	Y
Ensign	Y	N	Y	Y	Y	Y
NEW HAMPSHIRE						
Gregg	Y	N	Y	Y	?	?
Sununu	Y	Y	Y	Y	Y	Y
NEW JERSEY						
Lautenberg	Y	Y	N	Y	Y	?
Menendez	Y	Y	N	Y	Y	Y
NEW MEXICO						
Domenici	?	N	Y	Y	Y	Y
Bingaman	Y	Y	N	Y	Y	Y
NEW YORK						
Schumer	Y	Y	N	Y	Y	Y
Clinton	?	Y	N	Y	?	?
NORTH CAROLINA						
Dole	Y	N	Y	Y	Y	+
Burr	Y	N	Y	Y	Y	Y
NORTH DAKOTA						
Conrad	Y	Y	N	Y	Y	Y
Dorgan	Y	Y	N	Y	Y	Y
OHIO						
Voinovich	Y	N	N	Y	Y	Y
Brown	Y	Y	N	Y	Y	Y
OKLAHOMA						
Inhofe	Y	N	Y	Y	Y	Y
Coburn	Y	N	Y	Y	Y	Y
OREGON						
Wyden	Y	Y	N	Y	Y	Y
Smith	Y	Y	Y	Y	Y	Y
PENNSYLVANIA						
Specter	Y	N	N	Y	Y	Y
Casey	Y	Y	N	Y	Y	Y
RHODE ISLAND						
Reed	Y	Y	N	Y	Y	Y
Whitehouse	Y	Y	N	Y	Y	Y
SOUTH CAROLINA						
Graham	Y	N	Y	Y	Y	Y
DeMint	Y	N	+	?	?	Y
SOUTH DAKOTA						
Johnson	Y	Y	N	Y	Y	Y
Thune	Y	N	Y	Y	Y	Y
TENNESSEE						
Alexander	Y	N	Y	Y	Y	Y
Corker	Y	N	Y	Y	Y	Y
TEXAS						
Hutchison	Y	N	Y	Y	Y	Y
Cornyn	Y	N	Y	Y	Y	Y
UTAH						
Hatch	Y	N	Y	Y	Y	Y
Bennett	Y	N	Y	Y	Y	Y
VERMONT						
Leahy	Y	Y	N	Y	Y	Y
Sanders	Y	Y	N	Y	Y	Y
VIRGINIA						
Warner	Y	N	N	Y	Y	Y
Webb	Y	Y	N	Y	Y	Y
WASHINGTON						
Murray	Y	Y	N	Y	Y	Y
Cantwell	Y	Y	N	Y	Y	Y
WEST VIRGINIA						
Byrd	Y	Y	N	Y	Y	Y
Rockefeller	Y	Y	N	Y	Y	Y
WISCONSIN						
Kohl	Y	Y	N	Y	Y	Y
Feingold	Y	Y	N	Y	Y	Y
WYOMING						
Enzi	Y	N	Y	Y	Y	Y
Barrasso	Y	N	Y	Y	Y	Y

KEY	**Republicans**	Democrats	*Independents*

Y	Voted for (yea)	X	Paired against	C	Voted "present" to avoid possible conflict of interest
#	Paired for	–	Announced against		
+	Announced for	P	Voted "present"	?	Did not vote or otherwise make a position known
N	Voted against (nay)				

ND Northern Democrats, SD Southern Democrats
Southern states: Ala., Ark., Fla., Ga., Ky., La., Miss., N.C., Okla., S.C., Tenn., Texas, Va.

IN THE SENATE | By Vote Number

115. **HR 2881. FAA Reauthorization/Cloture.** Motion to invoke cloture (thus limiting debate) on the Rockefeller, D-W.Va., substitute amendment that would authorize the Federal Aviation Administration (FAA) through fiscal 2011. It would provide $290 million annually for air traffic control modernization by raising the fuel tax on high-end general aviation. It also would increase the tax on oil spills and use that revenue to replenish the Highway Trust Fund. Motion rejected 49-42: R 3-41; D 44-1 (ND 40-1, SD 4-0); I 2-0. Three-fifths of the total Senate (60) is required to invoke cloture. A "nay" was a vote in support of the president's position. May 6, 2008.

116. **S 2284. National Flood Insurance Program/Cloture.** Motion to invoke cloture (thus limiting debate) on the motion to proceed to the bill that would reauthorize the National Flood Insurance Program through fiscal 2013. Motion agreed to 90-1: R 43-1; D 45-0 (ND 41-0, SD 4-0); I 2-0. Three-fifths of the total Senate (60) is required to invoke cloture. May 6, 2008.

117. **S 2284. National Flood Insurance Program/Wind Insurance.** Wicker, R-Miss., amendment to the Dodd, D-Conn., substitute. The Wicker amendment would allow the National Flood Insurance Program to provide for an optional "multiperil" policy to cover wind and flood risk in one policy. The Dodd substitute would reauthorize the program through fiscal 2013 and establish a Commission on Natural Catastrophe Risk Management and Insurance. Rejected 19-74: R 12-34; D 7-38 (ND 3-37, SD 4-1); I 0-2. A "nay" was a vote in support of the president's position. May 7, 2008.

118. **S 2284. National Flood Insurance Program/Coverage Limits.** Vitter, R-La., amendment to the Dodd, D-Conn., substitute. The Vitter amendment would increase the coverage limits in the National Flood Insurance Program to $335,000 for residential properties, $135,000 for residential contents and $670,000 for non-residential properties. Rejected 27-66: R 11-35; D 16-29 (ND 12-28, SD 4-1); I 0-2. May 7, 2008.

119. **S 2284. National Flood Insurance Program/Risk Premium Rates.** Vitter, R-La., amendment to the Dodd, D-Conn., substitute. The Vitter amendment would allow the increases in risk premium rates to be phased in over five years instead of two years. Rejected 23-69: R 8-38; D 15-29 (ND 11-28, SD 4-1); I 0-2. May 7, 2008.

	115	116	117	118	119
ALABAMA					
Shelby	N	Y	N	N	N
Sessions	N	Y	N	N	N
ALASKA					
Stevens	N	Y	N	Y	N
Murkowski	N	Y	Y	Y	N
ARIZONA					
McCain	?	?	?	?	?
Kyl	N	Y	N	N	N
ARKANSAS					
Lincoln	Y	Y	Y	Y	Y
Pryor	Y	Y	Y	Y	Y
CALIFORNIA					
Feinstein	Y	Y	N	Y	Y
Boxer	Y	Y	N	Y	Y
COLORADO					
Allard	N	Y	N	N	N
Salazar	Y	Y	N	Y	N
CONNECTICUT					
Dodd	Y	Y	N	N	N
Lieberman	Y	Y	N	N	N
DELAWARE					
Biden	Y	Y	?	?	?
Carper	Y	Y	N	N	N
FLORIDA					
Nelson	Y	Y	Y	Y	Y
Martinez	N	Y	Y	Y	Y
GEORGIA					
Chambliss	N	Y	N	N	N
Isakson	N	Y	N	N	N
HAWAII					
Inouye	Y	Y	N	N	N
Akaka	Y	Y	N	N	N
IDAHO					
Craig	?	?	Y	N	Y
Crapo	N	Y	N	N	Y
ILLINOIS					
Durbin	Y	Y	N	N	Y
Obama	?	?	?	?	?
INDIANA					
Lugar	N	Y	N	N	N
Bayh	?	?	N	N	N
IOWA					
Grassley	N	Y	N	N	N
Harkin	Y	Y	N	Y	Y
KANSAS					
Brownback	Y	Y	N	N	N
Roberts	Y	Y	N	N	N
KENTUCKY					
McConnell	N	Y	N	N	N
Bunning	N	Y	N	N	N
LOUISIANA					
Landrieu	?	?	Y	Y	Y
Vitter	N	Y	Y	Y	Y
MAINE					
Snowe	Y	Y	Y	N	N
Collins	N	Y	N	N	N
MARYLAND					
Mikulski	Y	Y	?	?	?
Cardin	Y	Y	N	N	N
MASSACHUSETTS					
Kennedy	Y	Y	N	N	N
Kerry	Y	Y	N	N	N
MICHIGAN					
Levin	Y	Y	N	N	N
Stabenow	Y	Y	N	Y	Y
MINNESOTA					
Coleman	N	Y	N	N	N
Klobuchar	Y	Y	N	Y	N
MISSISSIPPI					
Cochran	N	Y	Y	Y	Y
Wicker	N	Y	Y	Y	Y
MISSOURI					
Bond	N	Y	N	N	N
McCaskill	Y	Y	N	N	Y

	115	116	117	118	119
MONTANA					
Baucus	Y	Y	N	N	N
Tester	Y	Y	N	N	N
NEBRASKA					
Hagel	?	?	?	?	?
Nelson	Y	Y	N	N	N
NEVADA					
Reid	N	Y	N	N	?
Ensign	N	Y	N	N	N
NEW HAMPSHIRE					
Gregg	N	Y	N	N	N
Sununu	N	Y	N	N	N
NEW JERSEY					
Lautenberg	Y	Y	Y	Y	Y
Menendez	Y	Y	Y	Y	Y
NEW MEXICO					
Domenici	N	Y	N	N	N
Bingaman	Y	Y	N	Y	N
NEW YORK					
Schumer	Y	Y	Y	Y	Y
Clinton	?	?	?	?	?
NORTH CAROLINA					
Dole	N	Y	N	N	N
Burr	?	?	N	Y	N
NORTH DAKOTA					
Conrad	Y	Y	N	N	N
Dorgan	Y	Y	N	N	N
OHIO					
Voinovich	N	Y	N	N	N
Brown	Y	Y	N	N	N
OKLAHOMA					
Inhofe	?	?	N	N	N
Coburn	N	N	N	Y	N
OREGON					
Wyden	Y	Y	N	N	N
Smith	N	Y	N	N	N
PENNSYLVANIA					
Specter	N	Y	N	N	N
Casey	Y	Y	N	N	N
RHODE ISLAND					
Reed	Y	Y	N	N	N
Whitehouse	Y	Y	N	N	N
SOUTH CAROLINA					
Graham	N	Y	Y	Y	N
DeMint	N	Y	N	N	N
SOUTH DAKOTA					
Johnson	Y	Y	N	N	N
Thune	N	Y	N	N	N
TENNESSEE					
Alexander	N	Y	N	N	N
Corker	N	Y	N	N	N
TEXAS					
Hutchison	N	Y	N	Y	Y
Cornyn	N	Y	N	N	Y
UTAH					
Hatch	N	Y	N	Y	N
Bennett	N	Y	N	N	N
VERMONT					
Leahy	Y	Y	N	N	N
Sanders	Y	Y	N	N	N
VIRGINIA					
Warner	N	Y	?	?	?
Webb	Y	Y	N	N	N
WASHINGTON					
Murray	Y	Y	N	Y	Y
Cantwell	Y	Y	N	Y	Y
WEST VIRGINIA					
Byrd	Y	Y	N	N	N
Rockefeller	Y	Y	N	N	N
WISCONSIN					
Kohl	Y	Y	N	N	N
Feingold	Y	Y	N	N	N
WYOMING					
Enzi	N	Y	N	N	N
Barrasso	N	Y	N	N	N

KEY **Republicans**   Democrats   *Independents*

Y	Voted for (yea)	X	Paired against	C	Voted "present" to avoid possible conflict of interest
#	Paired for	–	Announced against	
+	Announced for	P	Voted "present"	?	Did not vote or otherwise make a position known
N	Voted against (nay)		

ND Northern Democrats, SD Southern Democrats
Southern states: Ala., Ark., Fla., Ga., Ky., La., Miss., N.C., Okla., S.C., Tenn., Texas, Va.

IN THE SENATE | By Vote Number

120. **S 2284. National Flood Insurance Program/Purchasing Requirements Study.** Landrieu, D-La., amendment to the Dodd, D-Conn., substitute. The Landrieu amendment would strike the mandatory purchase provisions for property owners with land protected by levees and dams, and insert language that would require a study to assess the risk for properties that are protected by such structures. The Dodd substitute would reauthorize the program through fiscal 2013 and establish a Commission on Natural Catastrophe Risk Management and Insurance. Rejected 30-62: R 9-37; D 20-24 (ND 16-23, SD 4-1); I 1-1. May 7, 2008.

121. **S 2284. National Flood Insurance Program/Substitute.** Dodd, D-Conn., motion to waive pay-as-you-go rules with respect to the Coburn, R-Okla., point of order against the Dodd substitute. Motion agreed to 70-26: R 26-21; D 42-5 (ND 39-3, SD 3-2); I 2-0. A three-fifths majority (60) of the total Senate is required to waive the fiscal 2008 budget resolution. May 8, 2008.

122. **S 2284. National Flood Insurance Program/Premium Rates.** Durbin, D-Ill., amendment to the Dodd, D-Conn., substitute. The Durbin amendment would delay premium increases in the St. Louis District of the Mississippi Valley Division of the Corps of Engineers until the National Flood Insurance Program rate map is updated for that entire district. Adopted 68-24: R 25-21; D 41-3 (ND 36-3, SD 5-0); I 2-0. May 8, 2008.

	120	121	122			120	121	122
ALABAMA					**MONTANA**			
Shelby	N	Y	Y		Baucus	Y	Y	Y
Sessions	N	Y	Y		Tester	Y	Y	Y
ALASKA					**NEBRASKA**			
Stevens	N	Y	Y		Hagel	?	Y	N
Murkowski	N	Y	Y		Nelson	Y	Y	Y
ARIZONA					**NEVADA**			
McCain	?	?	?		Reid	?	Y	?
Kyl	Y	N	N		Ensign	N	N	?
ARKANSAS					**NEW HAMPSHIRE**			
Lincoln	Y	N	Y		Gregg	N	N	Y
Pryor	Y	N	Y		Sununu	N	N	N
CALIFORNIA					**NEW JERSEY**			
Feinstein	N	Y	Y		Lautenberg	Y	Y	Y
Boxer	N	Y	?		Menendez	Y	Y	Y
COLORADO					**NEW MEXICO**			
Allard	N	Y	N		Domenici	N	N	Y
Salazar	N	Y	Y		Bingaman	Y	Y	Y
CONNECTICUT					**NEW YORK**			
Dodd	N	Y	Y		Schumer	N	Y	Y
Lieberman	Y	Y	Y		Clinton	?	?	?
DELAWARE					**NORTH CAROLINA**			
Biden	?	Y	Y		Dole	N	Y	Y
Carper	N	Y	N		Burr	N	N	N
FLORIDA					**NORTH DAKOTA**			
Nelson	Y	Y	Y		Conrad	Y	N	Y
Martinez	Y	Y	Y		Dorgan	Y	N	Y
GEORGIA					**OHIO**			
Chambliss	N	N	Y		Voinovich	N	N	Y
Isakson	N	N	Y		Brown	N	Y	Y
HAWAII					**OKLAHOMA**			
Inouye	N	Y	Y		Inhofe	Y	N	N
Akaka	N	Y	Y		Coburn	N	N	N
IDAHO					**OREGON**			
Craig	N	N	Y		Wyden	N	Y	Y
Crapo	N	N	N		Smith	N	Y	Y
ILLINOIS					**PENNSYLVANIA**			
Durbin	Y	Y	Y		Specter	N	Y	Y
Obama	?	?	?		Casey	N	Y	Y
INDIANA					**RHODE ISLAND**			
Lugar	N	Y	N		Reed	N	Y	N
Bayh	N	Y	Y		Whitehouse	N	Y	Y
IOWA					**SOUTH CAROLINA**			
Grassley	N	N	Y		Graham	N	N	Y
Harkin	Y	Y	Y		DeMint	N	N	N
KANSAS					**SOUTH DAKOTA**			
Brownback	N	N	N		Johnson	N	Y	Y
Roberts	N	Y	N		Thune	N	N	N
KENTUCKY					**TENNESSEE**			
McConnell	N	N	Y		Alexander	N	Y	Y
Bunning	N	Y	N		Corker	N	Y	Y
LOUISIANA					**TEXAS**			
Landrieu	Y	Y	Y		Hutchison	Y	Y	N
Vitter	Y	Y	N		Cornyn	Y	Y	Y
MAINE					**UTAH**			
Snowe	N	Y	Y		Hatch	N	Y	Y
Collins	N	Y	N		Bennett	N	Y	Y
MARYLAND					**VERMONT**			
Mikulski	?	Y	Y		Leahy	N	Y	Y
Cardin	N	Y	Y		Sanders	N	Y	Y
MASSACHUSETTS					**VIRGINIA**			
Kennedy	N	Y	Y		Warner	?	?	?
Kerry	N	Y	Y		Webb	N	Y	Y
MICHIGAN					**WASHINGTON**			
Levin	Y	Y	Y		Murray	Y	Y	?
Stabenow	Y	Y	Y		Cantwell	Y	Y	Y
MINNESOTA					**WEST VIRGINIA**			
Coleman	Y	Y	Y		Byrd	N	Y	Y
Klobuchar	Y	Y	Y		Rockefeller	N	Y	Y
MISSISSIPPI					**WISCONSIN**			
Cochran	Y	Y	N		Kohl	N	Y	Y
Wicker	Y	Y	Y		Feingold	N	N	N
MISSOURI					**WYOMING**			
Bond	N	Y	Y		Enzi	N	N	N
McCaskill	Y	Y	Y		Barrasso	N	N	N

KEY	**Republicans**	Democrats	*Independents*		
Y	Voted for (yea)	X	Paired against	C	Voted "present" to avoid possible conflict of interest
#	Paired for	–	Announced against		
+	Announced for	P	Voted "present"	?	Did not vote or otherwise make a position known
N	Voted against (nay)				

ND Northern Democrats, SD Southern Democrats
Southern states: Ala., Ark., Fla., Ga., Ky., La., Miss., N.C., Okla., S.C., Tenn., Texas, Va.

IN THE SENATE | By Vote Number

123. **S 2284. National Flood Insurance Program/Energy.**
McConnell, R-Ky., perfecting amendment that would allow energy exploration in the Arctic National Wildlife Refuge and allow states to authorize oil drilling in offshore coastal waters currently subject to a federal moratorium. It also would promote development of clean-coal technology and suspend oil acquisition for the Strategic Petroleum Reserve for 180 days. Rejected 42-56: R 41-6; D 1-48 (ND 0-44, SD 1-4); I 0-2. (By unanimous consent, the Senate agreed to raise the majority requirement for adoption of the McConnell amendment to 60 votes. Subsequently, the amendment was withdrawn.) A "yea" was a vote in support of the president's position. May 13, 2008.

124. **S 2284. National Flood Insurance Program/Energy.** Reid, D-Nev., amendment to the Dodd, D-Conn., substitute. The Reid amendment would require the Energy and Interior secretaries to suspend acquisition of petroleum for the Strategic Petroleum Reserve through December 2008. Filling of the reserve could resume once the president notifies Congress that the 90-day average price of petroleum is $75 or less per barrel. The substitute would reauthorize the National Flood Insurance Program through fiscal 2013 and establish a Commission on Natural Catastrophe Risk Management and Insurance. Adopted 97-1: R 46-1; D 49-0 (ND 44-0, SD 5-0); I 2-0. (By unanimous consent, the Senate agreed to raise the majority requirement for adoption of the Reid amendment to 60 votes.) May 13, 2008.

125. **HR 3121. National Flood Insurance Program/Passage.** Passage of the bill that would reauthorize the National Flood Insurance Program through fiscal 2013. The bill includes provisions to forgive the $17.5 billion debt incurred by the program after the 2005 hurricane season. It would authorize $400 million annually to modernize all flood maps and to map the 500-year flood plain. As amended, the bill would establish a Commission on Natural Catastrophe Risk Management and Insurance. It also would temporarily suspend petroleum deposits into the Strategic Petroleum Reserve. Passed 92-6: R 45-2; D 45-4 (ND 44-0, SD 1-4); I 2-0. (Before passage, the Senate adopted the Dodd, D-Conn., substitute, as amended, by voice vote. The Senate then struck all after the enacting clause and inserted the text of S 2284 into the bill.) A "nay" was a vote in support of the president's position. May 13, 2008.

126. **HR 980. Public Safety Employees/Cloture.** Motion to invoke cloture (thus limiting debate) on the motion to proceed to the bill that would establish certain organized labor rights for state and local public safety officials, including police officers and firefighters. Motion agreed to 69-29: R 18-29; D 49-0 (ND 44-0, SD 5-0); I 2-0. Three-fifths of the total Senate (60) is required to invoke cloture. May 13, 2008.

127. **HR 980. Public Safety Employees/Military Education Benefits.** Reid, D-Nev., motion to table (kill) the Graham, R-S.C., amendment that would increase the Montgomery GI Bill's educational benefits for military veterans from $1,100 to $1,500 per month. It would require 12 years of service for the maximum benefit of $2,000 per month, with increases tied to the Consumer Price Index. National Guard and reserve members could transfer their education benefits to their spouses and children. Motion agreed to 55-42: R 6-42; D 47-0 (ND 42-0, SD 5-0); I 2-0. A "nay" was a vote in support of the president's position. May 14, 2008.

	123	124	125	126	127			123	124	125	126	127
ALABAMA							**MONTANA**					
Shelby	Y	Y	Y	N	N		Baucus	N	Y	Y	Y	Y
Sessions	Y	Y	Y	N	N		Tester	N	Y	Y	Y	Y
ALASKA							**NEBRASKA**					
Stevens	Y	Y	Y	Y	N		Hagel	Y	Y	Y	Y	Y
Murkowski	Y	Y	Y	Y	N		Nelson	N	Y	Y	Y	Y
ARIZONA							**NEVADA**					
McCain	?	?	?	?	?		Reid	N	Y	Y	Y	Y
Kyl	Y	Y	Y	N	N		Ensign	Y	Y	Y	N	N
ARKANSAS							**NEW HAMPSHIRE**					
Lincoln	N	Y	N	Y	Y		Gregg	Y	Y	Y	Y	N
Pryor	N	Y	N	Y	Y		Sununu	Y	Y	Y	N	N
CALIFORNIA							**NEW JERSEY**					
Feinstein	N	Y	Y	Y	Y		Lautenberg	N	Y	Y	Y	Y
Boxer	N	Y	Y	Y	Y		Menendez	N	Y	Y	Y	Y
COLORADO							**NEW MEXICO**					
Allard	Y	N	Y	N	N		Domenici	Y	Y	Y	Y	N
Salazar	N	Y	Y	Y	Y		Bingaman	N	Y	Y	Y	Y
CONNECTICUT							**NEW YORK**					
Dodd	N	Y	Y	Y	Y		Schumer	N	Y	Y	Y	Y
Lieberman	N	Y	Y	Y	Y		Clinton	N	Y	Y	Y	?
DELAWARE							**NORTH CAROLINA**					
Biden	N	Y	Y	Y	Y		Dole	N	Y	Y	N	N
Carper	N	Y	Y	Y	Y		Burr	Y	Y	Y	N	N
FLORIDA							**NORTH DAKOTA**					
Nelson	N	Y	N	Y	Y		Conrad	N	Y	Y	Y	Y
Martinez	N	Y	Y	Y	N		Dorgan	N	Y	Y	Y	Y
GEORGIA							**OHIO**					
Chambliss	Y	Y	Y	N	N		Voinovich	Y	Y	Y	Y	N
Isakson	Y	Y	Y	N	N		Brown	N	Y	Y	Y	Y
HAWAII							**OKLAHOMA**					
Inouye	N	Y	Y	Y	Y		Inhofe	?	?	?	?	N
Akaka	N	Y	Y	Y	Y		Coburn	Y	Y	N	N	N
IDAHO							**OREGON**					
Craig	Y	Y	Y	N	N		Wyden	N	Y	Y	Y	Y
Crapo	Y	Y	Y	N	N		Smith	N	Y	Y	N	Y
ILLINOIS							**PENNSYLVANIA**					
Durbin	N	Y	Y	Y	?		Specter	Y	Y	Y	Y	Y
Obama	N	Y	Y	Y	?		Casey	N	Y	Y	Y	Y
INDIANA							**RHODE ISLAND**					
Lugar	Y	Y	Y	N	N		Reed	N	Y	Y	Y	Y
Bayh	N	Y	Y	Y	Y		Whitehouse	N	Y	Y	Y	Y
IOWA							**SOUTH CAROLINA**					
Grassley	Y	Y	Y	Y	N		Graham	Y	Y	Y	N	N
Harkin	N	Y	Y	Y	Y		DeMint	Y	Y	Y	N	N
KANSAS							**SOUTH DAKOTA**					
Brownback	Y	Y	Y	N	N		Johnson	N	Y	Y	Y	Y
Roberts	Y	Y	Y	N	N		Thune	Y	Y	Y	N	N
KENTUCKY							**TENNESSEE**					
McConnell	Y	Y	Y	Y	N		Alexander	Y	Y	Y	N	N
Bunning	Y	Y	Y	Y	N		Corker	Y	Y	Y	N	N
LOUISIANA							**TEXAS**					
Landrieu	Y	Y	N	Y	Y		Hutchison	Y	Y	Y	N	N
Vitter	Y	Y	N	N	N		Cornyn	Y	Y	Y	N	N
MAINE							**UTAH**					
Snowe	N	Y	Y	Y	Y		Hatch	Y	Y	Y	N	N
Collins	N	Y	Y	Y	Y		Bennett	Y	Y	Y	N	N
MARYLAND							**VERMONT**					
Mikulski	N	Y	Y	Y	Y		Leahy	N	Y	Y	Y	Y
Cardin	N	Y	Y	Y	Y		Sanders	N	Y	Y	Y	Y
MASSACHUSETTS							**VIRGINIA**					
Kennedy	N	Y	Y	Y	Y		Warner	Y	Y	Y	N	Y
Kerry	N	Y	Y	Y	Y		Webb	N	Y	Y	Y	Y
MICHIGAN							**WASHINGTON**					
Levin	N	Y	Y	Y	Y		Murray	N	Y	Y	Y	Y
Stabenow	N	Y	Y	Y	Y		Cantwell	N	Y	Y	Y	Y
MINNESOTA							**WEST VIRGINIA**					
Coleman	N	Y	Y	Y	N		Byrd	N	Y	Y	Y	Y
Klobuchar	N	Y	Y	Y	Y		Rockefeller	N	Y	Y	Y	Y
MISSISSIPPI							**WISCONSIN**					
Cochran	Y	Y	Y	N	N		Kohl	N	Y	Y	Y	Y
Wicker	Y	Y	Y	N	N		Feingold	N	Y	Y	Y	Y
MISSOURI							**WYOMING**					
Bond	Y	Y	Y	N	N		Enzi	Y	Y	Y	N	N
McCaskill	N	Y	Y	Y	N		Barrasso	Y	Y	Y	N	N

KEY | **Republicans** | Democrats | *Independents*

Y Voted for (yea)	X Paired against	C Voted "present" to avoid possible conflict of interest
# Paired for	− Announced against	
+ Announced for	P Voted "present"	? Did not vote or otherwise make a position known
N Voted against (nay)		

ND Northern Democrats, SD Southern Democrats
Southern states: Ala., Ark., Fla., Ga., Ky., La., Miss., N.C., Okla., S.C., Tenn., Texas, Va.

IN THE SENATE | By Vote Number

128. HR 2419. Farm Bill Reauthorization/Conference Report Point of Order. Conrad, D-N.D., motion to waive the fiscal 2008 budget resolution with respect to the Gregg, R-N.H., point of order against the conference report on the bill that would reauthorize federal farm and nutrition programs for five years. Motion agreed to 74-21: R 27-20; D 45-1 (ND 40-1, SD 5-0); I 2-0. A three-fifths majority (60) of the total Senate is required to waive the fiscal 2008 budget resolution. May 15, 2008.

129. HR 2419. Farm Bill Reauthorization/Conference Report Point of Order. Harkin, D-Iowa, motion to waive Senate rules with respect to the McCaskill, D-Mo., point of order against the conference report. Motion agreed to 62-34: R 17-30; D 43-4 (ND 38-4, SD 5-0); I 2-0. (A three-fifths majority vote (60) of the total Senate is required to waive paragraph eight of Senate Rule 44. Under the rule, a senator may raise a point of order against provisions of a conference report that constitute new directed spending.) May 15, 2008.

130. HR 2419. Farm Bill Reauthorization/Conference Report. Adoption of the conference report on the bill that would reauthorize federal farm and nutrition programs for five years, including crop subsidies and food stamps, as well as conservation, rural development and agricultural trade programs. It would authorize a $10.4 billion increase for nutrition programs, offset by extending customs user fees. It also would cut direct payment subsidies overall by $313 million, in part by reducing the percentage of acres for which a farmer can collect those payments. Farmers making more than $750,000 a year in farm-related income and those with more than $500,000 a year in non-farm-related income would not be eligible for federal subsidies. Country-of-origin labels for all meat would be required by September 2008. Adopted (thus cleared for the president) 81-15: R 35-13; D 44-2 (ND 39-2, SD 5-0); I 2-0. A "nay" was a vote in support of the president's position. May 15, 2008.

131. S Con Res 70. Fiscal 2009 Budget Resolution/Motion to Instruct. Gregg, R-N.H., motion to instruct conferees to insist on provisions that include revenue levels consistent with the extension of current tax rates, rather than the revenue levels in the Senate- and House-adopted budget resolutions. Motion rejected 44-51: R 44-2; D 0-47 (ND 0-42, SD 0-5); I 0-2. May 15, 2008.

132. S Con Res 70. Fiscal 2009 Budget Resolution/Motion to Instruct. Boxer, D-Calif., motion to instruct conferees that no legislation providing for new mandates on greenhouse gas emissions should be enacted until it effectively addresses imports from China, India and other nations that have no similar emissions programs. Motion agreed to 55-40: R 8-38; D 45-2 (ND 41-1, SD 4-1); I 2-0. May 15, 2008.

	128	129	130	131	132		128	129	130	131	132
ALABAMA						**MONTANA**					
Shelby	Y	Y	Y	Y	N	Baucus	Y	Y	Y	N	Y
Sessions	N	N	Y	Y	N	Tester	Y	Y	Y	N	Y
ALASKA						**NEBRASKA**					
Stevens	Y	Y	Y	Y	N	Hagel	N	N	N	Y	N
Murkowski	N	Y	N	Y	N	Nelson	Y	Y	Y	N	Y
ARIZONA						**NEVADA**					
McCain	?	?	?	?	?	Reid	Y	Y	Y	N	Y
Kyl	N	N	N	Y	N	Ensign	N	N	N	Y	N
ARKANSAS						**NEW HAMPSHIRE**					
Lincoln	Y	Y	Y	N	Y	Gregg	N	N	N	Y	N
Pryor	Y	Y	Y	N	N	Sununu	N	N	N	Y	N
CALIFORNIA						**NEW JERSEY**					
Feinstein	Y	Y	Y	N	Y	Lautenberg	Y	Y	Y	N	Y
Boxer	Y	Y	Y	N	Y	Menendez	Y	Y	Y	N	Y
COLORADO						**NEW MEXICO**					
Allard	N	N	Y	Y	N	Domenici	N	Y	N	Y	N
Salazar	Y	Y	Y	N	Y	Bingaman	Y	Y	Y	N	Y
CONNECTICUT						**NEW YORK**					
Dodd	Y	Y	Y	N	Y	Schumer	Y	Y	Y	N	Y
Lieberman	Y	Y	Y	N	Y	Clinton	?	?	?	?	?
DELAWARE						**NORTH CAROLINA**					
Biden	Y	Y	Y	N	Y	Dole	Y	Y	Y	Y	Y
Carper	Y	N	Y	N	Y	Burr	N	N	Y	Y	N
FLORIDA						**NORTH DAKOTA**					
Nelson	Y	Y	Y	N	Y	Conrad	Y	Y	Y	N	Y
Martinez	Y	N	Y	Y	Y	Dorgan	Y	Y	Y	N	Y
GEORGIA						**OHIO**					
Chambliss	Y	Y	Y	Y	N	Voinovich	N	N	N	N	N
Isakson	Y	Y	Y	Y	N	Brown	Y	Y	Y	N	Y
HAWAII						**OKLAHOMA**					
Inouye	Y	Y	Y	N	Y	Inhofe	Y	N	Y	Y	N
Akaka	Y	Y	Y	N	Y	Coburn	N	N	N	Y	N
IDAHO						**OREGON**					
Craig	Y	Y	Y	Y	N	Wyden	Y	Y	Y	N	Y
Crapo	Y	Y	Y	Y	N	Smith	Y	Y	Y	Y	Y
ILLINOIS						**PENNSYLVANIA**					
Durbin	Y	Y	Y	N	Y	Specter	Y	N	Y	Y	Y
Obama	?	?	?	?	?	Casey	Y	Y	Y	N	Y
INDIANA						**RHODE ISLAND**					
Lugar	N	N	N	Y	N	Reed	Y	Y	N	N	Y
Bayh	Y	N	Y	N	Y	Whitehouse	Y	Y	N	N	Y
IOWA						**SOUTH CAROLINA**					
Grassley	Y	Y	Y	Y	N	Graham	Y	N	Y	Y	N
Harkin	Y	Y	Y	N	Y	DeMint	N	N	N	Y	N
KANSAS						**SOUTH DAKOTA**					
Brownback	Y	N	Y	Y	N	Johnson	Y	Y	Y	N	N
Roberts	Y	N	Y	Y	N	Thune	Y	N	Y	Y	N
KENTUCKY						**TENNESSEE**					
McConnell	Y	N	Y	Y	N	Alexander	Y	Y	Y	+	-
Bunning	N	N	Y	Y	N	Corker	Y	N	Y	?	?
LOUISIANA						**TEXAS**					
Landrieu	Y	Y	Y	N	Y	Hutchison	Y	N	Y	Y	N
Vitter	Y	N	Y	Y	N	Cornyn	Y	N	Y	Y	N
MAINE						**UTAH**					
Snowe	Y	Y	Y	N	Y	Hatch	N	N	Y	Y	N
Collins	N	N	N	Y	Y	Bennett	N	Y	N	Y	N
MARYLAND						**VERMONT**					
Mikulski	Y	Y	Y	N	Y	Leahy	Y	Y	Y	N	Y
Cardin	Y	Y	Y	N	Y	*Sanders*	Y	Y	Y	N	Y
MASSACHUSETTS						**VIRGINIA**					
Kennedy	Y	Y	?	N	Y	Warner	?	?	Y	Y	Y
Kerry	Y	Y	Y	N	Y	Webb	Y	Y	Y	N	Y
MICHIGAN						**WASHINGTON**					
Levin	Y	Y	Y	N	Y	Murray	Y	Y	Y	N	Y
Stabenow	Y	Y	Y	N	Y	Cantwell	Y	Y	Y	N	Y
MINNESOTA						**WEST VIRGINIA**					
Coleman	Y	Y	Y	Y	Y	Byrd	Y	Y	Y	N	Y
Klobuchar	+	Y	Y	N	Y	Rockefeller	Y	Y	Y	N	Y
MISSISSIPPI						**WISCONSIN**					
Cochran	Y	Y	Y	Y	N	Kohl	Y	Y	Y	N	Y
Wicker	Y	Y	Y	Y	N	Feingold	N	N	Y	N	Y
MISSOURI						**WYOMING**					
Bond	Y	N	Y	Y	N	Enzi	N	N	Y	Y	N
McCaskill	Y	N	Y	N	Y	Barrasso	N	N	Y	Y	N

KEY   **Republicans**   Democrats   *Independents*

Y Voted for (yea)	X Paired against
# Paired for	− Announced against
+ Announced for	P Voted "present"
N Voted against (nay)	

C Voted "present" to avoid possible conflict of interest

? Did not vote or otherwise make a position known

ND Northern Democrats, SD Southern Democrats
Southern states: Ala., Ark., Fla., Ga., Ky., La., Miss., N.C., Okla., S.C., Tenn., Texas, Va.

IN THE SENATE | By Vote Number

133. **S Con Res 70. Fiscal 2009 Budget Resolution/Motion to Instruct.** DeMint, R-S.C., motion to instruct conferees to adjust the budget resolution to require that if a deficit-neutral reserve fund for clean energy and environmental preservation remains in the resolution, then any legislation providing for new mandates on greenhouse gas emissions be contingent on enactment of similar mandates in China and India. Motion rejected 34-61: R 33-13; D 1-46 (ND 1-41, SD 0-5); I 0-2. May 15, 2008.

134. **S Con Res 70. Fiscal 2009 Budget Resolution/Motion to Instruct.** Vitter, R-La., motion to instruct conferees to insist that the conference report be adjusted to include a reserve fund for future legislation allowing increased outer continental shelf energy exploration. Motion rejected 44-51: R 41-5; D 3-44 (ND 1-41, SD 2-3); I 0-2. May 15, 2008.

135. **S Con Res 70. Fiscal 2009 Budget Resolution/Motion to Instruct.** Gregg, R-N.H., motion to instruct conferees to insist that the conference report be adjusted to reflect a $1 trillion cap on discretionary spending. Motion rejected 47-48: R 43-3; D 4-43 (ND 4-38, SD 0-5); I 0-2. May 15, 2008.

	133	134	135			133	134	135
ALABAMA					**MONTANA**			
Shelby	Y	Y	Y		Baucus	N	N	N
Sessions	Y	Y	Y		Tester	N	N	N
ALASKA					**NEBRASKA**			
Stevens	Y	Y	Y		**Hagel**	Y	Y	Y
Murkowski	N	Y	Y		Nelson	N	Y	N
ARIZONA					**NEVADA**			
McCain	?	?	?		Reid	N	N	N
Kyl	Y	Y	Y		**Ensign**	Y	Y	Y
ARKANSAS					**NEW HAMPSHIRE**			
Lincoln	N	N	N		**Gregg**	N	Y	Y
Pryor	N	N	N		**Sununu**	N	Y	Y
CALIFORNIA					**NEW JERSEY**			
Feinstein	N	N	N		Lautenberg	N	N	N
Boxer	N	N	N		Menendez	N	N	N
COLORADO					**NEW MEXICO**			
Allard	Y	Y	Y		**Domenici**	Y	Y	Y
Salazar	N	N	N		Bingaman	N	N	N
CONNECTICUT					**NEW YORK**			
Dodd	N	N	N		Schumer	N	N	N
Lieberman	N	N	N		Clinton	?	?	?
DELAWARE					**NORTH CAROLINA**			
Biden	N	N	N		**Dole**	N	N	Y
Carper	N	N	N		**Burr**	Y	Y	Y
FLORIDA					**NORTH DAKOTA**			
Nelson	N	N	N		Conrad	N	N	N
Martinez	N	N	Y		Dorgan	N	N	N
GEORGIA					**OHIO**			
Chambliss	Y	Y	Y		**Voinovich**	Y	Y	Y
Isakson	Y	Y	Y		Brown	N	N	N
HAWAII					**OKLAHOMA**			
Inouye	N	N	N		**Inhofe**	Y	Y	Y
Akaka	N	N	N		**Coburn**	Y	Y	Y
IDAHO					**OREGON**			
Craig	Y	Y	Y		Wyden	N	N	N
Crapo	Y	Y	Y		**Smith**	N	N	Y
ILLINOIS					**PENNSYLVANIA**			
Durbin	N	N	N		**Specter**	N	Y	N
Obama	?	?	?		Casey	N	N	N
INDIANA					**RHODE ISLAND**			
Lugar	Y	Y	Y		Reed	N	N	N
Bayh	N	N	Y		Whitehouse	N	N	N
IOWA					**SOUTH CAROLINA**			
Grassley	Y	Y	Y		**Graham**	N	Y	Y
Harkin	N	N	N		**DeMint**	Y	Y	Y
KANSAS					**SOUTH DAKOTA**			
Brownback	Y	Y	Y		Johnson	N	N	N
Roberts	N	Y	Y		**Thune**	Y	Y	Y
KENTUCKY					**TENNESSEE**			
McConnell	Y	Y	Y		**Alexander**	–	+	+
Bunning	Y	Y	Y		**Corker**	?	?	?
LOUISIANA					**TEXAS**			
Landrieu	N	Y	N		**Hutchison**	Y	Y	Y
Vitter	Y	Y	Y		**Cornyn**	Y	Y	Y
MAINE					**UTAH**			
Snowe	N	N	N		**Hatch**	Y	Y	Y
Collins	N	N	N		**Bennett**	Y	Y	Y
MARYLAND					**VERMONT**			
Mikulski	N	N	N		Leahy	N	N	N
Cardin	N	N	N		*Sanders*	N	N	N
MASSACHUSETTS					**VIRGINIA**			
Kennedy	N	N	N		**Warner**	N	Y	Y
Kerry	N	N	N		Webb	N	Y	N
MICHIGAN					**WASHINGTON**			
Levin	N	N	N		Murray	N	N	N
Stabenow	N	N	N		Cantwell	N	N	Y
MINNESOTA					**WEST VIRGINIA**			
Coleman	N	Y	Y		Byrd	Y	N	N
Klobuchar	N	N	Y		Rockefeller	N	N	N
MISSISSIPPI					**WISCONSIN**			
Cochran	Y	Y	Y		Kohl	N	N	N
Wicker	Y	Y	Y		Feingold	N	N	Y
MISSOURI					**WYOMING**			
Bond	Y	Y	Y		**Enzi**	Y	Y	N
McCaskill	N	N	N		**Barrasso**	Y	Y	Y

KEY	**Republicans**	Democrats	*Independents*		
Y Voted for (yea)		**X** Paired against		**C** Voted "present" to avoid possible conflict of interest	
# Paired for		**–** Announced against			
+ Announced for		**P** Voted "present"		**?** Did not vote or otherwise make a position known	
N Voted against (nay)					

ND Northern Democrats, SD Southern Democrats
Southern states: Ala., Ark., Fla., Ga., Ky., La., Miss., N.C., Okla., S.C., Tenn., Texas, Va.

IN THE SENATE | By Vote Number

136. Agee Nomination/Confirmation. Confirmation of President Bush's nomination of G. Steven Agee of Virginia to be a judge for the 4th Circuit Court of Appeals. Confirmed 96-0: R 48-0; D 46-0 (ND 41-0, SD 5-0); I 2-0. A "yea" was a vote in support of the president's position. May 20, 2008.

137. HR 2642. Supplemental Appropriations/Motion to Concur. Reid, D-Nev., motion to concur in the House amendment with an amendment. The Reid amendment would permanently expand education benefits for post-Sept. 11 veterans, temporarily extend unemployment insurance benefits and place a moratorium through March 2009 on seven Medicaid regulations proposed by the administration. It would provide $10.4 billion for hurricane recovery and other natural disasters, $1 billion for the Low Income Home Energy Assistance Program, and $1.25 billion for global food aid. Motion agreed to 75-22: R 25-22; D 48-0 (ND 43-0, SD 5-0); I 2-0. (By unanimous consent, the Senate agreed to raise the majority requirement to 60 votes.) A "nay" was a vote in support of the president's position. May 22, 2008.

138. HR 2642. Supplemental Appropriations/Motion to Concur. Reid, D-Nev., motion to concur in the House amendment with a second amendment. The amendment would express the sense of Congress that the mission of U.S. forces in Iraq should be transitioned by June 2009 to counterterrorism operations; training, equipping and supporting Iraqi forces; and force protection. It would provide $165.4 billion for the wars in Iraq and Afghanistan, with $99.5 billion in fiscal 2008 and $65.9 billion in fiscal 2009. It would require Congress to authorize any agreement between the U.S. and Iraqi governments committing U.S. forces, and prohibit permanent U.S. bases in Iraq. It would prohibit any unit not assessed as fully mission-capable from deploying to Iraq and limit deployment time, but would allow for presidential waivers. Motion rejected 34-63: R 6-41; D 28-20 (ND 24-19, SD 4-1); I 0-2. (By unanimous consent, the Senate agreed to raise the majority requirement for the motion to concur to 60 votes.) A "nay" was a vote in support of the president's position. May 22, 2008.

139. HR 2642. Supplemental Appropriations/Motion to Concur. Reid, D-Nev., motion to concur in the House amendment with a Reid amendment. The amendment would provide $165.4 billion for the wars in Iraq and Afghanistan, with $99.5 billion in fiscal 2008 and $65.9 billion in fiscal 2009. Motion agreed to 70-26: R 46-1; D 23-24 (ND 18-24, SD 5-0); I 1-1. (By unanimous consent, the Senate agreed to raise the majority requirement for the motion to concur to 60 votes.) A "yea" was a vote in support of the president's position. May 22, 2008.

140. HR 2419. Farm Bill Reauthorization/Veto Override. Passage, over President Bush's May 21, 2008, veto, of the bill that would reauthorize federal farm and nutrition programs for five years, including crop subsidies, food stamps, conservation and rural development. It would authorize a $10.4 billion increase for nutrition programs, offset by extending customs user fees. It would cut direct-payment subsidies overall by $313 million, in part by reducing the percentage of acres for which a farmer can collect the payments. Farmers making more than $750,000 a year in farm-related income and those with more than $500,000 a year in non-farm-related income would not be eligible for federal subsidies. Country-of-origin labels for all meat would be required by September 2008. Passed (thus enacted into law) 82-13: R 35-11; D 45-2 (ND 40-2, SD 5-0); I 2-0. A two-thirds majority of those present and voting (64 in this case for the Senate) of both chambers is required to override a veto. A "nay" was a vote in support of the president's position. May 22, 2008.

	136	137	138	139	140
ALABAMA					
Shelby	Y	Y	N	Y	Y
Sessions	Y	N	N	Y	Y
ALASKA					
Stevens	Y	Y	N	Y	Y
Murkowski	Y	Y	N	Y	N
ARIZONA					
McCain	?	?	?	?	?
Kyl	Y	N	N	Y	N
ARKANSAS					
Lincoln	Y	Y	Y	Y	Y
Pryor	Y	Y	Y	Y	Y
CALIFORNIA					
Feinstein	Y	Y	N	N	Y
Boxer	Y	Y	N	N	Y
COLORADO					
Allard	Y	N	N	Y	Y
Salazar	Y	Y	Y	Y	Y
CONNECTICUT					
Dodd	Y	Y	N	N	Y
Lieberman	Y	Y	N	Y	Y
DELAWARE					
Biden	Y	Y	Y	Y	Y
Carper	Y	Y	Y	Y	Y
FLORIDA					
Nelson	Y	Y	Y	Y	Y
Martinez	Y	Y	N	Y	Y
GEORGIA					
Chambliss	Y	Y	N	Y	Y
Isakson	Y	Y	N	Y	Y
HAWAII					
Inouye	Y	Y	Y	Y	Y
Akaka	Y	Y	Y	Y	Y
IDAHO					
Craig	Y	Y	N	Y	Y
Crapo	Y	Y	N	Y	Y
ILLINOIS					
Durbin	Y	Y	N	N	Y
Obama	?	Y	N	?	?
INDIANA					
Lugar	Y	N	N	Y	N
Bayh	Y	Y	Y	Y	Y
IOWA					
Grassley	Y	N	N	Y	Y
Harkin	Y	Y	N	Y	Y
KANSAS					
Brownback	Y	N	N	Y	Y
Roberts	Y	Y	N	Y	Y
KENTUCKY					
McConnell	Y	N	N	Y	Y
Bunning	Y	N	N	Y	Y
LOUISIANA					
Landrieu	Y	Y	Y	Y	Y
Vitter	Y	Y	N	Y	Y
MAINE					
Snowe	Y	Y	Y	Y	Y
Collins	Y	Y	Y	Y	N
MARYLAND					
Mikulski	Y	Y	Y	Y	Y
Cardin	Y	Y	N	N	Y
MASSACHUSETTS					
Kennedy	?	?	?	?	?
Kerry	Y	Y	N	N	Y
MICHIGAN					
Levin	Y	Y	Y	Y	Y
Stabenow	Y	Y	Y	Y	Y
MINNESOTA					
Coleman	Y	Y	N	Y	Y
Klobuchar	Y	Y	N	N	Y
MISSISSIPPI					
Cochran	Y	N	N	Y	Y
Wicker	Y	Y	N	Y	Y
MISSOURI					
Bond	Y	Y	N	Y	Y
McCaskill	Y	Y	Y	Y	Y

	136	137	138	139	140
MONTANA					
Baucus	Y	Y	Y	Y	Y
Tester	Y	Y	Y	Y	Y
NEBRASKA					
Hagel	Y	Y	Y	Y	N
Nelson	Y	Y	Y	Y	Y
NEVADA					
Reid	Y	Y	N	N	Y
Ensign	Y	N	N	N	Y
NEW HAMPSHIRE					
Gregg	Y	N	N	Y	N
Sununu	Y	Y	N	Y	N
NEW JERSEY					
Lautenberg	Y	Y	N	N	Y
Menendez	Y	Y	N	N	Y
NEW MEXICO					
Domenici	Y	Y	N	Y	N
Bingaman	Y	Y	N	Y	Y
NEW YORK					
Schumer	Y	Y	N	N	Y
Clinton	?	Y	N	N	Y
NORTH CAROLINA					
Dole	Y	Y	Y	Y	Y
Burr	Y	N	N	Y	Y
NORTH DAKOTA					
Conrad	Y	Y	Y	Y	Y
Dorgan	Y	Y	Y	Y	Y
OHIO					
Voinovich	Y	N	Y	Y	N
Brown	Y	Y	N	Y	Y
OKLAHOMA					
Inhofe	Y	Y	N	Y	Y
Coburn	Y	?	?	?	?
OREGON					
Wyden	Y	Y	N	N	Y
Smith	Y	Y	Y	N	Y
PENNSYLVANIA					
Specter	Y	Y	N	Y	Y
Casey	Y	Y	Y	Y	Y
RHODE ISLAND					
Reed	Y	Y	Y	N	N
Whitehouse	Y	Y	N	N	N
SOUTH CAROLINA					
Graham	Y	N	N	Y	Y
DeMint	Y	N	N	Y	P
SOUTH DAKOTA					
Johnson	Y	Y	N	Y	Y
Thune	Y	Y	N	Y	Y
TENNESSEE					
Alexander	Y	N	N	Y	Y
Corker	Y	N	N	Y	Y
TEXAS					
Hutchison	Y	Y	N	Y	Y
Cornyn	Y	N	N	Y	Y
UTAH					
Hatch	Y	N	N	Y	Y
Bennett	Y	N	N	Y	N
VERMONT					
Leahy	Y	Y	N	N	Y
Sanders	Y	Y	N	N	Y
VIRGINIA					
Warner	Y	Y	N	Y	Y
Webb	Y	Y	N	Y	Y
WASHINGTON					
Murray	Y	Y	Y	N	Y
Cantwell	Y	Y	Y	N	Y
WEST VIRGINIA					
Byrd	Y	Y	N	N	Y
Rockefeller	Y	Y	Y	Y	Y
WISCONSIN					
Kohl	Y	Y	Y	N	Y
Feingold	Y	Y	N	N	Y
WYOMING					
Enzi	Y	N	N	Y	Y
Barrasso	Y	N	N	Y	Y

KEY   **Republicans**   Democrats   *Independents*

Y Voted for (yea)	X Paired against	C Voted "present" to avoid possible conflict of interest
# Paired for	– Announced against	
+ Announced for	P Voted "present"	? Did not vote or otherwise make a position known
N Voted against (nay)		

ND Northern Democrats, SD Southern Democrats
Southern states: Ala., Ark., Fla., Ga., Ky., La., Miss., N.C., Okla., S.C., Tenn., Texas, Va.

IN THE SENATE | By Vote Number

141. **S 3036. Climate Change/Cloture.** Motion to invoke cloture (thus limiting debate) on the motion to proceed to the bill that would cap greenhouse gas emissions nationwide and set up a trading system for companies to buy and sell emission allowances. Motion agreed to 74-14: R 32-13; D 40-1 (ND 36-1, SD 4-0); I 2-0. Three-fifths of the total Senate (60) is required to invoke cloture. June 2, 2008.

142. **S Con Res 70. Fiscal 2009 Budget Resolution/Conference Report.** Adoption of the conference report on the concurrent resolution that would allow up to $1 trillion in discretionary spending for fiscal 2009, plus $70 billion for the wars in Iraq and Afghanistan, and $5.8 billion for hurricane recovery. It would assume $1.9 trillion in mandatory spending and allow for the statutory debt limit to increase by $800 billion to $10.615 trillion. It would create a "trigger" mechanism that would reinforce pay-as-you-go rules in the House. The measure assumes a one-year alternative minimum tax "patch" that would be offset. It also would create a 60-vote point of order in the Senate against legislation that increases the deficit by $10 billion in a year. Adopted (thus sent to the House) 48-45: R 2-44; D 44-1 (ND 39-1, SD 5-0); I 2-0. June 4, 2008.

143. **Procedural Motion/Require Attendance.** Reid, D-Nev., motion to instruct the sergeant at arms to request the attendance of absent senators. Motion rejected 27-28: R 0-28; D 25-0 (ND 23-0, SD 2-0); I 2-0. June 4, 2008.

144. **HR 6124. Farm Bill Reauthorization/Passage.** Passage of the bill that would reauthorize federal farm and nutrition programs for five years, including crop subsidies and food stamps, as well as conservation, rural development and agricultural trade programs. It would authorize a $10.4 billion increase for nutrition programs, offset by extending customs user fees. It would cut direct payment subsidies overall by $313 million, in part by reducing the percentage of acres for which a farmer can collect those payments. Farmers making more than $750,000 a year in farm-related income and those with more than $500,000 a year in non-farm-related income would not be eligible for federal subsidies. Country-of-origin labels for all meat would be required by September 2008. Passed (thus cleared for the president) 77-15: R 34-13; D 41-2 (ND 37-2, SD 4-0); I 2-0. A "nay" was a vote in support of the president's position. June 5, 2008.

145. **S 3036. Climate Change/Cloture.** Motion to invoke cloture (thus limiting debate) on the Boxer, D-Calif., substitute amendment that would cap greenhouse gas emissions nationwide and set up a trading system for companies to buy and sell emission allowances. Motion rejected 48-36: R 7-32; D 39-4 (ND 35-3, SD 4-1); I 2-0. Three-fifths of the total Senate (60) is required to invoke cloture. A "nay" was a vote in support of the president's position. June 6, 2008.

	141	142	143	144	145
ALABAMA					
Shelby	N	N	?	Y	N
Sessions	N	N	N	Y	N
ALASKA					
Stevens	Y	N	?	Y	?
Murkowski	?	N	N	N	?
ARIZONA					
McCain	?	?	?	?	+
Kyl	N	N	?	N	N
ARKANSAS					
Lincoln	Y	Y	Y	Y	Y
Pryor	Y	Y	Y	Y	Y
CALIFORNIA					
Feinstein	Y	Y	?	Y	Y
Boxer	Y	Y	Y	Y	Y
COLORADO					
Allard	N	N	N	Y	N
Salazar	Y	Y	Y	Y	Y
CONNECTICUT					
Dodd	Y	Y	Y	Y	Y
Lieberman	Y	Y	Y	Y	Y
DELAWARE					
Biden	+	+	?	?	+
Carper	Y	Y	?	Y	Y
FLORIDA					
Nelson	Y	Y	?	Y	Y
Martinez	Y	N	N	Y	Y
GEORGIA					
Chambliss	N	N	N	Y	N
Isakson	Y	N	?	Y	N
HAWAII					
Inouye	Y	Y	?	Y	Y
Akaka	Y	Y	?	Y	Y
IDAHO					
Craig	N	N	N	Y	?
Crapo	Y	N	?	Y	N
ILLINOIS					
Durbin	Y	Y	Y	Y	Y
Obama	?	Y	?	?	+
INDIANA					
Lugar	Y	N	N	N	N
Bayh	Y	N	?	Y	Y
IOWA					
Grassley	Y	N	N	Y	N
Harkin	Y	Y	Y	Y	Y
KANSAS					
Brownback	Y	N	?	Y	N
Roberts	Y	N	?	Y	N
KENTUCKY					
McConnell	N	N	N	Y	N
Bunning	N	N	?	Y	N
LOUISIANA					
Landrieu	?	Y	?	Y	N
Vitter	Y	N	N	Y	N
MAINE					
Snowe	Y	Y	N	Y	Y
Collins	Y	Y	N	N	Y
MARYLAND					
Mikulski	Y	Y	?	Y	Y
Cardin	Y	Y	?	Y	Y
MASSACHUSETTS					
Kennedy	?	#	?	?	+
Kerry	Y	Y	Y	Y	Y
MICHIGAN					
Levin	Y	Y	Y	Y	Y
Stabenow	Y	Y	?	Y	Y
MINNESOTA					
Coleman	Y	N	N	Y	+
Klobuchar	Y	Y	Y	Y	Y
MISSISSIPPI					
Cochran	Y	N	?	Y	N
Wicker	?	N	N	Y	N
MISSOURI					
Bond	Y	N	?	Y	N
McCaskill	Y	Y	Y	Y	Y
MONTANA					
Baucus	?	Y	Y	Y	Y
Tester	Y	Y	Y	Y	Y
NEBRASKA					
Hagel	Y	N	?	N	N
Nelson	Y	Y	Y	Y	Y
NEVADA					
Reid	Y	Y	Y	Y	Y
Ensign	Y	N	?	N	N
NEW HAMPSHIRE					
Gregg	Y	N	?	?	?
Sununu	Y	N	N	N	Y
NEW JERSEY					
Lautenberg	?	Y	?	Y	Y
Menendez	Y	Y	?	Y	Y
NEW MEXICO					
Domenici	Y	X	?	N	N
Bingaman	Y	Y	?	Y	Y
NEW YORK					
Schumer	Y	Y	Y	Y	Y
Clinton	?	?	?	?	+
NORTH CAROLINA					
Dole	Y	N	N	Y	N
Burr	?	N	N	Y	N
NORTH DAKOTA					
Conrad	Y	Y	?	Y	?
Dorgan	Y	Y	N	Y	N
OHIO					
Voinovich	Y	N	N	N	N
Brown	Y	Y	Y	N	Y
OKLAHOMA					
Inhofe	N	N	N	Y	N
Coburn	N	N	N	N	N
OREGON					
Wyden	?	Y	?	Y	Y
Smith	Y	N	?	Y	Y
PENNSYLVANIA					
Specter	Y	N	?	Y	?
Casey	Y	Y	Y	Y	Y
RHODE ISLAND					
Reed	Y	Y	Y	N	Y
Whitehouse	Y	Y	?	N	Y
SOUTH CAROLINA					
Graham	Y	N	N	Y	?
DeMint	N	N	N	N	?
SOUTH DAKOTA					
Johnson	Y	Y	Y	Y	N
Thune	Y	N	Y	N	N
TENNESSEE					
Alexander	Y	N	–	Y	N
Corker	Y	N	N	Y	N
TEXAS					
Hutchison	Y	N	N	Y	N
Cornyn	Y	N	?	Y	?
UTAH					
Hatch	N	N	?	N	N
Bennett	Y	N	?	N	N
VERMONT					
Leahy	Y	Y	Y	Y	Y
Sanders	Y	Y	Y	Y	Y
VIRGINIA					
Warner	Y	X	N	Y	Y
Webb	Y	Y	?	?	Y
WASHINGTON					
Murray	Y	Y	?	Y	Y
Cantwell	Y	Y	Y	Y	Y
WEST VIRGINIA					
Byrd	N	#	?	?	?
Rockefeller	Y	Y	?	Y	Y
WISCONSIN					
Kohl	Y	Y	Y	Y	Y
Feingold	Y	Y	Y	Y	Y
WYOMING					
Enzi	N	N	N	Y	N
Barrasso	N	N	N	Y	N

KEY	**Republicans**	Democrats	*Independents*		
Y	Voted for (yea)	X	Paired against	C	Voted "present" to avoid possible conflict of interest
#	Paired for	–	Announced against		
+	Announced for	P	Voted "present"	?	Did not vote or otherwise make a position known
N	Voted against (nay)				

ND Northern Democrats, SD Southern Democrats
Southern states: Ala., Ark., Fla., Ga., Ky., La., Miss., N.C., Okla., S.C., Tenn., Texas, Va.

IN THE SENATE | By Vote Number

146. **S 3044. Energy Prices/Cloture.** Motion to invoke cloture (thus limiting debate) on the motion to proceed to the bill that would repeal tax benefits for oil companies worth $17 billion over 10 years that were enacted in 2004 and 2005, as well as direct the money to renewable energy. It also would impose a profits tax on the largest oil companies. Motion rejected 51-43: R 6-41; D 43-2 (ND 39-1, SD 4-1); I 2-0. Three-fifths of the total Senate (60) is required to invoke cloture. A "nay" was a vote in support of the president's position. June 10, 2008.

147. **HR 6049. Tax Provisions Extension/Cloture.** Motion to invoke cloture (thus limiting debate) on the motion to proceed to the bill that would extend dozens of expired or expiring tax provisions for one year and create new energy-related tax incentives. Motion rejected 50-44: R 3-44; D 45-0 (ND 40-0, SD 5-0); I 2-0. Three-fifths of the total Senate (60) is required to invoke cloture. June 10, 2008.

148. **Davis Nomination/Confirmation.** Confirmation of President Bush's nomination of Mark S. Davis of Virginia to be a judge for the U.S. District Court for the Eastern District of Virginia. Confirmed 94-0: R 47-0; D 45-0 (ND 40-0, SD 5-0); I 2-0. A "yea" was a vote in support of the president's position. June 10, 2008.

149. **S 3101. Medicare Physician Payments/Cloture.** Motion to invoke cloture (thus limiting debate) on the motion to proceed to the bill that would prevent a 10.6 percent cut in Medicare physician payments scheduled to take effect on July 1, 2008, and would give the doctors a 1.1 percent increase in 2009. Motion rejected 54-39: R 9-38; D 43-1 (ND 39-1, SD 4-0); I 2-0. Three-fifths of the total Senate (60) is required to invoke cloture. A "nay" was a vote in support of the president's position. June 12, 2008.

	146	147	148	149			146	147	148	149
ALABAMA						**MONTANA**				
Shelby	N	N	Y	N		Baucus	Y	Y	Y	Y
Sessions	N	N	Y	N		Tester	Y	Y	Y	Y
ALASKA						**NEBRASKA**				
Stevens	N	N	Y	Y		Hagel	N	N	Y	N
Murkowski	N	N	Y	Y		Nelson	Y	Y	Y	Y
ARIZONA						**NEVADA**				
McCain	?	?	?	?		Reid	N	Y	Y	N
Kyl	N	N	Y	N		Ensign	N	N	Y	N
ARKANSAS						**NEW HAMPSHIRE**				
Lincoln	Y	Y	Y	Y		Gregg	N	N	Y	N
Pryor	Y	Y	Y	Y		Sununu	N	N	Y	?
CALIFORNIA						**NEW JERSEY**				
Feinstein	Y	Y	Y	Y		Lautenberg	Y	Y	Y	Y
Boxer	Y	Y	Y	Y		Menendez	Y	Y	Y	Y
COLORADO						**NEW MEXICO**				
Allard	N	N	Y	N		Domenici	N	N	Y	N
Salazar	Y	Y	Y	Y		Bingaman	Y	Y	Y	Y
CONNECTICUT						**NEW YORK**				
Dodd	Y	Y	Y	Y		Schumer	Y	Y	Y	Y
Lieberman	Y	Y	Y	Y		Clinton	?	?	?	?
DELAWARE						**NORTH CAROLINA**				
Biden	Y	Y	Y	Y		Dole	N	N	Y	N
Carper	Y	Y	Y	Y		Burr	N	N	Y	N
FLORIDA						**NORTH DAKOTA**				
Nelson	Y	Y	Y	Y		Conrad	Y	Y	Y	Y
Martinez	N	N	Y	N		Dorgan	Y	Y	Y	Y
GEORGIA						**OHIO**				
Chambliss	N	N	Y	N		Voinovich	N	N	Y	N
Isakson	N	N	Y	N		Brown	Y	Y	Y	Y
HAWAII						**OKLAHOMA**				
Inouye	Y	Y	Y	?		Inhofe	N	N	Y	N
Akaka	Y	Y	Y	Y		Coburn	N	N	Y	N
IDAHO						**OREGON**				
Craig	N	N	Y	N		Wyden	Y	Y	Y	Y
Crapo	N	N	Y	N		Smith	Y	Y	Y	Y
ILLINOIS						**PENNSYLVANIA**				
Durbin	Y	Y	Y	Y		Specter	N	N	Y	N
Obama	?	?	?	?		Casey	Y	Y	Y	Y
INDIANA						**RHODE ISLAND**				
Lugar	N	N	Y	N		Reed	Y	Y	Y	Y
Bayh	Y	Y	Y	Y		Whitehouse	Y	Y	Y	Y
IOWA						**SOUTH CAROLINA**				
Grassley	Y	N	Y	N		Graham	?	?	?	N
Harkin	Y	Y	Y	Y		DeMint	N	N	Y	N
KANSAS						**SOUTH DAKOTA**				
Brownback	N	N	Y	N		Johnson	Y	Y	Y	Y
Roberts	N	N	Y	Y		Thune	N	N	Y	N
KENTUCKY						**TENNESSEE**				
McConnell	N	N	Y	N		Alexander	N	N	Y	N
Bunning	N	N	Y	N		Corker	N	Y	Y	N
LOUISIANA						**TEXAS**				
Landrieu	N	Y	Y	+		Hutchison	N	N	Y	N
Vitter	N	N	Y	N		Cornyn	N	N	Y	N
MAINE						**UTAH**				
Snowe	Y	Y	Y	Y		Hatch	N	N	Y	N
Collins	Y	N	Y	Y		Bennett	N	N	Y	N
MARYLAND						**VERMONT**				
Mikulski	Y	Y	Y	Y		Leahy	Y	Y	Y	Y
Cardin	Y	Y	Y	Y		*Sanders*	Y	Y	Y	Y
MASSACHUSETTS						**VIRGINIA**				
Kennedy	?	?	?	?		Warner	Y	N	Y	N
Kerry	Y	Y	Y	Y		Webb	Y	Y	Y	Y
MICHIGAN						**WASHINGTON**				
Levin	Y	Y	Y	Y		Murray	Y	Y	Y	Y
Stabenow	Y	Y	Y	Y		Cantwell	Y	Y	Y	Y
MINNESOTA						**WEST VIRGINIA**				
Coleman	Y	N	Y	Y		Byrd	?	?	?	Y
Klobuchar	Y	Y	Y	Y		Rockefeller	Y	Y	Y	Y
MISSISSIPPI						**WISCONSIN**				
Cochran	N	N	Y	N		Kohl	Y	Y	Y	Y
Wicker	N	N	Y	N		Feingold	Y	Y	Y	Y
MISSOURI						**WYOMING**				
Bond	N	N	Y	N		Enzi	N	N	Y	N
McCaskill	Y	Y	Y	Y		Barrasso	N	N	Y	N

KEY   **Republicans**   Democrats   *Independents*

Y Voted for (yea)	X Paired against	C Voted "present" to avoid possible conflict of interest
# Paired for	– Announced against	
+ Announced for	P Voted "present"	? Did not vote or otherwise make a position known
N Voted against (nay)		

ND Northern Democrats, SD Southern Democrats
Southern states: Ala., Ark., Fla., Ga., Ky., La., Miss., N.C., Okla., S.C., Tenn., Texas, Va.

IN THE SENATE | By Vote Number

150. HR 6049. **Tax Provisions Extension/Cloture.** Motion to invoke cloture (thus limiting debate) on the motion to proceed to the bill that would extend dozens of expired or expiring tax provisions for one year and create new energy-related tax incentives. Motion rejected 52-44: R 5-43; D 45-1 (ND 40-1, SD 5-0); I 2-0. Three-fifths of the total Senate (60) is required to invoke cloture. June 17, 2008.

151. HR 6124. **Farm Bill Reauthorization/Veto Override.** Passage, over President Bush's June 18, 2008, veto, of the bill that would reauthorize federal farm and nutrition programs for five years, including crop subsidies and food stamps, as well as conservation, rural development and agricultural trade programs. It would authorize a $10.4 billion increase for nutrition programs, offset by extending customs user fees. It would cut direct payment subsidies overall by $313 million, in part by reducing the percentage of acres for which a farmer can collect those payments. Farmers making more than $750,000 a year in farm-related income and those with more than $500,000 a year in non-farm-related income would not be eligible for federal subsidies. Country-of-origin labels for all meat would be required by September 2008. Passed (thus enacted into law) 80-14: R 35-12; D 43-2 (ND 38-2, SD 5-0); I 2-0. A two-thirds majority of those present and voting (63 in this case for the Senate) of both chambers is required to override a veto. A "nay" was a vote in support of the president's position. June 18, 2008.

152. HR 3221. **Mortgage Relief/Low-Income Housing.** Bond, R-Mo., amendment to the Dodd, D-Conn., substitute amendment. The Bond amendment would clarify that Fannie Mae and Freddie Mac are not responsible for any payments to other housing entities under the new Affordable Housing Trust Fund. It also would bar the use of funds for soft program costs, including staff costs. The substitute would provide tax breaks for first-time homebuyers and for homebuilders, overhaul Fannie Mae and Freddie Mac, modernize the Federal Housing Administration and provide a $300 billion expansion of the FHA's insurance programs to help struggling borrowers refinance their mortgages. Rejected 11-77: R 11-32; D 0-44 (ND 0-39, SD 0-5); I 0-1. June 19, 2008.

153. HR 3221. **Mortgage Relief/Federal Housing Administration Expansion.** Bond, R-Mo., motion to waive the pay-as-you-go rules with respect to the Dodd, D-Conn., point of order against the Bond amendment to the Dodd substitute amendment. The Bond amendment would strike the HOPE for Homeowners Program, a new loan program that would provide a $300 billion expansion of the FHA's insurance programs to help struggling borrowers refinance their mortgages. Motion rejected 21-69: R 21-23; D 0-45 (ND 0-40, SD 0-5); I 0-1. A three-fifths majority (60) of the total Senate is required to waive the fiscal 2008 budget resolution. June 19, 2008.

154. HR 3221. **Mortgage Relief/Motion to Refer.** Bunning, R-Ky., motion to refer the House-passed bill to the Senate Committee on Banking, Housing and Urban Affairs with instructions to assess the potential financial benefits the legislation could provide to Countrywide Financial Corp. and other lenders. Motion rejected 11-70: R 11-30; D 0-39 (ND 0-36, SD 0-3); I 0-1. By unanimous consent, the Senate agreed to raise the majority requirement for the motion to refer to 60 votes. (Subsequently, the Bunning motion was withdrawn.) June 19, 2008.

	150	151	152	153	154			150	151	152	153	154
ALABAMA							**MONTANA**					
Shelby	N	Y	N	N	N		Baucus	Y	Y	N	N	N
Sessions	N	Y	N	Y	N		Tester	Y	Y	N	N	N
ALASKA							**NEBRASKA**					
Stevens	N	Y	N	Y	N		Hagel	N	N	N	N	N
Murkowski	N	N	N	Y	N		Nelson	Y	Y	N	N	N
ARIZONA							**NEVADA**					
McCain	?	?	?	?	?		Reid	N	Y	N	N	N
Kyl	N	N	?	?	?		**Ensign**	N	N	Y	Y	Y
ARKANSAS							**NEW HAMPSHIRE**					
Lincoln	Y	Y	N	N	N		**Gregg**	N	N	N	N	?
Pryor	Y	Y	N	N	P		Sununu	N	N	N	N	N
CALIFORNIA							**NEW JERSEY**					
Feinstein	Y	Y	N	N	N		Lautenberg	Y	Y	N	N	N
Boxer	Y	Y	N	N	P		Menendez	Y	Y	N	N	N
COLORADO							**NEW MEXICO**					
Allard	N	Y	N	Y	Y		**Domenici**	N	?	?	N	N
Salazar	Y	Y	N	N	P		Bingaman	Y	Y	N	N	N
CONNECTICUT							**NEW YORK**					
Dodd	Y	Y	N	N	N		Schumer	Y	Y	N	N	N
Lieberman	Y	Y	?	?	?		Clinton	?	?	?	?	?
DELAWARE							**NORTH CAROLINA**					
Biden	Y	Y	N	N	N		Dole	N	Y	N	N	N
Carper	Y	Y	N	N	N		Burr	N	Y	Y	Y	Y
FLORIDA							**NORTH DAKOTA**					
Nelson	Y	Y	N	N	N		Conrad	Y	Y	N	?	N
Martinez	N	Y	N	N	N		Dorgan	Y	Y	N	N	N
GEORGIA							**OHIO**					
Chambliss	N	Y	N	N	N		Voinovich	N	N	N	N	N
Isakson	N	Y	N	N	C		Brown	Y	Y	N	N	N
HAWAII							**OKLAHOMA**					
Inouye	Y	Y	N	N	N		**Inhofe**	N	Y	Y	Y	Y
Akaka	Y	Y	N	N	N		**Coburn**	N	N	Y	Y	Y
IDAHO							**OREGON**					
Craig	N	Y	N	Y	N		Wyden	Y	Y	N	N	N
Crapo	N	Y	N	Y	N		Smith	Y	Y	N	N	N
ILLINOIS							**PENNSYLVANIA**					
Durbin	Y	Y	N	N	N		Specter	N	Y	N	N	N
Obama	?	?	?	?	?		Casey	Y	Y	N	N	N
INDIANA							**RHODE ISLAND**					
Lugar	N	N	N	N	N		Reed	Y	N	N	N	N
Bayh	Y	Y	N	N	N		Whitehouse	Y	N	N	N	N
IOWA							**SOUTH CAROLINA**					
Grassley	N	Y	Y	Y	N		Graham	N	Y	N	N	N
Harkin	Y	Y	?	?	?		**DeMint**	N	N	Y	Y	Y
KANSAS							**SOUTH DAKOTA**					
Brownback	N	Y	?	?	?		Johnson	Y	Y	N	N	Y
Roberts	N	Y	?	?	?		**Thune**	N	Y	N	Y	Y
KENTUCKY							**TENNESSEE**					
McConnell	N	Y	N	Y	Y		Alexander	N	Y	–	–	–
Bunning	N	Y	Y	Y	Y		**Corker**	Y	Y	N	N	N
LOUISIANA							**TEXAS**					
Landrieu	Y	Y	N	N	N		**Hutchison**	N	Y	N	Y	N
Vitter	N	Y	Y	Y	Y		**Cornyn**	N	Y	N	Y	P
MAINE							**UTAH**					
Snowe	Y	Y	N	N	N		**Hatch**	N	Y	N	N	N
Collins	Y	N	N	N	N		**Bennett**	N	N	N	N	N
MARYLAND							**VERMONT**					
Mikulski	Y	Y	N	N	N		Leahy	Y	Y	N	N	N
Cardin	Y	Y	N	N	N		*Sanders*	Y	Y	N	N	N
MASSACHUSETTS							**VIRGINIA**					
Kennedy	?	?	?	?	?		**Warner**	N	Y	N	N	N
Kerry	Y	Y	N	N	N		Webb	Y	Y	N	N	?
MICHIGAN							**WASHINGTON**					
Levin	Y	Y	N	N	N		Murray	Y	Y	N	N	N
Stabenow	Y	Y	N	N	N		Cantwell	Y	Y	N	N	N
MINNESOTA							**WEST VIRGINIA**					
Coleman	Y	Y	N	N	N		Byrd	Y	?	N	N	?
Klobuchar	Y	Y	N	N	N		Rockefeller	Y	Y	N	N	N
MISSISSIPPI							**WISCONSIN**					
Cochran	N	Y	N	N	N		Kohl	Y	Y	N	N	N
Wicker	N	Y	N	N	N		Feingold	Y	Y	N	N	N
MISSOURI							**WYOMING**					
Bond	N	Y	Y	Y	Y		**Enzi**	N	Y	Y	Y	N
McCaskill	Y	Y	P	N	N		**Barrasso**	N	Y	Y	Y	N

ND Northern Democrats, SD Southern Democrats
Southern states: Ala., Ark., Fla., Ga., Ky., La., Miss., N.C., Okla., S.C., Tenn., Texas, Va.

IN THE SENATE | By Vote Number

155. **HR 3221. Mortgage Relief/Cloture.** Motion to invoke cloture (thus limiting debate) on the motion to concur in the House amendment with a Dodd, D-Conn., substitute. The substitute would provide tax breaks for first-time homebuyers and for homebuilders, overhaul Fannie Mae and Freddie Mac, modernize the Federal Housing Administration and provide a $300 billion expansion of the FHA's insurance programs to help struggling borrowers refinance their mortgages. Motion agreed to 83-9: R 35-9; D 46-0 (ND 41-0, SD 5-0); I 2-0. Three-fifths of the total Senate (60) is required to invoke cloture. June 24, 2008.

156. **White Nomination/Confirmation.** Confirmation of President Bush's nomination of Helene N. White of Michigan to be a judge for the 6th Circuit Court of Appeals. Confirmed 63-32: R 15-32; D 46-0 (ND 41-0, SD 5-0); I 2-0. A "yea" was a vote in support of the president's position. June 24, 2008.

157. **HR 3221. Mortgage Relief/Motion to Concur.** Motion to concur in the House amendment with a Dodd, D-Conn., substitute. The Dodd substitute would provide tax breaks for first-time homebuyers and for homebuilders, overhaul Fannie Mae and Freddie Mac, modernize the Federal Housing Administration and provide a $300 billion expansion of the FHA's insurance programs to help struggling borrowers refinance their mortgages. It would provide about $14.5 billion in housing-focused tax credits, authorize $3.92 billion in Community Development Block Grants to purchase and rehabilitate foreclosed properties and give mortgage relief to returning servicemembers. Motion agreed to 79-16: R 32-16; D 45-0 (ND 40-0, SD 5-0); I 2-0. A "nay" was a vote in support of the president's position. June 25, 2008.

158. **HR 6304. Foreign Intelligence Surveillance/Cloture.** Motion to invoke cloture (thus limiting debate) on the motion to proceed to the bill that would overhaul the Foreign Intelligence Surveillance Act, which governs electronic surveillance of foreign terrorism suspects. Motion agreed to 80-15: R 48-0; D 31-14 (ND 26-14, SD 5-0); I 1-1. Three-fifths of the total Senate (60) is required to invoke cloture. June 25, 2008.

159. **Lawrence Nomination/Confirmation.** Confirmation of President Bush's nomination of William T. Lawrence of Indiana to be a judge for the U.S. District Court for the Southern District of Indiana. Confirmed 97-0: R 48-0; D 47-0 (ND 42-0, SD 5-0); I 2-0. A "yea" was a vote in support of the president's position. June 26, 2008.

	155	156	157	158	159			155	156	157	158	159
ALABAMA							**MONTANA**					
Shelby	Y	Y	Y	Y	Y		Baucus	Y	Y	Y	Y	Y
Sessions	Y	Y	Y	Y	Y		Tester	Y	Y	Y	Y	Y
ALASKA							**NEBRASKA**					
Stevens	Y	Y	Y	Y	Y		Hagel	Y	Y	Y	Y	Y
Murkowski	Y	Y	Y	Y	Y		Nelson	Y	Y	Y	Y	Y
ARIZONA							**NEVADA**					
McCain	?	?	?	?	?		Reid	Y	Y	Y	Y	Y
Kyl	N	N	N	Y	Y		Ensign	N	N	N	Y	Y
ARKANSAS							**NEW HAMPSHIRE**					
Lincoln	Y	Y	Y	Y	Y		Gregg	Y	N	Y	Y	Y
Pryor	Y	Y	Y	Y	Y		Sununu	Y	N	Y	Y	Y
CALIFORNIA							**NEW JERSEY**					
Feinstein	Y	Y	Y	Y	Y		Lautenberg	Y	Y	Y	N	Y
Boxer	Y	Y	Y	N	Y		Menendez	Y	Y	Y	N	Y
COLORADO							**NEW MEXICO**					
Allard	?	N	Y	Y	Y		Domenici	Y	N	Y	Y	Y
Salazar	Y	Y	Y	Y	Y		Bingaman	Y	Y	Y	Y	Y
CONNECTICUT							**NEW YORK**					
Dodd	Y	Y	Y	N	Y		Schumer	Y	Y	Y	N	Y
Lieberman	Y	Y	Y	Y	Y		Clinton	?	Y	?	?	Y
DELAWARE							**NORTH CAROLINA**					
Biden	Y	Y	Y	N	Y		Dole	Y	N	Y	Y	Y
Carper	Y	Y	Y	Y	Y		Burr	Y	N	N	Y	Y
FLORIDA							**NORTH DAKOTA**					
Nelson	Y	Y	Y	Y	Y		Conrad	Y	Y	Y	Y	Y
Martinez	Y	N	Y	Y	Y		Dorgan	Y	Y	Y	Y	Y
GEORGIA							**OHIO**					
Chambliss	Y	N	N	Y	Y		**Voinovich**	Y	Y	Y	Y	Y
Isakson	Y	Y	Y	Y	Y		Brown	Y	Y	Y	N	Y
HAWAII							**OKLAHOMA**					
Inouye	Y	Y	Y	Y	Y		**Inhofe**	?	N	N	Y	Y
Akaka	Y	Y	Y	Y	Y		**Coburn**	?	N	N	Y	Y
IDAHO							**OREGON**					
Craig	Y	N	Y	Y	Y		Wyden	Y	Y	Y	N	Y
Crapo	N	Y	N	Y	Y		**Smith**	Y	Y	Y	Y	Y
ILLINOIS							**PENNSYLVANIA**					
Durbin	Y	Y	Y	N	Y		**Specter**	Y	N	Y	Y	Y
Obama	?	?	?	?	?		Casey	Y	Y	Y	Y	Y
INDIANA							**RHODE ISLAND**					
Lugar	Y	Y	Y	Y	Y		Reed	Y	Y	Y	Y	Y
Bayh	Y	Y	Y	Y	Y		Whitehouse	Y	Y	Y	Y	Y
IOWA							**SOUTH CAROLINA**					
Grassley	Y	N	Y	Y	Y		**Graham**	Y	N	Y	Y	Y
Harkin	Y	Y	Y	N	Y		**DeMint**	N	N	N	Y	Y
KANSAS							**SOUTH DAKOTA**					
Brownback	?	N	N	Y	Y		Johnson	Y	Y	Y	Y	Y
Roberts	Y	N	Y	Y	Y		**Thune**	Y	N	N	Y	Y
KENTUCKY							**TENNESSEE**					
McConnell	Y	N	Y	Y	Y		**Alexander**	Y	N	Y	Y	Y
Bunning	N	N	N	Y	Y		**Corker**	Y	N	Y	Y	Y
LOUISIANA							**TEXAS**					
Landrieu	Y	Y	Y	Y	Y		**Hutchison**	Y	N	Y	Y	Y
Vitter	N	N	N	Y	Y		**Cornyn**	Y	N	N	Y	Y
MAINE							**UTAH**					
Snowe	Y	Y	Y	Y	Y		**Hatch**	Y	Y	Y	Y	Y
Collins	Y	Y	Y	Y	Y		**Bennett**	Y	N	Y	Y	Y
MARYLAND							**VERMONT**					
Mikulski	Y	Y	Y	Y	Y		Leahy	Y	Y	Y	N	Y
Cardin	Y	Y	Y	Y	Y		*Sanders*	Y	Y	Y	N	Y
MASSACHUSETTS							**VIRGINIA**					
Kennedy	?	?	?	?	?		**Warner**	Y	Y	Y	Y	Y
Kerry	Y	Y	Y	N	Y		Webb	Y	Y	Y	Y	Y
MICHIGAN							**WASHINGTON**					
Levin	Y	Y	Y	Y	Y		Murray	Y	Y	Y	Y	Y
Stabenow	Y	Y	Y	Y	Y		Cantwell	Y	Y	Y	N	Y
MINNESOTA							**WEST VIRGINIA**					
Coleman	Y	Y	Y	Y	Y		Byrd	Y	?	?	?	Y
Klobuchar	Y	Y	Y	Y	Y		Rockefeller	Y	Y	Y	Y	Y
MISSISSIPPI							**WISCONSIN**					
Cochran	Y	N	Y	Y	Y		Kohl	Y	Y	Y	Y	Y
Wicker	Y	N	Y	Y	Y		Feingold	Y	Y	Y	N	Y
MISSOURI							**WYOMING**					
Bond	N	?	N	Y	Y		**Enzi**	N	N	N	Y	Y
McCaskill	Y	Y	Y	Y	Y		**Barrasso**	N	N	N	Y	Y

KEY	**Republicans**	Democrats	*Independents*	
Y Voted for (yea)	X Paired against		C Voted "present" to avoid possible conflict of interest
# Paired for	– Announced against		
+ Announced for	P Voted "present"		? Did not vote or otherwise make a position known
N Voted against (nay)			

ND Northern Democrats, SD Southern Democrats
Southern states: Ala., Ark., Fla., Ga., Ky., La., Miss., N.C., Okla., S.C., Tenn., Texas, Va.

IN THE SENATE | By Vote Number

160. **HR 6331. Medicare Physician Payments/Cloture.** Motion to invoke cloture (thus limiting debate) on the motion to proceed to the bill that would prevent a 10.6 percent cut in Medicare physician payments scheduled to take effect on July 1, 2008, by holding payments at current rates for 18 months. It would give doctors a 1.1 percent increase in payments in 2009 and provide $16.6 billion over 10 years for changes to Medicare beneficiary programs. Motion rejected 58-40: R 9-39; D 47-1 (ND 42-1, SD 5-0); I 2-0. Three-fifths of the total Senate (60) is required to invoke cloture. A "nay" was a vote in support of the president's position. June 26, 2008.

161. **HR 2642. Supplemental Appropriations/Motion to Waive.** Reid, D-Nev., motion to waive the fiscal 2008 budget resolution with respect to the Coburn, R-Okla., point of order against the Reid motion to concur in House amendments to the Senate amendment to the House amendment to the Senate amendment to the bill that would appropriate $161.8 billion for the wars in Iraq and Afghanistan, and $24.7 billion for domestic programs. Motion agreed to 77-21: R 28-20; D 47-1 (ND 42-1, SD 5-0); I 2-0. A three-fifths majority (60) of the total Senate is required to waive the budget resolution. June 26, 2008.

162. **HR 2642. Supplemental Appropriations/Motion to Concur.** Reid, D-Nev., motion to concur in House amendments to the Senate amendment to the House amendments to the Senate amendment to the bill that would appropriate $161.8 billion for the wars in Iraq and Afghanistan, including $95.9 billion for military operations for fiscal 2008 and $65.9 billion for fiscal 2009. It would provide $24.7 billion for domestic programs, including $2.7 billion for Midwest disaster relief and $5.8 billion for fiscal 2009 to rebuild levees destroyed by Hurricane Katrina. It would provide $4.6 billion for military construction and VA hospitals, and $10.1 billion over two years for the State Department, the U.S. Agency for International Development and international food aid. The bill also would bar permanent bases in Iraq and require the Iraqi government to match reconstruction aid. It would provide for a permanent expansion of education benefits for post-Sept. 11 veterans, extend unemployment insurance benefits for 13 weeks and place a moratorium through March 2009 on six Medicaid regulations proposed by the administration. Motion agreed to (thus clearing the bill for the president), 92-6: R 42-6; D 48-0 (ND 43-0, SD 5-0); I 2-0. A "yea" was a vote in support of the president's position. June 26, 2008.

	160	161	162			160	161	162
ALABAMA					**MONTANA**			
Shelby	N	Y	Y		Baucus	Y	Y	Y
Sessions	N	N	Y		Tester	Y	Y	Y
ALASKA					**NEBRASKA**			
Stevens	Y	Y	Y		**Hagel**	N	Y	Y
Murkowski	Y	Y	Y		Nelson	Y	Y	Y
ARIZONA					**NEVADA**			
McCain	?	?	?		Reid	N	Y	Y
Kyl	N	N	N		**Ensign**	N	N	Y
ARKANSAS					**NEW HAMPSHIRE**			
Lincoln	Y	Y	Y		**Gregg**	N	N	Y
Pryor	Y	Y	Y		**Sununu**	N	Y	Y
CALIFORNIA					**NEW JERSEY**			
Feinstein	Y	Y	Y		Lautenberg	Y	Y	Y
Boxer	Y	Y	Y		Menendez	Y	Y	Y
COLORADO					**NEW MEXICO**			
Allard	N	N	N		**Domenici**	N	Y	Y
Salazar	Y	Y	Y		Bingaman	Y	Y	Y
CONNECTICUT					**NEW YORK**			
Dodd	Y	Y	Y		Schumer	Y	Y	Y
Lieberman	Y	Y	Y		Clinton	Y	Y	Y
DELAWARE					**NORTH CAROLINA**			
Biden	Y	Y	Y		**Dole**	Y	Y	Y
Carper	Y	Y	Y		**Burr**	N	N	Y
FLORIDA					**NORTH DAKOTA**			
Nelson	Y	Y	Y		Conrad	Y	Y	Y
Martinez	N	Y	Y		Dorgan	Y	Y	Y
GEORGIA					**OHIO**			
Chambliss	N	N	Y		**Voinovich**	Y	N	N
Isakson	N	N	Y		Brown	Y	Y	Y
HAWAII					**OKLAHOMA**			
Inouye	Y	Y	Y		**Inhofe**	N	N	N
Akaka	Y	Y	Y		**Coburn**	N	N	N
IDAHO					**OREGON**			
Craig	N	N	N		Wyden	Y	Y	Y
Crapo	N	N	Y		**Smith**	Y	Y	Y
ILLINOIS					**PENNSYLVANIA**			
Durbin	Y	Y	Y		**Specter**	N	Y	Y
Obama	Y	Y	Y		Casey	Y	Y	Y
INDIANA					**RHODE ISLAND**			
Lugar	N	Y	Y		Reed	Y	Y	Y
Bayh	Y	Y	Y		Whitehouse	Y	Y	Y
IOWA					**SOUTH CAROLINA**			
Grassley	N	N	Y		**Graham**	N	N	Y
Harkin	Y	Y	Y		**DeMint**	N	N	N
KANSAS					**SOUTH DAKOTA**			
Brownback	N	Y	Y		Johnson	Y	Y	Y
Roberts	Y	Y	Y		**Thune**	N	Y	Y
KENTUCKY					**TENNESSEE**			
McConnell	N	Y	Y		**Alexander**	N	Y	Y
Bunning	N	Y	Y		**Corker**	N	N	Y
LOUISIANA					**TEXAS**			
Landrieu	Y	Y	Y		**Hutchison**	N	Y	Y
Vitter	N	Y	Y		**Cornyn**	N	Y	Y
MAINE					**UTAH**			
Snowe	Y	Y	Y		**Hatch**	N	N	Y
Collins	Y	Y	Y		**Bennett**	N	Y	Y
MARYLAND					**VERMONT**			
Mikulski	Y	Y	Y		Leahy	Y	Y	Y
Cardin	Y	Y	Y		*Sanders*	Y	Y	Y
MASSACHUSETTS					**VIRGINIA**			
Kennedy	?	?	?		**Warner**	N	Y	Y
Kerry	Y	Y	Y		Webb	Y	Y	Y
MICHIGAN					**WASHINGTON**			
Levin	Y	Y	Y		Murray	Y	Y	Y
Stabenow	Y	Y	Y		Cantwell	Y	Y	Y
MINNESOTA					**WEST VIRGINIA**			
Coleman	Y	Y	Y		Byrd	Y	Y	Y
Klobuchar	Y	Y	Y		Rockefeller	Y	Y	Y
MISSISSIPPI					**WISCONSIN**			
Cochran	N	Y	Y		Kohl	Y	Y	Y
Wicker	N	Y	Y		Feingold	Y	Y	Y
MISSOURI					**WYOMING**			
Bond	N	Y	Y		**Enzi**	N	N	Y
McCaskill	Y	Y	Y		**Barrasso**	N	N	Y

KEY	**Republicans**	Democrats	*Independents*		
Y	Voted for (yea)	X	Paired against	C	Voted "present" to avoid possible conflict of interest
#	Paired for	–	Announced against		
+	Announced for	P	Voted "present"	?	Did not vote or otherwise make a position known
N	Voted against (nay)				

ND Northern Democrats, SD Southern Democrats
Southern states: Ala., Ark., Fla., Ga., Ky., La., Miss., N.C., Okla., S.C., Tenn., Texas, Va.

IN THE SENATE | By Vote Number

163. **HR 3221. Mortgage Relief/Cloture.** Motion to invoke cloture (thus limiting debate) on the motion to concur in the House amendment to the Senate amendments to the bill. The House amendment would strike Titles VI through XI of the Senate amendments, including a clean-energy tax stimulus and other tax-related provisions, and an increase in the maximum assistance authorized for specially adapted housing benefits for disabled veterans. Motion agreed to 76-10: R 30-10; D 44-0 (ND 40-0, SD 4-0); I 2-0. Three-fifths of the total Senate (60) is required to invoke cloture. July 7, 2008.

164. **HR 6304. Foreign Intelligence Surveillance/Immunity From Civil Liability.** Dodd, D-Conn., amendment that would strike the provisions providing retroactive immunity from civil liability to telecommunications companies that have participated in the administration's warrantless surveillance program. Rejected 32-66: R 0-48; D 31-17 (ND 31-12, SD 0-5); I 1-1. A "nay" was a vote in support of the president's position. July 9, 2008.

165. **HR 6304. Foreign Intelligence Surveillance/Lawsuit Dismissal.** Specter, R-Pa., amendment that would prohibit the dismissal of lawsuits against telecommunications companies that have participated in the administration's warrantless surveillance program if a federal district court concludes that the assistance was provided in connection with an intelligence activity that violated the U.S. Constitution. Rejected 37-61: R 1-47; D 35-13 (ND 34-9, SD 1-4); I 1-1. (By unanimous consent, the Senate agreed to raise the majority requirement for adoption of the Specter amendment to 60 votes. Subsequently, the amendment was withdrawn.) A "nay" was a vote in support of the president's position. July 9, 2008.

166. **HR 6304. Foreign Intelligence Surveillance/Pending Lawsuits.** Bingaman, D-N.M., amendment that would stay all pending lawsuits against telecommunications companies that have participated in the administration's warrantless surveillance program until 90 days after Congress receives the required inspectors general report on the program. Rejected 42-56: R 1-47; D 40-8 (ND 37-6, SD 3-2); I 1-1. (By unanimous consent, the Senate agreed to raise the majority requirement for adoption of the Bingaman amendment to 60 votes. Subsequently, the amendment was withdrawn.) A "nay" was a vote in support of the president's position. July 9, 2008.

	163	164	165	166
ALABAMA				
Shelby	Y	N	N	N
Sessions	Y	N	N	N
ALASKA				
Stevens	Y	N	N	N
Murkowski	?	N	N	N
ARIZONA				
McCain	?	?	?	?
Kyl	N	N	N	N
ARKANSAS				
Lincoln	Y	N	N	Y
Pryor	?	N	N	N
CALIFORNIA				
Feinstein	Y	N	Y	Y
Boxer	Y	Y	Y	Y
COLORADO				
Allard	Y	N	N	N
Salazar	Y	N	N	Y
CONNECTICUT				
Dodd	Y	Y	Y	Y
Lieberman	Y	N	N	N
DELAWARE				
Biden	Y	Y	Y	Y
Carper	Y	N	N	N
FLORIDA				
Nelson	Y	N	N	Y
Martinez	Y	N	N	N
GEORGIA				
Chambliss	Y	N	N	N
Isakson	Y	N	N	N
HAWAII				
Inouye	Y	N	N	N
Akaka	Y	Y	Y	Y
IDAHO				
Craig	Y	N	N	N
Crapo	N	N	N	N
ILLINOIS				
Durbin	Y	Y	Y	Y
Obama	?	Y	Y	Y
INDIANA				
Lugar	Y	N	N	N
Bayh	Y	N	N	N
IOWA				
Grassley	Y	N	N	N
Harkin	Y	Y	Y	Y
KANSAS				
Brownback	Y	N	N	N
Roberts	Y	N	N	N
KENTUCKY				
McConnell	Y	N	N	N
Bunning	N	N	N	N
LOUISIANA				
Landrieu	Y	N	N	N
Vitter	?	N	N	N
MAINE				
Snowe	Y	N	N	N
Collins	Y	N	N	N
MARYLAND				
Mikulski	Y	N	N	Y
Cardin	Y	Y	Y	Y
MASSACHUSETTS				
Kennedy	?	?	?	?
Kerry	Y	Y	Y	Y
MICHIGAN				
Levin	Y	Y	Y	Y
Stabenow	Y	Y	Y	Y
MINNESOTA				
Coleman	+	N	N	N
Klobuchar	Y	Y	Y	Y
MISSISSIPPI				
Cochran	Y	N	N	N
Wicker	?	N	N	N
MISSOURI				
Bond	Y	N	N	N
McCaskill	Y	N	Y	Y

	163	164	165	166
MONTANA				
Baucus	Y	Y	Y	Y
Tester	+	Y	Y	Y
NEBRASKA				
Hagel	Y	N	N	N
Nelson	Y	N	N	N
NEVADA				
Reid	Y	Y	Y	Y
Ensign	?	N	N	N
NEW HAMPSHIRE				
Gregg	?	N	N	N
Sununu	Y	N	N	N
NEW JERSEY				
Lautenberg	Y	Y	Y	Y
Menendez	Y	Y	Y	Y
NEW MEXICO				
Domenici	Y	N	N	N
Bingaman	Y	Y	Y	Y
NEW YORK				
Schumer	Y	Y	Y	Y
Clinton	Y	Y	Y	Y
NORTH CAROLINA				
Dole	Y	N	N	N
Burr	N	N	N	N
NORTH DAKOTA				
Conrad	Y	N	Y	N
Dorgan	Y	Y	Y	Y
OHIO				
Voinovich	Y	N	N	N
Brown	?	Y	Y	Y
OKLAHOMA				
Inhofe	N	N	N	N
Coburn	N	N	N	N
OREGON				
Wyden	Y	Y	Y	Y
Smith	Y	N	N	N
PENNSYLVANIA				
Specter	Y	N	Y	Y
Casey	Y	Y	Y	Y
RHODE ISLAND				
Reed	Y	Y	Y	Y
Whitehouse	Y	Y	Y	Y
SOUTH CAROLINA				
Graham	?	N	N	N
DeMint	N	N	N	N
SOUTH DAKOTA				
Johnson	Y	N	N	Y
Thune	+	N	N	N
TENNESSEE				
Alexander	Y	N	N	N
Corker	Y	N	N	N
TEXAS				
Hutchison	Y	N	N	N
Cornyn	N	N	N	N
UTAH				
Hatch	Y	N	N	N
Bennett	Y	N	N	N
VERMONT				
Leahy	Y	Y	Y	Y
Sanders	Y	Y	Y	Y
VIRGINIA				
Warner	Y	N	N	N
Webb	Y	N	Y	N
WASHINGTON				
Murray	Y	Y	Y	Y
Cantwell	Y	Y	Y	Y
WEST VIRGINIA				
Byrd	Y	Y	Y	Y
Rockefeller	Y	N	N	N
WISCONSIN				
Kohl	Y	N	Y	Y
Feingold	Y	Y	Y	Y
WYOMING				
Enzi	N	N	N	N
Barrasso	N	N	N	N

KEY **Republicans**   Democrats   *Independents*

Y Voted for (yea)	X Paired against	C Voted "present" to avoid possible conflict of interest
# Paired for	– Announced against	
+ Announced for	P Voted "present"	? Did not vote or otherwise make a position known
N Voted against (nay)		

ND Northern Democrats, SD Southern Democrats
Southern states: Ala., Ark., Fla., Ga., Ky., La., Miss., N.C., Okla., S.C., Tenn., Texas, Va.

S-36 2008 CQ ALMANAC | www.cq.com

IN THE SENATE | By Vote Number

167. HR 6304. **Foreign Intelligence Surveillance/Cloture.** Motion to invoke cloture (thus limiting debate) on the motion to proceed to the bill that would overhaul the Foreign Intelligence Surveillance Act, which governs electronic surveillance of foreign terrorism suspects. Motion agreed to 72-26: R 48-0; D 23-25 (ND 18-25, SD 5-0); I 1-1. Three-fifths of the total Senate (60) is required to invoke cloture. July 9, 2008.

168. HR 6304. **Foreign Intelligence Surveillance/Passage.** Passage of the bill that would overhaul the Foreign Intelligence Surveillance Act (FISA), which governs electronic surveillance of foreign terrorism suspects. The bill would allow warrantless surveillance of foreign targets who may be communicating with people in the United States after the secret FISA court approves surveillance procedures; the administration can begin that surveillance before the FISA court review if the need is deemed urgent. The bill would require FISA warrants for surveillance of U.S. citizens overseas. It would allow federal district courts to waive existing lawsuits against companies that assisted President Bush's warrantless surveillance program. Passed (thus cleared for the president) 69-28: R 47-0; D 21-27 (ND 16-27, SD 5-0); I 1-1. A "yea" was a vote in support of the president's position. July 9, 2008.

169. HR 6331. **Medicare Physician Payments/Cloture.** Motion to invoke cloture (thus limiting debate) on the motion to proceed to the bill that would prevent a 10.6 percent cut in Medicare physician payments scheduled to take effect July 1, 2008, by holding payments at current rates for 18 months. It would give doctors a 1.1 percent increase in 2009 and provide $16.6 billion over 10 years for changes to Medicare beneficiary programs. The costs would be partially offset by provisions to reduce the cost of Medicare Advantage plans. Motion agreed to 69-30: R 18-30; D 49-0 (ND 44-0, SD 5-0); I 2-0. Three-fifths of the total Senate (60) is required to invoke cloture. (By unanimous consent, the motion to proceed was agreed to and the bill was passed by voice vote.) A "nay" was a vote in support of the president's position. July 9, 2008.

	167	168	169
ALABAMA			
Shelby	Y	Y	N
Sessions	Y	+	N
ALASKA			
Stevens	Y	Y	Y
Murkowski	Y	Y	Y
ARIZONA			
McCain	?	?	?
Kyl	Y	Y	N
ARKANSAS			
Lincoln	Y	Y	Y
Pryor	Y	Y	Y
CALIFORNIA			
Feinstein	Y	Y	Y
Boxer	N	N	Y
COLORADO			
Allard	Y	Y	N
Salazar	Y	Y	Y
CONNECTICUT			
Dodd	N	N	Y
Lieberman	Y	Y	Y
DELAWARE			
Biden	Y	N	Y
Carper	Y	Y	Y
FLORIDA			
Nelson	Y	Y	Y
Martinez	Y	Y	Y
GEORGIA			
Chambliss	Y	Y	Y
Isakson	Y	Y	Y
HAWAII			
Inouye	Y	Y	Y
Akaka	N	N	Y
IDAHO			
Craig	Y	Y	N
Crapo	Y	Y	N
ILLINOIS			
Durbin	N	N	Y
Obama	Y	Y	Y
INDIANA			
Lugar	Y	Y	N
Bayh	Y	Y	Y
IOWA			
Grassley	Y	Y	N
Harkin	N	N	Y
KANSAS			
Brownback	Y	Y	N
Roberts	Y	Y	Y
KENTUCKY			
McConnell	Y	Y	N
Bunning	Y	Y	N
LOUISIANA			
Landrieu	Y	Y	Y
Vitter	Y	Y	N
MAINE			
Snowe	Y	Y	Y
Collins	Y	Y	Y
MARYLAND			
Mikulski	Y	Y	Y
Cardin	N	N	Y
MASSACHUSETTS			
Kennedy	?	?	Y
Kerry	N	N	Y
MICHIGAN			
Levin	N	N	Y
Stabenow	N	N	Y
MINNESOTA			
Coleman	Y	Y	Y
Klobuchar	N	N	Y
MISSISSIPPI			
Cochran	Y	Y	N
Wicker	Y	Y	N
MISSOURI			
Bond	Y	Y	N
McCaskill	Y	Y	Y

	167	168	169
MONTANA			
Baucus	Y	Y	Y
Tester	N	N	Y
NEBRASKA			
Hagel	Y	Y	N
Nelson	Y	Y	Y
NEVADA			
Reid	N	N	Y
Ensign	Y	Y	N
NEW HAMPSHIRE			
Gregg	Y	Y	N
Sununu	Y	Y	N
NEW JERSEY			
Lautenberg	N	N	Y
Menendez	N	N	Y
NEW MEXICO			
Domenici	Y	Y	N
Bingaman	N	N	Y
NEW YORK			
Schumer	N	N	Y
Clinton	N	N	Y
NORTH CAROLINA			
Dole	Y	Y	Y
Burr	Y	Y	N
NORTH DAKOTA			
Conrad	Y	Y	Y
Dorgan	Y	N	Y
OHIO			
Voinovich	Y	Y	Y
Brown	N	N	Y
OKLAHOMA			
Inhofe	Y	Y	N
Coburn	Y	Y	N
OREGON			
Wyden	N	N	Y
Smith	Y	Y	Y
PENNSYLVANIA			
Specter	Y	Y	Y
Casey	Y	Y	Y
RHODE ISLAND			
Reed	N	N	Y
Whitehouse	Y	Y	Y
SOUTH CAROLINA			
Graham	Y	Y	N
DeMint	Y	Y	N
SOUTH DAKOTA			
Johnson	Y	Y	Y
Thune	Y	Y	N
TENNESSEE			
Alexander	Y	Y	Y
Corker	Y	Y	Y
TEXAS			
Hutchison	Y	Y	Y
Cornyn	Y	Y	Y
UTAH			
Hatch	Y	Y	N
Bennett	Y	Y	N
VERMONT			
Leahy	N	N	Y
Sanders	N	N	Y
VIRGINIA			
Warner	Y	Y	N
Webb	Y	Y	Y
WASHINGTON			
Murray	N	N	Y
Cantwell	N	N	Y
WEST VIRGINIA			
Byrd	N	N	Y
Rockefeller	Y	Y	Y
WISCONSIN			
Kohl	Y	Y	Y
Feingold	N	N	Y
WYOMING			
Enzi	Y	Y	N
Barrasso	Y	Y	N

KEY   **Republicans**   Democrats   *Independents*

Y Voted for (yea)	**X** Paired against	**C** Voted "present" to avoid possible conflict of interest
# Paired for	**−** Announced against	
+ Announced for	**P** Voted "present"	**?** Did not vote or otherwise make a position known
N Voted against (nay)		

ND Northern Democrats, SD Southern Democrats
Southern states: Ala., Ark., Fla., Ga., Ky., La., Miss., N.C., Okla., S.C., Tenn., Texas, Va.

IN THE SENATE | By Vote Number

170. **HR 3221. Mortgage Relief/Cloture.** Motion to invoke cloture (thus limiting debate) on the motion to disagree to the House amendments that added a new title and inserted a new section to the Senate amendment to the bill. The new title would provide a refundable tax credit for first-time homebuyers of up to $7,500 for joint filers, which would serve as an interest-free loan. It would provide a deduction in 2008 of up to $350 for individuals ($700 for married couples) for state and local property taxes. It also would increase temporarily the low-income housing tax credit. The new House section would clarify that no provision in the underlying bill or in two federal banking statutes — the Home Owners' Loan Act and the National Bank Act — could be construed to pre-empt any state law dealing with residential foreclosures. Motion agreed to 84-12: R 36-12; D 46-0 (ND 41-0, SD 5-0); I 2-0. Three-fifths of the total Senate (60) is required to invoke cloture. July 10, 2008.

171. **Petraeus Nomination/Confirmation.** Confirmation of President Bush's nomination of Gen. David H. Petraeus for reappointment to the rank of general and to be commander of the United States Central Command. Confirmed 95-2: R 48-0; D 45-2 (ND 40-2, SD 5-0); I 2-0. A "yea" was a vote in support of the president's position. July 10, 2008.

172. **Odierno Nomination/Confirmation.** Confirmation of President Bush's nomination of Army Lt. Gen. Raymond T. Odierno to the rank of general and commander of Multi-National Force-Iraq. Confirmed 96-1: R 48-0; D 46-1 (ND 41-1, SD 5-0); I 2-0. A "yea" was a vote in support of the president's position. July 10, 2008.

	170	171	172			170	171	172
ALABAMA					**MONTANA**			
Shelby	Y	Y	Y		Baucus	Y	Y	Y
Sessions	Y	Y	Y		Tester	Y	Y	Y
ALASKA					**NEBRASKA**			
Stevens	Y	Y	Y		Hagel	Y	Y	Y
Murkowski	Y	Y	Y		Nelson	Y	Y	Y
ARIZONA					**NEVADA**			
McCain	?	?	?		Reid	Y	Y	Y
Kyl	N	Y	Y		Ensign	N	Y	Y
ARKANSAS					**NEW HAMPSHIRE**			
Lincoln	Y	Y	Y		Gregg	Y	Y	Y
Pryor	Y	Y	Y		Sununu	Y	Y	Y
CALIFORNIA					**NEW JERSEY**			
Feinstein	Y	Y	Y		Lautenberg	Y	Y	Y
Boxer	Y	Y	Y		Menendez	Y	Y	Y
COLORADO					**NEW MEXICO**			
Allard	Y	Y	Y		Domenici	Y	Y	Y
Salazar	Y	Y	Y		Bingaman	Y	Y	Y
CONNECTICUT					**NEW YORK**			
Dodd	Y	Y	Y		Schumer	Y	Y	Y
Lieberman	Y	Y	Y		Clinton	?	Y	Y
DELAWARE					**NORTH CAROLINA**			
Biden	Y	Y	Y		Dole	Y	Y	Y
Carper	Y	Y	Y		Burr	Y	Y	Y
FLORIDA					**NORTH DAKOTA**			
Nelson	Y	Y	Y		Conrad	Y	Y	Y
Martinez	Y	Y	Y		Dorgan	Y	Y	Y
GEORGIA					**OHIO**			
Chambliss	Y	Y	Y		Voinovich	Y	Y	Y
Isakson	Y	Y	Y		Brown	Y	Y	Y
HAWAII					**OKLAHOMA**			
Inouye	Y	Y	Y		Inhofe	N	Y	Y
Akaka	Y	Y	Y		Coburn	N	Y	Y
IDAHO					**OREGON**			
Craig	Y	Y	Y		Wyden	Y	Y	Y
Crapo	N	Y	Y		Smith	Y	Y	Y
ILLINOIS					**PENNSYLVANIA**			
Durbin	Y	Y	Y		Specter	Y	Y	Y
Obama	?	?	?		Casey	Y	Y	Y
INDIANA					**RHODE ISLAND**			
Lugar	Y	Y	Y		Reed	Y	Y	Y
Bayh	Y	Y	Y		Whitehouse	Y	Y	Y
IOWA					**SOUTH CAROLINA**			
Grassley	Y	Y	Y		Graham	Y	Y	Y
Harkin	Y	N	N		DeMint	N	Y	Y
KANSAS					**SOUTH DAKOTA**			
Brownback	Y	Y	Y		Johnson	Y	Y	Y
Roberts	Y	Y	Y		Thune	Y	Y	Y
KENTUCKY					**TENNESSEE**			
McConnell	Y	Y	Y		Alexander	Y	Y	Y
Bunning	N	Y	Y		Corker	Y	Y	Y
LOUISIANA					**TEXAS**			
Landrieu	Y	Y	Y		Hutchison	Y	Y	Y
Vitter	N	Y	Y		Cornyn	N	Y	Y
MAINE					**UTAH**			
Snowe	Y	Y	Y		Hatch	Y	Y	Y
Collins	Y	Y	Y		Bennett	Y	Y	Y
MARYLAND					**VERMONT**			
Mikulski	Y	Y	Y		Leahy	Y	Y	Y
Cardin	Y	Y	Y		*Sanders*	Y	Y	Y
MASSACHUSETTS					**VIRGINIA**			
Kennedy	?	?	?		Warner	Y	Y	Y
Kerry	Y	Y	Y		Webb	Y	Y	Y
MICHIGAN					**WASHINGTON**			
Levin	Y	Y	Y		Murray	Y	Y	Y
Stabenow	Y	Y	Y		Cantwell	Y	Y	Y
MINNESOTA					**WEST VIRGINIA**			
Coleman	Y	Y	Y		Byrd	Y	N	Y
Klobuchar	Y	Y	Y		Rockefeller	Y	Y	Y
MISSISSIPPI					**WISCONSIN**			
Cochran	Y	Y	Y		Kohl	Y	Y	Y
Wicker	Y	Y	Y		Feingold	Y	Y	Y
MISSOURI					**WYOMING**			
Bond	N	Y	Y		Enzi	N	Y	Y
McCaskill	Y	Y	Y		Barrasso	N	Y	Y

KEY   **Republicans**   Democrats   *Independents*

Y Voted for (yea)	X Paired against	C Voted "present" to avoid possible conflict of interest
# Paired for	– Announced against	? Did not vote or otherwise make a position known
+ Announced for	P Voted "present"	
N Voted against (nay)		

ND Northern Democrats, SD Southern Democrats
Southern states: Ala., Ark., Fla., Ga., Ky., La., Miss., N.C., Okla., S.C., Tenn., Texas, Va.

IN THE SENATE | By Vote Number

173. **HR 3221. Mortgage Relief/Motion to Disagree.** Motion to disagree to the House amendments that added a new title and inserted a new section to the Senate amendment to the bill. The new title would provide a refundable tax credit for first-time homebuyers of up to $7,500 for joint filers, which would serve as an interest-free loan. It would provide a deduction in 2008 of up to $350 for individuals ($700 for married couples) for state and local property taxes. It also would increase temporarily the low-income housing tax credit. The new House section would clarify that no provision in the underlying bill or in two federal banking statutes, the Home Owners' Loan Act and the National Bank Act, could be construed to pre-empt any state law dealing with residential foreclosures. Motion agreed to 63-5: R 22-5; D 39-0 (ND 35-0, SD 4-0); I 2-0. July 11, 2008.

174. **S 2731. Global HIV/AIDS Program Reauthorization/Cloture.** Motion to invoke cloture (thus limiting debate) on the motion to proceed to the bill that would authorize $50 billion in 2009 through 2013 for programs under the President's Emergency Plan for AIDS Relief to fight AIDS, tuberculosis and malaria overseas. Motion agreed to 65-3: R 24-3; D 39-0 (ND 35-0, SD 4-0); I 2-0. Three-fifths of the total Senate (60) is required to invoke cloture. July 11, 2008.

175. **S 2731. Global HIV/AIDS Program Reauthorization/Funding Limitation.** Biden, D-Del., motion to table (kill) the DeMint, R-S.C., amendment that would authorize funding only for the 15 countries targeted under the 2003 global AIDS law. Motion agreed to 70-24: R 22-24; D 46-0 (ND 41-0, SD 5-0); I 2-0. July 15, 2008.

176. **S 2731. Global HIV/AIDS Program Reauthorization/Substitute.** Bunning, R-Ky., substitute amendment that would extend from fiscal 2009 through 2013 the $15 billion authorization level set in current law for programs under the President's Emergency Plan for AIDS Relief. Rejected 16-80: R 16-31; D 0-47 (ND 0-42, SD 0-5); I 0-2. July 15, 2008.

177. **HR 6331. Medicare Physician Payments/Veto Override.** Passage, over President Bush's July 15, 2008, veto, of the bill that would prevent a 10.6 percent cut in Medicare physician payments scheduled to take effect July 1, 2008, by holding payments at current rates for 18 months. It would give doctors a 1.1 percent increase in payments in 2009 and provide $16.6 billion over 10 years for changes to Medicare beneficiary programs. The costs would be partially offset by provisions to reduce the cost of Medicare Advantage plans. Passed (thus enacted into law) 70-26: R 21-26; D 47-0 (ND 42-0, SD 5-0); I 2-0. A two-thirds majority of those present and voting (64 in this case for the Senate) of both chambers is required to override a veto. A "nay" was a vote in support of the president's position. July 15, 2008.

	173	174	175	176	177
ALABAMA					
Shelby	?	?	Y	N	N
Sessions	Y	N	N	N	N
ALASKA					
Stevens	?	?	Y	N	Y
Murkowski	?	?	Y	N	Y
ARIZONA					
McCain	?	?	?	?	?
Kyl	N	N	N	Y	N
ARKANSAS					
Lincoln	Y	Y	Y	N	Y
Pryor	Y	Y	Y	N	Y
CALIFORNIA					
Feinstein	Y	Y	Y	N	Y
Boxer	?	?	Y	N	Y
COLORADO					
Allard	?	?	N	Y	N
Salazar	Y	Y	Y	N	Y
CONNECTICUT					
Dodd	Y	Y	Y	N	Y
Lieberman	Y	Y	Y	N	Y
DELAWARE					
Biden	Y	Y	Y	N	Y
Carper	Y	Y	Y	N	Y
FLORIDA					
Nelson	Y	Y	Y	N	Y
Martinez	?	?	Y	N	Y
GEORGIA					
Chambliss	?	?	N	Y	Y
Isakson	Y	Y	N	Y	Y
HAWAII					
Inouye	Y	Y	Y	N	Y
Akaka	Y	Y	Y	N	Y
IDAHO					
Craig	?	?	N	Y	N
Crapo	N	Y	N	Y	N
ILLINOIS					
Durbin	Y	Y	Y	N	Y
Obama	?	?	?	?	?
INDIANA					
Lugar	Y	Y	Y	N	Y
Bayh	Y	Y	Y	N	Y
IOWA					
Grassley	Y	Y	N	N	N
Harkin	Y	Y	Y	N	Y
KANSAS					
Brownback	Y	Y	Y	N	N
Roberts	Y	Y	Y	N	Y
KENTUCKY					
McConnell	Y	Y	N	N	N
Bunning	–	–	N	Y	N
LOUISIANA					
Landrieu	?	?	Y	N	Y
Vitter	?	?	N	Y	N
MAINE					
Snowe	Y	Y	Y	N	Y
Collins	Y	Y	Y	N	Y
MARYLAND					
Mikulski	Y	Y	Y	N	Y
Cardin	Y	Y	Y	N	Y
MASSACHUSETTS					
Kennedy	?	?	?	?	?
Kerry	Y	Y	Y	N	Y
MICHIGAN					
Levin	Y	Y	Y	N	Y
Stabenow	+	?	Y	N	Y
MINNESOTA					
Coleman	+	+	Y	N	Y
Klobuchar	Y	Y	Y	N	Y
MISSISSIPPI					
Cochran	Y	Y	Y	N	Y
Wicker	Y	Y	N	Y	Y
MISSOURI					
Bond	?	?	N	Y	Y
McCaskill	?	?	Y	N	Y
MONTANA					
Baucus	Y	Y	Y	N	Y
Tester	?	?	Y	N	Y
NEBRASKA					
Hagel	?	?	Y	N	N
Nelson	?	?	Y	N	Y
NEVADA					
Reid	Y	Y	Y	N	Y
Ensign	?	?	N	Y	N
NEW HAMPSHIRE					
Gregg	?	?	Y	Y	N
Sununu	Y	Y	Y	N	Y
NEW JERSEY					
Lautenberg	Y	Y	?	N	Y
Menendez	Y	Y	Y	N	Y
NEW MEXICO					
Domenici	Y	Y	Y	N	N
Bingaman	Y	Y	Y	N	Y
NEW YORK					
Schumer	Y	Y	Y	N	Y
Clinton	Y	Y	Y	N	Y
NORTH CAROLINA					
Dole	Y	Y	Y	N	Y
Burr	Y	Y	N	N	N
NORTH DAKOTA					
Conrad	Y	Y	Y	N	Y
Dorgan	Y	Y	Y	N	Y
OHIO					
Voinovich	Y	Y	Y	N	Y
Brown	Y	Y	Y	N	Y
OKLAHOMA					
Inhofe	?	?	N	N	N
Coburn	?	?	N	N	N
OREGON					
Wyden	Y	Y	Y	N	Y
Smith	Y	Y	N	N	Y
PENNSYLVANIA					
Specter	Y	Y	Y	N	Y
Casey	Y	Y	Y	N	Y
RHODE ISLAND					
Reed	Y	Y	Y	N	Y
Whitehouse	Y	Y	Y	N	Y
SOUTH CAROLINA					
Graham	Y	Y	N	N	N
DeMint	–	?	N	Y	N
SOUTH DAKOTA					
Johnson	Y	Y	Y	N	Y
Thune	N	Y	N	N	N
TENNESSEE					
Alexander	+	+	–	N	Y
Corker	?	+	?	N	Y
TEXAS					
Hutchison	?	?	Y	Y	Y
Cornyn	–	–	N	Y	Y
UTAH					
Hatch	Y	Y	N	N	N
Bennett	Y	Y	Y	N	N
VERMONT					
Leahy	+	+	Y	N	Y
Sanders	Y	Y	Y	N	Y
VIRGINIA					
Warner	Y	Y	Y	?	+
Webb	Y	Y	Y	N	Y
WASHINGTON					
Murray	?	?	Y	N	Y
Cantwell	Y	Y	Y	N	Y
WEST VIRGINIA					
Byrd	Y	Y	Y	N	Y
Rockefeller	Y	Y	Y	N	Y
WISCONSIN					
Kohl	Y	Y	Y	N	Y
Feingold	Y	Y	Y	N	Y
WYOMING					
Enzi	N	N	N	N	N
Barrasso	N	N	N	Y	N

KEY   **Republicans**   Democrats   *Independents*

Y Voted for (yea)	X Paired against	C Voted "present" to avoid possible conflict of interest
# Paired for	– Announced against	
+ Announced for	P Voted "present"	? Did not vote or otherwise make a position known
N Voted against (nay)		

ND Northern Democrats, SD Southern Democrats
Southern states: Ala., Ark., Fla., Ga., Ky., La., Miss., N.C., Okla., S.C., Tenn., Texas, Va.

IN THE SENATE | By Vote Number

178. S 2731. Global HIV/AIDS Program Reauthorization/Sunset

Commission. Cornyn, R-Texas, amendment that would establish a congressional "sunset commission" to review programs under the President's Emergency Plan for AIDS Relief and submit a legislative proposal that includes a time line for the commission's review and proposed abolishment of programs deemed ineffective by the Office of Management and Budget. Any selected program not reauthorized would be abolished two years after the commission completes its review. The amendment also would establish a process for expedited consideration of the commission's legislative recommendations. Rejected 32-63: R 32-15; D 0-46 (ND 0-41, SD 0-5); I 0-2. July 16, 2008.

179. S 2731. Global HIV/AIDS Program Reauthorization/Inspector

General. Gregg, R-N.H., amendment that would establish an inspector general at the Office of the U.S. Global AIDS Coordinator and authorize $10 million per year for fiscal 2009 through 2013 for the office. It also would strike the provision requiring the development of a coordinated oversight plan by the inspectors general at the departments of State and Health and Human Services and USAID. Rejected 44-51: R 40-7; D 4-42 (ND 4-37, SD 0-5); I 0-2. July 16, 2008.

180. S 2731. Global HIV/AIDS Program Reauthorization/

Authorization Level. Kyl, R-Ariz., amendment that would authorize $40 billion from fiscal 2009 through 2012, and $10 billion for fiscal 2013 for programs under the President's Emergency Plan for AIDS Relief. It would create a 60-vote point of order in the Senate against any legislation that exceeds the fiscal 2013 authorization level. Rejected 28-67: R 28-19; D 0-46 (ND 0-41, SD 0-5); I 0-2. July 16, 2008.

181. S 2731. Global HIV/AIDS Program Reauthorization/

Authorization Level. DeMint, R-S.C., amendment that would reduce the authorization level from $50 billion to $35 billion for fiscal 2009 through 2013 for programs under the President's Emergency Plan for AIDS Relief. Rejected 31-64: R 29-18; D 2-44 (ND 2-39, SD 0-5); I 0-2. July 16, 2008.

182. HR 5501. Global HIV/AIDS Program Reauthorization/

Passage. Passage of the bill that would authorize $48 billion in fiscal 2009 through 2013 for programs under the President's Emergency Plan for AIDS Relief to fight AIDS, tuberculosis and malaria overseas. The bill would replace the current requirement that one-third of all HIV prevention funding go to abstinence education with a requirement for balanced funding for abstinence, fidelity and condom programs. It also would authorize $2 billion for American Indian health programs. Passed 80-16: R 31-16; D 47-0 (ND 42-0, SD 5-0); I 2-0. (Before passage, the Senate struck all after the enacting clause and inserted the text of S 2731, as amended, into the bill.) A "yea" was a vote in support of the president's position. July 16, 2008.

	178	179	180	181	182
ALABAMA					
Shelby	Y	Y	N	N	Y
Sessions	Y	Y	Y	Y	N
ALASKA					
Stevens	N	N	N	N	Y
Murkowski	N	N	N	N	Y
ARIZONA					
McCain	?	?	?	?	?
Kyl	Y	Y	Y	Y	N
ARKANSAS					
Lincoln	N	N	N	N	Y
Pryor	N	N	N	N	Y
CALIFORNIA					
Feinstein	N	N	N	N	Y
Boxer	N	N	N	N	Y
COLORADO					
Allard	Y	Y	Y	Y	N
Salazar	N	N	N	N	Y
CONNECTICUT					
Dodd	N	N	N	N	Y
Lieberman	N	N	N	N	Y
DELAWARE					
Biden	N	N	N	N	Y
Carper	N	N	N	N	Y
FLORIDA					
Nelson	N	N	N	N	Y
Martinez	N	N	N	N	Y
GEORGIA					
Chambliss	Y	Y	Y	Y	Y
Isakson	Y	Y	Y	Y	Y
HAWAII					
Inouye	N	N	N	N	Y
Akaka	N	N	N	N	Y
IDAHO					
Craig	Y	Y	Y	Y	N
Crapo	Y	Y	Y	Y	N
ILLINOIS					
Durbin	N	N	N	N	Y
Obama	?	?	?	?	?
INDIANA					
Lugar	N	N	N	N	Y
Bayh	?	?	?	?	Y
IOWA					
Grassley	Y	Y	Y	Y	Y
Harkin	N	N	N	N	Y
KANSAS					
Brownback	N	Y	N	Y	Y
Roberts	Y	Y	N	Y	Y
KENTUCKY					
McConnell	Y	Y	Y	Y	Y
Bunning	Y	Y	Y	Y	N
LOUISIANA					
Landrieu	N	N	N	N	Y
Vitter	Y	Y	Y	Y	N
MAINE					
Snowe	N	Y	N	N	Y
Collins	N	Y	N	N	Y
MARYLAND					
Mikulski	N	N	N	N	Y
Cardin	N	N	N	N	Y
MASSACHUSETTS					
Kennedy	?	?	?	?	?
Kerry	N	N	N	N	Y
MICHIGAN					
Levin	N	N	N	N	Y
Stabenow	N	N	N	N	Y
MINNESOTA					
Coleman	N	Y	N	N	Y
Klobuchar	N	Y	N	N	Y
MISSISSIPPI					
Cochran	Y	Y	N	N	Y
Wicker	Y	Y	Y	Y	N
MISSOURI					
Bond	Y	Y	Y	Y	Y
McCaskill	N	Y	N	Y	Y
MONTANA					
Baucus	N	N	N	N	Y
Tester	N	Y	N	N	Y
NEBRASKA					
Hagel	N	N	N	N	Y
Nelson	N	N	N	Y	Y
NEVADA					
Reid	N	N	N	N	Y
Ensign	Y	Y	Y	Y	N
NEW HAMPSHIRE					
Gregg	Y	Y	Y	Y	N
Sununu	N	Y	N	N	Y
NEW JERSEY					
Lautenberg	N	N	N	N	Y
Menendez	N	N	N	N	Y
NEW MEXICO					
Domenici	N	N	N	N	Y
Bingaman	N	N	N	N	Y
NEW YORK					
Schumer	N	N	N	N	Y
Clinton	N	N	N	N	Y
NORTH CAROLINA					
Dole	N	Y	N	N	Y
Burr	Y	Y	Y	Y	Y
NORTH DAKOTA					
Conrad	N	N	N	N	Y
Dorgan	N	N	N	N	Y
OHIO					
Voinovich	Y	Y	N	N	Y
Brown	N	N	N	N	Y
OKLAHOMA					
Inhofe	Y	Y	Y	Y	N
Coburn	Y	Y	Y	Y	Y
OREGON					
Wyden	N	N	N	N	Y
Smith	N	Y	N	N	Y
PENNSYLVANIA					
Specter	N	Y	N	N	Y
Casey	N	N	N	N	Y
RHODE ISLAND					
Reed	N	N	N	N	Y
Whitehouse	N	N	N	N	Y
SOUTH CAROLINA					
Graham	Y	Y	Y	Y	N
DeMint	Y	Y	Y	Y	N
SOUTH DAKOTA					
Johnson	N	N	N	N	Y
Thune	Y	Y	Y	Y	Y
TENNESSEE					
Alexander	Y	Y	Y	Y	Y
Corker	Y	Y	Y	Y	Y
TEXAS					
Hutchison	Y	Y	Y	Y	N
Cornyn	Y	Y	Y	Y	N
UTAH					
Hatch	Y	Y	Y	N	Y
Bennett	N	N	N	N	Y
VERMONT					
Leahy	N	N	N	N	Y
Sanders	N	N	N	N	Y
VIRGINIA					
Warner	?	?	?	?	+
Webb	N	N	N	N	Y
WASHINGTON					
Murray	N	N	N	N	Y
Cantwell	N	N	N	N	Y
WEST VIRGINIA					
Byrd	N	N	N	N	Y
Rockefeller	N	N	N	N	Y
WISCONSIN					
Kohl	N	N	N	N	Y
Feingold	N	Y	N	N	Y
WYOMING					
Enzi	Y	Y	Y	Y	Y
Barrasso	Y	Y	Y	Y	N

KEY   Republicans **Democrats** *Independents*

Y Voted for (yea)	X Paired against	C Voted "present" to avoid possible conflict of interest
# Paired for	– Announced against	
+ Announced for	P Voted "present"	? Did not vote or otherwise make a position known
N Voted against (nay)		

ND Northern Democrats, SD Southern Democrats
Southern states: Ala., Ark., Fla., Ga., Ky., La., Miss., N.C., Okla., S.C., Tenn., Texas, Va.

IN THE SENATE | By Vote Number

183. **S 3268. Energy Futures Speculation/Cloture.** Motion to invoke cloture (thus limiting debate) on the motion to proceed to the bill that would increase staffing at the Commodity Futures Trading Commission and place more regulations on energy futures trading. Motion agreed to 94-0: R 46-0; D 46-0 (ND 41-0, SD 5-0); I 2-0. Three-fifths of the total Senate (60) is required to invoke cloture. July 22, 2008.

184. **S 3268. Energy Futures Speculation/Cloture.** Motion to invoke cloture (thus limiting debate) on the bill that would increase staffing at the Commodity Futures Trading Commission and place more regulations on energy futures trading. Three-fifths of the total Senate (60) is required to invoke cloture. Motion rejected 50-43: R 2-42; D 46-1 (ND 41-1, SD 5-0); I 2-0. July 25, 2008.

185. **HR 3221. Mortgage Relief/Cloture.** Motion to invoke cloture (thus limiting debate) on the motion to concur in the House amendment to the Senate amendment to the House amendments to the Senate amendment to the bill. The House amendment would grant authority to the Treasury Department to extend new credit and buy stock in Fannie Mae and Freddie Mac. It also would create an independent regulator for the two mortgage giants and the Federal Home Loan Bank System. It would overhaul the Federal Housing Administration and allow it to insure up to $300 billion worth of new, refinanced loans for struggling mortgage borrowers. It also includes a $7,500 tax credit for some first-time homebuyers, higher loan limits for FHA-backed loans, a standard tax deduction for property taxes and revenue-raisers to offset part of the costs. It also would authorize $3.9 billion in grants to states and localities to purchase and rehabilitate foreclosed properties, and increase the federal debt limit to $10.6 trillion. Motion agreed to 80-13: R 31-13; D 47-0 (ND 42-0, SD 5-0); I 2-0. Three-fifths of the total Senate (60) is required to invoke cloture. July 25, 2008.

	183	184	185			183	184	185
ALABAMA					**MONTANA**			
Shelby	Y	N	Y		Baucus	Y	Y	Y
Sessions	Y	N	Y		Tester	Y	Y	Y
ALASKA					**NEBRASKA**			
Stevens	Y	?	?		Hagel	?	N	Y
Murkowski	Y	N	Y		Nelson	Y	Y	Y
ARIZONA					**NEVADA**			
McCain	?	?	?		Reid	Y	N	Y
Kyl	Y	N	N		Ensign	Y	N	N
ARKANSAS					**NEW HAMPSHIRE**			
Lincoln	Y	Y	Y		Gregg	Y	N	Y
Pryor	Y	Y	Y		Sununu	Y	N	N
CALIFORNIA					**NEW JERSEY**			
Feinstein	Y	Y	Y		Lautenberg	Y	Y	Y
Boxer	Y	Y	Y		Menendez	Y	Y	Y
COLORADO					**NEW MEXICO**			
Allard	Y	?	?		Domenici	Y	N	Y
Salazar	Y	Y	Y		Bingaman	Y	Y	Y
CONNECTICUT					**NEW YORK**			
Dodd	Y	Y	Y		Schumer	Y	Y	Y
Lieberman	Y	Y	Y		Clinton	Y	Y	Y
DELAWARE					**NORTH CAROLINA**			
Biden	Y	Y	Y		Dole	Y	N	Y
Carper	Y	Y	Y		Burr	Y	N	N
FLORIDA					**NORTH DAKOTA**			
Nelson	Y	Y	Y		Conrad	Y	Y	Y
Martinez	Y	N	Y		Dorgan	Y	Y	Y
GEORGIA					**OHIO**			
Chambliss	Y	N	Y		Voinovich	Y	N	Y
Isakson	Y	N	Y		Brown	Y	Y	Y
HAWAII					**OKLAHOMA**			
Inouye	Y	Y	Y		Inhofe	Y	N	N
Akaka	Y	Y	Y		Coburn	Y	?	?
IDAHO					**OREGON**			
Craig	Y	N	Y		Wyden	Y	Y	Y
Crapo	Y	N	Y		Smith	Y	N	Y
ILLINOIS					**PENNSYLVANIA**			
Durbin	Y	Y	Y		Specter	Y	N	Y
Obama	?	?	?		Casey	Y	Y	Y
INDIANA					**RHODE ISLAND**			
Lugar	Y	N	Y		Reed	+	Y	Y
Bayh	Y	Y	Y		Whitehouse	Y	Y	Y
IOWA					**SOUTH CAROLINA**			
Grassley	Y	N	Y		Graham	Y	?	?
Harkin	Y	Y	Y		DeMint	Y	N	N
KANSAS					**SOUTH DAKOTA**			
Brownback	Y	N	Y		Johnson	Y	Y	Y
Roberts	Y	N	Y		Thune	Y	N	N
KENTUCKY					**TENNESSEE**			
McConnell	Y	N	Y		Alexander	+	N	Y
Bunning	Y	N	N		Corker	Y	N	N
LOUISIANA					**TEXAS**			
Landrieu	Y	Y	Y		Hutchison	Y	N	Y
Vitter	Y	N	N		Cornyn	Y	N	Y
MAINE					**UTAH**			
Snowe	Y	Y	Y		Hatch	Y	N	Y
Collins	Y	Y	Y		Bennett	Y	N	Y
MARYLAND					**VERMONT**			
Mikulski	Y	Y	Y		Leahy	Y	Y	Y
Cardin	Y	Y	Y		*Sanders*	Y	Y	Y
MASSACHUSETTS					**VIRGINIA**			
Kennedy	?	?	?		Warner	Y	N	Y
Kerry	Y	Y	Y		Webb	Y	Y	Y
MICHIGAN					**WASHINGTON**			
Levin	Y	Y	Y		Murray	Y	Y	Y
Stabenow	Y	Y	Y		Cantwell	Y	Y	Y
MINNESOTA					**WEST VIRGINIA**			
Coleman	Y	N	Y		Byrd	Y	Y	Y
Klobuchar	Y	Y	Y		Rockefeller	Y	Y	Y
MISSISSIPPI					**WISCONSIN**			
Cochran	Y	N	Y		Kohl	Y	Y	Y
Wicker	Y	N	Y		Feingold	Y	Y	Y
MISSOURI					**WYOMING**			
Bond	Y	N	N		Enzi	Y	N	N
McCaskill	Y	Y	Y		Barrasso	Y	N	N

KEY	Republicans		Democrats	*Independents*		
Y	Voted for (yea)	X	Paired against		C	Voted "present" to avoid possible conflict of interest
#	Paired for	–	Announced against			
+	Announced for	P	Voted "present"		?	Did not vote or otherwise make a position known
N	Voted against (nay)					

ND Northern Democrats, SD Southern Democrats
Southern states: Ala., Ark., Fla., Ga., Ky., La., Miss., N.C., Okla., S.C., Tenn., Texas, Va.

IN THE SENATE | By Vote Number

186. **HR 3221. Mortgage Relief/Motion to Concur.** Reid, D-Nev., motion to concur in the House amendment to the Senate amendment to the House amendments to the Senate amendment. The House amendment would grant authority to the Treasury Department to extend new credit and buy stock in Fannie Mae and Freddie Mac. It would create an independent regulator for the two mortgage giants and the Federal Home Loan Bank System. It would overhaul the Federal Housing Administration and allow it to insure up to $300 billion worth of new, refinanced loans for struggling mortgage borrowers. It also includes a $7,500 tax credit for some first-time homebuyers, higher loan limits for FHA-backed loans, a standard tax deduction for property taxes and revenue-raisers to offset part of the costs. It also would authorize $3.9 billion in grants to states and localities to purchase and rehabilitate foreclosed properties, and increase the federal debt limit to $10.6 trillion. Motion agreed to, thus clearing the bill for the president, 72-13: R 27-13; D 43-0 (ND 38-0, SD 5-0); I 2-0. A "yea" was a vote in support of the president's position. July 26, 2008.

187. **S 3186. Low-Income Energy Assistance/Cloture.** Motion to invoke cloture (thus limiting debate) on the motion to proceed to the bill that would provide $2.5 billion in fiscal 2008 emergency funds for the Low Income Home Energy Assistance Program, which helps low-income families pay home heating and cooling costs. Motion rejected 50-35: R 5-34; D 43-1 (ND 38-1, SD 5-0); I 2-0. Three-fifths of the total Senate (60) is required to invoke cloture. July 26, 2008.

188. **Procedural Matter/Require Attendance.** Reid, D-Nev., motion to instruct the sergeant at arms to request the attendance of absent senators. Motion agreed to 87-3: R 39-3; D 46-0 (ND 41-0, SD 5-0); I 2-0. July 28, 2008.

189. **S 3297. Omnibus Domestic and Foreign Policy Package/ Cloture.** Motion to invoke cloture (thus limiting debate) on the motion to proceed to the bill that contains the provisions of nearly three dozen measures. It includes proposals that would create a registry of those suffering from Lou Gehrig's disease; protect children from Internet predators; expand paralysis research at the National Institutes of Health; expand research on postpartum depression; authorize funding for investigations of pre-1970 civil rights crimes; and ban interstate sale or trade of monkeys and other non-human primates. Motion rejected 52-40: R 3-40; D 47-0 (ND 42-0, SD 5-0); I 2-0. Three-fifths of the total Senate (60) is required to invoke cloture. July 28, 2008.

190. **HR 6049. Tax Provisions Extension/Cloture.** Motion to invoke cloture (thus limiting debate) on the motion to proceed to the bill that would extend dozens of expired or expiring tax provisions for one year and create new energy-related tax incentives. Motion rejected 53-43: R 4-43; D 47-0 (ND 42-0, SD 5-0); I 2-0. Three-fifths of the total Senate (60) is required to invoke cloture. July 29, 2008.

191. **S 2035. Media Shield/Cloture.** Motion to invoke cloture (thus limiting debate) on the motion to proceed to the bill that would protect journalists, in some cases, from having to reveal the identity of their sources in court. Motion rejected 51-43: R 5-42; D 44-1 (ND 39-1, SD 5-0); I 2-0. Three-fifths of the total Senate (60) is required to invoke cloture. July 30, 2008.

	186	187	188	189	190	191		186	187	188	189	190	191
ALABAMA							**MONTANA**						
Shelby	Y	N	Y	N	N	N	Baucus	Y	Y	Y	Y	Y	Y
Sessions	Y	N	Y	N	N	N	Tester	Y	Y	Y	Y	Y	Y
ALASKA							**NEBRASKA**						
Stevens	Y	N	Y	N	?	N	Hagel	Y	N	?	?	N	Y
Murkowski	Y	N	Y	N	N	N	Nelson	Y	Y	Y	Y	Y	Y
ARIZONA							**NEVADA**						
McCain	?	?	?	?	?	?	Reid	Y	N	Y	Y	Y	N
Kyl	N	N	Y	N	N	N	Ensign	N	N	?	?	N	N
ARKANSAS							**NEW HAMPSHIRE**						
Lincoln	Y	Y	Y	Y	Y	Y	Gregg	Y	N	Y	N	N	N
Pryor	Y	Y	Y	Y	Y	Y	Sununu	Y	Y	?	?	N	N
CALIFORNIA							**NEW JERSEY**						
Feinstein	Y	Y	Y	Y	Y	Y	Lautenberg	Y	Y	Y	Y	Y	Y
Boxer	Y	Y	Y	Y	Y	Y	Menendez	Y	Y	Y	Y	Y	Y
COLORADO							**NEW MEXICO**						
Allard	?	?	?	?	N	N	Domenici	Y	N	Y	N	N	N
Salazar	Y	Y	Y	Y	Y	Y	Bingaman	Y	Y	Y	Y	Y	Y
CONNECTICUT							**NEW YORK**						
Dodd	Y	Y	Y	Y	Y	Y	Schumer	Y	Y	Y	Y	Y	Y
Lieberman	Y	Y	Y	Y	Y	Y	Clinton	Y	Y	Y	Y	Y	Y
DELAWARE							**NORTH CAROLINA**						
Biden	Y	Y	Y	Y	Y	Y	Dole	?	?	?	?	N	N
Carper	+	Y	Y	Y	Y	Y	Burr	?	?	Y	N	N	N
FLORIDA							**NORTH DAKOTA**						
Nelson	Y	Y	Y	Y	Y	Y	Conrad	Y	Y	Y	Y	Y	Y
Martinez	Y	N	Y	N	N	N	Dorgan	Y	Y	Y	Y	Y	Y
GEORGIA							**OHIO**						
Chambliss	Y	N	Y	N	N	N	Voinovich	Y	N	?	N	N	N
Isakson	Y	–	Y	N	N	N	Brown	Y	Y	Y	Y	Y	Y
HAWAII							**OKLAHOMA**						
Inouye	?	?	?	Y	Y	Y	Inhofe	?	?	Y	N	N	N
Akaka	Y	Y	Y	Y	Y	Y	Coburn	N	N	Y	N	N	N
IDAHO							**OREGON**						
Craig	Y	N	Y	N	N	N	Wyden	Y	Y	Y	Y	Y	Y
Crapo	Y	N	Y	N	N	N	Smith	Y	Y	Y	Y	Y	Y
ILLINOIS							**PENNSYLVANIA**						
Durbin	Y	Y	Y	Y	Y	Y	Specter	Y	N	N	N	N	Y
Obama	?	?	?	?	?	?	Casey	Y	Y	Y	Y	Y	Y
INDIANA							**RHODE ISLAND**						
Lugar	Y	N	Y	N	N	Y	Reed	Y	Y	Y	Y	Y	Y
Bayh	Y	Y	Y	Y	Y	Y	Whitehouse	Y	Y	Y	Y	Y	Y
IOWA							**SOUTH CAROLINA**						
Grassley	N	N	Y	N	N	N	Graham	?	?	Y	N	N	N
Harkin	?	?	Y	Y	Y	Y	DeMint	N	N	Y	N	N	N
KANSAS							**SOUTH DAKOTA**						
Brownback	Y	N	Y	N	N	N	Johnson	Y	Y	Y	Y	Y	Y
Roberts	Y	N	Y	N	N	N	Thune	N	N	Y	N	N	N
KENTUCKY							**TENNESSEE**						
McConnell	Y	N	Y	N	N	N	Alexander	Y	N	Y	N	N	N
Bunning	–	–	Y	N	N	N	Corker	N	N	Y	N	N	N
LOUISIANA							**TEXAS**						
Landrieu	Y	Y	Y	Y	Y	Y	Hutchison	N	N	Y	N	N	N
Vitter	N	N	N	N	N	N	Cornyn	N	N	Y	N	N	N
MAINE							**UTAH**						
Snowe	Y	Y	Y	N	Y	N	Hatch	N	N	Y	N	N	N
Collins	Y	Y	Y	N	Y	Y	Bennett	Y	N	N	N	N	N
MARYLAND							**VERMONT**						
Mikulski	Y	Y	Y	Y	Y	Y	Leahy	Y	Y	Y	Y	Y	Y
Cardin	Y	Y	Y	Y	Y	Y	*Sanders*	Y	Y	Y	Y	Y	Y
MASSACHUSETTS							**VIRGINIA**						
Kennedy	?	?	?	?	?	?	Warner	?	?	Y	N	N	N
Kerry	Y	Y	Y	Y	Y	Y	Webb	Y	Y	Y	Y	Y	Y
MICHIGAN							**WASHINGTON**						
Levin	Y	Y	Y	Y	Y	Y	Murray	?	?	Y	Y	Y	Y
Stabenow	Y	Y	Y	Y	Y	Y	Cantwell	Y	Y	Y	Y	Y	Y
MINNESOTA							**WEST VIRGINIA**						
Coleman	Y	Y	Y	Y	Y	N	Byrd	Y	Y	Y	Y	Y	Y
Klobuchar	Y	Y	Y	Y	Y	Y	Rockefeller	Y	Y	Y	Y	Y	?
MISSISSIPPI							**WISCONSIN**						
Cochran	Y	N	Y	N	N	N	Kohl	Y	Y	Y	Y	Y	Y
Wicker	Y	N	Y	N	N	?	Feingold	Y	Y	Y	Y	Y	Y
MISSOURI							**WYOMING**						
Bond	?	?	Y	N	N	N	Enzi	N	N	Y	N	N	N
McCaskill	Y	Y	Y	Y	N	?	Barrasso	N	N	Y	N	N	N

KEY Republicans Democrats *Independents*

Y Voted for (yea)	X Paired against	C Voted "present" to avoid possible conflict of interest
# Paired for	– Announced against	
+ Announced for	P Voted "present"	? Did not vote or otherwise make a position known
N Voted against (nay)		

ND Northern Democrats, SD Southern Democrats
Southern states: Ala., Ark., Fla., Ga., Ky., La., Miss., N.C., Okla., S.C., Tenn., Texas, Va.

IN THE SENATE | By Vote Number

192. **S 3335. Tax Provisions Extension/Cloture.** Motion to invoke cloture (thus limiting debate) on the motion to proceed to the bill that would extend dozens of expired or expiring tax provisions for one year and create new energy-related tax incentives. It also would appropriate $8 billion to the Highway Trust Fund. Motion rejected 51-43: R 5-42; D 44-1 (ND 39-1, SD 5-0); I 2-0. Three-fifths of the total Senate (60) is required to invoke cloture. July 30, 2008.

193. **HR 4040. Consumer Product Safety Commission Overhaul/Conference Report.** Adoption of the conference report on the bill that would authorize $626 million for the Consumer Product Safety Commission in fiscal 2010-14. The bill would set lower thresholds for lead in toys and ban certain phthalates, or plastic softeners, in products for children. It would require an online database of product-related injuries and risks, ban the sale of All-Terrain Vehicles that do not meet certain standards and provide whistleblower protections to certain employees. It also would provide states with increased consumer protection authority. Adopted (thus cleared for the president) 89-3: R 42-3; D 45-0 (ND 40-0, SD 5-0); I 2-0. July 31, 2008.

194. **HR 4137. Higher Education Reauthorization/Conference Report.** Adoption of the conference report on the bill that would reauthorize the Higher Education Act through fiscal 2012. The bill would increase the maximum Pell grant to $8,000 per year by the 2014-15 academic year. It would bar lenders from giving schools financial perks in order to get on a "preferred lender list." It also would penalize states that cut funding for institutions of higher education by withholding some federal funds if the state's funding for such institutions falls below the average amount allocated by the state over the last five academic years. It would establish a new loan-forgiveness program, providing up to $2,000 a year for five years for individuals such as nurses, early childhood educators and librarians serving in high-need areas. Adopted (thus cleared for the president) 83-8: R 36-8; D 45-0 (ND 40-0, SD 5-0); I 2-0. July 31, 2008.

195. **S 3001. Fiscal 2009 Defense Authorization/Cloture.** Motion to invoke cloture (thus limiting debate) on the motion to proceed to the bill that would authorize $612.5 billion for national defense activities in the Department of Defense and the Department of Energy in fiscal 2009, including $70 billion for war-related costs in Iraq and Afghanistan. Motion rejected 51-39: R 5-38; D 44-1 (ND 39-1, SD 5-0); I 2-0. Three-fifths of the total Senate (60) is required to invoke cloture. July 31, 2008.

196. **H Con Res 398. Adjournment/Adoption.** Adoption of the concurrent resolution that would provide for adjournment of the Senate until noon, Monday, Sept. 8, 2008, and the House until 2 p.m., Monday, Sept. 8, 2008. Adopted 48-40: R 1-40; D 45-0 (ND 40-0, SD 5-0); I 2-0. July 31, 2008.

	192	193	194	195	196
ALABAMA					
Shelby	N	Y	Y	N	N
Sessions	N	Y	N	N	N
ALASKA					
Stevens	N	Y	Y	N	N
Murkowski	N	Y	Y	N	N
ARIZONA					
McCain	?	?	?	?	?
Kyl	N	N	N	N	N
ARKANSAS					
Lincoln	Y	Y	Y	Y	Y
Pryor	Y	Y	Y	Y	Y
CALIFORNIA					
Feinstein	Y	Y	Y	Y	Y
Boxer	Y	Y	Y	Y	Y
COLORADO					
Allard	N	Y	Y	N	N
Salazar	Y	Y	Y	Y	Y
CONNECTICUT					
Dodd	Y	Y	Y	Y	Y
Lieberman	Y	Y	Y	Y	Y
DELAWARE					
Biden	Y	Y	Y	Y	Y
Carper	Y	Y	Y	Y	Y
FLORIDA					
Nelson	Y	Y	Y	Y	Y
Martinez	N	Y	Y	N	N
GEORGIA					
Chambliss	N	Y	Y	N	N
Isakson	N	Y	N	N	N
HAWAII					
Inouye	Y	Y	Y	Y	Y
Akaka	Y	Y	Y	Y	Y
IDAHO					
Craig	N	Y	Y	N	N
Crapo	N	Y	N	N	N
ILLINOIS					
Durbin	Y	Y	Y	Y	Y
Obama	?	?	?	?	?
INDIANA					
Lugar	N	Y	Y	N	Y
Bayh	Y	Y	Y	Y	Y
IOWA					
Grassley	N	Y	Y	N	N
Harkin	Y	Y	Y	Y	Y
KANSAS					
Brownback	N	Y	Y	N	N
Roberts	N	Y	Y	N	N
KENTUCKY					
McConnell	N	Y	Y	N	N
Bunning	N	Y	Y	–	–
LOUISIANA					
Landrieu	Y	Y	Y	Y	Y
Vitter	N	Y	Y	N	N
MAINE					
Snowe	Y	Y	P	N	Y
Collins	Y	Y	Y	Y	N
MARYLAND					
Mikulski	Y	Y	Y	Y	Y
Cardin	Y	Y	Y	Y	Y
MASSACHUSETTS					
Kennedy	?	?	?	?	?
Kerry	Y	Y	Y	Y	Y
MICHIGAN					
Levin	Y	Y	Y	Y	Y
Stabenow	Y	Y	Y	Y	Y
MINNESOTA					
Coleman	Y	?	?	?	?
Klobuchar	Y	+	+	?	?
MISSISSIPPI					
Cochran	N	Y	Y	N	N
Wicker	?	Y	Y	N	N
MISSOURI					
Bond	N	Y	Y	N	?
McCaskill	?	Y	Y	Y	Y

	192	193	194	195	196
MONTANA					
Baucus	Y	Y	Y	Y	Y
Tester	Y	Y	Y	Y	Y
NEBRASKA					
Hagel	N	?	?	?	?
Nelson	Y	Y	Y	Y	Y
NEVADA					
Reid	N	Y	Y	N	Y
Ensign	N	Y	Y	N	N
NEW HAMPSHIRE					
Gregg	N	Y	Y	N	N
Sununu	N	Y	Y	N	N
NEW JERSEY					
Lautenberg	Y	Y	Y	Y	Y
Menendez	Y	Y	Y	Y	Y
NEW MEXICO					
Domenici	N	?	?	?	?
Bingaman	Y	Y	Y	Y	Y
NEW YORK					
Schumer	Y	Y	Y	Y	Y
Clinton	Y	?	?	?	?
NORTH CAROLINA					
Dole	Y	Y	Y	N	N
Burr	N	Y	Y	N	N
NORTH DAKOTA					
Conrad	Y	Y	Y	Y	Y
Dorgan	Y	Y	Y	Y	Y
OHIO					
Voinovich	N	Y	Y	N	N
Brown	Y	Y	Y	Y	Y
OKLAHOMA					
Inhofe	N	Y	N	N	?
Coburn	N	N	N	N	N
OREGON					
Wyden	Y	Y	Y	Y	Y
Smith	Y	Y	Y	Y	N
PENNSYLVANIA					
Specter	N	Y	Y	N	N
Casey	Y	Y	Y	Y	Y
RHODE ISLAND					
Reed	Y	Y	Y	Y	Y
Whitehouse	Y	Y	Y	Y	Y
SOUTH CAROLINA					
Graham	N	Y	Y	N	N
DeMint	N	N	N	N	N
SOUTH DAKOTA					
Johnson	Y	Y	Y	Y	Y
Thune	N	Y	Y	N	N
TENNESSEE					
Alexander	N	Y	N	N	N
Corker	N	Y	N	N	N
TEXAS					
Hutchison	N	Y	Y	?	?
Cornyn	N	Y	N	N	N
UTAH					
Hatch	N	Y	Y	N	N
Bennett	N	Y	Y	N	N
VERMONT					
Leahy	Y	Y	Y	Y	Y
Sanders	Y	Y	Y	Y	Y
VIRGINIA					
Warner	N	Y	Y	Y	N
Webb	Y	Y	Y	Y	Y
WASHINGTON					
Murray	Y	Y	Y	Y	Y
Cantwell	Y	Y	Y	Y	Y
WEST VIRGINIA					
Byrd	Y	Y	Y	Y	Y
Rockefeller	?	Y	Y	Y	Y
WISCONSIN					
Kohl	Y	Y	Y	Y	Y
Feingold	Y	Y	Y	Y	Y
WYOMING					
Enzi	N	Y	Y	N	N
Barrasso	N	Y	Y	N	N

KEY	Republicans	Democrats	Independents	
Y Voted for (yea)		X Paired against		C Voted "present" to avoid possible conflict of interest
# Paired for		– Announced against		
+ Announced for		P Voted "present"		? Did not vote or otherwise make a position known
N Voted against (nay)				

ND Northern Democrats, SD Southern Democrats
Southern states: Ala., Ark., Fla., Ga., Ky., La., Miss., N.C., Okla., S.C., Tenn., Texas, Va.

IN THE SENATE | By Vote Number

197. **S 3001. Fiscal 2009 Defense Authorization/Cloture.** Motion to invoke cloture (thus limiting debate) on the motion to proceed to the bill that would authorize $612.5 billion for national defense activities in the Defense and Energy departments in fiscal 2009, including $70 billion for war-related costs in Iraq and Afghanistan. Motion agreed to 83-0: R 41-0; D 40-0 (ND 36-0, SD 4-0); I 2-0. Three-fifths of the total Senate (60) is required to invoke cloture. Sept. 8, 2008.

198. **S 3001. Fiscal 2009 Defense Authorization/Missile Defense.** Vitter, R-La., amendment that would authorize an additional $271 million for the Missile Defense Agency for programs to address and respond to near-term ballistic missile threats. It would be offset by making cuts to other unspecified military programs. Rejected 39-57: R 37-11; D 2-44 (ND 1-40, SD 1-4); I 0-2. Sept. 10, 2008.

199. **S 3001. Fiscal 2009 Defense Authorization/Survivor Benefits.** Nelson, D-Fla., amendment that would repeal the requirement that survivors of deceased military personnel who receive annuities under the Defense Department's Survivor Benefits Plan have those benefits reduced dollar for dollar by the amount received from the Department of Veterans Affairs' Dependency and Indemnity Compensation program. Adopted 94-2: R 46-0; D 46-0 (ND 41-0, SD 5-0); I 2-0. Sept. 10, 2008.

200. **S 3001. Fiscal 2009 Defense Authorization/Cloture.** Motion to invoke cloture (thus limiting debate) on the bill that would authorize $612.5 billion for national defense activities in the Defense and Energy departments in fiscal 2009, including $70 billion for war-related costs in Iraq and Afghanistan. Motion agreed to 61-32: R 15-31; D 44-1 (ND 39-1, SD 5-0); I 2-0. Three-fifths of the total Senate (60) is required to invoke cloture. Sept. 16, 2008.

201. **S 3001. Fiscal 2009 Defense Authorization/Passage.** Passage of the bill that would authorize $612.5 billion for defense programs in fiscal 2009, including $70 billion for the wars in Iraq and Afghanistan. Excluding the war funding, it would authorize $154 billion for operations and maintenance; $103.9 billion for procurement; $128.4 billion for military personnel; $24.8 billion for military construction, family housing and base closures; $79.7 billion for research development, testing and evaluation; and $24.8 billion for the Defense Health Program. It would authorize a 3.9 percent pay increase for military personnel. It would extend from three years to five years the statute of limitations on contractor fraud in theaters of war, including undeclared wars. Passed 88-8: R 43-5; D 44-2 (ND 39-2, SD 5-0); I 1-1. A "nay" was a vote in support of the president's position. Sept. 17, 2008.

	197	198	199	200	201			197	198	199	200	201
ALABAMA							**MONTANA**					
Shelby	Y	Y	Y	N	Y		Baucus	Y	N	Y	Y	Y
Sessions	Y	N	Y	N	Y		Tester	Y	N	Y	Y	Y
ALASKA							**NEBRASKA**					
Stevens	Y	N	Y	Y	Y		**Hagel**	Y	Y	Y	Y	Y
Murkowski	Y	N	Y	Y	Y		Nelson	Y	N	Y	Y	Y
ARIZONA							**NEVADA**					
McCain	?	?	?	?	?		Reid	Y	N	Y	Y	Y
Kyl	Y	Y	Y	N	Y		**Ensign**	?	Y	Y	N	Y
ARKANSAS							**NEW HAMPSHIRE**					
Lincoln	Y	N	Y	Y	Y		**Gregg**	Y	N	Y	N	Y
Pryor	Y	N	Y	Y	Y		**Sununu**	?	N	Y	Y	Y
CALIFORNIA							**NEW JERSEY**					
Feinstein	Y	N	Y	Y	Y		Lautenberg	Y	N	Y	Y	Y
Boxer	Y	N	Y	Y	Y		Menendez	Y	N	Y	Y	Y
COLORADO							**NEW MEXICO**					
Allard	Y	Y	Y	N	N		**Domenici**	Y	Y	Y	N	Y
Salazar	Y	N	Y	Y	Y		Bingaman	Y	N	Y	Y	Y
CONNECTICUT							**NEW YORK**					
Dodd	Y	N	Y	Y	Y		Schumer	Y	N	Y	Y	Y
Lieberman	Y	N	Y	Y	Y		Clinton	?	N	Y	Y	Y
DELAWARE							**NORTH CAROLINA**					
Biden	?	?	?	?	?		**Dole**	+	Y	Y	Y	Y
Carper	Y	N	Y	Y	Y		**Burr**	Y	Y	Y	N	Y
FLORIDA							**NORTH DAKOTA**					
Nelson	Y	N	Y	Y	Y		Conrad	Y	N	Y	Y	Y
Martinez	Y	Y	Y	?	Y		Dorgan	Y	N	Y	Y	Y
GEORGIA							**OHIO**					
Chambliss	Y	Y	Y	N	Y		**Voinovich**	Y	Y	N	N	Y
Isakson	Y	Y	Y	N	Y		Brown	Y	N	Y	Y	Y
HAWAII							**OKLAHOMA**					
Inouye	?	N	Y	Y	Y		**Inhofe**	Y	Y	Y	N	Y
Akaka	Y	N	Y	Y	Y		**Coburn**	Y	Y	Y	N	N
IDAHO							**OREGON**					
Craig	Y	Y	Y	N	Y		Wyden	?	N	Y	Y	Y
Crapo	Y	Y	Y	N	Y		**Smith**	Y	N	Y	Y	Y
ILLINOIS							**PENNSYLVANIA**					
Durbin	Y	N	Y	Y	Y		**Specter**	Y	Y	Y	Y	Y
Obama	?	?	?	?	?		Casey	Y	N	Y	Y	Y
INDIANA							**RHODE ISLAND**					
Lugar	Y	Y	Y	Y	Y		Reed	Y	N	Y	Y	Y
Bayh	Y	Y	Y	Y	Y		Whitehouse	Y	N	Y	Y	Y
IOWA							**SOUTH CAROLINA**					
Grassley	Y	Y	Y	N	Y		**Graham**	?	Y	Y	N	N
Harkin	Y	N	Y	Y	Y		**DeMint**	Y	Y	Y	N	N
KANSAS							**SOUTH DAKOTA**					
Brownback	?	Y	Y	N	Y		Johnson	Y	N	Y	Y	Y
Roberts	Y	Y	Y	Y	Y		**Thune**	Y	Y	Y	N	Y
KENTUCKY							**TENNESSEE**					
McConnell	Y	Y	Y	N	Y		**Alexander**	Y	Y	Y	N	Y
Bunning	Y	Y	N	N	Y		**Corker**	Y	N	Y	N	Y
LOUISIANA							**TEXAS**					
Landrieu	?	Y	Y	Y	Y		**Hutchison**	Y	Y	Y	N	Y
Vitter	?	Y	Y	N	N		**Cornyn**	Y	Y	Y	-	Y
MAINE							**UTAH**					
Snowe	Y	N	Y	Y	Y		**Hatch**	Y	Y	Y	N	Y
Collins	Y	N	Y	Y	Y		**Bennett**	Y	N	Y	N	Y
MARYLAND							**VERMONT**					
Mikulski	?	N	Y	Y	Y		Leahy	Y	N	Y	Y	Y
Cardin	Y	N	Y	Y	Y		*Sanders*	Y	N	Y	Y	N
MASSACHUSETTS							**VIRGINIA**					
Kennedy	?	?	?	+	?		**Warner**	Y	N	Y	Y	Y
Kerry	Y	N	Y	?	Y		Webb	Y	N	Y	Y	Y
MICHIGAN							**WASHINGTON**					
Levin	Y	N	Y	Y	Y		Murray	Y	N	Y	Y	Y
Stabenow	Y	N	Y	Y	Y		Cantwell	Y	N	Y	Y	Y
MINNESOTA							**WEST VIRGINIA**					
Coleman	Y	Y	Y	Y	Y		Byrd	Y	N	Y	Y	N
Klobuchar	Y	N	Y	Y	Y		Rockefeller	Y	N	Y	Y	Y
MISSISSIPPI							**WISCONSIN**					
Cochran	Y	Y	Y	Y	Y		Kohl	Y	Y	Y	Y	Y
Wicker	?	Y	Y	Y	Y		Feingold	Y	N	Y	N	N
MISSOURI							**WYOMING**					
Bond	Y	Y	Y	N	Y		**Enzi**	Y	Y	Y	N	Y
McCaskill	?	N	Y	Y	Y		**Barrasso**	Y	Y	Y	N	Y

KEY **Republicans** Democrats *Independents*

Y Voted for (yea)	X Paired against
# Paired for	– Announced against
+ Announced for	P Voted "present"
N Voted against (nay)	

C Voted "present" to avoid possible conflict of interest

? Did not vote or otherwise make a position known

ND Northern Democrats, SD Southern Democrats
Southern states: Ala., Ark., Fla., Ga., Ky., La., Miss., N.C., Okla., S.C., Tenn., Texas, Va.

IN THE SENATE | By Vote Number

202. **HR 6049. Tax Provisions Extension/Substitute.** Baucus, D-Mont., substitute amendment that would extend tax credits for wind and solar power, improvements in building efficiency, clean coal and biofuels, and other energy activities. The cost would be offset with revenue-raising provisions, including freezing a deduction for the sale of oil and natural gas, extending a federal unemployment surtax, eliminating the distinction between foreign oil and gas extraction income and other foreign oil-related income, and extending an oil spill tax. Adopted 93-2: R 45-2; D 46-0 (ND 41-0, SD 5-0); I 2-0. (By unanimous consent, the Senate agreed to raise the majority requirement for adoption of the Baucus amendment to 60 votes.) Sept. 23, 2008.

203. **HR 6049. Tax Provisions Extension/Alternative Minimum Tax.** Conrad, D-N.D., amendment that would provide a one-year adjustment to exempt more than 22 million taxpayers from paying the AMT on 2008 income. The exemption would be offset through imposing certain taxes on oil and natural gas produced from the outer continental shelf, a change in the rules for taxing deferred compensation, and other provisions. Rejected 53-42: R 5-42; D 46-0 (ND 41-0, SD 5-0); I 2-0. (By unanimous consent, the Senate agreed to raise the majority requirement for adoption of the Conrad amendment to 60 votes.) A "nay" was a vote in support of the president's position. Sept. 23, 2008.

204. **HR 6049. Tax Provisions Extension/Disaster Relief.** Baucus, D-Mont., motion to waive the Budget Act with respect to the Conrad, D-N.D., point of order against the Baucus amendment to the bill that would extend dozens of expired and expiring tax benefits, provide tax relief for victims of recent natural disasters and adjust the AMT for income earned in 2008. It would also require private insurance plans to put mental health benefits on par with other medical benefits. The tax cuts would be partially offset by revenue-raising provisions, including extending an oil spill tax and changing the rules for taxing deferred compensation. Motion agreed to 84-11: R 45-2; D 38-8 (ND 33-8, SD 5-0); I 1-1. A three-fifths majority (60) of the total Senate is required to waive the Budget Act. (Subsequently, the amendment was adopted pursuant to the previous order.) Sept. 23, 2008.

205. **HR 6049. Tax Provisions Extension/Passage.** Passage of the bill that would extend dozens of expired and expiring tax benefits, provide tax relief for victims of recent natural disasters and adjust the AMT for income earned in 2008. It would require private insurance plans to put mental health benefits on par with other medical benefits. The tax cuts would be partially offset by revenue-raising provisions, including extending an oil spill tax and changing the rules for taxing deferred compensation. Passed 93-2: R 47-0; D 44-2 (ND 39-2, SD 5-0); I 2-0. Sept. 23, 2008.

State / Senator	202	203	204	205		State / Senator	202	203	204	205
ALABAMA						**MONTANA**				
Shelby	Y	N	Y	Y		Baucus	Y	Y	Y	Y
Sessions	Y	N	Y	Y		Tester	Y	Y	Y	Y
ALASKA						**NEBRASKA**				
Stevens	Y	N	Y	Y		**Hagel**	Y	N	Y	Y
Murkowski	Y	N	Y	Y		Nelson	Y	Y	Y	Y
ARIZONA						**NEVADA**				
McCain	?	?	?	?		Reid	Y	Y	Y	Y
Kyl	N	N	Y	Y		**Ensign**	Y	N	Y	Y
ARKANSAS						**NEW HAMPSHIRE**				
Lincoln	Y	Y	Y	Y		**Gregg**	Y	N	Y	Y
Pryor	Y	Y	Y	Y		**Sununu**	Y	N	Y	Y
CALIFORNIA						**NEW JERSEY**				
Feinstein	Y	Y	Y	Y		Lautenberg	Y	Y	Y	Y
Boxer	Y	Y	Y	Y		Menendez	Y	Y	Y	Y
COLORADO						**NEW MEXICO**				
Allard	Y	N	Y	Y		**Domenici**	Y	N	Y	Y
Salazar	Y	Y	Y	Y		Bingaman	Y	Y	Y	Y
CONNECTICUT						**NEW YORK**				
Dodd	Y	Y	Y	Y		Schumer	Y	Y	Y	Y
Lieberman	Y	Y	Y	Y		Clinton	Y	Y	Y	Y
DELAWARE						**NORTH CAROLINA**				
Biden	?	?	?	?		**Dole**	Y	N	Y	Y
Carper	Y	Y	N	N		**Burr**	Y	N	Y	Y
FLORIDA						**NORTH DAKOTA**				
Nelson	Y	Y	Y	Y		Conrad	Y	Y	N	N
Martinez	Y	N	Y	Y		Dorgan	Y	Y	Y	Y
GEORGIA						**OHIO**				
Chambliss	Y	N	Y	Y		**Voinovich**	Y	Y	N	Y
Isakson	Y	N	Y	Y		Brown	Y	Y	N	Y
HAWAII						**OKLAHOMA**				
Inouye	Y	Y	Y	Y		**Inhofe**	Y	N	Y	Y
Akaka	Y	Y	Y	Y		**Coburn**	Y	N	Y	Y
IDAHO						**OREGON**				
Craig	Y	N	Y	Y		Wyden	Y	Y	Y	Y
Crapo	N	N	Y	Y		**Smith**	Y	Y	Y	Y
ILLINOIS						**PENNSYLVANIA**				
Durbin	Y	Y	Y	Y		**Specter**	Y	N	Y	Y
Obama	?	?	?	?		Casey	Y	Y	Y	Y
INDIANA						**RHODE ISLAND**				
Lugar	Y	N	Y	Y		Reed	Y	Y	Y	Y
Bayh	Y	Y	Y	Y		Whitehouse	Y	Y	N	Y
IOWA						**SOUTH CAROLINA**				
Grassley	Y	N	Y	Y		**Graham**	Y	N	Y	Y
Harkin	Y	Y	Y	Y		**DeMint**	?	?	?	?
KANSAS						**SOUTH DAKOTA**				
Brownback	Y	N	Y	Y		Johnson	Y	Y	Y	Y
Roberts	Y	N	Y	Y		**Thune**	Y	N	Y	Y
KENTUCKY						**TENNESSEE**				
McConnell	Y	N	Y	Y		**Alexander**	Y	N	Y	Y
Bunning	Y	N	Y	Y		**Corker**	Y	N	N	Y
LOUISIANA						**TEXAS**				
Landrieu	Y	Y	Y	Y		**Hutchison**	Y	N	Y	Y
Vitter	Y	N	Y	Y		**Cornyn**	Y	N	Y	Y
MAINE						**UTAH**				
Snowe	Y	Y	Y	Y		**Hatch**	Y	N	Y	Y
Collins	Y	Y	Y	Y		**Bennett**	Y	N	Y	Y
MARYLAND						**VERMONT**				
Mikulski	Y	Y	Y	Y		Leahy	Y	Y	Y	Y
Cardin	Y	Y	Y	Y		*Sanders*	Y	Y	N	Y
MASSACHUSETTS						**VIRGINIA**				
Kennedy	?	?	?	?		**Warner**	Y	N	Y	Y
Kerry	Y	Y	N	Y		Webb	Y	Y	Y	Y
MICHIGAN						**WASHINGTON**				
Levin	Y	Y	Y	Y		Murray	Y	Y	Y	Y
Stabenow	Y	Y	Y	Y		Cantwell	Y	Y	Y	Y
MINNESOTA						**WEST VIRGINIA**				
Coleman	Y	Y	Y	Y		Byrd	Y	Y	N	Y
Klobuchar	Y	Y	Y	Y		Rockefeller	Y	Y	Y	Y
MISSISSIPPI						**WISCONSIN**				
Cochran	Y	N	Y	Y		Kohl	Y	Y	Y	Y
Wicker	Y	N	Y	Y		Feingold	Y	Y	N	Y
MISSOURI						**WYOMING**				
Bond	Y	N	Y	Y		**Enzi**	Y	N	Y	Y
McCaskill	Y	Y	N	Y		**Barrasso**	Y	N	Y	Y

KEY	**Republicans**	Democrats	*Independents*		
Y	Voted for (yea)	X	Paired against	C	Voted "present" to avoid possible conflict of interest
#	Paired for	–	Announced against		
+	Announced for	P	Voted "present"	?	Did not vote or otherwise make a position known
N	Voted against (nay)				

ND Northern Democrats, SD Southern Democrats
Southern states: Ala., Ark., Fla., Ga., Ky., La., Miss., N.C., Okla., S.C., Tenn., Texas, Va.

IN THE SENATE | By Vote Number

206. **S 3604. Supplemental Appropriations/Motion to Proceed.**
Reid, D-Nev., motion to proceed to the bill that would extend unemployment benefits and provide additional fiscal 2009 funds for food assistance programs, infrastructure projects, state Medicaid plans and other programs. Motion rejected 52-42: R 6-40; D 44-2 (ND 39-2, SD 5-0); I 2-0. (By unanimous consent, the Senate agreed to raise the majority requirement for the motion to proceed to 60 votes.) A "nay" was a vote in support of the president's position. Sept. 26, 2008.

207. **HR 2638. Continuing Appropriations/Cloture.** Motion to invoke cloture (thus limiting debate) on the motion to concur in the House amendment to the Senate amendment to the bill. The House amendment would make fiscal 2009 appropriations through March 6, 2009. Motion agreed to 83-12: R 38-10; D 43-2 (ND 39-1, SD 4-1); I 2-0. Three-fifths of the total Senate (60) is required to invoke cloture. Sept. 27, 2008.

208. **HR 2638. Continuing Appropriations/Motion to Concur.**
Motion to concur in the House amendment to the Senate amendment to the bill. The House amendment would provide $41.2 billion in fiscal 2009 funding for the Homeland Security Department, $487.7 billion in discretionary funding for the Defense Department, $119.6 billion for military construction and veterans' programs and $22.9 billion for disaster relief. The amendment would appropriate funding through March 6, 2009, for programs covered by the nine unfinished fiscal 2009 appropriations bills. It also would provide extra funding, including $7.5 billion to support a $25 billion Energy Department auto company loan program and $2.5 billion above fiscal 2008 levels for Pell grants. Motion agreed to, thus clearing the bill for the president, 78-12: R 36-11; D 40-1 (ND 35-1, SD 5-0); I 2-0. Sept. 27, 2008.

209. **HR 2095. Federal Railroad Safety/Cloture.** Motion to invoke cloture (thus limiting debate) on the motion to concur in the House amendment to the Senate amendment to the bill. The House amendment would authorize $13 billion over five years for Amtrak and $1.6 billion for rail safety in fiscal 2008 through 2013. Motion agreed to 69-17: R 28-17; D 39-0 (ND 36-0, SD 3-0); I 2-0. Three-fifths of the total Senate (60) is required to invoke cloture. Sept. 29, 2008.

210. **HR 2095. Federal Railroad Safety/Motion to Concur.** Motion to concur in the House amendment to the Senate amendment to the bill. The House amendment would authorize $13 billion over five years for Amtrak and $1.6 billion for rail safety in fiscal 2008 through 2013. Motion agreed to 74-24: R 25-24; D 47-0 (ND 42-0, SD 5-0); I 2-0. Oct. 1, 2008.

	206	207	208	209	210
ALABAMA					
Shelby	N	N	N	N	N
Sessions	N	N	N	N	N
ALASKA					
Stevens	?	Y	Y	Y	Y
Murkowski	N	Y	Y	Y	Y
ARIZONA					
McCain	?	?	?	?	N
Kyl	N	N	N	N	N
ARKANSAS					
Lincoln	Y	Y	Y	Y	Y
Pryor	Y	Y	Y	Y	Y
CALIFORNIA					
Feinstein	Y	Y	+	Y	Y
Boxer	Y	Y	?	?	Y
COLORADO					
Allard	N	Y	N	N	N
Salazar	Y	Y	Y	Y	Y
CONNECTICUT					
Dodd	Y	Y	Y	Y	Y
Lieberman	Y	Y	Y	Y	Y
DELAWARE					
Biden	?	?	?	?	?
Carper	Y	Y	Y	Y	Y
FLORIDA					
Nelson	Y	Y	Y	?	Y
Martinez	N	Y	Y	Y	N
GEORGIA					
Chambliss	N	Y	Y	Y	N
Isakson	N	Y	Y	Y	Y
HAWAII					
Inouye	Y	Y	Y	Y	Y
Akaka	Y	Y	Y	Y	Y
IDAHO					
Craig	N	Y	Y	N	N
Crapo	N	Y	N	Y	Y
ILLINOIS					
Durbin	Y	Y	Y	Y	Y
Obama	?	?	?	?	Y
INDIANA					
Lugar	N	Y	Y	Y	Y
Bayh	N	?	Y	Y	Y
IOWA					
Grassley	N	Y	Y	Y	Y
Harkin	Y	Y	Y	Y	Y
KANSAS					
Brownback	N	Y	Y	N	N
Roberts	N	Y	Y	Y	Y
KENTUCKY					
McConnell	N	Y	Y	Y	Y
Bunning	N	N	N	N	N
LOUISIANA					
Landrieu	Y	N	Y	?	Y
Vitter	N	Y	N	N	N
MAINE					
Snowe	Y	Y	Y	Y	Y
Collins	Y	Y	Y	Y	Y
MARYLAND					
Mikulski	Y	Y	Y	Y	Y
Cardin	Y	Y	Y	Y	Y
MASSACHUSETTS					
Kennedy	?	?	?	?	?
Kerry	Y	Y	Y	Y	Y
MICHIGAN					
Levin	Y	Y	Y	?	Y
Stabenow	Y	Y	Y	Y	Y
MINNESOTA					
Coleman	Y	Y	Y	Y	Y
Klobuchar	Y	Y	Y	Y	Y
MISSISSIPPI					
Cochran	N	Y	Y	Y	Y
Wicker	N	Y	Y	Y	Y
MISSOURI					
Bond	N	Y	Y	?	N
McCaskill	N	Y	?	?	Y

	206	207	208	209	210
MONTANA					
Baucus	Y	Y	Y	Y	Y
Tester	Y	Y	Y	Y	Y
NEBRASKA					
Hagel	N	Y	Y	Y	Y
Nelson	Y	Y	Y	Y	Y
NEVADA					
Reid	Y	Y	Y	Y	Y
Ensign	N	N	N	?	N
NEW HAMPSHIRE					
Gregg	N	Y	Y	N	N
Sununu	N	Y	Y	?	N
NEW JERSEY					
Lautenberg	Y	Y	Y	Y	Y
Menendez	Y	Y	Y	Y	Y
NEW MEXICO					
Domenici	N	Y	Y	Y	Y
Bingaman	Y	Y	Y	Y	Y
NEW YORK					
Schumer	Y	Y	Y	Y	Y
Clinton	Y	Y	#	Y	Y
NORTH CAROLINA					
Dole	Y	Y	Y	Y	Y
Burr	N	N	X	N	N
NORTH DAKOTA					
Conrad	Y	Y	Y	Y	Y
Dorgan	Y	Y	Y	Y	Y
OHIO					
Voinovich	N	Y	Y	N	N
Brown	Y	Y	Y	Y	Y
OKLAHOMA					
Inhofe	N	Y	Y	N	N
Coburn	N	N	N	N	N
OREGON					
Wyden	Y	Y	Y	Y	Y
Smith	Y	Y	Y	Y	Y
PENNSYLVANIA					
Specter	Y	Y	Y	Y	Y
Casey	Y	Y	Y	Y	Y
RHODE ISLAND					
Reed	Y	Y	Y	Y	Y
Whitehouse	Y	Y	Y	Y	Y
SOUTH CAROLINA					
Graham	–	N	N	Y	N
DeMint	N	N	N	N	N
SOUTH DAKOTA					
Johnson	Y	Y	Y	Y	Y
Thune	N	Y	Y	N	N
TENNESSEE					
Alexander	N	Y	N	Y	Y
Corker	N	N	Y	Y	Y
TEXAS					
Hutchison	N	Y	Y	Y	Y
Cornyn	N	Y	Y	Y	Y
UTAH					
Hatch	N	Y	Y	Y	Y
Bennett	N	Y	Y	Y	Y
VERMONT					
Leahy	Y	Y	Y	Y	Y
Sanders	Y	Y	Y	Y	Y
VIRGINIA					
Warner	N	Y	Y	Y	Y
Webb	Y	Y	Y	Y	Y
WASHINGTON					
Murray	Y	Y	?	?	Y
Cantwell	Y	Y	Y	Y	Y
WEST VIRGINIA					
Byrd	Y	Y	Y	Y	Y
Rockefeller	Y	Y	Y	?	Y
WISCONSIN					
Kohl	Y	Y	Y	Y	Y
Feingold	Y	N	N	Y	Y
WYOMING					
Enzi	N	Y	Y	N	N
Barrasso	N	Y	Y	N	N

KEY	**Republicans**	Democrats	*Independents*		
Y	Voted for (yea)	X	Paired against	C	Voted "present" to avoid possible conflict of interest
#	Paired for	–	Announced against		
+	Announced for	P	Voted "present"	?	Did not vote or otherwise make a position known
N	Voted against (nay)				

ND Northern Democrats, SD Southern Democrats
Southern states: Ala., Ark., Fla., Ga., Ky., La., Miss., N.C., Okla., S.C., Tenn., Texas, Va.

IN THE SENATE | By Vote Number

211. **HR 7081. U.S.-India Nuclear Agreement/Passage.** Passage of the bill that would grant congressional approval to the U.S.-India nuclear cooperation agreement. It would require that the president determine and certify to Congress that certain actions have occurred, including that India has provided the International Atomic Energy Agency with a credible plan to separate civilian and military nuclear facilities, materials and programs, before the Nuclear Regulatory Commission can issue licenses for transfers of nuclear-related goods and services. Passed 86-13: R 49-0; D 36-12 (ND 31-12, SD 5-0); I 1-1. (By unanimous consent, the Senate agreed to raise the majority requirement for passage of the bill to 60 votes.) A "yea" was a vote in support of the president's position. Oct. 1, 2008.

212. **HR 1424. Mortgage-Backed Securities Buyout/Substitute.**
Dodd, D-Conn., substitute amendment that would allow the Treasury to use up to $700 billion, in installments, to buy certain mortgage assets. The amendment would require the Treasury to create a program to insure mortgage assets, would provide for congressional oversight and would limit compensation for executives of companies whose troubled assets are purchased. It would temporarily increase federal deposit insurance to $250,000 per bank account. It would extend dozens of expired or expiring tax provisions, provide a one-year adjustment to the alternative minimum tax, and require private insurance plans to put mental health benefits on par with other medical benefits. Adopted 74-25: R 34-15; D 39-9 (ND 36-7, SD 3-2); I 1-1. (By unanimous consent, the Senate agreed to raise the majority requirement for adoption of the Dodd substitute amendment to 60 votes.) Oct. 1, 2008.

213. **HR 1424. Mortgage-Backed Securities Buyout/Passage.**
Passage of the bill that would allow the Treasury to use up to $700 billion, in installments, to buy certain mortgage assets. The bill would require the Treasury to create a program to insure mortgage assets, would provide for congressional oversight and would limit compensation for executives of companies whose troubled assets are purchased. It would temporarily increase federal deposit insurance to $250,000 per bank account. It would extend dozens of expired or expiring tax provisions, provide a one-year adjustment to the alternative minimum tax and require private insurance plans to put mental health benefits on par with other medical benefits. Passed 74-25: R 34-15; D 39-9 (ND 36-7, SD 3-2); I 1-1. (By unanimous consent, the Senate agreed to raise the majority requirement for passage of the bill to 60 votes.) A "yea" was a vote in support of the president's position. Oct. 1, 2008.

214. **HR 6867. Unemployment Benefits Extension/Cloture.** Motion to invoke cloture (thus limiting debate) on the motion to proceed to the bill that would provide an additional seven weeks of unemployment benefits for workers who have exhausted their current compensation by March 31, 2009. The bill also would extend benefits for an additional 13 weeks, or half the duration of regular unemployment compensation, for workers in states with unemployment rates of 6 percent or higher. Motion agreed to 89-6: R 41-6; D 46-0 (ND 42-0, SD 4-0); I 2-0. Three-fifths of the total Senate (60) is required to invoke cloture. Nov. 20, 2008.

215. **HR 7005. Automobile Industry Loan Program Shell/Cloture.**
Motion to invoke cloture (thus limiting debate) on the motion to proceed to a bill on the alternative minimum tax, which would serve as the vehicle for an emergency loan package for domestic automakers. Motion rejected 52-35: R 10-31; D 40-4 (ND 36-3, SD 4-1); I 2-0. Three-fifths of the total Senate (60) is required to invoke cloture. A "yea" was a vote in support of the president's position. Dec. 11, 2008.

*Sen. Barack Obama, D-Ill., resigned Nov. 16, 2008, after winning the presidential election. The last vote for which he was eligible was 213.

ND Northern Democrats, SD Southern Democrats
Southern states: Ala., Ark., Fla., Ga., Ky., La., Miss., N.C., Okla., S.C., Tenn., Texas, Va.

	211	212	213	214	215
ALABAMA					
Shelby	Y	N	N	Y	N
Sessions	Y	N	N	Y	N
ALASKA					
Stevens	Y	Y	Y	Y	?
Murkowski	Y	Y	Y	Y	N
ARIZONA					
McCain	Y	Y	Y	Y	N
Kyl	Y	Y	Y	Y	N
ARKANSAS					
Lincoln	Y	Y	Y	+	N
Pryor	Y	Y	Y	Y	Y
CALIFORNIA					
Feinstein	Y	Y	Y	Y	Y
Boxer	N	Y	Y	Y	Y
COLORADO					
Allard	Y	N	N	Y	N
Salazar	Y	Y	Y	Y	Y
CONNECTICUT					
Dodd	Y	Y	Y	Y	Y
Lieberman	Y	Y	Y	Y	Y
DELAWARE					
Biden	Y	Y	Y	?	?
Carper	Y	Y	Y	Y	Y
FLORIDA					
Nelson	Y	N	N	Y	Y
Martinez	Y	Y	Y	Y	N
GEORGIA					
Chambliss	Y	Y	Y	?	N
Isakson	Y	Y	Y	Y	N
HAWAII					
Inouye	Y	Y	Y	Y	Y
Akaka	N	Y	Y	Y	Y
IDAHO					
Craig	Y	Y	Y	Y	?
Crapo	Y	N	N	Y	N
ILLINOIS					
Durbin	Y	Y	Y	Y	Y
Obama*	Y	Y	Y		
INDIANA					
Lugar	Y	Y	Y	Y	Y
Bayh	Y	Y	Y	Y	Y
IOWA					
Grassley	Y	Y	Y	Y	N
Harkin	N	Y	Y	Y	Y
KANSAS					
Brownback	Y	N	N	Y	Y
Roberts	Y	N	N	Y	N
KENTUCKY					
McConnell	Y	Y	Y	Y	N
Bunning	Y	N	N	Y	N
LOUISIANA					
Landrieu	Y	N	N	Y	Y
Vitter	Y	N	N	Y	N
MAINE					
Snowe	Y	Y	Y	Y	Y
Collins	Y	Y	Y	Y	Y
MARYLAND					
Mikulski	Y	Y	Y	Y	Y
Cardin	Y	Y	Y	Y	Y
MASSACHUSETTS					
Kennedy	?	?	?	Y	?
Kerry	Y	Y	Y	Y	+
MICHIGAN					
Levin	Y	Y	Y	Y	Y
Stabenow	Y	N	N	Y	Y
MINNESOTA					
Coleman	Y	Y	Y	Y	N
Klobuchar	Y	Y	Y	Y	Y
MISSISSIPPI					
Cochran	Y	N	N	Y	N
Wicker	Y	N	N	Y	N
MISSOURI					
Bond	Y	Y	Y	Y	Y
McCaskill	Y	Y	Y	Y	Y

	211	212	213	214	215
MONTANA					
Baucus	Y	Y	Y	Y	N
Tester	Y	N	N	Y	N
NEBRASKA					
Hagel	Y	Y	Y	Y	?
Nelson	Y	Y	Y	Y	Y
NEVADA					
Reid	Y	Y	Y	Y	Y
Ensign	Y	Y	Y	Y	N
NEW HAMPSHIRE					
Gregg	Y	Y	Y	Y	N
Sununu	Y	Y	Y	?	?
NEW JERSEY					
Lautenberg	Y	Y	Y	Y	Y
Menendez	Y	Y	Y	Y	Y
NEW MEXICO					
Domenici	Y	Y	Y	Y	Y
Bingaman	N	Y	Y	Y	Y
NEW YORK					
Schumer	Y	Y	Y	Y	Y
Clinton	Y	Y	Y	Y	Y
NORTH CAROLINA					
Dole	Y	N	N	Y	Y
Burr	Y	Y	Y	Y	N
NORTH DAKOTA					
Conrad	N	Y	Y	Y	Y
Dorgan	N	N	N	Y	Y
OHIO					
Voinovich	Y	Y	Y	Y	Y
Brown	N	Y	Y	Y	Y
OKLAHOMA					
Inhofe	Y	N	N	N	N
Coburn	Y	Y	Y	N	N
OREGON					
Wyden	Y	N	N	Y	+
Smith	Y	Y	Y	Y	?
PENNSYLVANIA					
Specter	Y	Y	Y	Y	Y
Casey	Y	Y	Y	Y	Y
RHODE ISLAND					
Reed	N	Y	Y	Y	Y
Whitehouse	N	Y	Y	Y	Y
SOUTH CAROLINA					
Graham	Y	Y	Y	Y	–
DeMint	Y	N	N	N	N
SOUTH DAKOTA					
Johnson	Y	N	N	Y	Y
Thune	Y	Y	Y	Y	N
TENNESSEE					
Alexander	Y	Y	Y	Y	N
Corker	Y	Y	Y	Y	N
TEXAS					
Hutchison	Y	Y	Y	Y	N
Cornyn	Y	Y	Y	Y	–
UTAH					
Hatch	Y	Y	Y	N	N
Bennett	Y	Y	Y	N	N
VERMONT					
Leahy	N	Y	Y	Y	Y
Sanders	N	N	N	Y	Y
VIRGINIA					
Warner	Y	Y	Y	Y	Y
Webb	Y	Y	Y	Y	Y
WASHINGTON					
Murray	Y	Y	Y	Y	Y
Cantwell	Y	N	N	Y	Y
WEST VIRGINIA					
Byrd	N	Y	Y	Y	Y
Rockefeller	Y	Y	Y	Y	Y
WISCONSIN					
Kohl	Y	Y	Y	Y	Y
Feingold	N	N	N	Y	Y
WYOMING					
Enzi	Y	N	N	N	N
Barrasso	Y	N	N	N	N

KEY **Republicans** Democrats *Independents*

Y Voted for (yea)	X Paired against	C Voted "present" to avoid possible conflict of interest
# Paired for	– Announced against	
+ Announced for	P Voted "present"	? Did not vote or otherwise make a position known
N Voted against (nay)		

Senate Roll Call Index by Subject

Appendix I

GENERAL INDEX

General Index

Justice Department grant peer review, 2-7

Media ownership, 2-15

Office of Federal Housing Enterprise Oversight
Mortgage industry regulation, 7-10

Office of Management and Budget
Budget deficit forecast, 4-6
Bush budget proposal, 4-3–4-4, 4-6
Highway Trust Fund, 3-19
Military Construction-VA, 2-25

Office of Personnel Management
Appropriations, 2-15–2-16

Ohio
Democratic electoral gains, 10-20
Special elections, 10-22
State and local elections, 10-24–10-25

Oil and gas industry
Biorefineries, 3-8
Economic stimulus, 7-18
Energy futures speculation, 8-4
Offshore drilling, 2-20, 2-21, 2-22, 8-3–8-5
Session overview, 1-3, 1-8–1-9
Refineries improvement tax break, 4-15

Oklahoma
State and local elections, 10-24–10-25

Olver, John W., D-Mass.
Transportation appropriations, 2-29

OMB. See Office of Management and Budget

Oregon
Congressional elections, 10-17

P

Packers and Stockyards Act
Annual report, 3-9

Palin, Gov. Sarah, R-Alaska
Offshore drilling, 1-9
Presidential election campaign, 10-4, 10-7
Republican National Convention address, D-23–D-25
Republican primary, 10-13

Pallone, Frank Jr., D-N.J. (6)
Tobacco regulation, 3-15

Party unity. See under Vote studies

Pastor, Ed, D-Ariz. (4)
Arizona attorney general prosecution rate, 2-7

Paterson, Gov. David A., D-N.Y.
Senate appointments, 10-18

Paul, Ron, R-Texas (14)
McCain Republican primary win, 10-13

Paulsen, Erik
Election victory, 10-22

Paulson, Treasury Secretary Henry M. Jr.
Automobile industry bailout, 7-20
Bush budget proposal, 4-6
Economic stimulus, 7-17
Fannie Mae and Freddie Mac, 7-9–7-13
Financial industries bailout, 1-9–1-10, 7-3–7-6

Pawlenty, Gov. Tim, R-Minn.
State elections, 10-25

Pearce, Gary
Hagan electoral victory, 10-17

Pearce, Steve, R-N.M. (2)
Election loss, 10-17
Reliable replacement warhead, 6-6

Pell grant program
Higher education reauthorization, 9-8–9-9, 9-10

Pelosi, Nancy, D-Calif. (8)
Automobile industry bailout, 7-20–7-22
Colombia trade agreement, 6-18–6-19
Congressional elections, 10-19
Economic stimulus, 1-9, 7-17
Farm bill, 3-4–3-5
Financial services bailout, 7-4
FISA overhaul, 6-15
Independent ethics office, 5-4
Labor-HHS-Education appropriations, 2-21
Offshore oil drilling, 8-3–8-4
Organizing for 110th Congress, 2nd session, 1-11, 10-3–10-9
Session overview, 1-3
Unemployment benefits, 9-11

Pence, Mike, R-Ind. (6)
Election as conference chairman, 1-11
Financial services bailout, 7-5
Global HIV/AIDS program reauthorization, 6-10
Iraq and Afghanistan supplemental appropriations, 2-33

Pennsylvania
State and local elections, 10-24–10-25

Perdue, Beverly
Gubernatorial election, 10-24

Perino, Dana
Global HIV/AIDS program reauthorization, 6-10

Peters, Secretary of Transportation Mary
Highway Trust Fund, 3-19

Peterson, Collin C., D-Minn. (7)
Farm bill, 3-5

Peterson, John E., R-Pa. (5)
Offshore drilling, 2-20, 2-22

Petraeus, Gen. David H.
Confirmation as Central Command head, 5-7

Pew Research Center
Offshore oil drilling, 8-3

Phillip Morris USA
FDA regulation, 3-14–3-16

Plouffe, David
Obama presidential campaign advice, 10-3

Poland
Anti-missile sites, 6-6, 6-7

Pollina, Anthony
Gubernatorial election, 10-25

Porter, Jon, R-Nev. (3)
Election loss, 10-19

Presidential elections
Budget resolution, 4-9–4-10
Bush budget proposal, 4-3, 4-6
Democratic ticket, 10-6
Election map, 10-5
Obama victory, 10-3–10-9
Overview, 1-11
Republican ticket, 10-7
Results, 10-8
Statistics, 10-4

Presidential support and opposition.
See under Vote studies

Preston, Steven C.
Confirmation as HUD secretary, 5-6–5-7

Price, David E., D-N.C. (4)
Border fence, 2-18
Military contractors as interrogators, 6-6

Price, Tom, R-Ga. (6)
Student aid, 9-10

Primaries
McCain wins, 10-13–10-15
Obama upsets Clinton for nomination, 10-10–10-12
Primary and caucus results, 10-11, 10-14

Prisons and prisoners
Iraq and Afghanistan supplemental appropriations, 2-33, 2-35

Project Bioshield
Appropriations, 2-17

Project on Student Debt
Higher education reauthorization, 9-9

Property taxes
Tax deductions, 4-15

Pryor, Mark, D-Ark.
Consumer Product Safety Commission reauthorization, 3-11–3-12

Public debt
Budget resolution, 4-8
Debt limit increase, 7-8, 7-10
Foreign-owned debt, 2-16

Public lands
Oil drilling, 8-4

Public laws
110-1 through 110-175, E-3–E-22

Public opinion
Bush and Cheney approval ratings, 10-10

R

R.J. Reynolds
Tobacco regulation, 3-14–3-16

Rahall, Nick J. II, D-W.Va. (3)
Offshore oil drilling, 8-5

Railroads. See also Amtrak
Commuter rail, 3-17
Safety, 3-17

Ramstad, Jim, R-Minn. (3)
Mental health parity, 9-5

Rangel, Charles B., D-N.Y. (15)
Ethics issues, 5-4–5-5
Highway Trust Fund, 3-19
Tax "extenders," 4-13
Tax credits for homebuyers, 7-11
Tobacco regulation, 3-14

Reading First
Appropriations, 2-22

Redistricting
State and gubernatorial elections, 10-24

Reed, Jack, D-R.I.
Iraq and Afghanistan supplemental appropriations, 2-33

Refugees. See Immigration

Reid, Harry, D-Nev.
Automobile industry bailout, 7-20–7-22
Bush budget proposal, 4-3
Climate bill, 8-6
Defense appropriations, 2-11
Defense authorization, 6-6
Economic stimulus, 7-18–7-19
FHA overhaul, 7-11
Financial services bailout, 7-3
Highway Trust Fund, 3-19
Iraq and Afghanistan supplemental appropriations, 2-34

Mental health parity, 4-13–4-14
Offshore oil drilling, 8-3
Pay inequality, 9-12
Physician Medicare payments, 9-3
Session overview, 1-3
Unemployment benefits, 9-11–9-12

Reliable replacement warheads
Appropriations, 2-13–2-14

Religion and religious organizations
Global HIV/AIDS program reauthorization, 6-9

Renewable energy. See also Energy
Appropriations, 2-12
Energy tax breaks, 7-18, 7-19

Renzi, Rick, R-Ariz. (1)
Ethics investigation, 5-5

Republican National Convention
McCain address, D-26–D-29
Palin address, D-23–D-25

Republican Party
Public opinion, 10-4–10-5

Republican State Leadership Committee
State and local elections, 10-24–10-25

Republican Study Committee
Iraq and Afghanistan supplemental appropriations, 2-33

Research and development
Agriculture and food research, 3-8
Biomass program, 3-8
Energy research, 3-4, 3-8
Minority researchers, 3-8
Tax credit, 4-4, 4-15

Restaurant industry
Tax breaks, 4-15

Retirement and pensions
IRAs, 4-15

Retirements (congressional)
Domenici, 2-14
List, 10-20–10-21

Reyes, Silvestre, D-Texas (16)
Intelligence authorization, 6-17

Rhode Island
State and gubernatorial elections, 10-24

Rice, Secretary of State Condoleezza
Nuclear cooperation with India, 6-12

Richardson, Gov. Bill, D-N.M.
Public opinion, 10-10

Rita. See under Hurricanes

Ritter, Gov. Bill Jr.
Senate appointments, 10-18

Robertson, Pat
McCain Republican primary win, 10-13

Rockefeller, John D. IV, D-W.Va.
Interrogation methods, 6-17
Unemployment benefits, 7-18
Warrantless wiretapping, 6-14

Rogers, Harold, R-Ky. (5)
Homeland security appropriations, 2-17, 2-18

Rogers, Mike, R-Mich. (8)
Tobacco regulation, 3-15

Rohrabacher, Dana, R-Calif. (46)
Global HIV/AIDS program reauthorization, 6-10

Romney, former Gov. Mitt, R-Mass.
McCain Republican primary win, 10-13

Ross, Mike, D-Ark. (4)
Tax "extenders," 4-14

Rossi, Dino
Gubernatorial election, 10-24

Royalties
Timber sales, 2-34